SKO   K

Afri

PROF. DR. D. B. BOSMAN
PROF. I. W. v. d. MERWE, M. A.

Bygewerk deur
DR. A. S. V. BARNES, M.A., M.ED.

PHAROS

ISBN 1 86890 008 8

Tiende uitgawe
in 1998 uitgegee deur
Pharos Woordeboeke,
'n afdeling van
NB-Uitgewers
Waalburg, Waalstraat 28
Kaapstad

Tiende uitgawe, eerste druk 1998
Tiende uitgawe, tweede druk 1999
Tiende uitgawe, derde druk 2000
Tiende uitgawe, vierde druk 2001
Tiende uitgawe, vyfde druk 2002
Tiende uitgawe, sesde druk 2002

Voorheen uitgegee deur
Nasou Beperk, Kaapstad

Kopiereg © 1998 streng voorbehou
Geen gedeelte van hierdie boek
mag sonder die skriftelike verlof
van die uitgewer gereproduseer of
in enige vorm of deur enige
elektroniese of meganiese middel
weergegee word nie, hetsy deur
fotokopiëring, plaat- of bandopname,
vermikrofilming of enige ander
stelsel van inligtingsbewaring

Gelitografeer en gebind deur Paarl Print,
Oosterlandstraat, Paarl
Suid-Afrika

NORTH TYNESIDE LIBRARIES	
012163342	
Cypher	24.05.03
439.368	£14.95
CEN	

Voorwoord

Hierdie *Tweetalige Skoolwoordeboek* is 'n verkorte uitgawe van die *Tweetalige Woordeboek* en is saamgestel veral met die oog op die behoeftes van leerlinge van die middelbare skool. Om die beperkte ruimte nie te oorskry nie, moes die samestellers natuurlik baie samestellinge en uitdrukkinge skrap wat in die *Tweetalige Woordeboek* opgeneem is, maar hulle strewe was steeds om dié woorde en uitdrukkinge te behou wat die leerling die meeste teëkom, in sy skoolwerk sowel as in die alledaagse lewe. Die aksent en die uitspraak word nie aangegee nie, omdat die prys van die woordeboek dan heelwat hoër sou gewees het. Wat die klemtoon van die Afrikaanse woorde betref, moet ons dus maar verwys na die *Tweetalige Woordeboek*, en wat die klemtoon en uitspraak van Engelse woorde betref, na die uitstekende verklarende Engelse woordeboeke van *The Oxford University Press*, naamlik, *The Little Oxford Dictionary*, *The Pocket Oxford Dictionary* en *The Concise Oxford Dictionary*.

D. B. BOSMAN
I. W. VAN DER MERWE

Voorwoord by die agtste uitgawe

By die aanvulling en modernisering van hierdie woordeboek het ek my deur die volgende oorweginge laat lei:

1. Hoewel ek met voordeel uit die jongste uitgawe van die TWEETALIGE WOORDEBOEK (Bosman, Van der Merwe en Hiemstra) kon put, is die Afrikaanse vorme vir talle Engelse woorde en uitdrukkinge nog nie opgeteken nie. Tipiese voorbeelde is ,,vertical take-off plane, aquaplane, minicar, minicopter, hovercraft, beer baron, poker-faced, cine-camera, claim-jumper, dodderer, gigolo, hoop-la, pinto, machan, play-boy, limp back (of an aeroplane), telstar, syncom, laser, beatnik, sweater-girl, on location" en nog baie meer. Die vertalings wat nou aan die hand gedoen word en nie in die smaak val nie, kan, sodra daar meer eenstemmigheid bestaan, deur doelmatiger Afrikaanse ekwivalente vervang word.

2. Die noodsaaklikheid om binne 'n bepaalde bestek te bly, het breedvoerigheid outomaties uitgeskakel. Gebrek aan ruimte het verder meegebring dat heelwat minder belangrike materiaal geskrap moes word om plek te maak vir nuwere begrippe.

3. By gebrek aan uitsluitsel moes daar ten opsigte van samekoppelinge 'n middeweg gevolg word tussen grammatiese beginsels (wat die voorkeur aan los skrywe gee) en skryfgewoontes (wat aaneenskrywe verkies). Koppeltekens is gebruik hoofsaaklik om onoorsigtelikheid en verwarring te vermy.

4. In ooreenstemming met die algemene gebruik in Engels is voorkeur gegee aan die spelling -IZE (-IZATION). Slegs in die volgende gevalle is -ISE behou: advertise, apprise, chastise, circumcise, comprise, compromise, demise, despise, devise, disguise, enterprise, excise, excercise, franchise, improvise, incise, paralyse, prise (open), supervise, televise, surmise, surprise.

5. By wyse van 'n tegemoetkoming is hier en daar ook sleng en gemeensame uitdrukkinge bygevoeg.

1964   A. S. V. BARNES

By die veertiende druk

Alle woorde wat aan een of ander deel van die bevolking aanstoot kan gee, is geskrap.

1981   A. S. V. BARNES

Afkortinge en Verduidelikinge

n., (*Lat.* nomen), *Afr.* selfstandige naamwoord, *Eng.* noun.
a., (*Lat.* adjectivum), *Afr.* byvoeglike naamwoord, *Eng.* adjective.
adv., (*Lat.* adverbium), *Afr.* bywoord, *Eng.* adverb
prep., (*Lat.* praepositio), *Afr.* voorsetsel, *Eng.* preposition.
conj., (*Lat.* conjunctio), *Afr.* voegwoord, *Eng.* conjunction.
interj., (*Lat.* interjectio), *Afr.* tussenwerpsel, *Eng.* interjection.
pron., (*Lat.* pronomen), *Afr.* voornaamwoord, *Eng.* pronoun.
v(ide), kyk.

Die verlede deelwoorde van werkwoorde word as volg aangedui:
(i) **loop**, (ge-) = (het) **geloop**;
(ii) **afkap**, (afge-) = (het) **afgekap**;
(iii) **verstaan**, (het) of net (—) = het **verstaan**.

Die (-*e*) of (-*s*) na 'n selfstandige naamwoord dui die meervoudsuitgang aan, bv. **hoed, (-e) = hoede** en **voël, (-s) = voëls.** Ander meervoudsuitgange word vollediger aangegee.

Die verbuiging van 'n byvoeglike naamwoord word net na die hoofwoord tussen hakies aangegee, bv., **lelik, (-e) = lelike; vol, (-, -le) = vol, volle**, bv. 'n **vol** rivier, 'n **volle** uur.

Waar samestellinge en afleidinge, veral afleidinge op **-er, -heid, -ing, -nis, -skap,** nie aangegee word nie, kan die vertaling meestal gevind word deur die *hoofwoord te raadpleeg*.

Woorde wat met ge- begin, is dikwels verlede deelwoorde of afleidinge van werkwoorde. As sulke woorde nie onder ge- verskyn nie, soek dan onder die werkwoord sonder ge-.

By refleksiewe werkwoorde word **sig** kortheidshalwe dikwels gebruik i.p.v. **jou, hom, haar,** ens. **Sig aan die letter hou** word dus aangegee i.p.v. **jou aan die letter hou; hom, haar aan die letter hou,** ens.

AFRIKAANS-ENGELS

# A

A, A; g'n – van 'n B ken nie, not know A from B; as jy – sê, moet jy ook B sê, in for a penny, in for a pound.
a, interj. ah!, oh!; – **ja** –, certainly, of course; – **nee** –, oh no, of course not.
aai, (-), n. caress, chuck, pat, stroke.
aai, (ge-), caress, pat, stroke.
aaklig, a. & adv. awful, beastly, ghastly, horrible, nasty, rotten, sick, wretched; 'n –e **skrif,** an awful scrawl; 'n –e **gedaante,** a ghastly apparition; –e **medisyne,** vile stuff; **ek is – daarvan,** it has made me feel sick (upset); – **skrywe,** write an awful hand; write badly (a bad style); – **bleek,** ghastly pale; – **vervelend,** horribly dull.
aakligheid, (-hede), awfulness, horribleness, nastiness, sickness, vileness; (pl.), horrors, terrors; **die –hede van die oorlog,** the horrors of war.
aal, (ale), eel; **so glad as 'n –,** as slippery as an eel.
aalagtig, (-e), eel-like, eely.
aalbes(sie), black-currant.
aalmoes, (-e), alms, charity; dole; **'n – vra,** ask (an) alms, ask for charity, beg; **van –e lewe,** live on charity.
aalmoesenier, (-s), almoner; chaplain.
aalwee, (alewee), (-s), aalwyn, (-e), aloe, bitter-aloe.
aalweebitter, aalwyn-, aloin.
aalweeboom, aalwyn-, aloe(-tree).
aalweehout, aalwyn-, eagle-wood.
aalweepil, aalwyn-, aloe-pill, aloin pill.
aam, (ame), aum; cf. **halfaam.**
aambeeld, anvil; incus (in ear); **op dieselfde – hamer,** harp on the same string.
aambei(e), haemorrhoids, piles.
aamborstig, (-e), shortwinded, wheezy, asthmatic; hoarse, husky.
aamborstig, asthma; short-windedness; throatiness, huskiness.
aan, prep, at, against, by, by way of, for, in, in the way of, near, next to, on, of, upon, with, to, up to; – **boord,** on board (ship); – **(die) brand,** on fire; – **die drank,** on the booze; **'n ring – sy vinger,** a ring on his finger; **'n prent – die muur,** a picture on the wall; – **wal,** on shore, ashore; – **land gaan,** go ashore; – **(die) slaap (raak),** (fall) asleep; – **(die) kant,** neat, tidied; – **(die) kant maak,** do (room); put in order, straighten, tidy (up); – **die deur,** at the door; – **die universiteit,** at (in) the university; – **tafel,** at table; – **die werk,** at work, busy; **hy is** – (die, 't) **skrywe,** he is (busy) writing; **met skoene – sy voete,** with shoes to (on) his feet; – **stukke trek,** pull to pieces; – **sy gesig sien,** see by his face; **hand – hand,** hand in hand; **kop –** (en) **kop,** neck and neck; – **die bewind,** in power; – **kontant,** in cash, **hy is – die tering dood,** he died of consumption.
aan, adv. in, on, onwards, upon; **daar is niks van – nie,** there is nothing in it; **daar is niks – nie,** that is nothing, it is quite easy; it isn't up to much; **ek het daar niks – nie,** it is of no value to me; **ek is daar nog nie – toe nie,** I am not so far yet; **dit kom nie daarop – nie,** it does not matter; **jy kan daarop –,** you can depend (up)on it; **die lig (pyp, vuur) is –,** the light (pipe, fire) is on (is burning); **sy skoene is –,** his shoes are on; **met sy skoene –,** in his shoes; **hy is (hoog) –,** he is tipsy; **jy is –,** you are on, it's your turn; **die kerk (skool) is –,** the service (school) has begun; **dit is weer – tussen hulle twee,** they have made it up again.

aanbousel

aan-aan: – **speel,** play (at) touch.
aanbak, (aange-), stick (to the pan); cake together (coal, etc.); get burnt.
aanbaksel, crust.
aanbel, (aange-), ring, give a ring.
aanbeland, (het –), arrive at, come to.
aanbelang, n. consequence, importance.
aanbelang, (het –): wat dit –, as regards this, as far as this is concerned.
aanbestee, (het –), put out to contract; call for tenders.
aanbetref, (het –), concern; **wat dit –,** as to this, as far as this is concerned.
aanbetrou, (het –), entrust to; confide to.
aanbeur, (aange-), struggle along.
aanbeveel, (het –), recommend; **sig – (aanbevole) hou,** recommend oneself, solicit the favour of.
aanbevelenswaardig, (-e), commendable.
aanbeveling, (-e, -s), recommendation; introduction, reference; **iemand 'n – gee,** recommend someone; **goeie –e,** good references (testimonials); **op – van,** on the recommendation of.
aanbevelingsbrief, letter of recommendation.
aanbevole, vide **aanbeveel.**
aanbid, (het –), adore, worship.
aanbiddelik, (-e), adorable, divine.
aanbidder, -bidster, (-s), adorer, admirer; worshipper.
aanbidding, (-e, -s), adoration; worship.
aanbie(d), aanbieë, (aange-), bid, offer, proffer; give, present, tender; volunteer; hand in; apply; render; **dienste –,** offer (proffer, tender, volunteer) services; **'n geskenk –,** make a presentation; **sy bedanking (ontslag) –,** tender one's resignation; **'n petisie –,** present a petition; **'n rekening –,** present a bill; **R1 vir iets –,** offer (bid) R1 for something; **'n telegram –,** hand in a telegram; **as die geleentheid hom –,** if the opportunity presents itself, **jou vir 'n betrekking –,** apply for a post.
aanbieding, (-e, -s), offer, overture, tender; presentation; vide **aanbod.**
aanbind, (aange-), bind, fasten, tie; **die stryd – met,** try conclusions with, join issue with.
aanblaas, (aange-), blow; fan, foment, stir up; **opstand –,** stir up rebellion; **die vuur –,** blow (fan) fire.
aanblaf, (aange-), bark at, bay at.
aanblaser, (-s), fomenter, instigator.
aanblasing, (-e, -s), blowing; instigation; **goddelike –,** divine inspiration.
aanblik, n. aspect; glance, look; sight, view; **by die eerste –,** at first sight.
aanblik, (aange-), glance (look) at, cast one's eyes (up)on; **iemand met liefde –,** beam lovingly upon someone.
aanbly, (aange-), continue, remain, stay; last; **in 'n betrekking –,** continue in office; **die kerk sal lank –,** the service will last long; **laat jou skoene –,** keep your shoes on.
aanbod, aanbot, (aanbiedinge, aanbiedings, aanbotte), offer, proposal, tender; supply; **'n – afslaan,** refuse an offer, turn down a proposal; **vraag en –,** demand and supply; vide **aanbieding.**
aanbons, (aange-), bump against.
aanbot, vide **aanbod.**
aanbots, (aange-), hit (knock, strike) against, collide with, be in conflict with.
aanbou, n. annex(e); construction, erection; **in –,** under construction.
aanbou, (aange-), build on to, add on (a new wing); build against (a wall).
aanbousel, (-s), annex(e), addition.

aanbrand, (aange-), burn, be (get) burnt; stick (to the pan).
aanbrandsel, (-s), crust, crustation.
aanbreek, n. beginning, commencement; dawn (of day); fall (of night).
aanbreek, (aange-), dawn (day); close in (night); open, broach; come, be at hand (time); cut into.
aanbrei, (aange-), knit on.
aanbring, (aange-), bring, bring on, bring with; construct (a wall), install; impart (knowledge); make (improvements); disclose, reveal (crime), tell (tales).
aanbringer, (-s), carrier; maker; denouncer, informer, talebearer; vide **aanbring**.
aanbruis, (aange-), roar (rush) along.
aanbyt, (aange-), bite (nibble) at.
aand, (-e), eve, evening, night; **die − tevore**, the evening (night) before, overnight; **die − voor die fees**, the eve of the festival.
aandadig, (-e); **− aan**, implicated in.
aandag, attention, notice; devotion; **die − trek**, attract attention; **die − vra**, invite attention; **die − boei**, hold the attention; **−!**, attention! **− gee aan**, pay attention to; **met −**, attentively; **onder die − bring van**, bring to the notice of; **die − vestig op**, draw attention to.
aandagstreep, dash.
aandagtig, (-e), a. attentive.
aandagtig(lik), adv. attentively, closely.
aandagtigheid, attention, attentiveness.
aandblad, evening-paper.
aanddiens, evening-service.
aandeel, allotment, part, portion, quota, share; **− hê in**, have a share in; **('n) − neem aan (in)**, participate in, take part in.
aandeelbewys, share-certificate, warrant.
aandeelhouers, shareholder.
aandelekapitaal, share-capital capital-stock.
aandelemaatskappy, joint-stock company.
aandenking, (-e, -s), memory, remembrance; memento, souvenir, keepsake; **'n − aan die oorlog**, a souvenir of the war; **in geseënde −**, in kind remembrance.
aandete, evening-meal, supper.
aandgodsdiens, evening-prayers.
aandien, (aange-), announce, usher in; **jou −send in one's name (card)**.
aandig, (aange-), impute.
aandigting, (-e, -s), imputation.
aandik, (aange-), thicken; underline, emphasise; exaggerate; **iemand se woorde −**, dot the i's and cross the t's of someone's words.
aandikking, (-e, -s), thickening; emphasis, stress(ing), underlining, exaggeration.
aandjie, (-s), social evening; night-out.
aandkerk, evening-service.
aandklas, evening-, night-class.
aandkostuum, evening-dress (-wear).
aandlied, evening-song.
aandlig, evening-light, twilight, dusk.
aandlug, evening-air; evening-breeze.
aandoen, (aange-, aangedaan), cause, give, affect, move, touch; call (touch) at (a port); **onaangenaam −**, displease, offend, grate (jar) upon; **eer −**, do honour to; **die waarheid geweld −**, stretch the truth.
aandoening, (-e, -s), emotion; affection, touch (of fever).
aandoenlik, (-e), moving, pathetic, touching; impressionable.
aandoenlikheid, pathos; sensitiveness.
aandpak, evening-dress.

aandpraatjies, vide **môrepraatjies**.
aandra(e), **aandraag**, (aange-), bring, carry, fetch; **nuus −**, tell tales.
aandraai, (aange-), fasten, fix on, tighten; turn on, switch on, crank (motor); **(die) briek −**, apply the brake; go slowly.
aandraer, carrier; telltale.
aandraf, (aange-), trot along.
aandrang, impetus, pressure; impulse, urge, insistence, instigation; urgency; **die − van die bloed**, blood pressure; **die − van die hart**, the impulse (promptings) of the heart; **met −**, insistently, urgently; **op − van**, at the instance (instigation) of; **uit eie −**, of one's own accord (free will).
aandrentel, (aange-), saunter along.
aandribbel, (aange-), trip (toddle) along.
aandrif, impulse, impetus.
aandring, (aange-), press, push, urge; **− op**, insist on; press ... for (payment).
aandrok, evening-dress.
aandruis, (aange-), roar up against.
aandruk, (aange-), clasp; hug; press against; press forward; **teen iemand −**, cuddle up against.
aandryf, **aandrywe**, (aange-), float ashore; float along; incite, prompt, urge (on).
aandrywer, driver; mover, instigator.
aandrywing, (-e, -s), driving, inciting, instigation, urge.
aandsitting, evening-, night-session.
aandskof, evening-, night-shift.
aandskool, evening-classes, night-school.
aandster, evening-star.
aandtabberd, **aandtawwerd**, evening-dress.
aandtoilet, evening-dress, evening-toilet.
aandui(e), (aange-), indicate, point out; describe, designate; bespeak, signify; specify; **'n eerlike inbors −**, argue an honest mind; **kortheidshalwe − as**, for the sake of brevity refer to as; **nader −**, specify; **iets terloops −**, (casually) refer to a thing.
aanduiding, (-e, -s), indication, description; sign.
aandurf, **aandurwe**, (aange-), dare, venture (upon); **'n taak −**, dare to undertake a task; **nie − nie**, fight shy of; **iemand −**, stand up to someone.
aandwandeling, evening-walk.
aandwind, evening-breeze, night-wind.
aaneen, vide **aanmekaar**.
aaneengeslote, **-gesluit**, coherent, connected, serried, united.
aaneenskakel, (aaneenge-), connect, link together (up), concatenate, couple.
aaneenskakelend, (e), copulative.
aaneenskakeling, concatenation, sequence, series, string; **'n − van ongelukke**, a series (chapter) of accidents; **'n − van leuens**, a string (tissue) of lies.
aaneensluiting, closing, joining, linking, uniting; rallying; joint union.
aangaan, (aange-), continue, go on, proceed; begin, commence; catch fire; carry on, go on (like mad); conclude (a treaty), incur (debts), enter into (partnership), lay (a wager), negotiate (a loan); concern, regard; call (on); **dit sal nooit − nie**, that won't do; **wat dit aangaan**, as regards this; **almal wat dit −**, all concerned; **wat my −**, as far as I am concerned; **wat kan dit my −?**, what business is that of mine?; **by iemand −**, call on someone, drop in at someone's house.
aangaande, as for (to), as regards, regarding, concerning, with regard to.

aangaap, (aange-), gape (stare) at; **'n afgrond het ons aange-,** an abyss was yawning in front of us.
aangalop(peer), (aange-), gallop along.
aangang, beginning, commencement.
aangebede, adored, idolised, worshipped.
aangebedene, (s), adored (one), idol.
aangebonde: kort -, short-tempered.
aangebore, inborn, innate, congenital (diseases), natural (taste), native (sagacity), hereditary (traits).
aangedaan, (-dane), affected; agitated.
aangee, (aangeë) n. pass (in football).
aangee, (aange-), give, hand, pass (on); record, register; allege (as reason); declare (goods); give notice of (birth), notify (a disease), state (particulars), set (the fashion); report (a matter); pass (in football); **jouself -,** give oneself up, report oneself (to the police); **iemand - by . . .,** lodge information against someone.
aangeebeweging, passing movement.
aangeër, -gewer, informer, reporter.
aangehuud, (-hude), related by marriage.
aangeklaagde, (-s), accused, defendant.
aangeklam, (de), slightly tipsy, squiffy.
aangekomene, (-s), newcomer, arrival.
aangeleë, adjacent, adjoining.
aangeleentheid, affair, matter; importance, moment.
aangeleer, (-de), acquired.
aangenaam, (-name), agreeable (person), pleasant (company, surprise), pleasing (sight), gratifying (result); acceptable (gift); **- (kennis te maak),** delighted (pleased) to meet you; **jou by iemand - maak,** make oneself agreeable to someone, ingratiate oneself with someone.
aangenaamheid, agreeableness, pleasantness; pleasure; comfort.
aangenome, a. accepted, received (opinion); assumed (name), adopted (child, country); taken on, contract (work); -!, agreed!, done!.
aangenome, conj. assuming, supposing.
aangesetene, (-s), guest (at dinner).
aangesien, considering, seeing (that), since.
aangesig, (-te), countenance, visage, face; **van - tot -,** face to face; **ondergang het hom in die - gestaar,** ruin stared him in the face.
aangeskote, vide **aangeklam.**
aangeskrewe, aangeskrywe, noted, reputed; **goed (sleg) - staan,** be in good (bad, ill) repute; **by iemand goed (sleg) - staan,** be in someone's good (bad) books; **'n - sirkel,** an escribed circle.
aangeslaan, (-slane), coated, blurred, tarnished; vide **aanslaan.**
aangeslote, aangesluit, vide **aansluit.**
aangespe(r), (aange-), buckle (gird) on.
aangeteken, (-de), noted; registered; **'n -de brief,** a registered letter; **- stuur,** send by registered post.
aangetroud, (-e), vide **aantrou.**
aangewese, (aangewys), dependent (up)on; obvious, right; **die - weg (middel),** the obvious (proper) way (means); **- (aangewys) op,** committed to; **op jouself - (aangewys),** thrown on one's own resources.
aangifte, declaration, notification, return; denunciation, information; **- doen van,** give notice of, declare (goods).
aangluur, (aange-), leer (peep) at; ogle.
aangolf, aangolwe, (aange-), roll on.
aangons, (aange-), buzz on (along).
aangooi, (aange-), cast (fling, throw) along (against, on), pass (throw) to; **'n baadjie -,** slip on a coat; **die geweer - (aan die skouer gooi),** aim (level) a gun,
aangord, (aange-), buckle (gird) on; brace up, take up; **die swaard -,** buckle (gird) on the sword; **die wapens -,** take up arms.
aangrens, (aange-), adjoin, border on.
aangrensend, (-e), adjacent, adjoining.
aangroei, (aange-), grow, increase, swell.
aangroeiing, accretion, growth, increase.
aangryns, (aange-), grin at; stare in the face.
aangryp, (aange-), catch (hold of), fasten upon (a pretext), grip; jump at (a chance); seize, take; fall upon (the enemy); affect (one's health); **met al twee hande -,** jump at.
aangrypend, (-e), gripping, touching.
aanhaak, (aange-), couple, fasten, hitch (hook) on (to); inspan.
aanhaal, (aange-), bring along, carry, fetch, draw tight(er); adduce, cite, instance (cases), set one's cap at (for),
aanhalerig, (-e), cajoling, coaxing, cuddlesome.
aanhalig, (-e), sweet, winning; coaxing.
aanhaling, (-e, -s), quotation; **'n afgesaagde -,** a hackneyed quotation, stock phrase, tag.
aanhalingstekens, inverted commas, quotation marks.
aanhang, n. adherents, clique, party; favour, support; **vind -,** find favour (support).
aanhang, (aange-), adhere (be attached, cling, stick) to; follow, hang on to, support; attach, tack on.
aanhanger, -ster, (-s), adherent, disciple, follower, partisan, supporter.
aanhangig, (-e), under consideration, pending; **'n saak - maak,** introduce a matter; institute legal proceedings; set a case down for trial; **- wees,** be pending.
aanhangmotor, outboard-motor.
aanhangsel, (-s), addendum, annexure, appendage, appendix (of a book), codicil (of a will), supplement.
aanhangwa, trailer, tow-car; side-car.
aanhanklik, (-e), affectionate, devoted.
aanhark, (aange-), rake along (up).
aanhê, (aangehad), have on; wear.
aanhef, n. beginning, exordium (of a speech), opening remarks; preamble.
aanhef, (aange-), begin, commence; raise, set up (a cry), strike up (a song).
aanheg, (aange-), affix, attach, fasten on.
aanhegsel, (-s), addendum, enclosure.
aanhegting, (-e, -s), affixture; attachment, fastening, sticking; insertion (bot.).
aanhegtingspunt, juncture.
aanhelp, (aange-), assist, help along (on).
aanhink, (aange-), hobble (limp) along.
aanhits, (aange-), egg on, incite, instigate, set on (a dog), stir up.
aanhitsing, (-e, -s), incitement, instigation.
aanhol, (aange-), run on (faster).
aanhoor, (aange-), give a hearing, listen to.
aanhoorder, hearer, listener; (pl.) audience.
aanhore: ten - van, in the hearing of.
aanhorige, (-s), relative; dependant.
aanhou, (aange-), continue, hold (on), insist, keep on, last, persevere, persist; arrest (a thief); detain (goods); hold, sustain (a note, tone), hold up (a train), keep (dog), keep (fire, light) burning, keep on (clothes); **- met,** keep on with, continue.
aanhoudelik, (-e), continual, repeated.
aanhoudend, (-e), constant, continuous, incessant, persistent.
aanhoudendheid, continuance, persistence.

aanhouding, continuance; detention; embargo, retention, seizure; **bevel tot –,** warrant (for arrest).
aanhouer, perseverer, sticker; – (aanhou) wen, dogged does it.
aanhuppel, (aange-), caper (hop, frisk, skip) along (on, faster).
aanja(ag), aanjae, (aange-), hurry (race, rush) on; drive (animals), urge on (a person); **skrik –,** frighten, strike terror into; **vrees –,** intimidate; **aangejaagde motor,** supercharged engine.
aanjaer, (-s), driver; inciter; supercharger.
aankant, (aange-): sig – teen, oppose.
aankap, (aange-), overreach, chafe (the fetlock).
aankla(ag), aanklae, (aange-): – **(weens),** accuse (of), charge (with).
aanklaer, -klaagster, accuser; prosecutor; open-bare –, public prosecutor.
aanklag, [-te(s)], accusation, charge, indictment; **'n – indien teen,** bring (prefer) a charge against; lodge a complaint against; **op – van,** on a charge of.
aanklam, (aange-), become moist, moisten.
aanklamp, (aange-), board (a vessel); accost, buttonhole; – **by,** hang (sponge) upon; make love to.
aankleding, clothing, get-up, make-up.
aanklee(d), (aange-), clothe, dress; get up.
aankleef, aanklewe, (aange-), adhere (stick) to.
aanklink, (aange-), rivet; clink (glasses).
aanklop, (aange-), knock (beat, rap) at the door; **by iemand – om geld,** apply to someone for money.
aanknoop, (aange-), button on (up), fasten (to); establish (relations), open (negotiations), begin; – **by,** join (link) up with; **'n praatjie –,** enter into a conversation.
aanknopingspunt, point of contact; starting point.
aankom, (aange-), come, come along (on, home, in); arrive, be born; begin; come on, improve; come round, call, drop in; matter; obtain, acquire, get at, touch; **die trein moet om vieruur –,** the train is due at four; **ek sien dit –,** I see it happen(ing); – **by,** arrive at; – **in,** arrive in; – **met,** come forward with; – **op,** arrive at; **dit kom nie daarop aan nie,** it does not matter; never mind!; **as dit daarop – (om),** if (when) it comes to a point; **waar dit op –,** the point at issue, what counts; **dit sal nie op geld – nie,** money is no object; **op tyd –,** arrive to time; **te laat –,** arrive (come in) late, be overdue; – **teen,** land (strike) against.
aankomeling, (-e), freshman, newcomer.
aankomend, (-e), arriving, coming; next; intending, prospective; **-e jaar,** next year; **'n -e onderwyser,** a prospective teacher; **die -e pos,** the incoming mail; **die -e gebeurtenisse,** coming events.
aankom(men)de, vide **aankomend.**
aankoms, arrival, coming (in).
aankondig, (aange-), announce, proclaim, notify, advertise; betoken, foreshadow, herald, predict, spell; write a notice of, review (a book).
aankondiger, (-s), announcer; compère; harbinger, reviewer; vide **aankondig.**
aankondiging, (-e, -s), announcement; notification; (press-)notice, review.
aankoop, n. acquisition, purchase.
aankoop, (aange-), acquire, purchase.
aankoopsom, purchase-price, -money.
aankoppel, (aange-), couple; join.
aankors, (aange-), crust, form a crust.
aankrui(e), (aange-), wheel, bring (in a wheelbarrow); struggle along.

aankruip, (aange-), crawl (creep) along; **teen iemand –,** nestle (cuddle) up to someone.
aankry, (aange-), get into, get on, (one's clothes), put on; get alight.
aankuier, (aange-), saunter (stroll), along; prolong a visit.
aankweek, n. cultivation; vide **aankweking.**
aankweek, (aange-), cultivate, grow, raise, rear; foster, nurture (feelings); train.
aankweking, cultivation, raising, nurture.
aankwispel, (aange-), wag on.
aankyk, (aange-), look at; **nie – nie,** cut (dead); **skeef –,** look askance at.
aanlaat, (aange-), leave on.
aanlag, (aange-), favour, smile at (upon); appeal to.
aanland, (aange-), arrive, land; **êrens –,** find oneself somewhere.
aanlanding, arrival, landing.
aanlap, (aange-), sew (tack) on; foist on.
aanlas, (aange-), add to; join on, lash on to; exaggerate (a story).
aanlê, aanheg, (aange-), aim, take aim; apply (a bandage, a standard); build; found, plan, fit up, install; draw up, make (a list); manage (things); moor, berth (a vessel); start (a collection); **dit so –,** contrive (manage) to; **dit verkeerd –,** set about the wrong way, **dit – op,** direct one's energies to, make it a point to; – **teen,** lie against, lean against; lay (place) against.
aanleer, (aange-), acquire, learn.
aanleg, n. arrangement, design, plan; installation, plant; ability, aptitude.
aanleg, (aange-), vide **aanlê.**
aanlegging, vide **aanleg,** n.
aanlegplaas, aanlêplaas, -plek; landing-place.
aanlei, (aange-), lead on; lead to.
aanleidende: – **oorsaak,** immediate (primary) cause; contributory cause.
aanleiding, (-e, -s), cause, inducement, motive, occasion; **na – van,** as a result of; in connection with; in pursuance of; with reference to; **sonder die minste –,** without the slightest provocation; – **gee tot,** give occasion (rise) to, lead to.
aanleg, (aange-), dilute, weaken.
aanlêplaas, -plek, vide **aanlegplaas.**
aanleun, (aange-): – **teen,** lean (recline) against; **jou iets laat –,** put up with a thing; take something as one's due.
aanliggend, (-e), contiguous (angle) adjacent (side).
aanlok, (aange-), attract, entice, tempt.
aanlokking, (-e, -s), allurement, attraction.
aanloklik, (-e), alluring, enticing, inviting, seductive, tempting.
aanloklikheid, alluringness, seductiveness.
aanloksel, (-s), bait, decoy, lure.
aanlonk, (aange-), smile at, ogle.
aanloop, n. patronage, run; preamble (of an act); rush (mil.); take-off; **'n – neem,** lead up to a subject; take off.
aanloop, (aange-), run (walk) along (on); call, drop in; – **teen,** collide with, run (up) against.
aanloophawe, port of call.
aanloopplank, spring-board.
aanlym, (aange-), glue on.
aanmaak, n. manufacture, preparation.
aanmaak, (aange-), manufacture, mix, prepare, light, make (up).
aanmaan, (aange-), admonish, warn; press (for payment); – **tot,** exhort (urge) to.
aanmaning, (-e, -s), exhortation; reminder; warning; relapse, recurrence, touch.

aanmars, advance, approach.
aanmarsjeer, (aange-), march on.
aanmatig, (aange-): hom –, arrogate to oneself, presume; pretend; usurp.
aanmatigend, (-e), arrogant, presumptuous.
aanmatiging, (-e, -s), arrogance, haughtiness, high-handedness, presumption.
aanmekaar, together; on end, consecutively; vide **mekaar.**
aanmekaar– ... vide **aaneen–** ... ; – bind, bind together; – **bly,** keep (remain, stick, hold) together; – **groei,** grow together; – **heg,** bind (stitch, sew, fasten, join) together; – **kleef, -klewe,** stick together, adhere (together); – **knoop,** tie together, button up (together); – **koppel,** couple (tie) together; – **las,** join together; dovetail, mortise, weld; – **plak,** stick together; glue (paste) together; – **raak,** start fighting, quarrel, go for one another; – **ry(e), ryg,** string (beads); baste (tack) together (clothes); – **voeg,** fit (join, piece, put) together.
aanmekaarhang, (aanmekaarge-), hang together; **van leuens –,** be a tissue of lies.
aanmekaarskryf, -skrywe, (aanmekaarge-), write as one word, join (letters).
aanmekaarspring, (aanmekaarge-), fight; vide **aanmekaar raak.**
aanmeld(e), (aange-), announce, report; **jou –,** come forward; apply; **iemand –,** announce a person; **jou laat –,** send in one's name (card).
aanmelding, (-e, -s), announcement, notice; application.
aanmeng, (aange-), mix; dilute, qualify.
aanmerk, (aange-), consider; observe, remark; note, mark; find fault with; **as 'n belediging –,** consider (as) an insult; **ek kan niks daarop – nie,** I have no fault to find with it; I have nothing to say to that.
aanmerking, (-e, -s), consideration; observation, remark; criticism, stricture, objection; **in – kom,** come into consideration; **in – neem,** take into consideration, make allowance for; **in – geneem (genome),** considering, in view of; **alles in – geneem (genome),** all things considered; **'n – maak,** make a remark; **–s maak op,** find fault with, criticize; **op- en –s,** suggestions and comments.
aanmerklik, (-e), considerable.
aanminlik, aanminnig, (-e), lovable, sweet.
aanmoedig, (aange-), encourage; give (moral) support to; give a fillip to (trade); tempt, lead on.
aanmoediging, (-e, -s), encouragement; countenance, (moral) support.
aanmonster, (aange-), enlist, sign on.
aanmonstering, enlistment.
aanmunt, (aange-), coin, mint, monetise.
aanmunting, coinage, coining, minting.
aannaai, (aange-), sew (stitch) on.
aanneem, (aange-, aangenome), accept, receive; take delivery of; adopt (name, child); assume (airs, a name, proportion), contract (a habit), take on (a colour); embrace (a faith); admit, confirm (as a member); assume, suppose, take for granted; agree to, carry (a motion), pass (a bill); undertake, contract for (a work); engage, take on (labourers); **'n voorstel –,** agree to a proposal; carry a motion; **g'n weiering – nie,** not take a refusal; **'n uitdaging –,** accept a challenge; **'n dreigende houding –,** adopt (take up) a menacing attitude; **as waar(heid) –,** accept as truth; **die notule –,** confirm the minutes; **ek wil – dat,** I take it for granted that; **algemeen word aange– dat,** it is generally believed that; **aange– dat,** vide **aangenome,** conj.
aanneemlik, (-e), acceptable; plausible.
aanneemlikheid, acceptability, reasonableness, plausibility, credibility.
aannemer, (-s), contractor; undertaker.
aanneming, acceptance; adoption; admission; confirmation (of church-members); passage (of a bill), carriage (of a motion); vide **aanneem.**
aannemingsdiens, confirmation-service.
aanpak, (aange-), seize (upon), catch hold of, grip; undertake; tackle, attack (an enemy); adhere to, form a crust; **'n onderwerp –,** tackle a subject; **verkeerd –,** set about (in) the wrong way; **ru –,** handle roughly; **die vuur –,** lay the fire.
aanpaksel, (-s), layer (of dirt, etc.), accretion tartar (of teeth).
aanpas, (aange-), fit (try) on (shoes); **jou – aan (by)** ..., adapt oneself to; **die straf aan die misdaad –,** suit the punishment to the crime.
aanpassing, (-e, -s), adaptation; accommodation; adjustment.
aanpassingsvermoë, adaptability.
aanpeiltoestel, homing device.
aanpiekel, (aange-), lug (drag) along.
aanplak, (aange-), paste (post) up.
aanplakbiljet, placard, poster, bill.
aanplakbord, notice-board, hoarding.
aanplant, n. planting; plantation.
aanplant, (aange-), plant, grow, cultivate; add to plantation.
aanplanting, vide **aanplant,** n.
aanpor, (aange-), jog up, spur on.
aanporring, (-e, -s), jogging, spurring on.
aanpraat, (aange-), talk into, persuade.
aanpresentasie, offer.
aanpresenteer, (aange-), offer.
aanprys, (aange-), extol, recommend, sing the praises of.
aanprysing, (-e, -s), (re)commendation.
aanraai, (aange-), advise; recommend.
aanraak, (aange-), touch.
aanrading, (-e, -s), advice; recommendation.
aanraking, (-e, -s), contact, touch; **in – bring met,** bring (put) into contact (in touch) with; **in – kom met,** come into contact with; **g'n punte van – hê nie,** have nothing in common.
aanrakingspunt, point of contact.
aanrand, (aange-), assault; hold up; attack.
aanrander, (-s), assailant, assaulter.
aanranding, (-e, -s), assault; hold-up.
aanreg, n. (kitchen-)dresser; slab.
aanreg, (aange-), dish up; prepare.
aanreik, (aange-), hand (on), pass, reach.
aanreken, (aange-), charge; **iemand iets –,** lay something to a person's charge; **as 'n verdienste –,** give credit for.
aanrig, (aange-), cause, bring about, do; **skade –,** cause (do) damage; **wat het jy aangerig?,** what have you been up to?
aanrigting, (-e, -s), doing, perpetration.
aanroei, (aange-), row along (on).
aanroep, (aange-), call, hail; challenge (a passer-by); invoke (God, the Muses).
aanroeping, hail(ing); invocation.
aanroer, (aange-), touch; mention, touch upon (a subject); hasten, hurry.
aanroering, mention.
aanrol, (aange-), roll along (on).
aanruis, (aange-), rustle on (along).
aanruk, (aange-), advance; **– op,** advance (march) upon, push on to.
aanrukking, advance, onward march.

aanry, (aange-), ride (drive) on (along); convey, transport; **êrens –,** pull up somewhere; **– teen,** crash (dash, run) into; **iemand –,** run into a person.
aanry(e), aanryg, (aange-), string (beads); baste, tack (a dress); lace (up) (boots).
aanryding, (-e, -s), collision, smash.
aans, by and by, presently; **– glo hy dit nog,** he may come to believe it.
aansê, (aange-), announce, inform.
aansegging, announcement, notification.
aanseil, (aange-), sail on (along).
aanset, aansit, (aange-), start (motor); sharpen, set (tools); incite, urge on.
aanset-, aansitmotor, starting-motor.
aansetter, aansitter, (-s), self-starter; rammer; inciter, instigator.
aansetting, starting; setting, sharpening.
aansien, n. appearance; complexion; prestige, respect; **dit gee die saak 'n ander –,** that puts another complexion on the matter; **in – wees,** be held in respect; **ten – van,** in (with) regard to; **van – ken,** know by sight; **'n man van –,** a man of consequence; **sonder – des persoons,** irrespective of persons.
aansien, (aange-), look at; consider, regard; **ek kan dit nie – nie,** I can't bear to look at it; **iemand – vir,** look upon someone as; take someone for; **met die nek –,** give the cold shoulder.
aansienlik, (-e), considerable; distinguished, notable; handsome, good-looking.
aansies = aans.
aansig, (-te), view, elevation.
aansit, (aange-), sit at table, sit down (to dinner); put on (a ring); add, join, sew on (buttons); set (dogs) on, incite, instigate; vide **aanset, (aange-).**
aansitmotor, vide **aansetmotor.**
aansittende, (-s), guest.
aansjou, (aange-), drag (lug) along.
aanskaf, (aange-), get, procure, purchase, provide oneself with, secure.
aanskaffing, getting, procuring.
aanskiet, (aange-), tumble into (clothes); **– op,** rush at (upon).
aanskoffel, (aange-), hoe on; dance on (along).
aanskommel, (aange-), waddle along; shuffle on.
aanskou, (het –), behold, view; **die lewenslig –,** see the light (of day).
aanskou(e)lik, (-e), clear; graphic (description); perceptible, visible; **–e onderwys,** object-teaching.
aanskou(e)likheid, clearness, vividness.
aanskouer, (-s), onlooker, spectator.
aanskouing, (-e, -s), observation.
aanskouingsles, object-lesson.
aanskouingsonderwys, object-teaching.
aanskroef, -skroewe, (aange-), screw on.
aanskry, (aange-), stride on (along).
aanskryf, -skrywe, (aange-, aangeskrewe), demand payment; summon; write on; vide **aangeskrewe.**
aanskrywing, (-e, -s), notification, letter of demand; summons, writ.
aanskuif, -skuiwe, (aange-), push (shove) on; come (go) shuffling along.
aanslaan, (aange-), touch, strike (a note); overreach, click (of a horse); present (arms); salute; start (of a motor); switch on (light); assess, rate (property, taxes); affix, post up (a notice); get blurred (steamy, thick) (of pane), get furred (of kettle, tongue), tarnish (of metal); knock on (in football); **– teen,** dash (strike) against; **die motor wil nie – nie,** the motor fails to start; **te hoog –,** overrate assess at too high a figure; **'n toon –,** strike a note; assume airs; **'n hoë toon –,** mount (ride) the high horse; **'n ander toon –,** sing another tune; **die regte toon –,** strike the right note (chord); **vir R10 –,** assess at R10.
aanslag, touch (piano); stroke; click; attempt, (bomb-)outrage; assessment; blacking; sediment; fur, furring, scale (in kettle); fur (on tongue); knock-on (in football); **'n – op iemand se lewe doen,** make an attempt on someone's life.
aanslagbiljet, notice of assessment.
aansleep, (aange-), drag (lug) along.
aanslib, (aange-), accrete, be deposited; silt (up).
aanslibbing, (-e, -s), accretion, deposit.
aanslibsel, (-s), deposit, silt.
aanslof, (aange-), shuffle along.
aansluip, (aange-), sneak along, approach stealthily; **– op,** steal upon.
aansluit, (aange-), connect, link; enrol, join; unite; **die geledere –,** close the ranks; **– by,** follow; join; link up with (a railway); **–** met, connect with, put through to (teleph.), link up with (train-service).
aansluiting, joining, junction, linking-up, connection, affiliation; **– kry,** get a connection; **in – aan,** with reference (further) to; **in – met,** relayed from (radio).
aansluitingspunt, point of junction.
aansluitstuk, adapter, nipple.
aanslyp, (aange-), sharpen.
aansmee(d), (aange-), forge (weld) on.
aansmeer, (aange-), smear (over); apply, put on (ointment); fob off (on).
aansmyt, (aange-), fling (throw) against (towards); slip (throw, whip) on (clothes).
aansnel, (aange-), hurry (run, rush) along (on).
aansnor, (aange-), whir (whiz) along (on).
aansny, (aange-), cut into.
aansoek, (-e), application, request, solicitation; proposal; **– doen om (vir) 'n betrekking,** apply for a post; **– doen om haar hand,** make a proposal (an offer of marriage).
aansolder, (aange-), solder on.
aanspeld(e), (aange-), pin on.
aanspoel, (aange-), drift (wash) ashore, wash up; be cast (washed) ashore (up).
aanspoeling, flotsam, jetsam; alluvium.
aanspoor, (aange-), spur on, urge on.
aansporing, (-e, -s), encouragement; incitement; incentive; stimulus.
aanspraak, claim, title; company; **– maak op iets,** claim, lay claim to; **sonder – wees,** be without company.
aanspraaklik(heid), vide **aanspreeklik(heid).**
aanspreek, (aange-), address, speak to; accost; **nog – bottel –,** crack another bottle; **sy kapitaal –,** draw on one's capital; **iemand om 'n skuld –,** dun a person.
aanspreeklik, (-e), accountable, answerable, liable, responsible; **– hou vir,** hold responsible for; **jou nie – hou nie,** take no responsibility.
aanspreeklikheid, liability, responsibility.
aanspring, (aange-), come (go) bounding (leaping, jumping, rushing) along.
aanstaan, (aange-), please, like, suit; stand ajar; **dit staan my nie aan nie,** I do not like it.
aanstaande, (-s), n. fiancé(e), intended.
aanstaande, a. next (week); (forth)coming (elections), approaching (marriage), prospective (father-in-law), impending (changes), imminent (danger); expectant (mother); **Kersfees is –,** Christmas is at hand.

aanstaar, (aange-), gaze (stare) at, stare in the face.
aanstalte(s), preparation(s); **- maak,** get ready, prepare.
aanstap, (aange-), step out, mend one's pace; walk on (along).
aansteek, (aange-), pin on (a flower), put (stick) on (a feather), put on (a ring); light (a lamp), kindle (a fire); set fire to; infect; get infection; **dit steek aan,** it is infectious.
aansteeklik, (-e), catching, infectious.
aansteeklikheid, infectiousness.
aansteking, kindling, lighting; infection.
aanstel, (aange-), appoint (to a post); behave, pretend; give oneself airs, put on; **hom baie -,** give oneself airs; **hom siek -,** pretend illness.
aansteller, (-s), pretender; swank.
aanstellerig, (-e), affected, full of airs.
aanstellerigheid, affectation, airs.
aanstellery, vide **aanstellerigheid.**
aanstelling, (-e, -s), appointment.
aanstellings, vide **aanstellerigheid.**
aansterk, (aange-), recuperate, recover.
aanstewen, (aange-), sail along (on); **- op,** bear down upon, make for.
aanstig, (aange-), instigate, set on foot.
aanstigting: op - van, at the instigation of.
aanstip, (aange-), jot down; touch (on).
aanstoker, agitator, firebrand, instigator.
aanstons, presently; vide **aans.**
aanstook, (aange-), kindle (fire), incite (to).
aanstoom, (aange-), steam on (along).
aanstoot, n. offence; **- gee,** give offence; **- neem,** take offence.
aanstoot, (aange-), push; jog, nudge; bestir oneself; clink (glasses).
aanstootlik, (-e), objectionable, offensive.
aanstootlikheid, indecency, offensiveness.
aanstorm, (aange-), charge (rush) on (along).
aanstreep, (aange-), underline; straggle on (along).
aanstrik, (aange-), fasten with a knot.
aanstrompel, (aange-), stumble (hobble) on (along).
aanstroom, (aange-), flow (rush, stream) on (along).
aanstruikel, (aange-), stumble along.
aanstryk, (aange-), walk (toddle) along (on).
aanstuur, (aange-), pass (send) on, forward to; **- aan (na),** forward (consign) to; **- op,** head (make) for, aim at.
aansuiwer, (aange-), pay (off), settle.
aansukkel, (aange-), struggle (jog) along.
aansweef, -swewe, (aange-), float (glide) along (on).
aansweep, (aange-), egg (goad) on, incite.
aanswel, (aange-), swell out, rise; increase.
aanswem, (aange-), swim on (along).
aanswewe, vide **aansweef.**
aanswoeg, (aange-), struggle along.
aansyn, being, existence, life; **(die) - gee aan,** give birth to, call into existence.
aantal, (-le), number.
aantas, (aange-), touch; affect; attack; **iemand in sy eer -,** injure a person's reputation; **sy gesondheid -,** affect (impair) his health; **die vyand -,** attack the enemy.
aantasbaar, (-bare), assailable.
aanteel, n. breed(ing); increase; **om die helfte van die -,** for half of the offspring.
aanteel, (aange-), breed, rear; increase.
aanteelmerrie, brood-mare.
aanteelvee, breeding cattle.
aanteken, (aange-), note down; mark; register (a letter); record, enter; score (a try); hoër be-

roep -, appeal; **protes - teen,** enter a protest against.
aantekening, note, annotation, record; **- hou van,** keep a record of; **-e maak,** take notes.
aantekeningboek, notebook; scribbler.
aantik, (aange-), knock (rap, tap) at (the door); tick off; clink (glasses).
aantog, approach, advance; **in -,** be approaching (advancing, coming on).
aantoon, (aange-), show; demonstrate, prove; indicate; **aantonende wys(e),** indicative (mood).
aantrap, (aange-), pedal along (on).
aantree, (aange-), fall in(to) line, line up.
aantref, (aange-), meet (with), find, come across (upon); stumble upon.
aantrek, (aange-), draw, pull; attract, appeal to; tighten, brace; put on (clothes), dress; **jou iets -,** take something to heart; take offence at something.
aantrekking, attraction; gravitation.
aantrekkingskrag, (power of) attraction, pull, gravity; appeal.
aantreklik, (-e), attractive; sensitive.
aantreklikheid, charm; sensitiveness.
aantrippel, (aange-), trip (amble) on (along).
aantrou, (aange-), obtain by marriage; **aangetroude familie,** relations by marriage; **'n aangetroude seun,** a son-in-law.
aantyg, (aange-), impute (to), accuse of.
aantyging, (-e, -s), imputation.
aanvaar, (aange-), sail along; **- op,** head (make) for; **- teen,** collide with.
aanvaar, (het -), set out on, begin; enter upon; accept (a position); face (the consequences).
aanvaarbaar, (-bare), acceptable.
aanvaarding, acceptance, accession, assumption, entrance upon.
aanval, n. attack, charge, assault; fit, stroke (of paralysis), bout, touch (of malaria); **tot die - oproep,** call to arms.
aanval, (aange-), attack, charge, assail; fall to (at table).
aanvallend, (-e), aggressive, offensive; **- optree,** take the offensive.
aanvaller, (-s), assailant, aggressor.
aanvallig, (-e), charming, lovely, sweet.
aanvalligheid, charm, loveliness.
aanvalsein, signal of attack.
aanvang, n. beginning, commencement, start; **'n - neem,** begin, commence; **by die -,** at the beginning (start).
aanvang, (aange-), begin, commence, start; **met hom kan 'n mens niks - nie,** he is utterly useless (intractable); **wat moet ek nou -?,** what am I to do now?; **wat het jy weer aangevang?,** what have you been up to again?
aanvangsalaris, commencing salary.
aanvangskapitaal, initial capital.
aanvanklik, (-e), initial, original; elementary.
aanvanklik, adv. at first, originally.
aanvaring, collision.
aanvat, (aange-), catch (get, lay, take) hold of, seize; start, begin, undertake.
aanvegbaar, (-bare), assailable, challengeable, contentious.
aanvegting, (-e, -s), fit, impulse; temptation.
aanverwant, (-e), allied, related.
aanverwantskap, affinity, relationship.
aanvleg, (aange-), plait on (to), braid on.
aanvlieg, (aange-), fly on (along); **- (op),** fly at, rush upon.
aanvloei, (aange-), flow along (on).
aanvly, (aange-), nestle (snuggle) against.
aanvoeg, (aange-), add, join; **-ende wys(e),** subjunctive (mood).

aanvoeging, addition.
aanvoegsel, addendum.
aanvoeg, (aange-), feel, touch; experience; sense, be attuned to.
aanvoeling, touch; experience; attunement.
aanvoer, n. supply.
aanvoer, (aange-), bring, convey; supply; import; advance, allege (reasons); raise (objections); adduce (proof); cite (a case); lead, command (an army), captain (a team); **ter verontskuldiging** –, plead in excuse.
aanvoerder, (-s), commander, leader.
aanvoering, command, leadership.
aanvoerpyp, feed-pipe.
aanvoor, (aange-), begin, start.
aanvra(ag), (aange-), apply for, request.
aanvraag, n. demand; request, requisition; **op – te toon**, to be shown on demand.
aanvraagformulier, application form.
aanvraer, applicant; caller (on teleph.).
aanvul, (aange-), replenish (one's stock), eke out (a meal); make up, make good; complete, supplement.
aanvulling, supplement, completion, amplification; replenishment.
aanvullingseksamen, supplementary examination.
aanvuring, incitement, stimulation.
aanvuur, (aange-), fire (the imagination), incite, inflame, inspire, stimulate.
aanwaai, (aange-), be blown towards; arrive at; **by iemand aange– kom**, blow in at someone's place.
aanwaggel, (aange-), reel (stagger, totter) along (on).
aanwakker, (aange-), animate, rouse; fan (a flame); stimulate, liven up; supercharge.
aanwakkering, fanning, stimulation.
aanwandel, (aange-), vide **aanloop**.
aanwas, n. growth, increase (of population); accretion; rise; deposit.
aanwas, (aange-), grow, increase; rise.
aanwen, (aange-), contract (a habit), fall into the habit of, get accustomed to; reclaim (land) increase.
aanwend, (aange-), apply, employ, take (pains); appropriate (money); bring into play; **'n poging –**, make an attempt; **alles –**, use every means.
aanwending, application, employment, use.
aanwensel, (-s), habit.
aanwerf, **-werwe**, (aange-), enlist, recruit.
aanwerk, (aange-), sew on (a button); work faster.
aanwerwing, enlistment, recruitment.
aanwesig, (-e), present; on hand.
aanwesiges, (pl.), those present.
aanwesigheid, presence; existence.
aanwinging, reclamation (of land).
aanwins, acquisition, asset; gain, profit.
aanwip, (aange-), call round, drop in.
aanwys, (aange-), indicate, point out; assign, allocate (money); read, register; **op mekaar aangewys**, thrown on each other's society; vide **aangewese**.
aanwysend, (-e), demonstrative (pronoun).
aanwyser, indicator; index, exponent (alg.).
aanwysing, direction, instruction; clue, hint; assignment, indication; index.
aanwysstok, pointer.
aanyl, (aange-), hurry (rush, tear) on (along).
aap, (ape), ape; monkey; **laat die – uit die mou**, let the cat out of the bag; **jy lyk 'n mooi –**, you look like doing it; **dit weet die – se stert**, everybody knows that.
aapagtig, (-e), apish, monkeyish.

aapkliere, monkey-glands.
aapmens, ape-man, pithecanthropus.
aapstert, monkey's tail; jackanapes!
aapstuipe: die – kry, fly into a passion.
aar, (are), ear (of corn); vein (in body, etc.); nerve (in leaf); underground watercourse; lode, seam (of ore).
aarbei, (-e), strawberry.
aarbeikonfyt, strawberry-jam.
aarbloed, venous blood.
aard, n. character, disposition, nature; kind, sort; **in die – van die saak**, in the nature of things; **uit die – van die saak**, from the nature of the case, naturally; **niks van die – nie**, nothing of the kind; **van allerlei –**, of all kinds (sorts); **driftig van – (geaardheid)**, of a hasty temper, quick-tempered.
aard, (ge-), thrive, get on well; **– na**, take after.
aardbaan, orbit of the earth.
aardbewing, (-e, -s), earthquake.
aardbewingsleer, seismology.
aardbewingsmeter, seismometer.
aardbewoner, dweller on earth, mortal.
aardbodem, earth, face (surface) of the earth.
aardbol, (terrestial) globe, the earth.
aarde, earth; mould, soil; **in goeie – val**, fall on good ground; **ter – bestel**, commit to the earth, inter; **hemel en – beweeg**, leave no stone unturned.
aard(e)draad, earth-wire, ground-wire.
aardgees, gnome, earth-spirit, goblin.
aardewerk, earthenware, crockery.
aardig, (-e), nice, pleasant; queer, disagreeable; **'n –e meisie**, a nice girl; **– voel**, feel queer (giddy, sick).
aardigheid, fun, joke, pleasantry, treat; **vir die –**, for fun, in sport.
aardjie; **'n – na sy vaartjie**, a chip of the old block; like father, like son.
aardkors, earth's crust, lithosphere.
aardkunde, geology.
aardkundige, (-s), geologist.
aardmannetjie, brownie, gnome, goblin; meercat.
aardmeetkunde, geodesy.
aardolie, petroleum, rock-oil.
aardoppervlakte, surface of the earth.
aardryk, earth; **die – nutteloos beslaan**, not be worth one's keep (salt).
aardrykskunde, geography.
aardrykskundige, (-s), geographer.
aards, (-e), earthly, terrestrial, worldly.
aardsgesind, (-e), worldly-minded.
aardsgesindheid, worldly-mindedness.
aardskok, earthquake-shock.
aardskudding, earth-tremor.
aardstorting, earthfall.
aardtrilling, earth-tremor.
aardverskuiwing, landslide, landslip.
aardwerke, (pl.), earthworks.
aardwolf, aard-wolf, striped hyena.
aars, (-e), arse, anus, rectum.
aarsel, (ge-), hang back, hesitate, waver.
aarselend, (-e), hesitating, wavering.
aarseling, (-e), hesitation, vacillation.
aartappel, ertappel, potato.
aartappelboer, potato-grower.
aartappelkop, blockhead, numskull.
aartappelland, potato-field.
aartappelloof, potato-leaves, -stalks.
aartappelmoer, seed-potato.
aartappeloes, potato-crop.
aartappelsak, potato-bag.
aartappelsiekte, potato-blight.
aartappelskil, potato-peel, -skin, -jacket.
aartappelskyfies, potato chips.

aartappelslaai, potato-salad.
aarts- . . ., arch-, consummate, regular.
aartsbedrieër, -bedrieger, arrant rogue, regular cheat.
aartsbisdom, archbishopric.
aartsbiskop, archbishop, primate.
aartsbiskoplik, (-e), archiepiscopal.
aartsdeken, archdeacon.
aartsdom, fearfully (very) stupid.
aartsengel, archangel.
aartshertog, archduke.
aartshertogin, archduchess.
aartsleuenaar, arrant (consummate) liar.
aartsluiaard, inveterate idler.
aartspriester, archpriest, high priest.
aartsskelm, -skurk, arrant knave.
aartsvader, patriarch.
aartsvaderlik, (-e), patriarchal.
aartsvyand, arch-enemy.
aas, (ase), n. ace (in cards).
aas, n. bait, carrion, prey; **rooi –**, red bait,
aas, (ge-), feed (prey) on.
aasblom, carrion-flower, toad-plant.
aasvoël, vulture; glutton.
aasvretend, (-e), necrophagous.
ab, (-te), abbot.
abacus, (abaci), abakus, (-se), abacus.
abattoir, (-s), abattoir, slaughter-house.
abba, (ge-), carry (a child) on one's back.
abba-vader, abba-father.
abc, abc, alphabet; **die – van**, the first principles of.
abc-boek, abc-book, primer.
abdikasie, abdication.
abdikeer, (ge-), abdicate.
abdis, (-se), abbess.
abdy, (-e), abbey, monastery.
abelspel, (mediaeval) secular drama.
aberrasie, (-s), aberration.
Abessiniër, (-s), Abyssinian.
abjater, (-s), scamp, urchin.
ablatief, (-tiewe), ablative.
ablaut, ablaut, vowel-gradation.
abnormaal, (-male), abnormal.
abnormaliteit, (-e), abnormality.
abnormiteit, (-e), abnormity.
abominabel, (-e), abominable.
abonneer, (ge-), subscribe to; **ge– wees op 'n koerant**, subscribe to a paper.
abonnement, (-e), subscription.
aborsie, abortion.
abrakadabra, abracadabra.
abrup, (-te), abrupt.
absensie, (-s), absence; non-attendance.
absent, opsent, absent; absent-minded.
absenteer, (ge-); jou –, absent oneself.
abses, (-se), abscess.
absint, absinthe, wormwood.
absolusie, absolution.
absoluut, (-lute), a. absolute.
absoluut, opsluit, adv. absolutely; **nie**, not at all, by no means.
absorbeer, (ge-), absorb; **–berende middel**, absorbent.
absorpsie, absorption.
abstraheer, (ge-), abstract.
abstrak, (-te), abstract; abstracted.
abstraksie, abstraction.
abstraktheid, abstractness.
absurd, (-e), absurd, preposterous.
absurditeit, (-e), absurdity.
abuis, error, mistake, oversight, slip; **per –**, by mistake, through an oversight.
abusieflik, -iewelik, by mistake.
Achille(u)s, Achilles.

Achilleshiel, Achilles' heel.
achromaties, (-e), achromatic.
activa, (pl.) assets.
adamsappel, Adam's apple.
adamsklere, -kostuum, -pak, Nature's garb.
adamsvy(g), Adam's fig.
adaptasie, adaptation.
adapteer, (ge-), adapt.
addendum, (-da), addendum.
adder, (-s), adder, viper; **'n – aan sy bors koester**, cherish (nourish) a viper in one's bosom.
adder(e)gebroed(sel), viperous brood.
addisioneel, (-nele), additional.
adekwaat, (-kwate), adequate.
adel, n. nobility; **van –**, of noble birth.
adel, (ge-), raise to the peerage; ennoble.
adelaar, (-s), eagle; vide **arend**.
adelaarsblik, eagle-eye; **met –**, eagle-eyed.
adelaarsnes, eyrie, eyry.
adelboek, peerage.
adelbors, midshipman; naval cadet.
adeldom, nobility.
adelheerskappy, aristocracy.
adellik, (-e), high-born, noble; titled.
adelikheid, nobleness.
adelstand, nobility, peerage; **tot die – verhef**, raise to the peerage.
adem, n., vide **asem**, n.
adem, (ge-), emanate, breathe.
ademhaling, vide **asemhaling**.
ademloos, (-lose), breathless.
ademtog, breath, gasp; respiration.
adenoïed, (-e), adenoïde, (-s), adenoid.
adep, (-te), adept.
ader- . . ., vide **aar- . . .**
adhesie, adhesion.
adieu, (-'s), good-bye.
adjektief, (-tiewe), adjective.
adjektiwies, (-e), adjectival.
adjudant, (-e), adjutant, aide-de-camp.
adjunk, (-te), adjunct, assistant, deputy.
administrasie, administration.
administrateur, (-s), administrator.
administratief, (-tiewe), administrative.
administreer, (ge-), administer, manage.
admiraal, (-s), admiral.
admiraalskip, flagship.
admiraliteit, admiralty.
admissie, admission.
admissie-eksamen, entrance-examination.
adolessensie, adolescence.
adolessent, (-e), adolescent.
adoons, monkey, jacko; ugly.
adopsie, adoption.
adopteer, (ge-), adopt.
adorasie, adoration, veneration.
adoreer, (-s), adore.
adoreerder, (-s), adorer, admirer.
adres, (-se), address; memorial; **per –**, care of; **dit is aan jou –**, that is meant (intended) for you.
adresboek, directory.
adressant, (-e), petitioner; sender.
adresseer, (ge-), address, direct, label.
adresverandering, change of address.
adventis, (-te), adventist.
adverbiaal, (-iale), adverbial.
adverbium, (-bia), adverb.
adverteer, (ge-), advertise.
advertensie, (-s), advertisement; announcement.
advertensieburo, advertising-agency.
advertensiekoste, cost of advertising.
advies, advice; opinion (of doctor, lawyer); **op – van**, on the advice of.
adviseer, (ge-), advise.

adviserend, (-e), advisory; consulting.
adviseur, (-s), adviser.
advokaat, (-ate), advocate, barrister, counsel; **vir – studeer**, study law; **'n – raadpleeg**, take legal advice.
advokatestreek, lawyer's trick.
aërodinamies, aerodynamic.
aërodinamika, aerodynamics.
aërostaat, aerostat.
af, off; down; from; **– en toe**, now and then; **goed (sleg) – wees**, be well (badly) off; **daarvan – wees**, have it off one's hands; **hy is van sy vrou –**, he is divorced; **op goeie geluk –**, trusting to luck; **van 50c –**, from 50c upwards; **van 1 April –**, from the 1st of April; **van die koning –**, from the king downwards; **van daardie dag –**, from that day onwards; **van my jeug –**, from my youth up; **van die pad –**, off the road; **van die eerste eeu –**, from the first century on.
afbaan, (afge-), mark off (out).
afbabbel, (afge-), talk over, discourse on.
afbaken, (afge-), mark (stake) out; delimit; define.
afbakening, demarcation, delimitation.
afbars, (afge-), burst (crack) off.
afbedel, (afge-), obtain by begging.
afbeeld, (afge-), depict, picture, portray.
afbeelding, (-e, -s), depiction, portrayal, portrait(ure), picture, representation.
afbeen, cripple(d).
afbeitel, (afge-), chip off (with a chisel).
afbel, (afge-), ring off.
afbestel, (het –), countermand; cancel.
afbetaal, (het –), pay off; pay on account.
afbetaling, payment; instalment; **op –**, on account.
afbetalingstelsel, instalment-system.
afbeul, (afge-), slave, work to death.
afbeur, (afge-), lift (drag) off.
afbid, (afge-), invoke, obtain by prayer, deprecate (God's judgment).
afbind, (afge-), tie up, ligate, underbind.
afblaas, (afge-), blow off.
afblok, (afge-), **jou –**, grind.
afbly, (afge-), keep off, leave alone.
afborsel, (afge-), brush (off), brush up.
afbou, (afge-), finish (building), complete.
afbraak, demolition; rubbish.
afbrand, (afge-), burn down; be burnt down.
afbreek, (afge-), break off, snap; break (a journey), divide (a word); interrupt (a story); sever (connections); pull down, demolish (a building), take down (scaffolding), strike (tents); run down (a book); break off, stop (short).
afbreking, demolition; vide **afbreek**.
afbreuk, damage, injury; **– doen aan**, be detrimental to, detract (derogate) from; **die vyand – doen**, inflict losses on the enemy; **sonder – te doen aan**, without detracting from.
afbring, (afge-), bring down, lead off; reduce; **iemand van iets –**, dissuade someone; **van die goeie pad (weg) –**, lead astray; **die gewig –**, reduce.
afbrokkel, (afge-), crumble away (off).
afbuie, **-buig**, (afge-), bend down, turn aside.
afbuitel, (afge-), tumble down.
afbyt, (afge-), bite off; clip (one's words); **die spit –**, bear the brunt.
afdaal, (afge-), come (go) down, descend; **– tot**, condescend to; stoop to.
afdak, lean-to, penthouse, shed.
afdaling, descent; condescension.
afdam, (afge-), dam up.

afdank, (afge-), dismiss, discharge; disband (troops); cast off (clothes); discard.
afdanking, (-e, -s), discharge, dismissal.
afdeel, (afge-), divide; graduate.
afdek, (afge-), clear (the table); cope (a wall).
afdeling, (-e, -s), division, portion, section, detachment; compartment; department; floor, ward; partition; **– ruitery**, body of horse; **– soldate**, detachment of soldiers.
afdelingsbestuurder, system-manager.
afdelingschef, **-hoof**, head of department.
afdelingsekretaris, departmental secretary.
afdelingsraad, divisional council.
afding, (afge-), bargain, haggle; **op iemand se verdienste –**, detract from someone's merits.
afdoen, (afge-, afgedaan), take off (clothes); detract from; settle (a business), get through (an amount of work); **dit doen daar niks aan toe of af nie**, that does not alter the case; **dit is afgedaan**, that is a thing of the past; **die saak is afge-**, the matter is settled; **as afgedaan beskou**, consider settled (closed).
afdoende, conclusive (proof), decisive (reply); effective (measures).
afdoening, settlement; disposal.
afdra, (afge-), carry down; wear out (clothes).
afdraai, (afge-), turn off (a tap); wring (neck); run off, show (a film); play (a record); rattle off (one's prayers); branch off (a road).
afdraand, **afdraans**, adv. downhill; **dit gaan – met hom**, he is on the downhill path.
afdraand(e), (afdraande(s), afdraans), decline, declivity, slope.
afdraf, **-drawwe**, (afge-), trot down (off).
afdreig, (afge-), extort, blackmail.
afdrink, (afge-); **dit –**, have a drink and be friends.
afdro(ë), **-droog**, (afge-), dry, wipe off.
afdruip, (afge-), drip (trickle) down; slink (sneak) away; gutter.
afdruk, n. copy, reproduction; print; imprint.
afdruk, (afge-), print, reproduce; impress; press down.
afdrukraam, printing-frame.
afdruksel, (-s), impression, print, mark.
afdrup(pel), (afge-), drip (trickle) down.
afdryf, **-drywe**, (afge-), drift (float) down (away, off); blow over.
afdryfsel, flotsam, jetsam; vide **opdrifsel**.
afdwaal, (afge-), stray; wander from (one's subject), ramble, digress; go astray, err.
afdwaling, digression; aberration; error.
afdwing, (afge-), extort, wring from; compel (admiration), command (respect); enforce (obedience).
afeet, (afge-), browse (eat) off.
aférese, **aphaeresis**, aphaeresis.
affektasie, affectation, mannerism.
affekteer, (ge-), affect.
affêre, (-s), affair, business, matter.
affiliasie, affiliation.
affilieer, (ge-), affiliate.
affodil, (-le), daffodil, asphodel, Lent lily.
affront, (-e), affront.
affronteer, (ge-), affront, insult.
affuit, (-e), gun-carriage.
afgaan, (afge-), go down; leave separate; **– op**, make for; depend (rely) on; **reg op die doel –**, go straight to the point; **die geweer sal –**, the gun will go off; **daar gaan niks van af nie**, there's no denying that; **-de op sy woorde**, judging by his words.
afgebroke, broken (words); intermittent.
afgedaan, vide **afdoen**.
afgedankste, confounded, severe.

afgee, (afge-), deliver, hand over (money); give up (a ticket); surrender (documents); give out (a smell); give off (smoke); stain; come off (of a colour; **jou – met iets**, meddle with something; **jou – met iemand**, associate with someone; **– op iemand**, run down someone.
afgeknot, (-te), maimed; stunted; topped.
afgeleë, distant, far-off, remote, out-of-the-way, outlying, off the beaten track.
afgeleef, (-de), decrepit, worn out.
afgelei, (-de), derived.
afgeleide, (-s), derivative.
afgelope, finished; ended, past (year).
afgemat, (-te), fagged, tired (worn) out.
afgematheid, exhaustion, fatigue.
afgemete, measured; stiff, formal.
afgemetenheid, formality, stiffness.
afgepas, (-te), measured (paces); apportioned (helpings); **in -te geld betaal**, pay the exact sum of money.
afgeplat, (-te), flattened; **-te bol**, spheroid.
afgerand, (-e), skirted (wool).
afgerem, (-de), worn out, fagged, jaded.
afgerond, (-e), rounded (narrative); round sum (figure); **'n -e geheel**, a whole in itself.
afgesaag, (-de), hackneyed, trite, stale.
afgesant, (-e), ambassador, messenger.
afgesien: – van, notwithstanding, apart from.
afgeskeidene, (-s), dissenter; member of the Reformed Church.
afgeskeidenheid, privacy, seclusion.
afgeskeie, separate(d); secluded, private; **– Kerk**, Reformed Church; **– van**, apart from.
afgesloof, (-de), fagged (out), jaded.
afgeslote, closed (in); secluded.
afgeslotenheid, seclusion.
afgesonder(d), (-de), isolated, lonely, retired, secluded, remote.
afgespe(r), (afge-), unbuckle, unclasp.
afgestomp, (-te), truncate; blunted, dulled.
afgestorwe, deceased, dead.
afgestorwene, (-s), the deceased (departed).
afgetob, (-de), harassed, weary, worn out.
afgetrokke, abstract; absent-minded; **– selfstandige naamwoord**, abstract noun.
afgetrokkenheid, absence of mind, detachment; abstractness.
afgevaardigde, (-, -s), delegate, deputy.
afgevallene, (-s), apostate, renegade.
afgewerk, (-te), fagged, tired; finished.
afgiet, (afge-), pour (strain) off; cast mould.
afgietsel, (-s), cast copy, mould.
afgietseldiertjies, infusoria.
afgifte, delivery; issue.
afglip, (afge-), slip down (off).
afglooi, (afge-), slope (down), shelve.
afgly, (afge-), glide (slide, slip) down (off).
afgod, idol; **'n – maak van**, idolize.
afgodediens, **afgodery**, idolatry.
afgodies, (-e), idolatrous.
afgodsbeeld, idol, image.
afgodsdienaar, idolater.
afgooi, (afge-), throw down (off); unseat.
afgord, (afge-), unbuckle.
afgraaf, **afgrawe**, (afge-), dig down; level.
afgraas, (afge-), browse, graze.
afgrond, abyss, chasm, gulf, precipice; **in die – stort**, ruin (wreck).
afgrou, (afge-), snub, snap (snarl) at.
afgryslik, (-e), ghastly, hideous, horrible.
afgryslikheid, ghastliness, horribleness.
afguns, envy, jealousy, spite.
afgunstig, (-e), envious, jealous, spiteful.
afhaak, (afge-), unhook; uncouple, detach, disconnect (railway-carriages); let go, let rip; get married.
afhaal, (afge-), bring (fetch) down; call for, meet; insult (a person).
afhaalwa, collecting-van.
afhaar, (afge-), depilate, unhair; string (beans).
afhak, (afge-), chop off, cut off, lop off.
afhandel, (afge-), conclude, settle.
afhandeling, dispatch, termination.
afhandig: – maak, filch, pilfer, trick out of relieve of.
afhang, (afge-), hang down, droop; depend (turn) on.
afhanklik, (-e), dependent; **– maak van**, make conditional on.
afhanklikheid, dependence.
afhap, (afge-), bite off.
afhaspel, (afge-), rattle off; scamp, bungle.
afheg, (afge-), cast off (knitting).
afhein, (afge-), fence in.
afhel, (afge-), slant, slope down, shelve.
afhelp, (afge-), help down (off); relieve of.
afhol, (afge-), rush (tear) down.
afhou, (afge-), keep off (from); **regs –**, turn to the right.
afhou, (afge-), = **afhak**.
afja(ag), **afjae**, (afge-), drive (chase) away.
afjak, (-ke), n. affront, insult; rebuff.
afjak, (afge-), snub, insult, rate, scold.
afjakker, (afge-), overwork; wear out.
afkabbel, (afge-), wash away; ripple down.
afkalf, **-kalwe(r)**, (afge-), cave (calve) in.
afkam, (afge-), comb off; run down.
afkantel, (afge-), topple (tumble) down.
afkap, (afge-), chop (cut, lop) off, cut (hew) down; abbreviate (a word).
afkappingsteken, apostrophe.
afkeer, n. dislike, aversion, repugnance.
afkeer, n. side-furrow.
afkeer, (afge-), avert, turn away; parry, ward off (a blow); turn aside (water).
afkeurig: – van, averse to.
afkeur, (afge-), disapprove; reject; ban, scrap; **jou – end uitlaat oor**, comment adversely upon.
afkeurenswaardig, (-e), blameworthy, censurable, objectionable, reprehensible.
afkeuring, censure, disapproval; rejection; **'n mosie van –**, a vote of censure.
afklap, (afge-), miss fire (of percussion-cap).
afklim, (afge-), climb down, descend.
afkloof, **afklowe**, (afge-), split (wood).
afklop, (afge-), flick (dust) away, dust (clothes); touch wood; pop off; peg out.
afklouter, (afge-), clamber (shin) down.
afkna(ag), **afknae**, (afge-), gnaw off.
afknabbel, (afge-), nibble (at); browse.
afknap, (afge-), snap off.
afknibbel, (afge-), nibble off; haggle.
afknip, (afge-), cut (snip) off; trim, flick off (ash of cigar); cut, crop (hair).
afknot, (afge-), lop off; truncate (a cone).
afknou, (afge-), gnawoff; hurt, bully.
afknyp, (afge-), pinch off.
afkoel, (afge-), cool (down); chill, refrigerate; calm down.
afkoeling, cooling, refrigeration; calming down.
afkom, (afge-), come down; **– van**, get off; get rid of; get out of (an engagement); be derived (descended) from; **daarvan –**, get off (escape); **– op**, go for; discover, catch.
afkoms, descent, parentage; origin.
afkomstig, descended from; **uit Engeland –**, of English origin; **is uit Latyn –**, derived from Latin; **bloed van 'n dier –**, blood of an animal.
afkondig, (afge-), declare, proclaim; **gebooie –**,

afkondiging

publish the banns.
afkondiging, (-e, -s), declaration, proclamation, promulgation, publication.
afkonkel, (afge-), coax (entice) away from.
afkook, (afge-), boil (bones,) decoct (herbs).
afkooksel, decoction.
afkoop, (afge-), buy off, redeem; ransom.
afkoppel, (afge-), disconnect, uncouple.
afkort, (afge-), abbreviate, abridge.
afkorting, abridg(e)ment, abbreviation, shortening; **op –,** in part-payment.
afkrap, (afge-), scrape (scratch) off; scribble (down).
afkruip, (afge-), creep down; crawl (a distance).
afkrummel, (afge-), crumble off.
afkry, (afge-), get down (off, out); get (someone) away from; get free (a day).
afkyk, (afge-), look down; copy, crib; spy.
aflaai, (afge-), discharge, unload, off-load.
aflaat, (-late), indulgence.
aflaat, (afge-), let down; leave away (off).
aflaatbrief, (letter of) indulgence.
aflaathandel, sale of indulgences.
aflê, -leg, (afge-), lay down (arms); discard; cover, do (forty miles), come (a distance); **dit –,** fail; **die lewe –,** lose (lay down) one's life; **dit teen iemand –,** be no match for a person; **'n gelofte –,** make a vow; **die eed –,** take the oath; **'n eksamen –,** pass an examination; **'n besoek –,** pay a visit, call; **getuienis –,** give evidence; **'n weg –,** describe a path (of a projectile); cover a distance.
afleer, (afge-), unlearn, break oneself of (a habit); overcome (one's stammering).
aflees, (afge-), read (off), read out.
aflegging, laying down; discarding; covering; taking (the oath); vide **aflê.**
aflei, (afge-), lead away (down); divert, conduct (lightning), distract (one's attention), avert (suspicion); conclude, infer, derive (words); trace back to.
afleiding, (-e, -s), diversion, distraction; derivation; deduction; **– soek,** seek diversion.
aflek, (afge-), (1) trickle down.
aflek, (afge-), (2) lick off.
aflewer, (afge-), deliver.
aflewering, delivery; instalment.
aflig, (afge-), (1) light down.
aflig, (afge-), (2) lift (take) off.
afloer, (afge-), watch, spy (out).
afloop, n. flowing off; expiration, termination; end; issue, result; slope; outlet.
afloop, (afge-), flow (run) down; expire, terminate; slope, shelve; wear out (down); scour, tramp; run down (clock); go off (alarm); gutter (candle); conclude, end, result; **goed –,** turn out well; **dit sal sleg met jou –,** you will come to a bad end; **die winkels –,** go from shop to shop; **die skool –,** pass through a school; **jou bene –,** walk oneself off one's legs.
aflos, (afge-), relieve, take turns; redeem (a loan), discharge.
aflosbaar, (-bare), redeemable.
aflossing, relief; redemption; discharge.
aflui, (afge-), ring off; signal off.
afluister, (afge-), overhear; eavesdrop.
afmaai, (afge-), mow; reap (corn); cut off.
afmaak, (afge-), finish, settle, dispatch, finish off (animals, persons); run down, slate (a book); **met iemand –,** make up with someone; **jou met 'n grap van iets –,** pass it off with a joke; **mielies –,** shell maize-cobs.
afmaker, sheller.
afmars, departure, start, marching off.
afmarsjeer, (afge-), file (march) off.

afroom

afmartel, (afge-), fret, torment, torture.
afmarteling, torture.
afmat, (afge-), fag, fatigue, exhaust.
afmattend, (-e), fatiguing, tiring; gruelling.
afmatting, exhaustion, fatigue, weariness.
afmeet, (afge-), measure off; proportion.
afmeting, dimension, measurement; **reusagtige –s aanneem,** assume enormous proportions; **van vier –s,** of four dimensions.
afmonster, (afge-), discharge; sign off.
afname, decline, decrease, diminution.
afneem, (afge-), remove, take down (away, off); deprive of; decrease, diminish; abate; subside; fall, sink; slacken; **die tafel –,** clear the table; **'n portret –,** take a photo(graph).
afneembaar, (-bare), detachable, removable.
afnemer, (-s), photographer.
afnommer, -nummer, (afge-), number off.
afoes, (afge-), reap.
afonie, aphonia, loss of voice.
aforisme, (-s), aphorism, adage.
afpaal, (afge-), fence in; peg (stake) out.
afpak, (afge-), pack off, unload, unpack.
afpeil, (afge-), gauge, fathom, sound.
afpen, (afge-), peg (stake) off (claims).
afperk, (afge-), peg (stake) out; fence in.
afperking, demarcation, limitation.
afpers, (afge-), draw (tears); extort (money).
afpersing, exaction, extortion; blackmail.
afpik, (afge-), peck off.
afplat, (afge-), flatten.
afpluis, (afge-), pick (give) off fluff.
afpluk, (afge-), pick (off), gather (flowers).
afpoets, (afge-), brush, clean, polish.
afpraat, (afge-), talk over; arrange, settle.
afprewel, (afge-), mumble.
afpynig, (afge-), torture; rack (one's brains).
afraai, (afge-), caution against, dissuade.
afraak, (afge-), get away (stray) from, get rid of; **van die drank –,** give up drink; **van mekaar –,** lose one another; get estranged.
aframmel, (afge-), reel off, gabble.
afrand, (afge-), edge (skirt) off.
afransel, (afge-), drub, lick, thrash, flog.
afranseling, drubbing, flogging, thrashing.
afraspe(r), (afge-), rasp off.
afraster, (afge-), fence (rail) in (off).
afrastering, fence railing.
afreën, afreent, (afge-), get washed out (off) by rain.
afreis, n. departure.
afreis, (afge-), depart, leave; **die land –,** tour the country.
afreken, (afge-), settle accounts (one's account).
afrekening, settlement; **op –,** on account.
afrig, (afge-), coach; train; break in (a horse).
afrigter, (-s), coach; trainer.
Afrika, Africa.
Afrikaan, (-kane), (native) African.
Afrikaans, (-e), n. & a. Afrikaans.
Afrikaner, (-s), Africander; marigold.
afrikanerbees, Africander (breed of cattle).
afrikanerskaap, fat-tailed South African sheep.
Afrikanervolk, South African nation.
afroei, (afge-), row down (the river); row off, start rowing; cover by rowing.
afroep, (afge-), call down; call from (one's work); call over (names); call out, announce; **'n staking –,** call off a strike.
afrokkel, (afge-), entice away, wheedle out of.
afrol, (afge-), roll down; unroll, unwind.
afrolmasjien, copying-machine.
afrond, (afge-), finish, round off.
afronding, finish, rounding off.
afroom, (afge-), cream, skim.

afros, (afge-), thrash, lick, wallop.
afroskam, (afge-), rub down; run down.
afruk, (afge-), pluck (pull, tear) down (off), snatch away; – op, advance on.
afry, (afge-), drive (ride) off (down); cover by driving (riding); override; wear out.
afsaag, afsae, (afge-), saw off.
afsaal, (afge-), off-saddle.
afsak, (afge-), come (slip) down, sag (down), subside; drop (float, sail) down; slide down; **jou laat –**, let oneself down; **as die son –**, when the sun sinks.
afsaksel, deposit, sediment, silt.
afsê, (afge-), cancel, countermand; break off an engagement with.
afsend, (afge-), consign, dispatch, forward.
afsender, consigner, sender, remitter.
afsending, dispatch, forwarding, shipment.
afsendingstasie, forwarding-station.
afset, n. sale, turnover, market.
afset, (afge-), victimize, swindle, fleece.
afsetgebied, market, opening, outlet.
afsetsel, trimming; layer; deposit.
afsetter, cheat, sharp(er), swindler.
afsettery, cheating, swindling.
afsetting, amputation; dismissal, removal.
afsien, (afge-), – **van**, abandon, give up (a plan); forgo, relinquish (a claim).
afsienbaar, (-bare), measurable.
afsigtelik, (-e), ghastly, hideous, ugly.
afsit, (afge-), dash off, start; remove, take off (from fire); amputate, cut off (a limb); deposit (sediment); close in, rope off (a space); down, drop (a passenger); trim (a dress); dismiss (from office), cashier (an officer), unfrock (a clergyman); dethrone (a king); switch off.
afsitter, starter.
afskaaf, afskawe, (afge-), plane down; abrade, bark, graze, chafe (one's skin).
afskadu, (afge-), adumbrate, foreshadow.
afskaduwing, adumbration, shadow.
afskaf, (afge-), abolish, do away with; abrogate, repeal (laws); give up (luxuries).
afskaffer, (-s), teetotaller; abolitionist.
afskaffing, abolition, abrogation, redress, repeal; abstinence, teetotalism.
afskaffingsbeweging, temperance movement.
afskawe, vide **afskaaf**.
afskeep, (afge-), ship; treat shabbily, fob off; neglect someone, botch (one's work).
afskeer, (afge-), shave off (beard); shear off (wool).
afskei(e), (afge-), separate; secrete (juices); extract; **jou – van**, secede, break away from; dissociate oneself from.
afskeid, departure, good-bye, leave-taking; – **neem**, say good-bye.
afskeiding, separation; secession; secretion; segregation; partition.
afskeidingsmuur, partition-wall.
afskeidsbesoek, leave-taking, farewell-call.
afskeidsgroet, farewell, send-off.
afskeidskus, parting-kiss.
afskeidsparty, farewell-party, send-off.
afskeidspreek, valedictory sermon.
afskeidsresepsie, farewell-reception.
afskeidsvoorstelling, farewell-performance.
afskeidswoord, parting-word.
afskeie, vide **afskei**.
afskeier, (-s), separator.
afskep, (afge-), skim (off), scoop off.
afskepery, neglect; negligence; botching.
afskeur, (afge-), peel (tear) off; secede.
afskeuring, tearing off; severing; secession.
afskiet, (afge-), discharge, fire; send up (rockets);
shoot down (a bird); shoot off (a limb); – **op**, pounce upon.
afskil, (afge-), peel, pare; skin; scale off.
afskilder, (afge-), depict, portray, describe.
afskilfer, (afge-), peel (off), flake away (off).
afskink, (afge-), pour off, decant.
afskoffel, (afge-), hoe away (off).
afskop, n. kick-off.
afskop, (afge-), kick off; kick down.
afskort, (afge-), partition off.
afskorting, partition; bulkhead; brattice.
afskot (-te), brattice; partition.
afskraap, (afge-), scrape (off); scale (fish).
afskraapsel, scrapings.
afskram, (afge-), glance off.
afskrif, copy, duplicate.
afskrik, n. horror: deterrent; aversion.
afskrik, (afge-), deter; frighten, dishearten.
afskrikwekkend, (-e), deterrent; terrifying; warning; prohibitive (price).
afskroef, afskroewe, (afge-), unscrew.
afskroei, (afge-), singe (off).
afskrop, (afge-), scrub, scour.
afskryf, afskrywe, (afge-), copy, transcribe; crib; cancel; break off an engagement with, finish; write off (debt).
afskryfbaar, expendable.
afskrywing, (-e, -s), copying; writing-off; depreciation; sack(ing); vide **afskryf**.
afsku, abhorrence, horror; **'n – hê van**, abhor, loathe; **'n voorwerp van –**, an abomination.
afskud, (afge-), shake off.
afskuif, afskuiwe, (afge-), slide, down; push off; slip (shift) off from oneself; **die skuld van hom –**, exculpate oneself.
afskuim, (afge-), skim, scum.
afskuimlepel, skimming-spoon, skimmer.
afskuiwe, vide **afskuif**.
afskut, (afge-), partition off, screen (off).
afskutting, fence, partition, railing.
afskuur, (afge-), scour off; abrade, graze.
afskuwelik, (-e), abominable, detestable, disgusting, hideous, vile, heinous (crime).
afskuwelikheid, atrociousness, hideousness.
afslaan, (afge-), beat (dash, knock, strike) off; repel, repulse (an attack); decline, refuse, reject; knock down, reduce (the price); branch (turn) off.
afslaer, (-s), auctioneer.
afslag, n. reduction; auction.
afslag, (afge-), flay, skin.
afsleep, (afge-), drag drown; pull (tow) off.
afslenter, (afge-), saunter down, knock about.
afsleur, (afge-), drag down.
afslinger, (afge-), hurl (toss, fling, sling) off; reel down; meander down.
afslof, (afge-), shuffle down; wear out.
afsloof, -slowe, (afge-),: **sig –**, drudge, fag, slave, toil (and moil), wear out.
afsluip, (afge-), slink (sneak) down (away).
afsluit, (afge-), lock (a door); cut (shut, turn) off; close, block (a road); fence, hedge (partition, rope), off; close (accounts); balance (books); conclude (a treaty); effect (an insurance); enter into (a contract); **jou –**, seclude oneself.
afsluitboom, bar barrier; gate-bar, boom.
afsluitdam, barrage, levee.
afsluiting, closing; balancing; conclusion; cutting off; enclosure.
afsluitklep, throttle-valve; stop-valve.
afsluitkraan, stop-cock.
afslyp, (afge-), grind down (off), polish.
afslyt, (afge-), wear away (out, down), waste.
afslyting, attrition, wear and tear.
afsmeek, (afge-), beseech, implore, invoke.

afsmeer, (afge-), rub off; palm off; – **aan**, palm (pass, fob), off on.
afsmeking, invocation, supplication.
afsmelt, (afge-), melt down (off).
afsmyt, (afge-), fling (throw, hurl) off.
afsnel, (afge-), rush down.
afsnoei, (afge-), lop (prune, clip) off.
afsnou, (afge-), snub, snap (snarl) at.
afsny, (afge-), cut, cut off, cut short, pare (nails), dock (a horse's tail), lop off (branches); intercept (a person); **iemand die pas** –, head a person off.
afsoek, (afge-), search, beat, scour.
afsoen, (afge-), kiss and be friends; kiss away.
afsonder, (afge-), separate, set apart; isolate, segregate.
afsondering, separation; segregation; seclusion.
afsonderlik, (-e), a. separate, individual, special.
afsonderlik, adv. separately, singly.
afspat, (afge-), fly (crack, chip) off.
afspeel, (afge-), finish, play off; take place.
afspel, (afge-), spell out.
afspeld, (afge-), pin off.
afspieël, (afge-), reflect, mirror.
afspieëling, reflection; mirror.
afspit, (afge-), dig away (off).
afsplinter, (afge-), splinter off.
afsplits, (afge-), split off.
afspoel, (afge-), rinse, wash; wash away.
afspons, (afge-), sponge down.
afspraak, appointment, engagement, agreement, arrangement; **'n – hou**, keep an appointment; **volgens –**, as agreed upon; by appointment.
afspreek, (afge-, **afgesproke**), agree upon, arrange; **vantevore afge-**, prearranged; **afge–!**, agreed!
afspring, (afge-), jump off, leap down; alight (from a horse); fly off; chip off; crack off; (negotiations) break down.
afspuit, (afge-), hose down.
afstaan, (afge-), cede, give up, yield, hand over, relinquish, surrender; – **van**, stand away (back) from.
afstam, (afge-); – **van**, be descended from, come off, spring from, be derived from.
afstammeling, (-e, -s), descendant.
afstamming, descent, extraction; derivation.
afstamp, (afge-), bump (dash, knock) off.
afstand, (-e), distance, range; interval; cession (of territory); abdication (from throne); relinquishment, renunciation, surrender (of rights); **op 'n –**, at a distance; **iemand op 'n – behandel**, be standoffish (distant) with someone; **op 'n – bly**, keep at a distance; keep aloof; **op 'n – hou**, keep at a distance; keep at bay; – **doen van**, renounce, forgo; – **doen van die troon**, abdicate the throne; – **doen van die wêreld**, renounce the world.
afstandbeheer, remote control.
afstandsrit, long-distance race.
afstap, (afge-), step off, dismount; walk; – **van**, go off (gold); drop (a subject).
afsteek, (afge-), cut (sods), mark out; deliver (a speech); **van wal –**, push off; **gunstig – by**, contrast favourably with; – **teen**, show up against.
afsteel, (afge-), steal from, rob of.
afstel, n. postponement, procrastination; **van uitstel kom –**, procrastination is the thief of time; **uitstel is geen – nie**, all is not lost that is delayed.
afstel, (afge-), adjust; disconnect.
afstem, (afge-), reject, turn down (a proposal); – **op**, tune in to.
afstempel, (afge-), stamp.

afsterf, **afsterwe**, (afge-), die, die off (organs mortify; lose touch with.
afsterwing, death, decease; mortification.
afstewen, (afge-), – **op**, bear down upon.
afstig, (afge-), secede.
afstof, (afge-), dust; wallop.
afstomp, (afge-), blunt; deaden, dull.
afstomping, blunting; dulling; obtusion.
afstoom, (afge-), steam away (down).
afstoot, (afge-), dash (knock, thrust) down (off); push (shove) off; repulse, rebuff; **mense van jou –**, alienate people.
afstootlik, (-e), repelling, repulsive.
afstootlikheid, repulsiveness.
afstorm, (afge-), rush down (the hill); – **op**, rush (storm) at, charge.
afstort, (afge-), tumble down; fling (hurl) down.
afstotend, (-e), vide **afstootlik**.
afstraal, (afge-), radiate, reflect.
afstraf, (afge-), punish, thrash; reprove.
afstraffing, punishment; reprimand.
afstraling, radiation, reflection, reflex.
afstroom, (afge-), flow (stream) down.
afstroop, (afge-), flay, skin; harry, ravage; roll down (sleeves).
afstryk, (afge-), iron off; wipe off; level off.
afstudeer, (afge-), complete one's studies.
afstuif, **afstuiwe**, (afge-), (rush, tear) off (down); – **op**, dash (rush) at.
afstuit, (afge-), rebound, glance off; ricochet; – **op**, glance off from; be frustrated by; **op teenstand –**, meet with opposition.
afstuur, (afge-), dispatch, send off; **van skool –**, expel from school; – **van**, steer away from; – **op**, head (make) for.
afstyg, (afge-), get (go) down; alight, dismount.
afsukkel, (afge-), trudge down; jog over (a road).
afswaai, (afge-), turn aside.
afsweer, (afge-), abjure, renounce.
afswem, (afge-), swim (down).
afswering, abjuration; renunciation.
afswoeg, **afswoeë**, (afge-), slave, toil.
aftak, (afge-), branch; shunt (off).
aftakel, (afge-), dismantle; criticize; thrash.
aftakking, branching, shunting.
aftands, (-e), long in the tooth, aged.
aftap, (afge-), draw off, tap; drain; trickle down; **iemand bloed –**, bleed a person.
afteken, (afge-), copy, sketch; delineate, portray; vis (a passport); endorse (a ticket); mark off; **afge– teen**, standing out against.
aftel, (afge-), count off; subtract; lift down.
aftelefoneer, (afge-), cancel by telephone.
aftelegrafeer, (afge-), cancel by wire.
aftelrympie, counting-out rhyme.
aftik, (afge-), tick off; type (out).
aftimmer, (afge-), knock up (off).
aftob, (afge-), fag, tire out, wear out.
aftog, retreat; **die – blaas**, beat (sound) the retreat; **die – dek**, cover the retreat.
aftoom, (afge-), unbridle.
aftop, (afge-), poll, prune, top (a tree).
aftorring, (afge-), unrip.
aftrap, (afge-), wear down (heels); step down; **'n stel –**, put one's foot into it.
aftreding, abdication, resignation, retirement.
aftree, (afge-), step down; retire, resign, abdicate; pace, step off.
aftrek, n. deduction, subtraction; demand; **'n goeie – vind**, be in great demand; **na – van**, after deducting.
aftrek, (afge-), deduct, subtract; extract (in chem.); pull down (off); trace; divert (someone's attention); fire, pull the trigger; withdraw, retire; **jou hande van iemand –**, wash

one's hands of a person.
aftrekker, subtrahend; puller.
aftrekking, deduction, subtraction.
aftrekkingsteken, minus sign.
aftrekpapier, tracing paper.
aftreksel, decoction, extract, infusion, tincture.
aftreksom, subtraction-sum.
aftrektal, minuend.
aftrippel, (afge-), trip down; amble.
aftroef, (afge-), trump; cut short.
aftuig, aftuie, (afge-), outspan, unharness.
aftuimel, (afge-), tumble down.
afvaardig, (afge-), delegate, depute.
afvaardiging, deputation, delegation.
afvaart, departure, sailing.
afvaartlys, list of sailing.
afval, n. refuse, rubbish, leavings, waste; tripe; defection; apostasy.
afval, (afge-), fall off, drop, fall (tumble) down; lose weight; secede (fall away) from.
afvalhoop, tip-mound, refuse-dump.
afvallig, (-e), disloyal, faithless, unfaithful.
afvallige, (-s), apostate, deserter, renegade.
afvalligheid, apostasy, defection, desertion.
afvalproduk, by-product; waste-product.
afvang, (afge-), catch (snatch) from; iemand 'n vlieg –, score off a person.
afvee(g), (afge-), wipe (off); dust, sweep.
afvlie(g), (afge-), fly away (off); be blown off; run down; take off.
afvloei, n. flowing-off, drainage.
afvloei, (afge-), flow down (off), drain.
afvloeiing, drainage; gradual dismissal.
afvoer, n. conveyance; discharge, outlet.
afvoer, (afge-), carry off; lead away; lead astray; convey, transport; abduct.
afvoerbuis, -pyp, outlet-, exhaust-, drain-pipe.
afvoerkanaal, drainage-canal; outlet; (excretory) duct (anat.).
afvoerpyp, vide **afvoerbuis**.
afvoersloot, catch-water drain (ditch).
afvra(ag), (afge-), ask (for), demand; ek vra myself af, I wonder (whether).
afvreet, (afge-), eat off, browse.
afvry, (afge-), cut out (with a girl).
afvryf, -vrywe, (afge-), rub, scour, polish.
afvuur, (afge-), discharge, fire (off).
afvyl, (afge-), file away (down, off).
afwaai, (afge-), blow off; be blown off.
afwaarts, downward(s), aside.
afwag, (afge-), await, wait for; wait (one's turn); bide (one's time).
afwagtend, (-e), waiting (attitude).
afwagting, expectation; in – van, pending, in expectation of.
afwas, (afge-), wash; wash away (off); wash up.
afwater, (afge-), drain; pour off; water down.
afwatering, drain(age); watering down.
afwateringsgebied, drainage-area.
afwateringskanaal, drainage-channel.
afwateringspyp, drain-pipe.
afwee(g), -weë, (afge-), weigh out.
afweek, (afge-), detach by soaking; unglue.
afweer, n. defence.
afweer, (afge-), avert; parry; keep off.
afweergeskut, -kanon, anti-aircraft gun.
afwei(e), (afge-), graze, browse.
afwen, (afge-); break (of a habit); wean from; jou –, get out of, unlearn; unreel, wind off.
afwend, (afge-), avert, turn aside (away); parry, ward off; divert (attention); stave off (defeat).
afwending, diversion; vide **afwend**.
afwentel, (afge-), roll back (off); shift off.
afwering, defence; prevention; resistance.
afwerk, (afge-), complete; finish (off), work off

(a debt); get through (a programme); jou –, overwork oneself.
afwerking, finish(ing); workmanship.
afwerp, (afge-), throw off; cast, shed; yield (profit); shake off (a feeling).
afwesig, (-e), absent.
afwesigheid, absence; non-attendance.
afwikkel, (afge-), unwind; wind up, liquidate (an estate).
afwikkeling, unwinding; liquidation.
afwimpel, (afge-), call off; fob off.
afwip, (afge-), skip down (off); tip off.
afwissel, (afge-), alternate, change, vary; iets –, (inter)change things; mekaar –, take turns; succeed each other.
afwisselend, (-e), alternate, diversified; met -e sukses, with varying success.
afwisseling, alternation, interchange, succession; change, variation; diversity, variety; by –, alternately, in turn, by turns; ter –, for (by way of) a change.
afwit, (afge-), whitewash.
afwring, (afge-), wring (wrench) off (from).
afwyk, (afge-), deviate, diverge; swerve (from); differ; dissent, disagree; geen duimbreed – nie, not budge an inch; van die regte pad –, go astray.
afwykend, (-e), divergent, different; dissentient (views); abnormal, anomalous.
afwyking, (-e, -s), deflection, deviation, divergence, difference; declination (of compass); departure (from tradition); dip (of the magnetic needle); (moral) aberration; in – van die reëls, in contravention of the rules.
afwykingshoek, angle of deflection.
afwys, (afge-), refuse admittance, turn away; reject; decline (an invitation), dismiss (a claim); scout (an idea); afge– word, fail, be rejected.
afwysend, (-e), negative.
afwysing, (-e, -s), denial, rejection, refusal.
ag, n. attention, care; – gee op, pay attention (give heed) to; in – neem, observe, practise; take into consideration; jou in – neem, be on one's guard; take care of oneself; gee ag! attention!
ag, (ge-), esteem, respect; consider, count, regard; – op, pay attention to; jou beledig –, feel offended.
ag(t), (ags, agte), n. eight.
ag(t), a. eight; oor – dae, this day week.
ag, interj. ah!, alas!, oh!
agaat, (agate), agate.
agbaar, (-bare), honourable, respectable.
agbaarheid, respectability; venerableness.
agdelig, (-e), consisting of eight parts.
agdubbeld, (-e), eightfold.
ageer, (ge-), act.
agenda, (-s), agenda.
agent, (-e), agent; constable, policeman.
agentskap, (-pe), agentuur, (-re), agency.
aggie, (-s), little eight.
agglomeraat, (-ate), agglomerasie, (-s), agglomerate, agglomeration.
agglutineer, (ge-), agglutinate.
aggregaat, (-ate), aggregate.
aggregasie, aggregation.
aggressie, aggression.
aggressief, (-iewe), aggressive.
aggressiwiteit, aggressiveness.
ag(t)hoek, octagon.
ag(t)hoekig, (-e), octagonal; octangular.
agie, (-s): nuuskierige –, Miss Curiosity, Paul Pry; inquisitive person.
agio, agio, premium.

agitasie, (-s), agitation; excitement.
agitator, (-s), agitator.
agiteer, (ge-), agitate; flutter, fluster.
agjarig, (-e), eight-year-old.
agmaal, eight times.
agnaat, (-ate), agnate.
agnosties, (-e), agnostic.
agnostikus, (-se), agnostic.
agnostisisme, agnosticism.
agpotig, (-e), octopod, eight-legged.
agrariër, (-s), agrarian.
agraries, (-e), agrarian.
agreëlig, (-e), of eight lines.
agretjie, (-s), mayflower.
agrimonie, agrimony.
agronomie, agronomy.
agronoom, (-nome), agronomist.
agste, (-s), eighth.
agsydig, (-e), eight-sided, octahedral; -e figuur, octagon.
agt, vide **ag**.
agteloos, careless, negligent; inattentive.
agteloosheid, carelessness, inattention.
agte(r)losig, (-e), careless.
agte(r)losigheid, carelessness.
agtenswaardig, (-e), estimable, respectable.
agtenswaardigheid, respectability.
agter, prep, behind; at the back of; – iemand se rug (om), behind a person's back; – slot, under lock and key; – die tralies, in jail; ek is daar –, I have found it out; ten –, behind, in arrear.
agter, adv. at the back; behind; my oorlosie is –, my watch is slow.
agteraan, behind, at the back, in the rear.
agteraankom, (agteraange-), come last, bring up the rear; be backward.
agteraf, adv. back, backward, in the rear; poor; out of the way; secretly; iets – hou, keep something back (quiet).
agteraf, a. backward, out-of-the-way; poor; jou – hou, keep aloof; – straat, back street; – mense, backward people.
agteras, rear- (back-)axle.
agterbak, dickey(-seat).
agterbaks, (-e), a. sly, underhand(ed).
agterbaks, adv. secretly, behind one's back.
agterband, rear-, back-tire (-tyre).
agterbank, back-seat.
agterbanker, back-bencher.
agterbeen, hind-leg.
agterbeweging, back movement (in football).
agterbly, (agterge-), remain (stay, drop) behind; be left behind, survive.
agterblyer, laggard, straggler; backnumber.
agterblywende, (-s), survivor.
agterboud, hind-quarter.
agterbuurt, slum(s), backstreet.
agterdeel, back-part, rear portion; buttocks.
agterdek, poop(-deck), quarter-deck.
agterdeur, n. back door; – oophou, keep a back door (loophole) open.
agterdoek, back-drop.
agterdog, suspicion.
agterdogtig, (-e), suspicious.
agterdogtigheid, suspiciousness.
agtereen, vide **aaneen & agtermekaar**.
agtereenvolgende, consecutive, successive.
agtereenvolgens, consecutively, successively.
agterend, -ent, back(-part); backside.
agtererf, backyard.
agtergeblewene, (-s), survivor.
agtergebou, back building, back premises.
agtergewel, back-gable.
agtergrond, background; back-drop.
agterhaal, (het –), overtake; hunt down.

agterhoede, rear(-guard).
agterhoek, outlying district.
agterhoof, -kop, back of the head occiput.
agterhou, (agterge-), keep (hold) back (behind), withhold; conceal, suppress.
agterhoudend, (-e), close, reserved.
agterhoudendheid, closeness, reticence.
agterhouding, keeping back; concealment.
agterhuis, back of house, back premises.
agterin, at the back.
Agter-Indië, Further India.
agteringang, rear entrance.
agterkant, back; reverse side, backside.
agterklap, calumny, backbiting, scandal; hindflap (of wagon, cart).
agterkleinkind, great-grandchild.
agterkom, (agterge-), discover, find out.
agterkop, vide **agterhoof**.
agterkwart, hind-quarter.
agterlaaier, breech-loader; frock-coat.
agterlaat, (agterge-), leave, leave behind; arm –, leave poorly off.
agterlamp, tail-, rear-lamp.
agterland, hinterland, interior, backveld.
agterlating, leaving behind; met – van, leaving behind, with abandonment of.
agterlig, tail-, rear-light.
agterlik, (-e), backward; behind the times.
agterlik, backwardness.
agterlosig(heid), vide **agtelosig(heid)**.
agterlyf, hind-quarter(s); buttocks.
agterlyn, base-line; back-line.
agtermekaar, a. spick and span, orderly, fine, up-to-date; neat, spruce.
agtermekaar, adv. on end at a stretch; one after (behind) the other, tandem; spick and span; in order; dinge – sit, put things in order; – loop, walk one behind the other, walk in single file; drie dae –, three days in succession.
agtermiddag, afternoon.
agtermiddags, in the afternoon.
agterna, after, behind; afterwards, later; – gaan, follow after; – kyk, gaze (look) after; – loop, follow (run) after; – roep, call after; – ry, ride after; – stuur, send after.
agternaam, family-name, surname.
agternasit, (agternage-), pursue.
agterneef, great-nephew; second cousin.
agternig(gie), great-niece, second cousin.
agterom, back, behind, round the back.
agteromkyk, (agteromge-), look back.
agteromloop, (agteromge-), walk round the back.
agteroor, back(wards), on one's back; – gooi, throw back(wards); – hang, hang (slant) back; – lê, lie back; lie on one's back; lean (recline) backwards; – leun, lean back; – val, fall backwards.
agterop, behind, at the back, in the rear; – ry, ride pillion. *
agteropskop, (agteroorge-), kick.
agteros, hind-ox; – kom ook in die kraal (juk), slow but sure.
agterossambok, ox-sjambok.
agterpant, hind-skirt, back-gore.
agterperd, hind-horse, wheel-horse.
agterplaas, backyard.
agterpoot, hind-leg; op sy –pote gaan staan, become unmanageable.
agterraak, (agterge-), drop (fall, lag) behind.
agterruim, afterhold.
agterryer, attendant, henchman.
agterskip, stern, poop.
agterskot, tail-board; (payment of) balance.
agterslag, thong (of whip).
agterstaan, (agterge-), be neglected; by ander –,

agterstallig be behind others, be handicapped; **by niemand – nie,** be second to none.
agterstallig, (-e), back, outstanding, in arrear; **– wees,** be in arrear(s).
agterstand, arrears, arrearage; backward position; backlog; **die – inhaal,** make up leeway.
agterste, (-s), n. back-part, backside.
agterste, a. hind, hindmost, last.
agterstel, n. back, tail(-end) (of wagon); rear-chassis (of motor); vide **agterste,** n.
agterstel, (agterge-), place (put) behind; handicap, place at a disadvantage; **– by,** subordinate to; pass over for.
agterstelling, subordination; neglect.
agterstevoor, hind-part foremost, the wrong way about (round), upside down, topsy-turvy; **– wees,** set about things in the wrong way.
agterstewe, -sten, stern, poop.
agterstraat, back-street.
agterstuk, hind-part; breech (of cannon).
agtertang, after-guide (of wagon).
agteruit, back, backward(s); **'n stap –,** a retrograde step; **hy is baie –,** he is very much worse; **– loop,** go (run, walk) backwards; **– ry,** reverse; **– sit,** sit back; **– stap,** step back; **– vlieg,** fly backwards.
agteruitboer, (agteruitge-), farm at a loss, do bad business.
agteruitdeins, (agteruitge-), start back.
agteruitgaan, (agteruitge-), go back(wards); move back recede, decline, get worse, fall off, be on the down-grade; come down in the world; deteriorate (of goods); degenerate (of morals); back, reverse (a motor).
agteruitgang, n. fall, decline, decay, deterioration, degeneration, retrogression.
agteruitgang, n. back door, rear exit.
agteruitsit, (agteruitge-), put back, throw back, make worse.
agteruitvlie(g), (agteruitge-), start back; recede.
agterveld, backveld.
agtervelder, backvelder.
agtervertrek, backroom.
agtervoeg, (agterge-), add, affix.
agtervoeging, addition, paragoge.
agtervoegsel, (-s), suffix.
agtervolg, (het –), pursue; persecute.
agtervolging, pursuit; persecution.
agterwaarts, adv. back, backwards.
agterwaarts, (-e), backward, retrograde.
agterweë, back; **– bly,** fail to turn up; remain in abeyance; **– hou,** keep back; **– laat,** drop.
agterwêreld, backveld; backside.
agterwiel, back- (hind-, rear-)wheel.
ag(t)tien, eighteen.
ag(t)tiende, eighteenth.
ag(t)tiende-eeus, (-e), eighteenth century.
agting, esteem, respect; estimation; **groot – geniet,** be held in high esteem; **met die meeste –,** respectfully (yours).
agt-in-lyn, straight eight.
ag(t)-urig, (-e), eight-hour.
agtuur, breakfast.
ag(t)-uur, eight o'clock.
agvlak, octahedron.
agvlakkig, (-e), octahedral.
agvoetig, (-e), of eight feet, octopod.
agvoud, eightfold, octuple.
agvoudig, (-e), eightfold, octuple.
agurkie, (-s), gherkin.
ai, interj. ah!, o(h)!; ow!, ouch!
aikôna, haikôna, oh no!; not at all.
aispaai, vide **aspaai.**
aits(a), my!, hallo!, look out!, sorry!

akademie, (-s), academy.
akademielid, member of the (an) academy.
akademieraad, council of the academy.
akademies, (-e), academic; **–e graad,** university-degree; **–e debat,** academic debate.
akademiestad, university town.
akasia, (-s), acacia.
akelei, (-e), columbine.
akke(r)dis, akkeldis, (-se), lizard; newt.
akker, (-s), 1. field, plot (of land); acre.
akker, (-s), 2. acorn.
akkerboom, oak(-tree).
akkerbou, agriculture.
**akkertjie, (flower-)bed, (vegetable-)bed.
akkerwanie, cuscus(-grass).
akklamasie, acclamation.
akklimatisasie, acclimatization.
akklimatiseer, (ge-), acclimatize.
akkolade, accolade; brace.
akkommodasie, accommodation.
akkommodasiewissel, accommodation-bill.
akkommodeer, (ge-), accommodate; focus.
akkompanjeer, (ge-), accompany.
akkompanjement, (-e), accompaniment.
akkoord, (-e). agreement; chord (mus.); **'n – aangaan (tref) met,** come to an arrangement with; **a gaan met,** agree to.
akkordeer, (ge-), agree; come to terms; get on with.
akkordeon, (-s), accordion.
akkrediteer, (ge-), accredit.
akkumulasie, accumulation.
akkumulator, (-e, -s), accumulator.
akkumuleer, (ge-), accumulate.
akkuraat, (-ate), accurate, precise.
akkusatief, (-tiewe), accusative.
akoestiek, acoustics.
akoesties, (-e), acoustic.
akoliet, (-e), acolyte.
akoniet, aconite.
akrobaat, (-ate), acrobat, tumbler.
akrobaties, (-e), acrobatic.
akrofobie, acrophobia.
akrostigon, (-s), acrostic.
aks, (-e), eighth (of an inch).
akselerasie, acceleration.
akselereer, (ge-), accelerate.
aksent, (-e), accent.
aksentuasie, accentuation.
aksentueer, (ge-), accent; accentuate.
akseptabel, (-e), acceptable.
akseptasie, acceptance.
akstepteer, (ge-), accept; allow (a claim).
aksidenteel, (-ele), accidental.
aksie, (-s), action; agitation; **–s (pl.) airs; met iemand –s hê,** be at loggerheads with someone.
aksioma, (-s), aksioom, (-iome), axiom.
aksiomaties, (-e), axiomatic.
aksionaris, (-se), shareholder.
aksyns, excise(-duty).
aksynskantoor, excise-office.
aksynspligtig, (-e), excisable.
akte, (-s), deed; diploma; act; **– van beskuldiging,** summons; indictment; **registrateur van –s,** registrar of deeds.
aktekantoor, deeds-office.
aktetas, brief-case, despatch-case.
akteur, (-s), actor, player.
aktief, (-iewe), active, energetic.
aktinies, (-e), actinic.
aktivis, (-te), activist.
aktivisme, activism.
aktiwiteit, (-e), activity.
aktrise, (-s), actress.
aktualiteit, (-e), actuality, timeliness.

aktuarieel 18 **allewêreld**

aktuarieel, (-iële), actuarial.
aktuari(u)s, (-se), actuary.
aktueel, (-uele), actual, topical.
akuut, (akute), acute.
akwaduk, (-te), aqueduct.
akwarel, (le), aquarelle, water-colour.
akwarium, (-s), aquarium, (-ia), aquarium.
al, (-le), a. all, each, every; – **drie,** all three; – **twee,** both; – **dae,** every day; **met klere en –,** clothes and all; **met dit –,** for all that.
al, adv. already, yet; – **eerder,** before now; **toe –,** then already; **dit is maar – te waar,** it's only too true; – **te bekommerd,** over-anxious; – **nader en nader,** nearer and nearer; – **dan nie,** whether or not; – **of nie,** yes or no; – **laggende,** laughing(ly); – **lank –,** long ago; for a long time (past); **geheel en –,** altogether; – **om die ander dag,** every second day.
al, conj. (al)though, even if, even though; – **is hy ook nog so arm,** however poor he may be.
alarm, (-s), alarm; tumult, uproar; **die – blaas,** sound the alarm; **vals –,** false alarm.
alarmeer, (ge-), alarm, give the alarm.
alarmerend, (-e), alarming.
alarmis, (-te), alarmist, panic-monger, scaremonger.
alarmisties, (-e), alarmist.
alarmkreet, cry of alarm.
alarmtoestel, alarm.
albakoor, albacore.
Albanees, (-nese), n. & a. Albanian.
albaster, (-s), marble; alabaster.
albatros, (-se), albatross.
albei, both.
albino, (-s), albino.
album, (-s), album, scrap-book.
alchemie, alchemy.
alchemis, (-te), alchemist.
aldaar, there, at that place (spot), over there.
aldag, al dae, every day.
aldeur, all the time, all along, right through.
aldra, soon, before long, presently.
aldus, so, thus, in this way, as follows.
aleer, before, ere.
aleksandryn, (-e), alexandrine.
alembiek, (-e), alembic, distilling-report.
alewee, vide **aalwee.**
alfa, alpha.
alfastraal, alpha ray.
alfaam, halfmaan, (-ame), half-aum.
alfabet, (-te), alphabet.
alfabeties, (-e), alphabetic(al).
algar, all, everybody, the whole lot.
algebra, algebra.
algebraïes, (-e), algebraic.
algeheel, (-hele), a. complete, utter.
algeheel, adv. completely, entirely, totally.
algemeen, n.: **in (oor) die –,** in general.
algemeen, (-mene), a. general; universal; common; public; indefinite, vague; **met –e stemme,** unanimously.
algemeen, adv. generally, commonly, universally; unanimously.
algemeenheid, commonness, universality; platitude.
algenoegsaam, (-same), all-sufficient.
Algeryns, (-e), n. & a. Algerian.
algorisme, algoritme, algorithm.
alheilmiddel, panacea.
alhier, here, at this place (spot), locally.
alhoewel, (al)though.
al-honderd-en-tien, all the same.
alias, (-se), n. alias.
alias, adv. alias, otherwise.
alibi, (-'s), alibi.

aliëneer, (ge-), alienate.
alikruikel, arikruikel, (-s), periwinkle.
alinia, (-s), paragraph.
aljimmers, always, ever, repeatedly.
alkali, (-ë, –'s), alkali.
alkalies, (-e), alkaline.
alkant, (on) all sides; – **selfkant,** six of the one and half a dozen of the other.
alklaps, every now and then.
alkohol, alcohol.
alkoholies, (-e), alcoholic.
alkoholis, alcoholic.
alkoholism, alcoholism, dipsomania.
alkoholvry, (-e), non-alcoholic.
alkoof, (-kowe), alcove.
alkoran, alcoran.
alla, allamapstieks, -mastig, -matjies, -mintig, -wêreld, gracious!, goodness!
alledaags, (-e), daily, ordinary, common(place).
alledaagsheid, commonness, triviality.
allee, (alleë), avenue; alley, walk.
alleen, alone, by oneself; lonely; single-handed; only; mere; in private; **iemand – spreek,** speak to a person in private; **die gedagte daaraan –,** the mere thought of it; **nie –, . . ., maar ook,** not only . . ., but also; – **maar omdat,** only because.
alleenhandel, monopoly.
alleenheerser, absolute monarch, autocrat.
alleenheerskappy, absolute power.
alleenlik, only, merely.
alleensaligmakend, (-e), only true.
alleenspraak, monologue, soliloquy.
alleenstaande, detached, isolated, single.
alleenverkoop, sole sale, monopoly.
alleenverteenwoordiger, sole agent.
alleenverteenwoordiging, sole agency.
alleenvlug, sole (solo) flight.
allegaartjie, (-s), hotch-potch, medley.
allegorie, (-ë), allegory.
allegories, (-e), allegoric(al).
allemansvri(e)nd, hail-fellow-well-met.
allemapstieks, ens., vide **alla-. . .**
allengs, by degrees, gradually, insensibly.
allenig, alone, lonely; vide **alleen.**
aller-. . ., the very . . ., the . . . of all, most.
alleraardigs(te), most charming(ly).
allerbekoorliks(te), most charming(ly).
allerbes(te), best of all, very best.
allereers(te), first of all, first and foremost.
allerergs(te), very worst, worst of all.
allergerings(te), least (lowest, smallest) possible (of all).
allergroots(te), very greatest (largest).
allerhande, of all sorts, (all and) sundry.
Allerheiligste, the Holy of Holies.
allerhoogs(te), highest of all, supreme.
Allerhoogste, n. the Most High.
allerlaas(te), very last; the very latest.
allerlei, (of) all sorts, miscellaneous.
allerliefs(te), most charming, dearest, sweetest; preferably, most of all.
allermees(te), most of all; the very most.
allermins(te), least of all; the very least.
allernaaste, nearest (of all); immediate.
allernodigs(te), most necessary; absolutely necessary (indispensable).
allernuutste, latest, newest; the very latest.
alleroudste, very oldest.
allersyds, allerweë, on all hands, everywhere.
alleryl: in –, in hot haste, at top speed.
alles, all, everything; **bo –,** above all; **van – wat,** something of everything.
allesbehalwe, anything but, far from.
allesins, in every respect; fully.
allewêreld, vide **alla . . .**

alliansie, (-s), alliance.
alliasie, (-s), alloy.
allieer, (ge-), ally; alloy (in metals).
allig, probably, possibly, perhaps.
alligator, (-s), alligator.
alliterasie, (-s), alliteration.
allitereer, (ge-), alliterate.
allooi, alloy; quality, standard.
allopatie, allopathy.
allures, (pl.) airs.
alluviaal, (-iale), alluvial.
almag, omnipotence.
almagtig, (-e), almighty, omnipotent.
almal, all, everybody; everything; **ons –**, all of us.
almanak, (-ke), almanac.
almaskie, all the same, nevertheless.
almelewe, always, for ever.
almoëndheid, almightiness, omnipotence.
alom, everywhere, on all sides.
alomteenwoordig, (-e), omnipresent, ubiquitous.
alomvattend, (-e), all-embracing.
alou(e), ancient, antique; time-honoured.
alpakka, alpaca (kind of wool).
alras, very soon.
alreeds, already.
alruin, mandrake, mandragora.
als(em), wormwood.
alsembeker, cup of bitterness.
als(em)kruid, wormwood.
alsiende, all-seeing.
also, thus, in this manner (way); so.
alsydig, (-e), all-round, many-sided, universal; versatile (sportsman).
alsydigheid, many-sidedness, versatility.
alt, (-e), also, contralto.
altaar, (-are), altar.
altaardienaar, acolyte.
altaardoek, altar-cloth.
altaarskildery, -stuk, altar-piece.
altans, at least, anyhow; at any rate.
altemit(s), perhaps, maybe.
alterasie, commotion, emotion, fright.
alternatief, (-iewe), alternative.
alterneer, (ge-), alternate.
altesaam, **altesame**, (al)together, all told.
altoos, always, ever; **vir –**, for ever.
altoosdurend, (-e), everlasting.
altruïsme, altruism.
altruïsties, (-e), altruistic.
altsangeres, contralto.
altyd, always, all along, for ever.
altyddurend, (-e), everlasting.
aluin, (-e), alum, alumen.
aluinagtig, **-houdend**, (-e), aluminous.
aluinlooiery, tawery, tawing.
aluminium, aluminium.
alvas, meanwhile.
alveolaar, (-are), n. alveolar.
alveolêr, (-e), a. alveolar.
alvermoë, omnipotence.
alvermoënd, (-e), omnipotent.
alverslindend, (-e), all-devouring, omnivorous.
alvleesklier, pancreas.
alvorens, before, preparatory to, until.
alwaar, where; wherever.
alweer, again, once more.
alwetend, (-e), all-knowing, omniscient.
alwetendheid, omniscience.
alweter, know-all.
Alwyse: die –, the All-wise.
alwysheid, supreme wisdom.
amalgaam, (-ame), amalgam.
amalgamasie, amalgamation.
amalgameer, (ge-), amalgamate.
amandel, (-s), almond; tonsil, amygdol.
amandelboom, almond(-tree).
amandelvormig, (-e), almond-shaped.
amanuensis, (-se), assistant, amanuensis.
amarant, (-e), amaranth, love-lies-bleeding.
amaril, emery.
amasone, (-s), amazon.
amasonekleed, riding-habit.
amateur, (-s), amateur, novice.
amateur(s)agtig, (-e), amateurish.
ambag, (-te), n. (handi)craft, trade, business, profession; **'n – leer**, learn a trade.
ambag, (ge-), do, be busy with.
ambagsjonge, **-leerling**, apprentice.
ambagskool, technical school, trade-school.
ambagsman, (-ne, **ambagslui**), artisan.
ambagsonderwys, technical instruction.
ambassade, (-s), embassy.
ambassadeur, (-s), ambassador.
amber, amber(gris).
ambergrys, ambergris.
ambieer, (ge-), aspire after.
ambisie, ambition.
ambisieus, (-e), ambitious; diligent.
ambraal, ill, sick, ailing.
ambrosyn, ambrosia.
ambulans, (-e), ambulance, field-hospital.
ambulansdiens, (field-)hospital service.
ambulanstrein, hospital-train.
ambulanswa, ambulance-wag(g)on.
amebe, amoeba.
amegtig, (-e), breathless, out of breath.
amen, (-s), amen; **sy woord is ja en –**, his word is law, you can depend on his word.
amendeer, (ge-), amend.
amendement, (-e), amendment.
Amerikaans, (-e), American.
Amerikaner, (-s), American.
ametis, (-te), amethyst.
ameublement, (-e), (set, suite) of furniture.
amfibie, (-ë), amphibian.
amfibies, (-e), amphibious, amphibian; **–e voertuig**, amphibian.
amfiteater, (-s), amphitheatre.
amfiteatersgewys(e), amphitheatrically.
amfora, (-s), amphora.
amikaal, (-ale), amicable, friendly.
ammoniak, ammonia.
ammonium, ammonium.
ammunisie, (am)munition.
ammunisiewa, ammunition wag(g)on, caisson.
amnesie, amnesia, loss of memory.
amnestie, amnesty; pardon.
amok, amuck; – **maak**, run amuck.
amorf, (-e), amorphous.
amortisasie, amortisation, redemption.
amortisasiefonds, sinking-fund.
amortiseer, (ge-), amortise, redeem, sink.
amp, (-te), function, office, post duty; **'n – beklee**, hold a post (an office).
ampel, (-e), a. & adv. ample (amply).
amper(tjies), almost, nearly.
ampère, (-s), ampère.
ampèremeter, (-s), ammeter.
ampgenoot, colleague.
ampie, (small) job.
amplitude, (-s), amplitude.
ampsaanvaarding, assumption of duty.
ampsbediening, **-bekleding**, discharge of duties, tenure of office.
ampsbekleër, incumbent (of office).
ampsduur, term (tenure) of office.
ampseed, oath of office.
ampsgeheim, official (professional) secret.
ampsgewaad, (official) robes, robes of office.
ampshalwe, officially, ex officio.

ampskleed, vide **ampsgewaad**.
ampsmisbruik, abuse of office (power).
ampsmisdryf, -oortreding, official misdemeanour, misfeasance, malfeasance.
ampsplig, official (professional) duty.
ampstyd, term (tenure, period) of office.
ampsversuim, misprision.
ampsvervulling, vide **ampsbediening**.
ampsweë: van –, vide **ampshalwe**.
amptelik, (-e), official; professional.
ampteloos, (-lose), out of office, retired; private.
amptenaar, (-are), civil (public) servant, functionary, official, officer, clerk.
amptenaardom, amptenary, officialdom.
ampul, (-s), ampulla; ampule.
amputasie, amputation.
amputeer, (ge-), amputate.
amulet, (-te), amulet, charm, talisman.
amusant, (-e), amusing, entertaining.
amuseer, (ge-), amuse; **jou –**, enjoy oneself.
amusement, (-e), amusement, entertainment.
anabaptis, (-te), anabaptist.
anabaptisme, (-e), anabaptism.
anabaptisties, (-e), anabaptist(ic).
anachoreet, (-ete), anchorite, hermit.
anachronisme, (-s), anachronism.
anachronisties, (-e), anachronistic.
analfabeet, (-bete), illiterate (person).
analise, analysis.
analiseer, (ge-), analyse.
analities, (-e), analytic(al).
analogie, (-ë), analogy; **na(ar) – van**, after the analogy of.
analities, (-e), analytic(al).
analogies, (-e), analogic(al).
analoog, (-loë), analogous, similar.
anapes, (-te), anapest.
anargie, anarchy.
anargis, (-te), anarchist.
anargisme, anarchism.
anargisties, (-e), anarchic(al), anarchist.
anatomie, anatomy.
anatomies, (-e), anatomical.
anatoom, (-tome), anatomist.
Andalusies, (-e), Andalusian.
ander, (-e), n. & a. another; other; **'n –, another; hy is 'n – mens**, he is a different person; **die – dag**, a few days ago; **'n – dag**, another day; **– week**, next week; **al om die – dag**, every other day; **nes al die –**, like the rest of them; **onder –(e)**, among other things; **met – woorde**, in other words; **die een die –**, each other, one another.
anderdeels: eensdeels, ...–, partly, ... partly.
anderhalf, (-halwe), one and a half.
anderkant, prep. across, beyond.
anderkant, on the other side.
anderland, abroad.
andermaal, again, once more, a second time.
anders, different; else, otherwise; **wie –**, who else; **dit is iets –**, that is another thing; **– sal ek**, else (otherwise) I shall . . .; **ek dink daar – oor**, I think differently (otherwise): **ek kan nie – nie**, I can do nothing else, I have no other choice; **net soos –**, just as usual; **– as sy vriende**, unlike his friends.
andersdenkend, (-e), of another opinion, different(ly) minded; dissentient.
andersgesind(e), vide **andersdenkend(e)**,
andersins, otherwise.
andersom, the other way about (round).
anderste(r), otherwise; different.
andersyds, on the other hand.
andoelie, (-s), andouille(-sausage).
anekdote, (-s), anecdote.

anekdoties, (-e), anecdotal.
anemie, anaemia.
anemies, (-e), anaemic.
anemoon, (-one), anemone, wind-flower.
aneroïed(-barometer), aneroid(-barometer).
anestesie, anaesthesia.
angel, (-s), sting (of bee); (fig.) barb.
angelier, (-e), carnation; **wilde –**, wild pink.
Angel-Sakser, (-s), Anglo-Saxon.
Angel-Saksies, (-e), n. & a. Anglo-Saxon.
Anglikaans, (-e), Anglican.
angliseer, (ge-), anglicise.
anglisisme, (-s), Anglicism.
angora, (-s), angora.
angorabok, Angora-goat.
angorahare, -wol, Angora-wool, mohair.
angssweet, cold perspiration (sweat).
angs, (-te), terror, anxiety, dismay.
angstig, (-e), afraid, fearful, terrified, anxious (moments).
angstigheid, fear, anxiety.
angsvallig, (-e), conscientious, scrupulous.
angsvalligheid, scrupulousness.
angsvol, (-te), anxious.
angswekkend, (-e), alarming.
anilien, aniline, aniline.
animalisme, animalism.
animeer, (ge-), animate, encourage.
animisme, animism.
animisties, (-e), animistic.
animo, energy, gusto, spirit, zest.
animositeit, animosity.
anioon, (-ione), anion.
anker, (-s), n. anchor; brace, tie (of wall); armature (of magnet); anker (liquid-measure); **die – laat val**, drop anchor; **die – lig**, weigh anchor; **voor – lê**, lie (ride) at anchor.
anker, (ge-), anchor, drop anchor; brace.
ankerblad, fluke.
ankerboei, anchor-buoy.
ankergeld, anchorage(-dues), groundage.
ankerhorlosie, -oorlosie, lever-watch.
ankerketting, anchor-chain, chain-cable.
ankerplek, anchorage.
ankertou, cable, hawser, mooring-rope.
ankerwikkeling, armature-coil.
anna, (-s), anna (a coin).
annale, (pl.) annals.
anneks, (-e), annex(e).
anneksasie, (-s), annexation.
annekseer, (ge-), annex; take.
annoteer, (ge-), annotate.
annuïteit, (-e), annuity.
annulleer, (ge-), annul, cancel, withdraw.
anode, (-s), anode.
anomalie, (-ë), anomaly.
anoniem, (-e), anonymous.
anonimiteit, anonymity.
anonimus, (-se, -mi), anonymous writer.
anorganies, (-e), inorganic.
ansiënniteit, seniority.
ansjovis, (-se), anchovy; white bait.
antagonis, (-te), antagonist.
antagonisties, (-e), antagonistic.
Antarkties, (-e), Antarctic.
antenne, (-s), aerial (wire); antenna.
antesedeer, (ge-), precede.
antesedent, (-e), antecedent; precedent.
anthr- ..., vide **antr- ...**
antibioties, (-e), a. antibiotic.
antibiotikum, n. antibiotic.
antichloor, antichlor, hypo.
antichris, Antichrist, (the) Beast.
antiek, (-e), antique.
antik(w)iteit, (-e), curio, relic; antiquity.

antik(w)iteitewinkel, antique-shop.
antiklimaks, anticlimax.
antikwaar, (-kware), second-hand bookseller; antiquarian; antiquary.
antikwariaat, (-ate), second-hand bookshop.
antikwaries, (-e), antiquarian; second-hand.
antikwiteit, vide **antik(w)iteit**.
antilogaritme, antilogarithm.
antiloop, (-lope), antelope.
antimakassar, (-s), antimacassar, tidy.
antimoon, antimony.
antinomie, (-ë), antimony.
antipasaat(wind), anti-trade(wind).
antipatie, (-e), antipathy, dislike.
antipatiek, (-e), antipathetic(al).
antipode, (-s), antipode.
antipodies, (-e), antipodal.
antirepublikein, anti-republican.
antirevolusionêr, (-e), anti-revolutionary.
antisemiet, (-e), anti-Semite.
antisemities, (-e), anti-Semitic.
antisepties, (-e), antiseptic.
antisipasie, anticipation.
antisipeer, (ge-), anticipate.
antitese, (-s), antithesis.
antiteties, (-e), antithetic(al).
antitoksien, (-e), **antitoksine**, (-s), antitoxin.
antraks, anthrax.
antrasiet, antracite.
antropofaag, (-fae), cannibal, man-eater, anthropophagite.
antropoïed, (-e), anthropoid.
antropologie, anthropology.
antropologies, (-e), anthropological.
antropoloog, (-loë), anthropologist.
antropomorf, (-e), antropomorphic.
antropomorfisme, anthropomorphism.
antroposentries, (-e), anthropocentric.
antwoord, n. answer, reply, response; **'n gevatte –**, a repartee; **'n skerp –**, a retort; **'n – op 'n –**, a rejoinder; **in – op**, in reply to.
antwoord, (ge–), answer, reply; retort; respond (to toast); **– op**, reply to; **daar val niks op te – nie**, that is unanswerable.
anys, anise.
anysolie, aniseed-oil.
anyssaad, aniseed.
aoris(tus), aorist.
apache, (-s), apache, hooligan.
apart, (-e), apart, aside, separate.
apatie, apathy.
apaties, (-e), apathetic.
apebroodboom, boabab, monkey-bread tree.
apegape: **op – lê**, be at the last gasp.
apekliere, monkey-glands.
apekool, bosh, nonsense, rubbish.
apeneute, **-note**, monkey-nuts, pea-nuts.
aperiodisiteit, aperiodicity.
aperitief, (-iewe), aperitif, appetizer.
apestreek, monkey-trick, monkeying.
aphaeresis, aferese, aphaeresis.
aphelium, afelium, aphelion.
apie, (-s), n. little monkey; **– op 'n stokkie**, jackanapes.
apodikties, (-e), apodictic.
apokalips(e), apocalypse; Revelation(s).
apokalipties, (-e), apocalyptic.
apokopee, apocope.
apokrief, (-iewe), apocryphal.
apologeet, (-ete), apologist.
apologetiek, apologetics.
apologeties, (-e), apologetic(al).
apologie, (-e), apology.
apopleksie, apoplexy.
apoplekties, (-e), apoplectic.

apostaat, (-state), apostate.
apostasie, apostasy.
apostel, (-s), apostle.
apostolaat, apostolate.
apostolies, (-e), apostolic.
apostroof, (-strowe), apostrophe.
aposteose, apostheosis, deification.
apparaat, (-ate), apparatus.
appartement, (-e), apartment.
appartementswoning, flat.
appel, (-s), apple; apple, ball, pupil (of the eye); **vir 'n – en 'n ei**, for a mere song; **'n suur – deurbyt**, swallow the pill, make the best of a bad job; **die – val nie ver van die boom (stam) nie**, he is a chip of the old block.
appèl, (-le, -s), appeal.
appelbloeisel, apple-blossom.
appelboom, apple-tree.
appelboord, apple-orchard.
appelde(r)liefde, Cape gooseberry.
appèlhof, court of appeal.
appelkoos, (-kose), apricot.
appelkoosboom, apricot-tree.
appelkooskonfyt, apricot-jam (-preserve).
appelkoossiekte, summer-diarrhoea.
appellant, (-e), appellant.
appelleer, (ge-), appeal (to a higher court).
appelliefie, (-s), Cape gooseberry.
appelmoes, mashed apples; apple-sauce.
appèlregter, judge of the appeal court.
appelskimmel, dapple-grey.
appeltjie, (-s), small apple; **'n – met iemand te skil hê**, have a bone to pick with someone.
appelwyn, cider.
appendiks, (-e), appendix.
appendisitis, appendicitis.
appersepsie, apperception.
appersipieer, (ge-), apperceive.
appliek, n. appliqué.
applikeer, v. appliqué.
applikant, (-e), applicant.
applikasie, (-s), application.
apploudisseer, (ge-), applaud, cheer, clap.
applous, applause, plaudits.
apposisie, apposition.
appresiasie, appreciation.
appresieer, (ge-), appreciate, value.
approbasie, approbation.
approksimasie, approximation.
approksimeer, (ge-), approximate.
approviandeer, (ge-), provision.
April, April.
Aprilgek, April-fool.
apteek, (-teke), chemist's (shop), pharmacy.
apteker, (-s), chemist, apothecary, druggist.
aptekersmaat, apothecaries' measure.
aptyt, appetite.
aptytlik, (-e), appetising.
aptytsnapsie, appetiser.
arabesk, (-e), arabesque.
Arabier, (-e), Arab.
Arabies, (-e), n. & a. Arabian; Arabic.
arak, arrack.
Aramees, (-ese), n. & a. Aramaic.
araroet, arrow-root.
arbei, (ge-), labour, toil, work.
arbeid, labour, toil, work.
arbeider, (-s), labourer, workman, hand.
Arbeidersparty, Labour Party.
arbeidsaam, (-same), diligent, industrious.
arbeidsaamheid, diligence, industry.
arbeidsbeurs, labour-exchange.
arbeidsburo, (-'s), labour-office.
arbeidsraad, labour-, trade-council.
arbeidsveld, field of activity, sphere of action.

arbeidsverdeling, division of labour.
arbeidsvermoë, energy, working-power; output; behoud van –, conservation of energy; – van beweging, kinetic energy.
arbeidsvraagstuk, labour-problem.
arbeidswetgewing, labour-legislation.
arbiter, (-s), arbiter, arbitrator.
arbitraal, (-ale), arbitral.
arbitrasie, arbitration; arbitrage.
arbitrasiehof, court of arbitration.
arbitreer, (ge-), arbitrate; umpire.
arbitrêr, (-e), arbitrary.
arch- ..., vide **arg-** ....
are, (-s), are.
arena, (-s), arena; ring.
arend, (-e), eagle.
arendsblik, eagle-eye; met –, eagle-eyed.
arendsjong, eaglet.
arendsnes, eagle's nest, aerie (eyrie).
arendsneus, aquiline nose.
arendsvlug, eagle's flight.
argaïsme, (-s), archaism.
argaïsties, (-e), archaic, archaistic.
argeloos, (-lose), guileless; unsuspecting.
Argentyns, (-e), Argentine.
argeologie, archaeology.
argeologies, (-e), archaeologic(al).
argeoloog, (-loë, -loge), archaeologist.
argief, (-iewe), archives; record-office.
argiefgebou, record-office; archives-building.
argipel, (-le), archipelago.
argitek, (-te), architect.
argitektonies, (-e), architectonic.
argitektuur, (-ture), architecture.
argivaris, (-se), archivist.
arglistig, (-e), cunning, crafty, guileful.
arglistigheid, cunning, guile.
argon, argon.
argument, (-e), argument, plea.
argumenteer, (ge-), argue, reason.
Argusoog, Argus-eye; met –oë, Argus-eyed.
argwaan, mistrust, suspicion.
argwanend, (-e), distrustful, suspicious.
aria, (-s), air, aria, song, tune.
Ariër, (-s), Aryan.
Aries, (-e), Aryan.
arig, (-e), queer, strange, unwell.
arikreukel, -kruikel, vide **alikruikel**.
aristokraat, (-ate), aristocrat.
aristokrasie, aristocracy.
aristokraties, (-e), aristocratic.
aritmeties, (-e), arithmetic(al).
ark, (-e), ark.
arkade, (-s), arcade.
arm, (-s), n. arm; branch; crank, lever; iemand in die – neem, consult someone; met die –s oor mekaar, with crossed (folded) arms; met oop –s ontvang, receive with open arms (cordially).
arm, a. poor, needy, indigent; (-e), unfortunate; –e drommel, unfortunate wretch, poor beggar; – aan, poor in; deficient in.
armada, (-s), armada.
armband, bracelet, bangle.
armbandhorlosie, -oorlosie, wrist-watch.
arm(e)blanke, (-s), poor-white.
arm(e)blankedom, poor-whites; poor-whiteism.
armbus, poor-box, charity-box.
armbuurt, poor-quarter(s).
arme- ..., vide **arm-** ...
arme, (-s), n. the poor.
armee, (-s), army.
Armeniër, (-s), Armenian.
Armenies, (-e), n. & a. Armenian.
armfonds, poor-relief fund.

armhuis, poor-house, almshouse, workhouse.
armkoshuis, poor hostel, charity-hostel.
armlastig, (-e), chargeable to the community.
armlastige, (-s), pauper.
armleuning, arm, elbow-rest.
armlik, (-e), needy, poor, shabby.
armoede, poverty, indigence, want; paucity (of ideas); tot – geraak (verval), be reduced to poverty; uit –, from poverty.
armoedig, (-e), poor, needy, shabby; humble; –e omstandighede, straitened circumstances; daar – uitsien, look shabby.
armoedigheid, poverty, poorness, penury.
armoedsaaier, starveling, pauper.
armpyp, brachial bone.
armrig, (-e), rather poor.
armsalig, (-e), poor, pitiful, pitiable, miserable; beggarly.
armsgat, armhole.
armslag, swing of the arm; elbow-room.
armslengte, arm's length.
armesorg, poor-relief.
armesorgkommisie, poor-relief commission.
armeversorging, vide **armesorg**.
armstoel, armchair, easy chair.
armvol, armful.
armwese, pauperism; poor-relief.
arnika, arnica.
aroma, (-s), aroma, fragrance.
aromaties, (-e), aromatic.
aronskelk, arum-lily, pig-lily.
arpuis, harpuis, resin (rosin).
arrangeer, (ge-), arrange; orchestrate.
arrangement, arrangement; orchestration.
arres, arrest; custody, detention; in – neem, place under arrest; take into custody.
arrestant, (-e), prisoner, arrested person.
arrestasie, arrest, apprehension.
arresteer, (ge-), arrest, take into custody.
arrie, (I) say!, heigh!, lo!, my!
arriveer, (ge-), arrive.
arrogansie, arrogance, presumption.
arrogant, (-e), arrogant, presumptuous.
arseen, arsenic.
arseer, (ge-), shade, hatch.
arsenaal, (-ale), arsenal, armoury.
arsenaat, (-te), arsenate.
artefak, artefact.
artesies, (-e), artisian; –e put, artesian well.
arties, (-te), artist.
artikel, (-s), article.
artikelsgewys(e), clause by clause.
artikulasie, articulation.
artikuleer, (ge-), articulate.
artillerie, artillery, ordinance.
artillerievuur, artillery-fire, gunfire.
artilleriewetenskap, gunnery.
artilleris, (-te), artilleryman, gunner.
artisjok, (-ke), artichoke.
artistiek, (-e), artistic, tasteful.
artistiekerig, (-e), would-be artistic.
artistisiteit, artisticity; artistry.
arts, (-e), doctor, physician; medical man.
artseny, (-e), medicine, medicament.
artsenybereiding, pharmacy.
artsenyberei(d)kunde, pharmaceutics.
artsenykunde, -leer, pharmacology.
artsenymiddel, drug.
as, (-se), n. ash, ashes; cinders; – is verbrande hout, if ifs and ands were pots and pans (there'd be no trade for tinkers); in die – lê, reduce to ashes; in sak en – sit, be in sackcloth and ashes; sy hand in die – slaan, oust (supplant, cut out) a rival; uit sy – verrys, rise from its ashes.

as, (-se, -te), n. axle; axle-tree (of wagon); axis (of figure, earth, etc.); shaft, spindle (of engine).
as, adv., conj. & prep. as, like, such as; in the capacity of; when; if; as if; – **'n kind**, as a child; **so oud** –, as old as; – **sodanig**, as such; – **volg**, as follows; – **'n ekskuus**, as an (by way of) excuse; – **vriende skei**, part friends; – **wat?**, in what capacity?; – **jy hom sien**, if (when) you see him; – **'t ware**, as it were.
asafstand, wheel base.
asalea, (-s), azalea.
asbaan, cinder-track; dirt track.
asbak, ash-pan; ash-bin.
asbakkie, ash-tray.
asbelasting, load on axle.
asbes, asbestos.
asblik, ash-bin.
Asdic, Asdic.
Asdic-straal, Asdic beam.
asem, (-s), breath; – **inhou**, hold one's breath; – **skep**, take breath, breathe; **buite (uit)** –, out of breath, winded; **in een** –, in one breath; **na** – **hyg (snak)**, gasp, pant for breath; **op** – **kom**, recover one's breath; **van lang** –, long-winded.
asem, (-ge), breathe, draw breath.
asemhaal, (asemge-), breathe.
asemhaling, breathing, respiration.
asemhalingsoefeninge, breathing-exercise.
asemloos, (-lose), breathless.
asemtog, breath, gasp of breath.
asepsie, asepsis, asepsis.
asepties, (-e), aseptic.
asetileen, asetylene.
asetoon, acetone.
asfalt, asphalt, butimen.
asfalteer, (ge-), asphalt.
asfaltpad, asphalt-road.
asfiksie, asphyxia(tion).
asfiksieer, (ge-), asphixiate.
as(se)gaai, (-e) assegai.
ashoop, ash-heap, scrap-heap, rubbish-dump.
Asiaat (-ate), Asiatic, Asian.
Asiaties (-e), Asiatic, Asian.
asiditeit, acidity.
asiel (-e), asylum; rescue-home; shelter; place of refuge, sanctuary.
asimmetrie, asymmetry.
asimmetrie, (-e), asymmetry.
asimmetries, (-e), asymmetric(al).
asimtoot, (-tote), asymtote.
asimtoties, (-e), asymtotic.
asimut, azimuth.
asindeties, (-e), asyndetic.
asindeton, asyndeton.
asjas, good-for-nothing, nincompoop.
askar, dust-cart, rubbish-cart.
Askari, Askari.
askeet, (-ete), ascetic.
askese, asceticism.
asketies, (-e), ascetic.
askleurig, ash-coloured.
askoek, ash-scon(e); imp, rogue, scamp.
asma, asthma.
asmaties, (-e), asthmatic.
asmede, as also, and also, as well as.
asnog, as yet.
asof, as if, as though; **maak** –, pretend.
aspaai, **aispaai**, I spy, hide-and-seek.
aspek, (-te), aspect.
aspersie, (-s), asparagus.
aspidistra, (-s), aspidistra.
aspirant, (-e), aspirant, applicant.
aspirant-kandidaat, (prospective) candidate.
aspirant-onderwyser, prospective teacher.
aspirasie, (-s), aspiration.
aspireer, (ge-), aspire; aspirate (a sound).
aspirien, (-e), aspirin(e).
aspis, (-se), asp (aspic).
aspoester(tjie), (-s), cinderella.
asreën, rain (shower) of ashes.
asseblief, (if you) please.
assegaai, vide **as(se)gaai**.
assertories, (-e), assertive.
assessor, (-e, -s), assessor; assistant.
assessorlid, assessor-member.
assimilasie, (-s), assimilation.
assimileer, (ge-), assimilate.
Assiriër, (-s), Assyrian.
Assiries, (-e), n. & a. Assyrian.
assisteer, (ge-), assist, help.
assistensie, assistance, help.
assistent, (-e), assistant.
assistente, (-s), lady-(assistant).
assistent-onderwyser, assistant-teacher.
assonansie, assonance.
assoneer, (ge-), assonate.
assoois, **assous**, (-e), smelt.
assosiasie, (-s), association; partnership.
assosiatief, (-iewe), associative.
assosieer, (ge-), associate; enter into partnership with.
assorteer, (ge-), assort.
assortiment, (-e), assortment, line.
assumeer, (ge-), co-opt.
assumpsie, assumption; co-option.
assuransie, assurance, insurance; insurance-policy.
assuransie-agent, insurance-agent.
assuransiemaatskappy, insurance-company.
assuransiepolis, insurance-policy.
aster, (-s), aster, chrysanthemum; girl, skirt.
asterisk, (-e), asterisk.
asteroïed, (-e), **asteroïde**, (-s), asteroid.
astigmaties, (-e), astigmatic.
astigmatisme, astigmatism.
astraal, (-ale), astral.
astraalluik, astral hatch, astrodome, astrohatch.
astrakan, (-s), astrakhan.
astrant, (-e), cheeky, pert, impudent.
astrantheid, coolness, cheek, impudence.
astrolabium, (-s), astrolabe.
astrologie, astrology.
astrologies, (-e), astrologic(al).
astroloog, (-loë, -loge), astrologer.
astronomie, astronomy.
astronomies, (-e), astronomic(al).
astronoom, (-nome), astronomer.
asuur, azure, sky-blue.
asvaal, ashen pale; ashen grey (colour); **jou** – **skrik**, turn pale with fright.
asyn, vinegar.
asynflessie, vinegar-cruet.
asyngees, acetone.
asynstandertjie, **-stelletjie**, cruet-stand.
asynsuur, n. acetic acid.
asynsuur, a. acetous; as sour as vinegar.
asynvat, **-vaatjie**, vinegar-vat.
atavisme, atavism, reversion (to type).
atavisties, (-e), atavistic.
ateïs, (-te), atheist.
ateïsme, atheism.
ateïsties, (-e), atheistic.
atelier, **ateljee**, (-s), studio.
Atheens, (-e), Athenian.
atheneum, athen(a)eum.
atjar, pickles.
Atlanties, (-e), Atlantic.
atlas, (-se), n. atlas.
atlas, n. satin, satin-tweel (-twill).

atleet, (-lete), athlete.
atletiek, athletics.
atleties, (-e), athletic.
atmosfeer, atmosphere.
atmosferies, (-e), atmospheric(al)
atomies, (-e), atomic.
atomiseer, (ge-), atomise.
atomisties, (-e), atomistic.
atonie, atony.
atonies, (-e), atonic.
atoom, (-tome), atom.
atoombom, A-bomb, atom(ic) bomb.
atoomgewig, atomic weight.
atoomneerslag, atomic fall-out.
atoomklowing, atom-splitting.
atoomkrag, atomic energy.
atoomleer, atomology.
atoomoorlog, atomic war.
atoomstapel, atomic pile.
atoomteorie, atomic theory.
atrofie, atrophy.
attarolie, attar, ottar (attar) of roses.
attensie, (-s), attention, consideration; considerateness, thoughtfulness.

attent, (-e), attentive; considerate, thoughtful; op iets – maak, draw attention to.
attes, (-te), **attestaat**, (-tate), certificate.
attestasie, attestation, certification.
attesteer, (ge-), attest, certify.
Atties, (-e), n. & a. Attic.
attraksie, (-s), attraction.
attribueer, (ge-), attribute.
attributief, (-iewe), attributive.
attribuut, (-bute), attribute, characteristic.
Augus(tus), August.
Augustyner, (-s), Augustine, Austin friar.
Australiër, (-s), Australian.
Australies, (-e), Australian.
aviatiek, aviation.
avokado, avocado.
Avondmaal, **Awendmaal**, the Lord's Supper, Holy Communion.
avonturier, **awenturier**, (-s), adventurer.
avontuur, **awentuur**, (-ture), adventure.
avontuurlik, **awentuurlik**, (-e), adventurous.
aweregs, (-e), inverted, wrong; perverse.
awery, average, damage.

B-dur, B sharp.
B-mol, B flat.
ba!, pshaw!, bah!
baadjie, (-s), coat, jacket; **iemand op sy – gee**, lick a person; **op jou – kry**, get licked.
baadjiepak, coat and skirt, costume.
baai, (-e), n. 1. bay.
baai, n. 2. baize.
baai, (ge-), bathe.
baai- . . ., vide **bad- . . .**
baaierd, chaos.
baaikostuum, bathing-costume.
baal, (bale), n. bale.
baal, (ge-), pack in bales.
baan, (bane), n. course, track; channel; orbit (of planet); trajectory (of projectile); panel, gore (of skirt); width, breadth (of cloth); court (for tennis); rink (for skating); floor (for dancing); – **breek**, pave the way; **sig – breek**, force (make) one's way; **ruim – maak**, clear the way; **op die lang – skuif**, put off indefinitely, shelve (plan); **van die – wees**, be off, be shelved; **kaatjie van die –,** cock of the walk; **'n – opskop**, kick up a row.
baan, (ge-), clear; pave (smooth) the way; **sig 'n weg – deur**, force one's way through; **gebaande weg**, beaten track.
baanbreker, pioneer.
baanbrekerswerk, pioneer-work.
baantjie, (-s), job, billet; **-s vir boeties**, jobs for pals.
baantjiesjaer, -soeker, job-hunter.
baantjiesjaery, job-hunting.
baanvak, section (of railway-line).
baanwagter, line-keeper; flagman.
baanwagtershuisie, line-keeper's cottage.
baanwerker, permanent-way worker.
baar, (bare), n. 1. wave, billow.
baar, (bare), n. 2. bier; stretcher.
baar, (-bare), n. 3. ingot, bar (of gold).
baar, a. raw, untrained, inexperienced.
baar, (ge-), bring forth, bear, give birth to; cause (anxiety); **opsien –**, create a stir, cause a sensation.
baard, (-e), beard; bit (of key); whiskers (of cat).
baard(e)loos, (-lose), beardless.
baardkoring, bearded wheat.
baardman(netjie), white-fish, barbel.
baarkleed, pail.
baarlik, (-e), incarnate (devil).
baarmoeder, womb, uterus.
baars, (-e), bass, perch.
baas, (base), master, boss; manager, head, chief; overseer; crack, champion.
baasbakleier, champion (crack) fighter.
baaskleremaker, master tailor.
baasraak, (baasge-), get the better of, overcome, defeat; master.
baasspeel, (baasge-), domineer, rule the roost; – **oor**, bully, boss, lord it over.
baasspeler, bully, blusterer; crack player.
baasspelerig, (-e), domineering, blustering.
baastimmerman, master carpenter.
baat, n. benefit, profit; – **vind by**, benefit by, derive benefit from; **te – neem**, avail oneself of; **bate**, assets.
baat, (ge-), avail; **wat sal dit jou –?**, what will you gain by it?; **wat – dit?**, what's the good (use)?
baatsugtig, (-e), selfish, egoistic.
baatsugtigheid, baatsug, selfishness, egoism.
baba(tjie), babe(tjie), (-s), baby, infant
babbel, (ge-), chatter, prattle; chat.
babbelaar, (-s), chatterbox; babbler, gossip.
babbelagtig, (-e), talkative, loquacious.
babbel(a)ry, chattering; tittle-tattle.

babbelbek, vide **babbelaar**.
babbeljoentjie, canopy (of bedstead).
babbelkous, vide **babbelaar**.
babbelry, vide **babbel(a)ry**.
babbelsiek, vide **babbelagtig**.
babbelsug, talkativeness.
babbelsugtig, (-e), talkative, loquacious.
baber, (-s), barbel, bagger
babetjie, vide **babatjie**.
Babiloniër, (-s), Babylonian.
Babilonies, (-e), Babylonian.
bad, (baaie), n. bath: **warm baaie**, hot springs, mineral baths; **'n – neem**, take (have) a bath; bathe (in the sea); **'n – gee**, bath (child).
bad, (ge-), bath (child); have (take) a bath; **gaan –**, go and have a bath.
badbroek, bathing-drawers.
badhanddoek, bath-towel.
badhokkie, bathing-cubicle, -box.
badhuis, bath-house, bathing-establishment.
badinrigting, bathing-establishment.
badjie, (-s) little bath.
badkamer bathroom.
bad-, baaikostuum, bathing-costume, -suit.
badkuur, stay at a health-resort.
badmus, baaimus, bathing-cap.
badpak, baaipak, vide **badkostuum**.
badplaas, -plek, bath, bathing-place, watering-place, seaside resort.
badseisoen, bathing-season.
bagasie, luggage, baggage.
bagasiebak, boot, luggage compartment.
bagasieburo, luggage-office.
bagasiedraer, luggage-carrier; porter.
bagasiekaartjie, luggage-ticket.
bagasiekamer, -kantoor, luggage-office, cloak-room.
bagasienet, cradle; luggage-rack.
bagasiewa, luggage-van.
bagatel, vide **bakatel**.
bagger, (ge-), dredge.
baggermasjien, dredger, dredging-machine.
baggernet, dredge, dredging-net.
baie, (meer, meeste), a., much; many; – **mense**, many people; – **vrugte**, much fruit; – **dankie!**, many thanks!, thank you very much!
baie, adv. very; much; many; far; frequently; – **moeilik**, very difficult; – **meer**, much (far) more; **many (far) more**; – **minder**, much less; far fewer, **dit gebeur –**, it happens frequently.
baiekeer, -maal, frequently, often.
bajonet, (-te), bayonet; **gevelde –**, fixed bayonet; – **op!**, fix bayonets!
bajonetaanval, bayonet-charge.
bak, (-ke), n. bowl; dish, basin; cistern, tank; bucket; trough (for pigs, sheep); (dust-)bin; (ash-)tray; tray; container; body (of car); hood (of snake); **in die – raak**, get behind (in arrears); **jou hande – maak**, cup one's hands; – **staan**, get down to it; **sy bene staan –**, he is bandy-legged; **sy ore staan –**, his ears stand out.
bak, (ge-), bake (bread), fry (egg, fish); bask (in the sun); **kluitjies –, make dumplings; fib; 'n poets –**, play a trick; – **en brou**, mess, jumble, muddle; intrigue, deal underhand.
bakatel, (-le), bagatelle, trifle.
bak(ke)baard, whisker(s).
bakbarometer, cistern-barometer.
bakbees, giant, colossus; whopper.
bakbene, bandy legs; – **hê**, be bandy-legged.
bakboord, port; **van – na stuurboord**, from pillar to post.
bakeliet, bakelite.

baken — **bankinstelling**

baken, (-s), beacon, landmark; buoy; – **steek**, come a cropper; **die –s versit**, change one's course.
baker, (-s), n. (dry-)nurse.
baker, (ge-), (dry-)nurse.
bakermat, cradle, birth-place.
bakersprokie, nursery-tale.
bakkebaard, vide **bak(ke)baard**.
bakker, (-s), baker.
bakkery, (-e), bakery; baking.
bakkie, (-s), small bowl; vide **bak**.
bakkies, (-e), phiz, mug.
bakkiesblom, red disa.
bakkiesdraai, (bakkiesge-), spin round, wheel.
bakkiespomp bucket-pump, Persian wheel.
bakkopslang, ringed cobra.
baklei, (ge-), fight, scuffle, scrap.
bakleier, (-s), fighter, bully.
bakleierig, (-e), quarrelsome, pugnacious.
bakleiery, fighting, fisticuffs, scrap.
bakleislag, fight, scrap.
bakoond, oven.
bakore, protruding ears.
bakpan, frying-pan; bread-pan.
bakpoeier, baking-powder.
baksel, (-s), batch, baking.
baksteen, brick.
baksteenoond, brick-kiln.
bakterie, (-ë, -s), bacterium (pl. bacteria).
bakteriologie, bacteriology.
bakteriologies, (-e), bacteriological.
bakterioloog, (-loë), bacteriologist.
baktrog, baker's trough.
bakvis(sie), flapper, bobby-soxer.
bal, (-le), n. 1. ball; **die – aan die rol bring (sit)**, set the ball rolling; **die – misslaan**, be beside the mark.
bal, (-s), n. 2. ball, dance.
bal, (ge-), clench (fist).
balalaika, balalaika.
balans, balance; balance-sheet.
balanseer, (ge-), balance, poise.
balansopruiming, stocktaking sale.
balansstaat, balance-sheet.
balboekie, (dance-)programme.
baldadig, (-e), rowdy, wanton; frisky.
baldakyn, (-e), canopy, baldachin.
balein, (-e), baleen, whale-bone; busk.
bal-en-kloupoot, ball and claw.
balhorig, balorig, (-e), refractory, stubborn.
balhorigheid, balorigheid, refractoriness.
balie, (-s), tub; bar, **tot die – toegelaat word**, be admitted (called) to the bar.
baljaar, (ge-), gambol, frisk, romp, play boisterously; kick up a row.
balju, (-s), sheriff.
baljuskap, post of sheriff, sheriffship.
balk, (-e), beam; rafter (for roof); (floor-) joist; staff, stave (mus.); bar (heraldry).
Balkan-, Balkan; **die Balkan**, the Balkans.
balkaniseer, Balkanize.
balkie, (-s), bar (on boot); vide **balk**.
balkon, (-ne-), balcony; platform (train, tram); dress-circle (in theatre).
balkostuum, dance-frock, ball-dress.
ballade, (-s), ballad.
ballas, ballast; lumber, encumbrance.
ballasmandjie, bushel-basket.
ballet, (-te), ballet.
balletdans, ballet-dancing.
balletdanseres, ballet-dancer, -girl.
balletliefhebber, balletomane.
balling, (-e, -s), exile.
ballingskap, exile, banishment.
ballon, (-ne, -s), balloon.

ballonband, balloon-tyre.
ballonversperring, balloon barrage.
ballotasie, ballot(ing).
ballotteer, (ge-), (vote by) ballot.
balorig(heid), vide **balhorig(heid)**.
balrok, dance-frock.
balsa, balsa.
balsaal, ballroom.
balsem, n. balm, balsam, ointment.
balsem, (ge-), embalm (corpse).
balsemagtig, (-e), balsamic, balmy.
balsemgeur, odour of balm, balsamic odour.
balseminie, balsemine, garden-balsam.
balsem-kopiva, copaiva balsam.
balspel, ball-game; playing at ball.
balsturig, (-e), refractory, obstinate.
balustrade, (-s), balustrade.
bamboes bamboo.
bamboesriet bamboo-reed.
ban, n. excommunication, ban; **in die – doen**, excommunicate; ostracise.
ban, (ge-), banish, exile, expel.
banaal, (-nale), banal, trite, trivial.
banaliteit, (-e), banality, platitude.
banana, (-s), banana.
banbliksem, anathema.
band, (-e), band (round arm, etc.); string (of apron); ribbon (for hair); tyre (of bicycle, motor-car); hoop (round barrel); bandage; tape (round parcel); binding, cover (of book); volume (book); belt; strap; sling (for arm); bond; tie (of friendship, blood); **–e van die liefde**, bonds of love; **hy is almal se –**, he is second to none; **aan –e lê**, keep in check; **uit die – spring**, kick over the traces.
bandelier, (-e, -s), bandoleer.
bandeloos, (-lose), lawless; unrestrained.
bandeloosheid, lawlessness, licence.
bandiet, (-e), convict.
bandmaat, tape-measure.
bandom, bantom, (-s), bantam.
bandopnemer, tape-recorder.
bandsaag, endless saw, belt-saw, band-saw.
bandvat, (bandge-), hold tight; pull up short.
bandyster, hoop-iron, brand-iron, hoops.
bang, (–, -e), afraid, frightened; cowardly, "funky", anxious, uneasy; **liewer – Jan as dooi Jan**, discretion is the better part of valour; **– maak**, frighten, scare; **– praat**, intimidate, overawe, scare; **– word**, become frightened (afraid), take fright; **– wees vir**, be afraid (scared) of, fear; fear for (one's life).
bangbroek, coward, poltroon, "funk".
bangerig, (-e), rather frightened (afraid); nervous; "funky" (player).
bangheid, fear; anxiety; cowardice.
bangmakery, intimidation, scaring.
bangpratery, intimidation.
banier, (-e), banner, standard.
banjo, (-'s), banjo.
bank, (-e), n. bench, seat; sofa, settee; pew (in church); form, desk (in school); bank (for depositing money; of sand, snow); ridge; **deur die –**, on an average; without exception; **in die – sit**, bank (money).
bank, (ge-), bank.
bankbiljet, banknote.
bankdiskonto, bank-rate.
banket, (-te), banquet; confectionery.
banketbakker, confectioner.
banketbakkery, confectioner's shop.
bankhouer, banker (gambling).
bankier, (-s), banker.
bankierskantoor, bank; banker's office.
bankinstelling, banking-house, -institution.

bankpapier, paper-currency.
bankrekening, banking-account.
bankroetier, (-s), bankrupt.
bankrot, bankrupt, insolvent; "broke".
bankrotskap, bankruptcy.
banksake, banking, banking-matters.
banksaldo, bank balance.
bankskroef, bench-vice, standing vice.
bankstaat, bank-statement.
bankstelsel, banking-system.
bankwerker, fitter, engine-turner.
bankwese, banking.
banneling, vide **balling**.
bantamhoendertjie, bantam(-cock, -hen).
bantom, **bandom**, (-s), bantam (pebble); striped, banded ox (cow).
banvloek, ban, anathema.
banvonnis, sentence of exile.
baobab(boom), cream of tartar tree, baobab.
baptis, (-te), baptist.
bar, (-re), a. barren; inclement, severe.
bar, adv. terribly, horribly.
barak, (-ke), barracks; hovel; hut; shed.
baratea, barathea.
barbaar, (-bare), barbarian, savage.
barbaars, (-e), barbarous, barbarian.
barbaarsheid, barbarousness, barbarity.
barbarisme, barbarism.
barber, (-s), vide **baber**.
barbier, (-s), barber, hairdresser.
barbierswinkel, barber's shop.
barbituraat, barbiturate.
barbituursuur, barbituric acid.
bard, (-e), bard.
barensnood, travail, labour; in -, in labour.
baret, (-te), beret; cap.
bargoens, jargon, gibberish.
barheid, inclemency, severity; vide **bar**.
baring, parturition, childbirth.
barium, barium (chem.).
bark, (-e), bark, barque.
barkas, (-se), launch, long-boat.
barlewiet, barley-wheat.
barmhartig, (-e), merciful, charitable.
barmhartigheid, mercy, charity.
barnsteen, amber.
barnsteenpyp, amber-pipe.
barok, baroque; grotesque.
barometer, barometer.
barometries, (-e), barometric.
baron, (-ne, -s), baron.
barones, (-se), baroness.
baroskoop, (-skope), baroscope.
barrikade, (-s), barricade.
barrikadeer, (ge-), barricade.
bars, (-te), n. crack; burst, split; chap (of skin); 'n - werk, work like blazes.
bars, (-, -e), a. harsh, rough, gruff.
bars, (ge-), burst, crack, split; chap (of skin); explode, burst (of shell); **my kop wil -**, my head is splitting; **- van die lag**, split one's sides; **buig of -**, bend or break, no matter what happens; **ons het ge-**, we had a hard (rough) time; **loop dat dit -**, run like mad (blazes).
barsheid, harshness, roughness; vide **bars**, a.
barshou, fine shot; **hy speel 'n -**, he is a crack player.
barstend, (-e), bursting; splitting.
barstens: **tot - toe**, bursting; **dit het - gegaan**, it was a devil of a job.
barsterig, (-e), cracky, full of cracks.

Bartholomeusnag, Massacre of St Bartholomew, St Bartholomew's Eve.
bas, (-se), n. (1) bass; - **sing**, sing bass.
bas, (-te), n. (2) bark (of tree); rind (of tree, plant); skin; **tussen die boom en die -**, betwixt and between; **iemand op sy - gee**, dust a person's jacket; **op jou - kry**, get one's jacket dusted.
basaar, (-s), bazaar.
basalt, basalt.
basboom, wattle.
baseer, (ge-): - **op**, base on, ground on.
basel, (ge-), talk rot (nonsense), twaddle.
basfluit, bass-flute.
basies, (-e), basic; **-e sout**, basic salt.
basil, (-le), bacillus (pl. basilli).
basilika, **basiliek**, (-e), basilica.
basilikum, basil; basilicum (ointment).
basilisk, (-e), basilisk.
basis, (-se), base; basis (fig.).
Baskies, (-e), Basque.
baskule, (-s), bascule, platform-scale.
Basoeto, (-'s), Basuto.
bas-relief, bas-relief, basso-rilievo.
bassleutel, bass-clef.
basstem, bass(-voice).
basta, stop; shut up! that's enough!
baster, (-s), bastard; half-caste, half-breed; hybrid; mongrel.
baster, adv. kind of; rather; quite.
baster, (ge-), hybridise; interbreed.
bastergensbok, roan (antelope).
bastergeslag, mongrel (degenerate) race.
basterkoedoe, nyala.
basterras, mongrel breed.
basterskaap, cross-bred sheep.
basterskap, bastardy.
bastersoort, hybrid.
bastertaal, mixed jargon, lingua franca.
basterkvloek(woord), mild oath.
bastervorm, hybrid (form).
basterwoord, hybrid (word); barbarism.
bastion, (-s), bastion.
basuin, (-e), trumpet; trombone.
basuingeskal, sound of trumpets.
basviool, contrabass, double bass.
Bataafs, (-e), Batavian.
bataljon, (-ne, -s), battalion.
Batavier, (-e), Batavian.
bate, asset; **ten - van**, for the benefit (good) of; in behalf of; in aid of (our school).
batig, (-e), **-e saldo**, credit-balance; surplus.
batik, (ge-), batik.
batikwerk, batik-work.
batis, batiste, lawn.
batisfeer, bathysphere.
batos, bathos.
battery, (-e), battery.
bauxiet, bauxite.
beaam, (-), assent to, approve of.
beaming, assent.
beampte, (-s), official, officer.
beangs, (-te), anxious, uneasy, alarmed.
beangstheid, anxiety, uneasiness.
beangstig, (-), alarm.
beantwoord, (-), answer; reply to: acknowledge (greeting); return (love); do, get on; thrive; **die ding sal nooit - nie**, this will never do; **- aan**, serve, answer (the purpose); answer to (the description); fulfil (conditions); correspond to.

beantwoording, answer(ing), reply(ing); ter – van, in reply to.
**bearbei, (–), work; cultivate (ground); treat (material); use one's influence with; try to pursuade; canvass (constituency, etc.); minister to the spiritual needs of.
**bearbeiding, canvassing; manipulation, ministration, ministering; vide bearbei.
beatnik, beatnik.
bebloed, (-e), blood-stained, bloody.
**beboet, (–), fine; met R1 –, fine R1.
beboeting, fining.
bebos, (–), afforest.
bebossing, afforestation.
bebou, (–), build (up)on; till, cultivate (land).
bebroei(d), (-de), hard-set (egg).
bebroeide–eiers, monkey-cap.
bebrou, (–), spoil, mess up.
bed, (-de, -dens), bed; bedside.
bedaar, (–), calm down; subside; drop (of wind); calm, quiet, soothe, pacify.
bedaard, (-e), calm, composed, tranquil.
bedag, mindful (of); prepared (for).
bedags, by day, during the day.
bedagsaam (-same), thoughtful; cautious; considerate.
bedank, (–), thank; resign (post); dismiss, discharge (employee); decline (honour); withdraw one's subscription; **as lid –,** resign one's membership; **vir 'n uitnodiging –,** thank (person) for invitation; decline invitation.
bedanking, thanking, resignation.
bedaring, abatement; calming down; **tot – bring,** pacify; soothe (child); **tot – kom,** calm down; vide **bedaar.**
beddegaanstyd, bedtime.
beddegoed, bedding, bed-clothes.
beddeken, blanket, quilt.
bedding (-s), bed (of river, of flowers), seam (of coal); layer, stratum (geol.).
beddinkie, (-s), bed (of flowers).
bede, (-s), prayer; entreaty, supplication.
bededag, day of prayer.
bedeel, (–), endow (with talents); **die armes –** bestow alms upon the poor.
bedeel(d), endowed, (blessed) with.
bedees, (-de), bashful, timid, shy.
bedeesdheid, bashfulness, timidity.
bedehuis, house of worship.
bedek, (-te), covered; concealed, disguised, veiled; covert (threat); **op –te wyse,** covertly.
bedek, (–), cover (up); conceal, hide.
bedekking, covering, cover.
bedekbloeiend, (-e), cryptogamous.
bedeksadig, (-e), angiospermous.
bedektelik, covertly.
bedel, (ge-), beg; ask alms; cadge.
bedelaar, (-s), beggar, mendicant.
bedelagtig, (-e), beggarly.
bedelares, (-se), beggar-woman.
bedel(a)ry, begging.
bedelbroe(de)r, mendicant.
bedeling, endowment; distribution of alms; (new) dispensation.
bedelmonnik, mendicant friar.
bedelorde, mendicant order.
bedelstaf: tot die – bring, reduce to beggary.
bedenking, (-e, -s), consideration; objection; **–e hê,** raise objections, object; **in – gee,** ask to consider, suggest.
bedenklik, (-e), critical (condition); dangerous; serious; doubtful (look); suspicious.
bedenklikheid, criticalness; vide **bedenklik.**
bede-oord, place of worship.

bederf, n. decay, putrefaction, decomposition; rot (in wood); corruption, depravity (of morals); deterioration; ruin.
bederf, bederwe, (–), go bad, rot, decay; spoil; ruin (health); corrupt (morals).
bederfbaar, (-bare), perishable.
bederflik, (-e), perishable; corruptible.
bederflikheid, corruptibility.
bederfwerend, (-e), preservative, antiseptic.
bederwer, (-s), spoiler; corrupter.
bedevaart, pilgrimage.
bedevaartganger, pilgrim.
bedevaartplek, -oord, place of pilgrimage.
bedgenoot, bedfellow.
bedien, (–), serve, attend to, wait upon, mind (machine); preach (the Gospel); **sig – (van),** help oneself (to); use; make use of, avail oneself of; **aan tafel –,** wait at table.
bedienaar, (-s), minister, preacher.
bediende, (-s), servant (in house); attendant, waiter; assistant (in shop).
bediening, service; serving; waiting, preaching; office.
bedil, (–) find fault with, carp at.
bedilsiek, (-e), fault-finding.
bedilsug, fault-finding.
beding, n. stipulation, condition.
beding, (–), stipulate.
beding, vide **beding, n.**
bedink, (–), bear in mind, remember; consider (matter); think out, contrive, invent (story); devise (ways and means); **sig –,** change one's mind, think better of.
bedinktyd, time for reflection.
bedissel, (–), adze; arrange, manage.
bedlêend, bedlêerig, (-e), bedridden, laid up.
Bedoeïen, (-e), Bedouin.
bedoel, (–), mean; intend; aim at, purpose; **wat – jy?,** what do you mean?; **ek het dit nie so (kwaad) – nie,** no offence was meant; **dit was goed –,** it was meant for the best; **goed –de,** well meant, well intentioned.
bedoeling, (-e) (-s), meaning; intention, object, purpose, aim; **met die beste –,** with the best intentions; **sonder kwaaie –e,** without meaning any harm.
bedol(d), mad, crazy.
bedolwe, buried.
bedompig, (-e), stuffy, fusty, close, sultry.
bedompigheid, stuffiness; sultriness.
bedonder(d), (-de), mad, crazy.
bedorwe, depraved; spoiled; bad; corrupt.
bedot, (–), trick, fool, take in.
bedra(ag), (–), amount to.
bedrag, (-drae), amount; **ten bedrae van,** to the amount of, amounting to.
bedreig, (–), threaten, menace.
bedreiging, (-e, -s), threat, menace.
bedremmeld, (-e), perplexed, bewildered.
bedrewe, skilled, skilful; practised, expert.
bedrewenheid, skill, proficiency.
bedrieë, bedrieg, (–), deceive, cheat, mislead, take in, impose upon, defraud.
bedrieër, (-s), deceiver, cheat, swindler.
bedrieëry, bedriegery, (–), deceit, fraud, deception, trickery, cheating.
bedrieglik, (-e), deceptive.
bedriegster, (-s), vide **bedrieër.**
bedroë, deceived, taken in; **– uitkom,** be disappointed.
bedroef, (-de), a. sad, grieved, sorrowing.
bedroef, adv. **: – min.** precious little (few); **– lelik,** awfully (frightfully) ugly.
bedroef, (–), grieve, distress.
bedroefdheid, grief, sorrow, sadness, distress.

bedroewend, (-e), sad, pitiful, saddening.
bedrog, (-drieërye), deceit, fraud, trickery.
bedruk, (-te). a. printed; depressed, dejected.
bedruk, (-), print on.
bedruktheid dejection, depression.
bedryf, (-drywe), deed; trade, business, profession; industry; act (of play); 'n – uitoefen, practise a trade.
bedryf, -drywe, (-), commit, perpetrate, do; rou –, mourn; vreugde –, rejoice; sonde –, commit sins.
bedryfseker, reliable.
bedryfskapitaal, working-capital.
bedryfskoste, working-expenses.
bedryfsleer, business-management; technology.
bedryfsleier, works-manager.
bedryfsvoorskrifte, service-instructions.
bedrywe, vide **bedryf**.
bedrywende vorm, active voice.
bedrywer, (-s), doer, perpetrator.
bedrywig, (-e), busy, active.
bedrywigheid, activity; stir; bustle.
bedsprei, coverlet, counterpane, bedspread.
bedstyl, bedpost.
bedug, afraid, apprehensive; – **dat**, apprehensive that; – **vir**, apprehensive for (person's safety); apprehensive of (danger).
bedugtheid, fear, dread, apprehension.
bedui(e), (-), mean, signify; portend, spell; indicate; make clear; point out; gesticulate; **die pad** –, direct, tell the way.
beduidend, (-e), considerable.
beduidenis, meaning.
beduimel, (-), thumb.
beduiwel(d), (-de), **beduweld**, (-e), mad, crazy, daft, possessed by the devil.
bedwang, control, restraint.
bedwelm, (-), daze, stun (by a fall); intoxicate (by strong drink); drug.
bedwelmend, (-e), intoxicating.
bedwelming, daze, stupefaction; intoxication.
bedwing, (-), control, check, curb; suppress (feeling, yawn, laughter); keep (hold) back, keep down; quell (insurrection); restrain (passions); contain (anger); sig –, restrain (control) oneself.
beëdig, (-), swear in; swear to.
beëdigde, sworn.
beëdiging, swearing in; putting to the oath.
beef, **bewe**, (-), tremble; shake (with fear); shudder (with cold, horror); shiver (with cold); quiver (of leaf, voice); – **by die gedagte**, shudder (tremble) at the thought.
beëindig, (-), finish, end, conclude.
beëindiging, termination, conclusion.
beek, (beke), brook, rivulet, rill.
beeld, (-e), n. image; reflection; statue (moulded figure); likeness, picture; figure of speech; conception; 'n – van 'n vrou, a picture of a woman.
beeld, (ge-), form, shape; depict, portray.
beelddienaar, image-worshipper; idolator.
beelddiens, idolatry, image-worship.
beeldenaar, (-s), head (on coin).
beeldende, plastic (art).
beelderig, (-e), sweet, lovely.
beeldestormer, iconoclast.
beeldhou, (ge-), sculpture, carve (wood).
beeldhouer, sculptor.
beeldhoukuns, sculpture.
beeldhouwerk, sculpture, statuary; carving.
beeldjie, (-s), image, statuette.
beeldradio, television.
beeldryk, (-e), ornate.
beeldrykheid, ornateness, floweriness.

beeldsend, (ge-), televise; telecast.
beeldskoon, (-skone), of rare beauty.
beeldskrif, picture-writing; hieroglyphics.
beeldsnyer, wood-carver.
beeldsnykuns, image-carving.
beeldsnywerk, carving.
beeldspraak, figurative (metaphorical) language metaphor.
beeldstormer, vide **beeldestormer**.
beeltenis, (-se), image, likeness, portrait.
been, (bene), leg; bone (of skeleton); side (of triangle); **jou bene dra**, leg it, take to one's heels; – **in die lug val**, come a cropper, fall flat on one's back; – **in die lug lê**, lie flat on one's back (with legs in the air); be laid up; **op drie bene spring**, limp badly; **op die – bly**, keep one's legs (feet); **hy is al weer op die** –, he is on his legs (about) again; **vroeg op die** –, up (stirring) early; **op die – bring**, raise (army); **op die – help**, help up; set (person) on his legs; **op jou laaste bene loop (wees)**, be on one's last legs; **op eie bene staan**, stand on one's own legs.
been-af, with a broken leg; in love.
beenagtig, (-e), bony, osseous.
beenbekleding, leggings.
beenbeskrywing, osteography.
beenbreuk, fracture (of bone, leg).
beeneter, necrosis, caries.
beenholte, bone-cavity.
beenkunde, beenleer, osteology.
beenloos, (-lose), boneless; legless.
beenmeel, bone-meal, bone-dust.
beenpyp, leg-bone.
beenskut, leg-guard, pad (in cricket).
beentjie, (-s), little leg; small bone, ossicle (anat.); **jou beste – voorsit**, put one's best foot foremost.
beenuitwas, bony excrescence.
beenvlies, periosteum.
beenvliesontsteking, periostitis.
beenvorming, bone-formation, ossification.
beenvreter, necrosis.
beenweefsel, bony (osseous) tissue.
beenwindsels, puttees.
beer, (bere); bear (wild animal); boar (male pig); **die Groot B-**, the Great Bear; **die Klein B-**, the Lesser Bear.
beërf, **beërwe**, (-), inherit.
beertjie, (-s), little boar (bear); Teddy bear.
beerwyfie, she-bear, female bear.
bees, (-te), beast; brute; **-te**, cattle; **jou –!**, you brute!; **ou –!**, splendid!; stout fellow!
beesagtig, (-e), beastly, brutal, bestial.
beesagtig, adv. beastly; tremendous, colossal.
beesagtigheid, beastliness, bestiality.
beesbak, vide **bakbees**.
bees(te)koper, cattle-dealer.
bees(te)kraal, cattle-kraal.
beeste, cattle.
beeste . . ., vide **bees-**.
beesteteelt, cattle-rearing.
beesvel, ox-hide.
beesvleis, beef.
beesvoer, cattle-fodder.
beeswagter, cattle-herd.
beet, (bete), 1. beetroot.
beet, n. 2. bite, hold, grip.
beethê, (beetgehad), have got hold of.
beetkry, (beetge-), get (take, seize) hold of, seize, grasp, grip.
beetneem, (beetge-), take in, deceive, make a fool of. Vide **beetpak**.
beetpak, (beetge-), lay hold of, seize, grab.
beetsuiker, beet-sugar (sugar-beet).
beetwortel, beetroot.

bef — **behang**

bef, (**bewwe**), **beffie,** (-s), (clerical, legal) bands; – **en toga,** bands and gown.
befaamd, (-e), renowned; notorius.
befaamdheid, fame; notoriety.
beffie, vide **bef.**
befoeter, (–), muck up.
befoeter(d), crazy, mad, daft.
befoeterdheid, craziness; cussedness.
begaaf, (-**de**), gifted, talented.
begaafdheid, ability, talent(s).
begaan, (-**gane**), a. beaten (track); anxious, concerned; **begane grond,** level ground; ground-level, ground-floor; – **wees oor,** be worried about; **op begane grond,** on terra firma.
begaan, (–), tread, go; make (mistake); commit (crime, blunder), perpetrate; **iemand laat –,** let a person have his way.
begaanbaar, (-**bare**), practicable, passable.
begaanbaarheid, practicability, passability.
begane, vide **begaan.**
begeef, begewe, (–), forsake, leave in the lurch, fail; **sy moed het hom –,** his courage failed him; **sig – in,** expose oneself to (danger); embark upon (engage in) (war); **jy weet nie waarin jy jou – nie,** you don't know what you are letting yourself in for; **sig in die huwelik –,** marry (get married); **sig – na,** go to (a place), proceed to; **sig op pad –,** set out; **sig ter ruste –,** retire to rest.
begeer, (–), desire, want, covet; **al wat 'n mens (se hart) kon –,** everything that one could wish for.
begeerlik, (-e), desirable; tempting, enticing; eager, greedy (eyes); covetous.
begeerlikheid, desirability; covetousness, greed-(iness), cupidity.
begeerte, (-s), wish, desire; eagerness; lust.
begelei, (–), accompany (to a place; on the piano); escort, attend.
begeleidend, (-e), accompanying; covering.
begelei(d)er, attendant; accompanist (mus.).
begeleiding, escort; accompaniment.
begenadig, (–), pardon, reprieve, grant an amnesty; grace, favour.
begenadiging, pardon, reprieve; favour.
begerig, (-e), desirous, eager; covetous.
begerigheid, eagerness; covetousness.
begiet, (–), drench, wet, sprinkle.
begiftig, (–), endow; – **met,** endow with; invest with (rank); confer upon.
begiftiging, donation, endowment.
begin, n. beginning, commencement; start, outset; **'n – maak,** begin, (make a) start; **aan, by die –,** at the beginning; at the outset; **in die –,** in the beginning; at first; **sommer in die –,** right from the start, at the very outset; **van die – (af),** from the beginning (start, outset); **van die – tot die end,** from beginning to end, from start to finish.
begin, beginne, begint, (–), begin, commence; set up, start (business); open (a school); set in of (rain); – **aan,** start, begin; – **met te sê,** begin by saying; **daarmee kan 'n mens niks – nie,** that is useless (no use); **met hom kan 'n mens niks – nie,** he is a good-for-nothing; it is impossible to deal (get on) with him.
beginkapitaal, principal, initial capital.
beginletter, initial (letter).
beginner, (-s), beginner; novice.
beginpaal, starting-post.
beginpunt, starting-point.
beginreël, opening line, first line.
beginsalaris, commencing salary.

beginsel, (-s), principle; **eerste –s,** first principles, rudiments (elements); **in (uit) –,** in (on) principle.
beginselloos, (-lose), without principles; unprincipled (conduct, person).
beginselloosheid, lack of principles.
beginselvas, (-te), of firm principles.
beginselvastheid, firmness of principles.
beginsnelheid, initial velocity (speed).
beginstadium, initial stage.
begluur, (–), spy upon; glare at; eye, ogle.
begoël, begogel, (–), bewitch, delude.
begoëling, begogeling, bewitchment, spell; delusion.
begonia, (-s), begonia.
begraaf, begrawe, (–), bury, inter.
begraafplaas, burial-place, cemetery.
begrafnis, (-se), funeral, burial, interment.
begrafnisdiens, burial-service.
begrafnisformulier, office of the dead.
begrafnislys, list of attendants at a funeral.
begrafnisondernemer, undertaker.
begrafnisonderneming, undertaker's business.
begrafnisplegtigheid, funeral-ceremony.
begrafnisstoet, funeral-procession.
begrens, (–), limit, bound.
begrensing, limitation, bounds.
begrepe, understood; – **in,** included in.
begrip, (-**pe**) idea, conception, notion; understanding, comprehension, apprehension; **dit gaan my – te bowe,** it passes my understanding; **nie die flouste – nie,** not the faintest idea (notion); **kort –,** summary, synopsis.
begripsleer, ideology.
begripsverwarring, confusion of ideas.
begroei, (–), overgrow.
begroet, (–), greet, salute; – **as,** hail as.
begroeting, greeting, salutation.
begroot, (–), estimate, rate.
begroting, (-s), estimate; **die –,** the budget, the estimates.
begrotingsdebat, budget-debate.
begrotingsrede, budget-speech.
begryp, (–), understand; comprehend, grasp, conceive; – **jou (aan)!,** just imagine (fancy, think of it)!; – **my good,** don't misunderstand me; – **jy wat ek bedoel?,** do you follow me?; **verkeerd –,** misunderstand; **alles – in,** include everything in; – **in,** contained in (maths.).
begryplik, (-e), comprehensible, understandable; conceivable; intelligent.
begryplikerwys(e), obviously.
begunstig, (–), favour; patronize.
begunstiger, (-s), patron; supporter.
begunstiging, favour; patronage; favouritism; **onder – van,** favoured by, under favour of.
begyn, (-e), **begyntjie,** (-s), beguine.
behaag, behae, (–), please.
behaaglik, (-e), pleasant; comfortable.
behaaglikheid, pleasantness; comfort.
behaagsiek, (-e), coquettish.
behaagsug, coquettishness.
behaal, (–), gain, win, (prize, victory), score; obtain (degree).
behaar(d), (-**de**), hairy, hirsute; pilose (bot.).
behae, n. pleasure; – **skep in,** take delight (pleasure) in, delight in.
behae, (–), vide **behaag.**
behalwe, except, but, save; **almal – een,** all but one; – **dit,** in addition to this; besides.
behandel, (–), treat; deal with (subject, case, person); do; handle, manage; attend; discuss.
behandeling, treatment; handling; hearing (of case); discussion.
behang, n., v. **behangsel.**

behang, (-), hang (decorate) with paper (a wall).
behanger, paper-hanger.
behangselpapier, wallpaper.
behartig, (-), look after; manage; cope with; attend to.
behartigenswaardig, (-e), worthy of consideration.
behartiging, looking after, furtherance, promoting (promotion); vide **behartig.**
beheer, n. management, administration, control, direction; **raad van -,** board of control.
beheer, (-), manage, control, administer.
beheerder, (-s), manager, director.
beheers, (-), control, master; govern, rule (people); dominate (a situation, a scene); **sig -,** control (command, restrain), oneself; **'n taal -,** have command of a language.
beheerser, (-s), master; ruler.
beheersing, control; command; domination.
beheks, (-), bewitch.
behelp, (-): sig -, manage, make shift.
behels, (-), embrace, comprise; contain.
behendig, (-e), dexterous, skilful, adroit.
behendigheid, dexterity, skill, deftness.
behep: - met, possessed by (with) (idea); afflicted (laden, burdened) with.
behoed(e), (-), protect; watch over, preserve; save.
behoeder, behoedster, (-s), protector, defender.
behoedsaam, (-same), cautious, wary, prudent, circumspect.
behoedsaamheid, cautiousness, caution.
behoef, (-), need, require, want; **jy - dit nie te doen nie,** you need not do it; **dit - nie, there** is no need to.
behoefte, (-s), need, want; **hê aan,** be in need (want) of, need; **voorsien in die - van,** provide for; **voorsien in 'n lang gevoelde -,** supply a long-felt want.
behoeftig, (-e), needy, poor, destitute.
behoeftigheid, neediness, destitution, indigence.
behoewe: ten - van, on behalf of.
behoor(t), (-), belong (to); be proper; **soos dit - te wees,** as it should be; **ek - nie hier nie,** this is no place for me; I do not belong here; **jy - dit te weet,** you should (ought to) know this; **- aan,** belong to; **- by,** go with; **- by mekaar,** go (belong) together; **- tot,** belong to; fall under, be among.
behoorlik, (-e), a. proper, becoming, fitting; decent, respectable.
behoorlik, adv. properly, decently, respectably; thoroughly, completely.
behoorlikheid, propriety.
behoorlikheidshalwe, for decency's sake.
behore: na -, properly, fittingly; respectably.
behou, (-), keep; retain; maintain; save.
behoud, retention; preservation; maintenance; conservation (of energy); salvation.
behoudend, (-e), conservative (party).
behou(d)er, (-s), preserver. Vide **behou.**
behoudenis, salvation.
behoudens, except (but) for; subject to.
behoue, safe, unhurt, unscathed.
behuis, (-de): ruim - wees, live in a large house.
behuis, (-), provide accommodation, house.
behuising, housing.
behuisingsplan, housing-scheme.
behulp: met - van, with the aid of.
behulpsaam, (-same), helpful; **- wees,** assist.
behulpsaamheid, helpfulness.
beiaard, (-s), chimes, carillon.
beiaardier, (-s), carilloneur.
beide, both; **een van -,** one of the two; either; **geen van -,** neither (of the two); **ons -r vriend,** our mutual friend.

beiderlei, of both sorts.
beidersyds, on both sides.
Beiers, (-e), Bavarian.
beïnvloed, (-), influence, affect.
beïnvloeding, influencing.
beitel, (-s), n. chisel; cutter.
beitel, (ge-), chisel.
bejaard, (-e), elderly, advanced in years.
bejaardheid, advanced (old) age.
bejag, pursuit (of).
bejammer, (-), pity; bewail; deplore.
bejammerenswaardig, (-e), pitiable; deplorable.
bejeën, (-), treat, use.
bejeëning, treatment.
bek, (-ke), mouth; beak, bill (of bird); snout (of animal); muzzle (of fire-arm), jaws (of vice); spout; opening; **'n groot - hê,** have plenty of jaw; **hard in die -,** hard-mouthed.
bek-af, down-hearted; dog-tired, worn out.
bekaaid: daar - (van) afkom, get the worst of it.
bekamp, (-), fight (against); combat.
bekeer, (-), convert; proselytize; reform.
bekeer(d), (-e), converted.
bekeerde, (-s), convert; proselyte.
bekeerling, (-e), convert; proselyte.
beken, (-), acknowledge, admit, confess, own up; see, make out; **kleur -,** follow suit; **nie kleur - nie,** revoke (cards); **skuld -,** plead guilty.
bekend, (-e), known; well known; familiar; **- om,** noted for; **- wees met,** be acquainted with, know; **dit is algemeen -,** it is common knowledge; **vir sover my -,** as far as I know, to my knowledge; **- maak,** announce, notify; **die uitslag - maak,** publish (announce) the result; declare the poll; **- staan as,** be known as; **- voorkom,** seem familiar; **- word,** become known; get abroad.
bekende, (-s), acquaintance.
bekendheid, name, reputation; acquaintance; **dit is van algemeen -,** it is (a matter of) common knowledge; **- verwerf,** become known, win a name for oneself.
bekendmaking, (-e, -s), announcement; notice; notification; publication.
bek-en-klousiekte, foot-and-mouth disease.
bekentenis, (-se), confession, admission.
beker, (-s), jug, mug; beaker; cup; **vir die -,** with might and main, like mad.
bekering, conversion;
bekeringswerk, proselytization; mission-work.
bekerwedstryd, cup-match.
bekken, (-s), basin; catchment-area; (baptismal) font; pelvis (anat.); cymbal (mus.).
bekkenbeen, pelvic bone.
bekkeneel, (-nele), skull.
bekkie, (-s), little mouth (beak); kiss.
bekla(ag), beklae, (-), pity (person); deplore, lament; bemoan (one's lot); **sig - oor,** complain of (to person).
beklaagde, (-s), accused; defendant.
beklaarlik, (-e), pitiable.
beklad, (-), blot; stain, sully; slander.
beklae, vide **bekla(ag).**
bekla(g)enswaardig, (-e), pitiable; lamentable.
beklag, complaint.
bekleding, covering; cover; upholstering; upholstery; lining; facing (of robe); tenure (of office); investiture (with office).
bekleed, beklee(d), (-), clothe; upholster, cover (furniture); drape (with cloth); case; line; panel (walls); fill, occupy, hold (post); invest (with power).
bekleedsel, cover(ing); upholstery.
bekleër, (-s), holder (of office); upholsterer.
beklem, (-), oppress; stress.

beklem(d), (-e), oppressed; heavy; accented.
beklemdheid, oppression, heaviness.
beklemming, oppression, heaviness, angina.
beklemtoon, (-), accent, stress (point).
beklim, (-), climb; ascend; scale.
beklimming, climbing, mounting, ascent.
beklink, (-), clinch, settle; drink to.
beklonke, settled, arranged, fixed up.
beklop, (-), tap (knock) on; percuss.
beklouter, (-), climb, scale. Vide **klouter.**
beknaag, (-), gnaw at.
beknabbel, nibble (at).
beknel, (-), pinch; oppress.
beknibbel, (-), barter down; stint; cut down.
beknop, (-te), a. concise (style); condensed, compact; poky (room); confined, cramped.
beknoptheid, conciseness; briefness, brevity; terseness, compactness; pokiness.
beknor, (-), scold, chide.
bekoel, (-), cool (down); flag.
bekom, (-), get, obtain; come round, recover (from); agree with (of food); **suur -,** regret.
bekommer: sig - oor (om), worry about, feel uneasy (concerned) about.
bekommer(d), (-de), worried, concerned.
bekommerdheid, uneasyness, anxiety.
bekommering, (-e), bekommernis, (-se), anxiety, trouble, worry; care.
bekoms: jou - eet, (hê), eat (have) one's fill.
bekonkel, (-de), a. muddled up; mad, daft.
bekonkel, (-), manoeuvre, scheme, wangle.
bekoop, (-): met die dood -, pay (with one's life).
bekoor, (-), charm, fascinate; appeal to.
bekoorlik, (-e), charming, enchanting.
bekoorlikheid, enchantment, fascination.
bekoorster, (-s), enchantress; temptress.
bekoring, charm, fascination, enchantment.
bekort, (-), shorten, cut short; abridge (book).
bekostig, (-), pay the expenses; afford.
bekostiging, defrayal.
bekragtig, (-), ratify, (compact); confirm (sentence, evidence); sanction (law).
bekragtiging, ratification; confirmation.
bekrans, (-), wreathe, adorn with garlands.
bekrap, bekras, (-), scratch (scribble) all over.
bekreun, (-), vide **bekommer.**
bekrimp, (-), cut down; **sig -,** stint oneself.
bekrimping, stinting oneself, scraping.
bekritiseer, (-), cry down, disparage.
bekrompe, a. confined (space); narrow-minded.
bekrompenheid, narrow-mindedness, narrowness.
bekroon, (-), crown; award a prize.
bekroning, crowning; award.
bekruip, (-), stalk, steal upon, surprise.
bekwaal(d), (-de), sickly.
bekwaam, (-kwame), a. competent, capable, efficient, fit; (of fruit) mature; ripe.
bekwaam, (-): sig -, qualify (for); train, study.
bekwaamheid, (-hede), ability, competence; capacity; skill; **bekwaamhede,** attainments.
bekwyl, (-), beslaver, beslobber.
bekyk, (-), look at, view (lit. & fig.).
bel, (-le), n. bell; ear-drop; wattle (of turkey); **die - aanbind,** bell (the cat).
bel, (ge-), ring; ring for (telephone).
belaai, (-), load; burden; **- met,** loaded with; **swaar -,** heavily laden.
belaglik, (-e), ridiculous, ludicrous; **- maak,** ridicule; **sig - maak,** make oneself ridiculous.
belaglikheid, ridiculousness.
beland, (-), land.
belang (-e), interest; importance; **- hê by,** be interested in; **- stel in,** take an interest in; be interested in; **in die - van,** in the interest(s) of; **van weinig (minder) -,** of little (minor) importance.
belangegemeenskap, community of interest.
belangeloos, (-lose), disinterested.
belangende, concerning.
belangesfeer, sphere of interest.
belanghebbend, (-e), a. interested; **die -e partye,** the parties concerned; **-e voorwerp,** indirect object.
belangrik, (-e), important; considerable.
belangrikheid, importance.
belangstellend, (-de), interested; sympathetic.
belangstelling, interest; sympathy; **- wek,** rouse interest.
belangwekkend, (-e), interesting.
belas, (-te), a. loaded; burdened; taxed; **- wees met,** have charge of; be burdened with; **erflik - wees,** be a victim of heredity.
belas, (-), load; burden; tax (the farmers); instruct, charge with; **sig - met,** take upon oneself.
belasbaar, (-bare), taxable; dutiable.
belaster, (-), slander, defame, blacken.
belastering, slandering, defamation.
belasting, (-s), taxation; tax; (local) rates; load, stress, strain; **-s hef,** levy taxes.
belastingaanslag, assessment.
belastingamptenaar, revenue-officer.
belastingbetaler, tax-payer; ratepayer.
belastingbiljet, notice of assessment.
belastingkantoor, revenue-office.
belastingopbrengs, tax-revenue.
belastingpligtig, (-e), ratable; taxable.
belastingpligtige, (-s), tax-payer; ratepayer.
belastingstelsel, system of taxation.
belastingvry, tax-free, duty-free.
belê, beleg, (-), trim (dress); cover; invest (money); call, convene (meeting); **belegde broodjie,** sandwich.
beledig, (-), offend, insult, affront.
beledigend, (-e), offensive, insulting.
belediging, (-e, -s), offence, insult, affront; **'n - aandoen,** insult, offend.
beleë, mature (wine), ripe (cheese).
beleef, belewe, (-), live to see; experience, go through; **hy - veel verdriet aan sy kinders,** his children cause him much sorrow.
beleef, (-de), a. polite, courteous, civil.
beleefdelik, politely, courteously, civilly.
beleefdheid, politeness, courtesy, courteousness, civility; decency; **beleefdhede,** civilities; compliments.
beleefdheidsbesoek, duty-call, courtesy-visit.
beleefdheidsfrase, complimentary phrase.
beleefdheidshalwe, out of politeness.
beleefdheidsvorm, formality, conventionality; polite form; **-e,** etiquette.
beleen, (-), pawn.
beleër, (-), besiege, lay siege to.
belêer, belegger, (-s), investor (of money); convener (of meeting).
beleëraar, (-s), besieger.
beleëring, siege.
beleëringsgeskut, siege-artillery.
beleëringsoorlog, siege-warfare.
beleg (-leëringe), n. siege.
beleg, vide **belê (-).**
belegging, (-e, -s), investment (of money); convening, convocation (of meeting), vide **belê.**
beleggingsfondse, investment-funds.
belegsel, (-s), trimming(s); facings.
beleid, management; discretion, tact; policy.
beleidvol, (-le), tactful, prudent.
belek, (-), lick (all over).

belemmer   **benoud**

belemmer, (-), impede, retard, hamper; obstruct (the way); stunt (growth).
belemmering, (-e, -s), hindrance, impediment (in one's speech); obstruction; stunting.
belendend, (-e), adjacent, adjoining.
belese, well-read.
belesenheid, reading.
belet, (-), prevent, put a stop to, stop (meeting), forbid (bullfights); preclude.
beletsel, (-s), impediment, hindrance.
belewe, vide **beleef.**
belg: ge- wees, be angry (offended).
Belg, (-e), n. Belgian.
Belgies, (-e), Belgian.
belhamel, bell-wether; ringleader.
belieg, (-), lie to (person).
beliewe, n. pleasure; **na –,** at pleasure.
beliewe, (-), please.
belig, (-), light; expose (photography), throw light on, elucidate, illuminate.
beliggaam, (-), embody.
beliggaming, embodiment, incarnation.
beligting, lighting; exposure; illumination.
belladonna, belladonna, deadly nightshade.
bellabaan, track (of a torpedo).
belletrie, belles-lettres, polite letters.
belletristies, (-e), bellestristic.
beloer, (-), watch, spy upon, peep at.
belofte, (-s), promise; **iemand aan sy – hou,** hold a person to his promise; **die land van –,** the promised land.
belommer, (-), shade.
beloning, (-e, -s), reward; remuneration.
beloof, belowe, (-), promise; **goed –,** be very promising.
beloon, (-), reward; recompense.
beloop, n. way, course; **die wêreld se –,** the way of the world; **op sy – laat,** let (things) take their course.
beloop, (-), walk; amount to; (**met bloed**) **belope oë,** bloodshot eyes.
belowe, vide **beloof.**
beluister, (-), listen to; overhear; auscultate (med.)
belus: – **wees op,** crave, be keen on.
belustheid, longing; lust.
bely, (-), profess (Christ); confess (sins).
belydenis, (-se), confession; creed, profession; denomination (sect); – **aflê (doen),** be confirmed.
belydenisskrifte, articles of faith.
bely(d)er, (-s), confessor.
belyn, (-), rule (paper); line; outline.
bemaak, (-), bequeath, leave, make over.
bemagtig, (-), take possession of; make oneself master of; seize; usurp; obtain, secure.
bemagtiging, seizure, seizing; usurpation.
beman, (-), man (ship); garrison (fort).
bemanning, (-s), crew (of ship); garrison.
bemantel, (-), cloak; gloss over, disguise.
bemas, (-), mast.
bemerk, (-), notice, observe, perceive.
bemerkbaar, (-bare), noticable, perceptible.
bemes, (-), fertilize, manure, dress.
bemesting, manuring, fertilization.
bemiddel, (-), mediate; settle (dispute).
bemiddelaar(ster), (-s), mediator, intercessor, intermediary.
bemiddeld, (-e), well-to-do, well-off, of means.
bemiddelend: **optree,** mediate.
bemiddeling, mediation, intercession; **deur – van,** by the instrumentality of, through the kind offices of.
bemin, (-), love, be fond of.
bemin(d), (-de), loved, beloved; **sig – maak,** endear oneself.

beminde, (-s), lover, sweetheart, loved one.
beminlik, (-e), lovable, amiable.
beminnenswaardig, (-e), lovable.
bemodder, (-), bemire, stain with mud.
bemoedig, (-), encourage, cheer up.
bemoedigend, (-e), encouraging, cheering.
bemoediging, encouragement.
bemoei: **sig – met,** meddle with, interfere with; – **jou met jou eie sake!,** mind your own business!
bemoeial, (-le), busybody, meddler.
bemoeienis, vide **bemoeiing.**
bemoeiing, (-e, -s), interference, meddling, intervention; effort, trouble.
bemoeilik, (-), make difficult, impede, hinder, hamper (progress); oppose, obstruct.
bemoeiliking, hampering; obstruction.
bemoeisiek, (-e), meddlesome.
bemoeisug, meddlesomeness.
bemoeisugtig, (-e), meddlesome.
bemors, (-), dirty, soil; beslaver.
bemos, (-te), mossy, moss-grown.
benaarstig: **sig –,** exert oneself, do one's best.
benadeel, (-), injure; harm, wrong (person); be injurious to; prejudice.
benadeling, injury; prejudice; vide **benadeel.**
benader, (-), approach; approximate.
benadering, (-e, -s), approximation; **by –,** approximately.
benaming, (-e, -s), name, appellation, denomination.
benard, (-e), critical; hard; straitened.
benardheid, distress; hardness (of times).
bende, (-s), gang, band; troop.
benede, adv. down, below; downstairs, **na –,** downstairs; down(wards); vide **onder.**
benede, prep. below; beneath; – **die waarde,** below the value; **dit is – my,** it is beneath me; – **alle kritiek,** below criticism, beneath contempt; – **pari,** at a discount.
benede-..., vide **onder-...**
benedeloop, lower course.
benediksie, benediction.
Benediktyner, (-s), Benedictine.
beneem, (-), deprive of; take (one's own life); obstruct (the view).
Benelux, Benelux.
benepe, cramped; small; petty, mean.
benepenheid, mean-spiritedness.
benerig, (-e), bony.
beneuk, (-te), mad, crazy.
benewel, (-), fog; befog, obscure, cloud; stupefy fuddle.
benewel(d), (-de), foggy, misty, hazy; muzzy (with drink), fuddled; clouded (intellect).
benewens, besides, together with.
Bengaals, (-e), Bengal.
bengel, (-s), n. urchin, rascal.
bengel, (-), dangle, swing.
benieu, (-),: **dit sal my –,** I wonder.
benieud, – **wees,** wonder.
benning, (-s), band.
benodig, (-de), wanted, required.
benodigdhede, requirements, necessaries; requisites; accessories, fittings.
benoem, (-), nominate, appoint.
benoembaar, (-bare), eligible.
benoem(d), (-de), nominated, appointed; **–de getal,** concrete number.
benoeming, (-e, -s), nomination, appointment.
benoorde, (to the) north of.
benou, (-), oppress.
benoud, (-e), close, oppressive, sultry; stuffy, suffocating, stifling; oppressed, tight in the chest; terrifying (dream); anxious, frightened;

'n -e oomblik, an anxious moment; die pasiënt is -, the patient's breathing is laboured; dit - kry, be suffocating; be hard pressed.
benoude-bors, asthma.
benoudheid, (-hede), sultriness; stuffiness, oppression, tightness of the chest; trouble; anxiety; vide benoud.
benouing, oppression.
benseen, benzene, benzol.
bensien, benzine, benzine.
benul, notion; nie die minste - nie, not the faintest (foggiest) notion (idea).
benut(tig), (-), make use of, utilise, avail oneself of, turn to account.
benuttiging, utilisation; vide benut(tig).
beny, (-), envy, be envious of.
benybaar, (-bare), enviable.
benydenswaardig, (-e), enviable.
beoefen, (-), practise (profession); cultivate (an art) study; exercise (patience).
beoefenaar, (-s), student; devotee, votary.
beoefening, pursuit, practice; cultivation; study; in - bring, put into practice.
beoog, (-), aim at, have in view.
beoordeel, (-), judge (person); adjudicate; review (book).
beoordelaar, (-s), judge; adjudicator (at eisteddfod); critic, reviewer.
beoordelaarster, (-s), vide beoordelaar.
beoordeling, judging; adjudicating; judg(e)ment; criticism, review.
bepaal, (-), fix; appoint; determine; stipulate; ascertain (value); define; lay down (by law); qualify, modify (gram.); sig - tot, confine oneself to.
bepaalbaar, (-bare), determinable, definable.
bepaal(d), (-de), a. fixed; specified; appointed (time); stipulated, stated (times); definite (reply, number); decided, distinct; 'n -e streek, a particular area; vide bepaal.
bepaald, adv. positively, decidedly, undoubtedly, unmistakably; nie - nie, not exactly (really); hy sal - daar wees, he is sure to be there.
bepaaldelik, specifically, particularly.
bepaaldheid, definiteness, positiveness.
bepak, (-), load, pack.
bepalend, (-e), defining; determining, qualifying, modifying; -e (bepaalde) lidwoord, definite article.
bepaling, (-e, -s), fixing; determination, extension (gram.); stipulation; regulation; (legal) provision.
bepantser, (-), armour.
bepeins, (-), ponder over, meditate on.
beperk, (-te), a. limited; confined, restricted.
beperk, (-), limit, confine; reduce (expenses); keep within limits; sig - tot, confine oneself to.
beperkend, (-e), limiting, restricting.
beperking, (-e, -s), restriction, limitation: reduction.
beperktheid, limitedness, restrictedness.
beplak, (-), paper (wall); paste over.
beplant, (-), plant.
bepleister, (-), plaster (over).
bepleit, (-), champion, plead, advocate.
bepleiter, (-s), pleader, champion, advocate.
beploe(g), beploeë, (-), plough.
bepoeier, (-), powder.
bepraat, (-), talk over, discuss; persuade.
beproef, beproewe, (-), attempt, try; test; afflict, visit.
beproef, (-de), tried; trusty, staunch (supporter); efficacious, (remedy); swaar -, sorely tried.
beproewing, (-e, -s), trial; affliction.

beraad, deliberation; na ryp -, after mature consideration.
beraadslaag, (-), deliberate; - met, consult with; - oor, deliberate (up)on.
beraadslaging, (-e, -s), deliberation, consultation.
beraam, (-), devise, contrive; plan (attack); estimate (damage).
beraming, (-e, -s), contriving; estimate.
berde: iets te - bring, bring a matter up.
bêre, berg, (ge-), put aside (away), store; hide; jou lyf -, save one's strength; loaf, laze; save oneself.
beredder, (-), put in order; administer.
beredderaar, (-s), administrator.
bereddering, arranging, arrangement; administration (of estate); fuss.
berede, mounted (police).
beredeneer, (-), argue, reason out; discuss.
beredeneer(d), (-de), reasoned (exposition).
bereg, (-), administer the last sacraments to; try (case); adjudicate.
beregting, administration of the last sacraments; trial; adjudication.
berei, (-), prepare; curry (leather); sig -, prepare (oneself), get ready.
bereid, prepared, ready, willing.
bereiding, preparation; dressing, currying.
bereidvaardig, -willig, (-e), willing.
bereidvaardigheid, -willigheid, willingness.
bereik, n. reach, range; grasp; buite -, beyond (out of) reach.
bereik, (-), reach; attain (a ripe age); gain, achieve (object).
bereikbaar, (-bare), attainable, within reach.
bereiking, attainment; achievement.
bereis, (-), travel (over, through).
bereis, (-de), (much-)travelled (man); much-frequented (region).
bereisbaar, (-bare), traversable, practicable.
bereken, (-), calculate, compute, charge; - op, calculate (compute) at.
bereken(d), (-de), calculated; deliberate; - vir sy taak, equal to his task.
berekenbaar, (-bare), calculable.
bérekenend, (-e), calculating, selfish.
berekening, (-e, -s), calculation.
bêrelaai, bottom drawer.
bêreplek, storeroom, shed.
berg, (-e), n. mountain, mount; 'n - van 'n molshoop maak, make mountains out of molehills; sy hare het te -e gerys, his hair stood on end.
berg, (ge-), salvage, salve (cargo); vide bêre.
bergaarde, ochre.
berg af, downhill, down the mountain; berg op en -, up hill and down dale.
bergagtig, (-e), mountainous.
bergamot-olie, bergamot-oil.
bergamot(peer), bergamot(-pear).
bergbeklimmer, mountaineer.
bergbewoner, mountain-dweller.
bergeend, shelduck.
bergengte, (narrow) mountain-pass.
berggees, mountain-spirit, gnome.
berghang, -helling, mountain-slope.
berging, salvage.
bergingsmaatskappy, salvage-company.
bergingswerk, salvage (operations).
bergkam, mountain-ridge, -crest.
bergkamer, storeroom.
bergketting, mountain-chain.
bergkloof, gorge, ravine, mountain-kloof.
bergkristal, rock-crystal.
bergkruin, mountain-top.
bergland, mountainous country.

berglandskap, mountain-scenery.
bergleeu, puma.
bergloon, salvage(-money, -charges).
berglug, mountain-air.
bergmannetjie, goblin.
bergolie, petroleum.
berg-op, uphill, up the mountain; vide **berg af**.
bergpad, mountain-road.
bergpas, mountain-pass.
bergpatrys, grey wing, Cape partridge.
bergplaas, **-plek**, vide **bêreplek**.
Bergrede, Sermon on the Mount.
bergreeks, mountain-chain (-range).
bergrug, mountain-ridge.
bergruimte, storeroom, storage-capacity.
bergskilpad, mountain-tortoise.
bergsolder, storage-loft.
bergsout, rock-salt.
bergspits, mountain-peak.
bergspoor(weg), mountain-railway.
bergstelsel, mountain-system.
bergstorting, landslip, rockslide.
bergstreek, mountainous region.
bergswa(w)el, bee-eater.
bergsysie, mountain-linnet.
bergtop, mountain-top.
bergverskuiwing, vide **bergstorting**.
bergvolk, mountain-people, -tribe.
bergwand, mountain-side.
berig, **(-te)**, n. tidings, news; report; notice; – **stuur**, send word; – **van ontvangs**, acknowledgment of receipt; **nagekome -te**, stop-press.
berig, (-), report; send word; notify.
beriggewer, correspondent; informant.
beril, **(-le)**, beryl.
berin, she-bear.
berisp(e), (-), reprimand, censure.
berispelik, **(-e)**, reprehensible, censurable.
berisping, reproof, rebuke, reprimand.
berk, **(-e)**, **berkeboom**, birch.
Berlyns, **(-e)**, Berlin.
berlyns-blou, Prussian blue.
bermotpeer, vide **bergamotpeer**.
beroem, (-): **sig** – **op**, pride oneself on, glory in; boast of (about).
beroemd, **(-e)**, famous, celebrated, illustrious; – **weens**, famous (noted) for.
beroemdheid, fame, renown, celebrity.
beroep, **(-e)**, n. calling, occupation; profession, trade, vocation; call (to minister of religion); **'n** – **doen op**, appeal to; **in hoër** – **gaan**, appeal to a higher court; **van** –, by profession; by trade.
beroep, (-), call (a minister of religion); **sig** – **op**, appeal to; call to witness; – **word**, receive a call.
beroepbaar, **(-bare)**, eligible.
beroepsdanser, professional dancer.
beroepsgeheim, professional secret.
beroepsiekte, occupational disease.
beroepskeuse, choice of a profession.
beroepsopleiding, vocational training.
beroepspeler, professional (player), pro.
beroepsrisiko, occupational hazard.
beroepswedder, bookmaker, bookie.
beroer, (-), stir, disturb, perturb.
beroerd, **(-e)**, miserable, wretched, rotten.
beroering, **(-e, -s)**, disturbance; commotion, unrest; **in** – **bring**, stir up; **in** – **wees**, be in a state of commotion.
beroerling, **(-e)**, rotter.
beroerte, apoplexy.
beroerte-aanval, paralytic stroke, seizure.
berokken, (-), cause, give, bring (upon).
berokkening, causing. Vide **berokken**.

beroof, **berowe**, (-), rob; deprive (of); **iemand van die lewe** –, take a person's life; **van sy sinne** –, bereft (out) of his senses.
berook, (-), (blacken with) smoke; fumigate.
berou, n. repentance, remorse; – **hê oor**, repent, regret.
berou, (-), repent, regret; rue.
berouvol, **(-le)**, penitent, repentant.
berowe, vide **beroof**.
berowing, robbing, robbery; deprivation.
berrie-berrie, beri-beri.
berug, **(-te)**, notorious, ill-famed.
berugtheid, notoriety, notoriousness.
beruik, (-), smell at.
berus, (-): – **by**, rest with (the Lord); be in the hands (keeping) of; be vested in; – **in**, acquiesce in; – **op**, rest (be based) on; **dit** – **op 'n misverstand**, it is due to a misunderstanding.
berustend, **(-e)**, acquiescent, submissive.
berusting, resignation, acquiescence.
bery, (-), ride (horse); drive (ride) over.
beryder, **(-s)**, rider.
berym, (-), rhyme, put into verse; **–de psalms**, rhymed version of the psalms.
beryming, **(-e, -s)**, rhyming; rhymed version.
bes, n. best; **jou** – **doen**, do one's best.
bes, adv. very well; – **moontlik**, quite possible, very likely.
besaai, (-), sow, strew, cover.
besadig, **(-de)**, cool(-headed), calm; moderate (politician); dispassionate.
besadigdheid, cool-headedness, calmness; moderation; dispassionateness.
beseël, (-), seal, put the seal on.
beseer, (-), injure, hurt.
besef, n. idea, notion, conception; realisation; **iemand tot 'n** – **bring van ...** , make a person realise; **tot die** – **kom**, realise.
besef, (-), realize.
beseil, (-), sail (the seas).
besem, **(-s)**, broom; besom (of twigs).
besembos. broom-bush.
besemgoed, broom-reeds.
besemgras, broomgrass.
besemsteel, broomstick.
besemstok, broomstick; **onder die** – **steek**, belabour with the broom-stick.
besending, **(-e, -s)**, consignment.
besering, **(-e, -s)**, injury.
beset, a. engaged, occupied; set (with gems); **die saal is goed** –, there is a good attendance.
beset, (-), occupy; cast (a play); set (with gems); line (with troops); garrison (fort).
besete, possessed (by the devil).
besetene, **(-s)**, one possessed.
besetsel, trimming.
besetting, occupation; garrison: strength (of orchestra); cast (of play).
besettingsleër, army of occupation.
besie, **(-s)**, cicada; small beast.
besiel, (-), inspire, animate, infuse (into); **wat het jou** –?, what possessed you?
besieling, inspiration, animation.
besien, (-), look at, view; **dit staan nog te** –, it remains to be seen.
besienswaardig, **(-e)**, worth seeing.
besienswaardigheid, something worth seeing; **die –hede**, the sights.
besig, **(-e)**, a. busy, engaged; – **aan**, busy at; – **met lees**, (busy) reading; – **houe**, keep busy; occupy (the mind); **sig** – **hou met**, occupy oneself with.
besig, (-), use, make use of.
besigheid, **(-hede)**, business; occupation.
besighou, **(besigge-)**, occupy.
besiging, using, use.

besigtig, (-), view, look at, inspect.
besigtiging, inspection; **ter -,** on view.
besin, (-), reflect; **- eer jy begin,** look before you leap; **sig -,** think the matter over; change one's mind.
besing, (-), sing (the praises of).
besink, (-), settle (down), subside, precipitate; sink in; **laat -,** let settle.
besinking, settling (down), precipitation.
besinksel, (-s), sediment, deposit, residue.
besinning, consciousness, senses, head; **tot - bring, kom,** bring (come) to one's senses.
besit, n. possession; asset(s); **in die - kom van,** obtain, get possession of; **in - neem,** take possession of.
besit, a. vide **beset.**
besit, (-), possess, have, own.
besitlik, (-e), possessive (pronoun).
besitster, (-s), owner; proprietress.
besitter, (-s), owner, proprietor.
besitting, (-e, -s), possession; property.
beskaaf, beskawe, (-), (lit.), plane; civilize.
beskaaf, (-de), civilised (nation); refined (manners), polished; cultured.
beskaafdheid, good manners, refinement.
beskaam, (-), put to shame, shame; falsify, disappoint (hope).
beskaam(d), (-de), ashamed; shamefaced; **- maak,** put to shame, make feel ashamed; **- wees,** be ashamed.
beskaamdheid, shame.
beskadig, (-), damage; injure.
beskadiging, damage; injury.
beskadu, (-), shade, overshadow.
beskaduwing, shading, overshadowing.
beskamend, (-e), humiliating.
beskaming, shame.
beskawe, vide **beskaaf.**
beskawing, (-e, -s), civilisation; refinement.
beskeid, answer; **- gee,** give a reply.
beskeidenheid, modesty; **in (met) alle -,** with due deference.
beskeidenlik, beskeielik, modestly.
beskei(e), (-), assign, allot; **sy - deel,** his allotted part.
beskeie, humble, modest; unassuming.
beskenk, (-), endow.
beskerm, (-), protect, shelter; patronise.
beskerm(e)ling, (-e), protégé.
beskermend, (-e), protective (duties), protecting (friendship).
beskermengel, guardian-angel.
beskermer, (-s), protector; patron (of art).
beskermheer, patron; sponsor.
beskermheerskap, patronage.
beskermheilige, patron-saint, patron.
beskerming, protection; patronage; shelter; guard; **in - neem,** take under one's protection; **onder - van,** under cover of; under the patronage (auspices) of.
beskermling, vide **beskerm(e)ling.**
beskermster, (-s), protectress; patroness.
beskermvrou, patroness.
beskiet, (-), fire at, shell, bombard.
beskieting, bombardment, shelling.
beskik, (-), arrange; dispose, determine; **die mens wik, God -,** man proposes, God disposes; **- oor,** have at one's disposal.
beskikbaar, (-bare), available; **- stel,** place at (person's) disposal.
beskikbaarheid, availability.
beskikker, (-s), disposer; dispenser.
beskikking, (-e, -s), disposal; decree; dispensation; **ter -,** available; **tot - van,** at the disposal of.

beskilder, (-), paint, paint over.
beskimmel, (-), grow mouldy.
beskimmel(d), (-de), mouldy; shy, bashful.
beskimp, (-), revile, taunt, scoff at.
beskimping, scoffing, abuse, taunt(ing).
beskinder, (-), slander, blacken.
beskoei, (-e), timber (mine-shaft).
beskonke, intoxicated, drunk.
beskonkenheid, intoxication, drunkenness.
beskore, allotted; **dit (die lot) is my -,** it is my fate (lot).
beskot, wainscoting; partition; bulkhead.
beskou, (-), look at, view, contemplate; regard, consider; **- as,** consider (as).
beskouend, (-e), contemplative.
beskouing, (-e, -s), looking at, contemplation, view (of the matter); **by nader -,** on closer examination; **buite - laat,** leave out of consideration.
beskrei(d), (-de), tear-stained.
beskroomd, (-e), shy, bashful, timid.
beskroomdheid, shyness, bashfulness.
beskry, (-), bestride.
beskryf, beskrywe, (-), write on; describe (a scene; geom. figure); draw (circle).
beskrywend, (-e), descriptive; generating (line).
beskrywing, (-e, -s), description.
beskrywingspunt, point for discussion.
beskuit, (-e), rusk; biscuit.
beskuitjie, (-s), biscuit.
beskuldig, (-), accuse, charge; incriminate; blame.
beskuldigde, (-s), accused.
beskuldiger, (-s), accuser.
beskuldiging, (-e, -s), accusation, charge; indictment.
beskut, (-), protect, shelter, screen; **- teen,** protect against (from), shelter from.
beskutting, protection, shelter.
beslaan, (-), shoe (horse); mount (with metal); get dimmed, tarnish (of metal); cover, extend over (fifty acres); occupy, take up (space); comprise, run to (many pages).
beslag, mounting, mount (ornamental metal parts); sheathing; fittings, furniture; clamps (of chest); clasps (of book); seizure (upon person, goods); embargo (on ship); **- lê op,** seize, confiscate (property); take possession of; put an embargo on (ship); **in - neem,** take up; absorb (attention); seize (goods).
beslaglegging, seizure, distraint; confiscation.
besleg, (-), settle (dispute).
beslegting, settlement.
beslis, (-te), a. decided, resolute; positive.
beslis, adv. decidedly, positively.
beslis, (-), decide, arbitrate.
beslissend, (-e), decisive (battle); conclusive, casting (vote); critical (moment).
beslistheid, resoluteness, firmness.
beslommering, (-e, -s), trouble, worry, care.
beslote, private; determined, resolved.
besluip, (-), stalk (game); steal upon.
besluit, (-e), conclusion; resolution, decision; **'n - neem,** decide; pass a resolution; **tot -, in conclusion; tot 'n - kom,** come to a decision.
besluit, (-), conclude, decide, resolve; pass a resolution; infer, conclude.
besluiteloos, (-lose), irresolute, wavering.
besluiteloosheid, indecision, irresolution.
besmeer, (-), (be)smear, grease; dirty.
besmet, (-te), a. infected; contaminated.
besmet, (-), infect; pollute (water); contaminate (lit. & fig.); defile.
besmetlik, (-e), contagious; infectious.
besmetting, infection, contamination.

besnaar 37 **bestrawwing**

besnaar, (-), string.
besnede, cut; circumcised; chiselled.
besneeu(d), **(-de)**, snow-covered.
besnoei, (-), prune, clip (hedge); curtail, reduce, retrench, cut down (expenses).
besnoeiing, pruning; reduction, retrenchment.
besnuffel, (-), sniff at; pry into.
besny, (-), circumcise: cut, carve.
besnydenis, circumcision.
besoedel, (-), soil, pollute, defile.
besoedel(d), **(-de)**, soiled; polluted, contaminated; guilty (conscience).
besoedeling, contamination, defilement.
besoek, **(-e)**, n. visit; call (of short duration); guests; **'n – aflê by**, pay a visit to; call on; **'n – beantwoord**, return a call; **op – wees by**, be on a visit to.
besoek, (-), pay a visit to, call on, go to see; attend (church); try, visit; **gereeld –**, frequent.
besoeker, **-ster**, **(-s)**, visitor, caller.
besoeking, visitation, affliction, trial.
besog, **(-te)**, visited; attended.
besoldig, (-), pay, salary.
besoldiging, pay, salary; wages.
besonder, n.: **in die –**, in particular.
besonder, **(-e)**, a. particular, special; individual; **niks –s nie**, nothing particular.
besonder, adv. particularly, exceptionally.
besonderheid, **(-hede)**, particular; **-hede**, details, particulars; **in –hede tree**, go into details.
besonderlik, vide **besonder**, adv.
besonders, **(-e)**, special, particular.
besondig, (-): **sig –**, sin; be guilty of.
besonke, well-considered (opinion).
besonne, staid; well-considered (attitude).
besope, drunk, tight, fuddled.
besorg, **besôre**, (-), attend to (horses); give, cause (sorrow, trouble); deliver; procure; provide; **iemand 'n betrekking –**, help a person to a post; **iemand tuis –**, see a person home.
besorg, **(-de)**, anxious, concerned (about).
besorgdheid, uneasiness, concern.
besorging, delivery. Vide **besorg**.
bespaar, (-), save; economize; spare.
besparing, saving.
bespat, (-), bespatter, splash.
bespeel, (-), play (the organ), play on.
bespeur, (-), observe, perceive, notice.
bespeurbaar, **(-bare)**, observable, noticeable.
bespied, (-), spy on, watch.
bespieder, **(-s)**, spy.
bespieëlend, **bespiegelend**, **(-e)**, contemplative; speculative (philosophy).
bespieëling, **bespiegeling**, contemplation; speculation.
bespoedig, (-), expedite, speed up.
bespoediging, speeding up.
bespoe(g), **bespu(ug)**, (-), spit at (upon).
bespoel, (-), wash.
bespot, (-), mock, scoff at, deride.
bespotlik, **(-e)**, ridiculous, ludicrous; **– maak**, ridicule, deride; **sig – maak (aanstel)**, make a fool of oneself.
bespotlikheid, ridiculousness, ludicrousness.
bespotting, ridicule, mockery, derision.
bespreek, (-), discuss, talk over; reserve (seats); review (book); exorcize (a toothache).
bespreekburo, booking-office.
bespreking, **(-e, -s)**, discussion; review (of book); booking (of seats).
bespring, (-), jump upon, assail.
bespringer, **(-s)**, assailant.
besprinkel, (-), (be)sprinkle, spray.
besproei, (-), spray; irrigate, water.
besproeiing, watering, irrigation.

besproeiingsraad, irrigation-board.
besproeiingswerke, irrigation-works.
besproke, reserved (seats); discussed.
bespu(ug), vide **bespoe(g)**.
bespuit, (-), spray, squirt (water) upon.
bessie, **(-s)**, berry.
bessiewas, berry-wax.
bestaan, n. being, existence; livelihood; **die stryd om die –**, the struggle for existence; **vyftigjarige –**, fiftieth anniversary.
bestaan, (-), exist; subsist, make a living; **– in**, consists in; **– uit**, consist of; **– van**, live on.
bestaanbaar, **(-bare)**, possible; reasonable; living (wage); **– met**, compatible with.
bestaanbaarheid, possiblity; compatibility.
bestaande, existing.
bestaansmiddel, means of livelihood.
bestaansreg, right of existence.
bestand, n. truce.
bestand, a: **– teen**, proof against.
bestanddeel, component, constituent.
beste, n. best; **die –!**, **alles ten (van die) –!** good luck!; **die – hoop**, hope for the best; **op sy –**, at one's (its) best; at most, at best; **ten – gee**, oblige with, give (a song).
beste, a. best; first class; dear (friend); **die eerste die –**, the first.
bestee, (-), spend; **– aan**, spend (money) on; devote (attention) to; bestow (care) on.
besteel, (-), rob, steal from.
bestek, **(-ke)**, space; scope; (builder's) specifications; **-ke**, bills of quantities; **buite die – van**, outside the scope of; **in 'n klein –**, in a small compass; **volgens –**, according to plan.
bestekopmaker, quantity-surveyor.
bestel, (-), order; make an appointment; deliver (letters).
bestelbiljet, order-form.
besteldiens, delivery-service.
bestelling, **(-e, -s)**, order; appointment; delivery; **op –**, to order; **volgens –**, as per order; **vol –s**, fastidious, hard to please.
bestelmotor, **-wa**, delivery-van.
bestem, (-), destine; set apart; fix (a day).
bestem(d), **(-de)**, destined; set apart; intended (for); appointed (day).
bestemming, destination; destiny, lot.
bestempel, (-), stamp; call, describe (as).
bestendig, **(-e)**, a. lasting; permanent; constant; steady; settled.
bestendig, (-), perpetuate, continue.
bestendigheid, durability, stability, permanence, constancy; steadiness.
bestendiging, perpetuation.
besterf, **besterwe**, (-), die (on one's lips).
bestialiteit, bestiality.
bestier, (-), guide.
bestierder, **(-s)**, ruler, guide.
bestiering, dispensation (of Providence), act of Providence; guidance.
bestook, (-), pelt, bombard.
bestorm, (-), storm, rush at, charge; bombard (with questions).
bestorming, storming, rush, charge.
bestorwe, deadly pale.
bestraal, (-), shine upon; X-ray.
bestraat, (-), pave.
bestraf, **-strawwe**, (-), reprimand, rebuke, reprove, scold; punish.
bestraffing, **-strawwing**, reprimand, scolding, rebuke; punishment.
bestraling, **(-e, -s)**, irradiation; X-ray treatment.
bestrating, paving; pavement.
bestrawwe, vide **bestraf**.
bestrawwing, vide **bestraffing**.

bestrooi, (–), bestrew, sprinkle, powder.
bestry, (–), combat; oppose (motion); dispute (statement); defray (expenses).
bestry(d)er, (-s), opponent, adversary.
bestryding, combating, defrayal.
bestryk, (–), stroke; spread (coat) with; cover, command (of artillery); **met salf –,** smear with ointment.
bestudeer, (–), study.
bestudering, study.
bestuif, bestuiwe, (–), cover with dust; pollinate (bot.).
bestuiwing, pollination (bot.).
besturing, driving; management.
bestuur, (-sture), n. management, direction; rule, government; committee; managing-board.
bestuur, (–), drive (motor-car); pilot (aeroplane); guide, direct; manage (business); control; rule, govern (country).
bestuurbaar, (-bare), manageable; navigable, dirigible (balloon).
bestuurder, (-s), driver, pilot (of aeroplane); manager, director.
bestuurskamer, committee-, board-room.
bestuurslid, committee-member, member of the board.
bestuursvergadering, committee-, board-meeting.
bestuursvorm, form of government.
besuinig, (–), economize, reduce expenses.
besuiniging, economizing, economy.
besuinigingsmaatreël, measure of economy.
besuip, (–), : sig –, fuddle oneself.
besuur, (–) : iets –, suffer (smart) for, rue.
beswaar, (-sware), n. objection; scruple; **– maak,** raise objections.
beswaar, (–), load; burden, weigh on.
beswaar(d), (-de), burdened, oppressed; **met 'n verband –,** mortgaged; **met 'n –de gemoed,** with a heavy heart; **sig – voel,** have scruples.
beswaarlik, hardly, with difficulty.
beswaarskrif, petition.
beswadder, (–), throw mud at, besmirch.
beswarend, (-e), aggravating (circumstances).
besweer, (–), swear; adjure, charge; exorcize, lay (ghost, wind); call up (ghost).
besweet, (beswete), perspring; in a sweat.
beswering, swearing; exorcism; adjuration.
beswil: vir jou eie –, for your own good.
beswyk, (–), succumb; yield; break down, collapse.
beswyking, succumbing, yielding.
beswym, (–), swoon, faint.
beswyming, swoon, fainting fit, black-out.
besyde, beside (the truth), alongside.
besyfer, (–), figure out, calculate.
bet, (ge-), dab, bathe (wound).
betaal, (–), pay, pay for; settle (account); **laat –,** make (person) pay, charge; **te veel laat –,** overcharge; **– met,** pay in (money); pay with (one's life).
betaalbaar, (-bare), payable.
betaaldag, pay-day; date of payment.
betaalmeester, paymaster.
betaalmiddel, means of payment; currency; **wettige –,** legal tender.
betaalstaat, pay-sheet.
betaam, (–), behove, become, be proper.
betaamlik, (-e), proper, fit(ting), becoming.
betaamlikheid, decency, propriety.
betakel, (–), dirty, begrime; besmear.
betaler, (-s), payer.
betaling, (-e, -s), payment, settlement.
betalingsvoorwaarde, condition of payment.
betas, (–), feel, handle, finger; palpate (med.).
betasting, feeling, handling; palpation (med.).

betastrale, beta rays.
bete, morsel (of bread).
beteken, (–), mean, signify; represent, stand for; cover with drawings; portend, spell (ruin); **dit – niks,** it is of no importance, that does not signify; it is no good.
betekenis, (-se), meaning, sense; significance, importance, consequence; **mense van –,** people of note; **– heg aan,** attach importance to; **dit is van geen – nie,** it is of no importance.
betekenisleer, semantics, semasiology.
betekenisvol, (-le), significant, important.
betelneut, betel-nut, areca-nut.
beter, a. & adv., better; **des te –,** so much the better; **dis maar – so,** it is just as well; **– maak,** make well again, make better; **– word,** improve; recover.
beterhand: aan die – wees, be getting better.
beterskap, improvement; recovery; **– belowe,** promise to turn over a new leaf.
beterwete: teen sy –, against his own better judgment.
beterweter, betweter, (-s), wiseacre, know-all.
beteuel, (–), restrain, curb; repress.
beteueling, restraint, check, curb.
beteuter(d), (-de), taken aback, perplexed.
beteuterdheid, perplexity; sheepishness.
betig, (–), charge (with), accuse (of).
betigting, imputation, accusation.
betimmer, (–), board, wainscot; hammer.
betimmering, wainscot(ing), woodwork.
betitel, (–), entitle; style, address.
betiteling, entitling, title, style.
betoë, vide **betoog,** v.
betoër, betoger, (-s), demonstrator.
betoging, (-e, -s), demonstration.
beton, concrete; **gewapende –,** reinforced concrete.
betoning, vide **betoon.**
betoog, (-toë), n. argument, demonstration; **dit behoef geen – nie,** it stands to reason.
betoog, (–), argue, demonstrate.
betooggrond, argument.
betoom, (–), restrain, curb; repress.
betoon, n. display, manifestation.
betoon, (–), (1) show; sig –, prove (oneself); **hulde – aan,** pay tribute to.
betoon, (–), (2) accent; accentuate.
betower, betoor, (–), bewitch, enchant; put a spell on; fascinate.
betower(d), (-de), bewitched, enchanted.
betowerend, (-e), bewitching; fascinating.
betowering, charm, spell, enchantment.
betraan(d), (-de), wet with tears, tearful.
betrag, (–), do; meditate, ponder.
betragting, discharge (of duty); meditation.
betrap, (–), catch, surprise, detect; **op heter daad –,** take (catch) red-handed (in the very act); **op diefstal –,** catch stealing; **op 'n fout –,** catch napping, catch out.
betrapping, detecting, detection.
betreding, treading (up)on; mounting.
betree, (–), set foot on; mount (platform).
betref, (–), concern, relate to; **wat dit – as to that,** for that matter; **wat my –,** for my part; as for me.
betreffende, concerning, regarding.
betrek, (–), (1) move into (a house); become overcast; cloud over (of face).
betrek, (–), (2) stalk (game); catch (person) off his guard; **iemand – in,** entangle (involve, implicate) a person in.
betrekking, (-e, -s), post, situation; relation; **sonder –,** out of employment; **– hê op,** refer to; **met – tot,** with reference to.

betreklik, (-e), a comparative, relative.
betreklik, adv. comparatively; relatively.
betreklikheid, relativity, relativeness.
betreur, (-), deplore, lament; regret.
betreurenswaardig, (-e), deplorable, regrettable, lamentable; pitiable.
betreurenswaardigheid, deplorability.
betrokke, overcast, clouded (sky): clouded (face); concerned; **die – amptenare,** the officials concerned; **– wees by (in),** be concerned in, be involved in.
betrokkene, (-s), person involved.
betrou, (-), trust.
betroubaar, (-bare), reliable, trustworthy.
betroubaarheid, reliability, trustworthiness.
betroubaarheidsrit, reliability run (trial).
Betsjoeana, Bechuana.
betuie, betuig, (-), testify; bear witness to; declare; express; profess (friendship).
betuiging, expression, profession.
betweter, vide **beterweter.**
betwis, (-), dispute, challenge; contest (seat in Parliament); deny.
betwisbaar, (-bare), disputable, debatable.
betwyfel, (-), doubt, (call in) question.
betwyfeling, doubting.
betyds, in time, in good time.
beuel, (-s), bugle; trigger-guard; **dit kan nie deur die – nie,** it cannot pass muster.
beuk, (-e), n. beech.
beuk, (-), beat, bang; pound, batter.
beukeboom, beech(-tree).
beukehout, beech(-wood); **wit –,** Cape beech.
beul, (-e, -s), executioner; brute, beast.
beulskneg, hangman's assistant.
beunhaas, quack; dabbler, rabbit.
beur, (ge-), drag, tug; lift; struggle, strive; **– so wat hy kan,** strain every nerve.
beurs, (-e), purse; scholarship; exchange.
beursberig, stock-exchange report.
beursie, (-s), purse.
beursnotering, stock-exchange quotation.
beursspekulant, stock-jobber.
beursvakansie, bank-holiday.
beurt, (-e), turn; innings (in cricket); **jou – afwag,** wait your turn; **hy is aan die –,** it is his turn; **by –e, om die –,** in turn; **dit het my te – geval,** it fell to my lot (share); **voor (na) jou –,** out of one's turn.
beurtelings, in turn, by turns, alternately.
beurtsang, antiphony; catch.
beusel, (ge-), trifle, dawdle.
beuselagtig, (-e), trivial, trifling, paltry.
beuselagtigheid, (-hede), triviality, trifle.
beuselary, trifle.
bevaar, (-), navigate, sail (the seas).
bevaarbaar, (-bare), navigable.
bevaarbaarheid, navigability.
beval, (-), (1) please; be to one's liking; **dit – my nie,** I do not like it.
beval, (-), (2) be confined, give birth (to).
bevallig, (-e), grace, charm, gracefulness.
bevalling, (-e, -s), confinement, delivery.
bevang, (-), overcome, seize.
bevange, overcome, seized (with, by); foundered (horse); lean (crops); stale (athlete); over-ridden (horse); grain-sick.
bevangenheid, seizure; body-founder; grain-sickness.
bevat, (-), contain, hold; comprehend.
bevatlik, (-e), intelligible, clear; intelligent.
bevatlikheid, intelligibility; intelligence.
bevatting, comprehension.
beveel, (-), command, charge; commend.
beveg, (-), fight (against), oppose.

bevegting, fighting (against).
beveilig, (-), safeguard, guard, protect.
beveiliging, safeguarding, protection.
bevel, (-e), command, order; **die – voer oor,** be in command of; **onder – van,** under the command of; **op – van,** by order of; **at the command of.**
bevelhebber, bevelvoerder, (-s), commander.
bevelskrif, warrant.
bevelvoerend, (-e), commanding.
bevestig, (-), fasten; confirm, corroborate (statement); affirm; strengthen, consolidate; prove; induct (minister of religion); ordain (elder); **met 'n eed –,** affirm with an oath.
bevestigend, (-e), affirmative; **– antwoord,** reply in the affirmative.
bevestiging, fastening; confirmation; induction; ordination; vide **bevestig.**
bevind, n.: **na – van sake,** according to circumstances.
bevind, find; **skuldig –,** find guilty; **hoe – jy jou?,** how are you?
bevinding, (-e, -s), finding; experience.
bevlag, (-), flag.
bevlek, (-), stain, soil; defile, sully.
bevlie(ë), bevlieg, (-), fly at, attack.
bevlieging, (-e, -s), whim, fancy; fit.
bevloei, (-), irrigate.
bevoeg, (-de), competent, qualified; authorized; **van –de sy,** on good authority.
bevoegdheid, (-hede), competence; ability; qualification; power; **– verleen aan,** authorise.
bevoel, (-), feel, finger, handle.
bevogtig, (-), moisten, wet, damp.
bevolk, (-te), a. populated; populous.
bevolk, (-), people.
bevolking, (-e, -s), population; peopling.
bevolkingsburo, registry-office.
bevolkingstatistiek, vital statistics.
bevolkingsyfer, number of the population.
bevoordeel, (-), benefit.
bevooroordeel(d), (-de), prejudiced, biased.
bevoorreg, (-te), a. privileged, favoured.
bevoorreg, (-), privilege, favour.
bevorder, (-), further, promote.
bevordering, promotion; furtherance; advancement (of science); vide **bevorder.**
bevorderlik, beneficial, (conducive) to.
bevrag, (-), load; charter (ship).
bevragting, loading; chartering.
bevredig, (-), satisfy, gratify; indulge (one's passions); appease (appetite).
bevredigend, (-e), satisfactory, gratifying.
bevrediging, satisfaction; gratification.
bevreem(d), (-): dit – my, it surprises me.
bevreemdend, surprising.
bevreemding, surprise; **– wek,** cause surprise.
bevrees, afraid (**of**), apprehensive (for).
bevreesdheid, fear, apprehension.
bevriend, bevrind, (-e), friendly.
bevries, (-te), a. vide **bevrore.**
bevries, (-), freeze; become frosted; freeze to death; be frozen over.
bevroed, (-), realize, suspect.
bevrore, frozen, frostbitten; frosted.
bevrug, (-te), a. impregnate, pregnant; fertilized.
bevrug, (-), impregnate; fertilize (bot.).
bevrugting, impregnation; fertilization.
bevry, (-), free, set free; rescue; deliver (from); rid (of); emancipate; liberate.
bevryder, (-s), rescuer, deliverer.
bevryding, setting free; rescue; release, emancipation; riddance.
bevuil, (-), dirty, foul.
bewaak, (-), guard, keep watch over.

bewaar, (-), save (coupons); keep (secret, commandments); maintain (one's self-possession); preserve, protect, save; **hemel - my!**, heaven forbid!
bewaarder, (-s), guardian; caretaker.
bewaarengel, guardian-angel.
bewaargeld, storage.
bewaarheid, (-), verify, confirm.
bewaarkluis, safe(-deposit).
bewaarplaas, -plek, storeroom, storehouse.
bewaarskool, infant-school.
bewaker, (-s), guard; keeper, caretaker.
bewaking, guard(ing), watch, custody.
bewandel, (-), walk in, walk upon.
bewapen, (-), arm.
bewapening, armament.
bewapeningstryd, armaments-race.
bewaring, custody, safekeeping; trust; preservation; **in - hê**, have charge of.
bewasem, (-), cover with vapour.
bewater, (-), water, irrigate; wet.
beweeg, (-), move; stir; shift, budge; persuade, prevail upon; **geen duimbreed - nie,** not budge an inch; **sig -,** move, stir; **hemel en aarde -,** move heaven and earth.
beweegbaar, (-bare), movable; moving.
beweegkrag, moving (motive) power.
beweeglik, (-e), movable; mobile; impressionable, sensitive; active.
beweeglikheid, movability; mobility; sensitiveness, susceptibility; liveliness.
beweegrede, motive, ground.
beween, (-), mourn for, lament.
beweer, (-), allege, aver, contend.
bewegend, (-e), moving; kinetic; dynamic.
beweging, (-e, -s), movement; motion; commotion; **arbeidsvermoë van -,** kinetic energy; **- neem,** take exercise; **in - bring,** start, put in motion; **in - kom,** begin to move; **in - kry,** get going; **in - wees,** be in motion; be astir; **uit eie -,** of one's own accord.
bewegingloos, (-lose), motionless.
bewegingskrag, impetus.
bewegingsleer, kinetics, kinematics.
bewegingsvryheid, freedom of movement.
bewer, (-s), beaver.
bewerasie, bibberasie, the shakes (shivers).
bewerig, (-e), shaking, shaky; doddering.
bewerigheid, shakiness; tremulousness.
bewering, (-e, -s), assertion, averment, contention; allegation.
bewerk, (-), work (mine); cultivate; treat (ore); shape; manufacture; adapt (play); remodel, revise; bring about, accomplish: manipulate, manage; canvass (voters).
bewerker, (-s), cause, author; adapter.
bewerking, (-e, -s), working; cultivation; adaptation; revision; manipulation; arrangement; accomplishment; vide **bewerk.**
bewerklik, (-e), laborious.
bewerkstellig, (-), bring about, accomplish.
bewerktuig, (-de), organized, organic.
bewertjies, quiver- (quaking-)grass.
bewese, proved; vide **bewys.**
bewierook, (-), incense; adulate, flatter.
bewillig, (-): **- in,** grant, consent.
bewillig, consent.
bewimpel, (-), gloze over, cloak.
bewimpeling, glossing over, explaining away.
bewind, government, administration; **aan die - wees,** be in power; **aan die - kom,** come into office (power).
bewindhebber, (-s), director, administrator.
bewindvoerder, commander.
bewing, trembling, quaking, shivering.

bewoë, moved, touched, affected.
bewolk, (-te), a. clouded, overcast.
bewolk, (-), cloud over; become cloudy.
bewonder, (-), admire.
bewonderaar, (-s), bewonderaarster, (-s), admirer.
bewonderenswaardig, (-e), admirable.
bewondering, admiration.
bewoner, (-s), inhabitant, occupant, tenant (of house); resident.
bewoning, occupation; inhabitation.
bewoon, (-), inhabit, occupy, dwell in.
bewoonbaar, (-bare), habitable, inhabitable.
bewoonster, (-s), vide **bewoner.**
bewoord, (-), word, phrase, put into words.
bewoording, (-e, -s), wording, phraseology.
bewus, (-te), conscious; **-te persoon,** person in question; **- van,** conscious of; **- of onbewus,** wittingly or unwittingly.
bewussyn, consciousness; **- verloor,** lose consciousness; **tot - kom,** regain consciousness.
bewusteloos, (-lose), unconscious, senseless.
bewusteloosheid, unconsciousness.
bewustheid, consciousness; **met -,** consciously, knowingly, wittingly.
bewys, (-e), n. proof, evidence; token (of affection); promissory note; receipt; voucher; certificate; testimony; **- van lidmaatskap,** certificate of membership; **- van ontvangs,** receipt; **- lewer van,** furnish evidence (proof) of.
bewys, (-), prove; demonstrate; substantiate (charge); do (a favour), render (a service), show (kindness); **hulde -,** pay homage; **eer -,** honour, pay tribute to.
bewysbaar, (-bare), capable of proof.
bewysbaarheid, demonstrability.
bewysgrond, argument.
bewysie, (-s), receipt; voucher; sign, trace.
bewyskrag, conclusiveness, cogency.
bewyslas, onus of proof.
bewysmiddel, proof.
bewysplaas, reference, quotation.
bewysstuk, document; exhibit.
bewysvoering, argumentation.
beywer, (-): **sig -,** exert oneself.
bibber, (-), shiver, tremble, quake.
bibberasie, vide **bewerasie.**
bibliofiel, (-e), bibliophil(e), book-lover.
bibliograaf, (-grawe), bibliographer.
bibliografie, bibliography.
bibliografies, (-e), bibliographic(al).
biblioteek, (-teke), library.
bibliotekaresse, (sg. & pl.), (lady-)librarian.
bibliotekaris, (-se), librarian.
bid(de), (ge-), pray, say one's prayers, beseech, beg, pray; say grace (at a meal), **(die) Onse Vader -,** say the Lord's prayer.
bidbankie, praying-stool.
biddag, day of prayer.
bidsnoer, rosary.
bidstond, biduur, prayer-meeting.
bied, (ge-), (1) offer (help), present (difficulty); **die hoof -, weerstand (teenstand) -,** offer resistance.
bied, bie(ë), (ge-), (2) bid; **hoër - as,** outbid; **- op,** (make a) bid for.
bieder, bieër, (-s), bidder.
bieding, biedery, bieëry, bidding.
bief, biefstuk, beefsteak.
bieg, n. confession.
bieg, (ge-), confess.
biegstoel, confessional (stall).
biegvader, confessor.
bier, beer.
bierbrouery, brewery.

bierbuik, -maag, pot-belly.
bierkan, -kruik, beer-jug.
bierparty, beer-drink.
biertjie, (-s) spot of beer.
biervat, beer-barrel, beer-cask.
bies(melk), beestings, colostrum.
biesie, (-s), (bul)rush, reed; whip; **sy -s pak,** clear off (out).
biesiegoed, -gras, rushes, reeds, coarse grass.
biesiepol, tussock (tuft) of reeds.
bietjie, (-s), n. little (bit); moment; **wag 'n -!,** wait a moment (bit); **by -s,** bit by bit, little by little; **maak 'n - die deur oop,** please open the door; **'n - Afrikaans,** a smattering of Afrikaans.
bietjie, adv. rather, somewhat, slightly.
bietjie-bietjie, a little at a time, bit by bit.
bifokaal, bifocal.
bigamie, bigamy.
bigamies, (-e), bigamous.
bigamis, (-te), bigamist.
biggel, (-), trickle.
bignonia, bignonia; trumpet-flower.
bigotterie, bigotry.
bikarbonaat, bicarbonate.
bikonkaaf, (-kawe), biconcave.
bikonveks, (-e), biconvex.
bikwadraat, biquadratic.
bilabiaal, (-ale), n. & a. bilabial.
bilateraal, (-ale), bilateral.
bilharzia, bilharzia.
biljart, n. billiards.
biljart, (ge-), play billiards.
biljartbok, cue-rest.
biljartkeu, -stok, billiard-cue.
biljartsaal, billiard-room.
biljartspeler, billiard-player.
biljartstok, billiard-cue.
biljet, (-te), poster; ticket; handbill; note.
biljoen, (-e), billion.
billik, (-e), a. reasonable, moderate; fair, just, unbiased, equitable.
billik, (ge-), approve of; consider fair.
billikerwys(e), in fairness.
billikheid, reasonableness; fairness.
billikheidshalwe, in (all) fairness.
billiking, approval.
biltong, (-e), biltong.
bimetallisme, bimetallism.
bind(e), (ge-), bind; fasten, tie (up); thicken (of soup); **sig -,** commit (bind) oneself; **- aan,** tie (fasten) to; tie (person) down to.
bindbalk, tie-beam, bond-timber, binder.
bindend, (-e), binding.
binder, (-s), binder.
bindery, (-e), binding; bindery.
bindgare, -garing, pack thread, string.
bindmiddel, agglutinant; cement; styptic.
bindsel, (-s) bandage.
bindspier, ligament.
bindvlies, conjunction (of eye).
binêr, (-e), binary.
binne, prep. within; inside.
binne, adv. in, inside, within; **daar -,** in there; **(kom) -!,** come in!, **na - gaan,** go in; enter; **te - skiet,** flash on; **van - en van buite,** inside and outside; **- bly,** stay in(doors) (down).
binneband, tube.
binnebrandmasjien, internal combustion engine.
binnebring, (binnege-), bring (take) in.
binnedeur, n. inner door.
binnedeur, adv.: **- gaan,** go through, take a short cut.
binnedring, (binnege-), penetrate into; invade (country); force one's way into.

binnegaan, (binnege-), go in; go into; enter.
binnegoed, entrails, intestines; works.
binnehaal, (binnege-), bring (fetch) in; gather (crops).
binnehoek, interior angle.
binnehof, inner court.
binnehou, (binnege-), keep in(doors) (down).
binnehuis, interior.
binne-in, (right) inside, within.
binnekamer, inner room.
binnekant, inside.
binnekom, (binnege-), come in; enter.
binnekoms, entry, entrance, coming in.
binnekort, ere (before) long, soon, shortly.
binnekruip, (binnege-), creep in.
binnekry, (binnege-), get in; get down.
binnelaat, (binnege-), let in, admit.
binneland, inland, interior; up-country.
binnelander, (-s), inlander.
binnelands, (-e), inland; internal, domestic; **-e oorlog,** civil war; **Minister van B-e Sake,** Minister of the Interior; **-e handel,** home-trade.
binnelei, (binnege-), usher in.
binneloods, (binnege-), pilot (ship) into port.
binneloop, (binnege-), walk in(to); put into port (of ship); draw in (of train).
binnemaat, inside measurement.
binnemeer, inland lake.
binnemeid(jie), housemaid.
binnemuur, inner wall.
binnenshuis, indoors.
binnenslands, in the country.
binnensmonds: - praat, mumble.
binne(n)ste, n. inside, interior; **in sy -,** in his heart (of hearts), deep down in his heart.
binne(n)ste, a. innermost, inner, inmost.
binne(n)ste-buite, inside out.
binne-om, round the inside.
binnery, (binnege-), ride in(to), drive in(to).
binneroep, (binnege-), call in.
binnesak, inside pocket.
binnesee, inland sea.
binneseil, (binnege-), sail into.
binnesleep, (binnege-), drag in(to); tow into port.
binnesmokkel, (binnege-), smuggle (in).
binnesool, inner sole, inside sole, in-sole.
binnestad, inner town.
binnestap, (binnege-), walk (step) into.
binneste- . . ., vide **binne(n)ste- . . .**
binnestoom, (binnege-), steam in.
binnestorm, (binnege-), rush (burst) in (into).
binnestroom, (binnege-), stream (flow, rush) in (into); flock in (into).
binnetelefoon, intercom.
binnetoe, in, inside.
binnetree, (binnege-), enter.
binnetrek, (binnege-), march (trek) in(to).
binneval, (binnege-), invade; drop in.
binneveermatras, inner-spring mattress.
binneveld, infield.
binneverbranding, internal combustion.
binnevet, fat around the intestines.
binnevra, (binnege-), ask in.
binnewaarts, (-e), a. inward.
binnewaarts, adv. inward(s).
binnewerk, inside (indoor) work, works watch).
binomies, (-e), binomial (theorem).
biochemie, biochemistry.
biograaf, (-grawe), biographer.
biografie, (-ë), biography.
biografies, (-e), biographic(al).
biologie, biology.
biologies, (-e), biological.

bioloog, (-loë, -loge), biologist.
bioskoop, (-skope), bioscope; cinema.
bioskoopvoorstelling, cinema show.
bisar, bizarre, grotesque.
bisdom, bishopric, diocese.
bisdomlik, (-e), diocesan.
biseps, (-e), biceps.
biskop, (-pe), bishop.
biskoplik, (-e), episcopal.
biskopsetel, bishop's see.
biskopstaf, bishop's staff, crosier (crozier).
bismut, bismuth.
bison, (-s), bison.
bisulfaat, bisulphate, hydrosulphate.
bits(ig), (-e), biting, cutting, bitter.
bits(ig)heid, acrimony, bitterness.
bitter, n. bitter; bitters.
bitter, (-, -e), a. bitter.
bitter, adv. bitterly; precious (little).
bitter, (ge-), take an appetiser (bitters).
bitteraarde, magnesia.
bitteramandel, bitter almond.
bitterappel(tjie), bitter apple.
bitterbessiebos, bitter berry.
bitterbossie, wild gentian, Christmas-berry.
bittereinder, (-s), die-hard.
bitterheid, bitterness; acerbity.
bitterkoekie, macaroon (biscuit).
bitterlik, bitterly.
bittersoet, bitter-sweet.
bitterwortel, bitterwort.
bitumen, bitumen.
bitumineus, (-e), bituminous.
bivak, (-ke), bivouac.
bivakmus, Balaclava cap.
bivakeer, (ge-), bivouac.
blaadjie, (-s) leeflet; petal (of flower), sheet (of paper); tract; paper; rag; 'n nuwe – omslaan, turn over a new leaf; by iemand in 'n goeie – staan, be in a person's good books.
blaai, (ge-), turn over the pages (leaves).
blaak, (ge-), burn, scorch; glow (with).
blaam, blame; reproach, blemish.
blaar, (blare), (1) leaf (of tree).
blaar, (blare), (2) blister, bleb.
blaar- . . ., vide **blad-** . . ., **blare** . . .
blaaragtig, (-e), leaflike, foliaceous.
blaarknop, leaf-bud.
blaarloos, (-lose), leafless.
blaarpens, manyplies, reticulum.
blaarryk, (-e), leafy.
blaarsel, leaf-cell.
blaarsiekte, leaf-blight.
blaarstand, phyllotaxy, disposition of leaves.
blaarsteel, leaf-stalk, petiole.
blaartabak, leaf-tobacco.
blaartjie, (-s), leaflet; little blister.
blaartrekkend, (-e), blistering, vesicant.
blaarvormig, (-e), leaf-shaped, foliated.
blaarvorming, foliation.
blaas, (blase), n. bag, bladder; cyst, bubble.
blaas, (ge-), blow (instrument); breathe, rest; spit (of cat); hiss (of goose); die perde laat –, rest the horses; – op, blow, sound (horn).
blaasbalk, bellows.
blaasinstrument, wind-instrument.
blaaskaak, windbag, gasbag.
blaas-op, toad-fish, toby.
blaasorkes, brass band, wind-band.
blaaspyp, -roer, blowpipe; pea-shooter.
blad, (blaaie), n. leaf (of book); sheet (of paper); (news)paper; shoulder(-blade); top (of table); surface (road); blade (of oar, saw, spring); van die – speel, play at sight.
blad- . . ., vide **blaar-** . . ., **blare-** . . .

bladaar, leaf-vein.
bladaarde, leaf-mould.
bladgoud, gold-leaf, leaf-gold.
bladgroen, chlorophyll.
bladluis, plant-louse, green fly, aphis.
bladrank, leaf-tendril.
bladsak, knapsack.
bladsiekte, **blaarsiekte**, leaf-blight.
bladsilwer, leaf-silver.
bladsteel, **blaarsteel**, leaf-stalk, petiole.
bladstil: dit was –, not a leaf stirred.
bladsy, page.
bladtin, tinfoil.
bladvulling, fill-up; padding.
bladwisselend, (-e), deciduous.
bladwisseling, shedding of leaves.
bladwyser, book-mark; index.
blaf, n. bark.
blaf, (ge-), bark; cough.
blafferig, (-e), inclined to bark.
blafon, vide **plafon**.
blakend, (-e), burning, glowing, ardent; in –e gesondheid, in the pink of health.
blaker, (-s), (flat) candlestick.
blaker, (ge-), (1) burn, singe, scorch, parch.
blaker, (ge-), (2) hit, strike.
blamaans, blancmange.
blameer, (ge-), blame, put the blame on.
blank, (a, -e), white; fair, pure, unstained; –e verse, blank verse.
blanke, (-s), a. white; die –s, the whites.
blanket, (ge-), rouge, paint.
blanketsel, rouge, cosmetic, paint.
blankheid, fairness, whiteness, pureness.
blanko, blank.
blare- . . ., vide **blaar-** . . ., **blad-** . . .
blaredak, canopy of leaves.
blaredos, **blaretooi**, foliage.
blas, dark, sallow (complexion).
blasie, (-s), little bladder; bubble.
blasoen, (-e), blazon, coat of arms.
blasoeneer, (ge-), blazon.
blatjang, chutney, ketchup.
bleek, **bleik**, n. bleaching; bleach-field.
bleek, a. pale, pallid; – word, turn pale.
bleek, (ge-), vide **bleik**.
bleekheid, paleness.
bleekmiddel, **bleik-**, bleaching-agent.
bleekpoeier, **bleik-**, bleaching-powder.
bleeksiekte, **bleeksug**, anaemia.
bleeksugtig, (-e), anaemic, chlorotic.
bleekveld, **bleik-**, bleach-field, bleach-ground.
bleik, **bleek**, (ge-), bleach, whiten.
blende, blende.
blêr, (ge-), bleat, bellow, cry, howl.
blêrfliek, the talkies.
blêrkas, juke-box.
bles, (-se), blaze; horse with a blaze; bald head.
blesbok, blesbuck.
bleshoender, red-knobbed coot; moor-hen.
bleskop, bald head, baldpate.
blesmol, mole-rat, sand-mole, star-mole.
blesperd, horse with a blaze.
bliep, bleep.
blik, (-ke), n. (1) tin.
blik, (-ke), n. (2) look, glance, gaze; 'n – slaan (werp), op, cast a glance at; breë –, a breadth of vision; helder –, keen insight.
blik, (ge-), look, glance; sonder (om te) – of bloos, unblushingly, without a blush.
blikbeker, tin-mug.
blikemmer, tin-pail. Vide **blikskottel**.
blikhuis, house of galvanised iron.
blikkantien, tin-can.

blikkie, (-s), (small) tin; **dit gaan jou –s!** good luck to you! cherio!
blikkiesbiltong, chipped beef.
blikkiesdorp, tin town; location; slums.
blikkiesgroente, tinned vegetables.
blikkieskos, tinned food.
blikkiesmelk, condensed (tinned) milk.
blikkiesvleis, tinned meat, bullybeef.
blikmes, -snyer, tin-opener.
bliksem, (-s), n. lightning; **soos die –,** quick as lightning, like blazes.
bliksem, (ge-), lighten; flash; fulminate.
bliksemafleier, lightning-conductor.
bliksemflits, flash of lightning.
bliksemslag, thunderclap; flash of lightning.
bliksemslig, flash of lightning.
bliksemsnel, quick as lightning, like lightning.
bliksemsnelheid, lightning-speed.
bliksemstraal, flash of lightning.
blikskater, (-s), vide **blikskottel.**
blikskater(s)!, the deuce!, hang it!
blikskêr, plate-shears.
blikskottel, (-s), tin-dish; blighter, rogue, rascal, devil, son of a gun.
blikskottel(s)!, vide **blikskater(s)!**
blikslaer, (-s), tin-smith; blighter.
blind, (-e), a. blind; **–e muur,** blank (dead) wall; **–e steeg,** blind alley; **–e toeval,** mere chance; **–e vertroue,** blind (implicit) faith; **– word,** become (go) blind; **– vir sy gebreke,** blind to his faults.
blind, adv. blindly.
blinddoek, n. bandage.
blinddoek, (ge-), blindfold; blind, hoodwink.
blinde, (-s), blind person; dummy (at cards); **in die –,** blindly, at random.
blindederm, appendix, caecum, blind gut.
blindedermontsteking, appendicitis.
blinde-instituut, institute for the blind, blind-school.
blindekas, wall-cupboard.
blindelings, blindly; (trust) implicitly.
blindemol, blind mole. Vide **blindemol(letjie).**
blindemol(letjie), blindman's buff.
blinder, (-s), stymie (golf). Vide **blinding.**
blindeskool, school for the blind.
blindeskrif, braille, writing for the blind.
blindeslang, blind snake.
blindevlieg, blind fly, sting-fly.
blindgebore, born blind, blind-born.
blindheid, blindness.
blinding, (-s), blind, shutter.
blink, a. shining, glittering, gleaming, bright; sleek (hair); **– vloer,** shining (polished) floor; **'n – gedagte,** a brain-wave.
blink, (ge-), shine, gleam, glitter.
blinkogies, cat's-eyes.
blinkoog: ou –, the devil.
blinkwater, will-o'-the-wisp.
blits, (-e), n. lightning; **soos (die) –,** quick as lightning, like blazes.
blits, (ge-), lighten; flash (of eyes).
blitsaanval, -oorlog, blitz.
blitspatrollie, flying squad.
blitspoeier, magnesium-powder.
blitssnel, adv. quick as lightning.
blitsstraal, vide **bliksemstraal.**
blitsvinnig, (-e), a. lightning-like.
blo, (ge-), vide **beloof.**
bloed, blood; **nuwe –,** fresh blood; **goed en –,** life and property; **kwaad – sit,** stir up ill feeling; **dit het my – laat kook,** it made my blood boil; **dit sit in die –,** it runs in the blood; **na – dors,** thirst for blood; **van koninklike –,** of royal blood.

bloedarmoede, anaemia.
bloedbad, massacre, slaughter, carnage.
bloedblaar, blood-blister.
bloeddorstig, (-e), blood-thirsty.
bloeddruk, blood-pressure.
bloeddruppel, drop of blood.
bloedeie: my – suster, my own sister.
bloed(e)loos, (-lose), bloodless.
bloederig, (-e), bloody; bloodstained.
bloedgeld, blood-money, price of blood.
bloedhond, bloodhound.
bloedig, (-e), a. bloody, sanguinary; scorching, blazing (sun).
bloedig, adv.: **ek was – kwaad,** I was furiously angry.
bloedig, bleeding, haemorrhage.
bloedjie, (-s), poor mite, little thing.
bloedjong, bloedjonk, very young.
bloedkleur, blood-colour.
bloedklont, clot of blood.
bloedlaat, (bloedge-), bleed, let blood.
bloedlating, bleeding, blood-letting.
bloedliggaampie, blood-corpuscle.
bloedloos, vide **bloed(e)loos.**
bloedloosheid, bloodlessness, anaemia.
bloedmenging, mixture of blood.
bloedmin, precious little (few).
bloedneus, bleeding nose; **iemand ('n) – slaan,** blood a person's nose.
bloedondersoek, blood-test.
bloedoortapping, bloodtransfusion.
bloedpens(ie), dysentery.
bloedpersie, -parsie, dysentery.
bloedplasma, blood plasm.
bloedrooi, blood-red; **– word,** turn scarlet.
bloedryk, sanguineous, full-blooded.
bloedserum, blood-serum.
bloedskande, incest.
bloedskuld, blood-guilt, blood-guiltiness.
bloedsomloop, circulation of the blood.
bloedspoor, blood-spoor, blood-trail.
bloedstorting, haemorrhage; bloodshed.
bloedsuier, leech; bloodsucker (lit. & fig.).
bloedsweet, bloody sweat.
bloedtransfusie, bloodtransfusion.
bloedvat, blood-vessel.
bloedvergieting, bloodshed.
bloedvergiftiging, blood-poisoning.
bloedverlies, loss of blood.
bloedverwant, (blood-)relation, relative.
bloedverwantskap, blood-relationship.
bloedvin, (-ne), -vint, (-e), boil, furuncle.
bloedwarmte, blood-temperature.
bloedweinig, vide **bloedmin.**
bloedwors, black-pudding, blood-sausage.
bloedwraak, blood-feud, vendetta.
bloei, n. bloom, blossom; florescence; prosperity; **in volle –,** in full bloom (blossom); **in die – van sy jare,** in the prime of his life.
bloei, (ge-), 1. blossom, flower; flourish.
bloei, (ge-), 2. bleed: **sy neus –,** his nose is bleeding, he bleeds at the nose.
bloeisel, (-s), blossom.
bloeityd, flowering-, blossoming-time; florescence; golden age, palmy days.
bloekom(boom), vide **blougom(boom)**
bloekomolie, eucalyptus-oil.
bloem, vide **blom.**
bloemis, (-te), florist.
bloemlesing, anthology.
bloemryk, (-e), flowery, florid, ornate.
bloemrykheid, floweriness.
bloes, (-e), bloese, (-s), blouse.
bloesem, (-s), n. blossom, bloom.
bloesem, (ge-), blossom, bloom.

bloesend, (-e), rosy, ruddy.
blok, (-ke), n. block; bloc; log (of wood); **dit was 'n – aan die been**, it was a handicap (an encumbrance); **'n – van 'n kêrel**, a giant.
blok, (ge-), cram, swot, grind (at).
blokbom, blockbuster.
blokdruk, block-printing.
blokhamer, mallet.
blokhuis, blockhouse; log-house.
blokkade, (-s), blockade.
blokkedoos, box of bricks, brick-box.
blokkeer, (ge-), blockade.
blokkie, (-s), square; cube.
blokletter, block-letter.
blokskoen, clog, wooden-soled shoe.
blokskrif, block-writing.
blokstelsel, block-system; cramming system.
blom, (-me), n. flower; blossom; flour (finer part of meal); – **van swa(w)el**, flowers of sulphur; **'n – maak**, make a splash (hit); **die – van die jeug**, the pick (flower, choice) of the youth.
blom, (ge-), flower; bloom, blossom (of tree).
blombak, flower-bowl.
blombed(ding), flower-bed.
blomblaar, petal.
blom(me)handelaar, florist.
blomkelk, calyx.
blomknop, flower-bud.
blomkool, cauliflower.
blomkroon, corolla.
blomkweker, florist, floriculturist.
blomkwekery, floriculture; nursery.
blommandjie, flower-basket.
blommehulde, floral tribute.
blom(me)meisie, flower-girl.
blommeprag, wealth of flowers.
blommetentoonstelling, flower-show.
blommeweelde, wealth of flowers.
blomperk, flower-bed.
blompot, flower-pot.
blomruiker, bouquet, bunch of flowers.
blomryk, vide **bloemryk**.
blomsaad, flower-seed.
blomtafel, flower-stand.
blomtyd, flowering-season.
blomtuin, flower-garden.
blomvaas, flower-vase.
blond, (-e), fair, blond(e).
blondharig, (-e), fair-haired.
blondine, (-s), blonde, fair-haired girl.
bloos, (ge-), blush, colour, flush.
bloot, (blote), a. bare, naked; very, mere (thought); bald (facts); naked (eye); **onder die blote hemel**, in the open.
bloot, adv. merely, only.
blootgee, (blootge-): **sig –**, lay oneself open; commit oneself.
blootlê, (blootge-), lay bare, expose; disclose, reveal plans.
blootlegging, exposure; vide **blootlê**.
bloots, a. unsaddled.
bloots, adv. bareback; – **ry**, ride bareback.
blootshoof(s), bare-headed.
blootsperd, barebacked horse; – **ry**, ride bareback.
blootsrug, bareback.
blootstaan, (blootge-), be exposed (to).
blootstel, (blootge-), expose, subject (to).
blootstelling, exposure.
blootsvoet(s), barefoot(ed), with bare feet.
blos, blush, glow, flush, bloom.
blosend, (-e), blushing; rosy, flushed.
blou, n. blue.
blou, a. blue; – **plekke**, bruises; **iemand 'n – oog slaan**, give a person a black eye; – **Maandag**, black Monday; **elke – Maandag**, once in a blue moon.
blouaap, vervet.
bloubaadjie, bluejacket.
Bloubaard, Bluebeard.
bloubes(bossie), bilberry, whortleberry.
bloublasie, (-s), Portuguese man-o'-war.
bloublommetjie, feeble excuse, story.
blou-blou: iets — laat, leave the matter there.
blouboek, blue-book.
bloubok, blue buck.
blouboontjie, ounce of lead, slub, blue pill.
bloudissel, -**distel**, Mexican thistle.
bloureën, wistaria.
blougom(boom), **bloekom(boom)**, bluegum(-tree).
blougrond, blue-ground.
bloukopkoggelmander, blue-headed lizard.
blou(kop)korhaan, blue bustard.
blou-oog, n. blue eyes.
blouoog-. . ., blue-eyed.
blousel, blue.
blouskimmel, grey, dapple-grey (horse).
blousuur, prussic acid, hydrocyanic acid.
bloute, blueness, blue.
bloutjie, (-s), 1. carbon-copy.
bloutjie, (-s), 2. **'n – loop**, gee, get, give the mitten.
bloutong, blue tongue (sheep's disease).
blouvlieg, blue-fly.
blouwildebees, blue wildebeest.
bluf, n. big talk, boasting, bragging.
bluf, (ge-), brag, boast, talk big.
blufferig, (-e), bragging, boasting.
bluffery, big talk, bragging.
blus, n. **sy – is uit**, he is finished (played out).
blus, (ge-), extinguish, put out; slake (lime).
blustoestel, (fire-)extinguisher.
bly, (–, -e), a. glad, pleased, happy.
bly, (ge-), stay, remain; live; keep; keep on; be killed; **waar – Jan?**, what has become of John?; **gesond –**, keep in good health; **goed –**, keep (of perishables); – **lewe**, live (on); **stil –**, keep quiet; – **staan**, remain standing; stand (still); – **steek**, stick; **6 van 8 – 2**, 6 from 8 leaves two; **laat (dit) maar –**, never mind that; – **by**, remain (stay) with; stick to (promise), adhere to (opinion), persist in; **en daarby het dit ge–**, and there the matter rested.
blydskap, joy, gladness.
blygeestig, (-e), cheerful, gay, merry.
blyheid, gladness, joy.
blyk, (-e), n. token, proof, mark, sign; – **gee van**, give evidence of; show signs of (fear).
blyk, (ge-), appear, be obvious (evident); **dit – dat . . .**, it appears that . . .; **dit moet nog –**, it remains to be seen; **laat –**, show (fear), betray, reveal.
blykbaar, (-bare), a. apparent, evident, obvious.
blykbaar, adv. apparently, evidently, obviously.
blykens, as appears from.
blymoedig, (-e), cheerful, joyful, jovial.
blymoedigheid, cheerfulness, joyfulness.
blyspel, comedy.
blyspeldigter, writer of comedies.
blystaan, (–), stick, get stuck (in the mud).
blywend, (-e), lasting (peace); enduring, permanent; **-e kleure**, fast colours.
bo, bowe, prep. above; over, past; beyond (one's income).
bo, bowe, adv. above; upstairs; at the top; on high; **hier –**, up here; **soos –**, as above; **na –**, up; upstairs; **te – gaan**, exceed, surpass, be beyond; **te – kom**, overcome, surmount; recover from (illness); **van –**, from above; from the top; **van – tot onder**, from top to bottom; from head to

foot; – **dryf,** **-drywe,** float on the surface; prevail.
bo-aan, at the top (of the page); at the head (of the table); – **staan,** be at the top of; head the list.
bo-aards, **bowe-aards,** **(-e),** supermundane; supernatural.
bo-af: van –, from the top; from above.
bo-arm, upper arm.
bobaadjie, jacket, coat.
bobaas, champion, master; top-dog.
bobbejaan, (-jane), baboon, monkey; **jy is (lyk) 'n mooi** –!, you look like it! Vide **bobbejaantjie.**
bobbejaanboud, "baboon's thigh", musket.
bobbejaandruiwe, wild grape-berries.
bobbejaankers, berg-cypress.
bobbejaanspinnekop, baboon-spider.
bobbejaanstuipe, hysterics, (hysterical) fits.
bobbejaantjie, (-s), little baboon; baby.
bobbejaantou, monkey-rope.
bobbejaanuintjies, monkey-bulbs.
bobbel, (-s), n. bubble, blister.
bobbel, (ge-), bubble, blister.
bobotie, "bobotie", curried minced meat.
bobou, superstructure.
bod, bot, (botte), bid, offer.
bode, (-s), messenger; servant.
bodeloon, messenger's fee (reward).
bodem, (-s), bottom; soil; territory; ship, vessel; **die** – **inslaan,** frustrate, knock on the head; **op vaste** –, on a firm (safe) foundation; on terra firma; **tot die** – **drink,** drain to the dregs.
bodemloos, (-lose), bottomless.
bodemsgesteldheid, nature of the soil.
bodeur, n. upper (part of a) door.
bodeur, through the top (of),
bodorp, upper town (village).
boe, bo(h); hy kan nie – **of ba sê nie,** he can't say bo to a goose; **hy het nie** – **of ba gesê nie,** he did not say a word.
Boeddha, Buddha.
Boeddhisme, Buddhism.
boedel, (-s), estate; property; – **oorgee,** surrender one's estate; puke, spew.
boedelbeheerder, trustee.
boedelberedderaar, administrator of an estate.
boedelbeskrywing, inventory.
boef, (boewe), villain, rogue, knave.
boefie, (-s), little rogue (villain), urchin.
boeg, (boeë), bow(s) (of ship); shoulder-joint, (of horse); **oor een ('n)** –, without a break; **dit oor 'n ander** – **gooi,** try another tack.
boeglam, dead beat, exhausted, played out.
boegoe, buchu.
boegoe-asyn, buchu-vinegar.
boegoeblare, buchu-leaves.
boegoebrandewyn, buchu-brandy.
boegseer, (ge-), tow (ship).
boegseerlyn, tow-line.
boegspriet, bowsprit.
boei, (-e), n. 1. handcuff(s); fetter.
boei, (-e), n. 2. buoy.
boei, (ge-), handcuff, put in irons; captivate, fascinate; hold the attention.
boeiend, (-e), captivating, fascinating; absorbing, gripping (tale); irresistible.
boeiekoning, escapologist.
boek, (-e), n. book; quire (of paper); **dit spreek soos 'n** –, it goes without saying; **dis 'n** –, that's a dead certainty; **hoog by iemand te** – **staan,** be in a person's good books; **te** – **staan as,** be known as; **te** – **stel,** (put on) record.
boek, (ge-), enter, book.
boekaankondiging, book-notice.
boekagtig, (-e), bookish.

boekanier, (-s), buccaneer.
boekbeoordeling, (book-)review, criticism.
boekbinder, bookbinder.
boekbindery, bookbinding; bookbinder's shop.
boekdeel, volume.
boekdrukkuns, art of printing.
boeke- . . ., vide **boek-** . . .
boekenhout, South African beech.
boekery, (-e), library.
boeket, (-te), bouquet (also of wine).
boekevat, (boekege-), hold family-prayers.
boekgeleerdheid, book-learning.
boekgeskenk, gift-book; gift of books.
boekhandel, book-trade; bookseller's shop.
boekhandelaar, bookseller.
boekhou, n. bookkeeping.
boekhou, (boekge-), keep an account of, keep accounts; keep the books.
boekhouding, bookkeeping, accountancy.
boekhouer, bookkeeper.
boekie, (-s), booklet, little book; **baie op sy** – **hê,** have much to answer for; **by iemand in 'n slegte** – **staan,** be in a person's bad books.
boeking, booking; entry.
boekjaar, financial year.
boekkas, bookcase.
boek(e)kennis, book-learning.
boek(e)lêer, book-mark.
boek(e)liefhebber, lover of books, bibliophil(e).
boekmerk, book-plate.
boe(k)pens, vide **boepens.**
boekrak, book-shelves, bookcase.
boeksak, book-bag, satchel.
boekstaaf, (ge-), put on record.
boekstalletjie, book-stall.
boekstander(tjie), book-stand.
boek(e)taal, bookish language.
boek(e)versamelaar, book-collector.
boek(e)versameling, collection of books.
boekweit, vide **bokwiet.**
boekwerk, bookwork.
boekwinkel, book shop.
boekwurm, bookworm.
boel, lot, crowd, heaps, lots; **'n** – **kinders,** lots of children; **die hele** –, the whole lot (caboodle); **die** – **in die war stuur,** make a mess of things.
boeljon, beef-tea, broth.
boeltjie: sy –, his traps (things).
boeman, bogy(-man).
boemel, n. spree; **aan die** –, on the spree.
boemel, (ge-), booze, spree; loaf about.
boemelaar, (-s), reveller; loafer, bum.
boemeltrein, slow train.
boemerang, (-s), boomerang.
boen, (ge-), polish, rub.
bo-end, -ent, head (of table); upper end.
boender, (-s), n. scrubbing-brush.
boender, (ge-), chase (drive) away, send packing, bundle off (out).
boe(k)pens, pot-belly, corporation, big paunch.
Boer, (-e), Boer.
boer, (-e), farmer; peasant; knave, jack (cards); **die** – **die kuns afvra,** try to worm a secret out of a person.
boer, (ge-), farm; stay, remain; **agteruit** –, at a loss; go downhill; **by 'n plek** –, frequent a place; **waar** – **jy teenswoordig?,** where do you hang out these days?
boerbiskuit, Boer-biscuit, rusk.
boerbok, Boer-goat.
boerboontjie, broad bean.
boerbot(t)er, farm-butter.
boere- . . ., vide **boer-** . . .
boerebank, rural bank.
boerebedrieër, confidence-trickster, swindler.

boerebedrog, humbug, swindling.
boerebedryf, farming.
boeredogter, farmer's daughter.
boeredorp, country-village.
boerelewe, country-life, farm-life.
boer(e)matriek, confirmation (church).
boeremeisie, country-girl, farm-girl.
boeremense, country-people.
Boere-oorlog, (Anglo-)Boer War.
boerestand, farmer-class, farming community.
boerevereniging, farmer's association.
boereverneuker, vide **boerebedrieër**.
boerkool, garden-kale, borecole.
boermeel, boer-meal, coarse meal.
boernôi, -nooi, vide **boeremeisie**.
boerperd, farm-horse.
boerplaas, farm.
boerplek, haunt; favourite spot.
boers, (-e), boorish, rustic.
boerseun, farmer's son, farm lad.
boersheid, boorishness, clownishness.
boertabak, boer-tobacco.
Boervolk, Boer-people (-nation).
boervrou, farmer's wife; country woman.
boerwors, home-made sausage.
boesel, (-s), bushel.
boesem, (-s), bosom, breast.
boesemsonde, secret sin.
boesemvriend(in), bosom-friend.
Boesman, (-s), Bushman.
Boesmanskildery, Bushman painting.
Boesmantaal, Bushman language.
Boesmantekening, Bushman drawing.
boet, n. brother.
boet, (ge-), pay, suffer; – **vir**, pay (atone) for.
boeta, boetie, (-s), brother, vide **baantjie**.
boete, (-s), fine, penalty; penance; – **oplê**, impose a fine; – **doen**, do penance; **op** – **van**, on penalty of.
boetebossie, "boetebossie", Xanthium spinosum.
boetedoening, penance; penitential exercise.
boeteling, (-e), penitent.
boetie, vide **boeta**.
boetpredikasie, penitential sermon.
boetpsalm, penitential psalm.
boetseer, (ge-), model.
boetseerklei, modelling-clay.
boetvaardig, (-e), penitent, repentant.
boetvaardigheid, penitence, repentance.
boewebakkies, gallows-face, sinister mug.
boewebende, pack of rogues (knaves).
boewestreek, knavery.
bof, (bowwe), n. den, home (in catch-games); tee (golf); base (baseball).
bof, (ge-), tee (golf).
bofbal, baseball.
bog, (-te), n. 1. bend, wind-curve; bight.
bog, n. 2. nonsense; litter; fool; bad sort; **jou** –!, you silly ass!; **pure** –!, sheer nonsense!; – **met jou!**, stuff and nonsense!
bog- . . ., worthless, useless, rotten.
bogedeelte, upper part.
bogenoemde, above(-mentioned).
boggel, (-s), hump, hunch.
boggie, (-s), little rogue (rascal); youngster.
bogkind, a mere child.
bogpraatjies, twaddle, senseless talk.
bogronds, (-e), overhead (wires); elevated.
bogterig, (-e), trifling, insignificant, paltry.
bogtery, nonsense; nuisance.
bohaai, pohaai, fuss, noise.
bohand, vide **bowehand**.
Boheems, (-e), Bohemian.
bohuis, upper part of a house; top house.
boikot, n. boycott.

boikot, (ge-), boycott.
bo-in, (in) at the top.
bok, (-ke), n. goat; (wild) buck; box (of coach); buck (of wagon); vaulting-buck (gymnastics); trestle, support; rest (billiards); young man; best girl; blunder, bloomer; **'n** – **skiet**, make a blunder.
bokaak, upper jaw.
bokaal, (-kale), goblet, beaker, drinking-cup.
bokamer, upper room, upstairs-room.
bokant, n. upper side, top (side).
bokant, prep. above, over (the door).
bokbaard(jie), goatee (beard).
bok-bok-staan-stil (-styf), high cockalorum.
bokerf, top notch; top-gear; – **trek**, strain under the load.
bokhaar, mohair.
bokhael, buckshot.
bokkapeter, "bokkapater", gelded goat.
bokkem, bokkom, (-s), mullet, Cape herring.
bokkesprong, caper; –e, antics.
bokkie, (-s), 1. kid, little goat; little buck; (wooden) trestle.
bokkie, (-s), 2. buggy.
bokknie, goat's knee; **die broek maak (het)** –**ë**, the trousers are baggy.
bokkom, vide **bokkem**.
boklam, kid.
bokleer, kid, buckskin.
boklere, upper clothes.
bokmakierie, bokmakiri, bush-shrike.
bokmelk, goat's milk.
bokom, (boge-), get to the top, get on top; come up, come to the surface.
bokooi, she-goat.
bokors, upper crust.
bokram, he-goat, billy-goat.
boks, (ge-), box.
bokseil, bucksail, tarpaulin.
bokser, (-s), boxer.
bokser(hond), boxer.
bokskryt, boxing-ring.
bokskyn, buckskin.
bok(s)leer, vide **bokleer**.
bokspring, (ge-), caper, buck-jump.
bokswedstryd, boxing-match.
Bokveld, Bokkeveld: – **toe gaan**, go west.
bokvet, goat-suet.
bokwa, buck-wagon.
bokwavrag, buck-load, buck-wagon-load.
bokwiet, boekweit, buckwheat.
bol, (-le), n. ball; globe; sphere; crown (of hat); bulb (of plant).
bol, (–, -le), a. convex (lens); bulging.
bol, (ge-), bulge; swell.
bolaag, top-layer, surface (upper) layer.
bolaken, top-sheat.
Boland, Western Province.
Bolander, (-s), inhabitant of the Western Province.
Bolands, (-e), of (from) the Western Province.
boldriehoek, spherical triangle.
boldriehoeksmeting, spherical trigonometry.
boleer, uppers, upper leather.
bolhol, convexo-concave.
bolig, skylight, fan-light.
bolip, upper lip.
bolkalander, boll-weevil.
bolla, (-s), bun (of hair), chignon.
bol(le)makiesie, head over heals; – **slaan**, turn a somersault; change front.
bol(le)makiesieslag, somersault.
bolletjie, (-s), bun.
boloop, upper course.
bolpen, ball-point pen.

bolrond, (-e), convex; globular; spherical.
bolsektor, sector of sphere.
Bolsjewiek, (-e), Bolshevik.
Bolsjewis, (-te), Bolshevist.
Bolsjewisme, Bolshevism.
Bolsjewisties, (-e), Bolshevistic.
bolug, upper air.
bolvorm, spherical shape.
bolvormig, (-e), spherical; bulb-shaped.
bolwerk, rampart; stronghold, bulwark.
bolyf, upper part of the body.
bolyfie, (-s), bodice.
bom, (-me), bomb, shell.
bomaanslag, bomb-outrage.
bombardeer, (ge-), bomb(ard), shell.
bombardement, (-e), bombardment.
bombardier, (-s), bombardier.
bombarie, bombalie, fuss, noise.
bombas, bombast.
bombasties, (-e), bombastic.
bomdop, bomb-shell.
bomenslik, (-e), superhuman.
bomgooier, bomb-thrower; bomber (machine).
bomvliegtuig, bomber, bombing-plane.
bomvry, shell-proof, bomb-proof.
bom(me)werper, vide **bomgooier.**
bo(we)natuurlik, (-e), supernatural.
bo(we)natuurlikheid, supernaturalness.
bond, (-e), bond, league, confederation.
bondel, (-s), bundle (of washing); sheaf (of papers); cluster, fascicle (bot.).
bondel, (ge-), bundle.
bondeldraer, pedlar, tramp.
bondgenoot, (-note), ally, confederate.
bondgenootskap, alliance, confederacy.
bondig, (-e), concise, brief, succinct, terse.
bondigheid, conciseness, terseness.
bondstaat, federal state.
bonk, (-e), n. lump; thump.
bonk, (ge-), thump; – **op,** thump.
bonkig, (-e), bony.
bons, (ge-), n. thump, bump, thud, bang.
bons, (ge-), bump, bang; throb (of heart).
bont, n. fur.
bont, (–, -e), a. pied, piebald (horse), spotted; variegated, gay (colours); motley (gathering); **– en blou slaan,** beat black and blue; **rond en –,** right and left; **'n bietjie te –,** a bit thick.
bontgoed, cotton-prints.
bontheid, variegation; vide **bont.**
bontjas, fur-coat.
bontkraag, fur-collar.
bontpraat, (bontge-), ramble; contradict oneself.
bontseep, mottled soap.
bontspan, particoloured team.
bontspring, (bontge-), jump about; vide **bontstaan.**
bontstaan, (bontge-), stir one's stumps; try different tacks; **lelik –,** leave no stone unturned.
bontwerk, fur-goods, furriery.
bontwerker, furrier.
bontwinkel, furrier's shop.
bonus, (-se), bonus.
boodskap, (-pe), n. message; errand; **blye –,** good news; **–pe doen,** run errands; go shopping.
boodskap, (ge-), bring word.
boodskapjong, errand-boy, messenger.
boodskapper, (-s), messenger, harbinger.
boog, (boë), n. bow (and arrow); arch (archit.); arc (geom.); curve; bind (mus.).
boog, (ge-): – **op,** boast of, glory in.
booggewelf, arched vault.
booggraad, degree of arc.
booglamp, arc-lamp.
booglyn, bowline, curvature.
boogpees, bowstring.

boogskiet, archery.
boogskoot, bow-shot.
boogskutter, archer.
boogvenster, arched window.
boogvormig, (-e), arched.
bo-om, round the top.
boom, (bome), n. 1. tree; barrier; punting-pole; **'n – van 'n kêrel,** a huge fellow, a giant.
boom, (bome), n. 2. bottom, seat (of trousers); **die – inslaan,** frustrate (plans).
boom, (ge-), punt.
boomagtig, (-e), treelike, arborescent.
boombas, tree-bark.
boomgaard, orchard.
boomgrens, tree-line.
boomklimmer, tree-climber.
boomkweker, nursery-man, arboriculturist.
boomkwekery, tree-nursery; arboriculture.
boomloos, (-lose), treeless.
boomluis, tree-louse.
boommos, tree-moss.
boomnimf, tree-nymph, dryad.
boompie, (-s), little tree, sapling.
boomplaas, wooded farm.
boomryk, (-e), woody, well-timbered.
boomskraap, a. finished, empty; broke.
boomskraap(sel), n. scrapings.
boomstam, tree-trunk.
boomstomp, tree-stump.
boomswam, tree-fungus.
boomvaring, tree-fern.
boomvormig, (-e), tree-shaped, arborescent.
boomwol, cotton; wood-wool.
boon, (bone), bean; **in die bone wees,** be in a fix; **boonop, bowenop,** besides, in addition.
boonste, n. top, upper part.
boonste, a. top, topmost, upper.
boontjie, (-s), bean; **– kry sy loontjie,** every dog has his day; **– kom om sy loontjie,** chickens come home to roost; **heilige –,** goody-goody.
boontjie-akker, bean-field.
boontjieso(e)p, bean-soup.
boontjiestoel, bean-stalk, -stool.
boontoe, upstairs; higher up; up(wards); **– roep,** swear, curse; call to heaven.
bo-oor, over the top; right (clean) over.
bop-op, at the top, on (the) top.
boor, (bore), n. 1. bit; drill; jumper, boring-machine; gimlet; borer.
boor, borium, n. 2. boron (chem.).
boor, (ge-), drill, bore; **in die grond –,** sink.
boord, (-e), n. 1. orchard.
boord, (-e), n. 2. border, edge; **aan –,** on board (ship); **oor– gooi,** throw overboard; **van – gaan,** go ashore.
boord(enste)vol, full to the brim.
boorder, (-s), borer; driller.
boordjie, (-s), collar; **hoë –,** stick-up collar.
boordjieknoop, collar-stud.
boord-lugprojektiel, air-to-air missile.
boordskutter, air gunner.
boorgat, bore-hole.
boorman, jumperman; borer.
boormasjien, boring-machine.
boorpoeier, boracic powder.
boorsalf, boracic ointment.
boorsel, edging, lacing, facing.
boortjie, (-s), gimlet.
boorwater, boracic lotion.
boorwydte, bore-width.
boos, (–, bose), angry, cross; wicked, evil (spirit); malignant (ulcer); **– word,** get angry.
boosaardig, (-e), malicious; malignant.
boosaardigheid, malice; malignity.
boosdoener, evil-doer, malefactor.

boosheid, anger; evil, wickedness.
booswig, (-te) criminal, villain.
boot, (bote) boat, steamer.
bootsman, boatswain.
boottog, boat-trip.
boottrein, boat-train.
bootwerker, dock-labourer.
boraam, upper window.
boraks, borax.
bord, (-e), plate (at table); (black)board.
bordeel, (-dele), brothel.
bordjie, (-s), small plate; notice-board; nameplate; **die –s is verhang**, the tables are turned.
bordpapier, cardboard, pasteboard.
borduur, (ge-), embroider (lit. & fig.).
borduurnaald, embroidery-needle.
borduurraam, embroidery-frame.
borduursel, embroidery.
borduurwerk, embroidery.
borg, (-e), n. surety, guarantee; security; guarantor; bail (law); (valve-)guard.
borgstaan, (**borgge-**), go (become) bail, stand surety (for person); – **vir**, vouch for.
borgsteller, surety.
borgstelling, security, surety, bail.
borgteken, (**borgge-**), vide **borgstaan**.
borgtog, surety, bail; **op – uit**, admitted to bail.
borium, boor, boron.
borok, skirt.
borrel, (-s), n. 1. bubble.
borrel, (-s), n. 2. gin, spot, sundowner.
borrel, (ge-), 1. bubble.
borrel, (ge-), 2. have a gin (sundowner).
borrelvink, red bishop-bird.
borrie, turmeric.
borriehout, lemonwood, wild lemon.
bors, (-te), breast; bosom; (weak) chest, brisket (meat); front (of shirt); **benoude –**, asthma; **dit stuit my teen die –**, it goes against the grain; **uit volle – sing**, sing at the top of one's voice.
borsbeeld, bust; effigy (on coin).
borsbeen, breast-bone, sternum.
borsel, (-s), n. brush; bristle (stiff hair).
borsel, (ge)- brush; give a whacking.
borselhare, bristles.
borselsak, brush-bag.
borsharnas, breastplate.
borshemp, dress-shirt.
borsholte, cavity of the chest.
borsie, (-s), little breast; shirt-front, dickey.
borskas, thorax, chest.
borskind, breast-fed child.
borsklontjie, lung-lozenge.
borskwaal, chest-trouble, -complaint.
borslap, bib (of child); chest-protector.
borslyer, consumptive patient.
borslyfie, bust-bodice.
borsplaat, breastplate; breast-piece (of harness).
borsriem, breast-strap; pole-strap.
bors(t)rok, corset, stays.
borsslag, breast-stroke.
borsspeld, brooch.
borsstuk, thorax; breastplate; brisket.
borssuiker, sugar-stick.
borstrok, vide **bors(t)rok**.
borsvlies, pleura.
borsvliesontsteking, pleurisy, pleuritis.
borswering, parapet, breastwork.
bos, (-se), wood, forest; bush, shrub; bunch (of carrots); bundle, sheaf, shock (of hair); **om die – loop (lei)**, cheat (take in, bluff).
bosaanplanting, afforestation.
bosaap, bush-baby.
bosagtig, (-e), woody.
bosbaadjie, lumber-jacket.

bosbewoner, forest-dweller.
bosbok, bush-buck.
bosbou(kunde), forestry, sylviculture.
bosbouskool, school of forestry, forestry-school.
bosbrand, bush-fire, forest-fire.
bosdruif, wild vine.
bosduif, speckled (rock-)pigeon.
bose: die B–, the Evil One.
bosgasie, **boskasie**, (-s), thicket, brushwood, underwood; shock (of hair), unkempt hair.
bosgod, faun, sylvan deity.
bosgodin, wood-nymph.
boskasie, vide **bosgasie**.
boskat, wildcat.
boskwartel, button-quail.
bosland, woodland.
boslanser, (-s), country-bumpkin, -cousin.
bosloerie, bush-lourie.
bosluis, (bush-)tick, tampan.
bosluiskoors, East Coast fever, tick-fever.
bosluisvoël, tick-bird, buff-backed egret.
Bosneger, bush-Negro, maroon.
bosopsigter, forester.
bosryk, (-e), woody, (well-)wooded.
bosrykheid, woodiness.
bosseer, (ge)-, mould in wax.
bosseleer, (ge-), emboss.
bossie, (-s), bush, shrub; bunch (of flowers). Vide **bos**; **geld soos –s**, pots (piles) of money; **dis alles –s!**, its all nonsense.
bossiedokter, herbalist.
bossiekop, shock of hair; bushy-maned pony.
bossiestee, bush-tea.
bostaande, **bowestaande**, above-mentioned; **die –**, the above.
bo-stel, body (of vehicle).
bostelegraaf, bush-telegraph.
bo-stuk, upper part (piece), top-part.
bosvark, bush-pig.
bosveld, bush-country.
Bosveld: die –, the Bushveld.
bosvoël, green bulbul.
boswagter, forester, ranger, keeper.
boswêreld, bush-country.
boswerker, lumberjack.
boswese, (department of) forestry.
bot, (-te), n. 1. flounder (fish).
bot, (-te), n. 2. bone.
bot, (–, -te), a. blunt, dull; sluggish.
bot, (ge-), bud, sprout.
bot-af, blunt(ly), curt(ly).
botand, upper tooth.
botanikus, (-se, -ici), botanist.
botanie, botany.
botanies, (-e), botanical.
botaniseer, (ge-), botanize.
boter, vide **botter**.
botheid, dul(l)ness; vide **bot**.
botoon, **boweton**, overtone; **die – voer**, dominate; set the pace, play first fiddle.
bots, (ge-), collide; clash, disagree; **– met**, collide (clash) with.
botsing, (-e, -s), collision; smash; impact, clash, conflict; **in – kom**, collide; clash.
botstil, stockstill, quite still.
bottel, (-s), n. bottle; **in die – kyk**, drink.
bottel, (ge-), bottle.
botter, butter; **– smeer op**, butter; **– by die vis**, touch pot, touch penny; **dit is – op sy brood**, that is grist to his mill; **met jou neus in die – val**, strike oil, have luck.
botterblom, buttercup, Cape daisy.
botterboer, dairy-farmer.
botterbroodjie, scone.

botterham(metjie), a slice of bread and butter; sandwich.
botterik, dunce.
botterkop, dunce, blockhead; hinny (mule).
bottermes, butter-knife.
botterpot(jie), butter-pot.
botterspaan, butter-scoop, -pat.
bottersuur, butyric acid.
bottervaatjie, butter-firkin, -tub.
bottervet, butter-fat.
botvier, (botge-), give rein to, indulge.
botweg, bluntly, flatly.
bou, n. build; make, construction; building, erection; structure; framework.
bou, (ge-), build; erect, construct; – **op,** rely on.
bou-aannemer, building-contractor.
boubedryf, building-trade.
boud, (-e), n. buttock; leg (of mutton), haunch; –**e,** hindquarters.
boud, a. bold.
boudjie, (-s), leg, drumstick; vide **boud.**
boudweg, boldly.
bouer, (-s), builder.
bouery, building; building-trade.
bougereedskap, building-implements.
bougrond, building-site, -ground; arable land.
bo-uit, above, out at the top.
boukoste, building-expenses.
boukunde, architecture.
boukundig, (-e), architectural; constructional (engineer).
boukundige, (-s), architect.
boukuns, architecture, architectural art.
boul, (ge-), bowl (cricket).
bouland, arable land.
bouler, (-s), bowler.
boulstreep, bowling-crease.
boumaatskappy, building-company, -society.
boumateriaal, building-materials.
bou-ondernemer, building and contractor.
bou-opsigter, building-inspector, clerk of works.
bouplan, plan (of house); building-scheme.
boustof, (building-)materials.
boustyl, style of building (architecture).
bout, (-e), bolt, rivet; pin; (soldering-)iron.
bouterrein, building-site, -plot.
boutjie, (-s), little pin (bolt), rivet.
bouvak, building-trade.
bouval, ruin(s).
bouvallig, (-e), dilapidated; decrepit.
bouvalligheid, dilapidation, decrepitude.
bouvereniging, building-society.
bouverordening, building-regulation.
bouwerk, building; building-operations.
bovenster, upper window.
boverdieping, upper storey, top-floor.
bovermeld, (-e), vide **bogenoemde.**
bowe, vide **bo.**
bo(we)bedoelde, above.
bowehand, bohand, upper hand; **die – kry,** get the upper hand.
bowendien, besides, in addition.
bra, really, very; **ek het – lus om . . .,** I have a good mind to . . .; **ek het nie – lus nie,** I don't quite feel like it; **ek kan dit nie – kleinkry nie,** I don't quite know what to make of it; **jy is – laat,** you are rather late; you've got a hope!
braaf, (brawe), virtuous, good; brave.
braafheid, bravery; honesty.
braai, (ge-), roast (in pot), grill (on grid-iron), fry (in pan), broil (meat on fire); toast (bread).
braaiboud, roast leg of mutton.
braairibbetjie, roast(ed) rib.
braaispit, spit.

braaivleis, roast (meat), barbecue; **-aand,** barbecue.
braak, a. fallow; **– lê,** lie fallow.
braak, (ge-), 1. break up, fallow (land).
braak, (ge-), 2. vomit; emit, belch.
braakland, fallow(-land).
braakmiddel, emetic, vomitive.
braam, (brame), blackberry; bramble.
brabbel, (ge-), jabber, chatter.
brabbeltaal, jargon, gibberish.
bragikefaal, (-sefaal), brachycephalic.
Brahmaan, (-mane), Brahman (Brahmin).
brak, (-ke), n. 1. pup; mongrel.
brak, n. 2. salt-lick, brackish spot.
brak, a. brackish, saltish, alkaline (soil).
brakbos(sie), lye- (salt-) bush, "brack" bush.
brakhond, brakkie, (-s), mongrel; vide **brak, n.**
brakplek, salt-lick.
brakslaai, ice-plant.
brakveld, brackish veld.
brand, (-e), n. fire, conflagration; burnt patch; blight, smut (in wheat); **– stig,** raise a fire; **aan – raak,** take (catch) fire; **aan (die) – steek,** set fire to, set on fire.
brand, (ge-), burn; be on fire; roast (coffee); scald (with hot water); brand (with hot iron); **my gesig –,** my face is burning; **– van verlange,** yearn.
brandaar, smut-ear (in wheat).
brandalarm, fire-alarm.
brandarm, penniless, as poor as a churchmouse.
brandassuransie, fire-insurance.
brandbaar, (-bare), combustible, inflammable.
brandbaar, blister; blister-bush.
brandblusapparaat, fire-extinguisher.
brandbom, incendiary bomb.
branddeur, emergency-exit; fireproof door.
brandemmer, fire-bucket.
brandend, (-e), burning; intense, ardent.
brander, (-s), 1. breaker, wave.
brander, (-s), 2. burner (of lamp).
brander, (-s), 3. letter of demand; rebuke.
branderig, (-e), burning (skin); burnt (taste).
branderplank, surf-board.
branders-ry, surf.
brandery, (-e), burning (of lime); lime-kiln.
brandewyn, brandy.
brandewynstokery, distillery.
brandewynvlieg, tippler.
brandgevaar, risk of fire; danger from fire.
brandglas, burning-glass, lens.
brandhout, firewood.
branding, breakers, surf.
brandkas, safe.
brandkluis, safe(-deposit).
brandlug, smell of burning.
brandmaer, skinny, scraggy, lean.
brandmerk, n. brand; stigma.
brandmerk, (ge-), brand; stigmatize.
brandnekel, (-netel), stinging-nettle.
brandoffer, burnt-offering.
brandpaal, stake.
brandplek, burn.
brandpolis, fire-policy.
brandpunt, focus, focal point; seat.
brandpuntafstand, focal length (distance).
brandsiekte, scab.
brandsiekte-inspekteur, scab-inspector.
brandsignaal, -sinjaal, fire-signal.
brandskade, damage caused by fire.
brandskerm, fire-curtain.
brandskilder, (ge-), enamel.
brandslaner, trouble-shooter.
brandslang, fire-hose.
brandsolder, fireproof ceiling.

brandspiritus, methylated spirits.
brandspuit, fire-hose, fire-engine.
brandstapel, funeral-pile; stake.
brandstigter, incendiary, arsonist, fire-bug.
brandstigting, arson, incendiarism.
brandstof, fuel.
brandtrap, fire-escape.
brandversekering, fire-insurance.
brandversekeringsmaatskappy, fire-insurance company.
brandvry, fireproof.
brandwag, outpost, picket, sentry, sentinel; – staan, stand sentry (sentinel).
brandweer, fire-brigade.
brandweerstasie, fire-station.
brandwond, burn; scald (from hot liquid).
brandyster, branding-iron; cauterising-iron.
bras, (ge-), revel, carouse, booze.
brasem, (-s), bream (fish).
Brasiliaans, (-e), Brazilian.
brasparty, brassery, (-e), orgy, drinking-bout.
braveer, (ge)-, defy, brave, face.
bravo, (-'s), n. bravo.
bredie, ragout, stew, "bredie".
breed, (breë), broad (chest), wide (road); **so lank as dit – is,** as long as it is broad; **in breë trekke,** in broad outline.
breedgebou(d), (-de), square-built.
breedgerand, (-e), broad-brimmed.
breedheid, breadth, width, broadness.
breedsprakig, (-e), verbose, prolix, long-winded.
breedte, (-s), breadth, width; latitutde (geogr.); **in die –,** broadwise.
breedtegraad, degree of latitude.
breedtesirkel, parallel of latitude.
breedvoerig, (-e), a. full, detailed.
breedvoerig, adv. at length, fully, in detail.
breedvoerigheid, fullness of detail.
breek, (ge-), break; be broken; smash, shatter; crush (stone); quarry (stones), refract (light); fracture (bone); snap (wire); become glassy (of eyes); burst (of dam); – met, break with (a person); give up (a habit).
breekbaar, (-bare), fragile, brittle.
breekgoed, crockery.
breekmielies, samp, split mealies.
breekspul, smash-up; mess.
breekyster, crowbar; jemmy (of burglar).
breërandhoed, broad-brimmed hat.
breëspoor, broad (normal) gauge.
brei, (ge-), 1. knit.
brei, (ge-), 2. prepare, curry, dress (skin); knead (clay); coach (athletes), train; harden.
breidel, (-s), bridle.
breidel, (ge-), bridle, curb.
breidelloos, (-lose), unbridled.
breier, (-s), 1. knitter; 2. skin-dresser; coach.
breigare, -garing, knitting-cotton.
breigoed, knitting; knitted things.
breiklip, dressing-stone, "brey-stone".
brein, (-e), brain, intellect.
breinaald, knitting-needle.
breipaal, "brey-pole".
breiwerk, knitting.
breking, breaking; refraction (of light-rays).
brekingshoek, angle of refraction.
breksie, breccia (geol.).
brem, broom.
bres, (-se), breach; **in die – tree vir,** step into the breach for.
breuk, (-e), break, breach; rupture; fracture (of skull); crack; fault (geol.); fraction (maths.); **egte (eintlike) –,** proper fraction; **onegte –,** improper fraction; **eenvoudige –,** simple fraction; **gewone –,** vulgar fraction; **samege-**
stelde –, complex fraction; compound fracture.
breukband, truss.
brief, (briewe), letter.
briefhoof, briewehoof, letter-heading.
briefie, (-s), note; promissory note; IOU.
briefkaart, letter-card.
briefkoevert, -omslag, envelope.
briefstyl, epistolary style.
briefwisseling, correspondence.
briek, (-e), n. brake; **die – aandraai,** apply the brakes; check; put one's foot down.
briek, (ge-), apply the brakes.
bries, (-e), n. breeze.
bries, (ge-), snort.
briesend, (-e), roaring; furious, raging.
briewebesteller, postman, letter-carrier.
briewebus, letter-box; pillar-box.
briewehoof, vide **briefhoof.**
brigade, (-s), brigade.
brigadegeneraal, brigadier-general.
bril, (-le), n. (pair of) spectacles (glasses); goggles (for motoring); seat of W.C.).
bril, (ge-), wear glasses (spectacles).
bril(le)huisie, spectacle-case.
briljant, (-e), brilliant.
bril(le)doos, vide **bril(le)huisie.**
brilskyfie, spectacle-case.
brilslang, spectacled snake, cobra.
bring, (gebring, gebrag), bring; take, convey, carry; see (take) (person to a place); **dit ver in die wêreld –,** go far, make a name for oneself; met sig –, entail; – my na mnr. X, take me to Mr X; dit – die getal op 100, that brings the total to 100; **iemand – op,** put a person onto; **iemand daartoe –,** get (induce, persuade) a person to; **dit tot hoofonderwyser –,** rise to be principal of a school.
bringer, (brenger), (-s), bringer.
brinjal, (-s), egg-plant.
Brit, (-te), Britisher, Briton.
Brits, (-e), British.
Brittannies, (-e), Britannic.
Brittanje, Britain, **Brittannië,** Britannia.
brodeloos, (-lose), breadless.
broeder, (-s), brother, (pl.: brothers, brethren).
broederhaat, fraternal hatred.
broederhand, hand of fellowship.
broederliefde, brotherly love.
broederlik, (-e), brotherly, fraternal.
broedermoord, fratricide.
broederskap, brotherhood, fraternity.
broedertwis, fraternal quarrel (feud).
broei, (ge-), hatch, brood, sit (on eggs); incubate; ferment (tobacco); get hot (heated); brew, gather; **daar – iets,** there is something brewing (afoot).
broeierig, (-e), stifling, sultry, close.
broeikas, hothouse.
broeimasjien, incubator, hatching-machine.
broeines, hot-bed, seed-bed (of vice).
broeis, broody (hen).
broeisel, (-s), set (sitting, clutch) (of eggs); brood (hatch) (of chickens).
broeishen, broody hen.
broeityd, brooding-time; incubation-period.
broek, (-e), (pair of) trousers; (riding) breeches; drawers, bloomers (female); back part (of harness); **ek voel dit aan my – (se naat),** I feel it in my bones; **dit sit nie in jou – nie,** you're not up to it.
broek(s)band, waist-band, trouser-band.
broekpers, trouser-press, -stretcher.
broeksak, trouser(s)-pocket.
broekferweel, corduroy.

broekskeur, tear in the trousers; – **gaan**, be a tough job, be hard pressed; have a rough time; – **deur 'n eksamen kom**, pass an examination by the skin of one's teeth.
broekspyp, trouser-leg; **sy –e het gebewe**, he was all of a tremble.
broer, (-s), brother; **ou –**, old fellow.
broerskind, nephew, niece.
broertjie, (-s), little brother; **'n – dood hê aan**, detest.
brok, (-ke), piece, lump, fragment.
brokaat, brocade.
brokkelrig, (-e), crumbling, crumbly.
brokkie, (-s), (little) bit, piece, morsel; **stukkies en as**, odds and ends.
broksgewys(e), bit by bit, piecemeal.
brokstuk, fragment, piece.
brom, (ge-), hum, drone (of insect); mutter, grumble (of person); growl (of animal); **jy – te veel**, you grouse too much.
bromfiets, buzz-bike.
bromied, (-e), **bromide**, (-s), bromide.
brommer, (-s), bluebottle, blowfly; grouser, grumbler.
brommerig, (-e), grumpy, grousing.
bromponie, motor scooter.
brompot, grouser, grumbler.
bron, (-ne), (hot) spring; well; source (of the Nile); origin, source; cause (of the evil); means (of living); **uit 'n goeie –**, from a reliable source.
bronaar, source, spring, fountain-head.
bronco, bronco.
brongitis, bronchitis.
bronkors, water-cress.
bronnestudie, original research.
brons, n. 1. bronze.
brons, n. 2. heat, rut.
bronsgieter, bronze-founder.
bronskleurig, (-e), bronze-coloured.
bronslaai, water-cress.
bronsperiode, bronze-age.
bronstig, (-e), on (in, at) heat, rutting.
bronstigheid, heat.
bronstyd, rut, rutting-season.
bronstydperk, vide **bronsperiode**.
brontosourus, brontosaurus.
brood, (brode), bread; loaf; **twee brode**, two loaves; **jou – verdien**, earn one's bread (a living); **wie se – 'n mens eet, die se woord 'n mens spreek**, one cannot quarrel with one's bread and butter; **die een se dood is die ander se –**, one man's meat is another man's poison; **by gebrek aan – eet mens korsies van pastei**, if you can't get crumb you must fain eat crust; **om den brode**, for a living; **dit kan jy op jou – smeer**, put that in your pipe and smoke it.
broodbakkery, bakery; bread-baking.
broodblik, bread-tin, -bin.
broodboom, (Kaffir) bread-tree.
brooddronke, wanton.
broodeter, bread-eater.
broodjie, (-s), roll; **mooi –s bak**, eat humble pie.
broodkas, bread-safe.
broodkors(ie), bread-crust.
broodnodig, (-e), absolutely (highly) necessary, badly needed, essential.
broodnyd, professional jealousy.
broodpap, bread-porridge; poultice.
broodplank, bread-platter, -trencher.
brood(s)gebrek, want of bread; starvation.
broodskrywer, penny-a-liner, hack-writer.
broodsop, bread-soup, panada.
broodtrommel, bread-bin.
broodvrug, bread-fruit.
broodwinner, breadwinner.

broodwinning, livelihood, means of living.
broodwortel, manioc, cassava-root.
broom, bromine.
broomsilwer, bromide of silver.
broomsout, bromic salt.
broos, (–, brose), a. brittle, fragile.
broosheid, frailty, fragility.
bros, a. brittle, friable, crisp, crumbly.
brosheid, brittleness, crispness, crumbleness.
brosjure, (-s), brochure, pamphlet.
broskoek, shortbread, shortcake.
brou, (ge-), brew (beer, mischief); bungle.
brouery, (-e), brewery; **lewe in die – bring**, put (some) life into things.
broukuip, brewing-tub.
brousel, (-s), brewing, brew; concoction.
brug, (brûe(ns), brugge), 1. bridge; parallel bars (gymnastics); gangway (leading to ship).
brug, 2. bridge (card-game).
brugbou, bridge-building.
brug(ge)hoof, bridgehead.
brugpad, road across a bridge.
brugreling, bridge-rail.
brugwagter, bridge-man.
bruid, (-e), bride.
bruidegom, (-s), bridegroom.
bruidsgoed, trousseau; bride's property.
bruidsjonker, best man.
bruidskat, dowry.
bruidskoek, wedding-cake.
bruidsmeisie, bridesmaid.
bruidspaar, bridal pair.
bruidsrok, wedding-dress.
bruidstoet, bridal procession.
bruikbaar, (-bare), serviceable, useful.
bruikleen, loan; **in – hê**, have on loan; lease-lend.
bruilof, (-te), wedding; **goue –**, golden wedding; **– hou**, celebrate a wedding.
bruilofsfees, wedding-party.
bruilofsgas, wedding-guest.
bruin, n. brown; Bruin (bear).
bruin, a. brown; fed-up, annoyed.
bruinbrood, brown bread.
bruine, (-s), brown one; **twee –s**, two brown horses.
bruinerig, (-e), brownish.
bruinhaar-. . ., brown-haired.
bruinkapel, brown cobra.
bruinkool, brown coal, lignite.
bruinoog, brown eyes; brunette.
bruinoog-. . ., brown-eyed.
bruintjie, (-s), brown one; Bruin (bear).
bruinvis, porpoise.
bruis, n. froth, foam.
bruis, (ge-), effervesce, fizz, bubble; boil, seethe (of waves, blood).
bruisend, (-e), foaming, fizzing; seething.
bruismelk, milk-shake.
bruispoeier, Seidlitz powder, effervescent powder.
brul, (-le), n. roar; bellow (of cattle).
brul, (ge-), roar; bellow (of cattle); **– soos hy lag**, roar with laughter.
brulpadda, bullfrog.
brulsand, roaring-sand, "brulsand".
brulvoël, bittern.
brunet, (-te), brunette.
Brussel, (-e), Brussels; **–e kant**, Brussels lace; **–e spruitjies**, Brussels sprouts.
brutaal, (-tale), impudent, insolent; audacious; cheeky, forward, saucy.
brutaliteit, impudence, audacity; cheek.
bruto, gross (weight).
bruto gewig, gross weight.
bruto ontvangste, gross receipts.

bruusk, (-e), brusque, off-hand, blunt.
bruut, (brute), brute.
bry, (ge-), speak with a burr, burr.
buffel, (-s), buffalo; bear, boor, churl.
buffelagtig, (-e), churlish, rude, boorish.
buffelsdoring, buffalo-thorn.
buffelgras, buffalo-grass.
buffelshoring, wild pomegranate.
buffer, (-s), buffer, bumper.
bufferstaat, buffer-state.
buffet, (-te), sideboard; (refreshment-)bar.
bui, (-e), shower (of rain); whim; mood, humour; fit (of coughing); **by -e,** by fits and starts.
buidel, (-s), bag, pouch.
buideldier, marsupial.
buidelrot, opossum.
buie, vide **buig.**
buierig, (-e), showery; fickle; moody.
buig, buie, (ge-), bend, bow; curve; stoop; **die knie -,** bow the knee; **sy wil -,** bend his will; **- voor,** bow to (the inevitable), submit to.
buigbaar, (-bare), flexible, pliable; declinable.
buigbok, bending-horse.
buiging, (-e, -s), bending; bend; bow; declension (gram.); modulation (of voice).
buigingsleer, accidence.
buigingsuitgang, (in)flexional ending.
buigingsvorm, (in)flexional form.
buigsaam, (-same), flexible, pliant; compliant.
buigsaamheid, flexibility; pliancy.
buik, (-e), belly; abdomen; venter (anat.); paunch, stomach; bottom (of wagon).
buikband, -gort, vide **buikriem.**
buikholte, abdominal cavity.
buiklanding, crash landing, belly-landing.
buikloop, diarrhoea.
buikplank, bottom-board, -plank, bed-plank.
buikpotig, (-e), gasteropodous.
buikpotiges, gast(e)ropoda.
buikriem, belly-band, girth (of horse).
buiksenuwee, abdominal nerve.
buikspier, abdominal muscle.
buikspraak, ventriloquy, ventriloquism.
buikspreker, ventriloquist.
buikvlies, peritoneum.
buikvliesontsteking, peritonitis.
buikvol, fed up.
buikwand, abdominal wall.
buil, (-e), boil; swelling.
builepes, bubonic plague.
buis, (-e), tube, pipe; duct (anat.); fistula (of insects).
buisie, (-s), tube; duct; tubule.
buisleiding, piping, pipe-line, system.
buisloos, (-lose), ductless (gland).
buisvormig, (-e), tube-shaped, tubular.
buit, n. booty, spoils, loot.
buit, (ge-), seize, capture, take.
buite, adv. outside; out of doors; in the country; **sig te - gaan,** go beyond the limit; drink (eat) too much; **van -,** from (on) the outside; **van - ken (leer),** know (learn) by heart.
buite, prep. outside; out of; beyond (my power); **- sigself van blydskap,** beside oneself with joy; **staan heeltemal -,** have nothing to do with; **- my om,** behind my back, without my knowledge; **hou (laat) my daar -,** leave me out of it; vide **buiten.**
buite-...., outside, outer; vide **buitenste,** a.
buiteband, (outer) tyre.
buiteboordmotor, outboard motor.
buitedeur, outer door; front-door.
buitedistrik, outlying district.
buitegebou, outbuilding, outhouse.
buitehoek, outer corner; exterior angle.

buitekamer, out-room, outer room.
buitekans, windfall, piece of luck.
buitekant, outside; vide **buite.**
buitekants(t)e, vide **buitenste.**
buiteklub, country club.
buiteland, foreign country; **in die -,** abroad.
buitelander, (-s), foreigner.
buitelands, (-e), foreign; exotic (fashions, plants); **-e sake,** foreign affairs; **'n -e reis,** a trip abroad.
buitelewe, outdoor life; country-life.
buitelid, country-member.
buitelug, fresh air; open air; country-air.
buitemense, country-people.
buiten, except, but; besides; beyond (the question); **- en behalwe,** over and above; **ek kan nie - hom klaarkom nie,** I cannot do without him; vide **buite** & **behalwe.**
buitenaatskoen, welted shoe (boot).
buitendien, besides, moreover; in addition.
buite(n)egtelik, (-e), (born) out of wedlock.
buitenissig, (-e), odd, eccentric, unusual.
buitenissigheid, (-hede), unusualness; fad, craze.
buitenshuis, out of doors.
buitelands, abroad.
buitensporig, (-e), excessive, exorbitant (price); extravagant, preposterous, outrageous.
buitensporigheid, excessiveness, extravagance vide **buitensporig.**
buitenste, n. outside, exterior, surface.
buitenste, a. outside, outer, exterior.
buitenstyds, out of season; out of hours.
buite(n)toe, outside, out.
buite-om, round (the outside).
buite-op, on the outside.
buitepasiënt, outpatient.
buiteplaas, farm.
buitepos, outpost; out-station.
buiteskool, country-school, farm-school.
buiteskop, n. touch(-kick).
buiteskop, (buitege-), kick touch; eject.
buitebesluit, (buitege-), exclude, shut out.
buitestaander, (-s), outsider.
buitevoorspeler, wing-forward.
buitewaarts, (-e), a. outward.
buitewaarts, adv. outwards.
buitewêreld, outside world, outer world.
buitewerk, outdoor work; outwork.
buitewerp, (buitege-), cast-out.
buitewyk, outlying district, suburb.
buitmaak, (büitge-), capture, loot, carry off.
buitstelsel, spoils-system.
buk, (ge-), bend, stoop, bow; **- vir,** bow before, submit to; **ge- gaan onder,** be bowed down by, suffer (labour) under.
buks, (-e), buksie, (-s), small rifle; little fellow.
bul, (-le), 1. (papal) bull; diploma.
bul, (-le), 2. bull; whopper, thumper; **ou -!,** good for you!; **hy is 'n -,** he is a great card (a ripper); **die - by die horings pak (vat),** take the bull by the horns.
bulder, (ge-), roar, rage; boom (of gun).
bulderend, (-e), roaring, raging.
bulderlag, roaring laugh.
Bulgaar, (-gare), Bulgaars, (-e) Bulgarian.
bulk, (ge-), bellow, low, moo.
bullebak, (-ke), bully, bear.
bulletin, (-s), bulletin.
bulperd, ripper, great card.
bulsak, feather-bed.
bult, (-e), n. bump, lump, protuberance, hunch, hump (on back); hill, ridge; **vol -e,** bumpy; dented (of metal); **ons is oor die -,** we are over the worst.
bult, (ge-), dent, indent.
bultenaar, (-s), hunchback.

bulterig, (-e), bumpy, lumpy; uneven; hilly.
bundel, (-s), n. collection, volume.
bundel, (ge-), collect, publish in bookform.
bunker, (-s), n. bunker.
bunker, (ge-), bunker.
buret, (-te), burette.
burg, (-e), 1. hog, barrow.
burg, (-te), 2. castle, stronghold.
burgemeester, mayor, burgomaster.
burgemeesteres, (-se), ladymayor.
burgemeestersamp, mayoralty.
burgemeestersvrou, mayoress.
burger, (-s), citizen; civilian, burg(h)er.
burgerdeug, civic virtue.
burgeres, (-se), citizenness.
burgerklas, middle class; burg(h)er-class.
burgerklere, civilian clothes.
burgerkryg, civil war.
burgerlik, (-e), civil; civilian; bourgeóis; –e civil law.
burgermag, civilian force(s); defence-force.
burgeroorlog, civil war.
burgerreg, civic right(s), citizenship; freedom of a city; burg(h)er-right(s); – **verleen aan,** enfranchise (a person); admit to the freedom (of a city); adopt (a word); – **verloor,** forfeit one's civil rights.
burgersin, civic spirit.
burgerskap, citizenship.
burgertwis, civil strife.
burgerwag, citizen-guard.
burggraaf, viscount.
burgravin, viscountess.
buro, (-'s), bureau.
burokraat, (-krate), bureaucrat.
burokrasie, bureaucracy.
burokraties, (-e), bureaucratic.
bus, (-se), 1. (omni)bus.
bus, (-se), 2. box, drum; tin.
bus, (-te), 3. bush; socket, box.
busdiens, bus-service.
buskruit, gunpowder.
buskruitverraad, gunpowder-plot.
busligting, collection (of letters).
butaan, butane.
buur, buurman, (bure), neighbour.
buurpraatjie, gossip, neighbourly talk.
buurskap, neighbourly intercourse.
buurt, (-e), buurte (-s), neighbourhood, vicinity; part, quarter.
buurvrou, neighbour, neighbour's wife.
buuste, (-s), bust.
buustelyfie, bra(ssiere).
buustepop, sweater girl.
by, (-e), n. bee.
by, prep. by, with, near, at; – **sy huis,** at his house; – **die huis,** at home; – **sy vader,** with his father; – **die vuur,** by the fire; – **dag,** by day; – **sy aankoms,** on his arrival; – **sy dood,** at his death; – **duisende,** in thousands, by the thousand; – **tye,** at times; **ek het dit nie** – **my nie,** I have not got it with (on) me; – **jou mening bly,** adhere to your opinion; **die geveg** – **Boomspruit,** the battle of Boomspruit; – **stormagtige weer,** in stormy weather; **iemand** – **sy naam noem,** call a person by name; **wat is ons land** – **so 'n ryk?,** what is our country in comparison with such an empire?; – **al sy slimheid,** with all his cleverness; – **die lugmag wees,** be in the air-force; **ek dink toe** – **myself,** then I thought to myself.
by, adv. present, there; **hy was nie** – **nie,** he was not there (present); **hy is nog nie** – **nie,** he has not come to (round) yet; **waar hy** – **was,** in his presence, to his face.
bybaantjie, extra work; sideline.
bybedoeling, ulterior motive; hidden meaning.
bybehorend, (-e), belonging to it, to match.
bybehorens, -behoorsels, accessories.
Bybel, (-s), Bible.
Bybelgenootskap, Bible Society.
Bybelkennis, knowledge of the Bible.
Bybels, (-e), biblical, scriptural.
Bybeltaal, biblical language.
Bybelvas, (-te), versed in Scripture.
Bybelverklaring, exegesis.
Bybelvertaling, translation of the Bible.
Bybelwoord, Holy Scripture; Bible-word.
bybestel, (–), order in addition.
bybetaal, (–), pay extra.
bybetekenis, secondary meaning.
byblad, supplement (of newspaper).
bybly, (byge-), keep pace with; stick in one's memory.
bybring, (byge-), bring forward; quote (examples); afford; bring (person) to (round); inculcate, instil (ideas); **ek kan dit nie** – **nie,** I cannot afford it; **ek kan hom dit nie** – **nie,** I cannot get him to understand.
bydam, (byge-), accost, button-hole, tackle.
byderhand, at hand.
bydra, (byge-), contribute (to).
bydraai, (byge-), heave to; come round.
bydrae, (-s), contribution.
bydraer, contributor.
by(e)brood, bee-bread.
byeen, together.
byeen- . . . , vide **bymekaar-** . . .
byeenkom, (byeenge-), come together, meet.
byeenkoms, (-te), meeting, assembly.
byeenroep, (byeenge-), call (meeting), convoke, call together, summon.
byekorf, by(e)nes, beehive.
bye-sel, bee-cell.
byeswerm, swarm of bees.
byeteelt, bee-culture, apiculture.
by(e)was, bees-wax.
by(e)werk, bees-wax.
byfiguur, minor character.
bygaande, accompanying; attached.
bygebou, annex(e) outbuilding.
bygedagte, by-thought; afterthought.
bygeloof, superstition.
bygelowig, (-e), superstitious.
bygelowigheid, superstitiousness.
bygenaamd, nicknamed; surnamed.
bygeval, in case, by any chance.
bygevolg, consequently, therefore.
bygooi, (byge-), add.
byhaal, (byge-), bring (drag) in.
byhou, (byge-), keep pace, keep up (with).
bykans, nearly, almost.
bykant, on-side (in cricket).
bykom, (byge-), get at, reach; come to (found), recover consciousness; he included (added); catch up, come up with; **dit moet daar ook nog** –!, this is the last straw!
bykomend, (-e), incidental (expenses); attendant (circumstances); additional.
bykomstig, (-e), subsidiary, accidental, minor, accessory.
bykomstigheid, (-hede), a matter of minor importance, non-essential; extra.
byl, (-e), axe, (light) hatchet, chopper.
bylae, (-s), appendix, enclosure.
bylange: – **nie,** not by long way.
bylas, (byge-), add, append.
bylbundel, fasces.

bylê, (byge-), make up, settle (dispute).
bylegging, settlement.
byltjie, (-s), chopper, little axe, hatchet; **die – daarby neerlê**, throw up the sponge.
bymaan, second (mock-)moon.
bymekaar, together; – **bly**, remain together; – **lê**, lie together; – **sit**, sit together; – **staan**, stand near each other (one another).
bymekaarbring, (bymekaarge-), bring together; collect, raise (money); raise (an army).
bymekaarhou, (bymekaarge-), keep together; **jou sinne –**, keep one's head.
bymekaarkom, (bymekaarge-), come together, meet, assemble.
bymekaarkomplek, meeting-place, rendezvous; junction (of rivers).
bymekaarkry, (bymekaarge-), get together; raise (money).
bymekaarmaak, (bymekaarge-), collect, save (money); round up (cattle); gather, collect (things).
bymekaarraap, (bymekaarge-), scrape together; **bymekaargeraapte span**, scratch team.
bymekaarroep, (bymekaarge-), call together, call (a meeting).
bymekaarsit, (bymekaarge-), put together.
bymekaarstaan, (bymekaarge-), stand together; unite forces.
bymekaartel, (bymekaarge-), add up, count together.
bymekaartrek, (bymekaarge-), contract, concentrate (of troops); add up, total.
bymekaarvoeg, (bymekaarge-), join together, unite.
bymeng, (byge-), mix with.
bymengsel, admixture.
bymot, bee-moth.
byna, almost, nearly; – **niks**, next to nothing.
bynaam, nickname; surname.
bynier, adrenal body.
byomstandigheid, accidental circumstance.
byoogmerk, ulterior motive, by-end.
byoorsaak, secondary cause.
bypaaltjie, leg-stump.
byplaneet, satellite.
byproduk, by-product.
byreken, (byge-), reckon in, add, include.
bysaak, matter of minor importance, sideline; **geld is –**, money is no object.
bysiende, short-sighted, near-sighted.
bysiendheid, short-sightedness, myopia.
bysin, subordinate clause.

bysit, (byge-), 1. add, contribute (R5); inter, lay to rest; **'n hand –**, lend a hand; **krag –**, add force to, reinforce.
bysit, (byge-), 2. sit by (near).
byskaduwee, penumbra.
byskilder, (byge-), touch up; paint in.
byskink, (byge-), add, fill up, pour in more.
byskrif, letterpress; inscription; postscript.
byskryf, -skrywe, (byge-), add; write up.
byskuif, -skuiwe, (byge-), push nearer; pull up (one's chair).
bysleep, (byge-), drag in.
bysmaak, tinge (lit. & fig.), flavour.
byson, parhelion, mock-sun.
byspring, (byge-), lend a hand.
bystaan, (byge-), help, assist, back up.
bystand, help, aid, assistance.
bystander, (-s), bystander.
byster, a.: **die spoor – wees**, have lost one's way; be at sea, be at a loss.
byster, adv.: **nie – goed nie**, not particularly good.
bystort, (byge-), make additional payment.
bysyn: **in die – van**, in the presence of.
byt, (-e), n. bite.
byt, (ge-), bite; – **na**, snap at; **in die stof –**, bit the dust; **op jou tande –**, clench one's teeth.
bytel, (byge), add, include; count in.
bytend, (-e), biting, caustic; corrosive.
bytoon, by-tone, secondary tone.
bytrek, (byge-), pull up (a chair).
bytsoda, caustic soda.
byvak, minor (subsidiary) subject.
byval, n. approval; applause; – **vind**, meet with approval.
byval, (byge-), remember; **dit het my bygeval**, it occurred to me.
byverdienste, extra earnings, sideline.
byvoeg, (byge-), add; enclose; append.
byvoeging, addition.
byvoeglik, (-e), adjectival; **-e naamwoord**, adjective.
byvoegsel, (-s), addition; appendix; supplement.
byvoorbeeld, for example, for instance.
byvorm, variant.
byvul, (byge-), fill up.
bywerk, (byge-), bring (books) up to date; touch up (picture).
bywoner, (-s), share-cropper, bywoner; squatter.
bywoon, (byge-), attend; be present at.
bywoord, adverb.
bywoordelik, (-e), adverbial.
bywyf, concubine.
bywyle, at times, now and then.

C

Vir woorde wat ontbreek onder **C**, kyk onder
K of **S**.
For words not found under **C**, see **K** or **S**.

cachet, kasjet, cachet, impress, mark, stamp.
café-chantant, café-chantant.
cairngorm, cairngorm.
caisson, (-s), caisson.
Calvinis, (-te), Calvinist.
Calvinisme, Calvinism.
Calvinisties, (-e), Calvinist; Calvinistic(al).
camouflage, camouflage.
camoufleer, (ge-), camouflage.
canna, (-s), canna (Canna indica).
canyon, (-s), canon (canyon).
caprice, (-s), caprice, whim.
Carbolineum, Carbolineum.
carnivora, (pl.), carnivora; vide **karnivoor**.
carte blanche, carte blanche; iemand – gee, give a person carte blanche (a free hand).
Carthaags, (-e), a. Carthaginian.
Carthago, Carthage.
casino, (-'s), casino.
causerie, (-ë,), causerie, talk.
causeur, (-s), talker, conversationalist.
cautie, bail, security, caution-money.
cédille, (-s), cedilla.
Cellophane, Cellophane.
centaur, (-e, -i), centaur.
centiem, (-s), centime.
centumvir, (-i), centumvir.
centumviraat, centimvirate.
cerebellum, cerebellum.
cerebrum, cerebrum.
Chaldeër, (-s), Chaldean.
Chaldeeus, (-ë), Chaldean.
chanson, (-s), chanson, song.
chaos, chaos.
chaoties, (-e), chaotic.
chaperon, (-s), chaperon.
chaperonneer, (ge-), chaperon.
charade, (-s), charade.
charlatan, (-s), quack.
charlatanerie, charlatanry, quackery.
charmeuse, (-s), charmer.
charter, (-s), n. charter.
charter, (ge-), charter.
chassis, chassis, frame(-work).
chauffeer, (ge-), drive (a motor-car).
chauffeur, (-s), chauffeur, driver.
chauvinis, (-te), chauvinist, jingo.
chauvinisme, chauvinism, jingoism.
chauvinisties, (-e), chauvinistic, jingoistic.
chemie, chemistry.
chemies, (-e), chemical.
chemikalieë, (pl.), chemicals.
chemikus, (-se, -ici), (general and analytical) chemist.
chic, (–, -e), a. chic, stylish, fashionable.
chicane, chicanery, trickery.
chiffon, chiffon.
Chileens, (-e), Chilian.
chinchilla, chinchilla.
Chinees, Sjinees, n. Chinese (language); (pl. -nese), Chinaman; (pl.) Chinamen, Chinese.
Chinees, Sjinees, (-nese), a. Chinese; Chinese tee, China-tea.
chirurg, (-e), surgeon.
chirurgie, surgery.
chirurgies, (-e), surgical.
chirurgyn, (-s), ship's doctor, surgeon.
chloor, chlorine.

chloorkalk, chloride of lime, bleaching powder.
chloormisetine, chloromycetin.
chloorwaterstof(suur), hydrochloric acid.
chloride, chloried, chloride.
chloriet, chlorite.
chloroform, n. chloroform.
chloroformeer, (ge-), chloroform.
chloroformkap, chloroform-mask.
chlorofil, chlorophyll.
cholera, cholera.
choleries, (-e), choleric.
Christelik, (-e), Christian(ly), Christianlike; –e jaartelling, Christian era; –e godsdiens (leer), Christianity.
Christelikheid, Christianity.
Christen, (-e), Christian.
Christendom, Christendom; Christianity.
Christenheid, Christendom.
Christenmens, Christian (soul); geen – nie, not a soul.
Christensiel, Christian (soul); geen – nie, not a soul.
Christin, (-ne), Christian (woman).
Christus, Christ.
Christusbeeld, image of Christ; crucifix.
chromaties, (-e), chromatic(ally).
chromo(litografie), chromolithograph; chromolithography.
chronies, (-e), chronic.
chronologie, chronology.
chronologies, (-e), chronological(ly).
chronometer, (-s), chronometer.
chroom, chromium, chromium.
chroomgeel, chrome(-yellow).
chroomkalfsleer, box-calf.
chroomleer, chrome-leather.
chroomstaal, chrome-steel.
Ciceroniaans, (-e), Ciceronian.
Ciprioot, Cypriot.
Ciprus, Cyprus.
Cirkassië, Circassia.
Cirkassiër, (-s), Circassian.
Cirkassies, (-e), Circassian.
Cisalpyns, (-e), Cisalpine.
cliché, (-s), n. block, plate, cliché (printing); hackneyed phrase.
cliché, a. hackneyed, stereotyped, cliché.
cochenille, cochineal.
Coliseum, Colosseum, Coliseum (Colosseum).
communiqué, (-s), communiqué.
confetti, (pl.), confetti.
consols, (pl.), consols.
contra, contra, against, versus.
convolvulus, convolvulus.
corps, (sing. & pl.), corps, body; **esprit de corps**, esprit de corps, fellow-feeling, team spirit. Vide **korps**.
corrigendum, (-da), corrigendum.
corsage, corsage, bodice; (bunch of) flowers.
coulisse, (–, -s), coulisse, side-scene, wing; **agter die –**, behind the scenes.
coup, (-s), coup, stroke.
crayon, (-s), crayon, chalk.
crèche, (-s), crèche, public nursery.
credo, (-'s), credo, creed, belief.
crème, n. crème, cream.
crème, a. cream(-coloured).
crêpe, crêpe; – de chine, crêpe de chine.
croquet, croquet (game).
croupier, (-s), croupier.
curiosum, (-osa), something unique.

D

daad, (dade), deed; act, action; move; exploit; **op die –,** at once, on the spur of the moment; **die – by die woord voeg,** suit the action to the word; **op heter – betrap,** catch in the act, take red-handed; **'n man van die –,** a man of action.
daadsaak, fact, reality.
daadwerklik, (-e), actual, real.
daagliks, daeliks, (-e), daily, everyday; **–e bestuur,** executive committee.
daags, by day; **een maal –,** once a day.
daai, ta!, thank you!
daal, (ge-), descend; sink, go down, drop; fall, decline; slump; **jou stem laat –,** lower one's voice.
daalder, (-s), one shilling and sixpence (old coin).
daar, adv. there; then; **wie praat –?,** who is that speaking?; **– gaan die deur oop,** then the door opened; **Krismis is alweer –,** Christmas is here again; **tot –,** as far as that; **van –,** from there.
daar, conj. as, because, since.
daaraan, by that, to that, attached to it, on it; **wat het ek –?,** of what use is that to me?
daaragter, behind it (that).
daarbenewens, besides, in addition to (that).
daarbinne, in there, within.
daarbo, up there, above; over and above.
daarbuite, outside.
daarby, besides, in addition; near it; **– kom nog dat,** add to this that; **ek bly nog –,** I still maintain (that); **hoe kom jy –?,** where do you get the idea from?
daardie, that; (pl.) those.
daarenbowe, besides, moreover.
daarenteë, -teen, on the contrary, on the other hand.
daargelate, leaving aside, let alone, apart from.
daarginds, -gunter, over there.
daarheen, there, thither, to that place.
daarin, in that, in there, therein; inside.
daarlaat, (daarge-), leave (it) at that.
daarlang(e)s, along there; somewhere there.
daarmee, with that, therewith.
daarna, after that, afterwards, next, then; **kort –,** shortly after, soon afterwards; **handel –,** act accordingly.
daarnaas, next to that; besides that.
daarnatoe, there, thither, in that direction; **dit is tot –,** that's that, it's neither here nor there.
daarnewens, besides, over and above that.
daarom, therefore, on that account.
daarom(heen), (round-)about it.
daaromstreeks, thereabouts.
daaromtrent, thereabout, as to that.
daaronder, under that; underneath, among them; thereby; down there.
daaroor, about (concerning) that, on that point; because of that; across (over) that.
daarop, (up)on that; thereupon, after that.
daaropvolgend, (-e), following, next.
daarso, there, at that place (spot).
daarsonder, without that.
daarstel, (daarge-), make, bring about; erect.
daarstelling, bringing-about, introduction, accomplishment; erection.
daarteë, -teen, against that.
daarteenoor, opposite; over against that.
daartoe, for that (purpose); to (as far as) that.
daartussen, among (between) them, in between; in the meantime.
daaruit, out of that, from that, thence.
daarvan, of that, from that, thereof.
daarvandaan, from there, thence; hence; **(van) – af,** from there on(ward); since then.
daarvoor, for that (purpose), therefore; for it.

daarvoor, before that; in front of that, there in front.
dadel, (-s), date; **daar kom –s van,** nothing of the kind (will happen).
dadelik, (-e), a. immediate, prompt.
dadelik, adv. immediate, directly, at once.
dadelikhede, blows.
dadelpruim, date-plum, prune.
dader, (-s), daderes, (-se), doer, author(ess).
daeraad, vide **dageraad.**
daeliks, vide **daagliks.**
dag, (dae), day; **– en nag,** night and day; **die hele –,** all day long; **die jongste –,** the Last Day; **die laaste der dae,** the last days; **– aan –,** day by day; **aan die – kom,** come to light; **aan die – bring,** bring to light, reveal; **aan die – lê,** display, evince, manifest; **by –,** by day, in the daytime; **by die – huur,** hire by day; **– in – uit,** day in day out; **in ons dae,** in our time; **met die – erger word,** get worse every day; **al om die ander –,** every alternate (second) day; **later op die –,** later in the day; **op jou ou –,** in one's old age; **op 'n goeie –,** one fine day; **vandag oor ag dae ('n week),** today week; **ten dae,** in the days of; **heden ten dae,** nowadays; **van dié – af,** since that day; **nuus van die –,** current news; **een van die dae,** one of these days; **van – tot –,** from day to day; **voor die – kom,** appear; become apparent; **die – tevore,** the previous day.
dagbestuur, executive.
dagblad, daily paper.
dagbladpers, daily press.
dagblindheid, day-blindness.
dagboek, diary; day-book (in bookkeeping).
dagbreek, daybreak.
dagbreker(tjie), (South African) stonechat.
dagdiens, day-service; day-duty.
dag-en-nagewening, equinox.
dageraad, daeraad, (-rade), dawn, daybreak; daggerhead (fish).
dagga, dagga, wild hemp.
daggasigaret, reefer.
daggeld, day's pay, daily wages.
daggie, day; **'n – af,** a short day off.
dagleerling, day-scholar.
daglig, daylight; **in 'n helder – stel,** throw a flood of light upon; **in 'n ander – stel,** put a different face (complexion) upon; **in 'n gunstige – stel,** place in a favourable light; **in 'n valse – stel,** put false colours upon.
dagloner, (-s), day-labourer, wage-earner.
dagloon, vide **daggeld.**
daglumier, dawn, daybreak.
dagmars, day's march.
dagorde, order of the day; order-paper.
dagorder, routine-order (mil.).
dagploeg, day-shift.
dagregister, daybook, journal, diary.
dagreis, day's journey; journey by day.
dagskolier, day-scholar.
dagskool, day-school.
dagsoom, outcrop.
dagtaak, day's work; daily task.
dagteken, (ge-), date.
dagtekening, date.
daguerreotipe, daguerreotype.
dagvaar, (ge-), summon(s), cite subpoena.
dagvaarding, (-e, -s), summons, subpoena.
dagverhaal, journal, diary.
dagverpleegster, day-nurse.
dagwerk, day-work; daily work, day's work.
dagwerker, day-labourer.
dahlia, (-s), dahlia.
dahliabol, dahlia-bulb.
dak, (-e, -ke), roof; **onder – bring,** house, shelter;

op iemand se – afklim (kom), come down on a person; **van die -e verkondig**, proclaim from the housetops.
dakgeut, gutter.
dakkamertjie, attic, garret.
daklat, roof-lath.
daklei, roof(ing)-slate.
daklig, skylight.
dakloos, (-lose), roofless, homeless.
daklose, (die –), homeless person, waif.
daknok, ridge of roof.
dakpan, (roofing-)tile.
dakpyp, gutter-pipe.
dakrand, eaves.
dakspaan, shingle; clapboard.
dakspar, rafter, spar; **kort –**, jack-rafter.
dakstrooi, thatch.
daktiel, (-e), **daktilus**, (-se, -tili), dactyl.
daktilies, (-e), dactylic.
daktuin, roof-garden.
dakvenster, attic-, dormer-, garret-window.
dal, (-e), valley, dale, glen.
daling, descent, drop, fall; decline, slump.
dalk, perhaps, maybe, possibly.
dalkies, by-and-by; before long, presently.
daltonisme, daltonism, colour-blindness.
dam, (-me), n. dam; reservoir; weir.
dam, (ge-), dam (up); crowd together.
dam, (ge-), play draughts.
damas, damask.
damaskusrooi, damask.
damaslinne, damask-linen.
damaspruim, damson.
damasroos, damask-rose.
damasseer, (ge-), damascene.
damassy, damask-silk.
dambord, draught-board.
dambordskyf, -stuk, draughts-piece.
dame, (-s), lady.
damesaal, side-saddle; lady's saddle.
damesakkie, lady's (fancy-, vanity-)bag.
damesfiets, lady's (bi)cycle.
dameskamer, powder-room.
dameskleermaker, ladies' tailor.
dameskoepee, ladies' compartment.
dameskostuum, lady's costume (suit).
damesperd, lady's mount.
dametjie, (-s), little lady.
damhert, fallow-deer; **jong –**, fawn.
damp, (-e), n. fume, smoke, steam, vapour.
damp, (ge-), smoke steam, emit steam (vapour); puff away (at one's pipe).
dampkring, atmosphere.
dampmeter, vaporimeter.
dampomp, outlet-pipe (of irrigation-dam).
dampvorming, vaporisation.
damskrop, dam-scraper.
damwal, embankment (wall) of dam.
damwater, water from a storage-dam.
dan, then; than; – **ook**, accordingly, consequently; **kom – tog**, do come!; **al – nie**, whether or not; **so nou en –**, now and then; **– en wan**, now and then, occasionally.
danig, (-e), a. thorough, strong.
danig, adv. very much; intimate; awfully; **hy is baie – met haar**, he is very familiar with her; **jy hou jou verniet so –**, don't give yourself airs.
dank, n. thanks, acknowledgment; **jou – betuig**, express one's thanks; **stank vir – kry**, get small thanks; **God sy –**, thank God; **– sy jou steun**, thanks to your support; **in – ontvang(e)**, received with thanks; **met – aanneem**, accept gratefully; **teen wil en –**, willy nilly, in spite of.
dank, (ge-), thank, give (render, return) thanks; say grace (at table); owe, be indebted to; **by**

kan sy sterre –, he can thank his lucky stars; **hy – sy sukses aan**, he owes his success to.
dankbaar, (-bare), grateful, thankful, appreciative (audience); responsive (pupil); **in dankbare aarde val**, be well received.
dankbaarheid, gratitude, thankfulness.
dankbetuiging, expression of thanks.
dankdag, thanksgiving-day.
dankdiens, thanksgiving-service.
danke: te – aan, due to; **dit het jy aan jouself te –**, you have yourself to thank for it; **dit was aan danke: te – aan**, due to; **dit het jy aan jouself te –**, **– nie**, quite welcome!, don't mention it!
dankfees, thanksgiving-feast.
dankgebed, (prayer of) thanksgiving.
dankie, thanks!, thank you!; **baie –!**, many thanks!
dankoffer, thankoffering.
dankse, (**dankge-**), thank, return thanks.
danksegging, thanksgiving.
dans, (-e), n. dance; ball; **die – ontspring**, escape (unhurt).
dans, (ge-), dance; **na iemand se pype –**, dance to someone's tune; **die poppe is aan die –**, the fat is in the fire.
danseres, (-se), (girl-)dancer.
danseuse, (-s), danseuse, ballet-dancer.
dansie, (-s), dance, hop.
dansinrigting, **-instituut**, dancing-academy.
dansles, dancing-lesson.
dansmeester, dancing-master.
dansparty, dance, ball; hop.
danssaal, ballroom.
dansskoen, dancing-shoe, (dancing-)pump.
danswoede, dancing-mania, rage for dancing.
dapper, n.: **met – en stapper**, on foot; **met – en stapper reis**, ride Shanks's mare.
dapper, a. brave, gallant, plucky, valiant; **jou – weer**, offer a stout resistance; **– veg**, put up a brave fight.
dapperheid, bravery, gallantry, valour.
darem, after all, all the same, surely, though; **– alte goed**, really too good (kind); **ek sal dit – maar doen**, I shall do it all the same; **hy het – maar ja gesê**, he agreed after all.
dartel, a. frisky, playful; wanton.
dartel, (ge-), frisk, dally, gambol, sport.
dartelheid, friskiness, playfulness, wantonness.
das, (-se), n. (neck-)tie; bow.
dassie, (-s), small rock-rabbit; "dassie"(-fish).
dasspeld, tie-pin, scarf-pin.
dat, that; so that, in order that.
data, data.
dateer, (ge-), date; **– van**, date from.
datief, (-tiewe), dative.
dato, date; **onder –**, dated, under date.
datum, (-s), date; **van gelyke –**, of even date; **sonder –**, undated.
datumstempel, date-stamp.
dawer, (ge-), boom, roar, rumble, thunder.
dawerend, (-e), roaring, thundering.
Dawid, David; **weet waar – die wortels gegrawe het**, know what's what.
de, the; **– duiwel in wees**, have one's monkey up; **hoe – duiwel?**, how the deuce?; **wat – ongeluk?**, what the deuce?
dè, here you are!; **–!** vat, here, take this!
dê, so there! **ek het dit tog gekry, –!**, I got it all the same, so there!
deballoteer, (ge-), blackball.
debat, (-te), debate, discussion; **die – sluit**, close the debate, apply the closure.
debatsvereniging, debating-society.
debatteer, (ge-), debate, discuss.
debatteerder, (-s), debater.

debet, debit.
debiet, sale, market.
debetsaldo, debit-balance.
debetsy, debit-side, debtor-side.
debiteer, (ge-), debit, charge (with).
debiteur, (-e, -s), debtor.
debutant(e), débutant(e).
debuteer, (ge-), make one's début.
debuut, début, first appearance.
decemvir, decemvir.
decemviraat, decemvirate.
décor, (-s), scenery (stage).
dedikasie, (-s), dedication.
deduksie, (-s), deduction, inference.
deduktief, (-tiewe), deductive.
deeg, dough.
deeglik, (-e), sound, substantial, thorough, solid, sterling; **ek meen dit wel –,** I do mean it; **hy het dit wel – gedoen,** he did it right enough; **dit is wel – so,** it is really so.
deeglikheid, soundness, thoroughness.
deel, (dele), n. deal, board, plank.
deel, (dele), n. part, portion; division, section; share; volume (of book); **sy – kry,** get one's share; **sy – ontmoet,** meet one's mate; **– uitmaak van,** form part of; **ten – val,** fall to, fall to one's share (lot); **ten dele, vir 'n –,** partly, in part; **vir 'n groot –,** to a large extent; **vir die grootste –,** for the greater part.
deel, (ge-), divide, participate, share; split (the difference); share (a person's views); participate (in someone's happiness); **iets – met iemand,** share something with a person; **gelykop –,** share and share alike.
deelagtig: – word, participate in.
deelbaar, (-bare), divisible, composite.
deelgenoot, partner, participator, sharer.
deelgenootskap, partnership; participation.
deelgeregtig, (-de), entitled to a share.
deellyn, bisector (of an angle).
deelneem, (deelge-): – aan, take part in, participate in, join in, take a hand in; enter (a war); be a party to (a plot).
deelnemend, (-e), sympathetic.
deelnemer, participant, competitor.
deelneming, participation; sympathy, compassion, commiseration; **– betuig,** condole with.
deels, partly, in part.
deelsgewys(e), bit by bit.
deelsom, division-sum.
deeltal, dividend.
deelteken, diaeresis; division-sign (in arith.).
deeltjie, (-s), particle, small part.
deelwoord, participle.
deemoed, humility, meekness.
deemoedig, (-e), meek, submissive.
deemoediging, humiliation, mortification.
Deen, (Dene), Dane.
Deens, (-e), n. & a. Danish.
deer, (ge-), harm, hurt.
deerlik, (-e), a. piteous, miserable.
deerlik, adv. badly, profoundly.
deernis, commiseration, compassion.
deerniswekkend, (-e), pitiful.
defek, (-te), n. hitch, fault; breakdown.
defek, (-te), a. defective, faulty, broken-down (car); punctured (tyre).
defensief, (-iewe), defensive; **– optree,** be (act, stand) on the defensive.
defileer, (ge-), defile, march (file) past.
definieer, (ge-), define.
definisie, (-s), definition.
definitief, (-iewe), definitive; definite, final; (permanent; decisive).
deflasie, deflation.

defleksie, deflection.
deflekteer, (ge-), deflect.
deftig, (-e), stately, dignified; fashionable, smart; **jou – hou,** give oneself airs.
deftigheid, (air of) distinction; dignity, stateliness; smartness.
degen, (-s), sword; foil.
degenerasie, degeneracy, degeneration.
degenereer, (ge-), degenerate.
degerig, (-e), doughy.
degradasie, degradation; disrating.
degradeer, (ge-), degrade; reduce to the ranks (mil.); disrate (mar.).
deikties, (-e), deictic.
dein, (ge-), heave, roll, surge, swell.
deining, (-e, -s), heave, roll, well.
deins, (ge-), shrink (back), recoil, retreat.
deïs, (-te), deist.
deïsme, deism.
deïsties, (-e), deistic.
dek, (-ke), n. cover, covering; deck (of ship).
dek, (ge-), cover; tile, slate, thatch (a house); defray (costs); make good (a loss), screen, shield (a person); **die aftog –,** cover the retreat; **die tafel –,** lay the table.
dekaan, (-ane), dean.
dekade, (-s), decade.
dekadensie, decadence.
dekadent, (-e), decadent.
dekagoon, (-one), decagon.
dekagram, decagram(me).
dekaliter, decalitre.
dekameter, decametre.
dekatlon, decathlon.
deken, (-s), counterpane.
dekgras, thatch.
dekking, cover; shelter, protection, guard.
dekkleed, cover, (horse-)cloth.
deklaag, upper layer, coping.
deklading, deck-cargo (-load).
deklamasie, declamation, recitation.
deklamator, (-s), declaimer, reciter.
deklameer, (ge-), recite, declaim.
deklarant, (-e), declarant.
deklarasie, (-s), declaration; entry (customs).
deklareer, (ge-), declare; enter.
deklinasie, declination.
deklinasiehoek, angle of declination.
deklinasienaald, declination-needle.
deklineer, (ge-), decline.
dekmantel, cloak; excuse, mask, pretext.
deknaald, thatching-needle.
dekolleteer, (ge-): jou –, wear a low-necked dress.
dekorasie, (-s), decoration.
dekoratief, (-iewe), decorative, ornamental.
dekoreer, (ge-), decorate.
dekorum, decorum; **die – in ag neem,** observe the proprieties (the decencies).
dekpassasier, deck-passenger.
dekplaat, coping-plate, capping.
dekpunt, cover-point (in cricket).
dekreet, (-ete), decree, edict, enactment.
dekreteer, (ge-), decree, enact, ordain.
dekriet, thatch(-reed).
dekseil, tarpaulin.
deksel, (-s), cover, lid, tap; **wat de (die) –?,** what the dickens . . . ?; **jou –!,** you dirty dog!
deksels, (-e), a. blessed, confounded; **die –e seun,** drat the boy!; **'n –e lawaai,** a devil of a noise.
deksels, interj. by gum!, by Jove!
dekstoel, deck-chair, canvas-chair.
dekstrien, dekstrine, dextrine.
dekstrooi, thatch(-grass).
dekstuk, abacus; cap, binder.
delegasie, (-s), delegation.

delegeer, (ge-), delegate.
deler, (s), divider; divisor; **grootste gemene –**, greatest common factor.
delf, delwe, (ge-), dig, mine.
delfstof, mineral.
delfstofkunde, mineralogy.
delfstofryk, mineral kingdom.
Delfts, (-e), Delft; **-e aardewerk**, Delft-ware.
delg, (ge-), discharge, redeem.
delging, payment, redemption.
delgingsfonds, sinking-fund.
deliberasie, (-s), deliberation.
delibereer, (ge-), debate, deliberate.
delik, (-te), delict, delinquency, offence.
delikaat, (-ate), delicate, ticklish (affair); delicious (savoury).
delikatesse, delicacy, dainty (bity); delikatessen.
delimitasie, delimitation.
delimiteer, (ge-), fix boundaries.
deling, (-e, -s), division; partition; fission (biol.).
delinkwent, (-e), delinquent, offender.
delirium, delirium.
delphinium, delphinium.
delta, (-s), delta.
deltastrale, delta rays.
delwer, (-s), digger.
delwerye, diggings.
demagogie, demagogy.
demagogies, (-e), demagogic.
demagoog, (-goë, -goge), demagogue.
demaskeer, (ge-), unmask.
demissie, demission.
demobiliseer, (ge-), demobilize.
demokraat, (-krate), democrat.
demokrasie, democracy.
demokraties, (-e), democratic.
demon, (-e), demon, devil.
demonies, (-e), demoniac(al).
demonstrasie, (-s), demonstration, exhibition.
demonstreer, (ge-), demonstrate.
demonteer, (ge-), dismount; dismantle.
demoraliseer, (ge-), demoralize.
demp, (ge-), fill up (a ditch); quell (a rebellion); dim (a light); extinguish, quench (fires); **die put – as die kalf verdrink is**, lock the stable after the steed is stolen; **met gedempte stem**, in a subdued voice, in an undertone.
demper, (-s), damper, silencer; mute (mus.).
den, (-ne), fir(-tree).
denaturaliseer, (ge-), denaturalize.
denatureer, (ge-), denature.
denkbaar, (-bare), conceivable, imaginable.
denkbaarheid, thinkableness, conceivability.
denkbeeld, idea, notion; view (on art).
denkbeeldig, (-e), imaginary; hypothetical.
denkkrag, power of thought.
denklik, (-e), possible, probable.
denkoefening, mental exercise.
denkvermoë, reasoning-capacity.
denkwyse, way of thinking; mental attitude.
dennebol, fir-cone.
denneboom, fir(-tree).
dennehout, fir-wood, pine-wood.
dennenaald, fir-needle.
dennepit, fir-cone pip.
denominatief, (-tiewe), denominative.
densiteit, density.
dentaal, (-ale), dental; dentary.
denudasie, (-s), denudation.
departement, (-e), department, office.
departementeel, (-tele), departmental.
dépêche, (-s), dispatch, message.
depolariseer, (ge-), depolarize.
deponeer, (ge-), put down, place; deposit (money); file, lodge (documents); have (a trade mark) registered.
deportasie, (-s), deportation; transportation.
deporteer, (ge-), deport; transport.
deposito, (-'s), deposit.
depot, (-s), depot; dump.
depresieer, (ge-), depreciate.
depressie, (-s), depression.
deprimeer, (ge-), depress.
deputasie, (-s), deputation.
deputeer, (ge-), depute.
derde, third; **'n –**, third (party); **ten –**, in the third place.
derdemag, cube.
derdemagsvergelyking, cubic equation.
derdemagswortel, cube-root.
derdemagsworteltrekking, finding the cube-root.
derderangs, (-e), third-rate.
derdeversekering, third-party insurance.
derf, derwe, (ge-), lack, miss, want.
dergelik, (-e), such(-like), like, similar.
derhalwe, consequently, so, therefore.
derm, (-s), intestine; gut; (pl.) entrails.
dermate, to such a degree (extent), so much.
dermatoloog, (-loë, -loge), skin-specialist.
dermontsteking, enteritis.
dermsnaar, catgut-string.
dermvlies, mesentery.
dermvliesontsteking, mesenteritis.
dertien, thirteen.
dertiende, thirteenth.
dertienjarig, (-e), of thirteen years.
dertig, thirty.
dertigjarig, (-e), of thirty years.
dertigste, thirtieth.
derwaarts, thither.
derwing, lack, want.
derwisj, (-e), dervish.
des, of the; **'n kind – doods**, a dead man; **– te beter**, all the better; **– te meer, omdat . . .**, the more so as . . .
desalnietemin, nevertheless, for all that.
desbetreffend, (-e), relating to the matter in question, relative.
dese, this; **na –**, after this.
Desember(maand), December.
desennium, (-s), decennium, (-ia), decade.
desentraliseer, (ge-), decentralize.
desepsie, (-s), deception.
deser, of this; **10de –**, tenth instant.
desersie, desertion.
deserteer, (ge-), desert; run away.
deserteur, (-s), deserter.
desgelyks, likewise.
desgewens, if required (necessary).
desideer, (ge-), decide.
desigram, (-me), decigram(me).
desiliter, (-s), decilitre.
desimaal, (-male), n. decimal place.
desimaal, (-male), a. decimal; **–male breuk**, decimal (fraction); **–male stelsel**, decimal system.
desimaal-, decimal point.
desimeer, (ge-), decimate.
desimeter, (-s), decimetre.
desinfeksie, disinfection.
desinfeksiemiddel, disinfectant.
desinfekteer, (ge-), disinfect.
deskundig, (-e), expert.
deskundige, (-s), expert.
desnieteenstaande, nevertheless.
desnietemin, for all that, nevertheless.
desnoods, if need be, in case of need.
desondanks, nevertheless.
desorganiseer, (ge-), disorganize.
desperaat, (-ate), desperate, despairing.

despoot, (-ote), despot.
despoties, (-e), despotic, tyrannic(al).
despotisme, despotism, tyranny.
dessert, dessert.
destyds, at that time.
desverkiesend, if desired; if so inclined.
desweë, on that account, for that reason.
detail, (-s), detail.
detektor, detector (radio).
determineer, (ge-), classify, identify (bot.).
detineer, (ge-), detain.
detonasie, detonation.
detoneer, (ge-), detonate, be out of keeping.
deug, (-de), n. virtue; excellence.
deug, (ge-), be good for, serve (a purpose); **nie – nie,** be no good; **– vir,** be good (fit) for; **jy – nie vir onderwyser nie,** you will never make a good teacher.
deugdelik, (-e), sound, reliable; solid.
deugdelikheid, soundness, reliability.
deugniet, (-e), good-for-nothing, rascal.
deugsaam, (-same), honest, virtuous.
deugsaamheid, probity, virtuousness.
deuk, (-e), n. dent, dint, cavity.
deuk, (ge-), dent, indent.
deuntjie, (-s), air, ditty, tune; **'n ander – sing,** sing a different tune.
deur, (-e), n. door; **aan die –,** at the door; **in die staan,** stand in the doorway; **met geslote –,** behind closed doors; **met die – in die huis val,** plunge straight into a matter; **voor die – staan,** be in store, be threatening; **voor jou eie – vee,** sweep before your own door.
deur, prep. through, throughout; by; on account of; **die hele land –,** all over the country; **die hele jaar –,** all the year round; **– die pos stuur,** send by post; **– die vyand gedood,** killed by the enemy; **ek kon – die stof die pad nie sien nie,** I could not see the road on account of the dust; **hy is –,** he is through, he has passed (his examination); **hy het die boek –,** he has finished the book.
deurbabbel, (deurge-), talk (chat) on.
deurbak, (deurge-), bake well.
deurbel, n. door-bell.
deurblaai, (deurge-), turn over the leaves of, glance at, skim (a book).
deurblaas, (deurge-), blow through.
deurboor, (deurge-), bore (drill) through, pierce.
deurboor, (het –), pierce, transfix, stab.
deurbraak, breaking through; breach.
deurbrand, (deurge-), burn on, keep on burning; burn through; fuse.
deurbreek, (deurge-), break (through); burst.
deurbring, (deurge-), waste, squander (one's money), spend, pass (the time).
deurbringer, spendthrift, wastrel.
deurbuig, (deurge-), bend; sag.
deurbyt, (deurge-), bite through.
deurdag, (-te), considered; well-planned.
deurdans, (deurge-), go on dancing; dance through; wear out with dancing.
deurdink, (deurge-), consider fully, think out; reflect on.
deurdraai, (deurge-), keep on turning; turn (wear) through; get through somehow.
deurdraf, -drawwe, (deurge-), trot on.
deurdring, (deurge-), penetrate, enter, pierce; ooze through; **dit het tot hom deurgedring,** it dawned on him.
deurdring, (het –), permeate, pervade, fill, impress; **iemand van iets –,** impress something on a person.
deurdringend, (-e), piercing, penetrating, searching (look), shrill (cry).

deurdringingsvermoë, penetrative power.
deurdronge: – van, alive to, convinced of.
deurdruk, (deurge-), press (push, squeeze) through; punch; go on printing; mackle (paper); persist, persevere.
deurdryf, -drywe, (deurge-), force (push) through; persist; **jou sin –,** carry one's point, have one's own way.
deurdrywer, headstrong person.
deurdrywery, persistence, obstinacy.
deur-en-deur, thoroughly, completely.
deurentyd, always, all the time.
deurgaan, (deurge-), go (pass) on; go through; keep on (raining); **die koop kan nie – nie,** the sale is off; **– vir,** pass for, be considered; pose as.
deurgaans, commonly, generally, usually; right through, all the way through.
deurgang, passage, corridor; thoroughfare.
deurgee, (deurge-), pass, pass on.
deurgelê, bedsore.
deurgestoke: 'n – kaart, a put-up job.
deurgraaf, -grawe, (deurge-), cut (dig) through.
deurgrawing, (-s), cutting, tunnel.
deurgrond, (het –), fathom, see through.
deurhaal, (deurge-), cross out, delete; put (a patient) through.
deurhak, (deurge-), cut (through); solve.
deurheen, through.
deurhelp, (deurge-), help (see) through.
deurhol, (deurge-), hurry (through).
deurja(ag), -jae, (deurge-), rush on (through).
deurkap, (deurge-), cut (through), split.
deurklief, -kliewe, (het –), cleave.
deurknaag, -knae, (deurge-), gnaw through (on).
deurknee, -knie(ë), (deurge-), knead thoroughly; keep on kneading.
deurknee(d), (-ede), versed (steeped) in.
deurknip, n. door-latch.
deurknip, (deurge-), cut (snip) (through).
deurknop, door-handle (-knob).
deurkom, (deurge-), get through; pass; pull through (an illness), survive, escape; **sy tande begin –,** he is teething.
deurkruip, (deurge-), creep (crawl) through; wear out by creeping (crawling).
deurkruis, (het –), cross; traverse.
deurkry, (deurge-), get (a pupil) through, pull (a patient) through.
deurkyk, (deurge-), look (go) through.
deurlaat, (deurge-), let through; transmit.
deurlê, (deurge-), become bedsore.
deurleef, -lewe (het –), go (live, pass) through, experience; survive.
deurlees, (deurge-), read through (on).
deurloop, n. passage; arcade.
deurloop, (deurge-), go (move, run, walk) on; wear out with walking; chafe; reprimand, thrash; **onder die voorslag –,** run the gauntlet; **laat – tot dag,** keep it up the whole night.
deurlopend, (-e), continuous, uninterrupted.
deurlug, (deurge-), aerate.
deurlugtig, (-e), illustrious.
deurlugtigheid, illustriousness; **Sy D–,** His Serene Highness.
deurlys, door-moulding.
deurmaak, (deurge-), vide **deurleef.**
deurmat, door-mat.
deurmekaar, in confusion, confused, higgledypiggledy; delirious; insane.
deurmekaarspul, confusion, chaos, mix-up.
deurnat, wet through, soaking (wet).
deurneem, (deurge-), take through.
deurplaat, finger-plate.
deurpos, door-post.

deurpraat, (deurge-), go on talking.
deurreën, -reent, (deurge-), keep on raining; let the rain through.
deurreis, n. passage; **op my –,** on my way through, en route.
deurreis, (deurge-), pass (travel) through.
deurreis, (het –), travel all over.
deurrit, passage.
deurroer, (deurge-), mix, stir (well).
deurroes, (deurge-), corrode, rust through.
deurry, (deurge-), ride (drive) on; ride (drive) through; wear out by riding, gall (a horse); **jou –,** get saddle-sore.
deursak, (deurge-), sag; sink (through).
deursein, (deurge-), signal through.
deursettingsvermoë, perseverance.
deursien, (deurge-), see through, sum up.
deursig, insight, penetration.
deursigtig, (-e), transparent (glass, pretext), obvious (excuse), lucid (exposition).
deursigtigheid, lucidity, transparency.
deursit, (deurge-), sit through, sit out (a meeting); **jou –,** sit oneself sore, get saddle-sore; **jou broek –,** wear through the seat of one's trousers; **iets –,** carry (see) a thing through.
deurskaaf, -skawe, (deurge-), plane through; chafe.
deurskemer, (deurge-), filter (glimmer) through; **laat –,** hint, intimate.
deurskeur, (deurge-), tear (to pieces).
deurskote: 'n – eksemplaar, an interleaved copy.
deurskrap, (deurge-), cross out.
deurskuif, -skuiwe, (deurge-), push through; slip through.
deurskuur, (deurge-), rub through; scour through; chafe.
deurskyn, (deurge-), shine (show) through.
deurskynend, (-e), transparent, translucent.
deurslaan, (deurge-), drive (knock) through; punch; knock in two; **jou daar –,** make one's way through.
deurslaande, conclusive (proof).
deurslaap, (deurge-), sleep on (through).
deurslag, punch; carbon-copy; boggy ground; decisive factor; **die – gee,** turn the scale, settle the matter.
deurslag- . . . , average; vide **deursnee.**
deurslagpapier, carbon-paper.
deurslagtig, (-e), boggy, marshy (ground).
deurslyt, (deurge-), wear through.
deursnede, deursnee, section; diameter; **in –,** in section; on an average.
deursnee- . . . , average.
deursneeprys, average price.
deursnuffel, (deurge-), nose through.
deursny, (deurge-), cut (in two); dissect.
deursny, (het –), cross, intersect.
deursoek, (deurge-), explore, search, scour.
deurspartel, (deurge-), struggle through.
deurspeel, (deurge-), play through (on).
deurspek, (-te), a. interlarded, larded.
deurspek, (het –), lard; interlard.
deurspring, (deurge-), jump through.
deurstaan, (deurge-, het –), endure, stand, pull through (an illness), weather (a storm); bear (comparison); stand (the test).
deurstap, (deurge-), walk on (through).
deursteek, (deurge-), cut, pierce, prick.
deursteek, (het –), stab, pierce.
deurstoot, (deurge-), push through (on).
deurstraal, (deurge-), shine through; **laat –,** intimate, give to understand.
deurstraal, (het –), light up, irradiate.
deurstroom, (deurge-), flow (run) through.
deurstuur,(deurge-), forward, send on.

deurstyl, jamb, door-post.
deurswoeg, swoeë, (deurge-), toil through (on).
deursyfer, (deurge-), trickle (ooze) through.
deurtas, (deurge-), take strong action.
deurtastend, (-e), drastic, thorough.
deurtastendheid, thoroughness, vigour.
deurtel, (deurge-), lift through.
deurtintel, (het –), thrill.
deurtog, march-through; passage, (right of) way.
deurtrap, (-te), crafty, consummate.
deurtraptheid, craftiness, cunning.
deurtrek, (deurge-), pull through, extend (produce a line); trek on (through).
deurtrek, (het –), pervade, permeate, soak.
deurtrokke: – van, imbued, saturated (with).
deurvaar, (deurge-), pass (sail) through; sail on.
deurvaart, passage.
deurval, (deurge-), fall through.
deurveg, (deurge-), fight on; fight through.
deurvleg, (deurge-), interlace, intertwine, interweave.
deurvlie(g), (deurge-), fly (rush) on; fly (rush) through.
deurvoed, (-e), well-fed.
deurvoer, n. transit.
deurvoer, (deurge-), convey (goods) in transit; carry (a plan) through; **te ver –,** push too far.
deurvoergoed(ere), transit-goods.
deurvreet, (deurge-), eat through; corrode.
deurwaad, (het –), ford, wade through.
deurwaadbaar, (-bare), fordable.
deurwaak, (deurge-), watch through.
deurwaarder, -wagter, (-s), doorkeeper.
deurweek, (-te), a. soaked, sodden.
deurweek, (het –), soak, moisten.
deurwerk, (deurge-), work on (through); finish; **iets laat –,** allow something to have its effect.
deurworstel, (deurge-), struggle through (on).
deurwrog, (-te), elaborate, studied.
deuskant, duskant, on this side of.
deuterium, deuterium.
Deuteronomium, Deuteronomy.
devaluasie, devaluation, depreciation.
devalueer, (ge-), depreciate.
deviasie, deviation.
devies, (-e), device, motto.
deviese, (pl.) foreign bills (paper).
dewyl, as, because, since.
diabolies, (-e), diabolic(al).
diadeem, (-eme), diadem.
diafragma, (-s), diaphragm.
diagnose, (-s), diagnosis.
diagnoseer, (ge-), diagnose.
diagonaal, (-ale), diagonal.
diagram, (-me), diagram.
diaken, (-s), deacon.
dialek, (-te), dialect.
dialektiek, dialectics.
dialekties, (-e), dialectal (pertaining to dialects); dialectic(al).
dialise, (-s), dialysis (chem.).
dialoog, (-loë, -loge), dialogue.
diamant, (-e), diamond.
diamantboor, diamond-drill.
diamantgruis, -poeier, diamond-powder, -dust.
diamanthandel, diamond-trade; **onwettige –,** I(llicit) D(iamond) B(uying).
diamantslyper, diamond-cutter.
diamantslypery, diamond-cutting factory.
diamantwerker, diamond-cutter.
diameter, (-s), diameter.
diapason, diapason.
diarree, diarrhoea.
diaspora, diaspore.
diastole, diastool, diastole.

Diatermie, diathermy.
diatonies, (-e), diatonic.
dictograph, Dictograph.
didaktiek, didactics.
didakties, (-e), didactic.
die, art. the.
dié, pron. (demon.), this (these); that (those).
diederdae: van – af, from days of yore.
diederik, (-e, -s), didric-cuckoo.
dieet, (diëte), diet, regimen.
dieetkunde, dietetics.
dieetkundige, dietician (dietitian).
dief, (diewe), thief.
diefagtig, (-e), thievish, larcenous.
diefstal, theft, robbery; larceny; **letterkundige –,** plagiarism, piracy.
diegene, he, she; those; **– wat,** whoever.
dien, (ge-), serve; wait on, attend to; **waarmee kan ek jou –?,** what can I do for you?; **daarmee is ek nie ge– nie,** that is of no use to me; **iemand van antwoord –,** reply to someone; **iemand van advies (raad) –,** advise a person; **– as,** serve for; **nêrens toe – nie,** serve no purpose; **jy – te weet,** you ought to know; **tot bewys –,** serve as proof.
dienaar, (-are, -s), servant; valet.
dienares, (-se), servant.
diender, (-s), constable, policeman.
diener, (-s), waiter; server (at tennis).
dienlik, (-e), serviceable.
dienooreenkomstig, accordingly.
diens, (-te), duty; function; service, **'n – bewys,** render a service; **– doen (as),** function (as); officiate (as); **– neem,** take service, join up; **die – opsê,** give notice; **die – verlaat,** retire; **in – gaan,** go into service; **in – neem,** engage, take into service; **in – stel** put into use; **op – wees,** be on duty; **ten –te van,** for the use of, at the service (disposal) of; **tot u –,** at your service; **uit die – tree,** retire; **van – wees,** be of use; **waarmee kan ek u van – wees?,** what can I do for you?; **– hê, be on duty; geen – hê nie,** be off duty; **sonder –,** out of employment; **In D–,** O(n) H(is)/H(er) M(ajesty.'s) S(ervice).
diensaanvaarding, entrance upon one's duties.
diensbaar, (-bare): – aan, subservient to; **– maak,** subjugate.
diensbaarheid, bondage, servitude, thraldom.
diensbataljon, service battalion.
diensbetoon, rendering of service.
diensbode, domestic (servant), servant.
diensdoende, acting; officiating; on duty.
diensjaar, year of service; financial year.
dienskneg, (man-)servant.
diensmaag(d), (maid-)servant; hand-maid.
diensmeisie, house-, nurse-, maid, maid-servant.
diensneming, acceptance of service; enlistment.
dienspersoneel, domestic staff.
diensplig, compulsory (military) service.
dienspligtig, (-e), liable to military service.
diensreëling, time-table.
diensregulasies, (service-)regulations.
diens(s)tasie, service-station.
dienstig, (-e), serviceable, useful.
dienstyd, term of office (service).
diensure, hours of attendance; working-hours.
diensvaardig, (-e), obliging, eager to serve.
diensvaardigheid, (-e), obligingness, readiness to serve.
diensverlating, desertion.
diensverrigting, discharge of one's duties.
diensvoorwaardes, conditions of service.
diensvry, exempt from (military) service.
diensweieraar, conscientious objector.
dienswillig, (-e), obedient.
dienswilligheid, vide **diensvaardigheid.**
diensywer, official zeal; professional zeal.
dientengevolge, in consequence, therefore.
dienvolgens, accordingly, consequently.
diep, n. deep.
diep, (–, -e), a. deep, profound (interest); low (bow); intense (scorn).
diep, adv. deeply profoundly; **– in gedagte,** deep in thought; **– in die skuld,** deep(ly) in debt; **– in die vyftig,** well on in his fifties; **tot – in die nag,** far on into the night; **– ongelukkig,** extremely unhappy.
diepbedroef(d), (-de), deeply afflicted.
diepbord, soup-plate.
diepgaand, (-e), thorough; deep-lying.
diepgang, draught (of ship).
diepgevoel(d), (-de), heartfelt.
diepgewortel(d), (-de), deep-rooted.
dieplood, sounding-lead, plummet.
diepsinnig, (-e), abstruse, deep, profound.
diepsinnigheid, abstruseness, profundity.
diepte, (-s), depth; the depth; profundity.
dier, (-e), animal, beast; brute.
dierasie, (-s), devil, virago, monster.
dierbaar, (-bare), beloved, dear.
diere-aanbidding, animal-worship.
dierebeskerming, protection of animals; **vereniging vir –,** S(ociety for the) P(revention of) C(ruelty to) A(nimals).
diere-epos, animal-epic, beast-epic.
dierelewe, animal-life.
diere-opstopper, taxidermist.
dierepark, zoo(logical garden).
dierereim, zodiac.
dierereyk, animal-kingdom.
dieretemmer, tamer of wild beasts.
dieretuin, zoo(logical garden).
dierkunde, zoology.
dierkundig, (-e), zoological.
dierkundige, (-s), zoologist.
dierlik, (-e), animal; bestial, brutal.
dierlikheid, animality; bestiality.
diersoort, species of animals.
dies, therefore; **wat – meer sy,** so forth.
dieselmasjien, diesel engine.
dieselfde, the same; **presies –,** the very same.
diesman, duusman, Dutchman; European.
diesulke, such(like).
diesvolk, Dutchmen; Europeans, white men.
diëteties, (-e), dietetic.
Diets, Middle Dutch; Pan-Dutch.
diets, iemand iets – maak, make a person believe something, gull a person.
diewebende, gang (pack) of thieves.
diewehol, thieves' den.
diewestreek, thievish trick, thief's trick.
dietaal, thieves' cant, argot.
differensiaal, (-iale), differential.
differensiaalrekening, (differential) calculus.
differensiasie, differentiation.
differensieel, (-iële), differential.
differensieer, (ge-), differentiate.
different, (-e), n. difference.
diffraksie, diffraction.
diffusie, diffusion.
diffuus, diffuse; **diffuse lig,** diffused light.
difterie, diphtheria.
diftong, (-e), diphthong.
diftongies, (-e), diphthongal.
dig, (-te), a. closed, shut; tight; dense (forest), compact (mass), thick (fog), close (texture); **– hou,** keep secret; **– maak,** seal; joint.
dig, (ge-), write poetry (verses).
digader, poetic vein.
digby, close by, close to, close upon, near.

**digestie, ** digestion.
**diggooi, (digge-), ** fill up; bang, slam.
**diggroei, (digge-), ** close (up), heal up.
**digkuns, ** (art of) poetry, poetic art.
**digmaak, (digge-), ** close; screw up; button up.
**digmaat, ** metre; **in –, ** in verse.
**dignaai, (digge-), ** sew up.
**digplak, (digge-), ** seal (up).
**digreël, ** (line of) verse.
**digskroei, (digge-), ** sear up (a wound).
**digsoort, ** kind of poetry.
digteby, ** vide **digby.
**digter, (-s), ** poet.
**digteres, (-se), ** poetess.
**digterlik, (-e), ** poetic(al).
**digtheid, ** closeness, compactness, density.
**digtrant, ** poetic style.
**digvorm, ** kind of poetry, poetic form.
**digvou, (digge-), ** fold up.
**digwerk, ** poem, poetical work.
**dik, ** thick; bulky; dense (fog); fat, stout; swollen; – **vriende, ** close friends; – **word, ** grow fat, put on flesh; – **wees vir iemand, ** be fed up with someone.
**dikbeksysie, ** (white-throated) seed-eater.
**dikbloedig, (-e), ** thick-blooded.
**dikbuik, ** pot-belly.
**dikbuikig, (-e), ** big-bellied, pot-bellied.
**dikderm, ** large intestine, colon.
**dik-dik, (-ke, -s), ** dik-dik (Rhynchotragus damarensis).
**dikhoofdig, (-e), ** thick-headed.
**dikhuid, ** pachyderm, thick-skinned person.
**dikhuidig, (-e), ** thick-skinned.
**dikkerd, (-s), ** fatty; chubby child.
**dikkerig, (-e), ** rather thick (fat, stout).
**dikkop, ** blockhead, numskull.
**dikkop- . . . , ** thick-headed (-skulled).
**dikkopvoël, ** thick-knee(d plover).
**diklip(pig), ** thick-lipped; sulky.
**dikmelk, ** curdled milk.
**dikneus(ig), ** thick-nosed, bottle-nosed.
diksak, ** vide **dikkerd.
**diksie, ** diction.
**diktaat, (-tate), ** dictation; notes.
**diktator, (-s), ** dictator.
**diktatoriaal, (-iale), ** dictatorial.
**diktatuur, (-ture), ** dictatorship.
**dikte, (-s), ** thickness.
**diktee, (-s), ** dictation.
**dikteer, (ge-), ** dictate.
**diktong(ig), ** thick-tongued.
**dikwang(ig), ** chubby, flabby-cheeked.
**dikwels, ** frequently, often.
**dilemma, (-s), ** dilemma.
**dilettant, (-e), ** dilettante, amateur.
**dilettanties, (-e), ** amateurish, dilettantish.
**dilettantisme, ** dilettantism, amateurishness.
**dimensie, (-s), ** dimension.
**diminutief, (-tiewe), ** diminutive.
**dinamies, (-e), ** dynamic.
**dinamiet, ** dynamite.
**dinamietaanslag, ** dynamite-outrage.
**dinamietdoppie, ** dynamite-cap.
**dinamietpatroon, ** dynamite-cartridge.
**dinamika, ** dynamics.
**dinamo, (-'s), ** dynamo.
**dinamometer, ** dynamometer.
**dinastie, (-ë), ** dynasty.
**dinastiek, dinasties, (-e), ** dynastic.
**dinee, (-s), ** dinner.
**dineebaadjie, ** dinner-jacket.
**dineer, (ge-), ** dine, have dinner.
**ding, (-e), ** n. thing, affair, matter, object.
**ding, (ge-): ** – **na, ** compete (sue, try) for.

**dinges, ** what-do-you-call-it, (Mr) So-and-So.
**dingesie, ** gadget; trifle.
**dingetjie, (-s), ** little thing, trifle; little child.
**dingo, (-'s), ** dingo.
**dink, (dag, dog; gedink, gedag, gedog), ** think; think of, intend (going); expect; **ek sou so –!, ** I should think so!; rather!; **dit laat 'n mens –, ** that sets one thinking; – **aan, ** think of; ek – **daar nie aan nie, ** it is out of the question; **laat – aan, ** make (a person) think of; remind (one) of; – **om, ** remember, mind; – **oor, ** think about (over); **daar anders oor –, ** think differently; – **van, ** think of; make of; believe of.
**dinosourus, (-se), ** dinosaur.
**Dinsdag, ** Tuesday.
**dioksied, (-e), diokside, (-s), ** dioxide.
**diorama, (-s), ** diorama.
**dip, (-pe), ** n. dip; dipping.
**dip, (ge-), ** dip.
**dipbak, ** dipping-tank.
**diphok, -kraal, ** dipping-pen.
**diploma, (-s), ** certificate, diploma.
**diplomaat, (-mate), ** diplomat(ist).
**diplomasie, ** diplomacy.
**diplomatiek, diplomaties, (-e), ** diplomatic.
**diplomeer, (ge-), ** certificate.
**dipstof, ** dip.
**direk, (-te), ** direct(ly), prompt(ly); at once.
**direksie, ** direction; management, board.
**direkteur, (-e, -s), ** director; manager.
**direktrise, (-s), ** manageress; matron.
**dirigeer, (ge-), ** direct; conduct (orchestra).
**dirigeerstok, ** baton, conductor's stick (wand).
**dirigent, (-e), ** conductor, choir-master.
**dis, ** n. table, board.
dis = **dit is, ** it is, that is.
**disa, (-s), ** disa (bot.).
**disharmonie, ** disharmony, discord.
**disharmonies, (-e), ** unharmonious, discordant.
**disintegrasie, ** disintegration.
**disintegreer, (ge-), ** disintegrate.
**diskant, (-e), ** descant, treble, soprano.
**diskoers, ** discourse, conversation.
**diskonteer, (ge-), ** discount.
**diskonto, ** discount.
**diskrediet, ** discredit; **in –, ** discredited.
**diskresie, ** discretion; modesty; secrecy.
**diskus, (-se), ** discus, disc (disk), quoit.
**diskussie, (-s), ** argument, discussion.
**diskuswerper, ** discus-thrower, discobolus.
**diskuteer, (ge-), ** argue, debate, discuss.
**diskwalifiseer, (ge-), ** disqualify.
**disnis: ** – **loop, speel, ** outdistance, outdo.
dispens, ** vide **spens.
**dispensasie, ** dispensation.
**disposisie, ** disposition; disposal.
**disputasie, (-s), ** argument, disputation.
**disputeer, (ge-), ** argue, dispute.
**dispuut, (-ute), ** controversy, disputation.
**dissel, (-s), ** n. adze.
**dissel, (ge-), ** adze.
**dissel, distel, (-s), ** n. thistle.
**disselboom, ** beam, shaft, thill.
**dissertasie, (-s), ** dissertation, thesis.
**dissimilasie, ** dissimilation.
**dissimulasie, ** dissimulation.
**dissipel, (-s), ** disciple.
**dissipline, ** discipline.
**dissiplineer, (ge-), ** discipline.
**dissiplinêr, (-e), ** disciplinary.
**dissonant, (-e), ** discord; jarring note.
**dissoneer, (ge-), ** be out of harmony, jar.
**dissosiasie, ** dissociation.
**dissosieer, (ge-), ** dissociate.
**distansie, (-s), ** distance.

distel — **distel-...**, vide **dissel**.
distillasie, (-s), distillation.
distilleer, (ge-), distil.
distilleerdery, distillery.
distilleerfles, **-kolf**, distilling-flask.
distilleerketel, stil.
distinksie, distinction.
distinktief, (-iewe), distinctive.
distorsie, distortion (radio).
distribueer, (ge-), distribute.
distribusie, distribution.
distrik, (-te), district.
distriksdokter, district-surgeon.
dit, this (these), it.
di(t)to, ditto, do.
diverse, sundries; nicidental expenses.
dividend, (-e), dividend.
dividendbewys, dividend-coupon.
divisie, (-s), division.
dobbel, (ge-), (play at) dice, gamble.
dobbel(a)ry, dicing, gambling.
dobbelspel, game of dice, gambling.
dobbelsteen, die, cube.
dobber, (-s), n. float; buoy.
dobber, (ge-), bob, drift; fluctuate.
dodder, cuscuta, dodder.
dodeakker, God's acre, cemetery, graveyard.
dodedans, death-dance, danse macabre.
dodekaëder, (-s), dodecahedron.
dodekagoon, (-one), dodecagon.
dodelik, (-e), mortal (fear), fatal (accident), deadly (poison), lethal (dose).
dodelys, death-roll, obituary.
dodemars, dead-march, funeral-march.
doderyk, realm of the dead.
dodo, (-'s), dodo.
doeane, custom-house; customs.
doeanebeampte, customs-officer.
doeaneregte, customs-dues.
doebleer, (ge-), double.
doeblet, (-e), doublet.
doedelsak, bagpipe.
doedoe, (ge-), sing to sleep; (go to) sleep.
doek, (-e), cloth, linen; canvas (of painter); painting; screen; napkin; **op die** – **gooi**, screen.
doekie, (-s), n. cloth; rag; **geen** –s **omdraai nie**, speak in plain terms.
doekie, (ge-), vide **doedoe**.
doel, (-e, -eindes), goal, object, purpose; butt, mark, target; goal (in football); **die** – **heilig die middele**, the end justifies the means; **'n** – **najaag** (beoog), have an end in view; **jou** – **bereik**, achieve one's end; **sy** – **mis**, miss one's mark; **die** – **tref**, hit the mark; **met die** – **om** ..., with a view to, for the purpose of; **reguit op die** – **afgaan**, go straight to the point; **jou ten** – **stel**, make it one's object to; **vir daardie** –, for that purpose.
doel, (ge-): – **op**, aim at; allude to, refer to.
doelaanwysend, (-e): –**e bysin**, final clause.
doelbewus, (-te), purposeful; unswerving.
doelbewustheid, fixity of purpose.
doeleinde, vide **doel**, n.
doelloos, (-lose), aimless, purposeless.
doelloosheid, aimlessness, uselessness.
doellyn, goal-line.
doelmatig, (-e), efficient, fit, practical.
doelmatigheid, appropriateness, efficacy.
doelpaal, goal-post.
doelpunt, goal, aim.
doeltreffend, (-e), effective, efficacious.
doelverdediger, goalkeeper.
doelwit, vide **doel**, n.
doem, (ge-), doom, condemn.
doemwaardig, (-e), damnable.

doen: **sy** – **en late**, his doings.
doen, (ge-, gedaan), do, make (a discovery), take (a step), ask (a question); **dit** – **'n mens nie**, it isn't done; **wat het jy vir hom ge–?**, what have you been doing to him?; **wat** – **hy?**, what is his business (profession)?; **niks te** – **hê nie**, be at a loose end; – **aan**, go in for (sport); **daar is niks aan te** – **nie**, nothing can be done about it; – **asof**, make as if (as though), pretend to; – **asof jy tuis is**, make yourself at home; **dit is nie daarom te** – **nie**, that is not the question (the point); vide **gedaan**.
doende, doing; **al** – **leer 'n mens**, practice makes perfect.
doenig, doing.
doenigheid, activity.
doening, act, deed; behaviour.
doenlik, (-e), feasible, practicable.
doepa, magic-potion, philtre, charm.
dof, (**dowwe**), dull (colour), faint (sound), dim (light, eyes).
dofheid, dullness, dimness, indistinctness.
dog, but, however, still, yet.
dogma, (-s), dogma.
dogmatiek, dogmatics.
dogmaties, (-e), dogmatic.
dogmatiseer, (ge-), dogmatize.
dogter, (-s), daughter; girl, girlie.
dok, (-ke), dock.
dokgeld, dockage, dock-dues.
dokter, (-s), n. (medical) doctor, physician.
dokter, (ge-), doctor; nurse; treat.
doktersbehandeling, medical treatment.
doktershande: **onder** – **wees**, be under the doctor, receive medical treatment.
dokterspraktyk, medical practice.
doktor, (-e, -s), doctor (of literature, etc.).
doktoraal, doctoral.
doktoraat, doctorate, doctor's degree.
doktoreer, (ge-), take a doctor's degree.
doktrinêr, (-e), doctrinaire.
dokument, (-e), document.
dokumenteer, (ge-), document; give documentary proof.
dokumentêr, (-e), documentary; –**e boek** (stuk, prent), documentary (n.).
dokwerker, docker, dock-labourer.
dol, (-le), a. mad; frantic, wild; crazy; **in** –**le vaart**, in headlong career; – **op wees**, be mad on, be crazy about; – **van woede**, mad with rage.
dolbly, overjoyed, as pleased as Punch.
doldraai, (dolge-), strip (a screw).
doldriftig, (-e), furious; hot-headed.
doleriet, dolerite.
dol(f)land, deeply trenched land.
dol(f)voor, trenched furrow.
dolfyn, (-e), dolphin.
dolgraag, very much, ever so much.
dolheid, folly; frenzy, fury; madness.
dolhuis, madhouse; bedlam, lunatic asylum.
dolk, (-e), dagger, dirk, poniard, stiletto.
dollar, (-s), dollar.
dolleeg, (-leë), absolutely empty.
dolliwarie: **in die** – **wees**, be in high feather.
dolomiet, dolomite, magnesian limestone.
dolos, knuckle-bone, dib, astragalus.
dolosgooier, Native witchdoctor.
dolsinnig, (-e), frantic, hare-brained, mad.
dolwe, **dolf**, (ge-), dig up (deeply), trench.
dom, (-me), n. cathedral(-church); dome.
dom, a. stupid, dense, silly.
dom-astrant, (-e), cheeky, impudent.
domein, (-e), domain; demesne.
domheid, (a piece of) stupidity.

dominee, (-s), clergyman, minister.
domineer, (ge-), domineer, predominate.
Dominikaan, (-ane), Dominican, Blackfriar.
domino(spel), (game of) domino(es).
domkerk, cathedral(-church).
domkop, blockhead, dud, fathead.
domkrag, jack(-screw), lifting-jack.
dommel, (ge-), doze, drowse.
dommelig, (-e), dozy, drowsy.
dommerik, (-e), vide domkop.
domoor, vide domkop.
dompel, (ge-), plunge.
dompeling, immersion.
domper, (-s), extinguisher; iemand die – opsit, repress (silence) a person.
don, (-s), don.
donasie, (-s), donation.
donateur, (-s), donor; contributor.
donder, n. thunder.
donder, (ge-), thunder; rave, storm.
donderbui, thunderstorm.
Donderdag, Thursday.
Donderdags, on Thursdays.
donderjaag, (ge-), bully.
donderjaer, bully.
donderpadda, bull-frog; rain-frog.
donderslag, thunderclap, peel of thunder.
donderstorm, vide donderbui.
donderweer, thundery weather.
donderwolk, thunder-cloud.
donga, (-s), donga, gully.
donker, n. dark, darkness; in die –, in the dark; die kat in die – knyp, do things on the sly; in die – tas, grope in the dark.
donker, a. dark; – maak, darken; dit word –, it's getting dark.
donkeragtig, (-e), darkish.
donkerte, dark, darkness; vide donker, n.
donkerwerk, work done in the dark; – is konkelwerk, bunglers work in the dark.
donkie, (-s), donkey; dunce.
donkiekraan, -lier, donkey(-crane).
dons, (-e), down, fluff.
dons(er)ig, donsagtig, (-e), downy, fluffy.
donshaartjies, donsies, fluff, fluffy hair (beard).
donsvere, flos (of ostrich).
donswol, fleecy wool.
dood, n. death, decease, demise; so bang as die – vir, mortally afraid of; 'n kind des –s, a dead man; die een se – is die ander se brood, one man's meat is another man's poison; die – sterf, die; duisende dode sterf, die a thousand deaths; 'n natuurlike – sterf, die a natural death; die – vind, meet one's death, find a grave; die – moet 'n oorsaak hê, there is an excuse for everything; – en verderf, death and destruction; die – op die lyf ja, frighten to death; by die – (omdraai), be at death's door; by die – van, at (on) the death of; deur die – verloor, lose through death; om die – nie, not for my (your) life; ten dode gedoem, doomed; ter – bring (veroordeel), put (sentence) to death; uit die – opstaan (verrys), rise from the dead.
dood, [dooi(e)], a. dead, deceased, defunct; so – as 'n mossie, dead as a doornail; – of lewend(ig), dead or alive; op sterwe na –, all but dead; – van die slaap, dead sleepy; 'n –(e) boel, a slow affair; – e gewig, dead weight; 'n –(e) kêrel, a muff; op 'n –e punt kom, reach a deadlock; –e tale, dead languages; –(e) vlees (vleis), proud flesh.
dood, (ge-), kill; slay; mortify (the flesh).
doodalleen, all (quite) alone.
doodarm, as poor as Job.

doodbaar, bier.
doodbaklei, (doodge-), fight to death.
doodbed, death-bed.
doodbedaard, (-e), as cool as a cucumber.
doodberig, vide doodsberig.
doodblaas, (doodge-), extinguish, blow out.
doodbloei, (doodge-), bleed to death; die down.
doodbrand, (doodge-), burn to death; cauterise.
doodbyt, (doodge-), bite to death.
dooddruk, (doodge-), press (squeeze) to death.
doodeenvoudig, (-e), quite simple.
doodeerlik, (-e), downright honest.
doodgaan, (doodge-), die.
doodgebore, still-born.
doodgegooi: – wees, be madly in love.
doodgerus, perfectly calm, quite unconcerned.
doodgewoon, (-gewone), quite common, ordinary, usual; very simple.
doodgoed, (-goeie), good to a fault, very kind.
doodgooi, (doodge-), kill (by throwing); squash, knock out, finish.
doodgrawer, grave-digger; sexton(-beetle).
doodhonger, a. very hungry, starving.
doodhonger, (doodge-), starve (to death).
doodhou, deathblow; knock-out blow.
doodjammer: dit is –, it is a great pity.
doodkalm, vide doodbedaard.
doodkis, coffin.
doodkry, (doodge-), kill.
doodlag, (doodge-), die with laughing.
doodlê, (doodge-), lie dead; overlie (a child).
doodloop, (doodge-), come to a dead end; jou –, walk oneself off one's legs.
doodlu(i)ters, -leuters, as innocent as a lamb.
doodmaak, (doodge-), kill.
doodmak, quite tame; as quiet as a lamb.
doodmaklik, (-e), quite easy, dead easy.
doodmartel, (doodge-), torture to death.
doodmoeg, dead-beat, tired to death.
doodongelukkig, (-e), perfectly wretched.
doodonskuldig, (-e), as innocent as a lamb.
dood-op, vide doodmoeg.
doodpraat, (doodge-), talk out; hush up.
doodry, (doodge-), ride (a horse) to death; run over (and kill) (a person).
doods, (-e), deathly, deathlike.
doodsangs, mortal fear; pangs of death.
doodsbang, mortally (deadly) afraid.
doodsbeendere, bones of dead bodies.
doodsbenoud, (-e), vide doodsbang.
doodsberig, death-notice, obituary notice.
doodsbleek, deathly pale.
doodsengel, angel of death.
doodsgevaar, danger of life, deadly peril.
doodsheid, deadness, desolateness; deathliness.
doodshoof, death's head, skull.
doodsiek, dangerously ill, sick to death.
doodskaam, (doodge-), jou –, die of shame.
doodskiet, (doodge-), shoot (dead).
doodskleed, shroud, winding-sheet; pall.
doodskleur, death-colour, deadly pallor.
doodsklok, death-bell.
doodskop, n. vide doodshoof.
doodskop, (doodge-), kick to death.
doodskrik, n. mortal fright.
doodskrik, (doodge-), jou –, be frightened to death, get the fright of one's life.
doodslaan, (doodge-), beat (batter) to death, kill, slay, squash.
doodslaap, death-sleep, sleep of death.
doodslag, homicide, manslaughter.
doodsnik, last gasp.
doodsnood, agony (of death), death-struggle; imminent danger.
doodsonde, mortal (deadly) sin.

doodsteek, n. death-blow, finishing-stroke.
doodsteek, (doodge-), stab to death.
doodstil, stock- (stone-)still, as still as death.
doodstraf, capital punishment.
doodstryd, death-struggle.
doodstyding, vide **doodsberig**.
doodsveragting, contempt of death.
dood(s)vyand, mortal enemy.
doodsweet, death-sweat, (cold) sweat of death.
doodtevrede, quite content.
doodtrap, (doodge-), trample to death.
doodval, (doodge-), drop (fall) dead.
doodvererg, mortally vexed.
doodvonnis, sentence of death.
doodvries, (doodge-), freeze to death.
doodwerk, (doodge-), work to death.
doof, (dowe), a. deaf; **so – as 'n kwartel, as deaf as an adder** (a post); – **wees vir**, be deaf to, turn a deaf ear to; **jou – hou**, pretend not to hear; **nie om (vir) dowe neute nie**, not to no purpose, not for dry beans.
doof, dowe, (ge-), put out; dim; deaden (a sound).
doofheid, deafness.
doofpot, extinguisher; **iets in die – stop**, hush up a thing, keep a thing dark.
doofstom, deaf and dumb, deaf-mute.
doofstominrigting, -instituut, institution (asylum) for the deaf and dumb.
doofstomme, (-s), deaf-mute.
dooi(e), vide **dood**, a.
dooi, (ge-), thaw.
dooier, (-s), door, (dore), yolk.
dooierig, (-e), lifeless, listless, slow.
dooi(e)mansdeur, voor – kom, find nobody at home.
dool, (ge-), roam, wander (about); err.
doolhof, maze, labyrinth.
doolweg, wrong way (path); **op die – geraak**, go astray.
doop, n. baptism, christening; **ten – hou**, present at the font.
doop, (ge-), baptise, christen; name (a ship); sop (bread in milk), dip (biscuit in tea); initiate (a student).
doopbak(kie), baptismal font.
doopgelofte, baptismal vow.
doopplegtigheid, christening ceremony.
dooprok(kie), christening-robe.
doopseel, baptismal certificate.
doopsertifikaat, vide **doopseel**.
doopsformulier, order of baptism.
Doopsgesind, (-e), Baptist.
doopsgetuie, sponsor, godparent.
door, vide **dooier**.
doos, (dose), box, case; **uit die ou –**, antiquated, old-fashioned.
doosbarometer, aneroid-barometer.
dop, (-pe), n. shell (of egg); husk (of seeds); pod (of peas); cap, top (of pen); tot; **in die –**, in the making, budding; **in sy – kruip**, draw in one's horns.
dop, (ge-), shell (peas, beans); fail (an examination).
dopemmer, milking-pail.
dopheide, bell-heather, bottle-heath.
dophou, (dopge-), hold the milking-pail; keep an eye on, watch.
Dopper, (-s), Dopper; member of the Reformed Church.
doppie, (-s), shell; cap, cover (of pipe); percussion-cap, detonator.
doppiemotor, bubble car.
dor, (-re), a. dry, barren, arid.
dor, (ge-), dry.
dorheid, dryness, barrenness, aridity.

Dories, (-e), n. & a. Dorian.
doring, (-s), thorn, prickle, spine; **'n – in die oog**, an eyesore, a thorn in the flesh; **'n ou –**, a brick.
doringagtig, (-e), thorny, spinous.
doringappel, thorn-apple.
doringboom, thorn-tree, acacia, mimosa.
doringdraad, barbed wire.
doringkroon, crown of thorns.
doringloos, (-lose), spineless.
doringstomp, thorn-tree stump.
doringstruik, thorn-bush.
dorp, (-e), village.
dorpenaar, (-are, -s), villager.
dorps, (-e), village-like, rustic.
dorpsbewoner, villager.
dorpsgrond, village-ground, commonage.
dorpskool, village-school.
dorpslewe, village-life.
dorpspastorie, village-parsonage.
dorpspraatjies, village-gossip.
dors, n. thirst; **– hê (kry)**, be (get) thirsty; **jou les**, quench one's thirst.
dors, a. thirsty; **ek is (het) –**, I am thirsty.
dors, (ge-), 1. be thirsty; **– na**, thirst for.
dors, (ge-), 2. thresh (thrash).
dorsaal, (-ale), dorsal.
dorser, (-s), thresher (thrasher).
dorsmasjien, threshing-machine.
dorstig, (-e), thirsty; vide **dors**, a.
dorstrek, trek through the desert.
dorstyd, threshing- (thrashing-)time.
dos, n. array, attire, dress, raiment.
dos, (ge-), array, attire, deck, dress.
doseer, (ge-), lecture, teach.
doseer, (ge-), dose (an animal).
dosent, (-e), lecturer, teacher, instructor.
dosie, (-s), (small) box (of matches).
dosis, (-se), dose, quantity.
dossier, (-s), dossier.
dosyn, (-e), dozen.
dot(jie), little dear, dot; bowler(-hat).
dou, n. dew.
dou, (ge-), dew.
doublom, sundew.
doudruppel, dew-drop.
doupunt, dew-point.
douspoor, track in the dew.
douvoordag, before daybreak.
douwurm, ringworm; vide **omloop**.
dowerig, (-e), slightly (somewhat) deaf.
dowwerig, (-e), rather indistinct; vide **dof**.
dra(ag), drae, (ge-), carry, bear, wear (clothes); discharge, run (of a wound); have a range (of gun); **ek kan dit nie langer – nie**, I cannot bear (stand) it any longer; **jou jare goed –**, carry your years well.
draad, (drade), thread; fibre, filament; grain (of wood); string (of pod); wire, strand (of wire); fence; **g'n – klere hê nie**, not have a rag; **die – kwytraak, (opneem)**, lose (pick up, resume) the thread; **'n – in die naald steek**, thread a needle; **teen die –**, against the grain; **tot op die – afgeslyt**, worn to a thread, worn threadbare; **kort van –**, cross-grained, short-tempered.
draadanker, wirewound armature.
draadgaas, wire-gauze; vide **gaasdraad**.
draadheining, wire-fence.
draadjie, (-s), filament; thin threat; **aan 'n – hang**, hang by a thread.
draadknipper, wire-clippers (-cutters).
draadloos, n. radio, wireless.
draadloos, (-lose), a. wireless.
draadloosstasie, wireless-station.
draadopnemer, wire recorder.

draadskêr, wire-cutters.
draadsnyer, screw-cutter.
draadsnymoer, die-nut.
draadspanner, wire-strainer; turn-buckle.
draadspyker, wire-nail.
draadtang, wire-pliers.
draadtrekker, wire-drawer (lit.); fence-strainer (lit.); wire-puller, schemer.
draadtrekkery, wire-straining (lit.); fencing (lit.); (political) wire-pulling.
draadversperring, wire-entanglement.
draadwerk, wire-work; filigree(-work); **vol – wees**, be full of fads and fancies.
draadwurm, thread-worm, round-worm.
draag, vide **dra**.
draagbaar, n. bier; litter, stretcher.
draagbaar, (-bare), a. bearable; portable; wearable (clothes).
draagbalk, supporting-beam, girder.
draagband, shoulder-tree; sling (for arm).
dra(ag)golf, carrier wave.
draaghout(jie), cross-bar, neck-bar.
draagkrag, bearing-powder; carrying capacity; range.
draaglik, (-e), bearable, tolerable.
draagloon, porterage.
draagriem, (neck-bar) strap; lanyard.
draagstoel, sedan(-chair); palanquin.
draagtyd, gestation(-period).
draagvermoë, vide **draagkrag**.
draagvlak, plane; bearing-surface.
draagwydte, range; import (of words).
draai, (-e), n. turn; kink, twist (of rope); bend, turning (of road); **'n – gee**, give a twist; **hy kan sy – nie kry nie**, he cannot find time to do it; **met 'n – loop**, not go straight to the point; be dishonest.
draai, (ge-), turn; spin (round); rotate, revolve (round a point); whirl; wind (of a road); shift, veer round (of the wind); linger, tarry, dawdle; roll (pills); wind (a piece of string); **my kop –**, my brain reels; **iets so – dat**, twist things in such a way that; **stokkies –**, play truant; **jou –**, turn, move; **alles – om my**, everything whirls round me; everything depends on me; **alles – om hierdie feit**, this is the crux of the whole question; **al om die punt –**, beat about the bush, hedge; **jou uit iets –**, wriggle out of something.
draaibaar, (-bare), revolving.
draaibank, lathe.
draaiboek, scenario.
draaiboekrak, revolving-bookstand.
draaiboom, turnstile, turnpike.
draaibrug, swing-bridge, swivel-bridge.
draaideur, revolving-door.
draaier, (-s), turner; shuffler; axis; loiterer.
draaierig, (-e), dizzy; loitering.
draaiery, turning-shop; delay, loitering.
draaihek, turnstile.
draaiing, turning, rotation; twist, gyration.
draaijakkals, long-eared fox.
draaikolk, whirlpool.
draaikous, dawdler, loiterer.
draaiorrel, barrel-organ.
draaisaag, circular saw; bow-saw, fret-saw.
draaisiekte, goggles, gid, staggers.
draaiskyf, rotating disc; turntable.
draaispieël, swing-glass, cheval-glass.
draaistoel, revolving-chair, swivel-chair.
draaitol, spinning-top, peg-top, whirligig.
draaitrap, spiral staircase.
draaiwissel, (turning-)points (railw.).
draak, (drake), dragon; **die – steek met**, poke fun at.
draal, (ge-), dawdle, delay, linger.

drabok, darnel, rye-grass, tares.
draderig, (-e), stringy; fibrous.
drae, vide **dra**.
draer, (-s), bearer, carrier, porter; exponent (of a principle); cross-bar (of wagon).
draf, n. draff, hogwash, swill.
draf, n. trot; **op 'n –**, at a trot.
draf, drawwe, (ge-), trot.
drag, (-te), costume, wear; burden, load; litter; crop; matter, pus (of a wound); **'n – slae**, a thrashing.
draggie, (-s), small load (bundle).
dragme, (-s), dram; drachma (coin).
dragonder, (-s), dragoon.
dragtig, (-e), with young.
drakebloed, dragon's blood; bloodwort.
drakerig, (-e), of the blood-and-thunder type.
dralend, dralerig, (-e), loitering, tarrying.
drama, (-s), drama, play.
dramaskrywer, dramatist, playwright.
dramatiek, (the) drama, dramatic art.
dramaties, (-e), dramatic.
dramatiseer, (ge-), dramatize.
dramaturg, (-e), dramatist.
drang, (-e), pressure; urgency; impulse, urge, craving; **– uitoefen op**, bring pressure to bear upon; **onder die – van omstandighede**, under the stress of circumstances.
drank, (-e), drink, beverage; draught (med.); (sterk) –, spirits, liquor; **aan die – wees**, be on the drink; **aan die – raak**, take to drink(ing); **aan die – (verslaaf) wees**, be addicted to drink.
drankbestryding, prohibition(ism).
drankhandel, liquor-trade.
drankoffer, drink-offering, libation.
dranksmokkelaar, liquor-runner.
dranksug, drink-craving, dipsomania.
dranksugtig, (-e), given to drink(ing).
dranksugtige, (-s), dipsomaniac.
drankverbod, prohibition; **voorstander van –**, prohibitionist.
drankverbruik, consumption of spirits.
drankverkoop, sale of liquor.
drankwet, liquor-law, licensing-act.
drapeer, (ge-), drape.
draperieë, hangings.
drassig, (-e), marshy, boggy.
drasties, (-e), drastic.
drawwertjie, (-s), (rufous) courser.
dreef, op – kom, get into one's stride, get one's hand in; **iemand op – help**, help a person on; **op – wees**, be in form.
dreg, (-ge), n. drag, grapnel.
dreg, (ge-), drag, trail.
dregnet, dragnet, trawl.
dreig, (ge-), threaten, menace; intend; **– om te kom**, intend to come.
dreigbrief, threatening letter.
dreigement, (-e), menace, threat.
dreigend, (-e), threatening, menacing, imminent (danger), impending (misfortune).
dreineer, (ge-), drain.
dreinering, drainage.
drek, filth, muck, ordure.
drel, (-le), dirty (indecent) woman.
drempel, (-s), threshold (fig.).
drenk, (ge-), drench (with blood); soak, steep.
drenkeling, (-e), drowning (drowned) person.
drentel, (ge-), loiter, lounge, saunter.
drentelaar, (-s), lounger, saunterer.
dresseer, (ge-), train, break in; coach.
dressuur, training; coaching.
dreun, n. boom, rumble; chant, drone.
dreun, (ge-), boom, roar, rumble; drone.

dreuning, (-se, -s), rumbling, **sy - (druiwe) teëkom,** get a nasty shock.
dribbel, (ge-), dribble.
drie, (-ë, -s), three; try (football); **een, twee, –,** in a trice; **drie-drie**, in three's; **– maal,** three times, thrice.
drie-ag(t)ste, three-eighth(s).
drie-aks, three-eighths (of an inch).
driebeen, three-legged; traid.
driedaags, (-e), three days'.
driedekker, three-decker; triplane.
driedelig, (-e), tripartite.
driedeling, division in three; tripartition.
driedimensionaal, (-ale), of three dimensions, **-e** meetkunde, solid geometry.
driedraads, three-ply.
driedubbel(d), threefold, treble, triple.
Drie-eenheid, (Holy) Trinity.
drie-enig, (-e), triune, three in one.
drieërlei, of three kinds (sorts).
driehoek, triangle; set-square.
driehoekig, (-e), triangular; three-cornered.
driehoeksmeting, trigonometry.
driehoeksverkiesing, three-cornered contest.
driejaarliks, (-e), triennial.
driejarig, (-e), of three years.
driekantig, (-e), three-sided, trilateral.
drieklank, triphthong (language); triad (mus.).
driekleur, tricolour.
driekleurig, (-e), tricolour(ed).
driekwart, three-fourths; three-quarter (rugby); three-quarters (of a mile).
driekwartsmaat, three-four time.
drieledig, (-e), threefold, tripartite.
drielettergrepig, (-e), trisyllabic.
drieling, (-e), triplets.
drielobbig, (-e), three-lobed, trilobate.
drieluik, triptych.
driemaandeliks, (-e), quarterly, three-monthly.
drieman, triumvir.
driemanskap, triumvirate.
driemaster, three-master.
driepoot-...., -potig, (-e), three-legged (chair).
driesaadlobbig, (-e), tricotyledonous (bot.).
driesnarig, (-e), three-stringed; trichord (piano).
driesprong, three-forked road; **op die –,** at the parting of the ways.
driestemmig, (-e), for three voices.
driesydig, (-e), three-sided, trilateral.
drietal, (number of) three, trio.
drietallig, (-e), ternary; ternate.
drietand, n. trident.
drieterm, trinomial.
drievoet, n. tripod; trivet.
drievoet-...., -voetig, (-e), a. three-legged.
drievoud, treble; triplicate.
drievoudig, (-e), threefold, triple, treble.
driewerf, three times, thrice.
driewieler, (-s), tricycle.
drif, (-te), n. anger, temper; haste; **in –,** in a fit of passion; **jou – beteuel,** keep one's temper.
drif, (-te, **driwwe**), ford, drift.
drifkop, hothead, spitfire.
driftig, (-e), passionate, quick-tempered; hasty; **jou – maak,** lose one's temper.
driftigheid, hot (quick) temper; haste.
dril, n. drill.
dril, (ge-), drill, train; coach; quiver, shake.
drilboor, drill, wimble.
drilmeester, drill-sergeant; coach, trainer.
drilsel, jelly, gravy-jelly.
drilsisteem, cramming-system.
drilvis, electric fish; electric ray (skate).
dring, (ge-), crowd, hustle, jostle, push, throng; press, urge, **die tyd –,** time presses.

dringend, (-e), pressing, crying, urgent.
drink, (ge-), drink; be given to drink(ing); **iets –,** have a drink; **iemand se gesondheid –,** drink a person's health.
drinkbaar, (-bare), drinkable, potable.
drinkbak, water(ing)-trough; water-bowl.
drinkbeker, beaker, cup, goblet.
drinkebroer, boozer, tippler, toper.
drinkgelag, carouse, drinking-bout.
drinklied, drinking-song.
drinkparty, drinking-party.
drinkwater, drinking-water.
drinkwatervoorsiening, (domestic) water-supply.
dro(ë), **droog**, (ge-), dry; become dry.
droë, n. dry land; **op die –,** on dry land; **jou skapie op die – hê,** have feathered one's nest.
droef, **(droewe)**, dejected, in low spirits, sad.
droef(e)nis, affliction, grief, sadness, sorrow.
droefgeestig, (-e), dejected, melancholy.
droefheid, sadness, sorrow.'
droëland, dry-land.
droëlandboerdery, dry-land farming.
droëlewer, dry-throated.
droëmaat, dry measure.
droëperskes, dried peaches.
droes, glanders.
droesem, dregs, lees; **tot die – ledig,** drink to the lees.
droewig, (-e), pityful, sad, sorrowful, sorry.
droë-ys, dry ice.
drogbeeld, chimera, illusion, phantom.
drogies, drily (dryly), with dry humour.
drogis, (-te), druggist.
drogistery, druggist's (shop), drug-store.
drogrede, fallacy, sophism.
drogredenaar, sophist.
drogredenering, sophistry.
drom, (-me), crowd, troop; drum.
dromedaris, (-se), dromedary.
dromerig, (-e), dreamy; far-away (look).
dromery, day-dream(ing), reverie.
drommel, (-s), beggar, wretch; deuce, devil; **arme –,** poor beggar (wretch); **wat die –,** what the deuce.
drommels, (-e), a. confounded, deuced.
dronk, n. drink, draught; toast.
dronk, a. drunken (attrib.), drunk (pred.), intoxicated; – **word van,** get drunk on.
dronkaard, (-s), drunkard, inebriate.
dronkenskap, drunkenness, intoxication, inebriety.
dronklap, drunkard.
dronksiekte, gid, sturdy (vet.).
dronkslaan, **(dronkge-)**, beat, dumbfounded, flabbergast; take one's breath away.
droog, **(droë)**, a. dry, arid, parched; dull.
droog, vide **dro(ë)**, **(ge-)**.
droogdok, dry-dock, graving-dock.
droogheid, dryness.
droogkomiek, a. droll, dryly humorous.
drooglê, **(droogge-)**, drain, reclaim; **make dry.**
drooglegging, draining, reclamation.
droogloop, **(droogge-)**, run dry.
droogmaak, **(droogge-)**, dry; cure (tobacco), season (wood); vide also **drooglê.**
droogoond, drying-kiln.
droogpomp, **(droogge-)**, pump dry.
droogpruim, dry (old) file; dry stick.
droogsit, **(droogge-)**, get the better of; oust (supplant) a rival.
droogstoppel, (Mr) Dryasdust.
droogte, (-s), drought, dryness.
droogvoets, dry-shod.
droogweg, drily (dryly); vide **drogies.**

droom, (drome), n. dream; **iemand uit die − help,** undeceive a person.
droom, (ge-), dream.
droombeeld, illusion, phantasm, vision.
droomgesig, vision.
droomland, dreamland.
droomuitlêer, -uitlegster, dream-reader, interpreter of dreams.
droomwêreld, dreamworld.
drop, liquorice (licorice).
dros, (ge-), desert, run away.
drosdy, (-e), dros(t)dy.
droster, (-s), runaway, deserter.
druïde, (-s), druid.
druif, (druiwe), grape; **die druiwe is suur,** the grapes are sour; vide **dreuning.**
druifluis, phylloxera.
druil, (ge-), mope, pout;
druilerig, (-e), moping, mopish, pouting.
druip, (ge-), drip (with blood); gutter, run (of candle); fail, be ploughed.
druipeling, (-e), failure (in an examination).
druipkelder, stalactite-cave.
druipnat, dripping(-wet), soaked, drenched.
druipsteen, sinter (deposits); stalactite (hanging); stalagmite (standing).
druipsteengrot, vide **druipkelder.**
druipstert, adv. sneaking; − **wegdros,** slink off (with the tail between one's legs).
druis, (ge-), roar, swirl, swish.
druiwekonfyt, grape-jam.
druiwekorrel, grape.
druiwe-oes, grape-harvest, vintage.
druiwepers, grape-crusher.
druiwepit, grape-stone.
druiweprieel, vine-bower, pergola of vines.
druiwerank, (vine-)tendril.
druiwesap, grape-juice.
druiwesteen, botryolite.
druiwestok, vine.
druiwetros, bunch of grapes.
druk, (-ke), n. pressure; burden, weight, squeeze (of the hand); print, type (of letter); edition, publication (of a book); **hoë (lae) −,** high (low) pressure; − **uitoefen op,** bring pressure to bear upon; **in −,** in print; **in − verskyn,** appear in print, be published; **uit −,** out of print, sold out.
druk, a. busy, lively; crowded; **dit − hê,** be very busy; **jou − maak,** get excited.
druk, (ge-), press, squeeze; push; weigh heavy upon; oppress (of thought); print (a book); **iemand se hand −,** press (squeeze) a person's hand; **iemand die hand −,** shake hands with a person; **iemand se voetstappe −,** follow (tread, walk) in a person's (foot)steps; **aan jou hart −,** fold (press) to one's heart; **in jou arms −,** clasp in one's arms, embrace (hug); **iemand iets op die hart (gemoed) −,** enjoin (impress, urge) something upon a person; **op 'n knoppie −,** press a button; **op 'n woord −,** emphasise (stress) a word; **hierdie wet − swaar op die armes,** this law bears heav(il)y upon the poor, this law is very oppressive to the poor.
drukbars, pressure burst.
drukfout, printer's error, misprint.
drukink, printer's ink, printing-ink.
drukkajuit, pressurized cabin.
drukkend, (-e), oppressive; close, sultry.
drukker, (-s), printer.
drukkersduiwel, printer's devil.
drukkery, (-e), printing-office, printing-works.
drukking, pressure, weight.
drukknoppie, press-button, press-stud.
drukkoste, printing-expenses.
drukkuns, printing, typography.

drukpers, (printing-)press.
drukpot, pressure cooker.
drukproef, printer's proof, proof(-sheet).
drukskrif, print-hand; letterpress.
drukspyker(tjie), thumb-tack.
drukte, bustle, excitement, fuss, stir, to-do.
druktemaker, noisy (fussy) person.
drukvas: −te vliegtuig, pressurized aircraft.
drukverligting, decompression.
drukvorm, printing-form.
drukwerk, printing, printed matter.
drumpel, (-s), threshold, doorstep; **iemand se − platloop,** frequent a person's house.
drup, drip; eaves.
drup, (ge-), drip, drop, trickle down.
druppel, (-s), drop; **'n − in die emmer,** a drop in the bucket; **soos twee −s water na (op) mekaar lyk,** be as like as two peas.
druppel, (ge-), drip, drop, trickle down.
druppelsgewys(e), drop by drop.
dryf, drywe, (ge-), float, swim (in butter), drift (ashore); drive; impel, urge hustle; conduct, run (a business); actuate, prompt; **handel −,** trade, carry on business; **die spot −,** mock, poke fun at; **iets te ver −,** carry things too far, go too far; **deur die begeerte (verlange) ge−,** actuated by the desire to . . . ; **iemand tot die uiterste −,** drive a person to extremities.
dryfas, driving-shaft (-axle).
dryfhou, drive (in tennis).
dryfhout, driftwood, flotsam, jetsam.
dryfjag, drive, battue, beat(-up); vide **klopjag.**
dryfkrag, driving-force; motive power.
dryfrat, driving-wheel, driver; impeller.
dryfriem, driving-band (belt).
dryfsand, driftsand, quicksand.
dryfstang, connecting-rod.
dryfstangkop, big-end.
dryfstok, driver (golf).
dryftol, whip(ping)-top.
dryfveer, spring; incentive, motive.
dryfwiel, driving-wheel, fly-wheel.
dryfys, drift-ice, floating ice, floe.
drywend, (-e), drifting; floating; swimming.
drywer, (-s), driver; embosser; fanatic.
drywery, driving; bigotry, fanaticism.
dualis, n. dual (number).
dualis, (-te), n. dualist.
dualisme, dualism.
dualisties, (-e), dualistic.
dubbel(d), duwwel(d), (-e), double, dual, twice; **'n −e betrekking,** a dual post; **'n −e spel speel,** play a double game; **− so duur,** twice as dear; **− en dwars,** over and again.
dubbelbrandpuntig, (-e), bifocal.
dubbeldooier, -door, double-yolked egg.
dubbelganger, double, second self; wraith.
dubbelhandig, (-e), ambidextrous.
dubbelhartig, (-e), double-faced.
dubbelkruis, double-sharp (mus.).
dubbelloop- . . . , double-barrelled.
dubbelloopgeweer, double-barrelled gun.
dubbelmol, double-flat (mus.).
dubbelpunt, colon; double-point (maths.).
dubbelsinnig, (-e), ambiguous; equivocal.
dubbelsinnigheid, ambiguity.
dubbelskroef, twin-screw.
dubbelslagtig, (-e), gynandrous.
dubbelspel, doubles.
dubbelspoor, doubletrack.
dubbelster, doublestar, binary star(s), twin-stars.
dubbelsweep, doublewhip.
dubbeltjie, duwweltjie, (-s), penny.
dubbeltjie, duwweltjie(doring), (-s), devil's thorn.
dubbelvoorploeg, gang-plough.

dubbelvorm, doublet.
dubieus, (-e), doubtful, dubious.
duel, (-le), duel, single combat.
duclleer, (ge-), (fight a) duel.
duellis, (-te), duellist.
duet, (-te), duet.
duetsanger, duettist.
dug, (ge-), apprehend, dread, fear.
dugtig, (-e), sound, strong, thorough.
dui(e), (ge-), – **op**, hint at, point to, suggest; **euwel (ten kwade)** –, take amiss, take in bad part.
duidelik, (-e), clear, plain; distinct; broad (hint); obvious, (reason); explicit (instructions); legible (handwriting).
duidelikheid, clearness, distinctness.
duiding, interpretation.
duif, (duiwe), dove; pigeon; **onder iemand se duiwe skiet**, trespass on a person's domain.
duig, (duie), stave; **in duie val**, fall to pieces, come to nothing, miscarry.
duik, vide **deuk**.
duik, (ge-), dive, dip, duck, plunge.
duikbombardering, dive-bombing.
duikbomwerper, dive-bomber.
duikboot, submarine.
duikbootjaer, submarine-destroyer.
duikel, (ge-), turn somersaults.
duikelaar, (-s), diver; tumbler (pigeon).
duikeling, (-e, -s), tumble; somersault.
duiker, (-s), diver; diving-bird; duiker (antelope); culvert; yorker (cricket).
duikergans, merganser.
duikertjie, dabchick; (Cartesian) devil (diver).
duikklopper, panel-beater.
duiklong, aqualung.
duikpak, diving-dress (-kit, -suit).
duikskyf, vanishing target.
duiktoestel, diving-apparatus, bathyscaph(e).
duikweg, subway.
duim, (-e), thumb; inch (measure); **iemand onder die – hou**, have someone under one's thumb; **iets uit jou – suie**, fabricate (invent, trump up) a story, draw on one's imagination.
duimbreed, an inch; **geen – wyk nie**, not budge an inch.
duimbreedte, the thickness of an inch.
duimgreep, thumb-index.
duimpie, (-s), (little) thumb; **(Klein) D–**, Tom Thumb; **iets op jou – ken**, have a thing at one's finger-ends, have a thing pat.
duimskroef, thumbscrew.
duimspyker, inch-nail, nail of one inch.
duimspykertjie, drawing-pin.
duimstok, footrule, inch-measure.
duin, (-e), dune, sand-hill.
duinagtig, (-e), dune-like.
duingras, beach-grass, bent-grass, lyme-grass.
duingrond, dune-soil.
duin(e)mol, dune-mole, sand-mole.
duinsand, dune-sand.
duintjie, (-s), n. small dune.
duintjie, vide **deuntjie**.
duisel, (ge-), get (grow) dizzy (giddy), reel.
duiselig, (-e), dizzy, giddy.
duiseligheid, dizziness, giddiness.
duiseling, dizziness (giddiness), vertigo.
duiselingwekkend, (-e), dizzy, giddy.
duisend, (-e), thousand; **die D– en een Nag**, the Arabian Nights Entertainments; **'n man –**, a superman, a rattling good fellow.
duisenderlei, of a thousand kinds.
duisendhoofdig, (-e), thousand-headed.
duisendjarig, millennial, of a thousand years, **die –e ryk**, the millennium.

duisendknoop, knotweed.
duisendmaal, a thousand times.
duisendpoot, millipede, centipede.
duisendskoon, sweet william, amarant(h).
duisendste, thousandth.
duisendtal, a thousand.
duisendvoud, n. multiple of 1,000.
duisendvoud(ig), a. thousandfold.
duisendwerf, a thousand times.
duiskoring, wheat.
duisman, duusman, vide **diesman**.
duister, n. dark, darkness; vide **donker**, n
duister, a. dark (night, future), obscure (style); gloomy (prospects); abstruse; **dit is vir my –**, it is inexplicable.
duisterheid, mystery, obscurity.
duisternis, dark(ness); **'n – van**, scores (crowds, a multitude) of.
duisvolk, duusvolk, vide **diesvolk**.
duit, (-e), farthing; **geen – besit nie**, be penniless; **geen (blou) – werd nie**, not worth a bean (brass button).
Duits, n. German.
Duits, (-e), a German.
Duitse masels, German measles, rubella.
Duitser, (-s), German.
Duitse sis, German print.
duiwehok, dove-cot(e), pigeon-house.
duiwemelk, pigeon's milk.
duiwel, (-s), devil; **arme –**, poor devil; **die – haal jou (sal jou ry!)**, the deuce take you!; **dan is die – los**, then the fat will be in the fire; **die – in maak**, put a person in a rage; **hy is 'n –**, he is a deuce of a fellow; he is a veritable devil; **hy is 'n – om te werk**, he is a glutton for work; **gee die – wat hom toekom**, give the devil his due; **hoe die – weet jy dit**, how the deuce do you know it?; **dank jou die –!**, I like that!, you bet!; **om die – nie!**, not for your life!; **op sy – kry**, get sound thrashing.
duiwelagtig, (-e), devilish, diabolical, fiendish.
duiwelin, (-ne), she-devil.
duiwels, (-e), devilish; diabolical, fiendish.
duiwelsbrood, death-cup.
duiwelsdoring, grapple-plant (-thorn).
duiwelsdrek, asafoetida, devil's dirt (dung).
duiwelskerwel, black-jack, sweetheart.
duiwelskind, child of the devil, imp.
duiwelskos, toadstool.
duiwelskunste, the black art, magic.
duiwelskunstenaar, magician, sorcerer.
duiwelsnaaigare, -garing, dodder.
duiwelsnuif, toadstool.
duiwelsterk, barbed-wire cloth; drill; corduroy.
duiwelstoejaer, factotum, jack-of-all-work.
duiwelswerk, a devil of a job; devil's work.
duiweltjie, little devil, imp; **– in 'n dosie**, jack-in-the-box.
dukaat, (-kate), ducat.
dukaton, (-s), ducatoon.
duld, (ge-), bear, endure, suffer (pain), tolerate (a person); stand, put up with (a treatment); **dit kan g'n uitstel – nie**, this brooks no delay.
dumdum(koeël), dumdum(-bullet).
dun, a. thin, slender (waist), rare (atmosphere); scanty (hair), sparse (population), clear (soup); **– voel**, be hungry; **– toeloop**, taper; **– gesaai**, rare, few and far between.
dun, (ge-), thin, deplete (the ranks).
dunbevolk, (-te), sparsely populated.
dunderm, small intestine.
dundoek, bunting.
dunheid, thinness; rarity; scarcity.
dunhuidig, (-e), thin-skinned, leptophylic.

dunk, idea, opinion; **'n hoë – hê van**, have a high opinion of, think highly of.
dunlippig, (-e), thin-lipped.
duntjies, thinly, lightly; slight(ly).
duo, (-'s), duo, duet.
duodesimo, (-s), duodecimo.
dupe, (-s), dupe, victim.
dupeer, (ge-), deceive, dupe; let down.
dupliek, (-e), rejoinder.
duplikaat, (-kate), duplicate.
dupliseer, (ge-), duplicate.
duplo, double; **in –**, in duplicate.
dur, sharp (mus.).
durabel, (-e), durable, lasting; expensive.
durf, n. pluck, daring, nerve.
durf, durwe, (ge-), dare; risk; venture.
durfal, dare-devil.
dus, consequently, so, therefore, thus.
dusdanig, (-e), such.
duskant, vide **deuskant**.
dusketyd, **om –**, about this time.
dusver, tot –, so far, thus far, hitherto.
dut, (ge-), doze, (take a) nap, snooze.
dutjie, (-s), doze, nap.
duur, n. duration; currency, life; **op die –**, in the long run; **van lange –**, of long duration; **hy het rus nog –**, he is very restless.
duur, **(dure)**, a. dear, expensive, costly; solemn (oath); **jou lewe – verkoop**, sell one's life dearly.
duur, (ge-), continue, last; endure; keep (of perishables).
duurkoop, dear; **goedkoop is –**, a bad bargain is dear at a farthing.
duursaam, (-same), durable, lasting.
duursaamheid, durableness, durability.
duurte, dearness, expensiveness; dearth.
duurtetoeslag, cost-of-living allowance.
duusman, duisman, vide **diesman**.
duusvolk, duisvolk, vide **diesvolk**.
dwaal, (ge-), roam, rove, wander; err.
dwaalbegrip, erroneous idea, fallacy.
dwaalleer, false doctrine, heresy.
dwaallig, will-o'-the-wisp, jack-o'-lantern.
dwaalspoor, false (wrong) track.
dwaalster, wandering star, comet.
dwaalweg, vide **dwaalspoor**.
dwaas, **(dwase)**, n. fool, silly fellow, ass.
dwaas, **(dwase)**, a. absurd, foolish, silly.
dwaasheid, folly, foolishness; piece of folly.
dwaaslik, foolishly, absurdly.
dwaling, (-e, -s), mistake; error; **in die – verkeer**, labour under a mistake (a misconception); **iemand uit die – help**, undeceive a person.
dwang, compulsion, coercion, constraint.
dwangarbeid, hard labour, penal servitude.
dwangarbeider, convict.
dwangbevel, warrant, writ.
dwangbuis, strait jacket.
dwangmaatreël, coercive measure.
dwangmiddel, means of coercion; coercive measure.
dwarrel, (ge-), whirl (round); flutter about.
dwarreling, whirl(ing); fluttering about.
dwarrelwind, whirlwind, tornado.
dwars, transverse, diagonal; cross, athwart, cross-grained, perverse, pig-headed; **iemand die voet – sit**, cross (thwart) a person; **dit sit my – in die maag**, it sticks in my gizzard.
dwarsbalk, cross-beam; cross-bar; collar-beam.
dwarsbank, cross-bench.
dwarsbanker, (-s), cross-bencher.
dwarsboom, (ge-), cross, obstruct, thwart.
dwarsdeur, right through, straight across.
dwarsdrywer, cross-patch, cross-grained fellow.
dwarsdrywery, contrariness, pigheadedness.
dwarsfluit, German flute.
dwarshou, cross-pass, cross-court shot.
dwarshout, cross-beam, cross-arm, cross-bar.
dwarskop, vide **dwarsdrywer**.
dwarskyker, grouser, grumbler.
dwarslêer, sleeper (railw.); cross-tie (architect).
dwarslyn, cross-line; transversal (maths.).
dwarsoor, right (straight) across.
dwarspaal, cross-bar.
dwarspad, cross-road.
dwarssaag, crosscut saw.
dwarsskip, transept.
dwarsskop, cross-kick, tally-ho (kick).
dwarssne(d)e, cross-section.
dwarsstraat, cross-street; side-street.
dwarsstreep, cross-line.
dwarste, in die –, across, athwart.
dwarstrek, **(dwarsge-)**, quarrel, squabble, thwart, pull (work) contrary.
dwarstrekker, vide **dwarsdrywer**.
dwarstrekkerig, (-e), contrary, cross-grained.
dwarsweg, iemand – antwoord, give a person a surly answer.
dweep, (ge-), be fanatical, gush, enthuse; **– met**, be enthusiastic about, be mad on, idolise.
dweepagtig, (-e), enthusiastic, gushing.
dweepsiek, (-e), fanatic.
dweepster, vide **dweper**.
dweepsug, fanaticism.
dweil, (ge-), n. floor-cloth; mop; swab.
dweil, (ge-), mop, scrub, wash, swab.
dwelmsmous, dope-peddler.
dwelmsugtige, dope-addict.
dwepend, (-e), fanatic(al).
dweper, (-s), fanatic; enthusiast; devotee.
dwepery, fanaticism; cult.
dwerg, (-e), dwarf, pigmy, midget.
dwergagtig, (-e), dwarfish, stunted.
dwergmotor, dustbug.
dwergvolk, dwarf-tribe, dwarfs, pigmean race.
dwing, (ge-), force, compel, constrain; nag; be on the point of; **tot betaling –**, enforce payment; **hy laat hom nie – nie**, he won't be driven; **die kind – daarom**, the child is nagging about it; **sy – om flou te word**, she is on the point of fainting.
dwingeland, (-e), tyrant.
dwingelandy, tyranny.
dwingerig, (-e), insistent; nagging.
dy, (-e), n. thigh.
dy, (ge-), thrive, prosper, succeed.
dybeen, thigh-bone, femur.
dyk, (-e), dyke, bank, embankment.
dyn(se)rig, (-e), cloudy, hazy, misty.
dyns(er)igheid, cloudiness, haziness.

E

ê(e), vide eg(ge).
eb, n. ebb(-tide).
eb, (geëb), ebb, flow back.
ebbehout, ebony.
eboniet, ebonite, vulcanite.
échec, (-s), check, setback; defeat, reverse.
edel, (-e), noble; generous; precious (metals); Sy Edele, His Honour.
edelaardig, (-e), noble, noble-minded.
edelagbaar, (-bare), honourable, worshipful; -bare, Your Honour (Worship, Lordship).
edeldenkend, (-e), high-minded.
edele(s), n. (pl.) the nobility, the nobles.
edelgesteente, gem, jewel, precious stone.
edelheid nobleness, nobility.
edelknaap, page.
edelman, (-ne), edelliede, edele(s), nobleman, noble.
edelmoedig, (-e), generous, magnanimous.
edelmoedigheid, generosity, magnanimity.
edelsteen, vide edelgesteente.
edelvrou, noblewoman, noble lady.
edelweiss, edelweiss, lion's foot.
edik, n. vinegar.
edik, (-te), n. edict, decree.
edisie, (-s), edition; issue (of a newspaper).
edukasie, education; vide opvoeding.
êe, vide eg(ge).
eed, (ede), oath; die – aflê, take the oath; die – afneem, administer the oath (to); swear (a witness); onder – (ede) verklaar, declare (state) on oath; onder ede staan, be on one's oath.
eedafneming, administration of the oath.
eedbreker, -breekster, perjurer.
eedbreuk, violation of one's oath, perjury.
eedformulier, (prescribed) oath.
eedgenoot, (-genote), confederate.
eedgenootskap, confederacy.
eekhorinkie, (-s), squirrel.
eeld, eelt, (-e), callosity, callus, horny skin.
eeld-, eeltagtig, -erig, (-e), callous, horny.
eeld-, eeltagtigheid, -erigheid, callosity.
eeld-, eeltsweer, bunion.
een, (ene, -s), n. & pro. one; someone; something; die – en ander, something, a thing or two; die – of ander, one (something) or other; ek ken – wat . . . , I know of someone who . . . ; iets –, twee, drie doen, do a thing in a trice (in a jiffy); hy is nie – om . . . , he is not one to . . . ; die – met die ander, one way and another; op – na; all except (but) one; the last but one; – vir –, one by one; vide een, ene, a.
een, ene, a. & adv. a, a certain one; man en vrou is –, husband and wife are one; – (ene) mnr. A., a certain Mr A.; – en al gehoor wees, be all ears; die ene modder (bloed), all mud (blood); die – of ander boek, some book (or other); van – leeftyd wees, be of the same age.
een-, mono-, uni-.
eenakter, one-act play, one-acter.
eenarmig, (-e), one-armed.
eenbeentjie, one leg; – speel, play hopscotch; – spring, hop on one leg.
eenbladig, (-e), one-leaved; monopetalous.
eenblommig, (-e), uniflorous, monanthous.
eend, (-e), duck; jong –, duckling.
eendaags, (-e), lasting a day; ephemeral.
eendag, once (upon a time), one day, some day.
eendagsvlieg, may-fly, ephemera.
eendagtig, (-e), ducklike.
eendeboud(jie), leg of a duck.
cendedam, duck-pond.
eendekker, (-s), monoplane.
eenders(ter), a. & adv. alike, similar.
eendjie, (-s), duckling.

eendrag, concord, harmony, union, unity; – maak mag, union is strength.
eendragtig(lik), (-e), united, unanimous.
eendstert, ducktail.
eendvoël, (wild) duck.
eenfasig, (-e), monophase.
eengalig, vide egalig.
eenhandig, (-e), one-handed.
eenheid, (-hede), unity; unit; unanimity.
eenheidsfront, united front.
eenhelmig, (-e), monandrous.
eenhoewig, (-e), one-hoofed.
eenhoofdig, (-e), monarchical (state); one head (management); monocephalous (bot.).
eenhoring, unicorn.
eenhuisig, (-e), monecious (bot.).
eenjarig, (-e), of one year, one year old.
eenkamerig, (-e), monothalamous (bot.).
eenkeer, vide eendag.
eenkennig, inkennig, (-e), shy, timid.
eenklank, unison (mus.); monophthong.
eenkleurig, (-e), of one colour, monochrome.
eenlettergrepig, (-e), monosyllabic.
eenling, (-e), individual; vide enkeling.
eenlobbig, (-e), monocotyledonous (bot.).
eenloop(geweer), single-barrelled (gun).
eenlopend, (-e), single, unmarried.
eenmaal, once; one day; – en andermaal, repeatedly; dit is nou – so, there it is; dit moet nou – gebeur, it is unavoidable.
eenmalig, (-e), single.
eenmannig, (-e), monandrous.
eenmiddelpuntig, (-e), concentric.
eenogig, (-e), one-eyed, single-eyed.
eenoog, one-eye, one-eyed person.
eenparig, (-e), unanimous(ly), with one accord, by common consent; –e beweging, uniform motion.
eenparigheid, unanimity; uniformity.
eenpersoonsbed, single bed.
eenpersoonsvliegtuig, single-seater (aeroplane).
eenrigtingstraat, one-way street.
eenrigtingsverkeer, one-way traffic.
eens, a. & adv. once (upon a time), one day, just; even; unanimous, of the same opinion; – op 'n goeie dag, one fine day; – en vir altyd, once and for all; nog – soveel, as much (many) again, twice as much (many); dit – wees, agree, be at one; ek is dit nie met myself daaroor – nie, I am in two minds about it; dit – word, come to an agreement (terms); hy kan nog nie – (eers) loop nie, he cannot even walk yet.
eensaadlobbig, (-e), monocotyledonous.
eensaadlobbiges, monocotyledons.
eensaam, (-same), solitary, lonely, secluded.
eensaamheid, loneliness, seclusion.
eensdelig, (-e), monispermic.
eensdeels, partly, on the one hand.
eensdenkend, (-e), of one mind, at one.
eensellig, (-e), unicellular, unilocular.
eenselwig, (-e), reserved, self-contained.
eenselwigheid, reserve.
eensgesind, (-e), of one mind, unanimous.
eensgesindheid, harmony, unanimity.
eenskalig, (-e), univalvular, univalve.
eensklaps, all at once, all of a sudden.
eenslag, once; one day.
eensluidend, (-e), verbally identical.
eensnarig, (-e), one-stringed.
eenstammig, (-e), monophyletic.
eenstemmig, (-e), a. unanimous; for one voice; – sing, sing in unison.
eenstemmigheid, agreement, unanimity.
eensydig, (-e), one-sided; unilateral; partial.
eensydigheid, one-sidedness, partiality.

eensyparkering, unilateral parking.
eentakkig, (-e), uniparous (bot.).
eenterm, monomial.
eentjie, one; **op jou –**, by oneself.
eentonig, (-e), monotonous; drab, tedious.
eentonigheid, drabness, monotony.
eenvormig, (-e), uniform; monotropic (maths.).
eenvormigheid, uniformity; monotropism.
eenvoud, simplicity.
eenvoudig, (-e), simple, plain, homely; **–e vergelyking**, equation of the first degree; **om die –e rede**, for the simple reason; **ek doen dit – nie**, I just won't do it; **dis – malligheid**, it is sheer madness.
eenvoudig, adv. simply, plainly.
eenvoudigheid, plainness, simplicity.
eenvoudigheidshalwe, for (the sake of) simplicity
eenvrugtig, (-e), monocarpous.
eenwiel- ..., **eenwielig**, (-e), one-wheeled.
eenwywig, (-e), monogynous.
eer, n. credit, honour, repute; **– aandoen (bewys)**, honour, do honour to, pay tribute to; **sy familie – aandoen**, be a credit to one's family; **die laaste – bewys**, render the last honours (to); **iemand die – gee van (vir)**, give a person the credit of (for); **die – hê om ...**, have the honour to inform you; **ek het die – u te berig**, I beg to inform you; **ek het die – my te noem u dienswillige**, I am, yours respectfully; **daar het jy – van**, that does you credit; **iemand se – te na kom**, wound a person's pride; **– in iets stel**, take a pride in something; **– aan wie – toekom**, honour to whom honour is due; **dit sal my 'n – wees**, I shall be honoured; **in alle – en deug**, in honour and decency; **in – hou**, honour, keep up; cherish; **jou met – kwyt van = met – afkom van**, acquit oneself with honour (credit); **op my –**, upon my honour, honour bright!; **ter ere van**, in honour of; **tot sy –**, in his honour, to his honour; **dit strek hom tot –**, it does him credit, it redounds to his honour; **iets tot iemand se – nagee**, give a person credit for something; **dit moet ek hom tot sy – nagee**, I'll say that (much) for him.
eer, adv. & conj. before; rather, sooner.
eer, (geëer), honour, respect, revere.
eerbaar, (-bare), good, honest, virtuous.
eerbetoon, **-betuiging**, **-bewys**, (mark of) honour, homage, tribute.
eerbied, respect, reverence; **met alle – vir**, with all (due) respect for.
eerbiedig, (-e), a. respectful; devout.
eerbiedig, (geëerbiedig), respect; defer to.
eerbiedigheid, respect; deference; devotion.
eerbiediging, respect; deference.
eerbiedwaardig, (-e), respectable, venerable.
eerbiedwekkend, (-e), imposing, impressive.
eerder, rather, sooner; **hoe – hoe beter (liewer)**, the sooner the better; **– meer as minder**, rather more than less.
eergestoelte, seat of honour.
eergevoel, sense of honour; pride.
eergevoelig, (-e), proud, touchy.
eergevoeligheid, sense of honour; pride.
eergierig, (-e), ambitious.
eergierigheid, ambitiousness.
eergister, the day before yesterday.
eergisteraand, **-middag**, **môre**, (-oggend), the night (afternoon, morning) before last.
eerherstel, rehabilitation.
eerlang, **-lank**, before (ere) long, shortly.
eerlik, (-e), a. & adv. honest, upright; honourable; fair, square; **– behandel**, give a square deal; **– bly**, keep straight; **'n –e kans**, a fair chance; **– waar (gesê)**, honestly, to tell the (honest) truth; **– wees teenoor jouself**, be candid (honest) with oneself.
eerlikheid, honesty, fairness; **– duur die langste**, honesty is the best policy; **in – teenoor hom**, in fairness to him.
eerloos, (-lose), dishonourable, infamous.
eerloosheid, infamy.
eerroof, calumny, defamation (of character).
eers, first, formerly; once; only; not even; before; **gister –**, not until yesterday, only yesterday; **as ek maar – daar kom**, once I get there; if I can only get there; **hy kan nog nie – (eens) loop nie**, he cannot even walk yet; **dit moet nog – blyk**, that remains to be seen; **ek moet nog – skrywe**, I have to write first; **nou –**, only now; **vir – = vereers**, for the time being, temporarily; at first.
eersaam, (-same), respectable; virtuous.
eersdaags, one of these days, shortly, soon.
eersgeboorte, primogeniture.
eersgeboortereg, birthright.
eersgebore, first-born.
eersgeborene, (-s), first-born (child).
eersgenoemde, first-mentioned; former.
eerskennis, defamation.
eerskomende, following, next.
eerste, a. & adv. first; chief; foremost; prime (minister), initial (expenses); maiden (speech, voyage); **die – die beste geleentheid**, the first opportunity (that offers itself); **– hulp (by ongelukke)**, first aid; **die –**, **die laaste**, the former, the latter; **– uitgawe**, first edition; initial expenses (outlay); **hy sou die – wees om ...**, he would be the first to ...; **in die – plek**, in the first place, first of all; **op die – gesig**, at first sight, on the face of it; **ten –**, firstly, in the first place.
eerstehands, (-e), first-hand (information).
eerstejaarkursus, first-year course.
eerstejaarstudent, freshman, first-year student.
eersteklas, adv. first-class; first-rate.
eersteklaskaartjie, first-class ticket.
eersteling, (-e), first-born, firstling; first-fruit(s); first work (of artist).
eerstemagsfaktor, **-funksie**, **-vergelyking**, linear factor (function, equation).
eerstens, first(ly), in the first place.
eersterangs, (-, -e), first-class, first-rate.
eersug, ambition.
eersugtig, (-e), ambitious.
eersvolgende, following, next.
eertyds, (-e), a. & adv. former(ly).
eervergete, devoid of honour, infamous.
eervol, (-le), honourable.
eerwaarde, reverend.
eerwaardig (-e) time-honoured (customs); venerable (man).
eerwaardigheid, venerableness.
eet, (geëet), eat; dine, take (have) one's meals; **lekker –**, enjoy a meal, do justice to a meal; **iemand die ore van die kop –**, eat a person out of house and home; **jou vol – aan iets**, eat one's fill of something; **by iemand –**, have one's meals with someone; have dinner with someone; **uit –**, dine out; **uit iemand se hand –**, feed out of someone's hand.
eetbaar, (-bare), eatable, edible.
eetbaarheid, eatableness, edibility.
eetbak feeding-trough.
eetgoed eatables; vide **eetwaar**.
eetkamer dining-room.
eetkamerstoel, dining-room chair.
eetlepel, tablespoon.
eetlus, appetite; **verandering van spys(e) gee –**, change of food whets the appetite.

eetmaal, meal; dinner, banquet.
eetplek, eating-house, restaurant.
eetsaal, dining-hall, dining-room.
eetsalon, dining-saloon (railway).
eetservies, dinner-set (-service).
eetstokkies, chopsticks.
eetwa, dinner-wag(g)on.
eetware, provisions, victuals.
eeu, (-e), century; age; **die goue –**, the golden age; **ek het jou in g'n – gesien nie**, I have not seen you for ages.
eeuelang, -lank, age-long, secular.
eeue-oud, (-oue), centuries old; time-honoured.
eeufees, centenary.
effe, level, flat, smooth; plain.
effek, (-te), effect, result; screw (on a ball); **op – bereken**, calculated for effect.
effekbejag, straining after effect, claptrap.
effekte, (pl.) shares, stocks, securities.
effektebeurs, stock-exchange, share-market.
effektehandel, stockbroking; (-jobbing).
effektehandelaar, stockbroker; (-jobber).
effektehouer, stockholder.
effektekoers, price of stocks.
effektemark, stockmarket.
effektief, (-tiewe), effective (mil.).
effektief, (-tiewe), a. effective, real.
effen, (geëffen), level, make even, smooth.
effenheid, evenness, smoothness.
effening, levelling.
effens, just; a little, slightly; a moment.
effentjies, vide **effens**.
effloresseer, (geëffloresseer), effloresce.
effloressensie, efflorescence.
effusiegesteente, effusive (extrusive) rocks.
efod, ephod.
eg, (-ge, êe), n. harrow.
eg, n. marriage, matrimony, wedlock; **in die – tree**, enter into matrimony.
eg, (-te), a. authentic, genuine, real, thorough, regular, proper; legitimate (child).
eg(ge), ê(e), geëg(ge), geê(e), harrow.
ega, (-s), consort, spouse.
egaal, (egale), even, level, smooth; **dit is my –**, it is all one (all the same) to me.
egalig, eengalig, (-e), smooth; uniform.
egalig, eengaligheid, levelness; uniformity.
egbreker, adulterer.
egbreuk, adultery.
eggenoot, (-note), husband, spouse.
eggenote, (-s), wife, spouse.
eggo, (-s), echo; vide **weerklank**.
eggolood, -soeker, echo-sounder.
Egiptenaar, (-nare, -s), Egyptian.
Egipties, (-e), Egyptian.
ego, ego, self; **sy alter –**, his alter ego (double).
egoïs, (-te), ego(t)ist, self-seeker.
egoïsme, ego(t)ism, selfishness.
egoïsties, (-e), ego(t)istic(al), selfish.
egosentries, (-e), self-centred.
egpaar, married couple.
egretreier, aigrette (egret).
egskeiding, divorce.
egskeidingsproses, divorce-suit.
egtelik, (-e), conjugal connubial, matrimonial; **die –e staat**, the wedded state.
egter, however, nevertheless, yet.
egtheid, authenticity, genuineness, legality, legitimacy; vide **eg**, a.
egverbintenis, marriage.
eie, own, private; innate, natural (gifts); peculiar; familiar, intimate; **vir – gebruik**, for one's private use; **jou – maak**, acquire, contract (a habit); master (a language); **die gewoonte is die mens –**, the habit is peculiar to man;

êrens – wees, be at home somewhere; **met iemand – wees**, be on familiar (intimate) terms with a person; **in – persoon**, in person, personally; **op – naam**, in one's own name; **op sy – (houtjie)**, off one's own bat; **uit – beweging**, of oneself, of one's own accord.
eiebaat, egoism, selfishness.
eiebelang, self-interest.
eiedunk, self-conceit.
eiegeregtig, (-(de)e), self-righteous.
eiegeregtigheid, self-righteousness.
eie(n)handig, (-e), autographic, in one's own hand(writing).
eieliefde, love of self, self-love, egotism.
eiemagtig, (-e), arbitrary, high-handed.
eien, (geëien), appropriate; recognise (a person).
eienaam, proper name.
eienaar, (-nare, -s), owner, proprietor (of a hotel); **van – verander**, change hands.
ei(g)enaardig, (-e), peculiar, singular.
ei(g)enaardigheid, peculiarity, idiosyncrasy.
einares, (-se); owner, proprietress.
eiendom, (-me), property, belongings, estate.
eiendom(me)lik, (-e), vide **ei(g)enaardig**.
eiendomsbewys, title-deed.
eiendomsreg, proprietary right.
eiehandig, vide **eie(n)handig**.
eienskap, (-pe), quality, property, attribute.
eier, (-s), egg; **'n halwe – is beter as 'n leë dop**, half a loaf is better than no bread; **op –s loop**, tread (walk) on eggs, go (walk) gingerly.
eierboer, egg-farmer, poultry-farmer.
eierboor, ovipositor.
eierbrandewyn, -drankie, egg-flip, egg-nog.
eierdans, egg-dance.
eierdooier, -door, yolk (of an egg).
eierdop, egg-shell.
eier-in-die-hoed, hat-ball (game).
eier-in-die-lepel, egg-and-spoon race.
eierkelkie, egg-cup.
eierkoek, egg-cake; omelette.
eierklitser, eierklopper, egg-beater, egg-whisk.
eierkokertjie, egg-glass, sand-glass.
eierleier, oviduct, Fallopian tube(s).
eierpannekoek, omelet(te).
eierplant, vide **brinjal**.
eierrond, eirond, (-e), egg-shaped, oval.
eiersel, egg-cell, oocyte; ovicell.
eierskuim, white-of-egg, froth.
eiersous, egg-sauce.
eierstandertjie, -stelletjie, egg-stand.
eierstok, ovary, ovarium.
eierstruif, omelet(te).
eiertjie, (-s), bird's egg; ovule.
eiervla, egg-custard.
eiesinnig, (-e), headstrong, self-willed.
eiesinnigheid, obstinacy, self-will.
eiewaan, conceitedness, self-conceit.
eiewaarde, self-esteem, self-respect.
eiewys, (self-)conceited, cocky; obstinate.
eiewysheid, obstinacy, self-conceit.
eigenaardig(heid), vide **ei(g)enaardig(heid)**
eik, (-e), oak(-tree).
eikeboom, oak-tree.
eikel, (-s), acorn; glans (anat.).
eikelaan, oak-avenue, avenue of oaks.
eiland, (-e), island; isle.
eilandbewoner, islander.
eiland(e)groep, group of islands, archipelago.
eilander, (-s), islander.
eilandryk, island-kingdom, island-empire.
eina!, interj. oh!, oh-oh!, ow!
eindbedrag, final sum.
eindbeslissing, final decision.
eindbestemming, (ultimate) destination.

einddiploma, final (leaving) certificate.
einddoel, ultimate object (aim).
einde, (-s), close, conclusion, end, termination; ending; **sy – nader, his end draws near; te dien –,** for that purpose, with that end in view; **ten –,** in order to, with a view to; **ek is ten – raad,** I am at my wits' end; **ten – loop,** draw to a close, come to an end; expire; **tot die – toe,** till the end, to the end; vide **end, ent.**
eindeksamen, final (leaving) examination.
eindelik, (-e), a. last ultimate.
eindelik, adv. last (lenth), finally, ultimately; **– en ten laaste,** at long last.
eindeloos, (-lose), endless, interminable.
eindeloosheid, endlessness, infinity.
eindig, (-e), a. finite; terminate.
eindig, (geëindig), (come to an) end, conclude, finish, stop, terminate; **– in,** end in; **– met,** end in; finish (wind) up with; result in; **– op,** end in.
eindigende: **– breuk,** terminating fraction.
eindigheid, finiteness.
eindklinker, final vowel.
eindlettergreep, final (last) syllable.
eindoogmerk, final purpose, ultimate aim.
eindoordeel, final judgment.
eindoorwinning, final victory.
eindpaal, goal, limit; winning-post.
eindpunt, end, farthest point; terminus.
eindreëling, final settlement.
eindresultaat, final result, upshot.
eindsitting, closing session, last meeting.
eindskikking, final arrangement.
eindstandig, (-e), end-: terminal (bot.).
eindstemming, decisive vote.
endterm, last term.
eindvlak, end-plane, base, terminal.
eindvonnis, final judgment (sentence).
eindwedstryd, final (match).
einste, same.
eintlik, -(e), a. actual, proper, real; **–e breuk,** proper fraction.
eintlik, adv. actually, properly, really; **dit is – jammer,** it is a pity when you come to think of it; **wat wil jy nou – van my hê?,** what exactly do you want of me?
eirond, vide **eierrond**.
eis, (-e), n. claim, demand; requirement, requisite; petition (for divorce): **– tot (vir) skadevergoeding,** claim for damages; **'n – instel,** bring (put in) a claim (for); **'n – teen iemand instel vir,** sue a person for; **hoë –e stel,** make high demands; require a high standard; **aan die –e voldoen,** come up to requirements; **na die –,** properly, as required; **na (volgens) die –e van die tyd,** up-to-date; **van sy – afsien,** waive one's claim.
eis, (geëis), claim, demand; require (attention).
eiser, (-s), **eiseres**, (-se), claimant, plaintiff.
eisteddfod, (-au, -s), eisteddfod.
eiwit, eierwit, white of an egg, albumen.
eiwithoudend, (-e), albuminous, glaireous.
eiwitstof, albuminold, protein.
ek, ekke, I; **die ek,** the self; **sy eie ek,** his own self; **ek vir my . . . ,** I for one.
ekheid, one's own self, the ego individuality.
ekkerig, (-e), egotistic, self-centred; subjective.
eklekties, (-e), eclectic.
eklektisisme, eclecticism.
eklips, (-e), eclipse.
eklipseer, (geëklipseer), eclipse.
ekonomie, economy; economics.
ekonomies, (-e), economic(al).
ekonomiseer, (geëkonomiseer), economize.
ekonoom, (-nome), economist.

eksak, (-te), exact, precise; strict.
eksaktheid, exactness, exactitude, preciseness, precision; strictness.
eksamen, (-s), examination; **'n – aflê (doen),** sit for an examination; pass an examination; **– afneem,** examine.
eksamengeld, examination-fee.
eksamenopgaaf, **-opgawe**, examination-paper.
eksamenstelsel, examination-system.
eksamenvak, subject of examination.
eksaminadus, (-di, -se), examinee, candidate for an examination.
eksaminator, (-e, -s), examiner.
eksamineer, (geëksamineer), examine.
eksegeet, (-gete), exegete, exegetist.
eksegese, exegesis.
eksegeties, (-e), exegetic.
eksekusie, (-s), execution.
eksekuteur, (-e, -s), executor.
eksekutrise, (-s), executrix.
eksellensie, (-s), excellency; **Sy (U) E–,** His (Your) Excellency.
eksellent, (-e), excellent.
eksemplaar, (-plare), specimen, sample; copy.
eksentriek, (-e), a. eccentric, odd; **'n –e persoon,** an eccentric person, a crank (faddist).
eksentries, (-e), eccentric.
eksentrisiteit, (-e), eccentricity.
eksepsie, (-s), exception; **– neem teen,** take exception to, take umbrage at.
eksepsioneel, (-nele), exceptional.
ekserp, (-te), excerpt, extract, abstract.
ekserpeer, (geëkserpeer), epitomize, make an abstract (excerpt, extract) of.
ekserseer, (geëkserseer), exercise, drill.
eksersisie, (-s), drill, exercise, practice.
eksersisieterrein, **-veld**, drill-ground.
ekses, (-se), excess.
eksessief, (-siewe), exessive.
ekshibisionis, (-te), exhibitionist.
eksie-perfeksie, perfect, smart; punctilious.
eksistensie, existence.
eksklusief, (-siewe), a. & adv. exclusive(ly).
ekskommunikasie, excommunication.
ekskommuniseer, (geëkskommuniseer), excommunicate.
ekskursie, (-s), excursion, outing, trip.
ekskursiekaartjie, excursion-ticket.
ekskuseer, (geëkskuseer), excuse, pardon.
ekskuus, (-kuse), apology; excuse, pardon; **– maak,** apologise; **ek vra u om –,** I beg your pardon.
eksodus, exodus, trek (to the coast).
eksoteries, (-e), exoteric.
eksoties, (-e), exotic.
ekspansie, expansion.
ekspansief, (-siewe), expansive.
ekspatriasie, expatriation.
ekspatrieer, (geëkspatrieer), expatriate.
ekspedisie, (-s), expedition; forwarding.
ekspedisieleër, expeditionary force.
eksperiment, (-e), experiment.
eksperimenteel, (-tele), experimental.
eksperimenteer, (geëksperimenteer), experiment.
ekspert, (-e), expert.
eksplikasie, (-s), explication, explanation.
ekspliseer, (geëkspliseer), explicate, explain.
eksploitasie, exploitation, working; **in –,** open to traffic; in operation.
eksploitasiekoste, working-expenses.
eksploiteer, (geëksploiteer), exploit (work), run (a railway-line); exploit; grind down (workers); trade on (a secret).
eksplorasie, exploration.
eksploreer, (geëksploreer), explore.

eksplosie, (-s), detonation, explosion.
eksplosief, (-siewe), explosive.
eksponeer, (geëksponeer), expose.
eksport, export(ation).
eksporteer, (geëksporteer), export.
eksporteur, (-s), exporter.
eksposant, (-e), exhibitor.
eksposeer, (geëksposeer), exhibit.
eksposisie, exhibition, show; exhibit.
ekspres, n. express (train).
ekspres, adv. expressly, intentionally, purposely, on purpose.
ekspressie, (-s), expression.
ekspressief, (-siewe), expressive.
ekspressionis, (-te), expressionist.
ekspressionisme, expressionism.
eksprestrein, express (train).
ekstase, ecstasy, rapture.
ekstaties, (-e), ecstatic, in ecstasy.
ekstensief, (-siewe), extensive.
ekster, (-s), magpie.
eksterieur, (-e), exterior.
ekstern, (-e), external.
ekstra, (-s), n. extra; spare.
ekstra, a. extra, additional, special.
ekstra, adv. specially, especially.
ekstraheer, (geëkstraheer), extract.
ekstrak, (-te), extract; excerpt (from a book).
ekstratjie, (-s), extra.
ekstremis, (-te), extremist.
ekstremisties, (-e), extremistic.
ekwator, equator; vide ewenaar.
ekwatoriaal, (-iale), equatorial.
ekwinoks, (-e), equinox.
ekwinoksiaal, (-iale), equinoctial.
ekwipasie, equipage, turnout; crew.
ekwivalent, (-e), equivalent.
el, (-le), ell; yard.
eland, (-e), eland (S.A.); elk (Eur).
elasties, (-e), n. elastic.
elasties, (-e), a. elastic.
elastisiteit, elasticity.
elders, elsewhere; êrens -, somewhere else; nêrens
 - nie, nowhere else; oral -, anywhere (everywhere) else.
elegansie, elegance.
elegant, (-e), elegant, stylish.
elegie, (-ë), elegy.
elegies, (-e), elegiac.
eleksie, (-s), election.
elektries, (-e), electric; -e kroonlamp, electrolier, -e sentrale, power-station; -e stroom, electric current.
elektries, adv. electrically.
elektrifikasie, electrification.
elektrifiseer, (geëlektrifiseer), electrify.
elektriseer, (geëlektriseer), electrify, electrize.
elektriseermasjien, electrical machine.
elektrisering, electrification; electrization.
elektrisiën, electrician.
elektrisiteit, electricity; deur - ontleed, electrolyse; deur - teregstel (dood), electrocute.
elektrode, (-s), electrode.
elektrokusie, electrocution.
elektroliet, (-e), electrolyte.
elektrolise, electrolysis.
elektroliseer, (geëktroliseer), electrolyse.
elektrolities, (-e), electrolytic.
elektromagnetisme, electro-magnetism.
elektrometer, electrometer.
elektromotor, electric motor.
elektron, (-e), electron.
elektrone-mikroskoop, electron microscope.
elektronies, electronic.
elektroskoop, (-skope), electroscope.

elektrotegniek, electro-technics, electrical engineering.
elektrotegnies, (-e), electro-technical; -e ingenieur, electrical engineer.
element, (-e), element; (electric) cell; constituent; in sy - wees, be in one's element.
elementêr, (-e), elementary.
elevator, (-s), elevator; lift.
elf, (elwe), n. elf, fairy; shad.
elf, (-s, elwe), n. & a. eleven.
elfde, eleventh; ter -r ure, at the eleventh hour, at the last minute.
elf-en-dertigste, op sy -, at a snail's pace, in a kind of way.
elfhoek, (h)endecagon.
elfie, (-s), shad.
elftal, eleven.
elfuur, eleven o'clock.
elfvoud, multiple of eleven.
elfvoudig, (-e), elevenfold.
elideer, (geëlideer), elide.
elikser, (-s), elixir.
eliminasie, elimination.
elimineer, (geëlimineer), eliminate.
elisie, (-s), elision.
elk, (-e), each, every, any; -e oomblik, any moment.
elkeen, each, everyone, anyone; dis - se gouigheid, it is everybody's lookout.
elkers, every now and then (again).
ellelang, -lank, long-drawn.
ellende, distress, misery, wretchedness.
ellendeling, (-e), villain, wretch.
ellendig, (-e), miserable, wretched; rotten; hy lê - siek, he is seriously ill.
ellendigheid, miserableness, wretchedness.
ellepyp, ulna.
ellips, (-e), ellipse; ellipsis (gramm.).
ellipsoïde, (-e), ellipsoid.
ellipties, (-e), elliptic(al); oval.
elmboog, (-boë), elbow; die - lig, „lift the elbow", be addicted to drink.
elmboogvet, elbow-grease.
elokusie, elocution.
elongasie, elongation, phase (astr.).
elpebeen, ivory.
els, (-e), awl.
els, (-e), alder(-tree).
Elsasser, (-s), Alsation.
Elsassies, (-e), Alsation.
elsie: bont -, avocet; rooipoot -, stilt.
elwedans, fairy-dance.
Elysies, Elisies, (-e), Elysian.
emalje, enamel.
emaljeer, (geëm-), enamel.
emansipasie, emancipation.
emansipeer, (geëmansipeer), emancipate.
embleem, (-bleme), emblem.
emblematies, (-e), emblematic(al).
embrio, (-'s), embryo.
embriologie, embryology.
embrionaal, (-nale), embryonic.
emendasie, (-s), emendation.
emendeer, (geëmendeer), emend.
emeritaat, superannuation.
emeritus, (-se, -ti), emeritus, retired.
emfase, emphasis.
emfaties, (-e), emphatic.
emigrant, (-e), emigrant.
emigrasie, emigration.
emigreer, (geëmigreer), emigrate.
eminensie, eminence; Sy E-, His Eminence.
eminent, (-e), eminent.
emir, (-s), emir.
emissie, issue.

emissiekoers, price of issue.
emmer, (-s), bucket, pail.
emoe, (-s), emu.
emolumente, emoluments; perquisites.
emosie, (-s), emotion.
emosioneel, (-nele), emotional.
empirie, empiricism.
empiries, (-e), empiric(al).
emplojeer, (geëmplojeer), employ.
en, and; – Jan – Piet, both John and Peter.
end, (eindes), end, close, conclusion, termination; daar het geen – aan gekom nie, there was no end to it; daar moet 'n – aan kom, that must stop; 'n – maak aan, put an end (a stop) to; terminate, bring to a close; 'n – neem, come to an end; nie die – van iets sien nie, see no end to a thing; op die ou –, at the end, at long last; sonder –, without end, endless; hy is sonder –, there is no end to him; teen die – van, towards the end of; tot die – toe, till the end; tot 'n – kom, come to an end, terminate; van die een – tot die ander, from end to end; vide **einde**, **entjie**.
end . . . , vide **eind-** . . .
endelderm, rectum.
endemie, endemic (disease).
endemies, (-e), endemic.
endossant, (-e), endorser.
endosseer, (geëndosseer), endorse.
endossement, endorsement.
endrym, eindrym, final rhyme.
endstasie, eindstasie, terminus.
end-uit, right to the end.
ene, vide **een** a. & adv.
ene male: ten –, absolute, altogether.
energie, energy.
energiek, (-e), energetic, active, pushing.
enerlei, of the same kind (soort).
eng, (-e), narrow, tight; narrow-minded.
engageer, (geëngageer), engage.
engel, (-e, -s), angel.
engelagtige, (-e), angelic, cherubic, seraphic.
engelagtigheid, angelic nature.
engelekoor, angelic choir, choir of angels.
engelgesang, hymn of angels.
engeleskaar, host of angels.
engelhaai, angel-fish.
Engels, (-e), n. & a. English; Aglican (Church); –e siekte, rickets; –e sleutel, monkey-wrench, shifting-spanner; –e sout, Epsom salt; –e vlag, Union Jack.
Engelsgesind, (-e), pro-English.
Engelsman, (Engelse), Englishman.
Engelssprekend, (-e), English-speaking.
enghartig, (-e), narrow-minded.
engheid, narrowness, tightness; vide **eng**.
engte, (-s), narrowness; defile (between mountains); strait (of the sea); isthmus.
enig, (-e), only, sole, one (hope); unique; – en alleen, simply and solely; – in sy soort, unique (of its kind).
enigeen, anyone.
enigermate, to some extent, somewhat.
eniggebore, only begotten (Bib).
enigheid, loneliness; in my –, by myself.
enigma, (-s), enigma, puzzle.
enigmaties, (-e), enigmatic, puzzling.
enigsins, somewhat, slightly, remotely, after a fashion; as dit – moontlik is, if it is at all possible.
enigste, only, sole; vide **enig**.
enjambement, enjambment.
enkel, (-s), n. ankle.
enkel, (-e), a. single; –e reis, single journey; 'n –e woordjie just one word; 'n – keer, once; –e ure, a few hours.

enkel, adv. only, merely, simply; – en alleen, simply and solely.
enkelbreed(te), single width.
enkeld, pred. a. single.
enkelgewrig, ankle-joint.
enkeling, (-e), individual.
enkelloop(geweer), single-barrelled gun.
enkelskut, ankle-guard.
enkelspel, single(s).
enkelspeler, singles-player.
enkelspoor, single-track.
enkelvoorploeg, single-furrow plough.
enkelvoud, singular (number).
enkelvoudig, (-e), singular; simple (fraction).
enklisis, enclisis; enclitic.
enklities, (-e), enclitic.
enorm, (-e), enormous.
enormiteit, (-e), enormity.
ensceneer, (geënsceneer), stage, stage-manage.
enscenering, staging.
ensikliek, (-e), encyclical (letter).
ensiklopedie, (-ieë), encyclopaedia.
ent, (-e), n. end; piece; length; distance, way; tail; 'n hele –, a long way; far on; daarmee kom ek 'n hele –, it will go far to (towards) . . . , 'n hele – in die sestig, well on in the sixties; aan die ander – van die wêreld, at the back of beyond; die kortste – trek, have the worst of it; aan die langste – trek, have the best of it, come out on top; jy het dit by die regte –, you are right.
ent, (-e), graft; inoculation; vaccination.
ent, (geënt), graft; inoculate; vaccinate.
enter, (-s), n. grafter; inoculator; vaccinator.
enter, (geënter), board (a ship).
enterhaak, grapnel, grappling-iron.
entiteit, (-e), entity.
entjie, end, stump, piece; short distance.
entmes, grafting-knife.
entoesias, (-te), n. enthusiast; fan.
entoesiasme, enthusiasm.
entoesiasties, (-e), enthusiastic.
entomologie, entomology.
entréegeld, admission-fee; entrance-fee (as member).
entrepôt, bonded warehouse.
entstof, vaccine.
entwas, grafting-wax.
envelop, (-pe), envelope; vide **koevert**.
eolies, (-e), aeolian (rocks).
eolusharp, Aeolian harp.
epentese, epenthesis.
epenteties, (-e), epenthetic.
epidemie, (-ë, -s), epidemic.
epidemies, (-e), epidemic.
epidiaskoop, (-skope), epidiascope.
epiek, epic poetry.
epies, (-e), epic.
epigram, (-me), epigram.
epigrammaties, (-e), epigrammatic.
epikuris, (-te), epicure.
epikurisme, epicurism.
epikuristies, (-e), epicurean.
epilepsie, epilepsy.
epilepties, (-e), epileptic.
epiloog, (-loë, -loge), epilogue.
episkopaal(s), (-se), episcopal.
episode, (-s), episode.
episodies, (-e), episodic.
epistel, (-s), epistle.
epiteel, epithelium.
epiteton, (-eta), epitheton, epithet.
epos, (-se), epic(-poem), epopee.
epoulet, (-te), epaulet(te); shoulder-knot.

erbarm, (het –): jou – oor, have (take) pity on, compassionate.
erbarming, compassion, pity; mercy.
erbarmlik, (-e), lamentable, miserable, pitiable, pitiful; rotten (road), wretched.
erbarmlikheid, wretchedness; vide **erbarmlik.**
erd, n. earth; clay; **van –,** of clay.
erd, n. fireplace; vide **haard, herd.**
erd, (geërd), earth (mould) up.
erd(e)- . . . , earth(en), clay.
erdepot, earthenware-pot.
erdeskottel, earthenware-dish.
erdewerk, crockery, earthenware, pottery.
erdvark, aardvark, ant-eater, ant-bear.
erdvarkgat, ant-eater hole, ant-bear hole.
erdwurm, earthworm.
ere, n. honour; glory; vide **eer,** n.
erebaantjie, post of honour, honorary post.
ereblyk, mark of honour.
ereboog, triumphal arch.
ereburger, freeman.
ereburgerskap, freedom (of a city).
erediens, public worship.
eredokter, doctor honoris causa.
eredoktoraat, honorary doctor's degree.
eregas, guest of honour.
eregraad, honorary degree.
erekroon, crown of honour.
erelid, honorary member.
erelidmaatskap, honorary membership.
eremedalje, medal of honour (merit).
erenaam, name of honour.
êrens, somewhere; **– mee belas wees,** be charged with something.
erepenning, medal of honour.
ereplaas, -plek, place of honour.
erepoort, vide **ereboog.**
erepos, vide **erebaantjie.**
erepresident, honorary president.
eresaak, affair of honour.
eresaluut, salute.
eresekretaris, honorary secretary.
ereskote, (pl.) salute.
ereskuld, debt of honour.
ereteken, mark of honour; badge of honour.
eretitel, title of honour, honorary title.
erevoorsitter, honorary president.
erewag, guard of honour.
erewoord, word of honour; parole (mil.).
erf, (erwe), n. erf, plot; premises.
erf, erwe, (geërf, geërwe), inherit, succeed to (a title).
erfdeel, heritage, (hereditary) portion.
erf(e)nis, heritage, inheritance.
erfgeld, money inherited; **– is swerfgeld,** lightly come, lightly go.
erfgenaam, (-name), heir.
erfgename, (-s), heiress.
erfgoed, estate, heritage, inheritance.
erflaatster, (-s), testatrix.
erflater, (-s), testator; devisor.
erflating, bequest, testation; legacy.
erflik, (-e), a. & adv. hereditary; **– belas wees,** be a victim to heredity; **–e eienskappe,** inherited characteristics.
erflikheid, heredity.
erflikheidsleer, genetics.
erfoom, legacy-uncle.
erfopvolger, successor.
erfopvolging, succession.
erfpag, quitrent-tenure; quitrent.
erfporsie, heritage, inheritance, share.
erfprins(es), hereditary prince(ss).
erfreg, law of succession, hereditary law, right of succession; hereditary right.

erfskuld, hereditary debt; hereditary sin.
erfsonde, original sin.
erfstuk, heirloom.
erftante, legacy-aunt.
erfvyand, hereditary enemy.
erg, n.; **sonder –,** unintentionally; unsuspectingly; without malice; **hy het daar g'n – in nie,** he is not aware of it.
erg, n. erg, ergon (unit of power).
erg, (-e), a. bad; ill; severe.
erg, adv. badly, severely, very; **al te –,** too bad; **– beskadig,** badly damaged; **hy maak dit te –,** he is going too far.
erg, (geërg), vide **erge(r), geërge(r).**
ergens, vide **êrens.**
erger, a. & adv. worse; **des te –,** so much the worse, vide **erg,** a. and adv.
erge(r), [geërge(r)], annoy, vex; shock, give offence; **jou –,** be annoyed.
ergerlik, (-e), annoying, provoking; offensive, scandalous, shocking.
ergerlikheid, annoyance, vide **ergerlik.**
ergernis, (-se), offence, scandal; annoyance, nuisance, vexation; **– gee,** give trouble; **tot groot – van,** to the great annoyance of.
ergo, ergo, therefore.
ergste, worst; **op die (sy) –,** at the (its) worst; **in die – geval,** if the worst comes to the worst.
erken, (het –), acknowledge, admit, grant; confess (guilt); **nie – nie,** repudiate.
erkende, acknowledged; admitted; approved.
erkenning, acknowledgment; admission; confession; **ter – van,** in recognition of.
erkentlik, (-e), grateful, thankful.
erkentlikheid, gratitude.
erkent(e)nis, acknowledgment; confession.
erlang, (het –), acquire, gain, obtain.
erns, earnest(ness), seriousness, gravity.
ernstig, (-e), a. and adv. earnest (endeavour); serious, grave (condition), severe (illness); grave (face); **iets – insien,** take a grave view of something; **nie – nie,** not really mean; **neem dit nie – op nie,** don't take it seriously.
ernstigheid, earnestness, gravity, seriousness.
erosie, erosion.
eroties, (-e), erotic.
ertappel, vide **aartappel.**
ertjie, (-s), pea.
ertjiedop, pea-pod, pea-shell.
ertjieso(e)p, pea-soup.
erts, (-e), ore.
ertshoudend, (-e), ore-bearing.
ertslaag, ore-deposit.
ertsstof, ore-dust.
erudisie, erudition.
erupsie, (-e), eruption.
eruptief, (-tiewe), eruptive.
ervaar, (het –), experience.
ervare, experienced, expert, practised.
ervarenheid, experience, skill.
ervaring, (-e, -s), experience; **uit (van) –,** by experience.
es, (-se), n. 1. fireplace, hearth.
es, (-se), n. 2. ash(-tree).
es, (-se), n. 3. sharp turn; **–se gooi,** take sharp turns.
esdoring, maple.
esel, (-s), ass, donkey; blockhead; dunce; easel.
eselagtig, (-e), asinine; stupid.
eselagtigheid, asinine behaviour, stupidity.
eselhings, jack-ass.
eselin, (-ne), eselmerrie, she-ass, jenny-ass.
eselsbrug, ass's bridge, pons asinorum.
esel(s)dom, (-me), asinine, stupid.
eselskop, ass's head (lit.); blockhead.

eselsoor, ass's ear; dog's ear (of pages).
eselwa, donkey-wag(g)on.
eshout, Cape ash, dog-plum.
eskader, (-s), squadron (naval).
eskadriel, (-le), eskadrielje, (-s), squadron (airforce).
eskadron, (-s), squadron (mil.).
eskalade, (-s), escalade.
eskapade, (-s), escapade.
Eskimo, (-'s), Eskimo (Esquimau).
eskort, (-e), escort.
eskorteer, (geëskorteer), escort.
esoteries, (-e), esoteric.
esp, (-e), asp(-tree), aspen.
esparto(gras), alfa, esparto, Spanish grass.
esplanade, (-s), esplanade.
essaai, (-e), assay.
essaieer, (geëssaieer), assay (essay).
essaieur, (-s), assayer (essayer).
essehout, vide eshout.
essens, essence.
essensie, essence, quintessence.
essensieel, (-siële), essential.
estafet, (-te), dispatch-rider, estafette.
ester, ester, ethereal salt.
estetiek, estetika, aesthetics.
esteties, (-e) aesthetic(al).
estetika, vide estetiek.
etagewoning, flat; apartment-house.
etalage, (-s), show-window; display.
etaleer, (geëtaleer), display.
ete, food, fare; meal, dinner; onder (na, voor) die –, during (after, before) meals.
etenstyd, meal-time, dinner-time.
etensuur, dinner-hour.
eter, (-s), eater.
eter, ether.
etergolf, ether-wave.
eteries, (-e), ethereal.
etery, eating.
Ethiopië, Ethiopia.
Ethiopies, (-e), Ethiopian.
etiek, vide etika.
eties, (-e), ethical; ethic (dative).
etika, etiek, ethics.
etiket, (-te), etiquette; label.
etiketjie, (-s), label, ticket.
etimologie, (-ë), etymology.
etimologies, (-e), etymological.
etimoloog, (-loë), etymologist.
etioleer, (geëtioleer), etiolate.
etiologie, etiology.
etlike, several, some.
etmaal, twenty-four hours.
etnograaf, (-grawe), ethnographer.
etnografie, ethnography.
etnografies, (-e), ethnographic(al).
etnologie, ethnology.
etnologies, (-e), ethnologic(al).
etnoloog, (-loë, loge), ethnologist.
ets, (-e), n. etching.
ets, (geëts), etch.
etsnaald, etching-needle.
etter, n. discharge, (purulent) matter, pus.
etter, (geëtter), fester, suppurate, ulcerate.
etteragtig, (-e), purulent.
eucharistie, eucharist.
eucharisties, (-e), eucharistic.
eufemisme, (-s), euphemism.
eufemisties, (-e), euphemistic.
eufonie, euphony.
eufonies, (-e), euphonic.
eugenetiek, eugenics.
eugeneties, (-e), eugenic.
eukaliptus, eucalyptus.

eukaliptusolie, eucalyptus-oil.
euntjie, uintjie, (-s), edible bulb.
eunug, (-e, -s), eunuch.
Eurasies, (-e), Eurasian.
euritmiek, eurhythmics.
euritmies, (-e), eurhythmic.
Europeaan, (-ane), European.
Europeër, (-s), European.
Europees, (-pese), European.
euwel, (-s), evil; defect, fault; – dui, take amiss.
euweldaad, crime, misdeed, outrage.
euwelmoed, insolence, wantonness.
evakueer, (geëvakueer), evacuate.
evangelie, (-s), gospel, evangel; dis nie alles – nie, it is not all gospel-truth; vir – aanneem, accept as gospel(-truth).
evangeliebediening, ministry (of the Gospel).
evangeliedienaar, minister of the Gospel.
evangeliegesinde, (-s), Evangelic(al).
evangelieprediker, preacher of the Gospel, evangelist.
evangelies, (-e), evangelic(al).
evangeliewoord, the Gospel.
evangelis, (-te), evangelist.
evangelisasie, evangelization.
evangelisties, (-e), evangelistic.
evenement, (-e), event, occurrence.
eventualiteit, (-e), contingency, eventuality.
eventueel, (-uele), a. & adv. possible, potential; by chance; eventuele onkoste sal vergoed word, any expenses will be made good; as hy – sou besluit, in case he should decide.
evolueer, (geëvolueer), evolve.
evolusie, evolution.
evolusieleer, theory of evolution.
evolusionisme, evolutionism.
ewe, n., dis my om die –, it is all the same to me; om die – wat, no matter what.
ewe, a. even; – of onewe, odd or even.
ewe, adv. as, even, just, equally, quite; hulle is – oud, they are of an age, they are of the same age; 'n – groot aantal, an equal number; hy is – ongeërg, he is quite unconcerned; ewe veel, as much; the same; ek hou van altwee –, I like both the same, I like the one as much as the other; ewe ver, equidistant, equally (just as) far.
eweas, ewenas, (just) as (like).
ewebeeld, likeness, picture, counterpart, image;
ewe-eens, eweneens, also, likewise, too.
eweknie, compeer, equal, match.
ewemaat, symmetry.
ewemagtig, (-e), proportional; – deel, aliquot part.
ewemens, fellow-man.
ewemin, just as little.
ewenaar, n. equator; tongue (of balance); swingle beam [of wag(g)on]; differential.
ewenaar, (geëwenaar), equal, be a match for.
ewenaarsratte, differential-gears.
ewenaaste, fellow-man, neighbour.
ewenagslyn, equator, equinoctial (line).
ewenas, vide eweas.
eweneens, vide ewe-eens.
ewe(n)wel, however, nevertheless, still, yet.
eweredig, (-e), proportional, proportionate, commensurate; –e verteenwoordiging, proportional representation.
eweredigheid, proportion; in omgekeerde –, in inverse ratio, inversely proportional.
eweseer, as much; alike; – as, as much as.
eweso, likewise; as.
ewewel, vide ewe(n)wel.
ewewig, balance, equilibrium, poise; labiele (onvaste, wankelbare) –, unstable equilibrium,

stabiele (vaste -), stable equilibrium; **die -bewaar, verloor,** keep (lose) one's balance; **die staatkundige -,** the balance of power; **in -,** in equilibrium.
ewewigsleer, statics.
ewewigspunt, centre of gravity.
ewewigstoestand, (state of) equilibrium.
ewewigtig, (-e), evenly balanced; level-headed.
ewewigtigheid, balance, level-headedness.
ewewydig, (-e), parallel.

ewewydigheid, parallelism.
ewig, (-e), a. & adv. eternal (life), perpetual (snow), perennial (youth), everlasting; **dit is - jammer,** it's a thousand pities; **ten -e dage,** for ever, for all time, in perpetuity; **vir -,** for ever.
ewigdurend, (-e), everlasting, perpetual.
ewigheid, eternity; **die - ingaan,** pass into eternity; **in der - nie,** never; **tot in (der) -,** to all eternity.
ewwa-trewwa, (-s), yellow orchid.

F

faal, (ge-), fail, be unsuccessful; miss.
faam, reputation, repute.
faas, (fase) fesse.
fabel, (-s), n. fable; fabrication, fiction.
fabel, (ge-), fable; romance; twaddle.
fabelagtig, (-e), fabulous; incredible.
fabelleer, mythology.
fabriek, (-e), factory, mill, works.
fabriek, (ge-), knock together, concoct.
fabriekmatig, (-e), a. & adv. machine-made, manufactured; mechanically.
fabrieksarbeid, factory-work.
fabrieksarbeider, factory-hand, -worker.
fabrieksgoed, manufactured articles (goods).
fabrieksmeisie, factory-girl, girl-hand.
fabrieksmerk, trade-mark.
fabrieksnywerheid, manufacturing industry.
fabriekstad, manufacturing-town.
fabrieksware, factory-goods.
fabriekswerker, vide **fabrieksarbeider**.
fabriekswese, factory-system; manufacturing industry.
fabriekswinkel, canteen.
fabrikaat, (-kate), manufacture, make; fabric.
fabrikant, (-e), manufacturer, maker.
fabrikasie, (-s), manufacture; fabrication.
fabriseer, (ge-), manufacture; concoct.
fabuleus, (-e), fabulous; incredible.
fagot, (-te), bassoon.
faikonta, as if, make believe, quasi.
fakir, (-s), fakir.
fakkel, (-s), torch, flare.
fakkeldraer, torch-bearer.
fakkel(op)tog, torchlight procession.
fakkelpistool, flare pistol.
faksie, (-s), faction.
faksimilee, (-s), facsimile.
faksimilee-telegrafie, phototelegraphy.
faktitief, (-tiewe), factitive.
faktor, (-e), factor; **enkelvoudige –**, prime factor; **ontbind in –e**, factorise.
faktotum, (-s), factotum, handyman.
faktureer, (ge-), invoice.
faktuur, (-ture), bill, invoice.
faktuurprys, invoice-price.
fakultatief, (-tiewe), facultative, optional.
fakulteit, (-e), faculty; board.
falanks, (-e), phalanx.
faljiet, bankrupt, insolvent.
falset, falsetto.
familiaar, (-iare), familiar, chummy, free, intimate; **– omgang met**, be on familiar (intimate) terms with.
familiariteit, (-e), familiarity; **jou –e veroorloof**, take liberties.
familie, (-s), family; relations, relatives; **ons is ver aangetroude –**, relations by marriage; **dit sit in die –**, it runs in the family.
familieaangeleentheid, family-affair.
familieband, family-tie.
familiebetrekking, relative, relationship.
familiedrama, domestic drama.
familiefees, family-feast (-gathering).
familiegek, overfond of one's relatives.
familiekring, family-circle, domestic circle.
familiekwaal, hereditary malady; family-failing, **dit is 'n –**, it runs in the family.
familielewe, family-life, domestic life.
familielid, member of a family; relative.
familienaam, family-name; surname.
familieomstandighede, family-affairs.
familiesake, family-matters.
familietrek, family-likeness.
familietrots, family-pride.
familiewapen, family (coat of) arms.

fanatiek, (-e), fanatic(al).
fanatikus, (-se, -ici), fanatic.
fanatisme, fanaticism.
fanfare, (-s), fanfare, flourish (of trumpets).
fantas, (-te), dreamer, phantast, visionary.
fantaseer, (ge-), indulge in fancies, imagine, romance, improvise (mus.).
fantasie, (-ë), fancy, imagination, phantasy; fantasia (mus.).
fantasie-artikels, -goed, fancy-articles.
fantasiekostuum, fancy-costume (-dress).
fantasmagorie, phantasmagoria.
fantasties, (-e), fantastic; wild (stories).
fantoom, (-tome), phantom.
farinks, pharynx.
fariseër, (-s), Pharisee; hypocrite.
farisees, (-sese), Pharisaic(al); hypocritical.
farmakologie, pharmacology.
farmakoloog, (-loë, -loge), pharmacologist.
farmaseuties, (-e), pharmaceutical.
Fascis, (-te), Fascist.
Fascisme, Fascism.
Facisties, (-e), Fascist.
fase, (-s), phase, stage (of an illness).
faset, (-te), facet.
fasiel, (-e), facile.
fasiliteit, (-e), facility.
fat, (-te), dandy, fop, nut (knut), swell.
fataal, (-ale), fatal.
fatalisties, (-e), fatalistic.
fataliteit, (-e), fatality.
fatsoen, (-e), n. fashion, form, make, shape, cut (of clothes); decency; decorum, good breeding (manners); **jou – ophou**, live up to one's station; keep up appearances; **met –**, decently, with decency; **uit sy –**, out of shape; **vir die –**, for form's sake.
fatsoeneer, (ge-), fashion, mould, shape.
fatsoenlik, (e), a. decent, respectable, proper (behaviour).
fatsoenlik, adv. decently, respectably.
fatsoenlikheid, decency, respectability.
fatsoen(likheid)shalwe, for decency's sake.
fatterig, (-e), dandified, flashy, foppish.
fatum, (fata) fate.
faun, (-e), faun.
fauna, fauna.
faveur, favour; **ten –e van**, in favour of.
favoriet, (-e), favourite.
favoritisme, favouritism.
Februarie, February.
federaal, (-ale), federal.
federalisme, federalism.
federasie, (-s), federation.
federeer, (ge-), federate.
fee, (feë), fairy.
feeagtig, (-e), fairylike.
feeks, (-e), shrew, termagant, virago, vixen.
feëland, feëryk, fairyland.
feëriek, (-e), fairylike; vide **feeagtig**.
fees, (-te), feast, festival, festivity, fête, treat.
feesdag, festival (-day).
feesdis, festive board.
feesdronk, toast.
feesgelag, symposium.
feesgesang, festive song.
feesmaal, banquet.
feesrede, speech of the day; inaugural speech.
feesredenaar, speaker of the day.
feesstemming, festive mood.
feestelik, (-e), a. & adv. festal, festive, **iemand – onthaal**, entertain (fête) someone.
feestelikheid, festivity, merrymaking.
feesvier, (feesge-), celebrate, feast, make merry.
feesvierder, reveller; celebrator.

feesviering, feasting; celebration.
feesvreugde, festive joy (mirth), revelry.
feil, (-e), n. fault; error; mistake.
feil, (ge-), err, go wrong, make a mistake.
feilbaar, (-bare), fallible, liable to error.
feilbaarheid, fallibility, liability to error.
feilloos, (-lose), faultless.
feilloosheid, faultlessness.
feit, (-e), fact.
feitekennis, knowledge of facts.
feit(e)lik, (-e), a. actual, real.
feitlik, adv. practically, as a matter of fact.
feit(e)likheid, (-hede), actually, reality.
fel, (-le), fierce, keen, sharp, violent.
felheid, fierceness, severity, violence.
felisitasie, (-s), congratulation.
felisiteer, (ge-), congratulate.
femelary, cant(ing), hypocrisy.
feminis, (-te), feminist.
feminisme, feminism.
feministies, (-e), feminist(ic).
fenasetien, fenasetine, phenacetin.
feniks, phoenix (phenix).
Fenisies, (-e), n. & a. Phoenician.
fenomeen, (-mene), phenomenon.
fenomenaal, (-ale), phenomenal.
feodaal, (-dale), feudal.
ferm, (-e), firm, steady, solid, strong.
fermentasie, fermentation.
fermenteer, (ge-), férment.
fermheid, firmness; vide ferm.
ferweel, corduroy; velvet; vide fluweel.
ferweelbroek, corduroy-trousers.
fes, (-se), fez.
festiwiteit, (-e), festivity.
festoen, (-e), festoon.
festoeneer, (ge-), festoon.
fetisj, (-e), fetish.
fetisjisme, fetishism.
feudal, vide feodaal.
feuilleton, (-s), serial (story), feuilleton.
fiasko, (-'s), fiasco.
fiber, (-s), fibre.
fideel, (-ele), jolly, jovial, merry.
fidei-commissum, fidekommis, filekommis, fidei-commissum.
fidusie, confidence, reliance, trust.
fidusiêr, (-e), fiduciary.
fiedel, (ge-), fiddle.
fiemies, nonsense, whims.
fier, (-e), high-minded, high-spirited, proud.
fierheid, pride; vide fier.
fieterjasies, superfluous ornaments, flourishes.
fiets, (-e), n. (bi)cycle.
fiets, (ge-), cycle.
fietsband, bicycle-tire.
fietser, (-s), cyclist.
fietspomp, (bi)cycle-pump, inflater.
fietsry, (fietsge-), vide fiets, (ge-).
fietsryer, vide fietser.
fietstog, cycling-tour.
figurant, (-e), cipher, figure, puppet.
figurasie, figuration.
figuratief, (-tiewe), figurative.
figureer, (ge-), figure, pose (as).
figuur, (-ure), figure; character (in drama); diagram (in maths.); 'n - slaan, cut a figure; 'n droewige - slaan, cut a sorry figure; 'n goeie - maak, make a fair show, show up well.
figuurlik, (-e), a. & adv. figurative(ly).
figuursaag, fret-saw, scroll-saw.
fiks, (e), healthy, quick, robust.
fikseer, (ge-), fix (a photo); stare at (a person).
fikseerbad, fixing-bath.

fiksheid, push, spirit; vide fiks.
fiksie, (-s), fiction; fabrication.
fiktief, (-tiewe), fictitious, imaginary.
filantroop, (-trope), philanthropist.
filantropie, philanthropy.
filantropies, (-e), philanthropic.
filatelie, philately.
filatelis, (-te), philatelist.
filatelisties, (-e), philatelic.
filekommis, vide fidei-commissum.
filiaalmaatskappy, subsidiary.
filigraan, filigree.
filippien, filippyn, philippine.
filister, (-s), philistine; townee.
Filistyn, (-e), Philistine.
Filistyns, (-e), Philistine.
film, (-s), n. film; screen.
film, (ge-), film.
filmoperateur, film-operator, cinematographer.
filmster, film-star.
filologie, philology.
filologies, (-e), philological.
filoloog, (-loë, -loge), philologist.
filosofeer, (ge-), philosophise.
filosofie, philosophy.
filosofies, (-e), philosophic(al).
filosoof, (-sowe), philosopher.
filter, (-s), percolator, strainer, filter.
filtraat, (-trate), filtrate.
filtrasie, filtration.
filtreer, (ge-), filter, filtrate, percolate, strain.
filtreerkan, percolator.
filtreerpapier, filter-paper.
Fin, (-ne), Finn, Fin(lander).
finaal, (-ale), final, total, complete.
finale, (-s), finale; final (in sport).
finansieë, finansies, finances; finance.
finansieel, (-siële), a. & adv. financial, monetary, pecuniary.
finansier, (-s), n. financier.
finansier, (ge-), finance.
finansies, vide finansieë.
finansiewese, finance.
finesse, (-s), finesse, nicety, subtlety.
fingeer, (ge-), feign, pretend; invent.
Fingo, (-'s), Fingo.
Finlander, (-s), Finlands, (-e), vide Fin, Fins.
Fins, (-e), n. & a., Finnic, Finnish.
fiool, (-ole), phial; vials (Bib.).
firma, (-s), firm, house, concern.
firmament, firmament, sky.
fisant, (-e), pheasant, red-necked francolin.
fisanthaan, cock-pheasant.
fisanthen, hen-pheasant.
fisiek, n. physique.
fisiek, (-e), a. physical; dit is - onmoontlik, it is physically impossible.
fisies, (-e), physical; -e aardrykskunde, physical geography.
fisika, physics.
fisiologie, physiology.
fisiologies, (-e), physiological.
fisioloog, (-loë, -loge), physiologist.
fisionomie, physiognomy.
fiskaal, (-ale, -s), fiscal; butcher-bird, shrike.
fjord, (-s), fjord (fiord).
fladder, (ge-), flit, flutter, flap; flow, stream.
flagrant, (-e), flagrant, glaring, notorious.
flair, flair.
flambou, (-e), torch.
flamink, (-e), flamingo.
flanelet, flannelette.
flank, (-e), flank, side.
flankaanval, flank-attack.
flans, (ge-), inmekaar -, knock together.

flap, (-pe), n. iris; widow-bird; bishop-bird; flap (of cart).
flap, (ge-), flap; vide **uitflap.**
flard, (-e), rag, tatter; **aan -e,** in rags (shreds).
flater, (-s), blunder, mistake.
flatteer, (ge-), flatter.
flegma, apathy, phlegm, stolidity.
flegmaties, (-e), phlegmatic, stolid.
fleksie, (-s), flection, (flexion).
flennie, flannel.
flens, (-e), flange.
flenter, (-s), n. rag, small piece, splinter; **g'n - omgee nie,** not care two hoots; **aan -s,** in rags (shreds); to smithereens; **fyn en -s slaan,** smash (in)to smithereens.
flenter, (ge-), gad (idle) about.
flenters, adv. in rags (shreds, tatters); in pieces (splinters, smithereens); **- slaan,** vide **flenter,** n.
flerrie, (-s), n. flirt, gadabout.
flerrie, (ge-), flirt, gad (idle) about.
fles, (-se), bottle; flask; **Leidse -,** Leyden jar.
flessie, (-s), small bottle, flask.
fiets, (-e), faded, pale; dim (eyes).
fietsheid, fadedness, paleness.
fleur, bloom, flower, heyday, prime.
fleurig, (-e), blooming, fresh, bright.
fleurigheid, bloom, prime; liveliness.
fliek, (-e), bioscope, cinema.
flik, (ge-), **aanmekaar -,** patch together.
flikflooi, (ge-), cajole, coax, flatter.
flikflooier, (-s), cajoler, flatterer.
flikflooiery, coaxing, flattering.
flikker, (ge-), glitter, sparkle; flicker; twinkle.
flikkering, (-e, -s), gleam, glint, glittering.
flikkers, capers; **- gooi (maak),** cut capers.
flink, (-, -e), a. fine, robust, spirited; energetic, pushing; considerable, substantial (sum); **- pak slae,** sound thrashing; **hy is nog -,** he is still hale and hearty.
flink, adv. energetically, soundly, thoroughly; pluckily; firmly; **iemand - die waarheid sê,** give a person a bit (piece) of one's mind.
flinkheid, push, spirit, thoroughness.
flint, flint.
flintgeweer, flint-lock.
flirt, (-e, -s), n. flirt.
flirt, (ge-), flirt.
flirtasie, flirtation.
flits, (-e), flash(light).
flits, (ge-), flash.
flitslig, flashlight.
flodder, (ge-), flounder, splash.
flodderig, (-e), baggy, floppy; dowdy.
flodderkous, dowdy, frump, slattern.
floers, (black) crape (crêpe).
floks, (-e), **floksie,** phlox.
flonker, (-s), sparkle, twinkle.
flonkering, sparkle, sparkling, twinkling.
flora, flora.
floreer, (ge-), flourish, prosper, thrive.
florerend, (-e), flourishing, thriving.
florissant, (-e), vide **florerend.**
floryn, (-e), florin.
flottielje, (-s), flotilla.
flou, (-, -e), flat, insipid, tasteless (food); feeble, poor, silly, (joke); dim (light); faint; remote (idea); weak (tea); dull (market); **- val,** faint, swoon.
flouhartig, (-e), faint-hearted.
flouheid, faintness; insipidity; vide **flou.**
flouiteit, (-e), foolish talk; poor (silly) joke.
flous, (ge-), cheat, deceive, let down.
floute, (-s), fainting-fit, faint, swoon.
floutjies, poor, feeble.
fluïdum, effluvium.

fluim, fleim, mucus, phlegm, slime.
fluister, (ge-), whisper,
fluisterend, (-e), in a whisper, under one's breath.
fluistering, (-e), whisper(ing).
fluit, n. whistle; flute (instr.).
fluit, (ge-), whistle; play on the flute; whiz, zip (of bullets); pipe (of birds); **sy bors (keel) -,** he is wheezing; **na iets -,** whistle for something.
fluit, (ge-), water, make water, urinate.
fluit-fluit, easily; **- wen,** win hands down.
fluitjie, whistle; pipe; mouth-organ.
fluitjiesriet, common reed.
fluitspeler, flute-player, flutist.
fluks, (-e), a. & adv. hard-working, willing; quick, smart; quickly; **hy het ons - gehelp,** he helped us very well (willingly); **dis - van jou,** that's fine (excellent).
fluktuasie, fluctuation.
fluktueer, (ge-), fluctuate.
fluoresseer, (ge-), fluoresce.
fluoressensie, fluorescence.
flus(sies), just now.
fluweel, velvet; vide **ferweel.**
fluweelagtig, (-e), velvety.
fnuik, (ge-), cripple, put down, break.
foefie, (-s), dodge, trick; pretext; gimmick.
foei!, fie!, for shame!
foeilelik, (-e), hideous, as ugly as sin.
foelie, n. mace; (tin)foil.
foelie, (ge-), silver, tinfoil.
foesel(olie), fusel-oil.
foeter, (ge-), bother, trouble; thrash.
fok, (-ke), n. foresail.
fok, (ge-), breed, rear; cultivate (a beard).
fokhings, stallion, stud-horse.
fokker, (-s), breeder, raiser (of animals).
fokkery, (stock-)breeding; stock-farm.
fokram, stud-ram.
foksia, fuchsia, (-s), fuchsia.
fokskape, stud-sheep.
fokus, (-se), focus.
fokvee, stud-animals, breeding-stock.
foliant, (-e), folio(-volume).
folio, (-s), folio.
foliopapier, foolscap(-paper).
folio-uitgawe, folio-edition, -volume.
folkloristies, (-e), folkloristic.
folter, (ge-), torment, torture; put on the rack.
folterbank, rack.
folterend, (-e), excruciating, racking.
foltering, (-e), torment, torture.
folterkamer, torture chamber.
folter(werk)tuig, instrument of torture.
fomenteer, (ge-), foment.
fondament, (-e), foundation; bottom.
fondeer, (ge-), found, lay the foundation.
fondering, (-e, -s), foundation.
fonds, (-e), fund; (pl.) funds; stocks.
fondskatalogus, publisher's catalogue.
foneem, (-neme), phoneme.
fonetiek, phonetics.
foneties, (-e), phonetic.
fonetikus, (-se), **foneticus, (-ici),** phonetician.
fonograaf, (-grawe), phonograph.
fonografies, (-e), phonographic.
fonogram, (-me), phonogram.
fontein, (-e), fountain, spring.
fooi, (-e), n. tip, gratuity.
fooi, (ge-), tip.
fooiestelsel, tipping-system.
foonsnol, call-girl.
fop, (ge-), cheat, let down, take in, fool, hoax.
foppertjie, (baby's) dummy.
foppery, cheating; fooling, trickery.
fopspeen, vide **foppertjie.**

forel   84   **fyn**

forel, (-le), trout.
formaat, (-mate), size; shape.
Formalin, Formalin.
formalisme, formalism.
formalisties, (-e), formalistic.
formaliteit, (-e), formality, (matter of) form.
formasie, (-s), formation.
formeel, (-ele), formal.
formeer, (ge-), create, form, mould, shape.
formeerder, (-s), moulder, shaper; creator.
formidabel, (-e), formidable.
formule, (-e), formula.
formuleer, (ge-), formulate, state, word.
formulering, statement, wording.
formulier, (-e), form; formulary (of church).
fors, (-, -e), bold, robust, vigorous.
forseer, (ge-), force, strain, compel.
forsgebou(d), (de-), powerfully built.
forsheid, robustness, strength, vigour.
fort, (-e), fort, fortress.
fortifikasie, (-s), fortification.
fortifiseer, (ge-), fortify.
fortuin, fortune; wealth.
fortuinlik, (-e), fortunate, lucky.
fortuinsoeker, fortune-hunter, adventurer.
fortuinsoekster, adventuress.
forum, forum.
fosfaat, (-fate), phosphate.
fosfor, phosphorus; phosphor.
fosforbrons, phosphor bronze.
fosforesseer, (ge-), phosphoresce.
fosforessensie, phosphorescence.
fosforsuur, phosphoric acid.
fossiel, (-e), fossil.
fossielkenner, fossilist.
foto, (-'s), photo(graph).
fotobeslissing, photo-finish.
foto-elektries, photo-electric.
fotograaf, (-grawe), photographer.
fotografeer, (ge-), photograph, take a photo.
fotografie, (-ë), photo(graph); photography.
fotografies, (-e), photographic.
fotogravure, photogravure.
fotomeisie, cover-girl.
fotosel, photo-electric cell.
fotostaat, photostat, phostatic copy.
fout, (-e), error, mistake; defect, fault.
fouteer, (ge-), go wrong, make a mistake.
foutief, (-tiewe), faulty, wrong.
fraai, (-e), pretty, fine, handsome.
fraaiheid, beauty, prettiness.
fraaigheid, fine thing.
fragment, (-e), fragment, piece.
fragmentaries, (-e), fragmentary, scrappy.
frailing, (-s), edging, fringe; tassel.
fraksie, (-s), fraction.
fraksioneel, (-ele), fractional.
fraktuur, (-ure), fracture (med.).
framboos, (-bose), raspberry.
Franciskaner, (-s), Franciscan; grey friar.
Frank, (-e), Frank.
frank, (-e), n. franc.
frank, a. frank, free, bold.
frankeer, (ge-), frank, stamp, prepay.
frankering, postage.
Frankfort: – se wors, frankfurter.
Frankies, (-e), Frankish, Franconian.
franko, franco, post-free, post-paid.
Frankryk, France.
Frans, (-e), n. & a. French; **die –e**, the French.
fransbrandewyn, French brandy, cognac.
Fransman, (-ne, Franse), Frenchman.
frappant, (-e), striking.
frappeer, (ge-), strike.
frase, (-s), phrase; **holle –s**, hollow phrases.

fraseologie, phraseology.
fraseur, (-s), phrase-monger.
frats, (-e), freak, whim; buffoonery.
fratsemaker, buffoon, clown.
fraude, fraud.
frauduleus, (-e), fraudulent.
freesia, (-s), freesia.
fregat, (-te), frigate.
frekwensie, frequency.
frekwensiemodulasie, frequency modulation.
frekwent, (-e), frequent.
frekwentatief, (-tiewe), frequentative.
frekwenteer, (ge-), frequent.
fresko, (-'s), fresco.
fret, (-te), ferret; gimlet.
fretsaag, fret-saw.
fries, (-e), frieze, moulding.
Fries, (-e), Frisian.
frikkadel, (-le), minced-meat, rissole.
frikkadelbroodjie, hamburger.
frikkeboortjie, gimlet.
friksie, friction.
fris, (-, -se), fresh, cool; refreshing (drink), fit, hale, hearty.
friseer, (ge-), crisp, curl, frizz(le).
friseertang, -yster, crisping-iron, curling-tongs.
friseur, (-s), hairdresser.
frisgebou(d), (-de), strongly built.
frisheid, coolness; freshness; vide **fris**.
frivool, friwool, (-ole), frivolous.
frivoliteit, (-e), frivolity.
froetang, (-e), frutang (froetang).
frok, (-ke), frokkie, (-s), vest.
frommel, (ge-), crumple, rumple; crease.
frons, (-e), n. frown; scowl.
frons, (ge-), knit one's brows, frown; scowl.
front, (-e), front; facade, frontage.
frontaansig, front-view.
frontaanval, frontal attack.
frontispies, frontispiece.
frontverandering, change of front.
fuchsia, vide **foksia**.
fuga, (-s), fugue.
fuif, (fuiwe), blow-out, bust, celebration, spree.
fuif, (ge-), carouse, feast, revel.
fuik, (-e), bow-net, fish-trap; hen-coop.
fulmineer, (ge-), fulminate, thunder, declaim.
fumigeer, (ge-), fumigate.
fundamentalisme, fundamentalism.
fundamenteel, (-tele), fundamental, basic.
fundasie, foundation; seating.
fundeer, (ge-), fund (a debt).
fungeer, (ge-), act (officiate) as.
fungerend, (-e), acting, deputy.
fungus, (gi) fungus.
funksie, (-s), function, capacity.
funksionaris, (-se), functionary.
funksioneel, (-ele), functional; functionary.
funksioneer, (ge-), function.
furie, (-s), fury.
furore, furore; – **maak**, create a furore.
fusie, fusion, amalgamation, merger.
fusileer, (ge-), shoot, fusillade.
fut, go, push, spirit, vim, dash, mettle.
futiel, (-e), futile, frivolous.
futiliteit, futility, frivolity.
futloos, (-lose), spiritless, spunkless.
futsel, (ge-), dawdle, fiddle, trifle.
futsel(a)ry, dawdling, fiddling, trifling.
futuris, (-te), futurist.
futurisme, futurism.
futuristies, (-e), futurist(ic).
fyn, (-, -e), fine; delicate; choice, exquisite (wines); smart, swell (party); refined (people);

fynbesnaard

subtle (distinction); **'n – gehoor**, a fine ear; **– maak**, crush, grind; **– druk**, mash (potatoes); **– vrywe**, pound, pulverise; **– uitgevat wees**, be smartly dressed; **– oplet**, attend carefully.
fynbesnaard, (-e), highly strung.
fynbesnede, fine-cut (features).
fynekam, fynkam, fine-comb; v. search narrowly.
fyngevoelig, (-e), delicate; sensitive.
fyngevoeligheid, delicacy; sensitiveness.
fynheid, fineness; nicety; delicacy; vide **fyn**.
fynighede, finesses, niceties, tricks.
fynmeel, flour.
fynproewer, connoisseur.
fyt, felon, whitlow.

G

ga!, faugh!
gaaf, (gawe), fine, good (fellow); excellent, sound (teeth); undamaged (wood).
gaafheid, excellence, soundness; vide **gaaf**.
gaan, (ge-), go; move, walk; **jou laat –**, let oneself go; **hoe – dit?**, how are you?; **dit – goed met hulle**, they are doing well; **dit – jou goed!**, good luck!; **as alles goed –**, if all goes well; **dit – nie**, it can't be done; that won't do; **so – dit maar**, that's the way of the world; **daar – hy!** here goes!; **as jy daaroor – nadink**, when you come to think of it; **– haal**, go and fetch; **daarvan ,– hou**, come to like it; **– slaap**, go to bed; **– trou**, get married; **– wandel**, go for a walk; **die wind het – lê**, the wind dropped (died down); **dit – jou nie aan nie**, it does not concern you; **dit – bo alles**, that comes before everything else; **daar kan 300 mense in die saal –**, the hall will hold (seat) 300 people; **na die josie (hoenders, maan) –**, go to the deuce (the dickens); **dit – om sy eer, lewe**, his honour (life) is at stake; **die kwessie waar dit om –**, the point at issue; **oor De Aar –**, go via De Aar; **Dr. R. – oor hom**, Dr R. attends him; **uit iemand se pad –**, get out of someone's way.
gaande, going; on foot; **wat is –?**, what is the matter?, what is up?; **– hou**, keep going, keep up; **– maak**, provoke; stir, rouse.
gaandeweg, by degrees, gradually, little by little.
gaans, 'n uur –, an hour's walk.
gaap, (gape), n. yawn, yawning.
gaap, (ge-), yawn; gape (with astonishment).
gaapsiekte, the gapes.
gaar, (well) cooked, done; **– rieme**, dressed thongs; **die broek is –**, the (pair of) trousers is worn threadbare; **iets – dra**, wear something till it falls to pieces; **te –**, overdone; **goed –**, well-done; **nie – nie**, underdone; **net –**, done to a turn.
gaarne, gladly, readily, willingly; vide **graag**.
gaas, gauze, netting.
gaasagtig, (-e), gauzy.
gaasdoek, cambric; gauze.
gaasdraad, wire-gauze.
gaatjie, (-s), little hole; finger-hole.
gaatjievisier, peep-sight.
gabardine, -dien, gabardine.
gade, (-s), consort, spouse.
gadeslaan, (gadege-), observe, regard, watch.
gading, taste, inclination, liking; **van sy –**, to his taste.
gaffel, (-s), prong; pitchfork; gaff (of ship).
gaffelvormig, (-e), forked, bifurcated.
gaip, (-e), uncouth person, boor, churl, lout.
gal, bile, gall; **sy – uitbraak**, vent one's spleen; **dis bo sy –**, it is more than he is capable of.
gala, (-s), festival, gala; **in –**, in full dress.
galabal, gala-ball, state-ball.
galafskeiding, secretion of bile.
galagtig, (-e), bilious (lit.); choleric (fig.).
galakleding, -kostuum, gala-dress, full dress.
galant, (-e), n. suitor.
galant, (-e), a. courteous, polite, gallant.
galanterie, courtesy, gallantry.
galanterieë, fancy-goods.
galavoorstelling, gala-performance.
galbessie, black nightshade.
galbitter, as bitter as gall.
galblaas, gall-bladder.
galbult, heat-bump, urticaria.
galei, (-e), galley.
galeiboef, -slaaf, galley-slave.
galeiproef, galley-proof (printing).
galery, (-e), gallery; drift-way, drive (mining).

galg, (-e), gallows(-tree), gibbet; **dis botter aan die – gesmeer**, it is labour lost; **so slim soos die houtjie van die –**, very cute; **vir die – grootword**, grow up for the gallows.
galgehumor, grim (morbid) humour.
galg(e)maal, last meal.
galg(e)tronie, gallows-face, hangdog look.
galgpaal, gallows-tree.
Galileër, (-s), Galilees, (-lese), Galilean.
galjoen, (-e), galleon (ship); galjoen (fish).
galkoors, biliary fever.
gallamsiekte, bovine parabotulism.
Gallië, Gaul; **Gallies**, Gallic, Gaulic.
Gallisisme, (-e), Gallicism.
gallon, vide **gelling**.
galm, (-e), n. boom, peal, reverberation.
galm, (ge-), bawl (of voice); (re)sound.
galon, (-s), braid, galloon, lace.
galonneer, (ge-), (trim with) braid (lace).
galop, n. galop (dance): gallop (of a horse).
galop, (ge-), galop (a dance); gallop (of horse).
galopdraf, canter.
galoppeer, (ge-), vide **galop, (ge-)**.
galoptering, galloping consumption.
galsiekte, bilious complaint (of humans), gall-sickness (of animals).
galsteen, gall-stone, biliary calculus.
galsterig, (-e), rancid, rank, strong.
galsug, bilious complaint.
galvanies, (-e), galvanic; **–e oortrekking**, electro-plating.
galvaniseer, (ge-), galvanize.
galvanisme, galvanism, voltaic electricity.
galvanometer, galvanometer.
galvanoskoop, (-skoop), galvanoscope.
gambiet, gambit (chess).
gamma, (-s, -te), gamma; gamut scale.
gammastraal, gamma ray.
gammat, (-s, -te), (young) Malay.
Gamsgeslag, blackamoor(s), Native(s).
gang, (-e), n. passage, corridor; gangway (railw.); drive tunnel (mining), dyke (geol.); canal, duct (anat.); gait (of a person); pace (of a horse); speed, velocity; running (of a machine); course (of a disease); trend (of a conversation); **daar sit g'n – in nie**, there is no go in it; **sy eie – gaan**, go one's own way; **gaan jou –!**, go ahead; **aan die – bly**, keep going; **aan die – gaan**, set to work; **aan die – help**, start, give a start; **aan die – hou**, keep going; **aan die – kry**, get going; **aan die – sit**, set going, start (up); **aan die – wees**, be at work; **die kerk is al aan die –**, church has already begun; **in volle –**, in full swing; **op – kom**, get going.
gangbaar, (-bare), current; valid; passable; **nog –**, still valid; **–e munt**, currency.
gangbaarheid, currency.
gangetjie, narrow passage; alley; jog-trot; **dit gaan so 'n –**, things are jogging on.
gangklok, hall-clock.
ganglamp, hall-lamp.
gangloper, passage-runner; hall-carpet.
gangmaker, pacemaker.
gangmat, hall-mat.
gangspil, bar-capstan.
gangstander, hallstand.
gangwissel, transmission; gear-lever.
ganna(bos), (-s), ganna, lye-bush.
gans, (-e), n. goose.
gans, (-e), a. all, entire, whole; **die –e dag**, the whole day, the livelong day.
gans, adv. absolutely, entirely, wholly; **– en al nie**, not at all, by no means; **– en gaar**, vide **gansegaar**.
gansbord, game of goose.

gansegaar, altogether; – **nie,** by no means.
gansie, (-s), gosling.
gansmannetjie, gander.
gansmars, in die –, single (Indian goose) file.
gansnek, goose-neck.
gansveer, goose-quill, goose-feather.
gapend, (-e), yawning (abyss), gaping (wound).
gaperig, (-e), yawny; sleepy.
gaping, (-e, -s), gap, hiatus, lacuna.
garage, (-s), garage.
garandeer, (ge-), guarantee, warrant.
garansie, (-s), guarantee, security.
garansiebewys, (certificate of) warranty.
garde, (-s), guard.
garderegiment, Guards-regiment.
garderobe, (-s), wardrobe; cloakroom.
gare, vide **garing.**
gareel, harness; **in die –,** in harness.
garing, gare, (cotton-)thread, yarn.
garingboom, agave, American aloe.
garingklip, asbestos.
garingtolletjie, cotton-reel.
garnaal, (-nale), shrimp.
garneer, (ge-), trim, garnish (a dish).
garneersel, garnering, (-s), trimming.
garnisoen, (-e), garrison.
garnisoenstad, garrison-town.
garnituur, (-ture), trimming; setting (of jewels).
gars, barley; **wilde –,** wild barley.
garsgerf, sheaf of barley.
garssaad, barley-seed.
gas, (-te), n. guest, visitor.
gas, (-se), n. gas.
gasaanval, gas-attack.
gasagtig, (-e), gaseous.
gasbom, gas-bomb.
gasbuis, gas-pipe.
gasdamp, gas-fume.
gasel, (-le), gazelle.
gaset, (-te), gazette.
gasfabriek, gas-works.
gas(t)heer, host.
gasie, (-s), pay, wage(s), salary.
gaskaggel, gas-heater.
gaskraan, gas-tap, gas-cock.
gaskroon, gaselier.
gasleiding, gas-main.
gasmaal, banquet, entertainment, feast.
gasmasker, gas-mask, gas-helmet.
gasmeter, gas-meter.
gasolien, gasoline.
gaspedaal, accelerator, throttle-pedal.
gasstoof, gas-stove.
gastehuis, guest-house.
gastheer, vide **gas(t)heer.**
gastronomie, gastronomy.
gastronomies, (-e), gastronomic(al).
gastronoom, (-nome), gastronomer.
gasvoorstelling, starring-performance.
gasvormig, (-e), gaseous.
gasvry, hospitable.
gasvryheid, hospitality.
gat, (-e), n. hole, gap, opening; **iemand 'n – in die kop praat,** talk a person round.
gaterig, (-e), holey, full of holes.
gat-gat, – speel, play holey-holey.
gawe, (-s), gift, talent; donation; **van gunste en – leef,** live on charity.
gawerig, (-e), excellent, fine, good, nice.
geaar, geader(d), (-de), veined; streaked.
geaard, (-e), disposed, natured, tempered.
geaardheid, disposition, nature, temper.
geadresseerde, (-s), addressee; consignee.
geaffekteerd, (-e), affected.
geaffekteerdheid, affectation.

geag, (-te), esteemed, respected; honourable; **Geagte Heer,** Dear Sir.
geagiteer(d), (-de), agitated, flustered.
geallieer(d), (-de), allied; **die –e(s),** the Allies.
geanimeer(d), (-de), animated.
geappel, (-de), dapple-grey, dappled.
gearm(d), (-de), arm-in-arm, armed.
geavanseer(d), (-de), advanced, modern.
gebaan, (-de), beaten (track).
gebaar, (-bare), gesture, gesticulation; **'n mooi –,** fine gesture; **gebare maak,** gesticulate.
gebabbel, chatter, gossip, prattle, tittle-tattle.
gebak, n. cake, pastry.
gebak, (-te), baked, fried (eggs); **met die -te pere bly sit,** be left to hold the baby.
gebaken(d), gebaker(d), kort – **wees,** be hasty (peppery, touchy).
gebarespel, pantomime, dumb-show.
gebaretaal, gesture-language.
gebasel, empty talk, silly prattle, twaddle.
gebed, (-e), prayer; grace (at table); **'n – doen,** say a prayer, pray.
gebedeboek, prayer-book.
gebedel, begging.
gebeente, bones; **wee jou –!,** heaven help you!
gebek, beaked; **elk voëltjie sing soos hy – is,** a bird is known by its note.
gebelg, (-de), angry, incensed, offended.
gebergte, (-s), mountain-range, mountains.
gebete, bit(ten); **op iemand – wees,** have a grudge against a person.
gebeur, (het –), happen, occur, chance, come about, come to pass; **wat – is, is –,** it is no use crying over spilt milk; **dit moet –,** it has to be done; **wat ook mag –,** come what may.
gebeurde, die –, the event (occurrence).
gebeurlik, (-e), contingent, possible.
gebeurlikheid, contingency, eventuality.
gebeurtenis, (-se), event, occurrence.
gebied, (-e), n. dominion, territory (of a state); area; department, domain, field, province, sphere; **op die – van die kuns,** in the realms of art; **op verstandelike –,** in the sphere of the intellect.
gebied, (het –), command, direct, order; **wat die plig –,** what duty dictates; **iemand hiet en –,** order someone about.
gebiedend, (-e), commanding, compelling; imperative, urgent; **–e wys(e),** imperative (mood); **– noodsaaklik,** imperative, urgently necessary.
gebieder, (-s), lord, master, ruler.
gebiedster, (-s), lady, mistress, ruler.
gebiedswaters, territorial waters.
gebit, (-te), (set of) teeth; bit (of bridle).
gebladerte, foliage, leaves.
geblaf, bark(ing).
geblêr, bleating.
geblinddoek, (-te), blindfolded.
gebloem(d), geblom, (-de), flowered (dress).
geblus, (-te), slaked; **te kalk,** slaked lime.
gebod, (-gebooie), command, injunction, order; decree; **die tien gebooie,** the ten commandments; **die gebooie laat gaan,** publish the banns.
geboë, arched, bent, bowed; curved.
gebonde, bound.
gebondenheid, lack of freedom.
geboomte, trees.
geboorte, (-s), birth; **by die –,** at birth, **in die – smoor,** kill at birth, nip in the bud; **van –,** by birth; **van hoë geboorte,** of high birth, high-born; **van sy – af aan,** from birth, from one's birth up.
geboortebewys, birth-certificate.
geboortegrond, native soil, home(land).

geboorteplek, birthplace.
geboortereg, birthright.
geboortestad, native town.
geboortesyfer, birth-rate.
geboortig, – uit S., native of S.
gebore, born; 'n – Brit, a Briton by birth; British-born; 'n – **onderwyser**, a born teacher; – en **getoë**, born and bred; 'n – **idioot**, a congenital idiot; nie – in staat wees nie om . . ., be not at all able to . . .
gebou, (-e), n. building, edifice, structure.
gebou(d), (-de), a. built; goed –d, well-built.
gebraad, roast (meat).
gebraai, (-de), broiled; grilled; roasted; parched; –de ribbetjie, grilled rib; vide **braai**.
gebrabbel, jargon, gibberish.
gebrand, (-e), burnt; –e glas, stained glass; –e kalk, burnt lime, quicklime; –e koffie, roasted coffee; vide **brand**, (ge-).
gebreek, (-te), broken; –te mielies, samp.
gebrei, (-de), knitted.
gebrek, (-e), lack, want, shortage, dearth, deficiency (of air); poverty; defect, failing, fault, flaw, shortcoming, die –e van die **ouderdom**, the infirmities of old age; die –e van sy **deugde**, the defects of one's qualities (virtues); 'n – **aan arbeid**, a dearth of labourers; geen – **aan kritiek nie**, no lack of criticism; **aan niks** – hê nie, want for nothing; – hê (ly), be in want, starve; by (deur, uit) – **aan**, for want (lack) of; **in** –e **bly om** . . ., fail, to default.
gebrekkig, (-e), defective, faulty, broken, imperfect (English); **jou** – **uitdruk**, express oneself badly (imperfectly).
gebrekkigheid, defectiveness, faultiness.
gebreklik, (-e), crippled, deformed, lame.
gebreklikheid, deformity, infirmity, lameness.
gebroeders, brothers; die – B., B. Bros.
gebroed(sel), (-s), brood.
gebroke, broken; – Engels, broken English; – **getal**, fractional number; 'n – **hart**, a broken heart; – **veld**, mixed pasturage.
gebrom, growling, grumbling; vide **brom**.
gebrons, (-de), bronzed; tanned.
gebruik, (-e), n. use (of one's limbs), custom, habit, practice, usage, application, function; consumption (of foodstuffs); – **maak van**, make use of, avail oneself of, utilise; **in** –, in use; **ten** –**e van**, for the use of; **vir** –, for use; **uitwendige** –, outward application.
gebruik, (-te), a. used, second-hand (car).
gebruik, (het –), use, employ, make use of; take (medicine), partake of (a meal); consume (coal); ek kan 'n paar pond –, I could do with a few pounds; ek – **nooit drank nie**, I never touch drink.
gebruiker, (-s), user; consumer.
gebruiklik, (-e), customary, usual.
gebruiklikheid, usage; use.
gebruiksaanwysing, directions for use.
gebruin, (-de), sunburnt, bronzed, tanned.
gebruis, effervescence; seething.
gebrul, howling, roaring.
gebukkend, (-e), crouching, stooping.
gebulder, boom(ing), roar(ing), rumble.
gebulk, bellowing, lowing, mooing.
gebundel(d), (-de), collected.
gedaagde, (-s), defendant; respondent.
gedaan, (-dane), done, exhausted, finished; hy is –, he is finished (done for); **ek voel** –, I feel fagged; gedane sake het g'n keer nie, what is done cannot be undone; **die watervoorraad is** –, the water-supply is exhausted.
gedaante, (-s), figure, shape; vision, apparition;

in die – van, in the shape of; **in sy ware** –, in his (its) true colours; van – **verander**, be transformed.
gedaanteverandering, -verwisseling, metamorphosis, transformation.
gedagte, (-s), idea, notion, thought; mind; memory, reflection; opinion; sy –s nie bymekaar hê nie, be absent-minded, be woolgathering; sy –(s) daaroor **laat gaan**, consider a matter; die – kry, get the idea; in –, in thought, in the spirit; in – hou, bear in mind, remember; in – (verlore) wees, absorbed in thought, in a brown study; **op twee** –s **hink**, be in two minds; op die – **bring**, suggest (the idea); tot ander –s kom, change one's mind; **uit die** – sit, put out of one's mind; van – **verander**, change one's mind; van – wees, be of opinion; (van) –s wissel, exchange views.
gedagtegang, order of thought; line of thought.
gedagteloos, (-lose), thoughtless.
gedagtenis, memory, remembrance; keepsake, memento, souvenir; ter – **aan**, in memory of.
gedagtestreep, dash.
gedagtewisseling, exchange (interchange) of ideas (thoughts, views).
gedagtig, mindful; – **aan**, mindful of.
gedamasseer(d), (-de), damascened.
gedans, dancing.
gedawer, booming, shaking, (re)sounding.
gedeelte, (-s), part, portion, section; share; vir die **grootste** –, for the greater part.
gedeeltelik, (-e), a. & adv. partial (eclipse); partly, partially.
gedek, (-te), covered, guarded.
gedekolleteer(d), (-de), décolleté, low(-necked).
gedelegeerde, (-s), delegate.
gedemp, (-te), filled up; op –te **toon**, in a muffled voice; vide **demp**.
gedenk, (het –), bear in mind, remember; commemorate.
gedenkboek, album, memorial volume.
gedenkdag, anniversary.
gedenknaald, memorial needle, monument.
gedenkpenning, commemorative medal.
gedenkplaat, memorial tablet.
gedenkrol, annals, record(s).
gedenkskrif, memoir.
gedenksteen, memorial stone (tablet).
gedenkstuk, **gedenkteken**, memorial, monument.
gedenkwaardig, (-e), memorable.
gedenkwaardigheid, memorableness.
gedeponeer, (-de), deposited; registered.
gedeporteerde, deportee.
gedeputeerde, (-s), delegate, deputy.
gedetailleer(d), (-de), detailed, in detail.
gedetermineer, (-de), classified (bot., etc.).
gedien: nie van iets – **wees nie**, not be prepared to put up with something.
gedienstig, (-e), obliging; officious.
gedienstigheid, obligingness; officiousness.
gedierte, (-s), creatures; vermin; monster.
gedig, (-te), poem.
geding, (-e), action, lawsuit; quarrel.
gediplomeer(d), (-de), qualified; certificated (teacher), chartered (accountant).
gedissiplineer(d), (-de), disciplined.
gedistingeer, (-de), distinguished.
gedistingeerdheid, distinction.
gedoe, bustle, concern, doings, fuss.
gedoë, gedoog, (het –), suffer, tolerate.
gedoente, (-s), vide **gedoe**.
gedomisilieer(d), (-de), domiciled.
gedoog, vide **gedoë**.
gedoriewaar, by gum!, really and truly.

gedra, (het -), behave, conduct oneself; **jou goed** -, behave well; render a good account of oneself; **jou sleg** -, misbehave.
gedraai, n. delay; turning, twisting.
gedraal, delay, lingering, loitering.
gedrag, behaviour, conduct, deportment.
gedragslyn, line of action, course.
gedrang, crowd, crush, squash, throng.
gedreun, din, drone, droning, shaking.
gedrewe, chased, embossed (gold); vide **dryf**.
gedrog, (-te), monster, monstrosity.
gedrogtelik, (-e), misshapen, monstrous.
gedronge, compact, terse (style); - **voel om** . . . , feel prompted to . . . , vide **dring**.
gedrongenheid, compactness; terseness.
gedruis, (-e), noise, roar, rumbling, rush.
gedruk, (-te), a. printed; depressed.
gedruktheid, dejection, depression, dullness.
gedug, (-te), formidable; severe, sound.
gedugtheid, formidableness; vide **gedug**.
geduld, forbearance, patience; - **verloor** lose patience, become impatient.
geduldig, (-e), patient.
geduldigheid, forbearance, patience.
gedurende, for (a fortnight); during.
gedurf, (-de), daring, reckless.
gedurfdheid, daring, recklessness, bravado.
gedurig, (-e), a. constant, continual; continued (fraction, product).
gedurig(lik), adv. constantly, continually.
gedwee, (**gedweë**), docile, meek, tractable.
gedweeheid, meekness, submissiveness.
gedweep, vide **dwepery**.
gedwonge, compulsory, enforced; forced (smile); forcible (feeding).
gedwongenheid, constraint, forcedness.
gedy, (het -), flourish, prosper, thrive.
gee, (ge-), give; afford; produce, yield; grant; give out (heat); deal (cards); **mag God – dat**, God grant that; **jou lewe** -, lay down one's life; **jou mening (oordeel)** -, express one's opinion; **jou(self) moeite** -, put oneself out; **dit gewonne** -, give it up; **dit** - **niks nie, it is no good**; **om iets'** -, care for something; **te dinke** -, give food for thought; **te kenne** -, intimate; **rekenskap** - **van**, account for; **jou rekenskap** - **van**, realize.
geel, n. yellow (colour); yolk (of an egg).
geel, a. yellow.
geelagtig, (-e), yellowish.
geelbaadjie: **die** - **aanhê**, be jealous.
geelbek, Cape salmon; yellow-billed duck.
geelblommetjie, Cape saffron.
geelborsie, icterine, warbler.
geelbruin, tawny.
geelhout, yellow-wood.
geelkapel, yellow cobra.
geelkoper, brass.
geelrys, curried rice.
geelslang, cobra.
geelsug, jaundice.
geelsysie, yellow seedeater, glass-eye.
geelvink, yellow weaverbird.
geelwortel, carrot.
geëmaljeer(d), (-de), enamelled.
geëmansipeer(d), (-de), emancipated.
geëmplojeerde, (-s), employee.
geen, g'n, a. & pron. no, not a, not any, not one, none; - **van beide**, neither (of them); - **woord nie**, not a word; **dit is** - **Engels nie**, that is not English; - **blou duit nie**, not a blessed farthing; - **stuk lollery nie!**, no nonsense!; **hy is** - **vriend van my nie**, he is no friend of mine; vide **g'n**, adv.

geeneen, no one, not one, none; **ek ken** - **van hulle almal nie**, I don't know any of them.
geensins, by no means, not at all.
geër, (-s), giver.
gees, (-te), spirit; mind; wit; genius; ghost, spectre, apparition; **die** - **van die taal**, the genius of the language; **die** - **van die tyd**, the spirit of the times; **'n groot** -, a mastermind; **die Heilige G-**, the Holy Spirit (Ghost); **soos 'n** - **lyk**, look like a ghost; **die** - **is gewillig, maar die vlees is swak**, the spirit is willing, but the flesh is weak; **die** - **gee**, breathe one's last, give up the ghost; **in** - **die** -, in the spirit; **in dieselfde** -, in the same strain, to the same effect; **na die letter en na die** -, in letter as well as in spirit; **teenwoordigheid van** -, presence of mind; **voor die** - **bring (roep)**, call to mind.
geesdodend, (-e), soul-deadening, dull.
geesdrif, enthusiasm, zeal.
geesdriftig, (-e), enthusiastic, zealous.
geesdrywer, fanatic, zealot.
geesdrywery, fanaticism, zealotry.
geeskrag, energy, spirit, strength of mind.
geesryk, (-e), witty; spirituous.
geestebanner, **geestebesweerder**, exorcist.
geestelik, (-e), spiritual; intellectual, mental (faculties); religious, sacred (songs); **-e afwyking**, mental aberration.
geestelike, (-s), divine, minister.
geestelikheid, clergy, spirituality.
geesteloos, (-lose), dull, insipid, spiritless.
geestesgawe, mental faculty, intellectual power.
geestesgesteldheid, state of mind, mentality.
geestesoog, the mind's eye.
geestestoestand, vide **geestesgesteldheid**.
geestesvoedsel, mental nourishment.
geestesweêreld, spirit-world.
geestig, (-e), bright, smart, witty.
geestigheid, joke, witticism; wit, wittiness.
geesverheffend, (-e), edifying, sublime.
geesvermoëns, (mental) faculties.
geesvervoering, ecstasy; trance.
geesverwant, n. kindred soul; adherent.
geesverwant, (-e), a. congenial, of like mind.
geesverwantskap, mental affinity.
geeu, (-e), n. yawn.
geeu, (ge-), (give a) yawn.
gefladder, flutter(ing), flitting.
geflikflooi, coaxing, fawning, wheedling.
geflikker, flash(ing), glitter(ing), sparkle, sparkling, twinkle, twinkling.
geflirt, flirtation, flirting.
gefluister, whisper(ing).
gefluit, whistling; warbling; catcalls.
gefoeter, botheration; nonsense.
gegalm, booming; chant; bawling, sing-song.
gegalvaniseer(d), galvanized.
gegeneer(d), (-**de**), embarrassed, uneasy.
gegewe, (-ns), n. datum, information; (pl.) data.
gegewe, a. given; **op 'n** - **moment**, at a given moment.
gegiegel, **gegiggel**, giggling, titter(ing).
gegiggel, vide **gegiegel**.
gegoed, (-e), well-off, well-to-do.
gegoedheid, affluence, wealth.
gegons, buzz(ing), hum, whirr.
gegote, cast (iron).
gegradueer(d), (-de), graduated.
gegradueerde, (-s), graduate.
gegrinnik, grin(ning).
gegroet!, hail!
gegrond, (-e), well-founded; legitimate (hope); sound (reasons); reasonable (doubt).
gegrondheid, justice, justness, soundness.

gehaas, hurry.
gehaastheid, hurry, hurriedness.
gehaat, (-hate), hated, hateful, odious.
gehalte, quality, grade, standard; proof (of alcohol); **innerlike** –, intrinsic value; **sedelike** –, moral worth; **van lae** –, of a low standard, low-grade.
gehamer, hammering.
gehandskoen(d), (-de), gloved.
gehard, (-e), tempered, hardened, hardy, seasoned (soldiers); inured (to pain); steeled (against adversity); **teen die klimaat** –, acclimatised.
gehardheid, temper; hardiness, inurement.
geharnas, (-te), armoured, in armour, mailed.
geharwar, bickering(s), wrangling.
gehawen(d), (-de), battered; in rags (shreds).
geheel, (gehele), n. whole; **in die** –, as a whole, in all; **in die** – **nie**, not at all; **in sy** –, in full; **die saak in sy** – **beskou**, look at the matter as a whole; **tien in die** –, ten in all; **oor die** –, on the whole, in the main.
geheel, (gehele), a. complete, entire, whole.
geheel, adv. all, completely, entirely, quite, wholly; – **en al**, altogether, entirely, quite.
geheelgetal, integer, integral (whole) number.
geheelonthouding, total abstinence, teetotalism.
geheelonthouer, total abstainer, teetotaller.
geheg: – **aan**, attached (devoted) to.
gehegtheid, attachment, devotion, fondness.
geheim, (-e), n. secret, mystery; **openbare (publieke)** –, an open secret, common knowledge; **'n** – **bewaar**, keep (guard) a secret; **'n** – **openbaar (verklap)**, divulge (let out) a secret; **in die** –, in secret, secretly.
geheim, (-e), a. secret; occult (science); clandestine (marriage); illicit (sale of liquors); **G-e Raad**, Privy Council; –**e sitting**, secret (private) session; –**e stemming**, voting by ballot; **iets** – **hou**, keep a thing secret (close, dark).
geheim(e)nis, (-e), mystery.
geheim(e)nisvol, (-le), mysterious.
geheimhouding, secrecy.
geheimsinnig, (-e), dark, mysterious.
geheimsinnigheid, mysteriousness.
geheimskrif, cipher, cryptogram, secret code.
geheimskrywer, (private) secretary.
gehekel, (-de): –**de werk**, crochet-work.
geheue, memory, mind, remembrance; **iets in die** – **hou**, keep something in mind; **iets in die** – **prent**, impress something on the mind (memory).
geheuenis, memory.
geheuewerk, memory-work.
gehinnik, neighing, whinny(ing).
gehoes, coughing.
gehol, running, scamper, scurry(ing).
gehoor, hearing; audience, hearers; **'n goeie** –, a good ear; a sympathetic audience; **g'n musikale** – **hê nie**, have no ear for music; – **gee aan**, listen; respond to; comply with; **geen** – **kry nie**, fail to get an answer; – **verleen**, give an audience; **op die** – **speel**, play by ear.
gehoorbuis, ear-trumpet; receiver (teleph.).
gehoorpyp, ear-trumpet; stethoscope.
gehoorsaal, auditorium.
gehoorsaam, (-same), a. dutiful, obedient.
gehoorsaam, (het –), obey, be obedient; submit to, answer to (the rudder).
gehoorsaamheid, obedience.
gehoorsafstand, hearing-distance; **binne (op)** –, within hearing, within earshot.
gehoorsenuwee, auditory, (acoustic) nerve.
gehoortoestel, otophone (for the deaf).
gehoorvlies, tympanum, eardrum.
gehou(e), bound to, obliged to.

gehoudenheid, obligation.
gehude, (-s), married person.
gehug, (-te), hamlet.
gehuigel, dissembling, hypocrisy.
gehuil, crying, howling, yelling.
gehumeur(d), (-de); **goed (sleg)** –, good-(ill-tempered.
gehunker, craving, hankering.
gehuppel, frisking, hopping; skipping.
gehuud, (-hude), married.
gehyg, gasping, panting.
Geiger-telbuis, Geiger counter.
geil, fertile, rank, rich (soil); lascivious.
geïllustreer(d), (-de), illustrated, pictorial.
geilsiekte, "geilsiekte" (stock disease).
geïnteresseer(d), (-de), interested; concerned, involved.
geiser, (-s), geyser.
geit, (-e), goat; girl.
geitjie, (-s), lizard; shrew, vixen.
gejaag, n. hurry(ing); racing.
gejaag, (-de), a. flustered, hurried.
gejaagdheid, agitation, flurry, fluster.
gejakker, scramble; vide **jakker**.
gejammer, lamentation(s), wailing(s).
gejeuk, itch(ing), psoriasis (sc.).
gejoel, cheering, shouting.
gejou, booing, hooting.
gejubel, cheering, cheers, applause, exultation.
gejuig, vide **gejubel**.
gek, (-ke), n. fool; lunatic; **'n halwe** –, an idiot, a half-wit; **hardloop soos 'n** –, run like mad; **met iemand die** – **skeer**, **iemand vir die** – **hou**, poke fun at (make a fool of) a person.
gek, (–, -ke), a. & adv. mad, crazy; foolish; queer, silly; funny, odd; **'n** – **(ke) uitdrukking**, a funny expression; **jou** – **hou**, sham madness; be foolish; **iemand** – **maak**, drive someone crazy; **jou** – **soek na**, look for (a thing) till one is half crazy; – **word**, go (run) mad; – **na**, fond of, partial to, mad on; – **van**, mad with.
gek, (ge-), joke, jest; **met iemand** –, make fun of a person, fool (kid) a person.
gekabbel, babbling, purling (of a brook).
gekant: – **teen**, antagonistic (hostile) to.
gekartel(d), (-de), jagged; wavy; crinkled.
gekekkel, cackle, cackling; tittle-tattle.
gekeper(d), (-de), twilled.
gekerm, groaning, lamentation, moaning.
gekheid, folly, foolishness; joking, fun; –**!**, nonsense!; **alle** – **op 'n stokkie (end)**, joking (jesting) apart; **sonder** –, jesting apart, really; **uit** –, for (in) fun.
gekibbel, bickering, squabbling.
gekir, cooing.
Gekkedag, All Fools' Day.
gekkehuis, bedlam, madhouse, lunatic asylum.
gekkepraatjies, (stuff and) nonsense.
gekkerny, jest, joke, joking, tomfoolery.
gekkewerk, folly, madness.
gekkigheid, folly, foolishness.
gekla(ag), geklae, geklag, complaining, complaints; moaning, wailing; lamentation.
geklap, clapping; cracking (of whip).
geklapper, flapping, chattering (of teeth).
geklee(d), (geklede), dressed; dressy.
geklepper, clatter(ing), clip-clop (of hoofs).
geklets, jaw, rot, rubbish, twaddle.
gekletter, clanging, clashing, clattering.
gekleur(d), (-de), coloured; –**e glas**, stained glass; –**e plate**, coloured plates.
geklik, (-ke), foolish, funny, silly, queer.
geklikklak, clattering, click-clack.
geklingel, jingle-jangle, jingling, tinkle.

geklop, knocking; throbbing (of the heart).
geklots, beating, dashing (of the waves).
geknabbel, gnawing, munching, nibbling.
gekneg, (-te), enslaved, subdued.
gekners, geknars, gnashing (of teeth).
geknetter, crackling.
gekneus, (-de), bruised.
geknip, (-te), cut; – **vir**, cut out for.
geknoei, bungling; plotting, scheming.
geknor, grunt(ing) of a pig; growling (of a dog).
gekommitteerde, (-s), delegate, deputy.
gekompromitteer(d), (-de), compromised.
gekonfyt, (-e), – **in**, well-versed (skilled) in.
gekonkel, vide **geknoei**.
gekostumeer(d), (-de), in costume; **–de bal**, fancy dress ball; **–de optog**, pageant.
gekrakeel, bickering, wrangling.
gekras, scratching; croaking, screeching.
gekrenk, (-te), hurt, offended; deranged (mind).
gekriebel, gekriewel, itching, tickling.
gekrioel, swarming.
gekroes (-te), crisped, crispy, curly (hair).
gekrui(d), (-de), seasoned, spiced; spicy.
gekruis, (-te), crossed; cross-bred (animals).
gekrul, (-de), curly, wavy, crisped, frizzled.
gekskap, fool's cap; tomfoolery.
gekskeer, (gekge-), banter, jest, joke; – **met, fool, kid, poke fun at; hy laat nie met hom – nie**, he will stand no nonsense.
gekskeerdery, fooling, jesting, skylarking.
gekuif, (-de), crested (waves); tufted (birds).
gekuip, intriguing, plotting, scheming.
gekuns, (-te), chaste, pure; **-te taal**, chastened language.
gekunsteld, (-e), artificial, mannered; **'n -e styl**, an artificial style.
gekunsteldheid, artificiality, mannerism(s).
gekwalifiseer(d), (-de), certificated, qualified.
gekwansel, bartering, haggling.
gekwes, (-te), wounded.
gekwets, (-te), offended (wounded).
gekyf, bickering, squabbling, wrangling.
gelaars, (-de), booted; **die Gelaarde Kat**, Puss in Boots.
gelaat, (-late), countenance, face, mien.
gelaatskleur, complexion.
gelaatstrek, feature.
gelaatsuitdrukking, facial expression.
gelag, n. score; **die – betaal**, pay the score (lit.); pay the piper (fig.).
gelag, n. laughing, laughter.
gelagkamer, bar(-room), taproom.
gelang: **na –**, according as; **na – van**, according (in proportion) to; **na – van omstandighede**, according to circumstances.
gelas, (-te), a. joined; welded.
gelas, (het, -), direct, instruct, order.
gelastigde, (-s), delegate, proxy, mandatory.
gelate, resigned.
gelatenheid, acquiescence, resignation.
gelatien, gelatine, gelatine (gelatin).
geld, (-e), n. money; **vals –**, bad money, base coin; – **soos water (bossies) verdien**, coin money; – **uit iemand se sak ja**, make someone spend money; – **slaan uit iets**, make money out of something; – **in die water gooi**, waste money; – **steek in iets**, invest money in something; **dit is met g'n – te betaal nie**, it is worth its weight in gold; **tot – maak**, convert (turn) into money; **vir g'n – ter wêreld nie**, not at any price, not for all the world; **nie vir – of goeie woorde nie**, not for love or money; **vir kwaadgeld rondloop**, go (wander) about aimlessly (idly).

geld, (ge-), apply, be in force, be valid, hold (good), obtain, count; apply to, concern; **die reël – sonder uitsondering**, the rule holds good (obtains) universally; **wie – dit?**, to whom does it apply?; **dit – sy eer**, his honour is at stake, **dit – ons almal**, it applies to all of us; **sy invloed laat –**, use one's influence; make one's influence felt; **sy regte laat –**, assert (enforce) one's rights; **dit – vir niks nie**, it counts for nothing; **die beurs – vir 'n jaar**, the scholarship is tenable for a year.
geldadel, moneyed classes, plutocracy.
geldbelegging, investment.
geldbeursie, purse.
geldboete, fine.
gelddors, lust for money, greed of gold.
geldduiwel, demon of money, mammon.
geldelik, (-e), monetary (reward), pecuniary (difficulties), financial (support).
geldend, (-e), current, ruling (prices); accepted, received (opinion).
geldgebrek, lack of funds, want of money; **– hê**, be short of money.
geldgierig, (-e), avaricious, covetous.
geldgierigheid, avarice, covetousness.
geldgod, mammon.
geldhandel, money-trade, banking.
geldhandelaar, money-dealer, banker.
geldig, (-e), valid (ticket, reason), binding (in law), legal, operative.
geldigheid, validity.
geldkas, cash-box, money-box; coffer, safe.
geldkissie, cash-box, till.
geldkoers, rate of exchange.
geldlaai, cash-drawer, till.
geldmakery, money-making, profiteering.
geldmiddele, finances, pecuniary resources.
geldmunter, coiner, minter.
geldnood, vide **geldgebrek**.
geldomloop, circulation of money.
geldprys, money-prize.
geldskaarste, scarcity of money.
geldskieter, (-s), moneylender.
geldsom, sum of money.
geldsorge, financial worries, money-troubles.
geldstuk, coin.
geldsugtig, (-e), vide **geldgierig**.
geldtrommel, cash-box.
geldverleentheid, pecuniary difficulties.
geldversending, remittance.
geldwêreld, world of finance.
geldwese, finance, monetary matters.
geldwinning, money-making.
geldwisselaar, money-changer.
geldwolf, money-grabber.
gelede, a. suffered; vide **ly, (ge-)**.
gelede, a. vide **geleed**.
gelede, adv. ago, past; **kort –**, recently; **lank –**, long ago.
geledere, vide **gelid**.
geleding, articulation, joint, hinge.
geleë, lying, situated; convenient; **dit is my nie – nie**, it does not suit me; **hoe dit daarmee – is**, how matters stand; **daar is bate aan –**, it is of great importance.
geleed, (gelede), articulate(d).
geleedpotig, (-e), -e diere, arthropoda.
geleentheid, occasion; opportunity; **– gee geneentheid**, opportunity makes the thief, as **die – hom aanbied**, as soon as opportunity offers; **die – aangryp**, seize the opportunity; **– kry om . . .**, get an opportunity to . . . ; **die – laat verbygaan**, let the opportunity slip; **by –**, on occasion, occasionally; **by die een of ander –**, as the occasion arises; **by die eerste –**,

at the first opportunity; **by elke –,** on every occasion; **in die – stel,** afford (give) an opportunity; **in die – verkeer (wees),** be in a position be able; **ter – van,** on the occasion of; **van die — gebruik maak,** avail oneself of the occasion (opportunity); **vir die –,** for the occasion.
geleentheidsgedig, occasional (topical) poem.
geleentheidstoespraak, speech for the occasion.
geleerd, (-e), learned (man), scholarly (work); trained (horse); **die –e wêreld,** the world of science.
geleerde, (-s), learned person, scholar.
geleerdheid, erudition, learning.
gelegener: ter – tyd, in due time.
gelei, n. jelly.
gelei, (het –), lead, escort, attend; convoy (ships); conduct (heat).
geleiagtig, (-e), jelly-like, gelatinous.
geleibrief, way-bill; permit; safe-conduct.
geleide, escort, guard, protection; **onder – van,** attended (chaperoned, escorted) by; **onder militêre –,** under military escort; **– projektiel,** guided missile.
geleidelik, gradual(ly), by degrees.
geleidelik, (-e), gradual.
gelei(d)er, (-s), conductor; guide, duct; **'n slegte –,** a non-conductor.
geleiding, conducting; conduction (of heat); (electric) wiring; conduit-pipes; main.
geleidingskoëffisiënt, coefficient of conduction.
geleidingsvermoë, conductivity.
gelei(d)ster, (-s), conductress, guide.
geleier, vide **gelei(d)er.**
gelerig, (-e), yellowish.
gelesene: die –, portion read; lesson.
geletter(d), (-de), lettered, literary.
gelid, (geledere), rank, file; generation; **in die – staan,** fall in, line up; **enkele –,** single file; **geslote, geledere,** serried ranks; **in die voorste geledere,** in the forefront; **tot in die derde –,** to the third generation; **uit die – tree,** fall out.
geliefde, (-s), beloved, dearest, sweetheart.
geliefkoosde, favourite.
geliewe, please; – my te berig, kindly inform me.
gelinieer(d), (-de), ruled (paper).
gelit, vide **geleed.**
gelling, gallon, (-s), gallon.
gelofte, (-s), solemn promise, vow.
gelol, botheration; vide **gefoeter.**
geloof, (-lowe), n. belief, faith; creed, religion; credit, credence, trust; **–, hoop en liefde,** faith, hope and charity; **– heg aan,** give credence to, believe; **'n blinde –,** implicit faith; **in die – verkeer,** be under the impression; **op goeie –,** (up) on trust.
geloof, gelowe, (het –), believe, credit, vide **glo.**
geloofbaar, (-bare), believable, credible.
geloofbaarheid, credibility.
geloofflik, (-e), vide **geloofbaar.**
geloofsartikel, article of faith.
geloofsbelydenis, confession of faith, creed.
geloofsbeswaare, religious scruples.
geloofsbriewe, credentials.
geloofsformulier, creed.
geloofsgenesing, faith-healing.
geloofslewe, inner life, religious life.
geloofsoortuiging, religious conviction.
geloofsvervolging, religious persecution.
geloofsvryheid, religious liberty (freedom).
geloofsywer, religious zeal.
geloofwaardig, (-e), credible, reliable.
geloofwaardigheid, reliability.
gelowig, (-e), believing, faithful, pious.
gelowige, (-s), believer; (pl.) the faithful.

gelowigheid, faithfulness, piety.
geluid, (-e), sound, noise.
geluiddemper, silencer, sordine, mute.
geluidsleer, acoustics.
geluidsmyn, acoustic mine.
geluidstrilling, sound-vibration.
geluidvry, (-e), sound-proof.
geluim(d), (-de): goed –, good humoured; **sleg –,** in a bad temper.
geluk, (-ke), n. bliss, felicity, happiness, joy; fortune, (good) luck; success; **huislike –,** domestic happiness; **wat 'n –!,** what a piece of luck!; **– hê,** be in luck, be fortunate (lucky); **jou – beproef,** try one's luck; **–, hoor!,** good luck!; congratulations; **veels –!,** hearty congratulations; **by –,** by chance, by good fortune; **op goeie – af,** at a venture, at random; **van – kan praat,** think oneself lucky, thank one's stars.
geluk, (het –), succeed, have luck; **as dit hom –,** if he succeeds; **dit het my – om . . . ,** I managed to . . .
gelukbrenger, –bringer, charm, mascot.
gelukkig, (-e), happy, fortunate, lucky; **'n –e afloop,** a happy ending; **'n –e toeval,** a lucky chance, fluke; **'n –e voorteken,** a good omen.
gelukkige, (-s), lucky person.
gelukkigerwys(e), fortunately, happily.
geluksalig, (-e), blessed.
geluksaligheid, bliss, blessedness, beatitude.
geluksbeentjie, merry-thought, wishing-bone.
geluksgodin, goddess of fortune, Fortune.
gelukskind, fortune's favourite, lucky dog.
gelukskoot, lucky shot; fluke, windfall.
gelukslag, piece of good luck, godsend.
geluksoeker, adventurer, fortune-hunter.
geluksoekster, gold-digger (woman).
gelukstaat, happiness, blessed state, bliss.
gelukster, lucky star.
geluksvoël, vide **gelukskind.**
gelukwens, n. congratulation.
gelukwens, (gelukge-), congratulate, wish good luck (happiness, joy).
gelukwensing, (-e, -s), congratulation.
gelyk, (-e), n. right; **iemand – gee,** agree that a person is right; **– hê,** be right; **– kry,** be put in the right; **in die – stel,** put in the right, justify.
gelyk, (-e), n. like; **daar is meer –e as eie,** appearances are deceptive.
gelyk, (-e), a. alike, equal, identical, same, flush, level; smooth; **as al die ander dinge – is,** other things being equal; **die gevalle is nie – nie,** the cases are not on all fours; **jouself – bly,** be consistent; **dit is my –,** it makes no difference to me; **in –e mate,** equally; **met –e munt betaal,** pay back in the same coin; **onder –e voorwaardes,** on equal terms; **op –e wyse,** in the same way; **van –e datum,** of even (same) date.
gelyk, adv. equally, similarly, alike; at the same time, simultaneously; vide **tegelyk.**
gelyk, (het –): – op, be (look) like, resemble; vide **lyk, (ge-).**
gelykbeduidend, –betekenend, (-e), synonymous.
gelykbenig, (-e), isosceles (triangle).
gelyke, (-s), equal; **jou –s,** your equals.
gelykend, (-e), like; **dit is 'n –e portret,** this photo is very like, this (photo) is a good likeness.
gelykenis, (-se), likeness, resemblance, similarity; parable (Bib.).
gelykerwys(e), just as, like(wise).
gelykgeregtig, (-de), of equal rank (status); with equal rights (title).
gelykgesind, (-e), like-minded, of one mind.
gelykgesindheid, unanimity.

**gelykheid, equality; similarity; evenness.
gelykhoekig, (-e), equiangular, isogonal.
gelyklik, equally, in equal parts.
gelykluidend, (-e), exact, consonant; homonymous (words); true (copy); of the same tenor.
gelykmaak, (gelykge-), equalize, equate; level, raze (to the ground), smooth.
gelykmaking, equalisation, equating; levelling, razing.
gelykmatig, (-e), equable; uniform; even; unruffled.
gelykmatigheid, equableness, uniformity.
gelykmiddelpuntig, (-e), concentric.
gelykmoedig, (-e), even-tempered.
gelykmoedigheid, equanimity.
gelyknamig, (-e), of the same name; like (poles); –e breuke, fractions with the same denominator; – maak, reduce (fractions) to the same denominator.
gelykop, equally; deuce (in tennis); – speel, draw, play a draw.
gelyksoortig, (-e), similar, of the same kind.
gelyksoortigheid, similarity.
gelykspel, draw, tie.
gelykstaan, (gelykge-), be equal; – met, be equal (equivalent) to, amount to.
gelykstel, (gelykge-), put on a par (with), place on the same level (as).
gelykstelling, equalisation, levelling.
gelykstroom, continuous (direct) current.
gelyksydig, (-e), equilateral (triangle).
gelykteken, sign of equality, equation-sign.
gelyktydig, (-e), simultaneously; contemporary.
gelyktydigheid, simultaneousness, synchronism.
gelykvloeiend, (-e), regular.
gelykvloers, on the ground-floor; on the same floor; homely, plain.
gelykvormig, (-e), similar; uniform.
gelykvormigheid, conformity, similarity.
gelykwaardig, (-e), equivalent; of equal value.
gelykwaardigheid, equivalence.
gemaak, (-te), ready-made; affected, studied, sham.
gemaaktheid, affectation.
gemaal, (-male, -s), n. consort, spouse.
gemagtigde, (-s), proxy; vide magtig.
gemak, comfort, convenience, ease, facility; leisure; met –, with ease, easily; op sy –, leisurely; op my dooie –, at my leisure; nie op sy – nie, uncomfortable; iemand op sy – laat voel, set a person at ease; vir die –, for convenience.
gemaklik, (-e), easy, comfortable.
gemaklikheid, ease, comfortableness.
gemakshalwe, for convenience' sake.
gemaksug, love of ease.
gemaksugtig, (-e), easy-going, ease-loving.
gemaksug, love of ease.
gemalin, (-ne), consort, spouse, wife.
gemanier(d), (-de), well-bred, mannerly.
gemanierdheid, mannerliness.
gemaniëreerd, (-e), mannered.
gemaniëreerdheid, mannerism.
gemarmer(d), (-de), marbled; mottled (soap).
gemasker(d), (-de), masked (ball).
gematig, (-de), moderate, temperate.
gematigheid, moderation; temperateness.
gemeen, (gemene), a. & adv., common; general, public; ordinary, usual, base, means, vulgar; gemene spel, foul play; gemene streek, dirty (shabby) trick; gemene saak maak met, make common cause with; niks – hê met nie, have nothing in common with; dit is –, it's a shame; iemand – behandel, treat a person meanly; gemene boedel, joint estate.
gemeengoed, common property.**

**gemeenheid, meanness, shabbiness; vulgarity.
gemeenplaas, commonplace, platitude.
gemeensaam, (-same), familiar, intimate.
gemeensaamheid, familiarity, intimacy.
gemeenskap, community, intercourse; communication; – van goedere, community of property; – hê (hou) met, have intercourse with.
gemeenskaplik, (-e), common, joint; collective community (singing).
gemeenskaplikheid, community.
gemeenskapskas, community-chest.
gemeenslagtig, (-e), of common gender.
gemeente, (-s), community, congregation.
gemeentegrond, church-ground; commonage.
gemeentelid, church-member.
gemeentelik, (-e), municipal.
gemelik, (-e), cross, morose, peevish.
gemelikheid, moroseness, peevishness.
gemenebes, (-te), commonwealth.
gemenereg, Common Law.
gemeng, (-de), mixed (miscellaneous); –de getal, mixed (fractional) number; met –de gevoelens, with mixed (mingled) feelings.
gemenigheid, shabby trick; scurrility.
gemes, (-te), fatted (calf); stalled (ox).
gemeubileer(d), (-de), furnished.
gemiddeld, (-e), average, mean, medium.
gemiddelde, (-s), average, mean.
gemis, lack, want.
gemmer, ginger.
gemmerbier, ginger-beer.
gemmerkoekie, ginger-nut.
gemmerkonfyt, ginger(-preserve).
gemodder, intriguing, plotting, scheming.
gemoed, (-ere), mind, heart; sy – het vol geskiet he was deeply moved; die –ere het in beweging gekom, feeling ran high; op sy – oortuig, convinced in his heart of hearts.
gemoedelik, (-e), genial, good-natured.
gemoedelikheid, good nature, joviality.
gemoedsaandoening, emotion, feeling.
gemoedsgesteldheid, attitude (frame) of mind.
gemoedsrus, peace of mind.
gemoedstemming, frame of mind, mood.
gemoedstoestand, state of mind.
gemoedstryd, internal struggle.
gemoei(d): mee –, at stake, involved.
gemors, mess(ing); filth.
gemsbok, vide gensbok.
gemunt, (-e), coined; – op, aimed at.
gemurmel, gurgling, murmuring.
gemurmureer, grumbling, murmuring.
gemymer, meditation, musing, reverie.
genaak, (het –), approach, come (draw) near.
genaakbaar, (-bare), accessible.
genaakbaarheid, accessibility.
genaamd, called, named, by name.
genade, grace; mercy; pardon; goeie –!, good gracious!; – betoon, pardon, show mercy to; geen – is gevra of gegee nie, no quarter was asked or given; – in sy oë vind, find favour in his eyes; aan die – van iemand oorgelewer wees, be at the mercy of someone; deur die – van God, by the grace of God; om – vra, pray for mercy; sonder –, without mercy, merciless; uit –, as an act of grace.
genadebrood, bread of charity.
genadedoder, humane killer.
genademiddel, (-e), means of grace.
genadeslag, death-blow, knock-out blow.
genadestaat, state of grace.
genadestoel, -troon, mercy-seat.
genadig, (-e), gracious, merciful; lenient; God sy my –!, God have mercy upon me!; – behandel, treat leniently.**

genadigheid, grace, mercy; clemency.
genant, (-e), namesake.
gene, yonder.
genealogie, (-ë), genealogy.
genealogies, (-e), genealogic(al).
genealoog, (-loë, -loge), genealogist.
geneë, disposed, inclined, ready, willing.
geneentheid, disposition, inclination, affection, attachment, liking, love.
geneer, (het –), inconvenience, incommode; **jou –,** feel ashamed; be shy.
genees, (het –), cure, heal; cover, get well again; be restored (to health); **iemand van sy siekte (kwaal) –,** cure someone of his disease.
geneesbaar, (-bare), curable, remediable.
geneesbaarheid, curability.
geneesheer, doctor, physician.
geneesinrigting, sanatorium.
geneeskrag, curative (healing) power.
geneeskragtig, (-e), curative; medicinal.
geneeskunde, medical science, medicine.
geneeskundig, (-e), medical.
geneeskundige, (-s), vide **geneesheer.**
geneeslik, (-e), geneesbaar.
geneesmeester, vide **geneesheer.**
geneesmiddel, medicine, remedy, physic.
geneesmiddelleer, pharmacology.
geneeswyse, method of medical treatment, cure.
geneig, disposed, inclined, prone, apt (to).
geneigdheid, inclination, disposition.
gener, van nul en – waarde, null and void.
generaal, (-s), general.
generaal-majoor, major-general.
generaliseer, (ge-), generalise.
generasie, (-s), generation.
generator, (-s), generator, producer.
genereer, (ge-), bring forth, produce.
generies, (-e), generic (biol.).
genesing, cure, healing, recovery.
Genesis, Genesis.
geneties, (-e), genetic.
genetika, genetica, genetics.
geniaal, (-ale), brilliant, gifted.
genialiteit, brilliance, giftedness, genius.
genie, (-ë), genius, man of genius.
geniekorps, corps of (military) engineers.
geniepsig, (-e), a. & adv. hurting, rough; malicious.
geniepsigheid, roughness; maliciousness.
geniet, (het –), enjoy; **'n goeie opvoeding –,** receive a good education; **ek het dit –,** I enjoyed it; I enjoyed myself.
genietbaar, (-bare), enjoyable.
genietbaarheid, enjoyableness.
genieting, (-e, -s), enjoyment; pleasure.
genietroepe, engineers (mil.).
genitief, (-tiewe), genitive.
genius, (genii), genius.
genoeë, genoege, (-ns), delight, joy, pleasure, liking; satisfaction; **dit doen (gee) my – om – ek het die – om . . . ,** it affords (gives) me pleasure to, I have pleasure in . . . ; **sal jy my die – doen om . . . ?,** will you oblige me with . . . ?; will you do me the favour (pleasure) of . . . ; – **neem met,** be content with, put up with; – **skep in,** take delight (pleasure) in; **met –,** with pleasure; **na –,** to one's liking (satisfaction); **tot – van,** to the satisfaction of.
genoeg, n., a. & adv. enough, sufficient; sufficiently; **dit is –,** that will do; **hy het swaar – gely,** he has suffered sufficiently; – **drink,** drink one's fill.
genoegdoening, satisfaction, reparation.
genoege, vide **genoeë.**
genoeglik, (-e), agreeable, enjoyable.

genoeglikheid, enjoyableness, pleasantness.
genoegsaam, (-same), sufficient.
genoegsaamheid, sufficiency.
genoem(d), (-de), called, named.
genooide, (-s), invited person, guest.
genoop, obliged; **jou – voel om . . . ,** feel compelled (obliged) to; vide **noop.**
genoot, (-note), companion, partner.
genootskap, associasion, company, society.
genot, (genietinge, genietings), delight, pleasure; enjoyment; possession; usufruct; – **verskaf,** afford (give) pleasure; **die – van die erflating,** the usufruct of the legacy; **dit is 'n – om . . . ,** it is a treat to . . . ; **onder die – van . . . ,** while enjoying . . . , over (a glass) . . . ; **tot – van,** to the delight of.
genote, enjoyed; **vir waarde –,** for value received.
genotmiddel, luxury.
genotryk, (-e), delightful, enjoyable.
genotsiek, (-e), genotsugtig, (-e), pleasure-loving.
genotsug, love of pleasure.
genotvol, (-le), vide **genotryk.**
genre, (-s), genre, kind, sort, style.
gensbok, gemsbok, gemsbok; (Cape) oryx.
gentiaan, gentian.
Genuees, (-uese), Genoese.
genugtig, goeie (my)–!, good gracious!
geodesie, geodesy.
geodeties, (-e), geodesic, geodetic (survey).
geoefen(d), (-de), drilled, practised, trained, expert (swimmer).
geofisika, geophysics.
geofisikus, geophysicist.
geograaf, (-grawe), geographer.
geografie, geography.
geografies, (-e), geographic(al).
geologie, geology.
geologies, (-e), geologic(al).
geoloog, (-loë), geologist.
geometrie, geometry.
geometries, (-e), geometric(al).
geoorloof, (-de), allowed, lawful, permissible; **-de middele,** lawful means.
gepaar(d), (-de), coupled; in pairs; – **gaan met,** be attended with, involve.
gepantser, (-de), armoured (train), armour-clad, iron-clad (ship); mailed (fist).
gepas, (-te), apt; becoming, fitting, proper.
gepassioneer, (-de), passionate.
gepasteuriseer(d), (-de), pasteurised.
gepastheid, aptness, fitness, propriety.
gepeins, meditation, reflection, reverie; **in – versonke,** absorbed in thought.
gepensioeneerde, (-s), pensioner.
gepeper, (-de), peppered, seasoned.
geperforeer, (-de), perforated.
gepers, (-te), pressed, compressed; ironed.
gepersonifieer, (-de), personified.
gepeupel, mob, populace, rabble, riff-raff.
gepeuter, fumbling; trifling.
gepikeer(d), (-de), offended, piqued.
geplaag, gepla(e), n. bothering, nagging.
geplaag, (-de), a. tormented, vexed.
geploeter, plodding, toiling.
gepolitoer, (-de), polished.
gepraat, talk, tittle-tattle.
gepreek, preaching, sermonising.
geprimediteer(d), (-de), premeditated.
geprewel, mumbling, muttering.
geprikkel(d), (-de), irritated.
gepromoveer, (-de), promoted (to degree).
gepromoveerde, (-s), graduate; doctor.
gepronk, ostentation, showing-off.
geprononseer(d), (-de), pronounced.
geproporsioneer(d), (-de), proportioned.

gepruttel, grumbling.
geraak, (-te), offended, vexed; **lig –**, ready to take offence, touchy.
geraaktheid, irritability, pique.
geraamte, (-s), carcass, skeleton; framework.
geraas, (-ase), din, hubbub, noise, roar.
gerade, advisable; **dit – ag**, think fit.
gerafel(d), (-de), frayed, unravelled.
geraffineer(d), (-de), refined (sugar); **'n –de skurk**, a thorough-paced villain.
geranium, (-s), geranium.
geratel, rattling.
geredekawel, arguing, logic-chopping.
geredelik, (-e), a. & adv. promptly.
gereed, ready; done, finished; prepared; **jou – hou = – staan**, hold oneself ready (in readiness); **– maak**, prepare, get ready.
gereedheid, readiness; **in – bring**, prepare.
gereedhou, (gereedge-), hold in readiness.
gereedmaak, (gereedge-), prepare, get ready.
gereedmaking, preparation.
gereedskap, implements, tools; utensils; tackle.
gereedskapskis, tool-box.
gereeld, (-e), fixed, orderly, regular.
gereeldheid, regularity.
gereformeerd, (-e), reformed.
gereg (-te), n. course, dish.
gereg, n. justice; court (of justice), tribunal; **jou aan die – oorgee**, give oneself up to justice; **voor die – bring**, bring into court, have up; **voor die – verskyn**, appear in court.
gereg, (-te), just, righteous.
geregsaal, lawcourt.
geregsbode, usher; messenger of the court.
geregsdienaar, officer of the court; policeman.
geregshof, court (of justice), lawcourt.
geregtelik, (-e), judicial (execution); legal (steps); forensic (medicine).
geregtig, entitled, justified, warranted.
geregtigheid, justice.
gerek, (-te), lengthy, protracted.
gereserveer(d), (-de), reserved; reticent.
gereserveerdheid, aloofness, reserve.
gereutel, death-rattle, ruckle.
gerf, (gerwe), sheaf.
geriatrie, geriatrics.
gerib, (-de), ribbed, channelled.
grief, (geriewe), n. convenience; gadget.
grief, geriewe, (het –), accommodate, oblige, be of service (to).
grieflik, (-e), comfortable, convenient.
grieflikheid, convenience, facility.
geriewe: ten – van, for the convenience of.
geriffel, (-de), corrugated, ribbed.
gerig, judgment; **die jongste –**, doomsday.
gerimpel, (-de), furrowed, wrinkled.
gering, (-e), slight, small, scanty, poor, trifling.
geringe -skat, (geringge-), disparage, hold cheap, underestimate.
geringagting, -skatting, underestimation; disparagement, disdain; **met – praat oor**, speak disparagingly of.
gerinkel, jingling, clank.
gerinkink, merry-making, loafing.
geritsel, rustle, rustling.
Germaan, (-mane), Teuton.
Germaans, (-e), Teutonic, Germanic.
Germanisme, (-s), Germanism.
germanium, germanium.
geroep, calling, cries, shouting, shouts.
geroepe, called upon; **jou – ag**, feel called upon; **kom of jy – is**, come in the nick of time.
geroesemoes, bustle, buzz, din, hurly-burly.
geroetineer(d), (-de), experienced, practised.
geroffel, roll, rub-a-dub (of drum).

geroggel, rattling, death-rattle; gurgling.
gerommel, rumbling.
gerond, (-e), rounded (vowel).
geronne, curdled (milk); clotted (blood).
gerooster, (-de), grilled, toasted (bread).
gerub, (-s -im), gerubyn, (-e), cherub.
gerug, (-te), report, rumour.
gerugmakend, (-e), sensational, epoch-making.
gerugsteun: – deur, supported (backed up) by.
geruime, considerable, ample, long (time).
geruis, rustle, rustling, rushing, swish.
geruisloos, (-lose), noiseless, silent.
geruit, (-e), n. check (material); gingham.
geruit, (-e), a. checked, chequered; **–e papier**, graph-paper, squared paper.
gerus, (-te), a. calm, easy, quiet; **'n – te gewete**, a clear conscience; **'n –te lewe**, a quiet life; **nie heeltemal – nie**, not altogether easy.
gerus, adv. safely, **kom –**, do come; **ek durf – beweer**, I can safely say; **jy kan dit – doen**, you can safely do it; you are welcome to doing it; please do it; **ewe –**, quite unconcernedly.
gerusstel, (gerusge-), reassure, relieve, set a person's mind at ease.
gerusstellend, (-e), reassuring (news).
gerusstelling, (-e, -s), assurance, relief.
gerustheid, confidence, comfort, easiness, peace, security; **met –**, confidently.
gerymel, doggerel, rhyming.
gesaaide, (-s), crop.
gesag, authority, power, prestige; **die – voer**, be in command; **met – praat**, speak authoritatively; **op – aanneem**, take on trust; **op – handel**, act on authority; **op eie –**, on one's own authority, off one's own bat; **'n man van –**, an authority.
gesaghebbend, (-e), authoritative; **in –e kringe**, in influential (leading) circles.
gesaghebber, (-s), commander.
gesagvoerder, (-s), commander.
gesalfde, (-s), anointed.
gesame(nt)lik, (-e), a. complete (works), total (amount), joint (owners), united (forces), concerted (action).
gesame(nt)lik, adv. collectively, in a body, jointly, together, unitedly.
gesang, (-e), song, hymn, warbling (of birds).
gesang(e)boek, -bundel, hymnbook.
gesanik, bother(ation), nagging, droning.
gesant, (-e), minister; ambassador.
gesantskap, (-pe), embassy, legation.
gesantskapsekretaris, secretary to an embassy (a legation).
gesê: jou nie laat – nie, not listen; disregard advice (warning).
geseën, (-de), blessed; fortunate; **–de ouderdom**, ripe old age; **– met wêreldse goedere**, blessed with worldly goods.
gesegde, (-s), expression, phrase, saying; predicate (gramm.).
geseglik, (-e), docile, tractable.
geseglikheid, tractability.
gesel, (-le), companion, fellow mate.
gesel, (-s), n. lash, scourge, whip.
gesel, (ge-), flog, lash, whip, scourge.
geseling, (-e -s), scourging, flogging.
gesellig, (-e), sociable; cosy, snug; social (intercourse).
geselligheid, conviviality, sociability; cosiness, snugness (of a room); social (meeting); **vir die –, for company**.
gesellin, (-ne), (female) companion.
geselroede, lash, scourge, rod.
gesels, (het –), chat, converse, talk.
geselserig, (-e), chatty; talkative.

geselsery, chatting, conversing, talking.
geselskap, (-pe), conversation; company, society; **iemand – hou**, bear (keep) a person company; **in – van**, in the company of; **in slegte – geraak**, fall (get) into bad company.
geselskapsjuffrou, lady-companion.
geselskapspeletjie, social game.
geselskapsreis, party-tour; guided tour.
geset, (-te), corpulent, stout, thickset; definite, fixed, regular, set (times).
gesete, seated; mounted.
gesetheid, corpulence, stoutness.
gesien, (-e), seen; esteemed, respected.
gesig, (-te), face countenance; view, prospect, sight, eyesight, vision; **–te trek**, pull (make) faces,; **jou – verloor**, lose one's sight; **by die – van**, at sight of; **in die –**, in view; **in die – kom**, come into sight (view); **in die – kry**, catch sight of; **in die – kyk**, look full in the face; **iemand in sy – prys**, praise a person to his face; **iemand iets in sy – sê**, tell someone something to his face; **op die eerste –**, at first sight; on the face of it; **uit die –**, out of sight; **uit die – verdwyn**, disappear (vanish) from sight; **uit die – verloor**, lose sight of; **iemand van – ken**, know a person by sight.
gesiggie, (-s), little face; pansy.
gesighou, uppercut.
gesigsbedrog, optical illusion.
gesigsbeeld, visual image.
gesigseinder, horizon, skyline.
gesigsenu(wee), facial (optic) nerve.
gesigskring, field (range) of vision; (intellectual) horizon, ken.
gesigspunt, aspect, point of view; **uit 'n ander – beskou**, viewed from a different angle.
gesigsveld, field of vision.
gesin, (-ne), family, household.
gesind, (-e), disposed, inclined, minded.
gesindheid, disposition, view; **godsdienstige –**, religious persuasion.
gesindte, (-s), denomination, persuasion; sect.
gesinshoof, head of the family.
gesinslede, members of the family.
gesinslewe, family-life.
gesitueeer(d), (-de), circumstanced, situated.
geskakeer(d), (-de), chequered, variegated.
geskal, flourish (of trumpets), clangour.
geskape, created; **dit staan so daarmee –**, such is the state of things.
geskeidenheid, separation; separateness.
geskeie, divorced; separated.
geskel, abuse, abusive language.
geskenk, (-e), gift, present; **ten –e gee**, make a present of, present with.
geskenkbewys, gift coupon.
geskerm, fencing, juggling (with figures).
gesketter, blare, flourish (of trumpets).
geskied, (het –), come to pass, happen, occur, take place; **U wil –**, Thy will be done; **reg moet –**, justice must prevail.
geskiedenis, (-se), history; story, tale; **'n lastige –**, an awkward affair; **'n mooi –**, a pretty kettle of fish; **nuwe –**, modern history; **ou –**, ancient history; **daar is 'n – aan verbonde**, thereby hangs a tale.
geskiedenisboek, history-book.
geskiedenisles, history-lesson.
geskiedenisonderwyser, history-master.
geskiedkundig, (-e), historical.
geskiedkundige, (-s), historian.
geskiedrol, historical record, (pl.) archives.
geskiedskrywer, **-vorser**, historian, historiographer.
geskiedskrywing, **-vorsing**, historiography.

geskiedverhaal, history.
geskiedvorser, **-vorsing**, vide **geskiedskrywer**, **skrywing**.
geskik, (-te), able, appropriate, capable, suitable; **'n –te kandidaat**, an eligible candidate; **'n –te kêrel**, a decent fellow; **'n –te persoon**, a fit person; **'n –te tyd**, a proper (suitable) time; **– om te eet**, fit to eat (to be eaten); **– vir**, adapted to.
geskiktheid, ability, capability; fitness.
geskil, (-te), difference, dispute, quarrel.
geskilpunt, matter (point, question) at issue.
geskipper, temporizing.
geskitter, glitter(ing), sparkle.
geskok, n. jolting, shaking.
geskok, (-te), a. shocked.
geskommel, rocking, swinging; fluctuation.
geskool(d), (-de), practised, schooled, trained; **–de arbeid**, skilled labour.
geskraap, scraping; money-grubbing.
geskree(u), crying; cries, shouting, shouts, shrieks.
geskrei, crying, weeping; wailing.
geskrif, (-te), document, writing; **in –te**, in writing on paper.
geskryf, scribbling; writing; polemic.
geskub, (-de), scaled, scaly.
geskut, n. artillery, guns, ordnance.
geskutpark, artillery-park, gun-yard.
geskutpoort, porthole.
geskutvuur, gunfire.
geslaag, (-de), successful.
geslag, (-te), n. family, race, lineage; gender, sex; generation; genus, tribe; **manlike –**, masculine gender; **die manlike –**, the male sex, **die menslike –**, the human race; **die skone –**, the fair sex; **die opkomende –**, the rising generation.
geslag(s)boom, family-tree, genealogical table
geslagkunde, genealogy.
geslagsattraksie, sex appeal.
geslagloos, (-lose), sexless; genderless.
geslagsmaniak, sex maniac.
geslag(s)register, genealogical table.
geslagsboom, vide **geslag(s)boom**.
geslagsdele, genital parts.
geslagsdrif, sexual passion.
geslagsnaam, family-name; genus-name.
geslagsorgane, vide **geslagsdele**.
geslagsregister, vide **geslag(s)register**.
geslagsryp, (-e), puberal.
geslagsverhouding, sexual relation.
geslagtelik, (-e), sexual; genital.
geslepe, cunning, sly; **– glas**, cutglass.
geslepenheid, cunning, slyness.
geslote, closed, locked, shut; reticent; **'n – boek**, a sealed book; **– geledere**, serried ranks; **agter – deure**, secretly, in camera.
geslotenheid, closeness, reticence.
gesluier(d), (-de), veiled; fogged, foggy.
gesmeek, entreaty, pleading, supplication.
gesmoor(d), (-de), suppressed; throttled (petrolfeed); strangled (voice); stewed (meat), fried (with onions).
gesnede, sliced (ham); graven (image); castrated.
gesneuwelde, (-s), person killed in action, (pl.) casualties, dead.
gesnork, snoring.
gesnuffel, sniffing; ferreting, rummaging.
gesnuif, sniffing; snorting (of a horse).
gesoebat, begging, coaxing, praying.
gesoen, kissing.
gesog, (-te), in demand, sought after; affected, far-fetched, forced, studied.
gesogtheid, affectation, far-fetchedness.

gesond, (-e), healthy, sound, wholesome; -e verstand, common sense; baie -, in the best of health; fris en -, hale and hearty; safe and sound; - bid, cure by prayer; - bly, keep fit (well); - hou, keep in health; - maak, cure, restore to health; - wees, be in good health, be well; - word, get well again, recover.
gesonde, (-s), healthy person.
gesonde, a. sent, dispatched; vide send.
gesondheid, health; healthiness, salubrity, soundness; saneness, sanity (of views); - in die rondheid!, here's (good luck) to everybody!; op iemand se - drink, drink (to) a person's health; vir die -, for the sake of one's health.
gesondheidsdiens, public health department; sanitary service.
gesondheidsertifikaat, certificate of health.
gesondheidshalwe, for the sake of one's health.
gesondheidsleer, hygiene, hygienics.
gesondheidsmaatreël, sanitary measure.
gesondheidsoord, health-resort.
gesondheidsredes, health-reasons.
gesondheidsreël, health-rule, regimen.
gesondheidstoestand, (state of) health.
gesorteer(d), (-de), assorted, graded.
gesout, (-e), salted; seasoned; cured (fish, ham); immunised (med.); -e perde, salted horses.
gespanne, stretched; bent (bow); strained (relations); rapt (attention); in - verwagting, in keen expectation; hulle verkeer op - voet, relations are strained between them.
gespannenheid, tenseness; tension; tightness.
gespartel, floundering, sprawling.
gespe(r), (-s), n. clasp, buckle.
gespe(r), (ge-), buckle, clasp; strap (on).
gespier(d), (-de), brawny, muscular, sinewy.
gespierdheid, muscularity; nervousness.
gespikkel(d), (-de), speckled, spotted.
gespits, (-te), pointed; met -te ore, with eager ears; with ears erect (animals).
gesplete, cleft (palate), split.
gespoor, (-de), spurred.
gesprek, (-ke), conversation, discourse, talk; 'n - voer, hold (carry on) a conversation; in -, in conversation; engaged (telephone).
gespuis, rabble, riff-raff, scum, vermin.
gestadig, (-e), constant; regular, steady.
gestadigheid, constancy, steadiness.
gestalte, (-s), build, figure, stature.
gestaltenis, (-se), figure, shape.
gestamel, stammering.
gestamp, n. pounding, trampling; pitching.
gestamp, (-te), a. -te mielies, samp.
gestand: sy belofte (woord) - doen, keep one's promise, redeem one's pledge.
gestasioneer(d), (-de), stationed.
geste, (-s), gesture.
gesteente, (-s), (precious) stones; rocks.
gestel, (-le), n. constitution, system.
gestel(d), (-de), a.: die magte oor ons -, the powers that be; dis daarmee so -, that is how matters stand; op iets - wees, be fond of something; stand on doing something; op sy waardigheid - wees, stand on one's dignity.
gestel(d), conj. suppose, supposing.
gesteldheid, condition, nature, character, state.
gestem(d), (-de), disposed; tuned.
gesternte, (-s), constellation, star(s); onder 'n gelukkige - gebore, born under a lucky star.
gesteur(d), gestoor(d), (-de), piqued, offended.
gestewel, (-de), booted.
gestig, (-te), n. institution, establishment, building, edifice; asylum, home.
gestikulasie, (-s), gesticulation.
gestikuleer, (ge-), gesticulate, make gestures.

gestileer(d), (-de), composed; conventionalized.
gestippel(d), (-de), spotted; dapple; pitted.
gestoei, romping.
gestoelte, (-s), seat.
gestol(d), (-de), congealed, curled, clotted.
gestommel, stumbling, row.
gestoor(d), vide gesteur(d).
gestotter, stammering, stuttering.
gestreep, (-te), striped, banded, streaked.
gestrek, (-te), stretched; -te hoek, straight angle; -te voet, linear foot; -te draf, full trot.
gestreng, (-e), severe; vide streng.
gestudeer(d), (-de), studied, of study.
gesuis, buzz(ing); singing (in ears); sough (of wind).
gesuiwer, (-de), purified; refined; fine, pure.
gesukkel, ailing; bungling; botheration.
gesusters, sisters.
geswam, gas, slush, tosh.
geswa(w)el, (-de), sulphured (lit.); tipsy.
geswel, (-le), growth, swelling, tumour.
geswets, blasphemy, swearing.
geswind, (-e), quick, rapid, swift, nimble.
geswoeg, drudging, drudgery, toiling.
geswolle, swollen (river); bombastic, stilted.
geswore, sworn; vide sweer, (ge-), (2).
getak, (-te), branched; forked (lightning).
getal, (-le), number; in groot -le, in great numbers; in (full) force; in groot -le voorkom, abound; ten -e van, to the number of ...
getallefaktor, numerical factor.
getalleleer, theory of numbers.
getalm, dawdling, lingering, loitering.
getalsterkte, numerical strength.
getand, (-e), edged, jagged, toothed; cogged (wheel); dentate(d); serrate(d).
geteken, (-de), marked.
getemper, (-de), moderate, temperate.
getik, n. ticking; rapping; clicking.
getik, (-te), a. crack-brained; tipsy.
getimmerte, (-s), building, structure.
getitel(d), (-de), entitled; titled (person).
getjank, crying, howling, whining.
getjilp, chirping, twittering (of birds).
getob, drudgery, toiling; bother, worry.
getoë, bred; gebore en -, born and bred.
getoeter, hoot(ing), toot(ing), tootling.
getokkel, thrumming.
getralie(d), (-de), grated, latticed, trellised.
getrappel, stamping, trampling.
getrippel, tripping.
getrokke, drawn (sword); vide trek, (ge-),
getroos, (-te), a. comforted; ewe -, quite coolly.
getroos, (het -), jou -, resign oneself to; jou baie moeite -, grudge (spare) no pains; jou ontberinge -, put up with privations.
getrou, (-e), faithful, devoted, loyal, reliable, true, trusty, close (paraphrase); exact (copy); - na die lewe, true to life.
getroud, (-e), married; -e lewe, married life.
getroude, (-s), married person.
getroue, (-s), faithful follower, supporter.
getrouheid, faithfulness, loyalty, reliability.
getuie, (-s), n. witness; deponent; second (at a duel); deur -(s) gestaaf, attested; tot - roep, call to witness; put in the (witness-)box; - wees van, be a witness of (to), witness.
getuie, **getuig**, (het -), testify, attest, depose, bear witness, give evidence, bear testimony; - teen, testify (give evidence) against; die feite - teen hom, the facts are against him; - van; testify, to argue, bespeak; - vir, speak (tell) in (one's) favour.
getuiebank, witness-box.
getuiegeld, witness-fee, (-money).

getuienis, (-se), evidence, testimony; deposition; – **aflê**, give evidence.
getuig, vide **getuie**, (het –).
getuigskrif, certificate; testimonial.
gety, (-e), tide.
getyeboek, breviary.
getygolf, tidal wave.
geul, (-e), channel, gully.
geur, (-e), n. perfume, scent, smell, aroma.
geur, (ge-), smell, give forth perfume (scent).
geurig, (-e), fragrant, sweet-smelling.
geurigheid, fragrance, perfume.
geurtjie, (-s), flavour; **daar is 'n – aan**, there is something strange about it.
Geus, (-e), Beggar, (Dutch) Protestant.
geut, (-e), gutter; drain, sewer; duct.
gevaar, (gevare), danger, peril, risk; – **loop**, incur (run) a risk; **in – bring**, endanger, imperil; **met – van**, at the hazard (peril, risk) of; **op – (af) van**, at the risk of.
gevaarlik, (-e), dangerous, perilous.
gevaarlikheid, danger(ousness).
gevaarte, (-s), colossus, monster; affair.
gevaarvol, (-le), vide **gevaarlik**.
geval, (-le), n. case; event, instance, matter, **by –**, in case; by chance; **in –**, in case; **in alle –**, = **in elk –**, in any case, at any rate; **in die ergste –**, if the worst comes to the worst, **in geen –**, in no case, on no account; **in die meeste –le**, in most cases; **in – van**, in case of; **in – van nood**, in case of need, in an emergency; **vir die – dat**, in case.
geval, (het –), please, suit; **dit – my nie**, I don't like it; **jou iets laat –**, put up with something.
gevalbeskrywing, case history.
gevallig, (-e), agreeable, pleasing.
gevange, captive, imprisoned; **jou – gee**, surrender; – **hou**, detain, keep prisoner; – **neem**, arrest; capture, take prisoner; – **sit**, be in prison; put in prison.
gevangebewaarder, jailer, warder.
gevangehouding, detention; imprisonment.
gevangene, (-s), captive, prisoner.
gevangeneming, arrest, capture.
gevangenis, (-se), gaol (jail) prison.
gevangenisstraf, confinement, imprisonment.
gevangeniswese, prison-system.
gevange(n)skap, captivity, imprisonment.
gevanklik, captive, as a prisoner; – **wegvoer**, carry off (as) a prisoner.
gevat, (-te), clever, quick-witted, smart; **'n –te antwoord**, ready retort, a repartee; **in goud –**, set in gold.
gevatheid, ready wit, smartness.
geveg, (-te), battle, engagement, fight; **buite(n) – stel**, put out of action.
gevegslinie, fighting-line.
gevegsterrein, battlefield; battle-zone.
geveins, n. dissimulation, hypocrisy.
geveins, (-de), feigned; pretended; hypocritical, assumed (indifference).
geveinsde, (-s), dissembler, hypocrite.
geveinsdheid, hypocrisy, simulation.
geves, (-te), hilt.
gevestig, (-de), fixed, established; **–de belange** (regte), vested interests.
gevier(d), (-de), fêted, popular.
gevin(d), (-de), finned, finny; pinnate.
gevlam, (-de), flamed, flamboyant.
gevlei, coaxing, flattering.
gevlek, (-te), speckled, spotted; stained; stretched (hide), (fish) cut open, "flekked".
gevleueld, (-de), winged.
gevloek, blasphemy, cursing, swearing.
gevoeglik, (-e), a. appropriate, decent.

gevoeglik, adv. appropriately, decently.
gevoeglikheid, appropriateness, decency.
gevoel, [-e(ns)], feeling, sensation, sense, touch; emotion, sentiment; **'n – hê asof**, feel like; **'n – van warmte**, a sensation of heat; **'n – vir die skone**, a sense of beauty; **met – praat**, speak feelingly, speak with emotion; **op die –**, to the touch; **op die – af**, by the feel; by the touch; **'n kwessie (saak), van –**, a matter of sentiment.
gevoel, (-de), a. felt (want).
gevoele, (-ns), feeling, opinion, sentiment, view; **ek is van – dat . . .**, I am of opinion that . . . ; **volgens sy –**, in his opinion, to his mind.
gevoelig, (-e), sensitive; susceptible; sharp (lesson); heavy (defeat); **'n –e klap**, a smart blow (lit.); a heavy blow (fig.); – **vir pyn**, sensitive to pain.
gevoeligheid, sensitiveness, susceptibility.
gevoelloos, (-lose), insensible; apathetic, callous, impassive, unfeeling; numb (off limb).
gevoelloosheid, callousness; insensibility.
gevoelsenu(wee), sensory nerve.
gevoelsin, sense of touch, tactile sense.
gevoelslewe, inner (emotional) life.
gevoelsmens, emotional person.
gevoelswaarde, emotional value.
gevoelvol, (-le), full of feeling, tender.
gevoer, (-de), fed (animal); lined (coat).
gevoelte, birds.
gevolg, (-e), consequence, effect, result; following, retinue; corollary (maths.); **oorsaak en –**, cause and effect; – **gee aan**, carry into effect, comply with; **met goeie –**, with success, successfully; **ten –e hê**, result in; **ten –e van**, in consequence of.
gevolgaanduidend, (-e), consecutive (gram).
gevolglik, accordingly, consequently.
gevolgtrekking, (-e, -s), conclusion, inference; –**e maak**, draw conclusions.
gevolmagtigde, (-s), proxy, person holding power of attorney; (minister) plenipotentiary.
gevonde, found.
gevorder(d), (-de), advanced; late (hour).
gevra, in demand, in request, wanted.
gevrees, (-de), dreaded.
gevreet, (gevrete), mug, phiz.
gevul(d), (-de), full; filled.
gevurk, (-te), forked; bifurcate.
gewaad, (gewade), attire, garb, raiment.
gewaag, (het –), – **van**, mention.
gewaag, (-de), a. risky; equivocal.
gewaagdheid, riskiness; vide **gewaag**.
gewaand, (-e), supposed.
gewaarmerk, (-te), hall-marked; certified.
gewaar, (gewaarge-) become aware of, perceive; find out.
gewaarwording, (-e, -s), feeling, perception, sensation; experience.
gewag, mention; – **maak van**, mention.
gewapen(d), (-de), armed (soldier); reinforced (concrete); **'n –de vrede**, a truce.
gewapper, fluttering, waving.
gewarrel, whirling.
gewas, (-se), growth; crop, harvest.
gewater(d), (-de), watered (silk).
gewatteer, (-de), padded; wadded.
geween, weeping.
geweer, (-s, gewere), gun, rifle; **na die – gryp**, take up arms.
geweerfabriek, small-arms factory.
geweermaker, gunmaker, gunsmith.
geweerskoot, rifle-shot, gun-shot.
geweerslot, gun-lock.
geweervuur, rifle-fire, musketry(-fire).
gewei, 1. antlers, horns.

gewei, 2. entrails, intestines.
gewel, (-s), façade, front; gable.
geweld, force, violence; **jouself – aandoen**, do violence to one's feelings, restrain oneself; **die waarheid – aandoen**, strain (stretch) the truth; **met –**, by force, forcibly; **met alle –**, by all means (by hook or by crook).
gewelddaad, act of violence, outrage.
gewelddadig, (-e), a. violent.
geweldenaar, (-s), oppressor, tyrant.
geweldig, (-e), a. enormous, powerful, mighty, prodigious, vehement, violent.
geweldig, adv. awfully, dreadfully.
geweldigheid, force, vehemence, violence.
geweldpleging, violence.
gewelf, (-welwe), arch., dome, vault.
gewellys, cornice.
geweltop, gable.
geweltrap(pie), corbie-step(s).
gewen, (het –), accustom, habituate; **jou – aan**, accustom oneself to.
gewen, accustomed, used to.
gewens, (-te), desired; desirable.
gewenstheid, desirability.
gewente, habit, custom.
gewer, (-s), donor, giver.
gewerskaf, bustle, to-do.
gewerwel(d), (-de), vertebrate.
gewes, (-te), province, region, territory.
gewese, former, late, ex.
gewesspraak, -taal, (regional) dialect.
gewestelik, (-e), regional, dialectal.
gewete, (-ns), conscience; **sy – pla hom**, he has a guilty conscience, **met jou – ooreenbring**, reconcile (square) with one's conscience; **op jou –**, on one's conscience.
gewete(n)loos, (-lose), unprincipled, unscrupulous.
gewete(n)loosheid, unscrupulousness.
gewete(n)saak, matter of conscience.
gewetensangs, qualms of conscience.
gewetensartikel, conscience-clause.
gewetensbeswaar, conscientious scruple.
gewetensdwang, moral constraint.
gewetensgeld, conscience-money.
gewetenswroeging, qualms of conscience, compunction, remorse.
gewetesaak, vide **gewete(n)saak**.
gewettig, (-de), justified, legitimate (hope).
gewig, (-te), weight; importance, moment; **soortlike –**, specific gravity; **– hê**, carry weight, be important; **– heg aan**, attach importance (weight) to; **– gee aan**, lend weight to; **– in die skaal lê**, carry weight; throw one's weight into the scale; **oor die –**, overweight; **'n man van –**, a man of weight (consequence).
gewigseenheid, unit of weight.
gewigstoot, n. putting the shot.
gewigstoot, (gewigge-), put the shot.
gewigtig, (-e), momentous, weighty.
gewigtigheid, importance, weight(iness).
gewiks, (-te), clever, knowing, sharp.
gewikstheid, quickness, sharpness, gumption.
gewild, (-e), in demand, popular; studied, laboured.
gewildheid, popularity.
gewillig, (-e), ready, willing; tractable.
gewilligheid, willingness; tractability.
gewin, n. advantage, gain, profit.
gewin, (het –), gain, win; beget (Bib.).
gewirwar, confusion.
gewis, (-se), a. certain, sure.
gewis, adv. certainly, surely, to be sure.
gewisheid, certainly, certitude.
gewis(se)lik, vide **gewis**, adv.

gewoë, weighed.
gewoel, bustle, stir; crowd, throng.
gewonde, (-s), wounded person.
gewonne, won; **dit – gee**, yield the point.
gewoon, (-wone), accustomed; common, normal, ordinary, regular, usual, customary; plain (food); vulgar (fraction); average (citizen); general (reader); **die gewone man**, the man in the street; **– raak (word) aan**, get used (accustomed) to.
gewoond, (– aan), accustomed, used to.
gewoonheid, commonness.
gewoonlik, (-e), a. & adv. common(ly), usual(ly).
gewoonte, (-s), habit, practice; custom, usage, use; **'n – word**, grow into a habit; **in die – wees**, be in the habit of; **na – = volgens –**, as usual, according to custom; **uit –**, by (from) habit.
gewoontereg, common (customary) law.
gewoonweg, downright, perfectly, simply.
geword, (het –), come to hand; **iemand laat –**, let someone have his way.
gewrig, (-te), joint; wrist.
gewrigsontsteking, arthritis.
gewrigsrumatiek, rheumatism in the joints.
gewrog, (-te), creation, production, affair.
gewronge, distorted: vide **wring**.
gewrongenheid, distortion.
gewyd, (-e), consecrated, sacred.
geyk, (-te), legally stamped; stereotyped.
ghantang, (-s), lover, suitor.
ghetto, (-'s), ghetto.
ghienie, (-s), guinea.
ghitaar, **kitaar**, (-s, tare), guitar.
ghnoe, (-s), gnu.
ghoem(a), whopper, spanker, anything big.
ghoen, (-e, -s), taw; (shooting-)marble.
ghoera, (-s), gorah (musical instrument).
ghoeroe, (-s), expert, master.
gholf, golf.
gholfbaan, golf-course, golf-links.
gholfbroek, plus-fours.
gholfveld, (golf-)links.
ghong, (-s), gong.
ghries, grease.
ghwano, guano, guano.
ghwar, (-re), lout, uncouth person.
ghwarrieboom, guarri-tree.
gids, (-e), n. guide; directory.
giegel, **giggel**, (ge-), giggle, snigger, titter.
gier, (-e), n. vulture.
gier, (-e), n. caprice, fancy; screech, yell.
gier, (ge-), scream, whistle (of wind).
gierig, (-e), avaricious, miserly, stingy.
gierigaard, (-s), miser.
gierigheid, avarice, stinginess.
giet, (ge-), pour (liquids); cast, mould.
gieter, (-s), watering-can; caster, moulder.
gietery, (-e), foundry.
gietkas, casting-box, casting-frame.
gietsel, (-s), casting; founding.
gietvorm, casting-mould, matrix.
gietyster, cast iron.
gif, (-te), n. gift, donation, present.
gif, n. poison, venom.
gifappel, apple of Sodom.
gifbeker, poison(ed)-cup.
gifgas, poison-gas.
gifklier, poison-gland.
gifleer, toxicology.
gifmenger, poisoner.
gifsakkie, poison-bag.
gifseer, -sweer, malignant ulcer.
gifstof, toxine.
giftig, (-e), poisonous, venomous; virulent.
giftigheid, poisonousness, virulence.

gifvry, (-e), non-poisonous.
gifwerend, (-e), antidotal, antitoxic.
giggel, vide **giegel**.
gil, (-te), n. scream, shriek, yell.
gil, (ge-), scream, shriek, yell.
Gila-akkedis, gila monster.
gilde, (-s), guild.
gimnasias, (-te), pupil of a gymnasium.
gimnasium, (-s), gymnasium.
gimnastiek, gymnastics.
gimnastiekles, gymnastic lesson.
gimnastiekoefening, gymnastic exercise.
gimnastiekrok, gym(-costume).
gimnastiekskoene, gym-shoes.
gimnastiekuitvoering, gymnastic display.
gimnasties, (-e), gymnastic.
gimnastiseer, (ge-), do (practise) gymnastics.
ginds, over there, yonder.
ginekologie, gynaecology.
ginnega(a)p, giggle, snigger, titter.
gips, gypsum; plaster of Paris.
gipsafgietsel, plaster-cast.
gipsmodel, plaster-cast.
gipsverband, plaster (of Paris) dressing.
giraf, (-fe), giraffe.
giroskoop, gyroscope.
gis, (-se), n. guess.
gis, n. yeast.
gis, (ge-), conjecture, guess.
gis, (ge-), ferment, rise, work.
gisbalie, **-kuip**, fermenting-vat.
gisp, (ge-), censure, blame.
gissing, (-e, -s), conjecture, guess, supposition; estimate; **na –**, roughly.
gisstof, ferment.
gister, yesterday.
gisteraand, yesterday evening, last night.
gistermiddag, yesterday afternoon.
gistermôre, **-oggend**, yesterday morning.
gisternag, last night.
gisting, ferment(ation); excitement.
git, jet.
gitswart, jet-black.
gla(a)s- . . . , vide **glas-** . . .
glaasogie, white-eye (bird).
gla(a)spypie, glass-tube.
glacé, kid (leather).
glacé-handskoene, kid gloves.
glad, (-de), a. smooth, plain (ring); slippery (floor); **so – soos seep**, as slippery as an eel; **– van tong**, glib, smooth-tongued.
glad, adv. altogether, quite; smoothly; **– nie**, not at all, by no means; **– vergeet**, clean forgotten; **– verkeerd**, altogether wrong.
glad en al, altogether, quite; vide **glad**, adv.
glad(dig)heid, smoothness, slipperiness.
gladiator, (-e, -s), gladiator.
gladiolus, (-se, gladioli), gladiolus.
glans, n. gloss, lustre; brilliancy, splendour, polish; **sy – verloor**, lose its lustre.
glans, (ge-), gleam, glisten; gloss, put a shine on (collars), polish.
glansend, (-e), gleaming, shining, lustrous.
glansend, adv. brilliantly.
glans(er)ig, (-e), glossy, shining.
glansloos, (-lose), lustreless, lacklustre (eyes).
glanspapier, glazed paper.
glansperiode, heyday (of life); golden age.
glanspunt, acme; crowning event, shining glory, star turn.
glansryk, (-e), brilliant, radiant.
glansrykheid, brilliance, splendour.
glas, (-e), glass; tumbler; **agter – sit**, glaze.
glasagtig, (-e), glassy, glasslike, vitreous.
glasblaser, glass-blower.

glasblaserspyp, blowpipe.
gla(a)sdak, glass-roof.
gla(a)sdeur, glass-door, French window.
glasekas, vide **glaskas**.
glaserig, (-e), glassy, glazed (eyes).
glasfabriek, glass-works.
gla(a)sgoed, glassware.
glashelder, as clear as glass, crystal-clear.
glasindustrie, glass-industry.
gla(a)skas, glass-case, display-case.
glasmaker, glazier.
gla(a)soog, glass-eye, artificial eye.
glasskerf, fragment of glass, glass-splinter.
glasskilder, painter on glass.
glasslyper, glass-grinder.
glassnyer, glass-cutter.
glassplinter, vide **glasskerf**.
glasuur, n. enamel (of teeth); glaze, glazing (of pottery); icing (of cakes).
glasuur, (ge-), glaze.
glaswol, glass wool.
gletser, (-s), glacier.
gleuf, (gleuwe), groove; slit.
glibber, (ge-), slip, slither.
glibberig, (-e), slippery, slithery, slimy.
glieps, **glips**, (-e), mistake, slip.
glim, (ge-), glimmer, gleam, shine.
glimlag, n. smile.
glimlag, (ge-), smile, give a smile.
glimlaggie, half-smile.
glimp, (-e), glimpse; gleam, glimmer.
glimwurm, glowworm, firefly.
glinster, (ge-), glint, glitter, sparkle.
glinstering, glittering, sparkling.
glip, (ge-), slide, slip.
glippe, **die –**, the slips (in cricket).
glipperig, (-e), slippery; vide **glibberig**.
glips, vide **glieps**.
gliserien, **gliserine**, glycerine.
glo, adv. evidently, presumably, seemingly.
glo, **geloof**, **gelowe** (ge-), **het geloof**, **– gelowe**), believe; trust; think; **iemand laat –**, make a person believe; **– dit as jy wil**, believe it or not; **ek wil –**, I dare say!, I should think so!; **– aan**, believe in; **– in**, believe in.
globaal, (-bale), a. general,-rough.
globaal, adv. roughly, in the gross.
globe, (-s), globe.
gloed, blaze, glow, heat; ardour, fervour; **in –**, aglow.
gloedvol, (-le), glowing (account).
gloei, (ge-), glow, be red-hot; be aglow; **– van**, glow with (enthusiasm), burn with (indignation).
gloeidraad, filament.
gloeiend, (-e), a. glowing; red-hot (iron); live coals); ardent (love); **– van**, ablaze with (anger).
gloeiend, adv. burning hot; red-hot; broiling.
gloeihitte, intense (red, white) heat, incandescence.
gloeilamp, incandescent lamp; electric bulb (lamp).
glooi, (ge-), slope, shelve.
glooiend, (-e), sloping, shelving.
glooling, (-e, -s), slope.
gloor, (glore), n. glow; lustre, splendour.
gloor, (ge-), glimmer; dawn, break (of day).
glorie, fame, glory, lustre.
glorieryk, (-e), glorious, famous.
glorieus, (-e), splendid.
glos, (-se), gloss, comment, marginal note; **–se maak op**, comment upon.
glossarium, (-ia, -s), glossary.
gluip, (ge-), sneak, spy, skulk.

gluiperig, (-e), furtive, sneaking.
glukose, glucose, grape-sugar.
gluten, gluten.
gluur, (ge-), peep, peer, pry; leer.
gly, (ge-), slide; glide; slip.
glybaan, slide.
glyer, (-s), glider; fricative, spirant (phon.).
glyerig, (-e), slippery.
glyvlug, glide, volplane.
g'n, vide **geen,** a. & pron.
g'n, adv. not, never; **hy sal dit – doen nie,** he will never do it.
gnomon, gnomon, sun-dial.
gnoom, (gnome), gnome, hobgoblin, elf.
gnosties, (-e), gnostic.
gnostisisme, gnosticism.
gô: sy – is uit, he is played out.
gobelin, gobelin (tapestry).
God, God; (pl. **gode),** god, idol; **van – nog Sy gebod weet,** be without religion; – **sy dank,** thank God; **as – wil,** God willing; – **bewaar, God (Heaven) forbid;** – **gee,** God grant; **so waarlik, help my –,** so help me God; **naas –,** under God; **om –s wil,** for God's sake.
goddank, thank God!, thank goodness!
goddelik, (-e), divine, godlike, sublime.
goddelikheid, divineness, divinity.
goddeloos, (-lose), a. godless, impious, wicked, naughty; **'n goddelose lawaai,** a dreadful noise.
goddeloos, adv. shamelessly; **hy kan – lieg,** he lies shamelessly.
goddeloosheid, n. godlessness, impiety, ungodliness, wickedness, naughtiness.
goddelose, die –, the wicked.
godedom, the gods.
godedrank, nectar.
godeleer, mythology.
godespys, ambrosia.
godeverering, idol-worship.
godewêreld, world of the gods, pantheon.
godganse(like), die – dag, the livelong day.
godgeklaag: dis –, it cries to Heaven.
godgeleerd, (-e), theological.
godgeleerde, (-s), divine, theologian.
godgeleerdheid, theology.
godgevallig, (-e), pleasing to God.
godgewyd, (-e), consecrated to God, sacred.
godheid, divinity, godhead, deity.
godin, (-ne), goddess.
godjie, (-s), little tin-god, tin-pot deity.
godloënaar, -logenaar, (-s), atheist.
godloëning, -logening, atheism, unbelief.
godsakker, cemetery, churchyard, God's acre.
godsalig, (-e), godly, pious.
godsaligheid, godliness, piety.
godsdiens, religion, faith; divine worship.
godsdiensleraar, minister of religion.
godsdiensloos, (-lose), unreligious.
godsdiensoefening, divine service.
godsdiensonderwys, religious instruction.
godsdiensplegtigheid, religious ceremony.
godsdienstig, (-e), devout, pious, religious.
godsdienstigheid, devotion, piety, religiousness.
godsdienstwis, religious dissension (quarrel).
godsdiensvryheid, religious liberty.
godsdienswaansin, religious mania.
godsdienswetenskap, divinity, theology.
godsdiensywer, religious zeal; fanaticism.
godsgerig, ordeal, divine judgment.
godsgesant, divine messenger; apostle.
godshuis, house of God, place of worship.
godsjammerlik, (-e), miserable, pitiable.
godslasteraar, blasphemer.
godslastering, blasphemy.
godslasterlik, blasphemous.

godsnaam, in –, for Heaven's sake.
godsonmoontlik, (-e), utterly impossible.
godsoordeel, vide **godsgerig.**
godspraak, oracle, prophecy.
Godsryk, kingdom of God.
godsvrede, truce of God; political truce.
godsvrug, devotion, piety.
godswil, om –, for God's (Heaven's) sake.
godvergete, -verlate, godforsaken.
godvresend, (-e), godfearing, devout, pious.
godvresendheid, devotion, godliness, piety.
godvrugtig(heid), vide **godvresend(heid).**
goed, n. 1. good; **– en kwaad,** good and evil; **veel –s hê,** have many good points; **iets –s,** something good (concr.); some good (abstr.); **jou te – doen,** do oneself well, **jou te – doen aan,** feast upon; **ten –e,** for the good; **ten –e of ten kwade,** for good or evil (ill); **ten – kom,** do good, benefit; come in handy; change for the good; **vir –,** for good (and all).
goed, (-ere), n. 2. goods, property; estate; material, stuff, things; luggage; wares; **– en bloed,** life and property, **aardse –ere,** wordly goods; **ver van jou –, naby jou skade,** the eye of the master makes the horse fat.
goed, (goeie), a. good; good-natured, kind, correct, right, proper; **'n goeie beloning,** a liberal reward; **op 'n goeie dag,** one fine day; **die goeie ou(e) tyd,** the good old days; **alles – en wel,** all well and good; **hy was baie – vir my,** he was very good (kind) to me; **dis –!,** that's good; all right!; **wees so – om . . . ,** be so kind as . . . ; **dis – so!,** well done!, serves you right!; **te –er trou,** honest, sincere; in good faith; vide **goed,** adv.
goed, adv. well; correctly, right; **– van iemand praat,** speak well of a person; **dit sal nie – bly nie,** that won't keep; **as die weer – bly,** if the weather holds; **dit gaan –,** I am fit, thank you; I am doing well; **dit gaan jou –!,** good luck to you!; **die pak sit –,** the suit fits well; **dit – hê,** be well-off; **as ek dit – verstaan het,** if I am not mistaken; **– verstaan,** understand aright; **so – as dood,** all but dead; **so – as seker,** practically certain; **so – as niemand nie,** next to nobody; **jou – hou,** keep a straight face; bear up, keep a stiff upper lip; vide **goed,** a.
goedaardig, (-e), good-natured, kind-hearted.
goedaardigheid, kind-heartedness.
goedag, (goedge-), think fit (proper).
goeddoen, (goedge-), do good, benefit.
goeddunke, pleasure; **na –,** at will; **na – handel,** use one's own discretion.
goedere, vide **goed,** n. (2).
goederekantoor, goods-office.
goedereloods, goods-shed.
goederetrein, goods-train.
goedereverkeer, -vervoer, goods-traffic.
goederewa, goods-van, truck.
goedertiere, merciful.
goedertierenheid, loving-kindness, mercy.
goedgebou(d), (-de), well-built.
goedgeefs, (-e), generous, lavish, liberal.
goedgeefsheid, generosity.
goedgehumeur(d), (-de), good-tempered.
goedgelowig, (-e), credulous, trusting.
goedgelowigheid, credulity.
goedgesind, (-e), favourable: well-disposed.
goedgesindheid, kindness, sympathy.
goedgunstig, (-e), kind, obliging.
goedgunstiglik, kindly.
goedhartig, (-e), kind-hearted.
goedig, goeiig, (-e), good-natured.
goedheid, goodness, excellence.

goedhou, (goedge-), keep (of perishables); **jou –**, control oneself.
goedjies, goods, things, knick-knacks, trifles.
goedkeur, (goedge-), approve (of), endorse, confirm; adopt (minutes); pass.
goedkeurend, (-e), approving(ly).
goedkeuring, approval, approbation; adoption (of minutes); (royal) assent, **sy – heg aan**, approve of; **sy – onthou**, withhold one's consent; **iemand se – wegdra**, meet with a person's approval; **ter – voorlê**, submit for approval.
goedkoop, cheap, inexpensive.
goedkoopheid, -koopte, cheapness.
goedlags, easily amused.
goedmaak, (goedge-), make good, make up for, repair (a mistake), make restitution for (a wrong), make amends for.
goedmoedig(heid), vide **goedaardig(heid)**.
goedpraat, (goedge-), explain away.
goedrond, (-e), frank, straightforward.
goedskiks, willingly, with a good grace.
goedsmoeds, cheerfully; deliberately.
goedvind, (goedge-), think fit; approve of.
goedvinding, approbation; discretion.
goedwillig, (-e), a. & adv. willing(ly).
goedwilligheid, willingness.
goeie, goodness!, **– weet!**, goodness knows!
goeie, vide **goed** 1.; **goed**, a.
goei(e)naand!, good evening!
goeiendag!, good day!
goei(e)middag!, good afternoon!
goei(e)n)môre!, **-more!**, good morning!
goei(e)(n)nag!, good night!.
Goeie Vrydag, Good Friday.
goël, **gogel**, (ge-), conjure, practise magic.
goëlaar, **gogelaar**, (-s), conjurer, magician.
goëlery, **gogelary**, conjuring, magic.
goëltoer, **gogeltoer**, conjuring-trick.
goeterig, (-e), fairly good, goody.
goeters, things; vide **goed**, 2.
goewerment, (-e), government.
goewermentsamptenaar, government-official.
goewermentsdiens, government-, civil-service.
goewermentskoerant, government-gazette.
goewermentskool, government-school.
goewernante, (-s), governess.
goewerneur, (-s), governor.
goewerneur-generaal, (goewerneurs-generaal), governor-general.
goewerneurshuis, -woning, residency.
gogel-, vide **goël-**.
gogga, (-s), insect; bogey.
goiensak, **goiingsak**, gunny-bag; hessian.
golf, (golwe), billow, wave; bay, gulf.
golf, **golwe**, (ge-), wave, undulate.
golfbeweging, wave-motion, undulation.
golfbreker, breakwater.
golflengte, wavelength.
golflyn, waving (wavy) line; wave-line.
golfslag, dash (wash) of the waves.
Golfstroom, Gulf Stream.
golwend, (-e), waving, wavy (hair); rolling, undulating; surging (crowd).
golwing, (-e, -s), undulation, waving.
gom, (me), n. gum.
gom, (ge-), gum, glue, close with gum.
gomboom, gum-tree.
gomlastiek, (India-)rubber.
gomlastiekskoene, rubber-shoes.
gompou, kori-bustard.
gomtor, lout, uncouth person.
gondel, (-s), gondola.
gondelier, (-s), gondolier.
gondellied, gondolier's song, barcarole.
goniometrie, goniometry.
goniometries, (-e), goniometric(al), **-e funksie**, trigonometrical function.
gons, (ge-), buzz, drone, hum.
gooi, (-e), n. throw, cast, fling; shy.
gooi, (ge-), cast, fling, pitch, throw; shy (at); **jy moet –**, it is your throw; **'n taal lekker –**, speak a language fluently; **met geld –**, burn money, play ducks and drakes with one's money; **uit die saal –**, unseat.
goor, (gore), dingy; putrid, rancid; sallow (face); threadbare (clothes).
goorderig, (-e), slightly dirty; vide **goor**.
goorheid, dirt(iness); rancidness; vide **goor**.
goormaag, congestion of the stomach.
Goot, (Gote), Goth.
gord, **gort**, (-e), n. band, belt, girdle.
gord, (ge-), gird, lace.
gordel, (-s), belt, circle, girdle; zone.
gordelroos, shingles.
Gordiaans, (-e); **die -e knoop deurhak (deurkap)**, cut the Gordian knot.
gordyn, (-e), curtain; blind.
gordynkap, pelmet.
gordynpaal, curtain-rod, curtain-pole.
gordyntjiekop, fringed head.
gordynvuur, curtain-fire, barrage.
gor-gor, grunter.
gorilla, (-s), gorilla.
gorra(tjie), (-s), waterhole (in riverbed).
gorrel, (-s), n. throat, larynx.
gorrel, (ge-), gargle, gurgle.
gort, vide **gord**.
gort, groats, grits; **die – is gaar**, the fat is in the fire.
gortso(e)p, barley-soup.
gortwater, barley-water.
Gotiek, Gothic style.
Goties, (-e), n. & a. Gothic.
gou, a. & adv. rapid, quick(ly), swift(ly); soon; **ek kom – terug**, I'll be back soon; **hy vergewe nie – nie**, he is slow to forgive; **sorg dat jy – maak**, be quick about it.
goud, gold; **alles wat blink is nie – nie**, all is not gold that glitters; **in – swem**, roll in money; **'n hart van –**, a heart of gold; **so goed as –**, as good as gold.
goudaar, gold-vein, gold-lode.
goudamalgaam, gold-amalgam.
goudblad, gold-leaf, gold-foil, leaf-gold.
goudborduursel, gold-embroidery.
goudbrokaat, gold-brocade.
goudbruin, auburn, chestnut.
gouddelwer, gold-digger.
gouddors, avarice, lust of gold.
goudduiwel, demon of gold, mammon.
gouderts, gold-ore.
goudfisant, golden pheasant.
goudgeel, gold-coloured, golden.
goudgehalte, percentage of gold.
goudgeld, gold-coin, gold.
goudgerand, (-e), gilt-edged (securities).
goudgrawer, gold-digger.
goudief, cutpurse, pickpocket.
goudkleur(ig), (-e), gold-colour(ed).
goudkoors, gold-fever.
goudkorrel, grain of gold.
goudlaag, auriferous formation.
goudland, gold-producing country.
goudmagnaat, gold-magnate, capitalist.
goudmyn, gold-mine.
goudopbrengs, -opbrings, gold-production.
goudoplossing, solution of gold.
goudranonkel, gaillardia.
goudreserwe, gold-reserve.
goudrif, gold-reef.

Goudse: – **kaas,** Gouda (cheese).
goudsertifikaat, gold-certificate.
goudsmid, goldsmith.
goudsoeker, gold-seeker.
goudstaaf, bar (ingot) of gold; bullion.
goudstuk, gold-piece.
gouduitvoer, gold-export (-efflux).
goudveld, gold-field.
goudvink, bull-finch; gold-finch.
goudvis(sie), gold-fish.
goudvleis, goldbeater's skin.
goudvoorraad, gold-stock (-supply).
goue, gold (coin); golden (hair, wedding).
gou-gou, quickly, in a jiffy (moment).
gouigheid, quickness; dexterity; **dis elke man se –,** first come first served; it's smartness that does it; **in die –,** quickly.
gousblom, calendula.
graad, (grade), degree, grade, rank; **'n – (be)-haal,** take one's degree; **in die hoogste –,** to the last degree.
graadboog, graduated arc; protractor.
graadverskil, difference in degrees.
graaf, (grawe), n. 1. earl; count.
graaf, (grawe), n. 2. spade.
graaf, (grawe), (ge-), dig, burrow.
graafskap, countship, earldom; (county).
graafsteel, spade-handle.
graafwerk, digging, excavation(s).
graag, gladly, readily, willingly.
graagte, eagerness.
graal, grail; **die Heilige Graal,** the Holy Grail.
graan, (grane), corn, grain; (pl.) cereals.
graanboer, grain-farmer.
graanbou, corn-growing (-cultivation).
graandistrik, corn-growing district.
graanhandelaar, corn-dealer.
graankorrel, grain of corn.
graanmark, corn-market, grain-market.
graanoes, grain-harvest.
graanskuur, granary.
graansolder, corn-loft.
graansuier, (grain-)elevator.
graanuitvoer, grain-export.
graas, (ge-), feed, graze.
graat, (grate), fish-bone.
graatjie, (-s), n. small fish-bone; thin child.
graatjie(meerkat), thin-tailed meercat.
grabbel, (ge-), scramble for.
gradedag, degree-day.
gradeer, (ge-), grade, gradate, graduate.
gradeermasjien, grader, sizer; graduator.
gradeplegtigheid, graduation-ceremony.
gradering, (-e, -s), grading; gradation; graduation.
graduandus, graduand.
gradueel, (-ele), a. gradual, in degree.
gradueer, (ge-), graduate.
graf, (-te), grave; sepulchre, tomb; **swyg soos die –,** be as silent as the grave; **aan die – = by die –,** at the graveside; **hy staan met een voet in die –,** he has one foot in the grave; **in sy – omdraai,** turn in his grave; **ten grafte daal,** sink into one's grave; **uit die – opstaan,** rise from the dead.
grafblom, candytuft.
grafdelwer, grave-digger.
grafiek, (-e), graph.
grafies, (-e), graphic.
grafiet, blacklead, graphite, plumbago.
grafkelder, vault.
grafmaker, vide **grafdelwer.**
grafnaald, sepulchral obelisk.
grafrede, funeral-oration.
grafskrif, epitaph.

grafsteen, gravestone, tombstone.
grafstem, sepulchral voice.
grafwaarts, to the grave.
grag, (-te), canal; ditch, moat.
gram, (-me), gramme.
gramadoelas, rough country.
gramkalorie, gramme-calorie.
grammaties, (-e), grammatical.
grammatika, (-s), grammar.
grammatikaal, (-ale), grammatical.
grammatikus, (-se), grammarian.
grammofoon, (-fone), gramophone.
grammofoonplaat, (gramophone-)record.
gramradio, gramradio.
gramskap, anger, ire, wrath.
gramstorig, (-e), angry, wrathful.
granaat, (-nate), pomegranate; grenade; shrapnel garnet.
granaatbom, (hand-)grenade.
granaatkartets, shrapnel.
granaatsteen, garnet.
granaatvuur, shell-fire.
grande, (-s), grandee.
grandioos, (-iose), grandiose.
graniet, granite.
granietblok, block (slab) of granite.
granuleer, (ge-), granulate.
grap, (-pe), fun, jest, joke; **–pe vertel,** crack jokes; **'n – en 'n half,** a good joke; an awkward situation; **'n mooi –,** a good joke; a nice to-do; **vir die –,** for fun, in sport.
grap(pe)maker, buffoon, joker, wag.
grapp(er)ig, (-e), amusing, comic, funny.
grapp(er)igheid, drollery, fun.
gras, (-se), grass; **g'n – onder jou voete laat groei nie,** not let the grass grow under one's feet; **van die – af,** dead.
grasangelier, pink.
grasbaan, grass-court.
grasduin, (ge-), browse, enjoy (a book).
grasetend, (-e), herbivorous, graminivorous.
grasgroen, grass-green.
grashalm(pie), grass-blade, blade of grass.
grasie, grace, pardon; gracefulness; **– verleen,** (grant) pardon; **by die – Gods,** by the grace of God; by divine right; **in die – wees,** be in (someone's) good graces.
grasieus, (-e), elegant, graceful.
grasig, (-e), grassy.
grasland, grass-land, pasture-land.
graslinne, grass-cloth, grass-linen.
grasparkiet, budgerigar.
grasperk, grass-plot, greensward, lawn.
grasrand, grass-border.
grassnyer, lawn-mower.
grassoort, kind of grass; (pl.) grasses.
graspriet(jie), vide **grashalm(pie).**
grasveld, grass-field.
grasvlakte, grassy plain, prairie.
grasweduwee, grass-widow.
graswewenaar, grass-widower.
graterig, (-e), bony (fish).
gratifikasie, (-s), gratuity.
gratis, free, gratis.
graveer, (ge-), engrave; sink (dies).
graveerder, (-s), engraver.
graveerkuns, (art of) engraving.
graveernaald, -stif, -yster, graving-tool.
graveur, (-s), engraver; die-sinker.
gravin, (-ne), countess.
gravure, (-s), engraving, print, plate.
graweel(steen), calculus, gravel, stone.
grawer, (-s), digger.
greep, (grepe), clutch, grasp, grip; hilt.
grein, (-e), grain.

**greinhout, deal.
greinhoutplank, deal-board.
greintjie, (-s), grain, scrap, shred.
grenadella, granadilla, (-s), granadilla (grenadilla), passion-flower; passion-fruit.
grenadier, (-s), grenadier.
grendel, (-s), n. bar, bolt.
grendel, (ge-), bolt.
grens, (-e),** n. boundary, frontier, border; bound, limit; **g'n -e ken nie,** know no bounds; **-e stel aan,** set bounds to; **êrens 'n - trek,** draw the line somewhere; **aan die -,** at the frontier; **binne sekere -e,** within (certain) limits; **op die - van,** on the borderline (verge) of; **oor die -e trek,** cross the frontiers (border).
grens, (ge-), - aan, adjoin, border on, be bounded by; verge upon.
grens, (ge-), cry, howl.
grensbalie, cry-baby.
grensbewoner, frontier-resident, borderer.
grens(e)loos, (-lose), boundless, unlimited; infinite (misery).
grens(e)loosheid, boundlessness.
grensgebied, border(-land), confines.
grensgeskil, boundary-dispute.
grensgeval, borderline case.
grenshou, boundary (in cricket).
grensloos(heid), vide **grens(e)loos(heid).
grenslyn,** boundary-line, frontier.
grenspaal, boundary-post (-mark).
grenspos, frontier-post.
grensregter, linesman (in football).
grenstraktaat, boundary-, frontier-treaty.
grenswag, frontier-guard.
Gresisme, (-s), Graecism.
gretig, (-e), desirous, eager; greedy.
gretigheid, eagerness; greediness.
grief, (griewe), n. grievance; offence, wrong.
grief, (ge-), gall, grieve, hurt.
Griek, (-e), Greek.
Grieks, (-e), n. & a. Greek; Grecian.
Griekwa, (-e), Griqua.
griep, influenza, flu.
griesel, (ge-), shiver, shudder.
grieselig, (-e), creepy, grisly, gruesome.
grieseligheid, gruesomeness, weirdness.
grieseltjie, particle; vide **krieseltjie.
griewend, (-e),** galling, mortifying.
grif, adv. promptly, readily.
grif, (ge-), engrave, impress.
griffel, (-s), slate-pencil.
griffeldosie, pencil-box.
griffie, (-e), vide **griffel.
griffier, (-s),** recorder, registrat.
griff(i)oen, (-e, -s), griffin.
grifweg, vide **grif,** adv.
gril, (-le), n. caprice, whim; shiver, shudder.
gril, (ge-), shiver, shudder.
grillerig, (-e), creepy, gruesome.
grillig, (-e), fanciful, faddy, fantastic, whimsical, fickle; fitful (weather).
grilligheid, fancifulness; vide **grillig.
grimas, (-se),** grimace.
grimeer, (ge-), make up.
grimlag, n. grin, sneer.
grimlag, (ge-), grin, sneer.
grimmig, (-e), angry, furious, grim.
grimmigheid, anger, fury, wrath.
grinnik, (ge-), chuckle, grin, sneer, snigger.
grint, gravel, grit; shingle.
grintpad, gravel-road, gravelled path.
grip(pie), furrow; vide **greppel.
groef, (groewe),** n. groove; furrow, wrinkle.
groef, groewe, (ge-), groove.
groefskaaf, fluting-, grooving-plane.

groei, n. growth; rising (of a river).
groei, (ge-), grow; rise; **- en bloei,** grow and thrive, **iemand verby -,** outgrow a person; **uit sy klere -,** grow out of one's clothes.
groeikrag, vital force, vitality, vigour.
groeipyne, growing-pains.
groeisaam, (-same), favourable to growth.
groen, n. green; greenery, verdure.
groen, a. green; fresh; immature, unripe.
groenagtig, (-e), greenish.
groenbemesting, green manuring.
groenblywend, (-e), evergreen.
groenboontjies, green (French, haricot) beans.
groendruiwe, green-grapes.
groene, (-s), fresher, freshman; vide **groentjie.
groenerig, (-e),** greenish.
groenerigheid, verdure; greenishness.
groenigheid, greenness; greengrass, greens.
groenmielies, green mealies.
groenpruim, greengage.
groenspaan, verdigris.
groente, vegetables.
groenteboer, vegetable-grower, market-gardener.
groenteboerdery, vegetable-growing.
groentemark, vegetable-market.
groenteso(e)p, vegetable-soup, julienne.
groentetuin, vegetable-garden.
groentewinkel, greengrocer's (shop).
groentjie, (-s), greenhorn; fresher.
groentyd, freshmanship, noviciate.
groenvlieg, Spanish fly.
groenvoer, fresh fodder, green stuff.
groep, (-e), group, clustre, clump (of trees).
groepeer, (ge-), group, classify.
groepering, (-e, -s), grouping, classification.
groepsgewys(e), in batches (groups).
groet, n. greeting: **sê - aan,** give my regards to: **met vriendelike -,** with kind regards.
groet, (ge-), greet, salute, take off one's hat, shake hands; say goodbye.
groete, groetnis, regards, greetings.
groewe, n. pit; quarry; grave.
grof, (growwe), coarse, rude (remarks), rough (road), gross (carelessness), big (lie), bad (blunder), harsh (voice); **- geskut,** heavy guns.
grofbrood, growwebrood, coarse (brown) bread.
grofgeskut, heavy ordnance (guns, artillery).
grofheid, coarseness, roughness, rudeness.
grok, (-ke), grog.
grom, (ge-), growl, grumble, snarl.
grond, (-e), n. ground, earth; soil; land, bottom; foundation; reason; (pl.) elements, rudiments; **vaste - onder die voete hê,** be on firm ground; **g'n - onder die voete hê nie,** have no ground under one's feet; have no legs to stand on; **goeie -e,** good grounds, sound reasons; **- vat,** touch ground, take root; **- verloor,** lose ground; **aan die - raak,** run aground; **bo die -,** above ground; **in die -,** at bottom; **in die - boor,** send to the bottom; **met -,** with good reason, with good grounds; **onder die -,** underground; **onder die - stop,** bury; **op gevaarlike -,** on thin ice; **op - van,** on the ground of, on account of; on the strength of, by virtue of; **sonder -,** without foundation; without rhyme or reason; **te -e gaan,** go to rack and ruin; **tot in die - bederwe,** spoil utterly; **uit die - van my hart,** from the bottom of my heart; **iets weer van die - af opbou,** start something again at the very beginning; **van alle - ontbloot,** without any foundation.
grond, (ge-), base, found, ground.
grondbeginsel, basic principle, rudiment.
grondbegrip, basic (fundamental) idea.
grondbelasting, land-tax.

grondbesit, landed property; land-tenure.
grondbesitter, landed proprietor, landowner.
grondbetekenis, original meaning.
grondboontjie, pea-nut, monkey-nut.
grond-eekhoring, gopher.
grondeienaar, vide **grondbesitter**.
grondeiendom, vide **grondbesit**.
grondeloos, (-lose), bottomless, abysmal.
gronderig, (-e), earthy (taste), muddy.
grondgebied, territory.
grondgetal, base.
grondhoop, earth-dump. (-mound).
grondig, (-e), thorough, searching.
grondigheid, thoroughness.
grondkleur, ground-colour, primary colour.
grondlaag, ground-layer; first coat (of paint).
grondlêer, (-s), founder.
grondlegging, foundation.
grondlugprojektiel, ground-to-air-missile.
grondlyn, base, basis, ground-line.
grondoorsaak, first (original, root-)cause.
grondplan, ground-plan, horizontal projection.
grondreël, maxim, principle.
grondslag, basis, foundation.
grondsoort, kind of ground (soil).
grondstelling, maximum, tenet; axiom (maths).
grondstof, element; raw material.
grondtaal, original language.
grondtal, base, basis, radix (maths.).
grondteks, original text.
grondtoon, keynote, dominant note.
grondtrek, characteristic feature, trait.
grondverf, ground-colour, first coat, priming.
grondversakking, depression, subsidence.
grondverskuiwing, landslide.
grondverspoeling, (soil-)erosion.
grondves, (ge-), found, lay the foundation of.
grondveste, foundations.
grondvester, (-s), founder.
grondvloer, earthen floor.
grondwaarheid, fundamental truth.
grondwerk, ground work; earthworks (railw.).
grondwet, constitution, fundamental law.
grondwet(te)lik, (-e), -wettig, constitutional.
grondwolf, landshark, landgrabber.
grondwoord, original word, radical.
grondys, ground-ice, anchor-ice.
groot, (grote), large vast; big, tall; grown-up; great; grand; **twee maal so – as**, twice the size of; **'n – man**, a great man; a tall man; **'n – menigte**, a large crowd, **die – moondhede**, the Great Powers; **– word**, grow up; **jy het – gelyk**, you are perfectly right; **te – lewe**, live beyond one's means; **die – publiek**, the general public; **soos 'n – speld verdwyn**, disappear unexpectedly.
grootbek, braggart, swaggerer.
grootboek, ledger.
grootbring, (grootge-), bring up, rear, raise.
grootgrondbesitter, large landowner.
groothandel, wholesale-trade.
groothandelaar, wholesale-merchant.
groothartig, (-e), generous, magnanimous.
groothartigheid, magnanimity.
grootheid, greatness, magnitude; quantity.
grootheidswaansin, megalomania.
groothertog, grand-duke.
groothertogin, grand-duchess.
grootindustrie, big industry.
grootjie, (-s), granny great-grandmother; great-grandfather; **loop na jou –!**, go to Jericho!, **na sy – wees**, be lost.
grootkanselier, Lord High Chancellor.
grootkruis, grand cross.
grootliks, to a great extent, largely.

grootmaak, (grootge-), vide **grootbring**.
grootmeester, grand-master.
grootmens, adult, grown-up.
grootmoeder, grandmother.
grootmoedig(heid), vide **groothartig(heid)**.
grootmogol, Great (Grand) Mogul.
grootouers, grandparents.
grootpad, high-road, main-road.
grootpraat, (grootge-), brag, boast.
grootpratery, boasting, bragging, swagger.
groots, (-e), grandiose, majestic; haughty; proud.
grootseëlbewaarder, (Keeper of the) Great Seal.
grootskeeps, (-e), on a large scale; princely.
grootspraak, boast(ing), brag, bravado.
grootsteeds, (-e), grand, of a large town.
grootte, (-s), bigness, extent, greatness, magnitude, size, tallness.
grootvader, grandfather.
grootvaderlik, (-e), grandfatherly.
grootvisier, grand-vizier.
grootvuur, hell(-fire).
grootwaardigheidsbekleër, high dignitary.
grootwild, big game.
grootwoord, blasphemy.
gros, (-se), gross, mass.
groslys, list of prospective candidates.
grot, (-te), cave, grotto.
grotbewoner, cave-dweller.
grotendeels, chiefly, largely, mainly.
grotesk, (-e), fanciful, grotesque.
grou, a. grey.
grou, n. growl, snarl.
grou, (ge-), growl, snarl.
groutjie, (-s), donkey.
growwebrood, vide **grofbrood**.
growwerig, (-e), rather coarse, rather rough.
gruis, grit; gravel.
gruisbaan, gravel-court; gravel-path.
gruiselemente: in –, to atoms (fragments).
gruisgat, gravel-pit (-quarry).
gruispad, gravelled path (road).
gruissif, screen.
grusaam, (-same), gruesome, horrible.
gruwel, (-s), abomination, crime, horror.
gruweldaad, atrocity, crime.
gruwelik, (-e), abominable, atrocious, naughty.
gruwelikheid, atrocity; horror; naughtiness.
gruwelstuk, atrocity; thriller; naughty prank.
gryns, (-e), n. grimace, grin, sneer.
gryns, (ge-), make a grimace, grin, sneer.
grynslag, n. sardonic smile; vide **gryns**, n.
grynslag, (ge-), vide **gryns**, (ge-).
gryp, (ge-), catch, clutch, grab, grasp, seize, lay hold of, snatch.
gryp-inbraak, smash-and-grab raid.
grys, (-e), grey, grey-headed; hoary; **die –e oudheid**, (verlede), remote antiquity, the dim past.
grysaard, (-s), grey-haired man, greybeard.
grysagtig, (-e), greyish, grizzly (beard).
grysappel, sand-apple.
grysbok, grysbuck.
gryserig, (-e), greyish, rather grey; vide **grys**.
grysheid, greyness; old age; antiquity.
gryskop, grey-head.
guano, vide **ghwano**.
guerrilla-oorlog, guer(r)illa-warfare.
guillotine, (-s), guillotine.
gul, (-le), cordial, frank, liberal.
gulden, (-s), n. guilder, Dutch florin.
gulde, a. golden; **die – eeu**, the golden age.
gulde snee, golden section (maths.).
gulhartig, (-e), vide **gul**.
gulhartigheid, **gulheid**, cordiality, generosity.

gulp, (-e), n. fly, trousers-slit.
gulp, (ge-), gush, pour forth, spout.
gulsbek, glutton.
gulsig, (-e), gluttonous, greedy.
gulsigaard, (-s), glutton.
gulsigheid, gluttony, greed(iness).
gulssak, **gulsbek**, glutton.
gulweg, frankly, genially, openly.
gummi, (India-)rubber.
gummistok, rubber-truncheon.
gun, (ge-), allow, grant; not to envy (grudge); ek – **jou dit**, you are welcome to it; it serves you right!; **jy – my ook nooit iets nie**, you always (be)grudge me everything.
guns, (-te), favour; kindness, patronage, support; iemand 'n – **bewys**, do a person a favour; **in iemand se – probeer kom**, ingratiate oneself (curry favour) with a person; **by iemand in die – staan**, be in a person's good books; om 'n – vra, beg a favour; **ten –te van**, in favour of; **uit die – wees**, be in disfavour; **van –te en gawe lewe**, live on charity.
gunsbejag, favour-currying.
gunsbetoon, favouritism; mark(s) of favour.
gunsbewys, favour, mark of favour.
gunsteling, (-e), favourite.
gunstig, (-e), favourable, propitious; – **geleë**, conveniently situated; **in die –ste geval**, at best; – **bekend staan**, enjoy a good reputation; – **stem**, propitiate.
gunstigheid, favourableness; vide **gunstig**.
gunter, yonder, over there.
gusooi, dry ewe, ewe not in lamb; barren ewe.
gusskape, sheep not in lamb, dry sheep.
gutturaal, (-ale), n. & a. guttural.
guur, bleak, inclement, raw, rough.
guurheid, bleakness, inclemency.
gyselaar, (-lare, -s), hostage; prisoner for debt.
gyseling, imprisonment for debt; **op – dagvaar**, summon(s) for debt.

H

ha!, ah!, ha!, oh!.
haagdoring, hawthorn.
haai, (-e), n. shark.
haai!, interj. hullo!, heigh!, I say!
haai-hoei, hoe(i)-haai, fuss.
haaivlakte, desolate plain, the open.
haak, (hake), hook, hasp, clasp; clamp; square; T-square; bracket; peg; gaff; crook, stake; in die –, square; in order; **'n ding in die** – **bring**, put (set) a thing right, square a thing; **uit die** –, out of square.
haak, (ge-), hook; crochet; catch; delay, be delayed; – **na**, crave (yearn) for, hanker after.
haakbus, arquebus.
haakdoring, hook-thorn; grapple-plant.
haak-en-steek(bos), umbrella-thorn.
haakkruis, hakekruis, (-e), swastika.
haakmes, hooked knife.
haakplek, difficulty, hitch, obstruction.
haaks, (-e), square(d), right-angle(d); **hulle is altyd** –, they are always at loggerheads.
haakspeld, safety-pin.
haakvormig, (-e), hooked, hook-shaped.
haakwurm, hookworm.
haal, (hale), n. pull; dash, stroke (of the pen); lash; stride.
haal, (ge-), fetch, go for, get; draw, pull; recover; catch; **laat** –, send for; **die trein** –, catch the train; **van die trein** –, meet at the station; **hy sal môre nie** – **nie**, he will not last (live) until tomorrow.
haan, (hane), cock, rooster; cock, hammer (of gun); **hy is 'n (ou)** –, he is a topper; **daar sal g'n** – **na kraai nie**, nobody will be the wiser; **hy moet altyd koning kraai**, he is cock of the walk.
haantjie, (-s), cockerel; – **die voorste**, cock of the walk.
haar, (hare), n. hair; **dit het g'n** – **geskeel nie**, it was touch and go; **hare op die tande hê**, know how to hold one's own; **g'n bang** – **op sy kop nie**, be afraid of nothing; **sy hare het orent (regop) gestaan**, his hair stood on end; **die hare laat waai**, make the sparks (pieces) fly; **met die hare daarby sleep**, drag in by the head and shoulders; **mekaar in die hare sit**, be at loggerheads; **mekaar in die hare vlie(g)**, fly at each other, come to blows; **op 'n** –, to a hair; **op 'n** – **na**, within an ace; **alles op hare en snare sit**, move heaven and earth.
haar, a right; **hot en** –, right and left.
haar, pro. pers. her.
haar, (hare), pro. poss. her; **dit is** – **boek**, it is her book; **dit is hare**, it is hers.
haar-af: **die perd gaan** –, the horse's hair is coming off; **hy kan nie hond** – **maak nie**, he is a good-for-nothing; **hy kon geen hond** – **maak nie**, he could do (achieve, effect) nothing.
haaragter, right-hind.
haaragtig, (-e), hairy, hairlike.
haarborsel, hareborsel, hairbrush.
haarbos, shock (tuft) of hair.
haarbreed(te), hair-breadth.
haarbuis(ie), capillary tube.
haard, (-e), fireplace, fireside, hearth; grate.
haardkleedjie, hearth-rug.
haardos, (head of) hair; wealth of hair.
haardrand, fender.
haardskerm, fire-screen.
haardstel, (set of) fire-irons.
haardyster, andiron, fire-dog; fender.
haarfyn, as fine as a hair; in detail.
haarkam, harekam, comb.
haarkant, right side, off-side.
haarkloof, –klowe, (ge-), split hairs, quibble.
haarklowery, hair-splitting, quibbling.
haarknipper, hareknipper, hair-clipper.
haarkrul, curl of hair.
haarlaat, (ge-): **hy moes** –, he had to pay (the piper).
haarlemmerolie, haarlemensis, Dutch drops.
haarlint, hair-ribbon.
haarlok, lock of hair.
haarloos, (-lose), hairless.
haarmiddel, hair-restorer.
haarnaald, hairpin.
haarnaasagter, second right-hind.
haarnaasvoor, second right-fore (-front).
haarom, to the right, clockwise.
haarpyn, chippiness, hot coppers.
haarsalf, pomade.
haarskeerder(spinnekop), barber-spider.
haarsnyer, haresnyer, hairdresser.
haartang(etjie), (pair of) tweezers.
haartooi(sel), headdress, coiffure.
haarvlegsel, braid, plait (of hair); pigtail.
haarvoor, right-fore (-front).
haarwas, shampoo.
haarwater, hair-wash.
haarwurm, wire-worm; thread-worm.
haas, (hase), n. hare; **so bang soos 'n** –, as timid as a hare; **so bang soos 'n** – **vir 'n hond wees**, be mortally afraid.
haas, in. haste, hurry, speed; **hoe meer** – **hoe minder spoed**, more haste less speed; **in** –, in haste; **in groot** –, in hot haste.
haas, adv. almost, nearly; practically.
haas, (ge-), hurry, make haste; – **jou nie!** take your time.
haasbek, having a tooth (teeth) missing.
haaslip, hare-lip.
haastig, (-e), hasty, hurried, in a hurry, speedy.
haastigheid, hastiness, hurry.
haat, n. hatred.
haat, (ge-), hate, detest.
haatdraend, (-e), vindictive, resentful.
haatdraendheid, malice, vindictiveness.
haatlik, (-e), detestable, odious; spiteful.
haatlikheid, malice, spite.
had, vide hê.
hadjie, (-s), hadji.
hael, n. hail; shot.
hael, (ge-), hail.
haelbui, hailstorm, shower of hail.
haelgeweer, shotgun.
haelkorrel, hailstone; grain (pellet) of shot.
haelpatroon, shot-cartridge.
haelstorm, hailstorm.
haglik, (-e), critical, desperate, precarious.
haglikheid, critical state, precariousness.
haikôna, aikôna, no, not at all, by no means.
hak, (-ke), n. heel; **die** –**ke lig**, take to one's heels; **nie by iemand se** –**ke kom nie**, not be in the same street with a person; **iemand op die** –**ke sit**, pursue a person closely; **van die** – **op die tak spring**, ramble.
hak, (ge-), chop, cut, hash, mince (meat).
hakerig, (-e), hooky; – **wees**, be at loggerheads.
hakhou, cut.
hakie, (-s), bracket; (little) hook; –**s en ogies**, hooks and eyes; **tussen** –**s**, in brackets, in parenthesis (lit.); by the way.
hakkel, (ge-), stammer, stutter; stumble.
hakkelaar, (are, -s), stammerer.
hakkelrig, (-e), stammering, stuttering.
hakkerig, (-e), inclined to hitch (stick).
hakskeen, heel.
hakskeensening, Achilles' tendon.
hal, (-le), hall.

half   108   **hand**

half, (halwe), half; semi-; **–een**, half past twelve; **daar slaan –**, the half-hour is striking; **halwe werk doen**, do one's work by halves, botch; **– en –**, nearly, not quite, partially; **ek het – sin om ...**, I have half a mind to ... ; **ek het nou – spyt daaroor**, I am rather sorry about it now.
halfaam, **alfaam**, half-aum.
halfaap, lemur.
halfag(t), half past seven.
halfbakke, half-baked, slack-baked.
halfbloed, n. & a. half-breed, halfcaste.
halfbroer, half-brother.
halfdeursigtig, (-e), semi-transparent.
halfdonker, n. & a. semi-darkness, twilight.
halfdood, half-dead, all but dead.
halfgaar, half-baked, half-done; dotty, half-gone.
halfgod(in), demigod(dess).
halfheid, half-heartedness, irresolution.
halfie, (-s), half a one.
halfjaar, half-year, six months.
halfjaarliks, (-e), half-yearly, every six months.
halfklaar, half-done.
halfkoord, vide **albekoor**.
halfkroon, half-a-crown.
halfmaan, half-moon; crescent, semicircle.
halfmaandeliks, (-e), fortnightly
halfmaantjie, half-moon (earmark).
halfmaanvormig, (-e), lunate, meniscate.
halfmas, half-mast.
halfpad, half-way.
halfrond, (-e), n. hemisphere.
halfrond, (-e), a. half-round, hemispherical.
halfskaduwee, penumbra.
halfslagtig, (-e), half-hearted.
halfslagtigheid, half-heartedness, indecision, irresolution.
halfslyt, second-hand, half-worn, part-worn.
halfsool, half-sole.
halfstok, vide **halfmas**.
halfsuster, halfsister.
halfuur, half an hour.
halfvokaal, semi-vowel.
halfwas, (-se), half-grown.
halfweg, half-way; mid-off (cricket).
halfwys, half-wit.
halfyster, mid-iron.
halleluja, (-s), hallelujah.
hallo!, hullo!
hallusinasie, (-s), hallucination.
halm(pie), (-s), blade, stalk.
halogeen, halogen.
hals, (-e), neck; **iemand om die – val**, fall upon a person's neck; **iets op die – haal**, let oneself in for something.
halsaar, jugular vein.
halsband, collar, neck-band; necklace.
halsbrekend, (-e), breakneck.
halskettinkie, necklet.
halskraag, collar; frill, ruff; gorget (of armour).
halslengte, neck-length; **met 'n – wen**, win by a neck.
halsoorkop, head over heels, precipitately.
halsslagaar, carotid (artery).
halssnoer, necklace; gorget.
halsstarrig, (-e), headstrong, obstinate, stubborn.
halsstarrigheid, obstinacy, stubbornness.
halsstuk, neckpiece; gorget; collar (of a stay).
halswerwel, cervical vertebra; **eerste –**, atlas.
halt!, halt!, stop!; **– hou**, call a halt.
halte, (-s), halt; stopping-place, stop.
halter, (-s), halter; **die – afhaal**, turn adrift.
halterriem, halter-strap, head-rope.
halveer, (ge-), bisect, halve.

halvering, halving, bisection.
halwe, (-s), half; **ten –**, by halves.
halwemaan, vide **halfmaan**.
halwerweë, half-way.
ham, (-me), ham.
hamel, (-s), wether, hamel.
hamer, (-s), n. hammer; mallet (of wood); **onder die – kom**, be put up to auction.
hamer, (ge-), hammer; **iemand –**, give someone a sound thrashing.
hamerkop, head of a hammer, mudlark.
hamerpik, poll-pick.
hamerslotgreep, hammer-lock.
hand, (-e), hand; handwriting; **die – gee**, shake hands; **– tuis**, hands off; **ek het my –e vol**, I have my hands full; **die – aan iets hou**, keep something up; enforce something; **die – bo iemand se hoof hou**, take a person under one's wing; **nie iemand se – kan hou nie**, be no match for a person; **die – lê op**, lay hands on; **die – aan jouself slaan**, lay violent hands upon oneself; **iemand se – in die as slaan**, oust someone (in love); **die – aan die ploeg slaan**, set to work; **sy –e staan verkeerd**, his fingers are all thumbs; **sy –e staan vir niks verkeerd nie**, he can turn his hand to anything; **die – uit die mou steek**, put one's shoulder to the wheel; **die – in die sak steek**, put one's hand in one's pocket, contribute towards something; **die – in eie boesem steek**, dive into one's own bosom; **die –e ineengeslaan**, throw up one's hands with wonder; **as die een – die ander was–**, word altwee skoon, one good turn deserves another; **iemand die vrye – laat**, give a person a free hand; **die laaste – aan iets lê**, put the finishing touches to something; **stem deur –e op te steek**, vote by show of hands; **geen – uitsteek nie**, not lift a finger; **jou – onder iets sit**, put one's hand to something; **'n – bysit**, lend a (helping) hand; **jou –e van iemand aftrek**, withdraw one's assistance from someone; **die –e slap laat hang**, remain inactive; **sy –e het gejeuk**, his fingers itched; **– en mond belowe**, promise faithfully; **aan die – van**, on the basis of; in view of; **aan –e en voete gebind**, bound hand and foot; **iets aan die – doen**, suggest something; **– aan – gaan**, go hand in hand; **by die –**, at hand; **in die –e kom**, be caught; **'n saak in –e hê**, have a case in hand; **in ander –e oorgaan**, change hands; **iemand iets in die – stop**, foist (palm) something off upon a person; **in verkeerde –e val**, fall (get) into the wrong hands; **in die – werk**, facilitate, promote; **iets met beide –e aangryp**, jump at a thing; **met – en tand beveg**, fight tooth and nail; **met die –e oormekaar**, with hands across; inactive; **met leë –e**, empty-handed; **met die –e in die hare sit**, be at one's wits' end, be at a loss; **met die –e in die skoot sit**, sit with, one's hands folded; **met die – op die hart**, sincerely, honestly; **iemand na jou – leer**, train a person to one's ways; **om haar – vra**, ask her hand (in marriage); **onder –e hê**, have in hand, be engaged in; **onder – neem**, take to task, haul over the coals; **– oor –**, hand over hand; **op die –e dra**, worship; **op –e en voete**, on all fours; **op –e wees**, be near at hand; **op iemand se – wees**, be on a person's side, side with a person; **ter – neem**, take in hand; **ter – stel**, hand over; **uit die eerste –**, at first hand; **uit die – verkoop**, sell by private contract (treaty); **uit die – raak**, become unmanageable; **van die – sit (doen)**, dispose of; **van die – in die tand lewe**, live from hand to

mouth; **van die – wys,** refuse, decline, dismiss (an appeal); **van – tot –,** from hand to hand; **alles wat voor die – kom,** everything that comes to hand; **dit lê voor die –,** it goes without saying, it is obvious.
handbagasie, hand-luggage.
handbeweging, motion of the hand, gesture.
handboeie, handcuffs, manacles, wristlets.
handboek, handbook, manual.
handbreed(te), hand's-breadth.
handbyltjie, hatchet, chopper.
handdoek, towel.
handdoekrak, towel-roller, towel-horse.
handdruk, handshake (-clasp, grasp, -grip).
handearbeid, manual labour, handicraft.
handel, n. commerce, business, trade; **iemand se – en wandel,** a person's conduct; **– drywe,** trade; **in die – bring,** put upon the market.
handel, (ge-), act; deal, carry on business, trade; **– in,** deal (trade) in; **– oor,** deal with, treat of; **ooreenkomstig jou belofte –,** act up to one's promise.
handelaar, (s), dealer, merchant, trader.
handelbaar, (-bare), docile, tractable.
handeldrywend, (-e), commercial, trading.
handelend: – optree, take action.
handeling, (-e), action; act; transaction; **die H–e van die Apostels,** the Acts of the Apostles.
handelsmaatskappy, trading-company.
handelsaak, business; commercial matter.
handelsaangeleentheid, business-matter.
handelsagent, commercial agent.
handelsagentskap, commercial agency.
handelsartikel, article of commerce, commodity.
handelsbalans, balance of trade.
handelsbank, commercial bank.
handelsberig, commercial report.
handelsbetrekkinge, commercial relations.
handelsekonomie, commercial economy.
handelsekretaris, commercial secretary; secretary of commerce.
handelsgebied; op –, in the domain of trade.
handelsgees, commercial spirit.
handelshuis, business-house, commercial house.
handelskool, commercial school.
handelskorrespondensie, commercial correspondence.
handelskringe, commercial circles.
handelslugvaart, commercial aviation.
handelsmerk, trade-mark.
handelsmonopolie, monopoly of trade.
handelsonderneming, commercial enterprise.
handelsonderwys, commercial education.
handelsooreenkoms, commercial agreement.
handelsreg, commercial law.
handelsreisiger, commercial traveller.
handelsrekenkunde, commercial arithmetic.
handelstad, trading-centre, commercial town.
handelstatistiek(e), trade-returns.
handelstelsel, commercial system.
handelsterm, business-term.
handelstraktaat, commercial treaty.
handelstransaksie, business-transaction.
handelsvennootskap, co-partnership.
handelsverkeer, commercial intercourse.
handelsvliegtuig, commercial plane.
handelsvloot, mercantile marine.
handelsvooruitsigte, commercial prospects.
handelsvryheid, freedom of trade.
handelsware, merchandise, commodities.
handelsweg, trade-route.
handelswet, commercial law.
handelswetenskap, commercial science.
handelswissel, trade-bill.
handelwyse, proceeding, procedure, behaviour.

hande-viervoet, on all fours.
handewerk, handiwork, handwork.
handgalop, hand-gallop, canter.
handgebaar, vide **handbeweging.**
handgeklap, applause, handclapping.
handgemeen: – raak, come to blows.
handgranaat, (hand-)grenade.
handgreep, grasp, grip; dodge, trick.
handhaaf, (ge-), maintain, vindicate; live up to; **jouself –,** hold one's own.
handhawer, (-s), maintainer, upholder.
handhawersbond, maintainers' league.
handhawing, maintenance, preservation.
handig, (-e), clever, handy, skilful; **– gedaan,** neatly done; **– wees in,** be a good hand at.
handigheid, adroitness, cleverness, handiness.
handjie, (-s), little hand; **'n – help,** give (lend) a hand.
handjie(s)klap, -plak, clapping of hands.
handjievol, handful.
handkarwats, riding-whip.
handkoffer, handbag, suitcase, portmanteau.
handlang, (ge-), help, assist.
handlanger, (-s), handyman; accomplice.
handleiding, guide, handbook, manual.
handmasjiengeweer, sub-machine-gun; tommy-gun.
handoplegging, laying on of hands.
handperd, led horse.
handreiking, assistance.
handrem, hand-brake.
handrug, back-hand.
handrughou, back-hand stroke.
handsaag, hand-saw.
handsak(kie), handbag; (lady's) vanity-bag.
handskêr, snips.
handskoen, glove; gauntlet: **die – opneem,** take up the gauntlet; **die – opneem vir iemand,** take up the cudgels for someone, espouse someone's cause; **iemand die – toewerp,** throw down the gauntlet (to someone); **met die – trou,** marry by proxy; **hy is nie iemand wat jy sonder – kan aanpak nie,** it is not easy to handle him.
handskoenhakie, glove-hook.
handskoenrekker, glove-stretcher.
handskoentjies, small gloves; honeysuckle.
handskrif, handwriting; manuscript.
handspieël, hand-mirror.
handtastelik: – word, begin to use one's hands; manhandle; come to blows.
handtastelikheid, (-hede), assault, violence; **tot –hede kom (geraak),** come to blows.
handtekening, signature.
handvat(sel), handle; ear, crutch (of spade).
handves, (-te), charter; covenant.
handvol, (handevol), handful.
handwerk, handicraft, handwork; needlework.
handwerker, hand-worker; manual labourer.
handwerkie, piece of needlework.
handwerksak(kie), sewing-bag.
handwerksman, artisan, workman, mechanic.
handwoordeboek, pocket-dictionary.
handwortel, carpus.
handwys(t)er, finger-post, signpost.
hanebalk, roof-beam, collar-beam, rafter.
hanegeveg, cock-fight(ing).
hanekam, cockscomb (coxcomb).
hanepoot, (lit.) cock's foot (claw); hanepoot (grapes); **hanepote en katteklou,** pot-hooks and hangers.
hanerig, (-e), cocky, quarrelsome.
hanetree(tjie), cock-stride, short distance.
hang, (-e), n. slope.

hang, (ge-), hang, be suspended; droop; suspend; be hanged; **sy kop (ore) laat –,** hang one's head (one's ears); **sy hart – daarna,** he has set his heart on it; **aan iemand se lippe (woorde) –,** hang on a person's words; **sy – alles aan haar lyf,** she spends all her money on dress; **hulle – aan mekaar,** they are bound up in each other; **dit – bo sy kop,** it is impending over him.
hangbrug, suspension-bridge.
hangend, (e), hanging, pending.
hanger, (-s), hanger; pendant; eardrop.
hangerig, (-e), drooping, languid, limp.
hangkas, wardrobe.
hangklok, wall-clock.
hanglamp, hanging-lamp.
hanglip, n. & a. hanging-lip; sulky; **– wees,** sulk.
hangmat, hammock.
hangoor, lop-ear, drooping ear.
hangslot, padlock.
hangspoor, suspension-railway.
hanou, honou!, whoa! (to oxen).
hans, orphan; **– grootmaak,** hand-feed.
hansie-my-kneg, jack-of-all-work.
hanslam, house-lamb, hand-fed lamb, cosset.
hanswors, (-te), buffoon, clown.
hansworstery, slapstick.
hanteer, (ge-), handle, operate, work.
hantering, handling, manipulation, operation, working.
hap, (-pe), n. bite; bit, morsel, mouthful.
hap, (ge-), bite, snap, snatch.
haper, (ge-), not function properly, miss, stick; **dit – aan geld,** funds are short; **sonder te –,** without a hitch.
hapering, (-e, -s), hitch, impediment.
happ(e)rig, (-e), eager, keen.
happie, (-s), titbit, morsel, small mouthful.
hara-kiri, hara-kiri, happy dispatch.
hard, (-e), a. & adv. hard, loud (voice), glaring (colours), stern (reality), uncharitable (feelings); heavily; fast; **'n –e kop,** very stubborn; **–e woorde,** hard (harsh) words; **dit was – nodig,** it was badly needed; **– ry,** ride fast; **– in die bek,** vide **hardbekkig; – hardloop,** run fast; **– reën,** rain heavily.
hard, (ge-), harden, steel (one's nerves).
hardbekkig, (-e), hard-mouthed.
hardebolkeil(tjie) bowler (hat).
hardepad, (hard) road; hard labour.
harder, (-s), n. mullet, Cape-herring.
harder, a. & adv. **vide hard.**
harderig, (-e), rather hard; vide **hard.**
hardhandig, (-e), hard-handed, harsh, rough, rude, violent
hardhandigheid, hard-handedness.
hardheid, hardness, sternness; vide **hard.**
hardhoofdig, (-e), headstrong, obstinate.
hardhoofdig, obstinacy, stubbornness.
hardhorend, -horig, (-e), hard of hearing.
harding, hardening, tempering.
hardkoppig, (-e), headstrong, obstinate.
hardkoppigheid, obstinacy, stubbornness.
hardleers, (-e), dull, slow of understanding.
hardleersheid, dullness, unteachableness.
hardloop, (ge-), run; hurry, make haste.
hardloper, runner, sprinter.
hardlopery, running; racing.
hardlywig, (-e), constipated, costive.
hardlywigheid, constipation, costiveness.
hardnekkig, (-e), obstinate (person), dogged (resolution), stubborn (fight), persistent (cough).
hardnekkigheid, obstinacy, stubbornness.
hardop, aloud, loud.

hardvogtig, (-e), heartless, unfeeling.
hardvogtigheid, hard-heartedness.
hareborsel, -kam, -knipper, vide **haarborsel, -kam, -knipper.**
harem, (-s), harem, seraglio.
ha(re)rig, (-e), hairy, hirsute, pilose.
ha(re)righeid, hairiness, pilosity.
haresnyer, vide **haarsnyer.**
haring, (-s), herring.
haringvangs, herring-fishery.
haringvisser, herring-fisher.
haringvloot, herring-fleet.
hark, (-e), n. rake.
hark, (ge-), rake.
harlaboerla, hurly-burly.
harlekinade, (-s), harlequinade.
harlekyn, (-e), buffoon, clown, harlequin.
harlekynspak, motley (suit).
harlekynstreke, buffoonery.
harmonie, (-e), harmony.
harmonieer, (ge-), harmonize, go together.
harmonieleer, theory of harmony.
harmonies, (-e), harmonious, harmonic.
harmonieus, (-e), harmonious.
harmonika, (-s), accordion, concertina.
harmoniseer, (ge-), harmonize (music).
harnas, (-se), n. armour; cuirass; **iemand in die – ja,** antagonize a person.
harnas, (ge-), (put on) armour; arm oneself.
harp, (-e), harp.
harpoen, (-e), harpoon.
harpoeneer, (ge-), harpoon.
harpoenier, (-s), harpooner.
harpspel, harp-playing.
harpspeler, -speelster, harp-player, harper.
harpuis, n. resin, rosin.
harpuisolie, resin-oil.
harpy, (-e), harpy.
hars-..., vide **harpuis.**
harsing, vide **hersen-, brein-.**
harsinggimnastiek, intellectual gymnastics.
harsingkoors, brain-fever.
harsingloos, (-lose), brainless.
harsingontsteking, inflammation of the brain.
harsingpan, skull.
harsingskudding, concussion of the brain.
harsingverweking, softening of the brain.
harsingvlies, cerebral membrane.
harsingvliesontsteking, meningitis.
harslag, (-te), pluck (of slaughtered animal).
harspan, head, skull; **iemand se – inslaan,** crack a person's skull (head).
hart, (-e), heart; mind; courage; core, centre; **sy – sit in sy keel,** he has his heart in his mouth; **hy het 'n klein –,** he is easily moved to tears; **sy – sak (sink) in sy skoene,** his courage fails him; **sy – sit op die regte plek,** he has his heart in the right place; **sy – lê op sy tong,** he wears his heart on his sleeve; **iemand 'n – onder die riem steek,** put heart into a person; **sy – lug (uitstort),** give vent to one's feelings, unbosom oneself; **sy – aan iets ophaal,** enjoy something immensely; **– en siel daarvoor,** wholeheartedly in favour of . . . ; **sy – op iets sit,** put (set) one's heart on something; **my – het in my keel geklop,** my heart leapt to my mouth; **waar die – van vol is, loop die mond van oor,** out of the full heart the mouth sings; **sy – was so vol dat hy nie kon praat nie,** he could not speak because of the fullness of his heart; **haar – is nog vry,** she is still fancy-free; **dit gaan my aan die –,** it goes to my heart; **dit lê my na aan die –,** it is near to my heart; **en niere,** to the backbone; **hy sê wat in sy – is,** he speaks his mind freely; **met – en siel,** heart and soul.

hartaandoening whole-heartedly; **'n man na my –,** a man after my own heart; **ek kon dit nie oor my – kry nie,** I could not find it in my heart to do it; **iemand iets op die – druk,** enjoy (impress, urge) something on a person; **iets op die – hê (dra),** have something on one's mind (in one's heart); **iemand se belange op sy – dra,** study a person's interests; **iets ter –e neem,** lay (take) a thing to heart; **van –e,** hearty; **van ganser –e,** with all one's heart; **dit gaan van my – af,** I part with it very reluctantly.
hartaandoening, affection of the heart.
hartbees, hartebeest.
hartbeeshuis, hartebeest-hut.
hartbrekend, (-e), heart-breaking (-rending).
harte-aas, hartenaas, ace of hearts.
hartebloed, heart's blood, life-blood.
harte(ns)boer, -(ns)heer, -(ns)vrou, jack (knave); king, ten, queen of hearts.
hartedief, darling, love, pet.
harteleed, heartfelt grief, heartache.
harteloos, (-lose), heartless.
harteloosheid, heartlessness.
hartelus: na –, to one's heart's content.
hartens, hearts (in cards).
hartepyn, vide **harteleed.**
hartewens, heart's desire, fondest wish.
hartewond, heart's wound.
hartgebrek, heart-ailment.
hartgrondig, (-e), cordial, heartfelt.
hartig, (-e), hearty.
hartjie, little heart (lit.); darling; **in die – van Afrika,** in the heart of Africa; **in die – van die winter,** in the dead (the depth, the middle) of winter; **in die – van die somer,** in the height of summer.
hartklep, heart-valve; suction-valve (of pump).
hartklop, heart-beat.
hartkloppings, palpitation of the heart.
hartkramp, spasm of the heart.
hartkwaal, heart-disease.
hartlam, darling, dearest.
hartlik, (-e), cordial, hearty.
hartlikheid, cordiality, heartiness, sincerity.
hart-longmasjien, heart-lung machine.
hartroerend, (-e), pathetic, touching.
hartseer, n. grief, sorrow; **van – sterwe,** die of a broken heart.
hartseer, a. sad, heartsore, grieved (at heart).
hartslag, heart-beat, pulsation of the heart.
hart(ver)sterkend, (-e), bracing, tonic.
hart(ver)sterking, bracer, cordial, tonic.
hartstog, (-te), passion.
hartstogtelik, (-e), passionate, impassioned; ardent, keen.
hartstogtelikheid, passion(ateness).
hartstreek, cardiac region.
hartsvanger, cutlass, hanger.
hartvergroting, dila(ta)tion of the heart.
hartverheffend, (-e), ennobling, elevating.
hartverlamming, heart-failure (-seizure).
hartverskeurend, (-e), heartrending, poignant.
hartversterkend, vide **hart(ver)sterkend.**
hartversterkinkie, (-s), cordial, drink, tot.
hartvormig, (-e), heart-shaped.
hartwerking, heart-action.
harwar, confusion; bickering, squabble.
hasepad: die – kies, take to one's heels.
hasie, (-s), young hare, leveret.
hasielip, haaslip, hare-lip.
hasie-oor, leapfrog.
haspel, (-s), n. reel.
haspel, (ge-), reel, bungle; bicker, wrangle.
hater, (-s), hater.
hawe, n. goods, property, stock; **– en goed,** goods and chattels; **lewende –,** livestock.
hawe, (-ns), n. harbour, port; dock; haven.
hawe-arbeider, dock-worker, docker.
hawegeld, dock-dues (-charges), dockage.
hawehoof, mole, pier, jetty.
haweloos, (-lose), poor, ragged, homeless.
haweplaas, port, seaport(-town).
hawer, oats; **iets van – tot gort (klawer) ken,** know all the ins and outs of a thing.
haweregte, port-dues.
hawergerf, oat-sheaf.
hawerkorrel, oat-grain.
hawerklap: om die –, every moment, for every trifle.
hawermeel, oatmeal.
hawermout, rolled oats; oatmeal-porridge.
hawersak, oat-bag; nose-bag (of a horse).
hawestad, port, seaport-town.
hawik, (-e), hawk, goshawk.
hawiksneus, hook-nose, aquiline nose.
hè!, my!, oh!
hê?, eh?, what?, eh?; hey!
hê, (had, gehad), have, possess; **daar het jy dit nou!,** there you are!; **gelyk –,** be right; **dit mis –,** be (in the) wrong; **dit wil ek –!,** I quite believe it; **iemand wil jou –,** you are wanted; **ek het nie geweet hoe ek dit het nie,** I didn't know what to make of it; **had ek dit maar gedoen,** if I had only done it; **jy weet nooit wat jy aan hom het nie,** one never knows where one is with him; **wat het jy daaraan?,** what is the good of it?; **ek het dit by my,** I have (got) it with me; **hoe het ek dit nou met jou?,** I cannot make you out; **hy het dit oor...,** he is talking about...; **ek het daar niks op teë nie,** I have no objection; **dit het jy daarvan,** that's all you get (by it); **dit goed –,** be well off; **hy kon dit gehad het,** he could have had it; **– is –, kry is die kuns,** possession is nine points of the law.
hebbelikheid, habit, peculiarity.
Hebreër, (-s), Hebrew.
Hebreeus, (-e), n. & a. Hebrew.
hebsug, covetousness, greed.
hebsugtig, (-e), covetous, grasping, greedy.
hebsugtigheid, vide **hebsug.**
hede, n. this day, the present; **tot op –,** up to the present.
hede, adv. to-day, at present; **– ten dae,** nowadays; **van – af,** from to-day onward.
hede!, oh my!, good heavens!
hedendaags, (-e), a. modern, present-day.
hedendaags, adv. nowadays, at present.
hedonisties, (-e), hedonistic.
heel, (hele), a. entire, whole; complete; **'n hele aantal,** a good many, **'n hele tyd,** quite a time; **deur die hele Europa,** throughout Europe.
heel, adv. quite, very; **– anders,** quite different; **– goed,** very well; **– veel,** a great many, a great deal.
heel, (ge-), cure, heal.
heel, (ge-), fence, receive (stolen goods).
heelal, universe.
heelbaar, (-bare), curable, healable.
heeldag, the whole day; frequently.
heelhuids, with a whole skin, unscathed.
heelkragtig, (-e), curative.
heelkunde, healing art, surgery.
heelkundig, (-e), surgical.
heelmeester, surgeon; **die H–,** the Healer.
heeltemal, altogether, entirely, clean, quite, utterly; **– alleen,** all alone; **– nie,** not at all; **nog nie – nie,** not quite; **– tot bo,** right to the very top; **ek het dit – vergeet,** I had clean forgotten it.

heelwat, a considerable number (of), a lot; – **moeite**, a lot of trouble, considerable trouble; – **meer**, a good deal (considerably) more; – **tyd**, quite a time.
heemraad, heemraad.
heen, away; **êrens** –, somewhere; **nêrens** – **nie**, nowhere; **oral(s)** –, everywhere; **waar gaan hy** –?, where are you off to?; **waar moet dit** –?, where is this to end?; **hy is ver** –, he is far gone; – **en terug**, there and back; – **en weer**, to and fro.
heen-en-weertjie: **'n** –, a moment; return-journey; return-ticket.
heengaan, n. death, departure, passing away.
heengaan, (heenge-), depart.
heenkome, refuge.
heenreis, n. outward voyage, forward journey.
heensit, (heenge-): **jou oor iets** –, get over something.
heenskeer, (heenge-), hurry off.
heensnel, -speed, (heenge-), run (speed) away, fly; **die tyd snel heen**, time flies.
heenswerf, -swerwe, (heenge-), wander away.
heer, (here), army, host.
heer, (here), gentleman; lord; master; king (in cards); **die** – **A.**, Mr A.; **die jong** – **A.**, Master A.; – **en meester**, lord and master.
Heer, Here, the Lord, God, the Almighty; **ons liewe** –, our (dear) Lord; **as die** – **wil**, God willing.
heeragtig, (-e), grand(ly), in a grand style.
heerleër, host.
heerlik, (-e), delicious (food), glorious, lovely (weather), delightful (time).
heerlikheid, glory, magnificence, splendour.
heerlik(heid)!, Great Scott!
heers, (ge-), reign, rule, govern; prevail, be prevalent.
heersend, (-e), ruling; prevailing; **die** –**e pryse**, ruling prices; **die** –**e winde**, the prevailing (prevalent) winds.
heerser, (-s), **heerseres**, (-se) ruler.
heerskaar, host; **die Heer van die** –**skare**, the Lord of Hosts.
heerskap, master, lord; gent, cove.
heerskappy, master, lord; gent, cove, sovereignty, **die** – **voer**, rule, hold sway.
heerssug, ambition, lust of power.
heerssugtig, (-e), ambitious.
heertjie, (-s), young gentleman; (young) blood.
hees, (–, **hese**), husky.
heesheid, hoarseness, huskiness.
heester, (-s), shrub.
heet, (**hete**), a. hot; burning; torrid (zone); bitter (tears); **op heter daad betrap**, take in the very act (red-handed).
heet, (ge-), call, name; be called (named); order, tell; **hoe** – **hy?**, what is his name?; **soos dit** –, on the pretence of; **hy** – **na my**, he is called after me; vide **hiet**.
heetgebaker(d), (-de), quick-tempered.
heethoof, hot-headed person.
heethoofdig, (-e), hot-headed.
heethoofdigheid, hot-headedness.
hef, (-te, **hewwe**), n. handle, haft; hilt (of sword); **die** – **in hande hê**, be in control.
hef, (ge-), lift, raise; impose, levy (taxes).
hefboom, lever; fulcrum (zool.).
heffing, (-e, -s), levying (of taxes); arsis (in verse).
heftig, (-e), heated, vehement, violent.
heftigheid, heat, vehemence, violence.
heg, (-ge), n. hedge; vide **haag**.
heg, (-te), a. firm, solid, staunch.
heg, (ge-), affix, attach, fasten, stitch (up); heat; **baie waarde aan** –, attach much importance (value) to; **jou** – **aan**, get attached to, attach oneself to; **jou handtekening** – **aan**, append one's signature to.
hegemonie, hegemony.
hegpleister, adhesive (sticking) plaster.
hegtenis, custody, detention; **in** – **neem**, take into custody; **in** – **hou**, keep in custody.
hegtheid, firmness, solidity, strength.
hei, **heide**, n. heath, heather; moor.
hei(de)blommetjie, heath(er).
heiden, (-e, -s), heathen, pagan.
heidens, (-e), heathen, pagan; **'n** –**e lawaai**, an infernal noise.
heidin, (ne), heathen(-woman), pagan (woman).
heil, good, welfare; salvation; – **in sien**, see the good of; **sy** – **in die vlug soek**, seek safety in flight; **tot** – **van sy siel**, for the salvation of his soul.
Heiland, Saviour.
heilbede, good wishes, God-speed.
heilbegerig, (-e), desirous of salvation.
heildronk, health, toast.
heilig, (-e), a. holy, sacred; **die H**–**e Franciscus**, St. Francis; **die H**–**e Gees**, the Holy Spirit (Ghost); –**e oortuiging**, firm conviction; **die H**– **skrif**, Holy Scripture; **die -e waarheid**, the gospel truth; **niks is vir hom** – **nie**, nothing is sacred to him; – **verklaar**, canonize; **jou** – **voorneem**, record a mental vow.
heilig, (ge-), hallow, sanctify; **die doel** – **die middele**, the end justifies the means.
heiligdom, (-me), sanctuary, shrine; sanctum.
heilig, (-s), saint.
heiligebeeld, image of a saint; icon.
heiligelewe, life of a saint.
heiligheid, holiness, sacredness, sanctity; **Sy H**–, His Holiness.
heiliging, hallowing, sanctification.
heiligmaking, sanctification.
heiligskennend, (-e), sacrilegious.
heiligskennis, desecration, sacrilege.
heiligverklaring, canonisation.
heilloos, (-lose), disastrous, fatal; impious.
heilsame, (-same), beneficial, salutary.
heilsaamheid, salutariness, wholesomeness.
Heilsleër, Salvation Army.
Heilsoldaat, Salvationist.
heilstaat, ideal state, Utopia.
heilwens, benediction, congratulation.
heimlik, (-e), secret; clandestine, private.
heimlikheid, secrecy.
heimwee, homesickness; – **hê**, be homesick.
heinde: – **en ver**, far and near (wide).
heining, (-s), enclosure, fence, hedge.
hek, (-ke), gate; boom.
hekatombe, (-s), hecatomb.
hekel, n. dislike; **'n** – **hê aan**, dislike, hate.
hekel, (ge-), crochet; heckle; censure, criticize, haul over the coals, satirize.
hekelaar, (-s), heckler; critic; satirist.
hekeldig, (-te), satire.
hekeldigter, satirist.
hekelnaald, -**pen**, crochet-needle.
hekelskrif, lampoon, satire.
hekelvers, satire, satiric poem.
hekelwerk, crochet-work, crocheting.
hekkies, hurdles.
hekkiesloop, n. hurdle-race.
heks, (-e), n. witch; vixen; **'n ou** –, a hag.
heks, (ge-), practise witchcraft, conjure.
heksaëder, (-s), hexahedron.
heksagonaal, (-ale), hexagonal.
heksagoon, (-gone), hexagon.
heksameter, (-s), hexameter.
heksedans, witches' dance.

hekseketel, witches' cauldron.
heksery, sorcery, witchcraft.
heksetoer, tough job.
heksewerk, sorcery, witchcraft; tough job.
heksluiter, last-comer, rear man; Benjamin.
hektaar, (-tare), hectare.
hektograaf, (-grawe), hectograph.
hektografeer, (ge-), hectograph.
hektogram, (-me), hectogramme.
hektoliter, hectolitre.
hektometer, hectometre.
hel, n. hell.
hel, a. bright, glaring.
hel, (ge-), dip, incline, shelve, slant, slope.
helaas, alas, unfortunately.
held, (-e), hero.
heldedaad, heroic deed, act of heroism.
heldedig, (-te), heroic poem, epic.
heldedigter, epic poet.
heldedood, heroic death, hero's death.
heldegeslag, heroic race, race of heroes.
heldemoed, heroism.
helder, (-e), clear, sonorous (sounds); vivid, bright lucid (style); **dit is – dag**, it is broad daylight; **– oordag**, in broad daylight; **hy het 'n – kop**, he is clear-headed; **'n – oomblik**, a lucid moment; **– wakker**, wide awake.
helderheid, brightness, clearness, lucidity.
helderklinkend, (-e), clear, ringing.
helderol, rôle of a hero.
heldersiende, clear-sighted; second-sighted.
heldersiendheid, clear-sightedness; clairvoyance.
heldesang, epic song (poem).
heldestryd, heroic struggle.
heldetyd, heroic age (time).
heldeverering, hero-worship.
heldevolk, heroic nation, nation of heroes.
heldhaftig, (-e), brave, heroic.
heldhaftigheid, bravery, heroism.
heldin, (-ne), heroine.
heler, (-s), healer; receiver, fence.
helfte, (-s), half; **die – meer**, half as much again; **die – minder**, less by half.
helhond, hell-hound, Cerberus.
helikopter, (-s), helicopter.
heliks, (-e), helix, (-ices), helix.
heling, healing; fencing, receiving.
heliografie, heliography.
heliogram, heliogram.
heliosentries, (-e), heliocentric.
helioskoop, (-skope), helioscope.
heliotroop, (-trope), heliotrope, turnsole.
helium, helium.
hellebaard, (-e), halberd.
hellebardier, (-s), halberdier.
Helleen, (-lene), Hellene.
Helleens, (-e), n. & a. Hellenic.
hellend, (-e), inclined, sloping.
Hellenisme, (-s), Hellenism.
hellevaart, descent into hell.
helleveeg, shrew, virago, vixen, hell-cat.
helling, (-e, -s), decline, slope; gradient.
helm, (-e, -s), helmet; helm; caul; **met die – gebore**, born with a caul.
helmdraad, (-e), galeate.
helmet, (-s, -te), helmet.
helmhoed, sun-helmet.
helmstylig, (-e), gynandrous.
heloot, (-lote), helot.
help, (ge-), aid, assist, help, succour; avail, be of use; attend to, serve; **dit – niks nie**, it's of no use, it's no good; **ek kan dit nie – nie**, I cannot help it; **– my onthou**, remind me; **alle bietjies –**, many a pickle makes a mickle; **iemand aan iets –**, help someone to something;

iemand by (met) iets –, help someone with (in) something; **iemand na die ander wêreld –**, send someone to Kingdom Come.
helpend, (-e), helping; **–e hand**, helping hand.
helper, -ster, (-s), assistant, helper, aid(e).
hels, (-e), devilish, hellish, infernal; **iemand – maak**, drive a person wild.
helsteen, lunar caustic, silver-nitrate.
Helveties, (-e), Helvetian.
hemdegoed, shirting.
hemel, (-e, -s), heaven; firmament, sky; tester (of bed); canopy (of throne); **goeie –!**, good heavens!; **die – bewaar ons**, Heaven (God) forbid, Heaven help us; **die – sy dank**, Heaven be praised; **die – weet**, Heaven (Goodness) knows; **aan die –**, in the sky (the heavens); **in die –**, in heaven; **in die – kom**, go to heaven; **onder die blote –**, in the open; **ten – vaar**, ascend to heaven; **tot die – (toe) prys**, laud to the skies, cry up; **tussen – en aarde**, between heaven and earth, in mid-air; **uit die – val**, drop from the blue.
hemelbestormer, heaven-stormer, Titan.
hemelbewoner, celestial, inhabitant of Heaven.
hemelbode, messenger from Heaven.
hemelboog, vault of heaven, firmament.
hemeldragonder, pulpit-thumper, sky-pilot.
hemelgewelf, vide **hemelboog**.
Hemelheer, Lord of Heaven.
hemelheer, celestial host.
hemelhoog, (-hoë), sky-high; **– prys**, laud to the skies, cry up.
hemeling, (-e), celestial, inhabitant of Heaven.
hemelledekant, tester-bed(stead).
hemelliggaam, celestial (heavenly) body.
hemelpoort, gate of Heaven.
hemelryk, Kingdom of Heaven.
hemels, (-e), celestial, heavenly.
hemelsblou, azure, sky-blue.
hemelsbreed, (-breë), wide (difference); **hulle verskil –**, there is all the world of difference between them; **dit maak 'n hemelsbreë verskil**, that makes all the difference.
hemel(s)breedte, astronomical latitude.
hemelsnaam: in –, for heaven's sake.
hemelstreek, zone; point of the compass.
hemelswil: om –, for heaven's sake.
hemelteken, sign of the zodiac.
hemeltergend, (-e), crying to heaven.
hemeltrans, vide **hemelboog**.
Hemelvaart, Ascension.
Hemelvaartsdag, Ascension Day.
hemelvuur, lightning.
hemelwaarts, heavenward(s).
hemisfeer, hemisphere.
hemp, (hemde), shirt; (lady's) chemise.
hempbroek, combination.
hempsboordjie, shirt-collar.
hempskakel, (shirt-)link, (cuff-)link.
hempsknoop, shirt-button.
hempsknopie, shirt-stud.
hempsmou, shirt-sleeve.
hen, (-ne), hen; **loop soos 'n – wat nes soek**, wander about aimlessly.
hengel, (ge-), angle.
hengelaar, (-s), angler.
hengelstok, angling-rod.
henna, henna.
hennep, hemp.
hennepsaad, hempseed.
hennetjie, (-s), pullet.
heradem, (het –), breathe again.
herademing, relief.
heraldiek, heraldry, heraldic art.

heraldies, (-e), heraldic.
herbarium, (-ia, -s), herbarium, herbal.
herbegraaf, -grawe, (het -), reinter.
herbegrafnis, reinterment.
herbenoem, (het -), reappoint.
herbenoeming, reappointment.
herberg, (-e), n. inn; accommodation.
herberg, (ge-), accommodate, house, lodge, put up; shelter; harbour (a fugitive).
herbergier, (-s), host, innkeeper, landlord.
herbergsaam, (-same), hospitable.
herbergsaamheid, hospitableness.
herbore, born again, reborn, regenerate.
herbou, n. rebuilding, reconstruction.
herbou, (het -), build again, rebuild.
herd, erd, (-e), fireplace, hearth; vide **haard.**
herdenk, (het -), commemorate.
herdenking, (-e, -s), commemoration; **ter - aan,** in commemoration of.
herdenkingsdiens, memorial service.
herdenkingsplaat, commemorative tablet.
herder, (-s), n. (shep)herd; pastor.
herderin, (-ne), shepherdess.
herderlik, (-e), pastoral.
herderloos, (-lose), without a shepherd (pastor).
herderroman, pastoral romance.
herdersdig, (-te), eclogue, pastoral (poem).
herdershond, shepherd's dog, sheep-dog.
herderspel, pastoral play.
herderstaf, shepherd's crook; crosier.
herdersvolk, pastoral (nomadic) people.
herdiskonteer, (het -), rediscount.
herdiskonto, rediscount.
herdoop, n. rebaptism.
herdoop, (het -), rebaptize, rechristen, rename.
herdruk, n. reprint, new edition.
herdruk, (het -), reprint.
Here, vide **Heer.**
hereboer, gentleman-farmer.
herefuif, stag party.
herekleding, (gentle)men's clothing.
hereksamen, re-examination.
hereksamineer, (het -), re-examine.
herenig, (het -), reunite.
hereniging, reunion.
herenigingskongres, reunion-conference.
herent, (het -), revaccinate; regraft.
herenting, revaccination; regrafting.
herereg(te), transfer-dues.
Herero, (-'s), Herero.
herfs, (-te), autumn.
herfsagtig, (-e), autumnal.
herfsblare, autumn-leaves.
herfsblommetentoonstelling, show of autumn(al) flowers.
herfsdraad, air-thread, gossamer.
herfskleur, autumnal colour (hue, tint).
herfsnagewening, autumnal equinox.
herfstint, vide **herfskleur.**
herfstyd, autumn-time, autumnal season.
hergiet, (het -), recast.
herhaal, (het -), repeat, reiterate, say over again; **jou -,** repeat oneself.
herhaalde, repeated, successive.
herhaaldelik, repeatedly, again and again.
herhaling, (-e -s), recapitulation, repetition, reiteration; **by -,** vide **herhaaldelik.**
herhalingsgetal, recurring number.
herhalingsles, repetition-lesson.
herhalingsteken, repeat (mus.).
herinner, (het -), jou -, call to mind, recall, recollect, remember; **as ek my goed -,** if I remember aright; **vir sover ek my -,** to the best of my recollection, **iemand aan iets -,** remind a person of something.

herinnering, (-e, -s), recollection, reminiscence, memory, reminder, memento, souvenir; **ter - aan,** in memory of.
herken, (het -), recognize; identify, know.
herkenbaar, (-bare), recognizable; identifiable.
herkenning, recognition.
herkenningsparade, identification-parade.
herkenningsteken, distinctive mark.
herkeuring, re-examination.
herkies, (het -), re-elect.
herkiesbaar, (-bare), eligible for re-election.
herkiesing, (-e, -s), re-election.
herkoms, derivation, extraction, origin.
herkomstig, descended (born, sprung) (from).
herkoop, repurchase.
herkou, (ge-), ruminate, chew the cud; repeat.
herkry, (het -), recover, regain, get back.
herkryging, recovery, recuperation.
herkulies, (-e), Herculean.
herleef, -lewe, (het -), live again, return to life, revive.
herlees, (het -), read again, reread.
herlei, (het -), reduce; convert (monkey); **- breuk na gemene deler,** reduce fractions to common denominator.
herleibaar, (-bare), reducible.
herleiding, reduction; deduction; conversion.
herlesing, rereading.
herlewing, rebirth, renascence, revival.
hermafrodiet, (-e), hermaphrodite.
hermelyn, ermine.
hermelynbont, ermine-fur.
hermeties, (-e), hermetic, airtight.
hermiet, (-e), hermit.
hermitage, hermityk, Hermitage(-wine).
herneem, (het -), take again; resume (one's seat); recapture (a fort).
herneming, recapture; resumption.
hernieu, hernu(we), (het -), renew, renovate; resume (old friendship); **die aanval -,** return to the charge.
hernuwing, renewal, renovation; resumption.
heroïes, (-e), heroic.
heroïsme, heroism.
heropen, (het -), reopen.
heropening, reopening.
herout, (-e), herald.
herower, (het -), reconquer, recover.
herowering, reconquest, recovery.
herplaas, replace.
herplant, (het -), replant.
herrangskikking, rearrangement.
herrie, row, uproar; confusion; **- maak (opskop),** kick up a row; **iemand op sy - gee,** give someone a thrashing.
herriemaker, rowdy; rioter.
herroep, (het -), recall, revoke; repeal (laws), countermand (an order); **sy woorde -,** retract (eat) one's words.
herroeping, revocation, recall, retraction.
herrys, (het -), rise again.
herrysenis, resurrection.
hersê, (het -), repeat, say over again.
hersen-, vide **harsing-.**
hersenskim, chimera, phantasm.
hersenskimmig, (-e), chimerical.
hersenskudding, vide **harsingskudding.**
hersien, (het -), revise, overhaul; reconsider (one's views).
hersiening, revision, reconsideration.
herskape, reborn, transformed.
herskat, (het -), revalue.
herskatting, revaluation.
herskep, (het -, het herskape), re-create, regenerate, transform, metamorphose.

herskepping, re-creation, transformation.
herstel, n. restoration, reinstatement; rehabilitation; recovery; reparation.
herstel, (het –), mend, repair; redress (grievances), restore (the monarchy), correct, rectify (a mistake), right (a wrong), make good (damage); re-establish, reinstate; recover (from illness); **jou –**, rally.
herstelling, correction; recovery, repair, restoration, re-establishment; reinstatement; vide **herstel**.
herstellingsoord, health-resort, sanatorium.
herstellingsteken, natural (mus.).
herstellingswerk, repair-work, work of repair, repairs.
herstelspan, breakdown gang.
herstem, (het –), vote again.
herstemming, second ballot.
hert, (-e), deer, hart, stag.
hertel, (het –), recount, count again.
hertelling, recount.
hertog, (hertoë), duke.
hertogdom, duchy.
hertogin, (-ne), duchess.
hertrou, (het –), remarry, marry again.
hervat, (het –), resume, restart.
hervatting, resumption, renewal.
herverseker, (het –), reinsure.
herversekering, reinsurance.
hervorm, (het –), reform, remodel.
hervorm(d), (-de), reformed.
hervormer, (-s), reformer.
hervorming, reform, reformation.
herwaarts, hither.
herwin, (het –), recover, regain; retrieve.
herwonne, regained, recovered.
heryk, (het –), regauge.
heserig, (-e), slightly hoarse (husky).
het, vide **hê**.
heterodoks, (-e), heterodox.
heterodoksie, heterodoxy.
heterogeen, (-gene), heterogeneous.
heterogeniteit, heterogeneity.
hetsy; – ... **of** (hetsy), either ... or; whether ... or.
hettete, **hittete: dit was so –**, it was touch and go, it was a near thing.
heug, n.: **teen – en meug**, reluctantly.
heug, (ge-): **dit – my nog**, I still remember.
heugenis, memory, remembrance.
heuglik, (-e), memorable; joyful, glad.
heul, (ge-), – **met**, collude (be in league) with.
heuning, honey; **iemand – om die mond smeer**, butter a person up, soft-soap a person.
heuningbakkie, nectary (bot.).
heuningdassie, honey-badger.
heuningdou, honey-dew, blight.
heuningklier, nectar-gland, honey-gland.
heuningkoek, honeycomb; honey-cake.
heuningkwas: die – gebruik, coax, flatter.
heuningvoël(tjie), honey-bird, honey-guide.
heup, (-e), hip (man), haunch (animal).
heupbeen, hipbone.
heupgewrig, hip-joint.
heupjig, hip-gout, sciatica.
heuppotjie, hip-cavity.
heuristies, (-e), heuristic.
heus, (-e), a. courteous, obliging, polite.
heus, adv. courteously; really, truly.
heusheid, courtesy, kindness.
heuwel, (-s), hill.
heuwelagtig, (-e), hilly.
heuwelrug, ridge of a hill.
hewel, (-s), n. siphon.
hewel, (ge-), siphon, draw off.

hewelbarometer, siphon-barometer.
hewig, (-e), violent, sharp, fierce, severe, vehement (protest).
hewigheid, fierceness, intensity, vehemence.
hiaat, (hiate), break, gap, hiatus.
hiasint, (-e), hyacinth.
hibride, (-s), hybrid.
hibridies, (-e), hybrid.
hidra, (-s), hydra.
hidraat, (-ate), hydrate.
hidrant, (-e), hydrant.
hidrochloorsuur, hydrochloric acid.
hidrodinamies, (-e), hydrodynamic.
hidrodinamika, hydrodynamics.
hidro-elektries, hydro-electric.
hidrofobie, hydrophobia.
hidroliese, hydrolysis.
hidrometer, hydrometer.
hidrosiaansuur, hydrocyanic (prussic) acid.
hidrostaties, (-e), hydrostatic.
hidrostatika, hydrostatics.
hidroterapie, hydrotherapy, water-cure.
hidroulies, (-e), hydraulic.
hiel, (-e), heel; vide **hak**.
hiëna, (-s), hyena.
hiep-hiep-hoera, hip, hip, hurrah!
hier, here; close by; **van – af**, from here; – **te lande**, in this country.
hieraan, at (by, on, to) this.
hieragter, behind this; here(in)after.
hiërarg, (-e), hierarch.
hiërargie, (-ë), hierarchy.
hiërargies, (-e), hierarchical.
hierbenede, (here) below, down here.
hierbinne, in here, within.
hierbo, up here, overhead; in heaven.
hierbuite, outside.
hierby, hereby, herewith; attached, enclosed (in letter); – **kom nog**, in addition to this, moreover.
hierdeur, by (in consequence of, owing to, through) this, through here.
hierdie, this (these).
hierheen, this way, hither.
hierin, in this, in here, herein.
hierjy, n. lout.
hierjy!, hullo!, I say!
hierlang(e)s, this way, along here; hereabout(s).
hiermee, with this, herewith.
hierna, after this, hereafter; according to this.
hiernaas, next to this, alongside; next door.
hiernamaals, hereafter; **die –**, the hereafter.
hiernatoe, this way.
hiernewens, annexed, enclosed (in letter).
hiëroglief, (-gliewe), hieroglyphic.
hiëroglifies, (-e), hieroglyphic.
hierom, for this reason.
hieromheen, round this; hereabout(s).
hieromstreeks, hereabout(s).
hieromtrent, with regard to this; hereabout(s).
hieronder, below, underneath; among these.
hieroor, about this, over this.
hierop, upon this, after this, hereupon.
hierso, here, at this place; **kom –!**, come here!
hierteen, against this.
hierteenoor, opposite, over the way; against this.
hiertoe, for this purpose; thus (so) far.
hiertussen, among (between) these; in between.
hieruit, from this, hence.
hiervan, of this, about this.
hiervoor, for this, in return for this.
hiervoor, in front; before this.
hiet, (ge-), order; – **en gebied**, order about (right and left); vide **heet**, (ge-).
higiëne, hygiene, hygienics.

higiënies, (-e), hygienic.
higroskoop, (-skope), hygroscope.
hik, (-ke), n. hiccup (hiccough).
hik, (ge-), hiccup (hiccough).
hikkerig, (-e), hiccuping.
hilariteit, hilarity, merriment.
himne, (-s), hymn.
hinder, n. hindrance, impediment, obstacle.
hinder, (ge-), hamper, hinder, inconvenience; trouble; annoy, worry; be in the way.
hinderlaag, ambush, ambuscade.
hinderlik, (-e), annoying, troublesome.
hindernis, (-se), hindrance, obstacle.
hindernis-wedloop, obstacle-race.
hinderpaal, bar, impediment, obstacle.
Hindoe, (-s), Hindu (Hindoo).
hings, (-te), stallion.
hingsel, (-s), handle; hinge; loop (of whip).
hink, (ge-), hobble, limp; op twee gedagtes –, be in two minds.
hinkspel, hopscotch.
hink-stap-spring, hop, skip and jump.
hinnik, (ge-), neigh, whinny.
hiper-Afrikaans, (-e), ultra-Afrikaans.
hiperbeleef, (-de), overpolite.
hiperbeskaafd, (-de), overcivilised.
hiperbolies, (-e), hyperbolic(al).
hiperbool, (-bole), hyperbole; hyperbola (maths).
hiperkrities, (-e), hypercritical.
hipermodern, (-e), ultra-modern.
hipersonies, hypersonic.
hipnose, hypnosis.
hipnoties, (-e), hypnotic.
hipnotiseer, (ge-), hypnotize.
hipnotiseur, (-s), hypnotist.
hipnotisme, hypnotism.
hipofosfiet, hypophosphite.
hipokonders, ipekonders, hypochondria; caprices, whims.
hipokondries, (-e), hypochondriac(al).
hipokriet, (-e), hypocrite.
hipokrities, (-e), hypocritical.
hipoteek, (-teke), mortgage.
hipoteekgewer, mortgager (mortgagor).
hipoteekhouer, hipoteeknemer, mortgagee.
hipotekêr, (-e), hypothecary, mortgage- . . .
hipotenusa, (-s), hypotenuse.
hipotese, (-s), hypothesis.
hipoteties, (-e), hypothetic(al).
hippodroom, (-drome), hippodrome.
hippopotamus, (-mi, -se), hippopotamus
hisop, hyssop.
histerie, hysteria, hysterics.
histeries, (-e), hysteric(al).
histologie, histology.
historie, (ë, -s), history; story.
histories, (-e), historical; historic.
historikus, (-se, -ici), historian, historiographer.
histrionies, (-e), histrionic.
hitsig, (-e), hot, lewd; in heat (animals).
hitte, heat.
hittegolf, heat-wave.
hittete, vide hettetè.
hitteslag, heat-stroke.
hittewerend, hittevas, heat-resistant.
ho!, ho!, stop!
hobbel, (ge-), rock, toss, jolt; seesaw; hobble.
hobbelagtig, (-e), bumpy, rough, uneven.
hobbelpaadjie, crazy path.
hobbelperd, rocking-horse.
hobbelrig, (-e), vide hobbelagtig.
hobo, (-'s), hautboy, oboe.
hoe, how; what; – so?, how do you mean?; – eerder – beter, the sooner the better; – dan ook, anyhow, anyway; – dit ook sy, be that as it may; – lank, how long, till when; – noem jy dit?, what do you call it?; – sien sy daaruit?, what is she like?
hoë, vide hoog.
hoed, (-e), n. hat; bonnet; hoë –, tophat; – vasdruk, run away, turn tail; met die – in die hand, hat in hand; die – laat rondgaan, pass (send) the hat round; jy kan jou – ook nog agternagooi, you can give your hat into the bargain.
hoed, (ge-), keep, tend, watch; guard, protect; jou – vir, guard against, beware of.
hoedanig, (-e), what, what kind (sort) of.
hoedanigheid, quality; capacity.
hoedband, hat-band.
hoede, care, guard, protection; aan sy – toevertrou, commit to his care; iemand onder sy – neem, take a person under one's protection; op jou – wees, be on one's guard.
hoededoos, hat-box.
hoedemaakster, milliner.
hoedemakery, millinery; hat-factory.
hoeder, (-s), guardian, keeper.
hoed(e)speld, hat-pin.
hoedestander, hallstand.
hoedewinkel, hatshop.
hoedlint, hat-band; bonnet-string.
hoef, (hoewe), n. hoof.
hoef, v. need; jy – dit nie te doen nie, you need not do it; vide behoef.
hoefgetrappel, tramp (clatter) of hoofs.
hoefslag, hoof-beat, thud of hoofs.
hoefsmid, farrier.
hoefspyker, horseshoe-nail.
hoefyster, horseshoe; 'n – verloor, cast a shoe.
hoegenaamd: – nie, not at all; – niks, absolutely nothing, nothing whatever (at all).
hoe(i)-haai, vide haai-hoei.
hoek, (-e), corner; angle; (fish-)hook; narrow glen; iemand in 'n – ja, corner a person; om die –, round the corner.
hoeka: van – (se tyd) af, (from) of old.
hoekafstand, angular distance.
hoekie, (-s), little corner; nook; die – van die haard, the chimney-corner, the inglenook; in 'n – wees, be in a tight corner; iets om die – doen, do something on the sly; uit alle –s en gaatjies, from every nook and corner; vide hoek.
hoekig, (-e), angular; jagged (rocks).
hoekkas, corner-cupboard, corner-cabinet.
hoeklyn, diagonal.
hoekmeetkunde, goniometry.
hoekmeter, goniometer; protractor.
hoekmeting, goniometry.
hoekom, why, for what reason; wherefore; om – nie reguit is nie, because Y is a crooked letter (and you cannot make it straight).
hoekpunt, angular point, vertex.
hoekskop, corner-kick.
hoeksteen, corner-stone; keystone.
hoekstenlegging, laying of the foundation-stone.
hoektand, eye-tooth, canine (tooth).
hoëlik, greatly, highly.
hoender, (-s), fowl; chicken; die –s in wees, have one's monkey up; iemand die –s in maak, put one's monkey up; loop na die –s!, go to the devil!
hoenderboer, poultry-farm(er).
hoenderboerdery, poultry-farm(-ing).
hoenderboud(jie), drumsticks.
hoenderdief, poultry-thief (-stealer).
hoendereier, hen's egg.
hoenderhaan, cock.
hoenderhen, hen.
hoenderhok, poultry-house, fowl-run.

hoenderkop: hy is –, he is tipsy.
hoendernes, hen's nest.
hoenderpastei, chicken-pie.
hoendervel: – kry, get goose-flesh.
hoendervlees, -vleis, chicken; – kry, get goose-flesh.
hoepel, (-s), n. hoop.
hoepel, (ge-), trundle a hoop; hoop (a cask).
hoepelbeen, bandy-leg, bow-leg, met –, bandy-legged.
hoepelrok, crinoline, farthingale.
hoepelstok, hoop-stick.
hoëpriester, high priest, pontiff.
hoer, (-e), harlot, whore.
hoër, vide **hoog;** – **jongenskool,** high school for boys; – **meisieskool,** high school for girls.
hoera!, hoerê!, hurrah!
hoereer, (ge-), commit adultery, whore.
Hoërhand: van –, from God.
Hoërhuis, Upper House, Senate.
hoërop, higher up.
hoërskool, high school.
hoes, (-te), n. cough.
hoes, (ge-), cough.
hoesbui, coughing-fit, spell of coughing.
hoesdrank(ie), cough-mixture.
hoeseer, however much, much as.
hoëskool, university.
hoesmiddel, cough-remedy, pectoral.
hoesterig, (-e), coughing.
hoeveel, how much, how many; – **is 2 en 3?,** what does 2 and 3 make?; – **ook,** however much (many).
hoeveelheid, amount, quantity.
hoeveelste: die – van die maand is dit?, what day of the month is it?; **die – keer is dit?,** how many times does this make?
Hoëveld, Highveld.
hoever, how far; **in –,** (as to) how far.
hoewel, although, though; vide **alhoewel.**
hof, (howe), court; garden; **die – van Eden,** the Garden of Eden; **die – van appèl,** the court of appeal; **'n meisie die – maak,** court a girl.
hofbal, court-ball, state-ball.
hofbeampte, court-official (-functionary).
hofdame, court-lady, lady-in-waiting; maid of honour.
hofdigter, poet laureate.
hofhouding, court, royal household.
hofie, (-s), small head; head(ing).
hofkapel, court-chapel; royal band.
hofkapelaan, court-chaplain.
hofkringe, court-circles.
hoflewe, court-life.
hofleweransier, purveyor to the court.
hoflik, (-e), courteous, obliging, polite.
hoflikheid, courtesy, courteousness.
hofmaarskalk, court-marshal.
hofmakery, love-making.
hofmeester, purser, steward; seneschal.
hofmeesteres, stewardess.
hofnar, court-jester, court-fool.
hofprediker, vide **hofkapelaan.**
hok, (-ke), n. kennel (for dogs), pen (for sheep), sty (for pigs), run, house (for poultry), cage (for wild animals); shed; den, dog-hole; quod; **in die – wees,** be at school, be in prison (in quod).
hok, (ge-), bymekaar, –, herd (huddle) together; **hulle is ge-,** they have been gated (put in bounds).
hokaai!, hookhaai!, halt there! (to oxen)
hokkerig, (-e), poky.
hokkie, n. hockey.
hokslaan (hokge-), hit calf from cow.

hokstok, milking-stick.
hokus-pokus, hocus-pocus, hanky-panky.
hol, (-e), n. hole; cave, cavern; den, lair.
hol, n. **op –,** running loose; **op – gaan,** bolt, stampede, **iemand se kop op – bring,** turn a person's head; **sy kop het heeltemal op –geraak,** he completely lost his head; **sy verbeelding is op –,** his imagination is running riot.
hol, (-le), a. hollow (tooth), empty (stomach), concave (lens); sunken (eyes).
hol, (-ge), run, rush, bolt, stampede.
holbewoner, cave-dweller.
holderdebolder, holderstebolder, head over heels, helter-skelter, pell-mell, topsy-turvy.
holheid, hollowness, emptiness; vide **hol,** a.
holklinkend, (-e), hollow-sounding.
Hollander, (-s), Hollander, Dutchman.
Hollands, (-e), n. & a. Dutch.
holligheid, cavity, hole; hollowness.
holograaf, (-grawe), holograph.
holoog– . . . , hologig, (-e), hollow-eyed.
holrug, hollow back; **'n teorie – ry,** ride a theory to death.
holster, (-s), holster, pistol-case.
holte, (-s), cavity, hollow, socket (of eye); pit (of stomach).
hom, him, it; **dit is van –,** that is typical of him.
hom(e)opatie, homoeopathy.
hom(e)opaties, (-e), homoeopathic.
Homeries, (-e), Homeric.
hommel, bumble-bee, humble-bee; drone.
homogeen, (-gene), homogeneous, uniform.
homogeniseer, homogenize.
homogeniteit, homogeneity.
homologeer, (ge-), homologate, sanction.
homoniem, (-e), n. homonym.
homoniem, (-e), a. homonymic.
homopatie(s), vide **hom(e)opathie(s).**
homoseksueel, homosexual, invert.
homp, (-e), chunk, hunk, lump.
hond, (-e), dog, hound; cur; **jong –,** pup(py); **baie –e is 'n haas se dood,** numbers count; **blaffende –e byt nie,** his bark is worse than his bite; **kommandeer jou eie –e en blaf self,** keep a dog and bark yourself; **kwaai –e byt mekaar nie,** dog will not eat dog; **so moeg soos 'n –,** dog-tired; **die – in die pot vind,** go without one's dinner; **elke – prys sy eie stert,** self-praise is no recommendation; **so siek soos 'n –,** (as) sick as a dog; **as jy 'n – wil slaan, kry jy maklik 'n stok,** give a dog a bad name and hang him; **'n mens moet nie slapende –e wakker maak nie,** let sleeping dogs lie; **hy lyk soos 'n – wat vet gesteel het,** he has a hangdog look; **hy kry – se gedagte,** his suspicion is aroused; **blaf met die –e en huil met die wolwe,** run with the hare and hunt with the hounds; **hy is oor die – se stert,** he is over the worst; **met die toewyding van 'n –,** with doglike devotion.
hondebaantjie, dog's job.
hondebelasting, dog-tax.
hondebyt, dog-bite.
hondedraffie, easy trot, dog-trot.
hondegeveg, dog-fight.
hondehok, (dog-)kennel.
hondelewe, dog's life, wretched life.
hondeliefhebber, dog-lover.
honderd, (-e), hundred; **'n man –,** a man in a thousand.
honderd-en-een: – moeilikheidjies hê, have a thousand and one troubles.
honderd-en-tien: al –, all the same.
honderdjarig, (-e), of a hundred years, centennial, centenary; **-e fees,** centenary.
honderdjarige, (-s), centenarian.

honderdmaal   118   **hoofpersoon**

honderdmaal, a. hundred times.
honderdponder, hundred-pounder.
honderdste, (-s), hundredth.
honderdtal, a hundred; a century.
honderdvoud, centuple.
honderdvoudig, (-e), hundredfold.
hondesiekte, distemper (in dogs).
hondesweep, dog-whip.
hondetentoonstelling, dog-show.
hondevleis, dog's flesh.
hondewag, middle-watch, midnight-watch.
hondeweer, beastly weather.
hondjie, (-s), little dog, doggie, pup, puppy.
hondmak, as tame as a dog.
honds, (-e), currish, churlish; brutal.
hondsdae, dog-days.
hondsdolheid, rabies; hydrophobia (in humans).
hondshaai, spotted dogfish.
hondsroos, dog-rose, briar-rose, dog-briar.
hondster, dog-star, Sirius.
Hongaar, (-gare), Hungarian.
Hongaars, (-e), Hungarian.
honger, n. hunger; – hê, be hungry; – **ly**, starve, be starving; **die – stil**, appease one's hunger; – **is die beste kok**, hunger is the best sauce; **my maag rammel van die –**, I am half starved; **van – sterf**, die of hunger, starve (be starved) to death.
honger, a. hungry; – **wees**, be hungry.
honger, (ge-), hunger.
hongerbetoging, hunger-march.
hongerdood, death from hunger (starvation).
hongerig, (-e), (slightly, a bit) hungry.
hongerkuur, fasting-cure.
hongerloon, starvation-wages.
hongerlyer, starveling.
hongersnood, famine.
hongerstaker, hunger-striker.
hongerstaking, hunger-strike.
honneurs, honours; **die – waarneem**, do the honours; **gelyke –**, honours easy; – **behaal**, obtain honours.
honorarium, (-ria, -s), fee, honorarium.
honoreer, (ge-), honour (a bill, a cheque).
honorêr, (-e), honorary.
honou!, vide **hanou**.
hoof, (-de), head; chief, leader; heading; principal; **gekroonde –de**, crowned heads; **'n – groter**, taller by a head; **die – bied**, brave, defy, face (danger), bear up against (misfortune); **die vyand die – bied**, put up a stubborn defence; **jou – breek oor**, cudgel, (rack) one's brains about; trouble one's head about; **die – buig**, bow one's head; submit; **die – laat hang**, hang one's head; **die – hoog hou**, hold up one's head; **die – ontbloot**, uncover one's head; **soveel –de, soveel sinne**, so many men, so many minds; **die –de bymekaar steek**, draw (lay, put) heads together; **aan die – staan van**, be at the head of, be in charge of; **dit hang jou bo die –**, it is hanging over your head (impending over you); **hy is nie goed (reg) by die –** nie, he has taken leave of his senses; **iemand 'n belediging na die – gooi**, fling an insult in a person's teeth; **onder 'n ander –**, under another heading; **iets oor die – sien**, overlook something; **iemand oor die – sien**, overlook (ignore, neglect) someone; **50c per –**, 50c a head; **verbruik per –**, per capita consumption; **uit –de van**, on account of, in consideration of; **uit die –de**, for the reason, on that account; **uit die – leer**, learn by heart; **uit die – speel**, play from memory; **van die – tot die voete**, from head to foot, from top to toe; **iemand iets voor die – gooi**, level an accusation at a person, fling something in a person's teeth; vide **kop**.
hoof-, ... chief, leading, main, principal.
hoofaanval, main attack.
hoofafdeling, main (principal) division.
hoofagent, chief agent, general agent.
hoofagentskap, general agency.
hoofamptenaar, high official, head of a department.
hoofartikel, leading article, editorial.
hoofbedekking, head-covering, headgear.
hoofbeginsel, fundamental principle.
hoofbestanddeel, chief ingredient, main constituent.
hoofbestuur, head-committee, executive.
hoofbestuurder, managing director; (general) manager.
hoofbestuurslid, member of the head-committee.
hoofbeswaar, chief objection.
hoofbrekens, -brekings, brain-racking, worry.
hoofbron, chief source, mainspring.
hoofburo, (-'s), head-office.
hoofdeel, main (principal) part.
hoofdek, main-deck.
hoofdelik, (-e), per head, per capita.
hoofdeug, cardinal virtue.
hoofdeur, main door (entrance).
hoofdoel, main object.
hoofeienskap, chief property (quality).
hoofeinde, head, top.
hooffaktor, main factor.
hooffiguur, central (principal) figure.
hoofgebeurtenis, chief event.
hoofgebou, main building.
hoofgeld, poll-tax, capitation-fee.
hoofgereg, chief (principal) dish.
hoofgetal, cardinal (number).
hoofgetuie, chief witness.
hoofingang, main entrance.
hoofingenieur, chief engineer.
hoofinspekteur, chief inspector.
hoofkaas, brawn.
hoofkantoor, head-office, headquarters.
hoofklerk, chief clerk.
hoofknik, nod (of the head).
hoofkomitee, head-committee.
hoofkommando, main commando.
hoofkommandant, chief commandant.
hoofkommissaris, chief commissioner.
hoofkommissie, general committee, head-committee.
hoofkondukteur, (chief) conductor.
hoofkonstabel, chief constable.
hoofkussing, pillow.
hoofkwartier, headquarters.
hoofleiding, supreme direction; main circuit.
hoofletter, capital (letter).
hooflyn, principal line; main line (railw.), trunk-line, records (teleph.).
hooflyngesprek, trunk-call.
hooflynoproep, long-distance call.
hoofmaaltyd, principal meal.
hoofmag, main body.
hoofman, captain, chief, leader, headman.
hoofmiddel: – **van bestaan**, chief (means of) support.
hoofmotief, leading (principal) motive.
hoofoffisier, chief officer.
hoofonderwyser, headmaster, principal.
hoofonderwyseres, headmistress.
hoofoogmerk, chief object, principal aim.
hoofoorsaak, main cause, mainspring.
hoofopsigter, head-overseer, chief inspector.
hoofpad, main road, high road.
hoofpersoon, principal person (character).

hoofposkantoor, general post-office.
hoofpunt, main point (feature).
hoofpyn, headache.
hoofpyp, main.
hoofredakteur, chief editor, editor-in-chief.
hoofreël, cardinal rule; headline.
hoofregter, chief justice, judge-president.
hoofreken(e), mental arithmetic.
hoofrol, leading (principal) part (rôle).
hoofs, (-e), ceremonious; courtly.
hoofsaak, main point (thing); (pl.) essentials; **in –**, in the main, in substance; **in – juis**, substantially correct.
hoofsaaklik, chiefly, mainly, principally.
hoofsetel, headquarters.
hoofsheid, ceremoniousness; courtliness.
hoofsin, principal clause (sentence).
hoofskedel, cranium, skull.
hoofskot(t)el, principal dish; staple dish (fare).
hoofskud, headshake, shake of the head.
hoofskuldige, chief culprit (offender).
hoofsom, capital (sum), principal; substance.
hoofsonde, deadly (mortal) sin.
hoofspoorweg, main line.
hoofstad, capital, metropolis.
hoofstraat, main street, principal street.
hoofstreke, cardinal points (of the compass).
hoofstuk, chapter.
hooftelwoord, cardinal (number).
hooftoon, main (principal) stress; keynote.
hooftrek, main feature, principal characteristic (trait); **in –ke**, in outline.
hooftribune, grand stand.
hooftroep, main body.
hooftyd, principal tense.
hoofvak, chief (major, principal) subject.
hoofvereiste, chief requisite.
hoofverkeersweg, arterial road, main road.
hoofverpleegster, head-nurse.
hoofvoedsel, principal (staple) food.
hoofvyand, chief enemy.
hoofwag, main-guard.
hoofweg, main road (route), high road.
hoofwerk, principal work; chief business; mental work.
hoofwindstreke, vide **hoofstreke**.
hoofwond, wound in the head, head injury.
hoog, (hoë), high, tall, lofty (ideals), high-pitched (voice); exalted (personage); **– aan iemand hê**, dislike a person; **– aan wees**, be tipsy; **– en droog**, high and dry; **– en droog sit**, be quite unconcerned; **hoë hoed**, top-hat; **'n hoë kleur**, a high colour; **'n hoë kleur kry**, get flushed, blush; **– in sy skik**; delighted; **– en laag sweer**, swear by all that is holy; **dit kan nie hoër of laer nie**, there is no way out of it; **'n hoë leeftyd**, a great age; **die gevoelens loop –**, feelings run high; **dit is – nodig**, it is imperative, it is urgently necessary; **hoër onderwys**, higher education; **hoë politiek**, high politics; **– prys**, praise highly, speak highly of; **hy ag hom nie te – nie om . . .**, he is not above . . . ; **dit is my te –**, it is above (beyond) me; **'n hoë toon aanslaan**, be high and mighty; **dit is – tyd**, it is high time; **vier verdiepinge –**, of four storeys; four storeys up; **hoë verwagtinge koester**, nourish high hopes; **dit het my –ste verwagtinge oortref**, it exceeded my wildest expectations; **– vlieg**, fly high; live above one's means; **hoër wiskunde**, higher mathematics; **ons het hoë woorde gekry**, we got (had) high words; **die hoë woord moet uit**, the truth must be admitted; **op hoë (hoog) bevel**, by order; by royal command; **van hoë afkoms**, of high descent; **van die –ste belang**, of the greatest importance; **– hou**, uphold; maintain; keep up; live up to.
hoogag, (hoogge-), esteem highly, respect.
hoogagtend: – die uwe, respectfully yours.
hoogagting, esteem, regard, respect; **met –**, vide **hoogagtend**.
hoogbejaard, (-e), advanced in years, aged.
hoogdrawend, (-e), high-flown, pompous.
hoogdrawendheid, bombast, pompousness.
Hoogduits, High German.
hoogedele, right honourable.
hoogeerwaarde, right (most) reverend.
hooggaande, heavy (sea); high (words).
hooggeag, (-te), esteemed; **H–te Heer**, Dear Sir.
hooggebergte, (high) mountains.
hooggebore, high-born; right honourable.
hooggeëerd, (-e), (highly) honoured (respected).
hooggeleë, elevated, high.
hooggeleerd, (-e), very learned.
hooggeplaas, (-te), highly placed, high.
hooggeregshof, supreme court.
hooggespan, (-ne), high(ly) strung; **sy verwagtings was –**, his hopes ran high.
hooggestem, (-de), high-pitched, high-toned; vide **hooggespan**.
hooggewaardeer, (-de), highly appreciated.
hooghartig, (-e), haughty, high and mighty.
hooghartigheid, haughtiness, hauteur.
hoogheid, highness; height; grandeur.
Hooghollands, High Dutch.
hoogland, highland, plateau.
hoogleraar, professor.
Hooglied, Solomon's Song, the Canticles.
hooglopend, (-e), vide **hooggaande**.
hoogmis, high mass.
hoogmoed, pride, haughtiness.
hoogmoedig, (-e), proud, haughty.
hoogmoedigheid, vide **hoogmoed**.
hoogmoënd, (-e), high and mighty.
hoognodig, (-e), urgently needed (necessary).
hoogoond, blast-furnace.
hoogpeil, high-water mark.
hoogs, extremely, highly; vide **hoogste**.
hoogseie: in – persoon, in his own person.
hoogskat, (hoogge-), esteem (value) highly.
hoogskatting, vide **hoogagting**.
hoogspanning, high tension (pressure).
hoogspring, n. high jump.
hoogspring, (hoogge-), do the high jump.
hoogstaande, eminent, of high standing.
hoogste, highest, sovereign, supreme; top, utmost; **op sy –**, at most; at its height; **ten –**, extremely, greatly, highly; vide **hoog**, **hoogstens**.
hoogstens, at best, at most, at the outside, at the utmost, up to, not exceeding.
hoogwaarskynlik, (-e), a. & adv. highly probable; most probably, as likely as not.
hoogte, (-s), height; altitude; pitch (of voice); highness (of prices); eminence; rise, hill; **dinge het so 'n – bereik**, things had come to such a pass; **in die – gaan**, advance, go up, rise, soar; **op dieselfde –**, at the same height; on a par; **op die – van Kaappunt**, off Cape Point; **op die – van die tyd**, up to date; **op die – bly**, keep abreast of the times; **op die – bring**, inform; **op die – hou**, keep posted (informed); **van iets op die – kom**, get to know (get knowledge of) something; **jou op die – stel van . . .**, make oneself acquainted with; **ter – van**, in height, (to) the height of; off (Cape Point); **tot op sekere –**, to a certain extent; after a fashion; **uit die – behandel**, treat off-handedly (condescendingly); **iets uit die – doen**, carry things with a high hand; **uit die – wees**, be

superior (uppish); **uit die – neersien op,** look down upon; **van goeie –,** of a good height.
hoogtegraad, elevation.
hoogtelyn, contour-line (on map); perpendicular, altitude (in triangle).
hoogtemeter, altimeter, height-recorder.
hoogtepunt, acme, culminating point, height, peak, pinnacle, zenith; high-water mark; crisis (of a disease); **sake het 'n – bereik,** matters have come to a head.
hoogterekord, altitude-record.
hoogteverskil, difference in altitude.
hoogtevrees, acrophobia.
hoogty; – vier, be rampant, reign supreme.
hoogverraad, high-treason.
hoogvlakte, plateau, tableland.
hoogvlieënd, (-e), high-flying, high-flown.
hoogwaardig, (-e), eminent, venerable.
hoogwaardigheid, eminence.
hoogwaardigheidsbekleër, dignitary.
hoogwater, high water, high tide.
hoogwaterlyn, high-water mark.
hooi, hay; **te veel – op die vurk hê,** have too many irons in the fire.
hooikoors, hay-fever.
hooimasjien, haymaker.
hooimied, -miet, haystack.
hooisolder, hay-loft.
hooiwa, hay-cart.
hook!, hookhaai!, hokaai!, whoa!
hoon, n. scorn, derision, jeer(s), taunt(s).
hoon, (ge-), deride, taunt, jeer (scoff) at.
hoongelag, scornful laughter.
hoop, (hope), n. 1. heap, pile; crowd, lot; **'n – geld,** heaps (pots) of money; pack (of lies); any amount (of work); **by hope,** in heaps, by the score; **geld by hope,** heaps of money; **alles op een –,** all of a heap; together; simultaneously.
hoop, n. 2. hope; **– gee,** give (hold out) hope; **alle – opgee,** abandon (give up) all hope; **jou – stel (vestig op),** place (set) one's hope on . . . ; **in die – dat,** in the hope that, hoping that; **op – van,** in the hope of; **op – van seën,** hoping for the best.
hoop, (ge-), hope; **die beste –,** hope for the best; **bly –,** keep on hoping; **teen beterwete in –,** hope against hope.
hoopsgewys(e), in heaps.
hoopvol, (-le), hopeful, sanguine; promising.
hoor, n. hearing.
hoor, (ge-), hear; learn; **– hier,** I say!, listen!; **ek het dit – sê,** I have heard it said; **ek het dit van – sê,** I have it on hearsay; **hy – moeilik,** he is hard of hearing; **– na,** listen to; **ek wil van geen weiering – nie,** not a word!, be quiet (silent).
hoorbaar, (-bare), audible.
hoorbaarheid, audibility.
hoorbuis, ear-trumpet, otophone.
hoorder, (-s), hoorderes, (-se), hearer, listener, auditor (auditress).
hoorsê, hearsay; **ek het dit van –,** I have it on hearsay.
hoor(t), v. **so – dit,** that's as it should be; **dit – nie hierby nie,** it does not belong to this; **dit – nie so nie,** it is not right (proper); vide **behoor(t).**

hoos, (hose), n. waterspout.
hoos, (ge-), bail, scoop.
hop, n. hop; **– pluk,** pick hops.
hopbrood, hop-bread.
hopeloos, (-lose), hopeless, desperate.
hopteelt, hop-growing.
horing, (-s), horn; bugle; hooter (of motor); receiver (of teleph.); **te veel op sy -s neem,** turn everything topsy-turvy; take possession of the house.
horingagtig, (-e), horny, hornlike.
horingdroog, (-droë), dry as dust (bone).
horinglaag, horny layer (of epidermis).
horingloos, (-lose), hornless.
horingoud, (-oue), as old as the hills.
horingslang, horned snake (viper).
horingsman, horned sheep; horned adder.
horingsman-ooi, horned ewe.
horingsteen, hornstone, chert, ceratite.
horingvee, horned cattle.
horingvlies, cornea (of the eye).
horingvormig, (-e), horn-shaped.
horison, (-te), horizon, skyline; **aan die –,** on the horizon; **onder die –,** below the horizon.
horisontaal, (-tale), horizontal, flat, level.
horlosie, oorlosie, (-s), watch; clock; **op jou – kyk,** look at your watch.
horlosie-, oorlosiebandjie, watch-ribbon.
horlosie-, oorlosieblom, passion-flower.
horlosie-, oorlosieketting, watch-chain.
horlosie-, oorlosiemaker, clock-, watchmaker.
horlosie-, oorlosierakkie, clock-stand.
horlosie-, oorlosiewinkel, watch-shop.
horlosie-, oorlosiewys(t)er, watch-hand.
hormoon, (-mone), hormone.
horoskoop, (-skope), horoscope; **iemand se – trek** cast a person's horoscope.
horrelpoot, crooked hoof, vide **horrelvoet.**
horrelpyp, hornpipe.
horreltjies!, time! (in games)
horrelvoet, clubfoot, stump-foot, talipes.
horries, horrors, delirium tremens.
horssweep, horsewhip.
horte, jerks; **met – en stote,** by fits and starts.
hortensia, (-s), hydrangea.
hortjie, (-s), blind, shutter.
hosanna, (-s), hosanna.
hospita, (-s), landlady.
hospitaal, (-tale), hospital; infirmary.
hospitaallinne, waterproof-, bed-sheeting.
hospitaaltrein, hospital-train, ambulance-train.
hospitaalverpleegster, hospital-nurse.
hospitaliteit, hospitality.
hostie, (-s), host, consecrated wafer.
hot, left, near (side); **– en haar,** right and left, higgledy-piggledy; **iemand – en haar stuur,** send someone from pillar to post; **– om,** to the left, round the left.
hotagter, left-hind; **dit – kry (hê),** have a rough time.
hotagteros, left-hind ox.
hotel, (-le, -s), hotel
hotelhouer, hotel-keeper, landlord, hotelier.
hotelwese, hotels.
hot en haar, vide **hot.**
hotnaasagter, second left-hind.
hotnaasvoor, second left-fore (-front).
hot-op-ses, sixth on the left.
hotvoor, left-fore (-front).

hou, (-e), n. blow, cut, lash, slash, stroke; **'n ou – slaan**, strike a hard blow; play a good shot; **'n – eet (leer, werk)**, eat a lot, study (work) hard.
hou: a. – **en trou**, loyal and true.
hou, (ge-), contain, hold, keep; fulfil; lash, strike; cut, hack, hew; deliver, make (a speech), give (an address), observe (the Sabbath); run (a shop); **jou – asof**, make as if, pretend to; **in bedwang –**, control; **hy het sy belofte ge–**, he kept his promise; **jou siek –**, pretended to be ill, sham illness; **jou doof –**, feign deafness; pay no attention; **jou goed –**, bear up well; **die weer het goed ge–**, the weather continued fair; **hierdie stof – goed**, this material wears well; **hy sal nog lank kan –**, he can hold out a long time yet; **– links!**, keep to the left; **hy – hom maar so**, he is only pretending; **hy is nie te – nie**, there is no stopping him; **staande –**, maintain; **jou aan 'n ooreenkoms –**, adhere to an agreement; abide by (a decision), keep to (the programme), stick to (one's word); **iemand aan sy belofte (woord) –**, hold a person to his promise; **jou by jou werk –**, stick to your work, **in toom –**, vide **in bedwang –**; **uit mekaar–**, tell apart, tell which is which; **– van**, be fond of, like; **dit daarvoor – dat . . .**, be of opinion that . . . ; **waarvoor – jy my?**, what do you take me for?
hou(d)baar, (-bare), tenable.
hou(d)baarheid, tenableness, tenability.
houding, (-e, -s), bearing, carriage; attitude, deportment; position, posture; poise; pose; conduct, demeanour; **'n – aanneem**, strike an attitude; **'n afwagtende – aanneem**, play a waiting game; **'n besliste – aanneem**, take a firm stand; **'n dreigende – aanneem**, assume a threatening attitude; **sy – bepaal**, define one's attitude; **in die – staan**, stand at attention (mil.).
houer, (-s), holder; bearer (of letter); licensee (of shop); container.
hout, (-e), wood; timber.
houtagtig, (-e), woody, woodlike, ligneous.
houtappel, crab-apple.
houtas, wood-ashes; wooden axle.
houtbekleding, boxing; panelling.
houtbeskot, wainscot(ing), panelling.
houtbewerking, woodwork; woodworking.
houtblok, wood-block, log of wood.
houtdruk, block-printing; block-print.
houtduif, wood-pigeon, stock-dove.
houtemmer, wooden bucket.
houterig, (-e), wooden; clumsy, stiff.
houterigheid, woodenness; clumsiness.
houtgees, wood-spirit, methyl-alcohol.
houtgerus, (-te), unsuspicious; unconcerned.
houtgraveerkuns, wood-engraving.
houtgraveur, wood-engraver, xylographer.
houtgravure, wood-engraving, woodcut.
houthakker, wood-cutter; **–s en waterputters**, woodcutters and drawers of water.
houthamer, mallet.
houthandel, timber-trade.
houtindustrie, timber-trade, -industry.
houtjie, (-s), bit (piece) of wood; **iets op eie – doen**, do something on one's own hook (off one's own bat).
houtkapper, woodcutter; woodpecker.
houtkatel, wooden bed(stead).
houtkewer, death-watch.
houtpakhuis, timber-warehouse.
houtpap, **houtpulp**, wood-pulp.
houtpop, wooden doll; **soos 'n – sit**, remain inactive.
houtsaagmeul(e), sawmill.

houtskool, charcoal.
houtsnee, woodcut.
houtsnip, woodcock, wood-snipe.
houtsnyer, wood-carver; wood-engraver.
houtsnywerk, wood-carving.
houtsoort, kind of wood.
houtstapel, wood-stack, pile of wood.
houtstof, lignin; wood-pulp.
houtsuiker, xylose.
houtswam, dry rot, wood-fungus.
houtvesel, wood-fibre.
houtvester, forester.
houtvorming, lignification.
houtvuur, wood-fire, log-fire.
houtwerf, timber-yard.
houtwerk, woodwork, timber-work.
houtwol, wood-wool, wood-fibre.
houtwurm, woodwurm, wood-fretter, borer.
houvas, (hand)hold, support; mainstay; **g'n – hê nie**, have nothing to go by (on).
houweel, (-wele), mattock, pickaxe, hack.
houwitser, (-s), howitzer.
hovaardig, (-e), haughty, arrogant.
hovaardigheid, hovaardy, arrogance, pride.
howeling, (-e), courtier.
howenier, (-s), gardener.
hu, (ge-), espouse, marry, wed; vide **trou**, **(ge)**.
hubaar, (-bare), marriageable.
Hugenoot, (-note), Huguenot.
huid, (-e), skin; hide (of animals); coat (of horse); **'n dik – hê**, be thick-skinned, **met – en haar**, hide and hair; **op die blote – dra**, wear next (to) the skin; **tot op die –**, to the skin; vide **vel**, n.
huidarts, skin-specialist, dermatologist.
huidmark, hide-market.
huidige, modern, present, of the present day; **tot op die – dag**, to this day.
huidjie, (-s), film, cuticle, skin, pellicle.
huidkleur, skin-colour; complexion.
huidsenuwee, cutaneous nerve.
huidsiekte, skin-disease.
huidsiekteleer, dermatology.
huidspesialis, vide **huidarts**.
huiduitslag, eruption (of the skin).
huidvlek, birth-mark, naevus, mole.
huidwurm, Guinea worm.
huig, (huie), uvula.
huigel, (ge-), feign, pretend, sham, simulate.
huigelaar(ster), (-s), dissembler, hypocrite.
huigelagtig, (-e), canting, hypocritical.
huigel(a)ry, cant, dissimulation, hypocrisy.
huigeltaal, cant, hypocritical language.
huik, (-e), clok; **die – na die wind hang**, trim one's sails to the wind.
huil, (ge-), cry, weep (of humans); howl, whine (of animals); bleed (of vines); **ek kon –**, **I felt like crying**; **help nie**, it's no good crying over spilt milk.
huilbui, crying-fit.
huilebalk, cry-baby, blubberer, weeper.
huilerig, (-e), tearful, whimpering.
huilery, crying, sobbing; whining, howling.
huis, (-e), n. house, dwelling, home; accommodation unit; household, family; firm; institution, **– en erf**, premises; **– en haard**, hearth and home; **met jou is daar nie – te hou nie**, you are impossible; **elke – het sy kruis**, there is a skeleton in every cupboard; **'n – soek**, be house-hunting; **by iemand aan – kom**, visit at a person's house; **met die deur in die – val**, blurt something out; go straight to business; **na – gaan = – toe gaan**, go home; **ten –e van**, at the house of; **van – gaan**, go from home, leave home; **van – uit**, by birth; originally.

huis, (ge-), house, be housed, lodge.
huisagent, (house-)agent.
huisaltaar, domestic altar; family-devotions.
huisapteek, (family-) medicine-chest.
huisarres, confinement to one's home, house arrest.
huisbaas, landlord.
huisbesoek, pastoral visit; house-to-house call.
huisbraak, housebreaking, burglary.
huisbybel, family-bible.
huisdier, domestic animal.
huisdokter, family-doctor.
huiscienaar, -eienares, house-owner.
huisgenoot, (-note), housemate, inmate; (pl.) household, family.
huisgesin, family, household.
huisgode, household-gods, gods of the hearth.
huisgodsdiens, family-devotions (-prayers).
huisheer, master of the house; landlord.
huishen, house-bird, stay-at-home.
huishou(e), (-ens), n. household; housekeeping; **die - doen**, keep house; **'n - begin**, set up house.
huishou, (huisge-), keep house, run the house; vreeslik - met, play havoc with; **daar is met jou nie huis te hou nie**, vide **huis**, n.
huishoudelik, (-e), household (expenses), domestic (affairs).
huishouding, vide **huishou(e)**, n.
huishoudkunde, domestic science.
huishoudskool, school for domestic science.
huishoudster, (-s), housekeeper.
huishougeld, housekeeping allowance.
huishuur, house-rent.
huisie, (-s), small house, cottage; box, case (of spectacles); shell (of snail); quarter, section (of orange); binnacle (of compass).
huisjong, house-boy.
huiskamer, sitting-room, living-room.
huiskneg, footman.
huislêer, stay-at-home; idler.
huislik, (-e), domestic; home-loving, homy, homely; **-e kring**, home-circle; **-e lewe**, home-life; **-e pligte**, household-duties; **-e twis**, domestic quarrel; **dit was baie -**, it was very homely.
huislikheid, domesticity, homeliness.
huismiddel, household remedy.
huismoeder, mother of the family; matron.
huismoederlik, (-e), housewifely; matronly.
huisnood, house-famine.
huisonderwys, private tuition.
huisplaag, house-pest.
huisraad, furniture; household-effects.
huissleutel, house-key, latch-key.
huissoeking, house-search.
huiswaeltjie, house-martin.
huisvader, father of a family; housemaster (of hostel).
huisves, (ge-), house, lodge, take in.
huisvesting, accommodation; housing.
huisvlieg, house-fly, domestic fly.
huisvlyt, home-industry.
huisvriend, family-friend.
huisvrou, housewife; wife.
huiswaarts, homeward(s).
huiswerk, homework; household-work.
huiwer, (ge-), shudder, tremble, shiver, hesitate.
huiwerig, (-e), afraid, hesitating; shivery.
huiwerigheid, hesitation; shiveriness.
huiwering, (-e, -s), hesitation; shudder.
huiweringwekkend, (-e), horrible.
hul, (ge-), envelop, wrap up; shroud, veil.
hul, vide **hulle**.
hulde, homage, tribute; **- bring aan**, pay homage (tribute) to.

huldebetoon, mark of esteem (homage).
huldeblyk, tribute; testimonial.
huldig, (ge-), pay homage to, honour; recognize.
huldiging, homage; recognition.
hul(le), pron. pers. they; them (acc.); **- sê**, people say.
hul(le), pron. poss. their; **dit is - s'n**, it is theirs, it belongs to them.
hulp, aid, assistance, help, support; succour, relief; rescue; **eerste - (by ongelukke)**, first aid; **iemand se - inroep**, call in a person's aid; **- verleen**, render help (assistance); **om - roep**, call for help; **sonder -**, unaided, single-handed; **iemand te - kom**, come to a person's aid (help, rescue).
hulpbattery, auxiliary (boosting-)battery.
hulpbehoewend, (-e), destitute, needy; helpless.
hulpbehoewendheid, destitution, helplessness.
hulpbetoon, assistance; succour.
hulpbron, resource.
hulpbrug, temporary bridge.
hulpeloos, (-lose), helpless.
hulpeloosheid, helplessness.
hulpgeroep, cry for help.
hulpkruiser, auxiliary cruiser.
hulpmiddel, expedient, makeshift; aids, means.
hulponderwyser(es), assistant (teacher).
hulpprediker, assistant minister.
hulptrein, breakdown train.
hulptroepe, auxiliary troops, auxiliaries.
hulpvaardig, (-e), helpful, ready to help.
hulpvaardigheid, helpfulness, readiness to help.
hulpwerkwoord, auxiliary (verb).
huls, (-e), case, shell, husk; holly.
hulsel, (-s), cover(ing), envelope, wrapper.
humaan, (-mane), humane.
humaniseer, (ge-), humanize.
Humanisme, Humanism.
humaniteit, humanity, humaneness.
humeur, (-e), humour, mood, temper; **in sy -**, in a good temper; **iemand uit sy - bring**, ruffle a person.
humeurig, (-e), moody; sulky.
humeurigheid, moodiness, sulkiness.
humor, humour.
humoresk, (-e), humoresque.
humoris, (-te), humorist.
humoristies, (-e), humorous, humoristic.
humus, humus, vegetable-mould.
Hun, (-ne), Hun.
hunker, (ge-), **- na**, crave for, hanker after.
hunkering, craving, hankering, longing.
huppel, (ge-), frisk, hop, skip.
hups, (-e), courteous, polite; lively, quick.
hupsheid, politeness; liveliness; vide **hups**.
hurk, (ge-), squat.
hurke, (pl.) haunches; **op sy - sit**, squat.
husaar, (-sare), hussar.
hut, (-te), cottage, hut, hovel; cabin (on board ship); shack (of wood); crib (mining).
hutjie, (-s), n. small cottage; vide **hut**.
hutpot, hotch-potch (hodge-podge).
huur, n. hire, rent; rental; lease; **huis te -**, house to let; **my - is in Desember om**, my lease expires in December; **die - opsê**, give notice.
huur, (ge-), hire, rent (a house), engage (a servant), charter (a ship), lease (on contract).
huurbaas, landlord.
huurder, (-s), hirer; lessee, tenant.
huurgeld, rent, rental.
huurhuis, hired (rented, tenanted) house.
huurkamer, room to let.
huurkantoor, registry(-office).
huurkoetsier, cabman, cabby.
huurkontrak, lease.

huurkoop(stelsel), hire-purchase (system), instalment-system.
huurling, (-e), hireling, mercenary.
huurmotor, hire-car, drive-yourself car.
huuropbrengs, -opbrings, rental.
huurprys, rent.
huurrytuig, cab.
huurtroepe, mercenary troops, mercenaries.
huurtyd, term of lease, tenancy.
huurvoorwaardes, terms of lease.
huwelik, (-e), marriage, wedding; matrimony, wedlock, 'n – om geld, a mercenary marriage; 'n – uit liefde, a love-match; 'n goeie – doen, marry well; die – **afkondig**, publish the banns; 'n – **sluit**, contract a marriage; jou in die – begewe = in die – tree, enter into matrimony, marry; 'n meisie ten – vra, ask in marriage; vide **trou**, n.
huweliksaankondiging, wedding-notice.
huweliksaansoek, proposal (of marriage).
huweliksafkondiging, banns.
huweliksakte, marriage-certificate.
huweliksbelofte, promise of marriage.
huweliksberig, vide **huweliksaankondiging**.
huweliksbevestiging, marriage-ceremony.
huweliksboot(jie), Hymen's boat; **in die – stap**, get married, get into double harness.
huweliksfees, wedding-party (-feast).
huweliksformulier, marriage-service.
huweliksgebooie, banns.
huweliksgeskenk, wedding-present.
huweliksinseëning, solemnisation of marriage.
huweliksknoop, wedding-knot, marriage-tie.
huwelikskontrak, marriage-articles (-contract).
huwelikslewe, married life.
huweliksliefde, conjugal (married) love.
huweliksplegtigheid, marriage-ceremony.
huweliksreis, wedding-trip, honeymoon (-trip).
huwelikstaat, married (wedded) state.
huweliksvoltrekking, solemnisation of marriage.
huweliksvoorwaarde(s), marriage-contract (-settlement); antenuptial contract.
hy, he; it; 'n – en 'n sy, a he and a she.
hyg, (ge-), gasp (for breath), pant.
hyging, gasp(ing), pant(ing); yearning.
hys, (ge-), hoist, pull (raise, haul) up.
hysbak, cage, skip.
hysblok, pulley-block, gin-block.
hyser, (-s), hoister; crane; lift.
hyskraan, (lifting-)crane.
hystoestel, crane, elevator.
hystou, hoisting- (winding-)rope, tackle.

I, (-'s), i; **die puntjies op die – sit**, dot one's i's.
Iberies, (-e), Iberian.
ibis, (-se), ibis.
ideaal, (-ale), ideal.
idealis, (-te), idealist.
idealiseer, (geïdealiseer), idealize.
idealisme, idealism.
idealisties, (-e), idealistic.
idee, (ideë, -s), idea, notion; opinion; **in die – dat**, thinking that; **met die – om**, with the idea of . . .; **na my –**, in my opinion; **op 'n – kom**, hit upon an idea.
ideël, (ideële), ideal, imaginary.
ideetjie, (-s), a bit of an idea; a suspicion.
ideëwêreld, world of ideas.
idem, ditto, idem, the same.
identiek, (-e), identical.
identifikasie, identification.
identifiseer, (geïdentifiseer), identify; **jou –**, establish one's identity.
identiteit, identity.
identiteitsbewys, proof of identity; identity-papers.
idille, (-s), idyll.
idillies, (-e), idyllic.
idiomaties, (-e), idiomatic.
idioom, (-iome), idiom.
idioot, (-iote), idiot; imbecile.
idiosinkrasie, (-ë), idiosyncrasy.
idioterig, (-e), (slightly) idiotic.
idiotisme, (-s), idiocy; idiotism (in language).
idool, (-le), idol.
ieder, (-e), each, every.
iedereen, anyone, everybody, everyone.
iegelik: **'n –**, everybody, everyone; **elk en 'n –**, one and all.
iemand, anybody, anyone, (some)one, somebody, a person; **– anders**, someone else.
iep(eboom), elm(-tree).
Ier, (-e), Irishman; (pl.) the Irish.
Iers, (-e), n. & a. Irish.
iesegrimmig, (-e), bearish, surly.
ietermago, **ietermagô**, (-s), **ietermagog**, (-ge, -s), pangolin.
iets, pron. anything, something; **– anders**, something else; **– nuuts**, something new.
iets, adv. a little, rather, somewhat, slightly.
ietsie, **'n –**, a bit, a shade, a trifle.
ietwat, slightly, somewhat.
iewers, somewhere.
ignoreer, (geïgnoreer), ignore.
igtiosourus, (-se, -ri), ichtyosaurus.
ikon, (-e), icon.
ikonometer, iconometer.
illuminasie, (-s), illumination.
illumineer, (geïllumineer), illuminate.
illusie, (-s), illusion; **iemand die – beneem**, disillusion a person; **jou g'n –s maak nie**, have no illusions.
illustrasie, (-s), illustration.
illustreer, (geïllustreer), illustrate.
imbesiel, (-e), imbecile, feeble-minded.
imitasie, (-s), imitation.
imiteer, (geïmiteer), imitate.
immanent, (-e), immanent.
immaterieel, (-iële), immaterial.
immens, (-e), immense, huge.
immer, ever, always.
immermeer, evermore.
immers, but, yet; indeed; **jy weet –**, you know, don't you?; vide **mos**, adv.
immigrant, (-e), immigrant.
immigrasie, immigration.
immigreer, (geïmmigreer), immigrate.
immobiel, (-e), immobile.

immoleer, (geïmmoleer), immolate.
immoreel, (-ele), immoral.
immuniseer, (geïmmuniseer), immunize.
immuniteit, immunity.
immuun, immune (from).
impala, (-s), impala.
imperatief, (-iewe), imperative.
imperfektum, (-ta), imperfect (tense).
imperfek, (-te)m imperfect.
imperfeksie, (-s), imperfection.
imperiaal, (-iale), imperial.
imperialis, (-te), imperialist.
imperialisme, imperialism.
imperialisties, (-e), imperialist(ic).
impertinensie, (-s), impertinence.
impertinent, (-e), impertinent.
impi, (-'s), impi.
implikasie, (-s), implication.
impliseer, (geïmpliseer), implicate; imply.
imponeer, (geïmponeer), impress (forcibly).
imponerend, (-e), imposing, impressive.
impopulariteit, unpopularity.
impopulêr, (-e), unpopular.
import, import; vide **invoer**.
importasie, importation.
importeer, (geïmporteer), import.
importeur, (-s), importer.
imposant, (-e), imposing, impressive.
impotensie, impotence.
impotent, (-e), impotent.
impregnasie, impregnation.
impregneer, (geïmpregneer), impregnate.
impressie, (-s), impression.
impressionabel, (-e), impressionable.
impressionis, (-te), impressionist.
impressionisme, impressionism.
impressionisties, (-e), impressionist(ic).
improduktief, (-tiewe), unproductive.
impromptu, (-s), impromptu.
improvisasie, (-s), improvisation, impromptu.
improviseer, (geïmproviseer), improvise, extemporize, speak extempore; vamp (mus.).
impuls, (-e), impulse.
impulsief, (-iewe), impulsive.
imputasie, (-s), imputation.
imputeer, (geïmputeer), impute.
in, prep. in, into, within; during; **– elk geval**, in any case; **– die rou**, in mourning; **dit sit – hom**, he has it in him; **– een slag**, at a blow; **goed – tale**, good at languages; **– die vakansie**, during the holidays; **daar was – die vyftig**, there were fifty odd; **dit wil by my nie – nie**, it won't go down with me; **– ag neem**, observe, practise; use (care), consider, take account of (facts); vide **ag, n**.
in, (geïn), collect (debts), cash (cheque).
inadem(ing), vide **inasem(ing)**.
inagneming, observance; **met – van**, with due observance of.
inakkuraat, (-ate), inaccurate.
inaktief, (-tiewe), inactive.
inaktiwiteit, inactivity.
inasem, (inge-), breathe, draw in, inhale.
inaseming, breathing, inhalation.
inbaar, (-bare), collectable, leviable.
inbaker, (inge-), swaddle; tuck in.
inbalsem, (inge-), embalm.
inbeeld, (inge-), **jou –**, fancy, imagine.
inbeelding, fancy, imagination; conceit.
inbegrepe, vide **inbegrip**.
inbegrip: **met – van**, inclusive of.
inbegryp, included, including.
inbeitel, (inge-), chisel in, engrave.
inbesitneming, occupation.

inbeslagneming, attachment, seizure; embargo (of ship); taking up (a person's time).
inbind, (inge-), bind (a book); take in; **jou –**, climb down, come down a peg or two.
inblaas, (inge-), blow into; suggest; breathe (infuse) into.
inblasing, instigation, suggestion.
inbly, (inge), stay indoors; stay in (school).
inboedel, furniture, household-effects.
inboek, (inge-), book, enter; indenture.
inboesem, (inge-), inspire into (with); **iemand belangstelling –**, interest a person.
inboeseming, inspiration.
inboet, (inge-), plant in between, fill in, replace; **die lewe –**, lose one's life.
inboorling, (-e), native, (pl.) aborigines.
inbors, character, disposition, nature.
inbou, (inge-), build in.
inbraak, burglary, housebreaking.
inbrand, (inge-), burn in(to).
inbreek, (inge-), break into, burgle (a house).
inbreekyster, jemmy.
inbreker, (-s), burglar, housebreaker.
inbreuk, infraction, infringement; **– maak op**, encroach upon.
inbring, (inge-), bring in; put forward; **– teen**, bring against; object to.
inbrokkel, (inge-), break (crumble) into.
inbuie, inbuig, (inge-), bend inward.
inburger, (inge-), become naturalized; become current; **jou –**, adapt oneself to.
inburgering, adaptation; naturalization.
inbyt, (inge-), bite into; corrode.
inchoatief, (-tiewe), inchoative (verb).
incognito, incognito.
indaba, (-s), indaba; Native council.
indagtig: – aan, mindful of; **iemand aan iets – maak**, remind a person of something.
indam, (inge-), dam, embank.
indeel, (inge-), class(ify), group; graduate; incorporate in (with).
indeks, (-e), index, table of contents.
indekssyfer, index-figure.
indelikaat, (-ate), indelicate.
indeling, (-e, -s), classification, division.
indemniteit, (-e), indemnity.
indink, (inge-): **jou – in**, realize, enter into; visualize.
independent, (-e), independent.
inderdaad, indeed, in (point of) fact, really.
inderhaas, in haste, in a hurry, hurriedly.
indertyd, at the time; formerly.
indeuk, induik, (inge-), dent, indent.
Indiaan, (-ane), (Red) Indian.
Indiaans, (-e), (Red) Indian.
indien, conj. if, in case.
indien, (inge-), bring in, introduce (a bill); lodge (a compliment), hand in, tender (one's resignation), move, put forward (a proposal), present (the budget); put in (a claim); present (a petition).
indiening, introduction, vide, **indien, (inge-)**.
indiensneming, employment.
indienstreding, commencement of duties.
Indiër, (-s), Indian.
Indies, (-e), Indian.
indigestie, indigestion.
indigo, indigo.
indikasie, (-s), indication.
indikatief, (-tiewe), indicative (mood).
indirek, (-te), indirect.
indiskreet, (-krete), indiscreet.
indiskresie, indiscretion.
individu, indiwidu, (-e, -'s), individual.
individualis, indiwidualis, (-te), individualist.

individueel, indiwidueel, (-ele), a. & adv. individual(ly).
indoen, (inge-), put in.
indoena, (-s), induna, Native councillor.
Indo-Germaans, (-e), Indo-Germanic.
indoktrineer, indoctrinate.
indolensie, indolence.
indolent, (-e), indolent.
indommel, (inge-), drop off, doze off.
indompel, (inge-), dip (steep) in, immerse.
indompeling, immersion.
Indonesies, (-e), Indonesian.
indoop, (inge-), dip in(to).
indoping, dipping in(to), immersion.
indra(ag), indrae, (inge-), carry in(to).
indraai, (inge-), turn into (a road); screw in (a nut); wrap up (a parcel).
indra(ag), indrae, (inge-), carry in(to).
indring, (inge-), break into, enter, penetrate into; **jou –**, intrude, obtrude oneself.
indringer, (-s), intruder, interloper.
indringerig, (-e), importunate, obtrusive.
indringerigheid, importunity.
indringing, intrusion; penetration.
indringingsvermoë, power of penetration.
indrink, (inge-), absorb, drink in, imbibe.
indruis, (inge-): **– teen**, clash (conflict, be at variance, jar) with.
indruk, (-ke), n. impression ('n) **– maak**, create (make) an impression; **hy maak op my die – van . . .**, he strikes me as . . . ; **onder die – verkeer**, be under the impression; **sterk onder die –**, deeply impressed.
indruk, (inge-), press (push) in; crush; impress; force one's way in(to).
indrukwekkend, (-e), imposing, impressive.
indrup, (inge-), drip (drop) in.
indryf, -drywe, (inge-), drive (force) in(to); float in(to).
induik, (inge-), vide **indeuk**.
induik, (inge-), dive (plunge) in(to).
induksie, induction.
induktief, (-tiewe), a. & adv. inductive(ly).
indulgensie, indulgence.
industrie, (-ë), industry.
industrieel, (-iële), n. manufacturer.
industrieel, (-iële), a. industrial.
industrieskool, industrial (technical) school.
industriestad, manufacturing town.
indut, (inge-), vide **indommel**.
inê, vide **ineg**.
ineen, close, together; vide **inmekaar**.
ineen- . . ., vide **inmekaar- . . .**
ineengedronge, close together; thickset.
ineenkrimping, contraction, shrinking; doubling up, writhing (with pain).
ineens, at once, immediately, suddenly.
ineensinking, collapse.
ineensluiting, fitting together, dovetailing.
ineensmelting, merging, fusion.
ineenstorting, break-up, collapse, crash.
ineenvlegting, interlacing, intertwining.
ineenvloeiing, blending, fusion, union.
ineg, (ingeëg), harrow in.
inent, (ingeënt), inoculate; vaccinate.
inersie, inertia, inertness.
inessensieel, (-iële), inessential.
infaam, (-fame), downright (lie), infamous.
infanterie, infantry, foot(-soldiers).
infanteris, (-te), infantryman.
infeksie, infection, contagion.
infekteer, (geïn-), infect.
inferieur, (-e), inferior, low-grade, poor.
inferioriteit, inferiority.
inferioriteitskompleks, inferiority-complex.

infiltreer, (geïn-), infiltrate.
infinitief, (-tiewe), infinitive (mood).
inflammasie, inflammation.
inflasie, inflation (of currency).
infleksie, (-s), inflection, (inflexion).
inflekteer, (geïn-), inflect.
infloressensie, inflorescence.
influensa, influenza, flu.
influenseer, (geïn-), affect, influence.
influister, (inge-), suggest, whisper to.
informaliteit, informality.
informasie, information; inquiry; **– inwin,** make inquiries; vide **inligting.**
informasieburo, inquiry-office.
informeer, (geïn-), inquire, inform.
infraksie, infraction.
infrarooi, infra-red.
infusie, infusion.
infusiediertjies, infusoria, diatoms.
ingaan, (inge-), enter, go in(to); take effect; **die ewigheid –,** pass into eternity; **die lewe –,** enter upon life; **die wêreld –,** set out into the world; **op iets –,** enter into a matter; **op 'n versoek –,** agree to (comply with) a request; **teen –,** oppose.
ingaande: – regte, import-duties; **– vanaf,** dating (with effect) from.
ingang, entrance, entry; way in; **– vind,** find acceptance; **met – van,** (as) from, with effect from.
ingebeeld, (-e), imaginary; conceited (fellow).
ingebore, inborn, innate, native.
ingedagte, absent-minded, lost in thought.
ingee, (inge-), administer, give; suggest.
ingehoue, pent-up, restrained.
ingekanker(d), (-de), deep-rooted, ingrained.
ingelas, (-te), inserted; interpolated.
ingelê, ingeleg, (-de), inlaid; canned, pickled; **ingelegde houtwerk,** marquetry; vide **inlê.**
ingelyf, (-de), embodied, incorporated.
ingenieur, (-s), engineer.
ingenieurswese, engineering.
ingenome: – met, charmed (taken up) with, **met jouself –,** self-complacent.
ingenomenheid, satisfaction; **dwase –,** infatuation; **– met jouself,** self-complacency.
ingerig, (-te), arranged, organized.
ingesetene, (-s), inhabitant, resident.
ingeskape, vide **ingebore.**
ingeskrewe, enrolled; inscribed.
ingeslote, enclosed; **– hoek,** contained angle; **koste –,** including costs.
ingesonde, contributed, sent in; **– stukke,** contributions; letters to the editor.
ingesonke, hollow (cheeks), sunken (eyes).
ingespanne, a. & adv. strenuous(ly).
ingetoë, modest, retired, reserved, sedate.
ingetoënheid, modesty, reserve.
ingeval, in case; vide **geval.**
ingeval(le), hollow, sunken, emaciated.
ingevolge, in accordance with.
ingewande, bowels, entrails, intestines.
ingewandskoors, enteric fever.
ingewikkel(d), (-de), complex, complicated, involved, intricate.
ingewikkeldheid, complexity, intricacy.
ingewing, (-e, -s), inspiration, suggestion; brainwave; **op die – van die oomblik,** on the spur of the moment.
ingewortel(d), (-de), engrained, deep-seated, inveterate.
ingewyde, (-s), adept, initiated.
ingiet, (inge-), pour in(to), infuse into.
inglip, (inge-), slip in.
ingly, (inge-), glide (slide, slip) in(to).
ingooi, (inge-), throw in(to), pour in; smash.

ingraaf, -grawe, (inge-), dig in; burrow.
ingrediënt, (-e), ingredient.
ingrif, (inge-), engrave, imprint.
ingroei, (inge-), grow in(to).
ingryp, (inge-), intervene, take action; encroach upon.
ingrypend, (-e), drastic, far-reaching.
ingryping, interference, intervention.
inhaak, (inge-), hook (hitch) in(to), take a person's arm; **ingehaak loop,** walk arm in arm.
inhaal, (inge-), bring (fetch, gather, haul) in; strike (a flag), take in (sails); draw in; receive in state; catch (up with), overtake, make up (for), recover (lost time).
inhaleer, (geïn-), inhale; draw (smoke).
inhalig, (-e), covetous, grasping, greedy.
inhaligheid, covetousness, greed.
inham, (-me), bay, creek, inlet.
inhamer, (inge-), hammer in; drum into.
inhê, (ingehad), contain, hold; **iets –,** be tipsy.
inheems, (-e), home, indigenous, native.
inheemsheid, indigenous origin; vide **inheems.**
inhegtenisneming, arrest, apprehension.
inherent, (-e), inherent.
inhibeer, (geïn-), inhibit.
inhol, (inge-), rush (tear) in(to); overtake.
inhou, (inge-), contain, hold; check, hold back, pull up, restrain; retain, keep down (food); cancel, stop (payment), deduct, dock (money); withdraw (from sale).
inhoud, contents; capacity; purport, tenor; **kort –,** abstract, summary; **kubieke –,** cubic content (capacity).
inhoudsmaat, cubic measure, (measure of) capacity.
inhoudsopgaaf, -opgawe, table of contents.
inhoudsregister, index, register.
inhuldig, (inge-), inaugurate, install.
inhuldiging, inauguration, installation.
inhumaan, (-ane), inhumane.
inhuur, (inge-), engage (hire) again, renew a lease.
inisiaal, (-iale), n. initial.
inisiatief, (-tiewe), initiative.
inja(ag), injae, (inge-), drive in(to); rush in(to); overtake; cause to take (medicine).
injeksie, (-s), injection.
injunksie, (-s), injunction.
ink, (-te), ink.
inkalf, -kalwe(r), (inge-), cave (calve) in.
inkamp, (inge-), enclose, fence in.
inkanker, (inge-), eat in(to), fester.
inkapabel, (-e), incapable.
inkapasiteit, incapacity.
inkarnaat, (-ate), carnation, flesh-coloured.
inkarneer, (geïn-), incarnate.
inkasseer, (geïn-), cash; collect.
inkbottel, ink-bottle.
inkeep, (inge-), indent, nick, notch, score.
inkeer, n. repentence; **tot – kom,** repent.
inkeer, (inge-), turn in(to); **tot jouself –,** commune with oneself.
inkennig, eenkennig, (-e), shy, timid.
inkennigheid, eenkennigheid, shyness.
inkeping, (-e, -s), indentation, nick, notch.
inkerf, -kerwe, (inge-), carve in, nick, notch.
inkfles, ink-bottle.
inkkoker, ink-pot, ink-well.
inklaar, (inge-), clear (goods).
inklam, (inge-), sprinkle (washing).
inklaring, clearance.
inkleding, clothing, wording, phrasing.
inklee(d), (inge-), clothe in words, phrase.
inklim, (inge-), climb in(to); rebuke, go for.
inklinasie, dip, inclination.
inklok, (inge-), clock in.

inklouter, (inge-), clamber in(to).
inkluis, included.
inklusief, (-iewe), inclusive.
inkom, (inge-), come in, enter, arrive.
inkome, (-ns), income; vide **inkomste.**
inkompetensie, incompetence.
inkompetent, (-e), incompetent.
inkompleet, (-ete), incomplete.
inkomste, earnings, income, revenue.
inkomstebelasting, income tax.
inkongruent, (-e), incongruent.
inkonsekwent, (-e), inconsistent, illogical.
inkonstitusioneel, (-ele), unconstitutional.
inkoop, (-kope), n. purchase; **inkope doen,** make one's purchases, go shopping.
inkoop, (inge-), buy, purchase; buy in.
inkoopsprys, cost-price, prime cost.
inkopies, small purchases; – **doen,** go shopping.
inkorporeer, (geïn-), incorporate.
inkorrek, (-te), incorrect.
inkort, (inge-), shorten; curtail.
inkorting, shortening; curtailment.
inkpot, ink-pot, ink-well.
inkpotlood, ink-pencil, indelible (pencil).
inkrap, (inge-), scratch in.
inkrimineer, (geïn-), incriminate.
inkrimp, (inge-), contract, shrink; reduce.
inkrimping, contraction; retrenchment.
inkrol, ink(ing)-roller, printing-roller.
inkruip, (inge-), creep (crawl) in(to); toady.
inkruiper, (-s), toady, squatter; intruder.
inkruiperig, (-e), fawning, toadyish.
inkruiperigheid, fawning, toadyism.
inkry, (inge-), get in; get down (food); get to take.
inkstandertjie, -stelletjie, ink-stand.
inkubasie, incubation.
inkuil, (inge-), ensilage, ensile, store in a silo.
inkuitveër, ink-eraser.
inkulpeer, (geïn-), inculpate.
inkvis, cuttle-fish, ink-fish, sepia, squid.
inkvlek, ink-blot (-stain).
inkwartier, (inge-), billet, quarter.
inkwisisie, inquisition.
inkwisitoriaal, (-iale), inquisitorial.
inlaai, (inge-), load, ship; entrain.
inlaat, (-ate), n. intake; inlet.
inlaat, (inge-), admit, let in; **jou – met meddle** (concern oneself) with; **jou met die politiek –,** go in for politics.
inlading, load(ing), shipment; entraining.
inla(g)e, (-s), enclosure (papers).
inlander, (-s), native.
inlands, (-e), inland, indigenous, native.
inlas, n. stop-press (news); inset (photo).
inlas, (inge-), insert, interpolate; mortise.
inlassing, insertion, interpolation; mortise.
inlê, (inge-), lay (put) in; deposit (money); can, preserve, pickle; inlay (with gold); **eer –,** gain honour.
inlêbottel, -fles, canning- (canned fruit) bottle.
inleef, -lewe, (inge-), adapt oneself (to), get accustomed (to); enter into.
inlêer, depositor (of money); layer (bot.).
inleggeld, stakes; deposit (in bank).
inlegwerk, inlaid work; marquetry; veneer.
inlei, (inge-), introduce, initiate; open; preface.
inleiding, (-e, -s), introduction; preface.
inleidingsartikel, leading-article, leader.
inleier, initiator, introducer, opener.
inlewer, (inge-), give (hand, send) in; present (a petition), lodge (documents) with; deliver up, surrender (arms).
inlewering, delivery, handing-in, surrender.
inlig, (inge-), enlighten, inform; **in goed ingeligte kringe,** in well-informed quarters.
inligting, (-e, -s), information.
inligtingsbeampte, public-relations officer.
inligtingsdiens, intelligence-department.
inloer, (inge-), peep (pry) in(to).
inlok, (inge-), entice into.
inloods, (inge-), pilot (into port).
inloop, n. catchment(-area).
inloop, (inge-), enter; call, drop in; overtake; **êrens –,** get caught, put one's foot into it; **teen mekaar –,** collide; **iemand – = iemand êrens laat –,** let a person down.
inlos, (inge-), redeem, take out of pawn.
inlossing, redemption.
inlui, (inge-), inaugurate, ring (usher) in.
inluister, (inge-), listen in.
inluisteraar, (angl.), listener-in.
inlyf, inlywe (inge-), annex, incorporate.
inlys, (inge-), frame.
inlywing, annexation, incorporation.
inmaak, (inge-), can, pickle, preserve, tin.
inmaakbottel, -fles, vide **inlêbottel.**
inmekaar, crumpled up, smashed; bent double, stooping.
inmekaar- . . . , vide **ineen- . . .**
inmekaardraai, (inmekaarge-), twist together.
inmekaarflans, (inmekaarge-), knock together.
inmekaarfrommel, (inmekaarge-), crumple up.
inmekaargroei, (inmekaarge-), grow together.
inmekaargryp, (inmekaarge-), interlock; engage; dovetail.
inmekaarkrimp, (inmekaarge-), shrink; double up, writhe (with pain).
inmekaarloop, (inmekaarge-), meet (of lines); communicate (of rooms); run into each other.
inmekaarpas, (inmekaarge-), fit together.
inmekaarrol, (inmekaarge-), roll up (together).
inmekaarsak, (inmekaarge-), collapse, cave in.
inmekaarsit, (inmekaarge-), assemble, build up, mount (machinery).
inmekaarskuif, -skuiwe, (inmekaarge-), slide (shove) into one another, telescope.
inmekaarslaan, (inmekaarge-), strike together, knock together; **die hande –,** join hands; **die hande van verbasing –,** throw up one's hands with wonder.
inmekaarsluit, (inmekaarge-), fit (dovetail) into each other.
inmekaarsmelt, (inmekaarge-), blend, fuse.
inmekaarstort, (inmekaarge-), collapse.
inmekaartrap, (inmekaarge-), kick (tread) to pieces.
inmekaarvleg, (inmekaarge-), interlace.
inmekaarvloei, (inmekaarge-), flow into one another; vide **inmekaarloop, -smelt.**
inmeng, (inge-), mix up with; interfere with.
inmenging, interference, meddling.
inmessel, (inge-), build in, immure.
inmiddels, meanwhile, in the meantime.
innaai, (inge-), sew, stitch (books).
inname, vide **inneming.**
inneem, (inge-), bring in; take in (a dress), take (medicine); load (cargo); occupy, take up (room); capture, take (a fortress); collect (tickets); charm; vide **ingenome.**
innemend, (-e), attractive, captivating, fetching, prepossessing, taking, winning.
innemendheid, charm, winning ways.
inneming, capture, taking; vide **inneem.**
inner, (-s), casher; collector.
innerlik, (-e), inner (life), internal (forces), intrinsic (merit), inward (eye).
innerlikheid, inwardness; vide **innerlik.**
innig, (-e), sincere, earnest, hearty.
innigheid, sincerity; vide **innig.**
inning, cashing; collection.

innooi, (inge-), invite in.
innovasie, innovation.
inoes, (inge-), gather in, reap.
inokuleer, (geïn-), inoculate.
inpak, (inge-), pack, do up (parcels); bale (goods); jou –, muffle (wrap) oneself up.
inpakking, packing (up).
inpalm, (inge-), haul in (a rope); captivate, ingratiate oneself with (a person); rope (a person) in; alles –, pocket everything.
inpas, (inge-), fit in.
inpekel, (inge-), pickle, salt.
inpeper, (inge-), pepper; iemand –, go for a person; give someone a hiding.
inperk, (inge-), fence in; curtail, restrict.
inperking, enclosure; curtailment, restriction.
inpers, (inge-), press (squeeze) in(to).
inpik, (inge-), nab, pinch, collar.
inplak, (inge-), paste in.
inplakalbum, paste in (on) album.
inplant, (inge-), plant; insert; implant, imprint.
inplanting, planting; inculcation.
inploe(g), inploeë, (inge-), plough in.
inpomp, (inge-), pump in; cram (drum) in.
inpompstelsel, cramming-system.
inpraat, (inge-), iets –, talk into doing something; iemand moed –, buoy a person up.
inprent, (inge-), impress, imprint, inculcate, instill, stamp (on the memory), drum, drill (into the head . . .).
inprenting, inculcation; vide inprent.
inprop, (inge-), cram into; stuff (food) into.
inreën, -reent, (inge-), rain in.
inreken, (inge-), add (to account); arrest.
inrig, (inge-), arrange, manage; fit (fix) up, furnish; jou lewe – na, adapt one's life to.
inrigting, (-e, -s), arrangement, organization; structure; furnishing, furniture, apparatus; establishment, institution.
inroep, (inge-), call in; enlist, invoke (help).
inrol, (inge-), roll in(to).
inruil, (inge-), trade in, barter, exchange.
inruiling, trading in, barter(ing), exchange.
inruim, (inge-); plek –, make room.
inruk, (inge-), drag (pull, snatch) in; march into break (ranks), dismiss.
inry, (inge-), ride in(to); break in (a horse); bring in.
inrybioskoop, drive-in theatre.
inruk, (inge-), drag (pull, snatch) in; march into;
inry(e), inryg, (inge-), lace (tightly); gather (a frill); tack (a dress), string (beads).
insa(g)e, inspection, perusal; ter –, for perusal; for inspection.
insak, (inge-), sink in; cave in, collapse; sag.
insakking, collapse; slump (of prices).
insamel, (inge-), collect, gather (in).
insê, (inge-): iemand –, give a person a bit of one's mind (a telling-off).
inseën, (inge-), consecrate; ordain (clergyman).
inseëning, consecration, induction.
inseep, (inge-), soap; lather (for shaving).
inseil, (inge-), sail into, enter (a harbour).
insek, (-te), insect.
insekdodende: – middel, insecticide.
insektekenner, entomologist.
insektekunde, -leer, entomology.
insektepoeier, insect-powder, insecticide.
insend, (inge-), hand (send) in; contribute.
insender, (-s), contributor; exhibitor.
insending, contribution; exhibit.
inset, stake(s); pool; put-up price.
insetsel, (-s), insertion, inset.
insetting, (-e, -s), decree (of heaven).
insgelyks, likewise, similarly.

insident, (-e), incident.
insidenteel, (-ele), incidental.
insien, (inge-), glance over, look into; see, come to realise; understand; dit kan ek nie – nie, I cannot see that; ernstig –, take a grave view.
insig, (-te), insight; opinion, view.
insinje, (-s), badge, (pl.) insignia.
insink, (inge-), give way, sink down (in); subside; slump; relapse; decline (of morality).
insinking, subsidence; slump; decline; relapse (of patient).
insinuasie, (-s), innuendo, insinuation.
insinueer, (geïn-), insinuate.
insit, (inge-), put in; set in; insert; start (bidding); stake (at games); strike up (a song); daar goed (warm) –, be well-off.
insitprys, starting-price (at sale).
inskakel, (inge-), switch on; engage; insert.
inskakelaar, switch; gear.
inskakeling, insertion; intercalation; switching on; throwing into gear.
inskeep, (inge-), embark; ship.
inskep, (inge-), ladle in; dish up (food).
inskeping, embarkation.
inskerp, (inge-): iemand iets –, impress (inculcate) something upon a person.
inskeur, (inge-), rend, slit, tear.
inskiet, (inge-), throw (thrust) in(to); try out (a gun); go by the board; jou lewe (geld) by –, lose one's life (money).
inskiklik, (-e), complaisant, obliging.
inskiklikheid, complaisance, obligingness.
inskink, (inge-), pour out (in).
inskop, (inge-), kick in.
inskrif, inscription.
inskripsie, (-s), inscription.
inskroef, -skroewe, (inge-), screw in.
inskryf, -skrywe, (inge-), enrol(l), enter; register; inscribe (one's name); subscribe (to a paper); tender, subscribe (to a loan).
inskrywer, applicant; tenderer.
inskrywing, (-e, -s), enrol(l)ment, registration; entry; tender; application (for shares); –s vra, ask for tenders.
inskrywingsgeld, registration-fee.
inskuif, -skuiwe, (inge-), shove (squeeze) in.
inskuiftafel, telescope-table.
inslaan, (inge-), drive in; batter (smash in); take, turn down (a road); strike (of lightning); catch on, take; sink in; swallow down; die regte (verkeerde) weg –, take the right (wrong) road (lit.); set about it the right (wrong) way (fig.); die bodem –, stave in (lit.); frustrate (fig.).
inslaap, (inge-), drop off to sleep; die, pass away; sleep in (on premises).
inslag, woof, weft.
insleep, (inge-), drag in(to).
insluimer, (inge-), doze off.
insluip, (inge-), creep (slip, steal) in(to).
insluit, (inge-), enclose, lock in, shut in; invest (a town), include; contain.
insluiting, locking in; investment (of a town); enclosure; encirclement, hemming in.
insluk, (inge-), swallow; sy woorde –, clip one's words; iemand sy woorde laat –, make a person eat his words.
inslukking, swallowing; absorption.
inslyp, (inge-), grind in.
insmeer, (inge-), grease, oil, smear; rub in.
insmokkel, (inge-), smuggle in.
insmyt, (inge-), fling (throw) in, smash.
insnoer, (inge-), constrict; string (beads).
insnuif, -snuiwe, (inge-), sniff in (up), inhale.
insny, (inge-), cut in(to), engrave, incise.
insnyding, cut, incision; indention.

insolvensie, (-s), insolvency, bankruptcy.
insolvent, (-e), insolvent, bankrupt.
insonderheid, especially, particularly.
insout, (inge-), salt; initiate (students).
inspan, (inge-), inspan; harness (horses); yoke (oxen); set (a person) to do something; exert (one's strength); strain (one's eyes).
inspannend, (-e), strenuous, trying (work).
inspanning, effort, exertion, strain.
inspeksie, (-s), inspection.
inspeksiereis, round (tour) of inspection.
inspekteer, (geïn-), inspect.
inspekteur, (-s), inspector; superintendent.
inspekteurskap, inspectorship.
inspektrise, (-s), (woman-)inspector.
inspin, (inge-), (form a) cocoon, wrap in (up).
inspirasie, inspiration.
inspireer, (geïn-), inspire.
inspraak, dictate(s) (of one's heart).
inspreek, (inge-): **iemand moed** –, put heart into (encourage) a person.
inspring, (inge-), jump (leap) in(to); bend inward; stand back; **vir iemand** –, take a person's place.
inspringend, (-e): –e **hoek**, re-entering angle.
insprinkel, (inge-), sprinkle.
inspuit, (inge-), inject, give an injection.
inspyker, (inge-), nail in (up).
instaan, (inge-): – **vir**, answer for, guarantee, vouch for; accept responsibility for, stand surety for.
instabiel, (-e), unstable.
installasie, (-s), installation; plant; inauguration, institution; induction.
installeer, (geïn-), fix up, install; furnish, induct; inaugurate.
instamp, (inge-), beat (ram) in.
instandhouding, conversation; maintenance; upkeep; preservation.
instansie, instance.
instap, (inge-), step in(to); walk in; get in; –!, all seats!
insteek, (inge-), put in; thread (a needle.)
instel, (inge-), establish, set up; institute, focus; adjust (instruments); propose (a toast).
instelling, (-e, -s), adjustment; institution.
instem, (inge-), agree; concur; chime in.
instemming, agreement, approval, assent, concurrence; **jou – betuig**, signify one's approval; **met algemene –**, by common consent.
instigeer, (geïn-), instigate.
instink, (-te), instinct.
instinkmatig, (-e), **instinktief**, (-tiewe), a. & adv. instinctive(ly).
institueer, (geïn-), institute.
institusie, (-s), institution.
instituut, (-ute), institute; institution.
instoom, (inge-), steam in(to).
instoot, (inge-), force, push (stave) in.
instop, (inge-), tuck (wrap) up, cram (stuff) in.
instorm, (inge-), rush (tear) in(to).
instort, (inge-), tumble down, fall in, collapse; relapse (of invalid).
instorting, collapse; break down; relapse.
instroming, inflow, influx.
instroom, (inge-), crowd (flock, flow, pour, stream) in(to).
instrueer, (geïn-), instruct.
instruksie, (-s), instruction, direction, order; **vir sy –**, for his guidance.
instrukteur, (-s), instructor; drill-sergeant.
instruktief, (-tiewe), instructive.
instruktrise, (-s), instructress.
instrument, (-e), instrument, implement, tool.
instrumentaal, (-ale), instrumental.

instrumentbord, instrument-board, dashboard.
instudeer, (inge-), practise, study, rehearse.
instuif, **-stuiwe**, (inge-), blow (rush) in.
instuur, (inge-), send in; vide **insend**.
insubordinasie, insubordination.
insuie, **insuig**, (inge-), suck in, absorb, imbibe.
insukkel, (Inge-), get in (down) with difficulty.
insulêr, (-e), insular.
insulien, **insuline**, insulin.
insurreksie, (-s), insurrection.
insuur, (inge-), prepare yeast.
insweer, (inge-), swear in, administer an oath.
inswelg, (inge-), devour, gulp down.
inswering, swearing in, administering an oath.
insyfer, (**insypel**), (inge-), infiltrate.
intak(t), intact, entire, unimpaired.
inteelt, inbreeding.
inteendeel, on the contrary.
inteer, (inge-), touch upon (use up) the capital.
integraal, (-ale), integral.
integraalrekening, integral calculus.
integreer, (geïn-), integrate.
integrerend, (-e), integral, component (part).
integriteit, integrity.
inteken, (inge-), subscribe to; mark (on a map).
intekenaar, (-are, -s), subscriber.
intekening, subscription; vide **inskrywing**.
intekenlys, subscription-list.
intellek, (-te), intellect.
intellektualisme, intellectualism.
intellektueel, (-uele), intellectual.
intelligensie, intelligence.
intelligensietoets, intelligence-test.
intelligent, (-e), intelligent; bright.
intens, (-e), intense.
intensie, (-s), intention.
intensief, (-iewe), a. & adv. intensive(ly).
intensiteit, intensity.
intersessie, (-s), intercession.
interdik, (-te), interdict.
interes, interest; **enkelvoudige**, **samegestelde –**, simple, compound interest; **met – terugbetaal**, return with interest; **– op –**, (at) compound interest.
interessant, (-e), interesting.
interesseer, (geïn-), interest; be interested in.
interieur, (-s), interior.
interim, interim; **ad –**, ad interim, pro tem.
interjeksie, (-s), interjection.
interkaleer, (geïn-), intercalate, interpolate.
interkollegiaal, (-iale), intercollegiate.
interkoloniaal, (-iale), intercolonial.
interkommunikasie, intercommunication.
intermediêr, (-e), intermediate.
intermezzo, (-s), intermezzo, interlude.
intermissie, intermission.
intern, (-e), internal.
internasionaal, (-ale), international.
internasionaliseer, (geïn-), internationalize.
internasionalisme, internationalism.
interneer, (geïn-), intern.
interneringskamp, internment-camp.
internis, (-te), specialist in internal diseases.
interpellasie, (-s), interpellation.
interpelleer, (geïn-), interpellate; question.
interplanetêr, interplanetary.
interpoleer, (geïn-), interpolate.
interpretasie, (-s), interpretation, version.
interpreteer, (geïn-), interpret.
interpunksie, punctuation.
interregnum, interregnum.
interrogatief, (-tiewe), interrogative.
interrogeer, (geïn-), interrogate.
interrupsie, (-s), interruption.
interseksie, intersection.

interuniversiteitswedstryd, intervarsity.
intervensie, (-s), intervention.
intestaat, (-ate), intestate.
inteuel, (inge-), curb, restrain.
intiem, (-e), intimate; – **wees met**, be on familiar terms with, be on terms of intimacy with.
intimideer, (geïn-), browbeat, intimidate.
intimiteit, (-e), intimacy.
intog, entrance, entry.
intoming, check, curbing, restraint.
intonasie, (-s), intonation.
intoneer, (geïn-), intone.
intoom, (inge-), pull up, rein in; curb, restrain.
intransitief, (-tiewe), intransitive.
intrap, (inge-), trample (tread) down, step (walk) in.
intraveneus, intravenous.
intrede, n. entrance (upon office), entry (into); advent (of spring).
intree, (inge-), enter; set in.
intreegeld, admission(-fee).
intreepreek, induction-sermon.
intreerede, inaugural lecture (speech).
intrek, n. **jou – neem by**, put up at (with).
intrek, (inge-), draw in, retract; march into; move into (a house); inhale (smoke); soak in; withdraw, repeal, cancel (leave, an order), retract (a statement), suspend (a licence); **iemand –**, cheat (deceive) a person; **by iemand –**, take up one's lodging with a person; **die land –**, trek into the country.
intrekking, cancellation, repeal, retraction; vide **intrek**.
intrigant, (-e), intriguer, plotter, schemer.
intrige, (-s), intrigue, plot.
intrigeer, (geïn-), intrigue, plot, scheme.
intrigeroman, novel with a plot.
intrinsiek, (-e), intrinsic.
introduksie, introduction.
introduseer, (geïn-), introduce.
introspeksie, introspection.
introspektief, (-tiewe), introspective.
intuïmel, (inge-), tumble in(to).
intuïsie, intuition; **by –**, intuitively.
intuïtief, (-tiewe), a. & adv. intuitive(ly).
intussen, meanwhile, in the meantime.
intyds, in time.
inundeer, (geïn-), flood, inundate.
invaar, (inge-), sail into; take possession of.
invaart, entrance.
inval, n. incursion, invasion, raid; brainwave, idea; incidence (of ray).
inval, (inge-), drop (fall) in(to); collapse, tumble down; set in (of night); invade (a country), raid (a club); join in (in singing): interrupt; start (work); occur to (one); **vir iemand –**, deputize for someone.
invalide, (-s), n. invalid.
invalide, a. incapacitated, invalid.
invaliditeit, invalidity, disablement.
invalparty, surprise party.
invalshoek, angle of incidence.
invasie, (-s), invasion.
inventaris, (-se), inventory.
inventarisasie, stocktaking.
inventariseer, (geïn-), make an inventory, take stock.
inventaris-uitverkoop, stocktaking sale.
inversie, (-s), inversion.
investituur, investiture.
invet, (inge-), grease, oil.
invitasie, (-s), invitation.
inviteer, (geïn-), invite.
invleg, (inge-), plait (weave) in; put in, introduce; **anekdotes in sy rede –**, intersperse one's speech with anecdotes.
invlieg, (inge-), fly in(to); go for (a person); **daar –**, be caught, walk into a trap; – **op**, fly (rush) at.
invloed, (-e), influence; **jou – aanwend (laat geld)**, bring one's influence to bear, use one's influence; – **hê op**, affect, influence; – **uitoefen**, exert (exercise) influence; – **uitoefen op**, affect, exercise influence (up)on; **onder die – van drank**, under the influence of (the worse for) drink.
invloedryk, (-e), influential.
invloedsfeer, sphere of influence.
invloei, (inge-), flow in(to).
invlug, (inge-), fly into.
invoeg, (inge-), insert, intercalate, put in.
invoeging, (-e, -s), **invoegsel**, (-s), insertion.
invoer, n. import(ation).
invoer, (inge-), import (goods); introduce.
invoerartikel, article of import, (pl.) imports.
invoerbelasting, import-duty.
invoerder, (-s), importer; introducer.
invoerhandel, import-trade.
invoerhawe, import-harbour.
invoering, importation; introduction.
invoerpremie, bounty on importation.
invoerreg, vide **invoerbelasting**.
invoerverbod, embargo (on importation).
invokasie, invocation.
involusie, (-s), involution.
invorder, (inge-), collect; recover (debts).
invorderaar, (-s), collector.
invorderbaar, (-bare), leviable; recoverable.
invordering, collection, levy; recovery (of debts).
invou, (inge-), fold in.
invreet, (inge-), bite (eat) into; corrode.
invreting, corrosion; erosion.
invryf, **-vrywe**, (inge-), rub in.
invryheidstelling, discharge, release.
invul, (inge-), fill in.
inwaai, (inge-), blow in, be blown in.
inwag, (inge-), await, wait for.
inwagting, awaiting.
inweef, **-wewe**, (inge-), weave in(to).
inweek, (inge-), soak (steep) in.
inwendig, (-e), a. inner, interior, internal, inward; **–e kwale**, internal complaints; **die –e mens**, one's inner man; **nie vir –e gebruik nie**, for external use only.
inwendig, adv. inwardly, internally.
inwerk, (inge-): – **op**, act upon, affect, influence; **jou êrens –**, get to know the ropes, master the details.
inwerking, action, influence.
inwerkingstelling, putting into operation.
inwerkingtreding, coming into force.
inwerp, (inge-), throw in(to).
inwikkel, (inge-), cover (wrap) up.
inwillig, (inge-), accede (agree) to, comply with, concede (demands), grant.
inwilliging, assent, compliance, consent.
inwin, (inge-), collect, gather; **raad –**, get (take) advice.
inwip, (inge-), whip (whisk) into (a hole); drop in (on a person).
inwissel, (inge-), cash (a cheque); change (a note); exchange (for something else).
inwisselling, cashing; exchange.
inwoner, (-s), inhabitant, resident (of city), inmate, occupant (of house), lodger.
inwoning, lodging; **kos en –**, board and lodging.
inwoon, (inge-), live in; live (lodge) with.
inwortel, (inge-), strike (take) root.
inwring, (inge-): **jou – in**, worm oneself into.

inwy, (inge-), inaugurate, consecrate (a church); iemand in iets –, initiate a person into something.
inwyding, (-e, -s), consecration; vide **inwy.**
inwydingsplegtigheid, inaugural ceremony.
inwydingsrede, inaugural address (speech).
ion, (-e), ioon (ione), ion.
Ionies, (-e), Ionian.
ioniseer, (geïoniseer), ionize.
ionium, ionium.
ionosfeer, ionosphere.
ipekonders, hipokonders, hypochondria.
Iraans, (-e), Iranian.
iris, (-se), iris.
ironie, irony.
ironies, (-e), ironical.
irrasioneel, (-ele), irrational.
irredentisme, irredentism.
irrigasie, irrigation.
irrigasiewerke, irrigation-works.
irrigeer, (geïr-), irrigate.
irritasie, irritation.
irriteer, (geïr-), irritate.
irrupsie, (-s), irruption.

is, vide **wees.**
iskias, sciatica.
Islam, Islam.
isobaar, (-bare), isobar.
isobarometries, (-e), isobaric.
isolasie, isolation; insulation.
isolasiemateriaal, insulating-material.
isolasionis, isolationist.
isolator, (-s), insulator; non-conductor.
isoleer, (geïso-), isolate; insulate.
isoleerband, insulating-tape.
isolement, isolation.
isoterm, (-e), isotherm.
Israel, Israel.
Israeliet, (-e), Israelite.
Israelities, (-e), Israelitish.
ismus, (-se), isthmus.
Italiaan, (-iane), Italian.
Italiaans, (-e), n. & a. Italian.
Italianer, (-s), Italian.
ivoor, ivory.
ivoorkleurig, (-e), ivory-coloured.
ivoorpapier, ivory-paper.
ixia, (-s), ixia.

ja, yes, ay(e); **op alles – en amen sê**, agree to everything.
ja(ag), **jae**, (ge-), chase, pursue; hurry; race, rush, tear; **iemand 'n koeël deur die kop –**, put a bullet through a person's head; **iemand op koste –**, put a person to expense; **na rykdom –**, hunt after riches; **alles deur die keel –**, pour everything down the throat.
jaagbesem, winnowing-fan.
jaagsiekte, droning-sickness (in sheep).
jaagspinnekop, jagspinnekop, hunting spider.
ja(a)psnoet, (-e), jackanapes; wiseacre.
jaar, (jare), year; **'n (per)**, –, a (per) year, per annum; **een – met die ander**, one year with another; **die hele – deur**, all the year round; **hy dra sy jare goed**, he carries his years well; **– in, – uit**, year in and year out; **een maal in die –**, once a year; **in die – onses Here(n)**, in the year of our Lord; **in die – nul**, in the year one; on the Greek calends; **– na –**, year after year; **op jare kom**, be getting on in years; **op jare wees**, be (well-)advanced in years; **tot voor enkele jare**, until a few years ago; **van – tot –**, from year's end to year's end; year by year; **hy is van my jare**, he is my age; **jonk vir sy jare**, young for his years.
jaarbeurs, annual fair.
jaarblad, annual.
jaarboek, year-book; (pl.) annals.
jaargang, volume (of a periodical).
jaargeld, annual allowance, annuity.
jaargety, season.
jaarhonderd, century; an age, ages.
jaar in –, jaar uit, year in and year out.
jaarlemoen, pom(m)elo, shaddock.
jaarliks, (-e), a. & adv. annual(ly), yearly.
jaarrapport, annual report.
jaarstaat, annual return(s).
jaart, (-s), yard.
jaartal, date.
jaartelling, era.
jaarvergadering, annual meeting.
jaarverslag, annual report.
jabroer, fellow without backbone, spunkless fellow.
jae, vide **ja(ag)**.
jaer, (-s), hunter; racer; vide **jagter**.
jag, (-te), n. hunt(ing); shooting; chase, yacht; **op (die) – gaan**, go out hunting (shooting); **op – na**, on the hunt for.
jag, (ge-), hunt, shoot, chase.
jagbombuis, proximity fuse.
jaggeleide, fighter escort.
jaggeselskap, hunting-, shooting-party.
jaggeweer, sporting-gun; fowling-piece.
jaghond, hunting-dog, pointer, setter.
jagklub, hunting-club; yacht-club.
jagliksens, -lisensie, hunting-licence.
jagongeluk, shooting-accident.
jagparty, hunting-party, shooting-party.
jagperd, hunting-horse, hunter.
jagspinnekop, jaagspinnekop, hunting-spider.
jagter, (-s), hunter, huntsman, sportsman.
jagtyd, shooting-season, open season.
jaguar, (-s), jaguar.
jagverhaal, hunting-story.
jagvermaak, field-sports, pleasures of the chase.
jagvliëer, fighter pilot.
jagvliegtuig, air fighter.
jagwet, game-act, game-law.
jak, (-s), yack.
jakaranda, (-s), jacaranda(-tree).
jakkals, (-e), jackal; **hy is 'n –**, he is a wily fox; **– prys sy eie stert**, he blows his own trumpet; **'n – verander van hare maar nie van streke** (nukke) **nie**, a leopard cannot change his spots; **dis bo my –**, that is beyond me.
jakkalsdraai, sharp turn; excuse, pretext.
jakkalsdraf(fie), fox-trot.
jakkalspruim, Cape sumach.
jakkalsstreek, artifice, cunning, shrewdness.
jakkalsvoël, jackal-buzzard.
jakker, (ge-), career along; gad about.
jakkie, (-s), coatee.
Jakobeaans, Jacobean.
Jakobiet, (-e), Jacobite.
jakob-regop, (-s), zinnia.
Jakobsleer, Jacob's ladder.
Jakobyn, (e), Jacobin.
jakopewer, (-s), Jacob Evertsen (fish).
jakopeweroë, protruding eyes.
jalap, jalap.
jaloers, (-e), jealous, envious.
jaloersheid, jaloesie, jealousy, envy.
jam, (-s), yam.
jamaikagemmer, Jamaica ginger.
jambe, (-s), iamb(us).
jambies, (-e), iambic.
jamboes, (-e), rose-apple.
jammer, a. sorry; **dit is –**, it is a pity; **ek is –**, I am sorry; **– genoeg**, more's the pity.
jammer, (ge-), lament, wail.
jammerhartig, (-e), compassionate, soft-hearted.
jammerhartigheid, soft-heartedness.
jammerklag, lamentation.
jammerlik, (-e), miserable, pitiable, pitiful.
jammerte, pity; sorrow.
jammertoon, tone of lamentation.
Jan, John; Jack; **– Rap en sy maat**; Tom, Dick and Harry; **– Pampoen**, nonentity, dunce; **liewer blo (bang) – as do (dooi) –**, better a living dog than a dead lion, discretion is the better part of valour; **bo – wees**, have turned the corner.
janblom, (-me, -s), rain-frog.
janboel, muddle.
ja-nee, sure!, that's a fact!
janfiskaal, (-ale, -s), butcher-bird, fiscal-shrike.
janfrederik, (-e, -s), Cape red-breast.
jangroentjie, (-s), sugar-bird.
janhen, (-ne), apron-husband, molly.
janklaassenspel, Punch and Judy show.
janmaat, (-s), bluejacket, Jack, jack-tar.
janpiedewiet, (-e, -s), **janpierewiet**, bokmakirishrike.
jansalie, (-e), stick-in-the-mud, spunkless fellow.
jansalieagtig, (-e), spiritless, spunkless.
jansaliegees, stick-in-the-mud spirit.
jantatara, jantatarat, (-s), vide **janfrederik**.
jantjie-trap-soetjies, (-e), chameleon.
Jan Tuisbly: **met – se kar ry**, stay at home.
Januarie(maand), (month of) January.
Japannees, (-ese), Japanese.
Japanner, (-s), Japanese, Jap.
Japans, (-e), Japanese.
japie, (-s), simpleton.
japon, (-ne), dress, frock.
japonika, (-s), japonica, camellia.
japsnoet, vide **jaapsnoet**.
jare lank, for years together (on end).
jargon, jargon.
jarig, (-e), a year old; **hy is vandag –**, it is his birthday today.
jarra, jarrah(-wood).
jas, (-se), greatcoat, overcoat.
jasmyn, jasmin(e), jessamin(e).
jaspis, jasper.
Javaan, (-ane), Javanese.
Javaans, (-e), Javanese.
jawel, indeed, yes.

jawoord, acquiescence, consent; promise (of marriage).
jazz, jazz.
jazz-orkes, jazz band.
jee!, o —!, o dear!
jeens, to, towards, by; with.
Jehova, Jehovah.
jekker(t), (-s), coat, jacket.
jellie, (-s), jelly.
jenewer, gin.
jenewerboom, -**struik**, juniper-tree.
jeremiade, (-s), jeremiad, lamentation.
jeremieer, (ge-), lament.
jeropiko, jerepigo, jeropigo.
jersie, (-s), jersey.
Jesuïet, (-e), Jesuit.
Jesuïties, (-e), Jesuitical.
Jesus, Jesus.
jeug, youth; **in sy prille —**, in his early youth.
jeugbeweging, youth-movement.
jeugdig, (-e), young, youthful.
jeugdigheid, youth(fulness).
jeugraad, Juvenile Affairs Board.
jeuk, n. itch(ing).
jeuk, (ge-), itch.
jeukerig, (-e), itching, itchy.
jeuking, itch(ing).
jeukpoeier, itching-powder.
Jiddisj, Yiddish.
jig, gout.
jigaanval, attack of gout.
jigagtig, (-e), gouty.
jiglyer, gouty patient, sufferer from gout.
jigpyne, gouty pains, twitches of gout.
jigtig, (-e), vide **jigagtig**.
jil, (ge-), jest, joke, play pranks, tease.
jilletjie, (-s), jest, joke, prank, trick.
jingo, (-s), jingo.
jingoïsme, jingoism.
jingoïsties, (-e), jingoistic.
Jobsbode, bringer of bad news.
Jobsgeduld, Job's patience.
Jobstrooster, Job's (poor) comforter.
Jobstyding, Job's news, message of ill-luck.
Jodebuurt, Jewish quarter, ghetto.
Jodedom, Judaism; Jewry, Jews.
Jodekerk, synagogue; **dit is 'n regte —**, it's bedlam broke loose, it's a regular bear-garden.
jodel, (ge-), yodel.
Jodestreek, Jewish trick, sharp practice.
Jodevervolging, persecution of the Jews, Jew-baiting; pogrom (in Russia).
Jodin(netjie), Jewess.
jodium, jood, iodine.
Joego-Slawies, (-e), Jugoslav, Yugoslav.
joejitsoe, ju-jitsu.
joeker, euchre.
joel, (ge-), bawl, shout.
joep-joep, (-s), jujube.
joernaal, (-ale), journal; log-book (mar.).
joernalis, (-te), journalist, pressman.
joernalisme, journalism.
joernalistiek, n. journalism.
joernalistiek, (-e), a. journalistic.
joggie, boy, kid, lad(die), sonny; caddy.
jogurt, yog(h)urt.
jok, (ge-), fib, tell fibs, tell stories.
jokkery, fibbing, story-telling; vide **jok**.
jokkie, (-s), jockey.
jol, (ge-), make merry.
jolig, (-e), jolly, merry.
jolyt, merry-making, jollity, feasting.
jong, (-ens), n. boy; **haai —!**, I say, man!
jong, (attrib.), **jonk**, (predic.), young; **in my —**

jare, in my young days: **die —ste berigte**, the latest news; **die —ste dag**, Domesday.
jong, (ge-), bring forth young.
jongedogter, (young) girl.
jongeheer, young gentleman; Master (in address).
jongejuffrou, young lady; Miss (in address).
jongeliede, **jongelui**, young people.
jongeliedevereniging, young people's association; **Christelike —**, Young Men's (Women's) Christian Association.
jongeling, (-e), young man, youth.
jongelingsjare, early manhood.
jongelingskap, adolescence, youth; young men.
jongelingsvereniging, vide **jongeliedevereniging**.
jongelui, vide **jongeliede**.
jongensagtig, (-e), boyish, boylike (girl).
jongensgek, (regular) flirt.
jongensklere, boys' clothing; boys' suit (outfit).
jongenskool, boys' school.
jongensleeftyd, boyhood.
jongensliefde, calf-love.
jongenspak, boy's suit.
jongenstehuis, boys' hostel.
jongenstreek, boy's trick, boyish trick.
jongetjie, (-s), boy, youth.
jongetjieskind, boy.
jonggesel, bachelor, single man.
jonggetroude, newly married (couple).
jongie, chappy, boy, laddie, sonny.
jongkêrel, young man; lover.
jongleer, (ge-), juggle; tour as minstrel.
jongleur, (-s), juggler; jongleur, minstrel.
jongman, young man, lad, stripling.
jongmeisie, young girl, lass.
jongmens, youngster, young person.
jongos, young ox; tolly; **—se inspan**, vomit.
jongosvleis, baby beef.
jongs: van — af, from childhood.
jongspan, children, kiddies, young folk.
jonk, vide **jong**, a.
jonker, (-s), (young) nobleman; junker (German).
jonkheer, "jonkheer"; baron.
jonkheid, youth.
jonkman, young man; lover.
jonkvrou, young lady, maiden; baroness.
jonkvroulik, (-e), maidenly.
jood, vide **jodium**.
Jood, (**Jode**), Jew, Hebrew.
Joods, (-e), Jewish; Judaic.
jool, fun, jollification, (students') rag.
joos: dit mag — weet, deuce (goodness) knows.
josie, the devil, the deuce; **die — in wees**, have one's monkey up.
jota, iota; **g'n — nie**, not an iota (jot).
jou, pron. pers. you; **— rakker!**, you rascal!
jou, jou(n)e, pron. poss. your; **jou(n)e**, yours.
jou, (ge-): **iemand —**, call a person thee or thou.
jou, (ge-), boo, hoot, barrack.
joviaal, (-iale), genial, jolly, jovial.
jovialiteit, joviality, geniality.
jubel, n. jubilation, shout(s) of joy.
jubel, (ge-), exult, jubilate, shout for joy.
jubeljaar, jubilee-year.
jubelkreet, cheer, shout of joy.
jubeltoon, vide **jubelkreet**.
jubilaris, (-se), person celebrating.
jubileer, vide **jubel**, (ge-).
jubileum, (-s), jubilee.
Judaskus, Judas kiss, traitor's kiss.
Judasstreek, Judas trick, treachery.
judisieel, (iële), judicial.
juffer, (-s), miss, mistress.
jufferagtig, (-e), finical, missish, prim.
juffertjie, (-s), missie; lassie.
juffertjie-in-die-groen, love-in-a-mist.

juffrou, lady; teacher; Miss, Madam.
juig, (ge-), exult, rejoice.
juigkreet, juigtoon, shout of joy.
juis, (-te), a. correct; exact, accurate, proper, right, precise.
juis, adv. exactly, precisely; – **gister**, only yesterday; – **daarom**, for that very reason: **waarom moet hy dit – doen?**, why should he do it rather than another?; **hy is – die man**, he is the very man.
iuistement, exactly, precisely, quite so.
juistheid, correctness, exactitude, precision.
juk, (-ke), yoke; beam (of balance); **in die – wees**, be in harness.
jukbeen, cheek-bone.
jukbout, trunnion.
jukskei, (-e), yoke-skey; **'n orige –**, a fifth wheel to a coach.
Julie(maand), (month of) July.
jul(le), pron. pers. you.
jul(le), pron. poss, your; – **s'n**, yours.

Junie(maand), (month of) June.
junior, junior.
Junior Sertifikaat(eksamen), Junior Certificate (Examination).
junksie, (-s), junction; joint.
jurie, (-s), jury.
juriebank, jury-box.
jurielid, member of the jury.
juridies, (-e), juridical; judicial.
juris, (-te), barrister, jurist, lawyer.
jurisdiksie, jurisdiction.
jurk, (-e), (night-)dress.
justisie, justice; law; judicature.
justisieel, (-iële), judicial.
jute, jute.
juts, adv., **so-ewe –**, prim and proper.
juweel, (-ele), jewel, gem; treasure (fig.).
juwelier, (-s), jeweller.
juweliersware, jewel(le)ry.
jy, you; – **weet nooit nie**, you never know.
jy-en-jou, (ge-): **iemand –**, call a person thee and thou, thou a person.

kaai, (-e), quay, wharf.
kaaigeld, wharfage, quayage, quay-dues.
kaaiman, (-ne, -s), cayman, alligator, lizard.
kaak, (kake), jaw; gill (of fish); mandible (of insect); **aan die – stel,** pillory, expose, show up; **die kake van die dood,** the jaws (maw) of death; **klem in die kake,** lockjaw.
kaal, (kale), bald (head); callow, unfledged (bird); shabby, threadbare (carpet); bare, leafless (tree); naked (person); barren (lands); **hoe kaler jonker, hoe groter pronker, (hoe kaler, hoe rojaler),** great boast, small roast; **daar – van afkom,** come off second best; **iemand – maak,** fleece (pluck) someone.
kaalgaar(tou), rope-yarn.
kaalheid, baldness; callowness; vide **kaal.**
kaalhoofdig, (-e), bald(headed).
kaalkar, open (hoodless) cart.
kaalkop, n. baldhead; tuskless elephant.
kaalkop, a. & adv. baldheaded; hatless, tuskless; **iemand – die waarheid sê,** go for someone baldheaded.
kaalperske, bald peach, nectarine.
kaalvoet, barefoot.
kaalwa, open (tentless) wagon.
kaambessie, wild plum, Kaffir plum.
kaap, (kape), n. cape, headland, point.
kaap, (ge-), capture; practise piracy.
Kaap: die –, the Cape (of Good Hope); Cape Town; the Cape Peninsula; the Cape Province; **'n mens kan op die mes – toe ry,** the knife is as blunt as a horse's back; **so oud as die –se pad,** as old as the hills.
Kaapkolonie, Cape Colony.
Kaapland, the Cape, Cape Province.
Kaapprovinsie, Cape Province.
Kaapse, (-e), Cape; **'n –e draai,** a sharp turn; **'n hele –e draai,** a roundabout way.
Kaapstad, Cape Town.
kaapstander, (-s), capstan.
Kaapvaarder, (-s), privateer; Cape trader.
Kaapvaart, privateering; trade to the Cape.
kaard, (ge-), card, tease (wool).
kaart, (-e), n. card; map; chart; ticket; **oop –e speel,** put (all) one's cards on the table; **'n doorgestoke –,** put-up job; **in – bring,** map out, chart; **in iemand se –e speel,** play into a person's hands; **nie op die – nie,** not on the map; **alles op een – sit,** stake everything on one throw.
kaart, (ge-), play at cards.
kaartkamer, card-room; chart-room.
kaartjie, (-s), card; ticket (railway).
kaartjie(s)knipper, ticket-collector.
kaartmaker, card-maker; cartographer.
kaartmannetjie, jack-in-the-box.
kaartspeel, (kaartge-), play (at) cards.
kaartspel, card-playing, game at (of) cards.
kaartstelsel, card-index system.
kaas, (kase), cheese; cheese-eater, Hollander.
kaasagtig, (-e), cheesy, cheese-like, caseous.
kaasdoek, butter-muslin.
kaasfabriek, cheese-factory.
kaashandelaar, cheesemonger.
kaaskop, blockhead; cheese-eater; **K–,** Hollander.
kaasmakery, cheese-making; cheese-factory.
kaasskottel, cheese-dish.
kaasstof, casein(e).
kaasstolp, cheese-cover, cheese-bell.
kaasstremsel, rennet.

Kaatjie: – Kekkelbek, chatterbox; **Ka(a)tjie van die baan,** cock of the walk.
kaats, (ge-), play (at) ball (tennis); **wie – moet die bal terug verwag,** if you play at bowls you must look out for rubbers.
kabaai, (-e), cabaya, gown.
kabaal, clamour, row, noise; **'n – opskop,** kick up a row; **daar was 'n helse –,** Bedlam seemed to have been let loose.
kabaalmaker, -skopper, rowdy fellow.
kabaret, (-te), cabaret; floor show.
kabbel, (-s), n. ripple, rippling.
kabbel, (ge-), babble, lap, purl, ripple.
kabbeling, (-e, -s), babbling, lapping.
kabel, (-s), n. cable; hawser.
kabel, (ge-), cable.
kabelballon, captive (observation) balloon.
kabelberig, -gram, cable(-gram).
kabeljou, (-e), cod(fish), Cape cod.
kabellengte, cable('s) length.
kabelnet, electric-mains.
kabelskip, cable-laying ship, cable-ship.
kabelspoor(weg), aerial (funicular) railway.
kabeltou, cable, cable-rope.
kabinet, (-te), cabinet, ministry; gallery.
kabinetmaker, cabinet-maker, joiner.
kabinetsbesluit dicision of the cabinet.
kabinetskrisis, cabinet-crisis.
kabinetsvergadering, cabinet-meeting.
kaboemielies, kaboe-mealies, boiled mealies.
kabouter(mannetjie), (-s) brownie; gnome.
kabriolet, cabriolet.
kadans, (-e), cadence.
kadawer, (-s), cadaver, corpse.
kade, vide **kaai.**
kader, frame, scheme.
kadet, (-te), cadet.
kado, (-'s), present.
kadriel, (-e), quadrille.
kaduks, in poor health, decrepit, seedy.
kaf, n. chaff; **praat (verkoop),** talk nonsense.
kaf, n. (-te), (book-)jacket, wrapper.
kafbaal, bale (bag) of chaff.
kafee, café, (-s), café, coffee-house.
kafeïen, kafeïne, caffeine.
kafeteria, cafeteria.
kafhok, chaff-barn.
kafloop, (kafge-), beat, give a hiding (thrashing); finish, polish off (food).
kafpraatjies, nonsense, trash, small talk.
kaftan, (-s), caftan.
kaggel, (-s), fireplace.
kaggelpyp, flue(-pipe); top-hat, chimney-pot.
kaiing, (-s), pl. greaves, brow(n)sels; **sy –s teëkom,** meet one's match.
Kainsmerk, -teken, brand (mark) of Cain.
Kaïro, Cairo.
kajapoet(olie), cajeput-, cajaput(-oil).
kajuit, (-e), cabin; wardroom.
kajuits(raad), council (of war).
kajuittrap, companion-ladder, -stairs, -way.
kakao, cocoa.
kakebeen, jaw(-bone), jowl.
kaketoe, kaketoea, (-s) cockatoo.
kakie, (-s), khaki; English soldier, tommy; Britisher, Englishman.
kakiebos(sie), khaki-bush; khaki-weed; Mexican marigold.
kakiehemp, khaki shirt.
kakiekombers, khaki (military) blanket.
kakkerlak, (-ke), cockroach.
kaktus, (-se), cactus.

Kalahari-woestyn, Kalahari Desert
kalamiteit, (-e), calamity.
kalander, (-s), (corn-)weevil; vine-calander.
kalant, (-e), (sly) fox, rogue, scamp.
kalbas, (-se), calabash, gourd.
kalbasdop, gourd; noddle, pate, nut.
kalbaspeer, winter-pear.
kalbaspyp, calabash-pipe.
kalbassies, orchitis (disease).
kaleidoskoop, kaleidoscope.
kaleidoskopies, (-e), kaleidoscopic.
kalender, (-s), almanac, calendar.
kalenderjaar, calendar-year.
kalerig, (-e), rather bald, etc; vide **kaal.**
kalf, (kalwers), n. calf; **kalwers inspan,** vomit, shoot the cat (slang); **met 'n ander se kalwers ploeg,** plough with another man's heifer; **die gemeste –,** the fatted calf; **as die – verdrink is, word die put gedemp,** when the steed is stolen the stable-door is locked.
kalf, kalwe, (ge-), calve (animals); cave in (ground).
kalfakter, (-s), n. jack-of-all-work; lick-spittle.
kalfakter, (ge-), drudge; toady.
kalfater, (ge-), caulk, repair, patch up.
kalfsboud, joint (leg) of veal.
kalfskop, calf's head; blockhead.
kalfsleer, calf(-skin), calf-leather.
kalfsoog, calf's eye; poached (fried) egg.
kalfsribbetjie, veal-cutlet.
kalfsvleis, kalwervleis, veal.
kali, potassium, potash.
kaliber, calibre; bore (of a gun).
kalibreer, (ge-), calibrate.
kalief, (-e), caliph, calif.
kalifaat, caliphate.
Kalifornies, (-e), Californian.
kaliko, calico
kalium, vide **kali.**
kalk, n. lime.
kalk, (ge-), lime-wash, whitewash.
kalkagtig, (-e), calcareous, limelike, limy.
kalkbank, limestone-reef.
kalkbrandery, lime-burning; limekiln.
kalkeer, (ge-), calk, trace.
kalkeerpapier, tracing-paper, transfer-paper.
kalkgrond, calcareous (limy) soil.
kalkhoudend, (-e), calciferous.
kalkklip, limestone.
kalklig, limelight.
kalkoen, (-e), turkey; **nie onder 'n – uitgebroei nie,** not as green as one looks.
kalkoeneier, turkey's egg; **'n gesig soos 'n –,** a freckled face.
kalkoenmannetjie, turkey-cock.
kalkoentjie, turkey-chicken; Cape pipit; (species of) gladiolus; **wilde –,** bald-ibis.
kalkoenwyfie, turkey-hen.
kalkoond, lime kiln.
kalkulasie, (-s), calculation.
kalkuleer, (ge-), calculate.
kalkverf, distemper.
kalkwater, limewater; whitewash.
kalligrafie, calligraphy.
kalligrafies, (-e), calligraphic(al).
kalm, (-e), calm; cool, quiet; collected, composed; **– bly, jou – hou,** keep cool (calm), keep one's temper; **dit – opneem,** take it philosophically; **– en bedaard,** cool and collected.
kalmeer, (ge-), calm down, compose oneself; calm, pacify, soothe.

kalmeermiddel, tranquillizer.
kalmerend, (-e), calming, soothing.
kalmoes, calamus, sweet flag, sweet sedge.
kalmoeswortel, orris-root.
kalmpies, calmly, quietly, steadily.
kalmte, calm(ness), composure.
kalmweg, calmly, coolly, quietly.
kalomel, calomel.
kalorie, (-ë), calorie (calory), heat-unit.
kalorimeter, (-s), calorimeter.
kalossie, vide **klossie.**
kalsineer, (ge-), calcine.
kalsium, calcium.
kalwerhok, -kraal, calves' kraal; **opdons tot by oom Daantjie in die –,** knock into a cocked hat, wipe the floor with (a person).
kalwerliefde, calf-love.
kam, (-me), n. comb; crest (of a hill), ridge; cam, cog (of a wheel); bridge (of a violin); **almal oor een – skeer,** treat all alike, lump all together.
kam, (ge-), comb; card (wool).
kamas, (-te), legging, gaiter, spat.
kam-as, thrust-shaft.
kambro, kambro (species of Fockea).
kamee, (-meë), cameo.
kameel, (-mele), camel; giraffe.
kameel(doring)boom, camelthorn(-tree).
kameelperd, giraffe, camelopard.
kameleon, (-s), chameleon.
kamelia, (-s), camellia.
kamenier, (-e, -s), -ster, (-s), waiting-woman.
kamer, (-s), chamber, room; ventricle (of the heart); **K– van Koophandel,** Chamber of Commerce; **K– van Mynwese,** Chamber of Mines; **–s te huur,** apartments (rooms) to let; **sy – hou,** be confined to one's room.
kamera, (-s), camera.
kameraad, (-rade), comrade; chum, pal.
kameraadskap, comradeship, companionship.
kameraadskaplik, (-e), companionable, chummy; **– omgaan met,** fraternise with.
kameraadskaplikheid, cameraderie.
kamerdienaar, man, valet; chamberlain.
kamerdoek, cambric.
kamergimnastiek, indoor gymnastics.
kamerheer, gentleman-in-waiting; chamberlain.
kamerhuur, chamber-rent, apartment-rent.
kamerjapon, dressing-gown.
kamermeisie, chambermaid.
kamermusiek, chamber-music.
kamerplant, indoor-plant.
kamertjie, little room, closet; cubicle.
kamerwag, orderly.
kamgare, -garing, worsted (yarn).
kamille, camomile.
kamilletee, camomile-tea.
kamma, kammakastig, -lielies, quasi, as if, make believe, would-be, pseudo; **hy het – gewerk,** he made a pretence of being at work.
kammetjie, small comb; freesia.
kamp, n. 1. combat, fight, struggle.
kamp, (-e), n. 2. camp; paddock; **– opslaan,** pitch camp; **– opbreek,** strike camp.
kamp, (ge-), camp, encamp; fight, combat, struggle; **te –e hê met,** have to contend with.
kampanje, (-s), campaign.
kampeer, (ge-), (en)camp, camp out, bivouac.
kampeerder, (-s), camper(-out).
kampement, (-e), camp, encampment.
kamperfoelie, kanferfoelie, honeysuckle.

kampioen, (-e), champion.
kampioenskap, championship.
kampplaas, -plek, battle-field; arena, lists, camp(ing)-site.
kampregter, umpire, referee.
kampvegter, fighter; champion, advocate.
kampvuur, camp-fire.
kamrat, cog(-wheel), mortice-wheel.
kamta(g), kamtig, vide **kamma.**
kamwol, comb(ing)-wool, top-wool.
kan, (-ne), n. can, jar, jug, mug, tankard.
kan, (kon), v. be able, can, may; **ek – nie meer nie,** I am finished; **dit – nie,** that is impossible, that won't do; **dit – so nie langer nie,** this can't go on; **hoe kon jy dit doen!** how could you possibly do it!; **dit het jy my kon sê,** you might have told me; **hy moes dit kon doen,** he should have been able to do this; **ek kon hom vermoor,** I felt like murdering him; **ek kon daar nie voor nie,** I could not help it; **so goed ek kon,** as best I could; **so al wat hy kon,** for all he was worth; **so kon hy urelank sit,** he would sit like that for hours; **hy – daar nie teë nie,** he can't stand it.
kanaal, (-nale), channel; canal; passage.
Kanaäniet, (-e), Canaanite.
Kanaänities, (-e), Canaanitish.
Kanadees, (-dese), Canadian.
kanaliseer, (ge-), channel, canalize.
ka(r)nalie, (-s), rascal, scamp.
kanapee, (-s), lounge, settee, sofa, couch.
kanarie, (-s), canary.
kanariebyter, butcher-bird, shrike.
kanariesaad, canary-seed.
Kanariese Eilande, the Canary Islands.
kandeel, caudle.
kandeelwyn, negus.
kandelaar, (-s, kandelare), candle-stick; agapanthus.
kandidaat, (-date), candidate, nominee, applicant (for a post); **– stel,** nominate, put up as candidate; **sig – stel,** contest a seat, stand (for); **– wees vir,** be a candidate for, be in the run for.
kandidaatstelling, nomination.
kandidatuur, candidature, nomination.
kandysuiker, candy-sugar, sugar-candy.
kaneel, cinnamon; **wilde –,** cassia.
kaneelblom, large brown africander.
kaneelkleurig, (-e), cinnamon(-coloured).
kaneelstokkie, cinnamon-stick.
kaneelsuiker, sugar and cinnamon.
kaneeltjie, vide **kaneelblom.**
kanfer, camphor.
kanferbrandewyn, camphorated spirits.
kanferfoelie, vide **kamperfoelie.**
kanferolie, camphor(ated) oil.
kangaroe, (-s), kangaroo.
kanis, (-se), dirty fellow.
kanker, cancer; (fig.), canker, pest.
kankeragtig, (-e), cancerous.
kankerbestryding, fight against cancer.
kankerbossie, cancer-bush.
kankergeswel, cancerous tumour, carcinoma.
kankerlyer, -pasiënt, cancer-patient.
kankerondersoek, cancer-research.
kankerplek, cancerous spot.
kankerroos, cocklebur(r).
kanna, (-s), canna.
kannetjie, cannikin, small can (jar, jug, mug).
kannibaal, (-bale), cannibal.
kannibaals, (-e), cannibalistic.

kannibalisme, cannibalism.
kanniedood, airplant.
kano, (-'s), canoe.
kanolpypie, Watsonia.
kanon, (-ne), cannon, gun.
kanon, (-s), canon.
kanongebulder, roar (booming) of the guns.
kanoniek, (-e), canonical.
kanoniseer, (ge-), canonize.
kanonkoeël, cannon-ball, shell.
kanonnade, (-s), cannonade, bombardment.
kanonneer, (ge-), bombard, cannonade, shell.
kanonneerboot, gunboat.
kanonnier, (-s), gunner.
kanonskootafstand, gunshot-range.
kanonvlees, (-vleis), -voer, cannon-fodder.
kanonvuur, cannonade; gunfire.
kanonwa, gun-carriage; caisson.
kans, (-e), chance, opportunity; risk; turn; **'n – hê,** stand a chance; **die –e staan gelyk,** the chances are equal, the odds are even; **'n – kry,** get an opportunity (a turn); **die – loop om te . . . ,** run the risk of . . . ; **die – waarneem,** seize the opportunity; **die – waag,** take one's chance; **– sien om iets te doen,** see one's way to doing something; **– op,** chance (prospect) of (success); risk of (failure); **daar is nog – op,** there is a (remote) possibility; **die – is verkyk,** the opportunity is lost; **die – skoon sien om . . . ,** see an opening (opportunity) to . . .
kansel, (-s), pulpit; **voor die – verskyn,** appear before the altar.
kanselary, (-e), chancery, chancellery.
kanselier, (-s), chancellor.
kanselrede, (pulpit-)oration, sermon.
kanselredenaar, pulpit-orator.
kanselstyl, -taal, pulpit-style.
kanselwelsprekendheid, pulpit-oratory.
kansrekening, theory of chances.
kansspel, game of chance (hazard).
kant, (-e), n. lace; **onegte –,** imitation-lace.
kant, (-e), n. side, border, edge, margin; direction, way; bank (of river); **daardie – van die saak,** that aspect of the matter; **elke saak het twee –e,** there are two sides to every question; **aan – (maak),** tidy; **aan die ander –,** on the other hand (side); **aan die een –,** on the one hand; **aan die klein –,** on the small side; **langs die –,** along the edge (border, side); **na die – swem,** swim ashore; **na daardie –,** in that direction; **na alle –e,** in all directions; **op sy – sit,** cant, tilt; **van alle –e,** on all sides, right and left; **ek, van my –,** I, for one; I, on my part; **van – maak,** do (make) away with; **– kies,** choose sides; **na die ou – toe,** well on in years.
kant – en klaar, quite ready, shipshape; **– en wal,** full to overflowing.
kant, (ge-): sig – teen, oppose.
kantate, (-s), cantata.
kantekleer, chanticleer, cock.
kantel, (ge-), topple over, capsize; tilt, tip.
kantgare, -garing, lace-thread.
kantien, (-e), canteen.
kantienhouer, (-s), canteen-owner.
kantig, (-e), angular, sharp-edged.
kantjie, (-s), edge, margin; **dit was op die – (af),** it was a close shave (a near thing).
kantlyn, marginal line; margin; **'n – trek,** rule a margin.
kanto, (-'s), canto.
kanton, (-s), canton.

kantonnement, (-e), cantonment.
kantoor, (-tore), office; aan die regte -, at the right address.
kantoorbehoeftes, stationery.
kantoorjonge, office-boy.
kantoorkruk, office-stool.
kantoorsaak, lawsuit.
kantoortyd, -ure, office-hours, business-hours.
kantoorwerker, white-collar worker.
kanttekening, marginal note, gloss.
kantwerk, lace(-work).
kantwerk(st)er, lace-worker, lace-maker.
kanunnik, (-e), canon.
kaoetsjoek, caoutchouc.
kaolien, kaolin, china-clay.
kap, (-pe), n. hood (of cart); cowl (of monk); shade (of lamp); cut (of axe); pawing (of horse); cowl (of chimney).
kap, (ge-), fell, cut down, chop; mince (meat); chip (in golf); chop (a ball in tennis); paw, hit out.
kapabel, (-e), able (to), capable (of).
kaparrang, (-s), wooden sandal, sabot.
kapasiteit, (-e), capacity, ability.
kapater, (-s), n. castrated goat, kapater.
kapater, (ge-), castrate.
kapblok, chopping-block.
kapel, (-le), 1. chapel.
kapel, (-le), 2. butterfly.
kapel, (-le), 3. cobra; geel, bruin —, Cape cobra.
kapel, (-le), 4. band, orchestra.
kapelaan, (-s, -lane), chaplain.
kapelmeester, bandmaster.
Kapenaar, (-s, -nare), Capetonian; inhabitant of Cape Colony (Western Province).
kaper, (-s), privateer, freebooter, raider.
kaphou, chop(-stroke) (tennis), chip (golf).
kapillêr, (-e), capillary.
kapitaal, (-tale), n. capital, principal.
kapitaal, (-tale), a. capital, excellent.
kapitaalheffing, capital-levy, levy on capital.
kapitaalkragtig, (-e), moneyed, rich.
kapitaalrekening, capital account.
kapitaaluitgawe, capital expenditure.
kapitalis, (-te), capitalist.
kapitaliseer, (ge-), capitalize; realize.
kapitalisme, capitalism.
kapitalisties, (-e), capitalist(ic).
kapiteel, (-tele), capital, head (of column).
kapitool, capitol.
kapittel, (-s), n. chapter.
kapittel, (ge-), read a lecture, take to task.
kapitelkerk, minster.
kapituleer, (ge-), capitulate.
kapkar, hooded cart.
kapmes, chopper, chopping-knife, bill-hook.
kapok, n. kapok, seed-cotton; snow.
kapok, (ge-), snow.
kapokboom, kapok-tree.
kapokhaantjie, bantam-cock; little spitfire.
kapokhoender, bantam(-fowl).
kapokkussing, kapok-cushion (-pillow).
kapokvoëltjie, Cape (penduline) tit.
kapot, broken, (gone) to pieces; done for, knocked up; in rags; out of order, gone smash.
kapper, (-s), hairdresser, barber.
kappertjie, (-s), orchid; nasturtium.
kappie, (-s), (sun-)bonnet; circumflex.
kapriol, (-le), caper; —le maak, cut capers.
kaprisieus, (-e), capricious.
kapsaag, tenon-saw.
kapsel, (-s), coiffure, hair-dress, headdress.

kapsie, (-s), -(s) maak, raise objections.
kapstewel, top-boot.
kapstok, hat-rack, hallstand.
kapsule, (-s), capsule.
kaptafel, dressing-table, toilet-table.
kaptein, (-s), captain; chief.
kapteinsrang, rank of captain.
kapteinsvrou, captain's wife; chief's wife.
Kapusyner, (-s), Capuchin, Franciscan.
kapwa, hooded wagon.
kar, (-re), cart; car (motor).
karaat, (-rate), carat.
karait, krait.
karabyn, (-e), carbine.
karaf, vide kraffie.
Karakoel(skaap), Karakul.
karakter, (-s), character; role (rôle).
karaktereienskap characteristic.
karakteriseer, (ge-), characterize.
karakterisering, (-e, -s), characterization.
karakteristiek, (-e), n. characterization, delineation; characteristic.
karakteristiek, (-e), a. characteristic.
karakterloos, (-lose), characterless; unprincipled.
karakterloosheid, characterlessness, lack of character; depravity.
karakterontleding, analysis of character.
karakterontwikkeling, development of character.
karakterskets, character-sketch.
karakterskildering, -tekening, characterization.
karaktertrek, characteristic, trait.
karakteruitbeelding, vide karakterskildering.
karaktervastheid, strength of character.
karaktervorming, character-building.
karamel, (-s), caramel, burnt sugar.
karavaan, (-vane), caravan.
karba, (-'s), carboy, demijohn, wicker bottle.
karbied, carbide.
karbol, carbol, carbolic (acid), phenol.
karboliseer, (ge-), carbolize.
karbololie, carbolic oil.
karbolsuur, carbolic acid, phenol.
karbonaat, carbonate.
karbonkel, (-s), carbuncle; garnet.
karburateur, (-s), carburettor.
kardinaal, (-nale), n. cardinal.
kardinaal, (-nale), a. cardinal, chief, vital.
kardoes, (-e), paper-bag, paper-cornet.
karee(boom), karee-(tree).
karet, (-te), 1. tailboard; luggage-carrier.
karet, (-te), 2. tortoise-shell.
kargadoor, (-s), shipbroker.
kariatide, (-s), caryatide.
kariboe, (-s), cariboo, caribou.
karie, krie, k(a)rie, mead, honey-beer.
kariemoer, k(a)rie-yeast.
karig, (-e), scanty, meagre, slender, frugal.
karigheid, scantiness, meagreness, frugality.
karikatuur, (-ture), caricature.
karikatuuragtig, (-e), caricaturish, exaggerated.
karikatuurtekenaar, caricaturist, cartoonist.
karikatuurtekening, caricature(-picture), cartoon.
kariljon, (-s), carrillon, chimes.
karkap, cart-tent (-hood).
karkas, (-se), carcass; skeleton.
karkatjie, (-s), sty(e), hordeolum.
karkiet, (-e), reed-bird, reed-warbler.
karkis, cart-box, box-seat.
karkoer, (-e), bitter melon, wild coloquint.
karmaker, cart-builder.
karmenaadjie, (-s), chop, cutlet.
karmosyn, crimson.

**karmosynbos, vegetable-kermes.
karmyn, carmine.
karnallie, vide ka(r)nallie.
karnaval, (-s), carnival.
karnivoor, (-vore), carnivore (pl. carnivora).
karnuffel, (ge-), cuddle, hug; bully.
Karoo, Karoo.
Karooveld, Karoo-veld.
karos, (-se), 1. kaross, skin-rug.
karos, (-se), 2. state-carriage, coach.
karper, (-s), carp.
karperd, cart-horse, dray-horse.
karpet, (-te), carpet.
karretjie, little cart, trap, gig.
karring, (-s), n. churn.
karring, (ge-), churn; aan iemand –, pester someone.
karringmelk, buttermilk.
karringsel, churning.
karspoor, cart-rut.
kartel, (-le), n. cartel, trust.
kartel, (-s), n. notch; wave, curl.
kartel, (ge-), notch; wave (hair); mill (coins).
kartelig, (-e), notched; wavy; milled.
karteling, (-e, -s), notch; wave; milling.
kartelrand, milling, milled edge.
kartets, (-e), grape-shot, canister-shot.
kartetsvuur, grape-shot fire.
kartografie, cartography.
karton, cardboard, pasteboard.
kartonneer, (ge-), board, put in boards.
kartonplank, hardboard.
kartonwerk, cardboard-work, (-modelling).
karvrag, cart-load.
karwats, (-e), n. riding-whip, hunting-crop.
karwats, (ge-), horsewhip.
karwei, n. job, piece of work.
karwei, (ge-), ride transport, convey (goods).
karweier, (-s), transport-rider; cartage contractor.
karweitjie, (-s), odd job.
karwy(saad), caraway(-seed).
kas, (-te), n. wardrobe; bookcase; cabinet, cupboard; case; cash; exchequer; box, chest; goed by – wees, in cash (in funds).
kas, (ge-), deposit (money).
kasarm, kasarring, (-s), barracks; die hele –, the ragtag and bobtail, the whole caboodle.
kasboek, cash-book.
kaserne, (-s), barracks.
kasjmier, cashmere.
kaskade, (-s), cascade.
kaskenade, (-s), prank, trick; to-do, uproar.
Kaspies, (-e): die –e See, the Caspian (Sea).
kasplant, hothouse-plant.
kasregister, cash-register, cash-till.
kasrekening, cash-account.
kassaldo, cash-balance.
kassawe, cassava.
kassier, (-s), cashier; banker.
kastaiing, (-s), chestnut; wilde –, horse chestnut; die –s uit die vuur haal (krap), pull the chestnuts out of the fire.
kastaiing- kastanjebruin, chestnut, auburn.
kaste, (-s), caste.
kasteel, (-tele), castle; citadel; rook (in chess).
kastegees, spirit of caste, caste-feeling.
kastekort, deficit.
kastelein, (-s), innkeeper, publican, landlord.
kastemaker, cabinet-maker.
kasterolie, castor-oil.
kastevooroordeel, class-prejudice.
kastig, quasi, as if (it were); vide kamma.
kastigeer, (ge-), castigate; expurgate.**

**Kastiliaans, (-e), Castilian.
kastreer, (ge-), castrate, geld; expurgate.
kastrol, (-le), stew-pan, saucepan, casserole.
kasty, (ge-), chastise, punish; chasten.
kastyder, (-s), chastiser, castigator.
kastyding, (-e, -s), chastisement; chastening.
kasuaris, (-se), cassowary.
kasueel, (-ele), casual, accidental.
kat, (-te), cat; 'n regte –, a regular cat; – en muis speel, play cat and mouse; as die – weg is, is die muis baas, when the cat's away the mice will play; soos – en hond lewe lead a cat-and-dog life; die – die bel aanbind, bell the cat; 'n – in die sak koop, buy a pig in a poke; die – in die donker knyp, do things on the sly; die – uit die boom kyk, wait to see which way the cat is going to jump; so nat soos 'n –, drenched to the skin.
katafalk, (-e), catafalque.
katagtig, (-e), catlike, feline.
katakombe, (-s), catacomb.
katalekties, (-e), catalectic.
katalepties, (-e), cataleptic.
katalogiseer, (ge-), catalogue.
katalogus, (-se), catalogue.
katapult, (-e), catapult.
katar, catarrh.
katarak, (-te), cataract.
katarraal, (-ale), catarrhal.
katastrofe, (-s), catastrophe.
katastrofies, (-e), catastrophic.
katderm, cat-gut.
katdoring, cat-thorn, wild asparagus.
kateder, (-s), cathedra; chair; desk.
katedraal. (-drale), cathedral (church).
kategismus, catechism.
kategorie, (-ë), category.
kategories, (-e), categorical.
katel, (-s), bedstead.
kater, (-s), tom-cat.
kateter, (-s), catheder, bougie.
katjang(boontjie), katjang-bean; monkey-nut.
katjie, (-s), kitten; vide kaatjie.
katjiepiering, (-s), gardenia.
katkisant, (-e), candidate for confirmation, catechumen.
katkisasie, catechism, confirmation(-class).
katkisasieboek, catechism(-book).
katkisasieklas, confirmation-class.
katkiseer, (ge-), catechize, give confirmation-classes; lecture, rebuke.
katkiseermeester, catechist.
katlagter, (-s), Cape ground-robin; maxim.
katode, (-s), cathode.
katoen, cotton.
katoenafval, cotton-waste.
katoenbou, cotton-growing.
katoenfabriek, cotton-factory (-mill).
katoenhandel, cotton-trade.
katoenindrustrie, cotton-industry.
katoennywerheid, cotton-industry.
katoenoes, cotton-crop (-harvest).
katoenpit, cotton-seed.
katoenplantasie, cotton-plantation.
katoenplanter, cotton-grower (-planter).
katoensaad, cotton-seed.
katoenspinnery, cotton-mill.
katoenwewery, cotton-mill.
katoliek, (-e), catholic; universal.
Katoliek, (-e), n. & a. (Roman) Catholic.
Katolisisme, (Roman) Catholicism.
katolisiteit, catholicity, universality.
katoog, cat's eye; sunstone; periwinkle.
katools, on heat, ruttish, lecherous.**

katrol   140   **kensketsend**

katrol, (-le), pulley.
kats, (-e), n. cat(-o'-nine-tails).
kats, (ge-), cat, thrash with the cat.
katstert, willow-herb, cat's tail; wild asparagus.
katswink, dazed, unconscious, in a swoon.
kattebak, dickey.
kattekruie, cat-mint.
kattekwaad, mischief, mischievous tricks, pranks.
kattemusiek, caterwauling.
katterig, (-e), cattish; chippy, seedy.
katuil, wood-owl, screech-owl.
katvel, cat-skin.
Kaukasies, (-e), Caucasian.
kavalier, (-s), cavalier.
kavalkade, (-s), cavalcade.
kavallerie, cavalry, horse.
kavalleris, (-te), cavalryman.
kaviaar, caviar(e).
keel, (kele), n. throat, gullet; gorge; gules (her.); **'n – opsit**, set up a cry; **die – smeer**, wet one's whistle; **alles deur die – jaag**, pour everything down the throat; **iemand na die – vlie**, fly at a person's throat; **sy eie – afsny**, cut one's own throat; **in die – bly steek**, stick in the throat; **iemand se – toedruk**, strangle someone.
keël, vide **kegel**.
keelaandoening, (-e, -s), affection of the throat.
keelaar, jugular vein.
keelgat, gullet; **in die verkeerde – kom**, go down the wrong way.
keelgeluid, guttural (sound).
keelholte, pharynx.
keelklank, guttural (sound).
keelklep(pie), epiglottis, throat-flap.
keelknop, Adam's apple.
keelkop, larynx.
keelontsteking, inflammation of the throat.
keelpyn, sore throat.
keelseer, sore throat.
keelspieël, laryngoscope.
keelvel, dewlap (cattle).
keep, (kepe), n. notch, nick; tally.
keep, (ge-), notch, nick, indent.
keer, (kere), n. change, turn; time; **'n enkele –**, once; **'n paar –**, once or twice; **op 'n –**, once, one day; **– op –**, time after time; **per –**, a time; **te – (kere) gaan**, take on, storm (rage).
keer, (ge-), turn, turn round; shrink back; prevent, stop; defend; oppose; turn back (the sheep); check (the enemy); stem (the flood); retire (shrink) into oneself; **– voor!**, stop him!; **per kerende pos**, by return (of post); **dit is nie te – nie**, it cannot be stopped (prevented).
keerdam, barrage, weir.
keerkring, tropic.
keerpunt, turning-point, crisis; apsis.
keersy, reverse; other side; back.
keertjie: **'n enkele –**, once in a blue moon.
keerwerk, defence, tackling.
kees, (kese), baboon; **dis klaar met –**, he is finished (done for), that's the end of him.
keeshond, keeshond.
kef, (ge-), yap, yelp, bark; squabble.
keffer(tjie), (-s), yapper; boaster; wrangler.
kegel, keël, (-s), n. cone; icicle; skittle.
kegel, keël, (ge-), play at skittles (ninepins).
kegel-, keëldeursnee, cone-section.
kegel-, keëlrat, conical (bevel-gear) wheel.
kegel-, keëlsnee, conic (section).
kegel-, keëlvlak, conical surface.
kegel-, keëlvormig, (-e), conical, cone-shaped.
keil, (-e), n. wedge; top-hat.
keil, (ge-), fling, pitch, shy; drive in a wedge.
keilskrif, cuneiform-writing (-characters).

keiser, (-s), emperor; **hy dink hy is die – (koning) se hond**, he thinks he is just it.
keiserin, (-ne), empress.
keiserin-weduwee, dowager-empress.
Keiserlik, (-e), Imperial.
keiserryk, empire.
keiserskroon, imperial crown; red crassula.
keiserstad, imperial city.
ke(r)jakker, (ge-), romp, gad about.
kekkel, (ge-), cackle; chatter, gabble, yap.
kekkel(a)ry, cackle, chit-chat, tittle-tattle.
kekkelbek, chatter-box, gossip.
kekkelpraatjies, chit-chat, gossip.
kelder, (-s), n. cellar.
kelder, (ge-), cellar, lay (store) up (in a cellar); slump, tumble, go down.
keldergat, air-, vent-hole.
kelderluik, cellar-flap, trapdoor.
kelderruimte, cellarage.
kelderverdieping, basement.
kelderwoning, basement(-house, -flat).
kelk, (-e), cup, chalice; calyx (of flower).
kelkblom, calyx.
kelkie, (-s), wineglass; moonflower.
kelkiewyn, (-e), (Namaqua) sandgrouse.
kelkvormig, (-e), cup-shaped, calyx-like.
kelner, (-s), waiter, steward.
Kelt, (-e), Celt.
Kelties, (-e), Celtic, Gaelic.
kemphaan, fighting-, game-cock.
ken, **kin**, (-ne), n. chin.
ken, (ge-), know, be acquainted with, recognise; **– u mekaar?**, have you met?; **iemand nie wil – nie**, give someone the cold shoulder, cut someone; **jou laat – as**, prove yourself a . . . ; **jou nie laat – nie**, not stand back; **te –ne gee**, give to understand; **'n wens te –ne gee**, express a wish; **iemand in iets –**, consult someone; **van buite – know by heart**; **uit mekaar –**, tell (them) apart.
kenbaar, (-bare), recognisable; **– maak**, make known.
kenketting, kinketting, curb(-chain).
kenlik, (-e), recognizable; visible, obvious.
kenmerk, (-e), n. distinguishing mark; characteristic (feature).
kenmerk, (ge-), mark, characterise.
kenmerkend, (-e), characteristic, distinctive; outstanding, salient.
kenner, (-s), connoisseur, judge, authority.
kennersblik, -oog, the eye of a connoisseur.
kennetjie, 1. little chin.
kennetjie, 2. tip-cat (game).
kennis, knowledge; acquaintance(ship); consciousness; **weer – aanknoop**, renew acquaintance; **– dra (hê) van**, have knowledge of; **– gee**, announce, notify; **– kry**, receive notice; **–se kry**, make acquaintances; **– maak met iemand**, meet someone; **met iets – maak**, learn (come across) a thing; **met die polisie – maak**, run foul of the police; **– neem van**, take cognisance (note) of; **by –**, conscious; **buite – wees**, be unconscious; **met iemand in – stel**, introduce to someone; **met – van sake**, with full knowledge of the facts, with authority; **ter – bring van**, bring to the notice of; **nader – maak**, improve one's acquaintance.
kennisgewing, (-e, -s), notice, announcement; **vir – aanneem**, note.
kennismaking, (-e, -s), (making) acquaintance, meeting; **by nadere –**, on closer acquaintance.
kennisneming, (-e, -s), (taking) cognizance; inspection; **ter –**, for information.
kenskets, (ge-), mark, characterize.
kensketsend, (-e), characteristic.

kenspreuk, motto.
kensyfer, index number.
kenta(g), kentang, afraid (to play), funky.
kenteken, n. distinctive mark, characteristic, token, badge; symptom.
kenteken, (ge-), characterize.
kenter, (ge-), turn.
kentering, (-e, -s), change, turn; transition.
kenwysie, signature tune.
keper, twill; **op die – beskou**, on close inspection.
keperstof, twill.
kepie, (-s), notch, etc. Vide **keep**, n.
keramiek, ceramics, ceramic art, potter's art.
kêrel, (-s), chap, fellow; boy, young man, lover; fiancé; **'n gawe –**, a fine fellow.
kerende, vide **keer, (ge-)**.
kerf, (kerwe), n. nick, notch, jag, incision; **bo sy –**, above his power, beyond him.
kerf, kerwe, (ge-), carve, notch, slash; cut (tobacco); slice.
kerfblok, cutting-, carving-block.
kerfie, (-s), little notch.
kerfstok, tally(-stick), nickstick; **baie op sy – hê**, have much to answer for.
ke(r)jakker, vide **kejakker**.
kerk, (-e), n. church; service; congregation; **sy – is uit**, he is finished.
kerk, (ge-), solemnize a marriage in church.
kerkbank, pew.
kerkbesoek, church-attendance.
kerkbus, poor-box (in church).
kerkdiens, divine service.
kerker, (-s), n. jail (gaol), prison, dungeon.
kerker, (ge-), imprison, incarcerate.
kerkfees, church-festival.
kerkgang, church-going, going to church.
kerkganger, (-s), church-goer, worshipper.
kerkgebou, church(-building); chapel.
kerkgenootskap, denomination, sect.
kerkgeskiedenis, ecclesiastical history.
kerkgoed, church-property.
kerkhervorming, reformation.
kerkhof, churchyard, cemetery, graveyard.
kerkklok, church-bell; church-clock.
kerkleer, church-doctrine.
kerklik, (-e), ecclesiastical, church- . . .
kerkmuis, churchmouse; **so arm soos 'n –**, as poor as a churchmouse.
kerkmusiek, church-music, sacred music.
kerkorrel, church-organ.
kerkpak, Sunday-suit.
kerkraad, church-council, consistory.
kerkraadslid, member of the consistory.
kerkreg, ecclesiastical law, church-law.
kerkregister, church-register.
kerkregtelik, (-e), according to church law.
kerks, (-e), churchy; devout, pious.
kerksaak, church-affair; church-trial.
kerksak, collection- (offertory-)bag.
kerkgesind, (-e), churchy; devout, pious.
kerksheid, churchiness; attachment to the church.
kerkskool, church-school.
kerktoring, church-tower; steeple.
kerktyd, time for church; service(-hours).
kerkvader, father of the church; church father, patriarch; **van die –s**, patristic.
kerkvergadering, church-meeting; synod; convocation.
kerkvoog, churchwarden; prelate.
kerkwaarts, churchward(s).
kerm, (ge-), groan, lament, moan, whine.
kermis, (-se), fair; **dit is nie elke dag – nie**, it is not all beer and skittles.
kermisbed, shakedown, made-up bed.

kermistent, (fair-)booth.
kern, (-s), kernel, pith, heart; nucleus (of a comet); gist, root (of a matter); **'n – van waarheid**, a grain of truth.
kernafval, atomic waste.
kernagtig, (-e), pithy, terse.
kernenergie, nuclear energy.
kernenergiesuil, reactor.
kerngesond, (-e), healthy to the core, hale and hearty; (fundamentally) sound.
kernkrag, nuclear power.
kernkragduikboot, nuclear-powered submarine.
kernneerslag, atomic fall-out.
kernreaktor, nuclear reactor.
kernsplyting, nuclear fission.
kernwapen, nuclear weapon.
kerrie, curry.
kerriekos, curry-dish, curried food.
kerriekruie, curry.
kerrierys, curry and rice.
kerrieso(e)p, mulligatawny, curry-soup.
kerrievis, curried fish.
kers, (-e), n. candle.
kers, (-e), n. cherry; vide **kersie**.
Kers, Christmas.
Kersaand, Oukersaand, Christmas Eve.
Kersboom, Christmas-tree.
kersbos, candlebush.
Kersdag, Christmas (Day); **eerste –**, Christmas Day; **tweede –**, Boxing Day.
kerse, vide **kersie-**.
kers(e)fabriek, candle-factory.
Kersfees, Christmas.
Kersgeskenk, Christmas-present, Christmas-box.
kershout, candlewood.
kersie, (-s), little candle; cherry.
kersie-, kerseboom, cherry-tree.
kersiepit, cherry-stone.
Kerslied, Christmas-carol.
kerslig, candlelight; **by –**, by candlelight.
Kersmis, Christmas.
Kersmisroos, Christmas-rose.
Kersmistyd, Christmas(-time).
Kersmisvakansie, Christmas-holidays.
Kersnag, Christmas Eve.
kersogie, white-eye; bush-warbler.
kerspit, candle-wick.
kerssterkte, candle-power.
kersten, (ge-), christianize.
Kerstyd, Christmas(-time).
Kersvakansie, Christmas-holidays.
kersvers, fresh, quite new, piping (red) hot.
kersvet, candle-grease, tallow.
kerwel, (-s), chervil; **dol(le) –**, (spotted) hemlock; **Kaapse –**, black jacks.
kerwer, (-s), carver; (tobacco-)cutter.
kês, boiled sour milk, lopperd (milk).
kesie-, kiesieblaar, mallow(s).
kêskuiken, (mere) chicken, child, youngster.
ketel, (-s), kettle; cauldron; boiler; **die pot verwyt die – dat dit swart is**, the pot calls the kettle black.
ketelbuis, boiler-tube.
ketellapper, tinker.
ketelmaker, boilermaker.
ketelmusiek, rough music, tin-kettling.
keteltrom, kettledrum; timpano.
keteltromslaner, kettledrummer.
keteltuit, kettle-spout.
ketelvormig, (-e), basin-shaped.
ketter, (-s), n. heretic.
ketter, (ge-), rage, storm; expound heresies.
ketterjaer, (-s), heretic-hunter, heresy-hunter.
ketterjag, heretic-hunt(ing), heresy-hunt(ing).
ketters, (-e), heretical.

kettery, (-e), heresy.
ketting, (-s), chain; –s, chains, bonds, fetters (of slavery); **in –s slaan**, put in(to) chains; **aan die –**, on the chain, chained up.
kettingbreuk, continued fraction.
kettingbrug, suspension-bridge.
kettingganger, (-s), chained convict.
kettinghandel, intermediary trade.
kettinghandelaar, intermediary, middleman.
kettingkas, gear-case (-box), chain-cover.
kettingkoeël, chain-shot, angel-shot.
kettingloos, (-lose), chainless.
kettingoorbringing, chain-drive.
kettingrat, chain-wheel.
kettingreaksie, chain reaction.
kettingsleep, (kettingge-), do (assist at) land-surveying.
kettingsluitrede, sorites, chain-syllogism.
kettingsteek, chain-stitch, lock-stitch.
kettingwiel, gear-wheel, chain-wheel.
kettinkie, (-s), chain(let).
keu, (-e, -s), (billiard-)cue.
keuken, (-s), kitchen; cuisine.
keukenmeester, head-cook, chef.
keur, (-e), n. choice, selection; pick, flower, hall-mark; charter; **te kus en te –**, in plenty.
keur, (ge-), try, test, inspect; assay (metals); taste, sample (wine, cigars); **iemand 'n blik waardig–**, deign to look at someone.
keurbende, picked men (troops).
keurboom, keurboom.
keurbundel, anthology, selected works.
keurder, (-s), inspector, assayer, taster.
keurig, (-e), exquisite, trim, dainty, natty; fine, choice.
keurigheid, exquisiteness, choiceness.
keuring, (-e, -s), examination, inspection, assaying, testing; tasting; vide **kleur**, (ge-).
keuringsdiens, food-inspection department.
keurkorps, picked body.
keurmerk, hallmark, stamp.
keurprins(es), electoral prince(ss).
keurslyf, bodice, corset, stays.
keurtjie, cancer-bush.
keurtroepe, picked troops.
keurvors, elector(al prince).
keus(e), choice, selection; option; **'n ruim (wye) –**, a large assortment (choice); **daar bly g'n ander – oor nie**, there is no alternative (choice, option); **vakke na –**, optional subjects; **uit vrye –**, by choice, of one's own free will; **voor die – stel**, give the choice, force to choose.
keuwel, (ge-), babble, prattle.
kewer, (-s), beetle.
kiaat(hout), teak(-wood); Cape teak.
kibbel, (ge-), bicker, squabble, wrangle.
kibbel(a)ry, squabble, wrangle, tiff.
kiek, (-e), n. snap(shot).
kiek, (ge-), snap, take a snap(shot).
kiektoestel, camera; kodak.
kiel, (-e), n. keel; valley (of roof); corner.
kiel (ge-), keel, careen, heave down.
kielhaal, (ge-), keelhaul.
kielhouer, pickaxe.
kielie, (ge-), tickle.
kieliebak, armpit.
kieliebeentjie, funnybone.
kielie-kielie, ketcher-kee!, tickle-tickle!
kielierig, (-e), ticklish.
kielwater, track, wake, dead water.
kiem, (-e), n. germ, embryo, seed, origin, **in die – dood (smoor)**, nip in the bud, stifle in its birth.
kiem, (ge-), germinate, sprout, shoot.
kiemdodend, (-e), germicidal, antiseptic.

kiemkrag, germinative power.
kiemkragtig, (-e), germinative, viable.
kiemsel, germ-cell.
kiemvry, (-e), germ-free, sterile, aseptic.
kiep!, shoo! (to fowls)
kiepersol(boom), umbrella-tree.
kiep-kiep, chick-chick!, chuck-chuck!
kierang, **kurang**, n. cheat(ing), deception; **dit is alles –**, it's all a cheat; **– sal braai**, you will be proved a cheat.
kierang, **kurang**, a. & adv. not fair, unfair; – **speel**, cheat, play false.
kierang, **kurang**, (ge-), cheat, play false.
kierie, (-s), kerrie, (knob-)stick.
kiertjie, chink; **op 'n – oop**, ajar.
kies, (-e, -te), n. 1. grinder; molar; cheek.
kies, n. 2. pyrites (mineral).
kies, (-e), a. delicate, considerate; nice.
kies, (ge-), choose, select; single (pick) out; elect; **tot voorsitter –**, elect chairman (to the chair); **sy woorde –**, pick one's words; **'n Volksraadslid –**, elect a member of Parliament; **niks te – hê nie**, have no option.
kiesafdeling, **-distrik- wyk**, constituency.
kiesbaar, (-bare), eligible.
kiesel, (-s), pebble; silicon.
kieselaarde, silica, siliceous earth.
kieser, (-s), constituent, voter, elector.
kieserslys, voter's roll, electoral list.
kiesheid, delicacy; considerateness.
kiesie-, **kesieblaar**, vide **kesieblaar**.
kieskeurig, (-e), fastidious, dainty, nice.
kieskeurigheid, fastidiousness, daintiness.
kiespyn, toothache.
kiesstelsel, electoral (election) system.
kiestand, molar(-tooth).
kieswet, election-law, ballot-act.
kiet(s), quits, even, equal.
kieu, (-e, **kuwe**), gill, branchia (pl.).
kieudeksel, gill-cover, gill-flap.
kieu-opening, **-spleet**, gill-slit (-cleft).
kiewiet, (-e), lapwing, plover, peewit.
kik, (-ke), n. sound; **nie 'n – gee nie**, not utter a sound; **g'n – nie**, mum's the word!
kik, (ge-), make a sound; **hy druf nie – of mik nie**, he daren't open his mouth.
kikker, (-s), frog.
kikkerland, frogland.
kikvors, (-e), frog.
kil, (-le), chilly, cold, shivery.
kilheid, chilliness.
kilo, (-'s), kilogram, (-me), kilogram(me).
kiloliter, kilolitre.
kilometer, kilometre.
kilowatt, kilowatt.
kim, (-me), n. 1. horizon; **aan die – verskyn**, appear above the horizon.
kim, n. 2. mould.
kim, (ge-), get (become) mouldy.
kimono, (-'s), kimono.
kin, **ken**, vide **ken**, n.
kina, quinine.
kinabas, cinchona-, Peruvian bark.
kinaboom, cinchona (-tree).
kinapil, quinine-pill (-tablet).
kin-, **kenband**, chin-strap.
kind, (-ers), child kid(dy); baby, babe, infant; **–ers bly – ers**, children will be children; **wie sy – liefhet**, **kasty hom**, spare the rod and spoil the child, **'n – des doods**, a dead man; **jy is 'n – by hom**, you cannot hold a candle to him; **g'n – of kraai hê nie**, have neither kith nor kin; **die – by sy naam noem**, call a spade a spade; **hy is nie meer 'n – nie**, he is no chicken; **nie**

vandag se – nie, an old fox (sly dog); 'n – van sy tyd, a product of the times.
kindeke: die – Jesus, the Infant Jesus.
kinderagtig, (-e), childish, puerile, silly.
kinderagtigheid, childishness, puerility.
kinderarbeid, child-labour.
kinderarts, children's specialist.
kinderbeskerming, child-welfare.
kinderbewaarplaas, creche, day nursery.
kinderboek, children's book; nursery-book.
kinderbybel, children's Bible.
kinderdief, child-stealer, kidnapper.
kinderdokter, children's specialist.
kinderfees, children's festival (party).
kindergees, child-mind.
kindergek, lover of children.
kindergoed, children's wear; baby-clothes.
kinderhart, heart of a child.
kinderjare, (years of) childhood, infancy.
kinderjuffrou, nursery-governess, mother's help.
kinderkamer, nursery.
kinderkerk, children's service.
kinderkleertjies, baby-clothes.
kinderkoor, juvenile choir.
kinderkwaal, children's ailment.
kinderleed, childish grief.
kinderlektuur, juvenile literature.
kinderlewe, child-life; childhood.
kinderliefde, love of (one's) children; filial love (affection).
kinderlik, (-e), childlike, filial, innocent.
kinderlikheid, childlike nature, artlessness.
kinderloos, (-lose), childless.
kindermaniere, childish manners.
kindermeel, infant's food.
kindermeid, nursemaid; (coloured) nurse-girl.
kindermeisie, nurse-maid (-girl).
kindermoord, child-murder, infanticide.
kinderplig, filial duty.
kinderpokkies, smallpox, variola.
kinderpraatjies, childish prattle.
kinderpreek, sermon for children.
kinderrym(pie), nursery-rhyme.
kinderroof, child-stealing, kidnapping.
kindersiekte, disease for children.
kinderskoen, child's shoe; die -e ontwas(se) wees, be a child no longer.
kindersorg, baby-care; child-welfare.
kinderspeelgoed, (children's) toys.
kinderspel(etjies), children's game, child's play; dit is g'n – nie, it is no child's play.
kindersprokie, nursery-tale.
kindersterfte, infantile mortality.
kinderstorie, children's tale, nursery tale.
kinderstudie, child-study.
kindertehuis, children's home.
kindertuin, kindergarten; children's garden.
kinderverlamming, infantile paralysis.
kindervers(ie), nursery-rhyme.
kindervriend, friend (lover) of children.
kinderwa(entjie), perambulator.
kinderwagter, baby-sitter.
kinderwelvaart, child-welfare.
kinderwêreld, child-world, child-land.
kinderwerk, child's (children's) work.
kindjie, (kindertjies), babe, infant; kid(dy); little child; dear, darling.
kindlief, dear, darling, child, deary.
kinds, (-e), childish, doting, senile.
kindsbeen: van – af, from childhood.
kindsdeel, -gedeelte, child's portion.
kindsheid, dotage, childishness; childhood.
kinema, (-s), cinema (kinema).
kinematies, (-e), cinematic (kinematic).
kinematograaf, (-grawe), cinematograph.

kineties, (-e), kinetic.
kinetika, kinetics.
kinien, quinine; vide kina.
kink, (-e), n. kink, hitch; knot; daar is 'n – in die kabel, there is a hitch somewhere.
kink, (ge-), turn, twist.
kinkel, (-s), vide kink, n.
kin-, kenketting, curb(-chain).
kinkhoes, (w)hooping-cough.
kinnebak, jaw(bone), mandible.
kiosk, (-e), kiosk.
kir, (ge-), coo.
kis, (-te), n. box, case; chest; coffin (for corpse); coffer (for valuables); kist (antique furniture).
kis, (ge-), (place in a) coffin.
kisklere, best clothes, Sunday-best.
kistemaker, box-maker; coffin-maker.
kitaar, ghitaar, (-are, -s), guitar.
kits: in 'n – , in a moment (jiffy).
kittelorig, (-e), touchy, short-tempered.
kittelorigheid, touchiness.
kiwi, (-'s), kiwi.
kla(e), klaag, (ge-), complain; grumble, lament, wail; dit is God ge–, it cries to Heaven; sy nood by iemand –, pour out one's troubles to someone; steen en been –, complain bitterly (loudly).
klaaglied, (song of) lamentation; elegy; K–ere, Lamentations (of Jeremiah); ou K–ere, querulous fellow.
klaaglik, (-e), doleful, plaintive.
Klaagmuur, Wailing wall.
klaagpsalm, penitential psalm.
klaagstem, -toon, plaintive voice (tone).
klaar, (klare), ready, finished; clear, limpid; evident; dis – met hom, met Kees, vide kees; gou – met 'n antwoord, prompt at an answer, quick at repartee; so – as die dag, as clear as daylight; –e onsin, sheer nonsense; – wakker, wide awake; – hê, have ready; – hou, keep ready (at hand); – lê, put ready, lay out; lie ready (waiting); – maak, get ready, prepare; dress; cook; make up; – sit, set out, put ready; – sit (staan) vir iemand, be ready; be at somebody's beck and call.
klaarblyklik, (-e), evident, clear; dit is – 'n fout, this is obviously a mistake.
klaarblyklikheid, obviousness, patency.
klaarheid, clearness, clarity; tot – bring, clear up; tot – kom, get to the bottom of.
klaarkom, (klaarge-), get (be) done; manage.
klaarkry, (klaarge-), get ready (done), finish.
klaarligte: dit is – dag, it is broad day.
klaarpraat, done, finished; dit is – met hom, he is finished, he is knocked up.
klaarsiende, clear-sighted, shrewd.
klaarspeel, (klaarge-), manage, bring (pull) it off, fix it up, do the trick.
Klaas Vaak, Klaas Vakie, Willie Winkie, sandman.
klad, (-de), n. blot, stain; blotch, rough draft; 'n – op iemand se eer werp, cast aspersions on a person's honour.
klad, (ge-), blot, stain; daub; scrawl.
kladboek, waste-book; scribbling-book.
kladnotule, draft-minutes.
kladpapier, blotting-paper, scribbling-paper.
kladwerk, rough copy, daub.
kla(e), vide klaag.
klaend, (-e), plaintive; complaining.
klaer, (-s), complainant; plaintiff (law).
klaerig, (-e), ill; peevish; seedy.
klag, (-te), klagte (-s), complaint; lamentation; accusation, charge.
klagteboek, complaint-book.

klakkeloos, (-lose), a. & adv., groundless; offhand, without more ado.
klam, (-me), clammy, damp, moist.
klammerig, (-e), a bit clammy (damp, moist).
klamp, (-e), clamp, cleat, bracket.
klamp, (ge-), clamp, cleat.
klandisie, custom, customers; patronage.
klank, (-e), n. sound, ring, tone; **ydel -e,** idle words; **hol(le) -e,** empty sounds.
klank, (ge-), sound, articulate, phone.
klankarm, tone-arm.
klankbord, sound(ing)-board.
klankdemper, silencer; sordine, damper; mute.
klankfilm, sound-film.
klankgrens, sound barrier.
klankkleur, timbre.
klankleer, phonetics.
klankloos, (-lose), toneless; silent.
klankmetode, phon(et)ic method.
klanknabootsend, (-e), onomatopoetic.
klanknabootsing, onomatopoeia, sound-imitation.
klankrolprent, sound-film.
klankryk, (-e), sonorous, full-sounding, rich.
klankrykheid, sonority, sonorousness.
klankstelsel, phonetic (sound) system.
klankverandering, sound-change.
klankverskuiwing, sound-shift(ing).
klankvol, (-le), vide **klankryk.**
klankvolume, volume of sound.
klankwet, sound-law, phonetic law.
klankwysiging, sound-change.
klant, (-e), customer, client; **'n ou -,** an old fox, a sly dog; vide **kalant & kliënt.**
klap, (-pe), n. slap, blow, smack, clout; lash, stroke, crack (of whip); **in een -,** at a (one) blow; **'n - in die gesig,** a slap in the face; **die - van die sweep ken,** know the ropes (the crack of the whip).
klap, (ge-), smack, clap; click (with the tongue); crack (with a whip); blab, tell tales; **hande -,** clap hands; **met die vingers -,** snap one's fingers; **uit die skool -,** blab, let the cat out of the bag.
klapbroek, flap-trousers.
klapdeur, flapdoor; swing-door.
klapklank, click, stop, explosive.
klapklapp(ertj)ie, Cape clapper-lark.
klaploop, (klapge-), sponge, cadge.
klaploper, sponger, cadger.
klapper, (-s), n. coconut.
klapper, (-s), n. tell-tale; index, register, cracker, stop, explosive (phonetics).
klapper, (ge-), rattle; flap; chatter (teeth).
klapperboom, coconut-tree (-palm).
klapperdop, coconut-shell; nut, numskull.
klapperhaar, coir.
klapperhaarmatras, coir-mattress.
klapperolie, coconut-oil.
klappertand, (ge-): hy het ge- van die kou, his teeth chattered with cold.
klapsoen, smack(ing) kiss.
klapstoel, folding-chair; flap-seat.
klaptafel, Pembroke table; folding-table.
klapwiek, (ge-), clap (flap) the wings.
klarigheid, readiness; **- maak,** prepare.
klarinet, (-te), clarinet.
klaroengeskal, clarion-call.
klas, (-se), class; form; grade; category.
klasboek, class-book.
klaskamer, classroom.
klasonderwyser, class-teacher.
klassehaat, class-hatred.
klassevooroordeel, class-prejudice.

klassiek, (-e), classic(al).
klassieke: die -, the classics.
klassifikasie, (-s), classification.
klassifiseer, (ge-), classify, sort.
klassikaal, (-kale), class (teaching); classical.
klassikus, (-se, -ici), classicist.
klassisisme, classicism.
klater, (ge-), rattle; splash.
klatergoud, tinsel.
klavier, (-e), piano(forte); vide **piano.**
klavierbegeleiding, piano-accompaniment.
klavierles, piano-lesson.
klavieronderwyser(es), piano-teacher.
klavierspeel, (klavierge-), play the piano.
klavierspel, piano-playing.
klavierstemmer, piano-tuner.
klavierstoel, piano-stool.
klawer, (-s), clover; **-s (pl.),** clubs (in cards).
klaweraas, ace of clubs.
klawerblad, clover-leaf, trefoil-leaf; trio.
klawerboer, knave (Jack) of clubs.
klawerheer, king of clubs.
klawersuring, wood-sorrel.
klawervrou, queen of clubs.
klaxon, klaxon.
kleding, clothes, dress, apparel.
kledingstuk, garment, article of dress.
klee(d), (ge-), dress, clothe; **dit - jou goed,** that suits you; **in mooi taal -,** express (couch) in beautiful language.
kleed, n. dress, garment; cover.
kleedgeld, dress-money, -allowance.
kleedjie, (-s), (table-)cloth, table-centre; saddle-cloth; rug; mat.
kleedkamer, dressing-room; cloakroom.
kleef, klewe, (ge-), cleave, cling, stick.
kleefpleister, adhesive (sticking-)plaster.
kleefstof, gluten.
kleermaker, vide **kleremaker.**
kleertjies, baby- (children's) clothes.
klei, clay.
kleiagtig, -erig, (-e), clayish, clayey.
kleigrond, clayey (loamy) soil (ground).
kleilat, clay-stick (in boy's games).
kleim, claim (mining).
kleimdief, claim-jumper.
klein, little, small; slight; petty; **- letter (druk),** small letter (print); **- treetjies,** short steps; **- en groot,** great and small; **- voel,** feel small; **van -s af,** from an early age (childhood, infancy); **die wêreld in die -,** the world on a small scale (in a nutshell); **daar is niks -s in hom nie,** there is nothing petty about him; **- begin, aanhou(er) win,** perseverance will be rewarded.
kleindogter, grand-daughter.
Klein Duimpie, Tom Thumb.
kleineer, (ge-), belittle, disparage, minimize.
kleingeestig, (-e), narrow-minded, petty.
kleingeestigheid, narrow-mindedness.
kleingeld, change; petty cash; **- van iemand maak,** make mincemeat of someone.
kleingelowig, (-e), lacking in faith.
kleingelowigheid, lack of faith.
kleingoed, kids, youngsters.
kleinhandel, retail-trade.
kleinhandelprys, retail-price.
kleinharsings, cerebellum.
kleinhartig, (-e), faint-hearted; petty.
kleinheid, smallness, littleness.
kleinhuisie, privy, W.C.
kleinigheid, (-hede), trifle, small thing.
kleinkind, grandchild.
kleinkinderskool, infant-school.

kleinkry, (kleinge-), master; understand.
kleinmaak, (kleinge-), change (money); break up; bring someone to his knees.
kleinmoedig, (-e), faint-hearted.
kleinneef, second cousin.
kleinood, (-ode), jewel, gem, treasure.
kleinpensie, reticulum.
kleinpinkie, little finger; vide **pink(ie)**.
kleinserig, (-e), easily hurt; touchy; – **wees**, be touchy; be a baby.
kleinserigheid, touchiness; babyishness.
kleinseun, grandson.
kleinsielig, (-e), petty, small-minded.
kleinsieligheid, pettiness.
kleinspan, vide **kleingoed**.
kleinste, smallest; slightest.
kleinsteeds, (-e), provincial, parochial.
kleinsteedsheid, provincialism, parochialism.
kleintjie, (-s), little one, baby; –**s**(pl.), youngsters; young (of animals); –**s kry**, bring forth young (animals).
kleintongetjie, uvula; **die** – **hang**, the palate is down.
kleinvee, small stock, sheep and goats.
kleinwild, small game.
kleiperd, clay-horse.
kleivloer, mud-floor.
kleiwerk, clay-modelling.
klem, (-me), n. accent, emphasis, stress; lockjaw; clamp, vice; **met** – (**van redes**), forcibly; **in die** – **kom** (**sit**), be in a fix; – **lê op iets**, stress something; – **in die kake(been)**, lockjaw.
klem, (ge-), pinch, jam (one's finger), clench (one's teeth), tighten, clamp; **aan die hart** –, clasp (press) to one's heart.
klemensie, clemency, mercy, indulgence.
klemmend, (-e), forcible, cogent.
klemteken, accent, stress-mark.
klemtoon, accent, stress; emphasis.
klep, (-pe), n. valve, flap (of bag); peak (of cap); damper (of fireplace); leaf (of gunsight).
klep, (ge-), clapper, clatter; clang, toll (of bell).
klepel, (-s), clapper, tongue.
klepkraan, valve cock.
klepligter, tappet.
kleploos, (-lose), valveless.
klepper, (-s), n. rattle; –**s** (pl.), clacks.
klepper, (ge-), rattle; chatter (teeth).
klepspeling, valve clearance.
klepsteel, valve stem.
klepstelling, valve adjustment.
klepstoter, valve tappet.
kleptomaan, (-mane), kleptomaniac.
kleptomanie, kleptomania.
klepvisier, leaf-sight.
klerasie, clothing, apparel, raiment.
klerasiewinkel, draper's (shop), drapery-store.
klere, clothes, garments; dresses; gowns; – **maak die man**, fine feathers make fine birds; **dit raak nie sy koue** – **nie**, that leaves him stone cold; **kinders in die** – **steek**, dress (clothe) children.
klereborsel, clothes-brush.
kleredrag, dress, clothing, fashion.
klerehaak, clothes-hook (-peg).
klerekas, wardrobe, clothes-press (-cupboard).
klerekoffer, (clothes-)trunk.
klerekoper, old-clothes man.
kleremaker, kleermaker, tailor.
klereprag, display of clothes, fine clothes.
klerewinkel, outfitter's shop.
klerikaal, (-kale), clerical.
klerk, (-e), clerk; –**e** (pl.), clerical staff.

klets, n. twaddle, piffle, tosh.
klets, (ge-), splash; talk rot.
kletser, (-s), twaddler, yapper.
kletsery, twaddle, talkee-talkee.
kletskous, chatterer, chatterbox.
kletsnat, wet through, soaking, soaked.
kletspraatjie(s), small talk, (idle) gossip.
kletter, (ge-), clash; pelt, clatter (rain).
kleur, (-e), n. colour; hue; complexion (of face); suit (of cards); – **beken**, follow suit (in card games); show one's colours; – **hou**, not fade; **'n** – **kry**, colour, flush; **van** – **verskiet**, change (lose) colour; **sy** –(**e**) **wys**, show his true colour(s).
kleur, (ge-), colour; dye; tone (phot.); flush, blush; **dit** – **daarby**, this colour matches that.
kleurblind, (-e), colour-blind, achromate.
kleurebeeld, spectrum.
kleuredruk, colour-printing.
kleureg, (-te), fadeless, fast-coloured.
kleuremengeling, blending of colours.
kleureprag, blaze (riot) of colour(s).
kleurerykdom, wealth of colour(s).
kleurespektrum, chromatic spectrum.
kleurespel, play of colours, iridescence.
kleurfikseerbad, toning and fixing bath.
kleurfilter, colour-filter.
kleurfotografie, colour-photography.
kleurgevoelig, (-e), orthochromatic.
kleurhoudend, (-e), fadeless.
kleurig, (-e), colourful, gay.
kleuring, coloration, colouring, pigmentation.
kleurkryt, coloured chalk.
kleurling, (-e), coloured person.
kleurloos, (-lose), colourless; drab (life).
kleurmenging, colour-blending.
kleurpotlood, colouring-pencil.
kleurryk, (-e), richly coloured, colourful.
kleursel, (-s), colouring; distemper.
kleurskakering, variation of colours, nuance.
kleurskema, colour-scheme.
kleurskifting, colour-dispersion; spectrum.
kleurslagboom, colour-bar.
kleurstof, colouring-matter, pigment, dye.
kleurvas, (-te), fadeless, fast-dyed.
kleuter, (-s), tot, toddler.
kleutertaal, baby-language.
klewerig, (-e), adhesive, sticky, gluey.
klewerigheid, adhesiveness, stickiness.
klief, **kliewe**, (ge-), cleave, split; plough, breast.
kliek, (-e), n. clique, coterie, set, party.
kliek, (ge-), form a clique.
kliekerig, (-e), cliquey.
kliekgees, cliquishness.
kliënt, (-e), client, customer.
klier, (-e), gland.
klik, (-ke), n. cleek (golf); click (with tongue).
klik, (ge-), tell tales, split; click (with tongue).
klikker, (-s), tell-tale; vide **klikspaan**.
klikklank, click.
klikspaan, (-spane), tell-tale, tale-bearer.
klim, n. climb; **'n harde** –, a stiff climb.
klim, (ge-), climb, ascend, mount; **die nood** –, the distress is increasing; **die son** –, the sun mounts; **in 'n boom** –, climb (up) a tree; **hy het ge**–, he rose (was promoted).
klimaat, climate.
klimaatgordel, zone.
klimaks, (-e), climax, culmination-point.
klimatologie, climatology.
klimatologies, (-e), climate, climatologic(al).
klimboontjie, runner-bean.
klimmend, (-e), ascending, increasing, rising
klimop, creeper, ivy, traveller's joy.

klimplant, climbing-plant, climber, creeper.
klimroos, rambler(-rose).
kling, (-e), blade, sword; **oor die – ja**, put to the sword.
klingel, (ge-), tinkle, jingle.
klingeling, (-e), ching-a-ling; jingling.
kliniek, (-e), clinic.
klinies, (-e), clinical.
klink, (-e), n. latch, catch.
klink, (ge-), sound; ring, clang, jingle; clink (glasses); clinch; rivet (bolts); nail; **vals –**, ring false; **vreemd in die ore –**, sound strange.
klinkbout, clinch-bolt, rivet, dowel.
klinkdig, (-te), sonnet.
klinkend, (-e), resonant, ringing, resounding; **–e munt**, hard cash.
klinker, (-s), vowel; clinker, hard brick.
klinkhamer, riveting-hammer, riveter.
klinkklaar, (-klare), pure; sheer; **–klare onsin**, sheer (downright, blatant) nonsense.
klink-klank, jingle(-jangle); mere words.
klinknael, rivet.
klinkslot, latch-lock.
klinometer, (-s), clinometer.
klip, (-pe, -pers), stone; pebble; rock; **stadig oor die –pe(rs)**, go slowly, mind your step; **slaap soos 'n –**, sleep like a top.
klipbaken, stone-beacon.
klipbank, stone-stratum (-reef); rocky ledge.
klipbok, "klipbok", chamois.
klipdas(sie), rock-rabbit, Cape dassie.
kliphard, (-e), very hard, as hard as stone.
klipkapper, stone-breaker (-dresser).
klip-klip, five stone(s) (a game).
klipkop, rocky hill; blockhead, obstinate person.
klipkous, ear-shell, sea-ear.
klipkrans, rock-ledge, krans (krantz).
klipmuur, stonewall.
klipperig, (-e), stony, rocky.
klippie, (-s, klippertjies), pebble; grit.
klipplaat, flat slabs (ledges) of rock.
klipsal(a)mander, rock-agama, (-lizard).
klipspringer, klipspringer.
klipsteen, stone, rock; idiot, numskull.
klipsteenhard, very hard, hard as stone.
klipsuier, sucker-fish.
klipvis, dried cod; klipfish.
klipwerktuig, stone-implement.
klisteerspuit, enema-syringe.
klits, (-e), n. bur(r); burdock; tangle (of hair); **aan iemand klou soos –**, stick to a person like a bur(r).
klits, (ge-), beat (eggs); thrash, smack.
klitsgras, -kruid, burdock, bur(r)weed.
klodder, (-s), n. clot, blob, dab.
klodder, (ge-), coagulate, clot; daub (with paint).
kloek, (-e), a. bold, brave, manly, stout, strong.
kloek, (ge-), cluck.
kloekhartig, (-e), vide **kloek**.
kloekheid, boldness, bravery, valour.
kloekhen, clucking-hen, mother-hen.
kloekmoedig(heid), vide **kloek(heid)**.
klofie, (-s), narrow ravine, little kloof.
klok, (-ke), clock; bell; bell-jar; receiver (of airpump); **hy het die – hoor lui, maar hy weet nie waar die bel (klepel) hang nie**, he has heard something, but he does not know the rights of it; **dit is alles werk wat die – slaan**, work is the order of the day; **hy kan nog nie op die – kyk nie**, he can't tell the time; **'n man van die –**, a punctual man; **met die –**, clockwise; **teen die –**, anti-clockwise.
klokblom, columbine; bell-flower.
klokboei, bell-buoy.
klokgelui, pealing; (chiming) of (the) bells.
klokgietery, bell-foundry.
klokkenis, (-te), carillonneur.
klokkespel, chimes, carillon.
klokkie, little clock (bell); bluebell, harebell.
klokkiesheide, bell-heath.
kloklied, chime(s).
klokluier, bell-ringer.
klokmaker, clockmaker.
klokslag, stroke of the clock.
klokspys, bell-metal.
kloktoring, bell-tower, steeple, belfry.
kloktou, bell-rope.
klokvormig, (-e), bell-shaped.
klomp, (-e), crowd, number, lot; lump.
klomp, (-e), clog, wooden shoe.
klompedans, clog-dance.
klompie, (-s), a bit, a little; small heap, handful; a few, some.
klont, (-e), n. lump, clod, nugget (of gold).
klont, (ge-), clot, curdle, coagulate, lump.
klonterig, (-e), clotted, clotty, lumpy.
klontjie, small lump, **(suur)–s**, (acid-)drops.
kloof, (klowe), n. chasm, gap, rift; gulf; ravine, kloof.
kloof, klowe, (ge-), cleave, split; chop (wood).
kloofsaag, rip-saw.
kloofsel, cleavage (diamonds).
klooster, (-s), cloister, abbey.
kloosterbroe(de)r, friar; lay-brother.
kloostergang, cloister.
kloosterkerk, convent-church, minster, abbey.
kloosterlewe, monastic (convent) life.
kloosterorde, monastic order.
kloosterreël, monastic rule.
kloosterskool, convent-school, cloister-school.
kloostertuin, monastery- (convent-)garden.
kloosterwese, monasticism.
kloot, (klote), ball, globe, sphere.
klop, (-pe), n. knock, tap, rap; throb, beat; **iemand – gee**, lick someone; **– kry**, get a licking.
klop, (ge-), knock, tap, rap (at the door); pat (on the back); beat (whip) up (eggs); beat, throb (of the heart); beat, lick, defeat (someone); agree (with), balance, tally; **die as uit die pyp –**, knock the ashes from the pipe; **daar word ge–**, there's a knock; **dit –**, that tallies; **dit – met sy gedrag**, that is of a piece with his conduct; **die syfers – nie**, the figures do not balance.
klopdans(ery), tap-dancing.
klophings, ridgel, cryptorchid.
klopjag, round-up; police-drive.
klopparty, fight(ing), scrap, scuffle.
kloppertjie, grass-warbler.
klopping, (-e, -s), beat(ing), throb.
klopplank, washing-plank.
klos, (-se), n. bobbin, spool; coil; lock (of sheep).
klos, (ge-), form locks, lock.
k(a)lossie, (-s), ixia.
klots, (ge-), lap, splash; kiss (in billiards).
klou, (-e), n. claw; paw; talon; fluke (of anchor); (bench-)clamp; **in die –e verval van**, fall into the cluches of; **hou jou –e van my af**, take your paws off me.
klou, (ge-), cling, stick; paw, clutch.
klouerig, (-e), sticky; flirty.
klouhamer, nail-puller, claw-hammer.
klouseer, -siekte, foot-disease (cattle).
klousule, (-s), paragraph, clause.
klouter, (ge-), clamber, climb, scramble.
klouteraar, (-s), clamberer, climber.
kloutjie, (-s), small claw (paw); hoof; vide **klou** n.
kloutjiesolie, neat's-foot oil.
klub, (-s), club.

klubgebou, club (building).
klug(spel), farce, low comedy; joke, scream.
klugspelskrywer, writer of farces.
klugtig, (-e), farcical, droll, comical.
klugtigheid, farcicalness, drollery, oddness.
kluif, (kluiwe), n. bone (to pick).
kluif, kluiwe, (ge-), pick (a bone), gnaw.
kluis, (-e), hermitage; safe, safe-deposit.
kluisenaar, (-s), anchorite, hermit, recluse.
kluisenaarshut, hermit's cell, hermitage.
kluister, (-s), n. chain, fetter, shackle.
kluister, (ge-), chain, fetter, shackle, trammel; **aan sy bed ge-**, bedridden.
kluit, (-e), clod, lump.
kluiterig, (-e), lumpy, cloddy.
kluitjie, (-s), small clod (lump); dumpling, fib, lie; **–s bak**, tell fibs; **met 'n – in die riet stuur**, fob off.
kluitjieso(e)p, dumpling-soup.
kluts: die – kwyt wees (raak), be at sea (all abroad), flurried.
kluwe, (-ns), ball (of wool), clew.
knaag, knae, (ge-), gnaw; prey (up)on; nag.
knaagdier, gnawer, rodent.
knaap, (knape), boy, lad; fellow, chap, page.
knabbel, (ge-), nibble, gnaw, peck at.
knae, vide **knaag**.
knaend, (-e), gnawing; dull; ceaseless(ly); poignant (grief); unending (rain); **-e pyn**, unabating (pain).
knaery, nagging.
knaging, (-e, -s), gnawing; pang, twinge.
knak, (-ke), n. crack, snap; blow, setback.
knak, (ge-), crack, snap; impair.
knaks, at loggerheads.
knal, (-le), n. bang, crack, clap, peal, pop.
knal, (ge-), bang, crack, crash, pop.
knaldemper, silencer, exhaust(-box).
knalgas, detonating gas.
knalpot, exhaust(-box), muffler, silencer.
knalsilwer, fulminating silver.
knap, (-pe), a. clever, smart; good-looking; neat, spruce; tight-(fitting).
knap, (ge-), snap; **'n uiltjie –**, take a nap.
knapbroekie, briefs.
knaphandig, (-e), dexterous, handy, skilful.
knaphandigheid, dexterity, skill.
knapheid, cleverness; good looks; vide **knap**, a.
knapie, (-s), little boy; vide **knaap**.
knappies, cleverly, skilfully; tightly.
knapsak, knapsack, wallet.
knars, (ge-), vide **kners**.
knarsetand, (ge-), gnash (grind) one's teeth.
knee, knie, (ge-), knead; fashion, mould.
knee(d)baar, (-bare), kneadable; plastic, pliable.
kneg, (-te), n. servant; slave; foreman.
kneg, (ge-), enslave.
knegs, (-e), servile.
knegskap, servitude, servility, slavery.
knel, (-le), n. pinch, difficulty; **in die – kom (sit)**, be in a fix (scrape, difficulty).
knel, (ge-), pinch, squeeze, jam; oppress.
knellend, (-e), oppressive.
knelling, (-e, -s), pinch(ing); restraint; oppression.
knelpunt, bottleneck.
knelter, vide **kniehalter**.
kners, (ge-), creak, grate; gnash, grind (teeth).
knersing, (-e, -s), gnashing, grinding.
knetter, (ge-), crackle, sputter; crash (thunder).
kneukel, (-s), knuckle.
kneus, (-e), n. bruise, contusion.
kneus, (ge-), bruise; contuse.
kneusing, (-e, -s), **kneusplek**, bruise; contusion.
knewel, (-s), n. moustache; whopper, stunner.

knewel, (ge-), gag; pinion, truss up; oppress.
knewel(a)ry, extortion, oppression.
knibbel, (ge-), haggle, higgle.
knibbelaar, (-s), haggler.
knibbel(a)ry, haggling, cheeseparing.
knie, (-ë), n. knee; **sy –ë dra**, skedaddle, cut and run; **die broek kry –ë**, the trousers are bagging at the knees; **iets onder die – kry**, master a thing, **op die –ë val**, go down on one's knees; **oor die –ë trek**, take across one's knee.
knie, (ge-), vide **knee**, (ge-).
kniebroek, knee-breeches, knickers; bloomers.
kniebuiging, genuflexion; bending of the knees.
kniediep, knee-deep, up to the knees.
kniehalter, knelter, (ge-), knee-halter; handicap (a person).
kniehalterslag, clove-hitch.
kniekop, knee-cap.
kniel, (ge-), kneel.
knies, (ge-), fret, mope, pine; brood, sulk.
knieserig, (-e), fretful, moping.
knieskut, knee-guard.
knieskyf, knee-cap; patella.
knieval, prostration; **'n – voor iemand doen**, throw oneself at a person's feet.
knik, (-ke), n. nod; rut (in a road).
knik, (ge-), nod; **sy knieë het ge-**, he gave at the knees; his knees were knocking together.
knikkebol, (ge-), nod, nid-nod.
knikker, (-s), n. marble.
knikspoor, cross rut (in a road).
knip, (-pe), n. cut, snip (with scissors); snare; catch (of door, purse); pinch (of salt); wink (of the eye).
knip, (ge-), cut, trim; pare (nails); punch (tickets); blink; wink (the eye); **hulle is vir mekaar ge-**, they were cut out for each other.
knipmes, clasp-knife, pocket-knife.
knipmesry, (knipmesge–), swank it on horseback.
knipogie, -oog, wink; glad-eye.
knippatroon, paper-pattern.
knipsel, (-s), cutting, clipping.
knipspeld, safety-pin.
knobbel, (-s), bump, knob; swelling.
knobbelrig, (-e), knotty, knobby, gnarled.
knoei, (ge-), mess, bungle; wangle, intrigue; **– met**, tamper with; **saam –**, intrigue.
knoeier, (-s), bungler; wangler.
knoeiery, bungling; wangling, jobbery.
knoeiwerk, bungling; wangling.
knoes, (-te), knot, gnarl, node.
knoesterig, (-e), knotty, gnarled; knobby.
knoet, (-e), knout.
knoffel, knoflok, garlic.
knok, (-ke), bone, knuckle.
knol, (-le), (old) crock (horse); bulb, tuber.
knolagtig, (-e), bulbous, tuberous.
knolgewas, tuberous plant.
knolkool, kohl-rabi.
knoop, (knope), n. button; stud (collar); knot (in rope); expletive, oath; (marriage-)tie; **die – deurhak**, cut the (Gordian) knot; **daar lê die –**, there lies the rub; **'n – gee**, swear, rap out an oath; **'n – losmaak**, undo a knot.
knoop, (ge-), knot, tie; net (a purse); make (nets); swear.
knoophakie, button-hook.
knooppunt, junction, centre; nodal point.
knoopsgatskêr, buttonhole scissors.
knoopwerk, tatting, macramé.
knop, (-pe), n. knob, handle (of door); peg (of hat rack); pommel (of a saddle); bump; lump (in the throat); (push-)button; switch (electric); bud (of a plant); **in –**, in bud; **'n digter in die –**,

a budding poet; iemand 'n – draai (steek), score a point against someone.
knop, (ge-), bud.
knopie, (-s), little button; small knot.
knopkierie, club, knobkerrie.
knopneus, large nose, conk; conky (person).
knor, n. growl, grunt; – kry, get a scolding.
knor, (ge-), growl, grunt; grumble; scold.
knorrig, (-e), peevish, testy, crusty, surly.
knorrigheid, peevishness; vide knorrig.
knot, (ge-), prune, poll, clip; curtail.
knots, (-e), bludgeon, (Indian) club.
knou, (-e), n. gnaw, bite; setback.
knou, (ge-), gnaw, munch; maul; injure.
knuis, (-te), fist; clutch; grasp.
knul, (-le), booby, duffer; lout.
knullig, (-e), doltish, awkward, loutish.
knuppel, (-s), n. club, cudgel; niblick (golf).
knuppel, (ge-), cudgel.
knuppeldik, quite satisfied, stuffed, loaded.
knuppelrym, -vers, doggerel(-rhyme, -verse).
knus, snug.
knutsel, (ge-), niggle (tinker) at.
knutselwerk, pottering; botchwork.
knyp, (ge-), n. pinch; in die – wees (sit), be in a fix (cleft, stick, scrape).
knyp, (ge-), pinch, squeeze.
knypbril, folders, nose-nippers, pince-nez.
knyper, (-s), clasper; claw; clip.
knyperig, (-e), stingy, mean; inclined to pinch.
knyptang, pincers (big), nippers (small).
koaguleer, (ge-), coagulate, clot.
koalisie, (-s), coalition.
koalisionis, (-te), coalitionist.
kobalt, cobalt.
kobold, (-e), kobold, (hob)goblin, brownie.
kobra, (-s), cobra.
koddig, (-e), droll, comic(al), funny, odd.
kode, (-s), code.
kodeks, (-e), codex.
kodifiseer, (ge-), codify.
koedoe, (-s), koodoo (kudu).
ko-edukasie, co-education.
koeël, (-s), n. bullet, ball; hy het die – gekry, he was shot; die – is deur die kerk, the die is cast.
koeël, (ge-), pelt, throw; shoot, fire upon.
koeëlbaan, trajectory, curve of projectile.
koeëlbui, rain of bullets.
koeëlgewrig, ball-and-socket joint.
koeëlklep, ball-valve.
koeëllaer, ballbearing.
koeëlrond, globular, spherical.
koeëltjie, (-s), pellet; globule.
koeëlvry, bullet-proof, shot-proof.
koëffisiënt, (-e), coefficient.
koei, (-e), cow; moenie ou –e uit die sloot haal nie, do not rip up old sores, let bygones be bygones; oor –e (koeitjies) en kalwers (kalfies) praat, talk about nothing in particular.
koeikamp, cow-paddock; cow-pasture.
koeimelk, cow's milk.
koeistal, cowshed, byre.
koeitjie, (little) cow; –s en kalfies, vide koei.
koejawel, (-s), guava.
koek, (-e), n. cake; alles vir soet – opeet, swallow everything.
koek, (ge-), cake, clot; knot; mat (hair); swarm together (bees); cling together.
koekbakker, confectioner, pastry-cook.
koekeloer, (ge-), peep, leer, peer, spy, pry.
koek(e)makranka, (-s), kukumakranka.
koekepan, (-ne), cocopan.
koekoek, (-e), cuckoo; Plymouth Rock.
koekoekhen, speckled hen.
koekoekhoender, Plymouth Rock.
koekoekklok, cuckoo-clock.
koeksaad, caraway-seed.
koeksoda, bicarbonate of soda.
koe(k)sister, (-s), cruller.
koel, (-e), a. cool, cold, fresh; in –en bloede, in cold blood; sy kop – hou, keep one's head; – klere, light clothes.
koel, (ge-), cool; vent (one's rage); wreak (vengeance); chill (foods).
koelbak, cooler, cooling-trough.
koelbewaring, cold storage.
koelbloedig, (-e), cold-blooded, in cold blood.
koelbloedigheid, cold-bloodedness.
koeldrank, cool drink.
koelerig, (-e), rather cool (chilly, fresh).
koelheid, coolness, coldness.
Koelie (-s), coolie; Asiatic, Indian.
Koeliewinkel, Indian store.
koelinrigting, cooling-plant.
koelkamer, cold-storage (chamber).
koelmiddel, coolant.
koeloond, cooling-furnace, annealing-oven.
koelte, (-s), coolness; breeze; shade; shady spot.
koeltrok, -wa, refrigerator(-truck).
koen, (-e), bold, brave, daring.
koenheid, boldness, bravery, daring, courage.
koenie-kannie: dit is –, the grapes are sour.
koens-, poenskop, hornless (ox, cow), pollard.
koenskopkoei, -ooi, pollard-cow (-ewe).
koepee, (-s), coupé.
koepeer, (ge-), cut (cards).
koepel, (-s), dome, cupola.
koepelvenster, bow-window.
koepelvormig, (-e), dome-shaped.
koeplet, (-te), couplet; stanza, verse.
koepon, (-s), coupon.
koer, (ge-), coo; make love.
koerant, (-e), newspaper, journal.
koerantartikel, newspaper-article.
koerantberig, newspaper-report.
koerantskrywer, journalist; newspaper-contributor (correspondent).
koerantstyl, -taal, journalistic style.
koerantuitknipsel, press-cutting.
koerasie, courage, pluck.
koerier, (-s), courier.
koers, (-e), n. course, direction, route; price; exchange, rate (money); teen die – van, at the rate of, – hou, keep straight; uit die – raak, be driven out of one's course; – kry, get going; van – verander, change one's course; change front; 'n nuwe – inslaan, strike out in a new direction, make a new departure.
koers, (ge-), head (make, steer) for.
koersberig, market-report; exchange-news.
koersnotering, (market-)quotation.
koersskommeling, fluctuation (in prices).
koersverlies, loss on exchange.
koersverskil, difference in the rate of exchange.
koe(t)s, (ge-), crouch, stoop, dodge, duck.
koe(k)sister, cruller.
koe(t)s-koe(t)s, continually dodging.
koester, (-s), n. lark, pipit.
koester, (ge-), cherish, entertain; coddle, pamper (children); bask (in the sun); 'n adder –, nourish a viper; die hoop –, cherish the hope; twyfel –, have doubts; die voorneme –, intend; 'n wrok –, bear (owe) a grudge.
koestering, cherishing; vide koester, (ge-).
koeterwaals, jargon, gibberish, double Dutch.
koets, (-e), n. coach, carriage; sedan (motor).
koets, (ge-), vide koes.
koetsier, (-s), driver; cabman; coachman.
koets-koets, vide koes-koes.

koetsperd, coach-horse.
koevert, (-e), envelope.
koevoet, (-e), crowbar, lever, jemmy.
koffer, (-s), box, trunk, suitcase.
kofferradio, portable radio.
koffertjie, (-s), small box, attaché-case.
koffie, coffee.
koffiebrandery, coffee-roasting (factory).
koffie-ekstrak, extract of coffee.
koffiehuis, coffee-house, café.
koffiekamer, coffee-room, refreshment-room.
koffietrommel, coffee-tin (-bin, -canister).
koffiekraam, coffee-stall.
koffiemelk, milk for coffee.
koffiemeul(e), coffee-mill(-grinder).
koffiemoer, coffee-grounds.
koffiepit, coffee-bean.
koffieplanter, coffee-planter (-grower).
koffiepot, coffee-pot.
koffiespaan, coffee-ladle.
koffietrommel, coffee-tin (-bin, -canister).
koffiewater, water for coffee, weak coffee.
koggel, (ge-), mimic, mock, imitate, tease.
koggel(a)ry, mimicking, mocking; teasing.
koggelmander, (-s), -mannetjie, (-s), S.A. rock-lizard, agama.
koggelstok, coupling-bar, tie-rod.
kohort, (-e), cohort.
kok, (-ke, -s), cook; caterer; **eerste –,** chef.
kokaïen, kokaïne, cocaine.
kokarde, (-s), cockade, badge, rosette.
koker, (-s), boiler; case, socket; quiver.
kokerboom, large aloe.
kokerjuffer, caddis-fly.
kokertjie, (-s), ocrea; small case (tube).
kokery, cooking; vide **kook**.
koket, (-te), n. coquette, flirt.
koket, (-te), a. coquettish.
koketteer, (ge-), coquet(te), philander.
koketterie, (-ë), coquetry.
kokkewiet, (-e) boubou shrike; gnome.
kokon, (-s), cocoon.
kokosneut, -noot, coconut.
kokospalm, coconut palm.
kol, (-le), n. spot; stain; star (on horse); bull's-eye (on target).
kol, (ge-), mark with a spot.
kolebak, vide **koolbak.**
kolf, (kolwe), n. bat (cricket), club; butt (-end) (of gun); (distilling) receiver, flask.
kolf, kolwe, (ge-), bat (cricket).
kolhaas, mountain-hare.
kolibrie, (-s), colibri, humming-bird.
koeliek, colic.
kolie(waar): by my –, upon my soul.
kolitis, colitis.
koljander, coriander.
kolk, (-e), n. eddy; abyss; (air-)pocket.
kolk, (ge-), yawn (abyss); eddy, whirl (water).
kol-kol, in patchess, here and there.
kollasioneer, (ge-), collate, check, repeat (telegr.).
kollega, (-s), colleague, confrère.
kollege, (-s), college; lecture.
kollegegebou, college(-building).
kollegiaal, (-ale), fraternal, as a colleague.
kollegialiteit, fraternity, fraternal spirit.
kolleksie, (-s), collection.
kollektant, (-e), collector; canvasser.
kollekte, (-s), collection.
kollektebus, collecting-box; offertory-box.
kollekteer, (ge-), collect, take up the collection (in church).
kollektesakkie, offertory-bag.
kollektief, (-tiewe), collective.
kolmol, star sand-mole.

kolokwint, (-e), coloquint, bitter-apple.
kolom, (-me), column; pillar.
kolon, (-ne), (army-)column.
kolonel, (-s), colonel.
koloniaal, (-ale), colonial.
kolonie, (-s), colony; settlement.
kolonis, (-te), colonist; settler.
kolonisasie, colonisation; settlement.
koloniseer, (ge-), colonise; settle.
kolonnade, (-s), collonnade, portico.
koloratuur, coloratura.
koloriet, coloration, colouring; hue, shade.
kolos, (-se), colossus.
kolossaal, (-sale), colossal, gigantic; thumping (lie); enormous (reduction).
kolperd, horse with a star.
kolporteer, (ge-), canvass, hawk (books).
kolskoot, bull's-eye; **'n – skiet,** hit the bull's-eye.
kolwer, (-s), batsman (in cricket).
kom, (-me), n. basin, bowl; wash-basin.
kom, (ge-), arrive, come; **laat –,** send for, call in (a doctor); order, send for (goods); **dit – duur uit,** it costs a lot (is expensive); **hoe het dit ge–?,** how did it come about?; **as hy te sterwe –,** in case of his death; **iets te wete –,** come (get) to know something; **te pas –,** be (come in) handy; **te kort –,** be deficient; be insufficient; fail; **aan geld –,** get (come by) money; **agter iets –,** find something out; **in die hemel –,** go to heaven; **ek kan nie op sy naam – nie,** I cannot hit upon (remember) his name; **daar niks van nie,** it is out of the question; **toe ek my – kry,** when I came to my senses.
komaan, come (along)!, cheer up.
komaf, descent, birth, class.
kombattant, (-e), combatant.
kombers, (-e), blanket.
kombinasie, (-s), combination; combine, ring.
kombinasieslot, combination lock.
kombineer, (ge-), combine.
kombuis, (-e), kitchen.
kombuis-Engels. kitchen-English.
kombuiskas, kitchen-dresser.
kombuistaal, kitchen-language; uneducated (vulgar) speech, patois.
komediant, (-e), comedian.
komedie, (-s), comedy; play; farce.
komediespel, comedy; farce, make-believe.
komediespeler, comedian; player, actor.
komeet, (komete), comet.
komfortabel, (-e), comfortable, snug.
komiek, (-e), n. low comedian, clown.
komiek(lik), (-e), comic(al), droll, queer, funny.
komieklikheid, comicality, drollery.
komies, (-e), comic(al), funny.
komitee, (-s), committee.
komkommer, (-s), cucumber.
komkommerslaai, cucumber-salad.
komkommertyd, silly season, gooseberry-season.
komma, (-s), comma.
kommandant, (-e), commandant; commander.
kommandeer, (ge-), command, give orders; commandeer, requisition; **ek laat my nie – nie,** I won't take orders from anybody.
kommandeur, (-s), commander.
kommando, (-'s), commando.
kommandovoël, stone-plover.
kommandowurm, army-worm, mystery-worm.
kommapunt, semicolon.
kommentaar, (-tare), comment(ary).
kommer, affliction, sorrow; distress, anxiety.
kommerlik, (-e), needy; scanty; anxious.
kommerloos, (-lose), carefree, untroubled.
kommernis, (-se), vide **kommer.**

kommersieel, (-siële), commercial.
kommervol, (-volle), distressful, wretched.
kommetjie, (-s), small basin; cup, bowl, mug.
kommissariaat, commissariat.
kommissaris, (-se), commissioner.
kommissie, (-s), commission; committee.
kommissielid, committee-member, member of (a) commission.
kommunikasie, (-s), communication.
kommunikasiemiddel, means of communication.
Kommunis, (-te), Communist.
Kommunisme, Communism.
kommunisties, (-e), communist(ic).
kommutator, (-e, -s), commutator.
kompak, (-te), compact.
kompanjie, (-s), company.
Kompanjiesdienaar, servant of the Company.
kompanjieskap, partnership.
Kompanjiestyd, (the) time of the East Indian Company, the Company's régime.
kompanjon, (-s), partner.
kompanjonskap, partnership.
komparant, (-e), appearer, party.
komparatief, (-tiewe), n. & a. comparative.
kompareer, (ge-), appear.
komparisie, appearance; meeting.
kompartement, (-e), compartment.
kompas, (-se), compass.
kompashuisie, binnacle.
kompasnaald, compass-needle.
kompasroos, compass-card, rhumb-card.
kompassie, compassion.
kompasstreek, point of the compass.
kompensasie, compensation.
kompensasieslinger, compensating pendulum.
kompenseer, (ge-), compensate, counterbalance.
kompeteer, (ge-), compete.
kompetent, (-e), competent.
kompetisie, (-s), competition; league.
kompetisiewedstryd, league-match.
kompilasie, (-s), compilation.
kompilator, (-e, -s), compiler.
kompileer, (ge-), compile.
kompleet, (-plete), a. complete; utter (failure); positive (scandal).
kompleet, adv. completely, utterly; just like; **hy is – sy vader,** he is just like his father.
kompleks, (-e), n. & a. complex; aggregate.
komplement, complement.
komplementêr, (-e), complementary.
kompleteer, (ge-), complete.
komplikasie, (-s), complication.
kompliment, (-e), compliment; **-e tuis,** remember me to all at home; **sonder -e,** unceremoniously; **vol -e,** full of whims; **iemand 'n – maak,** pay someone a compliment; **baie -e maak,** make a fuss.
komplimenteer, (ge-), compliment.
komplimenteus, (-e), complimentary.
kompliseer, (ge-), complicate.
komplot, (-te), plot, intrigue, conspiracy.
komplotteer, (ge-), plot, intrigue, conspire.
komponeer, (ge-), compose.
komponent, (-e), component.
komponis, (-te), composer.
komposisie, (-s), composition.
kompres, (-se), compress; fomentation.
kompressie, (-s), compression.
komprimeer, (ge-), compress.
kompromis, (-se), compromise.
kompromitteer, (ge-), compromise.
koms, arrival, coming; advent (of Christ); **op - wees,** be coming, be at hand.
kondensasie, condensation.
kondenseer, (ge-), condense.

kondisie, (-s), condition; form; **in goeie – bly,** keep fit.
kondisioneel, (-nele), conditional, qualified.
kondoleansie, (-s), condolence.
kondoleer, (ge-), condole.
kondor, (-s), condor.
konduksie, conduction.
kondukteur, (-s), conductor, guard.
kondukteurswa, guard's van.
konfederasie, (-s), confederacy.
konfedereer, (ge-), confederate.
konfereer, (ge-), consult, confer.
konferensie, (-s), conference.
konfessie, (-s), confession.
konfidensieel, (-siële), confidential.
konfigurasie, (-s), configuration.
konfirmasie, (-s), confirmation.
konfirmeer, (ge-), confirm.
konfiskasie, confiscation, seizure.
konfiskeer, (ge-), confiscate, seize.
konflik, (-te), conflict.
konfoor, (-fore), chafing-dish, brazier.
konform, in conformity with.
konfrater, (-s), colleague, confrère.
konfrontasie, (-s), confrontation.
konfronteer, (ge-), confront.
konfyt, (-e), n. jam, preserve, comfits.
konfyt, (ge-): ge– **wees in,** be accustomed to, be versed in; be an expert at.
kongestie, congestion.
konglomeraat, (-rate), conglomeration.
kongregasie, (-s), congregation.
kongregeer, (ge-), congregate.
kongres, (-se), congress.
kongruensie, (-s), equality and similarity.
kongruent, (-e), equal and similar, congruent.
konies, (-e), conic(al).
konifeer, (-fere), conifer.
koning, (-e, -s), king.
koningin, (-ne), queen.
koninginmoeder, queen-mother.
koninginweduwee, queen-dowager.
koningklipvis, kingklip.
koningsblou, royal blue, azure-blue.
koningsdogter, king's daughter, princess.
koningsgesind, (-e), royalist.
koningshuis, royal house, dynasty.
koningsmoord, regicide.
koningsmoordenaar, regicide.
koningsverjaardag, King's birthday.
koninkie, (-s), kingling, kinglet, petty king.
koninklik, (-e), royal, regal, kingly, kinglike; **van -e bloed(e),** of royal blood; **– lewe,** live like a king; **– onthaal,** entertain royally.
koninkryk, kingdom.
konjak, cognac, brandy.
konjektuur, (-ture), conjecture.
konjugasie, (-s), conjugation.
konjugeer, (ge-), conjugate.
konjunksie, (-s), conjunction.
konjunktief, (-tiewe), n. & a. conjunctive.
konjunktuur, (-ture), conjuncture.
konka, (-s), drum, tin.
konkaaf, (-kawe), concave.
konkel, (ge-), plot (and scheme), wangle, intrigue, botch, bungle.
konkel(a)ry, (-e), wangling: vide **konkel.**
konkelwerk, bungling, botching; wangling.
konklaaf, (-klawe), conclave.
konkludeer, (ge-), conclude, infer.
konklusie, (-s), conclusion, inference.
konkordaat, (-date), concordat.
konkordasie, (-s), concordance.
konkreet, n. concrete.
konkreet, (-krete), a. concrete.

konkurreer   151   **koolstofhoudend**

konkurreer, (ge-), compete.
konkurrensie, competition, rivalry.
konkurrent, (-e), competitor, rival.
konneksie, (-s), connection.
konsekreer, (ge-), consecrate.
konsekutief, (-tiewe), consecutive.
konsekwensie, (-s), consequence; consistency.
konsekwent, (-e), consistent, logical.
konsensie, conscience.
konsensieus, (-e), conscientious, scrupulous.
konsent, (-e), consent.
konsentrasie, concentration.
konsentrasiekamp, concentration-camp.
konsentreer, (ge-), concentrate, focus, fix.
konsentries, (-e), concentric.
konsep, (-te), concept, draft.
konsepordonnansie, draft-ordinance.
konsepsie, (-s), conception.
konsepwet, draft-act.
konsert, (-e), concert.
konsertganger, (-s), concertgoer.
konsertina, (-s), concertina.
konsertsaal, concert-hall (-room).
konsertsanger(es), concert-singer.
konservator, (-e, -s), custodian, curator.
konservatorium, (-s), conservatory.
konserveer, (ge-), preserve, keep; can, tin.
konserwatief, (-tiewe), n. & a. conservative.
konserwatisme, conservatism.
konsessie, (-s), concession.
konsiderasie, (-s), consideration; **in – neem**, take into consideration, make allowance for; **uit – vir**, in deference to.
konsiliasie, conciliation.
konsilieer, (ge-), conciliate.
konsipieer, (ge-), conceive; draft.
konsistorie(kamer), vestry.
konskripsie, conscription.
konsolidasie, consolidation.
konsolideer, (ge-), consolidate.
konsonant, (-e), consonant.
konsorte (pl.), associates, confederates.
konsortium, consortium.
konstabel, (-s), constable, policeman.
konstant, (-e), a. constant, uniform, steady.
konstante, (-s), n. constant.
konstateer, (ge-), state; establish (a fact); put on record; diagnose; declare, pronounce.
konstellasie, (-s), constellation.
konsternasie, consternation.
konstipasie, constipation.
konstipeer, (ge-), constipate.
konstitueer, (ge-), constitute.
konstitusie, (-s), constitution.
konstitusioneel, (-ele), constitutional.
konstrueer, (ge-), construct; construe.
konstruksie, (-s), construction; structure.
konstrukteur, (-s), constructor.
konsuis, kwansuis, quasi, professedly.
konsul, (-s), consul.
konsulaat, (-ate), consulate.
konsulent, (-e), relieving clergyman.
konsulêr, (-e), consular.
konsul-generaal, (konsuls-generaal), consul-general.
konsult, (-e), consultation.
konsultasie, (-s), consultation.
konsulteer, (ge-), consult.
konsumpsie, consumption.
kontak, (-te), contact, touch.
kontaklens, contact lens.
kontaminasie, contamination.
kontamineer, (ge-), contaminate.
kontant, (-e), n. (hard) cash, ready money.

kontant, (-e), a. cash; **– geld**, cash, ready money; **– waarde**, cash value.
konteks, context.
kontemplasie, contemplation.
kontensie, (-s), contention.
kontensieus, (-e), contentious.
kontinent, (-e), continent.
kontinentaal, (-ale), continental.
kontinuïteit, continuity.
kontrabande, contraband.
kontrabewys, counterfoil.
kontradiksie, (-s), contradiction.
kontraheer, (ge-), contract, shrink.
kontrak, (-te), contract, agreement.
kontrakbreuk, breach (violation) of contract.
kontraksie, contraction.
kontraktant, (-e), contractor, contracting party.
kontrakteer, (ge-), contract, make a contract.
kontrakteur, (-s), contractor.
kontraktueel, (-ele), contractual; by contract.
kontramine: in die – wees, be contrary, be contradictious.
kontrapunt, counterpoint.
kontrarevolusie, counter-revolution.
kontrarie, contrary, contradictious.
kontras, (-te), contrast.
kontrasteer, (ge-)-, contrast.
kontrei, (-e), country, part, region.
kontribuant, (-e), contributor.
kontribueer, (ge-), contribute.
kontribusie, (-d), contribution; subscription.
kontrole, control, check; supervision.
kontroleer, (ge-), control, check; supervise.
kontroleur, (-s), inspector, supervisor.
konus, (-se), cone.
konveks, (-e), convex.
konveksie, convection.
konvenieer, (ge-), be convenient to, suit.
konvensie, (-s), convention.
konvensioneel, (-ele), conventional.
konvergeer, (ge-), converge.
konvergensie, convergence.
konversasie, (-s), conversation.
konverseer, (ge-), converse.
konversie, conversion.
konverteer, (ge-), convert.
konvokasie, convocation.
konvooi, (-e), convoy.
konyn, (-e), rabbit, cony.
kooi, (-e), bed; cage; **– toe gaan**, turn in.
kooigoed, bed-clothes, bedding.
kook, (ge-), boil (water), cook (food); boil, fume, seethe (with rage).
kookboek, cookery-book.
kookkuns, cookery, art of cooking.
kookmelk, boiled milk; boiling milk.
kookpunt, boiling-point.
kooksel, (-s), boiling; decoction; batch; **die hele –**, the whole boiling.
kookskool, cookery-school.
kookwater, boiling water.
kool, (kole), n. 1. coal, carbon; **op hete –e sit (staan)**, be on pins and needles.
kool, n. 2. cabbage; **die – is die sous nie werd nie**, the game is not worth the candle.
koolaanpaksel, **-aanslag**, carbon-deposit.
kool-, **kolebak**, coal-box (-scuttle).
koolblaar, cabbage-leaf.
kooldruk, carbon-print(ing).
koolhidraat, carbohydrate.
koolkop, cabbage(-head).
koolmyn, coal-mine, colliery, coal-pit.
koolokside, **-okside**, carbonic oxide.
koolstof, carbon.
koolstofhoudend, (-e), carbonaceous.

koolstronk, cabbage-stalk (-stump).
koolsuur, carbonic acid.
koolteer, coal-tar.
kooltrok, -wa, coal-truck.
koolwaterstof, hydrocarbon.
koolwaterstofgas, hydrocarbon gas.
koop, n. purchase, bargain; **'n – sluit**, make a purchase; **te –**, for sale; **te – loop**, parade, show off, display; **op die – toe**, into the bargain.
koop, (ge-, gekog), buy, purchase.
koopbrief, deed of sale, purchase-deed.
koopdag, day of sale.
koöperasie, (-s), co-operation.
koöperatief, (-tiewe), co-operative.
koöpereer, (ge-), co-operate.
koophandel, commerce, trade; **kamer van –**, chamber of commerce.
koopkontrak, purchase-deed.
koopkrag, purchasing-, spending-power.
koopkragtig, (-e), able to buy (spend).
kooplustig, (-e), eager to buy; extravagant.
koopman, (-ne, -s, -liede, -lui), merchant.
koopmansgees, commercial spirit.
koopprys, purchase-price.
koopsom, purchase-price (-money).
koöptasie, co-op(ta)tion.
koöpteer, (ge-), co-opt.
koopvaardy, merchant service.
koopvaardyskip, merchantman.
koopvaardyvloot, mercantile marine.
koopvaart, mercantile navigation.
koopwaar, **-ware**, merchandise.
koor, (kore), choir (of singers); chorus (of song); **in die – sing**, sing in the choir; **in – sing**, sing in chorus.
koorbank, choir-stall.
koord, (-e), cord; chord (maths.).
koorddanser(es), rope-dancer (-walker).
koördinaat, (-nate), co-ordinate.
koördinasie, co-ordination.
koördineer, (ge-), co-ordinate.
koordirigent, choir-master.
koordjie, (-s), bit (length, piece) of string.
koorknaap, choir-boy, boy-chorister.
koorleier, choir-master.
koors, (-e), fever; **koue –**, ague, cold shivers.
koorsaanval, attack of fever; ague-fit.
koorsagtig, (-e), feverish; frenzied, hectic.
koorsagtigheid, feverishness.
koorsang, choral song; choral singing.
koorsanger(es), choralist; chorister (in church).
koorsblaar, blister, cold sore.
koorserig, (-e), feverish.
koorshitte, fever-heat.
koorsig, (-e), feverish, febrile, pyretic.
koorslyer(es), fever-patient.
koorspennetjie, **-pypie**, clinical thermometer.
koorssiekte, (enteric) fever; (malarial) fever.
koorsvry, (-e), free from fever.
koos, (ge-), caress, fondle; vide **liefkoos**.
kop, (-pe), n. head; hill, kopje; summit; cob (of maize); crest (of wave); hand, soul (on board); **sy – in 'n bynes steek**, bring a hornet's nest about one's ears; **geen – of stert van iets uitmaak nie**, make neither head nor tail of a thing; **sy – is op hol**, his head is turned; **sy – verloor**, lose one's head; **sy – bymekaar hou**, keep one's head; **die – laat hang**, lose courage; **sy – stamp (stoot)**, run one's head against a stone wall; **sy eie – volg**, go one's own way; **iemand se – was**, give someone a bit of your mind; **– tussen die bene steek**, buck; **– intrek**, draw in one's horns; **– uittrek**, back out (of something); **die – bo water hou**, keep one's head above water; **met iemand – in een mus wees**, be hand in glove with someone; **dan laat ek my – afkap**, I'll eat my hat (first); **die – indruk**, put down, suppress, knock on the head; **die – in die strop steek**, run one's head into a noose; **iemand sy – laat krap**, make someone think; **die – in die skoot lê**, give in, submit; **sy – staan soontoe**, he is bent in that direction; **hy het 'n goeie –**, he has a good head on his shoulders; **hy het (is) 'n stywe –**, he is stiffnecked; **– en (aan) – (hardloop)**, (run) neck and neck; **– en punt**, heads and feet together; **iets in die – kry**, get something into one's head; **'n gat in die – praat**, talk (someone) round; **met die – voor die bors**, dejected; ashamed; **op die – (af)**, exactly, precisely; **op iemand se – sit**, sit upon a person; **op sy – laat sit**, take things lying down; **die spyker op die – slaan**, hit the nail on the head; **op sy – staan**, stand on one's head; **kop – is topsy-turvy**; **al staan hy op sy –**, come what may; **op sy – kry**, get it in the neck, **op sy – gee**, give it him (in the neck); **per –**, per head, per piece; **uit die – ken (leer)**, know (learn) by heart; **iemand van – tot tone opneem**, eye a person from head to foot; **voor die – gooi**, cast in a person's teeth; vide **hoof**.
kop, (ge-), head (a ball); cob (maize); head (cabbage, etc.).
kop-af, head off.
kopbeen, scull.
kopdoek, kerchief, head-cloth; turban.
koper, (-s), n. buyer, purchaser.
koper, n. copper.
koperagtig, (-e), coppery; brassy.
koperdruk, copperplate (printing).
kopererts, copper-ore.
kopergeld, copper-coin (-money), coppers.
kopergoed, copper-(brass-)ware.
kopergravure, copperplate (-gravure).
kopergroen, verdigris.
koperkapel, (banded) cobra.
koperkies, copper-pyrites.
koperkleurig, (-e), copper-coloured; brazen (sky).
kopermyn, copper-mine.
koperoksied, cupric oxide.
koperoplossing, solution of copper.
koperroes, verdigris.
koperstaaf, bar-copper.
kopersuur, cupric acid.
koperware, copper-(brass-)ware.
koperwerk, copper-, (brass-)ware.
kopie, (-s), n. bargain.
kopie, (-ë), n. copy, duplicate; manuscript.
kopieer, (ge-), copy.
kopieerpapier, copying-paper.
kopieerwerk, copy-work.
kopiereg, copyright.
kopiis, (-te), copyist, transcriber.
kopkool, cabbage.
koplengte, head.
koplig, headlight (of motor).
koploos, (-lose), headless; acephalous.
koppel, (ge-), couple, join; engage (gear).
koppelaar, (-s), n. clutch.
koppelaar(ster), (-s), n. matchmaker.
koppeling, (-e, -s), clutch, coupling, linkage.
koppelriem, belt, coupling-strap.
koppelstang, coupling-rod; tie.
koppelteken, hyphen.
koppelwerkwoord, copula, copulative verb.
koppelwoord, copulative.
koppennent, head (of a bed).
koppesnel, (ge-), go scalp-hunting.
koppesneller, scalp-, headhunter.
koppie, (-s), small head; cup; hill, kopje.

koppig, (-e), headstrong, obstinate; heady (drink).
koppigheid, obstinacy, pigheadedness.
kopra, copra.
kopseer, headache.
kopskoot, shot in the head; floorer, knock-out.
kopsku, bridle-shy; shy, evasive, timid.
kopspeel, (ge-), prank.
kopstuk, head(piece), heading, leader; **die –ke van die party**, the great guns of the party.
koptelefoon, headphone.
Kopties, (-e), n. & a. Coptic.
kopuleer, (ge-), copulate.
koraal, (-rale), 1. coral.
koraal, (-rale), 2. choral(-song), chorale.
koraalboek, choral(e)-book, hymn-book.
koraaldier, coral-polyp, zoophyte.
koraaleiland, coral-island.
koraalgesang, choral-song (-singing), hymn.
koraalpoliep, coral-polyp.
koraalrif, coral-reef, atoll.
koraliet, corallite.
koralyn, coralline.
Koran, Koran (Alcoran, Alkoran).
Korana, (-s), **Koraner**, (-s), Korana.
kordaat, bold, firm, plucky, resolute.
kordaatstuk, feat, achievement, bold deed.
kordiet, cordite.
kordon, (-ne, -s), cordon.
Koreaans, (-e), n. Korean (Corean).
korente, **korinte**, (pl.) currants.
korente-, **korintekoek**, currant-, fruit-cake.
korf, (korwe), basket, hamper; (bee)hive.
korfbal, basket-ball.
korfbalspan, basket-ball team.
korhaan, (-hane), bustard.
koring, corn, wheat; **dit is – op sy meule**, that is grist to his mill.
koringaar, ear of wheat.
koringbeurs, corn-exchange.
koringblom, cornflower, bluebottle; Ixia.
koringbou, wheat-growing.
koringgerf, corn-sheaf, sheaf of corn.
koringhalm, corn-stalk.
koringhandelaar, wheat-merchant.
koringkriek, green grasshopper.
koringland, cornfield, wheatfield.
koringmied, -miet, wheat-stack.
koringoes, wheat-harvest (-crop).
koringsak, wheat-, grain-bag.
koringskuur, granary.
koringstoppel(s), corn-stubble.
korinte, **korente**, (pl.) currants.
Korinties, (-e), Corinthian.
kornet, (-te), cornet.
kornuit, (-e), comrade, companion, crony.
korporaal, (-s), corporal.
korporaalstrepe, corporal's stripes.
korporasie, (-s), corporation.
korps, **corps**, (-e), corps, body.
korpsgees, esprit de corps.
korpulensie, corpulence, stoutness.
korpulent, (-e), corpulent, fat, stout.
korrek, (-te), right, correct; proper.
korreksie, (-s), correction.
korreksioneel, (-nele), correctional.
korrektheid, correctness.
korrektief, (-tiewe), corrective.
korrel, (-s), n. grain, pellet; bead, sight (of gun); tuft (of hair).
korrel, (ge-), aim (at); pick (grapes).
korrelaat, (-late), correlate.
korrelatief, (-tiewe), correlative.
korreleer, (ge-), correlate.

korrelkop, touchy (peevish) fellow; tufted head (of Native); Native.
korrelrig, (-e), granular; crumbling; quarrelsome.
korreltjie, (-s), grain, granule; grape.
korrelvat, (korrelge-), aim (at).
korrespondeer, (ge-), correspond.
korrespondensie, correspondence.
korrespondensieskool, correspondence-school.
korrespondent, (-e), -dente, (-s), correspondent.
korridor, (-s), corridor.
korrigeer, (ge-), correct; set right.
korrigeerwerk, correction-work.
korrosie, corrosion.
korrup, (-te), corrupt.
korrupsie, (-s), corruption.
kors, (-te), n. crust; scab (on wound).
kors, (ge-), crust, form a crust.
korserig, vide **kors(t)erig**.
korset, (-te), corset, stays.
korsie, (-s), crust.
kors(t)erig, (-e), crusty.
korswel, n. fun, banter, joke; **uit –**, in jest.
korswel, (ge-), banter, jest, joke.
kort, (–, -e), a. short; brief; **– en bondig (kragtig)**, short and to the point, terse; **– en dik**, thickset; **maak dit –**, cut (make) it short; **– en klein slaan**, smash to smithereens; **– van stof (draad)**, short-tempered; **om – te gaan**, to make a long story short; **– daarna**, shortly after(wards); **– gelede**, a short time ago, lately; **in –**, in brief (short), briefly; **na –er of langer tyd**, sooner or later; **na mekaar**, within a short time; **iemand te – doen**, wrong someone; **die waarheid te – doen**, strain the truth; **te – skiet**, fall short (of the mark); **dit was hier te – en daar te lank**, he had a lot of petty excuses; **– begrip**, summary.
kort, (ge-), shorten; clip, beguile (while away) the time.
kortaf, abrupt, curt, blunt, short.
kortasem, short of breath, short-winded, puffed.
kortasemigheid, short-windedness.
kortbeen, short-legged.
kortgebonde, short-tempered, touchy.
kortgebondenheid, touchiness.
kortheid, brevity, shortness, briefness.
kortheidshalwe, for short, for briefness' sake.
korthoring, shorthorn.
korting, (-e, -s), reduction, discount.
kort-kort, frequently, every now and again.
kortliks, briefly, shortly.
kortlings, lately, recently, the other day.
kortling, swingle-tree.
kortom, in short, in brief, in a word; **– spring**, change front.
kortpad, short cut.
kortsigtig, (-e), short-sighted.
kortsigtigheid, short-sightedness.
kortsluiting, short-circuit(ing).
kortstondig, (-e), short, short-lived.
kortstondigheid, shortness, brevity.
kortweg, briefly, shortly, in short; curtly.
kortwiek, (ge-), clip the wings, frustrate.
korvet, corvette.
kos, n. food, fare, victuals; **– en inwoning**, board and lodging; **sy – verdien**, make (earn) a living; **dit is ou –**, that is an old story; **sy oë (die) – gee**, feed one's eyes (upon).
kos, (ge-), cost; **wat – dit?**, what is the price of this?; **dit sal sy lewe –**, that will cost him his life; **(laat) dit – wat dit wil**, whatever the cost, cost what it may; **baie moeite –**, give (cost) a great deal of trouble; **dit – tyd**, it takes time.
Kosak, (-ke), Cossack.

kosbaar, (-bare), expensive, costly; valuable (time); precious (stones).
kosbaarheid, expensiveness; preciousness.
kosganger, (-s), boarder.
kosgeld, board, boarding(-fee), boarding.
koshuis, boarding-house.
kosinus, (-se), cosine.
kosjer(vleis), kosher(-meat).
kosjuffrou, landlady.
kosleerling, (school-)boarder.
kosmetiek, cosmetic; cosmetics.
kosmetieksalon, beauty parlour.
kosmies, (-e), cosmic.
kosmogonie, cosmogony.
kosmografie, (-ë), cosmography.
kosmografies, (-e), cosmographic(al).
kosmopoliet, (-e), n. cosmopolitan.
kosmopolities, (-e), a. cosmopolitan.
kosmopolitisme, cosmopolitanism.
kosmos, cosmos.
kosprys, cost-price.
kosskool, boarding-school.
koste, cost(s), expense(s), expenditure; **ten – van**, at the expense of; **– aangaan (maak)**, incur expenses; **– meebring**, entail expense; **op eie –**, at one's own expense; **iemand op – ja**, put a person to expense; **lopende –**, running costs.
kosteberekening, calculation of costs.
kostelik, (-e), precious, splendid, excellent.
kostelikheid, preciousness; vide **kostelik**.
kosteloos, (-lose), free, gratis, free of charge.
koster, (-s), sexton, verger.
kosterekenmeester, cost accountant.
kostumeer, (ge-), dress up.
kostumier, wardrobe-mistress.
kostuum, (-s, -tume), costume; fancy-dress.
kosvrou, landlady.
kosvry, (-e), free of charge.
koswinner, breadwinner, wage-earner.
koswinning, livelihood.
kosyn, (-e), sash, frame.
kotangens, (-gente), cotangent.
kotelet, (-te), cutlet, chop.
koterie, (-ë), coterie, clique.
kots, (ge-), vomit.
kou, (-e), n. cage.
kou(e), n. cold; **– vat**, catch (a) cold.
kou, (ge-), chew, munch, masticate.
koubeitel, cold chisel.
koud, (kou(e)), cold, chilly; frigid; **–e lugstreek**, frigid zone; **dit laat my –, dit raak my –e klere nie**, it leaves me (stone) cold; **ek word daar – van**, it makes me go cold all over, it gives me the shivers; **die woord was nog nie – nie**, the word had scarcely been uttered.
koudbloedig, (-e), cold-blooded.
koudheid, coldness.
koudlei, (koudge-), cool (down); walk (a horse) up and down; gull (a person).
kouekoors, ague, shivering fit, the shivers.
kouelik, vide **kou(e)lik**.
kouerig, (-e), coldish, chilly.
kouevuur, gangrene, mortification.
kou(e)waterkompres, cold compress.
kougoed, something to chew.
kougom, chewing-gum
kou(e)lik, (-e), sensitive to cold, chilly.
kous, (-e), stocking; **–e** (pl.), hose; **met die – op die kop**, with a flea in the ear.
kousaal, (-sale), causal.
kousatief, (-tiewe), causative.
kousband, garter, suspender; garter-snake.
kousbandslang, garter-snake.
kousel, (-s), chew(ing), cud; mouthful.
kouswinkel, hosier's (shop).

kouter, (-s), coulter.
koutjie, (-s), 1. chew(ing), cud; mouthful.
koutjie, (-s), 2. cage.
kouvoël, kôvoël, tawny eagle.
kouwater, vide **kou(e) water**.
kraag, (krae), collar.
kraagjas, cape-coat; fur-collared coat.
kraagmannetjie, maned lion.
kraai, (-e), n. crow; **soveel van weet as 'n – van Sondag (godsdiens)**, not have the foggiest notion about a thing; **so maer as 'n – wees**, be as thin (lean) as a rake; **lyk of die –e sy kos opgeëet het**, look very dejected.
kraai, (ge-), crow; **sy haan – koning**, he is cock of the walk; **viktorie –**, shout victory.
kraaibek, parrot-fish; pipe-wrench.
kraaibessie, rub-rub berry.
kraaines, crow's-nest.
kraai-uintjie, crocus.
kraak, (krake), n. crack; flaw; fissure; **hy het 'n –**, he has a screw (tile) loose.
kraak, (ge-), crack; creak; (s)crunch (gravel); **dat dit (so) –**, like blazes, like one possessed.
kraakbeen, cartilage, gristle.
kraaksindelik, (-e), scrupulously clean.
kraakskoen, creaking shoe.
kraakstem, creaking (grating) voice.
kraal, (krale), n. bead; bead(ing) (of a board).
kraal, (krale), n. pen, fold, kraal; **dit is so in sy –**, that is food and drink to him, that is grist to his mill; **in iemand se – kom**, compete with someone; offend someone; **agteros kom ook in die – (juk)**, slow but sure.
kraalhek, kraal-gate.
kraalmis, kraal-dung (-manure).
kraalogie, beady eye; beady-eyed bird.
kraalskaaf, beading-, moulding-, ogee-plane.
kraaltjie, kraletjie, (-s), n. 1. (little) bead.
kraaltjie, (-s), n. 2. small kraal.
kraam, (krame), booth, stall; childbed; **dit kom in sy – te pas**, that suits his purpose.
kraambed, childbed.
kraaminrigting, maternity-home.
kraamkoors, puerperal fever.
kraamverpleegster, maternity-nurse.
kraamvrou, woman-in-childbed.
kraan, (krane), tap, stopcock; crane, derrick.
kraanbalk, (crane-)girder, cathead.
kraanvoël, crane.
krabbel, (-s), n. scratch; scrawl, scribble; sketch.
krabbel, (ge-), scratch; scrawl, scribble.
krabbelpoot, -skrif, scrawl, scribble.
krabbetjie, krawwetjie, (-s), earring.
kraffie, (-s), water-bottle; decanter (for wine).
krag, (-te), strength, force, vigour, power; energy; efficacy, virtue (of medicines); **– van wet**, the force of law; **al sy – daaraan gee**, devote (give) all his energy to something; **bo iemand se –**, beyond someone's strength; **in die – van sy lewe**, in the prime of his life; **met alle –**, with might and main; **op – kom**, regain one's strength; **op volle – werk**, work at full capacity; **uit – van**, in (by) virtue of; **van – wees**, be operative, be in force; **van – word**, come into force.
kragbesparing, conservation of energy.
kragdadig, (-e), energetic, vigorous; effective efficacious; powerful; potent.
kragdadigheid, vigour; efficacy; strength.
kragduik, power-dive.
krageenheid, unit of force, dynamic unit.
kragfiets, buzz-bike, moped.
kraginstallasie, (electric) power-plant.
kraglyn, line of force.
kragmeter, dynamometer.

kragmeting, trial of strength.
kragsentrale, (electric) power-station.
kragsinspanning, effort, exertion.
kragstasie, power-station.
kragverspilling, loss (waste) of energy.
kragteloos, (-lose), impotent, powerless, invalid; – **maak**, invalidate, nullify.
kragteloosheid, impotence; invalidity.
kragtens, by virtue of, on the strength of; – **hierdie wet**, under this act.
kragtig, (-e), a. strong, powerful, robust; nourishing, vigorous, strenuous, forcible (language).
kragtig!, interj. I am blessed!, great Scott!
kragtiglik, strongly, vigorously, forcibly.
kragtoer, tour de force, stunt.
kragvertoon, display of strength (power).
kragvoedsel, forcing food.
kragvol, (-le), forcible, powerful.
krakeel, (-ele), n. quarrel, wrangle.
krakeel, (ge-), quarrel, wrangle.
krakie, (-s), small crack, flaw; acidity (of wine); highness (of meat); **hy het 'n –**, he has a screw loose; vide **kraak**, n.
kraletjie, vide **kraaltjie**.
kram, (-me), n. staple; clamp, cramp.
kram, (ge-), cramp, clamp.
kramat, (-te), holy grave, kramat.
kramer, (-s), hawker, pedlar.
kramery, (-e), hawker's (pedlar's) wares.
kramhegter, stapler.
krammetjie, (-s), small staple (clamp).
kramp, (-e), cramp, spasm.
krampaanval, attack of cramp.
krampagtig, (-e), conclusive, spasmodic (jerks); desperate (attempts).
krampstillend, (-e), antispastic.
kranig, (-e), bold, dashing, crack; **hom – gedra**, give a good account of oneself.
kranigheid, boldness, dash.
krank, (-e), sick, ill.
krankbed, sick-bed.
kranke, (-s), patient, sick person.
krankheid, disease, illness, sickness.
kranksinnig, (-e), crazy, insane, lunatic.
kranksinnige, (-s), lunatic; maniac.
kranksinnigegestig, lunatic asylum, mental hospital.
kranksinnigheid, insanity; craziness.
krans, (-e), n. wreath, chaplet, garland.
krans, (-e), rock, ledge, krans.
krans, (ge-), wreathe, garland.
kransbal, (game of) ring-ball.
krap, (-pe), n. 1. crab(-fish).
krap, (-pe), n. 2. scratch.
krap, (ge-), scratch; claw; paw.
kras, (-, -se), a. strong, vigorous.
kras, (ge-), scrape; screech; croak.
krat, (-te), crate, skeleton-case, frame.
krater, (-s), crater.
kratervormig, (-e), craterlike (-shaped).
krawwetjie, **krabbetjie**, (-s), earring.
kreasie, creation.
kreatuur, (-ture), creature.
krediet, credit; – **gee**, allow credit; **op – koop**, buy on credit; **blanko –**, unlimited credit.
kredietbalans, credit-balance.
kredietbrief, credit-note, letter of credit.
kredietstelsel, credit-system.
kredietwaardig, (-e), solvent.
krediteer, (ge-), credit.
krediteur, (-e, -s), creditor.
kreër, (ge-), create.
kreef, (krewe), crayfish; lobster.
Kreefskeerkring, Tropic of Cancer.

kreefslaai, lobster-salad.
kreeftegang, backward-march; **die – gaan**, go (march) backwards.
kreet, (krete), cry, scream, shriek.
krematorium, (-s, -ria), crematorium.
kremeer, (ge-), cremate.
kremetart, cream of tartar.
kremetartboom, baobab, cream-of-tartar tree.
krenk, (ge-), hurt, injure, offend, mortify, wound; **ge– voel**, feel hurt (aggrieved); **sy verstand is ge–**, he is not right in his mind; **gekrenkte trots**, offended pride.
krenkend, (-e), insulting; mortifying.
krenking, (-e, -s), insult, mortification.
krenterig, (-e), mean, niggardly, stingy.
kreolien, **kreoline**, creolin(e).
kreoliseer, (ge-), creolize.
Kreool, (-ole), Creole.
Kreools, (-e), n. & a. Creole.
kreosoot, creosote.
Kretenser, (-s), Cretan.
Kretie: die – en Pletie, ragtag and bobtail.
kretinisme, cretinism.
kreton, (-s), cretonne.
kreuk, (-e), n. **kreukel**, (-s), crease, pucker.
kreuk, **kreukel**, (ge-), crease, crumple, pucker.
kreukelrig, (-e), crumpled, creased, wrinkled.
kreun, (-e), n. groan, moan.
kreun, (ge-), groan, moan.
kreupel, **kruppel**, a. cripple, lame, limping.
kreupel, **kruppel**, (ge-), limp; cripple.
kreupelbos, **-hout**, brushwood, underwood.
kreupele, **kruppele**, (-s), a. cripple, lame person.
kreupelrym, doggerel(-rhyme).
kriebel-, vide **kriewel**.
kriek, (-e), (house-)cricket.
krieket, cricket.
krieketbaan, cricket-pitch.
krieketkolf, cricket-bat.
krieketpaaltjie, wicket.
krieketspeler, cricketer.
krieketveld, cricket-field (-ground).
kriekie, (-s), (house-)cricket.
krielhaantjie, Bantam cock; pert (cocky) person.
kriesel(tjie), (-s), bit, particle, crumb; vide **griesel(tjie)**.
kriewel, **kriebel**, (ge-), tickle, itch; fidget.
kriewelkrappers, **kriebel-**, scrawls; caprices.
kriewelrig, **kriebelrig**, (-e), itchy; fidgety; nettled (at); **'n mens word daar – van**, it gets under your skin; it gets your dander up; it gives you the creeps.
krimineel, (-ele), criminal; outrageous; **dit het – gegaan**, it was a tough job.
krimp, (ge-), shrink, diminish, contract; – **van die pyn**, writhe with pain.
krimping, (-e, -s), shrinkage, contraction.
krimp(yster)varkie, small hedgehog.
krimpvry, unshrinkable.
kring, (-e), n. 1. circle, circuit, ring, orbit; quarter, walk of life; set; **blou (donker) –e onder die oë**, dark rings under the eyes; **in sekere –e**, in certain quarters; **in die hoogste –e**, in the upper circles; **in 'n – gaan staan**, form a circle.
kring, (-e), n. 2. carrion; beast, rotter.
kring, (ge-), curl, circle; form a circular stain mark with circles.
kringetjie, (-s), circlet, ring(let).
kringgat(bok), waterbuck.
kringloop, cycle, circuit, circular course; **noodlottige –**, vicious circle.
kringvormig, (-e), circular; rotary.
krink, (ge-), swing (round).
krinkel, (-s), n. crinkle.

krinkel, (ge-), crinkle.
krinolien, krinoline, crinoline.
krioel, (ge-), abound (swarm, teem) with.
krip, n. crape, crêpe.
krip, (-pe), n. manger.
kriptogram (-ame) cryptogram.
krisant, (-e), chrysanthemum; aster.
krisis, (-se), crisis, critical moment (point, stage), turning-point; **'n – bereik,** come to a crisis (a head); **'n – deurmaak,** pass through a critical stage.
kriskras, crisscross.
krismislelie, agapanthus.
krismisroos, Christmas-rose, hydrangea.
kristal, (-le), crystal.
kristalagtig, (-e), crystalline.
kristalbuis, transistor.
kristaldruiwe, crystal-grapes.
kristalhelder, as clear as crystal (daylight).
kristallisasie, kristallisering, crystallization.
kristalliseer, (ge-), crystallize.
kristalvormig, (-e), crystalline.
kristalwerk, crystal-ware.
kriterium, (-s), criterion.
kritiek, (-e), n. criticism; review; **– uitoefen,** criticize.
kritiek, (-e), a. critical, crucial.
krities, (-e), critical.
kritikus, (-se, -tici), critic.
kritiseer, (ge-), criticize; review (a book); censure, find fault with, disapprove of.
kroeg, (kroeë), bar, pub; students' club.
kroegloper, pub-loafer.
kroep, croup.
kroephoes, croup-cough.
kroes, crisp(ed), frizzled; **– voel,** feel seedy.
kroeshare, crisp (frizzy, woolly) hair.
kroeskop, curly-head; (person with) tufted hair.
kroeskopkêrel, curly-headed fellow.
kroketjie, (-s), croquette.
krokodil, (-le), crocodile.
krokodiltrane, crocodile-tears.
krokus, (-se), crocus.
krom, a. bent, crooked, curved; hooked (nose); **– lag,** double up with laughing; **– bene,** bandy legs; **– Afrikaans,** halting Afrikaans.
krom, (ge-), bend, bow, crook, curve.
krombeen-..., bandy-legged; knock-kneed.
krombek, pick; (crook)bill; pipe-wrench.
kromhals, retort.
kromheid, crookedness.
kromme, (-s), curve; **'n – teken,** plot a curve.
kromming, (-e, -s), bend, curve, turn.
kromneus, hook-nose, hooked nose.
krompasser, cal(l)iper-compasses.
krompraat, n. lisping, little language (of children); mutilated speech (of adults).
krompraat, (kromge-), lisp; speak (a language) imperfectly, mutilate a language.
kromprater, lisper; mutilator of a language.
kromtaal, jargon, mutilated language.
kroniek, (-e), chronicle; **K–e Chronicles (Bible);** **die –e voorlees,** read a lesson.
kroniekskrywer, chronicler.
kroning, coronation, crowning.
kroningsplegtigheid, coronation-ceremony.
kronkel, (-s), n. coil, twist(ing), kink.
kronkel, (ge-), coil, meander, twist, wind.
kronkelend, (-e), coiling, twisting, winding.
kronkelig, (-e), sinuous, tortuous.
kronkeling, (-e, -s), coil, kink, twist.
kronkelloop, winding (meandering) course.
kronkelpad, -weg, winding (tortuous) path.
kroon, (krone), n. crown; coronet; top; chandelier, gaselier, electrolier, lustre (light); corolla (of flower); **die – op alles sit,** crown (cap) everything; **dit span die –,** that caps everything, that is the limit; **na die – steek,** rival, vie with.
kroon, (ge-), crown.
kroonblaar, -blad, petal.
kroongetuie, witness for the crown.
kroongrond, crown-land.
kroonlys, cornice.
kroonprins, crown-prince, prince royal.
kroonprinses, crown-princess, princess royal.
kroonrat, crown-wheel.
kroontjie, (-s), coronet; cowlick, crown (in hair).
kroonslagaartrombose, coronary thrombosis.
kroonvervolger, public prosecutor.
kroos, n. 1. duck-weed.
kroos, n. 2. issue, offspring, progeny.
krop, (-pe), n. crop, gizzard; head (of lettuce); **dit steek hom in die –,** that sticks in his gizzard.
krop (ge-), cram; **ek kan dit nie – nie,** it sticks in my throat; I cannot stand it.
kropduif, cropper, pouter(-pigeon).
kropgans, pelican.
kropslaai, (cabbage-)lettuce.
krot, (-te), den, hovel, shanty, kennel.
krottebuurt, slums.
krui(e), (ge-), 1. season, spice; flavour.
krui(e), (ge-), 2. wheel, tundie (a barrow).
kruid, (kruie) herb; (pl.) spice.
kruidenier, (-s), grocer.
kruideniersware, groceries.
kruidenierswinkel, grocer's (shop), grocery-shop.
krui(d)erig, (-e), spiced, spicy.
kruidjie-roer-my-nie(t), (-s), touchy person; sensitive plant, touch-me-not.
kruie, vide **krui, kruid.**
kruiebrandewyn, spiced brandy.
kruiedokter, -kenner, herbalist.
kruier, (-s), barrow-man; (luggage-)porter.
kruik, (-e), jar, jug, pitcher; urn.
kruin, (-e), crown, top; summit; crest (of wave).
kruinael(tjie), (-s), clove.
kruip, (ge-), creep, crawl; cringe, grovel; **op hande en voete –,** go on all fours; **in sy skulp –,** draw in one's horns.
kruipend, (-e), creeping, crawling; **–e dier,** reptile.
kruiperig, (-e), cringing, fawning, servile.
kruiperigheid, servility, toadyism.
kruipmol, golden mole.
kruipplant, crawling plant, trailer.
kruis, (-e), n. cross; sharp (in music); croup (of horse), crupper; small of the back (of man); loin; affliction, trial; **'n – slaan,** cross oneself; **aan die – slaan,** nail to the cross; **– of munt,** heads or tails.
kruis, (ge-), cross; intersect; crucify; cruise; **sig –,** cross oneself; **die swaard –,** cross swords; **skape –,** cross sheep.
kruisbalk, cross-beam.
kruisbande, (pair of) braces.
kruisbeeld, crucifix.
kruisbeen, adv. with crossed legs.
Kruisberg, (Mount) Calvary.
kruisbestuiwing, cross-pollination.
kruisbevrugting, cross-fertilization.
kruisbloemig, (-e), cruciferous.
kruisboog, cross-bow; (diagonal) arch.
kruisbrug, fly-over bridge.
kruisdood, death on the cross.
kruiselings, vide **kruislings.**
kruisement, mint.
kruiser, (-s), cruiser.
kruishout, the cross, the tree, the rood.
kruisie, (-s), cross, mark; dagger (printing).
kruisig, (ge-), crucify.
kruisiging, crucifixion.

kruising, cross(-breeding); crossing.
kruiskerk, cruciform church.
kruislaag, broken course (in masonry).
kruis(e)lings, crossways, crosswise.
kruispad, crossroad.
kruispunt, (point of) intersection; junction.
kruisridder, knight of the cross, Crusader.
kruisstraat, cross-street.
kruisteken, sign of the cross.
kruistog, crusade; cruise.
kruisvaarder, Crusader.
kruisvaart, crusade.
kruisverhoor, cross-examination; **in - neem**, cross-examine, cross-question.
kruisvra(ag), (ge-), cross-examine.
kruisvraag, n. cross-question.
kruisvuur, cross-fire.
kruiswoordraaisel, crossword puzzle.
kruit, powder, gunpowder; **jou - drooghou**, keep one's powder dry; **jou - verspil**, waste powder and shot.
kruitdamp, (gun)powder-smoke.
kruitfabriek, powder-mill.
kruithoring, powder-horn (-flask).
kruitmagasyn, powder-magazine.
kruiwa, (wheel-)barrow; **'n - hê**, have powerful patronage (influential backing).
kruiwavol, (wheel)barrow-load.
kruk, (-ke), n. crutch; perch; crank; crock; stool; door-handle; **met -ke loop**, walk with (go on) crutches; **'n ou -**, an old crock; **hake en -ke**, game of leg-hooking.
kruk, (ge-), go on crutches; be ailing (crocked).
krukas, crankshaft.
krukkas, crankcase.
krukker, (-s), crock.
krukkerig, (-e), ailing, seedy; crocky.
krul, (-le), n. curl; shaving (of wood); flourish (of pen); scroll (ornamental).
krul, (ge-), curl; frizz, wave (hair).
krulhare, curly hair.
krulhou, curly ball (in cricket); screw.
krulkop, curly-head.
krulkopklonkie, curly-headed (native) boy.
krullebol, curly-head.
krullerig, (-e), curly.
krulletjie, (-s), (little) curl, ringlet.
krullyn, spiral line.
krulpen, curler.
krultang, -yster, curling-tongs.
krummel, (-s), n. crumb.
krummel, (ge-), crumble.
krummelrig, (-e), crumbly, crumby.
kruppel, vide **kreupel**.
kry, (ge-), get, receive, obtain, catch (a cold); have (a baby), acquire (knowledge); **longontsteking -**, contract pneumonia; **'n ongeluk -**, meet with an accident; **hoeveel - jy van my?**, how much do I owe you?; **iemand daartoe -**, get a person to do something; **dit is nie te - nie**, it is not to be had (not procurable); **ek sal hom -**, I'll pay him out; **ek kon hom nie te sien - nie**, I could not get hold of him; **mekaar -**, get married (in the end); **woorde -**, pick a quarrel; **iemand onder die klippe -**, throw stones at someone; **jy sal -**, you'll get a whacking; vide **kleinkry**.
kryg, n. fight, war; **- voer**, wage war.
kryg, (ge-), make (wage) war.
kryger, (-s), warrior.
krygsbasuin, war-trumpet.
krygsbende, band (troop) of soldiers.
krygsbevelhebber, military commander.
krygsdiens, military service.
krygsgevangene, prisoner of war.
krygsgevange(n)skap, captivity.
krygshaftig, (-e), bellicose, martial, warlike.
krygshaftigheid, martial spirit, valour.
krygskans, chance(s) of war.
krygskneg, soldier.
krygskunde, -kuns, military science, art of war.
krygskundig, (-e), military.
krygslewe, military life.
krygslied, war-song.
krygsliede, soldiers, warriors; vide **krygsman**.
krygslis, stratagem, strategy.
krygsmag, military force.
krygsman, (-ne, krygsliede), soldier, warrior.
krygsplig, military duty.
krygsraad, court-martial; council of war.
krygsreg, martial law.
krygstoerusting, equipment for war.
krygstog, campaign, expedition.
krygstug, military discipline.
krygsugtig, (-e), bellicose, warlike.
krygsugtigheid, warlike spirit.
krygsverrigtinge, military operations.
krygsvolk, soldiers, soldiery, the military.
krygsvoorraad, military stores.
krygswet, martial law.
krygswetenskap, military science.
krygsvoerend, (-e), belligerent.
krys, (ge-), scream, shriek, screech; cry; croak.
kryt, 1. chalk; crayon.
kryt, 2. arena; **in die - tree**, enter l theists.
krytagtig, (-e), chalky, cretaceous.
krytdoos, chalk-box.
krytstreep, chalk-line, white line.
kryttekening, crayon-drawing.
krytwit, chalk-white, as white as chalk.
Kuba, Cuba.
Kubaans, (-e), Cuban.
kubeer, (ge-), cube, raise to the third power.
kubiek, (-e), n. cube; **tot die - verhef**, cube.
kubiek, (-e), a. cube, cubic; **-e inhoud**, cubic content; **-e maat**, cubic measure.
kubiekgetal, cube-number.
kubiekwortel, cube- (cubic) root.
kubisme, cubism.
kubus, (-se), cube.
kubusvormig, (-e), cubical, cube-shaped.
kudde, (-s), flock.
kuddedier, gregarious animal.
kuddegees, -gevoel, -instink, herd-sense (-instinct).
kug, (-ge), n. (dry) cough.
kug, (ge-), cough; give a cough, hem.
kuier, n. visit, call, outing.
kuier, (ge-), call, visit; stroll.
kuiergas, guest.
kuif, (kuiwe), n. tuft, topknot; crest, hood.
kuif- . . ., crested, crowned, tufted.
kuifbal, shuttlecock.
kuifkopvoël, bulbul, topknot, blackcap.
kuiken, (-s), chicken; youngster.
kuikendief, Cape kite, harrier.
kuil, (-e), hole, pit; pool.
kuil, (ge-), put in pits, ensile, (en)silage, silo.
kuiltjie, (-s), hole: dimple.
kuilvoer, (en)silage, silo(-fodder).
kuip, (-e), n. tub; vat.
kuip, (ge-), cooper; scheme, intrigue.
kuipbalie, tub, vat.
kuiper, (-s), cooper; intriguer, schemer.
kuipersambag, -werk, cooper's work.
kuipery, coopery; intriguing, scheming.
kuiphout, staves.
kuis, (-e), chaste, virtuous, virginal.
kuisheid, chastity, purity.
kuit, (-e), n. 1. calf (of leg).
kuit, n. 2. roe, spawn (of fish).

kuitbeen, splint-bone, fibula.
kuitbroek, jeans.
kuitkouse, half-hose.
kuitspier, sural muscle.
kul, (ge-), cheat, deceive.
kullery, kulwerk, cheating, deceit.
kulminasie, culmination.
kulmineer, (ge-), culminate.
kultiveer, (ge-), cultivate.
kultureel, (-rele), cultural.
kultus, cult.
kultuur, (-ture), culture; cultivation.
kultuurgeskiedenis, cultural history.
kultuurhistories, (-e), socio-historical, from the point of view of cultural history.
kultuurmedium, culture-medium.
kultuurstelsel, culture-system.
kultuurvolk, civilized nation.
kunde, knowledge, learning, art.
kundig, (-e), able, experienced, skilful.
kundigheid, learning, knowledge, skill; **-hede** (pl.), accomplishments, attainments.
kunne, n. sex.
kuns, (-te), n. art; knack, trick, feat; **dit is die –**, that's the point; **hy verstaan die – om**, he knows how to; **–te en wetenskappe**, arts and sciences; **die beeldende –te**, the plastic arts; **die skone –te**, the fine arts; **die boer die – afvra**, ask too much.
kunsbeen, artificial leg.
kunsbeskermer, patron of art.
kunsbeskouing, conception of art.
kunsblom, artificial flower.
kunsbroe(d)er, brother-artist.
kunsgalery, art-gallery.
kunsgebit, (set of) artificial teeth, denture.
kunsgenootskap, society of arts.
kunsgenot, artistic enjoyment (pleasure).
kunsgeskiedenis, history of art.
kunsgevoel, artistic sense.
kunsgewrog, product of art, work of art.
kunsgreep, artifice, knack, trick.
kunshandel, trade in works of art; fine-art repository; **hy het 'n –**, he deals in works of art.
kunshandelaar, art-dealer.
kunshandwerk, art-needlework.
kunsie, (-s), feat, trick, knack, dodge.
kunsjuwele, costume jewellery.
kunskenner, art-connoisseur.
kunskring, art-circle, artistic society.
kunskritiek, art-criticism, criticism of art.
kunskritikus, art-critic.
kunsleer, imitation-leather, leatherette.
kunsliefde, love of art.
kunsliefhebber, art-lover, lover of art.
kunsliewend, (-e), art-loving, artistic.
kunslig, artificial light.
kunsmatig, (-e), artificial.
kunsmatigheid, artificiality.
kunsmiddel, artificial means, expedient; art(s).
kunsmis, artificial manure, fertilizer.
kunsnywerheid, industrial art, arts and crafts.
kunsproduk, product (work) of art.
kunsrubber, synthetic rubber.
kunsryk, (-e), artistic.
kunssin, artistic sense (judgment, talent, taste).
kunssinnig, (-e), artistic; art-loving.
kunssinnigheid, artisticity, artistic gift.
kunsskatte, art-treasures.
kunsskilder, artist, painter.
kunsskool, art-school, school of art.
kunssmaak, artistic taste.
kunsstuk, work of art; clever feat.
kunssy, artificial silk, rayon.
kunstand, artificial tooth.

kunsteloos, (-lose), artless, naïve.
kunstemaker, acrobat; juggler.
kunstenaar, (-nare, -s), artist.
kunstenares, artist(e).
kunstentoonstelling, art-exhibition.
kunstig, (-e), artful, skilful, clever; artistic.
kunstigheid, ingeniousness; artisticity.
kunstiglik, artfully, cleverly, ingeniously.
kunsvaardig, (-e), clever, skilful.
kunsvaardigheid, cleverness, skill.
kunsversameling, art-collection.
kunsvlieëry, aerobatics.
kunsvlug, flying-stunt.
kunsvol, (-le), artistic.
kunsvoorwerp, object of art.
kunsvorm, artistic form (shape).
kunswaarde, artistic value.
kunswerk, work of art.
kunswol, artificial (synthetic) wool.
kurang, vide **kierang**.
kuras, (-se), cuirass.
kurassier, (-s), cuirassier.
kurator, (-e, -s), curator, custodian.
kuriositeit, (-e), curiosity; relic, curio.
kuriositeitehandelaar, curio-dealer.
kurk, (-e), n. cork.
kurk, (ge-), cork, close (a bottle).
kurkdroog, (-droë), as dry as dust, bone-dry.
kurk(e)trekker, corkscrew.
kurper, (-s), carp.
kursief, (-iewe), in italics, italicized.
kursiveer, (ge-), print in italics, italicize.
kursories, (-e), cursory.
kursus, (-se), course, curriculum.
kurwe, (-s), curve, graph.
kus, (-se), n. 1. kiss.
kus, (-te), n. 2. coast, shore; **aan die –**, on the coast; **digby die –**, off the coast; **onder die –** inshore.
kus, n. 3. **te – en te keur**, in plenty, of a wide choice; **jy kan te – en te keur gaan**, you can pick and choose.
kus, (ge-), kiss.
kusbewoner, coast-dweller.
kusboot, coast- (coastal) steamer.
kusek, cusec.
kusgebied, coastal area (belt), littoral.
kushand(jie), hand-blown kiss; **'n – gee**, blow a kiss, kiss one's hand to.
kuslyn, coastline, shoreline.
kussing, (-s), cushion; pillow (of bed).
kussingband, balloon-tyre.
kussingsloop, pillow-case, pillow-slip.
kusstad, coast- (coastal) town.
kusstreek, coastal belt (area), littoral.
kusstrook, coastal strip (margin).
kusting, (-s), bond, mortgage.
kusvaarder, (-s), coaster, coasting-vessel.
kusvaart, coasting-trade.
kusverdediging, coast- (coastal) defence.
kuswag, coastguard.
kuur, (kure), cure; caprice, whim, freak.
kwaad, n. evil, wrong, harm, mischief; injury, damage; **goed en –**, good and evil; **– doen**, do wrong, be up to mischief; do harm, injure; **hy bedoel g'n – nie**, he means no harm; **– stig**, brew mischief; **sy saak – doen**, injure one's cause; **iets ten kwade dui**, take something ill (amiss); **van – tot erger**, from bad to worse; **– met goed vergeld**, return good for evil; **'n noodsaaklike –**, a necessary evil.
kwaad, a. & adv. angry, annoyed, cross, vexed; **iemand – maak**, make a person angry; rub someone up the wrong way; **– word**, get angry; **– wees op (vir)**, be angry with; **dit is nog nie so**

- **nie,** that is not half bad; **te kwader ure, in** an evil hour.
kwaadaardig, (-e), malicious, vicious; malignant, virulent (disease).
kwaadaardigheid, malignity; virulence.
kwaaddenkend, (-e), suspicious, prone to think ill (of someone).
kwaaddoener, (-s), evildoer; rascal, imp.
kwaaddoenerig, (-e), mischievous
kwaadgeld: vir – rondloop, loaf about.
kwaadheid, anger.
kwaadskiks, unwillingly.
kwaadspreek, (kwaadge-), talk scandal.
kwaadspreker, -spreekster, scandalmonger, backbiter.
kwaadstoker, -stookster, mischief-maker.
kwaadwillig, (-e), malevolent, ill-disposed.
kwaadwilligheid, malevolence; foul play.
kwaai, bad-tempered, ill-natured, vicious; harsh; strict.
kwaai(ig)heid, bad temper; strictness.
kwaaivri(e)nde, bad friends.
kwaaivri(e)ndskap, enmity, hostility; **in – lewe,** not to be on speaking terms.
kwaak, (ge-), croak; quack.
kwaal, (kwale), ailment, complaint, disease.
kwadraat, (-drade), n. square; **X-kwadraat,** X-squared; **tot die – verhef,** square.
kwadraat, a. square; quadratic.
kwadraatgetal, square number.
kwadraatsvergelyking, quadratic equation.
kwadraatwortel, square root.
kwadrant, (-e), quadrant.
kwadraties, (-e), quadratic.
kwadratuur, quadrature.
kwagga, (-s), quagga.
kwajong, (-ens), rascal, mischievous boy.
kwajongensagtig, (-e), boyish, mischievous.
kwajongensagtigheid, mischievousness.
kwajong(en)streek, boy's trick, practical joke.
Kwaker, (-s), Quaker.
kwakkel, (-s), quail.
kwaksalwe, (ge-), (play the) quack.
kwaksalwer, (-s), quack, charlatan.
kwaksalwersmiddel, quack-remedy.
kwaksalwery, quackery.
kwal, (-le), jellyfish.
kwalifikasie, (-s), qualification.
kwalifiseer, (ge-), qualify.
kwalik, hardly, scarecely; – **neem,** take amiss (ill), resent; **neem my nie – nie,** excuse me; **ek neem jou nie – nie,** I don't blame you; – **in staat om,** hardly (scarcely) able to.
kwalitatief, (-tiewe), qualitative.
kwaliteit, (-e), quality; capacity.
kwansel, (ge-), haggle, barter, truck.
kwanselaar, (-s), haggler, barterer.
kwansel(a)ry, bartering, truck, haggling.
kwansuis, vide **konsuis.**
kwantitatief, (-tiewe), quantitative.
kwantiteit, (-e), quantity, amount.
kwantum, (-s), quantum, amount.
kwarantyn, quarantine.
kwart, (-e), quarter; fourth part; quart; crotchet; – **oor een,** a quarter past one.
kwartaal, (-tale), quarter; (school-)term.
kwartaalrekening, quarterly account.
kwartaalsgewys, quarterly, every three months.
kwartel, (-s), quail.
kwartier, (-e), quarter of an hour, quarter (of moon); district (of town); (military) quarters, billet; **geen – gee nie,** give no quarter.
kwartiermeester, quartermaster.
kwartnoot, crotchet.
kwarto, (-'s), quarto.

kwarts, quartz.
kwas, (-te), 1. brush; tuft; tassel (ornament); knot (in wood), node; **dit is R5 aan sy –,** he'll have to pay up R5.
kwas, 2. (lemon-)squash.
kwasie, quasi, mock, pretend.
kwasterig, (-e), knotty, gnarled; difficult.
kweek, n. couch-, quick-grass.
kweek, (ge-), cultivate, grow (plants); breed (animals); foster (goodwill), nourish (hatred); train; **gekweekte rente,** accrued interest.
kweekgras, vide **kweek,** n.
kweekplaas, -plek, nursery; hotbed.
kweekskool, training-school (-college), (theological) seminary.
kweel, (ge-), carol, warble.
kween, (kwene), barren cow (mare, etc.).
kwekeling, (-e), pupil; apprentice; pupil-teacher.
kweker, (-s), grower; breeder; nurseryman.
kwekery, (-e), nursery.
kwel, (ge-), torment, annoy, vex, worry, nag, tease; **die gedagte – my,** the thought worries me (preys on my mind).
kwelgees, teaser, tormentor.
kwelling, (-e), (-s), torment, trouble, worry.
kweper, (-s), quince.
kweperheining, -laning, quince-hedge.
kweperlat, quince-stock; **onder die – deurloop, met die – kry,** be birched (licked).
kwe(t)s, (ge-), wound, hurt; bruise; grieve, offend.
kwe(t)sbaar, (-bare), vulnerable.
kwe(t)sbaarheid, vulnerability.
kwessie, (-s), matter, question; issue; quarrel; **geen – van nie,** that's out of the question; **'n – van tyd,** a matter (question) of time; **die saak in –,** the point at issue; **buiten die –,** outside the question; beyond dispute.
kwestieus, (-e), questionable; contentious.
kwets(baar), vide **kwes(baar).**
kwetsend, (-e), offensive, outrageous.
kwetsing, hurt, offence.
kwetsuur, (-sure), hurt, injury, wound.
kwetter, (ge-), chirp, twitter.
kwêvoël, grey lourie.
kwik, mercury, quicksilver.
kwikbarometer, mercury barometer.
kwikdamp, mercury-vapour.
kwikmyn, quicksilver-mine.
kwikoksied, kwikokside, oxide of mercury.
kwiksilwer, quicksilver, mercury.
kwikstertjie, (-s), wagtail.
kwiktermometer, mercury thermometer.
kwinkeleer, (ge-), carol, twitter, warble.
kwikslag, joke, quip, quiz, witticism, wisecrack.
kwint, (-e), fifth, quint (mus.); **vol -e wees,** be full of freaks (whims).
kwintessens, quintessence, pith, gist.
kwintet, (-te), quintet(te).
kwintsnaar, E-string.
kwispedoor, (-dore, -s), spittoon.
kwispel, (ge-), wag the tail.
kwispelstert, (ge-), wag the tail.
kwistig, (-e), lavish, liberal, prodigal.
kwistigheid, lavishness, prodigality.
kwitansie, (-s), receipt.
kwiteer, (ge-), receipt.
Kwomintang, Kuomintang.
kworum, (-s), quorum.
kwosiënt, (-e), quotient.
kwota, (-s), quota, contingent, share.
kwyl, n. drivel, slaver.
kwyl, (ge-), drivel, slaver, run at the mouth.
kwylbaard, kwyler, driveller, slobberer.
kwyn, (ge-), languish; wither (plants); flag (interest); fall into decline.

kwynend, (-e), languishing; vide kwyn.
kwyt, adv.: – raak, lose, get rid of.
kwyt, (ge-): jou – van . . . , acquit oneself of (a task), discharge, perform.
kwytbrief, receipt; acquittal.
kwyting, discharge, performance; payment.
kwytskel(d), (kwytge-), forgive (sins), let (someone) off; remit (taxes).
kwytskelding, absolution (of sins); acquittal, pardon; remission (of taxes, etc.).
kyf, (ge-), dispute, quarrel, wrangle.
kyfagtig, (-e), quarrelsome.
kyfsiek, (-e), quarrelsome.
kyk, n. aspect, look; view; sy – op die saak, his view of the matter; sy – op die lewe, his outlook (upon life); dit gee 'n – op . . . , it sheds light on . . . ; 'n – op iets kry, begin to see more clearly.
kyk, (ge-), look, see, view; pry; nou –!, fancy!; in die bottel (glas) –, be addicted to drink; – na, look at; look after, attend to; op sy neus –, look foolish; goed uit jou oë –, be very observant, watch your p's and q's.
kyker, (-s), looker-on, spectator; eye, pupil; spyglass, telescope; opera-glass.
kykgat, peephole, sight-hole.
kykie, (-s), look, peep, squint.
kyk-in-die-pot, Paul Pry, Miss Nancy.
kyklus, eagerness to see, inquisitiveness.
kyklustig, (-e), eager to see, inquisitive.
kykspel, peepshow; spectacular play.
kykuit, look-out, watching-tower.

L

laaf, lawe, (ge-), refresh; try to restore consciousness; **sig −,** refresh oneself; slake one's thirst.
laafnis, vide **lafenis.**
laag, (lae), n. layer; bed, stratum (geology); coat(ing) (of paint); course (of bricks); **lae van die samelewing,** social grades; **die volle −,** a broadside; **iemand lae lê,** lay snares for a person.
laag, (lae), a. & adv. low, base, infamous, mean, vile (creature); foul.
laag-by-die-grond, (-se), commonplace.
laaggeleë, low-lying (countries).
laaggety, ebb.
laaghartig, (-e), base, low, mean, vile.
laaghartigheid, baseness, vileness, meanness.
laagheid, lowness; meanness, baseness.
laagland, low land.
laagspanning, low voltage; low tension.
laagte, leegte, (-s), valley, dip, "laagte"; lowness; **oor hoogtes en deur −s,** up hill and down dale.
laagtetjie, leegtetjie, (-s), slight dip.
laagvlakte, low-lying plain.
laagwater, low tide; **by −,** at low tide.
laai, n. 1. in **ligte −(e),** ablaze, in a blaze.
laai, (-e), n. 2. drawer; till; stock (of gun).
laai, (-e), n. 3. custom, habit, trick, dodge; **dis sy ou −,** that is his usual trick.
laai, (ge-), load, charge.
laaigat, touch-hole.
laaikas, chest of drawers; box (mining).
laaiplek, loading-place, berth.
laaistok, ramrod; charging-stick (in mining).
laaitafel, chest of drawers; table with a drawer.
laaitjie, (-s), little drawer; till.
laak, (ge-), blame, find fault with.
laakbaar, (-bare), reprehensible.
laan, (lane), avenue.
laars, (-e), boot; **sewemylslaarse,** seven-league boots.
laas, last; **ek het hom lank − gesien,** it is a long time since I saw him last; **hy was − nog in Amerika,** the last time I heard (of him) he was still in America; **vir −,** for the last time; before we part.
laasgemelde, -genoemde, latter, last-named.
laaslede, last; **− Vrydag,** Friday last.
laaste, n. last one; **die −,** the last one; the latter; **op sy −,** at the point of death (vide **laat,** a.); **op die −,** at last; at the eleventh hour; **ten (lange) −,** at (long) last; **tot op die −,** to the last.
laaste, a. & adv. last; latest (reports); **die − maal,** the last time; **die − oordeel,** the last judgment; **ek het hom die − vyf dae nie gesien nie,** it is five days since I saw him last; **in die − tyd,** lately, recently, of late; **in die − jare,** of late years, in recent years.
laastelik, finally, lastly.
laat, (−, late), a. late; **hoe − is dit?,** what is the time?; **hoe − kom hy?,** what time is he coming?; **hy is −,** he hasn't got a hope; **jy's −!,** no fear!, you've got a hope!; **jy is − as jy dink jy kan my fop,** you are mistaken if you think you can cheat me; **beter − as nooit,** better late than never; **op sy (die) −ste,** at the (very) latest.
laat, adv. late; **− in die aand,** late at night; **te − om hom nog te sien,** too late to see him.
laat, (ge-), let; leave; allow, permit, let; leave off; stop; refrain from (doing); make (person do a thing); have (something) done; **met rus −,** leave in peace; **ons sal dit daarby −,** we'll leave it at that; **ek − my dit nie vertel nie,** I refuse to believe it; **− ons loop,** let us go; **− my dit doen,** let me do it; **iemand die tyd −,** allow a person the time; **'n pak klere − maak,** have a suit made; **ek het my goed daar − staan,** I left my things there; **− hom staan,** leave him (alone); **− val,** drop, let fall; **− weet,** let (person) know, send word; **− vra,** send to ask; **− haal,** send for; **− wag,** keep waiting; **waar het jy dit ge−?,** where did you leave (put) it?; **hy kan dit nie − nie,** he cannot help himself.
laatdunkend, (-e), conceited, arrogant.
laatdunkendheid, self-conceit, arrogance.
labiaal, (-ale), labial.
labiel, (-e), labile, unstable; **−e ewewig,** neutral equilibrium.
labirint, (-e), labyrinth.
laboratorium, (-s, -ria), laboratory, "lab."
Lacedemonies, (-e), Lacedaemonian.
lading, (-e, -s), load; cargo; charge.
ladingskoste, shipping-charges.
lae, vide **laag.**
laer, (-s), n. camp, lager; **− trek,** form a lager.
laer, a. lower; primary (education).
laer, (ge-), lager, go into camp.
Laerhuis, House of Assembly (S. Africa), Lower House, House of Commons (Eng.).
laerplek, (site of) lager (camp).
laerskool, primary school.
laerwal, lee-shore; **aan − wees,** be on the rocks, be on one's beam-ends.
laeveld, low veld, low country.
laf, (lawwe), silly; insipid; cowardly.
lafaard, (-s), coward.
lafbek, fool, silly fellow.
lafenis, laafnis, refreshment; relief.
lafhartig, (-e), cowardly.
lafhartigheid, cowardiness, cowardice.
lag, n. laugh, laughter; **uitbars van die −,** burst out laughing; **hy kon sy − nie hou nie,** he could not help laughing.
lag, (ge-), laugh; **stilletjie −,** chuckle; **sig 'n boggel (slap, dood) −,** split one's sides with; **− om,** laugh at; **dis om te −,** it makes one laugh; **− oor vir,** laugh at.
lagbui, fit of laughter.
lagerbier, lager beer.
laggas, laughing-gas.
laggend, (-e), a. & adv. laughing(ly).
laggerig, (-e), inclined to laugh, giggling.
laggery, laughing, laughter.
lag-lag, laughingly.
laglus, inclination to laugh, hilarity, risibility; **die − opwek,** provoke laughter.
laglustig, (-e), laughter-loving, hilarious.
lagsiek, giggling, given to laughter.
lagsiekte, "laughing sickness", giggles.
lagune, (-s), lagoon.
lagwekkend, (-e), laughable; ludicrous.
lak, n. sealing-wax; lac, lacquer (varnish).
lak, (-s), 1. seal (letter); lacquer, japan.
lak, (ge-), 2. tackle, bring down hard.
lakei, (-e), lackey, footman.
laken, (-s), cloth; sheet (for bed); **die −s uitdeel,** boss the show.
lakenhandel, cloth-trade.
lakense, cloth; **− pak,** cloth-suit.
lakenwewery, cloth-weaving; cloth-factory.
laker, (-s), fault-finder.
lakleer, patent leather.
lakmoes, litmus.
lakonie, (-e), a. & adv. laconic(ally).
laks, (−, -e), lax, slack.
laksheid, laxity, slackness.
lakskoen, patent-leather shoe.
laksman, executioner; butcher-bird.
lakune, (-e), gap, blank, lacuna.
lakwerk, lacquer(ing); lacquered ware.
lam, (-mers), n. lamb.

lam, a. paralysed; tired, weary, fatigued; sigh;
– skrik, be paralysed with fright.
lam, (ge-), lamb.
lama, (-s), 1. lama (priest).
lama, (-s), 2. llama (animal).
lambrisering, panelling, wainscoting.
lamenteer, (ge-), lament.
lamheid, paralysis; tiredness, fatigue.
lamlendig, (-e), miserable.
lammeling, (-e), miserable specimen.
lammeroes, a season's lambs.
lammerooi, ewe with lamb, lambing ewe.
lammertyd, lambing-season.
lammervanger, martial eagle.
lammerwol, lamb's wool, hoggets.
lammetjie, (-s, lammertjies), (little) lamb.
lamp, (-e), lamp; valve (wireless).
lampetbeker, -kan, toilet-jug.
lampetkom, wash(-hand)-basin.
lampglas, lamp-chimney.
lampion, (-s), Chinese lantern.
lampkap, lamp-shade.
lamppit, lamp-wick.
lamsak, (-ke), spunkless fellow, slacker.
lamsalig, (-e), miserable.
lamsboud, leg of lamb.
lamsiekte, "lamsiekte".
lamskotelet, lamb-cutlet.
lamslaan, (lamge-), paralyse; render helpless;
sig –, beat until one is tired; **ek was lamgeslaan**,
I was struck all of a heap.
lamvleis, lamb.
lamtyd, lammertyd, lambing-season.
land, (-e), n. land; field; country; shore; **my –**,
my country (native-land); **– en sand aanmekaar**,
endlessly, on end; **hy is lank in die –**,
he knows the ropes; **aan –**, on land; ashore;
aan – sit, put ashore; **op die –**, on land; in
the country; **te – en te water**, by land and sea;
hier te –e, in this country; **te –e kom**, land.
land, (ge-), land; disembark.
landarbeider, agricultural labourer.
landbesitter, landowner.
landbou, agriculture.
landboubedryf, agricultural industry.
landboudepartement, department of agriculture.
landbouer, (-s), farmer, agriculturist.
landbougereedskap, agricultural implements.
landboukollege, agricultural college.
landboukunde, agriculture, agricultural science.
landboukundige, (-e), agricultural.
landboukundige, (-s), agriculturist.
landboukursus, course in agriculture.
landbou-onderwys, agricultural instruction.
landbouproduk, agricultural product.
landbouskeikunde, agricultural chemistry.
landbouskool, agricultural college.
landboutentoonstelling, agricultural show.
landbouwetenskap, agricultural science.
landdag, diet.
landdros, (-te), landdrost, magistrate.
landeienaar, landowner.
landelik, (-e), rural; country- . . . ; rustic.
landengte, isthmus.
landerye, cultivated fields (lands).
landgenoot, (-note), (fellow-)countryman.
landgoed, (-ere), country-estate.
landheer, landlord.
landhuis, country-house.
landhuishoudkunde, rural economy.
landing, landing.
landingsbrug, gangway.
landingsbaan, runway.
landingsplaas, -plek, landing-place.
landingstrook, air-strip.

landkaart, map.
landklimaat, continental climate.
landloper, tramp, vagabond.
landmag, land-forces.
landman, farmer.
landmeet, (landge-), survey.
landmeetkunde, geodesy.
landmeetkundig, (-e), geodetic.
landmeetkundige, (-s), geodesist.
landmeter, (land-)surveyor.
landmeter-generaal, (landmeters-generaal), surveyor-general.
landmeting, surveying, land-survey.
landmyn, land-mine.
landontginning, land-reclamation.
landpaal, boundary(-post).
landreis, journey (by land), tour.
landroete, overland route.
landrot, land-rat; landlubber (naut.).
landsake, affairs of the country.
landsgeaardheid, nature of the country; national character.
landskap, (-pe), landscape.
landskapskilder, landscape-painter.
landskas, (national) treasury.
landsman, (landsliede, -lui), countryman.
landsplaag, general pest.
landsreën, -reent, general rain.
landsregering, government of the country.
landstaal, language of the country.
landstreek, region, district.
landsverdediging, national defence.
landtong, spit of land.
landverhuiser, emigrant.
landverhuising, emigration.
landverskuiwing, landslide, -slip.
landvoog, governor.
landwaarts, landwards.
landwerk, work on the land, field-labour.
landwind, land-breeze, -wind.
lanfer, crêpe (crape).
lang, (attrib.), **lank** (pred). long; tall (person);
– **jare gelede**, many years ago; **so lank as dit breed is**, as long as it is broad; vide **lank**.
langademig, (-e), long-winded.
langasemsprinkaan, cricket.
langbeen,, longshanks.
langbeenspinnekop, daddy-long-legs.
langdeling, long division.
langdradig, (-e), tedious, long-winded.
langdurig, (-e), long (illness); of long duration, long-standing, protracted.
langdurigheid, long duration.
langer, vide **lank**.
langeraad, middle-finger.
lang(e)s, vide **langs**.
langgerek, (-te), long-drawn-out.
langharig, (-e), long-haired.
langhoofdig, (-e), long-headed.
langlewend, (-e), long-lived.
langoog : – wees, be jealous (yellow-eyed).
langoor, long-ears; donkey.
langorig, (-e), long-eared.
langs, next (to), beside; alongside of; along;
die grond, op die grond –, along the ground;
– **my verby**, past me; – **die pad**, on the way;
– **die mure**, round the walls.
langsaam, (-same), a. slow, tardy, lingering.
langsaam, adv. slow(ly).
langsaan, next door to; **net –**, just next door.
langsamerhand, gradually, by degrees.
langsdeursnee, longitudinal section.
langskedelig, (-e), dolichocephalic.
langslewende, (-s), survivor.
langstert, long-tailed tit.

langwa, long wag(g)on, perch-pole.
langwerpig, (-e), oblong.
langwylig, (-e), long-winded, tedious.
laning, (-s), hedge.
lank, lang, long; a long time; **twee voet –**, two feet long; **'n tyd –**, for a time; **jare –**, for years; **sy (hele), lewe –**, his life long, all his life; **hy is al – siek**, he has been ill a long time; **jy moes dit al –(al) gedoen het**, you should have done it long ago; **– nie**, by no means, not by a long way; **– nie sleg nie**, not at all bad; **hoe langer hoe beter**, the longer the better; **hoe langer hoe vinniger**, faster and faster; **hoe langer hoe meer**, more and more; **op sy langste**, at the outside; **– laas**, vide **laas**.
lankal, long, long ago.
lankmoedig, (-e), long-suffering, patient.
lankmoedigheid, patience, long-suffering.
lank-uit, at full length.
lanolien, lanoline, lanolin.
lans, (-e), lance.
lanseer, (ge-), launch.
lanset, (-te), lancet.
lansier, (-s), lancer.
lanterfanter, (-s), idler, loiterer, loafer.
lanterfanter, (ge-), idle, loiter, loaf.
lantern, (-s), lantern.
lanternpaal, lamp-post.
lanternplaatjie, lantern-slide.
lap, (-pe), n. rag; cloth (for wiping, rubbing); patch; piece; remnant (of material); bandage (round finger); **iets op die –pe bring**, bring on the carpet, broach subject.
lap, (ge-), patch; mend; patch up.
lapel, (-le), lapel.
Lap(lander), Lapp, Laplander.
lapmiddel, patchwork, makeshift.
lappie, (-s), small piece (patch).
lappiesmous, ragman, pedlar.
lappop, rag-doll.
lapsus, slip, lapse, lapsus.
lapwerk, patchwork; tinkering.
lardeer, (ge-), lard.
larinks, (-e), larynx.
larwe, (-s), larva, grub.
las, (-se, -te), n. 1. weld, seam, joint.
las, (-te), n. 2. burden, load; cargo (of ship); nuisance, trouble; command, order; **bate en –te**, assets and liabilities; **– gee**, give instructions, order; **– veroorsaak**, give (cause) trouble; **– hê van**, be troubled with; **jou – dra**, bear your burden; **op (van) –**, by order (of); **ten –te lê**, charge with; **tot – wees**, be a burden; be a nuisance, give (cause) trouble.
las, (ge-), weld, join (together).
las, (ge-), instruct; vide **gelas**.
lasaret, (-te), lazaret(to).
lasarus, leprosy.
lasbrief, warrant, order, writ.
lasdier, beast of burden.
lasdraer, bearer of a load (burden).
laserstraal, laser beam.
lasgewer, principal.
lasgewing, instruction; mandate.
lasplek, joint, weld, rabbet.
laspos, (-te), nuisance, plague, bore.
lassie, (-s), vide **las**.
lasso, (-'s), lasso.
laster, n. slander, calumny; libel.
laster, (ge-), slander, defame; blaspheme.
lasteraar, (-s), slanderer, defamer; blasphemer.
lastering, slander; blasphemy.
lasterlik, (-e), slanderous, libellous; blasphemous (against God).
lasterpraatjie, slander, scandal.

lasterskrif, libel.
lastertaal, slander; blasphemy.
lastertong, slanderous tongue.
lastig, (-e), difficult, awkward; trying, delicate (question); troublesome; inconvenient; **– val**, trouble, pester.
lastigheid, troublesomeness; vide **lastig**.
lasuursteen, azure stone, lapis lazuli.
lat, (-te), cane, stick; lath (support); **onder die – kry**, cane.
latei, (-e), lintel.
latent, (-e), latent; **–e warmte**, latent heat.
later, adv. later; later on, afterwards; **hoe – hoe kwater**, worse and worse; the later the merrier.
lateraal, (-ale), lateral.
Latinisme, (-s), Latinism.
latitudinêr, (-e), latitudinarian.
latjie, (-s), little stick (cane).
latrine, (-s), latrine.
latwerk, lath-work, lattice-work; trellis.
Latyn, Latin.
Latyns, (-e), Latin.
laveer, (ge-), tack (about) (boat).
lavental, lavender.
laventelbos, (wild) lavender-shrub.
lawa, lava.
lawaai, n. noise, din, uproar, row, tumult.
lawaai, (ge-), make a noise, kick up a row.
lawaaierig, (-e), noisy, rowdy, uproarious.
lawaaierigheid, noisiness; vide **lawaaierig**.
lawaaimaker, rowdy, noisy person.
lawaaiwater, booze, spirits.
lawaglas, obsidian, vitreous lava.
lawastroom, lava-stream, lava-flow.
lawement, (-e), enema, lavement.
lawine, (-s), avalanche, snow-slide.
lawwigheid, silliness, foolishness.
lê, n. lie, lying; laying; **hy kon nie sy – kry nie**, he could not strike a comfortable position (in bed); **die henne is aan die –**, the hens are laying.
lê, **leg**, (ge-), put, place, lay; lie; **die fondament –**, lay the foundation; **gaan –**, go and lie down, drop (of wind); **laat –**, leave alone; **daar – die ding**, that's just it (the point); **dit – nie aan my nie**, it is not my fault; it does not rest with me; **dit – in my bedoeling**, I intend; **dit – in sy aard**, it is in his nature; **– op**, lie on; **uit die venster –**, lean out of the window.
lede, n. vide **lid**.
lede, a.: **met – oë**, regretfully.
ledegeld, subscription.
ledekant, bedstead.
ledelys, list of members.
ledemate, vide **lidmaat**.
ledetal, membership, number of members.
ledig, (-e), a. idle; **–e tyd**, spare time.
ledig, (ge-), empty.
lediganger, idler.
ledigheid, idleness.
leed, harm; sorrow, grief, pain, affliction; **dit doen my –**, I am sorry; it grieves me; **iemand – aandoen**, cause a person grief; vide **lief**.
leedvermaak, malicious joy.
leedwese, regret; **– betuig**, express regret.
leef, lewe, (ge-), live; **hulle kan goed –**, they are comfortably off; **– en laat –**, live and let live; **lank – die President!**, three cheers for the President!; **– van, lewe van**; **– volgens jou geloof**, live up to one's faith.
leefreël, diet; rule of life.
leeftog, subsistence; provisions.
leeftyd, lifetime; age; **op my –**, at my age.
leeftydsgrens, age-limit.
leefwyse, way (manner) of living.

leeg, (leë), a. empty; vacant (seat, house).
leeg, (ge-), vide **ledig**.
leegheid, emptiness; vide **leeg**.
leeghoofdig, (-e), empty-headed.
leegloop (leegge-), run dry; become deflated (of tyre); idle, loaf; **laat** –, empty, drain off; deflate.
leegloper, loafer, idler.
leeglopery, loafing, idling.
leegmaak, (leegge-), empty; clear (table).
leegsit, (leegge-), sit idle.
leegte, emptiness; blank; vide **laagte**.
leek, (leke), layman.
leem, loam, clay.
leemte, (-s), gap, blank, lacuna; void; 'n – **aanvul**, supply a deficiency.
leen, n. feudal tenure; **in** – **hê**, have the loan of; **te** – **gee**, lend; **te** – **kry**, get the loan of; **te** – **vra**, borrow.
leen, (ge-), borrow (from); lend (to); **sig** – **tot**, lend oneself (itself) to.
leenbank, loan-bank, credit-bank.
leendiens, feudal service.
leengeld, borrowed maney.
leengoed, feudal estate; borrowed things.
leenheer, feudal lord.
leenman, vassal.
leenreg, feudal right; feudal law.
leenstelsel, feudal system.
leenwese, feudalism.
leepoë, blear eyes.
leer, n. 1. leather; – **om** –, tit for tat.
leer, (lere), n. 2. ladder.
leer, n. 3. apprenticeship; doctrine; theory; teaching (of Christ); **in die** – **doen by**, apprentice to; **in die** – **wees by**, serve one's apprenticeship with.
leer, (ge-), teach (children); learn (language); **tot by st. VI** –, go as far as Std. VI; **hy het ver ge**–, he has had a good education; **van buite** –, learn by heart; **ek sal hom** –, I'll teach (show) him; **dit sal die tyd ons** –, time will show; **nood** – **bid**, neccessity is the mother of invention; – **ken**, get to know, become acquainted with; **vir dokter,** – study medicine.
leër, (-s), n. army; host, multitude.
leër, (ge-), encamp.
lêer, (-s), layer (hen); leaguer (for wine); sleeper (railway); file; register.
leeragtig, (-e), leathery.
leerband, strap.
leërbende, band (troop) of soldiers.
leërbereiding, leather-dressing, currying.
leerboek, text-book; school-book.
leerdig, didactic poem.
leergang, course of study.
leergeld, school-fees; tuition-fee; – **betaal**, learn something to one's cost.
leergierig, (-e), eager to learn, studious.
leergoed, leather-goods.
leerhandel, leather-trade.
leëring, **legering**, encampment.
leerjaar, year of study, year's course.
leerjare, years of apprenticeship.
leerjonge, (-ns), apprentice.
leërkorps, army-corps.
leerling, (–e), pupil; disciple.
leerling-klerk, indentured clerk, articled clerk.
leerling-onderwyser, pupil-teacher.
leerling-stelsel, apprentice-system.
leerling-verpleegster, probationer(-nurse).
leerlooier, tanner.
leerlooiery, tannery; tanning.
leerlus, studiousness, eagerness to learn.
leërmag, army (forces).
leermeester, teacher, tutor.
leermiddel, educational equipment.
leërorder, army-order(s), standing orders.
leërplaas, **-plek**, camp.
leerplan, syllabus, curriculum.
leerplig, compulsory education.
leerpligtig, (-e), of school-age.
leerrede, sermon.
leerryk, (-e), instructive.
leersaam, (-same), instructive; docile.
leersaamheid, instructiveness, docility.
leërskaar, host.
leerskool, school; **die** – **van beproewing**, the school of adversity.
leërstede, bed.
leerstellig, (-e), dogmatic.
leerstelling, (-e, -s), dogma, doctrine, tenet.
leerstelsel, system (of education).
leërsterkte, strength of the army.
leerstoel, leather-chair; professorate.
leerstof, subject-matter of teaching.
leerstuk, dogma, doctrine.
leertyd, time of learning; apprenticeship.
leeruur, study-hour.
leervak, subject (of study).
leervis, leerfish, garrick.
leerware, leather-goods.
leerwyse, method of teaching; method of studying (learning).
lees (-te), n. last, boot-tree; waist; **op dieselfde** – **geskoei**, cast in the same mould; **haar slanke** –, her slender waist.
lees, (ge-), read; **in iemand se hart** –, read a person's heart; **dit is (staan) op jou gesig te** –, it is written on your face.
leesbaar, (-bare), readable (book); legible (handwriting).
leesboek, reader, reading-book.
leesbril, reading-glasses.
leesgeselskap, reading-club.
leesinrigting, public library.
leeskaart, reading-chart.
leeskamer, reading-room.
leesles, reading-lesson.
leeslus, love of reading.
leesmetodes, method of reading.
leesoefening, reading-exercise; reading-practice.
leesonderwys, instruction in reading.
leessaal, reading-room; library.
leesstof, reading-matter.
leesteken, punctuation-mark.
leesuur, reading-hour.
leeswoede, mania for reading.
leeu (-e, -s), lion.
leeubekkie, snapdragon.
leeue-aandeel, lion's share.
leeuekuil, lion's den.
leeuemoed, lion's courage; **met** –, courageous(ly).
leeujagter, lion-hunter.
leeukooi, lion's cage.
leeumannetjie, lion.
leeutemmer, lion-tamer.
leeutjie, (-s), **leeuwelp**, ion's cub, little lion.
leeuin, (-ne), **leeuwyfie**, (-s), lioness.
leg, vide **lê**, (ge-),
legaat, (-gate), legacy; (papal) legate.
legaliseer, (ge-), legalize.
legaliteit, legality.
legasie, (-s), legation, embassy.
legateer, (ge-), bequeath.
legboor, ovipositor (zool.).
legendaries, (-s), legendary.
legende, (-s), legend.
legering, alloy.
legering, vide **leëring**.

leghen, lêhen, laying-hen, (good) layer.
legioen, (-e), legion.
legitiem, (-e), legitimate.
legitimasiebewys, identification-certificate.
legitimeer, (ge-), legitimate.
legitimiteit, legitimacy.
legkaart, jigsaw puzzle.
legplek, winter-pasture; vide **lêplek.**
legsel, number of eggs laid.
lêhen, vide **leghen.**
lei, (-e), n. slate.
lei, (ge-), lead, conduct, direct, guide; **'n armsalige lewe –,** lead a miserable life; **in versoeking –,** lead into temptation; **– tot, na,** lead to.
leiband, leading-strings.
leidak, slate-roof.
leidam, irrigation-dam.
leidend, (-e), leading (person); guiding.
leiding, lead; leadership, guidance, management; conductorship; line; piping; (take the) lead; **– gee,** give guidance, guide; **die – op sig neem,** take the lead; take charge of; **onder – van,** under the leadership (guidance) of.
leidraad, guiding line; guide, key, clue.
leidsman, leader, guide.
leidster, guiding-star, lodestar.
lei(d)ster, leader.
leier, (-s), leader; guide.
leikleurig, (-e), slate-coloured.
leiklip, slate.
leisel, (-s), rein; **die perde die –s gee,** give the horses the reins; **die –s vat,** take the reins; take charge (control).
leiselhouer, driver.
leisteen, slate.
leiwater, irrigation-water (-stream).
lek, (-ke), n, leak(age); puncture (tyre); **'n – kry,** spring a leak (of vessel); get a puncture.
lek, (ge-), 1. leak, be leaky.
lek, (ge-), 2. lick.
lekkasie, (-s), leak(age).
lekker, (-s), n. sweet.
lekker, a. & adv. nice, sweet, delicious; fine; tight, tipsy; **– koel,** nice and cool; **– ruik,** smell sweet; **– eet,** enjoy one's food; **nie – voel (wees) nie,** not feel well; **hy voel nie – daaroor nie,** he is not happy about it.
lekkerbek, epicure, gourmet.
lekkerbekkig, (-e), sweet-toothed, fastidious.
lekkergoed, sweets, sweetmeats.
lekkerheid, niceness, deliciousness; vide **lekker.**
lekkerkry, pleasure.
lekkerlyf, mellow, squiffy.
lekkerny, (-e), delicacy, dainty.
lekkers, vide **lekkergoed.**
lekkertjie, (-s), sweet(y).
lekkerwinkel, sweet-shop.
lekkery, 1. leak(ing).
lekkery, 2. licking, toadyism, fawning.
leksikograaf, (-grawe), lexicographer.
leksikografie, lexicography.
leksikografies, (-e), lexicographical.
leksikon, (-s, -ika), lexicon.
lektor, (-e, -s), lecturer.
lektoraat, (-rate), lectureship.
lektrise, (-s), (woman) lecturer.
lektuur, reading-matter; literature; reading.
lel, (-le), **lelletjie,** (-s), lobe, gill, wattle.
lelie, (-s), lily.
lelieagtig, (-e), lilly-like, liliaceous.
lelieblank, (-, -e), lily-white.
lelik, n. ugly(-face); vide **lelikerd.**
lelik, (-e), a. ugly; nasty (fall); bad (language).
lelik, adv. nasty, badly; **hy het – seergekry,** he is (got) badly hurt; **– skrik,** get a nasty fright;

ons moes – hardloop, we had to run for all we were worth.
lelikerd, (-s), ugly person, scarecrow, sight.
lelikheid, ugliness; vide **lelik.**
lem, (-me), blade.
lemmetjie, (-s), lime; vide **lem.**
lemoen, (-e), orange.
lemoenboord, orange-grove.
lemoenduif, lemon-, cinnamon-dove.
lemoenessens, lemon-essence.
lemoenhuisie, quarter of an orange.
lemoenkonfyt, marmalade.
lemoenskil, orange-peel.
lemoensap, -sop, orange-juice.
lemoenstroop, orange-syrup (-juice).
lemur, (-s), lemur.
lende, (-s, -ne), loin.
lendedoek, loin-cloth.
lendelam, hip-shot; ramshackle, rickety, crazy, shaky, tottering.
lendestreek, lumbar region.
lendestuk, loin-steak.
lengte, (-s), length; longitude (geogr.); height (of person); **in die –,** lengthwise, longitudinally; **in sy volle –,** full length; **tot in – van dae,** for many years to come.
lengtedeursnee, longitudinal section.
lengte-eenheid, unit of length.
lengtegraad, degree of longitude.
lengtemaat, linear measure.
lengtemeting, calculation of the longitude.
lengtesirkel, circle of longitude, meridian.
lengte-uitsetting, linear expansion.
lenig, (-e), a. lithe, supple.
lenig, (ge-), allay, alleviate (pain), relieve.
lenigheid, suppleness, litheness.
leniging, alleviation, relief.
lening, (-e, -s), loan.
leningsbegroting, loan-budget.
leningsfonds, loan-fund.
lens, (-e), lens.
lensie, (-s), lentil.
lensieso(e)p, lentil-soup.
lensopening, diaphragm.
lensvormig, (-e), lens-shaped.
lente, (-s), spring.
lenteagtig, (-e), springlike.
lentebode, harbinger of spring.
lentefees, spring-festival.
lentelied, spring-song.
lentemaand, month of spring.
lentemôre, -more, spring-morning.
lentenagewening, vernal equinox.
lepel, (-s), spoon; ladle; **met 'n – ingee (voer),** spoon-feed; vide **lepellê.**
lepel, (ge-), spoon (out, up).
lepelaar, (-s), spoonbill.
lepelbakkie, -dosie, spoon-dish, -box.
lepelboor, spoon-bit, shell-auger, gouge.
lepeleend, spoonbill-duck.
lepellê, (lepelge-), lie wedged up, lie bodkin.
lepelsgewyse, by spoonfuls.
lepelsteel, handle of a spoon.
lepelvol, (lepelsvol), spoonful.
lepelvormig, (-e), spoon-shaped.
lêplek, place (room) to lie down; den.
lepra, leprosy.
lepralyer, leproos, (-prose), leper.
leprosegestig, leper-hospital (-asylum).
leraar, (-s, lerare), minister; teacher.
leraar, (ge-), minister, preach; teach.
leraarsamp, -skap, ministry.
lering, (-e), instruction; **–e wek, voorbeelde trek,** example is better than precept.

les, (-se), n. lesson; lecture; – gee, give lessons; lecture; iemand die – lees, read a person a lesson; – opsê, say one's lesson; laat – opsê, take to task; ons moes – opsê vandag, we had a tough time today.
les, last; – bes, last but not least.
les, (ge-), quench (thirst), slake.
Lesbiër, (n.) Lesbian.
Lesbies, (-e), Lesbian.
lesenswaard(ig), (-e), worth reading, readable.
leser, (-s), leseres, (-se), reader.
lesing, (-e, -s), reading; lecture; version.
lessenaar, (-s), desk; writing-desk.
lessing, quenching, slaking.
lesuur, (teaching-)period, class-hour.
Let, (-te), Lett.
let, (ge-), 1. mind; – wel, please note, mind (you); – op, look after; heed, mind; – op my woorde, hoor!, mark my words!; op die gehalte –, look to the quality.
let, (ge-), 2. prevent; wat – my . . . ?, what prevents me (from)?
let(h)argie, (-e), lethargy.
Letlands, (-e), Latvian, Lettish.
letsel, (-s), injury; damage, harm; sonder –, unhurt, unscathed; unharmed.
letter, (-s), n. letter, character; type; -e, language and literature; die fraaie -e, belles-lettres; 'n dooie –, a dead letter; sig aan die – hou, stick to the letter; na die –, to the letter; na die – en na die gees, in letter and in spirit.
letter, (ge-), mark, letter.
letterdief, plagiarist.
letterdiefstal, -diewery, plagiarism.
lettergietery, type-foundry.
lettergreep, syllable.
lettergreepraaisel, charade.
letterhaak, composing-stick.
letterkas, type-case.
letterkeer, anagram.
letterknegtery, literalism.
letterkunde, literature.
letterkundig, (-e), literary.
letterkundige, (-s), literary man, literator.
letterlik, (-e), literal (translation).
letterlik, adv. literally; to the letter.
letterlikheid, literalness.
letterraaisel, word-puzzle.
lettersetter, compositor.
lettersettery, composing; composing-room.
lettersoort, type.
letterteken, character.
letterverbinding, letter-combination.
lettervers, acrostic.
lettervreter, bookworm, studious fellow.
Letties, (-e), Lettish, Latvian.
leuen, (-s), lie, untruth, falsehood; 'n onskuldige –(tjie), a white lie.
leuenaar, (-s), liar.
leuenagtig, (-e), untruthful, mendacious, false, untrue (account).
leuenagtigheid, untruthfulness, mendacity.
leuenares, (-se), liar.
leuentaal, lies, lying, mendacity.
leun, (ge-), lean; – op (teen), lean on (against).
leuning, (-s), back (of chair); rail(ing); support; banisters (staircase); balustrade.
leuningstoel, easychair, armchair.
leus, (-e), leuse, (-s), motto, device; slogan.
leuter, (ge-), linger, loiter; twaddle.
leuters, vide luters.
Levantyns, (-e), Levantine.
Leviet, (-e), Levite; die -e voorlees, admonish, read a lesson, take to task.
Levities, (-e), Levitical.

lewe, (-ns), n. life; quick; die – hiernamaals, the life hereafter; 'n nuwe – begin, begin a new life, turn over a new leaf; – gee aan, give life to; jou – laat, lay down one's life; lose one's life; 'n lekker – lei, lead an easy life; aan die lewe hou, keep alive; by sy –, during his life; nog in die –, still alive; in die – hou, keep alive; in die – roep, bring into being; institute; getrou na die –, true to life; om die – bring, kill; 'n stryd op – en dood, a life-and-death struggle; you naels in die – byt, bite one's nails to the quick; vir sy –, for life, as long as he lives.
lewend, (-e), living (language); in -e lywe, in the body; as large as life; die -es en die dooies, the quick (living) and the dead.
lewendig, (-e), a. living, live (animals); lively (description); active, full of life; spirited, frisky (horse); bright (eyes); busy, brisk (trade); keen (discussion).
lewendig-dood, more dead than alive.
lewendigheid, liveliness; vide lewendig.
lewensaand, evening of life.
lewensap, sap, vital juice.
lewensbeginsel, vital principle.
lewensbehoeftes, necessaries of life.
lewensbenodigheid necessity of life.
lewensberig, biographical sketch; obituary.
lewensbeskouing, philosophy of life.
lewensbeskrywer, biographer.
lewensbeskrywing, biography.
lewensbloed, life-blood.
lewensbron, source of life.
lewensdae, days of life; al my –, all my born days.
lewensdoel, aim in life; aim of life.
lewensduur, duration of life; span of life.
lewenselikser, elixir of life.
lewensessens, essence (elixir) of life.
lewensgeluk, joy of life, joy in life.
lewensgenot, enjoyment of life.
lewensgesel(lin), partner in life.
lewensgeskiedenis, life-story; biography.
lewensgevaar, peril of life; in –, in peril of one's life, met –, at the risk of one's life.
lewensgevaarlik, (-e), perilous.
lewensgroot, (-e), life-size (portrait), full-length.
lewensgrootte, life-size.
lewenskets, biographical sketch.
lewenskrag, vitality, energy; vital power.
lewenskragtig, (-e), vigorous, energetic.
lewenslang, (-e), -lank, lifelong, for life; lewenslank kry, get a life-sentence.
lewenslig, light of day.
lewensloop, career.
lewensloos, leweloos, (-lose), lifeless; inanimate (nature).
lewenslus, love of life; vol –, full of life.
lewenslustig, (-e), full of life, vivacious.
lewensmiddele, provisions, foodstuffs.
lewensmoed, courage to live.
lewensomstandighede, circumstances in life.
lewensonderhoud, livelihood, sustenance.
lewensopvatting, view of life.
lewenstaak, life-work.
lewenstandaard, standard of life.
lewensteken, sign of life.
lewensvatbaar, capable of maintaining life.
lewensvatbaarheid, vitality, vital power.
lewensversekering, life-insurance.
lewensversekeringsagent, insurance-agent.
lewensversekeringsmaatskappy, life-assurance (insurance) company.
lewensversekeringspolis, life-policy.
lewensvraag, vital question.
lewensvreugde, joy of living; joy in life.
lewenswandel, (conduct in) life.

lewensweg, path of life.
lewenswerk, life-work.
lewenswys(e), way of living; conduct.
lewenswysheid, wordly wisdom.
lewer, n. liver; **wat het oor jou – geloop?,** what's wrong (up) with you?
lewer (ge-), furnish, supply; deliver; do (good work); furnish (proof).
leweraandoening, liver-complaint (trouble).
leweransie, supply.
leweransier, (-s), furnisher, supplier; purveyor; stockist; caterer.
lewerbaar, (-bare), can be supplied.
lewering, delivery, supply.
leweringstermyn, term of delivery.
lewerik, (-e), lark.
lewerikie, lewerkie, (-s), lark.
lewerkoekie, liver-rissole, patty.
lewerkruid, agrimony, liverwort.
lewerkwaal, liver-disease, -complaint.
lewerpastei, liver-pie.
lewertraan, cod-liver oil.
lewerwors, liver-sausage.
lewewekkend, (-e), life-giving.
lewisiet, lewisite.
liaan, (liane), liana (liane).
lias, (-se), file.
liasseer, (ge-), file.
liasseerkas, filing cabinet.
liberaal, (-ale), liberal, broad-minded.
liberalisme, liberalism.
liberalisties, (-e), liberalistic.
liberaliteit, liberality.
libertyn, (-e), libertine.
libido, libido.
Libies, (-e), Libyan.
lid, (lede), limb (of body); member (of society); term (of ratio); lid (of eye); **onder lede hê,** be sickening for.
liddiet, lyddite.
liddoring, corn.
lidmaat, (-mate), 1. member (of church); – **word,** become confirmed.
lidmaat, (ledemate), 2. limb, member.
lidmaatskap, membership.
lidwoord, article.
lie(g), ge-), lie, tell lies.
lied, (-ere), song, hymn; **die ou –(tjie),** the same old story.
liederboek, -bundel, book of songs (hymns).
liederlik, (-e), dirty, filthy; obscene.
liedjie, (-s), tune, song, ditty; **'n ander – sing,** sing a different tune.
liedjiesanger, ballad-singer, minstrel.
lief, n.; – **en leed,** the bitter and the sweet; **in – en leed,** in joy and sorrow.
lief, (liewe), a. dear, sweet, kind, charming; **liewe hemel!,** good heavens!
lief, adv. sweetly, nicely; vide **lief, a.; hy sou net so – . . .,** he would just as soon.
liefdadig, (-e), charitable, benevolent.
liefdadigheid, charity; benevolence.
liefdadigheidsgenootskap, benevolent society.
liefdadigheidsinstelling, charitable institution.
liefdadigheidskonsert, charity-concert.
liefdadigheidsvoorstelling, charity-show.
liefde, love; **ou – roes nie,** old love never dies; **met alle –,** in all love; with the greatest pleasure; **uit – vir die spel,** for love of the game; **uit – trou,** marry for love.
liefdeband, tie of love.
liefdeblyk, token of love.
liefdediens, act of love; act of charity.
liefdedrank, love-potion.
liefdegawe, -gif, charity, alms.

liefdeloos, (-lose), loveless. unfeeling, cold.
liefdeloosheid, lovelessness; vide **liefdeloos.**
liefdepand, pledge of love.
liefderoes, transport of love.
liefderyk, (-e), loving, affectionate, kind.
liefdesbetuiging, declaration of love.
liefdeservaring, love-experience.
liefdesgeskiedenis, love-story; love-affair.
liefdesverklaring, declaration of love, proposal.
liefdevol, (-le), full of love, loving; **in –le herinnering,** in loving memory.
liefdewerk, work of charity.
liefhê, (liefgehad), love.
liefhebbend, (-e), loving, affectionate.
liefhebber, (-s), n. lover; enthusiast, fan, devotee amateur.
liefhebber, (ge-), dabble (in).
liefhebbery, (-e), hobby, fad.
liefhebberytoneel, amateur theatricals.
liefheid, sweetness; vide **lief.**
liefie, (-s), darling, love; sweetheart; mistress.
liefkoos, (ge-), caress, fondle.
liefkosing, (-e, -s), caress.
liefkry, (liefge-), grow fond of; fall in love with.
lieflik, (-e), lovely.
lieflikheid, loveliness.
liefling, lieweling, (-e), darling; favourite.
lieflingsdigter, liewelings-, favourite poet.
lieflingswerk, liewelings-, favourite work.
liefs, rather; – **nie,** rather not; **watter wil jy – hê?,** which do you prefer?
liefste, (-s), n. sweetheart, beloved; darling.
liefste, dearest, darling.
lieftallig, (-e), sweet, lovable, amiable.
lieftalligheid, sweetness, charm.
lieg, vide **lie(g),**
liemaak (liege-), fool, tease; sidestep, give (person) the dummy.
liemaakkuier, apology for a visit.
lier, (-e), lyre.
lierdig, lyric (poem).
lierdigter, lyric poet.
lies, (-te), groin.
lieweheersbesie, ladybird.
lieweling, vide **liefling.**
liewer(s), rather; preferably; – **nie gaan nie,** rather not go; – **water drink as wyn,** prefer water to wine; **sou – sterf as . . .,** would sooner die than . . .
liewerd(jie), (-s), darling.
liewerlede: van –, gradually.
liewigheid, sweetness, amenity.
lig, (-te), n. light; – **maak,** switch on the light, light lamp (candle), strike a light; **daar gaan nou vir my 'n – op,** it is beginning to dawn on me now; **die – sien,** see the light; be published; – **werp op,** shed (throw) light on; **aan die – bring,** bring to light; **aan die – kom,** come to light; **in die – gee,** publish; **in 'n vals – stel,** put false colours upon.
lig, (-te), a. light; bright; blond, fair; slight, mild; – **in die kop,** light-headed.
lig, adv. lightly; easily; **'n mens vergeet dit –,** one is apt to forget it; – **dink oor, – opneem,** make light of.
lig, (ge-), 1. lift, raise; weigh (anchor); clear (letterbox); **jou hoed –,** raise one's hat.
lig, (ge-), 2. give light; dawn; lighten.
liga, (-s), league.
ligawestryd, league-match.
ligbeeld, photograph; lantern-slide.
ligblond, (-e), light, fair.
ligblou, light-blue.
ligbreking, refraction of light.
ligbron, source of light.

ligbruin, light-brown.
ligbundel, beam of light, pencil of light-rays.
ligdag, daylight; **net voor –,** just before dawn; **helder –,** broad daylight.
ligeffek, light-effect.
liggaam, (-game), body; **vaste –,** solid.
liggaamlik, (-e), bodily; corporal (punishment); corporeal, material; physical (training); **– swak,** physically weak.
liggaampie, (-s), little body; corpuscle.
liggaamsbeweging, (bodily) exercise.
liggaamsbou, build, frame, stature.
liggaamsdeel, part of the body, limb.
liggaamsgebrek, physical defect.
liggaamshouding, carriage.
liggaamsoefening, physical exercise.
liggaamstraf, corporal punishment.
liggeel, pale, light-yellow.
liggebou, (-de), of slight build.
liggelowig, (-e), credulous; gullible.
liggend, (-e), lying, recumbent; prone.
liggeraak, (-te), touchy, oversensitive.
liggevoelig, (-e), sensitive to light.
liggewapen(d), (-e), light-armed.
liggewend, (-e), luminous, luminescent.
liggewig, light weight.
liggies, lightly; slightly.
ligging, (-e, -s), situation; site, position; lie.
liggolf, light-wave.
liggroen, light-, pale-green.
lighartig, (-e), light-hearted.
lighoofdig, (-e), light-headed.
liginstallasie, lighting-installation; light-plant.
ligjaar, light-year.
ligkant, bright side.
ligkewer, glowworm.
ligknippie, electric light-switch.
ligkoeël, fire-ball.
ligkrans, corona, glow; halo (round head).
ligkring, circle of light, luminous circle.
ligkroon, chandelier, electrolier, gaselier.
ligleiding, electric light-wiring.
ligmatroos, ordinary seaman.
ligmeter, photometer.
ligmis, (-se), libertine, rake.
ligplek, spot of light; flare-spot (photo).
ligpunt, luminous point; bright spot.
ligreklame, illuminated sign.
ligrooi, pink, light-red.
ligsein, light-signal.
ligsinnig, (-e), frivolous, flippant.
ligskerm, shade screen.
ligskip, lightship.
ligsku, (-we), shunning the light.
ligskuheid, photophobia.
ligspoorkoeël, tracer bullet.
ligsterkte, luminosity; candle-power.
ligstip, speck (dot) of light.
ligstraal, (beam) of light.
ligstreep, streak of light.
ligtekooi, prostitute, harlot.
ligtelaai(e): in –, in a blaze, ablaze.
ligtelik, slightly; lightly.
ligter, (-s), lift.
ligter(hout), lifter, lever.
ligterskip, lighter.
ligting, collection, clearance (of letters), draft levy (of soldiers); raising.
ligvaardig, (-e), rash, reckless, thoughtless.
likeur, (-e, -s), liqueur.
likeurstokery, liqueur-distillery.
likkebaard, -broer, gastronome, belly-god.
likkewaan, (-wane), iguana (leguan).
liksens, (-e), vide **lisensie.**
likwidasie, (-s), liquidation; settlement.

likwidateur, (-s), liquidator.
likwideer, (ge-), liquidate, wind up.
lila, lilac.
lilliputter, (-s), Lilliputian.
limf, lymph.
limiet, (-e), limit.
limiteer, (ge-), limit.
limonade, lemonade.
linde(boom), linden-tree, lime.
lindelaan, lime-tree avenue.
lineêr, (-e), linear.
linguistiek, linguistics.
liniaal, (-niale), ruler.
linie, (-s), line; equator.
linieer, (ge-), rule.
linieregiment, regiment of the line.
linieskip, ship of the line.
linker, left; near (foreleg, wheel).
linkerarm, left arm.
linkerhand, left hand; **op –,** on the left(-hand side); **met die – trou,** marry with the left hand.
linkerkant, left (side); **na die –,** to the left.
linkeroog, left eye.
linkersy, left side.
linkervleuel, left wing.
links, a. left-handed; **ook nie – wees nie,** be quick to seize the opportunity.
links, adv. to (on) the left; **– en regs,** right and left; **– laat lê,** leave on the left; ignore, take no notice of.
linksgesinde, leftist.
linkshandig, (-e), left-handed.
linksheid, left-handedness; awkwardness.
linne, linen; cloth (binding of book).
linnegoed, linen.
linnehandel, linen-trade.
linnekamer, linen-room.
linnekas, linen-press.
linnepers, linen-press.
linnewinkel, linen-, draper's shop.
linoleum, linoleum.
linotiep, linotipe, linotype.
lint, (-e), ribbon; tape.
lintgras, ribbon-grass.
lintjie, (-s), ribbon; order (of knighthood).
lintwurm, tape-worm.
lip, (-pe), lip; **die –pe optrek,** curl one's lip; **die –pe laat hang,** hang one's lip; **jou hart op die –pe hê,** wear one's heart on one's sleeve; **hy het nog niks oor sy –pe gehad nie,** nothing has passed his lips.
lipblommig, (-e), labiate.
lipletter, labial.
lip(pe)diens, lip-service.
lip(pe)taal, lip-language.
lipstif, lipstick.
lipstandletter, labio-dental.
lipvormig, (-e), lip-shaped, labiate, labial.
lira, (lire), lira.
liriek, lyric poetry, lyrics.
lirikus, (-se), lyricus, (-ici), lyric poet.
liries, (-e), lyric(al); **'n –e gedig,** a lyric.
lis, (-te), 1. trick, ruse, device.
lis, lus, (-se), 2. noose; loop; tag.
lisblom, iris.
lisensiaat, licentiate.
lisensie, (-s), liksens, (-e), licence.
lisensieer, (ge-), license.
lisensiehof, licensing court.
lispel, (ge-), lisp.
lissie, lussie, (-s), vide **lis** (2).
listig, (-e) canny, wily, craftly, artful.
listigheid slyness, wiliness, cunning.
listiglik cunningly, slyly; vide **listig.**

lit, (-te) joint; articulation; **uit –**, out of joint, dislocated.
litanie, (ë), litany.
Litauer, (-s), Lithuanian.
Litaus, (-e), Lithuanian.
liter, (-s), litre.
literaries, (-e), literary.
literator, (-e, -s), literary man, literator.
literatuur, literature.
literatuurgeskiedenis, history of literature.
literêr, (-e), literary.
litjiesgras, jointed grass.
litjieskaktus, jointed cactus.
litjieskweek, coarse quick.
litograaf, (-grawwe), lithographer.
litografeer, (ge-), lithograph.
litografie, lithography.
litografies, (-e), lithographic.
litotes, litotes.
litteken, scar, cicatrice (cicatrix).
liturgie, (-ë), liturgy.
liturgies, (-e), liturgical.
livrei, (-e), livery.
livreibediende, -kneg, livery-servant.
lob, (-be), lobe.
lobelia, (-s), lobelia.
loef, luff, windward side; **die – afsteek**, take the wind out of a person's sails.
loei, (ge-), low; roar.
loën, logen, (ge-), deny.
loënaar, logenaar, (-s), denier.
loënstraf, logenstraf, (ge-), belie, give the lie to (supposition); falsify.
loer, n.: **op die – lê**, lie in wait.
loer, (ge-), peep, peer; pry; lurk, watch.
loergat, peephole.
loerie, (-s), lory (lourie).
loesing, (-s), hiding, thrashing, spanking.
lof, n. praise, commendation; **iemand – toeswaai**, praise a person; **eie – stink**, self-praise is no recommendation; **met – praat van**, speak highly of; **met – deurkom**, pass with distinction; **dit strek hom tot –**, it does him credit.
lof, (lowwe), n. leaves, foliage, leafage.
lofdig, panegyric, laudatory poem.
lofdigter, panegyrist.
lofgesang, hymn of raise.
loflied, song (hymn, psalm) of praise.
loflik, (-e), praiseworthy, laudable.
lofpsalm, psalm of praise.
lofrede, panegyric, eulogy.
lofredenaar, panegyrist, eulogist.
lofsang, song (hymn) of praise; doxology.
lofspraak, praise, encomium.
lofuiting, (-e, -s), praise, eulogy.
lofwaardig, (-e), laudable, praiseworthy.
log, (-ge), n. log.
log, (–, -ge), clumsy, unwieldy.
logaritme, (-s), logarithm, log.
logaritmetafel, table of logarithms.
logaritmies, (-e), logarithmic.
logboek, log-book.
logheid, unwieldiness; vide **log**.
logen, vide **loën**.
logies, (-e), a. logical.
logika, logic.
logistiek, logistics.
lojaal, (jale), loyal.
lojalis, (-te), loyalist.
lojalisme, loyalism.
lojaliteit, loyalty.
lok, (-ke), n. lock, curl.
lok, (ge-), entice, lure, decoy.
lokaal, (-kale), n. room.
lokaal, (-kale), a. local.

lokaas, bait, lure, decoy.
lokaliseer, (ge-), localize.
lokaliteit, room, hall.
lokasie, (-s), location.
lokatief, locative.
loket, (-te), pigeon-hole; box-office window, ticket-window; booking-office; **aan (by) die —**, at the counter.
lokmiddel, bait, inducement, lure.
lokomotief, (-tiewe), locomotive, engine.
lokomotiefloods, engine-shed.
lokstem, lure, siren-voice, call.
lokvink, decoy, police-trap.
lokvoël, decoy(-bird).
lol, (ge-), be troublesome; nag; **– by iemand**, disturb (bother, pester, worry, trouble) a person.
lollerig, (-e), troublesome; nagging.
lollery, nagging; nuisance, bother.
lolpot, nuisance, bore.
lomerig, (-e), drowsy, sleepy; languid.
lomerigheid, drowsiness; languor.
lommer, foliage; shade.
lommerd, (-s), pawnbroker's shop.
lommeryk, (-e), shady.
lomp, (–, -e), a. clumsy, awkward.
lompe, n. rags; **in – gekleed**, clad in rags.
lomperd, (-s), bumpkin, clodhopper, lout.
lompheid, clumsiness; vide **lomp**.
Londenaar, (-nare, -s), Londoner.
long, (-e), lung.
longaandoening, affection of the lungs.
longkwaal, lung-disease (-trouble).
longlyer, consumptive.
longontsteking, pneumonia.
longpes, lung-plague.
longpyp, windpipe.
longsiekte, lung-sickness.
longtering, pulmonary consumption.
longvlies, pleura.
longvliesontsteking, pleurisy.
lonk, (-e), n. ogle, wink; leer.
lonk, (ge-), ogle, wink; give the glad eye.
lons, luns, (ge-), lunge; **'n perd (laat) –**, lunge a horse.
lonsriem, lunge (longe).
lont, (-e), fuse; **– ruik**, smell a rat.
lontstok, lintstock.
lood, n. lead; plumb-line; plummet, sounding-lead; **– om ou yster**, six of one and half a dozen of the other; **onder die – kry (steek)**, fire at, pepper; **uit die –**, out of plumb.
lood: **dit – kry (hê)**, have a gruelling time.
lood, (ge-), lead (panes); sound; let fly (at).
loodaar, lead-vein.
loodasetaat, lead-acetate.
loodagtig, (-e), leadlike, leaden.
looderts, lead-ore.
loodfoelie, lead-foil.
loodgieter, plumber.
loodgrys, lead-grey.
loodkleur, lead-colour.
loodkleurig, (-e), lead-coloured.
loodkoeël, lead-bullet.
loodlyn, perpendicular; plumb-line.
loodmyn, lead-mine.
loodpuntkoeël, soft-nose bullet.
loodpyp, lead-pipe.
loodreg, (-te), perpendicular, vertical.
loods, (-e), n. 1. pilot (of ship).
loods, (-e), n. 2. shed; hangar (for aeroplane).
loods, (ge-), pilot (ship); direct, conduct.
loodsboot, pilot-boat.
loodsekering, lead-fuse, -plug.
loodsulfaat, sulphate of lead.

loodsuur, plumbic acid.
loodsvlag, pilot-flag.
loodswaar, leaden, like lead.
loodswese, pilotage.
loodvergiftiging, lead-poisoning.
loodwit, white lead.
loof, n. foliage, leaves, leafage.
loof, lowe, (ge-), praise, glorify, extol.
loofboom, foliage-tree.
Loofhuttefees, Feast of Tabernacles.
loog, n. lye, lixivium, buck.
loog, (ge-), steep in lye.
loogas, lye-ashes, buck-ashes.
loogbak, -kuip, lye-tank, -trough.
loogsout, alkali.
loogwater, lye, lixivium.
looi, (ge-), tan; leather, thrash.
looibas, tanning-bark, wattle-bark.
looiery, tanning; tannery; tanner's trade.
looikuip, tan(ning)-vat.
looistof, tannin.
looisuur, tannic acid.
loom, (lome), drowsy; languid; heavy, dull.
loomheid, drowsiness; lassitude.
loon, (lone), n. wages, salary, pay; reward; **ondank is die wêreld se –,** the world pays with ingratitude; **dit is jou verdiende –,** it serves you right.
loon, (ge-), reward, pay; **dit sal die moeite –,** it is worth while.
loonarbeider, -dienaar, wage-earner.
looneis, demand for (higher) wages.
loongeskil, wage-dispute.
loonooreenkoms, wage-agreement.
loonraad, wage-board.
loonskaal, scale of wages.
loonstaking, strike for higher wages.
loonstryd, wage-war.
loonsverhoging, rise in wages.
loontjie: boontjie kry sy –, it serves you right; chickens come home to roost.
loontrekker, wage-earner.
loonwet, wage-act.
loop, n. walking; walk, gait; running (of machine); course (of events); (pl.: **lope**), barrel (of gun); spruit, stream; course (of river); **'n – se –,** an hour's walk; **die – van die treine,** the train-service; **die vrye – laat,** let . . . take its course; **die – neem,** take to flight, bolt; **in die – van die jaar,** in the course of (during) the year; **op – gaan (sit),** bolt (of horse).
loop, (ge-), walk; go; run; **ag –!,** go on!; **gaan –,** go for a walk; **die horlosie – goed,** the watch goes well; **hoog – met,** be taken up with; **gevoelens – hoog,** feeling is running high; **– in die honderde,** run into hundreds; **hy – na tagtig se kant toe,** he is getting on for eighty; **– om,** go (run) round; **dit – oor twee jaar,** it extends over two years; **waaroor – die gesprek?,** what is the conversation about?; **oor 'n wye gebied –,** cover a wide field; **teen iemand –,** walk close to a person; **vas teen iemand –,** bump into a person; **met jou kop teen die muur –,** run your head against the wall; **ten einde –,** draw a close.
loopbaan, career; orbit (of planet); track.
loopbrug, footbridge; gangway (of ship); cotwalk.
loopgraaf, trench.
loopjong, messenger-boy, office-boy.
looplys, cat-walk.
looppas, double quick (time).
loopplank, running-board; footboard; gangway.
loopplek, place for walking; pasturage; haunt, feeding-place.

loopprater, walkie-talkie.
loops, on heat, ruttish.
loopsheid, heat, rut.
looptyd, time to go; currency; gestation.
loopvlak, running-surface; tread (of wheel).
loopvoël, courser, cursorial bird.
loos, (lose), cunning, sly.
loot, (lote), n. shoot, sucker; offspring.
loot, (ge-), draw lots, raffle (for); toss.
lootjie, (-s), (lottery-)ticket; **–s trek,** draw lots.
lopend, (-e), running; current (month).
loper, (-s), walker; messenger; (carpet-)runner; master-key; bishop (chess); **–s,** buckshot, slugs.
lopie, (-s), run (mus., cricket); small stream.
lornjet, (-te), pince-nez, lorgnette.
lorrie, (-s), lorry.
los, (-se), n. lynx.
los, (–, -se), a. loose; extra, odd, spare (copy); undone, unfastened; detached, detachable; dissolute, wanton; free (person), **'n – gerug,** a wild rumour; **op –se gronde,** on insubstantial grounds; **'n – hotnot,** an odd hand, a casual labourer; a free man; **'n – lewe,** a loose life; **met – kruit,** with blank cartridges; **– werkies,** odd jobs; **– werkman,** casual labourer.
los, adv. loosely; **– voor wees,** be well ahead; **– en vas praat,** have a loose tongue; blow hot and cold; **– en vas lieg,** lie like a gas-meter; **– en vas koop,** buy right and left; **daarop – praat,** talk away; **daarop – slaan,** hit out; **– sit,** be loose (of tooth).
los, (ge-), fire (shot); discharge (ship); redeem (pledge); claim (goods); ransom (prisoner); release; let go.
losbaar, (-bare), redeemable.
losbandig, (-e), fast, dissipated, profligate.
losbandigheid, profligacy, dissipation.
losbars, (losge-), tear; burst out, explode, let fly; break (out); open fire.
losbarsting, (-e, -s), explosion, outbreak.
losbol, (-le), libertine, rake, profligate.
losbrand, (losge-), open fire, let fly, launch out.
losbranding, discharge; vide **losbrand.**
losbreek, (losge-), break loose; vide **losbars.**
losdraai, (losge-), undo, loosen; untwist, unscrew.
loseer, (ge-), board, put up, lodge.
loseergas, guest.
loseerkamer, visitor's room; boarding-house room.
losgaan, (losge-), become unfastened.
losgeld, ransom; unloading-charges.
losgespe(r), (losge-), unbuckle.
losgoed, movable property; loose stuff.
loshaak, (losge-), unhook, unhitch.
loshand(e), with hands free.
loshang, (losge-), hang loose, dangle.
losheid, looseness; slackness; laxity; vide **los.**
loshoofdig, (-e), flippant, frivolous.
losie, (-s), lodge; box (in theatre).
losies, board and lodging; accommodation; **– verskaf,** put up, provide board and lodging.
losieshuis, -plek, boarding-house.
losknoop, (losge-), unbutton; untie; undo.
loskom, (losge-), get loose (away); get free (off); be released (discharged); **sy tong het losgekom,** his tongue started wagging; he began to unbend.
loskoop, (losge-), buy off, ransom.
loskop, tailstock (lathe); loose head (rugby).
loskoppel, (losge-), disconnect.
loskry, (losge-), get loose; untie; unscrew.

loslaat, (losge-), let loose; release, discharge; let go.
loslating, release; vide **loslaat**.
losloop, (losge-), be at large; run free (loose); loaf about; idle; free-wheel.
loslopie, bye (cricket).
loslywig, (-e), having loose bowels.
losmaak, (losge-), loosen; disconnect; release; untie, undo, unfasten; loosen; sig –, free oneself.
lospitperske, free-stone peach.
losplek, discharging-berth.
losprys, ransom.
losraak, (losge-), get loose; become unfastened (detached, loose); get adrift.
losruk, (losge-), pull (tear) loose; break away.
losry(e), -ryg, (losge-), unlace, undo.
losserig, (-e), a. rather loose; vide **los**.
lossies, loosely; lightly.
lossing, discharge; redemption; vide **los**, v.
lossinnig, (-e), frivolous, flippant.
losskakel, fly-half, stand-off half (rugby).
losskeur, (losge-), vide **losruk**.
losskroef, -skroewe, (losge-), unscrew.
losskud, (losge-), shake loose (off).
losslaan, (losge-), knock loose; earn (money).
lossny, (losge-), unpin.
lossny, (losge-) cut (loos-).
losspeld(e), (losge-), unpin.
losspeler, loose (wing) forward.
losspring, (losge-), fly (spring) open.
lossteek, (losge-), dig loose; let fly (at), lash out, go for, belabour.
losstorm, (losge-): – **op**, rush upon (at).
lostorring, (losge-), unpick, undo (stitches).
lostrek, (losge-), pull (tear) loose; let out (fly).
losweg, loosely; lightly.
loswerk, (losge-), work loose; free oneself.
loswikkel, (losge-), unwrap, undo; loosen; sig –, free oneself.
lot, fate, destiny; lot; **aan sy – oorlaat**, leave to his fate (his own devices).
lot, (-e), lottery-ticket; vide **lootjie**.
lotery, (-e), lottery; raffle; gamble.
loterykaartjie, lottery-ticket.
lotgenoot, companion in adversity.
lotgevalle, adventures.
loting, draw, drawing of lots.
lotjie: 1. **van – getik wees**, have a screw loose.
lotjie: 2. vide **lootjie**.
lotsbestemming, destiny.
lotswisseling, vicissitude.
lotto, lotto.
lotus, lotus.
lou, lukewarm (lit. & fig.), tepid.
loudanum, laudanum.
louer, (ge-), crown with laurels.
louere, laurels; – **behaal**, reap laurels; **op jou – rus**, rest on one's laurels.
louerig, (-e), lukewarm(ish).
louerkrans, laurel-wreath.
louheid, lukewarmness.
lourier, (-e), laurel; **Kaapse –**, stinkwood.
lourierkrans, laurel-wreath.
louter, a. & adv. pure, sheer; – **deur toeval**, by the merest chance.
louter, (ge-), purify, refine, try, test.
loutering, purification, refining.
lower, foliage.
lowergroen, bright (fresh, vivid) green.
ludo, ludo.
lug, (-te), n. sky; air; atmosphere; scent, smell; **vars –**, fresh air; **die blou –**, the blue sky; – **gee**, air, give air; vent, give vent to (one's feelings); – **skep**, get fresh air; **die – kry van**, scent, get the wind of; **in die oop –**, in the open (air); **in die – laat vlieg**, blow up; **dit hang nog heeltemal in die –**, it is quite in the air as yet; **uit die – gegryp**, unfounded; **uit die – val**, drop from the skies.
lug, (ge-), air, ventilate; vent, give vent to (feelings, grievances); **jou kennis –**, air (parade) one's knowledge.
lugaanval, air-attack, air-raid.
lugafweer, air-defence.
lugballon, balloon.
lugband, pneumatic tyre.
lugblasie, air-bubble.
lugbom, air-bomb.
lugbrug, air-lift.
lugdiens, air-service.
lugdig, (-te), airtight; hermetically sealed.
lugdinamika, aerodynamics.
lugdraad, aerial, antenna; overhead wire.
lugdruk, atmospheric pressure.
lugeskader, air-squadron.
lugfilter, air-cleaner.
luggat, ventilator, air-hole; air-pocket.
luggekoel, air-cooled.
luggeveg, air-fight, -battle.
luggie, (-s), breath of air; whiff, scent.
lughartig, (-e), light-hearted, happy-go-lucky.
lughawe, airport.
lughou, lob (tennis); **'n – slaan**, lob.
lugkasteel castle in the air; air-castle.
lugklep, air-valve.
lugkoker, airshaft, ventilating shaft.
luglaag, layer of air.
luglaatklep, bleeder valve.
lugledig, n. vacuum.
lugledig, (-e), **lugleeg**, (-leë), exhausted, with no air inside; – **leë ruimte**, vacuum.
luglyn, air-line.
lugmag, air-force.
lug(mag)basis, air-base.
lugplant, aerial plant.
lugpomp, air-pump.
lugpos, air-mail.
lugposvliegtuig, airmail plane.
lugpyp, windpipe, trachea.
lugpypie, bronchial tube.
lugreëling, air-conditioning.
lugreis, air-trip, air-voyage.
lugreisiger, air-traveller; aviator.
lugrem, air-brake.
lugruim, atmosphere, space.
lugsak, air-pocket, -hole.
luggesteldheid, climate.
lugsiek, air-sick.
lugskip, airship, air-liner, zeppelin.
lugspieëling, -spiegeling, mirage.
lugspoor(weg), overhead (aerial) railway.
lugsteuring, -storing, atmospherics.
lugstreek, zone.
lugstroom, air-current.
lugtaxi, taxi plane.
lugtempering, air-conditioning.
lugter, (-s), candelabrum, electrolier.
lugtig, (-e), a. airy; light-hearted; nervous; cautious, funky.
lugtigheid, airiness; light-heartedness; flippancy, levity, cautiousness.
lugtoevoer, air-supply.
luguber, (-e), lugubrious, dismal, ghastly.
lugvaart, aviation, air-navigation.
lugvaartkunde, aeronautics.
lugvaartkundige, (-e), aeronautic(al).
lug(vaart)lyn, airline.
lugvaartuig, aircraft.
lugverdediging, air-defence.

lugverkeer, air-traffic.
lugverskynsel, atmospheric phenomenon.
lugverversing, ventilation.
lugvervoer, aerial transport.
lugvloot, air-force.
lugvry, (-, -e), air-free.
lugwaardig, (-e), airworthy.
lugwaardin, air hostess.
lugweerstand, resistance of the air.
lugweg, air-route; air-passage.
lugwortel, aerial root.
lui, n. folk, people.
lui, a. lazy, indolent, slothful.
lui, (ge-), ring (bell), sound, peal; toll; **dit – aldus**, it reads (runs) as follows; **soos die gesegde –**, as the saying goes.
luiaard (-s), lazy person, sluggard, lazybones; sloth (animal).
luid, (-e), loud; **met –er stem**, in a loud voice.
luidens, according to.
luidkeels, at the top of one's voice.
luidrugtig, (-e), noisy, boisterous, rowdy.
luidrigtigheid, noisiness, rowdiness.
luidspreker, loudspeaker.
luier, (-s), n. (baby's) napkin; diaper.
luier, (ge-), loaf, lounge, laze, idle.
luierig, (-e), rather lazy.
luierspeld, napkin-pin, safety-pin.
luiheid, laziness, sloth.
luik, (-e), n. shutter; hatch, trapdoor.
luik, (ge-), shut.
luilak, (-ke), n. sluggard, lazybones, idler.
luilak, (ge-), lounge (loaf, idle) about.
luilekkerland, Cockaigne, happy valley.
luim, (-e), mood, humour; whim.
luimig, (-e), humorous, witty; capricious.
luiperd, (-s), leopard, panther.
luis, (-e), louse.
luiskoors, typhus (fever).
luislang, python.
luister, n. splendour, lustre; **– bysit**, add lustre to.
luister, (ge-), listen; **– na**, listen to; **– na sy naam**, answer to his name; **– vir**, listen to, obey.
luisteraar, (-s), listener; eavesdropper.
luisterryk, (-e), splendid, brilliant.
luistervink, eavesdropper.
luitenant, (-e), lieutenant.
luitenant-generaal, (-s), lieutenant-general.
luitenant-ter-see, (luitenants-ter-see), naval lieutenant.
luiters, luters, innocent, unaware.
luitspeler, -speelster, lute-player.
luk, (ge-), succeed.
lukraak, (-rake), a. wild, random.
lukraak, adv. at random, haphazard.
lukwart, (-e), loquat.
lumier, n. break of day, dawn.
lumier, (ge-), break (of day), dawn.
lumineus, (-e), luminous, bright.
lummel, (-s), n. gawk, simpleton, booby.
lummel, (ge-), lounge (laze) about.
luns, (-e), lunspen, n. linch-pin, axle-pin.
lunsriem, axle-pin strap; dirty rascal.
lupien, (-e), lupine, (-s), lupin.
lus, (-te), n. 1. desire, appetite; liking, inclination; lust, passion, delight, joy, pleasure, treat; **'n – vir die oë**, a feast for the eyes; **dit is my – en my lewe**, it is the breath of life to me; **– hê**, feel inclined, have a mind to; **as jy – kry, if you feel like it; iets met – doen**, take pleasure in doing something; **jou – oormaak**, satisfy one's appetite.
lus, 2. vide **lis**, 2.
lus, (ge-), like, feel like, feel inclined (for).
lusern, lucern(e).

lushanger, strap-hanger.
lushof, pleasure-garden.
lusoord, pleasure-ground, beautiful spot.
lussie, lissie, vide **lis**, 2.
lusteloos, (-lose), listless, languid, dull.
lusteloosheid, listlessness, languor, lassitude.
luster, lustre.
lustig, (-e), cheerful, merry, gay.
lustigheid, cheerfulness; vide **lustig**.
lustrum, (-s, -tra), lustrum.
luters, vide **luiters**.
Luthers, (-e), Lutheran.
luttel, (-e), little.
luukse, luxury.
luukseartikel, luxury; –s, fancy goods.
luukse-uitgawe, edition de luxe.
luuksueus, (-e), luxurious.
ly, n. lee(-side).
ly, (ge-), suffer; bear, endure; **gebrek –**, suffer want; **honger –**, starve; **skipbreuk –**, be shipwrecked; **– aan**, suffer from; **– deur**, suffer as a result of; **– onder**, suffer under; **te – hê van**, suffer from; be afflicted with.
lydelik, (-e), passive.
lydelikheid, passiveness, passivity.
lydend, (-e), suffering; passive (voice); **die –e party**, the sufferer, the losing party.
lydensbeker, cup of bitterness.
lydensgeskiedenis, Passion (of Christ); tale of suffering (woe, misery).
Lydensweek, Passion- (Holy) Week.
lydensweg, way of suffering.
lyding, (-e), suffering.
lydsaam, (-same), meek, patient.
lydsaamheid, meekness, patience.
lyer, (-s), sufferer; patient.
lyf, (lywe), body; figure; **hoe voel jou –?**, how do you feel?; **jou – reghou**, prepare oneself (for); **jou – grootman hou**, boast, brag; **jou – spaar (wegsteek)**, shirk one's work; nurse one's strength; **jou – windmaker hou**, swank; **alles aan jou – hang**, spend everything on clothes; **nie 'n hemp aan jou – nie**, not a shirt to one's back; **aan die – (ge)voel**, experienced personally; **in lewende lywe**, in the flesh (body), as large as life; **om die –**, round the waist; **dit het nie veel om die – nie**, there is not much in it; **iemand die bene onder die – uitslaan**, bowl a person over; **'n skrik op die – ja**, give a fright; **iemand op die – loop**, run into (come across) a person; **te – gaan**, attack, go for; **bly van my – af**, leave me alone.
lyfarts, personal physician.
lyfband, belt, waist-band.
lyfblad, regular (news)paper.
lyfeiene, serf.
lyfeienskap, serfdom, bondage, servitude.
lyfie, (-s), little body; bodice.
lyfgarde, lifeguard, bodyguard.
lyfkneg, body-servant.
lyflik, (-e), bodily.
lyfrente, life-annuity.
lystraf, corporal punishment.
lyfwag, bodyguard, lifeguard.
lyk, (-e), n. corpse, dead body.
lyk, (ge-), look, seem, appear; **dit – so**, it looks like it; **jy – 'n mooi bog (daarna)**, you look like it!; **– na**, look like, resemble; **– baie na mekaar**, look very much alike; **dit – na reën**, it looks like rain; **dit – nà niks**, it is a washout; **– op**, look like, resemble; **dit – vir my**, it seems to me.
lykagtig, (-e), like a corpse, cadaverous.
lykdiens, funeral (burial) service.
lykdraer, bearer.

lykhuis, mortuary, morgue.
lykkleed, pall; shroud, winding-sheet.
lykkleur, livid colour.
lykkoets, hearse.
lykopening, autopsy.
lykrede, funeral service (oration).
lykskouer, coroner.
lykskouing, post-mortem (examination), autopsy; geregtelike –, inquest.
lykstasie, -stoet, funeral procession.
lykverbranding, cremation.
lykwa, hearse.
lym, n. glue; gum; bird-lime.
lym, (ge-), glue.
lymerig, (-e), gluey; sticky.
lympot, glue-pot, gum-pot.
lyn, (-e), n. line; string, rope, cord; **een – trek**, come into line, pull together; **– van gedrag**, line of action; **in 'n regte – afstam van**, be a lineal (direct) descendant of; **nie in my – nie**, not in my line; **in groot –e**, in broad outline; **op een – staan**, be on a level (with); **op een – stel met**, class (rank) with.
lyn, (ge-), rule; line.
lynboot, liner.
lynkoek, linseed-cake, oil-cake.
lynolie, linseed-oil.
lynreg, perpendicular, straight; **– in stryd met**, in direct opposition to.
lynsaad, linseed.
lynskip, liner.
lynstaan, (lynge-), line out; line up.
lyntjie, (-s), line; **iemand aan 'n – hou**, keep a person on a string.
lynvliegtuig, airliner.
lynwaad, linen.
lys, (-te), n. list, register; cornice, moulding; skirting-board; frame (of picture); ledge; (picture-)rail; **in 'n – sit**, frame; **op die – sit**, place on the list.
lys, (ge-), frame.
Lysol, Lysol.
lystemaker, maker of frames.
lywig, (-e), corpulent; bulky, voluminous.
lywigheid, corpulence; bulkiness.

M

ma, (-'s), mother, mummy, mam(m)a.
maag, (mae, mage), 1. stomach; corporation, tummy (colloq.); 'n goeie – hê, have a good digestion; **dit sit my dwars in die –**, it goes against my stomach, it sticks in my throat (gizzard); **jou – vashou van (die) lag**, shake with laughter.
maag, 2. kin(-sman, -swoman); **vriend nog – hê**, have neither kith nor kin.
maag, (-de), 3. vide **maagd.**
maagaandoening, affection of the stomach.
maagbom, dumpling, doughboy.
maagd, (maagde), maid(en), virgin; **die M– Maria**, the Virgin Mary.
maagdelik, (-e), maidenly, virginal.
maagdelikheid, maidenliness, virginity.
maagdepalm, periwinkle.
maagderei, chorus of virgins.
maagderoof, rape.
maagdokter, gastrologist, stomach-specialist.
maagdom, maidenhood, virginity.
maagholte, pit of the stomach.
maagkanker, cancer of the stomach.
maagkoors, gastric fever.
maagkramp, stomach-cramp.
maagkwaal, stomach-complaint.
maaglyer, stomach-sufferer, gastric patient.
maagpyn, stomach-ache.
maagsap, gastric juice.
maagsenuwee, gastric (stomachic) nerve.
maagsiekte, stomach-disease.
maagskap, kin, kindred, kinsfolk; kinship.
maagstreek, gastric (abdominal) region.
maagsuur, acidity of the stomach, heartburn.
maagsweer, gastric ulcer.
maagvol, satisfied; fed up.
maai, n. dam; **(loop na) jou –**, go to blazes; **hy is na sy –**, he is a goner.
maai, (ge-), cut mow, reap; **– en pagaai**, bustle and fidget; **– onder**, work havoc among.
maaier, (-s), 1. mower, reaper.
maaier, (-s), 2. maggot.
maaifoedie, (-s), scoundrel, blackguard.
maaimasjien, mowing-machine, harvester.
maaityd, reaping-time, harvest-time.
maak, n. making; **'n nuwe wêreld is in die –**, a new world is in the making; **ek het 'n pak in die –**, I am having a suit made.
maak, (ge-), make (a dress, a difference, points, runs, fortune, a name, enemies, laws, a journey, sounds); do (a job, sums); form (an idea of); **– dat jy wegkom!**, be off!; **hoe – jy dit?**, how are you (getting on)?; **alles wil – en breek**, act just as one pleases; **iemand aan die lag –**, make someone laugh; **erger –**, make worse; **moenie (so) lank – nie**, don't be (so) long; **met die hand gemaak**, hand-made, made by hand; **ja, maar hy – daarna**, yes, but he just asks for this world; **dit nie – nie**, not manage it; **dit – niks (nie saak) nie**, that doesn't matter; **hy kan my niks – nie**, he can't do anything to me; **hy het daar niks mee te – nie**, it's none of his business; **dit het daar niks mee te – nie**, that is beside (not) the point; **tot geld –, sell; iemand tot leuenaar –**, give someone the lie; **hom uit die voete –**, take to his heels; **ek het daarvan gemaak wat ek kon**, I made the best of it; **visite –**, (pay a) call; **jou oor iets vrolik –**, rejoice (laugh) at something; **(sy) werk daarvan – om ...**, make a point of ..., make it his job to ...
maakloon, charge for making.
maaksel, (-s), make, fashion; **eie –**, home-made.
maal, (male), n. 1. time; **een –, twee –, drie –**, once, twice, three times; **'n – of twee, drie**, two or three times.
maal, (male), n. 2. meal; **mosterd na die –**, after meat (comes) mustard.
maal, (ge-), 1. grind, mill; pulverize; **my kop –**, I feel dizzy; **jy –**, you're crazy; **aan sy kop – oor iets**, pester him for something; **eers(te) kom, eers(te) –**, first come first served.
maal, (ge-), 2. paint, picture.
maal, (ge-), 3. multiply.
maalgeld, miller's fee.
maalklip, grinding-stone.
maalstroom, maelstrom, whirlpool, vortex.
maalteken, multiplication-sign.
maaltyd, meal, repast.
maan, (mane), n. moon; **by donker –**, on a moonless night; **dis ligte (donker) –**, there is (no) moon, the moon is (not) shining; **die Halwe M–**, the Crescent; **glo dat die – van kaas gemaak is**, believe that the moon is made of green cheese; **met die – gepla wees**, be moonstruck; **gaan (loop, vlieg) na die –**, go to Jericho, go hang; **sy skool gaan na die –**, his school is going to the dogs (to rack and ruin); **die man(netjie) in die –**, the man in the moon.
maan, (ge-), warn, dun (for money).
maanbrief, dunning letter.
maand, (-e), month.
Maandag, Monday; **sy het 'n blou – by ons gekuier**, she stayed with us some short time; **(so) elke blou –**, once in a blue moon.
Maandagaand, Monday-night (-evening).
Maandagmiddag, Monday at noon; Monday-afternoon.
Maandags, (-e), a. & adv. (on) Monday(s); **die –e mark**, the Monday market.
maandberig, monthly report (statement).
maandblad, monthly (publication).
maandelang, (-e), a. **'n –e siekbed**, an illness lasting months.
maandelank, adv. for months.
maandeliks, (-e), a. & adv. monthly, once a month, every month.
maandgeld, monthly pay (allowance).
maandstaat, maandverslae, monthly return.
maangodin, moon-goddess.
maanhaar, mane; central ridge (in farm-track).
maanhaarjakkals, maned jackal, aardwolf.
maanhaarleeu, maned lion.
maanhaarpaadjie, farm-track (with ridge).
maankalf, moon-calf.
maankring, halo round the moon; lunar cycle.
maanlig, moonlight.
maanlignag, moonli(gh)t-night.
maanligstraal, moonbeam.
maanmaand, lunar month.
maansiek, (-, -e), lunatic, moonstruck.
maansiekte, lunacy.
maanskyf, disc of the moon, lunar disc.
maanskyn, moonlight.
maanskynaand, moonlight-night (-evening).
maansomloop, lunation, lunar revolution.
maansteen, moonstone.
maansverandering, change of the moon.
maansverduistering, eclipse of the moon.
maanvlek, moon-spot.
maanvormig, (-e), lunate.
maar, but, yet, merely, only, just; **– nee, dit sou nie**, but it was not to be; **vertel dit – aan my**, better tell it to me; you may tell me; **– alte graag**, all (only) too gladly; **dis – goed ook**, it's just as well; **soveel soos jy – wil**, as much as ever you want; **'n week of ook – 5 dae**, a week or even 5 days; **nog – 'n snuiter**, a mere youngster; **ons het nog – begin toe ...**, we

had just started when . . . ; **as hy – hier was!,** if only he were here!; **wag –!,** just you wait!; **toe –!,** all right! (don't worry; just you wait!)
maarskalk, (-e), n. marshal.
maarskalkstaf, marshal's baton.
Maart, n. March.
Maartlelie, amaryllis, belladonna-lily.
maas, (mase), n. mesh, stitch.
maas, (ge-), reknit, do "invisible mending".
maaswerk, network, tracery (archit.).
maat, (mate), 1. measure, size, gauge; time, bar (music); measure, metre (poetry); **mate en gewigte,** weights and measures; **iemand se – neem,** take someone's measure; **watter – dra jy?,** what size do you take?; **by die klein – verkoop,** retail; **bowe mate,** beyond measure, exceedingly; **in 'n hoë mate,** to a high degree; **in die hoogste mate,** to the last degree, in the extreme; **in meerdere of mindere mate,** more or less; **met mate,** in moderation; **'n pak klere na –,** a suit made to measure; **die – aangee,** mark (the) time; **die – slaan,** beat time; **die – hou,** keep time; know where to draw the line; **op die – van die musiek,** in time to the music; **uit (buite) die –,** out of time.
maat, (-s, maters), 2. mate, comrade, companion, partner; **met iemand maats wees,** be good friends with someone; **maats maak,** make friends; **ek is nie jou – nie!,** don't compare yourself to me!; **sy maters is (klein) dood,** no one can hold a candle to him; **ou –!,** old man!
maatband, tape-measure, measuring-tape.
maateenheid, unit of measure.
maatemmer, bucket-measure.
maatfles, measuring-flask.
maatgevoel, sense of rhythm.
maatglas, measuring-glass.
maatjie, (-s, matertjies), 1. little playmate.
maatjie, (-s), 2. small measure.
maatloos, (-lose): maatlose verse, free verse.
maatreël, measure, precaution; **–s neem (tref),** take steps (measures).
maatskaplik, (-e), social; joint (stock).
maatskappy, (-e), n. company; society.
maatslag, beat.
maatstaf, measure, scale; standard, criterion.
maatstok, yardstick; rule; (conductor's) baton.
maatstreep, bar(-line) (mus.).
maatvas, (-te), (steady in) keeping time.
macaroni, macaroni.
Macedonies, (-e), Macedonian.
Mach-getal, Mach number.
madam, (-s, -me), n. lady.
madeliefie, (-s), daisy.
Madonna, (-s), Madonna.
maer, lean, thin; (fig.) meagre, poor.
maerheid, n. thinness, leanness.
maermerrie, shin.
maerte, vide **maerheid.**
mag, (-te), n. power, might, force, strength; control; authority; **– gaan bo reg,** might is right; **die – in hande hê,** be in power (control); **die – van die gewoonte,** force of habit; **nie by magte wees om . . .,** be unable to; **omstandighede wat ek nie in my – het nie (omstandighede buite my –),** circumstances over which I have no control (beyond my control); **met – en krag, met (uit) alle –,** with might and main; **'n – der menigte,** heaps, lots, tons; **die 2de – van 5 is 25,** 5 squared (5 to the 2nd power) equals 25; **a tot die nde – verhef,** raise a to the nth power.
mag, (pret.: **mog**), may be allowed (permitted); **wat ook al – gebeur,** happen what may; **mog**

hy 'n saak daarvan maak dan . . ., should he go to law over it, then . . .; **mog dit die geval wees,** if so.
magasyn, (-e), n. store, warehouse; magazine.
magasyngeweer, magazine-rifle.
magbrief, warrant, power of attorney.
magdom, lot(s), heap(s), crowd(s).
maghebbend, (-e), having authority.
maghebber, (-s), authority, ruler.
magie, (-s), 1. tummy, corporation.
magie, 2. magic (art).
magiër, (-s), magician; **magiërs,** magi.
magies, (-e), magic(al).
magistraal, (-ale), magisterial, authoritative.
Magjaar, (-are), Magyar.
magnaat, (-ate), magnate, grandee; baron.
magneet, (-ete), magnet, lodestone.
magneetkanker, (magnetic) armature.
magneetnaald, magnetic needle.
magneetpool, magnetic pole.
magneetveld, magnetic field.
magneetyster, magnetic iron, magnetite.
magnesia, magnesia.
magnesium, magnesium.
magnesiumlig, magnesium-light, flashlight.
magneties, (-e), magnetic.
magnetiseer, (ge-), magnetize; mesmerize.
magnetiseur, (-s), magnetist, mesmerist.
magnetisme, magnetism.
magnetron, magnetron.
magnifiek, vide **manjifiek.**
magnolia, (-s), magnolia.
magaanwyser, exponent, index (alg.).
magsgebied, sphere of influence.
magsmisbruik, abuse of power.
magspreuk, authoritative utterance; catchword; silencer, clincher.
magsuitbreiding, expansion of power.
magsverheffing, involution.
magsvertoon, display (parade) of power.
magteloos, (-lose), powerless, impotent.
magteloosheid, powerlessness, impotence.
magtig, (-e), powerful, mighty, potent; **die omstandighede was my te –,** circumstances were too much for me; **'n taal – wees,** have command of a language; **hy is sy vak heeltemal –,** he has a perfect grasp of his subject.
magtig!, (interj.), Heavens!, Great Scott!
magtig, (ge-), authorise, warrant, empower.
magtiging, authorization, warrant.
magwoord, authoritative word; vide **magspreuk.**
mahem, (-me), n. crowned crane.
mahoniehout, mahogany.
mail- . . ., vide **pos- . . .**
mais, n. maize, mealies.
majesteit, (-e), majesty.
majesteitskennis, lese-majesty.
majestueus, (-e), majestic.
majeur, major (mus.); **a –,** A sharp; **– toonladder,** major scale.
majolika, majolica.
majoor, (-s, -ore), major.
majoorsrang, majorship, majority.
majoraat, (-ate), primogeniture.
majoriteit, (-e), majority.
mak, (–, -ke), tame, docile, manageable, tractable; **'n – perd,** a quiet horse; **so – soos 'n lam,** as quiet (meek and mild) as a lamb.
makeer, (ge-), ail; lack, be wanting; **hy – nooit nie,** he is never absent; **hy – nooit iets nie,** there is never anything wrong with him; **wat – jou?,** what is the matter with you?; **daar – drie skape,** there are three sheep missing.

makelaar, (-s), broker; – **in effekte,** stockbroker; – **in vaste goedere,** (real) estate-agent.
makelary, brokerage.
maker, (-s), author, creator; maker.
makheid, docility, tameness; vide **mak.**
maklik, (-e), easy, comfortable.
maklikheid, ease, easiness, facility, comfortableness.
makou, (-e), muscovy duck.
makriel, (-e), Cape mackerel.
makrolletjie, (-s), almond-cake, macaroon.
maksimum, (-s, -ima), maximum.
mal, (-, -le), mad, foolish; silly.
malagiet, (-e), malachite.
malaise, malaise, depression, slump.
malaria, malaria.
malariabasil, malarial (malaria-)germ.
malariamuskiet, malarial mosquito.
malariastreek, malaria region.
malariavry, free from malaria.
Malbaar, (-bare), native (slave) of Malabar.
Maleier, (-s), Malay.
Maleis, (-e), Malay.
Malgas, (-se), Malagasy.
malgas, (-se), n. malagash, Cape gannet.
Malgassies, Malagasy (language).
malheid, insanity, madness; folly, foolishness, nonsense, silliness.
malhuis, lunatic asylum.
malie, 1. money.
malie, 2. chucker (game of stone-quoits).
malie, 3. ring (of coat of mail).
malie, (ge-), play at chucker.
malieklip, chucker(-quoit).
maling: – **aan iets hê,** be fed up with a thing.
malisieus, (-e), malicious.
malkop, silly person, rattle-brain; tomboy; – **wees,** play the giddy goat.
malkopsiekte, (mad) staggers.
mallemeule, mallemole, merry-go-round.
malligheid, silliness; tomfoolery; nonsense.
malmok, (-ke), mallemuck; mollymawk.
malmokkie, marmotjie, (-s), guinea-pig.
malpraatjies, nonsense, stuff.
mals, (-e), lush (grass), tender (meat).
malsheid, softness, tenderness.
maltrap, vide **malkop.**
malva, (-s), geranium, mallow.
mama, (-'s), mamma, (-s), mam(m)a.
mama'tjie, (-s), mummy.
mamba(slang), mamba(-snake).
Mameluk, (-ke), Mameluke.
mammie, (-s), vide **mamaatjie.**
mammoet, (-e), mammoth.
mammonverering, mammon-worship.
man, (-ne -s), man; husband; – **en vrou,** husband and wife; **soos een** –, as one man, to a man, with one accord; **die gewone** –, the plain man, the man in the street; **die** – **(mannetjie) in die maan,** the man in the moon; **dit is my** –, he is my man, he is the man for me; **sy** – **staan,** hold one's own; **iets aan die** – **bring,** sell (dispose of) something; **as die nood aan die** – **kom,** when the worst comes to the worst; **met** – **en muis,** with 'all hands on board; **iets op die** – **af vra,** ask a straight question; **tot die laaste** –, to a man, every man Jack of them; **'n geveg van** – **teen man,** a hand-to-hand fight; – **vir** –, man for man.
manbaar, (-bare), marriageable, nubile.
mandaat, (-date), mandate.
mandaatgebied, mandated territory.
mandaathouer, mandatory.
mandaryn, (-e), mandarin.
mandataris, (-se), vide **mandaathouer.**

mandjie, (-s), basket, hamper.
mandjietjie, (-s), small basket, pottle.
mandjievol, (mandjiesvol), basketful.
mandolien, (-s), mandolin(e).
mandoor, (-dore, -s), foreman, mandoor.
mandragora, mandrake.
mandril, (-le), mandrill.
manel, (-le), frock-coat.
manelpant, (frock-) coat-tail.
maneskyn, moonlight, moonshine; **dit was alles roseguer en** –, everything was lovely in the garden; vide **maanskyn.**
maneuver, (-s), manoeuvre.
maneuvreer, (ge-), manoeuvre.
manewales, antics, capers.
mangaan, manganese.
mangat, manhole.
mangel, (-s), n. 1. tonsil.
mangel, (-s), 2. mangle, mangling-board.
mangel, (ge-), mangle.
mangelwortel, mangel(wurzel), mangold.
mango, (-'s), mango.
manhaftig, (-e), brave, manly; cheeky.
manhaftigheid, bravery, courage; cheek.
maniak, (-ke), crank, faddist, maniac.
manie, (-ë, -s), craze, fad, mania, rage.
manier, (-e), fashion, manner, way; **goeie -e,** good manners; **op hierdie** –, in this manner (way); **op die een of ander** –, in one way or another, somehow; **op 'n** –, after a fashion.
manierlik, (-e), polite, well-mannered.
manierlikheid, politeness, good manners.
maniertjie,(-s), mannerism.
manifes, (-te), manifest(o).
manifesteer, (ge-), demonstrate, manifest.
maniok, manioc.
manipuleer, (ge-), manipulate.
manjifiek, (-e), magnificent.
mank, (-e), crippled, lame, limping; **hy loop** –, he limps; **aan 'n euwel** – **gaan,** have a defect.
mankement, (-e), defect, trouble.
mankheid, lameness.
mankoliek(ig), crocked, ill, seedy.
mankpoot, cripple, dot-and-go-one.
manlief, hubby.
manlik, (-e), manly; masculine; male.
manlikheid, manhood; manliness; masculinity.
manmoedig, (-e), bold, brave, manful, manly.
manmoedigheid, boldness, bravery.
manna, manna.
mannekoor, male choir.
mannemoed, manly courage.
mannetaal, manly language.
mannetjie, (-s), male; chappie, little fellow.
mannetjiesagtig, (-e), termagant; **'n -e vrou,** a virago, a termagant.
mannetjie(s)bobbejaan, male baboon (monkey).
mannetjie-eend, mannetjieseend, drake.
mannetjie(s)gans, gander.
mannetjie(s)volstruis, male ostrich.
mannetjiesvrou, virago.
mannewerk, man's work.
mans: hy is – **genoeg om . . . ,** he is man enough to . . . , he is capable of holding his own.
manshand, man's hand(writing).
manshemp, man's shirt.
manshoogte, man's height.
mansiek, (-e), man-mad, mad after men.
mansjet, (-te), cuff.
mansjetknoop, (cuff-)link.
manskap, (-pe), crew; (pl.) men.
manskleding, -klere, male attire, men's clothes (dress), gentlemen's wear.
manslag, homicide, manslaughter; **strafbare** –, culpable homicide.

manslengte, man's height (length, size).
mansmens, -persoon, male (person), man.
mantel, (-s), cloak, mantle; cape; casing; jacket, shell; fire-screen; **jou – na die wind draai (hang),** trim one's sails to the wind, be a turncoat; **A se – het op B geval,** A's mantle has fallen on B; **iets met die – van die liefde bedek,** cover something with the cloak of charity.
manteldraaier, turncoat, weather-cock.
mantelkostuum, coat-and-skirt.
mantelpak, vide **mantelkostuum.**
mantelvlies, diaphragm.
manuaal, (-uale), finger-board, keyboard, manual.
manuskrip, (-te), manuscript.
man-uur, man-hour.
mapstieks!, by Jove!, my goodness!
maraboe, (-s), marabou.
marathonwedloop, marathon race.
marconigram, marconigram.
mare, maar, news, report, tidings.
maretak, mistletoe.
margarien, margarine, margarine.
marge, (-s), margin.
marginaal, (-ale), marginal.
margriet(jie), (-s), daisy, marguerite; **wilde wit –,** ox-eye daisy.
Maria, Maria, Mary.
Mariabeeld, image of the Virgin Mary.
Mariaverering, worship of the Virgin Mary.
marimba, marimba.
marine, navy.
marine-artillerie, naval artillery.
marineblou, navy-blue.
marine-instituut, naval college.
marine-offisier, naval officer.
marinestasie, naval station.
marinewerf, naval (dock)yard.
marinewese, navy, naval affairs.
marinier, (-s), marine(r).
marionet, (-te), marionette, puppet.
marionettespel, -teater, puppet-show.
maritiem, (-e), maritime.
mark, (-te), n. market.
mark, (-e), n. mark (German coin).
markant, (-e), conspicuous, salient.
markberig, market-report.
markdag, market-day.
markeer, (ge-), mark; **die pas –,** mark time.
markgeld, market-money; market-dues.
markgraaf, margrave.
markgravin, margravine.
markies, (-e), marquis.
markiesin, (-ne), marchioness; marquise.
markies(tent), marquee(-tent).
markmeester, market-master.
markplein, market-square.
markprys, market-price.
markwaarde, market-value.
marlyn, (-e), marline.
marmelade, marmalade.
marmer, n. marble.
marmer, (ge-), grain, marble.
marmer-aar, vein in marble.
marmeragtig, (-e), marblelike.
marmerbeeld, marble-statue.
marmerblad, marble-top.
marmergroef, marble-quarry.
marmerplaat, marble-slab.
marmersteen, marble.
marmot(jie), vide **malmokkie.**
maroela, (-s), marula.
Marokkaans, (-e), Moroccan.
Marokko, Morocco.
marokyn(leer), morocco(-leather).

mars, 1. top (marine).
mars, (-e), 2. march.
marsbanker, (-s), horse-mackerel, bastard mackerel, marsbanker.
marsbevel, order of march.
Marsbewoner, Martian.
marsepein, marchpane, marzipan.
marsiaal, (-iale), martial.
marsjeer, (ge-), march.
marskramer, (-s), hawker, pedlar.
marsorder, marching-order.
marstyd, march(ing)-time.
marsvaardig, (-e), ready to march.
martel, (ge-), rack, torture; torment.
martelaar, (-are, -s), martyr.
martelaarsbloed, martyr's blood.
martelaarskap, martyrdom.
martelaarskroon, martyr's crown.
martelares, (-se), (woman-)martyr.
martel(a)ry, torture; torment.
marteldood, martyr's death, martyrdom.
marteling, torture.
martelry, vide **martel(a)ry.**
martel(werk)tuig, instrument of torture.
martini, martini.
Marxisme, Marxism.
Marxisties, (-e), Marxian, Marxist.
mas, (-te), mast; pole (gymnastics); **sien om die – op te kom,** fend for oneself, fight one's own battle.
Masbieker, (-s), Mozambiquer.
masbos, fir-wood; forest of masts.
masels, measles; **Duitse –,** German measles (rubella).
mashout, fir-wood, pine-wood.
masjien, (-e), machine; engine.
masjienbou, engine-building, construction of machines; mechanical engineering.
masjiengaring, -gare, machine-cotton.
masjiengeweer, machine-gun.
masjienkamer, engine-room.
masjienolie, machine-oil, lubricating oil.
masjienskrif, typewriting.
masjienweiering, engine failure.
masjinaal, (-ale), a. & adv. mechanical(ly); automatical(ly).
masjinerie, machinery.
masjinis, (-te), engineer (on ship), engine-driver (on train); scene-shifter (in theatre).
maskara, mascara.
maskeer, (ge-), camouflage, cover, mask.
masker, (-s), n. mask; disguise; **iemand die – afdruk,** unmask a person; **onder die – van,** under the cloak (mask) of.
masker, (ge-), mask, veil.
maskerade, (-s), masquerade, pageant.
maskerbal, masked ball.
masochisme, masochism.
massa, (-s), crowd, mass, lot, lump; **die groot –,** the common herd, the masses.
massa-aanval, massed attack.
massaal, (-ale), wholesale.
massage, massage.
massaproduksie, mass-production.
masseer, (ge-), massage.
masseur, (-s), masseur, massagist.
masseuse, (-s), masseuse.
massief, (-iewe), massive, solid.
massiwiteit, massiveness, solidity.
mastig!, gracious!
mastik(boom), mastic(-tree).
mastodon, (-te), mastodon.
masurka, (-s), mazurka.
maswerkknoop, -slag, clove-hitch.

mat, (-te), n. mat, door-mat, floor-mat, bottom (of chair); **deur die – val**, come a cropper, make a blunder.
mat, (-te), a. languid, tired, weary; dead, dull (of gold); lustreless; dim; checkmate.
mat, (ge-), mat, rush, bottom (a chair).
matador, (-s), matador; pastmaster.
mate, degree, measure; **in die hoogste –**, to the fullest (extent, measure).
mateloos, (-lose), excessive, measureless.
matematies, (-e), mathematical.
matematikus, (-se, -ici), mathematician.
materiaal, (-iale), material(s).
materialis, (-te), materialist.
materialisme, materialism.
materialisties, (-e), materialist(ic).
materie, matter.
materieel, (-iële), a. & adv. material(ly).
maters: sy **– is dood**, he has no equal.
matesis, mathematics.
matglas, dull (frosted, ground) glass.
matheid, exhaustion, languor, lassitude, fatigue, weariness; dimness, dullness.
matig, (-e), a. moderate; abstemious, sober, temperate.
matig, (ge-), moderate, modify, mitigate; restrain (one's anger).
matigheid, moderation, temperance.
matigheidsgenootskap, temperance-society.
matiging, moderation, modification.
matinee, (-s), matinée.
ma'tjie, (-'s), mummy, little mother.
matjiesgoed, n. bulrush.
matjiesgoed!, interj. gracious!
matras, (-se), mattress.
matrasgoed, tick(ing).
matriargaal, (-ale), matriarchal.
matriargaat, matriarchy, mother-right.
Matriek(eksamen), Matric(ulation) examination.
matrikulasie, matriculation.
Matrikulasieraad, Matriculation Board.
matrikuleer, (ge-), matriculate.
matrone, (-s), matron.
matroos, (-ose), sailor; **vloek soos 'n –**, swear like a trooper.
matrooshoed, sailor-hat.
matrooslied, **matroselied**, sailors' song, sea-song.
matroospakkie, sailor-suit.
matrys, (-e), matrix; mould.
Mattheüs, Matthew.
matwerk, matting.
Mauser, (-s), Mauser.
mausoleum, (-lea, -s), mausoleum.
mauve, mauve.
mayonnaise, mayonnaise.
mebos, mebos, dried and sugared apricots.
meboskonfyt, mebos-jam.
medalje, (-s), medal.
medaljewenner, medallist.
medaljon, (-s), medallion.
Mede, **Medes**; **die wet van – en Perse**, the law of (the) Medes and Persians.
mede, vide **mee**.
mede- . . . , co-, fellow- (in compounds).
mede-aanspraaklik, (-e), co-responsible.
mede-aanwesig, (-e), likewise present.
mede-arbeider, fellow-worker.
medebelanghebbende, co-partner, sharer, party (person) also interested.
medebesitter, joint proprietor (owner).
medebestuurder, co-manager.
medebroeder, colleague; fellow-man.
medeburger, fellow-citizen.
mede-Christen, fellow-Christian.

mede-, **meedeelsaam** (-same), communicative; expansive; charitable, liberal, open-handed.
mede, **meedeelsaamheid**, communicativeness; charitableness, liberality.
mede-, **meedeling**, (-e, -s), announcement, communication, information.
mede-, **meedinger**, (-s), competitor, rival.
mede-, **meedinging**, competition, rivalry.
mededirekteur, co-director, co-manager.
mede-, **meedoë**, compassion, pity, sympathy.
mede-, **meedoënd**, **-dogend**, (-e), compassionate, sympathetic.
mede-eienaar, vide **medebesitter**.
mede-erfgenaam, co-heir, joint heir.
medegenoot, associate, consort.
medegetuie, fellow-witness.
medegevangene, fellow-prisoner.
mede-, **meegevoel**, fellow-feeling, sympathy.
medehelper, assistant, collaborator, co-operator, helpmate.
medekieser, fellow-elector.
medeklinker, consonant.
medekrygsman, fellow-soldier, fellow-warrior.
medelid, fellow-member.
medely(d)e, compassion, commiseration, pity, sympathy.
medelydend, (-e), compassionate.
medemens, fellow-man.
medeminnaar, **-minares**, rival.
mede-ondertekenaar, co-signatory.
mede-outeur, (-s), joint author.
medepassasier, fellow-traveller.
medepligtig, (-e), accessary (accessory); **hy was daaraan –**, he was a party to it.
medepligtige, (-s), accomplice.
medepligtigheid, complicity.
mederegter, fellow-judge.
medeseggenskap, co-partnership; right of say; participation.
medeskepsel, fellow-being.
medestander, partisan, partner.
medestryder, fellow-fighter, comrade.
medestudent, fellow-student.
mede-, **meewerkend**, (-e), co-operating.
medewerker, co-operator, co-worker, fellow-worker; collaborator; contributor (to a paper).
mede-, **meewerking**, assistance, collaboration, contribution, co-operation.
medewete, knowledge.
media, vide **medium**.
mediaan, (-iane), median.
mediaanletter, pica.
mediaanlyn, median (line).
mediateur, (-s), mediator, intercessor.
medies, (-e), medical.
medikament, (-e), medicament; medicine; drug.
medikus, (-se, -dici), medical man, medico, doctor, physician.
mediokriteit, mediocrity.
medisinaal, (-ale), medicinal.
medisyne, (-s), medicine.
medisynmeester, physician; **– genees jouself**, physician, heal thyself (Bib.); practise what you preach (fig.).
meditasie, (-s), meditation.
mediteer, (ge-), mediate.
Mediterreens, (-e), Mediterranean.
medium, (-dia), medium; means.
mee, **mede**, also, likewise, too; together; with; co-, fellow- (in compounds).
mee- . . . , vide **mede-** . . . .
mee-arbei, (meege-), co-operate.
meebring, (meege-), bring along, bring with one; entail (delay), involve (danger), cause (illness).

meedeel, (meege-), communicate (news), inform (a person), let (a person) know, record (one's experiences).
meedeling, vide **me(d)edeling**.
meeding, (meege-), compete.
meedinger, -dinging, vide **me(d)edinger, -dinging**.
meedoen, (meege-), join (in a game), take part, participate.
meedoënloos, (-lose), merciless.
meedra, (meege-), carry along.
meedrink, (meege-), drink with others.
meegaan, (meege-), accompany; keep pace (with the times), subscribe to (a view), fall in (with an arrangement).
meegee, (meege-), give, send along with; give way, yield.
meegevoel, vide **me(d)egevoel**.
meehelp, (meege-), assist, contribute.
meekom, (meege-), come along; accompany.
meel, meal; **fyn –**, flour.
meelagtig, (-e), mealy, floury.
meelblom, flour.
meelbol, "meelbol", ball of baked flour.
meeldou, blight, mildew.
meeldraad, stamen.
meeleef, -lewe, (meege-), – met, live the same life as, enter into the life (spirit) of, sympathise with.
meeloop, (meege-), acconpany; **dit het hom altyd meegeloop**, he has always been in luck.
meelpap, flourpaste; gruel.
meelsak, flour-bag.
meelsif, flour-sieve.
meelwurm, meal-beetle (-weevil, -worm).
meemaak, (meege-), go through, experience, take part in.
meen, (ge-), mean; intend; fancy, suppose, think; **ek – dit, I** am serious (in earnest), I mean it; **ek – dat ek jou gesê het**, I thought I had told you.
meeneem, (meege-), take along.
meent, commonage.
meepraat, (meege-), join (take part) in (a conversation); have a say in (a matter); put in a word.
meer, (mere), n. lake.
meer, a. & adv. more; – **as**, more than; **– as genoeg**, more than enough, too much; **des te –**, so much the more, the more so; **hy is g'n kind – nie**, he is no longer a child; **g'n woord – nie!**, not another word!; **hoe langer hoe –**, more and more, the longer the more; **dit is niks – as billik nie**, it is only fair (just); **nooit – nie**, never again; **steeds –**, more and more; **wat wil jy – hê?**, what more do you want?; **nee wat – is**, nay more, moreover; **dit smaak na –**, I should like some more; **sonder –**, without more ado; **ons kan dit nie sonder – aanneem nie**, we cannot accept that without comment; **te –**, the more so.
meerdere, (-s), superior.
meerderheid, majority; superiority.
meerderjarig, (-e), of age; **– word**, come of age, attain one's majority.
meerderjarigheid, majority.
meerderjarigverklaring, emancipation.
meerderman: **as – kom, moet minderman wyk**, honour comes first; the weakest goes to the wall.
meereis, (meerge-), travel with.
meereken, (meege-), count (in), include.
meergegoed, (-e), better-off.
meergemeld, **-genoemd**, (-e), above-named, before-mentioned.
meerkat, (-te), meercat.
meerkoet, (-e), coot.
meerlettergrepig, (-e), polysyllabic.
meermaal, -male, frequently, more than once, often.
meerman, (-ne), merman.
meermin, (-ne), mermaid.
meerpaal, mooring-post.
meerskuim, meerschaum.
meerslagtig, (-e), having more than one gender; polygenous.
meerstemmig, (-e), polyphonic; **'n –e lied**, a part-song.
meertou, mooring-cable.
meervoud, (-e), plural.
meervoudig, (-e), plural.
meervoudsuitgang, plural ending.
mees, (mese), n. titmouse, tomtit, tit.
mees, adv. most(ly).
meesal, vide **meestal**.
meesbegunstigde, most-favoured.
meesleep, (meege-), carry along, drag along; carry (sweep) before it; **hy het sy gehoor meegesleep**, he carried his audience with him.
meesmuil, (ge-), simper, smirk, sneer.
meespeel, (meege-), join in (a game), take part (a hand) in (a game).
meestal, meesal, mostly, usually.
meeste, greatest, most; **die – mense**, most (people); **ek hou hiervan die –**, I like this best; **op sy –**, at most, at the outside.
meestendeels, for the greater (the most) part; in the majority of cases.
meester, (-s), master; teacher; **baie tale – wees**, be master of many languages, have a command of many languages; **die toestand – wees**, have a situation in hand; **jou – maak van**, take possession of; **die oog van die – maak die perd vet**, the eye of the master makes the horse fat (the cattle thrive); **daar is altyd – bo –**, every man has his match.
meesteragtig, (-e), imperious; pedantic.
meesteres, (-se), mistress.
meestergoed, medicine.
meesterhand, master('s) hand.
meesterlik, (-e), excellent, masterly.
meestersanger, master-singer.
meesterskap, mastery.
meesterstuk, meesterwerk, masterpiece.
meet, n. starting-line, starting-point; **van – a aan**, from the beginning; **weer van – af aan begin**, start afresh.
meet, (ge-), measure, gauge; **jou met iemand –**, match (measure, pit) oneself against someone, measure one's strength against someone; **met die maat waarmee jy –, sal jy weer ge- word**, with what measure ye mete, it shall be measured to you again (Bib.); you will be judged by your own standard.
meetbaar, (-bare), measurable.
meetband, measuring-tape, measure.
meetel, (meege-), count, include.
meetinstrument, measuring-instrument.
meetketting, measuring-chain.
meetkunde, geometry.
meetkundig, (-e), geometrical.
meetkundige, (-s), geometrician.
meetlood, plummet.
meetlyn, measuring-line, -cord.
meetrek, (meege-), pull too, pull along.
meetstok, measuring-rod (-staff, -yard).
meeu, (-e), (sea-)gull, sea-mew.
meeval, (meege-), exceed one's expectations, cause agreeable surprise.
meevaller, (-s), piece of good luck, windfall.
meewarig, (-e), compassionate.

meewarigheid, compassion.
meewerk, (meege-), co-operate, collaborate, assist; contribute towards.
megafoon, (-fone), megaphone.
meganiek, mechanism; action; clockwork.
meganies, (-e), mechanical.
meganika, mechanics.
meganikus, (-se, -nici), mechanician.
meganisme, vide **meganiek.**
megaton, megaton.
Mei, May.
meiblom, May-flower.
meiboom, maypole.
Meidag, May Day.
meidoring, hawthorn, May-bush.
Meimaand, month of May.
meinedig, (-e), forsworn, perjured.
meineed, perjury.
meisie, (-s), girl; —s is nie handvol nie maar landvol, she is not the only pebble on the beach; dit bly onder ons —s, this is to be kept strictly secret.
meisiemens, woman, female.
meisie(s)agtig, (-e), girl-like, girlish.
meisiesdrag, girl's dress (costume).
meisiesgek, n. & a. (boy, man) fond of girls.
meisieshoed, girl's hat.
meisiesklere, girls' clothes.
meisieskool, girls' school.
meisiestem, girls' voice, girlish voice.
Meiviering, May Day celebration.
mejuffrou, Madam (address without name), Miss (address with name).
mekaar, each other, one another; met —, with each other; together, between them; **na** —, after each other, one after another; **onder** —, among (between) them; **op** —, one on top of the other.
Mekka, Mecca.
melaats, (-e), leprous.
melaatse (-s), leper.
melaatsheid, leprosy.
melancholie, melancholy.
melancholies, (-e), melancholy, depressed.
melasse, molasses.
meld(e), (ge-), announce, inform, mention, report, state; **baie gevalle word gemeld,** many cases are reported.
meldenswaardig, (-e), worth mentioning.
melding, mention; — **maak van,** mention, make mention of.
melerig, (-e), mealy, floury.
melk, n. milk; **'n land vloeiende van** — **en heuning,** a country (land) flowing with milk and honey.
melk, (ge-), milk; **iemand** —, fleece a person.
melkaar, lacteal vein.
melkafskeiding, (-e), lactiferous.
melkafskeiding, -afsondering, lactation.
melkagtig, (-e), milky.
melkbaard, down, soft beard; milksop.
melkbeker, milk-mug (-jug).
melkboer, dairy-farmer, dairyman.
melkbok, milch-goat.
melkbos, "milk-bush", Euphorbia spp.
melkbottel, milk-bottle.
melkdieet, milk-diet.
melkdissel, sow-thistle.
melkemmer, milk(ing)-pail.
melker, (-s), milker.
melkery, (-e), milking; dairy-farming; dairy (-farm).
melkkamer, dairy, milk-room.
melkkan, milk-jug; milk-can.
melkkar, milk-cart.
melkklier, lacteal gland.
melkkoei, milch-cow (also fig.).
melkkom, milk-basin, milk-bowl.
melkkoors, milk-fever, lacteal fever.
melkkos, milk-food, spoon-meat.
melkkwarts, milky quartz.
melkmeisie, milkmaid, dairy-maid.
melkmeter, lactometer.
melkooi, milch-ewe.
melkpap, milk-porridge.
melkpens, abomasum.
melksap, milky juice, latex.
melksuiker, milk-sugar, lactose.
melksuur, lactic acid.
melktand, milk-tooth.
melktert, milk-tart.
melktyd, milking-time.
melkvat, milk-tub, -vessel; (pl.) lacteals, lacteal vessels.
melkvee, dairy-cattle, milch-cattle.
melkweg, milky way, galaxy.
melkwit, milky white, as white as milk.
melodie, (-ë), air, melody, tune.
melodies, (-e), melodic.
melodieus, (-e), melodious, tuneful.
melodrama, melodrama.
melodramaties, (-e), melodramatic.
même, (-s), nurse.
memorandum, (-da, -s), memorandum.
memorie, (-s), document; petition.
memoriseer, (ge-), commit to memory, learn by heart, memorize.
meneer, (-ere), gentleman; Mr. (in address with name), Sir (in address without name); master; mister.
meng, (ge-), alloy (metals); blend (colours); mix (drinks); mingle (with people); adulterate, dilute; **jou — in,** join in (conversation), interfere in (quarrel), meddle with (other people's affairs).
mengbaar, (-bare), mixable.
mengbaarheid, mixability.
mengeldigte, miscellaneous poems.
mengeling, mixture.
mengelmoes, hodge-podge (hotch-potch), jumble, medley, mishmash, mixture.
mengelwerk, collectanea, miscellany.
mengmasjien, mixer.
mengsel, (-s), blend; mixture.
menie, minium, red-lead.
menige, many, several.
menigeen, many a one.
menigmaal, frequently, often.
menigte, (-s), crowd, great number, multitude.
menigvuldig, (-e), abundant, manifold.
menigvuldigheid, abundance, frequency, multiplicity.
menigwerf, vide **menigmaal.**
mening, (-s, -e), idea, opinion, view; intention; **die openbare —,** public opinion; **by jou — bly,** hold (stick) to one's opinion; **in die — verkeer,** be under the impression; **na my —,** in my opinion, to my mind (thinking); **van — verskil,** differ in opinion, hold different views; **van — wees dat,** be of opinion that, hold the view that; be under the impression that.
meningitis, meningitis.
meningsverskil, difference (divergence) of opinion, disagreement.
menner, driver; tamer; trainer.
mens, (-e), n. human being, man, person; (pl.) men, people; visitors; **'n goeie —,** a good soul;

mens ek is ook maar 'n –, I am only human; g'n –, nobody, no one; **ek het g'n – gesien nie**, I did not see a soul; **so is die –**, such is man; **wie is daardie –?, die –?**, who is that person?; **die – is sterflik**, man is mortal; **die –e sê**, people say, they say, it is said; **–e kry**, get visitors; **die – wik, God beskik**, man proposes, God disposes; **hy is 'n snaakse entjie –**, he is a strange specimen (bit, piece) of humanity; **die inwendige – versterk**, fortify (refresh) one's inner man; **'n – is maar 'n –**, to err is human; **na die – gepraat (gesproke)**, humanly speaking.
mens, pron. indef. one, you; **so iets sê – nie**, such things are not said; **dit doen – nie**, it is not done; **wat sal – daarvan sê?**, what can one say?
mensaap, man-ape, anthropoid (ape).
mensbloed, human blood.
mensdom, mankind, humanity.
mensegeslag, human race.
mensehaat, hatred of mankind.
mensehand, human hand.
mensehater, misanthrope.
menseheugenis, living memory.
mensekenner, judge of people.
mensekennis, knowledge of human character (of men).
mensekind, child of man, human being.
menseleeftyd, lifetime generation.
menselewe, human life.
menseliefde, humanity, love of mankind, philanthropy.
menseras, (human) race.
menseroof, kidnapping.
mens(e)sku, shy, timid, unsociable.
mensestem, human voice.
menseverstand, human understanding.
mensevrees, fear of men.
mensevri(e)nd, philanthropist.
mensewerk, work of man.
mensheid, humanity, mankind.
mensie, (-s), diminutive person, midget.
menskundig, (-e), knowing human nature.
mensliewend, (-e), humane, philanthropic.
menslik, (-e), human.
menslikerwys(e): **– gesproke**, humanly speaking.
menslikheid, humanity; human nature.
mensvlees, **-vleis**, human flesh.
mensvreter, man-eater, cannibal.
mensvreterhaai, man-eating shark.
menswaardig, (-e), worthy of a human being.
menswording, incarnation.
mentaliteit, mentality.
menu, (-'s), menu(-card), bill of fare.
menuet, (-te), minuet.
merendeel, greater part, majority.
merendeels, for the greater (the most) part, mostly; in the majority of cases.
merg, marrow; **dit dring deur – en been**, it goes (pierces) to the very marrow; **Afrikaans in – en been**, Afrikaans to the backbone (to the core).
meridiaan, (-iane), meridian.
meridiaansirkel, meridian circle.
meriete, merits.
merino, (-'s), merino.
merinoskaap, merino(-sheep).
merk, (-e), n. mark; brand (of articles), quality, sort; trade-mark; sign.
merk, (ge-), mark; notice, perceive, see; **jy moet niks laat – nie**, don't give yourself away.
merkbaar, (-bare), appreciable, noticeable, marked, perceptible.
merkink, marking-ink.
merkteken, mark, scar, sign, token.

merkwaardig, (-e), curious, noteworthy, remarkable.
merkwaardigheid, curiosity; remarkableness.
merrie, (-s), mare.
merrieperd, mare.
merrievul, filly.
mes, (-se), knife; **–se en vurke**, cutlery; **onder die – kry**, operate on; castrate; **die – sny aan albei kante**, it cuts both ways.
meshef, knife-handle, knife-haft.
meslem, knife-blade.
mesmeries, (-e), mesmeric.
mesmeriseer, (ge-), mesmerize.
mesmerisme, mesmerism.
meson, meson.
Mesopotamië, Mesopotamia.
messebak, knife-box, knife-tray.
messegoed, cutlery.
messel, (ge-), build, lay bricks.
messelaar, (-s), bricklayer, mason.
messelary, brick-work, masonry; brick-laying.
messelkalk, mortar.
messelwerk, brick-work, masonry.
mes(se)slyper, knife-grinder.
Messiaans, (-e), Messianic.
Messias, Messiah.
messing, brass.
messlyper, vide **mes(se)slyper**.
messteek, knife-thrust.
messtof, fertilizer, manure.
met, with; **'n sak – geld**, a bag of money; **– die dag**, day by day, every day; **– handevol**, by handfuls; **– Krismis**, at Christmas; **– ink**, in ink; **– dit al**, for all that, in spite of this; **– die spoor**, by rail.
metaal, (-ale), metal.
metaalaar, metallic vein, lode.
metaalagtig, (-e), metallic.
metaalgaas, wire-gauze, wire-netting.
metaalgieter, (metal-)founder.
metaalgietery, (metal-)foundry.
metaalglans, metallic lustre.
metaalindustrie, metallurgic industry.
metaalklank, metallic ring (sound).
metaalkunde, metallurgy.
metaalkundig, (-e), metallurgic(al).
metaalkundige, (-s), metallurgist.
metaalplaat, metal-sheet.
metaalskuim, dross.
metaalslak, scoria, slag.
metaalware, metal-ware, hardware.
metabolisme, metabolism.
metafisies, (-e), metaphysical.
metafisika, metaphysics.
metafoor, (-fore), metaphor.
metafories, (-e), metaphorical.
metallurgie, metallurgy.
metallurgies, (-e), metallurgic(al).
metamorfose, (-s), metamorphosis.
metatesis, metathesis.
meteen, at the same time.
meteens, (all) at once, all of a sudden, suddenly, immediately.
meteoor, (-eore), meteor.
meteoorsteen, aerolite, meteorite.
meteoriet, (-e), vide **meteoorsteen**.
meteorologie, meteorology.
meteorologies, (-e), meteorological.
meteoroloog, (-loë), meteorologist.
meter, (-s), measurer, gauger; meter (of gas); metre (unit of length).
meteropnemer, meter-inspector (-reader).
metgesel, (-le), companion, mate.
metgesellin, (-ne), vide **metgesel**.
meting, (-e, -s), measuring.

metode, (-s), method, plan, manner.
metodeleer, methodology.
metodiek, method.
metodies, (-e), methodical.
Metodis, (-te), Methodist.
Metodisme, Methodism.
metonimie, metonymy.
metriek, metrics, prosody.
metries, (-e), metric; metrical.
metropolis, (-se), capital (city), metropolis.
metropolitaans, (-e), metropolitan.
metrum, (-s, -tra), metre.
mette, matins; **kort – maak met**, make short work of, give short shrift to.
metterdaad, indeed, in fact, really.
mettertyd, in course of time, in due course, as time went on.
metterwoon: jou êrens – vestig, establish oneself (settle, fix one's abode, take up one's residence) somewhere.
Metusalem, Methusela.
meubel, (-s), article (piece) of furniture; (pl.) furniture.
meubelmaker, cabinetmaker, joiner.
meubelstuk, vide **meubel**.
meubileer, (ge-), fit up, furnish.
meubilering, furnishing; furniture.
méublement, furniture.
meul, (-e(ens)), **meule**, (-(n)s), mill; (game of) noughts and crosses; **dit is koring (water) op sy –**, that is grist to his mill; **eerste by die –, eerste maal**, first come, first served.
meulenaar, (-s), miller.
meulklip, -steun, millstone.
meulspeel, (meulge-), play (at) noughts and crosses.
mevrou, lady, Mrs (in address with name), Madam (in address without name); missus,
mezzosopraan, (-ane), mezzo-soprano.
miaau, (ge-), miaow, mew.
middag, midday, noon; **na die –**, in the afternoon; **voor die –**, before noon; **goeie –!**, good afternoon!
middagbreedte, latitude at noon.
middagdutjie, afternoon-nap, siesta.
middagete, midday-meal; lunch.
middaghoogte, meridian altitude.
middagmaal, vide **middagete**.
middagslapie, vide **middagdutjie**.
middaguur, noon(tide).
middagvoorstelling, matinée.
midde, middle; mean; **in ons –**, in our midst; **in die – laat**, leave undecided, pass over in silence; **te – van**, in the midst of.
middel, (-e, -s), means, expedient; remedy; instrument; centre, middle; waist; **'n – tot die doel**, a means to an end; **'n – van bestaan**, a means of livelihood; **g'n eie –e hê nie**, have no private means; **deur – van**, by means of; through; through the medium of (the Press); **in die – van die wêreld wees**, be at a loss.
middelaar, (-s), mediator.
middelaarskap, mediatorship.
Midde(l)-Afrika, Central Africa.
middelbaar, (-bare), average, intermediate, mean, medium, middle; secondary (school); **–bare leeftyd**, middle age; **van –bare leeftyd**, middle-aged.
middeldeur, across, asunder, in half, in two.
Middeleeue, Middle Ages.
Middeleeus, (-e), Mediaeval
Middelengels, Middle English.
middelerwyl, meanwhile.
Midde(l)-Europa, Central Europe.
middelgewig, middle-weight.

middelgrootte, medium size.
Middelhoogduits, Middle High German.
middelklas, intermediate (middle) class.
middelland, midland.
Middellandse: – See, Mediterranean (Sea).
middellyf, middle, waist.
middellyn, axis, centre-line, diameter.
middelmaat, medium size; average.
middelmannetjie, ridge (in road).
middelmatig, (-e), middling, moderate, indifferent, mediocre, so-so.
middelmatigheid, mediocrity.
middelmuur, partition(-wall).
Middelnederlands, Middle Dutch.
middelpunt, centre, central point; hub, pivot.
middelpuntsoekend, (-e), centripetal.
middelpuntvliedend, (-e), centrifugal.
middelrif, diaphragm, midriff.
middelslag, -soort, middling sort, medium, middlings.
midde(l)stand, middle classes.
middelste, middle, middlemost.
middelstuk, central (middle) piece.
middeltjie, (-s), 1. device, trick.
middeltjie, (-s), 2. slender waist.
middelvinger, middle finger.
midde(l)weg, middle course; mean; midway, **die gulde –**, the golden mean.
middernag, midnight; **om (te) –**, at midnight; **tot na –**, into the small hours of the night.
middernagson, midnight-sun.
middernagtelik, (-e), midnight (hour).
midskeeps, (-e), a. & adv. amidship(s).
midsomer, midsummer.
midwinter, midwinter.
mied, (-e(ns)), **miet**, (-e), heap, pile, (hay)stack.
mielie, (-s), maize, mealie, Indian corn; **gebreekte, gestampte –s**, samp.
mielie-afmaker, maize-sheller.
mieliebaard, mealie-beard (-awn).
mielieboer, mealie-farmer, mealie-grower.
mieliekop, mealie-cob.
mielieland, mealie-field.
mieliemeel, mealie-meal.
mielie-oes, mealie-harvest.
mieliepap, mealie(-meal) porridge.
mieliepit, mealie-grain, -seed.
mieliestronk, mealie-stalk.
mieliewurm, mealie-cob worm.
mier, (-e), ant; **–e hê**, be fidgety, fidget.
miereter, miervreter, ant-eater.
mierhoop, vide **miershoop**.
mierkat, vide **meerkat**.
mierkoningin, ant-queen.
mier(s)hoop, ant-hill.
miersuur, formic acid.
miet, n. vide **mied**.
miet, n. mite; tuberworm.
mik, (-ke), n. fork, forked post; forked stick (for catapult); vide **mikstok**.
mik, (ge-), aim.
mika, mica.
mikado, (-'s), mikado.
mikhout, forked stick, fork.
mikpunt, aim; butt, target.
mikrobe, microbe.
mikrofilm, microfilm.
mikrofoon, (-fone), microphone.
mikrogolf, microwave.
mikrokosmies, (-e), microcosmic.
mikro-organisme, micro-organism.
mikroskoop, (-skope), microscope.
mikroskopies, (-e), microscopic(al).
mikrostippel-kamera, microdot camera.
mikstok, forked stick.

mikstuur, (-ure), mixture.
Milaan, Milan.
Milanees, (-ese), Milanese.
mild, (-e), free-handed, generous, liberal; soft (rain); met –e hand, lavishly.
milddadig, (-e), generous, liberal.
milddadigheid, generosity, liberality.
mildelik, (-e), a. & adv. lavish(ly).
mildheid, generosity, liberality; mildness.
milieu, (-'s), milieu, atmosphere, environment, surroundings.
milisie, militia.
militaris, (-te), militarist.
militarisme, militarism.
militaristies, (-e), militarist(ic).
militêr, (-e), military man; die –e, the military.
militêr, (-e), a. military; –e diens, military service; –e dokter, army-doctor.
miljard, (-e), milliard.
miljoen, (-e), million.
miljoenêr, (-s), millionaire.
millinnium, (-s, -ia), millennium.
milligram, milligramme.
millimeter, millimetre.
milt, (-e), milt, spleen.
miltontsteking, splenitis.
mildsiekte, splenic fever; anthrax.
miltsteek, splenalgia.
miltsug, spleen.
miltvuur, anthrax.
mimiek, mimic art, mimicry.
mimies, (-e), mimic.
mimosa(boom), mimosa(-tree); wattle(-tree).
min, minne, n. love.
min, (-ne), n. (wet-)nurse.
min, a. & adv. few, little; less, minus; vyf – vier, five less (minus) four; – of meer, more or less; ek het R2 te –, I am R2 short; – dink van, think little (meanly) of.
minag, (ge-), be disdainful of, disregard, disdain, hold in contempt, despise.
minagtend, (-e), contemptuous, disdainful, slighting.
minagting, contempt, disdain.
minaret, (-s, -te), minaret.
minder, a. & adv. fewer, less; inferior, lower; – word, decrease, diminish; dis nou –, that is a detail, that is of minor importance; niemand – as ... nie, no less a person than ... ; niks – as ... nie, nothing less than ... ; hy kan dit nie hoor nie, nog – sien, he cannot hear, much less see it; van – belang, of minor (secondary) importance.
minder, (ge-), decrease, diminish, lessen.
mindere, (-s), inferior.
minderheid, minority; inferiority; in die – wees, be in the minority; be outvoted; be outnumbered.
minderheidsrapport, minority-report.
mindering, diminution; narrowing.
minderjarig, (-e), under age.
minderjarige, (-s), minor.
minderjarigheid, minority.
minderman, vide meerderman.
minderwaardig, (-e), inferior.
minderwaardigheid, inferiority.
minderwaardigheidskompleks, inferiority-complex.
mineraal, (-ale), mineral.
mineraalwater, mineral-water.
mineraleryk, mineral-kingdom.
mineralogie, mineralogy.
mineralogies, (-e), mineralogical.
mineraloog, (-loë, -loge), mineralogist.
mineur, miner (mil.); minor (mus.).

miniatuur, (-ure), miniature.
miniatuur-duikboot, minisub(marine).
miniatuurskilder, miniature-painter.
miniatuurskildery, miniature-painting, miniature.
miniem, (-e), small, slight; mean.
minikopter, minicopter.
minimaal, (-ale), minimal.
minimotor, minicar.
minimum, (-ima, -s), minimum.
minimum-loon, minimum-wage.
minister, (-s), minister; Eerste M–, Prime Minister, Premier; M– van Binnelandse Sake, Minister of the Interior; M– van Buitelandse Sake, Minister of Foreign Affairs; M– van Mynwese, Minister of Mines; M– van Openbare Werke, Minister of Public Works; M– van Volksgesondheid, Minister of Public Health.
ministerie, (-s), cabinet, ministry.
ministerieel, (-iële), ministerial.
ministerraad, cabinet-council.
minjonet, (-te), mignonette.
minlik, (-e), amicable, friendly.
minlikheid, amicableness, friendliness.
minnaar, (-s), lover.
minnares, (-se), lover, mistress, paramour.
minne: in der – skik, settle amicably.
minnebrief, love-letter.
minnedig, amatory poem, love-poem.
minnedigter, love-poet.
minnedrank, love-potion, philtre.
minnegod(in), god(dess) of love.
minnekoos, (ge-), bill and coo, dally.
minnelied, love-song.
minnepyn, pangs of love.
minnesang, vide minnelied.
minnesanger, minstrel.
minnetaal, language of love.
Minotaurus, Minotaur.
minsaam, (-same), affable, bland, gracious, kind, suave.
minsaamheid, affability, blandness.
minsiek, (-e), amorous, love-sick.
minste, fewest, least, slightest, smallest; hy het nie die – beswaar gemaak nie, he did not object at all; ek het nie die – idee gehad nie, I did not have the faintest notion; nie die – kans nie, not the ghost of a chance; nie te – nie, not at all, not in the least; op sy –, at the least; ten –, at least.
minstens, at least, at the least.
minstreel, (-ele), minstrel.
minteken, minus(-sign).
mintig!, gracious!, goodness!
minus, minus, less.
minusteken, vide minteken.
minuut, (-ute), minute.
minuutwys(t)er, minute-hand.
minvermoënd, (-e), indigent, poor.
mirakel, (-s), miracle, wonder.
mirakelspel, miracle-play.
mirakuleus, (-e), miraculous.
mirre, myrrh.
mirt, (-e), myrtle.
mirtekrans, myrtle-wreath.
mis, (-se), n. mass; die – bywoon, attend mass.
mis, (-te), n. fog. mist.
mis, n. dung, manure.
mis, a. & adv. amiss, wrong; – of raak, hit or miss; jy het dit –, you are mistaken, you are wrong; die skoot was –, the shot went wide; – gooi, miss (a throw); – gryp, fail to catch; – skiet, miss (a shot); – slaan, miss (a hit); – trap, make a false step; – skop, miss, fail (with a kick); – vat, miss (one's grip).

mis, (ge-), miss (the mark, the train); lose (the boat); spare, do without (money); lack (wisdom); **sy uitwerking –**, be ineffective.
misantroop, (-trope), misanthrope.
misantropie, misanthropy.
misantropies, (-e), misanthropic.
misbaar, clamour, uproar.
misbaksel, abortion, monster, monstrosity; churl, ill-bred fellow.
misbank, layer of fog, fog-bank.
misboek, mass-book, missal.
misbredie, pigweed, thorny amaranth.
misbruik, (-e), n. abuse, misuse; breach, betrayal (of trust); – **maak van**, abuse, take advantage of.
misbruik, (het –), abuse, misuse.
misdaad, crime, offence; **'n – begaan**, commit a crime.
misdadig, (-e), criminal (offence), culpable (negligence), guilty (pleasures).
misdadiger, (-s), criminal, evil-doer.
misdadigheid, criminality.
misdeel(d), (-de), destitute, poor; – **van verstand**, deficient in intellect, feeble-minded.
misdienaar, acolyte, server.
misdiens, (celebration of) mass.
misdoen, (het –), do wrong, offend.
misdra, (het –), misbehave.
misdryf, (-drywe), n. misdemeanour, offence, crime.
misdryf, -drywe, (het –), vide **misdoen**.
miserabel, (-e), miserable, rotten, wretched.
misgeboorte, abortion, miscarriage.
misgewas, bad harvest; deformity.
misgis, (het –), be mistaken; **jou –**, make a mistake.
misgreep, blunder, mistake, slip.
misgun, (het –), (be)grudge, envy.
mishaag, mishae, (het –), displease.
mishae, n. displeasure, annoyance.
mishandel, (het –), ill-treat, ill-use, maltreat.
mishandeling, ill-treatment, maltreatment.
mishoring, foghorn, siren.
misken, (het –), fail to appreciate.
miskenning, want of appreciation.
miskien, perhaps.
miskoop, bad bargain.
miskraam, abortion, miscarriage.
miskruier, dung-roller, tumble-bug.
miskyk, (misge-), look wrong.
mislei, (het –), deceive, mislead.
misleidend, (-e), deceptive, misleading.
mislei(d)er, deceiver, impostor.
misleiding, deceit, deception, imposture.
misluk, (-e), beastly, disgusting, nasty, rotten; nauseating; sick, bilious.
mislikheid, nausea, sickness.
misluk, (het –), come to naught, fail, miscarry; fall through; break down.
mislukking, (-e, -s), failure.
mismaak, (-te), a. deformed, misshapen.
mismaak, (het –), deform, disfigure.
mismaaktheid, deformity; disfigurement.
mismoedig, (-e), discouraged, disconsolate, disheartened, dejected.
mismoedigheid, discouragement, dejection.
misnoeë, displeasure, dissatisfaction.
misnoeg, (-de), displeased, disgruntled, discontented, dissatisfied.
misoes, bad harvest, failure of crops; failure; washout.
mispel, (-s), medlar.
misplaas, (-te), misplaced (faith), misdirected (sympathy).
misprys, (het –), disapprove of.

mispunt, blighter, good-for-nothing.
misreken, (misge-), miscalculate.
misreken, (het –), make a mistake.
misrekening, miscalculation.
missie, (-s), mission.
missit, (misge-), miss (one's seat); **die pot –**, come a cropper; be ploughed (exam.).
missive, (-s), missive, (official) letter.
misslag, miss; error, fault.
misstap, false step, misstep; **'n – doen**, make a false step; **'n – begaan**, do something wrong.
misstof, vide **messtof**.
mistas, (misge-), make a blunder.
mistel, (-s), n. mistletoe.
mistel, (misge-), miscount.
mistelling, miscount(ing).
misteltak, mistletoe(-bough, -branch).
misterie, (-ë, -s), mystery.
misteriespel, mystery(-play).
mistieureus, (-e), mysterious.
mistiek, n. mysticism.
mistiek, (-e), mystic(al).
mistifikasie, mystification.
mistifiseer, (ge-), mystify.
mistig, (-e), foggy, misty.
mistigheid, fogginess, mistiness.
mistikus, (-se), (-ici), mystic.
mistisisme, mysticism.
mistroostig, (-e), dejected.
mistroostigheid, dejection, sadness.
mistroue, distrust, mistrust, suspicion.
mistrouig, (-e), distrustful, suspicious.
misverstaan, (het –), misapprehend, misconstrue, misunderstand.
misverstand, misunderstanding.
misvloer, floor smeared with dung.
misvorm, (het –), vide **mismaak**.
misvorm(d), (-de), vide **mismaak**, (-te).
misvormdheid, vide **mismaaktheid**.
misvormig, (-e), vide **mismaak**, (-te).
misvorming, disfigurement; malformation.
miswurm, cutworm, caterpillar.
mite, (-s), myth.
mities, (-e), mythical.
mitologie, mythology.
mitologies, (-e), mythological.
mitoloog, (-loë, -loge), mythologist.
mits, provided (that), on the understanding that; **– dese**, hereby.
mitsgaders, together with.
Moabiet, (-e), Moabite.
Moabities, (-e), Moabite.
mobiel, (-e), mobile.
mobilisasie, mobilization.
mobiliseer, (ge-), mobilize.
mobiliteit, mobility.
modaal, (-ale), modal.
modaliteit, modality.
modder, mud, mire, ooze, sludge; **met – gooi**, fling (sling, throw) mud; **iemand uit die – help**, help someone out of trouble.
modderagtig, (-e), muddy, miry, oozy.
modderagtigheid, muddiness.
modderas, vide **modder**.
modderbad, mud-bath.
modderig, (-e), vide **modderagtig**.
modderplas, puddle.
modderpoel, quagmire, slough.
modderskerm, mudguard.
moddervet, as plump as a partridge.
mode, (-s), fashion, mode; style, vogue; **die – aangee**, set the fashion; **– word**, become the fashion; **in die – wees**, be in fashion, be fashionable; **met die – saamgaan**, follow the fashion; **na die –**, after the fashion; **uit die – raak**, go

out of fashion; **liewer dood as uit die –,** follow the fashion at any price.
mode-artikel, fancy-article, novelty.
modeblad, fashion-paper.
modeboek, book of fashions.
modegek, dandy, fop.
model, (-le), model, pattern; cut.
modelboerdery, model farm(ing).
modelleer, (ge-), model, mould.
modeltekening, model drawing.
modemaakster, -maker, dressmaker.
modeplaat, fashion-plate, fashion-sheet.
modepop, doll, fine lady; vide **modegek.**
modeprent, vide **modeplaat.**
moderasie, moderation.
moderator, (-e, -s), moderator.
moderatuur, executive church-council.
modereer, (ge-), moderate.
modern, (-e), modern.
moderniseer, (ge-), modernize.
modernisme, modernism.
modernisties, (-e), modernist.
moderniteit, modernity.
modieus, (-e), fashionable, stylish.
modifikasie, modification.
modiste, (-s), (up-to-date) dressmaker.
modulasie, modulation.
moduleer, (ge-), modulate.
moed, courage, heart, nerve, spirit; **sy – het hom begewe = sy moed het in sy skoene gesink = hy het – verloor,** his courage (heart) failed him, he lost courage (heart); **– bymekaarskraap,** muster (summon up) courage, pull oneself together; **– hou,** keep (a good, a stout) heart; **hou goeie –, die slegte kom vanself,** never say die!, keep your tail up!; **– inboesem = – gee = – inpraat,** buoy up, hearten, encourage, inspire with courage; **– skep (vat),** take courage (heart); **hy het die – van sy oortuiging,** he has the courage of his convictions.
moede: te –, at heart, in spirit; **bly te –,** in good spirits.
moedeloos, (-lose), crestfallen, dejected, despondent, discouraged, disheartened.
moedeloosheid, dejection, despondency.
moeder, (-s), mother; dam (of animals); **– Natuur,** Mother (Dame) Nature.
moederaarde, mother-earth.
moederbors, mother's breast.
moederdier, mother-animal.
moederhart, mother's heart.
moederkappie, grannie-bonnet (orchid).
moederkerk, mother-church.
moederland, mother-country, homeland.
moederliefde, maternal (motherly) love.
moederlik, (-e), maternal motherly.
moederlikheid, maternal nature.
moederloos, (-lose), motherless.
moedermaag(d), Holy Virgin.
moedermelk, mother's milk.
moedermoord, matricide.
moedernaak, (-te), -nakend, (-e), stark naked.
moeder-owerste, mother superior.
moederplant, parent-plant.
moedersielalleen, quite alone.
moederskant: van –, on the mother's side.
moederskap, motherhood, maternity; **opleiding in –,** training in mothercraft.
moederskoot, mother's lap; womb.
moedersmart, mother's sorrow.
moedersorg, maternal care, mother's care; maternity-welfare.
moedersy, vide **moederskant.**
moedertaal, mother- (native) tongue.
moedervlek, birth-mark, mole.

moedervreugde, mother's joy.
moedig, (-e), brave, courageous, plucky.
moedigheid, bravery, courage, pluck.
moedswil, petulance, wantonness; **met –,** on purpose; **uit –,** from love of mischief, wantonly.
moedswillig, (-e), a. & adv. petulant(-ly), wanton(ly), wilful(ly).
moedswilligheid, vide **moedswil**
moedverloor, despondency; **– se vlaktes,** fields of despondency.
moeg, (moeë), fatigued, tired, weary; **– vir die lewe,** tired of life; **jou – loop,** walk one's legs off.
moegheid, fatigue, weariness.
moeilik, (-e), a. & adv. difficult, hard (times), arduous (task), stiff (problem), heavy (road), uphill (work), tough (job), with difficulty; **– word,** lose one's temper.
moeilikheid, difficulty, scrape, trouble; **– soek,** look for trouble; **in – bring,** get into trouble; **in – verkeer,** be in trouble (a scrape, a fix).
moeisaam, (-same), fatiguing, laborious, tiring, tiresome.
moeite, difficulty, trouble; labour, pains; **dis die – werd,** it is worth while; **dis die – werd om te sien,** it is worth seeing; **as dit nie te veel – is nie,** if it is not too much trouble; **– doen,** take pains; exert oneself; **g'n – ontsien nie,** spare no pains; **sonder – het mens niks nie,** no gains without pains; no sweat, no sweet.
moeitevol, (-le), difficult, hard, toilsome, wearisome; laboured.
moenie!, don't!
moepel, (-s), (red) milkwood.
moer, (-e), mother, dam (of animals); dregs, grounds, lees, sediment (of liquids); matrix; womb, uterus; nut (on bolt); seed-potato.
moeras, (-se), marsh, bog, swamp.
moerasagtig, (-e), boggy, marshy.
moerasagtigheid, bogginess, marshiness.
moerasgas, marsh-gas, methane.
moerasland, marshland.
moerasplant, marsh-plant.
moerassig, (-e), vide **moerasagtig.**
moerbei, (-e), mulberry.
moerbeiboom, mulberry(-tree).
moerhamer, (adjusting) spanner.
moersleutel, spanner, screw-wrench.
moes, n. mash, pulp.
moes, vide **moet.**
moesie, (-s), mole; beauty-spot.
moeskruid, greens, pot-herbs, vegetables.
moesoek, moesoep, rival; superior.
moeselien, moeseline, muslin.
moet, (-e), mark, dent, spoor.
moet, (pret.: **moes**), must have to, be compelled (forced, obliged) to; should, ought to; **waar – die geld vandaan kom?,** where is the money to come from?; **dit –,** there is no help for it, it has got to be done; **hy moes geweet het,** he should have known; **ek moes sy moed bewonder,** I could not but admire his courage; **die trein – om tienuur aankom,** the train is due to arrive at ten.
mof, (mowwe), n. muff; sleeve, socket.
mof, (mowwe), n. bastard, cross-breed; undersized animal; undersized fellow.
mofbeeste, cross-bred cattle.
moffie, (-s), mitten.
mofskaap, merino-sheep, wool-sheep.
moggel, (-s), barber (barbel).
Mogol, Mogul.
Mohammed, Mohammed.
Mohammedaan, (-ane), Mohammedan.

Mohammedaans, (-e), Mohammedan.
Mohammedanisme, Mohammedanism.
mok, (ge-), pout, sulk.
moker, (ge-), hammer, strike, hit; give a thrashing; smash (tennis).
mokerhou, smash.
mokka, (koffie), Mocha (coffee).
mol, (-le), n. flat, minor key (mus.).
mol, (-le), n. mole; **so blind as 'n –,** as blind as a bat (beetle, mole).
Moldawië, Moldavia.
molekule, (-s), molecule.
molekulêr, (-e), molecular.
moles(te), trouble; **– maak,** cause trouble.
molesteer, (ge-), annoy, molest.
molibdeen, molybdenum.
mollig, (-e), chubby, plump, soft.
molligheid, chubbiness, plumpness.
molm, mould.
molsgat, mole-hole.
molshoop, mole-hill.
molslang, mole-snake.
molteken, flat (mus).
Molukke, the Moluccas, the Spice Islands.
molval, mole-trap.
molvel, moleskin.
molwa(entjie), trolley, light wagon.
mom, (-me), mask.
mombakkies, (-e), mask.
moment, (-e), moment.
momenteel, (-ele), a. & adv. momentary.
momentopname, instantaneous photo(graph), snap(shot).
mompel, (ge-), mumble, mutter.
mompeling, (-e, -s), muttering.
monarg, (-e), monarch.
monargaal, (-ale), monarchic(al).
monargie, (-ë), monarchy.
monargis, (-te), monarchist.
monargisties, (-e), vide **monargaal.**
mond, (-e), mouth; estuary (of a river), muzzle (of a gun); **het jy g'n – nie?,** have you lost your tongue?; **'n groot – hê,** have plenty of jaw (sauce); **jou – hou,** hold one's tongue; **hou jou –!, shut up!; so moet 'n – praat!,** that is the way to speak!; **nie jou – aan iets sit nie,** not touch food (a thing); **iemand se – snoer,** stop a person's mouth, shut a person up; **oral jou – insteek,** be given to gossip; **haar – staan nooit stil nie,** her tongue is incessantly going (wagging); **hy het sy – verbrand = hy het sy – verbygepraat,** he let his tongue run away with him, he committed himself, he put his foot in it, he gave away the show; **altyd die – vol van ander hê,** always be gossiping (about others); **met die – vol tande staan,** be tonguetied; **dit laat my – water,** it makes my mouth water; **ek het die versekering by –e van die voorsitter,** I have the personal assurance of the chairman; **iemand iets in die – lê,** put words into a person's mouth; **met oop – luister,** listen open-mouthed; **met twee –e praat,** blow hot and cold; **iemand na die – praat,** butter a person up; **nie op die – geval nie,** have a ready tongue, have a tongue in one's head; **iemand die woorde uit die – neem,** take the words out of a person's mouth; **van jou – 'n skoorsteen maak,** smoke like a chimney; **die nuus het van – tot – gegaan,** the news ran from mouth to mouth.
mondbehoeftes, food, provisions.
mondelik(s), mondeling(s), (-e), a. & adv. oral(ly), verbal(ly); **'n –e eksamen,** an oral examination.
mond-en-klouseer, foot-and-mouth disease.
mondering, (-e, -s), equipment.

mondfluitjie, mouth-organ.
mondhoek, corner of the mouth.
mondholte, mouth-cavity.
mondig, (-e), of (full) age, major.
mondigheid, majority.
monding, (-e, -s), mouth, estuary.
mondjie, (-s), (little) mouth; **sy is nie op haar – geval nie,** she has a ready tongue.
mondjievol, mouthful, tiny bit; **'n – Engels ken,** have a smattering of English.
mondklem, gag; lockjaw.
mondprop, gag.
mondprovisie, food, provisions, victuals.
mondspieël, mouth-glass, stomatoscope.
mondspoeling, mouth-wash, rinse.
mondstand, position of the mouth.
mondstuk, mouthpiece.
mondvol, (mondevol), mouthful.
mondwater, mouth-wash.
Mongolië, Mongolia.
Mongool, (-ole), Mongol, Mongolian.
Mongools, (-e), Mongolian.
monisme, monism.
monitor, (-s), monitor; prefect.
monnik, (-e), friar, monk.
monnikagtig, (-e), monastic, monkish.
monnikeklooster, monastery.
monnike-orde, monastic order.
monnikskap, monkhood; monk's cap (hood) cowl.
monnikskleed, monk's frock, cowl.
monochroom, (-ome), monochrome.
monodrama, monodrama.
monogaam, (-ame), monogamous.
monogamie, monogamy.
monografie, (-ë), monograph.
monogram, (-me), monogram.
monokel, (-s), monocle, eyeglass.
monoliet, (-e), monolith.
monolities, monolithic.
monoloog, (-loë, loge), monologue.
monomaan, (-ane), monomaniac.
monomanie, monomania.
monomiaal, (-iale), monomial.
monoplaan, (-ane), monoplane.
monopolie, (-s), monopoly.
monopolisasie, monopolization.
monopoliseer, (ge-), monopolize.
monosillabe, monosyllable.
monoteïs, (-te), monotheist.
monoteïsme, monotheism.
monoteïsties, (-e), monotheistic.
monotipe, monotype.
monotonie, monotony.
monotoon, (-one), monotonous.
Monroe-leer, Monroe doctrine.
monster, (-s), n. monster; freak.
monster, (-s), n. sample, specimen; pattern.
monster, (ge-), muster (soldiers); (pass in) review, inspect.
monsteragtig, (-e), monstrous.
monsteragtigheid, monstrousness.
monsterboek, pattern-book, book of samples.
monstering, (-e, -s), muster, review.
monsterrol, muster-roll; **die – teken,** sign the ship's articles.
monstervergadering, mass-meeting.
monstrans, (-e), monstrance.
montasie, montagé.
monteer, (ge-), mount, set up, assemble, erect, fit up, adjust; get up, stage (a play).
monteerbaan, assembly line.
monteerfabriek, -plek, erecting-shop, assemblingfactory.
monteer(werk)plaas, assembly plant.

Montenegro, Montenegro.
Montenegryn, (-e), Montenegrin.
montering, assembling, erecting, erection, fitting-up, installing, mounting.
monteur, (-s), erector, fitter, mounter.
monteur-draaier, fitter and turner.
montuur, (-ture), frame; setting.
monument, (-e), monument.
monumentaal, (-ale), monumental.
mooglik(heid), vide **moontlik(heid).**
mooi, a. & adv. beautiful, fine, handsome, nice, pretty; – so!, good!, right!, well done!; 'n – meisie, a pretty girl; 'n – man, a handsome man; die weer is –, the weather is promising; dit is – weer, the weather is fair (fine); dit is alles baie –, maar . . . , this is all very fine (very well), but . . . ; iemand – kry, let a person down; jou – maak, smarten (dress up) oneself, jy lyk 'n – een om dit te doen, I'd like to see you do it; jy is 'n – een!, you're a fine fellow!; nou nog –er!, well I never!, did you ever!; maar die –ste kom nog, but the best part is yet to come; – vergaan maar deug bly staan, beauty is only skin-deep.
mooibroodjies: – bak, curry favour.
mooidoenery, airs and graces put on.
mooie: jy is 'n –, you are a fine one; die – daarvan, the beauty of it.
mooiheid, beauty, fineness, handsomeness, prettiness; – vergaan maar deug bly staan, beauty is only skin-deep.
mooiigheid: iets met – verkry, get something done by gentle persuasion.
mooipraat, (mooige-), coax, beg; try to persuade.
mooipraatjies, coaxing, flattery.
mooiprater, flatterer, fawner, coax(er).
moois: iets –, something fine.
mooitjies, finely, prettily; hy moes dit maar – oordoen, he jolly well had to do it over again.
mooiweer: met iemand se goed – speel, play ducks and drakes with a person's things.
moondheid, power.
moontlik, (-e), a. & adv. possible; possibly, perhaps; – het hy my gesien, he may have seen me; al die –e doen, do everything possible; dit is bes –, it is quite possible; soveel –, as much (many) as possible.
moontlikheid, possibility, eventuality.
Moor, (More), Moor; blackamoor.
moor, (ge-), commit murder, kill, murder; maltreat, overwork; die werk – 'n mens, the work takes it out of you.
moord, (-e), murder; – en brand skreeu, raise a hue and cry, cry blue murder, make a fuss; die – steek, peg out; ek wou dat jy die – steek, go to blazes; van die hele – niks weet nie, know nothing about the matter.
moordaanslag, attempted murder, murderous assault.
moorddadig, (-e), murderous, slaughterous; cruel.
moorddadigheid, murderousness; cruelty.
moordenaar, (-s), murderer.
moordenares, (-se), murderess.
moordery, massacre, slaughter; maltreatment (of animals).
moordgeroep, -geskreeu, cry of murder.
moordgierig, (-e), bloodthirsty.
moordgierigheid, thirst for blood.
moordkuil: van jou hart g'n – maak nie, wear one's heart upon one's sleeve, speak one's mind freely.
moordlus, vide **moordgierigheid.**
moordsaak, murder-case.
moordtoneel, scene of a murder.

moordtuig, instrument of murder.
Moors, (-e), Moorish.
moot, (mote), fillet, slice; valley, glen.
mootjie, (-s), slice; "mootjie".
mootsaag, jack-saw, whip-saw, crosscut-saw.
mop, (-pe), n. 1. joke; hoax.
mop, (-pe), 2. pug(-dog).
mop, n. 3. grease (horse-sickness).
mopper, (ge-), grumble.
mopperaar, (ge-), grumbler.
mopperig, (-e), disgruntled, grumbling.
mops(hond) pug-dog.
mor (ge-), vide **mopper.**
moraal, moral.
moralis, (-te), moralist.
moralisasie, moralization.
moraliseer, (ge-), moralize.
moraliteit, (-e), morality; morality(-play).
moratorium, moratorium.
Morawië, Moravia.
Morawies, (-e), Moravian; die –e Broeders, the Moravian Brethren.
môre, more, (-s), morning, morrow; tomorrow; – is nog 'n dag, tomorrow is also a day (will do just as well); kom ek daar nie vandag nie, dan kom ek daar –, there is no need to hurry; – oor ag dae, tomorrow week; van die – tot die aand, from morning till night.
môre-, moreaand, tomorrow evening (night).
môre-, moreblad, morning-paper.
môre-, morediens, morning-service.
moreel, n. morale.
moreel, (-ele), a. moral.
môre-, moregebed, morning-prayer.
môre-, moregroet, morning-salute.
môre-, morelied, morning-hymn (-song).
môre-, morelig, morning-light, dawn.
môre-, morelug, morning-air.
môre-, moremaal, breakfast.
môre-, moreoggend, tomorrow morning.
môre-, morepraatjies, morning-talk; sy – en sy aandpraatjies kom nie ooreen nie, you cannot rely on his word.
môre-, moresang, morning-song.
môre-, moresitting, morning-session.
môre-, moreskemering, dawn.
môre-, moreson, morning-sun.
môre-, morester, morning-star; Lucifer.
môre-, morestond, (early) morning; die – het goud in die mond, the early bird catches the worm.
môre, more-uur, morning-hour.
môre-, morevroeg, tomorrow morning (early).
morfien, morfine, morphine, morphia.
morfologie, morphology.
morfologies, (-e), morphological.
morg, (-e), morgen (land-measure).
morganaties, (-e), morganatic.
Mormoon, (-one), Mormon.
Mormoons, (-e), Mormon.
moron, moron.
mors, (ge-), mess, make a mess; spill (milk), waste money.
morsaf, clean off, right through.
morsdood, stone-dead, stark-dead.
Morse-kode, Morse code.
morsery, messing, mess; wastage.
morsig, (-e), dirty, filthy, grimy.
morsigheid, dirt(iness), filth(iness).
morspot, messer, mucker.
mortaliteit, mortality.
mortel, mortar.
mortier, (-e, -s), mortar.
mos, (-se), n. moss.
mos, n. must, grape-juice, new wine.

mos, adv. indeed; ek het jou – gesê, I told you so, didn't I?; hy was – daar, he was there, wasn't he?; ek weet – nie, how can I know?
mosagtig, (-e), mossy.
mosaïek, mosaic.
Mosaïes, (-e), Mosaic.
mosbalie, must-vat.
mosbeskuit, must-bun (-rusk).
mosbolletjie, (-s), vide **mosbeskuit**.
mosdoppie, billycock.
moses, opponent, rival; master, superior; sy – is dood, he has no equal.
mosie, (-s), motion, vote; 'n – van dank, a vote of thanks; 'n – van vertroue, a motion of confidence; 'n – van wantroue, a motion of no-confidence.
moskee, (moskeë, -s), mosque.
moskonfyt, "moskonfyt", grape-syrup.
Moskou, Moscow.
Moskowië, Muscovy.
Moslem, Moslim, (-s), Moslem, Muslim.
mossel, (-s), mussel.
mosselskulp, mussel-shell.
mossie, (-s), Cape sparrow; so dood soos 'n –, vide **morsdood; hy verheug hom oor 'n dooi(e) –**, he has found a mare's nest and is laughing over the eggs.
moster(d), mustard; – na die maal(tyd), after meat (comes) mustard; too late.
moster(d)bad, mustard-bath.
moster(d)gas, mustard-gas.
moster(d)pap, mustard-poultice.
moster(d)saad, mustard-seed.
mot, (-te), moth.
motballetjie, moth-ball.
motby, death's-head moth, bee-moth.
motel, motel.
motief, (-iewe), motive; motif (mus.).
motiveer, (ge-), account for, give reasons for, motivate.
motjie, (-s), (little) moth; old coloured female.
motor, (-e, -s), motor; motor-car, automobile; engine.
motorbestuurder, motor-driver, chauffeur.
motorboot, motor-boat (-launch).
motorbril, goggles.
motorbus, motor-bus.
motordefek, motor-trouble, breakdown.
motorfiets, motor-cycle, motor-bike.
motorhek, grid, motor-gate.
motories, (-e), motorial, motory.
motoris, (-te), motorist.
motorjaer, racing driver, driving-ace.
motorjag, motor-yacht.
motorkap, bonnet.
motorkar, motor-car, automobile.
motorkas, motor-casing.
motorolie, motor-oil.
motorongeluk, motor(ing)-accident.
motor-torpedoboot, E-boat.
motorvragwa, motor-lorry.
motreën, motreent, n. drizzle.
motreën, motreent, (ge-), drizzle.
motreëntjie, motreentjie, (-s), slight drizzle.
motto, (-'s), device, motto.
mou, (-e), sleeve; **die –e oprol**, turn (roll) up one's sleeves; **die hande uit die – steek**, put the shoulder to the wheel; **iets uit die – skud**, turn out things by the dozen; do a thing off-hand.
mousgat, armhole, sleeve-hole.
mout, malt.
moutekstrak, malt-extract.
moveer, (ge-), attack, trouble, vex, bait; **wat het jou ge– om dit te doen?**, what actuated (moved) you to do this?, what made you do this?

mud, (-de(ns)), muid, bag.
mudsak, muid(-bag).
muf, (muwwe), fusty, musty, stuffy.
muggie, (-s), gnat, midge; van 'n – (vlieg, vlooi) 'n olifant maak, make a mountain of a mole-hill.
muil, (-e), 1. mule; half-caste.
muil, (-e), 2. muzzle, mouth.
muilband, (ge-), gag, muzzle.
muilesel, hinny; mule.
muis, (-e), mouse; **so stil soos 'n –**, as quiet as a mouse; **as die kat weg is, is die – baas**, when the cat is away the mice will play; **as die – dik is, is die koring (meel) bitter**, hunger is the best sauce; vide **muisie, muishare**.
muisgat, mouse-hole.
muis(hare), fetlock.
muishond, mongoose, weasel, polecat.
muisie, (-s), little mouse; **die – sal 'n stertjie hê**, this is not the end of the matter; **klein –s het groot (lang) ore**, little pitchers have long ears.
muisnes, mouse-nest; (pl.) musings; **sy kop is vol –te**, he has cobwebs (maggots) in his brain.
muistandjie, milk-tooth.
muisval, mouse-trap.
muisvoël, coly, mouse-bird.
muit, (ge-), mutiny, rebel, revolt.
muiter, (-s), mutineer, rebel.
muitery, mutiny, rebellion, sedition.
muitsug, rebellious spirit, seditiousness.
mulat, (-te), mulatto.
multimiljoenêr, multimillionaire.
mummel, (ge-), mumble.
mummie, (-s), mummy.
munisie, (am)munition.
munisiefabriek, munition-works.
munisiehandel, munition-trade.
munisietrein, munition-train.
munisiewa, ammunition-wag(g)on.
munisipaal, (-ale), municipal.
munisipaliteit, (-e), municipality.
munt, (-e), n. coin; coinage, money; mint, head; – **slaan**, coin money, strike coins, – **slaan uit**, make capital out of; **iemand met dieselfde (gelyke) – betaal**, pay a person back in his own coin; **kruis of –**, head or tail.
munt, (ge-), coin, mint.
munteenheid, monetary unit.
munter, (-s), coiner, minter.
muntgehalte, alloy (fineness) of coins.
muntgoud, standard gold.
muntkenner, numismatist.
muntkunde, numismatics.
muntpariteit, par rate.
muntreg, right of coinage.
muntspesie, specie.
muntstelsel, monetary system.
muntstempel, die, coin-stamp; stamp.
muntstuk, coin, piece of money.
muntversamelaar, coin-collector.
muntvervalser, debaser of coins; forger.
muntwese, vide **muntstelsel**.
murasie, (-s), dilapidated wall(s), ruins.
murg, marrow; – **in sy pype hê**, be very strong.
murgbeen, marrow-bone.
murg-van-groente, vegetable-marrow, squash.
murmel, (ge-), murmur; babble.
murmeling, murmur.
murmureer, (ge-), grumble, murmur.
murmurering, grumbling, grousing.
mus, (-se), cap, nightcap; bonnet; tea-cosy; **kop in een – wees**, be hand in glove (with).
muse, muse.
Muselman, (-ne), Musulman.
museum, (-s, -sea), museum.

musiek, music; piano; harmonium, organ; **toe was daar stille –**, the conversation broke off abruptly; **op – sit**, set to music.
musiekaand, musical evening.
musiekbeoordelaar, music(al) critic.
musiekboek, music-book.
musiekdoos, musical box.
musiekfees, musical festival.
musiekgeselskap, musical society.
musiekhandelaar, music-seller.
musiekinstrument, musical instrument.
musiekkorps, band.
musiekleer, theory of music.
musiekles, music lesson.
musiekliefhebber, lover of music.
musiekonderwys, musical instruction.
musiekonderwyser(es), music teacher.
musiekskool, school of music.
musiekstander, music-stand.
musiekstuk, piece of music.
musiekuitvoering, musical performance.
musiekwa, band-wagon.
musikaal, (-ale), musical.
musikaliteit, musicalness.
musikant, (-e), musician, player.
musikus, (-se), musician.
muskaat, nutmeg.
muskaatboom, nutmeg-tree.
muskaatneut, nutmeg.
muskadel, muscat(el), muscadel.
muskadeldruiwe, vide **muskadel**.
muskeljaat, civet; vide **muskus**.
muskeljaatkat, musk-cat, civet-cat.
musketier, (-s), musketeer.
muskiet, (-e), mosquito.
muskietbyt, mosquito-bite (-sting).
musieknet, mosquito-net.
muskus, musk.
muskushert, musk-deer.
muskusplant, musk.
muskusreuk, musky smell.
muskusroos, musk-rose.
mussie, (-s), small cap; bonnet; tea-cosy; vide **mus**.
mutasie, mutation.
mutileer, (ge-), mutilate.
muur, (mure), wall; **so vas as 'n –**, as firm as a rock; **mure het ore**, walls have ears; **met jou kop teen 'n – loop**, knock one's head against a stone wall.
muurblom, wallflower.
muurkas, (built-in) cupboard.
muurlamp, wall-lamp.
muurpapier, wall paper.
muurplaat, wall-plate.
muurskildering, wall-painting, mural painting.
muurtapyt, hanging, tapestry.
muurversiering, mural decoration.
muwwerig, (-e), rather musty.
muwwerigheid, mustiness.
my, pron. pers. me; **dit spyt –**, I am sorry; **– dunk**, I think, methinks.
my, pron. poss. my, mine; **dit is – boek = die boek is myne**, it is my book, this book is mine.
my (ge-), avoid, fight shy of, shun.
myl, (-e), mile; **baie –e lê tussen doen en sê**, it is deeds that count, not words.
mylgeld, milage.
mylpaal, milestone; landmark.
mylwys(t)er, speedometer.
mymer, (ge-), brood, muse, ponder, mediate, be lost in reverie (thought).
mymeraar, (-s), dreamer, muser.
mymering, (-e), day-dreaming, meditation, musing, reverie.
mymery, (-e), vide **mymering**.
myn, (-e), mine pit.
mynaandeel, mining-share.
mynbaas, mine-owner; mine-captain.
mynbou, mining(-industry).
mynboukunde, mining(-engineering).
mynboukundige, mining-engineer.
myndistrik, mining-district (-area).
myne, mine; **ek wil – hê**, I want mine.
myner: gedenk –, remember me.
mynersyds, on my part.
myngang, drift-way, gallery of a mine.
myngas, (fire-)damp, methane.
mynhout, pit-props (-timber).
myningenieur, mining-engineer.
mynlamp, miner's lamp.
mynmaatskappy, mining-company.
mynmagnaat, mining-magnate.
mynopsigter, mine-captain.
mynregte, mining-rights.
mynskag, mine-shaft.
mynstut, vide **mynhout**.
myntering, miner's phthisis.
mynveër, minesweeper.
mynverklikker, mine-detector.
mynwerker, miner, pit-man.
mynwerper, bomb-thrower.
mynwese, mining; **Kamer van M–**, Chamber of Mines.
myself, myself.
myter, (-s), mitre.

N

'n, a. an.
na, adv. near; – **aan**, near (to); **almal op een** –, all but one; **op een – die oudste**, the second oldest; **op verre – nie**, not by a long way; **te** –, too near; **iemand te – kom**, offend a person.
na, prep. after; on; – **mekaar**, one after the other; successively; – **dese**, from now on; – **tien**, past (after) ten (o'clock).
na, naar, prep. to; in, according to; after; at; of; – **my mening**, in my opinion; – **Kaapstad vertrek**, leave for Cape Town; – **brandewyn ruik**, smell of brandy; **smaak** –, taste like; taste of; **spring** –, jump at.
na, conj.: – **ons hoor . . .**, we are told that . . .
na-aap, (nage-), ape, mimic, imitate.
na-aapster, (-s), imitator.
naad, vide **naat**.
naaf, (nawe), hub, nave; boss.
naafband, nave-hoop, -ring, hub-band.
naafbus, axle-box, bush.
naafdop, axle-cap.
naai, (ge-), sew, stitch.
naaidoos, sewing-box.
naaigare, -garing, sewing-cotton.
naaigoed, sewing.
naaikissie, sewing-box.
naaimandjie, sewing-basket, work-basket.
naaimasjien, sewing-machine.
naairiempie, sewing-string, -riempie.
naaiskool, sewing-school.
naaister, (-s), seamstress, needlewoman.
naaiwerk, sewing, needlework.
naak, (-te), a. naked, nude, bare; **die -te waarheid**, the plain (bare) truth.
naak, (ge-), approach.
naakloper, nudist.
naaktheid, nakedness, nudity.
naald, (-e), needle (also of pine-trees, instrument, obelisk); **'n mens kan hom deur 'n – (ring) trek**, he is spick and span; **van 'n – tot 'n koevoet**, from a needle to an anchor; **op –e en spelde sit**, be on pins and needles.
naaldboom, needle-leaved tree, conifer.
naaldbossie, dysentery-herb.
naaldekoker, needle-case; dragon-fly.
naaldekussing, needle-cushion.
naald(e)werk, needlework, sewing.
naaldjie, (-s), little needle.
naaldsteek, (ge-), sound (person), throw out a feeler (hint).
naaldvormig, (-e), needle-shaped.
naaldwerk, vide **naald(e)werk**.
naam, (name), name; **hoe is jou** –?, what is your name?; **'n goeie (slegte)** –, a good (bad) name (reputation); **jou – hooghou**, keep up (maintain) one's reputation (good name); – **maak**, make a name for oneself, make one's mark; **by name**, namely; **by name noem**, mention specially; **iemand by sy – noem**, call a person by his name; **die kind by sy – noem**, call a spade a spade; **in** –, in name; **met name**, particularly, especially; **onder die – van liefdadigheid**, in the name of charity; **op iemand anders se – koop**, buy in another person's name; **sonder** –, without a name, nameless, anonymous; **uit my** –, in my name, from me; **uit – van**, on behalf of; **iemand van – ken**, know a person by name; **mense van** –, people of note.
naambord(jie), nameplate, door-plate.
naamgenoot, namesake.
naamkaartjie, visiting-card, card.
naamlik, namely, to wit, viz.
naamloos, (-lose), 1. nameless; anonymous (letter).
naamloos, nameloos, (-lose), 2. nameless, inexpressible, unutterable.
naamlys, list of names, register.
naampie, (-s), name.
naamplaat, nameplate, door-plate.
naamsiek, fond of one's own name.
naamstempel, stamp.
naamsverandering, change of name.
naamsyfer, cypher (cipher), initials.
naamval, case.
naamwoord, nomen; **selfstandige** –, noun.
naand, good evening!
na-aper, (-s), imitator, ape, mimic.
na-apery, imitation, imitating, aping.
naar, (nare), a. unpleasant; awful, horrible, terrible; disagreeable; nasty; foul; dismal, miserable, giddy, faint, queer; – **word**, faint; be sick; **dit lyk te** –, it looks too bad; **dit maak 'n mens** –, it makes one sick; **dit maak 'n mens – om te sien**, it makes one sad to see.
naar, prep.; vide **na**.
naargeestig, (-e), dreary, gloomy.
naargeestigheid, dreariness, gloom.
naarheid, unpleasantness; giddiness; **dis 'n** –, it is a terrible business; **hy lieg dat dit 'n** – **is**, it's terrible the way he lies; **jou** –!, you wretch (miserable specimen)! vide **naar**, a.
na(ar)mate, vide **namate**.
naarstig, (-e), diligent, assiduous.
naarstigheid, diligence, assiduity.
naas, next (to), beside, alongside of; next door to.
naasaan, next to.
naasagter, the second from the rear.
naasbestaande, (-s), next-of-kin.
naaseergister, three days ago.
naasgeleë, nearest.
naasmekaar, alongside one another; side by side, abreast.
naasoormôre, -more, three days hence.
naaste, (-s), n. neighbour, fellow-man.
naaste, a. nearest; next; – **bloedverwant**, nearest relation, next-of-kin; **die – pad**, the shortest road; **die – toekoms**, the near future.
naaste, adv. nearest.
naasteliefde, love of one's neighbour.
naaste(n)by, roughly, more or less.
naasvoor, the second from the front.
naat, (nate), seam; suture; weld; **op die – van jou rug**, flat on one's back.
naatloos, (-lose), seamless.
naatlos, torn in the seam(s); daft.
nababbel, (nage-), repeat words, echo, imitate.
nabehandeling, after-treatment.
naberig, postcript; epilogue.
nabestaande, vide **naasbestaande**.
nabestel, (—), repeat an order.
nabestelling, repeat-order.
nabetaal, (–), pay afterwards.
nabetragting, reflection, meditation.
nabetragtingsdiens, service after Holy Communion.
nablaf, (nage-), bark after.
nably, (nage-), stay behind; stay in.
nabloei, second blossom (bloom).
nabob, (-s), nabob.
naboots, (nage-), imitate, copy; mimic.
nabootsing, (-e, -s), imitation.
naburig, (-e), neighbouring.
nabuur, neighbour.
nabuurskap, neighbourship; vicinity.
naby, (-e), a. near; **die Nabye Ooste**, the Near East.
naby, adv. near, close by (to), near by, near at

hand; **van – bekyk**, look at closely; **van – ken**, know intimately; **– kom**, approach; come near.
naby, prep. near, close to; **– die kerk**, near the church; **hy het – die dood omgedraai**, he was at death's door; **hy kom nie – Piet nie**, he is not a patch on Piet.
nabygeleë, near-by, neighbouring.
nabyheid, neighbourhood, vicinity.
nadat, after.
nadeel, **(-dele)**, disadvantage; drawback; loss, detriment; harm; **in sy –**, to his disadvantage; **ten (tot) – van**, against, to the detriment of; **tot my eie –**, to my own cost.
nadelig, **(-e)**, disadvantageous, detrimental; injurious; **– wees vir**, **– werk op**, be detrimental to, have a bad effect on; **–e saldo**, debit balance, deficit.
nadeligheid, injuriousness; harmfulness.
nademaal, whereas.
nadenkend, **(-e)**, meditative, pensive.
nader, **(–, -e)**, a. nearer; further; **by – insien**, on second thoughts; **by – ondersoek**, on closer investigation.
nader, adv. nearer; **– kennis maak**, get better acquainted.
nader, **(ge-)**, approach, draw near.
naderby, nearer.
naderend, **(-e)**, approaching, coming.
naderhand, later on, afterwards.
naderhou, approach shot.
nadering, approach.
nadessert, dessert.
nadink, **(nage-)**, consider, reflect (upon); **ek moet daaroor –**, I must think it over (think about it); **sonder om na te dink**, without thinking.
nadir, nadir.
nadoen, **(nage-)**, imitate, mimic, copy.
nadors, after-thirst.
nadra(ag), **(nage-)**, carry after.
nadraai, sequel, after-effects, upshot.
nadraf, **-drawwe**, trot after.
nadrag, after-crop.
nadrentel, **(nage-)**, saunter (jog) after.
nadroe(jakkals), "nadroe".
nadruiwe, after-vintage.
nadruk, n. 1. emphasis, stress, accent; **– lê op**, emphasis, lay stress on.
nadruk, **(-ke)**, n. 2. reprint; pirated edition; **– verbode**, all rights reserved.
nadruk, **(nage-)**, reprint; pirate (book).
nadruklik, emphatic(ally).
nadruklikheid, emphasis, stress.
naduik, **(nage-)**, dive after.
nael, **(-e)**, n. nail; claw; rivet; **jou –s byt**, bite one's nails.
nael, **(ge-)**, 1. nail; **aan die grond ge–**, rooted to the spot (ground).
nael, **(ge-)**, 2. sprint, race, tear, fly.
na(w)el, navel; funicle: hilum.
na(w)elbank, navel-bandage.
naelblom, gilly-flower, dianthus.
naelbol, hyacinth-bulb; all-spice.
naelborsel, nail-brush.
na(w)elkruid, navel-wort.
na(w)ellemoen, navel-orange.
naelloop, sprint.
naelloper, sprinter.
naelskêrtjie, nail-scissors.
naelskraap: dit het – gegaan, it was a close shave (a near thing), it was touch and go; **die werk – klaarkry**, finish the work in the nick of time (only just in time).
na(w)elstring, umbilical cord.
naeltjie, **(-s)**, little nail; hyacinth; **–s**, cloves.
na(w)eltjie, **(-s)**, little navel.

naeltjieboom, clove-tree.
naeltjie(s)olie, oil of cloves, clove-oil.
naelvyltjie, nail-file.
naelwedloop, flat race.
nafta, naphtha.
naftalien, **naftaline**, naphthaline.
naftaline, vide **naftalien**.
nag, **(-te)**, night; **dit word –**, night is coming on; **so donker (swart) soos die –**, dark (black) as night, pitch dark (black); **so lelik soos die –**, as ugly as sin; **by –**, by night; **in die –**, during the night, at night; vide **vannag**.
nagaan, **(nage-)**, follow; trace; investigate; examine, check; **as jy nou –**, when you consider; **vir sover ek kan –**, as far as I can gather (ascertain).
nagaap, **-apie**, bush-baby, moholi lemur.
nagadder, night-adder.
nagalm, n. echo, reverberation.
nagalm, **(nage-)**, echo, reverberate.
nagana, nagana.
nagblindheid, night-blindness, nyctalopia.
nagblom, nocturnal flower.
nagdiens, night-duty; night-service.
nageboorte, afterbirth, placenta.
nagedagte, afterthought.
nagedagtenis, memory, commemoration; **ter – van**, in memory of.
nagee, **(nage-)**, charge (tax) with, blame for; **dit moet ek hom ter ere –**, I must (will) say this for him (to his credit).
nagemaak, **(-te)**, imitation (leather); counterfeit, artificial, mock; spurious.
nagenoeg, nearly, almost, more or less.
nagereg, dessert.
nageslag, posterity; **sy –**, his descendants.
nagewening, equinox.
naggewaad, nightdress, -attire.
naghemp, nightdress.
naghuisie, binnacle (on ship).
nagis, **(nage-)**, ferment again.
nagjapon, nightgown.
nagkar, **nagwa**, night(-soil)-cart.
nagkroeg, night-pub.
nagkwartier, night-quarters.
naglamp(ie), night-lamp.
naglewe, night-life.
naglig(gie), night-light.
nagloei, **(nage-)**, keep on glowing.
naglug, night-air.
Nagmaal, the Lord's Supper, Holy Communion.
Nagmaalsbeker, communion-cup, chalice.
Nagmaalsganger, communicant.
Nagmaalstafel, the Lord's table.
Nagmaalswyn, sacramental wine.
nagmerrie, nightmare; bugbear.
nagmus, nightcap.
nagploeg, night-shift.
nagportier, night-porter.
nagreier, night-heron.
nagronde, night-round.
nagrus, night's rest.
nagsê, **(nagge-)**, say good-night.
nagskade, **nagskaal**, common (black) night shade, bane-wort.
nagskuit, night-boat.
nagslang, night-snake; snake-flower.
nagslot, double lock.
nagsoen, good-night kiss.
nagsuster, night-sister, -nurse.
nagstuk, night-scene, nocturne.
nagswa(w)el, night-jar.
nagsweet, night-sweats.
nagtegaal, **(-gale)**, nightingale.
nagtegaalstem, voice of the nightingale.

nagtelik, (-e), nightly, nocturnal; –e **duister**, darkness of night; –e **aanval**, night-attack.
nagtrein, night-train.
naguil, night-jar.
nagverblyf, accommodation for the night.
nagvlinder, (fig.) night-bird.
nagvoël, night-bird.
nagwa, vide **nagkar**.
nagwaak, -wake, night-watch.
nagwag, night-watchman.
nagwandelaar, sleep-walker.
nagwerk, night-work.
nahol, (nage-), run after.
nahou, (nage-), keep in.
nahuppel, (nage-), hop after.
naïef, (naïewe), naive (naïve), artless.
naïwiteit, naivety, artlessness.
naja(ag), -jae, (nage-), run after, chase; seek (hunt) after, aim at; **kennis, plesier –**, pursue knowledge, pleasure.
najaar, autumn.
najaarsopruiming, -verkoping, autumn-sale.
najaarsweer, autumnal (autumn) weather.
najade, (-s), naiad.
najaging, pursuit; seeking after.
nakend, (-e), naked, bare.
naklank, echo (lit. & fig.).
naklink, continue to sound, resound.
naklip, "naklip", disintegrated rock.
nakom, (nage-), fulfil, keep; obey; do, perform; comply with; **jou verpligtinge –**, meet one's liabilities; keep one's promise (faith).
nakomeling, (-e), descendant.
nakomelingskap, offspring; posterity.
nakoming, fulfilment, performance.
nakroos, offspring, progeny, issue.
nakyk, (nage-), look at, watch; check, look over; look up; overhaul.
nalaat, (nage-), leave behind; neglect; stop; leave off; leave; bequeath; omit; **ek kan nie – om melding te maak van**, I cannot refrain from mentioning.
nalatenskap, estate; heritage, inheritance.
nalatig, (-e), negligent, careless.
nalatigheid, negligence, carelessness.
nalating, omission.
naleef, -lewe, (nage-), live up to; observe; comply with.
nalees, (nage-), read over; read up.
nalesing, perusal.
nalewing, observance.
naloer, (nage-), peer after.
naloop, n. faints, last runnings; drips.
naloop, (nage-), run after, follow.
naloper, follower.
namaak, n. imitation, counterfeit.
namaak, (nage-), copy, imitate, forge; counterfeit.
namaaksel, (-s), imitation, counterfeit.
Namakwa, (-s), Namaqua.
namakwaduif, Namaqua dove.
Namakwaland, Namaqualand.
Namakwalander, Namaqualander.
namakwapatrys, Namaqua partridge.
namate, **naarmate**, as, in proportion to.
name, vide **naam**.
nameet, (nage-), measure again, check.
nameloos, vide **naamloos** (2).
namens, on behalf of, for.
namiddag, afternoon.
namiddagdiens, afternoon-service.
nanag, after midnight.
nankink, nankeen.
na-oes, after-crop.
na-oog, (nage-), follow with one's eyes.

na-oorlogs, (-e), post-war.
nansoek, nainsook.
napalm, napalm.
Napels, Naples.
naploeg, (nage-), plough again.
napluis, (nage-), investigate, go into, thresh out.
Napoleonties, (-e), Napoleonic.
Napolitaans, (-e), Neapolitan.
napraat, (nage-), mimic; repeat words; echo; imitate the word (opinions) of.
naprater, parrot, imitator, echo.
napratery, parrotry, parrot-talk.
napret, fun (jollification) after the event.
nar, (-re), buffoon, jester, fool.
nardus, (spike)nard.
narede, epilogue.
nareken, (nage-), calculate; check.
narig, n. information.
narig, (-e), a. wretched, miserable.
narigheid, (-hede), misery; vide **naarheid**.
narkose, narcosis, anaesthesia; **onder – bring**, anaesthetize.
narkoties, (-e), narcotic.
naroep, (nage-), call after.
narol, (nage-), roll after.
narreskap, fool's cap.
narsing, (-s), narcissus.
nartjie, (-s), naartjie, mandarin(-orange).
nary, (nage-), ride (drive) after.
nasaal, (-sale), nasal.
nasaat, (-sate), descendant.
nasaleer, (ge-), nasalize.
Nasarener, (-s), Nazarene.
Nasaret, Nazareth; **kan daar iets goeds uit – kom?**, can there any good thing come out of Nazareth?
nasê, (nage-), say after, repeat.
nasie, (-s), nation; **die ou – is maar stadig**, they are a slow people.
nasie-eer, national honour.
nasie-gees, national spirit.
nasieheil, welfare of the nation.
nasien, (nage-), look over, read through, correct, go through; audit, do; overhaul, inspect.
nasietrots, national pride.
nasionaal, (-nale), national; **die Nasionale Party**, the National Party.
nasionalis, (-te), nationalist.
nasionaliseer, (ge-), nationalize.
nasionalisme, nationalism.
nasionalisties, (-e), nationalist(ic).
nasionaliteit, (-e), nationality.
nasionaliteitsgevoel, national feeling.
nasit, (nage-), chase, pursue, run after.
naskets, (nage-), sketch after; copy.
naskiet, (nage-), send a bullet after.
naskilder, (nage-), copy.
naskreeu, (nage-), shout (cry) after.
naskrif, (-te), postscript.
naskrif, -skrywe, (nage-), copy.
naslaan, (nage-), consult, look (turn) up.
naslaanboek, book of reference.
nasleep, n. train; aftermath, sequel, after-effects.
nasleep, (nage-), drag after (behind).
nasmaak, aftertaste; **'n bitter –**, a bitter taste in the mouth.
nasnuffel, (nage-), investigate, pry into (about), ferret into; running.
nasomer, latter part of summer.
naspel, n. postlude; afterpiece.
naspel, (nage-), spell after.
naspeur, (nage-), trace, investigate.
naspeuring, tracing, investigation.
naspoor, vide **naspeur**.
naspring, (nage-), jump (leap) after.

nastaar, (nage-), stare after.
nastamel, (nage-), stammer after.
nastoot, last (final) push.
nastreef, -strewe, (nage-), strive after, aim at, pursue; emulate.
nastuur, (nage-), forward, send on.
nasukkel, (nage-), struggle after.
nasweef, -swewe, (nage-), float after.
nat, n. wet, damp.
nat, a. wet; moist, damp; tight, tipsy; so – soos 'n kat, as wet as a drowned rat; nog – agter die ore, still a greenhorn, hardly out of one's shell.
Nat(te), (-s), Nat(ionalist).
nateken, (nage-), copy, draw from a model.
natel, (nage-), count over, check.
nathals, soaker, toper.
natheid, wetness, moistness, dampness.
natmaak, (natge-), wet; water.
natreën, -reent, (natge-), be (get) caught in the rain, get a soaking.
natrek, (nage-), trek (march) after, follow; copy, trace.
natril, (nage-), continue to vibrate.
natrium, sodium.
natron, natron.
natros(sie), bunch of late grapes; -s, gleanings (in vineyard).
natterig, (-e), rather wet (damp, moist), wettish; slightly tipsy.
nattigheid, vide natterigheid.
naturalis, (-te), naturalist.
naturalisasie, naturalisation.
naturaliseer, (ge-), naturalize.
naturalisme, naturalism.
naturalisties, (-e), naturalistic.
naturel, (-le), 1. Native.
naturel, (-le), 2. natural (mus.).
naturellebevolking, Native population.
naturellegebied, Native area (district).
naturellesake, Native affairs.
naturellevraagstuk, Native question.
natuur, nature; disposition; (natural) scenery; gewoonte is die tweede –, habit is a second nature; in die vrye –, in the open; van nature, by nature.
natuuraanbidder, nature-worshipper.
natuurbeskerming, protection of nature.
natuurbeskrywing, description of nature.
natuurdiens, nature-worship.
natuurdrif, instinct, sexual desire.
natuurgeneeswyse, -genesing, nature-cure.
natuurgenot, enjoyment of nature.
natuurgetrou, (-e), true to nature.
natuurgodsdiens, natural religion.
natuurhistorie, natural history.
natuurhistories, (-e), natural-historical.
natuurkenner, naturalist.
natuurkennis, natural history (science); knowledge of nature.
natuurkeus, natural selection.
natuurkind, child of nature.
natuurkrag, natural force.
natuurkunde, physics.
natuurkundig, (-e), physical.
natuurkundige, (-s), physicist.
natuurlewe, life of nature.
natuurliefde, love of nature.
natuurlik, (-e), a. natural; native; –e aanleg, natural ability, bent; –e dood, natural death; –e historie, natural history; –e kind, natural (illegitimate) child; natural (unaffected) child.
natuurlik, adv. naturally; –!, of course!
natuurlikerwys(e), naturally.
natuurlikheid, naturalness.

natuurmens, natural man.
natuurondersoeker, scientist, naturalist.
natuurramp, act of God.
natuurskoon, natural beauty, scenery.
natuurstaat, natural state.
natuurstudie, nature-study.
natuurtaf(e)reel, natural scene.
natuurverskynsel, natural phenomenon.
natuurvoórtbrengsel, natural product.
natuurvorser, scientist, naturalist.
natuurwet, law of nature, natural law.
natuurwetenskap, natural science.
natuurwetenskaplik, (-e), scientific; –e vakke, natural sciences.
natuurwonder, prodigy of nature.
navertel, (-), repeat.
naverwant, (-e), closely related.
naverwantskap, relationship.
navlieg, (nage-), fly after.
navolg, (nage-), follow; pursue; imitate.
navolgbaar, (-bare), imitable.
navolgenswaardig, (-e), worth following.
navolger, (-s), follower; imitator.
navolging, imitation.
navors, (nage-), investigate, inquire into; do research(work).
navorser, (-s), investigator; research-worker.
navorsing, investigation; research.
navorsingswerk, investigation; research-work.
navra, (nage-), inquire.
navraag, inquiry; demand; by –, on inquiry; – doen, make inquiries, inquire.
naweë, after-pains; after-effects.
naweek, week-end.
na(w)el-..., vide nael-...
nawerk, (nage-), work overtime; sy invloed het nagewerk, his influence made itself felt.
nawerking, after-effects.
nawinter, latter part of winter.
nawys, (nage-), point at.
naywer, jealousy, envy.
Nazi, Nazi.
nè?, isn't it (he, she)?; not so?; yes?; reken (raai) –!, just fancy (imagine)!
Nederduits, (-e), Low German; Dutch.
nederig, (-e), humble, modest, lowly.
nederigheid, humbleness, humility.
nederlaag, vide neerlaag.
nedersetter, settler.
nedersetting, (-e, -s), settlement.
ne(d)erwaarts, downward(s).
nee, no; ag –!, you don't say so!, well I never!; (ag) – wat!, no, darn (hang) it!; ag – moenie!, no, (please) don't; maar –!, but no!; – knik, shake one's head! – sê, say no, refuse.
neë, vide nege.
neef, (-s), nephew; cousin; middag, –!, good day "nephew" (friend).
neem, (ge-), take; book; engage; have; 'n einde –, come to an end; – soos dit kom, take things as they come (are); iets op jou –, undertake (take on) something, take something upon oneself.
neën-, vide negen-.
neer, down; op en –, up and down.
neer-, vide af-, om-, plat-.
neerbiggel, (neerge-), trickle down.
neerblik, (neerge-), look down.
neerbuig, (neerge-), bend down.
neerbuigend, (-e), condescending.
neerbuk, (neerge-), stoop down.
neerdaal, (neerge-), come down, descend.
neerdruk, (neerge-), press down; depress.
neerdrukkend, (-e), depressing.
neerdrup, (neerge-), drip (trickle) down.

neergeslaan, (-de), sad, heavy, doughy.
neergooi, (neerge-), throw (fling) down.
neerhaal, n. down stroke (of pen).
neerhaal, (neerge-), haul down; fetch down; pull down; lower.
neerhang, (neerge-), hang down, droop.
neerhangend, (-e), hanging, pendant.
neerhou, (neerge-), 1. keep down.
neerhou, (neerge-), 2. hew (cut) down.
neerdruk, (neerge-), squat (down).
neerkap, (neerge-), chop (cut) down.
neerkniel, (neerge-), kneel down.
neerkom, (neerge-), come down, descend, crash down; land; **dit sal alles op hom –,** he will have to bear the brunt of it; **dit kom hierop neer,** it amounts to this; **dit kom op dieselfde neer,** it works out the same in the end; **waar ek op –, is dat . . .,** my point is that . . ; **altyd op dieselfde ding –,** keep on harping on the same string.
neerkyk, (neerge-), look down.
neerlaag, nederlaag, (-lae), defeat, overthrow, reverse; **die – ly,** be defeated.
neerlaat, (neerge-), lower, let down.
neerlê, (neerge), 1. lie down.
neerlê, (neerge-), 2. put (lay) down; **jou betrekking –,** resign one's post; **sig – by,** acquiesce in, be satisfied with.
neerplof, (neerge-), fling down; flop down.
neerdruk, (neerge-), pull down.
neersabel, (neerge-), put to the sword.
neersak, (neerge-), sink down.
neersien, (neerge-), vide **neerkyk.**
neersink, (neerge-), sink down.
neersit, (neerge-), put down.
neerskiet, (neerge-), shoot down.
neerskryf, -skrywe, (neerge-), write down.
neerskud, (neerge-), shake down.
neerskyn, (neerge-), shine down.
neerslaan, (neerge-), strike (knock) down, fall down; cast down; beat down; turn down; deposit; **die koek is (het) neergeslaan,** the cake is sad (doughy, heavy); vide **afslaan.**
neerslag, down-beat; precipitate; downpour.
neerslagtig, (-e), depressed, despondent, dejected, downcast, downhearted.
neerslagtigheid, despondency, dejection.
neersmyt, (neerge-), fling (chuck) down.
neerstamp, (neerge-), push down; ram down.
neerstoot, (neerge-), push down.
neerstort, (neerge-), fall down, crash down, collapse; crash; come down in torrents.
neerstroom, (neerge-), stream down.
neerstryk, (neerge-), smooth down; come down, descend, alight; land.
neertel, (neerge-), 1. count down.
neertel, (neerge-), 2. lift down.
neertrap, (neerge-), trample underfoot.
neertrek, (neerge-), pull down; collar, tackle; **sig –,** lie down.
neertuimel, (neerge-), tumbledown.
neerval, (neerge-), fall (drop) down.
neervel, (neerge-), fell; strike down.
neervlieg, (neerge-), fly down.
neervloei, (neerge-), flow down.
neervly, (neerge-), lay down; **sig -,** lie down.
neerwaai, (neerge-), be blown down.
neerwerp, (neerge-), throw (fling) down.
neet, (nete), nit.
neewoord, refusal.
neffens, vide **naas.**
nefritis, nephritis.
negasie, negation.
negatief, (-tiewe), n. negative.
negatief, (-tiewe), a. negative.

nege, neë, nine.
negeer, (ge-), ignore; cut; disregard.
negehoek, neë-, nonagon.
negehoekig, neë-, (-e), nonagonal.
negejarig, neë-, (-e), nine years old, of nine (years), nine years' (war).
negemaal, neë-, nine times.
negende, (-s), neënde, ninth (part).
negentien, neëntien, nineteen.
negentiende, neëntiende, nineteenth.
negentig, neëntig, ninety.
negentigjarige, neëntig-, nonagenarian.
negentigste, neëntigste, ninetieth.
nege-oog, neë-, neën-, carbuncle.
Neger, (-s), Negro.
Negeragtig, (-e), Negrolike, negroid.
Negerdans, Negro dance.
Negerin, (-ne), Negress.
Negerlied, Negro song; Negro spiritual.
Negerslaaf, -slavin, Negro slave.
Negervriend, negrophil(e).
negetal, neë-, nine.
negetallig, neë-, (-e), nonary.
negevoud, neë-, (-e), multiple of nine.
negevoudig, neë-, ninefold.
negosie, wares, goods, trade.
negosiegoed, vide **negosieware.**
negosiekas, -kis, packing-case.
negosieware, storekeeper's stock-in-trade, merchandise.
negosiewinkel, general store.
Negrofilis, (-te), Negrophil(e).
negus, negus (hot wine); Negus.
neig, (ge-), bend, bow, incline; – **julle hart tot die Here,** incline your hearts unto the Lord; **ten einde –,** draw to a close; **ten val (ondergang) –,** be tottering; **ge– wees,** be inclined.
neiging, (-e -s), inclination, disposition, propensity; tendency, bent; **die hout het 'n – om skeef te trek,** the wood tends to warp; **'n – hê (vertoon),** be inclined (apt) to; **– tot,** inclination to; leaning towards.
nek, (-ke), neck; "neck" (between hills); **'n stywe –,** a stiff neck; **sy – breek,** break his neck; lead to his undoing, ruin him; **(die) – omdraai,** wring the neck of; **iemand die – vol lieg,** stuff a person, gull a person with lies; **deur jou – praat,** talk through one's hat; **jou – in (deur) die strop steek,** put one's head through a noose; bind oneself; **iemand in die – kyk,** do a person in the eye; **op iemand (anders) se – lê,** outstay (wear out) one's welcome; be a burden on someone.
nekkramp, (cerebro-spinal) meningitis.
nekrologie, necrology.
nekroloog, (-loë, -loge), necrologist.
nekromansie, necromancy.
nekslag, blow in the neck; death-blow, finishing (knock-out) blow; **die – gee,** finish, ruin, lead to the undoing of.
nekspier, neck (cervical) muscle.
nektar, nectar.
nekvel, skin of the neck; scruff of the neck.
nemer, (-s), taker; payee; buyer.
Nemesis, Nemesis.
neofiet, (-e), neophite.
neolities, (-e), neolithic.
neologisme, (-s), neologism.
nepotisme, nepotism.
Neptunus, Neptune.
nêrens, nergens, nowhere; **dit dien – toe nie,** serves no purpose.
nerf, (nerwe), n. vein, nervure (of leaf); grain (of wood, leather); skin; **op ('n) – na,** within

nerf — **neweproduk**

an ace of; **dit was so op ('n) – na**, it was touch and go, it was a near thing.
nerf, nerwe, (ge-), grain (leather); (strip of) skin, remove the grain.
nergens, vide **nêrens**.
nering, (-e, -s), trade; occupation; **die tering na die – sit**, cut one's coat according to one's cloth; **elkeen is 'n dief in sy –**, near is my shirt, but nearer is my skin.
neringloos, (-lose), without a trade.
nersderm, rectum.
nervatuur, nervation, venation, nervure.
nerveus, (-e), nervous.
nerveusheid, nervousness.
nes, (-te), n. nest; nidus (of insect), eyrie (of bird of prey); haunt; hole; hotbed (of vice); **jou eie – bevuil (vuilmaak)**, foul one's own nest; – **maak**, nest.
nes, adv. = **net soos**, just like; just as; as soon as; every time, whenever.
neseier, nest-egg.
nessie, (-s), (little) nest; nidulus.
nesskop, (nesge-), make a nest.
nestel, (ge-), nestle.
nesvere, first feathers.
net, (-te), n. net; netting; network; fruit-net, net-bag; **agter die – vis**, be too late, come a day after the fair; **iemand in jou – te vang**, ensnare (entrap, net) a person.
net, (–, -te), a. neat; smart; clean, tidy; exact, accurate; vide **netjies**.
net, adv. 1. neatly; vide **netjies**.
net, adv. 2. just, exactly; **dis – hy!**, that's the ticket!, this is the very thing; **– reg**, just right; **hy is nou – weg**, he has just left; **hy is – in sy skik**, he is quite pleased; – **(so)!**, exactly, precisely!; – **soos myne**, just like mine; – **soos hy my sien**, whenever he sees me; vide **nes**, adv.
netbal, netball.
netel, (-s), nettle.
neteldoek, muslin.
netelig, (-e), thorny, knotty; critical.
neteligheid, thorniness, knottiness.
netheid, neatness, tidiness; cleanliness.
netjies, (-e), neat, tidy; clean; smart, dainty, trim, spruce, neat.
netjies, adv. neatly; nicely.
netnou, just now; in a moment.
netskrif, fair copy; fair-copy book.
netto, net.
nettogewig, net weight.
netvlies, retina.
netwerk, network; meshwork.
neuk, (ge-), hit, strike, flog, trounce; **moenie so – nie!**, don't be such a nuisance!
neukery, (blinking) nuisance, mess-up.
neul, (ge-), be troublesome (a nuisance), nag; **by (met) iemand –**, annoy (pester, worry, bother) a person.
neulerig, (-e), troublesome, nagging.
neulery, nagging; vide **neul**.
neulkous, -pot, bore, plague, nuisance.
neuralgie, neuralgia.
neuralgies, (-e), neuralgic.
neurastenie, neurasthenia.
neurastenies, (-e), neurasthenic.
neurie, (ge-), hum.
neurities, (-e), neuritic.
neuritis, neuritis.
neurologie, neurology.
neurologies, (-e), neurological.
neuropaat, (-pate), neuropath.
neurose, neurosis.
neuroties, (-e), neurotic.

neus, (-e), nose; prow (of ship); nozzle (of pipe, tube); toecap (of shoe), toe; cape, point, shoulder (of mountain); **'n goeie – hê**, have a good nose; **sy – loop**, he runs at the nose; **jou – optrek vir**, sniff at, turn one's nose at; **wie sy – skend, skend sy aangesig**, he who cuts his nose spoils his face; **nie verder sien (dink) as sy – lank is nie**, not look beyond one's nose; **jou – steek in**, poke (thrust) one's nose into; **die – uitsnuit**, blow the nose; **dit is sy – verby**, he can whistle for it; it was a flash in the pan; **jou – verbypraat**, give the show away, let one's tongue run away with one; **iemand aan die – lei**, lead a person by the nose; **agter jou – aanloop**, follow one's nose; **deur jou – praat**, speak through one's nose; **die snuf in die – hê (kry)**, get wind of; **met jou – in die botter val**, be in clover (luck), be lucky, strike oil; **met jou – in die boeke sit**, pore over one's books; **iemand iets onder die – vrywe**, haul a person over the coals; **op jou – kyk**, feel (look) small (silly, a fool); **vlak voor jou –**, under your very nose.
neusaap, nose-monkey.
neusbeen, nasal bone.
neusbloeding, nose-bleeding.
neusgat, nostril.
neusgeluid, nasal sound.
neusgeswel, nasal tumour.
neushare, hair in the nostrils, vibrissae.
neusholte, nasal cavity.
neushoring, rhinoceros.
neushoringvoël, hornbill.
neusie, (-s), little nose; vide **neus**.
neuskatar, nasal catarrh.
neusklank, nasal sound.
neusletter, nasal letter.
neuspoliep, rhinopolypus.
neusriem, nose-band.
neusring, nose-ring.
neusslymvlies, mucous membrane.
neusspieël, rhinoscope.
neusspuit(jie), nasal syringe.
neusverkoue, -verkouentheid, snivels.
neusverstopping, snuffles.
neusvleuel, wing of the nose, nostril.
neuswarmer(tjie), nose-warmer.
neut, (-e), nut; nutmeg; **nie om dowe –e nie**, not for nothing; **'n harde – om te kraak**, a hard nut to crack.
neutboom, walnut-tree; nutmeg-tree.
neutdop, nutshell; cockle-boat.
neut(e)kraker, (pair of) nutcracker(s).
neutmuskaat, nutmeg.
neutraal, (-trale), neutral.
neutralisasie, neutralization.
neutraliseer, (ge-), neutralize.
neutraliteit, neutrality.
neutraliteitsreg, right of neutrality.
neutron, neutron.
newe(ns)gaand, (-e), enclosed, accompanying.
newe(ns)geskik, (-te), co-ordinate.
newel, (-s), mist, haze, fog.
newelagtig, (-e), misty, hazy, foggy.
newelagtigheid, mistiness, nebulosity.
newelbeeld, spectral image; mirage.
newelig, (-e), vide **newelagtig**.
newelster, nebulous star.
newelvlek, (-ke), nebula; –**ke**, nebulae.
newelvlekteorie, nebular theory.
newens, next to, beside.
newensgaand, (-e), vide **newe(ns)gaand**.
newensgeskik, (-te), vide **newe(ns)geskik**.
newe(n)skikkend, (-e), co-ordinate.
neweproduk, by-product.

nie, not; – **hy nie**, not he; **dis – waar –**, it is not true; – **beter as**, no better than; **sou dit – lekker wees –!**, wouldn't it be nice!; **hy het – eens geglimlag –**, he didn't even smile, he never even smiled.
nie-bestaande, non-existent.
nie-blanke, non-European.
nie-Engels, non-English.
nie-Europees, (-pese), non-European.
nie-lid, non-member.
niemand, no one, nobody, none; – **nie?**, nobody?; – **minder as**, no less a person than; – **anders as**, none other than.
niemandsland, no-man's-land.
niemendal, nothing at all.
nie-nakoming, non-fulfilment.
nie-oorlogvoerend, non-belligerent.
nier, (-e), kidney; nodule (ore).
niergruis, -steentjies, urinary calculi.
nierkoliek, renal colic.
nierkwaal, kidney-disease (-complaint).
nierlyer, nephritic sufferer.
nierontsteking, nephritis.
nierpyn, nephralgia, nephritic pain.
niersiekte, kidney-disease.
niersteen, renal calculus, stone in the kidney; nephrite.
niertjie, (-s), kidney.
nies, (ge-), sneeze.
nieshout, sneeze-wood.
nieskruid, hellebore.
niesmiddel, sternutative powder.
niespoeier, sneezing-powder.
niet, nothing, nothingness; **in die – verdwyn**, fade away, **in die – versink**, sink into nothingness; pale; **te – doen**, annul, cancel; do away with; undo; **te – gaan**, come to nothing; **tot – gaan**, perish, decay; go bad; **alles is tot –**, everything is lost, nothing remains.
nieteenstaande, nowithstanding, in spite of.
nietemin, nevertheless, none the less.
nietig, (-e), insignificant; paltry; trifling; miserable; – **verklaar**, declare null and void, annul.
nietigheid, (-hede), insignificance; invalidity, nullity (of marriage); trifle, trifling matter.
nietigverklaring, annulment, nullification.
niets-, vide **niks-**.
Nieu-Brunswyk, New Brunswick.
Nieu-Engels, modern English.
nieugebore, nu(ut)gebore, new-born.
Nieu-Guinea, New Guinea.
nieumodies, (-e), fashionable, new-fashioned, stylish.
Nieu-Seeland, New Zealand.
Nieu-Seelander, New Zealander.
niewers, vide **nêrens**.
nig, (-te), niggie, (-s), cousin; niece; **'n frisgeboude niggie**, a strapping (buxom) wench.
nihil, nil.
nihilis, (-te), nihilist.
nihilisme, nihilism.
nihilisties, (-e), nihilistic.
nikkel, nickel.
nikkelmunt, nickel coin.
nikotien, nikotine, nicotine.
nikotienvergiftiging, nicotine poisoning.
niks, nothing; – **meer nie**, nothing more, no more; **ek hou – meer daarvan nie**, I don't like it any more; – **mooier as**, no prettier than; – **mooiers**, nothing prettier; **dit beteken –**, it means nothing; it is no good; **dis –!**, it is nothing!, it doesn't matter!, never mind!; **daar kom – van nie!**, not a bit of it!; no, you don't!; **die ding is – werd nie**, this thing is worthless (no good); **ek het daar – aan nie**, it is useless to me, I don't care twopence about it; **vir –**, for nothing.
niksbeduidend, (-e), insignificant, trifling, worthless, good-for-nothing.
niksbetekenend, (-e), vide **niksbeduidend**.
niksdoen, idleness, doing nothing.
niksdoener, idler, loafer, do-nothing.
niksdoenery, idling, idleness, loafing.
niksnuts, good-for-nothing, rotten.
nimbus, (-se), nimbus, halo.
nimf, (-e), nymph.
nimfagtig, (-e), nymphlike.
nimfomaan, nymphomaniac.
nimmer, never.
nimmermeer, never again, never more.
nippel, (-s), nipple.
nippertjie: **op die –**, touch and go, in the nick of time.
Nippon, Nippon (Japan).
nirwana, nirvana.
nis, (-se), niche.
nitraat, (-trate), nitrate.
nitrogeen, nitrogen.
nitrogliserien-, gliserine, nitroglycerine.
niveau, (-x), level, plane.
nivelleer, (ge-), level, take a level.
nivelleerskroef, levelling-screw.
nivellering, levelling.
njala(bok), nyala.
Noag, Noah; **dit was saam met – in die ark**, it is as old as the hills.
nobel, (-e), noble.
Nobelprys, Nobel Prize.
node, reluctantly; **van –**, necessary; **van – hê**, need, require.
nodeloos, (-lose), needless, unnecessary.
nodeloosheid, needlessness.
nodig, (-e), necessary; requisite; – **hê**, need, require, stand (be) in need of, want; **hy het tien jaar – gehad om ...**, it took him ten years to ...; – **maak**, necessitate; – **wees**, be necessary; be needed (wanted); **daar is moed toe –**, it wants (needs) courage.
nodige, n. what is necessary, essential; necessaries of life.
nodigheid, necessity, need.
noem, (ge-), name, call, style; mention; **na sy oom ge–**, called after his uncle.
noembaar, (-bare), mentionable.
noemenswaard(ig), (-e), worth mentioning (speaking of).
noemer, (-s), denominator.
noen, noon.
noenmaal, lunch, midday-meal.
noeste, diligent, unflagging, unwearying.
nog, conj. 1. neither ... nor.
nog, a. & adv. 2. still, yet further; – **kos**, (some) more food; – **'n lemoen**, another orange; – **'n maal (keer)**, once more (again); – **nie**, not (just) yet; **ek wil – tien hê**, I want another ten; **hoeveel het jy – oor?**, how many (much) have you left?; **hy het – tien**, he has still got ten; **hoe lank –?**, how much longer?; – **iets**, something else; – **iets?**, anything else?; – **gister**, only yesterday; – **dieselfde dag**, that very day, that same day; – **lank nie**, not by a long way; – **maar jonk**, quite young, only a youngster; **ons het – maar pas begin**, we have only just started; – **net een dag**, only one more day; – **nooit nie!**, never!, not on your life!
nogal, rather, quite, fairly.
nogmaals, once again, once more.
nogtans, yet, nevertheless, still.
nôi, nooi, (-ens), sweetheart, (best) girl.

nôienshaar, nooiens-, maidenhair.
nôienslok, nooiens-, love-lies-bleeding.
nôiensuil, nooiens-, Cape barn-owl.
nôientjie, nooientjie, (-s), girl, young lady; vide nôi.
nok, (-ke), ridge (of roof); cam (of wheel).
nokbalk, ridge-beam, ridge-purlin, -piece.
nokpan, ridge-tile.
nokturne, (-s), nocturne.
nomade, (-, -s), nomad.
nomadevolk, nomadic people, nomads.
nomadies, (-e), nomad(ic).
nomenklatuur, nomenclature.
nominaal, (-nale), nominaal.
nominasie, nomination.
nominasiedag, nomination-day.
nominatief, nominative.
nomineer, (ge-), nominate.
nommer, (-s), number; size (of shoe); event (sport); item (on programme); issue, number (of magazine); – een, number one; top (of the class), first; dit kom – een, that comes first; dis (net) – pas, it fits like a glove, it is a perfect fit; op iemand se – druk (praat), call upon a person; urge (spur) a person on.
nommer, (ge-), number.
nommerplaat, numberplate.
non, (-ne), nun.
non-alkoholies, (-e), non-alcoholic.
nonchalance, nonchalance.
nonchalant, (-e), nonchalant, off-hand.
non-kombattant, non-combatant.
non-konformis, (-te), nonconformist.
nonnekleed, nun's dress.
nonneklooster, convent, nunnery.
nonne-orde, order of nuns.
nonnesluier, nun's veil.
nonnetjie, (-s), (little) nun; smew.
non-sektaries, (-e), undenominational.
nood, need, distress; necessity; emergency; daar is geen – nie, there is no hurry; geen – daarvoor nie, no fear of that; watter – het jy?, what's the hurry?; die – is hoog, things are black (indeed); the distress is great; – breek wet, necessity knows no law; – leer bid, need is the mother of invention; as die – aan die man kom, when the worst comes to the worst, if need be; jou – kla, pour out one's troubles, complain to (person); as die – die hoogste is, is die uitkoms die naaste, it is darkest just before the dawn; in –, in distress; in die –, anxious, uneasy, afraid; lelik in die – wees, be very much afraid; have the wind up; in die – leer 'n mens jou vriende ken, a friend in need is a friend in deed; in geval van –, in case of emergency.
noodanker, sheet-anchor.
noodbrug, temporary bridge.
nooddeur, emergency-door; fire-exit.
nooddrang, urgent need; compulsion.
nooddruf, want, destitution, poverty; necessaries of life, provisions.
nooddruftig, (-e), destitute, needy, poor.
nooddwang, vide nooddrang.
noodgedronge, -gedwonge, from sheer necessity, compelled by necessity.
noodgeroep, -geskree(u), cries (cry) of distress, cry (call) for help.
noodhulp, emergency-man; makeshift.
noodklok, alarm-bell.
noodkreet, cry of distress.
noodlanding, forced landing.
noodleuen, white lie.

noodlot, fate, destiny.
noodlottig, (-e), fatal; ill-fated.
noodlottigheid, fatality.
noodluik, escape hatch.
noodlydend, (-e), destitute; distressed.
noodrem, emergency-, safety-brake.
noodsaak, n. necessity.
noodsaak, (ge-), force, compel, oblige.
noodsaaklik, (-e), a. neccessary; essential.
noodsaaklikerwys(e), necessarily, of necessity.
noodsaaklikheid, necessity.
noodsein, signal of distress, S O S.
noodtrap, fire-escape.
noodvoor, stormwater ditch (channel).
noodwa, breakdown truck.
noodweer, stormy weather.
noodwet, emergency-law, -act.
noodwendig, (-e), a. necessary; inevitable.
noodwendig, adv. necessarily, of necessity; inevitable; dit volg –, it follows as a matter of course.
noodwendigheid, necessity; inevitability.
nooi, n. vide nôi.
nooi, (ge-), invite; moenie vir jou laat – nie!, help yourself!
nooiens-, vide nôiens-,
nooientjie, vide nôientjie.
nooit, never; nog so –, never as long as I live; so – as-te-nimmer, never.
noop, (ge-), compel, induce.
Noor, (Nore), Norwegian.
noord, north.
Noord-Amerika, North America.
Noord-Amerikaner, North American.
noorde, north; na die N– vertrek, leave for the North; ten – van, (to the) north of.
noord(e)kant, north (side).
noordelik, (-e), northern (hemisphere); northerly (direction).
noorderbreedte, north latitude.
Noorderhalfrond, Northern Hemisphere.
noorderlig, northern lights, aurora borealis.
noorderson: met die – vertrek, take French leave, abscond.
noordewind, north wind.
Noordkaap, North Cape.
noordkant, vide noord(e)kant.
noor(d)kapper, grampus.
noordkus, north-coast.
noordoos, north-east.
noordooste, north-east.
noordoostelik, (-e), north-eastern (parts), north-easterly.
noordoostewind, north-east wind.
Noordpool, North Pole.
Noordpoolgebied, -lande, Arctic regions.
Noordpoolreisiger, Arctic explorer.
Noordpoolsirkel, Arctic Circle.
Noordpoolstreke, Arctic regions.
Noordpooltog, Arctic expedition.
Noordpoolvaarder, Arctic navigator.
Noordsee, North Sea, German Ocean.
noordster, polar star; lodestar.
noordsy, north side.
noordwaarts, northward(s).
noordwes, north-west.
noordweste, north-west.
noordwestelik, (-e), north-west.
noorwestewind, north-west wind.
noorkapper, vide noordkapper.
Noorman, (-ne), Northman, Norseman.
Noors, (-e), Norse, Norwegian.
noors, (-, -e), vicious (bull); heavy, hard (soil); vide nors.

noorsdoring, hedgehog, euphorbia.
Noorweë, Norway.
Noorweegs, (-e), Norwegian.
Noorweër, (-s), Norwegian.
noot, (note), note; **hele** –, semibreve; **halwe** –, minim; **vierde** –, crochet; **agste** –, quaver; **sestiende** –, semiquaver; **twee-en-dertigste** –, demisemiquaver; **vier-en-sestigste** –, hemidemisemiquaver.
nop, burl; pile, nap (on carpet).
nopens, concerning.
noppies: in jou –, as proud (pleased) as Punch, mighty pleased.
norm, (-e), norm, standard.
normaal, (-male), n. normal.
normaal, (-male), a. normal; standard.
normaaldruk, normal pressure.
normaalskool, normal college.
normaalspoor, standard gauge.
normalisasie, **normalisering**, normalization.
normaliseer, (ge-), normalize.
normaliteit, normality.
Normandië, Normandy.
Normandiër, (-s), Norman.
Normandies, (-e), Norman.
norring, big lot, mob, crowd, swarm.
nors, **noors**, (–, -e), grumpy, morose, surly, sullen; vide **noors**.
norsheid, **noorsheid**, sullenness.
nosie, (-s), notion.
nostalgie, nostalgia, homesickness.
nota, (-s), note; note (from the government); – bene, nota bene, please note.
notabel, (-e), notable.
notabele, people of note, leading lights.
notariaat, notaryship.
notarieel, (-riële), notarial.
notaris, (-se), notary.
notariskantoor, notary's office.
notasie, notation.
note: werk dat jy die kromme – **haal**, work like blazes; **iemand slaan dat hy die kromme** – **haal**, beat a person black and blue.
notebalk, staff, stave.
notebeurs, notecase.
noteboom, vide **neutboom**.
notedop, cockle-shell, cockle-boat.
noteer, (ge-), note (down); quote (prices).
notepapier, music-paper.
notering, (-e, -s), noting (down); quotation (of prices).
noteskrif, staff-notation.
notifikasie, notification.
notisie, notice; –s, notes, jottings; – **neem van**, take note of.
notisieboek, notebook.
notule, minutes; **die** – **goedkeur**, confirm the minutes.
notuleboek, minute-book.
notuleer, (ge-), enter (record) in the minutes, minute.
nou, n. strait(s); **in die** –, in a fix.
nou, (–, -e), a. narrow; tight (clothes); **in** – **verband staan met**, be closely related (allied) to, be closely connected with.
nou, adv. 1. narrowly; tightly; – **sit**, sit close, sit squeezed (wedged) in; **die pak klere sit** –, the suit is tight.
nou, adv. 2. now, at present; – **en dan**, now and then, occasionally; – **of nooit**, now or never; **nie** – **nie**, not now; – **nog nie**, not yet; not at this stage; – **al moeg**, tired already; – **eers**, not until now, only now; **ons het** – **eers gekom**, we have only just arrived; **wat** –?, what next?, and now?; – **die dag**, the other day, recently.

nou, interj. well.
nou, conj. now (that).
nougeset, (-te), narrow-minded; conscientious, scrupulous.
nougesetheid, narrow-mindedness.
nouheid, narrowness, tightness.
noukeurig, (-e), a. exact, accurate, precise; careful; close.
noukeurig, adv. exactly, accurately; **tot 'n pennie** –, to the nearest penny.
noukeurigheid, exactness, accuracy, precision; vide **noukeurigheid**.
noulettend, (-e), precise, particular, strict, close; scrupulous.
noulettendheid, precision, strictness.
nouliks, hardly, scarcely, barely.
nou-nou, in a moment (minute).
nousiende, particular, fastidious.
nousiendheid, fastidiousness.
nousluitend, (-e), tight, close-fitting.
noustrop: – **trek**, work like a galley-slave, have a hard time, be hard pressed, be in deep water, struggle.
noute, (-s), narrowness; strait(s); (narrow) pass; **in die** –, in a tight corner.
novelle, (-s), short story, novelette.
novellis, (-te), writer of short stories.
November, November.
noviet, (-e), freshman.
nu: – **en dan**, now and then; vide **nou**.
nuanse, (-s), nuance, shade.
nuanseer, (ge-), shade.
nuansering, (-e, -s), nuance, shade.
Nubië, Nubia.
Nubiër, (-s), Nubian.
Nubies, (-e), Nubian.
nuffie, (-s), prude, pert girl.
nuffig, (-e), prudish.
nu(ut)gebore, vide **nieugebore**.
nugter, (–, -e), a. sober; sober-minded; level-headed; prosaic, matter-of-fact; – **weet (en dié is dronk)**, goodness knows; **op jou** – **maag**, on an empty stomach.
nugter, adv. soberly; in a matter-of-fact way; – **wakker**, wide awake.
nugterheid, soberness, sobriety.
nuk, (-ke), whim, caprice, freak; mood.
nukkerig, (-e), sulky, moody, sullen.
nukkerigheid, sullenness, moroseness.
nul, (-le), nought, cipher; zero (temperature); love (tennis); nil (rugby); **in die jaar** –, on the Greek calends; **hy is 'n (groot)** –, he is a nobody (nonentity); **van** – **en gener waarde**, null and void; valueless, worthless.
nulliteit, (-e), nonentity, nobody.
nullyn, zero-line.
nulpunt, zero (temp.); null-point.
nulstel, love-set (tennis).
Numeri, Numbers.
numeriek, (-e), a. numerical.
numeriek, adv. numerically.
nut, use; benefit, profit; **water** – **het dit?**, what is the use (good) of it?; **dit het geen** – **om . . .**, it is no good . . ., no useful purpose would be served by . . .; – **trek uit**, benefit (profit) by; **tot** – **van**, for the benefit of; **sig iets tot (ten)** – **maak**, turn something to advantage; **van** – **wees**, be useful (of use); **van geen** –, of no use, useless.
nuterig, (-e), vide **nuwerig**.
nutteloos, (-lose), useless, vain.
nutteloosheid, uselessness.
nuttig, (-e), a. useful; profitable; **eers die** –**e**, **dan die aangename**, business before pleasure.

nuttig, adv. usefully; profitably; **jou tyd – bestee**, spend your time profitably.
nuttig, (ge-), partake of (meal); **iets –**, take nourishment.
nuttigheid, usefulness; utility.
nuttigheidsleer, -stelsel, utilitarian doctrine, utilitarianism.
nuttiging, partaking (of meal).
nuus, news, tidings; **dit is ou –**, that is stale news; **geen – is goeie –**, no news is good news.
nuusberig, (news-)report, news-item.
nuusblad, newspaper.
nuusdraer, tell-tale.
nuuskierig, (-e), inquisitive; curious; **–e Agie**, Paul Pry, inquisitive person.
nuuskierigheid, inquisitiveness, curiosity.
nuus(rol)prent, newsreel.
nuut, (nuwe), new; modern; recent; fresh; **die hoed is –**, the hat is new; **dis 'n nuwe hoed**, it is a new hat; **iets –s**, something new; **niks –s onder die son nie**, nothing new under the sun; **van –s af**, from the beginning, (start) afresh.
nu(ut)- . . ., vide **nieu-** .
nuutheid, newness.

nuwe, vide **nuut**.
Nuwejaar, New Year.
Nuwejaarsdag, New Year's Day.
Nuwejaarspresent, New Year gift.
nuwejaarsvoël, black-crested cuckoo.
Nuwejaarswens, New Year wish.
nuweling, (-e), newcomer, beginner, novice; greenhorn; fresher, freshman.
nuwemaan, new moon.
nuwerig, (-e), newish, rather new.
nuwerwets, (-e), new-fashioned; new-fangled (ideas); modern, up-to-date.
nuwesiekte, (nauseatic) strangles.
nuwigheid, (-hede), novelty, innovation.
nydig, (-e), angry; **– wees op**, hate (like poison); be bitterly, jealous of.
nydigheid, anger; vide **nyd**.
nyg, (ge-), bow, curts(e)y.
nyging, bow, curts(e)y.
Nyl, Nile; **die –**, the Nile.
nylperd, hippopotamus.
nyweraar, (-s), manufacturer.
nywerheid, (-hede), industry.

o, oh!, ah!; – so!, aha!
oase, (-s), oasis.
Obadja, Obadiah.
obelisk, (-e), obelisk.
objek, (-te), object, thing.
objeksie, (-s), objection.
objekteer, (ge-), object, raise objections.
objektief, (-tiewe), objective.
objektiwiteit, objectiveness, objectivity.
oblietjie, (-s), rolled wafer.
obligasie, (-s), bond, debenture.
obliterasie, obliteration.
obool, (-bole), obol.
obseen, (-sene), obscene.
obseniteit, (-e), obscenity.
observasie, (-s), observation.
observatorium, (-s, -toria), observatory.
observeer, (ge-), observe.
obsessie, (-s), obsession.
obsidiaan, obsidian.
obskurantisme, obscurantism.
obskuriteit, obscurity.
obskuur, (-skure), obscure.
obstetrie, obstetrics.
obstinaat, (-nate), obstinate.
obstruksie, (-s), obstruction; constipation; – **voer**, practise obstruction.
oktavo, (-'s), octavo.
ode (-s), ode.
odeur, (-s), scent, perfume.
odeurflessie, scent-bottle.
Odyssee, Odyssey.
oë, vide oog.
oëdienaar, time-server, yes-man.
oefen, (ge-), practise, exercise, train.
oefengrond, training-ground.
oefening, (-e, -s), practice, exercise, training, prayer-meeting; – **baar kuns**, practice makes perfect.
oefenkamp, training-camp.
oefenskool, training-school.
oekase, (-s), ukase.
oënskou: in – **neem**, inspect; look at; review.
oënskynlik, (-e), a. apparent, ostensible.
oënskynlik, adv. apparently: ostensibly.
oer- . . ., primitive, primeval.
Oeralgebergte, the Ural Mountains.
oerbos, vide oerwoud.
Oergermaans, Primitive Germanic.
oermens, primitive man.
oeroud, (-oue), primeval, ancient.
oersel, primordial cell.
oertaal, primitive language.
oerteks, original text.
oertipe, archetype, prototype.
oertyd, prehistoric times.
oervolk, primitive race.
oerwoud, primeval forest, virgin forest.
oes, (-te), n. crop, harvest; output.
oes, a. bad, feeble, miserable, shabby; off colour, out of condition; 'n – **vent**, a miserable specimen, a sorry fellow.
oes, (ge-), reap, harvest, gather; earn; beat, lick.
oeslied, harvest-song.
oester, (-s), oyster.
oester, (-s), reaper, harvester.
oesterbed, oyster-bed.
oesterkweker, oyster-culturist.
oesterkwekery, oyster-culture.
oesterplaat, oyster-bank.
oesterskulp, oyster-shell.
oesterteelt, oyster-farming.
oestervergiftiging, oyster-poisoning.
oestervisser, oyster-fisher.

oestervissery, oyster-fishery.
oestyd, harvesting-season, reaping-time.
oesvolk, reapers, harvesters.
oëtroos, eyebright, euphrasy.
oëverblindery, make-believe, pretence, eyewash; deception, hallucination.
oewer, (-s), bank (of a river), shore.
oewerbewoner, riparian (proprietor).
of, or; whether; (as) if; but; X – Y, X or Y; **ja – nee**, yes or no; **min – meer**, more or less; **die een – die ander**, the one or the other; **dag – nag**, day or night; **(of) X – Y**, (either) X or Y; **'n dag – twee**, day or two; **'n stukses**, about six; **'n myl – tien**, ten miles or so; **'n dag – wat gelede**, some (a couple of) days ago; **jy sal moet gaan – jy lus het – nie**, you will have to go whether you like it or not; **hy loop (as) – hy nie gesond is nie**, he walks as if (as though) he were not well; **hy sien my nooit nie – hy probeer geld leen**, whenever he sees me he tries to borrow money; **dit het min geskeel – hy het 'n pak gekry**, he very nearly got a hiding; – **hoe?**, or what (do you say)?
offensief, (-siewe), n. offensive.
offensief, adv. on the offensive; – **optree**, take the offensive.
offer, (-s), n. sacrifice, offering; victim.
offer, (ge-), sacrifice, offer, immolate.
offeraar, (-s), immolator, sacrificer.
offeraltaar, sacrificial altar.
offerande, (-s), offering, sacrifice.
offerdier, victim.
offerfees, sacrificial feast.
offering, (-e, -s), offering.
offerlam, sacrificial lamb.
offerplegtigheid, sacrificial rites.
offerte, (-s), offer.
offervaardig, (-e), willing to make sacrifices.
offervaardigheid, willingness to make sacrifices.
offisieel, (-siële), a. official.
offisieel, adv. officially.
offisier, (-e, -s), officer.
offisiersrang, rank of an officer.
offisieus, (-e), semi-official.
ofskoon, (al)though.
oftalmie, ophthalmia.
oftalmoskoop, (-skope), ophthalmoscope.
ofte: **nooit – nimmer**, never, on no account; – **wel**, or; **of hy gaan – nie**, whether he goes or not; vide **of**.
og, oh!; – **kom!**, indeed!; you don't mean to say so!
oggend, (-e), morning.
oggendblad, morning-paper.
oggenddiens, morning-service.
oggendete, breakfast, morning-meal.
oggendstond, early morning.
ogie, (-s), little eye; –s **maak**, wink.
ogiesdraad, wire-netting.
oho, aha!.
oker, ochre.
okeragtig, (-e), ochreous, ochreish.
okkasie, (-s), occasion.
okkerneut, (-e), walnut.
okkerneuthout, walnut.
okkult, (-e), occult.
okkultisme, occultism.
okkupasie, (-s), occupation.
okkupeer, (ge-), occupy.
oksaalsuur, oxalic acid.
oksel, (-s), armpit, axil (bot.).
okshoof, (-de), hogshead.
oksidasie, oxidation.
oksideer, (ge-), oxidize.
oksied, (-e), okside, (-s), oxide.

oksimoron, oxymoron.
oktaaf, (-tawe), octave.
oktaëder, (-s), octahedron.
Oktober, October.
Oktobermaand, month of October.
oktogoon, (-gone), octagon.
oktrooi, (-e), charter, patent, grant.
oktrooibrief(we), letters patent.
oktrooieer, (ge-), (grant a) patent, charter; **geoktrooieerde maatskappy**, chartered company.
okulasie, (-s), inoculation, grafting.
okuleer, (ge-), inoculate, graft.
okulêr, (-e), n. ocular, eyepiece.
okulêr, (-e), a. ocular.
okulis, (-te), oculist.
oleander, (-s), oleander.
olie, (-s), n. oil; – **op (in) die vuur gooi**, pour oil on the flame; – **op die golwe giet**, pour oil on the waters.
olie, (ge-), oil, lubricate.
olieagtig, (-e), oily.
olieagtigheid, oiliness.
oliebol, doughnut.
olieboom, castor-oil plant.
oliebron, oil-well.
olie-en-asyn-stel(letjie), cruet-stand.
oliefabriek, oil-factory.
oliehoudend, (-e), oleaginous, oil-bearing.
oliekan, oil-can.
oliekoek, oil-cake; doughnut; simpleton.
olieleiklip, oil-shale.
oliemeul, oil-mill.
olienhout, **oliewenhout**, wild olive.
oliepak, oilskins.
oliesel, extreme unction.
oliesteen, oilstone.
olieverbruik, oil-consumption.
olieverf, oil-colours, oil-paint.
olieverfskildery, oil-painting.
olifant, (-e), elephant; **van 'n muggie (vlieg, vlooi) 'n – maak**, make mountains out of molehills.
olifantagtig, (-e), elephantine.
olifantjagter, elephant-hunter.
olifantsgras, elephant-grass.
olifantsroer, muzzle-loader.
olifantstand, elephant's tusk, ivory.
oligargie, (-ë), oligarchy.
oligargies, (-e), oligarchic(al).
olik, (-e), seedy, off colour, unwell.
olikheid, seediness, etc.; **na vrolikheid kom –**, after joy comes sorrow, after pleasure comes pain.
olim: **in die dae van –**, in the days of yore.
Olimpies, (-e), Olympic; **-e spele**, Olympic games.
olm, (-e), elm.
olyf, (olywe), olive.
olyfagtig, (-e), olivaceous.
Olyfberg, Mount of Olives.
olyfolie, olive-oil.
olyftak, olive-branch.
olyfvormig, (-e), olive-shaped, olivary.
om, adv. round; out; up, over; **die tyd is –**, time is up; – **en –**, round and round.
om, prep. round, about, at; for; – **die hoek (die hoek –)**, round the corner; – **vyfuur**, (at) five o'clock; – **en by die tagtig**, about eighty; – **die twee uur**, every two hours; **al – die ander dag**, every other day; – **die beurt**, in turn; **dit is my – die ewe**, it is immaterial to me; – **Gods wil**, for God's sake; – **hulp vra**, ask for help; – **die dokter stuur**, send for the doctor; **beroemd –**, famous for.

om te, to, in order to; – **lewe**, to live; **'n boek – lees**, a book to read; **nie – eet nie**, not to be eaten.
omarm, (–), embrace, fold in the arms.
omarming, (-e, -s), embrace, clasp.
ombabbel, (omge-), talk away (the time).
omber, umber (natural pigment).
omber(spel), (game of) ombre.
ombind, (omge-), bind (tie) round.
omblaai, (omge-), turn over (a leaf).
omblaas, (omge-), blow down (over).
omboor, (omge-), bind, hem, edge.
omboorsel, binding, edging, border.
ombring, (omge-), kill, put to death.
ombuig, (omge-), bend, turn (down, back, up), recurve.
omdat, because, since, as, seeing that.
omdoling, wandering, roaming.
omdop, (omge-), turn inside out; curl (up); double up; fall down (over).
omdraai, (omge-), turn round (back, about); turn over; wrap in; twist; **'n sleutel –**, turn a key; **iemand die nek –**, twist somebody's neck; **sig –**, turn round; turn over (on one's face).
omdraaiing, turning, rotation; change (of front), volte-face.
omdrentel, (omge-), lounge about; **die tyd –**, idle away the time.
omega, (-s), omega.
omelet, (-te), omelet(te).
omfloers, (–), cover, veil; muffle.
omgaan, (omge-), go round; take place, happen; associate (with), rub shoulders (with); pass; **'n draai –**, turn a corner; **niemand weet wat in sy gemoed – nie**, nobody knows what his feelings are; **met iemand –**, associate with somebody; **hy weet hoe om met daardie mense om te gaan**, he knows how to deal with those people; **met bedrog –**, practise deceit; **by die huis –**, call at the house; **per –de**, by return of post.
omgang, association, (social) intercourse, dealings; circuit, rotation; round, lap; – **hê met**, associate with; **hy is 'n gawe kêrel in die –**, he is a fine fellow to know, he is good company; **in die – genoem X**, generally known as X.
omgangstaal, colloquial language.
omgee, (omge-), care, mind; hand round, pass round.
omgeef, vide **omgewe**.
omgekeer(d), (-de), a. turned upside down (inside out); upturned, turned down; inverted; reversed; inverse.
omgekeer(d), adv. inversely; conversely; **en –**, and vice versa; **dit is net –**, it is just the other way round.
omgekeerde, n. the reverse; converse.
omgekrap, (-te), untidy; confused; riotous; unruly; irritable, upset, peeved.
omgewe, **omgeef**, (–), surround, encircle, enclose, encompass.
omgewing, environment; vicinity.
omgooi, (omge-), upset; throw down.
omgord, (–), gird; gird round; **die lendene –**, gird the loins.
omgord, (omge-), regird; gird round.
omgrens, (–), bound; confine, restrict.
omhaal, n. bustle, commotion, fuss, to-do; – **van woorde**, verbosity, prolixity; **sonder veel – van woorde**, without wasting words, without beating about the bush.
omhaal, (omge-), persuade; pull down.
omhang, (omge-), put on, throw (overcoat, etc.) over one's shoulders.
omhê, (omgehad), have on.

omheen, about, round about.
omhein, (-), fence in (round), enclose.
omheining, (-s), fence, enclosure.
omhels, (-), embrace.
omhelsing, embrace.
omhoog, aloft, on high; up(wards); **met sy hande -,** with his hands up.
omhoogstyg, (omhoogge-), rise, ascend.
omhou, (omge-), keep on; hold round.
omhul, (-), envelop, enwrap, enshroud.
omhulsel, (-s), wrapper, cover(ing); **die stoflike -,** the mortal remains.
omie, (-s), uncle.
omissie, (-s), omission.
omkantel, (omge-), fall over, topple over; tilt; upset, overturn, capsize.
omkap, (omge-), cut down, fell; whip.
om(me)keer, n. (complete) change, turn (of events); reversal; upsetting.
omkeer, (omge-), turn (up, out, down, over), turn upside down; invert; reverse; **jou sakke -,** turn out your pockets; **hooi -,** make hay, turn over hay; **hy het my omgekeer,** he made me turn back.
omkering, inversion, reversal.
omklem, (-), clasp, cling to, hug.
omklink, (omge-), rivet, clinch.
omknel, (-), hold (seize, grasp) tightly.
omknoop, (omge-), button up, tie round.
omkom, (omge-), come round; perish.
omkonkel, (omge-), talk over (round).
omkoop, (omge-), bribe; corrupt.
omkoopbaar, (-bare), corruptible, venal.
omkoopbaarheid, venality, corruptibility.
omkoper, briber.
omkopery, bribery, corruption.
omkrans, (-), wreathe.
omkrap, (omge-), throw into disorder (confusion), disarrange; make a mess of, bungle; **iemand -,** irritate (vex, upset) somebody; vide **omgekrap**.
omkruip, (omge-), creep round; drag.
omkrul, (omge-), curl up, bend back.
omkry, (omge-), get down; get round; get on; while away (the time).
omkyk, (omge-), look round, look back.
omlaag, (down) below; **na -,** down.
omlê, (omge-), lie down (flat), be upset (overturned, blown down); **laat -,** turn the edge of (knife).
omliggende, neighbouring, surrounding.
omloop, n. 1. circulation; rotation; **- van die bloed,** circulation of the blood; **geld in - bring,** circulate money; **die gerugte is in - dat . . .,** it is rumoured that . . .
omloop, (-lope), n. 2. ringworm.
omloop, (omge-), go (walk) round; stretch round; revolve; knock down, run down; cheat.
omlyn, (-), outline, define.
omlyning, outline (outlining).
omlys, (-), frame; set.
omlysting, frame; framing; setting.
om(me)keer, vide **omkeer**, n.
ommesientjie: in 'n -, in the twinkling of an eye (in a twinkle), in a jiffy.
ommesy, overleaf; **sien ommesy (S.O.S.),** please turn over (P.T.O.).
ommuur, (-), wall in.
omnibus, (-se), (omni)bus.
omnibus-uitgawe, omnibus edition.
omnivoor, (-vore), omnivorous animal.
ompad, roundabout way, detour.
omplant, (omge-), replant; plant round.
omploeg, (omge-), plough.
omplooi, (omge-), fold back (down, in).
ompraat, (omge-), persuade, talk over.

omreis, (omge-), travel round; make a detour, travel a roundabout way.
omring, (-), surround, encircle.
omroep, n. broadcasting (station).
omroep, (omge-), announce; broadcast.
omroeper, town-crier; announcer.
omroer, (omge-), stir.
omrol, (omge-), roll over.
omruil, (omge-), exchange; interchange; **plekke -,** change places.
omruk, (omge-), pull down, pull round.
omry, (omge-), knock down (over), run over; drive round.
omseil, (omge-), sail round.
omsendbrief, circular (letter).
omset, n. turnover; sale; returns.
omset, (omge-), turn over, convert into money; invert; transpose; vide **omsit**.
omsetting, inversion; transposition; conversion; transmutation; reversal.
omsien, (omge-), look back; **na iemand -,** look after somebody.
omsientjiestyd, short time; **in 'n -,** in no time, in a jiffy.
omsigtig, (-e), circumspect, cautious.
omsigtigheid, circumspection, caution.
omsingel, (-), surround, encircle, hem in.
omsit, (omge-), put round; sit round; turn round suddenly; transpose; transmute; invert; reverse, convert (into).
omskakel, (omge-), switch (change) over.
omskans, (-), fortify, entrench.
omskansing, (-e, -s), fortification, circumvallation, entrenchment.
omskep, (omge-), 1. transform, change.
omskep, (omge-), 2. ladle, transfer.
omskiet, (omge-), shoot down.
omskik, (omge-), rearrange.
omskop, (omge-), kick over (down).
omskryf, -skrywe, (-), paraphrase; define, describe; circumscribe (geom.).
omskrywing, (-e, -s), paraphrase; definition; description; circumscription.
omslaan, (omge-), strike (knock) down; fall down; capsize, overturn; turn over (page); fold down, turn down; turn up; fold (turn) back; change opinion, veer round.
omslag, 1. fuss, bustle, commotion; **- maak,** take trouble, put oneself out; **sonder veel -,** without much ado, without taking much trouble.
omslag, (-slae), 2. cover, jacket; wrapper (of newspaper); cuff; turn-up.
omslag, (-slae), 3. brace.
omslagboor, brace and bit.
omslagploeg, hillside-plough.
omslagtig, (-e), roundabout, long-winded, tedious, detailed; prolix; wordy; **- vertel,** tell in detail.
omslagtigheid, long-windedness, tediousness, wordiness, prolixity.
omslenter, (omge-), loiter about; **die dag -,** idle away the time.
omsluiter, (-), veil; conceal, cover.
omsluiering, veil; cover, disguise.
omsluip, (omge-), creep (crawl) round.
omsluit, (-), encircle, surround; grip, clasp; fit (tightly).
omsluiting, (-e, -s), enclosing, encircling; clasp; ring-fence, ring-wall.
omsmelt, (omge-), remelt, melt down.
omsmelting, re-fusing, melting down.
omsmyt, (omge-), knock down (over), upset, overturn.
omsnuffel, (omge-), pry (nose) about.
omsons, vain, fruitless, useless.

omsoom, (omge-), hem.
omsoom, (-), border, edge, fringe.
omspan, (omge-), change.
omspit, (omge-), dig (up).
omspoel, (omge-), rinse, wash; wash out (away).
omspring, (omge-), jump round; upset; manage; change one's opinion.
ontstaan, (omge-), stand about; move away, make room.
omstander, (-s), bystander, onlooker.
omstandig, (-e), a. detailed, circumstantial; **'n -e verhaal,** a circumstantial story.
omstandig, adv. in detail.
omstandigheid, (-hede), circumstance, circumstantiality; **sameloop van -hede,** coincidence, concurrence of events; **sy geldelike -hede,** his financial position; **in geseënde -hede,** with child, pregnant, in the family way; **onder (in) die -hede,** in the circumstances.
omstap, (omge-), walk round.
omstiksel, (-s), hem, stitching.
om soot, (omge-), push down; upset.
omstraal, (-), halo, surround with a halo.
omstreeks, about, more or less, in the neighbourhood of.
omstreke, (pl.), vicinity, neighbourhood, environs.
omstrengel, (-), twine, round, entwine; embrace.
omstroom, (omge-), flow round.
omstuur, (omge-), send (round).
omsukkel, (omge-), jog, about, trudge about.
omswaai, (-e), n. swinging round.
omswaai, (omge-), swing round; wheel round; veer round.
omswagtel, (-), swathe, bandage, swaddle.
omswem, (omge-), swim round.
omswerf, omswerwe, (omge-), wander (roam) about.
omswerwing, (-e, -s), wandering.
omswoeg, (omge-), toil, drudge, labour; **die tyd -,** toil through the days.
omtower, (omge-), transform (by, as if by, magic); transfigure.
omtrap, (omge-), kick over (down).
omtrek, (-ke), n. outline; circumference (of a circle); perimeter (geom.); vicinity, neighbourhood; **hier in die -,** in this neighbourhood; **myle in die -,** for miles around.
omtrek, (omge-), pull down; outflank (the enemy); "trek" round.
omtreklyn, contour-line.
omtrent, adv. about, nearly; extremely.
omtrent, prep. about; with regard to.
omtuimel, (omge-), tumble down, topple over.
omvaar, (omge-), sail round; run down.
omval, (omge-), fall down, topple over.
omvang, girth, circumference; range, extent; size; magnitude; **die - van die stem,** the range (compass) of the voice.
omvangryk, (-e), bulky; comprehensive.
omvangrykheid, comprehensiveness; extensiveness, great extent (range).
omvat, (-), include, comprise, embrace; take in; grip, clasp; span.
omvat, (omge-), clasp (take) round.
omvattend, (-e), embracing; (veel) -, comprehensive.
omver, over, down.
omvergooi, (omverge-), upset, knock over; frustrate, shatter (hopes).
omverloop, (omverge-), knock down.
omverry, (omverge-), knock down, run over.
omverstoot, (omverge-), push down.
omverwaai, (omverge-), blow down; be blown over, be blown off one's feet.

omverwerp, (omverge-), vide **omvergooi.**
omverwerping, upsetting; overthrow.
omvleg, (-), twine round, entwine.
omvleg, (omge-), plait round.
omvlie(g), (omge-), fly round; turn round suddenly; upset; **die tyd vlieg om,** time flies.
omvloei, (omge-), flow round.
omvorm, (omge-), transform, remodel.
omvou, (omge-), fold down (back), turn down.
omvroetel, (omge-), root up, dig (up).
omwaai, (omge-), vide **omverwaai.**
omwal, (-), circumvallate, wall in.
omwandel, (omge-), walk about; walk round, walk the earth, travel, sojourn.
omwandeling, sojourn(ing).
omweg, (-weë), roundabout way, detour; **iets langs 'n - hoor,** hear something indirectly.
omwend, (omge-), turn (round).
omwentel, (omge-), turn (round); rotate, revolve, move round axis.
omwenteling, (-e, -s), revolution; rotation; **die Franse O-,** the French Revolution; **'n - teweegbring in,** change radically, revolutionise.
omwentelingsas, axis of rotation.
omwerk, (omge-), refashion; reconstruct; border; rewrite; dig, plough, cultivate.
omwerking, recast, reconstruction; border; rewriting; recasting; cultivation.
omwikkel, (omge-), wrap round.
omwindsel, (-s), wrapper, wrapping(s).
omwissel, (omge-), change; exchange (for); alternate.
omwisseling, change; exchange.
omwoel, (omge-), dig up, turn up; stir; scatter; throw into disorder; wriggle round; wind round.
omwolk, (-), envelop (in clouds).
onaandagtig, (-e), inattentive.
onaandagtigheid, inattention.
onaandoenlik, (-e), unemotional, impassive; apathetic, indifferent.
onaandoenlikheid, impassiveness, etc.
onaangedaan, (-dane), unmoved.
onaangedien, (-de), unannounced.
onaangeklee(d), (-klede), undressed.
onaangemeld, (-e), unannounced.
onaangenaam, (-name), unpleasant, disagreeable, bad-tempered, unamiable.
onaangenaamheid, (-hede), unpleasantness, disagreeableness.
onaangeraak, (-te), untouched.
onaangeroer, (-de), untouched, intact.
onaangetas, (-te), untouched; not affected.
onaanloklik, (-e), unattractive.
onaanneemlik, (-e), unacceptable.
onaanneemlikheid, unacceptability.
onaansienlik, (-e), plain, unattractive; insignificant; inconsiderable.
onaansienlikheid, unattractiveness, etc.
onaanspraaklik, onaanspreeklik, not answerable (responsible).
onaanstootlik, (-e), inoffensive.
onaantasbaar, (-bare), unassailable; unimpeachable; inviolable.
onaantasbaarheid, unassailability, etc., inviolability.
onaantreklik, (-e), unattractive.
onaanvegbaar, (-bare), indisputable; unassailable; inviolable.
onaardig, (-e), unpleasant, not nice; **glad nie - nie,** not at all bad.
onaardigheid, unpleasantness, rudeness.
onafgebroke, incessant, unceasing, uninterrupted, continuous.
onafgedaan, (-dane), unfinished.

onafgedank, (-te), not dismissed.
onafgehaal, (-de), unclaimed.
onafgelos, (-te), unrelieved; unredeemed.
onafgemaak, (-te), unfinished.
onafgewerk, (-te), unfinished, rough.
onafhanklik, (-e), a. independent.
onafhanklik, adv. independently.
onafhanklikheid, independence.
onaflosbaar, (-bare), irredeemable.
onafrikaans, (-e), un-Afrikaans, not Afrikaans, not characteristic of the Afrikaner.
onafsienbaar, (-bare), interminable, immense, endless, vast.
onafskei(d)baar, (-bare), inseparable.
onafskeidelik, (-e), inseparable.
onafwendbaar, (-bare), unavoidable.
onafwendbaarheid, inevitability.
onafwysbaar, (-bare), that cannot be refused, peremptory, imperative.
onagsaam, (-same), careless, thoughtless, negligent, inattentive.
onbaatsugtig, (-e), unselfish, disinterested.
onbaatsugtigheid, unselfishness.
onbarmhartig, (-e), merciless, pitiless.
onbarmhartigheid, mercilessness.
onbeantwoord, (-e), unanswered (question, letter); unrequited (love).
onbebou(d), (-de), untilled; vacant.
onbedaarlik, (-e), violent, intense, uncontrollable, unceasing.
onbedag, (-te), thoughtless, incautious.
onbedagsaam, (-same), thoughtless, incautious, rash.
onbedagsaamheid, thoughtlessness.
onbedeel(d), (-de), not possessing.
onbedek, (-te), uncovered, bare.
onbederflik, (-e), imperishable.
onbedorwe, not decayed, not spoiled (unspoiled); innocent; unperverted.
onbedrewe, unskilled, inexperienced, untrained.
onbedrewenheid, inexperience, lack of skill, unskilfulness.
onbeduidend, (-e), insignificant, trifling, unimportant, trivial; 'n -e persoon, a nobody.
onbeduidendheid, insignificance, unimportance, triviality; trifle.
onbedwingbaar, (-bare), unrestrainable, indomitable; uncontrollable, ungovernable.
onbedwingbaarheid, indomitableness; irrepressibility, uncontrollableness.
onbedwonge, unsubdued, unconquered.
onbegaaf, (-de), untalented.
onbegaanbaar, (-bare), impassable.
onbegaanbaarheid, impassability.
onbegonne, not yet started (begun); dit is 'n – taak, that is attempting the impossible.
onbegrawe, unburied.
onbegrens, (-de), unbounded, unlimited, unrestricted, endless.
onbegrepe, not understood.
onbegryplik, (-e), inconceivable, incomprehensible.
onbegryplikheid, incomprehensibility.
onbehaaglik, (-e), disagreeable, unpleasant; uneasy; uncomfortable.
onbehange, unpapered.
onbeheer(d), (-e), uncontrolled; unattended; ownerless; without a guardian.
onbehendig, (-e), clumsy, unskilful.
onbehoedsaam, (-same), rash, reckless.
onbeholpe, clumsy, awkward, helpless; unpolished, crude.
onbeholpenheid, clumsiness.
onbehoorlik, (-e), improper, unseemly, indecent.

onbehoorlikheid, impropriety, unseemliness, indecency, unbecomingness.
onbehoue, rough, unhewn; uncouth, rude, illbred, unmannerly.
onbehouenheid, roughness, rudeness.
onbekeerbaar, (-bare), -lik, (-e), that cannot be converted, impervious.
onbekeer(d), (-e), unconverted.
onbekend, (-e), unknown; – maak onbemind, unknown, unloved; ek is – hier, I am a stranger here; dit is my –, I have never heard of it.
onbekende, (-s), unknown; stranger.
onbekendheid, strangeness; unfamiliarity; ignorance; obscurity (of a person).
onbeklaag, (-de), unlamented, unwept.
onbeklad, (-de), unsullied, unstained.
onbeklee(d), (-klede), unupholstered; vacant.
onbeklem(d), (-de), cheerful; unaccented.
onbeklimbaar, (-bare), unscalable, unclimbable, inaccessible.
onbekommerd, (-e), unconcerned, free from anxiety (care).
onbekommerdheid, unconcern.
onbekook, (-te), rash, thoughtless, not mature (digested), ill-considered.
onbekrompe, broadminded, liberal; generous; – lewe, live comfortably.
onbekwaam, (-kwame), unable, incapable; incompetent, unfit.
onbekwaamheid, inability; incompetence.
onbelangrik, (-e), unimportant, trifling.
onbelangrikheid, insignificance.
onbelas, (-te), unencumbered; unburdened; untaxed; unmortgaged.
onbelasbaar, (-bare), exempt from taxes.
onbeleef, (-de), impolite, rude, ill-mannered, uncivil.
onbeleefdheid, impoliteness, rudeness.
onbelemmerd, (-e), free, unimpeded, unhampered, unobstructed.
onbelesenheid, illiteracy, lack of reading.
onbeloon(d), (-de), unrewarded, unrequited.
onbemerk, (-te), unnoticed, unobserved.
onbemerkbaar, (-bare), imperceptible, unnoticeable.
onbemiddeld, (-e), without means, poor.
onbemin(d), (-de), not liked, unpopular.
onbeminlik, (-e), unamiable, not lovable.
onbenepe, large, spacious; frank, candid.
onbenewel(d), unclouded, clear.
onbenoem(d), (-de), unnamed; unappointed; –de getal, abstract number.
onbenullig, (-e), stupid, slow-witted, dull, fatuous; trifling, paltry.
onbenuttig, (-de), unused.
onbepaalbaar, (-bare), indeterminable.
onbepaald, (-e), indefinite; uncertain, not fixed; –e vertroue, complete (implicit) faith; –e mag, unlimited power; vir 'n –e tyd, indefinitely; –e wyse, infinitive (mood).
onbepaaldheid, indefiniteness; vagueness, uncertainty; unlimitedness.
onbeperk, (-te), unlimited, unrestricted.
onbeperktheid, boundlessness.
onbeplant, (-e), unplanted.
onbeproef, (-de), untested, untried.
onberade, ill-advised, rash, reckless.
onberadenheid, rashness, recklessness.
onberede, unmounted; unfrequented.
onberedeneer(d), (-de), unreasoned; thoughtless, unthinking, unreasoning.
onberedeneerdheid, thoughtlessness.
onbereid, (-e), unprepared.
onbereikbaar, (-bare), inaccessible, unattainable, unapproachable.

onbereis, (-de), untravelled (person); unfrequented (region, country).
onberekenbaar, (-bare), incalculable.
onberispelik, (-e), irreproachable, faultless, free from blame; immaculate.
onberispelikheid, irreproachability, faultlessness; immaculateness.
onberoepbaar, (-bare), cannot be called.
onberym(d), (-de), unrhymed.
onbesadig, (-de), rash, impetuous.
onbeseer(d), (-de), unhurt.
onbeset, (-te), unoccupied, vacant (post, chair); without a garrison.
onbesiens, unseen; iets – koop, buy something without having seen it.
onbeskaaf, (-de), uncivilised, savage; unrefined, unpolished.
onbeskaafdheid, lack of refinement (culture); unmannerliness.
onbeskaamd, (-e), impudent, impertinent, shameless, insolent, unabashed.
onbeskaamdheid, impudence, impertinence, insolence.
onbeskadig, (-de), undamaged.
onbeskeidenheid, immodesty; indiscretion.
onbeskeie, immodest; forward, impudent, indiscreet.
onbeskerm(d), (-de), unprotected, undefended, unguarded.
onbeskof, (-te), rude, uncouth, ill-mannered, unmannerly, impertinent.
onbeskoftheid, rudeness, impertinence.
onbeskrewe, blank, unrecorded; unwritten (law); not described.
onbeskroom(d), (-de), undaunted, outspoken, bold, fearless.
onbeskryflik, (-e), indescribable.
onbeskut, (-te), unprotected.
onbeslaan, (-beslae, -de), unshod.
onbesleg, (-te), not settled, undecided.
onbeslis, (-te), undecided; irresolute.
onbeslistheid, indecision, irresoluteness.
onbesmet, (-te), clean, pure, undefiled, uncontaminated; not infected.
onbesnede, uncircumcised; unregenerate.
onbesoedel(d), (-de), spotless, undefiled, unpolluted, unsullied.
onbesonne, thoughtless, unthinking, rash, wild, inconsiderate.
onbesonnenheid, rashness, indiscretion.
onbesorg, (-de), cheerful, light-hearted; unconcerned; undelivered (letter).
onbespreek, (-te), unreserved, unbooked (seats); not discussed, passed over.
onbesproke, unreserved; irreproachable.
onbestaanbaar, (-bare), not existing; impossible; incompatible.
onbestand, not proof (against).
onbestelbaar, (-bare), undeliverable; –bare brief, unclaimed letter.
onbestem(d), (-de), vague, indefinite.
onbestendig, (-e), unsettled, changeable, unstable, inconstant; –e persoon, fickle (inconstant) person.
onbestendigheid, changeability (changeableness), instability; inconstancy.
onbestorwe: 'n – weduwee, a grass-widow; – vleis, very fresh meat.
onbestrede, unopposed, undisputed.
onbestuurbaar, (-bare), unmanageable; undirectable; unsteerable.
onbesuis, (-de), reckless, rash, impetuous; unrestrained, ungovernable.
onbeswaar(d), (-de), unencumbered, clear, free from care; unmortgaged.

onbesweke, unyielding, unshaken.
onbetaal(d), (-de), unpaid, unsettled.
onbetaalbaar, (-bare), unpayable; priceless; –bare grap, priceless joke.
onbetaamlik, (-e), improper, unseemly, indecent, immodest, unbecoming.
onbetaamlikheid, unseemliness, indecency, immodesty, unbecomingness.
onbetekenend, (-e), insignificant, trivial.
onbeteuel(d), (-de), unbridled, unchecked, unrestrained.
onbetoombaar, (-bare), ungovernable.
onbetrede, untrodden.
onbetreur(d), (-de), unmourned.
onbetroubaar, (-bare), unreliable, untrustworthy.
onbetroubaarheid, untrustworthiness.
onbetuig: hy het hom nie – gelaat nie, he gave a good account of himself.
onbetwis, (-te), undisputed.
onbetwisbaar, (-bare), indisputable.
onbetwisbaarheid, unquestionableness.
onbetwyfelbaar, (-bare), unquestionable, undoubted, indubitable.
onbevaarbaar, (-bare), unnavigable.
onbevaarbaarheid, unnavigability.
onbevallig, (-e), uncomely, ungraceful.
onbevalligheid, ungracefulness.
onbevange, unbias(s)ed, impartial.
onbevangenheid, impartiality, fairness.
onbevatlik, (-e), incomprehensible; stupid; obtuse, dull.
onbevestig, (-de), unordained, not inducted; unconfirmed.
onbevlek, (-te), unstained, undefiled, clean, pure, spotless, immaculate.
onbevoeg, (-de), incompetent, unfit.
onbevoegde (-s), incompetent person.
onbevoegdheid, incompetence.
onbevolk, (-te), unpopulated.
onbevooroordeeld, (-e), unprejudiced, unbias(s)ed, fair, impartial.
onbevooroordeeldheid, impartiality.
onbevoorreg, (-te), unprivileged.
onbevredig, (-de), unsatisfied, ungratified, unfulfilled, unappeased.
onbevredigend, (-e), unsatisfactory.
onbevrees, (-de), undaunted, fearless.
onbevrug, (-te), unimpregnated.
onbewaak, (te), unguarded.
onbeweegbaar, (-bare), immovable.
onbeweegbaarheid, immovability.
onbeweeglik, (-e), motionless; steadfast, unmoved, unyielding, immovable.
onbeweeglikheid, immobility, firmness.
onbeween, (-de), unwept, unlamented.
onbewerk, (-te), untilled, uncultivated; uncured, undressed; unprepared; raw.
onbewese, unproved.
onbewimpeld, (-e), candid, outspoken, open, frank.
onbewoë, smooth, unmoved, untouched, calm, impassive.
onbewolk, (-te), cloudless; unclouded.
onbewoonbaar, (-bare), uninhabitable.
onbewoon(d), (-de), uninhabited; unoccupied, untenanted (house).
onbewus, (-te), a. unconscious; unaware (of).
onbewus, adv. unconsciously; unwittingly, unknowingly.
onbewustheid, unconsciousness.
onbewysbaar, (-bare), unprovable.
onbillik, (-e), unfair, unreasonable, unjust, not equitable.
onbillikheid, unfairness, unreasonableness, injustice.

onblusbaar, (-bare), unquenchable.
onboetvaardig, (-e), unrepentant.
onboetvaardigheid, impenitence.
onbrandbaar, (-bare), incombustible.
onbreekbaar, (-bare), unbreakable.
onbroederlik, (-e), unbrotherly.
onbruik, disuse, desuetude; in – raak, fall into disuse, become obsolete.
onbruikbaar, (-bare), useless; naughty, disobedient; unemployable.
onbruikbaarheid, uselessness, unserviceableness; naughtiness, disobedience.
onbuigbaar, (-bare), unbendable, inflexible; rigid; fixed (laws).
onbuigsaam, (-same), inflexible, unbendable; unbending, rigid, firm.
onburgerlik, (-e), uncivic.
onbybels, (-e), unbiblical.
onchristelik, (-e), unchristian(ly).
onchristelikheid, unchristianliness.
ondank, ingratitude, thanklessness; – is wêreldsloon, the world pays with ingratitude.
ondankbaar, (-bare), ungrateful, thankless; unprofitable; 'n ondankbare taak, a thankless task.
ondankbaarheid, ingratitude.
ondanks, notwithstanding, in spite of; des –, in spite of this.
ondeelbaar, (-bare), indivisible; ondeelbare getal, prime number.
ondeelbaarheid, indivisibility.
ondenkbaar, (-bare), inconceivable.
onder, adv. below; die son is –, the sun is set; na –, below, downstairs, down; van –, underneath; from below; from the bottom; rooi van –, red underneath; van – af op, from below; from the bottom; ten – bring, conquer, vanquish, subjugate; – aan, at the foot of; at the bottom of: – bly, remain under; stay below.
onder, prep. under, underneath, beneath; among; amid(st); – die mense, among the people; – die diens, during the service; – al die digters, of all the poets; – andere, among others; among other things; – mekaar, among themselves; – ons (gesê) en geblewe, between ourselves; – die lees, while reading; – trane, in tears; – skoot, in range.
onderaan, at the foot of (the page); at the bottom of.
onderaannemer, sub-contractor.
onderaards, (-e), subterranean, underground.
onderadjudant, orderly sergeant.
onderadmiraal, vice-admiral.
onderafdeling, subsection; subdivision.
onderarm, forearm.
onderbaadjie, waistcoat.
onderbalk, architrave, epistyle.
onderbevelhebber, second in command.
onderbewus, (-te), subconscious.
onderbewussyn, subconscious mind.
onderbibliotekaris, assistant librarian.
onderbind, (onderge-), tie under, tie on.
onderbootsman, boatswain's mate.
onderbou, substructure, substruction.
onderbreek, (–), interrupt; break.
onderbreking, interruption; pausé.
onderbring, (onderge-), (provide) shelter (for), accommodate; store, house.
onderbroek, drawers, pair of underpants.
onderbuik, abdomen.
onderburgemeester, deputy-mayor.
onderdaan, (-dane), subject.
onderdak, shelter, home, accommodation.
onderdanig, (-e), submissive, humble, obedient, meek and mild.

onderdeel, (-dele), lower part; subdivision; part.
onderdeur, n. lower door.
onderdeur, underneath; – wees, fail.
onderdeurloer, (onderdeurge-), look (at) from under your eyebrows.
onderdeurloop, (onderdeurge-), pass under; be reprimanded; be caned.
onderdeurspring, (onderdeurge-), pass under; iemand –, trick a person.
onderdirekteur, assistant director.
onderdoen, (onderge-): vir iemand –, yield to, be no match for.
onderdompel, (onderge-), immerse.
onderdompeling, immersion, plunge.
onderdruk, (onderge-), press down (under), hold down.
onderdruk, (–), oppress; suppress (a rebellion); crush, quell; smother; repress.
onderdrukker, oppressor; suppressor.
onderdrukking, oppression; suppression.
onderduik, (onderge-), dive, plunge.
onderduims, (-e), underhand, clandestine.
onderduimsheid, underhand dealings.
onderent, (-e), lower end, bottom end.
ondergaan, (onderge-), set (the sun); sink, go down (a boat); die, perish.
ondergaan, (–), undergo, endure, suffer.
ondergang, setting (of the sun); ruin, destruction; fall; downfall; undoing.
ondergeskik, (-te), subordinate; inferior; subservient; –te sin, subordinate clause; – maak aan, make subservient to; subordinate to; van –te belang, of minor importance.
ondergeskikte, (-s), subordinate, inferior; underling.
ondergeskiktheid, subordination.
ondergetekende, (-s), undersigned.
ondergoed, underclothes, underwear.
ondergoewerneur, vice-governor.
ondergooi, (onderge-), throw down; put beneath (at the bottom).
ondergraaf, -grawe, (–), sap, undermine.
ondergrond, subsoil; basis, foundation.
ondergronds, (-e), underground, subterranean.
onderhandel, (–), negotiate (with), discuss terms, confer.
onderhandelaar, negotiator.
onderhandeling, (-e, -s), negotiation; discussion; parley; in – tree met, enter into negotiations with.
onderhands, (-e), underhand, clandestine; private.
onderhawig, (-e), present; die –e saak, the case in question.
onderhemp, vest, undershirt.
onderhewig, liable (to); subject (to).
onderhoofman, sub-chief, assistant leader.
onderhorig, (-e), dependent, subordinate; inferior (officer); belonging to.
onderhorige, (-s), subordinate.
onderhorigheid, dependence, subordination, dependency (country).
onderhou, (onderge-), hold down.
onderhou, (–), support, keep, provide for; keep up (studies); gebooie –, keep commandments; 'n huis, paaie –, keep a house, roads, in repair.
onderhoud, 1. interruption, maintenance, upkeep; voorsien in die – van, provide for.
onderhoud, (-e), 2. interview, conversation.
onderhoudend, (-e), amusing, entertaining, interesting.
onderhoudskoste, maintenance cost, cost of upkeep.
onderhoudstoelae, subsistence allowance.
onderhuid, cutis, derm.
onderhuids, subcutaneous, hypodermic.

onderhuur, sub-tenancy.
onderhuurder, sub-tenant.
onderinspekteur, sub-inspector.
onderkakebeen, lower jaw.
onderkanselier, vice-chancellor.
onderkant, b. lower side, bottom.
onderkant, adv. below.
onderken, **-kin**, double chin.
onderkerk, lower church; crypt.
onderklas, sub-class.
onderkleed, undergarment.
onderklere, underclothing, underwear.
onderkome, shelter, accommodation.
onderkoning, viceroy.
onderkoningskap, viceroyship.
onderkruip, (-), undersell, undercut; blackleg; swindle.
onderkruiper, underseller; scab, blackleg (during strike); swindler.
onderkruipery, underselling, undercutting; blacklegging; swindling.
onderkry, (onderge-), get under; master, overpower, get the better of.
onderlaag, lower layer, substratum.
onderlangs, prep. along the foot.
onderlangs, adv. lower down; along the lower parts; – **nat**, wet up to the knees; **hy is altyd so –**, he can never look a person straight in the eyes.
onderleg: **goed – wees in**, have a good grounding in.
onderling, (-e), a. mutual.
onderling, adv. mutually; among (between) them; – **verdeeld wees**, be divided among themselves.
onderlinne, underlinen.
onderlip, lower lip; **sy – hang**, he is down in the dumps; he is sulking (in a bad temper).
onderloop, (onderge-), be inundated.
onderluitenant, sublieutenant.
onderlyf, lower part of the body.
onderlyfie, camisole, (under-)bodice.
ondermaans, (-e) sublunary, earthly, mundane.
ondermyn, (-), undermine, sap.
ondermyning, sapping, undermining.
onderneem, (-), undertake, attempt.
ondernemend, (-e), enterprising.
onderneming, (-e, -s), undertaking, enterprise, venture, risky undertaking.
ondernemingsgees, enterprise.
onderoffisier, non-commissioned officer.
onderonsie, family gathering, meeting of intimate friends; private business.
onderpand, pledge, guarantee.
onderploe(g), (onderge-), plough down.
onderregent, vice-regent.
onderrig, n. instruction, tuition.
onderrig, (-), teach, instruct; inform.
onderrigting, instruction; information.
onderrok, underskirt, petticoat.
onderseeboot, **onderseër**, (-s), submarine.
ondersees, (-sese), submarine.
onderskat, (-), underestimate, underrate.
onderskatting, underestimation.
onderskei(e), distinguish; discriminate; make out, discern; **'n perd van 'n koei –**, tell a horse from a cow; **sig –**, distinguish oneself, excel; **sig – van ander**, differ from others.
onderskeid, difference; distinction; discrimination; **almal sonder –**, all (without exception), each and all; **jare van – (jare des –s)**, years of discretion; – **maak tussen**, distinguish between.
onderskeidelik, respectively; severally.
onderskeiding, (-e, -s), distinction, esteem, honour, respect.

onderskeidingsteken, mark of distinction, badge, medal.
onderskeidingsvermoë, discriminative power, insight, discernment.
onderskeie, a. different; various.
onderskep, (-), intercept.
onderskepping, interception.
onderskikkend, (-e), subordinate.
onderskikking, subordination.
onderskraag, (-), prop (up); support.
onderskrif, letter-press, caption; inscription; motto, legend; signature.
onderskryf, **-skrywe**, (-), endorse, sign, confirm, endorse (a statement).
onderskuif, **-skuiwe**, (onderge-), shove under; introduce secretly, foist on.
ondersoek, n. investigation, examination, inquiry; – **doen na iets**, inquire into a matter; **by nader –**, on closer examination.
ondersoek, (-), investigate, inquire (look) into; examine; test; make researches; search, probe.
ondersoeker, investigator; researcher.
ondersoeking, (-e, -s), investigation, research.
ondersoekingsreis, (-tog), (research-)expedition.
onderspit: **die – delf**, be defeated.
onderstaande, under-mentioned.
onderstand, relief, aid, help, assistance.
onderstandsgeld, subsidy, grant, dole.
onderstandswerk(e), relief-works.
onderste, (-s), n. the bottom one; dregs, sediment.
onderste, a. lowest, bottom(most), undermost.
onderstebo, upside down, inverted; in confusion (disorder), upset; untidy.
ondersteek, n. bedpan.
ondersteek, (onderge-), shove under.
onderstel, n. lower frame(work), undercarriage, bogie, chassis.
onderstel, (-), presume, suppose.
onderstelling, (-e, -s), presumption, supposition, hypothesis.
ondersteun, (-), support, assist, aid.
ondersteuner, (-s), supporter.
ondersteuning, support; relief.
ondersteuningsfonds, relief-fund; provident fund.
onderstreep, (-), underline.
onderstroom, undercurrent.
onderstuk, bottom part; base, support.
onderstut, (-), support, prop (up).
onderstuurman, second mate.
ondertand, lower tooth.
onderteken, (-), sign.
ondertekenaar, signatory; subscriber.
ondertekening, signature; signing.
ondertitel, sub-heading, sub-title.
ondertoe, lower down, downward(s), to the bottom; – **gaan**, go down; go downstairs.
ondertrou, (-), intermarry.
ondertrouery, intermarriage.
ondertussen, meanwhile, in the meantime.
Ondervelds, up-country, the interior.
Ondervelds, (-e), from up-country.
onderverdeel, (-), subdivide.
onderverdeling, subdivision.
onderverhuur, (-), sublet.
ondervind, (-), experience, meet with; undergo, feel.
ondervinding, (-e, -s), experience; – **is die beste leermeester**, experience is the best teacher.
ondervoed, a. underfed, undernourished.
ondervoed, (-), underfed.
ondervoeding, underfeeding, malnutrition.
ondervoorsitter, vice-president, vice-chairman.
ondervra(ag), (-), (cross-)question, interrogate, (cross)examine.
ondervraer, interrogator, examiner.

ondervraging, interrogation.
onderweg, on the way.
onderwêreld, infernal regions, underworld.
onderwerp, (-e), n. subject, topic, theme.
onderwerp, (–), subject, subdue; submit; **jou aan jou lot –**, resign yourself to your fate.
onderwerping, subjection; submission.
onderwerpsin, subject-clause.
onderworpe, submissive, resigned to one's fate; **– aan**, subject to.
onderworpenheid, submissiveness.
onderwyl, (mean)while.
onderwys, n. education; teaching, instruction, tuition; **laer, middelbare, hoër –**, primary, secondary, higher education; **– gee**, teach.
onderwys, (–), teach, instruct.
onderwysdepartement, department of education.
onderwyser, teacher, master.
onderwyseres, (lady) teacher, mistress.
onderwysersamp, teaching profession.
onderwysersertifikaat, teacher's certificate.
onderwysersvereniging, teachers' association.
onderwysing, instruction.
onderwyssake, educational matters.
onderwysstelsel, system of education.
onderwysvraagstuk, problem of education; educational problem.
onderwyswet, education-act.
ondeug, vice; mischievousness, roguery (rouguishness); rascal, rogue.
ondeugdelik, (-e), unsuited, unsound.
ondeugsaam, (-same), not virtuous.
ondeund, (-e), naughty; mischievous.
ondeundheid, naughtiness; roguishness.
ondeurdag, (-te), thoughtless, rash; shallow, ill-considered, harebrained.
ondeurdringbaar, (-bare), impenetrable; impervious.
ondeurdringbaarheid, impenetrability.
ondeurgrondelik, (-e), unfathomable, inscrutable, impenetrable.
ondeurgrondelikheid, inscrutability.
ondeursigtig, (-e), untransparent.
ondeurskynend, (-e), opaque.
ondeurskynendheid, opacity.
ondeurwaadbaar, (-bare), unfordable.
ondienlik, (-e), unserviceable.
ondiens, disservice, bad (ill) turn.
ondienstig, (-e), useless, not serviceable.
ondienstigheid, uselessness.
ondiep, shallow.
ondiepte, shoal, shallow; shallowness.
ondier, monster, beast, brute.
ondig, (-te), leaky, not watertight.
ondigterlik, (-e), unpoetical.
ondigtheid, leakiness.
onding, rubbish, worthless (monstrous) thing, monstrosity; absurdity.
ondoelmatig, (-e), unsuitable, not serviceable.
ondoelmatigheid, unsuitability.
ondoenlik, (-e), impossible; impracticable; **dis vir my – om te gaan**, I cannot possibly go.
ondoenlikheid, impracticability.
ondraagbaar, (-bare), too heavy to be carried; unwearable; unbearable.
ondraaglik, (-e), unbearable, unendurable, intolerable, insufferable.
ondrinkbaar, (-bare), undrinkable.
ondubbelsinnig, (-e), unequivocal, plain, clear, unambiguous, unmistakable.
onduidelik, (-e), indistinct; faint, dim; not clear; obscure.
onduidelikheid, indistinctness.
ondulasie, (-s), wave; undulation.
onduldbaar, (-bare), intolerable, unbearable.

onduleer, (ge-), wave (the hair).
onedel, (-e), ignoble, dishonourable, base, mean; **–e metale**, base metals.
oneens, at variance; **– met sigself wees**, be unable to make up one's mind, be undecided.
oneer, disgrace, dishonour; **iemand – aandoen**, disgrace a person.
oneerbaar, (-bare), improper, immodest.
oneerbaarheid, immodesty, indecency.
oneerbiedig, (-e), disrespectful, irreverent.
oneerbiedigheid, disrespectfulness.
oneerlik, (-e), dishonest, insincere, unfair, fraudulent.
oneerlikheid, dishonesty, insincerity.
oneersugtig, (-e), unambitious.
oneetbaar, (-bare), uneatable, inedible.
oneffe, uneven; rough, bumpy.
oneffenheid, (-hede), unevenness.
oneg, (-te), illegitimate (child); false, sham, spurious (document, coin), artificial, counterfeit; **–te breuk**, improper fraction.
onegaal, (-gale), **onegalig**, (-e), uneven; varying, inconsistent, changeable.
onegtelik, (-e), illegitimate.
onegtheid, illegitimacy; artificiality.
onei(g)enlik, (-e), metaphorical.
oneindig, (-e), a. endless, boundless.
oneindig, adv. infinitely, endlessly.
oneindige, n. infinite, infinity; **tot in die –**, indefinitely, ad infinitum.
oneindigheid, boundlessness; infinity.
onenig, at variance, divided.
onenigheid, (-hede), discord, strife, dispute, variance, dissension, quarrel; **in – lewe**, be continually quarrelling, live in enmity.
onergdenkend, (-e), unsuspecting.
onerkentlik, (-e), ungraceful.
onervare, inexperienced
onervarendheid, inexperience.
onewe, odd (number).
oneweredig, (-e), disproportionate.
oneweredigheid, disproportion.
onfatsoenlik, (-e), unmannerly, rude; improper, indecent, unbecoming.
onfatsoenlikheid, rudeness; indecency.
onfeilbaar, (-bare), infallible, unfailing.
onfeilbaarheid, infallibility.
onfris, (-se), not fresh; unwell.
ongaar, (–, gare), raw, uncooked; underdone, slackbaked; stupid.
ongaarne, reluctantly, unwillingly.
ongasvry, (-e), inhospitable.
ongeag, (-te), a. unnoticed, not respected.
ongeag, prep. in spite of, notwithstanding.
ongebaan, (-de), untrodden, unbeaten.
ongebleek, **ongebleik**, (-te), unbleached.
ongeblus, (-te), unslaked (lime); unquenched (fire).
ongeboei(d), (-de), unchained, unfettered, not handcuffed.
ongeboet, (-e), unexpiated.
ongebonde, unbound; free, unrestrained, loose, licentious; **– styl**, prose.
ongebondenheid, freedom; licentiousness.
ongebordurd(d), (-de), unembroidered.
ongebore, unborn.
ongebou(d), (-de), unbuilt.
ongebrand, (-e), unburnt; unroasted.
ongebreidel(d), (-de), unbridled.
ongebroke, unbroken.
ongebruik, (-te), unused.
ongebruiklik, (-e), uncommon, unusual.
ongedaan, (-dane), undone; **dade – maak**, undo (past) actions.
ongedagteken, **ongedateer**, (-de), undated.

ongedeer(d), unscathed, unharmed.
ongedek, (-te), uncovered; unhatched (roof); not laid (table); uninsured.
ongedierte(s), vermin; wild beasts.
ongedoop, (-te), unchristened.
ongedop, (-te), unshelled (peas, beans).
ongedroom, (-de), undreamt of.
ongeduld, impatience.
ongeduldig, (-e), impatient.
ongeduldigheid, impatience.
ongedurig, (-e), restless, fidgety; fickle.
ongedurigheid, restlessness; fickleness.
ongedwonge, unrestrained, natural, unforced, spontaneous, easy.
ongeëer(d), (-de), unhonoured.
ongeërg, (-de), nonchalant, casual, cool, unmoved, calm, unconcerned.
ongeëwenaard, (-e), unequalled, unrivalled, unparalleled, unmatched.
ongefrankeer, (-de), unstamped.
ongegeneer(d), (-e), unceremonious; rude.
ongegis, (-te), unfermented.
ongegrond, (-e), unfounded, ungrounded.
ongeheilig, (-de), unhallowed, unsanctified.
ongehinder(d), (-de), undisturbed, unhindered, unmolested; unchecked.
ongehoor(d), (-de), unheard, not heard; unprecedented, unheard of.
ongehoorsaam, (-same), disobedient.
ongehoorsaamheid, disobedience.
ongehuud, (-hude), unmarried.
ongekam, (-de), uncombed, unkempt.
ongekap, (-te), unchopped.
ongekend, (-e), unknown; unparalleled.
ongeklee(d), (-klede), unclothed, undressed; in undress, in dishabille.
ongeknak, (-te), unbroken; unimpaired.
ongekneus, (-de), unbruised.
ongekook, (-te), uncooked, unboiled.
ongekroon, (-de), uncrowned.
ongekunsteld, (-e), simple, plain, unaffected, natural, artless.
ongekunsteldheid, simplicity.
ongekwes, (-te), unwounded, unhurt.
ongelaai, (-de), unloaded; uncharged.
ongeldig, (-e), invalid; – **verklaar**, declare invalid, annul, declare null and void.
ongeldigheid, invalidity.
ongeldigverklaring, annulment.
ongeleë, inconvenient, inopportune.
ongeleentheid, inconvenience; **iemand in (die) – bring**, inconvenience a person; put one in a fix.
ongeleer(d), (-de), unlearned (unlearnt); uneducated, illiterate; untrained, unbroken, not broken in.
ongeleerdheid, illiteracy, ignorance.
ongelees, (-lese), unread.
ongeletter(d), (-de), not marked (unmarked); uneducated, illiterate.
ongeloof, unbelief, disbelief.
ongeloofbaar, (-bare), **ongelooflik**, (-e), incredible, unbelievable.
ongeloofbaarheid, incredibility.
ongeloofwaardig, (-e), unreliable.
ongelouter(d), (-de), unpurified.
ongelowig, (-e), unbelieving, sceptical; incredulous.
ongelowige, (-s), unbeliever; infidel.
ongelowigheid, incredulity; scepticism.
ongeluk, (-ke), accident, mishap; misfortune; ill-luck; unhappiness; **die – wou dat (soos die – dit wou hê)**, as ill-luck would have it; **vir die – gebore wees**, be unlucky, be born under an evil star; **'n – kom nooit alleen nie**, it never rains but it pours, misfortunes never come singly; **per (by) –**, by accident, accidentally; **'n – kry (hê)**, meet with an accident; **by 'n – is daar altyd 'n geluk**, it is an ill wind that blows nobody good; **'n – begaan (aan iemand)**, injure (hurt, kill) a person; **wat die – wil jy hê?**, what the dickens (deuce, devil) do you want?; **die – sal jou haal**, there will be the devil to pay; **dit was sy –**, that was his misfortune (undoing); **die – is ek dat . . .**, unfortunately I . . .
ongelukkig, (-e), unhappy; unfortunate; unlucky.
ongelukkig, adv. unfortunately.
ongelukkigerwyse, unfortunately.
ongeluksbode, bringer of bad news.
ongeluksdag, unlucky day.
ongelukskind, unlucky person.
ongeluksvoël, bird of ill omen; unlucky person.
ongelyk, n. wrong; – **hê**, be in the wrong; **iemand – gee (iemand in die – stel)**, put a person in the wrong.
ongelyk, (-e), a. not level (smooth); uneven, unequal; not uniform; inconsistent; –**e getal**, odd number.
ongelykbenig, (-e), scalene (triangle).
ongelykheid, unevenness; bumpiness (of road) inequality, difference.
ongelykmatig, (-e), not uniform; uneven (temper, etc.); unequal; variable.
ongelyksoortig, (-e), dissimilar, heterogeneous.
ongelyksoortigheid, dissimilarity.
ongelyksydig, (-e), inequilateral.
ongelykvormig, (-e), dissimilar.
ongelykvormigheid, dissimilarity.
ongelyn, (-de), unglued.
ongelyn, (-de), unruled; –**de papier**, unruled (plain) paper.
ongemaal, (-de), unground.
ongemak, (-ke), discomfort, inconvenience.
ongemaklik, (-e), uncomfortable, difficult, troublesome.
ongemaklikheid, uncomfortableness.
ongemanierd, (-e), unmannerly, rude.
ongemanierdheid, unmannerliness.
ongematig, (-de), intemperate, immoderate, excessive, ultra.
ongematigheid, intemperance.
ongemeen, (-mene), uncommon, unusual.
ongemeld, (-e), not mentioned; unannounced.
ongemeng, (-de), unmixed.
ongemerk, (-te), unmarked; unnoticed, unperceived.
ongemeubileer(d), (-de), unfurnished.
ongemoei(d), (-de), undisturbed, untroubled.
ongemotiveer(d), (-de), not motivated, unwarranted, groundless; unsupported by reasons.
ongemunt, (-e), uncoined, unminted.
ongenaakbaar, (-bare), inaccessible; unapproachable (person).
ongenade, disfavour, displeasure; disgrace; **in – val**, be dismissed from favour; **in – wees (by iemand)**, not be in a person's good graces.
ongenadig, (-e), unmerciful, cruel, merciless; severe, violent.
ongeneë, disinclined, unwilling.
ongeneentheid, disinclination.
ongenees, (-nese), uncured.
ongeneesbaar, (-bare), incurable.
ongeneeslik, (-e), incurable, beyond (past) recovery.
ongeneeslikheid, incurability.
ongeneig, (-de), disinclined.
ongenietbaar, (-bare), unenjoyable, unpalatable.

ongenoeë, displeasure; **in – lewe met**, be continually at variance with.
ongenoeglik, (-e), unpleasant.
ongenoegsaam, (-same), insufficient.
ongenooi, (-de), uninvited, unasked; unwelcome; **–de gaste moet agter die deur staan**, come uninvited and you stay unserved.
ongeoefen(d), (-de), unpractised, inexperienced, untrained; out of practice.
ongeoefendheid, inexperience, want (lack) of practice (training).
ongeoorloof, (-de), forbidden, unlawful, illicit, not permitted (allowed).
ongeopenbaar, (de), unrevealed.
ongeopen(d), (-de), unopened.
ongeorden(d), unarranged; unordained.
ongeorganiseer(d), (-de), unorganized.
ongepas, (-te), improper, unbecoming, unseemly, indecorous.
ongepastheid, impropriety, unseemliness.
ongepermitteer(d), unpermitted.
ongeplak, (-te), unpapered (walls); unpasted, unmounted (stamps, etc.).
ongeplavei, (-de), unpaved.
ongepleister, (-de), unplastered.
ongeploeg, (-de), unploughed.
ongepoets, (-te), rude, ill-mannered.
ongepolys, (-te), unpolished.
ongerade, inadvisable.
ongereeld, (-e), irregular; confused, unregulated; rough-and-tumble.
ongereeldheid, (-hede), irregularity.
ongeregtig, (-e), 1. unjust, wicked.
ongeregtig, (-de), 2. unwarranted; **– tot**, not entitled to.
ongeregtigheid, unrighteousness, wickedness, iniquity; injustice.
ongereken(d), not taken into account.
ongerekend, (-e), careless; casual.
ongerep, (-te), untouched; pure, spotless; **–te sneeu, woud**, virgin snow, forest.
ongerief, inconvenience, discomfort; trouble; **iemand – veroorsaak**, put a person to inconvenience.
ongerieflik, (-e), inconvenient; uncomfortable.
ongerieflikheid, inconvenience.
ongeroer(d), (-de), unstirred; unmoved.
ongerus, (-te), anxious, uneasy; **– wees oor**, be worried about.
ongerustheid, anxiety, uneasiness, worry.
ongerymd, (-e), absurd, ridiculous, silly.
ongerymdheid, absurdity.
ongesê, unsaid.
ongeseël, (-de), unsealed; unstamped.
ongeseglik, (-e), refractory, unmanageable, disobedient, naughty, intractable.
ongesellig, (-e), unsociable (person); dull, gloomy, cheerless, dreary (place).
ongesien, unseen.
ongesiens, without having seen.
ongesif, (-te), unsifted.
ongeskeer, (-de), unshaven (chin); unshorn (sheep).
ongeskeie, unseparated, unparted.
ongeskik, (-te), unsuited, unfit, unsuitable, ill-mannered, rude; unmanageable, untamed (horse).
ongeskiktheid, unfitness, unsuitability; rudeness, unmanageableness.
ongeskil, (-de), unpeeled, unpared.
ongeskoei, (-de), unshod.
ongeskonde, undamaged, intact.
ongeskool, (-de), unskilled, untrained.
ongeskrewe, unwritten.
ongesog, (-te), natural, easy.

ongesond, (-e), unhealthy; insalubrious (climate); injurious to health; unwholesome (food); sickly (complexion); **—e lektuur**, harmful literature.
ongesondheid, ill-health, unhealthiness; insalubrity; unwholesomeness.
ongesout, (-e), unsalted (also fig.); not hardened; uninitiated.
ongestadig, (-e), inconstant, fickle, unsteady; unsettled (weather).
ongestadigheid, inconstancy, changeableness; unsettled state.
ongesteld, (-e), indisposed, unwell.
ongesteldheid, indisposition.
ongestem, (-de), untuned.
ongestempel, (-de), unstamped.
ongesteur(d), -stoor(d), (-de), undisturbed, uninterrupted.
ongestil, (-de), unappeased.
ongestoor(d), vide **ongesteur(d)**.
ongestraf, (-te), unpunished.
ongestyf, (-de), unstarched.
ongesuur, (-de), unleavened.
ongeteken(d), (-de), anonymous, unsigned.
ongetem, (-de), untamed.
ongetrou, (-e), unfaithful, disloyal.
ongetroud, (-e), unmarried, single.
ongetwyfeld, (-e), undoubted.
ongetwyfeld, adv. undoubtedly.
ongeval, (-le), accident, mishap.
ongevalleversekering, insurance against accidents, accident-insurance.
ongevallewet, Employers' Liability Act.
ongevee(g), (-de), unswept.
ongeveer, about, nearly; approximately.
ongeveins, (-de), unfeigned, sincere.
ongeveinsdheid, sincerity, genuineness.
ongevlek, (-te), spotless, unstained.
ongevoeglik, (-e), unbecoming, indecent.
ongevoelig, (-e), insensitive; insensible; impassive; unfeeling, cruel.
ongevoer, (-de), unlined; unfed.
ongevorm(d), (-de), unformed.
ongevra(ag), (-de), unasked, uninvited; uncalled for, unasked for.
ongewaardeer, (-de), unappreciated, unvalued; unestimated.
ongewapen(d), (-de), unarmed.
ongewas, (-te), unwashed; unshuffled.
ongewend, (-e), unaccustomed.
ongewens, (-te), unwished for, undesirable.
ongewerwel(d), (-de), invertebrate; **–de diere**, invertebrates (invertebrata).
ongewettig, (-de), unauthorized; unwarranted.
ongewild, (-e), unintentional; unpopular.
ongewillig, (-e), unwilling; obstinate.
ongewis, (-se), uncertain.
ongewond, (-e), unwounded.
ongewoon, (-wone), uncommon, unusual; unaccustomed, unfamiliar; **niks –s**, nothing unusual (out of the common).
ongewoond, unaccustomed.
ongewoonheid, unusualness.
ongewraak, (-te), unchallenged.
ongewyd, (-e), unhallowed, unconsecrated, profane; secular (music).
ongewysig, (-de), unmodified, unaltered.
ongoddelik, (-e), ungodly.
ongodsdienstig, (-e), irreligious.
ongodsdienstigheid, irreligion.
ongodvrugtig, (-e), impious, ungodly.
ongrammatikaal, (-kale), ungrammatical.
ongrondwettig, (-e), unconstitutional.
ongrondwettigheid, unconstitutionality.
onguns, disfavour.

ongunstig, (-e), unfavourable; adverse.
onguur, repulsive; coarse, rude; inclement (weather), sinister.
onhandelbaar, (-bare), unmanageable.
onhandelbaarheid, intractability.
onhandig, (-e), clumsy, awkward.
onhandigheid, clumsiness, awkwardness, unwieldiness.
onharmonies, (-e), inharmonious.
onhartlik, (-e), cold, not cordial.
onhebbelik, (-e), ill-mannered, rude, unruly (child); huge (piece).
onheelbaar, (-bare), incurable.
onheil, calamity, disaster, evil.
onheilig, (-e), unholy, wicked; profane.
onheilsaam, (-same), unwholesome, evil.
onheilsbode, bringer of bad news.
onheilsdag, unlucky day, fatal day.
onheilspellend, (-e), ominous.
onheilstigter, mischief-maker.
onherbergsaam, (-same), inhospitable.
onherbergsaamheid, inhospitality.
onherkenbaar, (-bare), unrecognisable.
onherleibaar, (-bare), irreducible.
onherleibaarheid, irreducibility.
onherroepbaar, (-bare), onherroeplik, (-e), irrevocable, unalterable.
onherroepbaarheid, onherroeplikheid, irrevocability.
onherroeplik, irrevocably; – **verby,** beyond recall.
onherstelbaar, (-bare), irreparable, irretrievable, irremediable.
onheuglik, (-e), immemorial; **sedert -e tye,** from time immemorial.
onhigiënies, (-e), unhygienic.
onhistories, (-e), unhistorical.
onhoflik, (-e), discourteous, uncivil.
onhoorbaar, (-bare), inaudible.
onhou(d)baar, (-bare), untenable.
onhou(d)baarheid, untenability.
onhuislik, (-e), not domestic, unhomely.
oniks, (-e), onyx.
oningebonde, unbound.
oningeënt, (-e), unvaccinated.
oningenaai(d), (-de), in sheets.
oningevul(d), (-de), not filled in, blank.
oningewy(d), (-de), not inaugurated, unconsecrated (church); uninitiated.
oninskiklik, (-e), unaccommodating.
onjuis, (-te), incorrect, inaccurate, false.
onjuistheid, incorrectness, erroneousness, inaccuracy; error, mistake.
onkant, off-side.
onkenbaar, (-bare), unknowable; unrecognisable.
onkerks, (-e), not devoted to the church, not churchy, not churchgoing.
onkies, (-e), immodest, indecent, improper, indelicate.
onkinderlik, (-e), unchildlike.
onklaar, unprepared, unfinished; out of order; – **(raak) trap,** kick over the traces; – **trap (in sy argumente),** become confused in his arguments.
onkleurspan, motley-team.
onknap: nie – nie, not incapable.
onkoste, expenses, charges.
onkosterekening, note of charges.
onkreukbaar, (-bare), unimpeachable.
onkreukbaarheid, unimpeachableness, integrity; uprightness.
onkruid, weeds; good-for-nothing; rascal; – **vergaan nie,** ill weeds grow apace.
onkuis, (-e), unchaste, impure.
onkuisheid, unchastity.
onkunde, ignorance.
onkundig, (-e), ignorant.

onkundigheid, ignorance.
onkwe(t)sbaar, (-bare), invulnerable.
onkwe(t)sbaarheid, invulnerability.
onlangs, (-e), a. recent.
onlangs, adv. recently, lately.
onledig: sig – hou met, busy oneself with, be busy with (in, at).
onleesbaar, (-bare), illegible (handwriting); unreadable (book).
onlesbaar, (-bare), unquenchable.
onliggaamlik, (-e), incorporeal.
onloënbaar, onlogenbaar, (-bare), undeniable, indisputable.
onlogies, (-e), illogical.
onlosbaar, (-bare), unredeemable.
onlus, (-te), dislike, aversion; listlessness; **-te,** riots, disturbances.
onlustig, (-e), listless, spiritless, dull.
onmaatskaplik, (-e), asocial; antisocial.
onmag, inability, impotence; swoon.
onmagtig, (-e), powerless; unable.
onmanierlik, (-e), unmannerly, rude.
onmanlik, (-e), unmanly.
onmatig, (-e), immoderate, intemperate, excessive; huge, unusually large.
onmatigheid, immoderateness.
onme(d)edeelsaam, (-same), stingy, miserly; uncommunicative.
onme(d)edoënd, -dogend, (-e), merciless.
onme(d)edoëndheid, (-dogendheid), ruthlessness, mercilessness.
onmeetbaar, (-bare), immeasurable.
onmeetbaarheid, immeasurability.
onmeetlik, (-e), immense, immeasurable.
onmens, (-e), monster, brute.
onmenslik, (-e), inhuman, brutal, cruel.
onmenslikheid, inhumanity, brutality.
onmerkbaar, (-bare), unnoticeable.
onmetodies, (-e), unmethodical.
onmiddellik, (-e), a. immediate, direct.
onmiddellik, adv. immediately, directly.
onmin, variance, discord, strife; **in – lewe,** be continually at variance, not get on well together.
onmisbaar, (-bare), indispensable, essential, necessary.
onmisbaarheid, indispensability.
onmiskenbaar, (-bare), unmistakable.
onmoederlik, (-e), unmotherly.
onmondig, (-e), under age; – **wees,** be under age, be a minor; **'n -e,** a minor.
onmondigheid, minority; pupil(l)age.
onmooglik, onmoontlik, (-e), a. impossible.
onmooglik, onmoontlik, adv. not possibly; **ek kan – langer bly,** I cannot possibly stay longer.
onmooglikheid, onmoontlikheid, impossibility.
onmusikaal, (-kale), unmusical.
onnadenkend, (-e), unthinking, inconsiderate, thoughtless, frivolous.
onnaspeurbaar, (-bare), onnaspeurlik, (-e), inscrutable, unsearchable.
onnatuurlik, (-e), unnatural; artificial, forced, affected.
onnatuurlikheid, unnaturalness.
onnavolgbaar, (-bare), inimitable.
onneembaar, (-bare), impregnable.
onnodig, (-e), unnecessary, needless.
onnoembaar, (-bare), unmentionable; unnamable, inexpressible; countless.
onnoemlik, (-e), unnamable; countless.
onnosel, (-e), stupid, silly; innocent.
onnoselheid, stupidity, silliness.
onnoukeurig, (-e), inaccurate, inexact.
onnoukeurigheid, inaccuracy, inexactitude (inexactness).

onnut, (-te), n. good-for-nothing, rogue.
onnut, (-te), a. useless, good-for-nothing.
onnutsig, (-e), naughty, mischievous.
onnutsigheid, naughtiness, disobedience.
onnuttig, (-e), useless.
onomatopee, (-peë), onomatopoeia.
onomatopeïes, onomatopoeic.
onomkoopbaar, (-bare), incorruptible.
onomkoopbaarheid, incorruptibility.
onomstootlik, (-e), irrefutable.
onomwonde, a. plain (truth), frank.
onomwonde, adv. plainly, frankly, without beating about the bush.
ononderbroke, uninterrupted; non-stop.
onontbeerlik, (-e), indispensable.
onontbindbaar, (-bare), indissoluble.
onontgin, onontgonne, uncultivated; unexploited; vide **ontgin**.
onontkombaar, (-bare), unescapable.
onontplofbaar, (-bare), inexplosive.
onontsyferbaar, (-bare), undecipherable.
onontvanklik, (-e), impervious (to), irresponsive (to).
onontvlambaar, (-bare), non-inflammable, uninflammable.
onontwerpbaar, (-bare), inextricable.
onontwikkeld, (-e), undeveloped; uneducated, illiterate.
onooglik, (-e), unsightly, unattractive.
onoorbrugbaar, (-bare), unbridgeable.
onoordeelkundig, (-e), injudicious.
onoorganklik, (-e), intransitive.
onoorkoomlik, (-e), insuperable, insurmountable.
onoorreedbaar, (-bare), unconvincible.
onoortrefbaar, (-bare), unsurpassable.
onoortroffe, unsurpassed.
onoortuigbaar, (-bare), unconvincible.
onoorwinlik, (-e), invincible, unconquerable.
onoorwonne, unconquered.
onopgeëis, (-te), unclaimed.
onopgehelderd(d), (-de), not cleared up.
onopgelos, (-te), undissolved, unsolved.
onopgemaak, (-te), not done; unmade (bed); not made up, not compiled; untrimmed, plain (hat).
onopgemerk, (-te), unnoticed.
onopgeplak, (-te), unmounted; not pasted (glued) on.
onopgesmuk, (-te), unadorned, unornamented; plain (truth).
onopgevoed, (-e), uneducated; ill-bred.
onophoudelik, (-e), incessant, unceasing.
onoplettend, (-e), inattentive.
onoplosbaar, (-bare), insoluble (salt, problem); unsolvable (problem).
onoplosbaarheid, insolubility.
onopmerksaam, (-same), unobservant.
onopreg, (-te), insincere.
onopsetlik, (-e), unintentional.
onordelik, (-e), disorderly, unruly.
onordelikheid, disorderliness, unruliness.
onordentlik, (-e), indecent, unmannerly.
onpaar, not a pair, odd; – skoene, odd shoes; – wees, not match, not be a pair.
onparlementêr, (-e), unparliamentary.
onpartydig, (-e), impartial, fair.
onpas: te –, out of season.
onpaslik, (-e), unsuitable, out of place.
onpassabel, (-e), impassable, unfordable.
onpedagogies, (-e), unpedagogical.
onpeilbaar, (-bare), unfathomable.
onpersoonlik, (-e), impersonal.
onplesierig, (-e), unpleasant.
onpoëties, (-e), unpoetical.
onprakties, (-e), unpractical.

onraad, trouble, danger; – bespeur (merk), become suspicious; daar is –, there is something wrong.
onraadsaam, (-same), unadvisable.
onredbaar, (-bare), irretrievable, beyond hope.
onredelik, (-e), unreasonable.
onreëlmatig, (-e), irregular.
onreëlmatigheid, (-hede), irregularity.
onreg, injustice, wrong; ten –te, wrongly, unjustly; – pleeg, do wrong; iemand – aandoen, do a person an injustice, wrong a person.
onregmatig, (-e), unlawful, illegal.
onregsinnig, (-e), heterodox.
onregverdig, (-e), unfair, unjust; unrighteous; wrongful (action).
onregverdigheid, (-hede), injustice.
onrein, (-e), unclean, impure.
onreinheid, uncleanness, impurity.
onridderlik, (-e), unchivalrous.
onroerend, (-e), immovable; –e goed, immovable property, immovables.
onrus, unrest, disturbance; anxiety; restlessness; balance, fly (of watch).
onrusbarend, (-e), alarming, disquieting.
onrusstoker, mischief-maker, agitator.
onrustig, (-e), restless; fidgety; uneasy, agitated, anxious, concerned.
onrustigheid, restlessness; anxiety.
onryp, unripe (lit. & fig.); immature.
onrypheid, unripeness; immaturity.
ons (-e), n. ounce.
ons, pers. pron. we, us.
ons, poss. pron. our; – s'n, ours.
onsag, (-te), not soft, hard; harsh.
onsalig, (-e), wretched, unholy, wicked.
onsamehangend, (-e), disconnected, disjointed; incoherent.
onsamehangendheid, disconnectedness.
onsedelik, (-e), immoral.
onsedelikheid, immorality.
onsedig, (-e), immodest.
onsedigheid, immodesty.
onseker(e), n. uncertainty, doubt; in die –e wees (verkeer), be in doubt.
onseker, (–, -e), a. uncertain, doubtful; unsteady, shaky, problematical; unsettled; unsafe.
onsekerheid, uncertainty; doubt.
onselfstandig, (-e), dependent.
onselfsugtig, (-e), unselfish.
onselfsugtigheid, unselfishness.
ons(e)-liewe-heersbesie, ladybird.
Onse Vader, the Lord's Prayer.
onsienlik, (-e), invisible.
onsierlik, (-e), inelegant, ungraceful.
onsigbaar, (-bare), invisible.
onsigbaarheid, invisibility.
onsimmetries, (-e), unsymmetrical.
onsimpatiek, (-e), unsympathetic.
onsin, nonsense, rubbish.
onsindelik, (-e), dirty, uncleanly.
onsindelikheid, dirtiness, uncleanliness.
onsinnig, (-e), foolish, absurd, idiotic.
onsinnigheid, (-hede), absurdity, nonsense, foolishness.
onskadelik, (-e), harmless, not injurious, innocuous; – maak, render harmless.
onskadelikheid, harmlessness.
onskaplik, (-e), unreasonable.
onskatbaar, (-bare), inestimable, invaluable.
onskei(d)baar, (-bare), inseparable.
onskei(d)baarheid, inseparability.
onskendbaar, (-bare), inviolable.
onskoon, (-skone), unbeautiful.
onskriftuurlik, (-e), unscriptural.

onskuld, innocence; **ek was my hande in –**, I wash my hands of it.
onskuldig, (-e), innocent, guiltless; inoffensive unoffending; harmless.
onslytbaar, (-bare), that cannot wear away (down, out).
onsmaaklik, (-e), unsavoury, unpalatable; unpleasant.
onsmaaklikheid, unsavouriness, etc.
onsmeltbaar, (-bare), infusible.
onstaatkundig, (-e), unstatesmanlike.
onstandvastig, (-e), inconstant, fickle, changeable, unstable.
onstandvastigheid, inconstancy.
onsterflik, (-e), immortal; undying.
onsterflikheid, immortality.
onstigtelik, (-e), unedifying, offensive.
onstigtelikheid, offensiveness.
onstoflik, (-e), incorporeal, spiritual.
onstuimig, (-e), stormy, rough, violent, boisterous; impetuous (person); vehement; dashing.
onstuimigheid, storminess, boisterousness; impetuosity; vehemence.
onsuiwer, (-, -e), impure; unrefined; untrue; flat, false (note); faulty; inexact; **–(e) leer**, unsound (fallacious) doctrine.
onsuiwerheid, (-hede), impurity.
onsydig, (-e), neutral (state), impartial, neuter (gender); neutral (bot.).
onsydigheid, neutrality, impartiality.
ontaalkundig, (-e), ungrammatical, unphilological.
ontaard, (-e), a. degenerate.
ontaard, (-), degenerate, deteriorate.
ontaardheid, degeneracy.
ontaarding, degeneration, deterioration.
ontak(t)vol, (le-), tactless.
ontasbaar, (-bare), intangible, impalpable.
ontasbaarheid, impalpability.
ontbeer, (-), lack, miss, do without.
ontbeerlik, (-e), dispensable.
ontbering, (-e, -s), want, privation.
ontbied, (-), summon, send for.
ontbind, (-), untie, undo; disband; dissolve; decompose; resolve (forces); **in faktore –**, factorize.
ontbinding, untying; disbandment; dissolution; decomposition; resolution (of forces); **tot – oorgaan**, decay, decompose.
ontbloot, (-blote), a. naked, bare; **– van**, devoid of, without; **van alle grond –**, altogether unfounded.
ontbloot, (-), uncover (head), bare, unsheathe (sword); reveal.
ontbloting, uncovering; revealing; stripping; exposure.
ontboesem, (-), unbosom, unburden.
ontboeseming, (-e, -s), effusion.
ontbos, (-), deforest (dis(af)forest).
ontbossing, dis(af)forestation.
ontbrand, (-), take fire, burst into flame, ignite; break out (of war); **in toorn –**, fly into a rage (passion).
ontbrandbaar, (-bare), combustible, ignitable; inflammable.
ontbranding, ignition; stirring up.
ontbreek, (-), be wanting, lack; **wie – nog?**, who is missing?; **die tyd – my**, I have not got the time; **woorde – my om . . .**, words fail me to . . .; **aan moed – dit hom nie**, he is not lacking in courage.
ontbreidel, (-), unbridle.
ontbyt, n. breakfast.
ontdaan, upset; divested.
ontdek, (-), discover; find out, detect.

ontdekker, (-s), discover.
ontdekking, (-e, -s), discovery, detection, revelation.
ontdekkingsreis, -tog, travel(s), voyage (of discovery), exploring-trip.
ontdekkingsreisiger, explorer.
ontdoen, (-), remove, strip (off), take off.
ontdooi, (-), thaw; unbend.
ontduik, (-), dodge; escape from, evade; elude.
ontduiking, (-e, -s), eluding, evasion.
onteenseglik, (-e), unquestionable.
onteer, (-), dishonour; violate, rape.
onteien, (-), expropriate; dispossess.
onteiening, expropriation; dispossession.
onteieningswet, expropriation-act.
ontelbaar, (-bare), countless, innumerable, numberless.
ontembaar, (-bare), untamable, indomitable; wild, violent, ungovernable.
onterf, **-erwe**, (-), disinherit.
onterwing, disinheritance.
ontevrede, discontented, dissatisfied.
ontevredenheid, discontentedness, discontentment, dissatisfaction.
ontferm, (-): **sig – oor**, take pity on.
ontferming, pity, commiseration.
ontfutsel, (-): **iemand iets –**, filch something from somebody.
ontgaan, (-), escape, elude, evade; **dit het (is) my –**, it has slipped my memory, I have forgotten it.
ontgeld(e), (-): **dit –**, pay (suffer) for it.
ontgin, (-), bring under cultivation, reclaim, break up; exploit, work (mine).
ontginning, reclaiming; exploitation.
ontglip, (-), slip from; escape; **hy het my –**, he has given me the slip; he has eluded my grasp; **die woord het my –**, the word slipped from my tongue.
ontgloei, (-), start to glow; burn (glow).
ontgogel, **-goël**, (-), disillusion.
ontgogeling, **-goëling**, disillusionment.
ontgonne, reclaimed, cultivated.
ontgrendel, (-), unbolt.
ontgroei, (-), outgrow; grow faster.
ontgroen, (-), initiate (a new student).
ontgroening, initiation.
onthaal, (-hale), n. entertainment; treat; regale; reception (lit. & fig.).
onthaal, (-), entertain, treat.
onthals, (-), behead.
ontharing, depilation.
ontharingsmiddel, depilatory.
onthef, (-): **– van**, exempt (free) from; relieve; **iemand van 'n amp –**, discharge a person.
ontheffing, exemption, exoneration; discharge, dismissal.
ontheilig, (-), desecrate, profane.
ontheiliging, desecration, profanation.
onthoof, (-), behead, decapitate.
onthoofding, beheading; decapitation.
onthou, n. remembering; **goed (sleg) van – wees**, have a good (bad) memory.
onthou, (-), withhold from, keep from; remember, bear in mind; **sig van stemming –**, refrain from voting; **iemand iets help –**, remind a person of something.
onthoudend, (-e), abstemious.
onthouding, abstinence, abstemiousness; refraining, withholding; abstention.
onthouer, (-s), abstainer.
onthul, (-), unveil; reveal, disclose.
onthulling, (-e, -s), unveiling; revelation, disclosure.
onthuts, (-te), a. upset, perplexed.

onthuts 214 **ontsien**

onthuts, (-), disconcert, bewilder.
ontken, (-), deny.
ontkennend, (-e), a. negative.
ontkennend, adv. negatively, in the negative.
ontkenning, (-e, -s), denial, negation; **die dubbele** –, the double negative.
ontketen, (-), unchain.
ontkiem, (-), germinate.
ontkieming, germination.
ontklee(d), (-), undress.
ontknoop, (-), unbutton; undo the knots; unravel, disentangle.
ontknoping, (-e, -s), unbuttoning; denouement; unravelling of the plot.
ontkom, (-), escape.
ontkoming, (-e, -s), escape.
ontkoppel, (-), unleash; declutch.
ontkroon, (-), discrown, depose (king).
ontkurk, (-), uncork.
ontlaai, (-), unload; discharge.
ontlading, unloading; discharge.
ontlas, (-), relieve; unburden; **sig** –, discharge itself (oneself); evacuate the bowels, relieve nature.
ontlasting, relief; discharge; evacuation of the bowels, motion; faeces, stool.
ontleder, (-s), dissector; analyser.
ontleding, (-e, -s), analysis (of sentences); parsing (of words); dissection.
ontleed, (-), dissect; analyse; parse.
ontleedkamer, dissecting-room.
ontleedkunde, anatomy.
ontleedmes, dissecting-knife, scalpel.
ontleedtafel, dissecting-table.
ontleen, (-): – **aan,** borrow from; derive from; –**de woorde,** loan-words.
ontlening, (-e, -s), borrowing; derivation, deriving; adoption.
ontlok, (-), draw out, evoke, elicit.
ontloop, (-), run away from, evade, escape, elude; avoid.
ontluik, (-), open; expand; bud.
ontluikend, (-e), opening; budding (author, etc.); dawning, nascent.
ontluiking, opening; budding, developing.
ontluis, (-), delouse.
ontluister, (-), tarnish.
ontmaag(d), (-), ravish, deflower, rape.
ontman, (-), castrate; weaken.
ontmanning, castration, emasculation.
ontmantel, (-), dismantle.
ontmasker, (-), unmask, expose.
ontmaskering, exposure, revelation.
ontmoedig, (-), discourage, dishearten.
ontmoediging, discouragement.
ontmoet, (-), meet (with); encounter; come across (a person); **lyne** –, lines meet; **iemand dikwels** –, see a person often.
ontmoeting, (-e, -s), meeting; encounter; adventure; accident.
ontneem, (-), deprive (of), take away.
ontnugter, (-), (make) sober; disillusion, disenchant.
ontnugtering, disillusionment.
ontoeganklik, (-e), inaccessible, inapproachable, unapproachable.
ontoeganklikheid, inaccessibility.
ontoegewend, (-e), unaccommodating, disobliging, unyielding, unpliable.
ontoegewendheid, unyieldingness.
ontoelaatbaar, (-bare), inadmissible.
ontoepaslik, (-e), inapplicable; irrelevant.
ontoereikend, (-e), insufficient, inadequate, deficient, not enough.

ontoerekenbaar, (-bare), not imputable (to); irresponsible (for something); **hy is** –, he is not answerable for his actions.
ontoeskietlik, (-e), vide **ontoegewend**.
ontologie, ontology.
ontologies, (-e), ontological.
ontoonbaar, (-bare), not fit to be shown (seen), unpresentable.
ontpers, (-), wring from; extort; draw from.
ontplof, (-), explode, detonate.
ontplofbaar, (-bare), explosive.
ontploffing, (-e, -s), explosion.
ontploffingsgeluid, explosive (phonetics).
ontplooi, (-), straighten; spread out, unfurl; unfold; reveal; develop, expand.
ontplooiing, unfolding; revealing.
ontpop, (-): sig –, creep (come) out of his shell; **sig** – **as,** turn out to be, blossom out into, reveal oneself as.
ontraadsel, (-), unravel.
ontraai, (-), dissuade (from).
ontrafel, (-), unravel (lit. & fig.).
ontredder, (-), disable, impair, damage.
ontredder(d), (-de), a. dismantled; damaged, disabled; **in** –**de toestand,** in a crippled state, disabled; in a mess.
ontreddering, confusion, disorganisation, breakdown, collapse.
ontreining, (-), defile, pollute.
ontrief, -we, (-), inconvenience; deprive of.
ontroer, (-), move, touch, affect.
ontroer(d), (-de), a. moved, touched.
ontroering, (-e, -s), emotion.
ontrol, (-), unroll, open, unfold.
ontroosbaar, (-bare), inconsolable, disconsolate.
ontroof, -rowe, (-), rob (of).
ontrou, n. infidelity, disloyalty.
ontrou, (-, -e,), a. unfaithful, disloyal, untrue.
ontrouheid, vide **ontrou,** n.
ontrowe, (-), vide **ontroof**.
ontrowing, (-e, -s), robbing, stealing.
ontruim, (-), vacate; evacuate.
ontruiming, (-), vacating; evacuation.
ontruk, (-), snatch away (from), wrench from; **aan die dood** –, snatch from the jaws of death.
ontsag, awe, respect; – **voel (hê, toon) vir,** show (have) respect for; hold (keep) in awe, stand in awe of.
ontsaglik, (-e), a. awful; vast, huge, tremendous, formidable; great (fun).
ontsaglik, adv. awfully; tremendously, terribly (cold, etc.), dreadfully.
ontsagwekkend, (-e), awe-inspiring, imposing.
ontsê, -seg, (-), deny; refuse; **iemand die huis** –, forbid a person the house.
ontsegging, denial; refusal; dismissal.
ontsenu, (-), unnerve, enervate; weaken; invalidate, refute.
ontsenuwing, enervation; refutation.
ontset, n. relief (of town, garrison).
ontset, a. horrified, terrified, aghast.
ontset, (-), dismiss, deprive of (an office); relieve (town); appal, horrify.
ontsettend, (-e), a. terrible, awful.
ontsettend, adv. terribly, dreadfully; – **snaaks,** screamingly funny.
ontsetting, (-e, -s), dismissal, deposition (from office); relief; consternation, horror, terror.
ontsiel(d), (-de), lifeless, inanimate.
ontsien, (-), stand in awe of; respect; spare (the feelings of); **die moeite** –, consider too much trouble; **geen geld, moeite, tyd** – **nie,** be regardless of (spare no) money, trouble, time; **hy** – **niks,** he is unscrupulous, he has no scruples; he has no respect for anything.

ontsier, (-), disfigure, deface, mar.
ontsiering, (-e, -s), disfiguration, disfigurement, defacement, marring.
ontsink, (-), sink, give way; **die moed het my –,** my courage failed me.
ontskeep, (-), disembark; discharge.
ontskeping, (-e, -s), disembarkation.
ontslaan, (-), dismiss, discharge; **uit die tronk –,** release from gaol; **van verantwoordelikheid –,** relieve of responsibility.
ontslaap, (-), pass away.
ontslae: – **van,** rid of, free from.
ontslag, discharge, dismissal; release; – **gee,** dismiss, discharge; **sy – indien, vra, versoek,** tender his resignation; – **neem,** resign.
ontslagbrief, notice of dismissal.
ontslape, passed away, deceased.
ontslapene, (-s), the deceased, the departed.
ontsluier, (-), unveil; disclose.
ontsluit, (-), unlock, open.
ontsluiting, opening, unlocking.
ontsmet, (-), disinfect, deodorize.
ontsmetting, disinfection.
ontsmettingsinrigting, disinfecting-establishment.
ontsmettingsmiddel, disinfectant, deodorant.
ontsnap, (-), escape.
ontsnapping, (-e, -s), escape.
ontsondig, (-), purge, cleanse.
ontspan, (-), unfasten; unbend; relax.
ontspanning, (-e, -s), relaxation, recreation.
ontsnappingslektuur, light reading.
ontspoor, (-), leave the rails, be derailed, **laat –,** derail.
ontsporing, (-e, -s), derailment.
ontspring, (-), jump away from; escape; rise (of river); be caused (by).
ontspruit, (-), sprout, shoot forth; – **uit,** be descended from; result from.
ontstaan, n. origin; development, rise.
ontstaan, (-), originate, begin; come into being; be formed; **laat –,** cause.
ontsteek, (-), light, ignite; inflame.
ontsteel, (-), steal from, rob off.
ontsteking, (-e, -s), lighting, kindling; ignition; inflammation (of wound).
ontstekingsklep, ignition-valve.
ontstekingsprop, sparking-plug.
ontstel, (-), upset, alarm, startle.
ontstel(d), (-de), a. upset, alarmed.
ontsteltenis, dismay, consternation.
ontstem, (-), untune, put out of tune (lit. & fig.); disturb, ruffle.
onstem(d), (-de), a. disturbed, ruffled.
ontstemming, bad mood (humour), vexation, discomposure.
ontsteltenis: by – van, failing, in default of.
ontstig, (-), offend, shock.
ontstoke, inflamed (wound); **sy toorn was –,** his wrath was kindled.
ontstry, (-), dispute.
ontstyg, (-), rise up from.
ontsyfer, (-), decipher, make out.
onttakel, (-), dismantle (ship).
onttrek, (-), withdraw; **sig – aan,** withdraw (retire) from.
onttrekking, withdrawal, retirement.
onttroon, (-), dethrone.
onttroning, (-e, -s), dethronement.
ontug, lewdness, prostitution.
ontugtig, (-e), lewd, lascivious.
ontugtigheid, lewdness, lasciviousness.
ontuig, rabble.
ontval, (-), fall from; **sy rykdom is hom –,** he has lost his riches; **al my vriende is my –,** I have lost all my friends.

ontvang, (-), receive; conceive; – **my dank,** accept my thanks.
ontvangdag, at-home, reception-day.
ontvangenis, conception.
ontvanger, (-s), receiver, recipient; consignee (of goods); receptacle.
ontvangerskantoor, revenue-office.
ontvangkamer, reception-room.
ontvangs, (-te), receipt; reception; –**te,** returns, takings; revenue; **na – van,** on receipt of; **in – neem,** receive.
ontvangsbewys, receipt.
ontvangstasie, receiving-station.
ontvangtoestel, receiving-set, receiver.
ontvanklik, (-e), receptive, susceptible.
ontvanklikheid, receptivity.
ontveins, (-), conceal, disguise.
ontvlam, (-), catch fire, burst into flame; flame up; inflame, stir up.
ontvlambaar, (-bare), inflammable.
ontvlambaarheid, inflammability.
ontvlamming, (-e, -s), bursting into flame; flaming up; inflammation.
ontvlees, (-de), a. fleshless.
ontvlees, (-), strip off the flesh.
ontvlied, (-), flee from.
ontvlug, (-), escape, flee (from).
ontvlugting, escape, flight.
ontvoer, (-), kidnap (child), abduct.
ontvoerder, (-s), kidnapper, abductor.
ontvoering, kidnapping, abduction.
ontvolk, (-), depopulate.
ontvolking, depopulation.
ontvonk, (-), set on fire, kindle.
ontvou, (-), unfold.
ontvouing, unfolding.
ontvreem(d), (-), pilfer, embezzle, steal.
ontvreemding, embezzlement, theft.
ontwaak, (-), awake, wake up.
ontwaar, (-), perceive, discern.
ontwaking, awakening.
ontwapen, (-), disarm; pacify.
ontwapening, disarmament.
ontwapeningskonferensie, disarmament-conference.
ontwar, (-), unravel, disentangle.
ontwasse, outgrown, past.
ontwel, (-), well up (out, forth).
ontweldig, (-), take by force from.
ontwen, (-), lose the habit of; (get) rid of the habit, unlearn.
ontwerp, (-e), n. plan, design; scheme; draft; sketch; (parliamentary) bill.
ontwerp, (-), plan, design; project; draft; draw up; devise.
ontwerper, (-s), designer; draftsman.
ontwikkel, (-), develop; generate (heat); unfold (plans); evolve.
ontwikkelaar, (-s), developer (photo).
ontwikkelbaar, (-bare), developable.
ontwikkeld, (-e), developed; educated.
ontwikkeling, (-e -s), development; evolution; generation; education.
ontwikkelingsgang, (process of) evolution (development).
ontwikkelingsleer, theory of evolution.
ontwikkelingsvermoë, power to develop; generating power.
ontwil, sake; **om my –,** for my sake; **om wie se –?,** for whose sake?
ontwoeker, (-): – **aan,** wrest from.
ontworstel, (-), wrest (wrench, tear) from.
ontworsteling, wrestling from, shaking off, breaking away.

ontwortel, (-), uproot (lit. & fig.), unroot, pull up by the roots.
ontwrig, (-), dislocate, put out of joint (limb, affairs), disjoint; disrupt.
ontwrigting, (-e, -s), dislocation; crippling (of trade); disintegration, disruption.
ontwring, (-), wrest (wrench) from.
ontwy, (-), desecrate, defile, profane.
ontwyding, desecration; unfrocking.
ontwyfelbaar, (-bare), undoubted, indubitable, unquestioned.
ontwyfelbaarheid, unquestionableness.
ontwyk, (-), avoid, keep clear of, shun, dodge, evade; **verantwoordelikheid** –, shirk responsibility.
ontwykend, (-e), evasive (answer).
ontwyking, (-e, -s), evasion, shunning.
ontydig, (-e), untimely, unseasonable; premature (birth); **tydig en** –, at seasonable and unseasonable times.
onuitblusbaar, (-bare), inextinguishable.
onuitbluslik, (-e), inextinguishable.
onuitgegee, (-gewe), unpublished.
onuitgemaak, (-te), unsettled, open (question).
onuitgesoek, (-te), unsorted.
onuitgevoer(d), (-de), unexecuted; unlined.
onuithou(d)baar, (-bare), unbearable.
onuithoudelik, (-e), unbearable.
onuitputlik, (-e), inexhaustible.
onuitroeibaar, (-bare), ineradicable, indestructible.
onuitspreekbaar, (-bare), unpronounceable.
onuitspreeklik, (-e), unspeakable, inexpressible.
onuitstaanbaar, (-bare), intolerable, unendurable, unbearable.
onuitvoerbaar, (-bare), impracticable.
onuitvoerbaarheid, impracticability.
onuitwisbaar, (-bare), indelible, ineffaceable.
onvaderlands, (-e), unpatriotic.
onvanpas, inconvenient; unsuited, unsuitable; out of place, inappropriate.
onvas, (-te), soft (ground); faltering (steps, voice), shaking, unsteady (hand); light (sleep); fickle, inconstant; uncertain.
onvatbaar, (-bare): – **vir**, impervious to, deaf to; insusceptible to; immune against (from).
onvatbaarheid, insusceptibility.
onveilig, (-e), unsafe, insecure.
onveiligheid, unsafeness, insecurity.
onveranderbaar, (-bare), unchangeable.
onveranderd, (-e), unchanged, unaltered.
onveranderlik, (-e), unchangeable, immutable, uniform, constant, invariable.
onverantwoord, (-e), unaccounted for.
onverantwoordelik, (-e), not responsible; irresponsible (person); inexcusable.
onverantwoordelikheid, irresponsibility.
onverbaster(d), (-de), pure-blooded; not interbred; uncorrupted.
onverbeter(d), (-de), uncorrected.
onverbeterlik, (-e), incorrigible; first-rate, "priceless".
onverbiddelik, (-e), inexorable, relentless.
onverbiddelikheid, inexorability.
onverbleekbaar, (-bare), unfadable.
onverbloem(d), (-de), a. undisguised, unvarnished (truth).
onverbloem(d), adv. plainly, straight out; – **die waarheid sê**, tell the plain truth.
onverboë, undeclined, uninflected.
onverbonde, unbandaged.
onverbrandbaar, (-bare), incombustible.
onverbreekbaar, (-bare), unbreakable; inviolable; indissoluble.
onverbreeklik(-e), inviolable.

onverbuigbaar, (-bare), indeclinable.
onverdag, unsuspected.
onverdedig, (-de), undefended.
onverdedigbaar, (-bare), indefensible.
onverdeelbaar, (-bare), indivisible.
onverdeel(d), (-de), a. undivided.
onverdeel(d), adv. entirely, wholly.
onverdelgbaar, (-bare), indestructible.
onverderflik, (-e), imperishable.
onverdien(d), (-de), unearned (wages); undeserved; –**de lof**, unmerited praise.
onverdienstelik, (-e), undeserving; **nie – nie**, not without merit.
onverdig, (-te), uncondensed; true.
onverdraagbaar, (-bare), unbearable.
onverdraagsaam, (-same), intolerant.
onverdraagsaamheid, intolerance.
onverdun(d), (-de), undiluted.
onverenigbaar, (-bare), that cannot be united; irreconcilable, incompatible.
onverflou(d), (-de), undiminished, unflagging, unabated.
onverganklik, (-e), imperishable, undying.
onverganklikheid, imperishability.
onvergeeflik, (-e), unpardonable.
onvergeetlik, (-e), unforgettable, never to be forgotten.
onvergelyklik, (-e), incomparable, matchless, unparalleled, peerless.
onvergenoeg, (-de), discontented, dissatisfied.
onvergesel, (-de), unaccompanied.
onvergete, unforgotten.
onvergewe, unforgiven.
onvergewensgesind, (-e), unforgiving.
onverglaas, (-de), unglazed.
onverhinderd, (-e), undisturbed.
onverhoeds, adv. unexpectedly; suddenly.
onverhole, undisguised, unconcealed.
onverhoop, (-te), unexpected, unhoped for.
onverhoor(d), (-de), unheard, unanswered (prayer); untried (case).
onverhuur(d), (-de), untenanted, unlet.
onverkiesbaar, (-bare), ineligible.
onverklaar(d), (-de), unexplained.
onverklaarbaar, (-bare), unaccountable, inexplicable.
onverkleinbaar, (-bare), irreducible.
onverkoop, (-te), unsold.
onverkoopbaar, (-bare), unsalable.
onverkort, (-e), unabridged.
onverkry(g)baar, (-bare), unobtainable.
onverkwiklik, (-e), unpleasant, unsavoury.
onverlaat, miscreant, villain, brute.
onverlig, (-te), unlighted (hall); unenlightened (person); dark.
onvermeld, (-e), unmentioned; – **laat**, leave unrecorded (unmentioned).
onvermeng(d), (-de), unmixed; unblended; sheer, pure (joy).
onverminder(d), (-de), unabated.
onvermoë, inability, incapacity; impotence; powerlessness.
onvermoeibaar, (-bare), indefatigable.
onvermoeid, (-e), untiring, tireless.
onvermoeidheid, tirelessness.
onvermoënd, (-e), unable, powerless; poor; impecunious.
onvermom, (-de), unmasked.
onvermurfbaar, (-bare), relentless, inexorable.
onvermydelik, (-e), inevitable, unavoidable; **die** –**e**, the inevitable.
onvernielbaar, (-bare), indestructible.
onvernietigbaar, (-bare), indestructible.
onverpoos, (-de), uninterrupted, unceasing, unabating.

onverrig, (-te), undone; **-ter sake,** without having achieved one's object.
onversaag, (-de), undaunted, fearless.
onversaagdheid, undauntedness.
onversadelik, (-e), insatiable.
onversadig, (-de), unsatisfied, unsated, unsatisfied.
onverseël, (-de), unsealed.
onverseker(d), (-de), uninsured.
onversetlik, (-e), stubborn, unyielding.
onversetlikheid, stubbornness, obstinacy.
onversier(d), (-de), plain, unadorned.
onversigtig, (-e), imprudent, rash.
onversigtigheid, imprudence, rashness.
onverskillig, (-e), indifferent; reckless (driver, etc.); careless, **dit is my –,** it is immaterial to me; **– vir die gevolge,** regardless of the consequences.
onverskilligheid, indifference; recklessness; carelessness.
onverskoonbaar, (-bare), unpardonable.
onverskrokke, undaunted, intrepid.
onverskrokkenheid, fearlessness.
onverslaan, (-de, -slane), unbeaten.
onverslae, undismayed, unabashed.
onverslap, (-te), unflagging, unabated.
onverslete, not threadbare; not worn out.
onverslyt, (-e, -slete), vide **onverslete.**
onverslytbaar, (-bare), not to be (not easily) worn out, everlasting.
onversoen(d), (-de), unreconciled.
onversoenlik, (-e), irreconcilable; implacable; **'n –e,** an irreconcilable.
onversoenlikheid, irreconcilability.
onversorg, (-de), uncared for, unprovided for; slovenly, untidy.
onverstaanbaar, (-bare), unintelligible; incomprehensible.
onverstand, unwisdom, folly.
onverstandig, (-e), unwise, foolish.
onverstandigheid, folly, imprudence.
onversteur(d), -stoor(d), (-de), undisturbed; unperturbed.
onversteurbaar, -stoorbaar, (-bare), imperturbable.
onverswak, (te), unweakened; undiminished; unimpaired.
onvertaal(d), (-de), untranslated.
onvertaalbaar, (-bare), untranslatable.
onverteer(d), (-de), undigested (food); unconsumed.
onverteerbaar, (-bare), indigestible.
onvertraag, (-de), not delayed, unremitting, unrelaxed.
onvervaard, (-e), undaunted.
onvervals, (-te), unadulterated, pure.
onvervreem(d)baar, (-bare), inalienable (possessions); indefeasible (rights).
onvervul(d), (-de), unfulfilled (promise); unexecuted (task).
onverwag, (-te), unexpected, sudden.
onverwags, unexpectedly, unawares.
onverwelk, (-te), unfaded.
onverwelkbaar, (-bare), unfadable, unfading; imperishable, everlasting.
onverwelklik, (-e), imperishable.
onverwerk, (-te), not worked out (up); unassimilated.
onverwinlik, (-e), invincible.
onverwisselbaar, (-bare), not exchangeable.
onverwoesbaar, (-bare), indestructible.
onverwyld, immediately, at once.
onvindbaar, (-bare), not to be found.
onvoegsaam, (-same), improper, indecent, unseemly.

onvoelbaar, (-bare), that cannot be felt (touched), impalpable.
onvolbrag, (-te), unperformed.
onvoldaan, (-dane), unsettled, unpaid; dissatisfied, displeased.
onvoldoende, insufficient, inadequate.
onvoldrae, premature, unripe.
onvolkome, imperfect, incomplete.
onvolledig, (-e), incomplete.
onvolledigheid, incompleteness.
onvolmaak, (-te), imperfect, faulty.
onvolmaaktheid, imperfection, deficiency.
onvolprese, beyond praise, surpassing.
onvoltooi(d), (-de), unfinished, incomplete; imperfect (tense).
onvoltrokke, unsolemnized (marriage); unexecuted.
onvolwasse, not full-grown, immature.
onvoorbedag, (-te), unpremeditated, not deliberate; unintentional.
onvoorbedagtelik, unintentionally.
onvoorbereid, (-e), unprepared; **'n –e toespraak,** an extempore speech.
onvoordelig, (-e), unprofitable.
onvoorsien, (-e), unexpected, unforeseen; **– van,** not provided with; **–e omstandighede,** unforeseen circumstances; **–e uitgawes,** incidental expenses.
onvoorsiens, unexpectedly.
onvoorspoedig, (-e), unlucky, unfortunate, not prosperous, unsuccessful.
onvoorwaardelik, (-e), unconditional, implicit (faith), absolute.
onvrede, strife, discord, feud, dispute.
onvri(e)ndelik, (-e), unkind, unfriendly.
onvri(e)ndelikheid, unkindness.
onvriendskaplik, unfriendly, in an unfriendly manner.
onvrou(e)lik, (-e), unwomanly.
onvrugbaar, (-bare), infertile (lit. & fig.); sterile (land, person, plant, discussion), unfruitful, unproductive, barren.
onvry, (–, -e), not free; not private.
onvrywillig, (-e), involuntary, compulsory.
onwaar, (–, -ware), false, untrue.
onwaardeerbaar, (-bare), invaluable, inestimable, priceless.
onwaardig, (-e), unworthy.
onwaardigheid, unworthiness.
onwaarheid, (-hede), falsehood, untruth.
onwaarneembaar, (-bare), imperceptible.
onwaarskynlik, (-e), improbable, unlikely.
onwaarskynlikheid, improbability.
onwankelbaar, (-bare), unshakable, steadfast, firm, unwavering.
onweegbaar, (-bare), unweighable.
onweer, unsettled (bad) weather, storm; **dit is elke dag –,** the weather is unsettled (bad) every day; **daar is – in die lug,** the weather is becoming unsettled; there is something afoot (brewing).
onweerlegbaar, (-bare), irrefutable, indisputable, irrefragable.
onweersbui, shower, (thunder)storm.
onweerspreekbaar, (-bare), onweerspreeklik, (-e), indisputable.
onweerstaanbaar, (-bare), irresistible.
onweersvoël, storm-bird, stormy petrel, bird of ill omen.
onweerswolk, stormcloud, thundercloud.
onwel, indisposed, unwell.
onwelkom, (-e), unwelcome.
onwellewend, (-e), ill-mannered.
onwelluidend, (-e), discordant, harsh (voice), inharmonious; cacophonous.

onwelluidendheid, inharmoniousness.
onwelriekend, (-e), evil-smelling.
onwelvoeglik, (-e), indecent, improper.
onwelwillend, (-e), discourteous, unkind, unsympathetic, disobliging.
onwenslik, (-e), undesirable.
onwerksaam, inactive.
onwenslik, (-e), unreal.
onwetend, (-e), ignorant; – **sondig nie**, doing wrong unwittingly is no sin.
onwetendheid, ignorance.
onwetenskaplik, unscientific.
onwetlik, (-e), illegal.
onwettig, (-e), illegal, unlawful, illicit; disobedient, naughty; illegitimate (child).
onwettigheid, illegability, unlawfulness; naughtiness, disobedience; illegitimacy.
onwil, unwillingness.
onwillekeurig, (-e), a. involuntary.
onwillekeurig, adv. involuntarily; **'n mens doen dit –**, one does it involuntarily, one cannot help doing it.
onwillig, (-e), unwilling, reluctant.
onwilligheid, unwillingness, reluctance.
onwis, uncertain.
onwraaksugtig, (-e), not vindictive.
onwrikbaar, (-bare), unshakable, steadfast, unyielding, firm, immovable.
onwys, (-, -e), unwise, foolish.
onwysgerig, (-e), unphilosophical.
oog, (oë), eye; fountain(head); pub, bar; **goeie, slegte, oë**, good, bad, eyesight; **'n blou –**, a black eye (as result of a blow); **sig die oë uit die kop (hoof) skaam**, be too ashamed to look a person in the face; **sy oë is te groot vir (groter as) sy maag**, his eyes are bigger than his belly; **vir iets geen – (oë) hê nie**, have no eye for (be blind to) something; **geen – toemaak nie**, not get a wink of sleep; **die oë vir iets sluit**, shut one's eyes to; **'n – in die seil hou**, keep a sharp lookout, be on the alert; **die – hou op**, watch, keep an eye on something; **die – op iets hê**, have an eye on something; **die – wil ook wat hê**, one must have something to look at too; **een en al oë wees**, be all eyes; **die oë knip, blink**; **oë knip vir**, make eyes at, wink at; **sy oë nie glo nie**, not believe his (own) eyes; **wat die – nie sien nie, deer die hart nie**, what the eye does not see the heart does not grieve over; **groot oë maak vir**, stare at; **die – van die meester maak die perd vet**, the eye of the master makes the cattle thrive; **sand in die oë strooi**, throw dust in the eyes; **dit steek my in die – (oë)**, this is an eyesore to me, in **my – (oë)**, in my eyes, in my opinion; **'n doring in die –**, an eyesore, a thorn in the flesh (side); **iemand in die – hou**, watch (keep an eye on) somebody; **in die – kry**, catch sight of; **in die – loop (val)**, strike the eye; **met die – op**, with a view (an eye) to; considering, in view of; **met die blote –**, with the naked eye; **met groot oë**, open-eyed; **iemand na die oë kyk**, be dependent upon a person, wait on a person's glances; **– om – en tand om tand**, an eye for an eye and a tooth for a tooth; **onder vier oë**, in private, privately; **onder iemand se oë kom**, be brought to a person's notice, meet a person's eye; **onder die oë kry**, see, set eyes upon; **feite onder die oë sien**, face facts; **op die –**, outwardly, on the face of it; **nie lelik op die – nie**, not bad to look at; **op die – hê**, have in mind; **uit die –, uit die hart**, out of sight, out of mind; **uit die – verloor**, lose sight of; **oneerlikheid kyk hom (by) die oë uit**, he has dishonesty written on his face; **net vir die –**, just for show; **iets voor oë hou**, bear in mind, be mindful of; **God voor oë hou**, fear God.

oogappel, eyeball, apple of the eye.
oogarts, oculist, ophthalmic surgeon.
oogbad(jie), eye-cup, eye-bath.
oogbal, eye-ball.
oogdokter, oculist, ophthalmic surgeon.
oogdruppels, eye-lotion, eyewash.
ooggetuie, eyewitness.
oogglas, eyeglass; monocle; eyepiece.
ooghaar, eyelash.
oogheelkunde, ophthalmology.
oogheelkundige, (-s), ophthalmologist.
ooghoek, corner of the eye.
oogholte, orbit, eye-socket, eye-pit.
oogkas, eye-socket.
oogklap, blinker; **–pe**, blinkers; **–pe aansit**, put blinkers on, blindfold; hoodwink, deceive.
oogklier, lachrymal gland.
oogkliniek, ophthalmological clinic.
oogknip, wink; **in 'n –**, in the twinkle of an eye.
oogkwaal, eye-disease.
ooglid, eyelid.
oogluikend: **– toelaat**, shut the eyes to, connive at, wink at.
ooglyer, eye-patient.
oogmerk, aim, intention, object.
oogmiddel, ophthalmic (remedy).
oogontsteking, inflammation of the eye.
oogopslag, glance.
oogpister, "eye-squirt".
oogpunt, visual point; point of view, viewpoint; **uit 'n ander – beskou**, look at from a different angle (point of view).
oogsalf, eye-ointment.
oogsenuwee, optic nerve.
oogsiekte, eye-disease, eye-trouble.
oogspieël, ophthalmoscope.
oogspier, muscle of the eye.
oogtand, eyetooth, canine.
oogvel, eyelid.
oogverblindend, (-e), blinding, dazzling.
oogvlek, spot on the eye.
oogvlies, tunic of the eye, tunicle.
oogwater, eye-lotion, eye-water.
oogwenk, -wink, wink; **in 'n –**, in the twinkling of an eye, in a moment.
oogwimpel, eyelash.
oogwit, white of the eye; goal, object.
ooi, (-e), ewe.
ooibok, she-goat.
ooievaar, stork.
ooievaarsbeen, stork's leg; **–bene**, long shanks.
ooievaarsbek, stork's bill; crane bill.
ooilam, ewe-lamb.
ooit, ever.
ook, also, as well, too, likewise, even; **en dit – nog**, and that too, and now (comes) this; **dit is – weer 'n mooi grap!**, well, I never!, that is a fine how-do-you-do!; **jy is – weer 'n mooie**, you are a fine one, (indeed) you are; **– so!**, same to you!; **hy weet dit nie en ek – nie**, he does not know and neither do I; **wat – al gebeur**, whatever happens, no matter what happens; **waar – al**, wherever; **wie – al**, whoever; **hoe dan –**, anyhow, no matter how; **hoe ek – al probeer**, no matter how I try; **dit kan my – nie skeel nie**, neither do I care; **dis my goed**, that suits me just as well; **jy is altyd laat**, really, you are always late; **hy weet – niks**, he never knows a thing; **dis – weer waar**, true again, so it is!

oom, (-s), uncle; – **Kool**, "our friend", rogue, knave, rascal; ace (of cards); **hulle sal – Kool**

oomblik nooit vang nie, they will never catch the rascal; they will never catch me!
oomblik, (-ke), moment, twinkling of an eye; **net 'n –(kie)**, one moment, just a moment; **in 'n – (se tyd)**, in a moment, in the twinkling of an eye; **op die –**, now, at once; at the moment, just now; **vir die –**, for the moment; for the present.
oombliklik, (-e), a. instantaneous; momentary; immediate; short-lived, fleeting.
oombliklik, adv. instantaneously, immediately, at once, instantly.
oompie, (-s), (little) uncle; mister.
oond, (-e), oven; furnace; (lime-)kiln.
oonddeksel, -deur, oven-door.
oondkoek, oven-bread, oven-cake.
oondskop, oven-shovel, peel.
oondstok, oven-rake; peel.
oop, ope, open; empty (seat); vacant (post); unbuttoned (coat); **die – lug,** the open (air); **'n ope brief,** an open letter (to the Press); **oop-en-toe aankom (hardloop),** run for all you are worth, be tearing.
oopbars, (oopge-), burst open, crack.
oopbreek, (oopge-), break open, force open (up); prize (box) open.
oopdraai, (oopge-), turn on, open.
oopdruk, (oopge-), push (force) open.
oopgaan, (oopge-), open.
oopgewerk, (-te), open-work.
oopgooi, (oopge-), throw open, fling open (door); spread out (rug).
oophang, (oopge-), hang open; **my mond het oopgehang (van verbasing),** I stared open-mouthed, I simply gaped.
oophou, (oopge-), open (hand); keep unlocked; hold (keep) open; keep vacant.
oopkap, (oopge-), hew open, chop down (open), cut down (trees).
oopknoop, (oopge-), unbutton, unfasten.
oopkry, (oopge-), get open.
ooplaat, (oopge-), leave open.
ooplê, (oopge-), lie open; lie uncovered (exposed); lay open; expose; **hardloop dat jy (so) –,** run for all you are worth.
oopmaak, (oopge-), open.
oopruk, (oopge-), tear (rip) open.
oopsit, (oopge-), open (door, window).
oopskeur, (oopge-), tear open.
oopskoen, slipper, open shoe.
oopskuif, -skuiwe, (oopge-), slide up (open); shove (move) up (back).
oopslaan, (oopge-), open (book); force (knock) open; **die deur het oopgeslaan,** the door flew open; **hy moes vir hom 'n pad –,** he had to fight his way through; **–de venster,** casement window; **–de deure,** folding doors.
oopsluit, (oopge-), unlock.
oopsmyt, (oopge-), fling open.
oopsny, (oopge-), cut open.
oopspalk, (oopge-), spread out, stretch out; open wide; **met oopgespalkte oë,** with dilated eyes.
oopsper, (oopge-), open wide; **oopgesperde neusgate,** distended nostrils.
oopsplits, (oopge-), split.
oopspring, (oopge-), burst open, fly open; crack; dehisce (bot.).
oopstaan, (oopge-), be open; **die deur staan oop,** the door is open; **die toekoms staan vir jou oop,** the future is yours; **die rekeninge staan nog oop,** the accounts are still unpaid.
oopstamp, (oopge-), knock (force) open.
oopsteek, (oopge-), prick, pierce, (pierce with) lance; pick (a lock); dig through.

oopstel, (oopge-), open; throw open.
oopstoot, (oopge-), push open.
oopte, (-s), open space.
ooptorring, (oopge-), unstitch, rip open.
ooptrap, (oopge-), kick open; tread open.
ooptrek, (oopge-), open (drawer, etc.); uncork, pull open; give a thrashing; **dit trek oop,** it is clearing up.
oopval, (oopge-), open automatically, fall open; become vacant.
oopveg, (oopge-), fight through.
oopvlieg, (oopge-), fly open.
oopvou, (oopge-), open, unfold.
oopwaai, (oopge-), be blown open.
oor, (ore), n. ear (of person, pitcher, etc.), handle; **eers ou (groot)mense, dan lang ore,** children must wait their turn; **die ore laat hang,** be downhearted, hang the head, **klein muisies het groot ore,** little pitchers have long ears; **die ore sluit vir,** be deaf to; **die ore tuit,** the ears burn; there is a tingling in the ears; **iemand die ore van die kop eet,** eat a person out of hearth and home; **die mure het ore,** walls have ears; **een en al ore wees,** be all ears; **dit gaan by die een – in en by die ander uit,** it goes in at the one ear and out the other; **'n ope – hê vir,** give a ready ear to; **die ore spits,** prick (up) the ears; **die – leen,** lend one's ears; **iemand aan die ore lol,** pester (worry) a person; **nog nie droog agter die ore nie,** inexperienced, still a greenhorn; **tot agter die ore rooi word,** blush to the roots of the hair; **in die – knoop,** make a mental note of; **hy het pluisies in sy ore,** his ears are plugged; he is deaf; **tot oor die ore verlief, in die skuld,** over head and ears in love, in debt; **tot oor die ore in die werk wees,** be up to the eyes (neck) in work; **iemand die vel oor die ore trek,** fleece a person; **dit het my ter ore gekom,** it has reached my ears; **iemand se kop tussen sy ore sit,** teach somebody a lesson.
oor, prep. over (head, shoulder, eyes, place); across (road, channel); more than, over (R6); beyond, above (a hundred); via, by way of (a place); (five minutes) past (the hour); **– dag,** by day, during the day; **– die tafel,** across the table; at table, (during meals); **– 'n maand,** a month hence; **– vyf minute,** in five minutes' time; **môre – ag dae,** tomorrow week; **– land,** by land; **– iets praat,** talk about (discuss) something; **– die geheel,** on the whole.
oor, adv. over; **– en weer,** to and fro, backwards and forwards; mutually; **daar is twee –,** there are two left; **hy het geld –,** he has money left; **die geveg is nog nie – nie,** the fighting has not ceased yet (is still going on); **hy is my –,** he is more than my match, I am not his equal.
oor, conj. because; **– ek arm is, verag hulle my,** they despise me because I am poor.
ooraandoening, ear-trouble.
oorarts, ear-specialist, aurist.
oorbaar, (-bare), becoming, proper.
oorbaarheid, seemliness, decency.
oorbagasie, excess luggage.
oorbak, (oorge-), bake again.
oorbekend, (-e), generally known; too well known.
oorbel(letjie), earring, eardrop.
oorbelas, (–), overtax; overload.
oorbelasting, overtaxation; overloading.
oorbeleef, (-de), too polite, ultra-polite, officious.
oorbelig, (-te), overexposed.
oorbeligting, overexposure.
oorbeskaaf, (-de), overcivilized; overrefined.

oorbeskawing, overcivilization.
oorbeskeidenheid, excessive modesty.
oorbeskeie, too modest, different.
oorbeurt, over (cricket).
oorbevolk, (-te), overpopulated.
oorbevolking, overpopulation; overcrowding.
oorbieg, auricular confession.
oorbietjie, oribie(tjie), (-s), oribi.
oorbind, (oorge-), tie (bind) over; tie (bind) again; rebind (books, etc.).
oorblaser, (-s), scandalmonger, gossiper.
oorbluf, (-), bluff, frighten, bully; fluster, ruffle; nonplus.
oorbly, (oorge-), remain, be left (over); stay; **drie dae in Parys –**, stay (remain) three days in Paris.
oorblyfsel, (-s), remainder, remnant; remains; relic.
oorblywend, (-e), remaining; **die –es**, the remainder, those left over (behind); the survivors.
oorbodig, (-e), superfluous, redundant; needless, unnecessary.
oorboord, overboard; **– gooi, val**, throw, fall overboard; **– gooi**, throw overboard (lit. & fig.), jettison; abandon.
oorborrel, (oorge-), bubble over.
oorbrei, (oorge-), knit again, reknit.
oorbring, (oorge-), take over (across); bring, convey, transport; transfer (to another post); carry over (forward); transmit (electricity); translate; transpose (term to other side of equation); take, deliver (message); tell (news, story); **'n siekte –**, transmit a disease; **groete –**, convey greetings; **ruik, klank –**, convey (transmit) smell, sound; **huisraad –**, remove furniture.
oorbringer, (-s), carrier, bearer, messenger; translator; telltale.
oorbringing, oorbrenging, transport(ation); transfer; transmission; translation.
oorbrug, (-), bridge.
oorbuig, (oorge-), bend over.
oord, (-e), place, region, (holiday) resort.
oordaad, excess, superabundance; **in – lewe**, live extravagantly, lead a prodigal life.
oordadig, (-e), a. excessive, extravagant.
oordadig, adv. excessively, to excess; **– lewe**, live in luxury, live extravagantly.
oordadigheid, excess, extravagance.
oordag, by (during the) day.
oordeel, n. judgement, sentence (passed by judge); verdict (of jury); opinion, view(s); **die laaste O–**, judgement day; **– uitspreek**, give (one's) opinion; pass sentence; **'n – vel**, pass judgement; **aan die – oorlaat van**, leave to the discretion of; **van – wees**, hold, be of opinion; **na my –**, in my opinion (judgment); **gesonde –**, sound judgement.
oordeel, (ge-), judge; be of opinion, consider, deem; **te – na**, judging from.
oordeelkundig, (-e), discerning, judicious; penetrating (criticism); sensible.
oordeelkundige, (-s), competent judge.
oordeelsdag, judgement-day, doomsday.
oordeelvelling, (-e, -s), judgement.
oordek, (-te), a covered (stand).
oordek, (-), cover (up).
oordek, (oorge-), thatch again, rethatch, thatch over; re-lay (the table).
oordelaar, (-s), judge.
oordenking, (-e, -s), consideration; meditation.
oordink, (-), consider, ponder over, reflect on, think (the matter) over.
oordoen, (oorge-), do over (again).

oordonder, (-), bluff, put out of countenance disconcert, overawe.
oordoop, (oorge-), rebaptize, rechristen.
oordra, (oorge-), carry over (across); assign, make over (personal property to); transfer (rights); cede; commit (authority to); let out a secret; **siekte –**, transmit disease.
oordraagbaar, (-bare), transferable.
oordrag, (-te), transfer, conveyance; cession; assignment.
oordragsbrief, (deed of) transfer, deed of assignment.
oordragtelik, (-e), metaphorical.
oordrewe, a. exaggerated; excessive; exorbitant (price), overdone.
oordrewe, adv. excessively; **– beleef(d) wees**, be painfully polite (overpolite).
oordrewenheid, exaggeration.
oordruk, (-ke), n. off-print, separatum, separate; surcharge (on postage-stamp).
oordruk, a. too busy, overbusy.
oordruk, (oorge-), press over; reprint (book); transfer (patterns); surcharge.
oordrukplaatjie, transfer.
oordryf, -drywe, (oorge-), drift across (the river); blow over (of weather).
oordryf, -drywe, (-), exaggerate, overdo, carry to excess.
oordrywing, (-e, -s), exaggeration.
oordwars, athwart, crosswise.
ooreen, vide compounds that follow.
ooreenbring, (ooreenge-), reconcile (with), make compatible, conciliate (conflicting statements).
ooreenkom, (ooreenge-), agree (with); correspond (to, with); **hierdie kleure kom nie goed ooreen nie**, these colours do not match, (these colours clash); **dit kom nie met sy beginsels ooreen nie**, it is against his principles; **met 'n beskrywing –**, answer to a description.
ooreenkoms, (-te), similarity, resemblance, likeness, agreement, mutual understanding, treaty contract.
ooreenkomstig, (-e), similar, corresponding, conformable; **– die wet**, according to (in accordance with) the law; **– sy wense**, in compliance with his wishes.
ooreenkomstigheid, similarity, conformability.
ooreenstem, (ooreenge-), agree, concur, be in unison; **– met**, agree (be at one, be in harmony) with (person); tally with (a description).
ooreenstemming, agreement, unison, harmony, concord; **in volkome –**, in perfect unison; **in – bring met**, harmonise (bring into harmony) with, fit in with, make to correspond (agree) with; **in – wees met**, be in accordance with, fit in with, be in keeping with; **tot – kom**, come to an agreement (understanding).
ooreet, (-): **sig –**, overeat oneself.
oor-en-oor, repeatedly, again and again.
oorerf, -erwe, (oorge-), inherit.
oorerflik, (-e), hereditary; inheritable.
oorerflikheid, heredity; hereditariness.
oorerwing, heredity; inheritance.
oorgaan, (oorge-), go across, cross; go over to another (party); pass off (of sensations); stop; clear up (of weather), blow over; be promoted, pass; **– in**, change into; **in ander hande –**, change hands; **– op**, pass to; **– tot**, pass on to; embrace, adopt; **ons het daartoe oorgegaan, we decided; tot stemming –**, proceed to the vote, vote.
oorgang, (-e), going across; crossing; going over; adoption; transition, change; transition (music); passage, transit.
oorgangseksamen, promotion-test.

oorgangsklank, glide.
oorgangsleeftyd, age of puberty.
oorgangspunt, transition-point.
oorgangsreg, right of transfer.
oorgangstoestand, state of transition.
oorgangstyd(perk), transition-period.
oorgansvorm, transition-form.
oorganklik, (-e), transitive (verb).
oorgat, ear-hole.
oorgawe, handing over; surrender; transfer, ceding, cession (of rights).
oorgedienstig, (-e), officious.
oorgee, (oorge-), pass over, hand, reach; yield, surrender; give up, part with; hand over (to the police); vomit, puke; **sig – aan**, surrender to, abandon (yield) oneself to, surrender oneself to, become a slave to (of).
oorgehaal, (-de), cocked (gun); prepared, ready, on the point of.
oorgelukkig, (-e), extremely happy.
oorgenoeg, more than enough.
oorgetuie, ear-witness.
oorgevoelig, (-e), oversensitive, hypersensitive; morbidly sensitive.
oorgevoeligheid, oversensitiveness.
oorgewig, overweight.
oorgiet, (oorge-), pour over (off).
oorgiet, (–), suffuse; – **met**, suffused with, coloured with.
oorgooi, (oorge-), throw over (across); pour into (off), decant (wine); vomit.
oorgord, surcingle, girdle.
oorgroot, (-grote), vast, huge, immense.
oorgrootouers, great-grandparents.
oorgrootvader, great-grandfather.
oorhaal, (oorge-), fetch (over); cock (a gun); persuade, talk over; **jou vir iemand –**, prepare yourself to face (confront) a person.
oorhaas, (–), hurry, drive, bustle.
oorhaastig, (-e), hurried, rash, reckless; **–e vlug**, precipitate flight.
oorhaastigheid, undue haste; rashness.
oorhand, upper hand, mastery, supremacy; **die – hê**, have the mastery (upper hand), **die – kry**, get the mastery (upper hand), get the better (of).
oorhandig, (–), hand (over), deliver.
oorhandiging, handing over, delivery.
oorhan(d)s, a.: **–e steek (oorhan(d)s-steek)**, top-sewing stitch.
oorhan(d)s, adv.: – **naai**, top-sew.
oorhan(d)snaat, top-sewn seam.
oorhang, (oorge-), hang over; incline, lean over, stand obliquely, beetle.
oorhanger, ear-drop.
oorhê, (oorgehad), have left (over, to spare); **alles vir iemand –**, assist a person in every possible way, sacrifice everything to help a person.
oorheelkunde, otiatrics.
oorheen, over, across.
oorheerlik, (-e), exquisite, too lovely.
oorheers, (–), dominate (a person), predominate (over).
oorheersend, (-e), (pre)dominant; prevailing, outstanding.
oorheerser, tyrant.
oorheersing, (-e, -s), domination.
oorhel, (oorge-), lean (hang) over, incline; heel; **– na**, lean to, have a tendency (leaning) towards (evil).
oorhelling, hanging over, leaning; inclination, disposition; heel (of ship).
oorhelp, (oorge-), help over.
oorhemp, shirt.

oorhoeks, (-e), a. diagonal; out of sorts; at loggerheads; **–e lyn**, diagonal.
oorhoeks, adv. diagonally.
oorholte, cavity of the ear.
oorhoop, in a heap; disarranged, in confusion; **– wees (lê) met mekaar**, be at loggerheads (variance).
oorhou, (oorge-), have left (over); save.
oorinspanning, overexertion.
oorjaag, -jae, (–), overdrive (horse, person), work (person) to exhaustion.
oorjaag, -jae, (oorge-), drive (chase) over (across); rerun (a race).
oorjas, overcoat.
oorkant, n. the other (opposite) side.
oorkant, prep. across, beyond.
oorkantel, (oorge-), topple over.
oorkants(t)e, opposite (bank).
oorkapitaliseer, overcapitalize.
oorklap, ear-flap.
oorkleed, n. upper-garment; overcarpet.
oorklee(d), (–), cover.
oorklim, (oorge-), climb over; change.
oorkom, (oorge-), come over (across), cross, get over, happen to, befall; **wat het hom oorgekom?**, what has happened to him?, what is the matter with him?
oorkom, (–), befall, happen to.
oorkoms, coming over; coming, visit.
oorkonde, (-s), document, deed; address.
oorkonkel, (-s), n. box on the ear.
oorkonkel, (ge-), box a person's ears.
oorkook, (oorge-), boil over, boil again.
oorkoomlik, -komelik, (-e), surmountable.
oorkrabbertjie, -krawwertjie, (-e), eardrop.
oorkrop, (-te), overburdened.
oorkruip, (oorge-), creep (crawl) over.
oorkruiper, earwig.
oorkruis, crosswise, diagonally.
oorkry, (oorge-), get over (across).
oorkussing, pillow; **ledigheid is die – van die duiwel**, Satan finds some mischief still for idle hands to do.
oorkyk, (oorge-), look beyond; look over; go (look, read) over, go through; correct.
oorlaai, (–), overload; overburden; overstock (market); deluge (with); shower (blessings upon), overwhelm (with praise); overcharge (description); overcrowd (canvas).
oorlaai, (oorge-), transfer the load, tranship; load over again, reload.
oorlaat, (oorge-), leave; entrust (to); **aan sy lot –**, leave to his fate; **aan jouself oorgelaat**, left to yourself, left to one's own devices.
oorlading, (-e, -s), overloading, overburdening; overcrowding; vide **oorlaai**.
oorlams, (–, -e), clever, smart, handy; cunning; sly; sharp; **'n – jong**, a trained boy, an old hand.
oorlamsheid, cunning; cleverness.
oorlas, nuisance, annoyance; **tot – wees**, be a nuisance, (burden), be in the way.
oorlê, -leg, (oorge-), put over; lean over; stop, wait, stay; **werk laat –**, let work stand over.
oorlê, -leg, (–), think over, deliberate; **nie weet hoe om iets te – nie**, not know how to set about doing something.
oorlê-dae, days of demurrage.
oorlede, deceased, the late; **– mnr. K**, the late Mr K.
oorledene, (-s), (the) deceased.
oorleef, -lewe, (–), survive, outlive.
oorleer, n. upper leather, vamp.
oorleer, (oorge-), learn over again.
oorlees, (oorge-), read over (through).

oorleg, deliberation, consideration; consultation; judgment; care; – **pleeg (in – tree) met iemand**, consult a person, discuss (matter) with a person; **in – met**, in consultation with; **met – te werk gaan**, act wisely (with discretion), use one's discretion.
oorlê, vide **oorlê**.
oorlê-koste, charges of demurrage.
oorlel(letjie), ear-lobe.
oorlepel, ear-prick.
oorlewe, vide **oorleef**.
oorlewer, (oorge-), give (deliver) up (over); hand down; – **aan**, hand over to; **oorgelewer wees aan**, be at the mercy of.
oorlewering, (-e, -s), handing over; tradition.
oorlog, (-loë), war; – **verklaar**, declare war; – **voer**, wage war; **Ministerie van O–**, War Office; **in – wees met**, be at war with.
oorlogsbasuin, trumpet of war.
oorlogsbelasting, war-tax.
oorlogsbuit, spoils of war.
oorlogsgerug, rumour of war.
oorlogsgevaar, danger of war.
oorlogsgod(in), war-god(dess).
oorlogskip, warship, man-of-war.
oorlogskorrespondent, war-correspondent.
oorlogskoste, expenses of war.
oorlogskreet, war-cry.
oorlogskuld, war debt.
oorlogslening, war-loan.
oorlogsmag, military forces.
oorlogsmoeg, war-weary.
oorlogspad, warpath.
oorlogsperd, warhorse.
oorlogsreg, law of war.
oorlogsrisiko, war-risk.
oorlogsterkte, fighting strength.
oorlogsterrein, theatre of war.
oorlogstoker, warmonger.
oorlogstoneel, theatre of war.
oorlogstuig, machinery of war.
oorlogstyd, time of war.
oorlogsugtig, (-e), warlike, bellicose.
oorlogsveld, field of battle.
oorlogsverklaring, declaration of war.
oorlogvoerend, (-e), belligerent; **-e moondhede**, powers at war.
oorlogvoering, waging war.
oorloop, n. overflow(ing); landing; crossing.
oorloop, (oorge-), cross; run (flow) over, overflow; go over; retouch; – **van geesdrif**, brim over with enthusiasm.
oorlooppyp, overflow-pipe.
oorloper, deserter.
oorlosie, vide **horlosie**.
oorlyde, death, decease.
oormaak, (oorge-), do over again; remake; stop (pain); transfer; remit; transmit.
oormaat, superabundance, excess; **tot – van ramp (ellende)**, to crown it all, to make matters worse.
oormag, superior power (numbers), odds; **voor die – swig**, succumb to superior numbers; **teen die – stry**, fight against odds.
oorman, (–), overpower, overcome.
oormatig, (-e), a. excessive; immoderate.
oormatig, adv. excessively, exceedingly; – **drink**, drink to excess.
oormatig, (-e), a. too moderate (temperate).
oormeester, (–), overpower, overmaster, overcome, get the better of.
oormeet, (oorge-), measure again.
oormerk, n. ear-mark.
oormerk, (oorge-), mark again.
oormoed, rashness: presumption.

oormoedig, (-e), rash, reckless, overbold; arrogant, presumptuous.
oormôre, -**môre**, the day after tomorrow; **môre –**, one of these (fine) days.
oormôreaand, -**moreaand**, the night after tomorrow night, two nights hence.
oornaai, (oorge-), sew again.
oornaat, overseam.
oornag, (–), pass the night.
oorname, taking over.
oorneem, (oorge-), take from; take over; adopt, borrow, derive; copy.
oornommer, (oorge-), number again, renumber.
oorontsteking, inflammation of the ear.
ooroorgrootmoeder, great-great-grandmother.
oorpak, (oorge-), repack, transfer.
oorpeins, (–), reflect on, contemplate.
oorpeinsing, (-e, -s), meditation, musing.
oorplaas, (oorge-), remove; transfer.
oorplak, (oorge-), repaper; paste over.
oorplant, (oorge-), transplant.
oorplasing, (-e, -s), removal, transfer.
oorpleister, (oorge-), replaster.
oorploeg, -**ploe(ë)**, (oorge-), replough, plough over again; plough too far.
oorpomp, (oorge-), pump over.
oorprikkel, (–), overstimulate; **-de senuwees**, overstrung nerves.
oorprikkeling, (-e, -s), overexcitement.
oorproduksie, overproduction.
oorpyn, ear-ache.
oorreding, persuasion.
oorredingskrag, persuasive powers.
oorredingskuns, art of persuasion.
oorredingsmiddel, inducement.
oorreed, (–), persuade, induce.
oorreedbaar, (-bare), persuadable.
oorreik, (oorge-), pass, hand.
oorrek, (oorge-), stretch again.
oorrek, (–), overstrain, **sig –**, overstretch (overreach) oneself.
oorreken, (oorge-), calculate again.
oorring, ear-ring.
oorroei, (oorge-), row across.
oorrok, overskirt.
oorrompel, (–), take by surprise, overwhelm, fall (swarm) upon, rush.
oorry, (oorge-), ride (drive) over (across).
oorry, (–), override; knock down.
oorryp, overripe.
oorrypad, road across; crossing.
oorsaak, (-sake), cause, origin; – **en gevolg**, cause and effect.
oorsaaklik, (-e), causal.
oorsaaklikheid, causality.
oorsê, (oorge-), say again, repeat.
oorsees, (-sese), oversea, transmarine.
oorseil, (oorge-), sail across (over).
oorsein, (oorge-), wire, telegraph, cable.
oorsend, (oorge-), dispatch; transmit.
oorsending, (-e, -s), sending, dispatch, remittance; transmission.
oorset, reset, vide **oorsit**.
oorsetting, (-e, -s), translation.
oorsiekte, ear-disease.
oorsien, (oorge-), see on the other side; excuse, overlook.
oorsig, (-te), view; synopsis, summary.
oorsigkaart, outline-map.
oorsigtelik, (-e), surveyable; giving an outline (synopsis, summary, account).
oorsilwer, (–), silver.
oorsing, (oorge-), sing over again.

oorsit, (oorge-), put over (across); take across, ferry over; promote (at school); translate, put into (another language).
oorskadu, (-), overshadow; outshine, eclipse; cloud, darken.
oorskat, (-), overestimate, overrate.
oorskat, (oorge-), estimate (value) again, re-estimate.
oorskatting, overestimation.
oorskatting, re-estimation, revaluation.
oorskeep, (oorge-), tranship.
oorskeer, (oorge-), shave again; shear (sheep) again.
oorskep, (oorge-), ladle over, spoon over.
oorskeping, (-e, -s), transhipment.
oorskiet, n. remains; remainder, rest; surplus, remnant; leavings.
oorskiet, (oorge-), remain, be left over.
oorskiet, (oorge-), shoot over again.
oorskietsel, vide oorskiet, n.
oorskilder, (oorge-), repaint, paint over.
oorskoen, galosh, overshoe.
oorskop, (oorge-), kick over, convert.
oorskot, (-te), vide oorskiet, n.; surplus; stoflike -, mortal remains.
oorskreeu, (-), shout (howl) down.
oorskry, (-), cross; overstep, pass beyond; exceed; violate, infringe.
oorskryf, -skrywe, (oorge-), rewrite; copy (out), transcribe; crib; transfer.
oorskuiwe, (oorge-), shift (move) across.
oorskut, ear-guard.
oorslaan, (oorge-), hit over; fold (turn) over, overflow (of river); skip, omit, leave out, miss out; miss (a meeting); pass (over) by; misfire (of motor, gun); – in, change into, turn to; – tot, turn to, change into.
oorslag, (-slae), overlapping part; hasp (and staple); flap.
oorsleep, (oorge-), drag across (over).
oorsmeer, (oorge-), smear again, butter (bread) again; put (smear) on.
oorspan, (-), span, extend across; overstrain; –ne, overstrung, overstrained.
oorspan, (oorge-), change (draught animals), stretch (span) over.
oorspanning, overstrain(ing), overexcitement, overexertion, overwork.
oorspel, vide owerspel.
oorspieël, otoscope.
oorsprei, n. bedspread, coverlet.
oorsprei, (oorge-), spread over.
oorspring, (oorge-), jump (leap) over; spark over, skip, omit.
oorsprong, (-e), origin, source.
oorspronklik, (-e), original; primordial.
oorspronklikheid, originality.
oorspuit(jie), ear-syringe.
oorstaan, n.: ten – van, in the presence of.
oorstaan, (oorge-), stand over; stop.
oorstap, (oorge-), cross, step across (over); change; pass over, disregard.
oorsteek, (oorge-), cross (the street).
oorstelp, (-), overwhelm; – met, shower (gifts) upon, load with (praise), heap upon, overwhelm with, swamp with.
oorstelping, overwhelming.
oorstem, (oorge-), tune again, retune (piano, etc.); vote again.
oorstem, (-), outvote; deafen, make (sound) inaudible.
oorstoot, (oorge-), push over.
oorstop, (oorge-), darn again.
oorstort, (oorge-), pour over; spill.
oorstroming, (-e, -s), overflowing; flood.

oorstroom, (oorge-), overflow; brim over.
oorstroom, (-), flood, inundate (lit. & fig.); deluge, swamp; overstock, glut.
oorstuur, upset; hy was –, he had lost control of himself, he was upset.
oorstuur, (oorge-), send over.
oorstryk, (oorge-), iron again.
oorstyg, (oorge-), cross.
oorstyg, (-), exceed, be beyond.
oorsuiker, (-), sugar.
oorsuising, (-e, -s), ringing in the ears.
oorswem, (oorge-), swim (across); swim again.
oorsy, opposite (other) side.
oortap, (oorge-), pour (transfer) into another vessel.
oorteken, (oorge-), redraw, draw over again; sign again; copy (a drawing).
oorteken, (-), oversubscribe (a loan).
oortel, (oorge-), (1) recount.
oortel, (oorge-), (2) lift over (across).
oortip, lobe of the ear.
oortog, (-te), passage, crossing.
oortollig, (-e), a. superfluous, redundant, unnecessary.
oortollig, adv. superfluously; – eet, drink, eat, drink to excess.
oortolligheid, superfluity.
oortreder, (-s), trespasser, transgressor, infringer (of law).
oortreding, (-e, -s), transgression, infringement, trespass(ing).
oortree, (-), transgress, infringe, break (rules), trespass against (the law).
oortree, (oorge-), step over.
oortref, (-), surpass, excel, outclass, outmatch; in getal –, outnumber.
oortreffend, (-e), superlative (degree).
oortrek, (-ke), n. cover, slip, casing.
oortrek, (oorge-), pull over; move (into another house); cross, trek over (across); blow over; trace (over); upholster (furniture), cover; 'n bed (skoon) –, change the bedclothes.
oortrek, (-), overdraw.
oortrektrui, pullover.
oortrekking, overdrawing, overdraught.
oortrekpapier, tracing-paper.
oortreksel, (-s), cover, slip, case.
oortroef, (-), overtrump; outbid, outdo.
oortrokke: – rekening, overdraft.
oortrou, (oorge-), go through the marriage ceremony again.
oortuie, -tuig, (-), convince.
oortui(g)end, (-e), convincing.
oortuiging, (-e, -s), conviction.
oortuiting, tingling of the ears.
oortyd, overtime.
oorvaar, (oorge-), cross; take across.
oorvaar, (-), run down (over).
oorvaart, passage, crossing.
oorval, (-le), surprise attack; fit.
oorval, (oorge-), fall (tumble) over.
oorval, (-), (take by) surprise, overtake; deur 'n rower –, attacked by a robber; deur die slaap –, overcome by sleep.
oorveeg, box on the ear.
oorverdowend, (-e), deafening.
oorverfyn, (-de) overrefined.
oorverhit, (-), overheat, superheat.
oorvermoeid, (-e), overfatigued.
oorvertel, (-), tell over again, repeat.
oorverf, (oorge-), repaint; redye.
oorversadig, (-), supersaturate; satiate, surfeit, cloy.
oorversadiging, supersaturation, surcharge; surfeit, satiation.

oorvleuel, (-), outflank; surpass.
oorvlie(g), (oorge-), fly over (across).
oorvlies, membrane of the ear.
oorvloed, abundance, plenty; **in** -, in profusion (plenty), galore; **in** - **lewe**, live in luxury; **die horing van** -, the horn of plenty, cornucopia.
oorvloedig, (-e), abundant, plentiful, copious, ample, profuse.
oorvloedigheid, abundance, plentifulness.
oorvloei, (oorge-), overflow, flow (run) over, brim over; flood, inundate; - **van**, bubble (brim) over with; be rich in, abound in.
oorvoed, (-), overfeed.
oorvoeding, overfeeding.
oorvoer, (oorge-), lead across (over); convey, transport, take across.
oorvoer, (-), overfeed; overstock.
oorvoering, transport, taking across.
oorvoering, overfeeding; glutting.
oorvol, overfull, brim-full; overcrowded.
oorvra, (oorge-), ask again.
oorvra, (-), overcharge.
oorvrag, excess-luggage.
oorwaai, (oorge-), blow over; pass off.
oorwaks, (-e), box on the ear.
oorwas, ear-wax.
oorweë, -**weeg**, (oorge-), weigh again, reweigh; be overweight.
oorweë, -**weeg**, (-), consider, think, (matter) over, weigh (consequences, etc.); turn the scale, decide the issue.
oorweg, n. level-crossing.
oorweg, adv.: **kom met**, get on with.
oorweging, (-e, -s), consideration; **in** - **gee**, suggest; **in** - **neem**, consider, take into consideration.
oorwegwagter, gatekeeper.
oorweldig, (-), overpower, overwhelm; conquer; seize; overcome.
oorweldigend, (-e), overpowering, intense, tremendous, overwhelming.
orweldiger, (-s), conqueror, usurper.
oorweldiging, overpowering.
oorwelf, (-), overarch, span, vault.
oorwelfsel, (-s), vault.
oorwen, vide **oorwin**.
oorwerk, n. overwork, overtime.
oorwerk, (oorge-), work overtime.
oorwerk, (-): **sig** -, overwork oneself.
oorwerp, (oorge-), throw (fling) over.
oorwig, preponderance; **die** - **hê**, preponderate.
oorwin, oorwen, (-), conquer, defeat, vanquish. overcome, master, get the better of.
oorwinlik, (-e), conquerable.
oorwinnaar, (-s), conqueror, victor.
oorwinning, (-e, -s), victory; **die** - **behaal oor**, gain the victory over.
oorwins, excess profit.
oorwinsbelasting, duty on excess-profits.
oorwinter, (-), winter, hibernate.
oorwintering, (-e, -s), wintering, hibernation.
oorwip, (oorge-), hop over; drop in.
oorwit, (oorge-), whitewash again.
oorwoë, considered.
oorwonne, conquered, defeated.
oorwonne, (-s), conquered (vanquished) person, loser.
oorwurm, ear-wig.
ooryling, hurry, precipitance, overhaste.
oorysten, casque.
oos, n. east; - **wes, tuis bes**, there is no place like home; east or west, home is best; vide **ooste**.
oos, a. east.
Oos-Afrika, East Africa.
Oos-Europa, Eastern Europe.

Oos-Indië, the East Indies.
Oos-Indies, (-e), East Indian; -**e Kompanjie**, East India Company.
Oos-Indiëvaarder, East-Indiaman.
ooskant, vide **oostekant**.
ooskus, east coast.
Ooskuskoors, East Coast Fever.
oosmoeson, dry monsoon.
oosnoordoos, east-north-east.
oospassaat, east trade-wind.
Oos-Pruisies, (-e), East Prussian.
Oossee: die -, the Baltic.
oossy, east side.
ooste, (the) east; **die O**-, the East.
oostekant, east (side).
oostelik, (-e), easterly, eastern.
Oostenryk, Austria.
Oostenryker, (-s), Austrian.
Oostenryk-Hongarye, Austria-Hungary.
Oostenryks, (-e), Austrian.
oostergrens, eastern border (frontier).
oosterkim, eastern horizon.
oosterlengte, eastern longitude.
Oosterling, (-e), Oriental; Eastener.
Oosters, (-e), Oriental, Eastern.
oostewind, east wind.
ooswaarts, (-e), eastward.
ootmoed, humility, meekness.
ootmoedig, (-e), humble, meek.
ootmoedigheid, vide **ootmoed**.
op, prep. on, upon, in, at; - **die muur**, on the wall; - **die platteland**, in the country; - **straat, kantoor**, in the street, office; - **skool**, at school; - **skool bly**, stay in; - **see**, at sea; - **wag**, on guard; - **tyd**, in time; - **'n dag**, one day; **twee maal** - **'n dag**, twice a day; - **die laaste**, at the latest; - **hande**, on hand; near; - **die end**, in the end, eventually; - **my ou dag**, in my old age; - **Engels**, in English; - **'n galop**, at a gallop; **almal** - **een na**, all but one; - **hierdie manier**, in this way; - **Oudtshoorn**, at Oudtshoorn; **die een** - **die ander**, one after the other.
op, adv. up, on; - **en neer**, - **en af**, up and down; **die trap** -, up the stairs; **van onder (af)** -, from below, from the bottom; **'n hoed** - **hê**, have a hat on; **dit is** -, there is nothing left, it is all gone (finished), it has run out; **hy is** -, he is up (out of bed); he is dead-beat, worn-out; - **en top**, all over, out-and-out; down-right.
opaal, (opale), opal.
opaalagtig, (-e), opal-like, opalescent.
opaalsteen, opal.
opbagger, (opge-), dredge up.
opbel, (opge-), ring up, give a ring.
opbêre, -**berg**, (opge-), put away; store.
opbeur, (opge-), lift up, drag up; cheer up, gladden, comfort.
opbeuring, comfort, consolation.
opbie(d), (opge-): - **teen**, bid against.
opbieg, (opge-), confess.
opbind, (opge-), tie (bind) up.
opblaas, (opge-), blow up, puff up, inflate; blast; **'n brug** -, blow up a bridge.
opblaassiekte, heaves, tympanites.
opbloei, n. revival; reawakening.
opbloei, (opge-), revive, begin to flourish.
opbly, (opge-), stay (wait) up; remain on.
opbod: by - **verkoop**, sell by auction.
opbondel, (opge-), bundle up.
opborrel, (opge-), bubble up.
opborreling, bubbling up, ebullition.
opborsel, (opge-), brush up.
opbou, n. building up; establishment, advancement; edification.

opbou, (opge-), build up; edify, benefit; **weer –**, rebuild.
opbouend, (-e), edifying; constructive.
opbouing, building up, construction; reconstruction; edification; cultivation.
opbrand, (opge-), burn (away, out), consume; press for payment.
opbrander, (-s), demand for payment.
opbreek, (opge-), break up; strike (tents); break (pull) up (street); disperse; raise (a siege); emit (wind), belch.
opbrengs, -brings, (-te), yield, crop (of wheat), output; produce; proceeds.
opbring, (opge-), bring up; serve (dinner); rear (child), educate; vomit; pay (taxes); yield (crop); bring in, realize; arrest, run in.
opbrings, vide **opbrengs**.
opbruis, (opge-), bubble up, effervesce, foam up, fizz, flare up.
opbruisend, (-e), effervescent; ebullient; hot-tempered.
opdaag, (opge-), arrive, turn up.
opdam, (opge-), dam up; block up.
opdamp, (opge-), vaporize; evaporate.
opdans, (opge-), dance up; wear out.
opdat, (in order) that; **– nie**, lest.
opdien, (opge-), dish up, serve up.
opdiep, (opge-), dig up (out), unearth.
opdis, (opge-), serve up, dish up.
opdoek, (opge-), furl (sails); clear out.
opdoem, (opge-), loom (up).
opdoen, (opge-), do (up) (the hair); come by, get; acquire (knowledge); catch (a cold); get, contract (disease).
opdok, (opge-), pay up; pay the piper.
opdomkrag, (opge-), jack up.
opdons, (opge-), let (a person) have it, dust (one's) jacket, go for (a person); do (things) anyhow, bungle along; **hy dons maar altyd op**, he is a devil-may-care (happy-go-lucky) sort of fellow.
opdra(ag), (opge-), carry up; wear out (clothes); instruct, charge; entrust (person) with (duty); dedicate (church, book to); **iemand die bevel –**, put a person in command.
opdraai, (opge-), turn higher; wind up.
opdraand, (-e), (pl. also **opdraans**), n. uphill path (road), rising ground; **steil –**, stiff climb.
opdraand, (-e), a. uphill, sloping upwards; **–e werk**, uphill work.
opdraand, -draans, adv. uphill; **dit – kry**, have a hard time.
opdrag, (-te), instruction, order, commission, charge; dedication (of church, book); **– gee**, instruct; **– kry**, be instructed (commissioned).
opdreun, (opge-), drone (on); make it hot for, drive (a person) on.
opdrifsel, (-s), drift, driftwood, debris.
opdring, (opge-), push on (forward); **iemand iets –**, force something upon, press something upon a person; **sig – aan**, force oneself upon, intrude upon (a person).
opdringer, (-s), intruder, obtruder.
opdringerig, (-iewe), intrusive, obtrusive.
opdringerigheid, intrusiveness.
opdrink, (opge-), drink up, finish.
opdroë, -droog, (opge-), dry up.
opdroging, drying up, desiccation.
opdruk, (-ke), n. imprint, surcharge.
opdruk, (opge-), press up, imprint (stamp) on; urge on hurry, drive.
opdryf, -drywe, (opge-), drive up; overdrive; overwork (person); force up.
opduik, (opge-), emerge, come to the surface; turn up, crop up.
ope, vide **oop**.

opêe, vide **opeg**.
opeen, one upon another, together.
opeendring, (opeenge-), crowd together.
opeenhoop, (opeenge-), heap up, accumulate.
opeenhoping, accumulation; mass, crowd; congestion (traffic).
opeenja(ag), (opeenge-), drive together.
opeenpak, (opeenge-), pack together.
opeenplak, (opeenge-), glue together.
opeens, suddenly, all of a sudden.
opeenstapel, (opeenge-), pile (heap) up, accumulate.
opeenstapeling, accumulation.
opeenvolg, (opeenge-), follow each other.
opeenvolgend, (-e), successive.
opeenvolging, succession, sequence.
opeet, (opgeëet), eat (up), finish; devour, consume; **sy (eie) woorde –**, swallow his own words, recant; **alles vir soet koek –**, swallow everything.
opeg, -êe, (opgeëg, opgeêe), harrow.
opeis, (opgeëis), claim, demand.
opeisbaar, (-bare), claimable.
opeising, (-e, -s), claim(ing), demand.
opelug, open air; **in die –**, in the open.
opelugspel, outdoor-game; open-air play.
opelugteater, open-air theatre.
opelyf, evacuation (of the bowels); **– kry (hê)**, have a motion.
open, (ge-), open.
openbaar, n. public; **in die –**, in public.
openbaar, (-bare), a. public; **–bare geheim, vyandskap**, open secret, enmity.
openbaar, (ge-), reveal, divulge, disclose.
openbaarmaking, (-e, -s), publication, divulgation (divulgement), disclosure.
openbaring, (-e, -s), revelation, manifestation, disclosure; **die O– van Johannes**, the Revelation of St. John; **dit was 'n –**, it was an eye-opener.
openhartig, (-e), frank, open(-hearted).
openhartigheid, frankness, candour.
opening, (-e, -s), opening; aperture, gap, passage, chink, slit, interstice; post-mortem.
openingsplegtigheid, opening ceremony.
openingsrede, opening address, inaugural address.
openinkie, (-s), little opening, gap, slit.
openlik, (-e), a. open, public.
openlik, adv. openly, publicly; frankly.
op-en-top, out-and-out.
opera, (-s), opera.
operagebou, opera-house.
operageselskap, opera-company.
operakoor, operatic chorus.
operasanger(es), operatic singer.
operasie, (-s), operation.
operasiekamer, operating-theatre (-room).
operasiemes, opereermes, operating-knife, surgeon's scalpel.
operasieplan, plan of campaign.
operasietafel, operating-table.
operateur, (-s), operator.
operatief, (-tiewe), operative, surgical.
operd, (opgeërd), earth up, bank up.
opereer, (ge-), operate.
operette, (-s), operetta.
operettegeselskap, operetta-company.
opflikker, (opge-), flicker (flare) up, blaze up, cheer (brighten) up.
opflikkering, (-e, -s), flicker(ing), flare-up; cheering up; flicker (of hope).
opfris, (opge-), refresh, revive; brush up, renew.
opfrissertjie, (-s), appetizer, pick-me-up.
opfrissing, refreshing; brushing up (of knowledge); refresher (drink).

opgaaf, (-gawe), **opgawe,** (-s), statement (of facts), account; (official) return, report, exercise, problem, (examination-)paper; hut-tax; **met – van redes,** stating reasons.

opgaan, (opge-), go up, ascend, rise; climb (mountain); run short; **in vlamme –,** go up in flames; **vir 'n eksamen –,** go in (enter) for an examination; **die verkeerde weg (pad) –,** take to (fall into) bad habits, be on the downward path; **in jouself –,** be self-absorbed; **in jou werk –,** be absorbed in one's work; **in 'n groot stad gaan hulle in die menigte op,** in a big city they are lost in the crowd; **die vergelyking gaan nie op nie,** the comparison does not hold good.

opgaande, going up, rising, ascending.
opgaar, (opge-), collect, store up.
opgang, (-e), rise; ascent; growth; success, fame; **– maak,** achieve success, rise in the world, become famous (popular).
opgeblaas, (-de, -te, -blase), blown up, puffed up, inflated; puffy.
opgeblase, puffed up, inflated.
opgeblasenheid, bloatedness; arrogance.
opgebruik, (–), use up, consume.
opgee, (opge-), pass (hand) up; give up, hand over; vomit, spit (blood); give, set (a problem); enumerate (items), state (reasons), specify (details); give up (patient, plan, hope), lose (courage); quit, stop (smoking); ask (riddle), give out (text), announce; **dit gee op,** it deceives the eyes; **hoog – van,** boast (brag) about, extol, praise; **my oë gee op,** my eyes are failing me.
opgeefsel, (-s), mirage.
opgehewe, raised; swollen, inflamed.
opgehoop, (-te), heaped up, accumulated.
opgekrop, (-te), pent-up (rage).
opgemaak, (-te), made up; used up, wasted; trimmed (hat); done up (hair); made (bed); instigated, put up.
opgeprop, (-te), crammed.
opgeruimd, (-e), cheerful, gay.
opgeruimdheid, cheerfulness.
opgeskeep: – **sit met iemand,** not know how to get rid of a person; – **sit met iets,** be saddled with something; **ek is – met my self,** I am at a loose end.
opgeskort, (-e), suspended (sentence).
opgeskote, grown-up (boy), adolescent.
opgeskroef, (-de), screwed up; stilted.
opgesmuk, (-te), showy, gaudy; embellished, bombastic (style).
opgeswel, (-de), swollen.
opgetoë, elated, exultant, in high spirits.
opgetoënheid, elation, delight, rapture.
opgewas(se): – **wees teen,** be a match for, be (somebody's) equal, be able to hold one's own against; **nie – teen die moeilikhede nie,** unable to cope with the difficulties.
opgewek, (-te), cheerful, gay, cheery.
opgewektheid, cheerfulness.
opgewonde, excited.
opgewondenheid, excitement.
opgooi, n. toss.
opgooi, (opge-), throw up, toss up; vomit, fetch up.
opgraaf, -grawe, (opge-), unearth, dig out; exhume (body); excavate.
opgrawing, (-e, -s), digging out (up); exhumation, excavation.
opgroei, (opge-), grow up.
ophaal, (-hale), n. hairline, upstroke.
ophaal, (opge-), draw up, pull up; hoist (flag); weigh (anchor); shrug (shoulders); fish (draw) out; turn up (the nose); collect (tickets); rake up, open up.
ophaalbrug, drawbridge.
ophaalgordyn, blind.
ophaalnet, square-net.
ophande, near at hand, approaching.
ophang, (opge-), hang; hang up, suspend; **sig –,** hang oneself.
ophap, (opge-), snap up.
ophark, (opge-), rake up, rake together.
ophê, (opgehad), have (a hat) on; have finished (one's food); **nie veel met iets – nie,** not care for something.
ophef, n. fuss.
ophef, (opge-), lift (up); raise (eyes, hand); abolish, repeal (law), revoke, annul; raise, (siege); remove (duties); elevate, lift, raise (socially).
opheffing, (-e, -s), lifting; abolition, raising; elevation, uplifting.
ophelder, (opge-), clear up; elucidate, illustrate; solve (mystery); brighten.
opheldering, (-e, -s), clearing up; elucidation, explanation, illustration.
ophelp, (opge-), help up, raise.
ophemel, (opge-), extol, sing the praises of, write up.
ophemeling, (-e, -s), praising, laudation.
ophits, (opge-), instigate, incite, stir up.
ophitser, (-s), instigator.
ophitsing, incitement, instigation.
ophoes, (opge-), cough up.
ophoop, (opge-), heap up, pile up, heap together accumulate; amass.
ophoping, (-e, -s), heap, accumulation.
ophou, n.: **sonder –,** without stopping.
ophou, (opge-), hold up; support; keep on (hat); hold (breath); retain (urine); detain, keep (waiting); arrest progress of; stop, leave off; keep up (one's position), uphold (honour); **hier hou die straat op,** this is the end of the street; **dit hou 'n mens lank op,** it takes up much time; **sig –,** stay, live, frequent, haunt; **daarmee hou ek my nie op nie,** I do not lend myself to that sort of thing.
ophouding, cessation, stopping.
opiaat, (opiate), opiate.
opinie, (-s), opinion.
opium, opium.
opiumhandel, opium-traffic.
opiumroker, opium-smoker.
opiumskuiwer, opium-smoker.
opiumsmokkelaar, opium-smuggler.
opja(ag), (opge-), drive (chase) up; speed up (the road); flush (birds), put up (game), rouse, start; frighten away; force up; force (bidding); raise (dust).
opkam, (opge-), comb up.
opkeil, (opge-), wedge up; drive (urge) on, chastise, give it (a person) hot.
opklaar, (opge-), clear up (of weather); brighten (of face); elucidate, solve.
opklim, (opge-), climb, ascend, mount (horse); rise, be promoted.
opklimming, (-e, -s), ascent; gradation, progression; **by –,** by degrees.
opklop, (opge-), knock up.
opklouter, (opge-), scramble up.
opknabbel, (opge-), nibble, munch.
opknap, (opge-), tidy up (oneself, table), trim up (person), make neat (tidy), clean up (room); renovate, do up (house), patch up, retrim (dress); put (matter) right; revive; **die sieke knap langsaam op,** the patient is gradually picking up.
opknappertjie, (-s), tonic.

opknoop, (opge-), tie up, button up.
opkom, (opge-), come up; get up, stand up; rise (of sun); shoot forth, sprout, come up (of grass); spring up (of breeze); come on (of storm); come on (the stage); attend (meeting), turn up; crop up, arise (of question); spring up; dit het nooit by my opgekom nie, it never struck (occurred) to me; – teen, make head against (the wind); take exception to, object to; – vir, take the part of, back up, stand up for (rights), champion.
opkomende, rising (sun, generation).
opkommandeer, (opge-), commandeer.
opkoms, rising (of sun); rise (of a statesman); beginning; attendance.
opkook, (opge-), boil up; boil, cook.
opkoop, n. buying up; forestalling.
opkoop, (opge-), buy up; forestall.
opkoper, buyer (up).
opkrimp, (opge-), shrink, shrivel up.
opkrop, (opge-), conceal, restrain, bottle up; opgekropte woede, pent-up anger.
opkruip, (opge-), creep (crawl) up.
opkrul, (opge-), curl up.
opkry, (opge-), get up; get on (a hat); use up, eat (drink) up, finish.
opkweek, (opge-), rear, educate; raise.
opkyk, (opge-), look up.
oplaag, impression, edition (of book).
oplaai, (opge-), (1) flame (blaze) up.
oplaai, (opge-), (2) load (up); give (person) a lift.
oplaas, finally, eventually, at last.
oplap, (opge-), patch up, repair, tinker up.
oplê (opge-), put on, apply; impose (tax) upon, lay on, inflict (punishment) on; set (person a task), command (to do); iemand die swye –, impose silence upon a person.
oplegging, imposition; infliction.
oplegsel, (-s), trimming (of dress).
oplei, (opge-), lead up; train (teacher), educate, bring up; vir 'n eksamen –, prepare for an examination.
oplei(d)er, trainer, coach.
opleiding, training, education.
opleidingskip, training-ship.
opleidingskool, training-college (-school).
oplek, (opge-), lick up, lap up.
oplet, (opge-), attend; watch.
oplettend, (-e), attentive.
oplettendheid, attentiveness, attention.
opleef, -lewe, (opge-), revive.
oplewer, (opge-), yield, bring in, produce, give; deliver; moeilikheid –, present difficulty.
oplewering, (-e, -s), yielding; delivery.
oplewing, revival.
oplig, (opge-), lift (up), raise; kidnap.
opligter, (-s), swindler, cheat.
oploop, n. tumult, riot; crowd.
oploop, (opge-), walk up, go up; slope upwards, rise; accumulate; contract (disease); get (a beating); sustain (injury); rekeninge laat –, run up accounts.
oplopend, (-e), sloping upwards.
oplopend, (-e), short-tempered, irascible.
oplopendheid, irascibility.
oplos, (opge-), dissolve; solve (problem); settle (dispute); work out.
oplosbaar, (-bare), soluble; solvable.
oplosbaarheid, solubility; solvability.
oplossing, (-e, -s), solution.
oplossingsmiddel, solvent.
oplug, (opge-), relieve.
oplugting, relief.
opluister, (opge-), adorn, add lustre to, shed lustre upon, illuminate; illustrate.

opluistering, adornment, illumination.
opmaak, (opge-), spend, use up; make (bed); do (up) (the hair); trim (hat); make up (in pages); compile; draw up (report), make out (list); stir up, incite; conclude; sig –, prepare oneself, get ready.
opmars, n. advance.
opmarsjeer, (opge-), march forward, advance.
opmeet, (opge-), measure; survey.
opmerk, (opge-), notice; observe.
opmerkenswaardig, (-e), noteworthy.
opmerker, (-s), observer.
opmerking, (-e, -s), remark, observation.
opmerkingsgawe, gift of observation.
opmerklik, (-e), remarkable, noteworthy.
opmerksaam, (-same), observant, attentive; iemand op iets – maak, draw a person's attention to something.
opmerksaamheid, attention.
opmessel, (opge-), build up.
opmeting, survey; measurement.
opmonter, (opge-), cheer up.
opnaaisel, (-s), tuck.
opname, (-s), taking; insertion; survey (of land); reception; record(ing); fotografiese –, photo.
opneem, (opge-), take up; pick up; take (temperature); count (votes); film, shoot; borrow (money); insert; put in; include; absorb (heat), assimilate; digest; admit; take in, adopt; look (person) up and down, take stock of; dit vir iemand –, take a person's part; verkeerd –, take amiss, misunderstand; iets goed –, take something in good part.
opnemer, registration-officer; counter.
opneming, borrowing; counting; admission; insertion; assimilation.
opnemingsvaartuig, survey(ing)-vessel.
opnemingsvermoë, receptivity.
opnoem, (opge-), name, mention, enumerate.
opnoeming, naming, enumeration.
opnuut, again, afresh, anew.
opoffer, (opge-), sacrifice, offer up.
opoffering, (-e, -s), sacrifice.
oponthoud, delay, stoppage; break down.
opossum, (-s), opossum.
oppak, (opge-), pack up.
oppas, (opge-), try on (hat); look after, take care of, tend (flock), herd (sheep), nurse (patient); be careful, take care, look out, mind; – vir, beware of.
oppassend, (-e), well-behaved; steady.
oppasser, (-s), nurse (of child); caretaker, keeper, attendant; servant.
oppas(sing), looking after, nursing; care.
opper, (-s), n. (hay)cock.
opper, (ge-), suggest, propose, raise (objection), broach (subject).
opperbes, excellent, first-rate, capital.
opperbestuur, supreme rule (direction).
opperbevel, supreme command.
opperbevelhebber, commander-in-chief.
opperbewind, vide opperbestuur.
oppergesag, supreme authority.
opperheer, sovereign, overlord; die O–, God.
opperheerser, sovereign.
opperheerskappy, sovereignty.
opperhoof, chief, head.
opperhuid, epidermis, cuticle, scarf-skin.
opperkamerheer, Lord Chamberlain.
opperkleed, upper garment.
opperleenheer, overlord.
oppermag, supremacy, supreme power.
oppermagtig, (-e), supreme, sovereign.
oppermajesteit, supreme majesty.
oppermens, superman.

opper-priester, high-priest.
oppers, (opge-), force up.
oppersaal, upper hall.
opperstalmeester, Master of the Horse.
opperste, uppermost, highest, supreme; 'n – skurk, an arch-rogue.
opperstuurman, first mate.
oppervlak, (upper) surface.
oppervlakkig, (-e), superficial, shallow, surface (impressions).
oppervlakkigheid, superficiality.
oppervlakte, surface; area; superficies.
Opperwese, Supreme Being, God.
oppik, (opge-), peck up; pick up.
opplak, (opge-), paste on; mount.
oppoets, (opge-), polish, brush up, clean.
oppomp, (opge-), pump up (liquid); inflate (tyre), pump up, blow up.
opponeer, (ge-), oppose.
opponent, (-e), opponent.
opportunis, (-te), opportunist.
opportunisme, opportunism.
opportunisties, (-e), opportunist.
opposisie, opposition.
opposisieblad, opposition-paper.
opposisiekant, the opposition.
opposisieparty, opposition.
opposisiestem, opposition-vote.
opprop, (opge-), cram, fill.
opraak, (opge-), run short, give out, be spent; my geduld het opgeraak, I lost patience.
opraap, (opge-), pick (snatch, take) up; 'n opgeraapte span, a. scratch team.
opraapsel, (-s), scraps, pickings; guttersnipe, street arab; mongrel.
oprakel, (opge-), poke up (fire); rake up.
opredder, (opge-), tidy up.
opreg, (-te), upright, sincere, straightforward, frank, open; genuine, pure.
opregtheid, uprightness; sincerity.
oprig, (opge-), raise, set (upright, help up; erect building); start, set up (business), found, (institution), establish, float (company), form (society).
oprigter, (-s), founder; promoter (of company); builder, erector.
oprigtersaandeel, founder's share.
oprigting, foundation, promoting; erection.
oproei, (opge-), row up.
oproep, (-e), n. summons; appeal; gehoor gee aan die –, answer the call, respond to the appeal.
oproep, (opge-), summon, call up(on); summons; call out (up); call (together).
oproeping, (-e, -s), summons, calling up.
oproer, (-e), revolt, rebellion, mutiny.
oproerig, (-e), rebellious, riotous.
oproerigheid, rebelliousness, riotousness.
oproerling, (-e), insurgent.
oproermaker, agitator, rioter.
oprol, (opge-), roll up; coil up.
oprook, (opge-), finish (smoking); al die sigarette –, smoke all the cigarettes.
oprui, (opge-), incite, instigate: -ende toespraak, inflammatory speech.
opruier, (-s), agitator, inciter, instigator.
opruiing, instigation, incitation.
opruim, (opge-), clear away, clear, tidy up; do away with.
opruiming, (-e, -s), clearing away, clearance; clearance sale; – hou, clear away things; get rid of completely.
opruk, (opge-), jerk, (pull) up; advance.
opryg, -rye, (opge-), tack; lace.
opsaal, (opge-), saddle.

opsê, (opge-), say (prayer); recite; call in (money); terminate (agreement); iemand die diens –, give a person notice.
opsegbaar, (-bare), terminable.
opsegging, notice; termination.
opseil, (opge-), sail up.
opsent, absent, absent; lost.
opset, (ground-)plan, outline, framework; purpose, intention, design; met –, on purpose, purposely, intentionally.
opsetlik, (-e), a. intentional, deliberate.
opsetlik, adv. on purpose, deliberately.
opsie, (-s), option; in – gee, give the refusal of.
opsien, n.: – baar, cause a sensation.
opsien, (opge-), look up; teen iemand –, look up to somebody; teen iets –, shrink from doing something.
opsienbarend, (-e), sensational.
opsiener, (-s), overseer, inspector; invigilator, commissioner.
opsier, (opge-), adorn, decorate.
opsiering, embellishment, adornment.
opsiersel, (-s), decoration, trimming.
opsig, (1), supervision.
opsig, (-te), (2) respect; ten –te van, in respect of, with regard to.
opsigselfstaande, isolated, separate.
opsigter, (-s), overseer; caretaker.
opsigtelik, (-e), showy, flashy, gaudy, loud (colour, dress, pattern).
opsigtig, (-e), vide opsigtelik.
opsigtigheid, showiness, flashiness.
opsioneel, (-nele), optional.
opsit, (opge-), (1) sit up; stay up; spoon; wait up.
opsit, (opge-), (2) put on (hat); cast on (knitting); swell (up); erect; raise (price); set up, start (business), establish; stake (money); 'n (groot) keel –, scream, cry, howl.
opskep, (opge-), scoop up, ladle out; serve up, dish up; brag, boast.
opskephou, drop-shot (tennis).
opskepper, (-s), ladle; braggart, boaster.
opskeploer, (opskepge-), sponge, cadge.
opskerp, (opge-), sharpen.
opskeur, (opge-), tear up.
opskiet, (opge-), shoot up; sprout; spend (ammunition); make progress; nie met iemand kan – nie, not be able to get on with a person.
opskik, n. finery, trimmings, trappings.
opskik, (opge-), dress up, trick out.
opskommel, (opge-), shake up.
opskop, (opge-), kick up.
opskort, (opge-), tuck up; reserve (judgement), postpone, defer, suspend (sentence); adjourn.
opskorting, (-e, -s), postponement, suspension, adjournment.
opskrif, (-te), inscription; heading (of chapter); caption; title.
opskrik, (opge-), start, be startled.
opskroef, (opge-), screw on; screw up.
opskryf, -skrywe, (opge-), write down, take down; enter, score; put down.
opskud, (opge-), shake up; hurry up.
opskudding, (-s), commotion, stir, bustle, confusion, fuss, sensation.
opskuif, -skuiwe, (opge-), push up; move up.
opslaan, (opge-), hit (strike) up; bounce; turn up (collar); put up (hood); cock (hat), turn up; raise (eyes); pitch (tent); raise (price); come up, shoot forth (out).
opslaangebou, prefab.
opslag, (-slae), up-stroke; rise, increase; ricochet, bounce; self-sown oats, barley, etc.; herbage, young grass; storage; – van die oog, look,

glance; **iemand slaan dat hy opslae maak,** send a person sprawling.
opslagkoeël, ricochet shot (bullet).
opslagplek, store, shed.
opslagruimte, storage-space.
opsluit, (opge-), shut up, lock up (in); imprison, confine; **wat lê hierin opgesluit (opgeslote)?,** what does this imply?
opsluit, adv. absolutely; **hy wou – saamgaan,** he insisted on going along.
opsluiting, (-e, -s), locking up (in); imprisonment, confinement.
opsluk, (opge-), swallow (up).
opslurp, (opge-), lap up; absorb.
opsmuk, n. finery, trimmings, trappings.
opsmuk (opge-), dress up, trick out (up), decorate; embellish (narrative); **opgesmukte styl,** ornate style.
opsmyt, (opge-), chuck (fling) up.
opsnap, (opge-), snap up.
opsny, (opge-), cut up; brag, boast.
opsnyer, boaster, braggart.
opsnyerig, (-e), boastful, bragging.
opsnuffel, (opge-), rummage out.
opsnuif, -snuiwe, (opge-), sniff up, inhale.
opsoek, (opge-), look up (a word); call on, look up (a person); look for.
opsom, (opge-), sum up; summarize.
opsomming, (-e, -s), summing up, enumeration; summary, précis.
opspaar, (opge-), save up, put by.
opspoor, (opge-), trace, track down, hunt down, find out.
opsporing, (-e, -s), tracing, tracking down; exploration.
opspraak, scandal; sensation; **in – kom,** become the theme of gossip; **– verwek,** cause a stir; **in – bring,** compromise.
opspring, (opge-), jump up; bounce; **van vreugde –,** leap for joy.
opstaan, (opge-), stand up, rise, get up; revolt, rebel; **uit die dood –,** rise from the dead.
opstaan-boordjie, stick-up collar.
opstal, (-le), (farm-)buildings, premises.
opstand, (-e), rebellion, revolt, rising, insurrection; **in – kom teen,** revolt against.
opstandeling, (-e), rebel, insurgent.
opstandig, (-e), insurgent, rebellious.
opstandigheid, rebelliousness.
opstanding, resurrection.
opstap, (opge-), walk up, walk on.
opstapel, -stawel, (opge-), build up; pile (heap) up, stack, accumulate.
opsteek, (opge-), pin up; put up (the hair); hold up (hand); prick up (ears); light (lamp); incite, instigate, urge on; **die weer steek op,** it is working up for rain.
opstel, (-le), n. composition, essay.
opstel, (opge-), place in position; mount (gun), erect (machinery); station, post; set up (theory); frame (rule), draw up (report), draft.
opsteller, (-s), framer, writer (of letter), draftsman.
opstelling, drawing up; placing in position; stationing (of troops).
opstelwerf, marshalling yard.
opstoker, (-s), instigator; agitator.
opstokery, instigation; incitement.
opstook, (opge-), stir (fire); instigate, incite, stir up.
opstoot, (opge-), push up; rise.
opstootjie, (-s), disturbance, riot, rising.
opstop, (opge-), fill, stop up, stuff (up).
opstopper, (-s), taxidermist; blow.
opstopping, stuffing; congestion; jam.

opstry, (opge-), contradict; dispute, argue away.
opstuif, -stuiwe, (opge-), fly up; flare up, flame up (into anger).
opstuur, (opge-), send up.
opstyg, (opge-), ascend, rise; mount.
opstyging, rising, ascent; mounting.
opsuig, -suie, (opge-), suck up (in); take up (liquid), absorb.
opsuip, (opge-), drink (booze) up.
opswaai, (opge-), swing up.
opsweep, (opge-), whip up; work up, incite, rouse up, inflame.
opswel, (opge-), swell (up).
opswelg, (opge-), swallow up.
opswelling, swelling, inflation.
optakel, (opge-), rig up; doll (trick) up.
optatief, (-tiewe), n. & a. optative.
opteken, (opge-), note (down), set (write) down, record, enter.
optekening, writing down, entering.
optel, (opge-), (1) add (up), total up.
optel, (opge-), (2) pick up; raise, lift; trouble, worry.
optelgoed, findings; rubbish.
optelkind, foundling.
optelling, (-e, -s), addition; counting up.
optelmasjien, adding-machine.
optelsom, addition-sum.
opties, (-e), optical.
optika, optics.
optikus, (-se, -tici), optician.
optimaal, a. optimum.
optimum, n. optimum.
optimus, (-te), optimist.
optimisme, optimism.
optimisties, (-e), optimistic.
optog, (-te), procession; approach.
optooi, (opge-), adorn, decorate, dress up.
optooisel, (-s), trimming, decoration.
optorring, (opge-), rip up.
optrede, appearance; behaviour, conduct, action, attitude.
optree, (opge-), appear; play (act) a part; take action, act; **as spreker –,** be the speaker, address the meeting; **handelend –,** take action, act.
optrek, (opge-), draw (pull) up; raise; shrug (shoulders); erect; add up; hoop (hoopingcough); lift, rise; **die neus vir iets –,** turn up the nose at; **teen die vyand –,** march against the enemy.
optuig, -tuie, (opge-), harness; rig.
opvaar, (opge-), sail up; ascend.
opval, (opge-), strike; **dit het my opgeval,** it struck me.
opvallend, (-e), striking, conspicuous.
opvang, (opge-), catch (snatch) up; catch (water); intercept; cut off (light); receive, check (blow).
opvangdam, catch-dam.
opvangdraad, aerial.
opvarende, (-s), passenger.
opvat, (opge-), take up; resume, continue; conceive (plan); understand; **iets verkeerd –,** take something in bad part; misinterpret something.
opvatting, (-e, -s), view, opinion, conception, idea.
opvee(g), (opge-), sweep up.
opveil, (opge-), sell by auction.
opveiling, (-e, -s), selling by auction, auction-sale.
opvis, (opge-), fish up (out); recover.
opvlam, (opge-), flare (flame) up.
opvlie(g), (opge-), fly up; jump up.

opvliegend, opvlieënd, (-e), quick-tempered, irascible.
opvliegendheid, opvlieëndheid, irascibility.
opvoed, (opge-), educate, bring up, train.
opvoeder, (-s), educator.
opvoeding, education, upbringing.
opvoedkunde, education, pedagogy.
opvoedkundig, (-e), pedagogic(al).
opvoedkundige, (-s), educationist.
opvoer, (opge-), (1) bring up; stage (play), produce, perform.
opvoer, (opge-), (2) consume; fatten.
opvoering, (-e, -s), performance.
opvolg, (opge-), succeed; obey, follow.
opvolger, (-s), successor.
opvolging, (-e, -s), succession.
opvorder, (opge-), claim, demand.
opvorderbaar, (-bare), claimable.
opvou, (opge-), fold up.
opvoubaar, (-bare), collapsible, foldable.
opvra, (opge-), withdraw (money), call in (money); claim.
opvreet, (opge-), devour.
opvrolik, (opge-), cheer up, gladden.
opvryf, -vrywe, (opge-), polish, rub up.
opvul, (opge-), fill up; stuff.
opvulsel, (-s), stuffing, filling.
opvysel, (opge-), extol, praise, cry up.
opwaai, (opge-), blow up; be blown up.
opwaarts, upward(s).
opwag, (opge-), wait for.
opwagting: sy – by iemand maak, wait (up)on somebody.
opwarm, (opge-), warm up.
opwas, (opge-), (1) wash up.
opwas, (opge-), (2) grow up.
opgwee(g), -weë, (opge-), – teen, counterbalance, make up for, be a setoff against.
opwek, (opge-), rouse, awake, wake up, raise from the dead; stir up; excite, provoke, stimulate; generate.
opwekkend, (-e), rousing, stirring, animating, exciting, stimulating.
opwekking, (-e, -s), rousing, stimulation, awakening, revival; resurrection; generation.
opwekkingsdiens, revival-meeting.
opwekkingsmiddel, stimulant, tonic.
opwel, (opge-), well up (out, forth), bubble up; –lende drifte, surging (rising) passions.
opwelling, (-e, -s), bubbling up, welling up, ebullition; outburst, flush (of joy), wave (of enthusiasm).
opwen, (opge-), wind up; excite.
opwerk, (opge-), work up; touch up.
opwerp, (opge-), throw up; build, make, erect; raise (question).
opwindend, (-e), exciting.
opwinding, excitement.
opwip, (opge-), tip up; rebound; jump up.
orakel, (-s), oracle.
orakelagtig, (-e), oracular.
orakelspreuk, oracle.
orakeltaal, oracular language.
oral(s), everywhere.
orang-oetang, (-s), orang-outang.
oranje, orange.
oranjeagtig, (-e), orange-like.
oranjebloeisel, orange-blossom.
oranjegeel, orange.
Oranje-huis, House of Orange.
Oranjerivier, Orange River.
Oranje-Vrystaat, Orange Free State.
orasie, (-s), (1) noise, row.
orasie, (-s), (2) oration.
oraties, (-e), oratorical.

orator, (-e, -s), orator.
oratorium, (-s, -toria), oratorio; oratory.
orde, (1) order; – hou (herstel), keep (restore) order; in 'n vergadering iets aan die – stel (bring), raise a question at a meeting; aan die – kom, come up for discussion; dit is aan die – van die dag, it is the order of the day; in – bring (maak), put in order, put right (straight), arrange, fix up; tot die – roep, call to order.
orde, (-s), (2) order (natural history): geestelike –, religious order.
ordebroer, brother.
ordeliewend, (-e), orderly, fond of order.
ordeliewendheid, love of order.
ordelik, (-e), orderly, well-behaved.
ordelikheid, orderliness.
ordeloos, (-lose), disorderly.
ordelys, order-paper.
orden, (ge-), put in order, arrange; ordain (minister of religion).
ordening, arrangement; ordination.
ordentlik, (-e), decent, respectable, fair, pretty good.
ordentlikheid, decency.
ordentlikheidshalwe, for decency's sake.
order, (-s), order, command; betaal aan K of –, pay to K or order; tot nader –, till further orders, until further notice.
orderbrief(ie), promissory note.
ordeteken, badge; –s, badges, insignia.
ordinaat, (-nate), ordinate.
ordinasie, (-s), ordinance (of God).
ordineer, (ge-), ordain.
ordinêr, (-e), ordinary, commonplace, everyday; vulgar, common.
ordinering, ordaining.
ordonnans, (-e), orderly.
ordonnansie, (-s), ordinance.
ordonneer, (ge-), ordain, decree.
oreer, (ge-), orate, hold forth.
orent, on end, upright, erect; – sit, sit up; place upright; – kom, get (stand) up; – staan, stand up.
orgaan, (-gane), organ.
organdie, organdie.
organies, (-e), organic.
organisasie, (-s), organization.
organisasietalent, organizing ability.
organiseer, (-s, -e), organizer.
organiseer, (ge-), organize.
organiseerder, (-s), organizer.
organisme, (-s), organism.
organsynsy, organzine.
orgelis, vide orrelis.
orgidee, (-deë), orchid.
orgie, (-s, -ë), orgy.
oribie, vide oorbietjie.
Oriënt, Orient.
oriëntaal, (-tale), oriental.
oriëntalis, (-te), orientalist.
oriëntasie, orientation.
oriënteer, (ge-): sig –, find one's bearings, orientate oneself.
oriëntering, orientation.
orig, (-e), (1) remaining; die –e, the remainder (rest).
orig, (-e), (2) meddlesome, intrusive.
origens, for the rest, otherwise.
origheid, meddlesomeness; vide orig (2).
originaliteit, originality.
origineel, (-nele), original.
orkaan, (-kane), hurricane.
Orkadiese Eilande, Orkneys.
orkes, (-te), orchestra.

orkesmusiek, orchestral music.
orkespartituur, orchestral score.
orkestoon(hoogte), concert-pitch.
orkestrasie, orchestration.
orkestreer, (ge-), orchestrate.
ornaat, official robes, canonicals.
ornament, (-e), ornament.
ornamenteel, (-tele), ornamental.
ornamenteer, (ge-), ornament, adorn.
ornamentiek, ornamental art.
orneer, (ge-), decorate.
ornitoloog, (-loë, -loge), ornithologist.
orrel, (-s), organ.
orreldraaier, organ-grinder.
orrelis, (-te), organist.
orrelklank, organ-sound.
orrelmaker, organ-builder.
orrelmusiek, organ-music.
orrelpyp, organ-pipe.
orrelregister, organ-stop.
orrelspel, organ-playing.
orrelspeler, organ-player, organist.
orrelstryk: – **gaan**, go on wheels, go smoothly (swimmingly).
orreltoon, organ-tone.
orreltrapper, organ-blower.
orreluitvoering, organ-recital.
ortodoks, (-e), orthodox.
ortodoksie, orthodoxy.
ortografie, orthography.
ortografies, (-e), orthographic(al).
ortopedie, orthopaedia.
os, (-se), ox; **jong –se inspan**, vomit; **nie al sy –sies in die kraal nie**, not in his senses, not all there; **soos 'n – neerslaan**, fall like a log; **van die – op die esel spring**, talk (write) disconnectedly, wander in (his) talk; **van die – op die esel**, by the way.
osbloed, blood of an ox, ox-blood.
oseaan, (-ane), ocean.
oskop, ox-head.
oskoper, buyer of oxen, ox-dealer.
osmium, osmium.
osmose, osmosis.
osmoties, (-e), osmotic.
osoon, ozone.
ossewa, ox-wag(g)on.
osstert, ox-tail.
ostentasie, ostentation.
osteologie, osteology.
ostong, ox-tongue; bugloss.
ostraseer, (ge-), ostracize.
osvel, ox-hide.
otjie,(-s), pig; chor-chor, grunter.
o-tjie, (-s), small o.
otter, (-s), otter.
Ottomaans, (-e), Ottoman.
Ottoma(a)n, (-ne), (-s), Ottoman.
Ottomanies, (-e), vide **Ottomaans**.
ou, (-es), n. (old) fellow; one, a man, a chap; **'n gawe –**, a good sort (chap).
ou, a. old (person, clothes, city, grudge, wine); ancient (history); **die – tale**, the classical languages; **die goeie – tyd**, the good old times; **– brood**, stale bread; **op sy – dag**, in his old age; **die – Adam**, old Adam; **op die – end**, at last, finally.
ou, (ge-), give.
oubaas, (old) boss, master; old gentleman (fellow, chap).
ouboet(a), ouboetie, eldest brother; (old) chum, mate.
oud, old, aged; **vyf jaar –**, five years old (of age); **– word**, grow old, live to a great age; **hy is – maar nog nie koud nie**, there is life in the old dog yet; **'n mens is nooit te – om te leer nie**, one is never too old to learn; **jonk en –**, young and old.
oud-, former, ex-, old (student).
oud-amptenaar, ex-official.
oudburgemeester, ex-mayor.
Ou(d)-Engels, n. & a. Old English.
ouderdom, (-me), age; old age; **– kom met gebreke**, old age has its infirmities.
ouderdomspensioen, old-age pension.
ouderlik, (-e), parental.
ouderling, (-e, -s), elder.
ouderlingskap, eldership.
ouderwets, (-e), old-fashioned, out-of-date, old-time; precocious (child).
oudgediende, (-s), veteran.
Ou(d)-Germaans, n. & a. Old Germanic.
oudheid, oldness; antiquity; **-hede**, antiquities.
oudheidkunde, archaeology.
oudheidkundig, (-e), archaeological, antiquarian.
oudheidkundige, (-s), archaeologist.
Ou(d)-Hollands, n. & a. Old Dutch.
oudiënsie, (-s), audience; **– verleen aan**, give audience to; **op – gaan by**, have an audience with.
oudiënsiesaal, presence-chamber.
ouditeur, (-e, -s), auditor.
ouditeur-generaal, auditor-general.
oud-leerling, old pupil; old boy.
Ou(d)-Noors, n. & a. Old Norse.
oudoom, grand-uncle.
oud-ouderling, ex-elder.
ouds: van –, formerly, of old.
oudsher: van –, from long ago.
oud-soldaat, ex-soldier.
oudste, (-s), oldest, eldest; (my) dear.
oud-stryder, ex-soldier, veteran.
oud-student, old student (boy).
oud-studente-unie, old-boys' union.
oudtante, greataunt.
oue, (-s), old one.
oueltjie, (-s), wafer; puff-ball.
Ou-Engels, vide **Ou(d)-Engels**.
ouer, (-s), n. parent; **–s vra**, ask parents' consent (to get married).
ouer, a. older; elder; **'n – suster**, an elder sister; **– wees as tien (twaalf)**, know a thing or two.
ouerhuis, parental home.
ouerig, (-e), oldish, not so young.
ouerliefde, parental love;
ouerlik, (-e), parental.
ouerloos, (-lose), parentless, orphan.
ouerloosheid, orphanhood, orphanage.
ouervreugde, parental joy.
Ou-Germaans, vide **Ou(d)-Germaans**.
Ou-Hollands, vide **Ou(d)-Hollands**.
Oujaarsdag, Old Year's Day.
Oujaars(dag)aand, New Year's Eve.
oujong, old coloured (native) man.
oujongkêrel, bachelor.
oujongmeisie, old maid, spinster.
oujongnôi, -nooi, vide **oujongmeisie**.
ouklip, gravel-stone.
oulaas: vir –, for the last time.
ouland, unsown land, fallow land.
oulik, (-e), precocious (child); cute, clever, tricky; neat, nice.
oulikheid, precocity; trickiness.
oulap, (-pe), penny; **vir 'n – en 'n bokstert**, dirtcheap, for a song.
ouma, (-s), grandmother.
oumannehuis, old men's home.
oumatjie, (-s), little grandmother.

oumense, aged parents.
oumenspeer, bon chretien pear.
oupa, (-s), grandfather.
oupatjie, (-s), little grandfather.
ousanna, (-s), matchlock, flintlock gun.
outentiek, (-e), authentic.
outentisiteit, authenticity.
outeur, (-s), author.
outeursaandeel, royalty.
outeurskap, authorship.
outeursreg, copyright.
outjie, (-s), (old) fellow, chap, boy, old man (woman); 'n klein –, a small one; a tiny tot; vide **ou**, n.
outo, (-s), motor-car.
outobiograaf, autobiographer.
outobiografie, autobiography.
outobiografies, (-e), autobiographical.
outodidak, (-te), self-taught man.
outografie, autography.
outokraat, (-krate), autocrat.
outokraties, (-e), autocratic.
outomaat, (-mate), automaton.
outomaties, (-e), automatic.
outomatisasie, automation.

outomobiel, (-e), automobile.
outonomie, autonomy.
outorisasie, authorization.
outoriseer, (ge-), authorize.
outoritêr, (-e), authoritative.
outoriteit, (-e), authority.
outosuggestie, autosuggestion.
outyds, (-e), old-fashioned; ancient.
ouverture, (-s), overture.
ouvolk, (kind of) lizard.
ouvrou, midwife.
ouvrou-onder-die-kombers, toad-in-the-hole.
ouwyf, iris.
ouwypepraatjies, idle talk, title-tattle.
ovaal, (-vale), oval.
ovasie, (-s), ovation.
owerheid, authorities, government.
owerheidspersoon, authoritative person.
owerigens, origens, for the rest, otherwise.
owermoed, vide **oormoed**.
owerpriester, high-priest.
owerspel, adultery.
owerspeler, adulterer.
owerspelig, (-e), adulterous.
owerste, (-s), chief; prior.

P

pa, (-'s), pa, dad.
paadjie, (-s), (foot-)path, track, trail; parting (of the hair).
paai, (-e), n. gaffer.
paai, (ge-), coax, soothe; pat, stroke.
paaiboelie, (-s), bugbear, ogre, bogey.
paaiement, (-e), instalment.
paal, (pale), pole, post, stake; **die – haal**, reach the (winning-) post, attain the goal; **– en perk stel aan**, set a check (bounds) to, put an end to; **dit staan soos 'n – bo water**, it is as plain as a pike-staff.
paalbewoner, lake-dweller.
paalhuis, pile-dwelling, lake-dwelling.
paalskerm, palisade, paling.
paalspring, n. pole-vault (-jump).
paalspring, (paalge-), do pole-jumping.
paaltjie, (-s), stake; (fencing-)standard; (cricket) stump.
paalvas, immovable, firm; incontestable.
paalwerk, paling, palisade.
paalwoning, pile-dwelling, lake-dwelling.
paalwurm, shipworm.
paap, (pape), pope; priest, parson.
paaps, (-e), papal, papist; popish.
paapsgesind, (-e), papist(ical).
paapsgesinde, (-s), n. papist.
paar, (pare), n. pair (of socks, eyes); couple (of people); **'n getroude –, tjie**), a married couple (pair); **'n – pond**, a couple of pounds, a pound or two; **'n – woorde**, a few words; **'n – keer**, a few (several) times, once or twice; **by pare**, **– vir –**, in pairs (couples, twos), two by two.
paar, adv. **– of onpaar**, odd or even.
paar, (ge)-, pair, mate, couple, unite; **ge–d gaan met**, go hand in hand with, be coupled with, be attended by.
paarsgewys(e), in pairs (couples).
paartjie, (-s), couple, pair.
paartyd, pairing-, mating-season.
Paasaand, Easter-eve.
paasblom, primrose; daisy.
Paasbrood, (Christian) Easter-loaf; (Jewish) Passover-bread.
Paasdag, Easter-day.
Paaseier, Easter-egg.
Paasfees, Easter; (Jewish) Passover.
Paaslam, paschal lamb.
Paasmaal, paschal repast.
Paasmaandag, Easter Monday.
Paassondag, Easter Sunday.
Paasvakansie, Easter holidays.
Paasweek, Easter-week.
pad, (paaie), road, way, path, walk (in garden); **groot –**, main-road; highway; **harde –**, hard (travelled) road; (imprisonment with) hard labour; **die – van die deug**, the road of virtue; **op die verkeerde – bring**, lead astray; **op die regte – hou**, keep to the right road; keep straight; **in iemand se – staan**, obstruct a person's way; **in die – steek**, sack, send packing.
padda, (-s), frog, toad; fishing frog; **opgeblaasde –**, swollen toad; conceited coxcomb.
paddaman, frogman.
paddaslyk, **-slym**, duckweed.
paddastoel, (edible) mushroom; (poisonous) toadstool.
paddavis, tadpole.
padgee, (pagde-), give way: make room.
padkos, provision for a journey.
padlang(e)s, with (along) the road; straight on; **– loop**, be straightforward; **– praat**, be outspoken (frank, candid).
padloper, tramp, vagabond; steam-roller.

padmaker, road-worker; road-builder.
padmakery, road-construction.
padteer, asphalt.
padverlegging, by-pass.
padvinder, path-finder; boy scout.
padwerker, road-worker.
pag, lease; (quit)rent; **in –**, on lease; **die wysheid in – hê**, have a monopoly of wisdom.
pag, (ge-), rent, lease.
pagaai, (-e), n. paddle.
pagaai, (ge-), paddle.
paganis, (-te), pagan.
paganisties, (-e), pagan.
pagbrief, contract (deed) of lease.
page, (-s), page, footboy; squire.
pageiendom, quitrent-property.
paggeld, rent; quitrent.
pagger, (-s), palisade.
pagina, (-s), page.
pagineer, (ge)-, page, paginate.
paginering, paging, pagination.
pagode, (-s), pagoda.
pagreg, right of lease; right of quitrent.
pagsom, rent, rental.
pagstelsel, leasing-system; land-tenure.
pagter, (-s), lessee; tenant(-farmer).
pagteres, (-se), lessee; tenant's wife.
pagtyd, period of lease.
pagvry, rent-free; exempt from quitrent.
pak, (-ke), pack, package, packet (of biscuits, candles), parcel, bundle (of papers); load, burden; suit (of clothes); hiding, thrashing, licking; **met sak en –**, with bag and baggage; **dit is my 'n – van die hart**, it is a load off my mind.
pak, (ge-), pack (up); wrap (up); seize, catch (hold of), grip, clutch; hold the attention, grip.
pakaters, capers; **sy – maak**, cut his capers.
pakdonkie, burro, packdonkey.
pakdraer, packman, pedlar.
pakesel, pack-mule, -donkey.
pakgaring, packthread, twine.
pakhuis, store, warehouse.
pakhuisruimte, store-room.
pakkamer, store-room.
pakkas, packing-case.
pakkasie, baggage.
pakkend, (-e), arresting, gripping, thrilling; catchy.
pakker, (-s), packer.
pakkery, packing; packing-room.
pakket, (-te), parcel.
pakketboot, packet(-boat).
pakketpos, parcel-post.
pakkie, (-s), packet; (small) parcel; bundle; **elkeen moet sy eie – dra**, every man must bear his own burden.
pakkiesdraer, porter, messenger-boy; pedlar.
pakking, packing, boxing, gasket.
pakkis, packing-case.
paklinne, packing-cloth.
paknaald, packing-needle.
pakos, pack-ox.
pakpapier, wrapping-paper.
pakperd, pack-horse.
paksaal, pack-saddle.
pakt, (-e), pact, agreement.
paktou, twine, packthread.
pakys, pack-ice.
pal, (-le), n. ratchet(-wheel), catch.
pal, adv. firm, fixed, immovable; **– staan**, stand firm; **hy moet – lê**, hy must keep his bed; **hy kom – te laat**, he is continually late; **– reën**, rain continuously.

paladyn — **papierplant**

paladyn, (-e), paladin.
palataal, (-tale), n. & a. palatal.
paleografie, pal(a)eography.
paleologie, pal(a)eology.
paleontologie, pal(a)eontology.
paleontoloog, (loë, -loge), pal(a)eontologist.
paleis, (-e), palace.
Palestina, Palestine.
Palestyns, (-e), Palestine.
palet, (-te), palette.
paletmes, palette-knife.
palimpses, (-te), palimpsest.
paling, (-s), eel.
palissade, (-s), palisade.
palissander(hout), black rose-wood.
paljas, charm, spell, magic-potion.
paljas, (-se), clown.
palladium, palladium.
palm, (-s), palm (of the hand).
palm, (-s), palm(-tree); palm-branch; **die –** wegdra, bear the palm.
palmblad, palm-leaf.
palmboom, palm-tree.
palmbos, palm-grove.
palmdraend, (-e), palmiferous.
palmhout, palm-wood.
palmiet, (-e), "palmiet," (bul)rush.
palmolie, palm-oil.
Palmsondag, Palm Sunday.
palmstruik, box-shrub.
palmtak, palm-branch.
palmwyn, palm-wine, toddy.
paltsgraaf, palsgrave, count palatine.
paltsgraafskap, palatinate.
pamflet, (-te), pamphlet; lampoon.
pamfletskrywer, pamphleteer.
pampa, (-s), pampa.
pampasgras, pampas-grass.
pampelmoes, (-e),, shaddock, pampelmoose, pomelo blue-fish (butter-fish.
pampelmoesie, (-s), Cape) gooseberry.
pamperlang, (ge-), cajole, wheedle, coax.
pampoen, (-e), pumpkin; bumpkin, awkward fellow; **vrot –**, rotten pumpkin; good-for-nothing.
pampoenkoekie, (-s), pumpkin-fritter.
pampoenkop, dunce, bumpkin.
pampoenpit, pumpkin-seed, -pip.
pampoenrank, pumpkin-shoot, -tendril.
pampoenskil, pumpkin-skin, -rind.
pampoenstoel, pumpkin-stool, -plant.
pampoentjies, (pl.), mumps.
pan, (-ne), (frying-)pan; tile; **in die – hak**, cut to pieces; **kruit op die – gooi**, prime (a gun).
Pan-Afrikaans, Pan-African.
Pan-Afrikanis, Pan-Africanist.
panama(hoed), panama(-hat).
Panama-kanaal, Panama-canal.
panchromaties, panchromatic.
pand, (-e), pledge, security; forfeit; **in – gee**, give as security, pledge.
pand, (ge-), pawn; pledge.
pandak, tile-roof.
pandbrief, bond; mortgage-bond.
pandemie, (-ë), pandemic.
pandemonium, pandemonium.
pandgeër, pawner.
pandhouer, pawnee.
pand(jies)huis, pawnshop.
pandnemer, pawnee.
pandoer, (-e, -s), pandour.
pandspeel, (pandge-), play (at) forfeits.
pandspel, (game of) forfeits.
paneel, (-nele), panel.
paneelbord, dash-board, fascia.

paneelkassie, -rak, cubby-hole.
paneer, (ge-), crumb.
paneermeel, (bread-)crumbs.
Pan-Germaans, (-e), Pan-Germanic.
pangeweer, flint-gun.
paniek, panic. scare.
paniekerig, (-e), panicky.
pankreas, pancreas.
panlekker, sponger.
pannekoek, pan-cake; **so plat as 'n –**, as flat as a pan-cake.
pannetjie, small pan.
panoptikum, (-s), panopticon.
panorama, (-s), panorama.
pant, (-e), (coat-tail), flap.
pantalon, (-s), trousers; pant(aloon)s.
pantbaadjie, tail-coat.
panteïs, (-te), pantheist.
panteïsme, pantheism.
panter, (-s), panther.
Pantheon, Pantheon.
pantoffel, (-s), slipper; **onder die – sit**, be henpecked.
pantoffelheld, henpecked husband.
pantomime, (-s), pantomime.
pantser, armour, mail, cuirass (for the breast); armour(-plating) (for ships).
pantser, (ge-), armour, plate (ships).
pantserdek, armoured deck.
pantserdier, armadillo.
pantserhemp, coat of mail.
pantsermotor, armoured car.
pantserskip, ironclad.
pantsertrein, armoured train.
pantservuis, bazooka.
pantserwa, armoured car; tank.
pap, n. porridge; poultice (on a sore); pap, pulp, mash; paste.
pap, a. & adv., soft, weak; flabby; punctured, deflated; **'n – kêrel**, a softy, a weakling; **ek voel –**, I feel done (knocked) up.
pap, (ge-), poultice (a sore); paste.
papa, (-'s), pappa, (-s), papa, daddy.
papaja, (-s), pa(w)paw.
papawer, (-s), poppy.
papaweragtig, (-e), papaverous, oppy-like.
papawerbol, poppy-head.
papawerolie, poppy-oil.
papawersaad, poppy-seed.
papbroek, softy, milksop, funk.
papbroekerig, (-e), soft, spunkless, spiritless, funky.
papbroek(er)igheid, spunklessness.
papegaai, (-e), parrot, polly.
papegaaiagtig, (-e), parrotlike.
papegaaisiekte, psittacosis.
papelellekoors, sham-fever; trembles.
papie, (-s), chrysalis; cocoon; **-s**, bot(t)s (horse-disease).
papier, (-e), paper; (pl.) papers; certificates, testimonials; documents; **op – sit**, put in writing; **– is geduldig**, all that's printed is not true; paper won't blush.
papieragtig, (-e), papery, papyraceous.
papierblom, artificial flower.
papierboom, paper-tree.
papierdrukker, paper-weight.
papierfabriek, paper-mill.
papiergeld, paper-money.
papierhandel, paper-trade; stationery.
papierklem, -knip(pie), paper-fastener.
papiermerk, watermark.
papiermes, paper-knife.
papiermeul, paper-mill.
papierplant, -riet, papyrus.

papies, (pl.), bot(t)s (horse-disease).
papil, (-le), papilla.
papirus, papyrus.
papis, (-te), papist.
papistery, papistry.
papisties, (-e), papist(ical).
papkuil, bulrush, (Thypha sp.).
paplepel, porridge-spoon; met die – voer, spoon-feed.
papnat, soaking (dripping) wet.
Papoea, (-s), Papuan.
pappa, (-s), papa, (-'s), papa, dad.
papperig, (-e), softish; pappy; sticky.
pappot, porridge-pot.
paprika, paprika.
papsaf, -sag, (-te), quite soft.
papsak, softy, milksop.
paraat, (-rate), ready, prepared.
parabel, (-s), parable.
parabolies, (-e), parabolical (in the form of a parable); parabolic (maths.).
parabool, (-bole), parabola.
parade, (-s), parade; op –, on parade.
paradeer, (ge-), parade; laat –, parade.
paradepas, parade-step.
paradigma, (-s), paradigm.
paradoks, (-e), paradox.
paradoksaal, (-sale), paradoxical.
paradys, (-e), paradise.
paradysagtig, (-e), paradisi(a)c(al).
paradysgeskiedenis, story of the fall.
paradysvoël, bird of paradise.
parafeer, (ge-), initial; paraph.
paraffien, paraffin(e).
paraffienblik, paraffin-tin.
paraffienlamp, paraffin-lamp.
paraffienolie, paraffin(-oil).
parafrase, (-s), paraphrase.
parafraseer, (ge-), paraphrase.
paragoge, paragoge.
paragraaf, (-grawe), paragraph; section.
paragrafeer, (ge-), divide into paragraphs (sections).
parallaks, (-e), parallax.
parallel, n. & a. (-e), parallel, 'n – trek, draw a parallel.
parallelisme, parallelism.
parallelklas, parallel class.
parallelogram, (-me), parallelogram.
parallelskool, parallel school.
paranoia, paranoia.
paranoïes, paranoic.
paranimf, (-e), paranymph.
paraplu, (-s), umbrella.
parasiet, (-e), parasite.
parasities, (-e), parasitic(al).
parasitisme, parasitism.
parasjutis, (-te), parachutist.
parasjuut, (-ute), parachute.
pardoems!, flop!, splash!
pardon, pardon; –!, I beg your pardon! geen – vra of gee nie, ask nor give quarter.
pareer, (ge-), parry, ward off.
parentese, parenthesis.
parenteties, (-e), parenthetic(al).
parfumeer, (ge-), perfume, scent.
parfumerie, (-ë), perfume, scent.
parfuum, n. perfume, scent.
pari, par; a, op, teen –, at par; bo –, above par; onder –, below par.
paria, (-s), pariah.
paring, paring, mating; vide paar, (ge-).
pariteit, parity.
park, (-e), park (also for motors).
parkeer, (ge-), park (motors).

parkeerplek, parking-place, -space; lay-by.
parket, parquet(-floor); front stalls; in 'n moeilike –, in a quandary.
parketvloer, parquet-floor; parquetry.
parkiet, (-e), parakeet.
parkopsigter, park-keeper, -caretaker.
parlement, (-e), parliament.
parlementêr, (-e), parliamentary.
parlementsgebou, -huis, house(s) of parliament, parliament-building.
parlementsitting, parliamentary session.
parlementslid, member of parliament.
parmant, (-e), cocky (cheeky) person.
parmantig, (-e), cocky, cheeky, jaunty, pert, impertinent, impudent.
parmantigheid, cheekiness, impudence.
parodie, (-ë), parody, travesty.
parodieer, (ge-), parody, travesty.
parogiaal, (-ale), parochial.
parogiaan, (-ane), parishioner.
parogie, (-ë), parish.
paroniem, (-e), n. paronym.
parool, parole, pass-word; word of honour, op –, on parole.
Pars, (-e), Parsee.
pars, (ge-), press; wyn –, press wine.
parsbalie, -kuip, winepress.
parsie, vide persie.
parsieel, (-siële), partial.
parstyd, winemaking season, vintage.
part, (-e), part, portion, share; vir my –, for my part; – nog deel hê in, have part nor lot in.
part, (-e), trick; iemand –e speel, play tricks on a person.
parterre, parterre; pit (of theatre).
partikel, (-s), particle.
partikularis, (-te), particularist.
partikulier, (-e), n. private individual.
partikulier, (-e), private, special.
partisan, partisan.
partituur, score.
partuur, vide portuur.
party, (-e), n. party; –e in 'n hofsaak, parties to a suit; – kies, choose sides; – kies vir (teen) iemand, side with (against) someone; iemand se – kies (opneem), side with someone; – trek van (uit), profit by, take advantage of, and turn to account; 'n hele –, a whole lot, quite a lot.
party, a. some; – (mense), some (people); – dae, some days.
partybelang, party-interests.
partydig, (-e), partial, prejudiced.
partydigheid, partiality, bias.
partydissipline, party-dicipline.
partyganger, (-s), partisan.
partygees, party-spirit, partnership.
partygenoot, member of the same party.
partykas, party-funds.
partykeer(s), sometimes, occasionally.
partyleier, party-leader.
partyleus, party-cry, -watchword.
partymaal, sometimes, at times.
partyman, partisan, party-man.
party-organisasie, party-organization.
partypolitiek, party-politics.
partystryd, party-strife; party-struggle.
partysug, party-spirit, faction-spirit.
partytjie, little party; game; – biljart (brug), game of billiards (bridge).
parvenu, (-'s), parvenu, upstart.
parvenuagtig, (-e), parvenu-, ..., upstart- ...
Parys, Paris.
parysblou, Paris-blue.
Paryse, Parisian; 'n –, a Parisienne.

Parysenaar, (-nare, -naars), Parisian.
pas, (-se), n. pace, step; gait, amble (of horse); (mountain) pass, defile, passage; pass, passport; **die – aangee,** mark time; set the pace; **die – hou,** keep step; **iemand die – afsny,** forestall a person; **in die – bly,** keep in step; **uit die – raak,** get (fall) out of step; **die perd loop 'n –,** the horse ambles.
pas, n.: **te – kom,** come in useful (handy), be of use; **as dit in sy kraam te – kom,** when it suits his purpose; **te – bring,** apply, introduce, bring up, make use of; **te – en te onpas,** in season and out of season.
pas, adv. (only) just; newly, just, only; scarcely hardly; **hy het – aangekom,** he has just arrived.
pas, (ge-), fit; fit on, try on (a coat); become, behove; suit, be convenient; pass (at cards); **die hoed – my net,** this hat fits me exactly; **so iets – 'n getroude vrou nie,** a thing like that does not become a married woman; **die tapyt – nie by die gordyne nie,** the carpet does not match the curtains, **die twee mense – nie by mekaar nie,** these two people do not suit one another (do not agree, are ill-matched); **dit lyk of die skoen jou –,** the cap seems to fit you.
Pase, Easter.
pasella, Passover.
Pasga, Passover..
pasganger, ambler.
pasgangetjie, amble.
pasgebore, new-born.
pasgehuud, (-hude), newly married.
pasgelê, (gelêde, gelegde), new-laid.
pasiënt, (-e), patient.
pasiënte, (-s), female (lady) patient.
pasifis, (-te), pacifist.
pasifiseer, (ge-), pacify.
pasifisme, pacifism.
pasifisties, (-e), pacifist, pacific.
pasja, (-s), pasha (pacha).
paskamer, fitting-room.
paskewil, (-le), to-do, bustle.
pasklaar, ready to try on; ready-made.
paskwil, (-le), lampoon; farce, mockery.
paslik, (-e), fitting, becoming; fair; in good condition, fit.
paslood, plummet.
pasmunt, (small) change.
pasoppens: in jou – bly, mind one's steps (p's and q's), look out.
paspoort, (-e), pass, passport.
passaat, (-sate), trade(-wind); passage.
passaatgeld, passage-money.
passaatwind, trade-wind.
passabel, (-e), passable.
passasie, (-s), passage.
passasiegeld, passage-money, fare.
passasier, (-s), passenger.
passasiersboot, passenger-boat.
passasiersdiens, passenger-service.
passasierslys, passenger-list.
passasierstrein, passenger-train.
passasierswa, passenger-coach, -saloon.
passeer, (ge-), pass (also in card-games), go past, overtake; pass by.
passement, braid, trimming.
passend, (-e), fitting, appropriate; **daarby –e sokkies,** socks to match.
passer, (-s), (pair of) compasses.
passerdoos, box of mathematical instruments.
passie, (-s), passion; craze.
passieblom, passion-flower.
passief, n. passive (voice).
passief, (-siewe), a. passive.
Passiespel, Passion-play.

passiwiteit, passivity.
pasta, paste.
pastei, (-e), pie, pastry, pasty.
pasteibakker, pastry-cook.
pasteideeg, paste.
pasteikors, pie-crust.
pasteitjie, (-s), patty.
pastel, (-le), pastel.
pasteltekenaar, pastel(l)ist.
pasteltekening, pastel(-drawing).
pasteuriseer, (ge-), pasteurize.
pastoor, (-tore), pastor; priest.
pastoraal, (-ale), pastoral.
pastorale, (-s), pastoral (poem).
pastorie, (-ë, -s), parsonage, rectory, vicarage.
pat, stale-mate.
Patagonië, Patagonia.
patat, patatta, (-s), sweet potato; block-head; **met die hele mandjie –s voor die dag kom,** blab out the whole secret; put one's cards upon the table.
patatkoekie, sweet potato fritter.
patatranke, sweet potato-runners (-slips, -vines).
patent, (-e), n. patent.
patent, (-e), a. patent; ingenious; capital, excellent.
patenteer, (ge-), patent.
patenthouer, -nemer, patentee.
patentmedisyne, patent medicine(s).
patentreg, patent-right.
patentwet, Patents' Act.
pater, (-s), father; priest.
paternoster, (-s), paternoster.
pateties, (-e), pathetic(al).
patois, patois.
patologie, pathology.
patologies, pathological.
patoloog, (-loë, -loge), pathologist.
patos, pathos.
patriarg, (-e), patriarch.
patriargaal, (-gale), patriarchal.
patriot, (-te), patriot.
patrioties, (-e), patriotic(ally).
patriotisme, patiotism.
Patriots, n. language of Die Patriot.
Patriots, (-e), a. of (like) Die Patriot.
patrisiër, (-s), patrician.
patrisies, (-e), patrician.
patrolleer, (ge-), patrol.
patrollie, (-s), patrol; **– ry,** patrol.
patrones, (-se), patroness, lady-patron.
patroon, (-one), cartridge, pattern, model; patron, patron saint; employer.
patroonband, bandolier, (bandoleer); feedband (for machine-gun).
patroondop, cartridge-case.
patrys, (-e), partridge, sandgrouse.
patrys, patrix (typog.).
patryshond, spaniel, pointer.
patrysjag, partridge-shooting.
patryspoort, port-hole.
paviljoen, pawiljoen, (-e), pavillion, stand.
pawee-, pawieperske, pavy(peach).
pawiljoen, vide **paviljoen.**
pê!, boo; **hy kan nie – sê nie,** he can't say boo to a goose.
pedaal, (-dale), pedal.
pedagogie(k), pedagogy (pedagogics), theory of education.
pedagogies, (-e), pedagogic(al).
pedagoog, (-goë, -goge), pedagogue, education(al)ist.
pedant, (-e), n. pedant.
pedanterie, (-ë), pedantry.
pedanties, (-e), pedantic.

peer, (pere), pear, testis; **met die gebakte pere laat sit**, leave in the soup (in the cart, in the lurch).
peer- pereboom, pear-tree.
peervormig, (-e), pear-shaped.
pees, (pese), tendon, sinew; string.
peesagtig, (-e), tendinous, sinewy.
peet, (pete), godfather, (-mother), sponsor; **– staan**, stand godfather, -mother; **loop na jou –**, go to blazes (the dickens).
peetdogter, goddaughter.
peetjie, (-s), godfather; **loop na jou –**, go to the dickens; **jou ou – af wag**, wait for a deuce of time.
peetkind, godchild.
peetoom, godfather.
peettante, godmother.
Pegasus, Pegasus.
peil, n. level, watermark, gauge; standard; **benede –**, below (not op to) standard (the mark); **op –**, up to standard (the mark); **op 'n hoë (lae) – staan**, be on a high (low) level; **op – bring (hou)**, bring (keep) up to the mark (standard); **– op iemand trek**, rely (depend) on someone.
peil, (ge-), gauge (a liquid, a character); fathom (seawater, misery); plump; sound, probe (a wound).
peilbaar, (-bare), fathomable.
peiler, (-s), sounder, gauger; direction-finder.
peilkraan, gauge-cock.
peillood, plummet, sounding-lead.
peilloos, (-lose), unfathomable.
peilskoot, sighting-shot.
peilstok, sounding-rod; gauging-rod.
peins, (ge-), meditate, ponder, muse.
peinsend, (-e), pensive, meditative.
peinser, (-s), meditator, muser.
peinsing, (-e, -s), meditation, musing.
peits, (-e), whip.
pekanneut, pecan nut.
pekel, n. pickle; **hy sit in die –**, he is in a nice pickle (in a sorry plight).
pekel, a. salt.
pekel, (ge-), pickle, salt, souse.
pekelagtig, (-e), salt(ish), briny.
pekelharing, salt-herring, pickle-herring.
pekelsonde, trifling sin; ancient sin.
pekelvleis, salt meat.
pekelwater, brine, pickle.
pelargonium, pelargonium.
pelgrim, (-s), pilgrim.
pelgrimsgewaad, -kleed, pilgrim's garb.
pelgrimsreis, -tog, pilgrimage.
pelgrimstaf, -stok, pilgrim's staff.
Pelgrimvader, Pilgrim Father.
pelikaan, (-kane), pelican.
Peloponnesies, (-e), Peloponnesian.
Peloponnesus, Peloponnesus.
peloton, (-s), platoon.
pels, (-e), fur; vide **bont**.
pelsdier, furred animal.
pelshandel, fur-trade.
pelshandelaar, furrier.
pelsjas, fur-coat.
pelskraag, fur-collar.
pelswerk, peltry, furriery.
peltery, (-e), peltry, furriery.
pen, (-ne), n. pen; nib; quill; spine; needle (for knitting); **die – op papier sit**, put pen to paper; **handig met die – wees**, have a ready (facile) pen; **in die – gee**, suggest, incite, dictate; **van sy – lewe**, make a living with his pen.
pen, (-ne), n. pin, peg, spike; **aan die – ry**, get into a fix, be caught.
pen, (ge-), pen, write.

penate, (pl.), penates, household gods.
pendant, (-e), pendant, complement.
pendoring, spike-thorn, long spine.
pendule, (-s), pendulum-clock.
penetrasie, penetration.
penetreer, (ge-), penetrate, pierce.
pen(ne)houer, penholder.
penisilline, (-ien), penicillin.
penitensie, penance; penitence.
penkop, youth, youngster, cub.
pen(ne)lekker, quill-driver, pen-driver.
pen(ne)naam, pen-name, pseudonym.
pennemes, pen-knife.
pen(ne)streep, stroke of the pen.
pennestryd, paper-war, controversy.
penneveër, pen-wiper.
pennevrug, product of the pen, book.
penning, (-e, -s), mite; penny; medal.
penningmeester, treasurer.
Pennsylvanië, Pennsylvania.
penorent, straight up, erect, upright.
penregop, straight up, erect, vertical.
pens, (-e), paunch, belly; **iets op jou – skrywe**, whistle for something.
penseel, (-sele), paint-brush; pensil.
penseelstreep, stroke of the brush.
pens-en-pootjies, n. tripe (and trotters).
pens-en-pootjies, adv. bodily, with body and limbs.
pensioen, (-e), pension; **– verleen**, grant a pension; **– neem**, take one's pension; **– kry**, receive a pension; **met – aftree**, retire on a pension; (mil.) go on retired pay.
pensioenbydrae, pension-contribution.
pensioeneer, (ge-), pension, grant a pension to, pension off.
pensioenering, retiring on pension, retirement; superannuation.
pensioenfonds, pension-fund.
pensioenraad, pensions-board.
pensioentrekkend, drawing a pension.
pensioentrekker, pensioner.
pensioenwet, pension act.
pensionaris, (-se), pensionary.
penswinkeltjie, pedlar's tray.
pentagoon, (-gone), pentagon.
pentameter, (-s), pentameter.
Pentateug, Pentateuch.
pentekenaar, black-and-white artist.
pentekening, ink-drawing, pen sketch.
penvoerder, penman, wielder of the pen.
penwortel, tap-root, main root.
peper, pepper; **dit is – en koljander, die een is soos die ander**, it is six of the one and half a dozen of the other.
peper, (ge-), pepper.
peperagtig, (-e), peppery.
peperboom, pepper-tree.
peperbos(sie), pepper-bush.
peperbus(sie), pepper-caster, -box.
peperduur, frightfully expensive.
peper-en-sout, pepper-and-salt.
peperkop, woolly-head.
peperkorrel, pepper-corn; **–s** (pl.), tufts of woolly hair.
peperment, (-e), peppermint.
peperwortel, horse-radish.
pepsien, pepsine, pepsin(e).
per, per, by; **– jaar**, per annum, a year, **– week**, per week, a week; **– abuis**, by mistake; **– boot**, by boat; **– pos**, by post; **– tjek**, by cheque; **– se**, by (in) itself.
perd, (-e), horse; knight (chess); (vaulting) horse; **te –**, on horseback; **'n verkeerde – opklim (ry)**, back the wrong horse; **'n gegewe – moet**

jy nie in die bek kyk nie, don't look a gift-horse in the mouth; die kar voor die -e span, put the cart before the horse; as die -e horings kry, when tortoises grow feathers.
perdeblom, dandelion.
perdeboer, horse-farmer, horse-breeder.
perdeborsel, horse-brush.
perdebos, horse-bush.
perdeby, wasp.
perdedief, horse-thief.
perdeduiwel, rough-rider; horse-bully.
perdefroetang, horse-frutang.
perdehaar, horse-hair.
perdehandelaar, horse-dealer.
perdehoef, horse's hoof.
perdejong, horse-boy, groom.
perdekoper, horse-dealer.
perdekrag, horse-power.
perdeliefhebber, lover of horses.
perdemark, horse-market, horse-fair.
perdemis, horse-dung (-manure).
perdepoot, horse's hoof.
perderas, breed of horses.
perderuiter, horseman, rider.
perdesiekte, horse-sickness.
perdeslagter, horse-butcher.
perdesmous, horse-dealer.
perdespoor, horse's hoofmark (spoor).
perdesport, horse-riding, horse-racing.
perdestal, (horse-)stable.
perdestamboek, studbook.
perdestapel, stock of horses, stable.
perdestert, horse's tail; horse-tail.
perdestoetery, stud, studfarm.
perdeteelt, horse-breeding.
perdetentoonstelling, horse-show.
perdetuig, horse-harness.
perdevleis, horse-flesh.
perdevlieg, horse-fly, botfly, cleg.
perdevy, horse-fig, Hottentot fig.
perdewa, horse-waggon.
perdewagter, horse-boy.
perde-yster, horse-shoe.
perdfris, healthy, hale and hearty.
perdgerus, calm, unconcerned, unsuspecting, at ease, at leisure.
perdjie, little horse; gou op sy - wees, be touchy, be quick to take offence.
perdry, n. (horse-)riding.
perdry, (perdge-), ride (on horseback); gaan -, go for a ride, go out riding.
peredrank, perry.
pêrel, (-s), pearl; -s voor die swyne werp (gooi), cast pearls before swine; - op die oog, cataract.
pêrel, (ge-), pearl, bead; sweet - op sy voorkop, perspiration beads (forms beads) on his forehead.
pêrelagtig, (-e), pearly, pearl-like.
pêrelbank, pearl-bank, (-bed).
pêrelduiker, pearl-diver.
pêrelgort, pearl-barley.
pêrelgrys, pearl-grey.
pêrelhoender, guinea-fowl.
pêrelkleurig, (-e), pearl-cloured.
pêrelmossel, pearl-mussel.
pêreloester, pearl-oyster.
pêrelskulp, pear-shell.
pêrelsnoer, string of pearls.
pêrelvisser, pearl-fisher.
pêrelvissery, pearl-fishing, pearl-fishery.
pêrelvormig, (-e), pearl-shaped.
perewyn, perry.
perfek, (-te), perfect.
perfeksie, perfection.

perforasie, (-s), perforation.
perforeer, (ge-), perforate, punch.
periferie, (-ë), periphery.
perifrase, (-s), periphrasis.
perihelium, perihelion.
perimeter, (-s), perimeter.
periode, (-s), period.
periodiek, (-e), periodical(ly).
periodisiteit, periodicity.
peripateties, (-e), peripatetic(ally).
peripetie, peripeteia, dénouement.
periskoop, (-skope), periscope.
perk, (-e), limit, bound; (flower)bed, (grass-)lawn, plot; arena; binne (buite) die -e, within (beyond) the bounds; die -e oorskry, exceed, ceed (go beyond) the bounds; dit gaan alle -e te buite, that exceeds all bounds, that is the limit; paal en - stel aan, limit, check, put an end to.
perkament, (-e), parchment, vellum.
perkamentagtig, (-e), parchment-like.
perkamentpapier, parchment-, vellum-paper.
perkamentrol, parchment-scroll.
perkussie, percussion.
perkuteer, (ge-), percuss, tap.
perlemoen, perlemoer, mother-of-pearl.
permanent, (-e), permanent, lasting.
permanganaat, permanganate.
permissie, permission, leave; met (u) -, by your leave.
permit, (-te), permit (Angl.).
permitteer, (ge-), permit, allow.
permutasie, (-s), permutation.
pernisieus, (-e), pernicious.
perorasie, (-s), peroration.
perpleks, confused, perplexed.
peroksied, perokside, peroxide.
perron, (-s), platform.
Pers, (-ë), Persian.
pers, (-e), n. press; in die -, ter -e, in the press; ter -e gaan, go to press.
pers, a. purple.
pers, (ge-), press, squeeze.
persbank, press-gallery (-seat).
persberig, press-report.
persburo, press-bureau.
perseel, (-sele), lot, allotment, plot.
persent, per cent.
persentasie, (-s), percentage; royalty.
persentgewys, pro rata, proportional(ly).
persepsie, perception.
perser, (-s), presser.
persgesprek, interview.
persie, parsie, (bloody) diarrhoea.
Persië, Persia.
persiflage, railery, banter, persiflage.
persifleer, (ge-), banter.
Persies, (-e), Persian.
persing, pressure, pressing.
perskaartjie, press-ticket.
perske, (-s), peach.
perskebloesem, -blom, peach-blossom.
perskeboom, peach-tree.
perskebrandewyn, peach-brandy
perskeblare, peach-down.
perskekonfyt, peach-jam.
perskepit, peach-stone.
persklaar, ready for the press.
persman, journalist, press-man.
personalia, personal news (matters).
personasie, (-s), person, personage.
personeel, personnel, staff.
personevervoer, passenger-traffic.
personifieer, (ge-), personify.
personifikasie, personification.

persoon, (-sone), person; head; player, actor, figure, appearance; **aangewese, -,** right man, proper person; **vorstelike -,** royalty; **per -,** per head; **'n gesin van ses persone,** a family of six (heads); **in eie -,** personally; **sonder aansien des -s,** without respect of persons; **klein van -,** of small figure, **die goedheid in -,** kindness itself.
persoonlik, (-e), personal(ly); **-e voornaamwoord,** personal pronoun; **ek ken hom -,** I know him personally.
persoonlikheid, (-hede), personality.
persoonsbelasting, personal tax.
persoonsverbeelding, personification.
persoorsig, press-review.
persorgaan, press-organ.
perspektief, (-tiewe), perspective; view.
perspektiwies, (-e), in perspective.
perspex, perspex.
persplank, pressing-board.
perspomp, force-pump.
perstelegram, press-telegram.
persverslag, press-, newspaper-report.
persvryheid, freedom of the press.
persyster, (tailor's) smoothing iron.
pertinent, (-e), pertinent, relevant, apposite, to the point.
Peru, Peru.
Peruaan, (-ane), Peruvian.
Peruaans, (-e), Peruvian.
pervers, (-e), perverse; perverted.
perversiteit, (-e), perversity, depravity.
pes, (-te), pestilence, plague; pest; **haat soos die -,** hate like poison.
pes, (ge-), pester, plague.
pesbasil, plague-bacillus.
pesbestryding, plague-fighting.
pesgeval, plague-case, case of plague.
peskiem, plague-germ.
peslug, pestilential air (vapour).
peslyer, plague-patient.
pespokke, pestilential pox.
pessimis, (-te), pessimist.
pessimisme, pessimism.
pessimisties, (-e), pessimistic.
pesstof, (plague-)virus.
pestilensie, (-s), pestilence, plague.
pet, (-te), cap.
petalje, (-s), stir, fuss, to-do, commotion, bustle, pl. antics, escapades, queer doings.
petieterig, (-e), small, tiny, weak.
petisie, (-e), petition, memorial.
petisionaris, (-se), petitioner.
petisioneer, (ge-), petition, request.
petrol, petrolie, petrol, motor-spirit.
petroleum, petroleum, oil.
petroleumbron, oil-, petroleum-well.
petroleummaatskappy, oil-company.
petroleumveld, oil-field.
petrol-, petroliepomp, petrol-pump, bowser.
petrol-, petrolietoevoer, petrol-supply.
petrol-, petrolieverbruik, petrol-consumption.
petunia, (-s), petunia.
peul, (-e), n. pad. husk.
peul, (-e), n. bolster, under-pillow.
peul, puil, (ge-), bulge, protrude.
peulvormig, (-e), pod-like.
peulvrug, leguminous plant, pulse.
peusel, (ge-), nibble, peck.
peuselwerk(ie), odd job.
peuter, (ge-), fiddle, potter, fuss, worry; tamper; **aan,** tamper with.
peuterig, (-e), petty, finical, trivial, nonsensical, fussy, pottering.
peuterwerk, small (odd) job.

phthisis, phthisis.
pianis, (-te), pianist.
pianiste, (pl.: pianistes), (lady-)pianist.
piano, (-'s), piano.
pianobegeleiding, piano-accompaniment.
pianola, (-s), pianola, player-piano.
pianoles, piano-lesson.
pianospeelster, (lady-)pianist.
pianospel, piano-playing.
pianospeler, pianist.
pianostemmer, piano-tuner.
piccolo, (-'s), piccolo, octave flute.
piedewiet, vide **pierewiet,**
piek, (-e), pike; peak.
piekel, (ge-), lug, drag, carry.
pieker, (ge-), worry, fret; puzzle.
piekfyn, grand, swell, spick and span.
piekniek, (-s), n. picnic.
piekniek, (ge-), picnic.
piekniekplek, picnic-spot.
pienang(bossie), quinine-bush.
pienangneut, areca-nut.
piep, n. pip, roup; **die - hê,** have the pip.
piep, (ge-), chirp, squeak, peep.
piep, interj. peep.
pieperig, (-e), squeaky, piping (voice); weak(ly), sickly (person), peaky, soft.
piepie, (-s), pee.
piepie, (ge-), pee, piddle.
piepjong, quite young, soft, tender.
piepkuiken, spring-chicken.
pier, (-e), n. pier, jetty.
pier, (-e), n. worm, grub.
pier, (ge-), diddle, cheat, swindle.
pierewiet, (-e, -s), pilawit.
piering, (-s), saucer.
piesang, (-s), banana.
piesangboer, banana-farmer; Natalian.
piesangskil, banana-peel.
Piet, Peter; **-, Paul en Klaas,** Tom, Dick and Harry; **'n hele -,** big bug.
piëteit, piety, reverence.
piëteitsgevoel, (feeling of) piety.
pieters(i)elie, parsley.
piëtis, (-te), pietist.
piëtisme, pietism.
piëtisties, (-e), pietist(ical).
pietjie-kanarie, siskin, chee-chee.
piet-my-vrou, (-e), robin-chat; whip-poor-will, "piet-my-vrou."
piets, (ge-), whip, flick.
pietsnot, nincompoop, duffer.
pigmee, (-meë), pigmy (pygmy).
pigment, (-e), pigment, dye.
pijama, (-s), pyjamas.
pik, (-ke), n. peck; pick(-axe).
pik, n. pitch; **wie met - omgaan, word met - besmeer,** sleep with dogs and you get up with fleas.
pik, (ge-), peck, bite; carp (at), nag (at); pick.
pikant, (-e), piquant, pungent, spicy.
pikanterie, (-ë), piquancy; pique.
pikbroek, Jack tar.
pikdonker, pitch dark.
pikdraad, waxed end (thread).
pikeer, (ge-), pique, nettle, wound.
piket, (-te), piquet (card-game); picket.
pikeur, (-s), riding-master; horse-breaker.
pikkenien, (-s), piccanin(ny).
pikkewyn, (-e), (jackass-)penguin.
pikkewyneier, penguin-egg.
pikriensuur, pikrinesuur, picric acid.
piksteel, pick-handle.
pikswart, pitch black, jet black.

pil, (-le), pill; die – verguld, to sugar (gild) the pill; **dit was 'n bitter – vir hom**, that was a bitter pill for him to swallow.
pilaar, (-are), pillar, column; stalwart.
pilaarbyter, church-hog, hypocrite.
pilaarheilige, pillar-saint, stylite.
pilaarkop, capital.
pilaarvoet, pedestal, base (of pillar).
pilaster, (-s), pilaster.
pilledosie, pill-box.
pilledraaier, pill-roller, pill-monger.
piloot, (-lote), pilot.
piment, allspice; pimento(-tree)
pimpel: – **en pers**, black and blue.
pimpernel, pimpernel.
pinkie, (-s), little finger; **as jy hom 'n – gee, vat hy die hele hand**, give him an inch and he'll take an ell; **iemand om jou – draai**, twist someone round your (little) finger.
Pinkster, Whitsuntide, Pentecost.
Pinksterbiduur, Whitsun(tide) prayer-meeting.
Pinksterdag, Whitsunday.
Pinksterfees, Whitsuntide.
Pinkstersondag, Whit Sunday.
pinksterroos, peony.
Pinksterweek, Whitsun-week.
pinotie(bossie), bur(r)weed.
pinsbek, pinchbeck.
pint, (-e), pint.
pioen(roos), peony.
pion, (-ne), pawn.
pionier, (-s, -e), pioneer.
pioniersgees, pioneer-spirit.
pipet, (-te), pipette.
piramidaal, (-dale), pyramidal; colossal.
piramide, (-s), pyramid.
Pireneë, Pyrenees.
piriet, (-e), pyrites.
pirouette, (-s), pirouette.
pis, n., piss, urine.
pis, (ge-), piss, pass water.
pisblaas, urinary bladder.
pisbuis, urethra.
pisglas, urinal.
pisgoed, piss-grass.
pisleier, ureter.
pispot, po, piss-pot; cry-baby.
pistool, (-tole), pistol (weapon.)
pistoolskoot, pistol-shot.
pit, (-te), stone (of peach), pip (of orange), kernel; core, pitch, marrow; wick (of a lamp); **geen – hê nie**, have no grit; **'n man met –te**, a man with tin (brass).
pitboom, seedling-tree.
pitkos, grain-food, concentrates.
piton, (-s), python.
pitso, (-'s), pitso, palaver, conference.
pits(w)eer, boil, furuncle.
pittig, (-e), pithy (speech), terse (expression), racy, snappy (style).
pittigheid, pithiness, terseness; body.
pittoresk, (-e), picturesque.
pitvoer, grain-food, concentrates.
pitvrug, stone-fruit.
pla(e), **plaag**, (ge-), plague, vex, annoy, tease, bother, chaff, banter, rally; **hy is met sinkings ge–**, he is troubled with neuralgia.
plaag, (plae), n. plague; nuisance; **die tien plae**, the ten plagues.
plaaggees, tease, teaser.
plaagsiek, (-e), fond of teasing; teasing.
plaagsug, love of teasing.
plaas, (plase), farm; place; **neem –**, take a seat; **– vind, gryp, hê**, take place happen, occur;
in – van, instead of, in place of; **in die eerste – (plek)**, in the first place, primarily.
plaas, (ge-), place, put, set (put) up, erect; locate, assign a place to, rank; insert, put in; accommodate; place (an order); station (troops).
plaas, vide **pleks**.
plaasbekleër, substitute, deputy.
plaasbeskrywing, topography.
plaasgebrek, want of space.
plaaskaffer, farm-boy (-Native).
plaaslewe, farm-life.
plaaslik, (-e), local.
plaasnaam, place-name.
plaasproduk, farm-product.
plaasruimte, space, room.
plaasvervangend, (-e), acting-, deputy.
plaasvervanger, deputy, substitute.
plaasvind, (plaasge-), take place, happen, occur.
plaasvolk, farm-Natives, -boys, -hands.
plaat, (**plate**), (door-, photographic, dental) plate; (marble-)slab, engraving, print, picture; (gramophone-)record; sheet (of iron); patch, stretch (of bush); **die – poets**, scoot.
plaatdruk, copper-plate.
plaatdrukkery, copper-plate printing (office).
plaatjie, (-s), little plate; disc, tag.
plaatyster, sheet-iron.
plae, vide **pla**.
plaerig, (-e), (fond of) teasing.
plaery, (-e), teasing, chaffing, banter.
plafon, **blafon**, (-ne, -s), ceiling.
plagiaat, plagiarism; – **pleeg**, plagiarize.
plagiaris, (-se), plagiarist, plagiary.
plak, (-ke), n. ferrule, strap, cane, stick; **onder die – deurloop**, get licked (caned); **onder die – sit**, be hen-pecked (domineered).
plak, (ge-), paste, glue, gum, stick, affix (stamp); paper (room); **op 'n stoel –**, slam (slap) on a chair.
plakalbum, **-boek**, scrap-album (-book).
plakkaat, (-kate), placard, poster; edict.
plakkaatboek, collection of edicts.
plakker, (-s), paperhanger; paster; hanger-on; squatter (on a farm).
plakkie, (-s), slice, slab.
plakkies, Crassula portulacea.
plakpapier, wall-paper.
plan, (-ne), plan, project, scheme, design; diagram; **'n – uitdink (beraam)**, devise a plan (scheme); **wat is jou –?**, what is your intention (idea)?; **van – wees om**, intend to, mean to; **met die – om**, with the intention of; **op 'n hoër – staan**, stand on a higher plane; **glad nie 'n slegte – nie**, not a bad idea.
planeer, (ge-), planish, smooth; size (paper), glide, plane (aeronautics).
planeet, (-ete), planet.
planeetbaan, orbit (of a planet).
planeetstelsel, planetary system.
planetarium, planetarium, orrery.
planimetrie, planimetry, plane, geometry.
plank, (-e), plank, board; shelf; deal; **op die boonste –**, on the top shelf; **op die –e**, on the stage; **'n stuk op die –e bring**, stage a play.
plank(e)koors, **-vrees**, stage-fright.
plankskutting, (wooden) hoarding.
plankvloer, wooden floor.
plankwerk, hoarding.
planmaak, (**plange-**), devise plans.
plan(ne)maker, man of ideas; schemer.
plant, (-e), n. plant, herb.
plant, (ge-), plant; transplant; tackle, collar, bring down (football).
plantaarde, mould.

plantaardig, (-e), vegetable.
plantasie, (-s), plantation.
plantbeskrywing, phytography.
plant(e)bus, botanical case.
plantegroei, vegetation.
plant(e)kenner, herbalist; botanist.
plant(e)kweker, nurseryman.
plant(e)kwekery, nursery(-garden).
plant(e)lewe, plant-life, vegetable-life.
planter, (-s), planter.
planteryk, vegetable-kingdom.
plantetend, (-e), herbivorous.
planteter, herbivore, plant-eter.
plant(e)wêreld, vegetable-world.
plantjie, (-s), (small) plant; seedling.
plantkunde, botany.
plantkundig, (-e), botanical.
plantkundige, (-s), botanist.
plantluis, plant-louse, aphis.
plantnaam, plant-name.
plantseisoen, planting-time (season).
plantsiekte, plant-disease.
plantsoen, (-e), pleasure-garden; plantation.
plantsoort, species (of plant).
planttyd, planting-time (season).
plas, (-se), n pool, puddle, plash.
plas, (ge-), splash, plash; pour (down); form pools.
plasreën, -reent, n downpour, heavy rain.
plasreën, -reent, (ge-), pour.
plasma, plasm(a) (cell-matter); plasma.
Plastisine, Plasticine.
plastiek, plastic art.
plastiek(stof), plastic.
plasties, (-e), plastic; **-e chirurg,** plastic surgeon.
plastisiteit, plasticity.
plat, flat (roof), horizontal; level, even, smooth; vulgar (language), course, broad; **- neus,** flat nose; **- taal,** vulgar language; slang; **- lê,** lie (down) flat, be prostrate, roll down, crush; run at full speed.
plataan, (-tane), platan(e), plane-tree.
platanna, (-s), clawed toad.
platdak, flat-roof.
platdakhuis, flat-roofed house.
platdruk, (platge-), squeeze flat, crush.
Platduits, (-e), Low-German.
platemusiek, recorded (canned), music.
platevoorspeler, disk-jockey.
platform, (-s), platform.
platgooi, (platge-), throw down; **jou -,** run as fast as you can; fling oneself down.
platheid, flatness; coarseness, vulgarity.
platina, platinum ore.
platinum, platinum.
platinumdraad, platinum-wire.
platineer, (ge-), platinize.
platjie, (-s), wag, rogue, scamp.
platkop, flat-head; catfish.
platkopspykertjie, tack, drawing-pin.
platloop, (platge-), overrun, sweep away, finish off; **die hele dorp -,** go (look) all over the town.
platluis, crab-louse.
platneus, flat nose, squat nose.
plato, (-'s), plateau.
platonies, (-e), platonic.
platriem, strap; **met die - gee,** give the strap.
platry, (platge-), travel across in all directions; ride upon, crush.
platsak, penniless, (stony-)broke; **- wees,** be hard-up (penniless, broke).
platskiet, (platge-), shoot down (people); level (town) with the ground.
plattegrond, (ground-)plan (of building, town); (seating-)plan.

platteland, country(-districts); backveld, rural parts.
plattelander, backvelder, countryman.
plattelandsgemeente, rural (country-) community (congregation, parish).
plat taal, slang.
plattrap, (platge-), trample under foot.
platvoet, flat-foot(ed person); plantain.
platweg, down-right, flatly; plainly.
plavei, (ge-), pave.
plaveisel, (-s), pavement; paving.
plaveisteen, paving-stone, flag-stone.
plaza, plaza.
plebejer, (-s), plebeian, commoner, pleb.
plebissiet, (-e), plebiscite.
plebs, rabble, (hoi-)polloi.
pleeg, (ge-), commit, perpetrate (crime); practise (deceit); be accustomed to, be in the habit of.
pleegkind, foster-child.
pleegmoeder, foster-mother.
pleegouers, foster-parents.
pleegseun, foster-son.
pleegsuster, foster-sister; nurse, sister.
pleegvader, foster-father.
pleganker, sheet-anchor.
pleggewaad, ceremonial dress (attire).
plegstatig, (-e), solemn, stately.
plegstatigheid, pomp, solemnity.
plegtig, (-e), solemn, dignified, ceremonious, stately, impressive; **-e stilte,** impressive (solemn) silence; **-e eed, belofte, waarskuwing,** solemn oath, promise, warning.
plegtigheid, (-hede), ceremony, rite, function; solemnity; stateliness.
pleidooi, (-e), plea, argument, address.
plein, (-e), square.
pleister, (-s), n. plaster; stucco (on wall).
pleister, (ge-), plaster, stucco.
pleisterbeeld, plaster-cast.
pleisterkalk, (lime-)plaster.
pleisterplank, (hand)hawk, mortar-board.
pleistertroffel, plastering trowel.
pleisterwerk, plastering, plaster.
pleit, n. plea, suit; **die - wen,** gain one's suit (point); **die - is beslis (besleg),** the matter is settled.
pleit, (ge-), plead; **dit - nie vir hom nie,** that does not speak in his favour; **hy het (onskuldig) ge-,** he pleaded (not) guilty.
pleitbesorger, counsel, advocate, lawyer; spokesman.
pleiter, (-s), pleader; counsel.
pleitrede, plea, argument, defence.
pleitsugtig, (-e), litigious.
Plejade, Pleiades.
plek, (-ke), place, spot; room, space; seat; post, position; **in jou, in die eerste, op die regte -,** in your, in the first, in the right place; **in (die) - van,** in place of, instead of; **op die -,** on the spot; there and then; **iemand op sy - sit,** put a person in his place; **stel jou in my -,** put yourself in my place; **op die - rus,** stand at ease; vide **plaas.**
pleks, plaas, instead of, in place of.
pleng, (ge-), shed (blood), pour out (wine); offer (a libation).
plengoffer, libation.
pleonasme, pleonasm.
pleonasties, (-e), pleonastic.
plesier, pleasure, fun, enjoyment, satisfaction; **met (alle) -,** with (the greatest) pleasure; **iemand 'n - doen,** do a person a favour; **baie - hê,** enjoy oneself; **ek het dit nie vir my - gedoen nie,** I did not do it for the fun of the thing.

plesier, (ge-), please.
plesierboot, launch, pleasure-boat.
plesierig, (-e), pleasant, happy; cheerful; **–e reis!**, happy voyage!; **'n –e kêrel**, a cheerful (jolly) chap.
plesierigheid, pleasantness, pleasure, joy; cheerfulness.
plesierjag, hunt for pleasure; launch.
plesierreis, pleasure-trip, jaunt.
plesierritjie, pleasure-ride; joy-ride.
plesiertog(gie), pleasure-trip (-ride).
plesiertrein, excursion-train.
plet, (ge-), flatten, roll out, planish.
pleuris, pleuritis, pleurisy, pleuritis.
plig, (-te), duty; **jou – doen (betrag, nakom, volbring, vervul)**, do (perform) one's duty; **jou – versuim**, neglect one's duty; **leamnd tot sy – bring**, teach someone his duty.
pligmatig, (-e), as in duty bound, conformable to one's duty, duteous.
pligpleging, (-e), ceremony.
pligsbesef, sense of duty.
pligsbetragting, devotion to duty.
pligsgevoel, sense of duty.
pligshalwe, as in duty bound, dutifully.
pligsversaking, neglect of duty.
pligsvervulling, performance of duty.
plint, (-e), skirting-board; plinth.
ploe(ë), ploeg, (ge-), plough.
ploeër, (-s), plougher, ploughman.
ploeëry, ploughing.
ploeg, (ploeë), n. plough; batch, team, gang, shift, **jou hand aan die – slaan**, put your hand to the plough.
ploeg, (ge-), vide **ploe(ë)**.
ploegbaar, (-bare), ploughable, arable.
ploegbaas, gang-boss, foreman; ganger.
ploegbalk, plough-tree, (-beam).
ploegland, ploughland, arable land.
ploegperd, plough-horse.
ploegskaar, ploughshare.
ploegstelsel, shift-system.
ploegstert, plough-handle(s); plough-tail; **die – hou**, hold the plough-handles.
ploegvoor, furrow (of a plough).
ploert, (-e), cad, blackguard.
ploertagtig, (-e), caddish.
ploeter, (ge-), plod, drudge.
ploeteraar, (-e), plodder, drudge.
plof, (plowwe), n. thud, flop.
plof, (ge-), thud, flop, thump.
plof!, interj. flop!, plop!
plombeer, (ge-), fill (tooth): seal.
plombeersel, filling; seal.
plomp, a. awkward, clumsy, stout.
plompheid, clumsiness, lumpishness.
plons, n. splash, plop.
plons, (ge-), splash, plop.
plooi, (-e), n. fold, pleat, crease (in trousers), wrinkle (in face, etc.).
plooi, (ge-), fold, crease, pleat; **hy het dit so gedat**, he contrived (manipulated, wangled) it so that.
plooibaar, (-bare), pliable, flexible (thing); pliant, compliant (character).
plooibaarheid, pliability; pliancy.
plooirok, pleated skirt.
plooisel, pleat(ing), tuck.
plotseling, (-e), a. sudden, abrupt.
plotseling, adv. suddenly, all at once.
plousibel, (-e), plausible.
pluche, plush.
pluiens, pluiings, (pl.), rags, tatters.
pluim, (-e), plume, feather, crest.
pluimasie, plumage.

pluimbal, shuttle-cock.
pluimbos, plume, crest.
pluimpie, little crest (plume); feather (in the cap), compliment.
pluimstryk, (ge-), flatter, fawn upon.
pluimstryker, (-s), fawner, toady.
pluimstrykery, toadyism, fawning.
pluimvee, poultry.
pluimveeboerdery, poultry-farming.
pluis, a. in order, as it should be; **dit is daar nie – nie**, matters are not as they should be.
pluis, (ge-), fluff, pick, make fluffy.
pluishoed, top-hat, topper.
pluisie, (-s), (bit of) fluff, plug (of wadding), wad, piece of cotton-wool.
pluiskeil, top-hat.
pluk, n. picking (fruit), plucking.
pluk, (ge-), pick, pluck; cull; fleece.
plukker, (-s), picker.
pluksel, (-s), picking, cullage; crop; lint.
plunder, (ge-), plunder, loot, pillage, ransack (a town); rob (a man).
plunderaar, (-s), plunderer, robber.
plundering, plundering, looting.
plunje, rags, togs. Vide **pluiens**.
plus, plus; **– minus**, approximately.
plusteken, positive sign, plus-sign.
Pluto, Pluto.
plutokraat, (-krate), plutocrat.
plutokrasie, plutocracy.
plutokraties, (-e), plutocratic.
plutonium, plutonium.
pneumaties, (-e), pneumatic.
podagra, podagra, gout.
podium, podium, platform.
poe!, ugh!, phew!
poedel(hond), poodle(dog).
poedelnaak, (-te), poedelnakend, (-e), stark naked.
poedelprys, booby-prize.
poeding, (-s), pudding.
poeëm, (poëme), poem.
poëet, (poëte), poet.
poef!, pop!, bang!
poeier, (-s), powder.
poeier, (ge-), powder.
poeierdoos, powder-box.
poeierkwas, powder-puff.
poeiervormig, (-e), in powder form.
poel, (-e), pool, puddle.
poelbetaan, (-tane), poelpetaat, (-tate), poelpetater, (-s), guinea-fowl.
poelsnip, poensnip, (-pe), snipe.
poema, (-s), puma, cougar.
poena(geweer), light rifle, small musket.
poenskop, (-pe), hornless (tuskless) animal, poll, pollard.
poe(n)skopbees, poll, pollard; **rooi –te**, redpolls.
poensnip, vide **poelsnip**.
poep, (-e), n. fart.
poep, (ge-), fart.
poësie, poetry.
poespas, jumble hotch-potch.
poëties, (-e), poetic(al).
poets, n. trick; **'n – bak**, play a trick.
poets, n. polish.
poets, (ge-), polish, clean, shine.
poetser, (-e), polisher, cleaner.
poetskatoen, cotton-waste.
poewasa, Ramadan.
pofadder, puff-adder.
pofbroek, knicker-bocker, plus fours.
poffertjie, fritter.
pofmou, puff(ed) sleeve.
poging, (-e, -s), attempt, try, effort, endeavour; **'n – doen**, make an attempt (effort).

pogrom, (-s, -me), pogrom.
pohaai, bohaai, fuss, noise, to-do.
pok, (-ke), pock; **die –ke**, smallpox.
pokagtig, (-e), pocky, pock-like.
pokdalig, (-e), pock-marked.
pokke-epidemie, small-pox-epidemic.
pokkel, (-s), lump of flesh, body.
pokkies, (pl.), smallpox.
pol, (-le), tuft, tussock, clump.
polarisasie, polarization.
polariseer, (ge-), polarize.
polder, (-s), polder.
polderland, polderland.
Pole, Poland; vide **Pool**.
poleer, (ge-), polish; smooth-bore.
poleersteen, polishing-stone.
polemiek, (-e), controversy, polemic.
polemies, (-e), controversial, polemic.
polemis, (-te), controversialist, polemic.
polemiseer, (ge-), engage in controversy.
polêr, (-e), polar; diametrical.
polgras, tuftgrass.
poliep, (-e), polyp(e) (animal); polypus.
poliëster, polyester.
poliets, smart, clever, knowing.
polietsheid, smartness, cleverness.
poligamie, polygamy.
poligamis, (-te), polygan st.
poliglot, (-te), polyglot.
poligoon, (-gone), polygon.
Polinesië, Polynesia.
polis, (-se), (insurance-)policy.
polishouer, policy-holder.
polisie, police; **geheime –**, secret police.
polisie-agent, policeman, constable.
polisieburo, police-office.
polisiedienaar, policeman.
polisiekantoor, police-office; charge-office.
polisiemag, police-force.
polisiespioen, trap, police-spy.
polisiewese, the police.
politegnies, (-e), polytechnic(al).
politeïs, (-te), polytheist.
politeïsme, polytheism.
politiek, n. politics; policy; **koloniale –**, colonial policy.
politiek, (-e), a. political; politic; wily.
politikus, (-se, -tici), politician.
politiseer, (ge-), politicize, talk politics.
politoer, n. polish.
politoer, (ge-), polish.
polka, (-s), polka.
polka-hare, bobbed hair.
polo, polo.
pols, (-e), pulse; **iemand se – voel**, feel a person's pulse (lit. & fig.).
pols, (-e), jumping-pole; sound a person.
polsaar, (radical) artery.
polsgewrig, wrist.
polshorlosie, -oorlosie, wrist-watch.
polshou, chip-shot.
polsmeter, pulsimeter.
polsslag, pulse(-beat), pulsation.
polsstok, jumping-pole.
polvy, (-e), heel (of boot).
polys, (ge-), polish (lit. & fig.), burnish.
pomelo, (-'s), grape fruit; pomelo.
pommade, (-s), pomade.
Pommere, Pomerania.
Pommers, (-e), Pomeranian.
pomp, (ge-), pump.
pomp, (ge-), pump; hit, strike.
pompe(l)moer(tjie), (Cape) gooseberry.
pompeus, (-e), pompous.

pompklep, pump-valve.
pompom, (-s), pompom, Maxim(-gun).
pompsuier, pump-piston.
pond, (-e), pound; **'n – vleis**, a pound of meat; **– vir – (stelsel)**, pound for pound (system).
pondok, (-ke), hut, hovel.
ponie, (-s), pony.
ponie-slagskip, pocket battleship.
pons, punch.
pont, (-e), pontoon; ferry(-boat).
pontak(wyn), pontac.
pontifikaal, (-kale), pontifical.
pontifikaat, pontificate.
ponton, (-s), pontoon.
Pontius, Pontius; **van – na Pilatus**, from pillar to post.
poog, (ge-), attempt, endeavour.
pook, (ge-), poke (up).
Pool, (Pole), Pole.
pool, (pole), pole.
poollande, polar regions.
poollig, northern (polar) lights.
poolreisiger, Arctic explorer.
Pools, (-e), Polish.
poolafstand, polar distance.
poolsee, polar (Arctic, Antarctic) sea.
poolshoogte, elevation of the pole, latitude.
poolsirkel, polar circle.
poolster, pole-star.
poolstreek, polar region; frigid zone.
poon, (pone), ponie, (-s), pony.
poort, (-e), gate(way), entrance; pass.
poortaar, portal vein.
poortwagter, gate-keeper.
poos, (pose), while, time, interval.
poot, (pote), paw, hoof, foot (of animal), leg (of animal, table, etc.); paw, fist (handwriting); **bly daar af met jou pote**, keep your paws off that; **sy redenering staan op pote**, there are no holes to pick in his argument; **op eie pote staan**, stand on one's own legs.
pootjie, (-s), (little) paw; gout.
pootjie, (ge-), trip (up).
poot-uit, exhausted, done up, dog-tired.
pop, (-pe), doll; puppet; figure-head; **toe was die –pe aan danse**, then the fat was in the fire.
popel, (ge-), flutter, beat fast.
popelien, poplin.
popgesig(gie), doll's face, puppet-face.
popgoed, doll's clothes; dolls, toys.
pophuis, doll's house.
pop-oë, doll's eyes.
poppekas, puppet-show; doll's house.
popperig, (-e), doll-like; dainty, trival.
poppie, (-s), dolly; popsy.
popspeel, (popge-), play with dolls.
populariseer, (ge-), polpularize.
populariteit, popularity.
populasie, population.
populêr, (-e), popular.
populier, (-e), poplar.
populierboom, poplar(-tree).
populierbos, poplar-grove.
popwaentjie, doll's pram.
popwinkel, doll-shop.
por, (-re), dig, thrust, poke.
por, (ge-), prod, poke; spur (egg) on.
poreus, (-e), porous.
poreusheid, porosity.
porfier(steen), porphyry.
porie, (-ë), pore.
pornografie, pornography.
pornografies, (-e), pornographic.
pors(e)lein, porcelain, china(-ware).

pors(e)leinaarde, china-clay, kaolin.
pors(e)leinbak, china-dish.
pors(e)leinfabriek, china-factory.
pors(e)leingoed, china-ware.
pors(e)leinkas, china-cabinet; **aap in 'n –**, unwelcome visitor, unwanted person.
pors(e)leinlak, porcelain-lacquer.
pors(e)leinwinkel, china-shop.
porsie, (-e), part, share; helping.
port, port(-wine).
port(o), postage.
portaal, (-tale), entrance-hall, lobby; porch, landing.
portefeulje, (-s), portfolio; brief-case; wallet; **– van Finansies**, portfolio of Finance.
portfisideur, folding-doors.
portiek, (-e), porch, portal.
portier, (-e, -s), porter; carriage-door.
portret, (-te), portrait, photo(graph).
portretalbum, photograph-album.
portretlys, photo-frame.
portretraam, photo, portrait-frame.
portretskilder, portrait-painter.
portretteer, (ge-), portray, paint.
Portugal, Portugal.
Portugees, (-gese), n. & a. Portuguese.
portuur, partuur, (-s), equal, match.
portvry, post-free.
portwyn, port-wine.
pos, (-te), post; post-office; mail; postman; postal delivery; **met die – kom**, come by post; **per – verstuur**, send by post; **per kerende –**, by return of post; **oor die –**, through the post; post, station; sentry, picket; situation, position, job; **op jou – wees**, be at one's post; **–te uitsit**, post pickets (sentries); **konstabels het voor die gebou op – gestaan**, policemen were stationed in front of the building; **'n belangrike – op die rekening**, an important item in the account; **'n – in die grootboek**, an entry in the ledger.
pos, (ge-), post (letters, pickets).
posagent, postal agent.
posbeampte, postal official.
posbestelling, mail-order.
posbewys, postal order, postal note.
posbode, postman.
posboot, mailboat.
posbus, (post-office) box; letter-box.
posdag, mail-day.
posdateer, (ge-), postdate.
posdiens, postal service.
posduif, carrier-pigeon.
poseer, (ge-), pose; sit (to a painter).
poseur, (-s), poser, attitudinizer.
posie, (-s), little while.
posisie, (-s), position, situation, status, degree; **– inneem (teen)**, take position, make a stand (against); **'n man van –**, a man of status.
positief, (-tiewe), n. positive.
positief, (-tiewe), a. & adv. positive; sure; **–tiewe trap**, positive degree (gram.); **ek is – seker**, I am positively certain.
positiewe, n. pl. senses; consciousness; **hy is nie by sy – nie**, he is not in his senses (not in his right mind); **hy het sy – verloor**, he lost his head; **toe hy weer by sy – kom**, when he regained consciousness.
positivis, (-te), positivist.
positivisme, positivism.
positivisties, (-e), positivistic(al).
poskaart, postcard.
poskantoor, post-office.
poskar, post-cart, mail-coach (-cart).
posmeester, postmaster.

posmerk, postmark.
pospakket, postal parcel.
posryer, driver of mail-cart; post boy.
possak, post-bag, mail-bag.
posseël, (postage-)stamp.
posseëlversamelaar, stamp-collector.
posspaarbank, post-office savings-bank.
posstempel, postmark.
postarief, postal rates, rates of postage.
poste restante, poste restante.
posterye: die –, the (General) Post Office, Posts.
posthuum, (-hume), posthumous.
postrein, mail-train, postal train.
postulaat, (-late), postulate.
postuleer, (ge-), postulate.
postuur, (-ture), figure, shape.
posvat, (posge-), take post, take root; take up one's position, post oneself.
posverbinding, postal communication.
posverkeer, postal (mail) traffic.
posvliegtuig, mailplane.
posvry, post-free.
poswese, postal service, postal affairs.
poswissel, postal order, money-order.
pot, (-te), pot, jar; chamber(-pot); game (tennis, etc.); pool, stakes; **–te en panne**, pots and pans; **die – verwyt die ketel**, the pot calls the kettle black; **al is 'n – nog so skeef, hy kry darem 'n deksel**, every Jack will have his Jill; **die – verteer**, pay the stakes (the piper), foot the bill.
pot, (ge-), hoard (up), save up.
potas, potash, potassium carbonate.
potbrood, potbread.
potdeksel, pot-lid.
potdig, (-te), tightly closed, air-tight.
potdoof, (-dowe), stone-deaf.
potensiaal, (-siale), n. potential.
potensialiteit, (-e), potentiality.
potensieel, (-siële), a. potential.
potentaat, (-tate), potentate.
pothingsel, pot-handle.
potjie, (-s), little pot (jar); socket (of hip); game; small pool; **jou eie – krap**, stand on your own legs; **uit die –**, out of joint; **met iemand 'n – loop**, pick a bone (fall out) with someone.
potklei, potter's clay; sticky mud.
potlepel, ladle.
potlood, (-lode), **potloot**, (-lote), lead-pencil.
potloodslyper, pencil-sharpener.
potpourri, potpourri.
potsierlik, (-e), grotesque; ridiculous.
potskerf, potsherd.
pottebakker, potter.
pottebakkerskyf, -wiel, potter's wheel.
pottebakkery, pottery.
potvis, cachalot.
pou, (-e), peacock, peafowl, peahen.
pou-eier, peahen's egg.
pouk, (-e), kettledrum.
pouoog, peacock-butterfly.
pouperisme, pauperism.
pous, (-e), pope.
pousdom, papacy; papal state.
pouse, (-s), interval, pause.
pouseer, (ge-), pause, stop for a while, break off.
pousgesind, (-e), a. papistical.
pousgesinde, (-s), n. papist.
pouslik, (-e), papal. pontificial.
poustert, peacock's tail; fantail-pigeon.
pouveer, peacock's feather.
power, poor, meagre, thin.
Praag, Prague.

praal, splendour, pomp, magnificence, glory; **prag en –,** pomp and glory.
praal, (ge-), boast, flaunt; glitter.
praalbed, bed of state; **op 'n – lê,** lie in state.
praalgraf, mausoleum.
praalsiek, (-e), ostentatious.
praalsug, ostentation.
praalsugtig, (-e), ostentatious.
praat, n. talk; **iemand aan die – hou,** detain in conversation, keep one busy (talking).
praat, (ge-), talk, chat, speak, converse; **jy kan maklik –,** it is all very well (for you to talk); **en die mooi klere! moenie – nie!,** and the fine clothes! I have no words to describe them!; **kan jy nie – nie?,** have you got nothing to say?; **in die wind –,** talk at random; **om iets heen –,** beat about the bush, shilly-shally, hedge; **– van die ding!,** yes, did you ever (hear the like)!
praatagtig, (-e), talkative, garrulous.
praatgraag, talkative person, tattler.
praatjie, (-s), talk, rumour, story; **-s,** gossip, tattle; **'n – maak,** have a chat; **dis sommer 'n –,** it is idle talk, it is a mere rumour; **-s vir die vaak,** nonsense, twaddle; **-s vul geen gaatjies,** talking mends no holes, fine words butter no parsnips.
praatjiesmaker, babbler; braggart.
praatkous, talker, tattler.
praatlustig, (-e), talkative, garrulous.
praatrolprent, talkie, speakie.
praatsiek, garrulous, loquacious.
praatstoel: op sy praatstoel sit, be in a talking mood, start spouting.
praatsug, garrulousness, loquaciousness.
praatsugtig, (-e), garrulous, loquacious.
prag, beauty, splendour, magnificence; **'n – van 'n . . . ,** a splendid (ripping, stunning). . . ; **– en praal,** pomp and glory (circumstance).
pragband, ornamental cover, edition de luxe.
prageksemplaar, beauty, fine specimen.
pragkêrel, fine type of man.
pragliewend, (-e), ostentatious.
pragmatiek, n. pragmatism.
pragmatiek, (-e), pragmatic.
pragmaties, (-e), pragmatic.
pragmatis, (-te), pragmatist.
pragmatisme, pragmatism.
pragstuk, beauty, masterpiece.
pragtig, (-e), fine, beautiful, splendid, lovely, grand.
praguitgawe, édition de luxe (de luxe edition), handsome edition.
pragwerk, masterpiece, beautiful piece of work; table-book.
praksasie, (-s), devising, contriving.
prakseer, (ge-), devise, contrive; cogitate, puzzle.
prakties, (-e), a. practical, workmanlike, workable; working; **-e kennis,** practical (working) knowledge **-e voorstel,** practical (workable) proposal.
prakties, adv. practically, virtually.
praktikus, (-se, **-tici**), practical man.
praktiseer, (ge-), practise.
praktiserend, (-e), practising; **-e geneesheer** general (medical) practitioner.
praktisyn, (-s), (legal, medical) practitioner.
praktyk, (-e), practice; **in die –,** in (actual) practice; **'n (druk) groot –,** a large practice; **'n – uitoefen,** practise; **slegte -e,** evil practices.
praler, (-s), braggart; swaggerer.
pralerig, (-e), bragging, swanking.
pralery, boasting, bragging, swaggering.
pram, (-me), bub, dug; teat, pap.

prang, (ge-), press, squeeze.
prater, (-s), talker, tattler.
praterig, (-e), talkative, garrulous.
pratery, talk(ing), tattle, gossip.
preadvies, (-e), report.
prebende, (-s), prebend.
predestinasie, predestination.
predestineer, (ge-), predestine.
predik, (ge-), preach.
predikaat, (-kate), predicate; attribute, title mark.
predikamp, ministry.
predikant, (-e), minister, clergyman, parson.
predikantswoning, parsonage.
predikasie, (-s), sermon; lecture.
predikasieboek, book of sermons.
predikatief, (-tiewe), predicative.
prediker, (-s), preacher; **(die boek) Prediker,** (the book of) Ecclesiastes.
prediking, preaching.
prediktor, predictor.
predileksie, (-s), predilection.
predisposisie, (-s), predisposition (to).
predominasie, predomination.
predomineer, (ge-), predominate.
preek, (preke), sermon, homily.
preek, (ge-), preach; sermonize, reprove.
preekbeurt, turn to preach; engagement to preach.
preekstoel, pulpit.
preektoon, pulpit-tone (-manner).
preektrant, manner of preaching.
preëminent, (-e), pre-eminent.
prefek, (-te), prefect.
prefektuur, (-ture), prefecture.
prefereer, (ge-), prefer; **– bo,** prefer to.
preferensie, (-s), preference.
preferent, (-e), preferential; **-e aandele,** preference shares, preferred shares; **-e skulde,** preferred debts.
prefiks, (-e), prefix.
pregnant, (-e), pregnant.
prehistories, (-e), prehistoric.
prei, leek.
prejudisieer, (ge-), prejudge; prejudice.
prekerig, (-e), preachy.
prelaat, (-late), prelate.
preliminêr, (-e), a preliminary.
prelude, (-s), **preludium,** (-s, **-dia**), prelude.
preludeer, (ge-), prelude; foreshadow.
prematuur, (-ture), premature.
premeditasie, premeditation.
premie, (-s), premium; bounty, bonus.
premielening, lottery-loan.
premier, (-s), premier, prime minister.
première, (-s), first night (performance).
premiestelsel, bounty-system; premium-system.
premis, (-se), premise (premiss).
prent, (-e), picture, illustration; print.
prent, (ge-), impress, imprint (on).
prentbriefkaart, picture-postcard.
prenteboek, picture-book.
prentebybel, pictorial Bible.
prentjie, (-s), picture.
prentkoerant, tabloid.
prenteverhaal, comic (strip).
preokkupasie, preoccupation.
preparaat, (-rate), preparation; slide.
preparasie, (-s), preparation.
prepareer, (ge-), prepare.
preposisie, (-s), preposition.
prêrie, prairie.
prerogatief, (-tiewe), prerogative.
pres, (ge-), press, force; crimp.

presbiter, (-s), presbyter.
Presbiteriaan, (-ane), Presbyterian.
Presbiteriaans, (-e), Presbyterian.
presedeer, (ge-), precede.
presedent, (-e), precedent.
presensie, presence.
presensiegeld, attendance-fee.
presensielys, attendance-register, roll.
present, (-e), n. present, gift; – gee, make a present, give as a present.
present, a. present.
presentabel, (-e), presentable, decent.
presentasie, (-s), presentation.
presenteer, (ge-), offer, hand-round; present; introduce.
presenteerblad, tray.
present-eksemplaar, presentation-copy.
preservasie, preservation.
preservatief, preserwatief, (-tiewe), preservative.
preserveer, (ge-), preserve.
presideer, (ge-), preside (at, over).
president, (-e), president; chairman.
presidentskap, presidency, presidentship.
presidentsverkiesing, presidential election.
presidium, presidium.
presies, (-e), a. precise, exact, accurate, regular; neat, tidy, cleanly, particular.
presies, adv. precisely, exactly; – om vyfuur, at five o'clock precisely (sharp).
presiesheid, preciseness; tidiness.
presieus, (-e), precious, affected.
presipitaat, (-tate), precipitate.
presipiteer, (ge-), precipitate.
presiseer, (ge-), state in detail, specify.
presisiegereedskap, precision tools.
preskripsie, (-s), prescription.
pressie, pressure; – uitoefen op, bring pressure to bear upon.
prestasie, (-s), achievement, feat.
presteer, (ge-), achieve, accomplish.
prestige, prestige, influence, reputation.
presumasie, (-s), presumption.
presumeer, (ge-), presume.
presumpsie, (-s), presumption.
pret, fun, pleasure; – maak, amuse, oneself, have lots of fun.
pretbederwer, spoil-sport, kill-joy.
pretendeer, (ge-), claim, pretend.
pretendent, (-e), pretender, claimant.
pretensie, (-s), pretence; pretension; sonder –, unpretentious, unassuming.
pretensieus, (-e), pretentious.
preteritum, preterite.
pretmaker, joker, jester; merrymaker.
prettig, (-e), pleasant, enjoyable, nice, jolly; – vind, enjoy, like.
preuts, (-e), prim and proper, prudish.
preutsheid, primness, prudishness.
preventief, (-tiewe), preventive.
prewel, (ge-), mutter.
prieel, (priële), prinjeel, (-jele), pergola, covered walk; arbour.
priem, (-e), awl, pricker; dagger.
priem, (ge-), pierce, prick.
priemgetal, prime number.
priester, (-s), priest.
priesteramp, priestly office.
priesterdom, priesthood, priestly order.
priesteres, (-se), priestess.
priestergewaad, priestly dress (garb).
priesterheerskappy, hierarchy.
priesterkleed, priestly dress.
priesterlik, (-e), priestly.
priesterorde, order of priesthood.
priesterskap, priesthood, priestly office.

priewie, (-s), privy, latrine.
prik, (-ke), prick.
prik, (ge-), prick; tingle.
prikkel, (-s), stimulus, incentive, spur; prick, goad; pricking; die versene teen die –s slaan, kick against the pricks.
prikkel, (ge-), excite, irritate, provoke; stimulate, incite; goad; tickle (the palate); sting.
prikkelbaar, (-bare), rritable, touchy.
prikkelbaarheid, irritability, touchiness.
prikkeldraad, barbed wire.
prikkelend, (-e), stimulating, exciting; irritating, provoking.
prikkeling, stimulus, stimulation; provocation, irritation; pricking, tickling.
prikkelpop, glamour-girl.
prik(vis), lamprey.
prill: –le jeug, early youth.
prima, prime, first-rate, A1, tiptop.
primaat, (-mate), primate.
prima-donna, prima donna.
prima(wissel), first of exchange.
primêr, (-e), primary (school, colours).
primitief, (-tiewe), primitive.
prinjeel, vide prieel,
prins, (-e), prince.
prinsdom, (-me), principality.
prinses, (-se), princess.
prins-gemaal, (-aals, -ale), prince-consort.
Prinsgesinde, (-s), adherent of the Prince; Orangist.
prinsiep, v. prinsipe.
prinsipaal, (-pale), principal.
prinsipe, (-s), prinsiep, (-e), principle; in –, in principle, uit –, on principle.
prinsipieel, (-ële), fundamental, basic, radical, essential.
prinslik, (-e), princely.
prins-regent, prince regent.
prior, (-s), prior.
prioraat, (-rate), priorate.
priores, (-se), prioress.
prioriteit, priority.
priorskap, priorate, priorship.
prisma, (-s), prism.
prismaties, (-e), prismatic.
prisonier, (-s), prisoner; convict.
privaat, (-ate), n. latrine, water-closet.
privaat, (-vate), a. & adv. private(ly).
privaatbesit, private property.
privaatgebruik, private use.
privaatles, private lesson(s).
privaatonderwyser(es), private teacher.
privaatreg, civil law.
privaat-sekretaris, private secretary.
privaatskool, private school.
privatief, (-tiewe), privative.
privilegi(i)e, (-s), privilege.
pro, prep. pro; – en contra, pro and con; – rata, pro rata, proportional(ly).
probaat, (-bate), efficacious, sovereign (remedy), proved (proven).
probeer, (ge-), try, attempt; test (a gun), try out (a machine), taste, sample (a cigar, wine).
probeerslag, attempt, trial, try.
probleem, (-bleme), problem, question.
problematies, (-e), problematic(al).
produk, (-te), product; (a literary) production; result, outcome; –te, products, produce.
produksie, production, output, yield.
produksiekoste, cost of production.
produktehandel, produce-trade.
produktehandelaar, produce-merchant.
produktemark, produce-market.
produktief, (-tiewe), productive.

produktiwiteit, productivity, productiveness, productive capacity.
produseer, (ge-), produce, turn out.
produsent, (-e), producer.
proef, (proewe), proof, test, trial, experiment; sample, specimen; dissertation; (phys.) experiment; (photog. & print), proof, copy; **iemand op die – stel**, put a person to the test; **iemand se geduld op die – stel**, tax one's patience; **die – deurstaan**, stand the test (proof); **dit is die – op die som**, that proves (settles) the matter; **'n – neem met iets**, give a thing a trial; **aan 'n – onderwerp**, subject to a trial; **op die – (huur, neem)**, (hire, take) on trial, on probation; **by wyse van –**, by way of trial, on trial.
proe(f), (ge-), taste; sample.
proef, (ge-), try, test, assay.
proefbalans, trial-balance.
proefballon, trial-balloon (kite).
proefbestelling, trial-order.
proefblad, proof-sheet; specimen-page.
proefdruk, proof.
proeffabriek, -installasie, pilot plant.
proefgewig, standard weight.
proefgoud, assay-gold.
proefhoudend, (-e), standard, genuine, proof; **– blyk**, prove genuine.
proefjaar, trial-year, probationary year.
proefleerling, probationer, apprentice.
proefles, trial-lesson.
proefleser, proof-reader.
proefmaand, trial-month.
proefmonster, testing sample.
proefmunt, sample-coin.
proefnaald, touch-needle.
proefnemer, experimenter.
proefneming, experiment.
proefnommer, specimen-copy.
proefondervindelik, (-e), experimental.
proefplaas, experimental station (farm).
proefpreek, probation-sermon, trial-sermon.
proefrit, trial-run, try-out.
proefskoot, trial-shot.
proefskrif, dissertation, thesis.
proefstasie, experimental station.
proefsteen, touchstone.
proefstuk, specimen, sample.
proeftyd, (time of) probation, probationary period, apprenticeship.
proefvel, proof-sheet.
proefvlug, trial-flight.
proefwedstryd, trial-match.
proes, (ge-), sneeze; burst out laughing; giggle; snort (of a horse).
proewe, (-s), sample, specimen.
proewer, (-s), taster.
profaan, (-fane), profane.
profanasie, (-s), profanation.
profeet, (-fete), prophet; **Saul onder die profete**, Saul among the prophets; **die ou profete is dood, en die jonges eet brood**, the gift of prophecy has gone with the prophets of old; **'n – is nie geëerd in sy eie land nie**, a prophet has no honour in his own country.
profesie, (-ë), prophecy.
professie, (-s), profession.
professioneel, (-nele), professional.
professor, (-s, -e), professor.
professoraal, (-rale), professorial.
professoraat, (-rate), professorship, chair.
profeteer, (ge-), prophesy.
profetes, (-se), prophetess.
profeties, (-e), prophetic.
profiel, profile, section, side-view.
profilakties, (-e), prophylactic.

profiteer, (ge-), profit (by), take advantage (of) avail oneself (of).
profyt, (-e), profit, gain.
profytlik, (-e), profitable.
prognose, prognosis.
program, (-me), program(me).
programmusiek, program(me)-music.
progressie, (-s), progression; graduation.
progressief, (-siewe), progressive.
prohibisie, prohibition.
prohibisionis, (-te), prohibitionist.
prohibitief, (-tiewe), prohibitive.
projek, (-te), project, design, scheme.
projeksielamp, projecting lantern.
projeksieskerm, screen.
projekteer, (ge-), project.
projektiel, (-e), projectile.
proklamasie, (-s), proclamation.
proklameer, (ge-), proclaim.
prokonsul, proconsul.
prokreëer, (ge-), procreate.
prokurasie, (-s), power of attorney, proxy, procuration.
prokurasiehouer, agent, proxy.
prokureur, (-s), attorney, solicitor.
prokureur-generaal, (prokureurs-generaal), attorney-general.
prokureurseksamen, law-examination.
prokureurskantoor, attorney's (solicitor's) office.
proleet, (-lete), vulgarian, plebeian.
proletariaat, (-ate), proletariat(e).
proletariër, (-s), proletarian.
proletaries, (-e), proletarian.
prolongeer, (ge-), prolong; renew.
proloog, (-loë, -loge), prologue.
promenade, (-s), promenade.
promenadedek, promenade-deck.
promesse, (-s), promissory note.
promosie, (-s), promotion, advancement, rise; graduation (at university).
promosiedag, degree-day.
promosielys, promotion-list.
promosieplegtigheid, graduation-ceremony.
promotor, (-s), (company-)promoter; professor presenting a candidate for a degree.
promoveer, (ge-), graduate, take one's (doctor's) degree.
promovendus, (-di), candidate for a (doctor's) degree.
promulgasie, promulgation.
promulgeer, (ge-), promulgate, proclaim.
pronk, show, ostentation; finery; pride.
pronk, (ge-), show off, parade; spread, buck, "pronk" (of a springbok).
pronkbed, bed of state.
pronkboontjie, scarlet runner.
pronker, (-s), fop, dandy, coxcomb.
pronkerig, (-e), foppish, showy.
pronk-ertjie, sweet pea.
pronkery, show, showing-off, parade.
pronkgewaad, state-dress, gala-dress.
pronkjuweel, (sparkling) gem, jewel.
pronkkamer, state-room, best room.
pronkstuk, show-piece, beauty, pride.
pronksug, ostentatiousness.
pront, prompt(ly), punctual(ly), regular(ly), glib(ly); **– ken**, know off pat, know by heart.
prontheid, promptness, readiness.
pront-uit, straight (out), directly, flatly, to one's face.
prooi, prey; **ten – val aan**, fall a prey to.
prop, (-pe), cork, stopper (of bottle); bung (of cask); gag; wad; plug (in hole); pellet; lump (in throat); tubby person, dump.
prop, (ge-), cram, stuff, plug, close up.

propaganda, propaganda; – **maak vir**, make (carry on) propaganda for, propagandize, agitate for.
propagadastuk, propagandist-piece.
propagandawerk, propaganda(-work).
propagandis, (-te), propagandist.
propagandisties, (-e), propagandist(ic).
propageer, (ge-), propagate, diffuse.
propedeuties, (-e), propaedeutic.
propgeweer, popgun.
proponent, (-e), candidate for the ministry, candidate minister.
proporsie, (-s), proportion.
proporsioneel, (-nele), proportionate(ly), in due proportion.
proposisie, (-s), proposition, proposal.
propskieter, popgun.
propvol, (-le), chock-full, crammed (with), stuffed (with).
prorogeer, (ge-), prorogue.
prosa, prose.
prosaïes, (-e), prosaic(ally); prosy.
prosaïs, (-te), prose-writer.
prosaskrywer, prosa-writer.
prosastyl, prose-style.
proscenium, (-s, -nia), proscenium.
prosedeer, (ge-), go to law, litigate.
prosedure, (-s), procedure.
prosekusie, (-s), prosecution.
proseliet, (-e), proselyte, convert.
proselietmaker, proselytizer.
proses, (-se), process, course (of action), method; lawsuit, legal proceedings; **kort – maak met**, give short shirt to, make short work of.
proseskoste, costs (of suit), legal expenses.
prosessie, (-s), procession.
prosesstuk, document (in a lawsuit).
proses-verhaal, official report, record.
prosodie, prosody.
prospekteer, (ge-), prospect.
prospekteerder, -teur, (-s), prospector.
prospektus, (-se), prospectus.
prostituee, (-s), prostitute.
prostitueer, (ge-), prostitute.
prostitusie, prostitution.
protégé (**protégée**), (-s), protége (protégée).
proteïen, (-e), **proteïne**, (-s), protein.
proteksie, protection; patronage.
proteksionis, (-te), protectionist.
protektoraat, (-rate), protectorate.
protes, (-te), protest, protestation; – **aanteken teen**, enter a protest against, protest against; **onder –**, under protest.
protese, prothesis.
Protestant, (-e), Protestant.
Protestantisme, Protestantism.
Protestants, (-e), Protestant.
protesteer, (ge-), protest; – **teen**, protest against, take exception to.
protesvergadering, protest-meeting.
protium, protium.
protokol, (-le), protocol.
protoplasma, protoplasm.
protospan, proto team.
prototipe, (-s), prototype.
protosoön, (-soa, -soë), protozoon.
Provensaals, (-e), Provencal.
proviand, provisions, victuals, stores.
proviandeer, (ge-), provision, victual.
provinsiaal, (-siale), provincial.
provinsialisme, provincialism.
provinsie, (-s), province.
provisie, (-s), provision, stock, supply.
provisiekamer, pantry, store-room.
provisiekas, cupboard, larder.
provisioneel, (-nele), provisional.
provokasie, (-s), provocation.
pruik, (-e), wig, periwig.
pruiketyd, age of the periwig.
pruikmaker, wigmaker.
pruil, (ge-), pout, sulk, be sulky.
pruilerig, (-e), pounting, sulky.
pruim, (-e), plum; quid, chew (tobacco); **gedroogde –**, prune; **hy lyk of hy nie – kan sê nie**, he looks as if he can't say boo to a goose.
pruim, (ge-), chew.
pruimbas, sumach.
pruimboom, plumtree; prune-tree.
pruimedant, (-e), prune.
pruimer, (-s), tobacco-chewer.
pruimpie, quid, chew.
pruimtabak, chewing-tobacco.
Pruis, (-e), Prussian.
Pruise, Prussia.
Pruisies, (-e), Prussian.
pruisiesblou, Prussian blue.
pruisiessuur, prussic acid.
prul, (-le), rubbish, trash.
pruldigter, poetaster, versifier.
prulding, trash, (piece of) rubbish.
prullerig, (-e), trashy, rubbishy.
prulwerk, trash, rubbish.
prunella, prunella.
prut, lees, sediment, dregs.
prutsel, (ge-), niggle, potter, tinker.
prutselwerk, tinkering (niggling) job.
pruttel, (ge-), grumble; simmer.
pruttelaar, (-s), grumbler.
pruttelrig, (-e), grumbling, grumpy.
pryk, (ge-), look splendid, shine, be resplendent; parade, show off; **bo aan die lys – sy naam**, his name heads the list.
prys, (-e), price, cost, figure, value; prize, reward; praise, commendation; **tot elke (iedere) –**, at any cost, at all costs; **onder die – verkoop**, sell below market-value; **op – stel**, care for, value highly, appreciate; – **op iets stel**, attach value (importance) to; **'n – behaal (toeken, trek, uitloof, wegdra)**, win (award, draw, offer, carry off) a prize; **'n – op iemand se hoof sit**, set a price on a person's head.
prys, (ge-), praise, extol, laud, glorify.
prys, (ge-), price, assign a price to.
prysaanvraag, enquiry (as to price)
prysbederwer, spoil-trade, underseller.
prysbepaling, fixing of prices.
prysdaling, fall (drop) in prices, slump.
prysenswaardig, (-e), praiseworthy.
prysenswaardigheid, praiseworthiness.
prysgee, (prysge-), abandon, deliver up (over), give up, hand over; **aan die bespotting –**, hold up to ridicule.
prysgeld, prize(-money).
prysgereg, prize-court.
pryshoudend, (-e), firm (in price).
pryskatalogus, **-koerant**, **-lys**, (priced) catalogue, pricelist.
prysnotering, quotation of prices.
prysopdrywing, forcing up of prices.
prysopgaaf, **-opgawe**, (-gawes), quotation.
prysregter, prize-judge.
prysskommeling, fluctuation of prices.
prysstyging, rise (increase) in price.
prysuitdeling, prize-distribution (distribution of prizes), prize-giving.
prysverbetering, advance (rise) in prices.
prysverhoging, increase, rise in price.
prysverlaging, **-vermindering**, price-reduction.
prysvraag, prize-question.
pryswenner, prize-winner.

psalm, (-s), psalm.
psalmberyming, versification of the Psalms.
psalmboek, psalm-book, psalter.
psalmdigter psalmist; psalmographer.
psalmgesing, psalm-singing; psalmody.
psalmis, (-te), psalmist.
pseudo-, pseudo-, bogus, pretended.
pseudoniem, (-e), pseudonym.
psige, psyche, soul, spirit, mind.
psigiater, (-s), psychiater, psychiatrist.
psigiatrie, psychiatry.
psigiatries, (-e), psychiatric(al).
psigies, (-e), psychic(al).
psigoanaliseer, psycho-analyse.
psigoanalise, psycho-analysis.
psigologie, psychology.
psigologies, (-e), psychological.
psigoloog, (-loë, -loge), psychologist.
psigopaat, (-pate), psychopath.
psigose, psychosis.
psittakose, psittacosis.
pst!, hist!
Psyche, Psyche.
Ptolemeïes, (-e), Ptolemaic.
ptomaïen, **ptomaïne**, ptomaine.
puberteit, puberty.
puberteitsjare, age of puberty.
publiek, n. public; audience; **in die –**, in public, publicly; **in die – optree**, appear publicly (before the public).
publiek, (-e), a. public; **–e leuen**, deliberate lie; **–e geheim**, open secret.
publiek, adv., publicly, in public; **– maak**, make public, publish; **– word**, become known; **– verkoop**, sell by public auction; **asof**, just (exactly) as if.
publikasie, (-s), publication.
publiseer, (ge-), publish, make public.
publisis, (-te), publicist.
publisiteit, publicity.
pueriel, (-e), puerile, childish.
puf, (ge-), puff, pant, blow.
puik, n. pick, elite, flower, cream.
puik, a. first-rate, choice, excellent.
puil, **peul**, (ge-), bulge, protrude.
puiloog, **peuloog**, goggle-eye.
puimsteen, pumice(-stone).
puin, ruins, debris; **in – val**, tumble in ruins; **in – lê**, lie (lay) in ruins.
puinhoop, (heap of) ruins.
puis, (-te), **puisie**, (-s), pimple, pustule.
pulp; pulp.
pulseer, (ge-), pulse, beat.
pulwer, powder; gunpowder.
Punies, (-e), Punic.
punktuasie, punctuation.
punktueer, (ge-), punctuate.
punt, (-e), point (of needle; in mathematics and sports); tip (of tongue finger); spot, dot, (full) stop; item; matter, question, issue; score, mark; **dubbele –**, colon; **skuldig op twee –e**, guilty on two counts; **–e maak (aanteken)**, score (points); **–e vir 'n opstel gee**, give marks for a composition; **geen –e behaal nie**, get (score) no marks; (sport) not score (a point); **'n netelige (teer) –**, a delicate matter, a tender subject; **– vir – bespreek**, discuss point by point (seriatim); **op die – om te vertrek**, on the point of leaving (departure), about to depart; **die besprekinge het 'n dooie – bereik**, the discussions have reached a deadlock.
punt, (ge-), point, sharpen.
puntbaard, pointed beard.
puntdig, (-te), epigram.
puntdigter, epigrammatist.

puntelys, score-sheet, mark-sheet; log.
puntene(u)rig, (-e), particular, fastidious, meticulous; squeamish, touchy.
puntgewel, gable.
puntig, (-e), pointed.
puntjie, (-s), point; **die –s op die i's sit**, dot one's i's (and cross one's t's).
puntkoeël, pointed bullet.
puntsgewyse, point by point, seriatim.
puntskoen, pointed shoe.
pupil, (-le), pupil.
puree, purée, mash(ed, potatoes).
purgasie, (-s), purgative; purgation.
purgasiemiddel, purgative, laxative.
purgatief, (-tiewe), purgative.
purgeer, (ge-), purge.
purgeermiddel, purgative.
puris, (-te), purist.
purisme, purism.
puristies, (-e), puristic.
Puriteit, (-e), Puritan.
Puriteins, (-e), Puritan.
purper, n. & a. purple; **met – beklee(d)**, clad in purple.
purperagtig, (-e), purplish, purply.
purperkleurig, (-e), purple.
purperkoors, the purples, purple-fewer.
purperrooi, purple.
purperslak, purple(-mollusc).
put, (-te), well, pit; **die – demp as die kalf verdrink is**, lock the stable-door after the steed is stolen; **'n – grawe**, dig (sink) a well; **'n – vir 'n ander grawe**, dig a pit for another.
put, (ge-), draw (water, inspiration).
putgrawer, well-sinker (-digger).
puthaak, well-hook, bucket-hook.
putjie, (-s), hole (golf).
puts, (-e), well; (tar-)pot, bucket.
putwater, well-water.
puur (pure), pure; sheer; all, nothing but; **pure onsin**, sheer (pure) nonsense; **'n pure man**, a true-blue, every inch a fine fellow.
py, (-e), cowl, gown.
pyl, (-e), arrow, barb, bolt, dart, shaft; **– en boog**, bow and arrow; **soos 'n – uit die boog**, as swift as an arrow; **hy het al sy –e verskiet**, he has shot all his bolts, he is at the end of his tether.
pyl, (ge-), dart, shoot, go straight, go swift; **hy – na die hek (op die hek af)**, he darts (makes straight) for the gate.
pyler, (-s), shaft, pillar, pier.
pylgif, arrow-poison.
pylkoker, quiver.
pylpunt, arrow-head.
pylreguit, straight as an arrow.
pylskrif, cuneiform characters.
pylsnel, swift as an arrow.
pylstert, sting-ray (fish); pin-tail.
pylvlerk, swept-wing.
pylvormig, (-e), shaped like an arrow.
pyn, pain, ache; **iemand – doen**, hurt a person.
pyn, (ge-), ache, hurt, smart, give pain, be painful.
pynappel, pine-apple.
pynbank, rack; **op die – lê**, rack, torture.
pynboom, pine-tree.
pynhars, pine-resin.
pynig, (ge-), torture, rack, torment.
pyniging, (-e, -s), torture, torment.
pynkamer, torture-room.
pynlik, (-e), painful, distressing, grievous, sad.
pynlikheid, painfulness.
pynloos, (-lose), painless.

pynstillend, (-e), analgesic (analgetic), anodyne, soothing.
pynstiller, pain-killer.
pyp, (-e), (tobacco-, water-, gas-, organ-)pipe; tube; (chimney-)flue; (trouser-)leg; (forearm-)tube; **iemand 'n lelike – laat rook**, do a person a bad turn.
pyp, (ge-), pipe; **na iemand anders se –e dans**, dance to somebody else's tune.
pypdop(pie), pipe-cover, -cap.
pypie, little pipe, tube; painted lady, africander.
pypkan, feeding-bottle.
pypkan, (ge-), fool, cheat, take in, diddle; (football) sell the dummy.
pypkaneel, (whole) cinnamon.
pypolie, pipe-oil.
pyprak, pipe-rack.
pypsleutel, pipe-wrench.
pypstander, pipe-stand.
pypsteel, pipe-stem; Cliffortia spp.
pypswa(w)el, roll-sulphur.

Q

quaestor, kwestor, (-s), quaestor.
quaestuur, kwestuur, quaestorship.
q'tjie, (-s), diminutive of letter q.
quidproquo, quid pro quo.
quiëtisme, quietism.
quiëtis, (-te), quietist.
Quintilianus, Quintilian.
quisling, (-s), quisling, traitor.
quodlibet, quodlibet, as you like it, potpouri.

R

r, (-'s), r.
ra, (-'s), yard (to support sail).
raad, (-gewinge, -gewings), (1) advice, counsel; my - aan jou is, I advise you; goeie - is hier duur, now we are (I am) in a dilemma (fix); buite (ten einde) - wees, be at one's wit's end; hy weet altyd -, he always knows what to do; geen - met jou geld weet nie, not know what to do with one's money; iemand met - en daad bystaan, assist a person by word and deed; by iemand te rade gaan, consult a person; vide raat.
raad, (rade), (2) council, board; Geheime, R-, Privy Council; R- van Handel, Board of Trade.
raadgewend, (-e) advisory (committee); consulting (engineer).
raadgewer, adviser, counsellor.
raadgewing, (-e, -s), advice, counsel.
raadhuis, council-house, town-hall.
raadkamer, council-chamber.
raadpleeg, (ge-), consult.
raadpleging, (-e, -s), consultation.
raadsaal, council-chamber.
raadsaam, (-same), advisable, expedient.
raadsaamheid, advisability.
raadsbesluit, decision (resolution) of the council; decree (of God).
raadsheer, councillor; bishop (chess).
raadsitting, council-meeting.
raadsliede, advisers.
raadsman, adviser, counsellor.
raadsvergadering, council-meeting.
raadsverkiesing, council-election.
raadsverslag, council's report.
raaf, (rawe), raven; 'n wit-, a white crow; al sou die rawe dit uitbring, even if the stones were to proclaim the truth.
raai, (ge-), advise; guess; iemand - om . . ., advise a person to . . .; iemand iets te - gee, leave a person to guess something; - na, guess at; nou -!, (just) fancy!
raaisel, (-e), riddle, puzzle, enigma; dit is vir my 'n -, that puzzles me, that is a problem to me; -s opgee, ask riddles.
raaiselagtig, (-e), enigmatic(al), puzzling.
raaiselagtigheid, incomprehensibility.
raak, (ge-), hit (mark); touch (ground); concern (person); van die spoor -, go off the track (off the scent); be derailed; van jou verstand -, lose one's reason, go out of one's mind; dit - jou nie, it does not concern you, you have got nothing to do with it; van sy stuk (die wysie) -, become embarrassed (upset); uit die mode -, cease to be fashionable, go out of fashion; slaags -, come to blows; aan die praat -, start (begin) talking.
raak, a. & adv. to the point, effective, telling (blow); 'n - antwoord, a hit, a reply that goes home; dit is -, that is a hit, that shot (blow) went home; - gooi, hit, strike; - skiet, hit, shoot straight; - vat, take (get) hold of; grasp firmly (properly); - ry, hit (in driving.)
raakloop, (raakge-), come across, meet.
raaklings, vide rakelings.
raaklyn, tangent.
raakpunt, tangent-point.
raaksien (raakge-), spot, espy.
raakskoot, hit; dit was 'n -, that was a hit, that shot went home.
raakvat, (raakge-), take (get) hold of; grasp (hold) firmly (properly).
raakvlak, tangent-plane.
raam, (rame), n. window; frame.
raam, (ge-), estimate; frame (picture).
raamkoord, sash-cord, sash-line.

raamkosyn, window-frame.
raamlood, sash-weight.
raamwerk, frame(work).
raap, (rape), n. turnip; rape.
raap, (ge-), gather, pick up; - en skraap, scrape together (up).
raapkoek, rape-cake.
raapkool, turnip-cabbage, kohl-rabi.
raapolie, rape-oil.
raapsaad, turnip-seed; rape-seed.
raar, (rare), a queer, strange, funny, odd, unusual.
raar, adv. strangely; daar sal hy - van opkyk, that will make him sit up.
raas, (ge-), make a noise, make (kick up) a row; rave, storm, rage.
raasbek, rowdy(-dowdy), windbag.
raasbessie, guarri (Euclea undulata).
raaskal, (ge-), rave, talk rubbish.
raaswater, rowdy(-dowdy); booze.
raat, (rate), remedy.
rabarber, rhubarb.
rabarberstroop, rhubarb-syrup.
rabat, (-tè), rebate, discount, reduction.
rabbedoe, (-ë, -s), rabbedoes, (-e), vide robbedoe(s).
rabbi, (-'s), rabbyn, (-e), rabbi.
rabbyns, (-e), rabbinical.
rad, vide rat.
radar, radar.
radarleiding, radar control.
radbraak, (ge-), break on the wheel; murder (language).
radeer, (ge-), etch; erase.
radeernaald, graver, burin.
radeloos, (-lose), desperate.
radeloosheid, desperation.
raderwerk, wheels, machinery.
radiaal, (-iale), radial.
radiator, (-s), radiator.
radikaal, (-kale), n. radical.
radikaal, (-kale), a. radical.
radikalisme, radicalism.
radio, (-'s), radio, wireless.
radioaktief, (-tiewe), radio-active.
radioberig, radio communication.
radiografie, radiography.
radiogram, (-me), radiogram (telegr.).
radio-isotoop, radio-isotope.
radiologie, radiology.
radioloog, (-loë, -loge), radiologist.
radioteks, radio script.
radiotelegram, radiotelegram, wireless message.
radioterapie, radiotherapy.
radium, radium.
radius, (-se), radius.
radja, (-s), rajah.
radys, (-e), radish.
rafel, (-s), n. ravel, thread.
rafel, (ge-), fray (out), ravel (out).
rafelrig, (-e), frayed.
rafelsy, ravelled silk.
raffia, raffia.
raffinadery, raffineerdery, (-e), (sugar-)refinery.
raffinadeur, raffineerder, (-s), refiner.
raffineer, (ge-), refine.
ragfyn, (-, -e), cobwebby, thin, filmsy.
ragitis, rickets.
ragout, ragout.
rak, (-ke), rack, shelf, bracket.
rakel, (ge-), rake; stir, poke.
rakelings: - verbygaan, graze past.
raket, (-te), racket (racquet); raket.
raket-aangedrewe, rocket-propelled.
raketbal, shuttle-cock.
raketmotor, rocket motor.

raketvliegtuig, rocket aircraft.
raketwerper, rocket-projector.
rakker, (-s), rascal, rogue, knave.
rakkie, (-s), bracket, little rack (shelf).
ram, (-me), ram, tup; die Ram, Aries; rammer; ou –!, hot stuff!
ram(e)nas, (-se), black radish, horse-radish; jointed charlock.
ramhok, ram-pen, ram-shed.
raming, (-e, -s), estimate, calculation.
ramkie, ramkie.
rammel, (ge-), rattle, clatter, clanck; chatter.
rammelaar, (-s), rattle.
rammeling, (-e, -s), rattling, clattering.
rammelkas, rattletrap, rumble-tumble, jalopy; rickety car; rattle-box.
ramp, (-e), disaster, catastrophe.
rampok, (-ke), gang.
rampokker, (-s), gangster.
rampsalig, (-e), wretched, miserable; doomed; fatal.
rampsaligheid, misery, wretchedness.
rampspoed, calamity, adversity.
rampspoedig, (-e), disastrous.
ramshoring, ram's-horn.
rancune, rancour, spitefulness, grudge.
rand, rand (decimal coinage).
rand, (-e), brim (of hat, cup); edge; brink (of precipice); margin (of paper); rim; border, boundary; fringe, edging; tot aan die – gevul, full to the brim, brim-full; aan die – van die graf, on the verge of death.
randeier, outer egg; wallflower.
randskrif, legend (on coin).
rantstaat, border-state.
randsteen, kerb-stone.
randversiering, ornamental border.
rang, (-e), rank, position, grade, degree, class, order; van die eerste –, of the first rank, first class; mense van elke – en stand, people of all ranks, people of every sort and kind.
rangeer, (ge-), arrange; shunt (train).
rangeerder, (-s), shunter.
rangeer-lokomotief, shunting-engine.
rangeerterrein, shunting-yard.
rangeerwissel, shunting-switch.
ranggetal, ordinal number.
ranglys, army-list; gradation-list.
rangorde, order.
rangskik, (ge-), arrange, put in order, range; classify; marshal.
rangskikkend, (-e), ordinal.
rangskikking, (-e, -s), arrangement; classification.
rangtelwoord, ordinal number.
rank, (-e), n. tendril, shoot; clasper.
rank, (-, -e), a. slender, thin, slim.
rank, (ge-), trail, shoot tendrils; twine.
rankboontjies, runner-bean, twining-bean.
rankroos, rambler, climbing-rose.
ranonkel, (-s), ranunculus.
ransel, (ge-), flog, thrash, lick.
ranseling, (-e, -s), flogging, thrashing.
ransig, (-e), rancid.
rant(jie), ridge.
rantsoen, (-e), ration, allowance; ransom; vide resoen.
rantsoeneer, (ge-), ration.
rapat, quick, agile, nimble, alert, nippy.
rapier, (-e), rapier.
rapport, (-e), report; – uitbring oor, report on; – maak van, report.
rapporteer, (ge-), report.
rapporteur, (-s), reporter.
rapportryer, (-s), dispatch-rider.
raps, (-e), flick, cut, lash, hit.

raps, (ge-), flick, hit, lash, strike.
rapsie, (-s), slight flick, etc.; a little.
rapsodie, (-ë), rhapsody.
rapsodies, (-e), rhapsodical.
rapsodis, (-te), rhapsodist.
rapsskoot, a near shot.
rarigheid, (-hede), rarity; queerness.
rariteit, (-e), curiosity, rarity, curio.
ras, (-se), n. race; strain, stock, breed; van gekruiste –, cross-bred.
ras, (-se), swift, quick; met –se skrede, swiftly, quickly.
raseg, (-re), thoroughbred; true to one's race, trueborn.
rasend, (-e), raving, raging, fuming, storming, wild, mad, furious; – e honger, roaring appetite; dis om 'n mens – te maak, it is enough to drive one mad.
raserig, (-e), noisy, rowdy, clamorous.
raserny, rage, fury, madness, frenzy.
rasgenoot, member of a race.
rashoender, pedigree-fowl.
rashond, thoroughbred (pedigree-)dog.
rasionaal, (-nale), rational.
rasionalis, (-te), rationalist.
rasionalisme, rationalism.
rasionalisties, (-e), rationalist(ic).
rasper, (-s), n. rasp, grater, scraper.
raspe(r), (ge-), rasp, grate.
rasperd, throughbred (pedigree-) horse.
rasse- . . ., vide ras- . . .
rassebeleid, race policy.
rassehaat, race-hatred, racialism.
rassehater, racialist.
rassestryd, racial struggle.
rassuiwer, (–, -e), purebred; true-born.
rasvee, pedigree-stock, purebred stock.
rasseverbeteringsleer, eugenics.
rasvermenging, mixture of races.
rat, (-te), (cog)wheel; iemand 'n – voor die oë draai, throw dust in a person's eyes; – van die fortuin, wheel of fortune.
ratel, (-s), n. (1) honey-badger, Cape badger.
ratel, (-s), n. (2) rattle.
ratel, (ge-), rattle.
ratelkous, chatterbox.
ratelslang, rattlesnake.
ratifikasie, (-s), ratification.
ratifiseer, (ge-), ratify.
ratio, (-'s), ratio.
ratjie, (-s), little (cog)wheel.
ratkas, gear-box.
rats, (–, -e), quick, swift, nimble, agile, nippy.
ratsheid, agility, nimbleness, quickness.
ratwerk, gearing, (the) wheels, gear.
ravot, (ge-), romp.
ravyn, (-e), ravine.
rawebek, raven's beak (bill).
reaal, (reale), real (coin).
reageer, (ge-), react.
reageerbuis, test-tube.
reageerpapier, test-paper.
reaksie, (-s), reaction.
reaksiespoel, reactor (radio).
reaksionêr, (-e), reactionary.
reaktor, reactor.
realis, (-te), realist.
realisasie, (-s), realization.
realiseer, (ge-), realize.
realisme, realism.
realisties, (-e), realistic.
realiteit, reality.
rebel, (-le), rebel.
rebelleer, (ge-), rebel, revolt.
rebellie, (-s), rebellion, revolt.

rebels, (-e), rebellious; furious; sulky.
red, (ge-), save, rescue, deliver; **uit die moeilikheid (nood)** -, help out of a difficulty.
redaksie, (-s), editorial staff; editorship; drafting, wording; **onder** – **van**, edited by.
redaksieburo, **-kantoor**, **-kamer**, editorial office.
redaksiewerk, editing.
redaksioneel, (-nele), editorial.
redakteur, (-s), editor.
redaktrise, (-s), editress.
reddeloos, (-lose), a. beyond help, irretrievable, irrecoverable.
reddeloos, adv. irretrievably; – **verlore**, irretrievably lost; past redemption.
redder, (-s), rescuer, saver, deliverer, saviour.
redding, (-e, -s), rescue, saving; salvation.
reddingsboei, life-buoy.
reddingsboot, life-boat.
reddingsgordel, life-belt.
reddingstoestel, life-saving, apparatus.
reddingswerk, rescue-work; salvage.
rede, (-s, -ene), 1. reason, cause; – **hê om . . .**, have reason to . . .; **om** – **van**, because of.
rede, 2. reason, understanding; **iemand tot** – **bring**, bring a person to reason; – **verstaan**, listen to reason.
rede, (-s), 3. speech, address, discourse; **in die** – **val**, interrupt.
rede, (-s), 4. ratio.
rede, (-s), 5. roadstead.
rededeel, part of speech.
redegewend, (-e), causal.
redekawel, (ge-), argue, reason.
redekaweling, reasoning.
redekundig, (-e), logical.
redekuns, rhetoric.
redelik, (-e), rational; reasonable, tolerable, fair.
redelikerwys, in reason, reasonably.
redelikheid, reasonableness.
redeloos, (-lose), irrational, not gifted with reason, brute; **die** **-lose diere**, brute creatures (creation).
redeloosheid, irrationality.
redenaar, (-s), orator.
redenaarstalent, oratorical gift (talent).
redenasie, (-s), argument, reasoning.
redeneer, (ge-), argue, reason.
redeneerkunde, logic.
redeneerkundig, (-e), logical.
redeneerkuns, art of reasoning; logic.
redeneertrant, manner of reasoning.
redenering, (-e, -s), reasoning.
reder, (-s), ship-owner.
redery, equipment (of ship); shipping-company.
rederyker, (-s), rhetorician.
rederykerskamer, guild of rhetoric.
rederykerskuns, rhetoric.
redetwis, n. dispute, disputation.
redetwis, (ge-), dispute.
redetwister, disputant.
redevoerder, (-s), speaker, orator.
redevoering, (-e, -s), speech, address.
redewisseling, conversation.
redigeer, (ge-), edit (newspaper); redact; compose, draw up (document).
redmiddel, remedy.
redoebleer, (ge-), redouble (bridge).
redster, (-s), saver, rescuer.
reduksie, (-s), reduction.
reduksiemiddel, reducing-agent.
reduplikasie, (-s), reduplication.
reduseer, (ge-), reduce.
ree(bok), roe(-buck).
reeds, already; **ek het hom** – **saamgeneem om . . .**, I purposely took him (in order) to . . . ; – **in die 17e eeu**, as far back as the 17th century.
reël, (reële), real.
reef, (rewe), reef.
reeks, (-e), series, succession, sequence; row; line; set; train (of events); – **berge**, chain of mountains; **rekenkundige** –, arithmetical progression.
reël, (-s), n. line; rule; **tussen die** –**s lees**, read between the lines; **in die** –, as a rule; **'n gulde** –, a golden rule; **die** – **van drie**, the rule of three.
reël, (ge-), arrange, settle, put in order; organize; adjust, regulate.
reëlaar, (-s), governor; regulator.
reëlbaar, (-bare), adjustable.
reëling, (-e, -s), arrangement; regulation(s), rule(s); adjustment; organization; **'n** – **tref**, make an arrangement.
reëlloos, (-lose), irregular, without rule.
reëlloosheid, irregularity.
reëlmaat, regularity, order.
reëlmatig, (-e), regular.
reëlmatigheid, regularity.
reëlreg, (-te), a. straight.
reëlreg, adv. straight(away); **iemand iets** – **sê**, tell a person something pointblank (straight out).
reëltjie, (-s), line.
reën, **reent**, (reëns), n. rain; **na** – **kom son(ne)skyn**, after rain comes sunshine.
reën, **reent**, (ge-), rain; **ou meide met knopkieries** –, rain cats and dogs; **dit** – **houe op my**, blows rain upon me.
reënagtig, (-e), rainy.
reënbak, **reent**-, rain-water tank (trough).
reënboog, **reent**-, rain-bow.
reënboogvlies, **reent**-, iris.
reënboogvoël, **reent**-, toucan.
reënbui, **reent**-, shower of rain.
reëndag, **reent**-, rainy day.
reëndig, **reent**-, (-te), rain-proof.
reëndruppel, **reent**-, rain-drop.
reënerig, (-e), rainy.
reënjas, **reent**-, mackintosh, rain-coat.
reënkaart, **reent**-, rain-chart.
reënmaker, **reent**-, rain-maker.
reënmeter, **reent**-, rain-guage.
reënskerm, **reent**-, umbrella.
reent, **reën**, n. & v.; vide **reën**, **reent**.
reenttyd, **reën**-, rainy season.
reentvlaag, **reën**-, shower of rain.
reentvoël, **reën**-, rainbird.
reentwind, **reën**-, rain-wind.
reentwolk, **reën**-, rain-cloud.
reentwurm, **reën**-, earth-worm.
reënval, rainfall.
reep, (repe), strip, string.
reet, (rete), split, crevice, fissure, rent.
referaat, (-rate), lecture, paper; report.
refereer, (ge-), refer.
referendaris, (-se), referendary.
referendum, (-s), referendum.
referensie, (-s), reference.
referent, (-e), speaker, lecturer; reporter.
referte, (-s), reference; **met** – **tot**, with reference to.
refleks, (-e), reflex (action).
refleksbeweging, reflex action.
refleksie, (-s), reflection.
refleksief, (-siewe), reflexive.
reflekteer, (ge-), reflect.
reflektor, (-s), reflector.
reformasie, reformation.
reformeer, (ge-), reform.
refraksie, refraction.
refrein, (-e), refrain, chorus.

reg, (-te), n. right, justice; claim; law; duty; **doen**, do justice; **dit is jou –**, you have the right; **– hê op**, have a right to; **– van opvoering**, stage-right; **geen – van bestaan hê nie**, not justify (its) existence; **die ongeskrewe –**, the unwritten law, common law; **die geskrewe –**, the written law, statue law; **Romeinse –**, Roman law; **sigself – verskaf**, take the law into one's own hands; **in die –te studeer**, student in the –te **wees**, study law; **met –**, justly, rightly; **na –**, by right; **iets tot sy – laat kom**, do justice to.
reg, (-te), a. right, correct; **hy is nie heeltemal – nie**, he has not got all his senses, he is not all there; **'n –te hoek** a right angle; **'n –te domoor**, a real dunce.
reg, adv. rightly; straight; **nie – verstaan nie**, not understand properly; **nie – weet nie**, not quite know; **– vorentoe**, straight on; **– hou**, keep straight (in order, in position); **– slaan**, hit (knock) into shape.
reg, (ge-), administer justice.
regaf, straight down.
regalia, regalia.
regbank, court of justice, tribunal, bench.
regeer, (ge-), rule, govern, reign; control, manage; rage (of disease).
regeerder, (-s), ruler.
regenerasie, (-s), regeneration.
regent, (-e), regent.
regentes, (-se), regent.
regentskap, regency.
regering, (-s), rule reign; government; **die – aanvaar**, come to the throne; come to power, assume office; **die – neerlê**, abdicate the throne; resign (from office).
regeringloos, (-lose), anarchic, without a government.
regeringsamp, government-post.
regeringsamptenaar, government-official.
regeringsbeleid, policy of the government.
regeringsblad, government-newspaper.
regeringskringe, government-circles.
regeringsparty, government-party.
regeringstelsel, system of government.
regeringsvorm, form of government.
regeringsweë: van –, officially.
reggeaard, (-e), right-minded.
reghebbende, (-s), rightful owner (heir).
reghoek, rectangle.
reghoekig, (-e), rectangular.
reghou, (regge-), keep ready.
regie, state control (monopoly); stage-management; **onder – van**, produced by.
regime, régime.
regiment, (-e), regiment.
regionaal, (-nale), regional.
regisseur, (-s), producer, stage-manager.
register, (-s), register; (organ-)stop; index, table of contents.
registrasie, registration.
registrasiekantoor, registry(-office).
registrasiekoste, registration-fee.
registrateur, (-s), registrar.
registreer, (ge-), register.
regkom, (regge-), come right; recover; **dit sal alles –**, everything will come right, all will be well; **kan jy –?**, can you manage?; **– met**, manage, handle; **met iemand –**, get on with a person.
reglement, (-e), rules, regulations; **– van orde**, standing orders.
reglynig, (-e), rectilinear, rectilineal.
regmaak, (regge-), mend, repair; correct; put right, rectify; arrange, settle; fix up.
regmakertjie, (-s), pick-me-up.

regmatig, (-e), rightful, lawful, fair.
regmatigheid, rightfulness, legitimacy.
regoor, right across; just opposite.
regop, erect, upright, perpendicular, vertical, straight up.
reg-reg, rêrig, very, really, terribly.
regressief, (-siewe), regressive.
rêrig?, really?; vide **regtig**.
regruk, (regge-), pull straight (into position), put straight.
regs, to the right; right-handed.
regsaak, lawsuit, case.
regsbedeling, administration of justice.
regsbegrip, sense of justice.
regsbevoegd, (-e), competent.
regsgebied, jurisdiction.
regsgebou, law-court(s), court-house.
regsgebruik, legal custom (practice).
regsgeding, lawsuit, case.
regsgeldig, (-e), legal, valid.
regsgeldigheid, legality, validity.
regsgeleerd, (-e), legal, versed in the law.
regsgeleerde, (-s), lawyer, jurist.
regsgeleerdheid, jurisprudence.
regsgevoel, sense of justice.
regsinnig, (-e), orthodox.
regsinnigheid, orthodoxy.
regskape, upright, just honest.
regskapenheid, uprightness, honesty.
regskoste, legal expenses.
regskundig, (-e), legal.
regskwessie, legal question.
regsomkeer, right about turn.
regsopvatting, legal opinion.
regspersoon, corporate body.
regspersoonlikheid, incorporation.
regspleging, administration of justice.
regspunt, point of law.
regspraak, administration of justice.
regspraktyk, legal practice.
regstaal, legal terminology (parlance).
regstandig, (-e), vertical, upright.
regsterm, law-term.
regstreeks, (-e), a. direct, straight.
regstreeks, adv. directly, straight.
regsverdraaiing, legal trickery.
regsverkragting, violation of justice.
regsvermoede, presumption of law.
regsvervolging, prosecution.
regsvordering, action.
regsvorm, form of judicature.
regsvraag, question of law.
regsweë: van –, according to law.
regswese, judicature.
regswetenskap, jurisprudence.
regte, n. right; law; duties.
regte, adv. really, very; vide **reg, a**.
regtens, by right(s).
regter, (-s), n. judge, justice.
regter-, a. right, off.
regteragterbeen, -**poot**, off hind leg.
regterarm, right arm.
regterhand, right hand (lit. & fig.).
regterkant, right side.
regterlik, (-e), judicial, of a judge.
regterstoel, judgement-seat, judge's seat, tribunal.
regtersy, right side.
regtervleuel, right wing.
regtervoet, right foot.
regtervoorbeen, off (right) front leg.
regtig, really, truly, indeed: **– (waar)?**, really?, indeed?; vide **reg-reg**.
reguit, straight (line, road): honest, frank, open, candid, straight.

regulariseer, (ge-), regularize.
regulasie, (-s), regulation.
reguleer, (ge-), regulate, adjust, time.
regulering, regulation, adjustment.
regvaardig, vide **regverdig.**
regverdig, -vaardig, (-e), a. just, righteous.
regverdig, -vaardig, (ge-), justify; sanctify; **sig –,** justify oneself; justifiable.
regverdige, (-s), righteous one.
regverdigheid, justice, righteousness.
regverdiging, justification.
rehabilitasie, (-s), rehabilitation.
rehabiliteer, (ge-), rehabilitate.
rei, (-e), chorus.
reier, (-s), heron.
reik, (ge-), reach, stretch; **– tot aan,** reach up to.
reikhals, (ge-): **– na,** yearn (long) for.
reikhalsend, (-e), yearningly, longingly.
reiling, vide **reling.**
rein, (–, -e), a. pure, chaste, clean, undefiled; **'n – gewete,** a clear conscience; **die –e waarheid,** the gospel truth.
reine, (-s), n. pure one; that which is pure; **vir die – is alles rein,** to the pure all things are pure; **weer in die – bring,** settle, put right.
reinheid, purity, chastity.
reinig, (ge-), purify, cleanse, clean.
reiniging, purification, cleaning.
reinigingsdiens, sanitary service.
reïnkarnasie, (-s), reincarnation.
reïnkarneer, (ge-), reincarnate.
reis, (-e), n. 1. journey (usually by land) trip; voyage (by sea); **-e (reisbeskrywinge),** travels; **'n – onderneem,** undertake a journey; **voorspoedige (aangename) –!,** prosperous (pleasant) journey!; **goeie –!,** a pleasant journey, good luck!; **op – gaan,** go on (undertake) a journey; **op – gaan na,** leave for; **op – wees,** be on a journey.
reis, n. 2. reis (Portuguese money).
reis, (ge-), travel, journey, tour.
reisang, chorus.
reisbenodigdhede, travelling-requisites.
reisbeskrywing, description of a journey, book of travel, itinerary.
reisbiblioteek, travelling-library.
reisburo, tourists' agency.
reisdeken, (travelling-)rug.
reisgeld, travelling-money (-expenses).
reisgenoot, (-genote), fellow-traveller.
reisgeselskap, touring-party.
reisgids, guide-book; time-table.
reisies, resies, races.
reisiesbaan, resies-, racecourse.
reisiesperd, resies-, racehorse.
reisiger, (-s), traveller.
reiskoffer, travelling-trunk.
reiskoste, travelling-expenses.
reiskostuum, travelling-costume.
reislus, love of travel.
reismaat, -makker, fellow-traveller.
reispas, passport.
reisplan, itinerary; intention of travelling.
reisroete, itinerary, route.
reisrok, travelling-costume (-dress), going-away dress.
reissak, travelling-bag, suitcase.
reistas(sie), suitcase.
reisvaardig, (-e), ready to start, on the point of leaving.
reisverhaal, account (story) of travel(s).
rek, (-ke), n. 1. elastic; catapult.
rek, n. 2. elasticity.
rek, (ge-), stretch; draw out; elongate, extend, prolong (discussion); protract (one's stay);

spin out; **die dae –,** the days are lengthening; **oë – van verbasing,** stare wide-eyed (at), stare (at) in amazement.
rekapitulasie, (-s), recapitulation.
rekapituleer, (ge-), recapitulate.
rekbaar, (-bare), elastic, ductile, extensible.
rekbaarheid, elasticity, ductility.
reken, (ge-), reckon, calculate, estimate, compute, cipher; count, consider, regard; **– op,** depend (rely) on, estimate at; **– tog ('n bietjie)!,** just imagine!; **deurmekaar ge–,** on average; **daar het ek nie op ge– nie,** I was not prepared for that, I did not bargain for that.
rekenaar, rekenaarster, (-s), reckoner, computer; arithmetician.
rekenbord, abacus, counting-frame.
rekenfout, miscalculation.
rekening, (-e, -s), calculation, computation, ciphering, reckoning; account, bill; calculus (maths.); **'n – vereffen,** pay a bill, settle an account; **–e maak,** run up bills; **– hou met,** take into consideration, take into account, make allowance for; **in – bring,** charge; **op – koop,** buy on credit; **per (op) slot van –,** ultimately, in the last resort; after all; **vir eie –,** on one's own account; **volgens –,** as per account.
rekening-koerant, account current.
rekenkunde, arithmetic.
rekenkundig, (-e), arithmetical; **–e reeks,** arithmetical progression.
rekenkundige, (-s), arithmetician.
rekenliniaal, sliding-rule, slide-rule.
rekenmasjien, calculating-machine, computer.
rekenmeester, accountant.
rekenraam, counting-frame, abacus.
rekenskap, account; **– gee van,** give an account of, account for; **– vra,** ask to account for; demand an account of; **sig – gee van,** get (form) an idea of, (try to) understand, realize.
rekensom, sum, problem in arithmetic.
rekker, (-s), elastic; garter; catapult; stretcher.
reklame, (-s), advertisement, puff(ing), pushing, boosting, réclame; claim; **– maak vir,** push, puff, advertise, boost.
reklame-afdeling, advertising-department.
reklame-agent, press agent.
reklamemaker, puffer, boomer, booster.
rekognisie(geld), rekonie(geld), quitrent.
rekommandasie, (-s), recommendation.
rekommandeer, (ge-), recommend.
rekonsiliasie, (-s), reconciliation.
rekonsilieer, (ge-), reconcile.
rekonstrueer, (ge-), reconstruct.
rekonstruksie, (-s), reconstruction.
rekord, (-s), record; **'n – slaan,** break a record.
rekreasie, (-s), recreation.
rekreëer, (ge-), recreate.
rekrimineer, (ge-), recriminate.
rekruteer, (ge-), recruit.
rekruut, (-krute), recruit.
rekstok, horizontal bar; catapult-handle.
rektifikasie, (-s), rectification.
rektifiseer, (ge-), rectify, correct.
rektor, (-s), rector, principal.
rektoraal, (-rale), rectorial, rector's.
rektoraat, (-rate), rectorship, rectorate.
rekwisisie, (-s), requisition.
relaas, (-lase), account, story, report.
relasie, (-s), relation.
relatief, (-tiewe), n. relative pronoun.
relatief, (-tiewe), a. relative.
relatiwiteit, relativity.
relatiwiteitsteorie, theory of relativity.
relegeer, (ge-), relegate.
relief, relief.

reliëfkaart, relief-map.
reliëfletter, embossed letter (type).
reliek, (-e), relic.
religie, (-ë), religion.
religieus, (-e), religious.
relikwie, (-ë), relic.
relikwieëkassie, reliquary.
reling, reiling, (-s), railing, rail.
relletjie, (-s), row, squabble.
rem, (-me), n. brake.
rem, (ge-), brake, apply (put on) the brakes; drag, pull, strain; curb.
remblok, drag, brake-block.
remedie, (-s), remedy.
remise, (-s), remittance.
remitteer, (ge-), remit.
remittent, (-e), remitter.
remketting, brake-chain, drag-chain.
Remonstrant, (-e), Remonstrant.
Remonstrants, (-e), Remonstrant.
remonstrasie, (-s), remonstration.
rempedaal, brake pedal.
remskoen, brake-shoe, (wheel-)drag, skid, stick-in-the-mud; obscurant(ist).
remskoenparty, conservative party.
remskoenpolitiek, obscurantism.
remtoestel, brake(s).
ren, (ge-), run, race.
Renaissance, Renaissance (Renascence).
renbaan, racecourse.
rendez-vous, rendezvous.
rendier, reindeer.
renegaat, (-gate), renegade.
renewasie, ruïnasie, ruination.
reneweer, ruïneer, (ge-), ruin, spoil.
renons, aversion, dislike, antipathy; **ek het 'n – daarin**, it is my pet aversion.
renonseer, (ge-), renounce; revoke.
renoster, (-s), rhinoceros.
renosterbos(sie), rhinoceros-bush.
renoveer, (ge-), renovate, do up, renew.
rens, sour (milk).
renserig, (-e), sourish.
rente, (-s), interest; **hy lewe van sy –**, he lives on the interest of his money; **'n boer wat van sy – lewe**, a retired farmer; **– op –**, compound interest.
rentebedrag, (amount of) interest.
rentegewend, (-e), interest-bearing.
rentekoers, rate of interest.
renteloos, (-lose), yielding no interest, interest-free; dead (capital).
rentenier, (-e, -s), n. retired person.
rentenier, (ge-), live on the interest of one's money; **hy –**, he has retired.
rentestandaard, rate of interest.
rentetafel, table of interest.
renteverlaging, lowering (fall in) the rate of interest.
renteverskil, difference in the rate of interest.
rentevoet, rate of interest.
rentemeester, steward, manager.
rentmeesterskap, stewardship.
reorganisasie, (-s), reorganization.
reorganiseer, (ge-), reorganize.
rep, n.: **in – en roer**, in confusion (commotion, tumult), in a stir.
rep, (ge-): **– van**, mention; **niks daarvan ge– nie**, never said a word; **sig –**, hurry, make haste.
reparasie, (-s), repair(s), repairing.
reparasiekoste, cost of repair.
repareer, (ge-), repair; mend.
repatriasie, repatriation.
repatrieer, (ge-), repatriate.
repertoire, (-s), repertoire, repertory.

repertoire-teater, repertory theatre.
repeteer, (ge-), repeat; rehearse (play); recur (of decimal).
repeteergeweer, repeating rifle.
repetisie, (-s), repetition; rehearsal.
repliek, (-e), rejoinder, reply, counterplea, replication; – **lewer**, reply.
repliseer, (ge-), reply.
representant, (-e), representative.
representasie, (-s), representation.
representatief, (-tiewe), representative.
repressie, (-s), repression.
reproduksie, (-s), reproduction.
reproduktief, (-tiewe), reproductive.
reproduktiwiteit, reproductiveness.
reproduseer, (ge-), reproduce.
reptiel, (-e), reptile.
republiek, (-e), republic.
republikanisme, republicanism.
republikein, (-e), republican.
republikeins, (-e), republican.
republikeinsgesind, (-e), republican.
republikeinsgesinde, (-s), republican.
republikeinsgesindheid, republicanism.
repudiasie, repudiation.
repudieer, (ge-), repudiate.
reputasie, (-s), reputation.
requiem, requiem.
rêrig, vide, **reg-reg, regtig**.
res, (-te), n. rest, remainder.
res, (ge-), remain, be left (over); **my – alleen nog (my – nog net) om . . .**, nothing remains for me but to . . .
reseda, (-s), mignonette.
resenseer, (ge-), review (book).
resensent, (-e), reviewer, critic.
resensie, (-s), review, critique.
resent, (-e), recent.
resep, (-te), recipe; prescription.
resepsie, (-s), reception.
reservasie, (-s), reservation.
reserveer, (ge-), reserve.
reservis, (-te), reservist.
reservoir, (-s), reservoir.
reserwe, (-s), reserve; reserves.
reserwebank, reserve bank.
reserwedele, spare parts.
reserwefonds, reserve-fund.
reserwemag, reserves, reserve-troops.
reserwetroepe, reserve-troops.
reserwewiel, spare wheel.
reses, (-se), recess; **op – gaan**, adjourn.
resgetal, remainder.
residensie, (-s), residence; residency.
resident, (-e), resident.
residu, (-'s), residue.
resies-, vide **reisies-**.
resiprositeit, reciprocity.
resitasie, (-s), recitation.
resitatief, (-tiewe), recitative.
resiteer, (ge-), recite.
resoen, (-e), measure (Bible); vide **rantsoen**.
resolusie, (-s), resolution.
resoluut, (-lute), resolute, determined.
resonansie, resonance.
respek(te), respect, regard; **met alle – vir**, with due respect to.
respektabel, (-e), respectable.
respekteer, (ge-), respect.
respektief, (-tiewe), respective, several.
respektieflik, -tiewelik, respectively.
respirasie, (-s), respiration.
respondeer, (ge-), answer, respond.
respondent, (-e), respondent.
respyt, respite, grace, rest, delay.

respytdae, days of grace.
ressort, (-e), province; jurisdiction.
ressorteer, (ge-): - onder, be classed among, come (fall) under.
restant, (-e), remainder.
restantverkoping, sale of remnants.
restaurant, restourant, (-e, -s), restaurant.
resteer, (ge-), remain.
restitusie, (-s), restitution.
restourasie, (-s), restoration, renovation; die R., the Restoration.
restoureer, (ge-), restore.
restriksie, (-s), restriction.
resultaat, (-tate), result, outcome, consequence, issue.
resultante, (-s), resultant (mech.).
resumé, (-'s), summary, résumé.
resumeer, (ge-), summarize, sum up.
resus(aap), rhesus.
resusfaktor, Rhesus (Rh.) factor.
retensie, retention.
retina, (-), retina.
retirade, (-s), lavatory.
retireer, (ge-), retreat, retire, step back.
retoer, return.
retoerkaartjie, return-ticket.
retoriek, rhetoric.
retorie, (-e), rhetorical.
retorika, rhetoric.
retort, (-e), retort.
retrospektief, (-tiewe), retrospective.
reuk, ruik, (-e), smell; scent; odour; in 'n slegte reuk staan by, be in bad odour with.
reukaltaar, incense-altar.
reukflessie, scent-bottle.
reukloos, (-lose), odourless, scentless.
reukoffer, incense-offering.
reukorgaan, organ of smell.
reuksin, sense of smell.
reuksout, smelling-salt(s).
reukvat, incensory, censer.
reukwater, perfumed (scented) water.
reukwerk, perfumery.
reun, (-s), gelding.
reunhond, dog.
reünie, reunion.
reunperd, gelding.
reus, (-e), giant; colossus.
reusagtig, (-e), gigantic, colossal, huge.
reusagtigheid, hugeness.
reuse-, gigantic, giant, mammoth-, huge.
reusarbeid, gigantic task.
reusegeslag, giant race, race of giants.
reusegestalte, gigantic stature.
reusekrag, Herculean (gigantic) strength.
reusel, (-s), (leaf-)lard.
reuseletters, huge letters.
reuseskrede, giant's stride; met -s vooruitgaan, go ahead by leaps and bounds.
reusestryd, tremendous (gigantic) struggle, battle of giants.
reusesukses, huge success.
reusetaak, Herculean task.
reveille, reveille.
revideer, (ge-), revise.
revisie, (-s), revision.
revokasie, (-s), revocation.
revolusie, (-s), revolution.
revolusiegees, revolutionary spirit.
revolusionêr, (-e), revolutionary.
rewolwer, (-s), revolver, pistol.
rib, (-be, -bes), rib; rib (of wood, iron).
ribbebeen, rib.
ribbekas, thorax, thoracic skeleton; iemand op sy - gee, dust a person's coat, strike (kick) someone in the ribs.
ribbetjie, (-s), (little) rib; gedroogde (gebraaide) -, sundried (roast) rib.
ribbok, rhebuck.
ribstuk, rib of beef, etc.
ridder, (-s), n. knight; tot - slaan, knight; dolende -, knight-errant; R. van die Kousband, Knight of the Garter.
ridder, (ge-), knight.
ridderdiens, service as a knight; chivalry.
riddereeu, age of chivalry.
ridderkruis, cross of the order of knights.
ridderlik, (-e), knightly; chivalrous.
ridderlikheid, chivalry, chivalrousness.
ridderorde, (order of) knighthood.
ridderroman, romance of chivalry.
ridderskap, knighthood; knightage.
ridderslag, accolade.
ridderspel, tournament.
ridderspoor, larkspur, delphinium.
ridderstand, knighthood; knightage.
riddertyd, age of chivalry.
ridderverhaal, tale (story) of chivalry.
ridderwese, chivalry.
ridikuul, (-kule), ridiculous.
riel, (-e), reel (dance).
riem, (-e), 1. thong, strap, riem; belt; jou -e styfloop, be up against it, find oneself in hot water, meet more than one's match; die -e neersit, (neerlê, bêre), take to one's heels; iemand 'n - onder die hart steek, cheer up (encourage) a person; uit jou -e uit wees, be in a huff; be in a bad temper.
riem, (-e), 2. oar.
riem, (-e), 3. ream (of paper).
riempie, (-s), thong, strap, riempie.
riempiesmat, riempie-seat.
riemspring, (riemge-), skip; iemand laat -, leather a person.
riemtelegram, a mere (false) rumour.
riet, (-e), reed, rush; thatch (of roof).
rietbok, reedbuck, rietbuck.
rietbos, reed-bush, clump of reeds.
rietdak, thatched roof.
rietfluitjie, reed-pipe.
riethaan, waterhen, reedhen; Cape rail.
rietjie, (-s), little reed.
rietperd, cane-horse, hobby-horse.
rietsanger, reed-warbler.
rietsap, cane-juice.
rietskraal, very thin, reedy.
rietstoel, wicker-chair.
rietsuiker, cane-sugar.
rietvink, masked weaver, reed-finch.
rietvlei, reed-marsh.
rif, (riwwe), reef (rock-formation); reel (of sail) ledge; ridge, edge.
riffel, (-s), n. wrinkle, fold, ridge, crinkle, ruffle, ripple; edge.
riffel, (ge-), wrinkle, ripple; corrugate.
riffelrig, (-e), crinkled, corrugated.
rig, (ge-), 1. aim, direct, dress (mil.); 'n brief aan iemand -, address a letter to somebody; 'n vraag - aan, put a question to; sig na iemand -, follow a person's example; jou skrede - na, turn your steps towards; - op, fix upon, aim at; almal se oë was op hom ge-, all eyes were turned towards him; sy gedagte - op, turn his thoughts to; die onderwys was ge- op . . ., education aimed at . . ., 'n geweer - op, point a gun at; - teen, direct against, aim at; sig tot iemand -, address oneself to a person; die woord tot die gemeente -, address the congregation.
rig, (ge-), 2. (act as) judge.

riggel, (-s), ledge, ridge, border; rail.
righoek, angle of sight.
rigsnoer, guide, directing principle, standard, rule, example, lead.
rigter, (-s), judge; **die Boek Rigters**, the book of Judges.
rigting, (-e, -s), direction; tendency, inclination; school (of philosophy etc.); **'n bepaalde – inslaan**, adopt a definite policy.
rikketik, tick-tick; pit-a-pat.
riksja, (-s), rickshaw.
ril, (ge-), shudder, shiver, tremble; **dis om van te –**, gives one the shudders (creeps).
rillerig, (-e), shivery, creepy.
rilling, (-e, -s), shudder, shiver.
rimpel, (-s), n. wrinkle, fold, line; ripple (of water); **vol –s**, wrinkled.
rimpel, (ge-), wrinkle, line; ripple; pucker (knit) (one's brow); pucker.
rimpeling, (-e, -s), wrinkling, wrinkle, puckering; ripple (of water).
rimpel(r)ig, (-e), wrinkled, puckered, rippled, ripply, shrivelled.
ring, (-e), ring; circle band; halo; presbytery, ring; **'n mens kan hom deur 'n – (naald) trek**, he is dressed up to kill, he looks as if he came out of a bandbox.
ringduif, ring-dove.
ringeloor, (ge-), bully, order about.
ringetjie, (-s), ringlet.
ringkop, ring-head, (Zulu) veteran.
ringmuur, ring-wall, circular wall.
ringvinger, ring-finger.
ringvormig, (-e), ring-shaped, ring-like.
ringwurm, ringworm (skin-disease).
rinkel, (ge-), jingle, chink.
rinkhals, ring-neck, ring-necked (animal).
rinkhalsslang, ring-necked snake (cobra).
rinkink, (ge-), jingle; rollick, romp; gallivant, gad about, make merry.
rioel, (-e), **riool**, (-ole), drain, sewer.
rioelpyp, **riool-**, sewer-pipe.
rioelstelsel, **riool-** drainage-system.
rioelwater, **riool-**, sewage.
rioleer, (ge-), drain.
riolering, (-e, -s), drainage, sewerage.
risiko, (-'s), risk: **op eie –**, at your own risk; **– loop**, run the risk.
riskant, (-e), risky, hazardous.
riskeer, (ge-), risk.
rissie, (-s), chilli; termagant, vixen.
rissiepeper, Cayenne pepper.
rit, (-te), journey, ride, drive, spin.
ritme, (-s), rhythm.
ritmiek, rhythmics.
ritmies, (-e), rhythmic(al).
rits, (-e), n. series, string, row.
ritseling, (-e, -s), rustling, rustle.
ritssluiting, zipper, zip-fastener.
ritsig, (-e), ruttish.
rittel, (ge-), shiver, shake, tremble.
ritteltit(s): **die – kry**, get the shivers; go into fits (hysterics).
rituaal, **(rituale)**, ritual.
ritualisme, ritualism.
ritueel, **(rituele)**, ritual.
rivier, (-e), river.
rivierbed(ding), river-bed.
riviergrond, river-soil; riverside.
rivierkant, riverside, bank of a river.
riviermond, river-mouth.
rivieroewer, river-bank, riverside.
rivierstelsel, river-system.
rob, (-be), seal.
robbedoe, (-ë, -s), robbedoes, (-e), tomboy,
hoyden, romp, boisterous person.
robbejag, seal-fishery, seal-hunt(ing).
robbespek, seal-blubber, seal-fat.
robbetraan, seal-oil.
robbevangs, seal-hunting.
robot, (-te), robot.
robuus, (-te), robust.
robyn, (-e), ruby.
Rococo, Rococo.
roebel, (-s), rouble.
roede, (-s), rod, cane, birch; road (1 of an acre); **wie die – spaar, bederf (haat) sy kind**, spare the rod and spoil the child.
roef, (roewe) 1. lid; deckhouse.
roef, (roewe), 2. notch.
roei, (-e), lattice.
roei, (ge-), row, pull.
roeibank, thwart, rowing-bench.
roeiboot, rowing-boat.
roeier, (-s), oarsman, rower; oar.
roeimik, rowlock.
roeipen, thole(-pin).
roeiriem, **roeispaan**, oar.
roeistok, gauging-rod.
roeitog, row, boat-excursion.
roeiwedstryd, boat-race, regatta.
roekeloos, (-lose), reckless, rash, foolhardy; wicked, sinful, profane.
roekeloosheid, recklessness.
roem, n. renown, praise, glory, fame; **eie – stink**, selfpraise is no recommendation.
roem, (ge-), boast; praise, laud, extol.
Roemeens, n. Roumanian.
Roemeens, (-e), a. Roumanian.
Roemenië, Roumania.
Roemeniër, (-s), Roumanian.
roemer, (-s), 1. boaster.
roemer, (-s), 2. rummer.
roemrugtig, vide **roemryk**.
roemryk, (-e), famous, renowned, glorious; splendid, magnificent.
roemsug, desire (thirst) for fame.
roemsugtig, (-e), thristing for fame.
roemvol, (-le), illustrious, renowned.
roep, n. call, cry.
roep, (ge-), call, cry, shout; **om hulp –**, cry for help; **'n dokter –**, call in (send for) a doctor; **my plig – my**, duty calls me; **iets in die lewe –**, call into being, create; **sig geroepe voel**, feel called upon.
roepende, (-s), one who calls; **soos die stem van die – in die woestyn**, like the voice of one crying in the wilderness.
roeper, (-s), crier, caller, megaphone.
roeping, (-e, -s), calling, vocation.
roepsek!, in you go!, in with you!.
roepstem, call, voice.
roer, (-e, -s), n. 1. rudder, helm; **jou – reg hou**, keep straight; **aan die – (van sake) staan (wees)**, be at the helm.
roer, (-s), n. 2. gun, rifle; **so reg soos 'n r̃**, as fit as a fiddle, as right as rain (a trivet); as straight as a die.
roer, n. 3. **in rep en –**, is a stir.
roer, (ge-), stir, move; touch; **– vir jou, – jou lyf**, bestir yourself, make haste; **– my net aan as jy durf**, just touch me if you dare!; **jou tong –**, wag one's tongue; **dit het my diep ge–**, I was deeply moved (touched) by it.
roerdomp, (-e), bittern.
roereiers, scrambled eggs.
roerend, (-e), a. touching; movable; **–e goedere**, movable property.
roerend, adv. touchingly; **ek is dit – met jou eens**, I heartily agree with you.

roerig, (-e), lively, active; restless.
roerigheid, liveliness; restlessness.
roering, stirring, motion; emotion.
roerloos, (-lose), 1. motionless.
roerloos, (-lose), 2. rudderless.
roerpen, tiller.
roersel, (-e, -s), motive; die -e van die hart, the promptings of the heart.
roerspaan, stirrer, stirring-rod; spatula.
roertoestel, stirring-apparatus.
roes, n. 1. intoxication; excitement; **jou - uitslaap**, sleep off one's debauch.
roes, n. 2. rust; blight, rust.
roes, (ge-), rust; corrode; **ou liefde - nie**, old love never dies.
roesagtig, (-e), rusty, like rust.
roesemoes, confusion, tumult.
roeserig, (-e), vide **roesterig**.
roeskleur, rust-colour.
roeskleurig, (-e), rust-coloured.
roesterig, (-e), rusty.
roesvlek, rust-stain.
roesvry, rust-proof, stainless.
roet, soot.
roete, (-s), route, road.
roeterig, (-e), sooty.
roetine, routine.
roetkleur, sooty colour.
roetswart, black as soot.
roetvlek, smut.
roffel, n. ruffle (of drum), roll.
roffel, (ge-), 1. beat a ruffle.
roffel, (ge-), 2. rough-plane.
roffelskaaf, trying-plane.
rofie, (-s), scab.
rofkas, n. rough-cast.
rofkas, (ge-), rough-cast.
rog, 1. rye; **wilde -**, wilde rye.
rog, (röe), 2. skate, spotted ray (fish).
rog(ge)brood, rye-bread.
roggel, (-s), n. phlegm; ruckle.
roggel, (ge-), expectorate; ruckle, rattle.
rogmeel, rye-meal.
rojaal, (-jale), royal; generous, liberal.
rojalis, (-te), royalist.
rojaliteit, generosity, lavishness, liberality.
rojeer, (ge-), expel; cancel, annul; disbar.
rok, (-ke), skirt, dress, gown; **die hemp is nader as die -**, charity begins at home; **hy dra die -**, he is hen-pecked.
rokband, waist-band, skirt-band.
rokbroek, divided skirt.
rokeer, (ge-), castle (chess).
roker, (-s), smoker.
rokerig, (-e), smoky.
rokery, smoking, smoking-habit.
rol, (-le), n. roll (of paper); scroll; register, list, roll; part (of an actor), rôle; cylinder, roller; **van die - skrap**, strike off the roll; **'n - speel**, play a part; **jou - ken**, know one's lines; **die -le verdeel**, assign the parts; **die -le omkeer**, turn the tables.
rol, (ge-), roll tumble; **met die oë -**, roll one's eyes; **jou geld laat -**, spend money like water
rolbed, trundle-bed.
rolfilm, roll-film.
rolgordyn, roller-blind.
rolhanddoek, roller-towel.
rollaag, upright course (masonry).
rollend, (-e), rolling; **-e materiaal**, rolling stocks; **'n -e klip vergaar geen mos nie**, rolling stones gather no moss.
roller, (-s), roller.
rolletjie, (-s), (small) roll; roller; castor; trundle;

reel (of cotton).
rolletjiestang, roller-bit.
rolnaat, run and fell seam.
rolpens, minced meat in tripe.
rolplek, rolling-place.
rolpoeding, roly-poly.
rolprent, film.
rolprentkamera, cine-camera.
rolprentprojektor, cine-projector.
rolprentster, film-star.
rolskaats, roller-skate; **-e ry**, rink.
rolslag, putt (gholf).
rolstoel, Bath chair, wheeled chair.
rolstok, rolling-pin.
roltabak, roll-tobacco, twist.
roltrap, escalator.
rolvark(ie), South African hedgehog.
rolverband, roller-bandage.
rolverdeling, cast.
rolwaentjie, trundle, truck.
Romaans, Romanic, Romance.
roman, (-s), 1. novel.
roman, (-ne, -s), 2. roman (fish).
romanheld, hero in a novel.
romanleser, novel-reader.
romanliteratuur, prose-fiction.
romanse, (-s), romance.
romanskryfster, (woman-)novelist.
romanskrywer, novelist.
Romantiek, Romanticism; Romantic Movement.
romanties, (-e), romantic.
romantikus, (-se, -tici), romanticist.
rombies, (-e), rhombic.
romboïde, (-s), rhomboid.
rombus, (-se), rhomb(us).
Rome, Rome; **- is nie in een dag gebou nie**, Rome was not built in a day; **so oud soos die weg (pad) na -**, as old as the hills.
Romein, (-e), Roman.
Romeins, (-e), Roman.
rommel, n. lumber, rubbish, trash.
rommel, (ge-), rumble; rummage.
rommel(a)ry, lumber, rubbish, litter.
rommel(r)ig, (-e), disorderly, untidy.
rommeling, (-e, -s), rumbling.
rommelkamer, lumber-room.
rommelrig, vide **rommelig**.
rommelverkoping, rummage-sale.
romp, (-e), trunk; hull; **- en stomp verkoop**, sell lock, stock and barrel.
rond, (-e), round; circular; **'n -e getal, som**, a round number, sum; **'n -e jaar**, a full year; **die -e waarheid**, the plain truth.
rondagtig, (-e), roundish.
rondas, (-se), shield.
rondawel, (-s), ("rondavel"), round hut (cottage).
rondbasuin, (rondge-), proclaim, blaze abroad, spread (news) about.
rondboog, round (Roman) arch.
rondborstig, (-e), open, candid, frank.
rondborstigheid, frankness, candour.
rondbring, (rondge-), take round.
ronddans, (rondge-), dance about.
ronddeel, (ronge-), hand round.
ronddien, (rondge-), hand (serve) round.
ronddobber, (rondge-), drift about.
ronddool, (rondge-), wander about.
ronddra, (rondge-), carry about.
ronddraai, (rondge-), turn (twist) round (about); gyrate; linger, loiter (round).
ronddraf, (rondge-), trot about.
ronddrentel, (rondge-), saunter about.
ronddryf, -drywe, (rondge-), drift about.
ronddwaal, (rondge-), wander about.

ronddwarrel, (rondge-), whirl about.
ronde, (-s), round; lap (of race-track); beat (of policeman); die berig doen die –, the news (story) is going around.
rondedans, ring-dance.
rondeel, (-dele), rondel.
rondfladder, (rondge-), flutter about.
rondgaan, (rondge-), go about (round).
rondgaande, travelling; – hof, circuit court; – brief, circular letter.
rondgang, circuit.
rondgee, (rondge-), pass (hand) round.
rondheid, roundness, rotundity.
rondhol, (rondge-), run (rush) about.
ronding, (-e, -s), rounding; camber.
rondjie, (-s), round.
rondkom, (rondge-), come round; make ends meet, manage.
rondkuier, (rondge-), go about visiting; stroll about.
rondkyk, (rondge-), look about.
rondlê, (rondge-), lie about.
rondlei, (rondge-), lead about; conduct, show (person) round (a place).
rondloop, (rondge-), walk about, go about; loaf about, gad about.
rondloper, tramp, vagrant, loafer.
rondo, rondeau.
rondom, on all sides (of) all round.
rondomtalie, pug-mill.
rondomtalie, round and round.
rondreis, n. tour, trip.
rondreis, (rondge-), travel about, tour.
rondry, (rondge-), drive (ride) about.
rondskarrel, (rondge-), fumble (potter) about.
rondskink, (rondge-), serve (drinks).
rondskrif, round hand.
rondskrywe, circular letter.
rondsleep, (rondge-), drag about.
rondslenter, (rondge-), saunter (idle, loaf) about.
rondslinger, (rondge-), fling about.
rondsluip, (rondge-), prowl about.
rondsmyt, (rondge-), fling about.
rondsnuffel, (rondge-), sniff about; nose (mouse) about; search about.
rondspring, (rondge-), jump about; beat about the bush.
rondstrooi, (rondge-), scatter; spread (news); die storie word rondgestrooi, it is rumoured.
rondstuur, (rondge-), send round.
rondswerf, -swerwe, (rondge-), roam (wander) about.
rondtas, (rondge-), grope about; in die duister –, grope in the dark.
rondte, (-s), roundness; round; circle; in die – draai, turn round and round; die – van vader Cloete doen, make one's rounds; al in die –, in a circle; vide ronde.
rondtrek, (rondge-), pull about; trek (journey, go wander) about.
ronduit, frankly, openly, candidly, straight out; – praat, speak out freely; – gesê, frankly, candidly.
rondvaar, (rondge-), sail about.
rondvertel, (rondge-), spread, circulate, reveal, let out, blab.
rondvlie(g), (rondge-), fly about.
rondvlug, circuit.
rondvra, (rondge-), inquire.
rondwandel, (rondge-), walk about.
rondweg, frankly.
rong, (-e), rung, upright, support.
ronk, (ge-), snore; drone, purr.
röntgen, röntgen.
Röntgenapparaat, X-ray apparatus (set).

Röntgenstraal, Röntgen ray.
röntgenologie, radiology.
Röntgenstrale, X-rays.
Roodhuid, Rooihuid, red Indian, redskin.
roodvonk, vide rooivonk.
roof, (rowe), n. 1. scab, crust.
roof, n. 2. plunder, robbery; booty.
roof, rowe, (ge-), plunder, rob, steal.
roofagtig, (-e), rapacious.
roofbou, overcropping.
roofdier, beast of prey.
roofgierig, (-e), rapacious.
roofpolitiek, policy of plunder.
roofridder, robber-knight.
roofsiek, (-e), rapacious.
roofsug, rapacity.
roofsugtig, (-e), rapacious.
roofsugtigheid, rapacity.
rooi, red; – word, turn red (scarlet), blush; so – soos 'n kreef ('n kalkoen), as red as a lobster (turkey cock).
rooi-aas, red-bait.
rooiagtig, (-e), reddish.
rooibaadjie, red-coat; voetganger (locust).
rooibeet, beet.
rooibekkie, waxbill, widow-bird.
rooibloedliggaampie, red corpuscle.
rooiblom, witchweed.
rooibok, impala.
rooibont, red and white.
rooiborsie, robin redbreast; Cape robin.
rooibos, red-bush (Combretum Zeyheri).
rooibostee, red-bush tea.
rooibruin, reddish-brown; bay (horse).
rooidag, dawn, day-break.
rooi-els, red-alder (Cunonia capensis).
rooierig, (-e), reddish.
rooihaar-, red-haired.
rooihaas, red-hare, rock-hare.
rooiharig, (-e), red-haired.
rooiheid, redness.
rooihond, prickly heat.
rooihout, red-wood.
Rooihuid, vide Roodhuid.
rooijakkals, red fox (jackal).
Rooikappie, Little Red Riding-hood.
rooikat, caracal, lynx.
rooiklei, red clay.
rooikleurig, (-e), red-coloured, reddish.
rooikool, red cabbage.
rooikop, red head, red-haired person.
rooikoper, copper.
rooimeerkat, -mierkat, bushy-tailed meercat.
rooimier, red ant.
Rooinek, "Rooinek" (Englishman).
rooipoot-elsie, black-winged stilt.
rooiskimmel, (strawberry-, red-) roan (horse), reddish-grey.
Rooitaal, English.
rooivalk, kestrel.
rooivink, red bishop-bird, red Kaffir finch.
rooivlerkspreeu, red-winged starling.
rooivonk, scarlet, scarlatina.
rooiwater, red-water, Texas fever.
rook, n. smoke; in – opgaan, end in (vanish into) smoke; geen – sonder vuur (daar is nooit 'n – nie of daar brand 'n vuurtjie), no smoke without a fire.
rook, (ge-), smoke; hy – soos 'n skoorsteen, he smokes like a chimney; daarvan sal die skoorsteen nie – nie, that won't keep the pot boiling.
rookgoed, smokables.
rookkamer, smoking-room.
rookloos, (-lose), smokeless.
rooklug, smell of smoke, smoky smell.

rookmis, smog.
rookspek, bacon.
rooktabak, smoking-tobacco.
rookvleis, smoked beef (meat).
rookvry, smokeless.
room, cream.
roomagtig, (-e), creamy.
roomafskeier, cream-separator.
roomkaas, cream-cheese.
roomkleur, cream-colour.
Rooms, (-e), Roman Catholic; Roman.
Roomsgesind, (-e), Roman Catholic.
Roomsgesinde, Roman Catholic.
Rooms-Katoliek, (-e), Roman Catholic.
roomtertjie, cream-tart.
roomys, ice-cream.
roos, 1. erysipelas, the rose.
roos, (rose), 2. rose; **'n − tussen twee dorings**, a rose between the thorns; **geen rose sonder dorings**, no rose without a thorn; **onder die −**, under the rose, sub rosa.
roosagtig, (-e), 1. like erypsipelas.
roosagtig, (-e), 2. rose-like; rosaceous.
roosboom(pie), rose-tree.
roosgeur, vide **rosegeur**.
rooskleur, rose-colour, pink.
rooskleurig, (-e), rose-coloured, rosy.
rooskleurig, (-e), bright.
roosknop, rose-bud.
rooskweker, rose-grower.
roosmaryn, rosemary.
roosolie, oil (attar) of roses.
roossteggie, rose-slip, rose-cutting.
roosstruik, rose-bush.
rooster, (-s), n. gridiron, grill (for roasting); grate (in fire-place); grating; time-table, roster.
rooster, (ge-), roast, grill, toast.
roosterbrood, toast.
roosterkoek, girdle-cake.
roostuin, rose-garden, rosary, rosarium.
ropy, (-e), rupee.
ros, (-se), n. steed.
ros, (-se), a. ruddy, reddish-brown.
rosegeur, perfume (scent) of roses; **die lewe is nie net − en maneskyn nie**, life is not all beer and skittles.
rosekrans, garland of roses; rosary.
roset, (-te), rosette.
roskam, n. curry-comb.
roskam, (ge-), curry; rebuke, take to task.
rosyn, (-e), **rosyntjie**, (-s), raisin.
rosyntjiebrood, raisin-bread.
rot, (-te), n. rat; **'n ou −**, an old hand.
rot, a, rotten, putrid.
rot, adv.: **iemand − en kaal steel**, steal everything a person possesses.
Rotariër, (-s), Rotarian.
Rotariërklub, Rotary Club.
rotasie, rotation, turn.
rotasiepers, rotary press.
roteer, (ge-), rotate.
rotheid, rottenness.
rots, (-e), rock, cliff.
rotsagtig, (-e), rocky.
rotsbank, layer of rock rocky ledge.
rotsblok, piece (lump) of rock, block.
rotseiland, rocky island.
Rotsgebergte, The Rocky Mountains.
rotsgevaarte, mass of rocks.
rotskristal, rock-crystal.
rotstuin, rockery.
rotsvas, (-te), firm as a rock, adamant.
rotswand, rock-face, krantz, precipice.
rottang, (-s), rat(t)an, cane.

rottangkierie, (rat(t)an-)cane.
rottegif, rat-poison.
rottejag, rat-hunting.
rottekruid, ratsbane, arsenic.
rotteplaag, -pes, rat-plague.
rot(te)val, rat-trap.
rot(te)vanger, rat-catcher.
rotting, putrefaction.
rou, n. mourning; **ligte (swaar) −**, half (deep) mourning; **− bedryf oor**, mourn for; **in die − wees**, be in mourning.
rou, a. raw, uncooked; hoarse (voice).
rou, (ge-), mourn; **− oor**, mourn for.
rouband, mourning-band.
roubedryf, mourning.
roubeklag, condolence.
roubrief, death-notice; mourning-letter.
roudiens, memorial service.
roudig, dirge, elegy.
roudraer, mourner.
rouerig, (-e), underdone, rawish.
roufloers, crape.
rougewaad, mourning-garb (-attire).
rouheid, rawness; vide **rou**, a.
rouklaag, (ge-), lament.
rouklag, lamentation.
roukleed, mourning-dress.
roukoop, smart-money.
roukrans, funeral wreath.
roupapier, mourning-paper.
rourand, black border.
rousool, untanned leather, raw hide.
rousluier, black crape veil, weeper.
rouvel, raw hide.
rowe, (ge-), vide **roof**, (ge-).
rower, (-s), robber, bandit, brigand.
rowerbende, gang (band) of robbers.
rowery, (-e), robbery.
ru (-we), rough (surface); raw (materials); crude (oil); coarse, unrefined, uncouth, rude.
rubber, rubber.
rubberboom, rubber-tree.
rubberlym, solution.
rubberplantasie, rubber-plantation.
rubriek, (-e), category, class; column (of a newspaper); heading, rubric.
rubriseer, (ge-), class, rubricate.
rudimentêr, (-e), rudimentary.
rûens, vide **rug**, 2.
rûensagteroor, right back.
rûensveld, hilly (ridgy) country.
rug, (-ge, rûe), 1. back; **iemand die − toekeer**, turn one's back on a person; **sy − is breed**, he has broad shoulders; **jy kan maar jou − vetsmeer**, prepare yourself for a good hiding; **agter iemand se −**, behind a person's back; **dit is gelukkig agter die −**, fortunately that is over; **in die − aanval**, attack from behind (in the rear); **die geld groei nie op my − nie**, I am not made of money.
rug, (-gens, rûens), 2. ridge, hill.
ru-gare, -garing, cotton-thread.
rugbaar, known; **− word**, become known, get abroad (about), leak out.
rugbaarheid, publicity; **− kry**, become known; **− gee aan**, make public.
rugby, rugby, rugger.
rugbyspeler, rugby-player.
rugbyvoetbal, rugby-football.
rug(ge)graat, backbone, spine.
rug(ge)graatsverkromming, curvature of the spine.
rugleuning, back (of chair, sofa).
rugmurg, spinal marrow.

rugmurgontsteking, inflammation of the spinal cord; poliomyelitis.
rugsaag, tenon-saw.
rugsak, rucksack.
rugspier, dorsal muscle.
rugsteun –, n. support.
rugsteun, (ge-), support, back.
rugstring, vertebral column; loin.
rugteken, (ge-), endorse (cheque).
rugwaarts, backward(s).
rugwerwel, dorsal vertebra.
ruheid, roughness; crudeness; rudeness.
ruig, (ruie), shaggy, hairy; shrubby, bushy, thickly overgrown.
ruigheid, shagginess; bushiness.
ruigte, underwood, undergrowth.
ruik, reuk, n. smell; scent; vide **reuk**.
ruik, (ge-), smell, scent; **na drank –**, smell of liquor; **lont –**, smell a rat.
ruiker, (-s), bunch of flowers, bouquet.
ruil, n. exchange, barter; **in – vir**, in exchange for; **'n goeie – doen (maak)**, make a good bargain.
ruil, (ge-), exchange, barter.
ruilbaar, (-bare), exchangeable.
ruilhandel, barter.
ruilmiddel, medium of exchange.
ruilnommer, exchange-copy.
ruim, (-e), n. hold (of a ship); nave.
ruim, (-, -e), a. spacious, large, roomy; wide, loose, not tight; ample, abundant; **die –ste betekenis**, the widest sense; **in 'n –(e) mate**, amply; **'n –(e) keuse**, a wide choice.
ruim, adv. amply, abundantly; **– R5**, fully R5; **– veertig jaar oud**, rather more than forty years old; **hulle het dit nie – nie**, they can hardly make ends meet.
ruim, (ge-), empty; ream, widen (hole); **uit die weg –**, remove clear away.
ruimer, (-s), reamer, rimer.
ruimnaald, priming-needle.
ruimskoots, amply, abundantly.
ruimte, (-s), room; gap; capacity; scope; breadth (of view); **– laat vir**, leave room for; **– van beweging**, elbow-room, scope.
ruimtemaat, cubic measure.
ruimteman, space-man.
ruimteskip, space-ship.
ruimtevaart, space travel.
ruimtevaartuig, space-craft.
ruimtevlieër, ruimreisiger, astronaut, cosmonaut.
ruïnasie, renewasie, ruination.
ruïne, (-s), ruins.
ruïneer, reneweer, (ge-), ruin.
ruis, (ge-), rustle, murmur.
ruising, rustling, rustle, murmur.
ruit, (-e), pane (of windows); rhomb(us); lozenge; rue (bot.) check (material); (pl. -e, -ens), diamond (cards).
ruite(n)aas, ace of diamonds.
ruitens, diamonds (cards).
ruite(n)vrou, queen of diamonds.
ruiter, (-s), rider, horseman.
ruiterbal, mounted (horseback-)rounders.
ruiterbende, troop of horsemen.
ruitergeveg, cavalry-fight.
ruiterlik, (-e), frank(ly), open(ly).
ruitersalf, mercurial ointment.
ruiterstandbeeld, equestrian statue.
ruitery, cavalry.
ruitjie, (-s), little pane; check.
ruitjiesgoed, check.
ruitjiespapier, squared paper.
ruitspuit, windscreen washer.
ruitveër, windscreen wiper.

ruitvormig, (-e), diamond-shaped.
ruk, (-ke), n. jerk, pull, tug; gust (of wind); time, while; **met –ke en stote**, pulling and pushing; by fits and starts.
ruk, (ge-), jerk, pull, tug; **iemand iets uit die hand –**, snatch (wrench) something from a person's hands; **– en pluk**, pull and tug; **woorde uit hulle verband –**, wrest words from their context.
ruk-en-pluk(dans), rock and roll.
rukkie, (-s), little pull (jerk): short while (time) moment.
rukwind, gust of wind, squall.
rum, rum.
rumatiek, rheumatism.
rumaties, (-e), rheumatic.
rumba, rumba.
rumoer, n. noise, row, hubbub, din.
rumoer, (ge-), make a noise.
rumoerig, (-e), noisy, rowdy, boisterous.
rumoerigheid, noisiness, boisterousness.
runderpes, rinderpest.
rune, (-s), runic letter.
runeskrif, runic writing.
runnik, (ge-), neigh, whinny.
Rus, (-se), Russian.
rus, n. rest, repose; peace; safety-catch; rest (mus.), pause, causura; **geen – of duurte hê nie**, not have a moment's peace; **hy kan nie sy – hou nie**, he cannot keep the peace; **in – en vrede lewe**, live in peace; **iemand met – laat**, leave a person in peace; **sig ter –te begeef**, go to rest; **ter –te lê**, lay to rest, bury; **tot – bring**, set at rest; **tot – kom**, settle down; find peace.
rus, (ge-), rest, repose; **wel te –te!**, good night!; **die saak laat –**, let the matter rest.
rusbank, couch, sofa, settee.
rusdag, day of rest, the Sabbath.
rusie, (-s), quarrel, dispute, squabble; **– hê**, quarrel; **– kry**, fall out, quarrel; **– soek**, pick a quarrel.
rusiemaker, quarrelsome person.
rusiemakerig, (-e), quarrelsome.
rusiesoeker, quarrelsome person.
ruskuur, rest-cure.
Rusland, Russia.
rusoord, place of rest.
ruspe(r), (-s), caterpillar.
rusplek, resting-place.
ruspunt, resting-point; pause.
Russies, (-e), Russian.
rusteken, rest (mus.).
rusteloos, (-lose), restless.
rusteloosheid, restlessness.
rustend, (-e), resting; retired; emeritus.
rustiek, (-e), rural; rustic (seat).
rustig, (-e), restful, quiet, tranquil, calm, peaceful.
rustyd, resting-time; half-time (games).
rusuur, hour of rest.
rusversteurder, -verstoorder, disturber of the peace.
rusversteuring, -verstoring, disturbance.
ry, (-e), n. row, line, string; series, suite, course (of bricks); **in die –, op 'n –**, in a row (line).
ry, (ge-), 1. ride, drive; **met die trein –**, go (travel) by train; **op 'n perd (te perd) –**, ride on horseback (a horse); **op skaatse –**, skate, rink; **die motor – lekker**, it is a comfortable car; **gaan –**, go for a ride (drive, spin); **iemand – maak it hot (unpleasant) for a person; **iemand in die wiele –**, put a spoke in somebody's wheel.
ry, (ge-), 2. vide **rye, ryg**.
rybaan, track; skating-rink.

rybaar, (-bare), practicable (road).
rybewys, driver's licence.
rybroek, riding-breeches.
rydier, riding-animal.
ry(e), ryg, (ge-), tack, shir(r), gather, run, baste; string (beads); lace (shoes).
rygdraad, tacking-thread.
rygnaald, bodkin.
rygsteek, gathering, running-stitch.
rygveter, lace.
ryhandskoen, riding-glove.
ryk, (-e), n. kingdom, empire, realm, sphere, province, domain; **die duisendjarige –, die – van die verbeelding (drome)**, the millenium; the realm of fancy (dreams).
ryk, (-, -e), a. rich, well-to-do, wealthy; fertile; copious.
rykaard, (-s), rich man, plutocrat.
rykdom, (-me), wealth, riches; abundance, profusion, richness.
ryke, (-s), rich person.
rykheid, richness.
ryklik, richly, abundantly, amply.
rykostuum, riding-habit, riding-dress.
ryksadelaar, imperial eagle.
ryksargief, public (state-)archives.
ryksdag, diet; **die R–**, the Reichstag.
rykskanselier, imperial chancellor.
Ryksconferensie, Imperial Conference.
rykuns, horsemanship, art of riding.
ryloop, hitch-hike.
rym, (-e), n. rhyme; **slepende (vroulike) –**, feminine rhyme; **staande (manlike) –**, masculine rhyme.
rym, (ge-), rhyme; agree, correspond, tally; **– met**, rhyme with; **nie met mekaar te – nie**, incompatible, irreconcilable.
rymbybel, rhymed bible.
rymelaar, (-s), rhymer, verse-monger.
rymelary, doggerel.
rymer, (-s), rhymer.
rymklank, rhyme,
rymkuns, art of rhyming.
rymloos, (-lose), rhymeless, blank.
rympie, (-s), short rhyme.
rymwoord, rhyme.

Ryn, Rhine.
Rynlands, (-e), Rhineland.
Ryns, (-e), Rhenish, Rhine.
Rynwyn, Rhine-wine.
ryp, n. hoar-frost; **wit van die –**, covered with frost.
ryp, (–, -e), a. ripe, mature; **–er jare**, riper years; **– oordeel**, ripe judgement; **die tyd is nog nie –nie**, the time is not yet ripe; **na – beraad**, after mature consideration; **vroeg –, vroeg rot**, soon ripe, soon rotten; **– word**, ripen; **– en groen**, ripe and unripe.
ryp, (ge-), frost; **wit ge–**, covered with frost.
ryperd, riding-horse, saddle-horse; **–!**, by Jove!, excellent!
rypheid, ripeness, maturity.
ryplank, surf-board.
ryplik, maturely.
rys, n. rice.
rys, (ge-), rise; **sy hare –**, his hair stands on end.
rysakker, rice-field.
rysbou, cultivation of rice.
rysig, (-e), tall.
ryskaaf, trying-plane.
ryskluitjie, rice-dumpling.
ryskool, riding-school.
ryskorrel, grain of rice.
ryskultuur, cultivation of rice.
rysmier, white ant, termite.
rysoes, rice-crop.
rysplantasie, rice-plantation.
rysso(e)p, rice-soup.
rystafel, rice-table, tiffin.
rysterplaat, rysterplank, mould-board.
rystoel, rocking-chair.
rysveld, rice-field, paddy-field.
ryswater, rice-water.
rysweep, riding-whip.
rytoer, drive, ride.
rytuig, (-tuie), vehicle; cab (for hire); coach, carriage.
rytuigmaker, wag(g)on- and cart-builder.
rytuigverkeer, vehicular traffic.
ryvernuf, road-sense.
ryweg, -pad, -baan, carriage-way.
rywiel, bicycle, cycle.

S

s, vide es (3).
sa!, catch him.
saad, (sade), saat, (sate), seed; semen; offspring; – skiet, (run to) seed.
saadakkertjie, seed-bed, seed-plot.
saadbed(ding), seed-bed.
saaddiertjie, spermatozoon.
saadhandelaar, seedsman.
saadhawer, seed-oats.
saadhuisie, seed-capsule, seed-vessel.
saadjie, saatjie, (-s), (grain of) seed.
saadkiem, germ.
saadkorrel, grain of seed, seed-corn.
saadlob, seed-lobe, cotyledon.
saadloos, (-lose), seedless.
saadolie, (rape)seed-oil.
saag, (sae), n. saw.
saag, sae, (ge-), saw, cut, rip; scrape.
saagbank, saw-bench, saw-horse.
saagblad, saw-blade.
saagbok, saw-trestle, saw-horse.
saagkuil, saw-pit.
saagmeul(e), saw-mill.
saagraam, saw-frame.
saagsel, saw-dust.
saagvis, saw-fish.
saagvormig, (-e), saw-like, saw-shaped.
saai, n. serge.
saai, a. & adv. dull, humdrum, tedious.
saai, (ge-), sow, scatter; tweedrag –, sow (the seeds of) dissension; wat jy –, sal jy ook maai, you must reap what you have sown; die vyand laat –, scatter the foe.
saaiboer, grain-farmer.
saaiboontjie, seed-bean.
saaier, (-s), sower.
saaiheid, dul(l)ness; vide saai, a. & adv.
saaikoring, seed-corn; wheat-seed.
saailand, sowing-land.
saaimasjien, seed-drill, sowing-machine.
saaisaad, sewing-seed.
saaisak, sower's bag.
saaityd, sowing-season, sowing-time.
saak, (sake), matter, business, concern, affair, case; cause; (law-)suit, (court-)case; hoe staan sake?, how are things?; dit is jou (my) –, that is your (my) business (concern, affair); bemoei jou met jou eie sake, mind your own business; dit maak geen – nie, it does not matter, it is of no importance; gedane sake het geen keer nie, it is no use crying over spilt milk; goeie sake doen, do good business; sake is sake, business is business; buitelandse sake, foreign affairs; 'n – maak, go to law, institute (legal) proceedings; vir 'n goeie –, die – van die vrede, for a good cause, the cause of peace; dis nie veel –s nie, it is not much to talk about, it is no great shakes; in sake, in the matter of, with reference to; ter sake, to the point, to the purpose; nie ter sake, not to the point, irrelevant.
saakgelastigde, (-s), agent, representative, deputy, commissioner.
saakkundig, (-e), expert.
saaklik, (-e), business-like, to the point, thorough; impersonal; concise; real.
saaklikheid, efficiency; conciseness.
saakkryk, (-e), full of matter, pithy.
saakwaarnemer, agent, representative.
saal, (sale), n. hall, room; ward (in hospital); 'n volle –, a full house.
saal, (-s), n. saddle; vas in die – sit, have a firm seat, be firmly seated, be saddlefast; in die – help, give a leg up; uit die – lig (werp), unsaddle, unhorse, unseat, dislodge, oust.
saal, (ge-), saddle.

saalboom, pommel; saddle-tree; – ry, cling to the pommel (saddle).
saalhuur, hall-rental.
saalklap, saddle-flap.
saalkleedjie, saddle-cloth.
saalknop, pommel.
saalkussing, saddle-cushion.
saalmaker, saddler.
saalmakery, saddlery.
saalrug, saddle-back.
saalsak, saddle-bag; tool-bag.
saalsuster, ward-sister.
saalvas, (-te), saddlefast.
saalvormig, (-e), saddle-shaped.
saam, same, together; algar –, all together; deur ons – betaal, paid by us jointly; ons het – 'n bottel bier gedrink, we drank a bottle of beer between us.
saam-..., vide same-... & mee-...
saambind, (saamge-), bind (tie) together; knit (bind) together (fig.).
saamblaf, (saamge-), bark (hunt) together, share in the attack (noise).
saambly, (saamge-), stay, live together.
saambring, (saamge-), bring (throw) together; bring along, bring.
saamdoen, (saamge-), join in, join hands.
saamdra, (saamge-), carry (take) along, bring (carry) together; pile up.
saamdruk, (saamge-), press (squeeze) together, compress.
saamdrukbaar, (-bare), compressible.
saamdryf, saamdrywe, (saamge-), drive together; float together.
saameet, (saamgeëet), eat (dine) together, join in a meal.
saamflans, (saamge-), flick together, knock together, patch up.
saamfrommel, (saamge-), crumple (rumple) up; make mincemeat of.
saamgaan, (saamge-), accompany, go along; go together, agree, go hand in hand; join in with; match; gaan jy saam?, are you coming (with me)?; ek het met hom saamgegaan stasie toe, I accompanied (went with) him to the station.
saam-, samegesteld, (-e), compound, complex, complicated; –e rente, compound interest; –e breuk, complex fraction (arith.); compound fracture.
saam-, samegesteldheid, complexity.
saamgesworene, (-s), confederate.
saamgroei, (saamge-), grow together.
saam-, samehang, (saamge-, samege-), hang together, cohere, be connected, be linked together; ten nouste met mekaar –, be closely bound up with one another, be interwoven.
saamhok, (saamge-), herd together.
saamhoop, (saamge-), heap up, pile up.
saamhoor(t), (saamge-), belong together.
saamhorig, samehorig, (-e), belonging together, related, homogeneous.
saamhorigheid, samehorigheid, solidarity, unity.
saam-, samehorigheidsgevoel, feeling of solidarity, communal sense.
saamhou, (saamge-), keep together.
saamkleef, -klewe, (saamge-), stick together, adhere.
saamklink, (saamge-), harmonize; sound together; rivet together.
saamknoop, (saamge-), tie together.
saamkom, (saamge-), come together, gather, assemble, meet, unite; go (come) with (a person), come too.
saamkoppel, (saamge-), couple.
saamleef, -lewe, (saamge-), live together, cohabit.

saamloop, (saamge-), meet, come together; accompany, go (come) with (a person), come too; **my hond het met my saamgeloop**, my dog followed (accompanied) me.
saamloop, n. vide **sameloop**.
saamneem, take (consider) together; take along.
saampak, (saamge-), pack together, pack up; gather, collect, crowd together.
saampers, (saamge-), press (squeeze) together, compress, condense.
saampraat, (saamge-), join in the conversation; have a say in the matter.
saamraap, (saamge-), scrape together.
saamroep, (saamge-), call together, convene, convoke.
saamrol, (saamge-), roll together.
saamrot, (saamge-), band together, assemble; conspire.
saamskool, (saamge-), band (flock) together, assemble, mob (together).
saamskraap, (saamge-), scrape together.
saamsmee(d), (saamge-), weld together.
saamsmelt, (saamge-), melt together, amalgamate, fuse, coalesce, merge.
saamspan, (saamge-), unite, co-operate join hands; conspire, plot (against).
saamspeel, (saamge-), combine (in play), play together, join (participate) in a play (game); act.
saamstel, (saamge-), compose, make up; put together, compile (a dictionary).
saamstem, (saamge-), agree; harmonize.
saamstroom, (saamge-), flow together, unite; flock together, assemble.
saamsweer, (saamge-), conspire, plot.
saamtrek, (saamge-), draw (pull) together; contract (muscles); concentrate (forces); draw (pull) along.
saamval, (saamge-), fall together, coincide; run concurrently; clash.
saamvat, (saamge-), take together; summarize; take along with one.
saamvleg, (saamge-), plait (braid, tie, string, weave) together, interlace.
saamvloei, (saamge-), flow together.
saamvoeg, (saamge-), join, unite.
saamvou, (saamge-), fold together (up).
saamwerk, n. co-operation; co-operative society.
saamwerk, (saamge-), work (act, pull) together, co-operate, join hands, collaborate; combine.
saamwoon, (saamge-), live together.
saans, in the evening, of an evening, at night.
saat, vide **saad**.
sabander, (ge-), clear out, scoot.
Sabbat, (-te), Sabbath.
Sabbatdag, Sabbath-day.
sabbatsjaar, sabbatical year.
Sabbatskender, Sabbath-breaker.
Sabbatskennis, Sabbath-breaking.
sabbatsreis, sabbath-day's journey.
Sabbatsrus, Sabbath-rest.
Sabbatariër, (-s), Sabbatarian.
sabel, (-s), n. 1. sable (fur; colour).
sabel, (-s), n. 2. sword, sabre.
sabelbont, sable(-fur).
sabeldier, sable.
sabelhou, sword-cut, sabre-cut, -thrust.
sabelkling, **sabellem**, sword-blade.
sabelskede, scabbard.
sabelvel, sable-skin.
sabotasie, rattening, sabotage.
saboteer, (ge-), ratten, sabotage.
saboteur, saboteur.
Sadduseër, (-s), Sadducee.
Saddusees, (-sese), Sadducean.

sadis, (-te), sadist.
sadisme, sadism.
sadisties, (-e), sadistic.
sae, vide **saag**, (ge-).
saer, (-s), sawyer.
saf, **sag**, (-te), soft; vide **sag**.
safari, safari.
saffier, (-e), sapphire.
saffraan, saffron.
saffraanagtig, (-e), like saffron.
saffraanhout, saffronwood.
saffraanpeer, saffron pear.
sag, **saf**, (-te), a. soft (in nearly all senses); light; gentle, mild, pliable; **sagte stap**, light step; **sagte windjie**, **wenk**, gentle breeze, hint; **sagte klimaat**, mild climate; **sagte leer**, pliable (soft) leather; **sagte humeur**, sweet temper.
sag, **saf**, adv. softly, gently, lightly; **sag loop**, tread (walk) softly; **sag oordeel**, judge leniently; **op sy sagste gesê (uitgedruk)**, to put it mildly; **sag ontslape**, passed away peacefully.
saga, (-s), saga.
sagaardig, (-e), mild, meek, gentle.
sagaardigheid, mildness, gentleness.
sage, (-s), legend, story; saga.
saggarien, (-ine), saccharine, vide **sakkarien**.
saggies, softly, gently, slowly; – **praat**, speak softly (low).
sagkens, gently, softly.
sagmoedig, (-e), mild, gentle, benign.
sagmoedigheid, gentleness, mildness.
sago, sago.
sagomeel, sago-flour.
sagopoeding, sago-pudding.
sagsinnig, (-e), gentle, mild.
sagsinnigheid, gentleness, mildness.
sagterig, (-e), softish, a bit soft.
sagtheid, softness, gentleness, mildness.
Sahara, Sahara.
sak, (-ke), n. sack (always big; of corn, coal), bag (generally big: of corn, coal; but also hand-, paper-bag); pocket (in clothes, but also: pocket of sugar); pouch (for tobacco, ammunition); **met – en pak**, with bag and baggage; **'n kat in die – koop**, buy a pig in a poke; **in – en as**, in sack-cloth and ashes; **iemand in jou – hê**, have a person in your pocket; **steek dit in jou –**, put it in your pocket; put that in your pipe and smoke it.
sak, (ge-), sink; drop, fall, subside, go down; give down milk; **pryse –**, prices fall (drop); **die weerglas –**, the barometer falls; **– in 'n eksamen**, fail in an examination; **laat –**, let down (a blind); **die kop laat –**, hang (sink) one's head; **'n kandidaat laat –**, plough (fail) a candidate.
sakboek, pocket-book.
sakdoek, handkerchief.
sake, vide **saak**.
sakebrief, business-letter.
sakekennis, **saakkennis**, practical (expert) knowledge, business-experience.
sakeman, business-man.
sakereis, business-tour.
sakewêreld, business-circles.
sakformaat, pocket-size.
sakgeld, pocket-money.
sakhorlosie, **-oorlosie**, watch.
sakie, (-s), little matter.
sakkammetjie, pocket-comb.
sakkarien, (-ine), saccharine, vide **saggarien**.
sakkerloot!, by gad!, by Jove!
sakkeroller, pickpocket.
sakmes, pocket-knife.
sakoorlosie, **-horlosie**, watch.

sakrament, (-e), sacrament.
sakramenteel, (-tele), sacramental.
sakristie, (-ë), sacristy, vestry.
Sakse, Saxony.
Sakser, (-s), Saxon.
Saksies, (-e), Saxon.
saksies-blou, Saxe blue.
sakspieël(tjie), pocket-mirror.
sakvol, (sakkevol), bagful, pocketful.
sakwoordeboek, pocket-dictionary.
sal, (past tense: sou), shall (should), will (would); ek (hy) sal môre kom, I shall (he will) come tomorrow.
sal(a)mander, (-s), salamander, lizard.
salammoniak, salmiak, sal-ammoniac.
salarieer, (ge-), pay (a salary), salary.
salaris, (-se), salary, pay.
salarisskaal, salary-scale, rate of pay.
salarisverhoging, increase in salary.
saldo, (-'s), balance; batige -, credit balance; nadelige -, debit balance; per -, on balance.
salf, n. ointment, unguent, salve; aan hom is geen - te smeer nie, he is past redemption (past praying for).
salf, salwe, (ge-), anoint; salve.
salfdoos, salve-box.
salfolie, anointing oil, unguent, chrism.
salfpot, ointment-pot, gallipot.
salie, sage; Salvia sp.
salig, (-e), blessed (blest); blissful; - maak, save; - word, be saved; - spreek, beatify; bless; dit is -er om te gee as om te ontvang, it is more blessed to give than to receive; - is die besitters, possession is nine points of the law; -er nagedagtenis, of blessed memory; 'n -e vakansie, a glorious holiday.
saligheid, salvation, blessedness, bliss, joy, beatitude.
saligmakend, (-e), saving, sanctifying.
Saligmaker, Saviour.
saligmaking, salvation, saving.
saligspreking, -verklaring, beatification.
salm, salmon.
salmiak, vide salammoniak.
salmiakgees, liquid ammonia.
salmkleur, salmon(-colour), salmon-pink.
salmvissery, salmon-fishery.
Salomo, Solomon.
salon, (-s, -ne), reception-room, drawing room; salon; saloon.
salonheld, carpet-knight.
salonrytuig, saloon-carriage.
salot, (-te), shallot.
salot-ui, shallot.
salpeter, saltpetre, nitre.
salpeter(agt)ig, (-e), nitrous.
salpetersuur, nitric acid.
salueer, (ge-), salute.
salutasie, salutation.
saluut, (-lute), n. salute.
saluutskoot, salute.
salvo, (-'s), salvo, volley, round.
salwe, vide salf, (ge-).
salwend, (-e), unctuous.
Samaritaan, (-tane), n. Samaritan; barmhartige -, good Samaritan.
Samaritaans, (-e), a. Samaritan.
samba, samba.
sambal, semball (sambal), (quince-)condiment.
sambalbroek, flap-trousers; bags.
sambok, (-ke), sjambok.
sambreel, (-brele), umbrella.
sambreelboom, cabbage-tree.
same, vide saam.

sameflansing, patching together; patchwork; tissue, conglomeration.
samegesteld, (-e), vide saamgesteld.
samehang, n. coherence, logic(alness), order; cohesion; connection; context.
samehang, (samege-), vide saamhang.
samehorig(heid), vide saamhorig(heid).
samekoms, meeting, gathering.
samekoppeling, coupling, linking.
samelewing, society; cohabitation.
sameloop, saamloop, n. confluence (of rivers); concourse (of people); - van omstandighede, coincidence.
samepersing, compression, condensation.
sameraapsel, (-s), mixture, medley; conglomeration, pack, tissue (of lies); motley crowd, rabble.
sameroeping, calling together, convening, convention, convocation.
samerotting, (-e, -s), conspiracy.
sameskikking, arrangement.
sameskoling, (-e, -s), flocking together, assemblage; conspiracy.
sameskraapsel, (-s), odd collection; scrapings; hoi polloi, rabble.
samesmelting, (-e, -s), fusion, amalgamation, coalition; combine, merger.
samespanning, (-e, -s), banding together, co-operation; conspiracy, plot.
samespel, combination, team-work.
samespraak, dialogue, conversation.
samespreking, conversation, discussion, interview; conference, meeting.
samestellend, (-e), component.
samesteller, (-s), compiler, composer.
samestelling, (-e, -s), composition; construction, assembly; compilation; texture; compound.
samestemming, agreement; harmony.
samesweerder, (-s), conspirator, plotter.
sameswering, (-e, -s), conspiracy, plot.
sametrekking, (-e, -s), contraction; concentration; pulling together.
samevatting, summary, résumé, epitome.
samevloeiing, confluence, junction.
samevoeging, union, junction; merger.
samewerking, co-operation.
samewoning, cohabitation; living together.
samoem, (-s), simoom.
samowar, (-s), samovar.
sampioen, (-e), mushroom, champignon.
sanatorium, (-s, -toria), sanatorium.
sand, sand; grit, dirt; (talryk) soos die - van die see, (numberless) as the sand(s) on the seashore; iemand - in die oë strooi, throw dust in a person's eyes; in die - (stof) byt, bite the dust; op - bou, build on sand.
sandaal, (-dale), sandal.
sand-aal, (-ale), sand-eel.
sandbad, sand-bath.
sandbak, sand-box.
sandbank, sand-bank, (sand-)bar, shoal.
sandbedding, sand-bed.
sandberg, sand-hill, mountain of sand.
sandblad, sand-leaf.
sandduin, sand-dune.
sandelhout, sandal(-wood).
sanderig, (-e), sandy; gritty.
sanderigheid, sandiness; grittiness.
sandglas, hour-glass, sand-glass.
sandgrond, sandy soil (ground).
sandhaai, sand-shark, dogfish.
sandheuwel, sand-hill.
sandhoop, sand-heap, sand-mound.
sandjie, (-s), grain of sand; piece of grit.
sandklip, sandstone.

sandkorrel, grain of sand.
sandlaag, layer of sand.
sandlelie, mauve africander.
sandlopertjie, sand-glass, hour-glass.
sandmannetjie, sandman.
sandpad, sandy road (path).
sandplaat, expanse of sand; sand-bank.
sandsak, sandbag.
sandsteen, sandstone.
sandstorm, sand-storm.
sandstuiwing, sand-drift, sand shift.
sandsuiker, crystallised sugar.
sandtrapper, country-bumpkin, yokel.
sandveld, sandveld(t), sandy parts.
sandvlakte, sandflats, sandy flat (plain).
sandvlooi, sand-flea.
sandwoestyn, sandy desert (waste).
sang, song, singing; canto, verse; poetry; – studeer, take (study) singing; 'n gedig in drie –e, a poem in three cantos.
Sangberg, Parnassus, Helicon.
sanger, (-s), singer; songster; songbird; poet, bard.
sangeres, (-se), singer; songstress.
sangerig, (-e), melodious, tuneful.
sangerigheid, melodiousness; lilt.
sanggeselskap, choral society, choir.
sanggod, god of song, Ap 'llo.
sanggodin, muse.
sangkoor, choir.
sangkuns, (art of) singing.
sangles, singing-lesson.
sanglus, love of singing (song).
sangmusiek, vocal music.
sangnommer, song(-item).
sangoefening, singing-exercise, -practice.
sangonderwys, singing, singing-lessons.
sangonderwyser(es), teacher of singing, singing-master, -mistress.
sangskool, school of singing.
sangspel, opera, musical comedy.
sangstuk, song.
sanguinies, (-e), sanguine.
sanguitvoering, vocal concert.
sangvereniging, choral society.
sangvoël, song-bird, singing-bird.
sangwedstryd, singing-competition.
sangwyse, tune; method of singing.
Sanhedrin, Sanhedrim (Sandhedrin).
sanik, (ge-), din, drone, bother, nag.
sanitêr, (-e), sanitary.
sanksie, (-s), sanction.
sanksioneer, (ge-), sanction; ratify.
Sanskrit, Sanscrit.
Sap, (-pe), Sap, South African Party (-man).
sap, (-pe), juice; sap.
sapgroen, sap-green.
saploos, (-lose), sapless.
sapperig, (-e), juicy; succulent, sappy.
sappeur, (-s), sapper.
sappig, (-e), juicy, luscious; succulent.
sappigheid, juiciness, lusciousness.
sapryk, (-e), sapful, sappy, juicy.
sar, (ge-), tease, nag, vex.
Saraseen, (-sene), Saracen.
Saraseens, (-e), Saracen(ic).
sardien(tjie), (-s), sardine.
Sardinië, Sardinia.
Sardiniër, (-s), Sardinian.
Sardinies, (-e), Sardinian.
sardonies, (-e), sardonic(ally).
sardoniks, (-e), sardonyx.
sardyntjie, sardine; little herring.
sarkasme, sarcasm.
sarkasties, (-e), sarcastic(ally).

sarkofaag, (-fae, -fage), sarcophagus.
sarsaparilla, sarsaparilla.
sarsie, (-s), charge, sally; volley, discharge; rally (tennis); 'n – maak, charge; fire a volley, have a go.
sassafras, sassafras.
sat, satiated, tired (of), sick (of); **ek is daar – van,** I am sick (tired) of it; **ek is –,** I have had my fill; **– van dae,** full of years.
Satan, Satan, the devil.
satanies, (-e), satanic(al), diabolical.
satans, (-e), satanic, hellish.
satanskind, child of the devil, imp; devil.
satanswerk, devilish work, hell of a job.
satelliet, (-e), satellite.
satellietstaat, satellite state.
sater, (-s), satyr.
Saterdag, Saturday.
Saterdags, every Saturday.
satheid, satiety; weariness, tiredness.
satire, (-s), satire.
satiriek, (-e), satiric(al).
satiries, (-e), satiric(al).
satirikus, (-se, -rici), satirist.
satisfaksie, satisfaction.
satraap, (-ape), satrap.
Saturnus, Saturn.
satyn, satin.
satynagtig, (-e), satiny, satin.
satynhout, satin-wood.
Savoje, Savoy.
savojekool, savoy-cabbage.
saxofoon, (-fone), saxophone.
scala, (-s), scale, gamut.
scenario, (-'s), scenario.
scriba, (-s), scriba, scribe.
scribent, (-e), pen-driver, hack-writer.
se, of, belonging to, **Pa (Ma) – hoed,** Father's (Mother's) hat.
sê, n. say; **sy – sê,** have his say.
sê, seg, (ge-), say, tell; **hy – dat** . . . , he says that . . .; **ek – (vir) jou** . . . , I tell you . . .; **wat (hoe) – jy?,** what do you say?; – **(maar) tien pond,** (let us) say ten pounds; **dis nou weer te –!,** well, I never!; **wat – jy daarvan?,** what do you think of (say to) that?; **hulle (die mense) –,** people say, it is said; – **dit maar reguit,** speak out, speak your mind; **ek het hom reguit gesê,** I told him straight (to his face); **dit mag jy wel –,** you may well say so; **jy moet dit maar –,** just say the word; **dit – nie,** that's nothing; **dit – niks,** that means nothing; **dit – vir my niks,** that conveys nothing to me; **ek – niks,** I have nothing to say; **jy het niks oor die geld te – nie,** the money is no business of yours (does not concern you); **dit – veel (baie),** it says a lot (much), it speaks volumes; **dit – nie veel nie,** that is not saying much; that means very little; **ek – nie te veel nie,** I do not exaggerate; **die waarheid –,** speak (tell) the truth; **dit wil –,** that is (to say), that means; **dit wil nie – nie** . . . , that does not mean (imply); **so gesê, so gedaan,** no sooner said than done; **soos reeds gesê,** as already stated; **onder ons gesê,** between ourselves (you and me); **ek het jou mos gesê,** I told you so; **so te –,** so to speak; – **en doen is twee,** promising is one thing, doing another; **daar is alles (niks) voor te – nie,** there is everything (nothing) to be said for it.
sebra, (-s), zebra.
sebra-oorgang, zebra crossing.
secunda(wissel), second of exchange.
sede, (-s), manner, custom, habit; (pl.) customs, habits; morals; **–s en gewoontes,** manners and customs.

sedebederf, corruption (of morals).
sedebederwend, (-e), corruptive.
sedeer, (ge-), cede, assign.
sedeleer, ethics, morality.
sedeles, moral lesson, moral.
sedelik, (-e), moral, ethical.
sedelikheid, morality.
sedelikheidsgevoel, moral sense.
sedelikheidswet, public morality act, moral law.
sedeloos, (-lose), immoral, dissolute.
sedeloosheid, immorality, profligacy.
sedemeester, moralist.
sedemisdryf, offence against public morals, act of indecency.
sedepreek, lecture in morals, sermon.
sedepreker, -prediker, moralist.
seder, (-s), cedar.
sederboom, cedar-tree.
sedert, since; for; – **die oorlog**, since the war; – **twee maande**, for (the past) two months.
sedertdien, since then.
sedewet, moral law (code).
sedig, (-e), modest, retiring, demure, coy; decorous.
sedigheid, modesty, coyness.
sediment, sediment.
sedimentêr, (-e), sedimentary.
sedisie, sedition.
sedisieus, (-e), seditious.
seduksie, seduction.
see, (seë), sea, ocean; flood, torrent, multitude; – **kies**, put (out) to sea; **'n – van trane** (lig, woorde), a flood of tears (light, words); **'n – van rampe**, a sea (multitude) of troubles; **aan (die) –**, at the seaside, by the sea; **reg deur – gaan**, steer a straight course; **in – steek**, put (out) to sea, launch out; **in volle –**, on the high seas; **na (die) – gaan**, go to the sea-side, go to sea; **op –**, at sea, on the sea; **oor – gaan**, go by sea, cross the sea (ocean); **ter – en te land**, by sea and land.
seë, sege, victory, triumph.
see-anemoon, sea-anemone.
see-arm, arm of the sea.
see-assuransie, marine insurance.
see-atlas, nautical atlas.
seebad, sea-bath, dip in the see.
seebadplek, watering-place.
seebamboes, sea-bamboo.
seebeer, small seal, sea-bear.
seebene, sea-legs.
seebeskrywing, oceanography.
seebewoner, inhabitant of the sea.
seebog, bight, bay.
seëboog, segeboog, triumphal arch.
seeboot, sea-boat.
seebreker, breakwater, mole.
seebries, sea-breeze.
seediens, naval service.
seediepte, depth of the sea.
seedier, marine animal.
seedorp, seaside-town (-village).
seedrif(sel), flotsam and jetsam.
seeduiker, diver, cormorant; shag.
seeduiwel, sea-devil, devil-fish.
see-eend, yellow-bill, sea-duck.
see-engel, angel-fish, sea-angel.
see-engte, strait.
seegesig, seascape.
seegeveg, sea-fight, naval battle.
seegod, sea-god.
seegodin, sea-goddess.
seegolf, sea-wave, ocean-wave, billow.
seegras, sea-grass; sea-weed.
seegroen, sea-green.
seehandel, (over)sea-trade.
seehawe, seaport, harbour.
seeheerskappy, naval supremacy.
seeheld, naval hero.
seehond, seal, sea-dog.
seehoof, pier, jetty.
seekaart, nautical chart.
seekant, seaside; **aan die –**, to seaward.
seekaptein, sea-captain, naval captain.
seekasteel, sea-castle, ship of war.
seekat, octopus; squid, cuttlefish.
seekoei, hippo(potamus); sea-cow, manatee.
seekoe(i)gat, hippo-pool, river-pool.
seekompas, mariner's compass.
seëkrans, segekrans, triumphal wreath.
seekreef, lobster.
seëkroon, segekroon, crown of victory.
seekus, sea-coast, seashore, seaside.
seel, (-s), 1. (birth-)certificate.
seël, (-s), 2. stamp; seal; **sy – druk op**, set one's seal to; **onder – van geheimhouding**, under seal of secrecy (silence).
seël, (ge-), seal (up); stamp (a letter).
seëlbelasting, stamp-duty.
Seëlbewaarder, Keeper of the Seal.
seeleeu, sea-lion, seal.
seëlied, segelied, song of victory.
seeliede, seelui, vide **seeman**.
seëllak, sealing-wax.
seëlmerk, seal.
seëlring, signet-ring.
seelug, sea-air.
seemag, sea-power; navy.
seeman, (seeliede, seelui), seaman, sailor.
seemanshuis, seaman's home.
seemanskap, seamanship.
seemanslewe, seafaring (sailor's) life.
seemanstaal, nautical language (slang).
seemanswoordeboek, nautical dictionary.
seemeermin, mermaid.
seemeeu, sea-gull.
seemonster, sea-monster.
seemoondheid, naval power.
seemyl, nautical mile, sea-mile.
seemsleer, chamois(-leather).
seën, (-s), drag-net, seine.
seën, (seëninge, seënings), n. blessing, benediction; godsend, boon, piece of luck; **sy – gee**, give his blessing; **die – uitspreek**, pronounce the benediction.
seën, (ge-), bless; **in geseënde omstandighede**, in a certain condition, in the family way.
seënbede, blessing, benediction.
seenimf, sea-nymph.
seëning, (-e, -s), blessing, benediction.
seënwens, blessing, benediction.
see-offisier, naval officer.
see-oorlog, sea-war, naval war.
seep, n. soap; **so glad soos –**, as slippery as an eel; **groen –**, soft soap.
seep, (ge-), soap (in); lather (the face).
seepagtig, (-e), soapy, saponaceous.
seepbakkie, soap-dish.
seepbel, soap-bubble.
seepbos, soap-bush, Noltea africana.
seepfabrikant, soap-manufacturer.
seepklip, saponite, soap-stone.
seepolis, marine policy.
seepos, overseas-mail.
seëpraal, segepraal, n. triumph, victory.
seëpraal, segepraal, (ge-), triumph (over), gain the victory.
seëpralend, segepralend, (-e), triumphant, victorious.
seepskuim, soap-froth, lather.

seepsoda, caustic soda.
seepsop, soap-suds.
seepwater, soapy water; soap-suds.
seer, (sere), n. sore; boil.
seer, a. sore, painful; – oë, sore eyes.
seer, adv. painfully; very (much), extremely, highly; – **maak**, hurt; **al te** –, (only) too much; – **kry**, feel much pain.
seeramp, shipping (naval) disaster.
seereg, maritime law.
seereis, voyage, sea-trip.
seereisiger, sea-traveller, voyager.
Seergeleerde, Very Learned; **Die – Heer, Dr. X, Dr X**.
seerheid, soreness, painfulness.
seerkry, (seerge-), get hurt.
seerob, seal, sea-dog; tar, old salt.
seeroë, sore eyes.
seeroof, piracy; – **pleeg**, commit piracy.
seeroos, sea-anemone.
seerower, pirate.
seerowery, piracy; vide **seeroof**.
seerrug, sore back; scalded back.
seesand, sea-sand.
seesiek, sea-sick.
seesiekte, sea-sickness.
seeskilpad, sea-turtle.
seeskuim, sea-foam.
seeskuimer, pirate.
seeskulp, sea-shell.
seeslag, naval battle, **sea-fight**.
seeslang, sea-serpent.
seesoldaat, marine.
seespieël, sea-level; **bo (onder) die** –, above (below) sea-level.
seester, sand-star, starfish.
seestorm, sea-storm.
seestraat, strait(s).
seestrand, seashore; beach, sands.
seestroming, ocean-current.
seëtog, segetog, triumphal procession.
seevaarder, (-s), navigator.
seevaart, navigation.
seevaartkunde, (art of) navigation.
seevaartkundig, (-e), naval, nautical.
seevaartskool, naval college.
seevaartuig, sea-vessel.
seevarend, (-e), sea-faring.
seevark, porpoise; porcupine-fish.
seeversekeraar, (marine) underwriter.
seeversekering, marine insurance.
seevesting, naval (coastal) fortress.
seëvier, segevier, (ge-), triumph (over), gain the victory (over); prevail.
seëvierend, segevierend, (-e), triumphant, victorious.
seevis, sea-fish; deep-sea fish.
seevoël, sea-bird.
seevrag, freight.
seewaardig, (-e), seaworthy.
seewaarts, (to) seaward.
seewater, sea-water, brine.
seeweg, sea-, ocean-route.
seewier, sea-weed.
seewind, sea-wind, -breeze.
sefier, (-s, -e), zephyr.
seg, vide **sê**.
sege-..., vide **seë-**...
seggenskap, say, voice.
seggingskrag, power of expression, expressiveness, command of words.
segment, (-e), segment, piece.
segregasie, segregation.
segregeer, (ge-), segregate.
segsman, informant.
segswyse, expression, saying.
seidissel, suidissel, sow-, milk-thistle.
seil, (-e), n. sail; tarpaulin; canvas; awning; **alle – byset**, crowd on (pack on), all canvas (all sail); make every possible effort; **onder – gaan**, set (get under) sail; **'n oog in die – hou**, keep a watchful eye (on a person); **jou – na die wind hang**, trim one's sails to the wind.
seil, (ge-), sail.
seilboot, sailing-boat.
seildoek, sail-cloth, canvas; oil-cloth.
seilgaar, (-gare), sail-thread, twine.
seiljag, sailing-yacht.
seilnaald, sail-needle, packing-needle.
seilskip, sailing-vessel.
seilslak, nautilus.
seilsport, yachting.
seilstoel, canvas-chair, deck-chair.
seiltog, sailing-trip, sailing-expedition.
seilvaartuig, sailing-vessel.
seilvliegtuig, glider.
seilwedstryd, yacht-race, regatta.
sein, (-e), signal.
sein, (ge-), signal; wire, telegraph.
seiner, (-s), signalman, signaller.
seinfout, telegraphic error.
seingeër, signaller; starter (at races).
seinhuis(ie), singal-box, -cabin.
seinontvanger, receiver (telegr.).
seinpaal, signal-post, semaphore.
seinskoot, signal-gun.
seinstasie, signal-station, -post.
seintoestel, signalling apparatus; transmitting apparatus (instrument).
seinvlag, signal-flag.
seinvuur, signal-fire, fire-signal.
seinwagter, signalman.
seis, (-e), scythe.
seismograaf, (-grawe), seismograph (instrument); seismographer (person).
seismografie, seismography.
seismologie, seismology.
seisoen, (-e), season.
seisoenkaartjie, (anglisisme), season-ticket.
seisoenwinde, periodical winds.
sekans, (-ante), secant.
sekel, (-s), sickle.
sekelbos, sickle-bush.
sekelmaan(tjie), sickle-moon.
sekelstert, sickle-tail.
seker, (–, -e), a. certain; sure, positive; **'n –e Van Zyl**, a certain Van Zyl, one Van Zyl; **op –e dag**, one day.
seker, adv. sure(ly), certain(ly), for sure, for certain, probably; **weet jy dit –?**, are you sure (certain) of it, do you know it for certain?; **jy is jou lewe hier nie – nie**, your life is not safe here; **hy is tog – nie so dwaas nie!**, surely he is not as foolish as that!; **hy is nou – tevrede**, I suppose he is satisfied now; **hy sal dit nou – nie meer weet nie**, he probably won't remember it any more; **hy het – gedink ek is gek**, he must have thought me mad; **ek hoef – nie te sê nie** ..., I need scarcely say ...
sekere, n. the certain.
sekerheid, certainty; assurance; sureness, accuracy; surety; security, safety; **die – gee**, give the assurance; **met – sê**, say definitely (for certain).
sekerheidshalwe, for safety's sake, to make quite sure.
sekering, (-e, -s), fuse (elec.).
sekerlik, certainly, surely, for sure.
sekondant, (-e), seconder; second.
sekonde, (-s), second.

sekondeer, (ge-), second.
sekondêr, (-e), secondary.
sekondewys(t)er, second-hand.
sekretaresse, (pl. idem), (lady-)secretary.
sekretariaat, (-ate), secretariat(e), office of secretary; secretaryship.
sekretaris, (-se), secretary.
sekretarisvoël, secretary-bird.
sekse, (-s), sex.
seksie, (-s), section (also mil.).
seksiekolonne, section-column.
sekstant, (-e), sextant.
sekstet, (-te), sextet.
seksualiteit, sexuality.
sekseel, (-ele), sexual, sex-...
sektaries, (-e), sectarian.
sektaris, (-se), sectarian.
sekte, (-s), sect.
sektegees, sectarianism.
sekteskool, denominational school.
sektor, (-e, -s), sector.
sekularisasie, secularization.
sekulariseer, (ge-), secularize.
sekulêr, (-e), secular.
sekundus, (-se, -di), secundus; proxy.
sekuriteit, (-e), surety, security.
sekuur, (-, -kure), a. accurate, precise.
sekuur, adv. accurately, precisely, punctiliously; – weet, know positively.
sekwestrasie, sequestration.
sekwestreer, (ge-), sequestrate.
sel, (-le), cell.
selde, seldom, rarely, infrequently.
seldery, selery, celery.
seldsaam, (-same), rare, scarce.
seldsaamheid, rareness, scarceness; rarity, scarcity; curiosity.
selebreer, (ge-), celebrate.
selebriteit, (-e), celebrity.
selei, sjelei, jam; jelly.
selek, (-te), select, choice.
selekant, coelecanth.
seleksie, (-s), selection.
selektief, (-tiewe), selective.
selektiwiteit, selectivity.
selenium, selenium.
selery, seldery, celery.
self, n. self, ego.
self, pron. self; *ek (jy, hy, sy, hulle)* –, I myself (you yourself, he himself, she herself, they themselves); *ek het dit – gesien*, I saw it myself; *hy moet – kom*, he must come in person; *ek – het hom gesien*, I saw him myself; *dit spreek van –*, it is (only) natural, of course, naturally; *die beleefdheid –*, politeness itself.
selfaansitter, self-starter.
selfbedieningswinkel, supermarket.
selfbedrog, self-deceit (-deception).
selfbedwang, self-restraint.
selfbehae, self-complacency.
selfbeheersing, self-control, self-possession, self-mastery.
selfbehoud, self-preservation, self-defence.
selfbeskikking, self-determination.
selfbeskikkingsreg, right of self-determination.
selfbespieëling, -bespieëling, introspection.
selfbestemming, self-determination.
selfbestuur, self-government.
selfbevlekking, onanism.
selfbewus, (-te), self-conscious; self-confident, self-assured.
selfbewussyn, self-consciousness.
selfbewustheid, self-confidence.
selfbinder, self-binder.
selfde, same, identical.

selfgenoegsaam, self-sufficient.
selfgenoegsaamheid, self-sufficiency.
selfgevoel, self-regard.
selfheid, selfhood, personality.
selfkant, selvedge (salvage); border, fringe; *alkant –*, it is immaterial, it is all the same.
selfkastyding, self-chastisement.
selfkennis, self-knowledge.
selfmoord, suicide, self-murder.
selfmoordenaar, -moordenares, suicide, self-murderer (-murderess).
selfonderrig, self-tuition, self-education.
selfondersoek, self-examination.
selfopofferend, (-e), self-sacrificing.
selfopoffering, self-sacrifice.
selfoorwinning, self-conquest.
selfportret, self-portrait.
selfregerend, (-e), self-governing.
selfregering, self-government.
selfrespek, self-respect, self-esteem.
selfrespekterend, (-e), self-respecting.
selfs, even.
selfstandig, (-e), a. independent, autonomous, self-reliant; self-supporting; substantive, substantival; *-e naamwoord*, substantive noun.
selfstandigheid, independence, autonomy; substance.
selfsug, selfishness, egoism.
selfsugtig, (-e), selfish, egoistic.
selfsugtige, (-s), egoist, selfish person.
selfsugtigheid, selfishness, egoism.
selfveragting, self-contempt, self-scorn.
selfverblinding, self-deception.
selfverbranding, spontaneous combustion.
selfverdediging, self-defence.
selfvergoding, self-idolization.
selfverheerliking, self-glorification.
selfverheffing, self-exaltation.
selfverloëning, self-denial.
selfvernedering, self-abasement, self-humiliation.
selfvertoningsdrang, exhibitionism.
selfvertroue, self-confidence, self-reliance.
selfverwyt, self-reproach.
selfvoldaan, (-dane), self-complacent.
selfvoldaanheid, self-complacency.
selfvoldoening, self-satisfaction.
selfwerksaamheid, self-activity.
selibaat, celibacy.
selibatêr, (-e, -s), celibate, celibatarian.
sellulêr, (-e), cellular.
selluloïed, selluloïde, celluloid.
sellulose, cellulose.
selonspampoen, (common) field-pumpkin.
selonsroos, Ceylon-rose, oleander.
seloot, (-lote), zealot, fanatic.
selstof, cellulose.
selstraf, solitary confinement.
selvormig, (-e), cellular, cellulate.
selwand, cell-wall.
selweefsel, cellular tissue.
semantiek, semantics.
semanties, (-e), semantic, semasiological.
semelagtig, (-e), bran-like, branny.
semelbroek, shy fellow, gawk.
semelbrood, bran-bread, bran-loaf.
semelmeel, pollard.
semels, bran.
semelwater, bran-water, bran-gruel.
sement, n. cement.
sement, (ge-), cement.
sementfabriek, cement-factory.
semester, (-s), semester, term, half-year.
Semiet, (-e), Semite.
seminarie, (-s), seminary.
Semities, (-e), Semitic, Semite.

senaat, (-nate), senate.
senator, (-e), (-s), senator.
send, (ge-), send, dispatch; vide **stuur**.
sendbrief, epistle.
sendeling, (-e), missionary.
sender, (-s), sender, consignor.
sending, mission, consignment; buitelandse –, foreign mission.
sendinggenootskap, missionary-society.
sendingstasie, mission-station.
sendingwerk, missionary-work, mission-work.
seneblare, senna.
seng, (ge-), scorch, burn, singe.
seniel, (-e), senile.
seniliteit, senility.
sening, (-s), sinew, tendon.
seningrig, (-e), sinewy, stringy, tough.
senior, senior.
senioriteit, seniority.
Senior-Sertifikaat-eksamen, Senior Certificate (examination).
senit, zenith.
senna, senna.
senotaaf, (-tawe), cenotaph.
sens, (-e), scythe.
sensasie, (-s), sensation, thrill.
sensasieberig, sensational news.
sensasieroman, sensation(al) novel, thriller.
sensasiewekkend, (-e), sensational.
sensasioneel, (-nele), sensational.
sensitief, (-itiewe), sensitive.
sensitiwiteit, sensitivity, sensitiveness.
sensor, (-s), censor, licenser.
sensoreer, (ge-), censor.
sensualis, (-te), sensualist.
sensueel, (-suele), sensual.
sensureer, (ge-), censure; censor.
sensus, census.
sensuskantoor, census-office.
sensuur, censure; censorship; **onder – plaas**, forbid the use of the sacraments.
sent, (-e), cent.
sentenaar, (-s, -nare), hundredweight.
senter, (-s), centre (football).
sentigram, (-me), centigram.
sentiliter, (-s), centilitre.
sentiment, (-e), sentiment.
sentimentaliteit, sentimentality.
sentimenteel, (-tele), sentimental.
sentimeter, (-s), centimeter.
sentraal, (-trale), central.
sentrale, (-s), (telephone-)exchange; power-station.
sentralisasie, centralization.
sentraliseer, (ge-), centralize.
sentrifugaal, (-gale), centrifugal.
sentrum, (-s, -tra), centre.
senu(wee)-aandoening, affection of the nerves.
senu-aanval, nervous attack.
senu(wee)agtig, (-e), nervous, nervy.
senu(wee)agtigheid, nervousness.
senu-arts, senudokter, nerve-specialist.
senugestel, nervous system.
senu-insinking, nervous collapse (breakdown).
senuknoop, ganglion, nerve-knot.
senu(wee)kwaal, nervous disease.
senulyer, neuropath, neurotic.
senu(wee)-ontsteking, neuritis.
senu-pasiënt, neurotic, nerve-patient.
senu(wee)prikkeling, irritation (excitation) of the nerves.
senu(wee)pyn, neuralgia.
senusiek, (–, -e), neurotic.
senusiekte, nervous disease (disorder).
senuskok, nervous shock.

senu(wee)stelsel, nervous system.
senutoeval, nervous fit, hysterics.
senu(wee)trekking, nervous twitch.
senuwee, (-s), nerve; **sy het dit op haar –s gekry**, she got a fit of nerves, she fell into hysterics.
senuweefsel, nervous tissue.
senuwee-orrel, nervous person.
senuweepyn, -stelsel, -trekking, vide **senu-** ...
separasie, separation.
separatis, (-te), separatist.
separatisme, separatism.
separatisties, (-e), separatist.
seperig, (-e), soapy.
sepia, sepia.
September, September.
septer, (-s), sceptre.
septies, (-e), septic.
Septuagint(a), Septuagint.
seraf, (-im, -s), seraph.
serebraal, cerebraal, (-brale), cerebral.
seremonie, (-s), ceremony; (pl.) formalities, ceremonial.
seremonieel, (-niële), n. & a. ceremonial.
seremoniemeester, master of ceremonies.
serenade, (-s), serenade.
serge, sersje, serge.
serie, (-ë, -s), series; break (billiards).
serieus, (-e), serious, (in) earnest.
sering, (-e), lilac; **wilde –**, wild lilac.
serk, (-e), (tomb)stone.
sermeinpeer, (Saint) Germain-pear.
sermoen, (-e), sermon, homily, lecture.
seroet, (-e), (1) cheroot, cigar.
seroet, (-e), (2) (native) grain-basket.
serp, (-e), scarf, muffler, sash.
serpent, (-e), serpent, snake; vixen.
serpentyn, (-s), serpentine; streamer.
sersant, (-e), sergeant.
sersant-majoor, (-s), sergeant-major.
sersje, serge, serge.
sertifikaat, (-kate), certificate.
sertifiseer, (ge-), certify.
serum, (-s), serum.
servet, (-te), table-napkin, serviette.
servetring, napkin-ring, serviette-ring.
servies, (-e), (tea-)set, (dinner-)service.
servomotor, servo-motor.
Serwië, Serbia.
Serwiër, (-s), Serbian.
serwituut, (-tute), servitude, casement, claim, charge.
ses, (-se), six.
sesam, sesame.
sesde, (-s), sixth.
sesdelig, (-e), (consisting) of six parts.
sesdubbel(d), (-e), sixfold.
sesessie, secession.
seshoek, hexagon.
seshoekig, (-e), hexagonal, six-sided.
sesjarig, (-e), six years old; sexennial.
seskantig, (-e), six-sided, hexagonal.
seslaag, six-ply.
sesmaandeliks, (-e), six-monthly.
Sesoeto, Sesuto, Sotho.
sesreëlig, (-e), of six lines.
sessie, (-s), session.
sessie, (-s), cession.
sessionaris, (-se), cessionary, assign.
sessydig, (-e), six-sided, hexagonal.
sestal, (-le), six; **'n –**, about six.
sestallig, (-e), senary.
sestien, sixteen.
sestiende, (-s), sixteenth.
sestig, sixty; **jy is –**, you are silly.
sestigste, (-s), sixtieth.

sestigvoudig, (-e), sixtyfold.
sesvlak, hexahedron.
sesvlakkig, (-e), hexahedral.
sesvoetig, (-e), six-footed; hexametric.
sesvoud, sextuple; multiple of six.
sesvoudig, (-e), sixfold, sextuple.
set, (-te), n. move, trick; set; putt (golf); **'n slim –,** a clever move.
set (ge-), set, mount; set up, compose (type); **in goud ge–,** mounted in gold.
setel, (-s), seat (in parliament); throne; see (of pope); headquarters.
setel, (ge-), reside, be resident; have its headquarters (seat); sit.
setfout, misprint, printer's error.
sethaak, composing-stick; boat-hook.
setlaar, (-s), settler, immigrant.
setmasjien, composing-machine, linotype.
setmeel, starch, amylum, farina.
setmiddel, setting-lotion.
setsel, (-s), type, matter, composition.
setter, (-s), compositor.
settery, (-e), composing-room.
seun, (-s), son; boy, chap, sonny; **die –s en die meisies (dogters) moet apart speel,** the boys and the girls must play separately.
seur, (-s), sir, master.
seur, (ge-), bother, nag; delay, dawdle.
seurderig, (-e), bothersome; tedious.
seurkous, bore, bothersome person.
sewe, (-s), seven.
sewedubbel(d), (-e), sevenfold.
Sewegesternte, Pleiades.
sewehoek, heptagon.
sewehoekig, (-e), heptagonal.
sewejaartjie, (-s), everlasting.
sewejarig, (-e), of seven (years), seven year(s) old; seven years'; septennial; **S-e oorlog,** Seven Years War.
sewemaands, (-e), of seven months.
sewemylslaarse, seven-league boots.
sewende, seventh; **in die – hemel wees,** be in the seventh heaven.
sewentien, seventeen.
sewentiende, seventeenth.
sewentig, seventy.
sewentigjarig, (-e), septuagenarian, of seventy years, etc. Cf. **sewejarig.**
sewentigjarige, (-s), septuagenarian.
sewentigste, seventieth.
sewentigvoudig, (-e), seventyfold.
Sewester, Pleiades.
sewetal, (-le), seven; **'n –,** about seven.
sewetallig, (-e), septenary.
sewevoud, (-e), multiple of seven.
sewevoudig, (-e), sevenfold.
sfeer, (sfere), sphere; (fig.) region, domain.
sferies, (-e), spherical.
sfinks, (-e), sphinx.
sfinksagtig, (-e), sphinxlike.
siaan, cyanogen.
Siam, Siam.
Siamees, (-mese), Siamese; **– kat,** Siamese cat.
sianied, cyanide:
Siberië, Siberia.
Siberies, (-e), Siberian.
sibille, (-s), sibyl.
Siciliaans, (-e), Sicilian.
Sicilië, Sicily.
sidder, (ge-), shiver, tremble, shake.
siddering, (-e, -s), shudder, trembling.
sie!, brr!, ough!, pf!
sieal, fey, doomed.
siebie, (-s), puppy, doggy.
siedaar!, there!, lo!, behold!

siedend, (-e), seething, boiling.
sie-jy!, go (get) away!, **– opstaan!,** will you get up!, get up at once!
siek, ill, sick, diseased; **– word,** be taken ill, fall ill, sicken; **jou – lag,** laugh till you cry.
siekbed, sick-bed.
sieke, (-s), sick person, invalid, patient.
siekefonds, sick-fund.
sieke(n)huis, hospital.
sieke-inrigting, nursing-home, hospital.
siek(e)kamer, sick-room.
siekelys, sick-list.
siekerig, (-e), ailing.
siekestoel, invalid-chair.
sieketrooster, sick-comforter.
siek(e)verpleegster, (sick-)nurse.
siek(e)verpleging, nursing.
siek(e)kamer, sick-room.
sieklik, (-e), ailing, suffering, in bad health, sickly; morbid.
sieklikheid, sickliness; morbidity.
siekte, (-s), illness, sickness, indisposition, disease, malady; ill-health; **gedurende sy –,** during his illness.
siektebeskrywing, pathography.
siektedraer, disease-carrier.
siektegeval, case (of illness).
siektekiem, germ of disease.
siekteleer, pathology.
siekteverlof, sick-leave.
siekteverloop, course of a disease.
siekteverskynsel, symptom (of disease).
siek(e)verpleging, nursing.
siel, (-e), soul; heart; spirit, mind; **hy is met hart en – in sy werk,** he is heart and soul in his work; **dit doen my – goed,** it does my heart good; **die – van die onderneming,** the (life and) soul of the enterprise; **geen lewende – nie,** not a living soul; **'n skip met 200 –e aan boord,** a ship with 200 souls on board; **iemand se – uittrek,** tease, pull a person's leg; **'n goeie ou –,** a good old soul; **by my –,** upon my soul!
sieldodend, (-e), soul-deadening; dull.
sieleadel, nobility of soul (mind, heart).
sieleheil, salvation (of one's soul).
sieleleed, heartache, sorrow, affliction.
sielelewe, spiritual (inner) life.
sielepyn, vide **sieleleed.**
sielestryd, inward struggle.
sieletal, number (of souls).
sieletroos, spiritual comfort.
sielevrede, spiritual (mental) peace.
sielevreugde, soul's delight.
sielig, (-e), miserable, pitiful.
sieling, sjieling, (-s), shilling.
sielkunde, psychology.
sielkundig, (-e), psychological.
sielloos, (-lose), soulless; lifeless, dead.
sielroerend, (-e), soul-stirring; touching.
sielsaandoening, emotion.
sielsangs, anguish (of the soul), agony.
sielsbedroef, (-de), distressed in mind.
sielsbegeerte, heart's desire.
sielsbeminde, dearly beloved.
sielsbly, heartily glad, overjoyed.
sielsgenot, soul's delight, joy.
sielsgesteldheid, state of mind.
sielsiek, (-e), mentally diseased; sick in mind, soul-sick.
sielsiekte, (-s), mental patient.
sielsiekte, mental disease (disorder).
sielskrag, strength of mind (soul).
sielskwelling, mental torment.
siel(e)smart, vide **sieleleed.**
sielsrus, peace of mind, spiritual peace.

sielstoestand, state of mind.
sielstrelend, (-e), gratifying to the soul.
sielstryd, vide **sielestryd**.
sielsverdriet, deep sorrow, affliction.
sielsverhuising, transmigration of the soul.
sielsverlange, heart's desire.
sielsverrukking, -vervoering, ecstasy, rapture, trance.
sielsverwantskap, affinity of soul.
sielsvriend(in), soul-mate, close friend.
sieltjie, (-s), (little) soul; – **sonder sorg**, happy-go-lucky person.
sieltogend, (-e), dying.
sielverheffend, (-e), inspiring, exalting.
sielverkoper, crimp.
siembamba, simbamba (picnic-dance).
sien, (ge-), see; notice, perceive, distinguish, make out; **jy kon geen hand voor jou oë – nie**, you could not see a thing; – **jy nou!**, I told you so!, there you are!; **ons sal –**, we shall see; – **(kyk) bo (bladsy 20)**, see above (page 20); **laat –**, show; **daar is niks te – nie**, there is nothing to be seen (to see); **iets te – kry**, get a sight (view) of something; **deur die vingers –**, overlook, condone; **die lewenslig –**, see the light, be born; **die lig –**, appear in print, be published; **die wêreld –**, see life, see something of the world; **iets oor die hoof –**, overlook (not notice) a thing; **dit was laaste – van-die blikkantien**, we never clapped eyes on him again.
siende, seeing; – **blind wees**, see and not perceive; **die blindes – maak**, make the blind see.
sienderoë, visibly, perceptibly.
siener, (-s), seer, prophet; visionary.
sienersblik, prophetic eye.
sienlik, (-e), visible, perceptible.
siens: tot –, so long, bye-bye, cheerio!
sienswyse, opinion, way of thinking.
sieps-en-braaibout, licking, thrashing.
sier, n. whit; **geen – nie**, not a whit.
sier, (ge-), decorate, adorn, embellish.
sieraad, ornament, trinket.
sier-ertjie, sweet pea.
sierkuns, decorative art.
sierlik, (-e), graceful, elegant.
sierlikheid, gracefulness, elegance.
sierplant, decorative plant.
siersel, (-s), decoration, ornament.
siertjie, (-s), whit, bit.
sies!, bah!, phew!, sis!
siësta, (-s), siesta, midday-nap.
sif, (-te, siwwe), sieve, strain, screen, sift.
sif, (ge-), sieve, strain, screen, sift.
sifdraad, (fine), gauze, wire-netting.
sifilis, syphilis.
sifilities, (-e), syphilitic.
sifon, (-s), siphon.
sifsel, (-s), sifting(s).
sifting, (-e, -s), sifting.
sig, n. sight, view; **in –**, in sight; **op – stuur**, send on appro(val); **wissel op –**, bill payable at sight.
sig, pron. oneself (him-, her-, -itself, themselves).
sigaar, (-gare), cigar.
sigaar-as, cigar-ash(es).
sigaar, sigarefabriek, cigar-factory.
sigaar-, sigarehandel, cigar-trade.
sigaar-, sigarehandelaar, tobacconist, cigar-merchant.
sigaar-, sigarekissie, cigar-box.
sigaarknipper, cigar-cutter.
sigaarkoker, cigar-case.
sigare ..., vide **sigaar ...**
sigaret, (-te), cigarette.
sigaret-aansteker, cigarette lighter.
sigaret-as, cigarette-ash(es).

sigaretbeentjies, spindle-shanks.
sigaretdosie, cigarette-box.
sigaretkoker, cigarette-case.
sigbaar, (-bare), a. & adv. visible; perceptible; clear, manifest; **hy was – aangedaan**, he was visibly moved.
sigbaarheid, visibility; perceptibility.
Sigeuner, (-s), gipsy.
Sigeunerin, (-ne), gipsy(-woman).
sigorei, chicory.
sigsag, zig-zag.
sigsag-blits, forked (chain) lightning.
sigself, oneself, itself (him-, herself, themselves); **op –**, in (by) itself.
sigwissel, sight-draft.
sikade, (-s), cicada.
sikkel, (-s), shekel.
siklies, (-e), cycle.
sikloïde, (-s), cycloid.
sikloon, (-lone), cyclone.
sikloop, (-lope), cyclop(s).
siklotron, cyclotron.
siklus, (-se, -kli), cycle.
siks: by my –!, upon my soul!
sikspens, (-e), sixpence; **lyk soos 'n splinternuwe –**, be as neat as a new pin; look nobby, be dressed up to the nines.
Silesië, Silesia.
Silesiër, (-s), Silesian.
Silesies, (-e), Silesian.
silhoeët, (-te), silhouette.
silhoeëteer, (ge-), silhouette.
silikaat, silicate.
silikon, silicon.
silikose, silicosis.
silinder, (-s), cylinder.
silinderpers, roller-press.
silindervormig, (-e), cylindrical.
silindries, (-e), cylindrical.
sillabe, (-e), syllable.
sillabies, (-e), syllabic.
sillabus, (-se), syllabus.
silt, (-e), briny, saltish.
silwer, silver; silverplate; silver coin.
silweraar, silver-vein.
silweragtig, (-e), silvery, silver.
silwerblad, silver-leaf, silver-foil.
silwerboom, silver-tree.
silwerbrokaat, silver-brocade.
silwerbruilof, silver wedding.
silwererts, silver-ore.
silwergehalte, percentage of silver.
silwergeld, silver coin (money).
silwergrys, silver(y) grey.
silwerkleurig, (-e), silver-coloured.
silwerling, (-e), silverling, silver coin.
silwermyn, silver-mine.
silweroplossing, silver-solution.
silwerpapier, silver-paper; tinfoil.
silwerpoeier, silver-dust; silvo.
silwerservies, silver-set, plate-set.
silwerskoon, as bright as silver; spotlessly clean.
silwersmid, silversmith.
silwerstuk, silver piece (coin).
silwervis, silver-fish.
silwervos, silver-fox.
silwerwerk, silverware.
simbaal, (-bale), cymbal.
simboliek, symbolism.
simbolies, (-e), symbolic(al).
simboliseer, (ge-), symbolise.
simbool, (-bole), symbol, emblem.
simfonie, (-ë), symphony.
simfonies, (-e), symphonic.
simmetrie, symmetry.

simmetries, (-e), symmetric(al).
simonie, simony.
simpateties, (-e), sympathetic (pain).
simpatie, (-ë), sympathy.
simpatiek, (-e), sympathetic.
simpaties, (-e), sympathetic (nerve).
simpatiseer, (ge-), sympathize (with).
simpel, (-e), silly, foolish, doting, dotty, simple, plain; mere.
simpelheid, silliness, dottiness.
simplisties, (-e), simple, superficial.
simptoom, (-tome), symptom.
Simson, Samson.
simuleer, (ge-), simulate.
sin, (-ne), n. sense; mind; wish, liking, taste, fancy; sentence; meaning; **die –ne**, the senses; **al jou –ne bymekaar hou**, keep one's head, be alert; **'n – vir humor**, a sense of humour; **hy het geen – vir kos nie**, he has no liking for food; **jou – kry**, have your way; **iemand sy – gee**, let one have one's way; **hy het geen – in die huis nie**, the house is not to his liking (taste); **as jy daar – in het**, if you like (care) to, if it is to your liking; **die – het geen – nie**, the sentence has no meaning; **nie goed by sy –ne wees nie**, not be in his right mind (senses); **weer by sy –ne kom**, return to consciousness; return to one's senses; **in letterlike –**, in a literal sense; **in sekere –**, in a (certain) sense, in a way; **iets in die – hê**, have in mind, drive at, be up to; **dit was so reg na my –**, that was exactly what I wanted; **ek kon geen hoed na my – kry nie**, I could not get a hat to suit me; **teen my –**, against (contrary) to my wishes; **ek het dit baie teen my – gedoen**, I did it very reluctantly; **hy is heeltemal van sy –ne**, he is quite out of his mind; **eens van – wees**, be of one (a) mind; **van –(s) wees**, intend, purpose.
sin, (ge-), muse, meditate, ponder.
sinagoge, (-s), synagogue.
sinchroonskakeling, synchromesh.
sindelik, (-e), clean, tidy; proper; serviceable.
sindelikheid, clean(li)ness, tidiness.
sindikaat, (-kate), syndicate, ring.
sindikalisme, syndicalism.
sinds, since; for; **– lank**, for a long time.
sindsdien, since.
sinekuur, sinecure.
sing, (ge-), sing; **die ketel –**, the kettle sings; **vals –**, sing false (out of tune), go flat; **aan die slaap –**, sing to sleep.
Singalees, (-lese), Cingalese, Ceylonese.
singenot, sensual enjoyment.
singer, (-s), singer.
sing-sing, singing; **– loop**, go singing.
sinies, (-e), ceynic(al).
sinikus, (-se), cynic.
sinisme, cynicism.
sinjaal, (-ale), signal, sign.
sinjaleer, (ge-), signal; signalize; point out, draw attention to.
sinjeur, (-s), fellow; sir, mister.
sink, n. zinc; galvanized iron.
sink, (ge-), sink; **sy moed het ge–**, his courage sank; **die skip het ge–**, the ship sank (went down, foundered); **die moed laat –**, lose courage; **'n skip laat –**, sink (scuttle) a ship; **in die niet –**, vanish into nothingness.
sinkdak, galvanized iron roof.
sinkdruk, zincography.
sinkerts, zinc-ore.
sinkhoudend, (-e), zinciferous.
sinkingkoors, rheumatic fever.
sinkings, neuralgia, rheumatic pains, rheumatism.

sinklaag, zinc-layer.
sinklood, sinker, sink.
sinkopasie, ragtime, syncopation.
sinkopee, syncope, elision, syncopation.
sinkopeer, (ge-), syncopate.
sinkplaat, n. (sheet of) galvanised (corrugated) iron; zinc-plate (elec.).
sinkplaat, a. corrugated; **die pad is baie –**, the road is badly corrugated.
sinkput, cess-pool, drainage-well.
sinksalf, zinc-ointment.
sinkspaat, zinc-spar.
sinksulfaat, zinc-sulphate.
sinledig, (-e), meaningless, nonsensical.
sinlik, (-e), sensual, carnal.
sinlikheid, sensuality, sensualism.
sinloos, (-lose), meaningless, senseless.
sinloosheid, senselessness.
sinnebeeld, emblem, symbol.
sinnebeeldig, (-e), symbolic(al).
sinnelik, (-e), of the senses, sensory.
sinnelikheid, sensuousness.
sinneloos, mad, insane, senseless.
sinnespel, morality-play.
sinnigheid, liking, inclination, fancy, mind; **geen – in hê nie**, have no mind to (inclination for).
sinodaal, (-dale), synodal, synodic(al).
sinode, (-s), synod.
sinoniem, (-e), n. synonym.
sinoniem, (-e), synonymous.
sinryk, (-e), full of (pregnant with) meaning, terse, significant.
sinrykheid, terseness, significance.
sinsbedrog, hallucination, illusion.
sinsbegogeling, delusion.
sinsbou, construction (of a sentence); syntax.
sinsdeel, part of a sentence, phrase.
sinsnede, clause, phrase, expression.
sinsontleding, analysis (of sentences).
sinspeel, (ge-), allude; **– op**, allude to.
sinspeling, allusion (to), hint (at).
sinspreuk, motto, maxim, device.
sinsteurend, **-storend**, (-e), confusing.
sinsverband, context.
sinsverbystering, bewilderment, stupefaction, daze; mental derangement.
sinswending, (turn of) phrase.
sint, (-e), saint.
sintaksis, syntax.
sintakties, (-e), syntactic(al).
sintel, (-s), cinder.
Sinterklaas, Santa Claus.
sintese, synthesis.
sinteties, (-e), synthetic(al).
sintuig, sense-organ, (organ of) sense; **sintuiglik**, (-e), sensory, sense- . . . ; **–e waarneming**, sense-perception.
sinus, (-se), sine, sinus.
sinverwant, (-e), synonymous.
Sion, Zion.
Sionisme, Zionism.
sipier, (-e, -s), gaoler, warder.
sipres(boom), cypress(-tree).
Sire, Sire, Your Majesty.
sirene, (-s), siren.
sirenesang, siren's song.
sirkel, (-s), circle, ring.
sirkelboog, arc of a circle.
sirkelgang, **-loop**, circular course, circle.
sirkelomtrek, circumference of a circle.
sirkelsaag, circular saw, buzz-saw.
sirkelsegment, segment of a circle.
sirkelvormig, (-e), circular.
sirkulasie, circulation.
sirkuleer, (ge-), circulate.

sirkulêre, (-s), circular (letter).
sirkumfleks, (-e), circumflex.
sirkus, (-se), circus.
sirokko, (-'s), sirocco.
sis, n. chintz, print.
sis, (ge-), hiss; sizzle.
sisal, sisal(-grass, -hemp).
sisklank, hiss, hissing sound, sibilant.
sisteem, (-teme), system, method.
sistematies, (-e), systematic(al).
sistematiseer, (ge-), systematize.
sit, n. comfortable sitting position; **hy kon sy – nie kry nie**, he could not strike a comfortable sitting position.
sit, (ge-), sit; put, place, stand; set; **bly –**, remain sitting (seated); fail; **in die modder bly –**, stick in the mud; **gaan –**, sit down, take a seat; **weer gaan –**, sit down again, resume one's seat; **die pak – goed**, the suit fits well; **die stoel – lekker**, the chair is comfortable; **hy – daar goed in**, he is comfortably off; **daar – die moeilikheid**, that is where the difficulty lies, there lies the rub; **tuis –**, stay at home; **daar – modder op jou skoene**, there is mud on your boots; **die boom – vol vrugte**, the tree is laden with fruit; **– en lees**, sit reading; **die Parlement (Sinode) –**, Parliament (the Synod) sits (is in session); **daar – iets 'ter**, there is something behind it; **agter iets aan –**, be after something; **in die moeilikheid –**, be in difficulty; **dit – in nie hom (sy broek) nie**, he hasn't got it in him; **dit – in die bloed (familie)**, it runs in the blood (family); **in die tronk –**, be in prison; put (throw) in prison; **in die koerant –**, put in the paper; **op musiek –**, set to music; **die besem teen die muur –**, put (stand) the broom against the wall; **uit die huis –**, eject from the house.
sitaat, (-tate), quotation, citation.
sitadel, (-le), citadel.
sitasie, (-s), citation.
sitbad, sitz-bath, hip-bath.
sitbank, seat, bench; settee.
sitdag, day of sitting (session).
siteer, (ge-), quote; cite (law).
siter, (-s), 1. citron.
siter, (-s), 2. cither.
sitkamer, drawing-room, sitting-room.
sito-sito, quick(ly), in no time.
sitplaas, -plek, seat; **die saal het – vir 1,000 mense**, the hall can seat 1,000 people.
sitroen, (-e), citron.
sitroenkleur, lemon-colour.
sitroenolie, citron-oil, lemon-oil.
sitroensuur, citric acid.
sitronella, citronella.
sitrus, citrus.
sitrusboerdery, citrus-culture.
sit-sit, (-e, -s), sitting; **– eet**, eat sitting; **– loop**, walk with an occasional rest.
sitstaking, sit-down strike.
sitstok, shooting-stick.
sittend, (-e), sitting, seated, sedentary.
sitter, (-s), sitter.
sitting, (-e, -s), sitting, session; seat, bottom (of a chair); **– hê in die raad**, have a seat on the Board; **die hof sal daar – hou**, the court will sit (hold session) there.
sittingsdag, day of session, sitting-day.
sittyd, (time of) session (sitting); term (of imprisonment).
situasie, (-s), situation, position.
situeer, (ge-), situate.
sitvlak, bottom, seat, buttocks.
sivet(kat), civet(-cat).
siviel, (-e), civil; **-e gyseling (reg, saak)**, civil imprisonment (law, action); **-e ingenieur**, civil engineer.
sjaal, (sjale), shawl, wrap.
sjabloneer, (ge-), stencil.
sjabloon, (-lone), pattern, stencil.
sjampanje, champagne.
sjarmant, (-e), charming.
sjarme, charm.
sjees, (ge-), send down, expel; fail.
sjef, (-s), chef (cook); chief.
sjeik, (-s), sheik(h).
sjelei, selei, jelly; jam.
sjerrie, sherry.
sjibbolet, (-s, -te), shibboleth.
sjiek, chic, (-, -e), chic, smart.
sjieling, sieling, (-s), shilling.
sjimpansee, (-s), chimpanzee.
Sjina, China.
Sjinees, Chinese.
sjokola(de), chocolate, cocoa; chocolates; **'n doos –**, a box of chocolates.
sjor, (ge-), lash, strap.
sjou, (ge-), drag, lug; carry.
sj(uu)t!, hist!, hush!
skaad, (ge-), harm, damage.
skaaf, (skawe), n. plane.
skaaf, skawe, (ge-), plane, smooth; rub, scrape, abrade, bark (one's skin).
skaafbank, carpenter's bench.
skaafmes, plane-iron.
skaafplek, abrasion, gall (on horse).
skaafsel, (-s), shaving.
skaafwond, gall, abrasion.
skaai, (ge-), pinch, pilfer.
skaak, n. chess; **– sit**, check.
skaak, (ge-), 1, play chess; check.
skaak, (ge-), 2. abduct, run off with.
skaakbord, chess-board; chequer.
skaakmat, checkmate; **jou opponent – sit**, (check-)mate your opponent.
skaakspel, (game of) chess; chess-board.
skaakspeler, chess-player.
skaakstuk, piece, chessman.
skaal, (skale), scale, pair of scales, balance; **die – laat oorslaan**, turn the scale; **op 'n – van 1 : 8**, to a scale of 1 : 8; **op groot –**, on a large (vast) scale; **op – geteken**, drawn to scale.
skaaldier, crustacean, shell-fish.
skaalverdeling, scale-division.
skaam, a. shy, bashful; ashamed.
skaam, (ge-), feel (be) ashamed, feel shame; **– jou!**, shame on you!, for shame!, fie!; **jy moet (behoort) jou te –**, you ought to be ashamed of yourself; **jou oor iets –**, be ashamed of something; **ek het my byna dood ge–**, I nearly died of shame; **ek – my die oë uit die kop**, I feel terribly ashamed.
skaamagtig, (-e), bashful, shy.
skaambeen, pubis, pubic bone.
skaamblom, mountain-rose, Protea rosacea.
skaamdele, private parts.
skaamheid, bashfulness, shyness.
skaamte, (sense of) shame; bashfulness, shyness; modesty; **het jy geen – nie?**, have you no sense of shame?
skaamtegevoel, sense of shame.
skaamteloos, (-lose), shameless.
skaamteloosheid, shamelessness.
skaap, (skape), sheep (also fig.); **een brandsiek – steek die hele trop aan**, one scabby sheep infects the whole flock, one rotten apple spoils the whole basket; **daar gaan baie mak skape in 'n kraal**, good sardines pack well; **die bokke van die skape skei**, separate the sheep from the goats.

skaapafval, (sheep's) tripe (and trotters).
skaapagtig, (-e), sheepish, sheeplike.
skaapboer, sheep-farmer.
skaapboerdery, sheep-farming.
skaapbos(sie), sheep-bush.
skaapboud, leg of mutton.
skaapherder, shepherd.
skaapkop, sheep's head; blockhead.
skaapkraal, sheep-kraal, sheep-fold, -pen.
skaaplam, lamb.
skaapluis, sheep-tick, -louse, ked.
skaapmis, sheep-dung, sheep-manure.
skaapooi, ewe.
skaapram, ram, tup.
skaaprib, sheep's rib.
skaapribbetjie, sheep's rib; rib-chops.
skaapskeerder, sheep-shearer.
skaapskêr, sheep-shears.
skaapsklere, sheep's clothing; 'n wolf in –, a wolf in sheep's clothing.
skaapsteker, rhombic, "sheep-sticker".
skaapvag, sheep's fleece.
skaapvel, sheepish.
skaapvlees, -vleis, mutton.
skaapwagter, shepherd.
skaapwagtertjie, capped wheat ear.
skaapwol, sheep's wool.
skaar, (skare), n. 1. (plough-)share.
skaar, (skare), n. 2. notch, chip; die lem het 'n –, the blade is notched (chipped).
skaar, (skare), skare, (-s), n. 3. crowd, host, multitude.
skaar, (ge-), range, draw up; sig – aan die sy van, range oneself on the side of, take the side of, join the ranks of.
skaars, (–, -e), a. scarce, rare; scanty.
skaars, adv. scarcely, hardly.
skaarsheid, scarcity, scantiness, paucity.
skaarste, scarcity, want.
skaats, (-e), skate, rink.
skaats, (ge-), skate.
skaatsbaan, skating ring.
skaatsry, (skaatsge-), skate, rink.
skaatsryer, skater, rinker.
skade, 1. damage, harm, injury, detriment, loss; – aanrig (doen), cause (do) damage, do harm; – ly, suffer (a loss), lose; deur – en skande word mens wys, experience makes fools wise; dis 'n hele – in die boedel, that is quite a loss; ver van jou goed, naby jou –, the eye of the master makes the horse fat.
skade, 2. shadow, shade.
skadelik, (-e), harmful, prejudicial, injurious, detrimental, noxious.
skadelikheid, harmfulness, injuriousness.
skadeloos, (-lose), harmless; iemand – stel, make reparations to, indemnify (compensate) someone.
skadeloosstelling, indemnification, reparation, compensation, reimbursement.
skadepos, loss, debit-entry.
skadevergoeding, indemnification, compensation, damages; – eis, claim damages, sue for damages.
skadu, (-'s), shadow; in die – stel, throw into the shade, outshine, eclipse.
skadubeeld, silhouette.
skadukant, shady side, dark side.
skaduloos, (-lose), shadowless.
skaduryk, n. realm of shades.
skaduryk, (-e), a. shady, shadowy.
skadusy, shady side, dark side.
skaduwee, (-s), shadow; nie in iemand se – kan staan nie, not be fit to hold a candle to someone.

skaduweekant, shadowy (shaded) side, shady side.
skaf, (ge-), furnish, give, provide.
skafie, (-s), small plane.
skaflik, vide skaplik.
skaftyd, -uur, knocking-off time.
skag, (-te), shaft (of mine, arrow); quill (of feather); shank (of anchor).
skakeer, (ge-), variegate, shade.
skakel, (-s), n. link; half-back (rugby); los-, stand-off half, fly-half.
skakel, (ge-), connect; switch (elec.); dial (teleph.).
skakelaar, (-s), switch.
skakelbord, switch-board.
skaker, (-s), abductor; chess-player.
skakering, (-e, -s), shade, nuance.
skaking, (-e, -s), abduction; elopement.
skalks, (-e), arch, roguish.
skalmei, (-e), reed-pipe, shawm.
skalpeermes, scalping-knife.
skalpel, (-s), scalpel.
skamel, (-s), n. footstool; bogie [of wag(g)on, truck]; transom.
skamel, (–, -e), a. poor, meagre, scanty, humble.
skamelbout, king-pin.
skamelheid, humbleness, scantiness.
skamelkar, springless cart.
skamerig, (-e), shy, bashful.
skamerigheid, shyness, bashfulness.
skamper, (–, -e), scornful, bitter.
skandaal, (-dale), scandal, disgrace.
skandalig, (-e), scandalous, disgraceful.
skandaliseer, (ge-), scandalise, shock.
skanddaad, outrage, scandalous deed.
skande, shame, disgrace, ignominy, reproach; armoede is geen – nie, poverty is no disgrace; in die – steek, disgrace, bring disgrace upon; put to shame; te – maak, put to shame; tot – strek, be a disgrace (reproach) to.
skandeer, (ge-), scan.
skandelik, (-e), disgraceful, shameful, scandalous, outrageous.
skandelikheid, disgracefulness.
skandering, scansion.
Skandinawië, Scandinavia.
Skandinawiër, (-s), Scandinavian.
Skandinawies, (-e), Scandinavian.
skandmerk, (-e), stigma.
skandpaal, pillory.
skandvlek, n. stigma, disgrace.
skandvlek, (ge-), brand, disgrace.
skans, (-e), rampart, bulwark, entrenchment, trench.
skansgrawer, sapper, trench-digger.
skanspale, palisade.
skapie, (-s), little sheep, lamb; my –, my lamb (darling, sweet); –s bymekaar ja, join in marriage; hy het sy –s op die droë, he has feathered his nest (made his pile).
skaplik, (-e), reasonable, fair, tolerable.
skaplikheid, reasonableness, fairness.
skapulier, (-e), scapular(y).
skarabee, (-beë), scarab.
skare, (-s), skaar, (skare), crowd, host, multitude.
skarlaken, scarlet.
skarlakenkoors, scarlet fever, scarlatina.
skarlakenrooi, scarlet.
skarnier, (-e), hinge.
skarniergewrig, hinge-joint, ginglymus.
skarrel, (ge-), search, rummage, ransack, philander, chase.
skarrelaar, (-s), dangler, chaser.
skat, (-te), treasure, wealth; darling.
skat, (ge-), estimate (number), value, assess

(property); esteem, appreciate; ek – die afstand op tweehonderd tree, I judge the distance to be two hundred yards; hoe hoog – jy die waarde van die eiendom?, at what (figure) do you value the property?; iemand hoog –, to esteem a person highly; te hoog –, overestimate, overrate; te laag –, underestimate, underrate.
skatbaar, (-bare), ratable, taxable.
skatbewaarder, treasurer.
skater, (ge-), roar with laughter, burst out laughing.
skaterlag, n. burst (peal) of laughter.
skaterlag, (ge-), roar with laughter.
skatgrawer, treasure-digger, -hunter.
skatjie, (-s), little dear (darling).
skatkamer, treasure-chamber, treasury, treasure-house (fig.), storehouse.
skatkis, treasure-chest; state-coffers, treasury, exchequer.
skatkisbiljet, treasury-bill; treasury-voucher, -note, -order, warrant-voucher.
skatkiswissel, treasury-bill.
skatlam, dearest, darling.
skatlik, (-e), dear, darling.
skatpligtig, (-e), tributary.
skatryk, very wealthy (rich).
skatter, (-s), appraiser, valuator.
skattig, (-e), dear, sweet.
skatting, (-e, -s), estimate, valuation; esteem; estimation; tribute.
skavot, (-te), scaffold.
skawe, (ge-), vide skaaf, (ge-).
skede, (-s), sheath; vagina.
skedel, (-s), skull, cranium.
skedelboor, trepan.
skedelbreuk, fracture of the skull.
skedelhuid, pericranium, scalp.
skedelkundige, craniologist, phrenologist.
skedelleer, craniology, phrenology.
skedelnaat, cranial suture.
skeef, (skewe), a. crooked, skew; oblique (angle, axis); sloping; distorted; skew, squinting (eyes); troddendown (heels); skewe voorstelling, misrepresentation; 'n skewe gesig trek, pull a wry face.
skeef, adv. crooked, askew, awry, amiss, wrong; – aankyk, look at askance, look on with distrust; – loop, walk lop-sidedly; (fig.) go wrong; jou das sit –, your tie is not straight (is skew); die hout begin – trek, the wood begins to warp; – voorstel, misrepresent.
skeefheid, crookedness, obliqueness.
skeel, a. & adv. squinting, squint-eyed; cock-eyed; – kyk, squint.
skeel, (ge-), differ; matter; dit – baie, it makes a great difference; dit – nie veel nie, there is little difference; dit het nie veel ge- nie of hy was gedood, he was within an ace of being killed; dit kan my nie – nie, I don't care (mind); wat – jou?, what is the matter (is wrong) with you?
skeelheid, squint, squinting, strabismus.
skeelkant, blind side; aan die –, on the blind side.
skeeloog, n. squint-eye, cock-eye.
skeen, (skene), shin; 'n blou – kry (oploop), get the mitten, be refused.
skeenbeen, shin-bone.
skeenskut, shin-guard.
skeepgaan, (skeepge-), embark.
skeepsagent, shipping-agent.
skeepsbemanning, crew, (ship's) company.
skeepsberigte, shipping-news.
skeepsbeskuit, ship('s) biscuit.
skeepsbou, shipbuilding.
skeepsboukundig, (-e), naval; –e ingenieur, naval architect.

skeepsboukundige, (-s), naval architect.
skeepsdokter, ship's surgeon.
skeepshelling, shipway, slipway.
skeepshorlosie, -oorlosie, chronometer.
skeepsjoernaal, ship's journal, log.
skeepskameraad, shipmate.
skeepskanon, naval gun.
skeepskaptein, ship('s) captain, skipper.
skeepskok, ship's cook.
skeepskompas, mariner's compass.
skeepslading, shipload.
skeepsmaat, shipmate.
skeepsmag, naval force(s), navy.
skeepsoffisier, ship's officer.
skeepspapiere, ship's papers.
skeepsramp, shipping-disaster.
skeepsreg, maritime law; derde maal is –, third time does the trick.
skeepsruim, ship's hold.
skeepsruimte, (cargo-)space, carrying capacity, tonnage.
skeepstimmerman, ship's carpenter.
skeepstimmerwerf, shipyard, dockyard.
skeepsvolk, crew; sailors.
skeepsvrag, shipment, shipload; freight.
skeepswerf, shipyard, dockyard.
skeepvaart, navigation; shipping, marine.
skeepvaartkunde, (science of) navigation.
skeepvaartlyn, shipping, shipping-line.
skeepvaartmaatskappy, shipping-company.
skeer, (ge-), shave (the beard), shear (wool), cut, trim (hair); – oor die water, skim the water.
skeerbekmuis, shrew(-mouse).
skeerder, (-s), shearer; barber, shaver.
skeergereedskap, -goed, shaving-set (-things).
skeergerei, shaving-kit.
skeerhok, shearing-pen.
skeerkwas, shaving-brush.
skeerlemmetjie, (safety razor-)blade.
skeermes, razor; (razor-)blade.
skeerriem, (razor-)strop.
skeersalon, shaving-saloon.
skeerseep, shaving-soap.
skeersel, clip (of wool); shearings.
skeertoestel, shaver.
skeertyd, shearing-season; time to shave.
skeervlug, hedge-hopping.
skeerwinkel, barber's shop.
skei, (-e), yoke-pin, skey.
skei(e), (ge-), part, divide, separate, divorce; hy het van sy vrou ge–, he obtained a divorce from his wife, he divorced his wife; van tafel en bed –, be divorced from bed and board.
skei(d)baar, (-bare), separable.
skeiding, (-e, -s), parting, division, separation; divorce; boundary; partition; – van tafel en bed, divorce from bed and board, judicial separation.
skei(ds)brief, bill of divorcement.
skeid(ing)slyn, dividing line, line of demarcation, boundary.
skeidsgereg, court of arbitration.
skeidsmuur, partition-wall, dividing wall; (fig.) barrier.
skeidsregter, n. referee, umpire; arbitrator.
skeidsregterlik, (-e), arbitral.
skeidsweg, cross-roads.
skeie, vide skei(e).
skeikunde, chemistry.
skeikundig, (-e), chemical.
skeikundige, (-s), chemist; analyst.
skel, (-le), n. bell; vide skelle.
skel, (-le), a. shrill (voice); glaring.
skel, (ge-), ring.
skel, (ge-), scold, abuse, call names.

skel(d)naam, nickname; abusive name.
skel(d)woord, term of abuse, abusive word; **-e**, abuse, abusive language.
skelet, (-te), skeleton.
skelheid, shrillness; glaringness, glare.
skelklinkend, (-e), shrill.
skellak, shellac.
skelle, (pl.), scales; **die – (skille) het hom van die oë geval**, the scales fell from his eyes.
skelling, (-s), twopence farthing.
skelm, (-s), rogue, rascal, knave, cunning (sly) person, thief.
skelm, a., sly, knavish, roguish, cunning; dishonest; furtive.
skelmagtig, (-e), dishonest, knavish.
skelmagtigheid, knavishness, dishonesty.
skelmery, (-e), dishonesty.
skelmpies, slyly, furtively.
skelm-skelm, furtively.
skelmstreek, -stuk, piece of dishonesty, underhand (sharp) dealing.
skel(d)naam, nickname; abusive name.
skelvis, haddock.
skel(d)woord, vide **skeldwoord**.
skema, (-s), scheme, outline, plan.
skematies, (-e), schematic, in outline.
skemer, n. dusk, twilight.
skemer, a., dusky, dim.
skemer, (ge-), grow dusk; dawn; glimmer, gleam, shine faintly.
skemeraand, twilight, dusk.
skemeragtig, (-e), dusky, shadowy, dim.
skemerdag, dawn.
skemerdonker, n., dusk, twilight.
skemerdonker, a., dusky, shadowy.
skemering, dusk, twilight; dawn.
skemerkelkie, sundowner.
skemerlamp, shaded lamp.
skemerlig, twilight; dawn; dim light.
skend, (ge-), disfigure, mutilate; violate; profane, desecrate; transgress (the law); defile, sully; break (the law, the Sabbath).
skendbrief, defamatory letter.
skender, skinder, (ge-), slander, backbite, gossip, talk scandal.
skenderaar, skinderaar, (-s), slanderer, backbiter, scandalmonger.
skenderbek, skinderbek, slanderer; scandalmonger gossip.
skenderpraatjies, skinderpraatjies, slander, backbiting, scandal, gossip.
skendertong, skindertong, vide **skenderaar**.
skending, violation, mutilation.
skenk, (ge-), give, grant, present (endow) with, make a gift of.
skenkelbeen, (-s), shank, femur.
skenker, (-s), donor, giver.
skenking, (-e, -s), grant, gift, endowment, donation.
skenkingsfonds, endowment fund.
skennis, violation, desecration.
skep, (-pe), n. scoop, ladle, shovel; spoonful (ladleful, spadeful): helping.
skep, (ge-), 1. scoop, ladle, dish up: bail (out of a boat); **Sannie het gaan water –**, S. has gone to fetch water; **vol –**, fill (up).
skep, (ge-), 2. create; establish, set-up.
skepbak, ladle, bucket, scoop.
skepdoel, drop-goal
skepel, (-s), bushed.
skepemmer, (well-)bucket, scoop-bucket.
skephou, half-volley (tennis).
skepie, skippie, (-s), little ship, toy-boat.
skeplepel, ladle.
skepnet, landing-net, dip-net.

skeppend, (-e), creative.
skepper, (-s), creator; scoop, dipper.
skeppie, (-s), spoonful, spadeful; helping.
skepping, (-e), creation.
skeppingsdag, day of creation.
skeppingsdrang, creative inpulse (urge).
skeppingsverhaal, story of creation.
skeppingsvermoë, creative power.
skeppingswerk, (work of) creation; creative work.
skeprat, paddle-wheel.
skepsel, (-s), creature, being, man, chap, coloured man, native.
skepskop, drop(-kick).
skepskoot, half-volley (tennis); drop-kick (football).
skepties, (-e), sceptical.
skeptikus, (-se, -tici), sceptic.
skeptisisme, scepticism.
skêr, (e), (pair of) scissors; (pair of) shears (for pruning, sheep-shearing).
skerf, (skerwe), (pot)sherd, fragment, piece, bit, splinter.
skering, warp; **– en inslag**, warp and weft (woof); **dit is by hom – en inslag**, it is the regular thing with him.
skerm, (-e, -s), screen (against light); curtain (in theatre); **agter die -e**, behind the scenes.
skerm, (ge-), fence, parry; flourish, parade; **met woorde –**, fence with words; **in die lug –**, bandy words, fight against windmills.
skermkuns, (art of) fencing.
skermles, fencing-lesson.
skermmaat, sparring partner.
skermskool, fencing-school.
skermutsel, (ge-), skirmish, have a brush, spar (with words).
skermutseling, (-e, -s), skirmish, brush.
skermvereniging, fencing-club.
skerp, (–, -e), a., sharp, cutting, keen, acute, severe; acrid; **– antwoord**, sharp (cutting) retort; **– bog (draai)**, sharp turn; **– hoek**, acute angle; sharp angle (corner); **– kant**, sharp (keen) edge; **– oë**, sharp (keen) eyes; **– pyn**, sharp (acute, severe) pain; **– ryp**, sharp (severe) frost; **– smaak**, sharp (acrid) taste; **– tong**, sharp tongue; **– verwyt**, sharp (severe) reproof; **– wind**, sharp (cutting) wind.
skerp, adv. sharply, severely, keenly, acutely, closely; **– aankyk**, look hard at; **'n –gestelde brief**, a strongly worded letter; **– maak**, sharpen.
skerpheid, sharpness, etc.; vide **skerp**, a.
skerphoek, acute angle.
skerphoekig, (-e), acute-angled.
skerpioen, (-e), scorpion.
skerpregter, executioner, hangman.
skerpsiende, sharp-sighted, keen-eyed, penetrating, acute.
skerpsiendheid, sharp-sightedness; penetration, acuteness.
skerpsinnig, (-e), sharp, sharp-witted, acute, penetrating, discerning.
skerpsinnigheid, acuteness, discernment.
skerpskutter, sharp-shooter; sniper.
skerpsnydend, (-e), sharp-edged.
skerpte, sharpness, edge; (fig.) acerbity.
skêrtjie, (-s), small (pair of) scissors.
skerts, n. joke, joking, jest, fun.
skerts, (ge-), joke, jest, make fun; **hy laat nie met hom – nie**, he is not a man to be trifled (fooled) with.
skertsend, (-e), joking(ly).
skertsenderwys(e), jokingly, jestingly.
skertsery, (-e), joke, jest, joking, fun.

skets, (-e), n. sketch, (rough) draft.
skets, (ge-), sketch, outline, picture.
sketsboek, sketch-book.
sketser, (-s), sketcher.
sketskaart, sketch-map, skeleton-map.
sketsmatig, (-e), sketchy.
sketstekening, sketch.
sketter, (ge-), blare; bray; rant; brag.
skeur, (-e), n. tear, rent (in cloth); crack, fissure; cleft, cleavage, split (in party), schism.
skeur, (ge-), tear (up), rend, rip; split, cleave, rupture (a party).
skeurbuik, scurvy.
skeurbuiklyer, scorbutic (patient).
skeuring, (-e, -s), split, rupture, cleavage, schism (in church).
skeurkalender, block-calendar.
skeurmaker, disrupter, schismatic.
skeurnael, agnail.
skeurpapier, waste-paper.
skeut, (-e), dash (of brandy); shoot.
skeutig, (-e), liberal, generous, free.
skewebek, **skeefbek**, wry face; – **trek**, pull faces (a wry face).
skielik, **skierlik**, (-e), a. sudden, quick.
skierlik, **skielik**, adv. suddenly, all at once, all of a sudden.
skie(r)likheid, suddenness.
skiereiland, peninsula.
skierlik, vide **skielik**.
skiet, n.: – (skot) gee, veer, slack.
skiet, (ge-), shoot, fire (a shot); blast (with dynamite) dart, rush; **laat** –, slack, pay out (a rope), give rope, let go; **geld** –, lend (advance) money; **die koring – mooi**, the wheat shoots well; **the wheat yields well**; **saad** –, go (run) to seed, seed; **strale** –, shoot rays; **wortel** –, take root; **die bloed het na haar wange ge-**, the blood rushed to her face; **na (op) iemand** –, shoot (fire) at a person.
skietbaan, rifle-range, shooting-range.
skietgat, loophole, embrasure.
skietgebed(jie), hurried (brief) prayer.
skietgoed, ammunition.
skietkatoen, gun-cotton.
skietlood, plumb, plummet.
skietoefening, shooting-, target-practice.
skietperd, shooting-horse, hunter.
skietspoel, shuttle.
skietterein, shooting-range, butts.
skiettog, shooting-trip, -expedition.
skietvereniging, rifle-club.
skietwedstryd, shooting-, rifle competition shooting match.
skietwond, shot-wound.
skif, (ge-), separate, sort out, sift; (milk) (begin to) run, curdle; (material) become thread-bare.
skifting, (-e, -s), sifting; curdling.
skig, (-te), arrow, bolt, dart; flash, ray.
skigtig, (-e), skittish, (inclined to) shy.
skigtigheid, skittishness.
skik, n. pleasure, enjoyment; **hy was baie in sy** –, he was very pleased (delighted).
skik, (ge-), arrange, manage, order; settle, make up; be convenient, suit; **'n saak** –, settle a matter; **as dit jou** –, if it suits you; **sig in jou lot (die onvermydelike)** –, resign oneself to one's fate (the inevitable); **sig – na die omstandighede**, adapt (accommodate) oneself to the circumstances; **blomme in 'n vaas** –, arrange flowers in a vase.
skikgodinne, the Fates, fatal sisters.
skikking, (-e, -s), arrangement; composition, settlement, agreement; **–e tref**, make arrangements, take steps; **'n – tref, tot 'n – kom**, come to an agreement. reach a settlement.
skiklik, (-e), obliging, accommodating.
skiklikheid, obligingness, complaisance.
skil, (-le), n. peel, rind, skin, scale; **–le**, **peels**, parings (of potatoes); **aartappels met die – kook**, boil potatoes in their jackets.
skil, (ge-), peel, pare, skin.
skild, (-e), shield, escutcheon; badge; **iets in die – voer**, be up to (drive at, aim at) something.
skilddraer, shield-bearer.
skilder, (-s), n. painter.
skilder, a. speckled, variegated.
skilder, (ge-), paint; depict, delineate, picture.
skilderagtig, (-e), picturesque.
skilderagtigheid, picturesqueness.
skilderboontjie, speckled bean.
skilderes, (lady) painter.
skildering, depiction, portrayal, picture, painting.
skilderkuns, (sort of) painting.
skilderkwas, paint-brush.
skildersesel, easel.
skilderskool, school of painting.
skilderstuk, piece, picture, painting.
skilderwerk, painting.
skildery, (-e), picture, painting.
skilderyversameling, collection of paintings.
skildklier, thyroid gland.
skildknaap, shield-bearer.
skildkraakbeen, thyroid cartilage.
skildvel, hide-shield.
skildvormig, (-e), shield-shaped; peltate (bot.); scutate (zool.); **–e kraakbeen**, thyroid cartilage.
skildwag, sentinel, sentry.
skildwaghuisie, sentry-box.
skilfer, (-s), dandruff (on the head); scale, flake, tuft.
skilfer, (ge-), scale, flake, give off scales.
skilfer(ag)tig, (-e), covered with dandruff, scaly, flaky.
skilpad, (paaie), tortoise (on land), turtle (in water); slowcoach; tortoise-shell; – **trek**, have a tortoise tug of war.
skilpadblom, ink-plant.
skilpaddop, tortoise-shell.
skilpaddraffie, jog-trot, lazy trot.
skilpadjie, ladybird.
skilpadso(e)p, turtle-soup.
skilpadtrek, tortoise tug of war.
skilpadvere, pigeon's milk; **loop pluk** –, go and buy pigeon's milk.
skim, (-me), shadow, spectre, ghost.
skimagtig, (-e), shadowy, spectre-like.
skimkabinet, shadow kabinet.
skimmel, (-s), mildew, mould; fungus; blight; grey (horse), roan (horse).
skimmel, a. mouldy, mildewy, musty, stale; bashful; roan, grey.
skimmel, (ge-), grow mouldy (mildewy).
skimmelagtig, (-e), (slightly) mouldy; greyish, roanish; vide **skimmel**, a.
skimmelbrood, musty (mouldy) bread; bashful person; gawk.
skimmelperd, roan horse, grey horse.
skimmeryk, realm of shades, Hades.
skimp, (-e), n. gibe, jeer; allusion, innuendo, oblique hint.
skimp, (ge-), gibe, scoff, jeer, flout; alude, make covert references.
skimpdig, (-te), satire.
skimper, (-s), giber, scoffer.
skimpery, (-e), scoffing; hinting.
skimpnaam, (abusive) nickname.
skimprede, invective, abusive speech.
skimpskeut, **-skoot**, vide **skimp**, n.

skimpskrif, lampoon.
skimpwoord, abusive word, gibe, taunt.
skinder, skender, (ge-), slander; backbite, etc.; vide **skender**.
skinder- ... vide **skender-** ...
skink, (ge-), pour; serve.
skinkbord, tray, salver.
skinker, (-s), butler, cup-bearer.
skinktafel, coffee, tea-stand, sideboard.
skip (skepe) ship, boat, vessel; nave (of church); **die – van die woestyn**, the ship of the desert; **die –, van Staat**, the ship of State; **sy skepe agter hom verbrand**, burn one's boats; **as my – met geld kom**, when my ship comes home; **skoon – maak**, clean out, make a clean sweep.
skipbreuk, shipwreck; **– ly**, be shipwrecked; fail, miscarry.
skipbreukeling, (-e), shipwrecked person, castaway.
ski-plank, aquaplane; **– ry**, aquaplane.
skipper, (-s), n. (sea)captain master.
skipper, (ge-), wangle, trim.
skipperaar, (-s), wangler, trimmer.
skippershaak, boat-hook.
skippie, skepie, (-s), small boat (vessel).
skisma, (-s), schism.
skismatiek, (-e), schismatic.
skitter, (ge-), sparkle, glitter, glister, scintillate, shine.
skitterend, (-e), sparkling, brilliant, splendid, magnificent, glorious.
skittering, sparkle, splendour, lustre.
skitterlig, flash, flare; flash-light.
skob, skub, (-be), scale; vide **skub**.
skobbejak, (-ke), scoundrel, rogue, bounder, scamp, rascal, bad egg (hat).
skoei, (ge-), shoe; **op 'n ander lees –**, cast in a different mould.
skoeisel, footwear.
skoe(n)lapper, (-s), butterfly.
skoen, (-e), boot, shoe; **as die – jou pas, trek hom aan**, if the cap fits, wear it; **die stoute –e aantrek**, pluck up courage, nerve oneself, take the bull by the horns; **hy weet waar die – hom druk**, he knows where the shoe pinches; **die moed het hom in die –e gesink**, his heart sank into his boots; **ek wil nie graag in sy –e staan nie**, I should not like to be in his shoes.
skoener, (-s), schooner.
skoen(e)winkel, boot-store, -shop.
skoengespe(r), shoe-buckle.
skoenlapper, cobbler; vide **skoelapper**.
skoenlees, shoe- boot-last.
skoenlepel, shoe-horn.
skoenmaker, bootmaker, shoemaker; **– hou jou by jou lees**, cobbler, stick to your last.
skoenmakery, (-e), boot-factory.
skoenpoets, boot-, shoe-polish.
skoenpoetser, boots, boot-, shoe-black.
skoenriem, boot-, shoe-lace, (-string); **nie werd om sy –e te ontbind nie**, not worthy to untie his shoestrings.
skoensmeer, boot-polish.
skoenveter, boot-, shoe-lace.
skoenwaks, boot-blackening, -polish.
skoenware, footwear.
skof, (skowwe), 1. hump, withers (horse), shoulders (ox).
skof, (skofte), 2. lap, stage, trek; shift.
skof, (-te), 3. scoundrel, blackguard.
skoffel, (-s), hoe, weeding-hook.
skoffel, (ge-), hoe, weed; dance.
skoffelpik, hoe.
skoffelploeg, cultivator.

skok, (-ke), shock, impact, concussion; jolt; jerk, jar; **elektriese –**, electric shock.
skok, (ge-), (give a) shock, shake jolt.
skokbreker, skokdemper, shock-absorber.
skokiaan, skokian.
skokkend, (-e), shocking, frightful.
skoktaktiek, shock tactics.
skolastiek, scholasticism.
skolasties, (-e), scholastic.
skolastikus, (-se, -ici), scholastic.
skolier, (-e), scholar, pupil.
skollie, (-s), hooligan, "skollie."
skommel, (-s), swing.
skommel, (ge-), swing, rock, oscillate, roll, wobble; (prices) fluctuate.
skommeling, (-e), rocking, oscillation; fluctuation; vide **skommel**, (ge-),
skommelrig, (-e), wobbly, rolling.
skommelsif, swinging screen, baby.
skommelstoel, rocking-chair.
skone, (-s), beauty, beautiful woman; **die –**, the beautiful, the beauty (of nature).
skoof, (skowe), sheaf.
skooi, (ge-), beg; "loaf"; cringe.
skooier, (-s), beggar, "loafer", tramp.
skool, (skole), school; shoal (of fish); **hoër–**, high school; **laer, primêre –**, primary (elementary) school; **middelbare, sekonêre –**, secondary school; **– gaan**, go to (attend) school; **– hou**, teach; **die – heropen**, (sluit), school re-opens, (breaks up); **in die –**, in school; **in (op) die – sit**, put (send) to school; **na(ar) – gaan**, go to school; **op – wees**, be at school; **uit die – klap**, blab, tell tales out of school.
skool, (ge-), flock together, shoal.
skoolbank, school-desk, -seat, -form.
skoolbehoeftes, (pl.), school-requisites.
skoolbesoek, school-attendance.
skool(besoek)beampte, (school) attendance-officer.
skoolbiblioteek, school-library.
skoolblad, school-magazine.
skoolboek, school-, class-book.
skooldag, school-day.
skooldwang, compulsory attendance.
skooleksamen, school-examination.
skoolfees, school-festival.
skoolgaan, (skoolge-), go to (attend) school.
skoolgebou, school-building(s).
skoolgebruik, use in schools; **vir –**, for use in schools, adapted for schools.
skoolgeld, school-, tuition-fees; **– betaal**, (also pay for one's experience.
skoolhoof, headmaster, principal.
skoolhou, (skoolge-), teach, give lessons.
skoolinspeksie, school-inspection.
skoolinspekteur, school-inspector.
skooljaar, school-year.
skooljuffrou, school-mistress, teacher.
skoolkamer, school-room.
skoolkind, school-child, pupil.
skoolkomitee, -kommissie, school-committee.
skoolkwartaal, school-quarter, -term.
skoollokaal, school-building; school-room.
skoolmaat, school-fellow, -mate.
skoolmeester, schoolmaster; pedant.
skoolmeesteragtig, (-e), pedantic.
skoolmeesteragtigheid, pedantry.
skollonderwys, school-teaching, -tuition.
skoolopsiener, school-caretaker.
skoolplig, compulsory attendance.
skoolraad, school-board.
skoolrapport, school-report.
skoolreis, education tour.

skools, (-e), scholastic, school- ... ; –e geleerdheid, book-learning, school-knowledge.
skoolseun, school-boy.
skoolsiekte, sham illness.
skooltug, school-discipline.
skooltyd, school-hours, -time; **gedurende die** –, during school hours; during term.
skoolure, (pl.), school-hours.
skoolvak, school-subject.
skoolvertrek, school-room.
skoolvos, pedant.
skoolwet, rule (regulation) of the school; education act.
skoolwysheid, book-, school-learning.
skoon, n. the beautiful; – **vergaan maar deug bly staan**, virtue is more lasting than beauty; **uiterlike – is slegs vertoon**, beauty is but skin-deep.
skoon, (–, skone), a. clean, pure; fine, beautiful, handsome; – **hemp**, clean shirt; **skone kunste**, fine arts.
skoon, adv., clean, quite, completely, absolutely; – **hou**, keep clean (fig. pure); – **maak**, clean, cleanse; **ek het dit – vergeet**, I clean (completely) forgot it.
skoondogter, daughter-in-law.
skoonheid, (-hede), beauty; cleanliness.
skoonheidsgevoel, skoonheidsin, sense (appreciation) of beauty, aesthetic sense.
skoonheidsleer, aesthetics.
skoonhou, (skoonge-), keep clean (pure).
skoonklinkend, (-e), fine-sounding, melodious. specious, plausible.
skoonmaak, n. clean-up, spring-cleaning.
skoonmaak, (skoonge-), clean, cleanse, clean out, clean up, weed (a garden-bed), dress, curry (a horse); gut (fish); dress, pick (salad).
skoonmaakdag, house-cleaning day.
skoonmoeder, mother-in-law.
skoonouers, (pl.), parents- in-law.
skoonseun, son-in-law.
skoonskip: – **maak**, make a clean sweep.
skoonskrif, calligraphy; copy-book.
skoonskrywer, calligraphist.
skoonskynend, (-e), specious.
skoonsuster, sister-in-law.
skoonteer, Stockholm tar.
skoontjies, nicely, neatly.
skoonvader, father-in-law.
skoonveld, n. (golf) fairway.
skoonveld, adv. clean gone.
skoor, n.: – **soek**, ask (look) for trouble, want to pick a quarrel.
skoor, (ge-), joke, tease; quarrel.
skoorsteen, chimney; funnel (of ship, engine); **daar sal die – nie van rook nie**, that won't keep the pot boiling.
skoorsteenmantel, mantelpiece.
skoorsteenpyp, (chimney-)flue.
skoorsteenveër, (chimney-)sweep.
skoorvoetend, reluctantly.
skoot, skot, (skote), shot; report, crack; time, turn; **toe die sko(ot) val**, when the shot rang out (was fired); **'n skoot skiet**, fire a shot; **die skoot hoog deur hê**, be the worse for liquor; **mooi skoot!**, good shot!, well done!; **onder skoot kom**, come within range; **onder skoot kry**, get within range.
skoot, (skote), lap, womb, bosom; fold; **verborge in die – van die aarde**, hidden in the bowels (depths) of the earth; **in die – van die Kerk**, in the bosom of the Church; **die hande in die – lê (vou)**, fold one's arms.
skoothond(jie), lap-dog.
skootvry, (–, -e), bullet-, bomb-proof.

skop, (-pe), n. showel; scoop; spade.
skop, (-pe), n. kick.
skop, (ge-), kick; recoil.
skopgraaf, shovel.
skoppe(ns), (pl.), spades (cards).
skoppe(n)aas, ace of spades.
skoppel-, skoppermaai, (-e), **skoppel-, skoppermaaier**, (-s), swing; – **ry**, swing.
skoppermaai(er), vide **skoppelmaai(er)**.
skop-skiet-en-donder-prent, blood and thunder film.
skor, (–, -re), hoarse, husky, rough.
skorheid, hoarseness.
skorrie-morrie, riff-raff, rabble.
skors, n. bark, rind.
skors, (ge-), suspend; adjourn.
skorsenier(wortel), salsify, scorzonera.
skorsing, suspension; adjournment.
skort, (-e), n. apron, pinafore.
skort, (ge-), be wrong, be wanting; **wat – daar?**, what is wrong?.
skorting, thing wanting; **wat is die –?**, what is wrong?, what is the matter?
skot: – (skiet) **gee**, veer (a rope), slack; relax, give play; (**pl. -te**), partition; bulkhead; vide **skoot**.
Skot, (-te), Scot, Scotchman.
skotig, (-e), gradually sloping; **'n –e afdraand**, a gradual declivity.
Skotland, Scotland.
Skots, (-e), Scotch, Scottish.
skotskar, scotch cart.
skotskrif, lampoon, libel, squib.
skottel, (-s), dish, basin.
skottelgoed, dishes and plates.
skottelgoedwater, dish-water, -wash.
skottelploeg, disc-plough.
skottelwiel, disc-wheel.
skotvry, scot-free, untouched.
skou, (ge-), view, inspect, survey.
skouburg, (-e), theatre.
skouburgbesoeker, theatre-goer.
skouburgpubliek, theatre-going public.
skouer, (-s), shoulder; **die –s ophaal**, shrug the shoulders; **die –(s) onder iets sit**, put the shoulders to the wheel; – **aan – staan**, stand shoulder to shoulder; **op die –s gedra word**, be carried shoulder high; **breë –s hê**, have broad shoulders.
skouerband, shoulder-strap.
skouerbeen, collar-bone.
skouerblad, shoulder-blade.
skouergewrig, shoulder-joint.
skouerriem, baldric.
skouspel, (-spele), spectacle, sight, scene.
skouspelagtig, (-e), spectacular.
skout, (-e), sheriff, bailiff.
skout-by-nag, rear-admiral.
skraag, (skrae), support, stay; trestle.
skraag, (ge-), support, prop (up).
skraal, (–, skrale), thin, lean, gaunt (of a person); poor (soil); bleak, cutting (wind); scanty, meagre (returns, hopes); **skrale troos**, poor consolation.
skraalhans, niggard.
skraalheid, thinness, poorness, poverty, bleakness, scantiness, meagreness.
skraalte, meagreness, scantiness.
skraaltjies, poor(ly), thin(ly).
skraap, (skrape), n. scratch.
skraap, (ge-), scrape; pursue, chase; **bymekaar –**, scrape together, **'n dam –**, excavate a "dam"; **die honde het hom ge–**, the dogs chased him.
skraapagtig, (-e), scraping, miserly.
skraapsel, (-s), scraping.

skraapsug | 282 | **skrywe**

skraapsug, stinginess, niggardliness.
skraapsugtig, (-e), stingy, niggardly.
skram, (-me), n. scratch, mark.
skram, (ge-), scratch, graze; (weg)-, be deflected.
skrams, grazingly; **die koeël het hom – geraak**, the bullet just grazed him.
skramsko(o)t, grazing shot, graze.
skrander, smart, clever, bright, sharp, sagacious, ingenious, shrewd.
skranderheid, cleverness, smartness.
skrap, adv., vide **skraps**.
skrap, (ge-), scratch, strike out, cross out, cancel.
skraper, (-s), scraper; dam-scraper.
skraperig, (-e), stingy; scratchy.
skrapie, (-s), scratch.
skrappies, vide **skraps**.
skrapping, (-e, -s), deletion, striking off, cancellation.
skrap(s), a. & adv. scarce(ly); barely.
skrede, (-, -s), step, stride; **met rasse –**, with rapid strides.
skree, (skreë), **skreeu**, (-e), n. shout, cry, scream; shriek; squeal (of a pig); bray (of a donkey).
skree, **skreeu**, (ge-), shout, cry, scream; shriek; bawl; squeal (of a pig); bray (of a donkey); croak (of a frog); – **soos 'n maer vark**, squeal like a stuck pig.
skree(u)balie, cry-baby.
skreër, **skreeuer**, (-s), howler, shouter.
skreërig, **skreeuerig**, (-e), crying, shouting; blatant; ranting.
skreëry, **skreeuery**, crying, shouting.
skreeulelik, (-e), n. ogre.
skreeulelik, (-e), a. frightfully ugly.
skrefie, chink, slit; **op 'n –**, ajar.
skrei, (ge-), cry, weep; **dit – ten hemel**, it cries to heaven.
skreiend, (-e,) crying, flagrant, shameful; **–e onreg**, glaring injustice.
skrif, (-te), writing, handwriting, exercise book; **die (Heilige) Skrif**, the (Holy) Scriptures, (Holy) Scripture.
skrifgeleerd, (-e), educated; cunning.
skrifgeleerde, (-s), scribe.
skrifkenner, student of Scriptures, scripturalist; palaeographer.
skrifkundige, (-s), handwriting-expert.
skriftelik, (-e), in writing, written; **–e eksamen**, written examination; **–e belofte**, written promise.
skriftuur, (-ture), scripture; document.
skriftuurlik, (-e), scriptural.
skriftuurplaas, text.
skrifuitlêer, (-s), exegete (exegetist).
skrifuitlegging, exegesis.
skrik, n. fright, terror, alarm, dread; **die – op die lyf ja(ag)**, – **aanja(ag)**, give a fright; **hy is die – van die woud**, he is the terror (dread) of the forest; **met – vervul**, fill with terror.
skrik, (ge-), start, be frightened (startled), get a fright; **ek het my dood ge–**, I was frightened to death; **wakker –**, awake, wake up; – **vir**, be frightened at, shy at.
skrikaanja(g)end, (-e), alarming, terrifying.
skrikagtig, (-e), vide **skrikkerig**.
skrikbarend, (-e), alarming, terrifying.
skrikbeeld, bugbear, bog(e)y, ogre.
skrikbewind, reign of terror.
skrikkeldag, leap-year's day.
skrikkeljaar, leap-year; **elke –**, once in a blue moon.
skrikkerig, (-e), jumpy, nervous, frightened, afraid; shy, skittish.
skrikkerigheid, jumpiness, nervousness.

skriklik, (-e), vide **verskriklik**.
skrikmaak, (skrikge-), startle; alarm, frighten, give a fright.
skrikwekkend, (-e), alarming, appalling.
skril, (–, -le), shrill; glaring (colours).
skrobbeer, (ge-), rebuke, reprove, reprimand; give a telling-of.
skrobbering, rebuke, reprimand, lecture; telling-off, dressing-down. ..
skroef, (skroewe), n. screw; propeller (of boat, aeroplane); (jaw-)vice; **daar is êrens 'n – los**, there is a screw loose somewhere.
skroef, **skroewe**, (ge-), screw.
skroefas, propeller-shaft.
skroefblad, propeller-blade.
skroefbout, screw-bolt.
skroefdraad, screw-thread, worm.
skroefhamer, wrench, spanner.
skroefsleutel, shifting spanner.
skroef(stoom)boot, screw-steamer.
skroefturbinemotor, prop-jet.
skroefvormig, (-e), screwshaped, spiral.
skroefwind, slip-stream.
skroei, (ge-), singe (hair); scorch (grass); cauterise (a wound).
skroewe, vide **skroef**, (ge-),
skroewedraaier, **skroefdraaier**, (-s), screwdriver.
skrofuleus, (-e), scrofulous.
skrok, (ge-), gorge; gulp (bolt) down.
skromelik, vide **skroomlik**.
skrompel, (-e), shrivel, wither.
skroom, n. diffidence, timidity, modesty.
skroom, (ge-), hesitate, dread, be afraid.
skroomagtig, **skroomhartig**, (-e), vide **skroomvallig**.
skroomlik, **skromelik**, (-e), shameful(ly), disgraceful(ly), bad(ly).
skroomvallig, (-e), diffident, timorous, bashful, shy.
skroot, grape-shot, slugs; scrap(iron).
skrop, (-pe), (dam-)scraper.
skrop, (ge-), scrub, scour; scratch; scrape.
skropborsel, scrubbing-brush.
skrum, (-s), scrum, scrummage.
skrum, (ge-), scrum.
skrumskakel, scrum-half.
skrupel, (-s), scruple (weight).
skrupule, (-s), scruple.
skrupuleus, (-e), scrupulous.
skry, (ge-), stride.
skryf, **skrywe**, (ge-), write; correspond.
skryfbehoeftes, **-benodighede**, writing-materials, stationery.
skryfblok, writing-pad (-block).
skryfboek, copy-book.
skryfburo, writing-desk.
skryffout, clerical error, slip of the pen.
skryfgereedskap, writing-materials.
skryfkramp, writer's cramp.
skryfkuns, art of writing; calligraphy.
skryflus, passion for writing.
skryfmasjien, typewriter.
skryfpapier, writing-paper, note-paper.
skryftaal, written language.
skryftafel, writing-table.
skryfwerk, writing, clerical work.
skryfwyse, style, manner (of writing); spelling, way of writing; notation.
skrylings, astride.
skryn, (ge-), smart, cause pain.
skrynend, (-e), smarting, painful.
skrynwerk, cabinet-work, joinery; carpentry.
skrynwerker, cabinet-maker, joiner; carpenter.
skrywe, n. letter; **u – van gister**, your letter (your favour, yours) of yesterday's date.

skrywe, vide **skryf**, (ge-),
skrywer, (-s), writer, author.
skrywery, writing.
sku, (-, -we), shy, bashful; reserved; unsociable; skittish (of horse, etc.).
skub, **skob**, (-be), scale, scutum.
skud, (ge-), shake; tremble; jolt; shuffle (cards); **die kop (iemand se hand) –**, shake the head (a person's hand); **– van die lag**, shake (be convulsed) with laughter.
skudding, (-e, -s), shaking; shock.
skuerig(heid), vide **skuwerig(heid)**.
skugter, (–, -e), timid, shy, coy.
skugterheid, timidity, shyness, coyness.
skuheid, shyness; skittishness.
skuif, (skuiwe), bolt (of a door), sliding-bolt; slide; slide-valve; puff (of smoke).
skuif, **skuiwe**, (ge-), push; shove; move; **die skuld op iemand anders –**, throw (fasten) the guilt on someone else.
skuifdak, sunshine roof.
skuifdeur, sliding-door, folding-door(s).
skuifel, (ge-), shuffle.
skuifgordyn, (sliding) curtain.
skuifklep, slide-valve.
skuifknoop, slip-knot, running-knot.
skuiflaai, drawer.
skuifmeul(e), (game of) noughts and crosses (lit.); excuse, pretext (fig.).
skuifraam, sash-window.
skuifspeld, paper-clip.
skuiftafel, sliding table, extension-table.
skuiftrompet, trombone.
skuifvisier, sliding sight.
skuil, (ge-), shelter, take over (shelter), hide; **daar – iets agter**, there is something behind it.
skuilgaan, (skuilge-), hide.
skuilhoek, hiding-place, cover.
skuilhou, (skuilge-), hide, keep hidden.
skuiling, cover, shelter; **– soek**, seek shelter, take cover (shelter).
skuilnaam, pen-name, pseudonym.
skuilplaas, **-plek**, hiding-place, cover, retreat, shelter, refuge, sanctuary.
skuim, n. foam (on liquids, horses, round the mouth); froth; lather (of soap); dross (of molten metal); scum; dress, refuse, offscourings; **die – van die golwe**, the foam of the waves; **die – van bier**, the froth of beer; **die – van die maatskappy**, the dregs of society.
skuim, (ge-), foam, froth; lather; skim; sparkle, bead; fume (with rage).
skuimagtig, (-e), foamy, frothy.
skuimbek, (ge-), foam at the mouth.
skuimerig, (-e), foamy, frothy.
skuimpie, **skuimtertjie**, meringue.
skuinspan, skimmer, skimming, ladle.
skuins, a. slanting, sloping, inclined, oblique; bevel(led).
skuins, adv. slantingly, obliquely; aslant, awry; askance; **– hou**, slant, tilt; **– kyk**, look askance; **– teenoor**, diagonally opposite; nearly opposite.
skuinsheid, slant, inclination.
skuinssy, hypotenuse.
skuinste, (-s), slope.
skuit, (-e), boat; **in dieselfde –(tjie), sit**, be in the same box.
skuiwe, vide **skuif**.
skuiwergat, scaffolding-hole, putlog-hole; scupperhole.
skuld, (-e), n. debt; fault, guilt; **agterstallige –e**, arrears; **R100 –**, a debt of R100; **– beken (bely)**, confess (admit) guilt, plead guilty; **– guilty; – dra (hê)**, be to blame; **dit is sy –**, it is his fault, he is to blame for it; **iemand die – gee**, put the blame on someone; **die – kry**, be blamed, be accused; **– maak**, run into (incur, make) debts; **– vergewe**, forgive trespasses (debts); **buite my –**, through no fault of mine.
skuld, (ge-), owe.
skuldbekentenis, confession of guilt.
skuldbelydenis, confession of guilt.
skuldbesef, consciousness of guilt.
skuldbewys, acknowledgement of debt, IOU.
skuldbrief, debenture.
skulddelging, debt-redemption.
skuldeiser, creditor.
skuldelas, burden of debt (sins).
skuldenaar, (-s, -nare), debtor.
skuldig, (-e), guilty; culpable; **– wees**, be guilty; owe (money); **– aan diefstal**, guilty of theft; **sig – maak aan**, commit, be guilty of; **die antwoord – bly**, fail to give an answer.
skuldige, (-s), offender, culprit.
skuldvergewing, **-vergif(fe)nis**, remission of debts (sins), pardon.
skuldvernuwing, renewal of debt(s).
skulelik, (-e), very ugly, awful, horrid.
skulp, (-e), shell; **in sy – kruip**, draw in one's horns.
skulpboor, shell-bit.
skulpdier, **skelpdier**, crustacean.
skulpkalk, shell-lime.
skulptuur, sculpture.
skulpvis, **skelpvis**, shell-fish.
skulpwerk, scalloping.
skurf, n. vide **skurfsiekte**,
skurf, (skurwe), mangy, scabby (in animals), chapped, rough (in human beings); scabious; scaly.
skurfagtig, (-e), **skurwerig**, (-e), slightly mangy (scabby); slightly chapped.
skurfsiekte, mange, scab (in animals); scabies, itch (in human beings).
skurfte, scabbiness; roughness; scab; itch.
skuring, friction, rubbing, chafing.
skurk, (-e), blackguard, villain, scoundrel, rogue.
skurkagtig, (-e), scoundrelly, vile.
skurkagtigheid, villainousness, villainy.
skurkery, **skurkstreek**, (piece of) villainy, blackguardly act (behaviour).
skurwejantjie, scaly, ant-eater, pangolin.
skurwerig, vide **skurfagtig**.
skut, (-s), n. shot, marksman.
skut, (-te), n. protection; screen; fence; pound (for stray animals).
skut, (ge-), protect; pound, impound.
skutblaar, **-blad**, bract (of plant).
skutblad, fly-leaf (of book).
skutgeld, poundage, pound-money, -fee.
skutkraal, pound.
skutmeester, pound-keeper.
skutsengel, guardian-angel.
skutsheer, patron.
skutsheilige, patron-saint.
skutspatroon, patron; patron-saint.
skutsvrou, patroness.
skutter, (-s), shot, marksman.
skutting, (-s), protection; fence, hoarding; impounding.
skutvee, impounded cattle.
skutverkoping, sale of impounded cattle.
skuur, (skure), n. barn, shed.
skuur, (ge-), rub; scrub; scour (pots); graze, chafe; **blink –**, polish.
skuurborsel, scrubbing-brush.
skuurlap, scouring cloth; emery-cloth.
skuurmiddel, abrasive.

skuurpapier, sand-paper, emery-paper.
sku(w)erig, (-e), (a bit) shy, bashful.
skyf, (skywe), target; slice (of watermelon), quater (of orange); disc; dial (of automatic telephone).
skyfie, (-s), slice; quarter (of orange).
skyfskiet, target-practice, -shooting.
skyfvormig, (-e), disc-shaped, discoid.
skyfwerper, discobolus.
skyfwiel, disc-wheel.
skyn, n. appearance, semblace; show, pretence; glimmer, glow; – **bedrieg**, appearances are deceptive; **– en wese**, shadow and substance; **– van waarheid**, semblance of truth; **die – red**, keep up appearances; **dit is alles –**, it is all outward show; **vir die –**, for the sake of appearances.
skyn, (ge-), shine; seem, look, appear; **'n –ende lig**, a shining light; **dit – dat**, it seems (would seem) that; **na dit –, weet hy dit nie**, he appears not to know it.
skynaanval, sham-attack, feigned attack.
skynbaar, (-bare), a. apparent, seeming.
skynbaar, adv. apparently, seemingly.
skynbeeld, phantom; virtual image.
skynbeweging, feint.
skynboks, shadow-boxing.
skyndeug, pretended (feigned) virtue.
skyndood, apparent (seeming) death, suspended animation, coma.
skyngeleerdheid, pseudo-learning, sciolism.
skyngeloof, simulated (pretended) faith.
skyngestalte, phase (of the moon).
skyngeveg, sham-fight, mock-fight.
skynheilig, (-e), hypocritical.
skynheilige, (-s), hypocrite, dissembler.
skynheiligheid, hypocrisy, simulation.
skynparlement, mock-parliament.
skynsel, glow, light, glimmer.
skyntjie, trifle, least bit.
skynvermaak, false pleasure.
skynvertoon, false show, sham, pretence.
skynvrede, false peace.
skynwaarheid, apparent truth.
skynwerper, search-light, reflector.
sla(e), (pl.) cuts, lashes, blows.
Slaaf, (Slawe), Slave, Slavonian.
slaaf, (slawe), n. slave; **hy is geen – van sy woord nie**, his word is not his honour.
slaaf, slawe, (ge-), slave, toil, drudge.
slaafs, (-e), slavish, servile.
slaafsheid, slavishness, servility.
slaag, (ge-), succeed; pass; **hy het daarin ge--om te . . .**, he succeeded in . . . , he managed to . . .
slaags: **– raak**, come to blows; (ships) join battle; **– wees**, be fighting.
slaai, lettuce; salad.
slaaibak, salad-dish.
slaaibos(sie), ice-plant.
slaaikrop, head of salad.
slaaiolie, salad-oil.
slaaisaad, lettuce-seed.
slaaisous, salad-dressing, mayonnaise.
slaaitjie, small lettuce; quid, chew.
slaak, (ge-), breathe, heave, utter.
slaan, slaat, (ge-), strike, beat, hit; thrash, flog; slap, flap; **die horlosie (klok) –**, clock strikes; **die pols –**, the pulse beats; **geloof aan iets –**, give credence to, believe; **die hand aan die lewe –**, commit suicide, take one's own life; **in die boeie –**, put in irons, handcuff; **'n spyker in die muur –**, drive a nail into the wall; **met die vuis op die tafel –**, hit (bang, thump) the table with one's fist; **jou arms om iemand –**, put your arms round a person; **'n blik op iemand –**, glance (cast a glance) at somebody; **die spyker op die kop –**, hit the nail on the head; **dit – op my**, that refers to me; **op die vlug –**, take to flight; **die arms (bene) oor mekaar –**, cross the arms (legs); **geld – uit**, make money out of; **munt – uit**, make capital out of, turn to account; **uit die veld –**, disconcert, discomfort, put out.
slaanbeurt, innings.
slaande, striking; **Sy – hand**, His chastising hand.
slaanding, something to hit with, cane.
slaap, sleep; (pl. **slape**), temple; **diep (ligte) –**, deep (light) sleep; **aan (die) –, in – raak**, val, fall asleep, go (drop off) to sleep; **aan die –, in – sus (wieg)**, lull (rock) ro sleep; **uit die – hou**, keep awake; **aan die – wees**, be asleep.
slaap, (ge-), sleep, be asleep; **my voet –**, my foot is all pins and needles (has gone to sleep); **jy kan maar gaan –**, you can give it up; **– soos 'n os**, sleep like a log; **ek sal daaroor –**, I shall sleep over (on, upon) it; **– gerus**, sleep well!
slaapbank, couch.
slaapdeuntjie, lullaby.
slaapdrank, sleeping-draught, soporific.
slaapgoed, night-wear, -things, -attire.
slaapkamer, bedroom.
slaapkamerameublement, -stel, bedroom-suite.
slaapkous, drowsy-head, sleepyhead.
slaaploos, slapeloos, (-lose), sleepless.
slaaploosheid, slapeloosheid, sleeplessness.
slaapmiddel, opiate, narcotic, soporific.
slaapmus, night-cap.
slaapplek, sleeping-accommodation.
slaapsaal, dormitory.
slaapsiekte, sleeping-sickness.
slaapster, sleeper; **die skone –**, the Sleeping Beauty.
slaapsug, sleepiness, sleepy sickness.
slaaptyd, bed-time.
slaapvertrek, bedroom.
slaapwandel, sleep-walking.
slaapwandelaar, -wandelaarster, sleepwalker, somnambulist.
slaapwekkend, (-e), soporific, somnolent.
slae, vide **sla(e)**,
slag, (slae), blow (of hand, sword); stroke (of clock, rower, swimmer); beat (of heart, pulse); lash (of whip); clap (of thunder); thump, thud, crash (of falling object); slap, smack (in the face); knack, trick, sleight of hand; turn, time; trick (in cardgames); kink, turn, twist (in a rope); battle; **dit was vir hom 'n harde, sware –**, it was a hard (terrible, crushing) blow for him; **dit is net 'n –, 'n mens moet daar – van hê**, it is only a knack, you have to get the feel (the hang, the way) of it; **– van iets kry**, get into (the way of) it; **die eerste –**, the first turn (time, occasion); **elke –**, every time; **'n – om die arm hou**, not commit oneself altogether; **– lewer**, give battle, fight a battle; **'n – slaan**, make a bargain (a hit); **sy – slaan**, make full use of one's opportunities; **met een –**, with (at) one blow (stroke); **op – kom**, strike form, get going; **op – wees**, be in form; **– op –**, blow upon blow; time after time, time and again; **van – afbring**, put out; **van – af wees**, be off colour, be in bad form; be out of strike (of a clock); **sonder – of stoot**, without striking a blow.
slag, n., kind, sort, ilk.
slag, (ge-), slaughter, kill; skin; **'n skaap –**, slaughter (kill) a sheep.
slagaar, artery.

slagaargeswel, aneurism.
slagbank, shambles.
slagbees, slaughter-ox (-cow); (pl.) slaughter-cattle, -stock, fat stock.
slagboom, barrier bar.
slagbyl, butcher's axe; battle-axe.
slagdier, slaughter-animal.
slagding, slaughter-animal.
slaggat, pot-hole.
slaggoed, slaughter-animals, -stock.
slaghoedjie, percussion-cap.
slaghuis, butcher's shop, butchery.
slagmes, butcher's knife.
slagoffer, victim.
slagorde, battle-order; -array.
slagos, slaughter-ox.
slagpale, abattoir, slaughter-house.
slagplaas, **-plek**, abattoir, shambles, slaughtering place.
slagreën, **-reent**, heavy rain, downpour.
slagroom, whipped cream.
slagsin (**-spreuk**), slogan.
slagskaap, slaughter-sheep.
slagskip, battle-ship.
slagtand, tusk; fang, canine (tooth).
slagter, (**-s**), butcher.
slagtersblok, chopping-block.
slagterswinkel, butcher's shop.
slagtery, (**-e**), butchery.
slagting, slaughter, butchery; **'n – aanrig onder**, slaughter.
slagvaardig, (**-e**), ready for the fray (for battle), game.
slagvee, slaughter-stock, fat stock.
slagveer, main spring, flight-feather.
slagveld, battle-field.
slagwerk, strike-mechanism.
slagyster, (spring-) trap.
slak, (**-ke**), snail, slug; (pl. also) slag, clinker (of metal).
slakkegang, snail's pace.
slak(ke)huisie, snail-house, -shell; cochlea (of the ear).
slak(ke)meel, basic slag.
slampamper, (**-s**), reveller, carouser.
slampamper, (**-ge**), revel, make merry.
slampamperliedjie, carousal-song.
slang, (**-e**), snake; (hose-)pipe; worm (of a still); **daar is 'n – in die gras**, there is a snake in the grass; **as dit 'n – was, het hy jou lankal gebyt**, look out, you are stepping on it.
slangagtig, (**-e**), snake-like, ophidian.
slangbyt, snake-bite.
slangdiens, snake-worship.
slang(e)besweerder, snake-charmer.
slangeier, snake's egg.
slangetjie, little snake; snake-fish.
slanggif, snake-poison.
slangkop, snake's head; blue weed.
slangkos, death-cup, toadstool.
slangmens, contortionist.
slanmuishond, snake-weasel, mongoose.
slangsteen, snake-stone, serpentine.
slangstert, snake's (serpent's tail.)
slangteengif, antivenene.
slangtuin, snake-park.
slangvel, snake-skin, slough.
slank, (**–**, **-e**), tall (and slim), willowy, of fine figure; slim, slender.
slankheid, tallness, slimness.
slap, a. & adv. slack (rope, discipline, morals); soft (collar, hat, tyre); weak (drink); (fig.) weak, slack, lax; flabby limp (figure; book-bindings); dull (trade); **– van die lag, limp**

(weak) with laughter; **– laat hang (lê)**, slack, not keep your end up.
slapeloos, slaaploos, (**-lose**), sleepless.
slapeloosheid, slaaploosheid, insomnia.
slaper, (**-s**), sleeper.
slaperig, (**-e**), sleepy, drowsy.
slaperigheid, sleepiness, drowsiness.
slapheid, slackness, laxity, softness.
slapie, nap, snooze, forty winks.
slappies, adv. slackly, weakly.
slapte, slackness, dullness. Vide **slap**.
slavin, (**-ne**), (female) slave.
Slavonië, Slavonia.
Savoniër, (**-s**), Slavonian.
Slavonies, (**-e**), Slavonian.
slawe, (ge-), vide **slaaf** (ge-),
slawearbeid, slave-labour; slavery.
slawe-eienaar, slave-holder, -owner.
slawehandel, slave-trade.
slawehandelaar, slave-trader, slaver.
slawejuk, yoke of slavery (bondage).
slawelewe, slave's life, life of slavery.
slawemark, slave-market.
slawerny, slavery, bondage, servitude.
slaweskip, slave-ship, slaver.
slawetyd, time when slaves were kept.
Slawies, (**-e**), Slav, Slavonic.
slee, (**sleë**), sledge; sleigh (for persons only); sled (for goods only); carriage.
sleep, n. drag, tow; train.
sleep, (ge-), drag, pull, draw, haul, trail, lug; tow, tug; go, ride; **na sig –**, cause, entail, bring in its train; **rok – in die stof**, skirt trails in the dust.
sleepboot, tug.
sleepdiens, towing-service.
sleepdraer, train-bearer.
sleepnet, drag-net, trawl-net.
sleeprok, train-dress; trailling skirt.
sleepsel, (**-s**), trail.
sleeptong: **– praat**, lisp.
sleeptou, tow-rope; **aan die (op) – hê (hou)**, have (keep) on a string; **op – neem**, take in tow.
sleepvoetend, (**-e**), shuffling, lagging.
Sleeswyk, Schleswig, Sleswick.
sleg, (**-te**), a. bad; evil; poor; rotten; **–te kind** (ruiter, maniere, keuse), bad child (rider, manners, choice); **–te kos**, bad (poor) food.
sleg, adv., badly, ill; poorly; **– eet**, have no appetite; **– aangetrek**, poorly (badly) dressed; **dit gaan – met haar**, she is in a poor (bad) way; **iemand –maak**, speak ill of a person; **iemand –sê**, give a person a piece of one's mind, scold a person; **– smaak**, have a bad taste; **–ste van iets afkom**, get off worst (second best).
sleg, (ge-), level, raze, demolish.
sleggerig, slegterig, (**-e**), poor(ly), rather poor(ly).
slegs, only merely, but.
slegste, worst; **op sy slegste**, at his (its) worst.
slegte, n. the bad.
slegterig, sleggerig, (**-e**), poor(ly).
slegtheid, badness, wickedness.
slegtigheid, weakness, worthlessness; rottenness.
slem, slam.
slemparty, carousal, drinking-bout.
slenter, (ge-), saunter, stroll; slouch.
slenteraar, (**-s**), saunterer; sloucher.
slentergang, saunter(ing) gait.
slentering, (**-e**, **-s**), saunter, stroll.
slenterslag, trick, dodge, roguery.
slet, (**-te**), slut, strumpet.
sleur, groove, rut, routine; **die ou – volg**, follow

the beaten track, move in the same old groove (rut).
sleur, (ge-), vide sloer, (ge-).
sleurgang, routine, humdrum.
sleurwerk, routine-work, grind.
sleutel, (-s), key; spanner; clef (music); sender, transmitter (telegr.).
sleutelbeen, collar-bone.
sleutelbos, bunch of keys.
sleutelgat, key-hole.
sleutelring, key-ring.
sleutelvormig, (-e), key-shaped.
sleutelwoord, key-word.
slib, silt, ooze, slime, mire.
slik, vide slib & slyk.
slik, (ge-), vide sluk (ge-).
slikgrond, vide slykgrond.
slim, (-, -me), smart, clever; crafty, cunning, slim; as jy nie sterk is nie, moet jy - wees, brain is better than brawn.
slimheid, cleverness; cuteness, cunning.
slimmerd, (-s), cunning fox, sly dog.
slimmigheid, smartness, astuteness.
slimpraatjies, clap-trap, glib talk.
slinger, (-s), pendulum; sling; (starting-)handle, crank; festoon.
slinger, (ge-), swing, oscillate; sway, reel, lurch, roll; wind; hurl, fling, buzz; so dronk dat hy -, so drunk that he reels (lurches); die skip -, the ship rolls; 'n beskuldiging - na, fling (level) a charge at.
slingeraap, spider-monkey.
slingeraar, (-s), slinger.
slingerbeweging, oscillating movement; reel, lurch; hurling motion.
slingering, (-e, -s), swing, oscillation; reel, lurch; roll; fling. Vide slinger.
slingerpad, winding-path, zig-zag path.
slingerplant, creeper, climbing plant.
slingertyd, time (period) of oscillation.
slingeruurwerk, pendulum-clock.
slingerwette, laws of oscillation.
slink, (ge-), shrink, diminish, dwindle.
slinks, (-, -e), underhand, clandestine, surreptitious.
slinksheid, cunning(ness), artfulness.
slip, (-pe), tail, flap (of a coat); slit; tip.
slip, (ge-), slip.
slipdraer, pall-bearer.
slipper, (-s), slipper.
slobber, (ge-), gobble, lap.
slobkous, spat; gaiter.
slorderig, (-e), slovenly, slatternly.
slodderjoggem, ragamuffin.
slodderkous, slattern, slut.
sloep, (-e), sloop, dinghy, long-boat.
sloer, (ge-), drag (on), dawdle, keep postponing (putting off); linger.
sloerie, (-s), slut, drab.
slof, (slowwe), n. slipper.
slof, (ge-), shuffle, shamble.
sloffie, (-s), slipper.
slok, (-ke), gulp, mouthful, swallow.
slons, (-e), slattern, slut.
slons(er)ig, (-e), slovenly, slatternly.
slons(er)igheid, slovenliness.
sloof, slowe, (ge-), drudge, toil, slave.
sloop, (slope), n. pillow-case, pillow-slip.
sloop, (ge-), level, demolish (a building); dismantle (a fort); break up; undermine; drain, sap (one's strength).
sloot, (slote), furrow, sluit, trench, ditch; hy kan 'n - eet, he eats like a horse.
slootgrawer, ditcher, trencher.

sloper, (-s), (house-, ship-)breaker, demolisher; wrecker.
sloping, demolition. Vide sloop, (ge-).
slordig, (-e), untidy, slovenly, dowdy; careless; shoddy, slipshod.
slordigheid, slovenliness; carelessness.
slorp, (ge-), gulp, guzzle. Vide slurp.
slot, end, conclusion; peroration; (pl. -te); lock (of door, gun); clasp (of book); castle; - volg, to be concluded; agter - (en grendel), locked up, under lock and key; aan die -, at the end (conclusion); op -, locked; op (per) - van rekening (sake), in the, end after all, ultimately; ten -te, lastly, finally, ultimately, in the end; tot -, in conclusion.
slotbedryf, last (final) act.
slotbewaarder, keeper of the castle.
slotgesang, closing hymn.
slothaak, pick-lock; hook-spanner.
slotklinker, final vowel.
slotmaker, lock-smith.
slotmedeklinker, final consonant.
slotnommer, -nummer, last item.
slotopmerking, closing (final) remark.
slotrede, peroration.
slotreël, last line.
slotsang, last canto; last hymn.
slotsin, closing sentence.
slotsom, conclusion.
slottoneel, closing (final) scene.
slotvers(ie), last verse.
slotwoord, conclusion, concluding word(s), peroration.
Slowaak, (-wake), Slovak.
Slowaaks, Slowakies, (-e), Slovak(ian).
Slowakye, Slovakia.
slowe, vide sloof, (ge-).
slu, (-(w)e), cunning, crafty, wily.
sluheid, craftiness, wiliness, cunning.
sluier, (-s), n. veil; fog; die - oplig, lift the veil; die laat val oor, draw the veil over.
sluier, (ge-), veil; conceal, cover.
sluiks: ter -, on the sly, stealthily.
sluimer, n. slumber.
sluimer, (ge-), slumber, doze.
sluimering, (-e, -s), slumber.
sluip, (ge-), slink, sneak, steal; prowl; slip (away) quietly.
sluipgat, loophole.
sluipkoors, slow fever.
sluipmoord, assassination.
sluipmoordenaar, assassin.
sluis, (-e), sluice; lock; die -e van die hemel (van die welsprekendheid), the flood-gates of heaven (eloquence).
sluisdeur, lock-gate.
sluiswagter, lock-keeper.
sluit, (ge-, geslote), close (door, book, eyes, meeting, account); lock; close down; conclude (treaty); prorogue (parliament); effect (insurance); make, conclude (peace); end, conclude (letter, speech); die geledere -, close the ranks; die oë - vir, close one's eyes to; connive at; iemand in die arms -, lock a person in one's arms; die skole -, schools break up; die vergadering het om 11-uur ge-, the meeting closed at 11 o'clock.
sluitboom, boom, barrier.
sluiter, (-s), shutter (of camera, etc.).
sluiting, closing, shutting; locking; closure (of debate in Parliament); break-up, closing (of school); prorogation (of Parliament); fastening.
sluitmoer, lock-nut.
sluitrede, syllogism.

sluitring, washer.
sluitstuk, breech-block.
sluk, slok, (-ke), n. swallow, gulp, mouthful, pull, draught; **in een –,** at one gulp; **'n goeie – op 'n bottel,** a considerable amount (part, quantity), a good deal; **dit skeel 'n – op 'n bottel,** it makes a good deal of difference.
sluk, slik, (ge-), swallow; put up with, endure; **'n belediging sluk,** stomach (pocket) an insult; **hy sluk alles wat jy hom vertel,** he swallows everything you tell him.
slukderm, gullet, oesophagus.
slurf, (slurwe), slurp, (-e), trunk.
slurp, (ge-), gulp, guzzle.
slyk, mire, slime, mud; silt; **aardse –,** filthy lucre; **met – gooi,** throw mud.
slykagtig, slykerig, (-e), slimy, muddy.
slym, phlegm, mucus, slime.
slymafdrywend, (-e), phlegm-expelling.
slymagtig, (-e), mucous, slimy.
slymerig, (-e), slimy, mucous.
slymhoes, catarrhal cough.
slymklier, pituitary gland; slime-gland.
slymvlies, mucous membrane.
slyp, (ge-), sharpen, whet, grind; cut (diamonds); polish (diamonds); **jou tande – vir iets,** lick one's chaps, enjoy in anticipation.
slyper, grinder, sharpener; cutter.
slypery, grinding; grinding-establishment; (diamond) cutting-works.
slypmasjien, grinding-machine.
slypmiddel, abrasive.
slypplank, knife-board.
slyppoeier, polishing powder.
slypsel, grindings.
slypsteen, grindstone, whetstone; **so bang as die duiwel vir 'n –,** as scared as the deveil is of holy water.
slyt, (ge-), wear out; pass, spend (one's days).
slytasie, wear (and tear), wastage.
slyting, erosion.
smaad, n. contumely, abuse, insult.
smaad, (ge-), malign, revile, deride.
smaadrede, invective, diatribe.
smaadskrif, libel, lampoon.
smaak, n. taste, relish, savour, flavour; liking; **die – van uie,** the taste (flavour) of onions; **'n man van –,** a man of taste; **– verskil,** tastes differ; **– in (vir) iets ontwikkel,** develop a taste (liking) for something; **in die – val by,** be to the taste of, find favour with; **met – eet,** enjoy one's food; **na my –,** to my taste (liking).
smaak, (ge-), taste; enjoy; appear, seem; **dit – lekker (soet, beter),** it tastes good (sweet, better), it is nice (sweet, better); **die wyn – heerlik,** the wine is excellent; **hoe – die wyn?,** how do you like the wine? how is the wine?; **dit – na meer,** one could do with another helping (glass); **– na,** taste like (of), savour of smack of; **dit – my asof,** it appears (seems) to me as if.
smaaklik, (-e), palatable, agreeable, delicious, enjoyable; **– ete!,** enjoy your dinner!, well may it become you!
smaakloos, (-lose), tasteless, without taste, insipid; in bad taste.
smaakloosheid, tastelessness; insipidity.
smaakvol, (-le), tasteful, in good taste.
smaal, (ge-), sneer.
smaalskrif, lampoon.
smadelik, (-e), derisive, scornful.
smadelikheid, derisiveness, scorn.
smag, (ge-), languish, pine; yearn (for).
smagtend, (-e), languishing; yearning.
smak, thud, crash; smack (of the lips).

smal, (–, -le), narrow.
smaldeel, squadron.
smalend, (-e), sneering, scornful.
smaler, (-s), railer, sneerer.
smalheid, smalligheid, narrowness.
smalkant, short side.
smalspoor, narrow gauge.
smarag, (-de), emerald.
smaraggroen, emerald-green.
smart, (-e), n. grief, sorrow, affliction, pain.
smart, (ge-), grieve, pain, give pain.
smarteloos, (-lose), painless.
smartlik, (-e), painful.
smartlikheid, painfulness.
smee(d), (ge-), forge, hammer, weld; invent (a lie), plan (conspiracy); coin.
smeedbaar, (-bare), malleable.
smeebaarheid, malleability.
smeehamer, forging-hammer.
smeek, (ge-), implore, supplicate, entreat, beseech, beg; **– om vergifnis,** implore (beg) forgiveness.
smeekbede, -gebed, supplication, entreaty.
smeekskrif, petition.
smeektaal, supplication, entreaty.
smeer, n. grease; smear, stain.
smeer, (ge-), grease, lubricate, oil (a motor); grease (leather); butter, spread butter on (bread); rub, embrocate, massage.
smeerboel, (dirty) mess.
smeerbus, grease-box, grease-cup.
smeerder, (-s), greaser.
smeergoed, liniment, ointment.
smeerlap, grease-rag; ragamuffin, dirty fellow, blackguard, swine, cad skunk.
smeermiddel, lubricant; liniment.
smeerolie, lubricating oil.
smeerpoets, dirty fellow, ragamuffin.
smeerpot(jie), grease-cup, lubricator.
smeersalf, ointment.
smeersel, rubbing; ointment; polish.
smee-yster, wrought iron.
smekeling, (-e), suppliant.
smekend, (-e), entreating; pleading.
smeker, (-s), suppliant.
smelt, (ge-), melt, liquefy; fuse (wire); melt down, render (fat); smelt (ore); merge, coalesce, fuse.
smeltbaar, (-bare), fusible, liquefiable.
smeltbom, fusion bomb.
smeltdraad, (-e), fus(-wire).
smelter, (-s), smelter; fusionist.
smeltery, (-e), foundry, melting-house, smeltingworks; fusion – business.
smelting, fusion, melting, liquation.
smeltkroes, crucible, melting-pool.
smeltoond, smelting-furnace.
smeltpommade, vanishing-cream.
smeltpunt, melting-point.
smerig, (-e), dirty, filthy, messy.
smerigheid, dirtiness, filth, dirt, shabbiness, meanness.
smering, lubrication.
smet, (-te), stain, blot, blemish, taint.
smetloos, (-lose), stainless, spotless, immaculate, free from blemishes.
smetstof, virus.
smetteloos, vide **smetloos.**
smeul, (ge-), smoulder, glow.
smeulstofie, slow combustion stove.
smid, (-s, smede), smit, (-te), (black)smith.
smiddags, in the (of an) afternoon; at noon, midday.
smidsambag, (black)smith's trade.
smidsoond, forge.

smidswinkel, smithy, blacksmith's shop.
smoel, (-e), mug; **hou jou –**, shut up!
smoelpleen, smoothing-plane.
smok, (ge-), smock.
smokkel, (ge-), smuggle, run (liquor, guns); cheat.
smokkelaar, (-s), smuggler, bootlegger.
smokkelary, smuggling.
smokkelhandel, smuggling.
smokkelwaar, contraband(-goods).
smoor, adv. very, exceedingly; **dit – kry**, have a hard time.
smoor, (ge-), smother, choke, throttle; stifle (sound); hush up (scandal); braise, stew, „smoor" (fish, meat).
smoordronk, dead drunk.
smoorheet, choking hot.
smoorhitte, broiling (sweltering) heat.
smoorklep, choke, throttle-valve.
smoorlik, deeply; **– verlief**, over head and ears (deeply) 'n love.
smoorverlief, deeply in love.
smoorvis, „smoorfish", stewed fish.
smoorwarm, chokingly hot, broiling.
smôrens, smorens: in the (of a) morning.
smous, (-e), n. pedlar, hawker, trader.
smous, (ge-), hawk; "smous(e)".
smousvraggie, pedlar's (hawker's) load, mixed merchandise; medley.
smouswinkel, trader's shop.
smout, grease, fat, lard.
smoutsetter, jobbing-compositor.
smoutwerk, table-work, jobbing.
smul, (ge-), feast, regale oneself.
smulpaap, gourmand, gastronomer.
smulparty, feast, spread, tuck-in.
smyt, (ge-), fling, hurl, cast, pitch.
s'n: **pa –**, pa's, father's; **wie – is dit?**, whose is it?
snaak, (snake), funny chap, wag.
snaaks, (-e), funny, comical, droll, queer, strange.
snaakserig, (-e), a bit funny.
snaaksheid, funny part, strangeness.
snaar, (snare), (pl.) n. string; lover, beloved; (pl. also) whims; **'n (gevoelige) – aanraak**, touch a (tender) string; **met – en st(r)amboel reis**, foot it.
snaar, (ge-), string (a racket, etc).
snaarinstrument, stringed instrument.
snags, in the (of a) night.
snak, (ge-), gasp (for breath); yearn.
snap, (ge-), catch; understand; babble.
snaphaan, flint-lock.
snap(sie), tot, spot, drop, drink.
snarespel, string-music.
snars, sners: **geen –**, not a thing, not a rap, not a hang.
snater, (-s), n. mug, jaw; **hou jou –**, shut up!, keep your jaw!
snater, (ge-), chatter, jabber
snawel, (-s), bill, beak.
snawelvormig, (-e), beak-shaped.
snedig, (-e), quick, smart, witty.
snedigheid, ready wit.
snee, (sneë), edge; caesura (in verse); **verguld op –**, gilt-edged.
Snees, (Snese), Chick, Chinaman.
sneespapier, India-paper, tissue-paper.
sneeu, n. snow.
sneeu, (ge-), snow.
sneeuagtig, (-e), like snow, snowy.
sneeubal, snowball.
sneeuberg, mound (mountain) of snow; snow-capped mountain.
sneeublind, (-e), snow-blind.
sneeubril, snow-goggles.

sneeubui, snow-fall, -shower.
sneeugrens, snow-line.
sneeuhoender, snow-grouse, ptarmigan.
sneeuhoop, mound (heap) of snow.
sneeuklokkie, snowdrop.
sneeulinie, -lyn, snow-line.
sneeuploeg, snow-plough.
sneeuskoen, snow-shoe.
sneeustrom, snow-storm, blizzard.
sneeuval, snowfall.
sneeuvlok(kie), snow-flake.
sneeuwit, snow-white.
Sneeuwitjie, Little Snow-white.
snekrat, (-te), fusee.
snel, (-, -le), a. & adv. fast, swift(ly), quick(ly), rapid(ly), speedy (speedily).
snel, (ge-), hurry, hasten, rush.
snelboot, speed-boat.
snelduik, crash-dive.
snelheid, speed (of car, train), velocity (of light, bullet); rapidity, quickness.
snelheidsbeperking, speed-limit.
snelheidsmeter, speedometer.
snellaaier, rapid-loading gun.
sneller, (-s), 1. trigger.
sneller, (-s), 2. sprinter; three-quarter.
snellont, runner-fuse.
snelpers, fly-press.
snelskrif, shorthand, stenography.
snelskrywer, stenographer.
sneltrein, express (train), fast train.
snelvaarder, speed-boat.
snelvarend, (-e), fast (sailing).
snelvoetig, (-e), fleet-, nimble-footed.
snelvuur, quick-firing, rapid fire.
snelvuurkanon, quick-firing gun.
snelweg, speedway.
snelwerkend, (-e), rapid, quick-acting.
snerp, (ge-), cut, bite, burn.
snerpend, (-e), biting, piercing (wind, cold); burning (pain).
snert, pea-soup; rot, rubbish, trash.
sneuwel, (ge-), fall, be killed (in action).
snik, (-ke), n. sob, gasp; **die laaste –**, the last gasp.
snik, (ge-), sob.
snikheet, snikkendheet, swelteringly hot.
snip, (-pe), snipe; perky (saucy) thing.
snipper, (-s), n. snippet, snip('ing), scrap, shred, chip.
snipper, (ge-), snip, cut up.
snipperig, (-e), perky, saucy.
snipperjag, paper-chase.
snippermandjie, waste-paper basket.
snippertjie, (-s), snippet, shred, scrap.
snipvis, sea-snipe.
snit, cut (of a garment); edge (of knive).
snoef, (ge-), boast, brag.
snoei, (ge-), prune (fruit-trees); trim, clip, lop; cut (expenses).
snoeier, (-s), pruner, trimmer.
snoeimes, pruning-knife.
snoeisel, (-s), pruning(s), trimming(s).
snoeiskêr, pruning-shears, garden-shears.
snoeityd, pruning-season, -time.
snoek, (-e), "snoek", pike (European).
snoep, a. greedy, grasping, having.
snoep, (ge-), sneak, pinch, eat furtively.
snoeper, (-s), pincher; rake, gallant.
snoeperig, (-e), (a bit) greedy.
snoepery, gallantry; sweets, eatables.
snoepgoed, sweets, eats.
snoepkroeg, snack bar.
snoepheid, greediness.
snoeplus, love of sweets.

snoer, (-e), n. line, string, lace; **die (meet)- -e, het vir my in lieflike plekke geval**, the lines are fallen unto me in pleasant places.
snoer, (ge-), tie, string (up); **iemand die mond –**, silence a person.
snoeshaan, boaster, swaggerer, windbag.
snoesig, (-e), dainty, ducky, sweet.
snoet, (-e), snout (of pig), muzzle, nose (of cat), trunk (of elephant); mug, jaw.
snoewer, (-s), braggart, boaster.
snood, (snode), evil (plans), base (ingratitude), heinous (crime).
snoodaard, (-s), villian, wretch.
snoodheid, baseness, heinousness.
snor, (-re), n. moustache.
snor, (ge-), drone; purr; whizz.
snorbaardjie, moustache; whiskers.
snork, n. snoring; snort (of horse).
snork, (ge-), snore; snort (of horse).
snorkery, snoring.
snorretjie, (little) moustache.
snot, snot, mucus of the nose.
snotneus, snotty nose; ninny, nincompoop, shipper – snapper, snot.
snou, (-e), n. snarl.
snou, (ge-), snarl (out), snap (out).
snuf, smell; **die – in die neus kry**, get wind of something, begin to suspect.
snuffel, (ge-), sniff, nose; snoop; ferret, pry, rummage; **– in ou boeke**, nose in old books.
snuffelaar, (-s), noser, Paul Pry.
snuif, n. snuff.
snuif, snuiwe, (ge-), take snuff; sniff.
snuifdoos, snuff-box.
snuifie, pinch of snuff.
snuiftabak, snuff-tobacco; snuff.
snuistery, (-e), knick-knack, gimcrack.
snuit, (-e), n. snout (of pig), trunk (of elephant), proboscis (of insect).
snuit, (ge-), blow one's nose; snuff.
snuiter, (-s), snuffers; kid, milksop.
snuitkewer, -tor, snout-beetle.
snuiwe, vide **snuif (ge-)**.
snuiwer, (-s), snuff-taker.
sny, (-e), n. cut gash, notch, slice.
sny, (ge-), cut, castrate, geld; sprint; **fyn –**, mince, cut up into small pieces; **hout –**, carve wood; **stukkend (aan stukke) –**, cut up; **vleis (vlees) –**, carve meat; **mekaar –**, (lines) intersect.
snybank, cooper's bench.
snyblom, cut flower.
snyboontjie, haricot-bean.
snydend, (-, -e), cutting, biting, sharp.
snyding, cutting, incision; intersection (maths), caesura (in verse).
snydokter, surgeon.
snyer, (-s), tailor; cutter, carver.
snyerspak, tailor-made suit.
snyerswinkel, tailor's shop.
snyervoël, tailor-bird.
snykamer, dissecting-room; operating-theatre.
snylyn, join, intersecting line, secant.
snymasjien, reaper, cutter, harvester.
snypunt, point of intersection.
snysel(tjie), dough-threads.
snytand, incisor.
snytjies, (-s), (little) cut; small slice.
snyvlak, cutting plane.
snywerk, carving.
snywond, incised wound, cut.
so, so, thus, (in) this (that) way, like this (that); **– groot**, so big, as big as this (that); **is dit al – laat?**, is it as late as that?; **– groot as**, as big as ; **– een**, one like that; **– iets**, something like that; **– iets het ek nog nooit gesien nie**, I

never saw anything like it (that); **goed mooi –**, that's right, (that) serves you right; **well done!**; **hoe –?**, in what way?, what do you mean?; **– is die lewe**, such is life; **– pas**, just now, only just; **– ja!**, that's right; that's that.
soas, vide **soos**.
sober, frugal; sober.
soberheid, frugality; soberness.
soda, soda.
sodapomp, soda-fountain.
sodanig, (-e), such, such like; **in such a way, as –**, as such, in that capacity.
sodat, so that.
sodawater, soda-water.
sodiak, zodiac.
sodiakaal, (-kale), zodiac(al).
sodoende, in this (that) way, thus so.
sodra, as soon as, the moment that.
soe!, ugh!, brr!, phew!
soebat, (ge-), coax, cajole; beg, implore, entreat.
soebattery, coaxing, begging, pleading.
Soedan, Soudan.
Soedannees, (-nese), Soudanese.
Soedans, (-e), Soudanese, Soudan.
soek, (ge-), look for (a pen, trouble), look (out) for (a job, a wife), look up (a word), seek (help), hunt for (a house), fumble for (the key); search; **Pa – jou**, Father wants you (is looking for you); **iets – wat jy nie verloor het nie**, wander about aimlessly; **êrens iets agter –**, be suspicious of a thing; **hulp –**, seek aid (help); **middele –**, devise means; **– na**, look for, look out for; **hy – nooit na 'n woord nie**, he is never at a loss for a word; **raad –**, seek advice; **rusie –**, seek (try to pick) a quarrel.
soeker, (-s), seeker, searcher; view-finder (on camera).
soeklig, search-light.
soel, (1) mild, soft; close, sultry.
soel, (2) sallow (of human complexion).
soen, (-e), n. kiss.
soen, (ge-), kiss.
soenbloed, blood of atonement.
Soenda, Sunda.
soendood, death of atonement.
soenerig, (-e), fond of kissing.
soenoffer, sacrifice of atonement; sin-offering.
soep, sop, soup.
so(e)pbord, soup-plate.
soepee, (-s), supper.
soepeer, (ge-), take (have) supper.
soepel, (-, -e), supple, pliant, lithe.
so(e)pkom, soup-tureen.
so(e)plepel, soup-spoon, soup-ladle.
so(e)pvleis, soup-meat.
soesie, (-s), (cream-)puff.
soet, sweet; **'n – kind**, a sweet (well-behaved, good) child ; **'n kind – hou**, keep a child quiet.
soetamaling, **soetemaling**, (-s), tuberose.
soetagtig, (-e), vide **soeterig**.
soetdoring, Karoo-thorn.
soeterig, (-e), sweetish, rather sweet.
soetheid, sweetness.
soethout, liquorice(-plant).
soethoutbossie, sweetroot-bush.
soetigheid, sweetness; sweets.
soetjies, suutjies, softly, gently, quietly.
soetkoek, sweet cookie(s); **vir – opeet**, swallow (believe) readily.
soetlemoen, orange.
soetlief, darling, sweetheart.
soetmelk, sweet milk, fresh milk.
soetolie, salad-oil, sweet oil.
soetriet, sugar-cane.

soetsappig, (-e), namby-pamby, sloppy, goody-goody, mealy-mouthed.
soetskeel, with a slight squint.
soetsopie, liqueur, sweet wine.
soetsuurdeeg, salt-rising yeast.
soetvlees, -vleis, fillet.
soetvloeiend, (-e), fluent, melodious.
soetvloeiendheid, fluency, melodiousness.
soetwater, sweet water, fresh water.
soetwatervis, fresh water fish.
so-ewe, just now a moment ago.
soewenier, (-s), souvenir.
soewerein, (-e), n., sovereign, ruler.
soewerein, (-e), a., sovereign..
soewereiniteit, (-e), sovereignty.
sofa, (-s), sofa.
sofis, (-te), sophist.
sofisme, sophism; sophistry.
sofisties, (-e), sophistical.
sog, (-ge, sôe), sow.
sog, wake (of a ship).
sogenaamd, (-e), a. so-called.
sogenaamd, adv., ostensibly, professedly; **dit is – selfstandige werk,** this is supposed to be original work.
soggens, in the (of a) morning.
soheentoe, soontoe, thither, there.
sojaboontjie, soy(a)-bean.
sok, (-ke), socket, sleeve; vide **sokkie.**
sokker, association-football, soccer.
sokkie, (-s), sock.
Sokrates, Socrates.
sol, sol (music).
solank, as long as.
solarium, (-ria), solarium.
sola(wissel), sole bill, sola (bill).
soldaat, (-date), soldier.
soldatelewe, a soldier's life, military life.
soldeer, (ge-), solder.
soldeerbout, soldering-iron.
soldeersel, solder, soldering.
soldeertin, tin solder.
soldeerwerk, soldering(-work).
solder, (-s), loft; ceiling.
soldering, ceiling.
solderkamer(tjie), attic, garret.
solderlig, sky-light.
solderraam, loft-window; dormer-window.
soldertrap, loft-stairs; garret-stairs.
soldervenster, = **solderraam.**
soldy, wage(s), pay.
solfametode, -musiek, tonic solfa.
solfa-skrif, tonic solfa notation.
solidariseer, (ge-), solidify, consolidate.
solidariteit, solidarity.
solidliteit, solidity; reliability.
solied, (-e), solid, substantial, reliable, respectable; sound, solvent.
solis, (-te), soloist.
sollisitant, (-e), candidate, applicant.
sollisitasie, (-s), application.
sollisiteer, (ge-), apply.
solo, (-'s,), solo.
solosang, vocal solo; solo-singing.
solosanger(es), soloist.
solovlug, solo-flight.
solsleutel, G. clef.
solusie, solution.
solvensie, solvency.
solvent, (-e), solvent.
som, (-me), sum; **–me maak,** do sums; **dit is die proef op die –,** that proves (settles) it.
somaar(so), vide **sommer(so).**
Somaliland, Somaliland.

somber, (–, -e), sombre, gloomy; **–(e) stemming,** dejection, sombreness.
somberheid, sombreness; melancholy.
sombrero, (-'s), sombrero.
somer, (-s), summer; **in die –,** in summer.
someraand, summer-evening.
someraster, (summer-)aster, Chinese aster.
somerdag, summer's day.
somerdrag, summer-wear.
somerhitte, summer-heat.
somerhuisie, summer-house.
somerklere, summer-clothes.
somermôre, -more, summer-morning.
someropruiming, summer-clearance (sale).
somerpak, summer-suit.
somerreis, summer-trip, -outing.
somers, (-e), sommer- . . . ; 'n –e dag, a summer's day, **–e weer,** summer-weather.
somerseisoen, summer-season, -time.
somerslaap, summer-sleep.
somersonnestilstand, summer-solstice.
somertyd, summer-time.
somervakansie, summer-holiday.
somerverblyf, summer-resort, -residence.
somerwarmte, summer-heat.
somer-weer, summer-weather.
somma, total (amount), sum (total).
sommasie, writ, summons.
sommeer, (ge-), summon.
sommer, somaar, for no particular reason; just, merely; without any difficulty, without further ado, straight off, immediately; **ek het – gestaan en kyk,** I was just (merely) looking on; **hy is – 'n lekker kêrel,** he is a real good sort.
sommerso, somaarso, simply, just (as it was); after a fashion, so-so, in an off-hand way; **hy het alles – laat staan,** he just left everything as it was; **ek laat my nie – vang nie,** I am not to be caught so easily.
sommige, some.
soms, sometimes, at times, now and then.
somtyds, somwyle = **soms.**
son, (-ne), sun; **in jou eie – staan,** stand in your own light, prejudice your own chances; **die – trek water,** the sun is westering (setting); **sy – is ondergegaan,** his sun is set.
son- . . . , vide **son(ne),. . .**
sonaanbidder, sun-worshipper.
sonaanbidding, sun-worship.
sonate, (-s), sonata.
sonbad, sunbath.
sonbesie, cicada.
sonbril, sun glasses.
sondaar, (-s), sinner; offender.
sondaarsbankie, stool of repentance.
Sondag, Sunday.
Sondagaand, Sunday-evening, -night.
Sondagdiens, Sunday-service.
Sondagnag, Sunday-night.
Sondags, (-e), a. Sunday- . . .
Sondags, adv. on Sundays.
Sondagkind, Sunday-child; (fig.) child born with a silver spoon in his mouth.
Sondagsklere, -pak, Sunday-clothes.
Sondagskool, Sunday-school.
Sondagskoolonderwyser(es), Sunday-school teacher.
Sondagsrus, Sunday-rest.
Sondagsviering, Sunday-observance.
sondares, (-se), sinner.
sonde, (-s), sin; trouble; **– doen,** commit a sin, sin; **hy veroorsaak gedurig –,** he is a continual nuisance.
sonde, (-s), probe.
sondebok, scape-goat.

sondeer, (ge-), probe, sound.
sondejammer: dit is –, it is a great pity, it is a sin and a shame.
sondelas, burden of sins.
sondeloos, (-lose), sinless.
sonder, without; – jou hulp, but for your help; – dat hy dit sien, without his seeing it.
sonderbaar, (-bare), strange, queer.
sonderegister, register of sins.
sonderling, (-e), queer, odd, peculiar, singular, eccentric.
sonderlingheid, singularity, peculiarity.
sondeval, fall of man, the Fall.
sondig, (-e), a., sinful.
sondig, (ge-), sin, commit a sin; offend.
sondigheid, sinfulness.
sondvloed, deluge.
sone, (-s), zone.
sonhelm, sun-helmet.
sonies, sonic.
sonkant, sunny side, side of the sun.
sonkwasriet, Sonqua-reeds, -thatch.
sonlig, sunlight.
sonloos, (-lose), sunless.
son(ne)- . . . , vide **son-** . . .
sonneblom, sunflower, helianthus.
son(ne)dag, solar day.
son(ne)diens, sun-worship.
son(ne)gloed, glow (blaze) of the sun.
son(ne)krag, solar energy.
son(ne)god, sun-god.
son(ne)hitte, heat of the sun.
son(ne)jaar, solar year.
sonnekeerkring, tropic.
sonneklaar, (-klare), as clear as the day; as plain as a pikestaff.
sonnekyker, helioscope.
son(ne)loop, course of the sun.
son(ne)sirkel, solar cycle.
son(ne)stand, sun's altitude.
son(ne)stelsel, solar system.
son(ne)stilstand, solstice, solstitium.
sonnet, (-te), sonnet.
sonnetskrywer, sonneteer.
son(ne)wa, chariot of the sun(-god).
son(ne)warmte, heat of the sun.
sonnewyster, sun-dial; gnomon.
sonnig, (-e), sunny.
sononder, n., sunset; adv., at sunset.
sonoor, (-nore), sonorous.
sonop, n. sunrise.
sonop, adv. at sunrise.
sonoriteit, sonority, sonorousness.
sonshoogte, sun's altitude.
sonskerm, sunshade, awning.
sonskyn, sunshine.
sonsondergang, sunset.
sonsopgang, sunrise; met –, at sunrise.
sonsteek, sunstroke.
sonstraal, sunbeam; sunstroke.
sonsverduistering, eclipse of the sun.
sontyd, solar time.
sonvlek, sun-spot.
sonwarmer, solar heater.
soog, (ge-), suckle, nurse, nourish.
soogdier, mammal.
soogvrou, wet-nurse.
sooi, (-e), sod; **onder die –e**, under the sod, in the grave.
sooibrand, heartburn.
sool, (sole), sole.
soolleer, shoe-leather.
soölogie, zoology.
soölogies, (-e), zoological.
soöloog, (-loge, -loë), zoologist.

soom, (some), hem, edge, border, fringe, outskirts.
soom, (ge-), hem, border.
soomnaat, hem.
soomsteek, hemstitch.
soontoe, soheentoe, thither, there.
soort, (-e), kind sort,, species, variety; **goed in sy –**, good of its kind; – **soek –**, birds of a feather flock together.
soortgelyk, (-e), of the same (that) kind, similar.
soort(e)lik, (-e), specific; –e **gewig**, specific gravity.
soortnaam, generic name.
soos, soas, as; like, such as, just as; **maak – ek**, do as I do, do like me; **mense – jy**, people like you; **behandel my – ek jou behandel**, treat me just as I treat you; **so gou – nou**, in no time.
sop, sap, juice. Vide **soep**.
sopie, (-s), drink, tot.
sopperig, sapperig, (-e), juicy; sloppy.
sopraan, (prane), soprano, treble.
sopraansangeres, soprano(-singer), sopranist.
sopraanstem, soprano(-voice), treble.
sorbet, sherbet; sorbet.
sôre, sorg(e), (ge-), mind, see; – **dat julle algar kom**, see that you all come, mind you all come; – **dat jy dit aanskaf**, be sure to get it; – **vir (daarvoor)**, take care of, mind, look after; provide for; supply; – **vir jou klere, jou tande**, take care of (look after) one's clothes, teeth; – **vir jou ouers**, provide for one's parents; **vir jouself –**, look after yourself; provide (shift) for yourself.
sorg, (-e), n. care; trouble, worry; anxiety, concern, solicitude; charge; **onnodige –e**, unnecessary worries (anxiety, concern); – **baar**, cause anxiety; – **dra vir iets**, look after (take care of) something; **aan sy – toevertrou**, entrust to his care, leave in his charge; **met –**, with care, carefully; **sonder –**, without a care, careless; **sieltjie sonder –**, happy-go-lucky person.
sorg(e), (ge-), vide **sôre**.
sorgbarend, (-e), alarming.
sorg(e)loos, (-lose), careless, thoughtless, unthinking; care-free.
sorg(e)looshied, carelessness.
sorgsaam, (-same), careful, attentive.
sorgvuldig, (-e), careful, thorough.
sorgvuldigheid, carefulness.
sorgwekkend, (-e), alarming, causing anxiety, precarious.
sorteer, (ge-), sort, assort; grade.
sorteerder, (-s), sorter; grader.
sorteerkamer, sortingroom.
sorteermasjien, grader, grading-machine.
sorteertafel, sorting-table.
sortering, sorting, grading; assortment.
sosatie, sosatie (sassate).
soseer, so much, to such an extent.
sosiaal, (-siale), social.
sosiaal-demokraat, social-democrat.
sosiaal-demokrasie, social-democracy.
sosialis, (-te), socialist.
sosialisasie, socialization.
sosialiseer, (ge-), socialize.
sosialisme, socialism.
sosialisties, (-e), socialist(ic).
sosiologie, sociology.
sosiologies, (-e), sociological.
sosioloog, (-loge, -loë), sociologist.
so-so, so-so, tolerably, after a fashion.
sosys, (-e), sausage, polony.
sot, (-te), n. fool.
sot, (–, -te), a. mad, crazy.

sotheid, madness, folly, craziness.
sotskap, cap and bells, fool's cap; fool.
sottepraatjies, nonsense.
sotterny, (-e), foolishness; tomfoolery.
sottin, (-ne), fool, foolish woman.
sou, vide **sal**.
souffleer, (ge-), prompt.
souffleur, (-s), prompter.
sous, n. gravy; sauce, relish; **die hele –**, the whole box and dice (caboodle).
sous, (ge-), sauce; rain, pour, drizzle.
sousboontjies, been-salad, salad-beans.
souskom, gravy-boat, sauce-boat.
souslepel, gravy-ladle, sauce-ladle.
sout, (-e), n. salt; **die – van die aarde**, the salt of the earth; **jou – verdien**, be worth one's salt; **'n sak – saam opeet**, live under the same roof, know one another intimately.
sout, a. salt, briny.
sout, (ge-), salt; initiate; **'n gesoute perd**, a salted horse; **gesout teen masels**, immune to (against) measels.
soutagtig, (-e), saltish, brackish.
soutbron, saline, spring.
souterig, (-e), saltish, brackish.
soutgehalte, percentage of salt, salinity.
southeid, saltness, salinity.
southoudend, (-e), saliferous.
soutigheid, saltness; something salt.
soutkorrel, grain of salt.
soutkors, crust of salt, salt-incrustation.
soutlaag, layer of salt, salt-stratum.
sout(e)loos, saltless; insipid, silly.
soutmyn, salt-mine.
soutoplossing, saline solotion.
soutpan, salt-pan.
soutpilaar, pillar of salt.
soutpotjie, salt-cellar.
soutribbetjie, salted (sun-dried) rib.
Soutsee, Dead Sea.
soutsuur, hydrochloric acid.
soutvaatjie, salt-tub.
soutvleis, salt(ed) meat.
soutwater, salt-water, brine.
soveel, (so veel), so much, so many; **– moontlik**, as much (many) as possible; as far as possible; **– te beter, erger**, so much the better, worse; **– te meer** all the more.
soveelste, umpteenth; **vir die – maal**, for the hundredth time, for the umpteenth time; **op die – van die maand**, on this or that day of the month.
sover, (so ver), so far, thus far; **in – dat**, in so far that, in that; **tot –**, so far; **vir –**, in so far as, as far as; **(nie) – as ek weet nie**, (not) as far as I know, (not) to my knowledge.
sowaar, actually, to be sure, as sure as fate; **ek het dit – nie gemeen nie**, I am sure I didn't mean it, I swear I didn't mean it.
sowat, about, more or less, roughly.
sowel: **– as**, as well as; **X – as Y**, X as well as Y, both X and Y.
Sowjet, (-s), Soviet.
spaan, (spane), scoop, ladle, skimmer; (roof) shingle; (for rowing) oar.
spaander, (-s), n. chip, splinter.
spaander, (ge-), scoot, skedaddle.
Spaans, n. Spanish.
Spaans, (-e), a. Spanish.
spaansriet, Spanish (Italian) reed.
spaanspek, musk-melon, sweet-melon.
spaansvlieg, Spanish fly, blister-beetle.
spaar, (ge-), save, put by reserve, husband; spare (one's life, costs, trouble); **– jouself die moeite**, save (spare) yourself the trouble;

jou kragte –, save (reserve, husband) your strength.
spaarbank, savings-bank.
spaarbankboekie, deposit-book.
spaarder, (-s), saver, depositor.
spaargeld, savings.
spaarpot, money-box.
spaarsaam, (-same), thrifty, economical, saving; **– wees met**, use sparingly.
spaarsaamheid, thrift, economy.
spaat, spar.
spade, late.
spaghetti, spaghetti.
spalk, (-e), n. splint.
spalk, (ge-), set (fractured leg,) splint, stretch (hides).
span, (-ne), n. team; gang; span (of oxen, of the hand).
span, (ge-), stretch (rope); strain (eyes, muscles, attention); draw, bend (a bow); hobble (a horse), strap (a cow); **'n strik –**, set a trap; **perde voor 'n kar –**, inspan horses, put (harness) horses to a cart; **die kroon –**, bear away the palm, cap, (top) everything; **gespanne verhouding**, strained relations; **op gespanne voet staan**, be at variance, disagree; **in gespanne verwagting**, with eager anticipation.
spanbroek, tights.
spandable, (-e), extravagant, wasteful.
spandabelheid, extravagance.
spandabelrig, (-e), extravagant.
spandeer, (ge-), spend.
Spanjaard, (-e), Spaniard.
Spanje, Spain.
spankrag, tensile, force, tension.
spannend, (-e), tight, tense; exiting, thrilling.
spanning, tension, strain, pressure; voltage, span (of bridge); suspense, exitement.
spanraam, tenter, stretcher, frame.
spanriem, hobbling; vide **spantou**.
spansaag, bow-, frame-saw.
spanskroef, stretching-screw.
spanspek, vide **spaanspek**.
spantou, milking-strap, knee-strap.
spanwedloop, team-race, relay-race.
spanwydte, span.
spar, (-re), rafter (of roof); spruce-fir.
Sparta, Sparta.
Spartaan, (-tane), Spartan.
Spartaans, (-e), Spartan.
spartel, (ge-), flounder, sprawl; struggle.
sparteling, (-e), sprawling; struggle.
spasie, (-s), space, room, opening.
spasieer, (ge-), space.
spasmodies, (-e), spasmodic.
spat, (-te), n. splash, spatter, stain, spot; **die – neem**, laat af, scoot, skedaddle, clear off.
spat, (ge-), splash, splutter, spatter; take to one's heels; **jy sal die vonke sien –**, you'll see sparks fly; **laat –**, take to one's heels.
spataar, varicose vein.
spatbord, splash-board, mud-guard.
spatel, (-s), spatula; patula.
spatsel, (-s), splash, spatter.
speaker, (-s), speaker.
speek, (speke), spoke; **iemand 'n – in die wiel steek**, put a spoke in someone's wheel.
speekbeentjies, spindle-shanks.
speeksel, spittle, saliva, sputum.
speekselafskeiding, secretion of saliva.
speekselklier, salivary gland.
speel, (ge-), play; act; chime; gamble; **klavier (voetbal, kaart), –**, play (the) piano (football, cards); **ek – maar**, I am only joking; **hy laat nie met hom – nie**, he is not to be trifled with;

speelbaar 'n rol –, play (act) a part; **watter stuk word daar in die teater ge–?**, what (piece) is on in the theatre; **sy – baie goed**, she acts very well; **die klokke –**, the bells chime; **groot man –**, play the big man; **met vuur –**, play a dangerous game; **die wysie het my deur die kop ge–**, the tune ran through my mind (head); **wie – saam?**, who are partners?
speelbaar, (-bare), playable.
speelbal, playing ball; sport; plaything, puppet.
speelbank, gaming-house.
speelding, toy, plaything.
speeldoos, musical box.
speelgeld, stakes, pool; gaming- (gambling-) money.
speelgenoot, partner; playfellow.
speelgoed, toys, playthings.
speelgoedwinkel, toy-shop.
speelgrond, playground.
speelhol, gambling-den, gambling-bell.
speelkaarte, playing-cards.
speelkamer, play-room; card-room.
speelmaat, playmate; partner.
speelman, musician, fiddler.
speelplek, playground.
speelruimte, playground; elbow-room, space, clearance, latitude (for activity); (free) play; **– laat aan**, allow full (free) play to.
speels, (-e), playful; on heat.
speelsgewyse, vide spelenderwys(e).
speelsheid, playfulness; heat, rut.
speelsiek, (–, -e), playful, frolicsome.
speelskuld, play-debt, gambling-debt.
speel-speel, playing; **jou werk – doen**, do one's work without exerting oneself; **hy het dit sommer – gedoen**, it was mere play to him.
speelsug, passion for gambling.
speelster, (-s), player; gambler; actress.
speelterrein, playground.
speeltoneel, stage.
speeltyd, playtime.
speen, (spene), n. nipple, teat.
speen, (ge-), wean.
speenvark(ie), sucking pig.
speer, (spere), spear; javelin.
speerpunt, spear-, javelin-head.
speervormig, (e), spear-shaped, hastate.
speg, (-te), woodpecker.
spek, bacon, pork, „spek"; blubber (of whale); **vir – en boontjies bysit**, act the mummer, play wallflower, be a mere cipher.
spekboom, spekboom, elephant's food.
spekskiet, (spekge-), draw the long bow, fib.
spekskietery, drawing the long bow, exaggeration, fibbing.
speksteen, soap-stone, steatite.
spektakel, (-s), scene, uproar, rumpus.
spektraal, (-trale), spectral.
spektroskoop, (-skope), spectroscope.
spektrum, (-s, -a), spectrum.
spekulant, (-e), speculator.
spekulasie, (-s), speculation; venture.
spekulateur, (-s), speculator.
spekulatief, (-tiewe), speculative.
spekuleer, (ge-), speculate.
spekvet, as plump as a partridge, fatted; in good health, looking well.
spekvreter, (familiar) chat.
spel, (-e), n. game; play, performance; playing; recreation, pastime; **vry – hê**, have a free hand; **hoe staan die –?**, what is the score?; **daar is jaloesie in die –**, jealousy plays a part in the matter; **daar is misdaad in die –**, foul play is suspected; **alles op die – sit**, stake everything;

jou naam is op die –, your reputation is at stake.
spel, spelle, (ge-), spell.
spelbederwer, -breker, spoil-sport.
speld, (-e), pin; **jy kon 'n – hoor val**, you might have heard a pin drop; **soos 'n groot – verdwyn**, abscond, levant, disappear on the sly; **op naalde en – sit**, be on pins and needles.
speld(e), (ge-), pin, fasten.
speldek(n)op, pin's head, pin-head.
speldekoker, pin-case.
speldekussing, pin-cushion.
speldeprik, pin-prick.
spelenderwys(e), speelsgewyse, playing, playfully, in play; jocularly.
speler, (-s), player; gambler; musician; actor; performer.
spelerig, (-e), playful, frolicsome.
speletjie, (-s), game; fun.
spelfout, spelling-mistake.
speling, play, allowance, scope.
spelkuns, orthography, art of spelling.
spelle, (ge-), vide **spel**.
spelleier, -leidster, producer (of a play).
spelletjie, (-s), game.
spelling, (-e, -s), spelling.
spellingsisteem, orthographical system.
spelmetode, spelling-method.
spelonk, (-e), cave, cavern.
spelonkbewoner, cave-dweller.
spelreël, spelling-rule.
spelt, spelt.
spelvorm, spelling.
spens, (-e), pantry.
sper, (ge-), bar, block; distend.
sperma, sperm.
spermaceti, spermaceti.
spervuur, barrage.
sperwel, sperwer, (-s), gos-hawk, sparrow-hawk.
spesery, (-e), spice.
speseryagtig, (-e), spicy.
Spesery-eilande, Spice Islands.
spesiaal, (-siale), special; (adv.) specially.
spesialis, (-te), specialist.
spesialiseer, (ge-), specialize.
spesialiteit, special(i)ty; specialist.
spesie, 1. specie.
spesie, (-s), 2. species, kind.
spesifiek, (-e), specific.
spesifikasie, specification.
spesifiseer, (ge-), specify.
speuls, (-e), rutting, on heat.
speur, (ge-), notice, discover, detect; trail, track.
speurder, (-s), detective.
speurhond, sleuth-hound.
speurverhaal, detective-story.
spieël, (-s), n. looking-glass, mirror; level (of the sea); stern (of a ship).
spieël, (ge-), mirror, reflect; **– jou aan hom**, take warning (a lesson) from him.
spieëlbeeld, image; illusion.
spieëleier, fried egg.
spieëlgeveg, mimic battle, sham-fight.
spieëlglad, (-de), as smooth as a mirror.
spieëlglas, plate-glass.
spieëlharpuis, colophony, fiddler's resin.
spieëlkas, mirrored wardrobe.
spieëllys, mirror-frame.
spieëlraam, -ruit, plate-glass window.
spieëlskrif, mirror-writing.
spieëltafel, dressing-table.
spieëlvlak, mirror-surface.
spier, (-e), muscle; **sonder om 'n – te vertrek**, without moving a muscle.
spierbundel, muscular fascicle.

spiering 294 **spook**

spiering, (-e, -s), smelt.
spierkrag, muscular strength.
spiernaak, (-te), -nakend, (-e), stark naked.
spierskede, muscle-sheath.
spiertrekking, muscular spasm (twitch).
spierverrekking, strain.
spierweefsel, muscular tissue.
spierwit, snow-white, pure white.
spies, (-e), spear, javelin, pike, lance.
spiesglans, (native) antimony.
spiesvormig, (-e), hastate, spear-shaped.
spigtig, (-e), peaky, spiky.
spikkel, (-s), n. spot, speck, speckle.
spikkel, (ge-), speckle.
spikkel(r)ig, (-e), speckled.
spiksplinternuut, (-nuwe), brand-new.
spil, (-le), pivot, axle; halfback.
Spilmoondhede, Axis powers.
spilsug, extravagance, prodigality.
spin, (ge-), spin; purr of a cat).
spinasie, spinach.
spinel, spinel.
spinet, (-te), spinet.
spinklier, spinning-gland.
spinmasjien, spinning-jenny.
spinnekop, (-pe), spider.
spinnekopblom, spider-flower.
spinner, (-s), spinner.
spinnerak, (-ke), cobweb; gossamer.
spinnerakdraad, spider-thread.
spinnery, spinning; spinning-mill.
spinnewiel, spinning-wheel.
spinsbek, pinchbeck.
spinsel, (-s), web, spinning; yarn.
spinwol, spinning-wool.
spioen, (-e), n. spy, scout.
spioen, (ge-), spy; scout.
spioenasie, espionage.
spioeneer, (ge-), spy; scout.
spiraal, spiral, coil, helix.
spiraalboor, twist-, spiral drill.
spiraalsgewys(e), spirally.
spiraalveer, coiled (spiral) spring.
spiraalvormig, (-e), spiral, helical.
spiritis, (-te), spiritism, spiritualist.
spiritisme, spiritism, spiritualism.
spiritisties, (-e), spiritualist(ic).
spiritualieë, spirits, alcoholic liquors.
spiritualis, (-te), spiritualist.
spiritualisme, spiritualism.
spiritualisties, (-e), spiritualist(ic).
spiritus, spirit(s).
spirituslamp, -stoof, spirit-lamp.
spit, (-te), n. spit; spadeful; crick, lumbago; die - afbyt, bear the brunt.
spit, (ge-), dig.
spits, n. point head; peak, summit, spire, pinnacle; van, forefront; aan die -, at the head; op die - drywe, bring to a head.
spits, (-, -e), a. pointed, sharp.
spits, (ge-), point; die ore -, prick up one's ears.
spitsbaard, pointed beard.
spitsboog, pointed (Gothic) arch, ogive.
spitsboor, common bit, pointed drill.
spitsbroe(de)r, comrade (in arms).
spitskonferensie, summit conference.
spitsmuis, shrew(-mouse).
spitsroei: - loop, run the gauntlet.
spitsvondig, (-e), subtle, ingenious, far-fetched, quibbling.
spitsvondigheid, subtleness, ingeniousness, quibble, subtle distinction.
spleet, (splete), crack, fissure, crevice.
spleethoewig, -potig, -voetig, (-e), fissiped, cloven-hoofed, -footed.

splinter, (-s), n. splinter, shiver, sliver, chip; hy sien die - in 'n nader se oog, maar die balk in sy eie oog merk hy nie, he beholds the mote in his brother's eye but perceives not the beam in his own eye.
splinter, (ge-), splinter, shiver.
splinternuut, (-nuwe), brand new.
splinterparty, splinter party.
split, (-te), slit, slash, vent.
split-ertjies, split peas.
splits, (ge-), split (up), cleave; splice.
splitsing, (-e, -s), splitting, division; splicing; cleavage; split; schism, rupture.
splyt, (ge-, gesplete), split, cleave; gesplete hoef, cloven hoof.
splytbaar, (-bare), cleavable, fissile.
splyting, cleavage, fission.
splytswam, fission-fungs, schizomycete.
spoe, vide spoeg.
spoed, n. haste, speed, expedition; haastige - is selde goed, the more haste the less speed; hoe meer haas hoe minder -, the more haste the less speed.
spoed, (ge-), speed, hasten, hurry.
spoedbestelling, rush-order; express-order; express-delivery.
spoedeisend, (-e), urgent.
spoedig, (-e), a. quick, speedy, early.
spoedig, adv. soon, quickly, speedily, at an early date, before long.
spoedvergadering, emergency-meeting.
spoe(g), spu(ug), n. spittle, spit, saliva.
spoe(g), spu(ug), (ge-), spit, expectorate; vuur en vlam -, be in a violent rage (in a towering passion).
spoe(g)-, spu(ug)bak, spittoon.
spoel, (-e), n. shuttle, spool, bobbin.
spoel, (ge-), flow, wash, rinse; die mond -, rinse (wash) one's mouth; skottelgoed -, rinse (wash) dishes.
spoelbak, wash-, rinsing-basin.
spoelbrug, causeway.
spoeldelwery, alluvial diggings.
spoeldiamant, alluvial diamond.
spoeling, rinsing, washing; swill(ings).
spoelkom, = spoelbak.
spoelmasjien, rinsing-machine.
spoelriolering, water-borne sewerage.
spoelwater, rinsing-water, dish-water; slops; floodwater.
spoetnik, sputnik.
spog, (ge-), boast, vaunt, brag, swank, show off; - met, boast (brag) of, show off.
spogding, show-article, swell thing.
spoggerig, (-e), boasting, boastful, bragging; showy; swanky.
spogperd, show-horse, swanky horse.
spogter, (-s), boaster, braggart; swank.
spogtery, boasting, bragging, swank.
spokery, appearance of a ghost, apparition; rumpus, row, fighting; het jy gehoor van die - in daardie huis?, did you hear that that house is haunted?
sponde, (-s), couch, bedside.
spondee, (-deë), spondee.
sponning, (-s), groove, rabbet, slot.
spons, (-e), n. sponge; bung.
spons, (ge-), sponge.
sponsagtig, (-e), spongy.
sponsgat, bung(-hole).
sponssiekte, black quarter, quarter evil.
spontaan, (-tane), spontaneous.
spontaneïteit, spontaneity.
spook, (spoke), n. ghost, spectre, apparition spook; fright, freak.

spook, (ge-), haunt, be haunted; struggle, fight; **hy – daar**, he haunts the place; **dit – in daardie huis**, that house is haunted.
spookagtig, (-e), spectral, ghostly.
spookgestalte, phantom, spectre.
spookhuis, haunted house.
spooksel, spook, ghost, spectre.
spookstorie, ghost-story.
spookverskyning, apparition, spectre.
spoor, (spore), n. (1) trace, track, trail, footmark, footprint; railway(-line), rails, track, mark, sign, trace, vestige, indication; rut, track (of a wagon); **breë (smal) –**, wide (narrow), guage; **die – byster raak**, get off the track (off scent); **– hou**, keep the trail, follow the track; **geen – nalaat nie**, leave no trace; **– sny**, track, follow the trail; **twee rye spore loop**, reel, lurch, stagger; **alle spore uitwis**, remove all traces, cover up all tracks; **die – vind**, pick up the scent, get on the trail; **die – volg**, follow a trail (a track); follow up a clue; **die spore van jou vader volg**, follow in the footsteps of your father; **in sy – trap**, mind his p's and q's, keep straight; **op die – bring**, put on the track (on the scent), give a hint (tip); **op die – kom**, get on the track, find a clue.
spoor, (spore), n. (2) spur; spore (bot.); **sy spore verdien**, earn (win) his spurs.
spoor, (ge-), (1) travel by rail; trail.
spoor, (ge-), (2) spur; ge-, spurred, **gestewel en ge–**, dressed from top to bottom, fully fressed.
spoorbaan, railroad, railway.
spoorbeampte, railway-official.
spoorboek, railway-guide, -timetable.
spoorbreedte, guage, width of wheels.
spoorbrug, railway-bridge.
spooelement, trace-element.
spoorloos, (-lose), trackless; **– verdwyn**, vanish into space.
spoorlyn, railway-line.
spoorslag, incentive, spur, urge.
spoorstaaf, rail.
spoortrein, railway-train.
spoorverbinding, railway-connection.
spoorvrag, railage, carriage.
spoorwa, railway-carriage, -truck.
spoorweg, railway.
spoor(weg)beampte, railway-official.
spoorwegdiens, railway-service.
spoorwegkaart, railway-map.
spoorwegkaartjie, railway-, train-ticket.
spoorwegleêr, sleeper.
spoorwegnet, network of railways.
spoorwegongeluk, railway-accident.
spoor(weg)oorweg, railway-crossing, level-crossing.
Spoorwegraad, Railway-Board.
spoorwegramp, railway-disaster.
spoorwegstasie, railway-station.
spoorwegverkeer, railway-traffic.
spoorwegvervoer, goods-traffic.
spoorwegwerkplaas, railway-workshop.
spoorwydte, gauge.
sporadies, (-e), sporadic(al).
sport, (-e), (1), rung; **hy het die hoogste – bereik**, he reached the top of the ladder (the tree).
sport, (2) sport.
sportbaadjie, sports-coat, -jacket, blazer.
sportblad, sporting-paper.
sportbyeenkoms, sports(-meeting).
sportgrond, vide **sportterrein**.
sportief, (-tiewe), sporting.
sportklub, sports-club.
sportkostuum, sports-suit, -costume.

sportkringe, sporting-circles.
sportliefhebber, sportsman.
sportliewend, (-e), sporting.
sportman, sportsman, sporting-man.
sportnuus, sporting-news.
sportterein, sports-ground(s).
sportwêreld, sporting-world.
spot, n. scorn, ridicule, derision, mockery, banter; **die – dryf met**, deride, mock at, laugh to scorn.
spot, (ge-), mock, scoff, jeer; jest, joke; **hy – my**, he is mocking me; **– jy of is dit erns?**, are you jesting or do you mean it?; **– met**, mock (scoff, jeer) at; deride, ridicule; **hy laat nie met hom – nie**, he is not to be trifled with, he stands no nonsense.
spotdig, (-te), satire, satrical poem.
spotdigter, satirist, satirical poet.
spot(goed)koop, dirt-cheap.
spotlag, laugh (smile) of derision, mocking (jeering) laugh (smile), jeer(s).
spotlus, love of mockery (teasing); inclination to satire.
spotnaam, nickname; byword.
spotprent, caricature, cartoon.
spotprentekenaar, caricaturist.
spotprys, bargain, bargain-price.
spotrede, denunciation, diatribe.
spotsiek (–, -e), (fond of) mocking (teasing); derisive, sarcastic, satirical.
spotsug, love of mockery (banter, teasing); love of satire.
spottend, (-e), mocking, jeering.
spottenderwys(e), mockingly, jeeringly.
spotter, (-s), mocker, scoffer; **– se huis brand ook af**, the mocker mocked.
spotterig, (-e), mocking, teasing.
spotterny, mockery; derision.
spotvoël, mocker, teaser.
spraak, speech; **hy het sy – verloor**, he has lost the power of speech.
spraakgebrek, defect of speech, defective speech, speech-defect.
spraakgebruik, (speech-)usage, language, idiom **in gewone –**, in every day speech, in common parlance.
spraaklank, speech-sound.
spraakkuns, grammar.
spraakleer, grammar.
spraakloos, sprakeloos, (-lose), speechless, dumb.
spraakorgaan, organ of speech.
spraaksaam, (-same), talkative, loquacious, garrulous, chatty, chattering.
spraakverlies, loss of speech.
spraakvermoë, power of speech.
spraakverwarring, confusion of speech (tongues), babel.
spraakwending, turn of speech, phrase.
sprake, talk, mention; **ter – bring**, raise, moot, broach; **ter – kom**, crop up, be raised; **daar is geen – van nie**, that is out of the question.
sprakeloos, vide **spraakloos**.
sprank(ie), spark; **geen – van vernuf nie**, not a spark of ingenuity (reason).
sprankel, (ge-), sparkle, scintillate.
sprankelend, (-e), scintillating.
spreek, [(sprak), ge-, gesproke,] speak; **hy is nie te – nie**, he is engaged, he cannot be seen now **dit – vanself**, it goes without saying, it stands to reason.
spreekbeurt, lecture, address, engagement to speak.
spreekbuis, speaking-tube, mouthpiece.
spreekfout, slip of the tongue.
spreekgestoelte, rostum, platform.
spreekkamer, consulting-room.

spreekles, elocution(-lesson), speech-training.
spreekoefening, speaking exercise, speech-training; conversation-lesson.
spreekster, (-s), (lady-)speaker.
spreektaal, spoken language.
spreektrant, manner of speaking.
spreekuur, consulting-hour(s).
spreekwoord, proverb, adage.
spreekwoordeboek, dictionary of proverbs.
spreekwoordelik, (-e), proverbial.
spreekwyse, manner of speaking (speech); idiom, expression.
spreeu, (-s), starling.
sprei, (-e), n. quilt, counterpane, coverlet.
sprei, (ge-), spread.
spreilig, flood-light.
sprekend, (-e), speaking; telling, striking; 'n -e gelykenis (ooreenkoms), a speaking (striking) resemblance.
spreker, (-s), speaker, lecturer.
spreuk, (-e), motto, maxim, adage, proverb; die Spreuke van Salomo, the Book of Proverbs.
spriet, (-e), blade (of grass); feeler, antenna (of insect); sprit (of ship).
sprietseil, sprit-sail.
sprikkel, (ge-), vide **spikkel**, (ge-).
spring, (-e), n., jump, leap, bound.
spring, (ge-), jump, leap, spring, bound; hop, skip, caper; snap, crack, burst; chap (of skin); play (of fountain); ver (hoog) –, do the long (high) jump; **hande en voete (-viervoet)** –, hop on all fours; **laat** –, blow up, blast; **die snaar het ge**–, the string has sprung (snapped); **in die saal** –, leap (vault) into the saddle; **oor die draad** –, clear (jump over) the fence.
springbok, springbok (springbuck).
springer, (-s), jumper; leaping-mullet.
springfontein, fountain.
springhaas, jumping-hare.
springlewendig, (-e), brisk, alive and kicking.
springmatras, spring-mattress.
springmielies, pop-corn.
springperd, vaulting-horse.
springplank, jumping-board, diving-board.
springstof, explosive.
springstok, jumping-, vaulting-pole.
springteuel, martingale.
springtou, skipping-rope.
springty, spring-tide.
springveer, spring.
springvloed, spring-tide.
sprinkaan, (sprinkane), locust, grasshopper.
sprinkaanbeampte, locust-officer.
sprinkaanplaag, locust-plague, -menace.
springkaanvoël, locust-bird, (large) white stork, (small) pratincole.
sprinkel, (ge-), sprinkle; damp.
sproei, spru, n. thrush, sprue.
sproei, (ge-), sprinkle, water; spray.
sproeier, (-s), sprinkler; spray-nozzle.
sproet, (-e), freckle.
sproeterig, (-e), freckled.
sprokie, (-s), fairy-tale; fable, fiction.
sprokiesagtig, (-e), fairy-like, fairy- ...
sprokiesland, fairy-land.
sprong, (-e), jump, leap, bound; caper, gambol, hop; 'n – **doen**, take a leap; 'n – **in die duister doen**, take a leap in the dark; **die** – **waag**, take the plunge; **in (met) één** –, at a bound; **met 'n** – **(met** –**e) vooruitgaan**, advance by leaps and bounds; **op stel en** –, immediately.
sprongsgewyse, by leaps and bounds.
sprook: hy sprak geen –, he said ne'er a word.
sprot,(-**te**), sprat.
spru, sproei, thrush, sprue.

spruit, (-e), n. shoot, sprout; offshoot, offspring; tributary, small stream, "spruit".
spruit, (ge-, gesprote), shoot, sprout; issue, descend (from).
spruitjie, little shoot (sprout).
spruitkool, (Brussels) sprouts.
spu(ug), vide **spoeg**.
spui, (-e), sluice.
spuigat, scupper-hole; **dit loop die** –**e uit**, that is the limit.
spuit, (-e), n. syringe, squirt; (water-)hose; fire-engine.
spuit, (ge-), spout, squirt; spray.
spuitfles, siphon.
spuitgat, blow-hole.
spuitslang, (water-)hose.
spuitwater, aerated water, soda-water.
spuitwaterfles, siphon; soda-water bottle.
spul, lot, caboodle; affair, case; quarrel.
spulletjie, (-s), affair, business.
spuug, vide **spoeg**.
spuugslang, spitting snake.
spuwing, spitting, expectoration.
spy, (-e), **spie**, (-ë), pin, wedge, cotter.
spyker, (-s), nail; 'n – **in sy doodkis**, a nail in his coffin; **die** – **op die kop slaan**, hit the nail on the head; –**s met koppe slaan**, take a strong line; deal straight blows.
spykerbalsem, Spykerointment.
spykerskrif, cuneiform writing.
spys, n. food; – **en drank**, meat and drink, solid and liquid food.
spys(ig), (ge-), feed.
spyskaart, -**lys**, menu, bill of fare.
spysvertering, digestion; **slegte** –, indigestion.
spyt, n. regret, repentance, sorrow; **jy sal daar nog** – **oor (van) kry (hê)**, you shall repent (regret) it; **ten** –**e van**, in spite of; **tot my (groot)** –, (much) to my regret; – **is 'n goeie ding, maar hy kom altoos te laat**, it is no use crying over spilt milk.
spyt, (ge-), regret, be sorry; **dit** – **my**, I am sorry.
spytig, (-e), regrettable.
st!, hist!, hush!
staaf, (stawe), n. bar, rod; bar, ingot (of gold, silver); brick (of copper).
staaf, **stawe**, (ge-), confirm, bear out, prove, substantiate (a claim, an argument, a charge).
staafgoud, bar-gold, gold in bars.
staafkoper, copper-bricks.
staafmagneet, bar-magnet.
staafsilwer, bar-silver, silver-ingots.
staak, (stake); n. stake, pole.
staak, (ge-), stop, knock off; **die werk** –, strike, go (come out) on strike; **betalinge** –, stop (suspend) payment; **bedrywighede ('n wedstryd)** –, abandon activities (a match); **die stemme** –, the votes are equally divided, there is a tie in the voting.
staal, (1) steel.
staal, (stale), (2) sample, pattern.
staal, (ge-), steel (the nerves).
staalagtig, (-e), steely, steel-like.
staalbad, steel-bath, chalybeate spring.
staalbalk, steel-girder.
staalblou, steel-blue, steely blue.
staaldraad, steel-wire.
staalfabriek, steel-works.
staalgietery, steel-foundry.
staalgraveur, steel-engraver.
staalgravure, steel-engraving.
staalgrys, steel-grey.
staalhoudend, (-e), chalybeate.
staalkaart, sample-card, pattern-book.
staalkleur, steely colour.

staalplaat, steel-engraving; sheet of steel.
staaltjie, (-s), sample; instance; yarn.
staalwyn, ferruginous wine.
staan, (staat), (ge-), stand, remain upright; be erect; exist; stop; **die horlosie notor (het gaan)** –, the clock, motor has stopped; **wat geskrewe** –, what is written; **wat – daar in die brief?**, what does the letter say?; **dit – in die Bybel**, it is written (it says) in the Bible; **– en lees**, stand up and read; read standing; **jy moenie vir my – en lag nie**, you must not laugh at me, don't stand there laughing at me; **bly –**, remain standing; stop (clock, etc.); **gaan –**, stand up, rise (to one's feet); come to a stop, stop; **goed –**, become, suit; **die kleur – jou goed**, the colour suits you; **ek – goed vir hom**, I'll answer (vouch) for him; **die koring – dun (sleg)**, the wheat is thin (poor); **laat –**, stand, leave alone, leave off, give up (a bad habit); **park (a car); sy vrou het hom laat –**, his wife left him; **hy betaal nie sy kruidenier nie, laat – sy kleremaker**, he does not pay his grocer, let alone (much less) his tailor; **jou man –**, stand firm, hold one's own; **sy kanse – goed**, he stands a good chance; **hoe – sake?**, how are things?, how is business?; **sy sake – sleg**, he is in a bad way financially; **toe ek sien hoe sake –**, when I saw how the land lay (how r atters stood); **dit – nog te besien**, that remains to be seen; **hy weet wat hom te doen –**, he knows how to act (his duty, what to do); **dit sal hom duur te – kom**, he will have to pay (dearly) for it; he will regret it; **voor 'n moeilikheid te – kom**, be faced with a difficulty; **iemand te woord –**, see a person, listen to a person, grant a person an interview; **opsy –**, stand aside; **terug –**, stand back; yield; **haar hande – vir niks verkeerd nie**, no work of any kind comes amiss to her; **sy oë – verwilderd**, he has a wild look in his eyes; **agter iemand –**, stand behind a person; urge a person on; back a person up; **die volk – agter hom**, he has the nation behind him; **bo iemand –**, stand above a person, be superior to a person; **by iemand –**, stand next to a person; back a person up; **in diens – van**, be in the employ (service) of, serve; **iemand in die weg –**, stand in a person's way; **hoe – dit met jou?**, how are you?; **hoe – dit nou met die geld wat jy my skuld?**, how about the money you owe me?; **onder iemand –**, stand (be) under a person; **dié afdeling – onder my**, I am in charge of that department; **onder die invloed – van**, be under the influence of, be influenced by; **onder water –**, be submerged (flooded); **op sy bene –**, stand up, keep on one's feet; **al – jy ook op jou kop**, do what you like; **op die punt – om te gaan**, be on the point of going; **op die wag –**, stand guard, be on duty; **hy – daarop**, he insists on it, he makes a point of it; **ek het hom presies gesê waar dit op –**, I told him exactly how matters stood (what it all amounted to); **– teenoor**, be faced (confronted) by; **hulle – teenoor mekaar**, they oppose each other; **tot – bring**, bring to a standstill, stop, check; **tot – kom**, come to a standstill; **dit – tot jou beskikking**, it is at your disposal; **armoede – ons voor die deur**, poverty stares us in the face (awaits us).
staandak, inclined roof, pitched roof.
staande, standing; permanent; **– leër**, standing army; **– mag**, permanent force; **– water**, still (stagnant) water; **sig – hou**, hold on, carry on; hold one's own.
staander, (-s), standard.
staangeld, grazing fee; stallage.

staanhorlosie, mantelpiece-clock; (groot) –, grandfather's clock.
staanlamp, standard-lamp, table-lamp.
staanplek, stand, parking area; standing room; **uit die –**, from the start.
staanspoor: uit die –, from the (very) start (beginning).
staan-staan, standing (stopping) every now and then, while standing; **– loop**, walk stopping every now and then; **– eet**, eat standing up.
staar, n. pearl-eye, cataract.
staar, (ge-), stare, gaze; **armoede – hulle in die gesig**, poverty stares them in the face.
staat, (state), n. state; condition; rank, position; statement, record, list, form; **– van beleg**, state of siege; **– van sake**, state (condition) of affairs; **egtelike –**, (state of) matrimony; **die kerklike –**, the Church, the ecclesiastical power; **minister van –**, minister of state; **om redes van –**, for state-reasons; **in – stel**, enable; **in – voel**, feel capable, feel up to; **in – wees**, be capable, be able.
staat, (ge-), vide **staan**.
staathuishoudkunde, political economy.
staathuishoudkundige, (-s), political economist.
staatkunde, (ordinary) politics; (farseeing) statesmanship.
staatkundige, (-e), political.
staatkundige, (-s), statesman.
staatlik, (-e), vide **statig**.
staatmaker, (-s), stalwart, man on whom one can depend, prop, mainstay.
staatsaak, state-affair, affair of state.
staatsaangeleentheid, affair of state.
staatsamp, government-post (-office), post in the civil service.
staatsamptenaar, (-nare), civil servant, government official.
staatsbank, state-bank.
staatsbedryf, government-undertaking.
staatsbegroting, (state)budget.
staatsbelang, interest of the state.
staatsbeleid, statesmanship; policy.
staatsbetrekking, vide **staatsamp**.
staatsblad, government gazette.
staatsburger, burgher, citizen.
staatsdienaar, civil servant.
staatsdiens, civil service.
staatseiendom, state-property.
staatsekretaris, secretary of state.
staatsfondse, government-securities.
staatsgeheim, state-secret.
staatsgesag, authority of the state.
staatsgevangene, prisoner of state.
staatsgevangenis, state-prison.
staatsgreep, coup (d'etat).
staatshulp, government-assistance.
staatsie, state, ceremony, pomp; procession.
staatsgebied, bed of state.
staatsiegewaad, -kleed, state-robes.
staatsinkomste, public revenue.
staatsinstellinge, public institution.
staatskas, public exchequer, treasury.
staatskoerant, government gazette.
staatskuld, public (national) debt.
staatsleer, political science.
staatslening, government-loan.
staatslotery, state lottery.
staatsman, statesman, politician.
staatsmansbeleid, policy, statemanship.
staatsmansblik, political insight.
staatsmanswysheid, statesmanship; **'n daad wat van – getuig**, a statesmanlike act.
staatsmisdaad, political offence.
staatsomwenteling, political revolution.

staatsonderneming, government-, state-enterprise (undertaking).
staatspapiere, government securities; state documents.
staatspoorweg, government-railways.
staatsprokureur, attorney-general.
staatsreg, constitutional law.
staatstoesig, government supervision.
staatsvorm, form of government, constitution.
staatsweë: van –, by (on behalf of) the government on authority (of the government).
staatswetenskap, political science.
stabiel, (-e), stable, steady, firm.
stabilisasie, stabilization.
stabiliseer, (ge-), stabilize.
stabiliteit, stability.
stad, (stede), city, town; **ek gaan na die –,** I am going (in) to town; **hy is uit die –,** he is out of town; **die hele – praat daarvan,** it is the talk of the town.
stade: te – kom, stand in good stead, be of good use, come in handy.
stadgenoot, fellow-townsman, fellow-citizen.
stadhouer, (-s), stadtholder.
stadhuis, hall, city-hall.
stadig, (-e), slow, lingering; **– aan,** slowly, gently.
stadigheid, slowness.
stadigies, slowly.
stadion, (-s), stadium.
stadium, (-s, stadia), stage, phase, period; stadium (length).
stadsaal, town-hall, city-hall.
stadsaanleg, town-planning.
stadsbestuur, municipality, town-, city-council.
stad(s)bewoner, townsman, town-, city-dweller.
stadsbou, town-planning.
stadsgebied, town-area.
stadshuis, town-house; town-hall, city-hall.
stadsklerk, town-clerk.
stadslewe, town-life, city-life, urban life.
stadsmense, townsfolk, city-dwellers.
stadsraad, municipality, town-council, city-coucil.
stadsriolering, city-sewerage.
stadstesourier, city-treasurer.
stadsvryheid, privilege of a city.
stadswapen, city coat of arms.
stadswyk, city-ward, town-quarter.
stadwaarts, townward(s), cityward(s), towards the town (city).
staf, (stawe), staff (support, sign of office or authority; body of officers, nurses, etc.); mace (in Parliament); (marshall's) baton; (bishop's) crozier; **my – en steun,** my staff and stay, my chief support; **die generale –,** the general staff.
stafdraer, mace-bearer.
stafkaart, staff-map, ordnance-map.
stafmusiek, regimental band (music).
stafoffisier, staff-officer.
stafrym, alliteration, initial rhyme.
stag, (-ge, stae), stay.
stagnasie, stagnation.
staker, (-s), striker.
staking, (-e, -s), cessation, stoppage (of activities); strike (of workmen); tie (of votes); suspension (of payment); **daar was 'n – van stemme,** the voting resulted in a tie.
stakingskomitee, strike-committee.
stakingsreg, right to strike.
stal, (-le), n. stable (for horses). cowshed (for cattle); **op – sit,** stable.
stal, (ge-), stable, put up.
stalagmiet, (-e), stalagmite.

stalaktiet, (-e), stalactite.
staldeur, stable-door.
stalhings, stallion.
stalhouer, stable-keeper.
staljong, stable-boy, groom.
stalles, (pl.) stalls (in theatre).
stalletjie, (-s), stall, booth; small stable.
stalmeester, master of the horse.
stalmis, stable-manure, -dung.
stalperd, stable-horse.
stam, (-me), n. stem (of tree, plant), trunk (of tree); tribe, clan (of people), stock, race; stem (of word);
stam, (ge-), form stems (a stem); **– van,** descend from; **– uit die tyd van,** date from the time of.
stamboek, genealogical register; pedigree-book, stud-book.
stamboekbeeste, blood cattle.
stamboekperd, thorough-bred-horse.
stamboekvee, pedigree-cattle.
st(r)amboel, vide **snaar,** n.
Stamboel, Istanbul, Constantinople.
stamboom, genealogical tree, pedigree.
stamel, (ge-), stammer (out), falter.
stamelaar, (-s), stammerer, falterer.
stamgenoot, (-note), fellow-tribesman, fellow-clansman.
stamgod, tribal god.
stamhoof, tribal chief.
stamhouer, son and heir.
stamhout, trunk-wood.
stamhuis, dynasty; ancestral home.
stamklinker, stem-vowel.
stamland, mother-country.
stammoeder, ancestress; first mother.
stamouers, acestors; first parents.
stamp, (-e), n. knock, blow; bruise; stamp (of foot); stamping.
stamp, (ge-), knock, pound, hit, give a blow; stamp; pound, crush; bruise; bump, jolt; thud; pitch (of ship); ram (into gun, throat); **fyn –,** pound, crush, bray; **gestampte mielies,** samp, stamped mealies; **met -e en stote,** jerkingly; with difficulty.
stampblok, pounding block.
stamper, (-s), pounder, stamper; jumper (-drill); stamp; pestle; rammer; pistol (of flower); **met – e en stoter,** on foot.
stamperboor, jumper-drill.
stamperig, (-e), bumpy, jolty.
stampkar, springless cart.
stampmeul, stamp-mill, crushing-mill.
stampmielies, samp, stamped mealies.
stampplek, bruise; jolty place (in road).
stampveer, bumper.
stampvoet, (ge-), stamp one's feet (in anger); (of horses) paw the ground.
stampvol, (-le), chock-full, crammed, packed, crowded.
stamregister, genealogical register.
stamtaal, parent-language.
stamvader, ancestor, progenitor.
stamverwant, (-e), akin, cognate, related; **–e woorde,** cognate words.
stamverwant, (-e, -es), n. blood-relation.
stamverwantskap, affinity, kinship, relationship, community of race.
stamwoord, root-word, stem.
stand, (-e), position, posture, attitude (of the body); state, condition, situation; degree, rank, standing, station (in life); class, circle, caste, order; position, level, height (of barometer); phase (of moon); score (in a game); **– van die partye,** position (strength) of the parties; **– van die spel,** score; **– van sake,** state

standaard (condition) of affairs; **hoë (lae) – in die maatskappy,** high (low) degree (rank, station) in life (society); **hoëre en laere –e,** higher and lower classes; **– hou,** hold one's own, hold out, stand firm; **die muur, sy geluk het – gehou,** the wall, his luck held (lasted); **bo sy – lewe,** live beyond his income; **in – bly,** remain intact, last, endure; **in – hou,** keep up, maintain; **tot – bring,** effect, bring about, achieve, accomplish; **tot – kom,** be effected (brought about); come about (into being).
standaard, (-e, -s), standard.
standaaardgewig, standard-weight.
standaardgoud, standard-gold.
standaardloon, standard-wage.
standaardprys, standard-price.
standaarduitgawe, standard-edition.
standaardwerk, standard-work.
standbeeld, statue.
stander, (-s), stand (for hats, umbrellas); cruet-stand; post, upright.
standerd, (-s), standard, class.
standertjie, (-s), cruet-stand.
standgenoot, (-note), man of one's own class, social equal.
standhou, vide **stand.**
standhoudend, (-e), lasting, permanent.
standjie, (-s), tiff, quarrel row.
standplaas, stand; station, post (of officer); place (of minister).
standpunt, standpoint, point of view.
standverskil, social inequality; class-distinction.
standvastig, (-e), steadfast, resolute, firm, constant.
standvastigheid, steadfastness, constancy.
stang, (-e), bit (of a birdle); rod, bar; **die – (tussen die tande) vasbyt,** become unmanageable, take one's own course.
stangkoeël, bar-shot.
stank, (-e), stench, stink; **– vir dank kry,** get more kicks than halfpence, be treated ungratefully.
stanniool, (-niole), tin-foil.
stansa, (-s), stanza.
stap, (-pe), n. step, pace, stride; footstep; **'n – agteruit, vooruit, in die regte rigting,** a step backward, forward, in the right direction; **die eerste – doen,** take the first step (the initiative); **by elke –,** at every step; **– vir –,** step by step.
stap, (ge-), walk, go on foot; hike, foor it, slog it; **'n entjie gaan –,** go for a walk; **op die trein –,** get on the train, take (board) the train; **– aan,** get along!
stapel, (-s), n. pile, stack, heap; stocks (shipbuilding); stock (of cattle); **van – laat loop,** launch; **van – loop,** be launched; **goed van – loop,** go (pass off) without, a hitch.
stapel, stawel, (ge-), stack, pile up, heap up; build.
stapelartikel, staple-commodity.
stapelgek, stawelgek, raving mad.
stapelgoed(ere), staple-commodities.
stapelhandel, staple-trade.
stapelplaas, -plek, staple(-place), emporium, dumping place (mil.).
stapelwolk, cumulus.
stapper, (-s), (fast) walker; hiker, footslogger; **met dapper en –,** on foot.
staptog, hike.
stapvoets, at a walking-pace.
star, (-re), stiff, fixed.
staroog, (ge-), stare (gaze) fixedly
stasie, (-s), station.
stasiegebou, station-building.
stasiemeester, station-master.

stasieweg, station-road.
stasioneer, (ge-), station.
stat, (-te), Kaffir-village (-kraal).
statebond, federation of states; **S–,** Commonwealth of Nations.
Statebybel, State-(translation of the) Bible, Authorised Version.
State-Generaal, States General.
Statevertaling, State-translation.
statika, statics.
staties, (-e), static.
statig, (-e), stately, solemn, dignified.
statigheid, stateliness, dignity.
statistiek, (science of) statistics; (pl. -e), statistics, returns, figures.
statisties, (-e), statistical.
statistikus, (-se, -ici), statistician.
status, status, position.
statuêr, (-e), statutory.
statuur, (-ture), stature, figure, build.
statuut, (-tute), statute, ordinance, regulation, articles (of association).
stawe, vide **staaf,** (ge-),
stawel, vide **stapel,** (ge-),
stawing, confirmation, proof, substantiation, support.
stearien, stearine, stearine.
stede, stee, stead, place; **in – van,** instead of.
stedebou, town-planning.
stedebouer, viceregent, governor.
stedelik, (-e), municipal, urban, civic.
stedeling, (-e), townsman, town-dweller.
stee, vide **stede.**
steeds, (-e), a. urban, town- . . .
steeds, adv. always, ever, constantly, still; **– bereid,** always ready.
steeg, (stege, steë), alley, lane.
steek, (steke), n. stitch; sting (from bee), stab, thrust (with dagger); dig, poke, prod (with finger); dig thrust (pointed remark); **– in die sy,** stitch in the side; **iemand 'n – onder water gee,** have a sly dig at a person; **'n – laat val,** drop a stitch; **dit was so donker dat ek geen – kon sien nie,** it was so dark that I could not see a thing; **geen – (werk) doen nie,** not do a stroke of work; **iemand in die – laat,** fail a person, leave a person in the lurch; **'n skip in die – laat,** abandon a ship; **die argument hou geen – nie,** the argument does not hold water.
steek, (ge-), prick, stab, jab (with a knife), thrust (with a sword); (insect) sting; (wound) burn, smart; (sun) burn, scorch; (pain) shoot, twitch; **bly –,** stick (fast), come to a (dead) stop, stop; **daar – iets agter,** there is something behind it; **geld in onderneming –,** invest (put) money in an undertaking; **hande in die sak –,** put (thrust, stick) hands in the pockets **jouself in die skuld –,** run into debt; **daar – geen kwaad in nie,** there is nothing wrong (no harm) in it.
steekbaard, prickly beard; whiskers.
steekbeitel, mortice-chisel, ripping-chisel.
steekdraad, barbed wire.
steekgras, „steekgras", stick-grass.
steekhaar, -hare, bristles.
steekhoudend, (-e), valid, sound.
steeklyn, pitch-line.
steekpalm, holly box.
steekpan, bed-pan.
steekpasser, -paster, (pair of) dividers.
steekproef, sample.
steekproefstem, straw vote.
steeks, (–, -e), jibbing; **die perd is –,** the horse jibs; **'n –(e) perd,** a jibbing horse, a jibber;

die arbeider is – by die werk, the labourer jibs at his work.
steeksheid, jibbing; repugnance, obstinacy
steekspel, tourney, tilt.
steekvlam, blowpipe-flame.
steekvlieg, gadfly.
steekwond, thrust-wound, stab-wound.
steel, (stele), n. handle (of tool); stem, stalk (of flower); stem (of pipe); shaft (of spear); van die – aftrek, stalk, strip; nou verstaan ek hoe die vurk in die – sit, now I gasp the ins and outs of the matter, now I see how the land lies.
steel, (ge-), steal.
steelkant, blind side.
steelloos, (-lose), stemless, stalkless.
steels, (-e), stealthy, furtive.
steelsgewyse, stealthily, on the sly.
steeltjie, stem, stalk (in plant); little handle; vide steel, n.
steen, (stene), brick; stone, rock; (dobbel)-, die; – (in die blaas), stone, calculus; – des aanstoots, stone of stumbling (Bib.), stumbling-block; – en been kla, complain endlessly; die eerste – werp (gooi), cast the first stone; met 'n hart van –, stony-hearted; geen – onaangeroer(d) laat nie, leave no stone unturned; geen – op die ander laat nie, not leave one stone upon the other.
steenagtig, (-e), stony, rocky.
steenagtigheid, stoniness.
steenarend, golden eagle.
steenbakker, brick-maker.
steenbakkery, brick-making; brick-field.
steenbok, steenbok (steenbuck).
steenboklopers, buck-shot.
Steenbokskeerkring, tropic of Capricorn.
steenboksuring, sheep-sorrel, dock.
steenbras, (-se), steenbras.
steendruk, lithograph; lithography.
steendrukkery, lithography; lithographic (printing) press.
steendrukkuns, lithography.
steendrukplaat, lithograph.
steeneik, holm-oak.
steen-es, (common) ash.
steengoed, earthenware crockery.
steengroef, -groewe, stone-quarry (pit).
steengrond, rocky ground.
steengruis, broken bricks; road-metal.
steenhoop, heap of bricks (stones).
steenhouer, stone-mason (-cutter).
steenkleuredruk, lithochromy.
steenkool, -kole, coal.
steenkoolas, coal-ashes, -dust.
steenkoolbak, coal-scuttle.
steenkoolformasie, carbonaceous system.
steenkoolgas, coal-gas.
steenkoolgruis, culm; coal-dust.
steenkoollaag, coal-seam, -layer.
steenkoolmyn, coal-mine, colliery.
steenkoolwa, coal-truck.
steenlaag, layer of bricks (stones).
steenlegging, laying of foundation-stone.
steenmos, rock-lichen.
steenolie, rock-oil, mineral-oil.
steenoond brick-kiln.
steenperiode stone-age.
steenpuis(ie), boil.
steenskrif, lapidary writing.
steensout, rock-salt.
steentydperk, stone-age.
steenuil, barn-owl.
steenvalk, stone-falcon (-hawk).
steenvink, sandpiper.
steenvlas, earth-flax, asbestos.

steenvorm, brick-mould.
steenvormig, lithification; lithiasis.
steenvrug, stone-fruit, drupe.
steenworp, stone's throw.
steg, (-ge), n. stile.
steg, (ge-), make slips (cuttings).
steggie, stekkie, (-s), cutting, slip.
steier, (-s), n. scaffolding, staging.
steier, (ge-), rear (of horse); stagger, walk unsteadily.
steierbalk, ledger.
steiergat, scaffolding-hole, putlog-hole.
steierpaal, scaffolding-pole.
steierplank, scaffolding-board.
steierwerk, scaffolding.
steil, steep, bluff; straight (hair).
steilte, (-s), steepness; incline, declivity.
stekelagtig, (-e), prickly; (fig.) stinging.
stekelagtigheid, prickliness; sharpness.
stekelbaars, (-e), stickle-back, minnow.
stekelig, (-e), sharp, stinging, acrimonious, prickly.
stekeligheid, sharpness; prickliness.
stekelrig, (-e), spiny (lobster).
stekelvark, porcupine.
steker, (-s), pricker, sticker, stabber.
stekkie, vide steggie.
stel, (-le), n. set; lot, bunch; under-carriage; suite (of rooms); 'n – aftrap, have a nasty experience; put one's foot into it; op – en sprong, without more ado, then and there.
stel (ge-), put, place; adjust, regulate, direct; fix; draw up, compose; 'n val –, set (lay) a trap; 'n wekker –, set an alarm-clock; iemand 'n taak –, impose a task on a person; (math.) – dat, let; gesteld dat, supposing that; – jou in my plek, put yourself in my place; in die lig –, bring to light; in vryheid –, set free (at liberty); alles in die werk –, employ every means, leave no stone unturned; die prys op 'n pond –, fix the price at a pound; ter hand –, hand (over) to; tevrede –, satisfy; stellende trap, positive degree.
steler, (-s), stealer, thief.
stelkunde, algebra.
stellasie, (-s), scaffolding, stand, structure, framework; (fruit-)tray.
steller, (-s), adjuster; trainer; writer.
stelletjie, stilletjie, commode, chamber-stool.
stellig, (-e), a. positive (assertion), definite (promise), firm, fixed, certain.
stellig, adv. positively, definitely; hy sal – kom, he is sure to come.
stelligheid, positiveness, certainty.
stelling, (-e, -s), proposition, theorem (math.); premise, supposition, hypothesis; thesis; (milit.) position; – neem teen, make a stand against, oppose.
stellingoorlog, position-war(fare).
stelmoer, adjusting-nut.
steloefening, composition-exercise.
stelp, (ge-), sta(u)nch, stop.
stelreël, maxim, principle, precept, rule.
stelsel, (-s), system.
stelselloos, (-lose), unsystematic.
stelselmatig, (-e), systematic.
stelskroef, set-screw, adjusting-screw.
stelsleutel, adjusting-wrench, -spanner.
stelt, (-e), stilt; op –e loop, walk on stilts; 'n plek op –e sit, cause an uproar in a place.
steltloper, stilt-walker.
stem, (-me), n. voice; vote; eerste (tweede) – sing, sing first (second) part; jou – uitbring, cast (record) your vote; die –me opneem, (tel), count the votes; met algemene – aanneem,

pass (agree to) ananimously (without a dissentient vote); **die – van die gewete,** the voice of conscience; **jou – verhef,** raise your voice; **met luider –,** in a loud voice.

stem, (ge-), vote, go to the poll, record (cast) one's vote; tune (a musical instrument); **treurig –,** make sad; **gunstig –,** incline favourably; **– oor,** vote on; **laat – oor,** put to the vote; **– teen,** vote against; **– voor,** vote for (in favour of).

stembande, (pl.), vocal chords.
stembandklapper, glottal stop.
stembiljet, ballot-paper, voting-paper.
stembrief(ie), ballot-paper, voting-paper, vote; **20 ongeldige stembriefies,** 20 spoilt votes (ballotpapers).
stembuiging, modulation, inflection (of the voice), intonation.
stemburo, (-'s), polling-station (-booth).
stembus, ballot-box, poll.
stemdag, polling-day, election-day.
stemdistrik, electoral division.
stemfluitjie, tuning-pipe.
stemgeluid, (sound of the) voice.
stemgeregtig, (-de), entitled to vote, having a vote, enfranchised.
stemgeregtigde, (-s), (registered) voter.
stemhamer, tuning-hammer.
stemhebbend, (-e), voiced.
stemloos, (-lose), voiceless, mute, dumb; voiceless (consonant); without a vote.
stem(me)werwer, canvasser (for votes).
stemmer, (-s), tuner; voter.
stemmig, (-e), sedate, quiet, staid, sober.
stemmigheid, sedateness, soberness.
stemming, (-e, -s), ballot, voting, vote, poll; mood, state of mind, humour, disposition; tuning; **in 'n feestelike –,** in a festive mood; **daar heers 'n flou (vaste) – op die mark,** the tone of the market is weak (firm); **die algemene – was daarteen,** the general feeling was against it, **'n – eis,** demand a division; **'n – skep,** create an atmosphere; **tot – oorgaan,** proceed to the vote.
stemoefening, voice-training, voice-production.
stemopnemer, teller (in Parliament); (at an election) returning-officer, polling-officer, scrutineer.
stempel, (-s), n. stamp; seal; impression, imprint, (post-)mark, stamp, seal; hall-mark; stigma (bot.); **–s van koper en van rubber,** copper- and rubberstamps; **sy – op 'n stuk afdruk,** put his seal to a document; **sy – op sy leerlinge afdruk,** leave his imprint (stamp, seal) on his pupils; **die – van die waarheid,** the stamp of truth; **'n man van die ou –,** a man of the old stamp.
stempel, (ge-), stamp; hall-mark; mark, brand.
stempelaar, (-s, -lare), stamper, chopper.
stempelafdruk, imprint, stamp, seal.
stempelband, cloth-binding.
stempeldatum, post-mark date.
stempelkussing, inking-pad.
stempelmasjien, stamping-machine.
stempelskroef, stamp-screw.
stempelsnyer, die-sinker, stamp-cutter, engraver, medalist.
stemplek, polling-station.
stemreg, franchise, suffrage, vote, right to vote; **algemene –,** universal suffrage; **– verleen,** enfranchise, give the vote.
stemregister, voters' list, polling-register.
stemregvrou, suffragette.
stemsleutel, tuning-key.
stemspleet, glottis; **van die –,** glottal.

stemval, cadence,
stemvee, polling-cattle.
stemverandering, change of voice.
stemverheffing, raising of the voice.
stemvorming, voice-production.
stemvurk, tuning-fork.
Sten-geweer, Sten (gun).
stenig, (ge-), stone (to death), lapidate.
steniging, stoning, lapidation.
stenograaf, (-grawe), stenographer, shorthand-writer.
stenografie, shorthand, stenography.
stenografies, (-e), stenographic.
stentorstem, stentorian voice.
steppe, (–, -s), steppe.
ster, (-re), star; luminary, shining light; **vallende –,** shooting star; **vaste –,** fixed star; **veranderlike –,** variable star; **met –re besaai,** star-spangled, studded with stars, starry; vide **sterretjie.**
stereofonies, stereophonic.
stereografie, stereography.
stereogram, stereogram.
stereometrie, stereometry.
stereometries, (-e), stereometric(al).
stereoskoop, (-skope), steroscope.
stereoskopies, (-e), stereoscopic(al).
stereotiep, (-e), a., stereotype.
stereotipeer, (ge-), stereotype.
sterf, sterwe, (ge-), die; **'n duisend dode –,** die a thousand deaths; **– aan 'n siekte,** die of a disease; **– aan sy wonde,** die from his wounds; **– op die brandstapel,** die at the stake; **op sterwe na dood,** on the point of death, all but dead; **– van armoede (dors, skrik, verdriet),** die of poverty (thirst, fright, grief).
sterfbed, death-bed.
sterfdag, day of one's death; **tot (aan) my –,** till my dying day.
sterfgeval, death.
sterfhuis, house of the deceased.
sterfjaar, year of one's death.
sterfkamer, death-chamber (-room).
sterflik, (-e), mortal.
sterflikheid, mortality.
sterfling, sterweling, (-e), mortal, mortal being; **daar was geen – nie,** there was not a soul.
sterf(te)lys, mortality-list, table of mortality, casualty-list (mil.).
sterfte, mortality, death-rate.
sterftelys, vide **sterf(te)lys.**
sterftestatistiek, mortality-returns.
sterftesyfer, death-rate.
sterfuur, dying-hour, hour of death.
ster(re)gewelf, starry vault (of heaven).
steriel, (-e), sterile, barren.
sterilisasie, sterilization.
steriliseer, (ge-), sterilize.
steriliteit, sterility, bareness.
sterk, (–, -e), a. strong; virile, robust, powerful; **'n – bewys, geheue, leër, skoen, vesting,** a strong proof, memory (also retentive), army, boot, fortress; **– drank,** strong drink, spirituous liquor; **'n – werkwoord,** a strong verb; **ek is nie – in Grieks nie,** Greek is not my strong point.
sterk, (ge-), strengthen; invigorate, encourage; **iemand – in sy kwaad,** encourage a person in the wrong.
sterkgebou(d), (-de), strongly built, well-built (-knit).
sterkgespierd, (-e), muscular.
sterking, strengthening.
sterkte, strength; fortress, stronghold; intensity (of light);

sterkwater, spirits (of wine), aqua fortis; **op – sit**, keep in spirits.
sterling, sterling.
sterlinggebied, sterling area.
ster(re)loop, course of heavenly bodies.
sterrebaan, orbit (course) of a star.
sterrebeeld, constellation.
sterredag, sidereal day.
sterrediens, star-worship.
ster(re)gewelf, starry vault (of heaven).
sterrehemel, starry heavens (sky).
sterrejaar, sidereal year.
sterrekunde, astronomy.
sterrekundig, (-e), astronomical.
sterrekundige, (-s), astronomer.
sterrekyker, telescope; star-gazer.
ster(re)loop, course of heavenly bodies.
sterrereën, sterrereent, meteoric shower.
sterretjie, little star; asterisk (printing); **iemand –s laat sien**, make a person see stars.
sterretyd, sidereal time.
sterrewag, (astronomical) observatory.
sterrewiggelaar, astrologer.
sterrewiggelary, astrology.
stert, (-e), tail, brush (of fox), pigtail; train, rear, back portion; **met die – tussen die bene**, with the tail between one's legs, with a crestfallen (hang-dog) air.
stertbeen, tail-bone, coccyx.
stertriem, crupper (of harness); loin-skin (of natives) pull-through; jockbelt.
stertster, comet.
stertstuk, tail-piece.
stertjie, tail, scut; ending (of word).
stertveer, tail-feather, rectrix.
stertvet, tail-fat.
stertvin, tail-fin, caudal fin.
stervormig, (-e), star-shaped, stellate.
sterwe, vide **sterf**.
sterweling, vide **sterfling**.
sterwend, (-e), dying, moribund.
sterwensnood, death-struggle.
sterwensuur, dying-hour, hour of one's death.
stetoskoop, (-skope), stethoscope.
steun, n. support, aid, assistance, help; stay; prop, **– verleen aan**, aid support, lend support to; **met – van**, with the support (assistance, help, aid) of.
steun, (ge-), 1. support, aid, assist, help; back (up), prop (up), support; speak in support of, support (a motion); **geldelik –**, finance, assist financially; **– op**, lean on (a stick), rely on (somebody's help).
steun, (ge-), 2. groan, moan.
steunbalk, supporting beam.
steunmuur, retaining wall.
steunpilaar, pillar, support; buttress.
steunpunt, point of support; fulcrum.
steunsel, support, prop, stay; bar.
steur, (-e), n. sturgeon.
steur, stoor, (ge-), disturb; be in the way, intrude; derange, inconvenience; **– aan**, mind, care about, take notice of; **– jou nie aan my nie**, never mind me; **ek sou my daar niks aan – nie**. I should not take any notice of it.
steurend, storend, (-e), disturbing, deranging, upsetting.
steuring, storing, (-e, -s), disturbance, introsion, inconvenience, nuisance; interference; **atmosferiese –e**, atmospherics.
steurnis, stoornis, (-se), disturbance, nuisance.
stewe, (-ns), prow.
stewel, (-s), boot; **vier –s in die lug lê**, fall right on one's back; drop dead.
stewelkneg, bootjack.

stewig, (-e), a. solid, stout, sturdy, strong, substantial; **'n –e handdruk**, a firm shake of the hand; **–e kos**, substantial food; **'n –e maal**, a hearty (substantial) meal.
stewig, adv. firm(ly), tight(ly), stiff(ly); **– drink**, drink hard; **– staan**, stand firm (fast).
stewigheid, solidity, sturdiness.
stiebeuel, (-s), stirrup-leather.
stiefbroer, stepbrother.
stiefdogter, stepdaughter.
stiefkind, stepchild.
stiefmoeder, stepmother.
stiefmoederlik, (-e), stepmotherly; **– behandel**, treat stepmotherly (harshly), neglect, pass over.
stiefseun, stepson.
stiefsuster, stepsister.
stiefvader, stepfather.
stiegriem, stirrup-leather.
stiekem, sneaking, underhand.
stier, (-e), bull; Taurus.
stiergeveg, bull-fight.
stiermens, minotaur.
stif, (-te, stiwwe), small rod, style, pencil; pin, peg; burin.
stiffie, (-s), small rod; small pin (peg).
stig, (ge-), found (a business, a college), establish, form (a society), plant (a colony), institute, raise, start (a fund), erect (a monument); edify; **brand – (in 'n winkel)**, raise a fire (in a shop), set (a shop) on fire; **goed, kwaad –**, do good, harm (evil); **onheil –**, brew evil, cause mischief; **oproer –**, stir up sedition; **tweedrag –**, cause (stir up) dissension; **vrede –**, make peace.
stigma, (-s, -ta), stigma.
stigmatiseer, (ge-), stigmatize.
stigtelik, (-e), edifying; **–e lektuur**, devotional literature (reading).
stigtelikheid, edification; edifying character.
stigter, (-s), founder, institutor.
stigting, (-e, -s), foundation; formation, institution, erection; edification.
stik, (ge-), (1) stitch (with a machine).
stik, (ge-), (2) suffocate, be suffocated, choke, be choked stifle, be stifled; rot, moulder; **ek –**, I am choking, I am suffocated (stifled).
stikbom, asphyxiating bomb.
stikdonker, a., pitch-dark.
stikdonker(te), n., pitch-darkness.
stikgas, asphyxiating gas.
stiklug, suffocating air.
stikmasjien, stitching-machine.
stiknaald, stitching-needle.
stiksel, stitching.
stikstof, nitrogen.
stikstofhoudend, (-e), nitrogenous.
stil, (–, -le), a., quiet, still, calm; silent; **–le aanbidding**, silent prayer; **'n –le hoop**, an unexpressed hope; **'n – rolprent**, a silent film; **'n – straat**, a quiet street; **'n –le vennoot**, a sleeping partner; **bly –!**, keep quiet!; **– gaan lewe**, retire (from business); **– hou**, keep quiet, be silent; **– lê**, lie still; lie idle; lie low; **– hou**, keep quiet (dark).
stil, (ge-), allay (fears, pain); quiet, hush (the conscience); alleviate, still (pain); satisfy, appease (hunger), quench (thirst); check.
stil, interj., hush! keep quiet!; shut up.
stilbly, (stilge-), keep (remain) quiet.
stileer, (ge-), formalize, stylize.
stilet, (-te), stiletto.
stilheid, quietness. Vide **stil**, a.
stilhou, (stilge-), stop, halt, come to a stop (halt). pull (draw) up.
stilis, (-te), stylist.

stilisties, (-e), stylistic.
stilletjie, stelletjie, chamber-stool, commode.
stilletjies, quietly, softly; **on the quiet, on the sly,** stealthily, secretly.
stillewe, still-life.
stilligheid, secrecy; **in die –,** secretly.
stilsit, (stilge-), sit still (quiet).
stilstaan, (stilge-), stand still (quiet); be at a standstill; **bly –,** stop, come to a stop (halt); **laat –,** stop, check, pull up; **die horlosie staan (stil),** the clock has stopped; **– by 'n gedagte,** pause (stop) at the thought, dwell on a thought; **my verstand staan daarby stil,** it passes my comprehension.
stilstaande, standing, stationary (car); stagnant (water).
stilstand, standstill, stop, stoppage; stagnation; **– van wapens,** armistice, truce; **tot – bring,** bring to a stop (standstill); calm down; **tot – kom,** come to a stop (standstill).
stilswy(g)e, silence; **die – bewaar,** keep (preserve) silence, remain silent.
stilswy(g)end, (-e), silent; taciturn; tacit; **– aanhoor,** listen to in silence; **– aanneem,** agree tacitly; take for granted.
stilswygendheid, taciturnity.
stilte, silence, stillness, quiet; **doodse –,** dead silence; **die – voor die storm,** the lull (calm) before the storm; **in –,** in silence, silently; **in die –,** secretly, on the quiet; privately.
stimulans, (-e, -lantia), stimulant.
stimulasie, stimulation.
stimuleer, (ge-), stimulate.
stimulus, (-se, -muli), stimulus; stimulant.
stingel, (-s), stem, stalk.
stingelloos, (-lose), stemless, stalkless.
stingelrig, (-e), stalked, stalky.
stingelvormig, (-e), stalklike, stemlike.
stink, a. stinking, evil-smelling, fetid.
stink, (ge-), stink, smell bad; **– na,** stink (smell) of.
stinkbesie, stink-bug, garden-bug.
stinkblaar, thorn-apple, stramony.
stinkbol, stink-ball.
stinkbom, stink-bomb.
stinkdas(sie), stinking rock-rabbit; stinking badger, teledu.
stinkdier, polecat, skunk.
stinkend, (-e), stinking; **sig – maak by,** stink in the nostrils of.
stinkerd, (-s), stinkard, stinker, stinkpot, skunk (also fig.).
stinkerig, (-e), smelly; cocky.
stinkhout, stinkwood.
stinkklier, scent-gland.
stinkkoeël, stink-ball.
stinkmuishond, Cape polecat.
stinkolie(blaar), (-boom), thorn-apple.
stinkpot, stink-pot; Cape hen
stinkstok(kie), stinking-weed, (penny-)stinker.
stinkvis, stink-fish, bamboo-fish.
stinkvlieg, stink-bug, stink-fly.
stip, (-pe), n., point, spot, dot.
stip, (-te), a. & adv., puntual, precise, accurate; strict; prompt; **-te aandag,** strict attention; **-te betaling,** prompt payment; **– op tyd,** punctually, to the minute; **– in die oë kyk,** look fixedly at a person.
stipendium, (-s, -dia), stipend; scholarship; bursary.
stippel, (-s), n., spot, speck, point, dot.
stippel, (ge-), dot, point, stipple.
stippellyn, dotted line.
stippeltjie, (-s), dot, speck, point.
stippie, (-s), speck, dot, point.
stiptelik, promptly, precisely, strictly.
stiptheid, punctuality; promptness.
stipulasie, (-s), stipulation, condition.
stipuleer, (ge-), stipulate, demand.
stoei, (ge-), wrestle, romp.
stoeier, (-s), wrestler; romper, tomboy.
stoeierig, (-e), romping.
stoeiery, (-e), wrestle, wrestling, romp, fray mêlée, rough-and-tumble.
stoeiwedstryd, wrestle, wrestling-match.
stoel, (-e), n. chair, seat; stool (also bot.); **hy wou op twee –e tegelyk sit,** he fell between two stools; **nie onder –e of banke wegsteek nie,** make no secret of.
stoel, (ge-), stool.
stoelgang, stool, motion.
stoelkleedjie, chair-cover.
stoelkussing, chair-cushion.
stoelleuning, chair-back.
stoelmat, chair-bottom.
stoelmatter, chair-bottomer.
stoep, (-e), stoep.
stoepkamer, stoep-room.
stoepsitter, stoep-fixture.
stoer, (-e), sturdy, hardy, stout.
stoerheid, sturdiness.
stoet, (-e), procession, train.
stoetery, (-e), stud; stud-farm.
stoetram, stud-ram.
stoets, (–, -e-), obtuse, blunt; **– hoek,** obtuse angle; **– neus,** stumpy nose.
stof, (stowwe), n. (1) dust, powder, (pl.) dust-storms; **die – van jou voete skud,** shake the dust from one's feet; **hardloop dat die – (so) trek (staan),** run like blazes; **– afvee(g),** dust remove the dust; **nie by 'n ander se – kom nie,** come nowhere near the other man; **in die – byt,** bite the dust; **in die – kruip,** grovel in the dust, lick the dust; **in die – vertrap,** trample in the dust; **iemand onder – loop,** bowl somebody over; **tot – vergaan,** turn to dust.
stof, (stowwe), n. (2) material, stuff; matter; subject-matter; **– tot nadenke,** food for thought; **lank van –,** long-winded.
stof, (ge-), dust, remove the dust.
stofbesem, hair-broom.
stofblik, dustpan.
stofbril, goggles.
stofdeeltjie, particle of dust; atom.
stofdig, (-te), dust-proof.
stofdoek, duster, dust-cloth.
stoffasie, (-s), material, stuff; calibre.
stoffeer, (ge-), upholster, furnish.
stoffeerder, (-s), upholsterer.
stoffeloos, (-lose), immaterial.
stoffer, (-s), duster.
stofferig, stowwerig, (-e), dusty.
stofferigheid, stowwerigheid, (-e), dustiness.
stoffering, upholstering; upholstery.
stoffie, (-s), speck of dust.
stoffig, stowwig, (-e), dusty.
stofgoud, gold-dust.
stofjas, dust-coat.
stoflik, (-e), material; tangible; **-e oorskot,** mortal remains.
stoflkheid, materiality.
stofloos, (-lose), dustless.
stofluis, book-louse.
stofnaam, name of material; (gram.) material noun.
stofnat, sprinkled, wet on top; **dit het net – gereent,** it was just a drizzle.
stofomslag, dust-cover.
stofreën, -reent, n. drizzle, sprinkle.
stofreën, -reent, (ge-), drizzle.

stofsuier, vacuum-cleaner.
stofwisseling, metabolism.
stofwolk, dust-cloud, cloud of dust.
Stoïes, (-e), Stoic(al).
Stoïsisme, Stoicism, Stoic philosophy.
Stoïsyn, (-e), Stoic, Stoic philospher.
stoïsyns, (-e), stoic(al).
stok, (-ke), n. stick, staff; pole; handle (of broom) stick, club (golf); pointer (in classroom); (wingerd) –, vine; **iemand 'n – in die wiel steek**, put a spoke in somebody's wheel; **met die –gee**, beat, cane, cudgel; **met die – kry**, get caned; **hy is nie met 'n – (met swaarde en –ke) weg te kry nie**, he is not to be shifted (moved) by any manner or means; **onder die – kry**, beat, cane, cudgel; **iemand**, **voor –**, kry, haul a person over the coals, rebuke a person; vide **stokkie**.
stok, (ge-), stop (of breath).
stokalleen, solitary, quite alone.
stokbewaarder, jailer.
stokblind, (-e), stone-blind.
stokdoof, (-dowe), stone-deaf.
stoker, (-s), stoker, fireman; distiller; firebrand.
stokery, (-e), distillery; mischief-making.
stokkerig, (-e), stalky, woody, stringy, fibrous; stocky.
stokkie, (-s), little stick; **'n – voor steek**, put a stopper on, make an end of, prevent, forestall; **–s draai**, play truant.
stokou, (predicatively: **stokoud**), very old.
stokperdjie, hobby-horse; hobby, fad.
stokroos, hollyhock.
stoksielalleen, all on his own, quite (all) alone.
stokstil, stock-still, motionless.
stokstyf, (-stywe), as stiff as a poker.
stokverf, stopverf, putty.
stokvis, stock-fish, hake.
stol, (ge-), clot, coagulate, congeal; freeze.
stolling, coagulation, congealment.
stolp, (-e), cover, bell-jar.
stolpplooi, box-pleat.
stom, (-me), dumb, mute, speechless; foolish, stupid, dull; poor, wretched, pitiable; **in –me verbasing**, in speechless amazement; **die –me dier**, the poor brute; **hy het geen –me woord gepraat nie**, he never said a word.
stomdronk, dead drunk.
stomheid, dumbness; stupidity.
stommekneg, dumb-waiter.
stommel, (ge-), clatter, clutter.
stommeling, (-e), (1) blockhead, ass.
stommeling, (-e), (2) cluttering, fuss.
stommerik, (-e), fathead, blockhead.
stommigheid, (-hede), stupidity.
stommiteit, (-e), blunder; stupidness.
stomp, (-e), n. stump, stub.
stomp, a. blunt, dull; snub, stumpy; obtuse (angle); **– maak**, take the edge off; **regter-oor –**, right ear cropped.
stompheid, bluntness, dullness.
stomphoek, obtuse angle.
stomphoekig, (-e), obtuse-angled.
stompie, (-s), small stump; end stub (of cigarette); fag-end; stub (of pencil).
stompneus, snub-nose, pug-nose; snub-nosed person; **rooi–**, red stump-nose.
stompoor, crop-ear; crop-eared sheep, etc.
stompsinnig, (-e), stupid, dense, dull.
stompstert, docktail; docktailed animal.
stompstertjie, (-s), crombec(k).
stonde, (-s), hour, time.
stonk, (ge-), roll, approach.
stoof, (stowe), n. stove.

stoof, stowe, (ge-), stew, braise, cook (meat), broil, swelter (in the sun).
stoofappel, cooking-apple, stewing-apple.
stoofpan, sewing-pan.
stoofvleis, stewed meat, stew.
stook, (ge-), fire, stoke (furnace); burn (coal); make (light) a fire; distil (spirits); **kwaad –**, make mischief, stir up strife.
stookgas, cooking-gas, heating-gas.
stookgat, stoke-hole.
stookoond, furnace.
stookplek, fire-place; stoke-hole.
stool, (stole), stole.
stoom, n. steam; **– afblaas**, blow off steam, **– maak**, get up steam; **onder –**, with steam up.
stoom, (ge-), steam; **vis –**, steam fish.
stoombad, steam-bath, vapour-bath.
stoomboor, steam-drill.
stoomboot, steamer, steamship.
stoomdruk, steam-pressure.
stoomfluit, steam-whistle, siren.
stoomhamer, steam-hammer.
stoomjag, steam-yacht.
stoomketel, boiler.
stoomklep, steam-valve, throttle-valve.
stoomkraan, steam-crane, steam-winch.
stoomkrag, steam-power.
stoommasjien, steam-engine.
stoommeul(e), steam-mill.
stoompers, steam-press.
stoomroller, steam-roller.
stoomskip, steamer, steamship.
stoomtrekker, steam-tractor.
stoomvaart, steam-navigation.
stoomvaartlyn, steamship-line.
stoomvaartmaatskappy, steamship-company, steam navigation-company.
stoomverwarming, steam-heating; central heating.
stoomwals, steam-roller.
stoomwassery, steam-laundry.
stoor, (ge-), vide **steur**.
stoornis, vide **steurnis**.
stoot, (stote), n. push, thrust, dig; shot, stroke (billiards); **'n – gee**, give a push; **die – ('n – vorentoe) gee**, give a fillip, set going, advance.
stoot, (ge-), push, thrust, knock, bump; jostle (in a crowd); butt, toss (with the horns); **gewig –**, put the shot; **teen die tafel –**, push (knock, bump) against the table.
stootband, binding, braid; cushion.
stootdemper, shock-absorber.
stootkant, false hem.
stootkarretjie, hand-cart, push-cart.
stootkussing, buffer.
stootplaat, guard (of rifle).
stootskraper, bull-dozer.
stootstoel, invalid-chair.
stootwaentjie, hand-cart; push-cart.
stop, (-pe), n. darn; plug; fill (of tobacco).
stop, (ge-), (1) stop (up), fill (up), plug (up) (a hole); fill (a pipe, a tooth); darn (a sock), stuff (birds, one's ears, a cushion); slip (into one's pocket); bundle (into a vehicle).
stop, (ge-), (2) stop, pull up, halt, come (bring) to a stop.
stopfles, stoppered bottle (jar).
stopgare, -garing, darning-thread.
stopkontak, (electric) plug, connection.
stoplap, filling, stop-gap, expletive.
stop-maar-in, hold all.
stopmiddel, (med.), astringent; stop-gap.
stopnaald, darning-needle.
stoppel, (-s), stubble.
stoppelbaard, stubble(-beard).

stoppelland, -veld, stubble-field.
stoppelrig, (-e), stubbly.
stopplek, (1) darn.
stopplek, (2) halt stop.
stopsel, filling, fill; plug, wad.
stopsetting, (-e, -s), stoppage, stopping.
stopsit, (stopge-), stop, close down; put an end (a stop) to.
stopsy, darning-silk.
stopverf, **stokverf**, putty.
stopwol, darning-wool.
stopwoord, expletive, stop-gap.
storend, vide **steurend**.
storie, (-s), story, tale, yarn; fib; –s **vertel**, tell stories (yarns; fibs); gossip.
storieboek, (angl.) story-book.
storing, vide **steuring**.
storm, (-e, -s), n. storm, gale, tempest; assault; 'n – in 'n glas water, a storm in a tea-cup; deur –e geteister, storm-beaten.
storm, (ge-), storm; 'n vesting –, storm a fortress, uit 'n kamer –, rush (tear, dash) out of a room.
stormagtig, (-e), stormy.
stormbui, squall.
stormdek, hurricane-deck.
stormenderhand, by storm.
storm en drang, (period of) storm and stress.
stormja(ag), (stormge-), storm.
stormjaer, (-s), stormer; dumping.
Stormkaap, Cape of Storms.
stormklok, alarm-bell, tocsin.
stormlamp, hurricane-lamp.
stormloop, (-lope), n., attack, assault, rush; run (on the bank).
stormloop, (stormge-), storm, attack, rush, charge.
stormpas, double quick march (step).
stormram, battering ram.
stormtroepe, storm-troops.
stormvoël, stormy petrel.
stormweer, stormy weather; gale.
stormwind, gale, tempest, wind-storm.
stort, (ge-), pour; spill (milk); shed (blood, tears); deposit, pay in (money); plunge (into water, misery); dit – buite, it is pouring outside; iemand in die ongeluk –, ruin a person.
stortbad, shower (-bath)
stortbui, shower, downpour, deluge.
storting, (-e, -s), deposit, part-payment; shedding, fall; vide **stort**.
stortreën, -reent, n. downpour, torrential rain, deluge (also fig.).
stortreën, -reent, (ge-), come down in torrents (buckets full).
stortsee, heavy sea, topping sea.
stortvloed, flood, torrent; deluge, mass.
stoterig, (-e), butting (bull); stuttering.
stotter, (ge-), stutter, stammer.
stotteraar, (-s), stutterer, stammerer.
stout, a. naughty, bad; bold, daring; die –(e) skoene aantrek, pluck up (screw up one's) courage, venture boldly.
stouterd, (-s), naughty boy (girl).
stoutheid, naughtiness; boldness, daring.
stoutigheid, naughtiness.
stoutmoedig, (-e), bold, daring.
stoutmoedigheid, boldness, courage.
stowe, vide **stoof**, (ge-).
stoww(er)ig, vide **stoff(er)ig**.
straal, (strale), n. beam, ray (of light, hope); flash (of lightning); stream, jet (of water); radius (of a circle); gleam, flicker, (of hope); 'n groot – water, a stream of water.
straal, (ge-), shine; beam, glow, glitter, flash, radiate.

straalaandrywing, jet propulsion.
straalaangedrewe, jet-propelled.
straalbreking, refraction.
straalbuiging, diffraction.
straalbundel, **stralebundel**, pencil of rays, luminous pencil.
straaldier, rayed animal.
straaldraadloos, beam-wireless.
straalpyp, jet-pipe, nozzle.
straalsgewys(e), radially.
straalstasie, beam-station.
straaltjie, (-s), small (feeble, weak) ray, beam, gleam, flicker; trickle (of blood, etc.), squirt (of water), small jet.
straalvegter, jet-fighter.
straalvliegtuig, jet aircraft.
straalvormig, (-e), radial.
straat, (strate), n. street; strait (of the sea); die – meet, stagger drunkenly; van die – opraap, pick out of the gutter.
straat, (ge-), face with stones, pave.
straatbelasting, street-tax, road-(construction-) charges.
straatbetoging, street-demonstration.
straatbord, notice-board.
straatbordjie, name-plate.
straatdeur, street-door; front-door.
straatgespuis, hooligans, street-roughs.
straatgeveg, street-fight.
straatjeug, street-urchins, street-arabs.
straatlawaai, street noise.
straatlied(jie), street song (-ballad).
straatmaker, road-maker, -mender.
straatmusikant, street-musician.
straatreiniger, street-orderly, scavenger.
straatrower, street-robber.
straatrumoer, street-noise.
straatsanger, street-singer.
straatskender, hooligan, street-rough.
straatsteen, pavingstone.
straattaal, street-jargon, vulgar language.
straatveër, street-sweeper, scavenger.
straatverkeer, street-traffic.
straatverligting, street-lighting.
straatweg, highroad.
straatwysie, street-tune, -ballad.
straf, (strawwe), n. punishment, penalty, chastisement; – ondergaan, verdien, undergo, deserve punishment; – kry, get punished (punishment); op – van, under penalty of; op – van die dood, under (on) pain of death; vir –, as a (by way of) punishment.
straf, (strawwe), a. & adv. severe (winter); severe, stern (tone); rigid; hard, stiff; dit het – gereën, it rained heavily; hy drink –, he is a heavy drinker.
straf, (ge-), punish, chastise.
strafbaar, (-bare), punishable; actionable; **strafbare daad**, punishable (indictable) offence.
strafbeding, -**bepaling**, penal (penalty-)clause; penal provision.
strafdoel, penalty-goal.
strafekspedisie, punitive expedition.
straf(fe)loos, (-lose), with impunity.
straf(fe)loosheid, impunity.
strafgerig, (divine) judgement.
strafheid, severity; vide **straf**, a.
strafkolonie, penal settlement (colony), convict-settlement.
strafloos(heid), vide **straffeloos(heid)**.
strafmaatreël, punitive measure.
strafmiddel, (means of) punishment.
strafpredikasie, admonition, lecture.
strafprediker, admonisher, moralist.
strafreëls, punishment-lines.

strafreg, criminal (penal) law.
strafregtelik, (-e), criminal, penal.
strafregter, criminal judge.
strafsaak, criminal case.
strafsitting, criminal session.
strafskop, penalty-kick, free kick.
strafskuldig, (-e), guilty.
straftyd, term (of imprisonment).
strafwerk, punishment-lines (-sums), imposition, detention.
strafwet, vide **strafreg**.
strafwetboek, penal code.
strafwetgewing, criminal legislation.
strak, (-, -ke), tight, taut, tense; severe, hard, fixed.
strakheid, tautness, tenseness; rigidity.
strakkies, presently, in a minute; perhaps.
straks, perhaps; presently; **tot** -!, so long!; bye-bye!
stralekrans, -kroon, halo, aureole.
stralend, (-e), beaming, radiant; –**e gesig**, beaming (radiant) face.
straling, radiation.
stram, (-, me), stiff, rigid.
stramheid, stiffness, rigidity.
stramien, (open) canvas; framework.
strammerig, (-e), slightly, stiff.
strammigheid, slight stiffness.
strand, (-e), n., beach, seaside; strand, seaside, resort.
strand, (ge-), strand, run ashore.
stranddief, beach-comber.
strandgas, seaside-guest.
strandgoed, flotsam, jetsam, wrecked goods.
strandhoof, beach-head.
strandhuis, seaside bungalow.
stranding, stranding.
strandjut, beech-comber; brown hyena.
Strandloper, Beachranger.
strandloper(tjie), sand-plover, -piper.
strandmeer, lagoon, coastal lake.
strandroof, beach-combing.
strandskoen, sand-shoe.
strandstoel, beach-chair.
strandvlooi, sand-flea, earth-flea.
strandwagter, coast-guard.
strandweg, marine-drive, seaside-road.
strandwolf, beach-hyena, brown hyena.
strateeg, (-teë, -tege), strategist.
strategie, strategy.
strategies, (-e), strategic(al).
stratifikasie, stratification, bedding.
stratosfeer, stratosphere.
strawasie, (-s), difficulty.
streef, strewe, (ge-), strive, endeavour; – **na**, strive after, aspire to, aim at, seek after (truth).
streek, (streke), region, track, area, part, point (of compass); trick, wile, artifice, dodge, joke; **'n gemene** –, a dirty trick; **hy is vol streke**, he is up to all kinds of tricks; he is a wily fellow; **streke uithaal**, play tricks; **iemand sy streke afleer**, cure a person of his tricks; **op** –, **van** –, vide **stryk**, n.
streekspraak, -taal, dialect.
streel, (ge-), fondle, caress, stroke; gratify; flatter (one's vanity).
streep, (strepe), n. stroke, line; stripe; streak (of light); dash; **hy het 'n** –, he is not all there; **iemand 'n** – **trek**, play a trick on someone; **do someone an ill turn; een** – **deur**, without a stop (break); **met strepe**, striped.
streep, (ge-), mark with a stripe; cane.
streepkoppie, Cape bunting.
streepmuis, striped field-mouse.

streepsak, grain-bag.
streepsiekte, streak (in sugar-cane).
streepsuiker, cane-juice, a thrashing.
strek, (ge-), stretch, reach, extend; last; **so ver sy invloed**, his influence extends (goes) so far; – **om**, serve to; – **tot**, stretch (etc.) to; conduce (tend) to; **dit** – **jou tot skande**, it is a disgrace to you; **dit** – **jou tot eer**, it does you credit.
strekker, (-s), (ex)tensor, protractor.
strekking, (-e, -s), tendency, drift, inclination; purport, tenor, sense, meaning; – **van**, purport of (a letter).
strekkingsroman, novel with a purpose.
strekspier, (ex)tensor, protractor.
strelend, (-e), caressing; flattering.
streling, (-e, -s), caress; gratification.
strem, (ge-), curdle, coagulate, hinder, retard, obstruct, hold up.
stremming, (-e), curdling, coagulation; hindrance, obstacle, obstruction; congestion, traffic-jam.
stremsel, (-s), curds; rennet.
streng, (–, -e), strict, severe (winter, judge, sentence), rigorous, stern, austere, close (supervision); – **bewaak**, guard closely (strictly); – **toepas**, apply (enforce) rigorously; – **verbode**, strictly prohibited.
strengle, (ge-), plait, twine, twist.
strengeling, intertwining, twisting.
strengheid, strictness, etc, Vide **streng**.
strepie, (-s), stripe, line.
strepiesgoed, striped material.
streptomisine, (-ien), streptomycin.
streukel, vide **struikel**.
strewe, vide **streef**.
strewer, (-s), trier; high-flier; member of an Endeavour Society.
Strewersvereniging, Endeavour Society.
striem, (-e), n., weal (wale), stripe.
striem, (ge-), castigate, lash, cut.
strignien, strignine, strychnine.
strik, (-ke), n., knot, bow; snare, noose, trap (for catching); snag; **'n** – **lê (span)**, lay (set) a snare.
strik, (-te), a. strict, rigorous, severe; precise, accurate.
strik, (ge-), tie (in a bow); snare.
strikdas, bow(tie).
strikkie, (-s), knot; ribbon; bow(-tie).
strikknoop, loop-knot.
striktelik, strictly.
striktheid, strictness; precision.
strikvraag, poser, puzzling question.
string, (-e), n., string; thread, skein (of yarn), strand (of rope); trace (of harness).
stroef, **(stroewe)**, stiff; rough; gruff, surly, roughmannered.
stroefheid, stiffness; gruffness.
strofe, (-s), strophe.
strofies, (-e), strophic.
stroming, (-e, -s), stream, current; tendency, drift, trend.
strompel, (ge-), stumble, hobble, limp.
strompelaar, (-s, -lare), stumbler.
strompeling, (-e), stumble, stumbling.
stronk, (-e), n. stalk; stump.
strontium, strontium.
strooi, n. straw.
strooi, (ge-), scatter (money, seeds); strew (flowers), sow (fertilizer); sprinkle, dredge (meal, sugar).
strooibiljet, hand-bill.
strooiblom, everlasting, immortelle.
strooidak, thatched roof.
strooidakhuis, house with thatched roof.
strooier, (-s), strewer, castor, sprinkler.

strooihalm, (blade of) straw.
strooihoed, straw-hat, boater.
strooihuis, stroois, struis, (-e), straw hut, Bantu hut, **hy het naby die** – **omgedraai**, he has a touch of the tar-brush.
strooijonker, best man.
strooikleurig, (-e), straw-coloured.
strooimandjie, flower-girl's basket.
strooimeisie, bridesmaid.
strooipop, straw-doll, figure-head.
stroois, vide **strooihuis**.
strooisand, fine sand.
strooisel(s), saw-dust, shavings; litter.
strooisuiker, castor-sugar.
strooitjie, (-s), little straw; **hy sal niemand 'n** – **in die weg lê nie**, he won't harm a fly.
strook, (**stroke**), n., strip, band, frill, flounce (needlework), couterfoil.
strook, (ge-), agree, tally, fit in; **dit** – **nie met my planne nie**, it does not agree (fit in) with my plans.
stroom, (**strome**), n., stream; current (in ocean, of electricity); flood (of light, tears); flow (of words); spate (of words); torrent; **strome reën**, torrents, of rain; **teen die** – **ingaan**, swim against the stream; try to stem the tide.
stroom, (ge-), stream, flow, rush, pour; **trane** – **oor haar wange**, tears run (course) down her cheeks, **die menigte** – **na die mark**, the multitude flocks to the market; **briewe** – **binne**, letters come pouring in.
stroomafwaarts, downstream.
stroombed, channel of a stream, river-bed.
stroombelyn, (-de), streamlined.
stroombelyning, streamlining.
stroombreker, contact-breaker, interruptor, cut-off starling (of a bridge).
stroomdraad, live wire; contact-wire.
stroomgebied, river-basin; catchment-area.
stroomgod, river-god.
stroomgodin, naiad.
stroomkring, (electric) circuit.
stroomlewering, current-supply.
stroomlyn, streamline.
stroommeter, ammeter.
stroomnimf, water-nymph, naiad.
stroomopwaarts, upstream; **altyd** – **wees**, be contrary (perverse).
stroompie, little stream, rivulet.
stroomsterkte, strength of current.
stroomverbruik, consumption of current.
stroomversnelling, rapid.
stroomwisselaar, commutator, reversing-switch.
stroop, n., syrup, treacle, love (tennis).
stroop, (ge-), pillage, plunder; strip; poach (game).
stroopagtig, (-e), like syrup, syrupy.
stroopbende, marauding band.
stroopkwas: met die – **werk**, butter up, flatter.
strooplekker, toady, lick-spittle.
strooppot, syrup-pot; love-game (tennis).
stroopsoet, as sweet as honey, honeysweet; very sweet (good) (of child).
stroopstel, love-set (tennis).
strooptog, raid, marauding expedition.
strop, (-pe), strap, brace, rope, halter; "strop" (for oxen); **jou nek in die** – **sit**, put your head in the noose; **tot die** – **veroordeel word**, be condemned to the gallows; **die** – **kry weens moord**, get the rope (swing) for murder; **vir die** – **groot word**, grow up for the gallows.
stroper, (-s), poacher; raider, marauder; combat.
stroperig, (-e), syrupy; cloying.
strot, (-te), throat.

strotaar, jugular vein.
strotklep, epiglottis.
strottehoof, larynx.
struif, **struis**, omelette.
struik, (-e), bush, shrub.
struikagtig, (-e), bushy, shrubby.
struikel, **streukel**, (ge-), stumble, trip.
struikelblok, stumbling-block, obstacle.
struikeling, (-e), stumble, trip.
struikgewas, shrubs, brushwood.
struikroos, bush-rose.
struikrower, robber, highwayman.
struikrowery, highway-robbery.
struis, vide **struif** & **strooihuis**.
struktuur, (-ture), structure, tecture.
struweling, stribbeling, (-e), difficulty, trouble, row. ruction.
stry, (ge-), fight, combat, contend, struggle; argue; quarrel; contradict, deny; **jy kan tog nie** – **(daarteen) nie**, you can't deny (contradict) that.
stryd, fight, battle, combat, struggle, conflict, war; **die** – **om die bestaan, die lewe**, the struggle for existence, life; **die** – **teen malaria**, the fight (war) against malaria; **'n** – **voer**, wage war; **die goeie** – **stry**, fight the good fight, **in** – **met my bedoelinge**, contrary to my intentions; **in** – **met die wet**, contrary to (against the law.
strydbaar, (-bare), fighting, efficient, capable of bearing arms; **elke strydbare man**, every man capable of bearings arms (fighting man).
strydbaarheid, efficiency, fitness (preparedness) for war; maritial spirit.
strydbyl, war-axe, battle-axe, tomahawk.
strydend, (-e), fighting, struggling, striving; militant (church); –e **burgers**, burghers in the field; conflicting (interests), incompatible.
stry(d)er, (-s), fighter, combatant, warrior.
strydgenoot, (-note), companion-, brother-in-arms, fellow-soldier.
strydig, (-e), conflicting, clashing, contrary; – **wees met**, conflict (clash) with, be inconsistent with.
strydigheid, incompatibility, inconsistency, discordance, disparity.
strydknots, -kolf, mace, war-club.
strydkrag, fighting-power; (pl.) military forces.
strydkreet, war-cry, battle-cry; slogan.
strydleus(e), slogan, watchword, motto.
strydlus, pugnacity, warlike (bellicose) spirit, fighting spirit.
strydlustig, (-e), bellicose, pugnacious, combative; **in 'n** – **e stemming**, in a fighting mood, spoiling for a fight.
strydmag, military force.
strydmakker, fellow-soldier, brother-, companion-in-arms.
strydmiddel, weapon.
strydperk, arena, lists.
strydros, battle-, war-horse, charger.
strydvaardig, (-e), ready (prepared) for war (battle), in fighting trim, game.
strydvraag, point (question) at issue (in dispute), moot point (question).
strydwa, (war-)chariot.
stryer, (-s), argumentative person; vide **stry(d)er**.
stryk, n. stroke; **een** – **deur**, without a stop (break); **dit gaan ou** –, it goes as usual (after the old style); – **hou**, keep going; keep straight; **op** – **kom**, get going, strike form, get into one's stride; (**weer**) **op** – **kom (raak)**, regain one's normal health; return to form; **van** – (**af**) **wees**, be off colour (out of form).
stryk, (ge-), 1. go, walk, stride, march.

stryk, (ge-), 2. smooth (one's hair); stroke (one's beard); iron (linen); draw the bow over the strings; strike (the flag); **die hand oor die hare –**, pass one's hand over (one's fingers through) one's hair; **oor (langs) die water –**, skim the water.
strykgoed, laundry.
strykinstrument, stringed instrument.
strykkonsert, concert for strings.
strykkwartet, string-quartette.
stryklaag, stretching course (of bricks).
strykorkes, string-band (-orchestra).
strykplank, ironing-board.
stryksteen, stretcher (brick); whet-stone.
strykstok, bow, fiddlestick.
strykvernis, liquid veneer.
strykyster, flat-iron, (solid) sad-iron.
stu, (ge-), push, press; stow (cargo).
studeer, (ge-), study; prepare, read (for an examination).
studeerkamer, -vertrek, study.
studeerlamp, study-lamp, reading-lamp.
student, (-e), student.
studente, (-s), woman-student.
studenteblad, university-magazine, students' quarterly (monthly, annual).
studentebond, student's union.
studentegrap, students' prank.
studentejool, students' rag.
studentelewe, student-life, college-, university-life.
studentelied, students' song.
studenteraad, students' representative council.
studentestreek, students' prank.
studentevereniging, students' society.
studentikoos, (-kose), student-like, student- . . ., undergraduate- . . .
studie, (-s), study.
studiebeurs, scholarship, bursary.
studieboek, text-book, manuel.
studiefonds, scholarship-fund.
studiejaar, year (of study).
studiekoste, college-expenses.
studiekring, study-circle.
studiereis, educational tour.
studietyd, (years of) study.
studieveld, field of study.
studieverlof, leave for purpose of study.
stug, (-, -ge), reserved, stiff, difficult to deal with, unfriendly, curt.
stugheid, reserve, curtness, coolness.
stuif, stuiwe, (ge-), be dusty; fly rush.
stuifmeel, pollen.
stuifsand, drift-sand.
stuifswam, puff-ball.
stuip, (generally pl. **-e**), convulsion(s), seizure, fit(s); **-e kry**, go off into convulsions (a fit), be seized with a convulsion, get a fit (seizure).
stuipagtig, (-e), convulsive.
stuiptrekking, (-e, -s), convulsion; **die laaste -e**, pangs of death, last agonies.
stuit, (ge-), check, arrest, stop; **so iets – my teen die bors**, that kind of thing is repugnant (revolting) to me; I dislike (detest) that kind of thing; **die vyand –**, check (arrest) the enemy; **op 'n moeilikheid –**, meet with a difficulty.
stuitend, (-e), objectionable, offensive, revolting.
stuiting, stuitlik, (-e), inept, objectionable; **moenie so – wees nie**, don't make yourself objectionable, don't be so silly.
stuitigheid, stuitlikheid, ineptitude, silliness, objectionableness.
stuitjie, (-s), **stuitjiebeen**, tail-bone, coccyx.
stuitjiestuk, aitch-bone.
stuiwe, vide **stuif**.

stuiwer, (-s), halfpenny; **sy – in die armbeurs (armbus) doen**, contribute his mite, also have a word to say.
stuk, (-ke), piece (of bread, furniture, ground, music, out of the Bible,) article (of clothing, furniture), fragment, splinter; paper, document, piece, man (at chess); play; piece, painting; gun, piece (of ordnance); patch, plot (of ground); **'n ingesonde –**, a contribution; **sy is 'n ou – van hom**, she is an old flame (sweetheart) of his; **'n – of tien**, nine or ten, about ten; **daar was tien –s**, there were ten of them; **100 –s vee**, 100 head of cattle; **aan –ke breek**, break to pieces; **voet by – hou**, stick to one's guns; **op sy –ke wees**, be at the top of one's form, be in good fettle; **op – van sake**, after all, in point (as a matter) of fact; **R1 per –**, R1 a (the) piece, R1 each; **'n man uit een –**, a man of sterling character; **iemand van sy –ke bring**, disconcert (upset) a person, put a person out; **– vir –**, one by one.
stukadoor, (-s), stucco-worker, plasterer.
stukadoorswerk, stucco-work.
stukkend, (-e), in pieces, broken; tattered, torn, out of order; **– breek**, break, (to pieces), smash; **– gaan**, go to pieces, break; **– gooi**, break (dash, throw) to pieces, smash; **– maak**, break (to pieces), smash; **– skeur**, tear up, tear to pieces; **– slaan**, knock to pieces; **– sny**, cut up, cut to pieces; **'n vinger – sny**, cut a finger; **– trap**, trample to pieces (under foot); **– val**, fall to pieces, smash; **– voel**, feel broken up; **– wees**, be the worse for liquor.
stukkenderig, (-e), rather broken; **– voel**, feel a bit broken up.
stukkie, (-s), little (small) piece, (little) bit; **'n – kos**, a bite, a feed; **van – tot beentjie (brokkie)**, from beginning to end in all detail; **– vir –**, bit by bit.
stukrag, propelling-force, force of propulsion; driving-force, -power.
stuksgewys(e), singly, one by one.
stukvat, "stukvat", vat.
stukwerk, piece-work; patch-work.
stukwerker, piece-worker.
stulp, (-e), lamp-shade; vide **stolp**.
stumperd, (-s), bungler; poor blighter; poor thing.
stumperagtig, (-e), stupid, bungling.
stustraal, ram-jet.
stustraalvliegtuig, ram-jet aircraft.
stut, (-te), n. prop. support, stay; buttress, stanchion; strut; truss.
stut, (ge-), prop (up), support, shore (up), buttress (up), truss (up).
stutbalk, supporting beam, joist, truss.
stutmuur, buttress.
stutpaal, shore, prop, stay.
stutsel, prop, etc. Vide **stut**, n.
stuur, (sture), n. (steering-)wheel; handles; tiller, rudder, helm (of ship); **aan (agter) die – sit**, be at the wheel.
stuur, (ge-), send, dispatch; drive (horses, motor); steer (ship); direct, guide; **– om 'n geweer**, send for a gun.
stuuras, steering-axle, -shaft.
stuurballon, dirigible balloon.
stuurboord, starboard.
stuurliede, -lui: vide **stuurman**.
stuurloos, (-lose), rudderless; out of control.
stuurman, (stuurliede, -lui), steersman, helmsman, man at the helm; (chief) mate cox(swain); **die beste stuurlui staan aan wal**, it is easier to criticize than to create, bachelor's wives are always best managed.

stuurmanskap, seamanship, navigation.
stuurmanskuns, art of navigation.
stuurrat, steering-wheel.
stuurs, (-e), curt, cool, stiff, reserved, unfriendly, gruff, surly.
stuursheid, curtness, etc,; vide **stuurs**.
stuurstang, steering-rod.
stuurstoel, cockpit.
stuurstok, control-lever, joy-stick.
stuurtoestel, steering-gear; controls.
stuurtou, tiller-rope.
stuwadoor, (-s), stevedore.
styf, (stywe), a. stiff, rigid, unbending; starched; firm; – **van die kou**, stiff with cold.
styf, stywe, (ge-), starch; (fig.) stiffen.
styfheid, stiffness.
styfhoofdig, (-e), obstinate, headstrong.
styfhoofdigheid, obstinacy.
styfkop, headstrong (obstinate) person.
styfkoppig(heid), vide **styfhoofdig(heid)**.
styfsiekte, stywesiekte, ,,stiff-sickness.''
styfte, stiffness.
styg, (ge-), rise, ascend; climb; (prices) go up, advance; **op 'n perd (te perd)**, –, mount (a horse).
stygbaan, air-strip.
styging, (-e, -s), rise, advance, increase.
stygkrag, -vermoë, lift, lifting-power.
styl, 1. style; **die ou –**, the old style.
styl, (-e), 2. post (of door, bed), jamb; strut; stanchion, support; style (bot).
stylblommetjie, flower of speech.
stylfout, bad-style, error in style.
stylleer, art of composition, stylistics.
styloefening, composition-exercise.
stylvol, (-le), in good style, elegant.
stysel, starch.
styselagtig, (-e), starchy.
styselfabriek, starch-factory.
stywe, vide **styf, (ge-)**.
stywerig, (-e), a bit stiff, stiffish.
stywing, stiffening; strengthening (of funds); **tot – van**, in support of.
subiet, suddenly; at once, straightaway.
subjek, (-te), subject (gram.).
subjektief, (-tiewe), subjective.
subjektiwiteit, subjectivity.
subjunktief, (-tiewe), subjunctive.
sub-kommissie, sub-committee.
subliem, (-e), sublime.
sublimaat, (-mate), sublimate.
sublimeer, (ge-), sublimate.
subordinasie, subordination.
subsidie, (-s), subsidy, grant(in-aid).
subsidieer, (ge-), subsidize, aid.
subsidiëring, subsidizing, subsidization.
subskripsie(geld), (angl.), subscription.
substansie, substance.
substantief, (-tiewe), substantive, noun.
substitueer, (ge-), substitute.
substitusie, substitution.
substituut, (-tute), substitute, deputy.
subtiel, (-e), subtle.
subtropies, (-e), sub-tropical.
suf, (suwwe), a. dull, muzzy, stupid, thickheaded; doting (from age).
sufferd, (-s), dunce, dullard, muff.
sufferig, (-e), dull, sleepy, muzzy.
suf(ferig)heid, dullness, muzziness.
suffiks, (-e), suffix.
suffrajet, (-te), suffragette.
sug, (-te), n. 1. sigh; desire, craving, appetite, thirst, love, passion; **'n – van verligting slaak**, heave a sigh of relief; – **na vryheid**, love of freedom; – **om te behaag**, desire to please.

sug, n. 2. pus, matter; (illness) dropsy.
sug, (ge-), sigh, heave a sigh; moan; sigh, sough (of wind); – **onder 'n juk**, groan under a yoke.
suggereer, (ge-), suggest.
suggestief, (-tiewe), suggestive.
suggestiwiteit, suggestiveness.
sugsloot, drain, drainage-channel.
suid, south.
Suid-Afrika, South Africa.
Suid-Afrikaans, (-e), South African.
Suid-Afrikaner, (-s), South African.
Suid-Amerika, South America.
Suid-Asië, Southern Asia.
suide: die –, the south; **na, uit die –**, to, from the south; **ten – van**, (to the) south of.
suideinde, south(ern) end.
suid(e)kant, south(side).
suidelik, (-e), south, southerly; southern; **'n –e wind**, a south(erly) wind.
suiderbreedte, south latitude.
suiderhalfrond, southern hemisphere.
Suiderkruis, Southern Cross.
suiderlig, southern lights, aurora australis.
Suidersee, Zuider (Zuyder) Zee.
suiderstrand, southern coast.
Suid-Europa, South(ern) Europe.
suidewind, south wind.
suidhoek, southern extremity (corner).
suidissel, seidissel, (-s), sow-, milk-thistle.
suidkant, vide **suidekant**.
suidkus, south coast.
suidoos, n. south-easter, south-east wind.
suidoos, adv. south-east.
suidoos(te), n. south-east.
suidoostelik, (-e), south-east(ern); south-easterly; **–e wind**, south-east wind; **–e rigting**, south-easterly direction.
suidooster, (-s), south-easter.
suidoostewind, south-east wind.
Suidpool, South Pole.
Suidpoolreisiger, Antarctic explorer.
Suidpoolsee, Antarctic Ocean.
Suidpooltog, Antarctic expedition.
suidpunt, souther(ern) point (extremity).
Suidsee: Stille –, Pacific Ocean.
Suidsee-eilande, South Sea Islands.
suidsuidoos, south-south-east.
suidwaarts, southward(s), to the south.
suidwes, adv. south-west.
suidwes(te), n. south-west.
Suidwes(-Afrika), South-West Africa.
suidwestelik, (-e), south-west(ern); south-westerly. Cf. **suidoostelik**.
suidwester, south-wester (sou'-wester).
suidwestewind, south-west wind.
suier, (-s), sucker; piston, plunger (of pump) sucker (of plant).
suierklep, piston-valve.
suierstang, piston-rod.
suig, suie, (ge-), suck; **'n verhaal uit jou vingers –**, fabricate (invent) a story; draw on one's imagination.
suigfles, feeding-bottle; suction-flask.
suig(e)ling, (-e), infant, baby.
suiggas, suction-gas.
suiging, suction.
suigklep, suction-valve.
suigkrag, suction-power, -force.
suig(e)ling, infant baby.
suigpomp, suction-pump.
suigvis, sucking fish, sucker.
suigwurm, fluke(-worm).
suiker, sugar.
suikeragtig, (-e), sugary.
suikerbakker, confectioner.

suikerbakkery, confectionery.
suikerbeet, sugar-beet.
suikerbekkie, sugar-bird, sun-bird.
suikerboontjie, sugar-bean.
suikerbos, sugar-bush, protea.
suikerbrood, sponge-cake; sugar-loaf.
suikerfabriek, sugar-factory, -mill.
suikergehalte, sugar-content.
suikerhandel, sugar-trade.
suikerhoudend, (-e), racchariferous.
suikerkan, Red Afrikander.
suikerklontjie, piece of lump-sugar; sugar-plum, mother's darling.
suikerkultuur, sugar-growing, -culture.
suikerkweker, sugar-grower.
suikerland, sugar-field, -plantation.
suikerlepeltjie, sugar-spoon.
suikermeter, saccharimeter.
suikernywerheid, sugar-industry.
suikeroes, sugar-crop, -yield.
suikeroom, sugar daddy.
suikerplantasie, sugar-plantation.
suikerpot(jie), sugar-basin.
suikerproduksie, sugar-production.
suikerraffinadery, sugar-refinery.
suikerraffinadeur, sugar-refiner.
suikerriet, sugar-cane, sweet cane.
suikersiekte, diabetes.
suikersoet, as sweet as sugar, sugary, sugared (words), honeyed.
suikerstrooier, sugar-castor, -sprinkler.
suikerstroop, molasses.
suikersuur, saccharic acid.
suikertand, sweet tooth; – e **uittrek**, stop taking (cut out) sugar (sweets).
suikertang(etjie), sugar-tongs.
suikervoël(tjie), sugar-bird, sun-bird.
suikerwater, sugar-water.
suil, (-e), pillar, column, obelisk, pile; – **van Volta**, Voltaic pile.
suilegalery, suilegang, colonnade, arcade.
suilvormig, (-e), columnar, pillar-like.
suinig, (-e), stingy, miserly, niggardly; parsimonious, frugal, thrifty, economical; **waarom is jy so – met jou lekkers?**, why are you so stingy of your sweets?; – **te werk gaan met**, use sparingly (of), economize (in), be chary of, be frugal with, go slow(ly) with, husband.
suinigheid, stinginess, parsimoniousness.
suip (ge-), guzzle, swill, tope, soak, booze; drink (of animals).
suiper = **suiplap**.
suipery, boozing.
suiping, watering-place (for animals).
suiplap, toper, boozer, soaker, tippler.
suipplek, drinking-place (also of animals); wateringplace (of animals).
suis, (ge-), buzz, sing, tingle (in the ears); sough, rustle, sigh, moan (of wind); whiz(z).
suising, buzzing, tingling; rustling.
suite, (-s), suite (of rooms; music).
suiwel, butter and cheese, dairy-products.
suiwelbedryf, dairying-industry.
suiwelbereiding, dairying.
suiwelboer, dairy-farmer.
suiwelfabriek, creamery, butter-and-cheese-factory.
suiwelproduk, dairy-product.
suiwer, (-, -e), a. pure, clean, plain (truth), clear; sheer, pure (nonsense), correct (pronunciation); **nie – in die leer nie**, not sound in the faith.
suiwer, (ge-), purify (blood, air, language), clean, cleanse, purge; refine (sugar); clear

(one's name); disinfect; – **van**, clear of, purge, cleanse (of sin).
suiweraar, (-s), purifier, purger, refiner.
suiwerend, (-e), purifying, cleansing.
suiwerheid, purity; correctness.
suiwering, purification; cleansing, clearing, clarification; purgation.
suiweringsmiddel, purgative, aperient (med.); clarifier (of liquid).
suiwer-uit, indeed, truly, really.
sukade, candied peel, lemon-peel.
sukkel, (ge-), plod (on), trudge (on), worry along, drudge, toil (and moil), plug; – **met**, worry at, plug away at, plod (toil) at; – **met jou gesondheid**, be in indifferent health.
sukkelaar, (-s), muff, bungler, noodle.
sukkelary, vide **sukkelry**.
sukkeldraffie, jog-trot.
sukkelgang, jog-trot.
sukkelrig, (-e), ailing, in indifferent health; ploddingly slowly.
sukkel(a)ry, (toiling and) moiling, plodding.
sukses, (-se), success, – **behaal**, achieve success, succeed, be successful.
suksessie, (-s), succession.
suksessiebelasting, death-duties, succession-, duties.
suksessief, (-siewe), successive.
suksessie-oorlog, war of succession.
suksessieregte, death-duties.
suksessiewet, settlement-act.
suksesvol, (-le), successful.
sulfa, sulfa (sulpha).
sulfaat, (-fate), sulphate.
sulfamiddel, sulfa (sulpha), drug.
sulfer, sulphur.
sulfied, (-e), **sulfide**, (-s), sulphide.
sulfiet, (-e), sulphite.
sulke, a. & pron., (pl. pron.: -s), such; (pl.) such ones; **more – tyd**, this time tomorrow.
sult, brawn.
sultan, (-s), sultan.
sultana(druiwe), sultana(-grapes).
sundgat, touch-hole, vent.
superfosfaat, superphosphate.
superheterodyn, superheterodyne.
superieur, (-e, -s), n. superior.
superieur, (-e, -a), superior.
superintendent, (-e), superintendent.
superioriteit, superiority.
superlatief, (-tiewe), superlative.
supersonies, supersonic.
supplement, (-e), supplement.
surigheid, something sour; pickles; unpleasantness.
suring, (-s), sorrel, sheep-sorrel, dock.
suringsout, salt of sorrel (lemoen).
suringsuur, oxalic acid.
surplus, (-se), surplus, excess.
surrealisme, surrealism.
surrogaat, (-gate), substitute, surrogate.
sus, n., sis, sister.
sus, adv., thus; – **of so**, this way or that way, one way or the other.
sus, (ge-), hush, quiet; pacify, calm; soothe (one's conscience).
suserein, (-e), suzerain.
susereiniteit, suzerainty.
suspendeer, (ge-), suspend.
suspisie, (-s), suspicion.
sussie, (-s), sis, little sister; (fish) shad.
sustentasie(fonds), sustentation(-fund).
suster, (-s), sister, (also) nurse.
susterliefde, sisterly love.
susterlik, (-e), sisterly.

**sustermoord, **sororicide.
**susterskind, **nephew, niece, sister's child.
**sustervereniging, **sister-society (-union).
**suur, (sure), **n., acid (chem.); heartburn, acidity (of the stomach).
suur, (-, sure), **a. sour, acid, acrid; peevish; unpleasant; – **smaak, **sour (acid) taste; **'n – (sure) **ondervinding, **an unpleasant experience.
**suuragtig, (-e), **sourish acid.
**suurdeeg, **yeast, leaven.
**suurderig, surerig, (-e), **sourish, acid.
**suurgehalte, **acidity.
**suurgesig, **sour-face, crabby-face.
**suurgras, **sour grass.
**suurheid, **sourness, acidity.
**suurk(a)nol, ,,suurknol''; **crabby fellow.
**suurklontjies, **acid-drops.
**suurkool, **sourcrout (sauerkraut).
**suurlemoen, **lemon; **'n gesig soos 'n –, **a wry face; a face as long as a fiddle.
**suurlemoensop, **lemon-juice; **daar loop – deur, **there is something fishy about it.
**suurmelk, **sour milk.
**suurmuil, **crab, sour-face.
**suurpol, **lemon-grass.
**suurpruim, **sour-face, kill-joy.
**suursoet, **sour-sweet, bitter-sweet.
**suurstof, **oxygen.
**suurstofverbinding, **oxide.
**suursuurdeeg, **yeast.
**suurtjie, **acid-drop; quarter (of lemon); **–s, **(pl.) (also) pickles.
**suurvorming, **acidification.
**suurvy(g), **sour fig.
suutjies, **vide **soetjies.
**swaai, (-e), **n. swing; sweep.
**swaai, (ge-), **swing, wield (a sceptre), wave, flourish; swing, sway (to and fro); reel; wheel (rugby).
**swaaibrug, **suspension-bridge.
**swaaideur, **swinging door.
**swaaiing, **swinging, waving, reel.
**swaaislag, **swing, swinging(-blow).
**swaan, (swane), **swan; **jong –, **cygnet.
**swaanhals, swanehals, **swan's neck; swanneck (Pear); goose-neck.
**swaap, (swape), **block-head, simpleton.
**swaapstreek, swapestreek, **stupid (foolish) prank.
**swaar, (-, sware), **heavy. big, massive; difficult, hard, onerous, arduous, stiff (examination); severe (illness, punishment); deep (voice); **wat die –ste is, moet die –ste weeg, **everything in order of merit; – **geskut, **heavy artillery; – – **kos, **heavy (stodgy) food; – **rou, **heavy mourning; – **slag, **heavy (cruel) blow; hard (loud) thunderclap; – **belaai, **heavily laden; – **beproef, **sorely (severely) tried; – **sondig, **sin grievously; – **in die rou, **in deep mourning; – **op die hand, **heavy in (on) hand, slow, dull; – **van tong, **slow of tongue.
**swaard, (-e), **sword; **die – aangord, **gird (take up) the sword; **deur die – val (gestraf word), **fall (perish) by the sword; **na die – gryp, **draw the sword.
**swaardblom, -lelie, **sword-lily, gladiolus.
**swaarddraer, **sword-bearer.
**swaardgekletter, **clash of swords; rattling of sabres.
**swaardlelie, **sword-lily, gladiolus.
**swaardskede, **sword-scabbard, sheath.
**swaardslag, **blow with the sword.
**swaardvegter, **swordsman; gladiator.
**swaardvis, **sword-fish.
**swaardvormig, (-e), **sword-shaped.

**swaargebou(d), (-de), **heavily-built, massive, stalwart, stocky, thickest.
**swaargewig, **heavy-weight.
**swaarheid, **heaviness, weight.
**swaarhoofdig, (-e), **pessimistic, despondent, gloomy; thick-headed.
**swaarlywig, (-e), **corpulent, stout.
**swaarlywigheid, **corpulence, stoutness.
**swaarmoedig, (-e), **melancholy, depressed.
**swaarmoedigheid, **melancholy, depression, hypochondria.
**swaarte, **weight, heaviness; worry.
**swaartekrag, **gravitation, force of gravity.
**swaartepunt, **centre of gravity; mair. point (of an argument).
**swaartillend, (-e), **gloomy, despondent.
**swaarwater, **heavy water.
**swaarweer, swareweer, **thundery weather, thunderstorm, -clap.
**swaarwigtig, (-e), **weighty, ponderous.
**swabber, (-s), **n. swab, mop.
**swabber, (ge-), **swab, mop.
**swa(w)el, (-s), **n. 1. swallow.
**swa(w)el, **n. 2. sulphur; **vuur en –, **fire and brimstone.
**swa(w)el, (ge-), **sulphur(ize); **wingerd –, **sulphur vines; **baie –, **drink heavily.
**swa(w)elagtig, (-e), **sulphureous, like sulphur, sulphurous.
**swa(w)elbad, **sulphur-bath, -spring.
**swa(w)elblom, **flowers of sulphur.
**swa(w)elbron, **sulphurspring.
**swa(w)ldamp, **sulphur-vapour.
**swa(w)elhoudend, (-e), **sulphurous.
**swa(w)elmelk, **milk of sulphur.
**swa(w)elnes(sie), **swallow's nest.
**swa(w)elruik, **sulphur(e)ous smell.
**swa(w)elstert, **dove-tail; swallow-tail; swallow-fork; V-shaped earmark; swallow-tail(ed coat).
**swa(w)elstertbaadjie, **swallow-tail(ed coat), evening-coat, tail-coat, tails.
**swa(w)elsuur, **sulphuric acid.
**swa(w)eltjie, (-s), **swallow; (sulphur-)match; **een – maak (nog) geen somer nie, **one swallow does not make a summer.
**swa(w)elverbinding, **sulphurcompound.
**swa(w)elwaterstof, **sulphuretted hydrogen, hydrogen sulphide.
**swaer, (-s), **brother-in-law.
**swagtel, (-s), **n. bandage, swathe.
**swagtel, (ge-), **bandage, swathe.
**swak, **n. weakness, soft spot; failing.
**swak, (-, -ke), **weak; feeble (voice); delicate (health, child); frail (health); poor, bad (chance, show, memory); gentle, soft(er), weaker (sex); faint; **in 'n – oomblik, **in a weak moment; **die – verbuiging, **the weak declension.
**swakheid, (-hede), **weakness, debility, feebleness, delicacy, poorness, faintness; failing, shortcoming.
**swakhoofdig, (-e), **feeble-minded.
**swakhoofdigheid, **feeble-mindedness.
**swakkeling, (-e), **weakling.
**swakkies, **weakly, faintly, feebly.
**swaksinnig, (-e), **mentally deficient (defective), feeble-minded.
**swaksinnige, (-s), **mentally defective.
**swaksinnigheid, **mental deficiency.
**swakte, **weakness; failing.
**swaik, (-e), **rove, roam, drift.
**swam, (-me), **fungus; spavin.
**swamagtig, (-e), **fungous.
**swamsiekte, **fungous disease.
**swamsteen, **mushroom-stone.

swanedons, swan's down.
swanehals, vide **swaanhals**.
swanesang, swan-song.
swang: in –, in vogue.
swanger, pregnant (also fig.).
swangerskap, pregnancy.
swareweer, vide **swaarweer**.
swarigheid, (-hede), difficulty, obstacle.
swart, n. black; **in (die)**, –, in black.
swart, (–, -e), a. black; – **brood**, black bread, ryebread; **die – kuns**; the black art, black magic; **die – lys**, the black list; **die Swart See**, the Black Sea; **iemand -smeer**, paint black, speak ill of; **ek wil dit – op wit hê**, I want it in black and white.
swartagtig, (-e), blackish.
swartbekboontjie, black-eyed bean.
swartbier, stout.
swartbont, black and white, pied.
swartbord, blackboard.
swarte, (-s), black one, a black.
swartgallig, (-e), pessimistic, melancholy.
swartgalligheid, pessimism, melancholy.
swartheid, blackness.
Swarthemp, Black Shirt.
swartkoors, black fever.
swartkop, black-haired child; black-headed sheep; Persian sheep.
swartkopskaap, black-headed sheep.
swartkraai, black crow.
swartkuns, black art, black magic.
swartoog, black eye.
swartoognôi, -nooi, black-eyed girl.
swartsel, blacking.
swartskaap, black sheep (also fig.).
swartsmeer, (swartge-), blacken; vilify.
swartspan, team of black oxen; body of church-wardens, church-council.
swartwaterkoors, black water fever.
swartwildebees, black wildebeest (gnu).
swartwitpens(bok), sable antelope.
Swazi, (-'s), Swazi.
Swaziland, Swaziland.
swawel, vide **swa(w)el**.
Swede, Sweden.
Sweed, (Swede), Swede.
Sweeds, (-e), Swedish.
sweef, swewe, (ge-), float, hover, be suspended; glide; flit (by, past); soar (aloft); **tussen lewe en dood** –, hover between life and death; **dit – my voor die gees**, I have a (faint) recollection of it.
sweefbaan, aerial railway.
sweefbrug, suspension-bridge.
sweefspoor, aerial railway.
sweefstok, trapeze.
sweefvliegtuig, glider.
sweefvlug, glide, volplane.
sweem, semblance, trace, shred.
sweem, (ge-), – **na**, look like.
sweep (swepe), whip.
sweepslag, lash.
sweepstok, whip-stick, -handle.
sweeptol, whipping top.
sweer, (swere), n. ulcer, tumour, abscess, sore.
sweer, (ge-), 1. fester, ulcerate.
sweer, (ge-), 2. swear, vow, take an oath; **dit – ek jou**, I swear; you bet!, you be sure!; **trou – aan die koning**, swear (take the oath of) allegiance to the king; **hy het haar trou ge-**, he plighted her his troth; **ek kan daar nie voor (op) – nie**, I cannot swear to it.
sweerlik, surely, certainly, without a doubt.

sweet, n. sweat, perspiration; **nat van die** –, streaming (wet through) with perspiration; **in die – van jou aangesig**, in (by) the sweat of one's brow.
sweet, (ge-), sweat, perspire; cure; **tabak (laat)** –, cure tobacco.
sweetbad, sweating-bath, sudatory.
sweetdoek, sweat-cloth; sudary (Bible).
sweetdrank, sudorific.
sweetdruppel, drop of perspiration.
sweetgat, (sweat-)pore.
sweethande, perspiring hands.
sweetkamer, sweating-room.
sweetkanaal, sweat-duct.
sweetklier, sweat-gland.
sweetkoors, sweating fever.
sweetlug, smell of perspiration.
sweetmiddel, sudorific.
sweetsiekte, sweating-sickness.
sweetvos, chestnut, sorrel.
sweis, (ge-), weld, forge.
swel, (ge-), swell, expand, dilate.
swelg, (ge-), swill (drink), guzzle (food).
swelgery, (-e), orgy.
swelgparty, orgy.
swelling, (-e, -s), swelling.
swelsel, (-s), swelling, tumour.
swem, (ge-), swim; **gaan** –, go for a swim; – **in die geld**, swim (roll) in money.
swembad, swimming-bath.
swembroek, bathing-trunks, -costume.
swemgat, swimming-pool.
swemgordel, swimming-belt, life-belt.
swemkuns, art of swimming.
swemmer, (-s), swimmer.
swemoefening, swimming-exercise.
swempak, swimming-, bathing-costume.
swempoot, swimming-foot, web-foot.
swemvlies, web; **met** –e, web-footed.
swemvoël, swimming-bird.
swemwedstryd, swimming-competition.
swendel, (-s), n. swindle, fraud.
swendel, (ge-), swindle.
swendelaar, (-s, -lare), swindler.
swendel(a)ry, (-e), swindle, fraud.
swendelmaatskappy, bogus-company.
swenk, (-e), n. turn, swerve, side-step.
swenk, (ge-), swerve; swing round, wheel (about); change about.
swenking, (-e, -s), swerve; change of front.
swerf, swerwe, (ge-), rove, wander, roam, stray, ramble, tramp.
swerfling, swerweling, (-e), wanderer; tramp, vagabond; stray (child, dog).
swerflus, roving disposition; wanderlust.
swerfsiek, of a roving disposition.
swerftog, peregrination, wandering(s), travel(s), ramble, roving expedition.
swerfvoël, migrant (bird).
swerk, firmament.
swerm, (-s), n. swarm; (bees in) hive.
swerm, (ge-), swarm, cluster, crowd.
swernoot, (-note), **swernoter**, (-s), scoundrel, skunk.
swernootjie, (-s), funny-bone.
swerwe, vide **swerf**.
swerweling, vide **swerfling**.
swerwend, (-e), wandering, nomadic.
swerwer, (-s) = **swerfling**.
swerwerslewe, wandering (roving) life.
sweserik, (-e), sweetbread.
swetrioel, swetterjoel, (-e), swarm, multitude, caboodle.
swewe, vide **sweef**.
swewer, glider pilot.

swiep, (ge-), swish.
swier, n. flourish, swagger, jauntiness; gracefulness, elegance.
swier, (ge-), glide, carry oneself gracefully; be (go) on the spree.
swierbol, (-le), rip, reveller.
swierig, (-e), dashing, jaunty, showy, stylish, graceful.
swierigheid, jauntiness, dash.
swig, (ge-), give way, yield.
swik, (-ke), n. (vent-)peg.
swik, (ge-), make a false step, stumble.
swikgat, vent-hole.
swingel, (-s), swingle(tree).
Switser, (-s), Swiss.
Switserland, Switzerland.
Switsers, (-e), Swiss.
swoeë, swoeg, (ge-), toil, labour, drudge; swot.
swoel, (-, -e), sultry, close.
swoelheid, swoelte, sultriness, closeness.
swye, n. silence; die – oplê, impose silence (upon); tot – bring, silence.
swye, swyg, (ge-), be (remain) silent, keep silence.
swy(g)end, (-e), silent, taciturn.
swy(g)er, silent person; Willem die Swyger, William the Silent.
swygsaam, (-same), silent, taciturn.
swym, swoon; in – val, swoon, faint.
swymel, n. dizziness; intoxication.
swymel, (ge-), be (become, feel) dizzy.
swyn, (-e), swine, pig.
swynagtig, (-e), swinish, piggish.
swynboel, dirty mess, piggery.
swynehoeder, swine-herd.
swynhond, dirty swine.
sy, n. 1. silk.
sy, (-e), n. 2. side; flank (of army), aan my –, at (by) my side; – aan –, side by side; met sy arms in sy –, with his arms akimbo; op – gaan, step aside, go to one (the) side; op – sit, put aside; sink (differences); put (one's pride) in one's pocket; op – stoot, push aside; van bevoegde – verneem ons, we can state on good authority.
sy, pers. pron. she.
sy, poss. pron. his, its.
sy, v. be; dit – so, so be it, so let it be; hoe dit –, however that may be.
syaansig, side-view.
syaanval, flank-attack.
syagtig, (-e), silky.
syaltaar, side-altar.
sybeweging, flank-movement.
sybok, angora-goat.
syde: ter –, aside, on one side; ter – staan, assist, support.

sydelings, (-e), sidelong; lateral; –e blik, side glance.
sydeur, side-door, -entrance.
syfabriek, silk-factory, -mill.
syfabrikant, silk-manufacturer.
syfer, (-s), n. figure; bogey (golf).
syfer, (ge-), 1. figure, reckon, calculate.
syfer, (ge-), 2. ooze, filter.
syg, (ge-), ooze, filter; sink down.
sygaas, silk-gauze.
sygalery, side-gallery.
sygang, side-passage; aisle; latteral gallery (in mine).
sygebou, annexe, wing.
syglans, silky lustre.
syhandel, silk-trade.
syhandelaar, silk-merchant, mercer.
sy-industrie, silk-industry.
sy-ingang, side-entrance.
sykamer, side-room.
sykanaal, side-channel; branch-canal.
sykultuur, silk-culture.
syleuning, side-rail, handrail; arm-rest.
sylig, side-light.
sylyn, branch-line, side-line (of railway).
symuur, side-wall.
syn, n. being.
syncom, syncom.
syne, s'n: dit is Pa, Ma –, it is Father's, Mother's dit is syne, it is his.
synersyds, on his part, from his side.
synsbaar, (-bare), tributary.
synsgelyke, his equal, his peer.
synywerheid, silk-industry.
sypaadjie,.-pad, by-path; pavement.
sypel, (ge-), vide syfer, (ge-), 2.
syrivier, tributary, branch.
syrok, silk dress.
sysie, (-s), (bird) seed-eater; siskin.
syspanwaentjie, side-car.
syspoor, side-track, siding.
sysprong, side-leap, side-step.
systappie, side-step.
systof, silk, silk-goods.
systraat, side-street, off-street.
sytak, side-branch; tributary (of river).
syteelt, silk-culture.
sywaarts, (-e), sideward; sideways.
syweg, side-way, by-way, -road.
sywewer, silk-weaver.
sywewery, silk-weaving, silk-mill.
sywurm, silk-worm.
sywurmteelt, silk-worm breeding.

T

t, (-'s), t.
ta, (-'s), tate, (-s), pa(pa), dad.
Taag, Tagus.
taai, (-, -e-), tough; sticky, viscous; wiry, hardy, tough; unyielding, dogged, tenacious; **iemand 'n – klap gee**, give a person a stinger; **hy is – (so – soos 'n ratel)**, he is a tough (hardy, wiry) fellow; **iemand – sê**, give a person a bit of one's mind.
taaibos, "taaibos", Rhus. sp.
taaierig, (-e), toughish; sticky.
taaierigheid, toughness; stickiness.
taaiheid, toughness; stickiness; tenacity.
taaiigheid, toughness; stickiness.
taaipit(perske), clingstone(-peach).
taak, (take), task; **iemand 'n – oplê**, set a person a task; **sig tot – stel**, set oneself the task.
taakmag, task force.
taal, (tale), language, tongue, speech; **– nog tyding ontvang**, receive no news whatever; **– nog teken**, no word or sign; **wel ter tale wees**, be a fluent speaker.
taalarmoede, poverty of language.
taalbeweging, language-movement.
taalboek, grammar, language-handbook.
taaleie, idiom.
taalfamilie, language-family.
taalfout, grammatical error, language-mistake.
taalgebied, language-zone.
taalgebruik, usage of language, use of words.
taalgeleerde, philologist.
taalgeskiedenis, history of (the) language.
taalgevoel, language-sense.
taalgerus, language-boundary.
taalhervorming, language-reform.
taalkaart, language-chart.
taalkenner, linguist.
taalkennis, knowledge of (the) language.
taalkunde, philology, linguistics.
taalkundig, (-e), philological, linguistic.
taalkundige, (-s), philologist, linguist.
taalles, language-lesson, grammar-lesson.
taaloefening, grammatical exercise.
taalonderwys, language-teaching.
taalreël, grammatical rule.
taalskat, vocabulary.
taalstryd, language-struggle.
taalstudie, study of language(s).
taalsuiwering, purism.
taalvereenvoudiging, simplification of the language.
taalvermenging, mixing of languages.
taalverskynsel, linguistic phenomenon.
taalvorm, grammatical form.
taalvorser, philologist, linguist.
taalwerk, language-work.
taalwet, linguistic law.
taalwetenskap, science of language, philology, linguistics.
taamlik, (-e), a. fair, passable.
taamlik, adv. fairly, passably, tolerably.
taan, (ge-), dim, pale, fade; wane.
taankleurig, (-e), tawny, tan-coloured.
tabak, tobacco; **– draai**, twist tobacco; **– kerf**, cut tobacco; vide **twak**.
tabak-as, tobacco-ashes.
tabakblaar, tobacco-leaf.
tabakboer, tobacco-grower, -farmer.
tabakbou, tobacco-growing.
tabakdraaier, tobacco-twister.
tabakfabriek, tobacco-factory.
tabakhandel, tobacco-trade.
tabakhandelaar, tobacconist.
tabakkerwer, tobacco-cutter.
tabakoes, tobacco-crop.
tabakplantasie, tobacco-plantation.
tabakrol(letjie), roll of tobacco.
tabakruik, smell of tobacco.
tabaksaad, tobacco-seed.
tabaksak(kie), tobacco-pouch.
tabakstoel, tobacco-stool, -plant.
tabakstronk, tobacco-stalk.
tabakwinkel, tobacconist's (shop).
tabberd, tawwerd, (-s), dress, skirt.
tabberd-, tawwerdgoed, dress-material.
tabel, (-le), table, list, index.
tabellaries, (-e), tabular, tabulated.
tabelleer, vide **tabuleer**.
tabernakel, (-s), tabernacle; **die fees van die –s**, the Feast of Tabernacles; **iemand op sy – gee**, dust somebody's jacket.
tablet, (-te), tablet; lozenge.
tabletvorm, tabular shape; tablet-form.
tablo, (-s'), tableau.
taboe, taboo.
tabuleer, (ge-), tabulate.
taf, taffeta.
tafel, (-s), table; index: **die – van die Here**, the Lord's table; **–s van die Wet**, tables of the Law; **–s van vermenigvuldiging**, multiplication-tables; **(die) – dek (afdek)**, lay (clear) the table; **aan – sit**, be at table; **ter – bring**, raise (a question), bring (a matter) up; **van – en bed skei**, separate from bed and board.
Tafelbaai, Table Bay.
tafelbediende, waiter.
Tafelberg, Table Mountain.
tafelblad, table-top.
tafeldans, table-lifting, -rapping.
tafeldrank, table-drink.
tafeldruiwe, table-grapes.
tafelgebed, grace (before or after meals).
tafelgereedskap, table-ware, cutlery.
tafelgoed, table-linen.
tafelkleedjie, table-cover, table-cloth.
tafellaai, table-drawer.
tafellaken, table-cloth.
tafelland, table-land, plateau.
tafellinne, table-linen.
tafelloper, table-centre, table-runner.
tafelmes, table-knife.
tafelpoot, table-leg.
tafelsilwer, silverplate, table-silver.
tafeltennis, table tennis.
tafelvormig, (-e), tabular.
tafelvreugde, pleasures of the table.
tafelwyn, table-wine.
taf(e)reel, [taf(e)rele], picture, description, scene, tableau.
tag(gen)tig, eighty.
tag(gen)tigjarig, (-e), octogenarian, eighty-year-old; **die T-e Oorlog**, the Eighty Years' War.
tag(gen)tigjarige, octogenarian.
tag(gen)tig maal, eighty times.
tag(gen)tigste, eightieth.
tak, (-ke), branch, bough; antlers (of stag); **van die hak op die – spring**, wander in one's discourse, ramble, talk disconnectedly; **hoog in die –ke**, three sheets in the wind, drunk; **met wortel en – uitroei**, root out.
tak(t), tact.
takbok, deer, stag.
takel, (-s), n. tackle; system of pulleys.
takel, (ge-), rig, tackle; knock about, dress down, maul, handle roughly.
takelasie, tackle-rigging, rig-out.
takelblok, tackle, block.
Takhaar, (-hare), Takhaar, Backvelder.
takkantoor, branch-office.
tak(t)loos, (-lose), tactless.
taklyn, branch-line.

taks, n. portion, share.
taks, (ge-), estimate, reckon.
taksasie, (-s), valuation, appraisal.
taksateur, (-s), appraiser, valuer.
takseer, (ge-), appraise, estimate, value.
taksie, (-s), taxi.
takt, vide **tak(t)**.
taktiek, tactics.
taktikus, (-se), tactician.
taktloos, vide **tak(t)loos**.
tak(t)vol, (-le), tactful.
tal, (-le), number; **sonder –**, numberless.
talent, (-e), talent; **met jou –e woeker**, use one's talents.
talentvol, (-le), talented, gifted.
talie, tackle.
talisman, (-s), talisman, amulet, charm.
talk, talc; tallow.
talkagtig, (-e), talcose (talcous).
talloos, (-lose), numberless, countless.
talm, (ge-), delay, linger, loiter, dawdle.
talm(e)rig, (-e), slow, lingering.
Talmoed, Talmud.
talryk, (-e), numerous, multitudinous.
talrykheid, numerousness.
tam, (-, -me), weary, tired, fatigued.
tamaai, huge, enormous, colossal, gigantic; **– groot**, very big, huge.
tamarisk (-e), tamarisk.
tamaryn, tamarind.
tamatie, (-s), tomato.
tamatiepruim, persimmon.
tamatiesous, tomato-sauce.
tamatiestraat: hy is in –, he is up the pole.
tamboekie(gras), tambookie-grass.
tamboer, (-e), drum; drummer.
tamboer, **-majoor**, (-s), drum-major.
tamboerslaner, drummer.
tamboeryn, (-e), tambourine.
tambotie, (-s), tambootie.
tameletjie, (-s), butter-scotch; **–s gee**, give (a person) strap-oil.
tamheid, fatigue, weariness, tiredness.
tampan, (-s), tampan(-tick).
tand, (-e), tooth; prong (of fork); cog; **–e kry, teethe**, cut one's teeth; **hare op die –e hê**, be able to hold one's own; **jou –e vir iets slyp**, look forward to someting; **die – van die tyd**, the ravages of time; **iemand aan die – voel**, test a person's knowledge of something; **met die mond vol –e staan**, have nothing to say; **met lang –e eet**, toy with one's food; **op jou –e byt**, set one's teeth; **tot die –e gewapen**, armed to the teeth.
tandarts, dentist, dental surgeon.
tandboor, dental drill.
tandeborsel, toothbrush.
tandedokter, dentist.
tandeloos, (-lose), toothless.
tand(e)poeier, dental powder.
tandestoker, toothpick.
tandetrekker, tooth-drawer; dental forceps.
tandglasuur, enamel (of tooth).
tandheelkunde, dentistry.
tandheelkundig, (-e), dental.
tandheelkundige, (-s), dental surgeon.
tandholte, cavity in a tooth.
tandkas, socket of tooth, alveolus.
tandletter, dental (letter).
tandpasta, dental cream, toothpaste.
tandpyn, tooth-ache.
tandrat, cog-wheel.
tandsteen, scale, tartar on teeth.
tandvleis, gums.

tandvormig, (-e), tooth-shaped.
tandvulling, tooth-filling, stopping.
tandwiel, cog-wheel.
tandwortel, root of a tooth.
tang, (-e), (pair of) pincers; tongs (for sugar, coal, hair); pliers; forceps (surgical); **'n mens kan hom nie met 'n – aanraak nie**, one wouldn't touch him with a barge-pole.
tangens, (tangente), tangent.
tangetjie, (-s), pincers, tweezers.
tango, ('s), tango.
tanig, (-e), tawny.
tannie, (-s), aunt(ie); missus, madam.
tannien, tannine, tannin.
tans, nowadays, now.
tantaliseer, (ge-), tantalize.
tant(e), (-s), aunt(ie), missus, madam.
tap, (-pe), n. tap; spigot, plug, bung; tenon; trunnion.
tap, (ge-), tap, draw.
tapbeitel, socket-chisel.
tapboor, tap-borer.
tapgat, mortise, tap-hole, bung-hole.
taphuis, public house, tavern.
tapioka, tapioca.
tapisserie, (-ë), tapestry.
tapper, (-s), tapster.
taptoe, tattoo; **die – slaan**, beat the tattoo.
tapyt, (-e), carpet; **op die – bring**, bring (a matter) up (on the carpet).
tapytfabriek, carpet-factory.
tarantula, (-s), tarantula, wolf-spider.
tarbot, (-te), turbot.
tarentaal, (-tale), guinea-fowl.
tarief, (-riewe), tariff; list (scale) of charges; rate, terms; fare.
tariewe-oorlog, tariff-war.
tarra, tare.
tart, (ge-), defy, dare, provoke.
Tartaar, (-tare), Tartar.
Tartaars, (-e), Tartar.
Tartarye, Tartary.
tarting, (-e, -s), provocation, defiance.
tartraat, tartrate.
tarwe, wheat.
tas, (-se), n. (1) bag, pouch, satchel, wallet.
tas, n. 2. **iets op die – (af) doen**, grope (feel) one's way.
tas, (ge-), grope, feel; touch; **– na**, grope for; **in die duister –**, grope in the dark.
tasal(letjie), tassall(-meat).
tasbaar, (-bare), palpable, tangible.
tasbaarheid, tangibility, palpability.
Tasmanië, Tasmania.
tasorgaan, tentacle.
tassin, sense of touch.
tastelik, (-e), tangible.
tate, (-s), vide **ta**.
tatoeëer, (ge-), tattoo.
tatoeëring, tattooing.
tawwerd, vide **tabberd**.
te, prep. at, in; to; **– Kaapstad**, in Cape Town; **– koop**, for sale; **– wete**, namely.
te, adv. too; **– vroeg**, too early.
teater, (-s), theatre.
teatraal, (-trale), theatrical.
teder, (-, -e), tender.
tee, tea.
teë, adv. against; **voor en –**, for and against, pro and con; **ek is daarop –**, I am against (opposed to) it; **– wees vir die kos**, be tired of the food; **– drink**, drink to satiety; **– eet**, have a surfeit of; **– maak**, (teëge-), nauseate,

give an aversion for; make fed up with; vide **teen**.
teë-...., vide **teen-**....
teë-aanval, teenaanval, counter-attack.
teëberig, teenberig, counter-report.
teëbeskuldiging, teenbeskuldiging, counter-charge, recrimination.
teëbevel, teenbevel, counter-order.
teëbewys, teenbewys, counter-proof.
teeblaar, tea-leaf.
teëblad, teenblad, counterfoil.
teebos(sie), tea-plant.
teebus, tea-canister.
teef, (tewe), bitch.
teëgaan, teengaan, (teëge-, teenge-), oppose, counteract, check, thwart.
teëgesteld, teengesteld, (-e), contrary, opposite; **die -e,** the opposite.
teëgif, teengif, antidote.
teegoed, tea-things, cups and saucers.
teëhanger, teenhanger, counterpart.
teëhou, teenhou, (teëge-, teenge-), check, obstruct, prevent, retard, impede; press against, support.
teëkandidaat, teenkandidaat, rival (opposing) candidate.
teëkanting, teenkanting, (-e, -s), opposition.
teëklink, teenklink, (teëge-, teenge-), resound, meet the ear.
teëkom, teenkom, (teëge- teenge-), come across, meet.
teekoppie, tea-cup.
teël, (-s), tile.
teel, (ge-), breed, raise (cattle); cultivate, grow (crop); beget (offspring).
teelaarde, humus, vegetable earth.
teëlag, teenlag, (teëge-, teenge-), smile (up)on (at).
teëlbakker, tile-maker.
teëldak, tiled roof.
teelepel, teaspoon.
teelkrag, procreative power, virility.
teëloop, teenloop, (teëge-, teenge-), go to meet, go wrong; **alles loop my teë,** I have no luck.
teelt, cultivation, culture; breeding.
teem, (ge-), whine, drawl.
teënmaatreël, teenmaatreël, (-s), counter-measure.
teëmiddel, teenmiddel, antidote.
teemus, tea-cosy.
teen, n.: **voor en -,** pro and con.
teen, prep. against; at; by; **vyf - een,** five to one; **- die einde van die week (reis),** towards the end of the week (journey); **- elfuur,** by eleven o'clock; **ek het daar niks - nie,** I have no objection to it; **iets - iemand hê,** have something against a person.
teen-, vide **teë-**.
teenaan, against.
teenaanval, vide **teë-aanval**.
teenberig, vide **teëberig**.
teenbeskuldiging, vide **teëbeskuldiging**.
teenbevel, vide **teëbevel**.
teenbewys, vide **teëbewys**.
teenblad, vide **teëblad**.
teendeel, contrary, opposite; **in -, on the contrary.**
teendraads, (-e), against the grain.
teeneis, counter-claim.
teengaan, vide **teëgaan**.
teengesteld, vide **teëgesteld**.
teengif, vide **teëgif**.
teenhanger, vide **teëhanger**.
teenhou, vide **teëhou**.
teenkandidaat, vide **teëkandidaat**.
teenkanting, vide **teëkanting**.
teenklink, vide **teëklink**.
teenkom, vide **teëkom**.

teennatuurlik, (-e), unnatural.
teenoffensief, teë-offensief, counter-offensive.
teenomwenteling, teë-omwenteling, counter-revolution.
teenoor, opposite; over against, in contrast with; **beleef -,** polite to.
teenoorgeleë, -liggende, opposite.
teenoorgestel(d), (-de), opposite, contrary, opposed; **die -de,** the opposite.
teenparty, teëparty, opposing party; opponent, enemy, rival, adversary.
teenpraat, teëpraat, (teenge-, teëge-), contradict.
teenprater, teëprater, contradictor.
teenpruttel, teëpruttel, (teenge-, teëge-), grumble, mutter objections.
teenrevolusie, counter-revolution.
teensin, teësin, dislike, distaste, antipathy, aversion.
teensit, teësit, (teenge-, teëge-): sig -, resist, offer resistance; bear up.
teenslag, teëslag, setback, reverse.
teenspartel, teëspartel, (teenge-, teëge-), struggle, resist; vide **teenstribbel**.
teenspioenasie, counter-espionage.
teenspoed, teëspoed, adversity, ill-luck.
teenspoedig, teëspoedig, (-e), unlucky, unfortunate; ill-fated; disastrous.
teenspraak, teëspraak, contradiction; **met sig self in - kom,** contradict oneself; **in - wees met,** contradict.
teenspreek, teëspreek, (teenge-, teëge-), contradict, deny.
teenstaan, teëstaan, (teenge-), resist; be repugnant (repulsive) to, nauseate.
teenstand, teëstand, resistance, opposition; **- bied,** resist, offer resistance.
teenstander, teëstander, (-s), opponent, adversary.
teenstelling. teëstelling, (-e, -s), contrast; **in - met,** in contrast with.
teenstem, teëstem, n. dissentient vote.
teenstem, teëstem, (teenge-, teëge-), vote against.
teenstribbel, teëstribbel, (teenge-, teëge-), struggle, resist, recalcitrate, jib.
teenstroom, teëstroom, counter-current.
teenstryd: in - met, in conflict with.
teenstrydig, (-e), conflicting (opinions), contradictory, clashing.
teenstrydigheid, (-hede), contradiction.
teenswoordig, (-e), a. present, present-day.
teenswoordig, adv. nowadays, at present.
teenval, teëval, (teenge-, teëge-), be disappointing; **hy het my teengeval (teëgeval),** I was disappointed in him.
teenvoerter, teëvoeter, (-s), antipode.
teenvoorstel, teëvoorstel, counter-proposal.
teenwerk, teëwerk, (teenge-, teëge-), work against, oppose, thwart.
teenwerking, teëwerking, (-e, -s), opposition, thwarting.
teenwerp, teëwerp, (teenge-, teëge-), object.
teenwerping, teëwerping, (-e, -s), objection; **-e maak,** raise objections.
teenwig, teëwig, counterpoise, counterbalance; **'n - wees,** counterbalance.
teenwind, teëwind, headwind.
teenwoordig, (-e), present.
teenwoordigheid, presence; **- van gees,** presence of mind.
teë-offensief, vide **teenoffensief**.
teë-omwenteling, vide **teenomwenteling**.
teë-party, vide **teenparty**.
teepot, tea-pot.
teëpraat, vide **teenpraat**.
teëprater, vide **teenprater**.
teëpruttel, vide **teenpruttel**.

teer, n. tar.
teer, (-, tere), a. tender; frail, delicate.
teer, (ge-), 1. tar; iemand – en veer, tar and feather a person.
teer, (ge-), 2.: – op, live on.
teeragtig, (-e), tarry.
teergevoelig, (-e), sensitive, touchy, tender, delicate, susceptible.
teerhartig, (-e), tender-hearted.
teerkwas, tar-brush.
teerling, die; die – is gewerp (geworpe), the die is cast.
teerolie, tar-oil.
teerpad, asphalt-road.
teerputs, tar-bucket.
teerseil, tarpaulin, buck-sail.
teësin, vide teensin.
teësit, vide teensit.
teëslag, vide teenslag.
teëspartel, vide teenspartel.
teëspoed, vide teenspoed.
teëspoedig, vide teenspoedig.
teëspraak, vide teenspraak.
teëspreek, vide teenspreek.
teëstaan, vide teenstaan.
teëstand, vide teenstand.
teëstander, vide teenstander.
teëstelling, vide teenstelling.
teëstem, vide teenstem.
teëstribbel, vide teenstribbel.
teëstroom, vide teenstroom.
teesuiker, sugar-candy.
teetafel, tea-table.
teetuin, tea-garden.
teëval, vide teenval.
teëvoeter, vide teenvoeter.
teëvoorstel, vide teenvoorstel.
teewater, tea-water.
teëwerk, vide teenwerk.
teëwerking, vide teenwerking.
teëwerp, vide teenwerp.
teëwerping, vide teenwerping.
teëwig, vide teenwig.
teëwind, vide teenwind.
tefgras, teff.
tegelyk, at once, at the same time, (all speak) together; in one batch.
tegelykertyd, simultaneously, at the same time; – met, together with.
tegemoetgaan, (tegemoetge-), go to meet; jou ondergang –, ride for a fall, be heading for disaster.
tegemoetkom, (tegemoetge-), come to meet; meet (person) half-way, (make a) compromise (with); satisfy, meet.
tegemoetkomend, (-e), obliging, compliant.
tegemoetkoming, (-e, -s), concession, allowance (kind) assistance, aid.
tegemoetloop, (tegemoetge-), go to meet.
tegemoettree, (tegemoetge-), go to meet.
tegniek, technique (in art); technics.
tegnies, (-e), technical.
tegnikus, (-se, -nici), technician; mechanic.
tegnologie, technology.
tegnologies, (-e), technological.
tegnoloog, (-loë, -loge), technologist.
tegoed, credit balance.
tehuis, (-e), home, hostel.
teiken, (-s), target, mark.
teikenskiet, (teikenge-), shoot at a mark (target), have rifle-practice.
teïs, (-te), theist.
teister, (ge-), ravage, devastate, afflict, harass, infest (a place); deur die storm ge–, storm-beaten.

teistering, (-e, -s), affliction, devastation, ravaging, scourge.
teken, (-s), n. sign; signal; mark, trace, symptom (of disease); token; die – gee om – . . ., give the signal (sign) to . . .; taal nog – gee, give no word or sign; 'n slegte –, a bad omen; ons tyd staan in die – van rekords slaan, record-breaking is the order of the day; as 'n – van, as a token of.
teken, (ge-), sign (one's name); draw, sketch; plot (curve); portray, delineate, describe.
tekenaap, pantograph.
tekenaar, (-s), drawer, draughtsman, designer caricaturist, cartoonist.
tekenagtig, (-e), picturesque.
tekenboek, drawing-book.
tekenend, (-e), characteristic; descriptive, telling.
tekenhaak, T-square.
tekening, (-e, -s), signing; signature; drawing; diagram; plan; marking.
tekenink, drawing-ink.
tekenkryt, crayon.
tekenkunds, art of drawing.
tekenles, drawing-lesson.
tekenmeester, drawing-master.
tekenonderwyser, drawing-master.
tekenpapier, drawing-paper.
tekenpen, crayon-holder; drawing-pen.
tekenplank, drawing-board.
tekenwerk, drawing; drawings.
tekort, (-e), deficit, deficiency, shortage.
tekortdoening, wronging, cheating (a person) out of something.
tekortkoming, (-e, -s), shortcoming, fault, imperfection.'
teks, (-te), text (of book, manuscript); words (of a song); letterpress.
teksboek, book of (Bible) texts; libretto.
tekskritiek, textual criticism.
tekstiel, (-e), textile.
tekstiel-nywerheid, textile industry.
tekstueel, (-tuele), textual.
teksuitgaaf, -gawe, original text edition.
teksverbetering, emendation.
teksverklaring, exegesis.
tekswoord, text.
tel, n. count; die – kwyt raak, lose count; in die – wees, be popular, be (keep) in (with); op jou –le pas, mind your P's and Q's.
tel, (ge-), count; number; ons stad – 'n miljoen inwoners, our city has a population of a million; iemand onder jou vriende –, regard (count) a person as one of your friends; hy – onder die knapste van sy tyd, he is regarded (looked upon) as one of the most brilliant men of his time; sy dae is ge–, his days are numbered.
telbaar, (-bare), numerable, countable.
telbord, score-board.
telefoon, (-fone), telephone.
telefoonaansluiting, telephone-connection.
telefoonboek, telephone-directory.
telefoondiens, telephone-service.
telefoondraad, telephone-wire.
telefoongesprek, conversation over the telephone; telephone-call.
telefoongids, telephone directory.
telefoonhokkie, telephone booth.
telefoonkantoor, telephone-office.
telefoonlyn, telephone-line.
telefoonnommer, telephone-number.
telefoonoproep, telephone-call.
telefoonsentrale, telephone exchange.
telefoneer, (ge-), telephone (phone).
telefonie, telephony.

telefonies, (-e), telephonic, telephone.
telefonis, (-te), telefoniste, (-s), telephonist, telephone-operator.
telefoto, telephoto.
telefotolens, telephoto lens.
telegraaf, (-grawe), telegraph.
telegraafdiens, telegraph-service.
telegraafdraad, telegraph-wire.
telegraafkantoor, telegraph-office.
telegraaflyn, telegraph-line.
telegraafpaal, telegraph-pole; longshanks.
telegrafeer, (ge-), telegraph, wire.
telegrafie, telegraphy.
telegrafies, (-e), telegraphic.
telegrafis, (-te), telegrafiste, (-s), telegraphist, telegraph-operator.
telegram, (-me), telegram, wire.
telegramadres, telegraphic address.
telegramvorm, telegraph-form.
telekstoestel, teleprinter, telex.
teleologie, teleology.
teleologies, (-e), teleologic(al).
telepatie, telepathy.
telepaties, (-e), telepathic.
teler, (-s), cultivator, grower; begetter; breeder (of animals).
teleskoop, (-skope), telescope.
teleskopies, (-e), telescopic.
teleurgestel(d), (-de), disappointed.
teleurstel, (teleurge-), disappoint.
teleurstelling, (-e, -s), disappointment.
televisie, television.
telg, (-e), shoot; descendant, scion.
telgang, amble, ambling gait.
telganger, (-s), pacer, ambler.
teling, breeding; procreation.
telkemaal, time and time, again and again, every now and then; every time.
telkens: – as, whenever.
teller, (-s), teller, counter; numerator.
telling, (-e, -s), counting, count; numeration; addition, census; score; elke tien –s, every now and then.
telraam, abacus, calculating-frame.
telstar, telstar.
telwoord, numeral.
tem, (ge-), tame, master, curb, subdue.
tema, (-s), subject, theme.
tembaar, (-bare), tamable.
Temboeland, Tembuland.
temerig, (-e), drawling.
temerigheid, drawling manner.
temmer, (-s), tamer.
tempel, (-s), temple.
Tempelier, (-e, -s), Templar.
Tempelorde, Order of Knights Templars.
temper, (ge-), temper, restrain; modify; mitigate; tone down, soften.
temperament, (-e), temperament; temper.
temperamentvol, (-le), temperamental.
temperatuur, (-ture), temperature.
temperatuursverhoging, rise of temperature.
tempering, tempering; assuagement; conditioning (of air).
tempermes, palette-knife.
tempo, (-'s), time, tempo; rate, pace.
temporêr, (-e), temporary.
temporiseer, (ge-), temporize.
temptasie, (-s), temptation; irritation.
tempteer, (ge-), vex, irritate, tease.
ten, to, at, in; – eerste, in the first place, firstly; – onder bring, vanquish, conquer, overcome; – onder gaan, be ruined, go to rack and ruin; – uitvoer bring, execute; – verderwe, to perdition.

tendens, (-e), tendency, purpose.
tendensieus, (-e), tendentious.
tendensroman, novel with a purpose.
tender, (-s), tender.
tenderlokomotief, tank-engine.
ten ene male, absolutely.
ten gevolge: – van, in consequence of.
tenger(ig), (-e), slender, fragile.
tenietdoening, annulment; destruction.
tenk, (-e, -s), tank.
tenkkuil, tank trap.
tenklandingsvaartuig, tank-landing craft.
tenkskip, tanker.
tenkvliegtuig, tanker.
ten minste, at least.
tennis, tennis.
tennisbaan, tennis-court.
tennisraket, tennis-racket.
tenoor, (-nore), tenor.
tenoorsanger, tenor(-singer).
tensy, unless.
tent, (-e), tent; booth (at fair); hood (of vehicle), tilt; awning (on vessel).
tentdak, tentroof; awning; tilt-roof.
tentdoek, tent-canvas.
tentoonsprei, (tentoonge-), display.
tentoonstel, (tentoonge-), show, exhibit.
tentoonstelling, (-e, -s), show, exhibition.
tentpaal, tent-pole.
tentwa, tent-wag(g)on.
tenue, uniform, dress.
teodoliet, (-e), theodolite.
teokrasie, theocracy.
teokraties, (-e), theocratic.
teologant, (-e), student of theology.
teologie, theology.
teologies, (-e), theological.
teoloog, (-loë, -loge), theologian.
teorema, (-s), theorem, proposition.
teoreties, (-e), theoretical.
teoretikus, (-se, -tici), theorist.
teoretiseer, (ge-), theorize.
teorie, (-ë), theory; in –, in theory.
teosofie, theosophy.
teosoof, (-sowe), theosophist.
tepel, (-s), teat, nipple.
ter, in (at, to) the; niks – wêreld, nothing on earth.
teraardebestelling, interment, burial.
terapie, therapeutics, therapy.
terdeë, thoroughly, soundly.
terdoodbrenging, execution.
têre, vide terg(e).
terg, rightly, justly.
teregbring, (teregge-), reclaim, win back (from vice) put right.
tereghelp, (teregge-), help out of a difficulty, set (person) right, direct.
teregkom, (teregge-), land, arrive; come right; daar sal niks van – nie, nothing will come of it.
teregstaan, (teregge-), stand one's trial, be tried.
teregstel, (teregge-), put on trial, try (a person); execute.
teregstelling, trial execution.
teregwys, (teregge-), reprove, reprimand; direct; show the way.
teregwysing, (-e, -s), reproof.
terg(e), têre, (ge-), tease, irritate, provoke, torment, exasperate.
tergend, (-e), provoking, irritating.
tergery, teasing, provoking.
terggees, tease.
tering, consumption, tuberculosis, phthisis;

die – na die nering sit, cut one's coat according to one's cloth.
teringagtig, (-e), consumptive.
teringlyer, consumptive.
terloops, (-e), a. casual, incidental.
terloops, adv. casually, incidentally.
term, (-e), term; expression.
termiet, (-e), termite, white ant.
terminologie, terminology.
terminologies, (-e), terminological.
terminus, (-se, termini), terminus, terminal.
termometer, thermometer.
termometries, (-e), thermometrical.
termonukleêr, thermo-nuclear.
termosfles, thermos-flask.
termoskoop, (-skope), thermoscope.
termyn, (-e), term, period, time; instalment; op kort –, at short notice.
termynbetaling, payment by instalments.
terneergedruk, (-te), dejected, downhearted, depressed, cast down.
terneergeslae, vide terneergedruk.
ternouernood, hardly, scarcely, barely.
terpentyn, turpentine.
terpentynboom, turpentine-tree.
terpentynolie, (oil of) turpentine.
terra-cotta, terra-cotta.
terras, (-se), terrace.
terrasvormig, (-e), terraced.
terrein, (-e), ground, (building-)site, plot; terrain, field, province (of thought, action), sphere, domain; verbode –, forbidden ground, die – verken, reconnoitre; see how the land lies; op gevaarlike –, on dangerous ground.
terreinkennis, knowledge of the ground.
terreur, terror.
terriër, (-s), terrier.
territoriaal, (-ale), territorial.
terroris, (-te), terrorist.
terroriseer, (ge-), terrorize.
terrorisme, terrorism.
terselfdertyd, at the same time.
terset, (-te), terzetto.
tersiêr, (-e), tertiary.
tersine, (-s), tercet.
tersluiks, stealthily, on the sly.
terstond, at once, immediately, directly.
tersy(de), aside.
tersy(de)stelling, putting aside, ignoring, disregard.
tert, (-e), tart.
tertbakker, pastry-cook, tart-baker.
tertdeeg, puff-pastry.
tertjie, (-s), tartlet.
terts, (-e), third (mus.); tierce.
terug, back, backward(s).
terugbesorg, (–), return, send back.
terugbetaal, (–), repay, refund.
terugbetaling, repayment, refund.
terugblik, n. retrospect; retrospection.
terugblik, (terugge-), look back (on).
terugbring, (terugge-), bring back.
terugdeins, (terugge-), shrink back.
terugdink, (terugge-), recollect, recall to mind, bring (call) to mind.
terugdraai, (terugge-), turn back.
terugdring, (terugge-), force back.
terugdryf, -drywe, (terugge-), drive back, repulse; float back.
terugeis, (teruggeëis), demand back.
teruggaan, (terugge-), return, go (turn) back; na huis –, return home.
teruggang, going back; decline.
teruggawe, giving back, restoration.
teruggee, (terugge-), give back, return.

teruggetrokke, self-contained, uncommunicative, of a retiring nature, reserved.
teruggetrokkenheid, reserve.
teruggroet, (terugge-), return a greeting.
terughaal, (terugge-), fetch back.
terughou, (terugge-), hold (keep) back.
terughoudend, (-e), reserved.
terughoudendheid, reserve.
terughouding, reserve; keeping back.
terugja(ag), (terugge-), drive (chase) back; hurry (race) back.
terugkaats, (terugge-), return (ball); reflect (light, sound), reverberate.
terugkeer, n. return.
terugkeer, (terugge-), return, go back.
terugkom, (terugge-), come back, return.
terugkoms, return.
terugkoop, (terugge-), buy back.
terugkrabbel, (terugge-), back out of.
terugkry, (terugge-), get back.
teruglei, (terugge-), lead back; reduce.
terugloop, (terugge-), walk back; flow (run) back.
terugmars, march back.
terugmarsjeer, (terugge-), march back.
terugname, taking back.
terugneem, (terugge-), take back; retract.
terugreis, n. return-journey, -voyage.
terugreis, (terugge-), travel (journey) back, return.
terugroei, (terugge-), row back.
terugroep, (terugge-), call back, recall.
terugry, (terugge-), drive (ride) back.
terugsetting, putting back; setback.
terugsien, (terugge-), look back (upon); see again.
terugsit, (terugge-), put back.
terugskiet, (terugge-), shoot back.
terugskrik, (terugge-), start back; – vir, shrink from.
terugskryf, -skrywe, (terugge-), write back.
terugslaan, (terugge-), hit (strike) back, return (a ball); repulse; revert.
terugslag, recoil(ing), repercussion; backswing; return-stroke; backfire; setback; reaction.
terugspring, (terugge-), jump (leap) back; recoil, rebound (after impact).
terugstoot, (terugge-), push back.
terugstotend, (-e), repulsive.
terugstuit, (terugge-), recoil, rebound; vir niks – nie, stick at nothing.
terugtog, retreat; return-journey.
terugtrap, (terugge-), kick back; back-pedal; step (fall) back.
terugtree, (terugge-), step back.
terugtrek, (terugge-), pull back, withdraw; retreat; stand down; retract.
terugtrekking, withdrawal; retreat.
terugval, (terugge-), drop (fall) back; relapse (into sin), backslide.
terugverlang, (–), want (wish) back; – na, long (yearn) for.
terugverwys, (–), refer back.
terugvind, (terugge-), find again.
terugvoer, (terugge-), carry back.
terugvorder, (terugge-), claim again, demand back.
terugvordering, (-e, -s), demand.
terugvra, (terugge-), ask back, demand.
terugwen, (terugge-), win back, regain.
terugwerk, (terugge-), work back; react.
terugwerkend, (-e), retrospective, retroactive; van –e krag, retrospective.
terugwerking, retroaction; reaction.
terugwerp, (terugge-), throw back.

terugwyk, (terugge-), retreat; recede.
ter wille: – van, for the sake of.
terwyl, while, whilst, whereas.
tes, (-se), fire-pan, chafing-dish.
tesaam, tesame, together.
tesis, (-se), thesis.
tesourie, treasury.
tesourier, (-e, -s), treasurer.
tessie, (-s), vide tes.
testament, (-e), testament, (last) will (and testament); die Nuwe (Ou) T–, the New (Old) Testament; jou – maak, make one's will; hy kan sy – maar laat maak, it is all up with him.
testamentêr, (-e), testamentary
testamentmaker, testator.
testateur, (-s), testator.
testatrise, (-s), testatrix.
tet, (-te), woman's breast, teat, dug.
tetanus, tetanus.
tetraëder, (-s), tetrahedron.
tetrarg, (-e), tetrarch.
teuel, (-s), bridle, rein; die –s kort (styf) hou, hold the reins tight; not give too much scope; die –s laat skiet, give (a horse) the reins; give rein (the reins) to, allow free scope.
teuelloos, (-lose), unbridled.
teug, (teue), drought; in een –, at a (one) draught, at a gulp.
Teutoons, (-e), Teutonic.
tevergeefs, in vain, vainly.
tevore, before, previously.
tevrede, satisfied, contented, content.
tevredenheid, contentment, contentedness, satisfaction.
tevrede stel, satisfy, please, content.
tewaterlating, launch(ing).
teweegbring, (teweegge-), bring about (to pass), cause.
tewens, at the same time, also.
Thessalonicense, Thessalonians.
Thomas, Thomas; 'n ongelowige –, a doubting Thomas.
tiara, (-s), tiara.
Tiber, Tiber.
tiekie, (-s), tickey.
tiekiedraai, (tiekiege-), "tiekiedraai", dance picnic dances.
tiemie, thyme.
tien, ten; elke – tellings, every now and then; – teen een, ten to one.
tiendaags, (-e), ten days', of ten days.
tiende, (-s), n. tenth, tithe.
tiende, a tenth.
tiendelig, (-e), having (consisting of) ten parts; –e stelsel, decimal (metric) system.
tienderjarige, teenager.
tiendubbel(d), tenfold.
tienduisendste, ten-thousandth.
tienhoek, decagon.
tienjarig, (-e), ten-year-old; decennial.
tien maal, ten times.
tienponder, ten-pounder.
tienpondnoot, ten-pound-note.
tiensnarig, (-e), ten-stringed.
tiental, (about) ten.
tienvoud, (-e), decuple.
tienvoudig, (-e), tenfold, decuple.
tiep, (-e), vide tipe.
tier, (-e, -s), n. tiger; South African leopard; iemand se – wees, be more than a match for a person.
tier, (ge-), 1. thrive, prosper, flourish.
tier, (ge-), 2. rage, bluster, storm.
tieragtig, (-e), tiger-like, tig(e)rish.

tierboskat, serval.
tierelier, (ge-), sing, warble.
tierjagter, tiger-hunter.
tierlantyntjie, (-s), flourish; bauble, fallal, gewgaw, showy trifle.
tierlelie, tiger-lily.
tiermannetjie, tiger.
tiermelk, tiger's milk; booze; hy het – gedrink, he is tight.
tiervel, tiger's skin.
tierwyfie, tigress.
tiet, teat, nipple, woman's breast.
tifeus, (-e), typhoid, enteric.
tifoon, (-fone), typhoon.
tifus, typhus (fever).
tik, (-ke), n. pat, tap, touch; rap; tick (of watch).
tik, (ge-), tick, click; pat, tap (on shoulder), touch; rap (over knuckles); type; iemand op die vingers –, give a person a rap on the knuckles; ge– wees, be tipsy.
tikkie, (-s), tick; pat, tap; tinge, touch, hint, trace; wee bit, trifle.
tikmasjien, typewriter.
tikskrif, typing; in –, typed.
tikster, (-s), (lady-)typist.
tiktak, tick-tick (of watch).
timbre, timbre.
timmer, (ge-), carpenter, do carpenter's work; build, construct; aan mekaar –, knock together.
timmerasie, (-s), framework (of roof), structure, scaffolding.
timmerhout, timber.
timmerman, (-s, -ne), carpenter.
tin, n. tin, pewter.
tinerts, tin-ore.
tinfoelie, tinfoil.
tingel, (ge-), jingle, tinkle.
tingeling(eling), ting-a-ling(-a-ling).
tinger, (–, -e), slender, slight, slim.
tingerig, (-e), slender, of slight build, slim, fragile, delicate, tender.
tingerigheid, slinderness, slimness.
tingieter, tinsmith, tinman.
tinkel, (ge-), tinkle.
tinktinkie, (-s), grass-warbler.
tinktuur, (-ture), tincture.
tinmyn, tin-mine.
tint, (-e), n. tinge, tint, hue.
tintel, (ge-), tint, tinge.
tintel, n. tingling.
tintel, (ge-), twinkle; sparkle; tingle.
tinteling, (-e, -s), twinkling, sparkle (sparkling); tingling; thrill (of joy).
tip, (-pe), n. tip, point.
tipe, (-s), tiep, (-e), type.
tipeer, (ge-), typify.
tipies, (-e), typical.
tipograaf, (-grawe), typographer.
tipografie, typography.
tipografies, (-e), typographic(al).
tippie, (-s), tip, point; op die – kom, come just in time.
tirade, (-s), tirade.
tiran, (-ne), tyrant.
tirannie, tyranny.
tiranniek, (-e), tyrannic(al).
tiranniseer, (ge-), tyrannize.
titanies, (-e), titanic.
titel, (-s), title; heading (of chapter).
titelblad, title-page.
titelplaat, frontispiece.
titelrol, title-rôle, name-part.
tittel, (-s), dot (on i, j); tittle; geen jota of –, not one jot or tittle.

titulatuur, titles, full title, style.
titulêr, titular.
tjalie, (-s), shawl.
tjank, (ge-), whine, yelp, howl, whimper.
tjankbalie, cry-baby, squealer.
tjap, (-pe), n. stamp; postmark.
tjap, (ge-), stamp.
tjek, (-ke, -s), cheque.
tjello, (-'s), cello (violoncello).
tjienkerientjee, (-s), chinkerinchee.
tjilp, (ge-), chirp, twitter.
tjingel, (ge-), jingle, tinkle.
tjoekie, quod, prison, choky.
tjoepstil, quite still (quiet).
tjokkerbek-aasvoël, black vulture.
tjokvol, chock-full, crammed full.
tjou-tjou, hotchpotch (hodge-podge), chow-chow, pickles.
tjou-tjouspul, a mixed (common, feeble) lot (crowd); hotchpotch, mixture.
tob, (ge-), toil, drudge, slave (away); – **oor iets**, worry about something.
tobber, (-s), toiler, drudge.
toboggan, (-s), toboggan.
toe, a. closed, shut; – **bly**, remain shut (locked); – **hou**, keep shut; – **kry**, get shut; – **laat**, leave shut; – **staan**, be shut, be unoccupied; – **motor, saloon**.
toe, adv. then, at that time, in those days, to(wards); **van – af**, from that time; **(na) Kaapstad –**, to Cape Town; **hy is daar sleg aan –**, he is badly off (in a bad way); –!, please!, do!; – **maar, go ahead!**, fire away; – **maar, alles sal regkom**, never mind, all will be well; – **tog!, please do!**; – **dan tog, kêrel!**, come along, man!
toe, conj. when; as, while.
toebedeel, (–), allot, mete out, assign.
toebehoor(t), (–), belong to.
toebehoorsels, belongings, accessories.
toebehore(ns), parts; vide **toebehoorsels**.
toeberei, (–), prepare; season, mature.
toebereiding, preparation; seasoning.
toebereidsels, preparations.
toebetrou, (–), entrust.
toebid, (toege-), pray (God) to . . .
toebind(e), (toege-), tie up, fasten.
toebou, (toege-), build in (round).
toebring, (toege-), give (strike) (a blow); inflict (defeat, loss).
toebroodjie, (-s), sandwich.
toedam, (toege-), dam (block) up; crowd round (a person).
toedeel, (toege-), allot, mete out.
toedek, (toege-), cover up; thatch.
toedien, (toege-), give (blow, beating), administer (medicine), mete out.
toedig, (toege-), impute (ascribe) to.
toeding-, toeringhoed, pointed hat.
toedoen, n. instrumentality, aid; **deur sy –**, with his aid, through him.
toedoen, (toege-): **dit doen daar niks (aan) toe nie**, that makes no difference.
toedra, (toege-), bear; **iemand agting –**, respect a person.
toedraai, (toege-), wrap up (parcel); turn (shut) off (tap).
toedrag: **die juiste – van die saak**, the ins and outs (all the particulars) of the case.
toedrink, (toege-), drink to.
toedruk, (toege-), shut, close.
toe-eie(n), [**toegeëie(n)**]: **sig –**, appropriate, usurp (power, property).
toe-eiening, appropriation.

toeërig, (-e), overcast, cloudy (sky); partly blocked (closed).
toef, toewe, (ge-), linger, tarry.
toegaan, (toege-), shut, close; heal.
toegang, entrance; admission, access; way in, approach; – **verleen**, admit, give access; – **weier, refuse admission**; **verbode –**, no admission (except on business), private; **vry –**, admission free.
toegangsbewys, -biljet, -kaart(jie), ticket of admission.
toegangsprys, (price of) admission.
toeganklik, (-e), accessible, approachable.
toeganklikheid, accessibility.
toegedaan: '**n mening – wees**, hold an opinion (a view).
toegee, (toege-), give extra (into the bargain); admit, grant, concede; yield, give way (in); **te veel –**, be too indulgent; – **aan jou luste**, indulge one's desires (passions); **ek gee dit graag toe**, I readily grant that.
toegeeflik, (-e), indulgent, lenient.
toegeeflikheid, indulgence.
toegeneë, affectionate.
toegeneentheid, affection.
toegepas, (-te), applied.
toegespe(r), [toegegespe(r)], buckle.
toegewend, (-e), indulgent, lenient; concessive (clause).
toegewendheid, indulgence, leniency.
toegif, extra; encore.
toegooi, (toege-), cover up; fill up; slam.
toegrendel, (toege-), bolt.
toegroei, (toege-), overgrow; heal.
toehaak, (toege-), hook, fasten.
toehoorder, listener, hearer.
toejuig, (toege-), cheer; welcome.
toejuiging, applause, cheers, cheering.
toeka: **van – se dae (tyd) af**, from the year one, from time immemorial.
toekeer, (toege-), turn to; **iemand die rug –**, turn one's back upon somebody.
toeken, (toege-), award (marks, prize), give, grant, allocate, allot; credit.
toekenning, (-e, -s), grant(ing), award.
toeknik, (toege-), nod to.
toeknoop, (toege-), button up.
toeknyp, (toege-), shut (eyes).
toekom, (toege-): **dit kom my toe**, it is my share, I have a right to it.
toekomend, (-e), future, next.
toekoms, future; **in die –**, in future.
toekomsdroom, dream of the future.
toekomstig, (-e), future.
toekos, side-dish; dessert; vegetables.
toekry, (toege-), get into the bargain (in addition, extra).
toekurk, (toege-), cork.
toekyk, (toege-), look on.
toekyker, onlooker, spectator.
toelaag, (-lae), **toelae**, (-s), grant, subsidy, allowance.
toelaat, (toege-), allow, permit; admit (to place class).
toelaatbaar, (-bare), permissible.
toelag, (toege-), smile at (on).
toelak, (toege-), seal (up).
toelating, permission; admission.
toelatingseksamen, entrance-examination.
toelê, (toege-): **sig – op**, apply oneself to, go in for.
toeleg, plan, attempt, design.
toelig, (toege-), explain, elucidate, illustrate.
toeligting, (-e, -s), explanation, illustration, elucidation.

toelonk (toege-), eye amorously.
toeloop, n. concourse, throng, crowd.
toeloop, (toege-), run up (to); swarm (throng) round; swoop upon.
toeluister, (toege-), listen.
toemaak, (toege-), shut, close; cover (up); put the lid on; button up; seal.
toemaakgoed, wraps, blankets.
toemeet, (toege-), meter (measure) out.
toemessel, (toege-), brick up, wall up.
toenaai, (toege-), sew up.
toenader, (toege-), approach.
toenadering, approach, advance; rapprochement; – soek, make overtures.
toename, increase.
toeneem, (toege-), grow, increase; become (grow) worse.
toeneming, increase, rise, growth.
toenmalig, (-e), then, contemporary; **die –e regeerder,** the then ruler.
toentertyd, at that (the) time.
toe-oog, with closed eyes; **iets – doen,** do something without any effort.
toepak, (toege-), cover with, heap upon.
toepas, (toege-), apply (rules); put into practice; enforce (law).
toepaslik, (-e), appropriate, suitable, apposite, applicable.
toepaslikheid, applicability, suitability.
toepassing, (-e, -s), application; **van – (op),** be applicable (to), apply (to); bring, put into practice.
toeplak, (toege-), close (seal) (letter); (glue) over, cover (hole).
toer, (-e), n. tour, trip; spin, ride, trick, feat; stunt
toer (ge-), tour, make a trip.
toereik, (toege-), pass, hand.
toereikend, (-e), adequate, enough.
toereikendheid, adequacy, sufficiency.
toereken, (toege-), impute (something to person), charge (person with something).
toerekenbaar, accountable, responsible.
toerekenbaarheid, responsibility.
toering-, vide **toedinghoed.**
toeris, (-te), tourist.
toernooi, (-e), tournament, tourney.
toeroep, (toege-), call (cry) to.
toerol, (toege-), roll up, wrap up.
toerus, (toege-), equip, fit out (up); **sig – vir,** prepare (get ready) for.
toerusting, (-e, -s), equipment, outfit, fitting out, preparation.
toery(e), -ryg, (toege-), lace (up).
toesê, (toege-), promise.
toesegging, promise.
toesien, (toege-), look on; take care; **ons moes maar –,** we had to make the best of a bad job.
toesig, supervision, surveillance, care; invigilation (at examination); **onder – van,** under the supervision of.
toeskiet, (toege-), dash (rush) at (up).
toeskietlik, (-e), accommodating, obliging, complaisant.
toeskouer, (-s), spectator, onlooker.
toeskroef, -skroewe, (toege-), screw down, screw on (lid), screw up (door).
toeskrywe: – **aan,** ascribe to; impute to.
toeskuif, -skuiwe, (toege-), close (window), draw (curtains).
toeslaan, (toege-), slam, bang (door); shut (book); knock down (to bidder).
toeslag, extra allowance, bonus.
toesluit, (toege-), lock (up).
toesmeer, (toege-), smear over.

toesnel, (toege-), dash (rush) up.
toesnoer, (toege-), lace up.
toesnou, (toege-), snarl (snap) at.
toespeld(e), (toege-), pin up.
toespeling, (-e, -s), allusion, hint, insinuation; **–s maak op,** hint at, allude to.
toespraak, (-sprake), speech, address.
toespreek, (toege-), address, accost.
toespyker, (toege-), nail up (down).
toespys, side-dish; dessert.
toestaan, (toege-), accede, grant (request), concede; permit, allow.
toestand, state (of affairs), position, condition; situation.
toestel, (-le), apparatus; appliance, device, contrivance, machine.
toestem, (toege-), consent; assent, grant.
toestemmend, (-e), affirmative; – **antwoord,** reply in the affirmative.
toestemming, consent, assent.
toestop, (toege-), stop (up), plug (hole).
toestroom, (toege-), flow (stream) towards; rush (flock) towards, come flocking in(to), pour in.
toet, n.: **hy is 'n man van –** (was hy beter dan was hy goed), he is a real nincompoop (ninny, dud).
toet, (ge-), hoot, toot, sound hooter.
toetakel, (toege-), maul, knock about, manhandle, belabour, flog.
toetas, (toege-), fall to, begin.
toeter, (-s), n. hooter, horn.
toeter, (ge-), hoot, toot.
toerhoring, hooter.
toetrap, (toege-), tread in (down); kick (door) to; do down.
toetree, (toege-), join (a society).
toetreding, joining.
toetrek, (toege-), shut, close, pull (door) to; swindle, cheat; **dit trek toe (die lug trek toe),** the sky is becoming overcast; **sy bors het toegetrek,** he has a cold on the chest; **my keel trek toe as ek net daaraan dink,** the very thought of it takes my breath away.
toets, (-e), n. test; assay; key (of piano); touch.
toets, (ge-), test, try; assay.
toetsbord, keyboard.
toetsnaald, touch-needle.
toetssaak, test-case.
toetssteen, touchstone.
toeval, n. chance, accident; fit; **by –,** by chance, accidentally.
toeval, (toege-), fall to, shut; fall on, cover; **ek word toegeval om ...,** people are crowding round me to ..., I am inundated (swamped) with (applications).
toevallig, (-e), a. accidental, casual, chance.
toevallig, adv. by chance, accidentally.
toevalligerwys, by chance.
toevallighied, coincidence, accident.
toeverlaat, refuge; support.
toevertrou, (–): **iemand iets –,** entrust a person with something; **iemand 'n geheim –,** confide a secret to a person.
toevloed, influx, flowing in; throng.
toevloei, (toege-), flock (flow) to (in).
toevlug, refuge, shelter; recourse; **tot iemand jou – neem,** seek a person's aid, take refuge with a person.
toevlugsoord, (house of) refuge.
toevoeg, (toege-), join; add; **iemand iets –,** say something to a person.
toevoeging, (-e, -s), addition.
toevoegsel, (-s), supplement, appendix.
toevoer, n. supply.
toevoer, (toege-), supply; **feed.**

toevou, (toege-), fold up (together).
toewe, vide **toef**.
toewens, (toege-), wish.
toewerp, (toege-), fling (throw) to (at).
toewuif, -wuiwe, (toege-), wave to.
toewy, (toege-), dedicate (to); consecrate; **sig – aan**, devote oneself to.
toewyding, dedicate (to); consecrate; **sig – aan**, devote oneself to.
toewyding, dedication; devotion.
toewys, (toege-), award, grant, allot.
toewysing, award, allotment.
toffie, toffee.
tog, (-te), n. journey, voyage, trip, expedition; draught.
tog, adv. yet, nevertheless, still, all the same; **dit kan – nie waar wees nie**, surely it cannot be true; **kom – hier!**, do come here!; **toe (asseblief) –!**, please do!; **ek is – alte jammer**, I am really very sorry; **wat makeer die man –?**, whatever is the matter with the man? **jy is – nie bang nie**, you are not afraid, are you?; **wat is sy naam – weer?**, what is his name again?; **maar –**, still, yet.
toga, (-s), gown, toga; soutane.
togganger, transport-rider; itinerant trader, trekker.
toggat, vent-hole; draughty hole.
toggie, (-s), trip, ride, outing.
togryer, transport-rider, trekker.
togtig, (-e), draughty; on heat.
togwa, transport-wagon, trekwag(g)on.
toienrig, toiingrig, (-e), ragged, tattered, torn, rent, frayed; **– voel**, be off colour.
toiens, toiings, rags, tatters.
toientjies, toiinkies, tatters, strips.
toilet, toilet; **– maak**, make one's toilet.
toiletartikel, toilet-article.
toiletbenodigdhede, toilet-requisites.
toiletdoos, dressing-case.
toiletemmer, slop-pail.
toiletseep, toilet-soap.
toiletstel, toilet-set.
toilettafel, dressing-table, toilet-table.
tokkel, (ge-), pluck (the strings), strum, twang (fiddle, lyre).
tokkelok, (-ke), theological student.
toksien, toksine, toxin.
toksikologie, toxicology.
toktokkie, (-s), tapping-beetle; tick-tock; **– speel**, play tick-tock.
tol, (-le), n. 1. top.
tol, n. 2. toll, duty (duties), customs; tollhouse; **– betaal**, pay toll; pay dearly; **die – aan die natuur betaal**, pay one's debt to nature.
tol, (ge-), spin.
tolbeampte, customs-house officer.
tolbossie, tumbleweed.
toleransie, tolerance.
tolerant, (-e), tolerant.
tolereer, (ge-), tolerate.
tolgeld, toll.
tolhek, toll-gate, toll-bar.
tolk, (-e), n. interpreter; mouthpiece.
tolk, (ge-), interpret.
tolkantoor, customs-house.
tollenaar, (-s, -nare), publican.
tolletjie, (-s), little top; reel, spool.
tollie, (-s), tollie, young ox.
tolpligtig, (-e), subject to toll, tollable.
toltarief, customs-tariff.
tolverbond, tariff-union, customs-union.
tolvry, toll-free, duty-free.
tombe, (-s), tomb.
tomeloos(heid), vide **toomloos(heid)**.

tommie, (-s), tommy (British soldier).
ton, (-ne), ton; barrel, cask.
tonaliteit, tonality.
toneel, (-ele), stage; scene; theatre; **op die – verskyn**, come on the stage; appear on the scene (stage).
toneelaanwysing, stage-direction.
toneelbenodigdhede, stage-properties.
toneeleffek, stage effect.
toneelgeselskap, theatrical company.
toneelkoors, stagefright.
toneelkritikus, dramatic critic.
toneelkuns, dramatic art; stage-craft.
toneellewe, stage-life.
toneelmatig, (-e), theatrical.
toneelmeester, stage-manager.
toneelskerm, (stage-) curtain; side-scene.
toneelskikking, setting of a play.
toneelskilder, scene-painter.
toneelskool, dramatic school.
toneelskrywer, dramatist, playwright.
toneelspeelster, actress.
toneelspel, play; acting.
toneelspeler, actor, player.
toneelstuk, play.
toneelvereniging, dramatic society.
toneelwese, stage.
tong, (-e), tongue; sole (fish); **'n gladde – hê**, have a fluent (ready) tongue; **jou – roer (laat gaan)**, wag one's tongue; **dit is (lê) op my –**, I have it on the tip of my tongue.
tongbeen, tongue-bone, hyoid (bone).
tongblaar, "tongblaar" (Rumex).
tongetjie, (-s), little tongue, tonguelet; **klein –**, uvula.
tongklier, lingual gland.
tongontsteking, glossitis.
tongpunt, tip of the tongue.
tongriem, fr(a)enum of the tongue.
tongsenuwee, lingual nerve.
tongval, dialect.
tongvis, sole.
tongvormig, (-e), tongue-shaped.
tongwortel, root of the tongue.
tonkaboontjie, tonka-bean.
tonnel, (-s), n. tunnel; subway.
tonnel, (ge-), tunnel.
tonnemaat, tonnage.
tonsuur, tonsure.
tontel, tinder.
tontelbos, tinder-bush.
tonteldoek, tinder.
tonteldoos, tinder-box.
tonyn, tornyn, (-e), porpoise.
tooi, n. finery, ornaments.
tooi, (ge-), decorate, adorn, deck, dress.
tooisel, (-s), ornament, trimming.
toom, (-s, tome), n. bridle; **in – hou**, keep in check.
toom, (ge-), curb, bridle.
toomloos, (-lose), unbridled, unchecked.
toomloosheid, unrestrainedness.
toon, (tone), n. 1. toe: **tone trap is rusie soek**, you're looking for trouble!; **op jou tone loop**, (walk on) tiptoe; **op iemand se tone trap**, tread on a person's toes (lit. & fig.); **van kop tot tone**, from head to foot, from top to toe.
toon, n. 2. tone; pitch (of voice); sound; tune; **die – aangee**, give the key-note; set the fashion, take the lead; **'n hoë – aanslaan**, ride the high horse, put on airs.
toon, n. 3.: **ten – stel**, vide **tentoonstel**.
toon, (ge-), show.
toonaangewend, (-e), leading (lights).
toonaard, key (mus.), tonality.

toonbaar, (-bare), presentable.
toonbank, counter.
toonbeeld, example, model; paragon.
toonbrood, shew-bread.
toondemper, mute, sordine.
toonder, (-s), bearer (of cheque).
toondigter, (musical) composer.
toonhoogte, pitch.
toonkamer, showroom.
toonkuns, music.
toonkunstenaar, musician, composer.
toonladder, scale.
toonloos, (-lose), toneless; unstressed, unaccented (syllable), mute (phon.).
toonset, (ge-), compose, set to music.
toonsetter, musical composer.
toonsetting, (-e, -s), composition.
toonskaal, scale.
toontjie, (-s), little toe.
toonval, cadence.
toonvas, (-te), keeping tune.
toor, (ge-), practise witchcraft, conjure, juggle; bewitch, put a spell on.
toorboek, conjuring-book.
toordery, witchcraft, sorcery, magic.
toordokter, witch-doctor, medicine-man.
toordrank, tower-, magic potion.
toorgoed, charms, magic objects.
toorkruid, tower-, magic herb.
toorkuns, tower-, witchcraft, magic.
toorlantern, tower-, magic lantern.
toormiddel, tower-, charm; talisman.
toorn, wrath, anger.
toornaar, towe(r)naar, (-s), magician.
toornig, (-e), wrathful, angry.
toorring, tower-, magic ring.
toorstokkie, magic wand (stock).
toorts, (-e), torch.
toortsdraer, torch-bearer.
toorwoord, tower-, magic word.
top, (-pe), n. top; peak, summit; tip (of finger); apex, vertex; **ten – styg,** reach its height; **van – tot toon,** from head to foot.
top, (ge-), 1. top, lop; clip, trim.
top, (ge-), 2. agree; **ek – dit nie,** I'm not on.
top, interj. all right!, right oh!, agreed!
topaas, (-pase), topaz.
tophoek, vertical angle.
topograaf, (-grawe), topographer.
topografie, topography.
topografies, (-e), topographic(al).
toppunt, top, peak, summit; apex; zenith, acme, height, pinnacle; **die – bereik,** reach the climax; **die – van domheid,** the height (limit) of stupidity.
topseil, topsail.
topswaar, topheavy.
tor, (-re), beetle; hawbuck, country-bumpkin, boor, clodhopper.
toreador, (-s), toreador.
toring, (-s), tower, steeple (of church)
toringhoog, (-hoë), as high as a steeple.
toringklok, tower-clock; tower-bell.
toringspits, spire.
toringvalk, staniel, kestrel.
toringwagter, tower-watchman.
torium, thorium.
tornado, (-'s), tornado.
tornyn, vide **tonyn.**
torpedeer, (ge-), torpedo.
torpedo, (-'s), torpedo.
torpedoboot, torpedo-boat.
torpedojaer, (torpedo-boat-)destroyer.
torrerig, (-e), uncouth, boorish, umkempt.
torring, (ge-), unpick, unstitch, rip open, trouble,
worry, pester, bother; **– aan,** meddle with, nag at.
torringmessie, ripper.
tors, (ge-), carry.
torso, (-'s), torso.
tortelduif, turtledove.
Toskaans, (-e), Tuscan.
Toskane, Tuscany.
tot, prep. till, until, to, as far as; **– hiertoe,** as far as this, thus far, so far; **– waar?,** how far?; **– sy middellyf in die water,** waist-deep in the water; **– voorsitter kies,** elect president; **– vrou neem,** take as (to) wife; **– en met,** up to and including.
tot, conj., until, till.
totaal, (-tale), n. total, total sum.
totaal, (-tale), a. total.
totaal, adv. totally, utterly, quite.
totaalindruk, general impression.
totalisator, (-s), totalizator.
totaliteit, totality.
totalitêr, totalitarian.
totem, (-s), totem.
totemisme, totemism.
tot nog toe, hitherto, up till now.
totstandbrenging, accomplishment.
totstandkoming, coming into being, realization, declaration; passing.
tou, (-e), n. string, twine, cord; **dik –,** rope; **daar is geen – aan vas te knoop nie,** I cannot make head or tail of it; **– opgooi,** give in, throw up the sponge; **die – vat,** lead (the oxen); take the lead; **aan die – praat,** speak (talk) like one possessed; **aan die – reent,** rain cats and dogs; **oor die –** (string, riem) **trap,** kick over the traces, get out of hand, misconduct oneself; **op – sit,** set on foot, start, get up, launch.
tou, (ge-), 1. taw (hide), dress.
tou, (ge-), 2. walk one after another.
tou, (ge-), 3. flog, beat.
touleer, rope-ladder.
toulei, (touge-), lead the oxen (team).
touleier, leader.
tou-opgooier, coward, faint-heart.
toustaan, (touge-), form a queue.
tou(tjie)spring, [tou(tjie)ge-], skip.
toutjie, (-s), string, cord; meat-strip.
toutologie, tautology.
toutologies, (-e), tautological.
toutrek, n. tug-of-war.
toutrek, (touge-), tug at the rope.
touwerk, ropes, rope-work; rigging.
touwys, broken in, tamed; more or less at home in (used to) work.
towe(r)naar, vide **toornaar.**
tower, (ge-), conjure, juggle; vide **toor.**
towerdrank, vide **toordrank.**
towerfee, fairy.
towergodin, fairy.
towerheks, witch.
towerklank, magic sound.
towerkruid, vide **toorkruid.**
towerkuns, vide **toorkuns.**
towerland, fairy-land.
towerlantern, vide **toorlantern.**
towermiddel, vide **toormiddel.**
towe(r)naar, vide **toornaar.**
towerring, vide **toorring.**
towerslag: soos met 'n –, as if by magic.
towerspreuk, charm; incantation.
towerstaf, magic wand.
towerwêreld, enchanted world.
towerwoord, vide **toorwoord.**
towery, magic; vide **toordery.**

traag, (trae), slow, indolent, lazy, sluggish, dull, apathetic, torpid.
traagheid, slowness, laziness.
traak, (ge-), concern; **dit – jou nie**, it is none of your business, you've got nothing to do with it.
traak-(my)-nie-agtig, (-e), happy-go-lucky.
traan, (trane), n. 1. tear; **trane stort**, shed tears; **lang trane huil**, cry bitter tears, weep bitterly; **tot trane beweeg**, move to tears.
traan, n. 2. train-oil, fish-oil.
traan, (ge-), water (of eyes).
traanbom, tear-bomb.
traanbuis, lachrymal duct.
traangas, tear-gas.
traanklier, lachrymal gland.
tradisie, (-s), tradition.
tradisioneel, (-nel), traditional.
trag, (ge-), endeavour, try, attempt.
tragedie, (-s), tragedy.
tragerig, (-e), rather slow (sluggish).
tragiek, tragedy.
tragies, (-e), tragic.
tragikomedie, tragicomedy.
trajek, (-te), stage, stretch, section.
traktaat, (-tate), treaty.
traktaatjie, (-s), tract.
trakteer, (ge-), treat; entertain; regale, stand treat.
traktement, (-e), pay, salary.
traktementsverhoging, increase of salary.
tralie, (-s), bar, spike; –s, trellis, railings, lattice; **agter die –s sit**, be behind bars, be locked up.
traliedeur, grated door.
tralievenster, lattice-window.
traliewerk, lattice-work, trellis, railings.
tranedal, vale of tears.
tranerig, (-e), watery, tearful.
tranevloed, flood of tears.
trankiel, (-e), tranquil, calm.
trans, (-e), pinnacle; firmament.
transaksie, (-s), transaction.
Transatlanties, (-e), transatlantic.
transendentaal, (-tale), transcendental.
transformasie, (-s), transformation.
transformator, (-s), transformer.
transformeer, (ge-), transform.
transfusie, (-s), transfusion.
transie, trassie, (-s), hermaphrodite.
transistor, transistor.
transitief, (-tiewe), transitive.
transito, transit.
transkribeer, (ge-), transcribe.
transkripsie, (-s), transcription.
transmigrasie, transmigration.
transparant, (-e), a. transparent.
transpirasie, perspiration.
transponeer, (ge-), transpose.
transport, 1. transport, carriage; **– ry**, transport goods, ride transport.
transport, (-e), 2. transfer; akte van **–**, deed of transfer.
transportasie, transportation.
transportband, conveyor belt.
transportbesorger, conveyancer.
transporteer, (ge-), convey, transport; carry forward (bookkeeping); transfer.
transportkoste, cost of transport; cost of conveyance (transfer).
transportpad, transport road, main road.
transporttryer, transport-rider.
transportskip, transport-ship (-vessel).
transportwa, transport-wagon.
transsubstansiasie, transubstantiation.
Transvaal, Transvaal.
Transvaals, (-e), Transvaal.

trant, manner, style, way, fashion, strain; **in die – van**, after the style of; **na (op) die ou –**, in the old way (style).
trap, (-pe), n. 1. stamp (with foot), trample, kick.
trap, (-pe), n. 2. step; staircase, (flight of) stairs; stepladder; degree step; **–pe van vergelyking**, degrees of comparison; **stellende (vergrotende, oortreffende) –**, positive (comparative, superlative) degree; **op 'n hoë – van ontwikkeling**, highly developed.
trap, (ge-), tread, trample, kick; pedal; blow (organ); thresh (thrash); scoot, skedaddle; **stukkend –**, trample (tread) to pieces; **ek moet –**, I must be off; **–!**, off with you!, be off!; **ek laat nie op my kop – nie**, I'll not be trampled upon.
trapbalie, winepress.
trapees, (-pese), trapeze; trapezium.
trapesium, (-s), trapezium; trapeze.
trapfiets, pushbike, pedal-cycle.
trapgewel, stepped gable.
trapleuning, banisters.
trapmasjien, threshing-machine, thresher (thrasher) treadle-sewing-machine.
trappel, (ge-), trample, stamp.
trapper, (-s), pedal (of bicycle); treadle; pedaller, blower, treader.
trappie, (-s), step.
trapsel, (-s), threshing (of wheat).
trapsgewys, (-e), a. gradual.
trapsgewys(e), adv. by degrees, step by step, gradually.
trapsoetjies, **-suutjies**, (-e), chameleon; slow-coach.
trapvloer, threshing-floor.
trassie, (-s), hermaphrodite.
travestie, (-s), travesty.
trawant, (-e), satellite.
tred, pace, tread; **gelyke – hou met**, keep pace with; **met vaste –**, with a firm step.
tredmeul, treadmill.
tree, (treë), n. pace, step; yard.
tree, (ge-), step, walk, tread; **nader –**, approach, go nearer; **na vore –**, come forward; stand out; **tussenbei –**, intervene; **in onderhandeling – met**, enter into negotiations with; **in diens – van**, take service with; **in die huwelik –**, marry; **in besonderhede –**, go into details.
treeplank, footboard.
treetjie, (-s), step.
tref, (ge-), strike, hit; find, meet, come across; come upon, attack, visit; **iemand tuis –**, find a person at home; **dit gelukkig (goed) –**, be fortunate (lucky); **'n ongeluk het hom ge-**, he met with an accident; **deur die ongeluk ge-**, overtaken by misfortune, hard hit; **'n ooreenkoms –**, come to an agreement; **maatreëls –**, take steps.
treffend, (-e), striking; touching.
treffer, (-s), hit; best-seller.
trefpunt, point of impact.
tregter, (-s), funnel; hopper (in mill).
tregtervormig, (-e), funnel-shaped.
treil, (-e), n. tow-line; drag-net.
treil, (ge-), tow.
treiler, (-s), trawler.
trein, (-e), train; retinue, following.
treindiens, train-service.
treingids, railway-timetable.
treinkondukteur, guard (conductor) on a train.
treinlading, trainload.
trainongeluk, railway-disaster, -accident.
treinreis, train-journey.
treinsiek, train-sick
treinspoor, railway(-line).

treiter, (ge-), plague, tease, annoy.
treiteraar, (-s), tease, nagger.
trek, (-ke), n. 1. pull, tug; haul; draught (of air); migration, trek, journey; stage; moving; stroke, flourish (of the pen); influx, rush (to a place; feature (of face); trait, characteristic; **'n paar –ke aan sy pyp,** a few puffs at his pipe; **die wrede – om sy mond,** the savage line of his mouth; **in breë (groot) –ke,** in broad outline; **met 'n paar vlugtige –ke skets,** sketch briefly.
trek, n. 2. appetite; inclination, desire.
trek, (ge-), pull, draw, tug, haul, drag; journey, travel, go, march, trek; migrate; move; be draughty, warp, become warped; twitch (of muscles); **blare –,** raise blisters; **die tee laat –,** allow the tea to draw, draw the tea; **'n salaris –,** draw a salary; **'n wissel –,** draw a bill; **'n tand laat –,** have a tooth extracted; **iemand se ore –,** pull somebody's ears; **– na,** move (journey, travel, trek) to; look like.
trekbees(te), cattle on trek; draught-oxen.
trekboer, trek-farmer, trekker.
trekbout, pitman, connecting-rod.
trekdier, draught-animal.
trekduif, migratory pigeon.
trekgat, draught-hole, vent-hole.
trekgees, trek-fever, trekking-spirit.
trekgoed, draught-animals; harness, gear, trek-things.
trekkebek, (ge-), bill and coo.
trekker, (-s), puller, trigger (of rifle); corkscrew; forceps; drawer (of bill); tractor, traction-engine; trekker.
trekkerig, (-e), draughty.
trekkerswee, woes of the trekker.
trekketting, pull-chain; trek-chain.
trekking, drawing; traction; twitch.
trekkings, convulsions, twitchings.
trekkrag, tractive power, tensile force.
treklus, trek-fever, desire to trek.
treknet, drag-net.
trekperd, draught-horse.
trekpleister, blister-plaster; attraction.
treksaag, cross-cut saw, whip-saw.
treksel, (-s), brew (of tea); enough coffee (tea) for a brew.
trekskaal, spring-balance.
trekskuit, draw-, tow-, track-boat, trawler.
trekspier, extensor.
treksprinkaan, flying locust.
trektou, trek-rope; tow(ing)-rope.
trekvee, trek-sheep, livestock on trek.
trekvis, migratory fish.
trekvoël, migratory bird, bird of passage.
trem, (-me, -s), tram(car).
trembus, trackless tram, trolley-bus.
trens, (-e), snaffle; loop.
trensriem, loop-strap, loop-riem.
trepaneer, (ge-), trepan.
trepaneerboor, trepan.
tres, (-se), tress.
tretter, vide **treiter.**
treur, (ge-), grieve, mourn, be sad, languish, pine.
treurdig, (-te), elegy.
treurig, (-e), sad, sorrowful, mournful; **'n –e gesig,** a sad face; a pitiful sight; **'n –e plek,** a miserable place.
treurigheid, sadness, sorrow; pitifulness; **dis 'n – soos hulle twis,** it is sad (pitiful) the way they quarrel; **o – op note,** alas!, woe is me!
treurlied, dirge, lament.
treurmare, sad tidings.
treurmars, funeral march, dead march.
treursang, elegy, dirge, lament.
treurspel, tragedy.

treurtoneel, tragic scene.
treurwilg(erboom), treurwilker(boom), weeping-willow.
trewwa, (-s), trewwa.
triangel, (-s), triangle (mus.).
triangulasie, triangulation.
tribunaal, (-nale), tribunal.
tribune, (-s), platform; gallery; stand.
tribuun, (-bune), tribune.
triestig, (-e), gloomy, dismal, dejected, miserable, dreary.
triesterig, (-e), vide **triestig.**
trigonometrie, trigonometry.
trigonometries, (-e), trigonometric(al).
tril, (ge-), tremble, vibrate, quiver, quake.
trilbeweging, vibratory motion.
trilgras, quaking-grass.
triljoen, (-e), trillion.
triller, (-s), trill, shake (mus.).
trilling, (-e, -s), trembling, vibration, quiver(ing), tremor, quaking; trill (mus.); thrill.
trillingsduur, period of vibration.
trilogie, (-ë), trilogy.
trilpopulier, trembling poplar, aspen.
trio, (-'s), trio.
triolet, (-te), triolet.
triomf, (-e), triumph; **in –,** in triumph.
triomfant(e)lik, (-e), triumphant; triumphal.
triomfboog, triumphal arch.
triomfeer, (ge-), triumph (over).
triomflied, triumphal song, paean.
triomfpoort, triumphal arch.
triomftog, triumphal procession.
triomfwa, triumphal car.
triplex, triplex (glass).
triplikaat, (-kate), triplicate.
triplo: in –, in triplicate.
trippel, n. tripple, amble.
trippel, (ge-), trip; amble, tripple.
trippelaar, (-s), trippler, ambler.
trippelmaat, triple time.
trippelpas, tripping step; amble.
trippens, (-e), threepence, tickey.
trits, (-e), trio, triplet.
triumviraat, triumvirate.
troebel, troewel, (–, -e), a. turbid, muddy, thick, cloudy.
troebelagtig, troewel-, (-e), (rather) muddy, turbid.
troebelagtigheid, troewel-, muddiness.
troebele, troewele, (pl.) disturbances.
troebelrig, troewel-, (-e), muddy, turbid, thick, cloudy.
troef, (troewe), n. trump(-card).
troef, (ge-), trump (lit. & fig.).
troefkaart, trump-card.
troei, vide **tru.**
troep, (-e), troop, company; troupe.
troepe, (pl.) troops, forces.
troepemag, (military) force(s).
troepleier, leader of a troupe; scoutmaster.
troepsgewys(e), in troops.
troetel, (ge-), caress, fondle, pet, pamper.
troetelkind, favourite, mother's darling.
troetelnaam, pet-name.
troetelwoord, term of endearment.
troewel, vide **troebel.**
troewelrig, vide **troebelrig.**
trofee, (-feë), trophy.
troffel, (-s), trowel.
trog, (-ge, trôe), trough.
trogee, (-geë), trochee.
trogeïes, (-e), trochaic.
troglodiet, (-e), troglodyte.
Trojaan, (-jane), Trojan.

Trojaans, (-e), Trojan.
Troje, Troy.
trok, (-ke, -s), truck.
trollie, (-s), trolley.
trom, (-me), drum.
trombone, (-s), trombone.
trombonis, (-te), trombonist.
trommel, (-s), n. drum; trunk, canister; tympanum, (ear-)drum.
trommel, (ge-), drum, beat the drum.
trommeldik, sated, full, filled.
trommelholte, tympanic cavity.
trommelslag, drum-beat.
trommelslaner, drummer.
trommelvlies, tympanum, ear-drum.
trommelvuur, drum-fire.
tromp, (-e), muzzle (of firearm); trunk (of elephant); trumpet; Jew's harp.
trompet, (-te), trumpet.
trompet(ter), (ge-), trumpet.
trompetblaser, trumpeter.
trompetgeskal, sound of trumpets.
trompetter, (-s), trumpet; trumpeter.
trompetter(blom), trumpet-flower; convolvulus.
trompie, (-s), Jew's harp.
tromp-op, directly, immediately; **iemand – loop**, go straight for a person.
tronie, (-s), face; phiz, mug.
tronk, (-e), gaol (jail), prison; **van nuuskierigheid is die – vol**, ask no questions, and you will hear no lies.
tronkbewaarder, jailer (jailor, gaoler).
tronkstraf, imprisonment.
tronkvoël, (angl.) gaolbird.
tronkwa, prison-van, black Maria.
troon, (trone), n. throne; **die – beklim (bestyg)**, ascend the throne.
troon, (ge-), reign; be enthroned.
troonhemel, canopy.
troonopvolger, heir to the throne.
troonrede, speech from the throne.
troonsaal, throne-room.
troonafstand, abdication.
troop, (trope), trope.
troos, n. comfort, consolation.
troos, (ge-), comfort, console.
troosbrief, letter of condolence.
troosprys, consolation-prize.
troosryk, (-e), comforting, consolatory.
troosteloos, (-lose), disconsolate, inconsolable; dreary, dismal, forlorn.
troostend, (-e), comforting, consoling.
trooster, (-s), comforter.
troosvol, (-le), vide **troostryk**.
trooswoord, comforting word.
trop, (-pe), flock (of birds, sheep; herd (of cattle); crowd, multitude, lot; covey (of partridges); pack (of dogs, fools); **'n – geld**, money galore, lots of money.
trope, (pl.) tropics.
tropies, (-e), tropical.
tros, (-se), n. bunch (of grapes), cluster (of flowers); batch (of children).
tros, (ge-), bunch, cluster.
trots, n. pride.
trots, a. (–, -e), proud, haughty.
trots, prep. in spite of, notwithstanding.
trotsaard, (-s), proud (haughty) person.
trotseer, (ge-), defy, dare, face, brave.
trotsering, defiance.
trotsheid, pride, haughtiness.
trou, n. fidelity, faithfulness, loyalty, faith; **– sweer**, swear allegiance, take the oath of allegiance; **goeie –**, good faith; **te goeder –**, in good faith.

trou, a. (–, -e), faithful; loyal; true, trusty; regular (visitor); accurate.
trou, (ge-), marry, be (get) married, wed; **– met**, marry, (get) married to; **getroud wees met**, be married to; be inseparable from; **– is nie perdekoop nie**, marry in haste and repent at leisure; **onder mekaar –**, intermarry.
trouakte, marriage-certificate.
troubaar, (-bare), marriageable.
troubadour, (-s), troubadour.
troubelofte, promise of marriage.
troubewys, marriage-certificate.
troubreuk, breach of faith.
troudag, wedding-day.
trouelik, faithfully.
troueloos, (-e), faithfulness, false, disloyal, perfidious.
trouens, indeed, as a matter of fact.
trouery, wedding.
troufees, wedding-feast.
trouhartig, (-e), true-hearted, candid.
trouhartigheid, true-heartedness.
trouklere, wedding-clothes.
troulustig, (-e), desirous of (keen on) getting married.
troupak, wedding-suit.
troupand, marriage-pledge.
trouparty, wedding-party.
trouplegtigheid, wedding(-ceremony).
trouring, wedding-ring.
trourok, wedding-dress.
tru, troei!, back!, wait!
tru, troei (ge-), reverse (car), back.
trui, (-e), sweater, jersey.
truitjie-roer-my-niet, touch-me-not, sensitive plant; hot-tempered (touchy) person, touch-me-not.
trust, (-s), trust.
trustakte, trust-deed.
trustee, (-s), trustee.
trustmaatskappy, trust-company.
tsaar, (tsare), czar (tsar).
tsamma, (-s), tsamma, wild melon.
tsetse(vlieg), tsetse-fly.
Tsjeg, (-ge), Czech.
Tsjeggies, (-e), Czech.
Tsjeggo-Slowakye, Czecho-Slovakia.
tsotsi, tsotsi.
tuba, (-s), tuba.
tuberkuleus, (-e), tubercular, tuberculous.
tuberkulose, tuberculosis.
tuf-tuf, tuff-tuff, motor-car, train.
tug, n. discipline; punishment; **die – handhaaf**, maintain discipline.
tug, (ge-), punish, chastise, discipline.
tughuis, house of correction.
tugmeester, disciplinarian.
tugordonnansie, discipline-ordinance.
tugroede, rod (of correction), cane.
tugteloos, (-lose), undisciplined, insubordinate; licentious, dissolute.
tugteloosheid, insubordination; dissoluteness.
tugtig, (ge-), punish, chastise.
tugiging, punishment, chastisement.
tug(tigings)ekspedisie, punitive expedition.
tuiemaker, harness-maker.
tuig, (tuie), harness; **in die –**, in harness.
tuimel, (ge-), tumble, topple (over).
tuimelaar, (-s), tumbler.
tuimeling, tumble, fall, somersault.
tuin, (-e), garden; **– maak**, garden, work in the garden, go in for gardening; **om die – lei**, hoodwink, deceive.
tuinargitek, landscape-gardener.
tuinbaas, gardener; garden-owner.

tuinbou, horticulture.
tuinboukundige, (-s), horticulturist.
tuinbouskool, horticultural school.
tuinboutentoonstelling, horticultural show.
tuinfees, garden-party.
tuingereedskap, gardening-tools.
tuingroente, vegetables.
tuingrond, garden-soil; garden-ground.
tuinhuis(ie), summer-house.
tuinier, (-e, -s), gardener.
tuiniersalmanak, gardener's calender.
tuiniersvak, gardening.
tuinman, gardener.
tuinpaadjie, garden-path.
tuinparty, garden-party.
tuinslang, garden-hose.
tuinwerk, gardening.
tuis, at home; **hy is nie – nie**, he is not at home (not in); **by die hotel – wees**, stay (stop) at the hotel; **hande –!**, hands off!; **sig – voel**, feel at home; **maak of jy – is**, make yourself at home; **goed – wees in 'n vak**, be at home in a subject; – **bly**, stay at home, stay in; – **bring**, bring home; see home; **ek kan hom nie – bring nie**, I cannot place him; – **gaan**, stay; – **hoort**, belong; **dit hoort nie hier – nie**, this does not belong here; this is out of place here; – **hou**, keep at home, keep in; **jou hande – hou**, keep your hands off (something); – **kom**, arrive home.
Tuisbly: met Jan – se karretjie ry, stay at home.
tuishuis, (farmer's) town-house.
tuiskoms, arrival, homecoming, return.
tuisreis, home(ward) journey.
tuiste, (-s), home.
tuit, (-e), n. spout (of tea-pot, etc.), nozzle, mouthpiece, point; pout; **trane met -e huil**, cry bitterly.
tuit, (ge-), tingle; **my ore –, my ears tingle**, (burn).
tuithoed, -kappie, poke-bonnet.
tulband, turban.
tulle, tulle.
tulp, (-e), tulip; poisonous tulip.
tulpbol, tulip-bulb.
tulphandel, tulip-trade.
tulpkweker, tulip-grower.
tuna, tuna.
tungolie, tung oil.
tuniek, (-e), tunic.
turbine, (-s), turbine.
turbineboot, turbine-steamer.
turbineskroef, turbo-prop.
turbineskroefvliegtuig, turbo-prop aeroplane.
turbinestraal, turbo-jet.
turbinestraalmotor, turbo-jet engine.
turf, peat; turf; clayey soil; **sy – sit**, that's got him beat, he is done for.
turfgrond, peat-ground; clayey soil.
Turk, (-e), Turk.
turkoois, (-e), turquoise.
Turks, n. Turkish.
Turks, (-e), a. Turkish.
turksvy(g), prickly pear.
Turkye, Turkey.
tussen, between; among, surrounded by.
tussenbei(e), so-so, passable, fair; – **kom (tree)**, interfere, intervene.
tussenboot, intermediate boat.
tussendek, between-decks.
tussendekspassasier, steerage-passenger.
tussendeur, n. communicating door.
tussendeur, adv. in between.
tussending, neither the one nor the other, hybrid, mongrel, cross.
tussengeleë, interjacent, intermediate.
tussengereg, intermediate course.

tussengevoeg, (-de), interpolated.
tussenhandel, intermediate trade.
tussenhandelaar, middleman.
tussenin, between the two; in between; parenthetic clause.
tussenkoms, intervention, intervening, mediation, agency.
tussenletter, medial letter.
tussenmuur, dividing wall, partition.
tussenpersoon, agent, broker, middleman, intermediary, mediator.
tussenpoos, interval.
tussenruimte, intervening space.
tussensoort, medium sort.
tussenspel, interlude.
tussentyd, interval, interim; **in die –**, meanwhile, in the meantime.
tussenverkiesing, by-election.
tussenvoeg, (tussenge-), insert.
tussenvoeging, insertion, interpolation.
tussenvoegsel, (-s), insertion, interpolation.
tussenvorm, intermediate form.
tussenwerpsel, (-s), interjection.
tuur, (ge-), peer (at); pore (over a book).
twaalf, twelve; **hy is ouer as –**, his head is screwed on the right way.
twaalfde, (-s), twelfth.
twaalfhoek, dodecagon.
twaalfhoekig, (-e), dodecagonal.
twaalfjarig, (-e), of twelve years.
twaalf maal, twelve times.
twaalfponder, twelve-pounder.
twaalftal, (about) twelve, dozen.
twaalfuur, twelve o'clock; midday-meal.
twaalfvingerig, (-e), twelve-fingered; **-e derm**, duodenum.
twaalfvlak, dodecahedron.
twaalfvoud, multiple of twelve.
twaalfvoudig, (-e), twelvefold.
twak, tobacco; **sy – is nat**, he is a goner, he is in a sorry plight, he is nowhere (no good); – **verkoop**, (talk) piffle, talk nonsense; **hy is 'n ou –**, he is a good-for-nothing (miserable specimen); **nie 'n pyp – werd nie**, not worth a damn (straw); vide **tabak**.
twakpraatjies, piffle, rubbish, nonsense.
twee, two; – **twee**, by (in) twos; **sê en doen is –**, fine words butter no parsnips, words are but wind; **so waar as twee maal – vier is**, as sure as eggs is eggs.
tweebeen . . ., two-legged.
tweebenig, (-e), two-legged.
tweedaags, (-s), of two days.
tweede, second; **ten –**, secondly.
tweedehands, (-e), second-hand.
tweedekker, (-s), biplane.
tweederangs, (-e), second-rate.
tweederlei, vide **tweërlei**.
tweedraads, two-ply (wool).
tweedrag, discord, dissension; – **saai**, sow the seeds of dissension.
tweedubbel(d), tweeduwwel(d), double.
tweegesprek, dialogue.
tweegeveg, duel, single combat.
tweehoekig, (-e), biangular.
tweehonderdjarig, (-e), two hundred years old, bicentenary (celebrations).
tweehoofdig, (-e), two-headed.
tweehoring(rig), (-e), two-horned, bicornous.
tweejarig, (-e), two-year-old, of two years, two years (war), biennial.
tweeklank, diphthong.
tweeledig, (-e), biarticulate; binary, binomial; double (meaning), dual.
tweelettergrepig, (-e) dis(s)yllabic.

tweeling, (-e), twins.
tweelingbroer, twin-brother.
tweelingwoord, doublet.
tweelobbig, (-e), bilobate.
tweeloop(sgeweer), double-barrelled gun.
twee maal, twice; vide twee.
tweemaandeliks, (-e), bimonthly.
tweemaster, two-master.
tweepersoonsbed, double bed.
tweepersoonsmotor, two-seater(-car).
tweeponder, two-pounder.
tweereëlig, (-e), of two lines.
tweërlei, of two kinds.
twee(saad)lobbig, (-e), dictotyledonous.
tweesang, duet.
tweeslag-, two-stroke.
tweeslagtig, (-e), bisexual, hermaphroditic; amphibious; double (life).
tweesnarig, (-e), two-stringed.
tweesnydend, (-e), double-edged.
tweesoortig, (-e), of two kinds.
tweespalk, -spalt, discord, dissension.
tweespraak, dialogue.
tweesprong, cross-roads.
tweestemming, (-e), for two voices.
tweestroompolitiek, two-stream policy.
tweestryd, duel; inward conflict; indecision.
tweesydig, (-e), two-sided, bilateral.
tweetal, two, pair.
tweetalig, (-e), bilingual.
tweetaligheid, bilingualism.
tweetallig, (-e), binary.
tweetandskaap, year-old sheep, yearling.
tweeterm, (-e), binomial.
tweevlakkig, (-e), dihedral.
tweevleuelig, (-e), two-winged.
tweevoetig, (-e), two-footed, biped(al); of two (metrical) feet.
tweevoud, (-e), double; multiple of two.
tweevoudig, (-e), double; twofold.
tweewieler, (-s), bicycle, two-wheeler.
tweewywery, bigamy.
twintig, twenty.
twintigjarig, (-e), twenty years old, of twenty years, twenty years (war).
twintig maal, twenty times.
twintigponder, twenty-pounder.
twintigste, twentieth.
twintingtal, score (about) twenty.
twintigvoud, multiple of twenty.
twintigvoudig, (-e), twentyfold.
twis, (-te), n. quarrel, dispute, strife; – soek, (try to) pick a quarrel.
twis, (ge-), quarrel, dispute.
twisappel, bone of contention, apple of discord.
twisgeskryf, controversy, polemic.
twisgierig, (-e), quarrelsome.
twispunt, point of issue.
twissaak, matter in dispute.
twissiek, (-e), quarrelsome, contentious.
twissoeker, quarrelsome person.
twisstoker, mischief-maker.
twisvraag, controversial question.
twyfel, n. doubt; dit ly geen – nie, daar is geen – aan nie, there is no doubt about it; buiten (sonder) –, undoubtedly, doubtless; in – trek, question, have doubts about it.
twyfel, (ge-), doubt; – aan, doubt, question, have doubts about.
twyfelaar, (-s), doubter, sceptic.
twyfelagtig, (-e), doubtful, dubious.
twyfelagtigheid, doubtfulness; questionableness.
twyfeling, doubt, hesitation.
twyfelmoedig, (-e), wavering, vacillating, halfhearted.

twyfelmoedigheid, irresoluteness.
twyfelsug, scepticism.
twyfelsugtig, (-e), sceptical.
twyg, [twy(g)e], twig; scion.
twyn, twine, twist.
ty, (-e), tide.
tyd, (tye), time; season; tense (gram.); die – sal dit uitwys (leer), time will tell (show); sedert onheuglike tye, from time immemorial; alles het sy – (daar is 'n – vir alles), there is a time for everything; dit is hoog –, it is high time; jou – afwag, bide one's time; kom –, kom raad, time will bring counsel; my –!, (o liewe –!), dear me!; die goeie ou –, the good old times (days); dit is –, it is time; time is up; hy het sy – gehad, he has had his day; 'n – gelede, some time ago; daar was 'n – toe, there was a time when, die – val my lank (ek kan die – nie omkry nie), time hangs heavy on my hands; dit kos baie –, it takes much time; wie nie pas op sy –, is sy maaltyd kwyt, those who don't come in time must forgo the meal; – maak, find time; by tye, at times, sometimes; in my –, in my time (day); in die laaste –, lately, of late; op –, in time; altyd presies op –, always punctual; alles op sy –, there is a time for everything; op vaste tye, at set times, at regular intervals; oor die – wees, be late (overdue); te eniger –, at some time or other; at any time; te alle tye, at all times; teen daardie –, by that time; van – tot –, from time to time; tot – en wyl, till; uit die – wees, be behind the times.
tydelik, (-e), temporary (office, relief); temporal (affairs).
tydelik, adv. temporarily, pro tem.
tydens, during.
tydgees, spirit of the times (age).
tydgenoot, contemporary.
tydig, (-e), a. timely, seasonable.
tydig, adv. in good time; – en ontydig, in season and out of season.
tydigheid, seasonableness, timeliness.
tyding, (-e, -s), news, tidings; geen – goeie –, no news is good news.
tydjie, (-s), short time, little while.
tydkorting, pastime.
tyd lank: 'n –, for a (some) time.
tydmaat, time, tempo.
tydmeter, chronometer.
tydopname, timing; time-exposure.
tydopnemer, timekeeper.
tydperk, period.
tydrekening, chronology; era.
tydrowend, (-e), taking up much time.
tydruimte, space of time, period.
tydsaam, (-same), slow, leisurely.
tydsbepaling, time-limit; fixing the time; adjunct of time.
tydsbestek, space of time.
tydsein, time-signal.
tydsgenoeg, slow, leisurely.
tydsgewrig, epoch, time; vide tydstip.
tydskrif, periodical, magazine.
tydsorde, chronological order.
tydstip, point of time; moment.
tydsverloop, course of time.
tydtafel, time-table; chronological table.
tydvak, period.
tydverdryf, pastime.
tydverlies, loss of time.
tydverspilling, waste of time.
tyk, tick(ing).
tym, vide tiemie.

U

u, pers. pron , you.
u, poss. pron., your.
U Edele, (U Ed.), Your Honour.
ui, (-e), onion; jest, joke.
uieagtig, (-e), onion-like.
uie-akker(tjie), onion-bed.
uielof, (-lowwe), onion-leaves.
uielug, onion-smell.
uier, (-s), udder.
uiereuk, -ruik, onion-smell.
uiesaad, onion-seed.
uieslaai, onion-salad.
uil, (-e), owl; **elkeen meen dat sy – 'n valk is,** everyone thinks his own geese swans; **soos 'n – onder die kraaie,** the laughing-stock of everyone; **soos 'n – op 'n kluit,** quite perplexed (lost in company).
uilagtig, (-e), owlish, stupid.
uilbek, owl-beak; forceps.
uiloog, owl's eye.
uilskuiken, blockhead, goose, numskull, nincompoop, simpleton.
Uilspieël, buffoon, joker, (little) rogue; **soos – in die maanskyn,** odd-looking, of singular appearance.
uiltjie, (-s), owlet; peacock-flower; **'n – knip,** take a nap.
uintjie, (-s), edible bulbous plant, Moraea edulis.
uit, prep., out of, on, in, of, through, by, from, among; – **liefde,** out of love; – **die mode,** out of fashion; – **beginsel,** on principle; – **wanhoop,** in despair; – **vriendskap,** in friendship; **een – duisend,** one in a thousand; – **edele ouers gebore,** born of noble parents; – **sy eie,** of his own accord; – **agteloosigheid,** through carelessness; – **ervaring,** by (from) experience; – **armoede (onkunde, vrees),** from poverty (ignorance, fear); – **'n glas drink,** drink from a glass; – **die vreemde,** from abroad; **een – baie,** one among many.
uit, adv. & a., off, out, over, up, on; **die verloofskap is –,** the engagement is off; **die kerk is –,** the service is over; **dit is – tussen ons,** it is all up between us; **hy is daarop – om . . . ,** he is bent on . . . ; – **eet,** dine out.
uit, (ge-), utter, express, voice.
uitadem, -asem, (uitge-), breathe out, expire, exhale.
uitademing, -aseming, (-e, -s), breathing out, expiration, exhalation.
uit-asem, adv. & a. out of breath.
uitasem, vide **uitadem.**
uitbagger, (uitge-), dredge.
uitbak, (uitge-), bake (fry) well; fall into disfavour, lose one's popularity.
uitbaklei, (uitge-), fight out.
uitban, (uitge-), banish, expel.
uitbars, (uitge-), burst (break) out, explode; **van die lag,** burst out laughing.
uitbarsting, (-e, -s), eruption, explosion, outbreak, outburst.
uitbasuin, (uitge-), trumpet forth; **sy eie lof –,** blow one's own trumpet.
uitbeeld, (uitge-), depict, delineate.
uitbeelding, (-e, -s), depiction, delineation, rendering.
uitbeitel, (uitge-), chisel out.
uitbestee, (–), put out to nurse, put out to board; give out on contract.
uitbetaal, (–), pay out (over, down), cash (a cheque); **ek sal jou (daarvoor) –,** I shall get even with you.
uitbetaling, (-e, -s), payment, settlement.
uitblaas, (uitge-), blow out; **die laaste asem –,** breathe one's last (breath).

uitblaker, (uitge-), blurt out; **hy het alles uitgeblaker,** he gave the whole show away, he let the cat out of the bag.
uitbleik, (uitge-), bleach; fade.
uitblêr, (uitge-), bleat out, blurt out.
uitblink, (uitge-), shine out; excel; – **bo,** eclipse, outshine.
uitblus, (uitge-), extinguish, quench.
uitbly, (uitge-), stay away; delay, tarry, fail to come.
uitboender, (uitge-), bundle out, expel.
uitboer, (uitge-), become bankrupt, come to the end of one's resources; lose favour.
uitboor, (uitge-), bore out, drill.
uitborrel, (uitge-), bubble out (up).
uitborsel, (uitge-), brush out, dust.
uitbot, (uitge-), bud, shoot, sprout.
uitbou, n. annex(e), wing, extension.
uitbou, (uitge-), enlarge, extend.
uitbraai, (uitge-), roast out.
uitbraak, n. escape; outbreak.
uitbraak, (uitge-), vomit, belch forth, disgorge.
uitbraaksel, (-s), vomit.
uitbrand, (uitge-), burn out; cauterize; be completely gutted.
uitbrander, (-s), scolding, reprimand.
uitbranding, (-s), cauterisation.
uitbreek, (uitge-), break (burst) out; originate.
uitbrei, (uitge-), spread, enlarge, extend.
uitbreiding, (-e, -s), extension, expansion.
uitbreidingsbeampte, extension-officer.
uitbreking, outbreak, eruption.
uitbring, (uitge-), bring, out, utter, disclose, record; **'n verslag –,** report; **'n stem –,** record a vote.
uitbroei, (uitge-), hatch; concoct.
uitbrul, (uitge-), roar out.
uitbuit, (uitge-), exploit.
uitbuiting, exploitation; advantageous use.
uitbulder, (uitge-), cease bellowing (blustering, raging); bellow, rave, roar, vociferate.
uitbundig, (-e), exceeding, excessive; enthusiastic, exuberant; boisterous.
uitbundigheid, exuberance, boisterousness. Vide **uitbundig.**
uitdaag, (uitge-), challenge; dare, defy.
uitdaagbeker, challenge-cup.
uitda(g)end, (-e), challenging, defiant, defying, provoking.
uitda(g)er, (-s), challenger.
uitdaging, (-e, -s), challenge.
uitdamp, (uitge-), evaporate; exhale; air.
uitdamping, evaporation; airing.
uitdeel, (uitge-), deal (dole, hand, serve) out, dispense, distribute.
uitdelg, (uitge-), destroy, exterminate, extirpate; wipe out (a debt).
uitdelger, (-s), destroyer, exterminator.
uitdelging, destruction, extermination.
uitdeling, distribution; dole; dividend.
uitdien, (uitge-), last (its time); serve (its purpose, one's time); **dit is uitgedien,** this has had its day.
uitdiep, (uitge-), deepen; excavate.
uitdink, (uitge-), contrive, devise, invent, think out.
uitdolf, -dolwe, (uitge-), dig up (out).
uitdoof, -dowe, (uitge-), extinguish, put out, quench.
uitdop, (uitge-), shell (peas).
uitdor, (uitge-), dry up (out), wither, shrivel (up).
uitdors, (uitge-), 1. thresh (out).
uitdors, (uitge-), 2. dry out, make thirsty.
uitdos, (uitge-), array, attire, deck out, dress up, trim out.

uitdra, (uitge-), carry out.
uitdraai, (uitge-), turn aside; turn out; switch off; shuffle (twist, worm, wriggle) out of; **op niks** –, come to nothing, fizzle out.
uitdraaipad, branch-road; cross-road; parting (of the roads).
uitdring, (uitge-), crowd out, press out.
uitdrink, (uitge-), empty, finish, drain.
uitdro(ë), -droog, (uitge-), dry up, run dry, become parched; desiccate; wipe dry (plate); wring out (clothes).
uitdruk, (uitge-), press (squeeze) out; express, put (in words).
uitdrukking, (-e, -s), expression, phrase, term, wording.
uitdrukkingsvermoë, power of expression.
uitdruklik, (-e), a. definite, emphatic, explicit, express, positive.
uitdruklik, adv. definitely, emphatically.
uitdruklikheid, explicitness.
uitdryf, -drywe, (uitge-), cast out, drive out, expel; exorcize (evil spirits).
uitdun, (uitge-), thin (out).
uitduur, (uitge-), last (out).
uitdy, (uitge-), swell; expand.
uiteen, apart, asunder.
uiteenbars, (uiteenge-), burst (asunder), crack, explode.
uiteendryf, -drywe, (uiteenge-), break up, disperse, scatter.
uiteengaan, (uiteenge-), break up, disperse, part, rise, separate.
uiteenhou, (uiteenge-), keep apart.
uiteenja(ag), (uiteenge-), break up, disperse, scatter.
uiteenloop, (uiteenge-), diverge.
uiteenlopend, (-e), divergent, different.
uiteensetting, explanation, exposition.
uiteensit, (uiteenge-), explain, expound, enunciate, set out, state; space.
uiteenspat, (uiteenge-), break up, burst (asunder), explode, disrupt.
uiteenval, (uiteenge-), disintegrate, fall apart, fall to pieces, break up.
uiteenvlieg, (uiteenge-), fly apart (to pieces), scatter, tumble to pieces.
uiteinde, end, extremity; finality; death.
uiteindelik, at last, finally, ultimately.
uiter, (ge-), vide **uit, (ge-).**
uiteraard, naturally, by nature, from the nature of the case.
uiterlik, n. appearance, exterior, looks.
uiterlik, (-e), a. & adv. apparent(ly), external(ly), outward(ly), at the latest, at the utmost.
uiterlikheid, exterior; superficiality.
uitermate, exceedingly, excessively, extremely, uncommonly, very.
uiters, utterly, extremely, supremely, very; to the last degree; at the latest.
uiterste, (-s), n. extreme, extremity, limit; death; **in die –s verval,** go to extremes; **op sy – lê,** be at death's door; **tot die –,** to the limit, to the utmost.
uiterste, a. extreme, farthest, last, outside, utmost, utter, very; **sy – bes,** one's utmost, one's very best; **die – nood,** in extreme distress; **in die – geval,** in case of need, in the last extremity.
uitflap, (uitge-), blab, blurt out, rap out.
uitfluit, (uitge-), hiss at, boo, hoot.
uitfoeter, (uitge-), swear at, scold; beat, thrash, lick, give a hiding.
uitgaaf, vide **uitgawe.**
uitgaan, (uitge-), go out; be over (church); end in; go out of, leave (room); emanate from;

op 'n klinker –, end in a vowel; **– van,** start out from.
uitgaande, outward, (mail); outward-bound (ship); pleasure-seeking.
uitgaansdag, day off, day out, off-day.
uitgang, exit, outlet, way out; egress; issue; ending, termination (of a word).
uitgangspunt, starting-point.
uitgawe, (-s), -gaaf, (-gawes), costs, expenditure, expenses; edition, publication.
uitgebak, (-te), found out, in disfavour.
uitgebrei(d), (-breide), broad, comprehensive, extensive, vast, wide.
uitgebreidheid, comprehensiveness, extensiveness, extent.
uitgedien, (-de), broken; worn out; obsolete.
uitgedruk, (-te), expressed; exact; **hy is A –,** he is the exact image of A.
uitgee, (uitge-), distribute (food), issue (tickets); spend (money); edit, publish (book); pass out (ball).
uitgeëet, (-geëte), overfed.
uitgehonger(d), (-de), famished, ravenous; underfed, starving.
uitgeknip, (-te), cut (pattern); **hy is A –,** he is the very image of A.
uitgelate, elated, exuberant, joyful, wanton.
uitgelatenheid, elation, exuberance.
uitgeleef, (-de), decrepit, worn out.
uitgeleide, conduct, escort; farewell; **iemand – doen,** escort a person; see someone off.
uitgelese, choice, picked, select.
uitgelesenheid, choiceness, selectness.
uitgemaak, (-te), established, settled; **dit is 'n uitgemaakte saak,** that is a foregone conclusion.
uitgenome, barring, except, save.
uitgerafel(d), (-de), frayed, worn.
uitgeslape, knowing, sly, shrewd.
uitgesonderd, barring, except, save.
uitgestel(d), (-de), postponed.
uitgestorwe, deserted (town); extinct (animal); deceased; **'n – boedel,** a deceased estate.
uitgestrek, (-te), extensive, large, vast.
uitgestrektheid, extensiveness; expanse, extent, stretch, sweep; vastness.
uitgeteer, (-de), emaciated, wasted.
uitgevreet, (-vrete), big and strong, well-fed.
uitgewekene, (-s), emigrant; refugee.
uitgewer, (-s), editor, publisher.
uitgewerk, (-te), detailed, elaborate(d); flat, dead (beer); extinct (volcano).
uitgewersaak, uitgewersfirma, -maatskappy, publishing-business (-company, -firm, -house).
uitgewery, publishing; publication; publishing-business; distribution.
uitgiet, (uitge-), empty, pour out.
uitgifte, (-s), issue; output.
uitgil, (uitge-), scream, yell.
uitglip, (uitge-), slip (out).
uitgly, (uitge-), slide, slip (out); skid.
uitgooi, (uitge-), eject, throw out, empty; spill.
uitgraaf, -grawe, (uitge-), dig out, dig up, excavate; exhume (corpse).
uitgrawing, excavation; exhumation.
uitgroei, (uitge-), grow; outgrow.
uitgroeisel, excrescence, outgrowth.
uithaal, (uitge-), draw (pull, take) out; root out; clean out; play (tricks); exert oneself.
uithaler, flashy, showy, smart.
uithalerperd, fine (lively, smart) horse.
uithang, (uitge-), hang out; play (a part); cut a dash, make a splash.
uithangbord, signboard.
uithangkas, show-window.

uitheems, (-e), foreign, exotic; outlandish; strange.
uithelp, (uitge-), help out.
uithoek, out-of-the-way place, remote corner, outlying district.
uithoes, (uitge-), cough up, expectorate.
uithol, (uitge-), 1. cut (dig, hollow, scoop) out, excavate.
uithol, (uitge-), 2. run out; outrun.
uithonger, (uitge-), famish, starve.
uithoor, (uitge-), draw, pump (someone); listen to the end (to someone).
uithou, (uitge-), 1. bear, suffer, stand, stick, endure; hold back (out).
uithou, (uitge-), 2. carve (out) hew (out); **in steen –**, carve in stone.
uithou(dings)vermoë, endurance, stamina, staying-power.
uithuil, (uitge-), have a good cry, cry (weep) oneself out.
uithuisig, (-e), from home, never at home, gadabout, not a home-bird.
uithuisigheid, gadabout habits (ways).
uithuwelik, (uitge-), give in marriage.
uiting, (-e, -s), expression, utterance; – **gee aan**, give expression to, voice.
uitja(ag), -jae, (uitge-), drive out, expel.
uitjie, (-s), small onion.
uitjou, (uitge-), boo, hoot, barrack.
uitjouery, barracking, hooting.
uitkaffir, (uitge-), scold severely, abuse.
uitkalf, -kalwe, (uitge-), cave in, hollow (wash) out (banks of a river), erode.
uitkam, (uitge-), comb out.
uitkap, (uitge-), carve out; cut out.
uitkeer, (uitge-), pay out, pay back; turn aside; head off (cattle).
uitkering, payment; dividend; dole.
uitkeringspolis, endowment policy.
uitkies, (uitge-), choose, pick out, select, single out.
uitklee, (uitge-), strip, undress.
uitklim, (uitge-), climb out, ascend.
uitklok, (uitge-), clock out.
uitklop, (uitge-), beat (out), dust, knock-out; defeat, beat, thrash.
uitklophou, knock-out blow.
uitknikker, (uitge-), bowl out, oust.
uitknip, (uitge-), cut out, clip out.
uitknipsel, clipping, cutting, scrap.
uitkoggel, (uitge-), deride, mock, mimic.
uitkom, (uitge-), appear, come out; (flowers) bud; (eggs) hatch; (facts) become known; (predictions) come true; turn out; work out; make ends meet; **laat –**, accentuate, emphasize; **met iets –**, bring to light; – **op**, open into, lead to; amount to; – **vir iets**, admit something; speak one's mind.
uitkoms(te), issue, outcome, result; deliverance, godsend, help, relief.
uitkook, (uitge-), boil out.
uitkoop, (uitge-), buy out, buy off.
uitkraai, (uitge-), crow (with delight).
uitkraam, (uitge-), display, parade, show off; reel off.
uitkrap, (uitge-), scratch out; erase.
uitkruip, (uitge-), creep out, get up; **vir sy sonde –**, suffer for one's sins.
uitkry, (uitge-), get out; finish.
uitkryt, (uitge-), cry out; denounce.
uitkuier, (uitge-), pay a long visit; outstay one's welcome.
uitkyk, n. lookout, prospect, view; outlook, viewpoint, attitude.

uitkyk, (uitge-), look out, watch, be on the lookout (watch); stare.
uitkyktoring, watch-tower.
uitlaat, n. outlet; exhaust.
uitlaat, (uitge-), leave out, omit, skip; let out, let off, release, express; let drop (a hint).
uitlaatpyp, exhaust-pipe.
uitlag, (uitge-), laugh at.
uitlander, (-s), alien, foreigner, outlander.
uitlands, (-e), foreign, outlandish.
uitlating, (-e, -s), letting out (of steam); omission; utterance, statement.
uitlê, lay out; extend; elucidate, explain, expound, interpret.
uitleef, -lewe, (uitge-), consume, spend; live one's own life.
uitleen, (uitge-), lend out, loan.
uitlêer, (-s), commentator, interpreter.
uitlees, (uitge-), finish; read out.
uitleg, lay-out; explanation, interpretation, construction, exposition; exegesis (of Scripture).
uitlegging, (-e, -s), vide **uitleg**.
uitlegkunde, exegesis, hermeneutics.
uitlegkundig, (-e), exegetic(al).
uitlei, (uitge-), lead out.
uitlek, (uitge-), 1. lick out, lick clean.
uitlek, (uitge-), 2. filter through, leak out, ooze out, trickle out; transpire.
uitlewe, vide **uitleef**.
uitlewer, (uitge-), deliver, hand over, surrender; exchange; extradite.
uitlewering, delivery, surrender; exchange; extradition.
uitleweringstraktaat, -verdrag, extradition treaty.
uitlig, (uitge-), lift out; oust.
uitlok, (uitge-), lure, tempt; elicit (an answer); call forth, evoke; ask for (trouble), provoke (a quarrel), court (disaster).
uitloof, -lowe, (uitge-), offer, promise.
uitloog, (uitge-), lixiviate, macerate.
uitlooi, (uitge-), tan, beat, thrash.
uitloop, n. overflow, outlet, spillway.
uitloop, (uitge-), go out, walk out; run out (liquids); bud, shoot, sprout; – **in**, empty (itself) into, run into, lead to; – **op**, lead to, end in; – **op niks**, come to nothing.
uitloopsel, (-s), bud, shoot, sprout; end.
uitloot, (uitge-), release (bonds); raffle (a prize).
uitloting, drawing (of bonds); raffle.
uitlowe, vide **uitloof**.
uitlowing, offering, promising.
uitlug, (uitge-), air, ventilate.
uitlui, (uitge-), ring out.
uitmaak, (uitge-), break off (an engagement); constitute, form; decide, settle; decry, denounce, call; **iemand vir 'n leuenaar –**, call someone a liar; **iemand vir al wat sleg is –**, call a person all sorts of names.
uitmeet, (uitge-), measure, measure off; mete out.
uitmekaar, apart, asunder.
uitmelk, (uitge-), milk dry (out), trip (a cow); pluck, skin (someone).
uitmergel, (uitge-), exhaust, impoverish.
uitmond, (uitge-), debouch into; discharge, empty (itself) into.
uitmonding, mouth, outlet.
uitmoor, (uitge-), butcher, massacre.
uitmunt, (uitge-), excel, surpass.
uitmuntend, (-e), excellent, eminent.
uitmuntendheid, excellence, eminence.
uitneem, (uitge-), take out.
uitnemend, (-e), excellent, eminent.
uitnemendheid, excellence, eminence; **by –**, par excellence, pre-eminently.

uitnodiging, invitation.
uitnooi, (uitge-), invite.
uitoefen, (uitge-), carry on, practise; exercise (influence); follow, pursue (a trade); hold, occupy (a post); discharge (duties); wield (power); **kritiek –,** criticise.
uitoefening, exercise, practice, execution, discharge; pursuit; vide **uitoefen.**
uitoorlê, (–), outmanoeuvre, outwit.
uitpak, (uitge-), unpack; pour out, unburden (one's heart), let out; **teen iemand –,** inveigh against someone.
uitpers, (uitge-), press (squeeze) out.
uitpeul, (uitge-), 1. peel, shell (peas).
uitpeul, 2. vide **uitpuil.**
uitpik, (uitge-), peck out; dig out with a pick; pick, select, single out.
uitplak, (uitge-), paper (a house, etc.).
uitplant, (uitge-), bed out, plant out.
uitpluis, (uitge-), sift (evidence), investigate (matter), scrutinize, thresh out (a subject); pick (coir).
uitpluk, (uitge-), pick out; pluck out.
uitplunder, (uitge-), loot, plunder, pillage, ransack, rob, sack, spoliate.
uitpomp, (uitge-), exhaust; pump out.
uitpraat, (uitge-), talk to the end; talk oneself out; have one's say; **iemand nie laat – nie,** cut someone short.
uitpuil, -peul, (uitge-), budge; (eyes) goggle, protrude.
uitpuiloë, goggle-eyes, pop-eyes.
uitpunt, (uitge-), scallop.
uitput, (uitge-), exhaust, wear out.
uitputting, exhaustion; enervation.
uitraak, (uitge-), get out; be broken off (engagement); go bankrupt.
uitraas, (uitge-), cease raging, rage out; blow (let) off steam, bluster.
uitrafel, (uitge-), fray, ravel out.
uitred, (uitge-), deliver, extricate, save.
uitredding, deliverance, escape.
uitreën, -reent, (uitge-), stop raining.
uitreik, (uitge-), present, confer (a prize), distribute, give away, hand out; issue.
uitreiking, award, bestowal, presentation; distribution, issue.
uitreis, n. outward journey (voyage).
uitreis, (uitge-), sail, start, set out.
uitrek, (uitge-), stretch (out); crane (one's neck); draw out, prolong.
uitrekbaar, (-bare), extensible, elastic.
uitreken, (uitge-), calculate, compute, figure (reckon, work), out.
uitrig, (uitge-), accomplish, do, perform.
uitroei, (uitge-), root out, uproot, eradicate, extirpate, weed out, exterminate, stamp out, annihilate.
uitroeiing, eradication, extermination.
uitroep, n. cry, exclamation, shout.
uitroep, (uitge-), call, cry, exclaim, shout; declare (a strike); proclaim.
uitroep(ings)teken, note of exclamation.
uitrol, (uitge-), roll out, unfurl, unroll.
uitrook, (uitge-), finish (pipe); fumigate, smoke out.
uitruil, (uitge-), barter, exchange.
uitruk, (uitge-), pluck (pull, tear) out.
uitrus, (uitge-), rest, have (take) a rest, repose; equip, fit out, rig (out).
uitrusting, equipment, outfit, kit.
uitsaag, -sae, (uitge-), saw out.
uitsaai, (uitge-), scatter; disseminate; broadcast.
uitsaaidiens, broadcasting service.
uitsaaistasie, broadcasting station.
uitsae, vide **uitsaag.**
uitsak, (uitge-), bag (bulge) out, sag; drop out; begin to rain.
uitsakking, bulging, falling, sagging; dropping out; downpour.
uitseil, (uitge-), sail (out), set sail.
uitsend, (uitge-), dispatch, send out.
uitset, n. trousseau, outfit.
uitsetting, enlargement, dilation, inflation; expansion; extension; diastole (of the heart); deportation, expulsion.
uitsettingskoëffisient, coefficien of expansion.
uitsettingsvermoë, power of expansion.
uitsien, (uitge-), look (out); look like; **– na,** look out for; long for, look forward to; **– op,** look out upon, face, overlook.
uitsif, (uitge-), sift, thresh out.
uitsig, prospect, view, vista; outlook; **– hê op,** face, overlook.
uitsing, (uitge-), finish (a song), sing to the end, sing out.
uitsinnig, (-e), crazy, demented, distracted, frantic, insane, lunatic, mad.
uitsit, (uitge-), sit out; serve one's time; expand, extend, distend, dilate; cut out (a rival); put out, post (a sentry); invest (money); put out, banish, deport, eject.
uitskakel, (uitge-), cut out, disconnect, switch off; declutch, eliminate, rule out.
uitskakelaar, circuit-breaker, cut-out.
uitskakeling, switching-off; elimination.
uitskater, (uitge-), burst out laughing.
uitskei(e), (uitge-), leave off, stop, knock off, chuck (drop) it; excrete; **skei tog uit!,** chuck it!, shut up!
uitskel, (uitge-), abuse, scold, revile.
uitskep, (uitge-), bail out (water), ladle out (soup), scoop out.
uitskeur, (uitge-), tear out.
uitskiet, (uitge-), shoot out; shoot (dash) away; slip bud, sprout.
uitskif, (uitge-), sift (out), single out.
uitskink, (uitge-), pour out.
uitskoffel, (uitge-), hoe out, weed out.
uitskop, (uitge-), kick out.
uitskot, cullings, offal, refuse, rubbish; tailings, dregs, rabble, riff-raff.
uitskraap, (uitge-), scrape (out), erase, scratch out.
uitskraapsel, scrappings, scrap(s).
uitskree(u), (uitge-), cry (scream) out.
uitskryf, -skrywe, (uitge-), write out, copy out; make out (invoice); issue (loan); call (election); '**n prysvraag –,** offer a prize.
uitskud, (uitge-), shake (out); strip to the skin; clean (clear) out; rob, win (someone's money).
uitskuif, -skuiwe, (uitge-), slide out; push out; draw out.
uitskulp, (uitge-), scallop.
uitskuur, (uitge-), scour (out).
uitslaan, (uitge-), beat (strike) out; knock out; spread (stretch) out (wings); beat (hammer) out (metals); break out (rash, flames); sweat, exude (of wall); **onverwags op die plaas –,** turn up unexpectedly on the farm.
uitslaap, (uitge-), sleep one's fill; sleep away from home; vide **roes.**
uitslag, 1. rash, eruption; efflorescence.
uitslag, 2. result, issue, outcome.
uitsluip, (uitge-), slip (sneak) out.
uitsluit, (uitge-), lock out; bar, debar, exclude; preclude (doubt); rule out (possibility).
uitsluitend, (-e), a. & adv. exclusive(-ly).

uitsluiting, lock-out; exclusion.
uitsluitlik, exclusively.
uitslyt, (uitge-), wear out.
uitslyting, wear (and tear).
uitsmyt, (uitge-), chuck out, eject.
uitsnik, (uitge-), sob (one's heart out).
uitsnuffel, (uitge-), ferret out, pry out.
uitsnuit, (uitge-), blow (one's nose).
uitsny, (uitge-), cut (out), excise; carve.
uitsnyding, cutting, excision.
uitsoek, (uitge-), choose, pick out, select; sort out, elect.
uitsoekerig, (-e), cliquish; fussy.
uitsonder, (uitge-), except, exclude.
uitsondering, exception; exemption; – **op die reël,** exception to the rule; **die – bevestig die reël,** the exception proves the rule; **by –,** by way of exception; **sonder –,** without exception; invariably.
uitsonderlik, (-e), exceptional.
uitspaar, (uitge-), economize, save.
uitspan, n. vide **uitspanning.**
uitspan, (uitge-), outspan, unharness, unyoke; stretch out; spread (sails).
uitspanning, outspan; recreation.
uitspanplek, outspan.
uitspansel, firmament, heavens, sky.
uitspat, (uitge-), splash (spurt) out; indulge in dissipation.
uitspattend, (-e), dissipated; excessive; loud.
uitspatting, (-e, -s), debauchery, dissipation, excess; **hom aan – oorgee,** live a dissolute life, indulge in excesses.
uitspeel, (uitge-), finish (game); play, lead (a card); **die een teen die ander –,** play one off against the other.
uitspel, (uitge-), spell (out).
uitspin, (uitge-), spin out.
uitspit, (uitge-), dig out, dig up.
uitspoe(g), -spu(ug), (uitge-), spit out.
uitspoel, (uitge-), wash out, rinse; be washed ashore; be laid bare.
uitspook, (uitge-), fight out, fight to the finish; settle by fighting.
uitspraak, pronunciation; pronouncement, utterance, finding, award, judgement, sentence, verdict; – **doen,** give (pass, pronounce) judgement; – **voorbehou,** reserve judgement.
uitspraakleer, phonetics, orthoepy.
uitspreek, (uitge-), pronounce; express, say, utter; have one's say; **'n mening –,** express an opinion.
uitsprei, (uitge-), spread (out), expand, unfold, unfurl, branch out.
uitspring, (uitge-), jump (leap, spring) out; jut out, project, protrude.
uitspringend, (-e), jutting out, projecting; **–e venster,** bay-, bow-window.
uitspruit, (uitge-), bud, shoot (up), sprout (out); result from.
uitspruitsel, bud, shoot, sprout, sprig.
uitspuit, (uitge-), spout (spurt, squirt) out; syringe (wound).
uitspu(u)g, vide **uitspoe(g).**
uitstaan, (uitge-), stand out; bulge out; be put out (at interest); bear, endure, stand, suffer; **iets nie kan – nie,** be unable to bear (stand) something; **niks met iemand uit te staan hê nie,** have nothing to do (no business) with someone.
uitstaande: – **gelde,** outstanding debts.
uitstal, (uitge-), display, put out (for sale); parade, show off.
uitstalkas, showcase, display-case.
uitstalling, display, parade, show; exhibits.

uitstalraam, -venster, show-window.
uitstamel, (uitge-), stammer (out).
uitstamp, (uitge-), stamp out; push out.
uitstap, (uitge-), alight, get off, get out, step out, walk out; change.
uitstappie, outing, excursion, tour, trip.
uitstedig, (-e), out of town.
uitsteek, (uitge-), jut out, project, protrude; rise above; extend, hold (reach, stretch) out (hand), put out (tongue), put forth, pop out (head).
uitsteeksel, projection; protuberance.
uitstek, projection; **by –,** par excellence, preeminently.
uitstekend, (-e), projecting; prominent.
uitstekend, (-e), excellent, first-rate.
uitstekendheid, excellence.
uitstel, n. delay, postponement, procrastination; respite; **van – kom afstel,** delays are dangerous, procrastination is the thief of time.
uitstel, (uitge-), defer, delay, postpone, put off.
uitsteldae, days of grace (respite).
uitsterf, -sterwe, (uitge-), die out, (species) become extinct.
uitstof, (uitge-), dust out; beat, lick.
uitstoom, (uitge-), steam out; draw (pull, steam) out (train from station); dry-clean (clothes).
uitstoot, (uitge-), push (thrust) out; expel, ostracise, turn out; ejaculate, utter (cries).
uitstort, (uitge-), pour out; spill (milk); unburden (one's heart); empty itself into.
uitstorting, effusion, outpour, pouring out; – **van die Heilige Gees,** descent of the Holy Spirit.
uitstraal, (uitge-), beam forth, emanate; emit, radiate (heat, light, love).
uitstraat, (uitge-), pave.
uitstraler, (-s), radiator.
uitstraling, emanation, emission, radiation.
uitstralingsteorie, theory of radiation.
uitstralingsvermoë, radiating capacity (power), radiation.
uitstralingswarmte, radiant heat.
uitstrek, (uitge-), expand; stretch out (hands); extend; **sig – tot,** stretch out (extend, reach) to.
uitstrooi, (uitge-), scatter, sow, strew; circulate, spread (rumours); disseminate (knowledge).
uitstrooisel, false report, rumour.
uitstroom, (uitge-), gush (pour, rush, stream) out (forth).
uitstryk, (uitge-), iron (smooth) out (clothes); outpace.
uitstudeer, (uitge-), complete one's studies.
uitstuur, (uitge-), steer out; send out, order out; emit.
uitsuie, -suig, (uitge-), suck (out); bleed (sweat) (labourers); drain, squeeze dry, impoverish (a country); extort (money).
uitsuier, extortioner, bloodsucker.
uitswa(w)el, (uitge-), sulphur, fumigate.
uitsweet, (uitge-), sweat out; exude.
uitswel, (uitge-), swell (out), bulge (out), expand, dilate.
uitswem, (uitge-), swim out; outswim.
uitsweting, exudation.
uitsyfer, (uitge-), figure out; vide **uitsypel.**
uitsypel, (uitge-), ooze (trickle) out.
uittart, (uitge-), challenge, defy, provoke.
uittarting, challenge, provocation.
uitteer, (uitge-), pine (waste) away.
uitteken, (uitge-), delineate, draw.
uittel, (uitge-), 1. count out.
uittel, (uitge-), 2. lift out.
uittering, emaciation, pining, wasting away; tabes; atrophy.

uittog, departure, exodus; flight.
uittorring, (uitge-), fray; unstitch, rip.
uittrap, (uitge-), tread out, stamp out; ease (shoes) by wearing.
uittreding, retirement, resignation.
uittree, (uitge-), retire, resign, withdraw; step out.
uittrek, (uitge-), pull out; pull off; take off (coat); draw, extract (tooth); strip (clothes), undress; **jou nie – voor jy gaan slaap nie**, not leave one's property to one's heirs before death; **– op**, march out on (an expedition).
uittreksel, extract; abridgment, digest, excerpt, epitome.
uittrektafel, extension-table.
uitvaagsel, (-s), dregs, riff-raff, scourings, scum.
uitvaar, (uitge-), sail (out), put to sea; blaze (fly) out, bluster, rant, storm; **– teen**, rail at, inveigh against, storm at.
uitvaardig, (uitge-), issue (order), enact (a law), decree.
uitvaardiging, (-e, -s), issue, promulgation, decree, enactment.
uitvaart, funeral, obsequies; departure.
uitval, n. sally, sortie; thrust; attack; outburst, quarrel.
uitval, (uitge-), drop (fall) out; come off (hair); make a sally (sortie); flare up, fly out; **goed (sleg) –**, pan (turn) out well (badly).
uitvars, (uitge-), freshen, refresh.
uitvee(g), (uitge-), erase (pencil-marks); sweep out (a room); wipe out (eyes).
uitveër, eraser, (india-)rubber.
uitveg, (uitge-), fight (have) it out.
uitverkies, (–, **uitverkore**), single out, choose; predestine.
uitverkiesing, election; predestination.
uitverkoop, n. sale, clearance-sale.
uitverkoop, (–), sell off, clear, sell out.
uitverkoping, vide **uitverkoop**, n.
uitverkore, chosen, elect, select, predestined; **die – volk**, the chosen people.
uitverkorene, (-s), chosen one, favourite.
uitvind, (uitge-), find out, discover; invent; ascertain.
uitvinder, discoverer; inventor.
uitvinding, invention.
uitvindsel, (-s), contrivance, device, invention.
uitvis, (uitge-), fish out, ferret out, scent out.
uitvlie(g), (uitge-), fly out.
uitvloei, (uitge-), flow out; issue, result.
uitvloeisel, (-s), outcome, result.
uitvloek, (uitge-), curse, swear at.
uitvlug, (-te), n. excuse, evasion, loophole, pretext, subterfuge.
uitvlug, (uitge-), escape (from).
uitvoer, n. export(s), exportation; **ten – bring**, carry into effect, execute, carry out.
uitvoer, (uitge-), export (goods); execute (an order), carry out (a plan), carry into effect, fulfill (a promise), perform (a task), administer, enforce (the law); line (a hat); **wat voer jy uit?**, what are you doing?; **niks – nie**, accomplish (do) nothing.
uitvoerartikel, article of export.
uitvoerbaar, (-bare), practicable.
uitvoerder, (-s), executor; exporter.
uitvoerhandel, export-trade.
uitvoerhawe, port of export(ation).
uitvoerig, (-e), ample (discussion), detailed (account), full (particulars), minute (description), copious (notes); lengthy (considerations), elaborate.
uitvoerigheid, ampleness, copiousness, fullness, minuteness.
uitvoering, (-e, -s), execution, performance (of duty, music); administration, enforcement (of a law); finish, workmanship; get-up (of book); **– gee aan**, carry out, carry into effect.
uitvoerreg, export-duty.
uitvoerverbod, prohibition of export.
uitvors, (uitge-), ferret (fish, hunt, search, spy) out, discover.
uitvra(ag), (uitge-), ask out, invite; examine, interrogate, pump, question; **van – is die tronk vol**, ask no questions and you will hear no lies.
uitvreet, (uitge-), eat away, corrode.
uitvroetel, (uitge-), scrape out, burrow out, rummage out; wriggle out.
uitvryf, -vrywe, (uitge-), rub out.
uitwaai, (uitge-), blow out; be blown out; **niks met iemand uit te waai hê nie**, have nothing to do with someone.
uitwaarts, outward(s).
uitwan, (uitge-), winnow.
uitwas, (-se), n. excrescence, outgrowth, protuberance, morbid growth.
uitwas, (uitge-), wash (out).
uitwasem, (uitge-), emanate; evaporate; perspire; exude, exhale, give off.
uitwaseming, emanation, evaporation, exhalation, exudation, perspiration.
uitweg, way out, outlet; escape, expedient, loophole; **geen ander – nie**, no other expedient (way out).
uitwei, (uitge-), digress; **– oor**, dilate (dwell, enlarge, expatiate) on.
uitweiding, (-e, -s), digression.
uitwendig, (-e), external, outward.
uitwendigheid, exterior, externals.
uitwerk, (uitge-), work out (sum); elaborate (scheme), develop (idea); calculate, work up (notes); squeeze out, oust; bring about, effect; cease fermenting.
uitwerking, working-out, elaboration; effect, result; **'n – hê**, be effective, produce a result, have an effect.
uitwerp, (uitge-), cast out, eject, expel, throw out.
uitwerpsel, (-s), excrement.
uitwiks, (uitge-), beat, thrash, lick.
uitwis, (uitge-), blot (wash, wipe) out, efface, erase, expunge, obliterate.
uitwissel, (uitge-), exchange, interchange (ideas); cash (cheque).
uitwisseling, exchange; cashing.
uitwoed, (uitge-), subside, abate.
uitwoel, (uitge-), cease tumbling about; burrow (root) up; chase out; rouse.
uitwring, (uitge-), squeeze (wring) out.
uitwyk, (uitge-), step aside; give way; swerve; dodge, emigrate, go into exile.
uitwyking, giving away; emigration; deviation.
uitwys, (uitge-), point out, show; prove; decide, pass judgment, banish, expel.
ulster, (-s), ulster.
ultimatum, (-s), ultimatum.
ultra, adv., excessively, extremely, too.
ultramaryn, ultramarine.
ultramodern, (-e), ultra-modern.
ultramontaan, (-tane), ultra-montane.
ultrarooi, ultra-red.
ultrasonies, ultrasonic.
ultraviolet, (-te), ultraviolet; **–te strale**, ultraviolet rays.
Umbries, (-e), Umbrian.
umlaut, umlaut, vowel-mutation.
unaniem, (-e), unanimous, of one accord.
unanimiteit, unanimity.
unie, union.
Uniegebou, Union-Buildings.

uniek, (-e), unique, unparalleled.
uniform, (-s), n. uniform; military dress.
uniform, (-e), a. uniform, flat (rate).
uniformiteit, uniformity.
universeel, (-sele), universal, general, sole; -sele erfgenaam, sole heir.
universiteit, (-e), university.
universitêr, (-e), university . . ., academic.
universiteitsgebou, university buildings.
universiteitskollege, university college.
universum, universe.
uraansuur, uranic acid.
Urania, Urania.
uranium, uranium.
Uranus, Uranus.
urbaan, (-bane), urbane, suave.
urbaniteit, urbanity, suavity, courtesy.
urelank, for hours.
urgent, (-e), urgent, pressing.
urien, vide urine.
urinaal, (-nale), urinal.
urine, urine.
urinebak, (-vat, -kom), urinary.
urineer, (ge-), urinate.
urn, (-e), urn.

usansie, usage, custom.
uso, usance.
usurpasie, usurpation.
usurpeer, (ge-), usurp.
ut, ut, do (in music).
utilitaris, (-te), utilitarian.
utilitarisme, utilitarianism.
utilitaristies, (-e), utilitarian.
utiliteit, utility.
utiliteitsbeginsel, utilitarianism.
utiliteitswa, jeep.
Utopie, (-ë), Utopia.
utopies, (-e), utopian.
uur, (ure), hour; sy laaste – het geslaan, his last hour has come; binne 'n –, within an hour; by die –, by the hour, hourly; om die –, every hour; om ses-, at six (o'clock); oor 'n –, in an hour; op die –, at that hour; hourly; punctually; ter elfder ure, at the eleventh hour.
uurglas, hour-glass, sand-glass.
uurwerk, clockwork; clock, timepiece.
uurwys(t)er, (-s), hour-hand.
uwe, yours; die –, yours truly (faithfully).
uwentwil: om –, for your sake.

vaag, (vae, vage), vague (idea, answer); hazy, indistinct, faint.
vaagheid, vagueness.
vaak, n. sleepiness; – **kry (hê)**, become (be) sleepy; **praatjies vir die –**, idle talk.
vaak, a. sleepy, drowsy.
vaak, adv. often.
vaal, ashen, ash-coloured, pale, tawny, sallow (skin), grey; faded, dull, drab; – **van die honger**, out of one's wits.
vaalagtig, (-e), ashen, greyish.
vaalblaarsiekte, septoria.
vaalbleek, greyish, sallow.
vaalbrak, salt-bush.
vaalbruin, dun, greyish-brown.
vaalgrys, greyish, mouse-coloured.
vaalhartbees, grey hartebeest.
vaalheid, tawniness, sallowness, drab.
vaalkorhaan, black-throated bustard.
vaalmol, grey mole.
Vaalpens, "Vaalpens".
vaalribbok, grey rhebuck.
Vaalrivier, Vaal river.
vaalstreep: die – vat, take the road.
vaalwater: in iemand se – kom, thwart a person; **uit iemand se – bly**, give a person a wide berth.
vaam, (vame), vide **vadem**.
vaan, (vane), banner, standard, flag, ensign.
vaandel, (-s), colours, flag, standard, banner; **met vlieënde –**, with flying colours.
vaandeldraer, standard-bearer.
vaandelparade, trooping the colours.
vaandrig, (-s), standard-bearer.
vaantjie, (-s), pennon; weathercock.
vaar, (-s), n. sire (male parent of horse).
vaar, (ge-), sail, navigate, voyage; **vinnig –**, travel fast; – **tussen Kaapstad en Robbeneiland**, ply between Cape Town and Robben Island; **hoe – jy?**, how do you do, how are you?; **sleg –**, fare badly, get the worst of it; **goed –**, be prosperous (successful); **laat –**, give up, drop, abandon; **die duiwel het in hom ge–**, the devil has taken possession of him; **ten hemel –**, ascend to heaven.
vaarder, (-s), seafarer, navigator, sailor.
vaardig, (-e), clever, dext(e)rous, skilful, deft, quick, facile; ready; – **met die pen wees**, have a ready pen.
vaardigheid, cleverness, skill, deftness, dexterity; readiness; ease, fluency.
vaarlandsriet, vaderlandsriet, common reed.
vaart, navigation; canal; speed; haste; course; **in sy – stuit**, check, stop; **in volle –**, at top speed, (at) full speed.
vaartjie: 'n aardjie na sy –, a chip of the old block, like father like son.
vaartrukking(s), speed wobble.
vaartuig, (-tuie), vessel.
vaarwater, fairway; vide **vaalwater**.
vaarwel, n. farewell; – **sê**, take leave of, say good-bye.
vaarwel, interj. farewell, good-bye!
vaas, (vase), vase.
vaatdoek, vide **vadoek**.
vaatjie, (-s), keg, little tub (barrel), firkin; pot-belly, corporation; fatty.
vaatstelsel, vascular system.
vaatwerk, vide **vatwerk**.
vabond, vagebond, (-e), rogue, rascal, scamp, knave; vagabond, tramp.
vadem, (-s), **vaam**, (-vame), fathom.
vader, (-s), father; sire (of horses); **die Hemelse V.** the Heavenly Father.
vaderhand, hand of a father.

vaderhart, paternal heart, heart of a father.
vaderhuis, paternal home.
vaderland, fatherland, native country.
vaderlander, (-s), patriot.
vaderlands, (-e), patriotic, nation (history); native (soil).
vaderlandsliefde, patriotism.
vaderlandsliewend, (-e), patriotic.
vaderlandsriet, vide **vaarlands-**.
vaderlief, father dear, dear father.
vaderliefde, paternal, (fatherly) love.
vaderlik, (-e), fatherly, paternal.
vaderloos, (-lose), fatherless.
vadermoord, parricide.
vadermoorder, (-s), parricide.
vaderplig, paternal duty.
vaderskant, paternal side, father's side.
vaderskap, fatherhood, paternity.
vadersorg, paternal care; paternal cares.
vaderstad, native town.
vadertrots, paternal pride.
vadoek, vaatdoek, (-e), dish-cloth, wash-cloth, facecloth.
vadsig, (-e), lazy, slothful, indolent.
vadsigheid, laziness, indolence.
va(g)evuur, purgatory.
vag, (-te), fleece, pelt.
vagebond, vide **vabond**.
vak, (-ke), pigeon-hole, compartment; square; panel; subject; profession; trade; **'n – leer**, learn a trade; **'n man van die –**, a specialist, an expert.
vakansie, (-s), holiday(s), vacation; **'n dag –**, a holiday; – **hou**, be on holiday, spend the holidays; – **neem**, take a holiday; **met –**, on holiday.
vakansiedag, holiday.
vakansiekursus, vacation-course.
vakansietyd, holiday-season, holidays.
vakant, (-e), vacant.
vakarbeider, skilled labourer.
vakature, (-s), vacancy.
vakbeweging, trade-unionism.
vakblad, professional paper (journal).
vakerig, (-e), drowsy, sleepy.
vakgeleerde, specialist.
vakgenoot, colleaque.
vakkennis, knowledge of a (the, one's) subject, professional knowledge.
vakkundig, (-e), expert, skilled.
vakleerling, apprentice.
vakman, expert, specialist.
vakonderwys, vocational instruction.
vakopleiding, vocational training.
vaksinasie, vaccination.
vaksine, vaccine.
vaksineer, (ge-), vaccinate.
vakskool, trade-school, vocational school.
vakterm, technical term.
vakuum, (-s), vacuum.
vakvereniging, trade-union.
val, (-le), fall; downfall; trap; slope; frill, valance; **ten – bring**, (bring to) ruin; overthrow, defeat; **'n – stel**, set a trap; **in die – loop**, walk into the trap, be trapped.
val, (ge-), fall; drop, come down; **die vesting het ge–**, the fortress surrendered; **die regering het ge–**, the government was overthrown (defeated); **dit – my swaar**, I find it difficult; **daar – weinig te sê**, there is little to be said; **daar – nie aan te dink nie**, it is out of the question; **dis net na dit –**, it (all) depends (how things turn out); **laat –**, drop, let fall, **'n woord laat –**, drop a word; **die prys laat –**, reduce the price; **in die oog –**, be conspicuous; **in die**

smaak –, be popular; vide **afval inval, opval,** etc.
valbrug, draw-bridge.
valbyl, guillotine.
valdeur, trap-door.
valensie, (-s), valency, valence.
valeriaan, valerian.
valerig, (-e), vide **vaalagtig.**
valgordyn, blind.
valhek, portcullis.
valhelm, crash-helmet.
valhoogte, drop.
validiteit, validity.
valies, (-e), travelling-bag, portmanteau.
valk, (-e), hawk, falcon, peregrine.
valk(e)blik, hawk's eye, eagle eye.
valkenier, (-s), falconer.
valk(e)jag, falconry, hawking.
valkoog, vide **valk(e)blik.**
vallei, (-e), valley; dale, vale.
vallend, (-e), falling; **–e siekte,** epilepsy, **–e ster,** falling (shooting) star.
valletjie, (-s), frill; vide **val,** n.
vallig, skylight.
valluik, trap-door.
valpoort, portcullis.
valreep, man rope; accommodation-ladder; **'n glasie op die –,** a stirrup-cup.
valreeptrap, accommodation-ladder.
vals, (–, e), a. false; counterfeit, base, spurious (coin), forged (signature); treacherous, deceitful; vicious (animals); **–e getuienis,** false evidence; **– ground,** boggy ground; **– lig,** deceptive light; **– sleutel,** skeleton key.
vals, adv. falsely; **– sing,** sing out of tune, sing flat; **– sweer,** swear falsely.
valsaard, (-s), perfidious (false) person.
Valsbaai, False Bay.
valsheid, falseness, falsity; treachery.
valskerm, parachute.
valskermsoldaat, -springer, parachutist.
valskermtroepe, paratroops.
valskyf, disappearing target.
valslik, falsely.
valstrik, trap, snare, pitfall; snag.
valuasie, (-s), valuation.
valueer, (ge-), estimate, value.
valuta, value; (rate of) exchange.
vampier, (-e), vampire; blood-sucker.
van, (-ne), surname.
van, prep. of: from, with, for; by; **– dag tot dag,** from day to day; **een – my vriende,** one of my friends; **'n vriend – my,** a friend of mine; **'n gedig – Celliers,** a poem by Celliers; **– hout gemaak,** made of wood; **beef – kwaadheid,** tremble with anger; **moeg – loop,** tired of walking; **huil – blydskap,** weep for joy; **groot – gestalte,** of tall stature; **– Kaapstad af,** from Cape Town; **– nuuts af,** anew, again; **van ouds,** of old; **– af,** from olden times.
vanaand, tonight, this evening.
vanaf, from.
Vandaal, (-dale), Vandal.
Vandaals, (-e), Vandalic.
vandaan, from; **waar kom jy –?,** where do you come from?; **hy kom ver –,** he has come a long way; **daar– (af),** from there.
vandaar, from there; hence.
vandag, to-day (today); **hy is nie – se kind nie,** he is no chicken; he knows a thing or two.
vandalisme, vandalism.
vandeesjaar, vandesejaar, (-maand, -week), this year (this month, this week).
vandisie, vendusie, (-s), auction (sale), public sale; **– hou,** sell by auction; sell out.

vaneen, asunder.
vaneenruk, -skeur, -trek, (vaneenge-), pull (tear) asunder, tear to pieces.
vaneffe, a minute ago, just now.
vang, (ge-), catch; capture, take prisoner, arrest.
vangarm, tentacle
vangdam, catch-dam.
vangdrade, (pl.) antennae, aerial.
vanggat, snare-hole, snare.
vanghou, catch.
vangriem, noose, lasso.
vangstok, noose-handle; noose.
vangwa, pick-up (van), squad car, black Maria.
vanielje, vanilla.
vanjaar, this year.
vanmekaar, asunder, to pieces.
vanmelewe, vans(e)lewe, in the old days, long ago, formerly; **– se dae,** the days of yore; **– se mense,** the people of old; **– se vrouens het nie gerook nie,** in the old days women did not smoke.
vanmôre, this morning.
vannag, tonight; last night.
vans(e)lewe, vide **vanmelewe.**
vanself, of one's (it's, his) own accord, of one self, by itself (oneself); **dit spreek –,** that stands to reason.
vanselfsprekend, (-e), obvious, self-evident.
vansgelyke, the same (to you).
vanslewe(se), vide **vanmelewe(se).**
vanwaar, from where, whence.
vanweë, on account of, owing to.
varia, miscellanies.
variant, (-e), variant, different type.
variasie, (-s), variation.
varieer, (ge-), vary; range.
variété, (-s), variety-theatre.
variëteit, (-e), variety.
variété-voorstelling, variety-show.
varing, (-s), fern, bracken.
vark, (-e), pig, swine, hog; **nie 'n – kan vang nie,** be bandy-legged; **al sy –e is nie op hok nie,** there is something wrong in his upper storey.
varkagtig, (-e), piggish, like a pig.
varkblom, arum-lily, pig-lily.
varkens– . . ., vide **vark– . . .**
varkhok, pigsty.
varkie, (-s), little pig, piggy, pigling; grunter; **hy het nie al sy –s in die hok nie,** there is something wrong in his upper storey.
varkkarmenaadjie, pork-chop.
varkkos, pig's food, pig's wash.
varkkotelet, pork-cutlet.
varkore, pig's ears.
varkpootjies, pig's trotters.
varkribbetjie, rib of pork.
varkslagter, pork-butcher; pig-killer.
varksnuit, pig's snout.
varksog, sow.
varkspek, bacon.
varkstert, pig's tail; pigtail (of hair).
varktrog, pig-trough.
varkvel, pigskin.
varkvet, lard.
varkvleis, pork.
varkwors, pork-sausage.
vars, fresh (meat, milk, air, flowers, egg); new-laid (eggs).
varsheid, freshness.
vas(te), n. fast(ing).
vas, (-te), a. fast, firm (hand, belief), fixed (price, abode, hour, deposit, star); permanent (appointment); **'n –te besluit,** a firm resolve; **'n –te geloof,** a firm belief; **'n –te gewoonte,** regular habit, established practice; **–te goed,**

immovable property; 'n –te klant a regular customer; –te kleure, fast (fadeless) colours; –te kos, solid food; 'n –te liggaam, a solid, –te oortuiging, firm conviction; –te reël, fixed rule; –te slaap, sound sleep; –te werk, regular employment; –te wil, firm will; vir –, definitely.
vas, adv. firmly, fast; – belowe, promise positively; – van plan wees, be firmly resolved; – slaap, sleep soundly.
vasal, (-le), vassal.
vasalstaat, puppet state.
vasberade, determined, resolute, firm.
vasberadenheid, determination, firmness.
vasbeslote, determined.
vasbind, (vasge-), tie (up) fasten.
vasbrand, (vasge-), burn (of food); seize (of engine); get stuck; be unable to pay; be unable to manage.
vasdag, fasting-day (fast-day)...
vasdraai, (vasge-), tighten (nut screw), screw down; tie, fasten; get stuck.
vasdruk, (vasge-), squeeze (tight), press firmly, hold tight, pin down.
vasel, (-s), fibre, thread.
vasgespe(r), (vasge-), buckle (up).
vasgoed, immovable property.
vasgroei, (vasge-), grow together.
vasgryp, (vasge-), grip, c` ch hold of.
vashaak, (vasge-), hook on (in, up).
vasheg, (vasge-), fix, fasten.
vashou, (vasge-), hold; hold fast (tight); hang on to; – aan, hold on to, grip, cling to.
vashoudend, (-e), tenacious; miserly.
vashoudenheid, tenacity.
vaskeer, (vasge-), corner, trap.
vasklamp, (vasge-): sig – aan, cling to.
vaskleef, -klewe, (vasge-), stick.
vasklem, (vasge-), hold tight; jam.
vasklink, (vasge-), rivet.
vasklou, (vasge-), cling to, stick to.
vasknel, (vasge-), hold tight; jam.
vasknoop, (vasge-), tie, fasten; button up (coat); – aan, tie (link) to.
vaskoppel, (vasge-), couple, fasten (link, tie) together.
vaslak, (vasge-), seal.
vaslê, (vasge-), be fastened; be chained (up); be moored; lie firm; pin (hold) down; fix, settle, determine.
vasloop, (vasge-), run aground (of ship); – teen, colide with; sig –, find one's way blocked, get stuck; come to the end of one's tether, be cornered, get into trouble.
vaslym, (vasge-), glue, fasten with glue.
vasmaak, (vasge-), fasten, make fast, secure, tie, button up (coat).
vasnaai, (vasge-), sew together.
vaspak, (vasge-), pack firmly.
vaspen, (vasge-), peg.
vasplak, (vasge-), stick, glue together.
vaspraat, (vasge-): iemand –, (drive a person into a) corner; sig –, get oneself into a corner, talk oneself into a tangle.
vasraak, (vasge-), become entangled, get stuck; run aground (of ship).
vasroes, (vasge-), rust, become rusted; vasgeroes in sy gewoontes wees, be unable to change one's habits.
vasry, (vasge-): – teen, collide with.
vassit, (vasge-), stick (fast); be (get) stuck, be fixed; fasten, fix, secure.
vasskroef, -skroewe, (vasge-), screw down (on, tight).
vasslaan, (vasge-), hammer in, nail down.

vasspeld(e), (vasge-), pin (up, together); – aan, pin on to.
vasspyker, (vasge-), nail (down).
vasstaan, (vasge-), stand firm(ly), stand fast; dit staan vas, it is a fact; dit staan by my vas, I am convinced of it; 'n –de feit, an established fact.
vasstamp, (vasge-), ram down.
vassteek, (vasge-), fasten, pin (on); halt, stop (dead, short); stick, get stuck.
vasstel, (vasge-), fix (price, place, date), determine (date), settle (day); ascertain; appoint (place, time); establish (fact); stipulate; lay down (rule).
vasstelling, fixing, fixation; determination; establishment; vide vasstel.
vasteland, continent.
vastelands, (-e), continental.
vastheid, firmness, fixedness; solidity, compactness; steadiness; certainty.
vastigheid, firmness; stability; certainty.
vastrap, n. hop-dance, "vastrap".
vastrap, (vasge-), tread (stamp) down; stand firm; be unwavering, give (person) a dusting (thrashing).
vastrapper, (-e), die-hard.
vastrek, (vasge-), pull tight; (drive into a) corner; swindle, take in.
vasval, (vasge-), stick (in the mud).
vasvraer, quiz master.
vasvrawedstryd, quiz contest.
vaswerk, (vasge), sew on, stitch up.
vaswoel, (vasge-), fasten, tie, lash.
vat, n. 1. grip, hold; dit gee jou 'n – op hom, it gives you a hold on a person; make no impression (be lost) on a person.
vat, (-e), 2. barrel, cask, vat, tun; vessel (anat.); heilige –e, sacred vessels; die swakke –, the weaker vessel; 'n uitverkore –, a chosen vessel.
vat, (ge-), take; seize, catch; grasp; understand, see; mount (in gold), set (in lead); kou –, catch cold; laat –, depart, go make off.
vatbaar: – vir, capable of; open to (conviction); susceptible to (cold, pain, kindness); susceptible of (impressions); amenable to; liable to.
vatbaarheid, capacity; susceptibility; amenability; liability.
vatemaker, cooper.
Vatikaan, Vatican.
vatterig, (-e), fond of touching.
vatwerk, casks, tubs; dishes and plates.
vaudeville, vaudeville.
Veda, (-s), Veda.
vee, stock, cattle.
vee(g), (ge-), sweep; voor jou eie deur –, sweep before one's own door.
veearts, veterinary surgeon.
veeartseny(kunde), veterinary science.
veeartsenykundig, (-e), veterinary.
veeartsenyskool, veterinary school.
veeboer, cattle-farmer, stock-breeder.
veeboerdery, stock-farming.
veedief, stock-thief, cattle-rustler, -lifter.
veediefstal, stock-theft, cattle-stealing.
veeg, (veë), n. wipe; swish (of tail), whisk; box, cuff (on the ear), slap; swipe.
veeg, (ge-), vide vee(g).
veeghou, (ge-), vide vee(g).
veeghou, swipe (cricket).
veegsels, sweepings.
veehandelaar, cattle-dealer, dealer in livestock.
veekoper, livestock-dealer, cattle-dealer.
veekraal, sheep-kraal; stock-yard.
veel, (-, vele), many; much; te –, too much (money); too many (people); veels te –, much

too much; far too many; te - om op te noem, too numerous to mention.
veel, adv. much; often; frequently.
veel, (ge-), stand, bear, endure.
veelal, often, mostly.
veelbelowend, (-e), promising.
veelbetekenend, (-e), significant, meaning.
veelbewoë, eventful, chequered (life); stirring, troublous (times).
veeleer, rather, sooner.
veeleisend, (-e), exacting.
veelgelese, widely read.
veelgodedom, veelgodery, polytheism.
veelheid, multitude, a large number, abundance, multiplicity.
veelhoek, polygon.
veelhoekig, (-e), polygonal.
veelhoofdig, (-e), many-headed; -e regering, polyarchy.
veeljarig, (-e), of many years; perennial.
veelkleurig, (-e), multi-coloured.
veellettergrepig, (-e), polysyllabic.
veelmannery, polyandry.
veelmannig, (-e), polyandrous.
veelmeer, rather.
veelomvattend, (-e), comprehensive, extensive; wide (knowledge).
veelpotig, (-e), multiped.
veels: - geluk!, heartly congratulations!; - te, far too; - te veel, far too much (many).
veelseggend, (-e), significant.
veelskrywer, polygraph.
veelsnarig, (-e), many-stringed.
veelsoortig, (-e), manifold, multifarious.
veelstemmig, (-e), many-voiced; polyphonic, polyphonous.
veelsydig, (-e), multilateral; many-sided, versatile; wide (knowledge).
veelsydigheid, many-sidedness, versatility.
veeltalig, (-e), polyglot.
veelvermoënd, (-e), powerful.
veelvlak, polyhedron.
veelvlakkig, (-e), polyhedral.
veelvoetig, (-e), polypod, multiped.
veelvormig, (-e), multiform.
veelvoud, (-e), multiple.
veelvoudig, (-e), manifold.
veelvraat, glutton (person); wolverene.
veelvuldig, (-e), frequent; manifold.
veelvuldigheid, frequency.
veelweter, (-s), know-all.
veelwywery, polygamy.
veemark, livestock-market.
veen, peat, peat-bog, peat-marsh.
veepos, outlying cattle-, sheep-station.
veer, (vere), n. 1. feather (of bird); spring (of car, watch); die vere maak die voël, fine feathers make fine birds; hy lê nog in die vere, he is still between the sheets; met 'n ander se vere pronk, adorn oneself with (strut about in) borrowed plumes.
veer, (vere), n. (2) ferry.
veer, (ge-), be springy (resilient); feather; die motor - goed, the car is well-sprung.
veeragtig, (-e), feathery.
veerbalans, spring-balance.
veerbed, verebed, feather-bed.
veerboot, ferry-boat.
veergewig, feather-weight.
veerkombers, (eider-down) quilt.
veerkrag, springiness; elasticity.
veerkratig, (-e), springy; elastic, resilient (lit. & fig.), buoyant.
veerman, ferryman.
veerslot, spring-lock.

veertien, fourteen; - dae, fourteen days, a fortnight.
veertiendaags, (-e), fortnightly; a fortnight's (rest).
veertiende, fourteenth.
veertienjarig, (-e), of fourteen (years).
veertiental, (about) fourteen.
veertig, forty.
veertigjarig, (-e), of forty years, forty years old, forty-year-old.
veertigponder, forty-pounder.
veertigste, fortieth.
veertigtal, (about) forty.
veertigvoud, multiple of forty.
veertigvoudig, (-e), fortyfold.
veertjie, (-s), little feather (spring).
veervoet, veerpoothoender, feathery-legged fowl.
veerwa, verewa, spring-wag(g)on.
veesiekte, stock-disease.
veestamboek, herd-book, stud-book.
veestapel, stock, livestock.
veeteelt, stock-breeding, cattle-breeding.
veetentoonstelling, livestock-show.
veevandisie, -vendusie, stock-fair.
veewagter, shepherd.
veg, (ge-), fight; - met, fight (with).
vegetariër, (-s), vegetarian.
vegetaries, (-e), vegetarian.
veggeneraal, field-general.
veglus, pugnacity, fighting spirit.
veglustig, (-e), pugnacious.
vegstellings, action stations.
vegter, (-s), fighter, combatant.
vegtersbaas, fighter, bully.
vegtery, fight, scuffle, tussle, fighting.
vegwa, tank.
veil, a. corruptible, venal; jou lewe - hê, be ready to sacrifice one's life.
veil, (ge-), sell by auction, put up for sale.
veilig, (-e), safe, secure.
veiligheid, safety, security; fuse.
veiligheidshalwe, for safety's sake.
veiligheidskeermes, safety-razor.
veiligheidsklep, safety-valve.
veiligheidsmaatreël, precautionary measure.
veiligheidspeld, safety-pin.
veiligheidswet, safety-law.
veiling, (-e, -s), public sale, auction.
veins, (ge-), simulate, feign, sham, pretend (to be); dissimulate.
veinsaard, (-s), hypocrite, dissembler.
veinsery, dissimulation, hypocrisy.
vel, (-le), n. skin (of person & animal), hide (of animal); sheet (of paper); 'n dik - hê, be thick-skinned; net - en been wees, be only skin and bone; iemand die - oor die ore trek, fleece a person; die - verkoop voor die beer geskiet is, count your chickens before they are hatched; uit jou - spring van blydskap, be beside oneself with joy.
vel, (ge-), cut down, fell (tree); couch (spear); hide, flog, lick; pass (sentence); 'n oordeel -, pass sentence, judge.
veld, (-e), veld; field; grazing, pasture, vegetation; die - behou, keep the field; hold one's ground (own); die - ruim, give ground, leave the field; - win (wen), gain ground; te -e trek teen, fight (take the field) against; strive against, oppose uit die - slaan, put out, disconcert, upset.
veldambulans, field-ambulance.
veldartillerie, field-artillery.
veldbattery, field-battery.
veldbed, camp-stretcher.
veldblom, wild flower.
veldbrand, veld-fire.

veldheer, general.
veldkornet, (-te), field-cornet.
veldkyker, field-glass.
veldmaarskalk, field-marshal.
veldmuis, field-mouse.
veldprediker, army-chaplain, padre.
veldrot, field-rat.
veldseer, veld-sore.
veldskans, field-work.
veldslag, battle.
veldspaat, felspar.
veldstoel, camp-stool.
veldstuk, field-piece, field-gun.
veldtent, (army)-tent.
veldtog, campaign.
veldtroepe, field-troops.
veldwerk, fielding (cricket).
veldwerker, field(er), fieldsman.
velerlei, all kinds of, various.
velhandelaar, dealer in hides (skins).
velkombers, skin-blanket, -rug.
vel(le)koper, buyer of skins (hides).
velletjie, (-s), (little) skin; skin (of fruit); film (on liquid); sheet.
velling, (-s), rim, fellow (felly).
velskoen, velskoen, veld(t)shoe.
velyn, vellum.
velynpapier, vellum-paper, satin-paper.
vendu-afslaer, auctioneer.
vendusie, vide **vandusie**.
veneries, (-e), venereal.
Venesiaan, (-ane), Venetian.
Venesië, Venice.
vennoot, (-note), partner.
vennootskap, (-note), partner.
venster, (-s), window; shelf (in wheatstack).
vensterbank, window-sill, -seat.
vensterblinding, (window-)shutter.
venstergordyn, window-curtain.
vensterkoevert, window-envelope.
vensterkosyn, window-frame.
vensterraam, window-frame.
vensterruit, window-pane.
venstertralie, window-bar.
vent, (-e), n. fellow, chap; bloke; 'n gawe -, a decent (nice) fellow (chap).
vent, (ge-), hawk, peddle.
venter, (-s), hawker, street-vendor.
ventiel, (-e), valve; ventil (in organ).
ventilasie, ventilation.
ventilasiesteen, air-brick.
ventilator, (-s), ventilator.
ventileer, (ge-), ventilate.
ventjie, (-s), little fellow (chap, man).
venyn, venom (lit. & fig.).
venynig, (-e), venomous; vicious, malignant, bitter, virulent.
venynigheid, venomousness; viciousness.
ver, (-, -re), a. far; distant; remote; 'n - ent, a long way, far; - familie, distant relative(s).
ver, adv. far; - weg, far away; te - gaan, go too far.
veraangenaam, (-), make pleasant.
veraanskoulik, (-), illustrate.
verademing, breathing-time; relief.
veraf, far (distant, away).
verafgeleë, far, distant, remote.
verafgoding, idolization.
verafgood, (-), idolize.
verafrikaans, (-te), a. Afrikanderized.
verafrikaans, (-), Afrikanderize, make Afrikaans; become Afrikaans.
verafrikaansing, Afrikanderization, Afrikaansification; becoming Afrikaans.
verafsku, (-), detest, abhor, loathe.

verag, (-), despise, look down upon, scorn, hold in contempt.
veragtelik, (-e), despicable, contemptible, vile; scornful (look).
veragtelikheid, despicableness.
veragtend, (-e), scornful, contemptuous.
veragter, (-s), n. despiser.
veragter, (-), decline, deteriorate, lag (fall) behind.
veragter(d), (-de), a. backward.
veragting, comtempt, scorn.
veral, especially, chiefly, above all; let - op, pay special attention to; - jy, you especially, you of all people.
veralgemeen, (-), generalize.
veramerikaans, (-), Americanize.
veranda, (-s), verandah.
verander, (-), change, alter; transform; dit - die saak, that alters the case; - in, change into; water in wyn -, turn water into wine.
verandering, (-e, -s), change, alteration, transformation.
veranderlik, (-e), changeable, fickle, inconstant, variable; unsettled.
veranderlikheid, changeableness, fickleness.
verantwoord, (-), account for, answer for, sig -, justify oneself; veel te - hê, have much to answer for.
verantwoordelik, (-e), responsible (to person, for a thing); answerable.
verantwoordelikheid, responsibility.
verantwoordelikheidsgevoel, sense of responsibility.
verantwoording, account for, answer for; ter - roep, call to account.
verarm, (-), impoverish, pauperize; become poor (impoverished).
verarming, impoverishment.
veras, (-), incinerate, cremate.
verassing, incineration.
verassureer, (-), insure.
verbaal, (-bale), verbal.
verbaas, (-de), a surprised, astonished.
verbaas, (-), surprise, astonish.
verbaasdheid, (-), surprise, astonishment.
verban, (-), banish, exile; expel.
verband, (-e), bond (of bricks); overlapping; bandage, dressing (of wound); ligature (of artery); bond (on property), mortgage; connection; context; met sy arm in 'n -, with his arm in a sling; in - met, in connection with; in - staan met, be connected with, have a bearing on; uit - ruk, take (wrest) from the context.
verbandgaas, sterilized gauze.
verbandgeër, mortgager (mortgagor).
verbandhouer, mortgagee.
verbandmiddele, dressings, bandages.
verbandnemer, mortgagee.
verbandstowwe, bandages, dressings.
verbandwatte, medicated cotton-wool.
verbanneling, (-e), exile.
verbanning, exile, banishment; expulsion.
verbasend, (-e), surprising, astonishing; marvellous (memory).
verbasing, surprise, amazement.
verbasingwekkend, (-e), amazing.
verbaster, (-), interbreed, degenerate.
verbastering, hybridization, interbreeding; degeneration.
verbeel, (-): sig -, imagine, fancy; wat - jy jou?, who do you think you are?; hy - hom nogal wat, he rather fancies himself, he is rather conceited.
verbeeld, (-), represent.

verbeelding, imagination, fancy.
verbeeldings, conceit, conceitedness; fancy, caprice, whims; **vol –,** conceited; capricious; hypochondriac(al).
verbeeldingskrag, (power of) imagination, imaginative power.
verbeid, (–), await.
verbelentheid, fancy, caprice, capriciousness, imagination.
verbena, (-s), verbena.
verberg, (–), hide, conceal.
verberging, concealment, hiding.
verbete, pent up, fierce, intense.
verbeter, (—), improve; make better; correct (proofs, essay); rectify (error); emend (text); reform (person); better.
verbeterhuis, house of correction.
verbetering, (-e, -s), improvement; correction; rectification; emendation; betterment; reformation.
verbeteringsgestig, reformatory.
verbeur, (–), forfeit; confiscate.
verbeurbaar, (-bare), forfeitable.
verbeurd, (-e), confiscated; **– verklaar**, confiscate.
verbeurdverklaring, confiscation, seizure.
verbeusel, (–), waste (time, money), fritter (idle) away (time).
verbied, (–), forbid, prohibit; place a ban on, ban (book, film); interdict.
verbind, (–), join, connect; link (up); put through (to number 63); bandage, dress (wound), tie up; retie, refasten; combine (chem.); **in die huwelik –,** join (unite) in marriage; **sig –,** commit (bind) oneself; ally oneself (with).
verbinding, (-e, -s), joining; linking (up); connection; junction (railway); dressing (of wound); communication (telegr.); compound, combination (chem.); union; **in – tree met,** communicate with, get into touch with.
verbindingskanaal, junction-canal.
verbindingskakel, connecting link.
verbindingslyn, line of communication.
verbindingsteken, hyphen.
verbindingstreep, hyphen; vinculum.
verbindingswoord, copulative.
verbintenis, (-se), union; alliance, bond; agreement; engagement; **'n – aangaan**, enter into an agreement.
verbitter, (–), embitter; exasperate.
verbitter(d), (-de), a. embittered.
verbitterdheid, bitterness, embitterment.
verbittering, vide **verbitterheid.**
verbleek, (-te), a. pale; faded.
verbleek, (–), turn (grow) pale; fade.
verbleik, (-te), a. faded.
verbleik, (–), fade, pale.
verblind, (-e), a. blinded, dazzled.
verblind, (–), blind, dazzle.
verblindheid, blindness; infatuation.
verbloem, (–), disguise, gloss over (facts), **palliate.**
verbloeming, glossing over, palliation.
verbluf, (-te) a. dumbfounded, nonplussed.
verbluf, (–), dumbfound, nonpluss.
verbluffend, (-e), startling, amazing.
verbly (–), gladden, delight; **sig –,** rejoice, be glad.
verblydend, (-e), gladdening, cheerful, joyful; hopeful (sign).
verblyf, n. residence, abode; stay; **– hou,** reside.
verblyf, (–), remain.
verblyfkoste, board and lodging expenses.
verblyfplaas, -plek, abode, residence.
verbod, prohibition; embargo; suppression; ban (on book, film).
verbode, prohibited, forbidden; **– boeke,** banned books; **– toegang,** no admission, private; **ten strengste –,** strictly prohibited.
verbodsbepaling, prohibition-regulation.
verboë, inflected, declined (gram.); **– vorm,** inflected form, inflexion.
verboemel, (–), squander, dissipate.
verbolge, wrathful, angry.
verbond, (-e), alliance, union, pact, league, coalition; covenant, treaty.
verbonde, bound up; allied; attached; **onafskeidelik aan mekaar –,** inseparable.
verbondsark, Ark of the Covenant.
verborge, concealed, hidden, secret (sin), latent; **in die -ne,** secretly, in secret.
verborgenheid, (-hede), secretary; mystery.
verbou, (–), rebuild; cultivate, grow.
verbouereerd, (-e), flurried, flustered, nervous, embarrassed.
verbouereerdheid, flurry, fluster, agitation, confusion.
verbouing, rebuilding; cultivation, growing (of vegetables).
verbrand, (–), burn, burn (be burnt) to death; cremate (corpse); **bruin – (deur die son),** tanned (by the sun), sun-burnt, **jou mond –,** drop a brick, put one's foot into it.
verbrande, burnt; confounded, bally.
verbranding, burning; cremation (of corpse), combustion (chem.).
verbrandingsoond, incinerator.
verbrandingsproduk, combustion-product.
verbrands: –!, confound it!, well I'm jiggered!; **– koud,** deuced(ly) cold.
verbree(d), (–), broaden, widen.
verbreek, (–), break; sever; violate.
verbrei, (–), spread (rumour); disseminate (doctrine), propagate.
verbrei(d), (-de), disseminated, propagated, widely spread, common (idea).
verbreiding, spread(ing); dissemination.
verbreker, breaker; violator.
verbreking, breaking, violation.
verbroeder, (–), fraternize.
verbroedering, fraternization, fraternizing, reconciliation.
verbrokkel, (–), crumble (to pieces) (lit. & fig.); disintegrate, break (up).
verbrokkeling, crumbling; disintegration.
verbrou, (–), make a mess (hash) of, spoil, bungle, misbehave (oneself).
verbruik, n. consumption, use; waste.
verbruik, (–), consume, use up.
verbruiker, (-s), consumer.
verbruiksartikel, article of consumption.
verbrysel, (–), smash, crush, shatter, break to pieces; break (heart).
verbryseling, smashing, shattering.
verbuie, -buig, (–), twist, bend; decline, inflect (gram.).
verbuigbaar, (-bare), declinable.
verbuiging, (-e, -s), declension, (in)flexion (inflection).
verbuigingsvorm, flexional form.
verby, prep. past, beyond; **– die kerk,** past the church; beyond the church.
verby, adv. past; over; at an end; **dit is alles –,** it is all over; that is a thing of the past; **– marsjeer,** march past, **– bring,** bring past; **– dra,** carry past.
verbydryf, -drywe, (verbyge-), drive past; float (drift) past; blow over.
verbygaan, n.: **in die –,** in passing.
verbygaan, (verbyge-), pass, pass (go) by pass (of time); pass over, omit; pass away; **stilswygend**

–, pass over in silence; **die geleentheid laat –**, miss the opportunity.
verbygaande, passing; transitory.
verbyganger, (-s), passer-by.
verbyglip, (verbyge-), slip past.
verbygroei, (verbyge-), outgrow.
verbykom, (verbyge-), pass, come past; **daar kom jy nie verby nie**, you cannot get past that; that cannot be argued (explained) away; **iemand laat –**, haul a person over the coals.
verbyloop, (verbyge-), walk past, pass.
verbypraat, (verbyge-): **sy mond –**, put one's foot in(to) it, drop a brick.
verbyry, (verbyge-), ride (drive) past.
verbysien, (verbyge-), overlook.
verbyskiet, (verbyge-), dash (shoot) past; overshoot (the mark).
verbysnel, (verbyge-), rush (hurry, run) past.
verbystap, (verbyge-), walk past, pass.
verbyster, (-), perplex, bewilder.
verbyster(d), (-de), bewildered.
verbysterend, (-e), perplexing, bewildering, baffling, puzzling.
verbystering, perplexity, bewilderment.
verbystreef, -strewe, (verbyge-), outstrip, outdistance; surpass.
verbystroom, (verbyge-), stream past.
verbyswem, (verbyge-), swim past.
verbytrek, (verbyge-), trek past; march past, pass; blow over.
verbyvlieg, (verbyge-), fly past.
verbyvloei, (verbyge-), flow past.
verdaag, (-), adjourn, prorogue, postpone.
verdag, (-te), suspicious; suspected (person, place); suspect (of statement), questionable (actions); **iemand – maak**, throw suspicion; on somebody; **– wees op**, be prepared for; **op iets – wees**, be prepared for something; expect it.
verdaging, adjournment, prorogation.
verdagmakery, **verdagmaking**, rousing of suspicion, insinuation.
verdamp, (-), evaporate.
verdamping, evaporation.
verdedig, (-), defend; stand up for.
verdedigbaar, (-bare), defensible.
verdedigend, (-e), defensive.
verdediger, (-s), defender; defending counsel, counsel for the defence.
verdediging, defence.
verdedigingsmag, defence force.
verdedigingstelsel, system of defence.
verdeel, (-), divide; distribute; assign (parts); **– onder**, distribute (divide) among; **– oor**, spread over.
verdeelbaar, (-bare), divisible.
verdeel(d), (-de), divided (lit. & fig.).
verdeeldheid, division, disagreement; discord, dissension.
verdeelskyf, distributor, division-plate.
verdek, under cover; **– opstel**, mask, place under cover; **sig – opstel**, make (lay an ambush, lie in ambush).
verdeksels, (-e), a. confounded.
verdeksels, adv. bally, confoundedly.
verdeler, (-s), divider.
verdelg, (-), destroy, exterminate.
verdelger, (-s), destroyer, exterminator.
verdelging, destruction, extermination.
verdelgingsoorlog, war of extermination.
verdeling, (-e, -s), division, distribution, graduation; partition.
verdelingsverdrag, partition-treaty.
verdenking, suspicion; **in – kom**, incur suspicion; **onder – staan**, be under suspicion.

verder, (-, -e), a. further, farther.
verder, adv. further, farther; **– moet jy beloof**, moreover (in addition) you must promise; **– wil ek niks hê nie**, I want nothing else; **en so –**, and so on, et cetera.
verderf, n. destruction, ruin; **in die – bring (stort)**, bring ruin upon, ruin; **ten verderwe lei**, lead to destruction.
verderf, -derwe, (-), ruin; corrupt.
verderfenis, vide **verderf**, n.
verderflik, (-e), pernicious, baneful.
verderflikheid, perniciousness, banefulness.
verdien, (-), earn (salary, a living); deserve (praise, honour); merit (reward); **hy – niks beters nie**, he does not deserve any better, he has got his deserts; **nie jou sout – nie**, not be worth one's salt.
verdien, (-de), earned, deserved; **dit is jou –de loon**, it serves you right, you have got your deserts.
verdienste, (-s), wages, earnings; profit; merit; **sonder –**, without income; unemployed; **iemand van groot –**, a person of great merit.
verdienstelik, (-e), meritorious, deserving; **sig – maak teenoor**, serve well.
verdienstelikheid, merit(oriousness).
verdiep, (-), deepen; **sig – in**, lose oneself in; **sig in die werk –**, plunge into the work; **– raak in**, become engrossed in, become absorbed in.
verdieping, (-e, -s), deepening; storey (story), floor; **benede –**, ground floor; **derde –**, third floor (storey).
verdiepingshuis, double-storey.
verdierlik, (-te), a. brutish, bestial.
verdierlik, (-), bestialize, brutalize.
verdierliking, brutalization.
verdig, (-te), a. 1. fictitious.
verdig, (-te), a. 2. condensed.
verdig, (-), 1. invent (story).
verdig, (-), 2. condense (of steam).
verdigsel, (-s), fiction; fabrication; fable.
verdigting, 1. fiction; fabrication.
verdigting, 2. condensation.
verdik, (-), thicken.
verdikking, thickening.
verdink, (-), suspect; vide **verdag**.
verdiskonteer, negotiate (bill), discount.
verdiskonteerbaar, (-bare), negotiable.
verdiskonteer(d), (-de), negotiated; **–de waarde**, present value.
verdoem, (-de), a. damned; doomed.
verdoem, (-), damn.
verdoemeling, (-e), reprobate.
verdoemenis, damnation.
verdoeming, damning; damnation.
verdoemlik, (-e), damnable.
verdoesel, (-), blurr; gloss over.
verdof, -dowwe, (-), tarnish; become faint; dim (light); deaden (sound).
verdonker, (-), darken, cloud, dim.
verdoof, -dowe, (-), dull, deaden (sound); tarnish; anaesthetize (surgery), render insensible; stupefy, stun.
verdool(d), (-de), stray, strayed.
verdooldheid, perversion.
verdor, (-de), a. withered, parched, shrivelled up.
verdor, (-), wither, parch, shrivel up.
verdorwe, perverted, depraved, corrupt.
verdorwenheid, perversion, depravity.
verdowe, vide **verdoof**.
verdowend, (-e), stupefactive; narcotic.
verdowing, deadening; vide **verdoof**; stupefaction, stupor; narcosis.
verdowingsmiddel, anaesthetic, narcotic.
verdowwe, vide **verdof**.

verdra(ag), (–), endure, tolerate, suffer, bear, stand (pain, nonsense).
verdraagsaam, (-same), tolerant, forbearing.
verdraagsaamheid, tolerance, forbearance.
verdraai, (–), twist (arm); dis ort (words), wrest (law, facts).
verdraai(d), (-de), twisted, distorted.
verdraaidheid, distortion.
verdraaiing, twisting, distortion; perversion, ~twist(ing), wresting.
verdrag, (-drae), treaty, agreement; 'n – **sluit (aangaan)**, conclude (enter into) a treaty; met –, gradually.
verdriedubbel, -voudig, (–), tripple, treble.
verdriet, sorrow, grief.
verdrietig, (-e), sorrowful, sad.
verdrietigheid, sorrow, sadness.
verdrievoudig, (–), treble, triple.
verdring, (–), push aside (away), jostle, crowd out; oust, supplant.
verdrink, (–), drown, be drowned.
verdroging, drying up.
verdroog, (-de), a. parched, dried up, shrivelled (up).
verdroog, -droë, (–), dry up, parch.
verdroom, (–), dream away.
verdruk, (-te), a. oppressed.
verdruk, (–), oppress; vide **verdring**.
verdrukking, oppression.
verdryf, -drywe, drive away (out) chase away (out); expel, eject, oust, turn out; pass (while away) (time); dissipate (cloud).
verdrywing, driving away; expulsion, ejection, dislodging (the enemy).
verdubbel, (–), double; **jou treë –**, quicken one's pace; **met –de krag**, with redoubled strength.
verdubbeling, doubling; redoubling.
verduidelik, (–), explain, elucidate, illustrate.
verduideliking, (-e, -s), explanation.
verduister, (–), darken, obscure; grow dark; embezzle (money), peculate, obscure (mind); darken, cloud.
verduistering, darkening; eclipse (of sun); clouding; embezzlement.
verduits, (–), Germanize.
verduiweld, (-e), devilish, confounded.
verduiwels, deuced, confoundedly; –!, the deuce!, the devil!; – **duur**, darned (jolly) expensive.
verdun, (–), thin, make thin; dilute (liquids); rarefy (air).
verdunning, thinning; dilution (of liquids); rarefaction, rarefication.
verdunningsmiddel, thinner(s).
verduring, enduring, endurance.
verduur, (–), endure, bear, suffer.
verduursaam, (-de), a. preserved.
verduursaam, (–), preserve, can.
verdwaal, (-de), a. stray (animal, bullet), strayed, lost (animal, person); – **raak**, lose one's way, get lost.
verdwaal, (–), lose one's way, get lost.
verdwaas, (-de), a. infatuated, silly.
verdwaas, (–), infatuate, knock silly.
verdwasing, infatuation, silliness.
verdwyn, (–), disappear, vanish; fade away; **uit die oog –**, pass out of sight.
verdwyning, disappearance, vanishing.
verdwynpunt, vanishing-point.
verebed, veerbed, feather-bed.
veredel, (–), improve (stock); refine (metals, language); elevate, ennoble.
veredeling, improvement, refining, elevation.
vereelt, (-e), a. horny, callous, hard.
vereelt, (–), make (become) horny (callous).
vereenselwig, (–), identify.

vereenselwiging, identification.
vereenvoudig, (–), simplify (matter, spelling); reduce (fraction).
vereenvoudiging, simplification.
vereer, (–), honour, reverence, worship.
vereerder, (-s), worshiper, admirer.
vereers, vide **vir**.
vereffen, (–), settle, pay (account), square; adjust, settle (matter).
vereffening, settlement (of account).
vereis, (–), demand, require; **dit – tyd**, it takes time; **die –te sorg**, the necessary care.
vereiste, (-s), requirement, requisite.
verengels, (-te), Anglicized, donationalized.
verengels, (–), Anglicize; become Anglicized.
verengelsing, Anglicization, Anglicizing.
verenig, (-de), a. united; amalgamated, combined; V –de Volke (**-Organisasie**), United Nations (Organization).
vereniging, (–), unite, merge, amalgamate, combine; incorporate (in one body); join; **in die eg –**, join in marriage; – **met**, unite with; reconcile with, make compatible with; **baie stemme op sig –**, poll (receive) many votes; **daarmee kan ek my nie – nie**, I cannot share that opinion (view).
verenigbaar, (-bare), can be united; – **met**, compatible (reconcilable) with.
vereniging, (-e, -s), union; amalgamation, combination; association, society.
verenigingslewe, corporate life.
vererf, vererwe, (–), bequeath.
vererg, (–), annoy, irritate, vex, make angry; **sig –**, become angry (annoyed).
vererger, (–), make worse, aggravate; grow (become) worse.
verergering, aggravation, change for the worse.
verering, worship(ping), veneration, reverance; devotion, cult.
vereuropees, (–), Europeanize; become Europeanized.
verewa, vide **veerwa**.
verewig, (–), immortalize, perpetuate; **jou naam –**, acquire undying fame.
verewiging, immortalization.
verf, (verwe), n. paint, colour; dye.
verf, verwe, (ge-), paint (woodwork); rouge (face), paint; dye (material).
verfdoos, colour-box, paint-box.
verfhandelaar, dealer in paints.
verfhout, dye-wood.
verfilm, (–), film.
verfkwas, paint-brush.
verflaag, coat of paint.
verflenter, (–), tear; become tattered.
verflenter(d), (-de), tattered, torn; – **wees**, be in rags.
verflou, (–), grow (become) faint; abate (of wind); fade; weaken (of energy); flag (of interest); slacken; cool down, diminish.
verflouing, fading; flagging, abatement.
verflug, smell of paint.
verfoei, (–), detest, loathe, abominate.
verfoeiing, detestation, loathing.
verfoeilik, (-e), detestable, abominable.
verfoeliesel, foil.
verfoes, (–), spoil, bungle, muddle.
verfomfaai, (–), crumple, ruffle.
verfomfaai(d), (-de), dishevelled, ruffled, untidy, unkempt; crumpled.
verfpot, paint-pot.
verfraai, (–), embellish, adorn.
verfraaiing, embellishment, adornment.
verfrans, (–), Frenchify; become French.
verfris, (–), refresh.

verfrissend, (-e), refreshing.
verfrissing, refreshment.
verfrommel, (-), crumple, crush.
verfstowwe, -ware, dyes (dye-ware); colours, paints.
verg, (ge-), demand, require; **dit is te veel ge-,** that is asking too much.
vergaan, n. passing away; loss (of ship).
vergaan, (-gane), a. perished (tyre), decayed, decomposed; lost, wrecked.
vergaan, (-), perish, decay, decompose; pass away; be wrecked (of ship); be lost; **hy het gedink die wêreld -,** he thought the world had come to an end; **van honger -,** die of hunger, be starving; **van koue -,** be perished with cold; **van dors -,** be parched with thirst, die of thirst; - **van hoogmoed,** be consumed with pride.
vergaar, (-), collect, gather; amass (money), store up, hoard.
vergaarbak, receptacle, reservoir, tank.
vergader, (-), collect, gather; meet, assemble.
vergadering, (-e, -s), meeting; assembly; gathering.
vergaderplek, meeting-place.
vergadersaal, meeting-room; assembly-hall.
vergal, (-), gall; embitter; spoil.
vergange, a. past, bygone.
vergange, adv. lately; the other day.
verganklik, (-e), perishable (goods); transient, transitory; **alles is -,** all things will pass away, nothing lasts.
verganklikheid, transitoriness, transience.
vergas, (-), 1. treat; - **op,** treat to.
vergas, (-), 2. gasify; vaporise.
vergasser, (-s), vergastoestel, (-le), carburettor; vaporizer.
vergeef, (-gewe), (-), forgive, pardon.
vergeeflik, (-e), pardonable, forgivable.
vergeeflikheid, pardonableness; venialty.
vergeefs, (-e), fruitless, futile, unavailing; **te -,** in vain, of no avail, to no purpose.
vergeefsheid, fruitlessness, futility.
vergeestelik, (-), spiritualize, sublimate.
vergeesteliking, spiritualization.
vergeet, (-), forget.
vergeetagtig, (-e), forgetful.
vergeetagtigheid, forgetfulness.
vergeet-al, forgetful person.
vergeetboek, oblivion; **in die - raak,** be forgotten, fall into oblivion.
vergeet-my-nietjie, (-s), forget-me-not.
vergeld(e), (-), repay, requite.
vergelding, reward, recompense, requital; retribution; reprisal; **die dag van -,** the day of reckoning.
vergeleke: - met, in comparison with.
vergelyk, (-e), n. compromise, agreement, settlement; **'n - tref,** make a compromise, come to an agreement; **tot 'n - kom,** compromise.
vergelyk, (-), compare; - **by,** liken to, compare to; - **met,** compare with.
vergelykbaar, (-bare), comparable.
vergelykend, (-e), comparative.
vergelykenderwys, by comparison.
vergelyking, (-e, -s), comparison; simile, equation (alg.); **trappe van -,** degrees of comparison; **'n - trek,** draw a comparison (parallel); **in - met,** in comparison with.
vergemaklik, (-), facilitate, make easier; **dit sal die saak -,** it will simplify matters.
vergemakliking, facilitation.
vergenoeg, (-de), a. contended, satisfied.
vergenoeg, (-), content; **sig - met,** be satisfied with, content oneself with.
vergenoegdheid, contentment.
vergesel, (-), accompany, attend.
vergesig, (-te), prospect; vista, view.
vergesog, (-te), far-fetched.
vergetelheid, oblivion; **aan die - onttrek (ontruk),** save from oblivion.
vergevorder(d), (-de), (far) advanced.
vergewe, 1. vide **vergeef.**
vergewe, (-), 2. poison; **vergewe wees van,** be overrun (infested) with, teem with (snakes).
vergewensgesind, (-e), forgiving.
vergewensgesindheid, forgiveness.
vergewing, pardon, forgiveness.
vergewis, (-): sig - van, make sure of, ascertain.
vergiet, (-e), n. strainer, colander.
vergiet, (-), shed (blood, tears); **jou bloed -,** shed one's blood.
vergieting, shedding.
vergif, (-te), poison; venom.
vergifboom, poison-oak, poison-tree.
vergif(fe)nis, forgiveness, pardon.
vergifstof, virus, toxin(e).
vergiftig, (-), poison; envenom.
vergiftiger, (-s), poisoner.
vergifting, poisoning.
Vergilius, Virgil.
vergis, (-): sig -, make a mistake, be mistaken; **jy - jou,** you are mistaken.
vergissing, (-e, -s), mistake, error.
verglaas, (-), glaze; vitrify.
verglaassel, glaze, enamel.
verglaser, (-s), glazer.
verglasing, glazing; virtrification.
vergoddelik, (-), deify.
vergoddeliking, deification.
vergoding, deification; idolization.
vergoed, (-), make good (loss, expense), compensate, indemnify; make it up to, repay.
vergoeding, compensation, indemnification, reimbursement; remuneration.
vergoedelik, (-), excuse, gloss (smooth) over, extenuate (conduct).
vergoeliking, extenuation, palliation.
vergote, spilt (spilled) (blood).
vergroei, (-), grow out of shape; outgrow; disappear (of scar).
vergroot, (-), enlarge (portrait); increase; augment; magnify; exaggerate; **vergrotende trap,** comparative degree.
vergrootglas, magnifying-glass.
vergroting, (-e, -s), enlargement; increase; magnifying; exaggeration.
vergruis, (-de), pulverized; shattered.
vergruis, (-), crush, pulverize; shatter, smash, break to bits.
vergryp, (-e), n. offence, transgression, misdemeanour.
vergryp, (-): sig - aan, transgress, infringe (law), violate; commit an offence against; lay hands on (person).
vergrys, (-de), (grown) grey.
vergrys, (-), become grey.
vergruis, (-de), abused; despised.
vergruis, (-), abuse, revile, vituperate.
vergruising, abuse, vituperation.
vergul(d), (-de), a. gilt.
vergul(d), (-), gild.
vergul(d)sel, gilt, gilding.
vergun, (-), permit, allow; grant.
vergunning, (-e, -s), permission; leave; concession; licence.
verhaal, (-hale), n. story, narrative, tale, account; redress, remedy; **sonder -,** without redress; **tot - kom,** recover, recuperate.
verhaal, (-), tell, narrate, relate.

verhaaltrant, narrative style.
verhaar, (-), lose the hair, change (renew) its coat (of horse, ox, etc.).
verhaas, (-), hasten, precipitate, expedite, accelerate.
verhaasting, hastening, precipitation.
verhalend, (-e), narrative.
verhalenderwys(e), narratively.
verhaler, (-s), narrator, story-teller.
verhalfsool, (-), half-sole.
verhandel, (-), negotiate (bill); barter (away); dispose of; discuss.
verhandelbaar, (-bare), negotiable; salable.
verhandeling, (-e, -s), treatise, essay, discourse, dissertation; lecture.
verhang, (-), rehang, hang otherwise.
verhard, (-e), a. hardened, callous, obdurate, hardhearted.
verhard, (-), harden; become (make) callous.
verhardheid, hard-heartedness, obduracy.
verharding, hardening; obduration.
verhaspel, (-), spoil, botch, garble.
verheel, (-), hide, conceal.
verheerlik, (-), glorify, extol.
verheerliking, glorification.
verhef, (-), lift (hand), raise (voice, eyes), lift up, elevate; extol; **tot die adelstand** -, raise to the peerage; **jou stem** - **teen**, protest against, raise one's voice against.
verheffend, (-e), elevating, ennobling.
verheffing, raising, elevation, elevating; uplift; rise.
verhelder, (-), brighten (of eyes, face); clear (up); make clear (bright); lighten; clarify; clear (mind).
verheldering, brightening; clearing.
verhelder, (-s), concealer.
verheling, concealment.
verhelp, (-), remedy, rectify, put in order; **dit kan nie** - **word nie**, there is no help for it.
verhelping, remedy.
verhemelte, (-s), palate, roof of the mouth.
verhemelteklank, palatal (sound).
verheug, (-de), a. pleased, glad, happy.
verheug, (-), gladden, delight; **dit** - **my om dit te hoor**, I am glad (delighted) to hear it; **sig** -, rejoice be glad (delighted).
verheuging, rejoicing, joy.
verhewe, elevated; embossed, in relief; swollen; lofty, exalted, elevated, fine, sublime; **bo gemeenheid** - **wees**, be above (superior to) meanness.
verhewenheid, loftiness (of style), sublimity, elevation.
verhinder, (-), prevent, hinder.
verhindering, hindrance, obstacle; prevention, preventing.
verhit, (-te), a. hot, heated; flushed.
verhit, (-), heat; inflame.
verhitting, heating.
verhoed, (-), prevent, avert, ward off; **mag God dit** -, God forbid.
verhoeding, prevention, preventing.
verhoging, (-e, -s), heightening; (raised) platform; elevation; promotion; increment, rise, increase (in salary); rise (in price, in temperature); cant (of rails); raising.
verhollands, (-), make (become) Dutch; turn into Dutch; Dutchify.
verhonderdvoudig, (-), centuple, multiply by a hundred.
verhonger, (-), famish, starve, be parished with hunger; **laat** -, starve.
verhongering, starvation, starving.
verhoog, (-hoë), n. platform, dais.

verhoog, (-), heighten, make higher; raise (salary), increase; promote; enhance (qualities); intensify; **sig** -, exalt oneself.
verhoogmeisie, show-girl.
verhoor, (-hore), n. hearing, trial, examination.
verhoor, (-), answer, hear (prayer); fulfil (wish); try (prisoner); examine.
verhouding, (-e, -s), relation; proportion, ratio (of numbers); –e, dimensions (of building); **buite alle** - **tot**, out of all proportion to; **in omgekeerde (regte)** - **tot**, inversely (directly) proportional to; **in** - **tot**, in proportion to; **na** -, proportionally, in proportion; relatively, comparatively; **na** - **van**, in proportion to.
verhuis, (-), move (into house), move in, remove; migrate (of birds); emigrate; pass away.
verhuising, moving, removal; migration (of birds); emigration.
verhuiswa, furniture-van, removal-van.
verhuring, letting, hiring out; leasing.
verhuur, (-), let (rooms), rent, let out; hire out; lease (farm); **sig** -, take service (with) go into service.
verhuurbaar, (-bare), rentable, lettable.
verhuurder, (-s), lessor; landlord.
verifieer, (-), verify, check; audit.
verifiëring verification, check(ing).
verifikasie vide **verifiëring**.
verinnerlik (-), deepen, spiritualize.
verja(ag), -jae, (-), drive (frighten, chase, scare) away; dislodge, drive out(enemy); disperse, dispel.
verjaar, (-), celebrate one's birthday; become superannuated; **hy** - **môre**, it is his birthday tomorrow; **'n** –**de tjek**, a stale cheque.
verjaar(s)dag, birthday; aniversary.
verjaarsfees, birthday-feast.
verjaarsmaal, birthday-dinner, -feast.
verjaarsparty, birthday-party.
verjaarspresent, birthday-present.
verjaging, chasing (driving) away.
verjaring, birthday; prescription (of debt.), superannuation (of judgement).
verjaringsreg, statute of limitations.
verjaringstermyn, (period of) limitation.
verjong, (-), rejuvenate, rejuvenize, make (become) young again.
verjonging, rejuvenation, rejuvenescence.
verjongingskuur, rejuvenating cure.
verkalk, (-te), a. calcified.
verkalk, (-), calcify, calcine.
verkalking, calcification, calcination; - **van die are**, arterial sclerosis.
verkap, (-te), disguised, veiled.
verkas, (-), shift, decamp.
verkeer, n. intercourse; traffic.
verkeer, (-), be (in a certain position); change; **hy** - **in 'n gevaarlike toestand**, he is (finds himself) in a dangerous position; **waar jy mee** -, **word jy mee geëer (besmeer)**, a man is judged by his friends; **aan die hof** -, move in court-circles; - **met**, associate (assort) with, mix with.
verkeerd, (-e), a. wrong, incorrect; troublesome, unreasonable, impossible; **die** –**e pad**, the wrong road; **'n** –**e woord**, a wrong word; a harsh word; **die** –**e keel**, the windpipe; **'n** –**e antwoord**, a wrong answer; a rude answer.
verkeerd, adv. wrong, wrongly; - **begryp**, misunderstand; - **doen**, do wrong; - **opneem**, take amiss; - **ry**, take the wrong road.
verkeerdelik, wrongly.
verkeerdeveeerhen, cross-feathered hen.
verkeerdheid, unreasonableness; perversity; **ek**

kan nie die – daarvan insien nie, I can see no wrong in it.
verkeersagent, traffic policemen.
verkeersknoop, traffic jam.
verkeerskring, traffic circle.
verkeerskonstabel, speed-cop.
verkeersmiddel, means of communication.
verkeersoutomaat, robot.
verkeersreëling, regulation of traffic.
verkeerstaal, common language.
verkeersvraagstuk, traffic-problem.
verkeersweg, thoroughfare; communication (-road).
verkeerswese, traffic, transport.
verken, (–), scout, reconnoitre.
verkenner, (-s), scout.
verkenning, scouting, reconnoitring; reconnaissance.
verkenningsdiens, scouting; scouting duty.
verkenningskorps, (body of) scouts.
verkenningstog, reconnoitring expedition.
verkenningsvliegtuig, scouting-plane, scout.
verkerf, -kerwe, (–), blunder; dit by iemand –, incur a person's displeasure.
verketter, (–), charge with (accuse of) heresy; denounce, cry down, decry.
verkettering, charging with (charge of) heresy; decrying, denouncing.
verkies, (–), elect, choose; return (as M. P.), prefer; – tot lid van die parlement, elect a member of parliament; doen (maak) soos jy –, do what you like; wat – jy?, what would you like?; what (which) do you prefer?
verkiesbaar, (-bare), eligible; sig – stel, stand for; seek election.
verkiesbaarheid, eligibility.
verkiesing, (-e, -s), election (by vote); wish, choice; na –, at will, at pleasure; uit eie –, of one's own free will.
verkiesingsagent, election-agent.
verkiesingsdag, polling-day.
verkiesingskomitee, election-committee.
verkiesingsleus, election-cry.
verkiesingsmanifes, election manifesto.
verkiesingsrede(voering), electioneering speech.
verkiesingstryd, election contest.
verkiesingsuitslag, election result.
verkiesingswet, electoral law.
verkieslik, (-e), preferable.
verkieslikheid, preferableness.
verkla(ag), -klae, (–), bring a charge (an action) against, lodge a complaint against; report, accuse, inform against.
verklaar, (-de), a. declared; avowed.
verklaar, (–), explain (meaning), make clear, elucidate; state, declare; testify, certify; oorlog –, declare war; skuldig –, find guilty; hoe – jy dit?, how do you explain that?; how do you account for that?; sig ten gunste – van, declare in favour of, side with.
verklaarbaar, (-bare), explicable; om – bare redes, for obvious reasons; moeilik –, difficult (hard) to explain.
verklae, vide verkla(ag).
verklaer, (-s), plaintiff, informer.
verklank, (–), express in music; voice.
verklap, (–), let out, blab; 'n geheim –, let out a secret; iemand –, give a person away.
verklapper, (-s), tell-tale.
verklarend, (-s), explanatory.
verklaring, (-e, -s), explanation, elucidation; statement, declaration; evidence; 'n – aflê, make a statement.
verklee(d), (–), disguise; change the clothes of; sig –, change one's clothes.

verkleef, devoted, attached.
verkleefdheid, devotion, attachment.
verklein, (-de), a. reduced (scale), diminished, vide verklein, (–).
verklein, (–), make smaller, diminish in size; reduce (fraction); cancel (arith.); decrease, lessen; disparage, belittle.
verkleinbaar, (-bare), reducible.
verkleineer, (–), belittle, disparage.
verkleinering, disparagement.
verkleining, diminution; simplification, reduction; disparagement.
verkleiningsuitgang, diminutive ending.
verkleinwoord, diminutive.
verkleur, (-de), a. faded, discoloured.
verkleur, (–), fade, lose colour, discolour, change (its) colour.
verkleuring, fading, discolouring.
verkleurmannetjie, chameleon.
verklik, (–), let out, tell, split on.
verklikker, (-s), tell-tale; detector.
verkluim, (-de), a. benumbed, numb with cold; totaal – wees, be frozen.
verkluim, (–), grow numb with cold, be benumbed, be perished with cold; die of the cold, perish in the cold.
verkneg, (–), enslave.
verkneukel, -kneuter, (–): sig –, chuckle, rub one's hands with joy.
verknies, (–), sig –, fret away one's life, mope.
verknip, (–), spoil in cutting.
verknoei, (–), spoil, make a mess of.
verknoeier, (-s), bungler.
verknog: – aan, attached (devoted) to.
verknogtheid, attachment, devotion.
verknorsing, sorry plight, fix; in die – wees (sit), be in a sorry (sad) pickle, be in (a fix) the soup.
verkoel, (–), cool (down) (lit. & fig.).
verkoeler, (–), radiator.
verkoeling, cooling; coolness.
verkoling, carbonization; charring.
verkondig, (–), preach (the Gospel), proclaim; expound (doctrine); advocate (policy); iemand se lof –, sing somebody's praises.
verkondiger, (-s), preacher, proclaimer.
verkondiging, preaching; proclamation.
verkook, (–), boil down (away).
verkool, (–), carbonize; char (wood); coke (coal); become carbonized.
verkoop, n. sale.
verkoop, (–), sell; dispose of; by afslag –, sell by Dutch auction; grappe –, crack jokes; kaskenades –, play tricks (the fool); leuens –, tell lies; uit die hand –, sell privately.
verkoopakte, deed of sale.
verkoopbaar, (-bare), salable, marketable.
verkoopbrief, deed of sale.
verkoopprys, selling-price.
verkoopprekening, account-sales.
verkoopster, (-s), saleswoman, seller.
verkoopwaarde, selling-value.
verkoopweerstand, sales resistance.
verkoper, (-s), n. seller; vendor (of small wares); salesman.
verkoping, (-e, -s), public sale, auction.
verkore, chosen (people), elect.
verkort, (-e), a. shortened; abbreviated; abridged (edition); contracted.
verkort, (–), shorten, make shorter; abbreviate (word); abridge (book); condense; while away (the time).
verkorting, (-e, -s), shortening; abbreviation; abridg(e)ment, abridged edition.
verkose, elected, chosen.

verkoue, n. cold, chill; – **kry,** catch cold; **'n swaar** – **hê,** have a severe cold.
verkoue, a. with cold; **'n** – **kind,** a child with a cold; – **wees,** have a cold.
verkouentheid, cold.
verkrag, (–), violate (law, conscience); ravish, force, violate, rape (woman).
verkragter, (-s), violator, ravisher.
verkragting, violation, rape, ravishing, ravishment.
verkreë, vested (rights).
verkreukel, (–), crumple, crush.
verkrimp, (–), shrink.
verkromming, curvature (of the spine).
verkrop, (-te), a. pent up (feelings).
verkrop, (–), swallow, put up with, bottle up, pocket (insults); restrain (feelings).
verkrummel, (–), crumble.
verkry, (–), obtain, get, acquire; gain; win (fame, honour).
verkrygbaar, (-bare), obtainable, procurable, to be had; **nie** – **nie,** unobtainable; **nie meer** – **nie,** out of stock; out of print.
verkryging, obtaining, getting.
verkul, (–), cheat, take in, trick.
verkwansel, barter away; throw away.
verkwik, (–), refresh.
verkwikkend, (-e), refreshing; comforting.
verkwikking, refreshment; comfort.
verkwiklik, (-e), refreshing; comforting.
verkwis, (–), waste, squander (money), dissipate, fritter away.
verkwistend, (-e), wasteful, extravagant.
verkwister, (-s), spendthrift, waster.
verkwisterig, (-e), vide **verkwistend.**
verkwisterigheid, wastefulness.
verkwisting, waste; extravagance.
verkwyn, (–), pine away, languish.
verkyk, (–): **sig** – **aan,** stare (gaze, gape) at.
verkyker, (-s), telescope, field-glasses.
verlaag, (–), lower; reduce (price); debase, disgrace, degrade.
verlaat, (-late), a. deserted, abandoned, derelict. (vessel); forsaken.
verlaat, (–), leave; deser (place, ship, post, wife); abandon (post); forsake (person); – **Kaapstad in die môre,** leave (depart from) Cape Town in the morning; **sig** – **op,** trust, depend (rely) on.
verlaging, lowering, reduction (of prices); degradation, debasement.
verlak, (-te), a. lacquered, japanned, varnished; –te **leer,** patent-leather.
verlak, (–), lacquer, japan, varnish.
verlakker, (-s), japanner, varnisher.
verlam, (-de), a. paralysed, palsied.
verlam, (–), paralyse; cripple.
verlamming, paralysis, palsy; crippling.
verlang, (–), want, desire; long, be longing; **alles wat 'n mens kan** – **(alles wat 'n mens se hart na** –), all that one can wish for; **ek** – **van jou dat . . .,** I want (expect) you to . . ., **wat** – **jy van my?,** what do you want (expect) me to do?; – **na,** long for; **na huis** –, be longing to go home.
verlange, (-ns), longing, desire; – **na,** longing for; **brand van** – **om . . .,** yearn (be burning or dying) to . . .
verlangste, (-s), longing, yearning.
verlate, lonely (spot, person); unfrequented (place); forsaken (by God).
verlatenheid, loneliness, forlornness.
verlating, desertion, abandonment, abandoning, dereliction; forsaking.
verlê, -leg, (–), shift, remove; lie (down) in a different position; divert (road); mislay (your gloves).
verlede, n. past; **in die** –, in the past.
verlede, a. past, last; – **deelwoord,** past participle; – **jaar, nag,** last year, night; – **Saterdag,** last Saturday.
verleë, bashful, timid; perplexed, embarrassed, confused; **iemand** – **maak,** embarrass a person; **heeltemal** – **wees,** be quite embarrassed; be completely at a loss; – **met iets wees,** not know what to do with a thing; – **wees om,** want badly, be in need of; **nooit om 'n antwoord** – **wees nie,** never be at a loss for an answer; – **om geld,** hard up, badly in need of money.
verleen, (–), give, grant (permission, aid), render (assistance); bestow (favour); lend.
verleentheid, bashfulness, timidity; perplexity, embarrassment, confusion; trouble, difficulty; **in (die)** – **wees,** be in trouble (a fix).
verleer, (–), unlearn (habit); forget.
verlei, (–), lead astray; seduce (woman); tempt, entice.
verleidelik, (-e), tempting, enticing.
verleidelikheid, allurement, seductiveness.
verlei(d)er, (-s), tempter, seducer.
verleiding, temptation; seduction.
verleidster, (-s), temptress, seducer.
verlekker, (–): **sig** – **in,** take (a) pleasure (a delight) in, delight in; **sig** – **op,** be keen on; depend on; **moet jou nie daarop** – **nie,** do not rely on that.
verleng, (–), make longer, lengthen; protract (visit); prolong, extend; produce (line); renew (bill).
verlenging, lengthening; producing; protraction; extension; prolongation.
verlengstuk, extension, lengthening-piece, -bar allonge, rider (commerce).
verlening, granting; rendering; lending.
verlep, (-te), a. faded, wilted, withered; –te **oë,** dull (filmy) eyes; **hy lyk** –, he looks pale (washed out).
verlep, (–), fade wilt, wither.
verlewendig, (–), revive; enliven (person, trade); animate, vivify, kindle, quicken, stimulate.
verlewendiging, quickening, stimulation.
verlief, (-de), a. amorous, in love; **'n** – **de paar,** (a couple of) lovers; –**de woorde,** sweet nothings **'n** – **de nôientjie,** a girl in love; – **op,** in love with; – **raak (word) op,** fall in love with.
verlief, adv.: – **neem,** put up with, not mind **ons sal dit maar** – **moet neem,** we'll have to rough it, we'll have to make shift.
verliefde, (-s), lover.
verliefderigheid, amorousness.
verliefdheid, amorousness, being in love.
verlies, (-e), loss; bereavement (through death) –**e,** losses; casualties; – **van sy oë,** loss of his eyesight; **'n** – **ly,** sustain a loss.
verlieslys, casualty-list.
verlig, (-te), a. lighted (lit) up; enlightened (person).
verlig, (–), 1. light (up), illuminate; enlighten (the people); **'n kamer (straat)** –, light a room (street).
verlig, (–), 2. lighten (burden); make easier; alleviate (distress), ease (pain), relieve.
verligting, 1. lighting, illumination; enlightenment.
verligting, 2. lightening (of burden); alleviation, relief.
verloën, -logen, (–), deny (God, one's parents), repudiate, disavow, renounce; **sig** –, deny oneself; belie oneself (itself, one's nature).
verloënaar, -logenaar, (-s), denier.

verloëning, **-logening**, denial, repudiation, renoucement, renunciation.
verlof, permission, leave; leave (of absence); furlough (of soldier); – **kry**, obtain (be granted) permission; obtain (be granted) leave; – **vra**, apply for leave; **met –**, on leave; **met – weens siekte**, on sick-leave; **met – gaan (wees)**, go (be) on leave.
verlofganger, soldier on furlough.
verlofpas, pass, permit.
verloftyd, leave, furlough.
verlogen, vide **verloën**.
verlok, (–), tempt, allure, entice.
verlokkend, (-e), tempting, alluring.
verlokking, tempting, temptation, enticement.
verloklik, (-e), tempting, alluring.
verloklikheid, enticement, seductiveness.
verloof, -lowe, (–), affiance, betroth; **sig –, – raak**, become engaged; **sig – aan (met)**, become engaged to.
verloofde, (-s), betrothed, affianced, fiancé (masc.), fiancée (fem.).
verloofring, engagement-ring.
verloop, n. course (of time, disease), progress (of disease); **die gewone – hê**, take the usual (normal) course; **die – van 'n saak vertel**, give particulars of the case (matter); tell the ins and outs of the matter; **na (met) – van tyd**, in course of time; **na – van 'n maand**, after a month had elapsed.
verloop, (–), pass, elapse (of time), expire (of period); go out (of tide); **hoe het dinge daar –?**, what happened there?
verloopte, runaway, vagabond; dissipated; **'n – kêrel**, a dissipated fellow, a down-and-out; **'n – matroos**, a wandering sailor.
verloor, (–), lose; **sig – in**, lose oneself (in the crowd).
verloorder, (-s), loser.
verlore, lost; **die – seun**, the prodigal son; **– gaan**, be (get) lost; be wasted (of fruit, food); **– raak**, get lost.
verlos, (–), save, deliver, set free, release, redeem.
verloskunde, midwifery, obstetrics.
verloskundig, (-e), obstric(al).
verloskundige, (-s), obstetrician.
verlosser, (-s), deliver, saviour, liberator; **die V–**, the Redeemer.
verlossing, deliverance, redemption.
verlossingswerk, (work of) redemption.
verlowe, vide **verloof**.
verlowing, (-e, -s), engagement.
verlowingsring, engagement-ring.
verlug, (-te), a. illuminated.
verlug, (–), 1. ventilate, air (room).
verlug, (–), 2. illuminate.
verlugting, 1. ventilation, airing.
verlugting, 2. illumination.
verluier, (–), idle away (time).
verlustig, (–), amuse; **sig – in**, take a delight (pleasure) in, revel in.
verlustiging, recreation, pleasure.
Vermaak, n.: 1. **ek is nie – se kind nie, you won't (can't) spite me**.
vermaak, (-make), n. 2. pleasure, amusement, delight; diversion, pastime; **tot – van die toeskouers**, to the amusement (delight) of the spectators.
vermaak, (–), alter (clothes); amuse, entertain, divert; bequeath, leave (by will); make (person) jealous; **sig –**, amuse oneself; **ek laat my nie van jou – nie, I can do (get on) without you, I don't need your assistance (permission); I won't be baffled by you.
vermaaklik, (-e), amusing, entertaining.

vermaaklikheid, amusingness; amusement, entertainment.
vermaaklikheidsbelasting, amusement-tax.
vermaan, (–), admonish, warn, exhort.
vermaard, (-e), renowned, famous, illustrious, celebrated.
vermaardheid, fame, renown; celebrity.
vermaer, (–), grow (become) lean (thin), become emaciated, lose flesh.
vermag, (–), have the power to; **niks – teen**, be powerless against.
vermaering, emaciation, losing (loss) of weight, (weight-)reducing.
vermaeringskuur, reducing-cure.
vermaking, bequest.
verman, (–): **sig –**, pull oneself together, summon up courage.
vermanend, (-e), exhortative.
vermaner, (-s), admonisher, exhorter.
vermaning, (-e, -s), admonition, exhortation; telling-off, talking-to.
vermeende, supposed (brother, heir), reputed, fancied, putative (father).
vermeer, vide **vomeer**.
vermeerder, (–), increase, augment, multiply; **–de uitgawe**, enlarged edition; increased expenditure.
vermeerdering, (-e, -s), increase (in numbers), addition, augmentation.
vermei, (–): **sig –**, disport oneself, enjoy oneself; **sig – in**, enjoy, revel in.
vermeld, (–), mention, state, record.
vermeldingswaar(dig), (-e), worth mentioning.
vermelding, mention; **eervolle –**, honourable mention; **eervolle – kry**, be mentioned in dispatches.
vermeng, (–), mix; blend (coffee, tea), **sig –**, mix; mingle.
vermengbaar, (-bare), miscible, mixable.
vermenging, mixing; mixture, blend.
vermenigvuldig, (–), multiply.
vermenigvuldigbaar, (-bare), multipliable, multiplicable.
vermenigvuldiger, (-s), multiplier.
vermenigvuldiging, multiplication.
vermenigvuldigtal, multiplicand.
vermetel, (–, e), audacious, bold.
vermetelheid, audacity, recklessness.
vermicelli, vermicelli.
vermiljoen, vermilion, cinnabar.
verminder, (–), diminish, decrease, essen, reduce, (numbers, price), lower, cut down (expenses), fall off (of numbers), slacken (speed); abate (of wind), remit (of pain).
vermindering, (-e, -s), diminution, decrease, reduction, drop (in price, temperature); cut (in salary, price).
vermink, (-te), a. mutilated, maimed, crippled; garbled (statement, facts).
vermink, (–), mutilate, maim, cripple; garble (statement).
verminking, mutilation; crippling.
vermis, (-te), a. missing.
vermis, (–), miss; **– word**, be missing.
vermiste, (-s), missing person.
vermits, whereas, since.
vermoë, (-ns), power; capacity; ability; riches, wealth, fortune; **na die beste van my –**, to the best of my ability.
vermoed, (–), suspect; presume, suppose, surmise.
vermoede, (-ns), suspicion; presumption, supposition, surmise.
vermoedelik, (-e), a. probable, presumptive, presumable.

vermoedelik, adv. probably, presumably.
vermoei, (-), tire, fatigue, weary.
vermoeid, (-e), tired, fatigued, weary.
vermoeidheid, fatigue, weariness.
vermoeiend, (-e), tiring, fatiguing; wearisome, tedious, tiresome.
vermoeienis, (-se), fatigue, weariness; languor, lassitude.
vermoeiing, fatigue, weariness.
vermoënd, (-e), rich, wealthy.
vermolm, (-de), a. mouldered.
vermolm, (-), moulder (away), rot.
vermolming, mouldering, dry rot.
vermom, (-de), a. disguised, masked.
vermom, (-), disguise, mask.
vermomming, disguise.
vermoor, (-), murder, kill.
vermoorde, (-s), murdered person.
vermoorder, (-s), murderer.
vermoording, murder(ing).
vermors, (-), waste.
vermorsel, (-), crush, pulverize, smash.
vermorseling, crushing, pulverization.
vermorsing, waste, squandering.
vermuf, (-te), a. musty, mouldy.
vermuf, (-), become (get) musty (mouldy).
vermuftheid, mustiness, mouldiness.
vermurf, -murwe, soften, become soft; make soft, molify.
vermurwing, softening, mollification.
vermy, (-), avoid, shun; steer clear of.
vermy(d)baar, (-bare), avoidable.
vermydelik, (-e), vide **vermy(d)baar**.
vermyding, avoiding, avoidance, evasion.
vernaam, (-name), a. important; prominent; distinguished; **die -ste punte**, the chief (main, principal) points; **die -ste kenmerk**, the outstanding characteristic.
vernaam, adv. especially, particularly.
vernaamheid, importance; prominence.
vernaamlik, especially, mainly, chiefly.
vernag, (-), pass (spend) the night.
verneder, (-), humble, humiliate, degrade, abase.
vernederend, (-e), humiliating.
vernedering, humiliation, mortification.
verneem, (-), hear, understand, learn; inquire (at the post-office); **na ons – kom hy nie**, we understand (hear) he is not coming; **– na**, inquire after.
verneembaar, (-bare), perceptible.
verneuk, (a), cheat, take in, diddle, do in the eye, swindle, defraud, trick, sell (person) a pup.
verneukbeentjie, funny-bone.
verneuker, (-s), cheat, swindler, fraud.
verneukery, swindle, fraud.
verniel, (-), destroy, ruin, wreck; ill-treat, overwork.
vernielagtig, (-e), destructive.
vernielbaar, (-bare), destructible.
vernielend, (-e), destructive.
vernieler, (-s), destroyer.
vernielery, destroying, destruction.
vernieling, destruction.
vernielingswerk, work of destruction.
vernielsiek, (-e), vide **vernielagtig**.
vernielsug, vandalism, destructiveness.
vernielsugtig, (-e), fond of destroying.
verniet, free (of charge), for nothing, gratis; in vain; **dis – om te argumenteer**, it is no use arguing; **dis nou net – of die kind wil luister**, do what you will (no matter what you do) the child refuses to obey.
vernietig, (-), destroy, wipe out; wreck out; annihilate; declare invalid, annul, reverse.

vernietigend, (-e), destructive; slashing, scathing; withering (look); crushing.
vernietigend, destruction, annihilation.
vernieu, vide **vernuwe**.
vernikkel, (-), nickel-plate.
vernis, n. varnish; veneer (fig.).
vernis, (-te), a. varnish; veneered.
vernis, (-), varnish; veneer (fig.).
vernoem, (-): **'n persoon –**, name a child after somebody.
vernou, (-), narrow; take in (dress).
vernouing, narrowing, contraction.
vern(ie)ubaar, (-bare), renewable.
vernuf, ingenuity, genius; wit.
vernuftig, (-e), ingenious; witty.
vernuftigheid, ingenuity.
vernuwe, vernieu, (a), renew; renovate.
vernuwing, renewal.
veronaangenaam, (-), make unpleasant.
veronagsaam, verontagsaam, (-), neglect (duty); slight (person), ignore, disregard.
veron(t)agsaming, neglect, disregard.
veronderstel (-), suppose; assume; **– dat . . .,** suppose (supposing); **ek – dit**, I suppose so.
veronderstelling, (-e, -s), supposition; **van die – uitgaan dat . . .**, assume that . . . , act on the assumption that . . .
verongeluk, be killed in an accident; be wrecked (train), meet with, disaster; be lost (of ship); perish (of people); fail, miscarry (of plan); **laat –**, wreck; **sig –**, kill oneself.
verongelyk, (-), wrong, do injustice.
verongelyking, wrong, injustice, injury.
veronika, veronica, speedwell.
veronreg, (-), vide **verongelyk**.
veronregting, vide **verongelyking**.
verontagsaam, vide **veronagsaam**.
verontheilig, (-), desecrate; profane.
verontheiliging, desecration; profanation.
verontreining, (-), pollute, defile, foul.
verontrus, (-), disturb, alarm, perturb.
verontrustend, (-e), disturbing.
verontrusting, alarm, perturbation.
verontskuldig, (-), excuse; **sig –,** excuse oneself, apologize.
verontskuldiging, (-e), apologetic.
verontskuldiging, (-e, -s), excuse; apology; **jou – e aanbied**, apologise, offer one's apologies.
verontwaardig, (-de), a. indignant.
verontwaardig, (-), make indignant.
verontwaardiging, indignation.
veroordeel, (-), condemn; sentence, convict; **tot die dood –**, sentence to death.
veroordeelde, (-s), condemned person.
veroordelaar, (-s), condemner.
veroordeling, condemnation; conviction.
veroorloof, (-de), a. allowed; permissible.
veroorloof, (-), permit, allow; **sig – om**, take the liberty to.
veroorlowing, permission, leave.
veroorsaak (-), cause, give rise to, occasion.
veroorsaking, bringing about, causing.
verootmoedig, (-), humiliate, humble.
verootmoediging, humiliation.
verorber, (-), eat up, dispatch, consume, put away.
verorden, (-), ordain, decree, order.
verordening, (-e, -s), regulation, order; rules; bylaw.
verordineer, (-), ordain, order.
verouder, (-), age, grow old; make older; become obsolete (of word).
verouder(d), (-de), obsolete (word), archaic (expression); discarded; exploded (theory); out of date, antiquated, old-fashioned.

verouderheid, obsoleteness.
veroudering, senescence; obsolescence.
verower, (-), conquer, capture.
veroweraar, (-s), conqueror.
verowering, (-e, -s), conquest.
verpag, (-), lease, put out to lease.
verpagter, (-s), lessor.
verpagting, leasing; farming out.
verpak, (-), pack; repack.
verpakker, (-s), packer.
verpakking, packing.
verpand, (-), pawn (one's furniture); mortgage (house); pledge (one's life).
verpander, (-s), pawner; pledger.
verpersoonlik, (-), personify.
verpersoonliking, personification.
verpes, (-), infect; contaminate, corrupt, poison; iemand se lewe –, plague (pester) a person.
verpestend, (-e), noxious, pernicious.
verpester, (-s), corrupter; vide **verpes.**
verpesting, infection; contamination.
verplaas, (-), shift, move, remove; transfer to another (post); sig in iemand se toestand –, put (imagine, place) yourself in another's position.
verplaasbaar, (-bare), removable.
verplant, (-), plant out, transplant.
verplantbaar, (-bare), transplantable.
verplanting, transplanting.
verplasing, shifting; displacement (of water); transfer.
verpleeg, **verpleë**, (-), nurse; care for.
verpleeginrigting, nursing-home.
verpleegster, (-s), nurse.
verpleër, **verpleger**, (-s), (male) nurse; assistant (attendant) in hospital.
verpleging, nursing.
verplegingsgestig, nursing-home.
verplegingsinrigting, vide **verpleeg-.**
verpletter, (-), crush, shatter, smash.
verpletterend, (-e), crushing (defeat); smashing; overwhelming; shattering.
verplettering, crushing, smashing.
verplig, (-te), a. obliged, compelled; compulsory (subject), obligatory; dit aan iemand – wees, owe it to a person; sedelik –, morally bound.
verplig, (-), force, compel, oblige; sig –, pledge (bind) oneself.
verpligtend, (-e), compulsory.
verpligting, (-e, -s), obligation; jou –e nakom, meet one's obligations; meet one's liabilities; die – rus op jou om dit te doen, it is incumbent (up)on you (it is your duty) to do it.
verpluk, (-te), dishevelled, untidy, unkempt.
verposing, relaxation, recreation, rest.
verpot, (-te), a. feeble, stunted, poor.
verpraat, (-), talk away (time); sig –, give oneself (the show) away, drop a brick; ons het dit weer –, talking about other things made us forget about it.
verraad, treason, treachery, betrayal; – pleeg, commit treason.
verraai, (-), betray; reveal.
verraaier, (-s), traitor, betrayer.
verraaiery, treachery, treason.
verraderlik, (-e), treacherous, traitorous, perfidious.
verraderlikheid, treacherousness.
verras, (-), surprise, take unawares (by surprise).
verrassend, (-e), surprising, startling.
verrassing, (-e, -s), surprise.
verre, far; – sy dit van my, far be it from me; op – na nie, not nearly.

verregaand, (-e), extreme (folly), outrageous, (almost) unheard of.
verreikend, (-e), far-reaching.
verrek, (-), strain (muscle), wrench (ankle), sprain (wrist); sig –, strain oneself.
verreken, (-), clear (cheques); sig –, miscalculate, calculate wrongly.
verrekenkantoor, clearing-house.
verrekking, straining, sprain(ing).
verreweg, far and away, by far.
verrig, (-), do, perform, execute; work.
verrigting, (-e, -s), execution, performance; transaction; –e, proceedings, transactions; meeting, function.
verrimpel, (-de), wrinkled.
verrinnewasie, **verruïnasie**, ruin(ation).
verrinneweer, **verruïneer**, (-), ruin.
verroer, (-), stir, move.
verroes, (-), rust, grow rusty.
verroesting, rustiness, rust(ing).
verrot, (-te), a. rotten, decayed, putrid.
verrot, (-), decay, putrefy.
verrotting, decay, putrefaction, rot(ting).
verruil, (-), exchange, barter.
verruiling, exchange, barter.
verruim, (-), widen, enlarge; broaden.
verruiming, widening, broadening.
verruïneer, vide **verrinneweer.**
verruk, (-te), a. enraptured, enchanted, rapturous.
verruk, (-), enrapture, enchant, ravish.
verrukkend, (-e), enchanting.
verrukking, rapture, ecstasy, enchantment.
verruklik, (-e), enchanting, charming, delightful, ravishing.
verryk, (-), enrich.
verryking, enrichment, enriching.
verrys, (-), rise; spring up, come into being.
verrysenis, resurrection.
vers, (-e), 1. verse; stanza; poem.
vers, (-e), 2. heifer.
versaag, (-), despair, flinch.
versaag, (-de), faint-hearted.
versaagdheid, faint-heartedness.
versaak, (-), forsake, desert, renouce (the world); neglect (duty).
versadig, (-), satisfy (appetite); saturate (chem.); sig –, satisfy one's appetite.
versadigbaar, (-bare), satiable; saturable.
versadigdheid, satiety; saturation.
versadiging, satiation; saturation.
versag, (-), make soft(er), soften (heart); ease, relieve (pain), alleviate, mitigate (grief); modify (expression).
versagtend, (-e), softening; alleviating, mitigating; –e middel, palliative; –e omstandighede, extenuating circumstances; –e uitdrukking, euphemism.
versagting, softening; alleviation, mitigation; euphemism; vide **versag.**
versaker, (-s), forsaker; renouncer.
versaking, forsaking, deserting; neglect (of duty); renouncing, renunciation.
versamel, (-), gather; collect (books, stamps, courage); assemble; amass, accumulate (riches); compile (volume of stories); store up.
versamelaar, (-s), collector; compiler.
versameling, (-e, -s), collecting (of books, stamps); gathering, collection, assemblage compiling; compilation.
versamelnaam, collective noun.
versamelplaas, -plek, meeting-place.
versand, (-), silt up.
versanding, silting up.
versbou, metrical construction.

versebundel, book of poetry (poems).
verseël, (-), seal (up).
verseëling, sealing.
verseg, (-), refuse point-blank.
verseil: – raak onder, get mixed up with, fall in with.
verseker, (-de), a. insured; assured; – wees van, be sure of.
verseker, adv. for sure (certain).
verseker, (-), assure; ensure, make certain; insure (life, etc.).
versekeraar, (-s), insurer; underwriter.
versekerbaar, (-bare), insurable.
versekerde, (-s), assured, insured.
versekerdheid, assurance.
versekering, assurance; insurance, assurance (life).
versekeringskantoor, insurance-office.
versekeringsmaatskappy, insurance-company.
versekeringspolis, insurance-policy.
versekeringspremie, insurance-premium.
versekeringswet, insurance-act.
versend, (-), send off, dispatch, consign (goods), transmit, forward.
versender, (-s), sender, consignor.
versending, (-e, -s), sending, dispatch; consignment, shipment (of goods).
versendingskoste, forwarding-charges.
versene: die – teen die prikkels slaan, kick against the pricks.
verseng, (-), singe, scorch.
verset, n. opposition, resistance; **lydelike** –, passive resistance; **in – kom teen**, oppose, resist; rebel (revolt, rise) against.
verset, (-): sig –, resist, offer resistance; **sig – teen**, resist, oppose; strive against (difficulty); bear up against (sorrow).
versie, (-s), 1. little poem (verse).
versie, (-s), 2. heifer.
vèrsiende, long-sighted, presbyopic.
vèrsiende, long-sightedness.
versier, (-), decorate, adorn; beautify; embellish (narrative); trim (dress).
versierder, (-s), decorator; trimmer.
versiering, (-e, -s), decoration, ornament, adornment; embellishment; trimming.
versieringskuns, decorative art.
versiersel, (-s), ornament.
versiersuiker, icing-sugar.
versifikasie, versification.
versigtig, (-e), careful, cautious.
versigtigheid, care, caution, prudence; – **is die moeder der (van die) wysheid**, prudence is the mother of wisdom; safety first!
versigtigheidshalwe, for safety's sake.
versigtigheidsmaatreël, precautionary measure.
versilwer, (-de), a. silver-plated.
versilwer, (-), silver.
versin, (-), fabricate, invent, concoct.
versink, (-), 1. sink; **in gedagtes –**, lost (absorbed) in thought.
versinsel, (-s), fabrication, concoction.
versit, (-), 1. move, shift; vide **verset**; **berge –**, remove mountains.
versit, (-), 2. shift (move) (up).
verskaal, (-de), a. flat, stale.
verskaal, (-), go stale (flat).
verskaf, (-), provide; furnish, give (an opportunity, pleasure), supply, afford.
verskaffer, (-s), provider.
verskaffing, provision, furnishing.
verskalf, heifer-calf.
verskalk, (-), outmanoeuvre, outwit.
verskans, (-), entrench.

verskansing, (-e, -s), entrenchment, rampart, earthwork, bulwark.
verskeep, (-), ship; tranship.
verskeidenheid, variety, diversity.
verskeidenheidskonsert, variety concert.
verskeie, several; different, various.
verskeper, (-s), shipper.
verskeping, shipment, shipping.
verskerp, (-), sharpen; become sharp(er); intensify, accentuate.
verskerping, sharpening, accentuation.
verskeur, (-de), a. torn.
verskeur, (-), tear (to pieces), tear up; devour, mangle; rend (heart).
verskeurdheid, laceration; affliction.
verskeurend, (-e), violent (pain); **-e diere**, beasts of prey.
verskiet, n. distance; perspective; view; prospect; **in die –**, in the distance; awaiting (in store for) you.
verskiet, (-), spend (cartridges); change colour, fade; shoot (of star); stop suddenly (of pain), shift (of pain).
verskil, **(le)**, n. difference; discrepancy; dispute; **die – deel**, split the difference.
verskil, (-), differ, vary.
verskillend, (-e), different, various; several; – **van**, different from (to).
verskilpunt, point of difference; controversial point.
verskimmel, (-de), a. mouldy; timid, shy.
verskimmel, (-), become mouldy.
verskoning, (-e, -s), change of clothes (linen); excuse; – **vra**, beg (person's) pardon, apologize.
verskoon, (-), change clothes (linen); excuse.
verskoonbaar, (-bare), pardonable.
verskoppeling, (-e), outcast.
verskrik, (-te), a. frightened, startled.
verskrik, (-), frighten, startle, terrify.
verskrikking, (-e, -s), terror, horror.
verskriklik, (-e), terrible, dreadful, horrible, frightful, awful.
verskriklikheid, terribleness.
verskroei, (-), scorch, singe.
verskroeiend, (-e), scorching, parching.
verskroeiing, scorching, parching.
verskrompel, (-de), a. shrivelled (up), withered, wrinkled, wizened.
verskrompel, (-), shrivel (up), wrinkle, wither, shrink.
verskuif, **-skuiwe**, (-), shift, (re)move, shove along (away), slide; postpone.
verskuifbaar, (-bare), removable.
verskuil, (-), conceal, hide.
verskuiwe, vide **verskuif**.
verskuiwing, shifting, sliding; fault (geology); postponement.
verskuldig, (-de), due, indebted; **met –de hoogagting**, yours respectfully; **met –de eerbied**, with due respect; yours respectfully; **baie aan iemand – wees**, owe a person much, be greatly indebted to a person.
verskuns, (art of) poetry.
verskyn, (-), appear; put in appearance; attend; be published.
verskyning, (-e, -s), appearance; apparition, ghost; publication (of book); **sy – maak**, put in an appearance; appear.
verskynsel, (-s), phenomenon.
verslaaf, (-de), a.: – **aan**, enslaved to, addicted to.
verslaaf, **-slawe**, (-), enslave; **sig – aan**, become addicted (a slave) to.
verslaafde, addict.
verslaafdheid, addiction, enslavement.
verslaan, (-de), a. beaten; stale.

verslaan, (-), beat, defeat; quench (thirst); go (turn) flat (stale); report.
verslaap, (-), sleep away; **sig -**, oversleep oneself.
verslae, dismayed, dumbfounded.
verslaen(t)heid, dismay, consternation.
verslag, (-slae), report, account; - **uitbring**, report.
verslaggewer, reporter.
verslap, (-), relax; slacken (of rope, trade); become weaker; flag (of interest), diminish.
verslapping, slackening, relaxation.
versleg, (-), make (grow) worse; degenerate; degrade; become feeble.
verslegting, deterioration, degeneration; degradation.
verslete, vide **verslyt**, a.
verslind(e), (-), devour (food, prey, book); swallow up, gorge; consume.
verslons, (-te), a. slovenly, untidy.
verslons, (-), ruin spoil.
versluk, (-), **sig -**, swallow the wrong way, choke.
verslyt, (-e), a. threadbare (clothes), worn (out, away, off), the worse for wear; hackneyed (expression), trite.
verslyt, (-), wear out (away, off); become threadbare; while away.
versmaad, -smaai, (-), scorn, despise, treat with contempt, be scornful of.
versmaat, metre.
versmade, scorned, despised.
versmading, scorn, disdain(ing).
versmag, (-), languish; waste (pine) away, **van dors -**, be parched with thirst; **van honger -**, starve.
versmagting, languishing, wasting.
versmal, (-), narrow, become narrower.
versmelt, (-), melt; smelt (ore); fuse; melt down (away); blend (colours).
versmoor, (-), smother, suffocate.
versmoring, smothering, suffocation.
versnapering, (-e, -s), titbit, delicacy, dainty, choice morsel.
versnel, (-), accelerate, quicken.
versneller, (-s), accelerator.
versnelling, (-e, -s), acceleration, quickening; gear; speed (of bicycle); rapids (in river); **hoogste -**, top gear.
versnellingsbak, -kas, gear-box.
versnipper, (-), cut into pieces (bits); fritter away; split; disintegrate.
versnippering, cutting up; frittering away.
versny, (-), cut to pieces; spoil in cutting.
versoek, (-e), n. request; petition; **'n - inwillig**, grant a request; **op -**, by (special) request.
versoek, (-), request; ask, invite; tempt; - **om**, ask for, request.
versoeker, (-s), tempter; petitioner.
versoeking, (-e, -s), temptation; **in - bring**, tempt; **in die - kom**, be (feel) tempted.
versoekskrif, petition.
versoen, (-), reconcile, conciliate; pacify, placate; - **raak**, become reconciled; - **met**, reconcile with; **sig met iets -**, become reconciled to something.
versoenbaar, (-bare), reconcilable.
versoendag, day of reconciliation; **Groot V-**, Day of Atonement.
versoendeksel, mercy-seat.
versoening, reconciliation, reconcilement.
versoeningsbloed, blood of atonement.
versoeningsbok, scapegoat.
versoeningsdood, expiatory death.
versoeningsoffer, sin-offering.
versoenlik, (-e), placable.

versoet, (-), sweeten.
versondig, (-), irritate, annoy, bother.
versonke, vide **versink**.
versool, (-), new-sole, resole; retread; - **de band**, retread.
versôre, sorg, (-), care for, attend to, provide for, look after, mind.
versorger, (-s), provider.
versorging, care, provision.
versot: - **op**, keen on, fond of; infatuated with (a girl).
versotheid, keenness; infatuation.
verspan, (-), change (oxen), change the position (of horse) in the team.
verspeel, (-), gamble away (a fortune); **die kans -**, lose the chance.
versper, (-), obstruct, bar, block.
versperring, (-e, -s), obstruction; barricade.
verspied, (-), scout, spy out.
verspieder, (-s), spy, scout.
verspieding, spying, scouting, espionage.
verspil, (-), waste, squander, dissipate.
verspilling, waste, squandering.
versplinter, (-), splinter, shiver.
verspoel, (-), wash away.
verspoeling, (-e, -s), washaway.
verspot, (-te), silly, foolish, ridiculous.
verspreek, (-): **sig -**, make a slip of the tongue; drop a brick, commit oneself, put one's foot into it.
versprei, (-), spread (rumour, news), diffuse (light heat); scatter (seed); propagate; disseminate.
versprei(d), (-de), a. spread; scattered; spares (population); dispersed.
verspreiding, spreading, scattering; distribution; dissemination; diffusion.
verspreking, slip of the tongue.
verspring, n. long jump.
verspring, (verge-), jump far; do the long jump.
verspring, (-), jump, spring; shift, move, leap; sprain (foot).
versreël, line of poetry.
verssoort, kind of poetry.
verstaan, (-), understand; **te - gee**, give to understand; **verkeerd -**, misunderstand; **rede -**, listen to reason; **wel te -**, that is to say.
verstaanbaar, (-bare), intelligible, comprehensible; **sig - maak**, make oneself understood.
verstaanbaarheid, intelligibility.
verstaander, (-s), one who understands; **'n goeie - het 'n halwe woord nodig**, a word to the wise is enough.
verstand, understanding; intelligence, intellect, mind, sense; **gesonde -**, common sense; **jou - verloor, van jou - af raak**, lose one's reason (wits), go off one's head; **- hê van iets**, know about something, have a knowledge of something; **jou - gebruik**, use your brains'; **my - staan stil, dit gaan bo my -, dit gaan my - te bowe**, it passes my understanding; **ek het my (ou) - af gepraat**, I talked until I was blue in the face; **jou -!**, you're mad!; **iemand iets aan die - bring**, make a person understand something; **by jou volle -**, in possession of all one's faculties, in one's senses, sane; **nie by jou volle - nie**, not sane, off one's head; **loop in (na) jou -!**, go to blazes, go to the devil.
verstandelik, (-e), intellectual.
verstandelikheid, intellectuality.
verstandeloos, (-lose), senseless.
verstandeloosheid, senselessness.
verstandhouding, understanding.
verstandig, (-e), a. sensible, wise, reasonable; intelligent.
verstandig, adv. sensibility, wisely.

verstandigheid, good sense.
verstandskies, wisdom-tooth.
verstandsmeting; measurement of the intellect (intelligence).
verstandsontwikkeling, intellectual development.
verstandstoets, intelligence-test.
verstar, (-de), a. inflexible, rigid.
verstar, (-), make rigid, stiffen.
versteek, (-), conceal, hide.
versteek, (-), 2. pin (peg) differently, shift (change) the peg(s).
versteen, (-de), a. petrified; fossil (fossilized); 'n -de hart hê, have heart of stone, be hardhearted.
versteen, (-), petrify; harden.
verstek, 1. default; by -, by default.
verstek, 2. mitre (carpentry).
verstekeling, (-e), stowaway.
verstekhaak, mitre square.
verstel, (-), (re)adjust; change gears, lever(s); mend, repair (clothes).
verstelbaar, (-bare), adjustable.
verstel(d), dumbfounded, nonplussed.
verstelwerk, mending.
verstening, (-e, -s), petrifaction; fossil.
versterf, n. death; by -, intestate.
versterf, -sterwe, die.
versterfreg, right of succession.
versterk, (-), strengthen; invigorate; fortify; reinforce (fortress, army); amplify (wireless); intensify (sound).
versterkend, (-e), strengthening; **-e middel**, restorative, tonic.
versterking, (-e, -s), strengthening; reinforcement; fortification (mil.).
versterkingsmiddel, restorative, tonic.
versterkingswerke, fortifications.
versterwing, death; mortification.
versteur, vide **verstoor**.
versteuring, vide **verstoring**.
verstik, (-), stifle, suffocate, choke.
verstikkend, (-e), stifling, suffocating.
verstikking, suffocation, asphyxia.
verstok, (-te), hardened (sinner), confirmed (gambler), inveterate.
verstoke: - van, deprived of.
verstoktheid, obduracy.
verstom, (-de), a. speechless, dumbfounded.
verstom, (-), render speechless, strike dumb; become speechless.
verstomp, (-), blunt, dull, deaden.
verstomping, blunting, dulling.
verstoor, -steur, (-), disturb, intrude upon (person, privacy), annoy, vex.
verstoor(d), -steur(d), (-de), a. disturbed; annoyed, vexed.
verstoorder, -steurder, (-s), disturber.
verstoordheid, -steurdheid, crossness.
verstoot, (-), cast off; repudiate; disown (child); ostracise.
verstop, (-te), a. stopped up; clogged, choked up; plugged; - **raak**, become clogged (blocked up); become constipated.
verstop, (-), stop (up); choke up, clog; plug; conceal, hide.
verstopping, obstruction, choking (up); constipation, costiveness.
verstoptheid, constipation, costiveness.
verstoring, -steuring, disturbance.
verstoteling, (-e), outcast, pariah.
verstout, (-), embolden; **sig -**, make bold.
verstrak, (-), become tense; set.
verstram, (-), make rigid, stiffen.
verstrek, (-), furnish, supply, provide, give (information).

verstreke, expired, elapsed.
verstrekkend, (-e), far-reaching.
verstrik, (-), trap, ensnare, entangle.
verstrooi, (-), scatter, disperse.
verstrooi(d), (-de), dispersed, scattered; absentminded.
verstrooidheid, absent-mindedness.
verstrooiing, scattering, dispersion; diversion; **die - van die Jode**, the Dispersion.
verstryk, (-), elapse, expire.
verstuif, -stuiwe, (-), pulverize; be scattered, be blown away, drift, shift.
verstuit, (-), sprain (wrist, ankle).
verstuiwing, scattering, dispersion, atomization; shifting, drifting.
verstyf, -stywe, (-), stiffen; grow numb.
verstywing, stiffening; benumbing.
versuf, (-te), a. dull; dazed; doting.
versuf, (-), grow (make) stupid (dull).
versuftheid, stupor, stupefaction, dotage.
versugting, (-e, -s), sigh.
versuiker, (-), saccharify; sugar (fig.).
versuikering, saccharification; sugaring.
versuim, n. omission; neglect; **sonder -**, without stopping; without delay.
versuim, (-), neglect; miss (chance); fail (to do); stop; stay, delay, wait.
versuip, (-), drown; be drowned; booze away (a fortune), soak to death.
versukkel(d), (-de), fagged (worn) out.
versuur, (-), sour (lit. & fig.); turn (become) sour; acidify.
versuur(d), (-de), a. soured.
versvoet, metrical foot.
verswaar, (-), make heavier; aggravate.
verswak, (-), weaken (constitution, eyes, heart), grow (become) weaker; grow dim (faint); enfeeble; enervate.
verswakking, weakening, debilitation.
verswaring, aggravation.
versweer, (-), fester, ulcerate.
verswelg, (-), swallow up.
verswering, (-e -s), festering, ulceration, suppuration.
verswik, (-), sprain.
verswye, -swyg, keep a secret, keep back, suppress (news).
verswyging, suppression, concealment.
vertaal, (-), translate.
vertaalbaar, (-bare), translatable.
vertaaloefening, exercise in translation.
vertaalreg, right of translation.
vertaalwerk, translation.
vertak, (-), branch out, ramify.
vertakking, (-e, -s), branching; ramification.
vertaler, (-s), translator.
vertaling, (-e, -s), translation.
verte, distance; **in die -**, in the distance; **uit die -**, from a distance, from afar; **nie in die verste - nie**, not at all, not in the least.
verteder, (-), soften (heart).
verteenwoordig, (-), represent.
verteenwoordigend, (-e) representative.
verteenwoordiger, (-s), representative.
verteenwoordiging, representation.
verteer, (-), consume, use up; spend; digest (food); waste away.
verteerbaar, (-bare), digestible.
verteerbaarheid, digestibility.
vertel, (-), tell, relate, narrate; **dit laat ek my nie - nie**, I refuse to believe that, you can tell that to the marines.
vertelkuns, art of story-telling.
verteller, (-s), narrator; story-teller.
vertelling, (-e, -s), story, narrative, tale.

vertelsel, (-s), story.
vertering, consumption; digestion.
vertienvoudig, (-), decuple.
vertikaal, (-kale), n. perpendicular.
vertikaal, (-kale), a. vertical.
vertikaalstyg-vliegtuig, vertical take-off plane.
vertin, (-), (coat with) tin.
vertinsel, tinning.
vertoef, -toewe, (-), stay, sojourn, wait, linger, tarry.
vertolk, (-), interpret; **die gevoelens -,** voice the feelings.
vertolker, (-s), interpreter; exponent.
vertolking, (-e, -s), interpretation; rendering; voicing (of feelings).
vertoning, (-e, -s), show, exhibition; performance; **'n treurige -,** a sorry sight (spectacle); **'n - maak,** present a fine sight, look pretty; give a good account of oneself.
vertoog, (-toë), representation, remonstrance, protest; expostulation.
vertoon, n. show, display; exhibition; presentation; **op -.betaalbaar,** payable at sight.
vertoon, (-), show; exhibit, display; screen, present; produce (play), perform.
vertoonbaar, (-bare), presentable.
vertoonkuns, showmanship.
vertraag, (-), delay; retard; slacken; **in jou ywer -,** relax one's efforts; **-de beweging,** retarted motion.
vertraging, delay; retardation.
vertrapping, trampling upon, treading underfoot.
vertree, (-), tread underfoot.
vertrek, (-ke), n. 1. room, apartment.
vertrek, n. 2. departure.
vertrek, (-), depart, leave, go away, set out, sail (of boat); distort, twist (face); shift, pull away; **nie 'n spier - nie,** not move a muscle.
vertrekking, distortion.
vertroebel, (-), make turbid (muddy); **die saak -,** confuse the issue.
vertroetel, (-), spoil, pamper.
vertroos, (-), comfort, solace, console.
vertroostend, (-e), comforting.
vertrooster, (-s), comforter.
vertroosting, comfort, consolation.
vertrou, (-), trust; **iemand -,** trust (put your trust in) a person; **- op,** rely on.
vertroubaar, (-bare), reliable.
vertroubaarheid, reliability.
vertroubaarheidstoets, reliability-trial.
vertroud, (-e), reliable, trustworthy, trusted, trusty; **- met,** familiar (conversant) with, at home in (a subject); **- raak met,** become conversant with.
vertroudheid, familiarity, conversance.
vertroue, confidence, faith, trust; **- hê in,** have confidence in; **- stel in,** have faith in, trust, put one's trust in; **jou - vestig op,** put one's faith in; **in - ,** in confidence, **iemand in jou - neem,** take a person into one's confidence.
vertrou(e)lik, (-e), a. confidential; intimate, private.
vertrou(e)lik, adv. confidentially.
vertrou(e)likheid, confidentiality.
vertroueling, (-e), confident, confidante.
vertroue-swendel, confidence trick.
vertwyfel, (-), despair.
vertwyfeld, (-e), desperate.
vertwyfeling, desperation, despair.
vervaag, (-), grow faint (dim).
vervaard, (-e), alarmed, frightened.
vervaardheid, alarm, fright.
vervaardig, (-), manufactured, make.
vervaardiger, (-s), manufacturer, maker.

vervaardiging, manufacture, making.
vervaarlik, (-e), awful, frightful.
vervaarlikheid, awfulness, hugeness.
verval, n. decline, decay; disrepair, dilapidation (of house); maturity (of bill); **die handel raak in -,** trade diminishes; **in - raak,** fall into decay.
verval, (-), decline, decay; become dilapidated, fall into disrepair; mature, become due (of bill); lapse (of life-policy); expire (of lease); fall. away; be dropped; **- in,** fall into; **in skulde -,** incur debt; **tot armoede -,** be reduced to poverty; **tot sonde -,** fall into sin.
vervaldag, -datum, day of maturity.
verval(le), a. decayed, dilapidated; tumbledown; expired (lease); lapsed (life-policy); due (bill); emaciated, decrepit, worn out.
vervallenheid, dilapidation; decrepitude.
vervals, (-), falsify; forgive (signature), counterfeit (coin); adulterate (wine).
vervalser, (-s), falsifier, forger.
vervalsing, falsification, forging.
vervang, (-), take the place of; supersede, replace; be substituted for; relieve; **deur 'n ander woord -,** substitute another word for.
vervanger, (-s), substitute.
vervanging, substitution, replacing.
vervat, (-), change one's grip; resume, begin (start) again (anew); continue; **- in,** included in.
verveel, (-), bore; tire.
verveer, (-), moult (of birds).
vervel, (-), change (cast) its skin, peel; slough (of snake).
vervelend, (-e), boring, wearisome, tiresome, tedious; **'n -e vent,** a. bore.
vervelendheid, tediousness, boredom.
vervelens: tot - (toe), ad nauseam, until one becomes bored (tired); **hy het tot - toe gepraat,** he talked until I could stand it no longer.
vervelig, (-e), vide **vervelend.**
verveligheid, vide **vervelendheid.**
verveling, boredom, tediousness, tedium.
vervelling, peeling, desquamation.
verversing, (-e, -s), refreshment.
verversingslokaal, -toonbank, canteen.
vervlaks, deuced, dashed, confoundedly, blooming; **-!,** hang it all, confound it!
vervlakste, confounded, blinking.
vervlieg, (-), fly (of time); vanish (of hope), evaporate.
vervloë, gone by.
vervloei, (-), flow away; run (of colour), fade; pass (fade) away.
vervloek, (-te), a. cursed; confounded.
vervloek, (-), curse, damn.
vervloeking, (-e, -s), curse, imprecation.
vervloeks, damned, blooming; **-!,** damn it!, damnation.
vervloekste, damned, confounded.
vervlugtig, (-), evaporate, volatilize.
vervlugtiging, volatilization.
vervoeg, (-), conjugate (verb).
vervoegbaar, (-bare), capable of being conjugated, conjugable.
vervoeging, (-e, -s), conjugation.
vervoer, n. transport, carriage, conveyance, transit.
vervoer, (-), convey, transport, carry.
vervoerbaar, (-bare), transportable.
vervoerder, (-s), transporter, conveyer.
vervoering, rapture, ecstacy, transport; **in - raak,** go into raptures.
vervoerkoste, carriage.
vervoermiddel, conveyance, vehicle.
vervoerwese, transport.

vervolg, n. continuation, sequel; **in die -**, in future, henceforth.
vervolg, (-), continue; persecute (the heretics); prosecute, institute legal proceedings against; haunt; plague, pester; purse (the enemy); **oortreders sal - word**, trespassers will be prosecuted; **word -**, to be continued.
vervolgbaar, (-bare), suable; actionable.
vervolgdeel, sequel.
vervolgens, further, then, thereupon.
vervolger, (-s), persecutor; prosecutor, pursuer.
vervolging, persecution; prosecution, pursuit.
vervolgingsgees, spirit of persecution.
vervolgingsreg, right of prosecution.
vervolgingswaansin, persecution-mania.
vervolglys, continuation-list.
vervolgstorie, -verhaal, serial (story).
vervolsug, spirit of persecution.
vervolmaak, (-), perfect.
vervolmaking, perfection.
vervorm, (-), transform, remodel.
vervorming, transformation.
vervreem, (-), estrange (person); alienate (property).
vervreem(d), (-de), a. estranged; alienated; **- raak**, become estranged.
vervreem(d)baar, (-bare), alienable.
vervreemding, estrangement, alienation.
vervroeg, (-), accelerate, fix at an earlier date (time, hour).
vervroeging, acceleration, anticipation.
vervrolik, (-), cheer up.
vervuil, (-de), a. filthy, dirty; rank; weedy; choked with weeds.
vervuil, (-), render (become, grow) filthy (dirty); grow rank (of plants, weeds); become choked with weeds, become weedy.
vervuiling, dirtiness, filthiness, weediness; becoming choked with weeds.
vervul, (-de), fulfilled.
vervul, (-), fill (position, a part); fulfil (promise, desire); do, discharge (duty); perform (task, duty); grant (wish); carry out; occupy (post); **- met die Heilige Gees**, filled with the Holy Ghost; **- wees van**, be obsessed by.
vervulling, fulfilment; realization; discharge (of duties).
vervyf, (-), convert (a try), goal.
vervyfskop, kick at goal.
verwaai, (-), blow away.
verwaai(d), (-de), a. blown about; dishevelled, ruffled, tousled.
verwaand, (-e), arrogant, bumptious, conceited, cocky, stuck-up.
verwaandheid, conceitedness; bumptiousness, arrogance.
verwaardig, (-): **sig - om**, condescend (deign) to.
verwaarloos, (-de), a. neglected; uncared-for.
verwaarloos, (-), neglect.
verwaarlosing, neglect.
verwag, (-te), expected.
verwag, (-), expect; look forward to; **ek - dat jy jou plig sal doen**, I expect you to do your duty.
verwagting, (-e, -s), expectation; **die - koester**, cherish (nourish) the hope, expect; **aan die - beantwoord**, come up to expectation; **bo -**, beyond expectation.
verwant, (-e), n. relative, relation.
verwant, (-e), a. related; kindred, allied; cognate (languages); congenial; akin.
verwantskap, relationship, kinship, affinity; congeniality.
verwar, (-), tangle, intertwine; confuse, mix up, muddle up; **met mekaar -**, mix up, confuse;

jy - hom met sy broer, you are mistaking him for his brother.
verwar(d), (-de), a. (en)tangled, intertwined; tousled, untidy; disarranged; confused (ideas), muddled; mixed up.
verwardheid, confusion.
verwarm, (-), warm heat.
verwarming, warming, heating.
verwarring, entanglement; confusion, muddle; perplexity, bewilderment; **in - bring**, confuse.
verwate, presumptuous, arrogant.
verwatenheid, presumption, arrogance.
verwater, (-), dilute (too much); water down (fig.).
verwater(d), (-de), a. watery, weak; watered down, watered.
verwatering, watering down.
verwe, vide **verf**, (ge-).
verwed, (-), bet; bet (gamble) away.
verweeklik, (-), make (become) effeminate enervate.
verweer, n. defence; resistance.
verweer, (-), 1. defend.
verweer, (-), 2. weather (of rocks), disintegrate.
verweer(d), (-de), a. disintegrated, weathered (rocks), weather-beaten.
verweerder, (-s), defendant; defender.
verweermiddel, means of defence.
verweerskrif, (written) defence.
verwek, (-), procreate, beget; generate; cause, raise (storm, laugh); stir up (mutiny); provoke (indignation); excite (feelings); rouse; produce (sensation); **tot toorn -**, rouse to anger.
verwekker, (-s), begetter; cause.
verwekking, procreation; stirring up.
verwelf, (-welwe), vault.
verwelk, (-te), a. faded, withered.
verwelk, (-), fade, wither, wilt.
verwelkbaar, (-bare), witherable.
verwelking, withering, fading, wilting.
verwelkom, (-), welcome, bid welcome.
verwelkoming, welcome.
verwen, (-), spoil (child); pamper.
verwen(d), (-de), spoilt.
verwens, (-), curse.
verwensing, (-e, -s), curse; execration.
verwer, (-s), painter; dyer.
verwerf, -werwe, (-), gain, win, achieve, obtain.
verwering, disintegration, weathering (of rocks); resistance; defence.
verwerk, (-), work up, elaborate, work out; assimilate (knowledge), digest.
verwerking, working up, elaboration, working out; assimilation, digestion.
verwerklik, (-), realize, materialize.
verwerp, (-), reject, repudiate; vote down; **die voorstel is -**, the motion was lost.
verwerping, rejection; repudiation.
verwerplik, (-e), objectionable, unacceptable, untenable, rejectable.
verwerwe, vide **verwerf**.
verwerwing, acquisition, gaining.
verwery, painting; dyeing, dye-works.
verwesenlik, (-), realize, actualize.
verwesenliking, realization.
verwikkel, (-), complicate; **- raak in**, become involved in.
verwikkeling, (-e, -s), complication.
verwilder, (-), run (grow) wild; chase (drive) away, frighten (scare) away.
verwilder(d), (-de), a. wild; thickly overgrown, neglected; unkempt.
verwildering, running (growing) wild; degeneration.
verwissel, (-), change; interchange, exchange;

commute; **die tydelike met die ewige –**, depart this life, pass away; **– van plek(ke)**, change places; **van klere –**, change one's clothes.
verwisselbaar, (-bare), interchangeable.
verwisseling, (-e, -s), change; interchange, exchange, alteration.
verwittig, (–), inform, notify.
verwittiging, notice, notification.
verwoed, (-e) fierce, furious, wild.
verwoedheid, fierceness, fury.
verwoes, (-te), a. destroyed; devastated.
verwoes, (–), destroy; devastate, ravage, lay waste (country); wreck, ruin.
verwoestend, (-e), destructive; ravaging, devastating.
verwoesting, destruction, havoc, devastation, ravage; **– aanrig**, work havoc.
verwond, (–), wound; hurt.
verwonder, (–), astonish, surprise; **dit – my nie**, I am not surprised; **sig – oor**, be astonished (surprised) at.
verwonder, (-de), a. surprised, astonished.
verwondering, surprise, astonishment, wonder.
verwonderlik, (-e), wonderful.
verwonding, wounding; wound, injury.
verword, (–), degenerate; change.
verwording, degeneration, deterioration.
verworpe, reprobate.
verworpeling, (-e), outcast, reprobate.
verworpenheid, depravity.
verwring, (–), twist, distort.
verwronge, twisted, distorted.
verwulf, vide verwelf.
verwurg, (-de), strangled, throttled.
verwurg, (–), strangle, throttle.
verwurging, strangulation, throttling.
verwyd, (–), widen; dilate; let out.
verwyder, (–), remove; get rid of, put out of the way; eliminate; estrange (people); **sig –**, go away, depart, with draw, leave, retire.
verwyder(d), (-de), a. remote (places), **– raak**, become estranged.
verwydering, removal; estrangement.
verwyding, widening; dilation (of eyes).
verwyf, (-de), a. effeminate.
verwyf, (–), make (become) effeminate.
verwyfdheid, effeminacy, effeminateness.
verwyl, n. delay.
verwyl, (–), stay; linger.
verwys, (–), refer; regelate.
verwysing, (-e, -s), reference; relegation.
verwyt, (-e), n. reproach, reproof, blame; **iemand 'n – van iets maak**, blame a person for something.
verwyt, (–), reproach, blame, upbraid.
verwytend, (-e), reproachful.
verwyting, reproach.
verydel, (–), frustrate, upset (plan), disappoint (hope), foil, ba(u)lk.
verydeling, frustration, upsetting.
vesel, (-s), fibre, filament, thread.
veselagtig, (-e), fibrous.
veselrig, (-e), fibrous; stringy, thready.
vesper, vesper, evensong.
Vestaals, (-e), Vestal.
vestibule, (-s), vestibule, hall, lobby.
vestig, (ge-), establish (business), foun-̈ settle; **jou hoop – op**, place one's hope on; **die oë – op**, fix the eyes upon; **die aandag – op**, draw (call) attention to.
vestiging, settlement, establishment.
vesting, (-e, -s), fortress, stronghold.
vestingbou, fortification.
vestingoorlog, siege-war.
vestingwerke fortifications.

Vesuvius, Vesuvius.
vet, (-te), n. fat; grease; **sagte –**, dripping, **harde –**, suet; **die – van die aarde**, the fat of the land; **so waar as –**, as sure as fate; **jou – sal braai**, your sins will find you out; **laat hom in sy eie – gaar kook**, let him stew in his own juice; **jy kan maar jou lyf – smeer**, there is a rod in pickle for you; **daar is geen – aan hom te smeer nie**, he is past (beyond) redemption.
vet, a. fat; fatty (food); greasy (hands); **– jare en maer jare**, fat years and lean years; **– druk**, fat (bold) type; **– grond**, rich (fertile, fat) soil.
vetagtig, (-e), fatty, fattish.
vetderm, rectum.
vete, (-s) feud, quarrel, enmity.
veter (-s), boot-lace; stay-lace.
veteraan, (-rane), veteran.
vetergat, eyelet.
veterinêr, (-e), veterinary.
vetheid, fatness; richness.
vetkers, tallow-candle, dip.
vetklier, sebaceous gland, fat-gland.
vetkoek, damper, dough-nut, "vetkoek".
veto, (-'s), veto.
vetoreg, right of veto.
vetplant, succulent.
vetpot, dripping-pot; grease-cup.
vetsak, fatty, roly-poly, fat-guts.
vetstert(skaap), fat-tailed sheep.
vetsug, obesity, fatty degeneration.
vetsuur, fatty acid.
vetterig, (-e), fat(ty); fattish; greasy.
vettigheid, fat(ness); **die – van die aarde**, the fat of the land.
via, via, by way of, through.
viaduk, (-te), viaduct.
vibreer, (ge-), vibrate, quaver.
vier, four; **onder – oë**, privately; **vier maal**, four times.
vier, (ge-), 1. celebrate (event); observe (Sabbath), keep.
vier, (ge-), 2. ease off, slack(en) (rope).
vierbenig, (-e), four-legged.
vierdaags, (-e), four days' of four days.
vierde, fourth; **ten –**, fourthly.
vierdelig, (-e), consisting of four parts, tetramerous, quadripartite.
vierdens, fourthly, in the fourth place.
vierderangs, (-e), fourth-rate.
vierdraads, (-e), four-ply.
vierdubbel(d), (-de), fourfold.
vierduims, four-inch.
vierendeel, (ge-), quarter.
vierhandig, (-e), four-handed.
vierhoek, quandrangle, quadrilateral.
vierhoekig, (-e), quadrangular.
viering, celebration; observance.
vierjaarliks, (-e), four-yearly.
vierjarige, (-e), four-year-old, of four years.
vierkant, (-e), n. square.
vierkant, a. square.
vierkant, adv. squarely; **– teen iets gekant wees**, be dead against something.
vierkantig, (-e), a. square.
vierkantig, adv. squarely; **sig – verset teen**, oppose with all one's might; **– weier**, flatly refuse.
vierkantsvergelyking, quadratic equation.
vierkantswortel, square root.
vierkleur, four-coloured flag, vierkleur.
vierkwartsmaat, quadruple time.
vierledig, (-e), consisting of four parts.
vierlettergrepig, (-e), four-syllabled.
vierling, (-e), quadruplets.
vierlobbig, (-e), four-lobed.

vierponder, four-pounder.
vierpotig, (-e), four-legged, tetrapod.
vierreëlig, (-e), of four lines, four-lined.
vierskaar, tribunal; **voor die – daag,** summon before the seat of judgment.
vierslag, four-stroke.
viersnarig, (-e), four-stringed.
vierspan, four-in-hand.
vierspel, foursome.
viersprong, cross-road(s); parting of the ways.
vierstemmig, (-e), four-part, for four voices.
viersydig, (-e), quadrilateral, four-sided.
viertal, four, tetrad.
vietalig, (-e), quadrilingual.
vieruur, four o'clock.
vieruurtjie, (-s), afternoon-lady.
viervingerig, (-e), four-fingered.
viervlak, tetrahedron.
viervlakkig, (-e), tetrahedral.
viervoetig, (-e), four-footed, quadruped.
viervors, tetrarch.
viervoud, (-e), quadruple.
viervoudig, (-e), fourfold, quadruple.
vies, a. & adv. annoyed, fed up, disgusted; dirty; offensive, nasty; foul; **iemand – maak,** put a person's back up, annoy a person; **– wees vir,** be cross (fed up) with; dislike; **– wees van,** be sick of.
vies, (ge-): **sig –,** be fed up.
vieserig, (-e), rather disgusted.
viesheid, annoyance, crossness.
vieslik, (-e), filthy, dirty, loathsome.
vieslikheid, filthiness, loathsomeness.
viets, smart, spruce, dapper.
Viking, (-s), Viking.
viktorie, victory.
vil, (ge-), fleece, strip, skin.
vilet, (-te), stock.
villa, (-s), villa.
vilt, felt.
vilthoed, felt hat.
vin, (-ne), fin, **nie 'n – verroer nie,** not stir a finger.
vind(e), (ge-), find; come across, meet with; consider, think, deem; **iets goed –,** approve of something; **– jy dit mooi?,** do you like it?, do you think it is pretty?; **hoe – jy dit?,** what do you think of it?; **baat – by,** benefit by; **genade – in die oë van,** find favour in the eyes of; **hulle kan dit nie met mekaar – nie,** they cannot hit it off (together); they do not see eye to eye.
vinder, (-s), finder.
vindikasie, vindication.
vinding, invention, discovery.
vindingryk, (-e), ingenious; resourceful.
vindingrykheid, ingeniousness.
vinger, (-s), finger (of hand, glove); digit; **nie 'n – verroer nie,** not stir a finger; **lang –s hê,** be light-fingered, have light fingers; **die –s verbrand,** burn one's fingers; **my –s (hande) jeuk om . . . ,** my fingers itch to . . . ; **gee hom die – (pinkie),** **dan neem hy die hele hand,** give him an inch, and he will take an ell; **iets deur die –s sien,** overlook (condone) something; **met die – na wys (wys na),** point one's finger at; **iemand om jou – draai,** twist a person round one's (little) finger; **iemand op sy –s tik,** rap a person over the knuckles.
vingerafdruk, finger-print.
vingeralleen, all by oneself, all alone.
vingerbakkie, finger-bowl, -glass.
vingerbeentjie, phalanx.
vingerbreedte, finger's breadth.
vingerdik, as thick as a finger.

vingerdoek(ie), doily, small napkin.
vingergewrig, finger-joint.
vingerglas, finger-bowl, -glass.
vingerhoed, thimble.
vingerhoedjie, fox-glove.
vinger(hoed)pol, Euphorbia spp.
vingerlit, finger-joint.
vingeroefening, five-finger exercise.
vingerplaat, finger-plate.
vingertaal, finger-language, -talk.
vingertop, finger-tip.
vingervormig, (-e), finger-shaped.
vingerwysing, (-e, -s), indication, warning.
vinhaai, dogfish.
vinjet, vignette.
vink, (-e), "fink", weaver(-bird) (S.A.); finch (Europe).
vinkel, (-s), fennel; **dis – en koljander, (die een is soos die ander),** it is six of the one and half a dozen of the other.
vinknes, fink's nest; finch's nest.
vinnig, (-e), fast, quick, swift, rapid; cutting, sharp; cross, angry.
vinnigheid, speed, quickness; sharpness.
vinvormig, (-e), fin-shaped.
viola, viola (mus.).
violet, (-te), n. violet.
violet, a. violet.
violetjie, (-s), violet.
violetkleurig, (-e), violet.
violier, (-e), stock(-gilliflower).
violis, (-te), violin-player.
violiste, (-s), (lady-)violinist.
violonsel, violoncello, 'cello.
viool, (viole), violin; **eerste (tweede) –,** first (second) violin; **eerste (tweede) – speel,** play first (second) fiddle.
vioolharpuis, colophony, violin-resin.
vioolkam, bridge (of violin).
vioolkis, violin-case.
vioolkonsert, violin-recital.
vioolsleutel, treble-clef.
vioolsnaar, violin-string.
vioolspel, violin-playing.
vioolspeler, -speelster, violinist.
vioolstuk, violin-solo; music for the violin.
viooltjie, (-s), violet; pansy; "viooltjie", groen –, wild hyacinth; **wit –,** chinkerinchee.
vir, for, to; **lag –,** laugh at; **– iemand sê,** tell a person; **dit lyk – my,** it seems to me; **een – een,** one by one; **ek – my,** I for one; **– sover ek weet,** as far as I know; **– eers (vereers),** for the present, for the time being; to begin with; **– altyd,** for ever, for all times; **eens – altyd,** once for all; **skaam – jou!,** shame on you, for shame.
Virgilius, vide **Vergilius.**
Virginië, Virginia.
viriel, (-e), virile.
viriliteit, virility.
virtuoos, (-tuose), virtuoso.
virtuositeit, virtuosity.
vis, (-se), n. fish; **– nog vlees,** neither fish, flesh, nor good red herring; **suip soos 'n –,** drink like a fish; **soos 'n – op droë (grond),** like a fish out of water; **gesond soos 'n –,** fit as a fiddle.
vis, (ge-), fish.
visaas, fish-bait.
visagtig, (-e), fishy, fish-like.
visafval, fish-offal.
visarend, osprey, sea-eagle, fishing-eagle.
visbank, fish-stall; fishing-ground(s).
vise-admiraal, vice-admiral.
viseer, (ge-), vise (a passport).
viseiers, spawn, roe.

**vise-konsul, vice-consul.
visentasie,** examination.
visenteer, (ge-), search, inspect.
visetend, (-e), fish-eating.
vise-voorsitter, vice-chairman.
visgereedskap, fishing-tackle.
visgereg, fish-course, -dish.
visgraat, fish-bone.
vishaak, fish-hook.
visie, (-s), vision.
visier, (-e, -s), 1. vizi(e)r.
visier, (-e, -s), 2. visor (of helmet); (back-)sight (of gun); **met hoë – skiet,** draw the long bow.
visioen, (-e), vision.
visioenêr, (-e), n. & a. visionary.
visitasie, visitation; search.
visite, (-s), call, visit; visitors.
visitekaartjie, visiting-card, calling-card.
viskar, fish-cart.
viskom, goldfish-bowl.
viskoper, fishmonger.
viskositeit, viscosity.
viskuit, vide **viseiers.**
vislym, fish-glue, isinglass.
vislyn, fishing-line.
vismark, fish-market.
vismes, fish-knife.
visnet, fishing-net.
visolie, fish-oil, cod-liver oil.
visreg, fishing-right.
visryk, (-e), abounding in fish.
visser, (-s), fisherman; fisher.
vissersdorp, fishing-village.
vissershawe, fishing-port.
visserskuit, fishing-boat.
visserslewe, fisherman's life.
vissersvloot, fishing-fleet.
vissersvolk, nation of fishermen.
vissersvrou, fisherman's wife.
vissery, (-e), fishery.
visskob, fish-scale.
vissmaak, fishy taste.
visteelt, fish-breeding, fish-farming.
vistraan, fish-oil.
visueel, (-suele), visual.
visum, (-s, visa), visa, visé.
visvalk, fish-hawk.
visvang, (visge-), fish; nod.
visvanger, (-s), fisherman; kingfisher.
visvangery, fishing.
visvangs, fishing.
visvrou, fish-woman, fishwife.
viswyf, fishwife.
viswywetaal, billingsgate.
vit, (ge-), find fault, cavil, carp; **– op,** find fault with, cavil at.
vitaal, (-tale), vital.
vitaliteit, vitality.
vitamine, (-s), vitamin.
vitrioel, vitriol.
vitrioelagtig, (-e), vitriolic.
vitsug, captiousness, censoriousness.
vitsugtig, (-e), captious, fault-finding.
vitter, (-s), fault-finder.
vitterig, (-e), fault-finding, captious.
vitterigheid, captiousness.
vittery, (-e), fault-finding.
viviseksie, vivisection.
vla, custard.
vlaag, (vlae), gust (of wind); shower (of rain); fit (of rage), paroxism; **by vlae,** by fits and starts.
Vlaams, (-e), Flemish.
Vlaamsgesind, (-e), pro-Flemish.
Vlaandere, Flanders.

vlag, (vlae), flag; colours; vane (of feather); **die wit – opsteek,** hoist the white flag; **die – stryk,** strike (lower) one's colours (the flag); **met – en wimpel,** with flying colours.
vlagdoek, bunting.
vlaggetjie, (-s), little flag; pennon.
vlaggie, vide **vlaggetjie.**
vlagsein, flag-signal; flag-signalling.
vlagskip, flag-ship.
vlagstok, flag-staff.
vlagswaaiery, flag-wagging, -waving.
vlagvertoon, showing the flag.
vlagvoerder, flag-ship; flag-officer.
vlak, (-ke), n. level (of sea); plane (geom.); face (geom.); surface, plain; flat (of the hand).
vlak, (–, -ke), a. shallow (water); flat; plane (geom.).
vlak, adv. flatly; **– by,** close (near) by; **iemand iets – in sy gesig sê,** tell a person something to his face; **– in die gesig raak,** strike (hit) full in the face; **– voor,** right in front of.
vlakhaas, Cape hare.
vlakheid, shallowness; flatness.
vlakte, (-s), plain; stretch.
vlaktemaat, square measure.
vlaktemeter, planimeter.
vlaktemeting, planimetry.
vlakvark, wart-hog.
vlakvoël(tjie), spike-heeled, lark.
vlam, (-me), n. flame; blaze; **sy ou –,** an old flame of his; **– vat,** catch fire; flare up; **in volle – staan,** be ablaze; **vuur en – wees,** be all in a flame, be on fire.
vlam, (ge-), flame, blaze; flash fire.
vlamblom, red-hot poker.
Vlaming, (-e), Fleming; **die –e,** the Flemish.
vlamkas, fire-box, combustion-chamber.
vlammend, (-e), flaming, blazing.
vlamwerper, flame-projector.
vlas, flax.
vlasagtig, (-e), flaxy, flaxen.
vlasbaard, flaxen beard; beardless boy.
vlasboerdery, -bou, flax-culture.
vlasbreker, flax-dresser.
vlashare, flaxen hair.
vlaskleurig, (-e), flaxen.
vlassaad, flax seed, linseed.
vlasspinnery, flax-mill; flax-spinning.
vlasvesel, flax-fibre.
vlees, flesh; meat (food); flesh, pulp (of fruit); **jou eie – en bloed,** one's own flesh and blood; **tot in die – (vleis) sny,** cut to the quick; **die weg van alle – gaan,** go the way of all flesh.
vlees-, vleiskleur, flesh-colour.
vleeslik, (-e), fleshly, carnal; **-e luste,** lusts of the flesh, carnal desires.
vlees, vleispot, flesh-pot; **die vleespotte van Egipte,** the flesh-pots of Egypt.
vlees-, vleiswond, flesh-wound.
vleeswording, incarnation.
vleg, (-te), n. tress, plait, braid.
vleg, (ge-), plait (hair, straw); twist (rope); wreathe (garland); make (basket); weave (mats); introduce (weave) details into story.
vlegel, (vleël), (-s), flail, shurl, gawk.
vlegsel, (-s), plait, tress, braid; pigtail.
vlegwerk, wicker-work; plaiting.
vlei, (-e), n. hollow, **shallow,** marsh, swamp, "vlei", (small) lake.
vlei, (ge-), flatter, wheedle, cajole.
vleiend, (-e), flattering.
vleier, (-s), flatterer, wheedler.
vleierig, (-e), flattering, coaxing.
vleiery, flattery, coaxing.
vleiloerie, coucal, rain-bird.

**vleinaam, **pet-name.
vleis, vlees, meat; **goed van** –, in good condition; **moenie die – braai voor jy die bok geskiet het nie,** don't count your chickens before they are hatched.
vleisafval, offal of meat.
vleisagtig, (-e), fleshy.
vleisblok, butcher's block.
vleisetend, (-e), carnivorous.
vleisekstrak, meat-extract.
vleisgereg, meat-dish, meat-course.
vleishandel, meat-trade.
vleiskas, meat-safe.
vleisloos, (-lose), meatless.
vleismark, meat-market.
vleismes, carving-knife; butcher's knife.
vleismeul(e), mincing-machine, mincer.
vleispastei, meat-pie.
vleispot, meat-pot; vide **vleespot.**
vleisskottel, meat-dish.
vleisso(e)p, meat-soup.
vleisvurk, meat-fork; carving-fork.
vleiswond, vide **vlees-.**
vleitaal, flattery, flattering words.
vlek, (-ge), n. stain, spot, smudge, smut (of soot); blot, blemish.
vlek, (ge-), 1. stain, soil, smudge.
vlek, (ge-), 2. flay, gut (fish).
vlek(ke)loos, (-lose), stainless, spotless.
vlek(ke)loosheid, spotlessness.
vlekkoors, spotted fever.
vlektifus, typhus fever.
vlekvry, stainless.
vlerk, (-e), wing.
vlerksleep, (vlerkge-), make love (to).
vlermuis, bat.
vlesig, (-e), fleshy; meaty; pulpy.
vleuel, (-s), wing (of bird, building, army); vane, blade (of wind-mill); leaf (of door); wingthree-quarter; **iemand onder jou –s neem,** take a person under one's wing.
vleueldeure, folding-doors.
vleuellam, winged, broken-winged.
vleuelpiano, grand piano.
vleuelskild, wing-case, wing-sheath.
vleuelslag, wing-beat, wing-stroke.
vleuelvormig, (-e), wing-shaped.
vleuelwydte, wing-spread.
vleug(ie), flicker.
vlie(g), (ge-), fly; **die tyd –,** time flies; **deur die strate –,** fly (tear, rush) through the streets; **in brand –, aan die brand –,** burst into flames.
vlied, (ge-), fly, flee.
vlieëbos, fly-bush; wild myrtle.
vlieëkas, meat-safe.
vlieënd, vliegend, (-e), flying; **in –e haas,** in a tearing hurry; **V–e Hollander,** Flying Dutchman; –**e katel,** flying bedstead; **met –e vaandel,** with flying colours; –**e piering,** flying saucer.
vlieënet, fly-net.
vlieënier, vide **vlieër,** 2.
vlieëpapier, fly-paper.
vlieëplak(kie), fly-swatter.
vlieër, (-s), 1. kite.
vlieër, (-s), 2. airman, aviator, flyer.
vlieëvanger, fly-catcher; sundew.
vlieëwaaier, fly-flap.
vlieg, (vlieë), n. fly; **hy sal nie 'n – kwaad doen nie,** he won't hurt a fly; **twee vlieë in een klap vang,** kill two birds with one stone; **dit lyk of 'n – oor sy neus (lewer) geloop het,** he is in a huff; **'n – in die salf,** a fly in the ointment; **iemand 'n – afvang,** steal a march on a person.
vlieg, (ge-), vide **vlie(g).**
vliegbaan, aerodrome.

vliegbyeenkoms, air-rally.
vliegdek, flight-deck.
vliegdekskip, aircraft-carrier.
vliegdiens, flying-service, air-service.
vliegend, vide **vlieënd.**
vliegenier, vide **vlieër,** 2.
vlieghawe, airport.
vliegie, (-s), little fly.
vliegkamp, aviation camp.
vliegklub, aeroclub.
vliegkorps, flying corps.
vliegkuns, aviation.
vliegmasjien, aeroplane, flying-machine.
vliegongeluk, flying-accident.
vliegskou, air display.
vliegsnelheid, flying-speed.
vliegterrein, aerodrome.
vliegtog, flying-expedition.
vliegtoggie, flip.
vliegtuig, aeroplane.
vliegtuigbestuurder, air-pilot.
vliegtuigbrandstof, air fuel.
vliegtuigloods, air-pilot; hanger, shed.
vliegveld, aerodrome.
vliegvertoning, air display (pageant).
vliegwedstryd, air-race.
vliegwese, flying, aviation.
vliegwerk: iets met kuns en – doen, do a thing by hook or by crook; do something with a lot of fuss (display).
vliegwiel, fly-wheel.
vlier(boom), elder.
vlierhout, elder-wood.
vliering, attic, garret.
vlies, (-e), fleece (of sheep); film (over eyes); membrane (in body); pellicle.
vliesagtig, (-e), fleecy; membranous.
vlies(er)ig, (-e), vide **vliesagtig.**
vliet, (-e), n. rivulet, brook.
vliet, (ge-), flow, run.
vlietend, (-e), flowing, running.
vlinder, (-s), butterfly.
vlinderagtig, (-e), butterfly-like.
Vlissingen, Flushing.
vloed, (-e), flood, flood-tide (opp. ebb), tide; river torrent, flow (of words).
vloeddeur, flood-gate.
vloedgolf, tidal wave.
vloei, (ge-), flow, run, stream; blot.
vloeibaar, (-bare), liquid, fluid.
vloeibaarheid, liquidity, fluidity.
vloeibaarwording, liquefaction.
vloeiend, (-e), flowing; liquid; fluent (style) speaker; smooth (style).
vloeiendheid, smoothness, fluency.
vloeiing, flowing, streaming.
vloeipapier, blotting-paper.
vloeispaat, fluorspar.
vloeistof, liquid.
vloek, (-e), n. curse, malediction; swear-word, oath, curse; **jou –!,** curse you!, you're a curse!
vloek, (ge-), swear, curse, damn; – **soos 'n matroos,** swear like a trooper; **iemand –,** curse (swear at) a person; **hierdie kleure – met (teen) mekaar,** these colours clash.
vloeker, (-s), swearer.
vloekwoord, oath, curse, swear-word.
vloer, (-e), floor, flooring; threshing-floor.
vloerbalk, flooring-beam, floor-joist.
vloerkleed, carpet, mat, rug.
vloerplank, flooring-board.
vloerseil, floor-cloth, linoleum.
vloerspyker, brad (nail).
vloersteen, paving-stone, flag-stone.
vlok, (-ke), flake (of snow); tuft.

vlokkig, (-e), flaky, flockly.
vloksy, floss-silk.
vlooi, (-e), flea; **van 'n - (muggie, vlieg) 'n olifant maak**, make mountains out of molehills.
vlooibyt, flea-bite.
vlooipoeier, flea-powder.
vloot, (vlote), fleet, navy.
vlootbasis, naval base.
vlootoefening, naval practice.
vlootvoog, commander of the fleet.
vlos, floss-silk.
vlossig, (-e), flossy.
vlossy, vide **vloksy**.
vlot, (-te), n. rath, float.
vlot, (-, -te), a. afloat, adrift; fluent (style), smooth, flowing; - **maak (kry)**, float (a vessel); - **pen**, a ready (facile) pen.
vlot, adv. fluently; - **gaan**, go without a hitch.
vlot, (ge-), float; go smoothly (swimmingly).
vlotbrug, floating bridge.
vlotheid, fluency, smoothness, readiness.
vlothout, drift-wood.
vlottend, (-e), floating; **-e bevolking**, floating population.
vlug, n. flight, escape; flight (of birds); wingspread; flock (of birds), covey (of partridges); **die - neem**, take to flight; **'n hoë - neem**, fly (soar) high; **in die - skiet**, shoot on the wing; **op die - ja**, put to flight; **op die - gaan (slaan)**, take to flight.
vlug, (-ge), a. fast, quick; swift, nimble (fingers, mind), agile; brisk (movement, pace); smart (boy, retort, walk); - **van begrip wees**, be quick-witted (smart), have quick wits.
vlug, adv. quick(ly), swiftly, briskly.
vlug, (ge-), flee, fly, take to flight.
vlughawe, port of refuge.
vlugheid, quickness, swiftness.
vlughou, volley.
vlugsand, quicksand.
vlugskrif, pamphlet.
vlugsout, sal volatile, smelling-salts, ammonium carbonate.
vlugteling, (-e), fugitive; refugee.
vlugtig, (-e), volatile (salts); cursory (glance); flying (visit); fleeting, transitory; hurried, rough (sketch); superficial; slight.
vly, (ge-), lay down, arrange; **sig -**, nestle (down, in(to), among).
vlym, (-e), lancet; fleam.
vlymend, (-e), acute, shooting, sharp; poignant (grief); scathing (sarcasm); stinging.
vlymskerp, (-, -e), razor-edged.
vlyt, diligence, assiduity, industry.
vlytig, (-e), diligent, assiduous, industrious, studious.
vlytigheid, vide **vlyt**.
vod, (-de, -dens), rag, tatter; **'n -jie papier**, a scrap of paper.
voddehandelaar, **-koper**, old-clothes-man, rag-dealer.
vodjie, vide **vod**.
voed, (ge-), feed; nourish (person, hatred); suckle, nurse (child); cherish, entertain (hope).
voeder, (-s), feeder.
voeding, feeding, nourishing; food, nourishment; nursing (child).
voedingskanaal, alimentary canal.
voedingsleer, dietetics, alimentology.
voedingsmiddel, article of food; **-s**, foodstuffs.
voedingsorgaan, nutritive organ.
voedingstof, nutritious substance.
voedingswaarde, nutritive value.

voedsaam, (-same), nutritious, nourishing, nutritive.
voedsaamheid, nutritiousness.
voedsel, food, nutrition, nourishment; - **vir die gees, geestelike -**, mental pabulum.
voedselskaarste, food-shortage.
voedster, (wet-)nurse, foster-mother.
voedsterkind, foster-child.
voeë, vide **voeg**, (ge-).
voeg, (voeë), n. joint, seam; **in dier -e**, in this (that) manner, accordingly; **in dier -e dat**, so that, so as to.
voeg, (voeë), (ge-), add; join, weld, seam, piece together; point (brickwork), flush; - **by**, add to; **sig - by**, join; **sig - na**, accede to, comply with.
voeg, (ge-), become, behave; **dit - jou nie om**, it does not become you to.
voege, vide **voeg**, n.
voeglik, (-e), becoming, proper, fit.
voegsaam, (-same), seemly, proper.
voegsaamheid, suitableness; seemliness.
voegwoord, conjunction.
voel, (ge-), feel; be aware (sensible) of, **wie nie wil hoor nie moet -**, he who will not be ruled by the rudder must be ruled by the rock; - **na**, fumble (feel) for; **ek - daar nie veel voor nie**, it does not appeal to me. I do not sympathise with (your sentiments).
voël, (-s), bird; **hulle is -s van een soort vere**, birds of a feather flock together; **een - in die hand is beter as tien in die lug**, a bird in the hand is worth two in the bush; **hy is soos 'n - op 'n tak**, he is as free as a bird on the wing; he is a bird of passage.
voelbaar, (-bare), perceptible; tangible.
voelbaarheid, perceptibility, tangibility.
voëlbek, beak, bill (of a bird).
voëleier, bird's egg.
voëlent, bird-lime; mistletoe.
voeler, (-s), feeler, tentacle, antenna.
voëlgesang, singing of birds.
voëlhandelaar, bird-fancier, bird-seller.
voelhoring, feeler, tentacle, antenna.
voeling, feeling; touch; - **hê met**, be in touch with; **uit - raak met**, lose touch with.
voëlkooi, **-kou(tjie)**, bird-cage.
voëlkunde, ornithology.
voëllewe, bird-life.
voëlliefhebber, bird-lover.
voëllym, bird-lime; mistletoe.
voëlmelk, star of Bethlehem.
voëlnes, bird's nest.
voëlopstopper, bird-stuffer; taxidermist.
voëlperspektief, bird's-eye view.
voëlspriet, feeler, antenna.
voëltjie, (-s), little bird, birdie; **ek het 'n - hoor fluit**, a little bird told me.
voëlverskrikker, scare-crow.
voëlvlug, bird's-eye view; **Kaapstad in - gesien**, a bird's-eye view of Cape Town.
voëlvry, outlawed; - **verklaar**, outlaw.
voëlvryverklaarde, outlaw.
voëlvryverklaring, outlawry.
voëlwiggelaar, ornithomancer.
voer, n. forage, fodder; (chicken-)food.
voer, (ge-), 1. feed (animals), fodder, forage; **vet -**, fatten.
voer, (ge-), 2. lead, conduct, take, bring, transport; bear (arms, name); make wage (war); carry on (conversation); wield (pen, sceptre); fly (a flag); **heerskappy -**, rule, hold sway (over); **die woord -**, speak.
voering, (-s), lining.
voeringstof, lining.

voerkuil, silo.
voerman, driver; wag(g)oner; feeder.
voersak, nose-bag; forage-bag.
voersis, printed calico.
voert!, away with you!, get (go) away!
voertaal, medium of instruction.
voertsek, -sik, vide **voert**.
voertuig, carriage, vehicle (lit. & fig.).
voet, (-e), foot (of human being, ladder, wall, mountain page, bed, stocking; metrical unit); bottom (-end), base; footing, foothold; **drie – nege duim**, three feet nine inches, **jou –!**, go away!, get along!, **–e kry**, vanish, disappear; **–e in die wind slaan**, take to one's heels; **– by stuk hou**, stick to one's guns, not budge; keep to the point; **vaste – kry**, get a firm footing; **met die verkeerde – uit die bed klim**, get out of bed with the left foot (leg) foremost, get out of bed on the wrong side; **met die –e vertrap**, trample underfoot, trample on; **onder die –e vertrap**, trample underfoot; **op blote –e**, barefoot; **op 'n groot – lewe**, live in grand style; **op gelyke –**, on equal terms, on an equal footing, on the same footing; **op goeie –**, on good terms; **op staande –**, at once, then and there, forthwith; **op vrye –e stel**, set at liberty, set free, liberate; **op die – volg**, tread upon the heels of; **te –**, on foot; **te – loop**, go on foot walk; **te – val**, throw oneself at the feet of; **sig uit die –e maak**, take to one's heels, run away; **geen rus vind vir die holte van jou – nie**, find no rest for the sole of your foot; **vir –**, step by step; **voor die –**, indiscriminately, without exception, without picking and choosing.
voetangel, man-trap; caltrop (mil.).
voetbad, foot-bath.
voetbal, football.
voetbalbroek, football-shorts.
voetbalskoene, football-boots.
voetbalspeler, football-player, footballer.
voetbalveld, football-ground.
voetbalwedstryd, football-match.
voetbank, foot-rest, foot-stool.
voetbreed: geen **– wyk nie**, not budge an inch.
voetbrug, foot-bridge.
voete-ent, voetenent, foot(-end).
voetganger, (-s), pedestrian; hopper, wingless locust; -s, infantry.
voetjie, (-s), little foot; **– vir –**, step by step, cautiously; at a snail's pace.
voetjie-voetjie: **– speel**, "tickle-toe", play "voetjie-voetjie".
voetjig, gout in the foot, podagra.
voetkleedjie, rug.
voetlig, footlights; **voor die – bring**, produce (a play), put on the stage.
voetlys, skirting-board.
voetoog: ou **–**, th bog(e)y-man.
voetpad, foot-path.
voetplaat, foot-plate.
voetplank, foot-board.
voetpunt, tip of the toes; nadir (astron.).
voetreis, journey on foot, walking-tour.
voetrem, foot-brake.
voetrus, foot-rest.
voetslaan, (voetge-), walk, foot it, slog.
voetslaner, slogger, hiker.
voetsoeker, squib, petrard.
voetsool, foot-sole.
voetspoor, foot-print, track; **die – volg van**, follow in the track of.
voetstap, footstep; **iemand se –pe druk**, follow in a person's footsteps.
voetstoof, foot-stove, foot-warmer.

voetstuk, pedestal base.
voetval, prostration; **voor iemand 'n – doen**, prostrate oneself before a person.
voetveeg, doormat; foot-cloth; **iemand se – wees**, be a person's slave (drudge, hack).
voetveër, foot-wiper.
voetvolk, foot-soldiers, infantry.
voetwassing, washing of the feet.
voetwortel, tarsus.
vog, (-te), liquid, fluid, moisture, damp.
voggehalte, percentage of moisture.
vogmaat, liquid-measure.
vogtig, (-e), damp; humid.
vogtigheid, dampness; moisture.
vogvry, damp-proof.
voile, voile.
vokaal, (-kale), n. vowel.
vokaal, a. vocal.
vokaalsisteem, vowel-system.
vokatief, (-tiewe), vocative.
vol, (-, -le), full (cup, stomach, name, moon, brother, speed, length), filled; **in die –le see**, in the open sea; **in –le bloei**, in full bloom; **'n –le uur**, a full (solid) hour; **in –le erns**, in all seriousness; **ten –le**, to the full, fully; (pay) in full; **– water**, full of water; **– skink**, fill to the brim; **– gooi**, fill (up); **– loop, maak**, fill; **– staan**, take up all the standing-room; pull (one's) weight.
volbek, full-mouthed (sheep); middle-aged.
volbloed, thoroughbred (animal); full-blooded.
volbloedig, (-e), plethoric.
volbloedigheid, plethora.
volbloedperd, thoroughbred horse.
volbring, fulfilment, accomplishment.
volbring, (–), fulfil, accomplish, perform, complete, execute, achieve.
voldaan, (-dane), n. receipt.
voldaan, (-dane), a. content, satisfied; paid.
voldaanheid, contentment, satisfaction.
voldoen, (–), satisfy, please, give satisfaction (to); **aan 'n belofte –**, fulfil a promise; **aan die verwagting –**, come up to expectation; **aan 'n wens, 'n versoek –**, comply with a wish, a request; **aan 'n bevel –**, obey a command; **aan die voorwaardes –**, satisfy the conditions.
voldoende, sufficient, adequate, enough.
voldoening, satisfaction; payment; atonement; **– vra**, demand satisfaction; **ter – aan**, in compliance with; **ter – van**, in settlement of.
voldonge: **– feit**, accomplished fact.
voleinder: V– **van die geloof**, Finisher of our Faith.
voleindig, (–), complete, finish.
voleindiging, completion, finishing.
volg(e), (ge-), follow; pursue (road, plan); **'n spoor –**, follow a track; follow up a clue; **klasse –**, attend classes; **daarop laat hy toe –**, he followed this up with the remark, thereupon he added; **soos –**, as follows; **slot –**, to be concluded (in our next issue).
volgeling, (-e), follower, supporter; adherent.
volgende, following, next.
volgenderwys, as follows.
volgens, according to; in accordance with; **–die jongste berigte**, according to the latest reports; **– die reëls**, in accordance with the rules; **– ons wet**, under (according to) our law.
volger, -(s), follower.
volgkaarte, sequence of cards.
volgnommer, consecutive number.
volgooi, (volge-), fill.
volgorde, order, sequence.
volgroeid, (-e), full-grown.

volgsaam, (-same), docile, obedient.
volgsaamheid, docility.
volhard, (-), persevere, persist.
volhardend, (-e), persevering, persistent.
volharding, perseverance, persistence.
volhardingsvermoë, power of endurance, perseverance.
volheid, ful(l)ness; plentitude.
volhou, (volge-), maintain (war, statement); keep up (pace, struggle); sustain (part, character); persevere, persist, hold out, stick to it; – **dat** . . ., insist (maintain) that . . .
volk, (-e, -ere), people, nation; **die uitverkore –**, the chosen people.
volkebeskrywing, ethnography.
Volke(re)bond, League of Nations.
volkekunde, ethnology.
volkereg, international law.
volkome, a. perfect; complete; absolute.
volkome, adv. perfectly, completely, absolutely, quite.
volkomenheid, perfection, completeness.
volkplanter, -planting, vide **volks-**.
volkryk, (-e), populous.
volksaak, popular cause; national question.
volksaard, national character.
volksbank, people's bank.
volksbestaan, national existence.
volksbeweging, popular (national) movement.
volksbewussyn, national consciousness, sense of nationhood.
volksboek, popular book.
volksbuurt, people's quarter.
volksdans, national dance.
volksdigter, popular poet; national poet.
volksdrag, national dress.
volksdrank, national drink.
volkseenheid, national unity.
volksetimologie, popular etymology.
volksfees, national festival.
volksgebruik, popular usage (custom).
volksgees, national spirit, spirit of the people.
volksgeloof, popular belief.
volksgesondheid, public health.
volksguns, public (popular) favour.
volkshaat, popular hatred.
volkshumor, national humour, popular wit.
volksinstelling, national institution.
volksklas(se), lower classes.
volksskool, national school, public school.
volkskunde, vide **volkekunde**.
volksleier, leader of the people.
volkslewe, life of the people.
volkslied, national anthem; national song, popular song, folk-song.
volksman, people's man, national favourite, leader of the people.
volksmenigte, crowd of people.
volksmening, public opinion.
volksmond: in die –, in the language of the people.
volksonderwys, national education.
volksoorlewering, popular tradition.
volksopruier, agitator.
volksparty, people's party.
volk(s)planter, settler, colonist.
volk(s)planting, settlement, colony.
volkspoësie, popular poetry.
Volksraad, House of Assembly.
volksregering, popular government, government by the people.
volkstaal, popular language, vernacular.
volkstam, tribe, race.
volkstelling, census; **'n – hou**, take a census.

volkstemming, plebiscite; public feeling.
vlokstrots, national pride.
volksvergadering, national assembly, meeting of the people.
volksverhuising, migration of the nations; general trek.
volksvermaak, public amusement.
volksverteenwoordiger, representative of the people.
volksvlyt, national industry.
volksvooroordeel, national prejudice.
volksvyand, enemy of the people.
volkswelvaart, national prosperity.
volkswil, will of the people, popular will.
volkswysie, popular air (tune).
volledig, (-e), full (account), complete (set).
volledigheid, completeness, ful(l)ness.
volledigheidshalwe, for the sake of completeness.
volleerd, (-e), accomplished, finished; **hy is –**, he has completed (finished) his education; **'n –e dokter**, a fully qualified doctor.
vol(le)maan, full moon.
vollersaarde, fuller's earth.
volmaak, (-te), a. perfect, consummate; – **teenwoordige tyd**, perfect tense; – **toekomende tyd**, future perfect tense; – **verlede tyd**, pluperfect tense.
volmaak, adv. perfectly.
volmaak, (-), perfect.
volmaaktheid, perfection.
volmag, (-te), power of attorney; full powers, plenary power; **by –**, by proxy; – **gee (verleen)**, authorize, give power of attorney.
volmagtig, (ge-), authorize.
volmondig, (-e), frank, candid; whole-hearted.
volop, plenty of, in plenty (abundance); – **geld**, pots (lots) of money, money galore, – **tyd**, plenty of time.
volprese: nooit –, surpassing, transcendent.
volprop, (volge-), stuff, cram.
volsin, sentence, period.
volslae, complete, absolute (fool, nonsense), perfect, utter (fool, misery, darkness); sworn (enemies).
volstaan, (-), suffice.
volstop, (volge-), stuff, cram.
volstrek, (-te), a. absolute (power); clear (majority).
volstrek, adv. absolutely, quite; – **nie**, on no account, certainly not, by no means.
volstrektheid, absoluteness.
volstruis, (-e), ostrich.
volstruisboer, ostrich-farmer.
volstruismaag, stomach of an ostrich; stomach of a horse.
volstruispolitiek, ostrich-policy.
volstruisvoël, ostrich.
volt, (-s), volt (electr.).
voltallig, (-e), full complete, fully attended (meeting), plenary (assembly).
voltalligheid, completeness.
voltameter, voltameter.
volte, ful(l)ness; crowd.
volteken, (-de), fully subscribed for.
voltmeter, voltmeter.
voltooi, (–), finish, complete; **–d verlede tyd**, pluperfect tense.
voltooiing, completion, finishing.
voltrek, (–), execute, (sentence); carry out solemnize, perform (marriage-ceremony).
voltrekker, executor; solemnizer.
voltrekking, execution; solemnization.
voltrokke, executed; carried out.
voluit, in full; at full length.
volume, (-s), volume.

volumetries, (-e), volumetric.
volumineus, (-e), voluminous, bulky.
volvet, full-cream (cheese).
volvoer, (-), fulfil, accomplish, perform.
volwasse, adult, grown-up, full-grown.
volwassene, (-s), adult, grown-up person.
volywerig, (-e), full of zeal, zealous.
vomeer, vermeer, (ge-), vomit.
vomitief, (-tiewe), emetic.
vondeling, (-e), foundling; **te – lê,** expose, abandon, lay on somebody's doorstep (child).
vonds, (-te), find, discovery; invention.
vonk, (-e), n. spark; **– e skiet,** sparkle; flash fire (of eyes).
vonk, (ge-), spark.
vonkdraad, ignition-wire.
vonkel (ge-), sparkle.
vonkeling, sparkling.
vonkie, (-s), spark, sparklet.
vonkontsteking, spark-ignition.
vonkprop, sparking-plug.
vonkvry, sparkless.
vonnis, (-se), n. sentence, judg(e)ment; **'n – vel (uitspreek),** pass sentence, pronounce judg(e)ment.
vonnis, (ge-), sentence, condemn.
vont, (-e), font (for baptismal water).
voog, (-de), guardian.
voogdes, (-se), guardian.
voogdy, guardianship.
voogdyskap, (-pe), guardianship.
voor, (vore), n. furrow; ditch.
voor, n: die – en teë (teen), the pros and cons.
voor, prep. in front of, before; before (Saturday); **– die kerk,** in front of the church; **– die deur, venster,** at the door, window; **tien minute – twaalf,** ten minutes to twelve; **hy stem daar –,** he votes for (in favour of) it.
voor, adv. in front; **my horlosie loop –,** my watch is fast; **– wees,** lead (tennis, cricket, etc.); be ahead of; forestall (person); **van – tot agter,** from front to rear (back).
voor, conj. before.
voor, (ge-), furrow.
vooraan, in front; in the forefront.
vooraand, eve.
vooraanstaande, leading, prominent.
vooraf, beforehand, previously; **– wil ek sê,** to begin with I wish to say.
voorafgaan, (voorafge-), precede; lead.
voorafgaande, preceding; foregoing.
voorarbeid, preparatory work.
voorarm, fore-arm.
vooras, front axle.
voorasnog, as yet.
voorbaan, front-width.
voorbaat: by **–,** in anticipation, in advance.
voorband, front tyre (tire).
voorbank, front seat (bench).
voorbarig, (-e), premature (decision); rash, hasty; presumptuous, arrogant.
voorbarigheid, prematureness; rashness.
voorbedag, (-te), premeditated; **met –te rade,** with premeditation.
voorbedagtelik, with premeditation.
voorbedagtheid, premeditation.
voorbede, intercession.
voorbeeld, (-e), example; model; illustration; instance; specimen; copy; **by –,** for example, for instance; **tot – strek,** serve as an example; **aan iemand 'n – neem,** follow a person's example.
voorbeeldeloos, (-lose), unparalleled.
voorbeeldig, (-e), exemplary.
voorbeeldigheid, exemplariness.

voorbeen, foreleg.
voorbehoedmiddel, preservative; preventive; contraceptive.
voorbehou, (-), reserve; **alle regte –,** all rights reserved.
voorbehoud, reserve, reservation; **sonder –,** unreservedly, unconditionally; **onder – dat . . . ,** provided that . . . ; **met hierdie –,** with this reserve.
voorberei, (-), prepare.
voorbereidend, (-e), preparatory; **–e werk,** preparatory work; spade-work.
voorbereiding, (-e, -s), preparation.
voorbereidingsdiens, preparatory service, service preparatory to Holy Communion.
voorbereidingskool, preparatory school.
voorbereidsel, (-s), preparation.
voorberig, preface, foreword.
voorbeskik, (-), predestine; (of God) predestinate, foreordain (person to).
voorbeskikking, predestination.
voorbestem, (-), vide **voorbeskik.**
voorbestem(d), (-de), predestined.
voorbid, (voorge-), lead in prayer.
voorbidder, intercessor, mediator.
voorbidding, intercession.
voorbly, (voorge-), maintain (keep) the lead, keep ahead of.
voorbode, precursor; omen, portent.
voorbok, bell-goat, leading goat; ringleader; **die –ke van die party,** the leaders (stalwarts) of the party.
voorbrand, fire-break.
voorbring, (voorge-), bring up (in court); propose, put forward; **'n saak –,** bring a matter up, broach a subject.
voordans, (voorge-), lead the dance; show how to dance; dance to.
voordanser, leader of the dance.
voordat, before.
voordateer, (voorge-), antedate.
voordeel, (-dele), advantage, benefit, profit; advantage (tennis); gain; **in jou –,** in your favour; to your advantage; **– oplewer,** yield profit; **– hê van,** profit by; **tot – strek van,** benefit, be to the advantage of.
voordek, forward deck.
voordelig, (-e), profitable, advantageous; **–e saldo,** credit-balance.
voordeligheid, profitableness.
voordese, before this.
voordeur, front door.
voordoen, (voorge-), do first; **sig – as,** pose (give oneself out) as, set up for (a teacher); **moeilikhede doen hulle voor,** difficulties arise (crop up); **die geleentheid doen hom voor,** the opportunity presents itself; **hy kan hom goed –,** he has a good address, he knows how to make an impression.
voordra, (voorge-), recite (poem), give a recitation; declaim; render (musical composition); do a turn; put (present) (the case of).
voordrag, (-te), (good, bad) delivery, elocution, diction; recitation; lecture, address, recital.
voordrag(s)kuns, elocution.
voordrag(s)kunstenaar, elocutionist.
vooreergister, three days ago.
voorent, fore-part, forefront.
voorgaan, (voorge-), walk (go) in front of; precede; lead the way; take precedence; **jou broers –,** be (set) an example to your brothers; **in die gebed –,** lead in prayer; **gaan jy maar voor,** after you!
voorgaande, preceding; **die –,** the foregoing.
voorgang, front passage; precedence.

voorganger, (-s), predecessor; minister.
voorgebed, opening prayer.
voorgebergte, promontory, cape.
voorgee, n. start.
voorgee, (voorge-), give a start; give odds; profess to be, pretend; – dat hy niemand liefhet, pretend (profess) to love a person.
voorgeewedstryd, handicap (-game, -match, -race).
voorgemeld, (-e), before-mentioned.
voorgenoem(d), (-de), vide **voorgemeld**.
voorgenome, proposed, intended.
voorgereg, hors d'oeuvre; entrée.
voorgeskiedenis, past history, antecedents (of person); prehistory.
voorgeskrewe, prescribed, set (book).
voorgeslag, ancestors, forefathers.
voorgestoelte, front seat; **die – (voorbanke) in die sinagoge**, the chief seats in the synagogue); **graag in die – wees**, like to be in the limelight.
voorgevoel, presentiment, foreboding.
voorgewel, front gable.
voorgewend, (-e), pretended, professed, feigned, simulated, sham.
voorgif, handicap.
voorgrond, foreground (lit. & fig.); forefront; **op die –**, in the foreground; **op die – raak**, come into prominence, come to the front; **op die – – tree**, come into prominence, come to the fore.
voorhaak, (voorge-), hitch on; lend a (helping) hand; lend, advance.
voorhamer, sledge-hammer.
voorhande, in stock (store), on hand; **nie meer – nie**, sold out, out of stock.
voorhang, n. veil, curtain.
voorhang, (voorge-), hang in front of.
voorhangsel, (-s), curtain, veil.
voorhê, (voorgehad), have before one; have on (apron); be up to, intend; **wat het hy voor?**, what is he after (up to)?, what are his intentions?
voorheen, formerly, in the past.
voorhistories, (-e), prehistoric.
voorhoede, van, vanguard; forwards.
voorhoef, fore-hoof.
voorhof, court (biblical), forecourt.
voorhoof, forehead.
voorhou, (voorge-), hold before; keep on (apron); **as 'n voorbeeld –**, hold up as an example; **dit word vir die kinders voorgehou dat . . .**, it is impressed on the children that . . . ; **iemand iets (slegte gedrag) –**, reproach a person with something, remonstrate with someone on something.
voorhuid, foreskin, prepuce.
voorhuis, vestibule, hall; dining-room.
voorin, in front.
voor-Indië, Hither India.
Vooringenome, prejudiced, bias(s)ed.
vooringenomenheid, prejudice, bias.
voorjaar, spring.
voorjaarsnagewening, vernal equinox.
voorjaarsopruiming, spring-sale.
voorjaarsweer, spring-weather.
voorjuk, front yoke.
voorkamer, front room; drawing-room, sitting-room.
voorkant, front(-side), face.
voorkeer, (voorge-), stop, bar (block) the way, obstruct; dam up (water); turn back (sheep).
voorkennis, prescience, foreknowledge.
voorkeur, preference; first choice; **– gee aan**, prefer, give preference to; **– geniet**, have preference; **by –**, preferably, by preference.

voorkeursreg, preference-duty.
voorkeurstarief, preferential tariff.
voorkis, front box, box-seat.
voorkom, (voorge-), 1. come to the front, gain the lead, get ahead; appear in court, be brought up; be found, occur; appear, seem; **wanneer kom sy saak voor?**, when does his case come up for hearing?; **dit kom my voor**, it seems to me.
voorkom, (–), 2. prevent; ward off (danger), obviate (danger, difficulty); avert (accident); forestall (person).
voorkome, **-koms(te)**, appearance, looks, air, complexion.
voorkomend, (-e), 1. occurring.
voorkomend, (-e), 2. obliging.
voorkomendheid, obligingness, affability.
voorkoming, prevention.
voorkoms(te), vide **voorkome**.
voorkry, (voorge-), get (20 yards) start, received odds (points); haul over the coals, reprimand, rebuke.
voorlaaier(geweer), muzzle-loader.
voorlaaste, last but one; **– lettergreep**, penultimate syllable.
voorlamp, head-light.
voorland, foreland; fate; **dood is jou –**, you are doomed to die; **wie weet wat my – is?**, who knows what is in store for me?
voorlê, (voorge-), 1. lie in front; **iemand –**, lie in wait for a person; **jy weet nie wat (vir) jou – nie**, you do not know what is awaiting (in store for) you.
voorlê, (voorge-), 2. put before, submit (plan), lay (facts) before (a person); put (question) to; state (a case to a person).
voorlees, (voorge-), read out; read to (person).
voorleser, reader.
voorlesing, (-e, -s), reading; lecture.
voorletter, initial; **-s**, initials.
voorliefde, predilection, liking, partiality; **'n – hê vir**, have a special liking for, be partial to.
voorlig, n. head-light.
voorlig, (voorge-), light; enlighten.
voorligting, enlightenment, information.
voorloop, (voorge-), walk in front; gain (of watch), go fast; lead (the way).
voorloper, leader; forerunner, precursor.
voorlopig, (-e), a. preliminary, provisional; temporary.
voorlopig, adv. for the present, for the time being, provisionally, as yet.
voorlyf, front part of the body.
voormalig, (-e), former, one-time, late.
voorman, foreman, leader.
voormas, foremast.
voormeld, (-e), before, above-mentioned.
voormiddag, morning, forenoon.
voornaam, Christian name.
voornaamwoord, pronoun.
voornag, first part of the night.
voorneem, (voorge-): **sig –**, resolve, make up one's mind, determine.
voorneme, (-ns), intention, resolve; **(van) –ns wees om**, intend to.
voornoem(d), (-de), above-mentioned.
voorondersoek, preliminary examination.
voorontsteking, pre-ignition.
vooroor, forward, leaning forward.
vooroorbuie, **-buig**, (vooroorge-), bend forward.
vooroorbuk, (vooroorge-), stoop, bend down.
vooroordeel, prejudice, bias.
vooroorhel, (vooroorge-), lean (forward) over, have a forward incline.

vooroorlê, (vooroorge-), lay prostrate; lie on one's face, lie prostrate.
vooroorloop, (vooroorge-), stoop.
vooroorstaan, (vooroorge-), stoop.
vooroorval, (vooroorge-), fall forward, fall head foremost (first).
voorop, in front.
vooropgeset, (-te), preconceived.
vooropstel, (vooropge-), postulate, premise;
voorgestelde mening, preconceived notion.
vooros, front ox, leader; forward.
voorou(d)erlik, (-e), ancestral.
voorouers, ancestors, forefathers.
voorpant, front panel (gore) (of skirt).
voorperd, front horse, leader; leading man; ringleader.
voorpoot, forepaw, foreleg.
voorportaal, porch, hall, vestibule.
voorpos, outpost.
voorpraat, (voorge-), stick up for, take the part (side) of; prompt.
voorpunt, front; point; van, forefront; **op die - loop**, walk right in front, lead, head (the procession).
voorraad, supply, store, stock; provisions; **in -**, in stock (store).
voorraadkamer, store-room.
voorraadskuur, store-house, granary.
voorradig, in stock (store); available.
voorrang, precedence; preference; **die - hê bo**, have priority over; **om die - stry**, vie with each other for the first place (the mastery, supremacy).
voorrede, preface; foreward.
voorreg, privilege; prerogative.
voorreken, (voorge-), figure out.
voorry, (voorge-), ride in front, lead.
voorsaal, antechamber, front hall.
voorsaat, (-sate), ancestor, forefather.
voorsanger, precentor.
voorsê, (voorge-), prompt, tell (a person) how to to say it, or; what to say.
voorsê, (-), prophesy, predict.
voorsegging, (-e, -s), prophecy.
voorsetsel, (-s), preposition.
voorsien, (-), foresee; provide, supply; **- van**, supply (provide) with; furnish (fit) with; **sig - van**, supply (provide) oneself with; **- in**, meet (wants), supply; **- in die behoeftes van**, provide for the needs of; **in 'n lang gevoelde behoefte -**, supply in a long-felt want; **in jou eie onderhoud -**, provide for oneself.
Voorsienigheid, Providence.
voorsiening, provision.
voorsing, (voorge-), lead the singing.
voorsinger, precentor; **- wees**, lead the singing.
voorsit, (voorge-), place in front of, put (something) before (a person); put forward; preside, take the chair.
voorsitster, chairman; **Geagte -**, Madam Chair.
voorsitter, chairman, president.
voorsitterskap, chairmanship.
voorsitterstoel, (presidential) chair.
voorskiet, (voorge-), advance, lend.
voorskieter, money-lender.
voorskip, foreship, forepart of a ship.
voorskoot, (-skote), apron.
voorskot, (-te), loan, advance.
voorskotbank, loan-office, -bank.
voorskrif, (-te), prescription (of doctor); nstruction, direction.
voorskryf, -skrywe, (voorge-), write (a copy); prescribe (medicine); dictate, prescribe; **boeke -**, prescribe books.
voorskyn: **te - bring**, produce; bring to light;

bring out; **te - kom**, appear, put in an appearance.
voorslag, whip-lash, "voorslag"; grace-note (mus.); proposal, suggestion; **soos 'n - wees**, be a real live wire, be lively (vigorous, full of life); **onder die - kry**, lash, whip, flog.
voorslagvel, buckskin used for whip-lashes.
voorsmaak, (fore)taste.
voorsnymes, carving-knife.
voorsomer, early summer.
voorsorg, provision, precaution.
voorsorgsmaatreël, precautionary measure.
voorspan, (voorge-), put (the horse) to the cart, inspan.
voorspanloko, banking-engine.
voorspel, n. prelude (mus.); introduction, prologue; voluntary (before church-services); forward-play (rugby).
voorspel, (voorge-), 1. spell (word) to.
voorspel, (-), 2. foretell, prophesy, predict; spell, portend, bode (well, ill); **dit - niks goeds nie**, that is a bad omen.
voorspeld, (voorge-), pin on.
voorspeler, forward (rugby).
voorspeller, prophet, predictor.
voorspelling, (-e, -s), prophecy, prediction, forecast (of result of match).
voorspieël, -spiegel, (voorge-), old out (hopes), delude (person with); **sig iets -**, promise oneself something, delude oneself into the belief that.
voorspieëling, delusion, false hope.
voorspoed, prosperity; **iemand - toewens**, wish a person success (best of luck); **alle -**, good luck!; **in - en teenspoed**, for better or for worse; through thick and thin.
voorspoedig, (-e), prosperous.
voorspooksel, (-s), ill omen; (also) good omen; **moenie -s maak nie**, don't meet trouble halfway.
voorspraak, mediation, intercession; mediator, intercessor.
voorspring, (voorge-), forestall, anticipate, steal a march on.
voorsprong, start; advantage; **- kry op sy mededingers**, get the start of his rivals.
voorspys, hors d'oeuvre, (also) entrée.
voorstaan, (voorge-), stand in front; advocate, champion, defend, stand for (equality); **dit staan my nog duidelik (lewendig) voor**, I remember it clearly, it stands out clearly in my mind.
voorstad, suburb.
voorstander, (-s), advocate, supporter, champion, elder.
voorstanderklier, prostate (gland).
voorste, first, foremost, front.
voorsteek, (voorge-), pin on; stick in front; **jou voet -**, trip up.
voorstel, (-le), n. fore-carriage, fore body; proposal; suggestion; motion; **'n - indien**, move a resolution.
voorstel, (voorge-), introduce; present (at court), represent (scene); play the part of, act (Othello); suggest; propose; move (adjournment of the debate); **wat stel dit voor?**, what does this represent (stand for, signify); **- dat van die punt afgestap word**, move that matter be dropped; **sig -**, introduce oneself; imagine, conceive of, picture to oneself, form an idea; **stel jou voor!**, just imagine!, just fancy!
voorsteller, (-s), proposer, mover.
voorstelling, (-e, -s), representation; introduction; performance; confirmation; conception, idea; **- aan die hof**, presentation at court;

sig 'n – maak van, picture, imagine, form an idea.
voorstellingswyse, way of representing things, method of representation.
voorstem, (voorge-), vote for.
voorsten, vide voorstewe.
voorstewe, stem, prow.
voorstraat, main street.
voorstudie, preparatory study.
voorstuk, front-piece; curtain-raiser.
voort, forward, on forth; away.
voortaan, in future, henceforth, from now on.
voortand, front tooth.
voortbestaan, n. survival.
voortbestaan, (–), survive, continue to exist.
voortbeweeg, (–), move (on); propel.
voortbeweging, locomotion; moving.
voortbou, (voortge-), go on building; – op, build on.
voortbrenging, production; creation.
voortbrengsel, (-s), product; –s, products; produce.
voortbring, (voortge-), produce, yield, bring forth; generate, beget.
voortdryf, -drywe, (voortge-), drive on, urge on; float along.
voortdurend, (-e), continuous, lasting, continual; constant; permanent.
voortdurig, continuation; continuance.
voortduur, (voortge-), last, continue.
voorteken, omen, augury, sign, portent; symptom (of disease).
voortgaan, (voortge-), continue, go on, proceed.
voortgang, progress; – maak, proceed.
voortgeset, (-te), continued; –te onderwys, post-primary (post-elementary) education; continuation classes.
voorthelp, (voortge-), help on.
voorthol, (voortge-), run on (along).
voortkanker, (voortge-), eat away (spread) like a cancer.
voortkom, (voortge-), get along; – uit, originate from (in), result from, spring from, arise from.
voortkruip (voortge-), crawl along.
voortlewe, (voortge-), live on.
voortmaak, (voortge-), hurry (up), be quick, make haste; vide vortmaak.
voortou, lead; die – neem, take the lead (initiative).
voortplant, (voortge-), propagate (disease, plant, race, belief); transmit (disease); sig –, breed, multiply, propagate; be transmitted.
voortplanting, propagation (of race); transmission (of sound).
voortreflik, (-e), excellent, first-rate.
voortreflikheid, excellence.
voortrek, n. forerunners of the Trek.
voortrek, (voorge-), favour (child); prefer; have higher opinion of.
Voortrekker, Voortrekker, pioneer.
voortrol, (voortge-), roll along (on).
voortruk, (voortge-), pull along; press (push) on.
voorts, further, besides; en so –, and so on, et cetera.
voortsê, (voortge-), repeat, pass on.
voortsetting, continuation.
voortsit, (voortge-), continue; pursue (inquiry); proceed on (journey); carry on.
voortskry, (voortge-), advance.
voortsleep, (voortge-), drag along; drag on (existence).
voortsluip, (voortge-), steal (sneak) along (forward).
voortsnel, (voortge-), rush (hurry) on.
voortspeel, (voortge-), play on.

voortspoed, (voortge-), speed on.
voortspruit, (voortge-): – uit, result (arise) from.
voortstap, (voortge-), walk on.
voortstrompel, (voortge-), stumble along.
voortsukkel, (voortge-), struggle along.
voortteel, (voortge-), breed, multiply.
voortvarend, (-e), impetuous, rash, impulsive; pushing.
voortvarendheid, impetuosity, rashness. – uit, flow
voortvloei, (voortge-), flow along (on); (result, arise, spring) from; hieruit vloei voort, from this follows.
voortvloeisel, (-s), result.
voortvlugtig, (-e), fugitive.
voortwoeker, (voortge-), spread, fester.
voortyd, prehistoric times, the dim (hazy) past.
voortyds, formerly.
voortyl, (voortge-), hurry on.
vooruit, (voortge-), in front of, before; forward; beforehand, in advance; –!, go ahead!, go it!, fire away!; jou tyd – wees, be ahead of one's time; – betaalbaar, payable in advance.
vooruitbepaal, (–), fix beforehand.
vooruitbestel, (–), order in advance.
vooruitbetaal, (–), pay in advance.
vooruitbetaling, payment in advance.
vooruitbeur, (vooruitge-), pull away, drag on; slog on (away), struggle on.
vooruitbring, (vooruitge-), bring forward; help on.
vooruitdink, (vooruitge-), think ahead.
vooruitdryf, -drywe, (vooruitge-), drive on (forward).
vooruitgaan, (vooruitge-), go first; get on, make progress; improve.
vooruitgang, progress, getting on; improvement (of patient); advance.
vooruithelp, (vooruitge-), help on.
vooruitja(ag), (vooruitge-), hurry on before, shoot ahead of.
vooruitkom, (vooruitge-), get on.
vooruitloop, (vooruitge-), walk on ahead of; go first anticipate; jou moeilikhede –, meetv you troubles half-way; die tyd –, anticipate erents.
vooruitry, (vooruitge-), ride on ahead.
vooruitsien, (vooruitge-), look ahead; foresee.
vooruitsig, prospect, outlook; goeie -te, good prospects; geen – op, no prospect of; in die –, in prospect.
vooruitskop, (vooruitge-), kick forward.
vooruitskuif, -skuiwe, (vooruitge-), push (move, shove) forward (along).
vooruitsteek, (vooruitge-), jut (stick) out, project; put out, thrust out.
vooruitstreef, -strewe, (vooruitge-), strive (to get on), forge ahead.
vooruitstrewend, (-e), progressive.
vooruitstuur, (vooruitge-), send on (ahead, in advance).
vooruitweet, (vooruitge-), know beforehand.
voorvader, forefather, ancestor.
voorvaderlik, (-e), ancestral.
voorval, (-le), n. incident, event.
voorval, (voorge-), happen, occur, take place.
voorvegter, champion, advocate.
voorvertrek, ante-room, antechamber.
voorvinger, forefinger.
voorvoegsel, (-s), prefix.
voorvoet, forefoot.
voorwaar, indeed, truly.
voorwaarde, (-s), condition, stipulation, term (of treaty); op – dat, on condition that, aan die –s voldoen, satisfy the conditions.
voorwaardelik, (-e), conditional.

voorwaarts, (-e), forward.
voorwedstryd, curtain-raiser.
voorwend, (voorge-), pretend, sham, feign; **voorgewende siekte**, sham illness.
voorwendsel, (-s), pretext, pretence; **onder – van**, on (under) the pretext of (that).
voorwêreldlik, (-e), prehistoric.
voorwerk, spade-work.
voorwerp, (-e), object, thing; **lydende –**, direct object **'n – van spot**, a subject for (an object of) ridicule.
voorwerplik, (-e), objective.
voorwerpsin, objective clause.
voorwiel, front wheel.
voorwinter, early winter.
voorwoord, foreword, preface.
voos, (-, vose), spongy, woolly.
voosheid, sponginess, woolliness.
vorder, (ge-), get on, (make) progress, make headway.
vorder, (ge-), demand, ask, expect.
vordering, (-e, -s), progress, headway, advance; improvement; demand, claim; **– maak**, get on, (make) progress.
vore: **na –**, to the front; **na – kom**, come forward; come to the fore.
vorentoe, a. forward (pass); progressive (farmer) smart, fine; first-class.
vorentoe, adv. forward; to the fore; **– gaan**, go (step) forward; get on, (make) progress; **– boer**, be a progressive farmer; get on; **dit smaak –**, it is jolly nice, it tickles the palate.
vorige, former, previous; last.
vorm, (-e, -s), n. form; shape; figure; mould (for cake); matrix (for type); voice (active & passive); formality, form; **– gee aan**, put (get) into shape; **'n vaste – aanneem**, take definite form (shape); **in die – van**, in the shape of.
vorm, (ge-), form; mould (lit. & fig.); shape, fashion; frame (theory, words).
vormbaar, (-bare), mouldable, plastic.
vormdrag, foundation garments.
vormend, (-e), forming; educative.
vormer, (-s), framer, former, moulder.
vorming, forming, formation, shaping, moulding; education.
vormkledingstuk, foundation garment.
vormklei, modelling-clay.
vormleer, accidence (gram.); morpology.
vormlik, (-e), formal, conventional.
vormlikheid, formality, conventionality.
vormloos, (-lose), formless, shapeless.
vormplank, modelling-board.
vormraam, moulding-frame.
vormverandering, change of form; transformation, metamorphosis.
vors, (-te), n. (1) ridge, capping.
vors, (-te), n. (2) monarch, sovereign; prince.
vors, (ge-), investigate, search.
vorstedom, principality.
vorstehuis, dynasty.
vorstelik, (-e), princely, royal (palace); **die –e huis**, the royal family; **–e beloning**, princely reward.
vorstelikheid, princeliness, royalty.
vorstenood, regicide.
vorsteseun, royal son.
vorstin, (-ne), queen, sovereign.
vort, **voort**, gone, away; **–!**, get (clear) out!, get a move on.
vos, (-se), fox; bay, sorrel.
voshare, red (ginger) hair.
vosperd, bay, sorrel (chestnut) horse.
votief, (-tiewe), votive.
vou (-e), n. fold; pleat (in cloth, skirt), crease (in trousers); **'n saak in die beste –e lê**, present the matter in the best light; make the best of a bad job.
vou, (ge-), fold.
voubaar, (-bare), foldable; collapsable (collapsible); pliable.
voubed, (camp-)stretcher.
voudeur, folding-doors.
voumasjien, folding-machine.
voustoel, camp-chair, folding chair.
vra, (ge-), ask; question; charge (price); invite (tenders); ask to marry, propose, call out (trumps); **– is vry (en (maar) weier daarby)**, there is no harm in asking; **dit – al my aandag**, it requires all my attention; **– dit!**, you may well ask!; **skoppens word ge–**, spades are led; **gevra: 'n bediende**, wanted: a servant; **– na**, inquire after (person); inquire about (thing); **hulle – na jou**, you are wanted; **na die pad –**, ask the way; **– om**, ask for; **om raad –**, ask advice.
vraag, (vrae), question; query; demand; **dit is nog die –**, that is a (the) question; that remains to be seen; **'n – doen**, ask a question; **– en aanbod**, supply and demand.
vraagal, inquisitive person.
vraagbaak, (-bake), book of reference, guide; oracle.
vraaggesprek, interview.
vraagpunt, point in question.
vraagsiek, inquisitive.
vraagsin, interrogative sentence.
vraagstuk, question, problem, rider.
vraagsug, inquisitiveness.
vraagteken, interrogation-mark, question mark; query; **'n – bysit**, query.
vraat, (vrate), glutton, gormandizer.
vraatsug, gluttony, voracity.
vraatsugtig, (-e), gluttonous, voracious.
vraeboek, catechism.
vraelys, questionnaire.
vraend, (-e), questioning, inquiring; interrogative (gram.).
vraenderwys, interrogatively.
vraer, (-s), questioner, interrogator.
vraestel, examination-paper.
vraetyd, question time.
vrag, (-te), load; cargo (of ship); freight (transport by water); carriage (by land); fare (for person).
vragboot, cargo-boat, freighter.
vragbrief, consignment-note (rail); bill of lading (boat).
vraggoed, cargo; goods.
vragmotor, motor lorry.
vragprys, carriage; freight; fare.
vragskip, cargo-boat, freighter.
vragtarief, rate of carriage, railway-tariff; freight-rate.
vragtrein, goods-train.
vragvliegtuig, freighter.
vragvry, carriage paid (free); freight paid; post-free.
vragwa, transport-wag(g)on; loaded wag(g)on; truck.
vrank, acrid, acid, tart, harsh, astringent.
vrat, (-te), wart.
vratjie, (-s), (little) wart.
vrede, peace; **– maak (sluit)**, make peace; **ek het daar – mee**, I don't mind (object, care); **iemand met – laat**, leave a person in peace.
vredefees, peace-celebration(s).
vredeliewend, (-e), peace-loving, peaceful.
vredeliewendheid, peacefulness, love of peace.
vredemaker, peacemaker.

vredeoffer, peace-offering.
vrederegter, justice of the peace.
vredesaanbod, peace-offer.
vredesengel, angel of peace.
vredeskonferensie, peace-conference.
vredesnaam: in –, for peace' (goodness', heaven's) sake.
vredesonderhandeling, peace-negotiations.
vredespaleis, palace of peace.
vredespyp, pipe of peace.
vredestempel, temple of peace.
vredestraktaat, peace-treaty.
vredestyd, time of peace.
vredesvoorwaardes, peace-terms.
vredevors, prince of peace.
vredig, (-e), peaceful.
vreedsaam, (-same), peaceful; peaceable.
vreedsaamheid, peacefulness.
vreemd, (-e), strange; foreign; queer, odd; exotic; –e tale, foreign languages; **die werk is my** –, the work is new to me.
vreemde, (-s), stranger; foreigner.
vreemde, strange part (thing); **in die** –, abroad, in foreign lands; **die – daarvan is ...**, the strange thing about (part of) it is ....
vreemdelegioen, foreign legion.
vreemdeling, (-e), stranger; foreigner; **'n – in Jerusalem,** a stranger in Jerusalem.
vreemdelingeboek, visitors' book.
vreemdelingeburo, tourist bureau.
vreemdelingelegioen, vide **vreemdelegioen.**
vreemdelingewet, Aliens' Act.
vreemdelingskap, alienship; **die jare van my** –, the years of my pilgrimage; **in** –, in exile.
vreemdheid, strangeness; oddness.
vreemdsoortig, (-e), strange, odd, queer; heterogeneous, motley.
vreemdsoortigheid, strangeness, oddness.
vrees, vrese, n. fear, dread; apprehension, **– vir honde,** fear of dogs; **– koester vir,** fear, be afraid of; **uit – dat,** for fear that, for fear lest; **uit – vir,** for fear of.
vrees, (ge-), fear, dread, be afraid of.
vreesaanja(g)end, (-e), terrifying.
vreesaanjaging, intimidation.
vreesagtig, (-e), afraid; timid.
vreesagtigheid, timidity.
vreeslik, (-e), terrible, awful, dreadful.
vreeslikheid, terribleness, dreadfulness.
vreeswekkend, (-e), awe-inspiring.
vreet, (ge-), feed on, eat (of animal); gorge, guzzle (of person).
vreetsak, glutton.
vrek, (-ke), n. miser, skinflint.
vrek, (ge-), die (of animals); **loop** –**!** go to blazes (the devil).
vrekagtig, vrekkerig, vrekkig, (-e), stingy, miserly.
vreksel, (-s), scoundrel, son of a gun.
vrekte, mortality (of animals); **hy het die** –, he is more dead than alive.
vreugde, joy, gladness; **hoe meer siele, hoe meer** –, the more the merrier.
vreugdebederwer, spoil-sport, kill-joy.
vreugdebedryf, -betoon, rejoycing.
vreugdedronk(e), mad with joy.
vreugdefees, festival, festivity, feast.
vreugdeklokke, joy-bells.
vreugdekreet, shout of joy.
vreugdelied, song of joy.
vreugdesang, song of joy.
vreugdeskote, (festive) salute.
vreugdeteken, sign of joy.
vreugdevol, (le), joyful, full of joy.
vreugdevuur, bonfire.

vriend, vrind, (-e), friend; **'n – in nood,** a friend in need (is a friend indeed); **dik –e wees,** be fast friends; **goeie –e wees, met,** be friends with, be on good terms with; **hulle is weer goeie –e,** they have made it up again; **iemand aan sy –e ken,** know a person by the company he keeps; **'n – van die spel,** a lover of the game; **tot – hou,** keep on good terms with.
vriendediens, friendly-service (turn).
vriendekring, circle of friends.
vriendelik, (-e), friendly, kind, amicable.
vriendelikheid, (-hede), kindness, friendliness.
vriendeloos, (-lose), friendless.
vriendin, (-ne), vriendinnetjie, (-s), (lady, woman) friend.
vriendjie, (-s), little friend.
vriendskap, friendship; favour good turn; **'n – bewys,** do a good turn; **– sluit met,** make friends with; **uit** –, for friendship's sake.
vriendskaplik, (-e), friendly.
vriendskaplikheid, friendliness.
vriendskapsband, tie of friendship.
vriendskapsbetrekking, friendly relation.
vriendskapsdiens, friendly service.
vries, (ge-), freeze.
vrieskamer, freezing-room (-chamber).
vriespunt, freezing-point.
vriesvlees, (-vleis), frozen meat.
vrind vide **vriend.**
vroe, vide **vroeg.**
vroed, (-e), wise.
vroedvrou, midwife.
vroeër, (–, -e), a. earlier; former (years), previous, bygone (days).
vroeër, adv. earlier; formerly, in former (bygone) days; before now, **– of later,** sooner or later.
vroeg, (vroeë), a. early; **vroeë perskes,** early peaches, **'n vroeë dood,** a premature death.
vroeg, adv. early; at an early hour; **– in die môre,** early in the morning; **– en laat,** at all hours; **te – doodgaan,** die before one's time; **as jy met hom te doen het, moet jy – opstaan,** you have to get up early (you will have to mind you P's and Q's) when you are dealing with him.
vroe(g)kos, breakfast.
vroegmis, early (morning) mass.
vroegryp, early (fruit); precocious.
vroegrypheid, precocity.
vroegste, earliest; **op sy (die)** –, at the earliest.
vroegte: in die –, early in the morning.
vroegtydig, (-e), a. early.
vroegtydig, adv. early, in good time, betimes.
vroe(g)-vroe(g), very early, in the small hours.
vroepampoen, vegetable-marrow, squash.
vrotel, (ge-), root (rout) (of pigs), turn up the ground; burrow; wriggle, fidget (of child); **– in (tussen),** rummage in.
vrome, (-s), pious person.
vrolik, (-e), merry, cheerful, gay, jolly; "happy", tipsy.
vrolikheid, cheerfulness, gaiety, hilarity, merriment jollification; vide **olikheid.**
vroom, (–, vrome), pious, devout.
vroomheid, (-e), devoutness, piety, godliness.
vrot, a. rotten, putrid, decayed.
vrot, (ge-), rot, decay, putrefy.
vrotpootjie(s), blackleg, root-rot (in potatoes); eelworm, root-gallworm.
vrotsig, (-e), rotten, worthless, beastly.
vrotsigheid, rottenness, worthlessness.
vrottigheid, rottenness, incompetence; clumsiness.
vrou, (-e, -ens), woman; wife, spouse (of husband); queen (cards); **die –e van Suid-Afrika,** the women of South Africa; **'n man mag nie**

twee -ens hê nie, a man is not allowed to have two wives; tot - neem, take to wife; die - van die huis, the lady of the house.
vrouagtig, (-e), effeminate, womanish, uxorious, fond of women.
vroue-aard, woman's nature.
vrouebeeld, statue (image) of a woman.
vrouebeweging, movement for women's rights, feminist-movement.
vrouebond, women's league (union).
vrouebors, woman's breast.
vrouedokter, gynaecologist; lady (woman) doctor.
vrouedrag, women's dress.
vrouhaar(varing), maidenhair(-fern).
vrouehaat, hatred of women.
vrouehater, woman-hater, misogynist.
vrouekiesreg, votes for women, woman-, women's suffrage.
vrouekleding, -klere, women's dress.
vroueliefde, women's love.
vrouelis, woman's cunning.
vrouenaam, woman's name.
vrouensaal, side-saddle.
vroueregering, petticoat-government.
vrouerower, abductor of women.
vrouesiekte, women's disease.
vroueskender, ravisher.
vroueskending, rape, ravishment.
vrouestem, woman's voice; women's vote.
vrouestemreg, votes for women.
vrouetehuis, women's hostel.
vrouevereniging, women's association.
vroulik, (-e), womanly (ways), feminine, female (opp. male); feminine (gender); -e dokter, woman (female, lady) doctor.
vroulikheid, womanliness, feminity.
vroumens, female, woman; daardie -, that hussy (vixen, she-devil).
vrouspersoon, female, woman.
vroutjie, (-s), little woman (wifie); met sy jong -, with his young wife.
vrug, (-te), fruit (lit. & fig.); foetus; aan die -te ken 'n mens, die boom, a tree is known by its fruit; -te dra, bear fruit (lit. & fig.); die -te pluk van, reap the fruits of; verbode -te smaak die lekkerste, forbidden fruit is sweet; stolen kisses are the sweetest; sonder -, fruitless.
vrugafdrywend, (-e), abortive; -e middel, abortificient.
vrugafdrywing, abortion.
vrugbaar, (-bare), fertile (soil, brain, imagination); fruitful (year); prolific (author); fecund; - maak, make fertile, fertilize.
vrugbaarheid, fertility, fruitfulness.
vrugbeginsel, ovary.
vrugdraend, (-e), fruit-bearing; fruitful.
vruggebruik, -genot, usufruct.
vrugkiem, embryo, germ.
vrugteboer, fruit-farmer.
vrugteboom, fruit-tree.
vrugteboord, orchard.
vrugtehandelaar, fruit-dealer, fruiterer.
vrugtekissie, fruit-tray, fruit-box.
vrugtekweker, fruit-grower, fruit-farmer.
vrugteloos, (-lose), a fruitless, futile, vain (effort).
vrugteloos, adv. in vain, fruitlessly.
vrugteloosheid, futility, fruitlessness.
vrugtesap, fruit-juice.
vrugteslaai, fruit-salad.
vrugtestalletjie, fruit-stall.
vrugtestellasie, (fruit-)drying-tray.
vrugtesuiker, fruit-sugar, glucose.
vrugtevlieg, fruit-fly.
vry, (-, -e), a. free; disengaged, at leisure, gratis;

empty, vacant (seat); - arbeid, free labour; 'n - middag, an afternoon free (off), a free afternoon; die -e hemel, the open sky; 'n - uitsig, a free (unobstructed) view; die -e woord, free (freedom of) speech; R1 in die maand en alles -, R1 a month and all found; die klawerboer is -, the knave of clubs is good (bridge); -(e) tyd, spare time, leisure; - ure, leisure hours; - wees, be free (disengaged); mag ek so - wees?, may I take the liberty?, I beg to (inform you); - van, free from; exempt from (taxes); - van diens, off duty; exempt from duty.
vry, adv. freely; fairly, pretty.
vry, (ge-), court, woo, make love; flirt, spoon; na 'n meisie -, court (make love to) a girl; - na 'n persoon (om 'n guns), try to get in a person's good books; na die stemme van sy kiesers -, try to catch the votes of his constituents.
vryasie, (-s), courting; flirtation.
vrybrief, (1) passport, permit; licence.
vrybrief, (2) love-letter.
vrybuiter, freebooter, filibuster.
vrybuitery, freebooting.
Vrydag, Friday; Goeie V., Good Friday.
vrydenker, free-thinker.
vrydenkery, free-thinking.
vrye, (-s), free-man, free one (person).
vryelik, freely.
vryer, (-s), lover, sweetheart; young man, best boy.
vryery, love-making, courtship; flirting.
vryf, vrywe, (ge-), rub; blink -, polish, make shine; fyn -, rub (reduce) to powder, pulverize.
vryfdoek, -lap, rubbing (polishing-)cloth; mop.
vryfplank, float (of mason).
vrygebore, free-born.
vrygee, (vryge-), give off (a day), let off; release, free.
vrygeestig, (-e), free-thinking.
vrygeleide, safe-conduct, escort.
vrygesel, bachelor.
vrygesellin, bachelor girl, spinster.
vrygewig, (-e), generous, liberal.
vrygewigheid, generosity.
vryhandel, free-trade.
vryheer, baron.
vryheid, (-hede), freedom, liberty; (poetic) licence; - van die pers, freedom of the press; - van (die) gewete, liberty of conscience; die - neem om ..., take the liberty to ...; meer - laat, allow more scope (latitude); sig vryhede veroorloof met, take liberties with; in - stel, release, set free.
vryheidliewend, (-e), liberty-loving.
vryheidsberowing, deprivation of liberty.
vryheidsin, spirit of freedom.
vryheidsliefde, love of liberty (freedom).
vryheidsoorlog, war of independence.
vryheidsug, love of liberty.
vryheidsvlag, flag of liberty.
vryhou, (vryge-), keep free.
vrykaart(jie), complimentary ticket.
vrykamer, spare (bed)room.
vrykom, (vryge-), escape; get off, be released; become vacant.
vrykoop, (vryge-), ransom, redeem.
vrylaat, (vryge-), let off (free), release; liberate, emancipate (slave); leave (person) a free hand.
vrylating, release; emancipation.
vryleen, freehold.
vryloop, (vryge-), (1) get off, escape.
vryloop, (vryge-), (2) free wheel.

vrymaak, (vryge-), (set) free; emancipate (slave); liberate.
vrymaking, emancipation.
Vrymesselaar, Freemason.
Vrymesselaarslosie, masonic lodge.
Vrymesselary, Freemasonry.
vrymoedig, (-e), frank, open, outspoken, bold, unabashed, unbashful, candid.
vrymoedigheid, frankness, boldness; ek het nie die – om . . . , I have not got the nerve (courage) to . . . , I don't feel at liberty to . . .
vrypleit, (vryge-), get (person) off, obtain person's acquittal (discharge).
vrypostig, (-e), bold, uppish, pert, forward, presumptuous.
vrypostigheid, boldness.
vrysinnig, (-e), liberal.
vrysinnigheid, liberalism.
vryskel(d), (vryge-), exempt; let off; die klasgeld –, excuse (exempt from) the class-fees.
vryspreek, (vryge-), acquit; absolve.
vryspring, (vryge-), get off, escape, dodge.
vrystaan, (vryge-), be permitted; dit staan jou vry om . . . , you are allowed (free, at liberty) to . . .
Vrystaat, Free State.
vrystad, city of refuge (Bib.).
vrystel, (vryge-), exemp' – van, exempt from, excuse (from).
vrystelling, exemption.
vry-uit, freely, frankly, openly.
vryveg, (vryge-): sig –, fight oneself free, obtain one's liberty by war.
vryverklaar, (–), declare free.
vryverklaring, release; emancipation.
vrywaar, (ge-): – teen (vir), safeguard against, protect (guard) against.
vrywaring, safeguard, security.
vrywe, vide vryf.
vrywel, well-nigh, practically; more or less.
vrywiel, free wheel.
vrywillig, (-e), free, voluntary.
vrywilliger, (-s), volunteer.
vrywilligheid, voluntariness.
vuig, (-e), base, sordid, vile.
vuil, n. dirt.
vuil, (–, -e), a. dirty; filthy; obscene (jokes), smutty; foul (linen; weather; talk), soiled (linen).
vuilbek, foul-mouthed person.
vuilgoed, dirt, muck, rubbish; pus.
vuilgoedblik, refuse-bin, dust-bin.
vuilgoedhoop, rubbish-heap, refuse-heap.
vuilgoedkar, dust-cart, refuse-cart.
vuilheid, dirtiness, filthiness; smuttiness.
vuiligheid, vide vuilheid.
vuilhoop, vuilishoop, rubbish-heap.
vuilis, vullis, dirt, rubbish, refuse; pus; dirty swine (skunk); vide vuilgoed.
vuilisbak, -blik, vide vuilgoedblik.
vuilishoop, vide vuilhoop.
vuiliskar, vide vuilgoedkar.
vuilsiekte, syphilis.
vuilspel, foul (dirty) play.
vuilwateremmer, slop-pail.
vuis, (-te), fist; met 'n yster–, with a grip of iron; in jou – lag, laugh in one's sleeve; voor die –, extempore, impromptu, offhand; 'n toespraak voor die – (uit die – uit) hou, make an impromptu speech; almal voor die – koop, buy without picking and choosing, buy the lot.
vuisgeveg, fisticuffs; boxing-match.
vuisslag, blow with the fist.
vuisvegter, boxer, prize-fighter.
vuisvol, (vuistevol), handful.

vul, (-le, -lens), n. foal; colt (male), filly (female).
vul, (ge-), (1) foal.
vul, (ge-), (2) fill (bottle, glass); stop, fill (tooth;) stuff (turkey, chair).
vulgariteit, vulgarity.
Vulgata, Vulgate.
vulgêr, (-e), vulgar.
vulkaan, (-kane), volcano.
vulkanies, (-e), volcanic.
vulkaniseer, (ge-), vulcanize.
vulletjie, (-s), (little) foal; side-car.
vullis, vide vuilis.
vulpen, fountain-pen.
vulsel, (-s), stuffing (of turkey; of furniture); filling (of tooth); padding.
vunsig, (-e), musty, fusty, mouldy.
vurig, (-e), fiery; ardent; fervent.
vurigheid, fieriness; fervour, ardour.
vurk, (-e), fork; pitchfork; weet hoe die – in die steel steek, know the ins and outs, know how the land lies.
vuur, (vure), n. fire; gangrene (med.); ardour, fervour; die – (aan)blaas, blow the fire; fan the flame (fig.); die – staak, cease fire; – en vlam wees, be all aflame, be on fire; – spuug, spit fire; – vat, catch fire (lit. & fig.); die – is in die gras, the fat is in the fire; hulle sit nie langs een – nie, they cannot hit it off together; die naaste aan (by) die – sit, sit nearest to the fire; be in a privileged position; vir iemand deur die – loop, go through fire for a person; in – en vlam, on fire; met – speel, play with fire; tussen twee vure sit, be between two fires (of soldiers); be between the devil and the deep sea.
vuur, (ge-), fire; – op, fire at.
vuuraanbidder, fire-worshipper.
vuurbaken, beacon-light.
vuurbol, fire-ball.
vuurbuis, fire-tube.
vuurdood, death by fire.
vuurdoop, baptism of fire.
vuur(h)erd, fire-place, hearth.
vuureter, fire-eater.
vuurgang, flue.
vuurgees, fire-spirit; salamander.
vuurgloed, glow (light) of the fire; glare.
vuurherd, vide vuur(h)erd.
vuurhoutjie, (-s), match.
vuurkas, fire-box.
vuurklip, flint(-stone).
vuurkoeël, fire-ball.
vuurkolom, pillar of fire (also bib.).
Vuurland, Terra del Fuego.
vuurlelie, fire-lily.
vuurlinie, firing-line.
vuurmaakplek, fire-place, hearth; bo my – wees, be beyond (too much for) me, beat me, pass my understanding.
vuurmeter, pyrometer.
vuurmond, (muzzle of a) gun (cannon).
vuurpeloton, firing-party, firing squad.
vuurplaat, furnace-plate.
vuurpoel, sea of fire, hell, inferno.
vuurproef, fire-ordeal; acid (crucial) test; die – deurstaan, stand the test.
vuurpyl, rocket; red-hot poker.
vuurrat, fire-wheel, Catherine-wheel.
vuurrooi, fiery (flaming) red.
vuursalamander, spotted salamander.
vuursee, sea of fire.
vuurskerm, fire-screen.
vuurslag, flint (and steel).
vuurspu(w)end, (-e), fire-spitting (-emitting); -e berg, volcano.

vuursteen, flint.
vuurstraal, flash of fire.
vuurtang, fire-tongs.
vuurtessie, chafing-dish, coal-pan.
vuurtoring, lighthouse.
vuurvas, (-te), fire-proof.
vuurvlieg(ie), fire-fly.
vuurvreter, fire-eater; hot-head.
vuurwapen, fire-arm.
vuurwarm, boiling hot; red hot; aflame; – **wees**, see red, be wild; be tight.
vuurwerk, fireworks, pyrotechnics.
vy(g), (vye), fig.
vyand, (-e), enemy, foe.
vyandelik, (-e), enemy, hostile (forces).
vyandelikheid, (-hede), hostility.
vyandig, (-e), a. hostile, inimical.
vyandig, adv. inimically, in a hostile way; – **staan teenoor**, be hostile to.
vyandigheid, hostility, enmity.
vyandin, (-ne), (female) enemy, foe.
vyandskap, enmity.
vyeblaar, **-blad**, fig-leaf (lit. & fig.).
vyeboom, fig-tree.
vyebossie, Mesembrianthemum.
vyf, (vywe), n. five.
vyf, num. five.
vyfblad, cinq(ue)foil.
vyfbladig, (-e), five-leaved.
vyfdaags, (-e), lasting five days.
vyfde, fifth; **die – wiel aan die wa**, the fifth wheel to the coach.
vyfdelig, (-e), quinquepartite; quinary.
vyfdens, fifthly, in the fifth place.
vyfdraads, (-e), five-ply.
vyfdubbel(d), five-fold.
vyfhoek, pentagon.
vyfhoekig, (-e), pentagonal.

vyfhonderdjarig, (-e), quincentenary.
vyfhoofdig, (-e), five-headed.
vyfjaarliks, (-e), five-yearly.
vyfjaarplan, five-year plan.
vyfjarig, (-e), of five years.
vyfkamp, pentathlon.
vyfkant, pentagon.
vyfkantig, **-sydig**, (-e), five-sided.
vyfledig, (-e), fivefold, quinquepartite.
vyflettergrepig, (-e), five-syllabled.
vyfling, (-e), quintuplets.
vyflobbig, (-e), five-lobed.
vyfmaal, five times.
vyfponder, (-s), five-pounder.
vyfreëlig, (-e), of five lines.
vyfsnarig, (-e), five-stringed.
vyftal, five; quintet(te).
vyftallig, (-e), quinary (system).
vyftien, fifteen.
vyftiende, fifteenth.
vyftienjarig, (-e), of fifteen years.
vyftiental, (about) fifteen.
vyftienvoud, fifteen times; multiple of fifteen.
vyftig, fifty.
vyftigtal, (about) fifty.
vyftigste, fiftieth.
vyfvingerig, (-e), five-fingered.
vyfvlak, pentahedron.
vyfvoetig, (-e), five-footed; **-e reëls**, pentameters.
vyfvoud, quintuple.
vyfvoudig, (-e), fivefold, quintuple.
vygie(s), "vygie" (Mesembrianthemum).
vyl, (-e), n. file.
vyl, (ge-), file.
vylsel, filings.
vysel, (-s), mortar; screw-jack.
vyselstamper, pestle.
vywer, (-s), pond.

wa, (-ens), wag(g)on, van, truck; (railway-) carriage, coach; chariot; **die – voor die osse span**, put the cart before the horse; **voor op die – wees**, make oneself too conspicuous.
waad, (ge-), wade, ford.
waadbaar, (-bare), fordable.
waag, wae, (ge-), risk, venture, hazard; **hy het sy lewe ge–**, he risked his life; **as jy dit tog durf –!**, just you dare (do it)!: **ek – my nie aan 'n uitleg nie**, I do not hazard an explanation; **wie nie – nie, wen nie**, nothing venture, nothing have; faint heart never won fair lady; **wie –, die wen**, fortune favours the bold.
waaghals, dare-devil.
waaghalsig, (-e), dare-devil, reckless, venturesome.
waaghalsery, (-e), **waaghalsigheid**, daredevilry; foolhardiness.
waagskaal, scale, balance; **hy het sy lewe in die – gestel**, he risked his life.
waagstuk, risk, hazardous undertaking, venture; daring deed, daring feat.
waai, (-e), n.: **die – van die been**, the bend (hollow) of the knee.
waai, (-e), n. slap, smack.
waai, (ge-), blow; float; flutter; fan; **sy – met haar sakdoek**, she is waving her handkerchief; **niks met iemand uit te – hê nie**, have no business (nothing to do) with a person; **jy sal –!**, I'll send you flying!
waaiboom, cabbage-tree.
waaier, (-s), fan.
waaierband, fan-belt.
waaierpalm, fan-palm, palmyra.
waaierstert, fan-tail, (pigeon).
waaiervormig, (-e), fan-shaped.
waak, (wake), n. watch.
waak, (ge-), watch; **by 'n sieke –**, sit up with a patient; **oor iemand se belange –**, look after the interests of a person.
waakhond, watch-dog, house-dog.
waaksaam, (-same), watchful, vigilant.
waaksaamheid, watchfulness, vigilance.
waaksaamheidskomitee, vigilance-committee.
Waal, (Wale), Walloon.
Waals, (-e), Walloon.
waan, n. delusion, erroneous idea; **in die – verkeer dat . . .** , labour under the delusion that . . . ; **iemand in die – bring dat . . .** , lead a person to believe that . . . ; **iemand in die – laat dat . . .** , leave a person under the impression that . . . ; **iemand uit die – help**, undeceive a person.
waan, (ge-), imagine, fancy, think.
waansin, madness, insanity, lunacy.
waansinnig, (-e), insane, demented, deranged, mad.
waansinnige, (-s), lunatic, maniac, madman, madwoman.
waansinnigheid, insanity, madness.
waanwys, (–, -e), opinionated, presumptuous, selfconceited, bumptious.
waanwysheid, presumption, self-conceit.
waar, (ware), n. goods, ware(s), merchandise.
waar, (–, ware), a. true; **'n – verhaal**, a true story; **die ware oorsaak**, the real cause; **'n ware las**, a regular nuisance; **'n ware seën**, a veritable boon; **die ware Jakob**, the real Simon Pure, Mr. Right; **op my ware woord**, upon my word of honour; **so – as padda manel (broek en baadjie) dra**, as sure as eggs is eggs; **hy is so – groter as sy vader**, he is actually taller than his father; **daar is niks van – nie**, there is not a word of truth in it; **dis voldoende, nie – nie?**, that is sufficient, isn't it? **jy het dit geskrywe, nie – nie?**, you wrote it, didn't you?; **jy sal jou woorde moet – maak**, you'll have to prove your words.
waar, adv. where; **– gaan jy heen?**, where are you going to?; **– kom jy vandaan?**, where do you come from? **– wil hy heen**, what is he driving at?
waar, conj. since, whereas.
waaraan, inter. pron. of (by, in, etc.) what?; **– herinner dit jou?**, what does it remind you of?; **– glo jy?**, what do you believe in?; **– het jy dit herken?**, what did you recognise it by?; **ek weet nie – dit lê nie**, I don't know where the fault lies.
waaraan, rel. pron. of (by, in, on, etc.) which (whom); **die kleur – ek dink**, the colour I am thinking of.
waaragter, inter. pron. behind what?
waaragter, rel. pron. behind which (whom).
waaragtig, (-e), a true, veritable, real.
waaragtig, adv. truly, really.
waaragtig, adv. truly, really; upon my soul, upon my word; **dit is – waar**, it is genuinely true; **hy het – gelyk gehad**, he was actually right; **ek weet dit – nie**, I'm blessed if I know; **hy weet – alles**, he knows positively everything; **– nie!**, certainly not!; **daar is hy –!**, there he is, sure enough.
waaragtigheid, trueness, veracity, truth.
waarbo(we), inter. pron. above (over) what?
waarbo(we), rel. pron. above (over) which (whom); **die stad – ons gevlie het**, the town above which we flew.
waarborg, (-e), n. guarantee, warrant, warranty, security; safeguard.
waarborg, (-ge), guarantee, warrant, safeguard.
waarborgfonds, guarantee-fund.
waarborgkapitaal, guarantee-capital.
waarborgsom, caution-money, security.
waarby, inter. pron. near (by, etc.) what, **– kan ek dit vergelyk?**, with what can I compare it?
waarby, rel. pron. near (by, etc.) which (whom); whereby; **die geleentheid –**, the occasion on which.
waard, (-e), host, landlord, innkeeper; **buiten die – reken**, reckon without one's host.
waarde, (-s), value, worth; **belasbare –**, ratable value; **innerlike –**, intrinsic value; **nominale –**, face-value; **– genote (ontvang)**, value received; **– hê**, be of value, have a value; **– heg aan, attach importance (value) to: in – verminder**, fall (diminish) in value; depreciate (of money); **na – skat**, estimate (rate) at its true (proper) value; **ter – van**, to the value of; **dinge van –, things of value, valuables**; **van nul en gener –**, null and void; worthless.
waarde, a. dear; **Waarde Heer**, (Dear) Sir.
waardebepaling, assessment of value.
waardeer, (ge-), appreciate, esteem, estimate, value, rate; appraise.
waardeerbaar, (-bare), valuable.
waardeleer, theory of values.
waardeloos, (-lose), worthless.
waardeloosheid, worthlessness.
waardemeter, standard of value.
waardering, appreciation; valuation, appraisal.
waarderingshof, valuation-court.
waardeur, inter. pron. through what.
waardeur, rel. pron. through (by) which.
waardevermindering, depreciation, fall in value.
waardevol, (-le), valuable.
waardig, (-e), worthy, dignified; **'n –e opvolger**, a worthy successor; **'n –e ou Boer**, a dignified (worthy) old Boer; **'n beter saak –**, deserving (worthy) of a nobler cause.

waardigheid, dignity; worthiness; **dit is benede my –**, it is beneath my dignity.
waardigheidsbekleër, dignitary.
waardiglik, worthily.
waardin, (-ne), hostess, landlady.
waardy, worth, value.
waarheen, inter. pron. where?, where ... to?, to what place?
waarheen, rel. pron. where, where ... to?
waarheid, (-hede), truth, veracity; **'n halwe –**, a half-truth; **die naakte –**, the naked (bare, cold, plain), truth; **die suiwere –**, the truth and nothing but the truth; **die – praat**, tell the truth; **iemand goed die – sê**, tell a person some home-truths; give a person a bit (a piece) of one's mind; **om die – te sê**, to tell the truth; **om die – te sê, moet ek lieg**, I really don't know; **agter die – kom**, find out (get at) the truth; **na –**, truthfully.
waarheidliewend, (-e), truthful, truth-loving, veracious.
waarheidsin, sense of truth.
waarheidsliefde, love of truth, veracity.
waarin, inter. pron. in what?; wherein?
waarin, rel. pron. in which.
waarlang(e)s, inter. pron. along (past, next to) what?; whereabouts?
waarlang(e)s, rel. pron. along (past, next to) which.
waarlik, truly, really, upon my word; actually.
waarmee, inter. pron. with what?
waarmee, rel. pron. with which.
waarmerk, (-e), n. stamp, hall-mark.
waarmerk, (ge-), stamp, authenticate, attest, validate, certify, hall-mark; **'n ge–te afskrif**, a certified copy.
waarna, after which, whereupon.
waarna(ar), inter. pron. at (to, etc.) what?; **– het jy geskiet?**, what did you shoot at?
waarna(ar), rel. pron. at (to etc.) which.
waarnaas, inter. pron. beside (next to, by the side of) what?
waarnaas, rel. pron. beside (next to, by the side of) which.
waarnatoe, inter. pron. where?, where ... to?, to what place?
waarnatoe, rel. pron. to which.
waarneem, (waargeneem), perceive, observe; watch; avail oneself of, make use of (an opportunity); perform, attend to (one's duty); hold a temporary appointment; **die beweging van 'n planeet –**, watch (observe) the movements of a planet; **jou kans –**, seize one's chance; **ds. X sal die diens –**, the Rev. Mr X will officiate; **die praktyk vir 'n dokter –**, take charge of a doctor's practice, act as a locum tenens.
waarneembaar, (-bare), perceptible.
waarneembaarheid, perceptibility.
waarnemend, (-e), acting, temporary.
waarnemer, observer; substitute, deputy, locum tenens.
waarneming, (-e, -s,) perception: observation.
waarnemingsvermoë, perceptive faculty, perceptivity; power of observation.
waarnewens, beside which.
waarom, inter. pron. round what?; why, what for?; **die –**, the why and (the) wherefore.
waarom, rel. pron. round which.
waaromheen, inter. pron. round what?
waaromheen, rel. pron. round which.
waaromtrent, inter. pron. about what?; **– het hulle gepraat**, what did you talk about?
waaromtrent, rel. pron. about which.

waaronder, inter. pron. under (beneath, among) what?
waaronder, rel. pron. under (beneath, among) whom (which); **tien gevangenes, – twee vroue**, ten prisoners, including two women.
waaroor, inter. pron. over (across, about, etc.) what?; **– is jy kwaad?**, what are you angry about, why are you angry?; **– het julle gepraat?**, what did you talk (were you talking) about?
waaroor, rel. pron. over (across, about, etc.) which; **die brug – ons gery het**, the bridge we crossed.
waarop, inter. pron. on (upon) what?; **– staan jy?**, what are you standing on?; **– wag jy?**, what are you waiting for?
waarop, rel. pron. on (upon) which; whereupon.
waarsê, (waargesê), tell fortunes.
waarsêer, (-s), fortune-teller, soothsayer, palmist.
waarsêery, fortune-telling.
waarsegster, (-s), fortune-teller.
waarsku, (ge-), warn, caution, admonish.
waarskuwing, (-e, -s), warning, caution, admonition; reminder; premonition.
waarskuwingsbord, caution-signboard.
waarskuwingsteken, danger-signal.
waarskuwingswoord, word of caution.
waarskynlik, (-e), a. probable, likely.
waarskynlik, adv. probably.
waarskynlikheid, (-hede), probability, likelihood; **na alle –**, in all probability.
waarso, where.
waarsonder, inter. pron. without what?, **– kan jy nie klaarkom nie?**, what is it you can't do without?
waarsonder, rel. pron. without which; **iets – ek nie kan klaarkom nie**, something I cannot do without.
waarteen, inter. pron. against what:? **– leun jy?**, what are you leaning against?
waarteen, rel. pron. against which.
waarteenoor, inter. pron. opposite (to) what?
waarteenoor, rel. pron. opposite (to) which, **– te sê is dat ...** , over and against which it can be argued that ...
waartoe, inter. pron. to (for) what?; **– dien dit?**, what purpose does this serve?
waartoe, rel. pron. to which.
waartussen, inter. pron. between (among) what.
waartussen, rel. pron. between (among), which.
waaruit, inter. pron. out of (from) what?; **– lei jy dit af?**, what do you deduce that from?
waaruit, rel. pron. out of (from) which.
waarvan, inter. pron. of (about, from, etc.) what?; **– het jy gepraat?**, what did you talk about?
waarvan, rel. pron. whose, of (about, from, etc.) which.
waarvandaan, inter. pron. from where, where ... from.
waarvandaan, rel. pron. from which; **die dorp waar hy vandaan kom**, the village he comes from.
waarvoor, inter. pron. for what?; **–?**, what for?; **– is jy bang?**, what are you afraid of?
waarvoor, rel. pron. for (before, etc.) which.
waas, haze (in the air); bloom (on fruit).
wa-as, axle-tree of a wag(g)on.
waatlemoen, vide **waterlemoen**.
waband, tire (tyre) of a wag(g)on-wheel.
waboom, wag(g)on-tree.
wabuik, wag(g)on-bed.
wadrywer, driver.
wae, (ge-), vide **waag, (ge-)**.
waenhuis, cart-shed, wag(g)on-house.
waentjie, (-s), little [wag(g)on]; toy-wag(g)on.

wafel, (-s), waffle; wafer.
wafelpan, -yster, waffle-iron; wafer-iron.
wag, (-te), n. watchman; sentry, guard; watch (on board ship); **die – aflos,** relieve guard; relieve the watch; **die – hou,** keep watch; **-te uitsit,** post sentries; **op – staan,** stand guard; stand watch.
wag, (ge-), wait; **– 'n bietjie,** wait a bit (a minute); **staan en –,** be waiting, stand and wait; **iemand laat –,** keep a person waiting; **'n swaar straf – jou (staan jou te –te),** a severe punishment awaits (is in store for) you.
waggel, (ge-), totter, stagger, reel; waddle; wobble, toddle; **'n –ende tafel,** a wobbly (rickety) table.
waghond, watch-dog.
waghuis, guard-house.
waghuisie, sentry-box.
wagkamer, waiting-room.
wag-'n-bietjie-(boom, -bos), Zizyphus spp.; Asparagus spp.; **kaffer- –,** cat-thorn, Acacia caffra.
wagparade, guard-parade.
wagplek, waiting-place, place of waiting.
wagpos, post.
wagter, (-s), watchman; shepherd.
wagtoring, watch-tower.
wagvuur, watch-fire.
wagwoord, password, parole, countersign; watchword, catchword.
wa-kap, wag(g)on-tilt, -hood.
wakend, (-e), wakeful, watchful, vigilant.
waker, (-s), watcher.
wa-kis, wag(g)on-box.
wakker, awake; vigilant, watchful, alert, active, energetic, brisk, smart, **helder (nugter) –,** wide-awake; **'n – boer,** an energetic (pushing) farmer; **– bly,** keep (stay) awake; **– lê,** lie awake; **– maak,** wake (up), (a)waken; **– skrik,** wake up (with a start); **– skud,** shake awake; rouse into activity; **– word,** wake up, awake.
wakkerheid, alertness, liveliness.
waks, n. boot-polish, blacking.
waks, (ge-), polish, black.
wal, (-le), bank, shore, coast; quay, embankment; rampart; **kant nog – raak,** be neither here nor there, be wide of the mark; **aan –,** ashore, on shore; **aan – gaan,** go ashore; **aan laer – geraak,** be thrown on one's beam-ends; **van die – in die sloot,** from (out of) the frying-pan into the fire; **van – steek,** push (put, set, shove) off.
walg, n. loathing, disgust, aversion.
walg, (ge-), loathe, nauseate, disgust; **dit – my (ek – daarvan, dit laat my –),** it nauseates (disgusts) me, it makes me sick, I loathe it; **tot –ens toe,** to loathing, ad nauseam.
walging, loathing, nausea, disgust.
walglik, (-e), loathsome, nauseating, disgusting, revolting, sickening.
walglikheid, loathesomeness.
Walhalla, Valhalla.
Walkure, Valkyrie.
Wallies, (-e), Welsh.
Wallis, Wales.
Walliser, (-s), Welshman.
walm, (-e, -s), n. dense smoke; reek.
walm, (ge-), smoke.
walrus, (-se), walrus.
wals, (-e), n. waltz; roller.
wals, (ge-), waltz; roll.
walvis, whale.
Walvisbaai, Walfish Bay.
walvisbaard, -been, whale-bone.

walvisspek, blubber.
walvistraan, whale-oil, train-oil.
walvisvaarder, whaler.
walvisvangs, whale-fishery, whaling.
wamaker, wag(g)on-builder.
wamakery, wag(g)on-builder's shop.
wan, (-ne), n. winnow, (winnowing-)fan.
wan, (ge-), winnow.
wanbegrip, false notion.
wanbeheer, mismanagement.
wanbestuur, misgovernment.
wanbetaler, defaulter.
wanbetaling, non-payment; **by –,** in default of payment.
wand, (-e), wall.
wandaad, misdeed, outrage.
wandel, n.: **handel en –,** conduct of life.
wandel, (ge-), walk, take a walk; promenade.
wandelaar, (-s), walker, promenader.
wandeldek, promenade-deck.
wandelend, (-e), walking, wandering; **die –e Jood,** the wandering Jew; **'n –e nier,** a floating kidney.
wandelgang, lobby.
wandeling, (-e), walk, stroll; **'n – doen (maak),** take (be out for) a walk (stroll); **in die – genoem,** popularly called.
wandelinkie, (-s), short walk.
wandelkostuum, -pak, walking-costume; lounge suit (of a man).
wandelstok, walking-stick, cane.
wandelweg, walk.
wandkaart, wall-map.
wandluis, bug.
wandversiering, mural decoration.
wang, (-e), cheek.
wangbeen, cheek-bone.
wangedrag, misbehaviour, misconduct.
wangedrog, monster, monstrosity.
wangeluid, dissonance, cacophony.
wanguns, envy, jealousy.
wanhoop, n. despair, desperation; **met die moed van (die) –,** with the courage (born) of despair.
wanhoop, (ge-), despair; **hy het aan sy lewe ge-,** he despaired of his life.
wanhoopsdaad, act of despair.
wanhopig, (-e), desperate, despairing.
wanhopigheid, desperation, despair.
wankel, (-e), a. & adv. unstable, unsteady, uncertain, rickety, wobbly.
wankel, (ge-), totter, stagger; waver, vacillate; **iemand aan die – bring,** make a person waver.
wankelbaar, (-bare), unstable, unsteady.
wankelend, (-e), tottering, staggering, wavering, vacillating.
wankeling, tottering; wavering.
wankelmoedig, (-e), irresolute, wavering, vacillating.
wankelmoedigheid, irresolution, wavering, vacillation.
wanklank, discordant sound, discord, dissonance; jarring (discordant) note.
wanklinkend, (-e), -luidend, (-e), dissonant, harsh sounding.
wanluidendheid, dissonance.
wanmasjien, winnowing-machine.
wanneer, adv. & conj. when.
wanorde, disorder, confusion.
wanordelik, (-e), disorderly.
wanordelikheid, disorderliness; **wanordelikhede,** disturbances, riots.
wans: uit (die) – (uit), then and there; **dit reën somaar uit – uit,** it is coming down buckets full, it's simply pouring.
wanskape, misshapen, deformed.

wanskapenheid, deformity, monstrosity.
wansmaak, bad taste.
wansmaaklik, (-e), in bad taste.
wanstaltig, (-e), misshapen, deformed.
wanstaltigheid, deformity, abnormity.
want, n. rigging, shrouds.
want, conj. because, as for.
wantrou, (ge-), distrust, mistrust.
wantroue, distrust, mistrust; **'n mosie van –, a** motion of no-confidence, a no-confidence vote.
wantrouend, (-e), wantrouig, (-e), distrustful, suspicious.
wantrouigheid, distrustfulness.
wanverhouding, disproportion; **die –e in die maatskappy,** social maladjustments.
wapad, wag(g)on-road.
wapen, (-s), n. weapon, arm; (coat of) arms; badge (school, etc.); **–s dra,** bear arms; **die –s neerlê,** lay down (surrender) arms; **die –s opneem,** take up arms; **na die –s gryp,** take up arms, rise in arms; **onder die –s,** under arms, (up) in arms.
wapen, (ge-), arm; reinforce (concrete).
wapenboek, armorial.
wapenbord, (e)scutcheon.
wapenbroe(de)r, brother (companion, comrade) in arms, fellow-soldier.
wapendos, full armour.
wapendraer, armour-bearer, squire.
wapenfabriek, (am)munition-works, -factory.
wapenfeit, feat of arms, martial exploit.
wapenkletter, clash (clang) of arms.
wapengeweld, force of arms.
wapening, arming, armament, equipment; reinforcing, reinforcement.
wapenkamer, armoury.
wapenkneg, armour-bearer, shield-bearer.
wapenkreet, call to arms, battle-cry.
wapenkunde, heraldry, armory.
wapenkundig, (-e), heraldic, armorial.
wapenkundige, (-s), heraldist, armorist.
wapenrusting, armour.
wapenskild, (e)scutcheon, coat of arms.
wapenskouing, review (of arms).
wapenspreuk, heraldic device.
wapenstilstand, armistice.
wapentuig, weapons, arms.
wapper, (ge-), flutter, float, fly, wave, stream (of flags, pennons, streamers, etc.).
war: in die –, in a tangle; in confusion, in a muddle; **in die – bring (maak),** throw into confusion, derange; confuse, put out; **in die – raak,** get entangled, be thrown into confusion; get flurried (confused); **iemand se planne in die – stuur,** upset (interfere with) a person's plans.
warboel, confusion, muddle, tangle.
ware, goods, wares: vide **waar,** n.
warehuis, department store.
wa-rem, wag(g)on-brake.
warempel, adv.; vide **waaragtig.**
warhoof, muddle-head, scatter-brain.
warhoofdig, (-e), scatter-brained.
warkop, vide **warhoof.**
warkruid, dodder.
warm, a. & adv. warm, hot; **kokend –,** boiling hot; **'n – aanhanger,** an ardent supporter; **'n – bron,** a hot (thermal) spring; **'n – ontvangs,** a warm reception; **'n – plek(kie) in jou hart vir iemand hê,** have a warm place (corner, spot) in one's heart for someone; **lekker –,** nice and warm; **ek sal dit vir hom – maak,** I'll make things hot for him; **jou – maak oor 'n saak,** get warm (warm up) over a question; **dit sal –**
toegaan, it will be hot work; **– word,** get angry (excited, hot).
warmbad, hot (thermal) spring; **die – by Caledon,** the warm baths at Caledon.
warmbloedig, (-e), warm-blooded.
warmpatat(s), hiding-the-thimble.
warmpies, vide **warm,** a.; **daar – insit,** be well-to-do.
warmte, warmth; heat; ardour; **gebonde (latente) –,** latent heat.
warmte-eenheid, thermal unit.
warmtegeleiding, conduction of heat.
warmtegeleier, conductor of heat.
warmtegraad, degree of heat (warmth).
warmtemeter, calorimeter; thermometer.
warmtetoevoer, heat-supply.
warmwaterkraan, hot-water tap.
warnet, maze, labyrinth.
warrel, (ge-), whirl, swirl; **dit – voor my oë,** things reel (swim) before my eyes.
warreling, whirl(ing), swirl(ing).
warrelwind, whirlwind.
wars: – van, averse to (from).
wartaal, incoherent talk, gibberish.
was, n. 1. wax.
was, n. 2. growth; rise (of river).
was, n, 3. wash(ing), laundry; **'n hemp in die – gooi,** send a shirt to the wash; **my hemp is in die –,** my shirt is in (at) the wash (at the laundry).
was, vide **is en wees.**
was, (ge-), 1. rise (of water), wax (of moon); **die –sende water,** the rising water; **die –sende maan,** the crescent (moon), the waxing moon.
was, (ge-), 2. wash; wash up (dishes), take in washing; **ek – my hande in onskuld,** I wash my hands in innocence, I wash my hands of it; **as die een hand die ander –, word albei skoon,** one good turn deserves another; **iemand se kop –,** give a person a rubbing down (a bit of your mind); **erts –,** wash ore.
wasafdruk, impression (imprint) in wax.
wasagtig, (-e), waxy.
wasbaar, (-bare), washable.
wasbak, wash-basin; washing-trough.
wasbalie, wash(ing)-tub.
wasbeeld, wax-figure.
wasbeker, ewer, (water-)jug, toilet-jug.
wasboom, wax-myrtle.
wasdag, washing-day.
wasdoek, washing-rag; oil-cloth.
wasdom, growth, increase.
was-eg, (-te), washable, washing-, fast-dyed.
wasem, n. vapour, steam; breath.
wasem, (ge-), steam.
wasgeld, laundry(-charges).
wasgoed, wash(ing), laundry.
wasgoedsak, soiled-linen bag.
washuis, wash-house.
wasig, (-e), hazy, vapoury; blurred.
wasinrigting, laundry(-works).
waskers, wax-candle, taper.
waskom, wash-basin.
waslap, wash-rag.
wasmandjie, soiled-linen basket.
wasmasjien, washing-machine.
wasmeid, washerwoman.
wasmodel, model in wax, wax-model.
waspoor, (cart-)rut, wag(g)on-track.
waspop, wax-doll.
wassend, (-e), waxing; rising.
wasser, (-s), 1. washer.
wasser, waster, (-s), 2. washer.
wassery, (-e), laundry(-works).
wasstel, toilet-set, toilet=service.

wastafel, 1. wash(ing)-stand, washhand stand.
wastafel, (2) wax-tablet.
waster, vide **wasser, 2.**
wasvrou, washerwoman, laundress.
wat, inter. pron. what?; – **is dit hier?,** what's all this?; – **makeer jou tog?,** whatever is the matter with you?; – **help dit?,** what good is it?; – **lag jy?,** what are you laughing at?; – **nou?,** what next?; – **was ek tog bly,** how glad I was; – **sou dit?,** what does it matter?; – **vir 'n geraas is dit?,** what noise is that?; – **vir man is hy?,** what manner (sort) of man is he?
wat, rel pron. who, that, which, what; **die man – gister hier was,** the man who was here yesterday; **die man – jy gister gesien het,** the man whom you saw yesterday; **alles – moontlik is,** everything possible; **al – ek het,** all (that) I have, my all; **al – Engels is,** everything (all things) English; **hy het gehardloop al – hy kon,** he ran as fast as he could.
wat, indef. pron. something; whatever; **van alles –,** something of everything; **alles en nog –,** all sorts of things (stuff); **'n stuk of –,** a few; **heel –,** a considerable number, quite a number (a lot); – **ook al mag gebeur,** come what may, whatever happens; **maak net – jy wil,** do whatever you like; – **al nie,** what not.
wat, interj.: **toe –!** please!, won't you?; **ag –, kom ons loop,** oh, let's go.
watent, wag(g)on-tilt, -hood.
water, (-s), n. water (also = urine); dropsy; **minerale –,** mineral water; **soet (vars) –,** fresh water; – **hê,** suffer from dropsy; – **in die knieë hê,** have water on the knees; **na mekaar lyk soos twee druppels –,** be as like as two peas (in a pod); **Gods – oor Gods akker laat loop,** let things slide (drift), wait and see; – **in 'n mandjie dra,** attempt the impossible; **dit is – op sy meul,** that brings grist to his mill; – **in die see dra,** carry coals to Newcastle; **daar sal nog baie – in die see moet loop,** much water will have to flow under the mill (bridges), **die son trek –,** the sun is setting; there are signs of rain; **stil –s het diep gronde (stille –s, diepe grond, onder draai die duiwel rond),** still waters run deep; – **trap,** tread water; **moenie vuil – weggooi voor jy skone het nie,** don't be off with the old love before you are on with the new; **jou kop bo – hou,** keep one's head above water; **geld in die – gooi,** waste one's money; **in troebel – vis vang,** fish in troubled waters; **so gesond soos 'n vis in die –,** as fresh as a fish; **hy kan nie sien dat die son in die ('n ander se) – skyn nie,** he is a dog in the manger; **onder – sit,** inundate, flood; **'n skip te – laat,** launch a boat; **'n skurk van die eerste –,** a rascal of the first water.
water, (ge-), water; make water, urinate; **my mond –,** my mouth waters.
wateraanvoer, water-supply.
wateraar, subterranean watercourse.
waterafvoer, water-drainage.
wateragtig, (-e), watery.
waterbak, cistern, tank; water-trough.
waterbewoner, aquatic (animal).
waterblaas, water-bubble; blister.
waterblommetjie, -euntjie, (-uintjie), Aponogeton spp.
waterbok, water-buck.
waterboukunde, hydraulics.
waterboukundig, (-e), hydraulic.
waterdamp, (water-)vapour, steam.
waterdier, aquatic animal.
waterdig, (-te), waterproof (clothes), watertight (compartment).

waterdokter, hydropathist, water-doctor.
waterdraer, water-carrier; drone.
waterdruppel, drop of water.
wateremmer, water-bucket, -pail.
watereuntjie, vide **waterblommetjie.**
waterfiskaal, water-superintendent.
watergas, water-gas.
watergat, water-hole.
watergebrek, water-famine.
watergehalte, water-percentage.
watergeneeskunde, -wyse, hydropathy.
watergeus, water-beggar, sea-beggar.
watergeut, gutter.
waterglas, tumbler, water-glass.
waterhof, water-court.
waterhoof, hydrocephalus; **hy het 'n –,** he has water on the brain.
waterhoos, water-spout.
waterig, (-e), watery; washy.
waterigheid, wateriness, washiness.
waterkan, (water-)jug, ewer; water-can.
waterkant, water-side; water-front.
waterkar, water-cart.
waterkers, 1. watercress.
waterkers, 2. (tallow-)dip.
waterkolom, column of water.
waterkom, water-basin, bowl.
waterkraan, water-tap; water-crane.
waterkraf(fie), water-bottle.
waterkrag, water-power, hydro-electric power.
waterkruik, pitcher.
waterkuip, water-tub.
waterkuur, water-cure, hydropathic cure.
waterkwekery, hydroponics.
waterland, watery country.
waterlander, tear; **toe kom die –s,** then the waterworks were turned on.
waterlei, irrigate, water.
waterleiding, waterworks, aqueduct; water conduit.
waterlelie, water-lily.
water-, waatlemoen, watermelon.
waterloop, watercourse.
waterloot, water-shoot.
waterlyn, water-line.
waterman, waterman; Water-bearer.
watermantel, water-jacket.
watermerk, watermark.
watermeter, water-meter; hydrometer.
watermeul, water-mill; drainage-mill.
waternat, soaking (streaming) wet, soaked (to the skin), wet through.
waternood, water-famine.
waterpas, n. (spirit-)level.
waterpas, a. level.
waterpeil, water-gauge; watermark.
waterpers, hydraulic press.
waterplant, water-plant, aquatic plant.
waterplas, -poel, pool, puddle.
waterpokkies, chicken-pox.
waterpolo, water-polo.
waterproef, water-proof.
waterput, draw-well.
waterpyp, water-pipe.
waterrat, water-wheel.
waterreg, water-law; **-te,** water-rights.
waterregter, water-judge.
waterryk, (-e), watery, abounding in (with an abundance of) water.
watersaak, water-suit.
waterskaarste, water-famine.
waterskeiding, watershed.
waterski, water ski.
waterskilpad, turtle.
watersku, afraid of water, hydrophobic.

waterskuheid, hydrophobia.
waterslag, water-hammer.
waterslang, water-snake; (water-)hose.
watersoeker, water-finder, water-diviner.
watersopnat, sopping (wet).
waterspieël, water-level.
watersport, water-sports, aquatics.
waterstand, water-level.
waterstof, hydrogen.
waterstofbom, H-bomb.
waterstraal, jet (spurt) of water.
waterstroom, stream of water, current.
watersug, dropsy.
watersugtig, (-e), dropsical.
watertand, (ge-): dit laat my –, it makes my mouth water.
watertrap, (waterge-), tread water.
wateruintjie, vide **watereuntjie**.
waterval, waterfall, cataract, cascade.
watervas, water-resistant.
watervat, water-cask.
waterverf, water-colour(s).
waterverfskildery, water-colour.
waterverkeer, traffic by water.
waterverplasing, displacement.
watervlak, sheet (stretch) of water.
watervliegtuig, hydroplane, water-plane, sea-plane.
watervloed, inundation, deluge.
watervoël, water-bird; –s, water-fowl.
watervoor, water-furrow.
watervoorraad, -voorsiening, water-supply.
watervrees, hydrophobia.
waterweg, waterway.
waterwerke, waterworks.
waterwyser, water-diviner.
watte, wadding; (med.) cotton-wool.
watteer, (ge-), wad, quilt.
wattelbas, wattle(-bark).
watter, what, which.
wavrag, wag(g)on-load.
wawiel, wag(g)on-wheel.
wawielore, ears like cart-wheels.
wawyd: – oop, wide open.
web, (-be), web.
wed, (ge-), bet. (lay a) wager.
weddenskap, (-pe), bet, wager; 'n – aangaan, make a bet, lay a wager.
wedder, (-s), better; bookie.
weder-, vide **weer-**.
wederdiens, return-service.
wederdoop, anabaptism.
wederdoop, anabaptism, rebaptism.
wederdoper, anabaptist.
wedergeboorte, rebirth, new birth, renascence, regeneration.
we(d)ergebore, born again, regenerate.
we(d)erhelf, better half.
wedekerend, (-e), reflexive (gramm.).
wederkerig, (-e), mutual, reciprocal.
wederkerigheid, reciprocity, mutuality.
we(d)erkoms, return; **die – van Christus**, the Advent (Second Coming) of Christ.
wederliefde, return of love, love in return, mutual love.
wederom: (tot) –!, see you again!
we(d)eropbou(ing), rebuilding.
we(d)eropsegging: tot –, until further notice.
we(d)eropstanding, resurrection.
wederparty, adversary, opponent.
wederregtelik, (-e), unlawful, illegal.
we(d)erspannig, (-e), recalcitrant, rebellious, refractory.
we(d)erspannigheid, recalcitrance, rebelliousness, refractoriness.

we(d)erstrewig, (-e), recalcitrant, rebellious refractory.
we(d)ersyds, (-e), mutual.
wedervaar, (het –), befall, happen to; **iemand reg laat –**, do justice to a person.
wedervare, -varing, experience.
wedervergelding, retaliation; reward.
wedervraag, counter-question.
wederwaardigheid, (-hede), vicissitude.
wedloop, race.
wedren, race.
wedstryd, match, competition, contest.
weduvrou, widow(-woman).
weduwee, widow; **'n onbestorwe –**, a grass-widow.
weduweeskap, widowhood.
weduwee(s)pensioen, widow's pension.
wedywer, n. competition, rivalry.
wedywer, (ge-), compete, vie; – met, compete (vie) with, rival, emulate.
wee, (weë), n. woe, grief, pain; – **en smart, grief and pain; wel en –**, weal and woe; **die weë**, the labour pains, the pains.
wee!, interj. – my!, woe is me!; – u!, woe be to you!; – **die man wat dit durf doen!**, woe betide the man who dares to do it!
weë, weeg, (ge-), weigh; **sulke dinge – nie swaar by my nie**, such things do not weigh heavily (do not count) with me; **jou woorde –**, weigh (measure) one's words; **ge– en te lig bevind**, weighed (in the balance) and found wanting.
wee(g)blaar, plantain.
weef, (ge-), weave.
weefgetou, weefstoel, (weaving-)loom.
weefkuns, textile art.
weefnywerheid, textile-industry.
weefsel, (-s), tissue, texture, fabric.
weefselleer, histology.
weefskool, textile-school.
weefspoel, shuttle.
weeg, vide **weë**.
weegbaar, (-bare), weighable.
weegbrug, weigh-bridge.
weeghaak, weigh-beam, steel-yard.
weegmasjien, weighing-machine.
weegskaal, (pair of) scales, balance.
weegtoestel, weighing-machine.
weeheid, faitness; mawkishness.
week, (weke), n. week; **ek het jou in geen weke gesien nie**, I have not seen you for weeks; **vandag oor 'n –**, today (this day) week; **'n babetjie van een –**, a week-old baby.
week, (–, weke), a. soft, tender.
week, n.: **in die – sit**, put in soak.
week, (ge-), soak, soften, steep.
weekblad, weekly (paper).
week(s)dag, vide **weeksdag**.
weekdiens, weekly service.
weekdier, mollusc.
weekgeld, weekly allowance; weekly (week's wages (pay).
weekhartig, (-e), tender-, soft-hearted.
weekhartigheid, tender-, soft-heartedness.
weekheid, softness, tenderness.
weeklag, -kla(e), (ge-), lament, wail; – **oor**, lament, bewail, bemoan.
weeklag, lamentation, lament, wailing.
weekliks, (-e), weekly.
weekloon, weekly (week's) wages.
week(s)dag, week-day.
weelde, luxury; luxuriance, profusion, abundance, wealth, affluence, opulence; luxuriousness; **in – lewe**, live in luxury; **wette teen die –**, sumptuary laws.

weelde-artikel, article of luxury, fancy-article; **-s**, fancy-articles, fancy-goods, luxuries.
weelderig, (-e), luxurious; luxuriant.
weelderigheid, luxuriousness, sumptuousness; luxuriance.
weeluis, bug.
weemoed, melancholy, sadness.
weemoedig, (-e), melancholy, sad.
ween, (ge-), weep, shed tears.
Weenen, Weenen.
weens, on account of, because of; for.
Weens, (-e), Viennese.
weer, n. weather; **mooi − speel met 'n ander se geld**, do the grand at another's expense; **deur die − getref**, struck by lightning.
weer, n.: **in die − wees**, be up and about, be busy, be astir.
weer, adv. again; **wat was dit ook −?**, what was it again?
weer, (ge-), avert; keep away (out, back), exclude; **sig −**, defend oneself; **tien weke lank het hulle die vyand ge−**, for ten weeks they held back (resisted) the enemy; **hy is uit die party ge−**, he was kept out of (excluded from) the party; **hy het hom tot die uiterste toe ge−**, he exerted himself to the utmost; **toe, − jou!**, hurry (buck) up, get a move on!; **hy het hom dapper ge−**, he put up a brave fight.
weerbaar, (-bare), defensible (of a fortress), able to bear arms (of men).
weerbaarheid, defensibility; ability to bear arms, ability to defend oneself.
weerbarstig, (-e), unruly, rebellious, refractory, recalcitrant.
weerbarstigheid, unruliness, recalcitrance, refractoriness, rebelliousness.
weerberig, weather-report.
weerga, equal, match, peer; **sonder −**, unequalled, matchless, peerless.
weergalm, n. echo, reverberation.
weergalm, (ge-), v. resound, re-echo, reverberate.
weergaloos, (-lose), matchless, peerless, unequalled, unparalleled, unrivalled.
weergawe, reproduction, rendering.
we(d)ergebore, born again, regenerate.
weergee, (weerge-), reproduce; render, interpret.
weerglans, reflection, lustre.
weerglas, barometer.
weerhaak, barb, barbed hook.
weerhaan, (lit. & fig.) weather-cock, weather-vane; (fig.) turn-coat.
we(d)erhelf, better half.
weerhou, (-), restrain, keep (hold) back; **jou van iets −**, abstain (refrain) from doing something.
weerkaats, (-), reflect (light, heat, sound), re-echo (sound).
weerkaatsing, reflection, reverberation, re-echo(ing) (sound).
weerklank, echo; **die oproep het oral − gevind**, the appeal met with (found) a wide response.
weerklink, (-), re-echo, resound, reverberate, ring again; **− van**, ring (resound) with.
we(d)erkoms, vide **wederkoms**.
weerkrag, military strength.
weerkry, (-), get-back.
weerkunde, meteorology.
weerkundige, (-s), meteorologist.
weerlê, **-leg**, (-), refute, disprove.
weerlegbaar, (-bare), refutable.
weerlegbaarheid, refutability.
weerlegging, (-s, -e), refutation.
weerlig, n. lightning.
weerlig, (ge-), lighten; **dit het ge− na die noorde**, there were flashes of lightning in the north.

weerloos, (-lose), defenceless.
weerloosheid, defencelessness.
weermiddel, means of defence.
weerom: tot −!, see you again!
weeromspel, return match.
we(d)eropbou(ing), rebuilding, reconstruction.
we(d)eroprigting, re-erection; re-establishment.
we(d)eropstanding, resurrection.
weerplig, compulsory military service.
weerprofeet, weather-prophet.
weergesteldheid, weather conditions, state of the weather.
weersien, n. meeting again; **tot −s!**, see you again!, see you later!, so long!
weersien, (weerge-), meet (see) again.
weersin, aversion, repugnance, loathing; **'n − in iemand hê**, loathe a person.
weersinwekkend, (-e), repugnant, repulsive, revolting.
weerskante: (aan) − van die pad, on either side of the road; **aan −**, on both sides, on either side.
weerskyn, reflection, reflex, lustre.
we(d)erspannig, (-e), vide **wederspannig**.
weerspieël, (-), reflect, mirror.
weerspieëling, (-s, -e), reflection, reflex.
weerspreek, (-), contradict, deny.
weerspreking, (-s, -e), contradiction.
weerstaan, (-), resist, withstand.
weerstand, resistance; opposition; **− bied**, offer resistance, make a stand.
weerstandsvermoë, (power of) resistance, endurance, stamina, staying-power.
weerstreef, **-strewe**, (-), oppose, resist, struggle against.
we(d)erstrewig, (-e), vide **wederstrewig**.
weersverandering, change of weather.
weersy, (-e), reverse, back.
we(d)ersyds, (-e), vide **wedersyds**.
weersy(e): (aan) −, on either side.
weervoorspelling, weather-forecast.
weerwil: in − van, in spite of, notwithstanding, despite.
weerwolf, wer(e)wolf; scarecrow, bugbear.
weerwoord, answer, reply.
weerwraak, revenge, retaliation.
wees, (wese), n. orphan.
wees, (is; was; ge-), be; **hy is in die oorlog vermink**, he was maimed in the war; **die dokumente was al geteken toe ek daar kom**, the documents had already been signed when I arrived; **as dit nie was dat . . .**, but (if it were not) for the fact that . . .
weesboom, "weesboom".
weesheer, master of the Supreme Court; member of the Orphanage-Board.
weeshuis, orphanage.
weeshuiskind, orphanage child.
wees(huis)vader, master (warden) of an orphanage.
weeskamer, orphan chamber.
weeskind, orphan.
weesmeisie, orphan-girl.
weesmoeder, matron of an orphanage.
weesvader, master (warden) of an orphanage.
weet, (wis, ge-), know, have knowledge of, be aware of; **hy − nie beter nie**, he knows no better; **Joos (nugter, die hemel) −**, goodness (heaven) knows; **dit moet jy −**, be sure of this!; **hy wis nie hoe om te begin nie**, he was at a loss how to broach the subject; **sy wil niks van hom − nie**, she will have none of (nothing to do with) him; **'n mens kan nooit − nie**, one never knows, you never can tell; **ek − seker nie**, I don't know for certain; **te**

wete, namely, viz.; **iets te wete kom**, come (get) to know (find out) something; **dis vir my om te – en vir jou om uit te vind**, you can go and find it out yourself; **hy wil nie – dat hy siek is nie**, he won't admit (acknowledge) that he is ill; **(vir) sover ek –**, as far as I know, to my knowledge.
weetal, (–), wiseacre, know-all.
weetgierig, (-e), eager to learn, with a thirst for information.
weetgierigheid, eagerness to learn.
weetlus, desire of (thirst for) knowledge.
weetniet, (-e), ignoramus.
weg, (weë), n. way, road, route; **die gebaande –**, the beaten road; **die – baan vir**, pave the way for; **iemand sy eie – laat gaan**, allow a person to go his own way; **'n – inslaan**, take a road; (fig.) adopt a course; **die – versper**, bar (block) the way; **die – van alle vlees gaan**, go the way of all flesh; **hy weet geen – daarmee nie**, he does not know what to do with it; **as niks in die – kom nie**, if nothing intervenes; **in die – staan**, be in the way; **op –**, on the (one's) way; **jou op – begewe**, set out; **moeilikhede uit die – ruim**, remove obstacles.
weg, adv. away; gone; lost.
weg, interj. away; **– daar!**, get off!, get away; **– met die kapitaliste**, down with the capitalists!
wegbêre, (wegge-), put away; tuck in.
wegbereider, pioneer, forerunner.
wegblaas, (wegge-), blow away.
wegbly, (wegge-), stay away.
wegbreek, (wegge-), break away.
wegbring, (wegge-), take away; **– na**, take to.
wegdink, (wegge-), think away, shut one's mind to.
wegdoen, (wegge-), do away (with).
wegdra, (wegge-), carry away (off); **die goedkeuring – van**, meet with the approval of.
wegdraai, (wegge-), turn away; branch off.
wegdring, (wegge-), push aside.
wegdros, (wegge-), run away, desert.
wegdruk, (wegge-), push away (aside).
wegdryf, -drywe, (wegge-), drive away; float away.
weggaan, (wegge-), go away, leave.
weggee, (wegge-), give away.
weggooi, (wegge-), throw away; lose; discard.
weggooi-ooi, ewe that refuses to suckle her lamb.
weghaal, (wegge-), take away, fetch.
weghardloop, (wegge-), run away (off), flee.
weghelp, (wegge-), help to get away.
weghol, (wegge-), run away (off), scurry off, take to flight (one's heels).
weghou, (wegge-), keep away.
wegja(ag), (wegge-), chase away (off), drive away; shoo away; expel.
wegkap, (wegge-), chop (hew, cut) away (off).
wegkom, (wegge-), get away; **maak dat jy –!**, clear off (out)!
wegkrimp, (wegge-), shrink away.
wegkruip, (wegge-), crawl (creep) away; hide oneself.
wegkrulpertjie, hide and seek; **– speel**, play at hide and seek.
wegkry, (wegge-), get away.
wegkwyn, (wegge-), pine (waste) away.
wegkyk, (wegge-), look away.
weglaat, (wegge-), leave out, omit.
weglating, omission, suppression.
weglatingsteken, caret; apostrophe.
weglê, (wegge-), put aside; **dit was nie vir hom weggelê om . . .**, it was not given to (reserved for) him to . . ., **– aan**, tuck in at (food).
weglei, (wegge-), lead away.

weglok, (wegge-), lure (entice) away.
wegloop, (wegge-), walk away (off); run away, make off, desert.
wegloper, deserter, run-away, absconder.
wegmaai, (wegge-), mow down.
wegmaak, (wegge-), do away with.
wegneem, (wegge-), take away; remove, **dit neem nie weg dat . . .**, that does not alter the fact that . . .
wegoorgang, (level) crossing.
wegpak, (wegge-), pack (put) away.
wegpluk, (wegge-), snatch away.
wegraak, (wegge-), get lost.
wegredeneer, (wegge-), explain away.
wegroep, (wegge-), call away.
wegrol, (wegge-), roll away.
wegruim, (wegge-), clear away.
wegruk, (wegge-), snatch away.
wegry, (wegge-), ride (drive) away (off); cart away.
wegsak, (wegge-), sink away, subside.
wegsink, (wegge-), sink away, subside.
wegsit, (wegge-), put away.
wegskeur, (wegge-), tear away.
wegskiet, (wegge-), shoot away.
wegskop, (wegge-), kick away.
wegskuif, -skuiwe, (wegge-), push away; move (shove) up (away).
wegskuil, (wegge-), hide (oneself).
wegslaan, (wegge-), strike (beat, knock) away (off); gulp down, swallow.
wegsleep, (wegge-), drag away.
wegslepend, (-e), fascinating.
wegsluip, (wegge-), steal (sneak) away.
wegsluit, (wegge-), lock away.
wegslyt, (wegge-), wear away (off).
wegsmelt, (wegge-), melt away.
wegsmyt, (wegge-), fling away.
wegsny, (wegge-), cut away.
wegspat, (wegge-), fly off (of sparks); **hulle het na alle kante toe weggespat**, they scattered in all directions.
wegspoel, (wegge-), wash away; be washed away.
wegspring, (wegge-), jump away; start off.
wegspringplek, start, starting-place.
wegstap, (wegge-), walk away (off).
wegsteek, (wegge-), hide.
wegsterf, -sterwe, (wegge-), die away.
wegstoot, (wegge-), push away.
wegstorm, (wegge-), dash (tear) away.
wegstuur, (wegge-), send away.
wegsyfer, (wegge-), eliminate; ooze away.
wegtoor, -tower, (wegge-), spirit away.
wegtrap, (wegge-), kick away.
wegtrek, (wegge-), pull away; leave, trek away; start, drive off.
wegval, (wegge-), fall away, drop off; be omitted.
wegveeg, (wegge-), sweep away; wipe away (tears).
wegvlie(g), (wegge-), fly away.
wegvloei, (wegge-), flow away.
wegvlug, (wegge-), flee.
wegvoer, (wegge-), lead away, carry away, carry off; abduct, kidnap.
wegvoering, leading away; abduction.
wegvreet, (wegge-), eat away, corrode.
wegwaai, (wegge-), blow away, be blown away, be carried off by the wind.
wegwerk, (wegge-), get rid of, clear away; smooth away.
wegwerp, (wegge-), throw (cast) away.
wegwerplik, (-e), rejectable.
wegwis, (wegge-), wipe away (off).
wegwyser, guide; signpost.
wei(de), (weides), meadow; pasturage.

wei, n. whey.
wei(e), (ge-), graze, feed.
weids, (-e), grand, stately.
weidsheid, grandeur, splendour.
weier, (ge-), refuse, decline, deny; refuse (to act), fail (to act); miss fire; **'n aanbod –**, refuse (decline, turn down) an offer; **'n tjek –**, dishonour a cheque; **vra is vry en – daarby, there is no harm in asking; die rewolwer het ge–**, the revolver missed fire.
wei(g)ering, (-s), refusal; misfire.
weifel, (ge-), waver, vacillate, hesitate, be in two minds.
weifelaar, (-s), waverer.
weifelagtig, (-e), wavering, vacillating.
weifelend, (-e), vide **weifelagtig**.
weifeling, (-e), wavering, vacillation, hesitation, irresolution.
weifelmoedig, (-e), irresolute, wavering.
weifelmoedigheid, irresolution.
weigeld, grazzing-fee.
wei(g)ering, vide **weiering**.
weiland, pasture(-land), grazing-land.
weinig, (-e), little few.
weireg, grazing-right.
weiveld, pasture-land; pasturage.
wek, (ge-), (a)wake, (a)waken, call, rouse, cause, create, excite (curiosity), raise (hopes), rouse (indignation), stir, call up.
wekker, (-s), alarm(-clock).
wekstem, clarion(-call), reveille.
wel, n.: **– en wee**, weal and woe.
wel, adv. well: – **ter tale wees**, be a fluent speaker; **dis alles goed en –, maar . . .** , its all very well; but . . . ; **as ek my dit – herinner**, if I remember rightly; **dit kan – wees**, that may be; **en – omdat**, and that because; **jy sal – moeg wees**, I dare say you are tired; **hy voel hom nie – nie**, he does not feel well.
welaan, well then, very well.
welbedag, (te), well-considered.
welbegrepe, well-understood.
welbehaaglik, (-e), comfortable; pleasant.
welbehae, pleasure; **in mense 'n –**, goodwill to man.
welbekend, (-e), well-known, familiar.
welbemind, (-e), well-beloved.
welbespraak, (-te), well-spoken, fluent.
welspraaktheid, fluency.
welbesteed, (-bestede), well-spent.
weldaad, benefit, boon, kind action.
weldadig, (-e), benevolent, charitable benecient; beneficial; **dit doen 'n mens – aan**, it does one good.
weldadigheid, benevolence, charity.
weldadigheidsvereniging, benevolent (charitable) society.
weldenkend, (-e), right-thinking.
weldeurdag, (-te), well thought-out.
weldoen, (welge-), do good.
weldoener, (-s), benefactor.
weldra, soon, presently, before long.
weledelagbare, -gestrenge: die – heer M. Brand, the Honourable M. Brand.
weledele: die – heer W. Smith, W. Smith, Esq.; **Weledele Heer**, Dear Sir.
weleer, formerly.
weleerwaarde: die – heer S. Botha, the Reverend S. Botha; **Sy Weleerwaarde**, His Reverence; **Weleerwaarde Heer**, Sir (form of address in letter).
welf, welwe, (ge-), vault, arch.
welgaan, (welge-), fare well; **mag dit jou –!**, good luck to you!
welgebore, well-born, high-born.

welgedaan, (-gedane), well-fed, plump.
welgeleë, beautifully situated.
welgeluksalig, (-e), blessed.
welgemanierd, (-e), good-mannered, well-behaved, well-bred.
welgemanierdheid, good manners.
welgemeen(d), (-de), well-meant.
welgemoed, (-e), cheerful.
welgesind, (-e), well-disposed.
welgeskape, well-formed, well-made.
welgesteld, (-e), well-to-do, well-off.
welgesteldheid, easy circumstances.
welgevalle, pleasure.
welgevallig, (-e), pleasing, agreeable.
welgevorm(d), (-de), well-formed.
welhaas, well-nigh, soon, shortly.
welig, (-e), luxuriant, rampant, rank.
weligheid, luxuriance.
welingelig, (-te), well-informed.
weliswaar, indeed, it is true, to be sure.
welk, (ge-), fade, wither.
welke, inter. pron. what, which.
welkom, (–, -e), welcome; **– tuis!**, welcome home!; **iemand – heet**, welcome a person, bid a person welcome.
welkoms, welcome.
welkomsgroet, welcome.
welkomsrede, address of welcome.
wellewend, (-e), well-bred; courteous.
wellewendheid, good breeding, courtesy.
wellig, perhaps, may be.
welluidend, (-e), melodious, sweetsounding, harmonious.
welluidendheid, melodiousness, euphony.
wellus, (-te), lust, voluptuousness, sensuality, delight, bliss.
wellusteling, (-e), sensualist, voluptuary.
wellustig, (-e), voluptuous, sensual.
wellustigheid, voluptuousness.
welmenend, (-e), well-meaning.
weloorwoë, well-considered, deliberate.
welopgevoed, (-e), well-bred; well-educated.
welp, (-e), cub.
welriekend, (-e), fragrant, sweet-smelling, sweet-scented.
welriekendheid, fragrance.
welsalig, (-e), blessed.
welsand, wilsand, quicksand.
welslae, success.
welsprekend, (-e), eloquent.
welsprekendheid, eloquence.
welstand, health; well-being, welfare.
welsyn, well-being, welfare; health.
weltevrede, well-satisfied.
welvaart, prosperity; welfare.
welvarend, (-e), prosperous, thriving, healthy, in sound (good) health.
welvarendheid, prosperity; good health.
welverdiend, (-e), well-deserved.
welvoeglik, (-e), becoming, proper, decent, seemly, decorous.
welvoeglikheid, propriety, decency.
welvoeglikheidshalwe, for the sake of propriety, for decency's sake.
welvoorsien, (-e), well-provided.
welwillend, (-e), benevolent, obliging.
welwillendheid, benevolence, goodwill.
welwing, (-s), vault.
wemel, (ge-), swarm, teem; **die opstel – van die foute**, the essay is bristling with mistakes; **die perske – van die wurms**, the peach is alive with worms.
wemeling, swarm.
wen, (-ne), windlass.
wen, (ge-), accustom to; **ek sal (my) nooit daar-**

wen   382   **werkersbond**

aan kan – nie, I shall never get accustomed (used) to it.
wen, win, (ge-), win, gain; gather (in), reap, harvest; **aan duidelikheid** –, gain in clearness.
wenakker, head-land.
wend(e), (ge-), turn; **jou skrede – na**, turn (direct) one's steps to; **jou tot iemand – om hulp**, turn (apply) to someone for assistance.
wendam, catch-dam.
wending, (-s, -e), turn; **'n gunstige – neem**, take a favourable turn (a turn for the better).
Wenen, Vienna.
wenhou, winning-stroke.
wening, weeping; **– en knersing van tande**, weeping and gnashing of teeth.
wenk, (-e), hint; **'n duidelike** –, a broad hint; **'n – opvolg**, take a hint, act on a suggestion.
wenner, vide **winner**.
wenpaalkamera, photo-finish camera.
wens, (-e), n. wish, desire; **my – is vervul**, I have my wish, my ambition is realized; **die – is vader van die gedagte**, the wish is father to the thought; **alles gaan na** –, everything is going well (smoothly).
wens, (ge-), wish, desire; **dit laat veel te –e oor**, it leaves much to be desired.
wenslik, (-e), desirable.
wenslikheid, desirability.
wentel, (ge-), revolve, rotate (on its own axis), welter (wallow, roll about).
wentelbaan, orbit; **in 'n – plaas**, put into orbit.
wenteling, (-s, -e), revolution, rotation.
wenteltrap, spiral (winding)staircase.
werd, a. worth; **niks – nie**, worth nothing; **dis nie die moeite – nie**, it's not worth while (the trouble).
werda!, who goes there?
wêreld, (-e), world, universe; part of country, region; **die ander** –, the next (other) world; **die hele** –, the whole world, all the world; **die Ou (Nuwe)** –, the Old (New) World; **Namakwaland is 'n droë** –, Namaqualand is a dry region; **die bose** –, the wicked world; **die geleerde (letterkundige, ens.)** –, the learned (literacy, etc.) world; **dit is die –s beloop**, that is the way of the world; **die (wye) – ingaan**, go out into the world; set out in life; **die – skeur (deel)**, take to one's heels; **die – is 'n speeltoneel**, all the world's a stage; **so gaan dit in die ou** –, such is the way of the world; **ter – bring**, bring into the world; **niks ter** –, nothing on earth; **vir niks ter – nie**, not for all the world; **hy is vir niks ter – bang nie**, he is afraid of nothing on earth; **my –!**, well I never!, good gracious!
wêreldas, axis of the world.
wêreldberoemd, (-e), world-famous (-famed), of world wide fame.
wêreldberoemdheid, world-wide fame.
wêreldbeskouing, view of life.
wêreldbewoner, inhabitant of the world.
wêreldburger, citizen of the world.
wêrelddeel, part of the world, continent.
wêreldgebeurtenis, world event.
wêreldgeskiedenis, history of the world.
wêreldhandel, world-trade.
wêreldheerskappy, world dominion.
wêreldhervormer, world reformer.
wêreldkaart, map of the world.
wêreldkampioen, world champion.
wêreldkennis, knowledge of the world.
wêreldkundig, (-e), known all over the world, universally known, notorious; **iets – maak**, make a thing public.

wêreldlik, (-e), worldly (goods); temporal (power); secular (music).
wêreldling, (-e), worldling.
wêreldmag, world power.
wêreldoorlog, world-war; **die W–**, the Great War.
wêreldorde, world order.
wêreldreis, world tour.
wêreldrekord, world record.
wêreldryk, world empire.
wêrelds, (-e), worldly; vide **wêreldlik**.
wêreldsee, ocean.
wêreldgesind, (-e), worldly(-minded).
wêreldgesindheid, worldliness.
wêreldsgoed, worldly thing(s), trash.
wêreldskokkend, (-e), world-shaking.
wêreldstad, metropolis.
wêreldstelsel, cosmic system.
wêreldtaal, world language.
wêreldtekort, world shortage.
wêreldtentoonstelling, international exhibition.
wêreldverkeer, world traffic.
wêreldvrede, world peace, universal peace, peace of the world.
wêreldwonder, wonder of the world.
wêreldwys, (-e), worldly-wise.
wêreldwysheid, worldly wisdom.
werf, (werwe), n. farmyard; shipyard.
werf, **werwe**, (ge-), recruit, enlist, enrol; **stemme** –, canvass for votes.
werfagent, recruiting-agent; canvasser.
wering, prevention; exclusion.
werk, (-e), n. work, labour, employment; works (of a watch, etc.); **die –e van Langenhoven**, the works of Langenhoven; **ons is 'n – van Gods hande**, we are of God's workmanship; **– soos bossies**, no end of work; **dis alles jou–!**, it's all your doing!; **'n – aanneem**, contract for a work; **iemand – gee**, give a person work, find work for a person; **hy gee aan 100 mense** –, he employs (gives employment) to 100 men; **geen – hê nie**, be out of work (employment); **ek sal daar – van maak**, I'll see to it; **– soek**, look for work; **aan die – gaan**, set (get) to work; **die hand aan die – slaan**, set to work; **alles in die – stel**, do one's utmost, leave no stone unturned; **sonder – wees**, be out of work (employment); **hy het glad verkeerd te – gegaan**, he set about it in quite the wrong way.
werk, (ge-), work; **– soos 'n esel**, work like an ox; **iemand te hard laat** –, overwork a person, work a person off his legs; **sy maag** –, he is suffering from diarrhoea; **die medisyne het al ge-**, the medicine has already acted (taken effect, operated, worked); **sy niere – nie goed nie**, his kidneys do not function properly; **die rem wou nie – nie**, the brake failed to act; **met 'n tikmasjien** –, work a typewriter; **dit – op die senuwees**, it works (acts) on (affects) the nerves; **hy – op my senuwees**, he gets on my nerves.
werkbaas, foreman.
werkbank, work-bench.
werkby, working-bee, worker.
werk(s)broek, working-trousers; overalls.
werkdadig, (-e), effective, efficacious.
werkdag, work(ing)-day, week-day.
werkdoos, work-box.
werkeloos, (-lose), idle, inactive.
werkeloosheid, idleness, inactivity.
werkend, (-e), working; active; efficious, effective; **die –e stand**, the working-classes.
werker, worker.
werkersbond, workers' league (union).

werkesel, drudge, slave, plodder; 'n regte –, a devil (fiend, demon, glutton) for work.
werkgewer, employer.
werkhuis, workhouse; penitentiary.
werkie, (-s), little job; los –s, odd jobs.
werking, working, action, operation; **buite – stel**, suspend (an act); put out of action; **in – stel**, put in(to) operation (the law); put into action, set going; **in – tree**, come into force, take effect.
werkkamer, work-room.
werk(s)klere, working-clothes, -kit.
werkkrag, working-power, energy; workman, hand labourer.
werkkring, sphere (field) of activity.
werkliede, workmen, labourers, hands.
werklik, (-e), a. real, actual, true.
werklik, adv. really, actually, truly.
werklikheid, reality; **in –**, in reality, in point of fact; **dis 'n hele –**, it means a lot of work.
werkloon, wage(s), pay.
werkloos, (-lose), out of work (employment) unemployed, workless.
werkloosheid, unemployment.
werkloosheidsuitkering, unemployment benefit.
werklus, zest (passion) for work.
werk(s)man, workman, labourer, hand.
werkmandjie, work-basket.
werknemer, employee.
werk(s)pak, working-suit (-clothes, -kit).
werkplaas, workshop, work-room.
werkplan, plan of work, working-plan.
werkrooster, time-table, work-schedule.
werksaam, (-same), industrious, active, diligent; **by 'n fabriek – wees**, work (be employed) at a factory.
werksaamheid, (-hede), industry, activity; (pl.) business, work, proceedings; **weens druk –hede**, owing to pressure of work.
werk(s)broek, working-trousers; overalls.
werk(s)klere, working-clothes, -kit.
werk(s)man, workman, labourer, hand.
werkstaker, striker.
werkstaking, strike; walk-out.
werkster, (-s), woman worker.
werkstuk, piece of work; problem.
werk(s)volk, workmen, labourers, hands.
werktafel, work-table.
werktuig, tool, implement, instrument.
werktuigkunde, mechanics.
werktuigkundig, (-e), mechanical.
werktuigkundige, (-s), mechanic(ian).
werktuiglik, (-e), mechanical, automatic.
werktyd, working hours.
werkuur, working-hour.
werkverskaffing, provision of employment (work); relief-work(s).
werk(s)volk, workmen, labourers, hands.
werkvrou, charwoman
werkwinkel, workshop.
werkwoord, verb.
werkwoordelik, (-e), verbal.
werkwyse, method of work; procedure.
werp, (ge-), throw, cast, hurl, fling; **anker –**, cast anchor; **'n blik op iets –**, cast an eye on (a glance at) something; **lig op iets –**, throw (cast, shed) light on something; **jou op jou knieë –**, go down on one's knees; **van jou –**, disclaim; repudiate.
werphout, boomerang.
werplood, sounding-lead.
werpskyf, discus.
werpspies, javelin.
werskaf, (ge-), be busily engaged; **wat – jy?**, what are you at?

werskaffery, to-do (ado), fuss.
werst, (-e), verst.
werwaarts, whither.
werwe, (ge-), vide **werf** (ge-),
werwel, (-s), vertebra; button.
werwelbeen, vertebra.
werweldier, vertebrate.
werwer, (-s), recruiter; canvasser.
werwing, canvassing; recruiting.
wes, n. vide **weste**.
wes, a. west.
Wes-Afrika, West Africa.
wese, (-ns), being, creature; face, looks, appearance; nature, character; substance; being, existence; **geen lewende – nie**, not a living soul; **skyn en –**, shadow and substance.
wesel, (-s), weasel.
wesen(t)lik, (-e), real; essential, fundamental, substantial, material.
wesenlikheid, reality, essentiality.
wesenloos, (-lose), vacant, blank (look, stare), expressionless.
wesenloosheid, vacancy, blankness.
wesentlik, vide **wesen(t)lik**.
Wes-Europa, Western Europe.
Wes-Europees, (-pese), West European.
Wesfale, Westphalia.
Wes-Gote, Visigoths.
wesie, (-s), little orphan.
Wes-Indië, the West Indies.
Wes-Indies, (-e), West Indian.
westekant, west-side.
weskus, west-coast.
Wesleyaan, (-ane), Wesleyan.
Wesleyaans, (-e), Wesleyan.
wesnoordwes, west-north-west.
wesp, (-e), wasp.
wespenes, wasps' nest, vespiary.
Wes-Pruise, West(ern) Prussia.
wessuidwes, west-south-west.
wes(te), west; **die Weste**, the West, the Occident; **na die –te**, to (towards) the west, westward(s); **ten –te van**, (to the) west of.
weste: **buite –**, unconscious.
westekant, west side.
westelik, (-e), westerly; **die –e halfrond**, the western hemisphere.
westergrens, western frontier.
westerlengte, west(ern) longitude.
Westerling, (-e), Westerner, Western.
Westers, (-e), Western, Occidental.
westewind, west-wind, westerly wind.
weswaarts, (-e), westward(s).
wet, (-te), n. law; act (of Parliament); **die Mosaïese –**, the Mosaic Law; **dit is geen – van Mede en Perse nie**, it is not a law of the Medes and Persians; **–te maak**, legislate, make laws; **'n – oortree**, violate a law; **iemand –te voorskrywe**, dictate to a person; **jou aan die – hou**, keep within the law; **by – bepaal**, enact by Statute; **– op besmetlike siektes**, Contagious Diseases Act; **–te teen die weelde**, sumptuary laws; **teen die –**, against the law; **volgens –**, according to law, **voor die –**, in the eye of the law.
wet, (ge-), whet, sharpen.
wetboek, code (of law); **– van strafreg**, criminal (penal) code.
wetbreuk, breach of the law.
wete, knowledge; **buite (sonder) my –**, without my knowledge, unknown to me; **nie by my – nie**, not that I know of; **na my (beste) –**, to (the best of) my knowledge; **teen beter – in**, against one's conscience (own better knowledge).
wetens, knowingly.
wetenskap, science; knowledge.

wetenskaplik, (-e), scientific.
wetenskaplikheid, scientific character.
wetenswaardig, (-e), worth knowing.
wetenswaardigheid, (-hede), thing worth knowing.
wetgeleerd, (-e), versed in law.
wetgeleerde, (-s), jurist, lawyer.
wetgeleerdheid, jurisprudence.
wetgewend, (-e), legislative.
wetgewer, legislator, law-giver.
wetgewing, legislation.
wetlik, (-e), legal; statutory; **-e erfdeel**, legitimate portion.
wetlikheid, legality.
wetsartikel, section (article, clause) of an Act (a law).
wetsbepaling, provision (stipulation) of a law (an Act).
wetskennis, legal knowledge.
wetsontwerp, bill; **'n - opstel**, draft a bill; **'n - indien**, introduce a bill.
wetsoortreding, breach (violation, transgression) of a law.
wetstaal, legal language (parlance).
wetsterm, law-term.
wetsvereniging, law society.
wetsverkragting, violation of the law.
wetsvoorstel, bill.
wetteloos, (-lose), lawless.
wetteloosheid, lawlessness.
wetties, (-e), adhering strictly to the letter of the law, strict, rigid.
wettig, (-e), lawful, legitimate, legal; **-e vrou**, lawful wife; **-e kind**, legitimate child; **-e eis**, legal claim; **-e betaalmiddel**, legal tender.
wettig, (ge-), legitimate, legitimatize (a child), legalize; justify, warrant.
wettigheid, legitimacy, legality.
wetverbreker, law-breaker.
wewe, vide **weef**.
wewenaar, (-s), widower.
wewenaars(gras), black-jack, beggar-ticks.
wewer, (-s), weaver.
wewertjie, (-s), weaver-bird.
wewery, (-e), weaving-mill.
whisk(e)y, whisk(e)y.
whist, whist.
Whitworth-draad, Whitworth thread.
wie, inter. pron. who, whom; **- praat?**, who is speaking?; **- se kind is jy?**, whose child are you?; **- van julle?**, which of you?; **maar - sê (so)?**, but no fear!, but nothing of the kind!
wie, indef. pron. (he) who; **- ook (al)**, who(so)ever.
wied, (ge-), weed.
wieë, wieg, (ge-), rock; **in slaap -**, rock (lull) to sleep; (fig.) lull (quiet).
wieg, (wieë), n. cradle; **vir iets in die - gelê wees**, be born to (destined for) something; **van die - tot die graf**, from the cradle to the grave.
wiegel, (ge-), wobble, rock.
wiegelied, cradle-song, lullaby.
wiek, (-e), wing (of bird); sail, wing, vane (of wind-mill); **op eie -e drywe**, paddle one's own canoe.
wiel, (-e), wheel; **die vyfde - aan die wa**, the fifth wheel to the coach; **iemand in die -e ry**, put a spoke in a person's wheel.
wielband, tyre (tire).
wiel(i)ewaai, (ge-), mill, wheel, circle spin.
wielewaal, (-wale), golden oriole.
wiel(i)ewalie, merry-go-round (game).
wielmaker, wheelwright.
wielryer, cyclist.
wier, sea-weed.

wierook, incense, frankincense; **- toeswaai**, praise to the skies.
wierookgeur, smell of incense.
wierookvat, censer, thurible.
wies(i)ewasie, (-s), trifle.
wig, (-te), baby, babe, child, bairn.
wig, (-ge, wie), wedge.
wigvormig, (-e), wedge-shaped.
wik, (ge-), weigh; **- en weeg**, weigh the pros and cons; **die mens -, maar God beskik**, man proposes (but) God disposes.
Wiking, (-e), Viking.
wikkel, (ge-), wrap, envelop, enfold, wind, swathe, swaddle; involve: shake; **in 'n stryd ge- raak**, get involved (mixed up) in a quarrel.
wikkelrig, (-e), wobbly.
wikkelwa: met die ounôi se - reis, train.
wiks, (-e), n. blow, stroke, slap, smack.
wiks, (ge-), slap, smack, beat, flog.
wil, n.: will, wish, desire; **'n eie - hê**, have a will of one's own; **sy laaste (uiterste) -**, his last will (and testament); **U - geskied**, Thy will be done; **die - vir die daad neem**, take the will for the deed; **waar daar 'n - is, is daar 'n weg**, where there is a will, there is a way, **buite my -**, without my (will and) consent; **met die beste - van die wêreld kan ek nie**, with the best will in the world (for the life of me) I cannot; **teen - en dank**, in spite of oneself, against one's wish; **ter -le van**, for the sake of; because of; **uit vrye -**, of one's own free will.
wil, (wou, ge-), want wish, like; intend, be on the point of; will; **die gerug - dat . . .** , it is rumoured (rumour has it, there is a rumour) that . . .; **as God -**, God willing; **die lot het dit anders ge-**, Fate has decreed otherwise; **die toeval wou dat . . .** , it so happened that . . .; **ek - liewer hier bly**, I prefer staying here; **jy wou mos bly**, well, you would stay; **wat - jy hê moet ek doen?**, what would you have me do?; what do you want me to do?; **wie wil, kan**, where there is a will, there is a way; **laat kom wat -**, (let) come what may; **dit - sê**, that is to say, that means; **hy weet wat hy -**, he knows his own mind.
wild, n. game.
wild, (-e), a wild (flowers, animals); savage (beasts); unruly; shy (birds, animals); fierce (passions); **-e vlees**, proud flesh; **in die -e (weg)**, at random; indiscriminately.
wild(s)bok, vide **wildsbok**.
wilddief, poacher.
wilddiefstal, **-diewery**, poaching.
wilde, (-s), savage.
wildeals, wild wormwood.
wilde-amandel, wild almond.
wildebees, gnu, wildebeest.
wilde-eend, wild duck.
wildegans, wild goose.
wildehawer, wild oats.
wildehoender, coot, moorhen.
wildehond, wild dog, **Cape hunting-dog**.
wildekat, wild cat.
wildeman, barbarian, savage.
wildepruim, sour plum.
wildernis, (-se), wilderness, waste.
wildevy(g), wild fig.
wildewingerd, Virginia-creeper.
wildheid, wildness, savageness.
wildpark, game-reserve.
wild(s)bok, buck; venison.
wildskut, hunter, game-killer.
wildstroper, poacher.
wild(s)vleis, venison, game.
wildtuin, game-reserve.

wildvreemd, (-e), quite strange; **'n -e,** a perfect (an absolute) stranger.
wildvuur, wildfire (in tobacco).
wilg, (-e), willow.
wilger-, wilkerboom, willow-tree.
willekeur, arbitrariness, high-handedness; **na -,** at pleasure, at (your own sweet) will, arbitrarily.
willekeurig, (-e), arbitrary, high-handed, despotic; voluntary (muscles).
willekeurig, arbitrariness.
willens: - en wetens, deliberately.
willig, (-e), willing.
willigheid, willingness.
willoos, (-lose), will-less.
wilsand, welsand, quicksand.
wilsbeskikking, last will, will.
wilskrag, will-power.
wimpel, (-s), pendant, pennon.
wimper, (-s), (eye)lash.
win, vide **wen.**
wind, (-e), wind; wind, fart; **-e,** flatulence, wind; **dis alles (pure) -,** it's all (mere) gas (wind), it's all empty boasting; **kyk uit watter hoek die - waai,** find out how the wind blows (how the land lies); **waai die - uit daardie hoek?,** is that how the land lies?; **daar waai geen - nie of dit is iemand van nut,** it's an ill wind that blows nobody good; **'n -jie hoor waai dat . . .,** hear a rumour that . . . ; **wie - saai, sal storm maai,** sow the wind and reap the whirlwind; **vir iemand - sny,** smooth the way for a person; **die wind van agter hê,** have a following wind; **die Eilande bo die Wind,** the Windward Islands; **deur die - wees,** be bewildered (dazed, confused, in a muddle); be three sheets in the wind; **in die - praat,** talk at random, talk nonsense; preach to the winds; **'n waarskuwing in die - slaan,** fling a warning to the winds; **iemand se raad in die - slaan,** flout a person's advice; **onder die -,** under the lee; **die Eilande onder die Wind,** the Leeward Islands; **onderkant die - hou,** keep on the leeside (of game); **vlak teen die -,** in the teeth of the wind; **'n mens kan van - alleen nie leef nie,** one can't live on air; **vir - en weer laat groot word,** leave children entirely un-cared for; **voor die - seil,** sail (run) before the wind; **dit gaan hom voor die -,** he is prospering; **-af,** before (down) the wind; **-op,** against the wind.
windblom, anemone, wind-flower.
windbreker, wind-screen.
windbui, gust of wind, squall.
windbuks, air-gun; gas-bag, braggart.
winddroog, (-droë), dried by the wind, air-dried; half dry.
winddruk, wind-pressure.
windeier, wind-egg.
winderig, (-e), windy; flatulent.
winderigheid, windiness, flatulence.
windgat, air-hole, wind-bag, gas-bag.
windgeweer(tjie), air-gun.
windhond, greyhound.
windhoos, windspout, tornado.
winding, (-s), winding, convolution (of shell), coil (of cable).
windjie, (-s), breath of air (wind).
windkant, wind-side, windward side.
windklep, air-valve, vent.
windmaak, (windge-), brag, boast, swank.
windmaker, (-s), braggart, gas-bag.
windmakerig, (-e), posh, swaggery.
windmeter, wind-gauge, anemometer
windmeul(e), windmill; **'n slag van die - weg hê,** have a tile loose; **teen -en(s) veg,** tilt at windmills.
windorrel, (fig.) gas-bag, wind-bag.
windrigting, direction of the wind.
windruk, gust of wind.
windsak, wind-bag, gas-bag.
windsel, (-s), bandage, swathe.
windskade, damage caused by wind.
windskeef, (-skewe), skew, slanting, crooked, on one side awry, lop-sided.
windskerm, wind-screen.
windskuif, wind-gauge (of a rifle)
windsnelheid, velocity of the wind.
windstil, (-le), calm.
windstilte, calm.
windstoot, gust of wind.
windstreek, point of the compass.
windsug, tympanites.
windswa(w)el, cliff-swallow.
windtonnel, wind-tunnel.
windvlaag, gust (blast) of wind, squall.
windwyser, weathercock.
wingerd, vineyard; **hy het deur die - geloop,** he has kissed the bottle.
wingerdluis, phylloxera.
wingerdsiekte, vine-disease.
wingerdstok, vine.
wingewes, conquered country; province.
wink, (-e), n. wink, nod.
wink, (ge-), beckon; wink.
winkbrou, (-e), eyebrow.
winkel, (-s), n. shop, store; (work-)shop.
winkel, (ge-), shop.
winkelbediende, shop-assistant.
winkeldief, shoplifter.
winkeldiefstal, shoplifting.
winkelhaak, (carpenter's) square; trapdoor (L-shaped tear in cloth).
winkelier, (-s), shopkeeper, shopman.
winkelklerk, shop-assistant.
winkelkykery, window-shopping.
winkellaai, till.
winkelmeisie, shop-girl.
winkelprys, retail price.
winkelraam, shop-window, show-window.
winkelruit, shop-window.
winkeluitstalling, shop-window display.
winkelvenster, shop-window.
winner, (-s), winner.
wins, (-te), profit, gain, return; winnings (at cards); **met - verkoop,** sell at a profit.
winsbedrag, profit.
winsbejag, greed of gain, profit-snatching; **uit -,** from motives of gain.
wins-en-verliesrekening, profit-and-loss account.
winsgewend, (-e), profitable, paying.
winsuitkering, distribution of profits.
winter, (-s), winter; **in die -,** in winter.
winteragtig, (-e), wintry.
winterappel, winter-apple.
winterdag, winter-day; **op 'n -,** on a winter's day.
winterdrag, winter-wear.
wintergesig, wintry scene.
winter(s)hande, chilblained hands.
winterklere, winter-clothes.
winterkoninkie, wren.
winterkwartiere, winter-quarters.
wintermaand, winter-month.
wintermôre, winter-morning.
winternag, winter-night.
winter(s)ore, chilblained ears.
winterpak, winter-suit.
winters, (-e), wintry.
winterseisoen, winter-season.
winter(s)hande, chilblained hands.

winterslaap, winter-sleep, hibernation.
wintersonstilstand, winter-solstice.
winter(s)ore, chilblained ears.
winter(s)voete, chilblained feet.
wintertyd, winter-time.
winterveld, winter-pasture.
winterverblyf, winter-residence.
winter(s)voete, chilblained feet.
wintervoorraad, winter-store.
winterweer, wintry weather.
wip, (-pe), n. seesaw; trap, gin (for catching birds); skip; in 'n –, in no time, in a jiffy.
wip, (ge-), (play at) seesaw; go up and down; wobble; tilt; whip, whisk, skip, hop; **'n kamer binne –**, whip (wisk) into a room; **die kar –**, the cart tilts.
wipbrug, bascule-bridge, drawbridge.
wipkar, tilt-cart, tip-cart.
wipneus, turned up (tip-tilted) nose.
wipperig, (-e), wobbly; (fig.) uppish, snobbish; **'n –e stappie**, a jumpy gait.
wipplank, seesaw.
wipstert, wagtail.
wirwar, whirl, jumble, tangle, muddle.
wis, (-se), a. certain, sure; – **en seker**, assuredly, as sure as fate, (as) sure as eggs (is eggs).
wis, (ge-), wipe.
wiskunde, mathematics.
wiskundig, (-e), mathematical.
wiskundige, (-s), mathematician.
wiskunstenaar, mathematician.
wiskunstig, (-e), mathematical.
wispelturig, (-e), fickle, freakish, inconstant, changeable.
wispelturigheid, fickleness, inconstancy.
wissel, (-s), n. bill (of exchange), draft; points, switch (railway); **'n – op Kaapstad**, a bill payable at Cape Town; **'n – honoreer**, honour (meet) a bill; **'n – trek**, draw a bill.
wissel, (ge-), exchange (letters, views, looks, blows), bandy (words), interchange; (change, give change for (money); cash cheque); shed (teeth); change, vary; **van plekke –**, (inter)change places.
wisselaar, (-s), money-exchanger.
wisselbank, bank of exchange.
wisselbeker, floating trophy, challenge-cup.
wisselboek, bill-book.
wisselbou, rotation of crops.
wisselhandel, bill-brokerage.
wisseling, (-e), change, fluctuation; exchange, interchange; **die – van die jaargetye**, the succession of the seasons; **die –e van die lot**, the vicissitudes of fortune.
wisselkantoor, exchange-office.
wisselkind, changeling.
wisselkoers, rate of exchange.
wisselmakelaar, bill-broker.
wisselrekening, exchange-account.
wisselrym, alternate rhyme.
wisselspoor, side-rail(s); siding; points.
wisselstroom, alternating current.
wisseltand, milk-tooth.
wisselvallig, (-e), uncertain, precarious.
wisselvalligheid, (-hede), uncertainty, precariousness; **die –hede van die lewe**, the vicissitudes of life.
wisselvervalsing, forging of bills.
wisselwagter, pointsman, switchman.
wisselwerking, interaction.
wit, n. white; **die – van 'n eier**, the white of an egg; **die – van die oog**, the white of the eye; **ek wil dit swart op – hê**, I want it put down in black and white.
wit, a. white; **die – vlag**, the white flag, the flag of truce; – **maak**, whiten, blanch; – **word**, turn pale, go white; grow (turn) white.
wit, (ge-), whitewash.
witagtig, (-e), whitish.
witbaard, white-beard.
witbloedig, (-e), white-blooded.
witbont, white-spotted, piebald.
witboom, silver-tree.
witborskraai, parson-crow.
witbrood, white bread.
wit-els, white-alder.
witgatboom, shepherd's tree.
witgatspreeu, pied starling.
witgepleister(d), (-de), whitewashed; **–de graf**, whited grave (sepulchre.)
witgloeiend, (-e), white-hot.
witgoud, platinum.
withaar-, white-haired.
witheid, whiteness.
without, Cape-holly (Ilex mitis).
witkalk, whitewash.
witkop, white-haired person; grey-head.
witkwas, distemper- (whiting-)brush; cow with white brush to tail.
witlag, (witge-), laugh happily.
witlood, white-lead.
witman, European; white man.
witmens, European, white man; **die –e**, the whites (white people, Europeans).
witmetaal, white metal (alloy).
wit-ogie, white-eye.
witroes, powdery mildew.
Witsee, the White Sea.
witseerkeel, diphtheria.
witsel, whiting, whitewash.
witskimmel, light-grey (horse).
witstam(boom), vide **witgatboom**.
witstertspreeu, vide **witgatspreeu**.
wittebroodsdae, **-weke**, honeymoon.
wittande: – **lag**, laugh contentedly.
witterig, (-e), whitish.
witvis, whiting, whitebait.
witvoet-, white-footed (horse, etc).
witvoetjie: by iemand – soek, toady to (fawn upon) a person, curry favour with a person.
witvoetsoeker, toady.
witwortel, parsnip.
wodka, vodka.
woed, (ge-), rage.
woede, rage, fury; **jou – op iemand koel**, vent your rage upon a person.
woedend, (-e), furious, (slang) wild; **iemand – aankyk**, look daggers at a person; **(verskriklik) – wees**, be in a (towering) rage.
woef!, bow-wow!
woeker, n. usury.
woeker, (ge-), practise usury; grow rank; **met jou talente –**, make the most of your talents.
woekeraar, (-s), usurer.
woekerdier, parasite.
woekergeld, money got by usury.
woekerhandel, usurious trade, usury.
woekerplant, parasitic plant; parasite.
woekerrente, usurious interest.
woekersugtig, (-e), usurious.
woekerwins, exorbitant profit.
woel, (ge-), bestir oneself, bustle, work hard, toss (about), fidget (about); burrow, grub, root (in soil), rummage (in papers); wind (round); **ek sal jou –**, I'll give it you hot.
woelerig, (-e), restless, fidgety (child).
woelgees, turbulent fellow, agitator.

woelig, (-e), restless, fidgety (child), lively, busy (street), turbulent.
woeligheid, restlessness, turbulence.
woeling, (-e, -s), agitation, turbulence, (plur.) disturbances.
woelsiek, (–, -e), restless, turbulent.
woelwater, fidget, restless person.
Woensdag, Wednesday.
woeps!, flop.
woerts!, whiz(z)!
woer-woer, whirr-whirr, whirligig.
woes, (-te), desolate, desert, waste (land, grounds); wild, savage (scenery), fierce, ferocious (looks struggle); – **te kere gaan**, behave riotously; – **ry**, ride (drive) recklessly; – **word**, become unruly.
woestaard, (-s), brute, yahoo, rough.
woesteling, (-e, -s), brute, rough.
woesteny, (-e), wilderness, waste (land), desolate (desert) tract.
woestheid, wildness; fierceness.
woestyn, (-e), desert.
wol, wool.
wolagtig, (-e), woolly.
wolbaal, bale of wool.
wolbereiding, wool-dressing.
woldraend, (-e), wool-bearing.
wolf, (wolwe), wolf; Lupus, Wolf; – **skaapwagter maak**, set the fox to keep the geese; **'n – in skaapsklere**, a wolf in sheep's clothing.
wolfabriek, woollen mill, wool-mill.
wolfabrikant, woollen manufacturer.
wolfagtig, (-e), wolfish.
wolfram, tungsten.
wolf(s)hond, wolf-hound (-dog).
wolfsvel, wolfskin.
Wolga, Volga.
wolgoed, woollens; woollen clothing.
wolhaar, woolly hair; **jou lyf – hou**, play the gallant.
wolhaarhond, woolly dog.
wolhaarpraatjies: wilde –, wild talk.
wolhandel, wool-trade.
wolhandelaar, wool-merchant.
wolk, (-e), cloud (also fig.); **in die –e wees**, be beside oneself with joy; **iemand tot in die –e verhef**, laud (extol) a person to the skies.
wolkaarder, wool-carder (-comber).
wolkagtig, (-e), cloudy, cloud-like.
wolkbank, bank of clouds.
wolkbreuk, cloud-burst.
wolk(e)krabber, sky-scraper.
wolkerig, (-e), cloudy, clouded.
wolkkolom, pillar of clouds.
wolkombers, woollen blanket.
wolkoper, wool-merchant.
wollerig, (-e), woolly.
wolmark, wool-market.
wolsak, wool-sack; big clumsy person.
wolskaap, wool-bearing sheep.
wolstof, woollen material.
Woltoon, (nickname for) inhabitant of the Eastern (Cape), Province.
wolveiling, wool-auction, wool-sale.
wolverwery, wool-dyeing; dye-works.
wolwassery, wool-refinery.
wolwegif, strychnine.
wolwehok, wolf-trap.
wolwejag, wolf-hunting.
wolweweer, wool-weaver.
wolwewery, wool-weaving factory.
wond, (-e), n. wound, injury; **ou –e oopkrap**, reopen old sores.
wond, (ge-), wound, injure, hurt.
wondbaar, (-bare), vulnerable.

wondbalsem, vulnerary balm (balsam).
wonder, (-s), n. wonder, marvel, miracle, prodigy; **die sewe –s van die wêreld**, the seven wonders of the world; **die –s in die Bybel**, the miracles in the Bible; – **bo –**, for a wonder, miracle of miracles; **–s doen**, work wonders; **is dit 'n – dat . . . ?**, is it any wonder (that) . . . ?
wonder, (ge-), wonder.
wonderbaarlik, (-e), miraculous, marvellous, wonderful.
wonderdaad, miracle, wonder.
wonderdier, prodigious beast, monster, monstrosity, freak.
wonderdoener, miracle-, wonder-worker.
wonderdokter, medicine-man, witch-doctor (among savages); quack.
wonderessens, wonder-essence.
wonderjaar, year of wonders.
wonderkind, infant-prodigy, wonder-child.
wonderkrag, miraculous power.
wonderland, wonderland.
wonderlik, (-e), wonderful, strange, queer; **die –e daarvan is dat . . .** , the wonderful part of it is that . . .
wonderlikheid, wonderfulness.
wondermag, miraculous power.
wondermens, human wonder, prodigy.
wondermiddel, wonderful remedy, panacea; quack-medicine.
wondermooi, (–, -e), exquisite, exceedingly (marvellously) beautiful.
wonderskoon, (–, -skone), exquisite, exceedingly (marvellously) beautiful.
wonderspreuk, magic formula.
wondersprokie, fairy-tale.
wonderteken, miraculous sign, miracle.
wonderwater, medicinal water.
wonderwerk, miracle.
wondheelkunde, surgery.
wondkoors, wound-fever.
wondkramp, tetanus.
wondmiddel, remedy (cure) for wounds.
wondnaat, suture.
wondpleister, vulnerary plaster.
wondsalf, healing ointment.
wondwater, (vulnerary) lotion.
wondyster, probe.
woning, (-s), residence, dwelling (-house), house.
woningnood, house-famine.
woningvraagstuk, housing-question.
woninkie, (-s), small (dwelling-)house.
woon, (ge-), live, stay, reside, dwell.
woonagtig, resident, living.
woonbuurt, residential quarter (area).
woonhuis, residence, dwelling-house, homestead.
woonkamer, living-room.
woonplaas, **-plek**, (place of) residence (abode), dwelling-place, home.
woonstede, vide **woonplaas**.
woonstel, flat; – **met bediening**, service flat.
woonvertrek, living-room.
woord, (-e), word, term; **die Woord (Gods)**, the Word (of God); **Gods Woord**, the Word of God; **jou – breek**, break (go back on) one's word; **'n – van dank**, a word of thanks; **die – doen**, he is never at a loss for a word, he has the gift of the gab, **ek gee jou my – van eer**, you may take my word for it; **iemand die – gee**, call upon a person to speak; **vir iemand 'n goeie – doen**, put in (say) a good word for a person; **mnr. X het die –**, I call upon Mr X to speak; **–e met iemand hê**, have words with a person; **jou – hou**, keep (make good stick to) one's word; **die – kry**, be called upon

(to speak); catch the Speaker's eye; **–e kry**, come to words; **die laaste – hê**, have the last word; have the final say; **sy laaste –e**, his dying words; **–e maak**, coin words; **jy neem die –e uit my mond**, you take the very words out of my mouth; **die – neem**, begin to speak; **die – tot iemand rig**, address a person; **–e soek**, pick a quarrel; **hy het g'n stom(me) – gesê nie**, not a word did he say; **jou –e terugtrek**, eat your words; **ek kon geen – uitbring nie**, I was speechless, I felt tongue-tied; **hy kon geen –e vind om . . .** , words failed him; **mnr. X sal die – voer**, Mr X will speak (address the meeting); **die – vra**, ask (beg) permission to speak; **–e wek, voorbeelde trek**, example is better than precept; **mnr. X is aan die –**, I call upon Mr X to speak; **Mr X is speaking**; **iemand aan sy – hou**, take a person at his word; hold (keep) a person to his word; **in een –**, in a (one) word; **met ander –e**, in other words; **met soveel –e**, in so many words; **onder –e bring**, put into words express, **op my – (van eer)**, upon my word (of honour); **jy kan op sy – reken**, his word is as good as his bond; **iemand te – staan**, give a person a hearing; **hy is 'n man van sy –**, he is as good as his word.
woordafleiding, etymology, derivation of words.
woordarmoede, paucity (lack) of words.
woordbetekenisleer, semantics.
woordbreuk, breach of promise (faith).
woordeboek, dictionary.
woordeboekmaker, lexicographer.
woordekeus, choice of words.
woordelik, (-e), literal, verbal; verbatim (report).
woordelys, vocabulary, glossary.
woordepraal, pomp of diction (words).
woordeskat, vocabulary, stock of words.
woordespel, punning, quibbling; pun.
woordestroom, flow (torrent) of words.
woordestryd, argument, dispute.
woordetwis, verbal difference, argument.
woordevloed, torrent (flow) of words.
woordewisseling, altercation, dispute.
woordherhaling, repetition of words.
woordjie, (-s), (little) word; **vir iemand 'n goeie – doen**, put in a word for a person; **daaroor kan ek 'n – saampraat**, I can speak from experience (with) authority) on that matter.
woordkuns, art of writing, literary art, word-painting.
woordkunstenaar, word-painter, literary artist.
woordomsetting, inversion (gram.).
woordontleding, parsing.
woordryk, (-e), verbose, voluble.
woordrykheid, verbosity, volubility.
woordsifter, quibbler, hair-splitter.
woordsmeder, word-coiner.
woordspeling, pun, play upon words.
woorduitlating, ellipsis.
woordverdraaiing, distortion of words.
woordverklaring, explanation (definition) of a word (of words).
woordvoerder, spokesman, mouthpiece.
woordvorming, word-formation.
word(e), ((werd-), ge-), become, get (angry, cold, dark), grow (old), go (blind, mad), turn (grey, pale), fall (silent, ill, in love); (pass, voice) be; **ys – water**, ice becomes (turns into) water; **dit – beweer dat . . .** , it is said that . . . ; **dit is beweer (ge-)**, it has been said.
wording, genesis, birth, origin.
wordingsgeskiedenis, genesis.
wors, (-te), sausage; **'n – het twee ente**, there are two sides to every question; **so skaars soos – in 'n hondehok**, very rare (scarce).
worsbroodjie, hot-dog.
worsderm, casing.
worsmasjien, sausage-machine.
worstel, (ge-), struggle, wrestle (also sport); **– met**, struggle (wrestle, contend, grapple) with (difficulties); **met die dood –**, struggle with (be in the grip of) death; **met God –**, wrestle with God (in prayer); **– teen**, struggle (wrestle, contend, fight, battle) against.
worstelaar, (-s), wrestler.
worsteling, (-s, -e), struggle, wrestle.
worstelkuns, (art of) wrestling.
worstelperk, (wrestling-)ring, -arena.
worstelstryd, struggle (for existence), contest.
wortel, (-s), n. root (also of tooth, tongue, nail; of word, number or quantity; of evil); carrot, parsnip; **– skiet**, take (strike) root; **die – trek uit**, extract the root of (a number); **(met) – en tak uitroei**, extirpate (destroy) root and branch, eradicate.
wortel, (ge-), (take) root; **– in**, root (be rooted) in.
wortelagtig, (-e), root-like.
wortelboer, carrot-grower.
wortelgroente, root-vegetables.
wortelgrootheid, radical quantity.
wortelhaar, root-hair, radical hair.
wortelklinker, radical vowel.
wortellof, carrot-leaves.
wortelskieting, taking root, radication.
wortelstelsel, root-system.
wortelteken, root-sign, radical sign.
worteltrekking, extraction of roots.
wortelvesel, root-fibre, fibril.
wortelvorm, radical quantity.
wortelwoord, root-word, radical (word).
woud, (-e), forest, wood.
woudbewoner, forest-dweller.
woudesel, wild ass, onager.
woudreus, giant of the forest.
wraak, n. revenge, vengeance; **my kom die – toe**, vengeance is mine; **jou – koel**, wreak one's vengeance; **– neem**, take revenge, retaliate; **– sweer**, vow (swear) vengeance; **– uitoefen**, take revenge; **om – roep**, cry for revenge; **uit –**, in revenge.
wraak, (ge-), disapprove of, object to, take exception to.
wraakbaar, (-bare), objectionable, blamable, challengeable.
wraakgevoel, feeling of revenge, revengeful feeling, vindictiveness.
wraakgierig, (-e), revengeful, vindictive.
wraakgierigheid, revengefulness.
wraakgodin, avenging goddess; **-ne, Furies**.
wraaklus, vide **wraakgierigheid**,
wraaklustig, (-e), revengeful, vindictive.
wraakneming, revenge, retaliation.
wraakoefening, revenge, retaliation.
wraaksug, thirst for revenge, vindictiveness, revengefulness.
wraaksugtig, (-e), vindictive.
wraaklustigheid, vide **wraaklustig**.
wraggies, wragtie, vide **waaragtig**.
wrak, (-ke), n. a wreck, derelict.
wrak, (-ke), rickety (furniture), crazy (boat), unsound, shaky, infirm.
wrakgoed, wreckage, flotsam and jetsam.
wrakhout, wreckage.
wraking, recusation, challenge.
wrang, (-e), bitter (fig.); vide **vrank**.
wrangheid, bitterness; vide **wrang**.
wreed, (wrede), cruel, inhuman, barbarous, ferocious; **die wrede werklikheid**, grim reality.

wreedaard, (-s), brute, cruel person.
wreedaardig, (-e), cruel, inhuman, barbarous, brutal.
wreedaardigheid, cruelty, ferocity.
wreedheid, (-hede), cruelty, savagery.
wreef, (wrewe), instep.
wreek, (ge-), revenge; avenge (a person, an insult); **jou oor iets op iemand –**, avenge (revenge) oneself for something (up)on a person.
wreker, (-s), avenger, revenger.
wrewel, resentment, annoyance, spite.
wrewelig, (-e), resentful, spiteful, rancorous, bitter; peevish, irritable.
wreweligheid, resentfulness, peevishness.
wrikbaar, (-bare), unstable.
wring, (ge-), wring (one's hands), wring (out) (clothes), twist (person's arm); **iets uit iemand se hande –**, wrest (wrench) something from a person; **jou – van pyn**, writhe (squirm) with pain; **jou deur 'n opening –**, wriggle through a hole.
wrintie, wrintig, wrintlik; vide **wraggies**.
wroeging, (-e, -s), remorse, compunction; **die – van jou gewete**, pangs (stings, qualms) of conscience.
wroet, (ge-), (fig.) burrow, grub; vide **vroetel**.
wrok, n. grudge, rancour.
wrok, (ge-), fret, fume, chafe.
wrywing, (-e, -s), friction (also fig.).
wuf, (-te), frivolous.
wuftheid, frivolity.
wuif, wuiwe, (ge-), wave.
wulps, (-e), lewd, lascivious.
wulpsheid, lewdness, lasciviousness.
wurg, (ge-), strangle, throttle; (intrans.) be strangled; **ek het gevoel of ek wou –**, I felt as if I was being strangled; **dit het dikwels ge– in tye van droogte**, we have often been hard put to it in times of drought.
wurggreep, deadly grip, strangle-hold.
wurging, strangulation.
wurgknoop, strangling-knot.
wurgpaal, strangling-post.
wurgpatat, choke-potato.
wurgpeer, choke-pear.
wurgsiekte, croup.
wurg-wurg: dit het dikwels – gegaan, at times it was as much as one could bear.
wurgyster, gar(r)otte.
wurm, (-s), n. worm, maggot, grub.
wurm, (ge-), worm, wriggle, twist.
wurmagtig, (-e), worm-like.
wurmhopie, worm-cast.
wurmmiddel, vermifuge, worm-killer.
wurmpie, (-s), small worm, wormling; **die arme –**, the poor (little) mite.
wurmvormig, (-e), vermiform.
wy, (ge-), ordain (priest), consecrate (bishop, king, church, bread, wine); **sy hele lewe was aan (die diens van) God ge–**, his whole life was dedicated (devoted) to (the service of) God; **jou tyd (kragte, lewe) aan die studie (die opvoeding van jou kinders) –**, devote one's time (energy, life) to study (the education of one's children); **ge– aan die nagedagtenis van**, sacred to the memory of.
wyd, (wye), wide, broad, spacious, roomy; **die baadjie sit te –**, the coat fits too loosely; **– en syd bekend**, known far and wide.
wydberoemd, (-e), far-famed.
wyders, moreover, further(more).
wydheid, wideness, broadness, roominess.
wyding, devotion; consecration, ordination.
wydlopig, (-e), verbose, prolix, diffuse, wordy, lengthy, long-winded.
wydlopigheid, verbosity, prolixity.
wydsbeen, astride, astraddle; **– ry**, sit astride a horse; **– staan (oor)**, straddle.
wydte, (-s), width, breath, gauge (railway), calibre (of a gun or tube).
wydvertak, (-te), wide-spread.
wyf, (wywe), vixen, termagant, shrew; **'n ou –**, an old woman (of a man).
wyfie, (-s), female (animal), cow (of elephant), hen (of birds).
wyfie-eend, (female) duck.
wyfie-olifant, female elephant.
wyfieskilpad, (female) tortoise.
wyk, (-e), n. quarter, district, ward; beat (of postman); **die – neem**, flee, make off; **die – neem na Holland**, take refuge in Holland.
wyk, (ge-), give way (ground), make way, yield, fall back, withdraw, retire; **hy – vir geen mens nie**, he gives way (yields to) nobody; **geen duimbreed – nie**, not budge an inch.
wykverpleegster, ward-, district-nurse.
wyl, n. while, (short) time; **by –e**, occasionally, now and then.
wyl, conj. since, as, because.
wyle, late, deceased; **– pres. Reitz**, the late Pres. Reitz; **– my oom**, my late uncle.
wyn, (-e), wine; **helder – skink**, speak plainly (openly), be frank; **– in die man, wysheid in die kan**, when wine (is) in, wit (is) out.
wynagtig, (-e), winy, vinous.
wynaksyns, duty (excise) on wine.
wynbeker, wine-cup.
wynboer, wine farmer, wine-grower.
wynbou, viticulture, wine-growing.
wyndruif, (wine-)grape.
wyngaard, (fig.) vineyard.
wyngees, spirit of wine.
wynglas, wine glass.
wynhandel, wine trade.
wynhandelaar, wine merchant.
wynkaart, wine-list.
wynkan, wine-jug, wine-can.
wynkelder, wine-cellar, wine-vault.
wynkelkie, wine-glass.
wynkenner, judge of wine.
wynkoper, wine merchant.
wynkraf(fie), wine-decanter.
wynkuip, wine-vat.
wynlug, winy (vinous) smell.
wynmeter, vinometer.
wynoes, vintage.
wynpers, wine press.
wynruit, rue.
wynruithaakdoring, hook-thorn.
wynsteen, tartar.
wynsteensuur, tartaric acid.
wynstok, vine.
wynvaatjie, wine-cask.
wynvervalsing, adulteration of wine.
wynvlieg, wine-fly; wine-bibber, tippler.
wynvomitief, ipecacuanha-wine.
wys(e), wyse, (wyses), n. manner, way fashion; mood (grammar); tune; **by wyse van proef**, by way of trial; **by wyse van spreke**, in a manner of speaking; **op gelyke wyse**, in like manner; **die wyse waarop**, the way in which; **aantonende –**, indicative mood; **bywoord van wyse**, adverb of manner.
wys, (–), a. wise, sensible; cross; ill-tempered (woman, child), vivious (horse); **'n – (e) staatsman**, a wise statesman; **hy is nie goed (reg) – nie**, he is not in his right mind (senses); **hulle sal nooit –er word nie**, they will never grow wiser (learn wisdom); **ek kan daar nie uit – word nie**, I can make nothing (neither head

nor tail) of it; I cannot make it out; **jy het baie – gehandel**, you acted very wisely; vide **wysmaak**.
wys, (ge-), show, point out; **iemand iets –**, point out something to a person; **die weerglas – mooi weer**, the barometer points to fine weather; **– na**, point to (at); **die pyltjie – na links**, the arrow points to the left; **iemand op iets –**, point out something to a person; **alles – daarop dat . . .**, everything points to the fact that . . .
wysbegeerte, philosophy.
wyse, vide **wys, n.**
wyse, (-s), wise man; **die Wyse(s) uit die Ooste**, the Wise Men of the East.
wyselik, vide **wyslik**.
wyser, vide **wyster**.
wysgeer, (-gere), philosopher.
wysgerig, (-e), philosophical.
wysgerigheid, philosophy.
wysheid, wisdom; **maak asof jy die – in pag het**, pretend to all knowledge.
wysie, (-s), tune, melody, air; **– hou**, sing in tune; **nie – hou nie**, sing out of tune; **op die – van**, to the tune of; **van die – raak**, loose the thread of one's discourse, get flurried; **hy is van sy – af**, he is not all there; **iemand van sy – afbring**, put a person out.
wysig, (ge-), modify, alter; amend.
wysiging, (-e, -s), modification, change; amendment; **'n – ondergaan**, undergo a change.
wys(e)lik, wisely.
wysmaak, (wysge-): **iemand iets –**, make a person believe something; **hy laat hom alles –**, he will swallow anything, he is very easily imposed upon; **hy het homself wysgemaak dat . . .**, he deluded himself into believing (into the belief) that . . .
wysneus, wiseacre, prig, pedant.
wysneusig, (-e), conceited, pedantic.
wysneusigheid, conceit, pedantry.
wys(t)er, (-s), hand (of watch), pointer (of balance, etc.); **die groot –**, the hour-hand; **die klein –**, the minute-hand.
wys(t)erplaat, dial.
wysvinger, forefinger, index.
wyt, (ge-): **iets aan iemand –**, blame a person for something; **dis aan sy onverskilligheid te –e dat . . .**, it is owing (due) to his carelessness that . . . ; **hy het dit aan homself te –e**, he has only himself to thank (blame) for it.
wywater, holy water.
wywepraatjie, idle gossip.

X

xenofobie, xenophobia.
Xhosa, (-s), X(h)osa.

xilofoon, (-fone), xylophone.
x-strale, X-rays, Röntgen-rays.

Y

ydel, (-e), vain (person, hope); idle (word), empty (talk).
ydelheid, (-hede), vanity; futility; – der ydelhede, vanity of vanities; alles is –, all is vanity.
ydellik: 'n naam – gebruik, take a name in vain.
ydeltuit, (-e), vain girl.
ydeltuitery, frivolousness, vanity.
yk, n. gauge, verification (stamping and verifying) of weights and measures.
yk, (ge-), gauge, stamp and verify; 'n ge–te term, a standing (standard) phrase.
yker, (-e), gauger, inspector of weights and measures.
ykkantoor, weights and measures office.
ykmaat, standard measure.
yl, a. thin (air, beard), rare, rarified.
yl, (ge-), (1) be delirious, wander (in one's mind), rave; –ende koors, delirium, delirious fever.
yl, (ge-), (2) hasten, hurry, rush.
ylbode, express-messenger, courier.
ylheid, thinness, rarity (of atmosphere).
ylhoofdig, (-e), light-headed, delirious, rattle-brained, scatter-brained.
ylhoofdigheid, light-headedness, delirium, empty-headedness, thoughtlessness.
ylings, hurriedly, hastily, in hot haste.
ys, n. ice; die – breek, break the ice.
ys, (ge-), shudder, shiver.
ysbaan, skating-rink (-course), ice-rink.
ysbeer, polar bear, white bear.
ysberg, iceberg.
ysig, (-e), icy, as cold as ice.
ysingwekkend, (-e), appalling, ghastly.
yskas, refrigerator, ice-safe.
yskegel, icicle.
yskoud, (-koue), icy-cold, ice-cold, icy; dit laat my –, it leaves me stone cold; ek het daar – van geword, it made me cold all over; I felt a chill down my spine.
Ysland, Iceland.
Yslander, (-s), Icelander.
Yslands, (-e), Icelandic.
yslik, (-e), horrible, frightful, terrible, ghastly, gruesome; huge, enormous; – groot, frightfully big.
yslikheid, (-hede), horror, ghastliness.
ysmasjien, freezing-machine.
ysmassa, ice-pack.
ysperiode, glacial period.
Yssee, Arctic Ocean.
yster, (-s), iron; (horse-)shoe; runner (of sledge); gegote –, cast iron; gesmede –, wrought iron; ou –, old iron, scrap-iron; ruwe –, pig-iron; 'n mens kan geen – met hande breek nie, one cannot make a windmill go with a pair of bellows; smee die – onderwyl dit heet is strike the iron while it is hot; make hay while the sun shines; te veel – in die vuur hê, have too many irons in the fire.
ystererts, iron-ore.
ysterfabriek, iron-works.
ysterghwano, basic slag.
ystergietery, iron-foundry, iron-works.
ystergordyn, iron curtain.
ysterhandel, iron-trade, iron-mongery.
ysterhandelaar, ironmonger.
ysterhoudend, (-e), ferriferous, ferrous.
ysterhout, ironwood.
ysterindustrie, iron industry.
ysterkatel, iron bedstead.
ysterkleurig, (-e), iron-coloured.
ysterklip, iron stone.
ysterklou: – in die grond slaan, take to one's heels; stand firm.
ysterlees, last, boot-tree.
ystermyn, iron-mine.
ysteroksied, -okside, ferric oxide.
ysterpaal, iron-post, iron-pole.
ysterperd, machine, bike, bicycle; railway-engine, locomotive; train.
ysterplaat, iron-plate, iron-sheet.
ystersmedery, (iron-)forge.
ystersmeltery, iron-foundry.
ystersmid, iron-smith, blacksmith.
ysterstaaf, iron bar.
ystersterk, strong as iron; 'n – gestel, an iron constitution.
ystersuur, ferric acid.
ystertydperk, iron-age.
ystervark, porcupine.
ysterverbinding, iron-compound.
ystervitriool, iron-sulphate, copperas.
ystervreter, fire-eater, swashbuckler.
ysterware, hardware, ironware.
ystyd, ice-age, glacial period.
ysveld, ice-field.
ysvorming, glaciation.
yswater, ice-water, iced water.
ywer, n. diligence, industry, zeal, fervour, ardour.
ywer, (ge-), be zealous; vir 'n saak –, be zealous for (devote oneself ardently to) a cause.
yweraar, (-s), zealot, fanatic, keen, partisan, zealous adherent.
ywerig, (-e), diligent, industrious, zealous; – besig met, busily engaged on, intent on, sedulously occupied with.
ywerigheid, diligence, zeal.
ywersug, jealousy, envy.
ywersugtig, (-e), jealous, envious.

Z

Zephyrus, Zephyr.
zeppelin, (-s), zeppelin.
zero, sero, (-'s), zero.
Zeus, Zeus.
zits, (ge-), whiz(z).

Zoeloe, (-s), Zulu.
zoem, (ge-), buzz, hum, drone, zoom.
zoemvlug, zoom.
Zwingliaan, (-ane), Zwinglian.

Enige Gebruiklike Afkortinge

A ampère.
aank. aankoms.
aanst. aanstaande.
aant. aantekening.
aanvr. aanvraag.
aanw. aanwysend.
A.A.U.B. Antwoord as u blief.
a.b. aan boord.
ACSV Afrikaanse Christen-Studentevereniging.
ACVV Afrikaanse Christelike Vrouevereniging.
A.D. Anno Domini.
a.d. ante diem.
adj. adjektief.
ad lib. ad libitum (**na wens**).
adv. adverbium.
adv. advokaat.
advt. advertensie.
afb. afbeelding.
afd. afdeling.
afl. afleiding.
Afr. Afrikaans.
agb. agbare.
Akad. Akademie.
akk. akkusatief.
al. alinea (paragraaf).
ald. aldaar.
alg. algebra; algemeen.
Am. Amerika; Amerikaans.
ANS Afrikaans-Nasionale Studentebond.
antw. antwoord.
A.N.V. Algemeen Nederlandsch Verbond.
appl. applous.
Apr. April.
art. artikel.
a.s. aanstaande.
ASB Afrikaanse Studentebond.
asb. asseblief.
asst. assistent.
ATKV Afrikaanse Taal- en Kultuurvereniging.
ATV Afrikaanse Taalvereniging.
a.u.b. as u blief.
Aug. Augustus.

B.A. Baccalaureus Artium.
bal. balans.
bb. of **brs.** broeders.
B.Com. Baccalaureus Commercii.
B.D. Baccalaureus Divinitatis.
bedr. bedrag; bedryf; bedrywend.
bekl. beklaagde.
bep. bepaald; bepaling.
bes. besending; besitlik; besonder.
besk. beskuldigde.
bes. vnw. besitlike voornaamwoord.
bet. betaal; beteken; betekenis.
betr. betreklik.
bg. bogenoemde.
bl. bladsy; bladsye.
B.Mus. Baccalaureus Musicae.
b.nw. byvoeglike naamwoord.
BO bevelvoerende offisier.
b.o. blaai om.
Br. Brits.
br. broeder.
brig.-genl. brigade-generaal.
brs. of **bb.** broeders.
B.Sc. Baccalaureus Scientiae.
burg. burgemeester.
bv. byvoorbeeld.
b.v.p. been voor paaltjies.
b.w. bywoord; bywoordelik.
byl. bylae.
byv. byvoeglik.
bw. bywoord; bywoordelik.

C Celsius.
ca. circa (ongeveer).
cap. caput (hoofstuk).
cf. confer(atur) (vergelyk).
cg sentigram.
Ch.B. Chirurgiae Baccalaureus.
CJV Christelike Jongeliedevereniging.
cl sentiliter.
cm sentimeter.
cm² vierkante sentimeter.
cm³ kubieke sentimeter.
cresc. crescendo.
c.s. cum suis.
CSV Christelike Strewersvereniging; Christen-Studentevereniging.

dat. datief; datum.
D.C. da capo (van die begin af).
D.D. Doctor Divinitatis.
d.d. de dato (vanaf datum).
def. definisie.
dekl. deklinasie.
del. deleatur (skrap).
dep. depot.
dept. departement.
Des. Desember.
dag dekagram.
dg desigram.
dgl. dergelike.
Di. Dinsdag.
d.i. dit is.
dial. dialek; dialekties.
dim. diminutief.
disk. diskonto.
dist. distrik.
dl desiliter; deel.
D.Litt. Doctor Litterarum.
dnr. dienaar.
Do. Donderdag.
do. dito.
dos. dosyn.
DPW Departement van Publieke Werke.
D.Phil. Doctor Philosophiae.
dr. dokter; doktor.
dr. debiteur.
Dr. Med. Doctor Medicinae.
Dr. Theol. Doctor Theologiae.
ds. dominus (Dominee).
D.Sc. Doctor Scientiae.
D.V. Deo Volente (as God wil).
dw. dnr. dienswillige dienaar.
d.w.s. dit wil sê.

e.a. en ander.
Ed. Edele.
ed. edisie.
e.d. en dergelike.
Ed.Agb. Edelagbare.
Ed.Gestr. Edelgestrenge.
e.d.m. en dergelike meer.
Eerw. Eerwaarde.
e.g. eersgenoemde.
e.k. eerskomende.
Eks. Eksellensie.
eks. eksemplaar.
Eng. Engeland; Engels.
ekv. enkelvoud.
ens. ensovoort(s).
e.s.m. en so meer.
Ev. Evangelie.
ev. eersvolgende; eventueel.
e.v. en volgende.

FAK Federasie van Afrikaanse Kultuurverenieginge.
Febr. Februarie.
fig. figuur; figuurlik.
fl. floryn (gulde).
fol. folio.
FM frekwensiemodulasie.
Fr. Frankryk; Frans.
fr. frank.
fut. futurum (toekomende tyd).

g gram.
geb. gebore; gebou; geboul.
Gebrs. gebroeders.
ged. gedagteken; gedateer; gedeelte.
geïll. geïllustreer.
gen. genitief.
genl. generaal.
geol. geologie; geologies.
Geref. Gereformeerd.
Ges. Gesang.
gesk. geskiedenis; geskiedkundig.
gest. gestorwe.
get. geteken; getuie.
gev. gevang.
gew. gewestelik; gewoonlik.
GGD grootste gemene deler.
ghn. ghienie.
goewt. goewerment.
Gr. Grieks.
GT Greenwichtyd.

H. Heilige.
ha hektaar.
h uur.
ha hektaar.
H.B.S. Hogere Burgerschool.
Hd. Hoogduits.
H.d.L. Heil die Leser.
Hebr. Hebreë(rs); Hebreeus.
H.Ed. Hoogedele.
H.Ed.Gestr. Hoogedelgestrenge.
H.Eerw. Hoogeerwaarde.
H.Eks. Haar eksellensie.
Herv. Hervormd.
hfst. hoofstuk.
hg hektogram.
H.H. Haar Hoogheid.
HH.EE. Hul Eksellensies.
HH.MM. Hul Majesteite.
HJS Hoër Jongenskool.
H.M. Haar Majestcit.
hm hektometer.
HMS Hoër Meisieskool.
HO Hoër Onderwys.
H.O.D. Hoër Onderwysdiploma.
Holl. Hollands.
Hott. Hottentot; Hottentots.
HPK Hoofposkantoor.
hs. handskrif.
hss. handskrifte.
hulpww. hulpwerkwoord.
h/v. hoek van.

ib(id). ibidem (op dieselfde plek).
ic. in casu (in dié geval).
id. idem (dieselfde).
i.e. id est (dit is).
iem. iemand.
i.e.w. in een woord.
imp. imperatief.
impf. imperfectum.
ind. indikatief.
inf. infinitief.
inkl. inklusief.

ins. insonderheid.
int. interes.
intr. intransitief.
i.p.v. in plaas van.
ir. ingenieur.
i.s. in sake.
Isr. Israelities(e).
It. Italiaans.
i.v.m. in verband met.

j jaar.
Jan. Januarie.
Jap. Japannees.
J.C. Jesus Christus.
jg. jaargang.
jhr. jonkheer.
jl. jongslede.
jr. junior.
Jul. Julie.
Jun. Junie.

kap. kapitaal; kapittel.
kapt. kaptein.
k.a.v. koste, assuransie, vrag.
k.b.a. kontant by aflewering.
kg kilogram.
KGV kleinste gemene veelvoud.
Kie. Kompanjie.
kl kiloliter.
km kilometer.
km/h kilometer per uur.
k.m.b. kontant met bestelling.
kol. kolonel.
komdt. kommandant.
komp. komparatief.
kon. koninklik.
konj. konjunksie; konjunktief.
kons. konsonant.
korr. korrespondensie; korrespondent
KP Kaapprovinsie.
kr. krediteer; krediteur.
k.s.b. kombuis, spens, badkamer.
kumek kubieke meter per sekonde.
KvK Kamer van Koophandel.
kW kilowatt.
kw. kwartaal.
kwal. kwaliteit.
kwant. kwantiteit.

l. lira.
l liter.
Lat. Latyn.
l.c. loco citato (op die aangehaalde plek).
lett. lettere; letterlik.
lg. laasgenoemde.
lidw. lidwoord.
Litt.D. Litterarum Doctor.
l.l. laaslede.
LL.B. Legum Baccalaureus.
LL.D. Legum Doctor.
LL.M. Legum Magister.
LO Laer Onderwys.
log logaritme.
LPR Lid van die Provinsiale Raad.
L.S. lectori salutem (heil die leser).
L.s.d. librae, solidi, denarii (ponde, sjielings, pennies).
luit. luitenant.
LUK Lid van die Uitvoerende Komitee.
LV Lid van die Volksraad.
L.W. let wel.
LWR Lid van die Wetgewende Raad.
LWV Lid van die Wetgewende Vergadering.

M. mark (Duitse munt).
m meter.
M.A. Magister Artium.
Ma. Maandag.
mag. magistraat.
maj. majoor.
maks. maksimum.
m.a.w. met ander woorde.
mbar millibar (*lugdrukeenheid*).
M.B. Medicinae Baccalaureus.
m.b.t. met betrekking tot.
M.Com. Magister Commercii.
M.D. Medicinae Doctor.
md. maand.
Me. Middeleeue.
med. medies; medisyne.
mej. mejuffrou.
mev. mevrou.
mevv. mevroue.
mg milligram.
mgr. monseigneur.
m.i. myns insiens.
min. minimum; minister.
min minuut.
ml milliliter.
ml. manlik.
Ml megaliter.
mm millimeter.
Mnl. Middel-Nederlands.
mnr. meneer.
mnre. menere.
MO Middelbare Onderwys.
mr. meester (in die regte).
Mrt. Maart.
ms. manuskrip; motorskip.
M.Sc. Magister Scientiae.
mss. manuskripte.
mus. musiek.
Mus.B. Musicae Baccalaureus.
Mus.D. Musicae Doctor.
mv. meervoud.
My. maatskappy.

N noord.
n. namens; neutrum; nomen.
N.A. Noord-Amerika; Noord-Amerikaans.
Nas. Nasionaal.
nat. natuurkunde; natuurkundig.
n.a.v. na aanleiding van.
N.B. nota bene.
NBr noorderbreedte.
n.C. na Christus.
Ndl. Nederlands.
Ned. Ger(ef). Nederduits Gereformeerd.
Ned. Herv. Nederduits Hervormd.
nl. naamlik.
nm. namiddag.
Nnl. Nieu-Nederlands.
NNO noord-noordoos.
NNW noord-noordwes.
NO noordoos.
no. numero, nommer.
NOIK Nederlandse Oos-Indiese Kompanjie.
nom. nominatief.
Nov. November.
nr. nommer.
Ns. Naskrif.
NUSAS Nasionale Unie van Suid-Afrikaanse Studente.
nv. naamval.
nw. naamwoord.
NW noordwes.

O oos.
o. of ons. onsydig.

o.a. onder andere.
ob. obiit (is oorlede).
obj. objek; objektief.
Oe. Ou(d)-Engels.
oef. oefeninge.
Ohd. Ou(d)-Hoogduits.
OI Oos-Indië; Oos-Indies.
o.i. onses insiens.
Okt. Oktober.
OL oosterlengte.
o.m. onder meer.
o/m omwentelinge per minuut.
On. Ou(d)-Noors.
onbep. onbepaald.
onderv. ondervoorsitter.
onderw. onderwerp.
ong. ongeveer.
ONO oosnoordoos(te).
ons. of o. onsydig.
ont. ontvang.
onvolm. onvolmaak.
onvolt. onvoltooi(d).
oorg. oorganklik.
oorl. oorlede.
oorspr. oorspronklik.
oortr. oortreffende.
OP Oostelike Provinsie.
op. opus (werk).
opm. opmerking.
opt. optatief.
ord. ordonnansie.
OSO oossuidoos(te).
oudhk. oudheidkunde; oudheidkundig.
oudl. ouderling.
OVS Oranje-Vrystaat.
OVSOV Oranje-Vrystaatse Onderwysersvereniging.
o.w. onder wie.

p. pagina; per; piano; pro.
p.a. per adres; per annum (per jaar).
par. paragraaf.
penm. penningmeester.
perf. perfectum.
pers. persoonlik.
pers. vnw. persoonlike voornaamwoord.
Ph.D. Philosophiae Doctor.
p.j. per jaar.
Pk. Poskantoor.
pk perdekrag.
pl. pluralis (meervoud).
p.m. per maand; per mensem; plus-minus.
PMG posmeester-generaal.
POA Portugees-Oos-Afrika.
Port. Portugees.
pp. paginas; pianissimo.
p.p. per persoon.
pqpf. plusquamperfectum.
PR Provinsiale Raad.
P.R. poste restante.
pred. predikaat.
pres. presens.
pres. president.
prim. primarius.
prof. professor.
proff. professore.
prok. prokureur.
prok-genl prokureur-generaal.
prop. proponent.
Prot. Protestant; Protestants.
prov. provinsiaal; provinsie.
P.S. postscriptum.
Ps. Psalm.
P.U. Potchefstroomse Universiteit.

q.q. qualitate qua (in die hoedanigheid van).
q.v. quod vide (kyk dié woord).

r. radius; reël.
RAK Raad vir Atoomkrag.
RDB Reddingsdaadbond.
red. redaksie; redakteur.
redupl. reduplikasie; redupliserend.
rek. rekening.
rel. relatief.
resp. respektiewelik.
R.I.P. requiescat in pace (rus in vrede).
RK Rooms-Katoliek.
RSA Radio Suid-Afrika; Republiek Suid-Afrika.
R.S.V.P. répondez s'il vous plaît (antwoord asseblief).
RVK rugbyvoetbalklub.

S suid.
s sekonde.
Sa. Saterdag.
SA Suid-Afrika; Suid-Afrikaans; Senior Advokaat.
SALM Suid-Afrikaanse Lugmag.
SALU Suid-Afrikaanse Landbou-Unie.
SAOU Suid-Afrikaanse Onderwysunie.
SAP Suid-Afrikaanse Party; Suid-Afrikaanse Polisie.
SAS & H Suid-Afrikaanse Spoorweë en Hawens.
SASM Suid-Afrikaanse Staande Mag.
SAVF Suid-Afrikaanse Vrouefederasie.
SBr suiderbreedte.
sc. scilicet (te wete).
SDB Spesiale Diensbataljon.
S.Ed. Sy Edele.
S.Ed.Agb. Sy Edelagbare.
S.Ed.Gstr. Sy Edelgestrenge.
S.Eerw. Sy Eerwaarde.
sekr. sekretaris.
Sekre. Sekretaresse.
S.Eks. Sy Eksellensie.
S.Em. Sy Eminensie.
sen. senator.
Sept. September.
sers. sersant.
sert. sertifikaat.
sg. sogenaamd.
S.H. Sy Heiligheid; Sy Hoogheid.
S.H.Ed. Sy Hoogedele.
S.H.Eerw. Sy Hoogeerwaarde.
s.i. syns insiens.
SM Staande Mag; stasiemeester.
S.M. Sy Majesteit.
s.nw. selfstandige naamwoord.
SO suidoos.
So. Sondag.
S.O.S. sien ommesy.
Sp. Spaans.
spes. spesiaal.
spr. spreker.
SR Studenteraad.
sr. senior.
ss. stoomskip.
SSO suidsuidoos.
SSW suidsuidwes.
St. Sint.
st. standerd; sterk.
sta. stasie.
sth. stemhebbend.
stl. stemloos.
str. straat.
subj. subjek; subjektief.
sup. superlatief; supra (bo).
s.v. sub voce (onder dié woord).
s.v.p. s'il vous plaît (asseblief).

SW suidwes.
sw. swak.
SWA Suidwes-Afrika.

t metrieke ton.
t.a.p. ter aangehaalde plaatse.
t.a.v. ten aansien van.
t.a.v. tout à vous (geheel die uwe).
teenw. teenwoordig.
tel. telefoon.
tel ad telegramadres.
telw. telwoord.
temp. temperatuur.
tes. tesourier.
Th(eol). D. Theologiae Doctor.
t.l. ten laaste.
TLU Transvaalse Landbou-Unie.
TO Transvaalse Onderwysersvereniging.
TOD Transvaalse Onderwysdepartement.
toej. toejuiging.
t.o.v. toejuiging.
TRUK Transvaalse Raad vir Uitvoerende Kunste.
t.t. totus tuus (geheel die uwe).
Tvl. Transvaal; Transvaals.
tw. tussenwerpsel.
t.w. te wete.

U Ed. U Edele.
uitdr. uitdrukking.
UK Uitvoerende Komitee; Universiteit van Kaapstad.
Univ. Universiteit.
UOVS Universiteit van die Oranje-Vrystaat.
UP Universiteit van Pretoria.
UR Uitvoerende Raad.
US Universiteit van Stellenbosch.
USSR Unie van Sosialistiese Sowjet-Republieke.

v. vers; vide (kyk).
v. of vr. vroulik.
v.a.b. vry aan boord.
vb. voorbeeld.
v.C. voor Christus.
v.d. van die.
V.D.M. Verbi Divini (Dei) Minister.
V.d.S. van die skrywer.
verb. verbuiging; verbum.
verg. vergadering.
verklw. verkleinwoord.
verl. verlede.
vert. vertaling; vertrek.
verv. vervroeging.
vgl. vergelyk.
v/h. voorheen.
Vl. Vlaams.
vlg. volgende.
VLV Vroue-Landbouvereniging.
vm. voormiddag.
vnw. voornaamwoord.
voegw. voegwoord.
VOC Vereenigde Oost-Indische Compagnie.
vok. vokaal; vokatief.
vol. volume.
volm. volmaak.
volt. voltooi(d).
voors. voorsitter.
voors. voorsetsel.
voorv. voorvoegsel.
voorw. voorwerp.
v.o.s. vry op spoor.
Vr. Vrydag.
vr. of v. vroulik.
vs. versus (teen).
VSA Verenigde State van Amerika.

VSB Vroue-Sendingbond.
VVO Verenigde Volke-organisasie.

W wes; watt.
WAT Woordeboek van die Afrikaanse Taal.
wdb. woordeboek.
wed. weduwee.
WelEd. Weledele.
WelEd.Gestr. Weledelgestrenge.

WelEerw. Weleerwaarde.
w.g. was geteken.
W.Germ. Wes-Germaans.
WL westerlengte.
wnd. waarnemend.
WNW wesnoordwes.
Wo. Woensdag.
wo. waaronder.
WP Westelike Provinsie.
ww. werkwoord.

Aardrykskundige Name

Abessinië, Abyssinia.
Adriatiese See, die –, the Adriatic Sea.
Afganistan, Afghanistan.
Afrika, Africa.
Agter-Indië, Further India.
Akadië, Acadia.
Aken, Aachen, Aix-la-Chapelle.
Albanië, Albania.
Alexandrië, Alexandria.
Algerië of Algerye, Algeria.
Algiers, Algiers.
Aliwal-Noord, Aliwal North.
Alpe, Alps.
Amasone, Amazon.
Amerika, America.
Andalusië, Andalusia.
Andes, Andes.
Antille: die –, the Antilles; Klein, –, Lesser Antilles.
Antiochië, Antioch.
Antwerpen, Antwerp.
Apennyne, Apennines.
Appalache, Appalachians.
Arabië, Arabia.
Ardenne, Ardennes.
Argentinië, the Argentine, Argentina.
Arkadië, Arcadia.
Armenië, Armenia.
Asië, Asia.
Asore, Azores.
Assirië, Assyria.
Athene, Athens.
Atlantiese Oseaan, Atlantic Ocean.
Atrecht, Arras.
Australië, Australia.

Babel, Babilon, Babel, Babylon.
Babilonië, Babylonia.
Baden, Baden.
Baleare, Baleariese Eilande, Balearic Islands.
Balkan: die –, the Balkans.
Basel, Basle, Bale.
Basoetoland, Basutoland.
Beaufort-Wes, Beaufort West.
Beiere, Bavaria.
België, Belgium.
Belgrado, Belgrade.
Beloetsjistan, Baluchistan.
Benede-Egipte, Lower Egypt.
Bengale, Bengal.
Beosië, Boeotia.
Bergen, Mons (in Belgium); Bergen (in Holland and in Norway).
Berlyn, Berlin.
Bethlehem (in O V S en V S A), Bethlehem.
Betlehem (in Palestina), Bethlehem.
Betsjoeanaland, Bechuanaland.
Birma, Burma.
Bisantium, Byzantium.
Biskaje: Golf van –, Bay of Biscay.

Blou Nyl, Blue Nile.
Boedapest, Budapest.
Bo-Egipte, Upper Egypt.
Boekarest, Bucharest.
Boergondië, Burgundy.
Boheme, Bohemia.
Bosporus: die –, the Bosp(h)orus.
Bosnië, Bosnia.
Botnië, Bothnia.
Botniese Golf, Gulf of Bothnia.
Brasilië, Brazil.
Brazzaville; die Republiek van die –, the Republic of Brazzaville (Congo).
Bretagne, Brittany.
Britannië, Britannia.
Brittanje, Britain.
Brugge, Bruges.
Brunswyk, Brunswick.
Brussel, Brussels.
Bulgarye, Bulgaria.

Carrara, Carrara.
Carthago, Carthage.
Celebes, Celebes.
Ceylon, Ceylon.
Charybdis, Charybdis.
Chili, Chile.
China, Sjina, China.
Cilicië, Cilicia.
Ciklade, Cyclades.
Ciprus, Cyprus.
Cirenaïka, Cyrenaica.
Cirene, Cyrene.
Cirkassië, Circassia.
Cochin-China, Cochin-China.
Colorado, Colorado.
Constantia, Constantia.
Cordova, Cordova.
Cornwallis, Cornwall.
Curaçao, Curacao.

Dacië, Dacia.
Dalmasië, Dalmatia.
Damaskus, Damascus.
Dardanelle, Dardanelles.
Delphi, Delphi.
Den Haag, The Hague.
Diewe-Eilande, Ladrone, Ladrones, Marianas.
Donau, Danube.
Dooie See, Soutsee, Dead See.
Doornik, Tournai.
Duinkerken, Dunkirk.
Duitsland, Germany.

Edenburg, Edenburg (in O F S).
Edinburgh, Edinburgh (in Scotland).
Edom, Edom.
Efese, Ephesus.
Egeïese See, Aegean Sea.
Egipte, Egypt.
Eire, Eire.

Elisium, Elysium, Elysium.
Elsas: die –, Alsace.
Elsas-Lotharinge, Alsace-Lorraine.
Engeland, England.
Estland, Est(h)onia.
Ethiopië, Ethiopia.
Etolië, Aetolia.
Etrurië, Etruria.
Eufraat, Euphrates.
Eurasië, Eurasia.
Europa, Europe.

Fenicië, Phoenicia.
Fidji-Eilande, Fiji Islands.
Filippynse Eilande, Philippine Islands.
Finland, Finland.
Florence, Florence.
Franke, Franconia.
Frankfort, Frankfort.
Frankryk, France.
Franschhoek, French Hoek.
Friesland, Friesland.
Frigië, Phrygia.

Galicië, Galicia.
Galilea, Galilee.
Gallië, Gaul.
Gambia, Gambia.
Gascogne, Gaskonje, Gascony.
Geel See, Yellow Sea.
Gelderland, G(u)elderland, Guelders.
Genève, Geneva.
Gent, Ghent.
Genua, Genoa.
Georgia, Georgia (in the U S A).
Georgië, Georgia (in Russia).
Germanië, Germania.
Geselskapseilande, Society Islands.
Goudkus, Gold Coast.
Granada, Granada.
's-Gravenhage, The Hague.
Griekeland, Greece.
Griekwaland, Griqualand.
Groenland, Greenland.
Groot-Brittanje, Great Britain.
Groot Karoo: die –, the Great Kar(r)oo.
Grootrivier, Orange River.
Guinee, Guinea.

Haag: Den –, The Hague.
Hamburg, Hamburg.
Hannover (in Duitsland), Hanover.
Hanover (in Suid-Afrika), Hanover.
Havana, Havana.
Hebride, Hebrides.
Helgoland, Heligoland.
Helsingfors, Helsinki, Helsingfors.
Helvesië, Helvetia.
Herzegowina, Herzegovina.
Hesperide, Hesperides.
Hesse, Hesse.
Hibernië, Hibernia.
Himalaja, Himalayas.
Hindoestan, Hindustan.
Holland, Holland.
Hongarye, Hungary.

Iberië, Iberia.
Ieperen, Ypres.
Ierland, Ireland.
Indië, India.
Ioniese See, Ionian Sea.
Irak, Iraq.
Iran (Persië), Iran (Persia).
Italië, Italy.
Ivoorkus, Ivory Coast.

Jamaika, Jamaica.
Japan, Japan.
Java, Java.
Jerusalem, Jerusalem.
Joego-Slawië, Yugoslavia.
Jordaan, Jordan.
Judea, Judea.
Jutland, Jutland.

Kaap die Goeie Hoop, Cape of Good Hope.
Kaapland, Kaapprovinsie, Cape Province.
Kaapstad, Cape Town.
Kaap-Verdiese Eilande, Cape Verde Islands.
Kaïro, Cairo.
Kalahari, Kalahari.
Kalabrië, Calabria.
Kalifornië, California.
Kameroen, the Cameroons.
Kameryk, Cambrai.
Kamperduin, Camperdown.
Kanaan, Canaan.
Kanada, Canada.
Kanariese Eilande, Canary Islands.
Kantelberg, Canterbury.
Karibiese Eilande, Caribbees.
Karibiese See, Caribbean Sea.
Karintië, Carinthia.
Karoo, Kar(r)oo.
Karpate, Carpathians.
Kasjmir, Kashmir.
Kaspiese See, Caspian Sea.
Kastilië, Castile.
KataloniCatalonia.
Kaukasus, ë, Caucasus.
Kenia, Kenya.
Keulen, Cologne.
Kleef, Cleves.
Klein-Asië, Asia Minor.
Klein Karoo: die –, the Little Kar(r)oo.
Koerland, Courland.
Kongo, Congo.
Koningsbergen, Koningsberg.
Konstantinopel, Constantinople.
Konstanz, Constance.
Kopenhagen, Copenhagen.
Korea, Korea.
Korinthe, Corinth.
Korsika, Corsica.
Kortryk, Courtrai.
Krakau, Cracow.
Kreta, Crete.
Krim: die –, the Crimea.
Kroasië, Croatia.
Kuba, Cuba.

Lacedemonië, Lacedaemon.
Lakkadive, Laccadives.
Laodicea, Laodic(a)ea.
Lapland, Lapland.
Leiden, Leyden.
Letland, Latvia.
Leuven, Louvain.
Levant: die –, the Levant.
Libanon, Lebanon.
Libië, Libya.
Lissabon, Lisbon.
Litaue, Lithuania.
Livorno, Leghorn.
Lombardye, Lombardy.
Londen, London.
Lotharinge, Lorraine.
Lourenço Marques, Lourenço Marques.
Luik, Liége.
Luxemburg, Luxemburg.
Luzern, Lucerne.

Lyfland, Livonia.
Lyon, Lyons.

Maagdenburg, Magdeburg.
Maas, Meuse, Maas.
Macedonië, Macedonia.
Madagaskar, Madagascar.
Mainz, Mainz, Mayence.
Majorka, Majorca.
Malakka, Malacca.
Malawi, Malawi.
Maledive, Maldives, Maldive Islands.
Maleise Skiereiland: die –, Malaya.
Manila, Manila.
Mantsjoerye, Manchuria.
Marathon, Marathon.
Mariane, Marianas.
Marokko, Morocco.
Marseille, Marseilles.
Masjonaland, Mashonaland.
Matebeleland, Matabeleland.
Mechelen, Malines, Mechlin.
Mekka, Mecca.
Mesopotamië, Mesopotamia.
Mexiko, Mexico.
Middellandse See, Mediterranean Sea.
Milaan, Milan.
Minorka, Minorca.
Moesel, Moselle.
Moldawië, Moldavia.
Molukke, Moluccas, Spice Islands.
Morawië, Moravia.
Mosambiek, Mozambique.
Moskou, Moscow.
München, Munich.

Namakwaland, Namaqualand.
Namen, Namur.
Nantes, Nantes.
Napels, Naples.
Nasaret, Nazareth.
Nederland, the Netherlands.
Nederlands-Indië, the Netherlands (Dutch) East Indies.
Neurenberg, Nuremberg.
Newfoundland, Newfoundland.
Nieu-Seeland, New Zealand.
Nieu-Guinee, New Guinea.
Nieu-Skotland, Nova Scotia.
Nieuwpoort, Nieuport.
Nigerië, Nigeria.
Ninevé, Nineveh.
Nizza, Nice.
Noord-Amerika, North America.
Noord-Holland, North Holland.
Noordkaap, North Cape.
Noordpoolsee, Noordelike Yssee, Arctic Ocean.
Noordsee, North Sea, German Ocean.
Noorweë, Norway.
Normandië, Normandy.
Nubië, Nubia.
Nuweveldberge, Nieuwveld Mountains.
Nyl, Nile.

Oekraine: die –, the Ukraine.
Oeral(gebergte), the Urals, the Ural Mountains.
Olyfberg, Mount of Olives.
Olympus, Olympus.
Oos-Afrika, East Africa.
Oos-Friesland, East Friesland.
Oos-Indië, the East Indies.
Oos-Londen, East London.
Oossee, Baltic Sea.
Oostenryk, Austria.
Oostenryk-Hongarye, Austria-Hungary.

Opper-Egipte, Upper Egypt.
Oranjerivier, Orange River.
Oranje-Vrystaat, Orange Free State.
Orkade, Orkadiese Eilande, Orkneys.
Oseanië, Oceania.
Ostende, Ostend.
Ouessant, Ushant.
Outeniekwaberge, Outeniqua Mountains.

Pakistan, Pakistan.
Palestina, Palestine.
Palts: die –, the Palatinate.
Panamakanaal, Panama Canal.
Pandjab: die –, Punjab.
Paraguay, Paraguay.
Parnas(sus), Parnassus.
Parys, Paris (in France), Parys (in the O F S).
Patagonië, Patagonia.
Peloponnesus, Peloponnesus.
Pennsilvanië, Pennsylvania.
Persië, Persia.
Peru, Peru.
Piëmont, Piedmont.
Pikardië, Picardy.
Pireneë, Pyrenees.
Pole, Poland.
Polinesië, Polynesia.
Pommere, Pomerania.
Pompeji, Pompeii.
Poolsee, Polar Sea.
Portugal, Portugal.
Posen (provinsie), Posen, Posnania.
Posen, (stad), Posen.
Praag, Prague.
Pruise, Prussia.

Regensburg, Regensburg, Ratisbon.
Reims, R(h)eims.
Rhodesië, Rhodesia.
Rhodus, Rhodes.
Rhône, Rhone,
Riebeek-Wes, Riebeek West.
Roemenië, R(o)umania.
Rome, Rome.
Rondebosch, Rondebosch.
Rooi See, Red Sea.
Rouaan, Rouen.
Rubicon, Rubicon.
Rusland, Russia.
Ryn, Rhine.
Rysel, Lille.

Sakse, Saxony.
Sakse-Weimar, Saxe-Weimar.
Salomonseilande, Solomon Islands.
Saloniki, Salonica.
Sarajevo, Sarajevo, Serajevo.
Sardinië, Sardinia.
Savoje, Savoy.
Scheide, Scheldt.
Scylla, Scylla.
Seeland (in Denemarke), Zealand.
Seeland (in Nederland), Zeeland.
Seepunt, Sea Point.
Sekoekoensland, Sekukuniland.
Senegambië, Senegambia.
Serawak, Sarawak.
Serwië, Serbia, Servia.
Sevilla, Seville.
Seweburge, Transsilvanië, Transylvania.
Siberië, Siberia.
Sicilië, Sicily.
Silesië, Silisia.
Singapoer, Singapore.
Sion, Zion.

Sirakuse (op Sicilië).
Sirië, Syria.
Sjina, China, China.
Skandinawië, Scandinavia.
Skithië, Scythia.
Skotland, Scotland.
Slawonië, Slavonia.
Sleeswyk, Schleswig.
Slowakye, Slovakia.
Slowenië, Slovenia.
Smirna, Smyrna.
Soedan: die –, the S(o)udan.
Soenda, Sunda.
Somerset-Oos, Somerset East.
Sont: die –, the Sound.
Soutrivier, Salt River.
Soutsee, vide Dooie See.
Sowjet-Rusland, Soviet Russia.
Spanje, Spain.
Spitsberge, Spitzbergen.
Sporade, Sporades.
Stamboel, Istanboel, Stamb(o)ul, Istanbul.
Stellenbosch, Stellenbosch.
St. Helena, (-baai), St. Helena (Bay).
Stiermarke, Styria.
Stille Oseaan, Pacific Ocean.
Stille Suidsee, South Pacific, Pacific Ocean.
Stockholm, Stockholm.
Straatsburg, Strasbourg, Strassburg.
Suez, Suez.
Suid-Afrika, South Africa.
Suid-Amerika, South America.
Suidelike Yssee, Suidpoolsee, Antarctic Ocean.
Suidersee, Zuider (Zuyer) Zee.
Suidsee: Stille –, Pacific Ocean, South Pacific.
Sumatra, Sumatra.
Suriname, Surinam.
Swabe, Swabia (Suabia).
Swart See, Black Sea.
Swart Woud, Black Forest.
Swaziland, Swaziland.
Swede, Sweden.
Switserland, Switzerland.
Syracuse (in die V S A), Syracuse.

Taag, Tagus.
Tafelbaai, Table Bay.
Tafelberg, Table Mountain.
Tanger, Tangier(s).
Tanzania, Tanzania.
Tartarye, Tartary.
Tasmanië, Tasmania.
Teems, Thames.
Tessel, Texel, Texel.
Thebe, Thebes.
Thermopylae, Thermopylae.
Thracië, Thrace.
Tibet, Tibet.
Tiger, Tigris, Tigris.
Tirol, Tyrol.

Tonga-Eilande, **Vriendskapseilande,** Tonga Islands, Friendly Islands.
Tongeren, Tongres.
Toskane, Tuscany.
Touwsrivier, Touws River.
Transsilvanië, vide **Seweburge.**
Transvaal, Transvaal.
Trier, Treves.
Triëst, Trieste.
Troje, Troy.
Tsjeggo-Slowakye, Czechoslovakia.
Turinge, Thuringia.
Turkye, Turkey.
Turyn, Turin.

Uganda, Uganda.
Umbrië, Umbria.
Uraquay, Uruguay.

Van Diemensland, Van Diemen's Land, Tasmania.
Venesië, Venice.
Venezuela, Venezuela.
Vereeniging, Vereeniging.
Verenigde State (van Amerika), United States (of America).
Vesuvius, Vesuvius.
Victoria, Victoria.
Virginië, Virginia.
Vlaandere, Flanders.
Vlissingen, Flushing.
Vogese, Vosges.
Voor-Indië, (Hither) India.
Vriendskapseilande, Tonga-Eilande, Friendly Islands, Tonga Islands.
Vuurland, Tierra del Fuego.

Waal (rivier), Waal.
Walagye, Wallachia.
Waleland, die –, **Wallonië,** Wallonia.
Wallis (in Brittanje), Wales.
Wallis (in Switserland), Valais.
Wallonië, Wallonia.
Warschau, Warsaw.
Weenen (in Natal), Weenen.
Weichsel, Vistula.
Wenen (in Oostenryk), Vienna.
Wes-Afrika, West Africa.
Wes-Europa, Western Europe.
Wesfale, Westphalia.
Wes-Indië, the West Indies.
Wit Nyl, White Nile.
Wit See, White Sea.
Wladiwostok, Vladivostok.
Wolga, Volga.
Wurtemberg, Wurtemburg, Württemberg.

Ysland, Iceland.

Zambezi, Zambezi, Zambesi.
Zambia, Zambia.
Zoeloeland, Zululand.

ENGELS-AFRIKAANS

A

a (an), 'n
aardwolf, aardwolf (erdwolf).
aback, agteruit; **taken** –, verbluf, verstom.
abacus, telraam; dekstuk.
abaft, agter, agteruit, op die agterdek.
abandon, v. opgee, verlaat, in die steek laat.
abandon, n. oorgawe; onverskilligheid.
abandoned, oorgegee, verlate; verdorwe.
abandonment, oorgawe, verlating; verlatenheid; losbandigheid; onverskilligheid.
abase, verneder, verlaag.
abasement, vernedering, verlaging.
abash, verleë maak; uit die veld slaan.
abashed, verleë, skaam, beskaamd; verbluf.
abashment, verleentheid; verbluftheid.
abate, verminder, afneem; afslaan; bedaar.
abatement, vermindering, matiging, bedaring.
abattoir, slagpaal, abattoir.
abbé, abbé, geestelike.
abbess, abdis.
abbey, abdy, klooster; kloosterkerk.
abbot, ab.
abbreviate, afkort, verkort; afsny, verklein.
abbreviation, verkorting, afkorting.
abc, abc, alfabet; eerste beginsel.
abdicate, afstand doen van, neerlê.
abdication, (troons)afstand, abdikasie.
abdomen, onderbuik, buik, maag.
abdominal, buik-...
abduct, ontvoer, skaak; wegvoer.
abduction, ontvoering, skaking.
abeam, opsy, in die dwarste.
aberration, afwyking, misstap.
abet, aanhits, opstook; help, steun.
abetment, aansporing; hulp, bystand.
abettor, opstoker; handlanger, medepligtige.
abeyance, opskorting; **in** –, buite(n) werking; opgeskort; in onbruik; onuitgemaak.
abhor, verafsku, verfoei, verag.
abhorrence, afsku, veragting, haat.
abhorrent, afskuwelik, afstootlik.
abide, vertoef, bly; volhard; wag op; verdra, uitstaan; – **by,** bly by; hou aan, onderwerp aan.
abiding, blywende, durende, vaste.
ability, bekwaamheid; gawe, talent.
abject, a. kruipend, laag; – **poverty,** volslae armoede.
abject, n. verworpeling.
abjectly, op 'n veragtelike (kruipende) manier.
abjectness, veragtelikheid; kruiperigheid.
abjuration, afswering, versaking.
abjure, afsweer, versaak.
ablative, ablatief.
ablaze, aan (die) brand, in vlam; glansend.
able, bekwaam, knap, kapabel; in staat.
able-bodied, sterk (geboud), weerbaar.
ablution, afwassing, reiniging, suiwering.
ably, knap, behendig, op 'n bekwame manier.
abnegate, verloën; laat vaar, afsweer.
abnegation, verloëning; versaking.
abnormal, abnormaal, onreëlmatig; misvorm(d); sieklik.
abnormality, abnormaliteit, onreëlmatigheid, misvormdheid, gebreklikheid.
aboard, aan boord; – **ship,** aan boord.
abode, verblyf, woning, tuiste.
abolish, afskaf; ophef; herroep; opgee.
abolishment, sien **abolition.**
abolition, afskaffing; opheffing; (die) opgee.
abolitionist, afskaffer (van die slawehandel).
A-bomb, atoombom.
abominable, afskuwelik, verfoeilik, gruwelik.
abominate, verafsku, verfoei, haat.
abomination, verafskuwing, gruwel.
aboriginal, a. oorspronklik, inheems, inlands.
aboriginal, n. oerinwoner, inboorling.
aborigines, oorspronklike bewoners.
abort, ontydig beval; misluk.
abortifacient, vrugafdrywende middel.
abortion, miskraam; vrugafdrywing; misbaksel, monster.
abortive, ontydig; misluk(te); vrugafdrywend.
abound, oorvloei, volop wees, wemel (van).
about, prep. om, rondom; omtrent, ongeveer; met betrekking tot, oor; aan, by, in; – **the house,** om die huis; – **8 o'clock,** omstreeks 8-uur; – **this matter,** met betrekking tot hierdie saak; – **town,** in die stad (rond); **what are you** –, wat voer jy uit?
about, adv. om, rond; **to walk** –, rondloop; **it is a long way** –, dit is 'n groot ompad; **to be (up and)** –, op die been wees; **to be** – **to,** op die punt staan om; **bring** –, veroorsaak; **come** –, gebeur; **go** –, rondloop; aanlê.
above, prep. bo, bo-oor, bo-op; bokant; meer as; – **the house,** bokant (bo-oor) die huis; – **water,** bo water; – **all,** veral, bowenal.
above, adv. omhoog, bo(we); **from** –, van bo(we).
above, a. bo(we)staande.
above-board, eerlik, reguit; rondborstig.
above-mentioned, bo(we)genoemd.
abracadabra, abrakadabra, toorwoord; wartaal.
abrade, afskawe, afskuur; afvrywe.
abrasion, afskawing, afslyting; skaafplek.
abrasive, n. skuurmiddel, slypmiddel.
abrasive, a. skuur-, slyp-, (af)skurend, (af)skawend.
abreast, naasmekaar; – **of,** op die hoogte van.
abridge, verkort, afkort, inkort, beperk.
abridgement, verkorting, inkorting; uittreksel.
abroach, oopgesit, oopgesteek.
abroad, van huis, buitenslands; **at home and** –, binne- en buitelands; **from** –, van die buiteland; **he was all** –, hy was die kluts kwyt; **the news is** –, die nuus is in omloop.
abrogate, herroep, intrek, ophef, afskaf.
abrogation, herroeping, intrekking, afskaffing.
abrupt, kortaf; skielik, plotseling; steil.
abruptness, kortaf manier; skielikheid.
abscess, geswel, verswering, abses.
abscond, op die vlug gaan, die plaat poets.
absence, afwesigheid; gebrek; verstrooidheid.
absent, a. afwesig; verstrooid.
absent, v. (sig) verwyder, wegbly.
absentee, afwesige; elderswonende eienaar.
absinth, als(em), absint; alsbrandewyn.
absolute, volstrek, onbeperk; totaal; absoluut.
absolutely, totaal, heeltemal, absoluut.
absoluteness, onbeperktheid; onbeperkte mag.
absolution, vergifnis, kwytskelding, absolusie.
absolve, kwytskeld, vryspreek, ontslaan.
absorb, opsuig, intrek, absorbeer; insluk, verslind; in beslag neem; – **ed in thought,** in gedagte versonke.
absorbent, n. opsuigmiddel, absorbeermiddel.
absorption, opsuiging, opneming, absorpsie.
absorptive, opsuigend, absorberend.
abstain, (sig) onthou; wegbly, (sig) onttrek.
abstainer, afskaffer, onthou(d)er; **total** –, geheelonthou(d)er.
abstemious, onthoudend, matig.
abstention, onthouding; onttrekking.
abstergent, suiwerend, reinigend, purgerend.
abstinence, onthouding; matigheid; **total** –, geheelonthouding.
abstinent, onthoudend; matig.
abstract, a. afgetrokke, teoretiese, abstrak; – **number,** onbenoemde getal.
abstract, v. afskei, af-, ont-, uittrek, abstraheer; uittreksel maak, ontleen, (sig) toeëien.

abstract, n. aftreksel, afkooksel; uittreksel, samevatting; afgetrokke begrip, abstraksie.
abstraction, aftrekking; afgetrokkenheid, abstraksie, afgetrokke denkbeeld; ontvreemding.
abstruse, verborge, diepsinnig, duister.
absurd, onsinnig, dwaas, ongerymd.
absurdity, onsinnigheid, ongerymdheid.
abundance, oorvloed, rykdom, menigte.
abundant, oorvloedig, ryk(lik), volop.
abuse, v. misbruik, mishandel; uitskel.
abuse, n. misbruik, mishandeling; skending; belediging, uitskelding; skeldtaal; **term of –,** skeldwoord.
abusive, verkeerd, onjuis; beledigend.
abut, grens (aan).
abutilon, bebroeide eier.
abutment, grens; steunpilaar.
abysm, sien **abyss.**
abysmal, grondeloos, onpeilbaar.
abyss, afgrond, bodemlose poel.
Abyssinia, Abessinië.
acacia, akasia.
academic(al), akademies; teoreties.
academics, akademiese drag.
academy, akademie; hoërskool; genootskap.
acanthus, akant.
acatalepsy, onbegryplikheid.
acataleptic, onbegryplik.
accede, toetree, aanvaar; instem, toestem; – to, voldoen aan, gehoor gee aan.
accelerate, versnel; verhaas, bespoed; vervroeg.
acceleration, versnelling; bespoediging.
accelerator, versneller.
accent, n. aksent, nadruk, klem(toon); uitspraak; klemteken; stembuiging, –s, taal, woorde.
accent, v. betoon, beklem(toon), nadruk lê op.
accentuate, betoon, beklem, nadruk lê op.
accentuation, aksentuasie, beklem(toning).
accept, aanneem, ontvang, aanvaar.
acceptability, aanneemlikheid.
acceptable, aanneemlik, welkom.
acceptance, ontvangs; aanvaarding; aksep(tasie) (van 'n wissel).
acceptation, gangbare betekenis, akseptasie.
accepted, aangenome; gangbaar.
acceptor, ontvanger, akseptant.
access, toegang, toename, vermeerdering; uitbarsting, aanval; **easy of –,** gemaklik toeganklik (genaakbaar).
accessary, a. medepligtig; bybehorend; sien **accessory.**
accessary, n. medepligtige; bybehoorsel.
accessible, toeganklik, genaakbaar; vatbaar; ontvanklik.
accession, toetreding; aanvaarding; (troons)bestyging; toestemming; aanwins.
accessory, a. bykomend, bykomstig.
accessory, n. bykomstigheid, vereiste, toebehoorsel, onderdeel; sien **accessary.**
accidence, vormleer, buigingsleer; beginsels.
accident, ongeluk; toeval; bykomstigheid.
accidental, toevallig; bykomstig; ondergeskik; – **death,** dood deur 'n ongeluk.
acclaim, v. toejuig, verwelkom.
acclaim, n. toejuiging.
acclamation, toejuiging, byval, applous.
acclamatory, van byval, byvals- . . .
acclimatization, akklimatisasie, aanpassing.
acclimatize, akklimatiseer; aanpas.
acclivity, opdraand, steilte.
accolade, (omhelsing by die) ridderslag.
accommodate, aanpas; versoen; voeg, skik; van diens wees; guns bewys; inneem, herberg, sitplaas verskaf, bevat; – **with,** voorsien van, help met.

accommodating, inskiklik, tegemoetkomend.
accommodation, aanpassing; skikking, akkoord; geleentheid; herberg, akkommodasie, slaapplek (sitplek); –s, geriewe; – **unit,** (woon)huis.
accompaniment, begeleiding, vergeselling; toebehore.
accompany, begelei, vergesel, in verband staan met, saamgaan.
accomplice, medepligtige, handlanger.
accomplish, uitvoer, vervul, tot stand bring.
accomplished, verfyn; begaaf; volmaak.
accomplishment, uitvoering; verrigting; verfyning; begaafdheid; handigheid.
accord, v. ooreenstem, akkordeer; toestaan, versoen; – **a welcome,** verwelkom.
accord, n. ooreenstemming, akkoord, ooreenkoms; **with one –,** eenparig; **of one's own –,** uit eie beweging, op eie houtjie.
accordance, ooreenstemming; **in – with,** ooreenkomstig, in ooreenstemming met.
according: – **as,** namate, na gelang; – **to,** volgens, ooreenkomstig.
accordingly, gevolglik, bygevolg, aldus.
accordion, akkordeon, (hand)harmonika.
accost, aanspreek; aanklamp.
accouchement, bevalling.
accoucheur, kraamverpleger, vroedmeester.
account, v. beskou, reken as, hou vir; – **for,** verklaar; verantwoord, omkap, afreken met.
account, n. rekening; rekenskap; verklaring; berig, verslag; **settle an –, square –s,** afreken, betos vereffen; **current –,** lopende rekening, rekening-koerant; **cash –,** kassa-rekening; **of no –,** van geen betekenis nie; **on no –,** onder geen omstandighede, in geen geval; **on – of,** weens, om, **on his own –,** op sy eie verantwoording, **call, bring to –,** ter verantwoording roep, **take into –,** in aanmerking neem, **leave out of –,** buite rekening laat; **give a good – of oneself,** (sig) flink gedra; **turn to –,** party trek van.
accountable, verantwoordelik, toerekenbaar.
accountancy, boekhoukunde.
accountant, boekhouer, rekenmeester.
accoutrement, uitrusting.
accredit, magtig, akkrediteer; geloof skenk, erken.
accredited, geakkrediteer, erken, toegelate.
accretion, aanwas, aansetsel; vermeerdering.
accrue, toeneem, oploop; voortspruit, **–d interest,** opgelope rente.
accumulate, ophoop; vermenigvuldig; opgaar.
accumulation, op(een)stapeling; hoop; opgaring.
accumulative, toenemend, akkumulatief.
accumulator, versamelaar; akkumulator, opgaarbattery.
accuracy, noukeurigheid, akkuraatheid.
accurate, noukeurig, nougeset, presies, akkuraat.
accursed, vervloek; ellendig.
accusation, beskuldiging, aanklag.
accusative, akkusatief.
accuse, beskuldig, aankla.
accused, aangeklaagde, beskuldigde.
accuser, beskuldiger, aanklaer.
accustom, wen, gewoon(d) maak; – **to,** wen aan, gewend raak aan; **–ed,** gewend, gewoon(d).
ace, aas, een; **within an –,** op 'n haar na.
acerbity, wrangheid, bitterheid; bitsigheid.
acetate, asynsuursout, asetaat.
acetic, suur, asynsurig; – **acid,** asynsuur.
acetone, asyngees, asetoon.
acetylene, asetileen (gas).
ache, v. seer wees, pyn ly.
ache, n. pyn; **heart –,** hartseer; **tooth –,** tandpyn.

**achieve, **uitvoer, verrig, volbring; bereik, presteer.
**achievement, **verrigting, daad; kordaatstuk, prestasie.
**Achilles, **Achille(u)s; –' **heel, **Achilleshiel.
**aching, **seer.
**achromatic, **kleurloos, achromaties.
**acid, **a. suur, wrang; skerp, bits(ig).
**acid, **n. suur.
**acidify, **suur maak; suur word, versuur.
**acidity, **suurheid; bits(ig)heid.
**acidulous, **suurderig.
**acknowledge, **erken, toegee; bedank vir.
**acknowledg(e)ment, **erkenning; bewys van erkentlikheid; berig van ontvangs.
**acme, **toppunt, hoogtepunt; keerpunt.
**acolyte, **altaardienaar; volgeling, aanhanger.
**aconite, **monnikskap, wolfswortel; akoniet.
**acorn, **akker, eikel.
**acotyledon, **onsaadlobbige plant.
**acoustic, **akoesties, gehoor(s)- . . . ; – **nerve, **gehoorsenu(wee); – **mine, **geluidsmyn.
**acoustics, **geluidsleer; klank; akoestiek.
**acquaint, **bekend maak, in kennis stel; **to be –ed, **ken, bekend wees.
**acquaintance, **kennis; bekendheid; kennismaking.
**acquiesce, **berus, (sig) skik; instem.
**acquiescence, **berusting; instemming.
**acquire, **verwerf, aanskaf; oploop, **–d taste, **aangeleerde smaak.
**acquirement, **verwerwing; aanwins; besit; **–s, **kennis, talente.
**acquisition, **aanskaffing; aanlering; aanwins.
**acquisitive, **begerig, hebsugtig.
**acquit, **vryspreek, ontslaan, (sig) kwyt.
**acquittal, **vryspraak, ontslag; verrigting.
**acquittance, **skuldbetaling; kwytskelding.
**acre, **akker.
**acreage, **grootte in akkers, oppervlakte.
**acrid, **bitter, wrang, skerp, bits(ig).
**acrimonious, **bitter, bits(ig).
**acrimony, **bitterheid, bits(ig)heid.
**acrobat, **kunstemaker, toudanser, akrobaat.
**acrobatic, **akrobaties, kunstemakers- . . .
**acrophobia, **hoogtevrees, akrofobie.
**acropolis, **burg, bowestad.
**across, **prep, oor; anderkant; deur; – **the face, **(dwars) oor die gesig; – **the road, **oorkant die pad; **come – someone, **iemand raakloop.
**across, **adv. oormekaar, oorkruis.
**acrostic, **naamdig, naamvers.
**act, **w. handel, te werk gaan; (sig) gedra, waarneem, optree; – **a part, **'n rol speel; – **as interpreter, **as tolk optree; – **up to, **nakom, handel volgens; **the brake –s, **die rem werk.
**act, **n. handeling, daad; bedryf; wet; **caught in the –, **op heterdaad betrap.
**acting, **a. agerend, waarnemend; werkend.
**acting, **n. (komedie)spel.
**action, **handeling, daad, optre(d)e, werking, (reg)saak; geveg; aksie; **man of –, **man van die daad; **put in –, **in werking stel; – **stations, **vegstellings.
**actionable, **strafbaar, aksionabel.
**active, **bedrywig, aktief, werksaam; werkend, effektief; – **voice, **bedrywende vorm.
**activity, **bedrywigheid, aktiwiteit, vlugheid.
**actor **toneelspeler, akteur, dader; bewerker.
**actress **toneelspeelster, aktrise; bewerkster.
**actual, **werklik, wesenlik; teenswoordig.
**actuality, **werklikheid, aktualiteit.
**actualize, **verwerklik, verwesenlik, aktualiseer.
**actually, **werklik, regtig, waarlik(waar).
**actuary, **wiskundige adviseur, aktuaris.

**actuate, **(aan)dryf, aansit, beweeg, moveer.
**acumen, **skerpsinnigheid, insig.
**acute, **skerp; fyn, skerpsinnig, gevat; akuut.
**adage, **spreekwoord, spreuk.
**adamant, **adamant, diamant; staal.
**adamantine, **klip(steen)hard; onvermurfbaar.
**adapt, **geskik maak; aangewend; aanpas (by).
**adaptability, **aanpassingsvermoë, geskiktheid.
**adaptation, **aanpassing; aanwending; bewerking.
**add, **byvoeg, optel; – **up, together, **optel, – **in, **byvoeg, meereken.
adder, **adder; slang; –'s tongue, **slangtong.
**addict, **wy, oorgee; **–ed to drink, **aan die drank verslaaf.
**addict, **n. verslaafde, –sugtige.
**addition, **toevoeging, vermeerdering, optelsomme, optelling; byvoegsel; **in –, **buitendien, boonop; **in – to, **behalwe.
**additional, **bygevoeg, ekstra, addisioneel.
**addle, **verwar; vrot (verrot).
**address, **v. (sig) wend tot, aanspreek; adresseer; toespreek; die woord voer.
**address, **n. adres, opskrif; toespraak, rede; behendigheid; **to pay –es to, **attensie bewys.
**addressee, **geadresseerde.
**adduce, **aanvoer, aanhaal, bybring.
**adenoids, **adenoïde.
**adept, **a. ervare, oulik, bedrewe.
**adept, **n. ingewyde, meester, bedrewene.
**adequacy, **geskiktheid; afdoendheid.
**adequate, **doeltreffend; genoegsaam, eweredig (aan).
**adhere, **aankleef, vaskleef; aanhang; bly by.
**adherence, **vasklewing; verkleefdheid, gehegtheid.
**adherent, **kleefstof, aanhanger, voorstander.
**adhesion, **vasklewing; verkleefdheid; instemming.
**adhesive, **klewerig, vaslewend; – **plaster, **hegpleister.
**adieu, **vaarwel, goeiendag.
**adipose, **vet; vetterig.
**adit, **toegang.
**adjacency, **nabyheid.
**adjacent, **aangrensend, belendend; naby.
**adjectival, **byvoeglik, adjektiwies.
**adjective, **byvoeglike naamwoord, adjektief.
**adjoin, **grens aan; aanheg.
**adjoining, **aangrensend, langsaan.
**adjourn, **verdaag, skors, uitstel; – **to a place, **(sig) begewe na 'n plek.
**adjudge, **beslis, oordeel; toewys, toeken.
**adjudicate, **beoordeel, bereg, verklaar.
**adjudication, **uitspraak, beslissing; toekenning.
**adjunct, **a. toegevoeg, adjunk- . . . ; **hulp- . . . ; – secretary, **hulpsekretaris.
**adjunct, **n. byvoegsel, aanhangsel; bykomstigheid.
**adjuration, **beswering; eed(oplegging), bede.
**adjure, **besweer; smeek.
**adjust, **skik, reël; (ver)stel, regstel.
**adjustable, **(ver)stelbaar.
**adjustment, **skikking; (ver)stelling; afrekening.
**adjutant, **adjudant.
**administer, **bestuur, beheer, waarneem, administreer; uitoefen; toepas, toedien; – **an oath, **'n eed afneem; – **to, **toedien, aanwend; aansmeer; bydra tot.
**administration, **bestuur, beheer, administrasie; toediening; toepassing.
**administrative, **besturend, administratief.
**administrator, **bestuurder, administrateur; boedelberedderaar.
**admirable, **bewonderenswaardig, uitstekend.
**admiral, **admiraal; admiraalskip.
**admiralty, **admiraalskap; admiraliteit.

admiration, bewondering; **to** –, onverbeterlik.
admire, bewonder, vereer, admireer.
admirer, bewonderaar, vereerder, aanbidder.
admissible, toelaatbaar, aanneemlik, geoorloof.
admission, toelating, aanneming; admissie; toegang; toegangsprys; erkenning; – **ticket**, toegangskaartjie.
admit, toelaat; aanneem; erken, toegee; toestaan.
admittance, toegang; toelating, aanneming.
admix, vermeng, bymeng.
admixture, (by)mengsel, toevoegsel.
admonish, vermaan, raai, waarsku, teregwys.
admonition, vermaning, teregwysing.
ado, gedoente, ophef; **much** – **about nothing**, veel geskreeu en weinig wol.
adolescence, ryper jeug, puberteitsjare.
adolescent, a. opgroeiend, opgeskote.
adolescent, n. jeugdige persoon.
adonize, opskik, mooimaak; laat bewonder.
adopt, aanneem; oorneem; kies; inneem; in besit neem.
adoption, aanneming, oorname, opname.
adoptive, aangenome.
adoration, aanbidding, verering.
adore, aanbid, vereer, afgod maak van, verafgood.
adorer, aanbidder, vereerder, vryer.
adorn, versier, tooi, opskik.
adornment, versiering, opskik.
adrift, drywend, los; **turn** –, aan sy lot oorlaat.
adroit, behendig; tak(t)vol, handig.
adroitness, behendigheid; tak(t), handigheid.
adscititious, ontleen, aangenome.
adulate, vlei, inkruip, lek.
adulation, vleiery, inkruipery, lekkery.
adult, a. volwasse, uitgegroei.
adult, n. volwassene, grootmens.
adulterate, vervals, knoei met; verdun; besmet.
adulteration, vervalsing; verdunning.
adulterer, owerspeler, egbreker.
adulteress, owerspeelster, egbreekster.
adulterous, owerspelig.
adultery, owerspel, egbreuk, ontug.
adumbrate, skets, aandui; voorafskadu; oorskadu.
adumbration, afskaduwing; skets, aanduiding.
advance, v. vooruitkom, vorder, nader; styg; vooruitbring; uitsteek; verhaas; bevorder, verhoog; voorbring, opper; voorskiet; **prices** –, pryse styg; – **in years**, ouer word; – **a meaning**, 'n mening opper; – **money**, geld voorskiet; – **upon**, opruk teen.
advance, n. vooruitgang, vordering; nadering; styging; oprukking; bevordering, verhoging; voorskot; **in** –, vooruit, by voorbaat; **in** – **of**, voor.
advancement, vordering, vooruitgang; bevordering; voorskot.
advantage, n. voordeel; voorsprong; **have the** – **of**, 'n voorsprong hê op; **take** – **of**, benut, te nutte maak; **take** – **of a person**, iemand fop, uitoorlê; **to turn to** –, party trek van.
advantage, v. bevoordeel, bevorder, baat.
advantageous, voordelig, bevorderlik.
advent, koms, nadering; advent (*R. Kerk*).
adventitious, toevallig, bykomstig.
adventure, n. onderneming, waagstuk, avontuur; voorval; –**s**, lotgevalle, avonture.
adventure, v. waag, op die spel sit.
adventurer, geluksoeker, avonturier.
adventuress, geluksoekster, avonturierster.
adventurous, avontuurlik, waaghalsig, gewaag, roekeloos; ondernemend.
adverb, bywoord.

adverbial, bywoordelik, adverbiaal.
adversary, teenstander, opponent, vyand.
adversative, teenstellend.
adverse, teengesteld; vyandig; ongunstig.
adversity, teenspoed, ongeluk.
advert, verwys, refereer.
advertise, aankondig, adverteer, reklame maak.
advertisement, aankondiging, advertensie.
advice, raad, meedeling, berig; advies.
advisable, raadsaam, gerade.
advise, (aan)raai, raadgee; laat weet, berig, meedeel; adviseer; – **with**, raadpleeg.
advised, welberade, oorwoë; **you are well** – **to**, jy doen verstandig om te.
advisedly, met opset; verstandiglik.
adviser, raadgewer, raadsman, adviseur.
advisory, raadgewend, adviserend.
advocacy, advokaatskap; bepleiting, voorspraak.
advocate, n. advokaat; voorstander, voorspraak.
advocate, v. bepleit, voorstaan, aanbeveel.
adze, dissel.
aegis, skild; beskerming.
aeon, eeu, onmeetlike tydperk, ewigheid.
aerate, lug; met koolsuur laai; –**d water**, spuitwater, sodawater.
aerial, a. lug- . . . ; gasvormig; eteries, onwesenlik; – **railway**, lugspoor, sweefspoor, kabelspoor.
aerial, n. opvangdrade, lugdrade.
aerobatics, kunsvlieëry.
aerodrome, vliegveld.
aerodynamic, aërodinamies.
aerodynamics, lugdinamika, aërodinamika.
aerolite, meteoorsteen.
aeronaut, lugskipper; vliegenier.
aeronautic, lugvaartkundig.
aeronautics, lugvaartkunde, vliegkuns.
aeroplane, vliegmasjien, vliegtuig.
aerostatics, ewewigsleer van gasse.
aesthetic, esteties, skoonheids- . . .
aesthetics, skoonheidsleer, estetiek.
aetiology, etiologie, oorsaakleer.
afar, ver, in die verte; **from** –, van ver af, uit die verte; – **off**, ver weg.
affability, minsaamheid.
affable, vriendelik, minsaam, inskiklik.
affair, saak, besigheid, affêre; **foreign** –**s**, buitelandse sake (aangeleenthede).
affect, voorgee, voorwend; hou van; raak, beïnvloed, werk op; **it does not** – **me**, dit maak vir my geen verskil nie.
affectation, aanstellings, gemaaktheid; voorwendsel.
affected, aanstellerig, gemaak; aangedaan; **well** –, goedgesind.
affectedness, aanstellerigheid, gemaaktheid.
affection, aandoening; liefde; siekte.
affectionate, toegeneë, liefhebbend; aandoenlik; minsaam.
affiance, n. troubelofte; vertroue.
affiance, v. verloof, trou belowe.
affianced, verloofde.
affidavit, beëdigde verklaring.
affiliate, aansluit, aanneem; erken (as kind).
affiliated, aangeslote, geaffilieer.
affiliation, aanneming; erkenning; aansluiting.
affinity, verwantskap; ooreenkoms; aantrekking.
affirm, bevestig; verseker; bekragtig.
affirmation, bevestiging, bekragtiging; versekering.
affirmative, bevestigend; **answer in the** –, bevestigend antwoord.
affix, v. aanheg, opplak; byvoeg; verbind.
affix, n. toevoeging, aanhangsel; agtervoegsel.
afflatus, inblasing, ingewing, inspirasie.

afflict, bedroef, kwel, teister, besoek.
affliction, droefenis, kwelling, besoeking, straf.
affluence, oorvloed, weelde, rykdom.
affluent, a. toevloeiend; oorvloedig; ryk.
affluent, n. sytak, spruit.
afflux, toevloei; stroom; vermeerdering.
afford, verskaf, gee; oplewer; **he can – to**, hy kan hom dit veroorloof; **I cannot – it**, ek kan dit nie bekostig nie; **can you – the time**, laat jou tyd jou dit toe?
afforest, bebos, bosse aanplant.
afforestation, bebossing, bosaanplanting.
affray, oploop, vegparty, bakleiery.
affright, skrikmaak, verskrik.
affront, v. beledig, affronteer; trotseer.
affront, n. belediging, affrontasie.
afield, in die veld; op die slagveld, te velde; **far –**, ver van huis.
afire, aan brand.
aflame, in vlam, aan brand, in ligtelaai; gloeiend.
afloat, drywend; op see; aan die gang; in (die) omloop.
afoot, te voet; op die been; aan die gang; in die maak; op tou.
afore, prep. voor.
afore, adv. eer.
afore-mentioned, voornoemd, voormeld.
afore-said, voornoemd.
aforethought, voorbedag, voorafberaam; **malice –**, bose opset.
afraid, bang, bevrees; **– of**, bang vir.
African, a. van Afrika.
African, n. Afrikaan; **South –**, Suid-Afrikaner.
Africander, Afrikaner, Afrikaner.
Afrikaans, Afrikaans.
aft, agter.
after, prep. na; agter; **– the war**, na die oorlog; **inquire –**, verneem na; **look –**, kyk na, oppas; **I come – you**, ek kom agter jou (*Plaas*); ek kom na jou (*tyd*); **– a fashion**, op 'n manier; **– all**, per slot van rekening, op die ou end.
after, adv. agterna, later.
after, conj. na(dat).
after, a. later, agter-, na- . . .; **in – years**, in later(e) jare.
afterbirth, nageboorte.
after-crop, na-oes.
after-dinner, na die maaltyd; **– speech**, tafelrede.
afterglow, (die) nagloei, naskynsel.
after-image, nabeeld.
after-life, later(e) leeftyd; lewe hiernamaals.
aftermath, na-oes, nasleep, nadraai.
aftermost, agterste.
afternoon, agtermiddag, namiddag.
afterthought, later oorweging; uitvlug.
afterwards, naderhand, daarna, later.
again, weer, nog eens, opnuut; verder; aan die ander kant; **– and –**, telkens weer, keer op keer; **time and –**, herhaaldelik; **now and –**, nou en dan, af en toe; **as much –**, nog 'n keer soveel; **half as much –**, anderhalf maal soveel; **what is his name –**, hoe heet hy ook weer?
against, teen; fight –, veg teen; **I am – it**, ek is daarteen; **– a dark background**, teen 'n donker agtergrond; **– his return**, teen sy terugkoms; **– a rainy day**, vir die ou dag; **to run (up) – a friend**, 'n vriend raakloop; (**over**) **–**, teenoor.
agapanthus, kandelaar, krismislelie, agapanthus.
agape, met ope mond, verstom, dronkgeslaan.
agate, agaat.
age, n. ouderdom, leeftyd, eeu; **of –**, mondig, meerderjarig; **over –**, oor die leeftyd; **– of discretion**, jare der onderskeids; **old –**, ouderdom, oudag; **Middle Ages**, Middeleeue; **to wait for –s**, eindeloos wag.

age, v. oud word, verouder; oud maak.
aged, oud, bejaard; **the –**, die oues van dae.
agency, agentskap; werking; bemiddeling.
agenda, agenda, (program van) werksaamhede; **point on the –**, beskrywingspunt.
agent, agent, saakwaarnemer; bewerker; werktuig; agens; middel.
agglomerate, v. op(een)hoop.
agglomerate, opeengehoop.
agglomeration, opeenhoping, versameling.
agglutinate, saamkleef, aaneenlym, verbind.
agglutinative, saamklewend; **– languages**, agglutinerende tale.
aggrandize, vergroot, verryk, verheerlik; verfraai.
aggrandizement, verryking, verheerliking.
aggravate, vererger, verswaar; treiter, terg.
aggravation, verergering; terging; oordrywing.
aggregate, v. saamvoeg; 'n totaal maak, beloop.
aggregate, a. gesamentlik, kollektief.
aggregate, n. versameling; totaal; geheel; **in the –**, oor die geheel, globaal.
aggression, aanval, aanranding; aggressie.
aggressive, aanvallend, parmantig, aggressief.
aggrieved, bedroef; gekrenk; benadeel, veronreg.
aghast, ontset, versteld.
agile, rats, vlug, lenig.
agility, ratsheid, vlugheid, lenigheid.
agio, opgeld, agio.
agitate, beweeg, skud; opwek, in beroering bring, verontrus; agiteer.
agitation, beweging; verontrusting; oproerigheid; agitasie.
agitator, oproermaker, onrusstoker, agitator.
aglet, aiglet, klossie, lowertjie; veterpunt.
aglow, gloeiend, verhit, warm; blosend.
agnail, geskeurde naelvelletjie, skeurnael.
agnate, a. verwant (van vaderskant).
agnate, n. verwante.
agnomen, bynaam.
agnostic, a. agnosties.
agnostic, n. agnostikus.
agnosticism, agnostisisme.
ago, gelede.
agog, opgewonde, verlangend, belus.
agonize, kwel, folter; worstel.
agony, pyn, angs, doodstryd; foltering, kwelling.
agrarian, a. agraries, landelik, boere-.
agrarian, n. agrariër, landbouverteenwoordiger.
agree, ooreenstem, instem, akkordeer, eens wees; harmonieer, oor die weg kom, stryk; **– on**, eens wees (word) oor; **fat does not – with me**, vet akkordeer nie met my nie.
agreeable, aangenaam, gewillig; ooreenkomstig; **if you are –**, as jy dit goed vind.
agreement, ooreenstemming, ooreenkoms, verdrag.
agricultural, landbou- . . ., landboukundige.
agriculturalist, landboukundige, landbouer.
agriculture, landbou, landboukunde.
agrimony, lewerkruid.
agronomy, landbou; landboukunde.
aground, aan die grond, gestrand.
ague, koors, kouekoors.
ahead, voor, vooruit, voorop, voorraad.
ahoy, heila, haai!
ai, aai, luiaard.
aid, v. help, bystaan; **– and abet**, hulp en bystand verleen.
aid, n. hulp, bystand, steun; **in – of**, ten bate van.
aide-de-camp, adjudant, aide-de-camp.
aiglet, sien **aglet**.
aigrette (egret), kuifreier; kuif; hoofsieraad.
ail, skeel, skort; siek wees.
ailing, sieklik, siekerig, sukkelend.

ailment, siekte, ongesteldheid.
aim, v. mik, korrel; – **at**, mik (streef) na.
aim, n. doel, oogmerk; **to take** –, korrelvat.
aimless, doelloos.
air, n. lug, windjie; houding, wysie, lied; **be in the** –, in die lug sit; **quite in the** –, onseker; **give oneself –s**, (sig) aanstel; – **display (pageant)**, vliegvertoning, vliegskou; – **fighter**, jagvliegtuig; – **fuel**, vliegtuigbrandstof; – **gunner**, boordskutter; – **hostess**, lugwaardin; – **rally**, vliegbyeenkoms; – **-to-** – **missile**, boord-lugprojektiel.
air, v. lug; droogmaak; lug gee aan; **to – one's views**, jou opinies lug.
air-, a. lug-..., wind-...
air-balloon, lugballon.
air-base, lug(mag)basis, vliegveld.
air-borne, in die lug; deur die lug vervoer.
air-break, lugrem.
air-brick, ventilasiesteen.
air-castle, lugkasteel.
air-cleaner, lugfilter.
air-conditioning, lugtempering, lugreëling.
air-cooled, luggekoel.
aircraft, lugvaartuig, (-tuie); vliegtuig, (-tuie); – carrier, vliegdekskip.
air-gun, windbuks, windgeweertjie.
airily, lugtig.
airiness, lugtigheid.
airless, bedompig.
air-lift, lugbrug.
airline, reguit lyn; lug(vaart)lyn.
airliner, lynvliegtuig.
airmail, lugpos.
airplant, kanniedood.
airport, vlieghawe, lughawe.
air-raid, lugaanval.
air-strip, stygbaan, landingstrook.
airtight, lugdig.
air-valve, lugklep.
airy, lugtig; yl; hoog in die lug.
aisle, vleuel; sygang, paadjie.
ajar, op 'n skrefie, op 'n kier.
akimbo: **with arms** –, met die hande in die sy.
akin, verwant.
alabaster, albas, albaster.
alack, helaas!
alacrity, lewendigheid; graagte, gretigheid.
alarm, n. alarm; skrik, angs; wekker; **to give the** –, alarm maak; **to take** –, skrikvat.
alarm, v. alarmeer, skrikmaak, ongerus maak.
alarm-clock, wekker.
alarming, verontrustend; onrusbarend.
alarmist, alarmmaker, skrikaanjaer.
alas, helaas!
alb, koorhemp.
albacore, albakoor, (halfkoord).
albatros, albatros, stormvoël.
albeit, (al)hoewel.
albino, albino.
album, album; gedenkboek.
albumen, wit van eier, eiwit.
alchemist, alchemis.
alchemy, alchemie.
alcohol, alkohol, wyngees; sterk drank.
alcoholic, alkoholies; – **drink**, sterk drank; n. alkoholis, dranksugtige.
alcove, alkoof; somerhuisie, prieel.
alder, els, elsboom.
alderman, raadsheer.
ale, Engelse bier; bierfees, fuif.
alembic, distilleerkolf.
alert, waaksaam, wakker, vlug, op die hoede.
alexandrine, aleksandryn.
alfresco, alfresco, buitelug-...

alga, seegras, seewier.
algebra, stelkunde, algebra.
algebraic, stelkundig, algebraïes.
Algerian, Algeryns.
algid, koud.
alias, alias.
alibi, alibi.
alien, a. vreemd, uitlands.
alien, n. vreemde, uitlander.
alienable, vervreembaar.
alienate, vervreem; ontvreem; afkonkel.
alienation, vervreemding; **(mental)** –, kranksinnigheid.
alienist, psigiater.
alight, v. afstyg, uitstyg; gaan sit, land, neerstryk.
alight, a. aan die brand.
align, in gelid stel, opstel, rig.
alike, a. gelyk, eenders.
alike, adv. eenders; gelykop; eweseer.
aliment, voedsel; steun, onderhoud.
alimentary, voedend; voedings-..., onderhouds-...; – **canal**, spyskanaal.
alimentation, voeding; onderhoud.
alimony, onderhoud, onderhoudskoste.
aliquot, opgaande; – **part**, opgaande deel.
alive, lewendig; in lewe; – **to**, bewus van, gevoelig vir; **be** – **with**, wemel van; **to look** –, gou maak.
alkali, alkali, loogsout.
alkaline, alkalies, loogsoutagtig.
all, a. alle, al die, algar; heel, die hele; – **the others**, al die ander; – **kinds of**, alle soorte (van); – **the world**, die hele wêreld; – **day**, die hele dag, heeldag; – **this**, dit alles; **for** – **his good looks**, al is hy so mooi.
all, pron. algar, alles; – **of you**, julle algar; – **of it**, alles; **take it** –, neem (dit) alles; **hang it** –!, vervlaks!; **after** –, per slot van rekening, op die ou end; **not at** –, heeltemal nie; **at** –, in enige opsig, ook maar enigsins; **ooit**; **did he ask you at** – **?**, het hy jou ooit gevra?; – **in** –, alles tesame; **for good and** –, eens en vir altyd; **one and** –, almal tesame.
all, adv. heeltemal, totaal; **dressed** – **in white**, heeltemal in wit gekleed; – **covered with mud**, ene modder; – **the better**, soveel te beter; – **the same**, tog, darem; almaskie; – **at once**, skielik, meteens; plotseling; – **along**, aldeur, al die tyd; – **over**, deur en deur; van kop tot toon; in alle rigtinge; in alle opsigte; **he was** – **but drowned**, hy was op 'n haar na verdrink
allay, verlig, versag, matig, verminder; bedaar.
allegation, bewering.
allege, beweer, aanvoer.
allegiance, trou, getrouheid.
allegoric, sinnebeeldig, allegories.
allegorize, sinnebeeldig (allegories) voorstel.
allegory, allegorie, sinnebeeldige voorstelling.
alleluia, halleluja, lofsang.
alleviate, verlig, versag, lenig.
alleviation, verligting, versagting, leniging.
alley, steeg, gang; **blind** –, blinde steeg.
alley, ally, ellie.
alliance, verbond, verwantskap; huwelik.
alligator, kaaiman, alligator.
alliterate, allitereer.
alliteration, alliterasie, stafrym.
alliterative, allitererend.
allocate, aanwys, toeken; plek aanwys.
allocation, aanwysing, toekenning.
allodial, vry van leenreg, allodiaal.
allopathy, allopatie.
allot, toewys, toeken, toedeel.
allotment, toewysing; aandeel; perseel.

allow   409   **amnesty**

allow, toestaan, toelaat, veroorloof, toegee, erken; – **for,** rekening hou met; – **of,** toelaat.
allowable, geoorlof, toelaatbaar.
allowance, vergunning; (aan)deel, porsie; toelae; afslag, rabat; **monthly –,** maandgeld, maandelikse toelae; **make – for,** rekening hou met.
alloy, n. mengsel; allooi, gehalte; kwaliteit.
alloy, v. meng, legeer; versleg; temper.
allright, goed, in orde!
all-round, a. alsydig, veelsydig.
all-round, adv. in die algemeen, vir algar.
allspice, Jamaikapeper, naelbol.
allude: – to, sinspeel (doel) op, bedoel.
allure, aantrek, aanlok, verlei.
allurement, verleidelikheid; lokmiddel.
alluring, aanloklik, verleidelik.
allusion, sinspeling, toespeling.
allusive, sinspelend; vol toespelinge.
alluvial, aangeslibte, rivier-...; – **diggings,** rivierdelwery; – **diamonds,** spoeldiamante.
alluvium, aanslibsel, slykgrond.
ally, v. verbind, verenig; **allied with,** gepaard met, verenig met.
ally, n. bondgenoot.
ally, sien alley.
almanac, almanak, kalender.
almighty, a. almagtig; tamaai, kolossaal, yslik; **the A.,** die Almagtige.
almond, amandel; mangel.
almoner, aalmoesenier.
almost, amper, byna.
alms, aalmoes, liefdegawe.
alms-house, armegestig.
aloe, aalwee (aalwyn), garingboom.
aloft, bo, omhoog, hoog; na bo, in die hoogte.
alone, alleen, eensaam; net, enkel; **leave –,** alleen laat, afbly.
along, prep. lang(e)s, lang(e)saan, naas(aan); – **the road,** lang(e)s (op) die pad.
along, adv. aan, vooruit, deur; **get –!,** vooruit!; **walk –,** aanstap; – **with,** saam met.
alongside, naas(aan), lang(e)saan.
aloof, apart, op 'n afstand, opsy; **stand –,** (sig.) afsydig hou.
aloofness, afsydigheid.
aloud, hard(op), luid.
alp, bergtop.
alpaca, lama; alpakka, lamawol.
alpha, alfa; – **ray,** alfastraal.
alphabet, alfabet, abc.
alphabetic, alfabeties.
Alpine, Alpe-...
Alpinist, Alpinis, bergklimmer.
Alps, Alpe.
already, al, (al)reeds.
Alsatian, Elsasser; Elsassiese (vrou); wolfshond.
also, ook; eweneens, insgelyks; verder.
altar, altaar; **family –,** huisaltaar, huisgodsdiens.
altar-piece, altaarskildery.
alter, verander, wysig.
alteration, verandering, wysiging.
altercate, twis, kibbel, krakeel.
altercation, woordewisseling, twis, rusie.
alternate, v. (mekaar) afwissel; (om)wissel, verwissel; **alternating current,** wisselstroom.
alternate, a. afwisselend; – **Sundays,** om die ander Sondag.
alternately, (af)wisselend, om die beurt.
alternation, (af)wisseling.
alternative, a. ander, alternatief.
alternative, n. alternatief, keus; **I had no –,** ek het geen keus(e) gehad nie.
although, al, (al)hoewel, almaskie, ofskoon.
altimeter, hoogtemeter, altimeter.
altitude, hoogte, diepte; hoë rang.

alto, alt (stem).
altogether, altesame; glad, totaal, heeltemal; oor die geheel.
altruism, altruïsme, onbaatsugtigheid.
alum, aluin.
aluminium, aluminium.
alveolar, alveolêr, tandkas-...
always, altyd, altoos, gedurig, aljimmer.
am, is.
amalgam, amalgaam, mengsel.
amalgamate, meng, amalgameer, saamsmelt.
amalgamation, amalgamasie, samesmelting.
amanuensis, amanuensis, assistent, sekretaris.
amarant(h), amarant.
amaryllis, narsinglelie.
amass, ophoop, versamel; **to – a fortune,** 'n fortuin maak.
amateur, amateur, dilettant, liefhebber.
amateurish, dilettanties, beginners-...
amatory, verlief(de), liefde(s)-...
amaze, verbaas, dronkslaan, verstom.
amazement, verbasing, verstomming.
amazingly, verbasend.
amazon, amasone; strydbare vrou.
ambassador, gesant, ambassadeur.
ambassadress, gesante; ambassadeursvrou.
amber, barnsteen, amber.
ambergris, ambergrys, grys amber.
ambidexter(ous), dubbelhandig, dubbelhartig.
ambient, omringend.
ambiguity, dubbelsinnigheid, onduidelikheid.
ambiguous, dubbelsinnig; twyfelagtig, onduidelik, duister.
ambit, omtrek, grens; strekking.
ambition, eersug, ambisie; doel, strewe.
ambitious, eersugtig, ambisieus; – **of,** begerig na.
ambitiousness, eergierigheid.
amble, v. pasgang (telgang), loop, trippel.
amble, n. telgang, pasgang, trippelgang.
ambrosia, godespys, ambrosyn.
ambulance, ambulans, veldhospitaal.
ambulatory, wandelend, trekkend, rondgaande.
ambuscade, hinderlaag.
ambush, n. hinderlaag, val; **lie in –,** in hinderlaag lê; **lay an –,** 'n val stel.
ambush, v. in hinderlaag lê; in 'n hinderlaag lok.
ameer, amir, emir (amir).
ameliorate, verbeter, versag.
amen, amen.
amenable, handelbaar, geseglik; – **to,** vatbaar vir; verantwoording, skuldig aan.
amend, verander, wysig; verbeter; amendeer.
amendment, wysiging; verbetering; amendement.
amends, vergoeding; **make –,** vergoed, goedmaak.
amenity, aangenaamheid, innemendheid; **amenities,** vriendelikhede; geriewe.
amerce, beboet, straf.
American, Amerikaner, Amerikaanse (vrou).
amethyst, ametis.
amiability, beminlikheid, minsaamheid.
amiable, vriendelik, beminlik, minsaam.
amicability, vriendelikheid, vriendskaplikheid.
amicable, vriendelik, vriendskaplik.
amid, amidst, tussen, onder, te midde van.
amidships, midskeeps.
amir, sien ameer.
amiss, verkeerd, onvanpas; **take –,** kwalik neem.
amity, vriendskap, vriendskaplikheid.
ammeter, ampèremeter.
ammonia, ammoniak, vlugsout.
ammunition, ammunisie, krygsvoorraad, skietgoed.
amnesia, geheueverlies.
amnesty, amnestie, vergifnis.

amoeba, amebe.
among, amongst, onder, tussen; **run in – the people**, onder (tussen) die mense in hardloop; **we possessed five pounds – us**, ons het tesame vyf pond besit; **they quarrelled – themselves**, hulle het onder mekaar rusie gemaak.
amorous, verlief(de), liefdes- . . ., minne- . . .
amorphous, vormloos, amorf.
amortization, skulddelging, amortisasie.
amount, v. bedra, beloop, kom (op); beteken; – **to the same**, op dieselfde neerkom.
amount, n. bedrag, som; opbrengs; hoeveelheid; **any – of money**, geld soos bossies.
amour, liefdesavontuur, minnary.
ampere, ampère.
amphibian, a. amfibies.
amphibian, n. amfibie; amfibiese voertuig.
amphibious, tweeslagtig, amfibies.
amphitheatre, amfiteater; strydperk.
amphora, amfora, vaas.
ample, ruim, wyd; breed(voerig); oorvloedig.
amplification, uitbreiding, vergroting, versterking, aanvulling; uitweiding.
amplifier, uitbreier; versterker.
amplify, uitbrei, aanvul, vergroot; uitwei.
amplitude, wydte, omvang; oorvloedigheid; slingerwydte.
amply, ruim, ruimskoots, volop.
ampoule, ampul.
ampulla, ampul, kannetjie.
amputate, afsit, afsny, amputeer.
amputation, afsetting, amputasie; besnoeiing.
amuck, amok; **run –**, amok maak.
amulet, amulet, geluksteentjie, toorhoutjie.
amuse, vermaak, amuseer; **to – oneself**, die tyd verdrywe, (sig.) vermaak.
amusement, vermaak, vermaaklikheid, tydverdryf.
amusing, vermaaklik, amusant, snaaks.
an, 'n.
anabaptism, wederdoop; anabaptisme.
anabaptist, wederdoper, anabaptis.
anachronism, anachronisme.
anachronistic, anachronisties.
anaemia, bloedarmoede, anemie.
anaemic, bloedarm, bloedloos, anemies.
anaesthesia, verdowing, gevoelloosheid, anestesie.
anaesthetic, a. verdowend.
anaesthetic, n. verdowingsmiddel.
anaesthetist, narkotiseur.
anaesthetize, verdoof, wegmaak, onder narkose bring.
anagram, letterkering, anagram.
analecta, analects, analecta, brokkies, bloemlesing.
analeptic, versterkend, opwekkend.
analogical, analogies, analoog, ooreenkomstig.
analogous, analoog, gelyksoortig.
analogy, analogie, ooreenkomstigheid, gelyksoortigheid.
analphabet, analfabeet, ongeletterde.
analyse, ontleed, oplos, analiseer; ondersoek.
analysis, ontleding, analise, opsomming.
analyst, ontleder; skeikundige.
analytical, analaties, ontledend; skeidend.
anapaest, anapes.
anapaestic, anapesties.
anarchic(al), regeringloos, wetloos, anargisties.
anarchist, anargis.
anarchy, regeringloosheid, anargie; wanorde.
anathema, vervloeking, banvloek, anatema.
anathematize, vervloek, die banvloek (oor) uitspreek.
anatomical, ontleedkundig, anatomies.

anatomist, ontleedkundige, anatoom.
anatomize, ontleed, anatomiseer.
anatomy, ontleedkunde, anatomie; ontleding; liggaam; geraamte.
ancestor, voorouer, voorvader.
ancestral, voorvaderlik, erf- . . .
ancestry, voorouers; afkoms; geboorte.
anchor, n. anker; toeverlaat: **cast –**, anker uitgooi; **weigh –**, anker lig; **at –**, voor anker, geanker(d).
anchor, v. anker; vasmaak.
anchorage, ankergrond; ankergeld; toeverlaat.
anchoress, kluisenares.
anchoret, anchorite, kluisenaar.
anchovy, ansjovis.
ancient, a. oud, outyds; ouderwets.
Ancients: the –, die Ou Volke.
ancillary, diensbaar, ondergeskik.
and, en; nice – thin, mooi dun, lekker dun; **try – come**, probeer (om te) kom.
Andalusia, Andalusië (*Sp.*).
Andalusian, n. Andalusiër.
Andalusian, a. Andalusies.
andiron, vuurbok, esyster.
anecdotage, spraaksame kindsheid.
anecdote, verhaaltjie, anekdote.
anemometer, windmeter.
anemone, anemoon, windroos; **sea –**, seeroos.
aneroid, doosbarometer, aneroïed-barometer.
anew, weer, weer oor, nog eens, opnuut.
anfractuosity, kronkeligheid; verdraaidheid.
angel, engel(tjie); **–'s food**, vrugteslaai.
angelic, engelagtig; engele- . . .
angelus, angelus; bedeklok.
anger, n. boosheid, gramskap, toorn.
anger, v. vertoorn, kwaad maak.
angle, n. hoek; (hoekige) punt; **right –**, regte hoek; **acute –**, skerp hoek; **oblique –**, skewe hoek; **obtuse –**, stomp hoek.
angle, v. vis, visvang; hengel.
angler, hengelaar, visser, visvanger.
Angles, Angele.
Anglican, Anglikaans.
Anglicism, Anglisisme.
Anglicize, verengels, angliseer.
Anglo . . ., Anglo- . . ., Angel- . . .
Anglo-Boer War, Engelse Oorlog, Tweede Vryheidsoorlog.
Anglo-Saxon, a. Angel-Saksies.
Anglo-Saxon, n. Angel-Sakser.
Angora, Angora; **– goat**, angorabok, sybok; **– wool**, angorahaar, bokhaar.
angry, kwaad, boos; **– about, at**, kwaad oor (om); **– with**, kwaad vir (op).
anguish, angs, benoudheid, pyn, foltering.
angular, hoekerig; maer; ongemaklik.
angularity, hoekigheid, hoekerigheid.
aniline, anilien.
anility, kindsheid.
animadversion, afkeuring, kritiek; berisping.
animadvert, aanmerkings maak, afkeur.
animal, n. dier.
animal, a. dierlik; **– kingdom**, diereryk.
animalcule, mikroskopiese diertjie.
animalism, dierlikheid; animalisme.
animality, dierlikheid; dierewêreld.
animate, v. besiel, aanspoor, opwek, animeer.
animate, a. lewend, lewendig.
animated, lewendig, opgewek, geanimeerd.
animation, lewendigheid; bemoediging; aansporing.
animosity, vyandigheid; verbittering.
animus, gees; vyandigheid.
anise, anys.
aniseed, anys(saad).

anker, anker.
ankle, enkel; – deep, tot aan die enkels.
ankle-guard, enkelskut.
anklet, voetring.
anna, anna (Indiese munt).
annalist, kroniekskrywer.
annals, kronieke, jaarboeke, annale.
anneal, temper.
annex, v. aanheg, toevoeg; inlyf, annekseer.
annex, annexe, n. aanhangsel, bylae; bygebou.
annexation, anneksasie, inlywing.
annihilate, vernietig, wegveeg, uitwis.
annihilation, vernietiging, uitroeiing.
anniversary, n. verjaar(s)dag, gedenkdag.
annotate, aantekeninge skryf (by); annoteer.
annotation, aantekening, verklaring; annotasie.
annotator, verklaarder, annoteerder.
announce, aankondig, (aan)meld.
announcement, aankondiging, bekendmaking.
annoy, lastig val, pla, terg, erger, kwaad maak.
annoyance, las, ergernis, hindernis.
annoying, lastig, ergerlik, hinderlik.
annual, a. jaarliks, jaar- . . .
annual, n. jaarboek, -blad; eenjarige plant.
annuity, jaargeld, lyfrente, pensioen.
annul, vernietig; nietig verklaar; afskaf, ophef.
annular, ringvormig, ring- . . .
annulation, ring.
annunciate, aankondig, boodskap.
annunciation, aankondiging, boodskap.
anode, anode.
anodyne, pynstillende middel.
anoint, salf, smeer.
anointed, gesalfde.
anomalous, onreëlmatig, afwykend; vals.
anomaly, onreëlmatigheid, anomalie.
anon, aanstons; ever and –, van tyd tot tyd.
anonymity, naamloosheid, anonimiteit.
anonymous, naamloos, anoniem.
another, 'n ander, 'n ander een; nog een; it was
– man, dit was 'n ander man; drink – cup of
tea, drink nog 'n koppie tee; one –, mekaar,
die een die ander.
anserine, gansagtig, dom, ganse- . . .
answer, n. antwoord; verdediging; oplossing.
answer, v. antwoord, beantwoord; – the bell
(door), die deur oopmaak; – for, verantwoord; instaan vir; – a purpose, aan 'n doel
beantwoord; that will not –, dit sal nie gaan
nie; – a description, klop met 'n beskrywing.
answerable, beantwoordbaar; verantwoordelik.
ant, mier.
antagonism, vyandskap; teenstrydigheid.
antagonist, teenparty, teenstander, antagonis.
antagonistic, vyandig; teenstrydig; antagonisties.
antagonize, teenwerk, bestry; in die harnas ja.
Antarctic, Suidpool–, Antarkties; – pole, Suidpool; – (Ocean), Suidelike Yssee.
antbear, -eater, erdvark, miervreter.
antecede, voorafgaan.
antecedent, a. voorafgaande.
antecedent, n. antesedent; –s, verlede.
antechamber, ante-room, wagkamer, voorvertrek.
antedate, vroeër dagteken; vervroeg; voorafgaan aan; vooruitloop op.
antediluvian, (van) voor die sondvloed, ante-
deluviaans.
antelope, antiloop, wildbok.
antemeridian, voormiddags.
antenatal, (van) voor die geboorte.
antenna, voelhoring; lugdraad, antenne.
antenuptial, van voor die huwelik, huweliks-
. . .; – contract, huweliksvoorwaarde(s).
antepenultimate, op twee na die laaste.

anterior, verder na vore, voor; vroeër.
ante-room, wagkamer, voorkamer.
anthem, lied, koorsang; national –, volkslied.
ant-hill, mier(s)hoop.
anthology, bloemlesing.
anthracite, antrasiet.
anthrax, miltvuur, miltsiekte.
anthropoid, antropoïed, mensagtig, mens- . . .
– ape, mensaap.
anthropologist, antropoloog.
anthropology, antropologie.
anthropomorphic, antropmorf, menslik.
anthropophagous, mensvretend, mensvreter- . . .
anthropophagus, mensvreter, antropofaag.
anti-aircraft gun, afweerkanon.
anti-bilious, galverdrywend, teen die gal.
antibiotic, n. antibiotikum (mv. . . . tika).
antibiotic, a. antibioties.
antic, a. snaaks, koddig, potsierlik.
Antichrist, Antichris.
Antichristian, Antichristelik, van die Antichris.
anticipate, voor wees, voorkom; vooruit oorweeg; voorsien, verwag; verhaas; antisipeer.
anticipation, die vooruitloop (op); voorkoming;
voorgevoel, verwagting; voorsmaak; antisipasie; in –, by voorbaat, vooruit.
anticlimax, antiklimaks.
antics, bokkespronge; kronkelinge; malstreke.
antidote, teengif.
antimacassar, antimakassar.
antimony, spiesglans, antimoon.
antimony, teenspraak, teenstrydigheid.
antipathetic, antipatiek, afstotend.
antipathy, antipatie, teensin, afkeer.
antiphony, beurtsang, teensang, wisselsang.
antipodes, teenvoeters, antipode.
antiquarian, a. oudheidkundig, antikwaries.
antiquarian, n. oudheidkundige, oudheidkenner,
antikwaar.
antiquary, oudheidkenner, antikwaar.
antiquated, verouderd, ouderwets, antiek.
antique, a. oud, ouderwets, antiek.
antique, n. ou, kunswerk, antik(w)iteit.
antiquity, die Oudheid; antik(w)iteit.
antirepublican, antirepublikeins.
antirrhinum, leeubekkie.
anti-Semitic, anti-Semities.
antiseptic, n. ontsmettingsmiddel, -stof.
antiseptic, a. antisepties, bederfwerend.
antithesis, teenstelling, antitese.
antithetic, teenstellend, antiteties.
anti-trade, antipassaatwind.
antivenene, (slang-)teengif.
antler, tak (van 'n gewei); –s, gewei.
anvil, aambeeld.
anxiety, angs, onrus; begeerte.
anxious, besorg; begerig; he was – to help me,
hy wou my baie graag help; an – business, 'n
benoude affêre.
any, enige; iedere, elke; soveel (-ver, -lank, ens.)
as jy wil; is there still – hope?, is daar nog
enige hoop?; – child knows that, elke kind
weet dit; you can come – day, jy kan kom
watter dag jy wil, jy kan enige dag kom; –
distance, so ver as jy wil; have you – cigars?,
het u (ook) sigare?; not –, geen . . . nie; I
cannot see – difference, ek kan geen verskil
sien nie.
anybody, iedereen, elkeen; iemand; not . . . –,
niemand . . . nie; – can see that, dit kan
iedereen sien; has – seen him?, het iemand
hom gesien?
anyhow, adv. sommerso, op 'n (onverskillige)
manier; in elk geval; he does his work –, hy
doen sy werk op 'n (onverskillige) manier; you'll

have to do it –, jy sal dit in elk geval moet doen.
anyhow, conj. hoe dit ook al sy, in elk geval.
anyone, iedereen (enigeen), wie ook, iemand; **not** . . . –, niemand . . . nie; **has – seen him?**, het iemand hom gesien?
anything, alles, enigiets; iets (in vraagsinne); **he'll do – for me**, hy sal enigiets vir my doen; **do you know – about it?**, weet jy daar iets van?; **not** . . . –, niks . . . nie.
anyway, hoe dit ook mag wees, in elk geval.
anywhere, orals, êrens; **you can buy it** –, jy kan dit orals koop; **can you buy it** –?, kan jy dit êrens koop?; **not** . . . –, nêrens . . . nie.
aorist, onbepaald verlede tyd, aoristus.
aorta, groot slagaar, aorta.
apace, snel, hard; by elke tree.
ap(p)anage, toelae; deel; eienskap.
apart, afsonderlik, apart; alleen; opsy, weg; **every one** –, iedereen afsonderlik; **I took him** –, ek het hom opsy geneem; **jesting** –, alle gekheid op 'n stokkie, in erns; **to take something** –, iets uitmekaar haal; **– from**, afgesien van; **to set** –, afsonder, opsy sit.
apartment, vertrek, kamer.
apathetic, ongevoelig; onverskillig, apaties.
apathy, ongevoeligheid; onverskilligheid, apatie.
ape, n. aap; na-aper.
ape, v. na-aap.
apercu, kort oorsig, samevatting.
aperient, purgeermiddel, purgasie.
aperitif, aperitief, aptytwekker.
aperture, opening.
apery, na-apery, dwase vertoning.
apex, punt, top, toppunt.
aphaeresis, voorafkapping.
aphis, bladluis.
aphorism, stelling; leerspreuk.
apiary, byehok, byehuis.
apiece, (per) stuk, elk.
apish, aapagtig, dwaas, verspot.
aplomb, sekerheid, selfvertroue, aplomb.
apocalypse, openbaring.
apocalyptical, apokalipties, openbarend.
apocope, agterafkapping, apokopee.
apocrypha, apokriewe boeke.
apocryphal, apokrief, twyfelagtig; verdag.
apod(e)ictic, onweerlegbaar, stellig, apodikties.
apologetic, verontskuldigend; apologeties.
apologize, (sig) verontskuldig, ekskuus (verskoning) vra (maak).
apologue, fabel.
apology, verontskuldiging, ekskuus, verskoning; verdediging, verweer(skrif).
apo(ph)thegm, sinspreuk.
apoplectic, apoplekties; – **fit**, beroerte-aanval.
apoplexy, beroerte; **fit of** –, beroerte-aanval.
apostasy, (geloofs)versaking, afval.
apostate, afvallige, versaker.
apostatize, versaak, afvallig word.
apostle, apostel, godsgesant, geloofsprediker.
apostolate, apostelskap, apostolaat.
apostolic, apostolies.
apostrophe, toespraak; afkappingsteken.
apostrophize, toespreek, (sig) wend tot.
apothecary, apteker.
apotheosis, vergoding; verheerliking, apoteose.
appal, ontstel, verskrik, ontset.
appalling, ontstellend, ontstellend.
appanage, sien **ap(p)anage**.
apparatus, toestel(le), gereedskap, apparaat.
apparel, n. kleding, drag, gewaad.
apparel, v. klee(d), aanklee(d), tooi.
apparent, duidelik, sigbaar, kenlik.
apparently, blykbaar; klaarblyklik; skynbaar.

apparition, verskyning; spook, gedaante.
apparitor, bode.
appeal, v. in beroep gaan, appelleer; **'n beroep doen (op)**; (sig) beroep (op); **– to the high court**, in beroep gaan na die hoër hof; **– to the country**, 'n beroep doen op die volk; **it does not – to me**, dit lok my nie aan nie; **that picture –s to me**, daardie skildery val in my smaak.
appeal, n. beroep; appèl; (smeek)bede.
appear, verskyn; blyk, skyn; lyk; optree.
appearance, verskyning, verskynsel; voorkome.
appease, bevredig; tot bedaring bring, kalmeer; stil, les; **– hunger**, honger stil; **– thirst**, dors les.
appellant, appellant.
appellate, appèl- . . . ; **– court**, appèlhof.
appellation, benaming, naam.
appellative, (soort)naam.
append, aanhang, toevoeg, byvoeg, vasknoop.
appendage, aanhangsel, byvoegsel.
appendicitis, blindedermontsteking, appendisitis.
appendix, aanhangsel; bylae; blindederm.
apperception, waarneming; appersepsie.
appertain, behoor (by, aan); betrekking hê (op).
appetite, eetlus, aptyt, sin, lus.
appetizer, aptytsnapsie, bittertjie, borrel.
appetizing, aptytlik, smaaklik; aantreklik.
applaud, toejuig; prys; apploudiseer.
applause, toejuiging, applous, handgeklap.
apple, appel; **– of discord**, twisappel.
apple-pie, appeltert; **in – order**, agtermekaar.
appliance, aanwending, toepassing, toestel.
applicable, toepaslik, bruikbaar.
applicant, sollisitant, applikant.
application, aanwending; aansoek; vlyt, ywer.
appliqué, n. appliek.
appliqué, v. applikeer.
apply, aanwend, toepas; gebruik (maak van); aansoek doen, aanvra; rig (tot), wend (tot); **– oneself to a task**, (sig) toelê op 'n taak; **– to the secretary**, aansoek doen by die sekretaris; **the argument does not** –, die redenering is nie van toepassing nie.
appoint, bepaal, vasstel; aanstel, benoem; uitrus.
appointment, bepaling; afspraak, bestelling; aanstelling, benoeming; uitrusting; **make an** –, 'n afspraak maak; **keep an** –, 'n afspraak hou; **break an** –, 'n afspraak versuim; **by** –, volgens afspraak.
apportion, toedeel, verdeel.
apportionment, toedeling, verdeling.
apposite, toepaslik, passend, gepas, geskik.
apposition, bystelling, aanhegting; apposisie.
appraise, takseer, waardeer, skat.
appraisement, skatting, taksasie.
appraiser, taksateur, skatter, waardeerder.
appreciable, merkbaar, aanmerklik; **– difference**, aanmerklike verskil.
appreciate, waardeer, op prys stel; vermeerder in waarde; appresieer.
appreciation, skatting, waardering, appresiasie.
apprehend, vang, arresteer; begryp; vrees.
apprehensible, bevatlik, begryplik.
apprehension, aanhouding, gevangeneming; bevatting, begrip; vrees.
apprehensive, bevrees, bang, bedug; **– of**, bang (bedug) vir.
apprentice, n. (vak)leerling, klerk; nuweling.
apprentice, v. 'n ambag laat leer, inboek.
apprenticeship, leertyd, leerjare; **serve an** –, leertyd deurmaak.
apprise, onderrig, meedeel, berig.
apprize, waardeer (teen).
approach, v. nader, nader kom.

approach, n. nadering; toegang; naderingswerke; – shot, naderhou.
approachable, toeganklik, genaakbaar.
approbation, goedkeuring, byval; aanbeveling.
appropriate, a. geskik, passend.
appropriate, v. (sig) toe-eien, beslag lê op; afsonder (vir).
appropriation, toe-eiening; afsondering; bestemming; aanwending; appropriasie.
approval, goedkeuring; on –, op sig.
approve, goedkeur; bevestig; – of, goedkeur.
approximate, a. by benadering, geraam.
approximate, v. naby kom; naby bring; raam.
approximately, by benadering, naastenby.
appurtenance, toebehore, aanhangsel.
apricot, appelkoos.
April, April; – fool, Aprilgek.
apron, voorskoot, skort.
apronstring, voorskootband; to be tied to the –s, aan die leiband loop.
apt, geneig (tot); geskik; bekwaam, vlug.
aptitude, geneigdheid; geskiktheid; aanleg.
aqualung, duiklong.
aquaplane, n. ski-plank.
aquaplane, v. ski-plank ry.
aquarelle, waterverfskildery, akwarel.
aquarium, akwarium (aquarium).
aquatic, a. water- ...
aquatic, n. waterplant; waterdier; –s, watersport.
aqueduct, waterleiding.
aqueous, waterig, wateragtig, water- ...
aquiline, geboë, arends- ...; – nose, arendsneus.
Arab, Arabier; Arabiese perd; street –, straatswerwertjie.
arabesque, arabesk, grillige versiering.
Arabian, Arabies; – Nights, Duisend-en-Een Nag.
Arabic, Arabies.
arable, ploegbaar, beboubaar, bewerkbaar; – land, beboubare grond.
arbiter, skeidsregter, arbiter.
arbitral, skeidsregterlik, arbitraal.
arbitrament, skeidsregterlike uitspraak.
arbitrariness, willekeur(igheid); eiemagtigheid.
arbitrary, willekeurig, eiemagtig, arbitrêr.
arbitrate, as skeidsregter optree, beslis.
arbitration, skeidsregterlike beslissing, arbitrasie.
arbitrator, skeidsregter, arbiter.
arbitress, skeidsvrou.
arboraceous, boomagtig; bebos.
arboreous, boomagtig, boom- ...; bebos.
arborescent, boom- ..., boomvormig.
arboriculture, boomkwekery, boomteelt.
arbour, prieel.
arc, boog.
arcade, booggang, winkelgang, arkade.
Arcadian, Arkadies.
arcanum, geheim; geheime middel.
arch-, a. aarts- ...; – knave, aartsskelm.
arch, a. skalks, skelm, ondeund.
arch, n. boog, gewelf.
arch, v. buig, welf.
archaeology, oudheidkunde, argeologie.
archaic, verouderd, oud, argaïsties.
archangel, aartsengel; engelduif.
archbishop, aartsbiskop.
archbishopric, aartsbisdom.
archdeacon, aartsdeken.
archduchess, aartshertogin.
archduchy, aartshertogdom.
archduke, aartshertog.
arched, gewelf, geboë; – neck, kromnek.
arch-enemy, aartsvyand.
archer, boogskutter.

archery, pyl-en-boogskiet, boogskietery.
archetype, oertipe, grondvorm; standaard.
arch-fiend, aartsvyand, Satan.
archiepiscopal, aartsbiskoplik.
archipelago, argipel, eilandsee; eilandgroep.
architect, boumeester, argitek.
architectonic, argitektonies, boukundig.
architecture, boukunde, boustyl, argitektuur.
archives, argief (argiewe); argiefgebou.
archivist, argivaris, argiefbewaarder.
archly, ondeund, skelmpies, skalks.
archness, ondeundheid, skalksheid.
archway, boog, gewelfde ingang (gang).
arc-lamp, booglamp.
arctic, noordelik, noordpool- ...; arkties; A– Circle, noordpoolsirkel; – expedition, noordpoolekspedisie; A– Ocean, Noordelike Yssee.
ardency, vurigheid, vuur, gloed, ywer.
ardent, vurig, gloeiend, blakend; – spirits, sterk drank; geesdrif.
ardour, warmte, hitte; gloed, ywer, vuur.
arduous, steil; moeilik; swaar, inspannend.
are, v. is.
are, n. are.
area, oppervlakte; gebied, wyk, ruimte.
arena, perk, strydperk, arena.
areometer, vogmeter, areometer.
argent, silwer.
Argentine, Argentynse Republiek, Argentinië.
argil, klei, potklei.
argol, wynsteen.
argon, argon.
Argonauts, Argonaute, vliessoekers.
argosy, ryk belade skip, geldskip.
argot, diewetaal, boewetaal, argot.
argue, redeneer, betoog; aandui; argumenteer.
argument, redenering, argument, bewys(grond); diskussie; inhoud.
argumentation, redenering, diskussie.
argumentative, betogend; redeneersiek.
Arian, Ariër.
arid, droog, dor, onvrugbaar.
aridity, dorheid, droogte.
aright, reg, tereg.
arise, opstaan, opkom; voortspruit, volg.
aristocracy, aansienlikes; adel; aristokrasie.
aristocrat, aristokraat; edelman.
aristocratic(al), aristokraties; adellik.
arithmetic, n. rekenkunde, rekenkundeboek.
arithmetic(al), a. rekenkundig, aritmeties.
arithmetician, rekenkundige, rekenmeester.
ark, ark; Noah's –, Noag se ark.
arm, n. arm; tak; mou; – in –, ingehaak, gearm(d); infant in –s, kind op die skoot, suigeling; keep at –'s length, op 'n afstand hou; with folded –s, met die arms (hande) oormekaar; with open –s, met ope arms.
arm, n. wapen; fire–, vuurwapen; small –s, kleingewere; bear –s, wapens dra; take up –s, wapens opneem; in –s, onder die wapens; up in –s, in opstand; lay down –s, wapens neerlê; under –s, onder die wapens; coat of –s, wapenskild, familiewapen.
arm, v. wapen, van wapens voorsien.
armada, vloot, armada.
armadillo, gordeldier, armadil.
armament, bewapening, oorlogstoerusting.
armature, bewapening; wapens; pantser; anker (van 'n magneet).
arm-chair, leun(ing)stoel, armstoel.
Armenian, Armenies.
armistice, wapenstilstand.
armlet, armband; armpie.
armorial, a. wapen- ...; – bearings, wapenskild.
armorial, n. wapenboek.

armour, n. harnas, wapenrusting, pantser.
armour, v. pantser, harnas.
armour-bearer, wapendraer, skildknaap.
armour-clad, a. gepantser(d).
armour-clad, n. pantserskip.
armoury, wapenkamer, wapenhuis, arsenaal.
armpit, armholte, oksel, kieliebak.
army, leër; menigte; **standing** –, vaste leër.
army-list, offisierslys.
arnica, wondkruid, arnika (tinktuur).
aroma, geur, aroma.
aromatic, geurig, aromaties.
around, prep. rondom, om, om . . . heen.
around, adv. rond; in die rondte.
arouse, wakker maak; in die lewe roep.
arquebus (harquebus), haakbus.
arrack, arak; palmbrandewyn.
arraign, aankla; in twyfel trek.
arraignment, beskuldiging; betwyfeling.
arrange, skik, rangskik, in orde maak, reël, inrig; ooreenkom, afspreek.
arrangement, skikking, rangskikking, reëling, inrigting; ooreenkoms, afspraak.
arrant, verstokte, deurtrapte, volslae.
array, v. opstel, skik; uitdos, opskik; kleed.
array, n. opstelling, rangskikkery; ry, reeks; slagorde; opskik, tooi.
arrear(s), agterstand, agterstallige; **in** –(s), agter, ten agter; **in** – **of,** agter.
arrest, v. teenhou, stut; in hegtenis neem, arresteer; – **attention,** aandag trek; **–ed development,** gestremde ontwikkeling.
arrest, n. inhegtenisneming; stilstand.
arrival, aankoms, aangekomene; aanvoer.
arrive, aankom, (aan)land; gebeur; **when the time –s,** as die tyd aanbreek.
arrogance, –cy, verwaandheid, aanmatiging.
arrogant, verwaand, aanmatigend, waanwys.
arrogate, (sig) aanmatig, (sig) toeëien.
arrogation, aanmatiging, toeëiening.
arrow, pyl.
arrowroot, pylwortel; araroet.
arsenal, arsenaal, wapenhuis.
arsenic, n. arsenicum, arseen, rottekruit.
arsis, (toon)heffing; betoonde lettergreep.
arson, (opsetlike) brandstigting.
arsonist, brandstigter.
art, v. is.
art, n. kuns, slag, streek, lis; **black –,** toordery, towery; **fine –s,** skone kunste.
artefact, artefak.
arterial, slagaar– . . .; – **road,** hoofverkeersweg.
artery, slagaar.
artful, kunstig; skelm, listig.
arthritis, jig, gewrigsontsteking.
artichoke, artisjok.
article, n. onderdeel, lid, stuk, artikel; lidwoord; **leading –,** hoofartikel; – **of dress,** kledingstuk; – **of furniture,** meubelstuk; – **of faith,** geloofsartikel.
article, v. verdeel; inskryf; aankla.
articulate, a. geleed; duidelik; geartikuleer(d).
articulate, v. van litte voorsien; duidelik uitspreek; artikuleer.
articulation, geleding, uitspraak; artikulasie.
artifice, lis, slimstreek, slenterslag.
artificer, handwerksman; uitvinder.
artificial, kunsmatig; gekunsteld, aanstellerig; – **flowers,** kunsblomme, papierblomme; – **teeth,** kunstande, valstande.
artillerist, artilleris, kanonnier.
artillery, artillerie; geskut; **heavy –,** grofgeskut.
artisan, handwerksman, ambagsman.
artist, kunstenaar; arties.

artistic, kunstig, kunsvol, kunssinnig, artistiek.
artless, kunsteloos; ongekunsteld, naïef.
arum-lily, varkblom, aronskelk.
as, adv. & conj. as, net as, soos, net soos, terwyl; aangesien; – **soon –,** sodra, so gou as; – **well –,** so goed as, so wel as; – **far –,** so ver as, tot aan; **you might – well help me,** jy kan my gerus help; – **you like,** soos jy wil; – **usual,** soos gewoonlik; **be so good –** . . ., wees so goed en (om te) . . .; – **I was speaking** . . ., terwyl ek aan praat was . . .; – **you are of age,** aangesien jy mondig is; – **regards,** wat betref, aangaande; – **yet,** tot nog toe; **I thought –** **much,** dit het ek gedag; **that – well,** dit ook (nog); – **it is,** onder die omstandighede, soos sake nou staan; – **it were,** as 't ware, so te sê, kan jy sê; – **for, – to,** wat betref; – **if,** asof, of; – **you were,** herstel!
as, pron. (as) wat; **the same difficulty – I had,** dieselfde moeilikheid (as) wat ek gehad het; **such things –,** dinge soos.
asafoetida, duiwelsdrek.
asbestos, asbes, steenvlas, garingklip.
ascend, opstyg, bestyg (op)klim, opvaar, opgaan, oploop, rys.
ascendancy, ascendency, oorwig, oorhand; **in the –,** aan die opgaan; aan die wenkant.
ascendant, a. opklimmend; oorheersend.
ascendant, n. oorwig, oorheersing; horoskoop; **in the –,** oorheersend; in die opgaan, aan die wenkant.
ascendency, sien **ascendancy.**
ascension, bestyging, hemelvaart; – **Day,** Hemelvaartsdag.
ascent, bestyging; opgang; steilte.
ascertain, uitmaak, vasstel, vergewis.
ascertainable, bepaalbaar.
ascertainment, vasstelling, bevestiging.
ascetic, a. selfverloënend; asketies; vroom.
ascetic, n. askeet, kluisenaar, boeteling.
asceticism, onthouding; boetedoening; askese.
ascribe, toeskryf, toeken.
ascription, toeskrywing.
Asdic, Asdic; – **beam,** Asdic-straal.
aseptic, a. asepties, steriel.
aseptic, n. ontsmettingsmiddel.
asexual, seksloos.
ash, as; cigar –es, sigaar-as.
ash, es, esboom; eshout.
ashamed, bekaamd; skaam, skamerig; **to be –** (sig) skaam.
ashen, es– . . ., van eshout.
ashen, asvaal, askleurig, as.
ashore, aan wal, aan land; gestrand.
Asia, Asië; – Minor, Klein-Asië.
Asian, n. Asiaat; **a.** Asiaties.
Asiatic, a. Asiaties.
Asiatic, n. Asiaat.
aside, adv. opsy, apart; **set – a verdict, 'n uitspraak te niet doen.
aside, n. tersyspraak.
asinine, eselagtig, esels– . . .; dom; koppig.
ask, vra; versoek; uitnooi; eis; **the matter –s, (for) attention,** die saak eis aandag; – **about (for),** vra na; – **for,** vra (om).
askance, skeef, skuins, van tersy.
askari, askari.
askew, skeef, skuins.
aslant, skuins, dwars.
asleep, aan die slaap, in slaap; **fall –,** aan (die slaap val (raak).
aslope, skuins, afdraand.
asp, adder, slang.
asparagus, aspersie(s); **wild –,** katdoring.

aspect, aanblik, voorkoms; uitsig; gesigspunt, oogpunt; aspek; another – of the question, ander kant van die saak.
aspen, (tril)populier, esp., abeelboom.
asperity, ruheid, skerpheid, strengheid.
asperse, besprinkel; beklad; beskinder.
aspersion, bekladding, belastering; laster, skindertaal; cast –s on, belaster.
asphalt, n. asfalt, padteer.
asphalt, v. asfalteer, teer.
asphodel, affodil, daglelie; asfodel, immortel.
asphyxia, verstikking; skyndood.
asphyxiate, (ver)stik.
aspic, vleisjellie, vleisdril.
aspirant, aspirant, kandidaat.
aspirate, v. aspireer; deursuig, uitsuig.
aspirate, n. h-klank, aspiraat.
aspiration, aspirasie; ambisie, strewe.
aspirator, suigbuis; lugsuier.
aspire, streef, begeer, aspireer.
aspiring, vooruitstrewend, ambisieus, eersugtig.
asquint, skeel, oormekaar.
ass, esel; domkop; make an – of oneself, jou belaglik maak, 'n stommiteit begaan.
assagai, as(se)gaai.
assail, aanval, aanrand, bestorm.
assailable, trefbaar, aantasbaar.
assailant, aanvaller, aanrander.
assassin, (sluip)moordenaar.
assassinate, vermoor, sluipmoord pleeg (op).
assassination, (sluip)moord.
assassinator, (sluip)moordenaar.
assault, v. aanval, aanrand, te lyf gaan.
assault, n. aanval, bestorming, aanranding.
assay, v. toets, keur; beproef; probeer.
assay, n. toets; proef, keuring.
assemblage, versameling; samekoms.
assemble, versamel, vergader, byeenkoms.
assembly, vergadering; resepsie; House of A–, Laerhuis; Legislative A–, Wetgewende Vergadering; – line, monteerbaan; – plant, monteer(werk)plaas.
assent, v. toestem, inwillig; instem.
assent, n. toestemming, instemming, goedkeuring; royal –, koninklike bekragtiging.
assert, laat geld; handhaaf; staan op; beweer, verklaar; – oneself, jou laat geld.
assertion, handhawing; bewering, verklaring.
assertive, uitdruklik, stellig; selfbewus.
assess, skat, raam; aanslaan, belas; beboet.
assessable, skatbaar; belasbaar.
assessment, skatting, (belastings)aanslag.
assessor, skatter; bysitter, assessor.
asset, bate, besit; –s and liabilities, bate en laste.
assever, asseverate, betuig, verseker.
asseveration, beswering, betuiging.
assiduity, volharding, ywer; aandag.
assiduous, volhardend, ywerig, aandagtig.
assign, toedeel, toewys; oormaak, vermaak; aangee, vasstel, bepaal; toeskryf.
assignable, aanwysbaar, bepaalbaar.
assignation, toewysing; oordrag, vermaking; bepaling; afspraak; toeskrywing.
assignee, gevolmagtigde, sessionaris.
assignment, toedeling; oordrag, akte van oordrag; toeskrywing; opnoeming; opdrag, taak.
assimilate, gelykmaak; gelyk word; opneem, verteer; opgeneem word; assimileer.
assimilation, gelykmaking; opname, verwerking; vereenselwiging; assimilasie.
assist, bystaan, help, ondersteun; teenwoordig wees, meedoen.
assistance, bystand, hulp, ondersteuning.
assistant, a. assistent-..., hulp-...
assistant, n. helper, handlanger, assistent.

assize, v. skat, raam; vasstel.
assize, n. vasstelling; –s, (rondgaande) hof.
associate, v. verenig, verbind; begelei; assosieer; – with, omgaan met; verbind met.
associate, a. verenigde, verbonde.
associate, n. deelgenoot, kompanjon; medepligtige; lid.
association, vereniging; verbinding; deelgenootskap, bond; omgang; assosiasie; –s, herinneringe; – (football), sokker (voetbal).
assonance, klinkerrym; assonansie.
assort, uitsoek, sorteer; saamvoeg, groepeer; bymekaar pas; – with, omgaan met; ill –ed, sleg passend; ongelyksoortig.
assortment, sortering, verskeidenheid; voorraad.
assuage, lenig; bevredig; kalmeer, bedaar; – pain, pyn lenig; – thirst, dors les.
assumable, assumedly, vermoedelik.
assume, aanneem, op (sig) neem, aanvaar; (sig) aanmatig; (sig) toeëien.
assumed, aangenome; voorgewend.
assuming, gestel(d); aanmatigend; – that, gestel(d) dat, laat ons aanneem dat.
assumption, veronderstelling, vermoede, aanvaarding; aanmatiging.
assumptive, (ver)ondersteld; aanmatigend.
assurance, versekering; selfvertroue; astrantheid; (lewens)versekering, assuransie.
assure, verseker, die versekering gee; seker maak; verassureer.
assuredly, verseker, stellig.
assurer, verassureerder; verassureerde.
Assyrian, Assiries.
aster, aster.
asterisk, sterretjie.
astern, agter; agteruit; op die agterkip.
asteroid, n. asteroïed, klein planeetjie.
asthma, asma, benoudebors.
asthmatic, asmaties, aamborstig, asma-.
astigmatic, astigmaties.
astigmatism, astigmatisme.
astir, op, in beweging, opgewonde.
astonish, verbaas, bevreem, dronkslaan.
astonishment, verbasing, bevreemding.
astound, verbaas, versteld laat staan.
astraddle, wydsbeen (wydsbene), skrylings.
astrakhan, astrakan(wol); karakoelwol.
astral, astraal, ster...; – hatch, astraalluik.
astray, verdwaal; go –, verdwaal; op die verkeerde pad gaan; lead –, op die verkeerde weg bring; verlei.
astriction, saamtrekking; (bloed)stelping.
astride, wydsbeen (wydsbene).
astringent, saamtrekkend; stelpend; streng.
astrodome, -hatch, see astral hatch.
astrolabe, astrolabium, (sterre)hoekmeter.
astrologer, astroloog, sterrewiggelaar.
astrological, astrologies.
astrology, astrologie, sterrewiggelary.
astronaut, ruimtevlieër, ruimreisiger.
astronomer, sterrekundige, astronoom.
astronomic, sterrekundig, astronomies.
astronomy, sterrekunde, astronomie.
astute, slim, slu, geslepe, oulik.
asunder, uitmekaar, aan stukke; tear –, uitmekaar skeur.
asylum, skuilplaas, toevlug(soord); mental –, gestig vir sielsiekes.
asymmetry, oneweredigheid, asimmetrie.
asymptote, asimptoot, amperraaklyn.
at, op, in, te, by; aan; na; met; teen; – Steynsrust, op Steynsrust; – Kimberley, op (in) Kimberley; – Cape Town, by Kaapstad; – a point, op 'n punt; – school, op (die) skool; – sea, op (die) see; in die war; – a distance, op

'n afstand; – home, by die huis, tuis; – work, aan die werk; – a great profit, met (teen) 'n groot profyt; snatch –, gryp na; aim –, mik na (op), laugh –, lag om (vir, oor); arrive –, aankom by (op, in); rush –, afvlieg op, storm; grumble –, brom oor; get –, bykom, in die hande kry; be busy –, besig wees met (aan); be impatient –, ongeduldig wees oor; be good – tennis, goed tennis speel; – first, eers, in die begin; – last, eindelik, op die end; – least, ten minste; – present, teenswoordig; – once, meteens, dadelik; – the latest, op sy laa(t)ste, uiterlik; – most, op sy meeste, uiterlik; – length, eindelik, einde ten laaste; – all, in die minste, ook maar enigsins; ooit; not – all, glad nie, volstrek nie.
atavism, atavisme, erflike neiging.
atheism, ongelowigheid, godloëning, ateïsme.
atheistic(al), ongelowig, godloënend, ateïsties.
athenaeum, letterkundige (wetenskaplike) vereniging; leessaal; athenaeum.
Athenian, a. Atheens.
Athenian, n. Athener; Atheense (vrou).
athirst, dors(tig), dorstend; verlangend.
athlete, atleet, sportman; kampvegter.
athletic(al), atleties, sport- . . .; gespierd.
athletics, atletiek, sport, kragsport.
at-home, resepsie(dag), ontvangs.
athwart, (dwars)oor; oordwars.
Atlantic, Atlantiese Oseaan.
atlas, atlas.
atmosphere, atmosfeer, dampkring; lug.
atmospherics, lugstoornis.
atom, atoom, stofdeeltjie; greintjie; – bomb, atoombom; – splitting, atoomklowing, -splitsing.
atomic(al), atoom- . . .; atomies; – theory, atoomteorie; – weight, atoomgewig; – energy, atoomkrag; – pile, atoomstapel; – fall-out, kernneerslag; – waste, kernafval; – warfare, atoomoorlog(voering).
atomism, atomisme, atoomleer.
atomistic(al), atomisties.
atomize, atomiseer, in atome split*; verklein; verstuif.
atomy, skelet, geraamte.
atomy, atoompie, klein wesentjie.
atone, boete doen, boet, goedmaak; versoen.
atonement, boetedoening; versoening; day of –, versoendag.
atonic, atonies, ongeaksentueerd; slap.
atop, bo-op.
atrabilious, swartgallig, melancholies; bitter.
atrocious, wreedaardig, snood, afskuwelik.
atrocity, wreedaardigheid; snoodheid; flater.
atrophy, uittering, wegkwyning, atrofie.
atropine, atropien.
attach, vasmaak, verbind, aanheg; in beslag (hegtenis) neem; – blame to, skuld gee aan; – importance to, waarde heg aan.
attachment, band, gehegtheid; beslag(legging); inhegtenisneming.
attack, v. aanval, bestorm; inwerk op, aantas.
attack, n. aanval, bestorming; aantasting.
attain, bereik, verkry; – to, bereik.
attainable, bereikbaar, verkrygbaar.
attainment, bereiking, verkryging; –s, bekwaamhede.
attaint, besmet, bevlek; aansteek; ontburger.
attar, roosolie, roosessens.
attempt, v. probeer, trag; aanslag doen op.
attempt, n. poging, onderneming; aanslag.
attend, ag gee, let op, pas op; bedien, verpleeg; begelei; bywoon; – to, let op, pas op; aandag gee aan; – (up)on, verpleeg, bedien; opwagting maak by; –ed with, vergesel van, gepaard met; – school, skoolgaan; – a patient, oor 'n pasiënt gaan.
attendance, bediening, verpleging; begeleiding; besoek, bywoning; opkoms, aanwesigheid; be in –, op diens wees, teenwoordig wees; oppas; school –, skoolbesoek; dance – on, orals naloop.
attendant, a. begeleidend; diensdoende; – circumstances, (bykomstige) omstandighede.
attendant, n. oppasser, bediende; begeleier.
attention, aandag, oplettendheid; give –, ag gee; attract –, aandag trek; –s, beleefdhede, attensies.
attentive, oplettend, aandagtig; beleef, attent.
attenuate, verdun, vermaer, verswak.
attenuation, verdunning, vermaering, verswakking.
attest, v. getuig, verklaar; – to, getuig van; besweer; sig laat inskryf; insweer, beëdig, die eed aflê.
attestation, getuienis, verklaring; bevestiging; getuigskrif, bewys; beëdiging; attes(tasie).
Attic, Atties; – salt, wit, Attiese gees.
attic, dakkamer(tjie), solderkamer(tjie).
attire, v. aanklee; optooi.
attire, n. kleding; tooisel, opskik.
attitude, houding, postuur; strike an –, 'n houding aanneem; – of mind, denkwyse.
attitudinize, gemaakte houding aanneem, poseer.
attorney, prokureur; saakwaarnemer; gevolmagtigde; power of –, volmag, prokurasie.
attorney-general, prokureur-generaal, staatsprokureur.
attraction, aantrekking(skrag); aantreklikheid, bekoring; – of gravity, swaartekrag.
attractive, aantreklik, bekoorlik.
attributable, toe te skrywe; te danke (aan).
attribute, v. toeskrywe; wyt (aan); toereken.
attribute, n. eienskap, kenmerk, hoedanigheid; byvoeglike bepaling; attribuut.
attribution, toeskrywing, toerekening.
attributive, a. attributief.
attributive, n. attributiewe woord, attribuut.
attrition, afslyting, vrywing; ligte berou.
attune, stem; in ooreenstemming bring.
auburn, goudbruin.
auction, verkoping, vandisie (vendusie), veiling.
auctioneer, vendu-afslaer, vandisiemeester.
auction-mart, verkooplokaal.
audacious, vermetel; brutaal; astrant.
audaciousness, vermetelheid; astrantheid.
audacity, stoutmoedigheid, vermetelheid.
audible, hoorbaar.
audience, gehoor; toehoorders; oudiënsie.
audit, n. verifikasie, ouditering.
audit, v. ouditeer, verifieer.
audition, gehoor.
auditive, gehoor(s)- . . .
auditor, (toe)hoorder; ouditeur.
auditory, gehoor(s)- . . .; (toe)hoorders.
auger, handboor.
aught, iets; for – I know, (vir) sover ek weet.
augment, n. ougment, voorvoegsel.
augment, v. vermeerder, vergroot, toeneem.
augmentative, vermeerderend.
augur, n. waarsêer, voëlwiggelaar.
augur, v. voorspel, waarsê; it –s well, ill (for), dit beloof veel, weinig (vir).
augury, waarsêery, voëlwiggelary, voorspelling; voorbode; voorgevoel; belofte.
August, n. Augustus(maand).
august, a. hoog, verhewe, groots.
Augustan, van Augustus; the – Age, die eeu van Augustus.

Augustine, Augustyns.
auk, alk, papegaaiduiker.
aum, aam.
aunt, auntie, tant(e), tannie.
aura, uitstraling, aura.
aural, oor-..., gehoor-...; – nerve, gehoorsenuwee.
aureole, oureool, stralekrans.
auricle, oor, buitenste oor; hartkamer.
auricular, oor-...; – confession, oorbieg.
auriferous, goudhoudend.
aurist, oorspesialis, oordokter.
aurora, oggendrooi, dagbreek, aurora; – borealis, noorderlig; – australis, suiderlig.
auscultation, ouskultasie; beluistering.
auspice, voorteken, voorspelling, waarsegging; –s, beskerming.
auspicious, veelbelowend, gunstig, gelukkig.
austere, streng; onkreukbaar; eenvoudig; vrank.
austereness, austerity, strengheid; eenvoudigheid; vrankheid.
austral, suidelik.
Australia, Australië.
Australian, Australiër; Australiese (vrou).
Austria, Oostenryk.
Austrian, Oostenryker; Oostenrykse (vrou).
authentic, outentiek, oorspronklik; betroubaar.
authenticate, staaf, bekragtig; legaliseer, waarmerk; die skrywer vasstel.
authenticity, egtheid; betroubaarheid; outentisiteit.
author, bewerker; dader; oorsaak; outeur.
authoress, bewerkster, daderes; skryfster.
authoritative, gesaghebbend; uit die hoogte.
authorities, owerheid, gesaghebbendes.
authority, gesag, aansien; volmag; segsman; outoriteit; **on good** –, uit betroubare bron.
authorization, magtiging, outorisasie; volmag.
authorize, magtig, outoriseer, reg gee.
authorship, outeurskap.
auto, sien **automobile.**
autobiographer, outobiograaf.
autobiographical, outobiografies.
autobiography, outobiografie.
autochthon, outochtoon, inboorling.
autochthonous, outochtoon, inheems.
autocracy, alleenheerskappy, outokrasie.
autocrat, alleenheerser, outokraat.
autocratic, outokraties, eiemagtig.
autogeny, spontane, generasie.
autograph, n. handskrif; handtekening.
autograph, v. eiehandig opstel; teken.
autogyro, outogiro.
automatic, werktuiglik; outomaties; n. outomatiese pistool.
outomation, outomatisasie.
automatism, werktuiglike handeling.
automaton, outomaat.
auto(mobile), outo(mobiel).
automobilism, outo(mobiel)sport, motorsport.
autonomous, selfregerend, selfbesturend.
autonomy, selfregering, selfbestuur.
autopsy, persoonlike ondersoek; lykskouing.
autotype, faksimilee, oerbeeld; outotipe.
autumn, herfs.
autumnal, herfs-..., herfsagtig.
auxiliary, a. hulp-...
auxiliary, n. helper, bondgenoot; hulpwerkwoord; **auxiliaries,** hulptroepe.
avail, v. baat, help; – **of,** benut, gebruik.
avail, n. baat, nut, voordeel; **of no** –, van geen nut; **without** –, vrugteloos, nutteloos; **to little** –, van weinig nut.

available, beskikbaar, voorhande; dienstig.
avalanche, sneeuval, lawine.
avarice, gierigheid, hebsug; vrekkigheid.
avaricious, gierig, hebsugtig, inhalig.
avaunt, weg, vort!
avenge, wreek, straf, wraak neem.
avenger, wreker.
avenue, toegang; laan.
aver, betuig, verseker; bewys; beweer.
average, n. gemiddelde, deursnee; awery; **on an** –, gemiddeld, in deursnee.
average, a. gemiddelde, deursnee-...
average, v. die gemiddelde bereken; 'n gemiddelde bereik; uitwerk op 'n gemiddelde.
averment, verklaring; bewering; bewys.
averse, afkerig, onwillig.
averseness, afkerigheid, onwilligheid.
aversion, afkeer, teensin (teësin); afsku.
avert, keer, afwend; afkerig maak, afkonkel.
aviary, voëlkooi, voëlhok.
aviate, vlieg, 'n vliegtuig bestuur.
aviation, vliegkuns; vliegsport; lugvaart.
aviator, vliegenier, vlieër; lugreisiger.
avid, begerig, gretig; gierig.
avidity, begerigheid, gretigheid; hebsug.
avocado, avokado.
avocation, afleiding; beroep; roeping.
avoid, vermy, ontwyk; ontduik.
avoidable, vermybaar, vermydelik.
avoidance, vermyding; ontduiking.
avoirdupois, Engelse gewig, avoirdupois.
avouch, bevestig, waarborg, instaan vir.
avow, erken, bely; –**ed enemy,** ope vyand.
avowal, erkenning, belydenis, bekentenis.
avowed, uitgesproke, verklaard.
avuncular, van 'n oom, ooms-...
await, opwag, wag op; te wagte wees.
awake, v. wakker word, ontwaak; opwaak, lewendig word; wakker maak, wek.
awake, a. wakker; lewendig; **be** – **to,** besef; op die hoede wees teen.
awaken, wakker maak, wek; wakker word.
award, v. toeken, toewys.
award, n. toekenning; uitspraak, vonnis; beloning, prys.
aware, bewus; **be** – **of,** bewus van wees.
away, weg; voort; **give** –, weggee; verraai; **fool** – **the time,** die tyd verbeusel; **out and** –, verwee; **fire** –!, vooruit!; **toe maar!**; **cannot** – **with him,** kan nie met hom oor die weg kom nie; **make** – **with,** uit die weg ruim.
awe, n. vrees, ontsag, eerbied; **stand in** – **of,** ontsag koester vir; **keep in** –, in bedwang hou.
awe, v. ontsag inboesem; bang maak.
awe-struck, vervaard, verskrik, spraakloos.
awful, skrikwekkend, verskriklik, ontsettend, ontsaglik, ontsagwekkend.
awfulness, verskriklikheid, ontsettendheid.
awhile, 'n tyd lank, (vir) 'n tydjie.
awkward, lomp, onhandig; lastig, vervelend; ongemaklik, moeilik; **an** – **customer,** 'n ongemaklike (gevaarlike) kêrel.
awkwardness, lompheid; lastigheid.
awl, els.
awn, baard (van koring).
awning, seil, skerm, skutting.
awry, skeef, skuins; verkeerd.
ax(e), byl; **have an** – **to grind,** eiebelang soek, persoonlike bybedoelinge hê.
axiom, aksioom, grondstelling.
axiomatic, aksiomaties; onbetwisbaar.
axis, as, spil; **A– powers,** Spilmoondhede.
axle, as.

axle-box, naaf, naafbus.
axle-pin, luns.
axle-tree, as.
ay(e), ja; **the ayes have it,** die meerderheid is daarvoor.

aye, vir altyd; altyd; ewig.
aye-aye, vingerdier.
azalea, asalea.
azimuth, asimut.
azure, asuur, hemelsblou.

B

baa, blêr, bê-maak.
babble, v. brabbel; babbel; klets; verklik, verklap; kabbel (van water).
babble, n. brabbeltaal; gebabbel; geklets; klikkery; gekabbel.
babbler, brabbelaar; babbelaar; verklikker.
babe, babetjie, suigeling; uilskuiken.
Babel, (toring van) Babel; lawaai; verwarring.
baboon, bobbejaan.
baby, babatjie, kindjie; kleintjie; skommelsif; **leave to hold (carry) the –**, in die steek laat, alleen laat, sien om die mas op te kom; **– beef**, jongosvleis.
babyhood, kindsheid, suigelingsjare.
Babylonian, Babiloniër, Babiloniese (vrou).
baby-sit, kinders bewaak.
baccalaureate, baccalaureus-graad.
Bacchanal, Bacchusfees; boemelparty.
Bacchanalia, Bacchusfees(te); swelgparty(e).
Bacchanalian, bacchanties, losbandig.
bachelor, vrygesel, oujongkêrel; **– of Arts (Science)**, Baccalaureus Artium (Scientiarum); **– girl**, vrygesellin.
bachelorship, oujongkêrelskap; baccalaureusgraad.
bacillary, basil- ... ; stafies- ...
bacillus, basil, bakterie.
back, n. rug; agterkant; agterspeler; **at the – of**, agter; **behind one's –**, agter iemand se rug (om), op agterbakse manier.
back, adv. terug, agteruit; gelede; **go – upon (from) one's word**, 'n belofte nie nakom nie; **– and forth**, heen en weer; **years –**, jare gelede.
back, v. (onder)steun; wed op; agteruit trap; agteruit laat gaan; **– up**, (onder)steun; **– out of**, kop-uittrek, terugtrek.
back, a. agterste; agterstallige; **– current**, teenstroom, terugstroming.
back-bencher, iemand uit die agterste rye, een van die mindere gode.
backbite, (be)skinder, (be)laster.
backbone, rug(ge)graat; beginselvastheid, pit; **to the –**, in merg en been.
back-fire, n. terugslag, terugplof.
back-fire, v. terugslaan.
back-drop, agtergrond (fig.); agterdoek.
backgammon, triktrak.
background, agtergrond.
backhand, n. handrug.
backhander, handrugspeler; handrughou.
backing, steun; ondersteuners; weddery.
backlog, agterstand.
backmost, agterste.
backnumber, ou aflewering; takhaar.
back-pedal, terugtrap.
backslide, terugval, afvallig word.
backslider, afvallige, oorloper.
backstairs, agtertrap, onderhands.
backveld, agterveld, platteland.
backward, a. agterwaarts; agterlik, traag.
backward, adv. agteruit; agteroor; **na agter**; **na die verlede**.
backwardness, agterlikheid.
backwards, sien **backward**, adv.; **– and forwards**, heen en weer, vooruit en agteruit.
backwash, terugspoeling, trek.
backwater, kielwater; dooi(e)water.
backwoods, bosveld; onbeskaafde dele.
backwoodsman, bosvelder.
backyard, agterplaas.
bacon, ontbytspek, (gerookte) spek.
bacteriology, bakteriologie.
bad, sleg, erg; stout; nadelig; naar, siek, ernstig (siek); ongunstig; vrot; vals; **– coin**, vals munt; **– debts**, oninbare skulde; **– shot**, mis

(geskiet, geraai); **– form**, gebrek aan goeie maniere; **– blood**, slegte gevoel; **– cold**, swaar verkoue; **– luck**, fortune, ongeluk; **– words**, skel(d)woorde; **to go –**, bederf, vrot word; be in a **– way**, daar sleg aan toe wees.
badge, ordeteken, onderskeidingsteken, kenteken; wapen.
badger, n. ratel.
badger, v. pla, tretter, sar, kwel; agtervolg.
badly, sleg, erg; hard; baie, gevaarlik; **– beaten**, erg geslaan; lelik uitgeklop; **want –**, baie nodig hê; baie graag wil hê; **be – off**, daar sleg aan toe wees.
badmash, bud-, skurk, deugniet.
badness, sleg(t)heid, slegtigheid; erns, gevaarlikheid; v(er)rotheid, verdorwenheid.
baffle, uitoorlê; verydel.
bag, n. sak, tas; uier; **– and baggage**, sak en pak; **it's in the –**, dis gewonne spel; ons het dit!
bag, v. in die sak stop; skiet; vang; inpalm; slap hang; knieë maak; sakkies maak.
bagatelle, bakatel; kleinigheid.
baggage, bagasie, reisgoed; parmant.
bagging, saklinne.
bagpipe, doedelsak.
bail, n. borg, borgtog; **be, become, go –**, borg staan; **admit to –**, onder borgtog vrylaat.
bail, v. borgstaan; onder borgtog uitlaat; **– out**, borgstaan vir.
bail, n. skutting; **–s**, balkies.
bail, n. hoepel, hingsel.
bailiff, balju; geregsbode; rentmeester.
bait, n. (lok)aas; verversing.
bait, v. aanhits; pla; tretter; lok; aas aansit.
baize, baai, groenlaken.
bake, bak.
bakelite, bakeliet.
baker, bakker; **–'s dozen**, dosyn en een.
Balaclava, Balaklawa, **– cap**, bivakmus, klapmus.
balalaika, balalaika.
balance, n. (weeg)skaal; vliegwiel; ewewig; (batige) saldo, oorskot; balans; **– of power**, magsewewig; **– of trade**, handelsbalans.
balance, v. weeg; balanseer; teen mekaar opweeg; slinger; vereffen, afsluit.
balance-sheet, balans(staat).
balcony, balkon.
bald, kaal, kaalkop; maak; **– facts**, naakte feite.
balderdash, wartaal, onsin; vuil taal.
baldhead, kaalkop; **go –ed**, kaalkop loop; iets blindelings doen, opdons.
baldpate, kaalkop.
baldric, skouerband.
bale, n. baal.
bale, v. in bale verpak, baal.
bale, v. uitskep, uithoos; **– out**, met 'n valskerm daal.
baleen, balein.
balefire, stapelvuur; sinjaalvuur.
baleful, nadelig, heilloos, verderflik.
balk, **baulk**, n. wenakker; hindernis; balk.
balk, **baulk**, v. versuim; wegvlieg, vassteek; in die weg staan; teenwerk; verydel.
Balkan, Balkan-.
Balkanize, balkaniseer.
ball, n. bal; bol; koeël; kluit; **keep the – rolling**, die saak aan die gang hou; **have the – at one's feet**, welslae vir die gryp hê; **– and claw**, balen -kloupoot.
ball, n. bal, dansparty; **open the –**, die bal open; die saak aan die gang sit.
ball, v. (in 'n bal) opdraai, tot 'n bal vorm.
ballad, ballade, lied.
ballad-monger, liedjiesdraaier.

ballast, n. ballas.
ballast, v. ballas inlaai.
ball-bearing, koeëllaer.
ballet, ballet, toneeldans.
balletomane, balletliefhebber.
balloon, (lug)ballon; – **barrage,** ballonversperring.
balloon-tyre, ballonband.
ballot, n. stembriefie; stemming; loting.
ballot, v. (met (stem)briefies) stem; loot.
ballot-box, stembus.
ballot-paper, stembrief(ie).
ball-point, bolpunt, rolpunt; – pen, koeëlstif, bolpen.
ball-room, balsaal, danssaal.
ball-valve, koeëlklep, vlotterklep.
bally, vervlakste, verbrande.
ballyhoo, bohaai, reklamelawaai.
balm, balsem, salf; troos.
balmy, balsemagtig; geurig; sag; kalmerend.
balsa, balsa.
balsam, balsem; smeergoed; balseminie.
Baltic, Balties; – Sea, Oossee.
baluster, styl, relingspaal.
balustrade, leuning, reling, tralie, borswering, balustrade.
bamboo, bamboes, bamboesriet.
bamboozle, fop, beetneem, in die nek kyk.
ban, v. verbied; ban, in die ban doen.
ban, n. ban, banvloek.
banal, banaal, alledaags, peuterig.
banana, banana, piesang.
band, n. band; dryfriem; bende; vereniging; musiekkorps, kapel.
band, v. 'n band omsit; verenig, verbind.
bandage, n. verband; blinddoek.
bandage, v. verbind; blinddoek.
bandbox, hoededoos, lintdoos.
bandit, (struik)rower.
bandmaster, orkesleier.
bandog, kettinghond.
bandoleer, –ier, bandelier.
bandstand, musiekkoepel, orkesverhoog.
band-wagon, musiekwa; reklamewa; **climb the –,** met die stroom meegaan.
bandy, n. hokkie; hokkiestok.
bandy, v. heen en weer kaats, wissel; – **words,** stry.
bandy-legged, hoepelbeen, met hoepelbene.
bane, vergif; verderf, vloek.
baneful, giftig, verderflik.
banewort, galbessie, nagskaal (nastergal).
bang, slaan, bons, toeklap; klop.
bang, n. slag, bons, knal.
bang, interj. bom!, boems!; **go –,** bars, ontplof, bankrotspeel.
bangle, armband; voetring.
banish, verban, verdryf, uitsit.
banishment, uitsetting, verbanning; ballingskap.
banister, styl; **–s,** trapleuning.
banjo, banjo.
bank, n. bank; wal: oewer; – **of a river,** rivierwal.
bank, v. wal maak, opdam; opstapel.
bank, n. bank, (speel)bank; pot.
bank, v. in die bank sit, deponeer; – **on,** staatmaak op, wed op.
bankbill, bankwissel.
bankbook, bankboekie.
banker, bankier; bankhouer.
bank-holiday, beursvakansie.
bankrupt, a. bankrot, insolvent.
bankrupt, n. bankroetier, bankrotspeler.
bankruptcy, bankrotskap, insolventskap.
banner, banier, vlag, vaandel.
banns, (huweliks)gebooie, huweliksafkondiging.

banquet, n. feesmaaltyd, banket.
banquet, v. feestelik onthaal; feesvier.
bantam, kapokhoendertjie; – **weight,** bantamgewig.
banter, n. gekskeerdery, skerts.
banter, v. gekskeer, skerts; terg, pla.
bantling, babetjie, snuiter.
banyan-tree, waringinboom.
baobab, kremetartboom, baobab.
baptize, doop; naam gee; onderdompel.
baptism, doop.
baptismal, doop- . . . ; – **ceremony,** doopplegtigheid.
baptist, doper; wederdoper; doopsgesinde.
bar, n. staaf, stand, tralie; slagboom; maatstreep (musiek); balk (heraldiek); regbank, balie; ,,bar'' buffet; kroeg, kantien; sandbank; hinderpaal; skoenbalkies; **horizontal –s,** rekstok; **parallel –s,** brug; **gold in –s,** baargoud, staafgoud; **be admitted to the –,** tot die balie toegelaat word.
bar, v. afsluit, uitsluit; hinder, verhinder, versper, belet; – **one,** op een na.
barathea, baratea.
barb, n. baard (van 'n vis); weerhaak; prikkel.
barb, v. met weerhake voorsien; **–ed wire,** doringdraad, hakiesdraad.
barbarian, a. barbaars, onbeskaaf.
barbarian, n. barbaar, onbeskaafde.
barbaric, barbaars.
barbarism, barbarisme; barbaarsheid.
barbarity, barbaarsheid, wreedheid.
barbarous, barbaars.
Barbary, n. Barbarye.
Barbary, a. Barbarys; – **ape,** magot, Turkse aap.
barbecue, groot rooster; braaivleis; braaivleisaand; vleisbraaiplek; vleisbraaistel.
barbel, baber.
barber, haarsnyer, barbier, kapper.
barbican, wagtoring.
barbiturate, barbituraat.
barcarole, dongellied.
bard, bard, digter, sanger.
bare, a. naak, kaal, bloot; leeg; skraal; **the – thought,** die blote gedagte; **the – truth,** die naakte waarheid.
bare, v. ontbloot, kaal maak.
barebacked, bloots, sonder saal; kaalrug.
barefaced, met onbedekte gesig; – **lie,** skaamtelose leuen.
barefooted, kaalvoet.
bare-headed, kaalkop, blootshoofs.
barely, ope(n)lik; enkel, alleen maar, skaars, ternouernood.
bareness, naaktheid, blootheid, kaalheid.
bargain, n. ooreenkoms; slag, kopie; **into the –,** op die koop toe; **strike a –,** ooreenkoms tref; 'n slag slaan.
bargain, v. onderhandel; ooreenkom; kwansel, knibbel; – **for,** reken op; beding.
barge, vragskuit, trekskuit; sloep.
bargee, skuitvoerder.
bar-iron, staafyster.
baritone, bariton.
bark, n. bars, skors, skil; vel, huid.
bark, v. bas afmaak; vel afskuur.
bark, n. blaf, geblaf; **his – is worse than his bite,** hy is nie so kwaai as hy lyk nie.
bark, v. blaf; hoes; knal.
bark, barque, 'n skuit, bark.
barker, blaffer, keffer; pistool; kanon.
barley, gars.
barley-sugar, borssuiker.
barley-water, grotwater.

barley-wheat   421   **bead-moulding**

barley-wheat, kaalgars, barlewiet.
barm, biergis, biermoer.
barmaid, buffetjuffrou.
barman, kantienman, buffetman.
barmy, gisterig, skuimerig; simpel, getik.
barn, skuur; – **dance,** boeredans.
barnacle, poolgans; eendmossel; neusknyper.
barnyard, werf, agterplaas.
barometer, weerglas, barometer.
barometrical, barometries, barometer- . . .
baron, vryheer; baron; **beer** –, biermagnaat.
baronage, vryheerskap; baronskap.
baroness, barones.
baronet, baronet; sir (seur).
barony, vryheerlikheid; baronie.
barrack, n. barak; –s, barakke; kaserne.
barrack, v. uitjou.
barrage, dam(wal); gordynvuur.
barrel, vat, vaatjie; (geweer)loop; buis; trommel (van 'n horlosie).
barrel-organ, draai-orrel.
barren, onvrugbaar; kaal.
barricade, n. barrikade, verskansing.
barricade, v. verskans, barrikadeer.
barrier, slagboom; grenspaal; tolhek; hinderpaal; hindernis, versperring.
barring, uitgeslote, behalwe.
barrister, advokaat.
barrow, kruiwa; draagbaar; stootkar.
barter, v. ruil, kwansel; verruil.
barter, 'n ruil, ruilhandel.
basalt, basalt, ystermarmer.
bascule, weegbrug, ophaalbrug.
base, a. snood, gemeen; laag; minderwaardig; onedel; – **metals,** onedele metale.
base, n. grondslag, basis, fondament, voetstuk, grondlyn; grondgetal.
base, v. (grond)ves, baseer, grond.
base-line, agterlyn.
basement, fondament; ondergrondse verdieping, kelder.
bash, (in)slaan, (in)deuk.
bashful, skaam, skamerig, verleë.
bashfulness, skamerigheid, verleentheid.
basic, basies, grond- . . .
basil, steentym; basilicum.
basilica, basiliek (basilika).
basilisk, basilisk, draak; kuifakkedis.
basin, kom; skottel; bekken; stroomgebied.
basis, grondslag, fondament, basis.
bask, (sig) koester, bak.
basket, mandjie, korf.
basket-ball, korfbal.
Basque, Baskies; Bask.
bas(s)-relief, basrelief.
bass, baars (soort vis).
bass, bas(stem).
basset, dassiehond.
bassoon, fagot.
bast, binnebas.
bastard, n. baster, halfnaatjie; onwettige kind.
bastard, a. baster- . . . ; oneg, nagemaak.
bastardy, basterskap; onwettigheid.
baste, bedruip (met vet); loesing gee.
baste, (aanmekaar) ryg.
bastinado, bastonnade; pak slae.
bastion, bastion, vestingbolwerk.
Basuto, Basoeto.
Basutoland, Basoetoland.
bat, n. vlermuis.
bat, n. (krieket)kolf; kolwer, slaner; **off his own** –, op eie houtjie.
bat, v. slaan (krieket), kolf.
Batavian, Bataafs; Bataaf, Batavier.
batch, baksel; klomp, bondel, stel, trop.

bate, v. opgee (hoop); inhou (asem); aftrek, verminder; **with** –**d breath,** met ingehoue asem, met gespanne aandag.
bate, n. loog.
bath, n. bad; badkuip; badwater; –**s,** badhuis; bad(plaas).
bath, v. bad.
bath-chair, rolstoel, siekewaentjie.
bathe, v. baai, swem; afwas, bet.
bathe, n. bad, (die) baai.
bathing-dress, baai-, swemklere, baai-, swempak.
bathing-place, baaiplek, swemplek; badplaas, strand.
bathing-tub, badkuip.
bathos, batos, antiklimaks.
bathyscaph(e), duiktoestel.
bathysphere, batisfeer, duikbol.
batiste, batis, fynlinne.
baton, (maarskalk)staf; (dirigeer)stok; polisiestok.
batsman, kolwer, slaner.
battalion, bataljon.
batten, vetmes; (sig) vetmes, swelg (in); vet word.
batter, v. rammel, beuk, deuk.
batter, n. deeg.
battering-ram, stormram.
battery, battery; aanranding, handtastelikheid.
battle, n. (veld)slag, geveg, stryd.
battle, v. veg, stry, slag lewer.
battle array, slagorde.
battle-axe, strydbyl.
battle-cry, strydkreet, strydleus.
battle-field, slagveld.
battle-ship, slagskip.
battue, klopjag, dryfjag.
bauble, prulding, speeldingetjie, tierlantyntjie.
baulk, sien **balk.**
bauxite, bauxiet, aluminiumerts.
Bavarian, Beiers; Beier.
bawd, koppelaarster; vuil praatjies.
bawdy, ontugtig.
bawl, hard skreeu, brul.
bay, n. baai, inham, golf.
bay, n. lourier(boom); louerkrans.
bay, n. nis, erker, losie; vak.
bay, a. rooibruin, vos.
bay, n. vosperd.
bay, n. blaf, geblaf; **be, stand at** –, (sig) te weer stel; **keep at** –, van die lyf hou; **in bedwang hou; drive, bring to** –, inhaal, vaskeer.
bay, v. blaf, aanblaf.
bayonet, n. bajonet.
bayonet, v. aan die bajonet ryg.
bay-window, uitspringende venster.
bazaar, basaar.
bazooka, pantservuis.
be, wees, bestaan; **do not** – **long,** moenie draai nie, maak gou!; – **off,** trap!, maak dat jy wegkom!; **to** – **for war,** ten gunste van oorlog wees; **let that** –, laat dit staan, bly daar af!; **the powers that** –, die oor ons gestelde magte.
beach, n. strand, kus, wal.
beach, v. op die strand laat loop (trek).
beach-comber, lang golf; strandjut(ter).
beach-head, strandhoof.
beacon, n. baken; sein(vuur); vuurtoring.
beacon, v. afbaken; voorlig.
bead, n. kraletjie; knoppie; (water)belletjie; druppel; korrel; kraallys; **draw a** – **on,** aanlê op.
head, v. inryg; krale (druppels)vorm.
beading, kraallys.
beadle, bode, pedel; (onder)koster.
beadledom, omslagtigheid, bemoeisug.
bead-moulding, kraallys.

beady, kraal- . . . ; – **eyes**, kraalogies.
beagle, speurhond; spioen; balju.
beak, bek, snawel; kromneus; tuit; boeg.
beaker, beker.
be-all, al, alles; **his** –, sy al.
beam, n. balk; ploegbalk; disselboom; straal.
beam, v. straal; – **on**, vriendelik toelag; – **with**, straal van.
beam-ends, sy, kant; **he was on his** –, hy was op sy laaste bene.
beam-system, straalstelsel.
bean, boontjie; –**s**, duite; **give** –**s**, inklim; **full of** –**s**, op sy stukke; **old** –, ou maat.
bean-feast, (jaar)fees, fuif.
bean-stalk, boontjiestingel.
bear, beer; brombeer; spekulant-op-daling.
bear, v. dra; gedra; verdra; toedra; baar, voortbring; – **children**, kinders baar (voortbring); – **in mind**, in gedagte hou; – **oneself well**, (sig) goed gedra; **bring to** –, aanwend, laat geld; **it was borne in upon me**, dit het tot my deurgedring; **I cannot** – **him**, ek kan hom nie verdra (uitstaan) nie; – **away**, wegdra, behaal; – **down**, onderdruk, oorwin; – **hard on**, swaar druk op, verdruk; – **out**, bevestig; – **up**, moed hou; – **up against**, die hoof bied aan; – **upon**, in verband staan met; – **with**, geduldig wees met, duld.
beard, n. baard.
beard, v. trotseer, uitdaag.
bearded, gebaard; – **corn**, baardkoring.
bearer, draer, bringer, houer, toonder; lykdraer.
bear-garden, beretuin; lawaaitoneel.
bearing, houding, gedrag; ligging, rigting; draplek; strekking; verhouding; –**s**, rigting; **armorial** –**s**, wapen.
bearing-rein, springteuels.
bearskin, beervel; kolbak.
beast, bees, dier; beesagtige mens.
beastliness, beesagtigheid.
beastly, beesagtig, dierlik; ellendig; – **scoundrel**, ellendige skurk.
beat, v. slaan, uitstof; wen, klop; klits; stamp; – **the air**, in die lug skerm; – **hollow**, ver uitstof; – **it**, maak dat jy wegkom; – **time**, tyd aangee; – **about the bush**, om 'n saak heenpraat, uitvlugte soek; – **a retreat**, die aftog blaas; **that** –**s everything**, dit is die toppunt!; **this** –**s me**, dit slaan my dronk.
beat, p.p. op, poot-uit; **dead** –, poot-uit.
beat, n. slag, klap; klop; tik; rondte; wyk.
beaten, geslaan; verslaan; gebaande (weg).
beatific, saligmakend; geluksalig.
beatification, saligmaking; geluksaligheid; heiligverklaring.
beatify, saligmaak; heilig verklaar.
beating, pak, loesing; getrommel.
beatitude, geluksaligheid.
beatnik, beatnik, defaitis.
beau, modegek; kêrel, vryer.
beautiful, pragtig, skitterend.
beautify, mooi maak, verfraai.
beauty, mooiheid, skoonheid, prag; **what a** –, dis 'n mooie!, **that's the** – **of it**, dis die mooiste daarvan; – **parlour**, kosmetieksalon, skoonheidsalon.
beauty-sleep, eerste slaap, voornagslaap.
beauty-spot, skoonheidsoord; moesie; skoonheidspleistertjie.
beaver, bewer; kastoorhoed.
becalm, bedaar; –**ed**, deur windstilte oorval.
because, omdat, oor; – **of**, om, weens, vanweë; – **of that**, daarom.
Bechuana, Betsjoeana.

beck, n. wink, knik; **at one's** –, tot iemand se beskikking.
beck, v. wink.
beckon, wink, knik, wuif, sein.
become, word; pas, goed staan; betaam.
becoming, gepas, betaamlik.
bed, n. bed, kooi; lêplek; bedding; **take to** –, gaan lê; – **and board**, tafel en bed; kos en inwoning.
bed, v. (in beddinkies) uitplant; 'n bed vorm.
bedabble, bespat.
bedaub, besmeer.
bed-chamber, slaapkamer.
bedclothes, beddegoed.
bedding, beddegoed.
bedeck, opskik, optooi, optakel.
bedevil, mishandel, uitskel; beheks, betoor; in die war jaag.
bed-fellow, bedgenoot, slaapmaat.
bedizen, opskik, optooi, optakel.
bedlam, gekkehuis; lawaaiboel.
bedlamite, kranksinnige, gek.
Bedouin, Bedoeïen, woestyn-Arabier.
bed-pan, steekpan, ondersteek.
bedpost, bedstyl.
bedraggle, besmeer, bevuil, betakel.
bedridden, bedlêend.
bedrock, rotsbed; grond; **get to** –, tot die grond van die saak deurdring.
bedroom, slaapkamer.
bedside, bed, sponde.
bedstead, ledekant, katel.
bed-time, slaaptyd.
bee, by.
bee-bread, broodheuning.
beech, beuk(e)boom.
beef, beesvleis.
beefsteak, biefstuk.
beef-tea, boeljon, vleesekstrak.
beefy, frisgeboud, gespierd.
beehive, by(e)nes, byekorf.
beer, bier; – **and skittles**, rosegeur en maneskyn.
beest, **beestings**, bies.
beet, beet.
beetle, n. kewer, tor.
beetle, n. stamper.
beetle, v. oorhang, vooruitsteek.
beetling, oorhangend.
beetroot, beet, beetwortel.
beeves, (sien **beef**), osse; os-karkasse.
befall, gebeur; oorkom, wedervaar.
befit, pas, voeg, betaam.
befool, vir gek hou.
before, prep. voor.
before, adv. voor, voorop, vooruit; tevore, voorheen.
before, conj. voor, voordat, eer.
beforehand, vantevore, vooraf, by voorbaat, vooruit; **be** – **with**, voor wees met; voorspring met.
befoul, bevuil.
befriend, vriendskap betoon, guns bewys.
beg, bedel; smeek; vra, versoek; – **for**, vra om; – **pardon**, verskoning (ekskuus) vra; – **leave**, vergunning vra; **I** – **to inform you**, ek het die eer om u te berig.
beget, verwek, verkry.
beggar, bedelaar; stumper; vent; **little** –, klein vabond, rakker.
beggar, v. tot die bedelstaf bring, reneweer; **it** –**s all description**, dit gaan alle beskrywing te bowe.
beggarly, armoedig, armsalig; gemeen.
beggary, armoede, bedelary.

begin, begin, aanvang, aan die gang sit; – **at**, begin by.
beginner, beginneling, groene.
beginning, begin, aanvang.
begone, maak dat jy weg kom! trap!
begonia, begonia.
begrime, besmeer, betakel.
begrudge, beny, misgun.
beguile, bedrieg, fop; **a the time**, die tyd verkort of verdryf.
behalf, belang; **in**, **on** – **of** X, om X ontwil; namens X.
behave, (sig) gedra; – **oneself**, (sig) netjies gedra, sy fatsoen bewaar.
behaviour, gedrag, houding.
behead, onthoof, kop-afkap.
behest, bevel, versoek.
behind, prep. agter; anderkant.
behind, adv. agter, agteraan, agterna, van agter, agterom; – **time**, (te) laat; – **the times**, uit die tyd, verouderd, ouderwets; – **one's back**, agter iemand se rug, agterbaks, onderduims.
behindhand, agter, agterstallig; agterlik.
behold, aanskou, beskou, sien.
beholden, dank verskuldig (aan).
beho(o)ve, betaam.
being, part, synde; **for the time** –, vir die oomblik, tydelik; **that** – **so**, aangesien dit so is.
being, n. bestaan; wese; skepsel, kreatuur; **in** –, in aansyn; **come into** –, ontstaan; **Supreme Being**, Opperwese.
belabour, bewerk; toetakel, afransel.
belated, vertraag, deur die donker oorval.
belch, v. wind opbreek, oprisp; uitbraak.
belch, n. wind, oprisₗing.
beldam(e), ou heks, helleveeg.
beleaguer, beleër, omsingel, insluit.
belfry, kloktoring; klokverdieping.
Belgian, a. Belgies.
Belgian, n. Belg.
belie, belieg; loënstraf, weerspreek.
belief, geloof, oortuiging, mening.
believe, geloof (glo), vertrou; meen; **make** –, wysmaak, voorgee, doen asof.
believer, gelowige.
belike, dalk, miskien.
belittle, verklein; kleineer, afkam.
bell, klok, bel; blomkelk.
belladonna, belladonna; nagskade.
bell-buoy, klokboei.
belle, mooi meisie; mooiste meisie.
bell-flower, klokblom, klokkie.
bell-foundry, klokgietery.
bellicose, oorlogsugtig, strydlustig.
belligerent, oorlogvoerend.
bell-metal, klokspys, klokmetaal.
bellow, v. brul, bulk, loei; bulder, dreun.
bellow, n. gebrul, gebulk; gebulder.
bellows, blaasbalk; **a pair of** –, 'n blaasbalk.
bell-pull, belknop.
bell-ringer, klokluier, klokspeler.
bell-wether, belhamel; leier, voorperd.
belly, n. buik, pens; (eet)lus; holte.
belly, v. opswel, uitstaan, bolstaan.
belly-ache, buikpyn.
bellyful, bekoms, buikvol.
belong, behoor(t) aan; tuisbehoor(t).
belonings, toebehorens, besittinge.
beloved, bemin(de).
below, prep. onder, benede, onderkant.
below, adv. onder, onderaan, aan die onderkant, benede omlaag, laer as.
belt, n. gord(el), lyfband; strook; riem; dryfriem.
belt, v. (om)gord; onder die riem kry.
bemoan, beklaag, bejammer.

bemuse, deurmekaar maak.
bench, bank, sitbank, draaibank, skaafbank; regbank.
bend, v. buig; span; buk; draai; knoop; **bent on**, daarop uit, vasbeslote.
bend, n. buiging, draai, kromming, bog.
beneath, prep. onder, benede.
beneath, adv. (na) onder, benede, ondertoe.
benediction, seëning, seën; gebed.
benefaction, weldaad; skenking.
benefactor, weldoener.
benefactress, weldoenster.
benefice, prebende, kerklike bediening.
beneficence, liefdadigheid, weldadigheid.
beneficent, weldadig; heilsaam.
beneficial, voordelig, heilsaam.
beneficiary, bedeelde.
benefit, n. voordeel, nut.
benefit, v. tot voordeel wees, baat, goeddoen; voordeel trek, profiteer.
benefit-night, benefiet, fondsaand.
benefit-society, onderstandsvereniging.
Benelux, Benelux.
benevolence, welwillendheid, weldadigheid.
benevolent, welwillend, weldadig; liefdadig; –, **fund**, liefdadigheidsfonds.
Bengalese, Bengaals.
benighted, deur die donker oorval; onwetend blind, onbeskaaf.
benign, minsaam; sagaardig; heilsaam.
benignant, liefderyk; heilsaam.
benignity, vriendelikheid; liefderykheid.
benison, seën, seëning.
bent, draai; neiging; **to the top of his** –, tot die uiterste, soveel as sy hart kon verlang.
benumb, verkluim, verlam, verdoof.
benzine, bensien.
benzoin, bensoë.
bequeath, vermaak, nalaat.
bequest, erf(e)nis, legaat, vermaking.
bereave, beroof; ontneem.
bereavement, verlies.
bergamot, bermot(peer); bergamot(sitroen).
beri-beri, beri-beri.
berry, bessie.
berserk(er), berserker.
berth, n. (aan)lêplek; kajuit; slaapbank; oortog; baantjie; **give a wide** –, uit die weg gaan.
berth, v. vasmaak, aanlê; lêplek gee.
beryl, beril(steen).
beseech, smeek.
beseem, pas, voeg, betaam.
beset, omring; aanval; –**ting sin**, boesemsonde; hoofgebrek.
beshrew, vervloek, verwens.
beside, naas, langs, digby; buite(n), behalwe; in vergelyking met; **that is** – **the question**, dit het met die vraag niks te maak nie; **be** – **oneself**, buite(n) sigself wees (van woede); – **the house**, langs die huis.
besides, buitendien; buite(n), behalwe, boonop.
besiege, beleër, omsingel; – **with requests**, oorlaai met versoeke.
beslaver, bekwyl; beflikflooi.
besmear, besmeer, bemors.
besmirch, bevuil, besmeer.
besot, verdwaas, verblind.
besotted, verdwaas, verblind.
bespangle, versier; optakel; besaai.
bespatter, bespat, beklad.
bespeak, bespreek; bestel; getuig van.
besprinkle, besprinkel, besaai.
best, a. beste; – **part**, grootste gedeelte, meeste.
best, n. bes(te), **with the** –, so goed as die beste; **have the** – **of it**, daar die beste van afkom;

make the - of it, jou skik na die omstandighede; at -, op sy beste, hoogstens; for the -, om beswil, met goeie bedoelinge; in his Sunday -, in sy kisklere; - man, strooijonker, bruidsjonker.
best, adv. liefs; I had, were - . . . , ek sou die verstandigste doen . . .
best, v. uitoorlê, oortroef; vir gek hou.
bestead, baat, help.
bested, geplaas, ill, hard, sore -, lelik in die nou, in die knyp.
bestial, beesagtig, dierlik.
bestialize, verdierlik.
bestiality, beesagtigheid, verdierliking.
bestir, roer.
bestow, (op)bêre; skenk, verleen.
bestowal, skenking, gif.
bestrew, bestrooi, rondstrooi.
bestride, bery; wydsbeen oor staan (sit).
bestseller, treffer, suksesboek.
bestudded, beslaan; besaai.
bet, v. wed; you -, dit kan jy glo!
bet, n. weddenskap.
beta, - rays, betastrale.
betake, wend.
betel, betel(noot).
betel-nut, arekaneut.
bethink, bedink, (sig) herinner.
betide, gebeur; woe - you, wee jou.
betimes, tydig, betyds.
betoken, beteken, voorspel, aandui.
betray, verraai; aandui, dui op.
betrayal, verraad; blyk.
betroth, verloof.
betrothal, verlowing.
betrothed, verloofde.
better, a. beter; - part, grootste gedeelte; - half, wederhelf.
better, adv. beter; liewer; you had - go, gaan maar liewers, dit is beter dat jy maar gaan; think - of it, van gedagte verander; - off, beter aan toe, ryker.
better, n. meerdere; oorhand; your -s, jou meerdere; get the - of, die oorhand kry oor, uitoorlê, baasraak; for -, for worse, in voorspoed en teenspoed, in lief en leed; a change for the -, 'n gunstige wending, 'n verbetering.
better, n. verbeter.
betterment, verbetering.
between, tussen, onder; - ourselves, onder ons; - you and me, tussen ons twee; - the devil and the deep blue sea, tussen twee vure.
betwixt, tussen; - and between, so-so, tussen die boom en die bas.
bevel, n. skuinste, hoek; winkelhaak.
bevel, v. skuins maak.
beverage, drank.
bevy, klompie, aantal, paar.
bewail, bejammer, beklaag, beween.
beware, oppas, op jou hoede wees.
bewilder, in die war bring, verbyster.
bewitch, beheks; bekoor, betower.
beyond, prep. anderkant, oorkant, buite(kant), oor, bo(kant), verby; - the river, anderkant (oorkant) die rivier; - the boundaries, buite(kant) of oor die grense; it is - me, dit is my oor of bokant my vuurmaakplek; - measure, bowemate, uitermate.
beyond, adv. verder.
beyond, n. oorkant; the -, die oorkant, die lewe hiernamaals; at the back of -, aan die ander end van die wêreld.
bezel, skuins kant; gleufie; kas.
bias, n. skuinste; oorhelling; vooroordeel.
bias, v. beïnvloed, bevooroordeel.

bib, n. borslap(pie).
bib, v. drink, suip.
bibber, drink(e)broer, suiplap.
Bible, Bybel.
Biblical, Bybels, Bybel- . . .
bibliographer, boekbeskrywer, bibliograaf.
bibliography, boekbeskrywing, bibliografie.
bibliomaniac, boekegek, bibliomaan.
bibliophile, bibliofiel, boekliefhebber.
bibulous, indrinkend; dranksugtig.
bicarbonate, bikarbonaat; dubbelkoolsuursoda; - of soda, koeksoda.
bice, bergblou(verf).
bicentenary, tweede-eeufees.
bicephalous, tweehoofdig.
biceps, biseps.
bicker, kibbel; klater, kletter.
bicycle, n. fiets, rywiel.
bicycle, v. fiets, fietsry.
bid, v. gebied, beveel; bie(d); heet, versoek; - fair, beloof, tekens gee.
bid, n. bod; make a -, 'n bod maak, 'n poging doen.
bidder, bieder (bieër).
bidding, bevel; bieëry; versoek.
bide, afwag.
biennial, tweejarig.
bier, baar.
biff, n. hou, klap.
biff, v. klap, slaan.
bifocal, bifokaal.
bifurcated, gevurk, gesplits.
bifurcation, splitsing, mik.
big, groot, dik; a - man, 'n groot man; 'n belangrike kêrel; - with young, dragtig; - with news, vol van gewigtige tydings.
bigamist, bigamis.
bigamous, bigamies.
bigamy, bigamie, tweewywery.
bight, bog, baai.
bigot, dweper.
bigoted, dweepsiek, bekrompe.
bigotry, dweepsug, bigotterie.
bike, fiets.
bilateral, tweesydig; dubbel; bilateraal.
bilbo, sabel; -es, boeie.
bile, gal; brommigheid.
bilge, n. buik, boom.
bilge, v. 'n lek kry; opswel.
bilge-water, ruimwater.
bilharzia, bilharzia.
biliary, galagtig.
bilingual, tweetalig.
bilious, galagtig, mislik; brommig.
bilk, fop.
bill, n. snawel, bek.
bill, v. met die bek streel, trekkebek; - and coo, liefkoos, minnekoos.
bill, n. (veg)byl; snoeimes.
bill, n. briefie; rekening; wissel; seël; plakkaat, aanplakbiljet; faktuur; wetsontwerp; aanklag; saak; - of fare, spyslys; - of lading, vragbrief; - of exchange, wisselbrief; - of costs, onkostelys; stick no -s, aanplak verbode.
bill, v. aanplak; aankondig.
bill-broker, wisselhandelaar.
billet, n. biljet, briefie; inkwartieringsorder; baantjie, betrekking.
billet, v. inkwartier; plaas.
billet, n. houtblok(kie).
billiards, biljart; play -, biljart speel.
billingsgate, viswywetaal.
billion, biljoen.
billow, n. golf, brander.
billow, v. golf, dein.

billowy, golwend.
bill-sticker, plakkaatplakker.
billy, kantien, kookblik.
billy-goat, bokram.
biltong, biltong.
bimetallism, bimetallisme.
bimonthly, veertiendaags, twee maal in die maand; tweemaandeliks.
bin, kas, kis, mandjie, bus, blik.
binary, binêr, tweetallig, tweeledig.
bind, bind, vasmaak, heg, verbind, inbind; verplig; bekragtig; – up, verbind; opbind; tesame inbind; – over, laat belowe *of* waarborg; I'll be bound, ek is seker, ek wed; he is bound to, hy sal stellig; hy is verplig om, hy moet; he is bound up with the matter, hy is in die saak betrokke.
binder, (boek)binder; verband, nawelband; bindmasjien.
binding, n. (boek)band; omboorsel.
binding, a. verpligtend, bindend.
bine, stam (van 'n klimplant); rank.
binnacle, kompashuisie.
binocular, verkyker, toneelkyker.
binomial, a. binomiaal, tweeledig.
binomial, n. tweeledige getal *of* grootheid, binomium.
biographer, biograaf, lewensbeskrywer.
biographic(al), biografies.
biography, biografie, lewensbeskrywing.
biological, biologies.
biologist, bioloog.
biology, biologie.
bioscope, bioskoop.
bipartisan: – policy, twee-partye-beleid.
biped, tweevoetige dier, tweevoeter.
biplane, tweedekker, dubbeldekker.
birch, n. berk(eboom); lat.
birch, v. onder die lat kry, klop, slaan.
bird, voël; kêrel, vent, nummer; –s of a feather, voëls van dieselfde pluimasie, mense van dieselfde slag *of* soort; – of paradise, paradysvoël; kill two –s with one stone, twee vlieë in een slag slaan; – of passage, trekvoël; – of prey, roofvoël.
bird-fancier, voëlverkoper.
birdie, voëltjie (ook in gholf).
bird-lime, voëllym.
bird's-eye, veronica; grofgekerfde tabak; – view of Cape Town, Kaapstad in voëlvlug.
birth, geboorte; stand, afkoms.
birth-certificate, geboortebewys.
birthday, verjaar(s)dag, geboortedag.
birthday-book, verjaar(s)dagalbum.
birth-mark, moedervlek.
birthplace, geboorteplek (-plaas).
birthrate, geboortesyfer.
birthright, geboortereg.
biscuit, beskuit; biscuit (biskwie), koekie.
bisect, halveer, in twee deel.
bisector, halveerlyn.
bisexual, twee(ge)slagtig, trassie- . . .
bishop, biskop; raadsheer (skaakspel); biskop- (wyn).
bishopric, bisdom.
bismuth, bismut.
bison, bison, buffel.
bisque, ongeglasuurde aardewerk.
bissextile, skrikkeljaar.
bit, n. hap, byt; bietjie, stukkie; brokkie; boor; stang; a –, 'n biet'ie, enigsins; not a –, heeltemal nie, volstrek nie; – by –, stukkie vir stukkie.
bit, v. stang *of* toom aansit; beteuel.
bitch, teef; feeks; slet.

bite, v. byt; invreet; (skroef) vat.
bite, n. byt, beet; hap; stukkie ete; greep, vat.
biting, bytend, skerp bits(ig).
bitten, gebyt; been-af, verlief; once –, twice shy, 'n esel stoot hom nie tweemaal aan dieselfde steen nie; the bitter –, die fopper gefop.
bitter, a. bitter, skerp, griewend.
bitter, n. bitter; –s, bitter.
bittern, roerdomp.
bitumen, asfalt, aardharpuis, bitumen.
bituminous, harpuisagtig, bituminieus.
bivalve, a. tweeskalig, tweekleppig.
bivalve, n. tweekleppige skaaldier; oester.
bivouac, n. kamp.
bivouac, v. bivakkeer, uitkamp.
biweekly, tweeweekliks, veertiendaags; twee maal weekliks.
bizarre, bizar, grillig, vreemd, ongewoon.
blab, verklap, verklik.
black, a. swart, donker, somber, duister; hit a – eye, blou-oog-slaan; look –, dreigend uitsien; be in one's – books, in diskrediet by iemand wees; – and blue, bont en blou; – arts, toorkuns, die swartekuns; – bread, rogbrood; – frost, kwaai ryp; – list, swart lys; – Maria, vangwa, nagwa; – market, swart-mark (handel).
black, n. swart; swartsel, swart verf; swart vlek; swartkoring, brandkoring; roet; swart klere, rouklere; Swartman; put down in – and white, swart op wit sit; op skrif stel.
black, v. swartmaak, swartsmeer; – out, uitvee(g).
blackball, afstem, lidmaatskap weier.
black-beetle, kakkerlak.
blackberry, braam(bes).
blackbird, n. swartvoël; lyster.
blackboard, skoolbord.
blackdeath, pes; die Swarte Dood.
black-draught, purgeermiddel, purgasie.
blacken, swartmaak, swartsmeer.
blackguard, n. skobbejak, smeerlap.
blackguard(ly), a. gemeen, skurkerig.
blackguard, v. uitskel; slegmaak.
blackhead, swartkoppie; vetwurmpie, mee-etertjie.
blacking, swartsel.
blackish, swarterig, swartagtig.
blacklead, potlood.
blackleg, onderkruiper; swendelaar.
black-letter, Gotiese letter; – day, ongeluksdag.
black-list, op die swart lys plaas.
blackmail, n. afpersing; brandskatting.
blackmail, v. afpers.
black-out, n. beswyming, breinfloute.
black-out, v. in 'n beswyming raak, flou word; uitvee; verdonker.
blackpudding, bloedwors.
Black Rod, stafdraer, seremoniemeester.
blacksmith, smid.
blackwood, rosehout.
blacky, swart skepsel; swartjie.
bladder, blaas; blaar; windsak.
blade, sprietjie; blad; halm; messie, lem; sabel; jolly –, vrolike vent.
blain, blaar, sweer.
blamable, laakbaar, afkeurenswaardig.
blame, n. skuld, blaam.
blame, v. beskuldig, blameer; laak, afkeur; be to –, skuld hê; afkeuring verdien.
blameless, onberisp(e)lik; onskuldig.
blameworthy, afkeurenswaardig, laakbaar.
blanch, bleik, witmaak; afskil; verbleek, wit word; – over, verbloem.

blanc-mange, blamaans (blanc-manger).
bland, innemend, beleef'; vleierig.
blandish, vlei, paai.
blandishment, vleiery, liewigheid; verlokking, verleidelikheid.
blank, a. blank, blanko; onbeskrewe, oningevul(d); leeg; wesenloos; – **space**, ledige ruimte; – **cartridge**, loskruitpatroon; – **wall**, blinde muur; – **verse**, rymlose verse.
blank, n. leegte, leemte; ruimte; weggelate woord, vloekwoord; 'n niet, 'n nul; **his mind was a** –, sy gedagte het stilgestaan; sy geheue was skoon weg.
blanket, n. kombers, deken; **wet** –, spelbederwer; droogstoppel, – **vote**, naturellestem.
blanket, v. toemaak, bedek; beesvel-gooi.
blankly, met die mond vol tande, beteurterd; – **deny**, kortweg ontken.
blare, v. sketter, lawaai maak, brul.
blare, n. gesketter, lawaai, gebrul.
blarney, n. flikflooiery, mooipraatjies.
blarney, v. mooipraat, flikflooi, vlei.
blaspheme, laster, spot, vloek.
blasphemous, (gods)lasterlik.
blasphemy, (gods)lastering.
blast, n. rukwind; windstroom; gesketter; ontploffing; verderf.
blast, v. in die lug blaas, laat spring; verskroei, verwoes; vervloek.
blasted, vervlakste, blikskaterse.
blast-furnace, smeltoond, hoogoond.
blatant, skeeuerig, lawaaierig; – **idiot**, volslae idioot, afgedankste gek.
blather, v. klets.
blather, n. geklets.
blaze, n. vlam, gloed; uitbarsting; –**s**, hel; **in a** –, in ligtelaai.
blaze, v. vlam, oplaai; skitter; opvlam, uitbars; losbrand, skiet.
blaze, n. bles.
blaze, v. bles, 'n wit streep maak op.
blaze, v. uitbassuin, rondvertel.
blazer, kleurbaadjie.
blazon, n. blasoen, wapen(skild), banier.
blazon, v. blasoeneer; versier, verlug; – **forth, out**, uitbasuin.
bleach, bleik, verbleik.
bleaching-powder, bleikpoeier.
bleak, a. kaal; guur; onherbergsaam.
blear, dof, glasig; – **eyed**, met waterige oë, met leepoë.
bleat, v. blêr, bulk; tjank.
bleat, n. geblêr; gebulk; getjank.
bleed, bloei, bloedstort; bloedlaat.
bleeder, bloeier; bloedlater; uitsuier, luglater; – **valve**, luglaatklep.
bleep, bliep.
blemish, vlek, klad, smet.
blench, terugdeins.
blend, v. vermeng, meng, berei; (wyn) versny.
blend, n. mengsel, soort; vermenging.
blesbok, –**buck**, blesbok.
bless, seën; loof; gelukkig maak; – **me!**, bewaar my!
blessed, **blest**, geseën, geloof, geluksalig; vervlakste; **he is a** – **fool**, hy is 'n verbrande gek; **the whole** – **day**, die godganse dag; **of** – **memory**, saliger nagedagtenis; **I'm** –, my mastig *of* magtig!
blessedness, geluksalighêid; **single** –, die ongehude gelukstaat.
blessing, seën, seëning; (tafel)gebed.
blest, sien **blessed**.
blether, sien **blather**.
blight, n. roes; verderf, plaag, pes.

blight, v. verskroei, verderf, verwoes.
blighter, rakker; skobbejak.
blind, a. blind, verblind; – **to**, blind vir, ongevoelig vir; – **side**, skeelkant; – **letter**, onbestelbare brief; – **door**, blindedeur; – **flying, instrumentevlieg**(kuns); – **alley**, blinde gang, omkeerstraatjie.
blind, v. blind maak, verblind; bedrieg.
blind, n. blinding, rolgordyn, luik, hortjie; skerm; blinddoek; oogklap; voorwendsel, oëverblindery.
blindage, blindwerk, blindering.
blindfold, v. blinddoek.
blindfold, a. & adv. geblinddoek; blindelings, in die blinde.
blindly, blindelings; roekeloos.
blindman, blindeman; –**'s buff**, blindemol.
blindness, blindheid, verblinding.
blink, v. knipoog; flits; die oë sluit vir.
blink, n. glimp, flits, glans, skynsel.
blinkers, oogklappe.
bliss, saligheid, geluk, heil, vreugde.
blissful, gelukkig, geluksalig.
blister, n. blaar; trekpleister.
blister, v. blare trek; trekpleister opsit; verveel.
blithe, bly, opgewek, lustig.
blithesome, vrolik, opgewek.
blitz, blitsaanval; blitsoorlog.
blizzard, sneeustorm, sneeujag.
bloat, sout en rook; opblaas; opswel.
bloated, opgeblaas; opgeblase; vertroetel(d), gerook.
bloater, gerookte haring, bokkem.
blob, bobbel, blaas.
bloc, blok (*fig*).
block, n. blok; vorm; katrol; drukplaat; obstruksie, hindernis; opblokking; blokgat (krieket).
block, v. versper, (ver)hinder, dwarsboom; obstruksie voer; blok (krieket); – **up**, versper, blokkeer.
blockade, n. blokkade, insluiting.
blockade, v. blokkeer, insluit.
blockade-runner, blokkadebreker.
block-buster, blokbom.
blockhead, domoor, klipkop, swaap.
blockhouse, blokhuis.
block-system, blokstelsel.
bloke, kêrel, vent; (gom)tor.
blond, blond, lig.
blonde, blondine, blonde meisie.
blood, n. bloed; sap; humeur, temperament; familie, verwantskap; **his** – **was up**, sy bloed het gekook; **in cold** –, koelbloedig, in koelen bloede; – **is thicker than water**, bloed kruip waar dit nie kan loop nie; **young** –, nuwe bloed *of* lewe; jeug; snuiter, fat; – **cattle**, stamboekbeeste.
blood, v. bloedlaat; bloed laat ruik.
blood-and-thunder film, skop-skiet-en-donderprent.
blood-feud, bloedvyandskap, bloedwraak.
blood-horse, volbloedperd.
bloodhound, speurhond, bloedhond.
bloodless, bloedloos; ongevoelig.
blood-pudding, bloedwors.
bloodshed, bloedstorting, bloedvergieting.
bloodshot, (bloed)deurlope, rooi.
bloodstained, met bloed bevlek.
blood-stock, volbloedperde; renperde.
bloodsucker, bloedsuier; uitsuier.
bloodthirsty, bloeddorstig, moordlustig.
blood-vessel, bloedvat, aar.
bloody, bloedig, bloederig; wreed; – **nose**, bloedneus.

bloom 427 **boil**

bloom, n. bloei, bloeisel; fleur, krag; blos, waas.
bloom, v. bloei, blom.
bloomer(s), rokbroek, kniebroek.
blossom, n. bloei(sel), blom, bloesem.
blossom, v. bloei, blom.
blot, n. klad, vlek; smet, skandvlek.
blot, v. klad; beklad; – out, uitwis, uitvee; uitdelg; kafloop; – **your copybook**, jou goeie naam bederf; 'n gekheid aanvang.
blotch, puis(ie); vlek, klad; vloeipapier.
blotting-paper, kladpapier, vloeipapier.
blouse, bloes; hempbaadjie.
blow, v. waai; blaas, hyg; snuit; eiers lê (van vlieë); – **hot and cold**, uit twee monde praat; – **a kiss**, 'n kushandjie gooi; – **off steam**, gemoed lug gee; – **over**, oorwaai, verbytrek; – out, uitwaai; uitblaas, doodblaas: bars; – **up**, opblaas, oppomp; in die lug laat spring; raas met.
blow, v. bloei, oopgaan.
blow, n. bloei, bloeisel.
blow, n. slag, klap, hou, raps, stoot; ramp, skok; **come to**, **exchange** –s, handgemeen raak, aanmekaar spring; **at one** –, in een slag, meteens.
blow-fly, brommer.
blown, uitasem; opgeswel; bederf; – **roses**, oop rose; – **horse**, flou perd.
blow-out, smulparty, fees, fuif.
blow-pipe, blaaspyp; blaasroer.
blowzed, **blowzy**, met 'n rooi gesig, verwaai, deurmekaar.
blub, huil, tjank, grens.
blubber, n. walvisspek; gegrens, getjank.
blubber, v. grens, tjank; huil-huil praat.
bludgeon, n. knuppel.
bludgeon, v. met 'n knuppel slaan.
blue, a. blou; geleerd; **look** –, senuweeagtig (bedruk) lyk; **every** – **moon**, elke bloumaandag; – **blood**, adellike bloed; – **devils**, neerslagtigheid.
blue, n. blou; blousel; die lug; die see; (**a fit of**) the –s, neerslagtige *of* vervelige bui, neerslagtigheid.
blue, v. blou maak; in die blousel sit.
blue-bell, klokkie; pypie.
blue-bottle, koringblom; brommer.
blue-gum, bloekomboom (blougom-).
blue-jacket, bloubaadjie, pikbroek.
blue-stocking, bloukous.
buff, a. stomp; kortaf, plomp; openhartig, hartlik.
bluff, n. (steil) wal, hang.
bluff, v. oorbluf; uitoorlê, grootpraat, opsny; bangmaak; wysmaak.
bluff, n. bangmakery; grootpratery, blur.
blunder, v. struikel; (sig) vergis, bok skiet, flater begaan, knoei; – **upon**, struikel op, by toeval op afkom.
blunder, n. flater, fout, bok.
blunderbuss, donderbus.
blunt, a. stomp, bot; kortaf, reguit.
blunt, v. stomp maak, bot maak, ongevoelig maak.
bluntness, stompheid; openhartigheid, eerlikheid.
blur, n. klad, vlek; warreling.
blur, v. klad, (be)vlek; onduidelik maak, verwar; uitwis, verdof.
blurt, in; – **out**, uitflap, verklap.
blush, v. blos, rooi word.
blush, n. blos; gloed; **without a** –, sonder blik of bloos.
bluster, v. storm, lawaai, raas; swets.
bluster, n. lawaai; geswets; bangmakery.
boa, boa; – **constrictor**, boakonstriktor, luislang.

boar, beer; wildevark.
board, n. plank; bord; karton, bordpapier; tafel; maaltyd, ete, losies, bestuur, raad, boord; **above** –, eerlik, ope(n)lik; **sweep the** –, alles opstryk; **go by the** –, oorboord val; uitgegooi word; **go on** – **ship**, aan boord gaan; – **and lodging**, kos en inwoning.
board, v. met planke bespyker; loseer, maaltye neem; losies gee, maaltye verskaf; enter, aanklamp; aan boord gaan.
boarder, kosganger; kosleerling.
boarding, losies.
boarding-house, koshuis, losieshuis.
boarding-school, kosskool.
board-wages, kosgeld.
boast, n. spoggery, grootpraat, roem, trots; **make a** – **of**, (sig) beroem op.
boast, v. spog, grootpraat; trots wees op die besit van, spog met; – **of**, spog met, roem op.
boat, n. skuit, boot, skip; souspotjie; **in the same** –, in dieselfde skuitjie vaar, in dieselfde omstandighede.
boat, v. roei, in 'n boot vaar.
boat-race, roeiwedstryd.
boatswain, bootsman.
bob, n. gewig (van 'n slinger, skietlood, ens.); (haar)bol; polkahare; pruik; stompstert.
bob, v. kortknip, in die nek afknip, ,,bob".
bob, v. dobber, duik; buig; hap.
bob, n. sjieling.
bob, v. raps; ruk, pluk.
bobbin, spoel(tjie), klos(sie).
bobbish, lekker fris.
bobby, konstabel; – **sox (socks)**, kort kouse.
bobby-soxer, bakvissie.
bob-sleigh, -sled, bobslee.
bobtail, stompstert; **tag-rag and** –, Jap Rap en sy maat; Piet, Paul en Klaas.
bob-wig, kort pruik.
bode, voorspel.
bodement, voorspelling.
bodice, lyfie.
bodiless, onliggaamlik, sonder liggaam.
bodily, a. liggaamlik, lyflik; – **fear**, liggaamsvrees, vrees vir die liggaam; – **presence**, aanwesigheid in lewende lywe.
bodily, adv. heeltemal, met huid en haar.
bodkin, rygnaald; dolk.
body, n. liggaam, lyf; lyk; romp; inhoud, hoofdeel; bak; mens, persoon; vereniging, mag, trop, bende, massa; **in a** –, gesamentlik (gesamelik); **in the** –, in die vlees; **heavenly** –, hemelliggaam.
body, v. beliggaam; – **forth**, beliggaam.
body-colour, dekkleur.
body-guard, lyfwag.
body-servant, lyfkneg.
body-snatcher, lykdief.
boffin, uitvinder; navorser.
bog, n. moeras.
bog, v. in 'n moeras dompel *of* versink.
bogey, syfer, ,,bogey" (gholf); sien **bogy**.
boggle, skrik, wegvlie; steeks word; met twee monde praat; knoei.
bogie, draaibare onderstel; trollie.
bogie, gees, voëlverskrikker.
bogus, vals, voorgewend, sogenaamd.
bogy (**bogey**), duiwel, gees; gogga, skrikbeeld.
boil, n. puis, sweer, bloedvint, pitsweer.
boil, v. kook; – **over**, oorkook; – **away**, verkook; deurkook; –**ed shirt**, borshemp; **keep the pot** –**ing**, die skoorsteen aan die rook hou.
boil, n. kook; **on the** –, aan die kook; **off the** –, van die kook af.

**boiler, koker; (stoom)ketel; warmwatertenk; kookgroente.
boisterous,** onstuimig; luidrugtig, rumoerig; ru.
bold, dapper, moedig, vermetel; skerp, duidelik; **make –,** so vry wees, die vryheid neem; **– type,** vet letter.
boldfaced, onbeskaamd, vrypostig.
bole, stam.
boll, (saad)bol.
bolster, n. peul, kussing; stut.
bolster, v. steun, opvul; **– up,** steun; stut, oplap.
bolster-bar, kussingslaanpaal; kussingslaan.
bolt, n. bout; knip, grendel; pyl; bliksemstraal; a **– from the blue,** 'n donderslag uit 'n helder hemel.
bolt, v. grendel, die knip opsit; vasskroef, vasbout; op loop gaan; haastig wegsluk.
bolt, n. vlug, wegspring.
bolt, adv. in; **– upright,** penregop.
bolt, boult, v. sif; ondersoek.
bomb, n. bom.
bomb, v. bombardeer; met handbomme gooi.
bombard, bombardeer.
bombardier, bombardier.
bombardment, bombardement, beskieting.
bombasine, bombasyn; ferweel.
bombast, bombas, hoogdrawende taal.
bombastic, bombasties, hoogdrawend.
bond, n. band; verbond; verband, hipoteek, skuldbrief; verpligting, verbintenis; entrepot, pakhuis.
bond, v. verbind, verband lê; verband neem op; in entrepot opslaan.
bondage, knegskap; gevangeskap; gebondenheid.
bondsman, kneg, slaaf, lyfei(g)ene.
bone, n. been; graat; **to the –,** in merg en been; **– of contention,** twisappel; **pick a –,** 'n appeltjie skil.
bone, v. bene uithaal, grate uithaal; wegskaai.
bone, a. van been, been- ...
bone-dust, beenmeel
bone-shaker, rammelkas.
bonfire, vreugdevuur.
bonnet, n. mus, kappie; kap (van lamp, skoorsteen, ens.); motordeksel; handlanger, lokvoël.
bonny, hups, aardig, lief, aanvallig.
bonus, bonus, premie, ekstra.
bony, benerig, graterig; langbeen- ... ; maer.
boo, v. boe, uitjou; bulk, loei.
booby, domoor, lummel, knul, esel.
booby-prize, poedelprys.
booby-trap, deurval, val op 'n deur.
book, n. boek; geskrif, werk; Bybel; wedrenprogram; teks, geskrewe woord; **– of reference,** naslaanwerk; **take a leaf out of somebody's –,** iemand navolg; **without –,** sonder gesag; **be in somebody's bad, good –s,** by iemand in 'n slegte, goeie blaadjie staan; **bring to –,** tot verantwoording roep; **kiss the –,** op die Bybel sweer.
book, v. inskryf, boek; bespreek.
bookcase, boekrak, boekkas.
bookie, sien **bookmaker.**
booking-clerk, kaartjiesbeampte.
booking-office, kaartjieskantoor.
bookish, boekagtig, geleerd, pedanties.
book-keeper, boekhouer.
book-keeping, boekhou.
bookmaker, beroepswedder.
bookman, letterkundige, boekwurm.
bookmark, boeklêer, bladwyser.
book-muslin, neteldoek.
book-plate, boekmerk, ex libris.
book-post, drukwerk (postarief).
book-rest, boekstandertjie.

bookseller, boekhandelaar.
bookstall, boekwinkeltjie.
bookworm, boekwurm.
boom, n. (versperrings)boom; spriet.
boom, v. dreun; oplecf, omhooggaan; ophemel, aanprys.
boom, n. oplewing; ophemeling.
boomerang, boemerang.
boon, n. seën, voordeel; hede; guns.
boon, a. gul; vrolik; **– companion,** lustige drinkebroer; lekker kêrel.
boor, lomperd, onbeskofte vent.
boot, n. stewel; bagasiebak.
boot, n. voordeel; **to –,** boonop, op die koop toe.
boot, v. baat.
bootee, vrouestewel, halfstewel; wolsokkie.
booth, tent, kraam.
bootjack, laarskneg, skoentrekker.
bootlace, skoenveter.
bootlegger, dranksmokkelaar.
boots, skoen(e)poetser, -skoonmaker.
boot-tree, lees, skoenvorm.
booty, buit, roof.
booze, v. drink, fuif, suip.
booze, n. drinkparty, fuif; drinkgoed, lawaaiwater.
boozy, drinklustig, hoenderkop.
bo-peep, wegkruipertjie, wegstekertjie.
boracic, boraks- ..., boor- ...
borax, boraks.
border, n. rand, kant; grens; soom.
border, v. grens, begrens; omrand, omsoom; **– (up) on,** grens aan.
borderland, grensland.
bore, v. boor, hol maak; opsy druk; nek uitrek.
bore, n. boorwydte; boorgat.
bore, n. las, vervelende persoon, klitsgras.
bore, v. verveel.
bore, n. vloedgolf.
boreal, noordelik, noorder- ...
borer, boor; boorder; boorwurm.
boric, boor- ... ; **– ointment,** boorsalf.
born, gebore; **– of,** geboortig van; **– again,** wedergebore; **– with silver spoon in the mouth,** gelukskind, sondagskind; **not – yesterday,** ouer as tien (twaalf).
borough, stad; kiesafdeling.
borrow, leen (van), ontleen (aan).
bort, diamantgruis.
bos, v. misskiet; 'n flater begaan, knoei.
bos, n. misskoot; flater, knoeiwerk.
bosh, bog, kaf, onsin.
bosky, bosagtig, skaduryk.
bosom, boesem, bors; skoot; hart; siel.
boss, n. knop, bobbel, bult.
boss, n. baas; bobaas; leier.
boss, v. baasspeel; beheer; **– the show,** lakens uitdeel, eerste viool speel.
bot(t), maaier, papie; **–s,** papies.
botanic(al), botanies, plantkundig.
botanize, botaniseer.
botanist, plantkundige, botanis.
botany, plantkunde, botanie.
botch, v. konkel, (ver)knoei.
botch, n. konkelwerk, knoeiwerk.
both, albei, altwee, beide; **– man and beast,** mens sowel as dier, beide mens en dier.
bother, v. hinder, pla, lol, neul; **– about,** (sig) bekommer oor.
bother, n. beslommering, geneul, geseur.
botheration, n. geneul.
bott, sien **bot(t).**
bottle, n. bottel, fles; pypkan.

bottle, v. bottel, in flesse tap; inmaak, inlê; – **up,** opkrop; vaskeer.
bottle, n. bondel; – **of hay,** hooibondel.
bottle-holder, sekondant, handlanger.
bottle-neck, knelpunt.
bottle-store, drankwinkel.
bottle-washer, handlanger; bottelspoeler.
bottom, n. boom, bodem; grond; agterst; onderste; onderent; kiel; sitting; **touch** –, grond raak; **from the** – **of my heart,** uit die grond van my hart; **what is at the** – **of it?,** wat sit daar agter?; **at** –, in die grond; in sy hart.
bottom, a. onderste; laaste; – **drawer,** onderste laai; bêrelaai.
bottom, v. boom insit; grond op; deurgrond.
bottomless, boomloos; bodemloos.
bottomry, bodemery.
bough, tak; galg.
boulder, klip, rots(blok).
bounce, v. opspring, terugstuit; huppel; grootpraat; (oor)bluf; **a** –**ing girl,** flink meisie.
bounce, n. terugslag, opslag; bluf, oordrywing.
bouncer, opslagskoot; 'n tamaaie, 'n knewel; aartsleuen(aar).
bound, n. grens, grenslyn, grenspaal; **out of** –**s,** buite(n) die perke; uit die gronde.
bound, v. begrens, beperk.
bound, v. opslag maak, terugkaats; huppel.
bound, n. sprong, opslag, terugkaatsing; **by leaps and** –**s,** met rasse skrede, sprongsgewyse.
bound, a. klaar (om te vertrek), bestem(d); – **for,** met bestemming (na).
bound, p.p. gebonde, verplig; **he is** – **to succeed,** hy sal stellig slaag; – **up with,** betrokke in, verbonde met.
boundary, grens, grenslyn; grenshou.
bounden, verplig; – **duty,** dure plig.
bounder, hierjy, skobbejak, rakker.
boundless, grens(e)loos, onbeperk.
bounteous, mild(dadig), weldadig.
bountiful, mild, ryk, oorvloedig.
bounty, mild(dadig)heid; gawe, weldaad; handgeld; premie.
bouquet, ruiker, bos; geur, bouquet.
bourn(e), grens, eindpaal, landpaal.
bourse, beurs, geldmark.
bout, pot(jie), beurt, rondjie.
bovine, osagtig, beeste- . . . ; vadsig, bot.
bovril, vleesekstrak, bovril.
bow, v. buig; laat buig; (sig) onderwerp; – **down,** neerdruk; neerbuig.
bow, n. buiging.
bow, n. boog; strykstok; strik, strikdas.
bow, v. stryk (met die strykstok).
bow, n. boeg.
bowels, ingewande; binneste, hart.
bower, somerhuisie; lushof; vrouevertrek.
bower(-anchor), boeganker.
bowl, n. kom, bak; beker; bole; pypkop.
bowl, n. rolbal; –**s,** rolbalspel.
bowl, v. rol, boul, balgooi; rol; – **out, uitboul;** – **down, omboul;** – **over,** onderstebo slaan.
bow-legged, hoepelbeen.
bowler, bouler; rolbalspeler.
bowler, hardebolkeiltjie, dophoedjie.
bowline, boeglyn.
bowling-club, rolbalklub.
bowling-crease, boulstreep.
bowling-green, rol(bal)baan.
bowman, boogskutter.
bow-saw, spansaag.
bow-sprit, boegspriet.
bow-string, boogsnaar, boogpees.
bow-window, (ronde) erker, kom-venster.
bowyer, boogmaker, boogverkoper.

box, n. doos, dosie, kis(sie), koffer, (teater)losie; bok, voorkis; afskorting; (kinder)speelkampie; huisie (naaf)bus; (geld)bus; **in the wrong** –, in moeilikheid.
box, n. boksboom; bokshout.
box, v. in 'n kis sit, wegbêre; afskort; – **the compass,** die 32 windrigtinge opsê; omspring, draai.
box, v. klap, opstopper gee; boks.
box, n. klap; – **on the ears,** klap om die ore.
box-calf, chroomkalfsleer.
boxer, vuisvegter, bokser; bokser(hond).
Boxing-day, Tweede Kersdag.
boxing-gloves, bokshandskoene.
boxing-match, bokswedstryd.
box-office, kaartjieskantoor; kas, loket.
box-tree, boksboom.
boy, jongetjie, knaap, seun; kêrel; **old** –, ou kêrel, jong.
boycott, boikot.
boyhood, jongensjare, kindsdae.
boyish, jongensagtig.
bra, buustelyfie, brassière.
brace, n. koppeling, klamp; koppel, paar; stut; omslag; bras; –**s,** kruisbande; – **and bits,** omslag en bore.
brace, v. vasmaak; versterk; **bracing air,** opwekkende lug; **to** – **yourself up,** jou inspan, jou regruk.
bracelet, armband; handboei.
bracken, varing.
bracket, n. rak(kie); klamp, arm, skraag; hakie; **income** –, inkomstegroep.
bracket, v. saamvoeg; tussen hakies sit.
brackish, brak, brakkerig.
bract, skutblaartjie.
brad, kleinkop-spykertjie; skoenspykertjie.
bradawl, els.
brag, v. grootpraat, bluf, windmaak.
brag, n. grootpraat, windmakery.
braggart, grootprater, windmaker.
braid, n. vlegsel; koord, omboorsel.
braid, v. vleg; omboor.
braille, braille-skrif, blindeskrif.
brain, n. brein, harsings; verstand.
brain-fag, oorspanning.
brain-wave, ingewing, blink gedagte.
brainy, slim, knap.
braise, smoor.
brake, ruigte, kreupelhout; varings.
brake, rem, briek.
brake, vlasbraak, vlasbreker; eg.
brake-lining, remvoering.
brake-lever, remhefboom.
bramble, braambos.
bran, semels.
branch, n. tak, vertakking; syrivier; sypa d, ens. bykantoor; vak, afdeling.
branch, v. vertak; – **off,** afdraai, vertak; – **out,** vertak, takke skiet.
brand, n. brandende hout; brandmerk; merk, soort, klas, kwaliteit; brand, roes; swaard
brand, v. brandmerk; inbrand, uitbrand; inprent; skandvlek.
brandish, swaai, slinger.
brand-new, splinternuut.
brandy, brandewyn.
brass, (geel)koper; geld, pitte, onbeskaamdheid, astrantheid.
brass-band, blaaskorps, benning.
brass-foil, klatergoud.
brass-works, kopergietery.
brat, snuiter, bengel, skreeuerd.
bravado, snoewery; uittarting, bravado.

brave 430 **brighten**

brave, a. dapper, moedig, onverskrokke; – **show**, mooi vertoning.
brave, n. krygsheld, dappere.
brave, v. trotseer, uitdaag; – **it out**, nie kopgee nie.
bravery, moed, dapperheid; opskik.
bravo, n. gehuurde moordenaar, bravo.
bravo, interj. mooi so!, bravo!
brawl, v. rusie maak, twis; bruis.
brawl, n. rusie, twis, relletjie.
brawn, spier; sult.
brawny, gespier(d).
bray, v. & n. runnik, balk; skree.
bray, v. (in 'n vysel) stamp, fynstamp.
braze, verbrons.
braze, soldeer.
brazen, koper- . . ., brons- . . . ; onbeskaamd, brutaal.
brazen, v. brutaal maak; – **out**, astrant hou, brutaal wees.
brazen-faced, astrant, onbeskaamd.
brazier, kopergieter, kopersmid.
brazier, konfoor.
breach, breking; breuk; deurbraak, verbreking, oortreding; verwydering, rusie; bres, gat; – **of faith**, troubreuk; – **of the peace**, rusverstoring, vredebreuk; – **of promise**, verbreking van (trou)belofte.
bread, brood; – **and butter**, botter en brood; – **of affliction**, brood der verdrukking; **better half a loaf, than no –**, beter 'n halwe eier as 'n leë dop; **quarrel with one's – and butter**, in jou eie lig staan.
breadfruit-tree, broodboom, baobab.
bread-stuffs, graan.
breadth, breedte, wydte; breë blik.
breadthways, -wise, in die breedte.
break, v. breek, aanbreek, afbreek, verbreek, stukkend breek; kleinmaak; – **on the wheel**, radbraak; – **ground**, aanvang, aanvoor; – **a journey**, 'n reis onderbreek; – **silence**, die stilte verbreek; – **news**, tyding meedeel; – **a bank**, 'n bank laat spring; – **a blow**, 'n slag opvang *of* versag; – **a horse**, 'n perd leer, 'n perd touwysmaak; – **a rebellion**, in opstand onderdruk *of* demp; – **a law**, 'n wet oortree; **weather –s**, weer verander; **ball –s**, bal swenk *of* draai; – **oneself of**, iets afleer, afwen; – **away**, losbreek, hande uitruk; afbrokkel; – **down**, afbreek, strand, bly staan, bly steek; in duie val; – **forth**, uitbars, lostrek; – **in**, inbreek, mak maak; – **into a house**, inbreek; – **off**, afbreek; uitmaak; – **out**, uitbreek; ontvlug; losbars; – **through**, deurbreek, deurbars; – **up**, opbreek, uitmekaar gaan, schools – **up**, skole sluit; – **with someone**, die vriendskap met iemand breek.
break, n. breuk; onderbreking, pouse; serie (in biljart); – **of day**, dagbreek.
breakage, (die) breek, brekasie; slytasie.
breakdown, instorting; vertraging, oponthoud, ongeluk; – **gang**, herstelspan; – **train**, hulptrein; – **truck**, noodwa, wegsleepwa.
breaker, brander.
breakfast, ontbyt, agtuur.
breakneck, halsbrekend, (lewens)gevaarlik; – **pace**, woeste *of* rasende vaart.
break-through, deurbraak.
break-up, splitsing; verval; sluiting.
breakwater, hawehoof, seehoof.
breast, n. bors; skoot; gemoed, hart; gewete; **make a clean –**, opbieg.
breast, v. braveer, die hoof bied aan.
breast-high, tot aan die bors.
breast-stroke, borsslag.

breath, asem (adem); luggie, windjie; woord; oomblik; **catch, hold –**, asem inhou; **take –**, asemhaal, rus; **out of –**, uit-asem.
breathe, asemhaal; laat blaas; – **one's last (breath)**, laaste adem uitblaas, die gees gee; – **again**, weer asemskep.
breathless, ademloos, ingespanne; uit-asem; lewensloos.
breech, n. agterste; agterstel (van 'n kanon); –**es**, broek.
breech, v. pakgee; broek aantrek.
breeching, pak slae; broek (van 'n tuig); kanontou.
breech-loader, agterlaaier.
breech-loading, agterlaaier- . . .
breed, v. verwerk, teel, fok, baar, kweek; uitbroei, voortbring, veroorsaak; oplei, opvoed.
breed, n. ras, soort, aanteel.
breeder, verwekker, fokker, kweker, boer; oorsaak; opleier.
breeding, opvoeding, beskawing.
breeze, bries; rusietjie, standjie.
breeze, perdevlieg.
breezy, winderig; lewendig.
breve, dubbele noot.
brevet, brevet, diploma.
breviary, brevier.
brevity, kortheid; beknoptheid.
brew, v. brou, meng; – **mischief**, kwaad stig.
brew, n. brousel, mengsel.
brewery, brouery.
briar, brier, wilderoos; doringstruik; heidepyp.
bribe, n. omkoopgeld, omkoopprys.
bribe, v. omkoop.
bribery, omkopery.
bric-a-brac, snuisterye.
brick, n. baksteen; blok; gawe kêrel, doring.
brick, v. messel; – **up**, toemessel.
brickbat, stuk baksteen.
brick-kiln, steenoond.
brick-layer, messelaar.
brickmaker, steenbakker.
brickwork, messelwerk.
bridal, a. trou- . . ., bruids- . . .
bridal, n. bruilof, troufees.
bride, bruid.
bridegroom, bruidegom.
bridesmaid, strooimeisie, bruidsmeisie.
bridge, n. brug; vioolkam; rug (van die neus).
bridge, v. oorbrug; 'n brug lê (oor).
bridge, n. brug (kaartspel).
bridge, v. brugspeel.
bridge-head, brug(ge)hoof.
bridle, n. toom, teuel; beteu(g)eling.
bridle, v. toom aansit, optoom; beteuel, breidel; – (**up**), kop in die nek gooi; vuurvat.
bridle-path, rypad, voetpad.
bridle-rein, toomteuel.
brief, a. kort; beknop.
brief, n. saakbrief, opdrag; instruksie; akte; **hold a – for**, as verdediger optree van; –**s**, knapbroekie.
brief, v. saamvat; as advokaat aanstel.
brief-case, portefeulje.
briefless, sonder praktyk.
brier, briar, wilderoos; doringstruik; heidepyp.
brig, brik.
brigade, brigade; afdeling.
brigadier, brigadegeneraal.
brigand, (struik)rower.
brigandage, struikrowery.
brigantine, brigantyn.
bright, helder, duidelik; lewendig; knap; opgeruimd.
brighten, verhelder, opklaar; opvrolik.

brightness, helderheid; vlugheid; opgeruimdheid.
brilliancy, skittering, glans; briljantheid.
brilliant, a. skitterend; briljant.
brilliant, n. briljant, geslypte diamant.
brim, n. rand, boord, kant.
brim, v. volskink; boorde(nste)vol wees.
brimful, boorde(nste)vol.
brimstone, swael (swawel), sulfer.
brindle(d), (bruin)gestreep.
brine, n. soutwater, pekel(water).
brine, v. pekel.
bring, bring, saambring, meebring, veroorsaak; – **home to**, aan die deur lê; oortuig; – **to pass**, tot stand bring; – **about**, veroorsaak; uitvoer; – **back**, terugbring; herinner; – **down**, afbring; neerskiet; – **down the house**, die gehoor verower, algemene byval vind; – **forth**, voortbring, te voorskyn bring; – **forward**, oordra, transporteer; voortbring; indien; – **in**, inbring; opbring; – **in a verdict**, uitspraak gee; – **off**, wegbring; red; uitvoer; – **on**, teweegbring; te voorskyn bring; – **out**, uitbring; uitdruk; uitgee, publiseer; in geselskap bring; – **over**, oorbring; oorhaal, bekeer; – **round**, omhaal, bybring; meebring; – **through**, deurhaal; – **to**, bybring; tot stilstand bring; – **under**, onderwerp; – **up**, opbring; tot anker bring; tot stilstand kom, inhou; – **up the rear**, die agterhoede vorm.
bringer, bringer (brenger).
brink, rand, kantjie.
briny, a. sout, pekel.
briny, n. die seewater.
brisk, a. lewendig, wakker, monter.
brisk, v. rondwoel, beweeg; – **up**, lewendig maak, opwek.
brisket, bors(vleis), borsstuk.
bristle, n. steekhaar, (borsel)haar.
bristle, v. stekelig maak; stekelig word; – **up**, vuurvat, opstuif; – **with**, wemel van.
Britain, **Britannia**, Brittanje.
Britannic, **British**, **Brits**, Brittanies.
Britisher, **Briton**, Brit.
brittle, bros.
broach, n. split; boor.
broach, v. aanbreek, (vat) oopslaan; aanroer.
broad, breed, wyd, ruim; liberaal; – **daylight**, volle daglig; helder oordag, klaarligte dag; – **facts**, hooffeite; – **hint**, duidelike wenk; **as – as it is long**, so lank as dit breed is, om die ewe.
broad-brimmed, breërand- . . .
broad-cast, a. & adv. wyd en syd.
broad-cast, v. uitsaai; uitbasuin.
broad-cloth, (swart)laken.
broaden, verwyd, verbreed; rek.
broadly, breed; naasteby; duidelik, reguit.
broadness, breedheid, grofheid, platheid.
broadside, volle laag.
broadsword, slagswaard.
brocade, brokaat, goudlaken.
brocaded, brokaat- . . ., goudlakens.
broccoli, spruitkool.
brochure, brosjure.
brock, dassie; stinkerd.
brogue, (soort) velskoen, „brogue"; Ierse aksent.
broil, n. rusie, lawaai, twis.
broil, v. braai, rooster; bak, blaker, brand; –**ing hot**, skroeiend warm.
broke, p.p. gebreek; platsak, bankrot.
broken, stukkend, gebroke.
broken-down, gebroke; ongesteld, sieklik; terneergeslae; gestrand.
broken-hearted, diepbedroef, terneergeslae.
brokenly, stukkie vir stukkie, onsamehangend.

broken-winded, uitasem, flou.
broker, makelaar; tussenhandelaar, agent.
brokerage, makelary, (makelaars)provisie.
broking, makelary.
bromide, bromied, (bromide).
bronchial, bronchiaal, van die lugpyptakke.
bronchitis, brongitis.
bronco, bronco.
bronco-buster, perdetemmer.
brontosaurus, brontosourus.
bronze, n. brons; bronsbeeld; bronskleur.
bronze, a. brons- . . . , bronskleurig.
bronze, v. verbrons, bronskleurig maak; verbruin, verbrand.
brooch, borsspeld.
brood, n. broeisel; gebroed, gespuis.
brood, v. broei, uitbroei; peins.
broody, broeis.
brook, n. spruit, beek.
brook, v. verdra, veel, gedoog.
broom, brem; besembos; besem.
broomstick, besemstok, besemsteel.
broth, sop, vleesnat.
brothel, bordeel.
brother, broer, boet(ie); broeder, gelyke; **–s**, broers . . . -genote; **brethren**, broeders; – **in arms**, wapenbroe(de)r.
brotherhood, broederskap.
brother-in-law, swaer, skoonbroer.
brotherly, broederlik.
brow, winkbrou; voorkop; rand, kruin.
browbeat, bars aanspreek, oordonder.
brown, a. bruin; donker; – **paper**, pakpapier; **in a – study**, diep in gedagte; – **hyena**, strandwolf, strandjut.
brown, n. die bruin, bruin kleur.
brown, v. bruineer; bruin word; –**ed off**, vies, buikvol.
brownie, kaboutertjie, aardmannetjie.
browse, n. jong lote, toppe; takvoer.
browse, v. knabbel; graas, wei, grasduin.
bruise, n. kneus(plek), stampplek.
bruise, v. kneus, indeuk; fynmaak.
brumby, ongetemde perd.
brunette, brunet, swartjie.
brunt, skok, ergste aanval; **bear the –**, die spit afbyt.
brush, n. borsel, kwas; besem; skermutseling.
brush, v. langes stryk, langes skuur; (af)borsel afvee(g); – **aside**, opsy stoot, verbygaan; – **away**, wegvee(g); geen notisie van neem nie; – **by**, rakelings by verbygaan; – **down**, afborsel; – **off**, afvee(g), wegvee(g); – **over**, langes stryk; oorverf; – **up**, opborsel; opfris.
brushwood, bossies, kreupelhout, ruigte.
brushy, stekerig, ruig.
brusque, kortaf; bruusk.
brutal, dierlik; onmenslik.
brutalize, verdierlik; ontaard.
brute, a. bruut, dierlik, onmenslik.
brute, n. (on)dier, wreedaard, onmens.
bryony, wilde-wingerd.
bubble, n. (water)blaas, lugbel, seepbel; – **and squeak**, koolbredie, hutspot; – **car**, doppiemotor.
bubble, v. borrel, kook; – **over with laughter**, uitbars van die lag.
bubbly-jock, kalkoenmannetjie.
bubonic, buile- . . . ; – **plague**, builepes.
buccaneer, boekanier, seerower.
buck, n. (wilde) bokram, mannetjie; wild; fat, modegek; **to pass the –**, om die verantwoordelikheid te ontduik.
buck, v. bokspring; vassteek, steeks wees; – **up**, gou maak; moed vat.

**buck-ashes, loogas.
bucked, opgemonter, uitgelate, gevlei.
bucket, emmer; bak; peitskoker, sweepkoker; kick the –, bokveld toe gaan.
bucket, v. vinnig ry, ja.
bucket-pump, bakkiespomp.
buckish, fatterig, hanerig.
buck-jump, bokspring.
buckle, n. gespe(r).
buckle, v. vasgespe(r); aangord; krombuig; omkrul; – to, flink aanpak, weglê (aan).
buckler, beukelaar, skild.
buckram, styflinne, gewasdoek.
buck-shot, bokhael, lopers.
buckskin, boksvel, bokskyn.
buck-waggon, bokwa.
buck-wheat, boekweit (bokwiet).
bucolic, herderlik, landelik.
bud, n. bot, knop, kiem; in –, in die knop; nip in the –, in die kiem smoor.
bud, v. bot, uitloop; ontluik; ent.
Budapest, Boedapest.
Buddha, Boeddha.
Buddhism, Boeddhisme.
budge, verroer, beweeg.
budget, n. sak, begroting.
budget, v. uittrek (op die begroting), voorsiening maak, begroot; – for, (be)raam, reken op.
budgerigar, grasparkiet.
buff, n. buffelleer; geel beesleer.
buff, a. dofgeel, seemkleurig.
buffalo, buffel.
buffer, stootkussing, stampveer; tussenstaat, buffer.
buffet, v. slaan, stamp, worstel met.
buffet, n. slag, stamp, stoot, hou.
buffet, n. buffet, (skink)toonbank.
buffoon, harlekyn, spotter.
buffoonery, gekskeerdery, grappemakery.
bug, weeluis; wandluis; kewer.
bugaboo, paaiboelie; gogga.
bugbear, paaiboelie; gogga.
buggy, bokkie.
bugle, beuel, trompet(ter).
bugler, trompetblaser.
build, v. bou, oprig, maak; – in, inbou, toebou; – (up)on, bou op; grond op, vertrou op; – up, opbou, tot stand bring.
build, n. bou; liggaamsbou, vorm.
builder, bouer, boumeester, kontrakteur.
building, gebou, bouery; – trade, bouvak; – plot, bouperseel, erf.
bulb, bol; electric –, gloeilamp.
bulbous, bolagtig; – plant, bolgewas, bolplant.
bulge, n. knop; buik (van 'n vat, ens.).
bulge, v. uitstaan, opswel, uitpeul, uitsit; laat uitstaan.
bulk, n. vrag, lading; omvang, grootte; massa; meerderheid; in –, by die groot maat.
bulk, v. vertoon, lyk; to – large, uitstaan, groot vertoon.
bulkhead, beskot, afskutting, afskorting.
bulky, groot, omvangryk, lywig, dik.
bull, n. bul, mannetjie; stier (sterreb.); spekulant op prysverhoging; kol.
bull, v. op prysverhoging spekuleer.
bull, n. (pouslike) bul.
bull, n. (Irish –), ,,bull'' lagwekkende teenstrydigheid.
bull-calf, bulkalf; stommerik.
bull-dog, bulhond.
bulldoze, gelyk stoot; oorrompel.
bulldozer, stootskraper.
bullet, koeël.
bulletin, bulletin, rapport.

bullet-proof, koeëlvry.
bullfight, stiergeveg.
bullfinch, bloedvink, rooivink.
bullfrog, brulpadda.
bullion, staafgoud, staafsilwer, ongemunte goud of silwer.
bullock, os.
bull's eye, lensvormige glas; handlantern; toorballetjies (soort lekkers); kol, kolskoot.
bully, n. ,,boelie'', baasspeler, bullebak.
bully, a. piekfyn, eersteklas, prima.
bully, v. baasspeel oor; afknou.
bully-beef, blikkiesvleis, boeliebief.
bulrush, biesie, matjiesgoed, papkuil.
bulwark, bolwerk, verskansing, skans.
bum, n. agterent; boemelaar; leegloper; suiper.
bum, v. klaploop; suip.
bumble, -bee, hommel.
bump, v. stamp, stoot; – off, vermoor.
bump, n. stamp, slag; knop, kneusplek; bult, knobbel.
bumper, n. stamper, stoter; opslagbal.
bumper, a. boorde vol glas (beker); – crop, buitengewoon ryk oes.
bumpkin, lomperd, skimmelbrood.
bumptious, verwaand, aanstellerig.
bumpy, stamperig, hobbelrig.
bun, bolletjie.
bunch, n. bos(sie), tros; bondel; klomp.
bunch, v. (in) bossies maak; tros, koek.
bundle, n. bondel, pak, hoop, gerf, rol.
bundle, v. saambind, saampak; op 'n hoop smyt, – out, uitboender.
bung, n. sponning, prop, tap; leuen.
bung, v. toestop, toekurk; (oë) toeslaan.
bungalow, buitehuis(ie), huthuis; seaside – strandhuis.
bungle, knoei, konkel, broddel; verknoei.
bungler, knoeier, broddelaar.
bunion, eeltswelsel, eeltsweer.
bunk, n. kooi, slaapbank.
bunk, v. klas versuim; dros, stokkiesdraai; – off, laat trap, die plaat poets; – the history class, van die geskiedenisklas dros.
bunker, n. bunker.
bunkum, onsin, bogpraatjies.
bunny, konyntjie.
bunt, buik.
bunting, vlagdoek, vlae.
buoy, n. seeboei, dryfton; life –, reddingsboei.
buoy, v. in; – up, ophou, drywende hou; opbeur.
buoyancy, dryfkrag; veerkrag(tigheid).
buoyant, drywend; veerkragtig; opgeruimd, lughartig; lewendig.
bur, burr, klits(gras); saadjie; kwas; (giet)naat; ruimyster; baard (van metaal).
burbot, barbot.
burden, n. las, vrag; inhoud; koor, refrein; beast of –, lasdier; – of proof, bewyslas.
burden, v. belas, belaai, bevrag.
burdensome, drukkend, swaar.
burdock, klitsgras.
bureau, skryftafel; kantoor; buro.
bureaucracy, amptenaredom; burokrasie.
bureaucrat, burokraat.
bureaucratic, burokraties.
burg, dorp, stad.
burgess, (stemgeregtigde) burger.
burglar, inbreker.
burglary, inbraak; huisbraak.
burgle, inbreek.
burgomaster, burgemeester.
burgundy, boergonje(wyn), (bourgogne)
burial, begrafnis.
burial-place, begraafplaas; kerkhof.

burial-service, lykdiens.
burin, graveernaald.
burlesque, a. bespottend; burlesk.
burlesque, n. bespotting; burlesk, grappigheid.
burlesque, v. parodieer, bespotlik voorstel.
burly, vors, groot, swaarlywig.
burn, v. brand, verbrand; aanbrand; bak; warm wees (ook in kinderspeletjies); gloei; sterk verlang; **ears** –, ore tuit; – **away, out**, verbrand, uitbrand; – **up**, verbrand, opbrand; – **down**, verbrand, afbrand; – **low**, flou brand; – **one's boats**, die terugtog onmoontlik maak.
burn, n. brandplek, brandwond.
burn, n. stroompie, spruitjie.
burner, brander, kop (van lamp, ens.).
burnish, polys, poets, vryf, skuur.
burp, wind opbreek.
burr, sien **bur**.
burr, n. newelkring; slypsteen; (die) bry.
burr, v. bry; onduidelik praat.
burro, (pak)donkie.
burrow, n. gat, hol, lêplek.
burrow, v. grawe, gat grawe; omvroetel, in 'n gat woon.
bursar, penningmeester; beurshouer.
bursary, (studie)beurs.
burst, v. bars; laat bars, oopbreek; **river** –s **its banks**, rivier oorstroom sy walle; **war, disease** –s **out**, oorlog, siekte breek uit; – **in**(to), binnestorm; oopbreek, indruk, in die rede val; –s **out**, uitbars, losbars, losbreek; – **up**, uitmekaar bars, ontplof, spring; bankrot speel; – **upon**, oorval, oorrompel; – **with**, bars van; **bud** –s, knop ontluik; **cloud** –s, wolk breek; **boil** –s, sweer breek oop.
burst, n. bars, skeur; uitbarsting, losbarsting; kragtige inspanning, spurt.
burthen, sien **burden**.
bury, begrawe; bedek; vergeet.
burying-place, begraafplaas.
bus, n. bus; **miss the** –, die bus mis; 'n kans laat glip; te laat kom; bedroë uitkom.
bus, v. met die bus gaan, busry.
busby, husare-mus.
bush, n. bos(sie), struik(e); bosveld; **beat about the** –, uitvlugte soek, om iets heen praat.
bush, n. (naaf)bus.
bush, v. 'n bus insit.
bushbuck, bosbok.
bushel, skepel, boesel.
bushman, (Australiese) bosvelder.
Bushman, Boesman.
bushranger, struikrower; boswagter.
bush-telegraph, bostelegraaf.
Bushveld, Bosveld.
business, besigheid; drukte; plig; saak, bedryf, beroep, handel; **to mean** –, in erns wees; sake wil doen; **mind your own** –, bemoei jou met jou eie sake; **send about his** –, in die pad steek; op sy plek sit; **you have no** – **to**, jy het geen reg nie om; **make it one's** –, sorg daarvoor, aandag aan gee.
business-hours, kantoorure, winkelure.
business-like, saaklik, saakkundig; pront.
business man, sakeman.
buskin, broos, toneellaars; tragedie.
bust, borsbeeld; bors.
bust, sien **burst**, n.
bustard, wilde pou.
bustle, v. woel, in die weer wees, werskaf; opdruk, aanja, haastig maak; – **about**, in die weer wees.
bustle, n. drukte, gewoel, bedrywigheid.
busy, a. besig, bedrywig, in die weer; beset; bemoeisiek; – **writing**, aan die skrywe.

busy, v. (sig) besig hou, (sig) bemoei.
busybody, bemoeial; kwaadstoker.
but, conj. maar, egter, dog.
but, prep. behalwe, buite(n); – **for**, as dit nie was dat *of* om; **the last** – **one**, op een na die laaste.
but, adv. maar, slegs.
but, n. maar; **but me no** –s, bespaar my jou „maar".
butane, butaan.
butcher, slagter; wreedaard.
butcher, v. slag; 'n slagting aanrig.
butcher-bird, janfiskaal, laksman
butchery, slagtery; slagting.
butler, bottelier, huiskneg.
butlery, provisiekamer, spens.
butt, n. skyf, mikpunt.
butt, n. kolf, agterent; stomp(ie).
butt, n. vat, pyp.
butt, v. stamp, stoot.
butte, spitskop.
butter, n. botter; vleiery, stroop.
butter, v. (botter op) smeer; heuning om die mond smeer.
butter-boat, souskommetjie, souspotjie.
buttercup, botterblom; aandblom.
butter-dish, botterpotjie.
butter-fingered, met botter aan die vingers, onhandig, lomp.
butterfly, skoe(n)lapper, vlinder.
buttermilk, karringmelk.
butter-muslin, kaasdoek.
butter-scotch, tameletjie.
buttery, spens, provisiekamer.
buttock, boud, agterste.
button, n. knoop; knop; dop(pie); –s, livreikneg.
button, v. (vas)knoop, toeknoop.
buttonhole, n. knoopsgat; ruiker.
buttonhole, v. aanklamp, ophou.
buttonhook, knoophakie.
buttress, n. stut(muur); steunpilaar.
buttress, v. steun, stut.
buxom, flink, mooi.
buy, koop; omkoop; – **in**, inkoop, terugkoop; – **off**, afkoop, loskoop; – **over**, omkoop; – **a pig in a poke**, 'n kat in die sak koop.
buzz, v. gons; – **off!**, trap! lastig val *(van vliegtuie)*.
buzz, n. gegons; gefluister; gewoel.
buzzard, (muis)valk.
buzz-bike, kragfiets, bromfiets.
buzz-saw, sirkelsaag.
by, prep. by; met; deur; op; na; volgens; per; – **day**, bedags, oordag; – **the nearest road**, langes *of* met die kortste pad; – **your leave**, met jou verlof *of* permissie; – **train**, met die trein; **written** –, geskrewe deur; – **land and sea**, op (die) land en op (die) see; – **the way**, – **the** –, tussen hakies, van die os op die esel; – **oneself**, alleen, op jou eie; **known** – **the name of**, bekend onder die naam (van); – **all means, seker**; – **no means**, volstrek nie; – **way of a joke**, by wyse van 'n grap; **cautious** – **nature**, versigtig van natuur; – **chance**, by toeval; – **next week**, teen aanstaande week; – **now**, teen hierdie tyd; **judge** – **appearances**, na die uiterlik(e) oordeel; **day** – **day**, dag vir dag; – **degrees**, trapsgewyse; – **heart**, van buite, uit die kop; – **cheque**, per tjek, met 'n tjek; – **rail**, per spoor.
by, adv. verby; opsy; **pass, go** –, verbygaan; **lay, put, set** –, opsy sit, opbewaar; – **and** –, strakkies, aanstons.
by(e), ondergeskik, onder- . . . , sydelings; –

effects, indirekte (sydelingse) gevolge; —election, tussenverkiesing.
bye, n. loslopie; to draw a –, vry loot.
bye-bye, tot siens!, dag!
bygone, n. wat verby is, 'n gedane saak; let –s be –s, moenie ou koeie uit die sloot grawe nie.
bygone, a. uitgesterf; verby, vervloë.
by(e)-law, regulasie, verordening.
bypass, n. padverlegging.
bypass, v. ompad om 'n dorp (plek) ry; 'n dorp (plek) verbyry.

bypath, sypad, dowwe paadjie.
byplay, stil spel; syspel.
by-product, byproduk, afvalproduk.
byre, koeistal.
by-road, ompad; dowwe paadjie.
bystander, toeskouer.
bystreet, agterstraatjie, systraat.
by-way, dowwe paadjie; kortpaadjie; onbekende terrein.
byword, spreekwoord; skimpnaam.
by-work, bywerk.

C

cab, huurrytuig, „keb".
cabal, kabaal, geheime kliek; politieke samespanning.
cabbage, kool, kopkool.
cabbage-lettuce, k(r)opslaai.
cab(b)ala, kabbala, geheime leer.
cabbalistic, kabbalisties, geheim.
cabby, (huur)koetsier.
cabin, n. kajuit, hut; hok.
cabin-boy, kajuitsjonge.
cabined, opgesluit, vasgekeer, gehok.
cabinet, kabinet; kantoor(tjie), hokkie; kas; ministerraad, ministerie.
cabinet-council, kabinetsraad, ministerraad.
cabinet-maker, skrynwerker.
cable, n. kabel.
cable, v. kabel, telegrafeer.
cablegram, kabel(gram).
cabman, (huur)koetsier.
caboodle, boel, spul, sous, rommel.
caboose, skeepskombuis; kondukteurswa.
cabriolet, kabriolet.
cab-stand, staanplek vir huurrytuie.
cache, n. wegsteekplek; wegsteekgoed.
cache, v. wegsteek.
cackle, v. kekkel; babbel, snater.
cackle, n. gekekkel; gebabbel, gesnater.
cacophonous, onwelluidend.
cacophony, wanklank, onwelluidendheid.
cactus, kaktus; **jointed** –, litjieskaktus; **spineless** –, kaalbladkaktus.
cad, ploert, skobbejak.
cadaverous, kadaweragtig; lykkleurig, doodskleur-...
caddie, (gholf)joggie.
caddish, gemeen, laag, ploerterig.
caddy, teebus.
cadence, kadans; ritme, maat, intonasie.
cadet, jonger seun; kadet.
cadge, bedel, klaploop; smous.
cadger, bondeldraer, smous; klaploper.
cadmium, kadmium.
cadre, kader; raam(werk).
caducous, swak, verbygaand; afvallend.
caecum, blindederm.
caesura, cesuur, ruspunt, verssnee.
café, kafee, koffiehuis.
cafeteria, kafeteria.
caffeine, kafeïen (kafeïne).
caftan, kaftan, ondertuniek.
cage, n. kooi, koutjie; hok; hysbak.
cage, v. in 'n koutjie (hok) sit, opsluit.
cagey, versigtig, omsigtig.
Cain, Kain; **raise** –, woes te kere gaan.
cairn, baken, klipstapel.
cairngorm, cairngorm, rooktopaas.
Cairo, Kaïro.
caisson, ammunisiewa, -kis; fondamentkas; dryfhek; caisson.
caitiff, ellendeling, lafaard.
cajole, vlei, flikflooi, omkonkel.
cajolery, vleiery, geflikflooi, konkelary.
cake, n. koek, gebak; broodjie; **that takes the** –!, dit is die toppunt!
cake, v. Koek; koek maak.
cakewalk, Negerdans, Kafferstap.
calabash, kalbas.
calamint, kattekruid.
calamitous, ongelukkig, rampspoedig.
calamity, onheil, ramp; rampspoed.
calcareous, kalkhoudend, kalk-...
calceolaria, mussie, pantoffelblom, calceolaria.
calciferous, kalkhoudend.
calcify, verkalk; tot kalk maak.
calcinate, verkalk.

calcine, verkalk; uitdroog; verbrand.
calcium, kalsium.
calculable, berekenbaar.
calculate, (be)reken, uitreken, (*Amer.*) dink, glo; – **upon**, reken op; –**d**, berekend; koelbloedig, voorbedag; –**d for, to**, bereken(d) om.
calculation, (be)rekening, kalkulasie.
calculator, rekenaar; rekenmasjien; rekentafel; **lightning** –, snelrekenaar.
calculus, graweel(steen); rekenmetode; **differential** –, differensiaalrekening; **integral** –, integraalrekening.
calendar, kalender, almanak; lys, rol.
calender, n. (mangel)pers, kalander.
calender, v. mangel, pers, kalander.
calends, calendae; **on the Greek** –, in die jaar nul, ad calendas Graecas.
calendula, gousblom.
calenture, ylende koors.
calf, n. kalf; kuit; snuiter.
calf-bound, in kalfsleer gebonde.
calf's, calves-foot, kalfspootjies; – **jelly**, sult, kalfsjelei.
calibre, kaliber, deursnee; gehalte.
calibrate, kalibreer.
calico, kaliko, katoen.
Californian, Kalifornies; Kaliforniër.
cal(l)iper, krom passer.
caliph, kalief.
caliphate, kalifaat.
calk, n. haak, klou (van 'n hoefyster).
calk, v. kalkeer, deurtrek, natrek.
call, v. roep, be-, byeen-, in-, op-, toeroep; uitlees; noem, heet; besoek aflê, aangaan; opbel; (troef) maak; – **attention to**, aandag vestig op; – **after**, naroep; heet (noem) na; – **at**, aangaan; – **back**, terugroep; herroep; –, **down**, afroep; afsmeek; – **for**, roep om; bestel; vereis; kom haal; – **forth**, te voorskyn roep; uitlok, veroorsaak; – **in**, oproep (geld); inroep (dokter); aanloop; – **in question**, in twyfel trek; – **into being**, in die lewe roep; verwek; – **off**, wegroep; – **names**, uitskel; – **on**, besoek, 'n beroep doen op; – **out**, uitroep; kommandeer (troepe), oproep; uitdaag; – **over**, aflees, uitlees; – **round**, aanloop; – **to**, toeroep, roep na; – **to account**, tot verantwoording roep; – **to mind**, (sig) herinner; – **up**, oproep; voor die gees roep; opbel; – **upon**, besoek; 'n beroep doen op; **feel –ed upon**, (sig) geroepe voel; – **a meeting**, 'n vergadering byeenroep; – **spade a spade**, 'n kind by sy naam noem; I – **that mean**, ek noem dit gemeen; – **a halt**, halt roep.
call, n. roep, geroep; (voël)gefluit; (trompet)sinjaal; (roep)stem; besoek; **no** – **to**, geen aanleiding tot (om); **at, within** –, beskikbaar, byderhand; **be at one's beck and** –, op iemand se wenke klaar staan; **pay a** –, 'n besoek bring.
caller, roeper; besoeker.
call-girl, foonsnol.
calligraphy, kalligrafie, skryfkuns.
calling, geroep; beroep; roeping.
cal(l)iper, krom passer.
callisthenics, ritmiese gimnastiek.
call-money, opvorderbare geld.
callosity, dikhuidigheid; eelt.
callous, gevoelloos, verhard; vereelt.
callow, kaal, sonder vere; baar, groen.
calm, n. kalmte, stilte.
calm, a. kalm, stil, bedaard.
calm, v. kalmeer, stilmaak, tot bedaring bring.
calomel, kalomel.

caloric, n. warmte(stof).
caloric, a. kalories, warmte.
calorie, calory, kalorie, warmte-eenheid.
calorimeter, warmtemeter, kaloriemeter.
caltrop, voetangel, klem; sterdissel.
calumet, (Indiaanse) pyp, kalumet.
calumniate, (be)laster, (be)skinder.
calumniator, belasteraar.
calumny, laster(ing), skindertaal.
calve, kalwe; – in, inkalwe.
calves-foot, sien calf's foot.
Calvinist, -ic, Calvinisties.
calx, kalsiumokside.
calyx, (blom)kelk.
cam, kam (aan 'n rat), nok.
camber, welwing, helling.
cambium, kambium, teeltweefsel.
Cambria, Kambrië, Wallis.
cambric, n. kamerdoek, batis.
cambric, a. kamerdoekse.
camel, kameel; it is the last straw that breaks the –'s back, dis die laaste druppel wat die emmer laat oorloop.
cameleer, kameeldrywer, -ryer.
camellia, kamelia, japonika.
camelopard, kameelperd, giraf.
camel's-hair, kameelhaar (kemelhaar).
cameo, kamee.
camera, kamera, kiek-, fotografeertoestel; in –, met geslote deure.
camisole, onderlyfie; kamisool.
camlet, kamelot, kameelhaarstof.
camomile, kamille.
camouflage, n. maskering, camouflage.
camouflage, v. maskeer, kamoufleer.
camp, n. kamp, laer.
camp, v. kamp(eer), laertrek; – out, kampeer.
campaign, n. kampanje, veldtog.
campaign, v. 'n veldtog (mee)maak.
campanile, kloktoring.
camp-bed, veldbed, voubed.
camp-fever, laerkoors.
camp-follower, laernaloper, leërsmous.
camphor, kanfer.
camphorated, kanfer- . . . ; – oil, kanferolie.
camp-meeting, kampdiens.
camp-stool, veldstoel, voustoel.
campus, skoolterrein, universiteitsterrein; die universiteitswêreld.
can, v. kan, in staat wees; mag.
can, n. kan(netjie), blik, kantien.
can, v. inlê, inmaak.
Canadian, Kanadees.
canal, kanaal; buis; groef.
canalize, kanaliseer.
canard, vals gerug, canard.
canary, kanarie; sysie; Kanariese wyn.
canaster, knaster, growwe tabak.
cancel, v. kanselleer; deurhaal; afsê, afskrywe; herroep, intrek; – out, teen mekaar wegval, kanselleer; – an appointment, 'n afspraak afskrywe (afsê).
cancellation, terugtrekking, kansellering.
cancer, kanker; Tropic of C–, Kreefskeerkring.
cancerous, kankeragtig.
cancroid, kreefagtig; kankeragtig.
candelabrum, kandelaber, (arm)kandelaar.
candid, openhartig, eerlik.
candidate, kandidaat; applikant, sollisitant.
candidature, kandidatuur, kandidaatstelling.
candied, versuiker(d); soet; vleiend; blink; – peel, suikerskil, sukade.
candle, kers; she cannot hold a – to her sister, sy kan nie in haar suster se skaduwee staan nie.
candlelight, kerslig.

candle-power, kerskrag.
candlestick, kandelaar, blaker.
candour, openhartigheid, eerlikheid.
candy, n. kandy(suiker), suikerklontjies.
candy, v. in suiker lê; versuiker.
cane, n. riet; bamboes; rottang; matwerk; lat, (wandel)stok, kierie.
cane, v. onder die lat kry; ('n stoel) mat.
cane-bottom, rietmat.
cane-sugar, rietsuiker.
canine, a. honds- . . . ; – tooth, hoektand.
canister, trommel, blik; – shot, skroot.
canker, n. (mond)sweer; hoefseer; kanker, pes, verpestende invloed.
canker, v. kanker, inkanker; verpes.
cankered, verkanker; ingevreet; venynig; verbitter(d).
cankerous, kankeragtig, venynig.
canna, kanna, blomriet.
canned: – music, platemusiek.
cannibal, kannibaal, mensvreter.
cannikin, kannetjie, kantientjie.
cannon, n. kanon; karambool (biljart).
cannon, v. karamboleer, bots.
cannonade, beskieting, kanonnade.
cannon-ball, kanonkoeël.
cannon-fodder, kanonvoer.
cannon-shot, kanonskoot; kanonkoeël.
canny, oulik, slim; versigtig; ca' –, stadig oor die klippe; oulik.
canoe, kano.
canon, kanon, wet, (kerk)reël; domheer, kanunnik; die kanonieke (Bybel)boeke.
cañon, canyon, diep kloof, sloot, canyon.
canonical, kanoniek; kerklik; kerk- . . .
canonicals, priestergewaad.
canonicity, kanonisiteit.
canonize, kanoniseer, heilig verklaar.
canopy, (troon)hemel, gewelf, dak.
cant, n. skuinste; skuinskant; stamp.
cant, v. skuins maak: (om)kantel.
cant, v. sektetaal, jargon; huigeltaal.
cant, v. mooipraatjies verkoop, huigel.
cantaloup, spanspek.
cantankerous, suur, brommig.
cantata, kantate.
canteen, kantien; veldkeuken; veldfles; fabriekswinkel; koskannetjie; verversingslokaal; verversingstoonbank; – of cutlery, tafelsilwerkis.
canter, n. huigelaar.
canter, n. handgalop, kort galoppie, win in a –, fluit-fluit wen.
canter, v. in (op) 'n handgalop loop (ry).
Canterbury-bell, klokkie.
cantharides, spaansvlieg.
canticle, (lof)sang; C–s, Hooglied.
cantilever, skraag, krombalk.
canto, kanto, sang.
canton, n. afdeling, wyk, kanton.
cantonment, soldatekwartiere, barakke.
canvas, seil; (skilder)doek; skildery.
canvass, bespreek, uitpluis; (stemme) werf; pols.
canvasser, (stemme)werwer.
canyon, sien cañon, diep kloof, sloot.
caoutchouc, kaoetsjoek, gomlastiek.
cap, n. pet; mus; baret; doppie; the – fits, die skoen pas; a feather in his –, 'n pluimpie; – and gown, toga en baret.
cap, v. 'n graad toeken; kies vir die eerste (internasionale) span; kroon, opsit troef, oortref; doppie opsit.
capability, bekwaamheid, geskiktheid.
capable, bekwaam; geskik, in staat, kapabel; vatbaar.
capacious, ruim, omvattend.

capacitate   437   **carriage**

capacitate, in staat stel.
capacity, bekwaamheid, vermoë; hoedanigheid, kapasiteit; inhoud, volume; **measure of** –, inhoudsmaat; **in the** – **of**, in die hoedanigheid van.
caparison, uitrusting, mondering.
cape, n. kaap: The Cape, die Kaap, Kaapland.
Cape, a. Kaaps; – **cart**, kapkar.
cape, mantel, kraag.
Cape Colony, Kaapkolonie.
caper, bokspring; **cut a** –, 'n flikker maak.
Cape Town, Kaapstad.
capillary, haarvormig; haarfyn; kapillêr; – **tube**, haarbuisie.
capital, n. kapiteel.
capital, a. hoof-...; kapitaal, uitstekend, eersteklas; – **fund**, hoofsom, kapitaal; – **offence**, halsmisdaad, misdaad waar die doodstraf op staan; – **punishment, sentence**, doodstraf; – **goods**, kapitaalgoedere.
capital, n. kapitaal, hoofsom; hoofstad; hoofletter; **make** – **out of**, munt slaan uit.
capitalism, kapitalisme.
capitalist, kapitalis.
capitalize, kapitaliseer, in geld omsit; benut.
capitally, uitstekend, eersteklas.
capitation, hoofbelasting; – **grant**, hoofdelike toelaag (bydrae).
Capitol, Kapitool; kongresgebou.
capitulate, kapituleer.
capitulation, kapitulasie, voorwaardelike oorgawe; opsomming; voorwaarde, ooreenkoms.
capon, gesnyde haan, kapoen.
caprice, gier, gril, kuur, nuk.
capricious, grillig, wispelturig, vol nukke.
capricorn, steenbok; **Tropic of C**–, Steenbokskeerkring.
capriole, n. kapriol, bokkesprong.
capriole, v. bokspring, kapriolle maak.
capsicum, rissies.
capsize, omslaan, omkantel, kapseis.
capstan, kaapstander.
capsule, doppie; skaaltjie; kapsule.
captain, n. kaptein.
captain, v. aanvoer.
captaincy, kapteinsrang, kapteinskap.
caption, titel; kapsie; arrestasie.
captious, spitsvondig, vitterig, twissiek.
captivate, bekoor, boei, inneem, vang.
captive, a. gevange; – **balloon**, kabelballon.
captive, n. gevangene; **hold, take** –, gevange hou, gevange neem.
captivity, gevangeskap, ballingskap.
captor, vanger, gevangenemer.
capture, n. vangs; gevangeneming; roof; inname; buit, prys.
capture, v. vang, gevange neem; roof, buitmaak; inneem.
Capuchin, Kapusyner(monnik).
car, rytuig, wa, motor(kar), trem(wa).
car(a)bineer, karabinier.
carafe, kraf(fie).
caramel, karamel; gebrande suiker.
carat, karaat.
caravan, karavaan.
caravanserai, karavansera.
caraway, karwy.
carbide, karbied, karbide.
carbine, karabyn, kort geweertjie. buks.
carbolic, n. karbol.
carbolic, a. karbol-...; – **acid**, karbolsuur, karbol; – **oil**, karbololie.
carbon, koolstof; – **dioxide**, kooldioksied, koolsuurgas; – **copy**, deurslag, bloutjie.
carbonaceous, koolstofhoudend.

carbonate, karbonaat.
carbon-copy, deurslag.
carbonic, koolsuur-...; – **acid**, koolsuur.
carbon-paper, deurslaanpapier, koolpapier.
carbuncle, karbonkel.
carburetter, -**or**, karburateur, vergasser.
carcase, carcass, karkas, geraamte.
card, n. kaart; re(i)siesprogram; **it is on the** –**s**, dit is moontlik *of* waarskynlik; **house of** –**s**, kaartehuis; **show one's** –**s**, sy plan openbaar; – **up one's sleeve**, 'n plan agter die hand.
card, n. & v. (wol)kaard, (wol)kam.
cardboard, bordpapier, karton.
card-case, visiteboekie.
cardiac, hart-...; hartkwaal-...
cardigan, wolonderbaadjie.
cardinal, a. kardinaal, vernaamste, hoof-... dieprooi; – **number**, hoofgetal; – **points**, hoofwindstreke.
cardinal, n. kardinaal.
card-sharper, valsspeler.
card-table, speeltafeltjie.
card-trick, kunsie met kaarte.
care, n. sorg; hoede; besorgdheid, ongerustheid; sorgvuldigheid; **take** –, oppas, versigtig wees; – **of**, per adres; **with** –!, versigtig! **take** – **of**, sorg vir; **under my** –, onder my hoede.
care, v. omgee, (sig) bekommer; – **for**, sorg vir; oppas; omgee vir, hou van; liefhê; – **about**, omgee vir; **I don't** –, dit kan my nie skeel nie, dit traak my nie; **for aught I** –, wat my betref; **he didn't** – **to go**, hy het nie lus gehad om te gaan nie.
careen, (laat) oorhel; kantel.
career, n. loopbaan; vaart; – **diplomat**, beroepsdiplomaat.
career, v. snel, vlieg, ja.
care-free, sorgvry, onbesorg.
careful, oppassend, sorgvuldig, versigtig.
careless, sorgeloos, onoplettend, slordig, onverskillig, roekeloos, agterlosig.
caress, n. liefkosing, streling.
caress, v. liefkoos, streel, paai, verwen.
caretaker, oppasser, opsigter.
care-worn, afgetob, vergaan van sorg.
cargo, lading, vrag, karga.
Caribbean, Karibiese Eilande.
caricature, karikatuur, spotprent.
caricaturist, spotprenttekenaar.
caries, beeneter.
carking, drukkend.
carmine, karmyn.
carnage, slagting, bloedbad.
carnal, vleeslik, sin(ne)lik; wêreldlik.
carnation, vleeskleur; ligrooi; angelier.
carnival, karnaval; feesviering.
carnivore, vleiseter.
carnivorous, vleisetend.
carol, n. vreugdelied; Kerslied.
carol, v. vreugdelied(ere) sing; kwinkeleer.
carotid, halsslagaar.
carousal, drinkgelag, boemelparty, fuif.
carouse, drink, suip, boemel, fuif.
carp, n. karper.
carp, v. vit, bedil, brom.
Carpathian, Karpaties; – **Mountains**, die Karpate.
carpenter, timmerman.
carpentry, timmermansambag; timmerwerk.
carpet, n. tapyt, **bring on the** –, op die tapyt bring.
carpet, v. met tapyte belê, bedek.
carpetbag, reissak, tapytsak.
carpetbagger, politieke hanslam.
carpet-dance, danspartytjie.
carpet-knight, saletjonker, salonheld.
carriage, rytuig, (trein)wa; onderstel; vervoer;

carriage-way 438 **catch**

vrag; vervoerkoste; houding; gedrag; – **free**, vragvry; – **paid**, vrag betaal(d); – **forward**, te betaal.
carriage-way, ryweg, -pad, -baan.
carrier, draer; karweier, vragryer; bagasierak; bomrak; draagsak; besteller, bagasiedraer; posduif; **aircraft-carrier**, vliegdekskip; – **wave**, dra(ag)golf.
carrion, aas.
carrot, (geel)wortel; –s, rooi hare.
carry, dra, vervoer; oorhou, oordra; (in)hou, bevat; – **all before one**, alle teenstand oorwin; – **coals to Newcastle**, water in die see dra; – **one's point**, jou doel bereik; – **a motion**, 'n voorstel aanneem; – **weight**, van betekenis wees; – **a fortress**, 'n vesting inneem; – **the day**, die oorwinning behaal; – **conviction**, oortuig; – **away**, wegvoer, -dra, -bring; – **back**, terugvoer, -dra, -bring; – **forward**, vooruit dra; oordra; – **into effect**, ten uitvoer bring; – **off**, wegvoer, wegdra; na die graf sleep; wen; – **on**, voortsit, vooruitbring; aangaan, te keer gaan; – **out**, uitvoer; – **over**, oordra; – **through**, deursnit.
cart, n. kar, voertuig, rytuig; **put the** – **before the horse**, agterstevoor te werk gaan.
cart, v. (met 'n kar) vervoer, ry; – **away**, wegry, wegkarwei.
cartage, vervoer; vrag, karweiloon.
cartel, uitdaging; ooreenkoms; kartel.
carter, voerman, karweier.
Carthaginian, Carthaags; Carthager.
cartilage, kraakbeen.
cart-load, karvrag, hele hoop.
cartoon, ontwerptekening; spotprent; tekenprent.
cartoonist, spotprenttekenaar.
cartridge, patroon; **blank** –, loskruit.
cartwright, wamaker, karmaker.
carve, (voor)sny, vleessny, uitsny; – **one's way**, (sig) 'n weg baan.
carver, (vleis)snyer; beeldsnyer; snymes; vleismes; leuningstoel.
carving-knife, vleismes, grootmes.
caryatid, caryatide.
cascade, watervalletjie; stroom; kaskade.
case, n. geval, saak; omstandigheid; hofsaak; naamval; **in** –, ingeval, **in any** –, in elk geval; **in every** –, in elke (iedere) geval; **in that** –, in daardie geval.
case, n. koffer, trommel, kis, doos; koker, huisie, sak, oortreksel, band; – **history**, gevalbeskrywing.
case, v. inwikkel, oortrek.
case-harden, verhard; verstok maak.
casein, kaseïen (kaseïne); kaasstof.
casemate, kasemat.
casement, raam; venster, draaivenster.
cash, n. kontant(geld); kas, kasgeld; **hard** –, klinkende munt, kontant; **in** –, in kontant; – **office**, kassierskantoor; – **discount**, kontantkorting.
cash, v. (in)wissel, inkasseer, trek; honoreer, uitbetaal.
cash-account, kasrekening.
cash-book, kasboek.
cashier, n. kassier.
cashier, v. afdank, afsit, ontslaan.
cashmere, kassemier (kasjmier).
cash-register, kasregister.
casing, oortreksel, koker, omhulsel.
casino, casino, speelbank.
cask, vat.
casket, dosie, kissie.
Caspian, Kaspies.
casque, helmet.

cassation, kassasie, vernietiging.
cassia, kassia (kassie); seneblare.
cassock, priesterrok, toga.
cassowary, kasuaris.
cast, v. gooi, werp, strooi; afwerp; vorm, rangskik, optel; rolle verdeel; – **lots**, lootjies trek; – **a vote**, 'n stem uitbring; – **doubt**, in twyfel trek; – **anchor**, anker uitgooi; – **in one's teeth**, iets voor die kop gooi; – **a spell on**, betower; – **the blame on**, die skuld gee; – **the skin**, vervel; – **figures**, syfers optel; – **about**, rondval; – **away**, verwerp, verkwis, wegwerp; – **down**, neergooi; neerdruk; ontmoedig; – **in one's lot with**, die kant kies van; – **out**, uitwerp, uitsmyt, verstoot; – **up**, opgooi; bereken, optel; – **off**, weggooi, afwerp; losgooi (skip).
cast, n. gooi; optelling; opwerpsel; rolverdeling; afgietsel; soort, slag; **have a** – **in the eye**, oormekaar kyk.
castanet, kastanjet, dansklepper(s).
castaway, skipbreukeling; verworpeling.
caste, kaste, stand; **lose** –, agteruitgaan.
castellated, gekanteel(d); kasteelagtig.
castigate, straf, tugtig; suiwer.
castigation, tugtiging; suiwering.
Castile, Kastilië; – **soap**, Spaanse seep.
casting-vote, beslissende stem.
cast-iron, n. gietyster; gegote yster.
cast-iron, a. yster- . . .; onveranderlik.
castle, n. kasteel, slot; – **in the air**, lugkasteel.
castle, v. rokeer (skaak).
castor, bussie; wieletjie, rolletjie.
castor-oil, kasterolie, wonderolie.
castor-sugar, strooisuiker.
castrate, sny, kastreer, ontman.
castration, (die) sny, kastrasie, ontmanning.
casual, toevallig, terloops; onverskillig.
casually, terloops, in die verbygaan.
casualness, toevalligheid; uitsonderlikheid; onverskilligheid.
casualty, ongeval; sterfgeval, verlies; dooies; **list of** –ties, verlieslys.
casuist, gewetensregter; drogredenaar.
casuistry, drogredenering, haarklowery.
cat, n. kat; kats (strafwerktuig); kennetjie; **it rains** –**s and dogs**, dit reent ou meide met knopkieries; **let the** – **out of the bag**, die aap uit die mou laat; **live like** – **and dog**, soos kat en hond lewe.
cat, v. jongosse inspan.
catachresis, woordmisbruik, katachrese.
cataclysm, oorstroming; omwenteling.
catacomb, katakombe, grafkelder.
catafalque, katafalk, doodkisverhoog.
catalectic, katalekties, onvolledig.
catalepsy, katalepsie, verstywing; begin.
catalogue, n. katalogus, lys, pryskoerant.
catalogue, v. katalogiseer.
catalysis, katalise.
catapult, katapult; rekker.
cataract, katarak, waterval; star.
catarrh, katar, sinkings.
catastrophe, katastrofe, ramp, onheil; ontknoping.
catastrophic, katastrofies, rampspoedig.
cat-burglar, klouterdief.
catcall, n. kattegetjank; gefluit, gesis.
catcall, v. tjank; uitfluit.
catch, v. vang, gryp, vat, vaspak; betrap; haal, inhaal; vashaak; besmetlik wees; raak; – **fire**, vuur vat; – **one's death**, jou die dood op die lyf haal; – **a train**, 'n trein haal; – **attention**, aandag trek; – **cold**, kou vat; – **the meaning**, die betekenis snap; – **at**, gryp na; betrap op; – **on**, pak, inslaan; – **up**, opneem; in die rede

val; inhaal; **you'll – it!,** jy kry!; – **a glimpse,** skrams raaksien.
catch, n. vangs, vang; vanger; strikvraag, strik; knip, haak.
catch-dam, wendam, opvangdam.
catching, besmetlik, aansteeklik; aantreklik; pakkend.
catchment, opvang(terrein).
catch-word, wagwoord, leus, lokwoord.
catchy, pakkend, aantreklik.
catechize, katkiseer, ondervra.
catechism, kategismus.
catechist, katkiseermeester, ondervraer.
catechumen, geloofsleerling, katkisant.
categorical, kategories, onvoorwaardelik, absoluut, beslis, uitdruklik.
category, kategorie, klas, soort.
catenate, aaneenskakel.
cater, voedsel (verversinge) verskaf; – **to the public taste,** die publieke smaak bevredig.
caterer, leweransier.
caterpillar, ruspe(r).
caterwaul, miaau, kattjank.
catgut, dermsnaar; snaar; strykinstrumente.
catharsis, reiniging, suiwering.
cat-head, kraan-, katrolbalk.
cathedral, n. katedraal, domkerk.
cathedral, a. katedraal- . . .
catheter, kateter.
cathode, katode, negatiewe pool.
catholic, a. algemeen omvattend, liberaal; katoliek.
Catholic, Katoliek.
Catholicism, Katolisisme.
catkin, katjie (aan 'n boom); saadjie.
cat-o'-nine-tails, kats.
cat's-eyes, katoë; blinkogies (in pad).
cat's-paw, katpoot; werktuig, iemand wa tvir 'n ander die kastaiings uit die vuur moet haal.
cattle, vee, beeste; stomme vee.
cattle-leader, neusring.
cattle-lifter, veedief, beessteler.
cattle-plague, runderpes, veesiekte.
cattle-rustler, veedief.
cattle-show, veetentoonstelling.
cat-walk, looplys; loopbrug (skip); kruipgang; brugvoetpaadjie.
Caucasian, Kaukasies; Kaukasiër.
caucus, koukus, partyvergadering.
caudle, kandeel.
caul, net; helm; **born with a –,** met die helm gebore.
cauldron, ketel, pot.
cauliflower, blomkool.
caulk, stop, kalfater.
causal, kousaal, oorsaaklik.
causality, kousaliteit, oorsaaklikheid, oorsaaklike verband.
causation, veroorsaking; oorsaaklike verband; oorsaaklikheidsleer.
causative, veroorsakend; oorsaaklik, redegewend, kousatief.
cause, n. oorsaak, rede, beweegrede, grond, aanleiding; (reg)saak.
cause, v. veroorsaak, teweegbring, bewerk, maak dat, laat.
causeless, sonder oorsaak, ongegrond.
causeway, causey, straatweg; spoelbrug.
caustic, a. bytend, brandend; skerp; – **soda,** bytsoda, seepsoda.
caustic, n. brandmiddel, helsteen.
cauterize, uitbrand, toeskroei.
cautery, brandyster; toeskroeiing.
caution, n. versigtigheid, omsigtigheid; ver-

maning, waarskuwing; skrobbering; borggeld; **he is a –,** hy is 'n skrik!
caution, v. vermaan, waarsku; skrobbeer.
caution-money, waarborgsom.
cautious, versigtig, omsigtig, behoedsaam.
cavalcade, ruiterstoet, kavalkade.
cavalier, n. ruiter, kavalier; begeleier, kêrel.
cavalier, a. ruiterlik; rojaal, los; swierig, windmakerig; hooghartig, kortaf.
cavalry, kavallerie, ruitery, perderuiters.
cave, n. spelonk, grot, gat; fraksie.
cave, v. uithol: inkalwe; uitdy; indeuk.
cave, interj. pas op!, kyk uit!
cave-man, grotbewoner, oermens; primitiewe mens; geweldenaar.
cavern, spelonk, grot, gat.
cavernous, spelonkagtig; hol.
caviar(e), kaviaar, sout viskuit.
cavil, v. vit, bedil, haarklower.
cavil, n. vittery, bedillery, haarklowery.
cavity, holte.
caw, kras, krys.
Cayenne, Cayenne; rooipeper, fyn rissies.
cayman, kaaiman.
cease, v. ophou, stop, staak, tot 'n end kom.
cease, n. staking; **without –,** onophoudelik.
ceaseless, onophoudelik.
cedar, seder(boom); sederhout.
cede, op-, afgee, afstand doen van; sedeer, oordra; toestaan.
ceiling, plafon, solder; hoogtegrens.
ceiling-board, plafonplank (blafon-).
celebrate, vier; herdenk; verheerlik.
celebration, viering; feesviering; herdenking; verheerliking.
celebrity, beroemdheid, vermaardheid.
celerity, spoed, snelheid.
celery, sel(d)ery.
celestial, hemels, hemel- . . .; – **bodies,** hemelliggame.
celibacy, selibaat, ongetroude staat.
celibate, selibatêr, oujongkêrel.
cell, sel; hokkie; vakkie; kluis; graf.
cellar, n, kelder; wynvoorraad.
cellar, v. in 'n kelder sit, kelder.
cellarage, kelderruimte; kelderhuur.
'cello, violoncel, tjello.
Cellophane, Cellophane.
cellular, sellulêr, selvormig, sel- . . .; – **tissue** selweefsel.
celluloid, selluloïed (selluloïde).
cellulose, sellulose, selstof; houtstof.
Celtic, Kelties.
cement, n. sement; band.
cement, v. sement; lym, bind, heg.
cemetary, begraafplaas, kerkhof.
cenotaph, gedenksteen; graf.
censer, wierookvat; bewieroker.
censor, sensor, keur-, sedemeester.
censorious, vitterig, bedillerig.
censorship, sensorskap; sensuur.
censurable, berispelik, afkeurenswaardig.
censure, n. berisping, afkeuring, sensuur.
censure, v. afkeur; berisp; sensureer.
census, sensus, volkstelling.
cent, sent; **per –,** per honderd, persent.
centaur, sentaur, perdmens.
centenarian, honderdjarige.
centenary, eeufees.
centesimal, honderddelig, honderdste.
centigrade, honderdgradig; **100 degrees –,** 100 grade Celsius.
centigramme, centigram.
centilitre, centiliter.
centimetre, centimeter.

centipede, duisendpoot.
centner, sentenaar.
central, sentraal, middel- . . ., midde- . . .; hoof- . . .; – **heating,** sentrale verwarming.
centralize, sentraliseer.
centre, n. middel, middelpunt, sentrum; spil; hoof; – **of gravity,** swaartepunt.
centre, a. midde, middelste.
centre, v. verenig; na die middel bring (stuur).
centre-bit, senterboor.
centre-piece, tafelloper.
centrifugal, middelpuntvliedend, sentrifugaal.
centripetal, middelpuntsoekend, sentripetaal.
centuple, a. honderdvoudig.
centuple, v. verhonderdvoudig.
centurion, hoofman (oor honderd).
century, honderd jaar, eeu; honderdtal.
ceramic, pottebakkers- . . .
ceramics, pottebakkerskuns; aardewerk.
ceramist, pottebakker.
cere, wasvlies.
cereal, a. graan- . . .
cereal, n. graansoort; –s, graan, grane.
cerebellum, kleinharsings, cerebellum.
cerebral, serebraal; brein- . . .
cerebrum, grootharsings, cerebrum.
cerement, wasdoek, grafdoek, lykkleed.
ceremonial, a. seremonieel, vormlik.
ceremonial, n. seremonieel, pligpleging.
ceremonious, vormlik, plegtig, statig.
ceremony, seremonie, pligtigheid; vormlikheid; **without** –, sonder pligpleginge; **master of** –**ies,** seremoniemeester; **stand upon** –, vormlik wees.
cerise, kersrooi.
certain, seker, gewis, stellig; **he is** – **to do it,** hy sal dit stellig doen; **for** –, stellig.
certainly, seker, ongetwyfeld; ja seker!
certainty, sekerheid; **to, for a** –, stellig, verseker, wis en warempel.
certificate, n. sertifikaat, getuigskrif, diploma.
certificate, v. diplomeer.
certify, verseker, verklaar, getuig; waarmerk; sertifiseer.
certitude, sekerheid, oortuiging.
cerulean, hemelsblou.
cess, skatting, belasting.
cessation, (die) ophou, staking, einde.
cession, afstand, sessie.
cessionary, sessionaris.
cesspool, sinkput; slykpoel.
Ceylon, Ceylon; – **rose,** selonsroos.
chafe, v. vryf, skuur, skaaf; erger, irriteer; wrewelig (ongeduldig) wees.
chafe, n. skaafplek; ergernis, ongeduld.
chafer, kewer.
chaff, n. kaf; bog, waardelose ding.
chaff, v. terg, pla, vir die gek hou.
chaffer, afknibbel, (af)ding, kwansel.
chaffinch, vink.
chafing-dish, konfoor.
chagrin, n. ergernis, teleurstelling.
chagrin, v. erger, verdriet aandoen.
chain, n. ketting; reeks; –s, boeie, bande, kettings; gevangenskap; – **lightning,** sigsagblits; – **reaction,** kettingreaksie.
chain, v. boei, aan die ketting lê.
chain-mail, maliënkolder.
chain-shot, kettingkoeël.
chain-stitch, kettingsteek.
chair, n. stoel; voorsitter(stoel); professoraat; **take a** –, neem plaas, gaan sit; **take the** –, die voorsitterstoel inneem; **appeal to the** –, (sig) op die voorsitter beroep; **go to the electric** –, deur elektrokusie ter dood gebring word.

chair, v. op 'n stoel (rond)dra; aanstel as voorsitter.
chairman, voorsitter.
chalcedony, melksteen, newelsteen.
Chaldean, Chaldeeus; Chaldeër.
chalice, kelk; (nagmaals)beker.
chalk, n. kalk; **by a long** –, vérweg.
chalk, v. kryt aansmeer; opteken.
chalky, krytagtig.
challenge, n. uitdaging; uittarting; (die) aanroep; protes, wraking.
challenge, v. uitdaag; uittart; aanroep, haltroep; protes aanteken, wraak.
challenger, uitdaer.
chalybeate, ysterhoudend.
chamber, kamer; slot, rewolwerloop; pot, uil; **of commerce,** kamer van koophandel.
chamberlain, kamerheer, kamerdienaar.
chambermaid, kamenier, kamermeisie.
chameleon, kameleon, trapsoetjies, verkleurmannetjie; oorloper.
chamfer, n. groef, gleuf; riggel.
chamfer, v. groef; skuinsmaak.
chamois, gensbok (gemsbok); – **leather,** seem(s)leer.
champ, kou, byt, knaag.
champagne, sjampanje.
champaign, vlakte, veld.
champion, n. kampioen, baas- . . . (-vegter, -hardloper); voorvegter.
champion, v. verdedig, veg vir, bepleit.
championship, kampioenskap; verdediging, bepleiting.
chance, n. kans, geleentheid; toeval, geluk, noodlot; **by** –, by toeval, toevallig; **stand a good** –, 'n goeie kans hê; **on the** –, op goeie geluk af; **take one's** –, 'n kans waag, riskeer.
chance, a. toevallig.
chance, v. gebeur; riskeer, waag; – **upon,** toevallig ontmoet; **to** – **one's arm,** dit waag.
chancel, koor.
chancellery, kanselary; kanselierskantoor.
chancellor, kanselier.
chancery, kanselary.
chancy, gevaarlik, gewaag.
chandelier, kroonkandelaar, lugter.
chandelier-lily, kandelaarblom.
chandler, kersmaker, kruidenier.
change, v. verander (van), verruil, omruil, verwissel; kleinmaak; ver-, omklee; oorstap; – **one's mind,** van gedagte verander; – **one's tone,** 'n ander toon aanslaan; – **hands,** in ander hande oorgaan; – **places,** plekke ruil; – **colour,** bloos, verbleek; – **front,** van standpunt verander, draai.
change, n. verandering; ruil, verwisseling; kleingeld; skoon klere; omkleding; oorstap(ping); **for a** –, ter wille van die afwisseling.
Change, n. die Beurs.
changeable, veranderlik.
changeling, wisselkind, omgeruilde kind.
channel, n. kanaal, sloot, bed(ding); groef.
channel, v. kanaleer, deurgrawe; groef.
chant, n. (koraal)gesang; dreun.
chant, v. sing; singende resiteer; opdreun; – **the praises of,** die lof sing van.
chanticleer, kantekleer.
chaos, chaos, warboel.
chaotic, chaoties, verward, wanordelik.
chap, n. kêrel, vent; **old** –, ou maat!
chap, v. bars, spring, skeur.
chap, n. bars, skeur.
chap (chop), n. wang, kaak; lip; **lick one's** –s jou lippe aflek.
chapel, kapel; kerk; kapeldiens; drukkery.

chaperon, n. chaperon, begelei(dst)er.
chaperon, v. chaperonneer, begelei.
chap-fallen, verleë, terneergeslaan.
chaplain, kapelaan.
chaplaincy, kapelaanskap.
chaplet, krans; rosekrans; snoer.
chapter, hoofstuk, kapittel; kerklike vergadering.
char(e), dagwerk doen.
char, (ver)brand, verkool, swartbrand.
char-a-banc, toerbus, charabanc.
character, n. karakter, kenmerk, stempel; hoedanigheid, soort; kenteken; letter(teken); rol; getuigskrif; reputasie; persoonlikheid.
character, v. teken; ingrif.
characterize, karakteriseer, kenskets.
characteristic, a. karakteristiek, kenmerkend, kensketsend, tekenend.
characteristic, n. karaktertrek, kenmerk, eienaardigheid; indeks.
characterless, gewoon, alledaags.
charade, charade, lettergreep-raaisel.
charcoal, houtskool.
charge, n. las; lading, skoot; sarsie, aanval; prys, koste; taak, opdrag; sorg, versorging; pleegkind; **-s,** beskuldiging(e); koste; **in the − of,** onder toesig van; **be in − of,** toesig hê oor; **give in −,** (aan die polisie) oorhandig; **lay to one's −,** beskuldig van.
charge, v. laai; oplaai, belas; opdra; vra, in rekening bring; aanval, beskuldig.
chargeable, verantwoordelik; te wyte (toe te skrywe) aan; wat ten laste kom; **shall I make it − to your account?,** sal ek dit op u rekening sit?
charger, ryperd, strydros.
chariot, strydwa, triomfwa.
charioteer, voerman, menner.
charitable, vrygewig; liefdadig; vriendelik.
charity, liefde, menseliefde; mensliewendheid; vrygewigheid, liefdadigheid; aalmoes; **− begins at home,** die hemp is nader as die rok.
charlatan, kwaksalwer.
charlatanry, kwaksalwery, boerebedrog.
Charles's Wain, die Groot Beer, die Wa.
charlock, geel mosterd.
charm, n. bekoring, betowering, sjarme; gelukbringer; toormiddel, -spreuk.
charm, v. bekoor, betower; sjarmeer; toor.
charmer, toorder; bekoorder (bekoorster).
charming, bekoorlik, betowerend.
charnel-house, beenderehuis; dodehuis.
chart, n. tabel; (see)kaart.
chart, v. in kaart bring.
charter, n. charter; grondwet; oktrooi.
charter, v. 'n charter (privilegie) toestaan; huur; bevrag.
charterer, bevragter.
charter-party, vragkontrak.
char-woman, werkvrou, skropvrou.
chary, versigtig; suinig, karig.
chase, n. jag; jagveld; wild; jagstoet; vervolging; **give −,** agtervolg, nasit.
chase, v. jag, jaag, najaag, agtervolg; agternaloop; **− from, out of, away,** verdryf, wegdryf, -jaag.
chase, v. graveer, siseleer; groef, keep.
chase, n. groef, bedding, kas.
chase, n. raam, vorm.
chased, gegraveer.
chasing, gravering.
chasm, kloof, afgrond.
chassis, onderstel, geraamte, raam.
chaste, kuis, rein; suiwer, gekuis.
chasten, kasty, tugtig; suiwer, kuis, temper.
chastise, kasty, straf, tugtig.

chastisement, kastyding, tugtiging, straf.
chastity, kuisheid, reinheid.
chasuble, kasuifel, altaargewaad.
chat, v. babbel, gesels.
chat, n. gebabbel, geselsery, praatjie.
chatelaine, sleutelketting; burgvrou.
chattel, hawe, besitting.
chatter, v. babbel; snater; klap(per)tand.
chatter, n. gebabbel, geklets; gesnater.
chatterbox, babbelbek, -kous, kekkelbek.
chatty, spraaksaam, babbelsiek, geselserig.
chauffeur, chauffeur, bestuurder, drywer.
chauvinism, chauvinisme, jingoïsme.
chauvinistic, chauvinisties, jingoïsties.
cheap, goedkoop; waardeloos; **hold −,** gering ag, verag; **dirt −,** spotgoedkoop; **on the −,** goedkoop, vir 'n prikkie; **feel −,** klein voel; **make oneself −,** jouself weggooi.
cheapen, goedkoop maak (word), afslaan.
cheat, v. bedrieg, fop, kul, flous.
cheat, n. bedrieër; bedrog, kullery; **you are a −,** jy fop (speel kurang).
check, n. skaakset(ting); stuiting; belemmering; teenslag; kontrole; bewys, waarmerk; **keep in −,** in toom hou.
check, v. skaaksit; stuit, stop; rem, weerhou, beteuel; kontroleer; toets, nareken; **− up,** optel, toets.
check, sien **cheque.**
check, n. ruit; geruit, geruite stof.
checker, kontroleur, opsigter.
checkmate, n. skaakmat.
checkmate, v. skaakmat sit; uitoorlê.
cheek, wang; astrantheid, onbeskaamdheid; koelbloedigheid.
cheek-bone, wangbeen.
cheeky, astrant, parmantig, brutaal.
cheep, piep.
cheer, n. stemming; opgeruimdheid; toejuiging; onthaal, spys; **be of good −;** opgeruimd wees; **make good −;** feesvier; **three −s,** drie hoera's.
cheer, v. bemoedig, opvrolik, (toe)juig, hoera roep, **− on,** aanmoedig; **− up,** moed skep; opvrolik.
cheerful, opgewek, blymoedig, opgeruimd.
cheerio, alles ten beste.
cheerless, troosteloos, neerslagtig.
cheery, blymoedig, opgeruimd.
cheesa-stick, aansteekstok, fakkelstok.
cheese, kaas.
cheesemonger, kaaskoper.
cheese-paring, n. kaaskors; suinigheid.
cheesy, kaasagtig; windmakerig.
cheetah, jagluiperd.
chemical, a. chemies, skeikundig.
chemical, n. skeikundige stof; **-s,** chemikalieë.
chemise, (vrouens)hemp, chemise.
chemist, apteker; skeikundige, chemikus.
chemistry, skeikunde, chemie.
cheque, tjek, wissel.
cheque-book, tjekboek.
chequer, v. ruit; skakeer.
chequered, geruit; geskakeer(d); **− life,** veelbewoë lewe.
chequers-dam, n. ruite, geruit; dambord.
cherish, koester, versorg; liefhê; op prys stel.
cheroot, seroet.
cherry, n. kers(ie), -boom.
cherry, a. kersrooi, kerskleurig.
cherub, gerubyn, engel(tjie).
cherubic, engelagtig.
chervil, kerwel.
chess, skaak(spel); **play −,** skaak speel.
chess-board, skaakbord.

chess-men, skaakstukke.
chest, kis, kas; bors(kas); – **of drawers**, laaikas, klerekas.
chestnut, n. kastaiing; sweetvos(perd); ou grap.
chestnut, a. kastanjebruin; sweetvos-. . .
cheval-glass, groot draaispieël.
chevalier, ridder; ruiter; galant.
chevron, moustreep, chevron.
chevy, chivy, n. jag; (jag)skreeu.
chevy, chivy, v. jaag, agternasit.
chew, kou; pruim; peins, oordink; – **the cud**, herkou.
chewing-gum, kougom.
chicane, a. sonder troefkaarte.
chicanery, foppery, slimstreke; haarklowery.
chick, kuiken; kind.
chicken, kuiken; hoender-, kuikenvlees; jong snuiter; **count one's –s before they are hatched**, die vel verkoop voor die bok geskiet is.
chicken-breasted, smalborstig.
chicken-hearted, kleinhartig; lafhartig.
chicken-pox, waterpokkies.
chicory, sigorei.
chide, berisp, knor, uitskel.
chief, a. vernaamste, belangrikste, hoof- . . . ; **Chief Justice**, hoofregter.
chief, n. leier, aanvoerder, hoofman, hoof.
chiefly, hoofsaaklik, vernaamlik, veral.
chief-magistrate, hooflanddros.
chieftain, hoof, opperhoof, kaptein.
chieftaincy, hoofmanskap.
chiffon, chiffon.
chilblain(s), winterhande, -voete.
child, kind; **from a –**, van kindsbeen af; **–'s play**, kinderspel(etjies).
childbed, kraambed.
child-birth, bevalling.
childhood, kindsheid, kindsdae; **second –**, kindsheid.
childish, kinderagtig; kinderlik.
childlike, kinderlik.
chili, rissie.
chill, n. kilheid; koudheid; kou(e); verkoue-(ntheid); koelheid, onvriendelikheid.
chill, a. koud, kil, fris; koel, onverskillig; ontmoedigend.
chill, v. kil (koud) maak (word); laat bevries; ontmoedig; neerdruk; afkoel; **–ed meat**, koelvleis.
chilly, kouerig; koulik, verkluimerig; koel, onhartlik.
chime, n. klokkie; klok(ke)spel; kloklied.
chime, v. lui, slaan, speel; klokke lui, klokke bespeel; ooreenstem; rym, saamstem; – **in**, inval.
chim(a)era, chimera, hersenskim, droombeeld.
chimerical, chimeries, hersenskimmig.
chimney, skoorsteen; lamppyp; opening.
chimney-hat, pluiskeil, kaggelhoed.
chimney-jack, skoorsteenkap.
chimney-piece, skoorsteenmantel.
chimney-sweep, skoorsteenveër.
chimpanzee, sjimpansee, mensaap.
chin, ken; **double –**, onderken; **up to the –**, tot oor die ore.
China, China (Sjina).
china, porselein; breekgoed.
china-cupboard, porseleinkas, glaaskas.
Chinaman, Chinees (Sjinees).
china-ware, porseleingoed, -waar.
chinchilla, chinchilla.
chine, rugstring.
Chinese, Chinees (Sjinees).
chink, n. spleet, bars.
chink, v. (laat) klink, rinkel.

chink, n. duite, pitte.
chintz, sis.
chip, n. spaander, splinter, snipper; **a – of the old block**, 'n aardjie na sy vaartjie; **he has a – on his shoulder**, hy is 'n kruidjie-roer-my-nie(t); **potato –s**, aartappelskyfies.
chip, v. afsny, afsplinter; (laat) spring; – **in**, inval.
chippy, splinterig; droog; brommig.
chip-shot, polshou.
ch(e)iromancy, handwaarsêery.
chiropodist, hande- en voetedokter.
chirp, piep, tjilp.
chirpy, vrolik, monter.
chirr, tjirr.
chirrup, piep, kweel; aanoedig.
chisel, n. beitel; **cold –**, koubeitel.
chisel, v. (uit)beitel; beeldhou; fop.
chit, kleintjie, meisietjie, snuiter.
chit, briefie; getuigskrif.
chit-chat, babbelary, gebabbel.
chitterling(s), binnegoed.
chivalrous, ruiterlik, ridderlik.
chivalry, ridderlikheid; ridderskap; **age of –**, riddertyd.
chivy, sien **chevy**.
chloral, chloraal.
chloride, chloried (chloride).
chlorine, chloor.
chloroform, n. chloroform.
chloroform, v. onder chloroform sit.
chloromycetin, chloormisetine.
chlorophyll, chlorophyl, bladgroen.
chlorosis, bleeksug, chlorose.
chock, wig.
chock-full, propvol, tjokvol.
chocolate, sjokola(de).
choice, n. keus, voorkeur; beste, keur; **take one's –**, kies, 'n keus doen; **for –**, by voorkeur; **have no – but**, geen ander uitweg hê nie as . . .
choice, a. uitgelese, uitgesogte, keurig.
choir, koor.
choke, v. (ver)stik, verwurg; smoor, demp; opstop, verstop; onderdruk; **– off**, afsnou, stilmaak.
choke, n. smoorder, smoorklep, demper.
choler, toorn, woede, kwaadheid.
cholera, cholera.
choleric, choleries, driftig, opvlieënd.
choose, kies, uit-, verkies; **there is nothing to – between them**, die een is so goed (sleg) as die ander.
chop, v. kap, hou, kloof; – **in**, inval.
chop, n. kap, hou; stuk; karmenaadjie, kotelet; golfslag.
chop, n. sien **chap**.
chop, v. ruil; – **and change**, weifel.
chop, n. tjap, (brand)merk, stempel.
chop-house, (goedkoop) eethuis.
chopper, kapper, houer; byl, vleisbyl.
chopping-block, stampblok, kapblok.
choppy, met kort golfslag.
chopstick(s), (Sjinese) eetstokkies.
choral, a. koraal, koor- . . .
choral(e), n. koraal(gesang), koor.
chord, snaar, koord; **touch the right –**, die regte snaar aanroer; **vocal –s**, stembande.
chord, akkoord.
chore, sien **char(e)**.
chorister, koorsinger, -knaap.
chorus, koor; refrein.
chorus-girl, koriste; balletdanseres.
chough, kou(voël).
chow-chow, mengelmoes; atjar.
chrism, chrisma, heilige olie, salfolie.

Christ, Christus, gesalfde.
christen, doop.
Christendom, Christenheid, Christendom.
christening, doop.
Christian, n. Christen; Christin.
Christian, a. Christelik; – name, voornaam; – era, Christelike jaarteiling.
christianize, bekeer.
Christianity, Christendom; Christelikheid.
Christmas, Kersfees, Kersmis.
Christmas-box, Kersgeskenk.
Christmas-card, Kerskaartjie.
Christmas carol, Kerslied.
Christmas-day, Kersdag.
Christmas eve, Kersaand; Oukersaand, dag voor Kersfees.
Christmas holiday, Kersvakansie.
Christmas-tide, Kerstyd.
Christmas-tree, Kersboom.
chromatic, chromaties, kleur- . . .
chromatics, kleureleer, chromatiek.
chrome, chroomgeel.
chromium, chromium.
chromolithography, kleursteendruk.
chronic, chronies, langdurig, slepend.
chronicle, n. kroniek; C–s, Kronieke.
chronicle, v. boekstaaf, te boek stel.
chronicler, kroniekskrywer.
chronological, chronologies, volgens tydorde.
chronology, chronologie, tydrekening.
chronometer, chronometer; skeepshorlosie.
chrysalis, papie.
chrysanthemum, krisant, aster.
chrysolite, chrisoliet, goudsteen, topaas.
chubby, mollig, rondwangig.
chuck, v. klop, tik (onder die ken); gooi, smyt; – away, wegsmyt; – out, uitsmyt; – up, opgooi; uitskei; – it, hou op, skei uit!
chuck, n. klop, tik; gooi.
chuck, v. aanspoor (van 'n perd); klok.
chuckle, stilletjies lag, grinnik; klok.
chuckle-head, domoor; stommerik.
chum, n. maat, vriend.
chum, v. maats maak; kamermaats wees.
chummy, vriendskaplik, intiem.
chump, stomp, blok; kop; off one's –, van lotjie getik, opgewonde.
chunk, stuk, klomp, brok.
church, kerk; enter the –, predikant word.
church-goer, kerkganger.
churchman, kerkman; geestelike.
church-mouse, kerkmuis; as poor as a –, so arm (kaal) as 'n kerkmuis.
churchwarden, kerkopsiener; langsteelpyp.
churchy, kerks.
churchyard, kerkhof.
churl, vent, lomperd; vrek.
churlish, lomp, onbeskof, honds; inhalig.
churn, v. karring, omroer; bruis, kook.
churn, n. karring.
churning, karringsel.
churn-staff, karringstok.
chut, sjt!
chute, stroomversnelling; glybaan.
chutney, blatjang.
chyle, chyl.
chyme, chymus, kospap (van die maag).
cicada, sikade, sonbesie.
cicatrice, litteken, wondmerk.
cicatrize, gesond word, toegroei; teken.
cicerone, gids, cicerone.
cider, sider, appelwyn.
cigar, sigaar.
cigarette, sigaret.
cigarette-case, sigaretkoker.

cigarette-holder, sigaretpypie.
cinch, buikgord; voordeel; seker ding.
cinchona, kina(bas).
cincture, gordel, band.
cinder, sintel, uitgebrande steenkool, as.
Cinderella, As(se)poester.
cinder-track, asbaan, sintelbaan.
cine-camera, rolprentkamera.
cinema, bioskoop, kinema.
cinematograph, bioskoop, kinematograaf.
cine-projector, rolprentprojektor.
Cingalese, Singalees.
cinnabar, sinnaber; vermiljoen.
cinnamon, kaneel.
cipher, n. syfer; nul; syferskrif; monogram.
cipher, v. syfer, reken, bereken; in syferskrif stel; – out, uitreken, bereken.
cipher-key, sleutel vir syferskrif.
Circassian, Cirkassies; Cirkassiër.
circle, n. sirkel, kring, omtrek; sirkelloop, geselskap; galery, balkon; run round in –s, doenig wees sonder om veel uit te voer.
circle, v. omsluit; omtrek; kringe maak, ronddraai; rondgaan; omsingel.
circlet, sirkeltjie; band, ring.
circuit, omtrek; rondreis; ompad; sirkelgang; stroomkring; short –, kortsluiting; on –, op die rondgaande hof; – court, rondgaande hof.
circuitous, onregstreeks, met draaie; wydlopig; a – road, ompad.
circular, a. sirkelvormig, kringvormig; rondgaande; – letter, sirkulêre, omsendbrief; – staircase, wenteltrap.
circular, n. sirkulêre, omsendbrief.
circularize, 'n omsendbrief rig aan.
circulate, rondgaan, in omloop wees, sirkuleer; laat rondgaan, in omloop bring; circulating decimal, repeterende breuk; circulating library, leeskring.
circulation, sirkulasie, omloop, verspreiding; – of the blood, bloedsomloop.
circumambient, omringend, omgewend.
circumcise, besny.
circumcision, besnydenis; besnyding.
circumference, omtrek.
circumflex, kappie, sirkumfleks.
circumfuse, omgiet, oorgiet.
circumgyrate, ronddraai, wentel.
circumjacent, omliggend.
circumlocution, omskrywing; omslagtigheid; ontwyking.
circumnavigate, omseil, rondom vaar.
circumscribe, omskryf; begrens, insluit; afbakend, beperk.
circumscription, omskrywing; omskrif; beperking; afbakening.
circumspect, omsigtig behoedsaam.
circumspection, omsigtigheid.
circumstance, omstandigheid; feit; besonderheid; omhaal; in, under the –s, in (onder) die omstandighede.
circumstantial, bykomstig; omstandig; – evidence, bykomende getuienis.
circumstantiate, (uit die omstandighede) bewys; uitvoerig beskryf.
circumvallate, omskans, omwal.
circumvent, uitoorlê, mislei, bedrieg.
circumvention, uitoorlegging, misleiding.
circus, sirkus; arena, strydperk; plein.
cirrus, hegrank; veerwolk.
cissy, melkdermpie, meisieagtige seun, moederskindjie.
cistern, tenk, bak; dam; spoelbak.
citadel, sitadel, burg, vesting.

citation, dagvaarding; sitasie; aanhaling, sitaat.
cite, dagvaar; aanhaal, siteer.
citizen, burger; stadsbewoner, inwoner.
citizenship, burgerskap, burgerreg.
citric, sitroen- . . .; – acid, sitroensuur.
citron, sitroen(boom), siter(boom); lemoenkleur, liggeel.
citronella, sitronella.
citron-wood, sitroenhout, geelhout.
citrus, sitrus.
city, stad; – of refuge, vrystad.
city hall, stadhuis, stadsaal.
civet, sivet(kat), muskeljaat(kat).
civic, burgerlik; – duty, burgerplig.
civics, burgerleer.
civil, burgerlik, burger- . . ., siviel; beleef, – case, siviele saak; – law, burgerlike wet; – service, staatsdiens; – war, burgeroorlog.
civilian, n. burger(man).
civilian, a. burger- . . .; – clothes, burgerklere.
civilization, beskawing, sivilasasie.
civilize, beskaaf, siviliseer.
civility, beleefdheid, vriendelikheid; civilities, gunste; beleefdheidsbetuiginge.
civility, beleef; as burger.
clack, n. klap; gebabbel; geklep.
clack, v. klap, klepper; babbel, kekkel.
claim, v. eis, aanspraak maak op; voorgee, beweer; – that, beweer dat.
claim, n. eis, vordering, aanspraak; bewering; kleim; lay – to, aanspraak maak op.
claimable, opeisbaar.
claimant, eiser.
claim-jumper, kleimdief.
clairvoyance, heldersiendheid.
clam, (soort) mossel.
clamant, luidrugtig; dringend.
clamber, klouter.
clammy, klam, vogtig, taai, klewerig.
clamour, n. lawaai, geroep, geskreeu.
clamour, v. roep, skreeu, lawaai maak; – for, skreeu om; – down, oorskreeu.
clamorous, lawaaierig, luidrugtig.
clam(p), n. kram; klem, skroef.
clamp, v. klem, (vas)klamp; las.
clan, stam; kliek; klas, soort.
clannish, stamvas; kliekerig.
clandestine, skelm, agterbaks, op bedekte manier, heimlik, ongeoorloof.
clang, n. geskal, gebons, gekletter; – of trumpets, trompetgeskal; – of arms, wapengekletter; – of bells, klokgelui.
clang, v. skal, bons, kletter, lui.
clangour, gekletter, geklank.
clank, v. rammel, raas, klink.
clank, n. gerammel, geklank.
clap, n. klap, slag, knal.
clap, klap; toejuig; toeslaan; – on, haastig aan-, opsit; – on all sail, alle seile bysit; – eyes on, in die oog kry; – into prison, in die tronk gooi.
clapper, klepel; voëlverskrikker.
clap-trap, effekbejag, mooipraatjies, vroompraatjies, boerebedrog.
claret, claret, bordeauxwyn; bloed.
clarification, opheldering, suiwering.
clarify, ophelder, opklaar, suiwer; helder word.
clari(o)net, klarinet.
clarion, klaroen, trompet.
clarity, helderheid, klaarheid.
clash, v. bots, stoot; klepper; klink; indruis (teen), in stryd wees met.
clash, n. bons, stamp; gekletter, gerammel; botsing; – of arms, wapengekletter; – of opinions, meningverskil.

clasp, n. klamp, haak, gespe(r), kram; hand druk; omhelsing.
clasp, v. vashaak, toegespe(r), omhels.
clasp-knife, knipmes, steekmes.
class, n. klas, rang, stand; orde; lesuur; kursus; – teaching, klassikale onderwys; upper –es, hoëre range (stande); working –es, arbeidende klasse; first –, eerste klas; no –, laag, sleg, benede peil.
class, v. klassifiseer, indeel.
classic, klassiek; –s, klassieke.
classical, klassiek.
classicism, klassisisme.
classify, klassifiseer, indeel, rangskik.
classy, van goede klas (stand), deftig.
clatter, v. kletter, rammel; trappel.
clatter, n. gekletter, gerammel.
clause, klousule; artikel; bysin, sinsdeel.
claustral, kloosterlik; bekrompe.
clavicle, sleutelbeen.
claw, n. klou, poot; knyper, haak.
claw, v. klou, krap.
clay, klei; stoflike oorskot; – pipe, erdepyp.
clayey, kleiagtig, kleierig, taai.
claymore, (Skotse) slagswaard.
clean, a. skoon, sindelik, suiwer, rein; netjies; show a – pair of heels, skoon weghardloop; – sweep, totale opruiming; make a – breast of, eerlik bekend.
clean, v. skoonmaak, suiwer, opruim, aan die kant maak, poets; – up, opruim, aan kant maak; – down, afstof, afveeg.
clean, adv. skoon; totaal, heeltemal, glad; – mad, skoon mal.
cleaning, skoonmaak, reiniging.
cleanliness, sindelikheid, reinheid.
cleanly, a. sindelik, netjies.
cleanly, adv. skoon, netjies; eerlik.
cleanness, skoonheid, sindelikheid; reinheid.
cleanse, skoonmaak; reinig.
clear, a. helder, klaar; duidelik, suiwer; skerp deurdringend; skoon; oop, vry; three days – drie volle dae; the coast is –, alles veilig.
clear, adv. skoon; helder, duidelik; totaal, glad; vry, los, opsy; stand –, weg staan; hang –, vry hang; steer –, verby stuur; get –, los raak.
clear, v. skoonmaak, ver-, ophelder; op-, wegruim; leegmaak; wegraak, trap; oorspring; in-, uitklaar; afbetaal, vereffen; (tafel) afneem; ooptrek, opklaar (van die weer); vryspreek, suiwer; uitverkoop; – the road, padgee; – the throat, keel skoonmaak; – out, leegmaak; trap, weggaan; – up, ophelder; opklaar; skoonmaak.
clearance, opruiming; opheldering; klaring (van wissels); – sale, uitverkoop, opruiming(suitverkoop).
clear-cut, skerp omlyn.
clear-headed, helder.
clearing, oop plek skoon plek; opruiming, klaring.
clearing-house, klaringskantoor.
clearness, helderheid, duidelikheid.
clearsighted, heldersiende.
cleavage, klowing, skeiding.
cleave, kloof, splits, skei; klief, deursny.
cleave, kleef, vaskleef; getrou bly.
clef, sleutel; bass –, F-, bassleutel; treble –, G-, sol-, vioolsleutel.
cleft, bars, spleet, kloof.
cleg, perdevlieg.
clematis, klematis, klimop.
clemency, genadigheid; sagtheid.
clement, genadig; sag.

clench 445 **clutch**

clench, clinch, (om)klink, ombuig; (tande) vasbyt; (vuiste) bal; beklink, beseël.
clepsydra, waterklok.
clergy, geestelikheid, geestelikes.
clergyman, predikant, dominee.
clerical, geestelik, klerikaal; klerklik; – **error,** skryffout; – **staff,** dienspersoneel, klerke.
clerk, klerk; – **of the works,** opsigter.
clever, slim, skrander, oulik, knap.
cleverness, slimheid, skranderheid, knapheid.
clew, bal, bol.
cleché, drukplaat, cliché; gemeenplaas.
click, v. tik, klik.
click, n. getik, geklik.
client, klant, kliënt.
clientele, gevolg; klante, kliënteel.
cliff, krans, rots, klip.
climateric, a. kritiek; klimakteries.
climateric, n. krisis, hoogtepunt; oorgangsleeftyd, klimakterium.
climate, klimaat; (lug)streek; **political** –, politieke gesindheid.
climatic, klimaat-...., klimaties.
climatology, klimatologie, leer van die luggesteldheid.
climax, klimaks, hoogtepunt, toppunt.
climb, v. klim, klouter; beklim, bestyg.
climb, n. klim.
climber, klimmer; klimplant.
clime, klimaat; streek, gewes.
clinch, sien **clench.**
clincher, (clencher), klinknael; doodskoot.
cling, vassit, (aan)kleef, (vas)klem.
clingstone, taaipitperske.
clinic(al), a. klinies; –**al thermometer,** koorspypie, -pennetjie.
clinic, n. kliniek.
clink, n. klink.
clinker, klinker, hardebaksteen.
clip, v. (af)knip, skeer, snoei; kortwiek; weglaat.
clip, n. skeersel.
clip, vasklou.
clip, n. klou, knip, tang.
clipper, knipper; skeermasjien, skêr; klipper (snel vaartuig); doring, haan.
clipping, (uit)knipsel, skeersel.
clique, kliek.
iquish, cliqu(e)y, kliekerig.
cloak, n. mantel; dekmantel.
cloak, v. (be)dek, bemantel.
cloakroom, klædkamer; bagasiekantoor.
clock, klok, horlosie; **what o'clock is it?,** hce laat is dit?; **six o'clock,** sesuur.
clock, v.: – **in,** inklok: – **out,** uitklok.
clock-face, wys(t)erplaat.
clocking-hen, broeihen.
clockwise, met die klok mee, vooruit.
clockwork, ratwerk; meganiek; **like** –, **so** gereeld as 'n klok.
clod, klont, kluit; blok, knul.
clodhopper, boerelummel, gomtor.
clog, n. blok (aan die been); klomp.
clog, v. belemmer; verstop; teenhou.
clogdance, klompedans.
cloggy, kluiterig, klonterig; klewerig.
cloister, n. klooster, kruisgang, suilegang.
cloister, v. in 'n klooster opsluit, afsonder.
close, a. toe, gesluit, dig; nou, bekrompe; bedompig; geheimsinnig, agterhoudend; suinig; naby, digby; dig op mekaar; getrou; – **prisoner,** streng bewaakte gevangene; – **season,** geslote jag; – **writing,** fyn skrif; – **texture,** fyn weefsel; **in** – **order,** in geslote geledere, kort op mekaar; **at** – **quarters,** op kort afstand; – **proximity,** onmiddellike nabyheid; **a** – **shave,** 'n nou(e) ontkoming; – **by, to, upon,** digby, naby; – **upon a hundred,** digby die honderd; – **resemblance,** groot ooreenkoms; – **victory,** naelskraapoorwinning; – **call,** noue ontkoming.
close, n. omheining; (speel)grond.
close, v. toemaak, sluit; besluit, afsluit, eindig; ooreenkom; – **in,** insluit; aansluit, geledere sluit, opskuif; – **up,** toemaak, toegooi; aansluit, opskuif; – **with,** handgemeen raak met; ooreenkom, akkordeer.
close, n. sluiting, slot, einde.
closed, gesluit, geslote, toe, dig; – **circuit,** geslote baan, geslote (stroom)kring.
close-fisted, suinig, inhalig, gierig.
closeness, nabyheid; nouheid; bedompigheid; agterhoudendheid; suinigheid.
close-stool, stelletjie.
closet, n. privaatkamer; gemakshuisie, kloset; blindeise.
closet, v. opsluit, afsonder.
close-up, vlakby(-opname).
closing, sluiting; – **hour,** sluitingsuur; – **scene,** slottoneel.
closure, n. sluiting, sluitingsreg.
closure, v. sluitingsreg toepas.
clot, n. klont, klodder, (bloed)stolsel; domkop.
clot, v. klont, saamplak; stol.
cloth, laken, tafellaken; amptelike gewaad; **lay the** –, tafeldek.
cloth-binding, linneband.
clothe, klee(d), beklee; inklee; bedek.
clothes, klere; beddegoed; linnegoed.
clothes-basket, wasgoedmandjie.
clothes-brush, klereborsel.
clothes-horse, droogstok.
clothes-line, droogtou, -lyn.
clothes-peg, wasgoedpennetjie.
clothes-press, klerekas.
clothier, lakenwewer; klerehandelaar.
clothing, kleding, klere.
cloth-merchant, lakenhandelaar, handelaar in kledingstowwe.
cloud, n. walk; **be in the** –**s,** in vervoering wees; **under a** –, onder verdenking; in onguns.
cloud, v. (be)wolk; oorskadu; verduister, benewel; – **over,** betrek.
cloud-burst, wolkbreuk.
cloud-capped, in wolke gehul.
clouded, bewolk; duister; bedruk.
cloud-hopping, wolkskuilingvlug.
cloudless, wolkloos, onbewolk.
cloudy, bewolk, newelagtig; wolkerig, troebel; duister, onduidelik.
clout, n. hou, slag; doek, lap.
clout, v. 'n hou gee.
clove, (krui)naeltjie; (gras)angelier.
cloven-footed, met gesplete hoewe.
clover, klawer; **live in** –, lekker lewe.
clown, nar, hanswors, harlekyn; lomperd.
clownish, dwaas, lomp, belaglik.
cloy, volprop, oorlaai; walg.
club, n. kierie, knots; gholfstok; klawer (kaart); klub, sosiëteit; **Indian** –, (swaai)knots.
club, v. (dood)slaan; – **together,** saamwerk, saamspan, 'n klub vorm.
clubfoot, horrelvoet.
club-house, klubhuis, -gebou.
cluck, kloek (van 'n hen).
clucking, broeis.
clue, draad; aanduiding, wenk; sleutel.
clump, bos, klomp; blok.
clumsy, onhandig, lomp.
cluster, n. tros, (bossie), trop, klompie.
cluster, v. 'n tros vorm, swerm, koek.
clutch, v. gryp, vat, ruk.

clutch, n. greep, gryp; klou; koppeling, koppelaar (van 'n motor).
clutch pedal, koppelpedaal.
clutter, n. geraas, warboel, verwarring.
clutter, v. stommel, rammel, lawaai.
clyster, lawement, spuitjie.
coach, n. koets, rytuig, (spoor)wa, poskar, -wa; breier, afrigter.
coach, v. (in 'n koets, rytuig) ry; voorberei, oplei; brei, afrig.
coach-horse, koetsperd, karperd.
coach-house, waenhuis.
coach-maker, wa-, rytuigmaker.
coachman, koetsier.
coachwork, koetswerk, bak(werk).
coadjutor, medewerker, handlanger.
coagulate, stol, strem, dik word, klont.
coagulation, stolling, stremming.
coal, n. (steen)kool; **heap -s of fire on,** vurige kole hoop op; **haul over the -s,** voor (die) stok kry; **carry -s to Newcastle,** water in (na) die see dra.
coal, v. kole inneem.
coal-box, kolebak.
coalesce, saamgroei, saamsmelt, verenig.
coalescence, samesmelting, samevloeiing.
coal-field, koleveld.
coal-gas, (steen)koolgas, liggas.
coalition, samesmelting; koalisie, bondgenootskap.
coal-mine, -pit, (steen)koolmyn.
coal-scuttle, kolebak, -emmer.
coal-shed, kolehok.
coal-shovel, (kool-) koleskop, -skep.
coal-tar, koolteer.
coal-vein, steenkoolaar.
coarse, grof, ru, lomp, onbehoorlik.
coarse-grained, grof van draad.
coast, n. kus; **the - is clear,** die kus is skoon.
coast, v. langes die kus vaar; afdraand rol.
coaster, kusboot, kusvaarder.
coastguard, kuswag.
coasting-vessel, kusvaarder.
coastwise, langes die kus.
coat, n. baadjie; manel; (oor)jas; (dames)mantel; bekleding; **- of arms,** wapen(skild), familiewapen; **- of mail,** pantser; **- of paint,** laag verf, verflaag; **cut one's - according to one's cloth,** die tering na die nering sit; - **and skirt,** baadjie-, mantelpak, mantelkostuum.
coat, v. beklee, bedek, oortrek; verf.
coated, beklee(d), oorgetrek; aangeslaan (van tong).
coatee, kort manteltjie.
coating, stof (vir klere); laag (verf).
coat-tail, (manel)pant.
coax, flikflooi, soebat, pamperlang.
cob, mannetjieswaan; poon; (mielie)kop.
cobalt, kobalt.
cobble, n. klip, kei; **-s,** kaggelkole.
cobble, v. (saam)lap, saamflans.
cobbler, (skoen)lapper; knoeier; ysdrank.
cobra, kobra; **banded -,** koperkapel; **brown -,** bruin kapel; **Cape -,** geelslang.
cobweb, spinnerak; net, web.
cobwebby, vol spinnerakke; (rag)fyn.
cocaine, kokaïen (kokaïne).
cochineal, cochenille.
cock, n. (hoender)haan; weerhaan; haan (van 'n geweer); haantjie, doring; kraan; **old -, ou kêrel; - of the walk,** katjie van die baan; **that - won't fight,** dit sal nie gaan (luk) nie; **- and bull story,** 'n opgemaakte verhaal; **at full -,** oorgehaal; **at half -,** in die rus.

cock, v. optrek; oorhaal; **- the ears,** die ore spits; **- one's eye,** 'n knipogie gee; **- one's hat,** sy hoed skuins sit (optoom); **- a gun,** 'n geweer oorhaal; **- one's nose,** sy neus optrek.
cockade, kokarde (kokarretjie).
cock-a-hoop, opgetoë, jubelend.
cockatoo, kaketoe.
cockatrice, basilisk, fabelmonster.
cock-brained, onbesonne, roekeloos.
cockchafer, (mei)kewer.
cock-crow(ing), haangekraai; dagbreek.
cocked, opgeslaan, opgetoom; oorgehaal; **- hat,** driekantige hoed, steek; opgeslaande hoed; **knock into a - hat,** papslaan.
cocker, v. vertroetel, verwen.
cockerel, haantjie.
cock-eye, skeeloog; uilskuiken, snoeshaan.
cock-eyed, skeel; skuins, krom.
cock-fight, hanegeveg.
cockle, n. koringblom, brand (in die koring).
cockle, n. skulp; mossel.
cockle, v. krul, skrompel.
cockle-burr, kankerroos.
cockpit, vegkamp; boegkajuit (op 'n skip); stuurstoel (op 'n vliegtuig).
cockroach, kakkerlak.
cocks-comb, hanekam.
cock-shy, kol, mikpunt; gooi.
cocksure, positief seker; aanmatigend.
cocktail, stompstert; 'n halfbloed-resieperd; parvenu; „cocktail" (soort drank), skemerkelkie.
cock-tailed, stompstert; stert in die lug.
cocky, cocksy, coxy, parmantig, verwaand.
coco(a), klapperboom, kokosboom; klapper; klapperdop.
cocoa, kakao.
cocoanut, klapper; klapperdop.
cocoanut-oil, klapperolie.
cocoanut-tree, klapperboom.
cocoon, papie.
cod, kabeljou.
coddle, vertroetel, verwen.
code, kode; wetboek, regulasies; **- of honour,** eerbegrip(pe).
codex, kodeks.
codfish, kabeljou.
codger, vent, kêrel.
codicil, kodisil, toevoegsel, aanhangsel.
codify, kodifieer.
codlin(g)-moth, kodlingmot, appelmot.
codliver-oil, visolie, lewertraan.
co-education, ko-edukasie.
coefficient, koëffisiënt; medewerker.
coelacanth, selakant.
co-equal, gelyk(waardig).
coerce, (af)dwing, beteuel, forseer.
coercion, dwang, beteueling.
coercive, dwang-..., beteuelend.
coeval, a. van dieselfde ouderdom, ewe oud.
co-executor, mede-eksekuteur.
coexist, gelyktydig bestaan.
coexistence, gelyktydige bestaan; saambestaan.
coextensive, van gelyke omvang; gelyktydig.
coffee, koffie.
coffee-bean, koffiepit, koffieboontjie.
coffee-ground, koffiemoer.
coffee-pot, koffiekan.
coffee-strainer, koffiesakkie, -siffie.
coffer, koffer, (geld)kas; **-s,** skatkis; fondse.
coffer-dam, kisdam.
coffin, n. (dood)kis; **that was a nail in his -,** dit was 'n spyker in sy doodkis.
coffin, v. kis, toespyker.
cog, n. kam, tand; kamrat, tandrat.

cogency, bewyskrag; bewyskragtigheid.
cogent, klemmend, oortuigend; dringend.
cogitate, peins, oorweeg, oordink.
cognac, konjak, fransbrandewyn.
cognate, verwant.
cognisance, kennis, kennisneming, waarneming; jurisdiksie; (regs)gebied; kenteken.
cognisant, bewus (van), gewaar, bekend (met).
cognition, kennis, bewustheid, waarneming.
cognomen, bynaam; van; naam.
co-guardian, medevoog, toesiende voog.
cog-wheel, kamrat, tandrat, -wiel.
cohabit, saamwoon; saamleef.
co-heir, mede-erfgenaam.
cohere, saamkleef, saamhang.
coherence, samehang, verband.
coherent, samehangend, duidelik.
cohesion, samehang, verband; kohesie.
cohort, kohort, (krygs)bende.
coiffeur, kapper, haarsnyer, barbier.
coiffure, kapsel.
coil, v. opdraai, oprol, slinger, kronkel.
coil, n. bog, kronkeling; rol; (haar)lok; (induksie)klos, -spoel.
coin, n. munt(stuk), geld(stuk); **pay one in his own –**, iemand met gelyke munt betaal.
coin, v. munt, geldslaan; geld soos bossies verdien; versin, uitdink; – **words**, woorde smee(d).
coinage, geldmunting; munt; versinsel.
coincide, saamval; ooreenstem.
coincidence, sameval, sameloop; ooreenstemming; toeval.
coincidental, toevallig; gelyktydig; ooreenstemmend.
coiner, munter; valse munter; versinner.
coir, klapperhaar.
coition, coitus, byslaap.
coke, kooks.
colander, vergiet(tes); haelvorm.
cold, a. koud; **throw – water on a plan**, 'n demper op 'n plan sit; **give the – shoulder to**, links laat lê, met die nek aankyk; **in – blood**, in koele bloede, koelbloedig, ewe goedsmoeds; – **comfort**, skraal troos; – **snap**, skielike koue; – **war**, koue oorlog; – **sore**, koorsblaar · – **storage**, koelbewaring.
cold, n. kou(e); verkoue; **catch a –**, kouvat; **to have a –**, verkoue wees; **leave out in the –**, geen notisie van neem nie, veronagsaam.
cold-blooded, koudbloedig (van diere); koelbloedig, onverskillig, ongevoelig.
cold-chisel, koubeitel.
coldhearted, koud, ongevoelig.
coldness, kou, koudheid; koelheid, onhartlikheid, ongevoeligheid.
colic, koliek.
colitis, kolitis.
collaborate, saam-, meewerk.
collaboration, mede-, saamwerking.
collaborator, medewerker.
collapse, v. inmekaarsak, in duie stort; opvou, inmekaarvou; misluk.
collapse, n. ineenstorting; mislukking.
collapsible, -able, (op)voubaar.
collar, n. boordjie, kraag; halsband; borsriem; ring, band.
collar, v. by die nek vat; vang, plant; skaai, inpalm.
collar-bone, sleutelbeen.
collate, vergelyk, kollasioneer.
collateral, sydelings, ewewydig, by- . . .; sy- . . .; kollateraal; – **branch**, sytak.
collation, vergelyking, kollasie; ligte maal.
colleague, kollega, ampgenoot.

collect, n. kort (voor)gebed, kollekte.
collect, v. versamel, bymekaarmaak, vergader; bymekaarkom; insamel, kollekteer; aflei; besluit; – **oneself**, jou selfbeheersing terugkry, bedaar.
collected, versamel(d); bedaard.
collectedness, bedaardheid, selfbeheersing.
collecting-van, oplaaiwa, afhaalwa.
collection, versameling, kolleksie; insameling, kollekte; inkassering; busligting.
collective, gesame(nt)lik, gemeenskaplik; kollektief, verenigde, versamel- . . .; – **noun**, versamelwoord, kollektief.
collector, versamelaar; kollektant; kaartjiesknipper, hekman.
college, raad, genootskap; kollege.
college cap, kollege-, studentepet, -baret.
collegial, kollege- . . .
collegian, kollegelid.
collegiate, kollege- . . .; geïnkorporeerde, korporasie- . . .
collide, bots, in botsing kom, aanvaar, aanry.
collie, Skotse herdershond, kollie.
collier, steenkoolgrawer, mynwerker; koleskip; matroos op 'n koleskip.
colliery, steenkoolmyn, kolemyn.
collision, botsing, aanvaring, aanryding.
collocate, plaas, rangskik, regstel.
collodion, kollodium (-ion).
collogue, die koppe saamsteek, saampraat.
collop, lappie vleis.
colloquial, gemeensaam, familiaar, tot die omgangstaal behorende; **in – language**, in die (gewone) omgangstaal; – **talents**, geselstalent.
colloquy, saamspraak, onderhoud.
collusion, onderhandse samewerking (verstandhouding), kollusie.
collusive, onderhands, skelm.
colocynth, kolokwint, bitter-, gifappel.
colon, dubbelpunt.
colon, dikderm.
colonel, kolonel.
colonelcy, -ship, kolonelskap.
colonial, a. koloniaal.
colonial, n. kolonis; kolonialer.
colonize, koloniseer, neerset.
colonist, kolonis, volksplanter, neersetter.
colonnade, suilery, suilegang, kolonnade.
colony, kolonie, volksplanting, nedersetting.
colophon, eindtitel; sluitsteen.
colophony, viool-, spieëlharpuis.
colo(u)ration, kleuring, kleursel.
coloratura, koloratuur.
colossal, kolossaal, reusagtig.
colossus, kolos, reus, gevaarte.
colour, n. kleur, tint; skyn, voorwendsel; –s, kleure; band; vlag; **change –**, verskiet, bleek word; **see in its true –s**, in sy ware lig sien; **put false –s upon**, in die verkeerde lig stel; **show one's –**, kleur beken; **nail –s to mast**, besliste standpunt inneem, voet by stuk hou; **come off with flying –s**, met vliegende vaandel deurkom; **under – of**, onder die skyn (voorwendsel) van.
colour, v. kleur, verf; oordryf, vermom, verdraai; kleur verleen; bloos.
colourable, skoonskynend, voorgewend.
colour-bar, kleurslagboom.
colour-blind, kleurblind.
colour-box, verf-, skilderdoos.
coloured, geverf, gekleurd.
colouring, kleur, kleursel, koloriet; valse skyn.
colourist, koloris.
colourless, kleurloos; karakterloos.

**colour-scheme, **kleurskema.
**colour-sergeant, **vlagsersant.
**colportage, **kolportasie, boeksmousery.
**colporteur, **kolporteur, boeksmous.
**colt, **jongperd; nuweling; slaanding.
**columbine, **klokblom, klokkie akelei.
**column, **kolom; pilaar; (leër)afdeling, kolonne.
**columnar, **pilaar-, kolomvormig.
**coma, **bedwelming, swym; koma.
**coma, **kuif; newelomtrek, koma.
**comatose, **katswink, slaapsugtig.
**comb, **n. kam; (heuning)koek.
**comb, **v. kam; kaard; skei, sif; fynkam, deursoek.
**combat, **n. geveg, stryd, kamp; **single -, **tweegeveg.
**combat, **v. (be)stry, (be)veg, worstel.
**combatant, **stryder, vegter, bakleier.
**combative, **strydlustig, veglustig, bakleierig.
**comber, **kammer; kaarder; brander.
**combination, **verbinding, vereniging, kombinasie; samespanning; hempbroek; - **lock, **kombinasieslot.
**combine, **v. verbind, verenig, saamvat; saamsmelt; kombineer.
**combine, **n. sindikaat, trust, kartel; stroper (by koringoes), snydorsmasjien, aarsnyer.
**combustible, **brandbaar, ontvlambaar.
**combustible, **brandstof; brandbare stof.
**combustion, **verbranding; brand.
come, **kom; - **undone, **losraak, -gaan; - **cheap, **goedkoop uitkom; - **true, **waar word; uitkom; **for a year to -, **vir die volgende jaar; - **(along), **kom saam; ag nee!; toe nou!; - **about, **gebeur; - **across someone, **iemand teenkom; - **across one's mind, **inval, te binne skiet; **not - amiss, **van pas kom; - **at, **bykom, in die hande kry; - **at the truth, **die waarheid agterkom; - **by, **verbykom; in die hande kry; - **down, **afkom; bydraai; - **down in the world, **agteruitgaan in die lewe; - **down upon, **op afkom; inklim; - **for, **kom om, kom haal; - **forward, **vorentoe kom; (sig) aanbied; - **in useful, **te pas kom; **where does the joke - in, **waar sit die grap, wat is nou snaaks daaraan?; **where do I - in, **waar bly ek, watter voordeel het ek daarvan?; - **in for, **('n deel) kry; erf; - **into one's own, **kry wat jou toekom; - **into power, **die mag in hande kry; - **near falling, **byna val; - **off, **wegkom; losraak; slaag; **when does the match - off, **wanneer vind die wedstryd plaas?; - **off badly, **daar sleg van afkom; - **on, **aankom, vooruitkom; opkom (bv. onweer); ter sprake kom; op die toneel verskyn; voorkom (bv. 'n hofsaak); - **on, **kom vooruit!; - **out, **uitkom; slaag; staak, uitwerk; verskyn; - **out with, **voor die dag kom met; - **over, **oorkom; oorloop; **a change has - over him, **hy het 'n verandering ondergaan; - **round, **aanloop; bykom (van 'n floute); bydraai; - **to, **bykom; - **to blows, **handgemeen raak; - **to hand, **aankom, sy bestemming bereik; **voor die hand kom; - **to light, **aan die lig kom, voor die dag kom; **it -s to this, **dit kom hierop heer; - **under, **val onder; - **under one's notice, **onder iemand se aandag kom; - **up, **opkom; ter sprake kom; - **up with, **inhaal; - **upon, **raakloop; aanval.
**comedian, **komediant; toneelspeler; blyspelskrywer.
**comedienne, **comédienne, komediante.
**come-down, **val, vernedering, agteruitgang.
**comedy, **komedie, blyspel.
**comely, **bevallig, aantreklik; gepas.

**comer, **aankomeling; **the first -, **die eerste die beste; **all -s, **die res; enigeen.
**comestible, **iets eetbaars; **-s, **eetware.
**comet, **komeet, stertster, roeister.
**comfit, **konfyt; gesuikerde vrugte.
**comfort, **n. troos, vertroosting; verligting; gemak, gerief; voldoening; komfort; welgesteldheid.
**comfort, **v. troos, vertroos, opbeur.
**comfortable, **gemaklik, gerieflik, behaaglik, komfortabel; **be comfortably off, **welgesteld wees; **feel -, **op jou gemak voel.
**comforter, **trooster, fopspeentjie; serp.
**comfortless, **troosteloos; ongerieflik.
**comic, **komiek, grappemaker; prentverhaal.
**comic(al), **komiek(lik), komies, grappig, snaaks, koddig; - **strip, **prentverhaal.
**comity, **hoflikheid.
**comma, **komma; **inverted -s, **aanhalingstekens.
**command, **v. beveel, gebied, kommandeer; aanvoer, die bevel voer oor; beheers; beskik oor; uitsig gee op, uitsien op; afdwing.
command, **n. bevel, gebod, las, opdrag; aanvoering; meesterskap, beheersing; beskikking; kommando; **at, by - of, **op bevel van; **have at -, **ter beskikking hê; **in - of, **aan die hoof van; **in die beste van; **great - of language, **groot meesterskap oor die taal; - **performance, **voorstelling (konsert) op hoë versoek (bevel); galakonsert.
**commandant, **bevelvoerder, kommandant.
**commandeer, **(op)kommandeer.
**commander, **bevelvoerder; -hebber; kommandeur; eerste offisier; kommandant.
**commander-in-chief, **opperbevelhebber.
**commanding, **bevelend; bevelvoerend; beheersend; indrukwekkend.
**commandment, **gebod.
**commando, **kommando.
**commemorate, **gedenk, herdenk, vier.
**commemoration, **herdenking, viering.
**commence, **begin, aanvang.
**commencement, **begin, aanvang.
**commend, **aanbeveel, prys; toevertrou; - **me to, **sê groetnis aan.
**commendable, **aanbevelenswaardig, loflik.
**commendation, **aanbeveling.
**commendatory, **aanbevelend, aanbevelens-...
**commensurable, **meetbaar, verdeelbaar, vergelykbaar; eweredig.
**commensurate, **eweredig; van dieselfde afmetinge.
**comment, **n. uitleg(ging); opmerking; aanmerking, kommentaar.
**comment, **v. aanmerk; - **on, **verklaar, aanmerkinge maak op, kritiseer.
**commentary, **verklaring, uitleg, kommentaar.
**commentator, **verklaarder, uitlêer, kommentator.
**commerce, **handel; verkeer; omgang.
**commercial, **kommersieel, handeldrywend, handels-..., verkeers-...; - **traveller, **handelsreisiger.
**commination, **(be)dreiging, vervloeking.
**comminatory, **bedreigend, dreig-...
**commingle, **(ver)meng.
**comminute, **verdeel, verklein.
**commiserate, **bekla, bejammer.
**commiseration, **medelye, beklag(ing).
**commissariat, **kommissariaat; voedselvoorraad.
**commissary, **afgevaardigde; koskommandant; verplegingsoffisier.
**commission, **n. las, opdrag; volmag; kommissie; (die) begaan, pleging; **on -, **in kommissie; volgens opdrag.
**commission, **v. opdra, las gee; magtig.

commission-agent, kommissie-agent.
commissioner, kommissaris; kommissielid; opsiener; **High C-**, Hoë Kommissaris.
commit, toevertrou; bedryf, begaan, pleeg; verwys; verbind; – **murder**, moord pleeg; – **to the care of**, aan die sorg toevertrou van; – **to memory**, van buite leer, uit die kop leer; – **to paper**, op skrif stel; – **for trial**, ter strafsitting verwys; – **oneself**, (sig) blootgee, (sig) kompromitteer; – **oneself to**, (sig) verbind tot.
commitment, (die) toevertrou; oordrag; verwysing; blootgewing.
committal, verbintenis; sien **commitment**.
committee, komitee, kommissie.
commode, klerekas, laaikas; stilletjie.
commodious, ruim.
commodity, gerief; handelsartikel.
commodore, commodore, bevelvoerder.
common, a. gewoon, algemeen; publiek; gemeenslagtig; ordinêr; laag, sleg; – **property**, gemeengoed; – **sense**, gesonde verstand; **make – cause**, gemene saak maak.
common, n. dorpsgrond, -veld; **in –**, gemeen(skaplik), gesame(nt)lik; **out of the –**, ongewoon, besonders.
commonage, weireg; dorpsgrond, meent.
commonalty, die (gewone) volk.
commoner, burger; lid van die Laerhuis.
commonly, gewoonlik, meestal, deurgaans; gewoon; gemeen, sleg.
commonplace, a. gewoon, alledaags.
commonplace, n. gemeenplaas.
common-room, geselskamer.
commons, burgery; rantsoen, kos, ete; **(House of) C-**, (Engelse) Laerhuis; **on short –**, op (half) rantsoen.
commonwealth, gemenebes,
commotion, beweging; opskudding; opstand.
communal, gemeenskaps- . . ., dorps- . . .
communalism, (leer van) plaaslike selfbestuur.
commune, n. gemeente, distrik; **The C-**, Die Commune.
commune, v. (siels)gemeenskap hê; saam oorlê; Nagmaal gebruik.
communicable, meedeelbaar; spraaksaam.
communicant, nagmaalganger; beriggewer.
communicate, meedeel; oorbring, Nagmaal bedien (gebruik); gemeenskap hou; in verbinding wees, oorlê; ineenloop (van vertrekke).
communication, meedeling; gemeenskap; verbinding; verkeermiddels, verkeersweë; kommunikasie.
communicative, meedeelsaam, spraaksaam.
communion, omgang; gemeenskap; Nagmaal.
communism, kommunisme, gemeenskapsleer.
communist, kommunis; a. kommunisties.
community, gemeenskap; ooreenkoms; – **of property**, gemeenskap van goedere.
commutation, (ver)wisseling; versagting.
commutator, (stroom)wisselaar.
commute, omset, verwissel; versag; daagliks trein ry.
compact, n. ooreenkoms, verdrag; poeierdosie.
compact, a. dig, beknop, kompak.
companion, n. metgesel, maat, kameraad, deelgenoot; geselskapsdame.
companion, a. bybehorende.
companion, v. vergesel; omgaan (met).
companion, n. kampanje(trap).
companionable, gesellig.
companionship, kameraadskap; geselskap.
company, n. geselskap; gaste; maatskappy, genootskap; bemanning; (kapteins)afdeling;

bear –, geselskap hou; **part –**, afskeid neem; **keep –**, omgang hou; gesels met; vergesel.
comparable, vergelykbaar, te vergelyk; **not – to**, nie te vergelyk met.
comparative, vergelykend; betreklik; – **degree**, vergrotende trap.
comparatively, in vergelyking, betreklik.
compare, v. vergelyk; wedywer; vergelyk word; trappe van vergelyking noem; – **notes**, aantekeninge (bevindinge) vergelyk.
compare, n. vergelyking; **beyond –**, sonder weerga.
comparison, vergelyking.
compartment, afdeling, vak; kompartement.
compass, n. omtrek; omvang, bestek; grens; bereik; kompas; **points of the –**, windrigtinge, hemelstreke.
compass, v. omvat, insluit; regkry.
compass-box, kompashuisie.
compass-card, kompasroos.
compasses, (pair of) –, passer,
compassion, medelyde, erbarming.
compassionate, a. medelydend.
compassionate, v. medelyde hê met.
compass-saw, sirkelsaag.
compatible, bestaanbaar, verenigbaar.
compatriot, landgenoot.
compeer, gelyke, ewekrie; maat.
compel, noodsaak, verplig; afdwing.
compendious, beknop, saaklik.
compendium, samevatting, kort begrip.
compensate, skadeloos stel, vergoed, vergeld; opweeg teen; **compensating pendulum**, kompensasieslinger.
compensation, skadeloosstelling, kompensasie.
compère, aankondiger, seremoniemeester.
compete, wedywer, konkurreer, meeding.
competence, **-cy**, bevoegdheid, geskiktheid; welgesteldheid; (middele van) bestaan.
competent, bevoeg, bekwaam; **it was not – to him to . . .**, dit was nie sy werk om . . .
competition, mededinging, wedywer; wedstryd; kompetisie.
competitive, mededingend, vergelykend.
competitor, mededinger, deelnemer.
compilation, kompilasie, versameling.
compile, versamel, saamstel, kompileer; bymekaarslaan (krieket).
compiler, versamelaar, kompilator.
complacence, **-cy**, inskiklikheid; selfgenoegsaamheid; genot.
complacent, (self)voldaan, tevrede; inskiklik.
complain, kla(e) (klaag).
complainant, klaer; eiser.
complaint, klag(te); aanklag; kwaal.
complaisance, tegemoetkomendheid; inskiklikheid.
complaisant, voorkomend, inskiklik.
complement, n. aanvulling; voltooiing; volle getal, taks; komplement (wiskunde).
complement, v. voltallig maak; kompleteer.
complementary, aanvullende, aanvullings- . . .; – **angle**, aanvullingshoek; – **colours**, komplementêre kleure.
complete, a. volledig, voltallig, kompleet; totaal, volkome, volmaak.
complete, v. voltooi; voltallig maak, kompleteer.
completeness, volledigheid; volmaaktheid.
completion, voltooiing; aanvulling.
complex, n. kompleks, geheel, samestel.
complex, a. ingewikkeld, samegestel(d), gekompliseer(d); – **sentence**, samegestelde sin.
complexion, (gelaats)kleur; aansien, voorkome.
complexionless, kleurloos.
complexity, ingewikkeldheid.

compliance, inskiklikheid; instemming; **in – with,** ingevolge, ooreenkomstig.
compliant, inskiklik, toegewend.
complicacy, ingewikkeldheid.
complicate, v. ingewikkeld maak; in die war stuur.
complicate, a. ingewikkeld, verward, gekompliseer(d).
complication, ingewikkeldheid; verwarring; komplikasie.
complicity, medepligtigheid.
compliment, n. kompliment, pluimpie; gelukwens; **–s,** komplimente, groetnis; beleefdheidsbetuiging(e); **no –s,** geen pligpleginge; **the –s of the season,** veels geluk (met Kersfees en Nuwejaar).
compliment, v. gelukwens; kompliment maak.
complimentary, gelukwensend; groetend; komplimenteus, hoflik; vol pligpleginge; **– ticket,** vrykaartjie.
comply, inwillig, toegee; **– with,** (sig) rig na; voldoen aan; toestem in.
component, a. samestellend.
component, n. bestanddeel.
comport, gedra; ooreenstem (met).
comportment, gedrag; houding.
compose, saamstel, (uit)maak; toonset; rangskik; skik, besleg; kalmeer; set (van drukwerk).
composedly, bedaard, rustig, kalm.
composer, samesteller; komponis, toonsetter; (letter)setter.
composite, samegesteld, gemeng.
composition, samestelling, verbinding; steloefening, opstel; toonsetting; (die) set, settery; geaardheid; vergelyk, ooreenkoms.
compositor, (letter)setter.
compost, mengsel; gemengde bemesting.
composure, gelatenheid, bedaardheid.
compound, v. verbind, saamstel; meng; berei; vergelyk tref, akkordeer.
compound, a. samegestel(d); **– interest,** rente op rente, samegestelde rente; **– addition,** optelling met ongelyknamige breuke.
compound, n. samestelling, mengsel.
compound, n. mynkamp, kafferkamp.
comprehend, begryp, verstaan; insluit.
comprehensible, begryplik, verstaanbaar.
comprehension, verstand, begrip; omvang; **above my –,** bo my verstand.
comprehensive, (veel)omvattend, uitgebreid.
compress, v. saamdruk; saampers; saamvat.
compress, n. kompres, nat verband.
compressible, saamdrukbaar, saam te druk.
compression, samedrukking, -persing; verdigting, kompressie; bondigheid.
comprise, v. omvat, insluit; bestaan uit.
compromise, n. skikking, vergelyk, ooreenkoms.
compromise, v. skik, vergelyk tref, akkoord maak; kompromitteer, in opspraak bring.
compulsion, dwang, geweld; **on – of gedwonge.**
compulsory, gedwonge, verpligtend; **– school attendance,** verpligte skoolbesoek, skooldwang, **– education,** leerplig, verpligt(end)e onderwys.
compunction, berou, wroeging.
computable, berekenbaar.
computation, berekening; skatting.
compute, bereken, uitreken; skat.
computer, rekenaar, berekenaar; skatter; rekenliniaal; rekenmasjien.
comrade, maat, kameraad; **—in-arms,** wapenbroeder, strydgenoot.
con, n.: pros and **–s,** voor- en nadele; die pro en contra.
con, v. bestuur; uitkyk.
con, v. bestudeer; leer.

conation, (die) strewe.
concentenation, aaneenskakeling.
concave, hol, holrond, konkaaf.
concavity, holte, holligheid.
conceal, verberg, verstop, wegsteek; bedek, verswyg, geheim hou.
concealment, verberging; verswyging, geheimhouding, **place of –,** skuilplek.
concede, toestaan, inwillig; opgee, oorgee.
conceit, verwaandheid, verbeelding; gril, gier; mening.
conceited, verwaand, eiewys.
conceitedness, verwaandheid, trots.
conceivable, denkbaar, begryplik.
conceivably, denklik, moontlik, allig.
conceive, opvat; swanger word; bedink, (sig) voorstel; glo, begryp; uitdink.
concentrate, saamtrek, konsentreer.
concentration, sametrekking, konsentrasie; inspanning.
concentric, konsentries, gelykmiddelpuntig.
concept, begrip; ontwerp, konsep.
conception, begrip, voorstelling, opvatting, konsepsie.
conceptual, begrips- . . ., voorstellings- . . .
concern, v. betref, aangaan, raak; **– oneself with,** (sig) bemoei (met); **the matter does not – me,** die saak gaan my nie aan nie; **that does not – you,** dit raak jou nie.
concern, n. saak; aangeleentheid; **of no –,** van geen belang nie; **feel – for,** bekommer(d) voel oor; **with deep –,** met groot besorgdheid; **no – of mine,** nie my besigheid nie; **the whole –,** die hele affère.
concerned, betrokke; besorg; **be – at,** begaan wees oor; **be – in,** betrokke wees in.
concerning, aangaande, met betrekking tot.
concernment, deelname; besorgdheid.
concert, n. samewerking; konsert.
concert, v. ooreenkom, beraam, oorlê.
concertina, konsertina.
concession, bewilliging; begunstiging; vergunning; konsessie.
concessionaire, konsessionaris, begunstigde.
conch, skulpdier, skelpvis.
conchology, skulpkunde.
conciliate, versoen, paai, oorhaal; konsilieer.
conciliation, versoening; bemiddeling; konsiliasie.
conciliator, bemiddelaar, vredestigter.
conciliatory, versoenend, bemiddelend.
concise, beknop, bondig.
conclave, (kardinaals)vergadering; **in secret –,** in geheime sitting.
conclude, besluit, eindig; aflei.
conclusion, slot, einde; gevolgtrekking, konklusie; **try –s with,** (sig) met mekaar meet, in die strydperk tree teen; **in –,** ten slotte, tot besluit.
conclusive, afdoende, oortui(g)end.
conclusiveness, afdoendheid.
concoct, saamflans; brou; smee(d), beraam.
concoction, brousel; versinsel.
concomitant, a. begeleidend, samehangend.
concomitant, n. begeleidende verskynsel.
concord, ooreenstemming, harmonie.
concordance, ooreenstemming; konkordansie.
concordant, ooreenstemmend, gelykluidend; harmonies; harmonieus.
concordat, konkordaat.
concourse, samestroming, toeloop, menigte.
concrete, a. konkreet; tasbaar, **– noun,** konkrete selfstandige naamwoord.
concrete, beton; **in the –,** in werklikheid.
concretion, samegroeiing, verdikking, verharding; gewas, verstening.

concubinage, samewoning, konkubinaat.
concubine, bywyf; bysit.
concupiscence, wellus, sondige begeerte.
concupiscent, sin(ne)lik, wulps; begerig.
concur, instem; saamstem; saamval.
concurrence, (die) saamval, samekoms; instemming.
concurrent, ewewydig; gelyktydig, samevallend; instemmend.
concurrently, gelyktydig.
concuss, skok; verontrus.
concussion, (hersen)skudding, skok; botsing.
condemn, veroordeel; afkeur.
condemnable, laakbaar, afkeurenswaardig.
condemnation, veroordeling; vonnis.
condensation, verdigting; saampersing; kondensasie.
condense, kondenseer, verdig; saampers.
condenser, kondensator.
condescend, neerbuig, (sig) verwaardig.
condescending, neerbuigend.
condescension, neerbuiging, (neerbuigende) vriendelikheid; minsaamheid.
condign, verdiende.
condiment, (kruie)sous.
condition, n. toestand, staat; voorwaarde, stipulasie; kondisie; rang, stand.
condition, v. bepaal, ooreenkom.
conditional, a. voorwaardelik, kondisioneel; **make – on**, afhanklik stel van.
conditional, n. voorwaardelike wys.
conditioned, gesteld; bepaal, beding; **well–, ill–**, in goeie, slegte staat.
condolatory, kondolerend, kondoleansie- . . .; **– letter**, brief van roubeklag, kondoleansiebrief.
condole, kondoleer, simpatie betuig.
condolence, kondoleansie, simpatiebetuiging, roubeklag.
condonation, vergifnis, kondonasie.
condone, vergewe; goedmaak.
condor, kondor, gier.
conduce, bydra (tot); bevorder, strek (tot).
conducive, bevorderlik (vir).
conduct, n. gedrag; bestuur, beheer; **safe –**, vrygeleide.
conduct, v. gedra; lei, bestuur; dirigeer.
conduction, geleiding.
conductor, geleier; bestuurder; kondukteur; orkesleier; bliksemafleier; geleidraad.
conduit, leikanaal; **– pipe**, leipyp, geleibuis.
cone, kegel (keël), keil; dennebol.
cone-shaped, kegelvormig.
confab(ulate), gesels, met mekaar oorlê.
confab(ulation), geselsery, samespreking.
confection, vervaardiging; suikergoed; lekkergoed; klaargemaakte kledingstuk.
confectionary, suikergoed- . . .; klaar gekoop.
confectioner, koekbakker, lekkergoedmaker.
confectionery, soetgoed; soetgebak; lekkers; lekkergoedwinkel; banketbakkery.
confederacy, verbond; (state)bond; konfederasie; samespanning.
confederate, a. verbonde.
confederate, n. bondgenoot; saamgesworene.
confederate, v. konfedereer.
confederation, bondgenootskap, konfederasie.
confer, toeken, verleen; beraadslaag, oorlê; **– an honour**, 'n eer bewys; **– together**, beraadslaag.
conference, byeenkoms, konferensie; onderhoud, bespreking, beraadslaging.
confess, erken, beken, bely, bieg; bieg afneem; **– sins**, sonde bely, sonde bieg.
confessedly, soos bekend is; volgens eie bekentenis.

confession, belydenis; bekentenis, erkenning; bieg; **– of faith**, geloofsbelydenis.
confessional, a. konfessioneel, bieg- . . .
confessional, n. biegstoel.
confessor, belyer; biegvader.
confidant, vertroude, vertroueling.
confide, vertrou, toevertrou, meedeel, opbieg.
confidence, (self)vertroue; vrymoedigheid; parmantigheid; **told in –**, in vertroue gesê; **– trickster**, swendelaar, opligter.
confidence trick, vertroue-swendel, swendelary.
confident, seker, oortuig; vrymoedig.
confidential, vertroulik, in vertroue; vertroud; geheim; konfidensieel.
configuration, skikking; gedaante; konfigurasie.
confine, n. grens, uiterste, oorgang.
confine, v. beperk, bepaal, begrens, insluit; opsluit, gevangegesit; **be –d**, beval, geboorte gee aan 'n kind.
confinement, beperking, opsluiting, gevangeskap; bevalling.
confirm, bevestig; goedkeur; versterk; aanneem; **– on oath**, onder ede bevestig; **– news**, berig bevestig.
confirmation, bevestiging; goedkeuring; versterking; aanneming.
confirmed, uitgesproke, besliste; verstokte.
confiscate, verbeurdverklaar, beslag lê op, konfiskeer.
confiscation, verbeurdverklaring, konfiskasie.
conflagration, verwoestende brand.
conflict, n. stryd, botsing, worsteling.
conflict, v. bots, in stryd wees (met).
confluence, samevloeiing.
confluent, a. saamvloeiend, meewerkend.
confluent, n. bystroom.
conform, vorm (na); skik (na), aanpas (by), voeg (na).
conformable, ooreenkomstig; passend; geskik, inskiklik.
conformation, bou, struktuur; aanpassing.
conformist, konformis.
conformity, ooreenkoms, gelykvormigheid; inskiklikheid, onderwerping; **in – with**, ooreenkomstig.
confound, in die war stuur; dronkslaan, verbluf laat staan; **– it**, vervlaks.
confraternity, broederskap; bende.
confront, teenoor mekaar stel; bymekaarbring, konfronteer; die hoof bied.
confrontation, konfrontasie; vergelyking.
confuse, verwar, deurmekaar maak.
confused, verwar(d), wanordelik, verleë.
confusion, verwarring, wanorde; verleentheid.
confutation, weerlegging.
confute, weerlê.
congeal, bevries, stol, dik (hard) word.
congelation, bevriesing, stolling.
congener, verwante, soortgenoot.
congenial, geesverwant, simpatiek; passend, geskik.
congeniality, geesverwantskap; geskiktheid.
congenital, aangebore, oorgeërf.
conger(-eel), seepaling.
congeries, versameling, hoop, massa.
congest, ophoop, saamhoop; strem; oorlaai.
congestion, ophoping, stremming; kongestie.
conglomerate, n. opeenhoping, konglomeraat.
conglomerate, v. opeenhoop, saamklont.
conglomeration, versameling, opeenhoping, massa; konglomerasie.
congratulate, gelukwens, felisiteer.
congratulation, gelukwens(ing); felisitasie.
congratulatory, gelukwensings- . . .; felisitasie- . . .
congregate, versamel, vergader, byeenkom.

**congregation, **vergadering; gemeente.
**congregational, **gemeentelik, gemeente- . . .
**congress, **kongres, byeenkoms.
**congruence, **ooreenstemming, ooreenkoms.
**congruent, **ooreenstemmend, passend, bestaanbaar (met); kongruent.
**congruous, **ooreenstemmend; passend.
**conic, **kegelvormig; – **section, **kegelsnee.
**conifer, **kegeldraende plant, konifeer.
**conjectural, **vermoedelik, volgens gissing.
**conjecture, **n. gissing, onderstelling.
**conjecture, **v. gis, (ver)onderstel, vermoed.
**conjoin, **aansluit; saamsluit, verbind.
**conjoint, **gemeenskaplike; toegevoegde.
**conjointly, **gemeenskaplik; gesame(nt)lik, mede.
**conjugal, **egtelik, huweliks- . . .
**conjugate, **v. vervoeg; een word.
**conjugate, **a. verbonde; saamgevoeg.
**conjugation, **vervoeging; samevoeging.
**conjunct, **a. verenig; toegevoeg.
**conjunct, **n. by-, toevoegsel.
**conjunction, **voegwoord; verbinding, vereniging; konjunksie (sterrek.).
**conjunctive, **a. (ver)bindend, aanvoegend; konjunktief.
**conjunctive, **n. aanvoegende wys; bindwoord.
**conjuncture, **tydsgewrig, sameloop van omstandighede, toestand van sake, krisis.
**conjuration, **smeekbede, beswering; toorwoord.
**conjure, **besweer; oproep, te voorskyn roep; toor, goël, oë verblind.
**conjurer, -or, **toornaar, goëlaar.
**conjuring trick, **goëltoer.
**conk, **voorgewel, neus.
**connate, **aangebore; gelyktydig gebore.
**connect, **verbind, aansluit.
**connected, **verbonde; samehangend; aaneengeskakel; **well –, **van goeie stand.
**connecting rod, **suierstang, dryfstang.
**connection, -nexion, **verbinding; verband; aansluiting; gemeenskap; samehang; betrekking; konneksie; **–s, **kennisse, konneksies; **in – with, **in verband met, met betrekking tot; **in this –, **in hierdie verband, in verband hiermee.
**connective, **a. verbindend; – **tissue, **bindweefsel.
**connective, **n. verbindingswoord.
connexion, **sien **connection.
**conning-tower, **uitkyk-, kommando-toring.
**connivance, **oogluikende toelating.
**connive: – at, **oogluikend toelaat; onder 'n geheime verstandhouding veroorloof.
**connoisseur, **kenner, fynproewer; connoisseur.
**connotation, **(by)betekenis; intensiewe betekenis; inhoudsbepaling; konnotasie.
**connote, **beteken; bybetekenis hê; insluit.
**connubial, **huweliks- . . ., egtelik.
conquer, **verower, oorwin, verslaan; **seëvier.
**conqueror, **oorwinnaar, veroweraar.
**conquest, **oorwinning; verowering.
**consanguineous, **(bloed)verwant.
**consanguinity, **bloedverwantskap.
**conscience, **gewete, konsensie; **guilty –, **skuldige gewete; **in all –, **op my woord; **have the – to, **die hart (astrantheid) hê om.
**conscience clause, **gewetensklousule.
**conscience money, **gewetensgeld.
**conscientious, **konsensieus, nougeset, pliggetrou; **– objections, **gewetensbesware; **– objector, **gewetensbeswaarde.
**conscientiousness, **nougesetheid, pliggetrouheid.
**conscious, **bewus; **– of, **bewus van; **– that, **bewus dat.
**consciousness, **bewustheid; bewussyn; **lose –, **bewussyn verloor, flou word.
**conscript, **dienspligtige.

**conscription, **opkommandering, konskripsie; verpligte krygsdiens.
**consecrate, **a. heilig, gewyd.
**consecrate, **v. heilig, wy; toewy; inseën.
**consecration, **wyding; toewyding; inseëning.
**consecutive, **opeenvolgend; gevolgaanduidend; **– number, **volgnommer.
**consecutively, **agtereenvolgens, na mekaar.
**consensus, **ooreenstemming, eenstemmigheid.
**consent, **v. in-, toestem, inwillig.
**consent, **n. in-, toestemming, inwilliging, konsent; **with one –, **eenparig; **silence gives –, **wie swyg stem toe; **– (to), **toestemming gee (tot).
**consequence, **gevolg, uitwerking; gevolgtrekking; belang, betekenis; **in –, **gevolglik; **in – of, **ten gevolge van; **of no –, **van geen betekenis nie; **money is of no –, **geld speel geen rol nie.
**consequent, **gevolglik, daaruit volgende; logies, konsekwent.
**consequential, **gevolglik; verwaand.
**consequently, **gevolglik, dientengevolge.
**conservation, **bewaring, behoud, beskerming, instandhouding, konservasie.
**conservative, **behoudend, konserwatief.
**conservatism, **behoudendheid, konserwatisme.
**conservator, **bewaarder, opsiener.
**conservatory, **broeikas; konservatorium.
**conserve, **n. ingelegde vrugte.
**conserve, **v. bewaar, instandhou; inlê.
consider, **beskou; in aanmerking neem; **oorweeg.
**considerate, **aansienlik, aanmerklik.
**considerate, **bedagsaam, voorkomend, hoflik.
**considerateness, **beleefdheid, voorkomendheid.
**consideration, **beskouing, oorweging; vergoeding; voorkomendheid, bedagsaamheid; betekenis, gewig; **take into –, **in aanmerking neem; **in – of, **om, vir, ter wille van.
**considering, **aangesien; (die omstandighede) in aanmerking geneem.
**consign, **toevertrou; oorlewer, oordra; afstuur, oorstuur, konsigneer.
**consignee, **geadresseerde, gekonsigneerde.
**consignment, **oordrag, oorlewering; afsending; (be)sending; **– note, **vragbrief.
**consignor, **afsender, konsinjant.
**consist, – of, **bestaan uit; **– in, **bestaan in.
**consistence, -cy **dikte, digtheid, vastheid, konsistensie; konsekwensie, beginselgetrouheid.
**consistent, **konsekwent, beginselgetrou; **– with, **in ooreenstemming (verenigbaar) met.
**consistory, **kerkraad; konsistorie.
**consolable, **troosbaar.
**consolation, **troos, vertroosting.
**consolation-prize, **troosprys, knolvoer.
**consolation-race, **knolwedloop, verloorderswedloop.
**consolatory, **troostend, troos- . . .
**console, **n. (draag)arm, stut.
**console, **v. (ver)troos, opbeur.
**consolidate, **vas word, **hard word; **versterk; bevestig; verenig, konsolideer.
**consonance, **gelykluidendheid; eenstemmigheid.
**consonant, **medeklinker, konsonant.
**consort, **n. gemaal (gemalin); metgesel.
**consort, **v. omgaan (met) vergesel, begelei; klaarkom (met); harmonieer (met).
**consortium, **konsortium, kartel.
**conspectus, **oorsig; (algemene) kyk.
**conspicuous, **opvallend, in die oog lopend; uitblinkend; opsigtig; **be – by absence, **skitter deur afwesigheid; **make oneself –, **opval; (sig) op die voorgrond dring; (sig) belaglik maak.
**conspicuousness, **opvallendheid; opsigtigheid.
**conspiracy, **sameswering, samespanning.
**conspirator, **samesweerder.

conspire, saamsweer, saamspan; beraam.
constable, konstabel, polisieagent.
constabulary, polisie(mag).
constancy, standvastigheid; bestendigheid; trou.
constant, a. standvastig; bestendig; trou; voortdurend, aanhoudend.
constant, n. konstante (rekenk.); onveranderlike waarde.
constantly, voortdurend; gedurig.
constellation, sterrebeeld, konstellasie.
consternation, ontsteltenis, verslaentheid.
constipate, hardlywig maak, konstipeer.
constipation, hardlywigheid, konstipasie.
constituency, kiesers; kiesafdeling.
constituent, a. saamstellend; kies- . . .; konstituerend.
constituent, n. bestanddeel; kieser.
constitute, saamstel, vorm, uitmaak; aanstel, benoem; stig; konstitueer.
constitution, samestelling; gesteldheid, gestel; staatsvorm; grondwet; konstitusie.
constitutional, a. gestels- . . .; grondwetlik; konstitusioneel.
constitutional, n. gesondheidswandeling.
constitutionalist, konstitusionalis, aanhanger van die grondwet.
constitutive, saamstellend; wesenlik, essensieel; wetgewend.
constrain, dwing; bedwing; verplig, noodsaak; vashou; gevangesit, opsluit.
constrained, gedwonge; onnatuurlik.
constraint, dwang; opsluiting; gedwongenheid.
constrict, toedruk, saamtrek, beperk.
constriction, saamtrekking; beknelling.
constrictor, sluitspier; luislang, konstriktor.
constringent, saamtrekkend, knellend.
construct, saamstel; maak, bou, oprig; konstrueer.
construction, samestelling; bou, oprigting; maaksel; uitleg; sinsbou; woordvoering; konstruksie.
constructive, opbouend; boukundig, bou- . . .; konstruktief; – **criticism**, opbouende kritiek.
constructor, oprigter; bouer, konstrukteur.
construe, uitlê, verklaar; opvat; verbind; konstrueer.
consuetude, gebruik, gewoonte(reg); omgang.
consul, konsul.
consular, konsulêr.
consulate, konsulaat, konsulaatskap.
consult, v. raadpleeg, beraadslaag; – **one's wishes**, iemand se wense in aanmerking neem.
consult, n. raadpleging, beraadslaging.
consultation, beraadslaging, konsultasie.
consultative, -**tory**, raadplegend, beraadslagend, konsulterend.
consulting, raadgewend; raadplegend; – **hours**, spreek-ure.
consume, verteer; verbruik; uitteer.
consumer, verbruiker; deurbringer.
consummate, a. volkome; volslae; deurtrap; – **scoundrel**, deurtrapte skurk.
consummate, v. voltrek, uitvoer.
consummation, voltooiing, voltrekking; einddoel, hoogste doel; toppunt.
consumption, vertering, verbruik; tering.
consumptive, a. verterend; teringagtig.
consumptive, n. teringlyer.
contact, aanraking; kontak; – **lens**, kontaklens; – **man**, kontakpersoon, tussenpersoon.
contagion, besmetting; besmetlikheid.
contagious, aansteeklik, besmetlik.
contain, inhou, bevat, insluit; bedwing.
container, doos, blik, bus, potjie; ding waar iets in gehou word, maathouer.

contaminate, besoedel, bevlek, besmet.
contamination, besoedeling, besmetting, kontaminasie.
contemn, verag, minag.
contemplate, beskou; (be)peins; van plan wees, beoog.
contemplated, voorgenome, beraamde; – **marriage**, voorgenome huwelik.
contemplation, oorpeinsing; oorweging; kontemplasie.
contemplative, peinsend, nadenkend.
contemporaneous, gelyktydig; van dieselfde tyd.
contemporary, a. gelyktydig.
contemporary, n. tydgenoot; kollega (nuusblad).
contempt, veragting, minagting; **beneath** –, benede kritiek; **hold in** –, verag; – **of court**, minagting van die hof.
contemptibility, veragtelikheid.
contemptible, veragtelik.
contemptuous, minagtend, smalend.
contemptuousness, minagtende houding.
contend, stry, worstel; wedywer; beweer.
content(s), n. inhoud; omvang.
content, a. tevrede, voldaan, vergenoeg; **rest** –, tevrede wees; genoeë neem (met).
content, n. tevredenheid, voldaanheid; **to one's heart's** –, na hartelus.
content, v. tevrede stel.
contended, tevrede, voldaan.
contentedness, tevredenheid, voldaanheid.
contention, twis; bewering; kontensie.
contentious, twissoekerig; betwisbaar; netelig; – **matter**, twispunt, saak wat bespreking uitlok.
contentment, tevredenheid, voldaanheid.
conterminous, aangrensend; saamvallend.
contest, n. geskil, stryd, kamp.
contest, v. bestry, beveg, betwis; stry.
contestable, betwisbaar.
contestant, teenstander; deelnemer.
context, verband, samehang.
contexture, weefsel; samestelling, bou.
contiguity, nabyheid, aangrensing; samehang.
contiguous, aangrensend; volgend.
continence, matigheid; kuisheid.
continent, a. matig, onthoudend; kuis.
continent, n. vasteland, kontinent.
continental, vastelands, kontinentaal.
contingency, toeval(ligheid); gebeurlikheid; gebeurtenis; onvoorsiene uitgawe.
contingent, a. gebeurlik, onseker; toevallig; afhanklik (van); voorwaardelik.
contingent, n. afdeling, kontingent.
continual, aanhoudend, voortdurend.
continuance, aanhoudendheid; voortduring; voortsetting; duur; verblyf.
continuation, voortsetting vervolg; aanhouding; voortduring; verlenging.
continue, aanhou, volhou; vervolg, voortsit; volhard; bly; verleng.
continued, voortdurend, aanhoudend; onafgebroke, voortgeset, vervolg- . . .; – **fraction**, gedurige breuk.
continuity, samehang, verband, aaneenskakeling; kontinuïteit.
continuous, onafgebroke, aanhoudend.
contort, verdraai, verwring.
contortion, verdraaiing, verwringing; –**s**, bogte.
contortionist, (woord)verdraaier; slangmens.
contour, omtrek, lyn, hoogtelyn.
contra, teen, contra.
contraband, a. verbode, smokkel- . . .
contraband, n. kontrabande, smokkelwaar; sluikhandel.
contrabandist, smokkelaar.
contrabass, kontrabas.

contract, n. ooreenkoms, verdrag, kontrak.
contract, v. ooreenkom; inkrimp, saamtrek; – marriage, huwelik aangaan; – habit, gewoonte vorm; – debt, skuld maak; – illness, siekte oploop.
contracted, saamgetrek; verkort; beknop.
contraction, saamtrekking, vernouing; verkorting; sluiting; vorming.
contractor, kontrakteur, aannemer; saamtrekspier.
contradict, weerspreek, ontken, teenspreek, teëpraat.
contradiction, weerspreking; teenspraak, teenstrydigheid.
contradictious, opstryerig, twissiek.
contradictory, teenstrydig; ontkennend; opstryerig.
contradistinction, teenstelling.
contradistinguish, onderskei.
contralto, contralto, diep alt(stem).
contrapuntal, kontrapunt-. . .
contrariety, teenstrydigheid; teenwerking.
contrariness, koppigheid, dwarstrekkerigheid.
contrariwise, inteendeel; omgekeerd, in omgekeerde rigting; koppig.
contrary, a. teenoorgesteld; teengesteld; dwars; koppig, eiewys; – wind, teenwind; – order, teenbevel; – to, in stryd met, in teenstelling met.
contrary, n. teenoorgestelde, teendeel; on the –, inteendeel.
contrast, n. teenstelling, kontras.
contrast, v. teenoorstel, vergelyk; verskil; afsteek (by); kontrasteer.
contravene, oortree; teenstaan, teenwerk.
contravention, oortreding; in – of, in stryd met.
contribute, bydra; meewerk.
contribution, bydrae, insending, kontribusie; medewerking; skatting.
contributor, insender, medewerker.
contributory, bydraend, meewerkend.
contrite, berouvol, boetvaardig, verslae.
contrition, berou, wroeging.
contrivance, bedenksel; versinsel; plan, streek, lis; toestel, middel.
contrive, beding, versin; regkry; bestuur.
control, n. beheer, toesig; beheersing, bedwang; teenrekening; kontrole.
control, v. beheers; bedwing, beteuel; toesig hou; nagaan; kontroleer.
controller, opsigter; kontroleur.
controversial, polemies; betwisbaar, stryd- . . . ; – correspondence, twisgeskryf, pennestryd.
controversialist, polemikus.
controversy, stryd(vraag), twispunt, geskil, twisgeskryf, polemiek; without –, ongetwyfeld, buiten kyf.
controvert, weerlê; betwis, bestry.
controvertible, betwisbaar.
contumacious, weerspanning, weerbarstig.
contumacy, weerspannigheid.
contumelious, beskimpend, honend.
contumely, smaad, hoon; skande.
contuse, kneus.
contusion, kneusing.
conundrum, raaisel, strikvraag.
convalesce, aansterk, beter word, opknap.
convalescence, herstel, beterskap.
convalescent, herstellend; – home, herstellingsoord.
convection, geleiding.
convene, saamroep, belê; vergader.
convener, saamroeper, belêer.
convenience, gerief, gemaak; geskiktheid; voordeel; at your –, op u gemak; wanneer dit u pas.

convenient, gerieflik; geskik; by die hand.
convent, klooster.
conventicle, heimlike samekoms; geheime vergaderplaas.
convention, byeenkoms; ooreenkoms; gebruik, tradisie; konvensie; sien **convene.**
conventional, konvensioneel, gebruiklik; vormlik; gewone (wapens).
conventionalize, konvensioneel maak; stileer.
conventionality, vormlikheid.
converge, (in een punt) saamloop, konvergeer.
convergent, saamlopend, konvergerend.
conversable, onderhoudend; geskik.
conversant, bekend (met), op die hoogte (van), bedrewe (in).
conversation, konversasie, gesprek.
conversational, gesellig, spraaksaam.
converse, v. praat, gesels, konverseer.
converse, n. gesprek; omgang.
converse, a. omgekeerde, teenoorgestelde.
converse, n. (die) omgekeerde, teenoorgestelde.
conversely, omgekeer(d).
conversion, omkering; bekering; omvorming, omsetting; omrekening; konversie.
convert, v. omsit, verander (in, tot), omwissel; bekeer; ('n drie) vervyf.
convert n. bekeerling, bekeerde.
convertible verwisselbaar; inwisselbaar; omkeerbaar.
convex, bol(rond), konveks.
convexity, bolheid, konveksheid.
convey, vervoer, (oor)dra, oorbring; meedeel, gee; sê, beteken; oormaak.
conveyance, vervoer; vervoermiddel; oordrag; transport.
conveyancer, transportbesorger.
conveyancing, transportbesorging.
conveyer, oorbringer, transporteur; – belt, transportband, (ver)voerband.
convict, n. bandiet, dwangarbeider.
convict, v. skuld bewys; skuldig vind; oortuig.
conviction, skuldigverklaring; veroordeling, vonnis; oortuiging.
convince, oortuig.
convincing, oortui(g)end.
convivial, a. feestelik, vrolik.
convivial, n. feestelikheid, gesellige aand.
conviviality, feestelikheid; tafelvreugde.
convocation, byeenroeping; vergadering; konvokasie.
convoke, byeenroep, belê.
convolvulus, convolvulus; slingerblom; winde, een-dag-mooi.
convoy, v. begelei, eskorteer.
convoy, n. konvooi; geleide.
convulse, skud; krampe veroorsaak; be –d with laughter, skud van die lag.
convulsion, skudding; skok; –s, stuipe.
convulsive, krampagtig; stuipagtig.
cony, coney, dassie; konyntjie.
coo, kir, koer; liefkoos.
cook, n. kok.
cook, v. kook; bewerk, vervals.
cooker, kooktoestel, kookding.
cookery, kookkuns.
cookery-book, kookboek.
cookie, koekie.
cooking-range, kookkaggel, stoof.
cooky, kok; kombuisbediende.
cool, a. koel; bedaard, kalm; onverskillig, lusteloos; astrant; – drinks, koue dranke; a – hundred rands, mooi netjies honderd rand.
cool, v. afkoel, verkoel; bekoel; – one's heels, sit en wag, ysbeer.
coolant, koelmiddel.

cooler, koelbak, -emmer; watersak.
coolie, koelie; werkjong.
coon, slimmerd; neger; **-s,** klopse; **- band,** klops.
coop, n. fuik, hoenderhok.
coop, v. opsluit.
cooper, n. kuiper, vatmaker.
cooper, v. kuip; inkuip; opknap.
co-operate, saamwerk, meewerk, koöpereer.
co-operation, samewerking; saamwerk(maatskappy); koöperasie.
co-operative, koöperatief; saamwerk- ...
co-operator, medewerker.
co-opt, koöpteer.
co-optation, koöptasie.
co-ordinate, a. gelyk, van dieselfde rang (orde, mag); newegeskik.
co-ordinate, v. gelykstel, neweskik; in onderlinge verband skik; koördineer.
co-ordinate, n. koördinaat.
co-ordination, gelykstelling; neweskikking; koordinasie.
coot, bleshoender.
cop, n. konstabel.
cop, v. vang, oppak; skaai; **- it, (slae) kry.**
copaiba, kopiva.
copal, kopal, (vernis)harpuis.
copartner, deelgenoot, kompanjon.
cope, n. mantel, kap; dek, deklaag.
cope, v. (af)dek, deklaag opsit; oorwelf.
cope, v. wedywer, meeding; **- with,** opgewasse wees teen; voldoen aan, raad weet met.
copeck, kopek.
coper, perdehandelaar, -koper, -smous.
Copernican, Copernicaans, van Copernicus.
coping, deklaag; **- stone,** deksteen; sluitsteen, kroon, toppunt.
copious, oorvloedig; uitvoerig; ryk.
copiousness, oorvloed(igheid); rykdom.
copper, koper; kopergeld; pennie.
copper, konstabel.
copperas, groenvitriool.
copperplate, koperplaat; kopergravure.
coppersmith, koperslaer.
coppice, kreupelbos, -hout.
copra, kopra, gedroogde klapper.
copse, kreupelbos, -hout.
Coptic, Kopties.
copula, verbinding; koppelwoord.
copulate, paar.
copulative, a. verbindend; parend.
copulative, n. verbindingswoord.
copy, n. kopie; afskrif; nabootsing, namaak; reproduksie; eksemplaar, nummer; kopie, manuskrip; **rough -,** klad; **clear, fair -,** netskrif.
copy, v. kopieer; afskrywe; naskrywe, oorskrywe; naboots, namaak.
copy-book, (skoon)skryfboek.
copying-ink, kopieer-ink.
copying-machine, afrolmasjien.
copyist, afskrywer, oorskrywer.
copyright, kopiereg.
coquet, a. koket, behaagsiek.
coquet, v. koketteer.
coquetry, koketterie, behaagsug.
coquette, koket, behaagsieke vrou.
coquettish, koket, behaagsugtig.
coral, koraal; **- island,** koraaleiland.
coraline, a. koraal- ..., koraalagtig.
coraline, n. koraalmos.
corbel, karbeel, kraagsteen.
corbie, raaf.
corbie-step, geweltrap.

cord, n. tou, lyn, koord, string, band; rib; **vocal -s,** stembande.
cord, v. (vas)bind, tou omsit.
cordage, touwerk, takelasie.
cordial, a. hartlik; hartsterkend.
cordial, n. hartversterking, versterkende medisyne.
cordiality, hartlikheid.
cordite, kordiet, toutjieskruit.
cordon, kordon; ring, ketting; muurlys.
corduroy, ferweel; ferweelbroek.
core, kern, pit, hart, binneste; **at the -,** van binne; **to the -,** deur en deur.
co-respondent, medeverweerder.
coriander, koljander.
Corinthian, Korinthies; Korinthiër.
cork, n. prop; kurk; dobber.
cork, v. toekurk, prop opsit; 'n kol gee.
corker, doodskoot, dooddoener; spekleuen; 'n grote, 'n kolossale.
corkscrew, n. kurktrekker.
corkscrew, v. slinger, draai; met 'n draai uittrek; (uit)wurm, krul.
cork-tipped, met kurk(mondstuk).
cormorant, seeraaf, visvanger.
corn, n. korrel; graan; koring; **Indian -,** mielies.
corn, v. insout.
corn, v. liddoring; **tread on one's -s,** iemand op die tone trap.
corn-chandler, graanhandelaar.
corn-cob, mieliekop.
cornea, horingvlies.
corned beef, soutvleis; blikkiesvleis.
corner, n. hoek; opkoop-spekulasie; **turn the -,** die krisis oorleef; **drive into a -,** vaskeer.
corner, v. vaskeer; in die hoek sit; opkoop.
corner-flag, hoekvlag.
corner-stone, hoeksteen.
cornet, kornet; kornetblaser; kardoes.
corn-exchange, graan-, koringbeurs.
cornfield, koringland, graanveld, -land.
corn-flour, mielieblo(e)m, fyn mieliemeel.
corn-flower, koringblom.
cornice, kroon(lys).
corn-sheaf, koringgerf.
corn-stack, koring-, graanmied.
corn-stalk, graanhalm, -stingel.
cornucopia, horing van oorvloed.
corn-weevil, kalander.
corny, laf, boers, slap, ouderwets.
corolla, blomkroon.
corollary, afleiding, gevolgtrekking, gevolg.
corona, ligkroon; kroonlys; korona *(astr.).*
coronal, kroon, krans.
coronary, kroon-; koronêr; **- thrombosis,** kroonslagaartrombose.
coronation, kroning.
coroner, lykskouer; **-'s inquest,** (geregtelike) lykskouing.
coronet, kroontjie.
corporal, corporeal, a. liggaamlik, stoflik, lyf- ...; **- punishment,** lyfstraf.
corporal, n. korporaal.
corporality, stoflikheid, liggaam(likheid).
corporate, verbonde, verenig, geïnkorporeerd.
corporation, korporasie, vereniging, liggaam, bestuur; buik, pokkel.
corporeal, liggaamlik; stoflik; tasbaar.
corps, korps, afdeling.
corpse, lyk, dooie liggaam.
corpulence, -cy, swaarlywigheid, gesetheid.
corpulent, swaarlywig, geset, korpulent.
corpus, liggaam; versameling.
corpuscle, liggaampie, stoffie, atoom.
corpuscular, atomies.

corral, kraal, kamp.
correct, v. verbeter, nasien, korrigeer; berisp.
correct, a. reg, juis, korrek, noukeurig, presies, netjies.
correction, verbetering, korreksie; berisping.
corrective, a. verbeterend, korrektief.
corrective, n. korrektief, middel tot verbetering.
correctness, juistheid, noukeurigheid, korrektheid.
correlate, n. korrelaat, wederkerige betrekking.
correlate, v. in wederkerige betrekking staan; in wederkerige betrekking bring, korreleer.
correlation, korrelasie, wederkerige betrekking.
correlative, a. korrelatief, in wederkerige betrekking.
correlative, n. korrelatief.
correspond, ooreenkom, ooreenstem; briefwisseling voer; korrespondeer.
correspondence, ooreenkoms; briefwisseling.
correspondent, a. ooreenkomstig.
correspondent, n. korrespondent; beriggewer.
corridor, gang, korridor.
corrigible, verbeterbaar; vatbaar vir verbetering.
corroborate, bevestig, bekragtig.
corroboration, bevestiging, bekragtiging.
corroborative, bevestigend.
corrode, wegvreet; verroes; vergaan.
corrosion, wegvreting; verroesting.
corrosive, a. wegvretend.
corrosive, n. bytende middel.
corrugate, rimpel; golf; –d iron, sink(plaat); –d iron roof, sinkdak; –d road, sinkplaatpad, riffelpad.
corrugation, rimpeling, golwing.
corrupt, a. bedorwe; omkoopbaar.
corrupt, v. bederf; verlei; omkoop.
corruptible, bederflik; omkoopbaar.
corruption, bederf; bedorwenheid; verdorwenheid; verbastering; verminking; omkoping; korrupsie.
corsage, lyfie, keurslyf.
corsair, seerower.
cors(e)let, (bors)harnas; borsstuk.
corset, bors(t)rok, korset.
cortege, stoet, gevolg.
cortex, bas, skors.
cortisone, kortisoon.
corundum, korund(um).
coruscate, flikker, blink, skitter, vonkel.
corvette, korvet.
cosecant, kosekans.
cosh, n. knuppel.
cosh, v. knuppel.
cosh-boy, rampokker.
cosine, kosinus.
cosmetic, kosmetiek, skoonheidsmiddel.
comic(al), kosmies, wêreld- . . .
cosmogony, kosmogonie.
cosmographer, kosmograaf.
cosmography, kosmografie.
cosmonaut, ruimreisiger.
cosmopolitan, a. wêreldburgerlik, kosmopolities.
cosmopolitan, n. wêreldburger, kosmopoliet.
cosmopolite, kosmopoliet.
cosmos, wêreldstelsel, heelal.
Cossack, Kosak.
cosset, vertroetel, verwen.
cost, n. prys, koste; –s, onkoste; at the – of, ten koste van; at any inkoopsprys; at any –, tot elke prys; to his –, tot sy skade; – accountant, kosterekenmeester; – price, inkoopsprys.
cost, v. kos, op te staan kom; prys vasstel.
costal, rib- . . .
costermonger, vrugtesmous; straatventer.

costive, hardlywig, verstop; suinig, vrekkig.
costly, duur; kosbaar.
costume, (klere)drag; kostuum, kleding; pak; rok; – jewellery, kunsjuwele.
cosy, a. behaaglik, gesellig; – corner, gesellige hoekie.
cosy, n. teemus.
cot, n. hok; hut.
cot, n. katel; hangmat; (kinder)bedjie; wieg.
cot(angent), kotangens.
cote, hok, skuur.
coterie, koterie, kliek.
cotillion, cotillon, kotiljons.
cottage, hutjie; villatjie; huisie.
cottar, **cottier**, bywoner.
cotter, spy, wig.
cotton, n. katoen; garing.
cotton, v. dik vriende wees; – up, maats maak, aanpap.
cotton-crop, katoenoes.
cotton-mill, katoenfabriek.
cotton-print, gedrukte katoen.
cotton-spinner, katoenwewer.
cotton-waste, poetskatoen.
cotton-wool, watte.
cotton-yarn, katoendraad.
cotyledon, saadlob, cotyledon.
couch, n. rusbank, sofa; bed, siekbed.
couch, v. neerlê, gaan lê; (spere) laat sak, vel; uitdruk, inklee (in woorde).
couchant, liggend, hurkend; couchant.
couch-grass, kweek(gras).
cough, hoes; – lozenge, hoespepermint, -klontjie.
coulomb, coulomb.
coulter, kouter.
council, raad; – of war, krygsraad.
councillor, raadslid.
counsel, n. raad, raadgewing, plan; beraadslaging; raadgewer, advokaat; take –, oorleg pleeg, konsulteer; keep one's (own) –, jou gedagte vir jouself hou.
counsel, v. raai, raad gee, aanraai.
counsellor, raadgewer, raadsman.
count, n. graaf.
count, v. tel, optel, meetel; reken, ag; – for, werd wees, beteken; – in, saamstel, meereken; – out, uit-, aftel; verdaag; – (up)on, reken op, staatmaak op; – up, optel, opsom.
count, n. tel, rekening; (punt van) aanklag; lose –, die tel kwyt raak.
countenance, n. gesig; uitdrukking; voorkoms(te); change –, van uitdrukking verander; his – fell, hy het 'n lang gesig getrek; keep –, goed hou; sy lag inhou; put out of –, verleë maak.
countenance, v. toelaat; begunstig, steun.
counter, n. blokkie, skyfie; toonbank.
counter, n. teller.
counter, a. teen- . . .; teenoorgestelde.
counter, v. teengaan; teenset doen, antwoord; pareer.
counter, adv. teen in, in die teenoorgestelde rigting; run – to, teen ingaan.
counteract, teenwerk; ophcf; verydel.
counter-attack, teenaanval.
counter-attraction, ander afleiding.
counterbalance, n. teen(ge)wig.
counterbalance, v. opwee(g) teen, ophef.
counterblast, antwoord, terugslag.
countercharge, teenbeskuldiging.
countercheck, rem, teenwig; kontrole.
counter-claim, teeneis.
counter-clockwise, teen die wysters van die klok in, agteruit.
counter-espionage, teenspioenasie.
counterfeit, n. namaaksel; afbeeldsel.

counterfeit, a. nagemaak, oneg, vals.
counterfeit, v. namaak, vervals; huigel.
counterfeiter, vervalser, namaker.
counterfoil, teenblad; kontrabiljet.
counter-jumper, winkelbediende.
countermand, v. herroep, teenbevel gee; bestelling intrek.
countermand, n. teenbevel.
counter-march, teenmars.
countermark, kontramerk.
countermine, n. kontramyn; teenlis.
countermine, v. kontramineer, ondergrawe.
counter-objection, teenbeswaar.
counterpane, deken, bedsprei.
counterpart, teenstuk; teenhanger; teenstem; ewebeeld, kopie.
counterplot, n. teenlis, teenkomplot.
counterplot, v. 'n teenlis smee, uitoorlê.
counterpoint, kontrapunt.
counterpoise, n. teen(ge)wig.
counterpoise, v. opwee(g) teen, ophef.
counterpoison, teengif (teëgif).
counter-revolution, teenrevolusie.
countersign, n. wagwoord; herkenningsteken, —woord.
countersign, v. mee-onderteken.
countess, gravin.
counting-house, (bankiers)kantoor.
countless, ontelbaar, talloos.
count-out, verdaging; uittel(ling).
countrified, boers, agtervelds.
country, land; landstreek; vaderland; platteland; go to the –, die kiesers raadpleeg; – **club,** buiteklub; – **cousin,** plaasjapie; – **life,** boerelewe.
country-dance, kontradans.
country-house, buiteverblyf, landgoed.
countryman, landgenoot; landbewoner.
country-people, buitemense.
country-seat, landgoed, buiteplaas.
country-town, dorp.
country, graafskap, provinsie, distrik.
coupé, koepee; geslote rytuigie.
couple, n. paar, span.
couple, v. verbind, in verband bring; koppel; paar.
coupler, koppelaar, koppeling.
couplet, koeplet, vers (van twee reëls).
coupon, koepon; rentebewys; kaartjie.
courage, moed, dapperheid, koerasie; **pluck up,** take –, moed skep; – **of one's opinions,** die moed van jou oortuiging.
courageous, moedig, dapper.
courier, koerier, boodskapper.
course, n. loop, gang; vaart; loopbaan, koers, rigting, (ren)baan; kursus, leergang; ry, reeks; laag; gereg; – **of events,** loop van gebeurtenisse; – **of nature,** gewone (be)loop (van omstandighede); – **of exchange,** wisselkoers; let it take its –, op sy beloop laat; – **of action,** handelwyse; **in** – **of erection,** in aanbou; **in due** –, mettertyd; **in** – **of time,** in die loop van tyd; **of** –, natuurlik; **matter of** –, gewone ding, vanselfsprekend.
course, v. jag; snel, vloei, loop.
courser, re(i)sie(s)perd.
court, n. hof; kantoor, hofsaal, geregshof, regbank; hofhouding; baan; agterplaas; – **of justice,** geregshof; **supreme** –, hooggeregshof; – **of appeal,** appèlhof; go to –, na die hof gaan, 'n saak maak; **pay one's** – **to,** die hof maak (aan); **settle out of** –, (in der minne) skik.
court, v. die hof maak; vry (na); uitlok, soek; – **trouble,** moeilikheid soek.

court-card, pop(kaart), honneurkaart.
courteous, beleef, hoflik, hoofs.
courtesy, hoflikheid; buiging; **by** – **of, deur die welwillendheid (van).**
courtier, howeling.
courtly, hoofs, hoflik.
court-martial, krygsraad.
courtship, hofmakery, vryery.
courtyard, agter-, binneplaas.
cousin, neef (niggie); oomskind; **first** –, volle neef (niggie); **second** –, agterneef (niggie).
cousinship, neefskap; bloedverwantskap.
cove, n. kreek, inham, baai; gewelf.
cove, v. welf.
cove, n. drommel, vent.
covenant, n. verbod, verdrag.
covenant, v. ooreenkom, 'n verbond sluit.
cover, v. (be)dek, oordek; beskerm; beheers, bestryk; aanlê op; betaal; dek; – **up,** toemaak; bedek; geheim hou.
cover, n. (be)dekking; deksel; band, omslag; skuilplaas; dekmantel; kreupelhout, bossies; reserwe, dekkingsfonds.
coverage, dekking; voorsiening; verslag; strekvermoë (verf).
cover-girl, fotomeisie.
covering, oortreksel, bedekking (om)hulsel.
coverlet, deken, sprei; dekkleed.
cover-point, dekpunt.
covert, a. bedek, geheim, onderlangs.
covert, n. skuilplaas; kreupelhout, bossies.
covertly, skelm(pies), onderlanges.
coverture, bedekking; staat van gehude vrou.
covet, begeer.
covetous, begerig; gierig, inhalig.
covey, vlug, broeisel (patryse); klompie.
cow, n. koei; wyfie.
cow, v. bang maak, oorbluf.
coward, lafaard, bangbroek.
cowardice, lafhartigheid.
cowardly, lafhartig.
cow-boy, beeswagter, „cowboy".
cow-catcher, baanveêr, kouter.
cower, koes, hurk, kruip; ineenkrimp.
cowherd, beeswagter.
cow-hide, koeivel; karwats; spantou.
cowl, kap; monnikskap.
cow-lick, kroontjie.
cow-pox, (koei)pokkies.
cowslip, sleutelblom.
cox, sien **coxswain.**
coxcomb, snuiter, windmaker, snoeshaan.
coxcombry, windmakerigheid, snoewery.
coxswain, bootsman, stuurman.
coy, sedig, skaam, bedees, verleë, afgeleë.
coyote, prairiewolf.
cozen, fop; – **into,** ompraat, (verlei) tot.
crab, n. krap; kreef; wen(as).
crab, n. wilde suurappel; iesegrim.
crab, v. baklei; bekritiseer, uitmekaartrek.
crabbed, nors, stuurs; onduidelik.
crack, n. (ge)klap; kraak, knak, bars; praatjie; doring, bobaas, uithaler; inbreker; inbraak.
crack, v. kraak, klap, bars, knap, skeur; grootpraat, windmaak; gesels; – **a joke,** 'n grap vertel; – **a bottle,** 'n fles knap; – **up,** ophemel.
crack, a. uithaler-...; baas-...
crack-brained, kranksinnig; roekeloos.
cracked, gekraak; gek, getik.
cracker, neutkraker; klapper; klinker.
crackle, kraak; knapper, knetter.
crackling, gekraak; geknetter; varkvel.
cracksman, inbreker.
cradle, n. wieg; bakermat; spalk, raamwerk; slee (op 'n skeepswerf).

cradle 458 **cricket**

cradle, v. wieg; in die wieg lê; beskerm.
craft, ambag, handwerk; vaartuig; behendigheid; lis(tigheid), geslepenheid.
craftsman, vakman, ambagsman.
crafty, handig, slim, slu, listig.
crag, krans, rots.
cragged, craggy, rotsagtig; steil.
cram, v. volstop, instop; inswelg, gretig sluk; inpomp, blok.
cram, n. geblok; gedrang; leuen.
cram-full, propvol, tjokvol.
cramp, n. kramp.
cramp, n. kram, klamp, (muur)anker.
cramp, a. onduidelik; nou, bekrompe.
cramp, v. kramp veroorsaak; belemmer, beklem; vaskram.
cramped, gedronge, beklem; onduidelik.
crampon, haak.
cranberry, bosbes.
crane, n. kraanvoël; kraan; hewel.
crane, v. (nek) uittrek; (met 'n hyskraan) oplig;. – at, vassteek vir.
cranial, skedel-. . .
craniology, skedelleer.
cranium, skedel.
crank, n. krukas; kruk; slinger, arm.
crank, v. draai, (aan)slinger.
crank, n. gril; 'n sonderling.
crank-case, krukkas.
cranking-handle, slinger.
crank-shaft, krukas.
cranky, sieklik; lendelam; eksentriek; slingerig; onvas, rank.
cranny, skeur, bars.
crape, krip, lanfer.
crapulence, onmatigheid; mislikheid.
crapulent, crapulous, dranklustig; mislik.
crash, v. raas; neerstort; verpletter; bots; bankrot gaan.
crash, n. geraas, lawaai; botsing; ineenstorting, val; bankrotskap.
crash, n. graslinne.
crash-dive, n. snelduik.
crash-helmet, valhelm.
crash-land, v. 'n buiklanding doen.
crass, grof, sterk, erg, kras.
crassitude, grofheid, lompheid, stomheid.
crassness, grofheid, krasheid; stomheid.
crate, krat, mandjie, kis, hok.
crater, krater.
cravat, krawat, das.
crave, bid, smeek, uitroep (om), verlang (na).
craven, n. lafaard.
craven, a. lafhartig.
craving, verlange, behoefte, begeerte, lus.
craw, krop.
crawfish, sien **crayfish.**
crawl, v. kruip; aansukkel; met die kruipslag; swem; – with, krioel van.
crawl, n. gekruip; sukkelgangetjie; kruipslag (by swem); gekriewel.
crawly, kriewelrig.
crayfish, (rivier)kreef.
crayon, n. (teken)kryt; pastel(tekening); koolspits.
crayon, v. kryttekening maak; skets.
craze, v. gekraak wees; afskilfer; gek maak.
craze, n. gekheid, gier, manie; mode.
craziness, kransinnigheid.
crazy, gek, waansinnig; lendelam; mal (oor iets of iemand); – **path,** hobbelpaadjie.
creak, v. kraak, knars, piep, skreeu.
creak, n. gekraak, geknars, gepiep.
cream, n. room; puik, blo(e)m; – **of tartar,** kremetart.

cream, a. roomkleurig, crême.
cream, v. room; afroom; room ingooi.
creamery, botterfabriek; melkinrigting.
cream-laid paper, crème geribde skryfpapier.
cream-separator, roomafskeier, roommasjien.
crease, n. vou, plooi, rimpel; streep (krieket).
crease, v. vou, plooi, rimpel, kreukel.
create, skep; in die lewe roep, voortbring; veroorsaak; benoem, kreëer.
creation, skepping; benoeming; werk; kreasie.
creative, skeppend.
creator, skepper; ontwerper.
creature, skepsel; kreatuur; mens; huurling, ondergeskikte dier.
credence, geloof, vertroue; **give** – **to,** geloof heg aan.
credentials, geloofsbriewe.
credibility, geloofwaardigheid.
credible, aanneemlik; geloofwaardig.
credit, n. vertrou, geloof;.reputasie, agting, aansien; eer; krediet; passiva; **give** – **to,** geloof heg aan; **get** – **for,** erkenning ontvang vir; **give** – **for,** eer gee vir; in staat ag, kapabel toe beskou; **it does him** –, dit strek hom tot eer; – **balance,** batige saldo.
credit, v. geloof, krediteer; – **with,** krediteer met; verwag van, in staat ag tot.
creditable, verdienstelik; fatsoenlik.
creditor, skuldeiser, krediteur.
credo, credo, geloof, geloofsartikels.
credulity, liggelowigheid.
credulous, lig-, goedgelowig.
creed, geloof, geloofsbelydenis.
creek, kreek, bog, baaitjie; sytak, spruit.
creel, vismandjie.
creep, v. kruip, sluip; vooruit-, aansukkel; kriewel, hoendervleis kry; dreg.
creep, n. krieweling; kruipgat; **give the** – kriewelrig maak; hoendervleis laat kry.
creeper, kruiper; slinger-, klimplant.
creepy, kruipend; grillerig.
cremate, verbrand, veras.
cremation, lykverbranding, verassing, kremasie.
crematorium, krematorium.
crenel(l)ated, gekanteel(d).
Creole, a. Kreools.
Creole, n. Kreool.
creosote, kreosoot; karbolsuur.
crêpe, lanfer, crêpe (krip); – **de chine,** crêpe de chine.
crepitate, kraak.
crepitation, kraakgeluid, krepitasie.
crescent, a. groeiend; halfmaanvormig.
crescent, n. groeiende maan; halfmaan.
cress, bronkors, waterkers.
cresset, lig-, vuurbaken.
crest, n. kuif; kam; pluim; maanhare; (skuim), top, kop, kruin; wapen, helmteken.
crest, v. kuif opsit; die top bereik; skuimkoppe vorm.
crested, gekuif, met 'n kuif.
crest-fallen, terneergeslae, druipstert.
cretaceous, krytagtig, kryt-. . . .
Crete, Kreta.
cretonne, kreton.
crevasse, ysskeur.
crevice, skeur, spleet, kloof.
crew, bemanning; trop, bende, gespuis.
crib, n. krip; stal; hutjie; bedjie; afskryfwerk, sleutelvertaling.
crib, v. in-, opsluit; skaai; afkyk, -skryf.
crib-biter, kripbyter.
crick, stywe nek; spit in die rug; kramp.
cricket, kriek(ie).
cricket, krieket.

cricketer, krieketspeler.
cricket-match, krieketwedstryd.
crier, omroeper.
crikey!, mastig!
crime, misdaad; wandaad.
Crimea, The, Die Krim.
criminal, misdadig; krimineel; – code, strafwetboek; – law, strafreg; – investigation department (C.I.D.), speurdiens.
criminate, aankla; berisp; skuldig maak.
crimination, beskuldiging; berisping.
criminology, kriminologie, misdaadleer.
crimp, n. matrose-, soldatewerwer, ronselaar.
crimp, v. werf, vang, ronsel.
crimp, v. plooi, krinkel, rimpel; krul.
crimson, a. karmosyn(rooi), hoogrooi.
crimson, n. karmosyn.
cringe, ineenkrimp; kruip; witvoetjie soek.
cringer, kruipeling, lekker, kalfakter.
crinkle, v. krinkel, frommel, kreukel.
crinkle, n. plooi, vou, krinkel, kreukel.
crinoline, hoepelrok, krinolien.
cripple, a. kreupel, mank.
cripple, n. 'n kreupele, 'n gebreklike, 'n manke.
cripple, v. kreupel, gebreklik maak; verlam; belemmer; onskadelik maak.
crisis, keerpunt, krisis.
crisp, a. kroes; krullerig; knappend, bros; fris, opwekkend; lewendig, beslis.
crisp, v. krul, golwe.
crispate, gekrul, omgekrul.
crispness, krullerigheid, kroeserigheid; brosheid; frisheid; beslistheid.
criterion, maatstaf, toets, kriterium.
critic, kritikus, resensent, beoordelaar.
critical, kritiek, haglik; krities; vitterig.
criticise, kritiseer, resenseer, beoordeel; vit.
criticism, beoordeling, resensie, kritiek; aanmerking, vuttery.
critique, kritiek.
croak, kwaak; naarheid voorspel; vrek.
croaker, ongeluksprofeet.
Croatia, Kroasië.
Croatian, Kroaties.
crochet, v. hekel.
crochet, n. hekelwerk.
crochet-hook, hekelpennetjie.
crock, v. breek, seermaak, kapotmaak.
crock, n. erdepot; knol, kruk; old –s, ou knolle.
crockery, erdegoed, breekgoed.
crocodile, krokodil.
crocodile tears, krokodiltrane.
crocus, krokus.
croft, lappie grond, kamp, land.
crofter, pagter, kleinboer.
crone, ou wyf, heks; ou-nooi.
crony, boesemvriend, boetie, kornuit.
crook, n. haak; staf; bog, buiging; bedrieër, opligter (Amer.); on the –, oneerlik, skelm.
crook, v. buig; oplig, bedrieg, fop.
crooked, krom, gebuie, verdraai; geboë, mismaak; slinks, oneerlik.
croon, v. binnensmonds sing, neurie, brom.
croon, n. geneurie, gebrom.
crop, n. krop; handvatsel, steel; rysweep; gewas, gesaaide, oes; knipsel; kortgeknipte hare, kaalkop.
crop, v. afsny; kort knip; afeet, afvreet; oes, pluk; dra (van gesaaide); – out, uitkom, opkom; – up, voor die dag kom, op die lappe kom.
crop-eared, stompoor.
cropper, knipper; vreter; draer; kropduif; come a –, baken steek, val; 'n ongeluk oorkom, jou rieme styfloop.

croquet, n. croquet.
croquet, v. wegstamp, wegslaan.
croquet(te), kroket.
crosier, biskopstaf.
cross, n. kruis; (ras)kruising; kruisproduk, baster; verneukery.
cross, v. kruis; deurkruis; met 'n kruis merk; oorgaan, oorsteek; dwarsboom, teenwerk; verbygaan by mekaar; – one's mind, deur jou gedagte gaan; – out, uitskrap, deurhaal.
cross, a. dwars, oorkruis; verkeerd; kwaad, kwaai.
cross-bar, dwarshout; swingel; draaghoutjie.
cross-beam, dwarsbalk, kruisbalk.
cross-bow, kruisboog, handboog.
cross-bred, van gekruiste ras, kruisras- . . .
cross-breed, n. gekruiste ras, kruisras.
cross breed, v. kruis.
cross-bun, paasbroodjie, -beskuitjie.
cross-country, oor heg en steg; – race, heg-enstegwedloop; – runner, veldloper.
cross-cut, dwarssny; – saw, dwarssaag, treksaag.
cross-entry, teenpos, kontraboeking.
cross-examination, kruisverhoor.
cross-examine, kruisvra(ag).
cross-eyed, skeel.
cross-fire, kruisvuur.
cross-grained, teendraads; dwars, stuurs.
crossing, kruising, kruispunt, oorgang; (die) oorsteek; dwarspad; -straat.
cross-legged, kruisbeen(s), met gevoude bene, met die bene oormekaar.
crossness, boosheid, kwaadheid; kwaaiigheid.
cross-purpose, teenstrydige doel; be at –, mekaar misverstaan; mekaar in die hare sit.
cross-question, n. kruisvraag.
cross-question, v. kruisvrae stel, kruisvra(ag).
cross-reference, verwysing.
cross-road, dwarspad; at the –s, op die tweesprong; op die keerpunt.
cross-section, dwarssnee; dwarsprofiel; deursneeproef (fig.).
cross-way, kruisweg, dwarspad.
cross-wind, teenwind; sywind.
crosswise, oorkruis.
crotchet, hakie; kwartnoot; gril, gier.
crotchety, vol grille, wispelturig, buierig.
crouch, hurk, buk; kruip.
croup, kroep.
croup(e), kruis; rug (van 'n saal).
crow, n. kraai; koevoet; as the – flies, in 'n regte lyn.
crow, v. kraai; babbel, brabbel; spog; vermaak; – over, windmaak oor, spog op.
crowbar, koevoet, breekyster.
crowd, n. menigte, klomp, hoop; gedrang op-loop.
crowd, v. (opeen)dring, druk, ophoop; vul; volprop; – into, indring; volstop; – out, uitdruk; – sail, alle seile bysit.
crow-foot, ranonkel; voetangel; hanepoot.
crown, n. kroon; krans; kruin; bol (van hoed); – land, staatsgrond; – prosecutor, publieke vervolger.
crown, v. (be)kroon; koning maak (in dambord); to – all, om die kroon op te sit; om die naarheid te kroon.
crowning, hoogste, grootste; – glory, hoogtepunt, toppunt.
crown-wheel, kroonrat, dryfrat.
crow's-feet, ouderdomsrimpels, oogrimpels.
crucial, kruisvormig; kritiek, beslissend.
crucible, smeltkroes; vuurproef.
crucifix, kruisbeeld; kruis.
crucifixion, kruisiging.

crucify, kruisig, kruis.
crude, ru; onbeholpe; onafgewerk; onryp; ongesuiwer(d).
crudeness, crudity, ruheid; onbeholpenheid; onsuiwerheid.
cruel, wreed, wreedaardig, onmenslik.
cruelty, wreedheid, onmenslikheid.
cruet, standertjie; kruikie.
cruet-stand, standertjie; asynstelletjie.
cruise, v. kruis, vaar.
cruise, n. tog, vaart.
cruiser, kruiser; – weight, ligswaargewig.
crumb, krummel.
crumble, krummel; (af)brokkel.
crummy, sag, mollig, lekker; ryk.
crumpet, plaatkoek.
crumple, kreukel, verfrommel.
crunch, v. kraak, hard kou, knars.
crunch, n. gekraak; geknars.
crupper, stertriem; kruis (van 'n perd).
crusade, kruistog, -vaart.
crusader, kruisvaarder.
crush, v. plat druk; onderdruk; verpletter, vermorsel; verkreukel.
crush, n. verplettering; gedrang; groot party.
crusher, stamper.
crush-hat, deukhoed.
crushing, verpletterend, verdrukkend.
crust, n. kors; roof; aanbrandsel; aansetsel.
crust, v. kors (vorm); aanbrand.
crustaceous, geskub, geskaal.
crusty, korsterig; korselig, brommig.
crutch, kruk; steun.
crux, crux (kruks), knoop, moeilikheid.
cry, n. skreeu, (ge)roep, kreet, gil; gehuil, geween; klag, bede, roepstem; geblaf; **within** –, binne stembereik; **a far** –, 'n groot afstand (verskil); – **of alarm,** noodkreet.
cry, v. roep, uitroep, skreeu; huil, ween; blaf; – **about,** huil om (oor); – **down,** afbreek, slegmaak; – **off,** terugstaan, kop uittrek; – **for,** huil (roep) om; – **out,** uitroep; – **out against,** die stem verhef teen; – **shame upon,** skande roep oor.
cry-baby, huilebalk; piepkindjie, tjankbalie.
crying, huilend, skreeuend; ergerlik, tergend; – **injustice,** skreiende onreg.
crypt, kelder; grafkelder; kripta.
cryptic, geheim(sinnig), duister.
cryptogram, -graph, stuk in geheimskrif, kriptogram.
crystal, a. kristal.
crystal, a. (kristal)helder.
crystalline, kristal- . . .; – **lens,** kristallens.
crystallize, kristalliseer; **–d fruit,** versuikerde vrugte.
cub, n. welp, (klein) leeutjie, beertjie, jakkalsie, ens.; ongepoetste vent; – **reporter,** onervare verslaggewer.
cubby-hole, hokkie; paneelvak, -kassie.
cube, n. kubus; kubiekgetal, derdemag; – **root,** kubiekwortel, derdemagswortel.
cube, v. tot die derdemag verhef; (kubieke) inhoud bereken; kubeer.
cubic(al), kubiek; – **content,** kubieke inhoud; – **equation,** derdemagsvergelyking.
cubicle, slaap-, baaihokkie.
cubism, kubisme.
cubit, ellemaat, voorarmslengte.
cuckold, n. horingdraer.
cuckold, v. horings opsit, bedrieg.
cuckoo, koekoek.
cucumber, komkommer; **cool as a –,** doodkalm.
cud, herkoutjie; **chew the –,** herkou; peins, prakseer.

cuddle, liefkoos, omhels, karnuffel; lepellê; – **up,** opgerol gaan lê; instop.
cudgel, n. kierie, stok; **take up the –s for,** verdedig, in die bres tree vir.
cudgel, v. afros, onder die kierie kry; – **one's brain,** jou kop breek, jou harsings pynig.
cue, wenk, aanwysing; wagwoord.
cue, keu; stert, haarvleg; biljartstok; tou; **stand in a –,** toustaan.
cuff, n. omslag, mansjet, (hemps)mou; **–s,** (hemps)moue; boeie.
cuff, n. klap, oorveeg, opstopper.
cuff, v. klap, oorveeg gee.
cuff-link, mansjetknoop, mouskakel.
cuirass, (bors)harnas, kuras.
cuirassier, kurassier.
cuisine, keuken; tafel.
cul-de-sak, blinde steeg, sakstraat.
culinary, kombuis- . . ., kook- . . .; – **art,** kookkuns.
cull, pluk; uitsoek, uitvang.
cullender, colander, vergiet(tes).
culls, n. uitskot, bog, uitvangskape.
culminate, die hoogtepunt bereik, kulmineer.
culmination, hoogtepunt, toppunt.
culpability, skuld, strafbaarheid.
culpable, skuldig, strafbaar; – **negligence,** strafbare versuim.
culprit, skuldige, boosdoener; beskuldigde.
cult, erediens, kultus, verering.
cultivate, bewerk; (aan)kweek, verbou; ontwikkel, beskaaf; beoefen, kultiveer.
cultivation, bewerking; verbouing; ontwikkeling, beskawing.
cultivator, kweker, verbouer; beoefenaar; beskawer; skoffelploeg, -eg.
cultural, kultuur- . . ., beskawings- . . ., beskawend; – **value,** kultuurwaarde.
culture, n. verbouing, kweking; veredeling, beskawing; ontwikkeling, kultuur.
cultured, bewerk; beskaaf, ontwikkel(d).
culvert, riool; spoelgat, duiksloot.
cumber, hinder, belemmer; belas.
cumbersome, cumbrous, lastig, hinderlik.
cumin-seed, komynsaad.
cumulate, ophoop, opstapel, vermeerder.
cumulation, ophoping, opstapeling, toename.
cumulative, ophopend; kumulatief; – **preferent shares,** kumulatief-preferente aandele.
cumulus, hoop, stapel; stapelwolk.
cuneiform, a. wigvormig.
cuneiform, n. spykerskrif.
cunning, a. slim, geslepe; bedrewe.
cunning, n. geslepenheid; bedrewenheid.
cup, n. koppie; beker; kelkie; kommetjie; **a bitter –,** 'n bittere beker.
cup, v. bloedlaat; 'n grondskoot slaan.
cup-bearer, skinker.
cupboard, kas, muurkas, koskas.
Cupid, Kupido.
cupidity, begerigheid, hebsug, inhaligheid.
cupola, koepel.
cur, brak(kie); skobbejak, skurk.
curable, geneeslik, geneesbaar.
Curaçao, Curaçao; curaçao (likeur).
curate, (hulp)predikant.
curative, genesend.
curator, opsigter; voog; kurator.
curb, n. kenketting; rem, beteueling; rand.
curb, v. inhou, beteuel; bedwing.
curb(stone), sien **kerb(stone).**
curd, dikmelk, stemsel.
curdle, dik word; stol (van bloed).
cure, n. (genees)middel; genesing.

cure, v. genees, gesondmaak; verhelp, regmaak; inlê, sout, rook, droogmaak.
curfew, aand-, nagklok.
curio, kuriositeit, kunsvoorwerp, curio.
curiosity, nuuskierigheid, weetgierigheid, kuriositeit, seldsaamheid, rariteit.
curious, weetgierig; nuuskierig; snaaks, merkwaardig, seldsaam
curl, n. krul; (haar)lok.
curl, v. krul, kronkel, draai; – up, opdraai; inmekaar sak, opvou.
curler, krulpen, -yster.
curlew, (soort) watersnip.
curling-pin, krulspeld, -naald, -pen.
curling-tongs, friseeryster, krultang.
curly, gekrul, krullerig, krul-...
curmudgeon, gierigaard, vrek.
currant, korent.
currency, omloop; gangbaarheid; munt.
current, a. lopende; in omloop, gangbaar; aangenome, algemeen.
current, n. stroom; stroming; loop, koers.
curriculum, kursus, leerplan.
currier, (leer)looier, -breier.
curry, n. kerrie.
curry, v. roskam; brei; vel, klop; – favour, witvoetjie soek.
curry-comb, roskam.
curse, n. vloek, vervloeking; straf.
curse, v. vloek, vervloek, laster; –d with, gestraf met, opgeskeep met.
cursed, vervloek(te), vervloekste.
cursive, lopend.
cursory, oppervlakkig, vlugtig; kursories.
curt, kortaf, bits(ig).
curtail, verkort, inkort, besnoei.
curtain, n. gordyn; skerm; klappie (van 'n kar); behind the –s, agter die skerme; lift the –, die sluier oplig; drop the –, die skerm laat sak.
curtain, v. met gordyne behang (afskei).
curtain-fire, skermvuur.
curtain-lecture, bedpreek, -sermoen.
curtain-raiser, voorstuk.
curtain-rod, gordynpaal; gordynstaaf.
curtilage, binneplaas.
curts(e)y, n. (knie)buiging, knieknik; drop a –, 'n buiging maak, deurknik.
curts(e)y, v. 'n buiging maak.
curvature, kromming; buiging.
curve, v. buig, draai, 'n bog maak.
curve, n. boog; kromme; bog, draai.
curvet, bokspring.
curvilinear, kromlynig.
cusec, kusek.
cushion, n. kussing; band (van biljarttafel).
cushion, v. opstop, van kussings voorsien; teen die band laat lê (biljart).
cusp, punt, keerpunt.
cuspidor, kwispedoor.
cuss, vloek; skepsel, vent.
cussed, vervloek(te); befoeterd.
cussedness, befoeterdheid.
custard, vla; baked –, vlapoeding.
custodian, bewaarder, opsigter.
custody, bewaring; hegtenis; voogdyskap; take into –, in hegtenis neem.
custom, gewoonte, gebruik; klandisie; –s, invoerregte, doeane.
customary, gebruiklik, gewoon.
customer, klant; an ugly –, 'n gevaarlike klant.
custom-house, doeanekantoor, tolhuis.
customs officer, tol-, doeanebeampte.
cut, n. sny; kap; slag, hou; raps; keep; snit fatsoen, vorm; short –, kort paadjie.
cut, v. sny; kerf; kap; raps, 'n hou gee; snoei; knip; klief; aanslaan; koepeer, afneem, afdek; grief, seer maak; – capers, flikkers maak; – a sorry figure, 'n treurige figuur slaan; – the teeth, tande kry; – to the heart, diep grief; – a person, iemand nie wil raak sien nie; – short, in die rede val; – across, oorsteek; – down, afkap; besnoei; – in, inval, in die rede val; – off, afkap; afsny; onderskep; stop; – off with a shilling, onterf; – out, uitsny; uitsit, hand in die as slaan; uitloot; have one's work – out, flink moet aanpak, homself moet ken; – up, in stukke sny; afmaak, hard behandel; feel – up, sleg voel; – up rough, kwaad word, uitvaar.
cut, a. gesny (gesnede); – and dried, kant en klaar; verouderd, ouderwets.
cut-away, swa(w)elstertbaadjie.
cute, oulik, slim, geslepe.
cut-glass, geslepe glas.
cuticle, opperhuid; vliesie.
cutlass, hartsvanger, kortelas.
cutler, messemaker.
cutlery, messeware, messegoed, tafelgereedskap
cutlet, kotelet, karmenaadjie.
cut-out, knalopening; uitskakelaar.
cut-purse, sakkeroller; dief.
cutter, snyer; snymasjien; kotter (boot).
cut-throat, n. moordenaar; skurk.
cut-throat, a. moorddadig; meedoënloos.
cutting, uitknipsel; uitgrawing; steggie.
cuttle-fish, inkvis.
cutty, stompie(pyp), neuswarmertjie.
cycle, n. kringloop; fiets, rywiel.
cycle, v. kringloop volbring; fiets, fietsry.
cyclic, siklies.
cyclist, fietsryer, fietser, wielryer.
cyclone, sikloon, warrelwind, windhoos
cyclopaedia, ensiklopedie.
cyclops, sikloop, eenoog.
cyclotron, siklotron.
cygnet, jong swaan.
cylinder, silinder.
cylindric, silindries, silindervormig.
cymbal, simbaal.
cynic, a. sinies; honds, bytend, skerp.
cynic, n. sinikus.
cynicism, sinisme.
cynosure, poolster; lei-ster, aantrekkingspunt.
cypher, sien cipher,
cypress, sipres.
Cypriot, n. Ciprioot.
Cypriot, a. Cipries.
Cyprus, Ciprus.
cyst, blaas, blaar, sak sist.
Czar, Tsaar.
Czech, n. Tsjek.
Czech, a. Tsjeggies.
Czechoslovakia, Tsjeggo-Slowakye.
Czechoslovak(ian), Tsjeggo-Slowaak.
Czechoslovakian, a. Tsjeggo-Slowaaks.

D

dab, v. tik; bet, aanstip.
dab, n. tikkie, kloppie; spatsel.
dabble, spat, plas; doen aan (bv. kuns).
dabchick, duikertjie.
dactyl, daktiel.
dad, daddy, pa, pappie.
daddy-longlegs, langbeenspinnekop.
dado, beskot, lambrisering.
daffodil, affodil, geel narsing.
daft, dwaas, gek, mal.
dagger, dolk; **be at -s drawn**, op voet van oorlog met mekaar wees.
daguerreotype, daguerreotipe.
dahlia, dahlia.
daily, a. & adv. daagliks, dag- . . . ; - **paper**, dagblad.
daily, n. dagblad.
daintiness, fynheid, kieskeurigheid.
dainty, n. lekkerny, delikates.
dainty, a. fyn, sierlik, delikaat; kieskeurig.
dairy, melkery, melkkamer.
dairy-farm, melkboerdery.
dairyman, melkboer.
dairy produce, suiwelproduk(te).
dais, verhoog; troonhemel.
daisy, madeliefie; margriet.
dale, dal, vlei, kom, leegte.
dally, dartel, speel; drentel, treusel.
dam, n. damwal; dam.
dam, v. opdam; stuit, keer.
dam, n. moe(de)r.
damage, n. skade; onkoste, skadevergoeding; **pay -s**, skadevergoeding betaal.
damage, v. beskadig, bederf; benadeel.
damascene, demasseer.
damask, n. damas; damaskusrooi.
damask, v. damasseer; met damaspatroon weef.
damask-rose, damasroos, muskaatroos.
damask-silk, damassy.
dame, dame; vrou; huisvrou; adellike dame.
damn, v. verdoem, veroordeel; benadeel, skend; afkeur, vloek.
damn, n. vloek; **not a -**, geen steek (flenter) nie.
damnable, verdoemlik; vervloeks(te).
damnation, n. verdoemenis; veroordeling.
damnatory, verdoemend, veroordelend.
damnify, beskadig, benadeel.
damp, n. vogtigheid, vog; neerslagtigheid.
damp, a. vogtig, klam.
damp, v. smoor; demp; laat bekoel, neerslagtig maak; klam maak, besprinkel.
damper, demper; skuif (in 'n kaggelpyp); teleurstelling, domper.
damsel, maagd, jonkvrou.
damson, damaspruim.
dance, v. dans; - **attendance upon**, agternaloop.
dance, n. dans; bal, dansparty; **lead one a -**, iemand die wêreld moeilik maak.
dancer, danser(es).
dancing, dans, gedans.
dancing-card, balboekie.
dancing-girl, balletdanseres.
dancing-room, danssaal, balsaal.
dandelion, perdeblom.
dander, slegte humeur, ergernis.
dandify, opskik, optakel.
dandle, wip, ry; wieg; troetel, verwen.
dandruff, skilfers.
dandy, n. fat, modegek, windmaker.
dandy, a. fatterig, windmakerig, keurig.
Dane, Deen; Noorman; Deense hond.
danger, gevaar, bedreiging; - **signal**, onveiligsein, gevaarsein.
dangerous, gevaarlik.

dangle, swaai, bengel, slinger; in uitsig stel; agternaloop.
dangler, naloper; slenteraar.
Danish, Deens.
dank, nat.
Danube, Donau.
dapper, vief, lewendig; agtermekaar.
dapple, v. (be)spikkel; vlek.
dapple, n. spikkel, vlek.
dapple, a. gespikkel, gevlek.
dapple-grey, appelskimmel.
darbies, boeie.
Dardanelles, Dardanelle.
dare, durf; waag, die moed hê; trotseer; **I - say**, ek veronderstel; dit wil ek glo!
dare-devil, waaghals.
dare-devilry, waaghalsery.
daring, n. durf, vermetelheid.
daring, a. koen, vermetel, astrant.
dark, a. donker; duister, geheim(sinnig); **nors**; onheilspellend; **keep -**, geheim hou; - **horse**, onbekende grootheid; nuweling; **D- Ages**, Middeleeue; - **lantern**, diewelantern.
dark, n. donker; duister(nis); duisterheid; skaduwee; **leap in the -**, sprong in die onbekende; **keep in the -**, in onwentenheid hou.
darken, donker word; donker maak, verdonker, verduister.
darkness, donker(te), duister(nis).
darkling, in die donker.
darling, n. liefling, liefste, skat, hartlam.
darling, a. skatlik, liefste, beminde.
darn, v. stop, heelmaak.
darn, n. stop(plek).
darn, v. vloek; - **it**, vervlaks!
dart, n. spies; pyl; sprong.
dart, v. gooi; skiet; straal; wegspring, pyl; - **a glance**, 'n blik werp.
dash, v. kletter, klets; klots; gooi, smyt; slaan; bespat; stuif, vlieg; neerslaan, die boom inslaan; - **off**, wegvlie, wegspring; afkrap, op die papier gooi; - **it!**, vervlaks!, verbrands!
dash, n. geklots; smeer, skeutjie; streep; aanval, stoot; swier, bevalligheid; omstuimigheid; **cut a -**, 'n flikker maak; **make a -**, op afvlieg, op afsnel; **a - of the pen**, 'n pennestreek; **c', c-dash**, c-aksent, c-streep.
dashboard, spatbord; instrumentbord, paneelbord.
dashing, swierig; onstuimig, voortvarend.
dashlamp, spatbordlamp.
dastard, lafaard, bloodaard.
data, sien datum.
dastardly, lafhartig, laag, gemeen.
date, n. dadel.
date, n. datum; dagtekening; jaartal; afspraak; **out of -**, ouderwets, uit die mode; **up to -**, nuwerwets, modern; **bring up to -**, bywerk; **from -**, vanaf datum.
date, v. dateer, dagteken; die stempel van sy tyd dra.
dative, datief.
datum, gegewe; **data** (pl.), gegewens, data.
daub, v. besmeer, bepleister, beklad.
daub, n. smeer(sel), klad; bepleistering.
daughter, dogter.
daughter-in-law, skoondogter.
daunt, verskrik, afskrik, uit die veld slaan; **nothing -ed**, onvervaard.
dauntless, onversaag, onvervaard.
dauphin, (Franse) kroonprins, dauphin.
davit, dawit.
daw, kou(voël).
dawdle, draai, seur, drentel, treusel.

**dawdler, **draaier, seurder, lanterfanter.
**dawn, **n. dagbreek, môreskemering.
**dawn, **v. lig word, daag, (dag) aanbreek; **it –ed on me, **dit het my duidelik geword.
**day, dag; daglig; dagbreek; all (the) –, **(die) heel dag; **at –, **teen dagbreek; **broad –, **helder-oordag; **one –, **op 'n dag; **the other –, **onlangs, 'n dag of wat gelede; **one of these (fine) –s, **een van die dae; **some –, **eendag; **at, to this –, **tot vandag toe; **this – week (fortnight), **vandag oor ag (veertien) dae; **– by –, **dag vir dag, **by –, **oordag(s); **for –s, **dae lank; **in my –, **in my tyd; **this –, **vandag; **the – before yesterday, **eergister; **the – after tomorrow, **oormôre; **every other –, **om die ander dag; **men of the –, **vooraanstaande manne; **–s of grace, **uitsteldae, respytdae; **carry, win the –, **die oorwinning behaal; **lose the –, **die stryd verloor; **call it a –, **dit daarby laat; aanneem dat 'n dag se werk verrig is.
**day-boarder, **tafel(kos)ganger.
**day-book, **dagboek, joernaal.
**daybreak, **dagbreek.
**day-dream, **lugkasteel, mymering.
**day-labourer, **dagloner.
**daylight, **(son)lig, daglig; dagbreek.
**day-time,, **dag(tyd); **in the –, **oordag, bedags.
**daze, **v. verbyster, bedwelm; verblind.
**daze, **n. verbystering, bedwelming.
**dazzle, **verblind, verbyster.
**deacon, **diaken; geestelike.
**deaconess, **diakones.
**dead, **a. dood; doods; styf, dom; dooierig, dof; **– as a doornail, **so dood as 'n mossie; **– letter, **dooie letter (van die wet); onbestelbare brief; **– sound, **dowwe geluid; **– weight, **dooie gewig; **– stock, **dooie kapitaal; **– season, **slap tyd van die jaar; komkommertyd; **– end, **dooie punt; **– stop, **skielike stilstand; **– certainty, **absolute sekerheid; **– earnest, **dodelike erns; **– shot, **dodelike skut; **they ran a – heat, **hulle het kop-en-kop uitgekom; **– fingers, **dom vingers; **– march, **treurmars, dodemars.
**dead, **adv. in erge graad; **– against, **sterk op teen; **– calm, **bladstil; **– drunk, **smoordronk; **– tired, **doodmoeg.
**dead, **n. die oorledene, die dooie; **from the –, **uit die dooie; uit die dood; **the – of night, **die middel (die holle) van die nag; **the – of winter, **die hartjie van die winter.
**dead-alive, **lewendig-dood.
**dead-beat, **poot-uit.
**deaden, **verdoof, temper; verstomp.
**deadlock, **dooie punt; **at, to a –, **op 'n dooie punt.
**deadly, **dodelik; **– sin, **doodsonde; **in – haste, **in doodshaas.
**dead-pan, **strak, uitdrukkingloos.
**dead-weight, **dooie gewig; drukkende las.
**deaf, **doof; **– as a post, **so doof as 'n kwartel; **turn a – ear to, **geen gehoor aan gee nie.
**deaf-and-dumb, **doofstom.
**deafen, **doof maak; verdoof.
**deaf-mute, **doofstom.
**deafness, **doofheid.
**deal, **n. deel, gedeelte, hoeveelheid, klomp, boel; beurt (om kaarte te gee); (handel)saak, slag; **a great –, **'n hele klomp, baie, heelwat; **a square –, **'n eerlike transaksie; **bring off a –, **'n slag slaan.
**deal, **v. deel, ver–, uitdeel, toedeel, gee, toebring; sake doen, handel; **– a blow, **'n slag gee; **– in, **handel drywe in; afgee met, inlaat met; **– with, **sake doen met; behandel; omgaan met; aandag gee aan.

**deal, **greinhout; deel, plank, balk.
**dealer, **handelaar; (kaart)geër.
**dealing, **(be)handeling, handelwyse; omgang; transaksie; **double –, **valsheid; **plain –, **eerlikheid, reguit manier (van sake doen).
**dean, **deken; fakulteitsvoorsitter, dekaan.
**dear, **a. lief, dierbaar; duur, kosbaar; **D– Sir, **geagte heer.
**dear, **n. skat, liefste.
**dear, **interj. allawêreld!, o hening! mastig!
**dearie, –y, **liefste, skat.
**dearly, **baie erg, teer; duur; **– beloved, **teerbeminde, dierbare.
**dearness, **dierbaarheid; duurte.
**dearth, **duurte; skaarste.
**death, **dood; sterfte; sterfgeval; (die) afsterwe, oorlye; **put to –, **ter dood bring; **catch one's –, **jou die dood op die lyf haal; **to the –, **tot in die dood; **tired to –, **doodmoeg; **at –'s door, **op die rand van die graf, in doodsgevaar; **sure as –, **so waar as ek leef!; **like grim –, **op lewe en dood; **condemn to –, **ter dood veroordeel; **frighten to –, **laat dood skrik.
**death-bed, **sterfbed.
**death-blow, **doodsteek, doodslag.
**death-duty, **sterfreg, suksessiereg.
**death-knell, **doodsklok; uiteinde.
**deathless, **onsterflik.
**deathlike, **doods; doodstil; doods- . . .
**deathliness, **doodsheid; dodelikheid.
**death-notice, **sterf-, doodsberig.
**death-rate, **sterftesyfer.
**death's head, **doodskop.
**death-warrant, **doodvonnis; eksekusiebevel.
**débâcle, **hopelose mislukking, fiasko, ineenstorting, debakel.
**debar, **uitsluit, verhinder, belet.
**debark, **ontskeep.
**debase, **verlaag, verneder; vervals.
**debasement, **verlaging, vervalsing.
**debatable, **betwisbaar, onuitgemaak.
**debate, **n. debat, bespreking.
**debate, **v. debatteer, bespreek, betwis.
**debater, **debatteerder, (publieke) spreker.
**debauch, **v. bederf, verlei; verliederlik.
**debauch, **n. uitspatting, brassery.
**debauchery, **losbandigheid, liederlikheid.
**debenture, **skuldbrief, obligasie.
**debilitate, **verswak.
**debility, **swakheid, kragteloosheid.
**debit, **n. skuld, debet.
**debit, **v. debiteer, boek teen; belas.
**debit balance, **nadelige saldo.
**debit entry, **skuldpos.
**debonair, **joviaal, opgewek, welgemoed.
**debouch, **uitmond; uitkom.
**debris, **puin; opdrifsels.
**debt, **skuld; **– of honour, **ereskuld; **– of nature, **tol van die natuur; **run into –, **skulde maak.
**debtor, **skuldenaar, debiteur.
**debunk, **ontmasker, aan die kaak stel.
**decade, **tiental; dekade.
**decadence, **verval, agteruitgang, dekadensie.
**decadent, **verwordend, dekadent.
**decagon, **tienhoek, dekagoon.
**decagram(me), **dekagram.
**decalitre, **dekaliter.
**decametre, **dekameter.
**decalogue, **die tien gebooie, dekaloog.
**decamp, **opbreek, afmarsjeer; verkas.
**decant, **(af)skink, afgiet.
**decanter, **kraf(fie).
**decapitate, **onthoof.
**decarbonize, **ontkool.
**decasyllabic, **tienlettergrepig.

decathlon, tienkamp. dekatlon.
decay, v. vergaan, verval; sleg word, bederf.
decay, n. verval, agteruitgang; verrotting, bederf; **fall into –,** in onbruik raak.
decease, v. oorly, sterf.
decease, n. oorlyding, sterwe, dood.
deceased, oorledene, afgestorwene.
deceit, bedrog, misleiding, bedrieglikheid.
deceitful, bedrieglik; vals.
deceive, bedrieg, mislei, fop; verlei.
deceiver, bedrieër, verleier.
decelerate, vertraag, vaart verminder.
December, Desember.
decemvir, lid van die tienmanskap, decemvir.
decemvirate, tienmanskap, decemviraat.
decency, fatsoenlik, betaamlikheid.
decennial, tienjarig.
decent, fatsoenlik, betaamlik; taamlik, ordentlik.
decentralise, desentraliseer.
deception, bedrog, misleiding.
deceptive, bedrieglik, misleidend.
decide, besluit, uitmaak, beslis; oordeel, uitspraak doen; **– on,** besluit om te . . .; **– against,** besluit om nie te . . .; uitspraak doen teen.
decided, beslis, bepaald; nadruklik.
decidedly, beslis, stellig.
deciduous, bladwisselend; afvallend.
decimal, a. tientallig; tiendelig; desimaal; **– system,** tientallige stelsel.
decimal, n. tiendelige (desimale) breuk.
decimate, desimeer; uitdun, wegmaai.
decipher, ontsyfer; uitmaak.
decision, beslissing, uitspraak, besluit; uitslag; beslistheid.
decisive, beslissend, afdoend.
deck, n. dek.
deck, v. dek, bedek; klee, tooi, uitdos.
deck-chair, dekstoel, seilstoel.
declaim, voordra, deklameer; uitvaar.
declamation, deklamasie; heftige toespraak.
declamatory, deklamatories, hoogdrawend.
declaration, verklaring; bekendmaking; deklarasie.
declare, verklaar; aankondig, bekend maak, aangee (by doeane); sê, troefmaak (by kaartspel); **– for, against,** party kies, voor, teen; **– off,** afsê, afskrywe.
declaredly, ope(n)lik, soos erken word.
declarer, aankondiger; troefmaker.
declass, afdaal, verlaag; deklasseer.
declension, afwyking; agteruitgang, verval; verbuiging, deklinasie.
declination, afbuiging; afwyking; verbuiging; deklinasie.
decline, v. afhel, afhang, afdraand loop; buig, laat hang; agteruitgang, afneem; weier, van die hand wys.
decline, n. verval, agteruitgang; afdraand.
declivity, afdraand, helling.
declutch, ontkoppel, uittrap.
decoct, afkook, brou.
decoction, afkooksel; brousel.
decode, ontsyfer.
decompose, oplos, ontleed; ontbind, vergaan.
decomposition, ontleding; ontbinding.
decompression, drukverligting; **– chamber,** drukverligtingsel, -skamertjie.
decontaminate, ontsmet, ontgas.
decorate, versier, tooi; dekoreer.
decoration, versiering, sieraad, dekorasie.
decorative, dekoratief, versierend, sier- . . ., versierings- . . .
decorator, versierder; plakker; huisskilder.
decorous, fatsoenlik, betaamlik, deftig.
decorum, fatsoen, welvoeglikheid; decorum.

decoy, v. verlok, lok.
decoy, n. lokmiddel; lokvoël; eendekooi.
decrease, v. verminder, afneem.
decrease, n. vermindering, afname.
decree, n. verordening, besluit, dekreet.
decree, v. verorden, bepaal, dekreteer.
decrepit, lendelam, gebreklik; afgeleef.
decreptitude, verval, afgeleefdheid.
decry, uitkryt, afkam, kleineer.
decumbent, liggend.
decuple, tienvoudig.
dedicate, (toe)wy, opdra.
dedication, (toe)wyding, opdrag.
dedicatory, inwydings- . . . ; **– sermon,** inwydingsrede.
deduce, aflei; gevolgtrekking maak; herlei.
deduct, aftrek.
deduction, aftrek(king), korting; gevolgtrekking; herleiding.
deductive, deduktief.
deed, daad, handeling; akte, dokument.
deeds office, registrasie-, aktekantoor.
deem, oordeel, dink, ag, meen.
deep, a. diep; diepsinnig; grondig; geheimsinnig, donker; innig; geslepe; **– insight,** grondige insig; **– thinker,** diepsinnige dinker; **– sigh,** swaar sug; **a – one,** 'n geslepe vent.
deep, n. diepte; see, golwe; **on the –,** op see.
deepen, diep maak, uitdiep; diep(er) word; versterk.
deepmost, diepste.
deep-rooted, ingewortel(d).
deep-seated, diepgewortel(d); ingekanker(d).
deer, hert, takbok.
deerhound, windhond, jaghond.
deer-lick, brakplek.
deface, skend, vermink; uitwis.
defacement, ontsiering, verminking; uitwissing.
defalcate, verduister, onwettig toeëien.
defalcation, tekort; verduistering.
defamation, belastering, bekindering.
defamatory, lasterlik, eerskendend.
defame, belaster, beskinder.
default, n. gebrek, versuim, ontstentenis; **– of payment,** wanbetaling; **in – of,** by gebrek aan, by ontstentenis van; **judgment by –,** vonnis by verstek.
default, v. versuim, in gebreke bly, nie verskyn nie; by verstek veroordeel.
defaulter, wanbetaler; oortreder; afwesige.
defeat, v. verslaan, (oor)win; verydel; vernietig, te niet doen.
defeat, n. neerlaag; verydeling; vernietiging.
defecate, suiwer; ontlas.
defecation, suiwering; ontlasting.
defect, gebrek, fout; tekort, defek.
defection, afval, ontrou, afvalligheid.
defective, gebrekkig, onvolledig; defektief.
defectiveness, gebrekkigheid, onvolledigheid.
defence, verdediging, teenstand; beskerming; verweer; verdedigingswerk, bolwerk.
defence force, verdedigingsmag.
defenceless, weerloos; onbeskermd.
defend, verdedig; teenstand bied, verweer; beskerm.
defendant, verweerder; verdediger.
defender, verdediger, beskermer.
defensible, verdedigbaar, houdbaar.
defensive, a. verdedigend, beskermend, defensief.
defensive, n. defensief; **stand, act on the –,** 'n verdedigende houding aanneem.
defer, uitstel, verskuiwe; draal, draai.
defer, eerbiedig, onderwerp (aan), neerlê (by).
deference, eerbied, ontsag, respek; onderworpen-

deferential   465   **demijohn**

heid; **in – to,** uit ontsag vir; **with due – to,** met alle respek vir.
deferential, eerbiedig, respekvol.
deferment, uitstel.
defiance, uittarting, trotsering; miskenning; **bid – to,** tart, trotseer; **in – of,** ondanks, ten spyte van.
defiant, uitda(g)end, tartend; wantrouig.
deficiency, gebrek, tekort; **make up a –,** 'n tekort aanvul.
deficient, gebrekkig, ontoereikend; **mentally –,** swaksinnig.
deficit, tekort, nadelige saldo, deficit.
defile, v. defileer, agter mekaar marsjeer.
defile, n. pas, kloof, engte.
defile, v. bevuil, besmet; onteer, besoedel.
defilement, verontreiniging, ontering.
definable, omskryfbaar, definieerbaar.
define, bepaal, omskrywe, duidelik maak; omlyn; definieer.
definite, bepaald; presies, noukeurig; **– article,** bepaalde lidwoord.
definition, bepaling, omskrywing, definisie.
definitive, bepalend, belissend, definitief.
deflate, afblaas, lug uitlaat.
deflation, (die) afblaas, uitlating; deflasie (van) geld.
deflect, wegbuig; afskram; deflekteer.
deflection, afwyking; (straal)breking; defleksie.
defloration, ontering; ontwyding.
deflower, onteer; ontwy.
deforest, ontbos, bome wegkap.
deform, vervorm, mismaak, skend.
deformation, vervorming; verminking; vormverandering; deformasie.
deformity, gebrek(likheid), mismaaktheid.
defraud, bedrieg.
defray, bekostig, (die koste) bestry, betaal.
defrayal, bekostiging, betaling.
deft, (knap)handig, knap, vaardig, netjies.
defunct, a. oorlede.
defunct, n. die oorledene.
defy, trotseer, tart, uitdaag, spot met.
degenerate, a. ontaard, gedegeneer(d).
degenerate, v. ontaard, verbaster, versleg, degenereer.
degeneration, degenerasie, ontaarding.
deglutition, (die) sluk, insluk, wegsluk.
degradation, verlaging, vernedering, degradasie; ontaarding.
degrade, verlaag, verneder, degradeer; ontaard.
degree, graad, trap; klas, rang; **to a –,** in hoë mate; **to a certain –,** tot op sekere hoogte; in sekere mate; **by –s,** trapsgewyse, geleidelik; **take a –,** 'n graad behaal; **honorary –,** eregraad.
degree day, gradedag, promosiedag.
dehumanize, ontmens, verdierlik.
de-ice, ontys.
de-icer, ontyser.
deictic, aanwysend, deikties.
deification, vergoding; vergoddeliking.
deify, vergood, vergoddelik; vereer, aanbid.
deign, (sig) verwaardig.
**deism, deïsme.
**deist, deïs.
deity, godheid.
dejected, neerslagtig, bedruk, bek-af.
dejection, neerslagtigheid, bedruktheid.
delaine, wolmoeselien.
delation, aanklag.
delay, v. vertraag, uitstel, verhinder, teenwerk; versuim, draai.
delay, n. vertraging, uitstel, oponthoud, versuim.

delectable, genoeglik, heerlik.
delectation, genoeë, genot; verrukking.
delegacy, afvaardiging; afgevaardigdes.
delegate, n. afgevaardigde, gemagtigde.
delegate, v. afvaardig; magtig, opdra.
delegation, afvaardiging; magtiging; afgevaardigdes, delegasie.
delete, uitkrap, deurstreep, uitwis.
deleterious, skadelik, nadelig; verderflik.
delf(t), Delftse aardewerk.
deliberate, v. beraadslaag; oorweeg.
deliberate, a. weloorwoë; opsetlik; bedaard, tydsaam; vasberade.
deliberately, met voorbedagte raad, opsetlik; tydsaam, op sy gemak.
deliberateness, opsetlikheid; beradenheid.
deliberation, oorweging, raadpleging, beraad; **take into –,** in beraad neem.
delicacy, fynheid, teerheid; tengerheid; fyngevoeligheid; lekkerny, versnapering.
delicate, fyn, teer; tenger; fyngevoelig; lekker; delikaat.
delicatessen, delikatesse.
delicious, heerlik, verruklik.
delight, n. genoeë, genot, behae, lus; **take – in,** behae skep in.
delight, n. genoeë (genot) verskaf; behae skep (in); verheug; **I shall be –ed,** dit sal my baie aangenaam wees; **–ed with,** opgetoë met, ingenome met.
delightful, genoeglik, heerlik, verruklik.
delimit, afbaken, delimiteer.
delimitation, afbakening, delimitasie.
delineate, afbeeld, teken, skets.
delineation, afbeelding, tekening.
delinquency, oortreding, pligsversuim.
deliquent, oortreder, skuldige.
deliquesce, smelt, vloeibaar word.
delirious, ylhoofdig, waansinnig; verruk.
delirium, ylhoofdigheid, raserny.
deliver, bevry, verlos; afgee; uitlewer; oorgee; voordra; **a speech,** 'n toespraak hou; **–ed of,** geboorte gee aan; verlos word van; **– judgment,** uitspraak gee; **– a battle,** 'n slag lewer; **– up,** oorhandig, afgee.
deliverance, bevryding, verlossend.
delivery, verlossing; bevalling; (af)lewering; afslaan (tennis); (boul)aksie (krieket); bal; toespraak; voordrag; **take –,** in ontvangs neem; **cash on –,** kontant by aflewering.
Delphian, Delphic, Delphies; duister.
delphinium, delphinium.
delta, delta; **– rays,** deltastrale; **– wing,** deltavlerk.
delude, mislei, fop.
deluge, n. vloed, oorstroming; sondvloed.
deluge, v. oorstroom; oorstelp.
delusion, misleiding; oogverblinding; waan.
delusive, misleidend, bedrieglik; waan- . . .
delve, grawe, delwe (dolwe).
demagogue, demagoog, volksredenaar.
demand, v. eis, vorder, verlang, vra.
demand, n. eis, vordering, (aan)vraag; **on –,** op aanvraag; **be in –,** gevra word, gesog wees, in trek wees; **supply and –,** vraag en aanbod.
demarcation, afbakening; grens.
demean, gedra.
demean, verlaag.
demeanour, gedrag, houding, handelwyse.
demented, gek, kranksinnig.
dementia, swaksinnigheid, dementia.
demerit, fout, gebrek.
demesne, eiendom; gebied.
demigod, halfgod.
demijohn, karba.

demi-monde   466   **derelict**

demi-monde, vrouens van verdagte sede, demi-monde.
demi-rep, vrou van verdagte sede, straatvlinder.
demise, n. vermaking; afsterwe.
demise, v. vermaak, oormaak, vererf.
demi-semi-quaver, 32ste noot.
demission, aftreding; ontslag; demissie.
demit, aftree, afstand doen, ontslag neem.
demobilize, demobiliseer, (leër) ontbind.
democracy, volksregering, demokrasie.
democrat, demokraat.
democratic, demokraties.
demolish, vernietig; sloop; verslind.
demolition, vernietiging; afbraak, sloping.
demon, bose gees, duiwel; skutsengel.
demoniac, besetene.
demoniacal, demonies, besete duiwels.
demonolatry, duiwelverering.
demonstrable, bewysbaar; onloënbaar.
demonstrate, uitlê, verklaar; aantoon; demonstreer.
demonstration, vertoning; bewys; verklaring; betoging; demonstrasie.
demonstrative, bewysend; aantonend; demonstratief.
demonstrator, betoger (betoër); assistent; demonstrateur.
demoralization, demoralisasie; ontmoediging.
demoralize, demoraliseer; bederf, verknoei; ontmoedig.
demur, v. beswaar maak; pruttel.
demur, n. beswaar, bedenking.
demure, sedig, stemmig; preuts, aanstellerig.
demurrage, oorlêgeld, lêkoste.
den, hol, lêplek; hok; bof.
denationalize, denasionaliseer.
denaturalize, denaturaliseer; dokter (bv. wyn).
denature, denatureer.
denial, ontkenning; wei(g)ering; (ver)loëning.
denigrate, swartsmeer, beklad.
denizen, n. bewoner; inheemse plant (ens.).
denominate, aandui; betitel, noem, benoem.
denomination, naam, benaming, betiteling; klas, grootheid; sekte; denominasie.
denominational, sektaries, sekte-...
denominative, naamgewend; denominatief.
denominator, aanduier; noemer (van 'n breuk), deler; **fractions with same (different)** –s, gelyknamige (ongelyknamige) breuke; **reduce to same** –, gelyknamig maak.
denotation, aanduiding; betekenis; denotasie.
denote, aandui, aanwys, bepaal; beteken; te kenne gee; die omvang bepaal.
denounce, aankla, veroordeel; aan die kaak stel; opsê.
denouncement, veroordeling, afkeur; aansegging.
dense, dig; dom, stom.
density, digtheid; stomheid.
dent, n. deuk (duik).
dent, v. (in)deuk (-duik).
dental, a. tande-...; – surgeon, tandedokter.
dental, n. tandletter, dentaal.
dentate, getand.
dentifrice, tandepoeier, -pasta, -poets.
dentine, tandbeen.
dentist, tandedokter, tandarts.
dentistry, tandheelkunde.
dentition, (die) tandekry; tandformasie.
denudation, ontbloting, blootlegging.
denude, ontbloot, blootlê; – of, ontbloot van.
denunciation, aanklag; veroordeling; (die) uitskel.
denunciate, sien **denounce**.
deny, ontken, verloën; ontsê; weier; – **access**, toegang weier; – **yourself pleasures**, jouself genoeëns ontsê.
deodar, (heilige) seder.
deodorize, reukloos maak; ontsmet.
depart, vertrek; heengaan; – **from**, afwyk van; – **this life**, heengaan, sterwe.
department, departement, afdeling; gebied; – **store**, warehuis, handelshuis.
departmental, afdelings-..., departementeel.
departure, vertrek; heengaan; afwyking.
depend, afhang; reken (op), staatmaak (op); **that –s**, dit hang daarvan af.
dependable, be-, vertroubaar.
dependant, -ent, n. afhanklike; ondergeskikte.
dependence, afhanklikheid; toevlug.
dependency, sien **dependence**; afhanklike staat.
dependent, afhanklik; onderhorig; ondergeskik.
depict, afteken, skilder, beskrywe.
depilate, onthaar, haar-af maak.
deplete, leeg maak, uitput; uitdun.
depletion, leegmaking; ontlasting; uitputting.
deplorable, betreurenswaardig, jammerlik.
deplore, betreur; bekla.
deploy, ontrol, ontplooi.
deponent, a.: – (**verb**), deponens.
deponent, n. getuie.
depopulate, ontvolk.
deport, (sig) gedra; uitsig, deporteer.
deportation, uitsetting, deportasie.
deportee, gedeporteerde, verbannene.
deportment, houding, gedrag.
depose, afsit; getuig; onder ede verklaar.
deposit, n. belegging; storting, deposito; neerslag, besinksel.
deposit, v. neersit, neerlê; stort, deponeer.
depositary, bewaarder.
deposition, afsetting; getuienis; belegging.
depositor, storter, belêer (belegger).
depository, bewaarplaas; sien **depositary**.
depot, opslagplaas, bêreplek; (hoof)kwartiere; depot.
depravation, ontaarding, bederf, verslegting.
deprave, versleg, (die sedes) bederf.
depraved, ontaard.
depravity, verdorwenheid, ontaarding.
deprecate, afkeur, opkom teen; afbid.
deprecation, afkeuring, protes; afbidding.
depreciate, agteruitgaan, depresieer; kleineer.
depreciation, waardevermindering, depresiasie; afskrywing; kleinering.
depredation, plundering, roof, verwoesting.
depress, af-, in-, neerdruk; verneder, verlaag; neerslagtig maak, deprimeer; –**ed classes**, parias.
depression, (neer)drukking, daling, druk; verslapping, slapte; laagte, kom; neerslagtigheid; lae druk; depressie.
deprivation, berowing; verlies; afsetting.
deprive, beroof, ontneem; afsit.
depth, diepte; diepsinnigheid; geslepenheid; **out of one's –**, in diep water; op glibberige terrein.
depuration, suiwering.
deputation, afvaardiging, deputasie.
depute, afvaardig; magtig; oordra.
deputy, plaasvervanger, gemagtigde, plaasvervangende, vise-...
derail, laat ontspoor; ontspoor; **be –ed**, ontspoor.
derailment, ontsporing.
derange, in die war stuur; ontrief, steur.
deranged, van die verstand af.
derangement, verwarring, wanorde; steuring, stoornis; sinsverwarring.
derelict, verlate, onbeheer(d).
derelict, n. verlate skip; versonkene, verstoteling.

dereliction, verlating; nalatigheid, pligsversuim.
deride, bespot, uitlag.
derision, bespotting, veragting; spot.
derisive, (be)spottend, honend, vermakerig.
derivation, afleiding, herleiding; herkoms, afkoms.
derivative, afgeleide woord; afleisel, afleiding.
derive, aflei; spruit uit; put uit, vandaan kry.
dermatology, dermatologie, huidsiekteleer.
derogate, te kort doen (aan), inkort, verklein, kleineer; (sig) verlaag.
derogation, afbreuk, inkorting, kleinering.
derogatory, benadelend; kleinerend, afkammend.
derrick, kraan, hyspaal; boortoring.
derringer, pistool.
dervish, derwisj, bedelmonnik.
descant, uitwei; – upon, uitwei oor.
descend, af-, neerdaal, afklim, afstyg, land, afkom; sink; afstam; – on, neerkom op; oorgaan op; – upon, oorval; – to, daal (verlaag) tot.
descendant, afstammeling, nakomeling.
descent, af-, neerdaling, afstyging, afsakking; afkoms, afstammeling; helling; afdraand; pad na onder; oorval; landing.
describe, beskrywe; omskrywe.
description, beskrywing; soort, slag.
descriptive, beskrywend.
descry, ontwaar, gewaar, ontdek, sien.
desecrate, ontheilig, ontwy.
desecration, ontheiliging, heiligskennis.
desert, n. verdienste; –s, verdiende loon.
desert, a. verlate, woes; dor.
desert, n. woestyn, woesteny, wildernis.
desert, v. verlaat; in die steek laat; oorloop; dros, deserteer.
deserter, droster, oorloper, deserteur.
desertion, verlating; verlatenheid; afval, oorloop, desersie.
deserve, verdien; – well of, diens bewys, (sig) verdienstelik maak teenoor.
deservedly, tereg; na verdienste.
deserving, verdienstelik.
desiccate, (uit)droë; opdroë.
desiderate, verlang (na), begeer, mis.
desideratum, vereiste, desideratum.
design, n. plan, ontwerp; opset; doel; **have –s on**, sy oog hê op.
design, v. ontwerp; bestem; beoog.
designate, aanwys, onderskei; bestem.
designation, aanwysing; naam; bestemming.
designedly, opsetlik, voorbedagtelik.
designer, ontwerper.
designing, arglistig, slu.
desirable, begeerlik, wenslik.
desire, n. begeerte, wens, verlange; versoek.
desire, v. begeer, verlang, wens; versoek, vra.
desirous, begerig, verlangend; **be – of**, begeer, verlang na.
desist, ophou (met), aflaat (van), uitskei (met).
desk, lessenaar; skoolbank; kateder.
desolate, a. eensaam, verlate; verval(le); troosteloos; desolaat.
desolate, v. verwoes; ontvolk; troosteloos laat.
desolation, verlatenheid; verwaarlosing; troosteloosheid; verwoesting.
despair, n. wanhoop, vertwyfeling.
despair, v. wanhoop, in vertwyfeling raak.
despairing, wanhopend; wanhopig.
despatch, **(dispatch)**, n. afsending, versending; (die) af-, doodmaak; verrigting; (die) wegsluk; haas, spoed.
despatch **(dispatch)**, v. afstuur; klaar maak, verrig; af-, doodmaak; wegsluk.
desperado, waaghals; woesteling.
desperate, wanhopig, radeloos; roekeloos.

desperately, hopeloos; verskriklik, uiters.
desperation, wanhoop, radeloosheid; woestheid, raserny.
despicable, veragtelik, gemeen, laag.
despise, verag, verfoei; versmaad.
despite, gekrenktheid; (in) – (of), ten spyte van.
despoil, plunder, beroof.
despoliation, plundering, berowing.
despond, wanhoop, moed verloor.
despondence, -cy, wanhoop, moedeloosheid.
despondent, wanhopig, moedeloos, neerslagtig.
despot, dwingeland, despoot, tiran.
despotic, despoties, eiemagtig, heerssugtig.
despotism, dwingelandy, despotisme.
dessert, nagereg, dessert.
dessert-spoon, dessertlepel.
destination, (plaas van) bestemming; lot.
destine, (voor)bestem, bedoel.
destined, (voor)bestem(d); voorbeskik.
destiny, bestemming, (nood)lot, voorland.
destitute, behoeftig; brandarm; verlate; – of, sonder, ontbloot van.
destitution, gebrek, armoede, ontbering.
destroy, verniel, vernietig, verwoes, te niet doen; – oneself, (sigself) vankant maak.
destroyer, vernieler; torpedojaer.
destruction, verwoesting; vernietiging; verderf.
destructive, verwoestend; vernietigend; dodelik.
destructor, vernieler; verbrandoond.
desuetude, onbruik; **fall into** –, in onbruik raak.
desultory, onsamehangend.
detach, losmaak, afsonder; uitstuur.
detachable, afneembaar, los.
detached, los; onbevange; – **house**, losstaande huis.
detachment, losmaking; losheid; onbevangenheid; afsydigheid; afdeling, detasjement.
detail, n. besonderheid, kleinigheid, detail; in –, (tot) in besonderhede; **that is a –**, dit is 'n kleinigheid.
detail, v. uitvoerig meedeel; opsom; afsonder.
detain, ophou, (ver)hinder, vashou; weerhou, agterhou; gevange hou; op skool hou.
detect, ontdek, gewaar word, agterkom; betrap.
detection, ontdekking, betrapping, opsporing.
detective, speurder.
detective story, speurverhaal.
detector, aanwyser; verklikker (masjien); detektor (radio).
detention, oponthoud, verhindering; opsluiting, hegtenis; agterbly (op skool); – **barracks**, detensiekaserne.
deter, terughou, weerhou, afskrik, keer.
detergent, suiwerend.
deteriorate, versleg, ontaard; bederf.
deterioration, agteruitgang, verslegting, ontaarding, degenerasie; bederf.
determinate, afgebaken, bepaald; beslis.
determination, bepaling, beslissing; beslistheid, vasberadenheid; beëindiging, end; afloop.
determinative, bepalend, karakteriserend.
determine, bepaal, vasstel; besluit, beslis; rigting gee; eindig.
determined, bepaal(d), vasgestel(d); beslis, vasberade, met mening.
deterrent, a. afskrikkend.
deterrent, n. afskrikmiddel; **act as a –**, weerhou.
detest, verfoei, verafsku.
detestable, verfoeilik, afskuwelik, mislik.
detestation, verfoeiing; **hold in** –, verafsku.
dethrone, onttroon, afsit.
detonate, ontplof; laat ontplof.
detonator, doppie; dinamietpatroon.
detour, omweg, ompad; uitweiding.
detract, te kort doen (aan), kleineer; laster.

detraction, kleinering, bekladding, lastering.
detrain, onttrein, aflaai (van die trein).
detriment, nadeel, benadeling, skade.
detrimental, nadelig, skadelik.
detrition, afslyting.
deuce, twee; gelyk (tennis).
deuce, duiwel, drommel, joos; – **alone knows**, die drommel alleen weet; **a – of a mess**, 'n verskriklike warboel.
deuterium, deuterium, swaarwaterstof.
Deuteronomy, Deuteronomium.
devastate, verwoes, verwoesting aanrig.
devastation, verwoesting.
develop, ontwikkel; onthul, ontvou.
developer, ontwikkelaar.
development, ontwikkeling; ontvouing.
deviate, afwyk, afdwaal.
deviation, afwyking.
device, leus, motto; gedagte; oogmerk; lis; uitvinding; middel; **left to one's own –**, aan jouself oorgelaat.
devil, n. duiwel; duiwelstoejaer; **poor –**, arme stumper; **like the –**, soos 'n besetene; **between the – and the deep sea**, tussen twee vure; **give the – his due**, gee die duiwel wat hom toekom; **play the – with**, ruïneer, roekeloos mee omspring; **– of a chap**, doring van 'n vent; **the – incarnate**, die waarlike duiwel; **–'s thorn**, duwweltjies, **–'s advocate**, duiwelsadvokaat; afkammer.
devil, v. slaaf; sterk krui, peper.
develish, duiwels, hels.
devil-may-care, onverskillig, roekeloos.
devilment, kwajongstreek, ondeundheid; spokery; **out of –**, uit ondeundheid.
devilry, -try, toordery; boosheid; kwajongstreke; roekeloosheid.
devious, slinger- . . ., kronkelend.
devise, versin, smee(d); vermaak, vererf.
devoid, ontbloot; – **of**, sonder, ontbloot van.
devolution, oordrag; teruggang; devolusie.
devolve, oormaak, afskuiwe; neerkom (op), te beurt val (aan).
devote, (toe)wy, oorgee, offer.
devoted, (toe)gewy, geheg, verknog; verslaaf.
devotedness, toegewydheid; verslaafdheid.
devotee, aanbidder; dweper; slaaf.
devotion, toewyding; verknogtheid; vroomheid; **–s**, gebede, godsdiens(oefening).
devotional, vroom, godsdienstig.
devour, verslind, verteer, verniel, opvreet.
devout, vroom, plegtig; opreg.
devoutness, vroomheid, godsvrug; eerbied.
dew, dou.
dew-lap, keelvel.
dewy, douerig; bedoud, nat gedou.
dexter, regs, regter.
dexterity, handigheid, ratsheid; regshandigheid.
dext(e)rous, regs; handig, behendig, rats.
diabetes, suikersiekte, diabetes.
diabolic, duiwels, hels, diabolies.
diabolism, toordery, duiwelskunste.
diabolo, diabolo.
diacritic, n. onderskeidingsteken.
diacritic(al), a. onderskeidend.
diadem, diadeem, kroon.
diaeresis, deelteken.
diagnose, diagnose maak, (siekte) konstateer.
diagnosis, diagnose, (siekte)bepaling.
diagnostic, simptoom, kenteken.
diagonal, a. diagonaal, oorhoeks.
diagonal, n. diagonaal, oorhoekse lyn.
diagram, figuur, tekening, diagram.
diagrammatic, skematies, grafies.
dial, n. sonnewyser; wyserplaat; (telefoon)-skyf.

dial, v. skakel; meet; aanwys.
dialect, dialek, tongval, streekspraak.
dialectal, dialekties.
dialectic, a. logies, redekundig; dialekties.
dialectic, n. dialektiek, redeneerkunde.
dialogue, dialoog, samespraak, tweespraak.
dial-plate, wys(t)erplaat.
diameter, middellyn, deursnee, diameter.
diametrical, diametraal; lynreg; **–ly opposed**, in lynregte teenstelling.
diamond, diamant; ruit; **rough –**, ongeslypte diamant; **cutting –**, glassnyer; **–s are trumps**, ruite is troef.
diamond-cutter, diamantslyper, -werker.
diamondiferous, diamanthoudend.
diamond-shaped, ruitvormig.
diapason, diapason; (toon)omvang; harmonie.
diaper, n. ruitjieslinne; banddoek; luier.
diaper, v. met figure weef.
diaphanous, deursigtig.
diaphragm, diafragma; middelrif.
diarist, dagboekskrywer.
diarrhoea, diarree; **blood –**, (bloed)persie.
diary, dagboek.
diastole, uitsetting, diastole.
diatonic, diatonies.
diathermy, diatermie.
diatribe, skotskrif, skimprede.
dibble, n. plantstok.
dibble, v. plant (met plantstok).
dice, v. dobbel; – **away**, verdobbel.
dice, n. sien **die**, dobbelstene.
dice-box, dobbelbeker, -dosie.
dicer, dobbelaar.
dichotomy, digotomie, gaffelsplitsing.
dichromatic, dichromaties, tweekleurig.
dickens, drommel, duiwel; **what the –**, wat die drommel.
dick(e)y, esel, donkie; borslappie; kattebak.
dick(e)y-bird, tinktinkie.
dick(e)-seat, kattebak, agterbak.
dictate, n. voorskrif, bevel; stem (van die gewete), ingewing (van die hart).
dictate, v. dikteer, voorlees; voorskrywe, beveel, ingee.
dictation, diktee; bevel; ingewing.
dictator, diktator, gebieder, heerser.
dictatorial, diktatoriaal, gebiedend, heersend.
dictatorship, diktatorskap.
diction, segging, voordrag; segswyse; diksie.
dictionary, woordeboek.
Dictograph, Dictograph.
dictum, gesegde, uitspraak.
didactic, didakties, lerend; – **poem**, leerdig.
didapper, duiker(tjie).
diddle, flous, fop, uitoorlê.
die, n. (pl. **dice**), dobbelsteen, teerling; (pl. **dies**), stempel; **the – is cast**, die teerling is geworpe; **straight as a –**, pylreguit.
die, v. sterf, doodgaan, vrek (van diere); – **down**, wegsterf; verflou; – **of**, sterf aan; – **off, out**, uitsterf; – **of laughter**, (sig) doodlag; **be dying for, to**, brand van verlange na (om); **never say –**, aanhou wen.
die-hard, onversoenlike, „bittereinder".
diesel: – **engine**, dieselmasjien.
diet, n. ryksdag.
diet, n. dieet; leefreël.
diet, v. op dieet stel, dieet hou.
dietary, a. dieetmatig, volgens voorskrif.
dietary, n. dieet.
dietetic, diëteties, dieetkundig.
dietetics, voedingsleer, dieetkunde.
dietician, dietitian, dieetkundige.

differ, verskil; **I beg to –**, ek is dit daar nie mee eens nie; **– by**, verskil met.
difference, verskil, onderskeid; geskil, onenigheid; **split the –**, die verskil deel.
different, verskillend, anders.
differentia, onderskeidingsmerk, kenmerk.
differential, a. differensieel; **– calculus**, differensiaalrekening.
differential, n. ewenaar, differensiaal.
differentiate, onderskei; verskil maak; begunstig; afgeleide vind (wiskunde).
differentiation, onderskeiding; begunstiging; differensiasie.
difficult, moeilik, swaar lastig.
difficulty, moeilikheid; beswaar.
diffidence, bedeesdheid, beskeidenheid, gebrek aan selfvertroue.
diffident, bedees, beskeie.
diffraction, breking.
diffuse, a. versprei(d); wydlopig, langdradig.
diffuse, v. versprei, uitsprei, uitgiet.
diffused, versprei(d); **– light**, gedempte lig.
diffuseness, verspreidheid; omslagtigheid.
diffusion, verspreiding, diffusie.
diffusive, uitspreidend, uitstralend; omslagtig.
dig, v. grawe, spit; snuffel; **– potatoes**, aartappels uithaal; **– up**, uitgrawe; omspit; **– in the ribs**, in die ribbe steek.
dig, n. stamp, stoot, steek.
digest, n. versameling; opsomming.
digest, v. verteer; verwerk, opneem; verkrop.
digestible, verteerbaar.
digestion, spysvertering; verwerking.
digestive, spysverterings- . . .; **– organs**, spysverteringsorgane.
digger, delwer.
diggings, delwery(e); kamer(s), woonplek.
digit, vinger, toon; vingerbreedte; syfer (onder 10).
digitalis, vingerhoedskruid.
dignified, waardig, deftig; verhewe.
dignify, vereer; deftigheid verleen.
dignitary, (hoog)waardigheidsbekleër.
dignity, waardigheid, deftigheid, adel; amp; **beneath his –**, benede sy waardigheid.
digraph, dubbelletter, digraaf.
digress, afdwaal, uitwei, afwyk.
digression, afdwaling, uitweiding, afwyking.
dik-dik, dik-dik.
dike, dyke, n. sloot; wal, dyk.
dike, dyke, v. indyk, walle gooi.
dilapidated, verval(le), bouvallig.
dilapidation, verval, bouvalligheid; verwaarlosing; agteruitgang.
dila(ta)tion, uitsetting, rekking; uitweiding.
dilate, uitsit, swel; rek, oopspalk; **– on**, uitwei oor.
dilatory, traag, draaierig, uitstellerig.
dilemma, dilemma, moeilikheid, verleentheid.
dilettante, dilettant, liefhebberaar.
diligence, ywer, vlyt; spoed.
diligent, ywerig, naarstig, vlytig.
dilly-dally, draai, sleur, treusel, talm.
dilute, verdun, verswak.
dilution, verdunning.
dim, a. dof, skemerig, flou, gedemp; **take a – view**, ontevrede wees; geen entoesiasme openbaar nie.
dim, v. dof word, verduister; dof maak, benewel; **– lights**, ligte demp.
dimension, afmeting, grootte, omvang.
diminish, verminder, afneem, inkrimp; **– by**, verminder met.
diminution, vermindering, verlaging.

diminutive, a. klein, gering; verkleinings- . . . diminutief.
diminutive, n. verkleinwoord(jie), diminutief.
dimple, n. kuiltjie.
dimple, v. kuiltjies maak (vertoon).
dimpled, met kuiltjies.
din, n. geraas, gedreun, lawaai.
din, v. raas, dreun, lawaai maak, verdoof; **– into one's ears**, in jou kop trommel.
dine, eet, dineer; ete verskaf; **– out**, uiteet.
diner, eter, dineerder; eetsalon.
ding-dong, tingeling, bim-bam; kling-klang; **–game**, op-en-af wedstryd.
dingey, dinghy, sloep(ie), skeepsbootjie.
dingle, dal, kloof.
dingo, (Australiese) wildehond, dingo.
dingy, donker; naar; vuil.
dining-car, eetsalon, restaurasiewa.
dining-room, eetkamer.
dining-table, eet(kamer)tafel.
dinner, n. middagete, eetmaal, dinee.
dinner, v. dineer, middageet.
dinner-hour, etensuur.
dinner-jacket, dineebaadjie, dineepak.
dinner-party, dinee(tjie); dineegeselskap.
dinner-service, -set, eetservies.
dinner-time, etenstyd, dinee-uur.
dinner-wag(g)on, dientafel, dienwaentjie.
dinosaur, dinosourus.
dint, n. slag, hou; deuk; **by – of**, deur middel van, deur (uit alle mag) te . . .; **by – of perseverance**, deur aan te hou.
dint, v. (in)deuk.
diocesan, bisdomlik, diosesaan.
diocese, bisdom, biskoplike gebied.
dioptrics, dioptriek, straalbrekingsleer.
diorama, diorama, kykspel.
dip, v. insteek, indompel; (vee) dip; (laat) sak; afhel, skuins loop; **– into**, insteek; uithaal; **– up**, op-, uitskep; **– into the future**, 'n blik slaan in die toekoms; **– into a book**, 'n boek deurblaai.
dip, n. indompeling, duik, bad; (vee)dip; skep, handvol; helling, skuinste; inklinasie (sterrek.); vetkers; **take a –**, induik, in die water spring; **– of horizon**, kimduiking.
diphtheria, witseerkeel, difterie.
diphthong, tweeklank, diftong.
diploma, getuigskrif, diploma.
diplomacy, diplomasie; oorleg.
diplomat, diplomaat.
diplomatic, diplomaties; diplomatiek; oulik, oorlams, poliets.
diplomatist, diplomaat.
dipper, duiker; skep(ding); (vee)dipper.
dipping-pen, diphok, kraal.
dipping-tank, dip, dipbak.
dipsomania, dranksug, dipsomanie.
dire, verskriklik, ontsettend, aaklig.
direct, a. direk, reguit, regstreeks; onmiddellik; lynreg(te); uitdruklik, ronduit.
direct, v. bestuur, reël, rig; aanwys, verwys; beveel; (brief) adresseer; **– attention to**, aandag vestig op.
direction, bestuur, direksie; rigting; aanwysing; bevel, las; voorskrif; opskrif, adres.
direction-finder, peiler (radio).
directly, adv. onmiddellik; aanstons; regstreeks; direk.
directly, conj. sodra, so gou as.
directness, rondborstigheid, direktheid.
director, direkteur, bestuurder, leier.
directorate, direkteurskap; raad van direkteure direksie.
directory, voorskrifboek; adresboek.

dirge, lyksang, klaagsang.
dirigible, a. (be)stuurbaar.
dirigible, n. bestuurbare lugballon.
dirk, dolk.
dirt, vullis (vuilis), vuilgoed, vuiligheid; modder, slyk; vuil praatjies; **fling** –, met modder gooi, beklad; **eat** –, belediginge sluk; – **track**, asbaan, sintelbaan; – **road**, grondpad.
dirt-cheap, spotgoedkoop.
dirt-heap, vullishoop, ashoop.
dirty, a. vuil, smerig, morsig; gemeen, liederlik, vieslik; – **work**, vuilwerk; skurkestreek.
dirty, v. vuil maak, besmeer; besoedel.
disability, onvermoë; ongeskiktheid, onbekwaamheid; gebrek.
disable, buite geveg stel, buite staat stel; vermink, wond.
disabuse, reghelp, uit die droom help.
disadvantage, nadeel; skade, verlies; **take at a** –, oorrompel, bekruip.
disadvantageous, nadelig, onvoordelig.
disaffected, misnoeg, ontevrede; ontrou.
disaffection, misnoegdheid, ontrou.
disagree, verskil (van mening), nie akkordeer (strook) nie; rusie maak; **fat –s with me**, vet akkordeer nie met my nie.
disagreeable, onaangenaam; onplesierig; nors.
disagreement, verskil; onenigheid, misverstand.
disallow, weier, afwys, verwerp, nie toestaan nie.
disappear, verdwyn, wegraak.
disappearance, verdwyning.
disappoint, teleurstel; fop; verydel.
disappointment, teleurstelling; verydeling.
disapprobation, afkeuring.
disapproval, afkeuring.
disapprove, nie saamstem nie; – **of**, afkeur.
disarm, ontwapen; paai, gerusstel.
disarmament, ontwapening.
disarrange, deurmekaar maak, in die war bring.
disarranged, deurmekaar, verwar(d).
disarrangement, verwarring, wanorde.
disarray, v. ontkleed; in wanorde bring.
disarray, n. wanorde.
disaster, ramp, ongeluk.
disastrous, noodlottig, rampspoedig.
disavow, loën, ontken; afkeur.
disavowal, loëning, ontkenning; afkeuring.
disband, ontbind, afdank; uiteengaan.
disbelief, ongeloof.
disbelieve, nie glo nie; betwyfel.
disburden, ontlas, verlig; lug; – **one's mind**, jou hart lug.
disburse, uitbetaal, opdok.
disc, sien **disk**.
discard, wegwerp, afdank; weggooi.
discern, onderskei, uitmaak, gewaar.
discernible, waarneembaar, sigbaar.
discerning, met deursig, oordeelkundig.
discernment, onderskeidingsvermoë, deursig.
discharge, v. los, aflaai; losbrand, aftrek; ontlaai; ontslaan, afdank; vryspreek, kwytskel; vervul, nakom; – **a gun**, 'n geweer aftrek; – **an accused**, 'n beskuldigde vryspreek; – **duties**, pligte vervul; – **a servant**, 'n bediende ontslaan.
discharge, n. lossing; ontploffing; ontlading; ontslag; ontheffing, vryspraak; vervulling, nakoming.
disciple, dissipel.
disciplinarian, bewaarder van die tug.
disciplinary, dissiplinêr.
discipline, n. dissipline, oefening; tug(tiging).
discipline, v. dissiplineer, dril; tugtig.
disclaim, afstand doen van; loën, teenspreek.
disclaimer, afstanddoening; ontkenning.

disclose, blootlê, aan die lig bring, openbaar.
disclosure, openbaarmaking, onthulling.
discolour, vlek; (laat) verkleur (verbleik).
discomfit, uit die veld slaan; verslaan; verydel.
discomfited, uit die veld geslaan, onthuts.
discomfiture, verbluftheid; ne(d)erlaag.
discomfort, n. ongemak, ongerief; onrus, kommer.
discomfort, v. ongemaklik maak, ongerief veroorsaak; bedroef.
discommode, lastig val, las veroorsaak.
discompose, verontrus; verbouereerd maak, in die war bring; erger, steur.
discomposing, verontrustend; verbouererend.
discomposure, verwarring, verleentheid; verontrusting; verbouereerdheid.
disconcert, verleë (verbouereerd) maak, uit die veld slaan; in die war stuur.
disconcernment, verleentheid, verbluftheid, verbouereerdheid.
disconnect, losmaak, loskoppel; ontbind, skei.
disconsolate, troosteloos, verslae.
discontent, ontevredenheid, misnoeë.
discontented, ontevrede, misnoeg, brommerig.
discontinuance, afbreking, (die) ophou, staking, (die) opgee.
discontinue, ophou, opgee, staak, uitskei; opsê.
discontinuity, onderbreking; onsamehangendheid.
discontinuous, onderbroke; onsamehangend.
discord, wanklank, disharmonie; onenigheid, tweedrag, twis; **apple of** –, twisappel.
discordance, wanklank; uiteenlopendheid.
discordant, wanluidend, onharmonies; onenig; uiteenlopend.
discount, n. korting, diskonto; **at a** –, benede pari; in diskrediet.
discount, v. (ver)diskonteer, inwissel; korting gee; buite rekening laat; met 'n greintjie sout neem.
discountance, ontmoedig, afkeur, teengaan.
discourage, ontmoedig, afskrik; teengaan, afraai.
discouragement, ontmoediging; afrading; moedeloosheid.
discourse, n. diskoers; redevoering, preek; verhandeling; gesprek, onderhoud.
discourse, v. voordrag hou, spreek; 'n gesprek voer; – **on**, bespreek, praat oor.
discourteous, onbeleef, onwellewend, lomp.
discourtesy, onbeleefdheid, onwellewendheid.
discover, ontdek, uitvind, agterkom; openbaar, aan die lig bring, verraai, onthul.
discovery, ontdekking, uitvinding; openbaarmaking; ontknoping.
discredit, n. diskrediet, oneer, skande.
discredit, v. oneer aandoen; betwyfel.
discreditable, weinig eervol, skandelik.
discreet, versigtig, tak(t)vol; swygsaam.
discrepancy, teenstrydigheid, verskil.
discrepant, teenstrydig, onverenigbaar.
discrete, onderskeie, apart; abstrak.
discretion, oordeel, oorleg; versigtigheid; willekeur, goeddunke; diskresie; **at** –, volgens goeddunke; **be at someone's** –, by iemand berus; **tot iemand se diens wees**; **years of** –, jare des onderskeids; **surrender at** –, op genade of ongenade oorgee; – **is the better part of valour**, versigtigheid is die moeder van die wysheid.
discretionary, willekeurig, na goeddunke.
discriminate, onderskei; – **against**, onderskeid maak ten koste van, te kort doen.
discriminating, onderskeidend; oordeelkundig.
discrimination, onderskeiding; onderskeidingsvermoë, oordeelkundigheid, oordeel.

**discursive, los, onsamehangend; beredeneerd.
discus, (werp)skyf; throwing the –, skyfwerp, discusgooi.
discuss, bespreek, beredeneer, uitpluis; ('n maaltyd, fles) aanspreek.
discussion, bespreking, beredenering, diskussie.
disdain, v. verag, versmaad, minag.
disdain, n. veragting, versmading, minagting.
disdainful, minagtend, veragtelik.
disease, siekte, kwaal.
diseased, siek, sieklik; bedorwe.
disembark, ontskeep, aan land sit; land.
disembarkation, ontskeping, landing.
disembarrass, uit (die verleentheid) help; bevry, verlos van, ontlas van.
disembodied, onliggaamlik; ontbonde.
disembody, van die liggaam bevry; ontbind.
disembogue, uitmond, (sig) ontlas; uitstort.
disembowel, die ingewande uithaal, ontwei.
disembroil, ontwar; uithelp, verlos.
disenchant, ontgoël (ontgogel), ontnugter.
disencumber, ontlas, onthef, verlos.
disengage, los-, vrymaak; ontslaan, bevry.
disengaged, vry, los; onbeset; ontslaan.
disengagement, vrysetting, bevryding; vryheid; ongedwongenheid; ontslag; afbreking (van verlowing).
disentangle, ontwar, ontknoop; vrymaak.
disestablish, afstig, (af)skei.
disfavour, n. ongenade, onguns, teensin; fall into –, in ongenade val.
disfavour, v. nie begunstig nie, teen wees.
disfiguration, vide disfigurement.
disfigure, vermink, skend, ontsier.
disfigurement, verminking, skending, ontsiering; mismaaktheid.
disforest, ontbos, bome afkap.
disfranchise, stemreg (burgerreg) ontneem.
disfranchisement, ontneming van stemreg (burgerreg).
disgorge, uitbraak, uitstort; teruggee.
disgrace, n. skande, skandvlek; ongenade; be in –, in ongenade wees.
disgrace, v. in die skande steek, skande (oneer) aandoen; be –ed, in ongenade val, uit die guns raak; – oneself, sig skandelik gedra.
disgraceful, skandelik, skandalig.
disgruntled, brommerig, misnoeg.
disguise, v. vermom, verklee; verbloem.
disguise, n. vermomming, mom; voorwendsel, dekmantel, masker; in –, vermom.
disgust, n. teensin, afkeer, walging.
disgust, v. erger, stuit, walg; be –ed with (at), walg van; maagvol wees vir (oor).
dish, n. skottel; gereg.
dish, v. opskep; uitoorlê; – up, opdien, opdis.
dishabille, des–, négligé, oggendkleding; en –, onaangetrek.
disharmonious, wanklinkend, vals.
disharmony, disharmonie, wanklank.
dish-cloth, vaatdoek (vadoek).
dishearten, ontmoedig; afskrik.
dishevelled, met die hare deurmekaar, verwaai.
dishonest, oneerlik, onopreg.
dishonesty, oneerlikheid.
dishonour, n. skande, oneer.
dishonour, v. onteer; oneer (skande) aandoen; ('n wissel) dishonoreer, weier.
dishonourable, eerloos; onterend.
dish-wash, dish-water, skottelgoedwater.
disillusion, ontnugter, ontgoël, die oë oopmaak; teenval.
disillusionment, ontnugtering, ontgoëling.
disinclination, ongeneigdheid, teensin, afkerigheid.**
**disincline, afkerig maak, teensin gee.
disinclined, ongeneig, afkerig, teensinnig.
disinfect, ontsmet.
disinfectant, ontsmettingsmiddel.
disinfection, ontsmetting.
disingenuous, onopreg, nie reguit nie.
disingenuousness, onopregtheid.
disinherit, onterf, ontmaak.
disinheritance, onterwing, ontmaking.
disintegrate, uitmekaarval; ontbind, oplos.
disintegration, verweer; ontbinding.
disinter, opgrawe; opdiep.
disinterested, belangeloos; onpartydig; onbaatsugtig.
disinternment, opgrawing.
disjoin, skei, losmaak.
disjoint, ontwrig, uit verband ruk, opbreek.
disjointed, ontwrig; onsamehangend.
disjunction, ontwrigting; skeiding, splitsing.
disjunctive, onwrigtend; skeidend; disjunktief.
disk, disc, skyf; diskus.
disk-jockey, platevoorspeler, musiekkletser.
disk-plough, skottelploeg.
disk-wheel, skottelwiel.
dislike, v. nie van hou nie, 'n afkeer van hê, 'n hekel aan hê.
dislike, n. afkeer, teensin, hekel.
dislocate, verplaas; ontwrig, verswik; he –ed his collar-bone, sy sleutelbeen het uit lid geraak, hy het sy sleutelbeen ontwrig.
dislocation, ontwrigting.
dislodge, verdryf, verjaag.
disloyal, ontrou, dislojaal.
disloyalty, ontrou(heid), dislojaliteit.
dismal, naar, aaklig, somber.
dismantle, ontakel, ontmantel; sleg, afbreek.
dismay, n. ontsteltenis, verslaentheid.
dismay, v. (laat) ontstel, onthuts, verslae maak; ontmoedig.
dismember, uiteenruk, verbrokkel, verdeel.
dismiss, wegstuur, laat gaan; ontbind, afdank, ontslaan; afsit, bedank; haastig afhandel; ('n plan) laat vaar; terugstuur (krieket).
dismissal, ontslag, afdanking, afsetting; ontbinding; (die) wegstuur; (die) uitkry, val.
dismount, afklim, afstyg; uitmekaar haal, demonteer.
disobedience, ongehoorsaamheid.
disobedient, ongehoorsaam.
disobey, ongehoorsaam wees aan, nie gehoorsaam nie, veronagsaam, nie na luister nie.
disoblige, onvriendelik behandel.
disobliging, onvriendelik, onbehulpsaam.
disorder, n. wanorde, verwarring; wanordelikheid, oproer; kwaal, ongesteldheid.
disorder, v. in die war maak, van stryk bring.
disordered, in die war, verward(d), van stryk.
disorderly, wanordelik, rumoerig.
disorganization, wanorde, desorganisasie.
disorganize, in wanorde bring, in die war stuur, deurmekaar maak, desorganiseer.
disown, weier om te erken, verloën, verwerp.
disparage, oneer aandoen; kleineer, neersien op.
disparagement, verlaging; kleinering, minagting, beskimping.
disparaging, kleinerend, skimpend.
disparate, ongelyk(soortig), disparaat.
disparity, ongelykheid, verskil.
dispassionate, bedaard, besadig.
dispatch, sien despatch.
dispel, verdryf, wegja; wegruim.
dispensable, ontbeerlik; verslapbaar.
dispensary, (arme)apteek.
dispensation, uitdeling; bedeling; beskikking; vrystelling, ontheffing, dispensasie.**

dispense, uitdeel; uitmeet, uitoefen; toeberei (medisyne); onthef, vrystel; – **with**, klaarkom sonder.
dispenser, uitdeler; bedeler; apteker.
dispersal, verstrooiing, verspreiding.
disperse, verstrooi, uitmekaar jaag; versprei.
dispersion, verstrooiing, verspreiding.
dispirited, moedeloos, neerslagtig.
displace, verplaas; vervang.
displacement, verplasing; vervanging; waterverplasing.
display, n. vertoning, uitstalling.
display, v. vertoon, uitstal, tentoonstel, openbaar, aan die dag lê.
display-cabinet, **-case**, vertoonkas.
displease, mishaag, ongenoeë doen, vererg.
displeasure, misnoeë, mishae; **incur** –, ongenoeë op die hals haal.
disport, v. (sig) vermaak, (sig) verlustig.
disposal, beskikking; reëling; verkoop, opruiming; **at your** –, tot u beskikking; **have the** – **of**, die beskikking hê oor.
dispose, skik, rangskik; reël, inrig; stem, in 'n stemming bring; beskik; – **of**, van die hand sit; wegruim; kafloop, afreken mee; (argumente) weerlê.
disposition, rangskikking; inrigting; geaardheid; disposisie; **(-s) reëlings**, voorbereidsels.
dispossess, (die besit) ontneem, onteien.
dispossession, onteiening, ontvreemding.
disproof, weerlegging, teenbewys.
disproportion, oneweredigheid, wanverhouding.
disproportionate, **disproportioned**, oneweredig, sleg, geproporsioneerd.
disprove, weerlê.
disputable, betwisbaar.
disputant, disputant.
disputation, redetwis, disputasie.
disputatious, twissiek, redeneersiek.
dispute, v. redetwis, disputeer, argumenteer; ontken, betwis; twis.
dispute, n. redetwis, dispuut; bespreking; geskil; twis; **point in** –, geskilpunt; **without** –, ongetwyfeld, buiten kyf.
disqualification, ongeskiktheid; gebrek; uitsluiting, diskwalifikasie.
disqualify, ongeskik maak; ongeskik verklaar, uitsluit, diskwalifiseer.
disquiet, v. ontrus, ongerus maak.
disquiet, n. onrus, ongerustheid.
disquieting, verontrustend, onrusbarend.
disquietude, ongerustheid, besorgdheid.
disquisition, verhandeling.
disregard, v. veronagsaam, geen notisie van neem nie; in die wind slaan.
disregard, n. veronagsaming, geringskatting.
disrepair, verval.
disreputable, berug, befaam.
disrepute, slegte naam, berugtheid.
disrespect, oneerbiedigheid.
disrespectful, oneerbiedig.
disrobe, ontklee(d).
disrupt, uiteenskeur.
disruption, skeuring, uiteenspatting.
dissatisfaction, ontevredenheid, onvoldaanheid.
dissatisfactory, onbevredigend.
dissatisfied, ontevrede, misnoeg, teleurgestel.
dissatisfy, teleurstel, mishaag, ontevrede maak.
dissect, ontleed; uitmekaar trek; **–ing knife**, ontleedmes; **–ing room**, ontleedsaal.
dissection, ontleding.
dissemble, veins, voorwend; ontveins.
dissembler, geveinsde, huigelaar.
disseminate, uitsaai, versprei, rondstrooi.
dissemination, verspreiding, uitstrooiing.

dissension, tweedrag, verdeeldheid.
dissent, n. meningsverskil; afskeiding.
dissent, v. van mening (gevoel) verskil; afskei.
dissenter, afgeskeidene, dissenter.
dissentient, a. andersdenkend, afwykend; – **vote**, teenstem.
dissentient, n. andersdenkende; teenstemmer.
dissertation, verhandeling; dissertasie.
disservice, ondiens.
dissidence, onenigheid, geskil.
dissident, onenig, andersdenkend.
dissimilar, ongelyk(soortig), uiteenlopend.
dissimilarity, ongelykheid, verskil.
dissimilitude, ongelykheid.
dissimulate, voorwend, veins; ontveins.
dissimulation, huigelary, geveinsdheid.
dissipate, verstrooi, verdryf; verkwis, deurbring; losbandig lewe.
dissipated, losbandig.
dissipation, verstrooiing; verkwisting, deurbringery; losbandigheid.
dissociate, losmaak, ontbind, (af)skei; – **oneself from**, nie mee instem nie.
dissociation, (af)skeiding, ontbinding.
dissoluble, oplosbaar, smeltbaar, ontbindbaar.
dissolute, losbandig, bandeloos, liederlik.
dissolution, oplossing, ontbinding, smelting; dood.
dissolve, oplos, ontbind, smelt; verdwyn; – Parliament, die Parlement ontbind.
dissolvent, oplossende (ontbindende) middel.
dissonance, wanklank, dissonans.
dissonant, wanluidend, vals, onharmonies.
dissuade, afraai, ontraai, uit die kop praat.
dissyllabic, tweelettergrepig.
dissyllable, tweelettergrepige woord.
distaff, spinrok; **on the** – **side**, van moederskant.
distance, n. afstand, distansie; verte; koelheid; terughoudenheid; **at a** –, op 'n afstand; in the –, in die verte; **keep one's** –, jou afstand bewaar.
distance, v. ver uitstof, disnisloop.
distant, ver, verwyder(d), weg; koel, terughoudend; **bear a** – **likeness**, enigsins lyk op.
distaste, afkeer, teensin.
distasteful, onsmaaklik.
distemper, n. kwaal; slegte humeur; hondesiekte.
distemper, v. deurmekaar maak; **–ed mind**, verwarde verstand.
distemper, n. muurkalk, kalkverf.
distemper, v. verf, wit, kalk.
distend, uitsit, swel, rek.
distension, uitsetting, rekking, opswelling.
distich, distigon.
distil, distilleer, oorhaal, stook; afdruppel.
distillation, distillasie; (die) stook, stoking.
distiller, distilleerder, stoker; distilleerketel.
distillery, stokery, distilleerdery.
distinct, onderskeie, afsonderlik; duidelik, helder; beslis, bepaald; **a** – **improvement**, 'n besliste verbetering.
distinction, onderskeiding; onderskeid, verskil; distinksie, vernaamheid; **in** – **to**, in teenstelling met, teenoor.
distinctive, kenmerkend; apart; vernaam.
distinctness, duidelikheid; beslistheid.
distinguish, onderskei; kenmerkend; uitmerker hou, onderken.
distinguishable, kenbaar, te onderskei.
distinguished, onderskeie; vernaam, beroemd.
distort, verdraai, verwring, skeef trek.
distorted, verwronge, verdraai, skeef.
distortion, verdraaiing, verwringing; verwrongenheid; distorsie (radio).
distortionist, spotprenttekenaar; slangmens.

distract, aftrek; aflei; verwar, gek maak.
distracted, verwar(d), kranksinnig, deurmekaar.
distraction, afleiding; kranksinnigheid; **to** -, om kranksinnig van te word.
distrain, in beslag neem, beslag lê op.
distraint, beslag(legging), inbeslagneming.
distraught, sien **distracted**.
distress, n. nood, benoudheid, ellende; beslag; - signal, noodsein.
distress, v. in nood (verleentheid) bring, kommer baar, kwel.
distressful, kommervol, rampspoedig; benoud.
distribute, uitdeel, (ver)deel, versprei; besorg; distribueer.
distribution, uitdeling, (ver)deling, verspreiding; besorging; distribusie.
distributive, ver-, toe-, indelend; distributief.
district, distrik; wyk, streek, gebied.
district surgeon, goewermentsdokter, distriksgeneesheer.
distrust, n. wantroue; verdenking, agterdog.
distrust, v. wantrou; verdink.
distrustful, wantrouig, agterdogtig.
disturb, steur (stoor), pla, hinder; verontrus; in die war bring.
disturbance, steuring, steurnis; verontrusting; rusverstoring, opskudding, oproerigheid.
disturber, (rus)verstoorder.
disturbing, storend; verontrustend.
disunion, tweedrag, onenigheid.
disunite, skei, verdeel; -**d**, onenig.
disuse, n. onbruik; ontwenning, ongewoonte.
disuse, v. ophou gebruik (toepas); afwen.
ditch, n. sloot, voor; **die in the last** -, volhard tot die bitter einde.
ditch, v. slote grawe; dreineer.
ditch-water, vuil water; **dull as** -, stom vervelend.
dither, bibber, beef.
dithyramb, ditirambe.
dithyrambic, ditirambies, vurig, rasend.
ditto, ditto (dito), dieselfde, van dieselfde.
ditty, liedjie.
diurnal, dag- . . ., daagliks.
divagate, (af)dwaal, uitwei.
divagation, afdwaling, afwyking, uitweiding.
divan, divan; raad(s)kamer.
dive, v. (in)duik, (in)dompel; insteek; (sig) verdiep (in), wegval (in); - **into your pocket**, jou hand in jou sak steek; - **into your memory**, in jou geheue rondval.
dive, n. duik; speelhol; **make a** - **for**, gryp na.
dive-bomber, duikbomwerper.
dive-bombing, duikbombardering.
diver, duiker.
diverge, splits, afwyk, uitmekaarloop; - **from**, afwyk van, verskil van.
divergence, splitsing, afwyking.
divergent, uiteenlopend.
divers, etlike, verskeie, verskillende, diverse.
diverse, verskillend, ongelyk.
diversify, afwissel, varieer, wysig.
diversion, afleiding; afwending; ontspanning.
diversity, verskeidenheid; verskil; - **of opinion**, verskil van mening.
divert, aflei; wegdraai, wegkeer; onttrek; afwend; vermaak, amuseer.
diverting, vermaaklik, amusant.
Dives, die ryk man.
divest, ontklee; ontdoen (van); beroof (van).
divestiture, **divestment**, ontkleding, ontbloting; berowing; afstand.
divide, v. (ver)deel; skei; sny, deurklief; verdeeld raak; verdeeld maak; - **by (into)**, deel deur (in).
divide, n. waterskeiding.

dividend, (wins)aandeel, dividend; deeltal.
dividend-warrant, dividendbrief, -koepon.
divider, deler; (verdeeldheid)stoker; -**s**, (verdeel)passer.
divination, voorgevoel; voorspelling; aanwysing.
divine, a. goddelik, godsdienstig; - **service**, godsdiens, kerkdiens.
divine, n. geestelike.
divine, v. 'n voorgevoel hê; vermoed; voorspel; (water) aanwys.
diviner, voorspeller, waarsêer; waterwyser.
diving-bell, duikerklok.
divining-rod, waterstokkie, wiggelroede.
divinity, goddelikheid; godgeleerdheid; godheid.
divisible, deelbaar; - **by**, deelbaar deur.
division, (\er)deling; deelsomme; afdeling; skeiding, grens; verdeeldheid; divisie; **long**, **short** -, lang-, kortdeling; - **sum**, deelsom.
divisional, afdelings- . . .; - **council**, afdelingsraad.
divisor, deler, divisor.
divorce, n. egskeiding; skeiding.
divorce, v. egskeiding verleen; laat skei; skei.
divorcee, geskeie persoon.
divulgation, sien **divulgence**.
divulge, openbaar, uitlaat, verklap.
divulgement, sien **divulgence**.
divulgence, openbaring, verklapping.
dixie, **dixy**, veldketel.
dizen, opskik, optooi.
dizziness, duis(e)ligheid, duis(e)ling.
dizzy, duis(e)lig, dronk, draaierig; duis(e)lingwekkend.
do, v. doen, maak, verrig, ten uitvoer bring, klaarmaak; - **honour**, **service**, eer, diens bewys; **it does him credit**, dit strek hom tor eer; - **harm**, kwaad doen; - **a room**, 'n kamer aan (die) kant maak; - **shopping**, inkope doen; - **one's hair**, jou hare opmaak; - **(out of)**, fop (uit); - **twenty miles**, twintig myl ry; - **ten years**, tien jaar tronkstraf uitdien; - **battle**, slag lewer; **how do you** -?, hoe gaan dit?; - **or die**, oorwin of sterf; **have done with it**, skei uit daarmee!; **that won't** -, dit sal nie gaan nie; **that'll** -, dis genoeg; - **you hear**, hoor jy?; **I** -, ja; **I** - **hope**, ek hoop werklik; **I did so**, ek het dit gedoen; - **tell me**, vertel my tog; **I don't like him**, - **you?**, ek hou nie van hom nie, en jy?; - **for**, genoeg wees vir; deug vir; - **away (with)**, wegdoen, afskaf; - **over**, oordoen; nasien; - **up**, herstel, regmaak; oprol, inpak; **be done up**, poot-uit wees; - **to death**, doodmaak; - **without**, klaarkom sonder.
do, n. foppery, bedriegery.
dobbin, knol, werksperd.
docile, leersaam, geseglik; mak.
docility, leersaamheid; volgsaamheid.
dock, n. wilde suring; tongblaar.
dock, v. stert afsny, stompstert maak; afkap, inkort.
dock, n. (skeeps)dok; **dry** -, droogdok; **floating** -, dryfdok.
dock, v. dok, in die dok bring.
dock, n. (beskuldigde)hok, -bank.
dockage, **dock-dues**, dokkoste, hawegeld.
docker, dokwerker.
docket, n. (dag)rol (van hofsake); uittreksel; etiket; kaartjie.
docket, v. op die rol plaas; uittreksel maak; opskryf; merk.
dockyard, skeepswerf.
doctor, n. dokter, doktor.
doctor, v. doktorsgraad verleen; dokter; regmaak.

doctoral, doktoraal, doktors- . . .
doctorate, doktoraat.
doctrinaire, doktrinêr, leerstellig(e).
doctrinal, leerstellig, dogmaties.
doctrine, leer(stelling), dogma; leerstelsel.
document, n. dokument, bewysstuk, akte.
document, v. dokumenteer.
documentary, n. dokumentêre boek, stuk, prent, ens.
documentary, dokumentêr.
dodder, n. duiwelsnaaigaring, dodder.
dodder, v. beef, tril; strompel, waggel.
dodderer, swak (sieklike, onbekwame) persoon; sukkelaar.
dodecagon, twaalfhoek.
dodge, v. draai, jakkalsdraaie maak; rondspring; uitoorlê; vryspring; verbyglip, ontduik.
dodge, n. draai, slenterslag, uitvlug.
dodger, jakkals, slimmerd, skelm.
dodo, dodo, walgvoël.
doe, hinde; haas-, konynwyfie.
doer, dader, verrigter; **evil- –**, boosdoener.
doff, afhaal; uittrek; afleer.
dog, n. hond; reun; kram, haak; **lucky –**, geluksvoël; **an old –**, 'n ou klant; **go to the –s**, na sy maai gaan, versleg; **throw to the –s**, wegsmyt; **every – has his day**, daar kom 'n dag vir iedereen; **die a –'s death**, 'n ellendige dood sterf; vrek soos 'n hond; **lead a –'s life**, 'n hondelewe lei; **let sleeping –s lie**, slapende honde nie wakker maak nie; **– in the manger**, iemand wat 'n ander die bene nie gun wat hyself geen tande het om af te eet nie; **rain cats and –s**, oumeide met knopkieries reent; **– latin**, potjieslatyn.
dog, v. agtervolg; opspoor; pak, vasvat.
dog-box hondehok; hondewa; hokkompartement.
dog-cake, hondebrood.
dogcart, hondekar.
dog-eared, flenters, beduimeld.
dogfight, hondegeveg; luggeveg.
dogged, (honds)taai, vasberade; **it's – does it**, aanhouer wen.
doggerel, kreupelrym, rymelary.
doggish, honds, hondagtig.
doggy, gek na honde; honde-.
dogma, dogma, leerstelling, leerstuk.
dogmatic, dogmaties, leerstellig; aanmatigend.
dogmatize, dogmatiseer.
dogmatism, dogmatisme, leerstelligheid.
dog's ear, vou, eselsoor.
dog-tired, doodmoeg, so moeg as 'n hond.
dog-trot, hondedraffie, sukkeldraffie.
dog-watch, platvoetwag.
doily, vinger(bak)doekie; kraaldoekie.
doing, werk, bedryf, doen en late; **it is all his –**, dit is alles sy werk; **your own –**, jou eie skuld; **nothing –**, pure verniet!
doit, duit, oortjie.
doldrums, windstilte; neerslagtigheid.
dole, n. lot; deel; uitdeling; aalmoes.
dole, v. uitdeel.
dole, n. droefheid; treurigheid; gejammer.
doleful, droewig, treurig.
dolerite, doleriet.
dolichocephalic, langskedelig.
doll, pop; **–'s clothes**, popgoed; **–'s house**, pop(pe)huis, klein woonhuisie.
dollar, daalder; (Amerikaanse) dollar.
dollop, klomp, klont, brok.
dolomite, dolomiet.
dolorous, pynlik, smartlik, klaaglik.
dolour, smart.
dolphin, dolfyn; aanlêpaal.

dolt, botterkop, uilskuiken.
doltish, onnosel, bot.
domain, domein; gebied.
dome, dom, koepel.
domestic, n. bediende, diensbode.
domestic, a. huis- . . ., huislik, huishoudelik; binnelands; **– animal**, huisdier; **– affairs**, huislike sake; binnelandse sake; **– economy**, huishoudkunde; **– science**, huisvlyt, huishoudkunde; **– war**, burgeroorlog.
domesticate, mak maak, tem; inburger.
domesticity, huislikheid; huislike lewe.
domicile, n. verblyf, woonplaas; domisilie.
domicile, v. (sig) vestig; **be –d**, woonagtig wees.
domiciliary, huis- . . . ; **– visit**, huissoeking.
dominant, (oor)heersend, dominerend; dominant.
dominate, oorheers, die botoon voer; uitsteek bo.
domination, be-, oorheersing; heerskappy.
dominator, beheerser.
domineer, oorheers, baasspeel.
domineering, heerssugtig, baasspelerig.
Dominican, a. Dominikaans.
Dominican, n. Dominikaner.
dominie, (skool)meester.
dominion, heerskappy; gebied; dominium, gewes.
domino, domino, vermomming; dominosteen.
dominoes, domino(spel).
don, n. don.
don, v. aantrek.
donation, skenking, gif, geskenk, donasie.
donga, donga, sloot.
donjon, toring, slot.
donkey, esel, donkie; botterkop, domkop; **–'s years**, 'n ewigheid.
donor, skenker, gewer.
doom, n. verordening; vonnis, oordeel; ondergang; **crack (day) of –**, laaste oordeel, oordeelsdag.
doom, v. veroordeel, vonnis, doem.
doomsday, oordeelsdag; **till –**, (vir) ewig.
door, deur; front –, voordeur; next –, naasaan, langesaan; **that is next – to . . .**, dit grens aan . . . ; **three –s off**, drie huise verder; **at death's –**, aan die rand van die graf; **show someone the –**, iemand die deur wys; **out of –s**, buite, in die ope lug; **within –s**, binnenshuis; **lay at the – of**, verwyt, toeskryf aan.
door-frame, (deur)kosyn.
door-handle, deurknop.
door-keeper, portier, deurwagter.
door-latch, deurknip, slot.
doornail, deurbout; **dead (deaf) as a –**, so doof soos 'n mossie; so doof soos 'n kwartel.
door-panel, (deur)paneel.
door-plate, naambord(jie).
door-post, deurstyl, kosyn.
door-sill, drumpel.
doorstep, drumpel; stoep; trappie.
doorway, ingang, deuropening.
dope, n. pap; bedwelmende middel; informasie.
dope, v. bedwelm; opkikker (renperd).
dope-addict, dwelmsugtige.
dope-peddler, dwelmsmous.
Dopper, Dopper.
Doric, Dories.
dormant, sluimerend, slapend, rustend, stil.
dormer(-window), dakvenster.
dormitory, slaapsaal.
dormouse, slaapmuis; marmotjie.
dormy, doedoe (in gholf).
dorsal, dorsaal, rug- . . .
dory, (geel)vis, goudvis, sonvis; sloepbootjie.
dose, n. dosis, dop.

dose, v. medisyne gee; meng; dokter.
doss, slaap.
doss-house, slaapgeleentheid.
dossier, dossier, register.
dot, n. punt, stippel; kleintjie, kindjie.
dot, v. stippel; puntjies opsit; – the **i**'s, puntjies op die i's sit; **–ted line**, stippellyn; **–ted with**, besaai met.
dotage, kindsheid, simpelheid; versotheid.
dotard, sufferd, simpel (kindse) mens.
dote, simpel (kinds) wees; – **on**, versot wees op.
doting, versot, gek; simpel, kinds.
dottle, pypmoer.
dotty, gespikkeld; simpel, getik.
double, a. & adv. dubbel(d), tweevoudig, tweeledig; twee maal; dubbelhartig; vals; **in –** (**quick**) **time**, in looppas (stormpas); soos die wind; **ride –**, agter mekaar ry; **see –**, dubbel sien; – **as bright**, twee maal so helder.
double, v. dubbel, verdubbel; doebleer (by kaartspel); pas versnel, hardloop; dubbel vou; omseil; omspring, terughardloop; – **one's fist**, vuis maak.
double, n. die dubbel(d)e; dubbelganger; dubbelspel (in tennis); (kort) bog of draai; – **or quits**, gelyk (kiet) of dubbel; **at the –**, in versnelde pas, in looppas.
double-barrelled, dubbelloop- . . ., tweeloop(s) . . .; dubbelsinnig.
double-bass, kontrabas.
double-cross, verraai, verneuk.
double-breasted: – **coat**, oorknoopbaadjie.
double-dealing, bedrieëry, verneukery; huigelary.
double-dyed, deurtrap, op-en-top.
double-edged, tweesnydend.
double-entry, dubbel boekhou.
double-faced, huigelagtig, geveins, vals.
double-quick, versnel, verhaas; **at the –**, in versnelde pas, in looppas.
double-storey, (twee)verdiepinghuis.
doublet, warmbuis; doeblet; paar.
double-tongued, met twee monde, huigelagtig.
doubloon, doebloen.
doubly, dubbel(d).
doubt, n. twyfel, weifeling; argwaan; **no –**, ongetwyfel; **without –**, ongetwyfeld; **there is no –**, dit ly geen twyfel nie; **cast – on**, in twyfel trek; **give him the benefit of the –**, die twyfel in sy voordeel oplos.
doubt, v. twyfel; weifel; betwyfel; argwaan koester, nie vertrou nie.
doubtful, twyfelagtig, onseker; weifelend.
doubtless, ongetwyfeld, bepaald, stellig.
douche, stortbad; spuit; douche.
dough, deeg.
doughnut, oliebol; stormjaer.
doughty, manhaftig, dapper.
dour, hard, streng; stuurs.
douse, begiet; (seile) neerlaat; (lig) doodmaak.
dove, duif.
dove-cot(e), duiwehok; **flutter the –s**, 'n beroering veroorsaak.
dovetail, n. swa(w)elstert.
dovetail, v. met 'n swa(w)elstert voeg.
dowager, adellike weduwee, douairière.
dowdy, n. sloerie, slons.
dowdy, a. slordig, slonsig, smaakloos.
dower, bruidskat, weduweegeld; gawe, talent.
down, n. duin.
down, n. dons(ies), donshaartjies, veertjies.
down, prep. af; van af; langes af; **up and –**, op en af; **he is going – town**, hy gaan af na die stad; – **the wind**, voor die wind uit; onderkant die wind.
down, adv. af, neer, (na) onder; **knock –**, neerslaan; **pull –**, aftrek, na onder trek; **the sun goes –**, die son gaan onder; **pay –**, aftel; **run –**, inhaal, vang; slegmaak; **be run –**, afgewerk wees; – **with**, weg met!; **he is – with fever**, hy lê aan die koors; **hand –**, oorlewer, nalaat; **wear –**, afslyt; uitput; **calm –**, afkoel, kalmeer; **be – on**, afklim op; – **to the ground**, heeltemal, uitstekend, eksie-perfeksie.
down, a. afgaande; afdraand; – **train**, afgaande trein; – **grade**, afdraand.
down, v. neerslaan, neergooi, „plant"; – **tools**, staak, die werk opskop.
down, n. teenslag; **ups and –s**, wederwaardighede.
downcast, terneergeslae, neerslagtig, mismoedig.
downfall, val; ondergaan.
downhearted, mismoedig, neerslagtig.
downhill, afdraand, berg af, bult af.
downpour, stortbui.
downright, regaf; volslae, pure; eerlik (waar), werklik; – **nonsense**, pure onsin.
downstairs, onder, benede; na onder, na benede; in 'n benedeverdieping.
downtrodden, verdruk, vertrap.
downward(s), na onder, ondertoe.
downy, donserig; oulik, slim.
dowry, bruidskat; gawe, talent.
dowse, sien **douse**.
dowse, waterwys (met die stokkie).
doxology, lofsang.
doxy, opinie, leer.
doyley, sien **doily**.
doze, dut, dommel, sluimer, visvang.
dozen, dosyn.
drab, n. hoer, slet, drel.
drab, a. vaal; grou; eentonig, vervelig.
drab, n. eentonigheid, verveligheid.
drabble, besmeer, bespat.
drachm, dragma, dragme.
draff, draf; oorskiet, afval; moer.
draft, (sien **draught**), n. afdeling, ligting, (bank)wissel; skets, ontwerp.
draft, v. opstel; ontwerp; detasjeer; uitstuur.
draft-act, **-law**, konsepwet, wetsontwerp.
draftsmen, opsteller; ontwerper.
drag, v. sleep; dreg; eg; rem; – **on**, voortsleep; omkruip; – **out**, uittrek; voortsleep.
drag, n. remskoen; blok aan die been; eg; dreg(net); sleepsel; vertraging.
draggle, (deur die modder) sleep; aansukkel.
drag-net, sleepnet, dreg(net).
dragoman, tolk, dragoman.
dragon, draak.
dragon-fly, naaldekoker.
dragoon, n. dragonder.
dragoon, v. (deur soldate) laat mishandel, vervolg; – **into**, dwing tot.
drain, v. afwater, aftap; leegdrink; drooglê; uitput; dreineer.
drain, n. riool, afvoersloot, dreineerpyp, sopie.
drainage, afwatering, drooglegging; riolering; dreinering.
drain-basin, opvanggebied.
drake, mannetjieseend.
dram, drachma (dragme); borreltjie, sopie.
drama, drama; toneelspel; dramatiese kuns.
dramatic, dramaties.
dramatize, dramatiseer; vir die toneel bewerk.
dramatist, toneelskrywer.
drape, oortrek, omhang; drapeer.
draper, klerasiehandelaar.
drapery, kledingstofhandel, klerasiehandel; kledingstowwe, klerasie; behang(sel), drapering.
drastic, drasties, deurtastend, effektief.
drat: – **it**, vervlaks!; – **the boy**, so 'n vervlakste kind!

draught, sien **draft**, n. trek, tog; teug, sluk; drank(ie); tapsel; skets, ontwerp; (vis)vangs, trek; diepgang (van 'n skip).
draught-bord, dambord.
draught-horse, trekperd.
draughts, dambord.
draught-screen, togskerm.
draughtsman, sien **draftsman**, tekenaar, ontwerper; (dambord)skyf.
draw, v. trek, aantrek, wegtrek; (rook) intrek; uittrek; skep, uitskep; uithaal, te voorskyn bring; (uit)rek, strek; (af)trek, teken; beskryf; opstel; – **breath**, asemhaal; – **bridle**, inhou; – **a conclusion**, 'n gevolgtrekking maak; – **a comparison**, 'n vergelyking maak (trek); – **inspiration**, inspirasie skep; – **trumps**, troewe (uit)vra; – **water**, water skep; – **it mild**, stadig oor die klippe!; – **near**, nader kom; – **off**, verder gaan; wegneem; – **to a close**, ten einde loop; – **up**, opstel; ontwerp; stilhou; – (**up**)**on**, ('n wissel) trek op; gebruik maak van; – **level**, kop-en-kop kom; – **a game**, gelykop speel; – **a line**, 'n grens trek.
draw, n. trek; skyfie (rook); pluk; aantreklikheid; uitloting; lotery; gelykspel.
drawback, beswaar, nadeel, skadusy.
drawbridge, ophaalbrug.
drawee, nemer, betrokkene.
drawer, trekker; tekenaar; laai; **chest of** –**s**, laaikas, -tafel; (**pair of**) –**s**, (onder)broek.
drawing, trek(king); tekening; tekenkuns.
drawing-board, tekenbord.
drawing-materials, tekengereedskap.
drawing-pin, drukspykertjie, duimspykertjie.
drawing-room, sitkamer, salon.
drawl, v. aanstellerig (temerig) praat.
drawl, n. aanstellerige (temerige) uitspraak.
drawn, sien **draw**, vertrokke, betrokke, gespanne; – **match**, onbesliste (gelykop) wedstryd.
dray, sleperswa.
dread, n. vrees, skrik, angs.
dread, v. vrees.
dread, a. gevrees(de), verskriklik.
dreadful, verskriklik, ontsettend, vreeslik.
dreadnaught, pantserskip.
dream, n. droom; hersenskim.
dream, v. droom; – **away**, verdroom; **I could not** – **that**, ek kon my nie verbeel dat ...
dreamy, dromerig; droom- ...
drear, naar, aaklig.
dreary, naar, aaklig; eentonig, vervelig.
dredge, n. dreg; baggermasjien, moddermeul.
dredge, v. dreg, bagger; met 'n baggernet vis.
dredge, v. (be)strooi, (be)sprinkel.
dredger, sien **dredge**, n. (meel)strooier.
dredging-machine, baggermasjien, moddermeul.
dreggy, moerderig.
dregs, moer; oorskot; uitskot; **to the** –, tot die droesem (bodem) toe.
drench, v. drenk, papnat maak, deurweek.
drench, n. stortbui; nat pak; sluk, sopie.
drencher, stortbui; stortbad.
dress, v. aantrek, klee; toilet maak; versier, optooi; (wond) verbind, behandel; leer, afrig, dresseer; regmaak; kam, roskam; klaarmaak, skoonmaak, gaarmaak; (hare, plante) knip, snoei; gelykmaak, gladmaak; bemes; – **up**, opskik; verklee, vermom; – **down**, roskam; afkam, skrobbeer.
dress, n. kleed; kleding, klere; kleredrag; rok; **full** –, gala-kleding, ampsgewaad.
dress-circle, (eerste) balkon (galery).
dress-coat, swa(w)elstertbaadjie; manel.
dresser, kombuisrak, -kas.

dressing, styflinne; verband(goed); smeersel; sous; vulsel; skrobbering; loesing.
dressing-case, toiletdoos.
dressing-gown, kamerjas, huisjas.
dressing-room, kleedkamer.
dressing-table, spieëltafel, toilettafel, kaptafel.
dressmaker, modemaker (-maakster).
dressmaking, modemakery.
dressy, keurig, smaakvol; spoggerig, windmakerig; goed gekleed.
dribble, n. gedruppel; vloei; kwyl; dribbel(werk).
dribble, v. druppel; kwyl; dribbel (in voetbal).
drib(b)let, druppeltjie; **by** –**s**, drupsgewyse.
drift, n. (die) drywe; trek; neiging; koers; bedoeling, strekking; (op)dryfsel; drif, deurgang.
drift, v. afdrywe, wegdrywe; meedrywe; ophoop.
drift-wood, dryfhout, wrakhout.
drill, v. boor; dril, oefen, ekserseer; in rye plant (saai).
drill, n. boor; dril, oefening, eksersisie; ry, voor.
drill, n. dril (stof).
drill-ground, drilveld, oefengrond, -terrein.
drill-hole, boorgat.
drill-plough, saaiploeg.
drill-sergeant, drilmeester; sersant-instrukteur.
drily, drogies, droog(weg).
drink, v. drink; opdrink; – **off**, **up**, uitdrink, wegslaan; – **in**, opsuig; opneem, indrink; – (to) **one's health**, (op) iemand se gesondheid drink; – **down sorrow**, verdriet verdrink; – **deep**, stewig drink.
drink, n. drank; **on the** –, aan die drank; **in** –, dronk; **the worse for** –, aangeskote, dronk; **strong** –, sterk drank; **stand a** –, op 'n glasie (borrel, sopie) trakteer.
drinkable, a. drinkbaar.
drinkable, –**s**, drinkgoed, drank.
drinker, drinker, dronklap, drinkebroer.
drinking-bout, drinkgelag, suipparty.
drip, v. drup; laat drup; druip.
drip, n. drup, gedrup, gelek; dakrand.
dripping, gedrup, gelek; braaivet.
drive, v. drywe, aan-, voortdrywe, aanja; leiselshou, stuur, bestuur, ry; ('n dryfhou) slaan; – **mad**, gek maak; – **a bargain**, 'n slag slaan; – **into a corner**, vaskeer; – **up**, voor die deur stilhou, voorry; – **up against**, teen (vas)ry, raakry; – **to despair**, tot wanhoop drywe; **what are you driving at**, wat bedoel jy?
drive, n. rit(jie), rytoertjie; pad; dryfjag; slag, hou; dryfhou (in tennis, gholf); krag, ywer; fondsinsameling.
drivel, v. kwyl; klets, basel.
drivel, n. kwyl; geklets, gebasel; kaf.
driver, bestuurder; koetsier; masjinis; dryfstok (in gholf); drywer (wa).
drizzle, mot-, stofreent.
drizzly, motreënerig.
droll, snaaks, koddig.
drollery, grappemakery; koddigheid.
dromedary, dromedaris.
drone, n. waterdraer, hommel; leegloper; gebrom, gegons; vervelige vent.
drone, v. brom, gons; voorsaag, opdreun.
drool, kwyl; klets.
droop, v. afhang; kwyn; sink; laat sak.
droop, n. slap houding; insinking.
drop, n. druppel; sopie; oorbel; drop (lekkers); klontjie; val, daling; skepskop; **acid** –**s**, suurklontjies.
drop, v. drup(pel); val; laat val; loslaat, laat vaar, opgee; ophou; – **a remark**, (sig) 'n opmerking laat ontval; – **a subject**, van 'n onderwerp afstap; – **a passenger**, 'n passasier aflaai; – **a letter**, 'n brief stuur, 'n reëltjie

skrywe; – **out**, uitval; agterraak; – **in**, inval; inloop; – **into a habit**, in 'n gewoonte verval; – it, hou op, skei uit!; **the wind –s**, die wind gaan lê; – **a perpendicular**, 'n loodlyn neerlaat.
dropper, afleier (paaltjie); dropbuisie; dropper; spar.
droppings, mis.
drop-shot, opskephou (tennis).
dropsical, watersugtig.
dropsy, water(sug).
dross, skuim; onsuiwerheid; vullis.
drought, droogte.
drove, trop, hoop.
drover, veedrywer; veesmous.
drown, verdrink, versuip; oorstem; **get, be –ed**, verdrink; **a –ing man**, 'n drenkeling.
drowse, suf (slaperig) wees, sluimer.
drowsy, slaperig, vaak, (slaap)dronk, lomerig.
drub, slaan, pak gee.
drubbing, pak slae, loesing.
drudge, n. sloof, werkesel.
drudge, v. sloof, slaaf, swoeg.
drudgery, sloofwerk, gesloof, sleur(werk).
drug, n. (genees)kruid; medisyne; bedwelmende middel; onverhandelbare artikel.
drug, v. 'n bedwelmende middel ingooi; 'n bedwelmende middel ingee, bedwelm maak.
druggist, drogis, apteker.
Druid, Druïde.
drum, trom(mel), tamboer; oortrommel; silinder; bus, blik; **with –s beating**, met slaande trom; **beat the –**, die trom roer.
drum, v. trommel, tamboerslaan; – **into**, intrommel, inhamer.
drumhead, trommelvel.
drum-major, tamboermajoor.
drummer, tamboer(slaner).
drumstick, tamboer-, trommelstok; hoenderboudjie.
drunk, a. dronk, beskonke; – **as a fiddler, so dronk soos 'n tol**.
drunk, n. suipparty; dronklap; dronkenskap.
drunkard, dronkaard, dronklap.
drunken, dronk; besope, beskonke.
drunkenness, dronkenskap.
drupe, steenvrug.
dry, a. & adv. droog, dor; dors(tig); nugter, ongeërg; frank (wyn); vervelig, swaar; – **goods**, droogware; weefstowwe; **run –**, droogloop, vasbrand; – **measure**, mate vir droogware; – **ice**, droë-ys.
dry, v. droë, uitdroog; droog word; droog maak; afdroë; – **up**, opdroë, uitdroë; die mond hou, stilbly.
dryad, bosnimf.
Dryasdust, Droogstoɪ pel.
dry-clean, (uit)stoom.
dry-dock, droogdok.
dryness, droogheid, dorheid; droogte; verveligheid.
dry-nurse, baker; kinderjuffrou.
dry-rot, vuur, molm, vrot; verrotheid.
dry-salter, handelaar in blikkiesgoed.
dry-shod, droogvoet(s).
dual, a. tweeledig, tweevoudig, tweetallig.
dual, n. tweetal, dualis; tweevoud.
dualism, dualisme; tweeledigheid.
duality, dualiteit.
dub, tot ridder slaan; bynaam gee; vetsmeer; 'n klankbaan aanbring.
dubbin(g), leervet.
dubiety, twyfel(agtigheid).
dubious, twyfelagtig, onseker, weifelend.
dubiousness, twyfelagtigheid; weifeling.
dubitation, twyfel, twyfeling; weifeling.

ducal, hertogelik, hertogs- . . .
ducat, dukaat; **–s**, dukate, geld.
duchess, hertogin.
duchy, hertogdom.
duck, n. eend; skat, hartlam; nul, eier; **play –s and drakes with**, deurbring, in die water gooi.
duck, v. (in)duik, wegduik; indompel; (weg)koes, (weg)buk.
duck, n. (die) duik, buk, koes.
duck, n. seildoek; **–s**, witbroek.
duckbill, voëlbekdier; rooi koring.
ducking, indompeling, bad.
duckling, jong eend.
duck-pond, eendedam(metjie).
duck's-egg, nul; eende-eier.
duckweed, eendekroos, paddaslym.
ducky, skat, hartlam.
duct, buis, pyp, kanaal; **biliary –**, galbuis.
ductile, smee(d)baar, buigbaar; buigsaam.
dud, n. waardelose ding (persoon), prul; **–s**, klere, spulle, toiings.
dud, a. waardeloos, onbruikbaar, prullerig.
dude, aansteller, windmaker.
dudgeon, toorn, ergernis, nydigheid.
due, a. skuldig, betaalbaar; passend, betaamlik; **in – time, course**, op sy tyd; **te syner (ter bekwamer) tyd**; **after – consideration**, na behoorlike oorweging; **the train is – in ten minutes**, die trein behoort oor tien minute aan te kom; – **to**, te danke (te wyte) aan; **he is – to speak tonight**, hy moet vanaand praat; – **east**, pal (reg) oos.
due, n. wat iemand toekom; **give everyone his –**, gee iedereen wat hom toekom; **–s**, tol, belasting; reg, geld.
duel, n. tweegeveg, duel; **fight a –**, duelleer, 'n tweegeveg hê.
duel, v. duelleer.
duenna, duenna, goewernante; chaperon.
duet(t), duet; woordstryd; paar.
duffel, duffle, duffel.
duffer, stommerik; bedrieër; vals munt.
dug, speen, tepel.
dug-out, kano; uitgeholde boomstam; loopgraaf, sloot.
duiker, duiker (boksoort).
duke, hertog.
dukedom, hertogdom.
dulcet, soet(klinkend).
dulcimer, hakkebord, dulsimer.
dull, bot, dom; dof; stomp; dooierig, vervelend, lusteloos; betrokke (lug); – **of hearing**, hardhorend.
dull, v. bot (dof, stomp) maak, verstomp; verswak, verdoof, verflou.
dullard, stommerik, botterik.
dull-brained, stom, swaar van begrip.
dull-eyed, met dowwe oog; dof van blik.
dul(l)ness, botheid, domheid, dofheid, loomheid; verveligheid.
duly, behoorlik, na behore, passend; op tyd.
duma, doema.
dumb, stom, spraakloos; stilswyend; **strike –**, dronkslaan, verstom(d) laat staan; – **show**, gebarespel.
dumb-bell, (hand)gewig, halter.
dumbfound, dronkslaan, verstom, verbluf.
dumbness, stomheid.
dumb-waiter, dientafeltjie.
dumdum, dumdum(koeël), loodneus(koeël).
dummy, n. stomme, pop; blinde(man) (in kaartspel); fopspeentjie; **act –**, stomme speel; **give the –**, liemaak, pypkan.
dummy, a. nagemaak, oneg, opgesteld.
dump, n. stompie; kort-dik ding.

dump, n. plof, bons; mynhoop.
dump, v. neerplof, aflaai, plemp, „dump" (op die mark).
dumpling, kluitjie, bolletjie.
dumps, bedruktheid, naarheid; in the –, bedruk.
dumpy, kort en dik, stomp.
dun, n. maner, skuldeiser.
dun, a. vaalbruin, donkerbruin.
dun, v. maan, lastig val, opdruk.
dunce, stommerik, domkop.
dunderhead, domkop, uilskuiken.
dune, duin.
dung, mis.
dung-beetle, miskruier.
dungeon, tronk, kerker; sien **donjon**.
dunghill, mishoop.
dunk, doop.
dunnage, pakgoed, stu-goed.
duodecimal, twaalftallig, duodesimaal.
duodecimo, duodesimo.
duodenum, twaalfvingerige derm.
dupe, n. slagoffer, dupe.
dupe, v. bedrieg, fop, beetneem, dupeer.
duplex, dubbel, tweeledig.
duplicate, a. dubbel, duplikaat– . ..
duplicate, n. duplikaat, afskrif.
duplicate, v. verdubbel; kopieer, dupliseer.
duplicator, kopieermasjien.
duplicity, dubbelhartigheid, valsheid.
durability, duursaamheid.
durable, duursaam, sterk; bestendig.
durance, hegtenis.
duration, duur, voortduring.
duress(e), dwang, geweld; gevangeskap.
during, gedurende, tydens.
dusk, skemer; halfdonker.
dusky, skemer(agtig), halfdonker.
dust, n. stof; bite the –, in die stof byt; – **devil**, stofstorm.
dust, v. afstof, bestrooi; uitstof.
dustbin, vullisbak, vuilgoedbak.
dust-bowl, woestyngebied.
dustbug, dwergmotor, snortjor.
dust-coat, stofjas, oorjas.
dust-cover, stofomslag.
duster, stoffer, stofdoek; stowwer, veër.
dustman, asryer; Klaas Vakie.
dusty, stowwig (stoffig), stowwerig (stofferig); not so –, nie so sleg nie.
Dutch, a. Hollands, Nederlands; – **uncle**, vermaner.

Dutch, n. Hollands, Nederlands; Holland –, Hooghollands, Cape –, Afrikaans(-Hollands); that's – to me, dis Grieks vir my.
Dutchify, verhollands.
Dutchman, Hollander, Nederlander; Afrikaner; I'm a – if I know, dit mag joos weet.
duteous, pligmatig, onderdanig.
dutiable, belasbaar, aan invoerreg onderhewig.
dutiful, dienswillig, onderdanig, pliggetrou.
duty, plig; wag, diens; belasting, invoerreg; – **call**, formele visite; **do – for**, diens doen vir, dien as; **be on –**, diens hê; **be off –**, geen diens hê nie; vry wees; – **free**, belastingvry.
dwarf, n. dwerg.
dwarf, a. dwergagtig, dwerg- . ..
dwarf, v. in die groei belemmer, agteruitsit; in die skaduwee stel.
dwarfish, dwergagtig, dwerg- . ..
dwell, woon, bly; – (up)on, druk op, nadruk lê op, stilstaan by.
dweller, bewoner, inwoner.
dwelling, woning, woonhuis.
dwelling-house, woonhuis, woning.
dwelling-place, woonplek, -plaas.
dwindle, agteruitgaan, verminder, inkrimp; – **away**, verskrompel, wegkrimp.
dye, n. kleurstof, verf; kleur.
dye, v. verf, kleur.
dying, a. sterwend(e), sterwens- . . ., sterf- . . ., doods- . . ., laaste.
dying, n. sterwe, dood.
dying day, sterfdag.
dyke, sien **dike**.
dynamic, dinamies, bewegings- . . .
dynamics, dinamika, bewegingsleer, kragteleer.
dynamite, n. dinamiet, springstof.
dynamite, v. laat spring, opblaas.
dynamo, dinamo (dynamo).
dynamometer, dinamometer, kragmeter.
dynast, heerser.
dynastic, stam- . . ., erf- . . ., dinastiek.
dynasty, dinastie, vorstehuis.
dyne, dine.
dysentery, buikloop, disenterie.
dyspepsia, -sy, slegte spysvertering, dispepsie.
dyspeptic, a. dispepties, lydende aan slegte spysvertering; neerslagtig.
dyspeptic, n. lyer aan slegte spysvertering; neerslagtige mens.

E

each, a. elke, iedere.
each, pro. elk, elkeen, iedereen; stuk; **they cost a cent –,** hulle kos 'n sent elk ('n sent stuk); **– other,** mekaar, die een die ander.
eager, gretig, begerig, verlangend; voortvarend, ywerig, vurig; **– to go,** gretig om te gaan; **– for,** after, begerig (verlangend) na, belus op.
eagerly, gretig(lik), ywerig, vurig(lik).
eagerness, gretigheid, verlange; ywer, drif.
eagle, arend, adelaar; arend (gholf).
eaglet, (jong) arendjie.
eagre, springvloed.
ear, n. oor; gehoor; **have an – for music,** 'n musikale oor (gehoor) hê; **prick up one's –s,** die ore spits; **over head and –s,** tot oor die ore; **set by the –s,** aanhits, aanmekaarsit; **send away with a flea in the –,** 'n uitbrander gee, die waarheid sê; **lend an –,** die oor leen, luister; **turn a deaf – to,** geen notisie van neem nie; **be all –,** aandagtig luister.
ear, n. aar; saad (saat); kop.
ear, v. in die aar kom (skiet).
ear-drum, oortrommel, trommelvlies.
ear-guard, oorskut.
earl, graaf.
ear-lap, oorlel.
earldom, graafskap.
early, vroeg (vroeë); **rise –,** vroeg opstaan; **the – part,** die begin; **the – bird gets the worm,** die môrestond het goud in die mond; **an hour –,** 'n uur te vroeg; **at your earliest convenience,** so gou as moontlik.
earmark, n. (oor)merk.
ear-mark, v. merk; **– a sum of money for,** 'n som geld opsy sit (bestem) vir.
earn, verdien; verwerf.
earnest, n. handgeld; voorsmaak.
earnest, n. erns; **in (good) –,** in (alle) erns; **be in –,** dit werklik meen.
earnest, a. ernstig; ywerig.
earnestly, ernstig; ywerig; in erns.
earnings, verdienste, loon.
ear-phone, koptelefoon.
ear-ring, oorring, krabbetjie.
earshot, gehoorsafstand.
earth, n. grond, aarde; gat, hol; grondsluiting, aardedraad.
earth, v. op-erd; begrawe; in die gat jaag (kruip); na die grond lei.
earth-born, aards; sterflik.
earthen, erde- . . ., van erd.
earthenware, n. erdegoed, aardewerk, breekgoed.
earthenware, a. erde- . . .
earthly, aards, aardsgesind; **of no – use,** van geen nut ter wêreld nie.
earthquake, aardbewing.
earth-tremor, aardtrilling.
earthwork, bolwerk, wal, skans.
earth-worm, erdwurm; nietige mens.
earthy, gronderig, grondagtig; aardsi
ear-trumpet, (ge)hoorpyp.
ear-wax, oorwas.
earwig, oorkruiper, oorwurm; vleier.
ease, n. gemak, rus, verligting; **feel at –,** op jou gemak voel; **stand at –,** op die plek rus; **ill at –,** nie op jou gemak nie.
ease, v. verlig, stil; gerusstel; laat skiet ('n tou); **– off,** draagliker word; verslap, laat skiet.
easel, (skilders)esel.
easily, (ge)maklik; fluit-fluit, op sy gemak.
east, oos; **to the – of,** oos (oostelik) van; **The Far East,** Die Verre Ooste; **The Near East,** Die Nabye Ooste; **-wind,** oostewind; **– coast fever,** ooskuskoors.

Easter, Pase; Paasvakansie; **– eggs,** Paaseiers; **– Sunday,** Paassondag.
easterly, oostelik.
eastern, a. oosters; oostelik.
East-India, Oos-Indië; **-man,** Oos-Indiëvaarder.
East-Indian, Oos-Indies.
eastward(s), ooswaarts.
easy, (ge)maklik; gerus; stil; **in – circumstances,** welgesteld; **honours –,** honneurs gelyk; **take it –,** op (sy) gemak doen, kalm opneem; **stand –,** rus!
easy-chair, gemaklike stoel, leun(ing)stoel.
easy-going, geskik, sorgloos, onbesorg.
eat, eet; **– away,** wegvreet; **– into,** invreet; **– up,** opeet, verteer; **–en up with pride,** verteer deur hoogmoed.
eatable, a. eetbaar.
eatables, n. eetgoed.
eau de Cologne, eau de Cologne (olie-kolonie), laventel.
eaves, (onderste) dakrand, geut.
eavesdrop, afluister, luistervink speel.
eavesdropper, luistervink.
ebb, n. eb; **at a low –,** op 'n lae peil.
ebb, v. eb, afneem, wegvloei; verval, agteruitgaan; **– away,** wegvloei, afloop.
ebb-tide, eb, ebgety.
E-boat, motor-torpedoboot.
ebonite, eboniet.
ebony, ebbehout.
ebullient, opborrelend, opbruisend.
ebullition, opborreling, opbruising; oproer.
eccentric, a. eksentries; sonderling, eksentriek.
eccentric, n. sonderling.
eccentricity, eksentrisiteit, sonderlingheid.
Ecclesiastes, Prediker.
ecclesiastic(al), a. kerklik, geestelik.
ecclesiastic, n. geestelike.
echo, n. weerkaatsing, weerklank, eggo.
echo, v. weerkaats, weerklink, weergalm; napraat.
echo-sounder, eggolood, eggosoeker.
eclectic, eklekties, uitsoekerig.
eclipse, n. verduistering, eklips.
eclipse, v. verduister; in die skadu stel; verdwyn.
ecliptic, a. eklipties.
ecliptic, n. aardbaan.
eclogue, herdersdig.
economic, ekonomies, staathuishoudkundig.
economical, ekonomies; spaarsaam.
economics, ekonomie, (staat)huishoudkunde.
economist, ekonoom, staathuishoudkundige.
economize, besuinig, bespaar.
economy, ekonomie, staathuishoudkunde; spaarsaamheid; besuiniging; inrigting.
ecstasy, vervoering, verrukking; ekstase.
ecstatic, verruk, in ekstase, opgetoë.
eczema, uitslag, ekseem.
eddy, n. maling, draaiing; warreling.
eddy, v. maal, draai, warrel.
edge, n. snee; skerp kant; skerpte; kant, rand; **set the teeth on –,** tande stomp maak; laat gril; **give an – to,** skerpmaak, slyp; **be on –,** opgewonde (senuweeagtig) wees; **have the – on someone,** 'n voordeel bo iemand hê.
edge, v. skerpmaak, slyp; afrand, met 'n rand afset; **– in a word,** 'n woord tussenin kry; **– on,** aanhits, aanspoor.
edged, skerp; gekant.
edgeways, -wise, op sy kant, skuins; **get a word in –,** 'n woordjie tussenin kry.
edging, rand; soom; omboorsel.
edgy, opgewonde, senuweeagtig.
edible, eetbaar.
edict, edik, verordening.

edification, stigting, opbouing, edifikasie.
edifice, gebou, gestig.
edify, stig.
edit, redigeer; persklaar maak.
edition, uitgaaf, druk, oplaag, edisie.
editor, redakteur.
editorial, a. redaksioneel.
editorial, n. hoofartikel.
educate, opvoed, oplei, onderwys; grootbring.
educated, opgevoed, ontwikkeld, geleerd.
education, opvoeding, opleiding; ontwikkeling, opvoedkunde.
educational, opvoedkundig, onderwys- . . .
education(al)ist, opvoedkundige.
educe, uittrek, aflei; afskei.
eduction, afvoering; afleiding; uitlating.
eel, paling, aal.
e'er, sien **ever**.
eerie, eery, huiweringwekkend, grillerig.
efface, uitwis, uitvee(g); te niet doen, in die skadu stel; – **oneself**, (sigself) op die agtergrond stel, (sigself) kleinmaak.
effacement, uitwissing; agterstelling.
effect, n. uitwerking, gevolg, uitslag, effek; indruk; –**s**, besittinge, goedere; **words to that** –, woorde met daardie strekking; **give** – **to**, uitvoering (gevolg) gee aan, ten uitvoer bring; gehoor gee aan; **take** –, uitwerking hê; in werking tree; **carry into** –, ten uitvoer (tot stand) bring; **to no** –, sonder uitwerking, vergeefs; **in** –, in werklikheid; vir praktiese doeleindes.
effect, v. uitwerk, bewerkstellig, teweegbring; ten uitvoer bring, verwesenlik.
effective, doelmatig, doeltreffend; geskik.
effectual, doeltreffend, afdoende; van krag.
effectuate, bewerk(stellig), uitrig.
effeminacy, verwyfdheid.
effeminate, meisieagtig, verwyf.
effervesce, opbruis, opborrel; werk.
effervescence, opbruising, opborreling.
effervescent, opbruisend, opborrelend.
effete, uitgewerk, afgewerk, afgeleef, poot-uit.
efficacious, werksaam, doeltreffend, kragdadig.
efficacy, werksaamheid; probaatheid.
efficiency, voltreffendheid, doeltreffendheid; geskiktheid, saaklikheid.
efficient, voltreffend, doeltreffend; kragdadig; geskik, saaklik.
effigy, beeld, beeltenis, afbeeldsel.
effloresce, ontluik, bloei; kristalliseer.
efflorescence, bloei; kristallisasie; skimmel.
efflorescent, ontluikend; kristalliserend.
effluence, uitvloeisel, uitstroming.
effluent, a. uitstromend.
effluent, n. uitloop.
effluvium, uitwaseming; reuk; effluvium.
efflux(ion), uitstroming, uitvloeiing; afloop.
effort, (krag)inspanning, poging; **make an** –, (sig) inspan; (sig) geweld aandoen.
effortless, sonder inspanning (moeite).
effrontery, astrantheid, parmantigheid.
effulgence, glans, skittering.
effulgent, stralend, skitterend.
effuse, uitgiet, uitstort; uitgee, versprei.
effusion, uitstorting; ontboeseming.
effusive, oorlopend; rojaal, hartlik; woordryk.
eft, (water)salamander.
egg, n. eier; **bad** –, vrot eier; niksnuts.
egg, v. – **on**, aanhits, aanspoor.
egg-cup, eierkelkie.
egg-flip, eierbrandewyn, advokaat.
egg-glass, sandlopertjie.
egg-head, slimkop.
egg-plant, brinjal

egg-whisk, eierklopper.
eglantine, eglantier; wilde kanferfoelie.
ego, ego, ek.
egoism, egoïsme, selfsug(tigheid).
egoist, egoïs, selfsugtige mens.
egoistic, egoïsties, selfsugtig.
egotism, selfingenomenheid, eiedunk, eiewaan.
egregious, kolossaal, reusagtig; opperste.
egress, uitgang.
egret, sien **aigrette**.
Egyptian, a. Egipties.
Egyptian, n. Egiptenaar.
eider, eider(gans); dons.
eider-down, dons; – **quilt**, veerkombers.
eight, ag; – **o'clock**, ag(t)uur.
eighteen, agt(t)ien.
eighteenth, agt(t)iende.
eighth, agste.
eighty, tag(gen)tig.
eisteddfod, eisteddfod.
either, a. & pro. albei; een van beide; (enig)een van twee.
either, adv., conj. of; **he is** – **drunk or mad**, hy is òf dronk òf gek; **not that** –, ook nie dit nie; **I shall not go** –, ek sal ook nie gaan nie.
ejaculate, uitroep; uitspuit, uitwerp.
ejaculation, uitroep, kreet; uitwerping.
ejaculatory, by wyse van uitroep.
eject, uitwerp, uitsit, uitskop; uitskiet; afgee.
ejection, uitwerping, uitsetting; (die) uitskiet.
ejectment, uitsetting.
ejector, uitskopper; uitsitter.
eke: – **out**, aanvul, vermeerder; – **out a livelihood**, op 'n manier 'n bestaan maak.
elaborate, a. uitvoerig; fyn afgewerk.
elaborate, v. (in besonderhede) uitwerk.
elaborateness, uitvoerigheid; afwerking.
elaboration, uitwerking; bewerking.
eland, eland.
elapse, verstryk, verloop.
elastic, a. rekbaar, elasties; veerkragtig.
elastic, n. rek, gomlastiek.
elasticity, rekbaarheid, elastisiteit.
elate, opwek; trots maak; verheug.
elated, verheug, uitgelate; opgeblase.
elation, uitgelatenheid; opgeblasenheid.
elbow, n. elmboog; bog, kromming; **at one's** –, byderhand; **out at** –**s**, verslete, armoedig.
elbow, v. stoot, dring, druk.
elbow-grease, swaar werk; spierkrag; kragsinspanning.
elbow-room, ruim baan, bewegingsvryheid.
elder, a. ouer; – **hand**, voorhand.
elder, n. ouderling; ouere.
elder, n. vlier(boom).
elderly, bejaard.
eldership, ouderlingskap.
eldest, oudste.
El Dorado, Eldorado.
eldritch, huiweringwekkend.
elect, a. uitverkore; gekose.
election, v. kies, uitkies, verkies.
election, (ver)kiesing, eleksie; keuse.
election day, stemdag.
electioneer, aan 'n verkiesingstryd deelneem, stemme werf.
elective, kies- . . . ; gekose.
elector, kieser, kiesgeregtigde; keurvors.
electoral, kies- . . . ; – **district**, kiesafdeling.
electorate, kiesers; keurvorstedom.
electress, kieseres; keurvorstin.
electric, **electrical**; – **eel**, sidderaal; – **jar**, Leidse fles; – **bulb**, gloeilamp; – **current**, elektriese stroom; – **motor**, elektromotor; – **plant**, el. aanleg.

electrical: – **engineer**, elektrotegniese ingenieur; – **engineering**, elektrotegniek.
electrician, elektrisiën.
electricity, elektrisiteit.
electrification, elektrifikasie; elektrisering.
electrify, elektrifiseer; elektriseer, skok.
electrocute, deur elektrisiteit ter dood bring (verongeluk).
electrocution, elektrokusie.
electrode, elektrode.
electro-dynamics, elektrodinamiks.
electrolier, elektriese kroonlamp.
electrolyse, elektroliseer.
electrolysis, elektrolise.
electro-magnet, elektromagneet.
electron, elektron; – **microscope**, elektronemikroskoop.
electronic, elektronies; – **brain**, elektroniese brein (rekenmasjien).
electroplate, v. versilwer.
electroplate, n. versilwerde ware.
electroscope, elektroskoop.
electrotype, elektrotipie.
electuary, lekstroop.
elegance, -cy, elegansie, swier; bevalligheid, sierlikheid; verfyning.
elegant, sierlik, bevallig, swierig, elegant.
elegiac, elegies; – **poem**, treurdig.
elegy, treursang, elegie.
element, element, bestanddeel, grondstof; beginsel; –**s**, (grond)beginsels.
elemental, wesenlik, fundamenteel.
elementary, elementêr, aanvangs- . . ., eenvoudig.
elephant, olifant.
elephantiasis, olifantsgeswel, elephantiasis.
elephantine, lomp; olifantagtig.
elevate, oplig, ophef; verhef, veredel.
elevated, verhewe; in die takke, aangeklam; – **railway**, lugspoorweg.
elevation, opheffing, veredeling; verhewenheid; hoogte; (elevasie)hoek; vertikale projeksie.
elevator, (hys)kraan, hystoestel; elevator; ligter, hyser; graansuier; hefspier.
eleven, elf; elftal (in krieket).
eleventh, elfde; **at the – hour**, ter elfder ure.
elf, elf, (berg)gees, kabouterjie.
elfin, a. elf- . . ., feëriek.
elfin, n. dwerg, kleuter.
elfish, plaagsiek, ondeund.
elf-lock, verwarde haarvleg.
elicit, uittrek, te voorskyn roep, uitlok, ontlok.
elide, weglaat, oorslaan.
eligible, verkiesbaar; verkieslik, geskik.
eliminate, verwyder, ophef, uitskakel; wegwerk; elimineer.
elimination, verwydering, uitskakeling; wegwerking; eliminasie.
elision, weglating, uitlating, elisie.
elite, elite.
elixir, elikser; afkooksel.
elk, elk, eland.
ell, el; **give him an inch and he'll take an –**, gee hom 'n vinger en hy neem die hele hand.
ellipse, ellips.
ellipsis, ellips (ellipsis, ellipse), uitlating.
ellipsoid, ellipsoïde.
elliptical, ellipties, ovaal.
elm, olm, iep.
elocution, voordragsleer, spraakles, elokusie.
elocutionist, voordragsleraar; voordraer.
elongation, verlenging; uitrekking; afstand.
elope, wegloop, (sig) laat skaak; skaak.
elopement, ontvlugting, vlug, verlating.
eloquence, welsprekendheid.
eloquent, welsprekend; veelseggend.

else, anders; **anyone –**, nog iemand, iemand anders, ieder ander; **anything –**, nog iets, iets anders, enigiets anders; **somewhere –**, êrens anders.
elsewhere, êrens anders, elders.
elucidate, ophelder, verhelder, toelig.
elucidation, verduideliking, toeligting.
elude, ontwyk; ontduik; ontsnap, ontvlug.
elusion, ontwyking; ontduiking; ontvlugting.
elusive, elusory, ontwykend; ontduikend; moeilik om te vat; misleidend.
Elysian, Elisies, geluksalig, hemels.
Elysium, Elysium, geluksalige oord.
emaciate, vermaer, uitteer.
emaciation, vermaering, uittering.
emanate, uitstraal, uitvloei; – **from**, uitgaan van, afkomstig wees van.
emanation, uitvloeisel, emanasie.
emancipate, vrystel, vrylaat; emansipeer.
emancipated, vry(gelaat); modern.
emancipation, vrystelling, bevryding; vrywording; emansipasie.
emancipator, vrymaker, bevryder.
emasculate, ontman, verslap, verswak.
emasculation, ontmanning; verwyfdheid.
embalm, balsem.
embank, indyk, afdam, inwal.
embankment, indyking; wal, dyk, kaai.
embargo, beslag, embargo.
embark, inskeep; – **in**, **(up)on**, onderneem, (sig begewe in.
embarkation, inskeping; onderneming.
embarrass, hinder, belemmer; verbouereerd (verleë) maak; bemoeilik.
embarrassed, belas, bemoeilik; verleë, verbouereerd, verward; in die skuld.
embarrassment, moeilikheid, hindernis; verbouereerdheid, verleentheid; skulde.
embassy, gesantskap; gesantskapsgebou.
embed, im-, insluit, vassit.
embellish, verfraai, opsier.
embellishment, verfraaiing, opsiering.
embers, (warm) as, (lewendige) kole.
embezzle, verduister, ontvreem.
embezzlement, verduistering, ontvreemding.
embitter, verbitter, vergal.
emblazon, blasoeneer; ophemel.
emblem, sinnebeeld, embleem.
emblematic(al), sinnebeeldig, emblematies.
embodiment, beliggaming, verpersoonliking.
embody, beliggaam, verpersoonlik; inlyf; omvat.
embog, in 'n moeras sink.
embolden, aanmoedig; verstout.
emboss, in reliëf bring, gedrewe werk maak.
embossment, reliëf, gedrewe werk.
embowel, die ingewande uithaal.
embrace, v. omhels, in die arms sluit; omvat, insluit; – **an opportunity**, 'n geleentheid aangryp; – **an offer**, 'n aanbod (met ope arms) aanneem; **the offer –s** . . ., die aanbod sluit in . . .
embrace, n. omhelsing, omarming.
embrasure, skietgat; afskuinsing.
embrocate, smeer, vrywe; bet; pap.
embrocation, smeergoed.
embroider, borduur; opsier.
embroidery, borduurwerk; opsiersel.
embroil, verwar; (in stryd) verwikkel.
embroilment, verwikkeling, rusie.
embryo, vrugkiem; **in –**, in wording.
embryologist, embrioloog.
embryology, embriologie.
embryonic, embrionaal.
emend, emendeer, verbeter.
emendation, emendasie, veelseggend.

emerald 482 **endive**

emerald, n. smarag.
emerald, a. smaraggroen; smarag-...
emerge, opkom, te voorskyn kom; voor die dag kom; blyk, uitkom.
emergence, verskyning.
emergency, (geval van) nood; dringende geval; in case of –, in geval van nood.
emergency-brake, noodrem.
emergency-meeting, spoedvergadering.
emeritus, rustend, emeritus.
emerods, aambeie.
emersion, (her)verskyning.
emery, polyssteen.
emery-paper, skuurpapier, poleerpapier.
emetic, braakmiddel, vomitief.
emigrant, emigrant, landverhuiser, trekker.
emigrate, emigreer, verhuis, trek.
emigration, emigrasie, landverhuising.
eminence, hoogte, verhewenheid; uitmuntendheid; hoogheid; eminensie.
eminent, hoog, verhewe; uitmuntend, uitstekend; eminent.
eminently, hoogs, besonder.
emir, emir.
emissary, afgesant; handlanger, spioen.
emission, uitgifte, uitsending; uitstraling.
emit, uitgee, uitsend, uitstraal, voortbring.
emollient, a. versagtend, verwekend.
emollient, n. versagtende middel, pap(omslag).
emolument, besoldiging, salaris; verdienste.
emotion, aandoening, ontroering, emosie.
emotional, gevoels-...; emosioneel, gevoelig; aandoenlik.
empanel, op die jurielys plaas.
emperor, keiser.
emphasis, klem, nadruk; klemtoon.
emphasize, nadruk lê op, beklem(toon).
emphatic, nadruklik, uitdruklik, emfaties.
empire, (keiser)ryk; gebied; heerskappy.
empiric, empiries, op ervaring gegrond.
empiricism, ervaringsleer, empirie.
empiricist, empirikus; kwaksalwer.
emplacement, terrein, grond; stelling.
employ, v. in diens neem (hê); gebruik, aanwend, besig; – your time, jou tyd bestee; –ed on, besig met.
employ, n. diens.
employee, werknemer, beampte, bediende.
employer, werkgewer, baas.
employment, diens, werk, besigheid, vak, bedryf; besteding, aanwending, gebruik; be out of –, werkloos wees.
empoison, vergiftig.
emporium, handelsentrum, markplaas; winkel.
empower, magtig, volmag gee; in staat stel.
empress, keiserin.
emptiness, leegheid, leegte; ydelheid, holheid.
empty, a. leeg; ydel, betekenisloos, hol.
empty, v. leegmaak; uitloop, (sig) ontlas.
empty-handed, met leë hande.
empty-headed, leeghoofdig, onnosel.
empyrean, n. hoogste hemel.
empyrean, a. hoogverhewe, hemelhoog.
emu, emoe.
emulate, nastreef, wedywer met; ewenaar.
emulation, wedywer, nastrewing; ewenaring.
emulous, (ywerig) nastrewend; naywerig; medidingend, wedywerend.
emulsion, emulsie.
enable, in staat stel, die geleentheid verskaf.
enact, verorden, bepaal, vasstel; opvoer.
enactment, verordening, bepaling.
enamel, n. erd, emalje, enemmel; – dish, enemmel-, erdeskottel.
enamel, v. vererd, enemmel, emaljeer.

enamour, verlief maak, bekoor; –ed of, verlief op, bekoor van (deur).
encage, opsluit, in 'n hok sit.
encamp, kamp opslaan, laer trek, kampeer.
encampment, kamp, laer; kampering.
encase, toemaak, insluit, toespyker, inwikkel.
encaustic, wasskildering, enkoustiek.
enceinte, swanger.
enchain, vasketen, boei, kluister.
enchant, betower, in verrukking bring; toor.
enchanter, towenaar; bekoorder.
enchanting, betowerend, bekorend, verruklik.
enchantment, betowering; bekoring.
enchantress, towenares; bekoorster.
encircle, insluit, omring, omsingel.
enclasp, omhels, omvat.
enclave, enclave, ingeslote grondgebied.
enclitic, enklities.
enclose, in-, insluit; omring; omhein, inkamp.
enclosure, afsluiting; kamp; hok; skutting; bylae.
encode, in kode skryf, kodeer.
encomium, lofrede, -sang, -tuiting.
encompass, omvat, omring, insluit.
encore, interj. nog eens! nogmaals! weer so!
encore, n. (geroep om 'n) toegif; applous.
encore, v. terugroep om 'n toegif.
encounter, v. tref, teenkom, ontmoet; slaags raak; – opposition, teenstand ondervind.
encounter, n. ontmoeting; geveg, slag, stryd.
encourage, aanmoedig; aanspoor; aankweek.
encouragement, aanmoediging, aansporing; bemoediging.
encroach, (– on), inbreuk maak (op), die grense oorskry, indring.
encroachment, inbreuk, oorskryding; aanmatiging.
encrust, (om-, toe-)kors, aanpak.
encumber, bemoeilik, belemmer, beswaar.
encumbrance, belemmering, las; verband.
encyclical, a. rondgaande, omgaande.
encyclical, n. (pouslike) brief, ensikliek.
encyclop(a)edia, ensiklopedie; leerkring.
encyclop(a)edic, ensiklopedies; veelsydig.
end, n. end (ent); einde; punt; doel; entjie (kers); (sigaret)stompie; to gain his –s, om sy doel te bereik; to what –, met watter doel; place on –, regop-sit, laat regop staan; world without –, tot in ewigheid; – on, met die punt vooruit; no – of, geweldig (eindeloos) veel; come to an –, opraak, op 'n end raak; in the –, op die (ou-)end, per slot van rekening; at one wits' –s, ten einde raad; put an – to, 'n end aan maak; make both –s meet, die tering na die nering sit; be at the end of one's tether, ten einde raad wees; poot-uit wees; go off the deep –, (sy) goeie humeur verloor, boos (ergerlik) word.
end, v. ophou, eindig, op 'n end raak, stop; 'n einde maak aan; – in, uitloop op; – in a vowel, uitgaan op 'n klinker; – in a point, in 'n punt uitloop; all's well that –s well, eind goed, al goed.
endanger, in gevaar bring.
endear, bemind maak.
endearment, bemindmaking; liefkosing; term of –, troetelnaampie.
endeavour, v. streef, trag, (sig) beywer; – to, streef om; – after, streef na.
endeavour, n. strewe, poging; – society, strewersvereniging.
endecagon, elfhoek.
endemic, a. inheems, endemies.
endemic, n. inheemse siekte, endemie.
ending, slot; afloop; uitgang; uiteinde.
endive, andyvie.

endless — **enterprising**

endless, eindeloos, sonder end.
endogamy, endogamie, stamhuwelik.
endorse, endosseer; onderskrywe; oormaak, oordra.
endorsement, endossement; onderskrywing.
endow, skenk, vermaak aan, toerus; –ed with, begaaf met.
endowment, skenking; begaafdheid; aanleg; – policy, uitkeringspolis; – fund, skenkingsfonds.
endue, voorsien (van), beklee (met).
endurance, uithoudingsvermoë; lydsaamheid.
endure, verdra, uitstaan; duur, aanhou.
enduring, blywend, durend.
endways, -wise, oorlangs; op sy kant.
enema, lawement, spuitjie.
enemy, n. vyand; duiwel.
enemy, a. vyandelik.
energetic, bedrywig, deurtastend, energiek.
energy, energie, (gees)krag; werksaamheid, ywerigheid; arbeidsvermoë, -krag.
enervate, verswak, verslap, ontsenu.
enervation, verslapping, ontsenuwing.
enfeeble, verswak, verslap.
enfeoff, met 'n leen begiftig.
enfilade, n. dwarsvuur, enfilade.
enfilade, v. onder dwarsvuur neem, enfileer.
enfold, toevou, inwikkel; omarm.
enforce, afdwing (gehoorsaamheid); krag bysit (aan 'n argument); – the law, die wet uitvoer (handhaaf).
enforcement, dwang; handhawing, uitvoering.
enfranchise, vry maak; stemreg verleen.
enfranchisement, vrystelling; verlening van stemreg.
engage, (ver)bind, verpand; verloof; in diens neem; bespreek, beset (sitplekke); in beslag neem; slaags raak, aanval; be –d, 'n afspraak hê; besig (beset) wees; verloof wees; be –d in, betrokke wees in; besig wees met, aan die ... wees; – in, (sig) inlaat met, (sig) begeef in; –d to, verloof aan (met).
engagement, verbintenis; afspraak; verlowing; besigheid; geveg, slag.
engaging(ly), innemend.
engender, voortbring, baar; veroorsaak.
engine, masjien; motor; lokomotief; middel, werktuig; fire –, brandspuit; steam –, stoommasjien, lokomotief; motor –, motor; – failure, masjienweiering; – trouble, motordefek; we had – trouble, die motor het onklaar geraak.
engine-driver, masjinis.
engineer, n. boukundige, ingenieur; civil –, boukundige (ingenieur), siviel-ingenieur; mechanical –, werktuigkundige (ingenieur).
engineer, v. lei; op tou sit, bewerk.
engineering, boukunde, ingenieurswese, -wetenskap; civil –, burgerlike boukunde; mechanical –, masjienboukunde, werktuigkunde; military –, (militêre) genie.
engine-house, lokomotiefloods; masjienkamer; brandweerstasie.
engirdle, omgord, omslinger.
England, Engeland.
English, a. Engels.
English, n. Engels; in plain –, in duidelike taal, onomwonde; Old –, Oud-Engels.
Englishman, Engelsman (pl. Engelse).
engraft, ent; inplant; imprent; inlyf.
engrain, in–, instamp, indruk; an –ed rogue, 'n deurtrapte skelm.
engrave, graveer, insny; imprent.
engraving, (die) graveer; plaat, gravure.
engross, in groot letters skrywe, grosseer; in beslag neem; –ed in, verdiep in; – attention, aandag in beslag neem.
engrossing, boeiend.
engulf, opsluk, verswelg; instort.
enhance, verhoog, verhef, vergroot, vermeerder.
enhancement, verhoging, vermeerdering.
enigma, raaisel, enigma.
enigmatic(al), raaiselagtig, geheimsinnig.
enjambment, enjambement, deurloop.
enjoin, gelas, beveel; op die hart druk, inskerp.
enjoy, geniet, hou van; I –ed myself immensely, ek het dit baie geniet.
enjoyable, genietbaar; genotvol, aangenaam.
enjoyment, genot, vermaak, plesier.
enkindle, aansteek; aanblaas, aanstook.
enlace, (om)snoer, omvat.
enlarge, vergroot, uitbrei; uitsit; oordryf; – upon, uitwei oor.
enlargement, vergroting; uitweiding.
enlighten, inlig, voorlig; verlig.
enlightenment, voorligting, inligting; ontwikkeling.
enlist, aanwerf, in diens neem; aansluit, diens neem; verkry.
enlistment, diensneming; verwerwing.
enliven, verlewendig, opwek; opvrolik.
enmesh, verstrik, vaswikkel, verwikkel.
enmity, vyandigheid; vyandskap.
ennoble, veredel; tot die adelstand verhef.
ennui, verveling.
enormity, ontsaglikheid; afskuwelikheid; gruweldaad.
enormous, ontsaglik, tamaai; ontsettend.
enough, genoeg, voldoende; – is as good as a feast, tevredenheid is beter as 'n erfenis; – and to spare, meer as genoeg.
enquire, sien inquire.
enrage, woedend maak, vertoorn, versondig.
enrapture, verruk, in verrukking bring.
enrich, verryk.
enrol, inskryf, inboek, registreer; te boek stel; diens neem, aansluit.
enrolment, inskrywing; diensneming.
ensconce, (sig) verskans, verskuil.
enshrine, bewaar, wegsluit.
enshroud, inwikkel, omhul.
ensign, teken; vaandel, standaard; vaandeldraer, vaandrig.
ensilage, n. inskuiling; kuilvoer.
ensilage, ensile, v. inkuil.
enslave, verslaaf; tot slaaf maak; –d to drink, verslaaf aan die drank.
ensnare, verstrik, in 'n val lok, verlok.
ensue, volg, voortvloei; – from, volg uit.
ensuing, daaropvolgende; gevolglike.
ensure, verseker; seker maak, bewerk; besorg.
entail, n. onvervreembare eiendom; fideicommis (filekommis).
entail, v. vassit, onder fideicommis vermaak; meebring, noodsaak.
entangle, verstrik, verwar, verwikkel.
entanglement, verwikkeling, verstrikking.
enter, in–, binnegaan, -tree, -vaar, -kom; binnedring; inskryf, opskryf; boek; – into, tree in, ingaan op, aangaan; deel uitmaak van; – into an agreement, 'n ooreenkoms aangaan; – (up)on one's duties, pligte aanvaar; – to, against, op rekening skrywe van; – for a race, (laat) inskrywe vir 'n wedstryd – a protest, protes aanteken.
enteric, ingewands- ...; – fever, ingewandskoors, tifus(koors).
enterprise, onderneming, waagstuk; ondernemingsgees.
enterprising, ondernemend.

entertain, **onderhou; onthaal; in oorweging neem; koester; – **guests, gaste onthaal; – **a feeling,** 'n gevoel koester.
entertainer, gasheer; onderhouer.
entertaining, onderhoudend, vermaaklik.
entertainment, onthaal, ontvangs; vermaak.
enthral(l), boei, kluister; verslaaf.
enthrone, op die troon plaas; installeer.
enthronement, troonsbestyging, kroning.
enthuse, dweep, geesdriftig word.
enthusiasm, geesdrif, ywer, entoesiasme.
enthusiast, geesdriftige, yweraar, entoesias.
enthusiastic, geesdriftig, ywerig, entoesiasties.
entice, verlok, verlei, in versoeking bring.
enticing, verleidelik, aan-, verloklik.
entire, heel, totaal, volledig; onbeskadig.
entirely, heeltemal, totaal, volkome, geheel en al.
entirety, geheel, volledigheid; **in its –,** in sy geheel.
entitle, noem; – **to,** reg gee op.
entitled, genaamd; **be – to,** reg hê op.
entity, wese, bestaan; geheel, entiteit.
entomb, inkelder, begrawe, byset.
entomological, insektekundig, entomologies.
entomologist, insektekundige, entomoloog.
entomology, insektekunde, entomologie.
entrails, ingewande, binnegoed, harslag.
entrain, op die trein klim, instap; oplaai; nasleep, meebring.
entrammel, hinder, belemmer.
entrance, n. ingang; binnekoms, opkoms; aanvaarding (van 'n amp); toegang, toelating, intree; portaal; intreegeld, toegang.
entrance, v. in verrukking bring, vervoer.
entrance examination, toelatingseksamen, admissie(-eksamen).
entrance-fee, intreegeld, inskrywingsgeld.
entrant, binnetredende; ingeskrewene.
entrap, verstrik, betrap, vang.
entreat, smeek, bid, soebat; bejeën.
entreaty, (smeek)bede, versoek.
entrench, verskans, ingraaf.
entrenchment, verskansing, loopgraaf.
entrust, in-, toevertrou; toebetrou, opdra.
entry, binnekoms, intog; ingang, toegang, aanvaarding; inskrywing; boeking, pos; **an – in ledger,** 'n pos in die grootboek.
entwine, deurvleg, omstrengel.
enumerate, opsom, tel.
enumeration, opsomming, optelling.
enunciate, uitdruk, uitspreek, formuleer.
enunciation, uitspraak, stelling, weergawe.
envelop, inwikkel, omwikkel, hul (in).
envelope, koevert, omslag; omhulsel.
envelopment, omhulsel; bekleding.
envenom, vergiftig; verbitter, vergal.
enviable, benydenswaardig beny(d)baar.
envious, jaloers, afgunstig.
enviousness, afguns, jaloesie, jaloersheid.
environ, omgeef, omring.
environment, omgewing; omstandighede.
environs, omstreke, omgewing.
envisage, voor oë stel.
envoy, gesant, verteenwoordiger.
envy, n. jaloesie, naywer, afguns, nyd; **to be the – of,** beny word deur.
envy, v. beny, jaloers (afgunstig) wees op.
enwrap, toedraai, inwikkel.
epaulet(te), rangstrepie; epaulet.
epergne, middelstuk (van tafelversiering).
ephemeral, eendaags, kortstondig, verbygaand(e).
ephod, fod.
epic, a. epies, verhalend; – **poem,** epos, heldedig.
epic, n. epos, heldedig.
epicure, epikuris, lekkerbek, smulpaap.

epicurean, epikuries; genotsugtig.
epicurism, epikurisme; genotsug.
epicycle, bysirkel, episikel.
epidemic, a. epidemies, heersend.
epidemic, n. epidemie, heersende siekte.
epidermis, opperhuid, epidermis.
epigram, puntdig, epigram.
epigrammatic, epigrammaties.
epigrammatist, puntdigter.
epigraph, opskrif; motto.
epilepsy, vallende siekte, epilepsie.
epileptic, a. epilepties; – **fit,** toeval.
epileptic, n. epileptikus, lyer aan vallende **siekte.**
epilogue, narede, slotrede, epiloog.
episcopacy, episkopaat; biskoplike regering.
episcopal, biskoplik, episkopaal(s).
episcopate, episkopaat; biskopsamp; bisdom.
episode, episode; voorval, geskiedenis.
episodic, episodies, bykomstig.
epistemology, kennisleer, epistemologie.
epistle, epistel, brief.
epistolary, brief- . . ., skriftelik; – **style,** briefstyl.
epitaph, grafskrif.
epithalamium, bruilofslied.
epithelium, opperste huidlaag, opiteel.
epithet, epiteton; bynaam.
epitome, uittreksel, samevatting, kort begrip.
epitomize, saamvat, uittreksel van maak.
epoch, tydstip, tydperk, tydvak.
epopee, heldedig, epopee.
epos, heldedig, epos.
Epsom salt, Engelse sout.
equability, gelyk(matig)heid, eweredigheid.
equable, eweredig, gelyk(matig).
equal, a. gelyk(waardig); – **to,** gelyk aan: opgewasse teen; **with – ease,** net so gemaklik.
equal, n. gelyke, partuur (portuur), weerga.
equal, v. gelyk wees aan; ewenaar; gelyk maak.
equality, gelykheid; gelykwaardigheid; **on an – with,** op voet van gelykheid met.
equalize, gelyk maak; ewenaar, gelykstel.
equally, ewe, net so, in gelyke mate; gelyklik; gelykop, regverdig.
equanimity, onverstoordheid; gelatenheid.
equate, gelykstel, gelyk maak.
equation, gelykstelling; vergelyking (in wiskunde).
equator, ewenaar, linie, ewenagslyn.
equatorial, ekwatoriaal, ewenaars- . . .
equerry, stalmeester.
equestrian, a. ruiter- . . .; – **statue,** ruiterstandbeeld.
equestrian, n. (perde)ruiter.
equidistant, op gelyke afstand, ewe ver.
equilateral, gelyksydig.
equilibrate, balanseer, in ewewig hou.
equilibrist, koorddanser, balanseerder.
equilibrium, ewewig, balans.
equine, perde- . . .
equinoctial, a. nagewenings- . . .; – **gales,** herfsstorme.
equinoctial, n. ewenagslyn.
equinox, nagewening.
equip, toerus; uitrus; beman; uitdos.
equipage, uitrusting; benodigdhede; gevolg; ek(w)ipasie (equipage).
equipoise, n. ewewig, balans; teenwig.
equipoise, v. in ewewig hou; teenwig vorm; in spanning hou.
equipollent, gelykwaardig, ekwivalent.
equitable, billik, regverdig, onpartydig.
equity, billikheid, regverdigheid, regmatigheid; **in –,** billikerwys.
equivalence, gelykwaardigheid.
equivalent, gelyk(waardig), ekwivalent.

equivocal — eucharist

equivocal, dubbelsinnig; twyfelagtig; verdag.
equivocate, dubbelsinnig praat, los en vas praat, uitvlugte soek.
equivocation, dubbelsinnigheid, uitvlug.
equivoque, dubbelsinnigheid; woordspeling.
era, tydperk; jaartelling.
eradicate, ontwortel, uitroei.
eradication, uitroeiing, vernietiging.
erase, uitwis, uitvee, uitkrap.
eraser, uitveër.
erasure, uitveging, uitwissing, uitkrapping.
ere, conj. eer(dat), voor(dat); – long, eerlang, binnekort; – while, eertyds, vroeër.
ere, prep. voor.
erect, a. (pen)regop, (pen)orent.
erect, v. oprig; stig, bou; opstel, opwerp.
erection, oprigting; stigting; opwerping.
erector, oprigter; trekspier.
eremite, kluisenaar.
erg, erg, eenheid van energie.
erf, erf.
ergot, roes, brand (in graan); brandkoring.
ermine, hermelyn; hermelyn(bont).
erode, uitvreet, wegvreet; verweer.
erosion, verwering, wegspoeling; erosie.
erosive, wegvretend; wegspoelend, verwerend.
erotic, eroties, liefde(s)- . . .
err, sondig; dwaal, 'n fout begaan, (sig) vergis.
errand, boodskap; opdrag, las; doel; **run –s**, boodskappe doen.
errand-boy, boodskapper, loopjong.
errant, dolend, swerwend.
erratic, onseker, wisselvallig, ongelyk.
erratum, (druk)fout, erratum.
erroneous, verkeerd, onjuis, foutief.
error, fout, vergissing; dwaling; sonde, vergryp.
ersatz, n. surrogaat.
ersatz, a. nagemaak, gesubstitueerde.
erst, eertyds, vroeër.
eructation, oprisping, sooibrand; uitbarsting.
erudite, geleerd, belese.
erudition, geleerdheid, belesenheid.
erupt, deurbreek, uitbreek; uitbars.
eruption, uitbarsting; uitslag; deurbraak.
eruptive, uitbarstend; vol uitslag.
erysipelas, roos.
escalade, beklimming, bestyging.
escalator, roltrap.
escapade, kwajongstreek, eskapade.
escape, v. ontvlug, ontsnap; uitspuit; **his name has –d me**, sy naam is my ontgaan; **it –d my attention**, dit het my aandag ontgaan; – notice, onopgemerk bly.
escape, n. ontkoming, ontsnapping; **a narrow –**, 'n noue ontkoming; **make one's –**, ontsnap; – hatch, noodluik; – **clause**, noodklousule.
escapement, uitlaatklep; échappement, gang (van 'n horlosie).
escape valve, uitlaatklep, veiligheidsklep.
escarp(ment), skuinste, glooiing, hang.
escheat, verval (aan); konfiskeer, beslag lê op.
eschew, vermy, sku.
escort, n. geleide, eskort.
escort, v. (be)gelei, vergesel, eskorteer.
escritoire, (skryf)lessenaar(tjie).
esculent, eetbaar.
Escurial, Eskuriaal.
escutcheon, skild, wapen; spieël (van 'n skip).
esoteric, ingewy; geheim; esoteries.
espalier, latwerk; opgeleide boom, leiboom.
esparto, spaanse gras, esparto.
especial, besonder, sien **special**.
espionage, spioenasie, bespieding.
esplanade, wandelplein, esplanade.

espousal, bruilof; huwelik; omhelsing, (die) voorstaan.
espouse, hu, trou; omhels, voorstaan.
espy, opmerk, in die oog kry.
esquire, skildknaap; **A. Brown, Esq.**, Die Weledele Heer A. Brown.
essay, n. proef; poging; opstel, verhandeling.
essay, v. toets, keur, beproef; onderneem, probeer.
essayer, assayer, keurder, essaieur.
essayist, skrywer (van kort verhandelinge), essayis.
essence, wese, kern; essens, aftreksel; geur; reukwerk; – of meat, vleesekstrak; – of life, lewensessens.
essential, a. wesenlik; noodsaaklik; essensieel; – oil, vlugtige olie.
essential, n. noodsaaklikheid, vereiste; wesenlike.
essentially, hoofsaaklik, in hoofsaak, in wese.
establish, vestig; stig, oprig; instel; vasstel, bewys, staaf; – **a fact**, 'n feit konstateer.
established, gevestig; bewese; – **church**, staatskerk.
establishment, stigting; nedersetting; instelling; bevestiging; vasstelling; gestig, inrigting; huishouding; saak; liggaam.
estate, rang, stand; boedel; besit, eiendom; landgoed; staat; – **of matrimony**, huwelikstaat; **man's –**, manlike leeftyd; **real –**, grondbesit, vasgoed; **surrender one's –**, boedel oorgee.
esteem, v. skat, ag; hoogag, waardeer.
esteem, n. agting, skatting; hoogagting.
Esthonian, Estlands; Estlander.
estimable, agtenswaardig.
estimate, n. skatting; begroting; prysopgaaf; **the –s**, die (lands)begroting.
estimate, v. skat, raam, waardeer; op prys stel.
estimation, mening; skatting, waardering, hoogagting; **in my –**, in my opinie.
estrange, vervreem.
estrangement, vervreemding, verwydering.
estuary, mond, monding.
esurient, hongerig; behoeftig; gulsig.
etch, ets.
etching, ets; etswerk.
eternal, a. ewig, ewigdurend.
Eternal, n. the –, die Ewige (God.)
eternalize, verewig.
eternity, ewigheid.
ether, eter; lugruim.
ethereal, eteries; vlugtig; lugtig; hemels.
etherealize, vergeestelik; vervlugtig.
etherize, eteriseer, eter gee.
ethic(al), eties; sedelik.
ethics, sedeleer, etiek.
ethnic, volkekundig; etnologies; heidens.
ethnographer, volkekundige, etnograaf.
ethnography, volksbeskrywing, etnografie.
ethnological, volkekundig, etnologies.
ethnologist, volkekundige, etnoloog.
ethnology, volkekunde, etnologie.
ethos, karakter, sede, gebruik.
ethyl, ethyl.
etiolate, verbleek, bleek maak, etioleer.
etiquette, etiket, wellewendheidsvorme.
etna, spiritusstofie, -lampie.
Etruscan, Etruskies.
etui, etwee, doos, dosie, koker, étui.
etymological, etimologies.
etymology, (woord)afleiding, etimologie.
eucalyptus, eukaliptus; gomboom; bloekomboom; – **oil**, bloekomolie.
eucharist, eucharistie; (R.K.) Avondmaal.

eugenics, rasverbeteringsleer, eugenetiek.
eulogise, prys, roem, ophemel.
eulogist, lofredenaar; ophemelaar.
eulogy, lof, lofspraak, -rede; ophemeling.
eunuch, eunug; ontmande persoon.
euphemism, eufemisme, verbloeming.
euphemistic, eufemisties, verbloemend.
euphonic, -ious, welluidend, eufonies.
euphony, welluidendheid.
euphorbia, noorsdoring, melkbos, vingerpol.
euphuism, bloemrykheid; euphuïsme.
Eurasian, halfbloed- . . ., Eurasies.
eurhythmic, euritmies.
eurhythmics, euritmiek.
Europe, Europa.
European, n. Europeaan, Europeër; Europese (vrou).
European, a. Europees.
evacuate, ontruim; leegmaak.
evacuation, ontruiming; ontlasting, lediging.
evade, (vraag) ontwyk, (wet) ontduik, ontsnap (aan).
evaluate, bereken, besyfer.
evaluation, berekening, besyfering.
evanesce, verdwyn, verdamp, verbygaan.
evanescence, kortstondigheid.
evanescent, vlugtig, verbygaand.
evangel, evangelie.
evangelic(al), a. evangelies.
Evangelic(al), n. Evangeliesgesinde.
evangelist, evangelis.
evangelistic, evangelisties.
evangelize, die evangelie verkondig; bekeer.
evaporate, verdamp, vervlieg; uitwasem.
evaporation, verdamping; uitwaseming.
evasion, ontwyking; uitvlug.
evasive, ontwykend; vol uitvlugte; vaag.
eve, aand; vooraand; **Christmas –**, aand voor Kers(mis); **New Year's –**, Oujaars(dag)aand; **on the – of**, aan die vooraand van.
even, n. aand.
even, a. gelyk, gelykmatig; eenvormig; glad; plat; ewe; **odd and –**, gelyk en ongelyk, ewe en onewe; **get – with**, uitbetaal, terugbetaal; **– money**, gelykop-weddenskap.
even, adv. selfs; **– so**, almaskie, selfs dan; **not –**, selfs nie, nie eers (eens) nie; **he cannot – write**, hy kan nie eers (eens) skryf nie; **– more**, (selfs) nog meer; **– now**, (selfs) nou nog; op hierdie oomblik; **– as**, net soos; **– though**, selfs as.
even, v. gelykmaak, effens; gelykstel; **– up**, gelyk kom.
evening, aand; **musical –**, musiekaand(jie); **of an –**, saans; **good –**, (goei)naand; **this –**, vanaand.
evening dress, aandpak; aandtoilet.
evenness, gelykheid; gladheid; platheid.
evensong, aanddiens; vesper.
event, gebeurtenis, voorval; geval; uitslag; (sport)nummer, wedstryd; **at all –s**, in elke geval; **after the –**, agterna; **in the – of**, in geval.
eventful, bewoë, ryk aan gebeurtenisse.
eventide, avondstond.
eventless, kalm, stil, rustig.
eventual, eventueel, moontlik, gebeurlik; eindelik, eind- . . .; gevolglik.
eventuality, gebeurlikheid.
eventually, uiteindelik, ten slotte.
eventuate, gebeur, uitkom, (so) loop (dat).
ever, altoos, ewig; ooit, weleens; **for –**, (vir) ewig, vir altoos; **– after**, daarna, van dié tyd af; **– and anon**, telkens, van tyd tot tyd; **did you – meet him?**, het jy hom ooit ontmoet?;

as well as – he could, so goed as hy maar (enigsins) kon; **as well as–**, so goed as ooit; **who- can it be?**, wie op aarde kan dit wees?; **– so much easier**, oneindig gemakliker; **thank you – so much**, baie, baie dankie; **if it costs – so much**, al kos dit nog soveel.
evergreen, bladhoudend, groenblywend.
everlasting, a. ewigdurend; knaend.
everlasting, n. ewigheid; sewejaartjie; kanniedood.
evermore, ewig, altyd.
every, elke, iedere, al; **– other day**, (al) om die ander dag; **– three days**, al om die derde dag; **– now and then (again)**, telkens, gedurig; **his – thought**, elke gedagte van hom; **– bit as much**, ruim soveel; **– bit**, elke stukkie, alles.
everybody, iedereen, elkeen.
everyday, adv. aldae, daeliks.
everyday, a. daeliks, gewoon.
everyone, iedereen, algar.
everything, alles.
everyway, in alle opsigte, allesins, ruim.
everywhere, oral(s), alom, allerweë.
evict, (geregtelik) uitsit; (geregtelik) ontset.
eviction, uitsetting; ontsetting.
evidence, getuienis; bewys; blyk(e); **give –**, getuienis aflê, getuig; blyk gee; **be in –**, op die voorgrond wees; **turn King's –**, kroongetuie word.
evident, duidelik, klaarblyklik.
evidently, klaarblyklik; blykbaar.
evil, a. sleg, kwaad, boos; **the E– One**, die Bose.
evil, adv. sleg; **speak – of**, sleg praat van, belaster, beskinder.
evil, n. kwaad, euwel; onheil; sonde; siekte.
evil-doer, boosdoener.
evil-minded, kwaaddenkend; van slegte inbors.
evilness, verkeerdheid, boosheid; sondigheid.
evil-speaking, a. lasterend, kwaadsprekend.
evil-speaking, n. kwaadsprekery, skindery, laster.
evince, openbaar, aan die dag lê; aantoon.
eviscerate, die ingewande uithaal, ontwei.
evocation, oproeping.
evoke, oproep, te voorskyn roep; uitlok.
evolution, ontwikkeling; evolusie; worteltrekking; swenking; **-s**, beweginge; ontplooiing.
evolve, ontvou, ontplooi, ontwikkel; aflei.
ewe, ooi.
ewer, lampetkan, waterbeker.
ex-, gewese, ou(d).
exacerbate, verskerp, vererger; verbitter.
exact, a. noukeurig, presies, stip, akkuraat, eksak; **– sciences**, eksakte wetenskappe.
exact, v. vorder, verg, eis; afdwing.
exacting, veeleisend, streng; **– circumstances**, moeilike omstandighede.
exaction, vordering, eis; afpersing.
exactitude, noukeurigheid; stiptheid.
exactly, adv. noukeurig, juis, presies; **not –**, nie juis nie, nie bepaald nie.
exactly, interj. presies, juistement!
exaggerate, vergroot, oordrywe.
exaggeration, vergroting, oordrywing.
exalt, verhef; ophemel, verheerlik.
exaltation, verheffing; verheerliking; vervoering, verrukking.
examination, eksamen; ondersoek; ondersoeking; verhoor; **– results**, eksamenuitslae.
examination-fee, eksamengeld.
examination-paper, vraestel.
examine, ondersoek, eksamineer, toets; verhoor, ondervra; visiteer.
examiner, eksaminator; ondervraer; kontroleur.
example, voorbeeld; model; eksemplaar; monster, staal; proef; **for –**, byvoorbeeld; **make**

an – of, voorbeeldig straf; **set an –,** 'n voorbeeld gee; **by way of –,** as voorbeeld.
exasperate, vererger; vererg(er), vertoorn, terg, kwaad maak.
exasperated, vererg, geprikkel, kwaad.
exasperating, tergend, ergerlik.
exasperation, vererging, verskerping, ergernis, versteurdheid; terging.
excavate, uitgrawe; uithol; opgrawe.
excavation, opgrawing; uitholling; gat, holte.
exceed, oortref; te buite gaan, oorskry; – **the speed-limit,** die snelheidsbeperking oortree.
exceedingly, uitermate, uiters, bowemate.
excell, oortref, uitmunt; uitblink.
excellency, uitmuntendheid, voortreflikheid.
excellency, voortreflikheid; **His E–,** Sy Eksellensie.
excellent, uitstekend, uitmuntend, voortreflik.
excelsior, excelsior.
except, v. uitsluit, uitsonder; objekteer.
except, -ing, prep. behalwe, uitgesonderd; **not –ing,** met inbegrip van.
except, conj. tensy.
exception, uitsondering; teenwerping; **the – proves the rule,** die uitsondering bevestig die reël; **take – to,** objekteer teen; **take – at,** kwalik neem, aanstoot neem (aan).
exceptionable, betwisbaar; aanstootlik.
exceptional, uitsonderlik, buitengewoon.
excerpt, n. uittreksel, ekserp.
excerpt, v. 'n uittreksel maak, ekserpeer.
excess, oormaat; oordaad; buitensporigheid, onmatigheid; gruwel(daad); oorskot; **in – of,** bo(kant), meer as; **carry on –,** oordrywe; **in, to –,** oormatig.
excessive, oordrewe, buitensporig, onmatig.
excessively, uiters, uitermate, oordrewe.
exchange, n. ruil(ing); uitwisseling, wisselkoers; hoofkantoor, sentrale; (geld)beurs; **rate of –,** wisselkoers; **bill of –,** (geld)wissel.
exchange, v. (om)ruil, verruil, wissel; – **blows,** handgemeen raak; – **words,** 'n woordewisseling hê.
exchangeable, (ver)ruilbaar, inwisselbaar.
exchequer, skatkis, tesourie; **chancellor of the –,** kanselier van die skatkis, minister van finansies.
excisable, aksynsbaar, aksynspligtig.
excise, n. aksyns; – **duties,** aksyns(belasting).
excise, v. aksyns laat betaal; oorvra.
excise, v. uitsny; skrap.
excise-office, aksynskantoor.
excise-officer, aksynsbeampte.
excision, uitsnyding; skrapping.
excitable, opgewonde, prikkelbaar.
excitation, aansporing, prikkeling.
excite, opwind; opwek, aanspoor; prikkel; gaande maak, aan die gang sit.
excited, opgewonde.
excitement, opgewondenheid, opwinding, spanning; prikkeling, aansporing.
exciting, opwindend, spannend.
exclaim, uitroep; – **against,** uitvaar teen.
exclamation, uitroep, roep, kreet; **note of –,** uitroepteken.
exclamatory, uitroepend, by wyse van uitroep.
exclude, uitsluit.
exclusion, uitsluiting.
exclusive, uitsluitend; apart, afsydig, eksklusief; – **of,** met uitsluiting van.
exclusively, uitsluitlik, uitsluitend.
exclusiveness, eksklusiwiteit, afsydigheid.
excogitate, uitprakseer, versin.
excommunicate, in die ban doen, ekskommuniseer.

excommunication, ban, ekskommunikasie.
excoriate, vel-af maak; afskil.
excrement, uitwerpsel, ontlasting.
excrescence, gewas, uitwas, uitgroeisel.
excrescent, oortollig.
excrete, uitwerp, afskei.
excruciate, pynig, folter, martel.
excruciating, pynigend, folterend; verskriklik.
exculpate, verontskuldig; vryspreek.
excursion, uitstap(pie), ekskursie; uitweiding, afdwaling; – **ticket,** vakansiekaartjie; – **train,** vakansietrein.
excursive, wydlopig, uitweidend.
excusable, vergeeflik, verskoonbaar.
excuse, v. verontskuldig, verskoon; – **me,** verskoon my, ekskuus, pardon; – **from,** vrystel van; **beg to be –d,** vra om verskoon te word.
excuse, n. verontskuldiging, verskoning; ekskuus.
execrable, ellendig, afskuwelik, verfoeilik.
execrate, vervloek; verfoei, verafsku.
execration, vervloeking, verfoeiing; gruwel.
executant, speler, singer, voordraer.
execute, uitvoer, volbring, ten uitvoer bring; voltrek ('n vonnis); teregstel, ter dood bring.
execution, uitvoering, volbrenging; voltrekking; teregstelling, eksekusie; **put into –,** in werking stel, ten uitvoer bring.
executioner, beul, laksman, skerpregter.
executive, n. uitvoerende mag (raad); dagbestuur; uitvoerende amptenaar.
executive, a. uitvoerend.
executor, uitvoerder; eksekuteur, boedelbesorger.
executrix, eksekutrise.
exegesis, (skrif)verklaring, eksegese.
exegetic, verklarend, eksegeties.
exemplar, voorbeeld; toonbeeld; tipe.
exemplary, voorbeeldig.
exemplification, opheldering, toeligting.
exemplify, met 'n voorbeeld toelig; as voorbeeld dien.
exempt, v. vrystel, onthef, ontslaan.
exempt, a. vrygestel, onthef, verskoon.
exemption, vrystelling, verskoning, ontheffing.
exequies, begrafnisplegtighede.
exercise, n. oefening; uitoefening; opgawe.
exercise, v. oefen; uitoefen; oefening neem; dril; besig hou; – **care,** sorg.
exercise-book, skrif.
exert, aanwend, te pas bring, uitoefen; – **oneself,** (sig) inspan, jou bes doen; – **influence,** invloed uitoefen.
exertion, uitoefening, aanwending; inspanning.
exfoliate, afskilfer.
exhalation, uitwaseming, uitademing.
exhale, uitwasem, uitasem, uitdamp; afgee.
exhaust, v. uitput; leegmaak, opmaak.
exhaust, n. afvoer; uitlaatpyp; knalpot.
exhausted, uitgeput; lugleeg; uitverkoop.
exhaustion, uitputting, afmatting.
exhaustive, uitputtend; volledig.
exhibit, v. tentoonstel, vertoon; uitstal; instuur (na 'n tentoonstelling); aan die dag lê.
exhibit, n. insending; uitstalling; (bewys)stuk.
exhibition, vertoning; uitstalling; tentoonstelling; beurs; **make an – of oneself,** jou belaglik maak.
exhibitioner, beurshouer.
exhibitionism, selfvertoningsdrang.
exhibitionist, ekshibisionis.
exhibitor, -er, insender; vertoner.
exhilarate, opvrolik, opwek, verfris.
exhilarating, opwekkend, verfrissend.

**exhilaration, **opgewektheid, frisheid, lewenslustigheid, opvroliking.
**exhort, **vermaan, waarsku; aanmaan, aanspoor.
**exhortation, **vermaning; aansporing; toespraak.
**exhortative, -tory, **vermanend; aansporend.
**exhumation, **opgrawing.
**exhume, **opgrawe.
**exigence, -cy, **nood, behoefte; geval van nood.
**exigent, **dringend; (ver)eisend; veeleisend.
**exiguity, **geringheid, onbeduidendheid.
**exiguous, **gering, klein.
**exile, **n. verbanning, ballingskap; balling.
**exile, **v. verban, uitban.
**exist, **bestaan, wees, leef, voorkom.
**existence, **bestaan, aansyn; **precarious –, **armoedige bestaan; **the best in –, **die beste wat daar bestaan.
**exit, **uitgang; dood; uitgangskaartjie.
**exodus, **uittog, eksodus.
**exonerate, **suiwer, vrypleit; ontlas, onthef.
**exoneration, **suiwering; ontheffing.
**exorbitance, -cy, **buitensporigheid.
**exorbitant, **buitensporig, verregaand.
**exorcise, **besweer, uitdryf, (uit)ban.
**exorcism, **(geeste)beswering, duiwelbanning.
**exorcist, **(geeste)besweerder, duiwelbanner.
**exordium, **aanhef, inleiding, eksordium.
**exoteric, **vir oningewydes, populêr.
**exotic, **uitheems, vreemd.
**expand, **uitbrei; ontwikkel; uitsit, swel; toeneem.
**expanse, **uitgestrektheid, oppervlakte.
**expansion, **uitbreiding; uitsetting, toename.
**expansive, **uitbreidend; rekbaar; uitgestrek; uitgebreid; omvattend; vertroulik.
**expatiate: – (up)on, **uitwei oor.
**expatiation, **uitweiding; omwandeling.
**expatriate, **verban, uitsit; verhuis.
**expect, **verwag; vermoed; **I – you to be punctual, **ek reken daarop dat jy betyds sal wees.
**expectance, -cy, **verwagting; vooruitsig.
**expectant, **verwagtend; aanstaande.
**expectation, **verwagting; vooruitsig; hoop; afwagting; **contrary to –s, **teen die verwagtinge (in); **in – of, **in afwagting van.
**expectorate, **spu (spuug); **expectorating prohibited, **verbode om te spu.
**expectoration, **spuwing, (die) spu.
**expedience, -ency, **dienstigheid, doelmatigheid; gerief; raadsaamheid.
**expedient, **a. dienstig, gerieflik, raadsaam.
**expedient, **n. (red)middel, plan, uitweg.
**expedite, **bevorder, bespoedig, aanhelp.
**expedition, **bevordering; aansending; spoed; onderneming; tog, ekspedisie.
**expeditious, **vlug, snel, glad, vlot.
**expel, **uitsit, wegja, verdryf, verban.
**expend, **bestee, spandeer, uitgee; verbruik.
**expendable, **misbaar, afskryfbaar.
**expenditure, **uitgawe, onkoste; verbruik.
**expense, **uitgawe (on)koste; **at the – of, **ten koste van; op koste van; **a joke at my –, **'n grap ten koste van my; **to go to –, **onkoste maak; **put one to –, **op (on)koste ja; **meet –s, **(on)koste bestry; **incidental –s, **onvoorsiene uitgawes.
**expensive, **duur, kosbaar, verkwistend.
**expensiveness, **duurte; verkwistendheid.
**experience, **n. ondervinding, ervaring; bevinding; **by –, **deur ondervinding; **man of –, **man van ervaring.
**experience, **v. ondervind, ervaar, belewe.
**experienced, **ervare, geoefend(e).
**experiment, **n. proef(neming), eksperiment.
**experiment, **v. proewe neem, eksperimenteer.
**experimental, **proefondervindelik; ervarings- . . .

**experimentalist, **proefnemer, ondersoeker.
**expert, **a. bedrewe; deskundig, vakkundig; – **at, in, **bedrewe op die gebied van.
**expert, **n. deskundige, vakman, ekspert.
**expertness, **bedrewenheid, vakkundigheid.
**expiate, **boet, boete doen, vergoeding doen.
**expiation, **boetedoening; versoening.
**expiatory, **boetend, versoenend.
**expiration, **uitademing; laaste ademtog; einde verval(tyd), afloop.
**expiratory, **uitademend, uitademings- . . .
**expire, **uitadem; doodgaan, die gees gee; verval; verstryk.
**expiry, **verloop, afloop, verstryk(ing).
**explain, **duidelik maak, verklaar, uiteensit; – **away, **wegredeneer; – **oneself, **(sig) nader verklaar.
**explanation, **verklaring, uitleg, uiteensetting, verduideliking; **in – of, **ter verklaring van; **come to an –, **'n misverstand opklaar; ooreenkom.
**explanatory, **verklarend, verduidelikend.
**expletive, **stopwoord; vloek, knoop.
**explicate, **verduidelik, ontvou.
**explication, **verklaring, verduideliking.
**explicatory, **verklarend.
**explicit, **uitdruklik, duidelik, stellig, bepaald.
**explicitness, **uitdruklikheid, volledigheid.
**explode, **ontplof, spring; uitbars; laat ontplof, laat spring.
**exploit, **n. prestasie, kordaatstuk.
**exploit, **v. eksploiteer, ontgin; uitbuit.
**exploitation, **ontginning; uitbuiting.
**exploration, **ondersoek(ing), verkenning.
**explorative, -atory, **ondersoekings- . . .
**explore, **ondersoek, navors, verken, eksploreer.
**explorer, **ondersoeker, vorser, reisiger.
**explosion, **uitbarsting, ontploffing; knal.
**explosive, **a. eksplosief, uitbarstend, ontploffings- . . ., ontplofbaar; – **cotton, **skietkatoen; – **gas, **knalgas.
**explosive, **n. ontploffingsmiddel.
**explosiveness, **ontplofbaarheid.
**exponent, **vertolker; beliggaming; wortelgetal.
**export, **v. uitvoer, eksporteer.
**export, **n. uitvoer, eksport.
**exporter, **uitvoerder, eksporteur.
**expose, **openbaar, blootlê; blootstel; ontbloot; aan die kaak stel; ten toon stel, vertoon; (fotografiese plaat) belig; (kind) te vondeling lê; – **one's life, **jou lewe blootstel.
**exposition, **uiteensetting; tentoonstelling; uitstalling; blootlegging.
**expositor, **uitleêr, verklaarder, vertolker.
**expostulate, **'n vertoog hou, vermaan; – **with, **vermaan, kapittel (oor).
**expostulation, **vertoog, teenwerping.
**exposure, **blootstelling; ontbloting; ontmaskering; beligting; beligtingstyd.
**expound, **uiteensit, uitlê, verklaar; vertolk.
**express, **a. uitgeknip, uitdruklik; uitgedruk; presies; spesiaal; ekspres.
**express, **n. ekspres(trein); spesiale boodskapper.
**express, **v. uitdruk; te kenne gee; vertolk; betuig.
**expression, **uitdrukking; gesegde; **beyond –, **onuitspreeklik.
**expressionism, **ekspressionisme.
**expressionist, **ekspressionis.
**expressionless, **uitdrukking(s)loos; toonloos.
**expressive, **vol uitdrukking; betekenisvol, veelseggend; nadruklik; ekspressief.
**expressly, **uitdruklik; spesiaal, ekspres; met opset.
**expropriate, **onteien, eksproprieer.

expropriation, onteiening; ekspropriasie.
expulsion, uitsetting, verdrywing; verbanning; ontsetting (uit eiendom).
expunction, skrapping, weglating.
expunge, skrap, uitvee(g), weglaat.
expurgate, suiwer; uitsny, skrap.
expurgation, suiwering; skrapping.
exquisite, uitgesog, uitgelese, voortreflik, keurig, fyn; – **pain,** hewige pyn.
exquisiteness, uitgelesenheid, keurigheid, fynheid; intensiteit, hewigheid.
extant, voorhaande, nog bestaande.
extemporaneous, onvoorberei, uit die vuis.
extempore, uit die vuis, onvoorbereid.
extemporise, uit die vuis praat; improviseer.
extend, uitsteek, uitbrei; (tydperk) verleng; (welkom) toeroep; **the runner was –ed to the utmost,** die renner moes al sy kragte inspan; – **over,** uitstrek oor.
extension, uitstrekking; uitrekking; uitbreiding; uitgebreidheid; verlenging; bepaling (in grammatika).
extension course, uitbreidingskursus.
extension lecture, buitelesing.
extension table, uitskuiftafel.
extensive, uitgebreid, omvattend, omvangryk; – **use,** gebruik op groot skaal.
extent, omvang; mate; uitgestrektheid; **to a great –,** in 'n groot mate, grotendeels; **to the – of,** tot die bedrag (grootte, omvang) van.
extenuate, versag, verminder, vergoelik.
extenuating, versagtend; vergoelikend.
extenuation, versagting, verkleining, verminderring verontskuldiging.
exterior, a. buitenste; van buite; uitwendig.
exterior, n. buitekant; uiterlik.
exterminate, uitroei, verdelg.
extermination, uitroeiing, verdelging.
external, buitekantse, buitenste; uitwendig; uiterlik; ekstern; **the – world,** die wêreld buite ons; die eksterne wêreld.
externals, uiterlikhede; bykomstighede.
exterritorial, eksterritoriaal.
extinct, uitgeblus, uitgedoof; uitgesterf; verouderd; afgeskaf; – **volcano,** uitgedoofde vulkaan.
extinction, uitdowing; uitsterwing; vernietiging.
extinguish, doodmaak, blus; doodblaas; vernietig; oorskadu; uitwis; (skuld) delg.
extinguisher, domper; blustoestel.
extirpate, uitroei, uitdelg.
extirpation, uitroeiing, verdelging.
extol, loof, verheerlik, ophemel.
extolment, ophemeling, verheerliking.
extort, afpers, afdwing; uitforseer.
extortion, afpersing; afsettery, uitsuigery.
extortionate, afpersings– . . .; buitensporig.
extra, a. ekstra; buitengewoon; addisioneel; – **special,** laaste uitgawe (van koerant).
extra, n. ekstra; toegif.
extract, n. ekstrak, aftreksel; uittreksel.
extract, v. uittrek; uittreksel maak; aftreksel maak; uithaal; aflei.

extraction, (uit)trekking; herkoms, geboorte.
extradite, uitlewer; uitlewering bewerk.
extradition, uitlewering.
extramural, buite– . . .; ⊥ lecture, buitelesing.
extraneous, vreemd, van buite.
extraordinary, buitengewoon; sonderling, snaaks.
extravagance, onmatigheid; buitensporigheid; verkwisting, oordaad; ongerymdheid.
extravagant, onmatig; buitensporig; verkwistend, oordadig; spandabel.
extreme, a. uiterste, verste, uiteindelike.
extreme, n. uiterste; **in the –,** in die ergste graad.
extremely, uiters, hoogs, uitermate.
extremist, ekstremis, ultra.
extremity, uiterste, eindpunt, uiteinde; uiterste nood; **–ies,** uiterste maatreëls; **the –ies,** die uiterste ledemate; **drive to –,** tot die uiterste dryf.
extricable, ontwarbaar; redbaar.
extricate, ontwar, losmaak; verlos, uitred.
extrication, ontwarring; uitredding.
extrinsic, buite– . . ., vreemd; bykomstig.
extrude, uitdryf, wegja, uitskop.
extrusion, verdrywing, uitstoting.
exuberance, weelderigheid; uitgelatenheid.
exuberant, weelderig, oorvloedig; uitbundig, uitgelate.
exudation, uitsweting.
exude, uitsweet, vog afgee.
exult, juig, jubel, koning kraai; – **over,** kraai oor, (sig) verheug oor.
exultant, jubelend, opgetoë, uitgelate.
exultation, gejuig, opgetoënheid.
exultingly, jubelend, triomfantelik.
exuviate, vervel.
eye, n. oog; **clap, set –s on,** in die oë kry; **up to the –s in work,** tot oor die ore in die werk; **make him open his –s,** skrikmaak, laat opkyk; **catch the –,** die oog tref; **have an – to,** 'n ogie hê op; **with an – to,** met die oog op; **keep an – on,** in die oog hou, dophou; **in the – of the law,** voor die wet; **in the mind's –,** voor die geestesoog; **see – to –,** eens wees, in ooreenstemming wees; **make –s at,** 'n knipogie gee; **before, under the –s of,** onder die oog van, ten aanskoue van; **see with half an –,** met 'n oogopslag sien.
eye, v. aanskou, waarneem, sien.
eyeball, oogappel.
eyebrow, winkbrou.
eye-flap, oogklap.
eye-glass, oogglas, monokel.
eyelashes, ooghare, wimpers.
eyelet, ogie.
eyelid, ooglid.
eye-opener, openbaring; **that was an – to him,** dit was 'n hele openbaring vir hom.
eyepiece, oogglas, okulêr.
eyeshot, gesig, gesigsafstand.
eyesight, gesig, oë; **bad –,** slegte oë (gesig).
eyesore, doring in die oog.
eyewitness, ooggetuie.
eyrie, eyry, (arends–, roofvoël–)nes.

F

fable, n. fabel, sprokie; versinsel; inhoud.
fable, v. fabel, fantaseer, versin, verdig.
fabric, weefsel, fabrikaat, stof.
fabricate, vervaardig, weef; versin.
fabrication, vervaardiging; versinsel.
fabulous, fabelagtig; legendaries; ongelooflik.
facade, (voor)gewel, voorkant, gesig; skyn (fig.).
face, n. gesig, voorkome; voorkant; sy(kant); wys(t)erplaat; onbeskaamdheid; **look one in the –**, iemand in die oë kyk; **show one's –**, (sig) vertoon, (sig) laat sien; **– to –**, van aangesig tot aangesig; onder vier oë, **set one's – against**, (sig) verset teen; **in – of**, reg teenoor; **in (the) – of**, ondanks; **to one's –**, in iemand se gesig; **make, pull a – (-s)**, gesigte trek; **have the –**, so astrant wees; **save one's –**, sy prestige red; **on the – of it**, na die skyn geoordeel; klaarblyklik; **put a new – on**, 'n ander kleur aan gee; **lose –**, aansien verloor.
face, v. in die oë sien; in die gesig staar; teenoorstel; staan teenoor; onder die oë sien, trotseer, die hoof bied; die gesig hê op, uitsien op; omkeer maak, draai; **– the music**, die storm verduur, die gevolge dra; **– down**, oorbluf, uit die veld slaan.
facer, klap, skok; gelol.
facet, vlak; hoeklys; faset.
facetious, grappig, geestig; snaaks.
face-value, nominale waarde.
facial, gesigs- . . ., gelaats- . . .; **– angle**, gesigs-, gelaatshoek.
facile, gemaklik, glad; vlot; inskiklik.
facilitate, vergemaklik; (aan)help.
facility, gemak; vaardigheid, vlotheid; geleentheid.
facing, n. belegsel, afsetsel, bekleding; voorkant; (boonste) laag.
facing, a. teenoor.
facing-board, skutlys, geutlys.
facsimile, faksimilee, reproduksie.
fact, feit, daadsaak; daad; **in –**, om die waarheid te sê; **in point of –**, in werklikheid; **the – of the matter**, die waarheid; **as a matter of –**, om die waarheid te sê; as iets doodgewoons.
faction, faksie, party; partygees.
factious, partysugtig, kliekerig; oproerig.
factiousness, partysug; tweedragtigheid.
factitious, (na)gemaak, gekunsteld.
factive, faktitief.
factor, aanleiding, oorsaak; agent; deler; faktor.
factorize, in faktore ontbind.
factory, (handels)kantoor, fabriek; faktory.
factory labourer, fabrieksarbeider.
factotum, faktotum, handlanger.
factual, feitlik, feite- . . .
facultative, fakultatief, opsioneel.
faculty, aanleg, geskiktheid; vermoë; bevoegdheid; fakulteit.
fad, idee, manie, gier, stokperdjie.
faddish, vol giere; dweepsugtig.
faddist, dweper, maniak.
fade, verbleek, verkleur; verlep, verwelk; verflou, kwyn; verswak (radio).
fadeless, kleurvas; onverwelklik.
faeces, moer; ontlasting.
fag, v. afjakker, uitput; vuilwerkies doen; joggie speel.
fag, n. koeliewerk, vuilwerk; moeite, las; groentjie; stinkstokkie; **too much –**, te veel moeite.
fag-end, oorskot; stert, slot; stompie.
fag(g)ot, bondel, bos, drag.
faience, faience(-aardewerk).
fail, n. feil, fout; **without –**, seker.
fail, v. ontbreek, in gebreke bly, tekort skiet, kortkom; verswak; faal; (motor) weier; mislui, misloop; in die steek laat; sak, druip; bankrot raak; **he cannot – to**, hy kan nie anders as.
failing, n. gebrek, tekortkoming, swak(heid).
failing, part, ontbrekend; agteruitgaande; **– subject**, hoofvak, druipvak; **– whom**, by wie se ontstentenis, in geval hy in gebreke bly; **– which**, anders, in gebreke waarvan; **never –**, onfeilbaar.
failure, mislukking; tekortkoming, versuim; gebrek, fout; weiering, (die) bly staan; bankrot.
fain: **I was – to**, ek was verplig om, ek moes wel; **I would – have gone**, ek sou graag wou gegaan het.
faint, a. flou, swak; dof, vaag; benoud; **– idea**, flou idee; **grow –**, flou word; **dof word**; moedeloos word.
faint, v. flou (bewusteloos) word; **–ing fit**, floute.
faint-hearted, flou(hartig), wankelmoedig.
faintness, flouheid, swakte; dofheid; vaagheid; slapheid; bangheid.
fair, n. kermis.
fair, a. mooi, fraai; blond, lig; taamlik, goed; suiwer, skoon, rein; regverdig, bilik; opreg, eerlik; **– copy**, skoon kopie; **– and square**, reguit, eerlik; **by – means or foul**, tot (teen) elke prys; **the – sex**, die skone geslag; **– weather**, mooi weer.
fair-haired, met ligte (blonde) hare.
fairish, taamlik, vrywel; taamlik blond.
fairly, sien **fair**; heeltemal, totaal, glad; taamlik, vrywel, goed; **he was – beside himself**, hy kon glad uit sy vel spring.
fairness, skoonheid; blondheid; eerlikheid; regverdigheid, billikheid.
fair-play, skoon spel; **that is not –**, dit is kurang.
fair-way, vaarwater; skoonveld (gholf).
fairy, n. (tower)fee.
fairy, a. tower- . . ., feeagtig.
fairyland, feëryk, towerland.
faith, geloof; vertroue; trou, (ere)woord; **pin one's – on**, vertroue stel in; **pledge –**, trou sweer; **keep –**, belofte hou; **good, bad –**, goeie, slegte trou; **in good –**, te goeder trou; **confession of –**, geloofsbelydenis.
faithful, getrou; gelowig.
faithfully, (ge)trou; **yours –**, u dienswillige; **promise –**, vas belowe.
faithless, ontrou, trouveloos; onbetroubaar.
fake, v. opdraai, oprol.
fake, n. bedrog; voorwendsel; vervalsing.
fake, v. voorwend, namaak, vervals.
fakir, fakir.
falchion, kromswaard.
falcon, valk.
falconer, valkenier.
falconry, valkejag.
falderal, tierlantyntjie, snuistery.
fall, v. val, daal, sink, stort, sak; **– to the ground**, in duie val; **– to pieces**; uitmekaar val; **– in love**, verlief raak; **– into a rage**, in woede uitbars; **– due**, verval; betaalbaar word; **– into conversation**, 'n gesprek aanknoop; **– into line**, in gelid val; meegaan; **– into a habit**, in 'n gewoonte verval; **– into debt**, in skuld verval; **– to fighting**, aan die veg raak; **– on**, tref; aanval; **– within**, val onder (binne); **– in with**, raakloop, teenkom, tref; instem met; **– astern**, agterbly; **– away**, afval; **– back**, terugval, -trek; **– back upon**, terugval op; **– behind**, agterraak, -bly; **– foul of**, deurmekaar raak met, in botsing kom met; **– off**, afval; verval; terugval; afvallig word; **– out**, rusie maak; gebeur; afloop; uitkom; **– short**, kortkom, -skiet; **– through**,

fall | 491 | **fast**

misluk, in duie val; nie deurgaan nie; – to, wegval.
fall, n. val; daling; instorting; afdraand, helling; waterval; reënval; lammeroes.
fallacious, bedrieglik, vals, verkeerd.
fallacy, bedrog; dwaalbegrip; onjuistheid.
fal-lal, snuistery, tierlantyntjie.
fallible, feilbaar.
fall-out, rusie; afval(stowwe); neerslag; **atomic** –, atoomneerslag.
fallow, a. braak; – **land,** driesland; braakland.
fallow, v. braak.
fallow, a. vaalbruin; – **deer,** damhert.
false, vals; verkeerd; onwaar; oneg; – **idea,** verkeerde idee; – **alarm, coin, hair, note, shame,** vals alarm, munt, hare, noot, skaamte; – **step,** misstap; – **pretences,** valse voorwendsels; – **position,** 'n skewe verhouding; – **bottom,** dubbele boom; **play** –, bedrieg, fop, kul; – **pretences,** valse voorwendsels.
false-hearted, vals.
falsehood, leuen; bedrog, valsheid.
falseness, valsheid.
falsification, vervalsing.
falsify, vervals.
falsity, valsheid; troueloosheid; leuen.
falter, stamel, hakkel; weifel; strompel.
fame, roem, vermaardheid; faam, gerug; **ill** –, berugtheid.
famed, beroemd, vermaard; – **for,** vermaard om; – be, bekend as.
familiar, a. (goed)bekend; gemeensaam, familiaar; vertroud; gebruiklik, alledaags; eie, tuis; – **language,** omgangstaal.
familiar, n. (huis)vriend; gedienstige.
familiarity, vertroudheid; bekendheid; gemeensaamheid; familiariteit; – **breeds contempt,** goedbekend maak sleggeërd.
familiarize, vertroud maak, gemeensaam maak.
family, (huis)gesin, familie; geslag; afkoms; **in a** – **way,** familiaar, op gemeensame manier; **in the** – **way,** in geseënde omstandighede.
family-doctor, huisdokter.
family-man, huisvader.
family-tree, stamboom.
family-worship, huisgodsdiens.
famine, hongersnood; gebrek, nood; **house** –, woningnood.
famish, verhonger.
famous, beroemd; vermaard; uitstekend.
famulus, gedienstige, handlanger.
fan, n. waaier; skroef.
fan, v. (koel) waai; aanblaas; uitwaai; – **discontent,** ontevredenheid aanblaas.
fanatic, a. fanatiek, dweepsugtig, dweepsiek.
fanatic, n. dweper, dweepsugtige, geesdrywer.
fanaticism, dweepsug, dwepery, fanatisme.
fan-belt, waaierband.
fancied, vermeende, ingebeelde; geliefkoosde.
fancier, liefhebber, fokker, kweker.
fanciful, vol giere, grillig; denkbeeldig.
fancy, n. verbeelding, fantasie; inbeelding, inval, gril; (voor)liefde, neiging; liefhebbery; **take a** – **to,** (for), neiging (begin) voel vir; geneentheid opvat vir; **catch the** – **of,** in die smaak val van; **strike one's** –, in iemand se smaak val; **he is not my** –, ek het nie veel met hom op nie.
fancy, v. verbeel; voorstel; dink, glo; ingenome wees met; kweek, fok; **just** –!, stel jou voor, verbeel jou!
fancy-dress, (fantasie)kostuum.
fancy(-dress) ball, gekostumeerde bal.
fancy goods, modeartikels.
fancy-name, fantasienaam, booknaam.
fancy price, buitensporige prys.

fancy-work, fraai handwerk.
fane, tempel.
fanfare, trompetgeskal, fanfare.
fanfaronade, windmakery, grootpraat.
fang, tand, slagtand; giftand; tandwortel.
fantast, dromer.
fantastic, denkbeeldig, hersenskimmig, fantasties; grillig, sonderling.
fantasy, fantasie; verbeeldingskrag; gril.
far, a. ver, afgeleë, verwyderd; **the** – **side,** die ander kant, oorkant.
far, adv. ver, ver(re)weg; baie, veel; diep; – **away,** ver weg; – **and away,** ver(re)weg; **(so)** – **from doing it,** wel ver van dit te doen; – **be it from me,** dit sy ver van my; **he will go** –, hy sal dit ver bring; **go** – **to,** veel help om, baie bydra tot; – **better, different,** baie beter, anders; – **the best,** verweg die beste; – **and near,** wyd en syd, heinde en ver; – **from it,** ver daarvan- (daan); – **more,** veel meer; – **off,** ver weg; **in so** – **as,** vir sover (as), namate.
far, n.: **by** –, verweg; **not by** –, op verre na nie; **from** –, van ver (weg).
farce, n. klug(spel).
farce, v. opstop, vul.
farcical, klugtig; belaglik.
fardel, las, pak.
fare, n. reisgeld, vragprys; passasiers; vrag; ete, gereg; **bill of** –, spyskaart.
fare, v. gaan, vaar; voed.
farewell, vaarwel.
far-fetched, vergesog.
farina, meel; stysel.
farinaceous, melerig; meel- . . .
farm, n. (boer)plaas, boerdery.
farm, v. boer; bebou; verhuur; uitbestee.
farmer, boer; landbouer; pagter.
farm-house, boerhuis, plaashuis.
farming, landbou, boerdery; **cattle** –, veeboerdery.
farmstead, opstal, plaasgeboue.
farmyard, werf.
Faroe Islands, Faroër-eilande.
farrago, brousel, mengelmoes, bredie.
farrier, hoefsmid; perdedokter.
farriery, (hoef)smidswinkel; perdedoktery.
farrow, v. jong(e), klein varkies kry.
farrow, n. worpsel.
farther, adv. sien **far;** verder, buitendien.
farther, a. sien **far;** verder, meer afgeleë.
farthest, verste; mees afgeleë; **at** –, op sy hoogs- (te), uiterlik.
farthing, oortjie; **does not matter a** –, maak geen duit verskil nie.
farthingale, hoepelrok.
fascia, lys; laag; band; swagtel, verband.
fascicle, bossie; bundel, deel.
fascinate, bekoor, betower, boei.
fascination, bekoring, betowering.
fascine, takbos.
Fascism, Fascisme.
Fascist, n. Fascis.
Fascist, a. Fascisties.
fashion, n. mode; manier; patroon, fatsoen; **after, in a** –, op 'n manier; **set the** –, **die toon** (mode) aangee; **in, out of the** –, in, uit die mode; **man of** –, man van stand; man van die mode.
fashion, v. vorm, fatsoeneer, vou, buig.
fashionable, na die mode, modieus.
fashion-plate, modeplaat.
fast, v. vas.
fast, n. vaste.
fast, a. vas, stewig; blywend; was-eg, kleurvas;

vinnig, snel, vlug; los(bandig); – **friendship**, troue vriendskap; – **colour**, was-egte kleur; **the door is** –, die deur is toe; **my watch is** –, my horlosie is voor; – **life**, los(bandige) lewe.
fast, adv. ferm; diep; styf; dig, vlak; **sleep** –, vas slaap; – **shut**, styf toe; – **by**, dig by.
fasten, vasmaak, toemaak; bevestig; vestig (op); – **eyes upon**, oë vestig op; – **quarrel upon**, rusie soek.
fastener, vasmaker; knip, haak, drukknopie.
fastening, sluiting; band; knip, haak, knoop.
fastidious, kieskeurig, lastig, punteneurig.
fastness, vastheid; vinnigheid, vlugheid; sterkte, vesting; los(bandig)heid.
fat, a. vet; dik; ryk; vrugbaar.
fat, n. vet; **the** – **is in the fire**, die grot is gaar, die poppe is aan die dans.
fat, v. (vet) mes, vet maak; vet word.
fatal, dodelik; noodlottig; fataal; beslissend.
fatalism, fatalisme.
fatalist, fatalis.
fatality, fataliteit; noodlottigheid; noodlot; (dodelike) ongeluk; onheil, ramp; **there were numerous –ties**, daar was baie dooies.
fate, noodlot; bestemming, lot; dood, einde; **the –s**, die skikgodinne.
fated, bestem(d), voorbeskik; gedoem.
fateful, noodlottig; beslissend; profeties.
fat-head, stompkop, uilskuiken.
father, n. vader.
father, v. verwek; vader staan; verantwoordelik wees vir.
fatherhood, vaderskap.
father-in-law, skoonvader.
fatherly, vaderlik.
fathom, n. vaam (vadem).
fathom, v. vadem; peil.
fathomable, peilbaar, deurgrondbaar.
fathomless, peilloos, bodemloos; onpeilbaar.
fatigue, n. vermoeienis; afmatting.
fatigue, vermoei, afmat, moeg maak.
fatiguing, vermoeiend, afmattend.
fatling, gemeste dier.
fat-tailed, vetstert- . . .
fatten, (vet) mes, vet (maak); vet word, bemes.
fatty, a. vetterig, vet(agtig).
fatty, n. vetsak.
fatuity, lafheid; onbenulligheid.
fatuous, laf, dwaas, onbenullig.
faucet, (tap)kraan.
fault, gebrek; fout; skuld; breuk, feil (geologie); lekplek (telegrafie); **he is generous to a** –, sy edelmoedigheid is 'n swakheid van hom; **find** – **with**, aanmerkings maak op, vit oor (op); **the** – **was mine**, dit was my skuld; **it will be our own** –, ons sal dit aan onsself te wyte hê; **be at** –, ongelyk hê; die spoor byster wees.
fault-finding, vittery.
faultiness, gebrekkigheid; verkeerdheid.
faultless, onberispelik; foutloos, feilloos.
faulty, gebrekkig; foutief; verkeerd.
faun, faun, bosgod, veldgod.
fauna, fauna; diere(wêreld).
favour, n. guns; begunstiging; beskerming; genade; toestemming; (geëerde) skrywe, brief; aandenking; voorkome; **do one a** –, iemand 'n guns bewys; **in** – **of**, ten gunste van; ten behoewe van; **find** –, genade vind; **do me the** –, bewys my die diens; **I have received your** – **of the 2nd**, ek het u geëerde skrywe van die 2de ontvang; **by your** –, met u verlof; **under** – **of the night**, onder begunstiging van die duisternis.
favour, v. begunstig; gunstig gesind wees; be-

voorreg; voortrek; bevorder; lyk na (op); – **with**, verleen; begunstig met.
favourable, gunstig; toestemmend; goedgesind; bevorderlik.
favoured, begunstig; bevoorreg; bedeel; **ill** –, ongunstig uitsiende.
favourite, n. gunsteling, liefling; kansperd.
favourite, a. geliefkoosde; begunstigde.
favouritism, voortrekkery, favoritisme.
fawn, n. jong hert.
fawn, a. vaalbruin.
fawn, v. stertwaai; pamperlang.
fay, fee.
fealty, trou; leenpligtigheid.
fear, n. vrees; angs; **for** – **of**, uit vrees vir (dat); **in** – **of his life**, bevrees vir sy lewe; **no** –, moenie glo nie!
fear, v. vrees, bang wees (vir); **never** –, wees maar nie bang nie; moenie glo nie!
fearful, verskriklik, vreeslik; bang; eerbiedig.
fearless, onbevrees, onverskrokke.
fearsome, skrikwekkend, vreeslik.
feasibility, uitvoerbaarheid.
feasible, uitvoerbaar, doenlik, prakties.
feast, n. fees; (fees)maal; onthaal.
feast, v. feesvier; smul; onthaal, fuif.
feat, kordaatstuk, prestasie; wapenfeit.
feather, n. veer; pluim; **show the white** –, lugtig word; **in high** –, in feestelike stemming; **birds of a** –, voëls van dieselfde vere; **birds of a** – **flock together**, soort soek soort; **a** – **in one's cap**, 'n pluimpie; **knock down with a** –, omblaas.
feather, v. met vere versier (vul, dek); – **one's nest**, sy skapies op die droë bring.
feather-bed, verebed, bulsak.
feather-brained, onnosel, pampoenkop- . .
feathered, geveer.
feather-weight, veergewig.
feathery, geveer(de); veeragtig.
feature, n. kenmerk; trek; hoofpunt; –**s**, (gelaats-)trekke.
feature, v. uitbeeld, teken; vertoon, in die hoofrol laat optree.
featureless, oninteressant, uitdrukkingloos.
febrifuge, koorsdrankie.
febrile, koors- . . ., koorsig.
February, Februarie.
feckless, flou, dooierig, futloos, swak.
feculent, moerderig, troebel, morsig.
fecound, vrugbaar.
fecundate, vrugbaar maak; bevrug.
fecundity, vrugbaarheid.
federal, verbonde, federaal, bonds- . . .
federate, federeer, 'n bondgenootskap sluit.
federation, (state)bond, federasie.
fee, n. honorarium, vergoeding; salaris; (skool-, eksamen-, inskrywings-)geld; leenbesit; **doctor's** –**s**, dokterkoste, -rekening; **lawyer's** –**s**, advokaatsonkoste.
fee, v. vergoed, (honorarium) bevat.
feeble, swak, flou; sleg, pap.
feeble-minded, swaksinnig; besluiteloos.
feebleness, swakheid; slegtigheid.
feed, v. voed; voer; kosgee; laat wei; vetmaak; – **eyes**, oë kosgee; – **on**, leef van; **be fed up with**, maagvol wees van (oor).
feed, n. voeding; maal, voer, kos; toevoer.
feeder, eter; vreter; pypkan; borslappie; sytak, spruit; voedingskanaal; sylyn.
feeding-bottle, pypkan.
feel, voel; betas; – **one's way**, op die tas af gaan; die terrein verken; – **for**, voel na; medelye hê met; voel vir; – **up to**, in staat voel tot.
feeler, voeler; voelhoring; proefballon.

feeling 493 **fiction**

feeling, n. gevoel; gevoeligheid; gesindheid; –s, gevoelens.
feeling, a. gevoelig; voelend; gevoelvol.
feign, voorgee, voorwend; veins, huigel.
feignedly, kastig, kwansuis (konsuis).
feint, n. skynbeweging; voorwendsel.
feint, v. liemaak, 'n skynbeweging maak.
feint, a. dof, onduidelik.
fel(d)spar, veldspaat.
felicitate, gelukwens, felisiteer (met).
felicitation, gelukwens(ing), felisitasie.
felicitous, gelukkig, toepaslik, raak.
felicity, geluk; toepaslikheid, raakheid.
feline, katte- . . ., katagtig, katterig.
fell, a. wreed, fel, woes.
fell, v. vel; om-, afkap; neerslaan; plat stik.
fellah, fella(h).
felloe, velling.
fellow, maat, kameraad; -genoot; kêrel; vent; lid; gelyke, weerga; **good** –, gawe kêrel; **a** – **can't work,** ('n) mens kan nie werk nie.
fellow-citizen, medeburger.
fellow-creature, medeskepsel, medemens.
fellow-feeling, meegevoel.
fellowship, kameraadskap; gemeenskap; geselskap; broederskap; lidmaatskap (van 'n kollege); beurs; **good** –, kameraadskap.
fellow-soldier, strydgenoot, medesoldaat.
fellow-worker, kollega, mede-arbeider.
felly, sien **felloe.**
felon, misdadiger; skurk.
felon, fyt.
felonious, misdadig; snood, skurkagtig.
felony, misdaad.
felt, n. vilt.
felt, a. vilt- . . .
female, a. vroulik; vroue- . . .; wyfie- . . .; – **child,** meisie(kind), kind van die vroulike geslag; – **suffrage,** vrouestemreg.
female, n. vrouspersoon, vroumens; vrou.
feminality, vroulikheid; vrouegoed, snuistery.
feminine, vroulik; verwyf; – **rhyme,** slepende rym.
femininity, vroulikheid; verwyfdheid; die vroulike geslag.
feminize, meisieagtig (verwyf) raak (maak).
femoral, dy- . . .
femur, dybeen, dy.
fen, moerasgrond, veengrond.
fence, n. draad, heining, skutting; skermkuns; beskutting; helder; **sit on the** –, die kat uit die boom kyk.
fence, v. draad span; skerm; pareer; – **about in, round, up,** omhein, inkamp, toespan; – **off, afweer;** – **with,** ontwyk; pareer.
fencer, skermer.
fencing, (die) skerm, skermkuns; omheining.
fend: – **off, afweer;** – **for,** sorg vir.
fender, skutyster; haardrand.
fennel, vinkel.
fenny, moerassig, moeras- . . .
feoff, sien **fief,** leen(goed).
feral, wild, woes.
ferment, n. suurdeeg, gis; gisting; woeligheid.
ferment, v. gis; laat gis; ophits; broei.
fermentation, gisting.
fern, varing.
fernery, varinghuis.
ferocious, wild, woes, wreed.
ferocity, wildheid, woestheid, wreedheid.
ferreous, yster- . . .; ysterhoudend.
ferret, n. fret; snuffelaar.
ferret, v. met frette jag; snuffel, opspoor.
ferret, n. floretband, -lint.
ferriage, pontvervoer; pontgeld.
ferric, yster- . . .

ferriferous, ysterhoudend.
ferruginous, ysterhoudend; roeskleurig.
ferrule, beslag, band (om 'n stok, ens.).
ferry, n. pont; oorbringvlug.
ferry, v. oorsit (met 'n pont); oorbring (vliegtuig).
ferry-bridge, treinpont.
ferry-man, veerman, pontbaas.
fertile, vrugbaar.
fertility, vrugbaarheid.
fertilization, vrugbaarmaking; bevrugting.
fertilize, vrugbaar maak; bevrug; bemes.
fertilizer, messtof, kunsmis; bevrugter.
ferule, plak.
fervent, gloeiend, vurig, brandend.
fervid, gloeiend, vurig.
fervour, ywer, (gees)drif; vuur, gloed.
festal, feestelik, fees- . . .
fester, v. etter, sweer, loop; kanker, vreet.
fester, n. sweer, verswering; kanker.
festival, n. feesdag; feesviering; fees.
festival, a. fees- . . ., feestelik.
festive, feestelik, fees- . . .
festivity, feestelikheid; feesvreugde.
festoon, n. festoen, loofwerk, slinger.
festoon, v. festoneer, met slingers versier.
fetch, v. haal, gaan haal; trek; behaal, opbring; – **a good price,** 'n goeie prys behaal; – **a sight,** 'n sug slaak; – **a breath,** asemhaal; – **a box on the ears,** 'n oorveeg gee; – **up,** opbring; oorgee, vomeer; tot stilstand kom.
fetch, n. slenterslag, lis, middeltjie.
fetching, aantreklik, innemend.
fete, n. fees(dag), fête.
fete, v. feestelik onthaal; huldig.
f(o)etid, stinkend.
fetish, fetisj, afgod.
fetishism, fetisjisme.
fetlock, muis(hare), vetlok.
fetter, n. kluister, boei; –s, bande.
fetter, v. bind, boei, kluister; belemmer.
fettle, kondisie; **in good** –, op sy stukke.
fetus, sien **foetus.**
feud, twis, vyandskap, vete.
feud, leen; leengoed.
feudal, feodaal, leen- . . .; – **system,** leenstelsel.
feudalism, leenstelsel; leenreg.
feuilleton, feuilleton.
fever, koors; opgewondenheid; **scarlet** –, skarlakenkoors; **typhoid** –, tifuskoors.
feverfew, moederkruid.
feverish, koorsagtig; koorsig.
few, min, weinig; **a** –, 'n paar, enkele; **a** – **people,** 'n paar mense; **only a** –, net 'n paar; **the** –, die weinige; **die minderheid; a good** –, 'n hele paar; **every** – **days,** elke paar dae; – **and far between,** seldsaam, dun gesaai.
fewness, geringe getal; seldsaamheid.
fey, veeg, bestem om gou te sterf; deurmekaar.
fez, fes, Slamaaiermus.
fiasco, mislukking, fiasko.
fiat, bevel; magtiging.
fib, n. kluitjie, jokkentjie; **tell** –, jok.
fib, v. jok. kluitjies vertel.
fib, n. slag, hou.
fib, v. slaan, 'n hou gee.
fibre, vesel; fiber.
fibre-trunk, fiberkoffer.
fibril, veseltjie, wortelhaar.
fibrous, veselagtig.
fibula, kuitbeen.
fichu, halsdoekie; kragie; manteltjie; fichu.
fickle, wispelturig, veranderlik, vol grille.
fickleness, wispelturigheid, onbestendigheid.
fiction, verdigsel, versinsel; verdigting; **fiksie;** roman(kuns), romanliteratuur.

fictitious, nagemaak, namaak- . . .; voorgewend; denkbeeldig, versonne, fiktief.
fictitiousness, denkbeeldigheid.
fiddle, n. viool; as fit as a –, so reg soos 'n roer; play first (second) –, eerste (tweede) viool speel.
fiddle, v. vioolspeel; beusel; – about, rondpeuter; – at, with, peuter met.
fiddle-bow, strykstok.
fiddlestick, 'n strykstok.
fiddlesticks, interj. onsin, gekheid, bog!
fiddling, peuterig.
fidelity, trou; getrouheid.
fidget, n. rusteloosheid; woelwater; he has the –, hy het miere.
fidget, v. woel, vroetel; lastig wees (val).
fiduciary, a. fidusiêr; vertroud, vertrouens- . . .
fiduciary, n. trustee; vertrouenspersoon.
fie, foei, sies!
fief, feoff, leen; leengoed.
field, n. veld; land; gebied; speler(s); veldwerker (krieket); take the –, te velde trek; op die veld stap; a good –, goeie mededinging; – of vision, gesigsveld.
field, v. veldwerk doen (krieket); (bal) vat (vang).
field-cornet, veldkornet.
field-day, wapenskouingsdag, kampdag.
fielder, veldwerker.
field-glass, verkyker, veldkyker.
field-hospital, veldambulans.
field-marshal, veldmaarskalk.
field-preacher, laerpredikant.
fieldsman, veldwerker (krieket).
field-sports, veldsport, jag en visvangs.
fiend, bose gees; besetene, woeste duiwel; dope –, dwelmsugtige.
fiendish, duiwels, hels, besete.
fiendishness, duiwelagtigheid, boosaardigheid.
fierce, woes, onstuimig, woedend; wreed.
fierceness, woestheid, verwoedheid.
fieriness, vurigheid, driftigheid.
fiery, vurig; brandend, vlammend; driftig; opvliegend; lewendig; ontplofbaar.
fiesta, feestelikheid; vakansie.
fife, fluit.
fifteen, vyftien; rugbyspan.
fifteenth, vyftiende.
fifth, a. vyfde; – column, vyfde kolonne.
fifth, n. vyfde (deel); kwint.
fifthly, in die vyfde plek, vyfdens, ten vyfde.
fiftieth, vyftigste.
fifty, vyftig.
fig, n. vy(g); vyeboom; I don't care a –, dit kan my geen duit skeel nie.
fight, v. veg; baklei (met); – a duel, duelleer; – a battle, 'n slag lewer; – out, uitbaklei, uitspook; – shy of, ontwyk, op 'n afstand bly.
fight, n. geveg, stryd; vegparty, bakleiery; twis.
fighter, vegter; bokser; jagvliegtuig; – escort, jaggeleide; – pilot, jagvlieër.
figment, versinsel; verdigsel.
figuration, vormbepaling; vorm, afbeelding.
figurative, beeldend; oordragtelik, figuurlik.
figure, n. gedaante, vorm, afbeelding, tekening, figuur; postuur, gestalte; beeld; syfer; a slim –, 'n slank figuur; cut a –, 'n figuur slaan, 'n vertoning maak; reach three –s, die honderd bereik; – of speech, figuurlike uitdrukking.
figure, v. afbeeld, teken; verbeel; verteenwoordig; versier; (uit)reken; – as, voorstel; – prominently, op die voorgrónd tree; it –s out at, dit werk uit op; – out, uitreken; – up, optel.
figurehead, skynhoof, strooipop.
filament, veseltjie, draad; gloeidraad; helmdraad.
filamentous, draderig, veselagtig.

filature, sy-spinnery.
filbert, haselneut; haselstruik.
filch, skaai, kaap, gap, steel.
file, n. vyl.
file, v. vyl; bywerk, polys.
file, n. papierhaak; lias; lêer; rol; ry, gelid, tou; rank and –, laer range; in single –, agtermekaar, op 'n (eende)streep; stand in –, toustaan.
file, v. inry(g), rangskik, laiasseer; oorlê, deponeer; in gelid marsjeer; – a complaint, 'n klag indien; – off, afmarsjeer.
filial, kinderlik.
filiation, afstamming; vertakking; spruit.
filibeg, rokkie (van die Skotse Hooglanders).
filibuster, vrybuiter; obstruksie(voerder).
filigree, filigraan.
fillings, vylsel.
filing (2), liasseerwerk; – cabinet, kaart-kas, lêerkas, liasseerkas; – clerk, liasseerklerk.
fill, v. vul, vol maak; vol word; ('n tand) stop; opvul; vervul; versadig; ('n pos) beklee, inneem; aanstel; – in, invul; – out, opvul; swel; – up, opvul; aanvul; toegooi demp.
fill, n. bekoms; drink one's –, jou vol drink.
filler, vuller; tregter; vulsel.
fillet, strook; lys, rand; haarband; filet; mootjie.
filling, vulsel, stopsel.
fillip, n. tik (met die vinger); slag; prikkel.
fillip, v. skiet (met die vinger); aanspoor.
filly, merrievul(letjie); wildebras.
film, n. laag, vlies; film; rolprent; sluier; talkie –, klankrolprent, klankfilm.
film, v. met 'n laag bedek (word); rolprentopname maak; verfilm (storie).
film-star, rolprentster.
filmy, wasig, newelig.
filoselle, flossy.
filter, n. filter (filtreerder); suiweringstoestel.
filter, v. filtreer; suiwer; deursyg; uitlek.
filter-paper, filtreerpapier.
filth, vuilgoed, vullis; smerigheid.
filthiness, vuilheid, smerigheid.
filthy, vuil, smerig; – lucre, vuil gewin.
filtrate, n. filtraat.
filtrate, v. filtreer.
filtration, filtrering, filtrasie.
Fin(n), Fin.
fin, vin.
final, a. laaste, slot- . . ., einde- . . ., beslissend; finaal; doelaanwysend.
final, n. eindeksamen; eindwedstryd; finale.
finale, finale; slot.
finality, afdoendheid; slot, besluit, eindpunt, oplossing.
finalize, afhandel; afrond.
finance, n. finansies; –s, geldmiddele, finansies; geldwese; minister of –, minister van finansies.
finance, v. finansier, kapitaal verskaf.
financial, geldelik, finansieel.
financier, n. geldman, finansier; geldbesitter.
financier, v. geldoperasies uitvoer; geldbedrog pleeg.
finch, vink.
find, v. vind, kry; aantref; bevind; verskaf, voorsien; –favour, genade vind; – necessary to, nodig vind om; I could not – it in my heart to, ek kon dit nie oor my hart kry nie om; – place, plaasvind; – guilty, skuldig verklaar; – one's feet, reg kom tuis raak; – yourself, in eie koste voorsien; – fault with, aanmerking maak op, vit op; – for the plaintiff, uitspraak doen ten gunste van die eiser; – out, uitvind, ontdek; betrap.
find, n. vonds; ontdekking; vangs; vindplek.
finder, vinder.

finding, uitspraak; bevinding; vonds.
fine, n. boete; **in** –, kortkom, ten slotte.
fine, v. beboet.
fine, a. fyn; dun, skerp; mooi, fraai, suiwer; edel; pragtig, heerlik, lekker; – **weather**, mooi weer; **one** – **day**, op 'n goeie dag; **the** – **arts**, die skone kunste.
fine, v. afsak, suiwer word (maak); – **away**, **down**, **off**, verfyn; skerp maak.
fine-draw, onsigbaar stop (naai).
fine-drawn, skerp, fyn; spitsvondig.
fineness, fynheid; mooihuid, fraaiheid; skerpte; geslepenheid.
finery, opskik, tooisel; swierigheid.
finesse, n. geslepenheid; finesse; sny (slag).
finesse, v. slu te werk gaan; sny (by kaartspel).
finger, n. vinger; **little** –, pinkie; **lay one's** – **on**, die vinger lê op; **turn round one's** –, om jou vinger draai; **stir a** –, 'n hand uitsteek; **his** –**s are all thumbs**, sy hande staan verkeerd; **have a** – **in the pie**, 'n hand in die spel hê; **have at one's** – **ends**, op sy duimpie ken.
finger, v. beduimel, bevoel, betas.
finger-board, toetse, manuaal.
finger-bowl, **-glass**, vingerbakkie.
fingering, betasting; vingersetting; kouswol.
finger-plate, deurbeslag.
finger-post, wegwys(t)er, handwys(t)er.
finger-print, vingerafdruk.
finical, kieskeurig, vol fiemies; gekunsteld.
finicking, **finikin**, sien **finical**.
finis, einde, slot.
finish, v. klaarmaak, voltooi, eindig; klaarkry, ophou, uitskei; afwerk; afmaak, doodmaak; opmaak, leegmaak; – **off**, **up**, klaarmaak; afwerk; – **by going**, eindig deur te gaan.
finish, n. einde, end, slot; afwerking; **fight to a** –, end-uit baklei, uitspook; polering, glans; wenpaal.
finished, klaar; afgewerk; volmaak, op-en-top.
finisher, voltooier; afwerker; genadeslag.
finishing, a. laaste, finale; – **stroke**, genadeslag; wenhou; **give the** – **touch**, die laaste hand aan lê.
finite, bepaald, begrens, definitief.
finiteness, eindigheid.
finlike, vinvormig, soos 'n vin.
Fin(n), **Fin**.
Finnish, **Fins**.
finny, gevin; vinvormig; visryk.
fiord, **fjord**, fjord.
fir, den(neboom); dennehout.
fir-apple, **-cone**, dennebol, denne-appel.
fire, n. vuur; brand; skietery; koors; drif, hartstog; ywer; vurigheid; **set on** –, **set** – **to**, aan die brand steek; **he will never set the Thames on** –, hy is nie die man wat buskruit uitgevind het nie; **catch**, **take** –, vuur vat, aan die brand raak; **open** –, die vuur open, lostrek; **under** –, onder vuur.
fire, v. aan die brand steek; ontvlam; skiet; losbrand; stook, opstook; aanspoor, aanwakker; afdank, uitskop; – **off**, afskiet, aftrek; – **a salute**, saluutskote skiet; – **away**, trek los, vooruit!
fire-alarm, brandsinjaal, brandklok.
fire-arm, vuurwapen.
fire-bomb, brandbom.
fire-band, brandende hout; onrusstoker.
fire-brick, vuurvaste steen.
fire-brigade, brandweer.
fire-bug, brand stigter.
fire-clay, vuurvaste klei.
fire-damp, myngas.
fire-dog, (h)erdyster.

fire-eater, vuurvreter.
fire-engine, brandspuit.
fire-escape, reddingstoestel; brandtrap.
fire-extinguisher, blustoestel.
fire-fly, vuurvlieg, glimwurm.
fire-insurance, brandassuransie.
fire-irons, vuur(h)erdysters, -stel.
fire-master, brandweerhoof.
fire-place, vuurmaakplek, vuur(h)erd, kaggel.
fire-plug, brandkraan.
fire-policy, brandpolis.
fire-proof, vuurvas, brandvry.
fire-screen, vuurskerm.
fireside, haard, vuurerd; hoekie van die haard.
fire-station, brandweerstasie.
fire-stone, vuurvaste (bak)steen.
firewood, vuurmaakhout, brandhout.
firework, vuurwerk.
firing, skietery, geskiet; uitbranding; vuurmaakgoed; sien **fire**, v.; – **squad (party)**, vuurpeloton.
firm, n. firma; (handels)naam.
firm, a. vas, hard, massief, stewig, heg; standvastig, vasberade, ferm; trou; **stand** –, vasstaan, pal staan; **op sy stukke staan**.
firm, v. vasstamp; styf word, hard word.
firmament, uitspansel, firmament.
firmness, vastheid, stewigheid, hegtheid; standvastigheid, vasberadenheid, fermheid.
first, a. eerste; vroegste; vernaamste; **at** – **sight**, op die eerste gesig; – **class ticket**, eersteklaskaartjie; – **hand**, uit die eerste hand; – **officer**, eerste stuurman; – **rate**, eersteklas-...; – **comer**, die eerste die beste; – **aid**, eerste hulp; – **cousin**, eie neef, volle neef.
first, n. die eerste; begin; **from the** –, van die begin af, uit die staanspoor uit; **from** – **to last**, van begin tot end; **at** –, eers, in die begin.
first, adv. eers, eerste; – **of all**, – **and foremost**, allereers, in die allereerste plek; – **come**, – **served**, wie die eerste kom, mag die eerste maal; **I would starve** –, ek gaan liewer dood van die honger.
first-born, eersgeborene.
firstling, eersteling.
firstly, eerstens, ten eerste, in die eerste plek.
firth, see-arm; riviermond.
fiscal, fiskaal.
fish, n. vis; **like a** – **out of water**, soos 'n vis op die droë, uit sy element; **neither**, – **flesh**, **nor good red herring**, (nog) vis nog vlees; **other** – **to fry**, iets anders in die oog; **a queer** –, 'n snaakse klant; **pretty kettle of** –, deurmekaarspul, lollery.
fish, v. vis, visvang; – **out**, opvis, uitvis; – **for**, vang; hengel na.
fish, n. & v. stut, las, klamp.
fish, n. pit, speelblokkie.
fish-bone, visgraat.
fish-carver, groot vismes.
fisherman, visser.
fishery, vissery.
fishing-boat, vissersboot, -skuit; visskuit.
fishing-line, vislyn.
fishing-net, visnet.
fishing-rod, visstok, hengelstok.
fishing-tackle, visgereedskap.
fishmonger, vishandelaar.
fish-pond, visvywer, visdam.
fishwife, visvrou, viswyf.
fishy, visryk; vis-...; verdag, twyfelagtig.
fissle, splitsbaar.
fission, splitsing; splyting (fis.).
fissure, bars, skeur; kloof, spleet; naat.
fist, n. vuis; poot; handskrif.

fist, v. slaan (met die vuis); vasvat.
fisticuffs, vuisslaan, vuisslanery, boks(ery).
fistula, fistel; (spuit)buis.
fit, n. toeval, skielike aanval; bui, nuk; **give one –**, iemand die skrik op die lyf ja; **by –s and starts**, met horte en stote.
fit, v. past; passend wees; passend maak; geskik maak; aanpas; **– on**, aanpas; aansit; geskik maak; **– out**, uitrus; **– together**, inmekaarsit, byeengevoeg; **–in with**, pas by, klop met.
fit, n. (die) pas, (die) sit; snit; **it is a good –**, dit pas (sit) goed.
fit, a. passend, gepas; geskik; in staat, bekwaam behoorlik; bruikbaar, dienstig; gesond; **think –**, goed dink; **– behaviour**, gepaste gedrag; **– to commit suicide**, bekwaam (in staat) om selfmoord te pleeg.
fitful, buierig, ongedurig, veranderlik.
fitly, passend, geskik, behoorlik.
fitness, gepastheid; geskiktheid.
fitter, uitruster; smid; passer; monteur; **– and turner**, monteur-draaier.
fitting, a. passend, gepas; aanpassend.
fitting, n. (die) pas, (die) aanpas, aansit; (sluit)stuk; **–s**, toebehore, benodigdhede.
five, vyf.
fivefold, vyfvoudig.
fiver, vyfpondnoot.
fix, v. vasmaak, -sit, -spyker, -heg; regmaak; reg kry; (be-)vestig; vasstel; beslis, keuse doen; styf word, dik word; fikseer; **– eyes (up)on**, oë vestig op; **– upon a day**, 'n dag vasstel; **– with one's eyes**, aanstaar, fikseer; **– up**, in orde bring, huisves.
fix, n. knyp, moeilikheid; **in a –**, in die knyp.
fixation, vasstelling; verdikking.
fixative, fikseermiddel.
fixed, vas; vasgestel(d); vasstaande; bepaald; **– idea**, idee fixe, vaste geloof.
fixedly, vas; strak; **gaze –**, strak kyk, staar.
fixings, toebehore, uitrusting; apparaat; garnering.
fixity, vastheid; onveranderlikheid.
fixture, (spyker)vaste voorwerp; vastigheid; (vasgestelde) datum; afspraak; wedstryd; **list of –s**, program (van voetbalwedstryde, ens.).
fizz, v. bruis, borrel; sis.
fizz, n. gebruis, geborrel; sjampie.
fizzle, v. sis, saggies bruis; **– out**, doodloop.
fizzle, n. gesis; mislukking.
flabbergast, dronkslaan, verbluf.
flabby, pap, papperig, slap, slapperig.
flaccid, pap, papperig, slap.
flaccidity, papheid, papperigheid, slapheid.
flag, n. vlag; **– of truce**, witvlag; **hoist the white –** die witvlag opsteek, oorgee; **lower, strike one's –**, die vlak stryk.
flag, v. vlag; afset (met vlae); sinjaleer, sein.
flag, n. swaardlelie; lis; **sweet –**, kalmus.
flag, n. plaveisteen; teël.
flag, v. plavei, uitlê.
flag, v. afhang, slap hang; verslap, verflou.
flagellate, gesel.
flagellation, geseling.
flageolet, flageolet, oktaaffluitjie.
flagon, flapkan, skinkkan; fles.
flagrancy, verregaandheid, skandelikheid.
flagrant, in die oog lopend; verregaand; flagrant.
flag-stone, plaveisteen.
flag-wagging, vlagswaaiery, ophitsery.
flail, dorsvleël, -stok.
flair, flair, aanleg; (goeie) neus.
flak, lugafweer(vuur).
flake, n. vlok; skilfertjie, stukkie; laag; gestreepte angelier.

flake, v. vlok; afskilfer.
flaky, vlokkig; skilferig.
flam, foppery, bedrog.
flambeau, flambou, fakkel, toorts.
flamboyant, gevlam, vlammend; opsigtig, swierig.
flame, n. vlam; hitte; vuur; **fan the –(s)**, die vuur aanwakker.
flame, v. vlam, brand; skitter, blink; **– forth, out, up**, op-, ontvlam; opvlieg; uitbars.
flamingo, flamink.
Flanders, Vlaandere.
flange, flens, rand (rant).
flank, n. flank, sy; kant, vleuel
flank, v. flankeer.
flannel, n. flanel; **—s**, flanel-onderklere; witbroek.
flannel, a. flanel- . . .
flannelette, n. flanelet.
flannelette, a. flanelet- . . .
flap, v. flap, klap, slaan, waai; opgewonde raak.
flap, m. flap, slag; klap; klep; slip; lelletjie; lappie; deksel; rant; opgewonde toestand.
flapdoodle, onsin, geklets, larie.
flapjack, plaatkoekie, (sak)poeierdosie.
flapper, vlieëplak; ratelaar; bakvissie.
flare, v. flikker, opvlam, gloei; **– up**, opvlam; opvlieg, uitbars; **–d dress (skirt)**, klokrok.
flare, n. flikkering, gloed; buiging, ronding; pronkery, vertoon fakkel; **– bomb**, fakkelbom; **– pistol**, fakkelpistool.
flare-up, opflikkering, opvlamming; uitbarsting; fuif.
flash, v. flikker, vonkel, skitter; glinster; opvlam; flits; **– in the pan**, doppie afklap; **his eyes –ed fire**, sy oë het vonke geskiet; **– past**, verby flits; **it –d upon me**, dit het my te binne geskiet.
flash, n. flikkering, flits, straal, skig; opsigtigheid; **a – in the pan**, 'n opflikkering; 'n fiasko **– of lightning**, blits, bliksemstraal; **– of hope**, flikkering van hoop; **in a –**, in 'n oogwenk, in 'n kits.
flash, a. windmakerig, opsigter; vals, nagemaak; onsedelik.
flash(ing)-point, ontbrandingspunt.
flash-light, skitterlig; blinkvuur; blitsig.
flashy, opsigtig, pronkerig, windmakerig.
flask, fles, veldfles; kruitbus, -horing.
flat, n. verdieping; verdiepinghuis, „flat."
flat, a. plat; gelyk; glad; eentonig; laf; reguit, onbewimpeld; **fall –**, plat val; misluk; **give a – denial**, beslis ontken; **that's –**, dis nie altemit nie, dis seker; **– beer**, verslaande bier; **with the – hand**, met die plat hand; **– race**, naelwedloop.
flat, v. platmaak.
flat, adv. plat; **sing –**, vals sing.
flat, n. platkant; gelykte; laagte; mol (musiek).
flat-bottomed, platboom- . . .
flat-footed, platvoet- . . .
flat-iron, strykyster.
flatly, plat; beslis, kortweg, botweg.
flatness, platheid; gelykheid; verveligheid.
flatten, platmaak; gelyk maak; plat word; gelyk word; verslaan; **– out**, plat maak (slaan); gelyk met die grond vlieg.
flatter, vlei, flikflooi; streel, flatteer.
flattery, vleiery, gevlei.
flattish, platterig.
flatulence, winderigheid; sooibrand; verwaandheid.
flatulent, opgeblaas, winderig; opgeblase, verwaand.
flaunt, spog (met); paradeer, vertoon; te koop loop (met); wapper, wuif.
flautist, fluitspeler.
flavour, n. geur; smaak; aroma.
flavour, v. krui; smaaklik maak; 'n geur gee.

flavouring, n. geursel, smakie.
flaw, n. bars, skeur; fout, gebrek.
flaw, v. bars, skeur; bederf.
flawless, foutloos, sonder gebreke; gaaf.
flax, vlas.
flaxen, vlas-..., van vlas, vlaskleurig, ligblond.
flay, afslag, afstroop, vel-aftrek; afskil; afkam.
flea, vlooi; a – in the ear, 'n afjak; 'n skrobbering.
flea-bite, vlooibyt; bakatel, kleinigheid.
fleam, vlym.
fleck, n. vlek; sproet; stippie, stippeltjie.
fleck, v. vlek; stippel.
flecked, gespikkel, gestippel.
flecker, stippel, vlek, bontmaak.
flection, sien flexion.
fledge, veer, beveer; begin vlie.
fledg(e)ling, jong voël; kuiken, snuiter.
flee, vlug; ontvlug, ontwyk; vermy.
fleece, n. vlies; vlag; skeersel; bossiekop.
fleecy, v. skeer; pluk, vel oor die ore trek.
fleecy, vliesagtig; – clouds, vlieswolkies.
fleer, spotlag, gryns.
fleet, n. vloot.
fleet, a. vlug, rats, geswind, vinnig.
fleet, v. vliet, vloei, heensnel.
fleeting, vlugtig, verbygaand; heenvloeiend; time is –, die tyd snel verby.
fleetingness, verbygaandheid, verganklikheid.
fleetness, vlugheid, ratsheid, vinnigheid.
Flemming, Vlaming.
Flemish, a. Vlaams.
Flemish, n. pl. (die) Vlaminge.
flench, flense, afslag; opsny.
flesh, n. vlees (vleis); – and blood, vlees en bloed; make his – creep, hoendervleis laat kry; lose –, maer word, afval; after the –, na(ar) die vlees; in the –, in lewende lywe; go the way of all –, die weg van alle vlees gaan.
flesh, v. bloed laat proe; prikkel, lusmaak; bloed laat drink.
flesh-colour(ed), vleeskleurig, vleeskleur-...
fleshy, vleeslik, sinlik.
flesh-wound, vleeswond.
fleshy, vlesig; dik, vet.
flex, v. buig.
flex, n. (elektriese) koord.
flexible, buigbaar; buigsaam, inskiklik.
flexion, flection, buiging; verbuiging; bog.
flexional, flectional, (ver)buigings-...
flexionless, flectionless, onverbuigbaar.
flexuous, kronkelend, bogtig.
flexure, buiging; kromming, bog.
flibbertigibbet, kekkelbek; floddermadam.
flick, tik; raps; klap.
flicker, v. flikker; fladder, wapper; tril.
flicker, n. geflikker; gefladder; trilling.
flier, vlieër; vliegenier; jaer; vlugteling.
flight, n. vlug; trek; vaart, loop; swerm; – of stairs, trap; – of steps, treetjies; – of time, loop van tyd; put to –, op die vlug jaag; take –, op die vlug gaan.
flight, v. in die vlug skiet.
flight-deck, vliegdek, landingsdek.
flighty, lighoofdig, lossinnig; wispelturig.
flimsy, a. dun; swak; flou.
flimsy, n. banknoot; kopieerpapier; kopie.
flinch, terugdeins; krimp; without –ing, sonder om te weifel; sonder om 'n spier te trek.
flinch, kyk flench.
fling, v. gooi, werp, slinger; vlieg, storm; — into prison, in die tronk gooi; — out of a room, 'n kamer uitstorm; – up heels, agteropskop; – into one's teeth, iemand voor die kop gooi; op – onseself into a person's arms, (sig) in iemand se arms werp; – to the ground, teen die grond gooi; afgooi.

fling, n. gooi; sprong; dans; have one's –, pret maak, die lewe geniet; have a – (at), 'n poging waag; 'n lopie neem (met); vir die gek hou.
flint, vuurklip.
flint-lock, vuurklipgeweer, flintroer.
flinty, kliphard; (vuur)klipagtig.
flip, n. skoot, raps; vliegtoggie.
flip, v. skiet, tik, raps.
flip-flap, buiteling, bolmakiesie; klapper.
flippancy, ligsinnigheid, onbesonnenheid.
flippant, ligsinnig, onverskillig, onbesonne.
flipper, poot; hand.
flirt, v. skiet; tik; fladder; koketteer, flirt.
flirt, n. wip, swaai, ruk; flirt; flirtery.
flirtation, geflirt, flirtery.
flit, v. sweef, fladder; swerf, trek.
flit, n. trek, verhuising.
flitch, syspek; skyf, stuk, mootjie.
flitter, fladder.
float, 'n dryfsel; vlot; dobber; blaas; vlotter, (in 'n tenk); vryfplank (van 'n messelaar).
float, v. drywe, swem, vlot, dobber; laat drywe; (maatskappy) oprig; op stapel sit; onder water sit; – a loan, 'n lening uitskryf.
floatage, opdryfsel; wrakgoed; dryfvermoë.
flo(a)tation, oprigting; uitgifte.
floating, dryf-..., drywend; vlottend; – debt, vlottende skuld; – dock, dryfdok; – population, vlottende bevolking.
flock, n. vlok, pluisie; –s, vlokwol.
flock, n. trop, swerm, skaar, kudde.
flock, v., – (together), bymekaarkom, saamstroom; – after, agternaloop; – in, instroom; – to, toestroom (na).
floe, ysskots.
flog, slaan, klop, uitstof; verkoop; – a dead horse, tevergeefse werk verrig.
flogging, pak (slae), afranseling, loesing.
flood, n. vloed; stroom; oorstroming; sondvloed; stortvloed.
flood, v. oorstroom; onder water sit; nat lei; laat oorloop; vloei.
flood-light, spreilig.
flood-tide, hoogwater, vloed.
floor, n. vloer, bodem; verdieping; take the –, uitstaan; die woord voer; ground –, onderste verdieping; – show, kabaret.
floor, v. vloer insit, bevloer; omgooi, platslaan; dronkslaan.
floorer, uitklophou.
flooring, vloer; vloerplanke; bevloering.
flop, v. swaai, slinger; plof; – down, neerplof.
flop, n. bons, plof, klap; mislukking, misoes.
floppy, slap pap(perig).
flora, flora, plante(wêreld).
floral, blom(me-)-..., plante-... ; – zone, plant(e)gordel.
Florentine, Florentyns.
florescence, bloei; bloeityd, opbloeiing.
floret, blommetjie.
floriculture, blom(me)-, blomkwekery.
florid, bloemryk; opsigtig; blosend, hoogrooi.
floridness, bloemrykheid; swierigheid; hoogrooi kleur.
florin, tweesjielingstuk; gulde(n); floryn.
florist, bloemis; blomkweker; blomkenner.
floss, vloksy; dons.
floss-silk, vloksy.
flossy, vlossig; donserig.
flotation, sien floatation.
flotilla, flottielje.
flotsam, wrakhout, opspoelsel; oesterkuit.
flounce, v. strompel, plof, struikel.

flounce, n. ruk, swaai, plof.
flounce, n. strook, belegsel, opnaaisel.
flounder, strompel, ploeter; sukkel, knoei.
flour, meelblom, fynmeel.
flourish, v. floreer, tier, welig groei; leef; spog (met); wuif, swaai met.
flourish, n. versiersel; stylblo(e)m; sierletter; swaai; geskal; – of trumpets, trompetgeskal.
floury, melerig; vol meel.
flout, v. hoon, met veragting behandel; – at, beskimp.
flout, n. spot, skimp.
flow, v. vloei; stroom; golf; ebb and –, daal en styg; – from, voortvloei uit; – over, oorloop, oorvloei.
flow, n. stroom; vloed; golwing; oorstroming; ebb and –, eb en vloed.
flower, n. blom (bloem); bloei; fleur; bloeisel; –s of sulpher, blo(e)m van swa(w)el; the – of life, die fleur van die lewe; in –, in bloei; the – of the nation, die keur van die nasie.
flower, v. bloei, blom.
flower-bed, blombedding, -akkertjie.
flowered, geblom.
flower-girl, strooimeisie; blommeverkoopster.
flower-show, blommetentoonstelling.
flowery, blo(e)mryk; blom- . . .
flowing, vloeiend; stromend; lopend; golwend.
flu, griep, influensa.
fluctuate, skommel; wissel; –ing prices, skommelende pryse.
fluctuation, skommeling; wisseling.
flue, dons, pluisies.
flue, skoorsteenpyp; lugkoker; windpyp.
fluency, vloeiendheid, vlotheid; vaardigheid; welbespraaktheid.
fluent, vloeiend;.vlot; vaardig; welbespraak.
fluff, dons, pluisie, vlokkie.
fluffy, donserig, dons- . . .
fluid, a. vloeibaar; beweeglik.
fluid, n. vloeistof; fluïdum.
fluidity, vloeibaarheid.
fluke, n. ankerblad; visstert; stertpunt; punt (van lans, harpoen, ens.).
fluke, n. gelukskoot.
fluke, v. geluk hê, gelukskoot skiet.
fluky, gelukkig, geluk- . . .
flummery, pap; komplimentjies, praatjies.
flummox, dronkslaan, uit die veld slaan.
flunkey, lakei; kruiper, lekker, kalfakter.
flunkeyism, kruipery, lekkery; kalfakterdom.
fluor, vloeispaat; fluor.
fluorescence, fluoressensie.
flurried, gehaas, gejaag; verbouereerd.
flurry, n. windvlaag; gejaagdheid.
flurry, v. aanjaag, verbouereerd maak.
flush, v. uitborrel, uitspuit; deurspoel; onder water sit; gloei; bloos; die bloed na die wange jaag; aanmoedig; –ed with victory, in die roes van die oorwinning; –ed with wine, deur wyn verhit; aangeskote.
flush, n. stroom, golf; deurspoeling; toevloed; roes, blydskap; opslag; gloed; blos.
flush, a. vol, boorde(nste)vol; goed voorsien, goed by kas; gelyk.
fluster, v. deurmekaar maak, in die war bring; dronk maak; woel; ongedurig wees.
fluster, n. gejaagdheid, woeligheid; agitasie.
flute, n. fluit; fluitspeler; groef(ie).
flute, v. fluitspeel; groewe maak, groef.
fluted, gegroef.
flutter, v. fladder; beef, tril; onduidelik klop (van die pols); swaai; verbouereerd maak, opwind.
flutter, n. gefladder; gejaagdheid, bewerasie.

fluvial, rivier- . . .
flux, n. vloeiing; vloed; bloedstorting; buikloop, wisseling; state of –, toestand van onvastheid.
flux, v. vloei; vloeibaar maak, smelt.
fluxion, vloeiing; verandering; fluksie; method of –s, differensiaalrekening.
fluxional, veranderlik; ongestadig; differensiaal.
fly, n. vlieg; – in the ointment, vlieg in die salf.
fly, v. vlie(g); vlug; waai, wapper; (vlag) laat waai, voer; — at, invlieg; op ols gaan; – into a passion, opstuif; – out, uitvlieg, losbars; make sparks –, die vonke laat vlieg; –ing visit, vlugtige besoek; send –ing, wegboender; let –, aftrek, lostrek; let – at, losbrand op; – off, wegvlieg; wegsnel; – the red flag, die rooi vlag voer; – the garter, hasie-oor spring; – the country, uit die land vlug; – danger, gevaar ontvlug; – in the face of, aanvlieg, te velde trek teen, (sig) teenworstel.
fly, n. vliegafstand; sprong; ligte karretjie; gulp; tentklep; vlagsoom; onrus (van 'n horlosie); vliegwiel.
fly, a. oulik, oorlams, geslepe.
fly-bane, vlieëbos.
fly-blown, bederf (bedorwe), vol maaiers.
fly-catcher, vlieëvanger.
flyer, sien flier.
fly-half, losskakel.
flying, n. (die) vlieg; vlieëry; vliegkuns; – deck, vliegdek; – operations, lugoperasies; – range, vlieglengte.
flying, a. vlieënd, vliegend; – bedstead, vlieënde katel; – box-car, transportvliegtuig; with – colours, met vlieënde vaandel; the F– Dutchman, die Vliegende Hollander; – saucer, vlieende piering; – squad, blitspatrollie; – start, aanloopwegspring, sterk voorsprong; – jump, sprong met aanloop.
flying-fish, vliegende vis.
flying-fox, vliegende hond; kalong.
flying-stunt, kunsvlug.
fly-leaf, skutblad.
flyman, koetsier; vliegwerker (in 'n skouburg).
fly-nut, vlerkskroef, vlerkmoer.
fly-over; – bridge, lugbrug, kruisbrug.
fly-paper, vlieëpapier.
fly-wheel, vliegwiel; onrus (van 'n horlosie).
foal, n. vul(letjie).
foal, v. vul.
foam, skuim; – at the mouth, skuimbek.
foamy, skuimend, vol skuim.
fob, n. horlosiesakkie.
fob, v. fop; – off upon, afsmeer aan.
focal, brandpunt- . . . , – length, brandpuntsafstand.
focalize, op een punt saamtrek.
fo'c'sle, sien forecastle.
focus, n. brandpunt, focus (fokus).
focus, v. instel; op een punt saamtrek.
fodder, voer.
foe, vyand.
foeman, vyand.
foetus, foetus (fetus), (ongebore) vrug.
fog, n. mis, newel; be in a –, benewel wees.
fog, v. mis; mistig maak; in die war maak, benewel.
fog-bank, misbank.
fog-bound, in die. mis gevang, vasgemis.
fogey, sien fogy.
foggy, mistig, newelagtig; vaag; beneweld.
fog-horn, mishoring.
fog(e)y; old –, ou-paai, verroeste kêrel.
foible, swak, swakheid; punt (van 'n swaard).
foil, n. blad; bladmetaal, foelie; teenstelling.
foil, v. (ver)foelie; afsit, uitbring.

foil, n. skermsabel, floret.
foil, v. van die spoor lei; uitoorlê; verydel.
foist, v.: – (up)on one, op iemand afskuiwe, iemand aansmeer.
fold, v. vou; – **in**, invou; insluit; omhels; – **together**, op-, saamvou; – **up**, opvou; – **arms**, arms oormekaarvou.
fold, n. vou; plooi; hoek.
fold, n. kraal; hok; kudde.
folder, vouer; voubeen; -s, lorgnet (lornjet).
folding-chair, voustoel.
folding-door, portfisiedeur, oopslaande deur.
folding-table, klaptafel.
foliaceous, bladvormig; blaar- . . . ; blad- . . .
foliage, blare, loof, gebladerte.
foliate, a. blaaragtig; blaar- . . . ; blarig.
foliate, v. blaar, skilfer, blare vorm; folieer.
folio, folio; foliant.
folk, mense; **old** –(s), oumense; **young** –(s), jongspan.
folk-lore, volkskunde.
folk-song, volksliedjie.
follicle, saadhuisie; blasie, follikel.
follow, volg, na-, opvolg; aanhang; – **the plough**, agter die ploeg loop, boer wees; – **a profession**, 'n bedryf uitoefen; – **the sea**, matroos wees; – **on**, aanhou; weer aan die beurt kom; – **out**, opvolg, uitvoer; voortsit; – **up**, navolg; laat volg op; ondersteun; agternasit; nabehandel volg (spoor).
follower, volgeling, aanhanger.
following, a. volgende; navolgende, onderstaande.
following, n. volgelinge, aanhang, gevolg.
folly, dwaasheid, gekheid, stommiteit.
foment, baai, pap, aankweek, aanstook.
fomentation, fomentasie; pappe, warm doeke; aanstoking, aankweking.
fond, dwaas, gek; verlief; liefhebbend; **be** – **of**, gek wees na, hou van, liefhê; –**est desire**, liefste wens; – **parents**, liefhebbende ouers.
fondant, fondant.
fondle, troetel, liefkoos, streel.
fondly, dwaas(lik); innig, vurig; liefderyk.
fondness, liefde, geneentheid; versotheid (op).
font, doopbakkie; wywaterbakkie; oliebakkie.
food, voedsel, spys, ete, kos; stof; – **for thought**, stof tot nadenking.
foodstuffs, eetware, eetgoed.
fool, n. dwaas, gek, sot, nar, idioot; **be a** – **to**, gek wees om; **play the** –, soos 'n dwaas aanstel; gekskeer; vir die gek hou; **make a** – **of**, vir die gek hou; **make a** – **of oneself**, jouself belaglik maak; **send on a** – **'s errand**, vir gek laat loop; **–'s paradise**, denkbeeldige hemel.
fool, v. gekheid maak; vir die gek hou; bedrieg, fop; – **away**, verbeusel.
fool, n. stoofvrugte, vla.
foolery, gekkerny; dwaasheid, gekheid.
foolhardy, onverskillig, roekeloos, waaghalsig.
foolish, dwaas, gek; dom, stom; stuitig.
foolishness, dwaasheid; stommiteit; stuitigheid.
fool-proof, bedryfseker, onverknoeibaar, onvernielbaar; **he is** –, hy laat hom niks wys maak nie.
foolscap, sots-, narrekap; folio(papier).
foot, n. voet; voetvolk, infanterie; onderent, voetenent; **swift of** –, vlug ter been, rats; **carry one off one's feet**, iemand se voete onder hom uitslaan; **be on one's feet**, op jou bene staan; **fall on one's feet**, op sy voete teregkom; **keep one's feet**, op die been bly; **put one's** – **down**, deurtas, 'n besliste houding inneem, sê waar dit op staan; **put one's** – **into it**, daar inloop, 'n flater begaan; **on** –, te voet; aan die gang; **set on** –, aan die gang sit, oprig; **tread under** –, met die voete vertrap; **put one's best** – **foremost**, sy beste beentjie voorsit.
foot, v. nuwe voet aanbrei, versool; – **it**, voetslaan, stap; skoffel, dans; – **the bill**, opdok.
foot-and-mouth (disease), mond-(bek-)en-klouseer.
football, voetbal.
footballer, voetbalspeler.
football match, voetbalwedstryd.
foot-board, voetplank, treeplank.
foot-boy, page; livreikneggie.
footfall, geluid van voetstappe; stapgeluid.
foot-fault, trapfout.
foothold, staanplek, vastrapplek.
footing, staanplek, vastrapplek; voet; voetstuk; **on an equal** –, op gelyke voet; **miss one** –**s**, mistrap.
footle, v. gekskeer, ligsinnig wees.
footle, n. dwaasheid, gekheid, onsin.
footlights, voetlig.
footman, livreikneg, lakei, huiskneg.
foot-mark, (voet)spoor.
foot-note, noot, aantekening, verwysing.
footpad, struikrower.
foot-plate, treeplank, voetplank, -bord.
foot-pound, voetpond.
footprint, (voet)spoor.
foot-rule, duimstok.
footsore, deurgeloop, seervoet.
footstep, voetstap; (voet)spoor.
footstool, voetbankie, stofie.
footwear, skoene, skoenwerk, skoeisel.
foozle, verbrou, verknoei.
fop, fat, modegek.
foppery, fatterigheid, opskik.
foppish, fatterig, windmakerig.
for, prep. vir; om; in plaas van; gedurende, once – **all**, eens vir altyd; – **example**, byvoorbeeld; – **his pains**, vir sy moeite; – **segregation**, ten gunste van segregasie; **they went** – **a walk**, hulle het 'n entjie gaan loop ('n wandeling gaan doen); – **her good**, om haar beswil; – **sale**, te koop; **send** – **the doctor**, stuur om die dokter; **die dokter laat haal**; – **nothing**, verniet; vir niks; **tevergeefs**; **not** – **the world**, vir niks ter wêreld nie; **pay** –, (daarvoor) betaal; **not** – **the life of me**, al slaan jy my dood; **leave** – **England**, na Engeland vertrek; **make** – **shelter**, skuiling soek; **go** – **him**, hom inklim; **it is getting on** – **two o'clock**, dit gaan twee-uur se kant toe; **care** –, omgee vir, hou van; sorg vir, kyk na; **long** –, verlang na; **fit** –, geskik (bekwaam) vir; **ready** –, klaar vir; klaar om te; **oh** – **wings**, o, as ek tog vlerke gehad het; **enough** –, genoeg om te; genoeg vir; **time** – **school**, tyd om skool toe te gaan; **time** – **the bell**, tyd om die klok te lui, tyd dat die klok lui; **there is nothing** – **it but**, daar staan niks anders op nie as; **it is** – **you to**, dit lê aan jou om; – **certain**, gewis, wis en seker; **mistook him** – **you**, hom vir jou aangesien; **shot** – **treason**, weens verraad doodgeskiet; **I** – **one**, ek vir my; – **fear of accidents**, uit vrees vir ongelukke; **notorious** – **his parsimony**, berug weens sy suinigheid; – **my sake**, om my ontwil; – **goodness' sake**, in hemelsnaam! – **shame**, skande!; skaam jou!; – **all you say**, ondanks alles wat jy sê; **were it not** –, **but** –, except – him, as dit nie vir hom was nie; **eye** – **eye**, oog om oog; **word** – **word**, woord vir woord; – **the rest**, vir die res, wat die res betref; – **my part**, wat my betref; – **all I know**, (vir) sover ek weet; – **months**, maandelank; – **long**, lank; – **two miles**, twee myl (ver); – **life**, lewenslank, vir sy lewe;

– **the present,** voorlopig, vir die teenswoordige; – **once,** (tog) een keer; – **all the world;** presies, net; – **God's sake,** om Gods wil; – **convenience' sake,** gemakshalwe; – **want of,** by gebrek aan; – **joy,** van blydskap.
for, conj. want, omdat, aangesien, omrede.
forage, n. voer.
forage, v. plunder, roof; snuffel; van voedsel voorsien.
forasmuch as, aangesien, nademaal.
foray, inval.
forbear, v. afsien van, nalaat, (sig) onthou van, stilbly; verdra.
forbearance, verdraagsaamheid; onthouding.
forbid, belet, verbied; **God –,** mag die Here dit verhoed!; – **the banns,** die gebooie stop.
forbidding, terugstotend, afskrikkend.
force, n. krag, mag; geweld; dwang; **–s,** kragte; strydmag(te); **in –,** in werking, van krag; in groot getal; **put into –,** van krag maak, in werking stel; **come into –,** in werking tree, van krag word; **by –,** met geweld; **by – of,** deur middel van, met behulp van; **by – of habit,** uit gewoonte; – **of circumstances,** dwang van omstandighede; **in great –,** in groot getalle; op sy stukke.
force, v. dwing, noodsaak; afdwing; geweld aandoen; verkrag; vermeester; oopbreek; – **one's hand,** iemand dwing; – **the pace,** die pas versnel; – **a smile,** gedwonge glimlag; **'n glimlag afdwing;** – **upon,** afdwing op; – **one's way,** jou weg (met geweld) baan; – **down,** afforseer; met geweld ingee (insluk).
forced, gedwonge; gesog, onnatuurlik, gemaak.
forceful, kragtig, gespierd.
forceps, tang.
force-pump, perspomp.
forcible, gewelddadig, kragdadig; pakkend.
forcibly, met geweld; op indrukwekkende manier.
ford, n. drif.
ford, v. deurwaad, deurgaan, oorgaan.
fore, a. voor- . . .
fore, n. voorpunt; boeg; voorgrond; **to the –,** byderhand; op die voorgrond.
fore, adv. voor; by; –!, pas op voor!
forebear, n. voorvader, voorsaat.
forbode, voorspel; 'n voorgevoel hê.
foreboding, voorspelling; voorgevoel.
forecast, v. voorspel; beraam.
forecast, n. voorspelling; beraming.
forecastle, fo'c'sle, bak, voorender.
fore-court, voorhof, voorplein, ingang.
fore-father, voorvader.
fore-finger, voorvinger, wysvinger.
fore-front, front, voorste gelid, voorhoede.
foregoing, voor(af)gaande.
foregone: – **conclusion,** uitgemaakte saak.
foreground, voorgrond.
forehand, n. voorhand, voorlyf (van 'n perd).
forehand, a. voorarm- . . . , – **play,** voorarmspel.
forehead, voorkop, voorhoof.
foreign, vreemd; buitelands, uitheems; – **office,** ministerie van buitelandse sake; – **parts,** vreemde lande.
foreigner, vreemde(ling), buitelander, uitlander.
foreknowledge, voorkennis; voorwetenskap.
foreland, landpunt, -tong; voorland.
forelock, voorste hare, kuif; **take time by the –,** die kans waarneem.
foreman, voorman; voorsitter (van die jurie).
foremast, voormas, fokmas.
foremost, voorste; mees vooraanstaande; **first and –,** in die allereerste plek.
forenoon, voormiddag.

forensic, geregtelik; – **medicine,** geregtelike geneeskunde.
fore-ordain, voorbestem, voorbeskik.
forepart, voorste gedeelte, voorstuk; voorstewe.
fore-run, voorafgaan, voorspel.
fore-runner, voorloper, voorbode, vóórspel.
foresee, voorsien, vooruit sien.
foreshadow, (voor)spel, die voorbode wees van.
foreshore, strand.
foreshorten, verkort; in perspektief teken.
foreshow, voorspel.
foresight, vooruitsiendheid; oorleg; voorvisier.
foreskin, voorhuid.
forest, woud, bos.
forestall, voorspring; voorkom; – **one's wishes,** iemand se wense voorkom.
forester, boswagter; houtvester; bosbewoner.
forestry, bosbou; bosboukunde; houtvestery.
foretaste, voorsmaak.
foretell, voorspel, voorsê, profeteer.
forethought, voorsorg, oorleg; voorbedagtheid.
forewarn, vooruit waarsku; **-ed is forearmed,** voorkennis maak voorsorg.
foreword, voorwoord, inleiding.
forfeit, n. pand; boete; verbeuring; **play –s,** pandspeel.
forfeit, v. verbeur, inboet; verbeurd verklaar.
forfeiture, verbeurling; verbeurdverklaring.
forfend, verhoed.
for(e)gather, vergader.
forge, n. smidswinkel; smidsvuurerd.
forge, v. smee(d); versin, bedink; namaak.
forge, v. (sig) vooruitwerk.
forger, vervalser; versinner, smeder.
forgery, vervalsing; vals handtekening; namaak; vervalste dokument.
forget, vergeet; – **oneself,** sy besinning verloor.
forgetful, vergeetagtig; **be – of,** vergeet.
forgetfulness, vergeetagtigheid, vegetelheid.
forget-me-not, vergeet-my-nietjie.
forgivable, vergeeflik.
forgive, vergewe, kwytskeld.
forgiveness, vergifinis; kwytskelding.
forgiving, vergewensgesind.
forgo, afsien van, (sig) ontsê, afstand doen van.
fork, n. vurk; gaffel; mik; **tuning –,** stemvurk.
fork, v. op die vurk neem; splits, vertak; – **out,** oorgee; opdok; opdiep.
forked, gesplits; mikvormig.
forlorn, verlate, verlore; hopeloos; moedverlore; – **hope,** gevaarlike onderneming; stormparty.
form, n. vorm, gedaante, fatsoen; orde; formaliteit; formulier; bank; klas; kondisie; – **and content,** vorm en inhoud; **sixth –,** sesde klas; **in due –,** in behoorlike orde; **fill in a –,** 'n formulier (vorm) invul; **good –,** goeie maniere, fatsoen; **in bad –,** ongemanierd, nie soos dit hoort nie; **out of –,** van stryk af; **in great –,** goed op stryk; opgewek; **a matter or –,** 'n blote formaliteit.
form, v. vorm; maak; set; kweek; oprig, stig; in gelid stel, rangskik.
formal, vormlik; formeel; uitdruklik.
formalism, formalisme, vormdiens.
formalist, formalis, vormdienaar.
formality, formaliteit, vormlikheid.
formation, vorming, formasie; oprigting.
formative, vormend, vorm- . . .
former, a. vroeër, vorige, gewese, voormalige.
former, pron. eerste, eersgenoemde.
formerly, vroeër, vanmelewe.
formic, miere- . . . ; – **acid,** mieresuur.
formidable, gedug; ontsagwekkend, formidabel.
formless, vormloos.
formula, formule; voorskrif, resep.

formulary, n. formulierboek.
formulate, formuleer, onder woorde bring.
fornicate, hoereer, boeleer, ontug pleeg.
fornication, hoerery, ontug.
fornicator, hoereerder, ontugtige.
forsake, verlaat, in die steek laat; versaak.
forsooth, warempel, sowaar; kastig.
forswear, afsweer; – **oneself**, vals sweer.
fort, fort, skans, vesting.
forte, sterkte, „fort."
forth, voort; vooruit; uit; voortaan; voorts, verder; **back and** –, heen en weer, vooruit en agteruit; **from this time** –, van nou af, voortaan; **and so** –, en so voorts; **bring** –, voortbring; te voorskyn bring; **come** –, uitkom, te voorskyn kom.
forthcoming, naderende, aanstaande; **be** –, voorhande wees.
forthright, reguit; meteens.
forthwith, onverwyld, op staande voet, meteens.
fortieth, veertigste.
fortification, versterking; verskansing; fortifikasie.
fortify, versterk; fortifiseer; aanmoedig.
fortitude, lewensmoed; vasberadenheid.
fortnight, veertien dae; **today** –, vandag oor veertien dae.
fortnightly, elke veertien dae; tweeweekliks.
fortress, fort, vesting, bolwerk.
fortuitous, toevallig.
fortunity, toeval; toevalligheid.
fortunate, gelukkig, voorspoedig; gunstig.
fortunately, gelukkig.
fortune, n. geluk, fortuin; kans; lot, voorspoed; vermoë, rykdom; **try one's** –, 'n kans waag; **tell one's** –, sy toekoms voorspel; **make a** –, 'n fortuin maak; **marry a** –, 'n ryk huwelik doen; – **favoured me**, die geluk het my gedien; **it was my good** –, ek het die geluk gehad.
fortune-hunter, geluksoeker.
fortune-teller, waarsêer (-segster).
fortune-telling, waarsêery, voorspellery.
forty, veertig; – **winks**, 'n dutjie.
forum, forum; markplaas; regsbank.
forward, a. voorste; voorwaartse; gevorderd; modern; vroegryp; voorbarig; vrypostig, **a – movement**, 'n voorwaartse beweging; – **behaviour**, vrypostige gedrag; **a – child**, 'n oulike kind; 'n vrypostige kind.
forward, n. voorspeler.
forward(s), adv. vooruit, (na) vorentoe, voorwaarts; **look** –, vooruit kyk; **come** –, na vore kom; **pass** –, vorentoe aangee; **from this day** –, van vandag af (aan); **put** –, aan die hand gee.
forward, v. bevorder; bespoedig; aanstuur.
forwarder, afsender; bevorderaar.
forwarding, versending; bevordering; – **agent**, versender.
forwardness, vrypostigheid; voorbarigheid; vroegtydigheid.
forwards, sien **forward**.
fosse, sloot.
fossil, a. versteen, fossiel.
fossil, n. verstening, fossiel.
fossilize, versteen; laat versteen.
foster, voed, kweek, koester, bevorder.
foster-brother, pleeg-, soogbroer.
foster-child, pleegkind, aangenome kind.
foster-daughter, pleegdogter, aangenome dogter.
foster-father, pleegvader.
fosterling, pleegkind, beskermling.
foster-mother, pleegmoeder.
foster-sister, pleegsuster.
foster-son, pleegsoon, aangenome seun.
foul, a. vuil, smerig; troebel; gemeen, vals,
skandelik, snood; onklaar; – **language**, vuil taal; – **air**, slegte lug; – **deed**, gemene daad; – – **play**, vuil spel; – **weather**, vuil weer; – **means**, ongeoorloofde middele.
foul, n. vuilspel; **commit a** –, vuil(spel) speel.
foul, adv. vuil; **play** –, vuil(spel) speel, kurang speel.
foul, v. vuil word; vuil maak; besmeer, onteer, onklaar maak; bots met.
foulard, foulard.
foully, op lae (gemene, snode, valse) manier.
foul-mouthed, vuilbekkig.
foulness, vuilheid, smerigheid; snoodheid; valsheid, gemeenheid.
found, grondves, stig, oprig; – **(up)on**, baseer op; laat rus op, grond op.
found, giet; smelt.
foundation, fondament, grondslag; stigting, **the report has no** –, die berig is ongegrond; – **garment**, vormkledingstuk; – **garments**, vormdrag.
foundation-stone, hoeksteen.
founder, n. stigter, oprigter, grondlêer.
founder, n. metaalgieter.
founder, v. vergaan; misluk; inmekaarsak; val; bly steek.
foundling, vondeling.
foundry, (metaal)gietery.
fount, bron(aar), wel, fontein; oorsprong.
fount, font, stel drukletters.
fountain, bron, (spring)fontein, oorsprong.
fountain-head, bron, oorsprong.
fountain-pen, vulpen.
four, vier; **go on all –s**, hande-(en)-viervoetloop: **be on all –s with**, klop met.
fourfold, viervoudig, vierdubbel.
four-footed, viervoetig.
four-in-hand, vierspan; **drive** –, met vier perde ry.
four-poster, ledekant (met vier style).
four-o'clock, vieruur; vieruurtjie.
fourscore, tag(gen)tig.
four-square, vierkant; rotsvas.
four-stroke, vierslag (motor).
fourteen, veertien.
fourteenth, veertiende.
fourth, vierde.
fourthly, in die vierde plek, vierdens.
four-whee(ler), vierwielrytuig.
fowl, n. voël, wildevoël; hoender.
fowl, v. voëls jag.
fowler, voëlvanger, -jagter.
fowling-piece, haelgeweer, voëlroer.
fowl-run, hoenderhok; -kamp.
fox, n. vos, jakkals; **set the** – **to keep the geese**, (van) wolf skaapwagter maak.
fox, v. skelmspeel, sy lyf jakkals hou; vlek.
foxglove, vingerhoedjie(s).
foxhound, jakkalshond.
fox-hunt, jakkals-, vossejag.
fox-terrier, foksterriër.
fox-trot, jakkalsdraf.
fox, jakkals- . . . ; slim, oulik, slu; rooibruin; vlekkerig; roesterig.
fracas, lawaai, rusie, bakleiery.
fraction, onderdeel, deeltjie; breuk; **vulgar** –, gewone breuk; **decimal** –, tiendelige breuk; **proper**, **improper** –, gebruiklike, ongebruiklike breuk; **simple**, **compound**, –, eenvoudige, saamgestelde breuk; **recurring (repeating)** –, repeterende breuk.
fractional, breuk- . . . ; – **part**, onderdeel.
fractious, weerspannig, twissiek.
fracture, n. breuk.
fracture, v. breek, bars.
fragile, teer, broos, swak; breekbaar.

fragility 502 **frigid**

fragility, teerheid, broosheid; breekbaarheid.
fragment, stuk, deel, fragment.
fragmentary, onvolledig, fragmentaries.
fragrance, -cy, geur, geurigheid.
fragrant, geurig, welriekend, lekkerruik- . . .
frail, n. (riet)mandjie.
frail, a. teer, tenger; swak; verganklik.
frailty, teerheid, broosheid, swakheid; swak.
frame, v. omlys, raam; ontwerp; vorm, skik; – **well**, veel belowe; vals beskuldig.
frame, n. lys, raam(werk); kosyn; gestel; inrigting, samestel; ontwerp; (gemoed)-stemming.
framer, ontwerper, opsteller; vervaardiger.
frame-saw, spansaag.
frame-up, valse beskuldiging.
framework, raam(werk), geraamte; opset.
franc, frank.
France, Frankryk.
franchise, stemreg; burgerreg; vrystelling.
frank, a. openhartig, eerlik, reguit.
frank, v. frankeer; portvry teken.
frankfurter, frankfortse wors.
frankincense, wierook.
frankness, openhartigheid, opregtheid.
frantic, wild, woes, rasend, waansinnig.
fraternal, broederlik.
fraternity, broederskap; gilde, gemeenskap.
fraternize, verbroeder; aanklamp.
fratricidal, broedermoordenaars- . . .
fratricide, broedermoord; broedermoordenaar.
fraud, bedrog; bedrieër; niksbeduiende persoon.
fraudulence, -cy, bedrog; bedrieglikheid.
fraudulent, bedrieglik.
fraudulenty, op bedrieglike wyse.
fraught, belaai (belade); – **with**, verbonde met; – **with danger**, gevaarvol.
fray, n. geveg, stryd; **eager for the –**, strydlustig.
fray, v. (uit)rafel, (ver)slyt.
freak, gier gril; wispelturigheid; – **of nature**, speling van die natuur.
freaked, bont gevlek.
freakish, grillig, vol giere, wispelturig.
freckle, n. sproet, vlek.
freckle, v. sproete gee; vol sproete word.
freckled, vol sproete, sproeterig; gespikkel.
free, a. vry; los, ongedwonge; vrypostig; kosteloos, verniet; gul, vrygewig; – **fight**, algemene vegparty; – **entrance**, vry toegang; – **translation**, vry(e)vertaling; – **and easy**, gemaklik in die omgang; **make – with**, vryhede neem met, op 'n ongeoorloofde manier gebruik; **it is – for him to do so**, dit staat hom vry om dit te doen.
free, v. vrymaak; bevry; losmaak;˙verlos.
freebooter, vrybuiter.
freebooting, vrybuitery.
freedom, vryheid; gemak; vrypostigheid; burgerskap.
freehand: draw –, uit die vrye hand teken.
freehanded, vrygewig, rojaal.
freehold, vry erfpag.
free-lance, onafhanklike joernalis (skrywer, ens.).
freely, vry, ope(nlik); geredelik; mildelik; erg.
freeman, vryburger.
freemason, vrymesselaar.
freeness, vrymoedigheid; vrypostigheid; vrygewigheid; openhartigheid.
freesia, kammetjié, aandblom, freesia.
freestone, sandklip; lospit.
free-thinker, vrydenker.
free-trade, vryhandel.
free-trader, vryhandelaar.
free-wheel, vrywiel.

freeze, v. vries; verkluim; ryp; (laat) bevries; **be freezing**, verkluim; – **one's blood**, jou bloed laat stol; – **prices**, pryse stabiliseer.
freeze, n. vors; ryp.
freezing, vries- . . . ; yskoud.
freezing-point, vriespunt.
freight, n. vrag, lading; vraggeld.
freight, v. bevrag, laai; ('n skip) huur.
freighter, versender; vragskip; vragvliegtuig.
French, a. Frans; **take – leave**, met die noordeson vertrek; **op die houtjie handel**; – **bean**, snyboontjie; – **window**, glasdeur(e).
French, n. Frans; **the –**, die Franse.
Frenchman, Fransman.
frenzied, waansinnig, rasend, dol.
frenzy, waansin, dolheid, raserny.
frequency, herhaling; veelvuldigheid; frekwensie; – **modulation**, frekwensiemodulasie.
frequent, a. herhaald; veelvuldig.
frequent, v. dikwels besoek, (daar) boer.
frequentation, (veelvuldige) besoek.
frequentative, a. herhalend, frekwentatief.
frequentative, n. frekwentatief.
frequented, besog.
frequenter, besoeker.
frequently, dikwels, herhaaldelik, baiemaal.
fresco, fresko(skildering).
fresh, a. fris; vars, nuut; parmantig; – **vegetables**, vars groente; – **water**, vars water; soetwater; – **arrival**, nuwe aankomeling; – **start**, nuwe poging (begin).
freshen, op-, verfris; ververs; opsteek (van wind).
fresher, groentjie, nuweling.
freshet, stroom; vloedwater, oorstroming.
freshly, onlangs, pas; opnuut.
freshmen, groentjie, nuweling.
freshness, frisheid; varsheid; oorspronklikheid.
fret, v. uitsaag; versier; ruit, skakeer.
fret, n. saagwerk; (Griekse) rand.
fret, v. vererg, prikkel; knies, (sig) bekommer; in-, wegvreet, knaag aan.
fret, n. ergernis, geprikkeldheid; kniesery; **be in a –**, geprikkel(d) wees.
fret, n. toetsbord.
fretful, brommig, lastig, prikkelbaar.
fret-saw, snysaag, figuursaag.
fretwork, saagwerk; snywerk.
friable, bros.
friar, monnik.
fribble, speel, ligsinnig wees.
fricassee, fricassee; fyn stoofvleis.
fricative, a. frikatief, skurend.
fricative, n. vryfklank, frikatief.
friction, wrywing, friksie.
frictional, wrywings- . . .
frictionless, sonder wrywing; glad.
Friday, Vrydag; **Good –**, Goeie Vrydag.
friend, vriend(in); **make –s with**, kennis maak; vriendskap sluit met; maats maak; **a – in need is a – in deed**, in die nood leer mens sy vriende ken.
friendless, sonder vriende, vriendeloos.
friendly, vriendelik; vriendskaplik.
friendship, vriendskap; vriendskaplikheid.
frieze, fries.
frigate, fregat; fregatvoël.
fright, skrik; voëlverskrikker; **take – at**, skrik vir.
frighten, skrikmaak, bangmaak; – **away**, afskrik, wegja, op die loop ja.
frightened, verskrik, bang.
frightful, verskriklik, vreeslik; afsigtelik.
frighfulness, verskriklikheid, afskuwelikheid.
frigid, koud; onvriendelik; vervelig; – **zone**, poolstreek.

frigidity, (ys)koudheid, koelheid.
frill, n. val(letjie); kraag; **put on -s,** aanstel.
frill, v. plooi, kartel, valletjies maak.
fringe, n. rand; fraiing; gordyntjiekop.
fringe, v. (met fraiings) afsit; afgrens.
frippery, tierlantyntjies.
Frisian, Fries.
frisk, huppel, dartel.
frisky, lewendig, uitgelate, dartel.
frit, frit.
fritter, v. snipper; **- away,** verspil.
fritter, n. snippertjie, skyfie; frituur; koekie.
frivolity, ligsinnigheid; beuselagtigheid; vermaak.
frivolous, ligsinnig; beuselagtig; vermaaksugtig; niksbeduidend, nietig.
friz(z), v. krul, kroes maak; afskraap.
friz(z), n. krulle; krulkop.
frizz, sis; spat; borrel; sputter (in die pan).
frizzle, v. krul.
frizzle, n. krulhare, krulkop.
frizzle, v. sissend bak.
fro: to and -, heen en weer.
frock, (monniks)py; manel; rok, kleed.
frock-coat, manel.
frog, padda; horingstraal (in 'n perdehoef).
frog, knooplus.
frogman, paddaman.
frolic, v. skerts, korswel; jakker.
frolic, n. vermaak, pret, plesiertjie.
frolicsome, vrolik, plesierig.
from, van, vanaf, vandaan, van uit; volgens; **- a child,** van jongs af; **be far - saying,** glad nie beweer nie; **apart, -,** afgesien van; **I could not refrain - laughing,** ek kon nie help (om te) lag nie; **- his looks,** te oordeel na sy voorkoms; **- of old,** van ouds af; **- under her spectacles,** onder haar bril uit; **painted - nature,** na die natuur geskilder; **suffer -,** ly aan; **- what he says,** volgens wat hy sê.
ont, n. voorkop; front; voorkant; bors (van hemp); ın -, voorop, op die voorpunt; **in - of,** voor; **come to the -,** na vore kom, op die voorgrond tree; **- and rear,** voor en agter.
front, v. teenoor staan; die hoof bied; **- (up)on to, towards,** uitsien op; **-ed with stone,** met die voorkant van klip.
front, front, voorkant; voorbreedte.
frontal, n. altaardoek, voorgewel.
frontal, a. voor- ...; voorhoofs- ...
front door, voordeur.
frontier, grens.
frontiersman, grensbewoner.
frontispiece, titleplaat, titelprent; voorgewel.
frontlet, kopband; gebedriem; altaardoek.
front room, voorkamer, voorste kamer.
front view, frontaansig, vooraansig.
frost, n. vors; ryp; mislukking, fiasko.
frost, v. ryp; doodryp; dof maak; (koek) glaseer; grys maak; (hoefysters) hake aansit.
frost-bitten, bevries, verkluim.
frost-bound, vasgevries, vasgeys.
frostiness, ryp(erigheid); kilheid, koudheid.
frosty, ryperig; wit van die ryp; op 'n afstand.
froth, skuim.
frothy, skuimerig; waardeloos.
froward, weerspannig.
frown, v. frons; **- at, (up)on,** suur aankyk; afkeur.
frown, n. frons.
frowst, bedompige lug.
frowsy, bedompig; slordig.
fructify, vrugte dra; vrugdra; bevrug.
fructose, vrugtesuiker, fruktose.
frugal, spaarsaam, matig; voordelig.

frugality, spaarsaamheid; matigheid.
fruit, vrug; vrugte; **first -s,** eersteling.
fruitage, vrugte.
frutarian, vrugte-eter.
fruit-bearing, vrugtedraend.
fruiterer, vrugtehandelaar.
fruitful, vrugbaar.
fruition, genot; verwerkliking; vrug(te).
fruitless, sonder vrugte; vrugteloos.
fruity, vrugte- ...; smaaklik; **- taste,** vrugtesmaak.
frumenty, furmety, koringpap.
frump, ou slons.
frustrate, dwarsboom, verydel, uitoorlê.
frustration, verydeling, verhindering.
frustum, stomp kegel.
frutex, struik, bos(sie).
fruticose, bossieagtig, struikagtig.
fry, n. klein vissies; **small -,** kleingoed; mindere gode.
fry, v. braai, bak; **have other fish to -,** ander dinge aan sy kop hê.
fry, n. braaivleis; harslag.
frying-pan, (braai)pan; **out of the - into the fire,** van die wal af in die sloot.
fuchsia, fuchsia.
fuddle, v. besuip; dronk maak; verwar.
fuddle, n. beskonkenheid; suipparty; verwarring.
fudge, interj. onsin, kletspraatjies, larie.
fudge, v. saamflans; vervals; bedrieg.
fudge, n. namaak, vervalsing, bedrog.
fuel, n. brandstof, vuurmaakgoed.
fuel, v. brandstof inneem.
fugacious, vlugtig, vervliegend; onhoubaar.
fugacity, vlugtigheid.
fugitive, a. voortvlugtig; vlugtig; onbestendig.
fugitive, n. vlugteling, wegloper, droster.
fugue, fuga.
fulcrum, steunpunt, fulcrum.
fulfil, vervul; verwesenlik, uitvoer; voldoen (aan); volbring, ten uitvoer bring.
fulfilment, vervulling; verwesenliking.
fulgent, skitterend, blinkend.
fulgurite, fulguriet, bliksembuis.
fuliginous, roeterig, roetagtig, donker.
full, a. volledig; voltallig; gevul; **- to the brim,** boorde(nste)vol; **- of water,** vol water; **- of the news,** vol van die nuus; **turn to - account,** die volste gebruik van maak; **- details,** volle besonderhede; **- brother,** eie broer; **of - age,** mondig; **- dress,** galakostuum; **- dress debate,** formele debat; **at -length,** in volle lengte; **- moon,** vol(le)maan; **at - speed,** in volle vaart; **- speed,** (in) volle vaart, **- stop,** punt.
full, adv. vol, ruim, heeltemal, ten volle, baie; **- many a,** menig; **- well,** baie goed; **- six miles,** (ten) volle ses myl; **- as useful as,** ruim so nuttig as; **- in the face,** reg in die gesig.
full, n. volheid; hoogtepunt; **in -,** ten volle, volledig, in sy geheel; **to the -,** ten volle, heeltemal; **at the -,** vol op sy hoogtepunt.
full, v. vol; **to - cloth,** om laken te vol.
full-back, heelagter.
full-blooded, volbloed- ...; volbloedig.
full-blown, in volle bloei; uitgegroei; volslae.
full-bodied, lywig.
fuller, (laken)voller; **-'s earth,** vollersaarde.
full-fledged, volslae; volleerd; formeel.
full-grown, uitgegroei, volwasse.
ful(l)ness, volheid; volledigheid.
fully, ten volle, volkome; ruim; **- fashioned,** gepasweef.
fulminate, bliksem; ontplof; uitvaar (teen).
fulmination, blikseming; knal; banvloek.
fulness, sien **fullness.**

fulvous, geelbruin.
fumarole, fumarole, rookgat, dampbron.
fumble, v. knoei, onhandig wees, modder.
fumble, n. geknoei, gemodder.
fume, n. damp, (uit)wasem(ing); –s of wine, wyndampe; in a –, woedend, briesend.
fume, v. berook, damp; kook (van woede), briesend wees; –d oak, gerookte eikehout.
fumigate, uitrook, ontsmet; bewierook.
fumigation, ontsmetting; bewieroking.
fun, pret, plesier, vermaak; grap, aardigheid; make – of, poke – at, vir die gek hou; for –, vir die grap; just for the – of it, net vir die aardigheid.
funambulist, koorddanser, draadloper.
function, n., werk; amp, waardigheid; plegtigheid, funksie.
function, v. werk; fungeer; funksioneer.
functionary, amptenaar; funksionaris.
fund, n. voorraad; fonds, kapitaal.
fund, v. konsolideer, in staatsfondse belê.
fundament, fondament, agterste.
fundamental, fundamenteel, grond- . . . ; prinsipieel; the – rules, die grondbeginsels.
fundamentally, in beginsel, prinsipieel.
fundamentals, grondslae, grondbeginsels.
funeral, a. begrafnis- . . . ; lyk-; – ceremony, begrafnisplegtigheid; – procession, lykstasie, -stoet; – march, dode-, treurmars.
funeral, n. begrafnis; lykstasie; that's your –, dis jou saak (sorg).
funereal, somber; begrafnis- . . . ; dode- . . .
fungicide, swamdoder.
fungous, swamagtig; kortstondig.
fungus, paddastoel; swam, fungus.
funicular, kabel- . . . ; – railway, kabelspoorweg.
funk, v. bang word (wees); weghardloop van.
funky, bang, lafhartig, skrikkerig, lugtig.
funnel, tregter; (lug-, skoorsteen-)pyp.
funniness, snaaksheid.
funny, snaaks, koddig, grappig.
funny-bone, kieliebeentjie; swernootjie.
fur, n. pels, bont; kim (op wyn); beslag (op die tong); ketelsteen; – coat, bontjas; – cloak, bont-, pelsmantel; – cap, pelsmus; then the – began to fly, toe was die poppe aan die dans.
fur, v. beklee met bont; beslaan, aanpak (van 'n ketel of die tong); skoonmaak (van 'n ketel).
furbelow, valletjie; tierlantyntjie(s).
furish, oppoets, opvrywe.
furcate, splits, afdraai (van 'n pad).
furious, woedend, woes, rasend; – mirth, woeste pret.
furl, opvou, oprol, inslaan.
furlong, furlong.
furlough, n. verlof; on –, op (met) verlof.
furlough, v. met verlof laat gaan.
furmety, sien frumenty.
furnace, oond; smeltkroes.

furnish, meubileer; uitrus; verskaf.
furnishing, uitrusting, toebehorens.
furniture, meubels, huisraad; toebehorens.
furniture-van, verhuiswa.
furore, groot byval.
furrier, bontwerker, -handelaar.
furrow, n. voor, sloot, grip; rimpel; riffel.
furrow, v. ploeg, vore maak; rimpel; riffel.
furry, bont- . . . ; met bont gevoer; aangepak.
further, a. & adv. verder, meer, nader; till – orders, tot nader order; – notice, nader kennisgewing; on the – side, anderkant.
further, v. bevorder, aanhelp, ondersteun.
furtherance, bevordering, steun.
furtherer, bevorderaar, ondersteuner.
furthermore, verder; boonop, bowendien.
furthermost, verste, uiterste.
furthest, verste, uiterste, at –, uiterlik.
furtive, heimlik, steelsgewyse.
furtively, skelm(agtig); tersluiks, onderlangs.
furuncle, bloedvin(t), nege-oog (neënoog).
fury, woede, raserny, drif; furie; helleveeg.
furze, brem.
fuse, v. smelt, saamsmelt; uitbrand.
fuse, n. lont; sekering(sdraad), smeltdraadjie; the – is blown, die sekering is uitgebrand.
fusee, kettingspil, snekrat; wasvuurhoutjie.
fusel (oil), foesel(olie).
fuselage, geraamte (van vliegmasjien).
fusible, smeltbaar.
fusil, geweer.
fusilier, fuselier.
fusillade, n. fusillade, geweervuur, -salvo.
fusillade, v. fusilleer, doodskiet.
fusion, smelting, fusie; samesmelting; – bomb, smeltbom.
fuss, n. drukte, lawaai, rumoer; ophef.
fuss, v. drukte (ophef, omslag) maak; lol, seur.
fussiness, drukte, omslagtigheid.
fuss-pot, lolpot, seurkous, ophefmaker.
fussy, druk, omslagtig, seurderig, lollerig.
fustian, ferweel.
fustic, (soort) geelhout; geelkleurstof.
fustigate, pakgee, uitlooi.
fusty, muf, vermuf.
futhorc, rune-alfabet.
futile, vergeefs, vrugteloos; beuselagtig.
futility, nutteloosheid; beuselagtigheid.
future, a. toekomstig; aanstaande; toekomende; – tense, toekomende tyd.
future, n. toekoms; vervolg; toekomende tyd; in –, in die vervolg, voortaan; for the –, in die vervolg; vir die toekoms.
futurism, futurisme.
futurist, futuris.
futurity, toekoms, toekomstigheid; hiernamaals.
fuzz, dons.
fuzzy, gerafel; donserig.
fylfot, swastika.

gab, gebabbel; **he has the gift of the –,** sy mondwerk is goed.
gabardine, gabardine, gabardien.
gabble, v. babbel; (af)rammel; mompel.
gabble, n. gebabbel, geklets, gesnater.
gaberdine, opperkleed, kaftan.
gabion, skanskorf.
gable, gewel(top).
gaby, uilskuiken, eselskop, domoor.
gad, interj. gits, hemel!.
gad, slenter; – **about,** rondslenter.
gadabout, slenteraar, lanterfanter.
gad-fly, perdevlieg; laspos; gier.
gadget, inrigting; uitvindinkie; gerief.
Gaelic, Gaelies.
gaff, n. vishaak; gaffel (van 'n skip).
gaff, v. (vis) haak.
gaffe, flater, stommiteit.
gaffer, ou paai, ou baas; voorman.
gag, v. knewel, muilband, die mond snoer; (woorde) inlas; fop.
gag, n. prop (in die mond); ingelaste woorde.
gage, n. (onder)pand; uitdaging, handskoen.
gage, v. verpand; insit, op die spel sit.
gaiety, vrolikheid; pret, vermaak; opskik.
gaily, sien **gay.**
gain, n. wins, profyt; baat.
gain, v. wen; profyt maak, voordeel trek; – **time,** tyd wen; – **the ear of,** gehoor vind by; – **the upper hand,** die oorhand kry; – **the day,** die oorwinning behaal; – **ground,** veld wen; – **ground upon,** wen op; 'n voorsprong kry up; – **one's object,** sy doel bereik; **what do you –by that,** wat bereik jy daarmee?; – **over,** oorhaal.
gainful, voordelig; inhalig.
gainings, wins(te).
gainsay, teenspreek, ontken.
gait, gang, stap, houding.
gaiter, slobkous, kamas, veerkous.
gala, gala, fees(telikheid).
galactometer, melkmeter.
gala-dress, gala-kleding, feesgewaad.
galantine, galantien.
galanty show, skimmespel.
galaxy, melkweg; skitterende geselskap.
gale, storm, sterk wind.
Galician, Galisiër, Galisiese (vrou).
Galilean, Galileër.
Galilee, Galilea.
galilee, voorportaal, kapel.
galjoen, galjoen.
gall, n. gal; – **and wormwood,** gal en alsem.
gall, n. skaafplek; puisie, seerplek; astrantheid.
gall, v. skaaf, skuur; seermaak, kwel, verbitter.
gall, n. galnoot.
gallant, a. galant, hoflik; dapper; fier, trots; statig, swierig.
gallant, n. galant, galante kêrel; minnaar.
gallant, v. die galant uithang; swier.
gallantry, galanterie, hoofsheid, dapperheid.
gall-bladder, galblaas.
gallery, galery; gang; (skildery)museum; **play to the –,** speel vir die publiek.
galley, galei; sloep; (skeeps)kombuis.
Gallic, Gallies.
Gallicism, Gallisisme.
gallinaceous, hoender- . . .
gallipot, salfpotjie.
gallivant, rondflenter, pierewaai.
gallon, gelling.
galloon, galon, boorband, boorsel.
gallop, n. galop; **at a –,** op 'n galop, in galop.
gallop, v. galop, galoppeer.
gallopade, galop(dans), galoppade.

galloway, (galloway)ponie.
gallows, galg.
gallows-bird, galgkos, -aas.
gall-stone, galsteen.
galop, galop(dans).
galore, volop, in oorvloed soos bossies.
galosh, golosh, oorskoen.
galvanic, galvanies.
galvanization, galvanisasie.
galvanize, galvaniseer; **–d iron,** sink(plaat); gegalvaniseerde yster.
galvanism, galvanisme.
galvanometer, galvanometer.
gambade, bokkesprong.
gambit, gambiet.
gamble, v. dobbel, speel; – **away,** verspeel.
gamble, n. dobbelary, dobbelspel; waagstuk.
gambler, dobbelaar.
gambling-hell, speelhol.
gambol, v. bokspring, huppel, buitel.
gambol, n. bokkesprong, buiteling, huppeling.
game, n. spel, spel(l)etjie; pot(jie); wedstryd; wild; **play the –,** eerlik speel; **play a double –** vals speel; **the – is up,** die spel is verlore; **have the – in your hands,** die spel in hande hê; **make – of,** vir die gek hou; **a – of billiards,** 'n potjie biljart; **the – is four all,** the spel staan (op) vier elk; – **all,** pot elk; **fair –,** geoorloofde wild; **the – is not worth the candle,** die kool is die sous nie werd nie; **to be off his –,** van stryk wees.
game, a. klaar, gewillig, bereid, sportief.
game, v. speel, dobbel.
game, a. lam, mank, kreupel.
game-cock, kemphaan.
game-keeper, jagopsiener, boswagter.
game-law, jag-, skietwet, wildwet.
gameness, gewilligheid, durf, sportiwiteit.
gamesome, dartel, speelsiek.
gamester, dobbelaar, speler.
gaming, (die) dobbel, dobbelary.
gaming-table, speeltafel.
gamma, gamma; – **ray,** gammastraal.
gammer, ou-maai.
gammon, n. agterkwart.
gammon, n. foppery.
gammon, v. fop.
gammy, mank.
gamp, tentsambreel.
gamut, toonladder, gamma; **the whole –,** die hele omvang.
gamy, wildryk, wild- . . . ; adelik.
gander, gansmannetjie.
gang, trop, bende; ploeg.
gang-board, loopplank.
gangling, lomp; – **fellow,** langderm.
ganglion, senu(wee)knoop; middelpunt.
gangrene, kouevuur.
gangster, rampokker, rower.
gangue, gangsteen, aar.
gangway, paadjie, deurloop; loopplank; **please,** gee pad asseblief.
gantry, stellasie.
gaol, (jail), n. tronk, gevangenis.
gaol, (jail), v. in die tronk sit, opsluit.
gaol-bird, (jail-bird), gewoontemisdadiger.
gaoler, (jailer), tronkbewaarder, sipier.
gap, opening; leemte, gaping; verskil.
gape, v. gaap; oopspalk; – **at,** aangaan.
gape, n. gaap; skeur, gat; **the –s,** gaapsiekte.
garage, n. garage, motorhuis; motorhawe.
garage, v. (motorkar) laat staan, stal.
garb, n. kleding, kleredrag, dos; inkleding.
garb, v. kleed, aantrek, uitdos; inklee.
garbage, afval, uitskot.

garble, sig; vermink, verdraai.
garden, n. tuin; lead up the – (path), bedrieg, mislei.
garden, v. tuinmaak, tuinier; kweek.
gardener, tuinier; tuinman.
garden-hose, tuinslang, -spuit.
gardenia, katjiepiering.
gardening, tuinmaak.
garden-party, tuinfees.
gargantuan, kolossaal, enorm.
gargle, v. gorrel.
gargle, n. gorreldrank.
gargoyle, dakspuier.
garish, opsigtig, helkleurig.
garland, n. krans; segekrans; bloemlesing.
garland, v. be-, omkrans.
garlic, knoflok (knoffel).
garment, kledingstuk; kleding, gewaad.
garner, n. (graan)skuur.
garner, v. versamel, vergaar, bêre.
garnet, granaat(steen).
garnish, v. garneer, versier.
garniture, garnituur; versiering; bybehorens.
garret, solderkamer.
garrison, n. garnisoen, besetting.
garrison, v. beset, in garnisoen lê.
gar(r)otte, verwurging; wurgstok.
garrulity, babbelsug, spraaksaamheid.
garrulous, babbelsiek, praatagtig, spraaksaam.
garter, kousband.
garth, agterplaas; kamp; hok.
gas, n. gas; wind, bluf; petrol; step on the –, versnel, trap op die versneller.
gas, v. gas, deur gas verstik; windmaak, bluf, grootpraat.
gas-bag, windbuks, bluffer, grootprater.
gasconade, windmakery, bluffery; kaskenade.
gaselier, gaskroon.
gas-engine, gasmotor.
gaseous, gas- ..., gasagtig.
gasfitter, gasfitter.
gash, n. sny, hou, keep.
gash, v. sny, 'n hou gee, 'n keep gee.
gasify, verdamp, in gas verander, vergas.
gasket, seising, vulsel, pakking, voering.
gas-main, gasleiding.
gasogene, sien **gazogene**,
gasoline, petrol.
gasometer, gashouer.
gasp, v. snak (na asem), hyg; met die oop mond staan; – out, hyg; – away, out life, die laaste adem (asem) uitblaas; he made me –, hy het my met die oop mond laat staan.
gasp, n. snak; snik, hyging, ademtog; last –, doodsnik, laaste ademtog.
gasping, hygend, snakkend; verbluf.
gas-stove, gaskaggel, -stel, stoof.
gassy, gas- ..., gasagtig; blufferig.
gastric, maag- ..., gastries; – juice, maagsap.
gastronomer, gastronoom; lekkerbek, smulpaap.
gastronomy, gastronomie; hoëre kookkuns; eetkuns.
gat, rewolwer; geweer.
gate, hek; poort; sluis; toegang; ontvangste.
gate-crasher, sosiale indringer.
gate-keeper, hekwagter, portier.
gateway, poort, ingang.
gather, vergader; versamel; pluk oes; plooi; verstaan; – information, inli.ding inwin; – flowers, blomme pluk; – the harvest, oes; we – that, ons verstaan dat; – strength, krag versamel; – way, vaart kry; – head, toeneem; the clouds –, die wolke pak saam; the sore –s, die seer sweer.
gathering, vergadering; insameling; sweer.

gathers, rimpels, plooie.
gaucherie, onhandigheid, lompheid.
gaud, opskik, siersel; –s, vertonings.
gaudiness, opsigtigheid.
gaudy, a. opsigtig, spoggerig.
gaudy, n. fuifmaal, feesmaal.
gauge, n. maat, standaard; spoorwydte; kalibermeter, take the – of, die maat neem van.
gauge, v. meet; peil; toets; yk.
gauging-rod, peilstok.
Gaul, Gallië, Galliër; Fransman.
Gaulish, Gallies; Frans.
gaunt, maer, skraal, uitgeteer, vervalle, hol.
gauntlet, handskoen; throw down the –, uitdaag; take up the –, die uitdaging aanneem.
gauntlet, run the –, spitsroei loop.
gauze, gaas; wasigheid, dynserigheid.
gauzy, gaasagtig; dynserig.
gavotte, gavot(te).
gawk, lomperd, skimmelbrood.
gawky, a. verskimmel, verleë, lomp.
gay, vrolik, plesierig; los(bandig); kleurig.
gaze, v. staar, strak kyk, tuur.
gaze, n. (starende) blik.
gazelle, gasel, springbok.
gazette, n. gaset; (staats)koerant.
gazette, v. bekend maak, aankondig, proklameer.
gazing-stock, aangegaapte (persoon).
gear, n. uitrusting; gereedskap; rat(te); in –, ingeskakel; out of –, uitgeskakel; uit orde; in top –, in die hoogste versnelling, in die boonste kerf; change –s, oorskakel.
gear, v. inspan; – up, optuig; inskakel; – up (down), in 'n hoër (laer) versnelling sit; – into, with, inskakel (met).
gear-box, ratkas; versnellingsbak.
gear-case, kettingkas.
gear-lever, versnellingsknop.
gee (whiz)!, (alle)maggies!
Geiger; – counter, Geiger-telbuis.
gelatine, gelatien (gelatine).
gelatinous, gelatienagtig, gelatien- ..
geld, sny, kastreer, kapater.
gelding, reun; (die) sny.
gelid, yskoud.
gelt-pig, burg(vark).
gem, edelsteen; juweel, kleinood; briljant.
geminate, verdubbel, twee-twee opstel.
gemma, bladknop; knop.
gemmiferous, ryk aan edelstene; knopdraend.
gemsbok, gemsbok.
gender, geslag.
genealogical, genealogies, stam- ...; – tree, stamboom.
genealogy, genealogie; afstamming, stamboom.
general, a. algemeen; gewoon; – rule, algemene reël; as a – rule, in die reël; in – terms, in algemene bewoordinge; in –, oor (in) die algemeen.
general, n. generaal; die groot publiek.
generalize, saamvat, generaliseer; veralgemeen.
generalissimo, hoofgeneraal, opperbevelhebber.
generally, algemeenheid; vaagheid; gros.
generally, gewoonlik, in die reël, oor (in) die algemeen, oor die geheel.
generalship, aanvoering, leiding; generaalskap.
generate, voortbring, veroorsaak; ontwikkel; opwek; –ing station, kragstasie.
generation, voortbrenging; veroorsaking; ontwikkeling; opwekking; geslag, generasie.
generative, voortbrengend; vrugbaar; geslags- ...
generator, voortbrenger; generator, dinamo.
generic, generies, generiek; algemeen.
generosity, edelmoedigheid; mild(dadig)heid.
generous, edelmoedig, mild; rojaal; oorvloedig.

genesis, genesis; oorsprong; wording, wordingsgeskiedenis.
genet, muskeljaatkat.
genetic, geneties, wordings- ...
geneva, jenewer.
genial, vriendelik, hartlik, joviaal; aangenaam.
geniality, gulheid, hartlikheid; opgewektheid.
genie, genius, gees.
genital, geslags- ..., teel- ...
genitals, geslagsorgane.
genitival, genitiefs- ...
genitive, genitief.
genius, genie; (beskerm)gees; genius.
genocide, volksmoord; groepsmoord; menseslagting.
gent, heer, witman, meneer.
genteel, fatsoenlik, deftig, beskaaf; lieftallig.
gentian, gentiaan; aambeibos.
gentile, a. nie-Joods, Christelik; heidens.
gentile, n. nie-Jood, Christen, heiden.
gentility, fatsoenlikheid, deftigheid.
gentle, a. sag; lief; deftig; – **reader**, welwillende leser; – sex, skone geslag.
gentle, n. maaier; –s, hoë mense.
gentle, v. mak maak, dresseer.
gentlefolks, deftige stande, hoë mense.
gentleman, heer; meneer; – **in waiting**, kamerheer; – **'s agreement**, eerbare verstandhouding.
gentlemanlike, – **ly**, soos 'n heer.
gentlemanliness, beskaafdheid, opgevoedheid; **show your** –, toon dat jy 'n heer is.
gentleness, sagtheid.
gentlewoman, dame.
gently, sag(gies).
gentry, burgermense; heerskappe.
genuflection, **-flexion**, kniebuiging, knieval.
genuine, waar, opreg, eg, onvervals.
genuineness, opregtheid, egtheid.
genus, geslag, soort, klas.
geocentric, geosentries, aardmiddelpuntig.
geodesy, landmeetkunde, geodesie.
geodetic, landmeetkundig, geodeties.
geographer, aardrykskundige, geograaf.
geographic(al), aardrykskundige, geografies.
geography, geografie; aardrykskunde; aardryksbeskrywing.
geological, geologies, aardkundig.
geologist, aardkundige, geoloog.
geology, aardkunde, geologie.
geometer, meetkundige; kruipruspe(r).
geometric(al), geometries, meetkundig.
geometry, meetkunde; **plane** –, vlak(ke) meetkunde; **solid** –, stereometrie.
geophysicist, geofisikus.
geophysics, geofisika.
georgette, georgette.
georgic, landelik; landbou- ...
geotropic(al), geotropies.
geranium, geranium; malva.
gerfalcon, giervalk.
geriatrics, geriatrie.
germ, n. kiem.
germ, v. (ont)kiem.
german: **cousin-german**, eie neef (niggie).
German, a. Duits; – **silver**, nuwesilwer.
German, n. Duitser; Duits; **High** –, Hoogduits; **Low** –, Nederduits; Platduits.
germane, verwant; in betrekking staande (tot).
Germanic, Germaans.
germanium, germanium.
Germany, Duitsland.
germicidal, **-cide**, a. kiemdodend.

germicide, n. kiemdoder.
germinal, kiem- ...; in die kiem aanwesig.
germinate, (ont)kiem, uitloop; voortbring.
germination, ontkieming, groei.
gerrymander, v. (kiesdistrikte) oneerlik afbaken; beknoei.
gerrymandering, afbakeningsknoeiery.
gerund, gerundium.
gerundive, gerundivum.
gesso, gips.
gestation, swangerskap, drag(tigheid).
gesticulate, gebare maak, gestikuleer.
gesticulation, gebaar, gestikulasie.
gesticulative, **-tory**, gebarend, gestikulerend.
gesture, gebaar, (hand)beweging.
get, v. (ver)kry, verwerf, behaal, in die hande kry; ontvang, verdien; hê; word, raak, maak; – **an advantage**, 'n voordeel behaal, – **the better of**, die oorhand kry oor; uitoorlê; – **a disease**, 'n siekte opdoen; – **knowledge, wind of**, agterkom; – **a living**, 'n bestaan maak; – **a start (on)**, 'n voorsprong kry (op); – **on one's nerves**, dit op die senuwees kry; – **by heart**, uit die kop leer; – **the worst of it**, daar die slegste van afkom; **it has got to be done**, dit moet gedaan word; – **ready**, klaarmaak; **I shall** – **my feet wet**, my voete sal nat word; – **going**, aan die gang kom; – **there**, jou doel bereik; slaag; **one** –s **to like it**, mens begin daarvan te hou; **they got talking**, hulle het aan die praat geraak; – **excited (drunk)**, opgewonde (dronk) word; – **well**, **better**, gesond, beter word; – **rid, quit of**, ontslae raak van; – **under way**, koers vat; – **done with**, klaarmaak met, 'n einde aan maak; – **married**, trou, getroud raak; – **about**, beweeg, loop; **op wees (na 'n siekte)**; **rugbaar word**; – **abroad**, rugbaar word; – **along**, oor die weg kom; loop!, maak dat jy weg kom!; – **at**, bykom; begryp; in die hande kry; – **away**, ontsnap; wegkom; **wegloop**; – **back**, terugkom; terugkry; – **down**, afklim; onder kry; – **in**, inkom; inklim; **binnekry**; – **your hand in**, op stryk kom; – **off**, ontsnap; wegspring; afklim; – **on**, vooruitkom, oor die weg kom; opklim; – **on one's feet**, opstaan om te praat; **be –ting on for forty**, veertig se kant toe gaan; – **out**, uitkom; uitlek, rugbaar word; uitklim; – **out of one's depth**, in diepwater raak; – **out of bed**, opstaan; – **out of hand**, hande uitruk; – **over**, agter die rug kry; (moeilikheid) oorkom; (van siekte) herstel; (van skrik, verwondering) bekom; ('n afstand) aflê; – **round**, verbykom by; ompraat; – **to business**, ter sake kom; – **through**, ('n wetsontwerp) deurkry; ('n eksamen) deurkom; – **through with**, klaarkry; – **to**, bereik; sover kom (om); – **together**, bymekaarkry; byeenkom; – **under**, baasraak, meester word; – **up**, opstaan; opstyg, opklim, ('n konsert) organiseer, op tou sit; opknap; (hare, linnegoed) opmaak; (toneelstuk) opvoer; (stoom) opkry; **I got his back up**, ek het hom kwaad gemaak.
get-at-able, bereikbaar, bykombaar.
getaway: **make a** –, ontsnap.
get-together, samekoms.
get-up, (die) opmaak; aankleding; uitvoering.
gew-gaw, tierlantyntjies, snuistery, prul.
geyser, geiser.
ghastly, aaklig, afgryslik; spookagtig; doodsbleek.
gherkin, agurkie.
ghetto, ghetto, Jodebuurt.
ghost, gees; spook; skaduwee; **give up the** –, die gees gee; **Holy G** –, Heilige Gees; **not the**

– of a chance, geen skyntjie kans nie; lay the –, 'n gees besweer; a – of his former self, 'n skaduwee van wat hy was.
ghostlike, spookagtig.
ghostly, geestelik; spookagtig.
ghoul, lykverslinder.
ghoulish, monsteragtig.
giant, n. reus.
giant, a. reusagtig, reuse.
giaur, ongelowige.
gib, sien **jib.**
gibber, v. brabbel, brabbeltaal (wartaal) praat.
gibber, n. gebrabbel, wartaal.
gibberish, koeterwaals, wartaal.
gibbet, n. galg; dood aan die galg.
gibbet, v. (op)hang; aan die kaak stel.
gibbon, gibbon, langarmaap.
gibbosity, bult, boggel.
gibbous, uitpuilend, bulterig, geboggel.
gibe, jibe, v. spot, skimp, uitkoggel.
gibe, jibe, n. spot, skimp.
giblets, (gans)afval, -ingewande.
giddy, a. duiselig, dronk; duiselingwekkend; ligsinnig; wispelturig.
gift ,n. gif, gawe, present; – **coupon (voucher),** geskenkbewys.
gift, v. begiftig, beskenk.
gifted, begaaf, talentvol; begiftig.
gift-horse, gegewe perd, presentperd.
gig, giek; sloep; (tweedisselboom)karretjie.
gigantic, reusagtig, reuse- . . .
giggle, v. giggel (giegel).
giggle, n. gegiggel (gegiegel).
gila monster, Gila-akkedis.
gild, v. vergul.
gild, n. sien **guild.**
gilding, vergulsel; (die) vergul.
gill, n. kieu (mv. kuwe); belletjie; kaak.
gill, v. skoonmaak, kaak.
gill, n. kloof; bergstroom.
gill, n. „gill", kwartpint.
gillie, agterryer; handlanger, visklonkie.
gillyflower, angelier; muurblom.
gilt, a. vergul(d).
gilt, n. vergulsel; skyn; – **edged,** goudgerand.
gimbal(s), kompasbeuel.
gimcrack, snuistery, tierlantyntjie.
gimlet, handboor.
gimmick, foefie; geheime toestelletjie.
gimp, gymp, gimp, passement, omboorsel.
gin, n. jenewer.
gin, n. strik, val; katrol, wen(as); suiwermasjien.
gin, v, vang, verstrik; suiwer, duiwel.
ginger, n. gemmer; vuur, moed; rooikop.
ginger, v. met gemmer krui; lewendig maak.
ginger-ale, gemmerlim.
ginger-beer, gemmerbier.
ginger-bread, n. peperkoek, gemmerbrood.
ginger-bread, a. opsigtig, prullerig.
gingerly, versigtig, behoedsaam.
ginger-nut, gemmerkoekie.
ginger-pop, gemmerbier.
gingery, gemmeragtig.
gingham, geruit, gestreepte katoen; sambreel.
gipsy, sigeuner(in), heiden (heidin).
gipsydom, -hood, -ism, sigeunerdom.
giraffe, kameel(perd).
girandole, draaivuurwerk; springfontein; armkandelaar.
gird, gord, opgord; aangord; wapen; – **(up) the loins,** die lendene omgord.
girder, dwarsbalk.
girdle, n. gordel, (broek)gord; buikriem.
girdle, v. omsluit; – **about, in, round,** omgord.
girdle, n. rooster.

girdle-cake, roosterkoek.
girl, meisie; nôi; **old** –, hartjie; – **friend,** nooi, vriendin.
girlhood, meisie(s)jare, meisieskap.
girlie, meisie(tjie), nôientjie.
girlish, meisie(s)agtig.
girth, n. buikgord; gordel, buikrem; omvang.
girth, v. omvang, insluit; (om)gord; meet.
gist, hoofsaak, kern.
gittern, sien **cithern.**
give, v. gee, aangee; meegee; insak; skiet (van 'n tou); – **as good as one gets,** in gelyke munt betaal; – **one his due,** iemand gee wat hom toekom; – **a jump,** (weg)spring; – **a piece of one's mind,** die waarheid sê; **I – you joy,** veels geluk!; – **a thought,** aan dink; – **oneself trouble,** moeite doen; **–s himself airs,** stel hom aan; – **chase,** agternasit; – **ground,** wyk; – **rise to,** aanleiding gee tot; – **way, padgee;** – **way to,** plek maak vir; toegee aan; (sig) oorgee aan; **–n to drink,** aan drank verslaaf; – **to the world,** bekend maak; – **to understand,** laat verstaan; – **away,** weggee; verklap – back, teruggee; weergee; – **forth,** uitgee; – – **in,** inlewer; kopgee, tou-opgooi; – **out,** uitgee; opraak; – **over,** opgee; oorhandig; **–n over to,** verslaaf aan; – **up,** opgee; afgee; oorlewer; – **it up,** dit opgee; – **oneself up to,** (sig) oorgee aan; (sig) wy aan.
give, n. (die) meegee, skot.
given, gegewe; – **to,** geneig tot; verslaaf aan.
giver, gewer.
gizzard, krop; **it sticks in his –,** dit steek hom in die krop.
glabrous, glad, kaal.
glacial, ys- . . . ; – **epoch,** ysperiode.
glacier, gletser.
glacis, glooiing, helling.
glad, bly, verheug.
gladden, verbly, verheug; opvrolik.
glade, oop plek (in 'n bos).
gladiator, gladiator, swaardvegter.
gladiolus, pypie, swaardlelie, gladiolus.
gladly, graag, met blydskap, met genoeë.
gladness, blydskap, opgewektheid.
glair, wit van eier, eiwit, (eiwit)lym.
glaive, swaard.
glamour, betowering, bekoring, aantreklikheid.
glamour-girl, prikkelpop.
glance, v. flikker, skitter; 'n blik werp; – **at,** 'n blik werp op; verwys na; – **off,** afskram; – – (one's eye) **over, through,** vlugtig deurkyk.
glance, n. blik, oogopslag; skramshou; flikkering, skynsel; **at a** –, met een oogopslag; **at first** –, op die eerste gesig.
gland, klier; sel.
glanders, droes.
glandiform, eikel-, akkervormig; kliervormig.
glare, v. flikker, fel skyn; woedend aankyk.
glare, n. skittering, felle lig; woeste blik.
glaring, verblindend; skreeuend; woes; – **injustice,** skreiende onreg.
glass, glas; spieël; verkyker; **weerglas;** raam; ruit; sopie; – **es,** bril; – **wool,** glaswol.
glass-blower, glasblaser.
glass-case, glaskas.
glass-eye, glaasoog.
glass-house, glaashuis; glasblasery; broeikas.
glass-ware, glasgoed, glaswerk.
glassy, glas(er)ig, glasagtig; glas- . . .; spieëlglad.
Glauber's salt(s), Glaubersout.
glaucoma, groen (grou) staar.
glaucous, grysgroen, seegroen.
glaze, v. glas (ruite) insit; verglaas; glans; glasig word; (oë) breek.

glaze

glaze, n. glans; glasuur; glasige blik.
glazed, verglaas; geglasuur; glasig; blink.
glazier, glasmaker; glaswerker; ruitwerker.
gleam, n. straal, skyn, flikkering; – of hope, straal van hoop.
gleam, v. straal, skyn, flikker, blink.
glean, versamel; optel, bymekaarskraap.
gleaner, areleser; versamelaar.
gleaning, (die) arelees, nalesing, versameling.
glebe, grond, land; pastoriegrond.
glee, rondsang; blydskap, vrolikheid.
glen, dal, vlei.
glib, glad, gelyk; los; welbespraak.
glibly, glad, los; oppervlakkig.
glibness, gladheid; welbespraaktheid.
glide, v. gly, skuiwe, sweef; sluip; sweef(vlieg).
glide, n. (die) gly; oorgang(sklank); sweefvlug.
glider, sweef(vlieg)tuig, – pilot, swewer, sweefvlieër.
glim, lig, kers, lantern.
glimmer, v. lig, skyn, flikker, skemer.
glimmer(ing), 'n skynsel, flikkering.
glimpse, n. glimp; vlugtige blik, kykie; catch a – of, skrams raak sien, 'n vlugtige blik op kry.
glimpse, v. skrams raak sien.
glint, n. glinstering, skynsel.
glisten, glinster, blink.
glister, vonkel, glinster.
glitter, v. skitter, glinster, vonkel.
glitter, n. skittering, glinstering.
glitter, n. skittering, glinstering.
gloaming, skemer.
gloat, lekkerkry; – over, (sig) vermei of verlustig in, met die oë verslind.
globe, bol, globe; oogbal; glaaskap.
globular, bolvormig.
globule, bolletjie; druppeltjie, koeëltjie.
gloom, n. donkerte, skemer; somberheid.
gloom, v. somber kyk (lyk), versomber.
gloomy, donker, somber, droefgeestig.
glorification, verheerliking; ophemeling.
glorify, verheerlik; prys, ophemel.
gloriole, stralekrans.
glorious, glorieryk; glansryk; salig (dronk).
glory, n. glorie; roem, eer; trots; stralekrans.
glory, v. (sig) beroem op; koning kraai.
gloss, n. kanttekening, glos; verdraaiing.
gloss, v. kommentarieer; verdraai.
gloss, n. glans, skyn, mooi uiterlik.
gloss, v. laat glans, poets; 'n skone skyn aan gee; – over, bemantel; doekies om draai.
glossary, glossarium; woordelys.
glossy, glansend, blink; skoonklinkend.
glottal, stemspleet; – stop, stembandklapper.
glottis, stemspleet.
glove, handskoen; throw down (take up) the –, die handskoen toewerp (opneem); fit like a –, pas of dit aangegiet is.
gloved, met handskoene aan, gehandskoen.
glover, handskoenmaker.
glove-stretcher, vingerstok.
glow, v. gloei, blaak, brand.
glow, n. gloed, vuur; be in a –, gloei.
glower, dreigend (swart) kyk.
glowing, gloeiend; vurig; lewendig.
glow-worm, vuurvliegie, glimwurm.
gloze, bewimpel, vergoelik, mooipraat.
glucose, glukose, druiwesuiker.
glue, n. lym.
glue, v. lym; vasplak; (oë) strak rig.
glue-pot, lympot.
gluey, lymerig, klewerig.
glum, bek-af, mismoedig, bedruk, stuurs.
glut, v. volprop, oorlaai; versadig.

glut, n. versadiging, oorlading.
gluten, kleefstof, gluten.
glutinous, klewerig, klewend.
glutton, vraat, gulsigaard, gulsbek.
gluttonous, vraterig; vraatagtig, gulsig.
gluttony, vraatsug, gulsigheid.
glycerine, gliserien; gliserol.
G-man, federale speurder.
gnarled, kwasterig, knoesterig.
gnash, kners; – the teeth, op die tande kners.
gnat, muggie.
gnaw, knabbel, knaag; wegvreet, verteer.
gnome, lyf-, sinspreuk, leus, gnomen.
gnome, aardmannetjie, kabouter.
gnomic, gnomies, spreuk-...
gnomon, gnomon; sonwyserpen.
gnostic, a. gnosties.
gnostic, n. gnostiek.
gnosticism, gnostisisme.
gnu, wildebees, ghnoe (gnu).
go, v. gaan; loop, wandel, reis; weggaan, verdwyn, val; reik; geldig wees; he will – far, hy sal dit ver bring; – straight, reguit gaan; reg deur see gaan; die regte weg bewandel; – for a walk (on a journey), 'n wandeling ('n reis) maak; (a rule) to – by, ('n reël) om na te volg, om jou aan te hou; nothing to – by, niks waarop jy kan afgaan nie; who –es there?, werda? wie's daar?; clock does not –, –es, well, die horlosie loop nie, loop goed; the story –es, die verhaal gaan; – by the name of, gaan onder die naam van, die naam voer van; the dance went well, die dansparty het goed van stapel geloop; one, two, three –!, een, twee, drie, af!; –es without saying, spreek vanself; – the way of all flesh, die weg van alle vlees gaan; – to pieces, stukkend breek; inmekaar sak; – to sea, matroos word; – on the stage, op die toneel gaan, toneelspeler (-speelster) word; now you have –ne and done it, daar het jy dit nou, nou het hy jou vasgeloop; – bail, instaan, borgstaan; – to war, oorlog maak, oorlog verklaar; – to work, aan die werk gaan; – all lengths, tot die uiterste gaan; – halves, (gelykop) deel; – to great expense, groot onkoste maak; – to the trouble of, die moeite doen om; – (one) better, oortroef; – to the bottom, sink, na die kelder (haaie) gaan; – – to one's heart, iemand ter harte gaan; –es a long way, help baie, skeel veel; – it, toe nou!; daarop losgaan; be –ne, trap, maak dat jy wegkom; far –ne, verheen; –ne on her, verlief op haar;
(go + prep.): – about, aanpak; – at, op los-gaan; inklim; – for, gaan haal, gaan om; op afgaan; invlie; – in for, (sig) toelê op, spesialiseer in, – into, (op) ingaan; – into hysterics, 'n senuwee-aanval kry; – off one's head, van jou verstand (af) raak; – over, nagaan, nasien; – through, nasien, deurleef; – with, gepaard gaan met; – without, sonder klaarkom.
(go + adv.): – about, rondgaan; 'n omweg maak; – ahead, aangaan; – back (up)on one's word, 'n belofte nie nakom nie; – by, verbygaan; – down, afgaan sink; daal; verloor, val; oorgelewer word; ingang vind; – in, ingaan; – in for, (sig) toelê op, (sig) wy aan; (mee)doen aan; aanskaf; – in for an examination, eksamen doen; – in for farming, boer, (sig) toelê op die boerdery; – in for law, (in die) regte studeer; – off, weggaan, verlaat; wegspring; heengaan; afgaan, ontplof; van stapel loop, gaan; – on, aangaan (met); te keer gaan; opkom (op die toneel); aan die beurt kom; 'n beurt kry; – on!, vooruit!;

hou op!, ag kom!; – **out**, uitgaan; doodgaan;
my heart –es out to her, ek het baie medelyde
met haar; – **over**, oorgaan; – **round**, ronddraai,
rondtrek, die rondte doen; uitkom, genoeg
wees; – **through with**, aangaan met; uitvoer;
– **to**, ag loop!; – **together**, saamgaan, pas
bymekaar; – **under**, te gronde gaan, verloop.
go, n. (die) gaan; wegspring; vaart; energie,
fut; **have a – at**, 'n poging waag; **on the –**,
in beweging; op stryk; aan die agteruitgaan.
goad, n. prikkel; slaanding, sambok.
goad, v. prikkel, aanspoor, drywe.
goal, n. doel, doelpunt, wen-, eindpaal.
goal, v. 'n doel behaal, 'n doel skop.
goalkeeper, doelverdediger.
goal-line, doellyn.
goat, bok, **he- –**, bokram; **she- –**, bokooi; **it gets
my –**, dit maak my vies.
goatee, bokbaardjie.
goatherd, bokwagter.
goatish, bokagtig.
goatskin, bokvel.
goatsucker, nagswa(w)eltjie, bokmelker.
gobble, v. skrok, inlaai; – **up**, wegslaan, kafloop.
gobble, v. koel-koel, klok.
gobblegook, amptenaretaal.
gobbler, skrokker, gulsigaard.
gobbler, kalkoen(mannetjie).
gobelin, gobelin, behangseltapyt.
go-between, tussenpersoon, bemiddelaar.
goblet, roemer, kroes, beker.
goblin, kabouter.
go-cart, stootkarretjie, -waentjie; dwergmotor.
god, (af)god; – **of war**, oorlogsgod; – **of love**,
god van die liefde; ye –**s!**, goeie gode!; –**s**,
engelebak (in teater).
God, God; **with –**, by die Here, in die Here
ontslape; –**'s truth**, so waar as God; – **forbid**,
mag God (dit) verhoed; – **grant**, God gee; –
– **bless my soul!**, wel allewêreld!; my alle-
magtig!; – **willing**, so die Here wil; **under –**,
naas God; met Gods hulp; **thank –**, God sy
dank, goddank; **for –'s sake**, om Gods wil.
god-child, peetkind.
god-daughter, peetdogter.
goddess, godin; aangebedene.
god-father, peetoom.
god-fearing, godvresend.
godhead, godheid.
godless, goddeloos; ongelowig.
godlike, goddelik.
godly, godvresend, vroom, godvrugtig.
god-mother, peettante.
godsend, godsgawe, uitredding.
godson, peetkind, -seun.
godspeed, goeie reis; veels geluk.
go-getter, deurdrywer, doring, voorslag.
goggle, skeelkyk, oormekaarkyk; uitpuil.
goggles, stofbril, oogklappe; dronksiekte.
goglet, **gugglet**, **gurglet**, gorletbeker.
going, n. (die) gaan, ry, hardloop; –**s-on**, gedrag, doen en late; kaskenades; **good –**, goeie
vaart; goeie grond (pad).
going, v. gaande; **set the clock –**, sit die horlosie
aan die gang; **one of the best things –**, een van
die beste dinge wat bestaan.
gold, n. goud; geld, rykdom; – **bloc**, goudblok;
go off –, die goudstandaard laat vaar.
gold, a. goud- . . ., goue.
gold amalgam, goudamalgaam.
gold-digger, goudgrawer; geluksoekster.
gold-dust, stofgoud.
golden, goue; gulde(n); goud- . . . ; goudkleurig;
the – age, die goue (gulde) eeu; – **mean**, gulde
middelweg; – **wedding**, goue bruilof.

gold-fever, gouddors.
goldfinch, geel-, goudvink.
goldfish, goudvis.
gold-foil, bladgoud.
gold-lace, goudboorsel, goudgalon.
gold-leaf, bladgoud.
gold-ore, gouderts.
gold-plate, goudwerk.
gold-rush, goudjag, goudstormloop.
goldsmith, goudsmid.
gold-wire, gouddraad.
golf, n. golf.
golf, v. gholfspeel.
golf-club, gholfklub; gholfstok.
golfer, gholfspeler.
golf-links, gholfgrond, -baan.
golliwog, nikkerpop; paaiboelie.
golly, hemel, hening!.
gondola, gondel.
gondolier, gondelier.
gong, ghong.
goniometer, hoekmeter, goniometer.
goniometric(al), goniometries.
goniometry, hoekmeting, goniometrie.
gonorrhoea, gonorr(h)ee, druiper.
good, a. goed; bekwaam, geskik; gaaf; eg; soet,
braaf; **in – spirits**, in 'n goeie bui, in 'n op-
gewekte stemming; **do a – turn**, 'n diens
bewys; **say a – word for**, 'n goeie woordjie
doen vir; **take in – part**, goed opneem;
be – at, uitmunt in; **in his – books**, in 'n
goeie blaadjie by hom; – **sense**, gesonde
verstand; **and a – thing too!**, en maar gelukkig ook!; **the rule holds –**, die reël is van toepassing; **have a – mind**, geneig voel; **as – as
his word**, 'n man van sy woord; **make –**, goedmaak; vergoed; vervul, uitvoer; die bewys
lewer; goed beantwoord; – **breeding**, fatsoen,
wellewendheid; – **for R10**, goed vir R10; –
– **looks**, mooi gesig, knapheid, mooiheid;
– **luck (to you)**, veels geluk!; – **humour**, goeie
luim; opgeruimdheid; – **nature**, goeie geaardheid; goedaardigheid; – **temper**, goeie
humeur; **too much of a – thing**, te veel van die
goeie, te erg.
good, n. (die) goeie; nut, welsyn; **the – and the
bad**, die goeie en die slegte; –**s**, goed, goedere;
for his own –, in sy eie belang; **what – will
it do?** watter nut sal dit hê?; **do –**, goeddoen,
weldoen; **R5 to the –**, R5 oor (te goed);
for – (and all), (eens en) vir altyd; **be no –**,
niks beteken nie; **he is up to no –**, hy voer iets
in die skild.
good afternoon, goei(e)middag.
good breeding, wellewendheid.
good-bye, vaarwel; **say –**, dagsê.
good evening, (goeie)naand.
good-fellowship, kameraadskap.
good-for-nothing, niksnuts.
good-humoured, goed geluim(d), vriendelik, goedhartig.
goodlooking, mooi, knap, aansienlik.
goodly, mooi, knap; taamlik, flink.
good-natured, goedaardig; goedig.
goodness, goedheid; geskiktheid, bekwaamheid;
deug, – **gracious**, goeie genade; – **knows**, die
hemel mag weet; **I wish to –**, ek wou in hemelsnaam!; **thank –**, die hemel sy dank!; **for –
sake**, in hemelsnaam.
goods, goed, goedere; **deliver the –**, doen wat
van jou verwag word.
goods-traffic, goederevervoer, vragvervoer.
goods-train, goederetrein, vragtrein.
goods-van, bagasiewa.
goodwife, huisvrou, moeder die vrou.

goodwill 511

goodwill, toegeneentheid; klandisie.
goody-goody, n. „vroom" kêrel, papbroek.
goof, n. stommerik.
goose, gans; uilskuiken, stommerik; parsyster.
gooseberry, appelderliefde (appelliefie).
goose-flesh, gansvleis, hoendervleis.
goose-neck, swanehals.
goose-quill, gansveer; veerpen.
goose-skin, hoendervleis.
goose-step, paradepas.
gopher, grond-eekhoring; goferboom.
Gordian, Gordiaans; **cut the – knot,** die Gordiaanse knoop deurhak.
gore, v. deurboor; stoot.
gore, n. dooi(e)bloed, (geronne) bloed.
gorge, n. keel, strot; kloof.
gorge, v. verslind, inswelg; volprop.
gorgeous, pragtig, skitterend; oordadig.
gorgeousness, prag; oorlading, oordaad.
gorilla, gorilla.
gorse, brem.
gory, bloed(er)ig.
gosh: by –, gits!
goshawk, patrysvalk.
gosling, gansie.
gospel, evangelie.
gospel oath, eed op die Bybel.
gospel truth, heilige waarheid.
gossamer, herfsdraad, spinnerak.
gossip, n. buur(vrou); praatjiesmaker, -maakster; buurpraatjies, skinderpraatjies.
gossip, v. babbel, skinder.
Goth, Got; **–s,** Gote.
Gothic, Goties; barbaars.
Gouda, Gouda (stad); **– (cheese),** Goudse kaas.
gouge, n. hol beitel, gutsbeitel.
gouge, v. uitbeitel, uithol; uitsteek.
goulash, ghoelasj.
gourd, komkommergewas; kalbaskruik.
gourmand, vraat, gulsigaard; smulpaap.
gourmet, fynproewer.
gout, jig; druppel; vlek.
gouty, jigtig, jigagtig.
govern, regeer, bestuur, lei, beheer, beheers; **–ing body,** bestuur(sliggaam).
governable, regeerbaar; handelbaar.
governess, goewernante, privaat-onderwyseres.
government, n. goewerment, regering.
government, a. regerings- . . ., staats- . . ., goewerments- . . .; **– house,** goewerneurswoning; **– securities,** staatspapiere.
governmental, goewerments- . . ., regerings- . . .
governor, goewerneur, bewindvoerder; oukêrel; reëlaar.
governor-general, goewerneur-generaal.
gowk, koekoek; lomperd; gek.
gown, n. rok, kleed; toga; (kamer)japon.
grab, v. gryp, skraap; vang, pak.
grab, n. (die) gryp; vangarm; **make a – at,** gryp na.
grace, n. guns, genade; grasie; bevalligheid, swier; fatsoen; uitstel; tafelgebed(jie); **have the – to,** so fatsoenlik wees om; **by the – of God,** deur die grasie (genade) Gods; **in the year of –,** in die jaar van onse Here; **a day's –,** 'n dag uitstel; **days of –,** respytdae, uitsteldae; **the –s,** die Grasieë; **say –,** bid of dank (oor die tafel).
grace, v. sier; vereer; begunstig.
grace-cup, afskeidsbeker.
graceful, bevallig, bekoorlik, grasieus.
graceless, lomp; onfatsoenlik; goddeloos.
grace-note, voorslag.
gracious, genadig; innemend; bevallig, grasieus; **good –,** goeie genade.

graciously, genadiglik, goedgunstiglik, innemende (bevallige) manier.
graciousness, genadigheid, goedgunstigheid, saamheid; bevalligheid.
gradate, gradeer.
gradation, gradering; volgorde; **–s,** grade.
grade, n. graad; gehalte; helling; **make th sukses behaal;** slaag; die top bereik.
grade, v. gradeer, rangskik; meng.
gradient, helling; hellingshoek; gradient.
gradual, n. graduaal.
gradual, a. geleidelik; trapsgewyse.
gradually, geleidelik; langsamerhand.
graduand, graduandus.
graduate, v, gradeer; gradueer.
graduate, n. gegradueerde; maatglas.
graduated, gegradeer; gegradueer.
graduation, gradering, indeling; graadverdeling; graadverlening; **– day,** gradedag.
graduator, gradueerder; graadmeter.
Gr(a)ecism, Gresisme.
graft, n. ent; oorentsel.
graft, v. ent; oorent.
graft, n. omkopery.
grail, graal, skottel.
grain, n. graan; korrel; grein(tjie); draad, nerf; **the – of the wood,** die draad van die hout; **against the –,** teen die draad in; **it went against the – with me,** dit het my teen die bors gestuit.
grain, v. korrel; haar-af maak; vlam; marmer; grein; aar.
grain-elevator, graansuier.
grainer, (marmer)skilder.
grainside, nerfkant.
grainstack, graanmied.
gram, gramme, gram.
graminaceous, gramineous, grasagtig.
graminivorous, grasetend.
grammar, grammatika, spraakkuns.
grammarian, grammatikus.
grammatical, grammatikaal, grammaties.
gramme, gram, gram.
gramophone, grammofoon.
grampus, noor(d)kapper, stormvis.
gramradio, gramradio.
granadilla, grenadilla, grenadella.
granary, graanskuur, -pakhuis.
grand, groot; groots; hoofs; pragtig, mooi, fraai, goed; **G.– Duke,** Groothertog; **– society,** hoë (hoofse) kringe; **– stand,** groottribune, -paviljoen; **– piano,** vleuel(piano).
grand-child, kleinkind.
grand-daughter, kleindogter.
grand-duchess, groothertogin.
grand-duke, groothertog.
grandee, edelman, grande.
grandeur, grootheid; grootsheid; prag.
grandfather, grootvader, oupa; **–'s clock,** (groot) staanhorlosie, staanklok.
grandiloquence, hoogdrawendheid.
grandiloquent, hoogdrawend; spoggerig.
grandiose, groots; spoggerig.
grandmother, grootmoeder, ouma.
grandson, kleinseun.
grand-uncle, oudoom.
grange, (plaas)opstal; skuur.
granite, graniet.
granivorous, graanetend.
granny, ouma.
grant, v. toestaan; vergun, veroorloof; skenk, verleen; toegee; toestem, erken; **–ed that, toegegee dat,** gestel(d) dat; **take for –ed,** aanneem, as uitgemaak beskou; **God –,** (mag) God gee.
grant, n. vergunning; toelae; verlening; skenking.

granular, korrelagtig, gekorrel.
granulate, korrels vorm; granuleer.
granule, korreltjie.
grape, druif.
grape-fruit, jaar-, bitterlemoen, pomelo.
grape-shot, skroot.
grape-vine, wingerdstok; along the –, met 'n riemtelegram.
graph, n. grafiese voorstelling, grafiek.
graphic(al), grafies; aanskoulik, lewendig.
graphite, grafiet, potlood.
graphology, grafologie, handskrifkunde.
graphotype, grafotipe; grafotiep.
grapnel, enterhaak; werpanker.
grapple, n. haak; greep; worsteling.
grapple, v. aanklamp; aanpak, beetpak.
grasp, v. vasgryp, vat, pak; begryp, vat.
grasp, n. greep; vashouplek; bereik; verstand; beyond, within one's –, buite, binne sy bereik; get a good –, 'n goeie houvas kry; 'n goeie begrip kry.
grasping, inhalig, skraapsugtig.
grass, n. gras; weiveld, -land; he does not let the – grow under his feet, hy laat daar geen gras oor groei nie; cut the – from under one's feet, iemand die gras voor die voete wegmaai.
grass, v. met gras beplant; teen die grond slaan; neertrek, plant; neerskiet.
grass-cloth, graslinne.
grasshopper, sprinkaan, sprinkaankriek.
grass-widow, grasweduwee.
grassy, grasryk; grasagtig; gras-...
grate, n. vuur(h)erd; rooster; tralie.
grate, v. rasper; knars; kras; kraak; skuur; – on the nerves, laat gril, die senuwees martel; – upon the ear, die oor pynig.
grateful, dankbaar, erkentlik; aangenaam, strelend.
gratefulness, dankbaarheid, erkentlikheid; aangenaamheid.
grater, rasper.
gratification, bevrediging; vergoeding.
gratify, bevredig; verheug; vergoed.
grating, a. krassend, knarsend.
grating, n. traliewerk, tralies.
gratis, gratis, verniet, kosteloos.
gratitude, dankbaarheid, erkentlikheid.
gratuitous, kosteloos, vry, gratis; ongevraag; ongegrond; onnodig.
gratuitously, verniet; ongevraag.
gratuity, gif, toelae, gratifikasie.
gratulatory, gelukwensend.
gravamen, beswaar(skrif); swaartepunt.
grave, n. graf, grafkuil,
grave, v. grif, graveer; inprent.
grave, a. swaar, gewigtig, ernstig belangrik; somber.
gravedigger, doodgrawer, grafmaker
grave, n. gruis; graweel(steen).
gravel, v. gruis; dronkslaan.
gravelly, gruisagtig, gruis-...
graven, gesnede; ingegraveer.
graver, graveerder; graveerstif, -naald.
gravestone, grafsteen.
graveyard, kerkhof, begraafplaas.
gravitate, graviteer; sak; oorhel, aangetrek word; (diamante) sif.
gravitation, swaartekrag; oorhelling.
gravity, erns; gewigtheid; swaarte, gewig; swaartekrag; centre of –, swaartepunt; specific –, soortlike gewig.
gravy, sous
gravy-boat, souskom(metjie), souspotjie.
gravy, sien grey.
graze, v. wei, graas; laat wei; vee oppas.

graze, v. skrams raak, skram; skaaf, skuur.
graze, n. skram, skaafplek.
grazier, slagveeboer, vetweier.
grazing, (die) wei; weiveld.
grease, n. vet, wa-smeer, teer, „ghries", mok (aan perdepote).
grease, v. smeer; – some one's palm, iemand iets in die hand stop.
grease-gun, ghriesspuit.
greasy, vetterig, olieagtig; smerig; lymerig, salwend; – wool, vetwol.
great, groot; lang; dik; they are – friends, hulle is groot (dik) vriende; a – age, 'n hoë ouderdom; a – painter, 'n groot (beroemde) skilder; – Scott, grote genade; that's –, dis mooi!; be – at, uitmunt in; – grandfather, oorgrootvader.
Great Britain, Groot-Brittanje.
greatly, grootliks, in hoë mate, baie.
greatness, grootheid, edelheid; grootte.
greave, beenskut.
greaves, kaiings, vetmoer, vetbesinksel.
Grecian, Grieks.
Greece, Griekeland
greed, hebsug, begerigheid; gulsigheid.
greediness, gulsigheid, snoepheid; hebsug.
greedy, gulsig, snoep; hebsugtig.
Greek, a. Grieks.
Greek, n. Griek; Grieks, die Griekse taal; it is – to me, dit is Grieks (Latyn, Hebreeus) vir my.
green, a. groen; onervare; fris, jong; the – light verlof om voort te gaan.
green, n. groen; groenigheid; groente; graskol; veld; setperk (gholf).
green, v. groen word (maak); iets wysmaak.
greener, nuweling, groene.
greenery, groen, loof, groenigheid.
green-fly, (blad)luis.
greengrocer, groentehandelaar.
greenhorn, groentjie; melkmuil.
greenhouse, glaasstoep, serre; broeikas.
greenkeeper, baanopsigter (gholf).
Greenland, Groenland.
green-room, artiestekamer.
green-sickness, bleeksug, -siekte.
greensward, groengras, grasveld.
greenwood, bosveld, woud, bosse.
green-yard, skut.
greet, groet, begroet, verwelkom.
greet, v. huil, ween.
greeting, groet, begroeting; –s, groete.
gregarious, kudde-...; gesellig; – instinct, kuddegevoel, -instink.
gregariousness, kudde-, gemeenskapsgevoel.
grenade, granaat.
grenadier, grenadier.
grenadella, granadilla, grenadella.
grey, a. grys, grou, vaal; – eyes, grou oë; – horse, (blou)skimmelperd.
grey, n. (die) grys, grou, vaal; gryskleur; grys (klere); (blou)skimmelperd.
grey-beard, grysbaard, grysaard.
grey-headed, grys, gryskop-...
greyhound, windhond.
greyish, grysagtig, grouagtig, vaal.
grid, rooster; tralie; motorhek.
griddle, koekplaat; rooster.
grid, rooster; tralie; motorhek.
grief, leed, droefheid, verdriet; come to –, verongeluk; skipbreuk ly, misluk; afval, in die verknorsing kom.
grievance, grief, krenking; beswaar.
grieve, bedroef; grief, krenk; treur.
grievous, ernstig; drukkend; smartlik.
griffin, griffon, gryphon, griffioen.
grill, n. rooster; braaivleis.

grill, v. (op die rooster) braai; kruisvra; – **ed**, **steak**, roosterbiefstuk.
grim, nors, grommig, streng; **hold on like – death**, op lewe en dood vasklou; **a – sight**, 'n huiweringswekkende gesig.
grimace, n. grimas, skewebek.
grimace, v. grimasse maak, gryns.
grime, vuiligheid, vuilgoed; roet.
grimy, vuil, besmeer, betakel,
grin, v. gryns, meesmuil, grinnik,
grin, n. gryns(lag), spotlag.
grind, v. maal; slyp; swoeg, blok; onderdruk; **– down**, onderdruk, afbeul; **– at Latin**, Latyn blok, swoeg oor Latyn; **– the teeth**, die tande knars.
grind, n. (die) maal; slyp; geswoeg.
grinder, meul; slyper; kies, maaltand; meulsteen; blokker, swoeger.
grindstone, slypsteen.
grip, n. (hand)greep, vat, houvas; hand(reiking); beheer; begrip; handvatsel.
grip, v. gryp, beetpak, vat; boei.
gripe, v. gryp, vasklou; koliek gee.
gripe, n. greep; mag; handvatsel; **–s**, koliek, krampe.
gripe-water, krampmiddel.
grisly, aaklig, afgryslik, grieselig.
grist, maalkoring, maalgraan; **all is – that comes to his mill**, alles is van sy gading.
gristle, kraakbeen.
grit, n. gruis; pit, fut, durf.
grit, v. knars, kraak.
gritty, sanderig.
grizzled, grys, peper-en-sout(kleurig).
grizzly, a. grys, gryserig, grou, valerig.
grizzly, n. grysbeer.
groan, v. kreun, steun, kerm.
groan, n. kreun, gesteun, gekerm.
groaningly, kreunend, kermend.
groats, grutte, gort.
grocer, kruidenier.
grocery, kruideniersware.
grog, n. grok.
groggy, aangeskote; slingerig; bewerig.
groin, lies, sy, graatrib.
groom, n. staljong, perdekneg; oppasser; kamerheer; bruidegom.
groom, v. roskam, versorg; oppas, bedien; **well –ed**, fyn uitgevat.
groove, n. groef, gleuf; (sleur)gang.
groove, v. groef, keep, uitgroef, uitkeep.
grope, (rond)tas, (in die donker) voel.
gropingly, tastend, soekend; op die tas.
gross, n. gros.
gross, a. groot; vet; grof; onbeskof; walglik; sinlik; **– error**, growwe fout; **– sum**, totale bedrag, bruto bedrag.
grot, grot.
grotesque, a. grotesk, pōtsierlik, grillig.
grotesque, n. grotesk.
grotto, grot.
ground, n. grond; **–s**, grond(e); moer; **touch –**, grond raak; **on the – of**, op grond van; **stand one's –**, jou man staan; **gain –**, veld wen; **lose –**, grond verloor; **give –**, padgee, wyk, toegee.
ground, v. grond, grondves; baseer; staaf; op die grond sit; na die grond lei; grondvat; strand; op die grond hou.
ground-floor, benedeverdieping, begane grond; **on the –**, gelykvloers.
ground-ice, grond-ys.
groundless, sonder rede, ongegrond.
ground-nut, grondboontjie.
ground-plan, plattegrond, grondplan.
ground-swell, (grond)deining.
ground-to-air missile, grondlugprojektiel.
groundwork, grondslag, grondwerk; geraamte.
group, n. groep; klomp(ie); party.
group, v. groepeer.
grouse, n. korhoenders.
grouse, v. brom, kla, mopper, murmureer.
grouser, brompot, mopperaar.
grove, bome, bos.
grovel, kruip, in die stof wentel.
grow, groei; laat groei, kweek, verbou; word; **– into one, together**, ineengroei; **– up**, opgroei, groot word; **– rich**, ryk word; **the habit –s on one**, die gewoonte raak ingewortel; **– potatoes**, aartappels kweek (verbou), met aartappels boer.
grower, kweker, boer; **this rose is a fast –**, dit is 'n roos wat vinnig groei.
growl, v. knor; brom, kla, mor; dreun.
growl, n. knor; gebrom, gemor; snou.
growler, brompot; vierwielrytuig.
grown, begroei; opgegroei, volwasse; **– up**, volwasse, opgegroei; opgeskote.
growth, groei, ontwikkeling, vooruitgang; wasdom; (die) kweek; gewas, gesaaide.
grub, n. wurm; maaier; sukkelaar; smerige vent; kos, eetgoed.
grub, v. (op)grawe; (grond) skoonmaak; snuffel; ploeter, swoeg; eet; kosgee.
grubby, vol wurms (maaiers); smerig.
grub-stake, n. kapitaal-aandeel.
grudge, v. misgun, nie gun nie.
grudge, n. pik, wrok, hekel; **bear someone a –**, 'n pik op (wrok teen, hekel aan) iemand hê.
grudgingly, met teensin, onwillig(lik).
gruel, gortwater; loesing, pak.
gruelling, n. pak slae, loesing, pak.
gruelling, a. moordend, uitputtend.
gruesome, aaklig, afskuwelik, afsigtelik.
gruff, nors, stuurs, bars, grof.
grumble, v. brom, pruttel, kla, mor; grom, knor; rommel, dreun.
grumble, n. gebrom; gerommel.
grumbler, brompot, pruttelaar, brommer.
grumbingly, brommend, pruttelend.
grumpy, a. brommerig, nors, knorrig.
grumpy, n. brompot, knor(re)pot.
grunt, v. knor, gor-gor; brom, grom.
grunt, n. (ge)knor, gegor; gegrom.
grunter, knorder; otjie.
guana, likkewaan.
guano, ghwano.
guarantee, n. garansie, waarborg; borg.
guarantee, v. garandeer, waarborg.
guarantor, borg, garant.
guaranty, garansie, waarborg.
guard, n. wag; kondukteur; bewaker; beskerming, hoede; **take –**, regstaan, in posisie gaan staan; **be on a**, wagstaan; **be on one's a**, op jou hoede wees; **mount –**, op wag gaan staan, die wag betrek; **relieve –**, die wag aflos; **– of honour**, erewag.
guard, v. oppas, bewaak, behoed; op jou hoede wees, waak (teen).
guard-boat, patrolleerboot, wagboot.
guard-chain, veiligheidsketting.
guarded, bewaak; versigtig, behoedsaam.
guard-house, waghuis.
guardian, bewaker; bewaarder, opsiener, oppasser; kurator; beskermer; voog; **– angel**, beskermengel; skutsengel.
guardianship, beskerming; voogdyskap.
guard-room, waglokaal, waghuis.
guard-ship, wagskip.
guardsman, garde, offisier, -soldaat.

guava, koejawel.
gudgeon-pin, stootpen.
guelder rose, gelderse roos.
guerdon, beloning, vergelding.
guer(r)illa, guer(r)illa(oorlog).
guess, v. raai, gis, skat; dink, glo.
guess, n. gissing; make a – at, raai na.
guess-work, gissing, skatting; raaiery.
guest, gas, kuiergas.
guest-house, gastehuis, rushuis.
guffaw, n. skaterende (luidrugtige) lag.
guffaw, v. brullend lag, brul, skaterlag.
guidance, leiding; bestuur.
guide, n. gids; leidsman; leidraad.
guide, v. lei, die weg (pad) wys, as gids dien; rondlei; raad gee; bestuur, stuur; guided missile, geleide projektiel; guided tour, geselskapsreis.
guide-book, reisgids.
guide-post, wegwys(t)er, handwys(t)er.
guide-rope, tentlyn; stuurlyn.
g(u)ild, gilde, vereniging.
guilder, gulde.
guile, lis, slimheid, bedrog.
guileful, arglistig, listig, vals.
guileless, arg(e)loos, onskuldig, eerlik.
guillotine, n. guillotine, valbyl; sluiting.
guilt, skuld.
guiltless, onskuldig; skuldeloos.
guilty, skuldig; – of, skuldig aan.
guinea, ghienie.
guinea-fowl, tarentaal, poelpetaat.
guinea-pig, marmotjie.
guise, kleding; mom, masker; in, under the – of, onder die masker van.
guitar, ghitaar (kitaar).
gulf, golf; draaikolk; afgrond; kloof.
Gulf-stream, Golfstroom.
gull, n. seemeeu.
gull, n. stommerik, uilskuiken, swaap.
gull, v. kul, fop.
gullet, slukderm, keel(gat); sloot, kloof.
gullible, liggelowig, simpel, onnosel.
gully, kloof, sloep(ie); sloot(jie), voortjie; sloep, gangetjie (krieket).
gulp, v. wegsluk; inswelg; – down tears, trane wegsluk.
gulp, n. sluk, mondvol, teug.
gum(s), n. tandvleis.
gum, n. gom; drag (van die oë).
gum, v. (vas)gom, lym; (vas)kleef.
gum, interj. by –, gits!
gumboil, sweer(tjie), abses.
gumption, oorleg, skranderheid; fut, pit.
gum-resin, gom(hars).
gum-tree, gomboom.
gun, geweer; kanon; rewolwer; skut; sure as a –, so waar as vet; stand, stick to one's –s, jou standpunt handhaaf; jou man staan.
gun-barrel, geweerloop.
gun-boat, kanonneerboot.
gun-carriage, kanonwa, affuit.

gun-metal, kanon-, geskutmetaal.
gunner, kanonnier, artilleris.
gunnery, geskutoefening.
gunny, goiing.
gun-port, geskutpoort.
gunpowder, (bus)kruit.
gun-running, geweersmokkelary.
gunshot, geweer-, kanonskoot(s)afstand.
gunsmith, geweermaker.
gun-stock, laaistok.
gun-stock, geweerkolf, -laai.
gunwale, gunnel, dolboord.
gurgle, v. borrel, klok.
gurgle, n. borreling, geklok.
gurlet, gugglet, goglet, gorletbeker.
gurnard, gurnet, knorhaan(vis).
gush, v. stroom, spuit, oorborrel; dweep.
gush, n. uitstroming; dwepery.
gusher, dweper; spuitbron, spuiter.
gushing, oordewe.
gust, ruk, vlaag, bui.
gustation, (die) proe.
gustatory, smaak- . . . ; – nerve, smaaksenuwee.
gusto, lus, genot, smaak, animo.
gusty, winderig, vlaerig, onstuimig.
gut, n. derm; (derm)snaar; –s, ingewande; he has no –s, hy het geen fut nie.
gut, v. ingewande uithaal; plunder; uitbrand; vreet.
gut-scraper, vioolkrapper, -krasser.
gutta-percha, gutta-percha.
gutter, n. geut, voortjie; modder(sloot).
gutter, v. uithol; afloop (van 'n kers).
gutter-child, -snipe, -walker, straatswerwer.
guttural, a. gutturaal, keel- . . .
guttural, n. keelklank, gutturaal.
guy, n. stuurtou; tentlyn.
guy, v. stuur; (tentlyne) span.
guy, n. gek, dwaas, voëlverskrikker.
guy, v. uitlag, vir die gek hou.
guzzle, gulsig eet en drink.
guzzler, vraat, suiplap.
gymkhana, sport; sportgrond.
gymnasium, gimnasium; gimnastiekkamer.
gymnastic, a. gimnasties, gimnastiek- . . .
gymnastic, -s, gimnastiek.
gymnospernous, naaksadig.
gynaecologist, ginekoloog, vrouedokter.
gynaecology, ginekologie, leer van die vrouesiektes.
gynandrous, helmstyl- . . . dubbelslagtig, trassie- . . .
gynocracy, vroueregering.
gyps(e)ous, gipsagtig, gips- . . .
gypsum, gips.
gyrate, rondomtalie draai, wielewaai.
gyration, ronddraaiing, (om)wenteling.
gyre, draai
gyromancy, giromansie, waarsêery.
gyroscope, giroskoop.
gyve, boei.

H

ha, ha!
haberdashery, garing en band, kramery.
habiliment, uitrusting; –s, kleding.
habit, n. gewoonte, gebruik; kleed, gewaad, kostuum; hebbelikheid; – of mind, gewoonte; geestesgesteldheid; riding –, rykleed, -kosstuum; by, from –, uit gewoonte; be in the –, gewoon(d) wees, die gewoonte hê.
habit, v. kleed; bewoon.
habitable, bewoonbaar.
habitat, woonplaas; verblyf, habitat.
habitation, bewoning; woonplaas.
habitual, gewoon, gebruiklik; – drunkard, gewoontedronkaard.
habitually, uit gewoonte, gereeld.
habituate, wen, gewend raak.
habitude, gewoonte; hebbelikheid.
hack, n. pik, byl, houweel; kap; skop.
hack, v. kap, keep, hou, skop; kug.
hack, n. knol; ryperd; broodskrywer.
hack, v. seerrug (holrug) ry.
hackle, hekel; veer.
hackle, v. kap, vermink.
hack-log, kapblok.
hackney, n. ryperd; sukkelaar, sloof.
hackney, v. holrug ry; -ed, afgesaag.
hack-saw, ystersaag.
hack-work, broodskrywery.
haddock, skelvis.
haematic, bloed- . . .
haematite, bloedsteen.
haemoglobin, bloedkleurstof.
h(a)emorrhage, bloeding, bloedvloeiing.
h(a)emorrhoids, aambeie.
haf, hef, handvatsel.
hag, heks, toorkol.
haggard, vervalle, ontdaan, verwilderd.
haggis, hartslag, „haggis".
haggle, v. afding; twis, kibbel.
haggle, n. knibbelary; rusie, getwis.
hagiocracy, heiligeregering.
hagiographer, gewyde skrywer.
hagiolatry, aanbidding van heilige.
hagiology, heiligelewens(beskrywinge).
Hague: The –, Den Haag (Die Haag).
hail, v. & n. hael.
hail, interj. heil, gegroet!; – fellow (well met), allemansvriend.
hail, v. begroet, verwelkom; (aan)roep praai; – from, afkomstig wees van.
hail, n. begroeting, verwelkoming; within –,binne beroep, te beroep.
hailstone, haelkorrel.
hair, haar (hare); keep your – on, bly bedaard; not turn a –, geen spier vertrek nie; it made my – stand on end, dit het my hare (te berge) laat rys; split –s, haarkloof; get by the short –s, (iemand) in jou mag hê.
hairbreadth, hair's breadth, vinger-, haarbreedte; – escape, nou(e) ontkoming.
hair-brush, haar-, hareborsel.
hair-do, kapsel, haardrag.
hairdresser, kapper.
hair-pin, haarnaald.
hair-raising, sensasioneel.
hair's breadth, sien hairbreadth.
hair-splitting, haarklowery.
hair-spring, onrusveer, spiraalveer.
hair-stroke, ophaal(lyn).
hair-trigger, sneller.
hairy, harig, behaard.
hake, stokvis.
halberd, hellebaard.
halberdier, hellebaardier.
halcyon, n. ysvoël.

halcyon, a. kalm, vredig, gelukkig.
hale, fris; – and hearty, fris en gesond.
half, a. half; – a loaf, 'n halwe brood.
half, n. helfte, halwe, halfie; give me –, gee my die helfte; give me a –, gee my 'n halwe ('n halfie); better –, wederhelf; too clever by –, veels te slim; – the men, die helfte van die manne; – a pound, 'n halfpond; go halves, gelykop deel; cry halves, die helfte eis.
half, adv. half: I – wish, ek wens half, ek wens eenkant; not – bad, glad nie sleg nie; – past two, halfdrie.
half-aum, halfaam.
half-back, skakel, spil.
half-baked, halfgaar; onbekook, onwys.
half-binding, halfleer(band).
half-bred, baster- . . .
half-breed, baster.
half-brother, stief-, halfbroer.
half-caste, a. baster- . . ., halfbloed- . . .
half-caste, n. baster, halfbloed.
half-cock, rus; at –, in die rus.
half-crown, halfkroon.
half-hearted, bedees; flou; nie van harte nie.
half-holiday, vry middag.
half-hose, sokkies.
half-length, halflyf- . . .
half-line, middellyn.
half-mast, halfstok.
half-mourning, ligte rou.
half-pay, waggeld; halfsalaris.
half-penny, halfstuiwer, halfpennie.
half-seas-over, aangeklam, hoenderkop.
half-sister, stief-, halfsuster.
half-sovereign, rand(stuk).
half-time, speeltyd; pouse; rustyd.
halfway, adv. halfpad, -weg.
halfway (house), uitspanplek; verversingstasie.
halfway line, middellyn.
half-witted, halfwys, getik, simpel.
half-yearly, halfjaarliks.
halieutics, visvangs, hengelkuns.
halitosis, slegte asem.
hall, saal; voorportaal; huis; hal.
hallelujah, halleluja.
hall-mark, stempel, yk, waarmerk.
hallo, hallo!
hallow, heilig, heilig verklaar.
hall-stand, (hoede)stander, hoederak, gangrak.
hallucination, sinsbedrog, waan, hallusinasie.
halma, halma.
halo, ligkring; stralekrans; halo.
halogen, halogeen.
haloid, sout- . . ., soutagtig.
halt, v. tot staan (stilstand) bring; stop, tot staan (stilstand) kom.
halt, n. halt, stop; halte, stopplek.
halt, v. kreupel (mank) loop, hink.
halt, a. kreupel, mank.
halt, n. kreupel-, mankstap.
halter, halter; strop.
haltingly, mank, kreupel; kreupel-kreupel, staanstaan.
halting-place, halte, uitspanplek.
halve, halveer, (gelyk) deel.
halyard, val.
ham, dy; ham.
hamadryad, bosnimf.
hamburger, frikkadelbroodjie.
hames, borsplaat; draagbors.
ham-fisted, onhandig; lomp.
Hamtic, Hamities.
hamlet, dorpie, gehug.

hammer, n. hamer; haan (van 'n geweer); – a tongs, met alle mag.
hammer, v. hamer, moker; – at, losslaan op; swoeg aan; – into, instamp.
hammer-head, hamerkop.
hammer-lock, hamerslot(greep).
hammock, hangmat.
hamper, n. mandjie; keldertjie (vir drank).
hamper, v. hinder, belemmer.
hamshackle, kniehalter.
hamster, hamster.
hamstring, n. knie-sening.
hamstring, v. die knie-sening deursny.
hand, n. hand, handbreedte; handvol; handtekening, handskrif; poot; wyster; werksman; **all –s,** alle hens, alle man (alman); **at first –,** uit die eerste hand; **he is a good – at,** hy is 'n doring in; **a new –,** nuweling; **an illegible –,** 'n onleesbare hand(skrif); **bear a –,** ('n handjie) meehelp; **come to –,** opdaag, ter hand kom; **lay –s on,** kry; in beslag neem; **take in –,** onderneem; **change –s,** van eienaar verander; **win –s down,** fluit-fluit wen; **–s off,** hande tuis; **–s up,** hensop, (steek jou) hande op!; **– in –,** hand aan hand; **– over –,** hand oor hand, handjie vir handjie; **– and foot,** hand(e) en voet(e); uit alle mag; **be – in glove with,** kop in een mus wees met; **at –,** byderhand; op hande; **by –,** met die hand; in hande; **from – to mouth,** van die hand in die tand; **in –,** in hande; onder hande; in voorbereiding; **off –,** uit die vuis, onvoorberei(d); **on –,** in voorraad; op hande; **on all –s,** aan alle kante; van alle kante; **on the one, the other –,** aan die een, die ander kant; **tell out of –,** voor die vuis sê; **get out of –,** onregeerbaar word; **to –,** binne bereik, byderhand; **to one's –,** kant en klaar; **your letter to –,** u brief ontvang.
hand, v. aangee, afgee; **– down,** oorlewer, oorhandig; **– in,** inlewer; **– out,** uitgee, -deel, -lewer; **– over,** oorhandig, -lewer; **– on,** aangee; **– up,** opgee, aangee.
hand-bill, strooibiljet.
handbook, handboek, -leiding.
handbreath, handbreedte.
hand-cart, stootkarretjie.
handcuff, n. (hand)boei.
handcuff, v. boei.
handful, handvol, handjievol.
handicap, n. voorgif; agterstand; nadeel, belemmering, las.
handicap, v. voorgee; agter-, terugsit; kniehalter.
handicapper, voorgeër.
handicap-race, voorgeewedstryd.
handicraft, hand(e)werk, ambag.
handicraftsman, ambagsman.
handiness, handigheid; behendigheid.
handiwork, hand(e)werk.
handkerchief, sakdoek.
handle, n. handvat(sel), steel, hingsel, kruk, oor, hef, stuur; vat.
handle, v. bevoel, betas; hanteer; baasraak; behandel; handel, handel drywe (in); – **roughly,** ru behandel, afknou.
handle-bar(s), stuur(stang).
hand-made, met die hand gemaak.
hand-organ, draaiorrel.
hand-rail, reling, leuning.
handsel, handgeld; voorsmaak.
hand-shake, handdruk.
handsome, knap, aansienlik; edelmoedig; rojaal **– is that – does,** mooi vergaan, maar deug bly staan.
handwriting, handskrif.
handy, handig, behendig, vaardig; **gerieflik,** geskik; byderhand; **come in –,** (goed) te pas kom.
handyman, hansie-my-kneg, slimjan.
hang, v. hang, ophang; behang; plak; **– the head,** die kop laat sak; **– fire,** afklap; draai, sloer; **time –s heavy on my hands,** die tyd val my lank; **the matter is hung up,** die saak is op die lang(e) baan geskuif; **– you, stik!; – it,** vervlaks!; **you be –ed,** loop na die maan; **– about,** rondstaan; **– back,** terugkrabbel; **– behind,** agterbly; **– on,** vashou; vasklem; **– out,** uithang; **where do you – out,** waar hang jy uit, waar is jy tuis?; **– together,** saamhang, saamgaan; **– up, ophang;** uitstel, op die lang(e) baan skuif.
hang, n. hang; **get the – of,** die slag van kry, verstaan; **not a –,** geen greintjie nie.
hangar, vlieg(tuig)loods, hangar.
hangdog, galgvoël, galgkind; **have a – look, lyk soos 'n hond wat vet gesteel het.
hanger, hanger; ophanger; haak; dolk.
hanger-on, aanhanger; afhanklike.
hangman, laksman, beul.
hank, string, knot.
hanker, hunker; **– after,** snak na.
hankering, hunkering, sug, begeerte.
hanky, sakdoek.
hanky-panky, hokus-pokus, flousery.
hap, gebeur, geskied.
haphazard, n. geluk, toeval; **at, by –,** lukraak, op goeie geluk af.
haphazard, a. toevallig; wild.
hapless, ongelukkig.
haply, miskien,; toevallig.
happen, gebeur, plaasvind, voorval, geskied; **– to,** oorkom, gebeur met; **– on,** (toevallig) teenkom; **I –ed to look up,** ek het toevallig opgekyk.
happiness, geluk.
happy, gelukkig, bly; **I shall be – to assist,** ek sal bly wees as ek kan help; **a – phrase,** 'n raak gesegde.
happy-go-lucky, onbesorg, sorgloos; onverskillig, dons-maar-op- . . .
hara-kiri, hara-kiri, selfmoord.
harangue, n. vurige toespraak.
harangue, v. 'n gloeiende toespraak hou; opsweep.
harass, lastig val, teister, bestook, kwel, pla, terg; vermoei.
harbinger, voorloper; aankondiger.
harbour, n. hawe; toevlugsoord.
harbour, v. herberg; koester.
harbourless, dakloos, sonder skuiling.
hard, a. hard, styf, dik; moeilik, swaar; hewig; streng, hardvogtig; skerp; **– cash,** klinkende munt; **– of hearing,** hardhorig (hardhorend); **– question,** moeilike vraag; **– master,** streng(e) meester; **– life,** moeilike (swaar) lewe; **– winter,** strawwe winter; **– consonant,** skerp medeklinker; **– labour,** hardearbeid, harde-pad; **– and fast rule,** vaste reël.
hard, adv. hard, swaar, moeilik; dig; **try –,** hard probeer; **run –,** hard hardloop; **it will go –,** dit sal swaar (moeilik) gaan; **– up,** platsak.
hard-bitten, taai.
hard-board, kartonplank.
hard-boiled, hardgekook (letterlik); hardgebak (fig.).
hard-earned, suur verdien.
harden, hard; hardmaak; hard word; verhard.
hardened, gehard; verhard; verstok.
hard-fisted, met goeie vuiste; suinig.
hard-headed, nugter, slim, oulik.
hard-hearted, hardvogtig.
hardihood, astrantheid; koenheid, moed.
hardiness, koenheid; gehardheid.

hard lines, teenspoed, 'n harde gelag; it was – on him, hy het dit ongelukkig getref; –!, jammer!
hardly, skaars, nouliks, ternouernood; – ever, byna nooit.
hardness, hardheid; strengheid.
hard-pressed, agtervolg, opgedruk; in nood; – for money, in geldnood.
hardship, teenspoed; ontbering.
hard-tack, skeepsbeskuit, klinkers.
hardware, ysterware.
hard-working, arbeidsaam, vlytig.
hardy, sterk, gehard; moedig.
hare, haas.
hare-bell, klokkie.
hare-brained, dwaas, roekeloos, onbesuis.
hare-lip, hasielip.
harem, harem, vroueverblyf.
haricot, bredie; –(bean), snyboontjie.
hark, luister; – back to, terugkom op; terugverlang na.
harlequin, harlekyn.
harlot, hoer.
harlotry, hoerery.
harm, n. skade, nadeel, kwaad.
harm, v. beskadig, skaad, benadeel.
harmful, nadelig, skadelik.
harmless, onskadelik; onskuldig.
harmonic, harmonies.
harmonica, harmonika; mondfluitjie.
harmonics, harmoniek, harmonieleer.
harmonious, harmonieus, welluidend; harmonies; eensgesind.
harmonize, harmonieer, ooreenstem; in ooreenstemming bring; harmoniseer.
harmonium, harmonium, serafyn.
harmony, harmonie; eensgesindheid.
harness, n. tuig; harnas, wapenrusting.
harness, v. optuig, inspan.
harp, n. harp.
harp, v. harpspeel; – on the same string, op dieselfde aambeeld hamer.
harpoon, n. harpoen.
harpoon, v. harpoen(eer).
harpsichord, klave-, klavier-simbaal.
harpy, harpy; vrek, grypvoël.
(h)arquebus, haakbus.
harridan, heks, feeks, teef.
harrier, wind-, jaghond; kuikendief.
harrow, n. eg.
harrow, v. eg; pynig, folter, kwel.
harrow, v. plunder, teister.
harrowing, folterend, martelend.
harry, plunder; bestook; beroof.
harsh, grof; vrank; fel, skel, rou; bars, nors, streng; wreed, hard.
harshness, ruheid; strengheid.
hart, hert.
hartebees, hartbees.
hartshorn, hartshoring.
harum-scarum, hals-oor-kop, onbesuis.
harvest, n. oes (figuurlik ook oogs).
harvest, v. oes; (in)oogs, insamel.
harvester, snyer, oester; snymasjien.
has-been, iemand uit die ou doos, fossiel, iemand wat sy tyd gehad het.
harsh, v. fynmaak, klein kap.
hash, n. fynvleis; opgwarmde kos; mengelmoes; make a – of, verbrou; settle a person's –, iemand sy vet gee.
hashish, hasjisj, (mak) dagga.
ha(r)slet, harslag; karmenaadjie.
hasp, n. knip, klink, neusie; string
hasp, v. grendel, op die knip sit.
hassock, knie- of knielkussing.

haste, haas, spoed; more – less speed, hoe meer haas hoe minder spoed.
hasten, gou maak, (sig) haas; haastig maak, aanja; verhaas, bespoedig.
hastily, haastig, gou.
hasty, haastig, gehaas, gejaag; vinnig, snel, ooryl(d), voortvliegend, driftig.
hat, hoed.
hatband, hoedlint, -band.
hatbox, hoededoos.
hatch, n. onderdeur; luik.
hatch, v. uitbroei.
hatch, n. broeisel; broeiery.
hatch, v. arseer, grif.
hatch, n. arsering.
hatchery, kwekery; broeiplek.
hatchet, byl.
hatchment, wapenbord.
hatchway, luikgat; valluik.
hate, haat.
hateful, haatlik; gehaat.
hatred, haat, wrok, vyandskap.
hatter, hoedemaker; hoedeverkoper; mad as a –, stapelgek; giftig kwaad.
hat-stand, kapstok.
hauberk, borsharnas, halsberg.
haugh, riviergrond.
haughty, hoog, trots, hoogmoedig; uit die hoogte.
haul, v. trek, hys, sleep; aanhaal; draai; vervoer, karwei.
haul, n. (die) trek, sleep; vangs, wins.
haulier, vervoerder, karweier.
haulage, sleep, vervoer; vervoergeld.
ha(u)lm, stam, steel, stronk halm; dekgoed, -strooi.
haunch, heup; boud; dy; sit on one's –es, op jou hurke sit.
haunt, v. (êrens) boer; ronddwaal; agternaloop; ghosts – the place, dit spook daar; the thought –s me, die gedagte vervolg my; –ed house, spookhuis.
haunt, n. lêplek, boerplek.
hautboy, hoboy, oboe, hobo.
have, v. hê, besit; kry, ontvang, neem, gebruik; beetneem, in die nek kyk, flous; you – me there, nou het jy my; you – been had, jy is geflous; I – my work to do, ek het my werk om te doen; I – to do my work, ek moet my werk doen; – in mind, in gedagte hê, aan dink; to – no doubt, nie twyfel nie; to – a game, 'n potjie speel; to – a try, 'n slag probeer; let him – it, gee hom dit; dons hom op; I shall – it removed, ek sal dit laat wegneem; – him up, bring hom voor die hof; – done, ophou, uitskei; – on, aanhê, dra; – it out, dit uitspook; ('n tand) laat uittrek; he has had it, dis verby met hom.
have, n. foppery, flousery.
haven, hawe; skuilplaas, toevlug.
haversack, rug-, knapsak, ransel.
having, n. hawe, besitting.
havoc, verwoesting; make – of, play – among, verwoesting aanrig onder.
haw, n. meidoring, haagdoringbessie.
haw, n. knipvlies, derde ooglid.
haw, v. hakkel; aanstellerig praat.
haw-haw, aanstellerig praat; runnik-lag.
hawk, n. vryf-, pleisterplank.
hawk, n. havik, valk.
hawk, v. smous; – about, (rond)vent.
hawk, v. die keel skraap, keel skoonmaak.
hawker, smous, venter, marskramer.
hawk-eyed, met valkoë, skerpsiende.
hawk-moth, aandskoenlapper, -vlinder.
hawk-nose, kromneus, arendsneus.
hawse, boeg, boeghout, voorpart.

hawser, kabel, tou, tros.
hawthorn, meidoring, haagdoring.
hay, hooi; **make – while the sun shines,** die yster smee solank as dit warm is.
hay-cock, hooihopie, opper.
hay-fever, hooikoors.
haymaker, hooimasjien, (wilde)swaaihou.
hayrick, -stack, hooimiet (-mied).
hazard, n. hasard-, dobbelspel; gevaar, risiko; kans, toeval; **at all –s,** tot elke prys, laat dit kos wat dit wil.
hazard, v. waag, riskeer; opper.
hazardous, gewaag, riskant, gevaarlik.
haze, waas, wasigheid, dynserigheid.
hazel, haselneutboom; haselneuthout.
haziness, wasigheid; vaagheid.
hazy, wasig, newelig, dynserig; vaal.
H-bomb, waterstofbom.
he, hy.
head, n. kop, hoof; verstand, lewe; oorsprong, bron; voorman, leier, bestuurder, prinsipaal; bo-ent, koppen-ent; punt, top; **he is off his –,** hy is nie goed by sy verstand nie; **the – of the school,** die hoof (prinsipaal) van die skool; **the – of the stairs,** die bo-ent van die trap; **the – of the bed,** die koppenent van die bed; **taller by a –,** 'n kop groter; **win by a –,** met 'n kop-lengte wen; **cannot make – or tail of it,** kan daar nie uit wys word nie; **–s or tails,** kop of let(ter), kruis of munt; **two pounds per –,** twee pond stuk; **twenty – of cattle,** twintig stuks vee; **come to a –,** ryp word (van 'n sweer); 'n kritieke punt bereik; **at the – of,** aan die hoof van; **keep one's –,** jou positiewe bymekaar hou; **lose one's –,** van jou positiewe raak, jou kop verloor; **turn some-one's –,** iemand se kop op hol maak; **make–,** vooruitgang maak; **make – against,** die hoof bied aan; **give him his –,** gee hom sy sin; **lay–s together,** die koppe bymekaar steek; **put into one's –,** iemand die idee gee; **– over heels,** hals-oor-kop, bolmakiesie; **over one's –,** oor jou kop (hoof); bokant jou vuurmaakplek; **be promoted over another's –,** oor iemand anders heen aangestel word; **from – to foot,** van kop tot tone, van bo tot onder; **over – and ears,** tot oor die ore; **under this –,** onder hierdie hoof.
head, v. eerste wees, lei; tot opskrif maak; kop; **chapter –ed,** hoofstuk getitel(d); **– back,** terugkeer, voorkeer; **– for,** rigting kies na; **– off,** afsny, afkeer.
headache, hoofpyn, kopseer.
head-boy, eerste in die klas, nommer een.
head-cheese, hoofkaas, sult.
head-dress, hoofdeksel; hooftooi(sel).
header, kopskoot.
head-hunter, koppesneller.
heading, opskrif, titel, hoof.
head-land, (land)hoof, punt; wenakker.
headline, hoof, kop, opskrif.
headlong, kop-vooruit; hals-oor-kop.
headman, (opper)hoof, hoofman.
headmaster, hoof(onderwyser).
headmistress, hoof(onderwyseres).
head-money, hoofgeld.
headmost, voorste.
head-on: – collision, kop teen kop botsing.
head-piece, kopstuk; helm; verstand.
headquarters, hoofkwartier.
headsman, laksman, beul.
headstall, kopstuk (van 'n toom).
headstone, grafsteen; hoofsteen.
headstrong, koppig, eiewys.
headway, vooruitgang; **make –,** vorder.
head-wind, wind van voor, teenwind.

heady, koppig, driftig.
heal, genees, gesond word; gesond maak.
heal-all, wondermiddel, geneesbossie.
healer, heler, heelmeester.
healing, gesondmaking; geneeskuns.
health, gesondheid, welstand; **officer of –,** gesondheidsbeampte; **to drink one's –,** op iemand se gesondheid drink.
healthy, gesond; welvarend.
heap, n. hoop; klomp, boel; **–s of times,** dikwels, herhaalde male; **struck all of a –,** uit die veld geslaan; kapot.
heap, v. stapel; **– up,** ophoop, opstapel; **– upon,** oorlaai met; oorstelp met.
hear, hoor, verneem; luister na; verhoor; **('n les) oorhoor.**
hearer, hoorder, toehoorder.
hearing, n. gehoor; verhoor; oor; **in my –,** waar ek by was; **in the – of,** ten aanhore van; **within –,** binne stembereik; **hard of –,** hardhorig (hardhorend).
hearken, luister, hoor.
hearsay, hore-sê; by, from, on –, van hore-sê.
hearse, lykwa; (dood)baar.
heart, hart; boesem; siel; gemoed; liefde; moed; kern; **lose one's – to,** verlief raak op; **lose –,** moed verloor; **take –,** moed skep; **cry one's – out,** jou doodhuil; **eat one's – out,** jou doodknies; **have the – to,** dit oor die hart kry om; **he was – and hand (soul) with us,** hy was hart en siel met ons; **have one's – in one's mouth,** jou hart in jou keel voel klop; **his – is in the right place,** hy dra sy hart op die regte plek; **wear one's – upon one's sleeve,** jou hart op jou tong dra; **after one's own –,** so reg na jou hart; **have at –,** op jou hart dra; **by –,** uit die kop, van buite; **in one's –,** in jou hart, innig; werklik; **heimlik; near (nearest, next) one's –,** na (naaste) aan jou hart; **lay to –,** ter harte neem; **take to –,** (sig) aantrek; **cut to the –,** aan die hart gaan; **with all one's –,** van (ganser) harte, met hart en siel; **– failure,** hartverlamming.
heart-ache, hartseer, harteleed, -pyn.
heart-beat, hartklop, polsslag.
heart-blood, heart's blood, hartebloed.
heart-break, hartseer.
heart-breaking, hartbrekend, hartverskeurend.
heart-broken, met gebroke hart; **he was –,** hy was ontroosbaar.
heartburn, sooibrand, suur.
heart-burning, afguns, ergernis.
heart-disease, hartkwaal.
hearten, opwek, moed inpraat.
heart-felt, innig, diepgevoelde.
heart-lung machine, hart-longmasjien.
hearth, (h)erd, haard.
hearth-rug, vuur(h)erdkleedjie.
hearth-stone, vuur(h)erdsteen; skuursteen.
heartily, hartlik, van harte; **– sick of,** sat van.
heartiness, hartlikheid.
heartless, harteloos, gevoelloos, wreed.
heart-rending, hartverskeurend.
heartsease, gesiggie, viooltjie.
heart-sick, neerslagtig; hartseer.
heartsore, hartseer; neerslagtig.
heart-strings, hartsnare.
heart-throb, hartklop; aangebedene, nooi.
heart-whole, onverlief; innig; moedig.
hearty, hartlik, opreg, innig; flink.
heat, n. hitte, warmte; vuur, opwinding; loopsheid; voorwedstryd; **red, white, –,** roodgloeiende, witgloeiende hitte; **specific –.** soortlike warmte; **prickly –,** uitslag.
heat, v. verhit; **get –ed,** driftig word.
heated, verhit, warm; driftig, vurig.

heater, verwarmer, stofie.
heat-resistant, hittewerend, hittevas, vuurvas.
heath, hei, vlakte; heide; erica.
heathen, n. heiden; ongelowige; **the** –, **die heidene**.
heathen, a. heidens.
heathendom, heidendom.
heathenish, heidens.
heather, heide(struik); hei, vlakte.
heat-stroke, hitteslag, „sonsteek".
heat-wave, hittegolf.
heave, v. (op)hef, (op)hys; dein, swel; kokhals, brul; gooi; slaak, uitstoot; – **a sigh**, 'n sug slaak; – **to**, bydraai, tot staan bring, stilhou.
heave, 'n rysing, deining; swelling.
heaven, hemel; lug(ruim); **good** –(s), goeie hemel!; **by** –(s), so waaragtig; **for** –'s **sake**, in hemelsnaam.
heavenly, hemels, goddelik; salig, heerlik; hemel-. . ., – **body**, hemelliggaam.
heavenward(s), hemelwaarts.
heaviness, swaarte; swaarheid.
heavy, swaar; moeilik; drukkend; bedruk; slaperig; – **crop**, ryk oes; – **guns**, grof geskut; – **water**, swaarwater.
heavy-laden, swaargelaai, swaarbelas.
heavy-weight, swaargewig.
hebdomadal, weekliks.
Hebraic, Hebreeus.
Hebrew, n. Hebreër; Hebreeus.
Hebrew, a. Hebreeus.
hecatomb, hekatombe, slagting.
heckle, uitslaan; hekel; ondervra; roskam.
heckler, hekelaar, uitslaner; ondervraer.
hectare, hektaar (hektare).
hectic, a. hekties, teringagtig; wild, woes; – **dance**, wilde dans.
hectogram(me), hektogram.
hectograph, hektograaf.
hectolitre, hektoliter.
hectometer, hektometer.
hector, n. baasspeler, bullebak.
hector, v. baasspeel (oor).
hedge, n. heg, heining, skutting.
hedge, v. afskut; heining plant; rondspring; bontpraat; – **in**, inkamp; omtrek, vaskeer; – **off**, afkamp; afsny.
hedgehog, krimpvarkie, rolvarkie.
hedge-hopping, skeervlug.
hedgerow, haag, laning.
hedonic, hedonisties, genotsugtig.
hedonism, hedonisme, genotleer.
heed, v. pas op, let op, ag gee op.
heed, n. ag, oplettendheid, hoede; **give, pay** –, ag gee, oplet; notisie neem; **take** –, oppas, op die hoede wees.
heedful, oplettend, oppassend.
heedless, agteloos, onverskillig, onoplettend, sorgloos; – **of**, onverskillig vir.
heel, n. hak, hiel; hoef; hakskeen, polvy; skobbejak; agterstuk, onderstuk, hieling; **head over** –**s**, bolmakiesie; halsoorkop; **kick one's** –**s**, staan en wag, ronddrentel; **show a clean pair of** –**s**, knie in die wind slaan; **take to one's** –**s**, die rieme neersit, laat spaander.
heel, v. hak aansit; uithak (voetbal); hak (gholf).
heel, oorhel, hiel; ('n skip) krink.
hefty, swaar, gewigtig; hard.
hegemony, hegemonie, heerskappy.
hegira, hedjra.
he-goat, bokram.
heifer, vers.
height, hoogte; hoogtepunt, toppunt; **at its** –, op sy hoogste, op sy hoogtepunt.
heighten, verhoog, vermeerder; verhef.

heinous, afskuwelik, verskriklik, snood.
heir, erfgenaam.
heir-apparent, erfopvolger.
heiress, erfgename, erfdogter.
heirless, sonder erfgenaam.
heirloom, erfstuk, familiestuk.
helianthus, sonneblom.
helical, spiraal-. . .
helicopter, helikopter, hefskroewer.
heliogram, heliogram.
heliograph, n. heliograaf.
heliograph v. heliografeer.
heliography, heliografie; sonbeskrywing.
helioscope, helioskoop, sonnekyker.
heliotherapy, heliotherapie, sonliggenesing.
heliotrope, heliotroop, sonsoekertjie.
heliotropic, heliotropies, ligsoekend.
heliotropism, heliotropisme, ligsoeking.
helium, helium, songas.
helix, heliks, skroeflyn, oorrand.
hell, hel; dobbelhol; **give someone** –, iemand opdonder; uitvreet.
hellebore, nieskruid.
Hellenic, Helleens.
hellish, hels.
helm, helmstok, roer(pen).
helm(et), helm(et), helmhoed.
helot, heloot; slaaf.
help, v. help, bystaan; (be)dien; **don't remain longer than you can** –, moenie langer bly as wat nodig is nie.
help, n. hulp, bystand; helpster; middel, raad.
helper, helper (helpster), hulp.
helpful, nuttig; behulpsaam.
helping, a. helpend, behulpsaam.
helping, n. hulp; porsie, (skeppie).
helpless, hulpeloos; onbeholpe.
helpmate, helpmeet, wederhelf.
helter-skelter, a. & adv. holderstebolder.
helter-skelter, n. gejaag, geharwar.
helve, steel.
hem, n. soom, kant, boord.
hem, v. (om)soom; – **in**, insluit.
hemisphere, halfrond, hemisfeer. .
hemistich, halfvers, halwe versreël.
hemlock, dollekerwel, giftige kerwel.
hemorr. . ., sien **haemorr**. . .
hemp, hennep; tou, galgtou; hasjisj.
hempen, hennep-. . . .
hemstitch, n. soomsteek.
hemstich, v. soomsteek, deurslaan.
hen, hen; in compp. -wyfie (wyfie-); **pea**—, pou-wyfie (wyfiepou).
henbane, dolkruid.
hence, hiervandaan af; van nou af; hieruit; daarom; **five years** –, oor vyf jaar.
henceforth, henceforward, van nou af, voortaan, hiervandaan af.
henchman, (lyf)dienaar, agterryer.
hencoop, hoenderhok, fuik.
hendecagon, elfhoek.
hendecasyllabic, elflettergrepig.
henna, henna.
hen-pecked, onder die plak (sittende); – **husband**, man onder die plak.
hen-roost, hoenderstellasie, -slaapplek.
hepatic, lewer-. . .
heptagon, sewehoek, heptagoon.
her, haar; **that is** –**s**, dit is hare.
herald, n. heraut; heraldikus; voorloper.
herald, v. boodskap, aankondig; inlui.
heraldic, heraldies, wapenkundig.
heraldry, heraldiek, wapenkunde.
herb, kruid, bossie.
herbaceous, kruierig; bossieagtig.

herbage — **hillock**

herbage, kruie; weireg.
herbal, a. kruie-...
herbal, n. kruieboek.
herbalist, kruiekenner; kruiedokter, drogis.
herbarium, herbarium; kruieversameling.
herbivorous, plantetend.
Herculean, Herkulies, Herkules-...
herd, n. kudde, trop.
herd, n. herder, (vee)wagter.
herd, v. oppas, kyk na; saamhok; – with, aansluit by; saamboer.
here, hier; hierheen, hiernatoe; **that is neither** – nor there, dit het niks met die saak te doen nie; – goes!, vooruit!, daar gaan hy!; **from** –, hiervandaan af.
hereabouts, hier rond, hier êrens.
hereafter, adv. hierna, voortaan; hiernamaals; verder op, agter in.
hereafter, n. the, –, die hiernamaals.
hereby, hierby, hierdeur, hiermee.
hereditability, erflikheid.
hereditary, erflik; oorgeërf, erf-...
heredity, erflikheid, oorerwing.
herein, hierin.
hereof, hiervan.
hereon, hierop.
heresy, kettery.
heretic, ketter.
heretical, ketters, ketter-...
hereto, hiertoe; tot hier.
heretofore, tot hiertoe, tevore, tot sover.
hereunder, hierna.
hereupon, hierop.
herewith, hiermee.
heritage, erf(e)nis, erfdeel, erfgoed.
hermaphrodite, n. trassie, hermafrodiet.
hermeneutics, uitlegkunde, hermeneutiek.
hermetic, hermeties, lugdig.
hermit, kluisenaar, hermiet.
hermitage, kluis, kluisenaarshut; **hermitage,** hermityk.
hero, held; halfgod, heros.
heroic, heldhaftig, dapper, helde-...; – **poem,** heldedig.
heroics, hoogdrawende taal, bombas.
heroine, heldin.
heroism, heldemoed, heldhaftigheid.
her(o)n, reier.
hero-worship, heldeverering.
herring, haring.
herring-bone, haringgraat; haringgraatsteek; visgraatverband.
herring-pond, visdammetjie, groot water.
herself, haarself; sy self; she said so –, sy het self so gesê; **by** –, alleen.
hesitancy, aarseling, weifeling.
hesitant, aarselend, weifelend.
hesitate, aarsel, weifel.
hesitation, aarseling, weifeling.
Hesperian, Hesperies, westers.
Hessian, Hes; Hessies.
hessian, goiingsak.
heterodox, onregsinnig, heterdoks.
heterodoxy, onregsinnigheid, heterodoksie.
heterogeneity, heterogeneousness, ongelyksoortigheid, heterogeniteit.
hew, v. kap; slaan; – **down, off,** af-, omkap; – **to pieces,** stukkend kap.
hewer, kapper; –s **of wood,** houthakkers.
hexagon, seshoek, heksagoon.
hexagonal, seshoekig, heksagonaal.
hexameter, heksameter.
hey, haai!; hê?
hey-day, bloei(tyd); hoogste punt.
hiatus, hiaat, gaping, leemte, breuk.

hibernate, oorwinter; luilak.
hibernation, oorwintering; winterslaap.
Hibernian, Hibernies, Iers.
hibiscus, vuurblom, hibiskus.
hiccough, hiccup, hik.
hickory, noteboom; notehout.
hide, v. verberg, wegsteek, weg-, verstop; wegkruip, verskuil; – **one's head,** jou kop laat hang.
hide, n. vel, huid.
hide, v. looi, tou, 'n loesing gee.
hide-and-seek, wegkruipertjie.
hide-bound, nou in die vel; bekrompe.
hideous, afskuwelik, afgryslik.
hiding, loesing, pak.
hiding, skuiling, skuilplaas; **remain in** –, verskuil bly, wegkruip.
hiding-place, skuilplaas, wegkruipplek.
hie, haas, jaag, rep.
hierarch, hiërarg, kerkhoof; aartsbiskop.
hierarchical, hiërargies.
hierarchy, hiërargie; priesterheerskappy.
hieroglyph, hiëroglief, beeldskrif.
hieroglyphic, hiëroglifies.
higgle, knibbel, ding, kwansel.
higgledy-piggledy, a. & adv. deurmekaar, onderstebo, hot en haar.
higgledy-piggledy, n. deurmekaarspul.
high, a. hoog; verhewe; adellik, sterk; hooglopend, hewig; – thoughts, verhewe gedagtes; – life, lewe in die hoë kringe; – meat, sterk (adelike) vleis; **in** – **favour,** hoog, in die guns; **in** – **spirits,** opgewek, uitgelate; – **words,** hooglopende woorde; – **and mighty,** uit die hoogte; – **road,** grootpad; – **sea,** swaar see, stortsee; – **seas,** oop see.
high, n. die hoë; **the Most H**–, die Allerhoogste; **the** – **and the low,** hoog en laag; **on** –, (daar)bo, in die hemel; na bowe, na die hemel; **from on** –, van bo af.
high altar, hoogaltaar.
high-backed, hoërug-...
high-ball, yssopie.
high-browed, geleerd, swaar, intellektueel.
high-faluting, -flown, bombasties, hoogdrawend; aanstellerig.
high-flyer, hoogvlieër.
high-handed, eiemagtig, outokraties.
high-hat, snob.
Highlander, Hooglander.
highlands, hooglande.
high-light, glanspunt, hoogtepunt; sterk laat uitkom.
highly, hoog, hoogs; hoëlik; **think** – **of,** baie van dink, 'n hoë dunk van hê; **esteem** –, hoog waardeer; **commend** –, sterk aanbeveel; – **seasoned,** sterk gekrui.
high-minded, edeldenkend, edelmoedig.
highness, hoogte; hoogheid.
high-pitched, hoog(gestem).
high-priest, hoëpriester.
high school, hoërskool.
high-spirited, fier; vurig, lewendig.
high-strung, hooggespanne; oorgevoelig.
high-water, hoogwater.
high-watermark, hoogwaterlyn; hoogtepunt.
highway, grootpad.
highwayman, padrower, struikrower.
hike, n. staptog, wandeltog.
hike, v. stap; n. wandeltog maak.
hiker, stapper, voetslaner.
hilarious, vrolik, opgeruim, uitgelate.
hilariousness, hilarity, vrolikheid.
hill, n. bult, heuwel, kop(pie), rantjie.
hillock, koppie, bultjie.

hillside, hang.
hilt, handvatsel, greep, geves, hef.
him, hom; **it's –,** dis hy.
Himalaya, Himalaya.
himself, hom, homself; self; **he hurt –,** hy het homself seergemaak; **he did it –,** hy het dit self gedoen; **by –,** alleen.
hind, n. hinde, ooi.
hind, a. agter- . . ., agterste; **– leg,** agterbeen.
hinder, v. hinder, belemmer; verhinder.
hind(er)most, agterste; verste.
hindrance, hindernis, belemmering.
Hindu, Hindoo, Hindoe, Indiër.
Hindustan, a. Hindoestaans.
hinge, n. skarnier, hingsel; spil.
hinge, v. draai, hang; rus op, afhang van.
hinny, n. muilesel.
hinny, v. runnik.
hint, n. wenk, toespeling; **take a –, 'n wenk** begryp.
hint, v. **'n wenk gee,** sinspeel op.
hip, n. heup; hoekspar (van dak).
hip-bath, sitbad.
hippo, sien **hippopotamus.**
hippocras, hippokras, kruiewyn.
hippodrome, sirkus; renbaan; hippodroom.
hippopotamus, seekoei.
hire, n. huur; loon, huurgeld; **for, on –,** te huur.
hire, v. huur; verhuur; **– out,** verhuur.
hire-car, huurmotor.
hireling, huurling.
hire-purchase, koop op afbetaling, huurkoop.
hire-purchase-system, huurkoop(stelsel).
hirer, huurder.
hirsute, harig, ruig.
his, sy, syne; **it is –,** dit is syne.
hiss, v. sis, fluit, blaas; uitfluit.
hiss, nl gesis, gefluit, gejou; sis-klank.
hist, st!; sjt!; sa!.
histology, weefselleer, histologie.
historian, geskiedkundige, historikus.
historic(al), geskiedkundig, histories.
historiographer, geskiedskrywer, historiograaf.
historiography, geskiedskrywing, historiografie.
history, geskiedenis; verhaal, storie; historie; **natural –,** natuurlike historie; **ancient, mediaeval, modern –,** ou, middeleeuse, nuwe (moderne) geskiedenis; **that is ancient –,** dit is ou nuus.
histronic, toneel- . . ., akteurs- . . ., histronies.
histronics, toneelspeelkuns, toneelspelery.
hit, v. slaan, moker; **'n klap (slag, hou) gee;** raak, tref; **– it off,** ooreenkom; **– (the nail) on the head,** die spyker op die kop slaan; reg raai; **– upon,** op kom, vind.
hit, n. hou, slag; raakskoot; steek, skimp; **make a –, 'n slag slaan;** raak.
hitch, v. vashaak; ruk; **– up,** optrek, opruk; **– on to,** vashaak aan.
hitch, n. ruk, pluk; slag, knoop; haakplek, hapering.
hitch-hike, ryloop, duimry, duimgooi.
hither, hierheen, hiernatoe; **– and thither,** heen en weer.
hitherto, tot hier toe, tot nog toe.
hitherward, herwaarts, hierheen.
hive, n. byekorf, by(e)nes; swerm.
hive, v. in 'n byekorf sit; huisves; instop; saamwoon; oppot.
hives, huiduitslag, galbulte.
hoar, a. grys, grou.
hoard, n. hoop, stapel, voorraad, skat.
hoard, v. ophoop, opstapel oppot.
hoarding, skutting.
hoarfrost, ryp.
hoariness, grysheid, grouheid.

hoarse, hees, skor.
hoary, grys, grou.
hoax, v. fop, om die tuin lei.
hoax, n. foppery, grap, vergekhouery.
hob, haardplaat; naaf.
hobble, v. strompel, hobbel; (perde) span.
hobble, n. strompeling; spanriem.
hobbledehoy, snuiter, penkop; lomperd.
hobble-skirt, hobbelrok, strompelrok.
hobby, stokperdjie, liefhebbery; ponie.
hobby-horse, hobbelperd; stokperdjie.
hobgoblin, kabouter; paaiboelie, spook.
hobnail, dikkopspyker.
hob-nob, saamdrink; **– together,** dik wees met mekaar, saamboer.
hock, hakskeensening; skenkel; pand.
hock, v. verpand.
hockey, hokkie.
hocus, vir die gek hou; bedwelm maak.
hocus-pocus, hokus-pokus, goëlery.
hod, kleibak, stenebak.
hodge-podge, sien **hotch-potch.**
hodman, handlanger.
hodometer, mylwys(t)er, afstandmeter.
hoe, v. skoffel; (grond) losmaak.
hoe, n. skoffel.
hog, (burg)vark; smeerlap.
hogget, jaaroud skaap; **–s,** lammerwol.
hogshead, okshoof.
hoist, v. ophys; opblaas.
hoist, n. (die) oplig; ligter, hystoestel.
hoity-toity, n. uitgelatenheid.
hoity-toity, a. uitgelate, vrolik; verwaand, uit die hoogte; brommerig.
hoity-toity, interj. hokaai!, stadig!
hokum, twak.
hold, v. hou, inhou, behou, vashou; besit, hê; daarvoor hou, meen; volhou; (plek) inneem, inbesitneem; (fees) vier; **– true, good,** waar wees, geld; **– back,** weerhou, aarsel; **– back from,** (sig) onthou van; **– water,** waterdig wees; steek hou; **– at bay,** terughou, weerstand bied; **– your own,** jou man staan; **– by,** bly by, hou by, staan by; **– forth,** uitwei, betoog; **– in,** inhou; **– on,** vashou; stop!; **– out,** uithou; uitstrek; **– over,** oorhou; verdaag; **– together,** saamhou; **– up,** ophou; beroof; aanhou, stop; **– with,** maats maak met; eens wees met.
hold, n. vat, greep; vatplek, houvas; **catch – of,** beetkry.
hold, n. (skeeps)ruim.
hold-all, reissak, stop-maar-in, reisrol.
holder, houer; besitter; bekleër (van 'n pos).
holding, eiendom; houvas; invloed.
hold-up, roofaanval, roofaanslag.
hole, n. gat; pondok; **pick –s in,** uitmekaar trek; gebreke aanwys in.
hole, v. gate maak; tonnel; inslaan, ingooi; **– out, 'n putjie maak (gholf).**
hole-proof, stopvry, steekvas.
holiday, vakansie(dag).
holiness, heiligheid.
holl(o)a, haai-roep, skree.
Holland, Holland; hollandslinne.
Hollander, Hollander.
Hollands, Hollandse jenewer.
hollow, a. hol; leeg; laag; oneg, vals geveins; **beat –,** uitstof, kafloop.
hollow, n. holte; leegte; laagte.
hollow, v. uithol; krom buig.
hollow-eyed, holoog.
hollowness, holheid; holte; onopregtheid.
holly, huls.
hollyhock, stokroos.
holocaust, groot brandoffer; groot slagting.

holograph, holograaf, eiehandig geskrewe dokument.
holster, holster, pistoolsak; saalsak.
holus-bolus, in een slag, almal saam.
holy, a. heilig, gewyd.
holy, n. Heilige; **H. of Holies**, Heilige der Heilige.
homage, hulde, eerbetoon.
Homburg: – (hat), deukhoed, sagte vilthoed.
home, n. tehuis, tuiste, huis, woonplek; bof, doel; – sweet –, oos wes, tuis bes; eie haard is goud waard; **at** –, tuis; resepsie, ontvangdag; **be at** –, tuis wees; op jou gemak wees.
home, a. huis- . . ., huislik; binnelands; raak; – comforts, huislike geriewe; – **industries**, inheemse nywerhede; – **consumption**, huishoudelike (binnelandse) verbruik; – **thrust**, raakskoot, raaksteek; – **truth**, harde waarheid; raaksteek.
home, adv. huis toe, na huis; tuis; raak; **come** –, kom huis toe; **come** – **to one**, tot iemand deurdring; **he is** –, hy is tuis; **the thrust went** –, dit was 'n raakskoot; **bring a charge** –, 'n skuld bewys; **ram** –, vasstamp; inpeper.
home-bred, tuis (in die moederland) gekweek (opgevoed); inheems; huislik.
home-coming, tuiskoms.
home-journey, tuisreis, terugreis.
home-made, eiegemaak; inheems.
homeless, (te)huisloos, sonder onderdak.
homely, huislik; eenvoudig; onaansienlik.
hom(o)eopathic, homopaties.
hom(o)eopathy, homopatie.
Homer, Homerus.
homer, posduif.
Homeric, Homeries.
home-rule, selfregering.
homesick, be –, heimwee hê.
homesickness, heimwee.
homestead, opstal, woonhuis.
homeward(s), huiswaarts, huis toe, na huis.
homework, huiswerk.
homicidal, moord- . . ., moorddadig.
homicide, manslag, doodslag; pleger van manslag.
homiletics, kanselwelsprekendheid.
homily, kanselrede; preek, predikasie.
homing: – **device**, aanpeiltoestel.
homing-pigeon, posduif.
hominy, growwe mieliepap.
homogeneity, homogeniteit, gelyksoortigheid.
homogenous, homogeen, gelyksoortig.
homogenize, homogeniseer.
homologate, homologeer, bekragtig.
homologous, homoloog, ooreenkomstig, ooreenstemmend; gelykstandig.
homology, homologie, ooreenstemming.
homonym, homoniem, gelykluidende woord.
homophone, homofoon, gelykklinkende woord.
homosexual, a. and n. homoseksueel.
homy, huislik.
hone, n. oliesteen.
hone, v. (op die oliesteen) slyp (aansit).
honest, eerlik, opreg; eerbaar; onvervals; – **Injun**, op my woord!
honesty, eerlikheid, opregtheid; eerbaarheid; regskapenheid; – **is the best policy**, eerlikheid duur die langste.
honey, heuning; soetigheid; soetlief, skat.
honey-buzzard, heuningvoël.
honeycomb, heuningkoek.
honeycomb-cream, heuningkoekpoeding.
honeyed, soet, stroperig, vleiend.
honeymoon, wit(te)broodsdae.
honey-suckle, kanferfoelie.
honey-sweet, heuningsoet.

honorarium, honorarium, vergoeding.
honorary, ere- . . .; – **secretary**, eresekreatris; – **degree**, eregraad.
honorific, agbaar, geëerd.
honour, n. eer; eerbewys; eergevoel; –s, eerbewyse; honneurs; **last**, **funeral** –s, laaste eer(bewyse); **do the** –s, die honneurs waarneem; –s **easy**, honneurs gelyk; **do** – **to**, eer bewys; **eer aandoen**; tot eer strek; **in** – **of**, ter ere van; **in his** –, tot sy eer; **be in** – **bound**, aan sy eer verplig wees; **be put to one's** –, jou eerwoord gee; **upon my** –, – **bright**, op my erewoord; **affair of** –, eresaak; **code of** –, eerbegrip; **debt of,** – ereskuld; **maid of** –, hofdame; **post of** –, erepos; **word of** –, erewoord; **Your H**–, Edelagbare.
honour, v. eer, respekteer; eer betoon; honoreer; – **a bill**, 'n wissel honoreer.
honourable, eervol; eerwaardig, agbaar; opreg, eerlik; vernaam; – **member**, agbare lid.
honourably, eervol, op eervolle manier, met eer.
hood, n. kap (van 'n mantel, kar, ens.).
hood, v. kap opsit (omhang); blinddoek.
hooded, kap- . . ., met 'n kap op; – **cart**, kapkar; – **snake**, kapelslang; – **waggon**, tentwa.
hoodoo, vloek (op); ongeluk (verbonde aan).
hoodwink, blinddoek; flous, fop, uitoorlê.
hoof, n. hoef; klou; poot.
hoof, v. voetslaan; – **out**, uitskop.
hook, n. haak, hakie, kram(metjie); vishoek; hoek, draai; sekel, sens; **by** – **or by crook**, op een of ander manier, op eerlike of oneerlike manier; **on one's own** –, op jou eie houtjie; –**s and eyes**, hakies en ogies.
hook, v. (aan)haak, vasmaak; skaai, inpalm; skram, trek (in golf, krieket); (uit)haak (in voetbal).
hooked, haak- . . ., met 'n haak, krom.
hooker, hoeker (skip); haker (in voetbal).
hook-nose, krom neus, haviksneus.
hook-worm, haakwurm.
hooligan, straatboef.
hooliganism, straatboewery.
hoop, n. hoepel; band, ring.
hoop, v. hoepelspeel; hoepels omsit; saamtrek, saambind.
hooping-cough, kinkhoes.
hoop-la, hoepelwerp.
hoopoe, hop, hoep-hoep.
hoot, v. jou, uitjou, uitfluit; toet; hoehoe.
hoot, n. gejou, gefluit, getoet, geblaas; gehoehoe.
hooter, fluit, sirene, toeter.
hop, n. hop(plant).
hop, n. sprong (spring), huppeling, huppelpas; dans, skoffelparty; vlug; –, **skip and jump**, hink, stap en spring.
hop, v. spring, hup; huppel; eenbeentjie-spring, hink; dans; – **the twig**, bokveld toe gaan.
hope, n. hoop, verwagting; –s, verwagtinge.
hope, v. hoop, verwag; – **for**, hoop op, verwag.
hopeful, hoopvol; veelbelowend.
hopeless, hopeloos; wanhopig.
hoplite, hopliet.
Hop-o'-my-Thumb, Klein Duimpie.
hopper, springer, huppelaar, hinker; danser; sprinkaan, vlooi; hopper (soort vaartuig; soort tregter).
hopscotch, hinkspel, klippiehink.
Horace, Horatius.
horde, horde, swerm, bende.
horizon, gesigseinder, kim, horison; gesigskring.
horizontal, a. horisontaal; gelyk, plat, waterpas; – **bar**, rekstok.
horizontal, n. horisontale lyn (vlak).
horn, n. horing; voelhoring; blaashoring; drink-

horing; punt; **draw in one's –s**, in jou skulp kruip; **on the –s of a dilemma**, voor 'n dilemma.
horn, v. horings opsit, van horings voorsien, met die horings steek.
horn-bill, horingvoël, neushoringvoël.
horned, horing(sman)- . . .; – **cattle**, horingvee; – ewe, horingsmanooi.
hornet, wesp; **bring –s' nest about one's ears**, jou in 'n wespenes begewe.
hornpipe, horingfluit; horrelpyp.
horny, horingagtig, horing- . . .
horology, uurwerkmakery; tydmeetkunde.
horoscope, horoskoop; **cast one's –**, iemand se horoskoop trek.
horoscopy, horoskopie, sterrelesery.
horrible, verskriklik, afskuwelik, aaklig.
horribly, verskriklik, vreeslik, afskuwelik.
horrid, aaklig, naar.
horrific, afskuwelik, afgryslik.
horrify, met afgryse vervul, afsku verwek; dronkslaan; aanstoot gee.
horror, afsku, afgryse, afgryslikheid, gruwel, rilling, huiwering.
horror-struck, met afgryse vervul, ontset.
horse, 'n perd, hings, reun; kavallerie, ruitery, perderuiters; (hout)bok; **to –!**, opsaal!, opklim!; **look a gift – in the mouth**, 'n gegewe perd in die bek kyk; **ride the high –**, 'n hoë toon aanslaan; **a – of another colour**, 'n totaal ander saak.
horse, v. 'n perd (perde) leen; abba; opklim; te perd ry (perdry).
horseback: **on a**, te perd.
horse-breaker, perdeleerder, -dresseerder.
horse-breeder, perdeboer, -teler.
horse-chestnut, wilde kastaiing.
horse-cloth, perdekombers.
horse-dealer, perdehandelaar.
horse-fly, perdevlieg.
horsehair, perdehaar.
horse-latitudes, perdebreedtes.
horse-laugh, runniklag.
horse-leech, groot bloedsuier; uitsuier.
horseman, (perde)ruiter.
horsemanship, rykuns.
horse-marines, berede marinier; **tell that to the –**, maak dit jou grootjie se kat wys.
horseplay, ruwe spel.
horse-power, perdekrag.
horse-race, perdereisies.
horse-raddish, rammenas, peperwortel.
horse-shoe, perde-yster, hoefyster.
horsewhip, n. horssweep, karwats.
horsewhip, v. onder die horssweep kry, uitlooi.
horsewoman, vrou te perd, ryster, dameruiter, amasone.
horsy, perde- . . ., stal- . . .
hortative, vermanend.
horticultural, tuinboukundig, tuinbou- . . .
horticulture, tuinbou.
horticulturist, tuinboukundige.
hosanna, hosanna.
hose, kous(e); broek; tuinslang; **half –**, sokkies.
hosier, koushandelaar, handelaar in ondergoed.
hosiery, kouse en ondergoed.
hospitable, gasvry, herbergsaam.
hospital, hospitaal, siekehuis; gashuis.
hospitality, gasvryheid, herbergsaamheid.
hospitalize, hospitaal toe stuur; in 'n hospitaal opneem.
hospital(l)er, hospitaalridder; -broeder, -suster; -kapelaan; **Knight H–**, hospitaalridder.
hospital-nurse, hospitaalverpleegster.
host, hostie.

host, leër, bende, skaar.
host, gasheer; waard, herbergier; **reckon without one's –**, buiten die waard reken.
hostage, gyselaar; pand.
hostel, herberg; losieshuis, koshuis, tehuis.
hostelry, herberg.
hostess, gasvrou; herbergierster, waardin.
hostile, vyandig, vyandelik.
hostility, vyandigheid, vyandelikheid.
hostler, stalkneg, perdekneg.
hot, warm, heet; vurig, hewig, kwaai; **nice and –**, lekker warm; **give it him –**, peper hom dit goed in; **in – haste**, in brandende haas, in vliegende vaart; **– blush**, vurige blos; **– dog**, worsbroodjie; **– spring**, warmbron; **– rhythm**, wilde ritme; **– money**, vlugkapitaal; wegsteekgeld.
hotbed, broeikas; broeines.
hot-blooded, warmbloedig; vurig.
hotch-potch, hutspot; mengelmoes.
hotel, hotel.
hotelier, hotelhouer.
hotfoot, in haas, in vliegende vaart.
hothead, heethoof, dwarskop.
hothouse, broeikas.
hotness, hitte, warmte; hitsigheid.
hot stuff, a. windmakerig, kranig, hanerig, warm, vrylustig.
hot water, warmwater; **get into –**, in die pekel raak.
hough, hekskeensening; skenkel.
hound, n. (jag)hond.
hound, v. agtervolg; **– on**, aanhits.
hour, uur; **at the eleventh –**, ter elfder ure; **in an evil –**, ter kwader ure; **keep early –s**, vroeg gaan slaap (en vroeg opstaan); **keep late –s**, laat na bed gaan; **after –s**, na kantoor-, skoolure.
hour-glass, uurglas.
hour-hand, uurwyser, kort wyser.
hourly, elke uur, om die uur, gedurig.
house, n. huis; parlementsgebou; vertoning saal; skouburg; **– of God**, Godshuis; **– of prayer**, bedehuis; **– of correction**, verbeterhuis; **H– of Assembly**, Volksraad, Laerhuis; **H– of Commons**, (Engelse) Laerhuis; **H– of Lords**, (Engelse) Hoërhuis; **keep –**, huishou; **keep the –**, binnebly, tuisbly; **keep open –**, baie ontvang, gasvry wees; **– arrest**, huisarres.
house, v. huisves, herberg, onder dak bring; woon; opbêre.
house-breaker, inbreker.
house-breaking, inbraak, huisbraak.
house-broken, **-trained**, sindelik.
house-dog, waghond.
house-famine, woningnood.
household, n. huisgesin; huis.
household, a. huislik, huis- . . ., huishoudelik; **– affairs**, huislike sake; **– gods**, huisgode; **–remedy**, huismiddel; **– troops**, lyftroepe; **– word**, ou bekende gesegde.
housekeeper, huishou(d)ster.
house-keeping, (die) huishou; huishouding.
houseless, dakloos, sonder onderdak.
housemaid, binnemeisie; **–'s knee**, kniewater; skropkneë.
housemaster, huisvader; inwonende onderwyser.
house-surgeon, inwonende dokter.
house-rent, huishuur.
house-top, dak, nok.
house-warming, inwy-fees, huisinwyding.
housewife, huisvrou; (hussif) naaidoos, werksakkie.
housewifery, huishoukuns.

housing, huisvesting; opberging; omhulsel.
hovel, pondok; afdak.
hover, fladder, sweef.
hovercraft, lugkussingvoertuig.
how, hoe; – are you, – do you do?, hoe gaan dit?; – now?, wat nou?; – so?, hoe so?; – about?, wat van?; – do you like it?, hoe geval dit jou, wat dink jy daarvan?; – he snores?, maggies, maar hy snork!
howbeit, nietemin, hoe dit sy.
howdah, olifantsaal.
however, egter, maar, ewewel, hoe dit sy.
howitzer, houwitser.
howl, v. tjank, huil, gier.
howl, n. getjank, gehuil, geskreeu; skreeu, gil.
howler, tjanker, skreeuer; bok, flater; **come a** –, in die verknorsing raak.
howsoever, hoe ook al, in elk geval.
hoyden, wildebras.
hub, naaf; spil, middelpunt; – **of the universe**, middelpunt van die heelal.
hubbub, kwaai, rumoer, geroesemoes.
huckaback, handdoeklinne, knoppiesgoed.
huckleberry, (soort) bloubessie, bosbessie.
huckle-bone, heupbeen; dolos.
huckster, n. smous, kwanselaar.
huckster, v. smous, kwansel; knibbel.
huddle, v. opeenhoop; oprol, inkrimp; halsoorkop doen; opeendring, koek.
huddle, n. bondel, hoop; warboel, drukte; **go into a** –, koukus hou.
hue, kleur(skakering), tint.
hue, – **and cry**, geskreeu, ophef; **raise a – and cry**, moord en brand skreeu, 'n lawaai opskop.
huff, v. tekeer gaan, kwaad word; aanstoot gee; (weg)blaas (by dambordspel).
huff, brombui, kwaai nuk.
huffish, huffy, brommerig, nukkerig.
hug, v. omhels, vasdruk, vasklem; – **the shore**, digby die wal bly.
hug, n. omhelsing; **give me a** –, pak my om die nek.
huge, tamaai, enorm, groot.
hugely, baie erg, besonder, vreeslik.
hugger-mugger, n. geheimdoenery.
hugger-mugger, a. geheim, deurmekaar.
hugger-mugger, v. konkel; wegmoffel.
Huguenot, Hugenoot.
hulk, (skeeps)romp; pakskip; bakbees.
bulking, lomp, log, swaar.
hull, dop; buitenste, rand, skil; romp.
hullaballoo, lawaai, geraas.
hullo(a), hallo!
hum, v. gons, brom, zoem; mompel; neurie; **make things** –, sake laat gons.
hum, n. gegons, brommery, gezoem; gemompel; geneurie; gehem.
human, a. menslik, mens(e)- ...
human, n. mens, menslike wese.
humane, menslievend, humaan; – **killing**, pynlose slag; – **killer**, genadedoder, sagslagter.
humanism, humanisme.
humanitarian, humanitêr.
humanity, mensheid; menslikheid; mensliewendheid; humaniteit; **the humanities**, die humaniora.
humankind, mensdom.
humanly, menslik; menslikerwys.
humble, a. nederig; eenvoudig, beskeie; onderdanig, dienswillig; **eat – pie**, soet broodjies bak.
humble, v. verneder, verootmoedig, kleinmaak.
humble-bee, waterdraer, hommel.
humbug, n. bedrog, foppery, kullery, verneukery, grootpratery, bog; bedrieër, grootprater.

humbug, v. kul, fop, bedrieg, swendel.
humdrum, a. eentonig, vervelig, saai.
humdrum, n. eentonigheid, saaiheid.
humerus, bo-armpyp, humerus.
humid, vogtig, kalm.
humidity, vogtigheid, klamheid.
humiliate, verneder, kleinmaak.
humiliating, vernederend.
humiliation, vernedering.
humility, nederigheid.
humming-bird, kolibrie.
humming-top, bromtol.
hummock, bultjie.
humorist, humoris; grappemaker.
humoristic, humoristies.
humorous, humoristies; grappig.
humour, n. bui, luim, humeur; humor; grappigheid; vog; **fighting** –, vegbui; **good** –, goedgehumeurdheid; goeie bui; **out of** –, **in an ill** –, in 'n slegte humeur, sleggehumeur(d).
humour, v. sy sin gee, sy gang laat gaan; paai.
hump, skof; boggel; bultjie, knoppie; **it gives me the** –, dit gee my die piep.
hump-backed, geboggel.
humpty-dumpty, diksak; wiedewietjie.
humus, teelaarde, humus.
Hun, Hun.
hunch, v. opbuig, kromtrek.
hunch, n. bult; boggel; dik stuk; suspisie.
hunchback, boggel(rug).
hunch-backed, geboggel.
hundred, honderd, honderdtal.
hundredfold, honderdvoud(ig).
hundredth, honderdste.
hundredweight, sentenaar.
Hungarian, Hongaar; Hongaars.
Hungary, Hongarye.
hunger, n. honger; lus, hunkering.
hunger, v. honger (na), hunker (na); honger hê; uithonger.
hunger-strike, hongerstaking.
hungry, honger, hongerig; hunkerend, begerig, lus; arm, dor.
hunk, dik stuk, klomp, klont.
hunkers: on one's –, op jou hurke.
hunks, vrek, skraper, bloedsuier.
hunt, v. jag; jaag; – **after, for**, soek na, jag maak op; – **down**, vang, vaskeer; opspoor; vervolg; – **out, up**, opspoor, opsoek.
hunt, n. jag; jagters, jaggeselskap; jagveld.
hunter, jagter; skietperd.
hunting-box, jaghuis(ie).
hunting-ground, skietveld, jagveld; **happy –s**, jagtershemel.
hunting-horn, jaghoring.
hunting-season, skiettyd, jagseisoen.
hunting-spider, ja(a)gspinnekop.
huntsman, jagter.
hurdle, hak(kie).
hurdle-race, hekkiespring, hekkiesreisies.
hurdy-gurdy, draai-orrel.
hurl, smyt, gooi, slinger; – **abuse at**, skeldwoorde slinger teen, uitskel.
hurly-burly, lawaai, rumoer, harlaboerla.
hurrah, hurray, hoera (hoerê)!
hurricane, orkaan.
hurriedly, haastig, halsoorkop, gejaag.
hurry, n. haas, haastigheid, gejaagdheid; **in a** –, haasting; in aller yl; you won't beat that in a –, jy sal dit nie sommer maklik klop nie; **be in a** –, haastig wees, haas hê.
hurry, v. haastig wees, gou maak, jaag, gejaag wees; aanjaag, haastig maak; – **away**, haastig weggaan; – **up**, aanjaag; gou maak, vortmaak.

hurry-scurry, n. deurmekaarspul, verwarring, haas.
hurry-scurry, v. halsoorkop te werk gaan, jaag.
hurst, bult, bos, lap bome.
hurt, n. seerplek, wond; kwaad, skade, nadeel.
hurt, v. seermaak, pyn doen; kwaad doen, benadeel; **my feet –,** my voete is (maak) seer; **feel –,** seer (gekrenk) voel.
hurtful, nadelig, sleg, skadelik.
hurtle, (aan)bons, smyt; vlieg; gons.
husband, n. man, eggenoot.
husband, v. spaar, suinig wees met.
husbandman, boer, landbouer.
husbandry, (kennis van) boerdery; spaarsaamheid.
hush, n. stilte.
hush, v. stilmaak; stilbly; **– up,** in die doofpot stop, stilhou.
hush-hush, geheim.
hush-money, omkoopgeld, steekpenning.
husk, n. skil, dop, buitenste.
husk, v. afskil, uitdop.
husky, vol doppe; dor; skor; sterk, taai.
hussar, husaar.
hussy, flerrie; snip.
hustings, verkiesinge; eleksieverhoog; eleksiekampanje.
hustle, v. stamp en stoot, dring, druk; woel, opkeil; jaag, gou maak.
hustle, n. gedrang, gedring, gestamp en gestoot.
hustler, aandrywer, woeler.
hut, hut, huisie, pondok.
hutch, hok; hut; kis.
huzza, hoesee!, hoera!
hyacinth, hiasint (blom en steen); naeltjie (blom).
hyaline, glasagtig, glashelder, glas- . . .
hybrid, n. baster, halfnaatjie, hibride.
hybrid, a. baster- . . ., hibridies.
hybridise, kruis, baster.
hydra, waterslang; hidra.
hydrangea, hortensia.
hydrant, brandkraan.
hydrate, n. hidraat.
hydrate, v. hidrateer.
hydraulic, hidroulies, water- . . .; **– brakes,** waterdrukremme, hidrouliese remme; **– press,** waterpers, hidrouliese pers.
hydraulics, hidroulika, vloeistowweleer, waterwerktuigkunde.
hydrocarbon, koolwaterstof.
hydrocephalus, waterhoof.
hydrochloric, hidrochloor- . . .; **– acid,** hidrochloorsuur, chloorwaterstof, soutsuur.
hydrocyanic, hidrosiaan- . . .; **– acid,** hidrosiaansuur, siaanwaterstof, blousuur.
hydro-electric, hidro-elektries; **– power,** waterkrag.
hydronamic(al), hidrodinamies.
hydronamics, hidrodinamika.
hydrogen, waterstof; **– bomb,** waterstofbom.
hydrographer, hidrograaf, seebeskrywer; seekaartmaker.
hydrographic(al), hidrografies.
hydrography, hidrografie, waterbeskrywing.
hydrology, hidrologie, watersamestellingsleer.
hydrolysis, hidrolise, watersplitsing.
hydrometer, hidrometer, watermeter.
hydrometric, hidrometries, watermeetkundig.
hydrometry, hidrometrie, watermeetkunde.
hydropathic, hidropaties, watergeneeskundig.
hydropathy, hidropatie, watergeneeskunde, -kuur.
hydrophobia, hidrofobie, watervrees, hondsdolheid.
hydroplane, hidroplaan, watervliegtuig.
hydroponics, waterkwekery, waterkultuur.
hydropsy, watersug.
hydrostatic, hidrostaties.
hydrostatics, hidrostatika, waterewewigsleer.
hydrotherapy, hidroterapie, watergeneeskunde.
hydrous, water- . . ., waterhoudend.
hy(a)ena, hiëna; **brown –,** strandwolf.
hygiene, gesondheidsleer, higiëne.
hygienic, higiënies, gesondheids- . . .
hygrometer, higrometer, vogmeter.
hygrometric(al), higrometries.
hygrometry, higrometrie, vogbepaling.
hygroscope, higroskoop.
hygroscopy, higroskopie.
hymen, huwelik, eg; maagdevlies.
hymn, n. himne, (lof)sang, gesang.
hymn, v. (lof)sing; gesange sing.
hymnody, himnodie; gesangdigting; gesangbundel.
hymnology, himnologie, gesangkunde.
hyp, sien **hip.**
hypallage, hippallagee, woordverwisseling.
hyperaesthetic, hiperesteties, oorgevoelig.
hyperbola, hiperbool.
hyperbole, hiperbool, oordrywing.
hyperbolic(al), hiperbolies, oordrewe.
hypercritical, hiperkrities.
hyperphysical, hiperfisies, bowenatuurlik.
hypersonic, hipersonies.
hypertrophy, hipertrofie, oorvoeding.
hypersonic, hipersonies.
hyphen, n. koppelteken.
hyphen, v. met 'n koppelteken verbind, koppel.
hypnosis, hipnose.
hypnotic, hipnoties, slaapwekkend.
hypnotize, hipnotiseer.
hypnotism, hipnotisme.
hypochondria, hipochondrie, hipokonders (ipekonders), swaarmoedigheid.
hypochondriac, a. hipochondries.
hypochondriac, n. hipochondris.
hypocrisy, skynheiligheid, huigelary.
hypocrite, skynheilige, huigelaar, veinsaard.
hypocritical, skynheilig, geveins, huigelagtig.
hypodermic, hipodermies, onderhuids; **– needle,** injeksienaald.
hypotenuse, hipotenusa.
hypothecate, verhipotekeer, verbind.
hypothesis, hipotese, onderstelling.
hypothetic(al), hipoteties, veronderstellend; veronderstelld.
hy-spy, I-spy, aspaai, wegkruipertjie.
hyssop, hisop.
hysteria, histerie.
hysteric(al), histeries.
hysterics, senu-aanval, histeriese aanval.

I, ek; the –, die ek, die ego.
iambic, jambies.
iamb(us), jambe.
Iberian, Iberies.
ibex, alpbok.
ibis, ibis.
ice, n. ys; break the –, die ys breek.
ice, v. ys; bevries; afkoel; (koek) glaseer.
ice-age, ysperiode.
iceberg, ysberg.
ice-cream, roomys.
ice-floe, ysblok, ysskots.
iceland, Ysland.
ichneumon, igneumon, faraosrot.
ichor, godebloed; bloedvog.
icthyography, visbeskrywing, igtiografie.
ichthyol, visolie, igtiol.
ichthyology, viskunde, igtiologie.
ichthyophagous, visetend, igtiofaag.
ichthyosaurus, visakkedis, igtiosourus.
icicle, yskegel, ysnaald.
icily, yskoud.
icing, glasering, versuikering; (koek)suiker.
icon, ikon, beeld.
iconoclast, beeldestormer, ikonoklas.
iconography, beeldebeskrywing, ikonografie.
iconometer, ikonometer.
ictus, slag; klem(toon), aksent, iktus.
icy, ysagtig; soos ys, yskoud; ys- . . .
idea, idee; denkbeeld, begrip, plan; have a high – of, 'n hoë opinie (dunk) hê van; what's the (big) – ? wat bedoel jy?; wat wil jy maak?
ideal, a. ideaal, volmaak; ideëel, denkbeeldig.
ideal, n. ideaal.
idealize, idealiseer.
idealism, idealisme.
idealist, idealis.
idealistic, idealisties.
identic(al), dieselfde, einste, identiek; identies (tweeling).
identify, vereenselwig; gelykstel; herken; aanwys; identifiseer.
identity, identiteit, eenselwigheid, gelykheid.
ideogram, ideograph, ideogram, begripteken.
ideography, ideografie, begriptekenskrif.
ideology, ideologie; ideëleer.
idiocy, idiootheid.
idiom, idioom, taaleie.
idiomatic, idiomaties.
idiosyncrasy, eienaardigheid, hebbelikheid.
idiot, idioot, dwaas, stommerik.
idiotic, idioot, ontsinnig, dwaas.
idle, a. ledig, werkloos; vry; ongegrond; ydel, nutteloos.
idle, v. leegloop, luilak; luier (mot.); – away, verbeusel.
idleness, ledigheid, luiheid; ydelheid.
idler, leegloper, luilak, niksdoener.
idly, ledig; gedagteloos; sommer.
idol, afgod; wanvoorstelling; dwaalbegrip.
idolater, afgodedienaar; aanbidder.
idolatress, afgodedienares; aanbidster.
idolatrous, afgodies.
idolatry, afgodediens; aanbidding, verering.
idolize, ver(af)good, aanbid, vereer.
idyl(l), idille.
idyllic, idillies.
if, as, indien, ingeval; of; try – you can, probeer of jy kan; as –, asof; – only not, as maar net nie; – but, as maar net; – not, so nie.
igneous, vuur- . . . ; vulkaan- . .
ignite, aan die brand steek; aan die brand raak, ontvlam.
ignition, ontbranding, ontsteking.
ignition-coil, ontstekingsklos, vonkspoel.

ignition-system, vonkstelsel, ontsteking.
ignoble, onedel, laag; skandelik.
ignobly, op 'n gemene manier, skandelik.
ignominious, skandelik, smadelik.
ignominy, smaad, skande, skandvlek.
ignoramus, stommerik, domoor.
ignorance, onkunde, onwetendheid.
ignorant, onkundig, onwetend; onbekend (met).
ignore, ignoreer, oor die hoof sien, verbysien.
iguana, likkewaan.
ilex, huls; steeneik.
Iliad, Ilias.
ilk, klas, soort.
ill, a. siek; sleg; be taken –, ongesteld raak; – temper, slegte humeur.
ill, adv. sleg; kwalik; moeilik; take –, kwalik neem; it becomes him –, dit pas hom sleg; – at ease, nie op sy gemaak nie.
ill, n. kwaad, euwel; –s, euwels, kwaad.
ill-advised, onbesonne, onbedag, onberade.
ill-affected, sleggesind, onvri(e)ndskaplik.
ill-assorted, sleg passend.
illation, gevolgtrekking.
ill-bred, onopgevoed, onmanierlik.
ill-breeding, onmanierlikheid, onopgevoedheid.
ill-disposed, sleggesind; sleggeaard.
illegal, onwettig.
illegality, onwettigheid.
illegally, onwettiglik.
illegibility, onleesbaarheid, onduidelikheid.
illegible, onleesbaar, onduidelik.
illegitimacy, onwettigheid; ongeoorloofdheid; onegtheid.
illegitimate, onwettig; ongeoorloof; oneg.
ill-fated, ongelukkig, rampspoedig.
ill-favoured, lelik; afstootlik.
ill-feeling, kwaaivri(e)ndskap, slegte gesindheid.
ill-gotten, onregverdig verkreë.
illiberal, bekrompe, kleingeestig; suinig.
illicit, ongeoorloof onwettig; – diamond buying, onwettige diamanthandel.
illimitable, onbegrens, grensloos.
illiteracy, ongeletterdheid, ongeleerdheid.
illiterate, ongeletterd, ongeleerd.
ill-judged, onbesonne, onwys.
ill-mannered, ongemanierd, onmanierlik.
ill-natured, sleggehumeurd, kwaadaardig.
illness, siekte, ongesteldheid.
illogical, onlogies.
ill-omened, ongelukkig, rampspoedig.
ill-starred, onder 'n ongelukkige gesternte gebore, ongelukkig.
ill-tempered, sleggehumeurd.
ill-timed, ontydig; ongeleë.
ill-treat, mishandel, sleg behandel.
illuminate, verlig, lig werp op; illumineer.
illumination, verligting; illuminasie.
illumine, sien illuminate.
ill-usage, slegte behandeling.
ill-use, mishandel, sleg behandel.
illusion, sinsbedrog, hersenskim, illusie.
illusionist, illusionis, goëlaar.
illusive, illusory, denkbeelding, bedrieglik.
illustrate, toelig, ophelder; kenskets; illustreer.
illustration, toeligting; voorbeeld; plaat, prent; illustrasie.
illustrative, verduidelikend; kensketsend.
illustrious, beroemd, deurlugtig, roemryk.
ill-will, teensin; kwaadwilligheid.
image, n. beeld; ewebeeld; afbeelding.
image, v. voorstel; afbeeld; weergee.
imagery, beeld; beeldspraak; verbeelding.
imaginable, denkbaar; moontlik.
imaginary, denkbeeldig.
imagination, verbeelding; verbeeldingskrag.

**imaginative, verbeeldings-...; ryk aan verbeelding; vindingryk.
imagine,** (sig) verbeel, (sig) voorstel, begryp.
imbecile, a. swaksinnig, idioot; imbesiel.
imbecile, n. swaksinnige, idioot, imbesiel.
imbecility, swaksinnigheid, swakhoofdigheid.
imbibe, indrink, insuie, opneem.
imbroglio, warboel; verwikkeling.
imbrue: – in, with, doop in.
imbue, indrink, opneem; deurtrek.
imitable, navolgbaar.
imitate, navolg; na-aap, naboots, imiteer.
imitation, navolging; nabootsing; namaak.
imitation..., namaak-...; – leather, namaakleer.
imitative, nabootsend; – of, in navolging van.
imitator, navolger; na-aper.
immaculate, onbevlek, rein; vlekloos, onberispelik.
immaculately, vlekloos; onberispelik.
immanence, immanensie, innerlikheid, inherensie.
immanent, immanent, inwonend, inherent.
immaterial, onstoflik; van geen belang; onverskillig.
immature, onryp, onvolgroei.
immeasurable, onmeetbaar; onmeetlik.
immeasurably, onmeetlik, oneindig.
immediate, onmiddellik; naaste; dadelik.
immediately, onmiddellik, dadelik.
immemorial, onheuglik; eeue-oud.
immense, ontsaglik, enorm; kolossaal.
immensely, ontsaglik, reusagtig; besonder.
immensity, ontsaglikheid.
immeasurably, onmeetbaar.
immerge, immerse, indompel; – in, dompel in; begrawe onder; verdiep in.
immersion, indompeling; verdieping.
immigrant, a. immigrerend, intrekkend.
immigrant, n. immigrant, landverhuiser.
immigrate, immigreer, intrek.
immigration, immigrasie, landverhuising.
imminence, naking, nabyheid.
imminent, nakend, ophande; dreigend.
immobile, onbeweeglik, immobiel.
immobilise, onbeweeglik maak, stop.
immobility, onbeweeglikheid, immobiliteit.
immoderate, onmatig, oordrewe, onredelik.
immoderation, onmatigheid, onredelikheid.
immodest, onbeskeie; onbetaamlik.
immodesty, onbeskeidenheid; onwelvoeglikheid.
immolate, (op)offer, immoleer.
immoral, onsedelik, immoreel; sedeloos.
immorality, onsedelikheid; sedeloosheid.
immortal, ensterflik; onverganklik.
immortalize, onsterflik maak, verewig.
immortality, onsterflikheid.
immortelle, sewejaartjie; strooiblom.
immovability, onbeweeglikheid, onwrikbaarheid.
immovable, onbeweeglik, onbeweegbaar, onwrikbaar.
immovables, onroerende eiendom, vasgoed.
immune, onvatbaar, immuun, vry.
immunity, onvatbaarheid; vrydom; immuniteit.
immure, in–, opsluit; inmessel.
immutability, onveranderlikheid.
immutable, onveranderlik.
imp, kwelgees, ondeug, vabond.
impact, botsing, skok, stamp, slag.
impair, benadeel; verswak.
impala, rooibok.
impale, deurboor.
impalpability, ontasbaarheid.
impalpable, ontasbaar; onbevatlik.
impalpably, ontasbaar; onmerkbaar.
imparity, ongelykheid.

impart, meedeel, deelagtig maak, oordra.
impartial, onpartydig.
impartiality, onpartydigheid.
impartially, onpartydig, gelyk-op.
impassable, ondeurganklik, ondeurwaardbaar, onpassabel, onbegaanbaar.
impasse, dooie steeg; dooie punt, impasse.
impassibility, ongevoeligheid, onaandoenlikheid.
impassible, ongevoelig, onaandoenlik.
impassion, aanvuur, opwek.
impassioned, hartstogtelik, vurig, opgewonde.
impassive, ongevoelig, onaandoenlik; lydelik.
impassivity, onaandoenlikheid; lydelikheid.
impatience, ongeduld(igheid); – of, afkeer van.
impatient, ongeduldig; onverdraagsaam; be – of, nie kan duld nie.
impeach, beskuldig, in twyfel trek.
impeachment, beskuldiging; verdagmaking.
impeccable, sonder sonde, onberispelik, volmaak.
impecuniosity, geldgebrek; onbemiddeldheid.
impecunious, onbemiddeld, sonder geld.
impede, hinder, belemmer, teenhou.
impediment, hindernis, hinderpaal; belemmering.
imperative, a. gebiedend; dringend; – mood, gebiedende wys, imperatief.
imperative, n. gebiedende wys, imperatief.
imperativeness, gebiedendheid.
imperceptible, onmerkbaar, onbespeurbaar.
impel, aanspoor, aandryf, moveer; voortbeweeg.
impend, hang (oor); bo die hoof hang, (be)dreig.
impending, dreigend, op hande (synde).
impenetrability, ondeurdringbaarheid.
impenetrable, ondeurdringbaar; ondeurgrondelik; ontoeganklik.
impenitence, onboetvaardigheid, verstoktheid.
impenitent, onboetvaardig, sonder berou.
imperceptibleness, onmerkbaarheid.
imperfect, a. onvolmaak, onvolkome; –tense, onvoltooid verlede tyd.
imperfect, n. onvoltooid verlede tyd.
imperfection, onvolmaaktheid; gebrek.
imperfectly, onvolmaak, op onvolmaakte manier; onduidelik, sleg.
imperial, keiserlik; vorstelik; ryks-...
imperialism, imperialisme, ryksgesindheid.
imperialist, imperialis, ryksgesinde.
imperialistic, imperialisties, ryksgesind.
imperil, in gevaar bring (stel).
imperious, heerssugtig; gebiedend.
imperiousness, gebiedenheid; heerssugtigheid.
imperishable, onvergangklik; onbederfbaar.
impermanent, tydelik, nie-blywend.
impermeable, ondeurdringbaar; (lug-, water-)dig.
impermissible, ontoelaatbaar.
impersonal, onpersoonlik.
impersonate, voorstel, verpersoonlik; (sig) uitgee vir; vertolk.
impersonation, verpersoonliking, uitbeelding, voorstelling, vertolking.
impersonator, vertolker, uitbeelder; the – of Mr X., die persoon wat hom uitgee vir mnr. X.
impertinence, astrantheid, onbeskaamdheid; onsaaklikheid, onvanpastheid; impertinensie.
impertinent, parmantig, onbeskaamd, astrant; indringerig; nie ter sake nie; impertinent.
imperturbability, onverstoorbaarheid.
imperturbable, onverstoorbaar.
impervious, ondeurdringbaar; ontoeganklik.
impetrate, afsmeek, verwerf, verkry.
impetuosity, onstuimigheid, voortvarendheid.
impetuous, onstuimig, voortvarend.
impetus, vaart, krag, beweegkrag; aandrang.
impi, impie, kafferregiment.
impiety, goddeloosheid; oneerbiedigheid.
impinge, raak, slaan (teen).

impious, goddeloos; profaan, heiligskennend.
impish, ondeund, rakkeragtig; duiwels.
implacability, onversoenlikheid.
implacable, onverbiddelik, onversoenlik.
implant, inplant; inprent.
implement, n. werktuig, (stuk) gereedskap.
implement, v. aanvul; vervul; uitvoer.
implicate, v. verwikkel; insluit, meebring; be –d in a crime, in 'n misdaad betrokke wees.
implication, verwikkeling; bedoeling; implikasie; by –, gevolglik; stilswygend.
implicit(ly), stilswygend; inbegrepe; onvoorwaardelik, blind.
implore, smeek, bid.
imploringly, smekend.
imply, insluit, behels; bedui; sinspeel op.
impolite, onbeleef, ongemanierd.
impolitic, onwys, onverstandig.
imponderable, onweegbaar; gewigsloos.
import, v. invoer; beteken, te kenne gee.
import, n. invoer; betekenis; belang(rikheid); –s, invoer, invoerartikels.
importance, belang(rikheid), betekenis.
important, belangrik, gewigtig, van betekenis.
importation, invoer, invoering.
importer, invoerder, importeur.
importune, lastig val, aandring, opdruk.
importunity, lastigheid, opdringerigheid.
importunate, lastig, dringerig.
impose, oplê; indruk maak op; – upon, om die tuin lei; misbruik maak van.
imposing, indrukwekkend.
imposition, oplegging; strafwerk; bedrog.
impossibility, onmoontlikheid.
impossible, onmoontlik; onuitstaanbaar.
impost, belasting; gewig, vrag.
impostor, bedrieër, opligter.
imposture, bedrog, bedrieëry.
impotence, magteloosheid, onmag.
impotent, magteloos, hulpeloos; impotent.
impound, skut, in die skut sit; beslag lê op.
impoverish, verarm; uitput.
impracticability, onuitvoerbaarheid; onbegaanbaarheid.
impracticable, onuitvoerbaar, ondoenlik; onprakties; onhandelbaar, onbegaanbaar.
imprecate, (ver)vloek, verwens; afsmeek.
imprecation, vervloeking, verwensing.
impregnable, onneembaar; onaantasbaar.
impregnate, a. swanger; deurtrokke (van).
impregnate, v. bevrug, swanger maak, laat deurtrek van, drenk in.
impregnation, bevrugting; drenking.
impresario, impresario.
impress, n. stempel, afdruk, indruk, merk.
impress, v. indruk, inprent; stempel; indruk maak op, tref; – something on a person, iemand iets op die hart druk.
impression, indruk; stempel; druk, oplaag.
impressionable, gevoelig, vatbaar (vir indrukke).
impressionism, impressionisme.
impressionistic, impressionisties.
impressive, indrukwekkend, aangrypend.
impressment, pressing.
imprint, n. stempel.
imprint, v. (af)druk, inprent; stempel.
imprison, gevangesit, in die tronk sit, opsluit.
imprisonment, opsluiting, gevangesetting, gevangeskap; tronkstraf.
improbability, onwaarskynlikheid.
improbable, onwaarskynlik.
improbity, oneerlikheid; goddeloosheid.
impromptu, a. & adv. uit die vuis, impromptu.
impromptu, n. improvisasie, impromptu.

improper, onbehoorlik, onfatsoenlik, ongepas; oneg, verkeerd; – fraction, onegte breuk.
improperly, onbehoorlik; ten onregte.
impropriate, toeëien; sekulariseer.
impropriety, onbehoorlikheid, onwelvoeglikheid.
improvable, verbeterbaar; bewerkbaar.
improve, verbeter; bewerk; – the occasion, gebruik maak van die geleentheid; – upon, verbeter; – upon the occasion, 'n stigtelike toespraak maak op die geleentheid.
improvement, verbetering; beterskap; vordering; bewerking; stigting.
improvidence, gebrek aan voorsorg; sorgeloosheid, verkwistendheid.
improvident, sorgeloos, verkwistend.
improvisation, improvisasie.
improvise, improviseer, uit die vuis lewer.
imprudent, onversigtigheid.
imprudent, onversigtig, onverstandig, onbesonne.
impudence, onbeskaamdheid, brutaliteit.
impudent, onbeskaamd, skaamteloos, brutaal.
impugn, bestry; in twyfel trek, betwis.
impugnment, bestryding, betwisting.
impuissance, magteloosheid.
impulse, (aan)drang, stoot; prikkel, aansporing; beweeggrond; opwelling.
impulsiveness, impulsiwiteit.
impunity, strafloosheid; with –, strafloos.
impure, onsuiwer, onrein; vervals; onkuis.
impurity, onsuiwerheid; onreinheid; onkuisheid.
imputable, toe te skrywe (aan), te wyte (aan).
imputation, toeskrywing; aantyging, beskuldiging.
impute, toeskryf (aan), wyt (aan); aantyg, ten laste lê, die skuld gee van.
in, prep. in, op, by; – itself, op sigself; – that, daarin; aangesien; he is not – it, hy tel nie mee nie, hy kom nie in aanmerking nie; as far as – me lies, so ver as in my vermoë is; – brown boots, met bruin skoene aan; one – a hundred, een op 'n honderd; – the day, oordag(s), in die dag, gedurende die dag; – three weeks, oor (binne) drie weke; – crossing the river, met die oorgaan van die rivier; believe –, glo in (aan); engage –, besig hou met; deel neem aan; rejoice –, (sig) verheug in (oor); be wanting – courage, tekort skiet in moed; seven – number, sewe in getal; four feet – width, vier voet wyd, vier voet in die wydte; – writing, op skrif.
in, adv. in, binne; come, send walk –, binnekom; -stuur, -loop; put –, insit; ingooi; lock –, in-, opsluit; he is –, hy is binne (tuis); he had only been – five minutes, hy was net vyf minute tuis (aan die slag, aan die beurt); the boat, train is –, die boot, trein is binne; keep the fire –, hou die vuur aan die gang; rub –, invryf; inpeper; you are – for it today, vandag sal jy dit hê, vandag is jy aan die pen; I am – for a race, ek neem deel aan 'n wedstryd; be, keep – with, op goeie voet wees, bly met; breed –, inteel.
in, a. binne; binnenshuis, inwonend.
in, n.: –s and outs, besonderhede, fyn puntjies.
inability, onbekwaamheid; onvermoë.
inaccessibility, ontoeganklikheid.
inaccessible, onbereikbaar, onbeklimbaar, ontoeganklik; ongenaakbaar.
inaccuracy, onnoukeurigheid.
inaccurate, onnoukeurig, foutief, verkeerd.
inaction, werkloosheid, inaktiwiteit.
inactive, werkloos, traag, flou, inaktief.
inactivity, werkloosheid, inaktiwiteit.
inadaptable, onaanwendbaar, ongeskik.
inadequacy, ontoereikendheid.

inadequate — 529 — **incompressible**

inadequate, ontoereikend, onvoldoende; – to, oneweredig aan.
inadmissibility, ontoelaatbaarheid.
inadmissible, ontoelaatbaar; onaanneemlik.
inadvertence, onopsetlikheid.
inadvertent, onopsetlik; onoplettend; agtelosig; onbewus, sonder te weet.
inalienable, onvervreembaar.
inalterable, onveranderlik.
inane, a. leeg; betekenisloos, sinloos, dwaas.
inane, n. ledige ruimte, leegte.
inanimate, lewensloos; doods.
inanimation, lewensloosheid; doodsheid.
inanition, leegheid; uitputting; gebrek.
inanity, leegheid; sinloosheid.
inappeasable, onbevredigbaar, onstilbaar.
inapplicability, ontoepaslikheid.
inapplicable, ontoepaslik, ongeskik.
inapposite, onvanpas, ongepas, ontoepaslik.
inappreciable, onmerkbaar; onwaardeerbaar.
inappreciative, nie-waarderend.
inapproachable, ontoeganklik.
inappropriate, misplaas, onvanpas, ongeskik.
inaptitude, ongeskiktheid.
inarticulate, ongeleed, sonder geledinge; onduidelik, onverstaanbaar; stom.
inartificial, ongekunsteld.
inartistic, onartistiek.
inasmuch: – as, aangesien, nademaal.
inattention, onoplettendheid.
inattentive, onoplettend, agtelosig; onattent, onhoflik.
inaudible, onhoorbaar.
inaugural, inwydings- . . . , intree- . . . , inougureel.
inaugurate, inwy, inhuldig; open.
inauguration, inwyding, bevestiging, inougurasie.
inauspicious, ongunstig.
inboard, binne(n)boord.
inborn, aan-, ingebore, ingeskape.
inbred, aangebore, ingeskape.
inbreeding, inteelt.
incalculable, onberekenbaar; ontelbaar.
incandesce, gloei; laat gloei.
incandescence, gloeihitte, gloeiing, gloed.
incandescent, gloeiend; – lamp, gloeilamp.
incantation, towerspreuk, beswering.
incapability, onvermoë, onbekwaamheid.
incapable, onbekwaam, nie in staat nie; onbevoeg; he was – of lying, dit was vir hom onmoonlik om te lieg.
incapacitate, ongeskik maak, buiten staat stel.
incapacity, onbekwaamheid; onbevoegdheid.
incarcerate, (in)kerker, gevangesit, opsluit.
incarceration, gevangesetting, opsluiting.
incarnadine, (bloed)rooi verf.
incarnate, a. vleeslik, in die vlees, vleesgeworde.
incarnate, v. beliggaam, gestalte gee.
incarnation, beliggaming, vleeswording.
incautious, onversigtig.
incendiarism, brandstiging; opruiing.
incendiary, a. brandstigtend; opruiend; – bomb, brandbom.
incendiary, n. brandstigter; opruier; brandbom; brandmiddel.
incense, n. reukwerk, wierook; bewieroking.
incense, v. kwaadmaak, vertoorn.
incentive, a. aansporend, prikkelend.
incentive, n. aansporing, spoorslag; dryfveer.
inception, begin, aanvang.
inceptive, beginnend, aanvangs- . . . ; inchoatief.
incertitude, onsekerheid.
incessant, onophoudelik, aanhoudend.
incest, bloedskande.

incestuous, bloedskendig.
inch, duim; by –es, by 'n paar duim; every – a Boer, 'n Boer van kop tot tone; within an – of his life, so ampertjies dood; op sterwe na dood; not depart an – from, geen duimbreed van afwyk nie.
inchoate, a. aanvangend; onontwikkeld.
inchoate, v. begin, aanvang neem.
inchoative, beginnend, inchoatief (inkohatief).
incidence, (die) val, (die) raak, (die) tref; tref-; raakpunt; trefwydte; invloedsfeer, gevolge; angle of –, hoek van inval; the – of the tax, die trefwydte van die belasting.
incident, a.: – to, gepaard gaande met; insidenteel; – upon, (in)vallend op.
incident, n. voorval, gebeurtenis, insident.
incidental, bykomstig, toevallig; – remark, terloopse opmerking; – to, gepaard gaande met.
incidentally, toevallig, terloops.
incinerate, (tot as) verbrand; veras.
incineration, verbranding; verassing, lykverbranding.
incipience, aanvang.
incipient, beginnend, in die beginstadium.
incise, insny, (in)kerf; graveer.
incision, insnyding, kerf, sny.
incisive, snydend; skerp; deurdringend.
incisor, snytand, voortand.
incite, aanspoor, opwek; aanhits, oprui.
incitement, aansporing; aanhitsing, opruiing.
incivility, onbeleefdheid; onhoflikheid.
inclemency, guurheid; onbarmhartigheid.
inclement, guur; onbarmhartig.
inclinable, geneig; geneë.
inclination, neiging; geneentheid; helling; angle of –, hellingshoek.
incline, v. (sig) buig neig; oorhel; – to, oorbuig tot; geneig wees tot; one's ear, die oor neig(tot); –d plane, hellende vlak.
incline, n. helling, skuinste af-, opdraand.
include, insluit, omvat, meetel; including the captain, die kaptein inbegrepe.
inclusion, insluiting.
inclusive, insluitend, inbegrepe, inklusief; pages 7 to 10 –, van bladsy 7 tot en met bladsy 10.
incognizant, onbewus (van).
incognito, incognito.
incoherence, onsamehangendheid.
incoherent, onsamehangend.
incombustible, onbrandbaar.
income, inkomste.
incoming, in-, binnelopend; intrekkend; opvolgend; uitstaande (geld).
incommensurable, (onderling) onmeetbaar; nie te vergelyk nie.
incommensurate, ongeëweredig (aan); (onderling) onmeetbaar.
incommode, ontrief, tot oorlas wees.
incommodious, ongerieflik; hinderlik.
incommunicable, onmeedeelbaar.
incommunicado, eensame opsluiting.
incommunicative, onmeedeelsaam, terughoudend.
incommutable, onveranderlik; onverwisselbaar.
incomparable, onvergelyklik, weergaloos.
incompatibility, onverenigbaarheid.
incompatible, onverenigbaar, onbestaanbaar met.
incompetence, -cy, onbevoegdheid; onbekwaamheid.
incompetent, onbevoeg; onbekwaam, ongeskik.
incomplete, onvolledig; onvoltallig.
incomprehensibility, onbegryplikheid.
incomprehensible, onbegryplik.
incomprehension, wanbegrip.
incompressible, onsaamdrukbaar.

incomputable, onbesyferbaar, onberekenbaar.
inconceivable, ondenkbaar, onbegryplik.
inconclusive, onoortuigend.
incongruity, onverenigbaarheid, ongerymdheid.
incongruous, onverenigbaar, onbestaanbaar met; misplaas.
inconsecutive, inkonsekwent, onlogies.
inconsequence, inkonsekwensie.
inconsequent, ontoepaslik, misplaas; inkonsekwent, onlogies; onsamehangend.
inconsiderable, onbeduidend; gering.
inconsiderate, onbedagsaam; onhoflik.
inconsideration, inconsiderateness, onbedagsaamheid; onhoflikheid.
inconsistency, ongelykheid; teenstrydigheid; inkonsekwensie.
inconsistent, ongelyk, veranderlik; teenstrydig, onverenigbaar (met); inkonsekwent.
inconsolable, ontroosbaar.
inconsonant, onharmonies; teenstrydig.
inconspicuous, onopvallend; beskeie.
inconspicuousness, onopvallendheid.
inconstancy, onbestendigheid.
inconstant, veranderlik, onbestendig, onstandvastig.
inconsumable, onverteerbaar.
incontestable, onbetwisbaar.
incontinence, onmatigheid, ontugtigheid; gebrek aan selfbeheersing; watervloed.
incontinent, onmatig; ontugtig; onbeheers.
incontinently, onmiddellik, op staande voet.
incontrovertible, onweerlegbaar.
inconvenience, ongemak, ongerief(likheid).
inconvenient, ongerieflik, ongemaklik, ongeleë lastig.
inconvertible, onverwisselbaar; onwisselbaar.
incorporate, a. ingelyf, geïnkorporeer.
incorporate, v. inlyf, verenig, inkorporeer.
incorporation, inlywing, opneming, inkorporasie.
incorporeal, onliggaamlik, onstoflik.
incorrect, onjuis, verkeerd, inkorrek.
incorrectness, onjuistheid, onnoukeurigheid.
oncorrigibility, onverbeterlikheid.
incorrigible, onverbeterlik, ongeneeslik.
incorruptibility, onverganklikheid; onomkoopbaarheid.
incorruptible, onverganklik; onomkoopbaar.
increase, v. vermeerder, vergroot, verhoog, verbeter.
increase, n. vermeerdering, toename; on the –, aan die toeneem.
increasingly, hoe langer hoe meer.
incredibility, ongelooflikheid.
incredible, ongelooflik, ongeloofbaar.
incredulity, ongelowigheid.
incredulous, ongelowig, twyfelsugtig.
increment, vermeerdering, (loons)verhoging, toelae; aanwas.
incriminate, beskuldig, betrek (in 'n beskuldiging), inkrimineer.
incriminatory, inkriminerend.
incrustation, kors; aansetsel.
incubate, uitbroei; broei; ontwikkel.
incubation, (uit)broei; inkubasie.
incubator, broeimasjien; kweektoestel.
incubus, nagmerrie, inkubus.
inculcate, inprent.
inculcation, inprenting.
inculpate, beskuldig, aankla; insleep.
inculpation, beskuldiging, aantyging.
incumbency, las, plig; kerklike amp.
incumbent, n. kerklike amptenaar, predikant.
incumbent: – (up)on, rustend op; it is – on you, dit is jou plig, jy behoort.
incur, (sig) blootstel aan, op die hals haal; –

danger, (sig) blootstel aan gevaar; – punishment, straf kry.
incurable, ongeneeslik.
incurious, onverskillig; oninteressant.
incursion, inval.
incus, aambeeld(beentjie).
indaba, indaba, bespreking, vergadering.
indebted, verskuldig; be – to, for, verskuldig wees weens.
indecency, onfatsoenlikheid.
indecent, onbehoorlik, onbetaamlik, onfatsoenlik, onwelvoeglik, onsedelik.
indecipherable, onontsyferbaar.
indecision, besluiteloosheid, onbeslistheid.
indecisive, onbeslis; besluitloos.
indeclinable, onverbuigbaar.
indecorous, onbehoorlik, ongepas; ondeftig.
indecorousness, onbehoorlikheid; ondeftigheid.
indecorum, ondeftigheid; ongepastheid.
indeed, werklik, regtig, inderdaad; who is he –?, wie is hy dan?
indefatigable, onvermoeibaar, onvermoeid.
indefeasible, onaantasbaar, onvervreembaar.
indefensible, onverdedigbaar.
indefinable, onbepaalbaar; nie te beskrywe nie; onduidelik, vaag.
indefinite, onbepaald, vaag, onduidelik; – pronoun, onbepaalde voornaamwoord.
indelible, onuitwisbaar; – pencil, inkpotlood.
indelicate, onkiesheid.
indelicate, onkies, tak(t)loos, indelikaat.
indemnification, skadeloosstelling; vrywaring.
indemnify, skadeloosstel; vrywaar.
indemnity, vergoeding, vrywaring, vrystelling.
indent, v. (uit)tand; (letters) inspring; bestel.
indent, n. inkerwing, insnyding; bestelling.
indent, v. (in)deuk; stempel, merk.
indent, n. deuk; stempel, merk.
indentation, onkerwing, kerf; inham.
indention, inspringing.
indenture, n. kontrak; dokument; bestelling, inkerwing, kerf.
indenture, v. inboek, inskryf.
independence, onafhanklikheid; eie inkomste.
independency, onafhanklike staat; onafhanklikheid.
independent, a. onafhanklik.
independent, n. onafhanklike.
indescribable, onbeskryflik; vaag.
indestructible, onvernielbaar, onverwoesbaar.
indeterminable, onbepaalbaar; onbeslisbaar.
indeterminate, onbepaald; vaag.
indetermination, besluiteloosheid.
index, n. wysvinger; wyser; inhoudsopgawe; klapper; magsaanwyser; eksponent (in algebra); indeks; – number, kensyfer, indekssyfer.
index, v. van 'n indeks voorsien; in die indeks opneem.
India, Indië; Further, –, Agter-Indië; British –, Brits-Indië.
Indiaman, Oosindiëvaarder.
Indian, a. Indies; Indiaans; Red –, Indiaan, Rooihuid; – corn, mielies; in – file, agter mekaar, tou-tou; – ink, Oosindiese ink.
India-paper, sneespapier, sypapier.
Indiarubber, gomlastiek, gummi; uitveër.
indicate, aandui, aan die hand gee.
indication, aanduiding, aanwysing, teken.
indicative, a. aantonend; be – of, dui op; – mood, aantonende wys, indikatief.
indicative, n. aantonende wyse, indikatief.
indicator, wyser; aanwyser; aangeër.
indict, beskuldig, aankla.
indictable, vervolgbaar, strafbaar.
indictment, beskuldiging, aanklag; verhoor.

Indies, Indië; East -, Oos-Indië; West -, Wes-Indië.
indifference, onverskilligheid.
indifferent, onverskillig; onpartydig; so-so, middelmatig.
indigence, -cy, behoeftigheid, armoede.
indigenous, inheems, inlands.
indigent, behoeftig, nooddruftig, arm.
indigested, onverteer(d); onverwerk.
indigestibility, onverteerbaarheid.
indigestible, onverteerbaar.
indigestion, slegte spysvertering, indigestie.
indignant, verontwaardig (oor).
indignation, verontwaardiging.
indignity, belediging; onwaardige behandeling.
indigo, blousel; indigo.
indigo-blue, indigoblou.
indirect, indirek, onregstreeks, sydelings, middellik; - **speech**, indirekte rede.
indirectly, indirek, op indirekte manier.
indiscernible, ononderskeibaar, nie waar te neem nie.
indisciplinable, ondrilbaar, onregeerbaar.
indiscreet, onbesonne; indiskreet, onbeskeie.
indiscrete, ongeskei, nie afsonderlik nie.
indiscretion, onbesonnenheid, indiskresie.
indiscriminate, sonder onderskeid, blind.
indiscriminately, blindelings, voor die voet.
indiscriminateness, -ation, gebrek aan onderskeiding; blindelingsheid.
indispensable, onmisbaar, onontbeerlik.
indispose, ongeskik maak; ongeneë, afkerig maak; ongesteld maak.
indisposed, ongeneë; ongesteld; afkerig.
indisposition, ongeneentheid; ongesteldheid; afkerigheid.
indisputable, onbetwisbaar.
indisputably, sonder twyfel, onteenseglik.
indissoluble, onoplosbaar; onverbreekbaar.
indistinct, onduidelik; dof, vaag; verward.
indistinctive, nie kenmerkend nie.
indistinctness, onduidelikheid.
indistinguishable, nie te onderskei nie; onsigbaar.
indite, opstel, saamstel.
individual, a. individueel; alleenstaande, afsonderlik; eienaardig.
individual, n. individu, enkeling.
individualize, individualiseer.
individualist, individualis.
individualistic, individualisties.
individuality, individualiteit, persoonlikheid.
individually, afsonderlik, persoonlik, individueel, apart.
indivisibility, ondeelbaarheid.
indivisible, ondeelbaar.
Indo-China, Agter-Indië, Indo-China.
indocile, ongeseglik, onhandelbaar.
indoctrinate, indoktrineer; onderrig; inpomp.
Indo-Germanic, Indo-Germaans.
indolence, traagheid; luiheid.
indolent, lui, traag, vadsig.
indomitable, ontembaar; onbuigbaar.
indoor, binne, huis-..., kamer-..., huislik; - **games**, huis-, kamerspeletjies; - **work**, huiswerk.
indoors, binnenshuis, binne.
indorse, endosseer, (rug)teken.
indorsee, geëndosseerde.
indubitable, ontwyfelbaar.
induce, oorhaal, beweeg, moveer, noop; veroorsaak, te voorskyn roep; aflei.
inducement, beweegrede, lokmiddel, verleiding.
induct, inlei; installeer; inwy; bevestig.
induction, inleiding; gevolgtrekking; induksie.
induction-coil, induksieklos.

inductive, induktief.
indulge, toegee aan, koester; die sin gee, verwen; die vrye loop gee; - **a hope**, 'n hoop koester; - **in a luxury**, (sig) die weelde veroorloof; te veel drink.
indulgence, toegeeflikheid; koestering; verwenning, bevrediging; guns; aflaat (R.K. kerk).
indulgence-money, aflaatgeld.
indulgent, toegeeflik, inskiklik, meegaand.
indurate, verhard, verstok word (maak).
induration, verharding, verstokking.
industrial, a. industrieel, industrie-..., nywerheids-...; - **school**, vakskool, industrieskool.
industrial, n. fabrikant.
industrialism, industrialisme; nywerheidspolitiek.
industrious, ywerig, vlytig, werksaam.
industry, industrie, nywerheid; ywer(igheid).
indwell, inwoon, huis (setel) in.
inebriate, a. dronk, beskonke.
inebriate, n. dronkman, beskonkene.
inebriate, v. dronk maak.
inebriety, dronkenskap; dranksug.
inedible, oneetbaar.
inedited, onuitgegee; ongeredigeer.
ineffable, onsegbaar, onuitspreeklik.
ineffaceable, onuitwisbaar.
ineffective, ondoeltreffend, vrugteloos, sonder uitwerking.
ineffectiveness, vrugteloosheid.
ineffectual(ly), sonder uitwerking, vrugteloos.
ineffectualness, vrugteloosheid, ondoeltreffendheid.
inefficacious, kragteloos, sonder uitwerking.
inefficiency, onbekwaamheid; ondoeltreffendheid.
inefficient, onbekwaam; ondoeltreffend.
inelegance, onbevalligheid.
inelegant, onbevallig, onsierlik, onelegant.
ineligible, onverkiesbaar; ongeskik, ongewens.
ineluctable, onontkombaar, onontwykbaar.
inept, onvanpas, ongeskik; ongerymd, dwaas; onbekwaam.
ineptitude, ongeskiktheid; ongerymdheid.
ineptness, onpaslikheid; dwaasheid.
inequality, ongelykheid; veranderlikheid.
inequilateral, ongelyksydig.
inequitable, onregverdig, onbillik.
inequity, onbillikheid.
ineradicable, onuitroeibaar, onuitwisbaar.
inert, traag, bewegingloos, log.
inertia, traagheid, bewegingloosheid; inersie.
inertness, traagheid, loomheid, inersie.
inessential, onessensieel, bykomstig.
inestimable, onskatbaar, onberekenbaar.
inevitability, onvermydelikheid.
inevitable, onvermydelik, noodwendig.
inexact, onnoukeurig, onjuis.
inexactitude, inexactness, onnoukeurigheid.
inexcusable, onverskoonbaar, onvergeeflik.
inexhaustible, onuitputlik.
inexorability, onverbiddelikheid.
inexorable, onverbiddelik.
inexpectant, niks (kwaads) vermoedend.
inexpediency, onraadsaamheid, ondienstigheid.
inexpedient, onraadsaam, ondienstig.
inexpensive, nie duur nie, redelik, billik.
inexperience, onervarendheid.
inexperienced, onervare, sonder ondervinding, rou.
inexpert, onvakkundig, onbedrewe.
inexpiable, onversoenbaar; onversoenlik.
inexplicable, onverklaarbaar.
inexpressible, onuitspreeklik, onnoembaar.
inexpressibles, beenkleding.

inexpressive 532 **inherit**

inexpressive, nikseggend, onbeduidend.
inextinguishable, onblusbaar, onuitbluslik.
inextricable, onontwarbaar; hopeloos.
infallibility, onfeilbaarheid; onbedrieglikheid.
infallible, onfeilbaar; onbedrieglik.
infallibly, onfeilbaar; vas en seker, sonder makeer.
infamous, skandelik, skandalig; berug.
infamy, skande(likheid), skandaligheid; berugtheid.
infancy, kindsheid, kinderjare; jeug.
infant, m. klein kindjie, babetjie, suigling.
infant, a. klein, jong, jeugdig, kleinkinder-...
infanta, infante.
infanticide, kindermoord; kindermoordenaar (kindermoordenares).
infantile, kinderlik, kinder-...; kinderagtig.
infantry, infanterie, voetgangers, voetvolk.
infantry-man, infanteris.
infant-school, kleinkinderskool, bewaarskool.
infatuate, versot maak, verdwaas, gek maak.
infatuated, versot, gek, verdwaas; verlief.
infatuation, versotheid; verliefdheid.
infect, aansteek, besmet, verpes.
infection, besmetting, verpesting, infeksie.
infectious, aansteeklik, besmetlik.
infelicitous, ongelukkig, onfortuinlik.
infelicity, ongeluk(kigheid).
infer, aflei, opmaak; bedoel.
inference, gevolgtrekking, konklusie.
inferential, afleibaar, konkludeerbaar.
inferior, a. laer; ondergeskik; minderwaardig; inferieur; onderstandig (in plantkunde).
inferior, n. ondergeskikte, mindere.
inferiority, ondergeskiktheid; minderwaardigheid.
inferiority-complex, minderwaardigheidsgevoel.
infernal, hels; ellendig, vervlaks(te); – machine, helse masjien.
inferno, inferno, hel.
infertile, onvrugbaar.
infest, teister, vervuil, verpes; thieves – the place, die plek wemel van diewe; –ed with flies, vervuil (verpes) van die vlieë.
infidel, n. ongelowige.
infidel, a. ongelowig.
infidelity, ongeloof; ontrou.
infield, binneveld (*kr.*).
infiltrate, insypel, deursyfer, deurdring.
infiltration, deursyfering, infiltrasie.
infinite, a. & adv. oneindig.
infinite, n. oneindigheid, die oneindige.
infiniteness, oneindigheid.
infinitesimal, oneindig klein.
infinitive, (die) infinitief, onbepaalde wys.
infinitude, oneindigheid.
infinity, oneindigheid.
infirm, swak.
infirmary, hospitaal, siekehuis; siekesaal.
infirmity, swakheid, gebrek, sieklikheid.
infix, v. inlas, invoeg, vassit; inprent.
infix, n. invoegsel.
inflame, (laat) ontvlam, (laat) ontbrand; verhit, aanvuur; ontstoke raak, inflammasie kry.
inflammability, ontvlambaarheid.
inflammable, brandbaar, ontvlambaar; opvlieënd, hartstogtelik.
inflammation, ontsteking, inflammasie; ontbranding, ontvlamming.
inflammatory, verhittend; opruiend, ontstekings-...
inflate, opblaas, oppomp; opgeblase maak; opdryf.
inflation, (die) opblaas (oppomp); opgeblasenheid; opdrywing, inflasie (van pryse).

inflect, buig, verbuig.
infected, verboë.
inflection, inflexion, verbuiging (gram.); buiging.
inflectional, inflexional, (ver)buigings-...
inflict, oplê, toebring, laat ondergaan.
infliction, oplegging; leed, kwelling, marteling.
inflorescence, bloei, blom, bloeiwyse.
inflow, instroming, invloeiing.
influence, n. invloed, inwerking; have – on, over, with, invloed hê op.
influence, v. beïnvloed, invloed (uit)oefen op, influenseer.
influential, invloedryk.
influenza, griep, influensa; nuwe-siekte (van perde).
influx, instroming, toevloed.
inform, meedeel, berig; – against, aankla, verklik.
informal, sonder seremonies, informeel; onreëlmatig.
informality, informaliteit; onreëlmatigheid.
informant, segsman, beriggewer; aanklaer.
information, inligting, informasie; klagte, beskuldiging; kennis; kennisgewing, berig.
informative, informatory, leersaam.
informed, op hoogte (van sake), onderleg.
informer, nuusdraer, aanklaer.
infra, benede; – dig, benede iemand se waardigheid, ongepas.
infraction, oortreding, skending, inbreuk.
infra-red, infrarooi.
infrequent, seldsaam.
infrequently, selde, nie dikwels nie.
infringe, oortree, breek, skend.
infringement, oortreding, skending, inbreuk.
infuriate, woedend (rasend) maak, vertoorn.
infuse, ingiet; inboesem; laat trek (van tee).
infusion, (die) ingiet; inboeseming; (dic) trek aftreksel, infusie.
infusoria, infusiediertjies.
ingathering, insameling, oes.
ingenious, oulik, vernuftig, vindingryk.
ingenuity, oulikheid, vernuftigheid.
ingenuous, ope(n)hartig; onskuldig, ongekunsteld.
ingenuousness, ope(n)hartigheid, opregtheid.
ingestion, opneming, inbrenging.
ingle, haardvuur (erdvuur).
ingle-nook, hoekie van die haard (vuurerd).
inglorious, roemloos; onroemrugtig, skandelik.
ingoing, a. ingaande.
ingoing, n. ingang, (die) ingaan.
ingot, staaf, baar.
ingrain(ed), in die wol geverf; ingeworteld.
ingrate, a. ondankbaar.
ingrate, n. ondankbare.
ingratiate, jou bemind maak; jou indring (in die guns).
ingratiating, innemend, beminlik; indringerig.
ingratitude, ondankbaarheid.
ingredient, bestanddeel, ingrediënt.
ingress, ingang, toegang.
ingrowing, ingroeiend.
inhabit, bewoon, woon in.
inhabitable, bewoonbaar.
inhabitant, inwoner, bewoner.
inhabitation, bewoning.
inhalation, inaseming, inhalasie.
inhale, inasem, intrek, insluk.
inharmonic, onharmonies.
inharmonious, onharmonieus, onwelluidend.
inhere, aankleef, saamgaan (met), berus by.
inherence, (die) samegaan, inherensie.
inherent, onafskeidelik verbonde (met), gepaard gaande (met), behorende by, inherent.
inherit, erf, oorerf.

inheritable   533   **inseparable**

inheritable, (oor)erflik, erfbaar.
inheritance, erfnis, erfporsie; oorerwing.
inheritor, erfgenaam.
inheritress, -trix, erfgename.
inhesion, samehang, inherensie.
inhibit, belet, verbied, stuit, terughou.
inhibition, verbod; stuiting, inhibisie.
inhibitory, stuitend, terughoudend, belettend.
inhospitable, ongasvry; onherbergsaam.
inhospitality, ongasvryheid.
inhuman, onmenslik.
inhumanity, onmenslikheid, gevoelloosheid.
inhume, ter aarde bestel, begrawe.
inimical, vyandig; skadelik, strydig (met).
inimitable, onnavolgbaar.
inimitably, op onnavolgbare manier.
iniquitous, onregverdig; verderflik.
iniquity, onregverdigheid; ongeregtigheid; verderflikheid; sonde.
initial, a. aanvangs- ..., begin- ..., eerste.
initial, n. voorletter.
initial, v. met die voorletters teken, parafeer.
initially, in die begin, in die eerste plek.
initiate, v. aanvang, begin; inwy, inlei; ontgroen.
initiate, a. & n. ingewyde.
initiation, inwyding; ontgroening; aanvang.
initiative, n. eerste stoot, inisiatief; ondernemingsgees.
initiative, a. inleidende, aanvangs- ...
inject, inspuit.
injection, inspuiting, injeksie.
injudicious, onverstandig, onoordeelkundig.
injudiciousness, onoordeelkundigheid.
injunction, opdrag, las (geregtelike) bevel.
injure, beseer; beskadig; verongelyk.
injured, beseer; verongelyk; beledig.
injurious, nadelig, skadelik; lasterlik.
injury, besering, wond, letsel; nadeel, skade, onreg, verongelyking.
injustice, onregverdigheid; onreg; **you do him an –,** jy doen hom onreg aan.
ink, n. ink.
ink, v. ink aansmeer; met ink merk.
ink-bottle, inkfles; inkpot.
inkling, idee, vermoede; **get an – of,** die snuf (lug) van kry.
ink-slinger, ink-wellusteling.
ink-stand, inkkoker.
inky, inkerig, inkswart.
inlaid, ingelê.
inland, n. binneland(e), onderveld.
inland, a. binnelands.
inland, adv. landwaarts, na die binneland.
inlander, binnelander.
inlay, v. inlê.
inlay, n. ingelegde werk; inlegsel.
inlet, opening, ingang; inham, kreek.
inlet-valve, inlaatklep.
inmate, huisgenoot, (mede)bewoner.
inmost, binneste; diepste, innigste.
inn, herberg.
innate, aan-, ingebore, ingeskape.
innateness, aangeborenheid, ingeskapenheid.
innavigable, onbevaarbaar.
inner, binne- ..., binneste, innerlik, inwendig; **the – man,** die inwendige mens.
innermost, binneste; diepste, innigste.
inner-spring: –mattress, binneveermatras.
innervation, senuwerking; besenuwing.
innervate, (die senuwees) krag gee, sterk.
innings, beurt(e).
innkeeper, herbergier.
innocence, onskuld(igheid); eenvoud(igheid).
innocent, a. onskuldig; eenvoudig, argeloos; onskadelik; **– of,** sonder skuld.

innocent, n. onskuldige; onnosele, simpele; **massacre of the –s,** kindermoord.
innocuous, onskadelik.
innovate, nuwighede invoer.
innovation, nuwigheid, verandering, afwyking.
innuendo, skimp, toespeling, insinuasie.
innumerable, ontelbaar; talloos.
inobservance, onoplettendheid; veronagsaming.
inoculate, (in)ent.
inoculation, (in)enting.
inodorous, reukloos.
inoffensive, onskuldig, argeloos; nie aanstootlik nie; nie onaangenaam nie.
inofficious, ongedienstig; funksieloos.
inoperable, onopereerbaar.
inoperative, buite werking; sonder uitwerking.
inopportune, ontydig, ongeleë.
inordinacy, buitensporigheid; ongereeldheid.
inordinate, buitensporig, oordrewe, ongereeld.
inorganic, onbewerktuig; anorganies; **– chemistry,** anorganiese skeikunde.
inpouring, instroming.
inquest, ondersoek, (lyk)skouing; **coroner's –,** geregtelike lykskouing.
inquietude, ongerustheid; onrustigheid.
inquire, enquire, verneem, navraag doen; **–** about, after, verneem na, navraag doen omtrent; **– for,** vra om; vra na; **– into,** ondersoek, ondersoek instel na; **–,** vra.
inquirer, enquirer, ondersoeker, (na)vraer.
inquiry, enquiry, navraag, ondersoek; **make inquiries (about, after),** navraag doen (omtrent).
inquiry-office, informasieburo.
inquisition, ondersoek; inkwissie.
inquisitive, nuuskierig.
inquisitiveness, nuuskierigheid.
inquisitor, ondersoeker, ondervraer, regter; inkwisiteur.
inquisitorial, inkwisitoriaal; nuuskierig.
inroad, inval, strooptog; inbreuk.
inrush, instroming.
insalubrious, ongesond.
insalutary, ongesond, nadelig.
insane, kranksinnig, gek, mal.
insanity, kranksinnigheid.
insanitary, ongesond, onhigiënies.
insatiability, onversadelikheid.
insatiable, onversadelik, onversadigbaar.
insatiate, onversadigbaar.
inscribe, inskryf, opskryf, graveer, ingrif; **opdra (aan); – in a circle,** beskryf in 'n sirkel.
inscription, inskrywing, opskrif; opdrag.
inscrutability, onnaspeurlikheid.
inscrutable, onnaspeurlik, ondeurgrondelik.
insect, insek, gogga.
insectarium, insektarium.
insecticide, insekpoeier, -gif; insektemoord.
insectivorous, insekte-etend.
insectology, insektekunde.
insect-powder, insekpoeier.
insecure, onveilig, onseker, los.
insecurity, onveiligheid, onsekerheid.
inseminate, saai; inplant, inprent.
insensate, gevoelloos; onsinnig, sinneloos.
insensibility, gevoelloosheid; ongevoeligheid; bewusteloosheid.
insensible, onmerkbaar, onwaarneembaar; gevoelloos; bewusteloos; onbewus.
insensibility, onmerkbaar.
insensitive, ongevoelig.
insentient, gevoelloos, lewensloos.
inseparability, onskeidbaarheid; onafskeidelikheid.
inseparable, onskeidbaar; onafskeidelik.

insert, insteek, invoeg, inlas; opneem, plaas.
insertion, inlassing, invoeging; plaatsing tussensetsel.
inset, byvoegsel, bylae, byblad, bykaart, byportret; tussenstrook, inlegsel.
inshore, dig by die kus, naby die wal.
inside, n. binnekant, binneste; middel; ingewande; **turn – out**, binneste buite draai.
inside, a. binne-..., binnekantse, binneste.
inside, adv. binne(kant), binnenshuis, binne-in.
inside, prep. binne, binne-in; – **of a week**, binne 'n week, in minder as 'n week.
insider, ingewyde, lid.
insidious, verraderlik; listig.
insidiousness, verraderlikheid; listigheid.
insight, insig.
insignia, ordetekens.
insignificance, onbeduidendheid.
insignificant, onbeduidend, niksbeduidend, onbetekenend, gering, nietig.
insincere, onopreg, onwaar.
insincerity, onopregtheid.
insinuate, te verstaan gee; indring, inwerk; insinueer.
insinuation, skimp, toespeling; toedigting; indringing; inwerking; insinuasie.
insinuative, insinuerend; indringend.
insipid, laf, flou, smaakloos.
insipidity, lafheid, smaakloosheid.
insist, aandring (op); aanhou, volhard (by); – **on a point**, nadruk lê (aandring) op 'n punt; – **on his innocence**, volhard by sy onskuld; – **on being present**, daarop staan om teenwoordig te wees.
insistence, aandrang, koppigheid.
insistently, voortdurend, met aandrang.
insobriety, onmatigheid.
insolence, parmantigheid, onbeskaamdheid.
insolent, parmantig, onbeskaamd, brutaal.
insolubility, onoplosbaarheid.
insoluble, onoplosbaar.
insolvency, bankrotskap, insolvensie.
insolvent, a. bankrot, insolvent.
insolvent, n. bankrotspeler, bankroetier.
insomnia, slaaploosheid, insomnia.
insomuch, is sover.
insouciance, onverskilligheid.
inspan, inspan.
inspect, ondersoek, nasien; inspekteer.
inspection, ondersoek, inspeksie; besigtiging.
inspector, inspekteur; opsiener.
inspiration, inaseming; ingewing, inspirasie, inspraak; besieling.
inspiratory, inasemings-..., inspiratories.
inspire, inboesem, besiel, aanvuur; inasem, intrek; inspireer.
inspissate, verdik, stol.
instability, onbestendigheid, onvastheid.
install, installeer; bevestig; inrig, maklik maak; aanlê.
installation, installasie; bevestiging; aanleg.
instalment, gedeelte; paaiement; aflewering; **in –s**, by gedeeltes; in paaiemente.
instance, n. voorbeeld, geval, instansie; versoek; **for –**, byvoorbeeld; **in the first –**, in die eerste plek (instansie); **at the – of**, op die versoek van; **in your –**, in u geval.
instance, v. as voorbeeld noem, aanvoer.
instant, a. dringend; onmiddellik, dadelik; **the 6th –**, die 6de deser, die 6de van hierdie maand.
instant, n. oomblik.
instantaneous, oombliklik.
instanter, op die daad.
instantly, onmiddellik, oombliklik, op die daad.

instead: – **of**, in plaas van, pleks; **in his stead**, in sy plek.
instep, wreef, voetrug.
instigate, opstook, aanspoor; op tou sit.
instigation, aansporing, aanhitsing, opstokery; **at the – of**, op aansporing van.
instigator, opstoker, ophitser.
instil(l), (laat) indrup; – **into**, inprent, besiel met.
instillation, **instilment**, (die) indrup; inboeseming.
instinct, n. natuurdrif, instink.
instinct, a. besiel.
instinctive, instinkmatig, instinktief, onwillekeurig.
institute, n. instelling; genootskap.
institute, v. stig, instel; vasstel; – **inquiry**, ondersoek instel.
institution, instelling, oprigting, stigting; institusie; aanstelling; instituut, inrigting; wet.
institutional, vasgestel.
instruct, onderwys gee, onderrig; in kennis stel; gelas.
instruction, onderwys, onderrig; –**s**, voorskrifte, opdrag, instruksies.
instructive, leersaam, instruktief.
instructor, leermeester, instrukteur.
instructress, instruktrise.
instrument, instrument; werktuig; middel; dokument, bewysskrif.
instrumental, instrumentaal; **be – to, in**, 'n middel wees tot, bydra tot.
instrumentalist, instrumentis.
instrumentality, middel, medewerking, bemiddeling; **by the – of**, deur bemiddeling van.
instrumentation, instrumentasie.
insubordinate, ongehoorsaam, weerspannig; **be –**, ongehoorsaam wees, sig verset teen.
insubordination, verset, insubordinasie.
insubstantial, onwesenlik; swak.
insufferable, onuitstaanbaar; ondraagbaar.
insufficiency, ontoereikendheid.
insufficient, ontoereikend, onvoldoende.
insular, van 'n eiland, insulêr; bekrompe.
insularity, insulariteit.
insulate, afsonder; isoleer.
insulation, isolering.
insular, isolator.
insulin, insulien.
insult, n. belediging, affrontasie.
insult, v. beledig, affronteer.
insulting, beledigend, honend.
insuperable, onoorkomelik.
insupportable, ondraaglik, onuitstaanbaar.
insurance, versekering, assuransie.
insurance agent, assuransie-agent.
insurance company, versekeringsmaatskappy.
insurance policy, versekeringspolis.
insure, verassureer; verseker.
insured, versekerde, verassureerde.
insurgency, opstandigheid.
insurgent, a. opstandig, oproerig.
insurgent, n. opstandeling, rebel.
insurmountable, onoorkoomlik.
insurrection, opstand, oproer.
insusceptibility, ongevoeligheid.
insusceptible, onvatbaar, ongevoelig.
intact, onaangeroer, ongeskonde, heel.
intaglio, gravuur, intaglio.
intake, (die) inloop; vernouing.
intangible, ontasbaar; onbevatlik.
integer, heel (integraal) getal; geheel.
integral, a. heel, volledig, integraal; – **part**, integrerende (essensiële) deel; – **calculus**, integraalrekening.
integral, n. integraal.
integrate, v. volledig maak; integreer.

**integration, **integrasie.
integrity, volledigheid, ongeskondenheid; onomkoopbaarheid; integriteit; regskapenheid.
integument, skil, dop, vel, vlies, omhulsel.
integumentary, bedekkend, dek-...
intellect, verstand, denkvermoë, intellek.
intellection, onderkenning, (die) verstaan.
intellectual, intellektueel, verstandelik; verstands:..., geestes-...; – **development,** verstandelike (intellektuele) ontwikkeling.
intellectualize, (ver)intellektualiseer.
intellectualism, intellektualisme.
intelligence, verstand, intellek; oordeel, begrip; vernuf; berig, tyding.
intelligence-office, informasieburo.
intelligencer, beriggewer; nuusdraer; spioen.
intelligent, skrander, intelligent.
intelligentsia, intellektuele.
intelligibility, verstaanbaarheid.
intelligible, verstaanbaar, begryplik, bevatlik.
intemperate, onmatig, oordadig, onstuimig; dranklustig.
intemperately, oormatig, buitensporig.
intend, van plan (voornemens) wees, meen, bestem (vir); **we – to go,** ons is van plan te gaan; **– no harm,** geen kwaad bedoel nie; **he is –ed for the Church,** hy is vir die Kerk bestem; **the cake is –ed for you,** die koek is vir jou bedoel.
intendant, opsigter, bestuurder.
intended, aanstaande.
intending, aanstaande; – **purchasers,** kooplustiges.
intense, intens, groot, lewendig, sterk, hewig, kragtig, diep.
intenseness, intensiteit, hewigheid, krag.
intensify, versterk, verdiep, verhoog, vererger.
intension, intensiteit, spanning, krag.
intensity, intensiteit, hewigheid, krag.
intensive, intensief; intens; kragtig, versterkend; – **agriculture,** intensiewe landbou.
intent, n. bedoeling, voorneme, oogmerk; **to all –s and purposes,** feitlik.
intent, a. vasbeslote; ingespanne; gespanne; – **on winning,** vasbeslote om te wen; – **on his reading,** verdiep in sy lektuur; **with – look,** met gespanne blik.
intently, ingespanne, ywerig; gespanne, strak.
intentness, vasbeslotenheid; (in)gespannenheid.
intention, bedoeling, oogmerk, plan.
intentional, opsetlik, moedswillig, ekspres.
inter, v. begrawe, ter aarde bestel.
inter, prep. inter, onder, tussen; – **alia,** onder andere.
interact, inwerk op mekaar.
interaction, wisselwerking.
interblend, meng, deurmekaar meng.
interbreed, kruisteel.
intercalary, ingevoeg, ingelas, ingeskuif.
intercalate, invoeg, inlas, inskuif.
intercede, bemiddel, as bemiddelaar optree, tussenbeide kom; voorspraak wees.
intercept, onderskep; afsny; teenhou, stuit.
interception, onderskepping; afsnyding; versperring.
intercession, bemiddeling, voorspraak.
intercessor, bemiddelaar, voorspraak.
intercessory, bemiddelend.
interchange, n. (uit)wisseling, ruil(ing).
interchange, v. (uit)wissel, (om)ruil, vervang.
interchangeable, wisselbaar; vervangbaar.
inter-collegiate, interkollegiaal.
intercolonial, interkoloniaal.
intercom, binnetelefoon.
intercommunicate, onderling gemeenskap aanknoop (hê), onderling van gedagte wissel.
intercommunication, onderlinge gedagtewisseling (gemeenskap), interkommunikasie.
intercommunion, onderlinge gemeenskap.
intercommunity, gemeenskaplikheid.
intercourse, gemeenskap, omgang, verkeer.
interdependent, onderling afhanklik.
interdict, n. verbod; skorsing; interdik.
interdict, v. verbied; skors; ontsê.
interdiction, interdiksie, verbod.
interdictory, verbods-...; skorsings-...
interest, n. belang; reg, aanspraak; deel; voordeel, belangstelling; rente; interes; **in your –,** in jou belang; **take an – in,** belang stel in; **at –,** op rente; **simple –,** enkelvoudige rente; **compound –,** samegestelde rente; **rate of –,** rentevoet; leningskoers.
interest, v. interesseer, belang inboesem; belangstelling opwek; – **oneself in,** belang stel in.
interested, belangstellend, geïnteresseer(d); belanghebbend; – **in,** geïnteresseer(d) in; betrokke by.
interesting, belangwekkend, interessant.
interfere, (sig) bemoei (inlaat) met, (sig) meng in; tussenbeide kom.
interference, bemoeiing, inmenging, tussenkoms.
interfering, bemoeisiek.
interfuse, saamsmelt, vermeng.
interim, n. tussentyd; **in the –,** in die tussentyd, intussen.
interim, a. tussentyds, interim-...; – **dividend,** tussentydse, dividend.
interior, a. binne-..., binnelands, inwendig, innerlik.
interior, n. binneste; binneland; interieur.
interjacent, tussenliggende, tussen-...
interject, tussengooi, tussenvoeg; uitroep.
interjection, tussenwerpsel, uitroep, interjeksie.
interjectional, by wyse van tussenwerping; – **sentence,** uitroepsin.
interlace, deurmekaar vleg, aanmekaar strengel; inmekaar gryp.
interlard, deurspek; opstop (met spek).
interleaf, tussenblad.
interleave, deurskiet; –**d copy,** deurskote eksemplaar.
interline, interlinieer, tussen die reëls skryf.
interlinear, interlineêr.
interlock, inmekaar (laat) gryp (sluit).
interlocution, samespraak, gesprek.
interlocutor, gespreksgenoot.
interlope, indring; onderkruip; smokkel.
interloper, indringer; onderkruiper.
interlude, tussenspel; pouse; tussenbedryf.
intermarriage, onderlinge huwelik.
intermarry, onder mekaar trou.
intermeddle, (sig) bemoei, inlaat (met).
intermeddler, bemoeial, bemoeisieke persoon.
intermediary, a. bemiddelend, tussen-...
intermediary, n. tussenpersoon, bemiddelaar.
intermediate, a. tussen-..., tussentyds; intermediêr; – **stage,** tussenstadium; – **boat,** tussenboot.
intermediation, bemiddeling.
interment, begrafnis, teraardebestelling.
intermezzo, intermezzo, tussenspel.
interminable, eindeloos.
intermingle, meng, vermeng.
intermission, onderbreking; tussenpoos, pouse; **without –,** sonder ophou.
intermit, afbreek, ophou, staak.
intermittent, by tussenpose (vlae), afwisselend.
intermix, meng.
intermixture, mengsel; vermenging.

intern, interneer, insper; [see **intern(e)**].
internal, inwendig; innerlik; binne-..., binnelands; intern; – **combustion**, binne-verbranding; – **combustion engine**, binnebrandmasjien.
international, a. internasionaal; – **law**, volkereg.
international, n. die internasionale (arbeidersvereniging); internasionale speler.
internationalize, internasionaliseer.
intern(e), intern; inwonende geneesheer; inwonende mediese student.
internecine, moorddadig mekaar verdelgend.
internuncio, internuntius.
interpellate, interpelleer, opheldering vra.
interpellation, interpellasie.
interpenetrate, (weersyds) deurdring.
interplanetary, interplanetêr.
interplay, wederkerige spel; wisselwerking.
interpolate, inlas, invoeg, interpoleer.
interpolation, invoeging, interpolasie.
interpolator, interpolator.
interpose, tussenskuiwe; tussenbeide kom; ('n woord) tussen voeg; in die rede val.
interposition, inlassing; tussenkoms.
interpret, (ver)tolk, verklaar, uitlê.
interpretable, verklaarbaar.
interpretation, uitleg, verklaring; vertolking.
interpreter, uitlêer, verklaarder; tolk.
interpretress, tolk(in); vertolkster.
interpunction, interpunksie, punktuasie.
interregnum, tussenregering.
interrelation, onderlinge betrekking.
interrogate, ondervra.
interrogation, ondervraging; vraag; mark; **note of –**, vraagteken.
interrogative, a. vra(g)end, ondervra(g)end.
interrogative, n. vra(g)ende voornaamwoord.
interrogatory, a. vra(g)end.
interrogatory, n. ondervraging, verhoor.
interrupt, onderbreek, steur, in die rede val.
interrupter, onderbreker; stroomverbreker.
interruption, onderbreking, stoornis, interrupsie; **without –**, sonder ophou, onafgebroke.
intersect, sny, kruis.
intersection, snypunt, kruispunt; snyding.
intersperse, strooi deurskiet; **–d with**, besaai (deurspek) met.
interspersion, (ver)menging, deurspekking.
interstate, tussen (twee) state.
interstice, tussenruimte, tussenvak; opening.
intertribal, tussen (twee) stamme onderling.
intertwine, deurmekaarvleg, inmekaarstrengel.
interval, tussentyd; pouse, rustyd; tussenruimte; toonafstand (musiek); **at –s**, by tussenpose; **at frequent –s**, telkens.
intervarsity, interuniversiteitswedstryd.
intervene, tussenbeide kom; ingryp; tussen kom; plaasgryp, gebeur.
intervening, -venient, tussenkomend.
intervention, tussenkoms.
interview, n. onderhoud, persgesprek; samekoms.
interview, v. 'n onderhoud (persgesprek) hê met.
interviewer, ondervraer, rapporteur.
interweave, deurmekaar vleg, inmekaar weef.
intestacy, testamentloosheid.
intestate, sonder testament, intestaat.
intestinal, derm-..., ingewands-...
intestine, n. derm; **–s**, derms, ingewande.
intestine, a. binne-..., inwendig; binnelands.
intimacy, vertroulikheid, gemeensaamheid, intimiteit; gemeenskap.
intimate, a. vertroulik; innig, diep, nou; intiem;

– **knowledge**, intieme kennis; **be – with**, gemeensame omgang hê met.
intimate, v. te kenne gee, laat verstaan.
intimately, innig; vertroulik; intiem.
intimation, kennis(gewing), wenk.
intimidate, bang maak, skrik aanja, intimideer.
intimidation, skrikaanjaery, intimidasie; bangheid.
intitule, betitel; **–d**, getitel(d).
into, in, tot in, **get – trouble**, in die moeilikheid kom; **come – property**, eiendom erf; **far on – the night**, tot diep in die nag; – **the bargain**, op die koop toe.
intolerable, ondraaglik, onuitstaanbaar.
intolerableness, ondraaglikheid.
intolerance, onverdraagsaamheid.
intolerant, onverdraagsaam.
intonation, stembuiging; klankvoortbrenging; aanhef; intonasie.
intone, intoneer, insit; uitspreek; sing-sing lees.
intoxicant, dronkmakend.
intoxicate, dronk maak, bedwelm.
intoxicated, dronk, beskonke, besope.
intoxication, dronkenskap, bedwelming, roes.
intractable, onhandelbaar, weerspannig.
intramural, binne die mure, binne-...
intransigent, onversoenlik, hard.
intransitive, a. onoorganklik.
intransitive, n. intransitief, onoorganklike werkwoord.
intravenous, binneaars, intraveneus.
intrepid, onverskrokke, onversaag, dapper.
intrepidity, onverskrokkenheid.
intricacy, ingewikkeldheid, verwikkeldheid.
intricate, ingewikkeld, verwikkeld, moeilik.
intrigue, v. konkel, knoei; nuuskierig maak; intrigeer.
intrigue, n. knoeiery, kuipery, intrige; minnary.
intriguer, kuiper, intrigant.
intrinsic, innerlik, werklik, intrinsiek.
introduce, invoer; voorbring, indien; voorstel; – **a bill**, 'n wetsontwerp indien; the word that **–s the sentence**, die woord wat die sin inlei; – a **lady**, 'n dame voorstel (introduseer).
introduction, invoering; inleiding; indiening; voorstelling; introduksie; **letter of –**, introduksie(brief).
introductory, inleidend.
intromission, toelating; invoeging.
intromit, inlaat, toelaat; invoeg.
introspect, jouself waarneem (ondersoek).
introspection, selfwaarneming, selfondersoek, selfbespieëling, introspeksie.
introspective, selfbespieëlend, introspektief.
introvert, v. na binne keer; intrek.
introvert, n. eenselwige.
intrude, opdring; indring, lastig val; ongeleë kom; – **oneself**, jouself indring; – **oneself, (up)on**, jouself opdring aan.
intruder, indringer, ongenooide gas.
intrusion, indringing; opdringing.
intrusive, indringerig; ingedronge.
intuition, intuïsie.
intuitive, intuïtief.
intumesce, (op)swel.
inundate, oorstroom; oorstelp.
inundation, oorstroming; (stort)vloed.
inurbanity, onhoflikheid.
inure, enure, gewend raak (aan), hard (teen).
inurement, enurement, gewenning, (die) harding.
inutility, nutteloosheid.
invade, inval (in); inbreuk maak op.
invalid, a. ongeldig.
invalid, a. siek, swak, invalide.
invalid, n. sieke, swakke, invalide.

invalid, v. siek maak; siek verklaar, met siekteverlof huis toe stuur.
invalidate, ongeldig verklaar; kragteloos maak, ontsenu.
invalidation, vernietiging; ontsenuwing.
invalidity, ongeldigheid; kragteloosheid.
invaluable, onskatbaar.
invariability, onveranderlikheid.
invariable, onveranderlik; konstant (matesis).
invasion, inval, strooptog; skending.
invective, skelwoorde, slegmakery.
inveigh, skel, slegmaak; – **against,** uitvaar teen.
inveigle, verlei, verlok, meesleep.
invent, uitvind; uitdink, bedink, versin.
invention, uitvinding; versinsel.
inventive, vindingryk.
inventor, uitvinder; versinner.
inventory, n. inventaris, lys; boedelbeskrywing.
inventory, v. inventariseer, 'n lys opmaak van.
inveracity, ongeloofwaardigheid.
inverse, a. omgekeer(d); – **ratio,** omgekeerde verhouding.
inverse, n. die omgekeerde.
inversion, omkering, omsetting, inversie.
invert, n. omgekeerde boog; homoseksueel.
invert, v. omdraai, omkeer, op sy kop sit; omsit; **-ed commas,** aanhalingstekens.
invertebrate, a. ongewerwel(d); papbroekerig.
invertebrate, n. ongewerwelde dier; papbroek.
invest, klee; omsingel, vaskeer; (geld) belê; – **in a tie,** 'n das aanskaf.
investigate, ondersoek, navors, uitpluis; – **into,** 'n ondersoek instel na.
investigation, ondersoek, navorsing.
investigator, navorser, speurder.
investiture, bekleding; bevestiging.
investment, (geld)belegging; beleg (van 'n stad); bekleding; kleding.
investor, belêer (belegger).
inveteracy, ingewortelheid; verstoktheid.
inveterate, ingeworteld; verouderd, verstok.
invidious, aanstootlik; onbenydenswaardig.
invidiousness, aanstootlikheid, onbenydenswaardigheid.
invigilate, toesig hou, oppas.
invigilation, toesig, opsig.
invigilator, opsigter, opsiener.
invigorate, versterk; verlewendig, opwek.
invigorating, versterkend; opwekkend.
invincibility, onoorwinlikheid.
invincible, onoorwinlik.
inviolability, onskendbaarheid.
inviolable, onskendbaar.
inviolacy, ongeskondenheid.
inviolate, ongeskonde.
invisibility, onsigbaarheid.
invisible, a. onsigbaar; – **ink,** simpa(te)tiese ink, geheim-ink.
invisible, n. die onsienlike.
invitation, uitnodiging, invitasie.
invite, v. (uit)nooi, vra; versoek; (aan)lok, uitlok; – **trouble,** moeilikheid soek.
invite, n. uitnodiging.
inviting, aanloklik.
invocation, aanroeping, gebed.
invoice, n. faktuur.
invoice, v. faktureer, op die faktuur sit.
invoke, aanroep; inroep; oproep; beroep op; afsmeek.
involuntarily, onwillekeurig, vansluif.
involuntary, onwillekeurig; onvrywillig.
involute, ingewikkeld; inmekaar gedraai; spiraalvormig.
involution, inwikkeling; ingewikkeldheid; magsverheffing (matesis).

involve, indraai; opkrul; betrek in, verwikkel in; meebring, tot gevolg hê.
involved, ingewikkeld; betrokke in.
invulnerable, onkwesbaar.
inward, a. inwendig, binne- . . . . ; innerlik, geestelik; na binne, binnewaarts.
inwardly, inwendig; innerlik; by (in) sigself.
inwardness, innerlike; innerheid.
inwards, n. ingewande, binnegoed.
inwards, adv. na binne, binnewaarts.
inweave, invleg, deurweef.
inwrought, ingewerk, ingeweef, deurvleg.
inyala, injala.
iodine, jodium, jood.
iodoform, jodoform.
ion, ioon.
Ionia, Ionies; Ioniër.
Ionic, Ionies.
ionize, ioniseer.
ionium, ionium.
ionosphere, ionosfeer.
iota, jota.
I.O.U., skuldbewys.
ipecacuanha, ipekakuana, braakwortel.
Iran, Iran.
Iranian, Iraans; Iraniër.
irascibility, sleggehumeurdheid, driftigheid.
irascible, sleggehumeurd, driftig, opvlieënd.
irate, kwaad, woedend.
ire, woede, toorn.
Ireland, Ierland.
iridescence, kleurespel; kleurwisseling.
iridescent, reënboogkleurig; wisselkleurig.
iridium, iridium.
iris, swaardlelie; iris.
Irish, Iers.
Irishman, Ier.
irk, vermoei, verveel, vererg.
irksome, vermoeiend, vervelend, ergerlik.
iron, n. yster; brandyster; strykyster; **the –s,** die boeie; **cast –,** gegote yster; **wrought –,** smee(d)yster; **a man of –,** 'n man van yster en staal; **strike while the – is hot,** die yster smee solank as dit warm is; **have too many –s in the fire,** te veel hooi op jou vurk hê; – **curtain,** ystergordyn.
iron, v. stryk; ('n perd) beslaan; met yster bedek; boei.
iron, a. yster- . . . . van yster; – **age,** eeu van yster; – **bar,** ysterroede, stuk yster.
iron-bound, met yster beslaan; rotsagtig; streng.
ironclad, a. gepantser(d).
ironclad, n. pantserskip.
iron-foundry, ystersmeltery, ystergietery.
iron-grey, ysterkleur.
ironic(al), ironies, spottend.
ironing-board, strykplank; stryktafel.
ironmonger, ysterhandelaar.
ironmongery, ysterhandel.
iron-ore, ystererts.
iron-stone, ysterklip.
ironwood, ysterhout.
ironwork, ystergoed; **–s,** ystergietery.
irony, ironie.
irradiate, uitstraal; (be)straal; (laat) straal.
irradiation, (uit)straling; bestraling; stralekrans.
irrational, onredelik; redeloos; irrasioneel; onmeetbaar (in matesis).
irrationality, onredelikheid; redeloosheid.
irreclaimable, onverbeterlik; onontginbaar.
irrecognisable, onherkenbaar.
irreconcilable, onversoenlik; onverenigbaar.
irrecoverable, reddeloos verlore; onherstelbaar; oninbaar.
irrecusable, onontwykbaar, onafwysbaar.

irredeemable, reddeloos (verlore); onverbeterlik; onherstelbaar; onaflosbaar; onafkoopbaar.
irredentism, irredentisme.
irreducible, onverminderbaar, laagste; onverkleinbaar (in matesis); onherleibaar; – **minimum**, absolute minimum.
irrefragable, onweerlegbaar, onwraakbaar.
irrefrangible, onskendbaar; onbuigbaar.
irrefutable, onweerlegbaar, onomstootlik.
irregular, a. onreëlmatig; ongereeld; ongelyk; wanordelik.
irregular, n. ongereelde; –s, ongereelde troepe.
irregularity, onreëlmatigheid; ongereeldheid; ongelykheid.
irrelevancy, ontoepaslikheid, onsaaklikheid.
irrelevant, nie toepaslik nie, nie ter sake nie, onsaaklik.
irreligion, ongodsdienstigheid; godsdiensloosheid.
irreligious, ongodsdienstig; godsdiensloos.
irremediable, onherstelbaar, ongeneeslik, onverbeterbaar.
irremissible, onvergeeflik; bindend.
irremovable, onverwyderbaar, onverplaasbaar.
irreparable, onherstelbaar.
irreplaceable, onvervangbaar, onherstelbaar.
irrepressible, onbedwingbaar.
irreproachable, onberispelik.
irresistibility, onweerstaanbaarheid.
irresistible, onweerstaanbaar; verleidelik.
irresistibly, op onweerstaanbare manier.
irresolute, besluiteloos.
irresolution, besluiteloosheid.
irresolvable, onoplosbaar.
irrespective: – **of**, afgesien van; – **of persons**, sonder aansien des persoons.
irresponsibility, onverantwoordelikheid.
irresponsible, onverantwoordelik.
irresponsive, ontoeskietlik, nie tegemoetkomend.
irretrievability, onherroeplikheid.
irretrievable, onherstelbaar; onherroeplik.
irreverence, oneerbiedigheid.
irreverent, irreverential, oneerbiedig.
irreversible, onveranderlik; onomkeerbaar.
irrevocable, onherroeplik.
irrigable, besproeibaar, irrigeerbaar.
irrigate, besproei, natlei, irrigeer.
irrigation, besproeiing, watervoorsiening; irrigasie.
irrigator, sproeier, irrigator.
irritability, prikkelbaarheid.
irritable, prikkelbaar, liggeraak, knorrig.
irritant, prikkelend, irriterend.
irritate, prikkel, vererg, ontstem, irriteer.
irritation, prikkeling; geprikkeldheid, ergernis, ontstemming, irritasie.
irruption, inval, inbraak, oorval.
is, sien **be**.
Isiah, Jesaja.
ischias, heupjig, iskias.
isinglass, vislym.
Islam(it)ic, Islams.
Islamite, Islamiet.
island, eiland.

islander, eilandbewoner.
isle, eiland.
islet, eilandjie.
isobar, isobaar.
isobaric, isobarometries.
isochromatic, isochromaties, gelykkleurig.
isochronous, isochronies, van gelyke duur.
isogonic, isogonies, gelykhoekig.
isolate, afsonder, afskei; isoleer.
isolation, afsondering, afskeiding; isolasie.
isolationist, isolasionis.
isolation ward, afsonderingsaal.
isolator, isolator, nie-geleider.
isometric, isometries.
isosceles, gelykbenig.
isotherm, isoterm.
isotope, isotoop.
Israelite, Israeliet.
Israelitish, Israelities.
issue, v. uit-, voortkom, **o**nt-, voortspruit, ontstaan; uitvaardig; uitgee; versprei; – **forth**, out, te voorskyn kom; – **from**, voortspruit uit; – **in**, uitloop op.
issue, n. uitvloeisel; uitgang; uitweg; nakomelingskap, kroos; uitslag, gevolg; uitkoms; (geskil)punt, strydvraag; uitgawe; uitreiking; without **male** –, sonder manlike nakomelinge; **it appears in the** –, die uitkoms toon aan; **point at** –, geskilpunt; **be at** –, dit oneens wees; **join** – **with**, die stryd aanbind met.
isthmus, landengte; ismus.
it, dit; hy; who is –?, wie is dit?; – **rains**, dit reent; go –, laat nael; steek los; **lord** – **over him**, baasspeel oor hom; **give** – **to him**, dons hom op.
Italian, Italiaan, Italianer; Italiaans.
italic, a. kursief, skuins.
italic, n. skuins letter; –**s**, kursiefdruk; **in** –**s**, kursief.
italicize, kursiveer.
Italy, Italië.
itch, n. (ge)jeuk; uitslag; sug, hunkering; **feel an** – **for**, jeuk om te.
itch, v. jeuk; his fingers – to, sy vingers jeuk om.
itchy, jeukerig.
item, n. nummer (op 'n program); pos (op 'n rekening); artikel (op 'n lys), besonderheid.
item, adv. eweneens, insgelyks.
iterate, herhaal.
iteration, herhaling.
iterative, herhalend, herhalings- . . .
itinera(n)cy, rondgang.
itinerant, rondreisend, rondtrekkend.
itinerary, n. reisplan; reisverhaal; reisgids.
itinerary, a. reis- . . . , rondreisend.
itinerate, rondtrek, rondreis.
its, sy, van hom, daarvan.
itself, self, homself; **in** –, op sigself.
ivory, n. ivoor, olifantstand; **black** –, ebbehout slawe; **ivories**, dobbelstene; biljartballe.
ivory, a. ivoor- . . . , olifantstand- . . .
ivory-black, ivoorswart.
ivy, klimop.
ixia, waardlelie, k(a)lossie, ixia.

jab, v. steek, stoot, sny.
jab, n. steek, hou.
jabber, v. babbel, ratel, snater, kekkel.
jabber, n. gebabbel, gesnater, gekekkel.
jabot, plooisel, strook, jabot.
jacaranda, jakaranda.
jacinth, hiasint.
Jack, Jan; **cheap –**, lappiesmous; **before you could say – Robinson**, so gou as blits, in 'n kits; **– of all trades**, iemand wat van alle markte tuis is, hansie-my-kneg; **every man –**, elke lewendige siel; iedere Piet, Paul en Klaas; **j– in the box**, kaartmannetjie; **j– pudding**, hanswors; **– Tar**, pikbroek; **j– o'lantern**, dwaallig.
jack, n. boer (kaartspel); vleisspit; domkrag; wen, windas; (hout)bok; (laarse)kneg.
jack, n. geus (vlag).
jack, v. opdomkrag; **– up**, tou opgooi; optrek.
jackal, jakkals; aanvoorder, handlanger.
jackanapes, aap; apekop; uilskuiken.
jackass, eselhings; domoor, uilskuiken.
jack-boots, kamaste.
jackdaw, kerkkraai.
jacket, baadjie; jekker; omslag; skil; vel; **dust his –**, sy baadjie vir hom uitstof, hom vel.
jack-knife, groot knipmes, herneutermes.
jack-plane, voorskaaf, grofskaaf.
jack-staff, vlagstok.
jack-towel, rolhanddoek.
Jacobean, Jakobeaans.
Jacobin, Jakobyn, Dominikaner.
jacobin, kappertjie(duif).
Jacobite, Jakobiet.
Jacob's-ladder, Jakobsleer.
Jacob's staff, pelgrimstaf; graadboog.
jaconet, jakonet.
jade, n. ou knol; vroumens, wyf, slet.
jade, n. niersteen, nefriet; liggroen.
jade, v. afjakker, uitput, flou ry.
jag, n. punt.
jag, v. skeur, kerf, inkeep, tand.
jagged, ru, skerp, ongelyk; vol skare.
jaguar, jaguar, (Suid-Amerikaanse) luiperd.
jail, sien gaol, n. tronk, gevangenis.
jail (gaol), v. in die tronk sit.
jail-bird (gaol-bird), tronkboef.
jailer (gaoler), tronkbewaarder, sipier.
jail-fever (gaol-fever), hospitaaltifus.
jalap, jalap.
jalopy, rammelkas.
jalousie, sonblinding.
jam, n. (fyn)konfyt.
jam, v. vasdruk, vasknyp; haak; volprop.
jam, n. gedrang, opstopping; geprop.
jamb, sykosyn, deurstyl.
jamboree, fees; kamp, laer, saamtrek.
jangle, v. rammel; krys; twis.
jangle, n. gerammel, lawaai; gekrys; twis.
janitor, deurwagter, portier.
janizary, **janissary**, janitsaar.
January, Januarie.
Jap, Japannees, Japanner.
Japan, Japan.
japan, n. lak.
japan, v. verlak; japanneer.
Japanese, a. Japannees, Japans.
Japanese, n. Japannees, Japanner; Japannees, Japans.
japanner, verlakker.
jape, v. 'n grap maak, gekskeer.
jape, n. grap.
Japhetic, Jafeties.
japonica, japonika; Japanse kweperboom.
jar, n. gekras, wanklank; skok; twis.
jar, v. knars, kras; twis; skok; **– upon the ear**, kras in die ore; **– upon the nerves**, dit op die senuwees laat kry; **– with**, vloek met; indruis teen.
jar, n. fles, kruik, pot.
jargon, jargon, brabbeltaal.
jarrah, (d)jarra, Australiese mahonie.
jarvey, huurkoetsier.
jasmin(e), **jessamin(e)**, jasmyn.
jasper, jaspis.
jaundice, n. geelsug.
jaundiced, afgunstig; verdraai.
jaunt, v. 'n uitstappie maak; op die swier gaan.
jaunt, n. uitstappie, plesierritjie; **on the –**, op die kuier; op die swier.
jaunty, lugtig, swierig.
Javanese, Javaan; Javaans.
javelin, werpspies.
jaw, n. kaak, kakebeen; bek; gepraat; **hold your –**, hou jou mond (bek).
jaw, v. babbel, klets, seur.
jaw-bone, kakebeen.
jaw-breaker, tongknoper.
jay, spotvoël, gaai, kletskous.
jay-walker, straatgans.
jazz, n., v., jazz, **– band**, jazz-orkes, lawaaibenning.
jealous, jaloers, naywerig, afgunstig; jaloers op; **– of his honour**, gesteld op sy eer.
jealousy, jaloesie, jaloersheid, afguns, naywer, nyd; gesteldheid, besorgdheid.
jeans, kuitbroek.
jeep, utiliteitswa.
jeer, v. spot, skimp (op), hoon.
jeer, n. spot, skimp, hoon.
Jehovah, Jehova.
jejune, skraal, dun; maer; droog.
jelly, (s(j)elei), jellie, drilsel; gelatienpoeding.
jelly-fish, seekwal; see-netel.
jeminas, rekkerskoene.
jemmy, breekyster; (gaar) skaapkop.
jennet, genet, Spaanse perdjie.
jenny, stoomkraan; spinmasjien; eselmerrie.
jenny-wren, winterkoninkie.
jeopardize, in gevaar stel, op die spel sit.
jeopardy, gevaar.
jerboa, springhaas.
jeremiad, jeremiade, klaaglied.
Jericho, Jericho; **go to –**, loop na die maan.
jerk, n. ruk; **by –s**, met rukke en plukke.
jerk, v. ruk, pluk; smyt, stamp, stoot.
jerk, v. droog; **–ed beef**, biltong.
jerkily, rukkerig, met rukke en plukke.
jerkin, (leer)baadjie.
jerky, rukkerig, stamperig, hortend.
jerry-builder, knutselbouer.
jersey, jersie, trui.
jessamine (jasmine), jasmyn.
jest, n. grap, gekheid, skerts, korswel; **in –**, vir die grap, uit korswel.
jest, v. skerts, korswel, gekheid maak; **–ing aside**, in erns; alle grappies op 'n stokkie; **no –ing matter**, niks om oor te lag nie.
jester, grapmaker.
jestingly, uit die grap, uit korswel, skertsend.
Jesuit, Jesuïet; **–'s bark**, kinabas.
Jesuitic(al), Jesuïties.
jet, got.
jet, n. straal; bek, tuit, kraan, spuit; **– aircraft**, straalvliegtuig; **– fighter**, straalvegter; **– propulsion**, straalaandrywing.
jet-propelled, straalaangedrewe.
jetsam, wrakgoed, seedrif, opdrifsel.
jettison, oorboord gooi.
jetty, hawehoof, pier, kaai.
Jew, n. Jood; **–'s harp**, trompie.

jew, v. fop, kul, verneuk.
jewel, n. juweel, kleinood, edelsteen; skat.
jewel, v. versier, opsier, met juwele behang.
jeweller, juwelier.
jewel(le)ry, juwele; juweliersware.
Jewess, Jodin.
Jewish, Joods.
Jewry, Jodedom; Jodebuurt.
jib, n. kluiwer; **the cut of his** –, sy tronie.
jib, vassteek, steeks word; omdraai; – **at**, bedank vir; skop teen.
jib-boom, kluifhout, kluiwerboom.
jiff(y), kits; **in a** –, in 'n kits.
jig, n. horrelpyp; horrelpypdeuntjie.
jig, v. horrelpyp dans; op en af wip; sif.
jigger, n. katrol; biljartbok; sifter.
jigsaw, figuursaag.
jigsaw-puzzle, legkaart.
jilt, n. flirt.
jilt, v. afsê, laat loop, fop.
jingle, n. geklingel, gerinkel; klinkklank.
jingle, v. klingel, rinkel; rymel.
jingo, jingo; **by** –, so by my kool.
jingoism, jingoïsme.
jingoistic, jingoïsties.
jinks: **high** –, reusepret, dolplesier.
jinricksha(w), riksja.
jinx, vloek, onheilbringer; towenaar.
jitter: **have the** –, die ritteltit kry; senuweeagtig wees.
j(i)u-jitsu, joejitsoe.
jive, n. wilde dans; v. wild dans.
job, n. (stuk) werk, karweitjie; baantjie; knoeiery; **bad** –, verspilde arbeid; **good** –, 'n goeie ding, 'n geluk; **make the best of a bad** –, jou daarna skik.
job, v. los werkies doen; uithuur, verhuur; agentswerk doen; knoeisake verrig.
job, v. steek, prik; in die bek ruk.
job, n. steek; ruk.
jobation, uitbrander, preek, vermaning.
jobber, karweiwerker; (rytuig)verhuurder; makelaar; konkelaar, knoeier.
jobbery, konkelwerk; knutselwerk.
job-lot, rommelspul.
job-work, stukwerk.
jockey, n. jokkie, reisiesjaer.
jockey, v. uitoorlê, fop.
jocose, grapperig.
jocoseness, **jocosity**, grapperigheid.
jocular, grapp(er)ig, skertsend.
jocularity, grapp(er)igheid, snaaksheid.
jocund, lustig, opgewek; aangenaam.
jocundity, vrolikheid, lustigheid.
jog, v. stamp, ruk; stoot, aanstoot; (geheue) opfris; – **along**, **on**, aansukkel.
jog, n. stamp, stoot, skud; sukkeldraffie.
joggle, v. waggel, strompel, sjok.
joggle, n. keep, inkerwing, las.
joggle, v. inkeep, inkerf.
jogtrot, sukkeldraf.
johnny, kêrel, vent; snuiter; fat.
join, v. (ver)bind, vasmaak, saamvoeg, vasknoop; aansluit (by), **toetree** (tot); (sig) verenig met; paar aan, gepaard gaan met; aangrens; – **hands**, die hande saamvou; mekaar die hand gee; saamwerk, gemene saak maak; – **battle**, slaags raak; – **the ranks**, aansluit; – **the Church**, lidmaat word van die Kerk; in die kerklike bediening gaan; **the Vaal –s the Orange River**, Vaalrivier val in Grootrivier; – **in a drink**, iets saamdrink; – **in a song**, saamsing; – **in a race**, deelneem aan 'n wedstryd; – **in the conversation**, deelneem aan die gesprek; – **up**, aansluit; – **with**, jou aansluit by; saammaak.

join, n. voeg, lasplek; verbindings(punt).
joiner, skrynwerker.
joinery, skrynwerk.
joint, n. voeg, las(plek); lit, gewrig; skarnier; verbinding; karmenaadjie; **out of** –, uit lit.
joint, a. gesame(nt)lik, gemeenskaplik, mede- ...; **on** – **account**, vir gesamentlike rekening; – – **owner**, mede-eienaar; – **stock**, es*tate*, gemeenskaplike kapitaal, boedel; – **stock company**, aandelemaatskappy; – **action**, gesamentlike optrede.
joint, v. las, voeg; deel, stukkend sny.
jointed, geleed, met litte.
jointer, voeër; voegskaaf; voegtroffel.
jointly, gesame(nt)lik, gemeenskaplik.
jointure, weduweegeld, -goed, -skat.
joist, n. dwarsbalk.
joist, v. van dwarsbalke voorsien.
joke, n. grap, gekheid; **it was no** –, dit was geen grap nie; **play a practical** – **on**, 'n poets bak; **as a** –, **for a** –, **in** –, uit of vir die grap.
joke, v. 'n grap (grappe, grappies) maak, gekskeer, korswel, speel; **joking apart**, sonder om te speel, in erns.
joker, grappemaker; vent, asjas; (swart) Piet boer (in kaartspel).
jokingly, vir die grap, skertsend, uit korswel.
jollification, pret, vreugde.
jollify, vrolik maak; lekker maak; feesvier.
jollity, joligheid, pret, feestelikheid.
jolly, jolig, vrolik, plesierig; lekker, aangeklam; – **fool**, mooi gek; **he will be** – **savage**, hy sal lekker kwaad wees; **you will** – **well have to**, jy sal tog maar mooi moet.
jollyboat, jol.
jolt, stamp, skok.
jolty, stamperig.
jonquil, sonkieltjie, narsing.
Jordan, Jordaan.
jorum, kom; pons, drank.
joss, josie.
josser, snuiter, asjas, uilskuiken.
joss-house, josietempel.
joss-stick, (Chinese) wierookstokkie.
jostle, v. stamp, druk, dring, stoei.
jostle, n. gedrang, gestoei, geworstel.
jot, n. jota; **not a** –, geen stukkie, geen jota.
jot, v. skryf; – **down**, opteken.
journal, joernaal, dagboek; (dag)blad, tydskrif.
journalese, joernalistejargon, koeranttaal.
journalism, joernalistiek, koerantskrywery.
journalist, joernalis, koerantskrywer.
journalistic, joernalisties, koerant- ...
journey, n. reis, tog; **a day's** –, 'n dagreis.
journey, v. reis, trek, 'n reis (tog) maak.
journeyman, vakman; huurling.
journey-work, dagwerk, loonwerk.
joust, n. toernooi, steekspel.
joust, v. deelneem aan 'n steekspel.
Jove, Jupiter; **by** –!, allemastig, mapstieks!
jovial, joviaal, lustig, gul.
joviality, jovialiteit, vrolikheid; gulheid.
jowl, kaak; wang; kop; krop; keelvel; **cheek by** –, sy aan sy; kop in een mus.
joy, n. vreugde, blydskap, genoeë; **I give you** –, ek wens jou geluk!; **it gives me** –, dit verheug my.
joy, v. juig, (sig) verheug; verbly.
joy-bells, vreugdeklokke.
joyful, bly, vreugdevol, vrolik.
joyfulness, blydskap, vrolikheid.
joyless, vreugdeloos.
joyous, bly, vrolik, vreugdevol; verblydend.
joy-ride, plesiertog(gie), steeltoggie.
joy-rider, plesierryer.

joy-stick, stuurstok.
jubilant, juigend, jubelend, triomfant.
jubilate, juig, jubel.
jubilation, gejuig, jubeling.
jubilee, jubeljaar; jubileum.
Judah, Juda, Judas.
Judaic, Joods.
Judaism, Judaïsme; Jodedom.
judge, n. regter; skeidsregter, beoordelaar.
judge, v. regspreek, uitspraak doen, oordeel; beoordeel; skat; – by, oordeel volgens.
judg(e)ment, oordeel; vonnis; mening; **the last** –, die laaste oordeel; **give** –, uitspraak doen, vonnis uitspreek; **in my** –, volgens my mening.
judgment-day, oordeelsdag.
judgment-seat, regterstoel, vierskaar.
judicature, regspleging, regspraak; regterlike mag.
judicial, regterlik; oordeelkundig; – **murder,** geregtelike moord; – **body,** regterlike liggaam.
judiciary, regs- . . ., regtelik.
judicious, oordeelkundig, verstandig.
judiciousness, verstandigheid, wysheid.
judo, see **ju-jitsu.**
jug, n. beker, kruik; tronk, tjoekie.
jug, v. stowe; in die tjoekie sit.
Juggernaut, Jaggernaut.
juggins, uilskuiken, stommerik.
juggle, v. goël, toor, knoei, verdraai; – **with figures,** goël met syfers.
juggle, n. goëlery, foppery.
juggler, goëlaar; bedrieër.
jugglery, goëlery, toordery; bedrieëry.
jugular, a. hals- . . .
jugular, n. halsaar, slagaar.
juice, sap (sop); **gastric** –, maagsap.
juiceless, saploos, droog.
juicy, sappig; smaaklik, gekrui(d).
jujube, bessie; taailekker, joepjoep.
juke-box, blêrkas.
julep, julep.
July, Julie; – **handicap,** Julie-perderenne.
jumble, v. deurmekaarhaspel, omwoel.
jumble, n. warboel, rommel; gehobbel.
jumble-sale, rommelverkoping.
jump, v. spring, opspring; oorspring; laat spring, voorspring; afhandig maak; – **a line,** 'n reël oorspring; – **the rails,** ontspoor; – **at,** hap na, gretig aanneem; – **down one's throat,** uitvaar teen iemand; – **for joy,** opspring van blydskap; – **(up)on an opponent,** 'n teenstander te lyf gaan; – **to a conclusion,** 'n oorylde gevolgtrekking maak; – **with,** ooreenstem met.
jump, n. sprong, spring; **high** –, hoogspring; **long** –, vérspring; **the** –**s,** bewerasie.
jumper, springer; springboor.
jumper, kiel, jakkie, jumper.
jumping-hare, springhaas.
jumpy, senuweeagtig, skrikkerig.
junction, vereniging, verbinding; bindplek, las; saamloop; knoop(punt) (van spoorlyne).
juncture, vereniging; voeg, naat, las; sameloop (van omstandighede), tydstip.
June, Junie.

jungle, boswêreld, wildernis; warboel.
junior, a. junior, jonger, jongste; – **partner,** juniorvennoot, jongste vennoot; – **clerk,** assistent, onderklerk.
junior, n. junior, jongere; **the** –**s,** die jongeres, die juniors.
juniper, jenewerbessie.
junk, n. touwerk; brok; afval; soutvleis.
junk, v. opkap, in stukke kap.
junk, n. jonk (Chinese skip).
junker, jonker.
junket, stremmelk; fuif, smulparty.
junta, junta.
junto, kliek, faksie.
judicial, geregtelik, wets- . . .
jurisconsult, juris, regsgeleerde.
jurisdiction, regsgebied; regspraak; regsbevoegdheid; jurisdiksie.
jurisprudence, regsgeleerdheid.
jurist, regsgeleerde, juris.
juror, jurielid, geswerone.
jury, jurie, geswerones.
jury-box, juriebank.
jury-man, jurielid.
jury-mast, noodmas, hulpmas.
just, a. regverdig; billik, gegrond; geregtig; verdiend; juis, presies; – **distribution,** regverdige verdeling; – **resentment,** billike verontwaardiging; – **fear,** gegronde vrees.
just, adv. net, presies, juistement; eenvoudig; – **now,** nou net; netnou; – **there,** net daar; – – **three o'clock,** presies drie-uur; – **so!,** presies, juistement!; – **splendid,** eenvoudig skitterend!
justice, geregtigheid, regverdigheid; reg; billikheid; justisie; regter; – **of the peace,** vrederegter; **administer** –, regspreek, die wet toepas; **court of** –, geregshof; **do** – **to,** reg laat wedervaar; **do oneself** –, sy beste gee; **in** – **to,** in billikheid teenoor.
justiceship, regterskap.
justiciary, a. regs- . . .
justiciary, n. regter, regspreker.
justifiable, verdedigbaar, te regverdig.
justification, regverdiging; wettiging.
justificatory, regverdigend, verskonend.
justifier, verdediger; vryspreker.
justify, regverdig, wettig; verdedig; verantwoord, verskoon, goedpraat; **the end justifies the means,** die doel heilig die middele.
justly, regverdig(lik), billik(erwyse) noukeurig(lik); met reg, tereg.
justness, regverdigheid, billikheid; gegrondheid; noukeurigheid.
jut, v. vooruitsteek, uitspring, oorhang.
jut, n. uitsteeksel, oorhangende gedeelte.
jute, goiing, jute.
juvenescent, jeugdig.
juvenile, a. jeugdig, jeug- . . . , vir die jeug; **J-Affairs Board,** Jeugraad.
juvenile, n. jeugdige persoon.
juvenility, jeugdigheid.
juxtapose, naasmekaarstel.
juxtaposition, naasmekaarstelling; nabyheid.

K

kaiser, keiser.
kale, kail, boerkool; koolsop.
kaleidoscope, kaleidoskoop.
kaleidoscopic(ally), kaleidoskopies.
kalong, kalong, vlieënde hond.
kangaroo, kangaroe.
kaolin, kaolien, porseleinaarde.
kapok, kapok(wol).
kaput, kapot, gedaan.
Karakul, Karakoel(skaap).
Karoo, Karoo.
kaross, karos.
katabolism, katabolisme.
kayak, kajak.
keck, kokhals, wurg in die keel.
kedge, werpanker.
kedgeree, kitsery.
keel, n. kiel; skip, vaartuig.
keel, v. kiel, kantel; – **over**, omkantel.
keel, n. koleskuit.
keelblock, kielblok.
keelhaul, kielhaal.
keen, n. (Ierse) lyksang.
keen, v. weeklaag.
keen, a. skerp; bytend; vurig; heftig; ywerig; belangstellend; begerig, happig, tuk; – **desire**, brandende verlange; – **interest**, lewendige belangstelling; – **sight**, skerp gesig; – **smell**, fyn reuk (ruik); – **supporter**, vurige ondersteuner; – **on**, versot op, gek na, happig op, tuk op, **I am not very** –, ek is nie baie happig nie, dit kan my nie soveel skeel nie, ek stel daar nie soveel belang in nie.
keenly, skerp; vurig; ywerig; besonder.
keenness, skerpte; vurigheid; belangstelling; gretigheid, happigheid.
keep, v. hou; behou; bewaar; oppas, beskerm; gehoorsaam, nakom, gestand doen, vervul, in ag neem; onderhou; in voorraad hou; goed bly; woon; **you** – **it**, hou jy dit; **God** – **you**, mag God jou behoed; – **the law**, die wet nakom; – **faith**, woord hou, trou bly; – **a promise**, 'n belofte hou (nakom); – **peace**, die vrede bewaar; – **an appointment**, (aan) 'n afspraak hou; – **goal**, doelwagter wees; – **house**, huishou; – **accounts**, boekhou; – **a family**, 'n familie onderhou; – **company**, geselskap hou; – **pace**, byhou, bybly, tred hou (met) – **step**, in die pas bly; – **time**, maat hou; – **watch, a look-out**, wag hou, op die wag staan, uitkyk, dophou; – **wicket**, paaltjiewagter wees; – **a secret**, 'n geheim bewaar; – **one's course**, jou koers hou, jou gang gaan; – **one's room**, in jou kamer (bed) bly; – **the saddle**, in die saal bly; – **the field**, die veld behou; – **one's seat**, bly sit; – **cool**, kalm bly; – **friends**, vriende bly; – **in good health**, gesond bly; **the meat won't** –, die vlees sal nie goed bly nie; – **late hours**, laat opbly; – **waiting**, laat wag; – **in mind**, onthou, daaraan dink; – **a shop**, 'n winkel hê; – **in clothes**, van klere voorsien; – **count, tel**; – **one's countenance**, 'n ernstige gesig bewaar; – **dark**, geheim hou; – **one's feet**, staande bly, op die bene bly; – **at**, aanhou met, deurgaan met; – **away**, weghou; wegbly; – **back**, terughou; agterbly; – **down**, onderhou; onderdruk, bedwing; – **expenses down**, uitgawes beperk, besuinig; – **from**, weghou van, afhou; (sig) onthou van; verswyg vir; – **in**, inhou; bedwing, in toom hou; op skool hou; binnebly; – **in with**, op goeie voet bly met; – **off**, afweer, op 'n afstand hou, van die lyf hou; – **on**, aanhou; vashou; – **out**, uithou; buite bly, buite hou, uitsluit; – **out of the way**, uit die weg hou (bly); – **to**, hou aan, bly by; – **together**, bymekaar hou (bly); – **under**, bedwing, onderdruk, in bedwang hou; – **up**, ophou; aanhou; onderhou; handhaaf, hooghou; volhou; – **up one's spirits**, opgeruimd bly, moed hou; – **up appearances**, die fatsoen (skyn) bewaar; – **up your Greek**, jou Grieks byhou; – **one's end up**, jou man staan; – **up with**, byhou, bybly; tred hou met.
keep, n. onderhou(d); bewaring; brug, kasteel; **(for)** –**s**, om te hou.
keeper, bewaarder, opsiener, oppasser, hoeder; – **of the archives**, argivaris; – **of the great seal**, rykseëlbewaarder.
keeping, bewaring; ooreenstemming; **in** – **with**, passend by, in ooreenstemming met; **in safe** –, in versekerde bewaring; **in his** –, in sy hoede, onder sy sorg.
keeping-room, sitkamer, voorkamer.
keepsake, aandenking, soewenier (souvenir).
keeshond, keeshond.
keg, vaatjie.
kelp, loogkruid; loogas.
kelpie, kelpy, watergees.
kelson, keelson, kolsem.
Kelt, sien Celt.
ken, n. gesig(skring), begrip, verstand; **in** –, in sig, sigbaar; **out of** –, onsigbaar; **beyond his** –, bo sy begrip.
ken, v. weet, verstaan.
kennel, n. hondehok; hok, pondok.
kennel, v. in 'n hok sit; in 'n hok woon.
kennel, n. geut, voor.
Kentish, Kenties.
kerb, rand van sypaadjie, trottoirband; sypaadjie.
kerbstone, randsteen, trottoirsteen.
kerchief, kopdoek, doek, sakdoek.
kerf, keep, kerf; kap-ent, saag-ent.
kermes, skildluis; karmosynbos.
kernel, pit; kern.
kerosene, paraffien, petroleum.
kerrie, kierie.
kersey, karsaai.
ketch, kaag.
ketchup, sampioensous, tamatiesous.
kettle, ketel; **pretty** – **of fish**, 'n mooi spul.
kettledrum, (ketel)tamboer, pouk.
kettledrummer, tamboer(slaner).
key, sleutel; verklaring, vertaling, antwoordboek; toonaard; trant; klawer, toets, noot; wig, pen.
key, v. vaswig; stem, aandraai; – **up**, opbeur; opskroef, opdryf.
key-board, toetsbord, klawerbord, klavier.
key-hole, sleutelgat.
key-note, grondtoon.
key-stone, sluitsteen.
khaki, kakie.
khedive, khedive, onderkoning.
kibe, wintervoet.
kibosch, onsin; **put the** – **on**, van kant maak.
kick, n. skop; skopper; krag, pit; **drop** –, skepskop; **penalty**, –, strafskop; **place** –, stelskop; **more** –**s than half-pence**, meer loesing as loon; **get the** –, uitgeskop word.
kick, v. skop; (sig) verset, (sig) teësit, ontevredenheid betuig; **(alive and)** –**ing**, springlewendig; – **the bucket**, bokveld toe gaan; – **one's heels**, staan en wag; – **up his heels**, agteropskop; – **downstairs**, die trap afsmyt; – **up a noise**, row, **shindy**, lawaai maak; – **over the traces**, uit die band spring, oor die tou trap.

kick, n. holte, siel (van 'n bottel).
kick-off, inskop, afskop.
kickshaw, kleinigheid; lekkernytjie.
kid, n. bokkie, boklammetjie; kidleer; (bog)-kind, snuiter; a mere -, 'n bogkind.
kid, v. lam; fop, flous, kul.
kid, n. bak, eetbak.
kidding, gekskeerdery, tergery.
kiddy, seuntjie (dogtertjie), snuiter.
kid-glove, kidleerhandskoen.
kidnap, skaak, ontvoer, pres.
kidnapper, skaker, ontvoerder; sielverkoper.
kidney, nier; slag, soort; a man of that -, 'n man van daardie slag.
kidney-bean, snyboontjie.
kill, v. doodmaak, vermoor; te niet maak, onderdruk, uit die weg ruim; be -ed, doodgemaak word; sneuwel; - off, uitroei, afmaak; - time, tyd doodslaan (omkry); - two birds with one stone, twee vlieë in een klap slaan; - time, tyd omkry.
kill, n. doodmaak, slagting; wildbraad.
killing, moordend, dodelik; hartverowerend, onweerstaanbaar; onbeskryflik.
killingly, hartverowerend; - funny, om jou dood oor te lag.
kill-joy, suurpruim, spelbederwer.
kiln, oond.
kilo-, kilo.
kilogram(me), kilogram.
kilometer, kilometre, kilometer.
kilowatt, kilowatt.
kilt, v. optel, opgord; plooi.
kilt, n. kilt, Skotse rokkie.
kimono, kimono.
kin, geslag, afkoms; next of -, nabestaande(s), bloedverwant(e).
kind, n. soort, klas, ras, slag; aard, natuur, aanleg; natura; what - of, watter soort; the human -, die menslike ras; something of the -, iets van die aard; men of that -, daardie slag van mense; a - of stockbroker, so iets as 'n makelaar; a - of millionaire, 'n bastermiljoenêr; I - of expected it, ek het dit so half verwag; after its -, in sy soort; volgens sy geaardheid; every - of, allerhande soort; pay in -, in natura betaal, ruil; repay in -, terugbetaal, in gelyke munt betaal.
kind, a. vriendelik, goedhartig, lief, liefdevol, beminlik; please be so -, wees asseblief so goed (vriendelik); with - regards, met vriendelike groete; - invitation, vriendelike uitnodiging.
kindergarten, kindertuin, kleinkinderskool.
kindle, aan die brand steek, laat ontvlam; aan die brand raak; ontvlam; opflikker.
kindliness, goedhartigheid, vriendelikheid.
kindly, goedhartig, sagaardig, welwillend.
kindred, n. (bloed)verwantskap; (bloed)verwante.
kindred, a. verwant; gelyksoortig; aangenaam.
kine, mv. van cow.
kinema, cinema, bioskoop.
kinematic, kinematies.
kinematics, kinematika, bewegingsleer.
kinematograph, sien cinematograph.
kinetics, kineties, bewegings- . . .
kinetics, kinetiek, bewegingsleer.
king, n. koning, vors; (by kaarte) heer; (by dambord en skaak) koning; -'s English, standaard-Engels; -'s evidence, kroongetuie.
king, v. koning maak; - it, koningspeel.
king-at-arms, wapenkoning.
kingbird, koningparadysvoël.
king-bolt, hoofbout.

king-cup, botterblom, gousblom.
kingdom, koninkryk; animal -, diereryk; mineral -, mineraleryk; delfstowweryk; vegetable -, planteryk; - come, die hiernamaals.
kingfisher, visvanger, ysvoël.
kinghood, koningskap.
kinglet, koninkie.
kinglike, koninklik, vorstelik.
kingly, koninklik, vorstelik.
king-post, hoofstyl.
kingship, koningskap.
kink, n. kink(el), slag; - in the brain, draai in die harsings, streep, nuk.
kink, v. 'n kink gee, 'n slag maak (in).
kinkajou, wikkelneus.
kinky, kinkelrig; vol nukke.
kinsfolk, familie, verwante.
kinship, verwantskap.
kinsman, bloedverwante, familielid.
kinswoman, bloedverwante, familielid.
kiosk, kiosk; tuinhuis; stalletjie; musiektent.
kipper, n. mannetjiesalm; gerookte haring.
kipper, v. sout en rook; -ed herring, gerookte haring.
kirk, kerk.
kirtle, rok, onderrok; baadjie, buis.
kismet, kismet, fatum, noodlot.
kiss, n. soen, kus; (kus)karambool.
kiss, v. soen, kus; (aan)raak; - and be friends, afsoen, afmaak; - the Books, op die Bybel sweer; - the dust, in die stof byt; - the ground, in die stof kruip; - hands, the hand, handkus gee; - the hand to, 'n kushandjie gee; - goodbye, afskeidsoen gee.
kiss-curl, koketkrulletjie, spoegkrulletjie.
kissing, gesoen, soenery.
kiss-in-the-ring, (soort) patertjie-spel.
kiss-me-quick, viooltjie, gesiggie; halfsluier; mus, kappie; snor.
kist, (ou-Hollandse) kis.
kit, vaatjie; ransel; uitrusting.
kitbag, knapsak, ransel, valies; reissak.
kitchen, kombuis.
kitchener, stoof; kok.
kitchenette, kombuisie.
kitchen-garden, groentetuin.
kitchen-range, kombuisstoof.
kite, kuikendief; vlieër; skraper, ,,haai"; proformawissel; fly a -, 'n proefballon oplaat.
kith, kennisse; - and kin, familie en kennisse; - nor kin, kind nog kraai.
kitten, n. katjie.
kitten, v. klein katjies kry, jong.
kittenish, katterig; speelsiek, baljaarderig.
kittle, lastig, moeilik, vol draadwerk.
kitty, katjie, kietsie; pot (geld).
kiwi, kiwi, (Nieu-Seelandse) snipstruis.
klaxon, klaxon.
kleptomania, kleptomanie, steelsug.
kleptomaniac, kleptomaniak.
knack, slag, kuns, handigheid; gewoonte; have the - of, die slag hê om.
knacker, perdeslagter; afbraakkoper.
knag, kwas, knoes.
knaggy, kwasterig, knoesterig.
knap, stukkend maak, breek, stamp.
knapsack, knapsak, ransel.
knapweed, knoopgras.
knar, kwas, knobbel.
knave, skelm, skobbejak, karnallie; boer (in kaartspel); - of hearts, harte(n)boer.
knavery, skelmstreke, skurkery.
knavish, skelm, skurkagtig.
knead, knee (knie); brei; kleitrap; masseer.

kneading, geknee, kneëry.
kneading-trough, kneebak.
knee, n. knie; hoek, bog; kniestuk; **go on one's** **-s**, op die knieë val; **bring to his -s**, onderwerp, kleinkry; **beg on both -s**, op blote knieë smeek; **housemaid's -s**, skrobknieë.
knee, v. knieë maak (van 'n broek).
knee-breeches, kuitbroek.
knee-cap, knieskyf; kniekap, knieskut.
kneed, met knieë.
knee-deep, kniediep, tot aan die knieë.
kneehalter, kniehalter.
knee-joint, kniegewrig.
kneel, kniel, op die knieë lê, op die knieë val; - to, kniel voor.
kneeler, knieler; knielkussing.
knee-piece, kniestuk.
knell, n. (klok)gelui; doodsklok.
knell, v. die doodsklok lui, uitlui; onheil spel, (met klokgelui) aankondig.
knickerbocker, pofbroek, gesperbroek.
knickers, sien **knickerbocker**.
knick-knack, snuistery, tierlantyntjie.
knife, n. mes; dolk; lem; **he has his - into you**, hy het die pik op jou; **war to the -**, stryd op lewe en dood; **before anybody could say -**, in 'n kits, soos die blits; **play a good - and fork**, fluks weglê.
knife, v. steek (met 'n mes).
knife-board, slypplank.
knife-edge, (mes)snee.
knife-rest, mesleêr.
knife-tray, mes(se)bak.
knight, n. ridder; perd (by skaakspel) **K-** **of the Garter**, Ridder van die Kous(e)band; - **of industry**, swendelaar, afsetter; - **of the pestle**, apteker; - **of the road**, padrower; - **of the rueful countenance**, ridder van die droewige figuur; - **of the stick**, lettersetter.
knight, v. ridder, tot ridder slaan.
knight-errant, dolende ridder.
knight-errantry, dolende ridderskap.
knighthood, ridderskap; ridderorde, ridderstand.
knightliness, ridderlikheid.
knightly, ridderlik, ridder- . . .
knight-service, ridderdies.
Knight-Templar, Tempelridder, Tempelier.
knit, brei; saamvleg, saambind; **- one's brows**, (die winkbroue) frons; **well - frame**, vasgeboude lyf; **- up**, toebrei; saambind.
knitter, breier, breister; breimasjien.
knitting, breiery; breiwerk; verbinding.
knitting-needle, breinaald.
knitting-wool, breiwol, breigaring.
knob, n. knop; klont; harspan, klapperdop; bult, knobbel; kwas.
knob, v. bulte gee; knoppe (in) maak.
knobbed, knopperig, bulterig, kwasterig.
knobble, knoppie, bultjie.
knobkerrie, knopkierie.
knobstick, knopkierie; onderkruiper.
knock, n. klop; stamp, stoot; slag, bons.
knock, v. klop; slaan, 'n hou gee, stamp, stoot, klap; dronkslaan; **what -s me is . . .**, wat my dronkslaan is . . .; **- about**, opdons; rondslenter; **a man who has -ed about the world**, 'n bereisde man, 'n man van ervaring; **- against**, stamp teen, bots met; **- the head against the wall**, met die kop teen die muur loop; **- at**, aanklop (by), klop op; **- down**, platslaan; omry; (pryse) afslaan; **down to**, toeslaan op; **- down with a feather**, omblaas; **- into**, inhamer, inklop; **- into a cocked hat**, kort en klein slaan, kafloop; **- off**, afslaan, wegslaan; **- spots off one**, iemand kafloop; **- off work**,

uitskei met werk; **- on the head**, op die kop slaan, uitklop; die kop indruk, verongeluk; **- out**, uitklop; uitklophou gee; **- the bottom out of**, in duie laat val; aan die kaak stel; **- over**, omry; onderstebo loop; **- together**, aanmekaar timmer, inmekaar slaan; **- under**, tou opgooi, ingee; **- up**, opklop; bymekaar klop; inmekaar sak; opdons; **be -ed up**, lelik toegetakel wees, poot-uit wees; **- up against**, toevallig op die lyf loop, raakloop.
knocker, klopper; **up to the -**, piekfyn.
knock-kneed, met aankapknieë.
knock-knees, aankapknieë, X-bene.
knock-on, aanslaan.
knock-out (blow), uitklophou.
knoll, n. bultjie, heuweltjie.
knoll, v. lui, uitlui.
knop, n. knop.
knot, n. knoop, strik, lissie; band, kwas, knobbel; bolla; groep, klampie; **undo a -**, 'n knoop losmaak; **cut the Gordian -**, die Gordiaanse knoop deurhaak; **ten -s an hour**, tien knope in die uur; **marriage -**, huweliksband; **I got myself tied into a -**, ek het myself lelik vasgepraat.
knot, v. knoop, aanmekaarknoop, vasbind; (ver)bind; verwikkel, in die war raak (bring); saamtrek, frons; **-ted brows**, gefronsde winkbroue.
knot-grass, duisendknoop, tongblaar.
knotting, n. knoopwerk, macramé.
knotty, geknoop; ingewikkeld; netelig.
knotwork, knoopwerk, macramé-werk.
knout, knoet.
know, n. weet; **be in the -**, ingewy wees.
know, v. weet, ken, herken, verstaan, besef; kan **I - it to be true**, ek weet dat dit waar is; **I - him well**, ek ken hom goed; **I knew him for an American**, ek het gesien dat hy 'n Amerikaner was; **shall you - him again?**, sal jy hom herken; **I - him by sight**, ek ken hom van sien; he -s **how to ride**, hy kan ry; **do you - what you are saying?**, besef jy wat jy sê?; **run for all you -**, hardloop so wat jy kan; **I knew better than that I should answer his questions**, ek was oulik genoeg om nie sy vrae te beantwoord nie; **not that I - of**, nie vir sover ek weet nie; he -s **what's what**, hy is ouer as tien; he -s **the ropes**, hy weet wat daar in die wêreld te koop is; **to - which is which**, van mekaar kan onderskei, uitmekaar ken; **- one's way about**, jou pad ken, jou weg kan vind; **to come to -**, leer ken, verneem; ervaar; **to - for certain**, seker weet, vervas weet; **to - by heart**, van buite ken, uit die kop ken; **before you - where you are**, as jy jou weer kom kry; **it was awful, you -**, dit was verskriklik, weet jy; **become -n**, bekend stel; **- by**, (her)ken aan; **- for a fact**, seker weet.
knowing, kundig; oulik, geslepe; veelseggend.
knowingly, op veelseggende manier; bewus, willens en wetens; **he winked - at me**, hy het op veelseggende manier vir my geknip; **I have never - injured him**, ek het hom nooit willens en wetens benadeel nie.
knowledge, kennis, verstand, wetenskap; **it came to my -**, ek het te wete gekom; **not to my -**, nie vir sover ek weet nie; **to the best of my -**, na my beste wete; **every branch of -**, iedere gebied van die wetenskap; **in the - that he was right**, in die bewussyn dat hy reggehad het; **without my -**, sonder my voorkennis (medewete); **it is common -**, dit is algemeen bekend, dit lê op die straat; **first-hand -**, eerstehandse kennis; **working -**, gangbare kennis.

knowledgeable, goed ingelig, belese.
knuckle, n. kneukel; skinkel(been); rap one's
 -s, iemand op die vingers tik.
knuckle, v. met die kneukels vrywe; - down,
 platskiet, hand-op-die-grond-skiet; - down
 (under) to, (sig) gewonne gee.
knuckle-bone, dolos; -s, dolosspel.
knuckle-duster, boksyster, boksring.
knuckle-joint, kneukelgewrig.
knur(r), knop, kwas, uitwas; houtbal.
knurl, knoop, knop, knobbel; rand.
knurled, knobberig, knoesterig.
knut, modegek, windmaker, fat.
kodak, kodak, kiektoestel.
kohlrabi, knolkool.
koodoo, kudu, koedoe.

kopje, koppie, koppie.
Koran, Koran.
kosher, kosjer.
kotow, v. salaam; grond lek, kruip.
kotow, n. salaam, voetval.
kourbasch, karwats, sambok.
kraal, n. kraal.
kraal, v. in die kraal ja.
krait, karait.
kraken, kraken.
kran(t)z, krans.
krone, kroon.
kudos, eer, roem.
kümmel, kummel.
Kuomintang, Kwomintang.

laager, n. laer; kamp.
laager, v. laer trek.
labefaction, verswakking, instorting.
label, n. etiket, kaartjie; seël.
label, v. etiket opplak, kaartjie aanbind; etiketteer, bestempel.
labial, n. lipklank, lipletter; labiaal.
labial, adj. labiaal, lip-...
labialization, labialisering, labialisasie.
labialize, labialiseer.
labiate, lipvormig; lipbloemig.
labio-dental, liptand-..., labio-dentaal.
laboratory, laboratorium, werkwinkel.
laborious, arbeidsaam; swaar, moeilik.
labour, n. werk, arbeid; taak; barenswee; arbeiders; **lost –,** vergeefse moeite; **a – of love,** 'n luswerk.
labour, v. werk, arbei; swoeg; sukkel; (grond) bewerk; **– under a mistake,** in dwaling verkeer; **– a point,** diep op iets ingaan.
laboured, uitgewerk; swaar, moeilik.
labourer, arbeider, dagloner, werksman.
Labourite, Arbeider; **–s,** Arbeiders(party).
laburum, goue-reën.
labyrinth, doolhof, labirint.
labyrinthine, soos 'n doolhof, verward.
lac, lak; lakwerk.
lace, n. veter; (ryg)band; kant; borsel.
lace, v. inryg, toeryg; vasryg; deurryg; borduur; met kant versier; omboor.
lacerate, (ver)skeur; seermaak, bedroef.
lachrymal, adj. traan-...
lachrymatory, a. traanwekkend, traan-...
lachrymatory, n. tranekruikie
lachrymose, tranerig, huilerig.
lacing, veter, boorsel, kantwerk.
lack, n. gebrek, behoefte, tekort, gemis.
lack, v. ontbeer; ontbreek, kortom, gebrek hê aan; **money was –ing,** geld het ontbreek; he **–s courage, he is –ing in courage,** dit ontbreek hom aan moed.
lackadaisical, onverskillig, slap; aanstellerig.
lackey, n. lakei, lyfkneg.
lackey, lacquey, v. slaafs volg, as lakei dien.
laconic, kort en bondig, lakoniek.
laconism, lakoniese uitdrukking (gesegde); pittige gesegde, lakonisme.
lacquer, lacker, n. vernis, lakwerk.
lacquer, lacker, v. verlak, vernis.
lacrosse, lacrosse.
lactation, soging, (die) soog; melkafskeiding; laktasie.
lacteal, adj. melk-..., melkhoudend.
lactescence, melkerigheid; melksap.
lactescent, melkagtig, melkerig, melk-...
lactic, melk-...; **– acid,** melksuur.
lactiferous, melk-..., melkafskeidend.
lactometer, melkmeter, laktometer.
lactose, melksuiker.
lacuna, hiaat, gaping, leemte.
lad, seun, knaap (knapie), kêreltjie.
ladder, n. leer.
ladder, v. lostrek, leer (van 'n kous).
ladder-stitch, dwarssteek.
laddie, knapie, mannetjie, kêreltjie.
lade, laai, bevrag.
la-di-da, n. aansteller; windmakerigheid.
la-di-da, adj. aanstellerig.
lading, lading, vrag; **bill of –,** vragbrief.
ladle, n. potlepel, soplepel.
ladle, v. skep; **– out,** uitskep.
ladleful, soplepelvol.
lady, dame, vrou (van die huis); lady; nôi, beminde; **Our Lady, Ons Liewe Vrou;** our sovereign **–, Haar Majesteit; your good –, mevrou.
ladybird, lieweheersbesie, boomskilpadjie.
lady companion, geselskapsjuffrou.
lady doctor, vroulike dokter.
lady-dog, teef, vroutjieshond.
lady-friend, vriendin.
ladyfy, -ify, 'n dame maak van; lady noem, as lady betitel; **ladified,** damesagtig.
lady-help, hulp in die huishouding.
lady-in-waiting, hofdame.
lady-killer, Don Juan, hartveroweraar.
ladylike, soos 'n dame; verwyf(d).
lady-love, beminde, geliefde, liefste, nôi.
lady's companion, naaiwerksakkie.
ladyship, ladyskap; **her –,** lady.
lady's-maid, kamenier, kamerjuffrou.
lady's man, damesvriend, meisiesgek.
lag, n. agterblyer; vertraging.
lag, v. agterbly; **– behind,** uitsak, agter raak.
lag, v. depoteer; oppak, arresteer.
lag, n. gedeporteerde, bandiet.
lager(beer), lagerbier.
laggard, n. draaikous, draler, agterblyer.
laggard, adj. traag, draaierig, treuselig.
lagger, sien **laggard,**
lagoon, -une, strandmeer, lagune.
laic, n. leek.
laic, adj. leke-...
laicize, sekulariseer.
laid, sien **lay.**
lain, sien **lie.**
lair, lêplek; afdak, skuur.
lair, v. lê, gaan lê.
laird, landheer, (Skotse) grondbesitter.
laity, die leke, lekedom.
lake, meer.
lake, karmosynverf.
lake-dweller, paalbewoner.
lake-land, lake-country, meerdistrik.
lam, afransel, uitlooi, pak gee.
lama, lama.
lamb, n. lam; skaapvleis, lamsvleis; **wolf, fox in –'s skin,** wolf in skaapsklere.
lamb, v. lam.
lambent, lekkend, spelend; sag glinsterend.
lamblike, soos 'n lam, sag.
lambskin, lamsvel.
lamb's-wool, lammerwol.
lame, adj. kreupel, mank, gebreklik; onbevredigend; hortend (van versmaat); **– of leg, mank; – duck,** verminkte persoon; ongelukkige stumperd; insolvente effektemakelaar.
lame, v. vermink, verlam, kreupel, maak.
lamella, skyfie, lagie, skilfer, lamel.
lameness, gebreklikheid, kreupelheid.
lament, n. weeklag, jammerklag; treurlied.
lament, v. betreur, beklaag, beween; weeklaag, lamenteer; **the late –ed,** wyle.
lamentable, betreurenswaardig, bekla(g)enswaardig, erbarmlik.
lamentation, klaaglied; weeklag; **Lamentations of Jeremiah,** Klaagliedere van Jeremia.
lamia, towerheks, vampiervrou.
lamina, plaatjie, lagie, skyfie, velletjie.
laminate, plet; splyt; in lagies pak; met plaatjies bedek (belê).
Lammas, St. Pietersdag, oesfees; **latter –,** in die jaar nul as die hingste vul.
lamp, lamp; **it smells of the –,** dit ruik na die lamp.
lamp-black, lampswartsel.
lamp-chimney, lampglas.
lampion, lampie.

lampoon 547 **larva**

lampoon, n. skimpskrif, skotskrif.
lampoon, v. skotskrif skrywe teen, hekel.
lamponeer, skotskrywer, hekelaar.
lamp-post, lamppaal.
lamprey, lamprei, prik.
lamp socket, lamphouer.
lance, n. lans; lansier.
lance, v. deursteek; (met 'n lanset) oopsny.
lance-corporal, vise-korporaal.
lance-fish, sand-aal.
lanceolate, lansetvormig.
lancet, lanset.
land, n. land, grond; grondbesit, landgoed; landstreek; landerye; how the − lies, hoe sake staan; − of promise, die beloofde land; the − of the living, die land der lewende; by −, oor land; te land.
land, v. land, aanland, aankom; aan wal sit, aflaai; neerstryk (vliegtuig); beland; grondvat, val; wen; uittrek, ophaal; besorg, bring; − a prize, 'n prys behaal; − in difficulties, in moeilikhede beland.
landau, landauer.
land-bank, landboubank; landbank.
land-breeze, landwind.
landdrost, landdros.
landed, grond-. . . ., grondbesittend, in grond (land) bestaande; geland; the − interest, die grondbesitters; − estate, property, grondbesit; − gentry, landadel; newly −, pas geland.
landfall, nadering van land.
land-grabber, grondwolf.
landgrave, landgraaf.
landgravine, landgravin.
landholder, grondbesitter.
landing, n. landing; landingsplek; lossing; trapportaal, oorloop.
landing, adj. landings- . . .
landing-stage, aanlegsteier.
land-jobber, grondspekulant.
landlady, kosjuffrou, losieshuishoudster, eienares van losieshuis; grondeienares, baas.
land-locked, deur land ingesluit.
landlord, kosbaas, hotelhouer, waard; grondeienaar, baas, landheer.
land-lubber, landrot.
landmark, baken, grenspaal; mylpaal.
landowner, grondbesitter.
landmine, landmyn.
landrail, kwartelkoning.
landscape, landskap.
landscape-painter, landskapskilder.
land-shark, matroosafsetter; grondwolf.
land-side, hoef, strykbord (van ploeg).
land-slide, grondverskuiwing; politieke omkeer.
landslip, grondverskuiwing.
landsman, landbewoner, landrot.
land-surveyor, landmeter.
land-tax, grondbelasting.
landward, landwaarts.
lane, pad (paadjie), steeg, deurgang; gang; vaarweg; it is a long − that has no turning, dit kan nie so aanhou nie.
lang syne, lank gelede, vanmelewe se dae.
language, taal, spraak; styl!; use bad −, vloek, lelik praat.
languid, loom, dooierig, mat, lusteloos, kwynend.
languish, verflou, wegkwyn, agteruitgaan; − for, smag na.
languishingly, kwynend, smagtend.
languishment, kwyning; versmagting.
languor, loomheid, lusteloosheid; drukkerigheid; sagtheid.
langurous, mat, lusteloos; drukkend; smagtend.

lank, dun, lank en skraal; sluik (hare).
lanky, sien lank.
lanner, lanneret, steenvalk.
lanolin, wolvet, lanolien.
lansquenet, lanskneg; lanskenet.
lantern, lantern; Chinese −, lampion; magic −, towerlantern; − lecture, lesing met ligbeelde.
lantern-slide, lanternplaatjie.
lanyard, taliereep; skouerriem, skouerband.
Laodicean, n. Laodiceër.
Laodicean, adj. onverskillig, lou.
lap, n. skoot; pand; klap; oorlel; holte.
lap, v. toedraai, wikkel; omgeef; uitsteek; − over, uitsteek, oorsteek.
lap, n. ronde (by wedrenne).
lap, v. (op)lek, opslorp; kabbel, spoel; − up, oplek, opslorp.
lap, n. sopperige kos; slap drank; kabbeling.
lap-dog, skoothondjie.
lapel, lapel, kraagpunt.
lapidary, adj. steen- . . . ; in steen gebeitel; lapidêr; − style, lapidêrstyl, kernagtige styl.
lapidary, n. steensnyer, graveur; steenkenner.
lapidate, stenig.
lapidity, (laat) versteen.
lapis lazuli, lasuursteen, lapis lazuli.
Lapp, n. Laplander, Lap.
Lapp, adj. Laplands.
lappet, pand, strook; oorlel; lapel; afhangende lint.
Lapponian, n. Laplander.
Lapponian, adj. Laplands.
lapse, n. fout; misstap, afdwaling, afwyking, glips, afval, val; verloop, verval; − of time, verloop van tyd; − from, afwyking (afdwaling) van.
lapse, v. afdwaal, val, verval, terugval; verloop, verbygaan; gly, glip; − into, verval tot, afdwaal tot; − from, afdwaal van.
lapsus, fout, vergissing, lapsus.
lapwing, kiewiet.
larboard, bakboord.
larcenous, diefagtig, diewe- . . .
larceny, diefstal.
larch, lork, lorkeboom, lariks.
lard, n. varkvet.
lard, v. lardeer, met spek stop: deurspek.
lardaceous, vetterig, vetagtig.
larder, koskas, provisiekamer.
large, adj. groot, ruim uitgestrek, breed, omvangryk, veelomvattend; tamaai; − of limb, grof gebou; − views, breë insigte.
large, n. : at −, vry, los op vrye voet; breedvoerig, in besonderhede; popular with the people at −, populêr by die volk in die algemeen; the public at −, die groot publiek; scatter insults at −, links en regs beledig; gentleman at −, man sonder beroep, rentenier; ,,los hotnot''; in −, op 'n groot skaal, by die groot maat.
large-hearted, groothartig, edelmoedig.
large-limbed, grofgebou.
largely, in groot mate, grotendeels, vernaamlik, hoofsaaklik; ruimskoots.
large-minded, sien large-hearted.
largeness, grootte, ruimte, uitgestrektheid.
largess(e), gif, geskenk; mildheid.
lariat, vangriem, lasso.
lark, laverock, n. lewerik (lewerkie).
lark, n. grap(pie), pret(makery).
lark, v. pret maak, gekskeer.
larkspur, ridderspoor.
larky, ondeund, vol streke, jolig.
larrikin, straatskender, kwajong.
larum, sien alarum.
larva, larwe.

laryngeal, laryngic, van die strottehoof.
laryngitis, ontsteking van die strottehoof.
laryngoscope, keelspieël, laringoskoop.
larynx, strottehoof; larinks.
Lascar, Oos-Indiese matroos, Laskar.
lascivious, wellustig, wulps, ontugtig.
lasciviousness, wellustigheid, wulpsheid.
laser: – **beam,** laserstraal, hipergekonsentreerde ligstraal.
lash, n. hou, raps; gesel, plak; voorslag; ooghaartjie; **under the** –, onder die plak.
lash, v. raps, slaan, onder die sambok laat deurloop, gesel; swiep, beuk; vasknoop, vassjor; – **at,** slaan na; gesel; – **down,** vasbind; – **out,** lossteek, agteropskop; hand uitruk, niks ontsien nie; moker; – **together,** aanmekaar bind.
lasher, slaner, geselaar; damwal.
lashing, geseling; sjorring, vasknopery.
lass, meisie(tjie), nôi(entjie).
lassie, sien **lass.**
lassitude, afgematheid, moegheid, loomheid.
lasso, n. vangriem, lasso.
lasso, v. met 'n vangriem (lasso) vang.
last, n. lees; **one must stick to one's** –, 'n skoenmaker moet hom by sy lees hou.
last, n. las (gewigsmaat, inhoudsmaat).
last, adj. laaste, verlede, jongslede; uiterste; – **but not least,** les bes; **the** – **but one,** op een na die laaste; – **Tuesday,** verlede Dinsdag; – **night,** gisteraand; verlede nag; **L**– **day,** die Oordeelsdag; **of the** – **importance,** van die uiterste belang.
last, n. laaste; **at (long)** –, eindelik (en ten laaste); **to, till the** –, tot (op) die laaste; **look one's** –, vir die laaste maal kyk (na); **we shall never hear the** – **of it,** daar kom nooit 'n einde aan nie.
last, adv. die laaste; eindelik, ten slotte; **when did you see him** –?, wanneer het jy hom laaste (laas) gesien?
last, v. aanhou; voortduur; goed bly; uithou; **this will** – **me eight months,** hiermee sal ek ag maande uitkom; **he cannot** – **long,** hy kan dit nie lank maak nie; **we could not** – **them out,** ons kon dit nie teen hulle volhou nie.
lastly, eindelik, ten laaste, ten slotte.
latch, n. knip, klink.
latch, v. op die knip sit.
latch-key, knipsleutel, klinksleutel.
late, adj. laat; te laat; vergevorder(d); vorige, gewese; oorlede, wyle; onlangs; **the** – **prime minister,** die gewese eerste minister; **my** – **husband,** my oorlede man; **of** – **years,** (in) die laaste paar jaar; **of** –, in die laaste tyd; **the** – **floods,** die oorstrominge van onlangs; **my** – **residence,** my woning tot onlangs; **at the latest,** op sy (die) laaste.
late, adv. laat, te laat; onlangs, vroeër, voorheen; **sooner or** –**r,** vroeër of later.
lately, onlangs; in die laaste tyd.
latency, verborgenheid; latentheid.
lateness, laatheid; **the** – **of the hour,** die late uur.
latent, verborge, onsigbaar, sluimerend, slapend, latent; – **heat,** latente warmte.
lateral, adj. sydelings, sy- . . . ; lateraal.
lateral, n. sytak, syspruit.
latex, melksap.
lath, n. lat, plankie.
lath, v. van latte voorsien.
lathe, draaibank.
lather, n. seepskuim, skuim (van 'n perd).
lather, v. inseep, seep smeer; skuim, uitlooi, afransel.
lathing, latte, latwerk.

Latin, n. Latyn.
Latin, adj. Latyns.
Latinism, Latynse spreekwyse, Latinisme.
Latinist, Latinis.
Latinity, Latynse styl; kennis van Latyn.
Latinize, verlatyns; Latynse vorme gebruik.
latish, laterig, 'n bietjie laat.
latitude, breedte(graad); omvang; speling.
latitudinarian, adj. vrydenkend, vrysinnig.
latitudinarian, n. vrydenker, liberaal.
latitudinarianism, vrysinnigheid.
latrine, latrine.
latten, latoen.
latter, laasgenoemde, tweede, laaste van twee, these – **days,** hierdie laaste dae; **the former** . . . **the** –, eersgenoemde . . . . laasgenoemde.
latter-day, hedendaags, modern; **the L**– **saints,** die Heiliges van die laaste dae.
latterly, onlangs, in die laaste tyd.
lattice, traliewerk, latwerk.
latticed, tralie- . . . , van traliewerk voorsien.
lattice-window, tralievenster; venster met ruitjies in lood.
latticing, tralies, traliewerk.
laud, v. prys, loof, verheerlik; ophemel.
laud, n. lofsang; –**s,** vroegmis, laudes.
laudability, lofwaardigheid, loflikheid.
laudable, lofwaardig, loflik; gesond.
laudanum, loudanum.
laudation, loftuiting, (lof spraak).
laudatory, lowend, prysend, lof- . . .
laugh, n. lag; gelag; **have, get the** – **of one,** iemand lekker uitlag; **join in the** –, saamlag, meelag; **laugh,** v. lag; **he** –**s best who** –**s last,** wie die laaste lag, lag die lekkerste; – **at,** uitlag, lag vir (oor, om); – **in one's sleeve,** in sy vuis lag; – **off,** laggend daarvan afmaak; – **on the wrong side of his mouth,** nie lus hê om te lag nie; – **over,** lag oor; – **to scorn,** bespot.
laughable, belaglik; lagwekkend, grappig.
laughing, n. lag, gelag.
laughing, adj. laggend, lag . . . ; **it is no** – **matter,** dit is geen grap nie.
laughing-gas, laggas.
laughingly, al laggend, lag-lag.
laughing-stock, voorwerp van bespotting.
laughter, gelag, laggery.
launch, v. werp, slinger; van stapel laat loop; uitstuur; aan die gang sit, op tou sit; – **forth,** van wal steek; – **out,** losbars, uitbars, laat rol; uitwei.
launch, n. barkas; plesierbootjie.
launder, was (en stryk).
laundress, wasvrou, wasmeid, skoonmaakster.
laundry, washuis, wassery, wasinrigting; waskamer; wasgoed.
laureate, adj. gelouerd; **poet** –, hofdigter.
laurel, n. lourier; lourierkrans; **rest on one's** –**s,** op jou louere rus; **look to one's** –**s,** sorg dat jy jou voorsprong behou.
laurel, v. louer, met 'n lourerkrans bekroon.
lava, lawa.
lavatory, waskamertjie, toiletkamer.
lave, was, bespoel, vloei langs.
lavement, inspuiting, lawement.
lavender, lavendel; laventelbos.
laver, wasbekken.
laverock, sien **lark.**
lavish, adj. kwistig; volop, oorvloedig.
lavish, v. met kwistige hand uitdeel; verkwis.
lavishly, kwistig, met kwistige hand.
lavishness, kwistigheid, verkwisting.
law, n. wet; reg; regspraak; baie; **the** – **of the Medes and the Persians,** die wet van die Mede en die Perse; – **of Moses,** Mosaïese wet; **Roman**

Dutch –, Romeins-Hollandse reg; **international** –, – **of nations,** volkereg, internasionale reg; **civil –,** burgerlike reg; **common –,** gemene reg; – **of nature,** natuurwet; **lay down the –,** die wet voorskrywe; **necessity knows no –,** nood breek wet; **go to –,** prosedeer; **have, take the** – **of one,** iemand voor die hof bring; **take the** – **into one's hands,** sigself reg verskaf; **study –,** in die regte studeer; **be at –,** in 'n hofsaak betrokke wees.
law-abiding, ordeliewend.
law-agent, wetsagent.
law-court, geregshof, magistraatshof, regbank.
lawful, wettig; wetlik, geoorloof.
lawgiver, wetgewer.
lawless, wetteloos, sonder wet; losbandig.
lawlessness, wetteloosheid; bandeloosheid.
law-maker, wetgewer.
law-merchant, handelsreg.
lawn, n. kamerdoek.
lawn, n. grasperk.
lawn-mower, grasmasjien.
lawn-tennis, tennis.
law-officer, regterlike amptenaar.
law-society, wetsvereniging.
law-student, student in die regte.
lawsuit, hofsaak, proses.
law-term, regsterm; sittingstermyn.
lawyer, advokaat, regsgeleerde, prokureur.
lax, los, slap, laks; nalatig, onverskillig.
laxative, adj. lakserend, purgerend.
laxative, n. purgeermiddel, lakseermiddel.
laxity, laksheid, slapheid, nalatigheid.
lay, n. lied, gesang.
lay, v. sien **lie.**
lay, adj. leke- ... ; wêreldlik.
lay, v. lê; neerlê; neerslaan, platdruk; laat bepaar; rig, mik; wed; ('n strik) span, ('n komplot) smee; ('n gees) besweer; – **siege to,** beeër; **the scene is laid in London,** die stuk speel in Londen; – **waste,** verwoes; – **the table,** tafel dek; – **a wager,** wed, 'n weddenskap aangaan; – **bare,** openbaar, toon; –**open,** blootlê; bloot laat; – **low,** verneder; plattrek, neertrek; – **claim to,** aanspraak maak op; – **snares,** strikke span; – **about one,** links en regs slaan; – **aside,** bêre, wegsit; **aflê,** laat vaar; – **at the door of,** beskuldig van; – **before** voorlê; – **by,** bêre, wegsit, aflê, laat vaar; – **down,** neerlê, neersit; laat vaar; begin bou, op stapel sit; voorskryf; – **down one's life,** jou lewe gee; – **in,** (sig) voorsien van, vergaar; – **into one,** iemand inpeper (invlie); – **off,** aflê; – **on,** ('n boete) oplê; (slae) toedien; die lat gebruik; aanlê; – **hold on, off,** (aan)gryp; – **one's hopes on,** jou hoop vestig op; – **hands on,** sig toeëien;– **hands on oneself,**die hand aan eie lewe slaan; – **it on thick,** – **it on with a trowel,** goed met die heuningkwas smeer; – **the blame on one,** iemand die skuld gee; – **out,** ('n tuin, 'n lyk) uitlê, vertoon, ten toon stel; – **oneself out to,** moeite doen om; – **over,** bedek, gooi oor; – **a spark to,** aan die brand steek; – **heads together,** koppe bymekaarsit; – **under an obligation,** iemand aan jou verplig; – **up,** wegsit, bymekaarmaak; **be laid up,** siek lê, in die bed lê; – **hands upon,** kry, vind.
lay brother, lekebroeder.
lay-by, parkeerplek; lêplek; spaargeld.
layer, n. laag; lêer (inlêer van plant).
layer, v. inlêer(s) maak; gaan lê (van graan).
lay figure, ledepop; nul.
layman, leek, oningewyde.
lay-off, tydelike ontslag.

lay-out, aanleg; uitrusting.
lazaret(to), lasaret, kwarantynhuis.
laze, n. luilekker, lewe, lanterfanter.
laze, v. lui wees, 'n luilekker lewe voer.
laziness, luiheid, vadsigheid, traagheid.
lazy, adj. lui, traag.
lazy-bones, luisak, luilak, luiaard.
lea, grasveld, weide, beemd.
leach, deurspoel; in die loog sit.
lead, n. lood, potlood; dieplood, peillood; **–s,** platdak; loodroeie, loodjies.
lead, v. met lood bedek; met lood beswaar; – **out,** spasieer.
lead, v. lei; (aan)voer; dirigeer; voor wees; uitkom, voorkom (by kaartspel); – **one a life,** die lewe vir iemand onaangenaam maak; – **the way,** voorgaan, voorloop; die voortou neem; – **the dance,** voordans; – **away,** weglei, wegvoer; – **by the nose,** by die neus lei; – **off,** begin aanknoop, aanvoer; – **on,** verder voer; – **to,** lei tot; aanleiding gee tot; beweeg om te; – **to expect,** die verwagting wek; – **to the altar,** na die altaar lei; – **up to,** lei (voer) tot; aanleiding gee tot; aanstuur op.
lead, n. leiding; watervoor; (koppel)riem; hoofrol; **take the –,** die leiding neem, die voortou neem; **it is your –,** jy moet uitkom, voorspeel; **return the –,** dieselfde kleur terugspeel.
leaden, lood- ... , loodswaar; loodkleurig.
leader, leier, voorman, aanvoerder; voorperd; dirigent; hoofartikel.
leaderette, (kort) hoofartikeltjie.
leadership, leiding, aanvoering.
leading, n. leiding.
leading, adj. vernaamste, voorste; – **article,** hoofartikel; – **lady, man,** eerste speelster, speelster, speler; **be** – **lady, man,** die hoofrol speel.
leading-strings, leiband; **be in –,** aan die leiband loop.
lead-pencil, potlood.
lead-works, loodsmeltery.
leaf, n. blaar; blad; velletjie; klep; **fall of the –,** as die blare val, najaar; **in –,** uitgeloop; **take a** – **out of a persons' book,** iemand tot voorbeeld neem; **turn over a new –,** 'n beter lewe begin.
leafage, loof.
leafless, blaarloos, sonder blare.
leaflet, blaartjie; blaadjie, traktaatjie.
leaf-mould, blaargrond.
leafy, blaar- ... , blaarryk.
league, n. (ver)bond, verbintenis; **L– of Nations,** Volkebond; **be with–,** bondgenoot wees van; kop in een mus wees met.
league, v. 'n verbond aangaan; **–d together,** verbonde; **–d with,** in bondgenootskap met.
leaguer, bondgenoot; lêer (inhoudsmaat).
leak, n. lekplek; **spring a –,** 'n lek kry.
leak, v. lek; – **out,** uitlek.
leakage, (die) lek, lekkasie.
leaky, lekkerig.
leal, lojaal, trou, eerlik.
lean, adj. maer, skraal, dun; – **years,** maer jare; – **mixture,** dun mengsel.
lean, n. maer vleis.
lean, v. leun, steun; laat (steun, rus); neig, geneig wees; oorhel; – **against,** (laat) leun teen; – **back,** agteroor leun; – **forward,** vooroor leun; – **on,** leun op; – **to,** partydig wees vir, oorhel na; – **upon,** steun op; – **over backwards,** baie tegemoetkomend wees.
leaning, (die) leun; oorhelling; neiging.
leanness. maerheid, maerte, skraalheid.

leant, sien lean.
lean-to, afdak.
leap, v. spring; oorsprong; laat spring; – **at,** bespring; – **over,** oorspring.
leap, n. sprong; a – **in the dark,** 'n sprong in die duister; **by –s and bounds,** met groot sprong, sprongsgewyse.
leaper, springer.
leap-frog, hasie-oor.
leapt, sien leap.
leap-year, skrikkeljaar.
learn, leer; verneem, te hore (te wete) kom; – **by heart, rote,** van buite leer.
learned, geleerd.
learner, leerling, beginneling, groene.
learning, geleerdheid, kunde; (die) leer.
lease, n. huur; huurkontrak; huurtyd; (die) verhuur; **put out to –,** verhuur, verpag; **take on –,** huur; **take a new – of life,** weer beter word; nuwe moed skep.
lease, v. huur; verhuur; pag; verpag; – **from,** huur van; – **to,** verhuur aan.
leasehold, huur, pag; verhuurde eiendom.
leaseholder, huurder, pagter.
lease-lend, bruikleen.
leash, n. koppel(riem); drietal (by die jag); **hold in –,** keer, in bedwang hou.
leash, v. vasbind, vaskoppel.
least, adj. minste, geringste, kleinste.
least, n. die minste; **to say the – of it,** om dit maar saggies uit te druk; **at –,** ten minste; **at the –,** op sy minste; **not in the –,** glad nie, hoegenaamd nie, volstrek nie, nie in die minste nie.
leastways, leastwise, ten minste.
leather, n. leer; leerwerk; riem; vel; **–s,** kamaste; rybroek; **give hell for –,** opdons tot by Oom Daantjie in die kalwerhok.
leather, v. met leer oortrek; afransel, uitlooi.
leatherette, kunsleer.
leathering, afranseling, loesing.
leathery, leeragtig, leer-...
leave, n. verlof; **by your –,** met u verlof; **be on –,** met (op) verlof wees, verlof(tyd) hê; – **of absence,** verlof; **take (one's) – (of),** afskeid neem (van).
leave, v. laat; nalaat; agterlaat; laat staan, laat lê, laat bly; verlaat; vertrek; – **alone,** alleen laat; – **behind,** agterlaat; nalaat; verbygaan; – **off,** ophou, uitskei; – **out,** uitlaat; verbygaan; – **over,** laat bly; – **him to himself,** hom laat begaan.
leaven, n. suurdeeg.
leaven, v. insuur; deurtrek.
leavings, oorskot, afval.
lecherous, ontugtig, wellustig.
lectern, koorlessenaar, lessenaartjie.
lecture, n. (voor)lesing; klas, kollege; vermaning, preek; **read somebody a –,** iemand die les lees.
lecture, v. 'n lesing hou; kollege gee, klas hê, die les lees, vermaan; – **on,** 'n lesing hou oor.
lecturer, lektor; spreker.
lecture-room, klaskamer, kollegesaal.
lectureship, lektoraat.
led, sien lead.
ledge, rotslys, (rots)bank; rant; rif; lys.
ledger, grootboek; steierplank; grafsteen.
lee, lykant; **under the – of,** onder beskutting van; – **shore,** kus aan die lykant; – **side,** lykant, lysy.
leech, bloedsuier; arts.
leek, prei; **eat the –,** belediging sluk.
leer, v. lonk; gluur; gryns.
leer, n. (die) lonk; gryns.
leery, geslepe, uitgeslaap.

lees, afsaksel, moer, grondsop; **drink to the –,** tot die bodem toe ledig.
leeward, onder die wind, lywaarts.
leeway, (die) afdrywe (van 'n skip); **make up –,** agterstand inhaal.
left, adj. linker: ... ; links; – **hand,** linkerhand; linkerkant.
left, adv. links, aan (na) die linkerkant.
left, n. linkerhand; linkervuis; linkerhou; **to the –,** links; aan die linkerkant.
left, sien leave.
left-handed, links; onhandig; twyfelagtig; – **compliment,** twyfelagtige kompliment; – **marriage,** morganatiese huwelik.
left-hander, linkerhou; 'n links persoon.
leftist, linksgesinde.
leg, been; poot (van 'n tafel); (broeks)pyp; **bound (vleis); pull one's –,** met iemand die gek skeer; **give one a – up,** hand bysit, help; **shake a –,** dans, skoffel; **take to one's –s,** die rieme neerlê, laat spaander; **on one's (hind) –s,** aan die praat; **be on one's –s,** op eie bene staan; **set one on his –s,** iemand op die been help; **stand on one's own –s,** op eie bene staan; **not have a – to stand on,** geen grond onder jou voete hê nie; **on one's last –s,** op sy laaste bene; **find one's –s,** regkom; **keep one's –s,** op die bene bly.
leg, v.: – **it,** voetslaan, hardloop.
legacy, legaat, nalatenskap, skenking.
legal, wettig, wetlik; regs- ...
legality, wettigheid, legaliteit.
legalization, legalisasie, wettiging.
legalize, wettig, legaliseer.
legate, v. bemaak, legateer.
legatee, legataris, erfgenaam.
legation, gesantskap, legasie.
legend, legende; opskrif, randskrif.
legendary, legendaries.
legerdemain, handigheid, goëlery, foppery.
legging, kamas; beenskut.
leg-guard, beenskut.
leggy, langbenig, langbeen- ...
legible, leesbaar.
legion, legioen; legio; **the number is –,** die getal is legio.
legionary, n. legioensoldaat.
legionary, adj. van 'n legioen, legioen- ...
legislate, wette maak.
legislation, wetgewing.
legislative, wetgewend.
legislator, wetgewer.
legislature, wetgewende mag.
legitimacy, egtheid, wettigheid.
legitimate, adj. eg, wettig; wetlik.
legitimate, v. wettig (eg) verklaar.
legitimation, wettigverklaring, legitimasie.
legitimist, legitimis.
legitimize, sien legitimate.
leg-pull, tergery, spottery.
legume, legumen, peul, peulvrug.
leguminous, peul- ..., peuldraend.
leisure, vry tyd, ledige uurtjies; **at your –,** op jou gemak.
leisured, met baie vry tyd.
lemon, suurlemoen; suurpruim.
lemonade, limonade, soetlimonade.
lemon-squash, kwas, suurlimonade.
lemur, lemur.
lend, leen, uitleen; – **one's ears to,** die oor leen aan; – **a hand,** hand bysit; – **a box on the ear,** 'n oorveeg toedien; – **itself to,** sig leen tot.
lender, lener.
length, lengte; afstand; duur; grootte; **go all –s,** tot die uiterste gaan; **go to great –s,** baie doen;

not go the - of, nie so ver gaan om; **at -,** (uit)eindelik; uitvoerig; **at full -,** uitvoerig; uitgestrek, languit; **at arm's -,** op armslengte; **keep one at arm's -,** iemand op 'n afstand hou.
lengthen, verleng; rek.
lengthening, verlenging.
lengthwise, in die lengte.
lengthy, lang, vervelend, omslagtig.
lenience, leniency, sagtheid, toegewendheid.
lenient, sag, genadig, toegewend.
lenitive, versagtend, pynstillend.
lenity, toegewendheid.
lens, lens.
lent, die vaste, vastyd.
lent, sien **lend.**
lenten, vas- . . . ; **have a - face,** triestig uitsien.
lentil, lensie.
leonine, leeu- . . . , leeuagtig.
leopard, luiperd; **the - cannot change his spots,** 'n jakkals verander van hare maar nooit van streke nie.
leper, melaatse.
leprosy, melaatsheid.
leprous, melaats.
Lesbian, n. Lesbier; Lesbiese vrou.
lesion, beskadiging.
less, adj. minder; kleiner.
less, prep. min; **- three,** min drie.
less, n. minder; **in - than no time,** so gou soos blits, in 'n oogwenk.
less, adv. minder.
lessee, huurder.
lessen, verminder.
lesser, minder.
lesson, les; leesstuk, leesgedeelte.
lessor, verhuurder.
lest, uit vrees dat (op)dat . . . nie.
let, n. net (by tennis).
let, v. laat; toelaat, toestaan; verhuur; **to -,** te huur; **- be,** laat staan; **- go,** (laat) los, laat loop; **- oneself go,** jou gemoed lug, lostrek; **- loose,** losmaak, loslaat; gaande maak; **- alone,** laat staan; **- down,** laat sak; teleurstel, in die steek laat; **- in,** binnelaat; insleep; **- into,** binnelaat; inwy, op die hoogte bring; **- off,** ('n geweer) aftrek, afskiet; vrylaat, laat loop; vrystel; (stoom) afblaas, uitlaat; **- on,** verklap; **- out,** uitlaat, laat uitkom; verklik, verklap; verhuur; lostrek.
let, n. (die) verhuur.
lethal, dodelik; **- chamber,** stikkamer.
lethargic, slaperig, dooierig; letargies.
lethargy, slaapsug, dooierigheid, letargie.
letter, n. letter; brief; **-s,** lettere; **man of -s,** geleerde; **to the -,** letterlik; **-s patent,** oktrooibriewe.
letter, v. letter, van 'n titel voorsien.
letter-balance, briefskaaltjie.
letter-box, briewebus.
letter-case, portefeulje, sakboekie.
lettering, die letters; die titel.
letter-perfect, rolvas.
letterpress, byskrif; kopieerpers; papierdrukker.
letterweight, briefweër; papiergewig.
letter-writer, briefskrywer; brieweboek.
lettuce, (krop)slaai.
Levant, maak dat jy wegkom, trap.
Levantine, Levantyns.
levee, (oggend)resepsie; hereresepsie.
level, b. waterpas, paslood; peil, standaard; vlak; **on a - with,** op gelyke hoogte as, waterpas met; op een lyn met; **on the -,** eerlik waar.
level, adj. horisontaal, waterpas, gelyk; egalig; gelykmatig; **do one's - best,** jou uiterste (bes) doen; **have a - head,** besadig (verstandig) wees;

keep - with, op die hoogte bly van, byhou; **it is a - race,** hulle loop kop aan kop.
level, v. gelykmaak, waterpas maak; nivelleer; mik, korrel vat, aanlê; **- at, against,** aanlê op; munt (doel, mik) op; **- down,** gelykmaak; nivelleer; **- to, with the ground,** met die grond gelykmaak; **- up,** ophoop, gelykmaak.
level-crossing, oorweg; spoor(weg)oorweg.
level-headed, besadig, ewewigtig, verstandig.
lever, n. hefboon; stelarm; ligter.
lever, v. (met 'n ligter) oplig, verskuiwe.
leverage, hefboomkrag; mag, invloed.
leveret, jong hasie.
lever-watch, ankerhorlosie.
leviathan, leviatan.
levigate, fyn maak, fyn druk; glad maak.
levin, blits, weerligstraal.
levitate, swewe, (laat) drywe.
Levite, Leviet.
Leviticus, Levitikus.
levity, ligsinnigheid, wuftheid; ligtheid.
levy, n. (die) opkommandeer, aanwerwing; heffing; ligting.
levy, v. hef, invorder; oproep, aanwerf; afpers; **- war upon,** oorlog voer teen; **- an army,** 'n leër op die been bring.
lewd, ontugtig, wellustig, wulps, onkuis.
lewisite, lewisiet.
lexical, leksikografies.
lexicographer, leksikograaf, woordeboekskrywer.
lexicography, leksikografie.
lexicon, woordeboek, leksikon.
Leyden, Leiden; **- jar,** Leidse fles.
liability, verantwoordelikheid; verpligting; **liabilities,** laste.
liable, verantwoordelik; **hold -,** aanspreeklik hou; **- to,** onderhewig aan; blootgestel aan; **difficulties are - to occur,** moeilikhede kan maklik voorkom; **the child is - to fainting fits,** die kind ly aan floutes.
liaison, liefdesverhouding, liaison; verbinding.
liana, liana, bobbejaantou, slingerplant.
liar, leuenaar.
lias, lias, blou kalksteen.
libation, plengoffer, drankoffer, libasie.
libel, n. laster; smaadskrif, skotskrif.
libel, v. belaster, beklad.
libeller, smaadskrifskrywer, belasteraar.
libellous, lasterlik.
liberal, adj. vrygewig, goedhartig; oorvloedig, vrysinnig; **- education,** breë (veelsydige) opvoeding.
liberal, n. liberaal.
liberalism, liberalisme.
liberality, vrygewigheid; vrysinnigheid.
liberate, bevry, vrylaat, vrymaak.
liberation, bevryding, vrylating.
libertine, vrydenker; losbandige, ligmis.
libertinism, losbandigheid; vrydenkery.
liberty, vryheid; **take liberties,** sig vryhede veroorloof; **at -,** in vryheid, vry; **set at -,** vrylaat, bevry.
libidinous, wellustig, wulps.
libido, libido, wellus; lewensdrif.
librarian, bibliotekaris.
library, biblioteek, boekery; uitgawe.
librettist, librettis.
libretto, operateks, libretto.
Libyan, Libies; Libiër.
lice, sien **louse.**
licence, verlof, vergunning; lisensie; diploma; losbandigheid; (digterlike) vryheid; **driver's -,** rybewys.
licence, verlof gee, 'n lisensie verleen, lisensieer.
licensee, lisensiehouer, gelisensieerde.

licensing court   552   **like**

licensing court, lisensiehof.
licentiate, lisensiaat.
licentious, losbandig, ongebonde; wellustig.
licentiousness, losbandigheid.
lichen, mos.
lick, v. lek; klop, 'n pak gee; – **one's chops (lips),** jou lippe aflek; – **the dust,** in die stof byt; **this –s me,** dit slaan my dronk; – **into shape,** vorm gee, brei, regruk.
lick, n. lek; lekplek; hou (met 'n lat); **at a great –,** **at full –,** in volle vaart.
lickerish, lickerous, versot op lekkergoed; gulsig, wellustig.
lickspittle, kruiper, lekker.
lictor, lictor, byldraer.
lid, deksel; lid.
lie, n. leuen; **act a –,** leuenagtig handel; **live a –,** 'n vals lewe lei; **tell a –,** lieg, 'n leuen vertel; **white –,** noodleuen; **give somebody the –,** iemand van leuentaal beskuldig; **give the – to,** loënstraf.
lie, v. lieg; **he –s like a gas-meter,** hy lieg op 'n streep; – **away,** aanhou met lieg; – **oneself out of,** (sig) loslieg.
lie, v. lê; rus; **let sleeping dogs –,** moenie slapende honde wakker maak nie; **find out how the land –s,** die kat uit die boom kyk; **as far as in me –s,** na my beste vermoë; – **about,** rondlê; – **back,** agteroorlê; – **down,** gaan lê; **take one's punishment lying down,** gedwee jou straf ondergaan; – **low,** wegkruip; jou tyd afwag; – **on,** lê op; – **over,** bly lê; – **under,** onder lê; **it –s with you,** dit berus by jou, dit is jou saak, jy behoort.
lie, n. ligging; die lê; rigting, koers; lêplek; – **of the land,** toestand van sake.
lief, graag; **I would as –...,** ek sou net so lief...
Liège, Luik.
liege, n. leenheer; koning; leenman, vasal.
liege, adj. leenpligtig; – **lord,** leenheer; vors, koning.
liegeman, vasal, leenman.
lien, pandreg, retensiereg.
lieu: in – of, in plaas van.
lieutenancy, luitenantskap.
lieutenant, luitenant.
lieutenant-colonel, luitenant-kolonel.
lieutenant-general, luitenant-generaal.
life, lewe; lewensbeskrywing; lewenswyse; lewende model; **for –,** lewenslank; **for one's –,** **for dear, –,** op lewe en dood, of jou lewe daarvan afhang; **not for the – of me,** om die dood nie; **as large as –,** lewensgroot; **taken from the –,** na die lewe geteken; **uit die lewe gegryp; come to –,** bykom, lewendig word; **the batsman was given a –,** die kolwer het 'n gelukkige ontkoming gehad; **everlasting –,** die ewige lewe; **the future –,** die (lewe) hiernamaals; **at his time of –,** op sy leeftyd; **see –,** die wêreld leer ken; **there was a great sacrifice of –,** daar is baie lewens opgeoffer, baie moes die lewe daarby inskiet; **all my –,** my hele lewe, my lewe lank; **escape with one's –,** met jou lewe daarvan afkom; **safe in – and limb,** ongedeerd; **the – and soul of the movement,** die siel van die beweging; – **sentence,** lewenslange gevangenisstraf.
life-belt, reddingsgordel.
life-blood, lewensbloed, hartebloed.
life-boat, reddingsboot.
life-buoy, reddingsgordel, -boei.
life-guard, lyfwag.
life-giving, lewewekkend, besielend.
life-assurance, lewensversekering.
lifeless, lewe(ns)loos.

life-like, wat sprekend lyk op, asof dit leef.
life-line, reddingstou.
lifelong, lewenslang.
life-preserver, reddingstoestel; mokerstok.
life-time, leeftyd, lewenstyd; **the chance of a –,** 'n kans wat jy nooit weer kry nie.
life-work, lewenstaak.
lift, v. (op)lig, (op)hef, optel; verhef; steel; (aartappels) uithaal; wegtrek (van mis en wolke); – **a hand against,** sy hand ophef teen; – – **up,** oplig, optel, ophef; – **up one's head,** jou kop oplig.
lift, n. (die) oplig, opheffing; ligter, hyser; bultjie; **give somebody a –,** iemand oplaai.
ligament, gewrigsband, ligament.
ligature, n. verband; band; afbinding, onderbinding; verbindingsteken.
ligature, v. afbind.
light, n. lig; lewenslig; vuurhoutjie; **see the –,** die lewenslig aanskou; **bring to –,** aan die lig bring; **come to –,** aan die lig kom; **act according to one's –s,** handel volgens die lig wat jou gegee is; **strike a –,** 'n vuurhoutjie trek.
light, adj. lig, ligkleurig.
light, v. opsteek; aan die brand steek; verlig; vuur vat; – **up,** opsteek.
light, adj. lig; bros, los; ligsinnig; vlug, onstandvastig; **make – of,** van geen belang beskou; – **of foot,** rats, vlug ter been; **he is a – sleeper,** hy slaap (baie) los.
light, adv. lig, los.
light, v. neerkom; – **(up)on,** neerkom op; gaan sit op; op die lyf loop.
lighten, ligter maak; ligter word; verlig; verhelder; weerlig, blits.
lighter, opsteker, aansteker; ligter(skip).
light-fingered, langvingerig.
light-footed, rats, vlug ter been, ligvoetig.
light-headed, lig in die kop; ylhoofdig.
light-hearted, opgewek, vrolik, lughartig.
lighthouse, vuurtoring.
lighting, (die) opsteek; verligting.
lightly, lig, saggies; maklik; ligsinnig.
light-minded, ligsinnig, sonder erns.
lightness, ligheid, gemak; ligsinnigheid.
lightning, weerlig, blits, bliksem; **like –,** soos blits; **with – speed,** bliksemsnel.
lightning-conductor, bliksemafleier.
lights, harslag, longe van diere.
light-weight, liggewig.
ligneous, houtagtig, hout-...
lignite, bruinkool, ligniet.
likable, beminlik, gaaf.
like, adj. soos; gelyk; eenders, dieselfde; **in – manner,** op dieselfde manier; **what is he –?,** hoe lyk hy?; **a man – you,** 'n mens soos jy; **something – R5,** 'n rand of vyf; **nothing – as good,** lank nie so goed nie; **feel – stopping work,** lus hê om op te hou werk; **it is just – him,** dit is net soos hy is; – **father – son,** die appel val nie ver van die boom nie; – **master – man,** soos die baas is, so is die kneg.
like, prep. soos, so; **do not talk – that,** moenie so praat nie; – **a shot,** op die plek; – **blazes,** anything, dat dit gons, dat dit 'n aardigheid is.
like, conj. soos; – **in August,** soos in Augustus.
like, adv.: **very –, – enough,** bes moontlik.
like, n. gelyke, weerga; iets soortgelyks; **the –s of me,** my soort; **and the –,** ensovoorts.
like, v. hou van; graag wil; aanstaan; **I should much – to come,** ek sou baie graag wil kom; **I do not – him,** hy staan my nie aan nie, ek hou nie van hom nie; **if – you,** as jy wil, as jy lus het; **I – that!,** dis 'n mooi grap!; **I – your cheek,** wat verbeel jy jou?; **how do you – it,** kyk hom.

like, n. voorliefde; **his –s and dislikes**, waar hy van hou en nie van hou nie; sy simpatieë en antipatieë.
likelihood, waarskynlikheid; **in all –,** na alle waarskynlikheid.
likely, waarskynlik, vermoedelik; geskik; aanneemlik; **his most – stopping-place,** die plek waar hy mees waarskynlik sal bly.
like-minded, eensgesind, een van sin.
liken, vergelyk.
likeness, gelykenis; gedaante; ewebeeld; portret; **take the – of,** afneem, fotografeer.
likewise, op dieselfde manier, net so; ook, insgelyks.
liking, sin, lus, smaak, voorliefde; geneentheid; **it is not to my –,** dit is nie na my sin nie.
lilac, n. sering(boom).
lilac, adj. lila, ligpers; **sering-** . . .
liliaceous, lelieagtig.
Lilliputian, Lilliputter; dwergie.
lilt, n. vrolike deuntjie (wysie); ritme.
lilt, v. 'n deuntjie (liedjie) sing.
lily, n. lelie; **– of the valley,** dallelie, lelietjie der dale.
lily, adj. lelieagtig, leliewit (lelieblank).
lily-livered, lafhartig, papbroekig.
lily-white, lelieblank.
limb, n. lit; tak; uitloper; deugniet; **– of the devil,** duiwelskind.
limb, v. vermink, uitmekaarskeur.
limber, n. voorstel (van 'n kanonwa).
limber, v. aanhaak.
limber, adj. buigsaam, lenig.
limbo, limbus; gevangenis; vergetelheid.
lime, n. kalk; (voël)lym; **slaked –,** gebluste kalk; **quick –,** ongebluste kalk.
lime, v. lym; met lym vang; kalk, in kalkwater laat lê; met kalk bemes.
lime, n. lemmetjie.
lime, n. lindeboom.
lime-kiln, kalkoond.
limelight, kalklig; **be in the –,** op die voorgrond wees, die aandag trek.
limestone, kalksteen, kalkklip.
limit, n. grens, grenslyn; toppunt, limiet; **this is the –,** dit is die toppunt, nou word dit darem te erg.
limit, v. begrens; bepaal, beperk, vasstel.
limitation, beperking, begrensing.
limited, beperk; **– liability company,** maatskappy met beperkte aanspreeklikheid.
limitless, onbegrens, grens(e)loos.
limn, skilder, teken.
limp, v. mank (kreupel) loop, mank wees; **– back,** terug sukkel (bv. skip).
limp, n.: **have a –,** mank loop.
limp, adj. slap, buigsaam; pap.
limpet, klipmossel; **stick like a –,** soos klitsgras vasklou.
limpid, helder, deurskynend.
limpidity, helderheid, klaarheid.
limy, kalkagtig, kalk- . . . ; lymerig, lym- . . .
linarias, weeskindertjies.
linchpin, luns, steker.
linden, lindeboom.
line, n. tou, lyn; streep, ry; reël; reeks; rigting, koers; ewenaar, linie; spoor; vak; besigheid; briefie, reëltjie; stoomvaartlyn; soort; gelid; **that is hard –s,** dit is jammer; **come into –,** inval, saamwerk; **all along the –,** langs die hele linie; **op alle punte;** dwarsdeur; **read between the –s,** tussen die reëls lees; **an essay of 50 –s,** 'n opstel van 50 reëls; **just a –,** net 'n reëltjie; **– of action,** gedragslyn; **– of communication,** verbindingsweg, kommunikasieweg;

that is not in my –, dit lê nie in my lyn nie; **keep to one's own –,** jou eie koers volg; **there I draw the –,** daar trek ek die grens; **a shop in the general –,** 'n winkel waar alles te koop is; **along these –s,** in hierdie rigting; op hierdie grondslag; **take a –,** 'n rigting inslaan, van mening wees; **in a – with,** op een lyn met; **stand in –,** in 'n ry staan, toustaan.
line, v. lyne (strepe) trek; linieer; afset; in gelid staan; in gelid stel; groef, rimpel; **– through,** deurhaal, 'n streep trek deur; **– up,** in gelid staan; in gelid stel; **a –d face,** 'n gerimpelde gesig, 'n gesig met vore deurploeg.
line, v. voer, uitvoer; vul, volprop.
lineage, afkoms, geslag, geslagsboom.
lineal, direk lynreg; **lyn-** . . . ; **– descendant,** direkte afstammeling.
lineament, trek, gelaatstrek.
linear, lengte- . . . , **lyn-** . . . , lineêr.
lineation, liniëring.
linen, linne; linnegoed.
linen-draper, linnehandelaar.
linen-press, linnekas.
liner, lynboot, lynskip; lynvliegtuig; linieskip (mil.); linievliegtuig.
linesman, liniesoldaat; grensregter.
linger, talm, toef; aarsel; kwyn, sukkel; **– on,** kwyn, aansukkel; **– over, (up)on a subject,** lank by 'n onderwerp stilstaan.
lingerer, draler, talmer, drentelkous.
lingerie, linnegoed, onderklere.
lingering, adj. draaierig, dralend; sukkelend; slepend; **a – disease,** 'n slepende siekte.
lingo, vreemde taal; koeterwaals, taaltjie.
lingual, tong- . . . ; taal- . . .
linguist, taalkenner; taalkundige.
linguistic, taalkundig, taal- . . . , linguisties.
linguistics, taalwetenskap, linguistiek.
liniment, smeergoed, smeersel.
lining, voering, bekleding.
link, n. skakel; **–s,** mouskakels, mansjetknope.
link, n. toorts, fakkel.
link, v. aaneenskakel, aanmekaarskakel, verbind; **– your arm in (through) another's,** by iemand inhaak; **– on,** aanhaak; aansluit (by); **– together,** verbind, aaneensluit, aanmekaarhaak.
links, gholfbaan.
linnet, vlasvink.
linoleum, linoleum.
linotype, setmasjien, linotipe.
linseed, lynsaad.
linseed-oil, lynolie.
linstock, lontstok.
lint, pluksel, verbandlinne.
lintel, latei.
lion, leeu; ('n) beroemdheid; **–'s share,** leeuedeel.
lioness, leeuwyfie; beroemde vrou.
lion-hearted, heldhaftig, met leeuemoed.
lion-hunter, leeujagter; iemand wat jag maak op beroemdhede.
lionize, soos 'n beroemdheid behandel, verafgood, ophemel.
lip, lip; astrantheid; rand; **bite one's –,** op jou lippe byt; **hang on one's –s,** aan iemand se lippe hang; **hang one's –,** die kop laat hang; **keep a stiff upper –,** moed hou; koppig bly; **none of your –!,** moenie vir jou astrant hou nie! **curl one's –,** die lippe optrek.
lip-homage, lippediens.
lipless, liploos, sonder lippe.
lipped, lipvormig, gelip, . . . -lippig.
lip-salve, lipsalf; vleiery.
lip-service, lippediens.

liquefaction, smelting.
liquefy, smelt.
liquescent, smeltend, maklik smeltbaar.
liqueur, likeur, soetsopie.
liquid, adj. vloeibaar; vloeiend; helder, deurskynend; onvas, veranderlik; likwied.
liquid, n. vloeistof.
liquidate, likwideer, vereffen; afwikkel; vernietig, uitwis.
liquidation, vereffening, likwidasie.
liquidator, likwidateur.
liquidity, vloeibaarheid.
liquor, vog; (sterk) drank; **in** –, **the worse for** –, onder die invloed van drank.
liquorice, licorice, drop, soethout.
liquorish, versot op drank.
lira, lira.
lisp, v. lispel, sleeptong praat.
lisp, n. gelispel.
lissom(e), lenig, slap, rats, vlug.
list, n. lys, rol; selfkant, band; **enter the** –**s**, in die strydperk tree; **wine** –, wynkaart.
list, v. 'n lys maak van, katalogiseer.
list, v. graag, wil.
list, n. oorhelling.
list, v. oorhel, oorhang, skuins hang.
listen, luister; – **in**, inluister.
listener, luisteraar,
listener-in, inluisteraar.
listless, lusteloos, dooierig, hangerig.
listlessness, lusteloosheid, dooierigheid.
lit, sien **light**.
litany, litanie.
literacy, lees-en-skryf-kennis.
literal, letterlik.
literalism, gebondenheid aan die letter, letterknegtery.
literalist, letterkneg.
literally, letterlik.
literary, letterkundig, literêr; geletterd.
literate, geletterd.
literati, geleerdes, geletterdes.
literature, letterkunde, literatuur, lettere.
lithe(some), buigsaam, lenig, slap.
lithium, litium.
lithograph, n. steendruk(plaat), litografie.
lithograph, v. litografeer.
lithographer, steendrukker, litograaf.
lithographic, steendrukkers- . . . , litografies.
lithography, steendrukkuns, litografie.
lithotomy, steensnyding, litotomie.
Lithuanian, Litaus; Litauer.
litigant, n. prosedeerder.
litigant, adj. prosederend.
litigate, prosedeer, 'n saak maak.
litigation, process, regsgeding, saak.
litigious, proses- . . . ; prosedeersugtig; betwisbaar.
litmus, lakmoes.
litotes, litotes.
litre, liter.
litter, n. draagbaar; ruigte, kooigoed; afval; rommel; werpsel, jongsel, kleintjies.
litter, v. kooi maak; deurmekaarmaak, 'n warboel maak van; rondgestrooi lê, oorhoop lê; jong, kleintjies kry; **the floor was** –**ed with papers**, die vloer was besaai met papiere.
little, adj. klein; weinig; kleinsielig, **the** – **ones**, die kleintjies; **wait a** – **(while)**, wag 'n bietjie; **a** – **way**, 'n (klein) entjie; **a** – **sugar**, 'n bietjie suiker; – **finger**, pinkie; – **man**, mannetjie, kêreltjie; **every** – **difficulty**, elke ou moeilikheidjie.
little, n. weinig, min; **a** –, 'n bietjie; **for a** –, 'n rukkie, 'n tydjie; – **by** –, langsamerhand,

by bietjies, trapsgewyse; **not a** –, nie min nie, nie 'n bietjie nie; **make a** – **go a long way**, ver kom met 'n klein bietjie.
little, adv. weinig; – –**known authors**, weinig bekende skrywers; **he** – **knows that**, weinig weet hy dat . . .
littleness, kleinheid, kleinte; kleinsieligheid.
littoral, adj. kus- . . . , langs die kus.
littoral, n. kusstrook, kusstreep.
liturgical, liturgies.
liturgy, liturgie, kerkgebruik.
livable, bewoonbaar, gesellig; die moeite werd (om te lewe).
live, adj. lewendig, lewend; gloeiend (van kole); onontplof; gelaai; onder stroom; **a real** – **burglar**, 'n inbreker in lewende lywe; **a** – **issue**, 'n brandende (aktuele) kwessie; **she is a real** – **wire**, sy is 'n wakker entjie mens, sy het gees genoeg, sy is 'n deurdrywer; – **broadcast**, direkte uitsending.
live, v. leef (lewe), bestaan, voortleef; woon; **and let** –, lewe en laat lewe; **where do you** –?, waar woon jy?; – **a blameless life**, onberispelik leef; – **and learn**, 'n mens word nooit te oud om iets te leer nie; – **by**, lewe van; – **down**, te bowe kom, oorkom; – **in**, woon in; inwoon; bewoon; – **on**, lewe van; voortlewe, aan die lewe bly; – **on air**, van die wind lewe; – **on one's reputation**, op jou roem teer; – **out**, buite woon; – **out the night**, deur die nag lewe; – **through**, deurlewe, deurmaak; – **to see it**, dit belewe; – **up to**, gestand doen, naleef; – **upon**, lewe van; lewe (op koste) van; – **with**, saamwoon met, (in)woon by; lewe met.
livelihood, broodwinning, bestaan.
liveliness, lewendigheid.
livelong, heel; **the** – **day**, die hele liewe dag.
lively, lewendig, vrolik, opgewek; **make it** – **for**, die wêreld moeilik maak vir, iemand laat hotagter kry.
liven, – **up**, opvrolik, opbeur.
liver, lewende; **a good** –, 'n deugsame persoon; **a fast** –, 'n losbol.
liver, lewer; white, lily –, lafhartigheid.
liveried, in livreidrag; – **servant**, livreibediende.
liverish, lewersugtig, deur die lewer gepla.
liverwort, lewerkruid.
livery, livrei; mondering.
livery-company, gilde.
livery-servant, livreikneg, levreibediende.
livery-stable, huurstal.
live-stock, lewende hawe, vee.
livid, blou, loodkleurig, doodsbleek.
lividity, doodsbleekheid, lykkleur.
living, adj. lewendig; lewend; **no man** –, geen lewende wese; **a** – **wage**, bestaanbare loon; **be** –, in lewe wees, nog lewe; **within** – **memory**, binne mensheugenis.
living, n. lewensonderhoud, broodwinning, bestaan; lewenswyse, lewe; standplaas (van 'n predikant); **make one's** –, 'n bestaan vind; **the land of the** –, die land der lewende.
living-room, woonkamer.
lixiviate, uitloog, was.
lizard, akkedis.
llama, lama.
lo, kyk!
load, n. vrag; las (masj.); gewig; pak.
load, v. laai, oplaai; bevrag; oorlaai; vervals; (met lood) swaarder maak, lood aansit; –**ed dice**, vals dobbelstene; –**ed with**, oorlaai met, oorstelp met.
load-line, laslyn.
loadstar, sien **lode**.
loadstone, magneetsteen, seilsteen.

loaf, n. brood; half a – is better than no bread, beter 'n halwe eier as 'n leë dop.
loaf, v. leegloop, rondslenter; jou lyf wegsteek; bedel, skooi.
loaf, n. (die) leegloop; on the –, aan die rondslenter.
loafer, leegloper, klaploper; skooier.
loaf-sugar, broodsuiker, klontjiesuiker.
loam, leem, teelaarde, klei.
loamy, kleierig; – soil, teelaarde, leem.
loan, n. lening; die geleende (geld); I want a – of R5, ek wil R5 leen; on –, te leen; (uit)geleen.
loan, v. uitleen.
loaner, uitlener.
lo(a)th, ongeneë, onwillig.
loathe, verafsku, verfoei, walg van.
loathing, weersin, walging, verafskuwing.
loathsome, weersinwekkend, walglik, afskuwelik, verfoeilik.
lob, v. 'n lugskoot slaan; voortsukkel.
lob, n. lugskoot, lugbal; lummel.
lobate, lobbig, gelob.
lobby, n. (voor)portaal, voorsaal; wandelgang (van parlementsgebou).
lobby, v. in die wandelgange boer.
lobbyist, wandelgangpolitikus.
lobe, lob; (oor)lel.
lobed, sien lobate.
lobelia, lobelia.
lobster, kreef; rooibaadjie.
lobular, lobvormig, gelob.
local, adj. plaaslik; lokaal; – colour, lokale kleur; – option, plaaslike keuse.
local, n. inwoner; –s, plaaslike eksamens.
locale, plaas (van handeling).
localism, gehegtheid aan 'n plek; bekrompenheid; plaaslike gebruik.
locality, plek; ligging, terrein; plaasgeheue, oriëntasievermoë.
localization, lokalisasie, beperking, binne sekere grense.
localize, lokaliseer, tot een plek beperk; desentraliseer.
locate, die plek aanwys; lokaliseer.
location, plekbepaling; lokasie; opsporing; plek, ligging; on –, op die verfilmingsterrein wees.
locative, n. lokatief.
locative, adj. plekaanduidend, lokatief.
loch, meer.
lock, n. (haar)lok, krul; –s, lokke, krulle.
lock, n. slot, klem (ook van 'n geweer); (kanaal)sluis; gedrang; under –, agter slot en grendel; –, stock and barrel, in sy geheel, die hele boel; romp en stomp.
lock, v. sluit, toesluit, opsluit, insluit, omsluit; mekaar vasgryp; – away, wegsluit; – in, opsluit, toesluit, insluit; – out, uitsluit, buite sluit; – up, opsluit; wegsluit; – the stable door after the horse has been stolen, die put demp nadat die kalf verdrink het; sell – stock and barrel, romp en stomp verkoop.
lockage, sluiswerk; sluisgeld, skutgeld.
lock-chain, sluitketting.
locker, toesluiter; kassie, laai, kis; not have a shot in the –, platsak wees.
locket, medaljon, hangertjie.
lock-jaw, klem (in die kake).
locksmith, slotmaker.
lock-up, sluitingstyd; opsluitplek.
locomotion, beweging, voortbewegingsvermoë; vervoer.
locomotive, adj. bewegings- . . . , voortbewegend;

– engine, lokomotief; – organs, bewegingsorgane.
locomotive, n. lokomotief.
locomotor, bewegings- . . . , lokomotories; – ataxy, verlamming van die bewegingsorgane, ataxie (ataksie).
locomotory, bewegings- . . .
locum tenens, plaasvervanger, locum tenens.
locus, meetkundige plek, lokus.
locust, sprinkaan.
locust-bird, sprinkaanvoël.
locution, spreekwyse, uitdrukking, lokusie.
lode, watervoor, sugsloot; metaalaar.
lodestar, **loadstar**, poolster, noordster.
lodestone, sien **loadstone**.
lodge, n. huisie; tuinierswoning, portiershuis; (vrymesselaars)losie; skuilplek.
lodge, v. huisves, losies verskaf, herberg; (klag) indien; deponeer; laat (bly); vassit, bly steek; a bullet –d in his brain, 'n koeël het in sy harsings bly sit; – in, huisves, herberg, vassit; laat (bly); – in the hands of somebody, in iemand se hande laat; – with, inlewer by; laat bly; inwoon by.
lodger, loseerder, kosganger.
lodging, huisvesting; woonplek, losies; indiening, inlewering; –s, huurkamers; board and –, kos en inwoning.
lodging-house, huurkamerhuis.
lodg(e)ment, skans; vaste voet; deposito; op(een)hoping; huisvesting; make, effect a –, vaste voet kry.
loft, solder; galery; duiwehok.
loftiness, hoogte; trotsheid, hoogmoed.
lofty, hoog; trots, hoogmoedig.
log, n. blok; log (van skip); logboek; spanstand, puntelys; log(aritme).
log, v. blokke kap; in die logboek aanteken; die opgetekende afstand aflê; beboet.
logarithm, logaritme.
log-book, logboek, skeepsjoernaal; dagboek; logaritmetafel.
log-cabin, blokhuis.
loggerhead, botterkop, dwaas, domkop; be at –s, haaks (knaks) wees, oorhoop lê.
loggia, loggia.
logic, logika, redeneerkuns.
logical, logies.
logicality, die logiese.
logician, logikus.
logistics, logistiek.
log-line, loglyn.
logomachy, woordetwis, woordestryd.
Logos, Logos, Die Woord.
log-rolling, wedersydse ophemeling.
logwood, campêche-hout; rooihoutjies.
loin, lendestuk; –s, lendene; gird up one's –s, die lendene omgord.
loin-cloth, lendekleed.
loiter, draal, draai, talm; slenter; – away one's time, jou tyd verbeusel.
loiterer, draler, talmer, treuselaar.
loitering, adj. dralend, talmend, slenterend.
loitering, n. (die) rondslente::; gedraai, gedraal.
loll, (uit)hang; laat (uit)hang; rondhang, lummel.
lollipop, suikerpoppie.
lollop, (rond)slof, (rond)slinger.
London, Londen.
Londoner, Londenaar.
lone, eensaam, verlate.
loneliness, eensaamheid, verlatenheid.
lonely, eensaam; verlate.
lonesome, sien **lonely**.
long, adj. lang; langdurig; (lang)gerek; – jump, verspring; take – views, (ver) in die

toekoms kyk, versiende wees; **the vacation is two months –,** die vakansie duur twee maande; he has a – arm, sy mag reik ver; **make a – arm,** probeer bykom; – **price,** hoë prys; – **custom,** ou gebruik; – **memory,** goeie geheue; **two – miles,** twee myl en nog 'n entjie; **he has a – head,** hy is uitgeslaap.

long, n. lang tyd; **before –,** een van die dae; **it will not take –,** dit sal nie lank duur nie; **not for –,** nie lank nie; **the – and the short of it is,** die saak kom hierop neer; om kort te gaan.

long, adv. lang; **I have – thought so,** ek het dit lankal gedink; **not be –,** nie lank wegbly nie; **not be – for this world,** dit nie lank meer maak nie; **all day –,** die hele dag, dwarsdeur die dag; **so –!,** tot siens!

long, v. verlang.
long-boat, sloep.
long-bow, boog; **draw the –,** spekskiet.
long-clothes, langklere, babaklere.
long-distance: – call, hooflynoproep; – **race,** afstandsloop, -rit; – **weather forecast,** weervoorspelling 'n paar dae vooruit.
long-drawn(-out), uitgerek, langgerek.
long-eared, langoor- . . . , met lang ore.
longer, langer.
longest, langste; **at –,** op sy langste.
longevity, hoë ouderdom, lang lewe.
longhand, gewone skrif.
long-headed, uitgeslape, oulik.
longing, adj. verlangend, hunkerend.
longing, n. verlange, hunkering, begeerte.
longish, langerig, taamlik lank.
longitude, geografiese lengte.
longitudinal, lengte- . . . , langs- . . . , sy- . . . , in die lengte; longitudinaal.
long-legged, langbeen .. , langbenig.
long-lived, langdurig, langlewend.
longshanks, langbeen, kiewietjie-langbeen.
long-shore, kus- . . . , langs die kus.
long-shoreman, dokwerker.
long-sighted, versiende.
long-standing, ou, van ou datum.
long-suffering, n. lankmoedigheid.
long-suffering, adj. lankmoedig.
long-winded, langasem- . . . ; omslagtig, langdradig, vervelend.
long-windedness, langdradigheid.
longways, longwise, in die lengte.
looby, (gom)tor, lummel.
look, v. kyk, sien; lyk; daar uitsien; deur jou gelaatsuitdrukking (blik) te kenne gee; – **before you leap,** besin eer jy begin; – **sharp,** gou maak; – **a fool,** soos 'n dwaas lyk, 'n gek figuur slaan; – **daggers,** lyk of jy kan moor; – **alive!,** maak gou!, vortmaak!; – **one's age,** so oud lyk soos jy is; – **like,** lyk na; – **about,** rondkyk, jou oë goed oophou; – **after,** kyk na, oppas; – **after the interests,** die belange behartig; – **ahead,** vooruitkyk; – **at,** kyk na, bekyk; beskou; – **back,** terugkyk, omkyk; – **back upon,** terugkyk op; – **behind,** omkyk; – **down,** afkyk; – **down upon,** neersien op; neerkyk op; – **for,** sock (na); verwag, uitsien na; – **forward to,** (verlangend) uitsien na; – **in,** inkyk; aanloop; – **into,** kyk in; ondersoek; – **on,** aankyk; beskou as; – **on with distrust,** wantrou; – **out,** uitkyk; uitsien; op die uitkyk staan; oppas; – **out for,** uitkyk na, verwag; – **out on,** uitsien op; – **over,** oorkyk, opneem; nasien; – **round,** omkyk; kyk hoe sake staan; – **through,** deurkyk; deursien; – **to,** oppas (sorg) vir; reken (staatmaak) op; verwag; die oë gevestig hou op; – **to it that,** sorg dat; – **to your manners,** dink aan jou gedrag; – **towards,** kyk na; uitsien op; – **up,** opkyk; opsien; opsoek, naslaan; besoek. opsoek; styg (van pryse); – **one up and down,** iemand van kop tot tone bekyk; – **up to,** opsien tot, vereer; – **upon,** neersien op, beskou as.

look, n. blik; gesig, gelaat; uitdrukking; voorkome; **good –s,** mooi (knap) uiterlik; **I don't like the – of him,** hy (sy gesig) geval my nie; **may I have a – at it?,** mag ek dit sien?
looker-on, toeskouer, omstander.
look-in, kans.
looking-glass, spieël; spieëlglas.
look-out, uitkyk; wag; uitsig; **keep a good –,** fyn oplet; **on the –,** op die uitkyk; **it's a bad – for him,** dit lyk nie mooi vir hom nie; **that is his –,** dit is sy saak.
loom, n. weef(ge)tou.
loom, v. opdoem, opskemer; – **large,** dreig, dreigend vertoon.
loon, deugniet, vreksel; kêreltjie.
loon, (see)duiker.
loony, luny, adj. mal(lerig), getik.
loony, luny, n. malle, mal mens.
loop, n. oog, lissie; hingsel; bog; – **the –,** bolmakiesie (in die lug) slaan.
loop, v. 'n oog (hingsel) maak, met 'n oog (lissie) vasmaak.
loop-hole, kykgat, skietgat; uitweg.
loose, adj. los; slap; ruim, wyd; loslywig; los(sinnig); **get –,** losraak; **at a – end,** met niks te doen nie; – **fish,** losbol.
loose, n.: **on the –,** aan die swier; **in the –,** in die losspel.
loose, v. losmaak, loslaat; aftrek, afskiet.
loose, n. uitdrukking; **give a – to one's feelings,** jou gemoed lug gee.
loosen, losmaak; los word; laat skiet.
looseness, losheid, slapheid; losbandigheid.
loosely, lossies.
loot, n. roof, buit.
loot, v. plunder, roof, buitmaak.
looter, buiter, rower, plunderaar.
lop, n. snoeihout, snoeitakke.
lop, v. afkap; snoei; **away,** wegkap, wegsnoei; – **at,** kap na.
lop, v. slap hang; laat hang; talm.
lop, v. klots (van water).
lop, n. geklots.
lope, v. lang hale gee, draf.
lope, n. lang spring (haal).
lop-ear, hangoorkonyn; –s, hangore.
lop-eared, hangoor- . . . , met hangore.
loppings, snoeihout, afgesaagde takkies.
lop-sided, (wind)skeef; onewewigtig.
loquacious, babbelsiek, praatlustig.
loquacity, babbelsug, spraaksaamheid.
loquat, lukwart; lukwartboom.
lord, n. heer, meester; lord; **the Lord,** die Heer (Here); **Lord!,** goeie genugtig! hemel!; **the Lord's Prayer,** die Onse-Vader; **the Lord's Supper,** Nagmaal, (die laaste) Avondmaal; **Lord have mercy, Lord bless me (us, my soul, you),** goeie genugtig!, goeie hemel!, liewe Vader!; – **and master,** heer en meester; **like a –,** soos wie, soos 'n groot meneer; **swear like a –,** vloek soos 'n matroos; **drunk as a –,** smoordronk; **my –,** edelagbare; **Lord Mayor,** burgemeester (van Londen en ander groot stede); **L– Lieutenant,** onderkoning; kommissaris.
lord, v. baasspeel; tot lord verhef; – **it over,** baasspeel oor.
lordling, lordjie, meneertjie.
lordly, heerssugtig, baasspelerig; vernaam, hoog, soos van 'n lord.

lordship 557 **lubricious**

lordship, heerskappy, mag; lordbesitting; lordskap; **his –,** sy lordskap.
lore, leer, kennis.
lorgnette, handbril; toneelkyker; lornjet.
lorn, eensaam, verlate.
lorry, vragmotor, lorrie.
lory, loerie.
lose, verloor; verlies(e) ly; kwyt raak; verbeur; laat verloor; agterloop (van horlosie); – **ground,** grond verloor; **be lost,** weg wees, verlore gaan; verdwaal wees; **the ship was lost,** die skip het vergaan; **the motion was lost,** die voorstel is verwerp; **be lost to a sense of shame,** geen skaamtegevoel meer hê nie; – **one's way,** verdwaal; – **the thread,** van die punt afraak, afdwaal; – **the train,** die trein mis, **that is lost upon him,** dit is bokant sy vuurmaakplek; – **oneself,** verdwaal; **lost in thought,** in gedagte verdiep, ingedagte.
loser, verloorder (verlieser); **be a –,** aan die verloorkant wees.
losing, adj. verloor-...., verliesend, wat verloor; hopeloos; – **side,** verloorkant; **play a – game,** geen kans hê om te wen nie; **he cannot play a,– game,** hy kan nie teen iemand verloor nie.
loss verlies, skade; **be at a –,** verleë sit; **never beat a – for,** nooit verleë wees om.
lost, sien **lose.**
lot, n. lot; (aan)deel; stuk grond, erf; klomp(ie), bossie, hoop (hopie), hoeveelheid, boel; belasting; **draw, cast –s,** lootjies trek, loot; **throw, cast in one's –,** jou lot inwerp met; **by –,** deur die lot; **no part nor –,** geen aandeel; **the – falls upon me,** die loot val op my; **it falls to my –,** dit is my lot; **the whole –,** die hele klomp; **–(s) of,** baie, hope, soos bossies; **a bad –,** 'n groot bog, 'n gemene vent; **two –s of potatoes,** twee hopies aartappels; **two –s of carrots,** twee bossies wortels.
lot, v.: – **out,** verdeel.
loth, sien **loath.**
lotion, wasmiddel, water, lawaaiwater.
lottery, lotery.
lottery ticket, loterykaartjie.
lotto, lotto(spel).
lotus, lotusblom; lotusstruik.
lotus-eater, lotuseter, gemaksugtige dromer.
lotus-eating, adj. gemaksugtig
loud, adj. luid, hard; luidrugtig, lawaaierig; – **colours,** opsigtige (skreeuende) kleure.
loud, adv. luid, hardop; **talk –,** hard praat.
louden, luider word.
loudness, luidrugtigheid; opsigtigheid; krag van stem (geluid).
lough, meer.
lounge, v. slenter, rondlê, drentel; rondhang; – **away one's time,** jou tyd verbeusel.
lounge, n. (die) slenter; lê-stoel; voorvertrek; geselskamer.
lounger, slenteraar, rondlêer.
lounge-suit, draagpak.
lour, lower, v. dreig; dreigend aankyk, frons.
lour, lower, n. dreigende blik (weer).
louse, luis.
lousy, vol luise, luisig; veragtelik.
lout, (gom)tor, boekkwagga, plaasjapie.
loutish, torrerig, takhaaragtig.
lovable, lief, beminlik.
love, n. liefde; min; liefling, skat, geliefde, beminde; nul (in tennis); **give my – to, sê groetnis vir; send one's –,** groetnis laat weet; **for the – of God,** om Godswil; **cannot get it for – or money,** kan dit nie vir geld of goeie woorde kry nie; **there is no – lost between them,** hulle kom nie goed met mekaar oor die weg nie; **play for –,** nie vir geld speel nie; **for – of the game,** uit liefde vir die spel; **in – (with),** verlief (op); **fall in –,** verlief raak; **make –,** vry, die hof maak; – **thirty,** nul, dertig; – **all,** nul, nul (in tennis); – **game,** strooppot.
love, v. liefhê, bemin, baie hou van, graag wil (hê); **Lord – you!,** goeie genugtig!, goeie (liewe) hemel!, allemastig!; **I should – to come,** ek sou baie graag wil kom; **children – to ape their elders,** kinders aap graag grootmense na; **he –s tennis,** hy speel baie graag tennis.
love-affair, liefdesgeskiedenis, -avontuur.
love-bird, dwergpapegaai; **–s,** verliefde paar.
love-child, onegte kind.
love-in-a-mist, duiwel-in-die-bos.
love-knot, liefdesknoop.
loveless, onbemin, liefdeloos.
love-letter, vrybrief, minnebrief.
love-lies-bleeding, rooi katstert.
loveliness, lieflikheid; heerlikheid.
love-lorn, smoorverlief; in die steek gelaat.
lovely, lieflik, heerlik; kostelik.
love-making, vryery, vry, hofmakery.
love-match, huwelik uit liefde.
love-philtre, love-potion, minnedrank.
lover, kêrel, vryer; liefhebber; minnaar; bewonderaar; **–s,** verliefde paar.
love-sick, smoorverlief.
love-song, minnelied.
love-story, liefdesgeskiedenis.
loving, liefhebbend; liefdevol, liefderyk; **in – memory,** in liefdevolle herinnering.
low, adj. laag; plat; sag; swak; nederig, gering; klein, min; gemeen; **in – spirits,** mismoedig, terneerdruk; – **tide,** laagwater; **run –,** op; raak, min word; **lay –,** omvergooi, platloop; **lie –,** uitgestrek lê; doodstil bly.
low, adv. laag, sag; **talk –,** saggies praat; – **down,** gemeen.
low, v. bulk, loei.
low-born, van lae afkoms.
low-bred, van lae afkoms; onopgevoed.
low-brow, filistyn; filistyns (adj.).
low-down, karig, skraal.
lower, adj. laer, swakker; nederiger, geringer; minder; benede-... ; – **deck,** benededek.
lower, v. neerhaal, stryk, laat sak; verlaag; daal, sak (van prys); verswak; verneder, verlaag; – **the voice,** sagter praat.
lower, sien **lour.**
lowermost, laagste.
low-grade, van lae gehalte.
lowing, (ge)bulk, geloei.
lowland, adj. laag, laevelds.
lowland, laagland, laeveld.
lowliness, nederigheid, geringheid.
lowly, gering, eenvoudig, nederig, beskeie.
low-minded, gemeen, laag.
lowness, laagheid, geringheid; swakheid.
low-spirited, terneergedruk, neerslagtig.
loyal, lojaal, getrou.
loyalist, lojalis, getroue aanhanger.
loyalty, lojaliteit, getrouheid.
lozenge, ruit; tablet(jie).
lubber, lomperd, tor.
lubricant, n. smeerolie, ghries.
lubricant, adj. gladmakend, smerend.
lubricate, olie, smeer, gladmaak; **lubricating-oil,** smeerolie.
lubrication, (die) olie, smering.
lubricator, smeermiddel; ghriespot(jie), oliekannetjie.
lubricity, glipperigheid, wellustigheid.
lubricious, lubricous, glyerig, glad; wellustig.

lucern(e) 558 **Lysol**

lucern(e), lusern.
lucid, helder, duidelik; blink(end).
lucidity, helderheid; blinkheid.
lucifer, (match), vuurhoutjie.
luck, geluk, toeval; **as — would have it,** soos die toeval dit wou hê; **be down on one's –,** in die verknorsing wees; **worse –,** ongelukkig; **try one's –,** dit waag (probeer); **be in –,** geluk hê; **good –!,** alle voorspoed!, alle sukses!; **bad –!,** dis jammer!, dis ongelukkig!; **just my –,** so gaan dit maar met my!
luckily, gelukkig; — **for me,** gelukkig.
luckiness, geluk.
luckless, ongelukkig.
lucky, gelukkig; — **hit, shot,** gelukskoot.
lucrative, winsgewend, voordelig.
lucre, wins, voordeel; **filthy –,** aardse slyk.
lucubrate, snags werk (swoeg).
lucubration, nagtelike studie (oorpeinsinge), nagwerk.
ludicrous, belaglik, lagwekkend, dwaas.
ludo, ludo.
luff, loef; die loef afsteek.
lug, v. sleep, trek; — **along,** piekel; — **at,** trek aan; — **in(to),** intrek, bysleep.
lug, n. ruk, pluk; loggerseil.
luggage, bagasie, passasiersgoed.
luggage-carrier, bagasiedraer, -rak.
luggage-office, bagasiekantoor.
luggage-ticket, bagasiekaartjie.
luggage-van, goederewa.
lugubrious, treurig, somber, luguber.
lukewarm, lou.
lull, v. sus; kalmeer, paai; bedaar.
lull, n. stilte, rus, verposing.
lullaby, wiegelied.
lumbago, lendepyn, spit (in die rug).
lumbar, lende- . . . , van die lende.
lumber, v. rammel, dreun; dreunstap.
lumber, n. rommel, prulle; timmerhout.
lumber, v. opstapel; vol stop; een kant gooi; (hout) kap.
lumberjack, boswerker.
lumber-jacket, bosbaadjie, windskerm.
lumberman, houtkapper.
lumber-room, rommelkamer, pakkamer.
luminary, lig, voorligter.
luminosity, helderheid, ligsterkte.
luminous, liggewend, skitterend, stralend, lumineus; ophelderend.
lump, n. stuk, klont; klomp, hoop; knop, bult; lummel, jandooi; — **in the throat,** knop in die keel; **in the –,** deur die bank.
lump, v. openhoop; bymekaargooi; hope (klompe) maak; — **down,** neerplak, neerplof; — **together, under,** saamgooi; oor een kam skeer.
lump, v. ontevrede wees oor; **if you don't like it, you may — it,** as jy dit nie wil hê nie, kan jy dit laat bly.
lumping, groot; volop.
lumpish, swaar, lomp; onnosel, dooierig.
lump-sugar, klontjiesuiker.
lumpy, bulterig; klonterig, onstuimig.
lunacy, kranksinnigheid.
lunar, maan(s) . . . , van die maan; — **eclipse,** maansverduistering.
lunarian, maanbewoner, maankenner.
lunate, halwemaanvormig.
lunatic, adj. kranksinnig, mal.
lunatic, n. kranksinnige, mal mens.
lunation, maansomloop.
lunch, n. middag ete, noenmaal.

lunch, middag eet; middagete verskaf.
lunette, lunet; brilskans.
lung, long.
lunge, longe, n. lonsriem.
lunge, longe, v. (laat) lons.
lunge, n. uitval; stoot, steek; sprong.
lunge, v. stoot, steek; (weg)spring; slaan; skop.
luny, sien **loony.**
lupin(e), wolfsboontjie, lupine.
lupine, wolfagtig, wolf- . . .
lupus, lupus.
lupous, lupusagtig, lupus- . . .
lurch, n.: **leave in the –,** in die steek laat.
lurch, n. steiering.
lurch, v. slinger, steier, eenkant toe rol.
lure, v. (aan)lok, weglok, wegrokkel; — **away,** weglok; — **on,** aanlok, verlok.
lure, n. lokaas, verlokking.
lurid, somber, aaklig, luguber; bruingeel.
lurk, v. skuil, op die loer lê.
lurk, n.: **on the –,** op die loer.
lurking-place, skuilplek.
luscious, suikersoet, lekker; oorlaai.
lush, adj. sappig, mals.
lush, n. lawaaiwater, tiermelk.
lush, v. dronk voer; suip.
lust, n. wellus, sinlike lus, begeerte; sug; — **of war,** oorlogsug.
lust, v. haak, snak (na).
lustful, wellustig, onkuis.
lustily, kragtig, flink, lewendig, fors.
lustiness, krag, flinkheid, opgewektheid.
lustration, reiniging, suiwering.
lustre, glans, skittering; luister, roem; lugter, kroonkandelaar, luster; lustre(stof); lustrum; **add — to,** luister bysit.
lustrine, glanssy, lustrine.
lustrous, luisterryk, glansryk, roemryk.
lustrum, lustrum.
lusty, sterk, fris en gesond, fors, kragtig, lewendig, opgewek, flink.
lute, n. luit.
lute, stopverf (stokverf), lym, klei.
lute-string, luitsnaar; glanssy.
Lutheran, Luthers; van Luther.
luxate, verstuit, ontwrig.
luxuriance, weelderigheid; geilheid; weligheid.
luxuriant, weelderig; geil, welig.
luxuriate, weelderig lewe; — **in, on,** swelg (sig vermei) in.
luxurious, weelderig; wellustig.
luxury, weelde, weelderigheid, oordaad, oorvloed; luukse, lekkerny; genot, weeldeartikel.
Lyceum, Lyceum.
lyddite, liddiet.
Lydian, Lidiër; Lidies.
lye, loog.
lying-in, bevalling; — **hospital,** kraaminrigting.
lymph, water, limf.
lymphatic, limfaties, limf. . .
lynch, lynch.
lynch-law, lynchwet.
lynx, rooikat.
lynx-eyed, met kat-oë.
lyre, lier.
lyric, n. liriese gedig; **–s,** liriek, liriese gedigte.
lyric(al), liries.
lyricism, liriese geaardheid, liriese vlug, verhewenheid, lirisme.
lyrist, lierspeler; lirikus.
Lysol, Lysol.

M

ma, ma
ma'am, mevrou; nôi.
macabre, aaklig, grieselig, dode-...
macadam, macadam.
macadamize, macadamiseer.
macaroni, macaroni; fat.
macaroon, makrolletjie, amandelkoekie.
macassar, makassar(olie).
mace, staf; roede; knots.
mace, foelie.
mace-bearer, stafdraer, roededraer.
Macedonian, Macedonies; Macedoniër.
macerate, laat week; vermaer; kasty.
Mach: – number, mach-getal.
machan, jagplatform.
Machiavellian, Machiavellisties, gewetenloos.
machicolate, van werpgate voorsien.
machinate, saamsweer, intrigeer.
machination, intrige, sameswering; konkelary.
machine, masjien, toestel; fiets; **bathing** –, badkoets; **sewing** –, naaimasjien; – **made,** masjinaal gemaak; – **gun,** masjiengeweer.
machinery, masjinerie; meganiek; opset.
machinist, masjinis; masjienmaker; naaister.
mackerel, makriel; – **sky,** met wolkies bedekte lug.
mackintosh, reënjas.
macramé, macramé.
macrocephalic, langhoofdig.
macrocosm, makrokosmos, heelal.
macula, vlek.
maculated, bevlek.
mad, a. gek, mal; kranksinnig, rasend; **like** –, soos 'n mal mens; – **as a March hare, as a hatter,** stapelgek; – **cap,** wildebras, malkop; **house,** malhuis; – **man,** kranksinnige; – **on,** versot op.
mad, v. mal maak; mal wees; **the –ding crowd,** die gewoel van die wêreld.
madam(e), madam, mevrou; juffrou.
madden, mal (woedend) maak; mal word.
madder, meekrap.
made, gemaak; **he is a** – **man,** hy is dwarsdeur, sy fortuin is gemaak; – **up,** gemaak; **a** – **up story,** 'n versinsel.
mademoiselle, mademoiselle, juffrou.
madly, mal, dwaas, soos 'n besetene; – **in love,** tot oor die ore verlief.
madness, kranksinnigheid, raserny; dwaasheid.
Madonna, Madonna; – **lily,** madonna-lelie.
madrigal, madrigaal; minnelied.
Maecenas, Maecenas, kunsbeskermer.
maelstrom, maalstroom, draaikolk.
Mae West, reddingsgordel.
magazine, tydskrif; pakhuis, loods; kruithuis.
magazine-gun, magasyngeweer.
mage, towe(r)naar; wyse; magiër.
magenta, magenta, skelrooi.
maggot, maaier; gier.
maggoty, vol maaiers; vol giere.
Magi, Magiërs; magi, wyse.
magic, n. towerkuns; heksery; toorkrag; **black** –, duiwelse towerkuns; **white** –, goëlery.
magic, a. toweragtig, betowerend.
magician, towe(r)naar.
magic-lantern, towerlantern.
magisterial, magistraats-...; meesteragtig; heersend; gesaghebbend.
magistracy, magistratuur, die magistrate; magistraatskap; magistraatsdistrik.
magistrate, magistraat, owerheid, landdros; –'s **court,** magistraatshof; –'s **office,** magistraatskantoor.
magnanimity, grootmoedigheid.
magnanimous, grootmoedig.

magnate, magnaat; geldman.
magnesia, magnesia.
magnesium, magnesium.
magnet, magneet.
magnetic, magneties; – **iron,** magneetyster; – **needle,** magneetnaald; – **north,** – **south,** magnetiese noorde, suide; – **pole,** magnetiese pool.
magnetize, magnetiseer, magneties maak; aantrek; mesmeriseer.
magnetism, magnetisme, aantrekkingskrag, **terrestrial** –, aardmagnetisme; **animal** –, dierlike magnetisme.
magnetron, magnetron.
magnificence, prag, luister, grootsheid.
magnificent, pragtig, heerlik; groots, manjifiek.
magnifier, vergroter, vergrootglas.
magnify, vergroot; groter maak; ophemel.
magnifying-glass, vergrootglas.
magniloquence, hoogdrawendheid.
magniloquent, grootsprakig, hoogdrawend.
magnitude, grootte; belangrikheid; **of the first** –, van die eerste grootte.
magnolia, magnolia.
magnum, magnumfles.
magpie, ekster; babbelaar.
Magus, Magiër, wyse; towe(r)naar.
Magyar, Magjaar; Magjaars; Hongaar; Hongaars.
maharaja(h), maharadja; opperkoning.
mahogany, n. mahoniehout(boom).
mahogany, a. mahonie-...
mahout, olifantdrywer.
maid, meisie(tjie); maagd; **old** –, oujongnôi; – **of honour,** hofdame; – **servant,** diensmeisie.
maiden, n. meisie, jongnôi; maagd; leë boulbeurt.
maiden, a. maagdelik; ongetroud; eerste; – **lady,** oujongnôi, ongetroude dame; – **name,** nôiensvan, meisiesnaam; – **speech,** eerste toespraak; – **voyage,** eerste seereis.
maidenhair, venushaarvaring.
maidenhead, maagdelikheid.
maidenhood, maagdelikheid; maagdskap.
maidenish, maagdelik, sedig, kuis, rein.
maidenly, maidenlike, sien **maidenish.**
mail, n. pos; possak; poskar; postrein; – **order,** posbestelling.
mail, per pos stuur; pos.
mail, n. pantser(hemp), harnas.
mail, v. bepantser, harnas.
mailbag, possak.
mailboat, posboot.
mailcart, poskar.
mail-clad, geharnas, gepantser.
mailed, gepantser; – **fist,** gepantserde vuis.
mail-service, posdiens.
mailtrain, postrein.
maim, n. verminking.
maim, v. vermink, skend; 'n knou gee.
main, n. krag; groot massa; die ope see; hoofleiding; **with might and** –, met mag en geweld; **in the** –, in hoofsaak, oor die algemeen.
main, a. vernaamste, grootste; eerste; **by** – **force,** met geweld; **the** – **force,** die hoofmag; – **line,** die hooflyn; – **point,** die vernaamste argument; – **switch,** hoofskakelaar.
main body, hoofmag.
main deck, hoofdek.
main entrance, hoofingang.
mainland, vasteland.
mainly, vernaamlik, in die eerste plaas (plek), hoofsaaklik.
mainmast, grootmas.
main road, hoofweg, grootpad.

main-spring   560   **manageableness**

main-spring, slagveer; dryfveer.
mainstay, grootstag; steunpilaar.
main street, hoofstraat.
maintain, volhou; handhaaf; in stand hou; ophou; voer; ondersteun; volhou.
maintainer, handhawer; verdediger; versorger.
maintenance, handhawing; onderhoud.
maison(n)ette, woninkie, kamerwoning.
maize, mielies.
maizena, maizena.
majestic, majestueus, groots, verhewe.
majestically, majestueus, groots, pragtig.
majesty, majesteit; **Your M–, U Majesteit.**
majolica, majolika.
major, n. majoor; mondige; senior; majeur, groot.
major, a. groter; hoof- . . ., groot; – **part**, grootste deel; – **course**, hoofkursus.
major-domo, hofmeester.
major-general, generaal-majoor.
majority, meerderheid; mondigheid; majoorskap; **absolute –**, volslae meerderheid.
majorship, majoorskap.
make, n. vorm; maaksel, fabrikaat; soort; natuur; **a man of his –**, 'n man van sy soort; **English –**, Engelse maaksel (fabrikaat); **your own –**, jou eie maaksel.
make, v. maak, vorm; vervaardig; doen; verhef; nader; opmaak; voorberei; (toespraak) hou; trek; aflê; (geld) verdien; (oorlog) voer; forseer; begaan; voorgee; – **a fire**, vuur opmaak; – **fun (game) of**, gekskeer met, spot met; – **peace**, vrede sluit; – **way**, padgee; – **friends**, vriende maak; – **an example of**, tot voorbeeld stel; – **a fool of**, belaglik maak, gekskeer met; – **much**, veel verdien; – **the best of**, jou daarin skik; **2 and 2 – 4**, 2 en 2 is 4; – **oneself scarce**, (sig) uit die voete maak; – **him repeat it**, laat hom dit herhaal; – **believe**, voorgee; **he –s a blunder**, hy begaan 'n fout; – **love**, die hof maak, vry; – **head**, vooruitgaan; – **as if**, voorgee; – **merry**, vrolik wees; – **away with**, uit die weg ruim; verkwis; – **for**, gaan na; – **off**, weghardloop; – **out**, uitskrywe (tjek ens.); **how do you – that out?**, hoe lê jy dit uit?, hoe kom jy daarby?; **I can't – him out**, ek kan hom nie verstaan nie; – **over**, oormaak; – **up**, ('n party) vol maak; berei; versin; aanvul; – **it up**, versoen; – **up one's mind**, voorneem, 'n besluit neem; – **up time**, verlore tyd inhaal.
make-believe, n. skyn.
make-believe, a. voorgewende.
maker, maker; skepper.
makeshift, hulpmiddel, noodhulp.
make-up, versinsel; vermomming, grimering; karakter.
making, maaksel, maak; –s, verdienste; aanleg, kwaliteite; **he has the –s of a soldier**, hy het soldateaanleg.
malachite, malagiet.
maladjustment, slegte inrigting (reëling).
maladministration, wanbeheer, wanbestuur.
maladroit, lomp, onhandig, onbeholpe.
maladroitness, onhandigheid, lompheid.
malady, siekte, kwaal.
malapert, n. wysneus.
malapert, a. brutaal, parmantig.
malapropos, ongeskik, onvanpas, ongeleë.
malaria, malaria.
malarial, malarious, malaria- . . .
Malay, n. Maleier; Maleis.
Malay(an), a. Maleis.
malcontent, n. ontevredene.
malcontent, a. misnoeg, ontevrede.

male, n. mannetjie, manspersoon.
male, a. manlik, mans- . . .; mannetjies- . . .; – **issue**, manlike afstammeling.
malediction, vervloeking, verwensing.
maledictory, verwensend, vervloekend.
malefactor, boosdoener, misdadiger.
maleficent, skadelik, verderflik; misdadig.
malevolence, boosaardigheid, kwaadwilligheid.
malevolent, kwaadwillig, boosaardig.
malfeasance, (amps)misdryf.
malformation, misvorming, wanstaltigheid.
malformed, misvormd, wanstaltig.
malice, kwaadwilligheid, (bose) opset; geniepsigheid; **bear –**, haat dra, wrok koester; **with – prepense**, voorbedag, met opset.
malicious, boos; kwaadwillig, boosaardig; voorbedag, opsetlik.
maliciously, kwaadwilliglik.
malign, v. kwaad praat van, beskinder, beklad.
malign, a. verderflik, nadelig; boosaardig.
malignancy, kwaadwilligheid; boosaardigheid, verderflikheid.
malignant, boosaardig; skadelik; kwaadaardig; kwaadgesind.
maligner, kwaadspreker; boosaardige persoon.
malignity, boosaardigheid; kwaadwilligheid.
malinger, siek aanstel, siekte voorwend.
malingerer, iemand wat hom siek aanstel.
mallard, wilde-eend.
malleability, smee(d)baarheid.
malleable, smee(d)baar; buigbaar, handelbaar.
mallet, (hout)hamer.
mallow(s), kiesieblaar, malva.
malmsey, malvesy(wyn).
malnutrition, ondervoeding.
malodorous, stinkend, slegruikend.
malodour, stank, slegte reuk.
malpractice, oortreding; verkeerde praktyk.
malt, n. mout; **extract of –**, moutekstrak.
malt, v. mout.
Malta, Malta; – **fever**, Maltakoors, bokkoors.
Maltese, Maltees; Malteser.
malt-liquor, moutdrank.
maltreat, sleg behandel, mishandel.
maltreatment, mishandeling.
malversation, (geld)verduistering; wanbeheer.
mamba, mamba(slang).
Mameluke, Mammeluk; slaaf; afvallige.
mamilia, tepel, speen.
mam(m)a, mama (mamma).
mamma, bors, uier.
mammal, soogdier; –**ia**, soogdiere.
mammon, mammon, rykdom, geld.
mammoth, mammoet.
mammy, mammie; aia, nenna.
man, n. man; mens; bediende; soldaat; die mens, die mensdom; stuk (in skaakspel); **the old –**, die oukêrel; die ou Adam; –**'s estate**, manlike leeftyd; **a – of property**, 'n vermoënde man; **the – in the street**, die gewone man; **the – of men**, die aangewese persoon; **I am – enough to**, ek is mans genoeg om; **so many men so many minds**, soveel hoofde soveel sinne; **a – of letters**, 'n geleerde man; – **for –**, een vir een; **per –**, per hoof; **to a –**, almal.
man, a. manlik, mans- . . .
man, v. beman, beset; moed inpraat.
manacle(s), n. boei(e), handboei(e).
manacle, v. boei.
manage, v. bestuur, lei; sôre; regkry; baasraak, beheer; behandel; **I can –**, ek sal klaarkom; **he is managing well**, hy kom goed reg.
manageable, handelbaar, regeerbaar.
manageableness, handelbaarheid.

management, bestuur, administrasie, beheer; oorleg, lis.
manager, bestuurder, direkteur, baas.
manageress, direktrise, hoof.
managership, leiding, bestuur, beheer.
managing, besturend; prakties.
managing director, (hoof)bestuurder.
man-at-arms, soldaat, krygsman.
manatee, seekoei.
Manchester: – **goods**, katoenstowwe, -ware.
manciple, provisiekoper, proviandmeester.
mandamus, bevelskrif.
mandarin, mandaryn; nartjie.
mandatary, gevolmagtigde, mandaathouer, mandataris.
mandate, n. mandaat; lasbrief; opdrag; volmag; –d territory, mandaatgebied.
mandatory, a. bevelend.
mandible, (onder)kakebeen.
mandolin(e), mandolien.
mandragora, mandrake, alruin, mandragora,
mandrel, -il, spil.
mandrill, mandril, woudduiwel.
manducate, kou.
mane, maanhaar, mane.
man-eater, mensvreter, kannibaal.
manège, ryskool.
manes, skimme, geeste.
manful, dapper, vasberade, manhaftig.
manfulness, dapperheid, manhaftigheid.
manganese, mangaan, bruinsteen.
mange, skurfte, onsuiwer(heid).
mangel(wurzel), mangelwortel.
manger, krip; trog.
manginess, skurfagtigheid, onsuiwerheid.
mangle, n. & v. mangel.
mangle, v. verskeur, vermink; verknoei.
mango, mango; mangoboom.
mangold, sien **mangel**.
mangosteen, mangostan.
mangrove, wortelboom.
mangy, skurf(tig); miserabel.
man-handle, toetakel, mishandel, karnuffel.
man-hole, mangat.
manhood, manlikheid; manlike jare; manne.
man-hour, man-uur.
mania, manie; gier; waansin.
maniac, n. waansinnige, maniak.
maniacle, waansinnig.
manicure, n. manikuur; manikuris.
manicure, v. manikuur.
manicurist, manikuris, naelpoetser.
manifest, n. manifes, verklaring.
manifest, a. duidelik, openbaar.
manifest, v. duidelik maak; bewys; openbaar, aan die dag lê; verskyn.
manifestation, betoging; openbaarmaking, openbaring, manifestasie.
manifesto, manifes.
manifold, a. menigvuldig, veelsoortig.
manifold, v. vermenigvuldig, hektografeer.
manifold, n. verdeelpyp; blaarpens.
manifold-writer, hektograaf, kopieertoestel.
manikin, mannetjie, dwergie; (hout)pop.
manilla, manilla(ring).
manioc, maniok, kassawe, broodwortel.
manipulate, hanteer, manipuleer; bewerk; knoei.
manipulation, bewerking, manipulasie; knoeiery; betasting.
manipulator, hanteerder, bewerker; knoeier.
mankind, mensdom, mensheid; die mense, die mansmense.
manlike, soos 'n man, manlik; mannetjiesagtig.
manliness, manlikheid; manmoedigheid.
manly, manlik, manmoedig, manne- . . .

manna, manna; geestelike voedsel.
manner, manier, wyse; aanwensel; soort, gewoonte; **good** –s, goeie maniere; –s **and customs**, sedes en gewoontes; after the – of, in die trant van; after this –, op hierdie manier; in a –, op 'n manier; to the – born, geknip vir soos dit behoort.
mannered, gemanierd; ill –, onmanierlik.
mannerism, gemaaktheid, aanwensel; gemanierdheid.
mannerliness, beleefdheid, goeie maniere.
mannerly, goedgemanierd, manierlik.
mannish, managtig, soos 'n man; onhandig.
manoeuvre, n. maneuver, krygsoefening; slim plan, kunsgreep.
manoeuvre, v. maneuvreer; intrigeer, bewerkstellig, manipuleer; to – somebody into . . . , iemand bewerk om te . . .
man-of-war, oorlogskip.
manometer, manometer.
manor, riddergoed, landgoed.
manor-house, herehuis; riddergoed.
manorial, landheerlik, ridder- . . .
man-power, leërsterkte, strydmag.
man-rope, valreep.
mansard(roof), mansardedak.
manse, pastorie, predikantshuis.
manservant, kneg, (manlike) bediende.
mansion, herehuis; woning.
mansion-house, landheerswoning; burgemeesterswoning.
manslaughter, manslag.
man-slayer, moordenaar, doodslager.
mansuetude, sagmoedigheid, sagtheid.
mantel(piece), skoorsteenmantel.
mantilla, sluier, mantel.
mantissa, mantisse.
mantle, n. mantel; dekmantel; bedekking.
mantle, v. bedek, verberg; kim, skuim; na die wange styg, (laat) gloei; (laat) bloos.
mantlet, manteltjie; koeëlskerm.
man-trap, val, voetangel.
manual, n. handboek; manuaal, toetse; –s, handgrepe.
manual, a. hand- . . . ; – **alphabet**, vingertaal; – **labour**, handearbeid; – **sign**, handtekening.
manually, met die hand.
manufactory, fabriek, werkswinkel.
manufacture, n. fabrikasie, vervaardiging; fabrikaat, maaksel.
manufacture, v. vervaardig, fabriseer, maak, bedink.
manufacturer, vervaardiger, fabrikant.
manumission, vrylating (van slawe).
manumit, (slawe) vrymaak.
manure, n. mis, messtof.
manure, v. bemes, misgee.
manuscript, n. manuskrip, handskrif.
manuscript, a. in manuskrip, manuskrip- . . .
many, n. die menigte, die algemeen; **a great** –, 'n groot hoeveelheid (menigte).
many, a. baie, veel; – **a man**, menigeen; – **and a time**, dikwels; **as** – **again**, nog 'n keer soveel; **one too** –, te veel.
many-coloured, veelkleurig, bont.
many-headed, veelhoofdig.
many-sided, veelsydig; ingewikkeld.
map, n. kaart, landkaart.
map, v. teken; – **out**, in kaart bring; ontwerp.
maple, esdoring, ahorn.
mar, skend, bederwe; **it will make or** – **me**, dit sal my maak of breek.
marabou, maraboe.
marabout, maraboet.

maraschino, maraschino (maraskyn).
marathon, – race, marathonwedloop.
maraud, plunder, steel, buit, stroop.
marauder, plunderaar, buiter.
marble, n. marmer; albaster.
marble, a. marmer-. . ., van marmer.
marble, v. marmer, vlam.
marble-topped, met marmerblad.
March, Maart; as mad as a – hare, stapelgek.
march, n. grens, grensland.
march, v. grens (aan).
march, n. mars; stap, skof; beloop, verloop, gang; **forced** –, geforseerde mars; **dead** –, dodemars, treurmars; – of time, verloop van tyd.
march, v. marsjeer; stap; laat marsjeer; – **against**, optrek teen; – **out**, uittrek; – **past**, defileer, verby marsjeer.
marching-order: in –, volledig uitgerus; –s, marsbevel.
marchioness, markiesin.
marchpane, marsepein.
marconigram, radiogram, marconigram.
marconi-operator, marconis.
mare, merrie; **find a** –'s **nest**, bly word oor niks; **shank's** –, dapper en stapper.
margarine, margarine, kunsbotter.
marge, sien **margin**.
margin, n. rand, kant; wins, oorskot; speling, (speel)ruimte; skeiding, grens; **leave a** –, kantruimte laat; (speel)ruimte laat; **rule a** –, 'n sylyn trek.
margin, v. rand laat.
marginal, aan die rand, marginaal; – **note**, kanttekening.
marginate, v. van rand voorsien.
margrave, markgraaf.
margravine, markgravin.
marguerite, margriet.
Maria, Maria, Marie; **black** –, tronkwa.
marigold, gousblom.
marijuana, dagga.
marimba, marimba.
marinade, v. marineer, inlê.
marine, n. marine, vloot; seesoldaat; **tell that to the** –**s**, maak dit vir jou grootjie wys.
marine, a. marine- . . ., see- . . ., skeeps- . . .
mariner, matroos, seevaarder.
marionette, marionet, pop.
marital, huweliks- . . .; van die man.
maritime, maritiem, see- . . .; – **insurance**, seeversekering; – **law**, seereg; – **power**, see-moondheid.
marjoram, marjolein.
mark, n. merk, merkteken; doelwit; kruisie; stempel; punt; spoor; blyk; – **of distinction**, onderskeidingsteken; – **of affection**, liefdeblyk; **hit the** –, die spyker op die kop slaan; **make one's** –, (sig) onderskei, 'n naam maak; **below the** –, benede peil; **beside the** –, nie ter sake nie; **mis**; **near the** –, naby die waarheid; **a man of** –, 'n man van betekenis; **to be up to the** –, op sy stukke wees; op peil wees; **within the** –, sonder te oordrywe; **gain 50 –s, 50** punte behaal.
mark, n. mark (Duitse munt).
mark, v. merk, stempel, teken; noteer; aangee; laat merk; afmerk; opmerk; oplet; markeer; punte gee; – **my words**, let op my woorde; – **me**, let op; – **time**, pas markeer; **a** –**ed man**, iemand wat in die oog gehou word; **a** –**ed difference**, 'n duidelike verskil; – **down**, noteer; – **off**, aftel, afsonder; – **out**, afsteek; afsonder;

– **up**, die prys verhoog; – **down**, die prys verminder.
marker, teller, opskrywer; pit; boekeleêr.
market, n. mark; navraag; afsetgebied; **(not)** in the –, (nie) in die handel (nie); put on the –, te koop aanbied; **no** – **for**, geen aanvraag vir nie.
market, v. verkoop, na die mark bring, bemark.
marketable, verkoopbaar, bemarkbaar.
market-gardiner, tuinier, groenteboer.
marketing, bemarking, verkoop.
market-hall, mark(gebou).
market-place, mark(plein).
market-trot, sukkeldraffie.
marking, merk(e), tekening.
marking-ink, letterink, merkink.
marksman, skutter, skerpskutter.
mark-up, prysverhoging; winsgrens.
marl, mergel.
marline, matlyn.
marlin(e)spike, marlpriem.
marmalade, marmelade; lemoenkonfyt.
marmoreal, marmer- . . ., marmeragtig.
marmoset, sy-apie.
marmot, marmot(jie).
maroon, n. bosneger; agtergelatene.
maroon, v. (op 'n verlate eiland) agterlaat; rondslenter, ronddwaal.
maroon, n. donkerrooi; klapper.
maroon, a. donkerbruin, kastanjebruin, donkerrooi.
marquee, markee, veldtent.
marquetry, inlegwerk.
marquis, **-quess**, markies.
marquise, markiesin; markiesinring.
marriage, huwelik, bruilof; eg; **take in** –, trou; **promise of** –, troubelofte; **civil** –, huwelik voor die magistraat; **ask in** –, ten huwelik vra (hand) vra; – **articles**, huweliksvoorwaardes
marriageable, troubaar, hubaar.
marriage-contract, huwelikskontrak.
marriage-licence, troulisensie.
married, getroud, huweliks- . . .; – **life**, getroude lewe, huwelikslewe.
marrow, n. murg (merg), pit.
marrow-bone, murgbeen; –s, knie.
marrowless, sonder murg; swak, laf.
marrowy, vol murg, murgryk; pittig.
marry, v. trou, in die huwelik tree; uithuwelik; – **a fortune**, 'n ryk vrou trou; **to** – **below one's station**, benede jou stand trou; **a** –**ing man**, 'n man om te trou.
marsh, moeras, vlei.
marshal, n. maarskalk; seremoniemeester.
marshal, v. (rang)skik, orden, opstel, lei.
marshaller, rangskikker; aanvoerder.
marshalling: – **yard**, opstelwerf, -terrein.
marshalship, maarskalkskap.
marsh-fever, moeraskoors.
marsh-marigold, vleigousblom.
marshy, moerassig.
marsupial, n. buideldier.
marsupial, a. buideldraend, buidel- . . .
mart, mark; vendusielokaal; handelsentrum.
martello, kusfort.
marten, marter; marterbont, marterpels.
martial, krygshaftig, oorlogs- . . ., krygs- . . .; – **law**, krygswet.
Martian, Marsbewoner.
martin, huisswaeltjie.
martinet, diensklopper, drilmeester.
martingale, springteuel; dubbele inset.
martini, martini (drankie).
Martinmas, St. Maarten(sfees).

martyr, n. martelaar, lyer; **make a – of oneself,** sigself opoffer.
martyr, v. martel, pynig, folter; opoffer.
martyrdom, marteling; martelaarskap.
martyrize, tot martelaar maak.
martyrology, martelaarsboek.
marvel, n. wonder; verbasing; **the – of Peru,** vieruurtjie.
marvel, v. wonder, verbaas wees (oor), (sig) verbaas (verwonder) (oor).
marvellous, wonderbaarlik, wonderlik.
marvellousness, wonderbaarlikheid.
Marxian, aanhanger van Marx, Marxiaan.
marzipan, marsepein.
mascara, maskara.
mascot, gelukbringer, talisman.
masculine, manlik; mannetjiesagtig, managtig; sterk, fors, ru; – **rhyme,** staande (manlike) rym; – **woman,** mannetjiesvrou.
masculinity, manlikheid; managtigheid.
mash, n. mengsel; mengelmoes; pap; fat, Don Juan.
mash, v. meng; fynmaak.
mash, v. verlief maak.
mashed, fyngemaak, gestamp; verlief.
masher, (hart)veroweraar, doring onder die nôiens, Don Juan; fat.
mask, n. masker; vermomming; mombakkies; maskerspel; gemaskerde; voorwendsel.
mask, v. vermom, verklee; bedek, verberg.
masked, vermom, gemasker; bedek; – **ball,** gemaskerde bal, maskerbal.
masker, masquer, gemaskerde (persoon).
masochism, masochisme.
mason, n. messelaar; **M–,** Vrymesselaar.
mason, v. messel.
masonic, messelaars- . . . ; **M–** lodge, Vrymesselaarslosie.
masonry, messelwerk; vrymesselary.
masque, maskerspel.
masquerade, n. maskerade; maskerbal.
masquerade, v. vermom, vermom loop; aan 'n maskerade deelneem; – **as,** (sig) uitgee vir, (sig) voordoen as.
mass, n. mis; **say –,** die mis lees; **high –,** hoogmis; **attend –,** na die mis gaan.
mass, n. massa; hoop, klomp; **in the –,** oor die algemeen; **in –,** en masse, tesaam; **the great –,** die massa; – **production,** massaproduksie.
mass, v. vergader, ophoop, konsentreer.
massacre, n. slagting, bloedbad, moord.
massacre, v. vermoor, bloedbad aanrig.
massage, n. massage, vrywe.
massage, v. masseer, vrywe.
masseur, masseerder, masseur.
masseuse, masseerster, masseuse.
massive, swaar, massief.
mass-meeting, monstervergadering.
massy, massief, swaar.
mast, n. mas; **sail before the –,** as gewone matroos vaar.
mast, v. mas; bemas.
mast, n. mas, varkenskos.
master, n. meester, baas; besitter; (huis)vader; kaptein; weesheer; werkgewer; bobaas; onderwyser; jongheer; **be – of,** baas wees van; beskik oor; beheer; **Master X,** die jongheer X; **English –,** Engelse onderwyser; – **of arts,** magister artium, M.A.; – **of ceremonies,** seremoniemeester; **like –, like man,** so die baas, so die kneg.
Master: the –, die Meester, Christus; – **of the supreme court,** die weesheer.
master, v. (oor)meester, meester maak van; onderwerp; baasspeel (oor); baas word (van);

baasraak; ('m taal) aanleer; heers; – **oneself,** (sig) beheers.
master-builder, boumeester, meesterbouer.
masterful, meesteragtig; eiemagtig; dominerend.
masterhand, hand van die meester.
master-key, loper.
masterless, sonder eienaar, onbeheer(d).
masterliness, meesterlikheid.
masterly, meesterlik, knap, voortreflik.
masterpiece, meesterstuk.
master-spirit, kopstuk, leier.
master-stroke, meesterwerk; meesterlike set; geniale inval.
mastery, beheer, oorhand, meesterskap.
mast-head, mastop.
mastic, mastik(boom); mastikgom.
masticate, kou, herkou.
mastication, (die) kou, kouery, mastikasie.
mastiff, waghond, slagtershond, kettinghond.
mastodon, mastodon.
masturbate, masturbeer.
masturbation, selfbevlekking, masturbasie.
mat, n. mat.
mat, v. met matte bedek; in die war maak.
mat, a. mat, dof.
mat, v. dof maak, matteer.
matador, matador; bobaas.
match, n. vuurhoutjie, swa(w)elhoutjie.
match, n. gelyke, partuur; wedstryd; (huweliks)party; **they will make a good –,** hulle sal 'n goeie paar uitmaak; **we shall never see his –,** ons sal nooit sy gelyke sien nie; – **point,** stelpunt.
match, v. verbind (in die huwelik); pas (by mekaar); teen mekaar opgewasse wees; **well –ed,** by mekaar passend; goed teen mekaar opgewasse, goeie partuurs; **ribbon to –,** lint wat daarby pas.
matchable, passend.
match-box, vuurhoutjiedosie.
matchless, weergaloos, onvergelyklik.
matchlock, snaphaan.
match-wood, hout vir vuurhoutjies; brandhout; **make – of,** kafloop; versplinter.
mate, n. maat; kameraad; man; mannetjie (wyfie); helper; hulp; stuurman; **cook's –,** koksmaat.
mate, v. trou, paar; geselskap hou; maats maak.
mate, n. (skaak)mat.
mate, a. skaak(mat).
mate, v. (skaak)mat sit.
mater, moeder.
material, n. materiaal, stof, boustof.
material, a. stoflik, materieel, liggaamlik; wesenlik, nodig (tot), belangrik; – **well-being,** liggaamlike welsyn.
materialization, verwesenliking; materialisasie.
materialize, verwesenlik (word), realiseer; voordeel lewer; materialiseer.
materialism, materialisme.
materialist, materialis.
materialistic, materialisties.
materiality, stoflikheid; wesenlikheid.
materially, materieel, stoflik; wesenlik, belangrik.
maternal, moederlik, moeder(s)- . . . ; – **love,** moederliefde; – **aunt,** tante van moederskant.
maternity, moederskap.
maternity home (hospital), kraaminrigting.
mathematic(al), wiskundig, matematies.
mathematician, wiskundige, matematikus.
mathematics, wiskunde, matesis; **pure –,** suiwere wiskunde; **applied –,** toegepaste wiskunde.
matins, vroegmette.
matinee, matinee, middagvoorstelling.

matriarch, stammoeder, aartsmoeder.
matriarchal, matriargaal.
matriarchy, matriargaat.
matric, matriek, matrikulasie.
matricide, moedermoord; moedermoordenaar.
matricidal, moedermoord- ...
matriculate, matrikuleer, as student ingeskryf word.
matriculation, matrikulasie; inskrywing (as student).
matrimonial, huweliks- ...; – duties, huwelikspligte.
matrimony, huwelik, eg.
matrix, baarmoeder; gietvorm; matrys.
matron, dame, huisvrou; matrone, huismoeder.
matronly, huisvroulik, deftig, statig.
matronship, betrekking van matrone (huismoeder); huismoederlikheid.
matter, n. stof, materie; inhoud; goed, ding, voorwerp, onderwerp, saak; etter; kwessie; **printed** –, drukwerk; **no** – **what**, dit kom daar nie op aan wat nie; **for that** –, wat dit betref; **what is the** –?, wat makeer?; **in the** – **of**, insake, wat betref; – **of course**, iets vanselfsprekends; **a** – **of fact**, 'n feit; **as a** – **of fact**, om die waarheid te sê, eintlik.
matter, v. van belang wees, op aankom; **it does not** –, dit kom daar nie op aan nie, dit maak geen saak nie.
matter-of-course, vanselfsprekend.
matter-of-fact, droog, saaklik, nugter.
matting, mat, matwerk.
mattock, houweel; bylpik.
mattress, matras; **spring** –, springveermatras.
maturate, ryp word.
maturation, rypwording; rypheid.
mature, v. ryp word, uitgroei, ontwikkel; ryp maak; (wissel) verval.
mature, a. ryp, uitgegroei, ontwikkel(d).
maturity, rypheid; vervaltyd (van wissel); **reach** –, tot volle rypheid kom.
matutinal, vroeg, môre- ..., matineus.
maudlin, sentimenteel, sentimenteel-dronk.
maul (mail), n. voorhamer, moker.
maul, v. slaan; moker; toetakel, kneus.
maulstick, skilderstok, maalstok.
maunder, sanik, seur.
maundy, aalmoes.
mausoleum, mausoleum, praalgraf.
mauve, ligpers, dofpers, mauve.
mavis, lyster.
maw, maag, pens; bek.
mawkish, sentimenteel; wee, naar, walglik.
mawkishness, sentimentaliteit; walglikheid.
maxilla, (boonste) kakebeen.
maxillary, kakebeen- ..., kaak- ...
maxim, meksim(kanon).
maxim, prinsipe, grondbeginsel; leus.
maximum, maksimum, grootste hoeveelheid.
May, n. Mei(maand); bloeityd.
may, **might**, v. mag, kan; **be that as it** –, hoe dit ook sy; **who** – **you be?**, wie is jy wel?; **you might have asked me**, jy kon my darem gevra het; **he** – **lose his way**, hy kan verdwaal; **you** – **meet somebody**, jy kan iemand teenkom.
may-be, miskien.
May-bug, meikewer.
May-day, Meidag, die eerste Mei.
May-flower, meidoring, meiblom.
mayhap, miskien, allig.
mayhem, besering.
mayonnaise, mayonnaise(sous).
mayor, burgemeester.
mayoral, burgemeesterlik.
mayoress, burgemeestersvrou; burgemeesteres.

mayorship, burgemeesterskap.
mazarine, donkerblou, diepblou.
maze, n. doolhof, labirint; warboel.
maze, v. verbyster, in verwarring bring.
mazurka, masurka.
mazy, verward, deurmekaar.
me, my; ek; **it's** –, dis ek.
mead, mee(drank), heuningdrank.
mead, weiland, weiveld, weide.
meadow, weiland, grasland, weide.
meagre, maer, arm, skraal, onvrugbaar, dor, armsalig; – **results**, skraal oes.
meagreness, skraalheid, onvrugbaarheid.
meal, meel.
meal, maal, maaltyd, voedsel, kos; **at** –**s**, aan tafel, by die maaltye.
mealie, mielie; **crushed** –**s**, gestampte mielies.
mealie-borer, mielierusper.
mealie-cob, mieliekop.
mealie-stalk, mieliestronk.
mealiness, melerigheid; krummelagtigheid.
meal-time, etenstyd.
mealy, melerig; krummelrig; bleek; vlekkerig.
mealy-mouthed, soetsappig; papbroekerig.
mean, n. middelweg, middelmaat; (die) gemiddelde; –**s**, middele; geld, rykdom; manier, wyse; **a man of** –**s**, 'n bemiddelde man; **by fair** –**s or foul**, op eerlike of oneerlike manier; **it has been the** –**s of helping me**, dit was die middel om my te help; **by no** (**manner of**) –**s**, in geen geval nie, volstrek nie; **by all** (**manner of**) –**s**, stellig, al te seker; **by** –**s of**, deur middel van; **the golden** –, die gulde middelweg, (middelmaat).
mean, a. gemiddeld, middel- ..., middelmatig; gemeen, laag; armoedig; suinig.
mean, v. bedoel; beteken; van plan wees, voornemens wees; bestem; – **to be used**, vir gebruik bestem; – **well to, by**, goed gesind wees teenoor, wel meen met; **what do you** – **by it?** wat bedoel jy daarmee?
meander, n. slingering, kronkeling; doolhof; –**s**, kronkelpaaie, slingerweë.
meander, v. kronkel, slinger, ronddwaal.
meandering, slingerend, kronkel- ...
meaning, n. betekenis; bedoeling; plan; sin; **with** –, met nadruk; met mening.
meaning, a. veelbetekenend, betekenisvol.
meaningless, niksseggend, sonder sin, niksbeduidend, betekenisloos.
meaningly, opsetlik; met mening.
meanly, sleg, min; **think** – **of**, sleg dink van; **pay** –, min betaal.
meanness, gemeenheid, laagheid.
means, middele; – **test**, middeletoets; rykdom, geld; manier.
mean-spirited, van lae inbors; lafhartig.
meantime, intussen; **in the** –, intussen.
meanwhile, intussen.
measles, masels; **German** –, Duitse masels.
measly, vol masels; armsalig, miserabel.
measurable, meetbaar, afsienbaar.
measure, n. maat; maatstaf; hoeveelheid; maatemmer, -glas; maatreël; metrum; grens, limiet; dans; **full** –, volle maat; **clothes made to** –, klere na (op) maat gemaak, aangemete klere; **take** –, maat neem; **tread a** –, dans; **take** –**s**, maatreëls neem; – **of capacity**, inhoudsmaat; **cubic** –, kubieke maat; **liquid** –, vogmaat; **lineal** –, lengtemaat; **square** –, vierkante maat; **greatest common** –, grootste gemene deler; **beyond** –, buitemate; – **for** –, leer om leer; **in a** –, in sekere mate, tot op sekere hoogte; **in a great** –, in groot mate, grotendeels; **within** –, redelik, matig.

measure, v. meet, maatneem; skat; af-, opmeet; goed bekyk; **he –d me with his eyes**, hy het my van die hoof tot die voete opgeneem; **– swords with**, degen kruis met, te staan kom teen; **– himself against**, hom meet met; **– 5 feet**, vyf voet lank wees.
measured, afgemete; weldeurdag.
measureless, onmeetlik.
measurement, maat, inhoud; (op)meting.
measuring-chain, landmetersketting.
measuring-glass, maatglas.
measuring-rod, maatstaf.
meat, n. vleis (vlees); kos; maaltyd, ete; **this was – and drink to him**, dit was net na sy smaak; **one man's – is another man's poison**, die een se dood is die ander se brood; **minced –**, gemaalde vlees; **salted –**, (in)gesoute vleis, soutvleis.
meat-chopper, vleisbyl.
meat-extract, vleisekstrak.
meat-offering, spysoffer.
meat-pie, (vleis)pastei(tjie).
meat-safe, vleiskas.
meaty, vleis- . . .., goed in die vleis; kragtig.
mechanic, n. ambagsman; werktuigkundige.
mechanic(al), a. meganies, werktuiglik, masjien- . . .; masjinaal, automaties.
mechanician, werktuigkundige.
mechanics, werktuigkunde, masjienleer.
mechanize, meganiseer, masjinaal maak.
mechanism, meganiek; meganisme; tegniek.
machinist, masjienmaker.
medal, erepenning, gedenkpenning, medalje; **the reverse of the –**, die ander kant van die saak.
medallion, medaljon.
medallist, muntkenner; medaljesnyer; medaljewenner.
meddle, bemoei (met), lol (met), inlaat (met), inmeng, torring (aan); **don't – with my affairs**, moet jou nie met my sake bemoei nie.
meddler, lolpot, bemoei-al.
meddlesome, lollerig, bemoeisiek, lastig.
Medes, Mede.
medi(a)eval, middeleeus.
medi(a)evalism, middeleeuse gees.
medial, middel- . . ., tussen- . . .
median, mediaan; mediaanaar.
mediant, mediant, middeltoon.
mediate, a. middellik.
mediate, v. bemiddel, tussenbei kom.
mediation, bemiddeling; tussenkoms.
mediator, (be)middelaar; voorspraak.
mediatorial, bemiddelend.
mediatrix, bemiddelaarster.
medicable, geneeslik.
medical, a. medies, geneeskundig, genees- . . .; **– man**, medikus, dokter; **– student**, mediese student; **– jurisprudence**, mediese reg.
medical, n. mediese student, medikus.
medicament, n. medisyne, medikament.
medicate, geneeskundig behandel; prepareer.
medicated, medisinaal toebereid; geprepareer; **– coffee**, geprepareerde koffie; **– water**, medisinale water.
medicinal, geneeskragtig, medisinaal; geneeskundig, medies.
medicine, n. geneesmiddel, medisyne, artseny; geneeskunde; toormiddel; **study –**, (in die) medisyne studeer; **take one's –**, die gevolge dra, die storm verduur.
medicine, v. medisyne toedien, dokter.
medicine-chest, huisapteek; medisynekas.
medicine-man, toordokter.
medico, medicus, dokter.

mediocre, middelmatig.
mediocrity, middelmatigheid.
meditate, oordink, (be)peins; voornemens wees, (planne) beraam.
meditation, (be)peinsing, gepeins.
meditative, (na)denkend, peinsend, dromerig.
Mediterranean (Sea), Middellandse (See); mediterreense (klimaat).
medium, n. middel; middelslag; hulp(middel); voertaal; mediaanpapier; medium; **by**, **through the – of**, deur bemiddeling (middel) van; **– of exchange**, ruilmiddel.
medium, a. middelmatig, deursnee- . . .; middelslag- . . .; **– wave**, middelgolf.
mediumistic, mediumisties.
medlar, mispel, mispelboom.
medley, n. mengelmoes, mengeling, potpourri.
medley, a. deurmekaar, gemeng, bont.
medulla, murg; pit.
medullary, murg- . . ., (merg- . . .).
meed, beloning, verdienste; geskenk.
meek, gedwee, sag(moedig), ootmoedig, **as – as a lamb**, so sag soos 'n lam.
meekness, sagmoedigheid, gedweeheid.
meercat, meerkat.
meerschaum, meerskuim; meerskuimpyp.
meet, n. (jag)byeenkoms; vergaderplek.
meet, a. paslik, gepas.
meet, v. ontmoet; teenkom; raakloop; tegemoetkom; voldoen aan, bevredig; byeenkom; **to – a person half way**, iemand tegemoetkom; **to – the eye (ear)**, sienbaar (hoorbaar) wees; **– expenses**, onkoste dek; **have I met you before?**, het ek u tevore ontmoet?; **more is meant than –s the ear**, daar steek meer agter as dit lyk; **it will – with your approval**, dit sal jou goedkeuring wegdra; **it –s the case**, dit los die saak op, dit is voldoende; **– one's liabilities**, jou verpligtinge nakom; **– at the station**, by die stasie afhaal; **– with an accident**, 'n ongeluk oorkom; **– with a loss**, 'n verlies ly; **– with a reverse**, 'n teenslag kry.
meeting, samekoms, byeenkoms, ontmoeting; samevloeiing; **he addressed the –**, hy het die gehoor toegespreek.
meeting-place, vergaderplek.
megalomania, grootheidswaan(sin).
megaphone, hardroeper, megafoon.
megass, uitgeperste suikerriet, ampas.
megaton, megaton.
megrim, (skeel) hoofpyn; gril; **–s**, malkopsiekte.
melancholia, swaarmoedigheid, melancholie.
melancholic, swaarmoedig, melancholies.
melancholy, n. swaarmoedigheid, bedruktheid, swartgalligheid, melancholie.
melancholy, a. swaarmoedig, droefgeestig, melancholies, swartgallig, treurig, droef.
melange, mengsel, mikstuur, mélange.
melee, skermutseling, deurmekaar geveg.
melinite, meliniet.
meliorate, verbeter, veredel; versag.
melioration, verbetering.
melliferous, heuningwekend, heuning- . . .
mellifluence, soetvloeiendheid.
mellifluent, heuningsoet, soetvloeiend.
mellifluous, sien **mallifluent**.
mellow, a. ryp, sappig; sag, mals, beleë; vrolik, aangeskote; mollig; **– wine**, beleë wyn; **– notes**, mollige klanke.
mellow, v. ryp word (maak); temper, versag.
mellowness, rypheid, sagtheid; molligheid.
melodious, welluidend, sangerig, melodieus.
melodiousness, welluidendheid, sangerigheid.
melodist, sanger; liederkomponis.
melodrama, melodrama.

melodramatic, melodramaties.
melody, (sang)wysie, melodie; gesang.
melon, spanspek.
melt, n. gesmelte metaal; smeltsel.
melt, v. smelt; verteder; oplos; ontdooi; – **away**, wegsmelt; – **down**, (ver)smelt; – **into tears**, in trane wegsmelt.
melting, n. smelting, smelt.
melting, a. smeltend, smelt-...; vertederend.
melting-point, smeltpunt.
melting-pot, smeltkroes; be in the –, deur die smeltkroes gaan.
member, lid, lidmaat; deel, afdeling; afgevaardigde; – **of Parliament**, Parlementslid; be – for, verteenwoordig.
membership, lidmaatskap; ledetal.
membrane, vlies, weefsel, membraan.
memento, herinnering, aandenke.
memoir, gedenkskrif; berig; verhandeling; –s, mémoires, lewensbeskrywing.
memorabilia, gedenkwaardighede.
memorable, (ge)denkwaardig, heuglik.
memorandum, memorandum, nota.
memorandum-book, notisie-, aantekeningboek.
memorial, n. gedenkteken; nota; herinnering; versoekskrif, adres; memorie; –s, gedenkstukke.
memorial, a. herinnerings-...; gedenk-...
memorialize, petisioneer; herdenk, vier.
memorialist, petisionaris; gedenkskrifskrywer.
memorize, opteken; van buite (uit die kop) leer.
memory, geheue, memorie; (na)gedagtenis; herinnering; **a good** –, 'n goeie geheue; **in** – **of**, ter gedagtenis aan.
men, mans, mense, hulle; sien **man**.
menace, n. bedreiging, dreigement.
menace, v. (be)dreig.
menacing, dreigend, onheilspellend.
menage, huishouding.
mend, n. lasplek, stopplek; **on the** –, aan die beterhand.
mend, v. heelmaak, regmaak, repareer; beter word, herstel; lap, las, stop; **to** – **one's ways**, 'n beter weg inslaan; **to** – **matters**, sake regmaak (verbeter); – **one's pace**, aanstap.
mendable, herstelbaar.
mendacious, leuenagtig, vals.
mendacity, leuenagtigheid, valsheid.
mender, heelmaker, stopper, hersteller.
mendicancy, bedelary, bedelstaf, armoede.
medicant, 'n bedelaar.
medicant, a. bedelend, arm, bedel-...; – **friar**, bedelmonnik.
mendicity, bedelary, armoede.
men-folk, mansmense.
menial, 'n diensbode, bediende, huurling.
menial, a. slaafs; diensbaar; laag.
meningitis, harsingvliesontsteking.
Mennonite, Doopsgesinde, Mennoniet.
menstrual, maandeliks; menstruasie-...
menstruate, menstrueer.
menstruation, maandstonde, menstruasie.
mensurable, meetbaar, mensurabel.
mensuration, oppervlakte- en inhoudsberekening; meting.
mental, geestelik, geestes-..., verstandelik, verstands-...; – **arithmetic**, hoofrekening; – **confusion**, begripsverwarring; – **reservation**, geheime voorbehoud; – **faculties**, gees(tes)vermoëns; – **hospital**, inrigting vir sielsiekes; – **defective**, swaksinnige; – **disease**, sielsiekte; – **gymnastics**, harsinggimnastiek.
mentality, mentaliteit; denkwyse.
mentally, geestelik; verstandelik; uit die hoof; – **deficient**, swaksinnig.

menthol, mentol.
mention, n. gewag, melding; **honourable** –, eervolle vermelding.
mention, v. (ver)meld, noem, melding maak van; verwys na; **don't** – **it**, nie te danke; **not to** –, afgesien van, laat staan.
mentionable, noemenswaardig.
mentor, raadgewer, leier, mentor.
menu, spyslys, spyskaart, menu.
mephitic, stinkend, verpestend.
mephitis, stank, stiklug.
mercantile, handels-..., koop-..., kommersieel, merkantiel; – **theory**, merkantiele teorie; – **marine**, handelsvloot; – **law**, handelsreg.
mercantilism, merkantilisme.
mercenary, n. huurling, huursoldaat.
mercenary, a. gehuur; omkoopbaar; inhalig, geldsugtig; – **troops**, huurtroepe.
mercer, handelaar in kosbare stowwe.
mercery, weefstowwe; weefstofhandel.
merchandise, koopware, negosie(goed).
merchant, (groot)handelaar, koopman.
merchant-man, koopvaardyskip.
merchant-prince, grootvors van die handel.
merchant-service, handelsvloot.
merciful, genadig, barmhartig.
mercilessness, opgenadig, meedoënloos.
mercurial, n. kwikmiddel.
mercurial, a. lewendig; wispelturig, veranderlik; kwikagtig.
mercury, kwik(silwer).
mercury-barometer, kwik-, bakbarometer.
mercy, genade, barmhartigheid; seën, geluk; **for** – **'s sake**, om Godswil; **that is a** –, dit is 'n seën; **have** – **on us**, wees ons genadig; **be at the** – **of**, oorgelewer wees aan die genade van; **I am thankful for small mercies**, alle bietjies help.
mercy-seat, genadetroon.
mere, n. meer, vlei.
mere, a. adv. net, louter, bloot, suiwer; **a** – **child**, 'n blote kind, 'n pure bog.
merely, net, louter, slegs.
meretricious, ontugtig; opvallend, opsigtig; oneg.
merganser, duikereend, duikergans.
merge, indompel; oplos; (laat) saamsmelt; be –d in, opgaan in.
merger, saamsmelting; oplossing.
meridian, n. middaglyn, meridiaan; hoogtepunt; – **altitude**, middaghoogte.
meridional, a. suidelik, meridionaal; – **distance**, lengteverskil.
meringue, skuimtert(jie), skuimpie.
merino, merino(skaap); merino(stof).
merit, n. verdienste, deug; verdienstelikheid, waarde; **the** –s **of the case**, die wesenlike van die saak; **to make a** – **of necessity**, van die nood 'n deug maak; **on his own** –s, op sigself, op sy eie.
merit, v. werd wees, verdien; **he has** –ed **well of the country**, hy het hom verdienstelik jeens die land gedra.
meritorious, verdienstelik.
meritoriousness, verdienstelikheid; verdienste.
merle, merel.
merlin, steenvalk, merlyn.
mermaid, meermin.
merman, meerman, triton.
Merovingian, Merovingies.
merrily, vrolik, prettig, opgeruimd, lekker.
merriment, vrolikheid, pret, plesier.
merry, vrolik, prettig, opgeruimd, plesierig; **to make** –, plesier maak; **a** – **Christmas to you!**,

merry-go-round gelukkige Kersfees!; make – over, lag om, spot met.
merry-go-round, mallemole, draaimole.
merry-making, pretmakery, feesviering.
merry-thought, geluksbeentjie.
mesa, tafelkop.
mesalliance, mésalliance, mishuwelik.
meseems, dit lyk my, dit kom my voor.
mesembryanthemum, vygie.
mesentery, dermvlies, mesenterium.
mesh, n. netwerk; maas; strik, val.
mesh, v. (in 'n net) vang, verstrik.
mesh-work, netwerk.
mesmeric, hipnoties.
mesmerize, hipnotiseer.
mesmerism, mesmerisme, hipnotisme, dierlike magnetisme.
mesmerist, hipnotiseur.
mesolithic, mesolities.
meson, meson.
mess, n. gereg, gemeenskaplike ete; hondekos; deurmekaarspul, warboel, wanorde; vuilgoed; vuilheid; **officer's** –, offisierstafel; – **of pottage,** lensiesop; **the house was in a pretty** –, die huis was in 'n mooi toestand; **to make a** – **of,** knoei, verknoei; **he got into a terrible** –, hy het hom in groot moeilikhede gedompel.
mess, v. saam-eet; knoei, verknoei, deurmekaar maak; bemors; – **with,** lol met; **to** – **(up) the whole business,** die hele spul verknoei.
message, boodskap, berig; **go on a** –, boodskap doen.
messenger, boodskapper, bode; voorbode; loopjong; – **of the court,** geregsbode.
messenger-boy, loopjong, boodskapper.
messiah, messias; **the M**—, die Messias.
mess-mate, tafelmaat.
mess-room, eetsaal, eetkamer.
Messrs, menere; – X and Y, die here X en Y.
messuage, geboue en erf, opstal.
messy, vuil, morsig, smerig; wanordelik.
metabolic, stofwisselend, metabolies.
metabolism, stofwisseling, metabolisme.
metacarpus, middelhand.
metal, n. metaal; klipgruis; glasspys; skeepskanon; –s, spoorstawe, treinspoor; **leave the** –, ontspoor; **base** –, onedele metaal.
metal, a. metaal-...
metallic, metaalagtig, metaal-...
metalliferous, metaalhoudend.
metallise, metalliseer; vulkaniseer.
metallography, metallografie, metaalbeskrywing.
metalloid, n. metalloïde.
metalloid, a. metaalagtig.
metallurgic, metallurgies.
metallurgist, metaalkundige, metallurgis.
metallurgy, metaalkunde; metallurgie.
metamorphic, metamorfies.
metamorphose, (van gedaante) verander, omskep, metamorfoseer.
metamorphosis, (vorm)verandering, gedaanteverwisseling, metamorfose.
metaphor, beeldspraak, beeld, metafoor.
metaphoric(al), figuurlik, oordragtelik.
metaphysical, metafisies; bo(we)natuurlik.
metaphysician, metafisikus.
metaphysics, metafisika.
metastasis, metastase.
metatarsus, middelvoet.
metathesis, letteromsetting, metatesis.
mete, v. meet, uitdeel; – **out,** toedeel.
metempsychosis, sielsverhuising, metempsigose.
meteor, meteoor; vallende ster; lugverskynsel.
meteoric, meteories, meteoor-; – **shower,** sterrereent; – **stone,** meteoorsteen.

meteorite, meteoorsteen, meteoriet.
meteorolite, meteoroliet, meteoorsteen.
meteorological, weerkundig, meteorologies.
meteorologist, weerkundige, meteoroloog.
meteorology, weerkunde, meteorologie.
meter, meter.
methinks, dit lyk my, ek dink, my dunk.
method, metode, manier; (leer)wyse, stelsel.
methodic(al), metodies, sistematies.
methodise, stelselmatig behandel, metodies rangskik.
Methodism, Metodisme.
Methodist, n. Metodis.
Methodist, a. Metodisties.
methodology, metodeleer, metodiek.
Methusela, Metusalem.
methyl, metiel.
methyl-alcohol, metielalkohol, houtgees.
methylate, met metiel meng; –**d spirits,** brandspiritus.
meticulous, nougeset, angsvallig, oordrewe presies.
metonic, maan-...; – **cycle,** maansirkel.
metonymy, metonimia.
metre, digmaat, versmaat, metrum.
metre, meter (lengtemaat).
metrical, metries; – **art,** metriek.
metrics, metriek.
metrology, maat- en gewigsleer, metrologie.
metronome, metronoom, tak(t)meter.
metropolis, hoofstad, metropool; middelpunt; aartsbiskopsetel.
metropolitan, n. aartsbiskop, metropoliet.
metropolitan, a. hoofstedelik; metropolitaans, aartsbiskoplik; **the** – **church,** die moederkerk, hoofkerk.
mettle, moed, energie, ywer, vuur, gees; **be on one's** –, op sy stukke wees; **a horse of** –, 'n vurige perd; **a man of** –, 'n staatmaker, 'n man van durf; **show one's** –, wys wat jy kan; **to try a person's** –, iemand op die proef stel.
mettlesome, vurig, driftig (van 'n perd).
mew, n. meeu.
mew, n. (valk)hok, (valk)kou; gevangenis; –s stal(le).
mew, v. in die hok sit, opsluit; verveer.
mew, v. miaau.
mewl, miaau; skree, tjank.
Mexican, Mexikaans, Mexikaner.
mezzanine, tussen-, insteekverdieping.
mezzo, mezzo; – **soprano,** tweede sopraan, mezzosopraan.
mezzotint, n. mezzo tint, swartkuns.
mezzotint, v. graveer in mezzo tint.
mi, mi (in musiek).
miaow, miaau, tjank.
miasm(a), smetstof, skadelike damp, miasma.
miasmatic, miasmaties, smetstof-...
miaul, miaau, tjank.
mica, mika.
Michaelmas, St. Michiel.
mickle, groot, baie.
microbe, mikrobe.
microcephalic, -**ous,** kleinskedelig, mikrosefaal.
microcosm, die wêreld in die klein, mikrokosmos; die mens; klein gemeenskap.
microcosmic, klein, mikrokosmies.
microdot: – **camera,** mikrostippel-kamera.
microfilm, mikrofilm.
micrometer, mikrometer.
micrometric, mikrometries.
micron, mikron.
microphone, mikrofoon.
microscope, vergrootglas, mikroskoop.
microscopic, mikroskopies, mikroskoop-...

**microscopy, **mikroskopie.
**microwave, **mikrogolf.
**mid, **a. middel, halfpad.
mid, prep. **sien **amid.
mid-air, **die lug; **in –, tussen hemel en **aarde.**
**midday, **n. middag.
**midday, **a. middag-...
**midden, **mishoop.
middle, **n. middel, midde, middelpunt, middelweg; **in the – **of,** in die middel van, onder, tussenin.
**middle, **a. middelste, middel-, tussen-; laag, middelmatig; – course, middelweg; **Middle High German, **Middelhoogduits; – **Ages, **Middeleeue; – **age (lIfe), **middelbare leeftyd; the – watch, die hondewag; – **stump, **middelste paaltjie; – **voice, **medium; – **classes, **middelstand, burgerklasse.
**middle-aged, **van middelbare leeftyd.
**middle-class, **middestand, burgerstand; tussensoort.
**middle-deck, **middeldek.
**middleman, **tussenpersoon, agent.
**middlemost, **middelste.
**middle-rate, **middelmatig.
**middle-sized, **middelsoort(ig).
**middling, **a., adv. middelmatig, so-so.
**middlings, **middelslag, tussensoort.
**midge, **muggie; dwergie.
**midget, **muggie; pikkie; dwergie; – **car, **dwergmotor.
**mid-iron, **middelyster, halfyster (in gholf).
**midland, **n. binneland, middelland.
**midland, **a. binnelands.
**midmost, **middelste.
**midnight, **n. middernag; pikdonkerte.
midnight, **a. middernag-, pikdonker; **burn the – **oil, **laat studeer.
**mid-off, **halfweg (in krieket).
**mid-on, **halfby (in krieket).
**mid-rib, **middelrib.
**midriff, **middelrif, diafragma, mantelvlies.
**midsea, **volle see, ope see.
**midshipman, **seekadet, adelbors, vlagjonker.
**midships, **midskeeps.
midst, **n. midde, middel; **in the – **of, **onder, tussen; **in our** –, in ons midde.
**midst, **prep. te midde van.
**midsummer, **hartjie van die somer; somersonstilstand; – **madness, **die toppunt van malligheid.
**mid-watch, **hondewag.
**midway, **halfpad, halwerweë.
**midwife, **vroedvrou, ou-vrou.
**midwifery, **verloskunde.
**midwinter, **hartjie van die winter; wintersonstilstand.
**mien, **voorkome, houding; gesig.
**miff, **n. rusietjie; slegte bui.
miff, **v. gesteur wees (oor); kwaad maak; **to be in a –, in 'n slegte bui wees.
might, **n. mag, krag, geweld, vermoë; **with – **and main, **met mag en geweld, uit alle krag.
might, **sien **may.
**mightiness, **magtigheid, mag; hoogheid.
mighty, **magtig, kragtig, geweldig, sterk; groot, massief, kolossaal; – **works, **wonderwerke; **that is – **easy, **dit is kinderspeletjies.
**mignonette, **minjonet, reseda; minjonetkant.
**migraine, **skeelhoofpyn, migraine.
**migrant, **n. swerwer; trekvoël.
**migrant, **a. rondtrekkend, trek-...
**migrate, **verhuis, trek, swerwe.
**migration, **verhuising, trek.

**migratory, **swerwend, trekkend, trek-...; – **birds, **trekvoëls, swerfvoëls.
**milch, **melk-...; – **cow, **melkkoei.
mild, **sag, sagaardig; goedaardig; mild, lig; flou; versagtend; **a – **climate, **'n sagte klimaat; – **cigars, **ligte sigare; **draw it** –, stadig oor die klippe.
**mildew, **n. skimmel weer.
**mildew, **v. (be)skimmel.
**mildewy, **skimmel, beskimmel(d).
mildly, **sag; lig(telik); **put it –, sag uitdruk.
**mildness, **sagtheid; goedaardigheid; ligtheid; toegewendheid, vriendelikheid.
mile, **myl; **nautical –, seemyl.
**mileage, **mylafstand; mylgeld.
**mile-stone, **mylpaal.
**militancy, **strydlus(tigheid).
militant, **vegtend, strydend; strydlustig; **the Church –, die strydende kerk.
**militarism, **militarisme.
**militarist, **militaris; krygskundige.
military, **n. militêr, soldaat; **the –, die militêre.
**military, **a. militêr, oorlogs-..., krygshaftig; – **duty, **oorlogsdiens; – **man, **militêr; – **art, **krygskuns; – **stores, **oorlogsvoorraad; – **chest, **leërkas.
**militate, **oorlog voer, stry; – **against, **stry teen, benadeel.
**militia, **burgermag, milisie.
**militiaman, **landweerman, burger(soldaat).
milk, **n. melk; **skimmed –, afgeroomde melk; **fresh** –, vars melk, soetmelk; **condensed** –, blikkiesmelk, gekondenseerde melk; **that is** – **for babes, **dis kinderkos; kinderspeletjies; – **and honey, **melk en heuning; **it is no use crying over spilt** –, dit help nie om oor gedane sake te treur nie; **not in** –, droog; – **of human kindness, **menslikheid, mensliewendheid.
**milk, **v. melk; – **the wires, **berigte tap.
**milk-and-water, **water-en-melk-praatjies.
**milker, **melker; melkkoei.
**milk-fever, **melkkoors.
**milkiness, **melkagtigheid; weekheid.
**milk-livered, **lafhartig, papbroekerig.
**milk-maid, **melkmeisie.
**milkman, **melker; melkjong; melkverkoper.
**milk-shake, **bruismelk, roomysmelk.
**milksop, **papbroek, melkmuil.
**milk-thistle, **melkdissel, suidissel.
**milk-tooth, **melktand, wisseltand.
**milk-van, **melkkar, melkwa.
**milk-white, **spierwit, melkwit.
**milk-weed, **melkbos.
**milky, **melkagtig, melk-...; troebel; swak, pap; **the Milky Way, **die Melkweg.
mill, **'n meul, fabriek; spinnery; **to go through the –, baie ondervind (deurmaak).
**mill, **v. stamp, maal; rondmaal; klits; afransel; (wol) vol; (munt) kartel.
**mill-board, **bordpapier, karton.
**milldam, **meuldam.
**mill-dust, **stuifmeel, meelstof.
**milled, **gemaal; gevol(d).
**millenarian, **duisendjarig; van die duisendjarige ryk.
**millenary, **n. millennium; duisendjarige gedenkfees; millennium-aanhanger.
**millenary, **a. duisendjarig.
**millennial, **duisendjarig; langdurig.
**millennium, **duisendjarige ryk, millennium.
**millepede, **duisendpoot.
**miller, **meulenaar.
**millesimal, **duisendste (deel).
**millet, **giers.
**mill-hopper, **meultregter.

milliard, miljard.
milligramme, milligram.
millilitre, milliliter.
millimetre, millimeter.
milliner, hoedemaker, hoedemaakster; modemaker, modemaakster, modiste.
millinery, hoedmakery, hoede, hoede-afdeling; modes, mode-artikels.
milling, malery, meulbedryf; freeswerk; walsery; – **machine**, frees(masjien).
million, miljoen.
millionaire, miljoenêr.
millionth, miljoenste.
mill-pond, meuldam.
mill-sluice, meulsluis.
millstone, meulsteen.
mill-wheel, meulrat.
millwright, meulmaker.
milreis, milreis.
milt, n. hom (van 'n vis); milt.
milt, v. bevrug, kuit laat skiet.
mime, n. gebarespel; gebarespeler; hanswors.
mime, v. mimeer, speel.
mimetic(al), na-apend, nabootsend.
mimic, n. na-aper, nabootser, uitkoggelaar.
mimic, a. na-apend, mimies; kastig, voorgewend; – **warfare**, spieëlgeveg.
mimic, v. namaak, na-aap, naboots; uitkoggel; presies op mekaar lyk.
mimicry, na-apery, nabootsing, mimiek; aanpassing.
mimosa, mimosa; doringboom.
minaret, minaret.
minatory, dreigend.
mince, n. (fyn)gemaalde vleis, frikkadel.
mince, v. (fyn)maal, kleinmaak; gemaak praat; trippel, gemaak loop; bedek, verskoon; **he does not – matters**, hy draai daar geen doekies om nie; – **one's steps**, trippel; – **words**, doekies omdraai; gemaak praat.
mince(d)-meat, gemaalde vleis, frikkadel, pasteivulsel.
mincemeat: to make – of, fynmaak, kafloop.
mince-pie, vleispastei(tjie); vrugtepastei.
mincer, vleismeul(e).
mincing, gemaak, geaffekteer; trippelend.
mind, n. verstand, intellek, gees; hart, gemoed; opinie, mening, opvatting; verlangste, sin; neiging, gevoelens, doel, voornemens; gedagte, herinnering, gedagtenis; **bear, keep in** –, onthou, bedink; **time out of** –, lank gelede; **I gave him a piece of my** –, ek het hom goed die waarheid gesê; **I have half a – to go**, ek het half lus om te gaan; **he has a – of his own**, hy weet wat hy wil; **to know one's own** –, weet wat 'n mens wil hê; **to change one's** –, van plan verander; **great –s think alike**, die kenners, stem ooreen; **set one's – on**, sy sinne (hart) sit op; **to follow one's** –, sy (eie) kop volg; **to be in two –s about something**, oor iets twyfel; **absence of** –, afgetrokkenheid; **presence of** –, teenwoordigheid van gees; **in body and** –, na siel en liggaam; **I have in** –, ek is voornemens; ek dink aan; **I am of your** –, ek stem met jou saam; **his – wanders**, sy gedagtes dwaal; **speak one's** –, jou eerlike mening sê, reguit praat; **put in** –, gedagtig maak aan; **that is a great thing off my** –, dit is 'n groot las van my hart; **I have something on my** –, ek het iets op my hart; **he is out of his** –, hy is nie reg nie, hy is van sy verstand af; **to my** –, volgens my mening, myns insiens.
mind, v. herinner, onthou; oplet oppas; sôre, na kyk; omgee; stem; – **your own business**, bemoei jou met jou eie sake; **would you** –

coming?, sal u asseblief kom?; **if you don't** –, as u nie omgee nie; –!, pas op!; **never – him**, steur jou nie aan hom nie; – **you**, sien jy, moet jy weet; – **yourself**, pas jouself op; **never** –!, dit kom nie op aan nie, dit maak nie saak nie, dis niks nie; **to – a child**, 'n kind oppas; **would you – telling me?**, gee u om om my te sê?
minded, gesind, geneig; **to be – to**, lus hê om.
mindful, oplettend, opmerksaam; indagtig; versigtig; – **of**, gedagtig aan.
mindless, dom; onoplettend, agteloos; onversigtig; – **of**, nie gedagtig aan nie, sonder om te dink aan.
mind-projection, telepatie.
mine, n. myn; bron (van rykdom ens.).
mine, v. grawe, delwe; ontgin; uithol; ondermyn; myne lê.
mine, pron. myne, my, van my.
mine-detector, myn(ver)klikker.
miner, delwer, mynwerker; mynlêer.
mineral, n. mineraal, delfstof, erts.
mineral, a. mineraal- . . ., delfstof- . . .; – **coal**, steenkool; – **water**, mineraalwater; – **spring**, mineraalbron.
mineralize, mineraliseer, versteen.
mineralogic, mineralogies, delfstofkundige, delfstof- . . .
mineralogist, mineraloog, delfstofkundige.
mineralogy, mineralogie, delfstofkunde.
mingle, meng, vermeng, deurmekaar maak, deurmekaar loop.
mingy, suinig.
miniature, n. miniatuur; **in** –, in 't klein.
miniature a. klein, miniatuur- . . .
miniature-painter miniatuurskilder.
mini-car, minimotor.
minicopter, minikopter.
minify, verklein, kleinmaak; verkleineer.
minim, halwe noot; minim.
minimal, minimaal, miniem.
minimise, verklein, laag aanslaan (skat); goedpraat.
minimum, n. minste, minimum.
minimum, a. minimaal, minimum- . . .
mining, n. mynbou, mynwese.
mining, a. myn- . . .; – **engineer**, myningenieur.
minion, gunsteling; kalfakter; flikflooier; –**s of fortune**, gunstelinge van die fortuin.
minish, verminder; sien ook **diminish**.
minister, n. minister; dienaar; gesant; predikant.
minister, v. (be)dien, versorg; verskaf; diens verrig; – **to**, voorsien in; voldoen aan; bydra tot; versorg; streel, bevredig.
ministerial, ministerieel; amptelik; geestelik; dienend; the – **benches**, die regeringsbanke; – **to**, bevorderlik aan.
ministerialist, regeringsman.
ministrant, n. dienaar.
ministrant, a. dienend.
ministration, bediening; diens; amp (van predikant); verskaffing; medewerking, hulp.
ministry, ministerie; ministerskap; bediening, ampsverrigting; geestelikheid; sorg; hulp, medewerking; **enter the** –, predikant word.
minisub(marine), miniatuur-duikboot, dwergduikboot.
mink, (soort) wesel; weselbont.
minnow, witvissie, grondeling.
minor, n. mindere; minderjarige; mineur.
minor, a. minder, kleiner; onmondig, junior; ondergeskik; onbeduidend, gering; van laer rang; minor; mineur; **Asia Minor**, Klein-Asië; – **poems**, kleiner gedigte; – **chord**, molakkoord; – **third**, klein terts; **in a – key**, in

mol, in mineur; op 'n klaende toon; – **term**, minor, minderterm.
minority, minderjarigheid; minderheid.
minster, munster, kloosterkerk.
minstrel, minnesanger, minstreel; digter; Negro **-s**, Negersangers.
minstrelsy, minnesangerkuns; die minnesangers; balladeversameling.
mint, n. munt; hoop; a – **of money**, 'n hoop geld.
mint, v. munt; uitvind, maak.
mint, n. kruisement.
mintage, munt; gemunte woord; muntgeld muntloon; muntreg.
minter, munter, muntmaker; uitvinder.
mint-master, muntmeester.
mint-sauce, kruisementsous.
minuend, aftrekgetal.
minuet, menuet.
minus, minus, min; sonder; waardeloos; negatief; I was – a few rands, ek was 'n paar rand armer; he came back – his hat, hy het teruggekom sonder sy hoed; a – **quantity**, 'n negatiewe hoeveelheid; – **sign**, minus-teken, aftrekteken.
minuscule, n. klein letter, minuskel.
minuscule, a. klein.
minute, n. minuut; oomblikkie; ontwerp; memorandum; **the –s**, die notule; **the – that**, op die oomblik dat; **this –**, op die daad; **just a –**, net 'n oomblikkie.
minute, a. klein, gering; haarfyn, presies.
minute, v. presies dateer; notuleer, afskrywe; – **down**, aanteken, notuleer.
minute-book, notuleboek; kladboek.
minute-glass, sandhorlosie, sandlopertjie.
minute-guns, minuutskote.
minute-hand, langwys(t)er.
minutely, haarfyn, presies, omstandig.
minuteness, kleinigheid, presiesheid.
minutiae, besonderhede, kleinighede.
minx, parmant, katjie; flerrie.
miracle, n. wonder, wonderwerk; mirakel; **to work –s**, wonderwerke doen; **to a –**, wondergoed.
miracle-play, mirakelspel.
miracle-worker, wonderdoener.
miraculous, wonderbaarlik, wonder-...; mirakuleus.
miraculousness, wonderbaarlikheid.
mirage, lugspieëling; waan, bedrog.
mire, n. modder; vuiligheid; **stick in the –**, in die verknorsing wees.
mire, v. besoedel, bemodder; in die modder laat val; in moeilikhede dompel.
mirror, n. spieël; toonbeeld.
mirror, v. weerspieël, weerkaats; met spieëls beklee.
mirth, vroulikheid, jolgheid.
mirthful, ongeruimd, jolig, plesierig.
mirthless, treurig, droef, droefgeestig.
miry, vuil, modderig.
misadventure, ongeluk, teenspoed.
misalliance, ongelyke huwelik, mésalliance.
misanthrope, mensehater, misantroop.
misanthropic, misantropies.
misanthropist, mensehater, misantroop.
misanthropy, mensehaat, misantropie.
misapplication, verkeerde toepassing, wanbeheer, verduistering.
misapply, verkeerd toepas; misbruik, sleg beheer, verduister.
misapprehend, verkeerd begryp, misverstaan.
misapprehension, misverstand.
misappropriate, misbruik, onwettig, toeëien.

misappropriation, misbruik, verduistering, wanbeheer.
misbecome, sleg staan, nie pas nie.
misbecoming, ongepas, onbetaamlik.
misbegot(ten), oneg, baster-...
misbehave, sleg gedra.
misbehaviour, wangedrag.
misbelief, ongeloof; wangeloof, dwaalleer.
misbeliever, dwaler, ongelowige.
miscalculate, misreken; verkeerd (be)reken.
miscalculation, misrekening, verkeerde berekening.
miscall, verkeerd noem.
miscarriage, mislukking; verlore-gaan (van 'n brief); wangedrag; miskraam; – **of justice**, geregtelike dwaling.
miscarry, misluk; verlore-gaan (van 'n brief); 'n miskraam kry.
miscasting, verkeerde optelling.
miscegenation, rasvermenging, verbastering.
miscellaneous, gemeng, deurmekaar; veelsydig; verskillend, veelsoortig.
miscellaneousness, verskeidenheid; veelsydigheid.
miscellanist, mengelwerkskrywer.
miscellany, mengelwerk; mengsel.
mischance, ongeluk; **by –**, per ongeluk.
mischief, kwaad, onheil, skade; kattekwaad, streke; **make –**, kwaad stook; **what the –!**, wat die drommel!; **the – of it is**, die ongeluk is; **out of pure –**, uit pure baldadigheid; **keep out of –**, g'n streke uithaal nie; **be up to –**, iets in die skild voer, vol kattekwaad wees.
mischief-maker, kwaadstoker, onheilstigter.
mischief-making, kwaadstokery.
mischievous, nadelig, verderflik, ondeund, gruwelik; – **rascal**, ondeunde rakker.
mischievousness, skadelikheid; ondeundheid.
miscible, mengbaar.
miscite, verkeerd aanhaal.
misconceive, verkeerd begryp, verkeerd opvat.
misconception, wanbegrip, verkeerde opvatting.
misconduct, n. wangedrag; wanbestuur.
miseonduct, v. sleg gedra; sleg bestuur.
misconstruction, verkeerde uitleg, verkeerde opvatting.
misconstrue, verkeerd uitlê, misdui, verkeerd opvat.
miscount, n. verkeerde telling.
miscount, v. verkeerd (op)tel; vertel.
miscreant, n. ellendeling, skurk; ongelowige.
miscreant, a. ellendig, laag; ongelowig.
miscreated, misvormd, wanskape.
miscue, misstoot (by biljart).
misdate, verkeerd dateer.
misdeal, (in kaarte) verkeerd gee (uitdeel).
misdeed, oortreding, misdaad.
misdemeanant, boosdoener, oortreder.
misdemeanour, wangedrag; oortreding, misdryf.
misdirect, verkeerd bedui, verkeerd rig, verkeerd lei; verkeerd adresseer.
misdirection, verkeerde aanduiding, verkeerde inligting; verkeerde adres.
misdo, kwaad doen, onreg doen.
misdoing, wandaad, verkeerde daad.
misdoubt, wantrou, verdink; betwyfel.
misemploy, misbruik.
misemployment, misbruik.
misentry, verkeerde boeking.
miser, vrek, gierigaard; ellendeling.
miserable, ellendig, ongelukkig; miserabel.
miserly, gierig, vrekkerig, suinig.
misery, ellende, armoede, nood.
misfeasance, magsmisbruik, ampsoortreding.
misfire, n. afklapskoot, ketsskoot.

misfire, v. doppie afklap, weier, kets; oorslaan.
misfit, n. slegpassende kledingstuk; **he is a social –,** hy pas nie in die maatskappy nie; that's a –, dit pas sleg.
misfit, v. sleg pas, sleg sit.
misfortune, ongeluk, ramp; **–s never come singly,** 'n ongeluk kom nooit alleen nie; by –, per ongeluk.
misgive: my mind –s me, ek vrees.
misgiving, argwaan; vrees, besorgdheid.
misgotten, onregverdig (ontvang).
misgovern, sleg bestuur, sleg regeer.
misgovernment, wanbestuur, wanbeheer.
misguidance, verkeerde leiding; misleiding.
misguide, verkeerd lei; mislei, verlei.
misguided, misleid; verdwaas, onwetend.
mishandel, sleg behandel; verkeerd aanpak.
mishap, ongeluk, ongeval.
mishmash, mengelmoes, warboel.
misinform, verkeerd inlig, mislei.
misinformation, verkeerde inligting.
misinterpret, verkeerd uitlê (vertolk), misdui.
misinterpretable, vir verkeerde uitleg vatbaar.
misinterpretation, verkeerde uitleg (vertolking), misduiding.
misjudge, verkeerd beoordeel; verkeerd oordeel, verkeerd bereken.
misjudg(e)ment, verkeerde beoordeling.
miskick, misskop.
mislay, verlê, op 'n verkeerde plek sit.
mislead, verlei, mislei; bedrieg, kul.
misleading, misleidend.
mismanage, sleg bestuur; verkeerd aanpak.
mismanagement, wanbeheer, wanbestuur; verkeerde behandeling.
misname, verkeerd (be)noem.
misnomer, verkeerde benaming; fout.
misogamist, huwelikshater.
misogamy, afkeer van die huwelik.
misogynist, vrouehater.
misogyny, vrouehaat.
misplace, verkeerd plaas, misplaas.
misprint, n. drukfout.
misprint, v. verkeerd (afdruk).
misprision, versuim, nalatigheid; – of treason, verheling van verraad.
misprize, onderskat, minag, verag.
mispronounce, verkeerd uitspreek.
mispronunciation, verkeerde uitspraak.
misquotation, verkeerde aanhaling.
misquote, verkeerd aanhaal.
misread, verkeerd lees; verkeerd uitlê.
misrepresent, verkeerd voorstel; verdraai.
misrepresentation, verkeerde voorstelling; verdraaiing.
misrule, n. wanbeheer, wanbestuur.
misrule, v. sleg regeer, sleg bestuur.
miss, n. juffrou, mejuffrou; nôi(entjie) kleinnôi; meisie; the **—es Lombaard**, die dames (nôiens) Lombaard.
miss, n. misskoot; gemis, verlies; a **– is as good as a mile,** amper is ver van stamper; **near –,** neweskoot; **it was a near –,** dit was amper raak.
miss, v. mis; verpas, versuim; vermy, ontbeer; mis skiet, mis slaan, mis stoot, uitlaat; – fire, doppie afklap, weier, kets; – a **blow,** misslaan; – a **mark,** mis skiet; –**one's step,** mis stap, gly; – a **train,** te laat kom vir die trein, die trein verpas; – **one's road,** verdwaal; – a **chance,** 'n kans laat verbygaan.
missal, misboek.
misshapen, mismaak, misvorm, lelik.
missile, werptuig, gooiding, projektiel.

missing, verlore, ontbrekend, weg, op soek; a **page is –,** daar makeer 'n blad; **the – link,** die ontbrekende skakel.
mission, sending, opdrag; roeping, bestemming; sendingpos; gesantskap; missie.
missionary, n. sendeling; gesant; bode.
missionary, a. sending- . . .
mission-church, sendingkerk.
missioner, sendeling; bode.
mission-school, sendingskool.
mission work, sendingwerk.
missive, bode; brief; sendbrief.
misspell, verkeerd spel.
misspend, verkwis, verkeerd bestee.
misstate, verkeerd voorstel, verdraai.
misstatement, verkeerde voorstelling, verdraaiing.
mist, n. mis, newel; motreën; waas.
mist, v. mis, motreën; benewel.
mistakable, (maklik) mee te verwar (vergis), onduidelik.
mistake, n. fout, vergissing, abuis; **and no –,** dit kan jy glo!; **by –,** per abuis; **make a –,** 'n fout maak, (sig) vergis.
mistake, v. verkeerd verstaan, misverstaan; verwar, verwissel; – **for,** verwar met, aansien vir, **there is no mistaking,** jy kan jou nie vergis nie.
mistaken, verkeerd; verkeerd begrepe; foutief, onjuis; **to be –,** dit mis hê, (sig) vergis.
mistakenly, by vergissing, verkeerdelik.
mister, meneer, heer, die heer.
mistime, op die verkeerde moment doen (sê); misreken.
mistimed, ontydig, misplaas, ongepas.
mistiness, newelagtigheid, mistigheid.
mistletoe, mistel(tak), voëlent, litjiestee.
mistral, mistral(wind).
mistranslate, verkeerd vertaal.
mistranslation, verkeerde vertaling.
mistress, mevrou, vrou; meesteres, nôi; onderwyseres; eienares; geliefde; **you are your own –,** jy is jou eie baas; **the – of the house,** die huisvrou. •
mistrust, n. wantroue, verdenking, argwaan.
mistrust, v. wantrou, twyfel aan, verdink.
mistrustful, wantrouig.
misty, newelagtig, mistig; onduidelik; vaag.
misunderstand, misverstaan, verkeerd begryp.
misunderstanding, misverstand, geskil, onenigheid.
misusage, verkeerde gebruik; mishandeling.
misuse, n. misbruik, verkeerde gebruik; mishandeling.
misuse, v. misbruik, verkeerd gebruik; mishandel.
mite, duit, penning; miet; kleinigheid; kleintjie; **not a –,** geen siertjie; **the widow's –,** die weduwee se penning.
mithridatize, immuun maak.
mitigant, versagtend.
mitigate, stil, versag, lenig; verlig, matig; – **pain,** pyn verlig (lenig); – **punishment,** straf ligter maak.
mitigation, versagting, verligting, leniging.
mitrailleuse, mitrailleur, snelvuurgeweer.
mitre, biskopshoed, myter.
mitre, lyshoek, verstek; – **box,** verstekblok.
mitt(en), moffie, duimhandskoen; **to get the –,** 'n bloutjie loop; **to give the –,** laat loop, nee sê; **to handle without –s,** hard aanpak.
mittimus, opsluitbevel, bevel tot gevangsetting; **to get one's –,** afgedank word.
mix, aanmaak, meng, deurmekaar maak; berei; omgaan; – **the cards,** die kaarte skommel; –

in society, in geselskap verkeer; – up, meng, vermeng, verwar; – with, meng met, omgaan met.
mixed, gemeng, deurmekaar gemaak; aangemaak; deurmekaar, van die kop af; to be – up with, betrokke wees in; – bathing, gemengde baaiery; – pickles, atjar; – race, gemengde ras, basterras; – doubles, gemengde dubbelspel (in tennis).
mixer, menger; mengmasjien; good –, iemand wat hom gemaklik aansluit.
mixture, mengsel; mikstuur; drankie.
mix-up, deurmekaarspul; mengelmoes.
miz(z)enmast, besaansmas.
miz(z)en-sail, besaan.
mizzle, motreën, stofreën.
mnemonic, geheue-. . . .
mnemonics, geheueleer, mnemoneutiek.
mnemotechny, geheueleer, mnemotegniek.
mo', oomblikkie; half a –, wag 'n bietjie.
moan, n. gekerm, geklaag, gesteun.
moan, v. kerm, steun; weeklaag; betreur.
moanful, klaend, weeklaend, jammerend.
moaning, gekerm, gejammer, gesteun.
moat, grag, sloot.
mob, n. gepeupel, gespuis; bende, menigte.
mob, v. naloop, molesteer; saamstroom.
mob-cap, mop(mus).
mobile, beweeglik; los; vlottend; mobiel.
mobility, beweeglikheid, mobiliteit.
mobilization, mobilisasie.
mobilize, mobiliseer, mobiel maak; losmaak.
mob-law, bendereg, volksjustisie.
mob-rule, gepeupelheerskappy.
moccassin, mokassin.
mock, n. bespotting; nabootsing.
mock, a. liemaak- . . ., namaak- . . ., skyn- . . .
mock, v. (be)spot, hoon; uitkoggel, naboots, namaak, na-aap; fop; verydel.
mocker, spotter, spotvoël; na-aper; bedrieër.
mockery, bespotting, (ge)spot, hoon, uitkoggelary, tergery, beskimping.
mock-fight, skyngeveg.
mocking, a. spottend, tergend, spotagtig.
mocking-bird, spotvoël, piet-my-vrou.
mock-moon, bymaan.
mock-parliament, skynparlement.
mock-sun, byson.
mock-trial, skynverhoor; skynhof.
mock-turtle: – soup, nagemaakte skilpadsop.
modal, modaal, van wyse.
modality, modaliteit.
mode, manier, wyse, vorm, modus; toon (in musiek); mode, gewoonte; all the –, die algemene mode.
model, n. model; voorbeeld; toonbeeld.
model, a. model . . ., voorbeeldig.
model, v. modelleer, vorm, boetseer; – after, on, vorm na; skoei op die lees van.
modeller, modelleerder, boetseerder.
modelling, modelleerkuns, boetseerkuns.
modelling-clay, modelleerklei, boetseerklei.
moderate, n. gematigde.
moderate, a. gematig, matig, middelmatig; taamlik; redelik; billik; – zone, gematigde (lug)streek.
moderate, v. matig, temper; in toom hou; (laat) bedaar, afslaan; afkoel; modereer.
moderately, gematig, matig, redelik.
moderateness, gematigdheid, matigheid.
moderation, matigheid, gematigdheid; matiging, maat; in –, met mate.
moderator, moderator, arbiter; demper, regulateur; moderateur.
modern, modern, nuwerwets, nieumodies.

modernism, modernisme.
modernist, modernis.
modernity, nuwerwetsheid.
modernization, modernisasie.
modernize, moderniseer.
modest, beskeie, sedig, ingetoë, teruggetrokke; fatsoenlik; matig.
modesty, beskeidenheid; eerbaarheid.
modicum, (klein) bietjie, minimum.
modification, verandering, wysiging; matiging; modifikasie.
modified, gewysig.
modify, wysig, verander; matig.
modish, modies, na die mode.
modishness, modesug; modiesheid.
modiste, modiste, klere- en hoedemaakster.
modulate, reguleer, stel, reël; moduleer.
modulation, regulering, reëling, modulasie; – of the voice, stembuiging.
modulator, reguleerder, modulator.
module, standaard, maatstaf.
modulus, modulus.
mohair, angorahaar, sybokhaar.
Mohammedan, n. Mohammedaan.
Mohammedan, a. Mohammedaans.
moiety, helfte, deel, gedeelte.
moil, swoeg, slaaf; to toil and –, slaaf en swoeg.
moire, n. moiré, gewaterde stof (sy).
moire, a. moiré, gewaterd.
moist, a. nat, vogtig, klam(merig).
moisten, natmaak, bevogtig; to – one's throat, keel natmaak, 'n dop steek.
moistness, nattigheid, vogtigheid, klamheid.
moisture, vog, vogtigheid, klamheid.
moke, esel; Neger.
molar, kiestand, maaltand.
molasses, stroop, suikerstroop, melasse.
mole, n. moesie, moedervlek.
mole, n. pier, hawedam, keerdam.
mole, n. mol.
mole, v. ondergrawe, uithol.
mole-cast, molshoop.
molecular, molekulêr, molekule- .
molecule, molekule, stofdeeltjie.
mole-hill, molshoop; to make a mountain of a – van 'n muggie 'n olifant maak.
moleskin, molvel.
molest, moveer, hinder, lastig val, molesteer.
molestation, hinder, kwellery, molestasie.
mole-snake, molslang.
moll, aanhangster (van boef).
mollient, versagtend.
mollify, versag, lenig, stil, bedaar.
mollusc, weekdier, mollusk.
molly-coddle, n. papbroek, meisietjie.
molly-coddle, v. (ver)troetel, verwen.
molten, gesmelte; sien ook melt.
moly, wilde knoflok.
molybdenum, molibdeen.
moment, oomblik; oogwenk; gewig, belang; one half a –, een oomblik; this –, onmiddellik, dadelik; men of the –, manne van die dag; men of –, gewigtige persone; of great –, van groot belang (gewig).
momentarily, elke oomblik; oombliklik; vir 'n oomblik; momenteel.
momentary, vir 'n oomblik; kortstondig, vlugtig.
momentous, gewigtig, belangrik.
momentousness, belangrikheid, gewigtigheid.
momentum, moment; dryfkrag, vaart.
monachism, kloosterlewe, kloosterwese.
monad, monade, eenheid.
monandrous, een-meeldradig.
monandry, monandrie, eenmannery.

monarch, monarg, koning, (alleen)heerser.
monarchic(al), monargaal.
monarchism, monargisme.
monarchist, monargis.
monarchy, monargie; koninkryk, keiserryk.
monastery, klooster.
monastic, klooster- . . .; monnike- . . .; – vow, kloostergelofte.
monasticism, kloosterlewe, kloosterwese.
Monday, Maandag; **black** –, eerste Maandag van die skoolkwartaal.
mondial, alom bekend.
monetary, geldelik, geld- . . .; – **value**, geldwaarde.
monetize, munt, in omloop bring.
money, geld, munt; betaalmiddel; **ready** –, baargeld, kontant; **time is** –, tyd is geld; **to make** –, geld verdien; **coin** –, grof geld verdien, geld soos bossies verdien; **for love of** –, vir geld of mooi woorde.
money-box, spaarpot, gelddosie.
money-broker, geldwisselaar, geldmakelaar.
moneyed, ryk, bemiddeld; geld . . .
money-grabber, **-grubber**, geldwolf, gierigaard.
money-lender, geldskieter.
moneyless, sonder geld, arm.
money-market, geldmark.
money-order, geldwissel.
money's-worth, geldwaarde, volle waarde.
moneywort, penningkruid.
Mongol(ian), Mongools; Mongool.
mongoose, igneumon, **faraosrat**, farao-rot.
mongrel, n. baster; basterhond.
mongrel, a. baster- . . .
monism, monisme.
monist, monis.
monistic, monisties.
monition, waarskuwing; dagvaarding.
monitor, n. vermaner; monitor.
monitor, v. afluister, opvang; as monitor optree.
monitory, vermanend, waarskuwend.
monk, monnik; drukkersklad.
monkdom, monnikedom.
monkery, monnikslewe, kloosterlewe; klooster; monnikedom.
monkey, n. bobbejaan; stamper, ramblok; waterkruik; R1,000; **to put his** – **up**, hom kwaad maak; **get one's** – **up**, kwaad word; **to play the** –, gekskeer, streke uithaal.
monkey, v. na-aap, uitkoggel; – **(about) with**, peuter met, speel met.
monkey-bread, baobabvrug, apebrood.
monkey-cap, bebroeide-eiers (plant).
monkey-jacket, matroosbaadjie.
monkey-nut, grondboontjie, apenootjie.
monkey-trick, bobbejaanstreek, kattekwaad.
monkey-wrench, Engelse sleutel.
monkhood, monnikskap; monnikestand; kloosterlewe; monnikedom.
monkish, monnikagtig, monnike- . . .
monocarpous, eenmaalbloeiend, eenjarig.
monocephalous, eenhoofdig, monosefaal.
monochord, monochordium.
monochromatic, eenkleurig, monochroom.
monochrome, n. skildery in een kleur, monochroom.
monochrome, a. eenkleurig, monochroom.
monocle, ooglas, monokel.
monocotyledon, eensaadlobbige plant.
monocotyledonous, eensaadlobbig.
monocular, eenogig, vir een oog.
monody, klaaglied; monodie.
monogamist, monogamis.
monogamy, monogamie.
monogram, monogram, naamsyfer.

monograph, n. monografie.
monographer, monografieskrywer.
monolith, monoliet.
monolithic, monolities.
monologue, alleenspraak, monoloog.
monomania, monomanie.
monomanic(al), monomaan.
monometallism, monometallisme.
monomorphic, **-ous**, eenvormig, monomorf.
monopetalous, eenblarig, monopetaal.
monophthong, monoftong, vokaal.
monoplane, eendekker.
monopolize, monopoliseer; in beslag neem.
monopolist, monopolis, alleenhandelaar.
monopoly, monopolie, alleenhandel; alleenreg.
monorail, eenspoortrein, enkelspoor.
monospermous, eensadig.
monosyllabic, eenlettergrepig, monosillabies.
monosyllable, monosillabe, eenlettergrepige woord; **to speak in** **–s**, kortaf praat.
monotheism, monoteïsme.
monotheist, monoteïs.
monotheistic, monoteïsties.
monotone, n.: **in** –, in een toon.
monotone, a. eentonig, vervelend.
monotonous, eentonig, vervelend, **monotoon**.
monotony, eentonigheid, monotonie.
monotype, monotiep, monotipe.
monsoon, moesson; reënseisoen.
monster, n. monster, gedrog.
monster, a. monsteragtig, reusagtig.
monstrance, monstrans.
monstrosity, monsteragtigheid, onmenslikheid; monster, gedrog.
monstrous, monsteragtig, gedrogtelik; afgryslik, onmenslik; reusagtig.
montagé, montage.
montane, bergagtig, berg- . . .
Montenegrin, Montenegryns; Montenegryn.
month, maand; **this day** –, vandag oor 'n maand.
monthlies, maandsiekte, menstruasie.
monthly, n. maandblad, maandskrif.
monthly, a. maandeliks, maand- . . .; – **pay**, maandgeld; – **return**, maandstaat; – **ticket**, maandkaartjie.
monument, monument, gedenkteken.
monumental, monumentaal; gedenk- . . .; groots, imposant; kolossaal; – **mason**, grafsteenmaker.
moo, loei.
mood, stemming, bui, luim, wyse, modus; **in the** –, in die stemming; **in a good** –, in 'n goeie bui (luim); **indicative** –, aantonende wys(e).
moodiness, knorrigheid, nukkerigheid.
moody, nukkerig, buierig; swaarmoedig.
moon, n. maan; **full** –, vol(le)maan; **new** –, nuwemaan; **once in a blue** –, so elke blou-Maandag.
moon, v. droom; ronddrentel; **to** – **away one's time**, sy tyd verdroom.
moonbeam, maanstraal.
moon-calf, maankalf, wangedrog; uilskuiken.
moonless, sonder maan, donker; **it was a** – **night**, dit was donkermaan.
moonlight, n. maanlig, maanskyn.
moonlight, a. maanlig- . . ., maanskyn- . . .; **a** – **night**, 'n maanligaand.
moonshine, maanskyn; onsin; smokkeldrank; **that's all** –, dit is alles bog.
moonshiner, dranksmokkelaar.
moon-stone, maansteen.
moon-struck, maansiek, mal, sentimenteel.
moony, soos die maan, maan- . . .; dromerig.
Moor, **Moor**.
moor, n. heide, heiveld; vlei, moeras.
moor, v. aanlê, vasmaak, anker.
moorage, ankerplek, aanlêplek; ankergeld.

moorings, meertoue, vasmaaktoue, aanlêplek.
Moorish, Moors.
moorland, heide, heiveld; vlei, moeras.
moose, (Amerikaanse) eland.
moot, betwisbaar, disputeerbaar.
moot, v. bespreek, ter sprake bring, opper.
mop, n. rabol, stokdweil.
mop, v. opvrywe, dweil; afvee; – **up**, insluk; opvang; opruim (mil.); – **the floor with somebody**, iemand kafloop, iemand vaatdoek maak.
mop, n. skewebek, grimas; –**s and mows**, grimasse.
mop, v. skewebek trek; – **and mow**, skewebek trek, grimasse maak.
mope, n. knieser; **the –s**, bedruktheid.
mope, v. (sig) verknies, druil.
mopped, kragfiets, bromfiets.
mop-headed, bossiekop- . . .
moping, **mopish**, knieserig.
moppy, bossiekop- . . .; geswael, aangeklam.
mop-stick, dweilstok; sukkelaar.
moquette, trypferweel.
moraine, moraine, gletserpuinhoop.
moral, n. moraal, les; ewebeeld; –**s**, sedes, sedelike gedrag; moraal.
moral, a. moreel, sedelik, moraal- . . .; sede- . . .; – **law**, sedewet; – **sense**, sedelikheidsgevoel; – **victory**, morele oorwinning; – **certainty**, uitgemaakte saak; – **philosophy**, sedekunde.
morale, n. moreel, moed, selfvertroue.
moralize, moraliseer; sedelik verbeter.
moralizer, sedepreker, sedemeester.
moralist, sedepreker, moralis.
morality, sedelikheid; sedekunde; sedelike gedrag; sinnespel; moraliteit.
morass, moeras.
Moravian, a. Morawies; Morawiër; Hernhutter.
morbid, sieklik, ongesond, siekte- . . .; – **anatomy**, patologiese anatomie.
morbidity, sieklikheid; siektesyfer; siektetoestand.
morbidness, sieklikheid.
mordacious, bytend; skerp; bitter.
mordant, n. bytmiddel, hegmiddel.
mordant, a. bytend, skerp.
more, meer, ander, nog, groter; **bring some** –, bring nog (meer); – **and** –, meer en meer; **as much** –, nog een keer soveel; **one** – **glass**, nog 'n glas; – **or less**, min of meer, ongeveer; **the** – . . ., **the** –, hoe meer . . ., des te meer; **so much the** –, des te meer; **never** –, nooit weer nie; **once** –, nog 'n keer; **no** –, nie meer nie; **the** – **the merrier**, hoe meer siele hoe meer vreugde; **what is** –, wat meer sê; en verder.
moreen, woldamas.
moreover, origens; daarenbowe, bowendien.
Moresque, Moors; arabesk.
morganatic, met die linkerhand, morganaties.
morgen, morg(e).
morgue, lykhuis.
moribund, sterwend, doodsiek.
morion, stormhoed.
Morisco, n. Moor; Moors; Moorse dans.
Mormon, Mormoon.
morn, môre, môrestond.
morning, n. môre, oggend, voormiddag; **in the** –, in die môre; **this** –, vanmôre; **tomorrow** –, môreoggend; **good** –, goei(e)môre; **of a** –, smôrens.
morning, a. môre.
morning-dress, oggendpak; pandbaadjie en broek; oggendrok.
morning-glory, purperwinde, eendagmooi.
morning-gown, kamerjas; kamerjapon.
morning paper, oggendblad.

morning prayers, oggendgodsdiens.
morning star, môrester, Venus.
morning-watch, dagwag.
Moroccan, Marokkaans; Marokkaner.
morocco, marokyn, marokynleer.
moron, moron; stommerik.
morose, stuurs, nors, stug.
morphia, morfia.
morphine, morfien.
morphinism, morfinisme.
morphology, morfologie, vormleer.
morphological, morfologies.
morris(-dance), Moorse dans; boeredans.
morrow, môre; **on the** –, die volgende dag; **on the** – **of the war**, na die oorlog.
Morse, Morse; Morse-toestel; – **code**, Morseskrif; – **alphabet**, Morse-alfabet.
morse, walrus.
morsel, stukkie, happie, brokkie.
mort, boel, menigte.
mortal, n. sterfling.
mortal, a. sterflik; dodelik; dood(s)- . . .; menslik, mense- . . .; – **enemy**, dood(s)vyand; – **combat**, stryd op lewe en dood; – **hurry**, vliegende haas; **any** – **thing**, enige ding onder die son; **a** – **shame**, 'n ewige skande; – **sin**, doodsonde; – **remains**, stoflike oorskot.
mortality, sterflikheid; mortaliteit; – **rate**, sterfte(syfer); mensdom.
mortally, dodelik; sterflik; menslik.
mortar, n. vysel; klei, messelkalk; mortier.
mortar, v. pleister.
mortar-board, pleisterplank; studentebaret.
mortgage, verband, hipoteek, kusting.
mortgage, v. verpand, verband neem (op).
mortgage-bond, verband, pandbrief, hipoteek.
mortgagee, verbandhouer, hipoteekhouer.
mortgager, -**or**, verbandgeër, hipoteekgeër.
mortice, sien **mortise**.
mortification, afsterwing; kastyding; vernedering, krenking, ergernis; mortifikasie; kouevuur.
mortified, gekrenk, beledig.
mortify, kasty; krenk, beledig, erger; afsterwe.
mortise, n. tapgat.
mortise, v. tap, inlaat, (in)voeg.
mortise-chisel, tapbeitel.
mortise-lock, inlaatslot.
mortuary, n. lykhuis; begraafplaas.
mortuary, a. dode- . . ., doods- . . ., sterf- . . ., begraaf- . . ., graf- . . .
mosaic, mosaïek.
Mosaic, Mosaïes.
moselle, mo(e)selwyn.
mosque, moskee.
mosquito, muskiet.
mosquito-net, muskietnet.
moss, n. mos; moeras; turf; **a rolling stone gathers no** –, 'n swerwer bly 'n derwer, 'n rollende steen vergaar geen mos nie.
moss, v. met mos bedek, bemos.
moss-clad, met mos bedek, bemos.
moss-rose, mosroos.
mossy, mosagtig, bemos, donserig.
most, a. meeste, uiterste, grootste; die meeste; **to make the** – **of**, die beste gebruik van maak; – **people**, die meeste mense; – **of us**, die meeste van ons; **at the** –, hoogstens; **for the** – **part**, grotendeels; – **of the time**, gewoonlik.
most, adv. die meeste, mees, hoogs, uiters; **what** – **annoys me**, wat my die meeste vererg; **ten at the** –, uiters tien; – **ludicrous**, uiters

belaglik; die belaglikste; – **certainly**, al te seker.
mostly, meestal, grotendeels, hoofsaaklik.
mote, n. stoffie, stofdeeltjie; siertjie, stipseltjie; splinter; – **in another's eye**, splinter in die oog van 'n ander.
motel, motel.
moth, mot, nagvlinder.
moth-ball, motballetjie; opgelê (van skepe).
moth-eaten, deur motte gevreet.
mother, n. moeder, ma; vroutjie, tante; abdis; huismoeder; **every** –**'s son**, elkeen sonder uitsondering; – **superior**, moeder-owerste.
mother, n. moer, droesem.
mother, v. bemoeder; vertroetel; in die wêreld bring; as kind aanneem.
mother-country, vaderland.
motherhood, moederskap.
mothering, moedersorg; troetelary.
mother-in-law, skoonmoeder.
motherless, moederloos.
motherly, moederlik, moeder-...
mother-of-pearl, perlemoen (perlemoer).
mother-tongue, moedertaal; grondtaal.
mother-wort, moederkruid.
mothy, vol motte; van motte gevreet.
motion, n. beweging; gang; gebaar; voorstel, mosie, aansoek; stoelgang; **of one's own** –, vrywillig; – **picture**, rolprent.
motion, v. (met 'n gebaar) wys, toewink.
motionless, beweegloos, doodstil, botstil.
motive, n. beweegrede, motief, dryfveer.
motive, a. bewegend, dryf-...; – **force**, dryfkrag.
motley, n. deurmekaarspul; narrepak.
motley, a. bont, deurmekaar, gemeng.
motor, n. motor, outo, motorkar; dryfkrag; – **cycle**, motorfiets; – **boat**, motorboot; – **bus**, motorbus; – **coach**, toerbus; – **launch**, motorbarkas; – **lorry**, vragmotor.
motor-car, motor, motorkar, outo.
motorist, motoris, motorbestuurder.
motor-spirit, petrol, motorbrandstof.
mottle, n. vlek, streep, kol.
mottle, a. gevlek, gestreep, bont.
mottle, v. vlek, streep, skakeer.
mottled, gevlek, bont, gemarmer, gestreep; **bluesoap**, blouseep.
motto, motto, leus, sinspreuk.
moujik, moezjiek.
mould, n. (los)grond, teelaarde.
mould, n. vorm; matrys; stempel; tipe.
mould, n. vorm, maak, giet, modelleer, knee.
mould, n. skimmel, kim.
mould, v. skimmel (word), kim.
mould, n. roes, roesvlek.
mould-board, rysterplank, rysterplaat.
moulder, verval, vergaan, vrot.
mouldiness, skimmelagtigheid.
moulding, lyswerk, lys, fries.
moulding-board, vloerlys; strykbord; knieplank.
moulding-plane, lysskaaf.
mouldy, skimmel, beskimmel; gekim; verouderd, uit die ou doos.
moult, verveer; verhaar; vervel; verloor.
moulting, (die) verveer; verhaar; vervel.
mound, n. hopie, heuweltjie; wal, skans.
mound, v. ophoop; omwal, verskans.
mount, n. berg, heuwel, kop.
mount, n. montering, karton; beslag; raam; ryperd; rit.
mount, v. monteer, insit; opplak; **to** – **in gold**, in goud vat; ('n aanval) loods.
mount, v. opklim, styg, rys; opstel, regsit; 'n perd verskaf; – **guard over**, (gaan) wag staan oor.
mountain, n. berg, kop; **to make** –**s of molehills**, van 'n muggie 'n olifant maak.
mountain, a. berg-..., bergagtig.
mountain-chain, bergreeks.
mountaineer, n. bergklimmer; bergbewoner.
mountaineer, v. bergklim.
mountaineering, bergklimmery.
mountainous, bergagtig, berg-..
mountain-pass, bergpas, poort.
mountain-range, bergreeks.
mountain-slide, bergstorting, bergverskuiwing.
mountebank, kwaksalwer, bedrieër.
mounted, berede, te perd; opgeplak; – **police**, berede polisie.
mounting, montering, beslag; (die) opklim.
mourn, treur, rou (oor), betreur, beween.
mourner, treurende, roudraer.
mournful, treurig, droewig, bedroef.
mourning, rou; rouklere; **deep** –, swaar rou, volle rou; **to be in** –, **out of** –, in, uit die rou wees.
mourning-paper, roupapier.
mouse, n. muis; blou-oog.
mouse-colour, muiskleur, vaal.
mouselike, so stil soos 'n muis.
mouser, muisvanger.
mouse-trap, (muis)valletjie; slagystertjie.
mousseline, moeselien.
moustache, snor(baard), knewel.
mousy, vol muise, muis-...
mouth, n. mond; bek; monding, uitloop; opening; stem; **from hand to** –, van die hand in die land; **he had his heart in his** –, sy hart het in sy skoene geklop; **my** – **waters**, my mond water, ek watertand; **he takes the words out of my** –, hy neem die woorde uit my mond; **give** –, blaf; **give** – **to**, uitspreek; **feel down in the** –, bek-af voel; **to make** –, skewebek trek; **he is everybody's** –, elkeen praat van hom; **to pass from** – **to** –, van mond tot mond gaan; **by word of** –, mondeling (mondeliks).
mouth, v. eet, vreet; proe aan; uitgalm, gemaak praat; skewemond trek.
mouther, grootprater; gemaakte prater.
mouthful, mondvol, hap, sluk.
mouth-organ, mondfluitjie, mondharmonika.
mouthpiece, mondstuk; woordvoerder.
mouthy, grootpraterig; vuilbekkig; prekerig.
movable, n. iets beweegbaars; –**s**, losgoed.
movable, a. beweeglik, los; roerend; verplaasbaar; – **property**, losgoed, roerende eiendom.
movableness, beweeglikheid, beweegbaarheid.
move, n. beweging; set, stoot; stap, maatreël; **to make a** –, 'n set doen; stoot; (van tafel) opstaan; **on the** –, aan die rondtrek, in beweging; **get a** – **on**, maak gou, vooruit!
move, v. beweeg, roer, gaan, loop; aandrywe; verplaas; marsjeer; trek, omtrek, stoot, set doen; groet, buig; werk; voorstel; – **heaven and earth**, hemel en aarde beweeg; **the spirit** –**s me**, die gees word vaardig oor my; – **away**, wegtrek; – **backwards**, teruggaan; – **down**, afgaan; – **into**, intrek; – **off**, wegtrek, wegloop; – **on**, verder gaan; – **on!**, voorwaarts!; – **out**, uittrek; **bowels** –, maag werk.
movement, beweging, gang; meganiek; opwelling; stap; tempo; ritme; motief; stoelgang, omset.
mover, beweger; voorsteller; drywer, dryfkrag; hoofoorsaak, dryfveer.
movies, bioskoop, fliek.
moving, beweeg; ...; roerend, aandoenlik;

dryf-...; – **force**, beweegkrag; – **spring**, dryfveer; – **pictures**, lewende beelde, bioskoop.
movingness, aandoenlikheid.
mow, n. hooi, maaisel, gemaaide; hooimied.
mow, v. maai, sny; hooimaak; – **down**, afmaai; wegmaai.
mower, maaier; snymasjien.
much, a. baie, veel, erg; **make – of**, baie hou van; **I – regret**, dit spyt my baie; **he is not – of a farmer**, as boer beteken hy nie veel nie; – **of a size**, omtrent ewe groot; **he is too – for me**, hy is my oor, hy is my baas; **I thought as –**, dit het ek wel gedag; **how –?**, hoeveel?; **as – again**, nog soveel; – **worse**, veel erger; – **the worst**, ver(re)weg die slegste; **not so – that**, nie eens dat; **so – so that**, soseer dat; – **the same**, omtrent dieselfde.
muchness, hoeveelheid; **much of a –**, peper en koljander, van dieselfde soort.
mucilage, gom; slym.
mucilaginous, gomagtig; slymagtig.
muck, n. vuilgoed, bog; mis; gemeenheid; gemors; aardse slyk; **it's all –**, dit is alles bog.
muck, v. mes, bemes; vuilmaak; verknoei; **he –s about**, hy slenter rond; – **up**, verknoei.
muck-heap, mishoop, vuilgoedhoop.
mucker, val.
muckle, baie, veel.
muck-worm, miswurm; gierigaard, vrek.
mucky, vuil, smerig; gemeen, laag.
mucosity, slymagtigheid, slym.
mucous, slymagtig, slymerig, slym-...; – **membrane**, slymvlies.
mucus, slym.
mud, modder, slyk; vuilgoed, vuilis; **fling – at**, deur die slyk haal, slegmaak; **to stick in the –**, vassit, agterbly.
muddle, n. deurmekaarspul, verwarring; knoeiwerk; **he made a – of it**, hy het dit verknoei; **in a –**, in die war.
muddle, v. verwar, knoei; troebel maak; dronk maak; meng; – **on**, aansukkel; – **through**, deursukkel.
muddle-head, uilskuiken, domkop.
muddle-headed, deurmekaar, onnosel.
muddler, knoeier.
muddy, n. modderig; troebel; vuil, morsig; onduidelik; deurmekaar; dik.
muddy, v. bemodder; troebel maak; benewel; bemors; deurmekaar maak.
mud-guard, modderskerm.
mud-lark, rioolwerker; straatslenteraar.
muezzin, gebedsroeper.
muff, n. mof.
muff, n. lomperd; domkop; mislukking.
muff, v. bederwe, verfoes; misvang.
muffin, muffin, teekoekie.
muffineer, suikerstrooier.
muffle, n. bek, snuit, bolip.
muffle, n. moffie, bokshandskoen; dwanghandskoen; omhulsel, doek; moffel.
muffle, v. toedraai, toemaak; demp; toesnoer; omfloers; blinddoek; mompel.
muffled, toegemaak; gedemp; **in a – voice**, met gedempte stem.
muffler, halsdoek; serp; bokshandskoen, demper.
mufti, mufti; burgerkleding.
mug, n. beker.
mug, n. uilskuiken, esel.
mug, n. blokker.
mug, n. gesig, smoel, bek, bakkies; **a –'s game**, gekkewerk.
mug, v. swoeg, blok; – **up**, blok.

muggins, uilskuiken; dominospel.
muggy, bedompig, swoel, broeierig.
mugwump, groot meneer, indoena; alleenloper.
muid, mud.
mulatto, baster, halfnaatjie, mulat.
mulberry, moerbei.
mulch, strooimis, dekblare.
mulct, n. geldstraf, geldboete.
mulct, v. beboet, straf.
mule, esel, muil; baster; styfkop; dommerik, fynspinmasjien.
mule-headed, koppig.
mule-jenny, fynspinmasjien.
muleteer, eseldrywer.
mulish, eselagtig, koppig.
mull, n. dun neteldoek.
mull, n. fiasko; misvat; **to make a – of**, verknoei.
mull, v. verfoes, verknoei; misvat.
mull, v. krui; **–ed wine**, gekruide wyn.
mullah, molla(h).
muller, maalklip.
mullet, mulvis, harder.
mulligatawny, kerriesop.
mulligrubs, maagpyn; terneergedruktheid.
mullion, (venster)roei.
mulangular, veelhoekig.
multeity, veelvuldigheid.
multi-coloured, veelkleurig, bont.
multifarious, veelvuldig, veelsoortig.
multiflorous, veelblommig.
multifold, veelvuldig.
multiform, veelvormig, veelsoortig.
multiformity, verworrigheid.
multilateral, veelsydig; multilateraal.
multimillionaire, multimiljoenêr.
multinomial, a. veelnamig; veeltermig.
multinomial, n. veelterm.
multiparous, meerbarig; meerkinderig.
multipartite, veeldelig.
multiped(e), n. duisendpoot.
multiped(e), a. veelvoetig.
multiple, n. veelvoud; **least common –**, kleinste gemene veelvoud.
multiple, veelvoudig, veelsoortig.
multiplex, veelvuldig, samegesteld.
multipliable, vermenigvuldigbaar.
multiplicand, vermenigvuldigtal.
multiplication, vermenigvuldiging; **– table**, vermenigvuldigingstafel.
multiplicative, vermenigvuldigend.
multiplicator, vermenigvuldiger.
multiplicity, menigvuldigheid, menigte, veelheid.
multiplier, vermenigvuldiger; versterker; multiplikator.
multiply, vermenigvuldig; vermeer(der); vergroot; **– by**, vermenigvuldig met.
multitude, menigte, hoop, skare.
multitudinous, menigvuldig, talryk; onmeetbaar, eindeloos.
multivalve, n. veelkleppige dier.
multivalve, a. veelkleppig.
multivocal, veelduidig, dubbelsinnig.
multocular, veelogig.
multure, maalloon; gemaal.
mum, stil; **to be –**, jou stilhou; **–'s the word**, stilbly; sst!
mumble, n. gemompel.
mumble, v. mompel, prewel; kou.
mumbling, n. gemompel, geprewel.
mumbling, a. mompelend, prewelend.
mumchance, stil.
mummer, vermomde (speler); skouspeler.
mummery, maskerade; komedie.
mummify, soos 'n mummie word (maak); verdroog, vermummie.

mummy, mummie; moes, pap; **beat to a –**, pap slaan.
mump, pruil; sedig kyk.
mump, bedel; fop, bedrieg.
mumping, mumpish, pruilend, knorrig, gemelik.
mumps, pampoentjies; pruilbui, slegte luim; **to be in one's –**, in slegte luim wees, pruil.
munch, vreet, hard kou, knabbel.
mundane, aards, wêrelds, mondaine.
municipal, munisipaal, gemeente-....; stads-...; stedelik; – **council**, stadsraad; – **tax**, munisipale belasting.
municipality, stadsraad, munisipaliteit.
munificence, vrygewigheid, milddadigheid.
munificent, vrygewig, milddadig, rojaal.
muniment, oorkonde, dokument.
munition, n. ammunisie, krygsvoorraad.
munition, v. ammunisie voorsien.
mural, muur-...; – **paint**, muurverf.
murder, n. moord; **commit –**, moord begaan; – **will out**, misdade kom aan die lig; **the – is out**, nou is die waarheid bekend; **cry blue –**, moord en brand skree.
murder, v. moor, vermoor; vernietig; radbraak; **he –s his Afrikaans**, hy radbraak sy Afrikaans.
murderer, moordenaar.
murderess, moordenares.
murderous, moorddadig, moord-...
mure, ommuur; opsluit.
muriate, chloried.
muriatic, sout-...; – **acid**, soutsuur.
murk, duisternis, donkerte.
murky, donker, duister; dik.
murmur, n. gemurmel; gemompel; gemor.
murmur, v. murmel, ruis; mompel, mor, murmureer; fluister.
murmurer, murmureerder.
murmuring, gemurmel, geruis; gemor.
murmurous, murmelend, ruisend; morrend.
murphy, ertappel.
murrain, veepes; – **take you!**, kry die pes.
muscadel, muscadine, muscat(el), muskadel; muskadeldruiwe; muskadelwyn.
muscle, spier; spierkrag; **he did not move a –**, hy het geen spier vertrek nie.
muscle-bound: he is –, hy het stywe spiere.
muscology, moskunde.
muscovado, moskovado, bruin suiker.
muscovite, mika.
Muscovite, van Moskou; Russies.
Muscovy, Moskovië, Rusland; – **duck**, makou; – **glass**, mika; – **leather**, Russiese leer.
muscular, gespierd; spier-...; – **strength**, spierkrag.
muscularity, gespierdheid, spierkrag.
musculature, spierstelsel.
Muse, Muse, sanggodin; **the –s**, die sanggodinne.
muse, v. peins, mymer; – **on**, oordink, bepeins.
museum, museum.
mush, pap, meelpap; moes; soetsappigheid.
mushy, soetsappig.
mushroom, n. paddastoel; sampioen; slangkos; sambreel; paddastoel(hoed); parvenu.
mushroom, v. paddastoele (sampioene) soek; platslaan (van 'n koeël).
mushy, papperig, pap, week; swak.
music, musiek; **sacred –**, gewyde musiek; **to make –**, (musiek) speel; **to set to –**, op musiek sit; **face the –**, die gevolge onder die oë sien; **rough –**, geraas, lawaai.
musical, musikaal, musiek-...; welluidend; – **instrument**, musiekinstrument; – **box**, speeldoos; – **chairs**, stoeldans; – **comedy**, operette, musiekblyspel.

musicale, musiekaandjie, privaatkonsert.
music-hall, variété-teater; konsertsaal.
musician, musikus; musikant.
music-lesson, musiekles.
music-master, musiekonderwyser.
music-mistress, musiekonderwyseres.
music-room, musiekkamer; konsertsaal.
music-stand, musiekstander; musiektent.
music-stoel, klavierstoel(tjie).
musing, gepeins, gemymer, mymering.
musk, muskus; -dier; -geur; -plant.
musk-cat, muskusdier.
musk-duck, makou.
musket, geweer, roer.
musket-ball, geweerkoeël.
musketeer, musketier.
musketry, infanterie; gewere; geweervuur.
musket-shot, geweerskoot.
muskmelon, spanspek.
musk-ox, muskusbees, muskusstier.
musk-plum, muskadelpruim.
musk-rat, muskusrot, bisamrot.
musk-rose, muskusroos.
musky, muskus-...; muskusagtig.
muslin, neteldoek; moeselien.
musquash, muskusrot; muskusrotbont.
mussel, mossel.
mussel-bed, mosselbank.
must, n. mos; jongwyn.
must, v. skimmel, skimmel word, kim.
must, v. skimmel, word, kim.
must, v. moet; verplig wees; mag; **you – never contradict**, jy mag (moet) nooit teenspreek nie.
must, n. **it is a –**, dit is 'n vereiste (noodsaaklikheid), dit moet volstrek gebeur.
mustang, mustang.
mustard, moster(d); – **gas**, mosterdgas.
mustard-poultice, moster(d)pleister.
muster, n. monstering; wapenskouing, inspeksie; **opkoms**; **pass –**, toets deurstaan; bymekaarskraap (versamel).
muster, v. versamel; toeloop; monster; – **(up) courage**, moed oproep; **I –ed my strength**, ek het al my krag ingespan.
muster-book, -roll, monsterrol.
mustiness, mufheid; skimmel.
musty, muf, (be)skimmel; verander.
mutability, veranderlikheid.
mutable, veranderlik, onbestendig, wispelturig.
mutation, verandering, wisseling; klinkerwisseling; stemverandering; mutasie.
mute, n. stomme; figurant; ontploffingsklank, klapper; toendemper; stomme kneg.
mute, a. stom, stil, sprakeloos; onuitgesproke; – **adoration**, stille aanbidding.
mute, v. (af)demp.
mutely, stil, swygend.
muteness, stomheid, sprakeloosheid.
mutilate, vermink, skend.
mutilation, verminking, skending.
mutineer, n. muiter, rebel, oproerling.
mutineer, v. opstaan, rebelleer, muit.
mutinous, oproerig, opstandig.
mutiny, n. opstand, oproer, muitery.
mutiny, v. opstaan, muit, oproerig word.
mutism, sien **muteness**.
mutt, gek, domkop, stommerik.
mutter, n. gemompel, gebrom; gerommel.
mutter, v. pruttel; prewel; mompel; rommel.
mutterer, mompelaar; murmureerder.
muttering, n. gemompel; gepruttel; gerommel.
mutton, skaap; skaapvleis; **dead as –**, so dood as

'n mossie; **to return to one's -s,** op die onderwerp terugkom.
mutton-chop, lamskotelet, karmenaadjie, skaapribbetjie; bakkebaard.
mutton-head, domkop, skaapkop.
mutual, wederkerig, wedersyds, onderling, gemeenskaplik; **our – interests,** ons gemeenskaplike belange; **– affection,** wedersydse liefde; **– friend,** gemeenskaplike vriend.
mutuality, wederkerigheid, wedersydsheid.
mutually, wederkerig, onderling, oor en weer.
muzz, suf maak, dikkop maak.
muzzle, n. snoet, bek; loop, mond (van geweer); muilband.
muzzle, v. muilband; besnuffel; stil maak; seil minder; opstopper gee.
muzzle-loader, voorlaaier.
muzzler, opstopper.
muzzy, suf; hoenderkop.
my, my; **(oh)–!,** goeie genade!
mycelium, swamvlok, miselium.
mycology, swamkunde, mikologie.
mycologist, swamkundige, mikoloog.
myology, leer van die spiere, miologie.
myope, bysiende persoon.
myopic, bysiende.
myopy, bysiendheid.
myosote, vergeetmynietjie.

myriad, n. miriade, tallose menigte.
myriad, a. ontelbaar, talloos.
myriapod, duisendpoot.
myrmidon, handlanger; huurling.
myrrh, mirre; Spaanse kerwel.
myrtle, mirte.
myself, ekself, myself; **I am not –,** ek is nie myself nie; **by –,** alleen.
mystagogue, misterievertolker.
mysterious, geheimsinnig, raaiselagtig.
mysteriousness, geheimsinnigheid.
mystery, misterie, geheim, raaisel, verborgenheid; sakrament, avondmaal; misteriespel.
mystic, n. mistikus (mysticus).
mystic(al), a. verborge, misties, geheimsinnig.
mysticism, mistisisme; mistiek.
mystification, foppery, kullery, mistifikasie.
mystify, fop, kul, mistifiseer.
mystique, 'n geheimsinnige atmosfeer.
myth, mite, fabel, storie, sage.
mythic(al), mities, fabel- . . .
mythographer, miteskrywer.
mythography, mitografie.
mythologic(al), mitologies.
mythologist, mitoloog.
mythology, mitologie, gode- en heldeleer.
mythus, mite, fabel.

nab, pak, betrap, arresteer.
nabob, n. nabob; rykaard.
nacre, perlemoen (perlemoer).
nadir, nadir, voetpunt, laagtepunt.
nag, n. ponie, bossiekop; ou knol.
nag, v. lol, sanik, pruttel, seur; **to** – **at somebody**, op iemand vit; **to** – **at something**, oor iets lol (sanik).
nagana, nagana.
nagging, a. pruttelagtig; kyfagtig.
nagging, n. gelol, gesanik, gepruttel.
naiad, najade, waternimf.
nail, n. nael; spyker; **as hard as** –s, kliphard; in uitstekende kondisie; **pay on the** –, op die dag betaal; **that is a** – **to her coffin**, dit is 'n spyker in haar doodkis; **to hit the** – **on the head**, die spyker op die kop slaan; **with tooth and** –, met hand en tand.
nail, v. vasspyker; beslaan; vang, betrap; aan sy woord hou; – **down**, toespyker, vasspyker; (iemand) vaskeer; – **an assertion**, 'n bewering op sy kop slaan; – **lie**, 'n leuen aan die kaak stel; **he stood** –**ed to the ground**, hy het aan die grond genael gestaan; – **to the counter (barn, door)**, aan die kaak stel; – **one's colours to the mast**, staan be jou beginsels.
nail-brush, naelborsel(tjie).
nailer, spykersmid, spykermaker; doring; **a** – **at running**, 'n duiwel om te nael.
nailing: – **good**, deksels (verbrands) goed.
nail-scissors, naelskertjie.
nainsook, nansoek.
naive, naïef, eenvoudig, ongekunsteld.
naivete, naivety, naïwiteit, eenvoudigheid.
naked, naak (nakend), bloot; onbeskerm(d); **with the** – **eye**, met die blote oog; **the** – **truth**, die naakte waarheid; **stark** –, poedelkaal; **strip** –, kaal uittrek, uitskud; – **light**, onbeskermde lig.
nakedness, naaktheid, kaalheid.
namable, noembaar.
namby-pamby, a. soetsappig, soetlik.
namby-pamby, n. soetpraatjies.
name, n. naam, benaming; **mention you by** –, by name noem; **call me by my** –, noem my by (op) my naam; **by** – **only**, alleen van naam; **by the** – **of John**, met die naam van Jan; **he called me** –s, hy het my uitgeskel; **give one's** –, jou naam sê; **give in one's** –, jou naam opgee; **leave one's** –, jou naam sê, jou kaartjie afgee; **send up your** –, jou laat aandien (aanmeld); jou laat inskrywe; **take in my** –, meld (dien) my aan; **a prince in** –, 'n prins in naam; **in the** – **of the king**, in die naam van die koning; **in the** – **of my father**, namens my vader; **he has a** – **for honesty**, hy is bekend vir sy eerlikheid; **become a** –, 'n leë klank word; **take God's** – **in vain**, Gods naam ydellik gebruik; **make a** – **for oneself**, naam maak, beroemdheid verwerf; **he has got a bad** –, hy het 'n slegte naam, hy is in slegte roep; **christian** –, voornaam; **family** –, van, familienaam; **maiden** –, nôiensvan; **the farm was put in his** –, die plaas is op sy naam gesit; **a cross was put to his** –, 'n kruisie is agter sy naam gemaak; **write the letter in my** –, skrywe die brief uit my naam.
name, v. noem, opnoem, benoem, vernoem; betitel; –**d after his grandfather**, na sy oupa vernoem; – **the day**, stel die dag vas; –**d by the Speaker**, deur die Speaker uit die Huis gestuur; **not to be** –**d (on) the same day**, kan nie in dieselfde asem genoem word nie; **the ship was** –**d by the Queen**, die skip is deur die Koningin gedoop; **he was** –**d as candidate**, daar was sprake van hom as kandidaat.

nameless, naamloos; onnoemlik, nameloos; onbekend.
namely, naamlik.
name-part, titelrol.
name-plate, (naam)bordjie, naamplaat.
namesake, naamgenoot, genant.
nankeen, nanking; –s, nankingse broek.
nanny(-goat), bokooi.
nap, n. dutjie, slapie; **take a** –, 'n dutjie doen, 'n uiltjie knap.
nap, v. dut, slaap, sluimer; **catch one** –**ping**, iemand betrap.
nap, n. nop (op klere); dons (op vrugte).
napalm, napalm.
nape, nekholte, nekbeen; **by the** – **of the neck**, aan die nek.
napery, tafellinne, servetgoed.
naphtha, nafta, steenolie.
naphthaline, naftalien.
napkin, servet; doek, luier.
napkin-ring, servetring.
napless, kaal, noploos, afgeslyt, blink.
Napoleonic, Napoleonties, van Napoleon.
nappy, skuimend, bedwelmend, sterk; wollerig.
nappy, n. luier.
narcissus, narsing.
narcosis, narkose, verdowing.
narcotic(al), narkoties, verdowend.
narcotic, slaapmiddel, verdowingsmiddel.
narcotize, onder narkose bring, narkotiseer.
nard, nardus, nardus(olie).
nark, n. polisiespioen.
nark, v. spioeneer.
narrate, vertel, verhaal, beskrywe.
narration, verhaal, beskrywing, relaas.
narrative, a. verhalend, vertellend.
narrative, n. verhaal, vertelling, relaas.
narrator, verteller, verslaggewer.
narrow, a. nou, smal, knap, eng; bekrompe, kleingeestig; **a** – **escape**, 'n noue ontkoming; **in** – **circumstances**, in behoeftige omstandighede; **a** – **compass**, 'n kort bestek; **the** – **side**, die smal kant; **a** – **majority**, 'n geringe meerderheid; – **gauge**, smalspoor; **in the** –**est sense**, in die engste sin; – **views**, bekrompe idees; **the** – **way**, die noue weg, die smal paadjie.
narrow(s), n. see-engte(s).
narrow, v. vereng, beperk, vernou; – **down**, beperk, verminder; – **in**, inkrimp.
narrow-brimmed, met 'n smal rand.
narrow-minded, kleingeestig, bekrompe.
narrow-mindedly, op kleingeestige wyse.
narrow-mindedness, kleingeestigheid, bekrompenheid.
narrowness, bekrompenheid; noute, smalheid.
narwhal, narwal.
nasal, n. neusklank, nasaal.
nasal, a. nasaal, neus- . . . ; – **cavity**, neusholte; – **sound**, neusklank.
nasalis, neusaap.
nasalize, nasaleer, deur die neus uitspreek.
nasally, deur die neus, met 'n neusgeluid.
nascency, ontstaan.
nascent, wordend, ontluikend, aan 't ontstaan.
nastiness, liederlikheid, morsigheid; onaardigheid; onaangenaamheid.
nasturtium, kappertjie, Oos-Indiese kers.
nasty, vuil, vieslik, morsig, smerig; onaangenaam, sleg; naar, onaardig, gemeen, lelik; **a** – **attack**, 'n kwaai aanval; **a** – **feeling**, 'n nare gevoel; **a** – **fellow**, 'n onaangename vent; – **weather**, miserabele weer; **don't be so** –, moenie so onaardig (naar) wees nie.
natal, geboorte- . . . ; – **hour**, geboorte-uur.
natality, geboortesyfer.

natation, swemmery, swemkuns.
nath(e)less, (des)nietemin, nieteenstaande.
nation, nasie, volk.
national, nasionaal, volks- . . ., staats- . . .; – **anthem**, volkslied; – **character**, volksaard, landaard; – **debt**, staatskuld; – **flag**, landsvlag.
national, n. burger.
nationalization, nasionalisasie; naturalisasie; onteiening (deur die staat).
nationalize, nasionaliseer; naturaliseer; onteien (deur die staat).
nationalism, nasionalisme.
nationalist, nasionalis.
nationality, nasionaliteit; volkskarakter.
native, a. aangebore, natuurlik; inheems; geboorte- . . .; – **country**, **land**, vaderland, geboorteland; – **language**, moedertaal; – **soil**, geboortegrond; – **wit**, natuurlike gevatheid.
Native, n. inboorling, naturel; – **council**, naturelleraad; indaba; – **education**, naturelleonderwys; – **hut**, naturellehut, strooihuis; – **policy**, naturellebeleid; – **problem**, naturellevraagstuk; **vote**, naturellestem.
nativism, nativisme, leer van aangebore ideë; inboorlingbegunstiging.
nativity, geboorte; herkoms.
natron, natron, loogsout.
natrium, natrium.
natter, babbel; brom, kerm.
nattiness, netheid, keurigheid.
natty, netjies, keurig, fyn; handig.
natural, a. natuurlik; ongekunsteld, ongedwonge; ongesog; natuur- . . .; – **child**, onegte kind; –**death**, natuurlike dood; – **history**, natuurlike historie; – **law**, natuurwet; – **phenomenon**, natuurverskynsel; – **philosophy**, natuurkunde; – **religion**, natuurlike godsdiens; – **science**, natuurwetenskap; – **state**, natuurstaat; – **world**, sigbare wêreld; **everything comes so** – **to him**, hy doen alles so ongedwonge; **in a** – **way**, op natuurlike wyse.
natural, n. idoot; naturel; herstellingsteken; wit noot (toets).
naturalization, naturalisasie.
naturalize, naturaliseer.
naturalism, naturalisme.
naturalist, natuurkundige; naturalis; dierehandelaar; diere-opstopper.
naturalistic, naturalisties.
naturally, natuurlik(erwyse); op natuurlike wyse; van nature.
nature, natuur; geaardheid, aard, inbors, karakter; soort; **good** –, goeie geaardheid; **against** –, teen die natuur, onnatuurlik, teennatuurlik; **by** – **bad**, van nature sleg; **freak of** –, speling van die natuur; **in**, **by**, **from the** – **of the case**, uit die aard van die saak; **to paint from** –, na die natuur skilder; **from its very** –, uit die aard van die saak; **in a state of** –, in natuurtoestand; **in** – **'s garb**, in Adamsgewaad; **anything in the** – **of**, enigiets wat lyk op; **true to** –, natuurgetrou; **in the course of** –, in die gewone loop van sake; **all** – **rejoices**, die hele skepping juig.
natured, geaard; **bad** –, sleggeaard.
nature-study, natuurstudie.
nature-worship, natuuraanbidding.
naught, nul, niks; **come to** –, op niks uitloop; **set at** –, in die wind slaan.
naughtiness, ondeundheid, kattekwaad.
naughty, ondeund, stout, onwettig, gruwelik.
nausea, mislikheid, seesiekte.
nauseate, walg, mislik maak, laat walg; **it** –**s me**, dit laat my walg, ek walg daarvan.
nauseous, walglik.
nautical, skeeps- . . ., see- . . ., seevaart- . . .;

almanac, seevaartkundige almanak; – **chart**, seekaart; – **compass**, skeepskompas; **a** – **man**, 'n seeman, seevaarder.
nautilus, nautilus.
naval, see- . . ., skeeps- . . ., marine- . . .; – **affairs**, vlootsake; – **architecture**, skeepsbou; – **battle**, – **engagement**, seeslag, seegeveg; – **officer**, marine-offisier; – **power**, seemag, seemoondheid; – **school**, seevaartskool; – **station**, vlootbasis; – **stores**, skeepsbehoeftes; – **term**, skeepsterm; – **victory**, oorwinning op see; – **war**, see-oorlog.
nave, naaf (van 'n wiel).
nave, skip (van 'n kerk).
nave-ring, naafband.
navel, na(w)el; nawellemoen; – **rupture**, na(w)elbreuk.
navel-string, na(w)elstring.
navicular, skuitvormig.
navigable, bevaarbaar (van water); bestuurbaar (van 'n skip, 'n ballon).
navigate, bevaar; stuur, stewe(n); vaar.
navigation, skeepvaart, seevaart; stuurmanskuns; **aerial** –, lugskeepvaart; **inland** –, binnelandse skeepvaart.
navigator, seevaarder.
navvy, dokwerker, slootgrawer, padwerker; (pl.) doodtrappers (skoene).
navy, vloot, seemag, marine; - **blue**, marineblou.
navy-office, admiraliteit; departement van marine.
navy-yard, marinewerf; arsenaal.
nawab, goewerneur; nabob.
nay, adv. nee; wat meer is.
nay, n. nee, weiering; **never said him** –, hom nooit iets geweier nie; **I'll take no** –, ek wil van geen weiering hoor nie.
Nazarene, Nasarener.
naze, kaap, landpunt, voorgebergte.
Nazi, n. Nazi.
Nazi, a. Nazisties, Nazi-.
Neapolitan, a. Napolitaans, Napels; Napolitaan.
neap-tide, dooie gety.
near, a. na, nabysynde, nabygeleë; nouverwant; dierbaar; suinig; – **akin**, nouverwant; **on a** –**er acquaintance**, by nadere kennismaking; **the** – **foreleg**, die hotvoorpoot; **in the** – **future**, in die nabye toekoms; **the** – **horse**, die hotagter perd; **the** –**est figure**, die naaste prys; – **prospect**, onmiddellike uitsig; **a** – **relative**, 'n naverwante; **it was a** – **thing**, dit het min geskeel.
near, adv. naby, digteby; byna; **to draw** –, nader kom, nader; – **at hand**, digby, ophande; **far and** –, wyd en syd; **he came** – **to breaking his neck**, hy het op 'n haar na sy nek gebreek.
near, prep. by, naby, digteby; na aan; **look** –**er at**, van naderby beskou; **that child lies** – **his heart**, daardie kind lê hom na aan die hart; **this matter lies** – **his heart**, hierdie saak gaan hom ter harte; – **the mark**, byna, amper maar nog nie.
near, v. nader, naby kom.
nearly, byna, amper(tjies), haas; van naby; **not** – **so tall**, lank nie so groot nie; – **related**, naverwant, nouverwant.
nearness, nabyheid.
near-sighted, bysiende.
neat, a. netjies; ordelik, sindelik; suiwer; keurig; **brandy** –, skoon brandewyn; **a** – **speech**, 'n keurige toespraak; – **style**, keurige styl.
neat, n. bees, grootvee.
neath, onder.
neatly, netjies, keurig.
neatness, netheid, sindelikheid, ordelikheid; knapheid, behendigheid.

neat's-foot, beespoot; –oil, kloutjiesolie.
neb, bek, snawel; tuit; neus.
nebula, newelvlek.
nebular, newelagtig, vaag; newel- . . ., wolk- . . .
nebulous, newelagtig; vaag.
necessarily, noodsaaklik(erwyse), noodwendig.
necessary, a. nodig, noodsaaklik, noodwendig.
necessary, n. benodigdheid, vereiste; **necessaries of life**, lewensbehoeftes.
necessitarian, determinis.
necessitate, noodsaak, dwing, verplig.
necessitous, behoeftig, nooddruftig.
necessity, noodsaaklikheid, behoefte, nood-(druf); **it is an absolute –**, dit is 'n absolute (gebiedende) noodsaaklikheid; **from –**, uit nood, weens behoefte; **of –**, noodwendig; **– is the mother of invention**, nood leer bid; **he is under the – to**, hy word genoodsaak om te; **make a virtue of –**, van die nood 'n deug maak; **– knows no law**, nood breek wet.
neck, nek, hals; pas, engte; **he came down – and crop**, hy het pens en pootjies neergeslaan; **– and –**, kop aan kop; **– or nothing**, daarop of daaronder; **to ride – or nothing**, uit alle mag jaag; **– of mutton**, skaapnek; **bow the –**, die hoof buig; **tread on the – of**, die voet op die nek sit.
neck-band, hempsboordjie; halsband.
neck-cloth, halsdoek, nekdoek.
neckerchief, halsdoek, nekdoek.
necklace, halsketting, halssnoer.
necklet, halskettinkie.
necktie, das.
necrologist, nekroloog.
necrology, sterftelys; doodsberig, nekrologie.
necromancer, geestebesweerder.
necromancy, swarte kuns, geestebeswering.
necromantic, toor- . . ., beswerings- . . .
necrophagous, lykvretend, wat op lyke aas.
necropolis, dodestad, begraafplaas.
necrosis, beeneter, nekrose.
nectar, nektar, godedrank.
nectarine, kaalperske, nektarien.
nectary, heuningpotjie (van blomme).
need, n. nood, behoefte, gebrek; **if – be**, indien nodig; **there is no – to worry**, jy hoef jou nie te kwel nie; **have – of**, nodig hê, behoefte hê aan; **a friend in – is a friend indeed**, in die nood leer 'n mens jou vriende ken; **at –**, desnoods, in geval van nood; **they suffer –**, hulle ly gebrek; **stand in – of**, nodig hê, behoefte hê aan.
need, v. nodig hê, (be)hoef, makeer; gebrek ly; **you are –ed here**, jy is hier nodig; **he –s a wife**, hy makeer 'n vrou; **it –s only . . .**, daar is maar net . . . nodig; **it –s not . . .**, dit hoef nie; **more than –s**, meer as nodig is; **as fast as –s be**, so vinnig soos kan kom.
needful, a. nodig, noodsaaklik, onmisbaar.
needful, n. die nodige; geld.
needfulness, noodsaaklikheid.
neediness, behoeftigheid, nooddruftigheid.
needle, v. irriteer; aanhits.
needle, naald; breipen, breinaald; kompasnaald, magneetnaald; **crochet –**, hekelnaald, hekelpen; **darning –**, stopnaald; **knitting –**, breipen, breinaald; **thatching –**, deknaald; **on pins and –s**, op hete kole; **look for a – in a haystack**, 'n onbegonne werk verrig.
needle-case, naaldekoker.
needleful, 'n draad gare.
needle-gun, naaldgeweer.
needle-point, naald se punt.
needless, onnodig, nodeloos; **– to say**, onnodig om te sê.
needlessness, nodeloosheid.

needlewoman, naaister, modemaakster.
needlework, naaldewerk; handwerk, naaigoed; **– lesson**, les in naaldewerk.
needs, adv. noodsaaklik; **he – must work**, hy is verplig om te werk; **he must – work**, hy wou met alle geweld werk.
needs, n. behoeftes, benodigdhede.
needy, behoeftig, hulpbehoewend.
ne'er, nooit; **– a penny**, nie 'n bloue duit nie.
ne'er-do-well, (-weel), niksnuts, deugniet.
nefarious, goddeloos, gruwelik.
negate, ontken, loën.
negation, ontkenning, negasie.
negative, a. negatief, ontkennend; **– answer**, ontkennende antwoord; **– quantity**, negatiewe hoeveelheid, minder as niks; **– electricity**, negatiewe elektrisiteit; **– voice**, vetoreg; **– vote**, teenstem; **– sign**, minusteken.
negative, n. ontkenning; veto(reg); negatief; **the answer is in the –**, die antwoord is nee.
negative, v. ontken; weerspreek; afstem; **his motion was –d**, sy mosie is afgestem.
neglect, v. verwaarloos, versuim, veronagsaam, nalaat.
neglect, n. verwaarlosing, versuim, veronagsaming, nalatigheid; **– of duty**, pligsversuim; **to the – of other duties**, met verwaarlosing van ander pligte.
neglectful, nalatig, agtelosig.
neglige, négligé; **in –**, in huisdrag.
negligence, nalatigheid, agtelosigheid.
negligent, nalatig, agtelosig.
negligible, onbeduidend, nietig; **a – quantity**, 'n onbeduidende hoeveelheid.
negotiable, verhandelbaar.
negotiate, verhandel, handel dryf; onderhandel; **– a bill**, 'n wissel verhandel; **– a marriage**, 'n huwelik tot stand bring; **– an obstacle**, 'n moeilikheid oorwin; **– a fence**, 'n heining neem.
negotiation, verhandeling; onderhandeling; totstandbrenging; **open –s**, onderhandelinge aanknoop.
negotiator, onderhandelaar.
negress, negerin.
Negro, Neger.
Negroid, Negroïde, Negeragtig.
Negro-minstrel, Negersanger.
negrophilist, Negervriend, Kafferboetie.
negrophobia, Negervrees, negrofobie.
negus, warm wyn, negus.
neigh, v. runnik, hinnik.
neigh, n. gerunnik.
neighbour, n. buurman, buurvrou; naaste; **next door –s**, naaste bure; **duty to one's –s**, plig teenoor jou naaste.
neighbour, v. grens aan; naby woon.
neighbourhood, buurte, nabyheid; omgewing, omtrek; **in the – of R20**, om en by R20; **live in a fine –**, in 'n mooi omgewing woon.
neighbouring, naburig, aangrensend.
neighbourly, vriendskaplik, gesellig.
neighbourship, buurskap.
neither, pron. geen (van twee), geneem.
neither, adv. ook nie, ewemin.
neither, conj.: **– . . . nor**, nog . . . nog.
Nemesis, Nemesis, vergelding.
neolithic, neolities, uit die latere steentydperk.
neologism, neologisme, nuwe woord; nuwe leer.
neologist, neoloog.
neology, neologie, neologisme.
neophyte, nefiet, nuwe bekeerling; nuweling.
neoteric, nuwerwets, modern.
nepenthe, vergetelheidsdrank.
nephew, neef, broerskind, susterskind.

**nephritic, nier-... , nefrities.
nephritis,** nierontsteking, nefritis.
nepotism, nepotisme, voortrekkery.
nervate, gerib, generf, (v. blare).
nerve, n. senuwee, lewe; krag, moed, durf; get it on one's –s, dit op die senuwees kry; strain every –, alle kragte inspan; have the – to, die moed (die onbeskaamdheid) hê om te.
nerve, v. sterk (maak), krag gee; – oneself, jou sterk maak, jou verman.
nerve-cell, senuwee-sel.
nerveless, kragteloos, pap, slap.
nervous, senuweeagtig, skrikkerig; – **system,** senu(wee)stelsel.
nervousness, senuweeagtigheid.
nervy, senuweeagtig; gespierd; brutaal.
nescience, onwetendheid.
nescient, onwentend, onkundig.
ness, voorgebergte, kaap.
nest, n. nes; feather one's –, jou skapies op die droë bring; – **of robbers,** rowerhol.
nest, v. nes maak; nes hê.
nest-egg, neseier.
nestle, nestle; nes skop; tuismaak; – **close to,** aanleun teen.
nestling, neskuiken; jongste (kind).
net, n. net; strik.
net, v. vang; knoop; binnehaal; **he –ted R10,** hy het R10 binnegehaal.
net(t), n. netto, suiwer; – **loss,** suiwer verlies; – **weight,** netto-gewig.
net-ball, netbal.
nether, onder(ste), laer benede; – **garments,** beenklere, broek; – **world,** die onderwêreld.
Netherlands, Nederland, die Nederlande.
nethermost, onderste, laagste.
netting, netwerk, gaas, sifdraad.
nettle, n. (brand)nekel, netel.
nettle, v. vererg, irriteer.
nettle-rash, netelroos, uitslag.
network, netwerk; gaas.
neuralgia, sinkings, senuweepyne.
neuralgic, neuralgies, senuwee-...
neurasthenia, senu(wee)swakheid, neurastenie.
neurasthenic, n. senu(wee)lyer.
neurasthenic, a. senu(wee)siek, neurastenies.
neuritis, neuritis, senuwee-ontsteking.
neurology, senuweeleer, neurologie.
neuropathy, neuropatie.
neurosis, senu(wee)siekte, neurose.
neurotic, n. senu(wee)lyer; senuweemiddel.
neurotic, a. senusiek, beuroties; – **complaint,** senu(wee)siekte, -kwaal.
neuter, a. onsydig; onoorganlik; geslagloos; neutraal.
neuter, n. onsydige geslag; neutrum.
neutral, a. neutraal, onsydig, onpartydig; vry (van motor); – **gear,** vryloop, neutrale stand.
neutral, n. neutrale, onpartydige.
neutrality, neutraliteit, onpartydigheid.
neutralization, neutralisasie; opheffing.
neutralize, neutraliseer, ophef; neutraal verklaar.
neutron, neutron.
never, nooit, nimmer; **now or –,** nou of nooit; **well I –!,** nou toe nou!; – **fear,** moenie glo nie; – **mind,** dis maar niks; dit maak geen saak nie; – **a word,** geen stomme woord nie; **be he – so smart,** al is hy ook hoe slim; **on the – – –,** tot in die oneindige; **the – – – system,** die nooitbetaalstelsel; die huurkoopstelsel.
never-ceasing, onophoudelik.
never-ending, eindeloos.
never-fading, onverwelklik; kleurvas.
never-failing, onfeilbaar.
nevermore, nimmermeer, nooit weer nie.
nevertheless, nietemin, almaskie.
never-to-be-forgotten, onvergeetlik.
new, nuut; vars; groen; – **bread,** vars brood; **a – student,** 'n groene; – **to the business,** nog baar; **turn over a – leaf,** 'n nuwe begin maak.
new birth, wedergeboorte.
new-blown, pas-ontloke.
new-born, pasgebore.
new-built, vernieu(de), herbou(de); pasgebou(de).
new-comer, nuweling.
new-fangled, nuwerwets.
new-fashioned, nuwerwets, nieumodies.
new-laid, vars(gelê).
newly, onlangs, pas.
new-made, vars, pas gemaak, pas klaar
newness, nuwigheid, nuutheid.
news, nuus, tyding, berig; **what's the –?,** watter nuus is daar; **that's – to me,** ek weet daar niks van af nie; **that is no –,** dit is ou nuus.
news-agent, koerantverkoper.
news-boy, koerantseun, koerantklonkie.
news-monger, nuuskramer.
new-sole, versool.
newspaper, koerant, nuusblad.
news-reel, nuus(rol)prent.
news-sheet, nuusblaadjie.
newt, watersalamander.
New-year, Nuwejaar.
New-year's day, Nuwejaarsdag.
New-year's eve, Oujaarsaand, Oujaarsdag.
New Zealand, Nieu-Seeland.
next, a. naaste, volgende, aanstaande, aankom(m)ende; langsaan; – **door,** langsaan, hiernaas, heffens; – **door neighbour,** naaste buurman; – **door to blasphemy,** nie veel anders as godslastering nie; – **to nothing,** so goed as niks, so te sê niks; **the – very – day,** net die volgende dag; **the – policeman I see,** die eerste die beste konstabel wat ek sien; – **best,** tweede beste.
next, adv. vervolgens, (daar)na; **what –?,** wat kom nou?; **mooier wil ek dit nie hê nie!;** – **to,** naasaan, langsaan; **the largest city – to London,** die grootste stad na(as) Londen; **when – I saw him,** toe ek hom weer sien.
next, prep. lang(e)s, langsaan, neffens, naasaan; **stand – him,** staan langes (naas) hom.
next, n. volgende; – **please,** die volgende, asseblief; **wie volg?**
nexus, verbinding; skakel; koppelteken.
nib, pen(punt), punt.
nibble, v. knabbel, peusel; vit.
nibble, n. geknabbel; mondjievol.
nibbling, geknabbel, gepeusel; vittery.
niblic, knuppel (gholf).
nice, lekker, aangenaam; mooi, gaaf, vriendelik, liefies; fyn; kieskeurig; **must not be too – about the means,** moenie te kieskeurig omtrent die middele wees nie; **a – distinction,** 'n fyn onderskeid; **a – ear,** 'n fyn oor; **a – mess,** 'n mooi boel; **you are a – one,** jy is 'n mooi een.
niceness, lekkerheid, aangenaamheid; gaafheid; vriendelikheid.
nicety, lekkerny; fynheid, noukeurigheid; **to a –,** op 'n haar, eksieperfeksie.
niche, nis; **a – in the temple of fame,** 'n plek in die heldery.
Nick: old –, die ou duiwel (josie).
nick, n. kerf, keep; **in the – of time,** op die tippie, net op die regte tyd.
nick, v. kerf (keep) insny; fop; vang.
nickel, n. nikkel.
nickel, v. vernikkel.
nickel-plated, versilwer(d).

nickel-silver, argentaan, nieusilwer.
nickname, n. bynaam.
nickname, v. bynaam gee; –d, bygenaamd.
nicotine, nikotien; pypolie.
nicotinism, nikotienvergiftiging.
nic(ti)tate, oë knip; – **membrane**, knipvlies.
niddle-noddle, knik; waggle.
nid-nod, gedurig knik, kopspeel.
nidus, broeines, kweekplek, haard.
niece, niggie, susterkind, broerskind.
niggard, n. gierigaard, vrek.
niggardly, inhalig, suinig, gierig.
niggle, beusel, peuter, sukkel.
nigh, naby, byna; **draw –**, nader kom.
night, nag, aand; **all –**, die hele nag; **by –**, in die nag, in die aand, snags; **have a good –**, 'n goeie nagrus hê; **make a – of it**, die nag deurfuif; **a – out**, 'n vry aand; 'n vrolike aandjie; **at –**, saans, snags; **last –**, gisteraand; verlede nag.
night-air, naglug.
night-bird, nagvoël; straatvlinder, asfaltblom.
night-cap, nagmus, slaapmus; nagsopie.
night-class, aandklas.
night-clothes, nagklere, slaapklere.
night-dress, slaapklere, naghemp.
night-fall, aand, skemerdonker.
night-float, nagpitjie.
night-gown, nagjurk, naghemp.
night-hag, nagmerrie.
nightingale, nagtegaal.
nightly, nagtelik, elke nag.
nightmare, nagmerrie.
night-piece, nagtoneel, naglandskap.
nightshade, (giftige) nastergal.
night-shelter, skuilplek vir die nag.
night-stool, stelletjie.
night-time, aand, nag; **in the –**, saans, snags.
nightwalker, slaapwandelaar.
night-watch, nagwag.
nighty, nagjurk, naghemp.
nigrescent, swarterig.
nigritide, swartheid.
nihilism, nihilisme.
nihilist, nihilis.
nil, nul, niks.
nimble, rats, vinnig, vlug, behendig; grif.
nimbleness, ratsheid, behendigheid.
nimbus, reënwolk; ligkrans; nimbus.
niminy-piminy, vol fiemies, aanstellerig.
nincompoop, bog, uilskuiken, niksnuts.
nine, nege (neë); – (o'clock), negenuur (neënuur it was a – day's wonder, dit het tydelik baie opspraak verwek; **possession is – points of the law**, salig is die besitters; **dressed up to the –s**, piekfyn aangetrek, fyn uitgevat; **the Nine**, die nege Muses.
ninefold, negevoudig.
ninepins, keëls (kegels).
nineteen, negentien.
nineteenth, negentiende.
nine-tenths, nege tiendes.
ninetieth, negentigste.
ninety, negentig; **in the nineties**, in die negentig; in die negentiger jare, tussen (18)80 en (18)90.
ninny, uilskuiken, bog, onnosele skaap.
ninth, negende.
ninthly, ten negende, in die negende plek.
nip, v. byt, knyp; – **in the bud**, in die kiem smoor; – **in**, inglip; – **off**, afbyt, afknip; **–ped by frost**, doodgeryp; – **up**, oppak.
nip, n. byt, knyp; bitsigheid; **a – in the air**, skerp luggie; **he is a –**, hy is 'n haan.
nip, n. kleintjie, kwartbotteltjie.

nipper, knyper; kêreltjie, seuntjie; (pl.) knyptang; knypbril.
nipping, bytend; bitsig.
nipple, tepel, speen; nippel, slagpennetjie.
Nippon, Nippon (Japan).
nippy, bytend; bitsig; rats; vinnig, glad.
nirvana, nirwana.
nit, neet.
nitrate, n. nitraat.
nitrate, v. nitreer.
nitre, salpeter.
nitric, salpeter- . . .; – **acid**, salpetersuur.
nitrite, nitriet.
nitrogen, stikstof.
nitrogenous, stikstofhoudend.
nitrous, salpeteragtig.
nitwit, domkop, onnosel.
nix, niks.
nix, waterfee, watergees.
no, a. geen (g'n); – **date**, ongedateer(d), **in – time**, in 'n kits; **there was – mistaking what he meant**, sy bedoeling was baie duidelik; – **ball**, blindebal; – **one**, niemand; – **thoroughfare**, geen deurgang; – **whit**, glad nie; – **go**, niks te maak nie; – **man's land**, niemandsland; **by – means**, glad nie, hoegenaamd nie; **to – purpose**, verniet, tevergeefs.
no, adv. nee; niks; – **better than before**, niks beter as tevore nie; – **sooner said than done**, so gesê, so gedaan; – **sooner had he said this than**, nouliks het hy dit gesê of; – **more**, nie meer nie.
nob, n. kop, klapperdop, bol.
nob, v. opstopper gee, teen die kop slaan.
nob, n. hoë heer, hele Piet.
nobble, bewerk; in die hande kry.
nobby, windmakerig.
nobiliary, adellik.
nobility, adel; edelheid; – **of mind**, sieleadel.
noble, n. edelman.
noble, a. adellik; edel, grootmoedig; groots; indrukwekkend.
nobleman, edelman.
noble-minded, edelmoedig, grootmoedig.
nobleness, edelheid; grootsheid.
nobly, edel; edelmoedig(lik).
nobody, niemand.
nock, keep, kerf.
nock, nok (van 'n seil).
noctambulism, slaapwandeling.
noctambulist, slaapwandelaar.
nocturnal, nagtelik.
nocturne, naglied, nokturne; nagskildery.
nod, v. knik; insluimer, visvang; **to sit –ding**, sit en visvang; **–ding acquaintance**, veraf kennis; **–ding plumes**, wuiwende vere (veerbos).
nod, n. (hoof)knik, wenk; **dependent on his –**, van sy wenke afhanklik; **a – is as good as a wink**, 'n goeie verstaander het maar 'n halwe woord nodig; **land of Nod**, land van Klaas Vakie.
nodal, knoop- . . .; – **point**, knooppunt.
noddle, n. kop, bol.
noddle, v. knik, (kop)skud.
noddy, domoor, esel.
node, knoes, kwas; knop; knoop, knooppunt.
nodose, **nodular**, knoesterig, kwasterig; knopperig.
nodule, knoesie, kwassie; knoppie.
nodus, knoop.
noetic, a. noëties; verstandelik.
noetic(s), n. noëtiek, verstandsleer.
nog, n. tap, houtprop.
nog, v. tap.

noggin, bekertjie, kommetjie.
nohow, glad nie; **look** –, oes lyk.
noise, n. geraas, lawaai, rumoer, gedruis; **make a** –, lawaai maak; opspraak verwek; **make** – – **about something**, 'n bohaai oor iets maak; **a big** –, 'n groot kokkedoor.
noise, v. – **it abroad**, dit uitbasuin.
noiseless, stil, geluidloos, geruisloos.
noisiness, luidrugtigheid, lawaai(erigheid).
noisome, nadelig, onaangenaam, walglik.
noisy, luidrugtig, lawaaierig, raserig.
nomad, n. nomade, swerwer, trekker.
nomad, a nomadies, swerwend.
nomadic, nomadies, swerwend, rondtrekkend.
nomadism, trekkerslewe.
nom de plume, skuilnaam, pennaam.
nomenclature, naam; benaming; naamlys; terminologie, nomenklatuur.
nominal, nominaal; in naam; naamwoordelik; – **value**, nominale waarde.
nominalism, nominalisme.
nominalistic, nominalisties.
nominally, in naam.
nominate, nomineer, benoem; noem, vasstel; – **a date**, 'n datum voorstaan.
nomination, nominasie, benoeming.
nominatival, nominatief- . . .
nominative, nominatief.
nominator, voorsteller; noemer (van 'n breuk).
nominee, genomineerde, kandidaat, benoemde.
non-acceptance, nie-aanneming, weiering.
non-activity, non-aktiwiteit.
nonage, minderjarigheid; kindsheid.
nonagenarian, negentigjarige.
nonagon, negehoek.
non-appearance, nie-verskyning, wegbly.
non-arrival, (die) wegbly.
nonary, a. negetallig.
nonary, n. negetal.
non-attendance, nie-bywoning, afwesigheid.
non-belligerent, nie-oorlogvoerend(e).
nonce: for the –, hierdie slag (keer).
nonce-word, geleentheidswoord.
nonchalance, onverskilligheid, nonchalance.
nonchalant, doodbedaard, onverskillig.
non-combitant, nie-vegter, non-kombatant.
non-commissioned, onder(offisier).
non-committal, vaag, niksseggend, tot niks verbindend, ontwykend.
non-compliance, nie-nakoming; weiering.
non-conducting, nie-geleidend.
non-conductor, nie-geleider.
non-conformist, nonkonformis.
nonconformity, nonkonformiteit; teenstelling, gebrek aan ooreenkoms.
nondescript, a. sonderling, vreemdsoortig.
nondescript, n. vreemdsoortige wese.
none, pron. geen een, niemand; niks; – **of this**, niks hiervan nie; – **of your impudence**, hou jou astrantheid vir jouself; – **of them**, geen een van hulle nie; – **of your business**, nie jou saak nie.
none, a. geen, niks; **I have** –, ek het niks; **he is** – **of my friends**, hy is geen vriend van my nje; **is** – **of the clearest**, nie eintlik van die helderste nie; – **other but**, niks (niemand) anders nie as; – **at all**, glad niks.
none, adv. niks; – **the better for it**, niks beter daarom nie; – **the worse for the accident**, ongedeerd deur die ongeluk; – **too fond of him**, nie te danig lief vir hom nie; **the pay is** – **too high**, die betaling is volstrek nie te hoog nie.
nonentity, onding; nul, nulliteit.
nones, none.

nonesuch, sien **nonsuch**.
non-European, nie-blanke.
non-existence, nie-bestaan.
non-existent, nie-bestaande.
non-interference, onthouding, non-intervensie.
non-member, nie-lid.
non-observance, nie-nakoming; nie-inagneming.
non-pareil, onvergelyklik, weergaloos.
non-payment, nie-betaling, wanbetaling.
non-performance, nie-vervulling; nie-optreding.
nonplus, n. verwarring, verleentheid; **at a** –, die kluts kwyt.
nonplus, verwar, verleë maak.
nonplussed, verwar, verleë; beteuterd.
non-resident, nie-inwonend, ekstern.
non-resistance, nie-verset, lydelikheid.
nonsense, onsin, dwaasheid, gekheid; – **verses**, onsinrympies.
nonsensical, onsinnig, gek, sot verspot.
non-stop, deurlopend, sonder stilhou.
non-subscriber, nie-intekenaar.
non-success, gebrek aan sukses.
non(e)such, man sonder waarga, iemand wie se maters dood is.
noodle, uilskuiken, onnosel bloed; noedel.
nook, uithoek, hoekie.
noon, middag, twaalfuur.
noonday, middag.
noontide, middaguur.
noose, n. strik, lis, strop.
noose, v. knoop, strik; in 'n strik vang.
nor, nog, ook nie; **neither** . . . –, nòg . . . nòg.
Nordic, Nordies.
norm, norm, standaard.
normal, a. normaal; – **college**, normaalskool, opleidingskollege.
normal, n. die normale, die loodregte.
Norman, Normandies, Normandiër.
Norse, Noors.
Norseman, Noorman, Noor.
north, n. die noorde; noordewind.
north, a. noord(e)- . . ., noordelik; – **pole**, noordpool; **North Sea**, Noordsee; – **side**, noordekant; – **wind**, noordewind; – **of**, noord van, ten noorde van; – **latitude**, noorderbreedte.
north, adv. noord, noordwaarts; **due** –, pal noord; **go** –, noordwaarts gaan.
north-east, noordoos.
north-easter, noordoostewind.
north-easterly, noordoostelik.
northerly, noordelik.
northern, noordelik noord(er)- . . ., uit die Noorde; – **lights**, noorderlig; – **hemisphere**, noordelike halfrond.
northernmost, noordelikste.
northing, noorddeklinasie.
north-light, noorderlig.
northwards, noordwaarts, na die noorde.
north-west, noordwes.
north-wester, noordwestewind.
north-westerly, noordwestelik.
Norway, Noorweë.
Norwegian, Noor; Noors; Noorweegs.
nor'-wester, noordwestewind; seemanshoed, suidwester; dop, borrel, oorlam.
nose, n. neus; reuk; tuit; **follow one's** –, agter jou neus aanloop; **poke one's** – **into**, jou neus insteek; **turn up one's** – **at**, jou neus optrek vir; **put someone's** – **out of joint**, 'n stok in iemand se wiel steek; **bite one's** – **off**, iemand se kop afbyt; **made to pay through the** –, jou vel oor jou ore trek; **lead by the** –, aan die neus lei; **under one's** –, vlak voor jou, onder iemand se neus.

nose   585   **nuisance**

nose, v. ruik, snuffel; – about, rondsnuffel; – at, ruik aan; – out, uitvis.
nose-bag, voersak.
nose-band, neusriem.
nose-dive, reg-af daling; **make a –**, kop tussen die bene steek.
nosegay, ruiker.
noseless, sonder neus, neusloos.
nose-monkey, neusaap.
nose-piece, neusstuk; tuit.
noser, teëwind, kopwind.
nose-rag, neuslap, sakdoek.
nostalgia, heimwee.
nostril, neusgat.
nostrum, kwaksalwersmiddel.
nosy, pure neus; sleg ruikend; nuuskierig.
not, nie; – **at all**, volstrek nie, glad nie; – **in the least**, nie in die minste nie; **I think –**, ek glo nie; **I hope –**, ek hoop van nee.
notability, beroemdheid; merkwaardigheid.
notable, a. vernaam; merkwaardig; merkbaar.
notable, n. hooggeplaaste (persoon), notabel.
notably, vernaamlik; merkbaar.
notarial, notarieel.
notary, notaris.
notation, notasie.
notch, n. keep, kerf, skaar (in 'n mes); **top –**, bokerf; eersteklas.
notch, v. keep, keep in maak, kerf; behaal; – **many points**, baie punte behaal.
note, n. noot (in musiek); toon; teken; nota, aantekening; briefie; **sound the – of**, die geroep laat boor; **strike the right –**, die regte toon tref; – **of exclamation**, uitroepteken; **make a – of**, nota (aantekening) maak van; kennis neem van; **make a mental – of**, in jou geheue prent; **a – of hand**, 'n wissel onder jou handtekening; **a man of –**, 'n man van betekenis; **worthy of –**, van belang om te weet; **circular –**, omsendbrief, sirkulêre.
note, v. oplet, kennis neem van; aanteken, opskrywe; – **down**, aanteken.
note-book, aantekeningboek, skryfboek.
note-case, notebeurs.
noted, beroemd, bekend, vermaard.
note-paper, briefpapier.
noteworthy, opmerkenswaardig.
nothing, niks, nul; glad nie; **he has – in him**, daar steek niks in hom nie; **there is – in it**, dit beteken niks; – **venture – have**, wie waag die wen; – **like trying**, probeer is die beste geweer; – **if not critical**, sterk krities; **there is – for it but to**, daar is geen ander genade nie as om te; **for –**, verniet; **it is – to you**, dit kan jou niks skeel nie maak; – **of it**, niks daarvan dink nie; niks daaruit wys word nie; **can make – of him**, kan hom nie begryp nie; kan niks met hom aanvang nie; **come to –**, op niks uitloop; **have – to do with**, niks daarmee te doen hê nie; – **like so good**, lank nie so goed nie; – **daunted**, onverskrokke; – **less than**, niks minder as.
nothing, n. nietigheid, nul; **a mere –**, 'n absolute nietigheid; **talk sweet –s**, komplimentjies maak; soet woordjies sê; **he is a –**, hy is 'n nul.
nothingness, nietigheid, onbeduidendheid.
notice, n. kennis, aandag, notisie, opmerksaamheid; kennisgewing, aankondiging, berig, waarskuwing; **brought to my –**, onder my aandag gebring; **take no – of**, geen notisie van neem nie; **please take – that**, geliewe kennis te neem dat; **give –**, kennis gee; (iemand) afdank; bedank; ('n betrekking,

huur) opsê; **he was given a month's –**, hy het 'n maand kennis gekry; **give – to quit**, (huur, huis, ens.) opsê; **take – of**, ag slaan op, notisie neem van; **at a moment's –**, dadelik, op staande voet; **till further –**, tot nadere kennisgewing.
notice, v. opmerk, merk, ag slaan op, notisie neem van.
noticeable, merkbaar; opmerklik.
notice-board, aanplakbord.
notifiable, wat moet gerapporteer word.
notification, kennisgewing, aankondiging.
notify, bekend maak, kennis gee, aankondig, meedeel, rapporteer.
notion, begrip, idee, denkbeeld; **not the slightest –**, nie die minste benul nie; **no – of obedience**, geen begrip van gehoorsaamheid nie.
notional, denkbeeldig, begrips- . . .
notoriety, berugtheid, befaamdheid.
notorious, welbekend (van feite); berug (van persone); **a – criminal**, 'n berugte misdadiger; – **for**, berug vir; **–ly stupid**, berug vir sy domheid.
notwithstanding, ondanks, nieteenstaande; nietemin, tog; **this –**, ondanks dit (alles); **he went there –**, hy het tog (nietemin) daarheen gegaan.
nought, niks; sien **naught**.
noun, selfstandige naamwoord.
nourish, voed; aankweek, koester.
nourishing, voedsaam.
nourishment, voedsel, kos.
nous, verstand, intellek, vernuf.
novel, a. nuut; eienaardig, vreemd; **a – feeling**, 'n vreemde gevoel.
novel, n. roman.
novelette, novelle.
novelist, romanskrywer.
novelty, nuwigheid.
November, November.
novice, novise; nuweling, groene.
noviciate, novitiate, novisiaat, proeftyd, groentyd; nuweling.
now, adv. nou; **but –**, so-ewe; **nou net**; **just –**, netnou; – **and then (again)**, nou en dan, af en toe; – **this**, – **that**, nou dit, dan weer dat.
now, conj. nou (dat); wel dan; – **then**, toe dan, toe nou; dus.
now, n. (die) hede, (die) teenswoordige.
nowadays, teenswoordig, hedendaags.
nowhere, nêrens, niewers; **be**, **come in –**, heeltemal uitval; nie kan saampraat nie; – **near**, glad nie in die nabyheid nie; lank nie.
nowise, glad nie, hoegenaamd nie.
noxious, skadelik, verderflik.
nozzle, neus, snoet; tuit, bek; mondstuk.
nub, kern (van 'n saak).
nubile, troubaar, hubaar.
nuclear, kern-; – **energy**, kernenergie; – **fission**, kernsplyting; – **power**, kernkrag; – **-powered submarine**, kernkragduikboot; – **reactor**, kernreaktor; – **weapon**, kernwapen.
nucleus, kern, pit; kop (van 'n komeet); nucleus.
nudation, ontbloting.
nude, a. kaal, naak, bloot.
nude, n. die naakte (model); naakfiguur, –skildery; naakte (vrou, man).
nudge, v. aanstoot, stamp (in die ribbe).
nudge, n. steek, stamp, stoot, prik.
nudity, naaktheid; naakstudie.
nugatory, beuselagtig, niksbeduidend; waardeloos, nie van krag nie.
nugget, klont, klomp.
nuisance, (oor)las, stoornis, plaag; laspos; **a private –**, 'n kruis; **a public –**, 'n openbare

hinder; **he is a regular** –, hy is 'n ware laspos; **it is a – having to**, dit is lastig om te moet; **commit no** –, verontreiniging verbode.
null, nietig, ongeldig, kragteloos; **– and void**, nietig, ongeldig, van nul en gener waarde.
nullification, verydeling, opheffing.
nullify, verydel, van nul en gener waarde maak, ophef; **– all his attempts**, al sy pogings verydel.
nullity, ongeldigheid, nietigheid; nul(liteit).
numb, a. gevoelloos, dood; **a – hand**, bottervingers; **my fingers are** –, my vingers is dood (verkluim).
numb, v. verstyf, verdoof; **–ed feelings**, gevoelloosheid, verstompte gevoel.
number, n. nommer, getal, klomp, aantal, party; –s, (ook) verse; **Numbers**, Numeri; **a great** –, 'n groot aantal (klomp); **the – of the house**, die nommer van die huis; **think of two** –s, dink aan twee getalle; **there are –s who**, daar is baie wat; **he was also among the** –, hy was ook daarby; **one of our** –, een van ons; **story issued in** –s, vervolgstorie, verhaal in afleweringe; **back** –, vorige aflewering; iemand (iets) uit die ou doos; **in** –, in getal; **the – of my enemies**, die getal van my vyande; **present in large –s**, in groot getalle aanwesig; **without** –, sonder getal, ontelbaar; **wrong** –, verkeerde nommer; **to the – of**, ten getalle van, tot 'n getal van.
number, v. numereer, nommer, tel; **I – him among my friends**, ek tel hom onder my vriende, ek reken hom tot my vriende; **his days are –ed**, sy dae is getel.
numberless, ontelbaar, talloos.
numb-fish, dril-vis.
numbness, styfheid, verkluimdheid; doodse gevoel.
numerable, telbaar.
numeral, telwoord; syfer; **– adjective**, telwoord.
numeration, telling; getalstelsel.
numerative, tel-...; **– system**, telstelsel.
numerator, teller.
numeric(al), numeriek, getal(s)-...; –al order, numerieke orde, getalsorde; –al strength, getalsterkte; –al superiority, groter getalsterkte, oorwig in getal.
numerous, talryk, baie; groot, sterk; **a – acquaintance**, 'n uitgebreide vriendekring; **a – family**, 'n groot huisgesin.
numismatic, numismaties, munt-...
numismatics, muntkunde.
nummary, nummulary, munt-..., geld-...
numskull, swaap, esel, uilskuiken.
nun, non; **–'s veiling**, kamerdoek.
nunciature, pouslike gesantskap.
nuncio, nuntius, pouslike gesant.
nuncupate, mondeling verklaar.

nuncupative, mondeling.
nunhood, nonskap.
nunlike, nonagtig.
nunnery, nonneklooster.
nunnish, nonagtig, nonnerig.
nuptial, huweliks-..., bruilofs-...
nuptials, bruilof.
nurse, n. verpleegster, suster; kinderoppasster, kinderjuffrou; ou-vrou, baker.
nurse, v. verpleeg, oppas; baker, soog, versorg; kweek (bv. plante); bewaar, opspaar, suinig mee te werk gaan (bv. geld); koester (bv. 'n grief); **– a sore leg**, 'n seer been verpleeg, met 'n seer been sit; **to – one's self**, goed vir jouself oppas.
nurse-child, pleegkind.
nursemaid, kinderoppasster.
nursery, kinderkamer; kwekery; kweekdam; kweekplaas.
nursery-governess, kinderjuffrou, goewernante.
nurseryman, blomkweker, vrugtekweker.
nursing-home, verpleegsinrigting.
nurs(e)ling, troetelkind, liefling, kwekeling.
nurture, v. kweek, opvoed, grootmaak, troetel; **to –a plan**, 'n plan koester.
nurture, n. aankweking, opvoeding, troeteling; voeding.
nut, neut; moer(tjie) (van 'n skroef); klont; modegek; **not for –s**, om niks ter wêreld nie; **a hard – to crack**, 'n harde neut (om te kraak); **be –s to**, in sy kraal wees, 'n genot wees; **be (dead) –s on**, versot wees op; **off his** –, mal, dronk.
nutate, die kop laat hang, verwelk.
nutation, verwelking.
nut-brown, ligbruin, kastaiingbruin.
nut-craker(s), neutkraker.
nutmeg, neut.
nutmeg-grater, neutrasper.
nutrient, voedend.
nutriment, voedingstof, voedsel, kos.
nutrimental, voedsaam.
nutrition, kos, voedsel; voeding.
nutritious, voedsaam.
nutritive, voedsaam.
nutshell, neutdop; **in a** –, in 'n paar woorde; in kort bestek.
nutting: **go** –, gaan neute pluk.
nut-tree, neutboom.
nutty, neutagtig; neut-...; verlief; dol, kranksinnig.
nut-weevil, neutmiet.
nuzzle, snuffel, vroetel; aankruip teen.
nymph, nimf; papie (bv. van 'n mot).
nymphlike, soos 'n nimf, nimfagtig.
nymphomania, nimfomanie, mansiekte.
nymphomaniac, nimfomaan.

o(h), o!
oaf, wisselkind; lomperd.
oafish, torrerig, stumperagtig.
oak, akkerboom, eik(eboom).
oak-apple, galappel.
oaken, eike- . . . van eikehout.
oakum, touwerk, pluisgoed.
oar, n. roeispaan, (roei)riem; rest on one's -s, uitrus; op jou louere rus.
oar, v. roei.
oarsman, roeier.
oarsmanship, roeikuns.
oasis, oase.
oast, (hop)oond; es.
oat-cake, hawerkoek.
oaten, hawer- . . .
oath, eed; vloek(woord); on -, onder ede; - of allegiance, eed van getrouheid.
oatmeal, hawermeel.
oats, hawer; sow one's wild -, 'n vrolike lewe lei.
obduracy, halsstarrigheid, verstoktheid.
obdurate, verhard, koppig, verstok.
obedience, gehoorsaamheid; in - to, ooreenkomstig; in gehoorsaamheid aan.
obedient, gehoorsaam; your - servant, u dienswillige dienaar.
obeisance, buiging; hulde.
obelisk, obelisk, gedenknaald.
obese, swaarlywig, geset.
obesity, swaarlywigheid.
obey, gehoorsaam (wees); luister na, gehoor gee aan.
obfuscate, verduister, verbyster.
obituary, n. sterflys; lewensberig; dood(s)berig.
obituary, a. sterf- . . ., dood(s)- . . ., - notice, dood(s)berig.
object, n. voorwerp; oogmerk, doel; plan, bedoeling; objek; money is no -, geld is bysaak.
object, v. beswaar maak; objekteer.
object-glass, objektief.
objection, beswaar, teenwerping, objeksie; raise -, beswaar maak.
objectionable, aanstootlik, laakbaar.
objective, a. objektief; - case, voorwerpsnaamval, 4de naamval.
objective, n. objektief; voorwerpsnaamval; mikpunt, doel.
objectivity, objektiwiteit.
object-lesson, aanskouingsles; aanskoulike voorstelling.
objector, beswaarmaker.
objurgate, berisp(e); bestraf, skrobbeer.
objurgation, berisping, skrobbering.
objugatory, berispend, verwytend.
oblate, n. oblaat, geestelike.
oblate, a. afgeplat.
oblation, offer(ande), oblaat; skenking.
obligate, verplig.
obligation, verpligting; verbintenis, obligasie; be under an -, (dank) verskuldig wees aan.
obligatory, verpligtend; bindend.
oblige, verplig; diens bewys, van diens wees; can you - me with a match?, kan u my asseblief 'n vuurhoutjie gee?; an answer will -, geliewe te antwoord; I shall be very much -d, ek sal baie bly wees, u sal my seer verplig; much -ed, baie dankie; - with a song, 'n sangstuk ten beste gee.
obligee, obligasiehouer, skuldeiser.
obliging, beleef(d) hulpvaardig.
obligor, skuldenaar.
oblique, skuins, skeef; afwykend; indirek; - cases, verboë naamvalle; - angle, skewe hoek.
obliquity, skuinsheid, skeefheid; afwyking; verkeerdheid, slegtheid.

obliterate, uitvee, uitwis; vernietig.
obliteration, uitwissing; vernietiging.
oblivion, vergetelheid; fall into -, in vergetelheid raak.
oblivious, vergeetagtig; ongevoelig; onbewus; - of, sonder inagneming van, onbewus van.
oblong, 'n langwerpige figuur, stuk.
oblong, a. langwerpig.
obloquy, laster, smaad.
obnoxious, aanstootlik, onaangenaam, onuitstaanbaar; skadelik.
oboe, hobo.
oboist, hobospeler.
obol, obool (obolus); penning.
obscene, vuil, liederlik, onkies, obseen.
onscenity, liederlikheid, onkiesheid.
obscurant, remskoen, domper.
obscurantism, obskurantisme, remskoenpolitiek.
obscure, a. duister; onduidelik, onbekend; afgeleë; obskuur.
obscure, v. verdof, verduister; verberg; in die skaduwee stel; die uitsig belemmer.
obscurity, onduidelikheid; onbekendheid; duisternis, donkerheid.
obsecration, smeekbede, smeking.
obsequies, begrafnis(plegtigheid).
obsequious, slaafs, onderdanig, kruiperig.
observance, waarneming, inagneming; viering; gebruik.
observant, oplettend, opmerksaam.
observation, waarneming, onservasie; opmerking, aanmerking.
observatory, sterrewag, observatorium.
observe, waarneem, gadeslaan, dophou; opmerk, aanmerk; vier; nakom, in ag neem, naleef; - silence, die stilwyse bewaar; - commands, bevele nakom; - the law, die wet in ag neem (nakom); - anniversary, jaardag vier.
observer, waarnemer, opmerker.
obsess, kwel, agtervolg; be -ed with, agtervolg word deur.
obsession, kwelling, las, obsessie.
obsidian, lawaglas, obsidiaan.
obsolescence, veroudering.
obsolescent, aan die uitsterf.
obsolete, verouder(d), uit die mode.
obstacle, hinderpaal, struikelblok.
obstacle-race, hindernis-wedloop.
obstetric(al), verloskundig.
obstetrician, verloskundige.
obstetrics, verloskunde.
obstinacy, koppigheid, hardnekkigheid.
obstinate, koppig, hardnekkig, halsstarrig, styfhoofdig, obstinaat.
obstreperous, lawaaierig; parmantig.
obstruct, belemmer; versper; dwarsstrek, obstruksie voer.
obstruction, belemmering; versperring; obstruksie.
obstructionist, dwarsdrywer, obstruksionis.
obstructive, belemmerend; versperrend; dwarstrekkerig.
obtain, (ver)kry, verwerf, behaal; geld.
obtainable, verkrygbaar.
obtrude, opdring, indring.
obtrusion, opdringing; opdringerigheid.
obtrusive, op-, indringerig.
obturate, toestop, toemaak, afsluit.
obtuse, stomp; dof; bot, dom, onnosel; - angle, stomp hoek.
obtuseness, stompheid; dofheid; botheid.
obverse, voorkant.
overt, omkeer, omdraai.
obviate, uit die weg ruim, verwyder; voorkom,

ontseil; – a difficulty, 'n moeilikheid ontkom of ontseil.
obvious, duidelik, vanselfsprekend.
ocarina, okarina, fluitjie.
occasion, n. geleentheid; aanleiding; okkasie; take – to, van die geleentheid gebruik maak om; on the – of his marriage, by geleentheid van sy huwelik; give – to, aanleiding gee tot; he rose to the –, hy het hom die geleentheid waardig betoon; when the – demands it, as die omstandighede dit vereis; (up)on –, van tyd tot tyd; as dit nodig blyk; –s, sake, besigheid.
occasion, v, aanleiding gee tot; noodsaak.
occasional, toevallig; af en toe, hier en daar.
occasionally, nou en dan, af en toe.
Occident, Weste.
Occidental, Westers, Westelik.
occipital, van die agterkop, agterkop- . . .
occlude, toestop, sluit; opvang.
occult, a. verborge, geheim, okkult.
occult, v. verberg, bedek, verduister.
occultation, verduistering, okkultasie.
occipital, van die agterkop, agterkop- . . .
occlude, toestop, sluit; opvang.
occult, a. verborge, geheim, okkult.
occult, v. verberg, bedek, verduister.
occultation, verduistering, okkultasie.
occultism, (leer van) die geheime wetenskappe, okkultisme.
occupancy, inbesitneming, betrekking.
occupant, besitter, bewoner; insittende.
occupation, inbesitneming, besetting; beroep, ambag.
occupational, beroeps-, – hazard, beroepsrisiko.
occupier, bewoner.
occupy, in besit neem, beset, ('n betrekking) beklee; bewoon; beslaan, inneem; in beslag neem; occupied with, besig met; – a chair, 'n stoel beset, op 'n stoel sit; – a post, 'n betrekking beklee; – a space, 'n ruimte beslaan.
occur, voorkom; opkom, byval; plaasvind; voorval; it –red to me, dit het by my opgekom, dit het my bygeval.
occurrence, gebeurtenis, voorval.
ocean, oseaan.
oceanic, van die oseaan, oseaan- . . .
oceanographer, oseanograaf, seebeskrywer.
oceanography, oseanografie, seebeskrywing.
ocelot, tierkat.
ochre, oker, geelklei; geelbruin.
o'clock, sien clock.
octagon, aghoek, oktogoon.
octagon(al), aghoekig, oktogonaal.
octahedral, agvlakkig.
octahedron, agvlak, oktaëder.
octant, oktant.
octave, oktaaf; agtal; ag(t)ste feesdag; ag(t)daagse fees; ag(t)dae.
octavo, oktaaf(formaat), oktavo.
octennial, ag(t)jaarliks; ag(t)jarig.
octet(te), oktet; oktaaf.
October, Oktober.
octogenarian, n. tagtigjarige.
octogenarian, a. tagtigjarig.
octopus, seekat, oktopus.
octosyllabic, ag(t)lettergrepig.
octosyllyable, ag(t)lettergrepige woord.
octuple, agvoudig.
ocular, oog- . . ., gesigs- . . ., okulêr.
oculist, oogdokter, -arts.
odd, ongelyk, onewe; orig; snaaks, sonderling, raar; – and even, gelyk en ongelyk, ewe en onewe, paar en onpaar; twelve pounds –, iets oor die twaalf pond; the – man, die orige kêrel;

in some – corner, êrens in 'n hoek; I have to do it at – moments, ek moet dit so tussenin doen, ek moet dit doen wanneer ek 'n oomblikkie vry het; – jobs, peuselwerkies, (los) werkies; the – trick, die sewende slag (by brugspel), een slag oor; – volumes, los dele.
oddish, snaaks(erig), komieklik.
oddity, sonderlingheid; eksentrieke mens; snaakse ding.
oddments, stukkies en brokkies, oorskiet.
odds, verskil; geskil, onenigheid; kanse, voordeel; oormag; what's the –, watter verskil maak dit; they are at –, hulle is dit met mekaar oneens; the – are in our favour, die voordeel is aan ons kant; fight against –, teen die oormag stry; the – are that he will do it, die kanse is dat hy dit sal doen; lay, give – of three to one, drie teen een wed; – and ends, stukkies en brokkies.
ode, ode.
odious, haatlik, verfoeilik.
odium, haat, veragting, blaam.
odor(ifer)ous, geurig, welriekend.
odour, ruik (reuk), geur; be in bad – with, in 'n slegte reuk staan by.
oecumenical, universeel, algemeen.
of, van, aan, deur, op, uit, in; – oneself, vanself, uit eie beweging; die –, sterwe aan; the city – – Rome, die stad Rome; he – all men, en dit nogal hy, dat dit nou juis hy moet wees; he is one – a thousand, hy is 'n man honderd, hy is een uit die duisend; – an evening, op 'n aand; – late, in die laaste tyd.
off, adv. af, weg; ver; be, make –, wegloop, maak dat jy wegkom; – with you!, maak dat jy wegkom!; three miles –, drie myl ver; we are – now, ons (ver)trek nou net; the engagement is –, die verloofskap is uit; fish is –, daar is nie meer vis nie, die vis is op; he is well –, hy sit daar goed in; he is badly –, hy is arm, hy lewe of kry swaar; – and on, af en toe, nou en dan; onseker; – with his head!, sy kop moet af!
off, prep van . . . af (weg); van; he fell – the ladder, hy het van die leer afgeval; I am glad the matter is – my hands, ek is bly dat ek van die las ontslae is (dat ek met die daak klaar het); he is – colour, hy is nie op sy stukke nie; – duty, vry; a street – Adderley Street, 'n dwarsstraat uit Adderleystraat; – shore, naby die land of kus.
off, a. ander; regter, haar; the – horse, die haarperd; the – front wheel, die haarvoorwiel; on the – side of the wall, anderkant die muur; on my next – day, as ek weer 'n dag vry het.
offal, afval; oorskiet, brokkies; aas.
off-chance, moontlikheid, geluk; on the –, met die hoop.
offence, aanstoot, ergernis; oortreding, misstap; no – was meant, daar was geen kwaad bedoel nie; he is too quick to take –, hy is te liggeraak, hy is te gou op sy perdjie; give – to, aanstoot gee, beledig.
offend, aanstoot gee, beledig; oortree.
offender, oortreder; belediger.
offensive, a. beledigend, aanstootlik; walglik; sleg, onaangenaam (van ruik); aanvullend, offensief; – language, beledigende taal.
offensive, n. aanval, offensief; act on the –, aanvallend optree.
offer, v. aanbied, (aan)presenteer; offer; opper, maak; – an opinion, 'n mening uitspreek; I – no apology, ek maak geen verskoning nie; as opportunity –s, wanneer die geleentheid daar is.
offer, n. aanbod; bod; voorstel; (huweliks)aanbod.

offering, offerande.
offertory, kollekte.
off-hand, voor die vuis, sonder om te dink; kortaf, onverskillig.
office, taak, plig; amp, betrekking; kantoor, buro; erediens; **take, enter upon** –, 'n betrekking (amp) aanvaar.
office-bearer, ampsbekleder; bestuurslid.
officer, n. amptenaar, beampte; bestuurslid; offisier; konstabel.
official, a. amptelik, amps- . . ., offisieel.
official, n. beampte, amptenaar.
officialdom, die amptenare; burokrasie.
officiant, dienswaarnemer.
officiate, 'n amp waarneem; 'n diens lei, voorgaan, voorsit; – **as,** optree as.
officinal, geneeskragtig, doelmatig.
officious, gedienstig, bemoeisiek, half-amptelik, offisieus.
offing, die oop see.
offish, hooghartig, ongenaakbaar.
off-print, afdruk.
offscourings, oorskiet, skuim, uitvaagsel.
offset, spruit, loot; teenstelling; teëwig; draai.
offshoot, loot, spruit.
off-side, onkant; ver kant, ander kant.
offspring, afstamming, spruit, kroos; gevolg.
oft, dikwels.
often, dikwels, baiemaal, herhaaldelik.
ogee, n. ojief.
ogive, spitsboog.
ogle, v. (toe)lonk, verliefderig aankyk.
ogle, n. lonk, wink, oogknip.
Ogpu, Ogpoe.
ogre, paaiboelie, mensvreter.
ogreish, ogrish, paaiboelieagtig, mensvreter- . . .
oh, o; ag, og.
ohm, ohm, eenheid van weerstand.
oil, n. olie; **strike** –, 'n oliebron ontdek; 'n geluk kry; – **of almonds,** amandelolie, –s, olieverf; oliepak, oliejas.
oil, v. olie, smeer; – **one's hand,** iemand se palms smeer; – **one's tongue,** mooi broodjies bak, met 'n heuningtong praat.
oil-cake, lynkoek, raapkoek.
oil-can, oliekan(netjie).
oil-cloth, wasdoek, seildoek.
oil-colour, olieverf.
oiled, aangeklam.
oiler, oliekan(netjie); smeerder.
oilman, oliehandelaar.
oil-painting, olieverf(skildery).
oil-press, oliepers.
oilskin, oliejas; wasdoek; –s, oliepak.
oilstone, oliesteen.
oily, olieagtig, olierig; salwend; glad.
ointment, salf, smeersel, smeergoed.
old, a. oud, ou; ouderwets, bejaard, afgeleef; verslete; ervare; – **age,** ouderdom, oudag; **he is an** – **woman,** hy is 'n ou vrou; – **bachelor,** oujongkêrel; – **chap,** ou kêrel, ou maat; – **maid,** oujongnôi, oujongmeisie; **be an** – **hand at something,** (ge)konft in iets wees; **as** – **as the hills,** so oud soos die Kaap se (wa)pad; **be an** – **bird,** 'n ou kalant (rot) wees.
old, n.: **of** –, vanmelewe(se); **people of** –, vanmelewe se mense; **of** – **there were giants,** vanmelewe was daar (nog) reuse.
old-clothes man, ouklerekoper.
olden, a. ou, vanmelewese, vroeër.
old-fashioned, ouderwets.
oldish, ouerig.
old-maidish, oujongnôiagtig.
oldster, 'n ou(erige) man, nie vandag se kind nie.
old-womanish, ouvrouagtig.

oleaginous, olieagtig, olierig, olie-.
oleander, oleander, selon(s)roos.
oleaster, wilde-olyfboom, oleaster.
oleograph, oleografie.
olfactory, a. reuk . . .; – **nerve,** reuksenuwee.
olfactory, n. reukorgaan.
oligarch, oligarg, lid van 'n oligargie.
oligarchic(al), oligargies.
oligarchy, oligargie, paarmansregering.
olio, mengelmoes.
olivaceous, olyfkleurig, olyfgroen.
olive, n. olyf(boom); olyftak; olyfkleur.
olive, a. olyfkleurig.
olive-oil, olyfolie, slaai-olie.
olive-tree, olyfboom; **wild,** –, wilde-olyfboom, olienhoutboom.
olivine, olivien.
olla podrida, sien **olio.**
olympiad, olimpiade.
Olympian, Olimpies.
Olympic, Olimpies; – **games,** Olimpiese spele.
ombre, omberspel.
omega, omega.
omelet(te), omelet, eier(panne)koek, struif.
omen, voorteken.
ominous, onheilspellend, dreigend.
omission, uitlating, weglating; nalatigheid.
omit, weglaat, uitlaat, oorslaan; nalaat, versuim.
omnibus, (omni)bus; – **edition,** omnibus-uitgawe.
omnifarious, allerhande, veelsoortig.
omnipotence, almag, alvermoë.
omnipotent, almagtig, alvermoënd.
omnipresence, alomteenwoordigheid.
omnipresent, alomteenwoordig.
omniscience, alwetendheid.
omniscient, alwetend.
omnium gatherum, deurmekaar klomp.
omnivorous, al(les)verslindend.
omphalos, na(w)el; middelpunt.
on, prep. op, by, aan, teen, met, na, oor, te; **have you a watch** – **you?,** het jy 'n horlosie by jou?; – **foot, horseback,** te voet, te perd; – **the wall,** aan of teen die muur; – **purpose,** met opset, opsetlik, moedswillig; – **account of weens;** – **no account,** volstrek nie, om die dood nie; – **the average,** gemiddeld; – **the minute,** die minuut; – **arriving,** by (my) aankoms; – **the sly,** stilletjies, agteraf; – **fire,** aan (die) brand; – **the watch,** op die uitkyk, op wag; **he is** – **duty,** hy het diens; – **the next day,** die volgende dag; **march** – **London,** teen Londen opruk.
on, adv. aan; deur, verder; **it is getting** – **for two o'clock,** dit gaan na twee-uur se kant toe; **from that day** –, van dié dag af; **he is rather** –, hy is bietjie hoenderkop (lekker); **work** –, deurwerk, aanhou werk; **Macbeth is** –, Macbeth word opgevoer.
onager, wilde esel, onager.
onanism, selfbevlekking, onanie.
once, adv. een maal, een keer; – **or twice,** een of twee maal, 'n paar keer; – **more, again,** nog 'n slag, nog 'n keer; – **for all,** eens vir altyd; **in a while,** 'n enkele maal, so nou en dan; – **upon a time,** eenmaal; **at** –, dadelik, onmiddelik, op die plek (daad); **don't all speak at** –, moenie almal gelyk praat nie; **for** –, ook 'n keer (tog) eenmaal; **for this** –, hierdie keer (tog).
once, conj. sodra, as; – **he stops,** sodra hy ophou, as hy eenmaal ophou.
once, n. ee**r**-maal; – **is enough for me,** ek het aan een maal genoeg.
once-over, vlugtige blik, vinnige ondersoek.
oncoming, a. naderende, aanstaande.
oncoming, n. nadering.

one, a. een; enigste; **for – thing, he drinks,** vereers al drink hy; – **of two people,** 'n paar ('n stuk of wat) mense; **the –** way, die enigste manier.

one, pron. ('n) mens; een; **dear –,** geliefde, beminde, liefste; – **and all,** soos een man, almal tesaam; – **by –,** – **after another,** een vir een, een na die ander; – **with another,** deur die bank, gemiddeld; **write to –** another, aan mekaar skrywe.

one, n. een; **write down a –,** skrywe 'n een; **they came by –s, and two's,** hulle het een-een en twee-twee gekom; **be at –,** dit eens wees, saamstem; **never a –,** ook nie een nie; **go – better,** oortroef; **that was –** too many **for him,** dit was meer as hy kon uitstaan, dit was bokant sy vuurmaakplek; **give somebody – in the eye,** iemand 'n hou op die oog gee; **it is all – to me,** dit maak vir my geen verskil nie, dit is vir my om die ewe; **become –,** een word, saamsmelt, verenig.

one-eyed, eenoog- . . ., met een oog; onbillik, eensydig.
one-handed, met een hand.
one-legged, eenbeen- . . .; met een been (poot).
one-man, eenpersoons- . . .
oneness, eenheid; eentonigheid.
oner, doring, bobaas; **a – at cards,** 'n baaskaartspeler; **he gave me a –,** hy het my 'n opstopper gegee.
onerous, swaar, drukkend, lastig.
oneself, jouself.
one-sided, eensydig, bekrompe, partydig.
one-way: – **street,** eenrigtingstraat.
onion, n. ui.
onlooker, toeskouer.
only, a. enigste; **the –** child, die enigste kind; **my one and –** hope, my enigste hoop.
only, adv. maar, slegs, net, pas, alleen; **I not – heard it, but saw it,** ek het dit nie alleen gehoor nie, maar ook gesien; **he has – just come,** hy het maar nou pas of net gekom; – **too glad,** maar alte bly.
only, conj. maar, alleen, as; **he is a good footballer, – he never practises,** hy is 'n goeie voetbalspeler, maar hy oefen nooit nie; – **that you would be bored, I should** . . ., as dit jou nie sou verveel nie, sou ek . . .
onomatopoeia, klanknabootsing.
onomatopoetic, klanknabootsend, onomatopeïes.
onrush, aanval, stormloop.
onset, aanval; **at the first –,** by die eerste stormloop; met die wegspring.
onslaught, aanval, stormloop.
onto, op, tot by, na.
ontology, ontologie.
onus, las, verantwoordelikheid, onus.
onward, a. voorwaarts.
onward(s), adv. voorwaarts, verder, vooruit.
onyx, oniks.
oof, geld, „pitte".
oof-bird, geldsak.
oofy, skatryk.
oolite, oöliet.
oomph, bekoring, bekoorlikheid.
ooze, n. modder, slyk; looiwater.
ooze, v. syfer, lek; uitsweet; **the secret –d out,** die geheim het uitgelek.
oozy, modderig, slykerig.
opacity, ondeurskynendheid; domheid.
opal, opaal.
opalescent, opaalagtig; halfdeursigtig.
opaque, ondeurskynend, donker; duister, onduidelik; dom, bot.
open, a. oop; blootgestel; openbaar, ope(n)lik; openhartig, rondborstig, vatbaar; **the –** air, die buitelug, die oop lug; **with an – mind,** onbevooroordeeld; – **to conviction,** vir oortuiging vatbaar; **an – question,** 'n onuitgemaakte saak; **I will be – with you,** ek sal openhartig met jou praat.
open, v. oopmaak; oopgaan; begin; blootlê, openbaar maak; inlei; – **fire,** losbrand; – **the debate,** die onderwerp inlei; **the door –s into the passage,** die deur kom (gaan) in die gang uit; – **out,** blootlê, oopgaan; ontwikkel, uitbrei; – **up,** bekend maak; toeganklik maak; – **up a mine,** 'n myn open (in bedryf stel); – **your shoulder,** jou bors uitsit.
open, n. ruimte; oop veld (lug); **in the –,** in die oop lug, onder die blote hemel.
open-eyed, waaksaam, wakker, met oop oë.
open-handed, vrygewig, rojaal.
open-hearted, openhartig.
opening, n. opening; aanvang, begin; inleiding; kans, geleentheid.
opening, a. openings- . . ., aanvangs- . . ., inleidend.
openly, ope(n)lik, rondborstig, openhartig.
open-minded, onbevooroordeeld.
open-mouthed, met oop mond, stom van verbasing, dronkgeslaan.
opera, opera.
opera-cloak, aandmantel, operamantel.
opera-glasses, toneelkyker.
opera-hat, klapkeil.
opera-house, opera(gebou).
operate, werk, uitwerking hê op; teweegbring, veroorsaak; werk met, bestuur; sny, operasie maak, opereer; – **upon,** werk op; beïnvloed; opereer.
operatic, opera- . . .
operating-room, operasiekamer, snykamer.
operation, werking; bewerking; handeling, werksaamheid; beweging; operasie; **come into –,** in werking tree.
operative, a. werkend, werkdadig, werk- . . .; prakties; snykundig, operatief.
operative, n. ambagsman, werkjong.
operator, werker; telegrafis, operateur.
opthalmia, oogontsteking, oogsiekte.
ophthalmic, n. oogmiddel.
ophthalmic, a. oog- . . ., oftalmies.
ophthalmoscope, oogspieël, oftalmoskoop.
opiate, slaapdrank, slaapmiddel.
opinie, van mening wees, 'n mening uitspreek.
opinion, mening, sienswyse, gedagte, opinie, gevoelens; advies; **in my –,** volgens my mening; **public –,** die openbare mening.
opinionated, eiewys, koppig, eiesinnig.
opium, opium.
opossum, opossum.
opponent, teenstander, teenparty, opponent.
opportune, geleë, gunstig, geskik.
opportuninsim, opportunisme.
opportunist, opportunis.
opportunity, geleentheid kans.
oppose, bestry, opponeer, teenwerk; stel teenoor; **be —d to,** gekant wees teen.
opposer, bestryder, teenstander.
opposite, a. teenoorgestel, ander; **in – directions,** in teenoorgestelde rigting; **the – sex,** die ander geslag; – **angle,** oorstaande (oorkantse) hoek; – **signs,** teengestelde tekens (in matesis).
opposite, n. die teenoorgestelde, teendeel.
opposite, adv. (aan die) anderkant (aan die) oorkant.
opposite, prep. regoor, teenoor, oorkant, anderkant.
opposition, teenstand, verset, weerstand; teen-

stelling, teenparty, opposisie; **leader of the –,** leier van die opposisie.
oppress, onderdruk, verdruk; swaar druk op.
oppression, onderdrukking, verdrukking; druk, terneergedruktheid; oppressie.
oppressive, onderdrukkend; tiranniek; benoud, drukkend.
oppressor, verdrukker, tiran.
opprobrious, beledigend, skimpend, skimp-..., skel(d)-...
opprobrium, smaad, skuld, blaam.
oppugn, betwis, bestry, weerlê.
optative, a. optatief, wensend.
optative, n. optatief.
optic, opties, gesig(s)-..., oog-...; **– angle,** gesigshoek; **– nerve,** gesigsenuwee.
optical, gesigs-..., **opties;** **– illusion,** gesigsbedrog.
optician, gesigkundige, optisiën.
optics, optika, gesigkunde.
optimism, optimisme.
optimist, n. optimis.
optimist(ic), a. optimisties.
optimum, n. optimum.
optimum, a. optimaal, gunstigste.
option, keuse; opsie, voorkeur; **local –,** plaaslike keuse.
optional, nie verpligtend nie, na keuse, opsioneel.
opulence, rykdom, weelde.
opulent, ryk.
opus, werk, opus.
or, of, anders; **either**...–, òf... òf.
oracle, orakel godspraak; **work the –,** 'n saak plooi, agterbaks konkel.
oracular, orakelagtig, geheimsinnig; dogmaties.
oral, mondeling; mond-...; **– examination,** mondelinge eksamen.
orange, n. lemoen; oranje(kleur); **–s and lemons,** aljanderspeletjie.
orange, a. oranje(kleurig).
Orange, n. Oranje.
orangeade, (soet)lemoensop.
orange-blossom, lemoenbloeisel.
orangery, lemoenboord, oranjerie.
orang-outang, orang-oetang.
orate, 'n toespraak afsteek, oreer.
oration, redevoering, toespraak, rede.
orator, redenaar, spreker.
oratorical, redenaars-..., oratories.
oratorio, oratorium.
oratory, welsprekendheid, redenaarskuns, retoriek.
oratory, bidvertrek, kapel.
orb, bol, sfeer; oog(appel); kringloop.
orbicular, sirkelvormig, kringvormig.
orbit, oogholte; baan, kringloop; wentelbaan; **put into –,** in 'n wentelbaan plaas.
orchard, boomgaard, (vrugte)boord.
orchestra, orkes.
orchestral, orkes-...
orchestrate, orkestreer.
orchestration, orkestrasie.
orchid, orgidee.
ordain, orden, inseën; bepaal, vasstel; bestem, beskik; beveel, verordineer.
ordeal, beproewing; vuurproef, toets; Godsoordeel.
order, n. orde; rang, stand; klas, soort; volgorde, skikking; bevel, las, gebod, order; bestelling; **out of –,** nie in orde nie; stukkend; **in (good) –,** reg, in orde, in die haak; **call to –,** tot die orde roep; **– of the day,** die orde van die dag; **in – to,** om te, sodat, ten einde; **by –,** op las; **made to –,** volgens bestelling (gemaak); **keep –,** die orde hou, die tug bewaar; **that is a**

large –, dit is veel geverg; **postal –,** poswissel; **take –s,** priester word; bevestig (georden) word.
order, v. gelas, beveel, gebied; voorskryf, baasspeel oor, kommandeer; bestel; inrig, reël, in orde bring; bepaal, bestem, beskik; **the doctor –ed a mustard plaster,** die dokter het 'n mosterdpleister voorgeskryf; **– about,** rondstuur, kommandeer; **– home,** gelas om huis toe te gaan, huis toe stuur.
order-book, bestelboek.
order-form, bestelbriefie.
orderliness, orderlikheid; reëlmatigheid.
orderly, a. ordelik, ordeliewend, op orde gesteld; gereeld, reëlmatig.
orderly, n. ordonnans; oppasser.
orderly-officer, ordonnansoffisier.
orderly-room, (kaserne)kantoor, -buro.
ordinal, a. rangskikkend.
ordinal, n. rangskikkende telwoord.
ordinance, ordonnansie, wet; instelling, reglement, ordinansie.
ordinary, a. gewoon, alledaags, gebruiklik, ordinêr; **in an – way I should refuse,** onder gewone omstandighede sou ek weier; **something out of the –,** iets buitengewoons; **the – dose,** die gewone (gebruiklike) dosis.
ordinate, ordinaat.
ordination, rangskikking; ordening; bepaling.
ordnance, artillerie, grofgeskut.
ordure, drek, vuil.
ore, erts.
oread, bergnimf.
organ, orrel; orgaan; mondstuk; **mouth –,** mondfluitjie; **–s of speech,** spraakorgane.
organ-blower, orreltrapper.
organ grinder, orreldraaier, draai-orrelis.
organic, organies.
organization, organisasie, reëling.
organize, organiseer, reël, inrig.
organism, organisme.
organist, orrelis.
organ-stop, orrelregister.
orgasm, hewige opwinding, aandrang, woede; orgasme.
orgy, drinkparty, swelg-, drinkgelag.
oriel, uitspringende venster.
Orient, n. die Ooste, Oriënt.
orient, n. glans.
orient, orientate, v. na die ooste keer (draai); die ligging bepaal; oriënteer.
Oriental, a. Oosters, Oriëntaal.
Oriental, n. Oosterling.
orientate, sien **orient,** v.
orientation, oriëntering.
orifice, opening, gaatjie, mond.
origin, oorsprong, afkoms; oorsaak.
original, a. oorspronklik, origineel, eerste; **– sin,** erfsonde.
original, n. origineel, (die) oorspronklike; eksentrieke mens.
originality, oorspronklikheid, originaliteit.
originally, oorspronklik, eers, in die begin.
originate, ontstaan, voortspruit; veroorsaak (word); voortbring.
origination, oorsprong, begin, ontstaan.
originator, ontwerper, bewerker.
orison, gebed.
orlop, onderste dek, oorloop, koeibrug.
ormolu, vergulde brons, goudbrons.
ornament, n. sieraad, versiering, ornament.
ornament, v. versier, tooi, ornamenteer.
ornamental, (ver)sier-..., sierlik, ornamenteel, dekorasie-..., dekoratief.

ornate — **outlook**

ornate, ryk versier(d), bloemryk.
ornithologist, voëlkenner, ornitoloog.
ornithology, voëlkunde, ornitologie.
orotund, hoogdrawend, geswolle.
orphan, n. wees(kind).
orphan, a. wees- . . ., ouerloos.
orphanage, ouerloosheid; weeshuis.
orrery, planetarium.
orthocentre, hoogtesnypunt.
orthocentric, ortosentries; – **triangle**, voetpuntsdriehoek.
orthodox, ortodoks, regsinnig.
orthodoxy, ortodoksie, regsinnigheid.
orthoepy, uitspraakleer, ortoëpie.
orthographic(al), ortografies, spel- . . .
orthography, ortografie, spelkuns.
orthopaedic, ortopedies.
orthopaedy, ortopedie.
oscillate, slinger, swaai, skommel; weifel, aarsel; osilleer.
oscillation, slinger(ing); skommel(ing); weifeling; osillasie.
oscillatory, swaaiend, slinger- . . .; weifelend.
osculate, oskuleer (in matesis); soen.
osier, wilger(boom), wilgerlat; mandjiesgoed.
osmium, osmium.
osmose, osmosis, osmose.
osmotic, osmoties.
osprey, see-arend; aigrette(pluim).
osseous, beenagtig, been-.
ossicle, beentjie.
ossification, beenwording, ossifikasie.
ossify, in been verander; verhard.
ossuary, knekelhuis, lykhuis.
ostensible, oënskynlik, kastig.
ostensibly, oënskynlik, kastig, konsuis.
ostentation, vertoon, pronkery; prag en praal, ostentasie.
ostentatious, spoggerig, pronkerig.
osteology, osteologie.
osteomyelitis, beenmurgontsteking.
ostler, staljong, -kneg.
ostracize, verban; uitsluit uitdrywe.
ostracism, verbanning, ostrasisme, skerfgerig.
ostrich, volstruis.
other, a. ander; anders; **every – day**, al om die ander dag; **the – world**, die hiernamaals; **the – day**, onlangs, 'n paar dae gelede; **some time or –**, een van die mooi dae, eendag; **some one or –**, een of ander.
other, n. ander; **you are the man of all –s**, jy is net die (regte) man.
otherwise, anders; op 'n ander manier; **he could not have acted –**, hy kon nie anders(ter) gehandel het nie; **do it now, – you will regret it**, doen dit nou, anders sal dit jou berou.
otiose, nutteloos, onbruikbaar; ledig.
otology, oorheelkunde.
otoscope, oorspieël, otoskoop.
otter, otter.
Ottoman, n. Ottoman, Turks.
Ottoman, a. Ottomaans, Turks.
ottoman, ottoman, sofa.
ought, n. nut.
ought, v. moet, behoort; **I – to have said it**, ek moes dit gesê het, ek behoort dit te gesê het.
ouija, ouija.
ouija-board, ouijabord.
ounce, ons.
ounce, sneeuluiperd, bergpanter.
our, ons (onse).
ours, ons s'n ons; **I like – better**, ek hou meer van ons s'n.
ourself, ourselves, ons, onsself; **we will see to it –**, ons sal self daarvoor sorg.

oust, uitdryf, verdryf, verdring, uitlig.
out, adv. uit, buite; dood; bekend; **father is –**, vader is uit, vader is nie tuis nie; **on the voyage –**, op die uitreis; **the miners are –**, die mynwerkers het gestaak; **the fire is –**, die vuur is dood; **I was – in my calculations**, ek het my misreken; **– and about**, op die been; **– and away**, verreweg; **– and –**, deeglik, eersteklas; **aarts- . . .; they are – to murder him**, hulle is daarop uit om hom te vermoor.
out, prep. uit; **from –**, (van)uit; **– of, uit**; buite, buitekant; van; **– of the house**, uit die huis (uit); **– of doors**, buitekant, in die oop lug; **– of sight**, uit die gesig (oog); **– of his mind**, van sy verstand af; **– of breath**, uit-asem; **– of work**, sonder werk, werkloos; **ten miles – of Boshof**, tien myl buitekant Boshof; **times – of number**, ontelbare male; **– of wedlock**, buitenegtelik; **be – of it**, uitgesluit wees, nie meetel nie; **die kluts kwyt wees, dit mis hê**; **– of date**, verouderd, uit die mode; **draw – of hand**, loshand teken; **– of print**, uitverkoop.
out, a. weg van huis; buitengewoon, groot; – **match**, wedstryd van huis af.
out-and-outer, doring, knewel; ekstremis.
outbalance, swaarder weeg as.
outbid, hoër bie(d) as; oortref.
outboard: – **motor**, buiteboordmotor, aanhangmotor.
outbound, op die uitreis.
outbreak, uitbarsting; oproer; (die) uitbreek.
outbuilding, buitegebou.
outburst, los-, uitbarsting.
outcast, verworpeling, verstoteling.
outclass, oortref, oorskadu.
outcome, uitslag, gevolg, resultaat.
outcrop, (die) opduik; resultaat; dagsoom (geol.).
outcry, geskreeu, lawaai, geroep.
outdistance, uit(hard)loop, disnis loop; verbygaan, agterlaat.
outdo, oortref, baasraak.
outdoor, buitelug- . . . opelug- . . ., buite- . . .; **– life**, buitelewe, lewe in die buitelug.
outer, buite- . . ., buitenste; uiterlik; **– world**, buitewêreld; **– darkness**, buitenste duisternis.
outermost, uiterste, buitenste.
outface, die oë laat neerslaan, trotseer, van die wysie bring.
outfall, uitloop (van 'n dam, ens.).
outfit, uitrusting, toerusting.
outfitter, uitruster, leweransier.
outflank, omtrek, uitoorlê.
outflow, uitloop; uitstroming.
outgeneral, in krygskuns oortref, uitoorlê.
outgoing, vertrekkende; aftredende.
outgoings, onkoste, uitgawe.
outgrow, uitgroei, verbygroei; vergroei.
outgrowth, uitgroeisel; resultaat.
outhouse, buitegebou.
outing, uitstappie, kuiertjie.
outlander, uitlander.
outlandish, uitheems, uitlands, vreemd.
outlast, oortref, langer uithou as.
outlaw, n. balling, voëlvryverklaarde.
outlaw, v. verban, voëlvry verklaar.
outlay, uitgawe, onkoste; ontwerp.
outlet, uitgang; uitweg; mond (van 'n rivier); afvoerpyp.
outline, n. omtrek, skets; **the –s**, die hoofpunte, algemene trekke.
outline, v. skets, die hooftrekke gee.
outlive, oorleef, langer leef as.
outlook, vooruitsig; uitkyk; uitsig, gesig; kyk; **his – on life**, sy kyk op die lewe.

outlying, afgeleë, ver.
outmanoeuvre, uitoorlê.
outmarch, uitmarsjeer.
outmatch, oortref, uitoorlê.
outmoded, verouderd, ouderwets, oudmodies.
outmost, verste, buitenste uiterste.
outnumber, oortref in getal.
outpace, uit-, verbyhardloop.
out-patient, buitepasiënt.
outpost, voorpos, buitepos.
outpouring, uitstorting, ontboeseming.
output, produksie, opbrings.
outrage, n. vergryp, aanranding, gewelddaad.
outrage, v. aanrand, beledig, verkrag, geweld aandoen, skend.
outrageous, gewelddadig, woes; skandelik, skandalig; beledigend.
outright, adv. heeltemal, skoon; ope(n)lik, rond-uit, rondborstig.
outright, a. deeglik, suiwer; ope(n)lik.
outrun, verbyhardloop; die grense oorskry.
outset, begin, aanvang, staanspoor; **at, from the –**, by (van) die begin, uit die staanspoor uit.
outshine, in die skadu stel, oortref.
outside, n. buitekant; uiterlik; uiterste; **hundred at the –**, honderd op sy hoogste.
outside, a. buite-. . .; buitenste, van buite; uiterste; **– prices**, hoogste of uiterste pryse; gering.
outside, adv. buitekant, na buite, buite(n)toe; **black –**, swart van buite.
outside, prep. buite, buitekant.
outsider, oningewyde, buitestaander, buiteperd.
outsize, groot nommer (maat); buitemaat.
outskirts, grense; uithoeke; rante.
ontspan, v. uitspan.
outspan, n. uitspanning, uitspanplek.
outspoken, rondborstig, reguit.
outstanding, uitstaande, onbetaal(d); prominent, buitengewoon.
outstay, langer bly as; oor jou tyd bly.
outstrip, verbyhardloop; verbystrewe.
outvie, oortref.
outvote, oorstem.
outward, a. uiterlik, uitwendig; buite-. . .; **– form**, die uiterlike.
outward, adv. na die buitekant.
outward, n. (die) uiterlike.
outward bound, op die uitreis.
outwardly, (na die) uiterlik.
outwards, buitekant toe, na buite.
outweigh, swaarder weeg as, van meer belang wees as.
outwit, fop, uitoorlê, te slim wees vir.
oval, a. ovaal, eiervormig.
oval, n. ovaal.
ovary, eierstok; vrugbeginsel.
ovation, ovasie, toejuiging, hulde.
oven, oond.
over, adv. oor; omver, onderstebo, om; verby; **ask somebody –**, iemand nooi; **– against**, teenoor, in teenstelling met; **it is all –**, dit is verby [klaarpraat, (af)gedaan]; **count, go, read –**, oortel, oorgaan, oorlees; **turn, blow, fall –**, omblaai, omwaai, omval; **– again**, nog 'n slag, nog 'n keer.
over, prep. oor, bo, by, oorkant; **– our heads**, bokant ons koppe; bokant ons vuurmaakplek; sonder om ons te raadpleeg; **– head and ears**, tot oor die ore; **all – the world**, die hele wêreld deur; **go to sleep – one's work**, by jou werk aan die slaap raak; **– and above**, boonop, buitendien behalwe; **– the way**, aan die oorkant; **– a glass of wine**, by 'n glasie wyn.
over, n. (boul)beurt.
over-all, totaal; **– dimension(s)**, totale maat.

overalls, oorbroek, oorpak, oorrok.
over-anxious, al te besorg; al te begerig.
overawe, ontsag (vrees) inboesem, bangmaak, oorbluf.
overbalance, die ewewig verloor; (laat) omtuimel; swaarder weeg as.
overbear, onderdruk, swaar druk op; platdruk, oorweldig; swaarder weeg as.
overbearing, baasspelerig, heerssugtig.
overboard, oorboord.
overburden, oorlaai, ooreis.
over-careful, te versigtig, te presies.
overcast, bewolk, betrokke, toegetrek.
over-cautious, te versigtig.
overcharge, n. te hoë berekening (prys), oorvraging; oorbelasting; te groot lading.
overcharge, v. te swaar laai, oorbelas, oorlaai; te veel vra (laat betaal).
overcloud, bewolk.
overcoat, jas.
overcome, v. oormeester, te bowe kom, oorman, die oorhand kry oor.
overcome, a. oorstelp, verslae; **– with, by emotion**, deur sy gevoel oorman.
over-confidence, oormoed.
over-confident, oormoedig.
overcrowded, te vol, oorvol; oorbevolk.
overdo, oordryf; te gaar kook; ooreis.
overdone, oordrewe; te gaar.
overdose, te groot dosis.
overdraft, oortrokke bankrekening.
overdraw, oortrek; oordrywe.
overdress, n. borok, bokleed; te windmakerige klere.
overdress, v. opsigtig aantrek.
overdrive, doodry, flou ry; ooreis; te ver slaan.
overdue, laat, oor sy tyd; agterstallig.
overeat, ooreet.
over-estimate, v. oorskat, te hoog skat.
over-estimate, n. oorskatting.
over-exertion, oorspanning.
over-expose, oorbelig; te veel blootstel.
over-exposure, oorbeligting.
overflow, v. oorloop, oorstroom.
overflow, n. (die) oorloop; oorstroming; oorvloed.
overgrow, toegroei, te vinnig groei.
overhand, oorhands.
overhang, oorhang; uitsteek; dreig.
overhaul, nakyk, regmaak, opknap; inhaal.
overhead, adv. bo jou kop, bo (in die lug).
overhead, a. lug-. . ., bogrondse; **– expenses**, administrasiekoste; **– wires**, lugdrade, luggeleiding.
overhear, afluister, hoor.
overheat, oorverhit.
overjoyed, opgetoë, in die wolke.
overland, oorland.
overlap, gedeeltelik dek, oormekaar val; gedeeltelik saamval.
overleaf, op die anderkantse bladsy.
overlive, oorleef.
overload, oorlaai.
overlook, uitkyk op; oor die hoof sien; opsig hou oor.
overlord, opper(leen)heer.
overmantel, skoorsteenspieël.
overmaster, oormeester, baasraak.
overmuch, te veel.
over-nice, te kieskeurig; te lekker.
overnight, die vorige aand; gedurende die nag die (vorige) nag, snags.
overpay, te veel betaal.
overplus, oorskot, surplus; oorvloed.
over-population, oorbevolking.

overpower, oorweldig, oormeester, bemagtig; oorstelp.
overpowering, onweerstaanbaar; oorstelpend.
overpressure, te groot (swaar) druk.
overproduction, oorproduksie.
overproof, te sterk.
overrate, oorskat, te hoog skat.
overreach, uitoorlê, fop, kul; aankap (van 'n perd).
override, onderstebo ry; vertrap; weier; tersy stel; baas wees oor; flou ry.
overripe, oorryp.
overrule, ('n voorstel) verwerp, uit die orde reël, te niet doen, van die hand wys.
overrun, oorstroom, platloop; vervuil, wemel (van ongedierte of onkruid); ooreis.
oversea(s), adv. oor (die) see.
oversea, a. oorsees.
oversee, toesig hê oor.
overseer, opsigter, opsiener.
overshadow, oorskadu, in die skadu stel.
overshoe, oorskoen.
overshoot, oorheen skiet; – **the mark,** – **oneself,** te ver gaan; jou mond verbypraat.
oversight, vergissing, versuim; toesig.
oversleep, verslaap.
overspend, te veel uitgee.
overspread, versprei, bedek.
overstate, oordryf, te sterk voorstel, te hoog opgee.
overstatement, oordrywing, oordrewe voorstelling.
overstep, oorskry, te buite gaan.
overstock, te groot voorraad hou; te veel vee aanhou; oorlaai.
overstrung, oorspanne; kruissnarig (van klavier).
overt, ope(n)lik, openbaar.
overtake, inhaal; oorval.
overtask, ooreis, oorlaai.
overtax, (die kragte) ooreis, te veel verwag van; te swaar belas.
overthrow, v. omvergooi; verslaan, tot 'n val bring.
overthrow, n. neerlaag, ondergang, val.
overtime, n. oorure, oorwerk.
overtime, adv. na ure; **work** –, oorwerk doen.
overtone, bowetoon; te donker kleur.
overtrain, te veel oefen, ooreis.
overtrump, oortroef.
overture, voorstel, aanbod, inleiding; voorspel.
overturn, v. omslaan; omgooi, onderstebo gooi; tot val bring, verslaan.
overturn, n. omkeer, omwenteling.
overweening, verwaand, aanmatigend.
overweight, oorgewig.
overweighted, te swaar (gelaai).
overwhelm, oorweldig, oorstelp.
overwhelming, oorweldigend, oorstelpend.
overwind, te styf opwen.
overwork, v. oorwerk.
overwork, n. 'n ekstra werk, oorwerk.
over-wrought, oorspanne; te uitgewerk.
oviform, eiervormig.
oviparous, eierlêend.
ovipositor, legboor.
ovoid, eiervormig.
ovum, eier.
owe, skuld; verskuldig wees, te danke hê; – **one a grudge,** 'n wrok teen iemand koester; **I** – **him much,** ek is veel aan hom verskuldig.
owing, a. (ver)skuldig; uitstaande, onbetaald.
owing to, prep. as gevolg van, weens, dank sy.
owl, uil.
owlet, (klein) uiltjie.
owlish, uilagtig, uil- . . .
own, a. eie; **hold one's** –, jou man staan; **on one's** –, eie houtjie; **a value all its** –, 'n besondere waarde.
own, v. besit; erken, beken, toegee; **he** –**s to having done it,** hy beken dat hy dit gedoen het; – **up,** beken, opbieg.
owner, eienaar, besitter, baas.
ownership, eiendomsreg.
ox, os.
oxalic, oksaal- . . .; – **acid,** oksaalsuur, suringsuur.
ox-eye, os-oog; margriet, gousblom.
Oxford, Oxford; **the** – **Group,** die Oxford-groep (Morele Herwapening).
oxherd, beeswagter.
oxhide, beesvel, osvel.
oxidation, oksidasie, versuring.
oxide, oksied, okside.
oxidize, oksideer.
oxidizing, oksideer- . . .; – **agent,** oksideermiddel.
oxtail, ossestert.
ox-waggon, ossewa.
oxy-acetylene, oksi-asetileen.
oxygen, suurstof.
oxygenate, met suurstof verbind, oksideer.
oxymoron, oksimoron.
oyster, oester.
oyster-farm, oesterkwekery.
ozone, osoon.

pa, pa.
pabulum, voedsel, kos.
pace, n. tree, stap; gang; vaart, snelheid; **keep – with,** gelyke tred hou met, byhou.
pace, v. stap; afstap; aftree; trippel, 'n pas loop; die pas aangee, gangmaak.
pace-maker, gangmaker.
pacer, trippelaar, pasganger; gangmaker.
pachydermatous, dikhuidig.
pacific, vreedsaam, vredeliewend; pasifiek; **P. Ocean,** Stille Oseaan.
pacification, versoening, pasifikasie.
pacificism, pacifism, vredeliewendheid, pasifisme.
pacificist, pacifist, pasifis, voorstander van wêreldvrede.
pacify, tot bedaring bring, kalmeer, paai; die vrede herstel, pasifiseer.
pack, n. pak, bondel; bende, klomp, trop; **a – of rouges,** 'n bende (klomp) skurke; **– of cards,** pak kaarte.
pack, v. pak, wegpak, inpak, verpak; volprop, volstop; **the hall was –ed,** die saal was stampvol; **– off, send –ing,** in die pad steek; **– up,** ingee, uit orde raak, gaan staan, onklaar raak (motor, masjien).
package, pak(kie), bondel; verpakking; pakloon; pakkasie.
packet, pakkie; pakket; pakketboot; groot som geld.
packet-boat, posboot, pakketboot.
pack-horse, pakperd.
packing-needle, seilnaald.
packman, pakkiesdraer, smous.
pack-saddle, paksaal.
packthread, seilgaring, pakgaring.
pact, ooreenkoms, verbond, verdrag.
pad, n. kussinkie; saaltjie; vulsel; beenskut; skryfblok; onderlêer; voetsool.
pad, v. (op)stop, opvul, beklee, uitvoer.
pad, v. loop, stap, te voet loop.
padding, stopsel, vulsel; bladvulling.
paddle, n. roeispaan, skepper(tjie), pagaai.
paddle, v. roei, pagaai; in die water plas, pootjies baai; waggel, strompel.
paddle-wheel, skeprat.
paddock, kamp; park; speelgrond.
padlock, n. hangslot.
padlock, v. (met 'n hangslot) toesluit.
paean, danklied, triomflied, loflied.
pagan, n. heiden.
pagan, a. heidens.
paganism, heidendom, paganisme.
page, n. sien **page-boy**.
page, n. bladsy, pagina.
page, v. pagineer.
pageant, vertoning, prag, praal; historiese optog.
pageantry, praalvertoning, prag en praal.
page-boy, page, livreikneg, (hotel)joggie, boodskappertjie; sleepdraertjie; edelknaap.
paginate, pagineer.
pagoda, (afgods)tempel; pagode.
pail, emmer.
paillasse, palliasse, strooimatras.
pain, n. pyn, leed, verdriet, smart; **–s, weë;** moeite, inspanning; straf; **take –s,** moeite doen; **under – of,** op straf van.
pain, v. pyn, pynig, seermaak; kwel; leed of smart veroorsaak.
painful, pynlik, seer.
pain-killer, pynstiller.
painless, pynloos.
painstaking, ywerig, werksaam; presies, noulettend.
paint, n. verf; blanketsel.

paint, v. verf, skilder; voorstel, beskrywe; **– the town red,** die dorp op horings sit.
painter, skilder.
painter, vanglyn, vangtou; **cut the –,** afskei, lossny.
painting, skildery; skilderkuns.
pair, n. paar; **a – of scissors, trousers,** 'n skêr, 'n broek.
pair, v. paar; twee-twee opstel; **– off,** afpaar.
pal, n. maat, vrind, vriend, boetie.
pal, v.: – up, maats maak.
palace, paleis.
paladin, paladyn, ridder.
pal(a)eographer, paleograaf.
pal(a)eography, paleografie.
pal(a)eolithic, van of uit die steenperiode, paleolities.
pal(a)eontologist, paleontoloog.
pal(a)eontology, paleontologie.
palankeen, -quin, draagstoel, palankyn.
palatable, smaaklik, lekker, aangenaam.
palatal, palataal.
palatalize, palataliseer.
palate, verhemelte; smaak; **not to my –,** nie na my smaak nie, nie van my gading nie.
palatial, paleis- . . ., paleisagtig; **a – dwelling,** 'n paleis (van 'n woning).
palatinate, paltsgraafskap, palatinaat.
palatine, a. paltsgraaflik.
palaver, n. bespreking, onderhandeling; gebabbel, geklets; mooipraatjies.
palaver, v. babbel; onderhandel, bespreek; mooipraat.
pale, n. paal(tjie); spar; grens; **within, beyond the –,** binne, buite die perke.
pale, a. bleek, vaal; dof, flou.
pale, v. bleek of dof word, verbleek, verdof, bleek maak; verskiet.
paleo-, sien **pal(a)eo-.**
paletot, oorjas, paletot.
palette, palet.
palette-knife, tempermes, paletmes.
palfrey, damesryperd.
palimpsest, palimpses.
paling, pale, paalheining, skutting.
palingenesis, herlewing, wedergeboorte.
palinode, herroeping, palinodie.
palisade, n. palissade, skanspale, paalwerk, skutting.
palisade, v. met skanspale afsluit, ompaal, verskans, palissadeer.
pall, n. doodskleed; (skouer)mantel.
pall, v. smaakloos word, walg.
palladium, bolwerk, waarborg, palladium.
palladium, palladium (metaal).
pall-bearer, slipdraer.
pallet, strooimatras; pottebakkerskyf.
palliasse, sien **paillasse.**
palliate, versag, verlig; verontskuldig, vergoelik, verbloem.
palliative, versagtend, verligtend; verontskuldigend, verbloemend.
pallid, bleek, asvaal.
pallor, bleekheid.
pally, bevriend, kameraadskaplik.
palm, n. (hand)palm; palm(boom); **bear the –,** die palm wegdra.
palm, v. betas, bevoel; verberg in die handpalm; omkoop; kul, fop; **– off,** afsmeer (aan).
palmer, pelgrim; ruspe(r); kunsvlieg.
palmetto, dwergpalm.
palmist, handkyker, goëlaar.
palmistry, handkykery; goëlery.
palm-oil, palmolie; omkoopgeld.
palm-stand, plantstander.

palmy, palmryk, palm-...; voorspoedig; -days, voorspoedjare, bloeitydperk.
palmyra, waaierpalm.
palpability, tasbaarheid, voelbaarheid.
palpable, tasbaar, duidelik.
palpate, betas, bevoel.
palpitate, klop, pols, tril.
palpitation, hartklopping; trilling.
palsgrave, paltsgraaf.
palsied, verlam, geraak.
palsy, n. verlamming, beroerte, geraaktheid.
palsy, v. verlam.
palter, rondspring, uitvlugte soek, onderduims te werk gaan, knoei; peuter.
paltriness, nietigheid, armsaligheid.
paltry, niksbeduidend, nietig, klein.
paly, blekerig.
pampa, vlakte, pampa.
pampas-grass, pampasgras.
pamper, vertroetel, verwen, bederwe.
pamphlet, pamflet, vlugskrif, brosjure.
pamphleteer, vlugskrifskrywer.
pan, n. pan.
pan, v.: – out, (goud) oplewer; – out well, slaag, geluk, goed uitval.
panacea, wondermiddel, panasee.
Pan-African, Pan-Afrikaans, Al-Afrikaans.
Pan-Africanist, Pan-Afrikanis.
Panama, Panama; **p-,** panamahoed.
pancake, pannekoek.
panchromatic, panchromaties.
pancreas, alvleesklier, pankreas, soetvleis.
pandects, pandekte.
pandemonium, pandemonium.
pander, n. koppelaar.
pander, v. as koppelaar optree; – to, na die mond praat, toegee aan, paai, voed.
pane, (venster)ruit, glasruit.
panegyric, n. lofrede.
panegyric(al), a. ophemelend, lof-...
panegyrise, ophemel, 'n lofrede hou oor.
panegyrist, ophemelaar, lofredenaar.
panel, n. paneel; naamlys, naamrol; baan, strook; span; **on the –,** op die rol.
panel, v. panele insit, van panele voorsien; bane of stroke inlas; op die rol sit.
panel-beater, duikklopper.
panelling, lambrisering, paneelwerk.
pang, skerp pyn, steek; kwelling, angs; **–s of conscience,** gewetenswroeging.
pangolin, miervreter.
panic, n. paniek, plotselinge skrik.
panic, a. panies.
panicky, paniekerig, verskrik.
panicle, pluim.
panic-monger, alarmmaker, skrikaanjaer.
panic-striken, deur skrik bevange.
pannier, (pak)mandjie, draagmandjie; rokhoepel; mandjierok.
pannikin, kommetjie, pannetjie.
panoplied, in volle wapenrusting.
panoply, wapenrusting.
panorama, vergesig, panorama.
pansy, gesiggie.
pant, v. hyg; snak (na); – **for, after** hunker na, snak na.
pant, n. (die) hyg, hyging.
pantalet(te)s, kantbroekie, rokbroek.
pantaloon, hanswors; **–s,** broek.
pantheism, panteïsme.
pantheist, panteïs.
pantheistic(al), panteïsties.
panther, panter, luiperd.
pantile, dakpan.
pantograph, tekenaap, pantograaf.

pantomime, gebarespel, pantomime.
pantomimic, pantomimies.
pantry, spens.
pants, broek; onderbroek.
pap, tepel; pap.
papa, pa(pa), pappie.
papacy, pousdom, pouslike mag.
papal, pouslik.
papaw, pawpaw, papaja.
paper, n. papier; koerant; vraestel; verhandeling; **–s,** dokumente; getuigskrifte; **commit to –,** opskrywe, op skrif stel; **send in one's –s,** jou ontslag indien; **on –,** op skrif; **read a – on a subject,** 'n verhandeling oor 'n onderwerp gee.
paper, v. in papier toedraai; plak.
paper-chase, snipperjag.
paper-clip, skuifspeld.
paper-currency, papiergeld.
paper-fastener, papierklem(metjie), -stekertjie.
paper-hanger, plakker.
paper-mill, papierfabriek, papiermeul.
paper-money, papiergeld, banknote.
paper-weight, papierdrukker.
papilionaceous, skoenlapperagtig, skoenlapper-..., vlinder-...
papilla, tepel, papil.
papillary, tepelvormig, tepel-...
Papist, Papis, pousgesinde; Roomse.
papistry, pousgesindheid; Rooms(gesind)heid.
papoose, rooihuidjie.
pappy, papperig.
paprika, paprika.
papyrus, papirus.
par, gelykheid, pari; **be on a – (with),** gelyk staan (met); **on a –,** gemiddeld; **at –,** teen pari; **below, above –,** onder (benede), bo pari.
parable, gelykenis, parabel.
parabola, parabool, kegelsne(d)e.
parabolic(al), parabolies, deur midde van 'n gelykenis uitgedruk.
parachute, valskerm.
parachutist, valskermspringer; -soldaat.
parade, n. wapenskouing, optog; vertoning; parade(plein); **make a – of one's virtues,** te koop loop met jou deugde.
parade, v. parade hou, (laat) marsjeer; te koop loop met, spog met, tentoonstel, lug; paradeer.
paradigm, modelwoord, paradigma.
paradise, paradys; hemel.
paradisic(al), paradysagtig.
paradox, paradoks.
paradoxical, paradoksaal.
paraffin, n. paraffien(olie), lampolie.
paraffin, v. lampolie aansmeer.
paragon, model; paragon.
paragraph, n. paragraaf.
paragraph, v. paragrafeer.
parakeet, paroquet, parkiet.
parallax, parallaks.
parallel, a. parallel, ewewydig; analoog, ooreenstemmend; – **bars,** brug.
parallel, n. parallel, ewewydige lyn; gelyke, weerga; vergelyking; **draw a –,** 'n vergelyking trek.
parallel, v. gelyk stel; ewewydig loop met; ooreenstem met; 'n soortgelyke geval noem.
parallelepiped, parallelepipedum, balk.
parallelism, ewewydigheid, ooreenkoms, gelykheid, parallelisme.
parallelogram, parallelogram.
paralogism, verkeerde gevolgtrekking, valse sluitrede, paralogisme.
paralyse, verlam; ontsenu, paraliseer.
paralysis, verlamming, beroerte; magteloosheid; paralisie.

paralytic, n. verlamde, paralitikus.
paralytic, a. (ver)lam, geraak, paralities; – stroke, beroerteaanval.
paramount, vernaamste, grootste, hoogste, opperste, opper- . . .; – chief, hoofkaptein.
paramour, minnaar (minnares).
paranoia, paranoia; vervolgingswaan.
paranoiac, paranoïes.
parapet, borswering, parapet.
paraphernalia, uitrusting, lyfgoed; mondering; rommel.
paraphrase, n. omskrywing, parafrase.
paraphrase, v. omskrywe, parafraseer.
paraplegic, n. lyer aan paraplegie; a. paraplekties.
parasite, parasiet; woekerplant, woekerdier, opskeploerder, klaploper.
parasitic(al), parasities.
parasol, sambreel, sonskerm, parasol.
paratroops, valskermtroepe.
parboil, half kook; verbrand.
parbuckle, n. skrooitou, roltou.
parbuckle, v. met 'n tou rol, skrooi.
parcel, n. pak(kie), pakket; stuk, deel.
parcel, v. verdeel; inpak; – out, verdeel, uitdeel.
parcel post, pakketpos, pakkiespos.
parcenary, mede-erfgenaamskap.
parcener, mede-erfgenaam.
parch, (ver)skroei, verdroog, verdor; braai; –ing heat, skroeiende hitte.
parchment, perkament.
pard, maat, vennoot.
pardon, n. vergifnis, kwytskelding, genade; pardon, ekskuus; aflaat; I beg your –, ekskuus, pardon.
pardon, v. vergewe, vryspreek, kwytskel(d).
pardonable, vergeeflik.
pare, (af)skil, afsny, (af)knip; snoei; afskaf; besnoei.
paregoric, pynstillende middel.
parent, ouer; bron, oorsaak; –s, ouers.
parentage, afkoms, geboorte, ouers.
parental, ouerlik.
parenthesis, tussensin, parentese; hakies.
parenthesize, (woorde) inlas of invoeg; tussen hakies plaas.
parenthetic(al), tussen hakies, parenteties.
par excellence, by uitnemendheid.
parget, v. pleister.
parget, n. pleisterwerk, pleistering.
parhelion, byson, parhelium.
pariah, paria; uitgeworpene, verstoteling.
pariah-dog, swerfhond, pariahond.
parietal, wand- . . .; – bone, wandbeen.
paring, skil, skaafsel.
parish, gemeente, parogie; – priest, pastoor (van 'n parogie); – register, kerkregister.
parishioner, gemeentelid.
Parisian, a. Paryse, van Parys.
Parisian, n. Parysenaar.
parisyllabic, gelyklettergrepig.
parity, gelykheid.
park, n. park; natuurtuin; wildtuin.
park, v. inpark, omhein, toemaak; parkeer.
parking area, staanplek, motorpark.
parky, koud, skerp.
parlance, gesprek; taal, uitdrukking; in common –, in gewone taal.
parley, n. gesprek, onderhandeling.
parley, v. onderhandel, bespreek, praat.
parliament, parlement.
parliamentarian, redenaar, spreker, debatteerder; parlementsgesinde.
parlour, voorkamer, sitkamer, ontvangkamer; salon; atelier.
parlour-boarder, inwonende kosleerling.

parlour-maid, binnemeisie.
parlous, gevaarlik; moeilik, lastig.
parochial, parogiaal; eng, bekrompe.
parochialism, parogialisme.
parodist, parodiemaker, parodieerder.
parody, n. parodie, spotdig; bespotting.
parody, v. parodieer.
parole, erewoord; wagwoord; parool.
paroquet, sien parakeet.
paroxysm, aanval, vlaag, paroksisme.
parquet, n. parketvloer.
parquet, v. parketeer, parketvloer insit.
parquetry, parketvloer.
parricidal, vadermoordenaars- . . .
parricide, vadermoord; vadermoordenaar.
parrot, n. papegaai; na-aper.
parrot, v. napraat, na-aap.
parry, v. afweer, keer, afwend, pareer.
parry, n. (die) pareer, afwering.
parse, (woorde) ontleed.
parsimonious, spaarsaam, suinig, gierig.
parsimony, spaarsaamheid; suinigheid.
parsing, woordontleding.
parsley, pieterselie.
parsnip, witwortel.
parson, predikant, dominee.
parsonage, pastorie.
part, n. deel, gedeelte, stuk, part; rol; aandeel; plig; kant, party; – and parcel of, 'n (onmisbare) deel van; I have done my –, ek het my plig gedoen; play a –, 'n rol speel; oneerlik te werk gaan; a man of good –s, 'n bekwame man; a stranger in these –s, 'n vreemdeling in hierdie streke; –s of speech, rededele; for the most –, grotendeels, hoofsaaklik; take – in, deelneem aan; take somebody's –, iemand se party kies; for my –, vir my part, wat my betref; in –, gedeeltelik; take in good –, goed opneem; on my –, van my kant.
part, v. (verdeel); uitmekaar gaan, skei, afskeid neem; breek; he –s his hair in the middle, hy kam sy paadjie in die middel; – company, uitmekaar gaan; – from, afskeid neem van, weggaan van; – with, afstand doen van, weggee.
partake, deelneem (aan); 'n deel hê in; geniet.
partial, partydig; eensydig; gedeeltelik; be – to, voortrek, 'n voorliefde hê vir.
partiality, partydigheid; voorliefde.
participant, deelnemer; deelhebber.
participate, deelneem aan, 'n deel hê in.
participation, deelneming.
participator, deelnemer.
participial, deelwoordelik.
participle, deelwoord, participium.
particle, deeltjie, stukkie, greintjie; partikel; a – of sense, 'n greintjie verstand.
particoloured, party-, bont, veelkleurig.
particular, a. besonder, spesiaal, buitengewoon; kieskeurig, puntenerig; for no – reason, om geen besondere rede nie.
particular, n. besonderheid; –s, besonderhede; in –, in die besonder, spesiaal.
particularize, spesifiseer, in besonderhede tree, een vir een noem.
particularism, partikularisme.
particularist, partikularis.
particularity, besonderheid, eienaardigheid, noukeurigheid.
parting, afskeid; skeiding; paadjie (in die hare); – of the ways, kruispad, skeiding van die weë.
partisan, -zan, partyman, volgeling.
partisan, partisan; aanhanger, voorstander; force, partisanemag.
partisanship, partydigheid; partygees.

partition, n. verdeling; afdeling; skeiding; afskorting.
partition, v. (ver)deel; 'n afskorting maak; afskei; – off, afskort, afskei.
partitive, (ver)delend; – **genitive,** partitiewe genitief.
partly, gedeeltelik, vir 'n gedeelte, deels.
partner, n. vennoot; maat.
partner, v. saamspeel of saamdans met, die maat wees van.
partnership, vennootskap; saamspel.
part-owner, mede-eienaar.
part-payment, paaiement; **in –,** in afbetaling.
part-time, deeltyds.
partridge, patrys.
parturition, baring, voortbrenging.
party, party; geselskap; gesellige byeenkoms, geselligheid; **be a – to,** 'n deel hê aan, medepligtig wees aan.
parvenu, parvenu, nuweling.
pasha, -cha, pasja.
pasquinade, skimpskrif, skotskrif.
pass, v. verbygaan, passeer; deurgaan; toelaat; aanneem; slaag, deurkom; te bowe gaan; aangee; stryk, trek; (vonnis) uitspreek; deurbring; pas (in kaartspel); – **away,** verbygaan; sterwe; – **by,** uitlaat, oorslaan; oor die hoof sien; verbygaan; – **by the name of,** deurgaan onder die naam van; – **for,** deurgaan vir; – **into,** oorgaan na (tot); – **off,** verdwyn, oorgaan; deurgaan; – **off well,** goed van stapel loop; – **off upon,** afsmeer (skuiwe) op; – **on,** aangee; verder gaan; oorgaan tot; – **over,** uitlaat, oorslaan; verbygaan; – **over in silence,** stilswyend verbygaan; – **through,** deurmaak, ondervind; deurgaan.
pass, n. (die) deurkom (slaag) (verlof)pas; handbeweging; toestand van sake; (die) aangee; **come to –,** gebeur, geskied; **come to such a –,** so 'n (ernstige) wending neem; **he does not expect to get a –,** hy verwag nie om te slaag nie; **free –,** vrybiljet, vrygeleide; **make a – at a girl,** by 'n meisie aanlê; opdringerig (vrypostig) word teenoor 'n meisie.
pass, n. (berg)pas, nek, deurgang.
passable, gangbaar, taamlik; begaanbaar.
passage, deurgang, -tog, -vaart, -reis; oorgang, -tog; passasie; reisgeld; gang; **bird of –,** trekvoël.
pass-book, bankboek(ie).
passenger, passasier, reisiger; meeloper.
passer-by, verbyganger.
passing, n. deurgang, (die) deurkom (slaag); (die) aanneem; dood; **in –,** in die verbygaan, terloops.
passing, a. verbygaande; kortstondig; terloops.
passing, adv. geweldig, baie; – **rich,** skatryk.
passion, hartstog, passie; drif, woede; lyding; **in a –,** driftig, woedend.
passionate, hartstogtelik, vurig; opvlieënd, driftig.
passion-flower, passieblom, Betlehem-ster.
Passion play, Passiespel.
Passion Week, Lydensweek.
passive, lydend; lydelik; passief; gedwee; – **resistance,** lydelike verset; – **voice,** lydende vorm, passief.
passivity, lydelikheid.
Passover, Joodse Paasfees; paaslam.
passport, paspoort.
password, wagwoord, parool.
past, a. verby; verlede; afgelope; oud- . . .; **the – month,** die afgelope maand; – **tense,** verlede tyd; – **student,** oud-student.

past, n. verlede; **a thing of the –,** iets wat tot die verlede behoort.
past, prep. oor, verby; **half – three,** halfvier; **five – two,** vyf (minute) oor twee; **he ran – the house,** hy het by die huis verby gehardloop; – **endurance,** ondraaglik.
past, adv. verby; **hasten –,** verby snel.
paste, n. deeg; pap; pasta; lym; kunssteen, kunsdiamant.
paste, v. plak, aanplak, vasplak; moker, slaan.
pasteboard, n. bordpapier; kaart(jie).
pastel, pastel.
pastern, kootbeen.
pasteurize, pasteuriseer.
pastil(le), pastille, pil(letjie), tabletjie.
pastime, tydverdryf spel, speletjie.
past-master, meester, bobaas, doring.
pastor, predikant, pastoor, herder.
pastoral, a. pastoraal, herderlik.
pastoral, n. herdersdig, pastorale.
pastorate, herdersamp; predikante(vereniging).
pastorship, herdersamp, pastoorskap.
pastry, pastei, gebak; koek.
pastry-cook, pasteibakker.
pasturage, (die) wei; weiveld, weiland.
pasture, n. wei(veld), weiplek, gras(veld).
pasture, v. laat wei, gaan wei met; wei.
pasty, n. vleis-, wildpastei.
pasty, a. deegagtig, deeg- . . .; bleek.
pat, n. tuk(kie), klappie; klontjie.
pat, v. tik, klop; platstryk; streel.
pat, adv. van pas, betyds; **he has the story –,** hy ken die verhaal op sy duimpie.
pat, a. toepaslik, geskik, geleë.
patch, n. lap; pleister; ooglappie; stuk(kie) (lappie); **he is not a – on his brother,** hy kom nie naby sy broer nie; **strike a bad –,** lydelik van stryk raak.
patch, v. lap, heelmaak; – **up,** oplap; skik, bylê ('n geskil); saamflans.
patchwork, lapwerk; knoeiwerk.
patchy, gelap; onsamehangend; ongelyk.
pate, kop, harspan.
paten, hostiebord, pateen; metaalband.
patent, a. gepatenteer(d), patent; duidelik, sigbaar; – **leather,** lakleer.
patent, n. patent, oktrooi.
patent, v. patenteer, patent (oktrooi) neem op.
patentee, patenthouer.
pater, ou-baas, ou-kêrel.
paternal, vaderlik, vader(s)- . . .; van vaderskant.
paternity, vaderskap; outeurskap; bron.
paternoster, Onse Vader, paternoster.
path, pad, weg.
pathetic, aandoenlik, pateties.
pathological, patologies.
pathologist, patoloog.
pathology, patologie, siekteleer.
pathos, die aandoenlike, patos.
patience, geduld, lankmoedigheid; volharding; **have no – with,** nie kan uitstaan nie; **I am out of –,** my geduld is op; **lose –,** geduld verloor.
patient, n. pasiënt, lyer, sieke.
patient, a. geduldig, lankmoedig, lydsaam, verdraagsaam; volhardend.
patois, dialek; kombuistaal; patois.
patriarch, aartsvader, patriarg.
patriarchate, patriargaat.
patriarchy, patriargale regeringsvorm.
patrician, n. patrisiër.
patrician, a. patrisies.
patricide, vadermoord; vadermoordenaar.
patrimonial, geërf, patrimoniaal.
patrimony, (vaderlike) erfdeel.

**patriot, patriot, vaderlander.
patriotic,** patrioties, vaderlandsliewend.
patriotism, vaderlandsliefde, patriotisme.
patristic, kerkvaderlik, patristies.
patrol, n. patrollie, rondte.
patrol, v. patrolleer, die rondte doen.
patron, beskermheer; patroon, beskermheilige; klant; –s, klandisie.
patronage, beskerming, ondersteuning; begunstiging; klandisie.
patroness, beskermvrou, patrones.
patronize, ondersteun, aanmoedig, hulp verleen, beskerm, begunstig.
patronymic, a. vader- . . ., familie- . . .
patronymic, n. vadersnaam, familienaam.
patten, kaparring, blok(skoen).
patter, n. gebabbel, gesnater.
patter, v. snater, babbel; aframmel.
patter, n. gekletter, geklater; getrippel, getrappel, geklap.
patter, v. kletter, ratel, klater; trippel, trappel, klap.
pattern, patroon, model; voorbeeld, toonbeeld; monster.
patty, pasteitjie, frikkadel(letjie).
paucity, skaarste, geringheid.
paunch, buik, pens.
pauper, arme, behoeftige.
pauperize, arm maak, tot die bedelstaf bring.
pauperism, armoede, armwese, pouperisme.
pause, n. poos; verposing, afbreking, pouse.
pause, v. wag, pouseer, rus, afbreek, stilbly; – upon, stilstaan by.
pave, plavei, (uit)straat, uitlê, bevloer; – the way, die weg baan.
pavement, sypaadjie; plaveisel, bestrating.
pavilion, pawiljoen, tent.
paw, n. poot, klou.
paw, v. kap, klou, krap; lomp hanteer, onhandig te werk gaan; ru beetpak.
pawky, slim; – humour, droë humor.
pawn, n. pion, boer (in skaakspel).
pawn, n. pand.
pawn, v. verpand, in pand gee.
pawnbroker, lommerhouer, pandjiesbaas.
pawnshop, pandjieswinkel, lommerd.
pawpaw, sien **papaw.**
pay, n. betaling, loon, besoldiging; in the – of, in diens van.
pay, v. betaal; beloon, vergeld; boet; – one in his own coin, iemand met gelyke munt betaal; – the piper, die gelag betaal; – attention to, ag gee op, aandag gee aan; – a compliment, 'n kompliment maak; – a visit to, 'n besoek bring aan, gaan kuier by; – away, ('n tou) laat skiet; – for, betaal; you will – for this, hiervoor sal jy boet; – in, deponeer; – off, afbetaal; afdank; – out, uitbetaal; he will – me out, hy sal my laat opdok of laat boet; – up, (af)betaal opdok.
payable, betaalbaar; winsgewend.
pay-box, loket, kaartjieskantoor.
payee, ontvanger, betaalde.
payer, betaler.
pay-master, betaalmeester.
payment, betaling, loon; vergelding; in – of, ter voldoening (vereffening) van.
pea, ertjie; green –s, dop-ertjies.
peace, vrede; rus, kalmte, stilte; hold one's –, stilbly, swyg; make one's – with, afmaak met, versoen raak met.
peaceable, vreedsaam; vredeliewend.
peaceful, vreedsaam, rustig, stil.
peacemaker, vredestigter.
peace-offering, soenoffer, dankoffer.

peach, n. perske; perskeboom; lieflike nooi; – Melba, Melbaperske.
peach, v. (ver)klap, (ver)klik, verraai.
peacock, pou(mannetjie).
peafowl, pou.
peahen, pouwyfie.
peak, n. punt, spits, (berg)top, piek.
peak, v. spits word, verkwyn, vergaan; – and pine, agteruitgaan, verkwyn.
peak, v. regop sit, regop laat staan.
peaked, spits, skerp, puntig, punt- . . .
peal, n. klokgelui; klokke; (donder)slag; sarsie, geratel; – of laughter, 'n skaterlag.
peal, v. lui, (weer)galm, (weer)klink.
peanut, grondboontjie, apenootjie.
pear, peer.
pearl, n. pêrel.
pearl, v. bepêrel, met pêrels versier.
pearl-barley. pêrelgars, gort.
pearl-diver, pêrelvisser.
pearl-shell, perlemoen (perlemoer).
pearly, pêrelagtig, pêrel- . . ., bepêrel(d).
pear-shaped, peervormig.
peasant, boer, landbouer.
peasantry, boerestand, boere.
peat, turf.
peat-bog, turfgrond, vleigrond.
pebble, kiesel(steen).
pebbly, kieselagtig.
pecan: – nut, pekanneut.
peccable, sondig.
peccadillo, sondetjie, oortredinkie.
peccancy, sondigheid.
peccant, sondig; sieklik.
peccary, pekari, bisamswyn.
peck, n. „peck".
peck, v. pik; – at, pik na; vit op.
peck, n. pik, hap; kos.
pectoral, a. bors- . . ., van die bors, pektoraal.
peculate, (geld) verduister.
peculiar, besonder, eienaardig; persoonlik; snaaks, raar, vreemd.
peculiarity, besonderheid, eienaardigheid; kenmerkende eienskap; sonderlingheid.
peculiarly, persoonlik; besonder; snaaks.
pecuniary, geldelik, geld- . . .
pedagogic(al), opvoedkundig, pedagogies.
pedagogue, pedagoog, skoolmeester.
pedagogy (pedagogics), opvoedkunde, onderwysleer, pedagogie.
pedal, n. pedaal; trapper.
pedal, v. die pedale gebruik; fiets.
pedal, a. voet- . . .
pedant, pedant; wysneus.
pedantic, skoolmeesteragtig, wysneusig, pedant(ies).
pedantry, pedanterie, wysneusigheid.
peddle, smous, bondel dra; peuter.
peddler, sien **pedlar.**
pedestal, voetstuk.
pedestrian, a. voet- . . ., voetganger(s)- . . ., loop- . . ., alledaags, vervelend.
pedestrian, n. voetganger.
pedicel, pedicle, stingeltjie, steeltjie.
pedigree, n. stamboom, geslagsboom.
pedigree, a. stamboek- . . .; – cattle, stamboekvee.
pediment, kroonlys.
pedlar, smous, bondeldraer.
pedlary, smousware; smousery.
pedometer, treemeter, pedometer.
peduncle, stingel, steel.
peel, v. (af)skil, afdop, bas afmaak; afskilfer, bas-afgaan; uittrek.
peel, n. skil, dop.
peeler, konstabel.

peep, v. piep.
peep, n. gepiep.
peep, v. loer, gluur, kyk.
peep, n. kykie, (die) loer; **the – of dawn, day**, dagbreek, môrelumier.
peeper, (be)loerder, afloerder; oog, kyker.
peer, n. weerga, gelyke; edelman.
peer, v. gelyk staan met, ewenaar.
peer, v. loer, kyk, gluur.
peerage, adelstand, adel; adelboek.
peerless, sonder weerga, weergaloos.
peevish, nors, stuurs, knorrig.
peewit, sien **pewit**.
peg, n. pen; kapstok; **take down a – or two, op sy plek sit; a – to hang on,** 'n voorwendsel.
peg, v. vaspen, met penne vasslaan; – **at**, slaan (steek) met 'n pen; vit op; – **away at something**, aan iets weglê; – **down**, beperk tot, bind aan; – **out**, afpen, afsteek; bokveld toe gaan.
pegamoid, imitasieleer, kunsleer.
pejorative, pejoratief; verergerend.
pekin, peking(sy).
pekoe, pekko-tee.
pelerine, skouermantel, kraag, pelerine.
pelf, duite, pitte, blik, aardse slyk.
pelican, pelikaan.
pelisse, damesmantel, pellies.
pellet, proppie; pilletjie; koeëltjie.
pellicle, velletjie, vliesie.
pell-mell, adv. deurmekaar, holderstebolder, onderstebo; halsoorkop.
pell-mell, a. deurmekaar, verward.
pell-mell, n. deurmekaarspul, warboel.
pellucid, helder, duidelik; deurskynend.
pelmet, gordynkap.
pelt, n. vel, huid.
pelt, v. gooi, koeël, aanval; neerkletter; **–ing shower**, kletterende reënbui.
peltry, velle, peltery, pelswerk.
pelvis, bekken.
pemmican, gedroogde vleis; pemmikan.
pen, n. hok, kraal; boerdery, plantasie.
pen, v. in die hok of kraal ja; opsluit.
pen, n. pen.
pen, v. skryf, neerpen.
penal, straf- . . .; strafbaar; – **laws**, strafwette; – **servitude**, dwangarbeid, hardepad.
penalize, straf, beboet.
penalty, straf, boete; – **(kick)**, strafskop.
penance, boetedoening, boete, straf.
pence, sien **penny**.
pencil, potlood; griffel; stralebundel.
pencil-case, potloodhouer, -koker, -dosie.
pendant, -ent, hanger(tjie); hangkroon; pendant, teëhanger; wimpel.
pendent, -ant, hangend, hang- . . ., oorhangend; onbeslis, hangende.
pending, a. hangende, onbeslis.
pending, prep. gedurende, hangende; – **his return**, totdat hy terugkom; – **these negotiations**, terwyl hierdie onderhandelinge nog hangende (aan die gang) is.
pendulous, (af)hangend, slingerend, slinger- . . .
pendulum, slinger.
penetrable, deurdringbaar.
penetrate, binnedring, deurdring; deurgrond, agterkom, uitvors.
penetrating, deurdringend, skerp.
penetration, (die) deurdring, (die) binnedring; skerpsinnigheid, deursig; uitvorsing.
penetrative, deurdringend, deurdringings- . . ., skerp.
penguin, pikkewyn.
penicillin, penisilline (penisillien).

peninsula, skiereiland.
peninsular, van 'n skiereiland.
penitence, berou, boetvaardigheid.
penitent, a. boetvaardig, berouvol.
penitent, n. boetvaardige, boeteling.
penitential, boet- . . .; boetvaardig; **the – psalms**, die boetpsalms.
penitentiary, n. verbeterhuis; tughuisstraf.
penitentiary, a. boetvaardig; verbeterings- . . ., verbeter- . . ., tug- . . .
penknife, sakmes, knipmes, pennemes.
penmanship, skryfkuns.
pennant, vlaggie, wimpel.
penniless, (brand)arm, sonder 'n duit.
pennon, wimpel, vlag, banier.
penny, pennie, oulap; **a pretty –,** 'n mooi sommetjie; **in for a –, in for a pound**, as jy A gesê het, moet jy ook B sê; **take care of the pence**, let op die kleintjies, spraaksaam wees wat die kleine betref; **to a –,** tot die laaste oulap.
penny dreadful, penny horrible, sensasieroman, moord-en-doodslag-roman.
pennyroyal, kruisementdrank; polei.
pennyweight, pennyweight (24 grein)
pensile, hangend.
pension, n. pensioen, jaargeld; losieshuis.
pension, v. pensioen toeken, op pensioen stel; – **off**, pensioeneer.
pensionable, op pensioen geregtig.
pensionary, a. pensioen(s)- . . .
pensionary, n. pensionaris, gepensioeneerde.
pensioner, gepensioeneerde.
pensive, peinsend, in gedagte versonke.
pensiveness, gepeins; swaarmoedigheid.
pent, opgesluit; – **up**, onderdruk, opgekrop.
pentad, vyftal.
pentagon, vyfhoek, pentagoon.
pentagonal, vyfhoekig.
pentameter, pentameter.
pentateuch, pentateug.
pentathlon, vyfkamp.
Pentecost, Pinksterfees, Pinkster.
Pentacostal, Pinkster- . . .
penthouse, afdak, skuur; dakwoning; bygebou.
penult(imate), a. voorlaaste.
penult(imate), n. voorlaaste lettergreep.
penumbra, halfskaduwee, byskaduwee.
penurious, behoeftig; karig; suinig.
penury, armoede, behoeftigheid; skaarste.
peony, pioenroos.
people, n. mense, persone; volk, nasie.
people, v. bevolk; bewoon.
pep, pit, vuur, fut; – **pill**, opwekpil; – **talk**, wekpraatjie,
pepper, n. peper
pepper, v. peper; inpeper, uitlooi; bestook.
pepper-castor, -er, peperbus.
peppercorn, peperkorrel.
peppermint, peperment.
peppery, peperagtig, peper- . . ., gepeper) bytend, bitsig, opvlieënd, kortgebonde.
pepsin, pepsine.
peptic, spysverterend, spysverterings- . . .
per, deur, per; – **annum**, jaarliks, per jaar; – **post**, per pos, met (oor) die pos; – **cent**, per honderd, persent.
peradventure, miskien.
perambulate, rondwandel.
perambulator, kinderwaentjie.
perceive, bespeur, bemerk, gewaar (word); sien; verstaan, begryp.
percent, persent, per honderd.
percentage, persentasie.
percept, waarnemingsinhoud, persep.
perceptible, waarneembaar, merkbaar.

perception, waarneming, gewaarwording; begrip; persepsie.
perceptive, waarnemend, waarnemings- . . .
perceptivity, waarnemingsvermoë.
perch, n. (dwars)stok, (dwars)houtjie (in 'n voëlhok), sitplek; verhewe posisie; roede (5½ jaart).
perch, v. gaan sit, sit; plaas; –ed on a hill, op 'n heuwel geleë.
perch, n. baars (vis).
perchance, dalk, altemit, miskien.
percipient, a. gewaarwordend, bewus(wordend).
percipient, n. waarnemer, persoon wat gewaar word.
percolate, deursyfer, filtreer.
percolation, (die) deursyfer, filtrasie.
percolator, filtreerkan, sif(fie).
percussion, slag, skok; perkussie.
percussion cap, (slag)doppie; slaghoedjie.
percussive, slag- . . ., skok-, . . .
perdition, verdoemenis, verderf.
perdurable, duursaam; ewig(durend).
peregrinate, rondreis, trek, swerf, dool.
peregrination, rondswerwing, swerftog.
peregrin(e), edelvalk.
peremptory, beslissend; gebiedend; dringend, absoluut noodsaaklik; **peremptorily dismissed**, sonder pligpleginge (op staande voet) afgedank.
perennial, a. standhoudend; altyddurend.
perennial, n. standhoudende plant.
perfect, a. volmaak, perfek, volkome; suiwer, presies; totaal, volledig; **I am a – stranger here**, ek is hier heeltemal vreemd; – **nonsense**, klinkklare onsin.
perfect, n. volmaak (voltooid) teenwoordige tyd, perfektum.
perfect, v. voltooi, deurvoer; volmaak, tot volmaaktheid bring; verbeter.
perfectible, volmaakbaar.
perfection, volmaaktheid, volkomenheid, perfeksie; voltooiing.
perfervid, vuurwarm, vurig.
perfidious, troueloos, vals, verraderlik.
perfidy, troubreuk, verraad, valsheid.
perforate, perforeer.
perforation, perforasie.
perforator, perforeermasjien.
perforce, noodsaaklikerwys, noodgedwonge.
perform, maak, doen, verrig; vervul, nakom, uitvoer; opvoer, speel, optree; – **your duty**, jou plig verrig; – **a play**, 'n (toneel)stuk opvoer.
performance, vervulling, (werk)verrigting; opvoering; vertoning, prestasie; **afternoon** –, middagvoorstelling.
performer, speler, voordraer.
perfume, n. geur, reuk; parfuum, reukwater.
perfume, v. parfumeer.
perfumery, parfumerie, reukwerk.
perfunctory, agtelosig, traak-my-nie-agtig, slordig; oppervlakkig.
pergola, prieel.
perhaps, miskien, altemit, dalk, straks.
pericardium, hartvlies, perikardium.
pericarp, saadhuisie; saadvlies.
pericranium, skedelvlies, harspan.
perigee, perigeum.
perihelion, perihelium.
peril, n. gevaar, risiko.
peril, v. aan gevaar blootstel.
perilous, gevaarlik.
perimeter, omtrek, perimeter; buiterand.
period, tydperk, periode, volsin, punt; –s, maandstonde; – **furniture**, stylmeubels; – **play**, kostuumstuk.
periodic(al), a. periodiek.

periodical, n. tydskrif.
periodicity, periodisiteit.
peripatetic, a. rondtrekkend; peripateties.
peripatetic, n. peripatetikus; rondwandelaar.
periphery, (sirkel)omtrek, periferie.
periphrasis, omskrywing, perifrase.
periphrastic, omskrywend, perifrasties.
periscope, periskoop.
perish, omkom, vergaan; bederf; –ed with cold, verkluim.
perishable, verganklik, aan bederf onderhewig.
perishables, bederfbare ware.
peristyle, suilegang, suilery.
peritonitis, buikvliesontsteking, peritonitis.
periwig, pruik.
periwinkle, alikruikel.
periwinkle, maagdeblom, maagdepalm.
perjure, vals sweer, 'n vals eed aflê.
perjured, skuldig aan meineed, meinedig.
perjurer, meinedige.
perjury, meineed; **commit** –, meineed pleeg.
perk, astrant word; – **up**, mooimaak; brutaal wees, die kop oplig.
perky, astrant, snipperig, parmantig.
perm, vaste golwing.
permanence, parmanency, duur, bestendigheid, vastheid.
permanent, durend, vas, blywend, permanent; – **wave**, vaste golwing; – **force**, staande mag; – **colour**, vaste kleur.
permeable, deurdringbaar.
permeate, deurdring, deurtrek.
permissible, geoorloof; toelaatbaar.
permission, toestemming, verlof, vergunning, permissie.
permissive, vergunnend.
permit, v. toelaat, toestaan, veroorloof, vergun, permitteer, duld.
permit, n. verlofbrief, pas.
permutation, permutasie, omsetting.
permute, omwissel, verwissel, permuteer.
pernicious, dodelik, verderflik, skadelik.
pernickety, punteneirig; lastig; delikaat.
perorate, 'n redevoering hou (eindig); peroreer.
peroration, slotrede, slotwoorde; redevoering, perorasie.
peroxide, perokside (peroksied).
perpendicular, a. loodreg, haaks, regstandig, vertikaal; regop, penorent.
perpendicular, n. loodlyn; loodregte stand.
perpetrate, pleeg, begaan, bedrywe.
perpetration, (die) begaan, pleging.
perpetrator, dader, pleger, bedrywer.
perpetual, ewigdurend, onophoudelik; lewenslank; – **motion**, ewigdurende beweging.
perpetuate, verewig, bestendig.
perpetuity, ewigdurendheid; lewenslange rente (besit); **in, to, for** –, vir ewig en altyd, in ewigheid.
perplex, in die war bring, verbyster, verleë maak, verbouereer.
perplexed, verslae, verbouereerd.
perplexity, verleentheid, verbouereerdheid.
perquisite, ekstra inkomste; fooi.
perry, peerwyn.
persecute, vervolg; lastig val, pla(e).
persecution, vervolging.
perseverance, volharding.
persevere, volhard, aanhou, volhou.
Persian, a. Persies.
Persian, n. Pers; Persies.
persiflage, jillery, korswel, persiflage.
persimmon, dadelpruim, tamatiepruim.
persist, volhard, volhou, aanhou.
persistence, volharding; hardnekkigheid.

persistent, volhardend; aanhoudend; hardnekkig.
person, persoon, mens; persoonlikheid; **in** –, 'n eie persoon, persoonlik.
personable, aansienlik, aanvallig.
personage, persoon, personasie.
personal, persoonlik; indiwidueel; eie; – **tax**, persoonsbelasting.
personality, persoonlikheid; indiwidualiteit; persoonlike belediging.
personality, persoonlike eiendom.
personally, persoonlik.
personate, die rol speel van; voorstel, (sig) uitgee vir, deurgaan vir.
personification, verpersoonliking, personifikasie
personify, verpersoonlik, beliggaam.
personnel, personeel, staf.
perspective, n. perspektief; perspektieftekening; gesig; vooruitsig, toekoms.
perspective, a. perspektiwies.
perspex, perspex.
perspicacious, skerpsinnig, skrander.
perspicacity, skranderheid.
perspicuity, duidelikheid, helderheid.
perspicuous, duidelik, helder.
perspiration, sweet, perspirasie.
perspire, (uit)sweet, uitwasem, perspireer.
persuade, oorreed, ompraat, oorhaal.
persuasion, oorreding; oortuiging, geloof, soort.
persuasive, a. oorredend, oortuigend; oortuigings-. . ., oorredings-. . .
persuasive, n. motief, beweegrede.
pert, astrant, vrypostig, permantig.
pertain: – **to**, behoort (pas) by; betrekking hê op, slaan op.
pertinacious, styfhoofdig, halsstarrig, eiesinnig; volhardend.
pertinacity, hardnekkigheid; volharding.
pertinence, pertinency gepastheid, saaklikheid.
pertinent, gepas, saaklik, pertinent.
perturb, verontrus.
perturbation, verontrusting.
peruke, pruik.
perusal, noukeurige lesing, studie.
peruse, sorgvuldig (deur)lees; noukeurig bekyk, ondersoek.
Peruvian, Peruaans.
pervade, deurtrek, deurdring.
pervasive, deurdringend.
perverse, verkeerd, dwars, eiewys; sleg, pervers.
perversion, verdraaiing; verleiding; verdorwenheid.
perversity, verkeerdheid, dwarsheid, verdorwenheid, perversiteit.
pervert, v. verdraai; verlei, op die dwaalspoor bring, misbruik maak van.
pervert, n. afgedwaalde; verdorwene; geperverteerde.
pervious, deurdringbaar.
peseta, peseta.
peso, peso.
pessimism, swartgalligheid, pessimisme.
pessimist, swartkyker, pessimis.
pessimistic. swaarmoedig, pessimisties.
pest, pes, plaag; plaaggees, kwelgees.
pester, lastig val, pla(e), tretter.
pestiferous, verpestend; verderflik.
pestilence, pes, pestilensie.
pestilent, skadelik, dodelik; verderflik; lastig, lollerig, neulerig.
pestilential, pes- . . ., verpestend.
pestle, stamper.
pet, n. hansdier; hanslam, ens.; liefling, gunsteling; **that is my** – **aversion**, daar het ek 'n besondere hekel aan; – **name**, troetelnaam; – **dog**, lieflingshond.
pet, v. (ver)troetel, verwen; liefkoos, streel; vry (met).
pet, n. slegte bui.
petal, blomblaartjie.
petard, bom, klapper.
peter; – **out**, opraak, doodloop.
petiole, blaarsteel, blaarstingel.
petition, n. versoek, versoekskrif, petisie.
petition, v. versoek; smeek; 'n versoekskrif (petisie) indien, petisioneer.
petitioner, eiser; petisionaris, ondertekenaar (van 'n petisie).
petrel, stormvoël.
petrifaction, verstening.
petrify, versteen; verstyf, verhard; laat lam skrik.
petrol, petrol, petrolie.
petroleum, petroleum.
petticoat, onderrok; vroumens.
pettifog, bogsakies waarneem; redetwis, kibbel; knoei, konkel.
pettifogger, bogadvokaatjie; knoeier, regsverdraaier, boereverneuker; vitter.
pettifogging, vitterig, peuterig, bog- . . ., knoei- . . .
pettiness, nietigheid, beuselagtigheid; kleingeestigheid.
pettish, liggeraak, prikkelbaar.
pettitoes, varkpootjies, varkafval.
petty, niksbeduidend, nietig, beuselagtig, kleingeestig, kleinsielig; onder- . . ., ondergeskik; – **cash**, kleingeld, los geld; **kleinkas**; – **officer**, onderoffisier.
petulance, prikkelbaarheid, knorrigheid.
petulant, prikkelbaar, ongeduldig, iesegrimmig.
petunia, petunia.
pew, (kerk)bank.
pewit, peewit, kiewiet.
pewter, piauter, tin; ou-tingoed.
phaeton, ligte koets, faëton; toermotor.
phalanx, falanks.
phantasm, hersenskim; geesverskyning.
phantasmagoria, geestesverskyning, fantasmagorie.
phantasy, sien **fantasy**.
phantom, spook(sel), skim, gedaante; hersenskim, droombeeld.
Pharisee, Fariseër; skynheilige.
pharmaceutic(al), artsenykundig, farmaseuties.
pharmaceutics, artsenybereikunde, faramsie.
pharmacologist, farmakoloog.
pharmacology, artsenyleer, farmakologie.
pharmacopoeia, artsenyhandboek, aptekersboek, farmakopea.
pharmacy, artsenybereikunde, farmasie; apteek.
pharos, vuurtoring.
pharynx, keelholte, farinks (pharynx).
phase, stadium; gestalte; fase.
pheasant, fisant.
phenomenal, waarneembaar; merkwaardig, verbasend, fenomenaal.
phenomenon, verskynsel; wonder, wondermens; fenomeen.
phial, flessie, botteltjie.
philander, vry, koketteer, flirt.
philanthropic, mensliewend, liefdadigheids- . . ., filantropie.
philanthropist, mensevriend, filantroop.
philanthropy, mensliewendheid, weldadigheid, filantropie.
philatelist, posseëlversamelaar, filatelis.
philately, (die) versamel van posseëls, filatelie.
philharmonic, filharmonies, musiekliewend.
philippine, filippyn.

Philistine, Filistyn; **p-,** bekrompe kêrel, filister.
phillipic, strafrede, heftige aanval, fillippika.
philological, taalkundig, filologies.
philologist, taalkundige, taalgeleerde, filoloog.
philology, taalkunde, taalwetenskap, filologie.
philosopher, wysgeer, filosoof.
philosophic(al), wysgerig, filosofies.
philosophize, filosofeer.
philosophy, filosofie, wysbegeerte.
philtre, -ter, minnedrank.
phiz, gesig, bakkies, tronie.
phlebotomy, bloedlating.
phlegm, slym; flegma, traagheid, onverskilligheid, koelheid.
phlegmatic, flegmaties, onverskillig, ongevoelig.
phlox, floks.
ph(o)enix, feniks.
phone, n. foneem, klank.
phone, n. telefoon.
phone, v. opbel, oplui.
phoneme, foneem.
phonetic, foneties.
phonetican, fonetikus.
phonetics, fonetiek, klankleer.
phon(e)y, vals, oneg, skyn-, bedrieglik.
phonic, klank- . . .
phonogram, fonogram.
phonograph, fonograaf.
phonography, fonografie.
phonology, fonologie.
phosgene, fosgeen.
phosphate, fosfaat.
phosphor, fosfor; – **bronze,** fosforbrons.
phosphoresce, glim, fosforeseer.
phosphorescence, fosforlig, fosforessensie.
phosphoric, fosfor- . . .; – **acid,** fosforsuur.
phosphorous, fosforig.
phosphorus, fosfor.
photo-electric, foto-elektries; – **cell,** fotosel.
photo-finish, fotobeslissing; – **camera,** wenpaalkamera.
photo(graph), n. portret, foto.
photo(graph), v. afneem, fotografeer.
photographer, afnemer, fotograaf.
photographic, fotografies.
photography, fotografie.
photogravure, fotogravure.
photometer, fotometer, ligmeter.
photosphere, ligkring, fotosfeer.
photostat, fotostaat; **-ic copy,** fotostaat(afdruk).
phototelegraphy, faksimilee-telegrafie.
phototherapy, ligterapie.
phrase, n. segswyse; uitdrukking; sinsnede, sinsdeel; frase.
phrase, v. uitdruk, bewoord.
phraseology, bewoording, woordekeus.
phrenetic, rasend, dol, fanatiek.
phrenologist, frenoloog, skedelkundige.
phrenology, skedelleer, frenologie.
phthisical, teringagtig.
phthisis, (myn)tering, ftisis.
phylactery, gebedsriem; talisman.
phylloxera, druifluis, filloxera.
physic, n. geneeskunde; medisyne.
physic, v. medisyne gee, dokter; karnuffel.
physical, natuurkundig, fisies; fisiek, liggaamlik, liggaams- . . .; – **exercise,** ligaamsoefening; – **culture,** (heil)gimnastiek; – **geography,** natuurkundige aardrykskunde.
physician, dokter, geneesheer.
physicist, natuurkundige.
physics, natuurkunde, fisika.
physiognomy, gelaat, gesig, voorkome, fisionomie; gelaatkunde, fisionomiek.
physiography, fisiografie, natuurbeskrywing.

physiologic(al), fisiologies.
physiologist, fisioloog.
physiology, fisiologie, natuurleer.
physique, liggaamsbou.
pianist, klavierspeler, pianis.
piano, klavier, piano.
pianola, pianola.
picaresque, skelm(e)- . . ., pikaresk.
picaroon, skelm; seerower.
piccalilli, atjar.
piccaninny, klonkie, pikkenien.
piccolo, piccolo.
pick, n. pik, kielhouer; tand(e)stoker.
pick, v. pik; steek, prik; skoonmaak; (af)pluk; (op)pik; peusel; kies, uitsoek; afkluif, afeet; – **and choose,** uitsoek; – **a quarrel,** rusie soek, twis soek; – **one's pocket,** iemand se sakke rol; – **a lock,** 'n slot oopsteek; – **off,** afpluk; wegskiet (omkap); – **out,** uitsoek, uitkies; uitmaak, onderskei; – **out with,** afset met; – **up,** oppik; optel, opraap; opneem; opvang (radio); oplaai; opdoen, leer, te wete kom; – **up a livelihood,** jou brood verdien; – **up knowledge,** kennis opdoen; – **up flesh,** groei, aansterk; – **oneself up,** weer orent kom, opstaan.
pick, n. keuse; (die) uitsoek; **the –,** die keur, die blom, die beste.
pickax(e), pik, kielhouer.
pickerel, jong snoek.
picket, n. paal, pen; (brand)wag, piket; pos.
picket, v. ompaal, met pale toemaak; op lyn staan; wagte pos; op wag staan.
picking, (die) pluk; **-s,** oorskiet, afval, stukkies en brokkies.
pickle, n. pekel; moeilikheid; stouterd; in die knyp; **-s,** atjar, suur.
pickle, v. inlê, inmaak; insout; **-d,** ingelê; nat, aangeskote.
pick-me-up, (hart)versterkertjie.
pickpocket, sakkeroller.
picnic, n. piekniek, veldpartytjie; **no –,** geen maklike taak nie.
picnic, v. piekniek maak.
picotee, donkerrand-angelier.
picric, pikrien- . . .; – **acid,** pikriensuur.
pictorial, a. geïllustreer(d), prent(e)- . . .; skilderagtig.
pictorial, n. geïllustreerde tydskrif.
picture, n. prent; skildery; beskrywing; toonbeeld; **her hat is a –,** sy het 'n beeld van 'n hoed op; **the very – of death,** 'n toonbeeld van gesondheid, sy verkeer in blakende gesondheid; **he was altogether out of the –,** hy het glad nie meegetel nie; **the (moving) -s,** die fliek, die bioskoop; – **window,** landskapvenster.
picture, v. voorstel, skilder, beskrywe.
picture-gallery, skilderyemuseum.
picture-hat, breërand-dameshoed.
picture-postcard, prentposkaart, -briefkaart.
picturesque, skilderagtig.
pie, pastei; **have a finger in the –,** in 'n saak betrokke wees.
piebald, bont.
piece, n. stuk, deel, lap(pie); kanon, geweer; **in -s,** uitmekaar, stukkend; **break to -s,** stukkend breek; **give a – of one's mind,** goed die waarheid sê; **5c a –,** 5c stuk (elk); **a – of impudence,** 'n ombeskaamdheid; **a – of road,** 'n ent pad; **all of a –,** algar van dieselfde soort.
piece, v. aanmekaar las, saamlap, heelmaak; – **out,** uitmaak, ontsyfer; – **up,** (op)lap, aanmekaar lap.
piecemeal, stuksgewyse, by stukkies en brokkies.
pier, seehoof, hawehoof; pilaar.
pierage, haweg_ld.

pierce, deursteek, oopsteek, deurboor, 'n gat steek in; deurdring.
pier-glass, penantspieël, stylspieël.
pierrot, pierrot, hanswors.
pietism, piëtisme.
pietist, piëtis; vrome, fyne.
piety, piëteit, vroomheid.
piffle, n. kaf, bog(praatjies).
pig, n. vark, otjie, swyn; varkvleis; huisie, skyfie; buy a – in a poke, 'n kat in die sak koop.
pig, v. jong, kleintjies kry; (soos varke) saampak.
pigeon, n. duif; swaap, uilskuiken.
pigeon, v. kul, fop.
pigeon-hole, 'n deurtjie, gaatjie; vakkie, hokkie.
pigeon-hole, v. in 'n vakkie wegsit; ('n saak) opsy skuif; in jou geheue prent.
pigeonry, duiwehok, -huis.
pigeon's-milk, kropkos; skilpadvere.
pigeon-toed: he is –, sy voete is inwaarts.
piggery, varkboerdery; varkhok.
piggish, varkagtig, vark- . . ., vuil, smerig, koppig; lastig.
piggy, varkie, otjie.
pigheaded, koppig, eiewys; dom.
pig-iron, ru-yster.
pigment, kleurstof, pigment.
pigmy, sien **pygmy**.
pigsty, varkhok.
pigtail, varkstert; pruikstert.
pigwash, skottelwater.
pike, piek, lans, spies; snoek.
pikestaff, lansstok; **as plain as a –**, so duidelik as die dag.
pilaster, pilaster.
pile, n. paal, balk.
pile, v. pale inslaan.
pile, n. hoop, stapel, klomp; brandstapel, stapelbou; rykdom, hoop geld; **make a –**, make one's –, ryk word, fortuin maak.
pile, v. opstapel, ophoop; – **it on**, oppak; oordryf, vergroot.
pile, n. nop (van tapyt), pluis.
piles, n. aambeie.
pilfer, ontfutsel, skaai, steel.
pilgrim, pelgrim.
pilgrimage, pelgrimstog, bedevaart.
pill, n. pil.
pill, v. pille ingee; afwys.
pillage, n. roof, buit, plundering.
pillage, v. plunder, verwoes.
pillar, n. (steun)pilaar; **from – to post**, van bakboord na stuurboord.
pillar, v. stut, steun.
pillar-box, briewebus.
pillion, vrouesaal, agtersaaltjie, duo(sitting).
pillory, n. skandpaal.
pillory, v. aan die skandpaal bind; aan die kaak stel.
pillow, n. kussing; peul.
pillow, v. kussing, as kussing dien; op 'n kussing (peul) rus.
pillow-case, kussingsloop.
pillow-fight, kussingslaan.
pilose, -ous, harig, wollerig.
pilot, n. loods; stuurman; vlieër (vlieënier); – car, vooruitgestuurde motor; – **light**, waarskuwingslig; – **plant**, proeffabriek, -installasie.
pilot, v. lei, stuur, loods; die pad wys.
pilotage, loodsgeld; loodswerk.
pil(l)ule, pilletjie.
pimento, jamaikapeper, piment.
pimp, n. koppelaar.
pimp, v. koppel.
pimpernel, pimpernel.
pimple, puisie.

pin, n. speld; pen, stif, spy, luns; **drawing –**, duimspykertjie; **quick on his –s**, rats (op sy bene); **on p–s and needles**, op hete kole.
pin, v. vassteek, vasspelde; deursteek; opsluit; – **down**, vasdruk; – **one down to a promise**, iemand aan sy belofte hou; – **one's faith on**, volle vertroue stel in, staatmaak op.
pinafore, voorskoot.
pincers, knyptang, tangetjie; knypers (krap).
pinch, n. knyp; knypie, snuifie; nood, verleentheid; **at a –**, as dit begin, as die nood aan die man kom.
pinch, v. knyp, druk, knel; afpers; suinig (vrekkig) wees; steel, skaai; vang; **that is where the shoe –es**, daar lê die knoop.
pinchbeck, pinsbek.
pine, n. denneboom, pynboom.
pine, v. kwyn, vergaan, versmag; – **for, after**, hunker na, smag na.
pine-apple, pynappel.
pine-cone, dennebol.
pinery, pynappelkwekery.
pinfold, skut(kraal).
ping, v. gons, fluit.
ping, n. gegons, (die) fluit.
ping-pong, tafeltennis, ping-pong.
pinion, v. vlerkpunt, slagveer; wiek, vleuel.
pinion, v. kortwiek; vasmaak, boei.
pinion, n. tandrat.
pink, v. deursteek; mooi maak; klop (motor).
pink, n. wilde angelier, grasangelier; angelierrooi, ligroos(kleur); die keur, toonbeeld; **be in the – of health**, 'n toonbeeld van gesondheid wees.
pink, a. angelierrooi, ligroos, rose.
pin-money, sakgeld.
pinnacle, n. torinkie, top; toppunt.
pin-point, stippel; presies aanwys.
pin-prick, speldeprik.
pint, pint.
pinto, bont perd.
piny, denne- . . ., denneagtig.
pioneer, n. baanbreker, pionier, voortrekker; padmaker.
pioneer, v. baanbrekerswerk doen.
pious, vroom, godsdienstig.
pip, n. piep (hoendersiekte).
pip, n. pit.
pip, v. dronkslaan; wegpiets.
pipe, n. pyp, buis; fluit; stop (tabak); **put that in your – and smoke it**, dit kan jy in jou sak steek.
pipe, v. fluit; piep; pype lê; – **down**, bly stil.
pipe-clay, pypaarde.
piper, fluitspeler; lokhond; **pay the –**, die gelag betaal.
pipe-rack, pyprakkie.
pipette, pipet.
pipe-wrench, pypsleutel, kraaibek.
piping, n. gepiep; boorsel; pyp(e).
piping, a. fluitend; – **times**, aangename dae; – **hot**, vuurwarm, kokendwarm.
pipkin, erdepannetjie, erdepotjie.
pip-squeak, bogsnuiter, klein twak.
piquancy, skerpheid, prikkeling.
piquant, skerp, prikkelend, pikant.
pique, v. beledig; wek, prikkel; pikeer; – **oneself on**, roem op.
pique, n. wrok, hekel, pik.
pique, n. pikee.
piquet, piketspel.
piracy, seeroof; nadruk, letterdiewery.
pirate, n. seerower; rowerskip; letterdief.
pirate, v. plunder, seeroof pleeg; letterdiewery pleeg.
piratic(al), seerowers- . . ., roof- . .

piscary, visreg.
piscatory, vis- . . ., visvangs- . .
pisciculture, visteelt.
piscivorous, visetend.
pish, ba! foei! ag!
pisiform, ertjievormig.
pismire, mier.
piss, v. water, pis.
piss, n. pis.
pistachio, groen-amandel.
pistil, stamper.
pistol, n. pistool, rewolwer.
pistol, v. met 'n pistool skiet.
pistole, pistool.
piston, suier; klep.
piston-rod, suierstang.
piston-wall, suierwand.
pit, n. put, kuil; myn; kuiltjie; gaatjie; afgrond; bak, parterre (in die skouburg); herstelkuil (motor); **the – of the stomach**, die maagholte, die krop van die maag.
pit, v. inkuil; gaatjies veroorsaak; – **against**, krag laat meet met.
pit-(a)-pat, doef-doef.
pitch, n. pik.
pitch, v. met pik smeer, teer.
pitch, v. (tent) opslaan; uitstal; (pad) uitstraat; gooi; maal (by albasterspel); stamp (van 'n skip); (storie) vertel; val, te lande kom; inklim; – **camp**, kamp(eer); a –ed battle, 'n gereelde slag; – **into**, invlie; te lyf gaan; – **into the food**, weglê aan die kos; – **in**, aanpak, fluks te werk gaan; – **upon**, kies.
pitch, n. (die) stamp (van 'n skip); gooi; (krieket)baan; hoogte; graad; toestand; toonhoogte; helling; staanplek.
pitch-dark, pikdonker.
pitcher, n. kruik, kan; **little –s have long ears**, klein muisies het groot ore.
pitchfork, n. gaffel, hooivurk.
pitchfork, v. met 'n vurk gooi.
pitch-pipe, stemfluitjie.
pitchy, pikdonker, pikagtig, pik- . . .
piteous, jammerlik, erbarmlik, ellendig.
pitfall, vanggat, strik, val; valstrik.
pith, pit, kern; murg; krag; energie.
pithecanthrope, aapmens.
pithiness, pitterigheid; pittigheid.
pithless, sonder pit, swak, futloos.
pithy, pitterig, pittig, kernagtig.
pitiable, bejammerenswaardig.
pitiful, medelydend; ellendig, treurig.
pitiless, meedoënloos, wreed.
pitman, steenkoolmynwerker; trekbout.
pittance, toelagie, deeltjie, bietjie.
pituitary, slymerig, slym- . . .
pity, n. medelyde, jammer(te), deernis; medelyde hê met; **for – 's sake**, in Hemelsnaam; **what a –**, hoe jammer (tog); **it is a thousand pities**, dit is alte jammer.
pity, v. bejammer, jammer kry, medelyde hê met, beklaag.
pivot, n. spil.
pivot, v. (om 'n spil) draai; laat draai.
pivotal, hoof- . . ., vernaamste.
pixy, fee.
placability, versoenbaarheid.
placable, versoenbaar, inskiklik.
placard, n. aanplakbiljet, plakkaat.
placard, v. aanplak; adverteer.
placate, paai, bevredig; versoen.
place, n. plek, plaas; woonplek, huis; posisie, stand; desimaal; **in the first –**, in die eerste plaas, eerstens, ten eerste; **in – of**, in plaas van; **take the – of**, vervang, die plek inneem van; **give – to**, padgee vir, plek maak vir; gevolg word deur; **take –**, plaasvind, voorval, gebeur; **out of –**, nie op sy plek nie, misplaas; onvanpas; **in –**, op sy plek; gepas, **put one in his –**, iemand of sy plek sit.
place, v. (neer)sit, plaas, regsit, aanstel; (geld) belê; 'n betrekking verskaf; verkoop, aan die man bring; tuisbring; – **confidence in**, vertroue stel in; – **an order**, bestel, 'n bestelling gee; **I cannot – him**, ek kan hom nie heeltemal eien nie; ek weet nie wat ek van hom moet dink nie.
placebo, troosmiddel, troosmedisyne.
place-kick, stelskop.
placenta, nageboorte; saadkoek.
placid, vreedsaam, stil; bedaard, kalm.
placidity, vreedsaamheid, stilte; rus.
placket, roksak.
placket-hole, slip.
plafond, plafon, solder; plafonskildering.
plagiarize, plagiaat pleeg.
plagiarism, plagiaat, letterdiewery.
plagiarist, plagiaris, letterdief.
plaque, n. plaag, pes; pestilensie; las; **a – on it**, na die duiwel daarmee!
plaque, v. (met plae) besoek, teister; lastig val, kwel, versondig.
plaguesome, lastig, vervelig.
plague-spot, pesbuil; pesplek; broeiplek, -nes.
plaguy, a. lastig; vervlakste.
plaguy, adv. baie, geweldig, verduiwels.
plaid, (Skotse) geruitmantel.
plain, a. duidelik, helder, verstaanbaar; eenvoudig; onaansienlik; gewoon, alledaags, rondborstig, eerlik; onversier(d), onopgesmuk; glad; – **words**, eenvoudige taal; **the – man**, die gewone man; – **dealing**, openhartigheid, opregtheid; **it was – sailing**, dit het glad gegaan, daar was geen moeilikheid nie; – **clothes**, burgerlike klere; – **cigarettes**, sigarette sonder mondstukke.
plain, adv. duidelik.
plain, n. vlakte.
plainly, duidelik; openhartig; eenvoudig.
plain-song, koraalgesang.
plain-spoken, openhartig, eerlik.
plaint, aanklag, beskuldiging; klag.
plaintif, eiser, klaer.
plaintive, klaend, klaag- . . .
plait, n. (haar)vlegsel; vou, plooi.
plait, v. vleg; vou, plooi.
plan, n. plan, bedoeling, voorneme, oogmerk; metode, manier; skets, ontwerp.
plan, v. planne maak, prakseer, oorlê, mik na, beoog; ontwerp.
planchet, muntplaatjie.
plane, n. plataan(boom).
plane, n. skaaf.
plane, v. skawe; – **down**, afskawe.
plane, v. vlak; gelykte; trap, peil, basis.
plane, a. vlak; – **geometry**, vlak(ke) meetkunde.
plane, n. vliegtuig.
planet, planeet; kasuifel (priesterkleed).
plane-table, meettafel(tjie).
planetarium, planetarium.
planetary, planeet- . . ., van die planete; aards; dolend, dwalend; – **system**, sonnestelsel, planeetstelsel.
planet-struck, **-stricken**, verskrik.
plane-tree, plataanboom.
plangent, kloppend, klotsend.
planimeter, vlaktemeter, planimeter.
planimetry, vlak(ke)meetkunde.
planish, planeer; uitklop; polys.
planisphere, planisfeer.

plank, n. plank; verkiesingsleus.
plank, v. planke lê, vloer insit (lê), bevloer; – **down,** neergooi.
plano-concave, plathol, plankonkaaf.
plano-convex, platbol, plankonveks.
planometer, planometer.
plant, n. plant, gewas; masjinerie, uitrusting, gereedskap.
plant, v. plant, beplant; vestig, stig; plaas, uitsit, pos teer; ('n slag) toedien; neersit; – **out,** verplant.
plantain, piesang(boom).
plantation, plantasie; volk(s)planting.
planter, planter, landbouer; setlaar.
plantigrade, n. soolganger.
plaque, plaatjie, medalje.
plash, n. geplas, gespat.
plash, v. plas, spat.
plasm, plasma.
plasma, groenkwarts, plasma.
plaster, n. pleister; pleisterkalk; – **of Paris,** (gebrande) gips.
plaster, v. (be)pleister; besmeer.
plasterer, pleisteraar, stukadoor.
plastic, n. plastiese kuns; plastiek(stof)
plastic, beeldend, plasties; – **arts,** beeldende kunste; – **surgeon,** plastiese chirurg.
plasticity, plastisiteit, vormbaarheid.
plasticine, boetseerklei, modelleerklei.
plastron, borsplant, borsstuk, bors(ie).
plat, lappie (stukkie grond).
platan, (Oosterse) plataanboom.
plate, n. plaat; bord; naambord; vaatwerk, goudwerk, silwerwerk, metaalwerk; beker; bekerwedren.
plate, v. versilwer, verguld, platteer.
plateau, tafelland, hoogvlakte, plato.
plate-glass, spieëlglas.
plat(t)en, druktafel, drukplaat.
plater, versilweraar.
platform, v. verhoog, tribune, platform.
plating, goudwerk, silwerwerk.
platinize, platineer, met platina bedek.
platinum, platina (erts); platinum (Pt).
platinum-points, platina-punte.
platitude, gemeenplaas.
platitudinarian, a. afgesaag, alledaags.
platitudinarian, n. gemeenplasekramer.
Platonic, Platonies.
platoon, peloton, afdeling.
platter, vlak skottel.
plaudit(s), toejuiging, applous.
plausibility, aanneemlikheid.
plausible, aanneemlik, plousibel; glad.
play, v. speel; baljaar; bespeel; laat speel; – **a part,** 'n rol speel; – **truant,** stokkies draai; – **a trick,** 'n poets bak; – **the fool,** gekskeer; – **the game,** eerlike spel speel, eerlik te werk gaan; – **about,** rondspeel, rondjakker; – **at,** speel; speel-speel doen; – **into the hands of,** iemand se planne bevorder, in iemand se kaarte speel; – **off one against the other,** die een teen die ander uitspeel; – **on,** spel op; laat speel op; –**ed out,** poot-uit, kapot; – **up to,** (onder)steun; in iemand se kaarte speel; pamperlang, flikflooi; – **upon words,** woordespelinge maak.
play, n. spel; vermaak; toneelstuk; speelruimte; **bring, call into** –, **te voorskyn roep;** aanwend, laat geld; **allow full – to,** skiet gee, die vrye loop laat; **at –,** aan die speel; – **on words,** woordspeling.
play-bill, aanplakbiljet.
play-boy, roekelose kêrel van die uitgaanslewe.
player, speler.

playfellow, speelmaat.
playful, uitgelate, dartel, vrolik, speels.
playgoer, skouburgbesoeker.
playground, speelplek, speelgrond.
playhouse, skouburg, teater.
playing-card, (speel)kaart.
playmate, speelmaat.
plaything, speeldingetjie; speelbal.
playtime, speeltyd.
playwright, toneelskrywer.
plaza, plaza, (stads)plein.
plea, pleidooi, argument; pleit.
pleach, deurvleg.
plead, pleit, smeek, soebat; 'n pleidooi hou; bepleit; – **guilty,** (skuld) beken.
pleading, (die) pleit, pleidooi.
pleasance, plesier, genot.
pleasant, aangenaam, lekker, genoeglik.
pleasantry, grappigheid, luimigheid.
please, beval, aanstaan, behaag, genoeë verskaf; – **yourself,** maak soos jy wil; **as many as you** –, soveel soos jy wil; **be** –**ed with,** in jou skik (ingenome) wees met; vermaak skep in; **I shall be only too** –**d to do it,** ek sal dit maar alte graag wil doen; **if you** –, asseblief; **ring the bell** –, lui asseblief die klok.
pleasing, aangenaam, innemend.
pleasurable, aangenaam, prettig.
pleasure, genot, genoeë, plesier, vermaak; begeerte, wens, welgevalle; **it is our – to,** dit behaag ons om; ons het die eer om; **take a – in,** behae skep in.
pleasure-boat, plesierboot.
pleasure-ground, (speel)park.
pleat, plooi, vou, plisseer.
plebeian, n. plebejer, burger.
plebian, a. burgerlik, plebejies; laag.
plebiscite, volksbesluit, volkstemming.
plectrum, plektron, speelpennetjie.
pledge, n. pand; onderpand; waarborg; belofte; **take, sign the** –, die onthoudingsbelofte aflê, afskaffer word.
pledge, v. verpand; jou woord gee.
pledgee, pandhouer.
Pleiades, Sewester, Plejade.
plenary, volkome, onbeperk, geheel; voltallig; – **power,** volmag.
plenipotentiary, gevolmagtigde.
plenitude, volheid; oorvloed.
plenteous, oorvloedig.
plentiful, oorvloedig, volop.
plenty, n. oorvloed; – **of,** volop, baie.
plenty, adv. oorvloedig, baie, volop.
plenum, volle vergadering; volte.
pleonasm, pleonasme.
pleonastic, pleonasties.
plethora, volbloedigheid; oorvloed.
pleura, borsvleis.
pleural, borsvlies- . . .
pleurisy, borsvliesontsteking, pleuris.
plexus, netwerk.
pliability, sien **pliancy.**
pliable, sien **pliant.**
pliancy, buigsaamheid; inskiklikheid.
pliant, buigsaam, slap; inskiklik.
plicated, geplooi, gevou, geplisseer.
pliers, knyptang, (draad)tang.
plight, v. verpand, belowe; – **one's troth, faith, word,** jou woord verpand (gee).
plight, n. belofte.
plight, n. toestand, posisie; **sorry** –, treurige toestand.
plinth, plint, lys; voetstuk.
plod, v. swoeg, beur, sukkel, sloof, ploeter, blok; – **along,** aansukkel.

plod, n. swaar werk, geswoeg.
plodder, ploeteraar, slower, sukkelaar.
plop, ploems, pardoems.
plot, n. erf, bouperseel, stuk(kie) grond; intrige, knoop (van 'n roman); komplot, sameswering.
plot, v. skets, (uit)teken, ontwerp, afbaken; saamsweer, planne smee.
plough, n. ploeg; dop (by 'n eksamen); **put one's hand to the –**, jou hand aan die ploeg slaan.
plough, v. ploeg (ploeë, ploe), omploeg; groef; klief; laat dop (by 'n eksamen); **– out, up**, uitploeë.
plough-beam, ploegbalk.
plough-boy, ploegleier.
plough-share, ploegskaar.
plough-tail, ploegstert.
plover, waterkiewietjie, strandloper.
pluck, n. ruk, pluk, trek; dop (by 'n eksamen); harslag; moed, durf.
pluck, v. (af)pluk; trek, ruk; fop, kaal maak; laat dop; **– away**, wegruk; **– up one's heart, spirits, courage**, moed skep.
plucky, moedig, dapper.
plug, n. prop, pen, tap, stop; pluisie; **sparkling –**, vonkprop.
plug, n. prop, pen, tap, stop; pluisie; **sparking –**, vonkprop.
plug, v. (toe)stop, 'n prop insteek, 'n tap inslaan; skiet; **– away at**, lostrek op.
plug-ugly, boef.
plug-wire, vonk(prop)draad.
plum, pruim; die beste.
plumage, vere.
plumb, n. skietlood; **out of –**, uit die lood, skuins, nie vertikaal nie.
plumb, a. vertikaal, loodreg, regop.
plumb, v. peil, meet; waterpas maak.
plumbago, potlood, grafiet.
plumbeous, loodagtig, lood- . . .
plumber, loodgieter.
plumber, persoon wat net vir een kandidaat stem; infame leuen.
plumbery, loodgietery.
plumb-line, loodlyn.
plume, n. pluim, veer, veerbos.
plume, v. van vere voorsien, bepluim; uitdos; (die vere) glad stryk; **– oneself on**, (sig) beroem op, pronk met.
plummet, dieplood, skietlood, peillood.
plummy, pruim- . . .; ryk, begeerlik.
plumose, geveer, gepluim; veeragtig.
plump, a. dik, rond, vet, geset; mollig.
plump, v. dik (vet) word, (op)swel.
plump, v.: **– down, upon**, neerplof; **– for**, stem vir (net een kandidaat).
plump, n. plof.
plump, adv. pardoems; botweg.
plum-pudding, rosyntjiepoeding.
plumule, pluimpie; donsie.
plumy, pluimagtig, pluim- . . .
plunder, v. roof, plunder, steel.
plunder, n. plundering; roof, buit; wins.
plunderage, roof, buit.
plunge, v. (in)spring, duik; onderdompel (in)stoot; vorentoe spring; woes dobbel; stamp; **– into the room**, die kamer binnestorm; **–d in darkness**, in duisternis gedompel.
plunge, n. sprong, indompeling; waagstuk; take the –, die sprong waag.
plunger, suier; dobbelaar; duiker.
pluperfect, voltooid-verlede (tyd).
plural, meervoud.
pluralize, meervoudig maak.
pluralism, meervoudigheid.
pluralist, pluralis.
plurality, pluraliteit; meerderheid; menigte, groot aantal; meervoudigheid.
plus, n. plus(teken).
plus, a. ekstra; positief (elektr.).
plus, prep. plus.
plus-fours, kardoesbroek; gholfbroek.
plush, pluis, ferweel, pluche.
Pluto, Pluto.
plutocracy, geldheerskappy, plutokrasie.
plutocrat, kapitalis, plutokraat.
plutocratic, plutokraties.
plutonic, plutonies, vulkanies.
plutonium, plutonium.
pluvial, reën- . . ., reënagtig.
pluviometer, reënmeter.
ply, n. laag, vou; dikte; aanleg, neiging; **two –**, dubbeldraad- . . ., dubbellaag- . . .; **three –**, driedraad- . . ., drielaag- . . .
ply, v. hanteer, gebruik; ('n beroep) uitoefen, (werk) doen, verrig; **– with questions**, met vrae bestook.
pneumatic, a. lug- . . ., **– tire**, lugband.
pneumatics, pneumatiek.
pneumonia, longontsteking.
pneumonic, long(ontstekings-) . . .
po, sien pot.
poach, v. eier sonder dop kook, kaal kook; **–ed egg**, kaalgekookte eier.
poach, v. steek; vertrap; stroop; oortree, steel, skaai.
poacher, stroper; wilddief; skaaier.
pock, pokkie.
pocket, n. sak; holte; **with an empty –**, platsak; **she has him in her –**, sy kan met hom maak net wat sy wil, sy het hom (skoon) in die sak; **put your pride in your –**, bêre maar jou hoogmoed tot later; **– battleship**, ponie-slagskip.
pocket, v. in die sak steek; skaal, (gevoelens) onderdruk; ('n belediging) sluk; stop (biljart).
pocket-book, sakboekie.
pocket-expenses, klein uitgawes.
pocket-knife, sakmes, knipmes.
pocket-money, sakgeld.
pocket-size, sakformaat.
pod, n. peul, dop.
pod, v. uitdop, uitpeul; peule dra.
podagra, jig, pootjie, podagra.
podded, peuldraend, peul- . . .
podge, dikkerd, vaatjie, vetsak.
podgy, dik, vet.
podium, verhoog, podium.
poem, gedig.
poesy, poësie.
poet, digter; **– laureate**, hofdigter.
poetaster, rymelaar, pruldigter.
poetess, digteres.
poetic(al), digterlik, poëties; dig- . . .
poetry, poësie, digkuns; gedigte.
poignancy, skerpheid.
poignant, skerp, bytend, bitsig; pynlik.
point, n. stippeltjie; puntjie; punt; teken, desimaalpunt, komma; top(punt) ent, eienskap; **–s**, wissel(spoor); **when it comes to the –**, as dit daarop aankom; **that is not his strong –**, hy munt nie daarin uit nie; **that is just the –**, dit is juis waar dit op aankom; **come to the –**, ter sake kom; **you must make a – of it**, jy moet dit vir jou ten doel stel, jy moet daar spesiaal aan dink; **at the – of death**, op sterwe; **– of view**, gesigspunt; **he did not see the –**, hy het nie begryp waar dit om gaan nie; **the – of no return**, die punt van waar jy slegs vorentoe kan gaan.
point, v. skerp maak; toelig; (messelwerk) voeg;

aanwys; – **at**, (met die vinger) wys na; mik na; – **out**, wys, aantoon; – **to**, wys na; die aandag vestig op.
point-blank, botweg, reguit, rondborstig, op die man af; horisontaal.
point-duty, verkeersdiens.
pointed, spits, skerp; gevat, raak.
pointer, wys(t)er; stok; jaghond; patryshond, naald.
pointless, stomp, sonder punt; betekenisloos, laf; nul-nul (van wedstryd).
pointsman, wisselwagter.
poise, v. balanseer; (laat) hang; swewe.
poise, n. ewewig; houding; onsekerheid.
poison, n. gif, vergif.
poison, v. vergiftig, vergewe; verpes, verbitter; **–ed arrow**, gifpyl.
poison-fang, giftand.
poisoning, vergiftiging.
poisonous, giftig; verpes; verderflik.
poke, n. sak; **buy a pig in a –**, 'n kat in die sak koop.
poke, v. stoot, stamp, steek; pook, roer; – **fun at**, gekskeer (spot) met.
poke, n. stoot, stamp, steek; tuit.
poker, vuuryster, pookyster; **as stiff as a –**, stokstyf.
poker, poker (kaartspel).
poker-faced, onbewoë, uitdrukkingloos.
pokerwork, brandwerk.
poky, nou, beknop; vuil, liederlik.
Poland, Pole.
polar, pool- . . . ; – **bear**, ysbeer; – **circles**, poolsirkels.
polarize, polariseer.
polarity, polariteit.
polder, polder.
pole, n. pool.
pole, n. paal, stok; disselboom.
pole, v. pale inplant.
Pole, Pool.
pole-ax(e), strydbyl, slagtersbyl.
polecat, muishond.
pole-jump(ing), polsstokspring.
polemic, a. polemies, twis- . . .
polemic, n. twisgeskryf, polemiek.
polemics, polemiek.
polemize, polemiek voer, polemiseer.
pole-star, poolster.
police, polisie.
police-court, magistraatshof.
policeman, polisieagent, konstabel.
police-officer, polisiebeampte.
police-station, polisiekantoor.
policlinic, polikliniek.
policy, staatsmansbeleid; staatkunde; politiek, gedragslyn; beleid, oorleg, verstandigheid.
policy, polis.
poliomyelitis, rugmurgontsteking.
polish, blinkmaak, opvrywe, polys, poleer, poets, verfyn, beskaaf; **–ed**, verfyn, beskaaf(d); blink; – **off**, afpiets, kafloop; – **up**, mooimaak, blinkmaak, oppoets.
polish, n. blinkheid, glans, skyn; smeer(sel), (skoen)waks, politoer; verfyning.
Polish, Pools.
polite, beleef, vriendelik, hoflik, galant; verfyn, beskaaf.
politic, verstandig; slim, slu, geslepe.
political, staatkundig, politiek.
politician, staatsman, politikus.
politics, politiek; staatkunde, staatswetenskap, staatsleer.
polity, regeringsvorm; staat.
polka, polka.

poll, n. kop, harspan; stemming; stembus; **there was a heavy –**, daar is druk gestem; **be returned at the head of the –**, die meeste stemme kry.
poll, v. top, afsny; (horings) afsae; stem; stemme opneem; stemme kry.
poll, a. poenskop- . . .
poll, n. poenskopbees.
pollard, n. poenskopdier; semels.
pollen, stuifmeel.
pollinate, bestuif.
polination, bestuiwing.
polling, stemming.
polling-booth, stemburo, stemplek, -bus.
polloi, gepeupel.
poll-tax, hoofbelasting.
pollute, besoedel, besmet; vuilmaak.
pollution, bevlekking, besmetting.
polo, polo.
polonaise, polonaise.
polony, wors, sosys, polonie.
poltroon, lafaard, papbroek, lamsak.
poltroonery, lafhartigheid.
polyandrous, veelmannig; veelhelmig.
polyandry, veelmannery, poliandrie.
polychromatic, veelkleurig.
polychrome, a. veelkleurig, polichroom.
polychrome, n. polichrome.
polychromy, polichromie.
polyester, poliëster.
polygamist, poligamis.
polygamous, veelwywig- . . .
polygamy, veelwywery, poligamie.
polyglot, a. veeltalig, poliglotties.
polyglot, n. poliglot, veeltalige persoon.
polygon, veelhoek, poligoon.
polygraphy, veelskrywery, poligrafie.
polyhedron, veelvlak, poliëder.
polyhistor, veelweter.
polymorphic, veelvormig, polimorf.
Polynesian, a. Polinesies.
Polynesian, n. Polinesiër.
polyp(e), veelvoet, poliep.
polyphagous, veelvretend; vraatsugtig.
polyphonous, veelstemmig, polifoon.
polypod, veelvoetig.
polysyllabic, veellettergrepig.
polysyllable, veellettergrepige woord.
polytechnic, politegnies.
polytheism, veelgodery, politeïsme.
polytheist, politeïs.
polytheistic, politeïsties.
pom, sien **Pomeranian**.
pomace, appelmoes; visafval.
pomade, n. pomade, (haar)salf, haarolie.
pomade, v. pomadeer, smeer.
pomatum, sien **pomade**.
pomegranate, granaat, granaatappel.
pomelo, pomelo; pompelmoes.
Pomeranian, a. Pommers.
Pomeranian, n. keeshond, spitshond; Pommer (Pommeriaan).
pomiculture, vrugtekwekery.
pommel, n. knop, swaardknop; saalknop.
pommel, v. slaan, karnuffel, klop.
pomological, pomologies.
pomology, pomologie, vrugtekunde.
pomp, prag, praal, vertoon.
pompier-ladder, brandleer.
pom-pom, pom-pom, bommaxim.
pompon, pompon, kwassie.
pomposity, verwaandheid, vertoon; praalsug; deftigheid; geswollenheid.
pompous, luisterryk, skitterend; deftig, verwaand; hoogdrawend, geswolle.
pond, dam, poel, vywer.

ponder, (be)peins, oordink; mymer.
ponderability, weegbaarheid.
ponderable, weegbaar.
ponderosity, swaarte: swaarwigtigheid.
ponderous, swaar, gewigtig; lomp; droog.
pongee, pongee, Chinese sy.
poniard, ponjaard, dolk.
pontifex, aartspriester, opperpriester.
pontiff, opperpriester; biskop; pous.
pontifical, hoëpriesterlik; pouslik; biskoplik; pontifikaal; dogmaties.
pontificate, hoëpriesterskap; pontifikaat.
pontoneer, pontonnier.
pontoon, pont(on).
pony, ponie, bossiekop; R50.
poodle, poedel(hond).
pooh, ag! bog!
pooh-pooh, die spot drywe met, lag vir.
pool, n. dam(metjie), poel, plas; kuil.
pool, v. grawe.
pool, n. pot, potgeld, inset; ring, trust.
pool, v. in die pot gooi; wins deel, saammaak.
poop, agterstewe, agterdek.
poor, a. arm, behoeftig, hulpbehoewend, armoedig; skraal, onvrugbaar, swak; gering, klein; armsalig, treurig; beskeie, nederig; ongelukkig; **that is a – consolation**, dit is maar 'n skraal troos; **– fellow**, stomme vent, arme kêrel!; **the –**, die arm mense, die armes.
poor-box, armbus.
poor-house, armhuis.
poorly, min, ellendig, armoedig; kaduks, siekerig; laag, gemeen, sleg.
poor-rate, armebelasting.
poor-spirited, lafhartig, papbroekerig.
pop, v. knal, skiet, klap, plof; skielik voor die dag kom; **– the question**, die jawoord vra; skielik met 'n versoek voor die dag kom; **– at**, skiet na; **– down**, skielik neersit; neerplof, neerval; **– in**, onverwags binnekom, inwip; **– off (the hooks)**, bokveld toe gaan, afklop; **– up**, opduik.
pop, n. klap, slag, knal, plof; kol, merk.
pop, interj. & adv. poef, klaps.
pop, n. volkskonsert.
pop-corn, springmielies
pope, pous; **–'s nose**, stuitjie.
popedom, pousdom.
popery, Roomse godsdiens, papistery.
pop-eyed, met puiloë; verstom, verbaas.
pop-gun, propgeweertjie, knalgeweertjie.
popinjay, papegaai.
popish, pouslik, paaps, Rooms.
poplar, populier(boom).
poplin, popelien.
poppet(-valve), stootklep.
popple, klots, slaan (van golwe).
poppy, papawer.
poppycock, pure bog, twak(praatjies).
popsy(-wopsy), skapie, hartlammetjie.
populace, volksmenigte, gepeupel.
popular; volks- . . ., gewild, populêr; gewoon, eenvoudig; **– prices**, lae pryse.
popularisation, popularisasie.
popularize, populêr maak, populariseer.
popularity, populariteit, gewildheid.
populate, bevolk.
population, bevolking, populasie.
populous, digbevolk, digbewoon.
porcelain, porselein.
porcelain-clay, porseleinaarde.
porcelainous, porselein- . . .
porch, (voor)portaal.
porcine, vark- . . ., varkagtig.
porcupine, ystervark.

pore, n. sweetgaatjie, porie.
pore, v. kyk, tuur, staar; **– at, on**, stip kyk na; **– over**, (in iets) verdiep wees, bepeins blok.
pork, varkvleis.
pork-butcher, varkslagter.
porker, voervark, slagvark.
porky, vark- . . ., varkerig; spekvet.
pornographic, pornografies.
pornography, pornografie.
porosity, poreusheid.
porous, poreus.
porphyry, porfier.
porpoise, seevark, to(r)nyn.
porridge, pap.
porringer, kommetjie, bakkie, diepbord.
port, n. hawe; hawestad.
port, n. poort, ingang; patryspoort.
port, n. houding, voorkome.
port, n. bakboord.
port, v. na bakboord draai.
port, n. portwyn.
portable, draagbaar, vervoerbaar; **– radio**, kofferradio; **– lamp**, handlamp, looplamp.
portage, vervoer(loon), draagloon.
portal, poort, portaal, ingang.
portal-vein, poortaar.
portcullis, valdeur, valpoort.
portend, voorspel, bedui, beteken.
portent, (voor)teken; wonder.
porter, deurwagter; draer, kruier.
porterage, dra(ag)geld, kruiersloon.
portfolio, briewesak; portefeulje.
port-hole, patryspoort, kajuitvenstertjie.
portico, portiek, (oordekte) suilegang.
portion, n. (aan)deel, porsie, erfdeel.
portion, v. verdeel; **– out**, uitdeel.
portliness, swaarlywigheid; deftigheid.
portly, geset, swaarlywig; deftig, statig.
portmanteau, handsak, reissak, valies.
portrait, portret; skildering, beeld.
portraiture, afbeelding; skildering.
portray, skilder, beskrywe; afbeeld.
portrayal, skildering; beskrywing.
Portuguese, Portugees.
pose, n. houding, pose; aanstellings.
pose, v. poseer; vasvra; plaas.
poser, raaisel, strikvraag, vasvraag.
position, posisie, stelling; ligging, plek; houding; status, rang, stand; betrekking; toestand; **I am not in a – to say**, ek is nie in staat (by magte) om te sê nie; **in –**, op sy plek, klaar, reg.
positive, a. positief, vas, bepaald, stellig; seker, oortuig, beslis; **he is a – nuisance**, hy is bepaald 'n las; **– sign**, plusteken; **– degree**, stellende trap.
positive, n. stellende trap; positief.
positivism, positivisme.
posse, mag, polisiemag.
possess, besit, hê, in besit wees van; beheers; **–ed by a devil**, deur 'n duiwel besete; **he is –ed with, by, this idea**, van hierdie gedagte kan hy nie loskom nie, hy maal gedurig oor hierdie een ding; **what –ed him to do such a thing?**, wat het hom makeer om so 'n ding aan te vang?; **like one –ed**, soos 'n besetene.
possession, besitting, eiendom; besit; **be in – of**, besit; **take – of**, in besit neem; **– is nine points of the law**, salig is die besitters.
possessive, besittend; besitlik; possessief; **– case**, tweede naamval.
possessor, eienaar, besitter.
possibility, moontlikheid; **he cannot by any – be in time**, hy kan onmoontlik betyds wees.
possible, a. moontlik, gebeurlik; doenlik; **only**

one – man among them, net een geskikte man onder hulle.
possible, n. uiterste; maksimum, hoogste aantal punte moontlik.
possibly, moontlik, dalk, miskien.
possum, buidelrot.
post, n. stut, paal, styl.
post, v. aanplak; bekend maak, opvysel; – up, aanplak.
post, n. pos; poskantoor, posdiens, poswese; by return of –, per omgaande, per (terug)kerende pos.
post, v. haas, jaag, gou ry; ('n brief) pos; (in)boek.
post, n. pos, posisie, betrekking; fort.
post, v. stasioneer; poste uitsit.
postage, posgeld.
postage-stamp, posseël.
postal, pos-. . .; – rate, postarief.
postal-order, posbewys, poswissel.
post-bag, possak.
post-box, briewebus.
post-boy, posjong, briewebesteller.
post-card, poskaart.
post-chaise, poskar, poswa.
postdate, later dateer, postdateer.
post-diluvian, na die sondvloed.
post-entry, later (laat) inskrywing.
poster, aanplakbiljet; aanplakker.
posterior, a. later; agter-. . ., agterste.
posterior, n. agterste, agterent.
posterity, nageslag, nakomelingskap.
postern, n. agterdeur, sydeur.
postern, a. agter-. . .; – gate, agterdeur.
post-free, franko, gefrankeerd, portvry.
post-graduate, a. nagraads; – work, navorsingswerk.
post-graduate, n. nagraadse student, gegradueerde.
posthumous, na die dood gebore; nagelate; postuum; – child, nakind; – writings, nagelate werke.
postil, kommentaar, kanttekening.
postil(l)ion, voorryer.
postman, posjong, briewebesteller.
postmark, posmerk, stempel.
postmaster, posmeester.
postmaster-general, posmeester-generaal.
post-meridian, na die middag.
post-mortem, lykskouing; nabetragting.
post-office, poskantoor.
post-office box, posbus.
post-paid, gefrankeer, porto betaald.
postpone, uitstel, verskuif.
postponement, uitstel.
postprandial, na die maaltyd, tafel-. . .; – speech, tafeltoespraak, tafelrede.
postscript, naskrif.
postulant, kandidaat, postulant.
postulate, n. stelling, postulaat.
postulate, v. (as vasstaande) aanneem, veronderstel, postuleer; eis.
postulation, veronderstelling; eis.
posture, n. houding, postuur; toestand.
posture, v. plaas, sit.
posy, ruiker; (ring)spreuk, ringvers.
pot, n. pot, kan; (kamer)uil; blompot; –s of money, geld soos bossies, geld lank; the – calls the kettle black, die pot verwyt die ketel (dat hy swart is); that won't keep the – boiling, daarvan sal die skoorsteen nie rook nie; go to –, na die maan gaan.
pot, v. inmaak, inlê; in 'n pot plant; neerskiet; inpalm.
potable, drinkbaar.
potash, potas.
potassium, kalium.
potation, drinkery; drinkparty; dronk.
potato, aartappel (ertappel); sweet –, patat.
pot-bellied, dikbuikig, boepens.
pot-boiler, broodskrywer; broodskryfsel.
potency, mag, vermoë.
potent, magtig, sterk.
potentate, heerser, potentaat, monarg.
potential, a. potensieel, latent, moontlik.
potential, n. potensiaal; moontlikheid.
potentiality, moontlikheid.
pother, n. rookwolk, stofwolk; lawaai, geraas, rumoer, bohaai; make a – about it, 'n bohaai daaroor maak.
pother, v. 'n bohaai maak, te kere gaan; lastig val, van die wysie bring.
pot-hole, slaggat (pad); maalgat.
pot-house, kroeg, drinkplek.
potion, drank, gifdrank.
pot-luck, wat die pot verskaf; (genoeë neem met) wat daar te ete is.
pot-pourri, potpourri, mengeling.
potsherd, potskerf.
pot-shot, potskoot; tromp-op-skoot.
pottage, so(e)p.
potter, n. pottebakker; –'s wheel, pottebakkerskyf.
potter, v. peuter, prutsel, sukkel.
pottery, pottebakkery; erdewerk.
potty, niksbeduidend, klein, bog-. . .; getik, dwaas.
pouch, n. sak(kie); patroonsak; tabaksak; beursie; buidel.
pouch, v. in die sak steek; vat, inpalm, toeëien; iets in die hand stop.
poult, kuiken, klein kalkoentjie, ens.
poulterer, pluimveehandelaar.
poultice, n. pap.
poultice, v. pap.
poultry, pluimvee.
pounce, n. klou; grypslag.
pounce, v. neerskiet op, bevlie, gryp; – upon, neerskiet op, gryp.
pounce, n. strooisand, houtskoolpoeier.
pounce, v. met houtskoolpoeier bestrooi.
pouncet-box, reukdosie.
pound, n. pond; five –s, vyf pond.
pound, n. skut, skutkraal, skuthok.
pound, v. skut, in die skut ja.
pound, v. (fyn)stamp; timmer, moker, met die vuis inklim, pap slaan; – to pieces, fyngoed maak van; flenters slaan.
poundage, skutgeld; pondgeld.
pounder, stamper.
pounder, ponder; ten –, tienponder.
pound-keeper, skutmeester.
pour, v. giet, gooi, (in)skink; stort, uitstort, stroom; stortreën; laat instroom; it never rains but it –s, 'n ongeluk kom nooit alleen nie; letters –ed in from all quarters, briewe het van alle kante ingestroom; the river –s itself into the sea, die rivier stort in die see (in); – forth, out, (laat) uitstroom; uitstort; (in)sking; – out the tea, die tee (in)skink; – oil upon troubled waters, olie op die golwe giet; – cold water on, kou(e) water gooi op; afkeur, doodpraat.
pour, n. stortbui.
pout, v. pruil, suur gesig trek.
pout, n. suur gesig, dik mond; in the –s, nors, stuurs, suur.
pouter, pruiler, kropduif.
poverty, armoede, gebrek; skaarste.
poverty-stricken, arm, armoedig.

powder, n. poeier; stof; (bus)kruit; baking -, bakpoeier.
powder, v. poeier; fynmaak, fynstamp.
powder-flask, powder-horn, kruithoring.
powder-magazine, kruithuis.
powder-puff, poeierkwas(sie).
powder-room, dameskamer.
powdery, poeieragtig, poeier- ...
power, mag, krag; vermoë, gesag, beheer, invloed; bekwaamheid; **more** - **to your elbow**, alle voorspoed!; **the party in** -, die regerende party; **the** -**s that be**, owerheid, die gesaghebbendes; **merciful** -**s**, goeie hemel, genadige gode!; - **of attorney**, volmag, prokurasie; - **of resistance**, weerstandsvermoë; **in one's** -, in jou mag.
power-dive, kragduik.
power-driven, met kragbediening; - **bicycle**, kragsfiets.
powerful, sterk, magtig; invloedryk.
powerless, magteloos, kragteloos.
powerloom, stoomweeftoestel.
power-station, kragsentrale, ,,kragstasie".
pow-wow, samespreking, konferensie, indaba.
pox, pokkies; sifilis; **small** -, kinderpokkies, **chicken** -, waterpokkies.
practicability, moontlikheid, uitvoerbaarheid.
practicable, moontlik, uitvoerbaar, doenlik; bruikbaar; begaanbaar, rybaar.
practical, prakties, doelmatig; werklik; **play a** - **joke**, 'n kool stowe, 'n poets bak.
practically, prakties; feitlik, so te sê; - **finished**, so te sê klaar.
practice, praktyk; oefening; gewoonte, gebruik; uitvoering; - **makes perfect**, oefening baar kuns, al doende leer mens; **in** -, in die werklikheid; **put into** -, in praktyk bring, ten uitvoer bring, toepas; **I am out of** -, ek het lank laas geoefen.
practician, praktikus.
practise, toepas, beoefen, uitoefen; praktiseer; oefen; - **upon his superstition**, misbruik maak van sy bygelowigheid.
practitioner, praktisyn; **general** -, praktiserende geneesheer.
praetor, pretor; landvoog.
pragmatic(al), pragmaties; dogmaties.
pragmatism, pragmatisme; bemoeisug.
pragmatist, pragmatis.
Prague, Praag.
prairie, prêrie, grasvlakte; - **schooner**, ossewa.
prairie-dog, prêrie-hond.
praise, n. lof, eer, roem; **he was loud in his** -**s of his friend's ability**, hy het sy vriend se bekwaamheid hoog geroem; - **be to the Lord**, die Here sy dank, die Here sy geloof.
praise, v. prys, opvysel, ophemel; loof.
praiseworthy, prysenswaardig, loflik.
pram, kinderwaentjie; melkkarretjie.
prance, steier, bokspring; spog, pronk.
prandial, maaltyd- ..., maal- ...
prang, pletter, verniel.
prank, n. grap, poets; kaskenade, streek.
prank, v. optooi, uitdos; spog.
prate, n. gebabbel, geklets, gesnater.
prate, v. babbel, klets, snater, sanik.
prater, babbelaar, snaterkous.
prattle, n. gebabbel, geklets, gesnater.
prattle, v. babbel, snater.
pravity, slegtheid, bedorwenheid.
prawn, seegarnaal.
praxis, praktyk; gewoonte, gebruik.
pray, bid, smeek; versoek, ernstig vra; - **be careful**, pas tog op; - **tell me**, sê my bietjie (asseblief).

prayer, gebed, bede, smeking, versugting; versoek; **The Lord's P**-, Onse Vader; **family** -**s**, huisgodsdiens.
prayer-book, gebedeboek.
prayer-meeting, biduur.
preach, preek; verkondig; - **up**, ophemel; - **down**, slegmaak.
preacher, predikant, pre(di)ker.
preachy, prekerig, preek- ...
pre-acquaintance, vroeëre kennis(making).
pre-admonish, vooraf vermaan (waarsku).
pre-admonition, voorafgaande waarskuwing.
preamble, inleiding, voorrede.
pre-appoint, vooraf aanstel (vasstel).
pre-arrange, vooraf skik (bepaal).
prebend, prebende.
prebendary, domheer.
precarious, onseker, twyfelagtig, wisselvallig; gevaarvol; **a** - **living**, 'n wisselvallige bestaan; - **assumption**, twyfelagtige veronderstelling.
precatory, versoek- ..., smeek- ...
precaution, voorsorg, voorbehoedmiddel, voorsorgsmaatreël.
precautionary, voorsorgs- ...; - **measures**, voorsorgsmaatreëls.
precede, voorgaan, voorafgaan, die voorrang kry bo; **the words that** - **this paragraph**, die woorde wat (aan) hierdie paragraaf voorafgaan.
precedence, voorrang, superioriteit.
precedent, n. voorbeeld, presedent; **it is without** -, daar bestaan nie nog so 'n geval nie, dit is ongeëwenaard.
precedent, a. voorafgaande.
preceding, voorafgaande, vorige.
precent, voorsing.
precentor, koorleier, voorsinger.
precept, bevel, voorskif, bevelskrif, oproep; **example is better than** -, leringe wek, voorbeelde trek.
preceptive, gebiedend, bevelend, voorgeskrewe, voorskrifs- ...
preceptor, onderwyser, (leer)meester.
precession, presessie.
precinct, gebied; -**s**, grens(lyn); **the** -**s of**, die grense van; die omgewing van.
preciosity, gemaaktheid, onnatuurlikheid, gesogtheid.
precious, a. kosbaar; kostelik; edel; opgesier, geaffekteer, gesog, presieus (van styl); - **metals**, edele metale; - **stones**, edelstene, edelgesteentes; **the** - **blood of Christ**, die dierbare bloed van Christus.
precious, adv. drommels, vervlaks; - **little**, bloedweinig.
precious, n.: **my** -, my liefste, my skat.
precipice, afgrond, krans, steilte.
precipitance, onbesonnenheid, oorhaasting.
precipitate, n. presipitaat, besinksel, afsaksel, neerslag, moer.
precipitate, a. (oor)haastig, onbesonne.
precipitate, v. (neer)stort, neergooi; aanja; versnel, verhaas, bespoedig; (laat) afsak, neerslaan, presipiteer, besink; - **the course of events**, die loop van sake verhaas.
precipitation, presipitaat, neerslag; gejaagdheid, oorhaasting; bespoediging.
precipitous, steil; oorhaastig.
precis, opsomming, kort inhoud, oorsig.
precise, presies, nougeset, sekuur; juis.
precisely, presies; juistement.
precisian, gewetensmens.
precision, stiptheid, juistheid, presiesheid, akku-

raatheid, eksaktheid; – **tools**, presisiegereedskap; – **bombing**, fynbomwerpery.
preclude, uitsluit; belet, voorkom.
preclusion, uitsluiting; voorkoming.
preclusive, uitsluitend; verhinderend.
precocious, vroeg (ryp); oulik, ouderwets, vrypostig, astrant.
precocity, vroegrypheid; vrypostigheid.
precognition, voorkennis.
preconceive, vooraf uitdink, vooraf begryp, ('n mening) vooraf vorm.
preconception, vooroordeel.
preconcert, vooraf oorlê, afspreek.
precondemn, vooruit veroordeel.
precondition, voorwaarde, vereiste.
precursor, voorloper, aankondiger.
precursory, inleidend, voorafgaande.
predacious, roof- . . .
predate, te vroeg dateer, antedateer.
predator, roofdier.
predatory, roof- . . ., roofsugtig.
predecease, v. eerder sterwe, vooroorly.
predecease, n. vroeër dood.
predecessor, voorganger; voorvader.
predestinarian, gelower in die voorbeskikkingsleer.
predestinate, voorbeskik, uitverkies.
predestination, predestinasie, voorbeskikking, uitverkiesing.
predestine, vooraf bepaal, voorbeskik.
predetermination, voorbeskikking.
predetermine, vooraf bepaal; predestineer.
predial, landelik, plaas- . . .
predicable, a. bepaalbaar, bevestigbaar.
predicable, n. kenmerk.
predicament, toestand; moeilike posisie.
predicate, n. gesegde; predikaat.
predicate, v. beweer, bevestig, vasstel.
predicative, bevestigend, predikatief.
predict, voorspel, voorsê.
predictable, voorsienbaar, voorspelbaar.
prediction, voorspelling, profesie.
predictor, voorspeller.
predilection, voorliefde; partydigheid.
predispose, voorbestem, predisponeer.
predisposition, aanleg, vatbaarheid, neiging, predisposisie.
predominance, oorhand, mag, gesag.
predominant, oorheersend.
predominate, die oorhand hê, oorheers, bobaas wees; in die meerderheid wees, die vernaamste deel uitmaak van.
pre-elect, vooraf (ver)kies.
pre-eminence, voortreflikheid; voorrang.
pre-eminent, uitstekend, voortreflik.
pre-empt, opsie verkry oor, vooruitkoop.
pre-emption, voorkoop, opsie.
preen, die vere gladstryk; – **onself**, jou uitvat (mooimaak).
pre-engage, vooraf verbind.
pre-establish, vooraf bepaal.
pre-establishment, voorafgaande vasstelling.
pre-exist, vooraf bestaan.
pre-existence, voorbestaan.
pre-existent, vooraf bestaande.
prefab, **prefabricated building**, opslaangebou.
preface, n. voorwoord, inleiding.
preface, v. inlei.
prefatory, inleidende, voorafgaande.
prefect, hoof, prefek; opsigter-leerling.
prefecture, prefektuur, prefeksamp.
prefer, verkies, voorkeur gee aan, meer hou van liewer wil hê, prefereer; bevorder; inlewer, indien; – **a statement**, 'n verklaring indien.
preferable, verkieslik.

preferably, liewers, by voorkeur.
preference, voorkeur; voorrang; preferensie; – **share**, preferente aandeel.
preferential, begunstigend, preferent; – **debts**, prioriteitskulde.
preferment, verhoging, bevordering.
prefiguration, voorafgaande voorstelling.
prefigure, vooraf voorstel.
prefix, n. voorvoegsel, prefiks.
prefix, v. vooraan voeg, vooraan plaas.
prefixion, vooraanvoeging.
preform, vooraf vorm.
pregnable, inneembaar, verowerbaar.
pregnancy, swangerskap; dragtigheid; betekenisvolheid, gewig(tigheid).
pregnant, swanger, in die ander tyd, dragtig, bevrug; vrugbaar; betekenisvol, veelbetekenend, veelseggend; – **with**, swanger van, vol (van).
prehensible, grypbaar.
prehensile, gryp- . . .; – **tail**, grypstert.
prehension, begrip.
prehistoric, voorhistories.
prehistory, voorgeskiedenis.
pre-ignition, voorontsteking.
prejudge, vooruit (ver)oordeel.
prejudice, n. vooroordeel, partydigheid; nadeel, skade; **to the – of**, tot skade van.
prejudice, v. afbreuk doen aan, benadeel; bevooroordeeld maak.
prejudiced, bevooroordeeld.
prejudicial, nadelig, skadelik.
prelacy, prelaatswaardigheid, prelaatskap; die prelate (biskoppe).
prelate, prelaat, kerkvader.
prelatess, abdis, priores.
prelature, prelaatsamp; die prelate.
prelect, n. voorlesing hou.
prelection, (voor)lesing.
prelibation, voorsmaak.
preliminary, n. inleiding, voorbereiding.
preliminary, a. voorafgaande, inleidend(e), voorbereidend(e), preliminêr.
prelude, n. inleiding, voorspel.
prelude, v. inlei; preludeer.
premature, voorbarig, ontydig; te vroeg.
prematurity, voorbarigheid, ontydigheid.
premeditate, vooraf bedink (beraam).
premeditated, met voorbedagte rade (gedaan), voorbedag; – **murder**, moord met voorbedagte rade.
premeditation, voorbedagtheid, opset, voorafgaande beraming, premeditasie.
premier, n. eerste minister, premier.
premier, a. eerste, beste, vernaamste.
première, eerste opvoering, première.
premiership, eersteministerskap.
premise, **premiss**, n. voorafgaande stelling, premis; –**s**, plek, huis en erf, gebou, werf; **will be sold on the –s**, sal op die plek (ter plase) verkoop word.
premise, v. vooropstel.
premium-rate, assuransietarief.
premium, beloning, prys; premie; onderriggeld; opgeld; **at a –**, bo pari.
premolar, voorkiestand.
premonition, waarskuwing, voorteken.
premonitory, waarskuwend.
prentice, sien **apprentice**.
preoccupation, vroeëre inbesitneming; vooroordeel; afgetrokkenheid.
preoccupied, afgetrokke, mymerend, in gedagte versonke.
preoccupy, vooraf in besit neem; in beslag neem; (die gedagte) besig hou.

preordain, vooraf bestem (bepaal).
preparation, voorbereiding; voorbereidsel, klaarmakery; preparaat.
preparative, voorbereidend.
preparatory, voorbereidings- ...; voorbereidend; – **school**, voorbereidingskool; – **to sending it**, voordat dit weggestuur word.
prepare, (voor)berei, gereed maak, klaarmaak, oplei; prepareer; **be –ed**, bereid wees; – **yourself for**, jou voorberei (klaarmaak) vir.
prepay, vooruitbetaal.
prepense, opsetlik, voorbedag; **of malice –**, met voorbedagte rade.
preponderance, oorwig.
preponderant, oorwegend.
preponderate, oorweeg, swaarder weeg, die deurslag gee; – **over**, in getal oortref; van groter belang wees as.
preposition, voorsetsel.
prepositive, voorgevoeg, vooraan geplaas.
prepositor, opsigter-leerling, prefek.
prepossess, beïnvloed, (vooraf) besit neem van.
prepossessing, innemend.
prepossession, vroeëre inbeslagneming; vooringenomenheid.
preposterous, ongerymd, belaglik, gek.
prepotent, oppermagtig.
prepuce, voorhuid.
prerequisite, a. noodsaaklik, vereis.
prerequisite, n. noodsaaklike vereiste.
prerogative, prerogatief, privilegie, reg, voorreg; **royal –**, prerogatief van die kroon.
presage, n. voorteken; voorgevoel.
presage, v. voorspel; 'n voorbode wees.
presbyopic, versiende.
presbyopia, versiendheid, presbiopie.
presbyter, ouderling, priester.
Presbyterian, a. Presbiteriaans.
Presbyterian, n. Presbiteriaan.
presbytery, (kerklike) ring; pastorie.
prescience, voorkennis, voorgevoel.
prescient, vooruitsiende, vooruitwetend, met die helm gebore.
prescind, afsny.
prescribe, voorskryf; voorskrifte neerlê.
prescript, wet, voorskrif, bevel.
prescription, resep, voorskrif; (die) voorskryf, gewoontereg, verjaring.
preselective, vooruitbepaalde.
presence, teenwoordigheid, aanwesigheid; houding, voorkome; – **of mind**, teenwoordigheid van gees; **a man of noble –**, 'n man van edel voorkome.
presence-chamber, oudiënsiesaal.
present, a. teenwoordig, aanwesig; teenswoordig, huidig; onderhawig; **in the – case**, in die onderhawige geval; **the – writer**, skrywer hiervan; – **tense**, teenwoordige tyd; **at the – day**, teenswoordig, hedendaags.
present, n. die teenwoordige, die hede; **at –**, nou, op die oomblik; **for the –**, voorlopig.
present, n. geskenk, present.
present, v. voorstel, introduseer; (ver)toon, wys; oplewer; indien, voorlê; aanbied, present gee; presenteer; – **oneself**, jou aanmeld; – **a ragged appearance**, 'n treurige vertoning maak; – **arms**, presenteer geweer; **when opportunity –s itself**, as die geleentheid hom voordoen; – **your compliments to**, jou klagte indien by.
presentable, presentabel, fatsoenlik.
presentation, aanbieding; voorstelling, vertoning; indiening; presentasie.
presentation-copy, presenteksemplaar.
presentee, voorgestelde; begiftigde, ontvanger van geskenk.

presentient, met 'n voorgevoel.
presentiment, voorgevoel.
presently, netnou, aanstons (aans), oor 'n rukkie, strakkies; dadelik daarop.
presentment, (klag)indiening; voorstelling.
preservation, bewaring, behoud, redding.
preservative, a. bewarend, behoudend, behoed- ...
preservative, n. voorbehoedmiddel, preservatief, bederfweringsmiddel.
preserve, n. konfyt, ingelegde vrugte; wildpark; visdam.
preserve, v. beswaar, beskerm, behoed, behou; inlê, inmaak.
preside, voorsit, die voorsitterstoel beklee, presideer; lei, bestuur.
presidency, voorsitterskap; presidentskap.
president, voorsitter; president.
presidential, voorsitters- ...
presidentship, presidentskap.
presidium, presidium.
press, n. gedrang, druk, drukte; drang, haas, gejaagdheid; menigte; pers; (druk)pers, drukkery; kas; **in the –**, word nou gedruk, ter perse; **go to –**, ter perse gaan; – **agent**, reklame-agent.
press, v. druk, pers; pars; platdruk, saamdruk; aandring; opdring, dwing, aanspoor, haastig maak; **time –es**, die tyd word kort, daar is haas; **I am –ed for space**, my ruimte is (baie) beperk; – **for an answer**, op 'n antwoord aandring; – **forward**, vooruitdring, vooruitbeur; – **on**, vortmaak, gou maak, opdruk; **hard –ed**, in die nou, in die knyp.
press-button, drukknop(pie); – **war**, drukknopoorlog.
press-cutting, koerantuitknipsel.
press-gallery, persbank.
pressing, dringend; dreigend; – **invitation**, dringende uitnodiging.
pressman, joernalis, persman; drukker.
pressmark, stempel, boeknommer.
pressure, druk, drukking; aandrang, pressie; moeilikheid; **atmospheric –**, lugdruk; **do something under –**, iets haastig doen; iets onder dwang doen; – **burst**, drukbars; – **cooker**, drukpot, drukkastrol.
pressure-gauge, drukmeter.
pressurize, drukvas maak; –**d cabin**, drukkajuit; –**d aircraft**, drukvaste vliegtuig.
prestidigitation, goëlery.
prestidigitator, goëlaar.
prestige, reputasie; prestige; gesag.
presto, vinnig, snel, presto.
presumably, vermoedelik.
presume, veronderstel vermoed, aanneem; waag, die vryheid neem; – (**up)on**, misbruik maak van.
presuming, verwaand, aanmatigend.
presumption, vermoede, veronderstelling; verwaandheid, onbeskaamdheid.
presumptive, waarskynlik, vermoedelik.
presumptuous, verwaand, vermetel, astrant, aanmatigend.
presuppose, aanneem, veronderstel.
presupposition, veronderstelling.
pretence, skyn, voorwendsel; reg, aanspraak; **under the – of**, onder voorwendsel van.
pretend, voorgee, maak asof, beweer; – **to something**, aanspraak maak op iets; – **to be clever**, voorgee om slim te wees; – **illness**, siekte voorwend, maak of jy siek is.
pretender, aanspraakmaker, pretendent.
pretending, aanmatigend; huigelagtig.

pretention, aanspraak, aanmatiging, pretensie; verwaandheid.
pretentious, pretensieus, aanmatigend; pronkerig; verwaand.
preterhuman, bomenslik.
preterite, preteritum, verlede tyd.
preterition, weglating, veronagsaming.
pretermission, uitlating, weglating.
pretermit, uitlaat, weglaat, veronagsaam, nalaat; oorslaan.
preternatural, bonatuurlik; onnatuurlik.
pretext, voorwendsel; ekskuus; **on**, **under**, **upon the** – **of**, onder die skyn (voorwendsel) van.
pretor, sien **praetor**.
prettily, mooi, smaakvol, netjies.
prettiness, mooiheid; gesogtheid.
pretty, a. mooi, lief, aanvallig, aansienlik; **you have made a** – **mess of things**, jy het sake mooi verbrou; **my** –, my liefie, my skatjie.
pretty, adv. taamlik; – **ill**, net (taamlik) siek; – **much the same**, min of meer (ongeveer) dieselfde.
pretty-pretty, oordrewe mooi, strooplief.
prevail, die oorhand kry; heers, in swang wees, algemeen wees; – **on**, ompraat, oorhaal.
prevailing, heersend, algemeen.
prevalence, oorhand, oorwig; (die) heers.
prevalent, oorwegend; heersend; **sickness is** – **here**, siekte heers hier.
prevaricate, rondspring, uitvlugte soek, jakkalsdraaie maak.
prevarication, uitvlugsoekery, bontpratery.
prevaricator, bontprater, uitvlugsoeker.
prevenient, voorafgaande, vorige.
prevent, verhinder, belet, verhoed; teëhou; voorkom.
preventative, sien **preventive**.
prevention, verhindering, verhoeding, afwering, voorkoming.
preventive, n. voorbehoedmiddel.
preventive, a. voorbehoed- . . ., voorsorgs- . . ., afwerend; – **custody**, preventiewe hegtenis.
preview, voorskou; voorvertoning.
previous, a. vorige, voorafgaande; voorbarig.
previous, adv. voor(dat); – **to my coming**, voor my koms.
previously, ventevore, vooraf, vooruit.
previse, vooruitsien, voorspel.
prey, n. prooi; buit, roof; slagoffer; **bird of** –, roofvoël.
prey, v.: – **upon**, roof, plunder, aas op, as prooi begeer; – **upon the conscience**, aan die gewete knae.
price, n. prys; waarde; **without** –, onbetaalbaar, nie vir geld te koop nie; **what is the** – **of it?**, wat kos dit?
price, v. prys vasstel; na die prys vra.
price-list, pryslys.
priceless, onbetaalbaar; kostelik.
prick, n. steek; prik; prikkel; stippeltjie, gaatjie; kwelling, wroeging; –**s of conscience**, gewetenswroeging.
prick, v. prik, steek, oopsteek, 'n gaatjie steek in; aanspoor, aansit; spits; kwel; knaag; – **up the ears**, die ore spits.
pricker, priem, prikkel, els, steekding.
prickle, n. prikkel, doring, pen.
prickle, v. steek, prik.
prickly, stekerig, steek- . . ., doringrig, doring- . . .; prikkelend, jeuk- . . .; – **heat**, rooihond; – **pear**, turksvy.
pride, n. hoogmoed, hovaardigheid; fierheid, trotsheid, trots; – **will have a fall**, hoogmoed kom voor die val; **take a** – **in**, trots wees op; **his mother's** –, sy ma se oogappel.

pride, v.: – **oneself (up)on**, jou roem op, trots wees op.
priest, priester, geestelike.
priestcraft, priesterlis, -beleid.
priestess, priesteres.
priesthood, priesterskap.
priest-in-the-pulpit, varkblom, geelpiet in die manteljas.
priestly, priesterlik, priester- . . .
priest-ridden, onder die priesterlike plak.
prig, pedant, wysneus; dief.
priggish, pedant(ies), verwaand, eiewys.
priggism, pedanterie, verwaandheid.
prim, presies, netjies, agtermekaar, piekfyn; styf gemaak, aanstellerig; – **and proper**, danig sedig.
prima, vernaamste, eerste, prima; – **donna**, eerste sangeres, prima donna.
primacy, primaatskap; voorrang.
primage, premie.
primal, primitief; vernaamste, grond- . . .
primary, vroegste, oorspronklike; eerste, primêr, elementêr; vernaamste; – **education**, laer onderwys; **of** – **importance**, van die grootste belang; – **school**, primêre skool, laerskool; – **colours**, primêre kleure, hoofkleure.
primate, aartsbiskop, primaat.
prime, n. begin, eerste stadium; lente; jeug, bloeityd; priemgetal; **the** – **of life**, die bloei van die lewe.
prime, a. vernaamste, belangrikste, eerste, prima, eersteklas; primêr; fundamenteel, oorspronklik; – **cattle**, eersteklas vee; – **number**, ondeelbare getal, priemgetal; – **cost**, inkoopsprys; – **mover**, voorman, leidende persoon; – **minister**, eerste minister.
prime, v. laai, kruit in die pan gooi; onderrig, afrig; inpomp; grondlaag gee.
primer, leesboekie, boek vir beginners; gebedeboek.
prim(a)eval, primitief, oorspronklik, eerste, oer- . . .; – **forest**, oerwoud.
priming, pankruit; grondverf.
primitive, oudste, oorspronklike, eerste, oer- . . .; outyds, primitief.
primogeniture, eersgeboortereg.
primordial, oorspronklik, eerste, oer- . . ..
primrose, sleutelblom.
prince, prins; vors, heerser; **P– of Peace**, Vredevors; – **of darkness**, vors van die duisternis; **P– of Wales**, Prins van Wallis; – **royal**, kroonprins; – **consort**, prins-gemaal; –**'s metal**, prinsmetaal.
princedom, prinsdom, vorstedom.
princely, vorstelik; skitterend.
princess, prinses; vorstin; – **royal**, kroonprinses.
principal, a. vernaamste, belangrikste, hoof- . . .; – **clause**, hoofsin(sdeel).
principal, n. hoof; hoofonderwyser, prinsipaal; hoofpersoon, baas direkteur, lasgewer; kapitaal; hoofsom.
principality, vorstedom.
principally, hoofsaaklik, grotendeels.
principle, beginsel, grondslag, grondbeginsel; prinsipe; **on** –, uit beginsel.
principled, beginselvas.
prink, opskik, uitdos; die vere gladstryk.
print, n. druk, afdruk; spoor, merk, teken; prent, plaat; sis; **out of** –, uitverkoop, nie te kry nie; **in** –, in druk, gedruk; nog verkrygbaar in die handel; – **dress**, sisrok.
print, v. afdruk, merk, stempel; druk, uitgee, publiseer; in drukletter skryf; inprent; –**ed matter**, drukwerk.
printer, drukker; –**'s error**, drukfout.

printing, druk; drukwerk.
printing-ink, drukink.
printing-press, drukpers.
prior, n. kloosterhoof, prior.
prior, adv. vroeër, voorafgaande, eerste.
prior, adv. vroeër voor; – **to his appointment**, voor sy aanstelling.
prioress, priores.
priority, prioriteit, voorkeur, voorrang.
priorship, prioraat, priorswaardigheid.
prise, sien **prize**.
prism, prisma.
prismatic, prisma- . . ., prismaties.
prison, gevangenis, tronk.
prisoner, gevangene, prisonier; bandiet; **take** –, gevange neem; – **of state**, politieke gevangene; – **of war**, krygsgevangene.
prison warder, tronkbewaarder, sipier.
pristine, vroeër, eerste oorspronklik, ou.
prithee: **tell me**, –, sê my tog.
privacy, afsondering, stilte, eensaamheid, geheimhouding.
private, a. privaat, persoonlik, eie; geheim, vertroulik, konfidensieel; afgesonder; – **clothes**, burgerklere; – **parts**, geslagsdele; – **property**, privaateiendom; – **law**, privaatreg; – **lesson**, privaatles; – **school**, privaatskool; **in** –, alleen, in die geheim; onder vier oë.
private, n. gewone, soldaat.
privateer, kaper, kaperskip.
privateering, kaapvaart.
privately, privaat, alleen, in die geheim.
privation, ontbering, gebrek.
privative, berowend; ontkennend.
privilege, n. voorreg; privilegie.
privet, liguster.
privilege, v. bevoorreg; vrystel.
privileged, bevoorreg.
privity, medewete; wetlike verhouding.
privy, n. privaat, sekreet, kleinhuisie.
privy, a. geheim, afgesonder(d), heimlik, verborge; **P– Council**, Geheimde Raad; – **seal**, geheimseël; **be – to**, bekend wees met; aandadig wees aan.
prize, n. prys, beloning; buit; prysskip.
prize, n. hefboom.
prize, a. bekroonde, prys- . . .; – **poem**, bekroonde gedig.
prize, v. waardeer, op prys stel, ('n skip) buit maak, prysmaak.
prize, v. oopmaak, oopbreek.
prize-fight, bokswedstryd, vuisgeveg.
prize-fighter, vuisvegter, bokser.
prizeman, pryswinner.
pro, n. sien **professional**.
pro, voor; – **and con**, voor en teë.
probability, waarskynlikheid; gebeurlikheid; **in all** –, na alle waarskynlikheid.
probable, waarskynlik.
probably, vermoedelik, waarskynlik.
probate, verifikasie van 'n testament.
probate-duty, boedelbelasting.
probation, proeftyd; ondersoek; voorwaardelike vrylating.
probationary, proef- . . .
probationer, proefleerling; leerling-verpleegster.
probative, proef- . . .
probe, n. peilstif, wondyster.
probe, v. peil, ondersoek; sondeer.
probity, opregtheid, eerlikheid.
problem, probleem, vraag(stuk), werkstuk, opgaaf; raaisel.
problematic(al), twyfelagtig, onseker, problematies.
proboscis, snuit, slurp, neus.

procedural, prosedure-, proses-.
procedure, handelwyse, werkwyse, metode, prosedure.
proceed, voortgaan, verder gaan, vervolg; te werk gaan; ontstaan, voortkom uit; – **against**, saak maak ('n aksie instel) teen; – **with the game**, die spel voortsit, verder gaan met die spel.
proceeding, handelwyse, gedragslyn; verrigting; –**s**, verrigtinge, handelinge; stappe, maatreëls; **institute legal –s against**, 'n aksie instel teen; –**s of the Royal Society**, handelinge van die Koninklike Genootskap.
proceeds, opbrings, wins(te).
process, loop, gang, voortgang, ontwikkeling; metode; hofsaak; regsgeding; proses; **in – of construction**, in aanbou; **in – of time**, met verloop van tyd.
procession, optog, stoet, prosessie; **funeral** –, lykstoet, lykstasie.
processional, a. prosessie- . . .
processional, n. prosessielied.
proclaim, aankondig, afkondig, bekend maak, proklameer, verklaar; uitroep.
proclamation, aankondiging, afkondiging, bekendmaking; proklamasie.
proclitic, proklities.
proclivity, neiging, oorhelling.
proconsul, prokonsul.
proconsulship, prokonsulskap.
procrastinate, uitstel, sloer, talm.
procrastination, uitstel, gesloer, getalm; – **is the thief of time**, van uitstel kom afstel.
procreate, verwek, teel, voortbring.
procreation, voortplanting, voortteling.
proctor, tugmeester; saakwaarnemer.
procumbent, vooroor, plat, uitgestrek.
procurable, verkrygbaar.
procuration, verkryging; volmag, prokurasie.
procurator, gevolmagtigde; prokurator.
procure, (ver)kry, besorg, verskaf; veroorsaak.
procurement, verkryging, verskaffing.
procurer, verskaffer, koppelaar.
procuress, koppelaarster.
prod, n. priem, steekding; prikkel.
prod, v. steek; aanspoor, aanpor.
prodigal, n. deurbringer, verkwister.
prodigal, a. deurbringerig, verkwistend, verspillend; oorloedig, rojaal; **the P– Son**, die Verlore Seun.
prodigalize, verspil, verkwis, deurbring.
prodigality, verspilling, verkwisting, deurbringerigheid; kwistigheid.
prodigious, wonderbaarlik, verbasend; enorm, ontsaglik, kolossal, ongehoord.
prodigy, wonder(mens), wonderkind.
prodrome, voorloper; voorteken, voorbode.
produce, n. produkte, voortbrengsels, oes; opbrings, produksie; resultaat.
produce, v. opbring, oplewer; veroorsaak, teweegbring; aanvoer, lewer; uithaal, toon, wys; opvoer, op die toneel bring; uitgee; verleng; voortbring, in die wêreld bring; produseer; – **a sensation**, 'n opskudding veroorsaak; – **a line**, 'n lyn verleng.
producer, produsent; opvoerder, regisseur; uitgewer.
product, produk, voortbrengsel.
production, voortbrenging, produksie; voortbrengsel, produk; opvoering, voorstelling; verlenging.
productive, produserend; produktief, vrugbaar.
productivity, produktiwiteit, vrugbaarheid.
proem, voorrede, voorwoord; proloog.
profanation, ontheiliging, skending.

profane, a. ongewyd; heidens; oneerbiedig, profaan; – **writer**, ongewyde skrywer.
profane, v. skend, ontheilig.
profanity, goddeloosheid, godslastering, heiligskennis, oneerbiedigheid.
profess, verklaar, erken; bely, betuig; voorgee, aanspraak maak **op**; les gee, onderwys, doseer.
professed, erkende; beweerde, verklaarde, aangegewe beroeps- . . .
professedly, kastig, openlik; oënskynlik.
profession, verklaring, belydenis, erkentenis; beroep, professie; **by** –, van beroep, beroeps- . . . .
professional, a. professioneel, beroeps- . . ., vak- . . .; – **men**, vakmanne; – **cricketer**, beroepskrieketspeler; – **jealousy**, broodnyd, beroepsnaywer.
professional, n. beroepspeler; vakman.
professionalism, beroepsport.
professor, belyer; professor, hoogleraar.
professorial, professoraal.
professorship, professorskap, professoraat.
proffer, n. aanbod.
proffer, v. aanbied, aanpresenteer.
proficiency, bekwaamheid, knapheid, bedrewenheid, meesterskap.
proficient, bekwaam, knap, bedrewe.
profile, n. profiel; vertikale deursnee; karakterskets.
profile, v. profileer, in profiel teken.
profit, n. wins, voordeel, profyt; nut; **at a** –, met wins; – **and loss**, wins en verlies.
profit, v. profiteer, wins maak, wen, voordeel trek uit; baat, help; **what will it** – **you**, wat sal dit jou baat?
profitable, voordelig, winsgewend.
profiteer, v. woekerwins maak, jou sal vul.
profiteer, n. profiteerder, woekerwinsmaker.
profiteering, woekerwins.
profligacy, losbandigheid, ontugtigheid.
profligate, a. losbandig, ontugtig.
profligate, n. losbandige, losbol.
profound, diep(gaande), diepsinnig; deeglik, grondig; **a** – **sleep**, 'n diep(e) slaap.
profundity, diepte, diepsinnigheid; deeglikheid; grondigheid.
profuse, mild, vrygewig, kwistig, oordadig; oorvloedig, volop.
profusion, mildheid; oorvloed, oordaad.
progenitive, teel- . . ., voortplantend, voortplantings- . . .
progenitor, voorvader, voorsaat.
progeniture, afstammelinge, nakomelingskap; verwekking.
progeny, nakomelinge, nageslag, kroos, afstammelinge; resultaat, gevolg.
prognathous, met uitsteek-kakebene.
prognosis, voorspelling, prognose.
prognostic, a. aanduidend, voorspellend.
prognostic, n. voorteken; voorspelling.
prognosticate, voorspel, aandui.
prognostication, voorteken; voorspelling.
prognosticator, voorsêer, voorspeller.
programme, program.
progress, n. vooruitgang, voortgang, vordering, ontwikkeling; reis; **now in** –, nou aan die gang.
progress, vooruitgaan, vordering maak, vorder.
progression, opklimming, reeks, progressie; **arithmetical** –, rekenkundige reeks.
progressional, vorderend, vooruitgaande.
progressionist, progressis, progressief.
progressive, n. sien **progressionist**.
progressive, a. progressief, vooruitstrewend;

toenemend; – **party**, progressiewe party; **a** – **nation**, 'n vooruitstrewende nasie.
prohibit, belet, verbied; **smoking is –ed**, hier word nie gerook nie, rook is verbode.
prohibition, prohibisie, (drank)verbod.
prohibitionist, afskaffer, prohibisionis.
prohibitive, verbiedend, belettend, verbod- . . ., prohibitief; – **prices**, onmoontlike pryse afskrikkende pryse.
project, n. plan, ontwerp, skema.
project, v. beraam, ontwerp, oorlê; uitskiet; projekteer, 'n projeksie-tekening maak; uitsteek.
projectile, n. projektiel; bom; gooiding.
projectile, a. skiet- . . ., voortdrywend.
projection, (die) uitgooi; ontwerp, projeksie, die uitsteek; (uitstekende) punt.
projective, projekterend, projeksie- . . .
projector, planmaker, beramer; projeksielamp.
prolapse, v. afsak, uitsak, val, (uit)glip.
prolapse, n. afsakking, breuk.
prolegomenon, inleiding.
prolepsis, prolepsis, antisipasie.
proletarian, n. proletariër, onbemiddelde.
proletarian, a. proletaries.
proletariat(e), proletariaat.
prolific, vrugbaar; **be** – **of**, veel oplewer, ryk wees aan.
prolix, langdradig, wydlopig, uitvoerig.
prolixity, langdradigheid, wydlopigheid.
prolocutor, voorsitter, woordvoerder.
prologue, voorspel, voorrede, inleiding, proloog.
prolong, verleng, langer maak, (uit)rek.
prolongation, uitstel, verlenging termynverlenging, prolongasie.
prolusion, proef, voorspel.
promenade, n. wandelpad, promenade.
promenade, v. op en neer loop, op en af kuier, wandel, promeneer.
prominence, uitstekendheid, vernaamheid, belangrikheid; beroemdheid; vername plek; punt; **give** – **to**, op die voorgrond bring, onder die aandag bring, goed laat uitkom.
prominent, eminent, uitstekend, voortreflik, hoog, vernaam; in die oog vallend; vooruitstekend.
promiscuity, deureenmenging, gemengdheid, verwarring.
promiscuous, deurmekaar; gemeng; verward; toevallig; – **massacre**, moord voor die voet.
promiscuously, voor die voet, sonder onderskeid, deurmekaar; toevallig.
promise, n. belofte; jawoord; **a player of great** –, 'n veelbelowende speler; **the land of** –, die beloofde land.
promise, v. belowe, toesê, verseker, jou woord gee; **I** – **you, it will not be so easy**, ek verseker jou dit sal nie so maklik gaan nie; **the –d land**, die beloofde land.
promisee, ontvanger (van 'n belofte).
promising, veelbelowend.
promiser, belower.
promissory, belowend, bindend; – **note**, promesse, skuldbewys.
promontory, kaap, voorgebergte.
promote, bevorder, verhoging gee, vooruithelp, oorsit; promoveer; bespoedig; oprig, op tou sit.
promoter, bevorderaar, voorstander; oprigter; promotor; bestuurder.
promotion, verhoging, bevordering, promosie.
prompt, a. vlug, snel, spoedig, onmiddellik, stip, pront, vaardig, fluks; kontant; – **payment**, stipte (kontante) betaling.

prompt, v. aanhits, aanspoor, aansit; inspireer, besiel; voorsê, influister.
prompt-box, souffleurshokkie.
prompter, voorsêer, souffleur.
prompting, aansporing, aanhitsing; (die) voorsê; –s, ingewing, stem.
promptitude, snelheid, vlugheid, vaardigheid, stiptheid, prontheid.
promulgate, bekend maak, afkondig; uitvaardig, proklameer; versprei.
promulgation, bekendmaking, afkondiging; uitvaardiging, proklamasie.
promulgator, bekendmaker, afkondiger.
prone, vooroor, plat (op die gesig), uitgestrek; afdraand, steil; – **to,** geneig tot; onderhewig aan.
prong, n. (hooi)vurk, ystergaffel; tand.
prong, v. (met 'n vurk) steek.
prong-buck, takbok, gaffelbok.
pronominal, voornaamwoordelik.
pronoun, voornaamwoord; **demonstrative** –, aanwysende voornaamwoord; **indefinite** –, onbepaalde voornaamwoord; **interrogative** –, vraende voornaamwoord, **personal** –, persoonlike voornaamwoord; **possessive** –, besitlike voornaamwoord; **relative** –, betreklike voornaamwoord.
pronounce, uitspreek, verklaar, uitspraak doen; – **sentence of death,** die doodvonnis uitspreek.
pronounceable, uitspreekbaar.
pronounced, beslis; sterk, skerp.
pronouncement, verklaring, uitspraak.
pronunciation, uitspraak.
pronouncing, (die) uitspraak; – **dictionary,** uitspraakwoordeboek.
pronto, op die daad, gou-gou.
proof, n. bewys(grond); blyk; proef, toets (druk)proef; sterktegraad; **in – of my statement,** as bewys van my bewering; **the – of the pudding is in the eating,** ondervinding is die beste leermeester; **bring to the –,** op die proef stel; **burden of –,** bewyslas.
proof, a. beproef, bestand; ondeurdringbaar, onkwesbaar; – **against the rain,** bestand teen die reën, waterdig.
proof, v. bestand maak teen; waterdig maak.
proofreader, proefleser.
proofsheet, drukproef.
prop, n. steun(pilaar), pilaar, stut; staatmaker; skroef; toneelrekwisiet.
prop, v. (onder)steun, stut.
propaedeutic, voorbereidend, inleidend.
propaedeutics, propedeutika.
propagandize, propaganda maak.
propagandist, propagandis.
propagandistic, propagandisties.
propagate, voortplant, versprei, propageer.
propagation, voortplanting, verspreiding.
propagator, voortplanter, verspreier, propageerder.
propel, (voort)dryf, vooruitstoot.
propellent, n. dryfkrag.
propellent, a. dryf– . . ., voortdrywend.
propeller, drywer; skroef (van stoomboot).
propensity, geneigdheid, neiging.
proper, eie; eintlik, reg, gepas, juis, geskik; eg; behoorlik, welvoeglik, fatsoenlik, betaamlik; – **name,** eienaam; – **fraction,** egte breuk; **literature** –, eintlike (werklike) letterkunde; **a – fight,** 'n egte bakleiery.
properly, behoorlik, fatsoenlik; eintlik; met reg.
property, eienskap, hoedanigheid; eiendom, goed, besitting; **properties,** eienskappe; toneelbenodigdhede; **immovable** –, vaste eiendom, vasgoed; **movable** –, roerende goed, losgoed.

prophecy, profesie, voorspelling, voorsegging.
prophesy, profeteer, voorspel, voorsê.
prophet, profeet, siener.
prophetess, profetes.
prophetic, profeties; **be – of,** voorspel.
prophylactic, n. voorbehoedmiddel.
prophylactic, a. voorbehoed– . . .
propinquity, nabyheid, buurt; ooreenkoms; verwantskap.
propitiate, versoen, paai, bevredig, gunstig stem, mak maak.
propitiation, versoening, bevrediging.
propitiatory, n. genadetroon.
propitiatory, a. soen– . . ., gunstig, stemmend, versoenend.
propitious, gunstig, genadig.
prop-jet, skroefturbinemotor.
propolis, byewas.
proportion, verhouding, eweredigheid, proporsie; deel; **in** –, na eweredigheid (verhouding); **out of all** –, buite alle verhouding, oneweredig; **in – as,** namate, na gelang; **–s,** afmetinge.
proportional, n. eweredige deel.
proportional, a. eweredig, proporsioneel; – **mean,** middeleweredige.
proportionally, na eweredigheid, eweredig, proporsioneel.
proportionate, a. eweredig, proporsioneel.
proportionate, v. eweredig maak.
proposal, voorstel, aanbod; aansoek.
propose, voorstel, aanbied; voornemens wees, van plan wees; ('n meisie) vra; – **the health of,** die heildronk instel op; **man –s, God disposes,** die mens wik, maar God beskik.
proposition, voorstel; aanbod; stelling, probleem; **a business** –, 'n handelstransaksie; **a paying** –, 'n betalende saak (onderneming).
propound, voorstel, aanbied, voorlê.
proprietary, a. eienaars– . . ., eiendoms– . . ., besittend; – **medicines,** patente medisyne; – **rights,** eiendomsregte.
proprietary, n. eiendomsreg; eienaar(s).
proprietor, eienaar, besitter.
proprietress, eienares.
propriety, juistheid, korrektheid; gepastheid; welvoeglikheid, fatsoenlikheid, behoorlikheid.
props, toneelbenodigdhede.
propulsion, voortdrywing, voortstoting, (die) drywe; dryfkrag; dryfveer.
propulsive, voortdrywend, dryf– . . .
propylaeum, tempelingang, voorhof.
prorogation, verdaging, opskorting.
prorogue, verdaag, opskort, uitstel.
prosaic, prosaïes, alledaags, gewoon.
prosaist, prosaskrywer, prosaïs.
proscenium, voortoneel, proscenium.
proscribe, verban, voëlvry verklaar, buite die wet stel; verwerp, veroordeel.
proscription, verbanning, voëlvryverklaring, veroordeling.
prose, n. prosa; alledaagsheid.
prose, a. prosa– . . .
prose, v. in prosa oorsit; sanik, seur.
prosector, prosektor.
prosecute, vervolg; voortsit; uitoefen; **trespassers will be –d,** oortreders sal vervolg word.
prosecution, vervolging; voortsetting; uitoefening; **the –,** die vervolging.
prosecutor, vervolger; **public** –, publieke aanklaer.
proselyte, bekeerling, proseliet.
proselytize, bekeer, bekeerlinge maak.
proselytism, proselietmakery.
prosify, in prosa oorsit; prosa skrywe.
prosodic, prosodies.

prosody, prosodie.
prospect, n. uitsig, vergesig; vooruitsig, hoop, verwagting, kans; 'n moontlike.
prospect, v. prospekteer, ondersoek; – **for**, soek na; – **well**, veel belowe.
prospective, te wagte; toekomstige, aanstaande; vooruitsiende; vooruitwerkend; **the – bridegroom**, die aanstaande bruidegom.
prospector, prospekteerder, prospektor.
prospectus, prospektus.
prosper, voorspoedig wees, bloei, floreer, vooruitgaan; begunstig, seën.
prosperity, voorspoed, bloei, welvaart.
prosperous, voorspoedig, bloeiend, florerend, welvarend; gunstig, gelukkig.
prostate, voorstanderklier, prostaat.
prosthesis, voorvoeging, protese.
prostitute, n. hoer, prostituee.
prostitute, v. onteer, aan ontug oorgee, prostitueer.
prostitution, ontering, prostitusie.
prostrate, a. uitgestrek; neergebuig; ootmoedig; verneder; uitgeput.
prostrate, v. neerwerp, onderwerp, verneder; neerbuig; verniel; uitput.
prostration, neerwerping; vernedering; neerbuiging, uitputting, swakheid.
prostyle, portiek.
prosy, vervelend, langdradig, saai.
protagonist, leier, voorman, hoofpersoon.
protasis, voorwaardelike sin, protasis.
protean, veranderlik, onbestendig.
protect, beskerm, bewaar, behoed, beveilig, vrywaar; ('n wissel) dek.
protection, beskerming, bewaring, beveiliging, beskutting; proteksie.
protectionism, proteksionisme.
protectionist, n. proteksionis.
protectionist, a. proteksionisties.
protective, beskermend; – **duties**, beskermende regte; – **custody**, beskermende bewaring.
protector, beskermer, beskermheer.
protectorate, protektoraat.
protectorship, beskermheerskap.
protectress, beskermster, beskermvrou.
protégé, beskermling, protégé.
protein, proteïen.
protest, n. protes, (teen)verklaring; **make a** –, protesteer, protes aanteken; **under** –, onder protes.
protext, v. protesteer; plegtig verklaar.
Protestant, n. Protestant.
Protestant, a. Protestants.
protestant, a. protesterend.
Protestantism, Protestantisme.
protestation, verklaring; protes.
prothalamium, bruilofslied.
protium, protium.
proto: – **team**, protospan.
protocol, protokol, akte, oorkonde.
protogenic, primêr.
protomartyr, eerste martelaar.
protoplasm, protoplasma.
prototype, model, prototipe.
protozoa, laagste dierklasse, protosoë.
protract, rek, verleng, uitstel; volgens skaal teken.
protractile, rekbaar, verlengbaar.
protraction, verlenging, rekking.
protractor, graadboog; strekker.
protrude, (voor)uitsteek.
protrusion, (die) vooruitsteek, vooruitsteking, uitsteeksel.
protrusive, vooruitstekend.
protuberance, knop, bult, swelsel.

protuberant, opgeswel, uitpuilend, uitpuil- . . ., uit-(peul- . . .), knop- . . .
proud, hoogmoedig, verwaand, hovaardig, trots, fier; groots; pragtig; **it was a – sight**, dit was 'n gesig waarop 'n mens kon trots wees; **you do me** –, jy doen my 'n groot eer aan; – **flesh**, nuwe vleis, welige vleis (by 'n genesende wond).
prove, bewys; openbaar, toon, wys; blyk; op die proef stel, probeer, beproef; – **to be true**, blyk waar te wees, bewaarheid word; – **to be a fool**, blyk 'n gek te wees.
provenance, herkoms.
provender, voer; kos, voedsel, proviand.
proverb, spreekwoord, spreuk; **Book of Proverbs**, Spreuke (van Salomo); **his laziness is a** –, sy luiheid is spreekwoordelik.
proverbial, spreekwoordelik.
proveant, proviand.
provide, voorsien, sorg vir, verskaf; voorsorg maak (vir); bepaal, neerlê; **I have to – against that**, ek moet maatreëls neem daarteen, daarvoor moet ek sorg; **I am –d for**, ek het al die nodige; **the law –s that** . . ., die wet bepaal dat . . .
provided, op voorwaarde dat, mits, as.
providence, voorsiening, voorsorg; **P**–, die Voorsienigheid.
provident, voorsienings- . . ., versigtig; spaarsaam; – **fund**, voorsieningsfonds.
providential, van die Voorsienigheid; wonderlik; gelukkig toevallig.
provider, verskaffer, besorger.
province, provinsie, gewes, afdeling; vak, gebied, sfeer, bestek; **that does not come within my** –, dit is buitekant my vak, dit val nie in my gebied nie.
provincial, provinsiaal; gewestelik.
provincialism, provinsialisme.
provision, n. voorsiening, voorsorg; bepaling; –**s**, voorraad kos, lewensmiddels, proviand, provisie.
provision, v. van lewensmiddels voorsien, mondvoorraad verskaf.
provisional, voorlopig, provisioneel.
proviso, bepaling, voorwaarde.
provisor, kerklike amptenaar, hoof.
provisory, voorwaardelik, voorlopig.
provocation, provokasie, uitdaging, uittarting; belediging; **without the least** –, sonder die minste aanleiding.
provocative, n. aanleidende oorsaak.
provocative, a. uitda(g)end, tergend; **be – of**, aanleiding gee tot, prikkel tot.
provoke, aanhits, prikkel, opwek; uitdaag, tart, gaande maak, uitlok; beledig, vererg.
provoking, tartend, prikkelend, ergerlik.
provost, hoof; opsiener; provoos.
prow, boeg, voorstewe.
prowess, dapperheid, moed.
prowl, n. rooftog, strooptog; loer; **on the** –, op die loer; op roof uit.
prowl, v. op roof uit wees, rondsluip.
proximate, naaste, eerste onmiddellik.
proximity, nabyheid; – **of blood**, bloedverwantskap; – **fuse**, jagbombuis.
proximo, aanstaande (maand).
proxy, volmag; gevolmagtigde; **get married by** –, by volmag trou, met die handskoen trou; **vote by** –, by volmag stem.
prude, preutse (dame).
prudence, versigtigheid, omsigtigheid; verstandigheid, wysheid.
prudent versigtig, omsigtig; verstandig.
prudential, versigtig, verstandig.

prudentials, verstandige maatreëls.
prudery, preutsheid, skynsedigheid.
prudish, aanstellerig, preuts, skynsedig.
prune, n. pruimedant; donkerrooi, pers.
prune, v. snoei; besnoei; sny.
prunella, wolstof; prunella.
pruning-knife, snoeimes.
pruning-shears, snoeiskêr, wingerdskêr.
prurience, pruriency, wellus, wulpsheid, vleeslike begeerte, jeukerigheid.
prurient, wellustig, wulps, jeukerig.
pruriginous, jeukerig, jeuk-...
prurigo, jeuksiekte, huidsiekte.
Prussian, n. Pruis.
Prussian, a. Pruisies; – **blue**, pruisiesblou, berlynsblou.
prussic acid, pruisiessuur, blousuur.
pry, tuur, nuuskierig kyk na, loer; – **into somebody's affairs**, jou neus in iemand se sake steek.
prying, snuffelend, nuuskierig, loer-...
psalm, psalm.
psalmist, psalmdigter, psalmis.
psalmodist, psalmdigter.
psalmody, psalmgesang, psalmodie.
psalter, psalmboek.
pseudo, oneg, vals; sogenaamd, pseudo.
pseudonym, skuilnaam, pen(ne)naam.
pseudonymous, pseudoniem.
pshaw, ba, ag!
psittacosis, papegaaisiekte.
psyche, gees, siel, psige.
psychiater, psychiatrist, psigiater.
psychiatric, psigiatries.
psychiatry, psigiatrie.
psychic, a. psigies, siels-..., spiritisties.
psychic, n. spiritistiese medium.
psychoanalyse, psigoanaliseer.
psychoanalysis, psigoanalise.
psychological, psigologies, sielkundig.
psychologist, psigoloog, sielkundige.
psychology, psigologie, sielkunde.
psychomancy, geestebeswering.
psychosis, psigose, sielsiekte.
ptarmigan, sneeuhoender.
pteridology, varingstudie.
Ptolemaic, Ptolemeïes.
ptomaine, ptomaïne; – **poisoning**, ptomaïnevergiftiging, voedselvergiftiging.
pub, kantien, drinkplek, kroeg.
puberty, puberteit, geslagsrypheid.
pubescence, geslagsrypheid; donsies.
pubescent, geslagsryp; donserig.
public, n. publiek; drinkplek; **the reading** –, die lesende publiek; **in** –, in die openbaar, in die publiek.
public, a. publiek, openbaar, algemeen; **a – enemy**, 'n volksvyand; – **school**, openbare skool, volkskool; – **spirit**, burgersin; **give – utterance**, in die openbaar verkondig, openbaar maak, wêreldkundig maak; – **relations**, skakeldiens; voorligting(swerk); – **relations officer**, inligtings-, reklamebeampte.
publican, kantienbaas, tollenaar.
publication, bekendmaking, openbaarmaking, uitgawe, publikasie.
public-house, kroeg, kantien, herberg.
publicist, joernalis, dagbladskrywer.
publicity, publisiteit, bekendheid, openbaarheid, rugbaarheid; – **agent**, reklameagent.
public-spirited, met 'n gevoel vir die algemene welsyn.
publish, bekend maak, rugbaar maak; uitroep, afkondig; publiseer, uitgee.
publisher, uitgewer.

puce, donkerbruin, persbruin.
puck, kabouter, elf; stouterd, ondeug.
pucker, n. rimpel, plooi.
pucker, v. vou, plooi, frons, rimpel.
pudding, poeding; (soort) wors; **black** –, bloedwors.
pudding-face, vollemaansgesig.
pudding-head, domkop.
pudding-heart, lafaard, bangbroek.
pudding-stone, poedingsteen.
puddle, n. modderplas, modderpoel; klei; warboel, deurmekaarspul; gemors.
puddle, v. plas, modderig maak; mors; poedel, pleister.
puddly, vuil, modderig.
pudency, beskeidenheid, nederigheid.
pudenda, skaamdele.
pudge, dikkerd, buks, vaatjie.
pudic, van die skaamdele.
puerile, kinderagtig; beuselagtig, niksbeduidend.
puerility, kinderagtigheid.
puerperal, kraam-..., geboorte-...; – **fever**, kraamkoors, bedkoors.
puff, n. rukwind; asemstoot; trek, haal; rookwolkie, damp; pof; poeierkwas; poffertjie; reklame, ophemeling.
puff, v. blaas, hyg, trek, pof, puf; opblaas; opswel; aanprys, ophemel, reklame maak; opja; **I was** –**ed**, ek was uit-asem; **he** –**ed at his pipe**, hy het aan sy pyp getrek; – **away the dust**, die stof wegblaas; –**ed up with conceit**, opgeblase van verwaandheid.
puff-adder, pofadder.
puffer, spogger, windsak; bluffer; opjaer.
puffin, seeduiker.
puffiness, winderigheid; swelsel.
puffy, winderig; kortasem; uit-asem; dik, opgeblaas, swaarlywig; bombasties.
pug, n. mopshond; jakkals.
pug, n. steenklei.
pug, v. klei aanmaak; met klei opvul.
pugg(a)ree, hoedwindsel, alabama.
pugilism, (die) boks, vuisvegtery.
pugilist, bokser, bakleier, vuisvegter.
pugilistic, boks-..., vuisvegters-...
pugnacious, vegterig, twissoekerig, bakleierig, strydlustig.
pugnacity, vegterigheid, strydlustigheid.
pug-nose, mopneus, stompneus, platneus.
puisne, van later datum; van laer rang; – **judge**, juniorregter.
puissance, mag, gesag.
puissant, magtig, invloedryk.
puke, opbring, vomeer, braak, opgooi.
pule, piep, tjank, huil, grens, skreeu.
pull, n. ruk, pluk, trek; trekker, knoppie (van 'n klokkie); trekskoot; roeitoggie; eerste drukproef; teug, sluk; voordeel, voorsprong; **it is a** –, dit is 'n lang roeitog; dit is 'n hele ent.
pull, v. ruk, pluk, trek; roei; – **his ears**, sy ore trek; **you are trying to – my leg**, jy probeer om met my die gek te skeer; – **something to pieces**, iets uitmekaar pluk; iets afbrekend beoordeel; – **faces**, gesigte trek, skewe-bek trek; – **about**, heen en weer pluk; **the building was** –**ed down**, die gebou is afgebreek; **I think he will – it off**, ek dink hy sal dit regkry; **he was so ill that I never thought he would – through**, hy was so siek dat ek nooit gedink het hy sou deur kom nie; **they don't – together**, hulle trek nie saam nie, daar bestaan geen samewerking tussen hulle nie; **he** –**ed himself together**, hy het nuwe moed geskep, hy het hom reggeruk; – **up**, stilhou; gaan staan; optrek; uittrek; op sy plek sit; – **up one's socks**, jou lyf roer, opdruk.

pull-back, remskoen, struikelblok.
pullet, jong hoender, kuiken.
pulley, n. katrol.
pulley, v. met 'n katrol ophys.
pullicate, gekleurde sakdoek.
Pullman-car, slaapsalon.
pull-over, oortrek-trui.
pullulate, uitspruit, uitloop, bot.
pulmonary, long- . . .; – **disease**, longkwaal; – **consumption**, longtering.
pulmonic, n. longmiddel; lyer aan longkwaal.
pulmonic, a. long- . . .
pulp, n. vleis (van vrugte), sagte massa, moes, pap, pulp.
pulp, v. pap maak; papsag word.
pulpit, preekstoel, kansel.
pulpous, pulpy, sag, pap.
pulsate, klop, slaan; tril.
pulsatile, slag- . . .
pulsation, slag, klop(ping), polsslag.
pulsatory, kloppend, klop- . . ., slag- . . .
pulse, n. pols, polsslag; trilling; **feel the** – die pols voel; pols.
pulse, n. peulvrug.
pulse, v. klop, slaan, pulseer; tril.
pulsimeter, polsmeter.
pulsometer, pulsometer.
pultaceous, pap, sag.
pulverization, fynmaking, fynstamping.
pulverize, fyn stamp, fyn maal, tot poeier maak; stof word; pulveriseer; verslaan, vernietig, vermorsel.
pulverulent, poeieragtig, fyn, bepoeier, vol stof; bros, krummelrig.
puma, poema, Amerikaanse leeu.
pumice, puimsteen.
pummel, moker, stamp, opdons.
pump, n. pomp; dansskoen.
pump, v. pomp, oppomp, uitpomp, leegpomp; uitvra, uithoor; **try to** – **it out of him**, hom probeer uitvra.
pump-handle, pompslinger.
pumpkin, pampoen.
pumpkin-fritter, pampoenkoek(ie).
pun, n. woordspelling.
pun, v. woordspelinge maak; vasstamp.
punch, n. deurslag, dryfyster; knipper; opstopper, vuisslag, hou; pons; dikkerd, diksak; hanswors; **he was as pleased as** –, hy was hoog in sy skik; **P- and Judy**, Jan en Tryn; **P- and Judy show**, poppekas, Jan Klaassenspel.
punch, v. gate inslaan, knip; steek; 'n opstopper gee, moker.
punch-bowl, ponskom.
puncheon, vat; stutpaal.
Punchinello, hanswors; dikkerd, vetsak.
punctate, gestippel, bont, skimmel.
punctilio, nougesetheid; formaliteit.
punctilious, puntenerig, nougeset.
punctual, presies, stip, noukeurig; op tyd.
punctuality, presiesheid, stiptheid.
punctuate, interpunkteer, leestekens insit, onderbreek, in die rede val; krag bysit, nadruk lê op.
punctuation, leestekens, interpunksie.
punctum, punt, stip, kolletjie.
puncture, n. prik, gaatjie, lek(plek).
puncture, v. prik, 'n gat insteek.
puncture-proof, lekvry.
pundit, geleerde.
pungency, skerpheid; bitsigheid.
pungent, skerp, bytend, prikkelend, pikant, bitsig, vinnig.
Punic, Punies.

punish, straf, kasty; toetakel, inpeper, bewerk, links en regs moker.
punishable, strafbaar.
punishment, straf, boete.
punitive, straffend, straf- . . .; – **expedition**, strafekspedisie.
punk, vrot hout; swam; hoer.
punka(h), waaier.
punner, (vas)stamper.
punster, maker van woordspelinge.
punt, n. pont, platboomskuit.
punt, v. voorstoot, vooruitboom.
punt, n. hoogskop.
punt, v. hoog skop.
punt, n. speler, wedder.
punt, v. vir geld speel; wed.
puny, klein, swak, tingerig, pieperig.
pup, n. klein (jong) hondjie; **in** –, dragtig; **conceited** –, verwaande snuiter; **sell somebody a** –, iemand in die nek kyk (beetneem).
pup, v. jong, kleintjies kry.
pupa, papie.
pupil, leerling, skolier; onmondige, minderjarige, pleegkind; oogappel; pupil.
pupil(l)age, leertyd; onmondigheid.
pupil(l)ary, minderjarig; oogappel- . . .
pupil(l)ise, onderrig gee, leer.
pupil-teacher, kwekeling (kwekelinge).
puppet, (draad)pop, marionet; speelbal; – **state**, vasalstaat.
puppet-play, poppespel.
puppet-show, poppespel.
puppetry, poppespel; skyn.
puppet-valve, springklep.
puppy, jong hond(jie); lafbek, snuiter.
puppyism, lafheid, lafbekkery.
purblind, half-blind, bysiende; bot.
purchasable, verkrygbaar, koopbaar.
purchase, n. koop, aankoop; verwerwing, (die aanskaf, verkryging; hefboom, katrol, meganiese krag; vat(plek); **by** –, deur aankoop; **make –s**, inkopies doen.
purchase, v. koop, verwerf, kry, aanskaf; optrek, oplig, ophys.
purchase-money, koopprys, inkoopsprys.
purchaser, koper.
pure, rein, suiwer, skoon; ongemeng; eg, kuis, vlekloos; louter, puur; – **mathematics**, reine wiskunde; – **nonsense**, pure onsin.
purfle, n. borduurkant.
purfle, v. versier, omboor, omsoom.
purgation, purgasie; suiwering.
purgative, n. purgeermiddel, purgasie.
purgative, a. purgeer- . . .; suiwerend.
purgatory, a. suiwerend, suiwerings- . . .
purgatory, n. va(g)evuur.
purge, v. skoonmaak, reinig, suiwer; – **the army**, skoonskip maak van ongewenstes in die leër.
purge, n. purgeermiddel; suiwering.
purification, reiniging, suiwering.
purificative, reinigend, suiwerend.
purificatory, sien **purificative**.
purifier, reiniger, suiweraar, skoonmaker.
purify, reinig, suiwer, louter.
Purim, Purim(fees), Hamansfees.
purism, purisme, taalsuiwering.
purist, purish, taalsuiweraar.
Puritan, n. Puritein.
Puritan, a. Puriteins.
Puritanical, Puriteins.
Puritanism, Puriteinse leer.
purity, reinheid, suiwerheid; kuisheid.
purl, n. borduurdraad; geborduurde (gestikte) rant; aweregse breisteek.
purl, v. borduur, omboor; aweregs brei.

purl, v. kabbel.
purl, n. gekabbel, gemurmel, kabbeling.
purlieu, grens, perk; –s, buitewyk, kant, rant; agterbuurte.
purlin, dwarsbalk, hanebalk.
purloin, steel, ontfutsel, skaai.
purple, n. purper, pers; purperkleed, konings-, kardinaalskleed, koninklike waardigheid; **be raised to the** –, tot kardinaal verhoog word; **born in the** –, koninklike afkoms.
purple, a. purper, pers.
purplish, persagtig, purperagtig.
purport, n. betekenis, bedoeling, sin.
purport, v. bedoel; behels, bevat.
purpose, n. oogmerk, plan, bedoeling, opset, doel, doeleinde; **it does not serve the** –, dit beantwoord nie aan die doel nie; **it will not alter my** –, dit sal my nie van plan laat verander nie; **a novel with a** –, 'n tendensroman; **on** –, opsetlik, met opset, ekspres; **to no** –, sonder gevolg, tevergeefs; **to the** –, ter sake.
purpose, v. beoog, van plan wees.
purposeful, doelbewus.
purposeless, doelloos, vrugteloos.
purposely, ekspres, opsetlik.
purpositive, doelbewus, met 'n doel.
purpura, purpelslak; binnehuidbloeding.
purpuric, purper-. . ., skarlaken-. . .; – **fever**, skarlakenkoors.
purr, spin, snor, snork.
purse, n. beursie, geldsakkie; beurs; som geld; sakkie; **he has a heavy, long** –, hy is 'n bemiddelde man, hy sit daar goed in; **put up a** –, prys uitloof.
purse, v. plooi, op 'n plooi trek, frons.
purse-bearer, penningmeester, tesourier.
purse-proud, trots op (jou) geld.
purser, betaalmeester, administrateur.
purse-seine, saknet.
purse-strings, die koorde van die beurs; **hold the** –, oor die geld beskik, die koorde van die beurs in hande hê; **tighten (loosen) the** –, suinig met die geld te werk gaan (die hand in die sak steek, ruimskoots gee).
purslane, porselein.
pursuance, uitvoering, nakoming, voortsetting; **in** – **of**, ingevolge.
pursuant, ooreenkomstig, ingevolge.
pursue, vervolg; nastreef, najaag; voortgaan met, voorsit, uitoefen; volg; nasit, agtervolg; – **one's object**, jou doel nastrewe.
pursuit, vervolging; najaging, nastrewing, voortsetting, uitoefening; agtervolging; –s, belange, arbeid, besigheid, werk, studie; **scientific** –s, wetenskaplike studies (navorsinge); – **of knowledge**, strewe na kennis; – **plane**, jagvliegtuig.
pursy, kortasem; dik, vet.
pursy, geplooi.
purtenance, harslag; ingewande.
purulence, etterigheid, vuilgoed.
purulent, etterig, etterend, swerend.
purvey, verskaf, lewer, voorsien (van).
purveyance, verskaffing; proviandering.
purveyor, leweransier, verskaffer; **p**– **to the royal household**, hofleweransier.
purview, inhoud, strekking, omvang.
pus, etter.
push, n. stoot, stamp druk; voorwaartse poging; volharding, deursettingsvermoë, pit; nood, moeilikheid, knel, knyp; bende; **if it comes to the** –, as dit begin knyp, as dit daarop aankom; **give the** –, die trekpas gee.
push, v. stoot, stamp, druk; aanhelp, aansit, voorthelp; deurdryf; bevorder; uitbrei, voort-
gaan met; aandring; – **one's way**, deurdruk; – **for payment**, op betaling aandring; **be** –**ed for time**, baie min tyd hê; – **away**, wegstoot, wegstamp; – **back**, terugstoot, terugstamp; – **down**, afdruk, afstoot; – **off**, afstoot; – **on**, aanspoor, aansit; aanstoot, deurdruk, opdruk; vooruitstoot; – **out**, uitsteek; uitstoot.
push-bike, trapfiets.
push-cart, stootkarretjie.
pushful, vooruitstrewend, haastig.
pushing, stoot-. . .; ondernemend, fluks, wakker; indringerig.
pusillanimity, lafhartigheid, papbroekerigheid, kleinmoedigheid.
pusillanimous, lafhartig, papbroekerig, lamsakagtig, kleinmoedig; kleinsielig.
puss, kat(jie), kietsie; haas; tier; meisie.
pussy, katjie, kietsie, kattie.
pussy-foot, saggies loop; versigtig handel.
pustular, vol puisies, puisieagtig.
pustule, puisie, vratjie, sweertjie.
put, n. (die) gooi, stoot (van 'n gewig).
put, v. sit, stel, plaas; steek; stoot; uitdruk, sê; **clearly** –, duidelik uitgedruk; – **about**, omdraai, laat omdraai; lastig val; – **across**, na die oorkant roei; laat inslaan, ingang laat vind; fop; – **away**, wegsit, bêre, spaar; opeet, wegslaan; opsluit; – **back**, terugsit; agteruitsit; weer op sy plek sit; – **by**, ontwyk; verbygaan; bêre, spaar, opsy sit, wegsit; – **down**, neersit, neerlê; onderdruk; op sy plek sit, afjak; neerskryf; – **down for**, beskou as, skat op; – **down to**, toeskryf aan; opskryf vir; – **forth**, uitsteek; uitvaardig; – **forth your strength**, al jou kragte inspan; – **forth buds**, uitloop, bot; – **forth leaves**, blare kry; – **forward**, voor die dag kom met, indien, huldig, verkondig; op die voorgrond dring; – **in**, insit, insteek; indien, voorlê; aanstel; aangaan, (by 'n hawe) aankom; – **in an appearance**, opdaag; jou gesig wys; – **in black and white**, neerskryf; – **in prison**, in die tronk sit; – **in order**, in orde bring, regmaak; – **in a word for one**, vir iemand 'n goeie woordjie doen; – **in a word**, ook 'n woordjie te sê kry; – **in a few hours**, 'n paar uur uur wy (bestee) aan; – **into English**, in Engels vertaal; – **into words**, in woorde uitdruk, onder woorde bring; – **a knife into**, met 'n mes steek; – **off**, uitstel; ontwyk; teleurstel, afskeep; uitvlugte soek; – **off from**, afraai; – **on**, aantrek; aanneem; aanstel; aan die werk sit; byvoeg; – **it on**, oordryf; te veel vra; – **on weight**, swaarder word; – **money on a horse**, op 'n perd wed; – **on a clock**, 'n horlosie vorentoe sit; – **out**, uit lit raak, verstuit; uitboul; doodmaak, doodblaas, (lig) afslaan, uitknip; blus; lastig val, ongerief veroorsaak; deurmekaar maak, verleë maak, van die wysie bring; (geld) belê, uitsit; – **out of countenance**, van die wysie bring; – **out of temper**, vererg, boos maak; – **out of the way**, ontslae raak van, doodmaak; – **a bullet through somebody**, iemand 'n koeël deur die lyf ja; – **me through to number 48**, sluit my met nommer 48 aan; – **to bed**, in die bed sit; – **to school**, in die skool sit, skool toe stuur; – **to good use**, goeie gebruik maak van; – **a stop to**, 'n einde maak aan; **I** – **it to you**, ek vra jou; – **to death**, om die lewe bring; – **to flight**, op die vlug ja; **he was hard** – **to it**, hy het dit benoud gehad; – **together**, saamstel, bymekaar sit; – **up**, op die toneel bring; opslaan (prys), duurder maak; opstuur; voorstel; afkondig; aanbied; bêre, wegsit; loseer, tuisgaan; bou; knoei; – **somebody's back up**, iemand die hoenders in maak; – **up for sale**, opveil; – **up**

with, verdra, verlief neem; – **up to**, aansit, aanhits; – **up banns**, gebooie afkondig.
putative, veronderstelde, vermeende.
putrefaction, verrotting; (die) vrot.
putrefactive, vrottend (verottend).
putrefy, bederwe, vrot (verrot), sleg word; sweer; ontaard.
putrescence, v(er)rotting.
putrescent, v(er)rottend, v(er)rottings- . . .
putrid, vrot (verrot), stink; bedorwe.
putridity, vrotheid (verrotheid).
putt, rolslag (gholf).
puttee, beenwindsel, beenband.
putter, rolstok.
putty, stopverf (stokverf).
puzzle, n. moeilikheid, verleentheid; vraagstuk, raaisel; knoop; sukkelspel.
puzzle, v. verwar, in die war bring, hoofbrekens gee; **be –d over a problem**, nie weet hoe om 'n vraagstuk op te los nie; – **out**, ontsyfer, oplos, uitpluis.
puzzle-head, warkop.
puzzle-headed, verward, deurmekaar.

pygmean, dwergagtig, dwerg- . . .
pygmy, n. dwerg, pigmee.
pygmy, a. dwerg- . . ., dwergagtig.
pyjamas, slaapklere, slaappak, pijamas.
pyramid, piramiede.
pyramidal, piramidaal.
pyre, brandstapel.
pyretic, koorswekkend; koors- . . .
pyrexia, koors.
pyrheliometer, (son)warmtemeter.
pyrites, piriet.
pyrogallic acid, pirogallol.
pyrolatry, vuuraanbidding.
pyromania, brandstigtingsmanie.
pyrometer, hittemeter.
pyrotechnic, n. vuurwerkkuns.
pyrotechnic, a. vuurwerk- . . .; skitterend.
pyrotechnist, vuurwerkmaker.
Pyrrhic, van Pyrrhus; – **victory**, Pyrrhusoorwinning.
python, luislang, piton.
pyx, monstrans; muntkissie.
pyxis, dosie, kissie.

Q

quack, n. gekwaak.
quack, v. kwaak.
quack, n. kwaksalwer; windbek, grootprater; – **remedies**, kwaksalwermiddels.
quack, v. kwaksalwer; grootpraat.
quackery, kwaksalwery; grootpratery.
quackish, kwaksalweragtig.
quad, sien **quadrangle**.
quadragenarian, a. veertigjarig.
quadragenarian, n. veertigjarige.
quadrangle, vierhoek; vierkant; binneplaas, binneplein.
quadrangular, vierhoekig; vierkantig.
quadrant, kwadrant, hoekmeter.
quadrantal, regsydig, kwadrant- . . .; – triangle, regsydige driehoek.
quadrate, n. vierkant.
quadrate, a. vierkant(ig).
quadratic, n. vierkantsvergelyking.
quadratic, a. vierkants- . . ., tweedemags- . . ., kwadraat; – **equation**, vierkantsvergelyking.
quadrennial, vierjaarliks; vierjarig.
quadrilateral, a. viersydig.
quadrilateral, n. vierhoek.
quadrilingual, viertalig.
quadrille, kadriel.
quadrillion, kwadriljoen.
quadripartite, vierdelig.
quadrisyllabic, vierlettergrepig.
quadrivium, quadrivium.
quadroon, halwe baster, kwartnaatjie.
quadrumanous, vierhandig.
quadruped, n. viervoetige dier.
quadruped, a. viervoetig.
quadruple, n. viervoud.
quadruple, a. viervoudig.
quadruple, v. viervoudig.
quadruplet, viertal; –s, vierling.
quadruplex, viervoudig.
quadruplicate, n. in –, in viervoudige kopie (afskrif).
quadruplicate, a. viervoudig.
quadruplicate, v. verviervoudig.
quadruplication, verviervoudiging.
quaestor, skatmeester, kwestor.
quaff, drink (met groot slukke), sluk.
quag, moeras, deurslag.
quagga, kwagga.
quaggy, moerasagtig, moeras- . . .
quagmire, moeras, vlei; modderpoel.
quail, n. kwartel.
quail, v. bang word, moedeloos word, beswyk, vrees inboesem.
quaint, eienaardig, raar, sonderling, ouderwets, snaaks.
quake, n. trilling, siddering, skud(ding).
quake, v. skud, bewe, sidder.
Quaker, Kwaker.
Quakerism, Kwakerleer.
Quaker's-meeting, Kwakersbyeenkoms.
quaking-grass, bewertjies.
qualification, kwalifikasie, bevoegdheid; bekwaamheid, vereiste, voorbehoud; modifikasie, wysiging, beperking; eienskap.
qualified, bekwaam, geskik, bevoeg, gekwalifiseer; geregtig.
qualify, bekwaam, (bevoeg) maak; jou bekwaam (vir 'n taak), finale eksamen aflê, eed aflê; kwalifiseer; beperk, wysig, matig; bepaal.
qualitative, kwalitatief.
quality, kwaliteit, gehalte; eienskap, kenmerk, hoedanigheid; kapasiteit, rang, stand; **the –
of his voice**, die toonkleur (timbre) van sy stem; **give a taste of one's –**, wys wat jy kan doen.

qualm, mislikheid; beswaar, wroeging; **–s of conscience**, gewetenswroeging.
qualmish, naar, mislik.
quandry, moeilikheid, verleentheid; **be in a –**, in die verleentheid wees, in die knyp (verknorsing) sit.
quant, stok, paal.
quantification, hoeveelheidsbepaling.
quantify, die hoeveelheid bepaal.
quantitative, kwantitatief.
quantity, kwantiteit, hoeveelheid, klomp menigte; **he is a negligible –**, hy kan buite rekening gelaat word.
quantity-mark, lengteteken.
quantity-surveyor, bestekopmaker.
quantum, hoeveelheid bedrag, kwantum.
quarantine, kwarantyn, afsondering.
quarantine, v. onder kwarantyn stel, isoleer, afsonder.
quarrel, n. twis, rusie, onenigheid, geskil; **pick a –**, rusie soek.
quarrel, v. twis, rusie maak, skoor, kyf; **don't – with jour bread and butter**, moenie in jou eie lig staan nie, moenie jou eie ruite stukkend gooi nie.
quarrelsome, rusiemakerig, twissiek.
quarry, n. prooi, slagoffer; wild.
quarry, n. steengroef, klipbreekgat.
quarry, v. (uit)grawe, (klippe) (uit)breek.
quarryman, klipbreker.
quart, kwart, ¼ gelling.
quarter, n. kwart, vierde deel; kwartier; kwartaal; wyk, buurt; verblyf; genade, pardon; **quarter**, 8 boesel; ¼ vadem; –s, kwartiere (van troepe); – **of an hour**, kwartier; – **past six**, kwart oor ses; **the wind blows from all four –s**, die wind waai uit alle hoeke (van al die kante af); **no help from that –**, geen hulp van daardie kant nie; **take up one's –s**, intrek neem; **at close –s**, digby, naby; tromp-op; **ask for –**, om genade smeek; **give no –**, geen kwartier gee nie; **high –s**, hoë kringe.
quarter, v. in vier verdeel; vierendeel; inkwartier; kwartier (wapenkunde).
quarterage, driemaandelikse betaling.
quarter-day, betaaldag.
quarter-deck, agterdek.
quarterly, n. kwartaalblad.
quarterly, a. driemaandeliks, kwartaal- . . .
quarterly, adv. elke drie maande, kwartaalsgewyse.
quarter-master, kwartiermeester.
quartet(te), kwartet, viertal.
quarto, kwarto(formaat); kwartyn.
quartz, kwarts.
quash, nietig verklaar, vernietig, verwerp; platdruk, verpletter.
quasi, kwasi, konsuis (kwansuis), sogenaamd, kastig.
quassia, bitterhout.
quarter-centenary, vierhonderdste verjaardag, vierde eeudag.
quarternary, viertal; vier.
quaternion, viertal.
quarternity, viertal.
quatrain, kwatryn, vierreëlige vers.
quaver, n. agste-noot; triller, trilling.
quaver, v. tril, vibreer, bewe.
quay, kaai, kade, hawehoof.
quayage, kaaigeld.
quean, slegte vrou, slet.
queasy, mislik, walglik; swak.
queen, n. koningin; vrou (in kaartspel); **the – of roses**, die pragtigste roos, pronkroos; – **of clubs**, klawervrou.

queen, v. die koningin speel; koningin maak (skaak); tot koningin kroon.
queen-bee, bykoningin, moederby.
queen-consort, gemalin van die koning.
queen-dowager, koningin-weduwee.
queenhood, koninginskap.
queenly, soos 'n koningin, vorstelik.
queen-mother, koninginmoeder.
queer, a. sonderling, wonderlik, snaaks, raar, eksentriek; verdag, naar, karig, duiselig; **in Q– street**, in die moeilikheid (knyp).
queer, v. bederwe, verbrou; – **the pitch**, die saak bederwe, die spul verbrou.
quell, onderdruk, oorrompel, demp.
quench, blus, doodmaak, uitdoof; les; onderdruk, bedwing, smoor; verminder; afkoel; tot swye bring, stilmaak; – **thirst**, dors les.
quencher, uitblusser; drank, groot glas.
quenchless, onlesbaar, onblusbaar.
querimonious, ontevrede, brommerig.
querist, vraer.
querulous, ontevrede, klaend, brommerig.
query, n. vraag; vraagteken.
query, v. vra, 'n vraag stel; betwyfel; 'n vraagteken by sit.
quest, n. ondersoek; soek; **in – of**, op soek na.
quest, v. soek na; opspoor.
question, n. vraag; kwessie, vraagstuk; twyfel; **put a –**, 'n vraag stel; **beyond all –**, sonder twyfel; **out of the –**, uit die kwessie, geen sprake van nie; **call in –**, betwyfel, in twyfel trek; **the matter in –**, die saak onder bespreking; **that is the –**, dit is die vraag, dit is waar dit op aankom; **put the –**, tot stemming bring; **without –**, sonder twyfel, ongetwyfeld, heeltemal seker.
question, v. vra; ondervra, onder verhoor neem; betwyfel, in twyfel trek, beswaar maak teen.
questionable, twyfelagtig, betwyfelbaar, verdag.
question-mark, vraagteken.
queue, n. haarvlegsel, stert; ry, streep, tou; **form a –**, in 'n ry staan, toustaan.
queue, v. in 'n ry staan, toustaan.
quibble, n. woordspeling, spitsvondigheid; ontwyking; woordestryd.
quibble, v. haarklowe; ontwyk, uitvlugte soek, jakkalsdraaie maak.
quick, n. lewe; **he bites his nails to the –**, hy byt sy naels tot op die lewe (tot op die vleis); **the insult stung him to the –**, die belediging het hom tot in die siel getref; **a republican to the –**, 'n republikein deur en deur (in murg en been).
quick, a. lewendig; gou, snel, vinnig, rats, vlug, skielik, haastig; **the – and the dead**, die lewendes en die dooies; **a – child**, 'n skrander kind; **he has a – temper**, hy is kort van draad (kortgebaken); **a – ear**, 'n fyn oor; **a – eye**, 'n skerp oog; – **to take offence**, liggeraak; **be –**, maak gou, roer jou.
quick, adv. gou, snel, vinnig.
quicken, opwek, aanspoor, aanvuur, aanmoedig; versnel, verhaas.
quickening, verlewendiging, opwekking.
quick-firer, (quick-firing), snelvuurkanon.
quick-grass, kweek.
quicklime, ongebluste kalk.
quickmarch, versnelde pas.
quicksand, wilsand, dryfsand.
quick-sighted, skerp van oog.
quicksilver, kwik(silwer).
quick-tempered, opvlieënd, kort van draad, kortgebaken (kortgebaker).
quick-witted, skerpsinnig, gevat.
quid, pond.
quid, pruim(pie) (tabak), slaaitjie.

quiddity, wesenlikheid; haarklowery.
quidnunc, storiemaker, nuusdraer.
quiescence, berusting, kalmte, stilte, rus.
quiescent, rustig, stil; sluimerend.
quiet, n. stilte, rus, kalmte, vrede.
quiet, a. stil, rustig, kalm, vreedsaam, gerus; bedaard, stemmig; **on the –**, stilletjies, in die stilligheid agteraf.
quiet, v. tot bedaring bring, stil maak, kalmeer; bedaar, stil word.
quietism, berusting, kwiëtisme.
quietist, kwiëtis.
quietude, rus, stilte, kalmte, vrede.
quietus, dood, uitvaart; genadeslag.
quil, n. slagveer, skag; veerpen; tandstoker; (ystervark)pen; fluit spoel.
quill, v. plooi; gare om 'n spoel draai.
quill-driver, klerk, pen(ne)lekker.
quillet, woordspeling, spitsvondigheid.
quilt, n. sprei, deken, veerkombers.
quilt, v. watteer, stik, deurnaai; klop.
quinary, vyftallig, vyfdelig.
quince, kweper; kweperboom.
quingentenary, n. vyfhonderdste gedenkdag, vyfde eeufees.
quingentenary, a. vyfhonderdjarig.
quinine, kinien (kina).
quinquagenarian, vyftigjarige.
quinquennial, vyfjaarliks; vyfjarig.
quinquennium, vyfjarige tydperk.
quinquelateral, vyfsydig.
quinsy, keelontsteking.
quint, kwint; vyfkaart.
quintal, 100 lb., sentenaar, kwintaal.
quintessence, kern, kwintessens.
quintet(te), kwintet; vyftal.
quintillion, kwintiljoen.
quintuple, n. vyfvoud.
quintuple, a. vyfvoudig.
quintuple, v. met vyf vermenigvuldig.
quintuplets, vyfling.
quip, raak gesegde, geestigheid, kwinkslag, spitsvondigheid; skimp.
quire, boek (24 vel papier); katern.
quirk, kwinkslag; uitvlug; streek; krul; streep (in karakter).
quirt, peits, rysweep.
quisling, quisling, (land)verraaier.
quit, a. vry, ontslae; **be – of**, ontslae wees van; **go –**, vry gaan.
quit, v. verlaat, laat vaar, opgee; vertrek, terugbetaal, vergeld; **death –s all scores**, die dood besleg alle geskille; **he –ted himself well**, hy het hom goed van sy taak gekwyt, hy het hom knap gedra.
quitch, kweek.
quite, heeltemal, geheel en al, glad, totaal, absoluut, volkome; – **a disappointment**, 'n hele teleurstelling; **I – like him**, ek hou bepaald van hom; **this is – the thing**, dit is net die ware Jakob; dit is die nuutste mode; – **so**, presies, juistement; – **three hours**, goed drie uur.
quitrent, erfpag, rekonie (rekognisie).
quits, kiet; **I will be – with him yet**, ek sal nog met hom afreken; **now we are –**, nou is ons kiet (gelyk); **cry –**, kiet wees; kiet wees; **they would not cry –**, hulle wou nie kop gee nie.
quittance, kwytskelding; kwitansie, betaling; vergelding.
quiver, n. pylkoker; **have an arrow left in one's –**, nog 'n plan hê, nog nie ten einde raad wees nie; **a – full of children**, 'n groot huisgesin, 'n tros kinders.
quiver, n. trilling, ritseling.
quiver, v. bewe, tril, ril, sidder, ritsel.

qui vive, werda; **on the –**, op die hoede.
quixotic, buitensporig, Don-Quichotterie.
quixotism, Don-Quichotterie.
quiz, n. eksentrieke mens, voëlverskrikker; spotvoël; grap, spotterny; – **contest**, vasvrawedstryd; – **master**, vasvraer, vraesteller.
quiz, v. gekskeer, terg; spottend aankyk.
quizzical, grappig, snaaks, spotlustig.
quizzing-glass, oogglas.
quod, tronk, tjoekie, hok.
quoin, hoek, hoeksteen; keil, wig.

quoit, n. gooiring; **–s**, ringgooi.
quoit, v. ringgooi; skyfgooi (speel).
quondam, gewese, voormalige.
quorum, kworum.
quota, kwota, deel, aandeel.
quotation, aanhaling, sitaat; prysopgawe.
quotation-mark, aanhalingstekens.
quote, aanhaal, siteer; (prys) opgee.
quoth, sê (het gesê).
quotidian, daagliks.
quotient, kwosiënt, uitkoms.

R

rabbet, n. sponning, groef; voeg (naat).
rabbet, v. (ineen)voeg; groef.
rabbi, rabbi, rabbyn.
rabbinical, rabbyns.
rabbinism, rabbinisme, rabbynse leer.
rabbit, konyn; beginner, nuweling; swak speler.
rabbit-hutch, konynhok.
rabble, gespuis, gepeupel, skorrie-morrie.
rabblement, rumoer, lawaai.
rabid, woes, rasend, mal, woedend, dol.
rabies, hondsdolheid.
race, n. snelle vaart; wedren, wedloop; loop; –s, resies(resies).
race, v. hardloop, jaag (ja(e), hol; (resies) ja; vinnig loop, vinnig laat loop.
race, n. ras, geslag, stam, familie, soort; afkoms; **the human** –, die menslik geslag; **of noble** –, van edele afkoms.
race, n. (gemmer)wortel.
racecourse, renbaan, reisie(s)baan.
racehorse, reisie(s)perd, renperd.
race-meeting, reisies (resies), perdewedren.
raceme, blomtros.
racemose, trosvormig.
racer, reisie(s)perd; snelfiets, snelmotor.
rachitis, regitis, Engelse siekte.
racial, ras-...; – **policy**, rassebeleid.
racialism, rassegevoel, rassehaat.
racialist, rassehater.
rack, n. drywende wolke; ondergang, verwoesting; **to go to** – **and ruin**, na die verderf gaan, ten gronde gaan.
rack, n. rak, kapstok; pynbank; **put on the** –, op die pynbank sit; **be on the** –, in die nood wees, in groot spanning verkeer.
rack, v. op die pynbank sit; folter, pynig, martel; afpers; uitput; **a** –**ing headache**, 'n folterende hoofpyn; – **one's brains about**, jou kop breek oor; **a** –**ing cough**, 'n kwellende (folterende) hoes.
racket, racquet, n. raket; –**s**, raketspel; – **press**, raketpers.
racket, n. rumoer, lawaai, geraas, opskudding, tumult; opgewondenheid, vrolikheid; plan, boel; proef; afpersery; swendelary; oneerlike geldmakery (bron van inkomste).
racket, v. lawaai maak.
racketeer, afperser.
racketeering, afpersing, afpersery.
rack-railway, tandratspoorweg.
rack-rent, woekerhuur.
rack-renter, afperser, woeker-huurbaas.
rack-wheel, kamrat, tandrat.
racy, geurig, sterk, kragtig, pittig, pikant, geestig, lewendig, raseg; – **style**, pittige styl; – **of the soil**, raseg.
radar, radar; – **control**, radarleiding.
raddle, n. rooiklei.
raddle, v. rooi verf, rooi smeer.
radial, straalvormig, radiaal, straal-...
radiance, glans, skittering, straling, prag.
radiant, n. uitstralingspunt.
radiant, a. (uit)stralend; skitterend, luisterryk; – **point**, uitstralingspunt; – **with joy**, stralende van geluk.
radiate, a. straalvormig, gestraal.
radiate, v. glinster, skitter; uitstraal; straal; versprei.
radiation, (u it)straling, straalwerping.
radiator, radiator, verwarmingstoestel, elektriese stoof; verkoeler (van 'n motorkar).
radical, n. wortel; grondstof; grondwoord; radikaal.
radical, a. radikaal, fundamenteel, volkome; wortel-..., stam-...; **a** – **change**, 'n radikale verandering; **the** – **idea**, die grondgedagte;– **reform**, algehele hervorming; – **sign**, wortelteken; – **word**, grondwoord.
radicate, laat wortel skiet, inplant.
radicle, worteltjie, wortelkiem.
radio, n. radio, radio(toe)stel; radiodiens, omroep; – **communication**, radioberig; – **operator**, marconis.
radio, v. uitsend, uitsaai; sein.
radioactive, radioaktief.
radiogram, radiogram (telegr.) gramradio.
radiograph, radiogram.
radiography, radiografie.
radio-isotope, radio-isotoop.
radiometer, radiometer.
radiotelegram, radiogram.
radiotherapy, bestraling, radioteropie.
radish, radys.
radium, radium.
radius, radius, straal; speekbeen; omtrek.
radix, wortel, basis.
raff, gespuis, skorriemorrie, gepeupel.
raffia, raffia.
raffish, losbandig, liederlik.
raffle, n. lotery.
raffle, v. loot; uitloot, verloot.
raffle, n. afval, vuilgoed, bog; rommel.
raft, n. vlot; dryfhout.
raft, v. vlot, dryf; op 'n vlot vervoer.
rafter, n. dakspar, kapstuk, balk.
rafter, v. van daksparre voorsien.
raftsman, vlotter.
rag, n. flenter, vod, lap, vadoek (vaatdoek); –**s**, toiings, flenters; **not a** – **of evidence**, nie 'n greintjie bewys nie; **he is the editor of this** –, hy is die redakteur van hierdie vod.
rag, n. leidakpanne, sandsteen.
rag, n. lawaaiparty, jool, luidrugtigheid.
rag, v. uitskel; terg; pla(ag); 'n lawaai maak, 'n plek op horings sit, jol.
ragamuffin, skobbejak, smeerlap.
rag-baby, lappop.
rag-bolt, takbout.
rage, n. woede, toorn, raserny; sug, begeerte, gier, manie; mode; **a grey suit is the** – **nowadays**, 'n grys pak is nou die nuutste mode.
rage, v. woed, raas, tier, tekere gaan; – **itself out**, uitraas.
rag-fair, rommelverkoping.
ragged, ru, ongelyk; gebrekkig; onreëlmatig; geskeur, stukkend, toiingrig, flenterig, verflenter; – **school**, armskool.
ragman, voddekoper, lappiesmous.
ragout, ragout, stoofvleis, bredie.
ragtag (and bob-tail), Jan Rap en sy maat; Piet, Paul en Klaas.
ragtime, sinkopasie; gesinkopeerde musiek.
rag-wheel, kamrat.
ragwort, kruishuid.
raid, n. inval, strooptog; opruiming.
raid, v. inval, 'n inval doen; roof.
rail, n. dwarshout, dwarspaal; leuning; latwerk; spoorstaaf; **off the** –**s**, van die spoor af; **by** –, per spoor.
rail, v. met traliewerk (latwerk) toemaak; per spoor reis (stuur).
rail, v. spot, smaal, beledig, skel, skimp.
rail-head, kopstasie, spoorweghoof.
railing, traliewerk, leuning, reling.
railing, spot, belediging.
raillery, korswel, skerts, jillery.
railroad, spoor(weg), treinspoor.
railway, spoorweg.
railway accident, spoorwegongeluk.
railway board, spoorwegraad.

railway bridge, spoorwegbrug.
railway carriage, spoorwa, treinwa.
railway compartment, (spoorweg)kompartement.
railway engine, lokomotief.
railway journey, treinreis.
railway line, spoorlyn.
railwayman, spoorwegman, -beampte, -werker.
railway rates, spoorwegtariewe.
railway station, spoorwegstasie.
railway ticket, treinkaartjie.
railway warrant, vrybrief, (spoorweg)magbrief, vrykaart.
raiment, kleding, gewaad.
rain, n. reën (reent); a – of **ashes**, 'n asreën.
rain, v. reën (reent); laat reën, laat neerdaal; it **–ed invitations**, uitnodiginge het ingestroom; it **–s cats and dogs**, dit reent oumeide met knopkieries, dit reent dat dit stort; **it never –s but it pours**, 'n ongeluk kom nooit alleen nie; **– blessings upon**, met seëninge oorlaai.
rain-bird, reënvoël.
rainbow, reënboog (reentboog).
rainfall, reënval.
rain-guage, reënmeter.
rain-water, reënwater (reentwater).
rainy, reënagtig, reënerig; **provide against a – day**, iets opsy sit vir die oudag, 'n appeltjie vir die dors bewaar.
raise, optel, oplig, ophelp, laat staan; opwek, oprig; bymekaarmaak, versamel; (op)bou; teel, verwek, aankweek; aanleiding gee tot, veroorsaak; verhoog, verhef, verhoging gee; **– from the dead**, uit die dode opwek; **– the dust**, stof maak; verwarring veroorsaak; **– an objection**, beswaar maak; **– a question**, 'n vraag opper; **no one –d his voice**, niemand het sy stem verhef nie; **– a loan**, 'n lening aangaan; **– an army**, 'n leër op die been bring; **– a siege**, 'n beleg opbreek; **– one's eyes**, opkyk.
raisin, rosyntjie.
raja(h), radja.
rake, n. hark; **as lean as a –**, so maer soos 'n kraai.
rake, v. hark, bymekaarskraap, op 'n hoop hark; naspeur, deursnuffel, oprakel, deursoek; bestryk (van 'n skip); **– up old grievances**, ou griewe oprakel.
rake, n. losbol, swierbol.
rake, n. helling; val; hellingsvlak.
rake, v. oorhang, oorhel.
rakehell, losbol, swierbol.
rakish, losbandig; swierig.
rakish, snelvarend; kaperagtig.
rake-off, kommissie, aandeel.
rally, n. (die) bymekaarkom, reunie, hereniging; herstel, herlewing; hernieude aanval; sarsie (ook in tennis).
rally, v. weer bymekaarbring bymekaarmaak; herenig; herstel; moed skep; moed inpraat; bystaan, te hulp kom; houe verwissel, 'n sarsie maak (tennis).
rally, v. spot, pla(ag), jil, korswel, terg.
ram, n. stormram, muurbreker; ramskip; stamper; ram.
ram, v. (vas)stamp, instamp, inslaan; inprop, instop, inbeur; **– the argument home**, die punt inhamer.
ramal, tak-...
ramble, n. uitstappie, swerftog.
ramble, ronddwaal, rondswerwe; 'n uitstappie maak; afdwaal, van die punt gaan, deurmekaar praat.
rambler, omswerwer; rankroos, klimplant.
rambling, omswerwend; verward, omsamehangend; rankend, klimmend, rank-..., slinger-...; onreëlmatig.

ramification, vertakking.
ramify, vertak, takke gee, takke uitskiet; in takke verdeel.
ram-jet, stustraal: **– aircraft**, stustraalvliegtuig.
rammish, stinkend, stink.
ramose, getak.
ramp, n. helling, skuinste; sprong.
ramp, n. afsettery.
ramp, v. steier; tekeer gaan, stoei.
rampage, n. vermaldheid, wildheid.
rampage, v. gaan tekere, raas, baljaar.
rampancy, verbreidheid, algemeenheid, toeneming.
rampant, heersend, algemeen; ongehinderd; welig, geil; steierend.
rampart, n. wal, skans, borswering.
rampart, v. verskans.
rampion, raponsie.
ramrod, laaistok.
ramshackle, bouvallig, vervalle, lendelam.
rance, gestreepte marmer.
ranch, veeplaas, veeboerdery.
rancher, veeboer.
rancid, galsterig, suur, sterk.
rancidity, galsterigheid.
rancorous, haatdraend.
rancour, haatdraendheid, vyandskap, wrok, bittere haat.
rand, sooltjie; rant (rand); rand **(geldeenheid)**; the **R.**, Witwatersrand, die Rand.
random, n. toeval, geluk; **at –**, op goeie geluk, wildweg, blindweg; los en vas.
random, a. toevallig; **a – shot**, 'n skoot op goeie geluk af, 'n blinde skoot.
randy, luidrugtig, lawaaierig, wild; loops.
range, n. ry, reeks, opeenvolging, aaneenskakeling; rigting, lyn; skietveld; wydte, omvang, perke, grens, bereik, gebied; afstand, draagkrag; kaggel, stoof **– of mountains**, bergreeks, bergteken; **the – of the voice**, die omvang van die stem; **the – of politics**, die gebied van die politiek; **Greek is out of my –**, Grieks is buitekant my gebied; **within –**, binne bereik, onder skoot.
range, v. in 'n ry plaas, (rang)skik; skaar, opstel, plek inneem; reik, uitstrek, loop; varieer; voorkom, te vinde wees; swerwe, dwaal; dra (van 'n geweer); vaar, seil; **his thoughts –d far**, sy gedagtes het ver gedwaal; **it –s over a mile**, dit strek 'n myl ver uit.
range-finder, afstandmeter.
ranger, veldwagter, boswagter; speurhond; swerwer.
rank, n. ry, gelid; rang, stand; graad; staanplek; **the front –**, die voorste ry; **– and file**, die laer rangs, die gewone soldate; die laer stande; **rise from the –s**, van onder af opkom; **join the –s**, soldaat word; aansluit; **people of all –s**, mense aan alle stande; **persons of –**, mense van hoë rang (stand); **give first – to**, die eerste plek toeken aan.
rank, v. (rang)skik, in orde stel, in gelid stel; klassifiseer; stel, plaas; beskou word, geag word; **–s among**, neem 'n plek in onder.
rank, a. welig, geil, vrugbaar, oormatig; galsterig, suur; walglik, onbeskof; wellustig, loops; flagrant, puur, duidelik; **– nonsense**, klinkklare onsin; **– treason**, lae verraad.
rankle, sweer, ontsteek, knaag.
ransack, deursoek, deursnuffel; plunder.
ransom, n. losprys, losgeld; bevryding.
ransom, v. los, vrykoop, bevry; boet.
rant, n. bombas, grootpraat.
rant, v. grootpraat; uitbulder, deklameer.
ranunculus, ranonkel.

rap, n. tik, slag, klop; duit, knip, die minste; **I don't care a –**, dit kan my nie die minste skeel nie.
rap, v. tik, klop; **– at the door**, aan die deur klop; **– out**, uitflap.
rapacious, roofgierig, roofsugtig; gierig.
rapacity, roofsug, gierigheid, hebsug.
rape, n. ontering, verkragting; wegvoering.
rape, v. onteer, verkrag; wegvoer.
rape, n. koolraap, kool(raap)saad.
rapid, n. snelstroom, stroomversnelling.
rapid, a. vlug, vinnig, snel.
rapidity, vlugheid, snelheid.
rapier, rapier.
rapine, roof, plundering.
rapport, mededeling; verband.
rapscallion, skurk, skelm, skobbejak.
rapt, weggevoer, meegesleep; verruk, opgetoeë; versonke; **listen with – attention**, met gespanne aandag luister.
raptorial, roof- ...
rapture, verrukking, ekstase, vervoering, geesdrif; **go into –s**, verruk wees.
raptured, in verrukking, in ekstase.
rapturous, verruk, opgetoeë.
rare, yl, dun; skaars; buitengewoon, seldsaam, ongewoon; pragtig.
rarebit, na-happie, braaikaas.
raree-show, kykkas; buitengewone gesig.
rarefaction, verdunning.
rarefy, verdun, yl maak (word); veredel, verfyn.
rarity, rariteit, seldsaamheid; skaarsheid, ylheid.
rascal, n. skurk, rakker, skelm, karnallie, vabond.
rascal, a. laag, gemeen.
rascality, skurkagtigheid; skurkstreek.
rase, sien **raze**.
rash, n. uitslag.
rash, a. onbesonne, roekeloos, haastig, oplopend, voortvarend.
rasher, snytjie ham (spek).
rasp, n. rasper.
rasp, v. rasper, skraap; kras, krap.
raspberry, framboos; **give someone a –**, iemand uitkoggel (hoon).
rat, n. rot; manteldraaier, oorloper; onderkruiper; **like a drowned, –**, soos 'n nat hoender; **smell a –**, lont ruik; **–s!**, kaf, onsin, bog!
rat, v. rotte vang; oorloop; onderkruip.
ratable, belasbaar.
ratafia, ratafia.
ratal, belasbare bedrag, valuasie.
rataplan, n. getrommel.
rataplan, v. tamboer slaan.
rat-catcher, rotvanger.
ratchet, ratch, vangrat, tandskyf, anker, pal.
rate, n. standaard, maatstaf; skaal, tarief, prys; belasting; tempo, snelheid; koers; graad, klas; **the death –**, die sterftesyfer; **– of interest**, rentekoers, rentevoet; leningskoers; **– of exchange**, wisselkoers; **at that –**, op daardie manier; **at the – of**, teen; **at any –**, in alle (elk) geval; **at a great –**, met 'n groot vaart; **at a high –**, teen 'n hoë prys; **at a – of six miles**, met 'n vaart (snelheid) van ses myl; **first –**, eersteklas; **–s**, plaaslike belastings.
rate, v. skat, waardeer, valueer, takseer, beskou, reken.
rate, v. uitskel, inklim.
ratel, ratel.
rather, liewer(s), eerder, meer; taamlik, nogal, bietjie, enigsins, vry; **– early**, bietjie vroeg; **she is – pretty**, sy is mooierig; **I – think you know him**, ek dink amper jy ken hom; **it was**
– good, dit was nogal goed; **–!**, alte seker! hoe dan anders! ek sou so dink! natuurlik?
ratification, bekragting, goedkeuring.
ratify, bekragtig, ratifiseer.
rating, skatting, valuasie; klas.
rating, teregwysing, skrobbering, afjak.
ratio, verhouding, ratio.
ratiocinate, logies redeneer.
ratiocination, gevolgtrekking, redenering.
ration, n. rantsoen, porsie; **–s**, mondvoorraad, kos, rantsoen.
ration, v. op rantsoen sit, rantsoeneer.
rational, redelik, met rede begaaf; billik, verstandig, rasioneel.
rationalize, verstandelik uitlê (verklaar).
rationalism, rasionalisme, redegeloof.
rationalist, rasionalis.
rationality, redelikheid.
ratlines, touleer, weeflyne.
ratlings, sien **ratlines**.
ratoon, suiker, soetrietspruit.
rat(t)an, rottang, bamboes, spaansriet.
ratten, saboteer, sabotasie pleeg.
rattle, n. ratel; geratel, gerammel; geraas; geroggel; gebabbel, geklets, gekekkel; babbelkous.
rattle, v. ratel, rammel, raas; voortbabbel, klets; aframmel; **– up the anchor**, die anker ophys (ophaal); **– a bill through**, 'n wetsontwerp deurjaag.
rattle-brained, leeghoofdig, ligsinnig.
rattlesnake, rattler, ratelslang.
rattletrap, rammelkas.
rattletrap, a. lendelam.
rattling, ratelend; vinnig, snel; uitstekend, deksels goed; **a – pace**, 'n vinnige vaart.
rat-trap, rotval.
raucous, hees, skor.
ravage, n. vernieling, verwoesting.
ravage, v. vernièl, verwoes, plunder.
rave, 'n reël, reling.
rave, n. geraas.
rave, v. raas, tekeer gaan, yl; uitvaar; dweep (met); in verukking wees (oor).
ravel, n. verwarring; knoop.
ravel, v. verwar; uitrafel, ontwar; **– out**, uitrafel, ontwar.
ravelin, ravelyn.
raven, n. raaf.
raven, a. pikswart.
raven, v. plunder, roof; verslind.
ravenous, vraatsugtig; uitgehonger.
ravin, roof, buit.
ravine, bergkloof, skeur, ravyn.
ravish, wegvoer, ontroof; verkrag, onteer; in verrukking bring, betower.
ravishment, ontrowing, verkragting, ontering, verrukking.
raw, n. seer plek; **touch one on the –**, 'n teer plek aanraak.
raw, a. rou, ongekook; ru, onbewerk; onervare, dom, baar, groen; seer, skrynerig; **– brick**, rou steen; **– hide**, ongebreide vel, rou vel; **– material**, grondstof, ruwe materiaal; **– deal**, onreg, onbillikheid.
raw-boned, brandmaer, vel-en-been- ...
raw-head and bloody bones, paaiboelie.
rawish, rouerig.
ray, n. straal, ligstreep.
ray, v. uitstraal, deurstraal, strale skiet.
ray, n. pylstert(vis), rog.
raze, rase, skawe; uitvee, uitkrap; verwoes, vernietig, met die grond gelyk maak.
razor, n. skeermes.
razor, v. skeer; sny.

razor-back, spitsrug; spitsrugwalvis.
razor-edge, skerp kant (van 'n skeermes).
razor-grinder, skeermesslyper.
razor-strop, slypriem.
razzle-dazzle, opgewondenheid, gewoel, drukte; drinkparty.
reabsorb, weer absorbeer.
reach, n. bereik; mag; omvang, uitgestrektheid, afstand; **out of** –, buite bereik; **within** –, binne bereik.
reach, v. uitstrek, uitsteek; bereik, bykom; aangee; – **out his hand**, sy hand uitsteek; **–es from the Cape to Cairo**, strek (uit) van die Kaap tot by Kaïro; – **forward to an ideal**, na 'n ideaal strewe; – **land**, land bereik; **I cannot – so high, ek kan nie so hoog bykom nie**; **as far as the eye could** –, so ver soos die oog kon sien; he **–ed down his coat**, hy het sy baadjie afgehaal.
reach-me-down: – **clothes**, klaargemaakte klere.
react, reageer, terugwerk, weerstaan.
re-act, weer speel, weer opvoer.
reaction, terugwerking, teenstand, reaksie.
reactionary, n. reaksionêr.
reactionary, a. terugwerkend, teenwerkend, reaksionêr.
reactor; reaktor; reaksiespoel (*radio*); reaksieketel; –toring; kernenergiesuil, –stapel.
read, lees; verklaar, uitlê; raai; lui; studeer; – **a dream**, 'n droom verklaar; – **the future**, die toekoms voorspel; – **the clock**, kyk hoe laat dit is; – **one a lesson**, iemand die les lees; – **for the examination**, vir die eksamen studeer; **the thermometer –s 30 degrees**, die termometer wys 30 grade; – **to me**, lees vir my voor; **the paragraph –s thus**, die paragraaf lui aldus.
readability, leesbaarheid.
readable, leesbaar; lesenswaardig.
readdress, heradresseer, nastuur.
reader, leser; persleser, proefleser, reviseur; lektor; leesboek.
readership, lektorskap.
readily, geredelik, graag; maklik.
readiness, gereedheid; gewilligheid, bereidwilligheid; vlugheid, vaardigheid; – **of wit**, skerpsinnigheid, gevatheid.
reading, n. belesenheid; lesing; verklaring, interpretasie, opvatting; (die) lees; lektuur, leesstof; **the third – of a bill**, die derde lesing van 'n wetsontwerp; – **of a thermometer**, die aflees van 'n termometer, stand van termometer.
reading, a. lesend, lees- . . .
reading-book, leesboek.
reading-desk, lessenaar.
reading-lamp, studeerlamp.
reading matter, leesstof, lektuur.
reading-room, leeskamer.
readjourn, nogmaals verdaag.
readjust, (weer) regmaak, herstel.
ready, a. klaar, gereed, bereid, gewillig; snel, vlug, vinnig; by die hand; geneig; **too – to get angry**, te gou op sy perdjie, te geneig om kwaad te word; **a – pen**, 'n vaardige pen; – **to depart**, op die punt om te vertrek; – **cash**, kontant; – **money**, kontantgeld.
ready, n. kontant.
ready-made, klaargemaak, klaargekoop.
ready-reckoner, rekenboekie.
reaffirm, opnuut bevestig (bekragtig).
reafforest, weer bebos.
reafforestation, weerbebossing.
reagent, reageermiddel, reagens.
real, n. reaal (muntstuk).
real, a. werklik, waar, wesenlik, eintlik, reëel, eg; – **money**, klinkende munt; **the – thing**, die ware Jakob, net hy; – **property**, vaste eiendom.

realgar, realgar, rooi swawel-arsenik.
realization, verwesenliking; tegeldemaking, realisering; besef.
realize, verwesenlik; besef; tot geld maak, ('n prys) haal, opbring; (wins) maak; realiseer.
realism, realisme.
realist, realis.
realistic, realisties.
reality, realiteit, werklikheid, wesenlikheid; **in** –, in die werklikheid.
really, werklik, waarlik, regtig.
realm, koninkryk, ryk, gebied, terrein.
realty, vaste eiendom.
realtor, eiendomsagent.
ream, n. riem (papier).
ream, v. ruim, wyer maak.
reamer, ruimer (boor).
reanimate, weer besiel, laat herlewe.
reanimation, herlewing.
reap, oes, inoes, maai; insamel; pluk; – **the fruits**, die vrugte pluk, die gevolge dra.
reaper, maaier; snymasjien.
reaping-hook, sekel.
reaping-machine, selfbindermasjien.
reappear, weer verskyn.
reappearance, weerverskyning.
reappoint, weer aanstel, herbenoem.
reappointment, herbenoeming.
rear, n. agterhoede; agtergrond, agterkant; **bring up the –**, die agterhoede vorm; **in the –**, van agter; **in die rug (aanval)**; **far in the –**, ver agter; **at the – of**, agter.
rear, v. grootmaak; oplei, vorm; teel; kweek, verbou; steier; opsteek; oprig; – **children**, kinders grootmaak; – **horses**, perde teel; **the horse –s**, die perd steier.
rear-admiral, skout-by-nag.
rearguard, agterhoede.
rearrange, omskik, verander, anders skik.
rearrangement, omskikking, verandering.
rearward, n. agterhoede; **to the – of**, agter.
rearward, a. agterste, in die agterhoede.
rearwards, na agter toe, agterwaarts.
reascend, weer (be)klim, weer opstyg.
reason, n. rede, verstand; dryfveer, motief, oorsaak, rede, aanleiding, grond; redelikheid, billikheid; **by – of**, as gevolg van; **he complains with –**, hy kla met reg; **he has lost his –**, hy is van sy verstand af; **anything in –**, alles wat redelik is (wat met billikheid kan verwag word); **it stands to –**, dit spreek vanself; **listen to –**, na rede luister; **speak –**, verstandig praat; **for that –**, om dié rede, daarom; **the woman's –**, vrouelogika, vroueredeneerkuns.
reason, v. redeneer, argumenteer; beredeneer; bespreek; – **a person out of his fear**, iemand sy vrees uit die kop praat; bereken.
reasonable, billik, redelik, verstandig.
reasoned, beredeneer(d).
reasoning, redenering.
reassemble, weer bymekaarmaak, weer bymekaarkom; weer inmekaarsit, hermonteer.
reassert, weer verklaar.
reassign, weer aanwys.
reassume, weer aanneem, weer aanvaar.
reassumption, hervatting.
reassure, weer verseker, gerusstel.
reattempt, weer probeer.
rebaptize, herdoop.
rebaptism, herdoop, weerdoop.
rebate, n. vermindering, korting, rabat.
rebate, v. verminder, korting gee.
rebel, n. rebel, opstandige, opstandeling.
rebel, a. opstandig, oproerig, rebels.
rebel, v. rebelleer, opstaan (teen).

rebellion, rebellie, opstand, oproer.
rebellious, oproerig, opstandig.
rebellow, hard weergalm.
rebind, herbind, weer bind.
rebirth, wedergeboorte.
rebound, v. terugspring, terugstoot, terugkaats.
rebound, n. terugslag, reaksie.
rebuff, n. afjak, affrontasie, teenstand, weiering, afwysing.
rebuff, v. verhinder, weier, afwys, afjak gee.
rebuild, herbou, weer opbou.
rebuke, n. berisping, teregwysing.
rebuke, v. bestraf, berispe, teregwys.
rebut, afweer, terugslaan; weerlê.
recalcitrant, a. weerspannig, weerbarstig, weerstrewig, balsturig.
recalcitrant, n. weerspannige.
recalcitrate, teëstribbel, teëspartel.
recall, v. terugroep; herroep, intrek; onthou, laat dink aan, herinner.
recall, n. terugroeping; herroeping; **beyond** –, onherroeplik.
recant, herroep, terugneem, intrek.
recantation, herroeping, terugtrekking.
recapitulate, beknop saamvat, rekapituleer; opsom.
recapitulation, samevatting, opsomming.
recapitulatory, herhalend, rekapitulerend.
recapture, v. herneem, weer gevange neem; herower.
recapture, n. herneming, herowering.
recast, opnuut giet, weer vorm; wysig, omwerk, verwerk.
recede, terugtree, terugwyk, terugtrek; daal, sak; verdwyn.
receipt, n. ontvangs; voldaan, bewys, kwitansie; resep; **on** – **of**, na ontvangs van; **be in** – **of**, in besit wees van.
receipt, v. voldaan maak.
receivable, aanneemlik, ontvangbaar.
receive, kry, ontvang, in ontvangs neem, aanneem; toelaat; onthaal, verwelkom; **news was** –**d yesterday**, berig het gister gekom.
receiver, ontvanger; hoorbuis; heler (van gesteelde goed); ontvangtoestel; vergaarbak.
recency, nuwigheid; resente dagtekening, onlangsheid.
recension, hersiening, hersiene uitgaaf.
recent, pas gebeur, onlangs, resent, van resente datum, nuut, vars; modern.
recently, onlangs, 'n tydjie gelede.
receptacle, (vergaar)bak; bewaarplek; vrugbodem.
reception, resepsie, ontvangs, onthaal, verwelkoming; **a warm** –, 'n hartlike ontvangs; 'n heftige teëstand; – **desk**, ontvangstoonbank.
reception-room, ontvangkamer.
receptive, ontvanklik, vatbaar; opnemings- . . .
receptivity, vatbaarheid, ontvanklikheid.
recess, vakansie, reses; terugwyking; hoek, alkoof; skuilplek; –**es of the heart**, skuilhoeke van die hart.
recession, terugwyking, terugtrekking; afstand, (die) afsien van; handel (slapte).
recessional, reses- . . . ; slot- . . .
recharge, weer vul; weer beskuldig; weer aanval; weer laai, herlaai.
recheck, weer kontroleer.
rechristen, herdoop.
recidivist, residivis, terugvaller.
recipe, resep, voorskrif, preskripsie.
recipient, a. ontvangend; ontvanklik.
recipient, n. ontvanger, resipiënt.
reciprocal, a. wederkerig, wedersyds.
reciprocal, n. omgekeerde.

reciprocate, heen en weer gaan; vergeld, vergoed op gelyke wyse behandel.
reciprocity, wederkerigheid, weervergelding, resiprositeit, wisselwerking.
recital, opsomming, verhaal; uitvoering.
recitation, resitasie, voordrag; opsomming.
recitative, resitatief.
recite, opsê, resiteer, voordra; opsom.
reciter, voordraer; voordragbundel.
reck, omgee, skeel.
reckless, roekeloos, onverskillig, onversigtig, onbesonne; **he is** – **of danger**, hy gee niks vir gevaar om nie.
reckon, reken; tel; beskou, veronderstel, dink, meen; – **with**, rekening hou met; afreken met; – **without the host**, jou misreken, buite die waard reken – **among**, tel onder.
reckoning, (af)rekening; berekening; gissing; **day of** –, dag van vergelding, dag van afrekening; **you are out in your** –, jy het verkeerd gereken.
reclaim, terugwin, red, hervorm, verbeter; mak maak; terugvorder, terugkry; ontgin, bewerk, droogle.
reclamation, terugwinning, terugvordering, verbetering; eis; ontginning.
recline, lê, leun, rus, agteroorlê; laat rus; – **upon**, lê op; vertrou op.
reclothe, opnuut klee(d),
recluse, n. kluisenaar, heremiet.
recluse, a. eensaam, kluisenaars- . . .
reclusion, eensaamheid, afsondering.
recognizable, herkenbaar.
recognizance, verbintenis, verklaring; skuldbekentenis; borgtog.
recognize, herken; besef.
recognition, herkenning; erkenning, waardering; **in** – **of his services**, uit waardering vir (ter erkenning van) sy dienste.
recoil, v. terugslaan, teruspring, skop; terugtree, terugskrik, terugdeins.
recoil, n. terugslag, terugsprong, skop.
recoin, weer munt, hermunt.
recollect, (sig) herinner, onthou; weer versamel, herversamel.
recollection, herinnering; herversameling; **it is in my** –, ek onthou dit, ek herinner my dit.
recommence, weer begin, hervat.
recommencement, hervatting, heropening.
recommend, aanbeveel, aanprys; rekommandeer, aanraai.
recommendation, aanbeveling; rekommandasie **letter of** –, aanbevelingsbrief.
recommendatory, aanbevelings- . . .
recommit, weer begaan; terugverwys.
recompense, n. beloning, vergoeding, vergelding; skadeloosstelling.
recompense, v. beloon, vergoed, vergeld.
recompose, weer saamstel; weer komponeer.
reconcilable, versoenbaar; verenigbaar.
reconcile, versoen; ('n geskil) bylê; verenig (met) in ooreenstemming bring (met); **he** –**d himself to his fate**, hy het hom geskik in sy lot.
reconciliation, versoening, rekonsiliasie.
reconciliatory, versoenend.
recondite, geheim(sinnig), verborge; duister.
reconduct, teruglei.
reconnaissance, verkenning, spioentog.
reconnoitre, v. verken, spioen.
reconnoitre, n. verkenning(stog).
reconquer, herwin, herower.
reconsider, weer oorweeg.
reconstruct, rekonstrueer, weer saamstel; herbou, weer bou.
reconversion, weerbekering, herbekering.

reconvert, opnuut bekeer, herbekeer.
record, n. offisiële afksrif; register; gedenkskrif, dokument, geskiedrol; getuienis; verslag; gedenkteken; rekord; plaat; –s, argief; **the only case on** –, die enigste bekende geval; **it is on** –, dit is bekend (opgeteken); **keep a** – **of,** aanteken, opskrywe; **gramophone** –s, grammofoonplate; **hold the** –, die rekord hou; **to break a** –, 'n rekord slaan; (tel.) **give me** –s, hooflyn asseblief!; **for the** –, om die feite te gee; **off the** –, nie-amptelik.
record, v. opteken, aanteken, noteer, opskryf, boekstaaf, vermeld; registreer; opneem; – **your vote,** jou stem uitbring.
recorder, argivaris, geskiedskrywer; opvangtoestel, registrasietoestel.
record-room, argief.
recount, verhaal, meedeel, vertel; oortel.
recoup, aftrek; vergoed; skadeloos stel.
recourse, toevlug; **have** – **to,** toevlug neem tot.
recover, terugkry, terugvind, herwin; herstel, gesond word, beter word; laat herstel; bykom, inhaal; goed maak; (skadevergoeding) kry; – **one's breath,** asem kry; – **consciousness,** bykom; – **one's legs,** weer op die bene kom; – **lost time** verlore tyd inhaal.
recover, weer toemaak; weer beklee.
recovery, terugkryging; herstel, genesing, beterskap; **past** –, onherstelbaar.
recreant, n. afvallige, lafaard.
recreant, a. afvallig, troueloos.
recreate, vermaak, verlustig; ontspanning neem; weer skep, herskep.
recreation, ontsnapping, vermaak, verlustiging, tydverdryf; herskepping.
recreative, ontspannend, ontspannings- . . .
recrement, afval; skuim.
recriminate, oor en weer beskuldig.
recrimination, teëbeskuldiging.
recrudesce, weer uitbreek; weer oplewe.
recrudescence, hernieude uitbreking; hernieude uitbarsting, heroplewing.
recruit, n. rekruut; nuweling.
recruit, v. (aan)werf, rekruteer; aanvul; versterk; opknap, sterk word.
recruiting-officer, werfoffisier.
rectangle, reghoek.
rectangular, reghoekig.
rectifiable, herstelbaar.
rectification, verbetering, herstelling, rektifikasie; suiwering.
rectifier, gelykrigter (elek.).
rectify, regmaak, herstel, verbeter, in orde bring; suiwer, distilleer.
rectilinear, reglynig.
rectitude, opregtheid, eerlikheid.
rector, rektor, hoof; predikant.
rectorial, rektoraal.
rectorship, rektoraat; leraarskap.
rectory, pastorie; rektorswoning.
rectum, endelderm, nersderm, rectum.
recumbency, leunende houding.
recumbent, rustend, (agteroor-)leunend.
recuperate, herstel, opknap, beter word.
recuperation, herstel.
recuperative, herstellend, versterkend.
recur, terugkom op; te binne skiet, byval; weer voorkom, terugkeer, weer gebeur; –**ring decimals,** repeterende breuke.
recurrence, terugkeer; herhaling.
recurrent, terugkerend, terugkomend.
recurvature, terugbuiging.
recurve, ombuig, terugbuig.
recusancy, weerspannigheid; weiering.
recusant, n. weerspannige; weieraar.

recusant, a. weerspannig; weierend.
red, a. rooi; **grow** –, rooi word, bloos, kleur; **R- Cross,** Rooi Kruis, ambulans; – **man,** Rooihuid; **this is a** – **rag to him,** hy kan dit net so min verdra as 'n bul 'n rooi doek (kan verdra); **R- Riding Hood,** Rooikappie; see –, woedend word.
red, n. rooie; rooi, rooiheid; **in the** –, in die skuld
redact, redigeer, persklaar maak.
redaction, (die) redigeer.
red-breast, rooiborsie.
red-coat, rooibaadjie.
redden, rooi word, bloos; rooi maak.
reddish, rooiagtig, rooierig.
reddish-brown, rooibruin.
reddle, rooiklei, rooigrond.
redeem, terugkoop; vrykoop; verlos; goedmaak; inlos; vervul, nakom; – **a promise,** 'n belofte nakom; **his only** –**ing feature,** al wat in sy guns kan gesê word, sy enigste goeie punt.
Redeemer, Verlosser, Heiland.
redeliver, weer aflewer; weer bevry.
redemand, terugeis, terugvorder.
redemption, verlossing, bevryding, redding; **past** –, hopeloos verlore.
redemptive, verlossings- . . ., verlossend.
redemptory, verlossings- . . ., – **price,** losprys.
redescend, weer afdaal.
red-handed, op heter daad; **caught** –, op heter daad betrap.
red herring, bokkem (bokkom); **neither fish, flesh nor good** –, vis nog vlees.
red-hot, gloeiend warm.
redintegrate, herstel, heelmaak, vernuwe.
redirect, aanstuur, heradresseer.
redistribute, weer verdeel, herverdeel.
redistribution, herverdeling, redistribusie.
red-letter, gedenkwaardig, besonder, gelukkig; – **day,** gedenkwaardige dag.
redolence, geur, welriekendheid.
redolent, geurig, welriekend; **be** – **of,** ruik na; herinner aan.
redouble, verdubbel, vermeerder; aangroei; redoebleer (by brugspel).
redoubt, vesting, skans, redoute.
redoubtable, gedug, gevrees.
redound, bydra, strek; terugval; terugkom; voortvloei.
redraft, n. nuwe ontwerp; retoerwissel.
redraft, v. weer opstel, weer ontwerp.
redraw, oorteken.
redress, n. herstel, vergoeding, redres.
redress, v. verhelp, herstel, vergoed, goedmaak, regstel.
Redskin, Rooihuid, Indiaan.
red tape, rooi lint; burokratisme, amptelike omslagtigheid.
reduce, terugbring; reduseer, herlei; verneder, verlaag, ten onder bring, onderwerp, verminder, afslaan, minder maak; klassifiseer; degradeer; – **something to powder,** iets fynmaak (vergruis); – **to submission,** tot onderwerping dwing; **-d to despair,** tot wanhoop gedrywe; – **to poverty,** tot armoede (die bedelstaf) bring; **-d prices,** verminderde pryse; –**d circumstances,** armoedige omstandighede.
reducible, herleibaar; verminderbaar.
reduction, vermindering, afslag, reduksie; inkorting, beperking; onderwerping; herleiding.
redundance, redundancy, oortolligheid, oorbodigheid; oorvloed(igheid).
redundant, oortollig, oorbodig.
reduplicate, verdubbel, redupliseer.
reduplication, reduplikasie, verdubbeling.

re-echo, v. weegalm, weerklink; weerkaats; herhaal.
re-echo, n. weerkaatsing; naklank.
reed, riet; mondstuk, rietjie, tongetjie; fluit; wewerskam; –s, riete, biesies, matjiesgoed; **lean on a –,** op sand bou, op 'n gekrookte riet steun.
reed-babbler, rietvink.
re-edify, weer opbou, herbou.
reedy, riet- . . ., rietagtig; skraal, tingerig; swak, krassend.
reef, n. reef.
reef, v. die seile inbind, reef.
reef, n. rif; rotsbank, rotslaag.
reefer, daggasigaret.
reek, n. rook, walm, wasem; stank.
reek, v. rook, wasem; – **of,** ruik na.
reeky, vuil, swart gerook, rokerig.
reel, n. rolletjie, tolletjie, klos; **off the –,** vlot sonder om te haak.
reel, v. oprol, opdraai, opwen; – **off,** afrol, afdraai; aframmel.
reel, n. wankelende (waggelende) gang.
reel, v. wankel, waggel, slinger; duiselig word; **his head –s,** sy kop draai, hy word duiselig.
reel, n. riel (dans).
reel, v. 'n riel dans.
re-elect, herkies.
re-election, herkiesing.
re-eligible, herkiesbaar.
re-embark, (sig) weer inskeep.
re-emerge, weer te voorskyn kom.
re-enact, weer bepaal, weer vasstel.
re-enter, weer binnekom, terugkom.
re-establish, weer oprig, herstel.
reeve, n. vrederegter, balju.
reeve, v. inskeer, reef.
re-examination, hereksamen; nader ondersoek.
re-examine, weer ondersoek; weer eksamineer.
re-export, heruitvoer.
refashion, verander, vervorm.
refection, verversing; ligte maaltyd.
refectory, eetsaal.
refer, refereer, verwys; toeskryf (aan); voorlê, op dra, in hande stel; (sig) beroep op; betrekking hê (op); melding maak (van), aandag vestig (op); **I – myself to your generosity,** ek beroep my op u goedhartigheid; – **to his notes,** sy aantekeninge raadpleeg; – **the matter to a committee,** die saak na 'n komitee verwys; **these remarks only – to certain instances,** hierdie opmerkinge het alleen betrekking op sekere gevalle; **the place –red to,** (die) genoemde plek.
referee, n. skeidsregter.
referee, v. as skeidsregter optree.
reference, verwysing; verband, verhouding, betrekking; melding, gewag; beslissing, uitspraak; bewysplaas, aanduiding; getuigskrif; referensie; **with – to,** met verwysing na, wat betref, met betrekking tot; **for –s please apply to the manager,** wend u asseblief tot die bestuurder om inligting; **books of –,** boeke om te raadpleeg, naslaanboeke.
reference library, naslaanboeke.
reference number, aanwysingsnommer.
referendary, skeidsregter; referendaris.
referendum, volkstemming; referendum.
refill, weer volmaak.
refine, suiwer, louter, raffineer; verfyn, veredel; suiwer (beskaaf) word.
refined, gesuiwer, geraffineer; beskaaf, verfyn; – **manners,** beskaafde maniere; – **sugar,** geraffineerde suiker.

refinement, suiwering, loutering; beskawing, verfyning, veredeling.
refiner, suiweraar, raffinadeur; verfyner.
refinery, suiweringsfabriek, raffinadery.
prefit, weer aanpas; repareer, in orde bring, opknap; weer uitrus.
reflect, weerkaats, weerspieël; peins, nadink; – **upon,** jou ongunstig uitlaat oor, laak; bepeins, oordink.
reflection, weerkaatsing, weerspieëling, refleksie; oorweging, gedagte; blaam, verwyt, skimp; **on –,** by nadere oorweging; **angle of –,** hoek van uitval.
reflective, weerkaatsend, weerspieëlend; peinsend, dinkend; wederkerend.
reflector, reflektor, weerkaatser.
reflex, n. weerkaatsing; weerspieëling, weerkaatste lig; refleksbeweging; **conditioned –,** aangeleerde refleks.
reflex, a. teruggekaats; bespieëlend; reagerend; – **action,** refleksbeweging.
reflexibility, weerkaatsbaarheid.
reflexible, weerkaatsbaar.
reflection, sien **reflection.**
reflexive, wederkerend, refleksief; – **verb,** wederkerende werkwoord.
refluent, terugvloeiend.
reflux, terugvloeiing, eb.
re-form, v. weer vorm.
reform, v. verbeter, hervorm; afskaf; **R–ed Church,** Gereformeerde (Hervormde) Kerk.
reform, n. verbering, hervorming.
reformation, verbetering, hervorming, reformasie; **the R–,** die Hervorming.
reformative, hervormend, verbeterings- . . .
reformatory, n. verbeteringsgestig.
reformatory, a. sien **reformative.**
reformer, hervormer.
refract, breek (van strale).
refraction, straalbreking, refraksie.
refractive, brekings- . . ., straalbrekend.
refractor, refraktor.
refractory, koppig, hardnekkig, weerbarstig, weerspannig, onbuigsaam.
refrain, n. refrein.
refrain, v. bedwing, beteuel, inhou; – **from,** nalaat (sig.) onthou van.
refrangible, breekbaar.
refresh, verkwik, verkoel, verfris, opfris.
refresher, opknappertjie, versterkertjie.
refreshment, verversing, verkwikking.
refrigerant, n. verkoelende middel.
refrigerant, a. verkoelend.
refrigerate, v. koud maak, verkoel.
refrigeration, afkoeling, verkoeling.
refrigerator, yskas; koel-, ysmasjien; koelyskamer; koeltrok.
refrigeratory, n. koelkamer, yskamer.
refrigeratory, a. verkoelend, koel- . . .
reft, beroof.
refuge, toevlug, skuilplek, toevlugsoord; **seek –** toevlug neem tot, 'n skuilplek soek; **city of –** vrystad.
refugee, vlugteling, uitgewekene.
refulgence, glans, skittering.
refulgent, skitterend, blink, glinsterend.
refund, n. terugbetaling.
refund, v. terugbetaal, teruggee.
refusal, weiering; keuse, opsie.
refuse, n. oorskiet, afval, vuilgoed.
refuse, a. vuilgoed- . . ., waardeloos.
refuse, v. weier, van die hand wys, bedank, verwerp.
refutable, weerlegbaar.
refutation, weerlegging.

refute, weerlê, teëspreek.
regain, terugkry, herwin; – **consciousness**, weer tot bewussyn kom, bykom; – **one's feet**, weer op die been kom.
regal, koninklik, vorstelik.
regale, n. feesmaal, onthaal; lekker geur.
regale, v. onthaal, trakteer, vergas.
regalement, onthaal.
regalia, onderskeidingstekens; regalia.
regality, koninklike voorreg (waardigheid).
regard, n. agting, eerbied, ontsag; verband, opsig; notisie, aandag; **in this** –, in hierdie opsig; **in – to**, met betrekking tot; **pays no – to**, neem geen notisie van nie, gee niks om nie; **have great – for**, hoog ag, groot agting hê vir; **have no – for his advice**, geen ag slaan op sy raad nie; **kind –s**, beste groete.
regard, v. bekyk, beskou; in aanmerking neem; ag slaan op; (hoog) ag; aangaan; omgee; **as –s**, wat betref.
regardful, met inagneming; oplettend, aandagtig; – **of the consequences**, met inagneming van die gevolge.
regarding, betreffende, wat betref.
regardless: – **of**, sonder om te let op, onverskillig omtrent; **be – of expense**, geen onkoste ontsien nie.
regatta, seilwedstryd, roeiwedstryd.
regelate, aaneenvries.
regelation, aaneenvriesing.
regency, regentskap.
regenerate, a. wedergebore.
regenerate, v. laat herlewe, met nuwe lewe besiel, opwek, hervorm.
regeneration, herlewing, wedergeboorte; hervorming; regenerasie.
regent, n. regent (regentes); ryksbestuurder, bewindhebber.
regent, a. regerend, heersend; **prince r.**, prinsregent.
regerminate, weer ontkiem.
regicide, koning(s)moord; koning(s)moordenaar.
regime, (regering)stelsel, beheer; instelling; regime; **under the old** –, onder die ou regering (stelsel).
regimen, stelsel; dieet; lewenswyse.
regiment, regiment.
regimental, regiments- . . .
region, streek, landstreek, gewes, gebied; **the lower –s**, die hel; doderyk, onderwêreld; **the upper –s**, die lug; die hemel; **the – of metaphysics**, die gebied van die metafisika.
register, n. register; lys, kieserslys, rol.
register, v. registreer, inskryf; boek, aanteken; aanwys; – **a letter**, 'n brief laat aanteken (registreer); **I want to –**, ek wil my laat inskryf.
register office, registrasiekantoor.
registrar, registrateur.
registration, registrasie, inskrywing; – **fee**, inskrywingsgeld.
registry, inskrywing; registrasiekantoor.
regnal, regerings- . . .
regnant, regerend, heersend.
regorge, vomeer, uitbraak; verswelg.
regress, n. teruggang.
regress, v. agteruitgang, agteruitbeweeg.
regression, teruggang, agteruitgang.
regressive, terugkerend, regressief.
regret, n. verdriet, hartseer, smart; teleurstelling; spyt, leedwese; **hear with –**, met leedwese verneem.
regret, v. treur oor; spyt hê oor, betreur; **I – to state**, dit spyt my om te sê.
regretful, berouvol.
regrettable, te betreur, betreurensw aardig, spytig.

regroup, opnuut groepeer, hergroepeer.
regulable, reguleerbaar.
regular: **–s**, gereelde troepe.
regular, a. gereeld, reëlmatig; vas; – **soldiers**, gereelde troepe; – **army**, 'n staande leër; – **rascal**, 'n egte skurk.
regularity, gereeldheid, reëlmatigheid.
regulate, reguleer; regsit; reël.
regulation, regulasie, reëling, skikking; reglement, voorskrif, bepaling.
regulative, reëlend, reëlings.
regulator, reëlaar; slinger; regulateur.
regurgitate, terugstroom; uitbraak.
regurgitation, terugstroming; uitbraking.
rehabilitate, rehabiliteer, herstel.
rehabilitation, herstel(ling), rehabilitasie.
rehash, v. weer opdis; opwarm.
rehash, n. opgewarmde kos.
rehearsal, repetisie; herhaling.
rehearse, opsê; herhaal, opsom; repeteer.
reign, n. regering, bestuur.
reign, v. regeer, heers.
reignite, weer aan brand steek.
reimburse, terugbetaal, vergoed.
reimbursement, terugbetaling.
reimport, weer invoer, weer importeer.
rein, n. leisel, teuel; beheer; **draw –**, stilhou, inhou; inkort; **give a horse the –s**, 'n perd die die teuels gee (sy gang laat gaan); **give – to the imagination**, die verbeelding vrye vlug gee; **assume the –s of government**, (die teuels van) die bewind aanvaar.
rein, v. stuur, leisels hou; beteuel.
reincarnate, reïnkarneer.
reincarnation, reïnkarnasie.
reincorporate, weer inlyf.
reindeer, rendier.
reinforce, versterk; – **one's argument**, nuwe bewyse aanvoer; **–d concrete**, betonyster, gewapende beton.
reinforcement, versterking.
reinsert, weer plaas; weer insteek.
reinspire, weer inspireer, weer besiel.
reinstate, herstel, weer in besit stel.
reinsure, weer verassureer, herverseker.
reinvest, weer belê, herbelê, weer uitsit; weer beklee, weer verleen.
reinvigorate, weer krag gee, weer versterk.
reissue, n. nuwe uitgawe.
reissue, v. weer uitgee.
reiterate, herhaal.
reiteration, herhaling.
reject, verwerp; verstoot; weier, afwys, van die hand wys, afslaan; opbring.
reject, n. afgekeurde; **–s**, fabrieksuitskot.
rejectable, verwerplik.
rejectamenta, afval, vuilgoed, uitwerpsel; uitspoelgoed, strandgoed.
rejection, verwerping, weiering.
rejoice, verbly, bly maak, bly (verheug) wees.
rejoicing(s), blydskap, vreugde, gejuig.
rejoin, antwoord; weer inhaal, weer bykom, weer aansluit; weer verenig.
rejoinder, antwoord; dupliek.
rejuvenate, verjong, weer jonk maak.
rejuvenation, verjonging.
rekindle, weer aansteek; weer aanvuur.
relapse, v. terugval; weer instort.
relapse, n. terugval; instorting.
relate, verhaal, vertel; in verband bring (met), in verband staan (met).
related, verwant; – **groups**, verwante groepe; – **to me**, familie van my; **closely –**, na verwant (aan mekaar).
relation, betrekking, verhouding; verwantskap;

relationship familiebetrekking, bloedverwant; verhaal; **out of all –,** buite alle verhouding; **bear – to,** betrekking hê op.
relationship, verwantskap.
relative, n. familiebetrekking, bloedverwant; betreklike voornaamwoord.
relative, a. betreklik, relatief; respektief; **– to,** met betrekking tot.
relativity, betreklikheid, relatiwiteit.
relax, verslap, verflou; versag; laat skiet; ontspan; **don't – your grasp,** moenie laat skiet (loslaat) nie; **– the attention,** die aandag laat verflou.
relaxation, verslapping, verflouing; ontspanning.
relay, n. voorspanning; vars span, aflosspan; heruitsending, ploeg.
relay, v. voorspanning gee, aflos; heruitsaai.
re-lay, v. weer lê.
relay-race, afloswedstryd, afloswedloop.
release, n. bevryding, loslating, vrylating, verlossing; ontslag; afstand.
release, v. loslaat, vrystel, verlos; losmaak; afstaan, oormaak; onthef.
relegate, verban; verplaas; verwys.
relegation, verbanning; verwysing.
relent, toegee, week word, vriendeliker word, bedaar, meer gematig word.
relentless, meedoënloos, onverbiddelik.
relevance, -cy, verband, toepaslikheid.
relevant, toepaslik, vanpas, ter sake.
reliability, vertroubaarheid; **– trial,** betroubaarheidsrit, (-toets).
reliable, vertroubaar, betroubaar, deeglik.
reliance, vertroue; **place – upon,** vertroue hê op (in).
relic, reliek; oorblyfsel; aandenking; **–s,** stoflike oorskot; oorskiet, oorblyfsels.
relict, weduwee.
relief, n. verligting, versagting; onderstand, ondersteuning; ontset; aflossing; afwisseling; **– fund,** ondersteuningsfonds; **– works,** onderstandswerke; **the – of Ladysmith,** die ontset van Ladysmith; **the – of the guard,** die aflossing van die wag; **– map,** reliëfkaart.
relief, n. reliëf, verhewe beeldwerk; **stand out in –,** duidelik uitkom; **bring out in full –,** in 'n duidelike lig stel, duidelik laat uitkom.
relieve, verlig, versag, lenig; help, ondersteun; bevry; aflos; ontset; ontlas, lug gee aan; laat uitkom; afwissel; **the town was –d,** die stad is ontset; **– the feelings,** aan die gevoelens lug gee; **– the guard,** die wag aflos; **black –d with white,** swart met wit afgesit; **relieving army,** ontsettingsleër; **relieving officer,** armeversorger; **relieving staff,** aflospersoneel.
religion, godsdiens, geloof; **he makes a – of it,** dit is vir hom 'n gewetesaak.
religionism, oordrewe godsdienswyer.
religionist, godsdienswyeraar, dweper.
religiose, oordrewe godsdienstig.
religiosity, godsdienswyer.
religious, godsdienstig, godvresend, vroom; godsdiens- . . . ; stip, streng.
relinquish, opgee, laat vaar, laat staan; afsien van; loslaat.
relinquishment, afstand(doening).
reliquary, relikwieëkassie.
relish, n. smaak, geur; genot, behae; **play loses its – after childhood,** speel verloor sy aantrekkingskrag as 'n mens groot word; **eat with –,** met smaak eet; **read with –,** met lus lees.
relish, v. behae skep in, hou van, in die smaak val; smaak na; smaaklik maak.
relishable, smaaklik.
relive, herlewe.

reload, weer laai, herlaai.
relucent, blink, skitterend, glansend.
reluctance, teësin, huiwerigheid; weerstrewigheid, teëstribbeling.
reluctant, teësinnig, huiwerig, onwillig.
relume, weer aansteek; weer verlig.
rely, vertrou (op), (sig) verlaat (op), steun (op), staatmaak (op), bou (reken) (op); **you may – upon it,** jy kan daarop reken (staatmaak).
remain, v. oorbly, oorskiet; bly; **what -s is easily told,** wat volg, kan maklik vertel word; **– three weeks in Paris,** drie weke in Parys vertoef; **this –s to be seen,** dit moet nog bewys word, dit moet ons nog sien.
remain(s), oorblyfsels, oorskiet; stoflike oorskot; ruïne; nagelate werke.
remainder, res, oorskiet, die orige; resgetal.
remake, weer maak, oormaak.
remand, v. terugstuur (na die gevangenis), roep.
remand, n. terugsending; voorarres.
re-mark, v. weer merk, oormerk.
remark, v. opmerk; aanmerk; **– on,** opmerking (aanmerking) maak oor.
remark, n. opmerking; aanmerking; **worthy of –,** opmerklik, merkwaardig.
remarkable, opmerklik, merkwaardig.
remarry, weertrou, hertrou.
remediable, herstelbaar.
remedial, heilsaam, genesend, herstellend.
remedy, n. geneesmiddel, (hulp)middel.
remedy, v. genees; verhelp, herstel.
remember, onthou, (sig) herinner; byval, te binne skiet; gedagte kry; dink aan; **he begs to be –ed to you,** hy stuur die beste groete; **he –ed himself,** hy het hom bedink; **I don't – having met him,** ek kan my nie herinner dat ek hom ontmoet het nie; **I –ed suddenly,** dit het my skielik bygeval.
remembrance, herinnering, geheue; aandenking; gedagtenis; **–s,** komplimente, groete.
remind, herinner, help onthou, indagtig maak; **this –s me,** dit laat my dink (aan); **– me of it,** herinner my daaraan, help my onthou.
reminder, herinnering; wenk; aanmaning; **a gentle –,** 'n vriendelike waarskuwing (aanmaning).
reminiscence, herinnering.
reminiscent: be – of, herinner aan, laat dink aan.
remise, afstand doen van.
remiss, agtelosig, nalatig; traag, lui.
remissible, verskoonbaar, vergeeflik.
remission, vergifnis; kwytskelding; vermindering, afslag; verslapping.
remit, vergewe, kwytskeld; afneem, verminder, verslap, verflou; terugstuur; oormaak, remitteer; uitstel.
remittal, kwytskelding, vergifnis.
remittance, betaling, oormaking, remise.
remittee, ontvanger (van 'n remise).
remittent, afwisselend (van koors).
remitter, afsender, remittent.
remnant, oorblyfsel, oorskiet; stukkie, brokkie; lap; restant.
remnant sale, restantverkoping.
remodel, vervorm, omwerk, verwerk.
remonstrance, protes, remonstransie.
remonstrant, a. protesterend.
remonstrant, n. remonstrant.
remonstrate, protesteer, beswaar maak, teenwerpinge maak; betoog; teregwys.
remora, suigvis.
remorse, berou, gewetenswroeging.
remorseful, berouvol.
remorseless, meedoënloos, onbarmhartig.
remote, afgeleë, afgesonder, ver (van mekaar),

ver verwyder; gering, min; **the -st parts of the earth**, die uithoeke van die wêreld; **memorials of - ages**, gedenktekens van die gryse verlede; **he is a - kinsman of mine**, hy is ver langes familie van my; **our - ancestors**, ons voorouers uit die verre verlede; **not the -st conception**, nie geringste begrip nie; **- control**, afstandbeheer, -reëling; afstandreëlbaar.
remoteness, afgeleënheid, groot afstand.
remould, weer vorm, vervorm.
remount, v. weer opklim, weer bestyg (beklim); remonteer; van perde voorsien.
remount, n. 'n vars perd, remonte.
removable, a. verplaasbaar; afsitbaar.
removal, verplasing; ontslag; verwydering; verhuising; wegruiming.
remove, verplaas; ontslaan, afsit, afdank; wegneem, verwyder, verskuiwe, uit die weg ruim; verhuis, oorbring; **- from mountains**, berge versit, wonderwerke verrig; **- from office**, afsit; **- from school**, uit die skool haal; **- from Capetown to Wellington**, van Kaapstad na Wellington verhuis; **not many degrees -d from the ape**, baie na aan 'n aap; **my first cousin once -d**, my kleinneef (-niggie); **- one's hat**, jou hoed afhaal.
remove, n. gereg; bevordering; graad.
remunerate, beloon, betaal; vergoed.
remuneration, beloning, vergoeding, betaling, remunerasie.
remunerative, winsgewend, voordelig.
renaissance, herlewing; **R-**, Renaissance.
renal, nier- . . .
rename, hernoem.
renascence, wedergeboorte; **R-**, Renaissance.
renascent, herlewend.
rencounter, toevallige ontmoeting; botsing, geveg, skermutseling.
rend, (stukkend) skeur, losskeur, uitmekaar ruk (skeur); uitruk; verdeel; **a shout rent the air**, 'n geroep het deur die lug weerklink.
render, teruggee, vergeld; oorgee, oorlewer; gee, oplewer; maak, bewys; weergee, vertolk; vertaal, oorsit; uitbraai, suiwer; aangooi, pleister; **- thanks**, dank betuig; **- good for evil**, kwaad met goed vergeld; **account -ed**, gelewerde rekening; **Handel's Largo was well -ed**, Largo van Handel is goed gespeel (vertolk); **age has -ed him peevish**, ouderdom het hom iesegrimmig gemaak.
rendezvous, vergaderplek, rendezvous.
rendition, oorgawe, uitlewering; weergawe, vertolking.
renegade, renegaat, afvallige, verraaier.
renew, vernuwe, hernuwe (hernieu); herhaal; hervat, weer begin; verlewendig, laat herlewe, versterk; lap, heelmaak.
renewable, vernubaar.
renewal, vernuwing, hernuwing.
reniform, niervormig.
rennet, stremsel.
rennet, renetappel.
renounce, afstand doen van, afsien van, opgee, laat vaar; versaak, verwerp, verloën; **- friendship**, vriendskapsbande verbreek; **- the world**, die wêreld vaarwel sê.
renouncement, afstand(doening), versaking; verloëning.
renovate, repareer, regmaak, vernuwe.
renovation, reparasie, vernuwing.
renown, roem, vermaardheid, faam.
renowned, beroemd, vermaard.
rent, sien **rend**.
rent, n. skeur, opening, bars.
rent, n. huur, pag.

rent, v. huur, pag; verhuur, verpag.
rentable, huurbaar; verhuurbaar.
rental, huur(geld).
rent-free, vry, kosteloos; huurvry.
renunciation, afstand; selfverloëning.
reobtain, terugkry, weer verkry.
reoccupy, weer beset; weer intrek neem in.
reopen, weer oopmaak, begin, heropen.
reorganization, reorganisasie.
reorganize, reorganiseer.
repair, v. repareer, regmaak, heelmaak, verstel; vergoed, goedmaak, herstel.
repair, n. herstel; reparasie; **the house needs -**, die huis moet reggemaak word; **out of -**, sleg onderhou, stukkend; **vervalle; in bad -**, sleg onderhou; **it is under -**, dit word gerepareer, dit is in reparasie.
repair, (sig) begewe (na); besoek.
repaper, weer plak, oorplak.
reparable, herstelbaar.
reparation, reparasie, herstel; vergoeding, skadeloosstelling, kompensasie.
repartee, gevatte antwoord; gevatheid; **quick at -**, gevat.
repast, maal(tyd).
repatriate, repatrieer.
repatriation, repatriasie.
repay, terugbetaal; vergeld, beloon.
repayable, terugbetaalbaar.
repayment, terugbetaling.
repeal, v. herroep, intrek; afskaf.
repeal, n. herroeping; afskaffing.
repealable, herroeplik.
repeat, v. herhaal; nasê, nadoen, oordoen; oorvertel, navertel, repeteer.
repeat, n. herhaling; herhalingsteken; nabestelling.
repeatedly, herhaaldelik, herhaalde male.
repeater, opsêer; herhaler, repetisiehorlosie; repeteergeweer.
repeating, repeterend; **- decimal**, repeterende breuk; **- rifle**, repeteergeweer; **- watch**, repetisiehorlosie.
repel, terugdryf, verslaan, afweer, afslaan; weerstaan; afstoot.
repellent, terugdrywend; afwerend; afstotend, afstootlik.
repent, berou hê; spyt voel; **you shall - this**, dit sal jou berou.
repentance, berou.
repentant, berouvol, boetvaardig.
repeople, weer bevolk.
repercussion, terugslag, skop; terugkaatsing; reaksie.
repercussive, terugkaatsend; terugslaand.
repertoire, repertoire.
repertory, lys, register; repertoire (van toneelgeselskap); **- company**, vaste toneelgeselskap; **- theatre**, repertoire-teater.
repetition, herhaling, repetisie; kopie.
repine, treur, knies; ontevrede wees, kla.
replace, terugsit; opvolg; vernuwe, vervang; in die plek stel van.
replacement, terugbetaling, vernuwing, vervanging; verplasing; **-s**, vervangingstroepe; **-dele**.
replant, oorplant, verplant.
replay, n. herhaalwedstryd.
replenish, (weer) volmaak; aanvul.
replete, vol, gevul; goed voorsien (van); **- with**, sat van; voorsien van, uitgerus met.
repletion, volheid, oorlading, satheid.
replica, kopie; faksimilee, nabootsing.
replication, antwoord, repliek; kopie.
reply, v. antwoord (gee), repliseer.
reply, n. antwoord; repliek; **in - to**, in antwoord

repolish   636   **reseize**

op; **he said nothing in – to that,** hy het daarop niks geantwoord nie; **make no –,** nie antwoord nie.
repolish, weer poleer, oor vrywe.
report, v. rapporteer, verslag gee; berig, vertel; (sig) aanmeld; **it is –ed,** dit word gesê, die gerug lui; **– all details,** alle besonderhede meedeel; **I'll – you to the chief,** ek sal jou by die hoof aangee (verkla); **– to the magistrate,** jou by die landdros aanmeld.
report, n. gerug; verslag, rapport; berig, tyding; knal, skoot; **the – goes,** die gerug lui, die mense sê; **of good –,** goed aangeskrewe, met 'n goeie naam; **faithful through good and evil –,** getrou deur dik en dun (in voor- of teenspoed).
reporter, verslaggewer, beriggewer.
repose, v. rus, uitrus, neerlê, lê; berus; vertrou (op); **– on,** berus op.
repose, n. rus, verposing, kalmte, stilte.
reposeful, rustig, kalm, stil.
repository, bewaarplek, pakhuis; begraafplaas; vertroueling.
repossess, weer in besit neem; weer in besit stel.
reprehend, bestraf, berispe, blameer.
reprehensible, berispelik, laakbaar.
reprehension, blaam, berisping.
represent, voorstel; beweer, voorgee; verteenwoordig; **– a constituency,** 'n kiesafdeling verteenwoordig.
representation, voorstelling; verteenwoordiging.
representative, a. verteenwoordigend; representatief; voorstellend, tipies; **– government,** verteenwoordigende bestuur.
representative, n. verteenwoordiger.
repress, onderdruk, in toom hou, teëgaan, in bedwang hou.
repression, onderdrukking, beteueling.
repressive, onderdrukkend, onderdrukkings- . . ., beteuelings- . . .
reprieve, v. uitstel, opskort (van voltrekking van vonnis).
reprieve, n. uitstel, opskorting (van vonnis); **grant a –,** begenadig.
reprimand, n. teregwysing, berisping.
reprimand, v. teregwys, bestraf, berispe, skrobbeer.
reprint, herdruk.
reprisal, weerwraak, wraakoefening, vergelding; **make –s,** weerwraak neem.
reproach, v. beskuldig, verwyt, berispe; **his eyes –ed me,** hy het my verwytend (beskuldigend) aangekyk.
reproach, n. beskuldiging, verwyt, berisping; skande; **the state of the roads is a – to those responsible,** die toestand van die paaie strek die verantwoordelike persone tot skande; **abstain from –,** moenie verwyte maak nie; **heap –es on him,** beskuldiginge voor sy kop gooi.
reproachful, verwytend; skandelik.
reprobate, v. verwerp, afkeur; verdoem.
reprobate, n. verworpeling, goddelose, deugniet, slegte mens.
reprobate, a. verworpe, goddeloos.
reprobation, verwerping; verdoeming.
reproduce, weer voortbring; reproduseer, kopieer; weergee; vermenigvuldig.
reproduction, reproduksie; kopie; voortplanting; weergawe.
reproductive, reproduktief, voortplantings- . . .
reproof, berisping, skrobbering.
reprove, berispe, bestraf, skrobbeer.
reptile, n. kruipende dier, reptiel; wurm.
reptile, a. kruipend; laag; kruiperig.
reptilian, a. kruipend.

reptilian, n. kruipende dier.
republic, republiek, gemenebes.
republican, a. republikeins.
republican, n. republikein.
republicanize, republikeinsgesind maak.
republicanism, republikanisme.
republication, nuwe uitgawe, herdruk.
republish, weer uitgee.
repudiate, verwerp; ontken; repudieer.
repudiation, verwerping; loëning, ontkenning, weiering; repudiasie.
repugnance, afkeer, weersin, teensin.
repugnant, teenstrydig; afkerig, aanstootlik; walglik, stuitend.
repulse, v. terugdrywe, verslaan; afskrik; afslaan, van die hand wys.
repulse, n. terugdrywing, terugslag; weiering, afwysing; **he suffered, met with a –,** hy is teruggeslaan; (sy versoek) is botweg geweier; hy het 'n klap in die gesig gekry ('n bloudjie geloop).
repulsion, terugstoting; afkeer, afsku.
repulsive, terugstotend; afstootlik, haatlik, walglik.
repurchase, v. weer koop, terugkoop.
repurchase, n. terugkoop.
repurify, weer suiwer.
reputable, fatsoenlik, agtenswaardig.
reputation, goeie naam, reputasie, eer; **of –,** mense van naam en faam; **he has a – for dishonesty,** hy staan bekend as 'n oneerlike man; **a bad –,** 'n slegte naam (reputasie).
repute, v. ag, beskou, reken; **his –d father,** sy beweerde (vermeende) vader.
repute, n. naam, reputasie; **a man of ill –,** 'n man met 'n slegte naam.
request, n. versoek; versoekskrif, petisie; bede; **at his –,** op sy versoek; **by –,** op versoek; **make a – for,** aanvraag doen om, versoek om; **be in great –,** gesog (veel aanvraag voor) wees.
request, v. versoek, vra; verlang, begeer; aanvraag doen om.
requiem, sielmis, requiem.
require, eis, vorder, vereis; begeer, wil hê; nodig hê; **it –s an army,** dit vereis 'n leër; **how much do you –,** hoeveel het jy nodig?; **what do you – of him,** wat wil jy van hom hê?
requirement, vereiste; behoefte; **–s,** benodigdhede, behoeftes.
requisite, a. nodig, vereis.
requisite, n. vereiste; benodigdheid.
requisition, n. aansoek, eis; opeising; oproep; rekwisisie.
requisition, v. eis, vorder; versoek.
requital, vergelding, beloning; wraak.
requite, vergeld, beloon.
reread, oorlees, herlees.
reredos, altaarskerm.
resaddle, weer opsaal.
resale, weer verkoop, herverkoop.
rescind, herroep, nietig verklaar; afskaf.
rescission, herroeping, nietigverklaring, opheffing, afskaffing.
rescript, beslissing; edik; reskrip.
rescue, v. red, bevry, verlos.
rescue, n. (uit)redding, bevryding; hulp; **he came to our –,** hy het ons te hulp gekom.
research, n. navorsing, ondersoek(ing).
research, v. navors, navorsingswerk doen, ondersoek, naspoor.
reseat, van nuwe sitplek(ke) voorsien; ('n broek) 'n nuwe boom insit.
reseda, reseda.
reseize, weer in besit neem.

resell, weer verkoop, herverkoop.
resemblance, ooreenkoms, gelykenis.
resemble, lyk na, aard na, trek na.
resent, kwalik neem, beledig voel oor.
resentful, boos, beledig; haatdraend.
resentment, geraaktheid, gebelgdheid, boosheid; haatdraendheid, wrok.
reservation, voorbehoud, reservasie; plekbespreking.
reserve, v. terughou, agterhou; bewaar; reserveer; bespreek; voorbehou; bestem.
reserve, n. reserwe; voorraad; voorbehoud; terughoudendheid; beskeidenheid, ingetoënheid, stemmigheid; **without** –, sonder voorbehoud (onvoorwaardelik); **with all proper** –s, met die nodige voorbehoud; **the -s**, die reserwetroepe.
reserved, besproke (bespreekte); terughoudend, ingetoë; gereserveer(d).
reservoir, dam, reservoir; bak.
reset, weer insit; weer skerp maak; weer styf word.
reship, verskeep, weer inskeep.
reshuffle, weer skommel (skud).
reside, woon, bly; berus; – **in**, berus by; word aangetref in (by); woon in.
residence, woning, verblyf(plek), woonplek, (woon)huis; inwoning; residensie; **he took up** –, hy het hom (metterwoon) gevestig; **beautiful – for sale**, pragtige woonhuis te koop.
residency, residensie.
resident, a. woonagtig; inwonend; resident- . . . ; – **in Cape Town**, in Kaapstad woonagtig; – **doctor**, inwonende dokter; – **bird**, standvoël, voël wat nie trek nie.
resident, n. inwoner, bewoner.
residential, wonings- . . ., woon- . . ., huis- . . ., verblyf- . . ., inwonend; – **allowance**, (huis)huurtoelae, verblyftoelae; – **quarters**, woonwyke.
residual, a. oorblywend.
residual, n. res, oorskot, oorblyfsel.
residuary, orig, oorblywend.
residue, oorblyfsels, res; besinksel.
residuum, besinksel, residu; oorskot.
resign, bedank, aftree; neerlê, afstand doen van; (sig) onderwerp aan, oorgee; – **oneself to another's guidance**, jou aan 'n ander se leiding oorlaat; **I** –ed **myself to my fate**, ek het my aan my lot onderwerp.
re-sign, weer teken.
resignation, bedanking, ontslag; afstand; gelatenheid, berusting, onderwerping; **send in one's** –, jou bedanking instuur, jou ontslag indien.
resilience, elastisiteit; veerkrag.
resilient, elasties, veerkragtig.
resin, n. harpuis; gom, hars.
resin, v. met harpuis smeer (bestryk).
resinous, harpuisagtig, gomagtig.
resinaceous, sien **resinous**.
resipiscence, inkeer, skulderkenning.
resist, weerstaan, weerstand (teëstand) bied, (sig) verset teen; – **temptation**, versoeking weerstaan; **cannot** – **a joke**, kan nie nalaat om 'n grap te maak nie.
resistance, weerstand, teëstand, verset; **passive** –, lydelike verset; **the line of least** –, die maklikste weg.
resistibility, weerstandsvermoë.
resistible, weerstaanbaar.
resistless, onweerstaanbaar.
resistor, weerstand.
resole, versool.
resoluble, oplosbaar.

resolute, vasberade, vasbesluit (vasbeslote), onverstrokke, resoluut.
resolution, resolusie, besluit; voorneme; vasberadenheid; onverskrokkenheid oplossing; ontleding; ontbinding; **good** –s, goeie voornemens.
resolutive, oplossend.
resolvable, oplosbaar.
resolve, besluit, 'n besluit neem; laat besluit, oplos, ontbind, ontleed; **the House** –d **itself into a commmittee**, die Raad het in Komitee gegaan; –d **into various elements**, opgelos in verskillende bestanddele.
resolve, besluit; **she kept her** –, sy het by haar besluit gebly.
resolved, vasberade, basbeslote.
resolvent, oplosmiddel.
resonance, weerklank, resonansie.
resonant, weerklinkend, weergalmend; **be – with**, weerklink van.
resonator, resonator; klankbord.
resorbtion, herabsorbering.
resort, v. toevlug neem (tot), (sig) begewe (na); **visitors** –ed **to the sea-side by the hundred**, honderde besoekers het hulle na die strand begewe; – **to force**, toevlug tot geweld neem.
resort, n. toevlug, uitvlug, uitweg, redmiddel; samekoms, sameloop; bymekaarkomplek; oord; **in the last** –, in die laaste instansie; **holiday** –, vakansieplek, -oord; **seaside** –, strad(plek).
re-sort, v. weer sorteer.
resound, weergalm, weerklink; uitbasuin.
resource, hulpmiddel, redmiddel, toevlug; vindingrykheid; –**s**, middele, geld; **at the end of one's** –**s**, ten einde raad; **be full of** –, vindingryk wees.
recourceful, vindingryk.
resourceless, hopeloos, radeloos.
respect, n. agting, eerbied, ontsag, respek; opsig; betrekking; **with** – **to his salary**, met betrekking tot sy salaris; **without** – **to the results**, sonder om die gevolge in aanmerking te neem; – **of persons**, aansiens des persoons, partydigheid; **in all** –**s**, in alle opsigte; **admirable in** – **of style**, bewonderenswaardig wat die styl betref; **give him my** –**s**, komplimente (groete) aan hom.
respect, v. respekteer, ag, eerbiedig, hoogag; ontsien; betrekking hê op; **you must** – **his old age**, jy moet sy ouderdom ontsien.
respectability, fatsoenlikheid, agtenswaardigheid, aansien; agtenswaardige persoon, iemand van aansien.
respectable, fatsoenlik, agtenswaardig, respektabel, ordentlik; aansienlik.
respectful, eerbiedig, beleef(d).
respectfully, beleef(d), hoogagtend; **yours** –, u dienswillige dienaar, hoogagtend die uwe.
respective, onderskeie, respektief, besonder, eie; A and B celebrated the – sums of 4c and 3c. A en B het respektiewelik 4c en 3c bygedra.
respectively, onderskeidelik, respektiewelik (respek)tieflik.
respiration, asemhaling.
respirator, respirator, asemhalingstoestel.
respiratory, asemhalings- . . .
respire, asemhaal, uitasem, inasem; asemskep.
respite, n. uitstel, respyt; verposing, rus.
respite, v. uitstel, verdaag.
resplendence, glans; luister.
resplendent, glinsterend, skitterend.
respond, (be)antwoord; reageer (op); vatbaarheid (belangstelling) toon; gehoor gee (aan); **he does not** – **to kindness**, vriendelikheid maak geen indruk op hom nie.

respondent, n. verweerder, gedaagde; respondent, verdediger.
respondent, a. gedaag(de); **be – to,** gehoor gee aan; antwoord gee op.
response, antwoord; beurtsang, responsorie; **make no –,** geen antwoord gee nie; **called forth no – in his breast,** het geen snaar in sy hart aangeroer nie, het hom koud gelaat.
responsibility, verantwoordelikheid, aanspreeklikheid; **on his own –,** op eie verantwoordelikheid, op sy eie houtjie.
responsible, verantwoordelik, aanspreeklik; – **government,** verantwoordelike bestuur.
responsive, antwoordend; vatbaar; simpatiek; **be – to,** reageer op.
responsory, beurtsang, teensang.
rest, v. rus, uitrus; laat rus, rus gee; leun, steun; berus (op); baseer (op); **the matter cannot – here,** die saak kan nie hierby gelaat word nie; **are you quite –ed,** is jy heeltemal uitgerus?; – **one's elbow on the table,** met jou elmboog op die tafel leun.
rest, n. rus; slaap; kalmte; ruspunt, steun(punt); pouse; bok (by biljart); **day of –,** rusdag; **at –,** stil, rustig, kalm; **set person's mind at –,** iemand gerusstel; **lay to –,** ter aarde bestel, begrawe; stil 'n end aan maak; **retire to –,** gaan rus, (sig) ter rus begewe.
rest, v. oorbly, oorskiet; – **assured,** gerus wees, seker wees; **it –s with you,** dit is jou saak, dit hang van jou af, dit berus by jou.
rest, n. oorskiet (oorskot), res.
restaurant, restaurant (restourant), eethuis.
rest-cure, ruskuur.
restful, rustig, stil, kalm; rusgewend.
resting-place, rusplek, rusplaas.
restitution, teruggawe, vergoeding, herstel; restitusie; – **of conjugal rights,** herstel van huweliksregte; **make –,** teruggee, vergoed.
restive, koppig, eiewys, steeks.
restless, rusteloos, onrustig, woelig.
restorable, herstelbaar.
restoration, herstel(ling); teruggawe; restourasie.
restorative, a. genesend, versterkend.
restorative, n. versterkmiddel.
restore, teruggee; herstel; vernuwe, regmaak; restoureer, genees; verhelp; terugbring, terugsit; – **to health,** genees, gesond maak.
restrain, in toom hou, inhou, bedwing, beteuel, beperk.
restrainable, bedwingbaar, beteuelbaar.
restraint, dwang, beperking, bedwang, verbod; selfbeheersing; **without –,** onbeperk, vry.
restrict, beperk, bepaal; inkrimp.
restriction, beperking, bepaling, restriksie; inkrimping; voorbehoud.
restrictive, beperkend, bepalend.
result, v. uitloop (op), lei (tot); volg, voortvloei; voorspruit; – **in failure,** op 'n mislukking uitloop.
result, n. resultaat, uitslag; gevolg, uitwerking, effek; **without –,** tevergeefs.
resultant, a. voortspruitend.
resultant, n. resultante; resultaat.
resume, v. terugkry; terugneem; hervat, weer begin, vervolg; weer inneem; saamvat, opsom, resumeer.
résumé, n. opsomming, saamvatting.
resummon, opnuut dagvaar.
resumption, hervatting; herneming.
resumptive, hervattend.
resupinate, onderstebo.
resurge, herlewe, weer opstaan.
resurrect, opwek; opgrawe; oprakel.
resurrection, herrysenis, opstanding.

resurvey, v. weer ondersoek; weer opmeet.
resurvey, n. nuwe opmeting.
resuscitate, laat herlewe, opwek.
resuscitation, herlewing, opwekking.
ret, rate, rait, (vlas) week; vrot, stik.
retail, n. kleinhandel; **sell by –,** by die kleinmaat (in die klein) verkoop.
retail, v. by die kleinmaat (in die klein) verkoop; in besonderhede vertel.
retail dealer, kleinhandelaar.
retain, hou, behou; onthou; terughou; in diens neem, aanhou.
retainer, volgeling, onderhorige; retensie, retensiereg; honararium.
retaining fee, honorarium.
retake, terugneem, weer neem.
retaliate, terugbetaal, vergeld; weerwraak neem.
retaliation, weervergelding, wraakneming, weerwraak.
retaliatory, wraaknemend, vergeldings- ...
retard, vertraag, ophou, teëhou; uitstel; agteruitsit; belemmer.
retardation, vertraging; uitstel.
retch, kokhals, brul.
retention, behoud; terughouding, agterhouding, onthouvermoë.
retentive, vashoudend; **a – memory,** 'n goeie (sterk) geheue.
reticence, terughoudendheid, swygsaamheid; verswyging.
reticent, terughoudend, swygsaam, stil.
reticle, kruisdraad.
reticular, netvormig.
reticulate, netvormig verdeel.
reticulation, netwerk.
reticule, damessakkie, werksakkie.
reticulum, blaarpens(ie), kleinpensie.
retiform, netvormig.
retina, netvlies (van die oog), retina.
retinitis, netvliesontsteking, retinitis.
retinue, stoet, gevolg.
retire, v. terugwyk, vlug, retireer; (sig) terugtrek (onttrek, afsonder); (sig) verwyder; aftree, bedank, uit diens tree; stil gaan lewe, gaan rentenier, besigheid opgee; na bed gaan; – **into oneself,** afgetrokke (stil) wees; – **to bed,** na bed gaan; – **from business,** uit die besigheid tree; – **from the army,** militêre diens verlaat, uit diens gaan.
retire, n. aftog; **sound the –,** die aftog blaas.
retired, stil, afgetrokke; afgesonder; gewese, aftrede, gepensioeneer(d); **a – general,** 'n gepensioeneerde generaal; – **pay,** pensioen; **a – farmer,** 'n rentenierende boer, 'n boer wat van sy rente lewe.
retirement, afsondering, eensaamheid, teruggetrokkenheid; uitdienstreding.
retiring, stil, teruggetrokke, ingetoë; beskeie; – **room,** toiletkamer; privaat.
retort, v. vinnig (gevat) antwoord.
retort, n. vinnige (gevatte) antwoord; teëwerping; teregwysing.
retort, retort, retort, kromhals, kolffies.
retorted, omgebuie.
retortion, ombuiging; weerwraak.
retouch, v. weer aanraak; bywerk, retoucheer, finale verbeteringe aanbring.
retouch, n. bywerking.
retrace, naspoor, weer nagaan; weer oortrek; – **one's steps,** teruggaan.
retract, intrek; terugtrek; herroep.
retractable, terugtrekbaar.
retraction, herroeping.
retraction, intrekking; terugtrekking, herroeping.
retractile, intrekbaar.

retractor, terugtrekkende spier.
retread, v. versool.
retread, n. versoolde band.
retreat, v. terugwyk, terugtrek, retireer; **a –ing forehead**, 'n skuins voorkop.
retreat, n. terugtog, aftog, terugwyking; afsondering, eensaamheid, stil verblyfplek; skuilplek, rusplek; **sound the –**, die aftog blaas; **beat a –**, die aftog blaas, terugtrek, terugwyk; **they made good their –**, hulle het gesorg dat hulle veilig wegkom; **in full –**, in volle aftog.
retrench, verminder, inkort, inkrimp, beperk, besuinig, besnoei; verskans.
retrenchment, vermindering, inkorting, besuiniging, besnoeiing; verskansing.
retribution, vergelding, beloning.
retributive, vergeldings- . . ., wraak- . . .
retrievable, herstelbaar.
retrieval, (die) terugkry; herstel.
retrieve, v. terugvind, terugkry; herstel, vergoed; red; opspoor.
retrieve, n. herstel; **beyond –**, onherstelbaar.
retriever, jaghond.
retroact, terugwerk.
retroaction, terugwerking.
retroactive, terugwerkend.
retrocede, terugtree, terugwyk.
retrocession, terugtreding, terugwyking, (weer)-afstand.
retrogradation, agteruitbeweging; agteruitgang, ontaarding.
retrograde, a. agterwaarts, teruggaand(e), agteruitgaand(e), ageruit.
retrograde, v. agteruitgaan, terugwyk, teruggaan; versleg, ontaard.
retrogress, agteruitgaan; ontaard.
retrogression, teruggang; agteruitgang.
retrospect, terugblik; oorsig.
retrospection, terugblik; (die) terugkyk.
retrospective, terugwerkend; terugblikkend; terug- . . ., retrospektief.
return, v. terugkom, teruggaan, terugkeer; teruggee, terugstuur, terugbetaal; vergeld; terugslaan; **– to the subject**, op die saak (onderwerp) terugkom; **– a profit**, wins oplewer; **– a ball**, 'n bal teruggooi (terugslaan); **– like for like**, met gelyke munt betaal; **– a blow**, terugslaan; **– thanks**, (be)dank; **– partner's lead**, in jou maat se kleur terugspeel; **the Labour member was –ed by a big majority**, die Arbeiderslid is met 'n groot meerderheid gekies; **– to dust**, tot stof wederkeer; **– a visit**, 'n teenbesoek aflê.
return, n. terugkoms, terugkeer, tuiskoms; voordeel, wins, profyt; terugbetaling, teruggawe, (die) terugstuur, terugbesorging; verkiesing; rapport, statistiek, verslag, opgawe, retoerkaartjie; **empty –s**, leë goed; **– of post**, kerende pos; **many happy –s of the day**, nog baie jare, veels geluk; **he got nothing in –**, hy het niks daarvoor gekry nie; **– journey**, terugreis; **– ticket**, retoerkaartjie; **– cargo**, retoervrag; **– match**, kontrawedstryd, teen westryd.
reunion, reunie, hereniging.
reunite, herenig, versoen.
rev, laat draai; **– up**, vinnig laat loop.
revaccinate, weer ent, oorent.
revalue, weer skat, oorskat, herskat.
reveal, openbaar, aan die lig bring, bekend maak, uitbring; verraai.
revel, v. pret maak, uitgelate wees; drink, oordadig eet en drink, swelg; **– in**, (sig) verlustig in, geniet.
revel, n. luidrugtigheid, uitgelatenheid; fees, swelgparty, drinkparty.

revelation, openbaring; ontdekking, bekendmaking, onthulling.
reveller, pretmaker, losbol, swierbol.
revelry, luidrugtigheid; feestelikheid.
revendication, terugreis, terugkry(ging).
revenge, v. wreek, wraak neem; **– oneself**, wraak neem, jou wreek.
revenge, n. wraak, wraakneming; wraaksug; **I will have my –**, ek sal my wreek; **in –**, uit wraak.
revengeful, wraakgierig, wraaksugtig.
revenue, inkomste.
revenue officer, belastingbeampte.
revenue stamp, belastingseël.
reverberant, weerkaatsend; weergalmend.
reverberate, weerkaats; weergalm.
reverberation, weerkaatsing; weergalm.
reverberator, weerkaatser.
reverberatory, a. weerkaatsend.
revere, vereer; eerbiedig, eer, hoogag.
reverence, n. eerbied, ontsag; verering; **hold in –**, vereer
reverence, v. eerbiedig, vereer.
reverend, a. eerwaardig; eerwaarde; **the R- Mr Murray**, dominee (eerwaarde) Murray.
reverent, eerbiedig.
reverential, sien reverent.
reverie, mymering, gepeins, gemymer.
reversal, onderwerping, herroeping, vernietiging; om(me)keer.
reverse, a. teenoorgestel(de), omgekeer; **the – side**, die keersy; **– fire**, rugvuur.
reverse, v. omdraai, onderstebo draai, omkeer; omsit; agteruit ry, ruggel, ('n motor) tru; herroep, nietig verklaar.
reverse, n. teenoorgestelde, omgekeerde; keersy, agterkant; teenspoed; wederwaardigheid; neerlaag.
reversible, omkeerbaar, dubbelkantig, wat omgedraai kan word; herroepbaar.
reversion, terugval(ling); atavisme.
reversionary, terugvallend; atavisties.
revert, terugval; terugkeer, terugkom.
revertible, terugvallend.
revet, beklee, bemantel.
revetment, bekledingsmuur, revêtement.
review, n. hersiening; wapenskouing, parade; oorsig; resensie, (boek)beoordeling, (boek)-beskouing; tydskrif.
review, v. hersien, nagaan, deurkyk; terugkyk op; beoordeel, resenseer; inspeksie hou.
reviewer, resensent, beoordelaar.
revile, beskimp, slegmaak, uitskel.
revisal, hersiening.
revise, v. nalees, nasien, hersien, verbeter, korrigeer, wysig.
revise, n. hersiening; tweede drukproef.
revision, hersiening; revise.
revisit, weer besoek.
revisory, hersienings- . . .
revival, herlewing; opwekking; herstel.
revive, herlewe, weer oplewe; weer opwek, verlewendig, weer aanvuur; weer in die lewe roep.
reviver, opwekker; opknappertjie.
revivification, weeropwekking, herlewing.
revivify, weer opwek, met nuwe lewe besiel, weer aanwakker, verlewendig.
reviviscence, oplewing, herlewing.
revocable, herroeplik.
revocation, herroeping, revokasie.
revoke, herroep, intrek, terugtrek; renonseer, nie beken nie (kaartspel).
revolt, v. rebelleer, opstaan (in opstand kom) teen, opstandig word, oproerig word; (sig) verset; walg.
revolt, n. opstand, oproer, rebellie.

revolter, oproermaker, opstandeling.
revolting, opstanding, oproerig; walglik.
evolution, omwenteling; omloop; opstand, revolusie.
revolutionary, a. revolusionêr (rewolusionêr), opstandig.
revolutionary, n. oproermaker, opstandige.
revolutionize, omwenteling teweegbring, 'n om(me)keer veroorsaak.
revolutionist, oproerling, revolusionêr (rewolusionêr).
revolve, draai, omdraai; oorweeg, oorpeins, oordink; **the earth –s round the sun**, die aarde draai om die son.
revolver, rewolwer.
revulsion, om(me)keer, plotselinge verandering; onttrekking; afleiding.
revulsive, afleidend, afdrywings- . . .
reward, n. beloning, vergelding.
reward, v. beloon, vergoed; vergeld.
rewin, herwin.
reword, anders stel, anders uitdruk.
rewrite, oorskryf, weer skryf, omwerk.
Reynard, Reinaard, Broer Jakkals.
rhabdomancy, wateraanwysing.
rhapsode, rapsodis.
rhapsodical, rapsodies; onsamehangend
rhapsodist, rapsodis.
rhapsody, rapsodie.
rhebuck, ribbok.
Rhenish, a. Ryn- . . .
Rhenish, n. Rynwyn.
rhesus, resus(aap); **R– factor**, resusfaktor.
rhetor, r(h)etor, redenaar.
rhetoric, retorika (retoriek), welsprekendheid- (sleer); deklamasie.
rhetorical, retories.
rhetorician, r(h)etor; redenaar.
rheum, verkoue; slym; kwyl.
rheumatic, a. rumaties; – **fever**, sinkingkoors.
rheumatic, n. rumatieklyer; –**s**, rumatiek.
rheumatism, rumatiek.
rheumy, klam, vogtig; druip- . . .
rhinal, neus- . . .
Rhine, Ryn.
rhino, renoster.
rhinoceros, renoster.
rhinoscope, neusspieël, r(h)inoskoop.
rhinoscopy, ondersoek van die neus.
rhizome, wortelstok.
rhodium, rodium (metaal).
rhodium, rodiumhout.
rhododendron, rododendron.
rhomb, ruit, rombus.
rhombic, ruitvormig.
rhomboid, n. romboïde.
rhomboidal, a. ruitvormig, romboïdaal.
rhombus, rombus, ruit.
rhubard, rabarber.
rhumb, windstreek, kompasstreek.
rhyme, **rime**, n. rym; rympie; rymwoord; berymde verse; **nursery** –, kinderversie; **without** – **or reason**, totaal onverklaarbaar, ongerymd.
rhyme, **rime**, v. rym; laat rym; op rym sit; –**d verse**, berymde verse.
rhymer, versemaker, rymer, rymelaar.
rhymeless, rymloos.
rhythm, maat, ritme.
rhythmic(al), ritmies; gelykmatig.
riant, vrolik, bly, laggend.
rib, n. rib(betjie); ribbetjie; ribbebeen.
rib, v. riffel; van ribbetjies voorsien.
ribald, liederlik, vuil, smerig.
ribaldry, vuil (gemene) taal.

riband, s. ribbon.
ribbed, geriffel.
ribbon, lint, band; **torn to** –**s**, flenters (toiings) geskeur; – **development**, strookbou.
rice, rys.
rice-bird, rysvoël.
rich, ryk, vermoënd, bemiddeld; vrugbaar; kostelik; kragtig; klankryk, klankvol; – **food**, kragtige kos.
riches, rykdom.
rick, mied (miet).
rickets, Engelse siekte, rachitis.
rickety, swak, lamlendig, lendelam.
ricksha(w), riksja.
ricochet, n. opslagkoeël, opslag(skoot).
ricochet, v. wegskram, opslaan.
rictus, gaap; mondwydte.
rid, bevry, ontslaan, verlos; **be** – **of** ontslae wees van, kwyt wees.
riddance, bevryding, verlossing; **he left this morning and good** – **too**, hy is vanoggend weg, en ek is maar dankie bly!
riddle, n. raaisel.
riddle, v. oplos, raai; raaiselagtig praat.
riddle, n. sif.
riddle, v. sif, uitsif; vol gate skiet; uitmekaar trek, met feite weerlê.
ride, v. ry, laat ry; – **a ford**, 'n drif (te perd) deurgaan; – **a child on one's back**, 'n kind abba (op jou rug laat ry); – **one's horse**, jou stokperdjie ry; – **at anchor**, voor anker lê; – **somebody down**, iemand inry, iemand onderstebo ry; – **for a fall**, onverskillig ry; moeilikheid soek; onverstandig (roekeloos) te werk gaan; – **out a storm**, 'n storm afry, veilig deur 'n storm kom; – **to death**, doodry; holrug ry, altyd weer daarop terugkom.
ride, n. rit, toertjie; rypad; **go for a** –, ('n entjie) gaan ry, 'n ritjie maak; **take for a** –, gaan ry met, laat saamry; om die bos lei; van kant maak.
rider, ruiter, ryer; bygevoegde klousule; meetkundige vraagstuk, probleem.
ridge, n. rug, rant, begrug; rif, kam; vors, nok; maanhaar (in 'n pad); hart (van 'n omgeploegde akker).
ridge, v. rimpel, vore trek; akker(tjies) maak.
ridgel, klophings.
ridge-piece, **-pole**, **-tree**, nok(balk).
ridgy, heuwelagtig; geriffel.
ridicule, n. belaglikheid; spot, bespotting; **hold up to** –, bespotlik maak.
ridicule, v. belaglik maak, bespot.
ridiculous, belaglik, bespotlik, verspot.
riding, (die) ry; rypad.
riding-breeches, rybroek.
riding-habit, rykostuum.
riding-whip, karwats, sambok, rysweep.
rife, heersend, algemeen; **be** –, baie voorkom, algemeen wees, heers; **be** – **with**, vol wees van, wemel van.
riff-raff, gepeupel, skorriemorrie, gespuis.
rifle, v. roof, plunder; buit maak; 'n geweerloop groef; skiet.
rifle, n. (koeël)geweer; **mounted** –**s**, berede skutters.
rifle club, skietvereniging.
rifleman, (skerp)skutter.
rifle range, skietbaan; skietafstand.
rift, n. bars, skeur, kraak; **there is a little** – **within the lute**, daar is iewers 'n krakie.
rift, v. bars, skeur, kraak, klowe.
rig, v. ('n skip) optuie, optakel; – **out**, uitdos, aantrek; – **up**, aanmekaar timmer; aantrek; optooi.

rig, n. tuigasie, touwerk; uitrusting, opskik.
rig, grap, poets, streek; bedrieëry.
rigging, touwerk, tuigasie.
right, a. reg, regverdig, billik; juis, waar; regter, haar; **a - angle, 'n regte hoek; at - angles,** haaks, reghoekig; **in one's - mind,** by sy volle verstand; **as - as a trivet, as rain,** so reg soos 'n roer; **set, put -,** in orde bring; **- eye,** regteroog; **all -, - oh, - you are,** goed in orde, afgesproke, mooi!
right, v. in orde bring, verbeter, herstel, regmaak; reg laat wedervaar; regsit, regop laat staan; **it will - itself,** dit sal vanself regkom.
right, n. reg, aanspraak; regterkant; regterhand; **might is -,** mag is reg; **by -(s),** na regte, eintlik; **he is in the -,** hy het gelyk; **on your -,** aan jou regterkant; **- and wrong,** reg en onreg, goed en kwaad; **he has no - to it,** hy het geen aanspraak daarop nie; **the -s of the case,** die ware toedrag van sake; **set, put to -s,** regmaak, in orde bring; **- of way,** voorrit, reg van deurgang, reg om voor te gaan.
right, adv. presies, reg; regs; behoorlik; regverdig; **turn - round,** heeltemal omdraai; **- in the middle,** reg in die middel; **it serves him -,** dit is sy verdiende loon; **if I remember -,** as ek dit wel het; **left and -,** hot en haar, links en regs.
right-about, regsom.
righteous, regverdig, regskape.
rightful, wettig, regmatig; regverdig.
right-handed, regs.
rightly, regverdig; behoorlik; tereg.
right-minded, reggeaard.
rightness, juistheid, billikheid.
rigid, styf, onbuigsaam; streng; stip.
rigidity, styfheid; strengheid; stiptheid.
rigmarole, n. kafpraatjies, geklets, onsin.
rigorous, streng, straf, hard.
rigour, strengheid, hardheid, stiptheid.
rile, boos maak, die siel uittrek.
rill, stroompie, beek.
rim, n. kant, rand; raam, lys; velling.
rim, v. omraam, omlys; 'n velling insit.
rime, sien **rhyme.**
rime, ryp.
rimose, rimous, gebars, vol barste.
rimy, vol ryp; witgeryp.
rind, n. skil; bas; kors; buitenste.
rind, v. afskil, bas afmaak.
rinderpest, runderpes.
ring, n. ring; kring, sirkel; kartel, kombinasie; vuisvegtery, boks(kuns) boksers; beroepswedders; **make -s round a person,** iemand disnis loop.
ring, v. 'n ring in die neus sit, 'n ring aansit; draaidraai hardloop; **- about, in, round,** insluit, 'n kring maak om.
ring, lui, klink; weerklink; bel; **- curtain down,** lui om die skerm te laat sak; **- for supper,** (die klok) vir die aandete lui; **- in,** inlui; **- in one's ears,** in jou ore weerklink; **- off,** afbel, aflui; **- out,** uitlui; weerklink; **- up,** opbel, oplui; **- with,** weerklink van.
ring, n. (ge)lui; toon, klank.
ring-bolt, ringbout.
ring-bone, ringbeen.
ring-dove, ringduif.
ringed, gering, ring- . . ., met ringe.
ringleader, belhamel, voorperd.
ringlet, ringetjie.
ringworm, douwurm, omloop.
rink, n. skaatsbaan, ysbaan.
rink, v. skaats, op (rol)skaatse ry.
rinse, uitspoel, afspoel.

riot, n. drinkgelag, uitspatting, buitensporigheid; oproer, opstand, muitery; **run -,** uit die band spring, uitspat, uitspattinge begaan, niks ontsien nie.
riot, v. wild lewe, buitensporighede begaan; oproer maak, oproerig word.
rioter, oproermaker; rusverstoorder.
riotous, oproerig; losbandig.
riotry, oproerigheid; losbandigheid.
rip, n. knol; losbol, niksnuts.
rip, v. (oop)skeur, (los)skeur, (af)skeur, oopsny, (los)torring; **- up old quarrels,** ou koeie uit die sloot haal.
rip, n. skeur, sny.
riparian, a. oewer- . . ., wal- . . .
riparian, n. oewerbewoner.
ripe, ryp; soon -, soon rotten, vroeg ryp, vroeg rot, **- age,** hoë ouderdom.
ripen, ryp word; laat ryp word.
riposte, n. terugsteek; raak antwoord.
riposte, v. gevat antwoord, terugsteek.
ripper, oopskeurder, oopsnyer; doring, haan; gawe nôi; (iets) van die fynste.
ripping, oopskeurend; fyn, gaaf, eersteklas.
ripple, n. (ge)kabbel; rimpeling; **- cloth,** ribbelstof.
ripple, v. kabbel, rimpel, golf.
rip-saw, kloofsaag, treksaag.
rise, v. opstaan; opkom, opgaan, rys, styg; in opstand kom; vooruitgaan, toeneem; ontspring, begin; voortspruit, ontstaan; opvlie; **- from the dead,** uit die dode opstaan; **if the wind should -,** as die wind opkom (opsteek); **the bread will not -,** die brood wil nie rys nie; **-s before the mind,** kom (rys) voor die gees; **the water -s,** die water styg; **- in the world,** vooruitkom in die wêreld, opgang maak; **does not - above mediocrity,** verhef (sig) nie bo die middelmatige nie; **- to the occasion,** jou die geleentheid waardig betoon, opgewasse vir die taak; **prices -,** pryse styg; **- in arms,** die wapens opvat, in opstand kom.
rise, n. opgang, styging; promosie, verhoging, bevordering; opkoms; opdraand, hoogte, bult; **give - to,** aanleiding gee tot; **- in prices,** prysverhoging; **prices are on the -,** pryse is aan die styg.
risibility, laglus; belaglikheid.
risible, laggerig, lagwekkend, belaglik.
rising, a. opgaande, opkomende, opstygende.
rising, n. (die) opstaan; opgang; opdraand, heuweltjie; opstand, oproer, opstootjie; opstanding.
risk, n. gevaar, risiko, waagstuk; **run the -,** die gavaar loop; **take -s,** waag (riskeer); **at the - of his life,** met lewensgevaar; **at your -,** op eie risiko.
risk, v. riskeer waag, op die spel sit; **- one's life,** jou lewe waag.
risky, gevaarlik, gewaag, riskant.
rissole, frikkadelletjie.
rite, (kerk)gebruik, plegtigheid, ritus.
ritual, a. ritueel.
ritual, n. rituaal, voorskrif, bepaling.
ritualism, ritualisme.
rival, n. mededinger; medeminnaar; **he is without a -,** hy is sonder weerga.
rival, a. wedywerend, mededingend; **- candidate,** teenkandidaat.
rival, v. wedywer, meeding.
rivalry, rivalship, wedywer, mededinging; konkurrensie.
rive, skeur, splyt, splits, klowe.
river, rivier, stroom.
river-basin, stroomgebied.

river-bed, rivierbedding.
river-horse, seekoei, rivierperd.
riverside, rivieroewer, rivierwal.
rivet, n. klinknael, bout.
rivet, v. (vas)klink, vasnael; boel; – **the attention**, die aandag boei; –**ed to the ground**, aan die grond genael; – **the eyes upon**, stip kyk na.
rivulet, stroompie, riviertjie.
rix-dollar, riksdaalder.
road, pad, weg; rede, ankerplek; **on the** –, op pad; **rules of the** –, rywette, verkeersregulasies; **take the** –, op reis gaan.
road-book, roeteboek.
road-hog, doldrywer, ryduiwel.
road-metal, padmateriaal.
road-sense, ryvernuf, padvernuf.
roadside, die kant van die pad.
roadstead, ankerplek, rede.
roadster, (op die rede) geankerde skip; ryperd; fiets; ervare reisiger.
roadworthy, in staat om te reis; bruikbaar.
roam, swerf, ronddool, rondtrek.
roan, a. rooiskimmel.
roan, n. rooiskimmel(perd).
roan, n. skaapleer, basaanleer.
roan-antelope, bastergensbok.
roar, v. brul; bulder, raas, dreun.
roar, n. (ge)brul; gebulder, geraas, gedreun; geskater.
roaring, brullend; dreunend; **a** – **night**, 'n stormagtige nag; **in** – **health**, in blakende gesondheid; **they drive a** – **trade**, hulle doen voordelige sake, hulle maak geld soos bossies.
roast, v. braai; rooster, (koffie) brand; spot dryf met.
roast, n. braaivleis; braaiery; **rule the** –, baasspeel.
roast, a. gebraaide, braai-...
roaster, braaier; koffiebrander; braaioond, brandoond; braaivark.
rob, (be)steel, (be)roof, ontroof, plunder.
robber, rower, dief.
robbery, rowery, diefstal.
robe, n. tabberd, mantel, kleed, damesjapon, gewaad; toga.
robe, v. aantrek, aanklee.
robin, rooiborsie.
roborant, versterkend, verstrek-...
robot, robot, verkeerslig, -outomaat.
roburite, roburiet.
robust, sterk, kragtig, robuust, gesond, gespier(d), frisgebou.
robustious, luidrugtig, lawaaierig.
roc, rok, reusevoël.
rochet, koormantel, koorhemp.
rock, n. rots, klip, steen(rots); **built on the** –, op vaste fondament gebou; **on the** –**s**, platsak, bankrot.
rock, v. wieg, skud, skommel; wankel, waggel; – **to sleep**, aan slaap wieg; – **and roll**, ruk-en-pluk(dans).
rock-crystal, bergkristal.
rocker, wieg, rystoel; **off his** –, van lotjie getik.
rockery, rotswerk, rotstuin(tjie).
rocket, vuurpyl, raket; – **aircraft**, raket-vliegtuig; – -**propelled**, raket-aangedrewe; – **motor**, raketmotor; – -**projector**, raketwerper.
rock-garden, kliptuin, rotstuin.
rock-hewn, uit klip gekap.
rocking-chair, skommelstoel, rystoel.
rocking-horse, gobbelperd.
rock-oil, steenolie, petroleum.
rock-pigeon, klipduif.
rock-rabbit, (klip)dassie.
rock-salt, klipsout.

rocky, rotsagtig.
Rococo, Rococo.
rod, roede; stok, staf, meetroede; staaf, stang, trekbout, (van pomp); **make a** – **for one's own back**, moeilikheid op jou hals haal; **I have a** – **in pickle for him**, ek sal met hom afreken, ek het nog 'n appeltjie met hom te skil (**Usher of the**) **Black R**–, Draer van die Swart Roede.
rode, sien **ride**.
rodent, knaagdier.
rodomontade, n. grootpraat, windmaak, spoggery, rodomontade.
roe, ree.
roe, viskuit, viseiertjies.
rogue, skurk, skelm; vabond, karnallie, rakker.
roguery, skurkstreke, skelmstreke, skelmery; ondeundheid.
roguish, skelmagtige, skurkagtig; guitig.
roister, lawaai maak, raas.
roisterer, lawaaimaker, boemelaar.
roistering, lawaaierig, luidrugtig.
role, rol.
roll, n. rol; register, naamlys; silinder, (ronde) broodjie; **call the** –, die presensielys opmaak, die register (af)lees.
roll, v. rol, oprol, inrol, platrol; laat rol; draai; slinger; – **cigarettes**, sigarette draai; – **along**, voortrol; – **by**, verbyrol; **years** – **by**, jare gaan verby; – **down**, afrol; **he** –**s in money**, hy het geld soos bossies; **saint and philosopher** –**ed into one**, heilige en filosoof in een persoon verenig; – **on**, voortrol; verbygaan; – **out**, plat rol, uitrol; ooprol; laat rol; – **over**, omrol; – **up**, oprol; **hundreds** –**ed up**, honderde het opgedaag.
roll, n. (die) rol, gerol; gerommel.
roll-call, appèl, naamaflesing.
roller, roller; rolstok; rol; groot golf.
roller-bandage, rolverband.
roller-blind, rolgordyn.
roller-skate, rolska.
roller-towel, rolhanddoek.
rollick, v. pret maak, baljaar, fuif.
rollick, n. uitgelatenheid, pret, fuif.
rollicking, dartel, uitbundig, uitgelate.
rolling, rollend, golwend.
rolling-pin, rolstok.
rolling-press, rolpers.
rolling-stock, rollende materiaal.
roly-poly, n. rolpoeding; vetsak.
roly-poly, a. vet, plomp, dik.
Roman, a. Romeins; **Rooms**; – **Catholic**, Rooms-Katoliek.
Roman, n. Romein.
Romance, a. Romaans.
Romance, n. Romaanse taal.
romance, n. romanse; verdigting, verhaal; romantiek, die romantiese.
romance, v. oordryf, vergroot.
romancer, romansier, romanskrywer.
Romanic, a. Romaans.
Romanize, romaniseer; Rooms word (maak).
romantic, romanties, avontuurlik.
romanticism, romantiek, romantisme.
romanticist, romantikus.
Rome, Rome; – **was not built in a day**, Keulen en Aken is nie op een dag gebou nie; môre is nog 'n dag; **do in** – **as the Romans do**, skik jou na die omstandighede.
romp, v. baljaar, stoei, jakker, ravot; – **past**, verbyskiet, verbyglip.
romp, n. robbedoe(s); stoeiery.
rompy, wild, uitgelate.
rondel, rondeel.
roneo, afrol, kopieer.

röntgen, röntgen; R– **ray,** Röntgenstraal, X-straal.
rood, roede; kruis.
roof, n. dak; verhemelte; – **of the mouth,** verhemelte; **a** – **of foliage,** 'n blaredak.
roof, v. dak opsit, onder dak bring; – **in over,** bedek, 'n dak vorm oor.
roofing, dakwerk.
roofless, sonder dak, dakloos.
roof-tree, nokbalk.
rook, n. roek, kraai, raaf; bedrieër.
rook, v. bedrieg, kurang speel, oneerlik speel; geld afpers, pluk.
rook, n. kasteel (skaakspel).
rook, v. rokeer (skaakspel).
rookery, kraaines; agterbuurte, armebuurte, diewenes.
room, kamer, vertrek; plek, ruimte, spasie; geleentheid, aanleiding; **plenty of** –, baie plek; **make** –, pad gee, plek maak; **no** – **for dispute,** geen aanleiding tot onenigheid nie.
roominess, ruimheid.
roomy, ruim.
roost, n. stok, steier, stellasie; slaapplek; **go to** –, op stok gaan, gaan slaap, inkruip; **at** –, op stok; in die vere; **come home to** –, hok toe kom; op jou eie kop neerkom; **your chickens come home to** –, jou sonde vind jou.
roost, v. op stok gaan; gaan slaap.
rooster, haan.
root, n. wortel; oorsprong, bron, oorsaak; stam; **take** –, wortel skiet; – **and branch,** wortel en tak; **the** – **of all evil,** die wortel van alle kwaad; **get to the** – **of the matter,** tot die grond van die saak deurdring, die saak grondig ondersoek; **square** –, vierkantswortel.
root, v. wortel skiet; ingewortel(d) wees; laat wortel vat; toejuig, ondersteun; –**ed to the ground,** aan die grond genael; – **out,** uitroei; – **up,** ontwortel, met wortel en al uitruk.
root, rout, vroetel; – **out,** uitsnuffel; – **up,** omvroetel; uitsnuffel.
rootlet, worteltjie.
root-rot, vrotpootjie.
rope, n. tou, lyn; **know the –s,** op hoogte van sake wees, goed ingelig wees; **put one up to the –s,** iemand goed touwys maak; **give him plenty of** –, hom baie skiet gee (sy vrye gang laat gaan).
rope, v. vasmaak, vasbind; trek (met 'n tou); – **in,** omspan, omlyn; (met 'n tou) vang, nader trek, binnehaal.
rope-dancer, koorddanser(es).
rope-ladder, touleer.
rope-walk, lynbaan.
rope-walker, sien **rope-dancer.**
rope-yarn, kaalgaar.
ropy, draderig, klewerig.
rorqual, vinvis, walvis.
rosarian, rooskweker.
rosarium, roostuin, rosarium.
rosary, roostuin; rosekrans; paternoster.
rose, n. roos; roset; rooskleur; sproeier; **gather life's –s,** die lewe geniet; **no** – **without a thorn,** geen roos sonder dorings nie; **life is not always a bed of –s,** die lewe is nie altyd enkel sonskyn nie; **under the –s,** in die geheim, stilletjies, sub rosa.
rose, a. rooskleurig.
roseate, rooskleurig.
rosebud, roosknop.
rose-bush, roosboom, rosestruik.
rose-coloured, rooskleurig.
rose-diamond, rosetsteen.
rosemary, roosmaryn.

roseola, uitslag, rooihond.
rosette, roset, kokarde.
rose-wood, rooshout.
rosin, harpuis.
rosiny, harpuisagtig, harpuis- . . .
roster, rooster, lys.
rostral, snawelvormig, snawel- . . .
rostrated, gesnawel.
rostrum, spreekgestoelte, snawel, bek.
rosy, rooskleurig; blosend, rose- . . .
rot, n. vrotheid, v(er)rotting, (die) vrot; lewersiekte (by skape); kaf, onsin, geklets; **dry** –, vermolming; **a** – **set in,** die naarheid het begin.
rot, v. vrot, sleg word, vergaan, bederwe; wegkwyn; pla, terg, die gek skeer; – **off,** afvrot.
rota, rooster, lys.
Rotarian, Rotariër.
rotary, draaiend, rondgaande; rotasie- . .
Rotary-club, Rotariërsvereniging.
rotate, draai; laat draai; (af)wissel.
rotation, (om)draaiing, wenteling, rotasie; afwisseling; **in, by** –, om die beurt; – **of crops,** wisselbou.
rotator, omdraaier; draaispier.
rotatory, draaiend, draai- . . .
rote, gewoonte; **know by** –, van buite ken.
rotten, vrot; beroerd, sleg; korrup.
rotter, deugniet, niksnuts, vrotterd.
rotund, rond; deftig; plomp, vet.
rotunda, rotonde.
rotundity, rondheid.
rouble, roebel.
rouge, a. rooi.
rouge, n. (rooi) blanketsel, rouge.
rouge, v. verf, blanket.
rough, a. grof, ru, hard; wild, woes, ongemanierd; ongelyk, hobbelagtig, onagfewerk; onstuimig; vrank; – **manners,** onbeskaafde maniere; – **sea,** ruwe (onstuimige) see; **have a** – **time,** swaar kry; **be** – **on somebody,** iemand laat swaar kry; **I can make a** – **guess,** ek kan min of meer raai; **a** – **sketch,** 'n ruwe skets (ontwerp); **it is only a** – **estimate,** dit is maar by benadering geskat, dit is maar 'n globale raming; – **house,** moles, tumult, bakleiery.
rough, n. oneffenheid, hobbelagtigheid, deugniet, skurk; **over** – **and smooth,** oor klippe en bosse; **the** – **and smooth of life,** die suur en soet van die lewe; **in the** –, onafgewerk; in die natuurlike staat.
rough, v. 'n ruwe skets (ontwerp) maak; dresseer, touwys maak; **we'll have to** – **it,** ons moet maar deurdruk, ons moet dit maar verlief neem; – **somebody up the wrong way,** iemand die hoenders in maak.
roughage, ru-kos, ru-voer; veselstof.
rough-and-ready, ongeërg; primitief; ondeurdag, oppervlakkig; grof.
rough-and-tumble, a. slordig, onordelik, wild; ongereeld, deurmekaar.
rough-and-tumble, n. vegparty, stoeiery.
roughcast, a. gerofkas.
roughcast, n. grintspatpleister.
roughcast, v. grintspat.
rough-hew, ru bekap (behou).
rough-hewn, ru, ongepolys; onafgewerk.
rough-house, hard(handig) aanpak.
roughly, ru, naasteby, min of meer; – **speaking,** in die algemeen.
rough-neck, ruwe vent.
rough-rider, perdetemmer, jongperd-ryer.

roughshod, skerp beslaan; **ride – over**, baasspeel oor, nie ontsien nie.
rough-wrought, grof bewerk, onafgewerk.
roulade, toonloper, roulade.
rouleau, rolletjie.
roulette, roulette (roelet).
Roumanian, n. Roemeniër; Roemeense (vrou); Roemeens.
Roumanian, a. Roemeens.
round, a. rond, bolvormig, sirkelvormig, kringvormig; welluidend, vol; vloeiend; rondborstig, openhartig.
round, n. kring, bol; omgang, omloop; rondte; sport, rondelied; **the daily –**, daaglikse arbeid; **go one's –s**, die ronde doen; **story goes the –**, dit word vertel; **never fired a single –**, nie 'n enkele skoot geskiet nie; **two –s of toast**, twee snye geroosterde brood; **twenty –s of cartridges**, twintig patrone; **a – of drinks**, 'n rondjie.
round, prep. (rond)om.
round, adv. om; **all the year –**, die hele jaar deur, dwarsdeur die jaar; **go a long way –**, 'n groot draai loop; **show –**, laat sien, wys.
round, v. afrond, rond maak; insluit, omring; omseil; **– up**, bymekaar maak; gevange neem.
roundabout, n. ompad, omweg; draaimeul.
roundabout, a. wydlopig; omslagtig.
roundelay, rondedans; voëlgesang.
rounders, honkbal.
roundly, kortaf, ronduit, botweg; sirkelvormig.
rouse, wakker maak; wakker word; opwek, aanspoor; opja.
rousing, opwekkend, besielend, inspirerend; kragtig.
roustabout, dokwerker; handlanger.
rout, n. lawaai, rumoer, oproer; algemene vlug, verpletterende neerlaag; **put to –**, totaal verslaan, op die vlug ja.
rout, v. verslaan, op die vlug ja.
route, weg, pad, koers, roete; **en –**, op pad; op weg, en route.
routine, sleur, gewoonte; roetine.
rove, v. (rond)swerf, dwaal, ronddool.
rover, rondswerwer; seerower; losspeler.
roving: **– commission**, uitgebreide opdrag; **– correspondent**, reisende verslaggewer.
row, n. ry; reeks; **in a –**, op 'n ry.
row, v. roei.
row, n. (die) roei; roeitoggie.
row, n. rusie, twis; rumoer, lawaai, opskudding; **get into a –**, in die ongeleentheid kom.
row, v. rusie maak; 'n skrobbering gee.
rowdy, a. luidrugtig, lawaaierig.
rowdy, n. lawaaimaker, raasbek.
rowdyism, lawaai, herrie; oproerigheid, luidrugtigheid; wanordelikheid.
rowel, n. spoor(ratjie), wieletjie.
rowel, v. spoor, die spore gee.
rowing, n. (die) roei.
rowing, a. roei- . . .
rowlock, roeimik, roeiklamp, roeipen.
royal, koninklik, vorstelik; van die koning; rojaal, uitstekend, eersteklas.
royalist, n. koningsgesinde, rojalis.
royalist, a. koningsgesinde, rojalisties.
royalty, koningskap; die vorstelike huis; outeursaandeel, tantième, honorarium.
rub, v. vrywe, skuur; skawe; polys, opvrywe, blink maak; **– one's hands**, jou hande vrywe; **– shoulders with**, in aanraking kom met; **begin to – noses with**, op vriendskaplike voet kom met; **– somebody the wrong way**, iemand verkeerd aanpak (vererg); **– in**, invrywe;

inpeper; **please don't – it in**, moet my dit nie onder die neus vrywe nie.
rub, n. (die) vrywe, vrywing; moeilikheid, hinderpaal, knoop; **give the table a –**, vrywe die tafel bietjie op; **there's the –**, daar sit die knoop, daar lê die moeilikheid.
rub-a-dub, getrommel, geroffel.
rubber, n. vrywer; masseur; vryfdoek; rubber, gomlastiek; uitveër, gummi.
rubber, n. rubber (by brugspeel).
rubbish, vuilgoed, vullis, afval; rommel; prulwerk, waardelose goed; onsin, kafpraatjies, geklets.
rubble, afval; steengruis.
rubefy, rooi maak.
Rubicon, Rubicon; **cross the –**, die beslissende stap doen, die teerling werp.
rubicund, rooi.
rubidium, rubidium.
rubiginous, roeskleurig.
rubric, rubriek, afdeling, hoofstuk.
rubricate, in rubriek verdeel.
ruby, n. robyn; (rooi) puisie.
ruby, a. robynkleurig.
ruck, n. trop, hoop, klomp, massa.
ruck, ruckle, v. kreukel, plooi, vou.
ruck, ruckle, n. kreukel, plooi, vou.
ruckle, n. (ge)roggel.
ruckle, v. roggel.
rucksack, rugsak, bladsak.
ruction, onenigheid, twis, rusie; rumoer.
rudder, roer, stuur.
ruddle, n. rooisel, rooiklei.
ruddle, v. met rooiklei maak.
ruddle, v. met rooiklei merk.
ruddock, rooiborsie.
ruddy, rooi; blosend; **– health**, blakende gesondheid.
rude, ru, grof; woes; onbeskof, ongepoets, onmanierlik, onbeleef; onbeskaaf, primitief.
rudiment, grondslag; rudiment; **–s**, eerste beginsels, grondbeginsels.
rudimentary, rudimentêr; elementêr.
rue, v. betreur, berou hê oor; **you shall – the day** jy sal die dag betreur.
rue, n. berou, leedwese.
rue, n. wynruit.
rueful, verdrietig, treurig, bedroef.
ruff, geplooide kraag; ringnekduif.
ruffian, n. booswig, skurk, woestaard.
ruffian, a. skurkagtig, woes, gemeen.
ruffle, v. deurmekaar maak, frommel; plooi, rimpel; vererg, verstoor; in die war bring, ontstel; **his temper was –d**, hy was uit sy humeur; **–d hair**, kroes hare.
ruffle, n. rimpeling; plooi; storing, beroering, verwarring; twis, rusie.
rufous, rooibruin.
rug, reiskombers; reisdeken; vloermatjie.
rugby (football), rugbyvoetbal.
rugged, ruig, ru; ongelyk, hobbelagtig, skurf; nors, hard, streng; onbeholpe, lomp; kragtig, sterk.
rugger, rugby.
rugose, gerimpel.
rug-strap, kombersriem.
ruin, n. verderf, ondergang, ongeluk, val; ruïne, puinhoop, bouval, murasie; **tumble in –s**, in puin stort, verval; **bring to –**, in die ongeluk stort, ruïneer.
ruin, v. ruïneer (reneweer), tot 'n val bring, in die ongeluk stort, bederf; vernietig, verniel; **his hopes were –ed**, sy verwagtinge is die bodem ingeslaan.

ruination, ongeluk, verderf, ondergang, verwoesting, vernieling, renewasie.
ruinous, verderflik, nadelig, noodlottig.
rule, n. reël, bepaling, reglement; maatstaf, standaard; voorskrif; bestuur, beheer, gesag, regering, heerskappy, bewind; liniaal, maatstock, duimstok; **as a –**, in die reël, gewoonlik; **I know it by – of thumb**, ek ken dit uit die praktyk; **deduce –s of action**, 'n vaste gedragslyn neerlê.
rule, v. regeer, bestuur, beheer, heerskappy voer oor; bedwing, beheers; bepaal, vasstel; linieer, lyn trek; **–d him out of order**, het hom buite die orde verklaar; **– out**, buite beskouing laat, nie in ag neem nie.
ruler, heerser, vors; duimstok, liniaal.
ruling, a. heersend; **– prices**, markpryse, heersende pryse.
ruling, n. beslissing, uitspraak.
rum, n. rum.
rum, rummy, a. sonderling, snaaks.
rumba, rumba.
rumble, v. rommel, dreun; ratel, raas.
rumble, n. gerommel, gedreun; geratel.
rumble-tumble, rammelkas; gerammel.
rumbustious, rumoerig, luidrugtig.
rumen, pens.
ruminant, n. herkouer, herkouende dier.
ruminant, a. herkouend; peinsend.
ruminate, herkou; **– about, of, on, over**, oorpeins, diep dink oor.
rumination, herkouing; oorpeinsing.
rummage, v. visenteer, deursnuffel, omkrap.
rummage, n. (die) deursoek; rommel.
rummage-sale, rommelverkoping.
rummer, wynglas, roemer.
rumour, n. gerug.
rumour, v. uitstrooi, rugbaar maak, rondvertel.
rump, stuitjie, agterste, agterste deel.
rumple, kreukel, vou, verfrommel.
rumpsteak, biefstuk.
rumpus, oproer, rumoer; rusie.
run, v. hardloop, hol; loop; laat loop; laat wei; laat oploop; stroom, vloei; traan, drup; in omloop wees, versprei word; lui; smokkel; **– to meet one's troubles**, jou moeilikhede vooruitloop; **tune –s in the head**, die deuntjie draai in die kop; **feeling –s high**, die gemoedere is gaande; **his eyes –**, sy oë traan; **– short**, opraak, kort kom; **– messages**, boodskappe dra; **he –s a chance of being . . .**, dit is moontlik dat hy . . .; **he –s this whole show**, hy is die baas hier, hy het alles te sê; **one's blood –s cold**, dit laat jou gril (ys); **the story –s**, dit word vertel; **– a race**, reisies hardloop, aan 'n wedren deelneem; **– about**, rondhardloop, rondloop; **– across somebody**, iemand op die lyf loop (toevallig ontmoet); iemand onderstebo ry; **– after**, agternaloop; nastrewe, najaag; **– one's head against the wall**, jou kop teen die muur stamp; **– one's eyes along, down, over**, jou oë laat gaan oor; **– at**, stormloop; **– away**, weghardloop; die spat neem; **don't – away with the idea**, moet dit nie so gou glo nie; **– down**, onderstebo loop, in botsing kom met; inhaal, vang; slegmaak; **my watch is – down**, my horlosie is afgeloop; **he looks – down**, hy lyk gedaan (afgewerk); **– in**, vlugtige besoek aflê; aanloop; in die tronk sit; inklim, inpeper; **it –s in the family**, dit sit in die familie; **– in**, aanloop; gevange neem; inry (motor); inloop (masjien); **– into**, vasloop teen; **– off**, weghardloop; afdwaal; aframmel; **– on**, voorthardloop; voortbabbel, aframmel; **– out**, uitloop (krieket), opraak;

– oneself out, jou flou hardloop; **– over**, oorloop; oorgaan, nagaan; omry, onderstebo ry; **– one's fingers over**, jou vingers laat gaan oor; **– through**, deurloop; deursteek; deurhaal, uitkrap; **– up**, oploop, opja; optel; opskiet; **– up accounts**, op rekening koop; **– to extremes**, tot uiterstes gaan.
run, n. lopie; toeloop; aanvraag; wedren; ritjie, toggie, uitstappie; verloop, gang; soort, klas; (hoender)hok; weiveld; vry gebruik, toegang; **we were allowed the – of their house**, hulle het ons vry toegang tot hulle huis gegee; **on the –**, op die vlug; in die hardloop; **in the long –**, op die duur; **– of the mill**, gewoon, gemiddeld.
runabout, (rond)swerwend.
runagate, droster, wegloper.
runaway, n. vlugteling, wegloper.
runaway, a. op loop, weghollende.
rune, runeskrif.
rung, sport.
runic, a. rune- . . .
runic, n. runeskrif.
runlet, wynvat.
runlet, stroompie.
runnel, riviertjie, stroompie; geut.
runner, hardloper; boodskapper, bode, agent; loper; rank, spruit; skuifring.
running, n. (die) loop; (die) hardloop; **he is out of the –**, hy het geen kans nie, hy tel nie mee nie.
running, a. lopend; **– account**, lopende rekening; **– commentary**, deurlopende kommentaar; **ours was a – fight**, ons het veg-veg gevlug (gehardloop); **– knot**, skuifknoop; **three days –**, drie dae agtereen.
running-board, treeplank.
runway, baan; landingsbaan; glyplank; groef.
rupee, n. breuk; tweespalk, skeuring.
rupture, v. verbreek; 'n breuk kry.
rural, plattelands, landelik.
ruse, streek, lis, krygslis.
rush, biesie; **not worth a –**, nie 'n blou duit werd nie.
rush, v. hardloop, storm, hol; bestorm, stormloop; jaag, voortsnel; **I refuse to be –ed**, ek laat my nie aanja nie; **– at**, bestorm, stormloop; **– into the room**, die kamer binnestorm; **– into extremes**, van die een na die ander uiterste spring; **– into print**, na die pers hardloop, haastig laat druk.
rush, n. vaart, haas; stormloop; toestorming, toeloop; drukte; **make a – for the train**, na die trein storm.
rusk, beskuit.
russet, rooibruin.
Russia, Rusland.
Russian, n. Rus; Russies.
Russian, a. Russies.
rust, n. roes.
rust, v. roes, verroes; laat roes.
rustic, a. landelik; plattelands; lomp, boers; onvervals, eenvoudig; rustiek.
rustic, n. landbewoner, boer, takhaar.
rusticate, buite gaan woon; verboers raak.
rusticity, landelikheid; eenvoud.
rustle, v. ritsel, ruis; steel.
rustle, n. geritsel, geruis.
rustler, veedief.
rusty, geroes, verroes; stram; ouderwets, uit die mode; krassend, skor; roeskleur; **my Latin is a little –**, my Latyn het ek al bietjie vergeet.
rut, n. wielspoor, moet, groef; gewoonte, gebruik; roetine, sleur.
rut, v. spore trek (maak), moete maak.

rut, n. bronstyd.
rut, v. brons wees.
ruth, meegevoel.

ruthless, meedoënloos, wreed.
rye, rog.
rye-bread, rogbrood.

Sabaism — salary

Sabaism, sterreverering.
Sabbatarian, n. Sabbatariër.
Sabbatarian, a. Sabbataries.
Sabbath, Sabbat(dag), rusdag; **keep the –,** die Sabbat vier (heilig).
Sabbath-breaker, Sabbatskender.
Sabbath-day, Sabbatdag.
Sabbatic(al), Sabbat- . . .; **– year,** Sabbatjaar.
Sabian, Sabiër.
Sabine, n. Sabyn.
Sabine, a. Sabyns.
sable, n. sabel(dier); sabelbont.
sable, swart, donker kleur; swartwitpens; – antelope, swartwitpens(bok).
sabot, klomp, blokskoen, houtsoolskoen.
sabotage, sabotasie.
sabotage, v. saboteer.
saboteur, saboteur.
sabre, n. sabel.
sabre, v. neersabel.
sabulous, sanderig, sand- . . .; korrelrig.
sac, sak.
saccharic, suiker- . . .; **– acid,** suikersuur.
sacchariferous, suikerhoudend.
saccharify, (ver)suiker.
saccharine, a. suiker- . . ., suikeragtig.
saccharine, n. sakkarien(-ine), saggarien(ine).
sacciform, sakvormig.
sacerdocy, priesterskap, priestersamp.
sacerdotage, priestergees; priestersamp.
sacerdotal, priesterlik, priester- . . .
sack, n. sak; **give the –,** in die pad steek; afsê.
sack, v. in sakke gooi; ontslaan; afsê.
sack, n. plundering, verwoesting.
sack, v. plunder, verwoes.
sackcloth, sakgoed; **in – and ashes,** in sak en as.
sack-race, sakloop.
sacrament, sakrament.
sacramental, sakramenteel, sakraments-.
sacred, heilig, gewyd; onskendbaar; **– music,** gewyde musiek.
sacrifice, n. offerande, offer; opoffering; verlies; **at the – of,** ten koste van.
sacrifice, v. offer; afstaan.
sacrificial, offer . . .
sacrilege, heiligskennis, ontheiliging.
sacrilegious, ontheiligend, heiligskennend.
sacristan, koster.
sacristy, sakristie.
sacrosanct, heilig, onskendbaar.
sacrum, heiligbeen.
sad, treurig, droewig, bedroef, neerslagtig, verdrietig, terneergedruk.
sadden, bedroef, treurig stem; droewig word.
saddle, n. saal; rugstuk; bergrug; stut; **in the –,** in die saal; aan die bewind; **put the – on the wrong horse,** die skuld op die verkeerde persoon pak.
saddle, v. opsaal; belas; **– somebody with the responsibility,** die verantwoordelikheid op iemand skuiwe; **be –ed, with** opgeskeep sit met.
saddle-back, saalrug.
saddle-backed, holrug.
saddle-bag, saalsak, holster.
saddle-bow, saalknop.
saddle-cloth, saalkleedjie.
saddle-horse, ryperd.
saddler, saalmaker, tuiemaker.
saddlery, saalmakery.
saddle-tree, saalboom.
Sadducee, Sadduseër.
sadism, sadisme.
safari, safari; jagekspedisie.
safe, n. brandkas, geldkas; (bewaar)kluis; koskas, spenskas; vlieëkas; **– deposit,** (brand)kluis, bewaarkluis; versekeringsloket.
safe, a. veilig, seker; ongedeerd; **it is – to say,** 'n mens kan met sekerheid sê; **– and sound,** fris en gesond; **a – statesman,** 'n betroubare staatsman; **– from,** vry van, beveilig teen; **– custody,** versekerde bewaring.
safe-conduct, vrygeleide.
safeguard, n. beskerming; vrygeleide.
safeguard, v. beskerm, beveilig; verseker.
safekeeping, bewaring.
safely, veilig; gerus.
safety, veiligheid, sekerheid; **play for –,** versigtig te werk gaan (speel).
safety-belt, reddingsgordel, reddingsboei.
safety-bolt, rus (van 'n geweerslot).
safety-chain, veiligheidsketting.
safety-curtain, brandskerm.
safety-lamp, veiligheidslamp.
safety-lock, nagslot; veiligheidslot; rus.
safety-match, vuurhoutjie.
safety-pin, haakspeld, knipspeld.
safety-razor, veiligheidskeermes.
safety-valve, veiligheidsklep.
saffian, saffiaan, marokynleer.
saffron, n. saffraan; saffraankleur.
saffron, a. saffraan, saffraankleurig.
saffrony, saffraanagtig, saffraan.
sag, v. uitsak, afsak, afhang, skiet, pap (slap) hang; laat afsak; daal.
sag, n. afsakking, deursakking; daling.
saga, saga; sage, legende.
sagacious, skerpsinnig, slim, skrander.
sagacity, skerpsinnigheid, skranderheid.
sage, a. wys, verstandig.
sage, n. wyse, wysgeer.
sage, n. salie.
sago, sago.
Sahara, Sahara; woesteny.
said, sien say.
sail, n. seil; skip; seiltog(gie); **(in) full, – met volle seile; go for a –,** op 'n seiltog(gie) gaan; **take in –,** die seile inbind; stadig oor die klippe gaan.
sail, v. seil, vaar; laat seil; gly, trek.
sail-cloth, seil(doek).
sailer, seilskip.
sailing, (die) seil; vertrek (van skip); **it's plain –,** dit is maklik genoeg.
sailor, seeman, matroos; **I am a very bad –,** ek word baie gou seesiek.
saint, a. heilig; sint.
saint, n. heilige, vrome.
sainted, heilig; vroom.
saint-like, heilig, vroom.
saintliness, heiligheid, vroomheid.
saintly, vroom.
Saint-Vitus's-Dance, senuweetrekkings, danssiekte, Sint-Vitusdans.
sake: for the – of, ter wille van; **for my –,** ter wille van my; om my ontwil; **for peace' –,** om vredeswil; **for goodness' –,** om liefdeswil, in hemelsnaam; **for any –,** in hemelsnaam.
salaam, n. groet, buiging, salaam.
salaam, a. groet, buiging, salaam.
salable, verkoopbaar; verkoop- . . .
salacious, wellustig, ontugtig.
salad, slaai.
salad-days, onervare jeug, domdae.
salad-dressing, slaaisous.
salad-oil, soetolie, slaai-olie.
salamander, salamander; vuurgees.
salamandrine, salamanderagtig.
sal-ammoniac, salmiak (salammoniak).
salary, n. salaris, loon, besoldiging.

salary 648 **sanguineous**

salary, v. salarieer, besoldig.
sale, verkoping, verkoping, uitverkoop; afset; vendusie, veiling; **for –**, te koop; **put up for –**, opveil; **deed of –**, koopbrief; **–s resistance**, verkoopweerstand.
salesman, verkoper; winkelklerk.
saleswoman, verkoopster.
Salic, Salies; **– law**, Saliese wet.
salient, uitspringend; opvallend.
saliferous, southoudend.
saline, a. sout -. . ., soutagtig.
saline, n. sout; soutpan; soutbron.
salinity, southeid; soutgehalte.
salinometer, soutmeter, salinometer.
saliva, spu(spuug), speeksel.
salivary, spu- . . ., speeksel- . . .; **– gland**, speekselklier.
salivate, kwyl; laat kwyl.
salivation, kwyl; speekselafskeiding.
sallow, n. waterwilg, dwergwilg.
sallow, bleek, geel sieklik.
sally, m. uitval; uitstappie, uittog; kwinkslag, raak gesegde.
sally, v. uitstorm, 'n uitval maak; **– forth, out**, daarop uitgaan, uittrek.
sally-port, uitvalpoort.
salmon, n. salm.
salmon, a. salmkleurig.
saloon, salon, saal; drinkplek; salonrytuig, passasierswa; toe motor.
saloon-carriage, salonwa.
saloon-rifle, salongeweertjie: kleingeweertjie.
salt, n. sout; soutvaatjie; gevatheid; geestigheid; pikbroek, seerob; **eat one's –**, iemand se brood eet; iemand se gas wees; **he is not worth his –**, hy verdien nie sy sout nie; **take with a grain of –**, nie al te letterlik opvat nie; **the – of the earth**, die sout van die aarde; **in –**, ingesout; **an old –**, 'n seerob.
salt, a. sout, gesout; pekel; skerp; gekrui.
salt, v. sout, insout, pekel; **– an account**, 'n rekening dik maak; **– the books**, ontvangste aandik.
saltation, spring, dans; sprong.
saltatory, springend.
salt-cellar, soutvaatjie.
salted, gesout.
salter, southandelaar; insouter.
saltigrade, n. springspinnekop.
saltigrade, a. spring- . . .
saltish, soutagtig, souterig, sout.
salt-lick, brak, soutlekplek, brakplek.
saltpetre, salpeter.
salt-works, soutmakery.
salty, souterig, brak.
salubrious, gesond, heilsaam.
salubrity, heilsaamheid, gesondheid.
salutary, heilsaam, voordelig, gesond.
salutation, groet, begroeting.
salutatory, (be)groetend.
salute, v. groet, begroet; salueer, aanslaan; ereskote los (afskiet).
salute, n. groet, begroeting; saluut, saluutskoot; kus; a **– of seven guns was fired**, sewe saluutskote is afgeskiet; **take the –**, die saluut beantwoord.
salvable, redbaar; bergbaar.
salvage, n. berging; bergloon.
salvage, v. red, berg.
salvation, redding, verlossing, heil, behoud, saligheid.
Salvation Army, Heilsleër.
Salvationist, Heilsoldaat.
salve, n. salf, smeersel; balsem.
salve, v. salf, insmeer; heel; red.

salver, (skink)bord, skottel.
salvo, salvo, sarsie; **– of applause**, dawerende toejuiging.
sal volatile, vlugsout.
salvor, berger, redder (van wrakgoedere).
Samaritan, n. Samaritaan; **good –**, barmhartige Samaritaan.
Samaritan, a. Samaritaans.
samba, samba.
same, (die)selfde; einste; genoemde; eentonig; **the very –**, die einste; **one and the –**, presies dieselfde; **she was always the –**, sy was altyd eenders; **it is all the – to me**, dit is vir my om die ewe; **much the –**, min of meer dieselfde; **at the – time**, terselfdertyd; tog, nieteenstaande; tegelykertyd; **all the –**, almaskie, tog.
sameness, gelykheid; eentonigheid.
samp, breek-, stampmielies (gebreekte, gestampte mielies).
sample, n. monster, staaltjie; voorbeeld.
sample, v. monsters (staaltjies) neem (uitdeel); probeer, toets, proe.
sampler, monster; borduurlap; toetser.
Samson, Simson.
sanative, **-tory**, genesend, genees- . . .
sanatorium, sanatorium.
sanctification, heiliging, wyding.
sanctified, heilig; geheilig; skynheilig.
sanctify, heilig, heilig maak, wy.
sanctimonious, skynheilig, skynvroom.
sanctimony, skynheiligheid.
sanction, n. goedkeuring, toestemming, bevestiging, strafmaatreël, sanksie.
sanction, v. goedkeur, bekragtig.
sanctitude, heiligheid.
sanctity, heiligheid, onskendbaarheid; reinheid.
sanctities, heilige pligte.
santuary, heiligdom; toevlugsoord.
sanctum, heiligdom.
sand, n. sand; **–s**, sandstreek; sandbank; sandkorrels; **the –s are running out**, die tyd is byna om; **built on –**, op sand gebou.
sand, v. met sand bestrooi; met sand skuur; onder sand begrawe.
sandal, sandaal.
sandal(wood), sandelhout.
sandbag, n. sandsak.
sandbag, v. sandsakke pak; met 'n sandsak slaan.
sand-bank, sandbank.
sand-bath, sandbad.
sand-blind, bysiende.
sand-box, sandkoker.
sand-glass, sandloper.
sand-hill, sandduin, sandbult.
sandiness, sanderigheid.
sandman, Klaas Vakie.
sandpaper, n. skuurpapier.
sandpaper, v. met skuurpapier vrywe.
sand-pit, sandgat.
sand-shoe, strandskoen.
sandstone, sandsteen.
sand-storm, sandstorm, stofstorm.
sandwich, n. toebroodjie.
sandwich, v. tussenin sit, inskuif, insluit.
sandy, a. sanderig; rooierig.
sandy, n. rooikop, „rooihaas".
sane, by jou volle verstand; verstandig.
sangaree, kruiewyn.
sang-froid, koelheid, bedaardheid.
sanguification, bloedvorming.
sanguinary, bloedig; moorddadig, wreed.
sanguine, bloedryk; optimisties, hoopvol; **vurig**, hartstogtelik; bloedrooi.
sanguineous, bloed- . . .; bloedkleurig, bloedrooi; bloedryk; sanguïnies.

**Sanhedrim, Sanhedrin, Joodse Raad.
sanitary, gesondheids- . . .; higiënies, sanitêr; –
officer, gesondheidsbeampte.
sanitate, higiënies verbeter.
sanitation, higiëniese versorging.
sanity, gesondheid van verstand; verstandigheid, gematigdheid.
Sanskrit, -scrit, Sanskrit.
Santa Claus, Sinterklaas.
sap,** n. sap, vog; lewenskrag.
sap, v. tap; droog maak; ondermyn.
sap, n. ingrawing, loopgraaf, myngraaf, sappe, ondermyning.
sap, v. loopgrawe maak, sappeer; ondergrawe; uitkalwe; ondermyn, verswak.
sap, v. blok.
sap, n. blokker; swaar werk; moeite.
sapid, geurig, smaaklik.
sapidity, smaaklikheid, geurigheid.
sapience, wysheid; eiewysheid.
sapient, eiewys, waanwys; verstandig.
sapless, saploos; droog; swak, uitgeput.
sapling, boompie.
saponaceous, seepagtig, seep-.
saponification, verseping.
saponify, verseep.
sapor, geur, smaak.
sapper, myngrawer, sappeur.
sapphire, saffier.
sapphirine, saffier- . . ., saffieragtig.
saraband, sarabande.
Saracen, n. Saraseen.
Saracen, a. Saraseens
sarcasm, sarkasme, bytende spot.
sarcastic, sarkasties, bytend, spottend.
sarcophagus, sarkofaag.
sarcous, vleis- . . ., spier- . . .
sardine, sardientjie.
sardonic, bitter, sinies, spottend, sardonies; – laugh, grynslag.
sardonyx, sardoniks.
sarong, sarong.
sarsaparilla, sarsaparilla.
sarsenet, voeringsy, sarsenetsy.
sartorial, kleermakers- . . .
sash, serp, gord, lyfband, seintuur.
sash, (skuif)raam.
sash-window, skuifraam.
Satan, Satan.
satanic(al), satanies, duiwels, hels.
satanism, boosheid, duiwelstreke.
satchel, sakkie, boeksak.
sate, versadig; oorlaai, volprop, walg.
sateen, linne-, wolsatyn.
satellite, satelliet, byplaneet; handlanger; – state, satellietstaat.
satiable, bevredigbaar, versadigbaar.
satiate, a. versadig, bevredig; sat.
satiate, v. versadig, bevredig; sat maak.
satiation, versadiging; satheid.
satiety, satheid, volheid, versadigheid; to –, tot satwordens toe.
satin, n. satyn.
satin, a. satyn- . . .
satin, v. glad en blink maak, satineer.
satinet(te), satinent.
satin-finish, satynglans, satynafwerking.
satin-paper, satynpapier.
satin-wood, satynhout.
satiny, satynagtig.
satire, satire, spotskrif, hekelskrif, hekeldig.
satiric(al), satiries, bytend, spottend.
satirise, hekel, spot met.
satirist, satirikus, hekeldigter; spotter.
satisfaction, voldoening, bevrediging, satisfaksie;

genoeë; betaling; if you can prove it to my – as jy my 'n bevredigende bewys kan lewer.
satisfactory, bevredigend; voldoende.
satisfy, bevredig, voldoen, tevrede stel; oortuig, gerusstel; versadig; I am satisfied, ek is tevrede; – the requirements, aan die eise voldoen; – onseself, jouself oortuig.
satrap, goewerneur, satraap.
saturable, deurweekbaar, versadigbaar.
saturate, deurweek, deurtrek; versadig.
saturation, deurweking; versadiging.
Saturday, Saterdag.
Saturn, Saturnus.
saturnalia, Saturnalieë, Saturnusfees; uitgelate pret, uitspattinge.
saturnalian, uitgelate, uitspattig, dol.
Saturnian, a. Saturnies.
Saturnian, n. bewoner van Saturnus.
saturnine, somber, swaarmoedig; lood- . . .; – symptoms, simptome van loodvergiftiging.
saturnism, loodvergiftiging, saturnisme.
satyr, sater, bosgod; wellusteling.
satyric, saters- . . ., van saters.
sauce, n. sous; vrypostigheid; hunger is the best –, honger is die beste kok; none of your –, moenie vir jou so astrant hou nie!
sauce, v. smaaklik maak; sous, kruie; astrant (vrypostig) wees.
sauce-boat, souskommetjie, souspotjie.
sauce-box, brutale vent, parmant.
saucepan, kastrol.
saucer, piering.
saucy, astrant, brutaal; piekfyn.
saunter, v. slenter, drentel, kuier.
saunter, n. slentergang; slenterdans.
saurian, a. akke(r)dis- . . ., akke(r)disagtig.
sausage, wors, sosys.
sausage-machine, worsmasjien.
savage, a. wild, woes, barbaars; wreed; boos, woedend; naak.
savage, n. barbaar, onbeskaafde, wilde mens; woestaard, wreedaard.
savagery, barbaarsheid, woestheid.
savanna(h), grasvlakte.
savant, geleerde.
save, v. red, verlos; salig maak; behoed; bewaar; spaar, opsy sit, wegsit; – us, die Hemel bewaar ons!; God – the King, God behoede die koning; – appearances, die skyn bewaar (red); – one's breath, stil bly; you may – your pains, spaar jou die moeite, dit is moeite tervergeefs.
save, prep. behalwe, behoudens.
save, conj. tensy, behalwe dat.
saving, a. reddend, verlossend; spaarsaam; a clause, stipulasie, voorbehoud.
saving, prep. behalwe, uitgenome, uitgesonder; – your reverence, met alle eerbied vir u.
saving, n. redding, verlossing; besparing; reservasie; –s, spaargeld.
savings-bank, spaarbank.
Saviour, Heiland, Verlosser, Saligmaker;
saviour, redder.
savour, n. geur; smaak.
savour, v. smaak; ruik; – of, ruik na, laat dink aan.
savouriness, smaaklikheid, geurigheid.
savoury, smaaklik, geurig, lekker.
savoy, savojekool.
saw, n. spreekwoord, segswyse, spreuk.
saw, n. saag; cross-cut –, treksaag.
saw, v. saag(sae).
sawder: soft –, mooipraatjies.
saw-dust, saagsel.
saw-fish, saagvis.
saw-frame, saagraam.

saw-horse, saagbok.
saw-mill, saagmeul.
saw-pit, saagkuil.
saw-set, tandsetter, saagsetter.
sawyer, saer; drywende boom.
saxe-blue, saksies-blou.
Saxon, n. Angel-Saksies.
Saxon, a. Saksies.
saxophone, saxofoon.
say, v. sê, beweer; opsê; – **a good word for somebody**, vir iemand 'n goeie woordjie doen; – **grace**, bid (voor die ete); **that is to** –, dit wil sê, met ander woorde; – **one's lesson**, jou les opsê they –, dit word gesê; **jou may well – so**, dit mag jy wel sê; –**s you!**, sou jy dink!; **I cannot** –, ek weet nie; **I** –, **what a beauty**, maar hoor, dis 'n pragstuk!; **it –s in the Bible**, die Bybel sê, in die Bybel staan; – **out**, reguit (ronduit) sê; – **over**, herhaal, nog 'n slag sê.
say, n. mening, bewering; **let him have his** –, laat hom uitpraat (klaar praat); **I had no – in the matter**, ek het geen seggenskap (niks te sê) gehad in die saak nie.
saying, gesegde, spreekwoord; sê; **as the –is**, soos die spreekwoord sê; **that goes without** –, dit spreek vanself; **there is no – who it was**, dit is uiters moeilik om te sê wie dit was.
scab, skurfte, brandsiekte; kors, roof; onderkruiper.
scabbard, skede.
scabby, skurf, brandsiek.
scabies, skurfte.
scabious, skurf.
scabrous, skurfagtig, ongelyk; lastig.
scaffold, n. skavot; steier, stellasie.
scaffold, v. van 'n steier voorsien, stut.
scaffolding, steierhout, stellasie.
scalable, beklimbaar.
scalariform, leervormig.
scalawag, -lly-, deurgniet, niksnuts.
scald, v. (met kookwater) brand, skroei.
scald, n. brandwond, brandplek.
scald, n. oud-Noorse digter, skalde.
scalding, gloeiend, brandend, skroeiend; – **tears**, hete (brandende) trane; – **hot**, kokend-heet, gloeiendheet.
scale, n. skob (skub); skilfer; lagie; dop.
scale, v. skobbe (skubbe) afkrap; afskilfer, opskilfer; uitdop, afdop.
scale, n. (weeg)skaal; **turn the** –, die deurslag gee; **pair of –s**, (weeg)skaal.
scale, v. weeg (weë); trek, haal.
scale, n. skaal; toonskaal, toonladder; stelsel; maatstaf; **the social** –, die maatskaplike leer; **on a large** –, op groot skaal; – **of wages**, loonskaal.
scale, v. beklim, opklouter.
scale-armour, geskubde harnas.
scalene triangle, ongelyksydige driehoek.
scaling-ladder, stormleer.
scallop, scollop, n. kammossel; skulp; skulpwerk.
scallop, v. uitskulp; in die skulp kook.
scallywag, sien **scalawag**.
scalp, n. skedel; kopvel.
scalp, v. skalpeer, die kopvel afslag.
scalpel, ontleedmes.
scaly, skubbig.
scamp, skurk, skelm, vabond.
scamper, v. hardloop, weghol; galop.
scamper, n. galop, draf; vlugtige toer.
scan, skandeer; noukeurig ondersoek, bekyk, beskou.
scandal, skandaal, skande; aanstoot; kwaadpraat, skindery, laster.

scandalize, belaster; aanstoot gee, beledig, ergernis verwek.
scandalmonger, kwaadprater, skindertong, storiemaker, kekkelbek.
scandalous, skandelik, lasterlik.
Scandinavian, n. Skandinawiër; Skandinawies.
Scandinavian, a. Skandinawies.
scansion, skandering.
scansorial, klim-. . ., klimmend.
scant, a. karig, armoedig, skraal, gering; – **of breath**, kortasem; **with** – **courtesy**, met weinig beleefdheid.
scant, v. beperk, knap toemeet.
scantily, karig, skraal, effentjies, dun, armoedig; – **fed**, karig gevoed; – **clad,** armoedig gekleed; met min klere aan.
scantling, bietjie, stukkie, klein hoeveelheid; staaltjie; balkie.
scanty, skaars, karig, skraal, min.
scapegoat, sondebok.
scapegrace, deugniet, niksnuts.
scapula, skouerblad.
scapular, a. van die skouerblad.
scapular, n. skapulier; rugveer.
scar, n. merk, litteken.
scar, v. (met littekens) merk; gesond word, 'n litteken vorm.
scar, scaur, krans, steilte.
scarab, skarabee; kewer.
scaramouch, bluffer, grootprater.
scarce, skaars; seldsaam; **make jourself** –, trap maak dat jy wegkom.
scarcely, nouliks, ternouernood, skaars.
scare, v. skrik maak, bang maak, laat skrik; afskrik; – **away**, wegja, verwilder, op loop ja.
scare, n. vrees, skrik, paniek.
scarecrow, voëlverskrikker.
scaremonger, alarmblaser, skrikverwekker, onrussaaier, alarmis.
scarf, n. serp, halsdoek.
scarf, n. naat, las.
scarf, v. las, saamvoeg.
scarf-pin, daspeld.
scarification, insnyding; kerwing.
scarify, insnydinge in die vel maak; eg, loswerk; kwel, seer maak; hekel.
scarlatina, roodvonk, skarlakenkoors.
scarlet, n. skarlaken, skarlakenrooi.
scarlet, a. skarlakenrooi, helderrooi, – **fever**, skarlakenkoors.
scarp, n. steilte, skuinste; eskarp (muur).
scarp, v. skuins maak, eskarpeer.
scathe, v. beskadig, kwes, beseer.
scathe, n. letsel; **without** –, onbeskadig, sonder letsel, ongedeerd.
scatheless, ongedeerd.
scathing, vlymend, skerp, vernietigend, verpletterend; – **sarcasm**, vlymende sarkasme.
scatter, n. verspreiding; spreiding.
scatter, v. strooi, verstrooi, rondstrooi, versprei; uiteendrywe (hoop)verydel.
scatter-brain, warhoofdige, warkop.
scatter-brained, waarhoofdig.
scavenge, straat vee, opruim, skoonmaak.
scavenger, straatveër.
scavenger-beetle, miskruier.
scenario, draaiboek.
scene, toneel, tafereel; voorval, standjie; **the** – **is laid in India**, die stuk speel in Indië **the** – **of the disaster**, die toneel van die ramp; **the third** – **of Act 2**, die derde toneel van die tweede bedryf; –**s of clerical life**, sketse uit die predikantslewe; **behind the** –**s**, agter die skerms; **change of** –, verandering van toneel; **quit the** –, van die toneel verdwyn; sterwe; **don't make**

scene-painter   651   **scorn**

a –, moenie opvlieënd word nie, moenie 'n lawaai maak nie.
scene-painter, toneeldekorateur.
scenery, natuurtonele, natuurskoon; toneel, toneeldekorasie, dekoratief.
scene-shifter, masjinis, toneelhandlanger.
scenic, toneel- . . ., dramaties; skilderagtig; – **drive**, landskapspad; – **railway**, panoramaspoor.
scenography, perspektieftekening.
scent, v. ruik; insnuif; met geur vul; parfumeer; vermoed; **the rose –s the air,** die roos vul die lug met sy geur; **–ed cigarettes,** geparfumeerde sigarette; – **out,** uitsnuffel.
scent, n. ruik (reuk), geur; ruiksin; laventel, ruikgoed; odeur; lug, spoor; **follow up the –,** die spoor volg; **on the –,** op die spoor; **put off the –,** van die spoor bring; **get the – of something,** iets in die neus kry.
scent-bottle, reukflessie, odeurflessie.
sceptic, n. twyfelaar.
sceptical, skepties, ongelowig.
scepticism, skeptisisme, twyfelsug.
sceptre, septer, staf.
schedule, n. lys, opgaaf, staat; **on –,** op tyd.
schedule, v. op die lys plaas; **–d time,** die bepaalde tyd.
schematic, skematies.
scheme, n. skema, plan, ontwerp, skets; voorneme; – **of colour,** kleurskema.
scheme, v. planne maak (beraam); intrigeer, knoei, konkel.
schemer, planmaker; intrigant, knoeier.
schism, skeuring, verdeeldheid.
schismatic, n. skeurmaker, verdeler.
schismatic, a. verdelend, skeurmakend.
schist, leisteen.
scholar, skolier, leerling; geleerde.
scholarly, geleerd, knap, wetenskaplik.
scholarship, geleerdheid; studiebeurs.
scholastic, a. skolasties; skools.
scholastic, n. skolastikus.
scholasticism, skolastiek.
scholium, verklarende aantekening.
school, n. skool, skoolgebou; leerskool, oefenskool; **go to –,** skoolgaan, skool toe gaan; **in the – of adversity,** in die skool van beproewing.
school, v. leer, onderrig, onderwys, oefen, dril; tug, vermaan, bestraf; – **oneself to patience,** leer om geduldig te wees.
school, n. skool (van visse).
school, v. skole vorm.
school-board, skoolraad.
schoolboy, skoolseun.
school-days, skooldae.
schoolfellow, skoolmaat.
schoolhouse, skool(gebou).
schooling, opvoeding, onderwys.
school-inspector, skoolinspekteur.
schoolmaster, skoolmeester, onderwyser.
schoolmistress, onderwyseres.
schoolroom, klaskamer, skoollokaal.
school-teacher, onderwyser(es).
schooner, skoener.
sciagraphy, Röntgenfotografie.
sciatic, heup- . . .; aan heupjig lydend.
sciatica, heupjig, iskias.
science, wetenskap; kunde, kennis; natuurwetenskap.
science-building, gebou vir natuurwetenskappe.
science-master, onderwyser in die natuurwetenskap.
scientific, (natuur)wetenskaplik.
scientist, (natuur)wetenskaplike natuurkundige.
scimitar, (Oosterse) krom sabel.

scintilla, vonkie; greintjie; **not a – of evidence,** geen sweempie bewys nie.
scintillate, vonkel, flikker, skitter.
scintillation, vonkeling, skittering.
sciolist, skyngeleerde, halfgeleerde.
scion, spruit, ent, steggie; afstamming.
scirrhus, bindweefselgewas.
scissel, metaalafknipsel.
scission, (die) sny, snyding, splitsing.
scissor, knip; – **out,** uitknip.
scissor-bill, skêrbek.
scissors, skêr; **pair of –,** 'n skêr; **buttonhole –,** knoopsgatskêr.
sclerosis, weefselverharding.
scobs, saagsel, krulle, skaafsel; uitskot.
scoff, n. spot, skimp, bespotting.
scoff, v. spot, skimp, bespot.
scoffer, spotter.
scold, v. uitskel, raas met, berispe, 'n uitbrander gee, inklim.
scold, n. helleveeg, heks, rissie.
scoliosis, ruggraatverkromming.
scollop, sien **scallop.**
scolopendrine, duisendpootagtig.
sconce, n. lantern; blaker; skans; harspan, kop, skedel; boete; stuk dryfys.
sconce, v. straf, beboet.
scone, botterbroodjie.
scoop, n. skop, koolskop, skepper, skeplepel, skepemmer; nuustreffer, alleenberig; wins, slag; **at one –,** met een skep (slag); **make a big –,** 'n goeie slag slaan; 'n groot skep maak.
scoop, v. (uit)skep, uithol; 'n slag slaan.
scoop-net, sleepnet, skepnet.
scoop-wheel, skerprat.
scoot, laat spat, weghol, jou knieë dra.
scooter, eenstapper, trapwiel, skopfiets; **motor –,** brompoonie.
scope, (speel)ruimte, geleentheid, kans; vryheid; bestek; gesigskring; doel; **beyond my –,** buitekant my bestek; **ample –,** oorgenoeg vryheid (ruimte); **an undertaking of wide –,** 'n onderneming van groot omvang.
scorbutic, n. skeurbuiklyer.
scorbutic, a. aan skeurbuik lydend.
scorch, brand, (ver)skroei, verseng; nael, woes (wild) ry; **–ed earth,** verskroeide aarde.
scorcher, n. mooie, pragstuk; naelryer.
score, n. keep, kerf, snytjie; streep, skraap, merk, hou; rekening, gelag; partituur; telling, (aantal behaalde) punte; twintigtal; **pay one's –,** betaal wat jy skuldig is; **pay off old –s,** afreken (met); **three – and ten,** swentig; **–s of people,** hope mense; **on the – of,** op grond van, weens; **on that –,** wat dit betref, in daardie opsig; **the – is,** die telling is nou; **what is the – now?,** hoe staan die spel nou?, hoe tel dit nou?; **will you keep the –?,** sal jy tel, sal jy die punte opskryf?; **lose (count of) the –,** die tel kwytraak.
score, v. inkeep, kerfies maak; slaan; opskryf, tel, die tel hou, opteken, boek; (punte) behaal; op musiek sit; **has –d success,** het sukses gehad; **our team failed to –,** ons span het geen punte behaal nie; **we shall – by it,** ons sal daardeur wen; **that is where he –s,** dit is waar hy die voorsprong het; – **out words,** woorde deurhaal; – **up,** opskrywe.
scorer, teller.
scoria, lawastukkies, metaalskuim.
scoriaceous, slakagtig.
scorn, n. veragting, hoon, versmading; **a – to,** 'n voorwerp van veragting vir; **laugh to –,** uitlag.

scorn, v. verag, versmaad, minag; **he –s lying,** hy ag dit benede hom om te lieg.
scornful, veragtelik, vol veragting.
scorpion, skerpioen; gesel.
Scot, Skot.
Scotch, n. Skots; **the –,** die Skotte.
Scotch, a. Skots.
scotch, kerf, jeep; wond.
Scotchman, Skot, Skotsman.
scot-free, ongedeerd, vry, ongestraf.
Scotland, Skotland.
Scottish, sien **Scotch.**
scoundrel, skurk, skobbejak, skelm.
scour, n. (die) skuur, vrywing; spoeling, buikloop, dun (by vee).
scour, v. (1) skuur, vrywe, suiwer.
scour, v. (2) deurkruis, rondsoek, rondtrek, rondswerwe; – **the coast,** langs die kus vaar.
scourge, n. gesel, roede; plaag.
scourge, v. gesel; kasty, teister.
scout, n. verkenner, spioen; **boy –,** padvinder; **on the –,** verkenning uit.
scout, v. verken, spioen.
scout, v. met minagting verwerp.
scoutmaster, padvinderleier.
scowl, v. frons, suur (boos) (aan)kyk.
scowl, n. frons, suur gesig.
scowling, fronsend, boos, suur, kwaad.
scrabble, v. krabbel, krap; skarrel.
scrabble, n. gekrabbel; geskarrel.
scrag, skrale, maere; maer vis.
scrag, v. nek omdraai; ophang.
scraggy, maer, skraal, net vel en been.
scramble, v. klouter; spook, oor mekaar val, worstel, woel; – **for places,** oor mekaar val om plekke te kry; **–d eggs,** roereiers.
    cramble, n. geklouter; gespook, gestoei, geworstel, oor-mekaar-vallery, gewoel.
scrap, n. stukkie, brokkie; uitknipsel; vodjie; **–s,** stukkies en brokkies, afval; – **of paper,** vodjie papier.
scrap, v. weggooi, afkeur.
scrap, n. bakleiery, rusie.
scrap, v. baklei.
scrap-book, snipperboek, uitknipselboek.
scrape, v. skraap, krap; kras; polys, skuur, galdmaak; **work and – as you may,** arbei en besuinig soveel as jy wil; – **one's boots,** jou voete afvee; – **one's feet,** met jou voete skuiwe; – **against,** krap teen; – **away,** afkrap, afskraap; – **down,** afkrap; – **off,** afskraap, afkrap; – **out,** uithol, uitskraap; **he –d through,** hy het net deurgeglip; – **together,** bymekaarskraap; – **up,** byeenskraap.
scrape, n. gekrap, gekras; moeilikheid, verleentheid; **be in a –,** in die knyp sit.
scraper, krapper, skraper; skraapyster.
scrap-heap, vuilgoedhoop.
scrapings, snippers, skraapsel.
scrap-iron, ou-yster, ysterafval.
scrappy, onsamehangend, fragmentaries.
Scratch, n.: **Old –,** die josie.
scratch, v. krap, skrap, skraap; afkrabbel; uitskraap, uithol; terugtrek, skrap; – **one's head,** jou kop krap; met die hande in die hare sit; – **along,** aansukkel, voortskarrel; – **out,** **through,** deurhaal; – **together,** bymekaarskraap.
scratch, n. krap, skrapie, skram; streep; pruikie; **come up to the –,** by die streep gaan staan; jou man staan; **in this race I am –,** in hierdie wedloop kry ek niks voor nie; **start at –,** by nul (niks) begin (tennis).
scratch, a. deurmekaar, bymekaargeskraap, saamgeraap; **a – team,** 'n deurmekaarspan.

scratch-race, gelykstaanwedren.
scratchy, sleg geteken, onduidelik; krassend; deurmekaar, saamgeraap.
scrawl, v. onleesbaar skrywe, krap.
scrawl, n. gekrap, hanepote.
scream, v. skree(u), gier, gil; **–ing fun,** allerdolste pret; – **out an order,** 'n bevel uitgil.
scream, n. skree(u), gil; **–s of laughter,** 'n uitbundige geskater, laggille; **it was a perfect –,** dit was om jou slap te lag.
screamingly, dol; – **funny,** vreeslik snaaks.
screech, n. skreeu, gil.
screech, v. gil, skreeu, gier.
screech-owl, kerkuil.
screed, tirade, lang redevoering.
screen, n. skerm; beskutting; doek, voorruit; sandsif; groot sif; **under – of night,** onder beskerming van die duisternis.
screen, v. beskerm, beskut, verberg; sif; vertoon; verfilm.
screen-wiper, ruitafveër (van motor).
screw, n. skroef; vrek; salaris; ou knol; **there is a – lose,** daar is iets verkeerd, daar is iets nie pluis nie; **put the – on,** opkeil, die duimskroef aansit.
screw, v. (vas)skroewe; opdruk, opkeil; gierig wees; uitsuig, afpers; (die gesig) vertrek; swenk draai, krul; **his head is –ed on the right way,** hy weet wat hy doen; – **out of,** afpers; – **up one's courage,** moed vat; – **a ball,** 'n bal laat krul.
screwdriver, skroewedraaier.
screw-jack, domkrag.
screw-key, skroefsleutel.
screw-propeller, skroef (van 'n skip).
screw-wrench, skroefhamer.
scribble, v. krap, afkrabbel.
scribbel, n. gekrap, (ge)krabbel.
scribe, skrywer, klerk; skrifgeleerde.
scrim, voering.
scrimmage, scrummage, stoeiery, bakleiery, skermutseling; skrum.
scrimp, vrekkig wees; afskeep.
scrimpy, vrekkig, suinig.
scrimshaw, (skulpe, ivoor ens.) versier.
scrip, sak(kie), tas.
scrip, voorlopige aandeelsertifikaat, recepis.
script, manuskrip; skrif, handskrif; skryfletter; eksamenboek; **radio –,** radioteks.
scriptural, Skriftuurlik, Bybels.
Scripture, die (Heilige) Skrif, die Bybel.
scrivener, skrywer, opsteller, notaris, makelaar; **–'s palsy,** skryfkramp.
scrofula, klierswelling, kliersiekte.
scrofulous, klieragtig, skrofuleus.
scroll, rol, perkamentrol; lys; krul.
scrotum, balsak, skrotum.
scrub, n. ruigte, struikgewas; (stomp) besem, borsel; stumper, sukkelaar; armoedige dier; dwerg; (die) skrop.
scrub, v. skrop, skuur, feil; swoeg.
scrubbing-board, wasplank.
scrubbing-brush, skropborsel.
scrubby, dwergagtig, klein, niksbeduidend, met struikgewas begroei, ruig.
scrub-oak, dwergeik.
scruff, nek; **take by the – of the neck,** agter die nek beetkry.
scrum, skrum; – **half,** skrumskakel.
scrummage, sien **scrimmage.**
scruple, n. beswaar, aarseling, gewetensbeswaar, skrupule; **make no – to do it,** nie ontsien om dit te doen nie, sonder die minste kwelling doen; **a man of no –s,** 'n gewetelose kêrel.
scruple, v. aarsel, swarigheid sien, beswaar maak.

scrupulosity, scrupulousness, nougesetheid, stiptheid, skroomvalligheid.
scrupulous, nougeset, sorgvuldig, versigtig, stip, noukeurig; – **honesty,** stipte eerlikheid; –**ly clean,** silwerskoon, buitengewoon skoon.
scrutineer, stemopnemer.
scrutinize, goed deurkyk (bekyk), noukeurig ondersoek, navorser, natel.
scrutiny, noukeurige ondersoek (beskouing); (die) ņagaan (van stemme).
scud, v. vlieg, voorstsnel, gly.
scud, n. vlug, vaart; drywende wolke.
scuffle, n. stoeiery, worsteling, deurmekaarbakleiery, geharwar.
scuffle, v. worstel, baklei, stoei.
scull, roeispaan, skulriem.
scullery, opwasplek, bykombuis.
scullion, kombuisjong; skottelwasser.
sculp, beeldhou.
sculptor, beeldhouer.
sculptural, beeldhou- . . .
sculpture, n. beeldhoukuns.
sculpture, v. beeldhou, uithou; graveer.
scum, n. skuim; uitvaagsel, uitskot.
scum, v. skuim; afskuim.
scummy, skuimagtig, skuim- . . .
scupper, spuitgat.
scurf, rofie; skilfer; korsie; skurfte.
scurfy, vol skilfers (rofies) skurf.
scurrility, laagheid, gemeendheid.
scurrilous, laag, gemeen, vuil, plat, grof.
scurry, v. (weg)hardloop, wegyl.
scurry, n. haas; geloop, gejaag.
scurvy, a. gemeen, laag, veragtelik.
scurvy, n. skeurbuik.
scut, stompstert(jie).
scutcheon, (wapen)skild, wapenbord; naamplaatjie; sleutelgatplaatjie.
scutellum, doppie.
scuttle, n. koolbak, koolemmer.
scuttle, n. luik.
scuttle, v. gate inboor, laat sink.
scuttle, n. haas vlug, (die) hardloop.
scuttle, v. hardloop, yl, die spat neem.
scuttle-fish, inkvis.
scutum, skild; knieskyf; dop, skob.
scythe, sens (seis).
sea, see, oseaan; golf, deining; **by – and land,** op land en see; **on the –,** op see, aan die see; **go to –,** op see gaan, matroos word; **follow the –,** matroos wees; **put to –,** van wal steek; **at –,** op see; **I was completely at –,** ek was totaal in die war (die kluts kwyt); **the high –s,** die oop see; **there was a heavy –,** die see was onstuimig; **half –s over,** aangeklam, lekker, getik; **a – of troubles,** moeilikheid sonder end.
sea-air, seelug.
sea-anemone, see-anemoon.
seaboard, seekus.
sea-born, uit die see gebore.
sea-borne, oorsees, uit verre lande.
sea-breeze, seewind.
sea-coast, seekus.
sea-dog, (see)rob, seehond.
sea eagle, see-arend.
seafaring, seevarend; – **man,** seeman.
sea-fight, seegeveg, skeepsgeveg.
sea-fowl, seevoël.
seafront, seekant (van 'n stad).
sea-gauge, diepgang.
sea-girt, deur see omring.
seagoing, seevarend, see- . . .
sea-green, seegroen.
sea-gull, seemeeu.
sea-hog, to(r)nyn, seevark.

sea-horse, seeperd, walrus.
seal, rob, seehond.
seal, n. seël; stempel; bevestiging; **given under my hand and –,** deur my geteken en geseël; **set one's – to,** sy seël heg aan, goedkeur; **the Great S.,** die Rykseël, die grootseël.
seal, v. seël, verseël, lak; **it is a –ed book to me,** dit is vir my 'n geslote boek; **his fate is –ed,** sy lot is beslis; – **up a tin,** 'n blik toesoldeer; **the windows must be –ed up,** die vensters moet toegeplak word.
sea-legs, seebene; **he has not yet got his –,** hy het nog nie sy seebene nie.
sealer, robbevanger; robbeskip.
sea level, seespieël, seevlak.
sea-line, horison, kim.
sealing-wax, lak.
sealskin, robbevel; robbeveljas.
seam, n. naat; litteken; (kool)laag.
seam, v. met littekens bedek; aanmekaar naai (stik) groef.
seaman, matroos, seeman.
seamanship, seemanskap.
sea-mark, baken (in see).
seamless, sonder naat, naatloos.
seam-presser, persyster.
seamstress, naaister.
seamy, met nate; **the – side,** die verkeerde kant; die keerkant.
sea-nymph, seenimf.
sea-piece, seegesig.
seaplane, watervliegtuig.
seaport, seehawe.
sear, a. (ver)droog, dor.
sear, v. brand, skroei, verseng; ongevoelig maak, toeskroei.
search, n. soek; ondersoek, naspeur; deursoek, visenteer; peil; deurdring; **– a wound,** 'n wond peil; – **somebody's heart,** iemand se hart deurgrond; – **for something,** na iets soek; – **me!** nou is ek dom.
search, n. soek; ondersoek; huissoeking; **I am in – of something,** ek is op soek na iets, ek soek na iets.
searching, a. deurdringend; noukeurig.
searching, n. ondersoek; –**s of the heart,** gewetenskwelling.
searchlight, soeklig.
search-party, soekgeselskap.
search-warrant, magtiging tot huissoeking, visentasiemagsbrief.
searing-iron, brandyster.
sea-scape, seegesig.
sea-serpent, seeslang.
seashore, seekus.
seasick, seesiek.
seaside, strand; seekant.
season, n. seisoen; jaargety; tyd; geskikte tyd; **a word in –,** 'n woordjie op sy tyd; **in – and out of –,** te pas en te onpas; **it is not the – now,** dit is nie nou die tyd nie; **holiday –,** vakansietyd; **the four –s,** die vier jaargetye; **shooting –,** oop jag, jagtyd.
season, v. geskik maak; laat gewoond word aan; laat ryp word; (laat) droog word; smaaklik maak, kruie (ingooi); temper, matig; **–ed soldiers,** geharde soldate; **highly –ed food,** sterk gekruide kos.
seasonable, geleë, gepas, geskik; tydig.
seasoning, tobereiding; kruie, sous.
season-ticket, abonnement(skaartjie), ,,seisoenkaartjie".
seat, n. sitplek, bank, stoel; setel; sitting; toneel; landgoed, buiteplaas; sit, boom (van 'n broek); **take a –,** gaan sit, plaas neem; **the – of the war,**

die oorlogstoneel; a – on the board, sitting ('n setel) op die raad; the disease has its – in the liver, die siekte setel (het sy oorsprong) in die lewer.
seat, v. laat sit, plaas, plek aanwys; van sitplekke voorsien; ('n stoel) mat; ('n broek) 'n boom insit; be –ed, plaas neem, gaan sit; – oneself, gaan sit; the church is –ed for 2,000, die kerk het sitplek vir 2,000 mense.
seating accommodation, sitplek.
sea-urchin, see-egel.
seaweed, seegras, seewier.
seaworthy, seewaardig.
sebaceous, vet-. . .
secant, a. snydend, sny-. . .
secant, n. snylyn, sekans.
secede, afskei, terugtrek, sedeer.
secernent, a. afskeidend, afskeidings- . . .
secernent, n. afskeidingsorgaan.
secession, afskeiding, sesessie.
seclude, uitsluit, buitesluit; afsonder.
secluded, afgesonder, stil, rustig.
seclusion, afsondering.
second, a. tweede; ander; ondergeskik; on – thoughts, by nader beskouing; he is – to none, hy doen vir niemand onder nie, hy staan vir niemand agteruit nie; habit is – nature, gewoonte is die tweede natuur; play – fiddle, tweede viool speel, 'n ondergeskikte rol speel; – cousin, kleineef, kleinniggie.
second, n. tweede, ander; tweede stem; helper, sekondant, getuie; sekonde; in this race he was a good –, in hierdie wedloop was hy kort agter die wenner; wait a –, wag 'n oomblikkie.
second, v. bystaan, steun; sekondeer.
secondary, a. sekondêr; ondergeskik, bykomend; – education, middelbare onderwys.
secondary, n. afgevaardige; satelliet.
second-best, op een na die beste; come off –, aan die kortste ent trek.
second-class, tweede klas.
seconder, sekondant.
second-hand, tweedehands, uit die tweede hand, halfslyt, gebruik; van hoor-sê; – clothes, halfslytklere; – bookseller, tweedehandseboekhandelaar; I have it at –, ek het dit van hoor sê.
secondly, in die tweede plek, ten tweede.
second-mourning, ligte rou.
second-rate, tweederangs, tweedeklas.
second sight, heldersiendheid.
secrecy, geheimhouding; verborgenheid; heimlikheid; in –, in die geheim, heimlik; you can rely on his –, jy kan daarop reken dat hy dit geheim sal hou.
secret, a. geheim; bedek, verborge, heimlik; – treaty, geheime verdrag; – sin, verborge sonde.
secret, n. geheim; keep it a –, dit geheim hou; keep a –, 'n geheim bewaar; it is an open –, dit is 'n publieke geheim, almal weet dit; in –, in die geheim, stilletjies.
secretarial, van die sekretaris, sekretaris- . . .
secretariate, sekretariaat, sekretarisskap.
secretary, sekretaris; minister; honorary –, eresekretaris; S– of State for Foreign Affairs, Minister van Buitelandse Sake (Br.).
secretary-bird, sekretarisvoël, slangvreter.
secrete, wegsteek, versteek; afskei.
secretion, verberging; afskeiding; afgeskeie vog, sekresie.
secretive, geheim, stil, geheimsinnig; afskeidings- . . ., afskeidend.
secretly, stilletjies, in die geheim.
secretary, afskeidings- . . .
sect, sekte.

sectarian, a. sektaries.
sectarian, n. sekte-aanhanger, sektaris.
sectarianism, sektegees, sekte-ywer.
section, verdeling; deel; afdeling, paragraaf, deursnee; seksie; horizontal –, horisontale deursnee; transverse –, dwars deursnee.
sectional, afdelings- . . ., van 'n seksie (afdeling).
sector, sektor.
secular, wêreldlik, tydelik, sekulêr; honderdjarig; eeue-oud; blywend; – change, gestadige verandering; – cooling, langsame afkoeling; – fame, blywende roem; – clergy, sekuliere, wêreldlike geestelikes; – music, ongewyde musiek.
secularization, sekularisasie.
secularize, sekulariseer.
secularity, wêreldsgesindheid.
secure, a. veilig; seker; gerus; vas.
secure, v. beveilig, beskerm, in veiligheid stel; vasmaak, toemaak, sluit; vrywaar, waarborg, verseker, (ver)kry, bereik; – your ends, jou doel bereik; – two seats, twee sitplekke kry.
securiform, bylvormig.
security, sekuriteit, waarborg, borg, pand; veiligheid, sekerheid; in –, in veiligheid; in – for, as pand vir, as waarborg vir; collateral –, saaklike onderpand.
sedan, sedan, toe motor.
sedan(-chair), draagstoel.
sedate, bedaard, stemmig, kalm.
sedative, a. pynstillend, kalmerend.
sedative, n. pynstillende (kalmerende) middel.
sedentary, a. sittend, sedentêr; loerend.
sedentary, n. sittende persoon; loerspinnekop.
sedge, watergras, rietgras.
sediment, afsaksel, besinksel, moer, grondsop, sediment.
sedimentary, sedimentêr; afsak- . . .
sedition, opruiing, opstoking, ophitsing, oproer, opstand, muitery, sedisie.
seditious, oproerig, opstandig; opruiend.
seduce, verlei, verlok.
seducer, verleier.
seducible, verleibaar.
seduction, verleiding, verlokking.
seductive, verleidend, verleidelik.
sedulity, ywer, vlyt, naarstigheid.
sedulous, ywerig, vlytig, naarstig.
see, v. sien, kyk, aanskou; begryp, insien, verstaan; sorg, oppas; besoek; – the light, die eerste lewenslig aanskou; I cannot – my way to . . ., ek sien nie kans om . . .; I – what you mean, ek begryp wat jy bedoel; – whether it is there, kyk of dit daar is; as far as I can –, sover soos ek kan insien; when will you come and – us?, wanneer kom jy kuier (ons opsoek)?, may I – you?, mag ek u spreek?; – a doctor, 'n dokter raadpleeg; – somebody on business, met iemand oor besigheid praat; – somebody home, iemand na huis bring (vergesel); – that it is done, sorg dat dit gedoen word; – you don't catch your foot, pas op dat jou voet nie haak nie; let me –, laat ek eers dink, wag net so 'n bietjie; he has –n life, hy ken die lewe; he refused to – me, hy het geweier om my te ontvang; will you – them to the door?, sal jy met hulle saamgaan deur toe?; you will never – the day, jy sal die dag nooit belewe nie; I must have the money, you –, ek het die geld nodig, verstaan jy?; I saw red, ek het gevoel of ek kon moor; I'll – about it, ek sal daarvoor sorg; ek sal daaroor dink; – after, kyk na, oppas; I must – into it, ek moet die saak ondersoek; – somebody off at the station, iemand by die stasie gaan dagsê (groet); – over

a house, 'n huis bekyk; I can – through it, ek begryp wat daaragter skuil; – the matter through, die saak deursit; – to it, sorg.
see, n. bisdom; pouslike hof.
seed, n. saad; nakomelinge, afstammelinge; gekeurde speler; go, run to –, saadskiet; the –s of vice, die kiem van die kwaad.
seed, v. saadskiet; saai; ontpit; keur (sport).
seed-bed, saadakkertjie.
seed-bud, saadknop.
seed-corn, saadkoring.
seeding-plough, planter.
seedling, plantjie, saaiplant.
seed-lobe, saadlob.
seed-plot, saadakkertjie; broeines.
seed-potato, aartappelmoer.
seedsman, saadhandelaar.
seed-time, saaityd.
seedy, vol saad, in die saad; siekerig, kaduks; oes; toiingrig.
seed-vessel, saadvlies.
seeing, n. (die) sien.
seeing, conj.: – that, aangesien.
seek, v. soek; probeer, poog; beoog, verlang, begeer; he –s my life, hy probeer om my om die lewe te bring; come to – advice, kom raad vra; – one's bed, jou bed opsoek; an efficient leader is yet to –, 'n bekwame leier ontbreek nog; it is sought after by everyone, daar is groot aanvraag na; – after, soek na; – out, uitkies; opspoor.
seem, lyk, skyn; die skyn hê van, deurgaan vir; the man who –ed the leader, die man wat blykbaar die leier was; I – deaf to-day, ek moet glo doof wees vandag, dit smaak my ek is doof vandag; I – to see him still, dit is my of ek hom nog sien; I do not – to like him, hy staan my nie intlik aan nie.
seeming, skynbaar, oënskynlik.
seemingly, in skyn, na dit skyn, oënskynlik.
seemly, betaamlik, welvoeglik, gepas.
seep, sypel, syfer.
seer, siener, profeet.
see-saw, n. wipplank.
see-saw, v. wip, wipplank ry; op en neer gaan.
seethe, kook, sied.
seething, kokend, siedend.
segment, segment; gedeelte.
segregate, afsonder, isoleer, afskei.
segregation, afsondering, afskeiding, segregasie.
seine, n. sleepnet, treknet.
seismic, aardbewings-...., seismies.
seismograph, seismograaf.
seismography, seismografie.
seismology, seismologie, aardbewingsleer.
seizable, grypbaar, neembaar.
seize, vat, gryp, neem; vasbrand (motor); in beslag (in besit) neem, beslag lê op; konfiskeer; vasbind; – a fortress, 'n vesting (in besit) neem; –d by apoplexy, deur beroerte getref; – upon a chance, die geleentheid aangryp; –d with panic, skrikbevange.
seizure, beslaglegging, inbesitneming; aanval (van siekte).
seldom, selde, min.
select, a. uitgesoek, uitgelese; selek; keurig; – committee, gekose komitee.
select, v. uitsoek, uitkies, kies.
selection, keuse; seleksie; versameling.
selectivity, selektiwiteit.
selenium, selenium.
selenography, maanbeskrywing.
self, self, eie persoonlikheid, individualiteit, ekheid, eie-ek; the consciousness of –, selfbewussyn; the love of –, eieliefde.

self-abasement, selfvernedering.
self-abhorrence, selfveragting.
self-abuse, selfbevlekking, onanie.
self-accusation, selfbeskuldiging.
self-acting, selfwerkend, outomaties.
self-adjusting, selfregulerend.
self-assertion, aanmatiging.
self-assurance, selfvertroue.
self-binder, selfbinder.
self-centred, in sigself gekeerd.
self-colour, egalige (natuurlike) kleur.
self-coloured, eenkleurig.
self-command, selfbeheersing.
self-communion, selfbetragting.
self-complacency, selftevredenheid.
self-conceit, verwaandheid, eiedunk.
self-confidence, selfvertroue.
self-concious, selfbewus; verleë.
self-contained, stil, afgetrokke, ongesellig; op sigself staande; afgesonder.
self-contempt, selfveragting.
self-control, selfbeheersing.
self-deception, selfbedrog.
self-defence, selfverdediging; in –, uit selfverdediging.
self-denial, selfverloëning.
self-destruction, selfmoord, selfvernietiging.
self-determination, vrye wil; eie keuse.
self-devotion, selfopoffering, toewyding.
self-esteem, selfagting, selfrespek.
self-evident, klaarblyklik, vanselfsprekend.
self-examination, selfondersoek.
self-glorification, selfverheerliking.
self-help, eiehulp.
self-importance, verwaandheid, eiedunk.
self-imposed, selfopgelegde.
self-interest, eiebelang.
selfish, selfsug, baatsugtig.
selfishness, selfsug, baatsugtigheid.
self-knowledge, selfkennis.
selfless, onbaatsugtig.
self-love, eieliefde, selfsug.
self-made man, iemand wat homself opgewerk het.
self-opinion, eiewaan.
self-opinionated, eiewys, wysneusig.
self-possession, selfbeheersing.
self-praise, eielof.
self-preservation, selfbehoud.
self-reliance, selfvertroue.
self-renunciation, selfverloëning.
self-reproach, selfverwyt.
self-restraint, selfbeheersing.
self-righteous, eiegeregtig.
self-sacrifice, selfopoffering.
selfsame, einste, presies, dieselfde.
self-satisfaction, selfvoldoening.
self-satisfied, selfvoldaan.
self-seeking, a. selfsugtig.
self-seeking, n. selfsug(tigheid).
self-service, selfbediening; – shop, selfhelpwinkel; – system, selfdienstelsel.
self-sown, opslag-...
self-starter, outomatiese aansitter.
self-styled, selfbetitelde.
self-sufficiency, selfgenoegsaamheid.
self-sufficient, selfgenoegsaam, verwaand.
self-torture, selfkastyding.
self-will, koppigheid, eiesinnigheid.
self-willed, eiegeregtig, koppig, eiewys.
sell, v. verkoop, van die hand sit; verraai; kul, fop, bedrieg; – off, uitverkoop; – out, verkoop; uitverkoop; – down the river, verraai, aan jou vyande oorlewer.
sell, n. bedrog, kullery, foppery.

selvage, -edge, selfkant.
semantics, betekenisleer, semantiek.
semaphore, semafoor, seintoestel.
semasiology, semasiologie, betekenisleer.
semblance, skyn, voorkome.
semen, saad.
semester, semester, halfjaar.
semi-annual, halfjaarliks.
semi-barbarian, halfbarbaars.
semibreve, hele noot.
semi-circle, halwe sirkel (halfsirkel).
semi-curcular, halfsirkelvormig.
semi-civilised, halfbeskaaf(d).
semicolon, kommapunt.
semi-detached, half-alleenstaande; − **house,** koppelhuis.
semi-final, halfeindwedstryd.
semilunar, halfmaanvorming.
semi-mute, halfstom.
seminal, saad- . . ., kiem- . . .
seminary, seminarie, kweekskool.
semination, saadvormig.
semi-official, half-amptelik, offisieus.
semiquaver, sestiende noot.
Semitic, Semities.
semitone, halwe toon (halftoon).
semi-transparent, halfdeurskynend.
semi-vowel, halvokaal, halfklinker.
semolina, griesmeel, semolina.
senate, senaat; hoërhuis.
senator, senator.
senatorial, senaats- . . ., van die senaat.
send, stuur, uitstuur, wegstuur, (ver)send; − **word,** berig stuur, laat weet; **it almost sent him mad, crazy,** dit het hom byna mal gemaak; − **flying,** (uitmekaar) laat spat, laat spaander; laat vlieg; − **him rolling down the stairs,** hom die trap afsmyt; − **one about his business,** iemand in die pad steek, gou-gou ontslae raak van iemand; − **away,** wegstuur; − **back,** terugstuur; − **down,** wegja; verminder (koors); − **for the doctor,** stuur om die dokter, die dokter laat haal; − **forth,** uitstuur; ('n ruik) versprei; − **forth buds,** bot; − **in,** instuur; − **in one's name,** jou laat inskryf; − **off,** wegstuur; afskeidsgroet bring; − **out,** uitstuur; ('n ruik) versprei; − **up,** opstuur; laat styg; − **up one's name,** jou naam laat inskryf.
sender, (af)sender.
send-off, afskeid; afskeidsfuif.
senescence, verouding.
senescent, verouderend, bejaard.
senile, ouderdoms- . . ., seniel.
senility, ouderdomswakte, seniliteit.
senior, a. senior; ouer, oudste; hoër in rang; − **clerk,** hoofklerk; − **partner,** hoof van die firma, hoofvennoot; **two years − to me,** twee jaar ouer as ek, twee jaar voor my.
senior, n. ouer (persoon); superieur, hoof, eerste in rang, senior student; **he is two years my −,** hy is twee jaar voor my (ouer as ek).
seniority, voorrang; hoër ouderdom.
senna, seneblare; **senna-pods,** senepeule.
sensation, gewaarwording, gevoel, aandoening; sensasie, opskudding; **created a −,** opskudding veroorsaak.
sensational, opsienbarend, sensasioneel; gevoels- . . .
sensationalism, sensasiebejag; sensasionalisme, sinnelike-gewaarwordingsleer.
sense, n. sin, sintuig; gevoel, gewaarwording; besef, begrip, verstand; betekenis; **the five −s,** die vyf sintuie; **are you out of your −s,?** is jy nie by jou volle verstand nie, is jy mal?; **we must bring him to his −s,** ons moet hom tot besinning bring; **frighten him out of his −s,** hom kapot (lam) laat skrik; − **of shame,** skaamtegevoel; **a keen − of humour,** 'n fyn sin vir humor; **a man of −,** 'n verstandige man; **now you are talking −,** nou praat jy (verstandig)!; **what is the − of talking like that?** wat help dit om so te praat?; **it does not make −,** dit het geen sin nie, dit is onverstaanbaar; **in the strict −,** in engere sin; **in every −,** in elke opsig.
sense, v. gewaar(word), voel, aanvoel.
senseless, gevoelloos, bewusteloos; dwaas.
sensibility, gevoeligheid, ontvanklikheid, vatbaarheid; fyngevoeligheid.
sensible, waarneembaar, merkbaar; bewus; verstandig.
sensitize, gevoelig maak.
sensitive, fyngevoelig, liggeraak, sensitief; − **plant,** kruidjie-roer-my-niet.
sensitivity, gevoeligheid, sensitiwiteit.
sensorium, setel van die gewaarwordinge.
sensory, sensorial, sintuiglik, sensories.
sensual, sinlik, wellustig, vleeslik.
sensualize, versinlik.
sensualism, sinlikheid, wellus.
sensualist, wellusteling.
sensuality, sinlikheid, wellus.
sensuous, sin- . . ., van die sinne, sinnelik.
sentence, n. vonnis, uitspraak; (vol)sin.
sentence, v. veroordeel, vonnis.
sententious, bondig, kernagtig, pittig; orakelagtig, verwaand.
sentience, waarnemingsvermoë, gevoel.
sentient, voelend, met gevoel.
sentiment, gevoel, sentiment; mening, gedagte, idee; heildronk.
sentimental, sentimenteel, oorgevoelig.
sentimentalize, oorgevoelig wees.
sentimentalism, oorgevoeligheid.
sentimentalist, oordrewe gevoelsmens.
sentimentality, oorgevoeligheid, sentimentaliteit.
sentinel, n. wag, brandwag, skildwag.
sentry, wag, brandwag.
sentry-box, (skild)waghuisie.
sepal, kelkblaar.
separability, skei(d)baarheid.
separable, skei(d)baar.
separate, a. afsonderlik, apart, afgesonder, afgeskei.
separate, n. afdruk.
separate, v. skei, afskei, verdeel, afsonder; uitmekaar gaan.
separation, skeiding, afsondering.
separatist, a. separatisties.
separatist, n. separatis; afgeskeidene.
separator, afskeier; roomafskeier.
separatum, afdruk.
sepia, sepia, bruin waterverf; inkvis.
sepoy, sipoy (sepoy, sipahi),
sepsis, (ver)rotting, bloedvergiftiging.
septangle, sewehoek.
septangular, sewehoekig.
September, September.
septenary, sewetallig, sewejarig.
septennial, sewejaarliks, sewejarig.
septic, bederfbevorderend, septies.
septuagenarian, sewentigjarige.
Septuagint, Septuagint.
septuple, a. sewevoudig.
septuple, v. versewevoudig.
sepulchral, graf- . . .; van die graf; − **voice,** grafstem; − **customs,** begrafnisplegtighede.
sepulchre, n. graf; **whited −,** witgepleisterde graf.
sepulchre, v. begrawe.
sepulture, begrafnis.

sequacious, volgsaam, slaafs, gedwee.
sequacity, volgsaamheid, gedweeheid.
sequel, gevolg, resultaat, uitvloeisel, nasleep vervolg.
sequence, reeks, opvolging, opeenvolging, volgorde; sequens (in musiek); – **of events**, opeenvolging van gebeurtenisse; – **of cards**, volgkaarte; **give the facts in historical** –, die feite in geskiedkundige volgorde aangee; – **of tenses**, ooreenstemming van tye.
sequent, volgend.
sequential, opvolgend.
sequester, afsonder, isoleer; in beslag (bewaring) neem, sekwestreer; afstand doen van; **a –ed life**, 'n afgesonderde lewe, 'n lewe van afsondering.
sequestrate, sekwestreer, beslag lê op.
sequestration, beslaglegging, inbeslagneming, sekwestrasie; afsondering.
sequestrator, beslaglêer, sekwestreerder.
sequin, lowertjie, blinkertjie.
seraglio, seraglio; harem.
seraph, seraf, engel.
seraphic, serafies, engelagtig, hemels.
Serb, n. Serwiër.
Serb, a. Serwies.
serenade, n. serenade.
serenade, v. 'n serenade bring.
serene, helder; kalm, stil; bedaard, rustig; deurlugtig.
serenity, helderheid; kalmte, rus.
serf, slaaf, lyfeiene.
serfdom, lyfeienskap.
serge, serge (sersje).
sergeant, sersant; deurwaarder.
sergeant-at-arms, stafdraer.
sergeant-major, sersant-majoor.
serial, a. in (opeenvolgende) afleweringe; periodiek; **a – story**, 'n vervolgstorie.
serial, n. vervolgverhaal, feuilleton.
serially, in afleweringe; reeksgewyse.
seriatim, een na die ander, agter mekaar.
series, reeks, serie; aaneenskakeling.
serinette, voëlorreltjie.
serious, ernstig; stemmig; belangrik, gewigtig; gevaarlik; deeglik; **are you –?** is dit jou erns? meen jy wat jy sê?
seriously, ernstig, in (alle) erns; **take it –**, dit ernstig opneem.
seriousness, erns.
sermon, preek, leerrede, predikasie; vermaning, teregwysing; **S– on the Mount**, Bergrede, Bergpredikasie.
sermonize, preek; vermaan, bestraf.
serous, serumagtig; waterig.
serpent, slang; serpent (blaasinstrument); vuurpyl, voetsoeker.
serpent-charmer, slangbesweerder.
serpentine, a. slangagtig, slang- . . .; kronkelend; vals, slu; – **dance**, slangdans, kronkeldans.
serpentine, n. serpentyn(steen).
serpentine, v. kronkel, draai.
serrate, getand, saagvormig.
serried, vas teen mekaar, aaneengeslote; – **ranks**, aaneengeslote geledere.
serrulate (serrulated), fyn getand.
serum, serum, entstof.
serval, tierboskat.
servant, bediende, diensmeisie, kneg, diensbode; dienaar, dienares; amptenaar; **railway –s**, spoorwegamptenare; **your obedient –**, u dienswillige dienaar (dienares).
serve, v. dien, van diens wees, diens bewys, bedien; help, baat; voldoende wees; uitdien;

dek; afslaan (in tennis); – **at table**, by die tafel bedien; **not – the purpose**, nie geskik vir die doel nie; **to – his own ends**, om sy eie planne te bevorder; – **an apprenticeship**, in die leer wees, as leerjong dien; – **his sentence, time**, sy straf, tyd, uitdien; **dinner is –ed**, die ete is op tafel; **that –s him right**, dit is sy verdiende loon; –.a trick, 'n poets bak; – **shamefully**, skandelik behandel; – **out**, uitgee, uitdeel; – **up**, opskep, op tafel sit; – **with the same sauce**, met gelyke munt terugbetaal; – **the city with water**, die stad van water voorsien.
server, afslaner (in tennis).
Servia, Serwië.
Servian, n. Serwiër; Serwies.
Servian, a. Serwies.
service, diens, diensbaarheid; (kerk)diens, stel, servies; (die) afslaan (in tennis); **take – with**, in diens gaan by; **at your –**, tot u diens; **will you do me a –?**, sal u my 'n diens bewys?; **can I be of – to you?**, kan ek u van diens wees?; **divine –**, kerkdiens, godsdiensoefening; – **flat**, woonstel met bediening.
serviceable, nuttig, bruikbaar, dienlik.
service-station, motorbedienplek, garage, diens(s)stasie.
serviette, servet.
servile, slaafs, onderworpe; kruiperig.
servility, slaafsheid, onderworpenheid.
servitude, slawerny; serwituut.
service-station, motorbedienplek, garage, diensstasie.
servo-motor, servomotor.
sesame, sesamplant; **open –**, sesam, gaan **oop**.
sessile, sonder steel, steelloos.
session, sitting, sessie.
sestet, sekstet.
Sesuto, Sesoeto.
set, v. sit (set), plaas, stel; aansit; bepaal, reël, skik; spalk; (die toon) aangee; styf word, hard word; ondergaan (van die son); – **a hen**, 'n hen laat broei, 'n hen op eiers sit; – **eggs**, eiers in die broei sit; – **a watch**, 'n horlosie regsit; – **a razor**, 'n skeermes aansit; – **the table**, tafel dek; – **a leg**, 'n been spalk; – **an example**, 'n voorbeeld wees (gee); – **the fashion**, die toon aangee; – **questions**, vrae opstel; – **a saw**, 'n saag stel; – **sail**, onder seil gaan, vertrek; – **one's teeth**, op jou tande byt; – **one right**, iemand op sy plek sit; iemand reghelp; – **about**, begin, aanstalte maak; aanpak; – **against**, plaas teenoor; – **oneself against**, weerstand bied, gekant wees teen; – **apart**, apart hou; reserveer; – **aside**, opsy sit, bêre; verwerp, buite beskouing laat; – **person's heart at rest**, iemand gerusstel; – **at liberty**, in vryheid stel, vrylaat; – **at naught**, bespot; ignoreer, minag; – **back**, terugsit; agteruitsit; – **by**, bêre, spaar; – **down**, neerskrywe, opteken; – **down to**, toeskrywe aan; op rekening sit van; – **down as**, beskou as; – **forth**, bekend maak, openbaar maak, vermeld, uiteensit; op reis gaan, vertrek; – **in**, begin; **reaction – in**, daar het 'n reaksie gekom; – **off**, versier; laat uitkom; aan die lag (praat) sit; op reis gaan, vertrek – **on**, aanhits, aanpor, aanspoor, aansit; – **eyes on**, te sien kry, onder die oë kry; **I have – my heart, mind on it**, ek het my hart daarop gesit; – **a movement on foot**, 'n beweging op tou sit; – **out**, vertrek, op reis gaan; uiteensit; versier; tentoonstel; – **one's hand to the task**, die hand aan die ploeg slaan, die werk aanpak; – **fire, to** aan die brand steek; – **up**, oprig, begin; opsit; weer op die been bring; ('n geskreeu)

aanhef; – **up as a dentist,** as tandarts begin praktiseer.
set, n. stel; services; set (hare); groep, klompie, span; kliek; kring; plantjie, steggie; ondergang (van die son); rigting; neiging; houding; snit (van klere); stel (in tennis); broeisel (eiers); **make a dead – at,** 'n heftige aanval maak teen; **a – of teeth,** 'n stel tande.
set, a. vas, bepaal(d), gereeld, vasgestel; onbeweeglik; **a – face,** 'n strak gesig; **– phrases,** vaste uitdrukkinge.
setaceous, harig, borselrig.
set-back, teenslag, klap, knou.
set-down, teregwysing, skrobbering.
set-off, kontras; versiersel.
set-out, begin, aanvang; vertoning.
set square, teken-driehoek.
settee, rusbank, sofa, sitbank.
setter, jaghond, patryshond.
setter-on, aanhitser, opstoker.
setting, raam, omlysting, montering; broeisel eiers; toonsetting; toneelskikking.
setting-lotion, setmiddel.
settle, n. leuningbank.
settle, v. (sig) vestig; tot bedaring kom, tot bedaring bring; bepaal, vasstel, reël, in orde bring, regmaak, vereffen; gaan sit; afsak, helder word; koloniseer; **– down to dinner,** aan tafel gaan sit; **cannot – down to work,** kan nie aan die werk kom nie; **let the excitement – down,** laat die opgewondenheid bedaar; **– the day,** die dag bepaal; **– quarrel,** 'n rusie uit die weg ruim, afmaak; **that –s the question,** daarmee is die saak afgehandel; **– his affairs,** sy sake in orde bring; **I shall soon – him,** ek sal hom gou-gou op sy plek sit; **– an account,** 'n rekening betaal (vereffen); **the mud –s,** die modder sak af.
settled, vasgestel; gereeld, bestendig; betaal; afgehandel, afgedaan.
settlement, skikking, reëling; volksplanting, nedersetting, kolonie; vereffening, betaling; kontrak; **in – of,** ter voldoening (vereffening) van.
settler, kolonis, nedersetter, setlaar.
set-to, bakleiery.
seven, sewe; **– of hearts,** harte-sewe.
sevenfold, sewevoudig.
seven-league boots, sewemylslaarse.
seventeen, sewentien.
seventeenth, sewentiende.
seventh, sewende.
seventy, sewentig.
seventieth, sewentigste.
sever, skei; afskeur, afkap, afsny.
several, a. verskeie; indiwidueel; respektief; eie; afsonderlik; **they went their – ways,** elkeen het sy eie pad gegaan; **all of us in our – stations,** elkeen van ons op sy eie plek.
several, pron. verskeie.
severally, (elkeen) afsonderlik (op sy eie).
severance, (af)skeiding, skeuring.
severe, straf, hard, streng; wreed; ernstig, swaar; **a – winter,** 'n strawwe winter; **a – attack of gout,** 'n swaar aanval van jig; **a – test,** 'n swaar toets; **– remarks,** skerp aanmerkinge.
severity, strengheid, hardheid; erns.
Seville, Sevilla; **– orange,** bitterlemoen.
sew, naai; **– on,** aannaai; **– up,** toenaai.
sewage, rioolslyk, rioolvullis.
sewer, n. riool (rioel).
sewer, v. rioleer, dreineer.
sewerage, rioolstelsel, riolering.
sewer-gas, rioolgas.

sewing, naaldwerk, naaiwerk; (die) naai.
sewing-machine, naaimasjien.
sex, geslag, sekse; **– appeal,** geslagsattraksie; **– maniac,** geslagsmaniak.
sexagenarian, sestigjarige.
sexagenary, sestigjarig; sestigdelig.
sexangular, seshoekig.
sex-appeal, geslagsattraksie.
sexcentenary, seshonderdjarig.
sexennial, sesjaarliks; sesjarig.
sexless, geslagloos, seksloos.
sextant, sekstant, hoogtemeter.
sextet(te), sekstet.
sexton, koster.
sextuple, sesvoudig.
sexual, seksueel, geslags- . . ., geslagtelik; **– organs,** geslagsorgane; **– passion,** geslagsdrif.
sexuality, seksualiteit.
shabby, laag, gemeen, veragtelik; armoedig, slordig, verslyt, armsalig, kaal.
shackle, n. boei, skakel, kram, koppeling; **–s,** boeie; belemmering.
shackle, v. boei; belemmer, hinder.
shaddock, pampelmoes.
shade, n. skaduwee; koelte; tint, kleur(skakering); skerm, kap; skim; ietsie, tikkie; **the –s,** die skimmeryk; **throw into the –,** in die skaduwee stel; **different –s of purple,** verskillende skakeringe van pers; **delicate –s of meaning,** fyn betekenisverskille (-nuanses); **a – better,** 'n ietsie beter.
shade, v. beskadu, oorskadu; beskerm, beskut, bedek; versomber; skakeer, skadu, donker kleur; **– off into,** langsaam oorgaan in; **he –d his eyes with his hand,** hy het sy hand oor sy oë gehou.
shadiness, skadurykheid; verdagtheid.
shadow, skaduwee, skadubeeld; gees, spook; skim; beskerming; aanduiding, bewys, spoor; **without a – of doubt,** sonder die minste twyfel; **catch at –s,** die skyn vir werklikheid aansien; **– cabinet,** skimkabinet.
shadow, v. oorskadu; stilletjies volg, dophou, in die oog hou.
shadow-boxing, skynboks.
shadowy, skaduagtig, skaduryk; vaag.
shady, lommerryk, skaduryk; beskadu; duister, oneerlik, verdag.
shaft, spies; pyl; disselboom; steel; skag, mynput; as; ligstraal.
shag, ruie hare; pluis; kerftabak.
shaggy, harig, wolhaar; ruig.
shagreen, sagryn(leer).
shah, vors van Persië, sjah.
shake, v. skud, ruk, skok; uitskud; bewe, bibber, tril; laat wankel; verswak; **– hands,** met die hand groet, handgee; **his hand –,** sy hand bewe; **– the head,** die kop skud; **– down,** afskud; uitsprei; inskud; tuis raak; **his faith in X was –n,** sy vertroue in X is geskok; **– off,** afskud; ontslae raak van; **– out,** uitskud; **– up,** opskud; wakker skud; **– with fear,** bewe van angs; **– with cold,** bewe (rittel) van die koue; **it shook me,** dit het my onthuts.
shake, n. skok, ruk, skud(ding); bewing, trilling; (hand)druk; triller; skeur (in hout); **in two –s of a lamb's tail,** in 'n kits, in 'n wip, in a japtrap; **he is all of a –,** hy het die bewerasie; **he is no great –s,** hy is nie wat wonders nie.
shakedown, kermisbed.
shaking, skudding, (die) skud; **he deserves a good –,** hy behoort terdeë deurmekaar geskud te word.
shako, sjako.
shaky, onvas, wankelbaar, wikkelrig; bewerig;

shale 659 **sheer**

swak, onseker; a – **house**, 'n bouvallige huis; he looks –, hy sien daar vaal (sleg) uit; **I feel** –, ek voel bewerig (skrikkerig).
shale, leiklip.
shall, sal; moet.
shallop, sloep.
shal(l)ot, salot.
shallow, a. vlak, ondiep; oppervlakkig.
shallow, n. vlak plek, sandbank.
shallow, v. vlak word; vlak maak.
shallow-brained, dom, onnosel.
shallowness, vlakheid; oppervlakkigheid.
sham, v. voorgee, veins, aanstel, liemaak, maak as of; fop, bedrieg; **he –s illness**, hy hou hom siek, hy maak of hy siek is; **he is only –ming**, hy hou hom maar so, dit is maar net aanstellery van hom.
sham, n. bedrog, foppery; voorwendsel, liemakery, skyn, bluf; **pillow** –, kussingkleedjies, vals sloop.
sham, a. vals, geveins, aanstellerig.
shamble, v. sleepvoet loop, slof.
shamble, n. slofgang.
shambles, slagpale, slagplek; bloedbad.
shambling, waggelend, sloffend.
shame, n. skaamte; skande, oneer; **for** –, skaam jou! foei tog!; – **on you**, skaam jou!; **put to** –, in die skande steek, beskaamd maak; **a** – **to his parents**, 'n skande vir sy ouers.
shame, v. beskaam, beskaamd maak, oneer aandoen; skaam wees.
shamefaced, bedees, beskroom, skamerig.
shameful, skandelik.
shameless, onbeskaamd, skaamteloos.
sham-fight, spieëlgeveg, skyngeveg.
shammer, aansteller, bedrieër, fopper.
shammy, shamoy, gensbok; seemsleer.
shampoo, v. hare was.
shampoo, n. haarwasmiddel; sjampoe.
shamrock, klawer.
shanghai, met geweld aanwerf, pres.
shank, been, skeen; steel, stingel; **Shanks's mare**, snel en geduld, snaar en st(r)amboel, dapper en stapper.
shanty, pondok, hutjie; hok.
shape, v. vorm, maak, fatsoen gee, fatsoeneer, modelleer; uitwerk, uitdink; inrig, reël; **–d like a pear**, peervormig; **the full-back** – **well**, die heelagter kom mooi op stryk.
shape, n. fatsoen, vorm, model; gedaante, gestalte; soort; **spherical in** –, bolvormig; **get his ideas into** –, sy gedagtes agtermekaar kry; **give** – **to**, vorm gee aan; **out of** –, uit fatsoen.
shapeless, vormloos, uit fatsoen.
shapely, mooi gevorm, mooi gebou.
shard, sherd, potskerf; eierdop.
share, n. deel, gedeelte, porsie; aandeel; – **and** – **alike**, gelykdop verdeel(d); **go** –s, billik verdeel; **had a large** – **in bringing it about**, het baie te doen gehad met die totstandkoming daarvan.
share, v. deel, verdeel, uitdeel; 'n deel hê in; **we must** – **alike**, ons moet gelykop deel; **I** – **your opinion**, ek stem met jou saam; – **a room with him**, met hom saam in een kamer bly.
share, n. (ploeg)skaar.
shareholder, aandeelhouer.
share-pusher, aandeelsmous.
sharer, deelhebber, deelgenoot.
shark, n. haai; woekeraar, uitsuier.
shark, v. uitsuig, woekerwins neem, swendel; insluk.
sharp, v. bedrieg, fop, skelm speel.
sharp, a. skerp, spits, puntig; bitsig, venynig; bytend; deurdringend; stemloos; skerpsinnig,

slim, vlug; oulik, geslepe, listig; vinnig, haastig, snel; **a** – **turn**, 'n skerp bog, 'n kort draai; **a** – **cry**, 'n deurdringende skreeu; **a** – **tongue**, 'n skerp tong, 'n tong soos 'n vlym; **a** – **attack of gout**, 'n hewige aanval van sinkings; **a** – **contest**, 'n hewige (vinnige) stryd; **keep a** – **look-out**, jou oë goed oophou, fyn oplet; **he was too** – **for me**, hy was te oulik vir my; – **practices**, slim streke, knoeiery; –**'s the word**, gou maak!
sharp, adv. gou; presies; **six o'clock** –, sesuur presies, sesuur op die kop; **look** –! gou nou! vortmaak! oppas!; **sing** –, te hoog sing!
sharp, n. kruis (in musiek); **B**– **major**, Bis; **B**– **minor**, bis.
sharpen, skerp maak, slyp.
sharper, bedrieër; kaartknoeier.
sharp-shooter, skerpskutter.
sharp-sighted, skerp van oë; skerpsinnig.
sharp-witted, skerpsinnig, skrander.
shatter, verpletter, verbrysel, ruineer; uitmekaar ja; skok; verydel, die bodem inslaan.
shave, v. skeer; skawe; stryk langs, verbyskram, verbyglip; in repies sny.
shave, n. (die) skeer; noue ontkoming; skaafmes; bedrog, foppery, versinsel; **I want a** –, ek wil my laat skeer; **it was a close** –, dit was 'n nou ontkoming, dit het weinig geskeel, dit het naelskraap (broekskeur) gegaan.
shaver, skeertoestel, skeerapparaat.
shaving, (die) skeer; krul, skaafsel.
shaving-brush, skeerkwas(sie).
shaving-horse, skaafbank.
shaving-kit, skeergerei.
shawl, tjalie, sjaal.
she, sy.
sheaf, n. gerf; bondel.
sheaf, v. (in gerwe) bind.
shear, skeer; knip, sny; kaalmaak, pluk; **he came back shorn**, hy het kaal daarvan afgekom.
shear-bill, skêrbek.
shears, (tuin)skêr, skaapskêr.
sheath, skede, huisie; vlerkskild, dop.
sheathe, in die skede steek; klee.
sheathing, bekleding.
sheave, (in gerwe) bind.
she-bear, berin, beerwyfie.
she-cat, wyfiekat.
shed, v. stort, vergiet; verloor; (ver)sprei, werp, uitstraal; – **tears**, trane stort; **the tree** –**s its leaves**, die boom verloor sy blare, die blare val van die boom af; **the snake** –**s its skin**, die slang vervel; – **light on**, lig werp op.
shed, n. skuur, afdak; loods; werkplek.
sheen, glans, skittering, glinstering.
sheeny, glansend, skitterend.
sheep, skaap, skape; **cast** –**'s eyes at**, verliefderig aankyk.
sheep-dip, skaapdip.
sheep-dog, skaaphond.
sheep-farmer, skaapboer.
sheep-fold, skaapkraal.
sheep-hook, haakkierie, haak(stok).
sheepish, skaapagtig; onnosel, dom.
sheep-run, skaapveld, skaapplaas.
sheep-shearing, (die) skaapskeer.
sheepskin, skaapvel.
sheep-tick, skaapluis, brandsiekteluis.
sheep-walk, skaapveld.
sheep-wash, skaapdip.
sheer, a. louter, puur, suiwer, absoluut; loodreg, regaf, steil; – **nonsense**, klinkklare (pure) onsin.
sheer, adv. loodreg, regaf.
sheer, v. uit die koers raak, gier; – **off**, wegdraai pad gee.

sheer, n. afwyking.
sheet, n. laken, bed(de)laken; plaat; vlak, oppervlakte; vel (papier); between the −s, in die vere, in die bed; three −s in the wind, aangeklam, in die takke; with flowing −s, met volle seile; the rain came down in −s, die reën het in strome geval, dit het gestortreën; a − of snow, in sneeulaken.
sheet, v. in lakens toedraai, met 'n laken toemaak.
sheet-anchor, noodanker; toeverlaat.
sheet-copper, bladkoper.
sheeting, lakenlinne.
sheet-iron, plaatyster.
sheet-lightning, weerlig.
sheik(h), sjeik.
shekel, sikkel; −s, geld, pitte, duite.
sheldrake, wilde-eend.
shelf, rak; plank; laag, bank (van 'n krans); sandbank; on the −, opgebêre, opsy gesit, klaar met, vergeet.
shell, n. dop, peul, skil; skulp; geraamte; binneste doodkis; bom; notedop, ligte roeibootjie; vertoon, skyn; come out of his −, uit sy dop (skulp) kruip.
shell, v. uitdop; bombardeer, beskiet; − off, afskilfer; − peas, ertjies (uit)dop.
shellac, skellak, gomlak.
shell-back, ou seerob, pikbroek.
shell-fish, skulpvis.
shell-lime, skulpkalk.
shell-proof, bomvry.
shell-work, skulpwerk.
shelly, vol. skulpe; skulpagtig, skulp- . . .
shelter, n. beskutting, beskerming, skuilplek; skerm; take −, skuiling soek, skuil; under −, beskut, onder dak.
shelter, v. beskut, beskerm; − oneself, skuil.
shelterless, onbeskut, sonder dak.
shelve, op die rak sit; rakke insit; op die lange baan skuif, uitstel.
shelve, skuins afloop, afhel.
shelving, n. rakke; rakplanke.
shepherd, n. skaapwagter, herder, oppasser; the Good S−, die Goeie Herder.
shepherd, v. oppas.
sheperdess, herderin.
shepherd's crook, herderstaf, haakkierie.
sheriff, balju, skout; fiskaal.
sherry, sjerrie.
Shetland, Shetland.
shew, sien **show,**
shewbread, toonbrood.
shibboleth, sjibbolet, wagwoord.
shield, n. skild; wapenskild; skerm.
shield, v. beskut, beskerm.
shift, v. verskuiwe, versit, verplaas; verander; omruil, vervang; verhuis; − one's lodging, verhuis; − the scene, die toneel verander; he tried to − off the responsibility, hy het probeer om die verantwoordelikheid van hom af te skuiwe; the wind −s round to the east, die wind draai oos; he must − for himself, hy moet maar sien om reg te kom.
shift, n. verandering, afwisseling; ploeg (werksmense), klompie; skof; plan, uitvlug, lis; redmiddel, hulpmiddel; must make a − without it, moet maar daarsonder klaarkom.
shifting, a. veranderlik, verganklik.
shifting, n. verandering, verplasing; trek.
shiftless, radeloos, hulpeloos, onbeholpe.
shifty, skelm, oulik; − eyes, skelm oë.
shilling, sjieling.
shilly-shally, aarsel, weifel.
shim, keil, wig.

shimmer, n. glans, glinstering.
shimmer, v. glinster, glans, skemer.
shimmy, hemp(ie); drildans; wielslingering.
shin, skeen, maermerrie.
shindy, lawaai, geraas, bakleiery; kick up a −, lawaai maak.
shine, v. skyn, blink, glinster; blink maak; uitblink.
shine, n. glans, skyn; rain or −; reent of mooiweer (sonskyn); put a good − on the boots, die stewels mooi blink maak; take the − out of, van sy glans berowe; in die skadu stel; take a − to someone, tot iemand aangetrokke voel.
shiner, muntstuk; −s, geld, pitte, duite.
shingle, n. dakspaan; ,,shingle''-haardrag.
shingle, v. met dakspane dek; (hare) skuins knip, ,,shingle''.
shingle, n. ronde klippies.
shingles, gordelroos.
shin-guard, beenskut, skeenskut.
shining, blink, skitterend, glansend.
shiny, glansend, blink.
ship, n. skip, vaartuig; when my − comes, as my skip met geld kom; they took −, hulle het hul ingeskeep; on board −, aan boord.
ship, v. laai, (met 'n skip) wegstuur, verskeep; aan boord neem; inskeep; aanmonster.
ship-biscuit, skeepsbeskuit.
ship-broker, skeepsmakelaar.
shipbuilder, skeepsboumeester.
shipbuilding, skeepsbou.
ship-chandler, skeepsleweransier.
ship-load, skeepsvrag, skeepslading.
shipmate, skeepskameraad.
shipment, lading, besending; verskeping.
shipper, verskeper, skeepsagent.
shipping, skepe, skeepsmag (handels)vloot, marine; verskeping, versending.
shipping-agent, skeepsagent.
shipshape, agtermekaar, in orde.
ship's papers, skeepspapiere.
ship-way, skeepshelling.
shipwreck, n. skipbreuk.
shipwreck, v. (laat)skipbreuk ly.
shipwright, skeepstimmerman.
shipyard, skeepstimmerwerf.
shire, graafskap.
shirk, v. ontduik, ontvlug, versuim (werk, plig, ens.), vermy, ontseil.
shirk(er), n. pligversaker; lamsak.
shirt, hemp; near is my −, but nearer is my skin, die hemp is nader as die rok.
shirt-front, (hemps)borsie.
shirt-sleeve, hempsmou.
shirting, hemdelinne, hemdegoed.
shiver, v. bewe, ril, sidder, huiwer.
shiver, n. rilling; it gives me the −s, ek kry die bewerasie daarvan; cold −s, kouekoors.
shiver, n. stukkie, brokkie, splinter.
shiver, v. versplinter, flenters breek.
shoal, a. vlak, ondiep.
shoal, vlak plek, sandbank.
shoal, n. menige, hoop, klomp, trop; skool (visse).
shoal, v. wemel, saamskool.
shoaly, vol sandbanke, vlak.
shock, n. botsing; skok; slag; − tactics, skoktaktiek.
shock, v. skok; aanstoot gee, 'n skok gee, teen die bors stuit, vererg; −ed to hear it, verstom om dit te hoor.
shock, n. hopie gerwe.
shock, v. gerwe opper (in oppers sit).
shock, n. deurmekaar hare; − head, wolhaarkop, kroeskop.

shock-absorber, skokdemper, skokbreker.
shocker, prul; sensasieroman.
shock-headed, wolhaarkop- ...
shocking, a. ergerlik, aanstootlik, verskriklik; ongehoord, gruwelik.
shocking, adv. beroerd.
shoddy, n. bog, prulle; uitgepluiste wol.
shoddy, a. nagemaak, prullerig, bogterig.
shoe, n. skoen; hoefyster; remskoen; **that's another pair of** –s, dis glad 'n ander saak; **be in somebody's** –s, in iemand se skoene staan; that's where the – **pinches**, daar lê die moeilikheid, daar sit die knoop; **put the – on the right foot**, die kind by sy regte naam noem, nie doekies omdraai nie.
shoe, v. beslaan; skoei; **shod feet**, geskoeide voete.
shoeblack, skoenskoonmaker.
shoeblacking, skoensmeer, -poets, waks.
shoe-buckle, skoengespe(r).
shoe-horn, skoenlepel.
shoelace, skoenveter.
shoe-leather, skoenleer.
shoemaker, skoenmaker.
shoe-string, skoenveter; **on a** –, op die goedkoopste (manier).
shoo, v. ja; – **away**, wegja.
shoot, v. skiet, doodskiet; bot, uitloop; uitspruit; fotograveer, opneem; steek; vlieg, trek; afneem, kiek, draai; **my corn** –s, my liddoring steek; – **a bolt**, 'n grendel (toe)skuif; **he has shot his bolt**, hy het sy ergste gedoen, sy rol is uitgespeel; – **ahead**, vooruitskiet; verbyhardloop; **I'll be shot if** ..., mag ek doodval as ... ;) **a match**, aan 'n skietwedstryd deelneem; – **out**, uitskiet; uitsteek; uitspring; – **through**, skiet deur; trek deur; – **up**, skielik styg; opskiet; **prices shot up**, pryse het skielik gestyg.
shoot, n. spruit, loot; stroomversnelling; glyplank; jagtog; skietwedstryd.
shooter, skutter; skietertjie; blaaspyp.
shooting, a. skietend, skiet- ... ; – **star**, vallende verskietende) ster.
shooting, (die) skiet; jag, jagreg.
shooting-box, jaghuis(ie).
shooting-range, skietbaan, skietterrein.
shooting-stick, sitstok, stoelkierie.
shop, n. winkel; werkplek; talk –, oor jou werk (vak) praat; **shut up** –, die hortjies toemaak, sluit; tou opgooi; **all over the** –, links en regs, hot en haar, deurmekaar.
shop, v. inkopies doen, winkel toe gaan.
shop-boy, winkelbediende, loopjonge.
shopkeeper, winkelier.
shoplifter, winkeldief.
shopping, (die) inkopies doen; **go** –, gaan inkopies doen, winkel toe gaan.
shopwalker, klerkopsigter.
shop-window, winkelvenster.
shop-worn, verkleur, verbleik.
shore, n. kus, strand, oewer; **on** –, aan wal, aan land.
shore, n. balk, stut.
shore, v. stut.
shoreward, landwaarts, na die kus.
short, a. kort, klein; kortaf; bros; beknop, skrap; – **story**, kortverhaal; – **circuit**, kortsluiting; **a** – **cut**, kortpad; – **rib**, kort rib, vals rib; **make** – **work of**, gou speel met; **he has a** – **temper**, hy is kort van draad (kortgebonde); **we ran** – **of tea**, ons tee het opgeraak; **in** –, kortom, om kort te gaan; **fall** –, nie daarby haal nie, (te) kort skiet; **cut** –,
afbreek; in die rede val; **by a** – **head**, met 'n kort kop; – **leg**, kortby (kr.).
short, adv. plotseling, skielik; **stop** –, skielik stilbly (stilstaan, stilhou).
shortage, tekort.
shortbread, broskoek, krummelkoek, sprits.
short circuit, kortsluiting.
shortcoming, tekortkoming.
shorten, verkort, korter maak; korter word.
shorthand, snelskrif, stenografie.
shorthand-writer, snel(skrif)skrywer.
shorthorn, korthoring(bees).
short-lived, kortstondig, kort van duur.
shortly, binnekort, spoedig; kortliks.
shorts, kort broek.
short-sighted, kortsigtig; bysiende.
short-spoken, kortaf, lakoniek.
short-tempered, kortgebonde (kortgebaker), kort van draad, opvlieënd.
short-winded, kortasem.
shot, n. skoot; hael; skutter; hou; (rolprentkamera-)opname; **you made a bad** –, jy het swak geraai; **I'm going to have a** – **at it**, ek gaan probeer; **he is a crack** –, hy is 'n baasskut; **within** –, onder skoot; **like a** –, soos 'n koeël uit die roer; al te graag; –!, mooi skoot!
shot, v. sien **shoot**; – **silk**, weerskynsy.
shot-free, skotvry.
shotgun, haelgeweer.
shotproof, koeëlvas, koeëlvry.
should, sien **shall**; behoort, moet.
shoulder, n. skouer; skouerstuk; skof; blad; – **of mutton**, skaapblad; – **to** –, skouer aan skouer; **put one's** – **to the wheel**, skouer teen die wiel sit; **give him the cold** –, hom die rug toedraai; **he has broad** –s, sy skouers is breed, hy kan die verantwoordelikheid dra; **rub** –s **with**, in aanraking kom met; **straight from the** –, op die man af; vry-vuis.
shoulder, v. (met die skouer) stamp; op die skouer neem; (las, verantwoordelikheid) dra (op jou neem).
shoulder-belt, bandelier.
shoulder-blade, skouerblad.
shoulder-strap, skouerriem; skouerstrook; skouerlus.
shout, v. skree (skreeu), hard roep; juig; – **for joy**, juig van blydskap; – **with laughter**, skaterlag.
shout, n. geskree(u), geroep; gejuig.
shove, v. stoot, stamp, skuif; – **it in the drawer**, stop (gooi) dit maar in die laai; – **off**, afstoot; van wal steek.
shove, n. stoot, stamp.
shovel, n. skop, skopgraaf.
shovel, v. skep.
shovelful, skopvol, skopgraafvol.
show, **shew**, v. wys, toon, laat sien; tentoonstel, vertoon; bewys, aantoon; **he hardly ever** –s **himself**, hy laat hom byna nooit sien nie; – **fight**, regstaan, 'n verdedigende houding inneem, (sig) verset; – **mercy**, genadig wees; – **kindness**, vriendelikheid betoon; **it** –s **white**, dit lyk wit; – **somebody the door**, iemand die deur wys; **he** –**ed us round the house**, hy het ons die huis laat sien (gewys); – **in**, binnelaat; – **off**, windmaak, spog; te koop loop met; – **out**, uitlaat; die deur wys; – **up**, (laat) uitkom; aan die kaak stel; opdaag.
show, n. vertoning, tentoonstelling; voorstelling; skyn; praal, vertoon; onderneming; **just for** –, net vir die skyn; net om 'n vertoon te maak, net om te spog; **he gave away the** –, hy het die aap uit die mou gelaat, hy het die spul bederf; **he had no** – **at all**, hy het hoege-

naamd geen kans gehad nie; **he made a poor –,** hy het 'n treurige vertoning gemaak; **vote by – of hands,** stem deur hande op te steek; **be on –,** vertoon word; **let's do a –,** laat ons 'n vertoning (opvoering) bywoon.
show-down, kragmeting, beslissende stryd.
show-case, uitstalkas.
shower, n. (reën)bui; stroom
shower, v. reent, neerstroom; – **upon,** oorlaai met oorstelp met.
shower-bath, stortbad.
showery, buierig, reënagtig, reënerig.
show-girl, verhoogmeisie.
showing, vertoning; bewys, verklaring.
showman, sirkusbaas.
showmanship, vertoonkuns; reklamekuns; windmakery.
show-room, toonkamer, uitstalkamer.
show-window, uitstalvenster.
showy, windmaker(ig), spoggerig.
shrapnel, granaatbom, skrapnel.
shred, n. flenter, stukkie, lappie, repie; **tear to –s,** (aan) flenters skeur; **not a – of evidence,** nie 'n greintjie bewys nie.
shred, v. stukkend sny (skeur).
shrew, wyf, heks, helleveeg.
shrewd, skrander, slim; listig, slu.
shrewish, kyfagtig, twissiek.
shrew-mouse, spitsmuis.
shriek, v. gil, skree(u); – **with laughter,** gier van die lag, skaterlag.
shriek, n. gil, skree(u).
shift, absolusie, bieg; **give short –,** gou speel met, kort werk maak van.
shrike, janfiskaal, laksman.
shrill, deurdringend, snerpend, skerp.
shrimp, garnaal; dwergie, kleintjie.
shrine, relikwieëkassie; altaar; heiligdom, heilige graf; tempel.
shrink, krimp, inkrimp, ineenkrimp; laat krimp; – **from,** terugdeins vir; – **back,** huiwer, terugdeins; – **into oneself,** in sy skulp *of* dop kruip.
shrinkage, (in)krimping; vermindering.
shrive, absolusie gee; die bieg afneem.
shrivel, krimp, verskrompel, uitdroë.
shroud, n. omhulsel; kleed; lykkleed.
shroud, v. omhul; verberg, bedek, wegsteek, in 'n doodskleed wikkel.
shrub, struik, bossie, heester.
shrubbery, struikgewas, bosgasie.
shrubby, struikagtig, ruig, bosagtig.
shrug, v. die skouers ophaal (optrek).
shrub, n. skouerophaling.
shrunk(en), sien **shrink.**
shuck, n. dop, peul.
shuck, v. uitdop.
shudder, v. huiwer, sidder, gril, ril, ys.
shudder, n. huiwerig, rilling, gril.
shuffle, v. skuif, slof; (deurmekaar) skud, verwar; jakkalsdraaie maak, uitvlugte soek, onderduims wees; – **the feet,** die voete heen en weer skuif; – **the cards,** die kaarte skommel; – **off responsibility,** die verantwoordelikheid afskuif; – **along,** aansukkel, aanslof.
shuffle, n. geskuif; geslof, slofgang; (die) skud, (die) was (van kaarte); uitvlug, veranderlikheid, draai, jakkersstreek.
shuffler, bedrieër, „jakkals".
shuffling, sloffend, slof- . . .; listig.
shun, vermy, ontwyk.
shunt, v. rangeer, op 'n syspoor bring, uit die pad stoot, regstoot; uitstel, op die lang(e) baan skuiwe; afsien van.
shunt, n. wisseling, (die) rangeer.

shut, v. sluit, toemaak; toegaan; – **the eyes,** die oë toemaak; – **the door upon,** buitesluit, uitsluit; onmoontlik maak; **the door – with a bang,** die deur het toegeklap; **the lid –s automatically,** die deksel gaan vanself toe; – **his teeth,** sy tande op mekaar byt (klem); – **down,** toemaak, toetrek; stopsit, sluit; – **in,** opsluit; insluit, omring; – **off,** afsluit; – **off from,** uitsluit; – **out,** uitsluit; – **up,** opsluit; toesluit; – **up shop,** winkel toemaak; tou opgooi; **will you – up,** sal jy jou mond hou?
shut, a. toe, gesluit; **the door is –,** die deur is toe (gesluit); **a – door,** 'n toe (geslote) deur.
shutter, hortjie, luik, blinding; sluiting; sluiter.
shuttle, (skiet)spoel.
shuttle-cock, pluimbal, kuifbal.
shy, a. sku, skaam, skamerig, verleë, eenkennig, beskroomd; agterdogtig; **–shy** (e.g. **work-shy),** -sku (bv. werksku).
shy, v. skrik, wegvlie(g), wegspring.
shy, n. sysprong.
shy, v. gooi, smyt, slinger.
shy, n. gooi; **have a – at,** gooi na.
shyster, beginsellose persoon (prokureur).
si, si (in musiek).
Siam, Siam.
Siamese, Siamees; – **cat,** Siamese kat; – **twins,** Siamese tweeling.
Siberian, a. Siberies.
Siberian, n. Siberiër; Siberiese vrou.
sibilant, a. sis- . . ., sissend.
sibilant, n. sisklant.
sibilate, sis, sissend uitspreek.
sibyl, sibille, profetes, waarsegter.
sibylline, profeties, sibillyns.
siccative, opdroënde middel, sikkatief.
Sicilian, a. Siciliaans.
Sicilian, n. Siciliaan; Siciliaans.
Sicily, Sicilië.
sick, a. siek, ongesteld; mislik, naar; **be – of fever,** die koors hê; – **at heart,** hartseer, weemoedig, treurig gestem; **I feel –,** ek is siek (naar); – **of waiting,** moeg (sat) van wag.
sick, n.: **the –,** die siekes.
sick, v.: – **him, sa!,** vat hom.
sickbed, siekbed.
sicken, siek word; mislik (naar) word; mislik maak, walg; **the child is –ing for something,** die kind het iets onder lede; **–ed of trying to make peace,** moeg geprobeer om vrede te maak.
sicken, siek word; mislik maak, walg.
sickle, sekel.
sick-leave, siekteverlof.
sick-list, siekelys.
sickly, sieklik, swak; walglik; **a – smile,** 'n flou glimlag.
sickness, siekte; mislikheid.
side, n. sy, kant, rant; helling; houdings, aanstellings; **the light –,** die ligsy; **the dark –,** die donker kant; – **of a mountain,** berghelling; – **by –,** sy aan sy, skouer aan skouer; **on one –,** eenkant, opsy; **study all –s of the question,** die saak grondig ondersoek; **on both –s,** aan albei kante; **take –s,** party kies; **Ceres has a strong –,** Ceres het 'n sterk span; **this – of,** duskant; **on the right,** wrong **– of forty,** onder, oor die veertig jaar; **on the mother's –,** van moederskant; **he puts on too much –,** hy is te aanstellerig; – **bet,** byweddenskap.
side, v. party trek, party kies.
side-arms, sygeweer.
sideboard, buffet.
side-car, sywaentjie, syspanwaentjie.
side-dish, bygereg.

side-drum, tamboertjie.
side-face, profiel.
side-issue, bysaak, ondergeskikte saak.
sidelight, (sy)lig; syraam; sylantern; sydelingse informasie; **throw a curious − on,** 'n snaakse lig werp op.
side-line, byverdienste; liefhebbery.
sidelong, sydelings.
side-note, kanttekening.
sidereal, sterre- . . ., sideries.
side-saddle, meisiesaal.
side-show, byvertoning, ekstra vertoning.
side-slip, glips; loot, spruit.
side-splitting, om jou 'n boggel oor te lag.
side-step, n. trappie; systap; swenk.
side-step, v. verbyspring.
side-stroke, syslag, kanthou.
side-track, n. syspoor, wisselspoor.
side-track, v. op 'n syspoor bring; uitstel, opsy skuif.
side-view, profiel; **get a − of,** van die kant te sien kry.
side-walk, sypaadjie.
sideward(s), sydelings, sywaarts.
sideways, sydelings, skuins.
side-whiskers, bakkebaard.
side-wind, sywind.
siding, (spoorweg)halte; syspoor, wisselspoor.
sidle, skuins loop, skeef loop.
siege, beleg, beleëring; **lay − to,** beleër; **raise the −,** die beleg opbreek.
sierra, (berg)reeks.
siesta, middagslapie, middagrussie.
sieve, n. sif.
sieve, v. sif.
sift, sif; ondersoek, uitpluis, naspeur; uitvra, uithoor; **− out,** uitpluis.
sigh, v. sug; **− for,** smag na.
sigh, n. sug.
sight, n. (die) oë; (die) sien; gesig; vertoning; visioen; skouspel; besienswaardigheid; visier, korrel (van 'n geweer); **short −,** slegte oë; kortsigtigheid; **he has lost his −,** hy het sy oë (gesig) verloor; **he has a good −,** hy het skerp oë, hy kan fyn sien; **I know him by −,** ek ken hom van sien; **lose − of,** uit die oog verloor; **catch − of,** in die oog kry, sien; **at −,** op sig; **plays music at −,** speel musiek van die blad; **at first −,** op die eerste gesig; **she found favour in his −,** sy het genade gevind in sy oë; **in −,** sigbaar, onder die oë; **out of −,** onder die oë uit; **out of − out of mind,** uit die oog, uit die hart; **out of my −!,** weg onder my oë, maak dat jy wegkom; **the flowers were a −,** dit was 'n lus om die blomme te sien; **his face is a perfect −,** jy moet sy gesig sien!, hy lyk soos 'n voëlverskrikker; **as soon as we came in − of the town,** sodra ons die dorp kon sien; **don't make a − of yourself,** moet jou nie belaglik maak nie; **a long − better,** 'n hele end (skoot) beter; **be careful − before firing,** hy het sekuur korrel gevat voor hy skiet; **I can't stand the − of him,** ek kan hom nie onder my oë verdra nie; **it is a − for sore eyes,** dit is 'n lus vir die oë; **back −, front − of a rifle,** visier, korrel van 'n geweer.
sight, v. sien, in die oog kry; waarneem; korrel aansit; stel; korrelvat, mik.
sightless, blind.
sightly, mooi, aangenaam vir die oog.
sight-seeing, (die) kyk na besienswaardighede; toerisme.
sight-seer kykgierige; toeris.
sigmate, s-vormig.

sign, n. teken, merk; voorteken; wagwoord; uithangbord; simbool, sinnebeeld.
sign, v. teken, onderteken; 'n teken gee; **− away,** oordra; **− off,** afteker; **ophou uitsend; − on,** aansluit; aanmonster; jou verbind, teken; **− assent,** toestemmend knik.
signal, n. teken, sein, sinjaal; **− of distress,** noodsein.
signal, a. duidelik, beslis, onmiskenbaar, sprekend, merkwaardig, skitterend.
signal, v. sein, sinjaleer; 'n teken (wenk) gee, aankondig.
signal-box, -cabin, seinhuisie.
signal-gun, seinskoot.
signalize, kenmerk; onderskei; beskrywe.
signal-man, seiner; seinwagter.
signatory, ondertekenaar.
signature, naamtekening, ondertekening, teken voorteken(ing) (musiek); **− tune,** kenwysie.
sign-board, uithangbord.
signet, seël.
signet-ring, seëlring.
significance, betekenis, gewig, belang.
significant, betekenisvol, gewigtig, veelbetekenend; **it is − of,** dit dui aan, dit is kenmerkend van.
signification, betekenis.
signify, aandui; beteken; te kenne gee.
signor, meneer.
signora, mevrou.
signorina, mejuffrou.
sign-painter, dekorateur, skilder van uithangborde.
signpost, uithangbord; wegwys(t)er.
silage, n. ingekuilde voer, kuilvoer.
silage, v. inkuil.
silence, n. stilte; stilswye, stilswyendheid; geheimhouding; vergetelheid; **pass over in −,** stilswyend verbygaan; **put to −,** stil maak, laat swyg.
silence, v. stil maak, die swye oplê.
silencer, knalpot, (knal)demper.
silent, stil; **remain −,** stilbly, swyg; **− partner,** tillevennoot; **− film,** stil prent.
Silesia, Silesië; Silesiese linne.
Silesian, a. Silesies.
Silesian, n. Silesiër; Silesies.
silhouette, n. silhoeët, skadubeeld.
silhouette, v. silhoeëtteer.
silica, kieselaarde, kieselsuur.
silicate, silikaat, kieselsuursout.
silicon, kiesel, silikon.
silk, n. sy, systof; **−s,** syklere; systowwe.
silk, a. sy- . . .
silken, sy; syagtig.
silk-stockings, sykouse.
silkworm, sywurm.
silky, syagtig, sag; glad, stroperig.
sill, vensterbank; drumpel (drempel).
siller, silwer; geld.
silly, verspot, laf, stuitig; onnosel, dom.
silo, n. silo, voerkuil.
silo, v. inkuil.
silt, n. modder, slyk (slik), slib.
silt, v. toedrywe, vol modder (slyk) loop, versand; **− up,** toedrywe.
Silurian, a. Siluries.
Silurian, n. Siluriër.
silvan, sylvan, bosagtig; landelik.
silver, n. silwer; silwergeld; silwergoed.
silver, a. silwer; **− screen,** rolprentskerm.
silver, v. wit (grys) word; versilwer.
silver-fish, silwervis.
silver-fox, silwerjakkals.
silver-gilt, vergulde silwer.

silver-grey, silwergrys.
silver-plated, versilwer(d).
silversmith, silwersmid.
silver-tree, witboom, silwerboom.
silver-ware, silwergoed, tafelsilwer.
silvery, silweragtig, silwer- . . .; wit.
simian, a. aapagtig, aap- . . .
simian, n. aap.
similar, eenders, ooreenkomstig, gelyksoortig; gelykvormig.
similarity, eendersheid, ooreenkoms, gelyksoortigheid; gelykvormigheid.
similarly, op dieselfde manier, net so.
simile, vergelyking.
similitude, vergelyking, gelykenis; ewebeeld.
simmer, borrel; sing (van ketel); saggies (effentjies) kook.
simony, simonie.
simoon, samoem, woestynwind.
simper, v. aanstellerig glimlag.
simper, n. aanstellerige glimlaggie.
simple, a. eenvoudig; enkel, skoon, louter; enkelvoudig; onskuldig; onnosel, simpel; – sentence, enkelvoudige sin; – equation, eenvoudige vergelyking; he is too – to understand it, hy is te onnosel om dit te verstaan; – life, eenvoudige lewenswyse; her – efforts, haar nederige poginge.
simple-hearted, eenvoudig, opreg.
simple-minded, eenvoudig; swaksinnig.
simpleton, lummel, swaap.
simplicity, eenvoud(igheid), natuurlikheid, onskuld.
simplification, vereenvoudiging.
simplify, vereenvoudig.
simply, enkel, eenvoudig, louter, niks anders as, puur.
simulacrum, skyn(beeld), beeltenis.
simulant, gelykend op wat lyk na.
simulate, veins, voorgee, voorwend, simuleer; naboots, namaak.
simulation, voorwendsel; nabootsing.
simultaneity, gelyktydigheid.
simultaneous, gelyktydig.
sin, n. sonde, oortreding; deadly, mortal –, doodsonde; his besetting –, sy swakheid (kwaal).
sin, v. sondig.
sinapism, mosterdpleister.
since, adv. van toe af, daarna; gelede; how long is it –, hoe lank gelede is dit?
since, prep. sedert, sinds, van . . . af; he has eaten nothing – yesterday, hy het niks geëet van gister af nie.
since, conj. nadat, sedert, sinds; aangesien, daar, omdat, nademaal.
sincere, openhartig, opreg, eerlik; eg.
sincerely, openhartig, opreg; – yours, jou (u) toegeneë.
sincerity, opregtheid, openhartigheid.
sine, n. sinus.
sinecure, sinekuur; voordelige amp.
sinew, sening, spier.
sinewy, seningagtig; seningrig; sterk, gespier(d), kragtig.
sing, v. sing; besing; gons; suis; – another tune, 'n ander toon aanslaan; 'n ander wysie sing; – small, mooi broodjies bak; – out, uitsing; uitskree, uitgalm; hard sing, uit volle bors sing.
singe, skroei, seng, afbrand; – the hair, die hare skroei.
singer, sanger(es).
singing, (die) sing; getuit, gesuis (in die ore); sanglesse, sangkuns.

single, a. enkel; enkelvoudig; eenlopend, ongetroud, alleen; eenpersoons- . . .; – game, enkelspel; – court, enkelbaan; – ticket, enkelkaartjie; – bed, eenpersoonsbed; inspired with a – purpose, met een doel voor oë; in a – sum, in een bedrag.
single, n. enkelspel; een lopie (krieket).
single, v.: – out, uitkies, uitsoek.
single-breasted, met een ry knope.
single-eyed, met een doel voor oë.
single-handed, alleen; met een hand.
single-hearted, eerlik, opreg, heelhartig.
single-heartedness, openhartigheid.
singlet, onderhempie, frokkie.
singleton, enetjie.
singly, een vir een, afsonderlik, alleen.
singsong, eentonige wysie, eentonigheid; saamsing, sangoefening.
singular, a. enkelvoudig; buitengewoon; vreemd, sonderling; seldsaam.
singular, n. enkelvoud.
singularity, sonderlingheid, eienaard'gheid, enkelvoudigheid.
sinister, onheilspellend, rampspoedig; kwaadaardig; linker; sinister.
sink, v. sink, sak, daal, val, laat sink; laat sak; laat val; laat hang; swak word, agteruitgaan, beswyk; grawe; my spirits sank, my moed het my begewe; the sick man is –ing, die sieke is sterwende; his cheeks have sunk, sy wange het ingeval (hol geword); here goes, – or swim, daarop of daaronder; nou of nooit; – a well, 'n put grawe; it –s into the memory, dit bly in die geheue geprent; – one's own interests, jou eie belange op die agtergrond skuiwe; – all differences, alle geskille laat vaar (rus); – money in, geld belê in, geld steek in; – one's head, jou kop laat sak; – a fact, 'n feit verswyg.
sink, n. afwasbak, wasbak; vuilwaterbak; riool; poel; sinkput.
sinker, dieplood, sinklood.
sinking, sinkend; afnemend.
sinking-fund, amortisasiefonds.
sinner, sondaar.
sin-offering, soenoffer.
sinuate, gekartel, gegolf.
sinuosity, karteling, golwing; kronkeling, bogtigheid, bog, kromming, draai.
sinuous, kronkelend, bogtig.
sinus, holte; baie, bog; opening; fistel; sinus.
sip, v. slurp, insuie, met teugies drink.
sip, n. slukkie, mondjievol.
siphon, n. sifon, hewel; spuitwaterfles.
siphon, v. opsuig, hewel, aftap, oortap.
sir, meneer, seur; sir.
sirdar, opperbevelhebber, sirdar.
sire, n. voorvader; vader (van 'n perd bv.); S–, Majesteit.
sire, v. teel, die vader wees van.
siren, verleister; mishoring; sirene.
sirloin, lendestuk (van beesvleis).
sirocco, sirokko, woestynwind.
sirrah, vent, kêrel.
siskin, sysie.
sissy, sien cissy.
sister, suster; non; pleegsuster, hoofverpeegster; the Fatal Sisters, die Skikgodinne.
sisterhood, susterskap.
sister-in-law, skoonsuster.
sisterly, susterlik.
Sistine, Sixtyns.
sit, sit; sitting hê (hou); pas; broei; poseer; shoot a bird –ting, 'n voël in die sit skiet; the hen wants to –, die hen is broeis; –s the wind

there, waai die wind van daardie kant af?; **he sat himself next to me**, hy het langs my kom sit; hy het hom langes my neergeplak; – **tight**, vastrap, hou wat jy het, jou nie laat bang maak nie; vas in die saal sit; nou aan die lyf sit; – **at home**, by die huis sit (lê), 'n huishen wees; – **down**, gaan sit; – **for one's portrait**, poseer; – **for an examination**, eksamen doen; – **on the fence**, die kat uit die boom kyk; – **on a committee**, lid wees van 'n komitee, sitting hê in (op) 'n komitee; – **out**, bly sit, nie deelneem aan ('n dans) nie; buitekant sit; langer bly (as die ander); uitsit, bly tot aan die einde (van 'n opvoering, ens.); – **up**, regop sit; opbly; waak; skrik, verbaas wees; **make somebody – up**, iemand hotagter laat kry; iemand verbaas laat staan; **he wants –ting upon**, hy moet kort gevat word; – **up and take notice**, bewus word en oplet; aandag gee aan die saak.
sit-down: – **supper**, volledige soepee; – **strike**, sitstaking.
site, ligging; (bou)terrein.
sitter, sitter; model; broeihen; **that's a –**, dit is 'n maklike hou (skoot).
sitting, n. sitting; broeisel eiers; sitplek; **at a –**, in een slag.
sitting, a. sittend; – **hen**, broeihen.
sitting-room, sitkamer, voorkamer; sitplek.
situated, **situate**, geleë.
situation, ligging; posisie, toestand, omstandighede, situasie; betrekking, pos.
six, ses; **it is – of one and half-a-dozen of the other**, dit kom maar op dieselfde neer; **at –es and sevens**, in die war, deurmekaar, oorhoop.
sixfold, sesvoudig.
sixfooter, sesvoeter.
six-ply, seslaag.
sixteen, sestien.
sixteenth, sestiende.
sixth, sesde.
sixthly, in die sesde plek.
sixtieth, sestigste.
sixty, sestig.
sizable, groot.
size, n. grootte, omvang, maat; nommer; formaat; **of vast –**, ontsaglik groot; **that's about the – of it**, dit kom daarop neer.
size, v. sorteer, klassifiseer, rangskik; – **up**, takseer, 'n oordeel vorm omtrent.
size, n. gomwater, lym.
size, v. lym.
size-stick, maatstok.
sizy, taai, klewerig, lymerig.
sizzle, braai, spat, sputter.
sjambok, sambok.
skate, n. skaats.
skate, v. skaatse ry, skaats; – **over thin ice**, jou op gevaarlike terrein begewe.
skating-rink, skaatsbaan.
skedaddle, trap, die spat neem.
skein, string; knoop, warboel.
skeletal, van 'n geraamte, geraamte- . . .
skeleton, geraamte, skelet; skets; **a – at the feast**, skelet agter die deur, stille kwelling (sorg); – **in the cupboard**, family –, familiegeheim, die kruis van die familie.
skeleton-key, loper, slotoopsteker.
sketch, skets.
sketch-book, sketsboek.
sketch-map, sketskaart.
sketchy, onafgewerk, vlugtig geteken (geskets), los, onsamehangend.
skew, skeef, skuins.

skewbald, bont.
skewer, vleispen, sosatiepen.
skew-eyes, skeel.
ski, n. ski, sneeuskaats.
ski, v. sneeuskaats ry.
skid, n. rem, briekblok; (die) gly.
skild, v. rem; gly, uitgly, glip, skuiwe.
skiff, n. bootjie, skuitjie, skif.
skiff, v. skifroei.
skilful, bekwaam, knap, bedrewe.
skill, bekwaamheid, knapheid, handigheid, bedrewenheid.
skilled, bekwaam, bedrewe, ervare, geskool; – **labour**, geskoolde arbeid.
skim, v. afskuim, afskep, afroom; vlugtig deurlees (deurkyk); gly oor (deur); – **along**, gly langs; – **the cream off**, afroom.
skim, a. afgeroom; – **milk**, afgeroomde melk.
skimmer, skuimspaan.
skimp, suinig wees, afskeep.
skimpy, skrap, skraal.
skin, n. vel, huid; skil, vlies; **only – and bone**, net vel en been; **with a whole –**, heelhuids, sonder klereskeur; **save one's –**, heelhuids daarvan afkom; jou lyf wegsteek; **I would not be in his –**, ek sou nie graag in sy skoene wil staan nie; **he escaped with the – of his teeth**, hy het ternouernood ontkom, dit was so hittete of hy het nie vrygekom nie; **he has a thick –**, hy is dikhuidig (onbeskaamd); **get under one's –**, jou vererg; jou belangstelling aangryp; jou diep aantas.
skin, v. met 'n rofie bedek; toegroei; die vel afstroop; pluk, plunder; afslag; uitsuig, afset; **keep your eyes –ned**, goed dophou.
skin-deep, oppervlakkig, vlak.
skinflint, vrek, geldwolf.
skinful, trommeldik.
skinner, afslagter; afsetter, velkoper.
skinny, (brand)maer, benerig.
skip, v. spring, huppel; riemspring; oorslaan, uitlaat, oorspring.
skip, n. springetjie, sprongetjie.
skipjack, springkewer, kniptor.
skipper, skipper; kaptein; springer.
skipping-rope, springtou, springriem.
skirmish, n. skermutseling.
skirmish, v. skermutsel.
skirt, n. rok; pant, slip; vroumens, „aster"; kant, rant, soom; **divided –**, rokbroek, harembroek.
skirt, v. langs die kant gaan, omsoom.
skirting-board, (voet)lys, plint.
skit, parodie, spotskrif.
skittish, (kop)sku, skrikkerig; uitgelate; wispelturig; ligsinnig; vryerig.
skittle-alley, kegelbaan.
skittle-pin, kegel.
skive, sny, splits; slyp.
skiver, dun leer; mes.
skivvy, diensmeid.
skulduggery, swendelary, kullery, gemene praktyk.
skulk, loer, sluip, skuil; ontwyk.
skull, skedel, kopbeen.
skull-cap, kalotjie, mussie.
skunk, muishond; smeerlap, vuilgoed.
sky, n. lug, hemel; **under the open –**, onder die blote hemel; **laud to the skies**, ophemel, opvysel.
sky, v. in die lug gooi (slaan, skop).
sky-blue, hemelsblou.
sky-clad, nakend.
sky-high, hemelhoog.
skylark, n. lewerkie.

skylark, v. strewe uithaal, kattekwaad aanrig, poetse bak, pret maak.
skylight, dakvenster, dakraam, vallig.
sky-line, kim, gesigseinder, horison.
sky-pilot, hemelloods.
sky-rocket, vuurpyl.
sky-scape, luggesig.
sky scraper, wolkekrabber, hemelboorder.
skyward, hemelwaarts.
slab, plat klip, steen, plaat.
slack, a. slap, los; traag, lui, laks; **a – rope,** 'n slap tou; **keep a – hand,** laks wees, sake hulle eie gang laat gaan.
slack, n. slaphangende ent (van 'n tou); slap tyd, slapte; steenkoolgruis.
slack, v. verslap; vertraag; laat skiet.
slack-baked, halfgebak, halfgaar.
slacken, slap word, laat skiet; verslap, verminder.
slacker, luiaard; pligversaker, papbroek.
slag, metaalskuim, slak; sintel.
slain, sien **slay; be –,** sneuwel.
slake, les; blus; **–d lime,** gebluste kalk.
slam, v. toeklap, toeslaan (van 'n deur).
slam, n. harde slag, skoonskip maak (kaartspel).
slander, n. laster, skinderpraatjies.
slander, v. (be)laster, (be)skinder.
slanderer, kwaadprater, skindertong.
slanderous, lasterlik, laster- . . .
slang, plattaal, ,,slang".
slant, v. skuins (skeef) loop (staan).
slant, n. skuinste, helling; **on a –,** skuins; **kyk** (op), opvatting (van).
slant, a. skuins, skeef.
slanting, skuins, skeef.
slap, v. slaan, klap (gee).
slap, n. klap, slag.
slap, adv. plotseling; reg; – **in the eye,** reg in die oog.
slap-bang, met geweld; halsoorkop, holderstebolder; pardoems.
slapdash, met geweld; haastig, halsoorkop, onverskillig.
slapstick, n. hansworstery; growwe humor.
slapstick: – **comedy,** dolle klug.
slap-up, modern, piekfyn.
slash, v. sny; slaan, raps.
slash, n. hou, sny.
slashing, skerp; kras, vernietigend; – **criticism,** vernietigende kritiek.
slat, lat, plankie.
slate, n. leiklip; lei.
slate, a. lei- . . ., leikleurig.
slate, v. streng kritiseer, hekel; uitskel.
slate-coloured, leikleurig.
slate-pencil, griffel (griffie).
slattern, slonsige (slordige) vrou, slet.
slatternly, slonsig, slordig, liederlik.
slaughter, n. slagting; bloedbad.
slaughter, v. vermoor; slag.
slaughter-cattle, slagvee.
slaughterer, slagter; bloedvergieter.
slaughter-house, slagplek, slagpaal.
slaughterous, moorddadig.
Slav, n. Slaaf.
Slav, a. Slawies.
slave, n. slaaf, slavin; **he is a – to drink,** hy is verslaaf aan die drank.
slave, v. sloof, swoeg.
slave-born, in slawerny gebore.
slave-holder, slawe-eienaar, slawehouer.
slaver, n. slaweskip; slawehandelaar.
slaver, n. kwyl.
slaver, v. kwyl, bekwyl.
slavery, slawerny.

slave-trader, slawehandelaar.
Slavic, Slawies.
slavish, slaafs.
Slavonian, a. Slavonies; Slawies.
Slavonian, n. Slavoniër; Slaaf.
Slavonic, Slavonies; Slawies.
slay, doodmaak, vermoor.
sleazy, dun, flou; slordig; miserabel.
sled, sledge, sleigh, slee.
sledge(-hammer), voorhamer.
sleek, a. glad, glansend, blink, sag.
sleek, v. glad (blink) maak.
sleep, n. slaap, vaak; **go to –,** gaan slaap; **aan slaap raak.**
sleep, v. slaap; rus; **let –ing dogs lie,** moenie slapende honde wakker maak nie; – **the hours away,** die tyd verslaap; – **on, upon, over something,** oor iets slaap; – **off his debauch,** sy roes uitslaap.
sleeper, slaper; dwarslêer.
sleeping accommodation, slaapplek.
sleeping-car(riage), slaapwa.
sleeping-draught, slaapdrank.
sleeping-partner, rustende (stille) vennoot.
sleeping-sickness, slaapsiekte.
sleeping-suit, slaappak, slaapklere.
sleepless, slaaploos.
sleep-walker, slaapwandelaar.
sleepy, vaak, vakerig, slaperig; stil, vervelend, dooierig.
sleepyhead, slaapkous, jandooi.
sleet, n. nat sneeu, hael en reent, kapok.
sleet, v. sneeu (hael) en reent deurmekaar.
sleeve, mou; huis; **laugh in one's –,** in sy vuis lag; **have something up one's –,** iets in die mou hê; **turn up one's –s,** jou moue oprol; vir jou klaar maak; **wear one's hart upon one's –,** die hart op die tong hê.
sleeveless, sonder moue.
sleeve-link, mouknoop, mansjetknoop.
sleigh, sien **sled.**
sleight, handigheid, behendigheid, streek; – **of hand,** handigheid, goëltoertjie.
slender, dun, skraal, maer, rank; slank; gering, min, armsalig, klein.
sleuthhound, bloedhond, speurhond.
slice, n. sny, skyf; vislepel; vuurskop; deel; **a – of the profits,** 'n deel van die wins; **a – of bread,** 'n sny brood.
slice, v. skywe sny, dun sny.
slick, a. handig, rats, glad; puur, louter.
slick, adv. reg, vlak, mooi, skoon, glad.
slide, v. gly, glip; skuiwe; laat gly, laat glip; **let things –,** sake hulle gang laat gaan; – **over a delicate subject,** 'n delikate saak effentjies aanraak; – **into sin,** in sonde verval.
slide, n. (die) gly (glip); skuinste, helling; glybaan; plaatjie; knip, skuif; grond-, aardverskuiwing.
slide-rule, rekenliniaal.
slide-valve, skuifklep.
sliding, glyend, glippend, skuiwend, gly- . . ., skuif- . . ., wissel- . . .
sliding-door, skuifdeur.
sliding-rule, skuifliniaal, rekenliniaal.
sliding-scale, wisselende loonskaal.
sliding-seat, glybank.
slight, a. tinger, swak; klein, gering, min, bietjie; oppervlakkig; **a – cold,** effentjies verkoue.
slight, v. minag, gering ag, beledig, versmaad, veronagsaam.
slight, n. minagting, belediging.
slightly, effe(ntjies), bietjie.
slily, op listige (skelmagtige) wyse.

slim, dun, skraal, maer, tinger, slank; oulik, geslepe, slim.
slim, v. verslank.
slime, slym, slyk, modder.
slimy, slymerig, glyerig, glipperig, glad.
sling, v. swaai; slinger, gooi.
sling, n. slinger; doek, draagband; riem.
slink, v. (weg)sluip.
slink, v. voor die tyd kalwe (jonge).
slinky sluipend; slank; tenger; – **dress**, nousluitende tabberd.
slip, v. gly, glip, glibber; ontglip; 'n fout maak, jou vergis (verspreek); laat glip, laat gly; **it –ped my memory**, dit het my ontgaan; **the cow –ped its calf**, die koei het voor die tyd gekalwe; – **across to the bakers**,, gou na die bakker oordraf (oorwip); – **along**, vlie, seil oor die grond; – **in**, insluip, inglip; – **a coin into the hand of somebody**, iemand 'n geldstuk in die hand stop; – **off**, wegsluip; afgooi, gou-gou uittrek, uitruk; afskuif; – **a ring off the finger**, 'n ring van jou vinger afskuif; – **on**, inskuif; haastig aantrek; – **out**, uitglip; **the opportunity –ped through his fingers**, hy het die kans laat verbygaan; – **up**, 'n fout begaan.
slip, n. fout, vergissing, abuis; (kussing)sloop; onderlyfie; onderrok, voeringrok; voorskoot; (bad)broekie; skeepshelling; ketting (riem) vir honde; stukkie, strokie papier; spruit, steggie; (die) gly (glip); **it was a – of the tongue on his part**, dit was 'n vergissing van hom; hy het sy mond verby gepraat; hy het hom verspreek; **a – of the pen**, 'n skryffout; **he gave me the –**, hy het my ontglip; **there's many a – 'twixt the cup and the lip**, tussen die bord en die mond val die sop (pap) op die grond; **–s**, glippe (krieket).
slip-cover, oortreksel, stoelkleed.
slip-dock, skuins dok, hellende dok.
slip-knot, skuifknoop.
slipper, n. pantoffel, sloffie.
slippered, met pantoffels aan.
slippery, glipperig, glyerig, glad; onseker; listig, slu.
slipshod, sloffig.
slipslop, soppies; slordige werk, prulwerk; sentimentele gepraat (geskryf).
slip-stream, skroefwind.
slit, v. (aan repe) sny, skeur, splits, kloof.
slit, n. sny, skeur, slip; spleet.
slither, gly, glip.
sliver, n. splinter, spaander.
sliver, v. aan spaanders breek (sny).
slobber, v. kwyl, bekwyl, bemors; knoei.
slobber, n. kwyl; sentimentele gesanik.
slobbery, kwylerig, kwylend.
sloe-eyed, donkerogig.
slog, hard slaan, moker; – **away**, vooruitbeur, opdruk; daarop los moker.
slogan, strydkreet; wagwoord, leuse, slagsin, slagspreuk.
sloop, sloep.
slop(s), n. vuil water; sop, slap drank; pap kos.
slop, v. mors, stort.
slop-basin, spoelkom.
slope, n. helling, skuinste, afdraand.
slope, v. skuins (afdraand) loop, skuins hou; skuins maak.
sloping, skuins, opdraand, afdraand.
slop-pail, toiletemmer, vuilwateremmer.
sloppy, modderig, nat, morsig, slordig; week, oordrewe.
slot, n. gleuf, sleuf; valdeur.
slot, v. van 'n gleuf voorsien.
slot, n. spoor (van hert).

sloth, luiheid, traagheid; luiaard.
slothful, lui, traag.
slouch, v. slap (pap) bang; neerplak, onmanierlik sit; slof; (hoed) in die oë trek.
slouch, n. slofgang, geslof; (die) gebukkend loop; slofkous; knoeier.
slouch-hat, hangrand-, afrandhoed.
slough, n. (modder)poel, moeras.
slough, n. slangvel; roof, kors.
slough, v. vervel.
sloughy, modderig, moerasagtig.
Slovak, n. Slowaak.
Slovak, a. Slowakies.
Slovakia, Slowakye.
sloven, slons, morspot, vark, sloerie.
slovenly, slordig, liederlik, vuil, morsig.
slow, a. stadig, langsaam; lomerig, traag; vervelend; agter; – **but sure**, stadig maar seker; **be – to anger**, nie gou kwaad word nie; **twenty minutes –**, twintig minute agter; **not – to defend himself**, gou klaar om homself te verdedig; – **of wit**, dom, bot; **a – affair**, 'n vervelende boel; – **combustion stove**, smeulstofie; **in – motion**, in vertraagde tempo.
slow(ly), adv. stadig, suutjies.
slow, v. die vaart (snelheid) verminder, stadiger gaan (loop).
slowcoach, druiloor, draaikous, jandooi.
slow-match, lont.
slow-motion picture, vertraagde (rol)prent.
slubber, (be)mors; knoei.
sludge, modder, klei.
sludgy, modderig.
slug, n. slak; loper.
slug, v. slakke vang.
sluggard, luiaard, leegleêr.
sluggish, traag, lui, langsaam vloeiend.
sluice, n. sluis; sluiswater; watervoor.
sluice, v. van 'n sluis voorsien; laat uitloop (uitstroom); spoel; – **out**, uitstroom, uitspoel.
sluice-gate, sluisdeur.
sluice-way, watervoor.
sluit, sloot.
slum, v. die agterbuurte besoek.
slumber, v. sluimer, slaap.
slumber, n. sluimer, sluimering.
slumb(e)rous, sluimerend; slaapwekkend.
slump, n. slapte, slap tyd; daling.
slump, v. daal, skielik sak (van pryse).
slur, v. mommel, slordig (onduidelik) uitspreek (skrywe); beklad; sleep, trek, uitrek (van 'n noot); – **over**, net aanraak.
slur, n. klad, smet, skandvlek; verwyt, blaam; slordige uitspraak; slegte skrif; verbindingsteken; **it is no – upon his reputation**, dit is geen klad op sy naam nie.
slush, modder, slyk, nat, sneeu.
slushy, modderig, slykerig.
slut, slons, slordige vrou, sloerie.
sluttish, slordig, morsig, slonserig, vuil.
sly, skelm, listig, slu, geslepe, oorlams; **on the –** stilletjies, in die stilligheid.
slyboots, ka(r)nallie, skelm.
smack, n. klap, slag; klapsoen; **a – in the face**, 'n klap in die gesig.
smack, v. klap (gee), slaan; (met 'n sweep) klap; met die lippe klap.
smack, adv. reg, pardoems; – **into the water**, pardoem in die water; – **on the nose**, mooi reg op sy neus.
smack, n. smakie, geur; ietsie, tikkie; **a – of pepper**, 'n tikkie (knypie) peper.
smack: – **of**, smaak na.
smack, n. smak (bootjie).

smacker, klapsoen; harde slag; taai klap, pragstuk, 'n mooie.
small, a. klein, gering, weinig, min; niksbeduidend; kleingeestig, bekrompe; **he lives in a – way**, hy lewe maar eenvoudig; **he thinks no – beer of himself**, hy dink hy is watterhoed se kêrel; **– craft**, klein vaartuie (skuitjies); **– talk, klets-, kafpraatjies**; **– hours of the morning**, na middernag; **– beer**, dun bier; **– hand**, klein skrif; **– hail**, fyn hael.
small holder, kleinboer.
small holding, (klein) hoewe.
smallish, kleinerig.
small-minded, kleingeestig, bekrompe.
smallpox, kinderpokkies.
smalt, kobaltglas, smalt.
smart, v. pynig, seer maak, brand; smart veroorsaak, ly; **my finger –s**, my vinger brand (steek); **you shall – for this**, jy sal hiervoor boet.
smart, n. smart, pyn.
smart, a. skerp, vinnig; oulik, geslepe, slim, gevat, fluks, knap; agtermekaar, netjies, viets, piekfyn; modieus, deftig, swierig; **a – pace**, 'n vinnige pas; **a – retort**, 'n gevatte antwoord; **a – lad**, 'n knap (oulike) seun; **– dealing**, slim planne; **a – house**, 'n agtermekaar huis; **the – set**, die windmaker-klas.
smart-money, roukoop.
smash, v. (flenters, stukkend) breek, stukkend slaan, stukkend gooi, verbrysel, verpletter; totaal verslaan; moker (tennis); **– into**, vasloop teen; **a –ing blow**, 'n doodhou; **– -and-grab raid**, gryp-inbraak.
smash, n. vernieling; botsing, ongeluk, ramp; breekspul; bankrotskap; mokerhou (tennis); **go to –**, in duie val, 'n totale mislukking wees.
smash, adv. reg, vierkant.
smasher, doodhou; doodsê.
smashing, wonderlik, skitterend; verpletterend; buitengewoon; **– success**, reusesukses.
smash-up, vernieling; breekspul; botsing; totale mislukking, ineenstorting.
smattering, mondjievol; bietjie.
smear, v. smeer, bestryk; besmeer.
smear, n. vlek, vuil kol, veeg.
smell, n. ruik, geur; **take a – at it**, daaraan ruik; **– of brandy**, brandewynruik, brandewynlug.
smell, v. ruik; snuffel; **– a rat**, lont ruik; **– about**, rondsnuffel; **– out**, uitsnuffel, naspeur, opspoor.
smelling-bottle, ruikflessie.
smelling-salts, ruiksout, vlugsout.
smelly, stink(end), met 'n slegte ruik.
smelt, n. spiering (soort vis).
smelt, v. (metaal) smelt.
smew, (soort) wilde-eend, duikeend.
smile, n. glimlag.
smile, v. glimlag; **– at his behaviour**, lag oor sy gedrag; **– appreciation**, glimlaggend goedkeur; **– a sarcastic smile**, sarkasties glimlag; **– (up)on**, toelag.
smirch, v. besmeer; bevlek, beklad.
smirch, n. vlek, klad, smet; kol, veeg.
smirk, v. glimlag, onnatuurlik glimlag.
smirk, n. glimlag, gemaakte laggie.
smite, v. slaan; tref; verslaan, vernietig; kasty, straf; bots, slaan teen; **– his hands together**, sy hande saamslaan; **– hip and thigh**, ongenadiglik klop, 'n verpletterende neerlaag toedien; **his conscience smote him**, sy gewete het hom gekwel; **a city smitten with plague**, 'n stad deur 'n plaag geteister.
smite, n. slag, hou; poging.
smith, smid (smit).
smithereens, stukkies, flenters, gruis.
smithy, smidswinkel.
smock, n. oorbroek, voorskoot, jurk.
smock, v. smok.
smog, rookmis.
smoke, n. rook, damp; **end in –**, in rook en damp opgaan; **he wants a –**, hy wil rook; **no – without fire**, daar is nie 'n rokie nie of daar is 'n vuurtjie.
smoke, v. rook, damp; uitrook; **put that in your pipe and – it**, dit kan jy in jou sak steek.
smoked, gerook; **– glass**, berookte glas; rookglas; **– glasses**, sonbril; **– meat**, rookvleis.
smoke-dried, gerook.
smokeless, rookloos.
smoker, roker; rookkoepee; rookkonsert.
smoking, rook; rookbaadjie.
smoking, a. rokend, rook- . . .
smoking-carriage, rookkoepee.
smoking-concert, rookkonsert.
smoking-jacket, rookbaadjie.
smoking-room, rookkamer.
smoky, rokerig, rook- . . ., berook.
smooth, a. glad, sag, gelyk, soetvloeiend; beleef, vleierig; **a – passage**, 'n aangename (kalm) seereis; voorspoedige verloop; **say – things**, vlei, heuning om die mond smeer.
smooth(e), v. gelykmaak, glad maak, glad stryk; maklik maak; bedek, bewimpel; **– away difficulties**, moeilikhede uit die weg ruim; **– the way**, die pad skoonmaak, die weg baan; **– over the matter**, die saak bewimpel (in die beste voue lê).
smoothfaced, skyn-vriendelik.
smooth-tongued, vleiend, glad van tong.
smother, n. rook, stof.
smother, v. (ver)smoor, (ver)stik; onderdruk; geheim hou; **– a yawn**, 'n gaap onderdruk; **–ed curses**, binnensmondse vloeke; **– with gifts**, met geskenke oorlaai.
smothery, verstikkend, benoud.
smoulder, smeul.
smudge, smutch, v. (be)mors, (be)smeer; (be)vlek, (be)klad, besmet.
smudge, n. vuil kol, klad; vlek, smet.
smudge, n. smeulvuur; muskietrook.
smudgy, vuil, smerig, bemors.
smug, a. burgerlik, selfvoldaan.
smug, n. jansalie, selfvoldane persoon.
smuggle, smokkel; **– in**, binnesmokkel.
smuggler, smokkelaar.
smut, n. roetvlek, roet; vuil taal; brand (in koring).
smut, v. vlek, vuil maak; (laat) brand kry.
smutch, sien **smudge**.
smutty, vuil, morsig; vol roet.
snack, happie, ligte maaltyd; **go –s**, deel; **–s**, eetgoedjies; **– bar**, snoepkroeg; snelkafee.
snaffle, trens(toom).
snaffle, v. steel.
snag, stomp, knoes, punt; belemmering, moeilikheid; haakplek, struikelblok; (val)strik; **what is the –?**, waar sit die knoop?
snagged, snaggy, kwasterig, vol knoeste, vol stampplekke.
snail, slak; slakvormige rat, snekrat; **–'s pace**, slakkegang.
snail-wheel, slakratjie.
snake, slang; **there's a – in the grass**, daar is 'n slang in die gras, daar skuil gevaar; **cherish a – in one's bosom**, 'n adder aan jou bors koester.
snake-charmer, slang(e)besweerder.
snake-stone, slangsteen.
snaky, slangagtig, slang- . . .
snap, v. hap, snap, gryp; knal, klap; laat klap (knal); toeklap; knip; breek; afneem, kiek;

aftrek; toesnou; – **the fingers**, met die vingers klap (knip); – **the fingers at**, bespot, uitlag; – **at**, hap (byt) na; – **at an offer**, 'n aanbod gretig aanneem; – **off**, afbyt; afknap, afbreek; – **to**, toeklap; – **up**, opraap, gryp, opvang; – **into it**, toe maak gou; – **out of it**, word wakker, vergeet maar daarvan.
snap, n. klap, knal, slag; hap, byt; snap; portretjie, kiekie; pit, fut; veerkrag; **a cold** –, 'n skielike koue.
snapdragon, leeubekkie.
snappish, vinnig, bitsig, snipperig.
snappy, lewendig, opgewek, fluks.
snapshot, n. kiekie; blinde skoot.
snare, n. strik, wip, val; valstrik.
snare, v. in 'n strik vang, verstrik.
snarl, v. knor; grom, (toe)snou, afsnou.
snarl, n. knor, snou.
snarl, v. verwar, deurmekaar raak.
snarl, n. verwarring.
snarler, brompot, knorder.
snatch, v. gryp, vat, wegruk; – **off**, afruk; – **from death**, aan die dood ontruk; – **a kiss**, 'n soen steel; – **at an offer**, 'n aanbod aangryp.
snatch, n. gryp, greep, ruk; stukkie, brokkie; **make a** – **at it**, daarna gryp; **by –es**, by rukke (tussenpose); **a** – **of song**, 'n liedjie, 'n stukkie (van 'n lied).
sneak, v. sluip, kruip, stilletjies gaan; skaai, steel; verklik, verklap; – **away, off, out**, stilletjies wegloop (wegsluip).
sneak, n. sluiper, gluiper, valsaard; verklikker, nuusdraer.
sneak-thief, insluipdief, goudief.
sneer, v. (be)spot, uitlag, spottend lag, die neus optrek.
sneer, n. grens(lag), spot(lag), hoonlag.
sneering, spottend, spot- . . ., honend.
sneeze, v. nies; **not to be –d at**, nie te verag nie, glad nie so danig sleg nie.
sneeze, n. nies.
sneeze-wood, nieshout.
snick, 'n kerfie sny; sny.
snicker, saggies runnik.
sniff, v. snuiwe; snuffel; – **at**, ruik (snuffel) aan; die neus optrek vir.
sniff, n. gesnuiwe, gesnuffel; snuffie.
sniffy, veragtend, smalend.
snigger, v. giggel, grinnik.
snigger, n. gegiggel, gegrinnik.
snip, v. (af)sny, (af)knip.
snip, n. sny, knip; snipper; knipsel; **it's a** –, dis doodseker.
snipe, n. (poel)snip.
snipe, v. snippe skiet; skiet; steelskiet.
sniper, skerpskutter, sluipskutter.
snippet, snipper, stukkie.
snivel, v. snotter; grens, huil, tjank.
snivel, n. snot; gegrens; huigelary.
snob, snob, inkruiper, ploert.
snobbery, snobisme.
snobbish, snobagtig, ploerterig.
snood, haarlint.
snook, snoek.
snook: **cut, make a** –, uitkoggel; **–s**, vrek!
snoop, snuffel, afloer; neus insteek.
snooper, (rond)snuffelaar, spioen, bemoeial.
snooty, verwaand.
snooze, v. 'n uiltjie knap; dut; leeglê; – **the time away**, die tyd verdroom.
snooze, n. dutjie, slapie.
snore, v. snork; – **awake**, wakker snork.
snore, n. snork, gesnork.
snort, v. snork, proes, snuif.
snort, n. snork, proes.

snorter, snorker; stormwind; doodhou.
snot, snot; snotneus.
snotty, a. snotterig; gemeen; boos, kortgebonde; minagtend.
snotty, n. snotneus.
snout, snoet, snuit, neus.
snouted, met 'n snuit, snuit- . . ., gebek.
snow, n. sneeu, kapok; **–s**, sneeuvelde.
snow, v. sneeu, kapok; **soos neeu val**; **–ed in**, toegesneeu; **–ed up**, toegesneeu, vasgesneeu.
snowball, sneeubal; **he has not got a** – **'s hope**, sy twak is nat.
snow-blind, sneeublind.
snow-blink, sneeu-, ysblink, sneeuglans.
snow-boots, oorstewels, sneeustewels.
snow-bound, vasgesneeu.
snow-capped, met sneeu bedek, besneeu.
snow-drift, sneeuval, sneeuhoop.
snow-drop, sneeuklokkie.
snow-flake, sneeuvlokkie.
snow-grouse, sneeuhoender.
snow-line, sneeugrens.
snow-plough, sneeuploeg.
snow-shoe, sneeuskoen.
snow-slip, sneeustorting.
snow-storm, sneeustorm.
snow-white, sneeuwit, spierwit.
snowy, sneeuagtig, sneeu- . . ., spierwit.
snub, v. afsnou, afjak.
snub, n. afjak, berisping, snou.
snub, a. stomp.
snub, n. stompneus.
snub-nosed, stompneusig, stompneus.
snuff, v. snuit; – **a candle**, 'n kers snuit; – **out**, bokveld toe gaan; **I was nearly –ed out**, dit was byna klaarpraat met my.
snuff, n. snuitsel.
snuff, v. snuiwe; snuffel, ruik aan.
snuff, n. snuif; snuf.
snuff-box, snuifdoos.
snuffers, snuiter.
snuffle, v. snuiwe; deur die neus praat.
snuffle, n. gesnuiwe.
snuffy, snuif- . . ., snuifagtig.
snug, lekker, warm; beskut, toe; aangenaam, gesellig.
snuggery, private kamertjie, hok(kie).
snuggle, inkruip, nader kruip; vasdruk teen; **the mother –d her child close to her**, die moeder het haar kind teen haar vasgedruk; – **up to the fire**, nader by die vuur kruip.
so, so, sodanig; dus; **you are talking** – **much rubbish**, jy praat pure kaf; **I told you** –, ek het jou dit gesê; **quite** –, presies, juistement; **send me half–a–dozen or** –, stuur vir my so 'n stuk of ses; – **forth and** – **on**, ensovoorts; – **and** –, die en die, dinges; **ever** – **much better**, oneindig beter; **you don't say** –, ag nee? regtig? waarlik?; **not** – **much as thanked me**, my nie eens bedank nie? – **you took it?** jy het dit dus geneem?; **how** –? **hoe dan? hoe so?**; – **much for that**, hiermee het ons nou klaar; – **far**, tot dusver; – **long as**, as . . . maar; – **long!**, tot siens!
soak, v. week, deurweek; drink, suip; – **in**, insuig, intrek, deurdring.
soak, n. (die) week; drinkparty.
soaker, suiplap, dronklap; stortbui.
soaking, deurdringend, deurwekend; – **wet**, papnat, deurnat.
soap, n. seep.
soap, v. inseep, seep smeer.
soap-bubble, seepblaas, seepbel.
soap-suds, seepsop.
soap-works, seepfabriek.

soapy, seep- . . ., seepagtig, seperig.
soar, swewe, hoog vlie(g), opstyg, seil.
sob, v. snik; – out, uitsnik.
sob, n. snik.
sober, a. nugter; matig; verstandig, gematig, bedaard, kalm; as – as a judge, volkome nugter (kalm); he is a – man, hy drink nie.
sober, v. bedaar, kalm (besadig) word; tot bedaring bring; ontnuger.
sober-minded, bedaard, kalm, besadig.
sober-sides, stil Jan, stilomdraai.
sobriety, soberheid, nugterheid.
sobriquet, bynaam.
so-called, sogenaamd.
soccer, sokker.
sociability, geselligheid.
sociable, a. gesellig, aangenaam.
social, a. gesellig; maatskaplik, sosiaal; – science, sosiale wetenskap; his – position, sy stand in die samelewing; – intercourse, gesellige verkeer; – evils, maatskaplike euwels.
social, n. gesellige byeenkoms.
socialism, sosialisme.
socialist, n. sosialis.
socialist(ic), a. sosialisties.
socialite, uitgaande persoon.
society, samelewing, maatskappy, gemeenskap; vereniging, genootskap; geselskap; die deftige kringe, die elite, die hoë lui, die groot wêreld.
society people, die deftige lui (mense).
sociologist, sosioloog.
sociology, sosiologie.
sock, n. sokkie; binnesool; toneelskoen; pull up your –s, word wakker, roer jou riete; jy moet verbeter.
socket, holte; kas (van 'n oog); potjie; pyp; mof, kousie (aan 'n waterpyp).
socket-joint, koeëlgewrig.
socle, sokkel, voetstuk, suilvoet.
Socratic, Sokraties.
sod, n. sooi; under the –, onder die grond (kluite), in die graf.
sod, v. met sooie belê, besooi.
soda, soda; caustic –, seepsoda; bicarbonate of –, koeksoda.
soda-fountain, sodapomp, bruisbron.
sodality, broederskap, genootskap.
soda-water, spuitwater, sodawater.
sodden, a. deurweek, deurtrek, deurnat, papnat; klam, kleierig (van brood); voos, sakkerig (van 'n dronkaard).
sodden, v. deurweek, papnat word.
sodium, sodium, natrium.
sodomy, sodomie.
sofa, sofa, rusbank.
soft, a. sag (saf), pap, week; soetsappig; goedhartig, teer, simpatiek; onnosel; – goods, weefstowwe; a – heart, 'n teer hart; – nothings, verliefde praatjies; a – job, maklike (lekker) baantjie.
soft, n. sukkelaar, stumper, goeierd.
soften, sag (week) maak; sag (week) word; versag; temper.
softening, n. versagting, verweking.
softening, a. versagtend, versagtings- . . .
soft-hearted, teerhartig.
soft-sawder, vleiery, mooipraatjies.
soft-soap, n. groen seep; vleiery.
soft-soap, v. vlei.
soft-spoken, sag, vriendelik.
softy, sukkelaar, stumper, papbroek.
soggy, papnat, deurweek.
soil, n. grond, bodem; –s, grondsoorte.
soil, v. vlek, vuil maak; besmet.
soil, n. vlek, smet.

soil, v. (vee) met groenvoer voer.
soiree, soiree, aandparty.
sojourn, v. vertoef, verbly.
sojourn, n. verblyf.
sojourner, reisiger, besoeker, gas.
solace, n. troos, vertroosting.
solace, v. (ver)troos, opbeur.
solar, son(s)- . . ., van die son; – eclipse, sonsverduistering; – system, sonstelsel; – year, sonjaar; – energy, son(ne)krag; – heater, sonwarmer.
solarium, sonbadkamer.
solder, n. soldeersel.
solder, v. soldeer.
soldering-iron, soldeeryster.
soldier, n. soldaat, krygsman.
soldier, v. as soldaat dien, krygsdiens verrig; tired of –ing, moeg van krygsdiens.
soldierly, soldaat- . . ., krygsmans- . . .
soldiery, krygsvolk, soldate.
sole, n. sool; voetsool.
sole, v. versool.
sole, n. tong(vis).
sole, a. enigste, enkel.
solecism, vergryp; taalfout.
solemn, plegtig, indrukwekkend, ernstig; deftig, statig.
solemnize, vier; voltrek.
solemnity, plegtigheid; statigheid.
solfa, sien tonic-solfa.
solicit, versoek, vra, smeek, aansoek doen (om); lastig val, aanspreek (op straat).
solicitant, aansoeker, sollisitant; vraer.
solicitation, versoek, aansoek.
solicitor, prokureur.
solicitor-general, prokureur-generaal.
solicitous, begerig, verlangend; bekommerd, begaan, besorg.
solicitude, besorgdheid, bekommerdheid.
solid, a. vas, solied, sterk, stewig, massief; onverdeeld, eenparig; gegrond, deeglik, eg; kubiek; – food, vaste kos; be – for, eenparig ten gunste wees van; – tyres, soliede bande; three – hours, drie volle ure; – angle, liggaamshoek; – measure, kubieke maat.
solid, n. vaste liggaam.
solidarity, solidariteit, eenheid.
solidification, vaswording, verdigting.
solidify, verdig, vas (styf) maak (word).
solidity, vastheid, stewigheid; grondigheid, deeglikheid, egtheid; soliditeit.
soliloquize, 'n alleenspraak hou; met jouself praat, alleen praat.
soliloquy, alleenspraak.
solitaire, solitêrspel; solitêrsteen.
solitary, eensaam, verlate, afgesonder, alleenstaande; enkel; – confinement, afsonderlike opsluiting.
solitude, eensaamheid.
solo, solo; – flight, solovlug.
soloist, solosanger, solospeler, solis.
Solomon, Salomo.
so-long, tot siens, tot straks.
solstice, sonstilstand.
solstitial, van die sonstilstand.
solubility, oplosbaarheid.
solube, oplosbaar.
solution, oplossing, ontbinding; tire –, rubbergom, bandlym.
solvability, oplosbaarheid.
solvable, oplosbaar.
solve, oplos, verklaar, uitlê, ophelder.
solvency, betaalvermoë, solventskap.
solvent, a. oplossend, oplossings- . . .; in staat om te betaal, solvent.

solvent, n. oplosmiddel.
somatic, liggaamlik.
sombre, somber, donker, duister.
sombrero, sombrero, breërand-hoed.
some, a. sommige, party, enige; een of ander, sowat, ongeveer, omtrent; bietjie; – **book** (or other), een of ander boek; – **experienced person**, een of ander persoon wat ondervindinge het; **drink – water and eat – bread**, drink bietjie water en eet 'n stukkie brood; **bring – pens**, bring 'n stuk of wat penne; – **years ago**, enige jare gelede, 'n jaar of wat gelede; – **twenty minutes**, sowat twintig minute; **we had to wait – time**, ons moes 'n tydjie wag; **we must do it – time**, ons moet dit op een of ander tyd doen; **that was – joke**, dit was vir jou 'n grap.
some, pron. sommige, party; iets; bietjie.
somebody, iemand, een of ander.
somehow, op een of ander manier.
someone, sien **somebody**.
somersault, n. bolmakiesie(slag), bolmakiesieslaan; **turn a –**, bolmakiesie slaan.
somersault, v. bolmakiesie slaan.
something, iets, wat; **he is – in the civil service**, hy het een of ander betrekking in die staatsdiens; – **of a carpenter**, so 'n halwe timmerman; **a bishop or –**, 'n biskop of so iets; – **like seventy-five**, so ongeveer vyf-en-sewentig; **a drop of –**, 'n snapsie; – **awful**, iets verskrikliks.
sometime, voormalig, vorig, vroeër.
sometimes, somtyds, soms, partymaal.
someway, op een of ander manier.
somewhat, enigsins, 'n bietjie.
somewhere, êrens, iewers.
somnambulism, slaapwandeling.
somnambulist, slaapwandelaar.
somniferous, slaapwekkend.
somniloquism, **somniloquence**, slaappratery.
somniloquist, slaapprater.
somnolence, **somnolency**, slaperigheid.
somnolent, vaak, slaperig.
somnolism, hipnose.
son, seun (soon); **S. of God**, Seun van God; – **of Mars**, krygsman; – **of a sea-cow**, hierjy, uilskuiken; **–s of liberty**, kinders van die vryheid.
sonant, a. stemhebbend, sonanties.
sonant, n. stemhebbende klank, sonans.
sonata, sonate.
song, lied, sang, sangstuk; poësie; kleinigheid; **sell for an old –**, vir 'n appel en 'n ei verkoop; **S– of Solomon**, Hooglied van Salomo; **folk –s**, volksliedjies; **make a – about something**, 'n ophef maak van iets.
song-bird, sangvoël.
songster, sanger, sangvoël.
sonic, sonies; – **barrier**, klankgrens.
soniferous, klinkend, welluidend.
son-in-law, skoonseun.
sonnet, sonnet, klinkdig.
sonneteer, sonnetskrywer, sonnetdigter.
sonny, ou seun, jongie, boetie.
sonometer, klankmeter, sonometer.
sonorific, klinkend, klankgewend.
sonority, welluidendheid, klankrykheid.
sonorous, welluidend, klankryk, sonoor.
soon, gou, spoedig, weldra, binnekort; – **after four**, kort na vier; **I would –er die than**, ek sou liewer sterwe as; **we had no –er sat down than**, ons het nouliks gaan sit of; **no –er said than done**, so gesê, so gedaan; **the –er the better**, hoe eerder hoe beter; **–er or later**, vroeg of laat, eendag.
soot, roet.

sooth, waarheid, werklikheid; **in (good) –**, voorwaar, waarlik.
soothe, kalmeer, versag, stil; paai, sus.
soothsayer, waarsêer.
sooty, roetagtig, vol roet, vuil, roet- . . .
sop, n. sop, geweekte brood; troosmiddel, paaimiddel; omkoopmiddel.
sop, v. week, doop; papnat maak, sop; **–ping wet**, papnat.
sophism, sofisme, drogrede.
sophist, sofis, drogredenaar.
sophistic(al), sofisties, bedrieglik.
sophisticate, vervals; mislei, bedrieg; oulik maak; veroulik.
sophisticated, oulik, ouderwets, gekunsteld.
sophistication, vervalsing; sofisme.
sophistry, drogredenering, sofistery.
soporiferous, slaapwekkend.
soporific, a. slaapwekkend, slaap-.
soporific, n. slaapmiddel.
soppy, nat, sopperig.
soprano, sopraan.
sorbet, vrugtedrank, sorbet.
sorcerer, towenaar.
sorceress, towenares.
sorcery, toordery (towery).
sordid, laag, gemeen, vuil; vrekkig.
sore, a. seer, pynlik; gevoelig; swaar, hewig; **touch him on a – place**, hom op 'n teer plek aanraak.
sore, n. seer, wond; **reopen old –s**, ou wonde oopmaak, ou koeie uit die sloot grawe.
sororicide, sustermoord; sustermoordenaar.
sorrel, n. suring.
sorrel, a. rooibruin; vos.
sorrel, n. rooibruin; vosperd.
sorrow, n. smart; droefheid, verdriet.
sorrow, v. treur; – **at**, **over**, treur (hartseer wees) oor.
sorrowful, treurig, verdrietig, droewig.
sorry, jammer, spyt; ellendig, treurig, armsalig; **I am – to hear it**, dit spyt my om dit te hoor; **–!**, **ekskuus! jammer!**; **a – fellow**, 'n treurige vent; **a – excuse**, 'n flou ekskuus; **a – plight**, 'n betreurenswaardige toestand.
sort, n. soort, klas; **nothing of the –**, niks van die aard nie; **moenie glo nie**; **I – of expected it**, ek het dit so half-en-half verwag; **an awfully good –**, 'n baie gawe kêrel; **after a –**, op 'n manier; **feel out of –s**, siekerig (uit jou humeur) voel.
sort, v. sorteer, uitsoek.
sorter, sorteerder.
sortie, uitval; krygsvlug.
so-so, so-so, so op 'n manier.
sot, dronklap, suiplap.
sottish, besope.
Soudan, Soedan.
Soudanese, Soedannees.
SOS, noodsein, noodroep.
sough, n. gesuis, sug.
sough, v. suis, sug.
soul, siel; wese, skepsel; **not a –**, nie 'n lewende wese nie; **upon my –**, by my siel, by my kool.
soulful, (siel)verheffend, hartroerend.
soul-stirring, sielroerend.
sound, a. gesond, sterk, gaaf, goed; gegrond, deeglik; vas, solied; gedug; **a – flogging**, 'n gedugte pak slae; **a – sleep**, 'n vaste slaap.
sound, adv.: **– asleep**, vas aan die slaap.
sound, n. klank, geluid, toon; **– barrier**, klankgrens.
sound, v. klink, lui; laat klink; laat hoor, uitbasuin, verkondig; toets, ondersoek, beklop; **– a note of warning**, 'n waarskuwende stem laat

hoor; – the retreat, die aftog blaas; – his praises, sy lof uitbasuin.
sound, v. (die diepte) peil; sondeer; ondersoek; uithoor, pols.
sound, n. sondeerstif, peilstif.
sound, n. see-engte.
sound-board, klankbord.
sounder, ontvangtoestel; peiler.
sounding, a. klinkend, klank . . .
sounding, a. peilend, peil- . . .
sounding, n. peil(ing); take –s, peil.
sounding-board, sien sound-board.
sounding-lead, dieplood.
sounding-line, skietlood, loodlyn.
soundly, terdeë, flink, vas; gaaf, goed.
sound-proof, geluid-vry.
soup, sop (soep); in the –, in die verknorsing, in die knyp, in die sop.
soup-kitchen, so(e)pinrigting.
soup-ladle, so(e)plepel.
soup-plate, diepbord, so(e)pbord.
sour, a. suur; nors, stuurs.
sour, v. suur maak (word); verbitter.
source, oorsprong, bron.
sour-dock, suring.
sourish, suuragtig, suurderig.
souse, n. pekelsous, pekelkos; onderdompeling.
souse, v. (in)pekel; indompel; oorgooi; –d, besope.
south, adv. suidwaarts.
south, a. suidelik, suid(e)- . . .; S– Sea, Suidsee, Stille Oseaan.
south, n. suide.
south-east, suidoos.
southeaster, suidoostewind, Kaapse dokter.
south-easterly, suidoostelik.
southerly, suidelik.
southern, a. suidelik; S– Cross, Suiderkruis.
southernmost, suidelikste.
southpaw, linksspeler; linksbokser; linkshandige.
South Pole, Suidpool.
southward, suidwaarts.
south-west, n. suidweste.
south-west, adv. rigting, suidwes.
southwester, suidwes(tewind).
south-westerly, suidwestelik.
souvenir, aandenking, soewenier, gedagtenis.
sovereign, a. soewerein, oppermagtig, opper- . . .; voortreflik, uitstekend.
sovereign, n. vors. heerser; pond.
sovereignty, soewereiniteit, oppermag.
sow, v. saai, strooi; versprei.
sow, n. sog; you have the wrong – by the ear, jy het dit by die verkeerde ent beet.
sower, saaier; saaimasjien.
sow-thistle, suidissel (seidissel).
soy(a), soja; – -bean, sojaboon(tjie).
sozzled, besope.
space, n. ruimte, plek, spasie, afstand; duur tyd(jie), in the – of an hour, binne 'n uur se tyd; after a short –, na 'n rukkie; – -craft, ruimtevaartuig; – -ship, ruimteskip; – -man, ruimteman, ruimtevaarder; – travel, ruimtevaart; – traveller, ruimtereisiger.
space, v. spasieer.
spacing, spasiëring.
spacious, ruim, groot; uitgetrek.
spade, graaf, skop(graaf); skoppe(n); call a – a –, die kind by sy naam noem, nie doekies omdraai nie; ace of –s, skoppenaas.
spadeful, graafvol.
spade-work, graafwerk; aanvoor-werk.
Spain, Spanje.
spall, n. stukkie, splinter, spaander.
spall, v. fynmaak, vergruis.

span, v. span, afspan, afmeet; oorbrug.
span, n. span; spanning (van 'n brug, ens.) kort tyd (duur); our life is but a –, ons lewe is kort van duur.
spangle, n. goud-, silwerversierseltjie.
spangle, v. versier; skitter.
Spaniard, Spanjaard; Spaanse vrou.
spaniel, patryshond; vleier, kruiper.
Spanish, a. Spaans; – fly, spaansvlieg.
Spanish, n. Spaans.
spank, v. pak gee, looi, ransel.
spank, n. klap, plak.
spanker, knewel, 'n kolossale, reus.
spanking, n. pak (slae), loesing.
spanking, a. gaaf, eersteklas; sterk, groot.
spanless, onmeetlik.
spanner, skroefhamer, (skroef)sleutel, moerhamer; throw a – into the works, 'n stok in die wiel steek.
span-roof, spitsdak.
spar, n. spar, paal; spriet, mas.
spar, n. spaat (soort mineraal).
spar, v. skerm; redetwis; –ring partner, skermmaat.
spar, n. (die) skerm; vuisgeveg.
spare, a. skraal, maer; vry; orig; a man of – frame, 'n skraal geboude man; – time, vry(e) tyd; – room, vrykamer; a – wheel, 'n orige wiel, ekstra wiel, reserwewiel; – parts, onderdele, orige dele, reserwedele.
spare, v. spaar, bespaar; klaarkom sonder, mis; ontsien; I cannot – him just now, ek kan nie nou sonder hom klaarkom nie; can you – me a rand? het jy 'n rand vir my? enough and to –, meer as genoeg; a few envelopes to –, 'n paar orige koeverte; he did not – my feelings, hy het my gevoelens nie ontsien nie.
spare wheel, reserwewiel, orige wiel, noodwiel.
sparing, spaarsaam, suinig, karig.
spark, n. vonk; sprankie, greintjie.
spark, v. vonke afgee, vonk.
spark, swierbol, windmakerige kêrel.
spark-control, vonkreëling, vonkreëlaar.
sparking, ontsteking.
sparking-plug, ontstekingsprop, vonkprop.
sparkle, v. vonkel, skitter, flikker, vonke skiet; skuim, bruis (van drank).
sparkle, n. glans, flikkering, flonkering, geskitter, gevonkel; vonk.
sparklet, koolsuurdoppie, koeëltjie; vonkie, sprankie, greintjie.
sparring, skerm; – partner, skermvennoot, -maat.
sparrow, mossie.
sparrow-hawk, sperwel, (wit)valk.
sparry, spaat- . . ., spaatagtig.
sparse, dun, skaars, versprei, yl.
Spartan, a. Spaartans.
Spartan, n. Spartaan.
spasm, kramp, trekking.
spasmodic, krampagtig; van kort duur, met rukke en stote.
spastic, n. spastikus.
spastic, a. spasties.
spat, n. saad (van oesters).
spat, v. saadskiet.
spat, n. slobkous.
spatchcock, n. spithoender.
spatchcock, v. aanvul, inlas.
spate, vloed, oorstroming.
spatial, ruimte- . . .
spatter, spat, bespat, bemors.
spatula, spatel, tempermes; strykmes.
spatulate, spatelvormig.
spawn, n. eiertjies, kuit; gebroed(sel).

spawn, v. eiers lê, uitbroei.
speak, praat, spreek; sê; **this photograph –s,** hierdie portret is sprekend; **– your mind,** sê ronduit wat jy dink; **roughly –ing,** so min of meer; **legally –ing,** van 'n geregtelike standpunt beskou; **so to –,** (om)so te sê; **–s volumes,** spreek boekdele; **nothing to – of,** niks om van te praat nie; **– out,** harder praat; jou gevoelens lug, reguit sê wat jy dink; **– to,** praat met; **– up,** harder praat.
speaker, spreker; **S–,** Spreker (Volksraad).
speaking, a. sprekend, pratend; **we are not on – terms,** ons praat nie met mekaar nie.
speaking, n. (die) praat.
speaking-tube, praatbuis.
spear, n. spies, lans, speer.
spear, v. (met 'n spies) steek.
spearhead, speerpunt; spits, wig (fig.).
spearman, lansier, speerdraer.
spec, sien **speculation.**
special, a. spesiaal, besonder.
special, n. ekstratrein; ekstrablad, spesiale uitgawe; spesiale pas.
specialize, spesialiseer; **– in,** jou toelê op, spesialiseer in.
specialist, spesialis, spesialiteit.
speciality, specialty, spesialiteit; besonderheid.
specie, spesie, klinkende munt.
species, soort; geslag; spesie(s).
specific, spesifiek, bepaald, soortlik; **the – name of a plant,** die soortnaam van 'n plant; **– gravity,** soortlike gewig.
specification, spesifikasie, (noukeurige) opgawe; **–s,** bestek.
specify, spesifiseer, in besonderhede noem.
specimen, monster, proef, spesimen; staaltjie, voorbeeld; eksemplaar; **– page,** proefblad; **what a –,** wat 'n spektakel.
specious, bevallig; skoonklinkend.
speck, n. stippel, spikkel, kolletjie; stukkie, deeltjie; vlekkie.
speck, v. (be)spikkel.
speckle, n. spikkel, vlekke.
speckle, v. (be)spikkel; **–d,** bespikkel(d).
spectacle, skouspel, toneel, vertoning, spektakel; **a pair of –s,** 'n bril.
spectacled, met 'n bril, gebril; bril– . . . .
spectacular, pragtig, skitterend; aanskoulik; toneelmatig; **a – play,** 'n kykstuk; **– football,** aanskoulike voetbal.
spectator, toeskouer, aanskouer.
spectral, spookagtig, spook– . . .; van die spektrum, spektraal– . . .
spectre, spook, gees.
spectroscope, spektroskoop.
spectrum, spektrum.
specular, spieël– . . ., soos 'n spieël.
speculate, bepeins, bereken, uitreken, bespieëlinge maak; spekuleer.
speculation, oorpeinsing, berekening, bespieëlinge, beskouing; spekulasie.
speculative, spekulatief; bespieëlend.
speculator, spekulant.
speculum, spieël; tregter.
speech, spraak, taal; aanspraak, toespraak, redevoering; **parts of –,** rededele; **– from the throne,** troonrede; **after-dinner –,** tafeltoespraak.
speechify, 'n toespraak afsteek.
speechless, spraakloos, stom.
speed, n. snelheid, vaart; spoed, haas; **more haste less –,** hoe meer haas hoe minder spoed; **at full –,** in volle vaart; **good –,** alle heil, alle voorspoed; **a wobble,** vaartrukking(s).
speed, v. snel, spoed, jaag; gou maak, bevorder,

die snelheid reguleer; **– up,** verhaas, bespoedig; gou maak.
speed-boat, snelboot.
speed-cop, verkeerskonstabel.
speed-limit, maksimum-snelheid, snelheidsbeperking.
speedometer, mylmeter, snelheidsmeter.
speed-trial, snelheidstoets.
speedway, jaagbaan, snelweg.
speedy, spoedig; vinnig; haastig.
spell, n. towerspreuk, towerformule; betowering, aantrekkingskrag.
spell, v. spel; beteken.
spell, n. poos, tyd(jie), ruk(kie); beurt.
spel, v. aflos.
spellbound, betower, in verrukking.
speller, speller; spelboek.
spelling, spelling.
spelling-bee, spelwydstryd.
spelt, spelt (soort koring).
spend, uitgee; bestee; spandeer, verkwis, verteer; deurbring; **our ammunition was all spent,** al ons ammunisie was op; **candles – fast in a draught,** in die trek brand kerse gou uit; **how do you – your time,** hoe bring jy jou tyd deur?; **the storm is spent,** die storm is uitgewoed; **his anger will soon – itself,** sy kwaai bui sal gou oor wees.
spendthrift, n. deurbringer, verkwister.
spendthrift, a. verkwisterig.
spent, uitgeput, klaarpraat; **– cannonball,** flou kanonkoeël; sien **spend.**
sperm, saad, sperma.
sperm(-whale), potvis.
spermaceti, spermaceti.
spermatic, saad– . . .
spew, opbring, uitspu(ug).
sphenoid, wigvormig.
sphere, bol, bal, globe; hemelliggaam; sfeer, (werk)kring, omgewing, gebied, omvang; **within his peculiar –,** binne sy besondere kring; **a wider – of work,** 'n uitgebreider arbeidsveld.
spheric, hemels, verhewe.
spherical, bolvormig, sferies, bol– . . .; **– trigonometry,** boldriehoeksmeting; **– triangle,** boldriehoek.
spheroid, sferoïde.
spheroidal, sferoïdaal.
sphinx, sfinks.
spice, n. spesery, kruie; smakie.
spice, v. krui(e), smaak gee aan.
spicery, spesery(e).
spick and span, piekfyn, agtermekaar.
spicy, speseryagtig, spesery– . . .; gekrui; geurig, smaaklik; pikant, skerp; netjies, piekfyn; onbetaamlik.
spider, spinnekop; spaaider (soort rytuig).
spiderlike, spinnekopagtig, spinnekop– . . .
spider-monkey, slingeraap.
spider-web, spinnerak.
spidery, spinnekopagtig.
spigot, prop, spons, swik.
spike, n. skerp punt, lang spyker; aar.
spike, v. vasspyker, vaspen.
spikelet, aartjie.
spikenard, nardus.
spiky, skerp, puntig, spits.
spile, pen, prop; paal.
spilling, paalwerk.
spill, v. stort, mors, uitgooi; afgooi; **it is no use crying over spilt milk,** gedane sake het geen keer nie, wat verby is, is verby; **– the beans,** die aap uit die mou laat.
spil, n. val.
spillway, uitloop(voor).

spin, v. spin; laat draai, in die rondte draai, tol (in die rondte); tol(vlieg) vertel; – **a yarn**, 'n storie vertel; **the blow sent him –ing**, die slag het hom soos 'n tol in die rondte laat draai; – **a top**, 'n tol gooi.
spin, n. draai; ritjie, toertjie; **go for a –**, ('n entjie) gaan ry.
spinach, spinage, spinasie.
spinal, van die ruggraat, ruggraat- . . .; – **column**, ruggraat.
spindle, n. spoel; spil, as.
spindle-shanked, met speekbene.
spindle-shanks, speekbene.
spindrift, waaiskuim.
spine, ruggraat, rugstring; doring.
spinel, spinel.
spineless, sonder ruggraat; pap, slap, papbroekig; doringloos.
spinet, spinet.
spiniferous, doringrig, doring- . . .
spinner, spinner; spinmasjien.
spinneret, spinorgaan, spinnertjie.
spinning-jenny, spinmasjien.
spinning-wheel, spinwiel.
spinosity, doringrigheid.
spinster, oujongnôi (oujongnooi).
spiny, doringrig, vol dorings; lastig.
spiracle, luggat, lugopening.
spiral, a. spiraalvormig, skroefvormig; – **spring**, spiraalveer; – **staircase**, wenteltrap.
spiral, n. spiraal.
spiral, v. draai, kronkel, krul; in 'n spiraal styg.
spirant, glyer, spirant, frikatief.
spire, toringspits, top, spits punt.
spire, n. spiraal, kronkeling.
spirit, n. gees; moed, lewenskrag, energie, geesdrif; siel, inspirasie; aard; –**s**, sterk drank, spiritualieë; stemming; **in high –s**, opgetoë (neerslagtig); – **of wine**, alkohol, wynspiritus; **in the –**, in die gees; **the Holy S–**, die Heilige Gees; **he infused – into his men**, hy het sy manskappe moed gegee (geïnspireer); **the animating – of the rebellion**, die siel van die rebellie; – **of the times**, die tydgees; **he took it in the wrong –**, hy het dit verkeerd opgeneem.
spirit, v. aanvuur, opbeur; – **away**, **off**, wegvoer, laat verdwyn; – **up**, aanmoedig, besiel, moed inpraat.
spirited, vurig, opgewek, lewendig.
spirit-lamp, spirituslamp.
spiritless, sonder gees, slap, bot.
spirit-level, waterpas.
spirit-rapper, geesteklopper.
spirit-rapping, geestekloppery.
spirit-stove, spiritusstofie.
spiritual, geestelik, onstoflik, geestes- . . .; – **interests**, geestelike belange; n. Negergesang.
spiritualize, vergeestelik, verhef; besiel.
spiritualism, spiritisme; spiritualisme.
spiritualist, spiritis, spiritualis.
spirituality, geestelikheid, onstoflikheid.
spirituous, sterk, alkoholies.
spirt, **spurt**, v. spuit, spat, uitbars.
spirt, **spurt**, n. uitspuiting, straal.
spiry, spiraalvormig; spits, puntig.
spit, n. braaispit; landtong.
spit, v. aan 'n spit steek; deursteek.
spit, v. spu, spoeg (spuug); blaas; – **out**, uitspu; – **it out**, sê dit reguit; – **upon**, spu op.
spit, n. spu (spuug), spoeg.
spit-curl, spuugkrul, -lok.
spite, n. wrok, kwaadaardigheid, nyd; **have a – against somebody**, 'n wrok teen iemand koester; **he did it from pure –**, hy het dit uit pure wrok (kwaadaardigheid) gedoen; **in – of**, in weerwil van, ten spyte van.
spite, v. dwarsboom; vererg, kwaad maak, vermaak; **cut off one's nose to – one's face**, uit kwaadaardigheid (wraaksugtigheid) jou eie nadeel bewerk.
spiteful, haatlik, nydig, boosaardig.
spitfire, drifkop, heethoof, rissie.
spittle, spu(ug), spoeg.
spittoon, spu(ug)bakkie, kwispedoor.
splash, v. plas, spat; bespat, natspat; in groot letters druk, inksmeer.
splash, n. geplas, gespat, plons; spatsel, plekkie; vertoning; **make a –**, opsien baar; **make a – of**, in groot letters druk, inksmeer.
splash-board, modderskerm, spatbord.
splasher, plasser; modderskerm.
splashy, modderig, spatterig, bespat.
splatter, plas, spat.
splatter-dash, geraas, lawaai, rumoer.
splay, v. skuins maak.
splay, n. skuinste.
splay, a. plat; na buite gekeer.
splay-foot, plat uitstaande voet.
splay-footed, met plat, uitstaande voete.
splay-mouth, skewe mond.
spleen, milt; swaarmoedigheid; neerslagtigheid; miltsug; slegte luim, humeurigheid; **a fit of –**, 'n slegte (kwaai) bui; **vent one's –**, aan jou ergernis lug gee.
spleenful, **spleenish**, **spleeny**, swaarmoedig, neerslagtig; brommerig, gemelik.
spleenwort, miltkruid.
splendent, glinsterend, blink, skitterend.
splendid, pragtig, skitterend, kostelik, groots, luisterryk; uitstekend.
splendour, prag, luister, praal, luisterrykheid, grootsheid, glans.
splenetic, a. sleggehumeurd, knorrig.
splenetic, n. lyer aan miltkwaal; swaarmoedige; middel teen miltkwaal.
splenic, milt- . . .; – **fever**, miltvuur.
splenitis, miltontsteking.
splice, v. splits, las; trou; **when did they get –d?**, wanneer is hulle gekoppel?
splice, n. splitsing, las.
splint, n. spalk, splinter; kuitbeen; knoppie, splint (aan 'n perd se been).
splint, v. spalk.
splint-bone, kuitbeen.
splinter, v. (ver)splinter.
splinter, n. splinter, splint, spaander; – **party**, splinterparty.
splinter-bar, swingelhout.
splinter-proof, skerfvry.
splintery, splinterig, vol splinters.
split, v. splits, bars, skeur, kloof (klowe); verdeel; – **up**, verdeel; – **one's vote**, vir albei kante stem; – **the difference**, die verskil deel; – **the job**, die werk verdeel; – **hairs**, vit, haarklowe; **he nearly – his sides**, hy het hom byna 'n boggel gelag; **my head is –ting**, my kop wil bars (van pyn); – **on**, verklap, verklik, gaan verkla(e).
split, a. gesplits, gebars, geskeur; – **infinitive**, geskeie infinitief; – **peas(e)**, split-ertjies.
split, n. spleet, skeur, bars; skeuring, tweespalk, verdeeldheid, onenigheid.
splotch, **splodge**, vlek, vuil kol.
splotchy, gevlek, beklad.
splutter, sien **sputter**.
spoil, n. (oorlogs)buit, roof; voordeel.
spoil, v. bederwe, verniel; verfoes; berowe; **he was –ing for a fight**, sy hande het gejeuk om te baklei.

**spoiler, bederwer; plunderaar.
spoil-sport, pretbederwer, spelbreker.
spoke, speek; put a – in one's wheel, iemand dwarsboom (in die wiele ry).
spokeshave, skaafmes.
spokesman, woordvoerder.
spoliation, plundering, verwoesting.
spoliator, plunderaar, berower.
spondaic, spondeïes.
spondee, spondee.
spondulic(k)s, pitte.
sponge, n. spons; geryste deeg; parasiet, klaploper, opskeploer(der); he threw up the –, hy het tou opgegooi; hy het hom oorgegee, hy het hom gewonne gegee; let us pass the – over it, laat ons daaroor maar nie meer praat nie; – rubber, skuimrubber.
sponge, v. spons, afspons; afvee, uitvee (met 'n spons), uitwis; optrek, opsuie; – on, klaploop, opskeploer.
sponge-cake, suikerbrood.
sponge-cloth, wisser.
sponger, klaploper, opskeploerder.
spongy, sponsagtig, sponserig.
sponsion, borgtog.
sponsor, peetvader (peetoom), peetmoeder (peettante), doopgetuie; borg; beskermheer, uitsaai-adverteerder.
sponsorial, van 'n doopgetuie (borg).
sponsorship, peetskap.
spontaneity, spontaneïteit.
spontaneous, spontaan, vrywillig, ongedwonge; instinktief; natuurlik; – combustion, selfverbranding.
spontaneously, vanself, spontaan.
spoof, v. kul, fop, verneuk.
spoof, n. kullery, verneukery.
spook, spook.
spookish, spooky, spookagtig, spokerig.
spool, spoel, rolletjie, tolletjie.
spoon, n. lepel.
spoon, v. (met 'n lepel) skep; sag slaan.
spoon, n. sukkelaar, stumperd; smoorverliefde vryer; be –s on, smoorverlief wees op.
spoon, v. vry, vlerksleep.
spoonbeak, spoonbill, lepelaar.
spoonerism, spoonerisme.
spoon-feed, met 'n lepel voer.
spoonful, lepelvol.
spoon-meat, lepelkos.
spoony, gek, sentimenteel; been-af.
spoor, n. spoor.
spoor, v. die spoor volg, die spoor sny.
sporadic, sporadies, versprei.
spore, spoor; saad, kiem.
sporiferous, spoordraend.
sport, n. pret, korswel, vermaak; speletjie, tydverdryf; sport; make – of, vir die gek hou, belaglik maak; in –, vir die aardigheid, uit die grap; he is a real –, hy is 'n gawe kêrel; old –, ou maat, ou kêrel; –s, sport.
sport, v. jou verlustig (vermaak), speel; vertoon spog met.
sportful, vrolik, speels, dartel.
sporting, spelend; sportief, sport- . . .; a – fellow, 'n sportiewe kêrel; take a – chance, 'n kans waag; a – offer, 'n gawe aanbod; the – world, die sportwêreld; – of him, sportief (gaaf) van hom.
sportive, vrolik, dartel, spelerig.
sports coat, sportbaadjie.
sportsman, sportman, sportliefhebber.
sportsmanlike, sportief.
sporule, spoortjie.
spot, n. plek; plekkie, kolletjie, merkie, vlek;** klad, smet; a black tie with white –s, 'n swart das met wit kolletjies; on the –, op die plek, dadelik; onmiddellik, sonder versuim; be on the –, op stryk wees; jou man staan; al jou varkies bymekaar hê; our men were on the –, ons kêrels was daar (by); knock –s out of, kafloop, deeglik op sy baadjie gee.
spot, v. merk, bespikkel; beklad, besmet; raaksien, bespeur, agterkom.
spot-cash, kontant.
spotless, vlekloos; silwerskoon.
spot-light, soeklig; draailamp.
spotted, gespikkel, bont.
spotty, gespikkel, vol vlekke.
spousal(s), n. bruilof, huwelik.
spousal, a. bruilofs- . . ., huweliks- . . .
spouse, eggenoot, eggenote.
spout, v. spuit; deklameer, oreer, „spoeg"; verpand.
spout, n. tuit, pyp, geut; straal; up the –, in die pandjieswinkel; he was up the –, hy was in die knyp.
sprag, remblok.
sprain, v. verstuit, verswik, verrek.
sprain, n. verstuiting, verrekking.
sprat, sprot; throw a – to catch a whale, herring, mackerel, 'n spiering uitgooi om 'n kabeljou te vang.
sprawl, uitrek, uitgestrek lê; spartel; uitsprei; send one –ing, iemand laat ploeë in die grond.
spray, n. takkie.
spray, n. sproeiwater, spuitwater, bruiswater, stofreën; skuim; sproeier.
spray b. (be)sproei, spuit.
spread, v sprei, versprei, uitsprei, uitbrei, rondstrooi, uitstrooi; uitstrek; ontplooi, ontvou, ooprol, oopgooi; smeer; – butter on bread, botter op brood smeer; – out a rug, 'n kombers oopgooi; – out on the table, ooplê op die tafel; a table – with every luxury, 'n tafel met allerlei lekkernye belaai.
spread, n. omvang; uitgestrektheid; uitgebreidheid; verspreiding; sprei, tafelkleed; fees, maaltyd; arches of equal –, boë met gelyke spanning; we had no end of a –, dit was 'n etery van die ander wêreld.
spread-eagle, n. arend met uitgespreide vlerke.
spread-eagle, a. grootpraterig.
spread-eagleism, grootpratery.
spreader, verspreier; rondstrooier.
spree, n. pret, fuif, drinkpartytjie.
spree, v. fuif, boemel, „sprie".
sprig, n. takkie, twygie, loot, spruit; spykertjie; versiersel, aigrette; –ged muslin, geblomde neteldoek.
sprig, v. met takkies versier.
sprightly, vrolik, lewendig, opgeruimd.
spring, v. spring, opspring; voortkom, ontspruit, ontstaan; krom trek, bars, (wild) opja; veer; – a leak, 'n lekplek kry; – at somebody's throat, iemand na die keel vlie; – away, wegspring; – back, terugspring; – from a false conviction, spruit uit 'n valse oortuiging voort; – surprises on, verras; – to the assistance, te hulp snel; – up, opspring; voor die dag kom, verskyn; verrys; ontstaan; a breeze sprang up, 'n windjie het opgesteek; my car is well sprung, my kar veer goed.
spring, n. spring, sprong; lente, voorjaar; bron, fontein; veer; veerkrag, dryfveer, motief; oorsprong; his muscles have no – in them, sy spiere het geen veerkrag nie; watch –, horlosieveer.
spring-balance, trekskaaltjie.
spring-bed, springmatras.

spring-blade, veerblad.
spring-board, springplank, duikplank.
springbok, springbok.
spring-carriage, veerrytuig, veerkoets.
spring-chicken, piepkuiken.
spring-cleaning, huisskoonmaak.
spring-clean, huis skoonmaak.
springe, strik, val, wip.
springer, springbok; jaghond.
springiness, elastisiteit, veerkrag.
spring-leaf, veerblad.
springless, sonder veer (vere).
springlike, lenteagtig, lente-...
spring-tide, springvloed; lente.
springtime, lente.
spring-water, bronwater, fonteinwater.
springy, elasties, veerkragtig.
sprinkle, v. sprinkel, strooi; stofreent.
sprinkle, n. mot-, stofreent; sprinkeling.
sprinkling, sprinkel(ing); a − of Scotchmen, 'n stuk of wat Skotte.
sprint, v. nael, (hard) hardloop, sny.
sprint, n. naelwedloop.
sprinter, naelloper, hardloper.
sprit, spriet, boegspriet.
sprite, fee, kabouter; spook, gees.
spritsail, sprietseil.
sprocket, tand.
sprout, v. opkom, groei, uitspruit, uitloop, opskiet; laat groei.
sprout, n. spruit, loot; (Brussels) −s, spruitkool.
spruce, a. netjies, piekfyn, agtermekaar.
spruce, v. opskik, mooimaak.
spruce, n. denneboom, spar.
spry, lewendig, vlug, wakker, rats.
spud, grafie; diksak, „vaatjie"; aartappel.
spume, n. skuim.
spume, v. skuim.
spumescence, skuim.
spumous, skuimend, skuim-...
spunge, sien **sponge**.
spunk, koerasie, moed, vuur, gees, fut.
spunky, vurig.
spur, n. spoor; spoorslag, aansporing; uitloper (van 'n berg); **win his −s**, sy spore verdien; **on the − of the moment**, dadelik, op die oomblik, sonder om na te dink.
spur, v. die spore gee; (aan)spoor, aansit, aanja; van spore voorsien, spore aansit; − **forward**, aanja, vinnig ry; − **on**, aanspoor.
spurious, oneg, vals, vervals.
spurn, v. versmaad, verag, verstoot.
spurn, n. veragting, verwerping.
spurt, v. spat, spuit; laat nael, laat spat.
spurt, n. uitbarsting, uitspuiting, sterk straal; kragsinspanning.
spurwheel, tandrat.
sputnik, spoetnik, kunsmaan.
sputter, v. spat, spu; sputter; babbel.
sputter, n. gebrabbel, gesputter.
sputum, sputum; fluim (fleim).
spy, n. spioen, bespieder.
spy, v. spioen, bespied; afloer; in die oog kry; uitvis, uitvind, agterkom; **quick at spying your neighbour's faults**, gou om jou bure se gebreke agter te kom; − **out**, uitvis, agterkom, uitvors; − **into a secret**, 'n geheim probeer agterkom; − **upon somebody**, iemand afloer.
spyglass, verkyker.
spyhole, kykgat.
squab, a. kort, dik, vet.
squab, n. vetsak; jong duif; kussing.
squabble, v. rusie maak, twis, skoor, kibbel, dwarstrek.
squabble, n. rusie, twis, dwarstrekkery.

squad, seksie, klompie; afdeling; span; **flying − car**, blitsmotor; **flying −**, blitspatrollie.
squadron, eskadron (van leër); eskader (van vloot) eskadrielje (van lugmag).
squalid, vuil, liederlik, smerig, morsig.
squalidity, smerigheid, vuilheid.
squall, v. skreeu, gil.
squall, n. windvlaag, bui; skreeu, gil.
squally, stormagtig, winderig, buierig.
squalor, sien **squalidity**.
squaloid, haaiagtig, haai-...
squamose, squamous, skobbig.
squander, verkwis, deurbring, mors.
square, n. vierkant; (vierkantige) blok (huisie); plein; ouderwetse persoon; winkelhaak; tweede mag, vierkantgetal, kwadraat; ruit; **out of −**, nie haaks nie, nie reghoekig nie; **the − of X is X^2, X kwadraat is X^2**.
square, a. vierkantig, reghoekig; in orde, in die haak; eerlik, billik; gelyk, kiet, niks skuldig nie; − **foot**, vierkante voet; − **measure**, vlaktemaat; − **root**, vierkantswortel; − **number**, kwadraatgetal; **a − peg in a round hole**, die verkeerde man op die verkeerde plek; **get things −**, sake in orde bring (reël); **he met with a − refusal**, dit is hom botweg geweier; **a man of − frame**, 'n sterk geboude man; **a − deal**, 'n eerlike behandeling (transaksie); **I must get − with him**, ek moet hom betaal (met hom afreken); **we are − now**, ons is nou kiet, ons skuld mekaar nou niks; **a − meal**, 'n stewige maal.
square, v. vierkantig (reghoekig) maak; tot die tweede mag verhef; vereffen, betaal; omkoop; in orde bring; voeg (na), aanpas (by); **3 −d is 9**, die tweede mag van 3 is 9; − **accounts with**, afreken met; **he −d himself**, hy het sy lyf reggetrek.
square, adv. vierkant, reg; eerlik; − **on the jaw**, mooi reg op die kakebeen; **treat −**, eerlik behandel.
square-built, breed, vierkantig, sterk.
square-rigged, met ra-seile.
square-sail, ra-seil.
square-shouldered, breed geskouerd.
square-toed, stompneus, styf, gemaak.
squash, v. plat (pap druk), fyn maak, moes maak, verbrysel, kneus; doodsê, doodsit; − **into the car**, in die kar inbeur.
squash, n. vroeëpampoen, murg-van-groente, skorsiemoes; pulp; gedrang; kwas; **lemon −**, kwas, suurlemoensop.
squash-hat, paphoed.
squashy, sag, pap, papperig.
squat, v. (neer)hurk, op die hurke sit; kruip; − **down**, gaan sit, plak.
squat, a. gehurk; kort, dik.
squat, n. gehurkte houding; vetsak.
squatter, plakker; neerhurker; kolonis.
squaw, (Indiaanse) vrou, meid.
squawk, skree(u).
squeak, v. piep; skree(u), knars; verkla, verklik.
squeak, n. gepiep, gil; **a narrow −**, 'n nou ontkoming, so hittete.
squeaker, pieper; jong duif.
squeaky, piep-...; krakend.
squeal, v. gil, skree(u), tjank; verkla.
squeal, n. gil, skree(u).
squealer, skreeuer; jong duif; verklikker.
squeamish, mislik; nougeset, kieskeurig.
squeeze, v. druk; afpers; druk uitoefen op; afdruk; −**d orange**, uitgedrukte lemoen; −**d to death**, doodgedruk; **he −d himself into the room**, hy het in die kamer ingebeur; − **money**

squeeze   677   **stamp-duty**

out of, geld afpers van; – the government, druk uitoefen op die regering.
squeeze, n. druk; afdruk; gedrang; a – of the hand, 'n handdruk; it was a tight –, dit het broekskeur gegaan.
squeezer, drukker; pers.
squelch, v. verpletter; onderdruk; stilmaak, doodsê.
squelch, n. doodhou; doodsê.
squib, voetsoeker, klapper; skotskrif.
squid, pylinkvis.
squill, see-ajuin.
squint, v. skeel kyk, skeel wees, oormekaarkyk; – at, skuins kyk na; loer na.
squint, n. skeel kyk, skeel oë; he has a fearful –, hy kyk geweldig skeel.
squint, a. skeel.
squint-eyed, (soet)skeel, skeeloog- . . .
squire, landedelman, landjonker; skildknaap; – of dames, dameskêrel.
squirrel, eekhorinkie.
squirt, v. spuit.
squirt, n. spuit; straaltjie; windbuks.
stab, v. steek, doodsteek, deursteek.
stab, n. steek, dolksteek, messteek; wond; belediging, belastering; a – in the back, 'n steek in die rug.
stability, stabiliteit; standvastigheid.
stable, a. vas, solied, stabiel, duursaam; standvastig, vasberade.
stable, n. stal, (resies)perde.
stable, v. op stal hou, in die stal sit, in die stal staan.
stable-boy, staljong.
stable-horse, stalperd.
stabling, stalling; stal, staanplek.
stack, n. mied (miet); hoop, stapel; klompie regopstaande gewere; groep skoorstene.
stack, v. mied pak; opstapel; stapel, op verskillende hoogtes laat vlieg.
stack-stand, miedkraal.
stad(t)holder, stadhouer.
staff, n. stok, staf, paai; stut, steun; staf, personeel; bread is the – of life, sonder brood kan die mens nie lewe nie.
staff, v. van personeel voorsien.
staff-notation, balkskrif.
staff-officer, stafoffisier.
stag, takbok, hert; – party, herefuif, rampartytjie.
stage, n. toneel; steier, stellasie; stadium, fase, trap, punt; he went on the –, hy het toneelspeler geword (op die toneel gegaan); quit the –, van die toneel verdwyn, die toneel verlaat; at this –, op hierdie stadium, op hierdie punt; the first – ends here, dit is die einde van die eerste trek.
stage, v. opvoer, op die toneel (planke) bring.
stage-coach, poswa.
stage-direction, toneelaanwysing.
stage-fever, toneelmanie.
stage-fright, plankekoors.
stage-management, régie; toneelleiding.
stage-manager-, toneeldirekteur, regisseur.
stage-painter, toneelskilder.
stage-right, reg van opvoering.
stage-struck, toneelmal.
stage-whisper, hoorbare fluistering.
stagger, v. wankel, waggel, slinger; laat wankel (waggel); aarsel, weifel; oorbluf, verstom, skok; (ver)sprei; completely –ed him, het hom totaal uit die veld geslaan; a –ing blow, 'n geweldige slag; –ed holidays, gespreide vakansies.
stagger, n. waggelende gang, waggeling.

staghound, windhond, jaghond.
staging, opvoer(ing); steier, stellasie.
stagnancy, stilstand; luiheid, traagheid.
stagnant, (stil)staand(e), stil; lui, traag; – water, staande water.
stagnate, stilstaan; lui (traag) wees.
stagnation, (die) stilstaan, stilstand.
stagy, teatraal, toneel- . . .
staid, bedaard, stemmig; solied, nugter.
stain, v. vlek; besmet, besoedel, beklad; verf, kleur; –ed glass, gekleurde (beskilderde) glas; –ed wallpaper, gekleurde plakpapier.
stain, n. vlek; smet, klad, skande, skandvlek; kleur, verf, tint.
stainer, verwer; besmetter, bevlekker.
stainless, onbevlek, rein, skoon, smetloos, onbesmet; vlekvry, roesvry.
stair, trappie, treetjie; –s, trap; a flight of –s, 'n trap; up –s, op solder, bo; down –s, onder; go up –s, down –s, die trap op (die trap af) gaan.
stair-carpet, traploper.
staircase, trap.
stair-rod, traproei.
stair-runner, traploper.
stake, n. paal, stok; brandstapel; marteldood; inset, wedgeld; aandeel; –s, potgeld, inset; at –, op die spel; perish at the –, op die brandstapel sterwe.
stake, v. met pale stut; ompaal, afbaken, pale omsit; waag; wed, insit.
stake-net, staaknet.
stalactite, stalaktiet, druipsteen.
stalagmite, stalagmiet, druipsteen.
stale, a. oud, muf; afgesaag; bevange; verswak, verflou; get – with too much exercise, bevang raak weens te veel oefening; – news, ou nuus; – joke, afgesaagde grap.
stale, v. bevange raak, verswak; oud (muf, afgesaag) word.
stalemate, n. pat (in skaak).
stalemate, v. pat sit; vaskeer.
stalk, v. deftig stap; kruip, bekruip.
stalk, n. deftige stap.
stalk, n. stingel, steel.
stalking-horse, jagperd, skietperd.
stall, n. stal, hok, vak; stalletjie, toonbank, kiosk, kraam; koorstoel; –s, stalles (in die skouburg).
stall, op stal sit, op stal hou; gaan staan, stop; in die modder vassit.
stallage, markgeld, staangeld.
stall-feed, (op stal) vetvoer.
stallion, hings.
stalwart, a. sterk gebou, fris, stoer; stoutmoedig, standvastig, dapper.
stalwart, n. staatmaker, getroue.
stamen, meeldraad.
stamina, uithouvermoë.
staminate, meeldraad- . . .
stammer, v. hakkel, stamel, stotter.
stammer, n. gehakkel, gestotter.
stamp, v. stempel, tjap, merk; bestempel; frankeer, seël, 'n posseël sit op; fynmaak, fyn stamp; stamp, trap; – out, doodtrap; – on the memory, in die geheue geprent.
stamp, n. stempel, seël, tjap; posseël; soort, aard, karakter; stamper; stamp, trap; men of his –, manne van sy soort; bear the – of, die stempel dra van.
stamp-act, seëlwet.
stamp-collector, posseëlversamelaar.
stamp-duty, seëlreg.

stampede, n. dolle vlug, plotselinge skrik; toeloop.
stampede, v. op loop sit; op loop ja.
stamp-mill, stampmeul.
stamp-office, seëlkantoor.
stance, houding, posisie.
stanch, staunch, laat ophou, stelp.
stanchion, n. pilaar, stut, paal.
stanchion, v. stut; vasmaak.
stand, v. staan; gaan staan; uithou, uitstaan, verdra; van krag wees (bly); deurstaan; neersit; laat staan; – **easy**, rus!; – **at ease**, op die plek rus!; **he –s six foot three**, hy is ses voet drie duim (lank); **don't – there arguing**, moenie staan teenpraat nie; – **firm**!, staan vas!; **it –s to reason**, dit spreek vanself; **this paragraph must –**, hierdie paragraaf moet onveranderd bly; **he –s in need of help**, hy het behoefte aan hulp; **the matter –s thus**, die saak staan so; – **in awe of somebody**, vir iemand bang wees; **I want to know where I –**, ek wil weet wat my posisie is, ek wil weet waar ek staan; – **clear**, uit die pad staan, opsy staan; – **it against the wall**, sit dit teen die muur; **I could never – the fellow**, ek kon die vent nooit verdra nie; – **at ease**, op die plaas rus; **he failed to – the test**, hy kon die toets nie deurstaan nie; – **one's ground**, pal staan, jou man staan, vastrap; – **a treat**, trakteer; **you'll – the drink**, jy sal die drank betaal; – **by**, ondersteun, bystaan; naby staan; toeskouer wees; – **by his promise**, sy belofte hou; **free trade –s for a great deal more than that**, vryhandel beteken baie meer as dit; **will not – for it**, sal dit nie duld nie; – **for parliament**, kandidaat vir die Volksraad wees; **he –s for free trade**, hy is 'n voorstander van vryhandel; – **in good stead**, goed te pas kom; – **in for**, kos; waarneem vir (iemand); **if you – on it**, as jy daarop aandring; – **on ceremony**, op die vorm (uiterlikheid) gesteld wees; – **out**, uitsteek; uitmunt, volhou, volhard; – **out for**, verlang, wil hê, ywer vir; **this must – over**, dit moet bly oorstaan (gelaat word tot later); – **to**, gestand doen, bly by; stand hou, voet by stuk hou; – **to sea**, in see steek, afvaar; – **up**, opstaan, regop staan; – **up for**, ondersteun, opkom vir; – **up to**, weerstand bied, sy man staan teen; – **well with**, goed aangeskrywe staan by.
stand, n. stilstand, halt; stelling, posisie, staanplek, standplaas; weerstand; standertjie; tafeltjie, kassie, rak(kie) stalletjie, kraam; tribune, paviljoen, verhoog; **come to a –**, tot staan kom, tot stilstand kom; **make a – against**, (sig) verset teen, weerstand bied; **he took his – near the door**, hy het naby die deur gaan staan; **I take my – on**, ek baseer my argument op; **brought to a –**, tot stilstand gebring.
standard, n. vlag, vaandel, banier, standerd; standaard, peil, maatstaf, gehalte; paal; stander; **does not come up to the same –**, bereik nie dieselfde standaard nie; – **four**, standerd vier.
standard, a. standaard-. . . ; stam-. . . , hoogstammig; staan-. . . ; – **work**, standaardwerk; – **rose**, stamroos.
standard-bearer, vaandeldraer.
standardization, vasstelling, standaardisasie, standaardisering.
standardize, standaardiseer, vasstel.
standing, n. (die) staan; stand, rang, naam, posisie; duur; **a person of high –**, 'n persoon van naam; **a dispute of long –**, 'n ou twis;

students of three years' –, derdejaarstudente.
standing, a. staand(e); vas, bestaand(e), bepaal, oud, erken(de); **a – rule**, 'n erkende (vaste) reël; **a – joke**, 'n vaste (ou) grap; – **army**, staande leër; – **orders**, reglement van orde; leërorder, legorder (handelsterm), vaste bestelling; – **water**, staanwater, staande water.
standing-room, staanplek.
stand-off: – **half**, losskakel.
stand-offish, eenkant, terughoudend.
standpoint, standpunt.
standstill, stilstand; **come to a –**, tot stilstand kom.
stand-up, reg-op; hewig; **a – fight**, 'n hewige bakleiery.
staniel, toringvalk.
stannery, tinmyn.
stannic, tin- . . . ; – **acid**, tinsuur.
stanniferous, tinhoudend, tinbevattend.
stanza, stansa, vers, koeplet.
staple, kram.
staple, n. vernaamste produk; mark; ruwe materiaal; hoofbestanddeel; draad; **wool of fine –**, wol van fyn draad.
staple, a. vernaamste, hoof- . . . , stapel- . . .
staple, v. klassifiseer, sorteer; vaskram, draadheg.
stapler, kramhegter, draadhegter.
star, n. ster; sterretjie; kol (voor 'n perd se kop); **shooting –**, verskietende ster; **unlucky –**, ongelukster; **you may thank your –s**, jy kan die hemel dank.
star, v. met sterre versier; met 'n sterretjie merk; as hoofakteur (-aktrise) optree; – **ring Sofia Loren**, met Sofia Loren in die hoofrol.
starblind, bysiende.
starboard, stuurboord.
starch, n. stysel; formaliteit.
starch, v. stywe.
starched, styf, gestywe.
starchy, stysel- . . . , vol stysel; styf.
stare, v. tuur, staar, aangaap; – **at**, aan gaap; **famine –d them in the face**, honger het hulle in die aangesig gestaar; **it –s you in the face**, dit is so duidelik as die dag; dit is vlak voor jou.
stare, n. getuur, starende blik.
star-fish, seester.
star-gazer, sterrekyker.
stark, a. styf; puur, bloot, louter; – **and stiff**, stokstyf, styf en strak; – **madness**, louter kranksinnigheid.
stark, adv. gans, totaal, geheel en al; – **mad**, stapelgek; – **naked**, poedelnaak.
starlight, sterlig.
starlike, soos 'n ster, ster- . . .
starling, blinkvlerkspreeu.
starling, stroombreker (by 'n brug).
starlit, sterverlig.
starry, ster(re)- . . . , met sterre besaai.
starry-eyed, met skitterende oë; alte idealisties.
star-spangled, met sterre besaai.
start, v. skrik, opspring; begin (maak) 'n aanvang maak; vertrek; opja (van wild); aan die gang (loop) sit; op tou sit; (laat) wegspring; **my car would not –**, my motor wou nie vat nie; – **on a journey**, afreis, op reis gaan, 'n reis begin; – **up**, opspring, skrik; aan die gang sit; to – **with**, om mee te begin; in die eerste plek.
start, n. skielike beweging, spring, sprong; skrik; begin, aanvang; (die) wegspring; wegspringplek; voorsprong; **by fits and –s**, met rukke en stote; **make an early –**, vroeg begin; **difficult at the –**, moeilik in die begin; **give**

ten yards –, tien tree voorgee; **he has got the – of his rivals,** hy het 'n voorsprong op sy mededingers; **he gave me a –** *(in life),* hy het my aan die gang (op die been) gehelp; **gave me such a –,** dit het my so laat skrik; **from the –,** uit die staanspoor.
starter, aansitter; deelnemer; seingeër.
starting-crank, -handle, slinger.
starting-place, beginplek, wegtrekplek.
starting-point, uitgangspunt; staanspoor, wegtrekplek, wegspringplek.
startle, skrikmaak, laat skrik, ontstel.
startler, verrassing; ontnugtering.
startling, ontstellend, verrassend.
starvation, uit-, verhongering, gebrek, hongersnood; hongerdood; **– wages,** hongerloon.
starve, van honger omkom; honger ly, gebrek ly, verhonger; honger wees; uithonger, laat gebrek ly; **I am simply starving,** ek is dood van die honger; **– for sympathy,** hunker na simpatie.
starveling, hongerlyer, uitgehongerde mens (dier).
state, n. toestand, staat, stemming; staat; waardigheid, rang; prag; luister; **he was in quite a – about it,** dit het hom heeltemal opgewonde gemaak; **befitting his –,** soos dit by sy stand pas; **lie in –,** op 'n praalbed lê; **live in great –,** op 'n groot voet lewe; **the king and queen appeared in –,** die koning en koningin het in staatsie (gala) verskyn.
state, a. staats- . . . ; staatsie- . . . , gala- . . . , hof- . . . ; **– criminal,** politieke misdadiger.
state, v. (ver)meld, verklaar, uiteensit, sê, opgee; vasstel; **– Boyle's Law,** gee die wet van Boyle; **the time was not –d,** die tyd is nie aangegee (bepaal nie); **the case clearly,** die saak duidelik stel (uiteensit).
state affairs, staatsake.
state aid, staatsubsidie; **–ed of schools,** subsidieskole.
state ball, hofbal.
statecraft, staatkunde, diplomasie.
stateliness, statigheid, deftigheid.
stately, statig, deftig, waardig, imposant, groots; pragtig, luisterryk.
statement, verklaring, bewering, gesegde; opgaaf, staat.
state prison, staatsgevangenis.
stateroom, praalkamer; private kajuit.
statesman, staatsman.
statesmanlike, soos dit 'n staatsman betaam, diplomaties, takties.
statesmanship, staatkunde, staatsmansbeleid.
static(al), staties, gewigs- . . .
statics, statika (statica), ewewigsleer.
station, n. standplaas, standplek, pos; stasie; status; posisie, stand.
station, v. plaas, stel, stasioneer.
stationaries, vaste troepe.
stationary, stilstand, blywend, vas; **the balloon was now –,** die ballon het nou stilgestaan; **– troops,** vaste troepe; **the temperature is –** die temperatuur bly onveranderd.
stationer, handelaar in skryfbehoeftes.
stationery, skryfbehoeftes.
station-master, stasiemeester.
statistical, statisties.
statistician, statistikus.
statistics, statistiek(e).
statuary, n. beeldhouer; beeldhoukuns; beeldegroep, beeldhouwerk.
statue, standbeeld.
statuesque, soos 'n standbeeld.
statuette, beeldjie.

stature, lengte, gestalte.
status, status, stand, rang, posisie.
statute, wet, statuut, instelling; **– law,** die geskrewe wet.
statutory, wetlik, volgens wet, wets- . . .
staunch, stanch, trou, betroubaar.
stave, n. duig, plankie, houtjie, sport; stansa, vers; balk (in musiek).
stave, v. in duie slaan, 'n gat inslaan; duie insit; **– off,** afweer, afwend.
stay, v. teëhou, weerhou, stuit, in bedwang hou; uitstel, opskort; ondersteun, stut; uithou, volhou; bly, loseer; vertoef, wag, **– at the hotel,** loseer (bly) by die hotel; **– in,** binnebly (tuis bly); op skool bly, skoolsit; **– on,** langer bly; **– up,** opbly; stut; **couldn't – the pace,** kon die vaart nie volhou nie.
stay, n. verblyf; uitstel, opskorting; hinderpaal; uithouvermoë; steun, stut; **your – has been very short,** jou kuiertjie was maar kort.
stay, n. stag, mastou.
stay-at-home, huishen, tuissitter.
staying-power, uithouvermoë.
stay-lace, bors(t)rokband, -veter.
stays, bors(t)rok, korset.
staysail, stagseil.
stead, stede plaas, plek; diens, nut; **stand in good –,** goed vanpas kom; **in his –,** in sy plek; **in – of,** in plaas van.
steadfast, standvastig, onwankelbaar.
steady, n. vaste nooi.
steady, a. vas; gereeld, gestadig, egalig, besadig; oppassend, solied; not **– on his legs,** nie vas op sy bene nie; **– increase,** 'n gestadige vermeerdering; **we had a – wind against us,** die wind het een stryk deur van voor gewaai; **a – pace,** 'n gereelde pas; **–!,** stadig (oor die klippe)!
steady, v. bestendig (besadig) maak (word), tot bedaring bring (kom); **steadied himself and dropped a goal,** vasgetrap en 'n skepdoel geskop.
steak, biefstuk, stuk (vleis).
steal, steel; sluip, kruip; **– a march on somebody,** iemand die pas afsny; **– in, out, away,** stilletjies in-, weggaan (in-, uit-, wegsluip); **– a person's heart,** iemand se hart verower; **– a glance at,** skelmpies kyk na.
stealth, geheime handelwyse, geheimhouding; onderduimsheid; **by –,** stilletjies, op onderduimse manier.
stealthy, skelm, onderduims, slinks.
steam, stoom, wasem, damp; **blow off –,** stoom afblaas; **get up –,** stoom maak.
steamboat, stoomboot.
steam-boiler, stoomketel.
steam-engine, stoommasjien.
steamer, (stoom)boot, stoomskip; stoomketel, stoomkoker.
steam-gauge, stoomdrukmeter.
steam-hammer, stoomhamer.
steam-heat, stoomverwarming.
steam-jacket, stoommantel.
steam-laundry, stoomwassery.
steam-navigation, stoomvaart.
steam-power, stoomkrag.
steam-roller, stoomwals; v. met geweld deurdruk.
steamship, stoomskip.
steamy, stomend, wasemend; vol stoom.
stearing, stearine, vet- . . .
steed, (stryd)ros.
steel, n. staal; swaard; slypstaal; **– wool,** staalwol.
steel, a. staal, van staal.

steel, v. staal, verhard; – **one's heart**, jou hart verhard.
steel-clad, gepantser(d).
steel-engraving, staalgravure.
steely, staal, (staal)hard.
steelyard, unster, Romeinse balans.
steep, a. steil; kras, kwaai (van pryse).
steep, n. steilte, hoogte, helling.
steep, v. indoop, week, dompel; **–ed in misery**, in ellende gedompel; **–ed in Greek and Latin**, gedrenk (gekonfyt) in Grieks en Latyn.
steepen, steiler word.
steeper, kuip, bak.
steeple, toring.
steeplechase, heg-en-steg-ren.
steepled, met torings.
steeplejack, toringwerker.
steepy, steilerig.
steer, v. stuur; koers vat; – **clear of**, vermy, ontwyk, buite bereik bly van.
steer, bulletjie; tollie, jong ossie.
steerage, (die) stuur; tussendek; – **passenger**, tussendekspassasier.
steering-gear, stuurtoestel.
steering-rod, stuurstang.
steering-wheel, stuurrat, stuurwiel.
steersman, stuurman.
steeve, hel, duik.
stellar, van die sterre, sterre- . . .
stellate(d), stervormig.
stellular, stervormig.
stem, n. stam, stingel, steel; gesag; boeg (van 'n skip), voorstewe; **from – to stern**, van voor tot agter.
stem, v. afstroop (van tabakblare).
stem, v. stuit, teëhou; opdam.
stemma, stamboom, afstamming.
Sten (gun), Sten-geweer.
stench, stank.
stencil, n. uitgesnyde patroonplaat (tekenpatroon); sjabloneer(werk).
stencil, v. sjabloneer.
stenographer, stenograaf, snelskrywer.
stenography, stenografie, snelskrif.
stentorian, stentor- . . ., hard, luid, bulderend; – **voice**, bulderende stem.
step, v. stap, tree, loop; – **this way, please**, kom hiernatoe (hierlanges) asseblief; – **aside**, opsy tree (stap); – **across the road**, oor die pad loop; – **back**, agteruittree; – **down**, afstap, afklim; – **in**, binnestap, binnetree; tussenbeide tree; – **out**, buitentoe gaan; aanstap, die treë rek.
step, n. tree, stap, pas; voetstap; treetjie, trappie; sport; trapleer; – **by** –, trapsgewyse; versigtig, voetjie vir voetjie; **it is but a – to my house**, dis maar 'n hanetreetjie na my huis toe; **turn one's –s**, 'n rigting inslaan, jou skrede rig; **in, out of –**, in, uit die pas; **keep –**, in die pas bly; **break –**, uit die pas raak; **take –s**, stappe doen; **on the top – of the ladder**, op die boonste sport van die leer.
stepbrother, stiefbroer.
stepchild, stiefkind.
stepdance, solodans.
stepdaughter, stiefdogter.
stepfather, stiefvader.
step-ladder, trapleer.
stepmother, stiefmoeder.
steppe, steppe, hoogvlakte.
stepping-stone, oorspringklip; stap, oorgang, middel.
stepson, stiefseun.
stereogram, stereogram.
stereometer, stereometer.
stereometry, stereometrie.
stereophonic, stereofonies.
stereoscope, stereoskoop.
stereoscopic, stereoskopies.
stereoscopy, stereoskopie.
stereotype, stereotiepplaat, stereotiepdruk.
stereotyped, stereotiep, vas, onveranderlik.
sterile, onvrugbaar, skraal, maer, dor, steriel; kiemvry, gesteriliseer.
sterilization, sterilisasie.
sterilize, steriliseer, kiemvry maak, kieme doodmaak; onvrugbaar maak.
sterility, onvrugbaarheid, dorheid.
sterling, sterling; eg, onvervals, suiwer; **a – fellow**, 'n gawe kêrel; – **area**, sterlinggebied.
stern, a. ernstig, streng, stug, stroef.
stern, n. agterstewe.
sternum, borsbeen.
sternutation, (die) nies.
sternutative, sternutatory, a. nies- . . .
sternutative, sternutatory, n. niesmiddel.
stertorous, snorkend.
stethoscope, stetoskoop.
stethoscopic, stetoskopies.
stevedor, stuwadoor.
stew, v. stowe; **let him – in his own grease**, laat hom in sy eie sop gaar kook; **–ing pears**, stoofpere.
stew, n. gestoofde vleis (stoofvleis), bredie; **be in a –**, in die knyp sit.
steward, rentmeester, bestierder; kelner; seremoniemeester.
stewardess, waardin; **air –**, lugwaardin.
stick, v. steek, vassteek; vasklewe, vassit, vasplak; aanhou; getrou bly; **–s like a bur**, sit soos klitsgras aan jou vas; – **fast**, vassit, bly steek; **cannot – it any longer**, kan dit nie langer uithou nie; – **at nothing**, vir niks terugdeins nie; – **in your pocket**, in jou sak steek; – **indoors**, by die huis sit; – **in the mud**, in die modder vassit; 'n remskoen wees; nie met die tyd saamgaan nie; **it –s in his gizzard**, hy kan dit nie verkrop nie, hy kan dit nie kleinkry nie; – **out**, uitsteek; – **it out**, volhou nie opgee nie; – **to**, vassit aan, vasklewe aan; getrou bly aan; – **to a promise**, 'n belofte hou (nakom); – **to it**, volhou, nie opgee nie; **together**, aanmekaar plak; bymekaar bly, mekaar getrou bly; **the name stuck to him**, hy het die naam bly behou; – **up**, regop staan, regop sit; laat sukkel, moeite gee; – **up for somebody**, vir iemand opkom.
stick, n. stok, wandelstok, kierie, lat; string (bomme); pyp; droogstoppel, jandooi, lummel; **a few –s of furniture**, 'n paar stukkies huisraad.
sticker, aanplakker; aanhouer.
stickiness, taaiheid, klewerigheid.
sticking-plaster, hegpleister.
stick-in-the-mud, remskoen, jandooi.
stickle-back, stekelbaars.
stickler, puntene(u)rige persoon; voorstander, yweraar; **a great – for precision**, erg gesteld op presiesheid.
stick-up, opstaande; – **collar**, opstaanboordjie, hoë (stywe) boordjie.
sticky, klewerig, taai; moeilik; onsimpatiek; hoogs onaangenaam.
stiff, styf, stram, onbuigsaam; moeilik, swaar; sterk; **a – examination**, 'n moeilike eksamen; **a – price**, 'n kwaai prys; **he met it with a – denial**, hy het dit ten ene male ontken; **a – hinge**, 'n stram skarnier; – **climb**, taamlik steil.
stiff, n. niksnuts.

stiffen, styf maak (word); stywe; koppig (onhandelbaar) word.
stiff-necked, hardnekkig, koppig.
stifle, v. (ver)stif, versmoor; onderdruk.
stifle, kniegewrig, lit.
stigma, brandmerk, skandvlek; stempel.
stigmatization, bestempeling, (die) brandmerk.
stigmatize, brandmerk, bestempel.
stile, trappie, oorklimtrap.
stiletto, stilet, dolkie.
still, a. stil; kalm; – **waters run deep**, stille water diepe grond; – **life**, stillewe; – **as the grave**, stil soos die graf; **as – as a mouse**, doodstil.
still, v. stil, stilmaak, kalmeer, bedaar.
still, adv. nog, nog altyd; nogtans.
still, n. distilleerketel; stilte; stilfoto.
stillborn, doodgebore.
still-room, stookkamer, distilleerkamer.
stilt, n. stelt; **on –s**, op stelte.
stilt, v. op stelte sit (loop).
stilted, op stelte; hoogdrawend.
stilt-walker, steltloper.
stimulant, a. prikkelend, opwekkend.
stimulant, n. opwekkende middel, prikkel, versterking, stimulans; alkohol.
stimulate, prikkel, aanspoor, opwek, aansit, stimuleer.
stimulation, prikkeling, aansporing.
stimulus, prikkel, aansporing, stimulus.
stimy, 'n blinder (gholf).
sting, v. steek, prik; brand; pyn (wroeging, leed) veroorsaak; ruk (met geld); **his conscience stung him**, sy gewete het hom gekwel.
sting, n. angel; steek; prikkel; knaging, wroeging; – **of hunger**, knaende honger; **the bowling has no – in it**, die boulwerk is maar slappies; **the air has a – in it**, die lug is skerp.
stinger, taai klap, seer hou.
stinginess, suinigheid, vrekkigheid.
stinging-nettle, brandnekel.
stingy, suinig, vrekkig, inhalig, gierig.
stink, v. stink, sleg ruik; – **somebody out of the house**, iemand deur 'n slegte ruik uit die huis dryf.
stink, n. stank.
stinkard, stinkerd; stinkdier.
stinkball, stinkbom.
stinker, stinkerd; stinkdier; stinkstok; nare vent; 'n duiwel (vraestel).
stinkwhoop, stinkhout.
stint, v. beperk; suinig (spaarsaam) wees, skrap uitdeel, afskeep; – **oneself**, jouself te kort doen.
stint, n. karigheid, suinigheid; bekrimping; deel, rantsoen; **without –**, volop, mild, rojaal.
stipend, besoldiging, loon, salaris.
stipendiary, a. besoldig, loontrekkend.
stipendiary, n. gesalarieerde.
stipulate, stipuleer, bepaal, vasstel.
stipulation, stipulasie, bepaling.
stir, v. roer, verroer, beweeg; omroer, in beweging bring; **without –ring a foot**, sonder om 'n voet te verroer; **the people are not –ring yet**, die mense is nog nie op nie; – **your stumps**, jou lyf roer, jou knieë dra; – **your tea**, jou tee omroer; **a –ring life**, 'n veelbewoë (druk) lewe; **it –red my blood**, dit het my bloed laat kook, dit het die bloed vinniger deur my are laat stroom; – **somebody's wrath**, iemand boos maak; **not a breath is –ring**, daar trek nie 'n luggie nie; **–ring music**, aangrypende musiek; – **up**, omroer; aanhits, aanspoor, oprui; verwek; – **up discontent**, ontevredenheid verwek; – **up curiosity**, nuuskierigheid

gaande maak; **he wants –ring up**, hy moet wakker geskud word.
stir, n. beweging, opskudding, opgewondenheid, drukte, gewoel; **there was not a –**, dit was doodstil.
stirrup, stiebeuel.
stirrup-cup, afskeidsglasie.
stirrup-iron, stiebeuel.
stirrup-strap, **stirrup-leather**, stiegriem.
stitch, n. steek; **a – in time saves nine**, betyds keer is 'n goeie geweer; **he has not a dry – on him**, hy het nie 'n droë draad aan sy lyf nie; **drop a –**, 'n steek laat val; – **in the side**, steek in die sy.
stitch, v. naai, stik; – **up**, toenaai.
stiver, stuiwer, sent, duit.
stoat, hermelyn.
stock, n. stomp, stam; steel, handvatsel; geslag, ras, familie; vee(stapel), stok; voorraad, kapitaal; effekte; – **of an anvil**, voetstuk van 'n aambeeld; **lock**, – **and barrel**, romp en stomp, met wortel en tak; **live –**, lewende hawe; **in –**, in voorraad, voorhande; **take –**, die voorraad opneem; inventaris opmaak; **take – of somebody**, iemand noukeurig beskou; **–s**, aandele, effekte; violette, somerviolliere.
stock, a. oud; **a – joke**, 'n ou grap.
stock, v. in voorraad hou, in voorraad hê, voorsien van, die nodige aankoop; **we do not – boots**, ons hou nie stewels in voorraad nie; – **his farm**, sy plaas van vee voorsien („stok").
stockade, verskansing, skanspale.
stock-breeder, veeteler.
stockbroker, effektemakelaar.
Stock Exchange, (effekte)beurs.
stockfish, stokvis.
Stockholm, Stockholm; – **tar**, skoonteer.
stockinet(te), stokkinet.
stocking, kous.
stock-in-trade, voorraad; gereedskap.
stockist, leweransier.
stockjobber, effektehandelaar.
stockjobbing, spekulasie in effekte.
stock-market, veemark; effektemark.
stock-pile, n. voorraadstapel.
stock-pile, v. voorrade stapel.
stock-still, doodstil, botstil, stokstil.
stock-taking, voorraadopname; – **sale**, inventarisuitverkoop.
stock-whip, karwats, plak.
stockyard, veekraal; slagkraal.
stocky, kort en dik, geset.
stodge, n. swaar kos.
stodge, v. gulsig eet, inprop, wegslaan.
stodgy, swaar; tjokvol, oorlaai.
stoep, stoep.
stoic, n. stoïsyn.
stoic, a. stoïsyns.
stoicism, stoïsynse leer.
stoke, stook.
stoke-hole, stookgat.
stoker, stoker.
stole, n. mantel, stool; lang bont.
stolid, flegmaties, ongevoelig, bot.
stolidity, botheid; koppigheid.
stolon, uitloper, spruit.
stomach, n. maag, pens (van diere); eetlus; neiging, lus.
stomach, v. sluk; **he could not – that**, hy kon dit nie sluk (verkrop) nie.
stomach-ache, maagpyn.
stomachic, a. maag- . . ., spysverterings- . . .
stomachic, n. maagmiddel.
stone, n. klip, steen; pit; haelsteen; „stone" (ge-

wigsmaat: 14 pond); **leave no – unturned,** hemel en aarde beweeg, niks onbeproef laat nie.
stone, v. stenig; pitte uithaal; straat.
stone, a. klip- . . ., steen- . . .
stone-blind, stokblind.
stone-broke, platsak, boomskraap.
stone-coal, antrasiet.
stone-dead, morsdood.
stone-deaf, stokdoof.
stone-fruit, pitvrugte.
stone-mason, messelaar, steenwerker.
stone-pit, klipgat. steengroef.
stone-work, messelwerk.
stony, klipperig: klip- . . .; ongevoelig.
stooge, gek; skyf (van komediant); verteenwoordiger, handlanger.
stool, n. stoeltjie; ontlasting; stoel; **go to –,** stoelgang doen, jou ontlas.
stool, v. stoel.
stool-pigeon, lokvoël, lokduif.
stoop, v. buk, vooroorbuig, krom loop, vooroor loop; jou verlaag.
stoop, n. krom houding; **he has a bad –,** hy loop erg krom.
stop, v. stop, toestop; stelp; vul; belet, verhinder, 'n einde maak aan; keer; laat stilstaan; stopsit; inhou, terughou; ophou; stilhou, gaan staan; bly; – **work,** staak, ophou werk; – **a hole,** 'n gat toestop; – **a tooth,** 'n tand stop (vul); – **a wound,** die bloed stelp; – **a horse,** 'n perd keer; – **short,** skielik ophou (vassteek); **do – that noise,** hou tog op raas; **my watch has –ped,** my horlosie het gaan staan; **I shall – at home,** ek sal tuis bly; – **him from doing it,** hom belet om dit te doen; **the matter won't – there,** daarmee is die saak nog nie klaar nie; – **over,** oorbly.
stop, n. end; stilstand; halte; leesteken; klep, register (van 'n orrel); klapper, ontploffingsgeluid; **put a – to,** 'n end aan maak; **bring to a –,** tot stilstand bring; **full –,** punt; **come to a full –,** heeltemal ophou; **without a –,** sonder ophou, sonder om stil te hou.
stopcock, afsluitkraan.
stop-gap, stoplap, noodhulp.
stoppage, (die) stop, (die) ophou; stilstand, staking; skorsing.
stopper, prop.
stopple, prop.
stop-press (news), nagekome berigte, laat berigte.
stop-watch, chronometer, stophorlosie.
storage, pakhuisgeld, pakhuishuur, berglloon, bewaargeld; berging; bêreplek; **cold –,** koelkamers, koelbewaring.
store, n. voorraad, oorvloed; pakhuis, winkel; **you never know what the future has in –,** jy weet nooit wat die toekoms sal oplewer nie; **in –,** in voorraad; **set – by,** op prys stel, waarde heg aan.
store, v. bêre, opbewaar, wegpak (in 'n pakhuis); opgaar, insamel, binnehaal; voorsien van hou, bevat; – **up something in your heart,** iets in jou hart bewaar.
storehouse, pakhuis, loods, voorraadskuur; skatkamer.
storekeeper, winkelier.
store-room, pakkamer, bêreplek.
storey, verdieping; **be a little wrong in the upper –,** nie al die varkies in die hok hê nie; **first –,** eerste verdieping.
storied, beroemd, besonge, in die geskiedenis beskrywe.
storied, met verdiepinge.
stork, ooievaar; groot sprinkaanvoël.

storm, n. storm, orkaan, stortbui; aanval, bestorming; **by –,** stormenderhand; – **and stress,** storm en drang; **a – of applause,** dawerende toejuiging.
storm, v. storm, woed, hard waai; tier, raas; storm, stormja, stormloop.
storm-beaten, deur storm geteister(d).
storm-tossed. deur die storm geteister.
stormy, stormagtig, ontstuimig, hewig.
story, geskiedenis, storie, verhaal, vertelling, sprokie; **to make a long – short,** om kort te gaan, in een woord; **the –** goes, dit word gesê (vertel); **according to his own –,** volgens sy eie verhaal; **short –,** kortverhaal; **serial –,** vervolgstorie; **don't tell stories,** moenie jok nie.
story-book, storieboek.
story-teller, verteller; leuenaar.
stout, a. kragtig, sterk, dapper; geset, fris, swaarlywig.
stout, n. swartbier, stout.
stout-hearted, dapper, kloekmoedig.
stoutish, taamlik geset, fris.
stove, n. stoof.
stow, bêre, wegsit.
stowage, bêreplek; pakhuisgeld.
stowaway, blinde passasier, verstekeling.
straddle, wydsbeen staan (loop); – **a target,** 'n doelwit invurk.
straggle, afdwaal, swerwe, verdwaal; versprei raak, streep-streep loop.
straggler, verdwaalde, agterblyer, swerwer; uitloper, loot, spruit.
straggling, versprei, verstrooi.
straight, a. reguit; opreg, eerlik, openhartig; glad; in orde; **he gave us a – talk,** hy het openhartig met ons gepraat; **put things –,** sake in orde bring; – **thinking,** logies (helder) dink; – **flush,** vyf volgkaarte in een kleur (kaartspel); – **eight,** agt-in-lyn; **kept a – face,** het ernstig gebly.
straight, adv. reguit, onmiddellik, direk; – **from Paris,** direk van Parys af; – **out,** ronduit; – **away,** onmiddellik, dadelik; – **off,** dadelik; – **in the eyes,** reg in die oë.
straight, n. reguit stuk; volgkaart (kaartspel); pylvak (atletiek); **out of the –,** nie in 'n lyn nie.
straighten, reguit maak; reg trek, glad stryk; in orde bring, opknap.
straightforward, eerlik, padlangs, rondborstig, openhartig.
strain, v. trek, rek, span; oorspan, ooreis, forseer; verrek; filtreer, deurgooi; – **every nerve,** alle kragte inspan; – **one's eyes,** jou oë ooreis; – **the voice,** die stem forseer; – **the ears,** die ore spits; **you – the point,** jy gaan te ver, jy oordrywe; **a –ed laugh,** gedwonge laggie; –ed **his leg,** sy been verrek; **the rowers – at the oar,** die roeiers beur aan die roeirieme; – **under a heavy load,** onder 'n swaar las swoeg.
strain, n. inspanning, sterk poging, kragtige strewe; oorspanning; spanning, druk; verreking; trant, manier, toon; wysie; neiging, karaktertrek; familie, ras; **the – of modern life,** die druk van die hedendaagse lewe; **the – on my attention was too great,** dit het te veel aandag van my geverg; **all his senses were on the –,** al sy sintuie was tot die uiterste gespan; **he comes of a good –,** hy is van goeie familie; **in another, the same –,** in 'n ander, dieselfde trant.
strained, gespan(ne); onnatuurlik, gemaak, geforseer.
strainer, suigdoek, deurgooidoek; siffie.
strait, a. nou, eng; beperk; bekrompe.

strait, n. seestraat; –s, moeilikheid.
straiten, beperk; in die moeilikheid bring; –ed circumstances, armoedige omstandighede; be –ed for, gebrek hê aan, sleg voorsien wees van.
strait-jacket, dwangbuis.
strait-laced, streng, nougeset, bekrompe.
stramineous, strooikleurig, strooiagtig.
strand, n. strand, kus.
strand, v. strand; –ed, gestrand; in die moeilikheid; we were –ed, ons kon nie verder nie, ons was in die knyp.
strand, n. string, draad.
strange, vreemd, onbekend; eienaardig, sonderling, buitengewoon, snaaks; I feel –, ek voel nie lekker nie, ek voel naar; ek voel ontuis; it feels –, dit is vreemd; he is quite – here, hy is hier heeltemal vreemd (onbekend); I am – to the work, die werk is vir my vreemd.
stranger, vreemdeling, vreemde, onbekende; uitlander; you are quite a –, 'n mens sien jou byna nooit; he is a – to fear, hy ken geen vrees nie.
strangle, (ver)wurg; onderdruk.
strangles, droes; nuwesiekte.
strangulate, vasbind, toebind; (ver)wurg.
strangulation, wurging; (die) vasbind.
strap, n. riem, platriem; gord; aansitriem, skeerriem; lis.
strap, v. vasgord, vasmaak, vasbind met 'n riem; aansit, skerp maak; (met 'n riem) slaan, afransel, uitlooi.
strap-oil, streepsuiker, sieps-en-braaiboud.
strapping, groot, sterk, frisgebou.
strata, sien **stratum**.
stratagem, krygslis, slim plan (streek).
strategic, strategies; krygskundig.
strategist, krygskundige, strateeg.
strategy, strategie, krygskuns.
stratification, stratifikasie, laagvorming.
stratify, in lae op mekaar lê, lae vorm.
stratigraphy, stratigrafie.
stratosphere, stratosfeer.
stratum, laag, stratum.
stratus, wolklaag, wolkbank, stratus.
straw, n. strooi; strooitjie; kleinigheid, nietigheid; draw –s, lootjies trek; catch at a –, aan 'n strooihalm vasklem; don't care a –, kan my nie die minste skeel nie; not worth a –, nie 'n duit werd nie; man of –, strooipop; – vote, steekproefstem.
straw, a. van strooi, strooi.
strawberry, aarbei.
straw-coloured, strooikleurig.
straw-hat, strooihoed.
strawy, strooi- . . ., stooierig.
stray, v. dwaal, afdwaal, verdwaal, swerwe, wegloop, wegraak.
stray, n. verdwaalde dier (kind).
stray, a. afgedwaal, verdwaal, verlore; los, sporadies; – thoughts, los gedagtes; – visitors, toevallige kuiergaste.
streak, n. streep; strook; like a – (of lightning), soos blits, bliksemsnel; a – of lightning, weerligstraal; a – of humour, 'n tikkie humor.
streak, v. streep, merk; (voort)snel.
streaked, gestreep.
streaky, gestreep, vol strepe.
stream, n. stroom; stroming; rivier, spruit; up –, stroom-op, teen die stroom (op); down –, stroom-af, met die stroom saam; go with the –, met die stroom saamgaan.
stream, v. stroom, vloei, loop; wapper.
stream-anchor, werpanker.
streamer, wimpel, vlag; lint, papierlint.
streamlet, stroompie.
street, n. straat; on the –s, op straat; not in the same –, kom daar nie naby nie, nie van dieselfde kaliber nie.
street-arab, straatkind.
street-door, voordeur.
street-walker, straatloper; straatvlinder.
strength, sterkte, krag, mag; on the – of, kragtens. op grond van, na aanleiding van; in full –, met man en mag; voltallig.
strengthen, versterk, sterk maak.
strenuous, energiek, wakker, ywerig, onvermoeid, kragtig; swaar.
streptomycin, streptomisine (-ien).
stress, n. drang; inspanning; spanning; klem, nadruk; klemtoon, aksent; under – of weather, as gevolg van ongunstige weer; under – of poverty, deur armoede (daartoe) genoodsaak; lay – on, nadruk lê op.
stress, v. beklem, nadruk lê op, klem lê op, aksentueer.
stretch, v. rek, trek; uitrek; tyd lank in die tronk; uitstrek, uitsteek; geweld aandoen, oordrywe; – one's legs, jou bene rek, jou litte losmaak; – the truth, die waarheid geweld aandoen, oordrywe; you are –ing your powers, jy gaan jou bevoegdheid te buite; don't – the point, moenie oordrywe nie; – out, die treë rek; uitstrek; (die hand) uitsteek.
stretch, n. rek; spanning; uitgestrektheid; ten hours at a –, tien uur sonder ophou; a long – of road, 'n lang ent pad.
stretcher, rekker; draagbaar; kateltjie.
strew, strooi, bestrooi, besaai.
stria, strepie, groefie, skrapie.
strict, streng, stip, presies, strik, noukeurig; eng; keep a – watch, goed uitkyk; streng toesig hou; in the – sense, in die enge betekenis.
stricture, afkeuring, aanmerking, ongunstige kritiek; saamtrekking, vernouing.
stride, v. lang treë gee, stap.
stride, n. stap, skrede, tree; with rapid –s, met rasse skrede; if he gets into his –, as hy eers op stryk kom.
strident, skerp, krassend, deurdringend.
strife, stryd, twis, onenigheid, tweedrag.
strike, v. slaan; stoot, stamp, bots; tref; trek; (die vlag) stryk; lyk, skyn, (werk) staak; struck by lightning, deur weerlig getref; – home, 'n kopskoot gee, raakslaan; stricken in years, hoogbejaard; a stricken heart, 'n gebroke hart; – coins, munte slaan; – a bargain, 'n slag slaan; – a match, a light, vuurhoutjie trek; the clock –s, die horlosie slaan; the hour has struck, die horlosie het geslaan; die uur het aangebreek; – me dead!, mag ek doodval!; it struck me, dit het my getref; it –s me, dit kom my voor; an idea struck him, 'n gedagte het hom te binne geskiet; how does it – you?, wat dink jy daarvan?; – one's flag, die vlag stryk; – root, wortelskiet; – one blind, iemand met blindheid slaan; the tallest man I've yet struck, die langste man wat ek nog ooit teëgekom het; – at the root, die wortel raak; – back, terugslaan; – down, plat slaan, teen die grond slaan; – terror into the heart, die hart met skrik vervul; struck with terror, deur skrik bevang; – into, ('n pad) inslaan; na binne slaan; – off, afkap, afslaan; skrap; afdruk; – off a name, 'n naam skrap; – out a name, 'n naam skrap; – up, begin speel; – upon an idea, op 'n gedagte kom; the light –s upon it, die lig val daarop.
strike, n. (werk)staking; vonds; byt (vis); slag; aanslag; aanvat; they are on –, hulle het gestaak.
strike-a-light, vuurslag.

striker, staker.
striking, treffend, opvallend.
string, n. lyn, tou, riempie; snaar; snoer, string; reeks, streep; **pull the –s**, die drade trek; **touch a –**, 'n snaar aanroer; **harp on one –**, altyd op dieselfde aambeeld slaan; **the –s**, die snaarinstrumente; **for –s**, vir strykorkes; **a – of beads**, 'n kralesnoer.
string, v. (in)rye; snare insit; (snare) span; afhark, afhaar, afdraad (van boontjies); **he was strung up to do the deed**, hy was oorgehaal om die daad te pleeg; **a highly strung person**, 'n uiters senuweeagtige persoon, iemand met oorspanne senuwees.
string-band, strykorkes.
stringed, snaar– ..., besnaar; **– instrument**, snaarinstrument.
stringency, strengheid, stiptheid; skaarste.
stringent, streng, bindend, nadruklik, strik; deur geldskaarste belemmer.
stringy, draderig, seningrig, touerig.
strip, v. uittrek (van klere); afstroop, kaal maak; uitmelk, plunder, berowe (van); **–ped**, poedelnakend; **– off**, afruk, afskeur, afstroop.
strip, n. strook, streep; **(comic) –**, prentverhaal.
stripe, streep; slag, striem; **get one's –s**, jou strepe kry, verhoging kry.
striped, gestreep, streep– ...
stripling, opgeskote seun.
stripy, met strepe, gestreep.
strive, strewe, trag, poog; worstel, sukkel; stry; wedywer; **– against temptation**, teen die versoeking stry.
stroke, n. hou, slag; aanval (van siekte); haal, streep, trek; **a – of apoplexy**, 'n aanval van beroerte; **finishing –**, die genadeslag; **give the finishing –s**, afwerk; **not a – of work**, nie 'n steek werk nie; **one – of the pen**, een haal van die pen; **on the – of six**, op die kop sesuur, klokslag sesuur; **row –**, die slag aangee, slag roei; **killed by a – of lightning**, deur die blits (weer) doodgeslaan; **two- – motor**, tweeslagmotor.
stroke, v. die slag aangee, slag roei.
stroke, v. streel, liefkoos, stryk.
stroke, n. liefkosing, streling.
stroll, v. loop, kuier, slenter, drentel.
stroll, n. wandeling; **go for, take a –**, 'n entjie gaan loop.
strong, sterk, kragtig; hewig, geweldig; kras; **by the – arm**, met geweld; **how many are you –?**, hoeveel (man) is julle?; **he used – language**, hy het hom kras uitgedruk; **give – support to**, kragtig ondersteun; **he is still going –**, hy hou nog een stryk deur aan.
strong-box, brandkas.
stronghold, sterkte, vesting.
strong-minded, manlik, beslis, sterk.
strong-room, kluis, brandkamer.
strontium, strontium.
strop, n. skeerriem, slypriem.
strop, v. aansit, slyp, skerp maak.
strophe, strofe.
strophic, strofies.
structural, wat die bou betref, bou– ...
structure, bou, struktuur; gebou.
struggle, v. worstel, spartel, sukkel; **– and kick**, spartel en skop; **he –d to control his feelings**, hy het sy gevoelens met moeite onderdruk; **– with difficulties**, met moeilikhede te kampe hê; **– along**, aansukkel.
struggle, n. worsteling, stryd, geveg.
strum, v. kras, sae, hamer, tjingel.
strum, n. gekras, getjingel.
struma, kliergeswel.

strumous, klieragtig, klier– ...
strumpet, hoer, slet.
strut, n. deftige stap.
strut, v. trots en deftig stap, pronk.
strut, n. & v. stut.
strychnia, strychnine, strignien, wolwegif.
stub, n. stomp(ie), entjie; teenblad; **– axle**, stomp as.
stub, v. uitkap, uitgrawe, skoon kap.
stubble, stoppels.
stubble-field, stoppelland.
stubbly, stoppel– ..., stoppelagtig.
stubborn, hardnekkig, koppig.
stubby, stomp, dik.
stucco, v. met stukadoorskalk pleister.
stuck-up, verwaand, hoogmoedig, trots.
stud, n. grootkopspyker; knop; nael; hempsknopie, halsknopie, boordjieknopie; paal, stut.
stud, v. spykers inslaan; met knoppies versier; **–ded with stars**, met sterre besaai.
stud, n. stoetery.
stud-book, stamboek.
student, student, leerling; navorser.
stud-farm, stoetery.
stud-horse, dekhings; volbloedperd.
studied, opsetlik, moedswillig; bestudeer(d), gestudeer(d).
studio, ateljee; klanksaal (radio); werkvertrek.
studious, vlytig, ywerig, naarstig, leergierig, fluks; opsetlik; **be – of**, strewe na.
stud-ram, stoetram.
study, n. studie; studeerkamer; skets, oefening; **in a brown –**, in diep gepeins; **make a – of**, 'n studie maak van; **his face was a –**, dit was die moeite werd om sy gesig te sien; **a – of a head**, 'n studiekop; **his studies are exquisite**, sy sketstekening is pragtig.
study, v. studeer, bestudeer; strewe na; rekening hou met, in aanmerking neem; **– law**, in die regte studeer; **– up**, blok; **– his own interests**, aan sy eie belange dink; **– out**, uitvors, naspeur; **– the convenience of others**, aan die gegrief van ander mense dink.
stuff, n. stof, goed, materiaal; **– and nonsense**, alles pure kaf; **what – he writes**, skrywe hy nie bog nie!; **he has good – in him**, daar steek heelwat in hom; **this is good –**, dit is goeie goed; **hot –!**, mooi so! ryperd!
stuff, v. stop, opstop, volstop, volprop; voorlieg; **–ed birds**, opgestopte voëls; **a head –ed with facts**, 'n kop vol feite geprop; **– one's ears with wool**, wol in die ore stop; **–ed turkey**, gestopte kalkoen; **–ed veal**, gelardeerde kalfsvleis; **you can't – me**, jy kan my nie alles wysmaak nie.
stuffing, vulsel; opstopsel.
stuffy, bedompig, benoud.
stultify, belaglik maak; tot niet maak; kragteloos maak.
stum, mos, ongegiste druiwesop.
stumble, v. struikel, strompel; flaters maak; **– across upon somebody**, iemand op die lyf loop; **– along** voortstrompel.
stumple, n. struikel(ing).
stumbling-block, struikelblok, hinderpaal.
stump, n. stomp, stompie; paaltjie (krieket).
stump, v. swaar stap, strompel; (paaltjie) stamp, uitstamp (krieket); doesel; **be –ed**, verleë wees, in die moeilikheid wees; **this question has –ed me**, hierdie vraag is bokant my vuurmaakplek; **– up**, opdok.
stump-oratory, verkiesingswelsprekendheid.
stumpy, stomp, kort, dik, geset.
stun, verdoof; dronkslaan, oorbluf; bedwelm, bewusteloos maak.

stunner, geweldige slag, doodhou.
stunning, bedwelmend; uitstekend.
stunt, v. die groei belemmer, teëhou, knot.
stunt, n. kordaatstuk, kaskenade, (uithaler)-streek; gier, streek.
stunted, klein dwergagtig, verpot.
stunt-flying, kunsvlieëry.
stupe, n. warm kompres.
stupe, v. warm kompresse opsit.
stupefaction, bedwelming, verdowing.
stupefactive, bedwelmend, verdowend.
stupefier, verdowingsmiddel.
stupefy, bedwelm, verdoof; dronkslaan, bot (suf) maak, gevoelloos maak.
stupendous, ontsaglik, verbasend, ontsettend, kolossaal.
stupid, a. dom, onnosel, stom, bot.
stupid, n. domkop, esel, pampoenkop.
stupidity, domheid, onnoselheid.
stupor, bedwelming, gevoelloosheid, verdowing; verbasing.
sturdy, a. kragtig, stoer, fors, sterk.
sturdy, n. dronksiekte, draaisiekte.
sturgeon, steur.
stutter, v. hakkel, stotter, stamel.
stutter, n. gehakkel, gestotter; **he has a bad –,** hy hakkel erg.
stutterer, hakkelaar, stotteraar.
sty, varkhok.
sty, stye, n. karkatjie.
style, n. skryfstif; styl; skryfwyse, skryftrant, wyse, manier; mode; naam, titel; soort; **in grand –,** op grootse manier, skitterend; **what – of house do you require,** hoedanige huis wil jy hê?; **they do things in –,** hulle doen alles volgens die mode; wat hulle doen, moet alles in die haak wees.
style, v. betitel, bestempel, noem.
style, n. styl (in botanie); wys(t)erplaat.
stylet, stilet, priem.
stylish, deftig, nuwerwets, fyn, na die mode, in die haak, agtermekaar.
stylist, stillis.
stylistic, stilisties.
stylograph, stilograaf(pen).
styptic, bloedstelpend, bloedstoppend.
Styx, Styx.
suable, vervolgbaar.
suasion, oorreding.
suave, vriendelik, sag, goed, lief; tegemoetkomend, beleef, paaiend.
suavity, vriendelikheid, sagtheid.
subacid, suuragtig.
subaltern, ondergeskikte.
subaquatic, onder die water.
subclass, onderafdeling.
subcommittee, onder-, subkomitee.
subconscious, halfbewus, onderbewus; **– mind,** onderbewussyn.
subcutaneous, onderhuids, onder die vel.
subdivide, onderverdeel.
subdivision, onderverdeling, onderafdeling.
subdue, ten onder bring, oorwin, onderwerp, onderdruk, beteuel; mak maak, tem; versag, temper.
subdued, stil, gelate, onderworpe, tevrede; getemper.
subeditor, subredakteur.
subereous, suberose, kurkagtig, kurk- . . .
subjacent, laer geleë, onderliggend.
subject, a. onderworpe; onderhorig; **a – province,** 'n onderhorige provinsie; **– to France,** onderhorig aan Frankryk; **– to the laws of nature,** onderworpe aan die natuurwette; **– to,** vatbaar vir; blootgestel aan, onderhewig aan; **– to**
ratification, onderworpe aan bekragtiging.
subject, n. onderdaan; onderwerp; vak; tema; voorwerp; ekheid; **– and predicate,** onderwerp en gesegde; **– and object,** subjek en objek (in metafisika); **– of discussion,** onderwerp van bespreking; **– of study,** leervak; **what is the – of the poem,** waaroor handel die gedig?; **– for dissection,** lyk, kadawer, liggaam.
subject, v. onderwerp, tot onderworpenheid dwing; **– to,** blootstel aan, laat ondergaan.
subjection, onderwerping; onderworpenheid.
subjectivity, subjektiwiteit.
subject-matter, onderwerp, stof.
subjoin, byvoeg, aanlas, toevoeg.
subjugate, onderwerp, ten onder bring.
subjugation, onderwerping.
subjunctive, n. aanvoegende wyse.
subjunctive, a. aanvoegend.
sublease, onderkontrak, onderhuur.
sublessee, onderhuurder.
sub-let, onderverhuur.
sublimate, v. sublimeer; veredel, verfyn.
sublimate, n. sublimaat.
sublimation, sublimering; veredeling.
sublime, a. subliem, hoog verhewe.
sublime, n. die sublieme, die verhewene.
sublime, v. sublimeer; louter, veredel.
sublimity, sublimiteit, verhewenheid.
sublunary, ondermaans, aards.
sub-machine-gun, handmasjiengeweer.
submarine, a. ondersee- . . ., ondersees.
submarine, n. duikboot, onderseeboot.
submerge, onder water sit, onderdompel, laat oorstroom.
submersion, onderdompeling, oorstroming.
submission, onderwerping; onderdanigheid, nederigheid; voorlegging.
submissive, onderworpe, onderdanig.
submit, (sig) onderwerp; voorlê, indien; beweer.
subordinate, a. ondergeskik; **– clause,** ondergeskikte sin, bysin.
subordinate, n. ondergeskikte.
subordinate, v. ondergeskik maak (aan).
subordination, ondergeskiktheid.
subpoena, n. dagvaarding.
subpoena, v. dagvaar.
subreption, verkryging deur valse voorwendsels, aftroggeling.
subscribe, onderteken; onderskrywe; bydra; inteken; **I cannot – to that,** dit kan ek nie onderskrywe nie, daarmee kan ek nie saamstem nie; **– to a fund,** tot 'n fonds bydra; **– to a newspaper,** op 'n koerant inteken.
subscriber, intekenaar; ondertekenaar.
subscription, subskripsiegeld, intekengeld; intekening; bydrae, kontribusie.
subsequence, opvolging.
subsequent, daaropvolgende, volgende; **– to that,** daarna.
subsequently, daarna, naderhand.
subserve, dien, bevorderlik wees.
subservience, bevorderlikheid, dienstigheid, onderdanigheid, diensbaarheid.
subservient, dienstig, behulpsaam; diensbaar, onderdanig, kruiperig.
subside, sak, sink; insak, wegsak; bedaar.
subsidence, sak(king); bedaring.
subsidiary, a. hulp- . . ., bykomend; **– troops,** hulptroepe.
subsidiary, n. hulp, plaasvervanger; filiaalmaatskappy.
subsidize, subsidieer, subsidie gee (aan), (geldelike) hulp verleen, ondersteun.
subsidy, subsidie, geldelike steun, ondersteuning, onderstandsgeld.

subsist, bestaan, lewe, aan die lewe bly.
subsistence, bestaan, broodwinning; – **allowance**, onderhoudstoelae.
subsoil, onderlaag, ondergrond.
substance, stof; selfstandigheid; kwintessens, pit, kern; wese; hoofbestanddeel; inhoud; werklikheid; vermoë; substansie; **agree in** –, in hoofsaak saamstem; **give the** – **of**, die inhoud gee van; **the** – **of religion**, die wese van die godsdiens; **a man of** –, 'n vermoënde man.
substantial, werklik, wesenlik; belangrik; aansienlik; vas, sterk, solied; kragtig, voedsaam; vermoënd, welgesteld.
substantiality, werklikheid, wesenlikheid; vastheid, krag; aansienlikheid.
substantiate, bewys, bevestig, staaf.
substantive, a. selfstandig; onafhanklik; – **rank**, effektiewe rang.
substantive, n. substantief, selfstandige naamwoord.
substitute, n. plaasvervanger, substituut.
substitute, v. in die plek stel, vervang.
substitution, (plaas)vervanging.
substratum, onderlaag; basis.
substructure, fondamant, onderbou.
subtenant, onderhuurder.
subtend, onderspan, teenoorstaan.
subterfuge, uitvlug, voorwendsel.
subterranean, onderaards.
subtitle, ondertitel; byskrif (in rolprent).
subtle, subtiel, fyn, teer; skerp; spitsvondig; slu, slim, geslepe, listig.
subtlety, fynheid; spitsvondigheid; listigheid, geslepenheid, sluheid; subtiliteit.
subtract, aftrek, verminder (met).
subtraction, aftrekking, vermindering.
subtropic(al), subtropies.
suburb, voorstad.
suburban, voorstedelik.
subvention, subsidie, onderstand.
subversion, omverwerping.
subvert, omverwerp, omvergooi, omkeer.
subway, tonnel, onderaardse deurgang, duikweg.
succedaneum, plaasvervanger; noodhulp.
succeed, opvolg; volg op; slaag, geluk, sukses hê; **day** –**s day**, een dag volg op die ander; **he** –**ed in achieving his aim**, hy het daarin geslaag (dit het hom geluk) om sy doel te bereik.
success, sukses, gunstige uitslag, welslae, voorspoed; **inquired without** –, het tevergeefs navraag gedoen; **nothing succeeds like** –, hoe meer jy het, hoe meer sal jy kry; welslae boesem vertroue in; **the** – **of the undertaking**, die welslae van die onderneming.
successful, suksesvol, voorspoedig, gelukkig, geslaag.
succession, opvolging, suksessie, troonopvolging; reeks, opeenvolging; **in** –, na mekaar; **a** – **of disasters**, 'n reeks rampe; **War of the Spanish S**–, die Spaanse Suksessie-oorlog.
successive, agtereenvolgend, opeenvolgend, na mekaar.
successor, opvolger.
succinct, kort, beknop, bondig, pittig.
succour, v. help, te hulp kom, steun.
succour, n. hulp, steun, bystand.
succulence, sappigheid, sopperigheid.
succulent, sappig, sopperig, sapryk; – **plants**, sappige plante, vetplante.
succumb, beswyk; swig.
such, a. sodanig, sulke, so; van so 'n aard; **don't be in** – **a hurry**, moenie so haastig wees nie; – **big ones**, sulke grotes; **it was** – **an enjoyable conversation**, dit was tog so 'n aangename gesprek; – **and** – **a person**, die en die, die en daardie; – **and** – **a thing**, dit en dat.
such, pron. sulkes, sulke mense (dinge); – **was not my intention**, dit was nie my bedoeling nie; **as** –, sodanig; **none** –, sonder gelyke.
suck, v. suig, uitsuig; insuig; drink; suip; – **in**, opsuig, insuig, opslurp.
suck, n. (die) suig, gesuig; **give** –, laat drink.
sucker, suier; loot, suier (van plante); pypkan; suigvis; suiglekker; dwaas.
sucking, sui(g)end, suig- . . .
sucking-disk, suigorgaan.
sucking-pig, speenvark.
suckle, laat drink, soog.
suckling, suigeling.
sucrose, rietsuiker.
suction, suiging, (die) suig.
suction-pump, suigpomp.
sudation, sweet.
sudatorium, warm lugbad, sweetbad.
sudatory, a. swetend, sweet- . . .
sudatory, n. sweetmiddel; sweetbad.
sudden, skie(r)lik, plotseling, onverwags; **of a** –, eensklaps, skie(r)lik; – **death**, skielike dood; onmiddellike beslissing.
sudorific, n. sweetmiddel.
sudorific, a. sweet- . . .
suds, seepsop, seepwater, seepskuim.
sue, (geregtelik) vervolg, eis, dagvaar, aanskrywe; versoek om, ding na (die hand); – **for damages**, dagvaar vir skadevergoeding, 'n eis tot skadevergoeding instel teen.
suede, suède.
suer, eiser.
suet, niervet.
suffer, ly; uithou, dra; (straf) ondergaan, boet; gedoog, toelaat, duld; – **defeat**, neerlaag ly; – **punishment**, straf ondergaan; **the engine** –**ed severely**, die lokomotief is erg beskadig; **he will** – **for it**, hy sal daarvoor boet; – **them to come**, laat hulle kom.
sufferable, toelaatbaar, te duld.
sufferance, toelating, toestemming; **on** –, nog geduld (gedoog).
sufferer, lyer; slagoffer.
suffering, a. lydend.
suffering(s), n. lyding.
suffice, voldoende wees, genoeg wees; – **it to say that**, dit is voldoende om te sê dat.
sufficiency, genoeg, voldoende hoeveelheid; genoegsaamheid; bekwaamheid.
sufficient, a. genoeg, genoegsaam, voldoende; – **unto the day is the evil thereof**, elke dag het genoeg aan sy eie kwaad.
sufficient, n. genoeg.
suffix, n. agtervoegsel, suffiks.
suffix, v. agtervoeg.
suffocate, (ver)stik, versmoor.
suffocation, verstikking.
suffrage, stemreg; stem; goedkeuring; **woman** –, vrouestemreg.
suffragette, stemregvrou.
suffragist, voorstander van uitbreiding van die stemreg.
suffuse, sprei oor, oordek; kleur; loop oor, stroom oor.
suffusion, kleur, blos, tint; verspreiding.
sugar, n. suiker; mooipraatjies; – **daddy**, suikeroom.
sugar, v. versuiker, suiker bygooi.
sugar-basin, suikerpot.
sugar-bean, suikerboontjie.
sugar-bird, suikerbekkie, jangroentjie.
sugar-candy, suikerklontjies, kandysuiker.
sugar-cane, suikerriet.

sugar-loaf, suikerbrood.
sugar-mill, suikerfabriek.
sugar-plantation, suikerplantasie.
sugar-refinery, suikerraffinadery, witsuikerfabriek.
sugar-tongs, suikertangetjie.
sugary, suikeragtig, suikerig, suiker-...
suggest, aan die hand gee, voorstel, aanraai; opper; suggereer; op die gedagte bring; **the thought –ed itself to me,** die gedagte het by my opgekom.
suggestion, suggestie, ingewing; wenk, raad, plan, voorstel.
suggestive, suggestief; suggererend; **be – of,** laat dink aan.
suicidal, selfmoord-...., noodlottig.
suicide, selfmoord; selfmoordenaar; **commit –,** selfmoord pleeg.
suit, n. regsgeding, proses; versoek (huweliksaansoek); kleur (in kaartspel); pak (klere); uitrusting, stel; **press one's –,** met aandrang vra (versoek).
suit, v. pas; voeg; geskik wees; voldoen, bevredig; **– the action to the word,** die daad by die woord voeg; **he is not –ed for an engineer,** hy is nie aangelê vir ingenieur nie, hy deug nie as ingenieur nie; **– yourself,** net soos jy wil, soos jy verkies; **that date will –,** dit is 'n geskikte datum; **red does not – her complexion,** rooi pas nie by haar gelaatskleur nie; **the part –s him admirably,** hy is uitgeknip vir daardie rol; **when it –s you,** wanneer dit vir u (jou) pas (gerieflik, geleë is); **that –s me down to the ground,** dit is net so na my sin, dit kon my nie beter pas nie.
suitability, geskiktheid; gepastheid.
suitable, geskik, geleë; gepas, behoorlik.
suitcase, handkoffer, valies.
suite, gevolg; stel, reeks; **– of furniture,** meublement; **a – of rooms,** 'n stel kamers, 'n suite.
suitor, versoeker; eiser; vryer.
sulfa, see **sulpha.**
sulk, v. pruil, mok, nukkerig wees.
sulk(s), n. nukkerigheid; **in the –s,** nukkerig, dikmond, pruilend.
sulky, a. nukkerig, pruilerig, nors.
sullen, knorrig, stuurs, nors, suur, ongesellig, somber; kwaaikoppig.
sully, besmet, besoedel, bevlek.
sulpha, sulfa; – drug, sulfamiddel.
sulphate, sulfaat, swawelsuursout.
sulphide, sulfide.
sulphur, n. swa(w)el, sulfer; **flowers of –,** blom van swa(w)el.
sulphur, v. swa(w)el.
sulphureous, swa(w)el-....; swa(w)elagtig swa(w)elkleurig.
sulphuretted hydrogen, swa(w)elwaterstof.
sulphuric, swa(w)el-...; **– acid,** swa(w)elsuur.
sultan, sultan.
sultana, sultana(rosyntjie).
sultaness, sultane.
sultry, drukkend, bedompig.
sum, n. som; bedrag; totaal; **– total,** totaal; **in –,** kortweg gesê, om kort te gaan.
sum, v. optel; **– up,** optel; saamvat, opsom, resumeer.
summarily, beknop, kortweg, vlugtig; sonder pligpleginge, op staande voet.
summarize, opsom, (kort) saamvat.
summary, a. kort, beknop; kortaf, bot; **– dismissal,** ontslag op staande voet.
summary, n. opsomming, samevatting.
summer, somer.
summer, dwarsbalk, dwarsstuk.

summer-house, somerhuisie.
summersault, -set, see **somersault.**
summer-time, somer(tyd).
summery, someragtig, somer-...
summit, hoogste punt, top, toppunt; **– conference,** spitskonferensie.
summon, dagvaar; oproep, bymekaarroep, laat roep, ontbied; opeis; **– up courage,** moed bymekaarskraap.
summons, n. dagvaarding; oproep.
summons, v. dagvaar.
sumptuary, weelde-..., weeldebeperkend; **– laws,** weelde(beperkings)wette.
sumptuous, weelderig, kosbaar, duur.
sun, n. son; sonlig, sonskyn; **rise with the –,** douvoordag opstaan; **nothing new under the –,** niks nuuts onder die son nie; **mock –,** byson; **hold a candle to the –,** water in die see dra.
sun, v. in die son sit, staan, lê, ens.; aan die son blootstel; **– oneself,** in die son sit, (sig) koester (in die son).
sun-bath, sonbad.
sunbeam, sonstraal.
sun-blind, rolgordyn.
sun-bonnet, kappie.
sunburnt, (deur die son) verbrand.
Sunday, Sondag; **– best,** kisklere.
Sundayschool, Sondagskool.
sunder, skei, (ver)breek; afkap, afsny.
sun-dial, son(ne)wys(t)er.
sundown, sononder, sonsondergang.
sundowner, aandsopie, skemerkelkie.
sun-dried, in die son gedroog, droog; **– fruit,** droëvrugte.
sundries, allerhande klein dingetjies, diverse kleinigheidjies, ekstras.
sundry, verskillende, diverse, allerhande; **all and –,** elkeen en almal.
sunfish, sonvis.
sunflower, sonneblom.
sun-glow, sonkring.
sun-god, songod.
sunken, hol, ingeval; **– eyes,** (met) oë agter in die kop, hol oë.
sunless, sonder son, sonloos.
sunlight, sonlig.
sunlit, deur die son verlig, sonbestraal(d), sonnig.
sunny, sonnig; bly, vrolik, opgewek, opgeruimd; **the – side of a house,** die sonkant van die huis; **the – side of life,** die ligte kant van die lewe.
sunrise, sonsopgang, sonop.
sunset, sonsondergang, sononder.
sunshade, sambreel, sonskerm.
sunshine, sonskyn; mooi weer; **– roof,** skuifdak.
sun-spot, sonvlek.
sunstroke, sonsteek, sonstraal.
sun-worshipper, sonaanbidder.
sup, aandete gebruik, soepeer.
super, kostelik, heerlik, prima.
superable, oorkoomlik.
superabound, oorvloedig (volop) wees.
superabundance, groot oorvloed.
superabundant, oorvloedig.
superaddition, verdere byvoeging.
superannuate, pensioneer, op pensioen afdank.
superannuation, pensioen, pensioenering; **– fund,** pensioenfonds.
superb, pragtig, skitterend, voortreflik.
supercharge, aanwakker; aanja (motor); **–d engine,** aangejaagde motor.
supercharger, (druk)aanjaer.
supercilious, trots, verwaand.
superciliousness, trots, aanmatiging.

supererogation, oordrewe pligsbetragting; oorgedienstigheid; **works of** –, oortollige (goeie) werke.
superexcellence, buitengewone voortreflikheid.
superexcellent, buitengewoon voortreflik (uitmuntend).
superficial, oppervlakkig; vlak; **a – wound**, 'n vlak wond; – **knowledge**, oppervlakkige kennis.
superficiality, oppervlakkigheid.
superfine, prima, eersteklas.
superfluity, oortolligheid, oorvloed.
superfluous, oortollig, oorbodig.
superheat, oorverhit.
superheterodyne, superheterodyn.
superhuman, bo(we)menslik.
superimpose, bo-op sit.
superincumbent, bo-op liggend.
superintend, toesig hou, toesig hê.
superintendence, toesig.
superintendent, superintendent; toesighouer.
superior, a. hoër, beter, superieur; groter; opper; uitstekend; verhewe (bo); bostandig (in botanie); – **numbers**, oormag; **made of – leather**, van die beste leer gemaak; – **to bribery**, bo omkopery verhewe; – **air**, verwaande houding; – **rank**, hoër rang.
superior, n. meerdere, superieur.
superiority, hoër rang, hoër gesag; superioriteit, uitstekendheid, voortreflikheid; voorrang.
superlative, n. oortreffende trap.
superlative, a. oortreffend; voortreflik.
superlunar, bo-aards.
superman, oppermens.
supermarket, selfbedieningswinkel.
supermundane, bo-aards.
supernal, hemels, goddelik, verhewe.
supernatural, bo(we)natuurlik.
supernaturalness, bo(we)natuurlikheid.
supernumerary, a. ekstra, orige.
supernumerary, n. ekstra-amptenaar.
supernutrition, oorvoeding.
superphosphate, superfosfaat.
superpose, bo-op sit.
superprime, ekstra prima.
supersaturate, oorversadig.
superscription, opskrif, adres.
supersede, vervang; afdank, ontslaan; afskaf; die plek inneem van.
supersensitive, oorgevoelig.
supersession, vervanging; afdanking.
supersonic, supersonies.
superstition, bygeloof, bygelowigheid.
superstitious, bygelowig.
superstratum, boonste laag.
superstructure, bo(we)bou.
super-tax, ekstrabelasting, superbelasting.
supervene, onverwags gebeur; tussen(beie)kom.
supervention, onverwagte verandering (wending); tussenkoms; verrassing.
supervise, toesig hê (oor), toesig hou (oor), opsig hê (oor).
supervision, opsig, toesig.
supervisor, opsigter, opsiener.
supine, a. agteroor; traag, lusteloos.
supine, n. supinum.
supper, aandete, soepee.
supper-time, tyd vir aandete.
supplant, verdring, uitoorlê, onderkruip.
supple, slap, buigsaam, soepel; sag, meegaande, gedwee, vleierig.
supplement, n. aanhangsel, byvoegsel, aanvulling; supplement (in geometrie); byblad, bylae.
supplement, v. byvoeg, aanvul.
supplementary, supplementêr, aanvullings- . . ., aanvullend; – **examination**, hereksamen.

suppliant, a. smeek- . . ., smekend.
suppliant, n. smekeling.
supplicate, smeek, bid, soebat.
supplication, smeekgebed, smeking; smeekskrif, versoekskrif.
supplicatory, smeek- . . ., smekend.
supplies, benodigdhede; voorraad; toelaag; toegestane gelde, middele.
supply, v. voorsien, verskaf, sorg vir, lewer; aanvul; die plek vervul van; – **a loss**, 'n verlies vergoed.
supply, n. leweransie, lewering, verskaffing, voorsiening; voorraad; toevoer; demand and –, vraag en aanbod; **water –**, watervoorraad.
support, v. steun, ondersteun, hulp verleen aan, help; hou, dra, stut; van die nodige voorsien, onderhou; verdra, uithou; bewys, staaf; aanmoedig, versterk, krag gee, laat uithou; **too little food to – life**, te min kos om aan die lewe te bly; **unable to – a family**, nie in staat om 'n huisgesin te onderhou nie; – **an actor**, 'n toneelspeler bystaan; – **a motion**, ten gunste van 'n voorstel praat; – **a speaker**, saam met 'n spreker op die verhoog verskyn.
support, n. steun, ondersteuning, hulp, bystand; onderhoud; stut, voetstuk, voet; **give – to**, ondersteun, hulp verleen aan; **the chief – of our party**, die steunpilaar van ons party.
supporter, ondersteuner, helper.
supposable, onderstelbaar.
suppose, veronderstel, aanneem; vermoed, meen; – **it was so**, gesteld (laat ons aanneem) dat dit so was; – **your father saw you**, sê nou jou pa sien jou; – **we went for a walk**, hoe sal dit wees as ons gaan stap; **what do you – he meant**, wat dink jy het hy bedoel?; **you will be there, I –**, jy sal seker daar wees, nie waar nie?; **his –d brother**, sy vermeende broer.
supposition, (ver)onderstelling, mening, vermoede.
suppositional, vermoedelik.
supposititious, nagemaak, oneg, vals.
suppress, onderdruk, 'n einde maak aan; bedwing, inkrop; terughou, agterhou, terugtrek, verswyg, geheim hou.
suppression, onderdrukking; geheimhouding, verswyging, weglating.
suppurate, (ver)sweer, etter.
suppuration, verswering, ettering.
suppurative, verswerend.
supramundane, bo-aards.
supremacy, (opper)heerskappy, oppergesag, oppermag.
supreme, hoogste, opperste, uiterste; oppermagtig; grootste, belangrikste; **S– Court**, Hooggeregshof; **S– Being (the S–)**, die Allerhoogste; **the – test**, die hoogste toets.
sural, van die kuit, kuit- . . .
surcharge, n. oorlading (oorlaaiing); ekstra betaling, ekstra bedrag, ekstraport; opdruk, posseël met opdruk.
surcharge, v. oorlaai; oorversadig; ekstra laat betaal, ekstra bereken.
surcingle, (buik)gord.
surcoat, oorkleed, opperkleed.
surculose, -lous, met suiers, suier- . . .
surd, wortelvorm, onmeetbare getal.
sure, a. seker, gewis; onfeilbaar; veilig; **are you –**, is jy seker!; **he feels – of success**, hy voel oortuig dat hy sal slaag; **put it in a – place**, sit dit op 'n veilige plek; **he is a – shot**, hy is 'n wis skut, hy is seker van sy skoot; **you would be – to dislike him**, jy sal stellig nie van hom hou nie; **one thing is –**, een ding staan vas (is seker); **to be –**, ongetwyfeld; warempel, wrag-

gies, waarlik; **well, I'm –!, well to be –!, nou kyk!, nou toe!, waarlik!; be – to do it,** jy moet dit seker doen; **I want to make – of it,** ek wil sekerheid hê daaromtrent, ek wil myself oortuig daaromtrent; **as – as eggs is eggs, as – as a gun,** so waar soos padda manel dra, so waar soos vet.
sure, adv. seker, waarlik; **he will come – enough,** hy sal wis en seker kom.
sure-footed, vas op sy voete; eerlik.
surely, seker; tog; **there is no truth in it –?,** maar dit is tog seker nie waar nie; **– I have met you before?,** maar ek het jou (tog) vantevore ontmoet, nie waar nie?
surety, borg; waarborg, pand; sekerheid; **stand –,** borg teken, borg staan.
surf, branders, branding.
surf, v. branders-ry; branderplank ry.
surface, n. oppervlakte; vlak; oppervlak; uiterlike, buitekant; **his politeness is only on the –,** sy beleefdheid is maar net skyn; **a plane –,** 'n plat vlak; **– of contact,** aanrakingsoppervlak; **– soil,** bogrond; **– mail,** voertuigpos.
surface, v. glad (sag) maak; opkom.
surface-tension, oppervlaktespanning.
surf-board, branderplank, swemplank.
surfeit, n. oorversadiging, satheid.
surfeit, v. (sig) ooreet, oorlaai.
surge, n. golf; golwende beweging.
surge, v. golf, dein.
surgeon, snydokter, chirurg; **dental –,** tandarts, tandedokter.
surgery, heelkunde, chirurgie; spreekkamer, apteek (van 'n dokter).
surgical, heelkundig, chirurgies.
surliness, norsheid, stuursheid.
surly, nors, stuurs, kortaf.
surmise, n. vermoede, gissing.
surmise, v. vermoed, gis, raai.
surmount, te boewe kom, oorwin.
surmountable, oorkoomlik, oorwinbaar.
surname, van, familienaam; bynaam.
surpass, oortref, uitblink bo.
surpassable, oortrefbaar.
surpassing, uitstekend, ongeëwenaard.
surplice, koorkleed, koorhemp.
surpliced, met 'n koorkleed aan.
surplus, oorskot, orige, surplus; **– population,** oorbevolking.
surprise, n. verrassing; verbasing, verwondering; **to my –,** tot my verbasing; **the enemy took us by –,** die vyand het ons verras (oorrompel).
surprise, v. verras; verbaas, verstom, verwonder; oorrompel; **– in the act,** op heter daad betrap; **I am –d,** dit verbaas my.
surprise-packet, verrassinkie, verrassingspakkie.
surprise-party, invalparty, instuif.
surprise-visit, onverwagte besoek.
surprising, verbasend, verbasingwekkend.
surrealism, surrealisme.
surrender, v. oorgee; hensop; afstand doen van, laat vaar; uitlewer; **– oneself to,** jouself oorgee aan; **– an insurance policy,** 'n assuransiepolis afkoop; **– hopes,** hoop opgee; **– an estate,** boedel oorgee.
surrender, n. oorgawe; afstand; uitlewerig (die) afkoop (van 'n polis).
surrender-value, afkoopwaarde.
surreptitious, onderduims, slinks.
surreptitiously, agteraf, stilletjies, op onderduimse (slinkse) manier.
surrogate, surrogaat, plaasvervanger.
surround, omgewe, omring, omsingel, insluit; **the –ing country,** die omliggende land, die omgewing.

surroundings, omgewing.
surtax, n. ekstra belasting, superbelasting.
surtax, v. ekstra belas.
surveillance, toesig, bewaking.
survey, v. bekyk, beskou, besigtig, opneem; noukeurig ondersoek; opmeet.
survey, n. oorsig; besigtiging; ondersoek; opmeting.
surveying, landmeting; landmeetkuns.
surveyor, inspekteur; landmeter.
surveyor-general, landmeter-generaal.
survival, oorlewing, behoud; oorblyfsel; **– of the fittest,** behoud (standhouding, oorlewing) van die geskikste.
survive, oorlewe, nog lewe, behoue bly, nog bestaan, langer lewe as; **– one's contemporaries,** jou tydgenote oorlewe; **– all perils,** alle gevare deurlewe.
survivor, langslewende; oorblywende, oorlewende, oorgeblewene.
susceptibility, vatbaarheid, gevoeligheid.
susceptible, vatbaar, gevoelig; liggeraak; sensitief; **– to female charms,** nie bestand teen die behoorlikheid van die vrou nie; **not – to kindness,** nie vatbaar vir vriendelikheid nie.
susceptive, vatbaar.
suspect, v. vermoed; verdink, wantrou; **you, I –, don't care,** jy, veronderstel ek, gee nie om nie; **– the authenticity of,** twyfel aan die egtheid van.
suspect, a. verdag.
suspect, n. verdagte persoon.
suspend, ophang, hang; uitstel, opskort; skors, suspendeer; **–ed particles of dust,** drywende stofdeeltjies; **a balloon –ed in air,** 'n swewende ballon; **– one's judgment,** jou oordeel opskort; **–ed sentence,** opgeskorte vonnis; **– payment,** betaling staak.
suspender, ophanger; kous(op)houer, sokkiehouer.
suspense, spanning, spannende afwagting, onsekerheid, twyfel; opskorting.
suspension, (die) (op)hang; uitstel, opskorting; skorsing; staking.
suspension-bridge, hangbrug, swaaibrug.
suspensory, hangend, hang-...
suspicion, argwaan, verdenking, agterdog, suspisie, vermoede; tikkie, bewysie; **not a – of,** nie die minste bewys(ie) van; **above –,** bo alle verdenking; **I have a – that,** ek vermoed dat.
suspicious, agterdogtig; verdag.
sustain, dra, steun; help, krag gee, aanmoedig; uithou, deurstaan, verduur; aanhou, volhou; handhaaf; ly; bewys, staaf; **– a defeat,** 'n neerlaag ly; **– a note,** 'n noot aanhou; **a –ed note,** 'n lang aangehoue noot.
sustainment, hulp, ondersteuning.
sustenance, voedsel, kos, lewensmiddelde; (lewens)onderhoud; **there is no – in it,** dit besit geen voedende waarde nie.
sustentation, onderhoud, hulp; **– fund,** steunfonds, sustentasiefonds.
susurration, fluistering, gefluister.
susurrous, fluisterend; ritselend, ruisend.
suture, naat; vasnaaiing, vashegting.
suzerain, opperleenheer, suserein.
suzerainty, susereiniteit.
swab, n. skropbesem, swabber; doek, feillap, pluisie, prop.
swab, v. skrop, feil, opvee; opneem.
Swabian, a. Swabies.
Swabian, n. Swaab.
swaddle, toedraai.

swaddling-bands, -clothes, doeke, windsels; luiers; bande, belemmering.
swag, gesteelde goed, roof.
swagger, v. grootpraat, windmaker wees, windmaker stap, spog.
swagger, n. windmaker-stap, grootpratery, spoggerigheid, blufpraatjies.
swagger, a. windmaker, spoggerig.
swagger-cane, (spog)kierietjie.
swain, boerkêrel; kêrel, vryer.
swallow, v. sluk, insluk; verswelg; he will – anything you tell him, alles wat jy hom vertel, sal hy vir soetkoek opeet.
swallow, n. sluk.
swallow, n. swa(w)el.
swallow-tail, swa(w)elstert; – coat, swa(w)elstert(baadjie).
swamp, n. vlei, moeras.
swamp, v. in 'n moeras vassit (sink); laat sink, wegspoel, oorstroom, vol water (laat) loop; oorstelp; oorrompel; insluk, verswelg; –ed with work, oorstelp met werk, toe onder die werk.
swampy, moeras-...., moerasagtig.
swan, swaan; a black –, 'n wit raaf (fig.).
swank, v. spog, windmaker wees.
swank, n. spoggerigheid, windmakerigheid; spogter, windmaker-persoon.
swanky, windmaker, spoggerig, uithaler.
swan's-down, swanedons.
swan song, swanesang.
sward, grasveld.
swarm, n. swerm; menigte.
swarm, v. swerm; krioel, wemel.
swarthy, donker, bruin, blas, swart.
swash, slaan; klots, kabbel, plas; –ing blow, dugtige hou, taai hou.
swashbuckler, baasspeler, twissoeker.
swat, slaan.
swath, strook, ry.
swathe, verbind; vasbind; toedraai.
swatter, vlieëslaner, -plakkie.
sway, v. swaai, slinger, oorhel; hanteer; regeer, heers, beheers; – the sceptre, die septer swaai, regeer; be –ed by, jou laat lei deur.
sway, n. swaai; heerskappy, gesag, mag.
sway-backed, holrug-...
Swazi, Swazi.
swear, v. sweer, 'n eed aflê, onder 'n eed verklaar (bevestig); beëdig; vloek, swets, ,,knoop", boontoe roep; why do you – at me?, waarom vloek jy my?, waarom skel jy my uit?; – a witness, 'n getuie die eed afneem; – a person to secrecy, iemand laat sweer om iets geheim te hou; sworn enemies, geswore vyande; – by, swear by; – in, die eed afneem; – off, afsweer.
swear, n. vloek.
swear-word, vloekwoord.
sweat, n. sweet; harde werk; a – will do him good, dit sal hom goed doen om te sweet; all of a –, nat van die sweet.
sweat, v. sweet; uitsweet, afgee; laat sweet; swaar werk, swoeg; uitbuit, hongerloon betaal; hongerloon ontvang.
sweater, uitbuiter, bloedsuier; oortrui; sweettrui; – girl, buustepop, kleeftruipop.
sweat-gland, sweetklier.
sweating-bath, sweetbad.
sweating-iron, roskam.
sweating-room, sweetkamer.
sweating-sickness, sweetsiekte.
sweating-system, hongerloonstelsel.
sweaty, sweet-...., natgesweet.
Swede, Sweed; s–, Sweedse raap.

Swedish, n. Sweeds, die Sweedse taal.
Swedish, a. Sweeds.
sweep, v. vee, wegvee, uitvee, skoonvee; vinnig verbyvlie(g), storm; meevoer, wegvoer, saamsleep; trek, stryk, gly; die oë laat gaan oor, vlugtig beskou; bestryk; – the seas, die see deurkruis; die see skoonvee; – the board, alles wen; the battery swept the streets, die battery het die strate bestryk; – the horizon, die hele horison in die oog hou; – along, saamsleep, meevoer; – away, wegvee; meevoer; saamsleep; – away the bridge, die brug meevoer (wegspoel); the plain –s away to the sea, die vlakte strek na die see toe uit; – down on, (be)storm; – all obstacles from one's path, alle struikelblokke uit die weg ruim; the plague swept off thousands, die pes het duisende afgemaai; – past, verbyvlie(g), verbyskiet, verbystuif; – up, opvee, wegvee, uitvee.
sweep, n. swaai, draai; veeg; bereik; uitgestrektheid, omvang; skoorsteenveër; a – of the arm, 'n swaai van die arm; beyond the – of (the eye), buite die bereik van (die oog); give this room a –, vee hierdie kamer uit; make a clean – of, algehele opruiming hou van, heeltemal ontslae raak van.
sweeper, veër.
sweeping, veënd; algemeen, (alles)omvattend; make – statements, generaliseer; – reductions, algemene prysverminderinge.
sweepings, vuilgoed, vullis.
sweep-net, sleepnet.
sweepstakes, insetgeld, wedlootjie; wedrenne.
sweet, a. soet; lekker, aangenaam, lieflik; vars; he has a – tooth, hy is 'n lekkerbek; it smells –, dit ruik lekker; – stuff, lekkergoed; – temper, saggeaardheid, vriendelikheid; a – girl, 'n liewe meisie; be – on, been-af wees op; water, vars water; – one, soetlief.
sweet, n. soet; lekker; –s, lekkers, lekkergoed; poeding, nagereg, dessert; the –(s), and the bitter(s), die lief en die leed.
sweetbread, sweserik.
sweeten, soet maak; veraangenaam.
sweetheart, liefling, soetlief, skat; nooi (nôi), kêrel, vryer.
sweetish, soeterig, soetagtig.
sweetmeat, lekker, lekkergoed.
sweet-natured, saggeaard, vriendelik.
sweet-oil, soetolie.
sweet-pea, pronk-ertjie, ertjieblom.
sweet-potato, patat.
sweet-scented, welriekend, lekkerruik-...
sweety, lekkertjie; liefste, liefling.
swell, v. swel, opswel; uitdy; vermeerder, toeneem, groei, groter word; opgeblase (verwaand) wees; – into a roar, tot 'n gebrul aangroei; the wind –s the sails, die wind vul die seile; small items – the total, die kleinighede laat die totaal oploop; –ed head, verwaandheid; – with pride, iets wil oorkom van hoogmoed.
swell, n. (die) swel, swelling, swelsel; styging; deining; vername persoon; ,,haan", ,,doring"; what a – you are, maar hoor jy is fyn uitgevat!
swell, a. fyn, piekfyn; vernaam.
swelling, n. swelsel, geswel.
swelter, v. bedompig (benoud, drukkend) wees; versmoor, verskroei, verstik, versmag; the city –ed in the plain, die stad het in die vlakte lê en skroei.
swelter, n. bedompigheid, skroeihitte.
swept-wing, pylvlerk.

swerve, v. afwyk; opsy spring, verby spring, padgee, swenk; kantel.
swerve, n. swaai; syspring, swenking.
swift, a. vlug, gou, rats, vinnig, snel; be - to anger, gou kwaad word.
swift, adv. gou, vinnig.
swift, n. muurswa(w)el; akke(r)dissie.
swift-footed, gou, vinnig, rats.
swig, sluk, teug.
swill, v. spoel, uitspoel; suip.
swill, n. skottelwater, vuilwater; spoeling; give it a -, spoel dit uit.
swim, v. swem; drywe; draai; - with the tide, met die stroom saamgaan; my head -s, ek word duiselig, ek voel dronk in my kop, alles draai voor my oë; eyes -ming with tears, betraande oë.
swim, n. (die) swem; be in the -, weet wat gaande is, op hoogte van sake wees, meedoen.
swimmer, swemmer.
swimming, (die) swem; duiseligheid.
swimming-bath, swembad.
swimming-belt, swemgordel.
swimming-bladder, swemblaas.
swimmingly, lekker, fluks; everything went -, alles het so glad soos seep gegaan, alles het voor die wind gegaan.
swindle, v. bedrieg, fop, swendel, verneuk, 'n knop steek.
swindle, n. bedrog, skelmstuk, verneukery, swendelary.
swindler, bedrieër, skelm, verneuker.
swine, vark(e), swyn(e).
swine-fever, varkpes.
swine-herd, varkwagter.
swine-pox, waterpokkies.
swing, v. swaai, slinger, skommel; hang; he shall - for it, daarvoor sal hy hang; the door swung to, die deur het toegeklap; he swung out of the room, swaai-swaai is hy die kamer uit; hy het die kamer uitgestorm.
swing, n. swaai; gang; skoppelmaai, skommel; the work is in full -, die werk is in volle gang; get into the - of, op stryk kom; let him have his -, laat hom maar begaan, gee hom maar die vrye teuel; it goes with a -, daar sit lewe (beweging) in; beware of the - of the pendulum, oppas vir die terugslag.
swing-bridge, draaibrug.
swingle, swingel.
swingle-tree, swingelhout, swingel.
swipe, v. hard slaan, vee(g) (tennis); steel.
swipe, n. harde slag, veeghou (tennis).
swirl, v. draai, warrel.
swirl, n. draaikolk, warreling.
swish, v. ransel; swiets, suis, ruis.
swish, n. gesjiep, geswiep, ritseling; hou.
Swiss, n. Switser.
Swiss, n. Switsers; - roll, rolkoek.
switch, n. loot, lat; vals haarvlegsel; wisselskakelaar, stroomwisselaar, (elektriese) knoppie.
switch, v. pak gee, afransel; vinnig swaai (gryp); wissel, ('n trein) op 'n ander spoor bring; inskakel, uitskakel, omskakel; - the light off, on, die lig uitknip (afdraai, afslaan) aandraai (aanslaan).
switchback, roetsbaan, hobbelbaan.
switchboard, skakelbord.
switchman, wisselwagter.
swivel, draaiskyf, skyf.
swivel-chair, draaistoel.
swivel-eye, skeeloog.
swivel-eyed, skeel.
swizzle, yssopie; - stick, roerstokkie.
swollen, sien swell.

swoon, v. flou (word), beswym.
swoon, n. floute, beswyming.
swoop, v. neerskiet, neerstryk, skielik neervlie; - up, skielik gryp.
swoop, n. (die) neerskiet; the hawk came down with a -, die valk het neergeskiet; with one -, met een slag.
swop, swap, ruil, omruil.
sword, swaard, sabel; cross, measure -s, kragte meet; put to the -, oor die kling jaag, om die lewe bring; draw, sheathe the -, die swaard trek, in die skede steek.
sword-arm, skermarm.
sword-blade, swaardlem, swaardkling.
sword-cut, sabelhou.
sword-dance, sabeldans.
sword-fish, swaardvis.
sword-knot, sabelkwas.
sword-law, die reg van die swaard.
swordsman, swaardvegter.
swordsmanship, skermkuns.
swot, v. blok, pomp.
swot, n. blokker; blokker.
sybarite, sibariet; wellusteling.
sybaritic, sibarities; wellustig, verwyf.
sycamore, wildevyeboom.
sycophancy, gemene vleiery, lekkery, kruiperigheid.
sycophant, gemene vleier, kruiper.
sycophantic, vleierig, kruiperig.
syllabic, sillabies, lettergrepig.
syllable, lettergreep, sillabe.
syllabus, sillabus, leerplan.
syllogism, sillogisme, sluitrede.
syllogistic, sillogisties.
sylph, luggees, luggodin.
sylvan, sien silvan.
symbol, simbool, sinnebeeld, (ken)teken.
symbolic(al), simbolies, sinnebeeldig.
symbolization, sinnebeeldige voorstelling.
symbolize, simboliseer, sinnebeeldig voorstel, as simbool dien.
symbolism, simboliek, simbolisme.
symbolist, simbolis.
symmetrical, simmetries, eweredig.
symmetry, simmetrie, eweredigheid.
sympathetic, simpatiek; medelydend; simpaties; - ink, simpatetiese ink; - pain, simpatetiese pyn.
sympathize, simpatiseer, medelyde hê.
sympathy, simpatie, meegevoel, medelyde.
symphonic, simfonies.
symphonious, welluidend.
symphony, simfonie.
symposium, drinkgelag, drinkparty; samespreking; simposium.
symptom, simptoom, teken, verskynsel.
symptomatic, simptomaties, aanduidend.
synagogue, sinagoge.
synchromesh: - gears, sinchroonskakeling.
synchronize, op dieselfde tyd plaasvind, saamval; reguleer, regsit; sinchroniseer.
synchronism, gelyktydigheid.
synchronous, gelyktydig.
syncom, syncom, sin-kom.
syncopate, sinkopeer, saamtrek.
syncope, sinkopee; floute, beswyming.
syndicate, sindikaat, kartel.
synod, sinode.
synodal, sinodaal.
synonym, sinoniem.
synonymous, sinoniem, sinverwant.
synonymy, sinonimie, sinverwantskap.
synopsis, oorsig, kort begrip.

synoptic, sinopties, oorsigtelik.
syntactic, sintakties.
syntax, sintaksis, sinsleer.
synthesis, sintese, samevatting.
synthetic, sinteties; – **fibre,** kunsvesel; – **rubber,** kunsrubber.
syphilis, vuilsiekte, sifilis.
syphilitic, sifilities.
syphon, sien **siphon.**
syren, sien **siren.**
Syrian, n. Siriër; Siries.
Syrian, a. Siries.

syringe, n. spuit; **hypodermic** –, onderhuidspuitjie.
syringe, v. spuit, inspuit.
syrup, stroop; **golden** –, gouestroop.
syrupy, stroperig, stroopagtig.
system, sisteem, stelsel; metode; gestel, konstitusie; formasie; – **of government,** regeringstelsel; **mountain** –, bergreeks; **solar** –, sonnestelsel.
systematic, sistematies, stelselmatig.
systematize, sistematiseer.
systole, sametrekking, krimping.

T

t, t; cross the –'s, die puntjies op die i's sit; **to a –,** op 'n haar, op 'n druppel water; – **square,** tekenhaak.
tab, strokie, stukkie; tongetjie (oor) klappie; veterpunt; **keep –s on,** oplet, die oog hou op.
tabby, gewaterde sy; (Ciperse) kat.
tabefaction, wegkwyning, uittering.
tabernacle, tabernakel; tent, hut; liggaam; **Feast of –s,** loofhuttefees.
tabes, wegkwyning, (uit)tering, tabes; **dorsal –,** rugtering, rugmurgtering.
tabetic, n. teringagtige, teringlyer.
tabid, uitgeteer.
tablature, beeld, afbeelding; tablatuur.
table, n. tafel; plato, hoogland; tabel, lys, register; **at–,** aan tafel; **he keeps a good –,** hy het 'n welvoorsiene tafel; **the —s are turned,** die rolle is omgekeer; **multiplication –,** tafel van vermenigvuldiging; **lay on the –,** vir 'n onbepaalde tyd uitstel; ter (op die) tafel lê; **– tennis,** tafeltennis.
table, v. op die tafel (ter tafel) lê; uitstel; rangskik, tabelleer.
tableau, tablo.
table-boarder, dagloseerder.
table-boarding, daglosies.
table-centre, tafelloper, middelkleedjie.
table-cloth, tafellaken, tafeldoek.
table-flap, tafelklap.
table-knife, tafelmes.
tableland, plato, hoogvlakte.
table-lifting, tafeldans.
table-linen, tafellinne.
table-moving, -rapping, tafeldans.
table-spoon, eetlepel.
tablet, tablet; steen(tjie); **memorial –,** gedenksteen.
table-talk, tafelgesprek.
table-tipping, -turning, tafeldans.
table-ware, tafelgoed.
tabloid, tablet, pilletjie; prentkoerant.
taboo, n. verbod; taboe.
taboo, a. heilig, verbode; taboe.
taboo, v. verbied.
tabor, tamboertjie, tamboeryn.
tabouret, sitbankie, stoeltjie, taboeret; borduurraam; naaldekussing.
tabular, tafel–..., tabellaries.
tabulate, v. tabelleer.
tabulate, a. plat.
tachometer, snelheidsmeter, tagometer.
tacit, stilswy(g)end; – **consent,** stilswy(g)ende instemming.
taciturn, stil, onspraaksaam, swygsaam.
taciturnity, stilswy(g)endheid, swygsaamheid.
tack, n. platkopspykertjie; rygsteek; hals (van 'n seil); rigting, koers, pad; kos, ete; **on the wrong –,** op die verkeerde spoor; **we must change our –,** ons moet 'n ander koers inslaan; **soft –,** brood, lekker kos.
tack, v. vasspyker, vasslaan; vasryg (vasrye), aanmekaar heg; laveer; van koers verander, 'n saak anders aanpak.
tackle, n. takel; hystoestel; gereedskap.
tackle, v. aanpak, aanvat, onder hande neem, plant, lak, neertrek (voetbal).
tackling, gereedskap, tuig; (die) aanpak; (die) plant (voetbal).
tact, tak(t), slag.
tactful, tak(t)vol.
tactical, takties.
tactician, taktikus, krygskundige.
tactics, taktiek, krygskunde.
tactile, gevoels–...; voelbaar, tasbaar.
tactless, tak(t)loos.

tadpole, paddavis(sie).
tael, tael.
taenia, rolverband; lintwurm; haarband.
taffeta, taf.
tag, n. veterpunt, riempunt; lissie; adreskaart, etiket; fraiing, rafel; aanhangsel; stertpunt; slottoespraak; ou gesegde, stokperdjie; refrein; aan-aan (kinderspeletjie).
tag, v. vasbind, vasheg; agternaloop.
tag-end, slot, stert, agterent.
tag-rag (and bobtail), Jan Rap en sy maat.
tagtail, wurm; inkruiper, lekker.
tail, n. stert; haarvlegsel; pant, slip; keersy (van muntstuk); agterent; gevolg; **–s,** swaelstert-(pak); **with the – between the legs,** stert tussen die bene; **turn –,** omspring, die hasepad kies; **the – of the eye,** die hoek van die oog; **the – (end),** die agterent (agterpunt).
tail, v. 'n stert aansit; – **after,** op die hiele volg, agteraan tou; – **away, off,** uitsak, agterbly.
tail-board, karet, agterplank.
tailcoat, swa(w)elstert(baadjie).
tailed, met 'n stert, stert–...
tail-end, agterste punt, agterent, stert.
tailing, binnekop (van 'n baksteen).
tailings, vuilgoed; afsaksel, onderste, oorskiet, gewaste grond.
tailless, sonder stert, stompstert.
tail-light, agterlamp; remlamp.
tailor, n. kleremaker.
tailor, v. klere maak, kleremaker wees; **well –ed,** goed gemaak; goed gekleed.
tailoring, kleremakery; maaksel, snit.
tailor-made, aangemeet; snyers–...
tail-spin, draaiduik.
taint, n. vlek, smet, besmetting; teken, bewys, blaam.
taint, v. bevlek, besmet, besoedel; bederwe; aansteek.
taintless, vlekloos, onbevlek, skoon.
take, v. neem, vat, gryp, pak; wen, bemagtig; kry, ontvang, trek; verstaan, vat, begryp, snap; aanneem; opneem; afneem; betrap; **–n in a trap,** in 'n val (wip) gevang; – **him in the act,** hom op heter daad betrap; **he was –n ill,** hy het siek geword; **it –s my fancy,** dit trek my aan, ek hou baie daarvan; – **degree,** 'n graad behaal; – **a holiday,** gaan vakansie hou; **I am not taking any,** nee dankie, (so laat ek my nie fop nie); – **seats in advance,** plekke vooruit bespreek; – **the opportunity,** van die geleentheid gebruik maak; – **a cup of tea,** 'n koppie tee drink; – **the cup,** die beker wen; – **your time,** moet jou nie haas nie; – **legal advice,** geregtelike advies inwin; **it –s a lot of doing,** dit is nie sommer eke man se werk nie; **these things – time,** hiervoor het 'n mens tyd nodig; – **offence,** aanstoot neem; **I took no notice of it,** ek het my nie daaraan gesteur nie; – **for granted,** aanneem; **do you – me for a fool,** sien jy my vir 'n gek aan; **not – it ill of him,** hom dit nie kwalik neem nie; – **my advice,** luister na my raad; **you may – it from me,** jy kan vir my glo, ek sê vir jou; – **sides,** party kies; – **notes,** aantekeninge maak; – **a walk,** gaan loop; – **the evening service,** die aanddiens waarneem; **the horse will not – the fence,** die perd wil nie oor die heining spring nie; – **an oath,** sweer, 'n eed aflê; – **account of,** rekening hou met; – **aim,** korrel vat, mik; – **care,** oppas; – **one's chance,** dit waag, riskeer; – **earth,** wegkruip, in 'n gat kruip; – **one's life in one's hand,** jou lewe in gevaar stel; – **God's name in vain,** die Heer se naam ydellik gebruik; – **place,** plaasvind, gebeur; **he took his seat,** hy het

plaasgeneem, hy het gaan sit; – **after**, aard na; I – you at your word, ek hou jou aan jou woord; – **back**, terugtrek; terugneem; – **down**, afhaal, wegneem; afskryf, opskryf; – **in**, fop, kul, bedrieg; glo, sluk, as soet koek opeet; verstaan, begryp; inneem; insluit, omvat; aanneem (van wasgoed, naaiwerk, ens.); ontvang; – **in boarders**, kosgangers hou; – **into one's confidence**, in jou vertroue neem; – **into one's head**, in jou kop kry; – **off**, (hoed) afhaal, (klere) uittrek, afkom, (prys) laat val; wegspring; opstyg; na-aap, naboots; **he took himself off**, hy het gemaak dat hy wegkom; – **on**, aanneem (werk, ens.); – **somebody out for a walk**, met iemand 'n entjie gaan loop; **I must – that obstinacy out of you**, ek moet jou daardie koppigheid afleer; – **out a stain**, 'n vlek wegmaak; – **it out of**, uitput; inpeper; wraak neem, iemand „kry"; – **out a patent**, 'n patent neem; – **over a business**, 'n saak oorneem; – **to bad habits**, slegte gewoontes aankweek; – **up**, opneem; oplig, optel; in beslag neem; **it –s up all my time**, dit neem al my tyd in beslag; – **up with**, omgaan met; **he took the matter up**, hy het hom met die saak bemoei; – **up an attitude**, 'n houding aanneem; – **up a profession**, 'n beroep kies; – **up passengers**, passasiers oplaai; – **up a speaker**, 'n spreker in die rede val.
take, n. vangs; ontvangste; opname.
take-in, kullery, bedrieëry.
take-off, karikatuur; wegspringplek.
taker, nemer; aannemer.
taking, innemend, bekoorlik, aanloklik; aansteeklik.
takings, ontvangste.
talc, talk, talkaarde.
talcose, talcous, talkagtig, talk- . . .
tale, verhaal, vertelling, vertelsel, storie, sprokie; getal, aantal; **tell –s out of school**, uit die skool klap; **the thing tells its own –**, die saak het geen verklaring nodig nie.
talebearer, nuusdraer, verklikker.
talebearing, nuusdraery.
talent, talent, gawe, begaafdheid; talent.
talented, begaaf, talentvol.
taleteller, verteller; verklikker.
talion, weervergelding, vergeldingsreg.
taliped, a. horrelvoet- . . .
taliped, n. horrelvoet.
talipod, waaierpalm.
talisman, talisman.
talk, v. praat, gesels; – **a person round**, iemand ompraat (oorhaal); – **a horse's hind leg off**, 'n sloot in die grond praat; – **about**, bespreek, gesels (praat) oor; **I do not want to be –ed about**, ek wil nie hê die mense moet van my praat nie; – **away**, daarop los praat; – **back**, brutaal (astrant) antwoord; – **down**, doodpraat, onderstebo praat; – **ing of tennis . . .**, van tennis gepraat . . .; – **out a motion**, 'n voorstel doodpraat; – **over**, bespreek; oorhaal, ompraat; – **round the subject**, al om die punt praat; – **to**, praat met, gesels met; onder hande neem, goed die waarheid sê; – **(cold) turkey**, die volle waarheid vertel.
talk, n. gesprek; praatjie; **they are the – of the town**, iedereen in die stad het die mond vol van hulle.
talkative, praatsiek, spraaksaam.
talker, prater; grootprater.
talkie, praatprent, -film.
talking, a. sprekend, pratend, praat- . . .
talking, n. gepraat, praat, pratery.
talking-to, skrobbering; **give somebody a –**, iemand goed die waarheid vertel.

tall, groot, lang, hoog; spoggerig; kras; **six feet –**, ses voet lank; **that's a – order**, dit is 'n bietjie kras, dit is 'n bietjie te veel geverg; – **talk**, grootpratery, bluf.
tallow, kersvet, harde vet; talk.
tallow-candle, vetkers.
tallow-chandler, (vet)kersmaker.
tallow-faced, bleek.
tallowish, tallowy, vetagtig; talkagtig.
tally, n. kerfstok; rekening; keep, kerf; getal, bordjie.
tally, v. op die kerfstok sit; ooreenstem, klop, strook (met).
tally-ho, interj. sa!
tally-shop, winkel waar kort krediet gegee word, kerfstokwinkel.
Talmud, Talmoed.
Talmudist, Talmoedis.
talon, klou.
taloned, met kloue.
tamability, tembaarheid.
tamable, tembaar.
tamarind, tamarinde.
tamarisk, tamarisk(boom).
tambour, borduurraam; borduurwerk.
tambourine, tamboeryn.
tame, v. tem, mak maak.
tame, a. mak, getem; onderdanig, gedwee; suf, slap, tam, swak; vervelend.
tamer, temmer.
tam-o'-shanter, wolmus.
tamp, instamp, vasstamp.
tampan, tampan(luis).
tamper: – **with**, knoei aan; peuter aan; omkoop; slinks te werk gaan.
tampion, prop, geweerprop.
tampon, n. tampon, prop, stopsel.
tampon, v. tamponneer, toestop.
tan, v. looi; verbrand, bruin brand, bruin word; ransel, uitvel.
tan, n. (looi)bas; bruin, taankleur.
tan, a. bruin, taankleurig.
tandem, tandem.
tang, n. punt, stiffie, tongetjie, hefpunt.
tang, n. smaak, geur; eienaardigheid.
tang, n. seebamboes.
tang, v. klink.
tang, n. klank.
tangent, raaklyn, tangens; **go off at a –**, van die os op die esel spring.
tangibility, tasbaarheid.
tangible, tasbaarheid.
tangible, tasbaar, voelbaar.
tangle, v. deurmekaar maak, knoop; in die war raak, deurmekaar raak, verwar; **–d affair**, 'n warboel.
tangle, n. verwarring, warboel, deurmekaar spul, knoop; **in a –**, in die war.
tangly, in die war, deurmekaar.
tango, tango.
tank, tenk; waterbak, reservoir; pantserwa; – **landing craft**, tenklandingsvaartuig; – **trap**, tenkkuil.
tankage, inhoud van tenk; tenkgeld.
tankard, drinkkan.
tanker, tenkskip; tenkwa; tenkvliegtuig.
tanner, looier.
tannery, looiery.
tannic, looi- . . .; – **acid**, looisuur.
tannin, looisuur, tannien.
tan-pit, looikuip.
tantalization, tantalisasie, tempering.
tantalize, tantaliseer, tempteer.
tantamount, dieselfde as; **be – to**, gelyk staan met.

tantrum, slegte luim; she is in her –s, sy het haar kwaai-mus op.
tap, n. kraan, tap (in 'n vat); drank; drinkplek, kantien; **liquor on** –, drank uit die vat.
tap, v. 'n kraan (tap) inslaan; tap, uittap; aanvoor; – somebody, iemand die water aftap; iemand uitvra; – **the telegraph wires**, die telegraafdrade tap.
tap, v. tik, klop.
tap, n. klop, tikkie; **I heard a** – **at the door**, ek het iemand hoor klop.
tap-dancing, klopdans(ery).
tape, n. band, lint; papierstrook; maatband, maatlint; telegrafiese koersberig; **breast the** –, 'n wedloop wen; – **recorder**, bandopnemer, -opneemtoestel.
tape, v. vasmaak, vasbind; **have someone (something)** –d, iemand (iets) haarfyn ken.
tape-line, tape-measure, maatband.
taper, a. spits.
taper, v. spits uitloop; spits maak (word).
tapering, spits.
tapestried, met behangsel, behang.
tapestry, behangsel.
tape-worm, lintwurm.
tapioca, tapioka.
tapir, tapir.
tapis, tapyt; **on the** –, op die tapyt.
tappet, klepligter.
tap-room, drinkplek, tappery, kantien.
tap-root, penwortel.
tapster, skinker, tapper, kantienhouer.
tar, n. teer; **he has a touch of the** –**brush**, sy wieg het naby die struispaal gestaan, hy het naby die stroois omgedraai.
tar, v. teer, teer smeer; – **and feather**, teer en veer; –**red with the same brush**, voëls van dieselfde vere.
tar (Jack Tar), pikbroek.
tarantula, tarantula.
tarboosh, fes.
tar-brush, teerkwas.
tardiness, traagheid, stadigheid.
tardy, traag, stadig, langsaam; laat.
tare, n. onkruid.
tare, n. tarra; **average** –, gemiddelde tarra; – **and tret**, tarrarekening.
target, skyf, teiken; mikpunt.
tariff, tarief; – **wall**, tolmuur.
tariff union, tolverbond.
tarlatan, tarlatan, moeselien.
tarnish, n. vlek, smet; verbleking.
tarnish, v. dof maak, dof word, aanslaan; bevlek, besoedel; verbleek.
taroc, -ot, tarok (in kaartspel).
tarpaulin, teerseil, bokseil; matrooshoed.
Tarpean, Tarpejes.
tarry, a. teer-..., geteer, teeragtig.
tarry, v. wag; vertoef, draal, draai.
tarsus, voetwortel.
tart, a. suur; bitsig, skerp.
tart, n. tert(tjie); flerrie, vryerige meisie.
tartar, n. wynsteen; aanpaksel (aan tande) tandsteen; **cream of** –, kremetart.
Tartar, n. Tartaar (Tater); woestaard; **catch a** –, jou moses teenkom.
Tartar, a. Tartaars.
tartaric, wynsteen-...; – **acid**, wynsteensuur.
Tartarus, Tartarus, hel.
tartlet, tertjie.
tartness, suurheid, rankheid; bitsigheid.
task, n. taak, werk, arbeid; **take somebody to** –, iemand berispe (bestraf), iemand voor stok kry (die les lees); – **force**, taakmag.
task, v. 'n taak oplê; (te veel) eis van.

taskmaster, baas, werkgewer; opsiener.
tassel, n. klossie; bladwys(t)er(lintjie).
tastable, smaaklik; proebaar.
taste, v. proe; smaak; ondervind; **it** –**s of**, dit smaak na.
taste, n. smaak; voorliefde; happie, slukkie, proefie; **he has no** – **for sweet things**, hy hou nie van soetgoed nie; **not to my** –, nie na my sin nie; **the remark was in bad** –, die aanmerking het van slegte smaak getuig.
tasteful, smaakvol; smaaklik.
tasteless, smaakloos; laf.
taster, proeër; proe(f)glas; kaasboor.
tasty, smaaklik, lekker.
tatter, lap, toiing, flenter, vod.
tatterdemalion, verflenterde vent.
tattered, verflenter, flenterig, toiingrig.
tatting, knoopwerk.
tattle, v. babbel, klets; kekkel, skinder.
tattle, n. gebabbel, geklets; gekekkel.
tattler, babbelaar; kekkelbek.
tattoo, n. taptoe; **beat the devil's** –, met die vingers tamboerspeel.
tattoo, v. tatoeëer.
tattoo, n. tatoeëring, tatoeëermerke.
taunt, v. beskimp, hoon, terg, tretter.
taunt, n. smaad, hoon, belediging, verwyt, spot.
taunting, honend, beledigend, tergend.
taurine, bul-...; stier-...; bees-...
taut, styf, gespanne; in goeie toestand.
tauten, styf span; styf word.
tautological, toutologies.
tautology, toutologie.
tavern, kroeg, drinkplek.
tavern-keeper, kroeghouer.
taw, v. witlooi.
taw, n. albasterspeletjie; albaster, tooi, ghoen; stonkstreep.
tawdriness, opsigtigheid, bontheid.
tawdry, opgeskik, opsigtig, uitspattig.
tawer, witlooier.
tawny, geelbruin, taankleurig.
tax, v. belas, belasting oplê; op die proef stel; – **with**, verg van; beskuldig van.
tax, n. belasting; las, proef; **it will be a heavy** – **upon him**, dit sal hom swaar op die proef stel.
taxability, belasbaarheid.
taxable, belasbaar.
taxation, belasting.
tax-collector, ontvanger van belastings.
tax-free, belastingvry.
tax-gatherer, ontvanger van belastings.
taxi, taxi; – **plane**, lugtaxi; – **rank**, staanplek vir taxi's.
taxidermist, diere-opstopper.
taxidermy, die kuns om diere op te stop.
taxidriver, taxibestuurder.
taximeter, taximeter, afstandsmeter.
taxpayer, belastingbetaler.
tea, tee.
tea-caddy, teeblik.
teach, leer, onderwys gee, skoolhou, onderrig gee; **where does he** –? waar hou hy skool? waar gee hy onderwys?; **he** –**es Greek**, hy gee onderwys in Grieks.
teachable, leergierig; onderwysbaar.
teacher, onderwyser(es), (skool)meester.
tea-chest, teekis.
teaching, n. onderwys; leer.
teaching, a. onderwys-...
tea-cloth, tee(tafel)kleedjie.
tea-cosy, teemus.
tea-cup, teekoppie; **it was a storm in a** –, dit was 'n lawaai oor niks, hulle het van 'n muggie 'n olifant gemaak.

tea-garden, teetuin.
teak, kiaathout.
tea-kettle, teeketel.
teal, wilde-eend, taling.
tea-leaves, teeblare.
team, n. span; ploeg.
team, v. inspan; werk laat aanneem.
teamster, voerman, drywer.
tea-pot, teepot.
tear, v. skeur; ruk, losruk; trek, pluk; vlie(g), ja, storm; – **one's hair**, jou hare uitruk; **I could not** – **myself away**, ek kon my nie (van die plek) losskeur nie; – **at**, ruk aan, pluk aan; – **down**, afskeur (afruk); – **down the hill**, die heuwel afstorm; – **from**, wegskeur, wegruk; ontruk; – **off**, afskeur; – **out a page**, 'n blad uitskeur.
tear, n. skeur.
tear, n. traan.
tearful, treurig; vol trane, betraan.
tear-gas, traangas.
tearing, skeurend; geweldig; rasend; **a** – **pace**, 'n vlieënde vaart; **in a** – **rage**, rasend van woede.
tear-jerker, tranerige stuk (rolprent).
tearless, sonder trane, onbetraan.
tea-room, kafee, teehuis.
tear-stained, betraan.
tease, v. terg, pla, versondig; uitkam.
tease, n. plaaggees, terggees.
teasel, wolkam, wewerskam.
teaser, plaaggees, kwelgees; moeilikheid, lastigheid, neukery.
tea-service, tea-set, teeservies.
teaspoon, teelepel.
teat, tepel, tiet; speen, uier.
tea-table, teetafel.
tea-things, teegoed.
technical, tegnies.
technicality, tegniese uitdrukking; tegniese besonderheid; formaliteit.
technician, tegnikus.
Technicolor, kleur; kleur-.
technique, tegniek.
technological, tegnologies.
technologist, tegnoloog.
technology, tegnologie.
tectonics, boukuns.
tectorial, dek- . . .
ted, omkeer, oopsprei.
tedious, vervelend, vermoeiend, lastig.
tedium, verveling.
tee, n. (letter) T; T-stuk, T-buis.
tee, n. bof (in gholf); pen (in koits).
tee, v. bof.
teem, wemel, krioel; – **with**, wemel van.
teenager, tienderjarige.
teens, jare tussen 13 en 19, tienderjare; **she is still in her** –, sy is nog nie 20 jaar nie, sy was maar pas 13.
teeny, klein.
teethe, tande kry.
teething, tandekry.
teetotal, afskaffers- . . .; algeheel; – **meeting**, vergadering van afskaffers.
teetotalism, geheelonthouding.
teetotaller, afskaffer, geheelonthouer.
teetotum, A-al-tolletjie, dobbeltolletjie.
tegular, teëlagtig, teëlvormig, teël- . . .
tegument, vel, huid, omhulsel.
telecast, n. beeldsending.
telecast, v. beeldsend.
telegram, telegram, draadberig.
telegraph, n. telegraaf.
telegraph, v. telegrafeer.

telegrapher, telegrafis.
telegraphic, telegrafies.
telegraphist, telegrafis.
telegraph office, telegraafkantoor.
telegraph wire, telegraafdraad.
telegraphy, telegrafie.
teleological, teleologies.
teleology, teleologie.
telepathic, telepaties.
telepathy, telepatie.
telephone, n. telefoon; – **booth**, telefoonhokkie; – **directory**, telefoongids; – **exchange**, telefoonsentrale.
telephone, v. telefoneer, opbel, oplui.
telephonic, telefonies, telefoon- . . .
telephony, telefonie.
telephoto, telefoto; – **lens**, telefotolens, telelens.
teleprinter, telekstoestel, teledrukker.
telescope, n. teleskoop, verkyker.
telescope, v. inmekaar skuif, inmekaar sluit.
telescopic, teleskopies; inskuifbaar.
televise, beeldsend.
television, beeldradio, televisie.
telex, n. teleks(toestel).
telex, v. per teleks stuur.
tell, vertel, verhaal; sê, meedeel, meld; bepaal; onderskei; verseker; tel; – **me what you want**, sê vir my wat jy wil hê; – **the truth**, die waarheid praat; **you are** –**ing me!**, of ek dit nie weet nie!; **I cannot** – **them apart**, ek ken hulle nie uit mekaar uit nie; **don't** – **on me**, moet my nie gaan verklik nie; **we were 15 men all told**, ons was altesaam 15 man; – **it not in Gath**, verkondig dit nie in Gat nie; **you never can** –, 'n mens weet nooit; **every blow told**, elke skoot was raak; **have your fortune told**, jou toekoms laat voorspel; – **off**, aftel; gelas; aanwys; **the burden began to** – **upon him**, die las het swaar op hom begin druk; **you are** –**ing me!**, of ek dit nie weet nie!
teller, verteller; teller, kassier; stemopnemer.
tell-tale, nuusdraer, verklikker.
tellurian, a. aard- . . ., aards.
tellurian, n. aardbewoner.
telotype, druktelegraaf; gedrukte telegram.
telstar, telstar.
temerity, vermetelheid, roekeloosheid.
temper, v. aanmaak, brei (van klei); hard maak, hard word; temper, matig, versag; tot bedaring bring.
temper, n. humeur; gemoedstoestand, stemming; slegte humeur; mengsel; hardheid; **in a good, bad** –, in 'n goeie, slegte luim (bui); **lose one's** –, uit jou humeur raak, kwaad word; **keep one's** –, bedaard (kalm) bly; **he has a** –, hy word gou kwaad.
temperament, temperament, geaardheid.
temperamental, temperamenteel.
temperance, matigheid, gematigdheid; – **society**, matigheidsgenootskap; – **movement**, matigheidsbeweging, drankbestryding.
temperate, matig, gematig; bedaard; **the** – **zone**, die gematigde lugstreek.
temperature, temperatuur, warmtegraad.
tempered, getemper(d); gehumeur(d).
tempest, storm, orkaan.
tempestuous, stormagtig, onstuimig.
templar, tempelier.
temple, tempel.
temple, slaap (aan die kop).
tempo, tempo, maat.
temporal, slaapbeen.
temporal, a. tydelik; wêreldlik.
temporary, tydelik.
temporization, gésloer, uitstel.

**temporize, tyd wen, uitstel, draal, sloer, jou na die omstandighede skik.
tempt,** in die versoeking bring, verlei, versoek, verlok, beproef.
temptation, versoeking, verleiding, verlokking.
tempter, versoeker, verleier.
tempting, verleidelik, aanloklik.
temptress, verleidster, verlokster.
ten, tien.
tenability, houbaarheid.
tenable, houbaar; verdedigbaar; **the scholarship is – for three years,** die beurs word vir drie jaar toegeken; **the office is – for five years,** die dienstyd strek oor 'n tydperk van vyf jaar.
tenacious, hardnekkig, taai; klewerig; sterk; **a – memory,** 'n sterk geheue; **be – of,** hardnekkig vashou aan.
tenacity, hardnekkigheid, taaiheid.
tenancy, huur, pag.
tenant, n. huurder, pagter.
tenant, v. huur, in die huur hê.
tenantable, verhuurbaar, verpagbaar.
tenant farmer, huurboer, pagter.
tenantless, onverhuur, onbewoon, leeg.
tenantry, huurders, pagters.
tend, gaan, beweeg; geneig wees, strek, dien; bydra (tot).
tend, oppas, kyk na, versorg (versôre).
tendency, neiging, strekking.
tender, n. koolwa, tender; oppasser.
tender, v. aanbied; inskrywe, „tender"; – **one's services,** jou dienste aanbied; – **one's resignation,** jou bedanking indien.
tender, n. aanbod; inskrywing, „tender"; betaalmiddel.
tender, a. teer, sag; swak, tingerig; teergevoelig; delikaat; **a – heart,** 'n teer hart; – **meat,** saggekookte vleis.
tender-hearted, teerhartig.
tendon, sening.
tendril, rank.
tenebrous, donker, duister.
tenement, verblyf, woonhuis; huurkamers; paggrond, huurgrond.
tenement-house, huurhuis.
tenet, leer, beginsel.
tenfold, tienvoudig.
tenner, tienpondnoot; tienponder.
tennis, tennis.
tennis-court, tennisbaan.
tenon, tap, pen.
tenon-saw, tapsaag.
tenor, koers, gang, rigting, loop; inhoud, strekking; afskrif; tenoor; altviool.
tense, n. tyd, tempus.
tense, a. styf; gespanne.
tensibility, rekbaarheid, spanbaarheid.
tensile, rekbaar; – **force,** spankrag.
tension, spanning; gespannenheid; spankrag; opgewondenheid; inspanning.
tensor, trekspier.
tent, tent; kap.
tent, n. pluksel.
tentacle, voelhoring, tasorgaan, voelorgaan.
tentative, a. proef-. . ., tydelik, „tentatief".
tentative, n. proefneming, poging.
tenter, n. spanraam.
tenterhook, spanhaak; **be on –s,** op hete kole sit.
tenth, a. tiende.
tenth, n. tiende, die tiende deel.
tenthly, in die tiende plek, ten tiende.
tenuis, tenuis.
tenuous, tingerig, dun, klein, fyn.
tenure, eiendomsreg, besit; – **of office,** dienstyd.
tepee, Indiaanse hut, wigwam.

tepefy, lou word; lou maak.
tepid, lou.
tepidity, louheid.
tercel, mannetjie(s)valk.
tercentenary, a. driehonderdjarig.
tercentenary, n. derde eeufees.
tercet, terset, tersine.
terebinth, terpentynboom.
teredo, paalwurm.
tergal, rug-. . .
tergiversate, om die bos spring, uitvlugte soek, jakkalsdraaie maak.
tergiversation, jakkalsdraaie, uitvlugte.
term, n. perk, grens; tydperk, termyn; kwartaal, semester; sitting; term, uitdrukking; lid; bewoording; –s, uitdrukkinge, bewoordinge; voorwaardes; prys; **in the most flattering –s,** in die vleiendste bewoordinge; **our –s are very reasonable,** ons betalingsvoorwaardes is baie billik; **his –s are 2 guineas a lesson,** hy vra 2 ghienies 'n les; **come to –s,** dit eens word, 'n vergelyk tref; **bring somebody to –s,** iemand noodsaak om jou voorwaardes aan te neem; **on good –s with,** op goeie voet met; **we are not on speaking –s,** ons praat nie met mekaar nie; – **of office,** dienstyd; **reduce to lowest –s,** in die eenvoudigste vorm weergee, soveel soos moontlik vereenvoudig; **reduce a fraction to its lowest –s,** 'n breuk verklein; **–s of reference,** opdrag.
term, v. noem; **I forget what he –s it,** ek het vergeet wat hy dit noem.
termagancy, twisterigheid, kyfagtigheid.
termagant, n. kyfagtige vrou, heks.
termagant, a. kyfagtig, luidrugtig.
terminable, begrensbaar, bepaalbaar; opsegbaar.
terminal, a. eind-. . . (ent-. . .), grens-. . .; termyn-. . .; terminaal; – **subscription,** termynsubskripsie; – **account,** termynrekening.
terminal, n. uiterste, eindpunt, ent (einde); klem, klemskroef; terminus.
terminate, v. eindig, ophou; afloop; 'n einde maak aan, afbreek; begrens; – **in,** eindig op (met), uitgaan op.
termination, einde; grens; beëindiging, afbreking; uitgang; **bring to a –,** 'n einde maak aan, afbreek.
terminator, grenslyn; stopsetter; opsêer.
terminological, terminologies; – **inexactitude,** onjuistheid.
terminology, terminologie.
terminus, terminus, eindpunt.
termite, witmier, termiet, rysmier.
termless, onbegrens, onbeperk.
ternary, a. drietallig, ternêr.
ternary, n. drietal.
ternate, drietallig, drie-drie.
Terpsichorean, van Terpsichore, dans-. . .; – **art,** danskuns.
terra, aarde; – **firma,** vaste grond; – **incognita,** onbekende land.
terrace, n. terras.
terrace, v. terrasse maak.
terra-cotta, terra-cotta.
terrain, terrein.
terrapin, varswaterskilpad.
terraqueous, uit land en water bestaande.
terrene, aards.
terrestrial, a. aards, ondermaans, aards-. . .; – **animals,** landdiere.
terrestrial, n. aardbewoner.
terrible, vreeslik, verskriklik; yslik.
terrier, terriër.
terrific, verskriklik, skrikwekkend.

terrify, verskrik, die skrik op die lyf ja, laat skrik, bang maak.
terrigenous, grond- . . .; aard- . . .
territorial, territoriaal, van 'n grondgebied, grond- . . .; landweer- . . .; – waters, kussee; gebiedswaters.
territory, grond(gebied), landstreek.
terror, vrees, skrik, ontsteltenis; gruwel, onnut; Reign of T-, Skrikbewind.
terrorism, skrikbewind, terrorisme.
terrorize, skrik aanja, terroriseer.
terror-stricken, terror-struck, deur skrik bevang, met skrik vervul.
terse, pittig, kort en bondig, beknop.
tertiary, van die derde orde; tersiër.
tessellar, geruit.
tesselated, geruit, mosaïk- . . .
tessera, teëltjie; dobbelsteen.
test, b. toets, toetssteen; proef; reagens; smeltkroes; toetswedstryd; **put to the** –, op die proef stel; **stand the** –, die proef deurstaan; – **case**, 'n proef, 'n toetssaak.
test, v. op die proef stel, toets, ondersoek.
testable, toetsbaar.
testaceous, skaal- . . ., skulp- . . .
testament, testament.
testamentary, testamentêr.
testate, n. testament nalatend.
testator, erflater, testateur.
testatrix, erflaatster, testatrise.
tester, toetser.
tester, dak (hemel) van 'n ledekant.
testicle, (teel)bal, saadbal.
testiculate, balvormig.
testify, getuig; getuienis aflê; plegtig verklaar.
testimonial, getuigskrif; huldeblyk.
testimony, getuienis, verklaring, betuiging; **call him in** –, hom tot getuie roep; **produce** – **of**, bewys lewer van; **bear** – **to**, getuig van; **on the** – **of**, op die verklaring van.
test-match, toetswedstryd.
test-tube, proefglasie, reageerbuisie.
testudo, skilpad.
testy, prikkelbaar, liggeraak.
tetanic, klem- . . .
tetanus, klem, kramp, tetanus.
tête-à-tête, private gesprek, gesprek onder vier oë, tweepersoonsrusbank.
tether, n. tou, riem (om 'n dier op lyn te sit); **that was beyond his** –, dit was bokant sy vuurmaakplek; **he was at the end of his** –, hy was ten einde raad, hy het sy rieme styfgeloop.
tether, op lyn sit (slaan).
tetragon, vierhoek.
tetragonal, vierhoekig, tetragonaal.
tetragram, vierletter-woord; vierhoek.
tetrahedron, viervlak; tetraëder.
tetrameter, viervoetige versreël.
tetrapodous, vierpotig.
tetrarch, viervors, tetrag.
tetrasyllabic, vierlettergrepig.
Teutonic, Teutoons (Teutonies); Germaans.
text, teks; onderwerp.
text-book, handboek, leerboek.
text-hand, grootskrif.
textile, a. weef- . . .; geweeg(de), tekstiel-.
textile, n. weefstof.
textual, tekstueel, teks- . . ., in die teks.
textualist, skrifgeleerde.
texture, weefsel, samestelling, bou.
Thalia, Thalia (muse van die blyspel).
than, as, dan; **drier** –, droër as.
thank, bedank, dank, dankie sê; – **you**, dankie; he has only himself to – for that, dit is sy eie skuld.
thankful, dankbaar.
thankless, ondankbaar.
thank-offering, dankoffer.
thanks, dank, dankbetuiging; dankie; – **to your obstinacy**, dank sy jou hardkoppigheid; **will you return** –? sal jy asseblief dank?; **small** – I got for it, bloedweinig dank het ek daarvoor gekry; – **awfully**, baie dankie!
thanksgiving, danksegging; – **service**, dankseggingsdiens.
that, pron. daardie, dié; wat; who is – woman? wie is daardie vrou?; like –, so; **responsibility and all** –, verantwoordelikheid en dergelike dinge; –'**s right**, mooi so!; **this** –, **and the other**, alles en nog wat, hiervan en daarvan.
that, adv. so.
that, conj. dat, sodat, opdat.
that, adj. sodanig, soveel.
thatch, n. dekstrooi, dekgras, dekriet; strooidak, grasdak; (die) dek; bos hare.
thatch, v. dek; –**ed roof**, strooidak, rietdak.
thaumatrope, wonderwiel.
thaumaturge, wonderdoener.
thaumaturgy, wonderdoenery.
thaw, v. smelt, dooi; ontdooi.
thaw, n. dooi, warm weer.
the, die; **4c** – **pound**, 4c die pond; **16 oz. to** – **pound**, 16 ons op 'n pond; – **more he gets**, – **more he wants**, hoe meer hy kry, hoe meer wil hy hê; – **sooner** – **better**, hoe eerder hoe beter; **that makes it all** – **worse**, dit maak dit des te erger.
theatre, teater, skouburg; toneel; gehoorsaal; **the** – **of war**, die oorlogsfront, die oorlogsveld, die oorlogstoneel; **operating** –, operasiesaal.
theatre-goer, skouburgbesoeker.
theatre-going, skouburgbesoekend; **the** – **public**, die skouburgpubliek.
theatrical, a. teatraal, toneel- . . .
theatrical(s), n. toneelvoorstelling(e).
thee, u.
theft, diefstal.
theine, teïen (theïne).
their, hul(le); –**s**, hulle s'n.
theism, teïsme.
theist, teïs.
them, sien **they**.
thematic, tematies.
theme, tema, onderwerp; opstel; – **song**, wederkerende wysie (in 'n rolprent).
themselves, hul(le), hul(le)self; **they know it** –, hulle weet dit self.
then, adv. toe; dan; daarna, vervolgens; **now and** –, nou en dan, af en toe; **every now and** –, kort-kort; **by** –, teen dié tyd; **from** –, van toe af; **till** –, tot dié tyd; **there and** –, op die plek, onmiddellik, dadelik.
then, a. toenmalig, destyds; **the** – **secretary**, die toenmalige sekretaris.
then, conj. dus, dan.
thence, daarvandaan af, van daar, daaruit, derhalwe.
thenceforth, thenceforward, van toe af, van dié tyd af, sedert dié tyd.
theoeracy, teokrasie, godsregering.
theocratic, teokraties.
theodolite, hoogtemeter, teodoliet.
theologian, teoloog, godgeleerde.
theological, teologies.
theology, teologie, godgeleerdheid.
theorem, stelling, teorema.
theoretical, teoreties.
theoretics, teorie.
theorist, teoretikus.
theorize, teoretiseer.

**theory, **teorie.
theosophical, teosofies.
theosophist, teosoof.
theosophy, teosofie.
therapeutic, terapeuties, geneeskundig.
therapeutics, terapie, geneeskuns.
there, adv. daar, daarso; daarheen, daarnatoe, soontoe (soheentoe); **I agree with you –**, op daardie punt is ek dit eens met jou; **I go – every day**, ek gaan elke dag daarnatoe; **I don't think he will get –**, ek glo nie hy sal dit maak nie; **– and back**, heen en terug; **he is not all –**, hy het nie al sy varkies in die hok nie, hy is nie heeltemal reg nie; **he is all –**, hy weet wat hy doen, hy is nie onder 'n kalkoen uitgebroei nie; hy is danig op die voorgrond.
there, interj. –!, daar het jy dit!
thereabout(s), daaromtrent, daar iewers, daar rond, daar in die buurt; ongeveer, omtrent, naasteby.
thereafter, daarna; daarvolgens.
thereby, op dié manier, daardeur.
therefore, daarom, derhalwe, dus.
therefrom, daarvan.
therein, daarin.
thereof, daarvan, hiervan.
thereto, daartoe; boonop, behalwe.
thereupon, daarna, daarop.
therewithal, buitendien, daarby.
therm, warmte-eenheid, term.
thermal, termaal, warmte- . . ., warm; **– unit,** warmte-eenheid; **– springs,** warm bronne.
thermic, warmte- . . .
thermo-dynamics, termodinamika.
thermo-electricity, termo-elektrisiteit.
thermogenesis, warmteverwekking.
thermometer, termometer.
thermo-nuclear, termonukleêr.
Thermos flask, Thermosfles, warmfles.
these, hierdie, die.
thesis, stelling; tesis, dissertasie.
thews, senings, spiere; sedelike krag.
thewy, gespier, sterk.
they, hulle (hul); **– say,** die mense sê.
thick, a. dik, dig; troebel; bot, dom; intiem, kop-in-een-mus; **a bit –**, 'n bietjie kras; **as – as thieves,** baie kop-in-een-mus.
thick, n. dikte; hewigste; **through – and thin,** deur dik en dun; **the – of the fight,** die hewigste van die geveg.
thicken, dik word; dik maak, verdik; aangroei, toeneem.
thicket, ruigte, bossies.
thickhead, dikkop, domkop.
thickheaded, dom, bot.
thickish, dikkerig.
thickness, dikte; digtheid.
thickset, digbegroei; geset, dik, fris.
thick-skinned, dikhuidig.
thick-skulled, dom, bot, dikkop- . . .
thick-witted, dom, bot, stom.
thief, dief.
thieve, steel.
thievery, diewery, diefstal.
thieving, a. diewe- . . ., steel- . . ., stelend.
thieving, n. stelery, diewery.
thievish, diefagtig.
thigh, dy.
thigh-bone, dybeen.
thimble, vingerhoed.
thimbleful, 'n vingerhoed(vol).
thin, a. dun; maer, skraal; yl; flou; deursigtig; swak; **a – excuse,** 'n flou eksuus.
thin, v. dun (yl, maer) word (maak); verdun.
thine, u, van u.

thing, ding; iets; saak; **poor –!; arme ding! arme drommel!; isn't she a dear little –?** is sy nie 'n klein skat nie! **you nasty –?** jou naarheid!; **old –?** ou kind! skat!; **pack up your –s,** pak in jou goed; **it was a foolish – to do,** dit was dom om so iets te doen; **don't take –s too seriously,** moet sake nie te ernstig opneem nie; **you've made a mess of –s,** jy het alles verbrou; **an unusual –,** iets buitengewoons; **it is the latest – in hats,** dit is die nuutste mode wat hoede betref; **I am not feeling at all the –,** ek voel nie danig lekker nie; **that is not the same –,** dit is nie dieselfde nie; **he knows a – or two,** hy is ouer as twaalf; **do the handsome – by,** rojaal behandel; **that's the very – I want,** dit is net wat ek wil hê; **that is not quite the –,** dit is nie heeltemal soos dit behoort te wees nie; **as –s are,** soos sake nou staan.
thingamy, thingumajig, thingumbob, thingummy dinges, hoe-se-naam.
things, goed, goeters.
think, dink; ag, meen, glo, beskou; van plan wees; 'n denkbeeld vorm (van); **the child thought no harm,** die kind het geen kwaad vermoed nie; **I don't – so,** moenie glo nie, aikôna!; **if you – it fit,** as jy dit goed vind; **I thought so,** dit kon ek dink; **I don't – so,** ek glo nie; **– of,** dink van; dink aan; bedink; **I couldn't – of his name,** ek kon nie op sy naam kom nie; **he –s nothing of 30 miles a day,** 30 myl op 'n dag is vir hom niks; **– out,** uitdink; oorweeg; **– over,** nadink oor; **I must – it over,** ek moet daaroor nadink.
thinkable, denkbaar.
thinker, dinker (denker).
thinking, a. dink- . . ., dinkend, redelik.
thinking, n. gedagte; mening; dink; **to my –,** na my mening, myns insiens.
thinly, dun, dunnerig.
thinner(s), verdunningsmiddel.
thin-skinned, dun van vel; prikkelbaar, liggeraak, fyngevoelig.
third, a. derde; **the – degree,** afdreiging van bekentenis.
third, n. 'n derde, derde deel; terts (in musiek).
third-class, derdeklas; goedkoop.
thirdly, in die derde plek, ten derde.
third-party insurance, derdeversekering.
third-rate, derderangs, minderwaardig.
thirst, n. dors; **– after, for, of,** dors na.
thirst, v. dors hê; **– after, for,** dors na, vurig verlang na.
thirsty, dors, dorstig.
thirteen, dertien.
thirteenth, a. dertiende.
thirteenth, n. dertiende (deel).
thirtieth, a. dertigste.
thirtieth, n. dertigste (deel).
thirty, dertig.
this, dit; hierdie, dié; **like –,** so; **I knew all –,** ek het dit alles geweet; **in these days,** in ons dae; **–, that and the other,** alles en nog wat; **– day,** vandag, hede; **– morning,** vanmôre (vanoggend); **– day fortnight,** vandag oor veertien dae; **he ought to be ready by – time,** hy moet nou al klaar wees; **I have been asking for it these three weeks,** ek vra nou al die afgelope drie weke daarna.
thistle, dissel.
thistly, vol dissels, disselagtig.
thither, daarheen, daarnatoe, soontoe.
thole, roeipen, dol(pen).
thong, riem; voor-, agterslag.
thoracic, bors- . . .
thorax, bors(stuk), borsharnas; borskas.

thorium, torium.
thorn, doring; doringbos, doringstruik; **a − in one's flesh, side**, 'n doring in die vlees; **sit on −s**, op hete kole sit.
thornback, stekelvis.
thorn-hedge, doringheining.
thorny, vol dorings, doringrig, doringagtig, moeilik, lastig.
thorough, deeglik, grondig; volkome, algeheel, volledig; **a − scoundrel**, 'n deurtrapte skurk.
thoroughbred, a. volbloed-, opreg geteel; welopgevoed; **− horse**, volbloedperd.
thoroughfare, deurgang; (hoof)straat; **no −**, geen deurgang, deurgang verbode.
thorough-going, radikaal, deurtastend.
thoroughly, terdeë, deur en deur.
thorough-paced, volleer; volmaak; **a − rascal**, 'n deurtrapte skurk.
those, sien that; die, daardie, diegene.
though, ofskoon, alhoewel, al; **it looks as −**, dit lyk (as)of; **he acts as − he were mad**, hy gedra hom soos 'n mal mens; **what − the way is long**, al is die weg ook lank; **I wish you had told me, −**, ek wens tog dat jy my gesê het; **even −**, al.
thought, gedagte; oorweging; oorpeinsing; gepeins; idee, inval; bietjie, 'n ietsie; **after serious −**, na ernstige oorweging; **he acts without −**, hy handel sonder om na te dink; **a happy −**, 'n gelukkige nval ; **he had some −s of resigning**, hy was half en half van plan om te bedank; **his one − is to get away**, al waar hy aan dink, is hoe om weg te kom; **a − shorter**, so 'n ietsie korter; **quick as −**, so gou soos blits; **take no − of the morrow**, bekommer jou nie oor die dag van môre nie; **on second −s**, na verdere oorweging; **in deep −**, in diep gepeins, ingedagte.
thoughtful, bedagsaam; peinsend, nadinkend; vol gedagtes, suggestief; bedag (op); **he is never − of others**, hy dink nooit aan ander nie.
thoughtless, onbesonne, onbedagsaam; gedagteloos; onagsaam.
thought-reader, gedagteleser.
thought-transference, telepatie.
thousand, duisend; **a − times easier**, oneindig makliker, honderd maal makliker; **one in a −**, een uit die duisend; **it is a − pities**, dit is tog alte jammer; **a − thanks**, duisend maal dank.
thousandfold, duisendvoudig.
thousandth, duisendste.
thraldom, slawerny, knegskap.
thrall, n. slaaf; slawerny.
thrall, v. tot slaaf maak.
thrash, (uit)dors; slaan, uitklop, afransel; oortref, kafloop; **− out**, uitpluis, agter die waarheid kom.
thrasher, thresher, dorser; dorsmasjien.
thrashing, (die) dors; pak slae, loesing.
thrashing-floor, dorsvloer, trapvloer.
thrashing-machine, dorsmasjien, trapmasjien.
thread, n. draad; **the − of life**, die lewensdraad; **he lost the − of his argument**, hy het die draad kwytgeraak; **hang by a −**, aan 'n draadjie hang; **resume, take up the −**, vervat, vervolg.
thread, v. draad deursteek (insteek); inryg; 'n weg baan deur; **− beads**, krale inryg; **− my way through**, tussen die mense deurvleg.
threadbare, verslyt (verslete); afgesaag.
threadiness, draderigheid.
thread-worm, draadwurm.
thready, draderig.
threat, dreigement, bedreiging.
threaten, bedreig; dreig (met).
threatening, n. dreigement, bedreiging.

threatening, dreigend; **a − letter**, 'n dreigbrief, 'n brander.
three, drie; **T− in One**, die Drie-eenheid; **the − R's**, lees-, skryf- en rekenkuns.
three-cornered, driehoekig, driekantig; **a − contest**, 'n driehoekige verkiesing.
three-decker, driedekker.
three-fold, drievoudig.
three-forked, drietand- . . .
three-handed, driehand- . . .; driemans- . . .
three-legged, driebeen- . . .; **− race**, driebeenwedloop, spanbeenwedloop.
threepence, trippens.
three-ply, driedraads, drielaag- . . .
three-quarter, agterspeler; driekwart.
threescore, sestig.
threesome, driespel (gholf).
threnode, threnody, klaagsang, lyksang.
thresh, sien **thrash**.
threshold, drumpel; drempel (fig.); aanvang, begin, ingang; **on the − of**, aan die vooraand van.
thrice, drie maal.
thrift, spaarsaamheid, suinigheid.
thriftiness, sien **thrift**.
thriftless, verkwistend.
thrifty, spaarsaam; voorspoedig.
thrill, v. tril, ril, sidder; laat tril (ril), deurdring; deurhuiwer; **− with horror**, laat sidder van afsku; **his voice −ed the listeners**, sy stem het 'n rilling deur die toehoorders laat gaan.
thrill, n. trilling, rilling, spanning, siddering, huiwering; tinteling; sensasiewekkende verhaal, sensasie; triller; **a − of joy**, 'n tinteling van blydskap; **it gave him a −**, dit het hom laat lekker kry.
thrilling, trillend, rillend; spannend, opwindend, aangrypend; sensasioneel; **a − experience**, 'n opwindende (spannende) ondervinding.
thrive, vooruitkom, voorspoedig wees; floreer; goed aard, geil groei.
thriving, voorspoedig, bloeiend.
throat, keel; noute, ingang, uitgang; **cut one's own −**, jou eie keel afsny; jou eie ondergang bewerk; **cut one another's −s**, mekaar die keel afsny; mekaar benadeel; **he lies in his −**, hy lieg op 'n streep; **spring at the − of**, na die keel vlie; **thrust a thing down one's −**, iets aan jou opdring; **jump down somebody's −**, iemand invlie; **clear one's −**, jou keel skoonmaak; **be full to the −**, buikvol wees.
throaty, keel- . . ., gutturaal.
throb, v. klop, pols, slaan; bewe, ril.
throb, n. klop, klopping, slag.
throe(s), wee (weë), barensnood; pyn, (doods)angs; **in the −s of (writing)**, hard besig met (skrywe).
thrombosis, trombose, aarverstopping.
throne, n. troon; **come to the −**, die troon beklim, die regering aanvaar.
throne, v. op die troon sit (plaas).
throng, n. gedrang, menigte.
throng, v. toestroom, verdring; **the streets were −ed**, die strate het gewemel (van mense).
throstle, lyster; spinmasjien.
throttle, n. lugpyp, keelgorrel; smoorklep, stoomklep, gasklep.
throttle, v. verwurg, die gorrel toedruk, versmoor, verstik, laat stik; smoor.
throttle-valve, smoorklep, stoomklep.
through, prep. deur; uit; **it was all − you**, dit was alles net jou skuld; **− shame**, uit skaamte.
through, adv. deur, tot die einde; deur en deur; **he looked me − and −**, hy het my van kop tot tone beskou; **it lasted all −**, dit het dwarsdeur

(aan)gehou; **are you – with that job,** het jy daardie werk klaar?; **I am – with you,** ons twee is klaar met mekaar.
through, a. deurgaande, deur- . . .
through freight, deurvrag.
throughout, adv. dwarsdeur, deurgaans, deur en deur, geheel en al; in alle opsigte.
throughout, prep. dwarsdeur.
through train, deurgaande trein.
throw, v. gooi, werp, smyt; afgooi; ondergooi; vleg, draai (van sydrade, ens.); **you must not – stones,** jy moenie met klippe gooi nie; **– a party,** 'n partytjie reël; **– a fit,** die stuipe kry (lett. en fig.); **– at,** gooi na; **– away,** weggooi, laat verlore gaan; **he threw away an excellent chance,** hy het 'n uitstekende kans laat verlore gaan; **– back,** terugaard (na voorouers); **he threw a glance backwards,** hy het vinnig omgekyk; **– down,** omgooi, omvergooi, neergooi; **– into the bargain,** op die koop toegee; **– in one's lot with,** gemene saak maak met, die lot deel van, lief en leed deel met; **– in the teeth of,** voor die kop gooi; **– into confusion,** in die war stuur; **– oneself into,** met hart en siel meewerk aan; **– off,** ontslae raak van, kwytraak; afgooi; lewer; begin, 'n aanvang maak; **– off poems,** gedigte fluit-fluit afmaak, gedigte uit die mou skud; **– on your clothes,** jou klere gou-gou aantrek; **– light on,** lig werp op; **he threw himself upon the mercy of,** hy het hom beroep op die barmhartigheid van; **– open,** oopgooi, oopmaak, oopsit, oopstel; **– open the door,** die deur oopmaak; die pad oopmaak, dit moontlik maak; **– out,** uitgooi; verwerp; van die wysie bring, deurmekaar maak; insinueer; opper; **– over,** verlaat, in die steek laat, afsê; **– overboard,** oorboord gooi; **– up,** opgee, laat vaar; neergooi; (hande) opsteek; opbring; **he was thrown upon his own resources,** hy moes sien dat hy regkom; **– up one's hands,** hensop, jou hande opsteek.
throw, n. gooi, worp; **it is merely a stone's –,** dit is maar net so ver soos jy met 'n klip kan gooi.
thrum, n. fraiing, draad; **thread and –,** goed en sleg, almal voor die voet.
thrum, tokkel, trommel, tjingel.
thrush, spru.
thrush, lyster.
thrust, v. stoot; steek; **– forth,** uitstoot, uitgooi; uitsteek; **he was – from his rights,** sy regte is hom met geweld ontneem; **– oneself,** one's nose in, jou neus steek in, jou bemoei met; **– into, insteek; instop; – through,** deursteek; **he tried to – his way through,** hy het hom 'n weg probeer baan deur; **I don't want it – upon me,** ek wil dit nie aan my opgedring hê nie.
thrust, n. stoot; steek; stamp; druk.
thud, n. dowwe slag, plof, bons.
thud, v. neerdoef, neerplof, (neer)bons.
thug, sluipmoordenaar, skurk; wurger.
thumb, n. duim; **hold somebody under your –,** iemand onder die duim hou.
thumb, v. beduimel, vlek; betas; trommel.
thumb-index, duimgreep.
thumb-latch, deurknip.
thumb-mark, vingervlek.
thumb-nail, duimnael; **– sketch,** miniatuurtekening, penkrabbel.
thumb-screw, duimskroef.
thumb-stall, duimhoedjie, skot.
thumb-tack, drukspyker(tjie).
thump, v. stamp, slaan, moker.
thump, n. stamp, slag, hou.
thumper, grote, reusagtige, yslike.

thumping, stampend; geweldig, groot; **a – lie,** 'n yslike leuen.
thunder, n. donder, donderweer; donderslag; **steal someone's –,** die wind uit iemand se seile haal.
thunder, v. donder; bulder, brul, **it –s,** die weer dreun, dit donder.
thunder-bolt, donderslag, weerlig(straal), blits; banbliksem.
thunderclap, donderslag; **the news came on me like a –,** soos 'n donderslag het die nuus my getref.
thunder-cloud, donderwolk.
thunderer, donderaar.
thundering, a. donderend.
thundrous, donderend.
thunderstorm, donderstorm.
thunder-struck, deur die weerlig getref; oorbluf, verstom.
thundery, donderagtig, donder- . . .
thurible, wierookvat, reukvat.
thurification, bewieroking.
Thursday, Donderdag.
thus, dus, aldus, op dié manier; so; **– far, tot sover.**
thwack, sien, **whack.**
thwart, a. dwars.
thwart, v. dwarsboom, teenwerk, in die wiele ry.
thy, u.
thyme, tiemie.
thyroid, skildvormig; **– gland,** skildklier.
thyself, uself.
tiara, tiara.
tibia, skeenbeen.
tibial, skeenbeen- . . .
tic, senuweepyn, -trekking.
tick, v. tik; **– off,** aanstreep, merk.
tick, n. tik; merkie, strepie; **to the –,** presies, op die minuut; **in two –s,** in 'n kits, in 'n jap-trap.
tick, n. luis, bosluis, skaapluis.
tick(ing), tyk (in materiaal).
tick, n. krediet; **on –,** op skuld.
ticker, tikker; horlosie.
ticket, kaartjie, toegangskaartjie, reiskaartjie, etiket; **that's the –,** daar's hy mos, dit is die ware Jakob, ditsit, net hy; **that's not quite the –,** dit is nie eintlik wat dit moet wees nie.
ticket-collector, kaartjiesknipper, kaartjiesontvanger.
ticket-examiner, kaartjieskontroleur.
ticket-office, kaartjieskantoor.
ticket-punch, kaartjiesknipper.
ticking, tyk.
ticking, tik, getik.
tickle, v. kielie; streel; **my foot –s,** dit kielie onder my voet; **I was –ed at this,** ek het groot lag gekry hieroor; **I wonder what is tickling his fancy,** ek wil graag weet wat hom so amuseer; **it –s the palate,** dit smaak na teer (ek wens na meer), dit smaak fyn.
tickle, n. kielierige gevoel, gekielie.
ticklish, kielierig; moeilik, lastig.
tick-tack, doef-doef, tik-tak.
tidal, gety- . . . ; **– harbour,** getyhawe, vloedhawe; **– wave,** vloedgolf.
tide, n. gety, ty, eb en vloed; tyd; stroom; **high –,** hoogwater; **low –,** laagwater; **go with the –,** met die stroom saamgaan; **the – has turned,** die kans het gekeer.
tide, v. met die stroom saamdrywe; **– over difficulties,** moeilikhede te bowe kom.
tide-gate, sluisdeur, getysluis.
tide-gauge, peilskaal, getymeter.
tide-lock, skutsluis.
tidily, netjies, sindelik.

tidings, tyding, nuus, berig.
tidy, a. netjies, sindelik; mooi, ordentlik; gesond, lekker; **a – sum**, 'n mooi sommetjie.
tidy, n. antimakassar, oortreksel; voorskootjie; rommelsakkie, bakkie.
tidy, v. aan kant maak, opruim; opknap.
tie, v. bind, vasbind, vasmaak, vasknoop; knoop, strik; gelyk wees, gelykop speel; ewe veel punte behaal; verbind; beperk; **– a persons's tongue**, iemand die mond snoer; **– your –**, jou das knoop; **– it in a bow**, strik dit; **I don't want to be –d down**, ek wil my nie laat bind nie; **Gardens and Maitland –d**, Tuine en Maitland het gelykop gespeel; **– up**, vasbind, vasmaak; verbind; opbind; toebind; vassit.
tie, n. band, knoop; das; verpligting; verbindingsbalk; gelykspel; **– of friendship**, vriendskapsbande; **play off a –**, 'n beslissende wedstryd speel.
tie-beam, dwarsbalk; dwarslêer.
tier, ry, reeks.
tierce, terts; drie volgkaarte.
tie-rod, (stuur)koppelstang, koggelstok.
tie-up, stilstand; staking.
tiff, n. teug, slug; slegte bui; rusie.
tiff, v. beledig wees; rusie.
tiffin, ligte middagmaal.
tige, steel, stingel.
tiger, tier; grootprater, twissoeker; duiwel.
tiger-cat, tierkat.
tiger('s)-eye, tieroog ('n edelsteen).
tiger-lily, tierlelie.
tight, a. styf, vas, stewig; dig; nou; styf(gespan); netjies, fyn, agtermekaar; getik, aan, lekker; skaars; **the cork is too –**, die prop sit te styf; **be in a – corner**, in die knyp sit; **that's a – fit**, dit sit baie nou (van klere); dit kan net so skaars-skaars in.
tight, adv. styf; **hold –**, hou styf vas.
tighten, stywer (nouer) maak, stywer trek; **– one's belt**, jou maag ingord, sonder kos bly.
tight-fisted, gierig, vrekkig, inhalig.
tight-laced, styf vasgery(g); bekrompe.
tights, 'n spanbroek; 'n vleispakkie.
tigress, tierwyfie.
tigrish, tieragtig.
tike, smeerlap, skurk.
tile, n teël; (dak)pan; **have a – loose**, nie al die varkies in die hok hê nie.
tile, v. met panne dek; met teëls belê.
tiler, pannedekker.
tiling, teëls; dakpanne.
til, v. bewerk, bebou, omploeë.
till, n. geldlaai, toonbanklaai.
till, prep. tot; **wait – then**, wag tot dan; **not – ten o'clock**, nie voor tienuur nie.
till, conj. tot, totdat.
tillable, beboubaar, bewerkbaar.
tillage, akkerbou, bewerking, bebouing.
tiller, n. landbouer.
tiller, n. roerpen.
tiller-rope, stuurtou.
tilt, n. kap, tent, seil.
tilt, v. met 'n seil toemaak.
tilt, v. skuins staan, skuins hou, (een kant) oplig; wip, laat wip; met 'n lans steek na; slaan, smee; **– at**, steek na; iemand 'n steek gee; **– at the ring**, ringsteek.
tilt, n. helling, skewe (skuins) ligging, skuinste; steekspel; smeehamer; **give it a –**, hou dit skuins, lig een kant op; **run full – against**, stormloop, in volle vaart aanstorm op; lynreg teen ingaan.
tilt-boat, tentskuit.
tilt-hammer, smeehamer.

tilt-yard, toernooiveld.
timbal, keteltrom.
timber, hout, timmerhout; bos, woud.
timber-headed, dom, bot.
timber-yard, houtwerf.
timbre, timbre, toonkleur.
timbrel, tamboeryn.
time, n. tyd; keer, maal; maat, tempo; **the good old –s**, die goeie ou tyd; **it will last our –**, dit sal hou solank soos ons lewe; **now is your –**, nou is jou kans, **I must bide my –**, ek moet my tyd afwag; **– is up!** die tyd is om!; **my – is drawing near**, my tydjie word kort, my einde nader; **he is doing his –**, hy moet sy tyd uitsit (in die tronk); **he is serving his –**, hy dien as leerjong; **I had the – of my life**, dit was vir my 'n heerlike tyd; **what a – you will have getting him home**, wat sal dit jou 'n moeite kos om hom by die huis te kry!; **the first –**, die eerste maal (keer); **–s out of number**, tallose male; **– and again**, keer op keer, herhaaldelik; **many a –**, dikwels; **– after –**, keer op keer; **ten –s two**, tien maal twee; **what is the –**, hoe laat is dit?; **this – of the day**, nou nog, op hierdie stadium; **two at a –**, twee op 'n slag; **work against –**, werk dat dit kraak (om betyds klaar te kom); **he was ahead of his –**, hy was sy tyd vooruit; **at the same –**, terselfdertyd; aan die ander kant; tog; **at –s**, soms, nou en dan; **from – to –**, van tyd tot tyd, so nou en dan; **in –**, op tyd, betyds; mettertyd; **in no –**, in 'n ommesiensstyd, in 'n japtrap; **beat –**, tyd hou; **keep –**, die maat hou; in die pas bly; **my watch keeps good –**, my horlosie loop goed; **out of –**, uit die maat; uit die pas; onvanpas; **from – immemorial**, sedert onheuglike tye; **the – of day**, die uur; **so that's the – of day!** is dit sulke tyd!; **you are behind the –**, jy is uit die tyd; **by that –**, teen daardie tyd, dan; **for a –**, 'n tydjie; **in – to come**, in die toekoms; **at the present –**, vandag; **– lag**, vertraging.
time, v. reël, reguleer; die tyd bereken; die maat aangee; die maat hou; regsit; **you must – your blows**, sorg dat jy elke hou net op die regte tyd slaan; **– him**, kyk hoeveel tyd hy nodig het.
time-card, werkuurregister, uurkaart.
time-fuse, maatlont.
time-honoured, eerbiedwaardig, eeue-oud.
time-keeper, tydaangeër; tydopnemer; horlosie; **that watch is a good –**, daardie horlosie loop goed.
timely, tydig, betyds, net op tyd.
time-piece, uurwerk, horlosie, klok.
time-server, verkleurmannetjie; **he is a –**, hy is soos die wind waai.
time-serving, a. veranderlik, onbestendig.
time-table, rooster, "tydtafel"; spoorboek.
time-worn, verslyt (verslete), oud.
timid, skamerig, bedees; bangerig.
timidity, beskroomdheid, bedeesdheid, skamerigheid, skugterheid.
timing, regulering; tydopname.
timocracy, timokrasie, besittersregering.
timorous, skroomvallig, beskroom; skrikkerig, bangerig.
timpano, keteltrom.
tin, n. tin; blik; geld, "pitte".
tin, a. tin-...; blik-...; **T– Lizzie**, 'n rammelkas, tjorrie; **– foil**, tin bladtin, foelie; blinkpapier; **– foil**, v. in bladtin toedraai.
tin, v. vertin; inmaak; **–ned meat**, blikkiesvleis.
tinctorial, kleur-..., verf-...
tincture, n. tinktuur; tikkie; tint.
tincture, v. effe kleur (verf) tint; 'n smakie gee.
tinder, tonteldoek, tontel.

tinder-box, tonteldoos.
tinder-bush, tontelbos.
tine, tand (van vurk, eg. ens.); punt.
ting, n. geklingel, tingeling.
ting, v. klingel, klink.
tinge, v. tint, kleur; 'n smakie gee.
tinge, n. tint, kleur; tikkie; smakie.
tingle, v. suis, tuit, jeuk, prikkel; **it –d in his ears,** dit het sy ore laat tuit.
tingle, n. prikkeling, getuit, gesuis.
tingling, tinteling, getuit, gesuis.
tin-god, afgodjie.
tin-hat, staalhelm.
tinker, n. ketellapper, blikslaer.
tinker, v. heelmaak, lap; knoei, konkel.
tinkle, v. klink, tingel; laat klingel.
tinkle, n. geklink, getingel, geklingel.
tinman, tingieter, blikslaer.
tinnitus, gesuis.
tinny, tin-..., tinagtig.
tin-opener, blikmes.
tin-ore, tinerts.
tin-pan: – **alley,** tingeltangelkring.
tin-plate, blik.
tinsel, n. klatergoud, verguldsel.
tinsel, a. klatergoud-..., vals, skyn-...
tin-smith, blikslaer.
tint, n. tint.
tint, v. tint, kleur.
tintinnabulation, geklingel, getjingel.
tinty, slordig, getint.
tin-ware, blikgoed.
tiny, klein; gering.
tip, n. punt, top, tip; **I had it on the – of my tongue,** dit was op (die punt van) my tong.
tip, v. 'n punt aansit; **cork –ed,** met 'n kurkmondstuk.
tip, v. wip, laat wip; skeef (skuins) hou, (laat) omkantel; gooi; fooi, 'n fooi gee; 'n snuf in die neus gee; 'n wenk gee; – **us your fin,** gee hier jou blad!; **you might have –ped me the wink,** jy kon my daarop verdag gemaak het; – **over,** kantel; – **up,** skuins hou; – **off,** waarsku, 'n wenk gee.
tip, v. fooi(tjie); wenk; stootjie, tikkie; vuilgoedhoop; **I can give you the straight –,** ek kan jou net sê wat jy wil weet; **miss one's –,** die bal mis slaan; **why didn't you take my –?** waarom het jy nie na my geluister nie, waarom het jy nie op my wenk ag gegee nie?
tip-cart, wipkar, skotskar.
tip-cat, kennetjie (spel).
tippet, pelskraag, bontkraag.
tipple, v. dopsteek, die elmboog lig.
tipple, n. sterk drank.
tippler, dopsteker, drinkebroer.
tipsify, dronk maak, lekker maak.
tipsy, dronk, lekker, aan, getik.
tipsy-cake, wynkoek, lekkermaakkoek.
tiptilted, opwip-...; wip-...; – **nose,** wipneus.
tiptoe, adv. op (die punte van) die tone.
tiptoe, v. op die tone loop.
tiptop, n. die beste, die mooiste.
tiptop, a. prima, eersteklas.
tip-up, wip-..., opklap-...; – **seat, (op)klap**stoel.
tirade, tirade; woordevloed.
tire, moeg word, teë word (van); moeg maak, vermoei, verveel.
tire, tyre, n. (buite)band.
tire, n. (hoof)tooisel.
tire, v. uitdos, klee.
tired, moeg, tam.
tireless, onvermoeid.
tiresome, vermoeiend, afmattend.

tiro, tyro, beginner, nuweling, 'n groene.
tirwit, klap-klappie.
'tis, dis.
tissue, weefsel; goudlaken; aaneenskakeling, reeks; **a** – **of lies,** 'n aaneenskakeling van leuens.
tissue-paper, sypapier, sneespapier.
tit, tepel, tiet.
tit, tinktinkie.
tit: – **for tat,** leer om leer, botter vir vet, **tik jy my dan pik ek jou.**
titan, titan; reus; **the T–s, die Titane.**
titanic, titanies, reusagtig, geweldig.
titbit, lekkernytjie, lekker happie.
tithe, tiende, tiende deel.
tithing, tiendeheffing.
Titian, Titiaan; – **hair,** goudbruin hare.
titillate, kielie; streel.
titillation, kielierige gevoel; streling.
titivate, tittivate, mooimaak; **he was busy tit(t)ivating himself,** hy was besig om hom mooi te maak (uit te vat, reg te piets).
title, n. (ere)titel; opskrif, naam, titel; aanspraak, eiendomsreg, eiendomsbewys; goudgehalte; **have a** – **to,** geregtig wees op.
title, v. betitel, noem.
title-deed, eiendomsbewys; kaart en transport.
titleless, sonder titel.
title-page, titelblad.
title-role, titelrol, naamrol.
titling, titeldruk; betiteling.
titrate, titreer.
titter, giggel.
tittle, tittel, jota, stippie.
tittle-tattle, v. babbel, klets, kekkel.
tittle-tattle, n. geklets, gebabbel.
tittup, bokspring, huppel.
titubation, kriewelrigheid, rusteloosheid.
titular, titulêr, in naam; – **saint,** beskermheilige.
to, prep. na, tot, na ... toe; vir; voor; aan; **on his way** – **the station,** op pad stasie toe; – **bed with you!** kooi toe, jy!; – **arms!** te wapen!; **I told him** – **his face,** ek het hom dit in sy gesig gesê; **all** – **no purpose,** alles tevergeefs; – **a hair's-breadth,** op 'n haar; **he drank himself** – **death,** hy het hom doodgedrink; **this is nothing** – **what it might be,** dit is niks in vergelyking met wat dit kon wees nie; **true** – **life,** lewensgetrou, lewenswaar; **ten** – **one,** tien teen een; – **his liking,** na sy sin; **compared** –, in vergelyking met; **lend it** – **me,** leen dit vir my; **write** – **somebody,** aan (vir) iemand skrywe; **apply** – **the secretary,** aansoek doen by die sekretaris – **my mind,** volgens my mening; **pleasant** – **the taste,** lekker; **what's that** – **you,** wat kan dit jou skeel; **here's** – **you!** gesondheid!; **next door** – **us,** naas ons; **not a cent** – **his name,** nie 'n sent op sy naam nie; **five minutes** – **six,** vyf minute voor ses; **there is no end** – **it,** daar is geen end aan nie; **that's not** – **the point,** dit is nie ter sake nie.
to, (+ infinitief) te, om te; **he declines** – **go,** hy weier om te gaan; **I want** – **know,** ek wil weet; **he was seen** – **fall,** hulle het hom sien val; **he was made** – **repeat it,** hy moes dit herhaal; **allow me** – **remind you,** mag ek jou daaraan herinner; **difficult** – **explain,** moeilik om duidelik te maak; **you promised** –, jy het dit beloof; **I have never known it** – **fail,** sover soos ek weet, het dit nog altyd geluk.
to, adv. toe; – **and fro,** heen en weer; **pull the door** –, die deur toetrek.
toad, padda; 'n haatlike mens, 'n pes; – **in the hole,** pasteitjie, ouvrou-onder-die-kombers.
toad-eater, vleier, inkruiper.

toad-eating, a. inkruiperig, laagvleierig.
toad-eating, n. inkruiperigheid, lekkery.
toad-stone, paddasteen.
toadstool, paddastoel.
toady, n. inkruiper, witvoetjie-soeker, lekker.
toady, v. inkruiperig (laagvleierig) wees, witvoetjie soek, lek.
toadyism, inkruiperigheid.
toast, n. gebraaide brood, braaibrood, roosterbrood; heildronk.
toast, v. rooster, braai; warm maak; die heildronk instel, die gesondheid drink van.
toaster, broodbraaier.
toasting-fork, roostervurk.
toast-master, seremoniemeester.
toast-rack, braaibroodstandertjie.
tobacco, tabak (twak).
tobacco heart, rokershart.
tobacconist, tabakhandelaar.
tobacco-pouch, tabaksak (twaksak).
tobacco-stopper, pypstoppertjie.
toboggan, n. toboggan.
toboggan, v. toboggan-ry.
tocsin, alarmklok, alarmteken, alarmgelui; **sound the –,** die alarm blaas.
today, vandag; teenswoordig.
toddle, v. waggel; **– round,** rondslenter, rondkuier.
toddle, n. waggelende gang; klein kindjie, kleuter.
toddler, kleintjie, kleuter.
toddy, sopie, grok, „toddy".
to-do, ophef, opskudding, gedoente.
toe, n. toon; little **–,** kleintoontjie; **turn up one's –s,** afkop, bokveld toe gaan; **from top to –,** van kop tot tone; **tread on somebody's –s,** iemand te na kom, iemand aanstoot gee, iemand op die tone trap.
toe, v. die toon (van skoen, ens.) heelmaak; skop, „oorleer"; op die streep staan (voor 'n wedren); **– the line,** na die pype van jou leier dans.
toe-cap, neus, neusleer (van 'n skoen).
toed, met tone.
toe-drop, voetverlamming.
toe-nail, toonnael.
toff, grootmeneer, haan, windmaker.
toffee, toffy, toffie.
tog(s), n. klere, mondering; sport-, voetbalklere.
tog, v. aantrek.
toga, toga.
together, saam, bymekaar, gelyk; **both – exclaimed,** albei het gelyk uitgeroep; **compared –,** vergelyk (vergeleke) met mekaar; **– with,** saam met, behalwe nog.
toggle, pen; dwarsstuk.
toil, v. swoeg, sloof, arbei, sukkel, swaar werk; **– up the hill,** teen die opdraand uitbeur.
toil, n. swaar werk, geswoeg.
toil(s), n. net, strik.
toiler, werkesel, swoeger.
toilet, toilet; toilettafel; **make one's –,** toilet maak.
toilet-jug, lampetkan.
toilet-paper, klosetpapier, toiletpapier.
toilet-set, wastafelstel.
toilsome, swaar, vermoeiend, moeilik.
token, aandenking, gedagtenis; teken; kenteken; bewys; **– payment,** formele betaling.
tolerable, draaglik, redelik, taamlik.
tolerance, verdraagsaamheid; toleransie; vergunning, dulding.
tolerant, verdraagsaam.
tolerate, verdra, duld, toelaat, uitstaan.
toleration, verdraagsaamheid; toelating.
toil, n. tol, tolgeld; **take – of,** eis, verg.

toll, v. tol betaal; tolgeld eis.
toll, v. (stadig) lui, slaan, klepper.
toll, n. klokgelui, slag, geklepper.
tollable, tolpligtig, belasbaar.
toll-bar, toll-gate, tolhek.
toll-house, tolhuis.
Tom: –, Dick and Harry, Piet, Paul en Klaas; Jan Rap en sy maat; **– Thumb,** Kleinduimpie.
tomahawk, strydbyl, tomahawk.
tomato, tamatie.
tomato sauce, tamatiesous.
tomato stew, tamatiebredie.
tomb, graf, graftombe, grafkelder.
tombac, tombak.
tomboy, rabbedoe(s) (robbedoe(s)), wilde meisie.
tombstone, grafsteen.
tom-cat, mannetjie(s)kat.
tome, lywige boekdeel.
tomentose, tomentous, harig, wollerig.
tomfool, gek, uilskuiken, dwaas.
tomfoolery, gekkestreke, lawwigheid.
tommy, tommie (Britse soldaat).
tommy-gun, hand-masjiengeweer.
tommy-rot, kaf, bog, twak.
tomnoddy, swaap, domkop, stumperd.
tomorrow, môre; **the day after –,** oormôre.
tomtit, winterkoninkie.
tomtom, trom, tomtom.
ton, ton; **–s of money,** geld soos bossies; **I have asked him –s of times,** ek het hom al honderde male gevra; **–s of people,** hope mense.
tonal, toon- . . ., klank- . . .
tonality, tonaliteit, toonaard; kleurafwisseling, kleurnuansering.
tone, n. toon, klank; klem; aard; kleur, tint, kleurskakering; gees, aard; **the – of the nation,** die volksgees; **the – of the school,** die gees in die skool.
tone, v. stem; die regte toon gee; kleur; **– down,** versag, temper; bedaar; minder skerp kleur; bietjie sagter uitdruk; **– up,** 'n skerper kleur gee; meer krag bysit; die krag herstel van; hoër stem.
tone-arm, klankarm.
tone-poem, toondig.
tongs, tang(etjie).
tongue, tong; taal, spraak; tongetjie (van gêspe(r), 'n skoen, ens.), klepel (van 'n klok); landtong; **he has a ready –,** hy is glad met sy mond, hy is gevat; **the mother –,** die moedertaal; **confusion of –s,** spraakverwarring; **he couldn't find his –,** sy tong wou nie losraak nie, hy kon nie woorde kry nie; **hold one's –,** stilbly, jou mond hou; **with one's – in one's cheek,** ironies, spottend; **wag one's –,** los en vas praat; it is on the **–s of men,** almal het die mond daarvan vol; **keep a civil – in one's head,** beleef bly.
tongued, met 'n tong.
tongueless, sonder tong; spraakloos.
tongue-tied, swaar van tong (spraak); sonder 'n woord te kan uitkry; stom; gebonde, gemuilband.
tonic, a. versterk- . . ., tonies; toon- . . .; **– solfa,** letter-note, solfa-note, solfa-notering.
tonic, n. versterkmiddel, opknappertjie; tonika.
tonicity, toon; veerkrag.
tonight, vanaand, vannag.
tonka-beam, tonkaboontjie.
tonnage, ton(ne)maat; skeepsruimte; tonnegeld.
tonometer, toonmeter, stemvurk.
tonsil, mangel.
tonsillitis, mangelontsteking, tonsilitis.
tonsorial, skeer- . . ., barbiers- . . .
tonsure, n. tonsuur.
tonsure, v. die kruin skeer.

too, te, alte, ook; **that is – much of a good thing**, dit is bietjie te erg.
tool, n. gereedskap; werktuig; **carpenter's –s**, timmermansgereedskap.
tool, v. bewerk; (met 'n beitel) regkap.
toot, v. blaas, toeter.
toot, n. geblaas, getoeter.
tooth, n. tand; **artificial teeth**, vals tande; **cast a thing in a person's teeth**, iets voor iemand se kop gooi; **in the teeth of**, nieteenstaande, trots; **in the teeth of the wind**, reg teen die wind; **in the teeth of the chief's instructions**, lynreg teen die bevele van die hoof in; **armed to the teeth**, tot die tande gewapen; **cut one's eye-teeth**, oogtande kry; **escape by the skin of one's teeth**, naelskraap (ternouernood) ontkom; **fight – and nail**, hand en tand veg; **he began to show his teeth**, hy het sy tande begin wys, sy maanhare het begin rys.
tooth, v. tande aansit.
toothache, tandpyn.
tooth-billed, saagbek- ...
tooth-brush, tandeborsel.
toothed, getand.
toothful, mondjievol, slukkie.
toothing-plane, tandskaaf.
toothless, sonder tande, tand(e)loos.
tooth-paste, tandepasta.
toothpick, tandestoker, tandeskoonmaker.
tooth-powder, tandepoeier.
toothsome, lekker, smaaklik.
tootle, toet, blaas.
tootsy(-wootsy), voetjie, pootjie.
top, n. top, hoogste punt, kruin; hoof, bo-ent (van 'n tafel); kap; toppunt, hoogtepunt; mars (skeepsterm); **at the – of the tree**, in die top van die boom, bo in die boom; op die boonste sport; **at the – of his class**, eerste in sy klas; **at the – of the table**, aan die koppenent (bo-ent) van die tafel; **at the – of his voice**, so hard soos hy kan; **come to the –**, na bo kom; alle ander oortref; **on – of this**, boonop; **from – to bottom**, van kop tot tone, van bo tot onder; **at the – of his speed**, so vinnig soos hy kon.
top, a. hoogste, boonste, eerste, beste; **the – rail**, die boonste spoor; **at – speed**, so vinnig soos moontlik; **– gear**, hoogste versnelling, bokerf.
top, v. 'n kap opsit, 'n punt aansit; top, snoei; die top bereik, tot bo klim; hoër wees as; oortref, uitmunt bo, klop; **mountains –ped with snow**, berge met sneeubedekte kruine; **– the list**, eerste op die lys staan; **that –s everything**, dit oortref alles.
top, n. tol; **sleep like a –**, slaap soos 'n klip.
topaz, topaas.
top-boots, kapstewels.
top-dog, bobaas.
top-dress, bobemesting gee.
top-dressing, bobemesting.
tope, v. suip, te veel drink.
toper, dronklap, suiplap.
topgallant, bramsteng.
topgallant sail, bramseil.
top-gear, hoogste versnelling, bokerf.
top-hat, pluiskeil, hoëhoed.
top-heavy, topswaar.
top-hole, eersteklas, uitstekend.
topiary, snoei- ...; **– art**, snoeikuns.
topic, onderwerp.
topical, plaaslik; aktueel; **a subject of – interest**, 'n onderwerp van aktuele belang; **a – allusion**, 'n toespeling op plaaslike omstandighede; **a – song**, 'n geleentheidslied.
topknot, strik; kuif.
topman, boonste saer; bobaas.
topmost, boonste, hoogste.
topographer, topograaf.
topographical, topografies.
topography, topografie.
topper, pluiskeil; gawe vent.
topping, uitstekend, allergaafs, heerlik; **it was –**, dit was van die fynste.
topple, (laat) omval, omkantel, omtuimel.
top-side, bokant.
topsy-turvy, adv. onderstebo, been in die lug; deurmekaar, agterstevoor.
topsy-turvy, a. onderstebo; deurmekaar.
toque, toque.
torch, toorts, fakkel; **hand on the –**, die vuur aan die lewe hou; **electric –**, toorts, flitslig.
torch-bearer, fakkeldraer.
torch-light, toortslig, fakkellig; **– procession**, fakkeloptog.
toreador, toreador.
torfaceous, moeras- ...
torment, n. kwelling, foltering, pyniging, marteling; **this child is a positive –**, hierdie kind trek 'n mens se siel uit.
torment, v. kwel, folter, pynig, martel, pla.
tormentor, kwelgees, plaaggees.
tormina, koliek, maagpyn.
tornadic, tornado- ..., orkaan- ...
tornado, tornado, orkaan.
torpedo, n. torpedo; knalsinjaal.
torpedo, v. torpedeer.
torpedo-boat, torpedoboot.
torpedo-catcher, torpedojaer.
torpedo-net, torpedonet.
torpid, slapend; styf; verstyf; langsaam, stadig, traag; ongevoelig.
torpidity, slaap; styfheid; traagheid; ongevoeligheid, doodsheid.
torpor, sien **torpidity**.
torque, torc, halsband; torsie.
torrefaction, uitdroging, (die) brand.
torrefy, uitdroë, brand, rooster.
torrent, stroom; stortvloed; **it rained in –s**, die reën het in strome geval.
torrential, in strome, geweldig; **– downpour**, stortreën.
Torricellian, van Torricelli; **– vacuum**, Torricelli-vakuum.
torrid, versengend, skroeiwarm, brandend; **– zone**, versengende lugstreek.
torridity, skroeihitte, versenging.
torsel, krul.
torsion, draai(ing), kronkeling; torsie; **– balance**, torsiebalans, torsieskaal.
torsional, draai- ..., kronkel- ..., torsie.
torso, romp; tors(o).
tort, onreg, verongelyking, nadeel; **law of –s**, delikte-reg.
torticollis, stywe nek.
tortile, gedraai, spiraalvormig.
tortious, onregmatig, oneerlik.
tortoise, skilpad.
tortoise-shell, skilpaddop.
tortuosity, kronkeling; jakkalsdraaie.
tortuous, gekronkel, gedraai; slinks.
torture, n. foltering, marteling; pyniging; **be put to the –**, gemartel word.
torture, v. martel, pynig, folter.
torturer, folteraar, pyniger.
Tory, Tory, konserwatief.
tosh, kaf, onsin, geklets.
toss, v. gooi, opgooi, rondgooi, rondsmyt; rondrol, heen en weer rol (in die bed); hot en haar slinger, heen en weer skud; loot; **– a person in a blanket**, iemand laat beesvel ry; **I'll – you for it**, laat ons loot daarvoor; **– one's head**,

toss   706   **toxic**

jou kop agteroor gooi; **the child –es in its bed,** die kind rol rond (woel) in sy bed; – **away, aside,** weggooi, wegsmyt, opsygooi; – **off,** gou-gou klaarmaak, afpiets; – **off a beer, 'n** glas bier wegslaan; – **up,** ('n geldstuk) opgooi; – **for sides,** vir kante loot.

toss, n. (die) opgooi (van geldstuk); loot, gooi; **win the –,** die opgooi wen; die loot wen; **with a – of the head,** met die kop in die lug; **take a –,** „plaas koop", baken steek.

toss-up, onsekerheid; opgooi; **it is quite a –,** dit is 'n dubbeltjie op sy kant, dit is nog heeltemal onseker.

tot, n. kleutertjie, klein kindjie; sopie, doppie, slukkie; **a tiny –,** 'n ou kleintjie.

tot, v. optel; – **up,** optel; oploop.

total, a. totaal, (ge)heel; – **eclipse,** algehele sonsverduistering; – **abstainer,** geheelonthouer, afskaffer.

total, n. totaal, volle som (bedrag).

total, v. optel, bymekaartrek; beloop, bedra, oploop tot.

totalitarian, a. totalitêr.

totality, totaliteit, die totaal.

totalizator, totalisator.

totalize, optel, die totaal bereken.

totem, totem.

totemism, totemisme.

totter, (wiggel-)waggel, wankel, slinger.

tottering, onseker, onvas, waggelend, wankelend.

toucan, toekan.

touch, v. (aan)raak, vat aan, aanroer, voel aan; tik; aanslaan; bykom; tref, aandoen, roer; – **pitch,** met pek omgaan, jou hande vuil maak; – **on the shoulder,** op die skouer tik; **I wouldn't – him with a barge-pole,** ek sou nie met 'n tang aan hom wil raak nie; **he –ed his hat,** hy het aangeslaan (sy hoed gelig); – **wood,** (ongeluk) aftik; **he –ed the bell,** hy het op die klokkie gedruk; **no one can – him,** niemand kan naby hom kom nie, sy maters is dood, hy moet sy moses nog kry; **it –ed me to the heart,** dit het my diep geroer; **it –ed him to the quick,** dit het hom geraak; **it –es you too,** dit raak jou ook; **he refuses to – beer,** hy wil sy mond nie aan bier sit nie; **he merely –ed the subject,** hy het net die onderwerp aangeroer; – **at,** aandoen, aangaan by; – **down,** druk, afdruk, dooddruk (voetbal); – **on, upon,** aanraak, aanroer; – **off,** vlugtig skets, gou afmaak; – **up,** opknap, regpiets; bywerk; oppoets; – **up the memory,** die geheue bietjie opfris.

touch, n. aanraking; tikkie; gevoel, tassin; trek; ietsie, bietjie, sweempie; aanslag; styl; buitelyn (voetbal); buiteskop; **a – of salt,** 'n knypie sout; **a – of rheumatism,** 'n ligte aanval van jig; **a – of sadness,** iets treurigs; **Rachmaninoff's masterly –,** Rachmaninoff se meesterlike aanslag; **the piano is wanting in –,** die klavier het nie 'n goeie aanslag nie; **keep in – with,** in voeling bly met; **put to the –,** op die proef stel; **a near –,** 'n nou ontkoming; **put the finishing –es to the work,** die laaste hand aan die werk lê; **kick into –,** uitskop; **game of –,** aan-aan.

touchable, voelbaar, aan te raak.

touch-and-go, a. haastig, vlugtig; onseker, waagsaam; **it was –,** dit was so hittete, dit was so byna-byna (op die nerf na).

touch-and-go, n. onsekerheid, waagstuk.

touch-down, dooddruk.

toucher, aanraker; **that was a near –,** dit was 'n noue ontkoming.

touch-hole, laaigat.

touching, a. roerend, aandoenlik.

touching, prep. betreffende, met betrekking tot.

touch-line, buitelyn.

touch-me-not, kruidjie-roer-my-nie.

touch-needle, toetsnaald.

touch-pan, kruitpan.

touch-paper, salpeterpapier.

touchstone, toetssteen.

touchwood, swam.

touchy, fyngevoelig, liggeraak, kruidjie-roer-my-nie-agtig; kort van draad.

tough, taai; hard, styf; koppig; moeilik, lastig; **the –est steel,** die sterkste staal; **as – as leather,** so taai soos leer; **a – customer,** 'n lastige vent, 'n moeilike klant.

toughen, taai(er) maak (word).

toughish, taaierig.

toupee, pruikie.

tour, n. rond(reis), toer; – **de force,** uithalerstreek, kragtoer.

tour, v. rondreis, deurreis, 'n (kuns)reis maak; op toer gaan, toer.

tourer, toeris; toermodel (motor).

tourist, toeris.

tourmaline, toermalyn.

tournament, steekspel, toernooi; wedstryd(e).

tourney, steekspel, toernooi.

tourniquet, aar-afbinder, aarpers.

tournure, ronding; draai; kussinkie.

tousle, ronddruk; deurmekaar pluk, verfrommel, (hare) deurmekaar maak; – **d hair,** deurmekaar hare.

tousy, deurmekaar, (wind)verwaaid.

tout, v. (perde) beloer, op die loer lê.

tout, n. klantelokker; perdespioen.

tow, v. trek, sleep, op sleeptou neem.

tow, n. (die) trek (sleep); **take, have in –,** op sleeptou neem.

tow, n. growwe vlas, (tou)werk.

towage, sleeploon; (die) sleep.

toward(s), prep. na, na . . . toe; teen, teenoor; tot; naby; **his attitude – the Native question,** sy houding met betrekking tot die naturellevraagstuk; **your behaviour –,** jou gedrag teenoor; – **noon,** teen die middag (se kant); **contribute something –,** iets bydra tot.

towel, n. handdoek; **roller –,** rolhanddoek; **throw in the –,** tou opgooi.

towel, v. (met 'n handdoek) afdroë; slaan, ransel.

towel-horse, handdoekrak.

towelling, handdoekgoed; afdroging.

tower, n. toring; vesting, kasteel; toevlug; **a – of strength,** 'n steunpilaar, 'n egte staatmaker.

tower, v. hoog uitsteek bo; hoog in die lug vlie, regop vlie; **he –s above his contemporaries,** hy steek ver bokant sy tydgenote uit.

towering, baie hoog; geweldig, hewig; **he was in a – rage,** hy was woedend.

towery, met torings.

tow(ing)-line, sleeptou.

tow(ing)-net, treknet.

town, dorp, stad; **it is the talk of the –,** die hele dorp het die mond daarvan vol; **in –,** in die stad; **man about –,** windmakerige leeglêer (niksdoener); **paint the – red,** die dorp (stad) op horings sit.

town clerk, stadsklerk.

town council, stadsraad.

town councillor, stadsraadslid.

town hall, stadsaal, stadhuis.

town house, huis in die stad, dorpshuis.

townplanning, stadsaanleg(plan).

townsfolk, stedelinge, dorpelinge.

township, dorpie; stadsgebied.

townspeople, stedelinge, dorpelinge.

toxaemia, bloedvergiftiging.

toxic, giftig; gif- . . .; vergiftigings- . . .

toxicant, n. gif.
toxicant, a. giftig.
toxicological, toksikologies.
toxicologist, toksikoloog.
toxicology, toksikologie.
toxin, toksien (toksine), gif.
toxophilite, boogskutter.
toy, n. speelding(etjie); speelbal; –s, speelgoed.
toy, v. speel.
toy dog, skoothondjie.
toyingly, speel-speel.
toy soldier, popsoldaatjie.
trace, v. natrek, oortrek, traseer; 'n plan ontwerp, skets, teken; afbaken, neerlê; opspoor, die spoor volg, die spoor sny; naspoor, nagaan; – a plan, 'n plan ontwerp; **the policy –d out by him**, die gedragslyn deur hom aangedui (neergelê); – **it back to . . .**, dit nagaan tot . . .; – **a map**, 'n kaart natrek.
trace, n. spoor, voetspoor; teken, bewys; –s of Italian influence, spore (bewys) van Italiaanse invloed; **a – of salt**, 'n tikkie sout.
trace, n. string; **in the –s**, in die tuig; **kick over the –s**, onklaar trap, hand-uit ruk, onregeerbaar word.
traceable, opspoorbaar.
trace-element, spoorelement.
tracer, opspoorder; ondersoeker; natrektekenaar; aanwyser; – **bullet**, ligspoorkoeël.
tracery, trasering; netwerk.
trachea, lugpyp; lugbuis, tragea.
trachitis, lugpypontsteking.
trachoma, tragoom.
tracing-paper, kalkeerpapier, aftrekpapier.
track, n. spoor; pad, weg; spoor(weg), spoor(baan); renbaan, reisiesbaan; **we are on his –**, ons is op sy spoor; **follow in his –**, sy voetspore volg; **the – of a comet**, die baan van 'n komeet; **the beaten –**, die gebaande weg; **double –**, dubbelspoor; **single –**, enkelspoor; **make –s**, die rieme neerlê, knie in die wind slaan; **off the –**, van die spoor af.
track, v. opspoor, die spoor volg, spoor sny; naspoor, nagaan; – **down**, opspoor, vang.
tracker, opspoorder; speurder.
trackless, spoorloos, sonder spore; onbegaan, ongebaan; – **tram**, trembus.
tract, streek.
tract, traktaatjie.
tractability, geseglikheid, inskiklikheid.
tractable, geseglik, gewillig, gedwee, inskiklik, gehoorsaam.
tractate, verhandeling.
traction, (voort)trekking, traksie; saamtrekking; – **steam –**, stoom(trek)krag.
traction-engine, treklokomotief, straatlokomotief, trekker.
tractive, trek-. . . .
tractor, treklokomotief, straatlokomotief; trekmotor, trekker.
trade, n. handel, bedryf, ambag, beroep; **the –**, die handel; die handelaars; **the trick of the –**, die geheime van die vak, die fyn puntjies; **a butcher by –**, 'n slagter van beroep; **a roaring –**, 'n bloeiende handel; **the –s**, die passaatwinde.
trade, v. handel, handel drywe; – **on**, eksploiteer.
trade mark, handelsmerk.
trade name, handelsnaam.
trade price, groothandelprys.
trader, handelaar; handelskip.
tradesman, handelaar; werksman.
trade union, vakunie, vakvereniging.
trade-unionism, vakuniestelsel.
trade wind, passaatwind.

trading, n. (die) handel(drywe).
trading, a. handeldrywend; handels-.
tradition, tradisie, oorlewering.
traditional, tradisioneel.
traditionalism, tradisieverering.
traduce, belaster, beskinder.
traducer, (be)lasteraar, skindertong.
traffic, n. handel; verkeer; – **jam**, verkeersknoop – **circle**, verkeerskring.
traffic, v. handel drywe, handel; verkwansel.
traffic control verkeersreëling.
trafficker handelaar.
tragedian, treurspelskrywer; treurspelspeler.
tragedienne, treurspelspeelster.
tragedy, tragedie, treurspel.
tragic, tragies.
tragicomedy, tragikomedie.
tragicomic, tragikomies.
trail, n. (na)sleep; streep; stert (van 'n komeet), sleepsel; rank; spoor; pad; **on the –**, op die spoor; **off the –**, die spoor kwyt.
trail, v. sleep; trek, 'n (voet)pad trap, plat trap; los hang; opspoor; rank, kruip.
trailer, rankplant, sleepkar(retjie), –wa(entjie), aanhangwa(entjie); lokprent (in bioskoop).
trailing-wheel, agterwiel.
trail-net, treknet.
train, v. leer, oplei, oefen, brei; dresseer; dril; snoei, lei; lok; met die trein reis; **a –ed nurse**, 'n opgeleide verpleegster; **a –ed eye**, 'n geoefende oog; **a –ed dog**, 'n gedresseerde hond; – **horses**, perde dresseer (mak maak, leer); **–ed for the ministry**, as predikant opgelei; – **a gun upon**, 'n kanon stel (rig) op.
train, n. sleep; nasleep; stert; gevolg, stoet, reeks, streep, ry, opeenvolging, aaneenskakeling trein; **a – of events**, 'n reeks gebeurtenisse form part of his –, deel uitmaak van sy gevolg – **of thought**, gedagtegang.
trainable, oefenbaar; sien **train**.
train-bearer, sleepdraer.
trainer, afrigter, instrukteur, drilmeester; breier.
training, oefening, opleiding, (die) brei; **go into –**, begin oefen; **be in –**, geoefen word, gebrei word.
training-college, opleidingskool.
training-ship, oefenskip, opleidingskip.
train-oil, traanolie.
trait, (karakter)trek, eienskap; trek; streep.
traitor, verraaier.
traitorous, verraderlik.
traitress, verraaister (verraaier).
trajectory, baan; koeëlbaan.
tram, trem; koolwa.
tramcar, trem(rytuig), tremwa.
tramway, tramline, tremspoor.
trammel, n. net, span; –s, hindernisse, belemmeringe, boeie.
trammel, v. belemmer, hinder, bind.
tramontane, transalpyns; uitlands.
tramp, v. swaar stap, stamp; stap, loop, voetslaan; rondloop; **–ed the whole country**, die hele land platgeloop.
tramp, n. gestamp, getrap, voetstap; hoefslag; voetreis, wandeltog; rondloper, landloper; vragsoeker (boot).
trample, v. trap, vertrap; – **on**, vertrap, trap op; – **to death**, doodtrap; – **under foot**, met die voete vertrap.
trample, n. getrap, (die) trap.
trance, ekstase, verrukking; beswyming, skyndood; hipnose.
tranquil, kalm, stil, rustig; **he preserved a – state of mind**, hy het kalm en bedaard gebly.
tranquillization, gerusstelling, sussing.

tranquillize, kalmeer, stil, sus, gerusstel.
tranquillity, kalmte, rus, stilte; gerustheid.
tranquillizer, kalmeermiddel.
transact, afhandel, verrig, doen; onderhandel;
– **with**, sake doen met.
transaction, verrigting, transaksie, saak; onderhandeling; handeling; skikking; vergelyk, ooreenkoms; **the Transactions of the Royal Society**, die Handelinge van die Koninklike Genootskap.
transactor, verrigter, onderhandelaar.
transalpine, transalpyns.
transatlantic, transatlanties.
transcend, oortref, to bo(we) gaan.
transcendence, voortreflikheid.
transcendent, voortreflik, uitstekend.
transcendental, transendentaal.
transcontinental, transkontinentaal.
transcribe, afskryf, oorskryf, transkribeer.
transcriber, afskrywer, oorskrywer.
transcript, afskrif, geskrewe kopie.
transcription, transkripsie, oorskrywing; oorsetting; afskrif, kopie.
transection, deursnee.
transept, dwarsskip, dwarsvleuel (van kerk).
transfer, v. oordra, transporteer; oorplaas, verplaas; oordruk, afdruk.
transfer, n. oordrag, transport; verplasing; afdruk-(prent).
transferability, oordraagbaarheid.
transferable, oordraagbaar, verhandelbaar, **not** –, persoonlik.
transferee, persoon aan wie iets oorgedra word; transportnemer.
transfer-ink, oordrukink.
transfer-paper, oordrukpapier.
transfiguration, verheerliking (van Christus op die berg), gedaantewisseling.
transfigure, van gedaante verander (verwissel), vervorm, verheerlik.
transfix, deursteek, deurboor; **–ed**, deursteek, deurboor(d); aan die grond genael.
transfixion, deurboring, deursteking.
transform, (van vorm) verander, van gedaante wissel, vervorm.
transformable, vervormbaar, veranderbaar.
transformation, gedaantewisseling, vervorming, verandering; transformasie, metamorfose; omsetting.
transformer, transformator (elektr.); vervormer.
transformism, ontwikkelingsleer.
transfuse, oorgiet, oorstort; oortap; oorbring; – **into**, meedeel, aansteek met; inprent; laat deurtrek van; **–d with**, deurdring van, deurtrek van.
transfusion, oorgieting, oorstorting; deurtrekking; inprenting, transfusie.
transgress, oortree, sondig.
transgression, oortreding, sonde.
transgressor, oortreder.
transience, kortstondigheid.
transient, verbygaand; kortstondig, verganklik; – **note**, oorgangsnoot; **a** – **glance**, 'n vlugtige blik.
transistor, transistor, kristalbuis.
transit, vervoer, deurvoer; oorgang; verkeersweg; **the** – **of a planet**, die oorgang van 'n planeet.
transit duty, deurvoerbelasting, -reg, transitoreg.
transition, oorgang; – **stage**, oorgangstydperk; – **point**, oorgangspunt.
transitional, oorgangs- . . .
transitive, oorganklik, transitief.
transitoriness, kortstondigheid, verganklikheid; vlugtigheid.

transitory, kortstondig, verganklik, van korte duur, vlugtig.
translatable, vertaalbaar.
translate, vertaal, oorsit; verklaar, opvat; oorplaas, verplaas; oorneem; sein; ten hemel voer; **–d from the** French, uit die Frans vertaal; **kindly –**, vertaal asb.; sê asb. wat jy daarmee bedoel; **–d from one art into another**, uit die een kuns in die ander oorgebring.
translation, vertaling, oorsetting; verplasing; oorbrenging; oordrag.
translator, vertaler.
translucence, deurskynendheid.
translucent, deurskynend.
transmarine, oorsees.
transmigrant, landverhuiser.
transmigrate, verhuis; oorgaan.
transmigration, (land)verhuising, oorgang; – **of the soul**, sielsverhuising.
transmission, (die) aanstuur; oorhandiging; oorerwing; deurlating; – **of heat**, voortplanting van hitte.
transmit, aanstuur, deurstuur, oorstuur; laat erwe, nalaat; deurlaat; oorplant, voortplant; – **a parcel**, 'n pakkie deurstuur; **the disease was –ted to his descendants**, sy afstammelinge het die siekte oorgeërwe.
transmitter, aanstuurder; voortplanter.
transmutable, veranderbaar.
transmutation, verandering, vormwisseling.
transmute, verander, omwissel.
transoceanic, oorsees, anderkant die oseaan; – **flight of birds**, die trek van voëls oor die oseaan.
transom, latei; dwarshout, dwarsbalk.
transparency, deursigtigheid, deurskynendheid; transparant.
transparent, deursigtig, deurskynend.
transpierce, deursteek, deurboor.
transpiration, uitdamping, uitwaseming, sweet; (die) uitlek.
transpire, uitwasem, uitsweet; uitlek, rugbaar word.
transplant, verplant; oorplaas.
transplantation, verplanting; oorplasing.
transplanter, verplanter.
transport, v. vervoer, transporteer; wegvoer; deporteer; in vervoering bring; **–ed with joy**, verruk van blydskap.
transport, n. vervoer, transport; gedeporteerde; verrukking, vervoering; transportskip; **in –s**, in verrukking.
transportable, vervoerbaar.
transportation, transport, vervoer.
transporter, vervoerder, transportryer.
transposal, omsetting, omruiling.
transpose, omruil, omwissel, omsit; oorbring; transponeer.
transposition, omsetting; oorsetting, transposisie (van musiekstuk).
trans-ship, oorskeep, oorlaai.
transubstantiate, van vorm verander.
transubstantiation, transubstansiasie.
transude, uitsweet, uitsyfer.
transversal, a. dwars- . . ., transversaal.
transversal, n. dwarslyn.
transverse, dwars- . . ., transversaal.
trap, n. strik, wip; val, vanggat, vanghok, slagyster; valstrik, hinderlaag; trep(karretjie); lokvoël; diener; **walk into the –**, in die val loop.
trap, v. (in 'n strik) vang; betrap.
trap, n. trapsteen; **–s**, trapleertjie.
trap, v. versier, optooi.
trap, n.: **–s**, goed; **pack up your –s**, vat jou goed.
trap-door, valdeur.
trapeze, sweefstok, trapesium.

trapezium   709   **trespasser**

trapezium, trapesium.
trapezoid, trapesoïde.
trapper, strikspanner; pelsjagter.
trappings, tuig; tooisel, opskik.
trash, weggooigoed, vuilgoed, afval; snoeisels; prul; bog, kaf.
trashiness, prullerigheid.
trashy, niksbeduidend, prullerig, bog- . . .
travail, n. barenswee; trawal, afmattende arbeid.
travail, v. in barensnood verkeer; swoeg.
travel, v. (rond)reis, deurreis; gaan, beweeg, loop; (laat) trek; afdwaal; **light –s faster than sound**, lig word vinniger voortgeplant (trek vinniger) as klank; – **100 miles a day**, 100 myl op 'n dag aflê; **this iron –s in a groove**, yster beweeg in 'n groef; **a –led man**, 'n bereisde man; – **out of the record**, van die onderwerp afdwaal.
travel, n. reis; reisverhaal; beweging, loop, swaai, slag (van masjiendele); **he cannot read –s**, hy hou nie van reisverhale nie; **he has changed the – of the valves**, hy het die slag van die kleppe verander, hy het die kleppe anders gestel.
traveller, reisiger; **a –'s tale**, 'n kluitjie, jagterslatyn; –**'s joy**, (soort) klimop.
travelling, n. reis.
travelling, a. reis- . . ., reisend; – **expenses**, reiskoste.
travel-stained, vuil van die reis, verreis.
traverse, n. dwarshout, dwarsbalk; dwarslyn; dwarsgalery; dwarsbeweging, dwarsgang; dwarswal.
traverse, v. aflê, afreis, reis deur; deurreis, deurkruis; dwarsboom, teëwerk, in die wiele ry; draai; dwarsloop; – **a subject**, die hele onderwerp bespreek (behandel).
traverser, draaiskyf.
traverse-table, draaiskyf.
travesty, v. belaglik voorstel, parodieer.
travesty, n. belaglike voorstelling, parodie, travestie.
trawl, v. treil, trek.
trawl, n. treil, sleepnet.
trawler, treiler; sleepnettrekker.
trawl-net, treil, sleepnet.
tray, skinkbord; bak (bv. in 'n reiskoffer); platkissie (vrugte); droogstellasie.
treacherous, verraderlik; vals; – **memory**, onvertroubare geheue.
treachery, verraad; troueloosheid.
treacle, stroop.
treacly, stroopagtig, stroperig.
tread, v. trap, loop, stap; betree; – **lightly**, saggies loop; versigtig te werk gaan; – **grapes**, druiwe trap; – **the boards, stage**, toneelspeler wees, toneelspeel; **op die toneel verskyn**; – **water**, water trap; – **down**, vastrap, plattrap, trap op; verpletter; – **in**, (in die grond) vastrap; – **in somebody's footsteps**, iemand se voetspore druk; – **on**, trap op; – **on somebody's corns, toes**, op iemand se liddorings, tone trap; iemand te na kom; – **on the heels of**, onmiddellik volg op, op die hakke volg; – **on the neck of somebody**, iemand die voet op die nek sit; **he seemed to – on air**, hy was opgetoë; – **out**, blus; demp, onderdruk; uittrap; – **under foot**, met die voete vertrap.
tread, n. stap, trap; tree, skrede.
treadle, trapper; pedaal.
treadmill, trapmeul; sleurwerk.
treason, verraad; **high** –, hoogverraad.
treasonable, verraderlik; skuldig aan verraad.
treasure, n. skat; rykdom.

treasure, v. (as 'n skat) bewaar; opgaar, bymekaarmaak, versamel.
treasure-house, skatkamer.
treasurer, penningmeester, tesourier.
treasureship, penningmeesterskap.
treasure trove, vonds, gevonde skat.
treasury, skatkamer; skatkis; tesourie.
treasury note, skatkisbiljet.
treat, v. behandel; onthaal, trakteer; – **it as a joke**, dit as 'n grap beskou; **it must be –ed with sulphuric acid**, daarna moet dit aan die werking van swawelsuur blootgestel word; **I will – you all**, ek sal julle almal trakteer; – **of**, behandel; handel oor, gaan oor; – **with**, onderhandel met; behandel met.
treat, n. onthaal; genot, traktasie.
treatise, verhandeling.
treatment, behandeling.
treaty, verdrag, traktaat; ooreenkoms; **be in – with**, in onderhandeling wees met.
treble, a. drievoudig; hoog, sopraan; – **clef**, sopraan-sleutel.
treble, v. verdrievoudig.
treble, n. (die) drievoudige, drie maal soveel; eerste stem, sopraan.
trebly, drie maal, drievoudig.
tree, boom; as; swingelhout; lees; saalboom; **be up a –**, in die knyp wees; **at the top of the –**, op die boonste sport.
tree-fern, boomvaring.
tree-nail, houtpen.
tree-snake, boomslang.
trefoil, klawer.
trek, v. trek, op trek gaan.
trek, n. trek.
trellis, n. traliewerk, latwerk, prieel.
trellis, v. 'n prieel maak, traliewerk (lat-) omsit.
tremble, v. bewe, sidder, gril; **in trembling uncertainty**, in kwellende onsekerheid; **I – for his safety**, ek vrees vir sy veiligheid; **his life –s in the balance**, sy lewe hang aan 'n draadjie.
tremble, n. bewing, trilling; –**s**, trekkings; **a – in her voice**, 'n trilling in haar stem; **he was all of a –**, hy het die bewerasie gehad, hy het gebewe soos 'n riet.
trembler, elektriese klokkie.
trembly, bewerig.
tremendous, verskriklik, vreeslik, geweldig, yslik.
tremolo, tremolo, triller, trilling; tremulant, trilregister.
tremor, bewing, trilling, siddering, rilling; huiwering.
tremulous, bewend, trillend; huiwerend.
trench, v. ('n sloot) grawe; diep omspit, omdol- (we); loopgrawe maak.
trench, n. sloot, voor; loopgraaf.
trenchancy, snydendheid, skerpheid.
trenchant, skerp, snydend, vlymend, kragtig, beslis.
trencher, houtbord, broodbord; grawer.
trend, v. loop, gaan; **the coast –s towards the south**, die kus strek na die suide uit.
trend, n. loop, neiging, rigting; **the – of events**, die loop van gebeurtenisse.
trepan, n. trepaan, skedelboor.
trepan, v. die skedel deurboor.
trepan, v. vang, in 'n strik lok.
trepidation, ontsteltenis, angs; bewerasie, trilling.
trespass, v. oortree; inbreuk maak (op); sondig; misbruik maak van; – **on somebody's hospitality**, van iemand se gasvryheid misbruik maak; – **against the law**, die wet oortree.
trespass, n. oortreding; sonde; **forgive us our –es**, vergeef ons ons skulde.
trespasser, oortreder.

trespass-offering, soenoffer.
tress, haarlok, haarkrul, vlegsel; –es, lokke, krulle, vlegsels.
tressy, krul-..., gekrul.
trestle, bok, stut.
triad, drietal, groep van drie; drieklank.
trial, toets, proef, proefneming, eksperiment; verhoor, proses, geregtelike ondersoek; beproewing; **make a – of somebody's strength**, iemand se krag op die proef stel; **put to –**, op die proef stel; **make a – ascent with an aeroplane**, 'n proefvlug met 'n vliegmasjien doen; **take it on –**, dit op proef neem; **I'll give you a –**, ek sal jou 'n kans gee; **old age has many –s**, ouderdom kom met baie gebreke; **be on stand, undergo –**, verhoor word, voorkom; **commit for –**, ter strafsitting verwys; **– match**, proefwedstryd; **by – and error**, deur die proefmetode; **– run**, proefrit.
trial balance, proefbalans.
tricar, driewielmotor.
trial trip, proeftog.
triangle, driehoek; triangel.
triangular, driehoekig; **a – treaty**, 'n driehoeksverdrag.
triangulation, triangulasie.
trias, trias(formasie).
tribal, stam-...; **– feud**, stamtwis.
tribalism, stamorganisasie.
tribe, stam; geslag, familie.
tribesman, lid van 'n stam.
tribulation, beproewing, wederwaardigheid, verdrukking, tribulasie.
tribunal, regterstoel, regbank; geregshof.
tribune, tribuun, volksverteenwoordiger.
tribune, spreekgestoelte, verhoog.
tributary, a. skatpligtig; tak-..., sy-...
tributary, n. skatpligtige; takrivier, syrivier, spruit.
tribute, skatting; skatpligtigheid; huldeblyk, hulde; **under –**, skatpligtig.
trice, v. ophaal, ophys; vaskoppel.
trice, n. oomblik, kits; **in a –**, in 'n kits, in 'n oomblik, so gou soos nou.
triceps, a. driehoofdig.
triceps, n. driehoofdige spier.
trichord, n. driesnarige instrument.
trichord, a. driesnarig.
trick, n. lis, skelmstreek; toer, behendigheid, kunsie; gewoonte, aanwensel, manier; poets, streek; slag (kaartspel); **he will not serve me that – twice**, hy sal my nie nog 'n keer so fop nie; **conjurer's –s**, goëltoertjies; **learn the –**, die slag kry; **play a dirty –**, 'n lelike poets bak; **this ought to do the –**, dit behoort te werk.
trick, v. kul, fop, bedrieg, kool stowe; streke uithaal; **– out, up**, uitdos, versier, opskik, optooi; **– somebody out of something**, iemand uit iets fop.
tricker, fopper, bedrieër.
trickery, foppery, kullery, skelmstreke.
trickish, bedrieglik.
trickle, v. drup, tap; rol, biggel; uitlek; **tears –d her cheeks**, trane het oor haar wange gerol (gebiggel); **the information –d out**, die inligting het uitgelek.
trickle, n. drupstraaltjie, sypeltjie, syferstraaltjie.
tricksy, oulik, lewendig; snaaks.
tricky, vol streke; bedrieglik; oulik, oorlams; netelig, lastig.
tricolo(u)r, a. driekleurig.
tricolo(u)r, n. driekleur.
tricot, tricot, (masjien)breigoed.
tricycle, driewieler.
trident, drietand.

triennial, a. driejaarliks; driejarig.
triennial, n. driejarige plant; driejaarlikse herdenking(sfees).
trier, ondersoeker; proef; aanhouer.
trifle, n. nietigheid, kleinigheid, beuselagtigheid, bakatel; koekpoeding.
trifle, adv. bietjie; effe; **a – angry**, bietjie vererg.
trifle, v. speel, spot, korswel; verspeel, verbeusel, mors; **he is not to be –d with**, hy laat nie met hom speel nie; **– away time, energies, money**, tyd mors, kragte verspil, geld verskwis.
trifler, beuselaar.
trifling, klein, niksbeduidend, beuselagtig.
trifoliate, driebladig.
trig, a. netjies, viets, agtermekaar.
trig, v. rem.
trig, n. rem, remblok.
trigger, sneller, trekker.
trigon, driehoek.
trigonal, driehoekig.
trigonometrical, trigonometries.
trigonometry, driehoeksmeting, trigonometrie.
trike, driewieler.
trilateral, driesydig.
trilingual, drietalig.
trill, v. tril, vibreer.
trill, n. trilling; triller; r-klank.
trilling, drieling.
trillion, triljoen.
trilogy, trilogie.
trim, a. netjies, fyn, viets; in orde, mooi gerangskik.
trim, v. in orde bring; regmaak; knip, snoei; ('n kers) snuit; mooimaak, opskik, optooi, versier, opmaak; (bome) fatsoeneer; nog vis nog vlees wees; bestraf; **– someone's jacket**, iemand op sy baadjie gee; **– the sails**, die seile volgens die wind span; **– off, away**, snoei; afknip; afskaaf; **– with lace**, met kant afset (opmaak).
trim, n. toestand, staat; tooi(sel), drag; **everything was in perfect –**, alles was in die haak; **I am in no – for this kind of work**, my klere is nie geskik vir hierdie werk nie; my gesondheid sal nie hierdie soort werk toelaat nie; **in fighting –**, klaar vir die geveg; strydvaardig; **in, out of –**, in, uit orde; in, uit die haak.
trimeter, drievoetige versreël.
trimmer, opmaker; knipper, snoeiskêr; „verkleurmannetjie".
trimming, opmaaksel, belegsel, garneersel; toebehoorsels.
trinal, drievoudig.
trine, a. drievoudig.
trinity, drietal; drie-eenheid; **Holy Trinity**, Heilige Drie-eenheid.
trinket, sieraad, versierseltjie, snuistery, kosbaarheidjie.
trinket-box, juweelkissie.
trinomial, drieterm(ig).
trio, trio; drietal.
trip, v. trippel; struikel; 'n misstap begaan; pootjie; betrap; die anker lig; 'n uitstappie maak; **catch sombody –ping**, iemand op 'n fout betrap; **– over something**, oor iets struikel; **– up**, pootjie; betrap.
trip, n. uitstappie, toggie, seereis; passie; misslag, misstap, val; vangs; **a round –**, heen-en-terugreis, rondreis.
tripartition, verdeling in drie, driedeling.
tripe, ingewande, binnegoed, pens; afval; bog, kaf.
triphthong, drieklank, triftong.
triplane, driedekker.
triple, a. drievoudig; **T– Alliance**, Drievoudige Verbond; **– time**, drieslagsmaat.

triple, v. verdrievoudig.
triplet, drietal; drieling; triool (musiek).
triplex, triplex (glas).
triplicate, a. drievoudig; in triplikaat.
triplicate, n. triplikaat.
triplicate, v. verdrievoudig, tripleer.
triplication, verdrievoudiging.
tripod, drievoet.
triptych, triptyque, triptiek.
trireme, trireem.
trisect, in drie (gelyke dele) verdeel.
trisection, driedeling.
trisyllabic, drielettergrepig.
trisyllable, drielettergrepige woord.
trite, afgesaag, alledaags, uitgedien.
tritium, tritium.
Triton, Triton, seegod; **he is a − among the minnows**, in die land van die blinde is eenoog koning.
triturate, fyn maal, fyn kou.
triumph, n. triomftog, seëtog (segetog); triomf, oorwinning, seëpraal; oorwinningsvreugde; **he returned home in −**, sy terugkeer was 'n (ware) triomftog.
triumph, v. seëvier (segevier), triomfeer; koning kraai; hoerê skree.
triumphal, seë− . . ., (sege−), oorwinnings− . . ., triomf− . . .; **− car**, segekoets; **− progress**, triomftog, seëtog; **− arch**, triomfboog.
triumphant, seëvierend, triomferend.
triumvir, drieman, triumvir.
triumvirate, driemanskap, triumviraat.
triune, drieënig.
trivet, drievoet; **as right as a −**, so reg soos 'n roer.
trivial, niksbeduidend, beuselagtig; oppervlakkig; alledaags; **− matters**, kleinighede.
triviality, trivia, niksbeduidendheid, beuselagtigheid; alledaagsheid.
troat, skreeu, blêr.
trochaic, trogeïes.
trochee, trogee.
troglodyte, grotbewoner; troglodiet.
troglodytic, grotbewoners− . . . .
Trojan, a. Trojaans.
Trojan, n. Trojaan; **they fought like −s**, hulle het soos helde geveg; **he works like a −**, hy is 'n werkesel; hy werk oor 'n boeg.
troll, v. (binnensmonds) sing; visvang.
troll, n. rondgesang, deuntjie, wysie.
troll, n. dwerg (in Skandinawiese mitologie).
trolley, −ly, trollie; molwa; beuel, rolkontak, glykontak (van 'n trem).
trollop, slofkous; straatmeisie.
trombone, trombone, skuiftrompet.
trombonist, trombonis.
troop, n. klomp, trop, hoop; troep; **−s**, troepe, troepemag; **a − of schoolchildren**, 'n klomp skoolkinders.
troop, v. in 'n trop loop, in klompe bymekaarkom; **− away, off**, haastig vertrek, op 'n streep weggaan; **− the colours**, vaandelparade hou.
trooper, ruiter; transportskip; kavallerieperd, troepperd; **swear like a −**, vloek soos 'n matroos.
troop-horse, kavallerieperd, troeppperd.
troopship, transportskip, troepeskip.
trope, redefiguur, troop.
trophy, trofee, seëteken, ereteken, prys; beker; **floating −**, wisselbeker, -prys.
tropic, n. keerkring; **T− of Capricorn**, Steenbokskeerkring; **T− of Cancer**, Kreefskeerkring; **the −s**, die trope, die keerkringe.
tropic, a. tropies.

tropical, tropies; keerkrings- . . .; **− diseases**, tropiese siektes.
trot, v. draf, laat draf, op 'n draf trek, afdraf; **− along**, aandraf, wegdraf; **I −ted him off his legs**, ek het hom disnis geloop; **− out**, ('n perd) laat draf; ten toon stel, pronk met, voor die dag bring; probeer.
trot, n. draf; **at a swift −**, op 'n vinnige draf; **keep somebody on the −**, iemand gedurig besig hou, iemand aan die loop hou.
troth, waarheid; **in −**, regtig, op my woord; **plight one's −**, jou woord (van eer) gee.
trotter, drawwer; poot(jie); voet; **sheep's −s**, (skaap)pootjies, (skaap)afval.
trottoir, sypaadjie.
troubadour, troebadoer.
trouble, v. verontrus, kwel; pla; lastig val, (las) veroorsaak; **don't let it − you**, moet jou nie daaroor kwel nie; **a −d countenance**, 'n besorgde gelaat; **how long has this pain been troubling you?** hoe lank pla die pyn jou al?; **may I − you for the mustard?** sal jy asb. die mosterd aangee?; **sorry to − you**, dit spyt my om jou lastig te val; **don't − to explain**, moenie die moeite doen om 'n uitleg te gee nie; **I did not − to go**, ek het dit nie die moeite geag om weg te gaan nie.
trouble, n. sorg, kwelling, verdriet; moeilikheid, moeite, las, ongerief; kwaal; **liver −s**, lewerkwaal; **his old −**, sy ou kwaal; **I shall not put you to any −**, ek sal jou nie die minste las veroorsaak nie; **he will never take the −**, hy sal hom nooit die moeite getroos nie; **it is no − at all**, dit is hoegenaamd geen moeite nie; **be in −**, in die moeilikheid sit; **get into −**, in die moeilikheid kom.
trouble-shooter, brandslaner.
troublesome, lastig, moeilik.
troublous, moeilik; **− times**, veelbewoë tye.
trough, bak, trog, bakkis.
trounce, ransel, uitklop; 'n kafferpak gee.
trouncing, 'n gedugte pak; 'n kafferpak.
troupe, geselskap, troep.
trouper, toneelspeler, (-speelster); staatmaker op die toneel.
trouser(s), broek; **a pair of −s**, 'n broek.
trouser-button, broeksknoop.
trousered, met 'n broek aan, gebroek.
trousering, broekstof.
trouser-leg, broekspyp.
trouser pocket, broeksak.
trousseau, uitset, uitrusting (van 'n bruid).
trout, forel (vis).
trout-coloured, (blou)skimmel.
troutlet, forelletjie.
trowel, troffel; **lay it on with a −**, dik opsmeer, goed gebruik maak van die heunigkwas.
troy (weight), troois gewig, fyn gewig.
truancy, stokkiesdraaiery, werkversuim.
truant, n. stokkiesdraaier, werkversuimer, **play −**, stokkies draai, werkversuim.
truant, a. skelm, lui, stokkiesdraaierig, ronddrentelend; dwalend.
truce, wapenstilstand; verposing, rus; **− of God**, godsvrede.
truck, v. handel, (ver)kwansel, (ver)ruil; smous, met smousware rondtrek.
truck, n. ruilhandel; smousware, negosiegoed; kaf, bog; **have no − with a person**, niks met iemand te doen hê nie.
truck, n. trok, goederewa; onderstel (van 'n spoorwegwa, ens.); vragwa, bokwa; stootwaentjie.
truck, v. (in 'n trok) laai, per goederewa vervoer.
truckle, n. rolletjie, wieletjie.

truckle, v. inkruip, lek.
truckle-bed, rolbed.
truck-system, dwangkoopstelsel.
truculence, wildheid, woestheid.
truculent, wild, woes, wreed.
trudge, v. voort-, aansukkel, voortstrompel.
trudge, n. sukkelgang, gesukkel.
true, a. waar; suiwer, eg; getrou, opreg, standvastig; juis; in die haak; **his words have come –**, sy woorde is bewaarheid; –, **it will cost more**, seker, dit sal meer kos; **a – judgment**, 'n suiwer oordeel; **the – heir**, die ware (regte) erfgenaam; **– to type**, raseg; tipies, normaal.
true, v. waterpas stel, haaks maak.
true-blue, a. eerlik, opreg, getrou.
true-blue, n. 'n ware Jonatan, 'n egte staatmaker, 'n Israeliet in wie geen bedrog is nie.
true-born, eg.
true-bred, raseg.
true-love, skatlief, soetlief.
truffle, truffel.
truism, ou bekende waarheid; gemeenplaas, afgesaagde uitdrukking.
trull, hoer, slet.
truly, waarlik, regtig, werklik; trou; volgens die werklikheid; **yours (very) –**, met (die meeste) hoogagting, hoogagtend; **it has been – said**, dit is tereg gesê.
trump, v. – **up**, versin, uit die duim suie.
trump, n. troef(kaart); 'n staatmaker; **put a person to his –s**, iemand dwing om sy troewe uit te speel; iemand se planne laat opraak, iemand raad-op maak; **turn up –s**, troewe omdraai; 'n geluk tref; goed uitval.
trump, v. troef; 'n troefkaart speel.
trump-card, troefkaart.
trumpery, n. klatergoud; prulle; kaf.
trumpery, a. waardeloos, prul- . . .
trumpet, n. trompet; trompetgeskal; **blow one's own –**, jou eie lof uitbasuin.
trumpet, v. uitbasuin, trompet.
trumpet-call, trompetsinjaal.
trumpeter, trompetblaser; trompetvoël; **be one's own –**, jou eie lof uitbasuin.
trumpet-flower, trompetblom.
truncal, romp- . . .; stam- . . .
truncate, top, snoei, afknot, afkap.
truncheon, stok, knuppel, mokerstok (van 'n konstabel); staf.
trundle, n. wieletjie; rolwa.
trundle, v. rol.
trundle-bed, rolbed.
trunk, stam, stomp; romp (van die liggaam); hooflyn; trommel, koffer; slurp (van olifant); koker; blaaspyp.
trunk-call, hooflyngesprek.
trunk-line, hooflyn.
trunk-road, hoofweg.
trunnion, tap, spil.
truss, v. stut; vasbind, opbind.
truss, n. stut; draagsteen; bondel; tros; breukband.
trust, n. vertroue; geloof; krediet; toevertroude pand; trust; kartel; bewaring; **put – in**, vertroue stel in; **he takes everything on –**, hy neem alles op goeie geloof aan; **a position of –**, 'n verantwoordelike betrekking; **in –**, in bewaring; **– money**, toevertroude geld, trustgeld; **– deed**, akte van oordrag, trustakte.
trust, v. vertrou; toevertrou (aan); **do not – him with your typewriter**, laat hom nie toe om jou skryfmasjien te gebruik nie; **– one with something**, iets aan iemand toevertrou; **I – he is not hurt**, ek hoop tog hy het nie seer gekry nie; **– in**, vertrou op; **you can't – to your memory**, jy kan jou nie op jou geheue verlaat nie; **let's – to luck**, laat ons hoop alles sal regkom; **– me for that**, laat dit maar aan my oor.
trustee, trustee; kurator.
trustful, vol vertroue.
trustiness, getrouheid; vertroubaarheid.
trustworthy, vertroubaar.
trusty, vertroubaar, trou.
truth, waarheid; eerlikheid; **there is – in what he says**, daar sit iets in wat hy sê; **the – is that I forgot**, om die waarheid te sê, ek het vergeet; **I told him a few home –s**, ek het hom goed die waarheid gesê; **in –**, waarlik, werklik, om die waarheid te sê.
truthful, waarheidliewend.
truthless, vals, ontrou.
try, probeer, poog, trag; op die proef stel, 'n proef neem, toets; ondersoek, in verhoor neem; suiwer, kook, uitbraai; **– your hand at**, probeer om te; **– one's patience**, jou geduld op die proef stel; **– how far you can throw**, probeer (kyk) hoe ver jy kan gooi; **be tried**, voorkom; **be tried for**, voorkom weens; **– for**, mik na, probeer om te kry; **– on clothes**, klere aanpas; **it is no use –ing it on with me**, dit help nie om sulke streke by my uit te haal nie; **– out**, suiwer; uitbraai, uitkook; probeer.
try, n. probeerslag, kans, poging; 'n drie (voetbal); **have a – at it**, probeer 'n slag; **score a –**, 'n drie maak; **convert a –**, 'n drie vervyf.
trying, lastig, moeilik; uitputtend, afmattend, vermoeiend.
try-square, winkelhaak.
Tsar, Tsaar.
tsetse, tsetsevlieg.
t-square, tekenhaak.
tub, vat, balie, kuip; badkuip.
tuba, tuba.
tubby, vatvormig; rond (en dik).
tube, buis, pyp; binneband; ondergrondse spoorweg, tonneltrein.
tube-colours, tubeverf.
tuber, knol; aartappel; knop, geswel.
tubercle, knoppie; puisie.
tubercular, tuberkuleus; vol knoppies.
tuberculosis, tuberkulose; tering; **pulmonary –**, longtering.
tuberculous, tuberkuleus.
tuberiferous, knoldraend.
tuberose, a. knopperig; knopvormig, knolvormig; knoldraend.
tuberose, n. soetemaling.
tuberosity, knopperigheid; knop-, knolvormigheid; knop, geswel.
tuberous, sien **tuberose**.
tubing, (stuk) pyp (buis); slang.
tub-thumper, skreeuer, seepkisredenaar.
tubular, buisvormig; buis- . . ., pyp- . . .; **– boiler**, vlampypketel.
tuck, v. opnaaisels maak (insit); plooi; omslaan, inslaan, oprol; intrek; lekker toemaak (toedraai), inrol; **– away**, bêre, wegstop, wegsteek; **– in**, intrek; instop, wegbêre, (kos) wegslaan; inrol, lekker toemaak; **– up**, ophang; **the bird –s his head under his wing**, die voël steek sy kop onder sy vlerk in.
tuck, n. opnaaisel, pylnaat; lekkergoed, snoepgoed; **make a – in**, 'n opnaaisel insit.
tuck-shop, snoepwinkel.
Tudor, Tudor.
Tuesday, Dinsdag.
tufa, tufsteen.
tufaceous, tufkrytagtig.
tuff, tufsteen.

tuft, n. bossie; klossie; kwassie; kuif(ie); trossie, graspolletjie.
tuft, v. klossies aansit; in trossies (bossies) groei; ('n matras) deurnaai.
tufty, trossierig; geskuif.
tug, v. trek, ruk, pluk; sleep.
tug, n. ruk, trek; kragsinspanning, kragtige poging; sleepboot; oog, lissie (van 'n tuig).
tug-boat, sleepboot.
tug-of-war, toutrek.
tuition, onderrig, onderwys; skoolgeld, klasgeld.
tulip, tulp.
tulle, netsy, tule.
tumble, v. tuimel, val; rol; val-val loop (hardloop); deurmekaar maak; onderstebo gooi, rondgooi; neertrek, neerskiet; akrobaattoere uithaal, bolmakiesie slaan; – **down**, omval, omtuimel; aftuimel; omgooi, omsmyt; – **in**, na buite tuimel; inkruip, kooi toe gaan; – **out**, na buite tuimel; uitsmyt, uitgooi; – **out of bed**, uit die bed rol, opstaan; – **over**, omval, omtuimel; omgooi; – **to**, begryp, vat, snap.
tumble, n. val, tuimeling; bolmakiesieslag; warboel, deurmekaarboel.
tumble-bug, miskruier.
tumble-down, bouvallig, lendelam.
tumbler, akrobaat; tuimelaar(duif); (water)glas.
tumbly, ongelyk, hobbelagtig, stamperig.
tumefaction, opswelling, geswel, swelsel.
tumefy, (laat) opswel.
tumescence, opswelling.
tumescent, opswellend.
tumid, (op)geswel; bombasties.
tumidity, hoogdrawendheid, bombas.
tummy, magie, boekpensie.
tumour, geswel.
tumult, tumult, opskudding, lawaai, rumoer, oploop; **the – within him**, die storm in sy gemoed.
tumultuous, oproerig, rumoerig, woes.
tumulus, grafheuwel.
tun, n. vat, ton.
tun, v. in 'n vat (ton) gooi.
tuna, tuna, to(r)nyn.
tunable, stembaar.
tundra, moeras, toendra.
tune, n. toon, melodie, wysie, deuntjie; gemoedstemming; **he sings out of –**, hy sing vals; **learn to sing in –**, leer om reg te sing (om die wysie te hou); **be out of – with the surroundings**, nie met die omgewing harmonieer nie; **totally out of –**, totaal ontstem, heeltemal van die wysie af; **change one's –**, **sing another –**, 'n ander liedjie sing, 'n ander toon aanslaan; **in – with**, in harmonie (gelykgestem) met.
tune, v. stem; (laat) harmonieer (met); sing; **the lark –s his song**, die lewerkie sing sy lied; – **up**, stem (van 'n orkes); begin speel (sing); aan die huil gaan; – **with**, harmonieer met.
tuneful, melodieus, welluidend, musikaal.
tuneless, klankloos; wanluidend.
tuner, stemmer; (radio) insteller.
tung-oil, tungolie.
tungstate, tungstaat.
tungsten, wolfram.
tunic, tuniek; soldaatbaadjie; vlies, vel.
tunicle, tunika; vliesie, velletjie.
tuning-fork, stemvurk.
tuning-hammer, stemhamer.
tunnel, n. tonnel; mynskag.
tunnel, v. tonnel grawe deur; – **through**, deurgrawe, deurtonnel.
tunnel-borer, tonnelboor.
tunny, to(r)nyn.
tup, ram; slaankant (van stoomhamer).

turban, tulband.
turbaned, met 'n tulband op, getulband.
turbid, troebel, modderig, vuil.
turbidity, modderigheid, troebelrigheid.
turbinate, tolvormig, keëlvormig.
turbine, turbine.
turbine-boat, turbine-boot.
turbo-jet, turbinestraal; – **engine**, turbinestraalmotor.
turbo-prop(eller), turbineskroef; – **aeroplane**, turbineskroefvliegtuig.
turbot, tarbot.
turbulence, onstuimigheid; woeligheid; oproerigheid, opstandigheid.
turbulent, onstuimig, in beroering; woelig; oproerig, opstandig.
turd, drol, mis, drek, a.
tureen, so(e)pkom.
turf, n. turf, kweek; grasveld; baan; kweekgrond; turfsooi, kweeksooi; **the –**, die renbaan, re(i)siesbaan, re(i)sies.
turf, v. besooi; met gras beplant.
turfy, sooierig, kwekerig.
turgescence, swelling; hoogdrawendheid.
turgescent, swellend; hoogdrawend.
turgid, hoogdrawend, opgeswel.
turgidity, geswollenheid, bombas, (op)swelling.
Turk, Turk; harde kop.
Turkey, n. Turkye.
Turkey, a. Turks; – **red**, Turkse rooi.
turkey, kalkoen.
turkey-cock, kalkoenmannetjie.
turkey-hen, kalkoenwyfie.
turkey-poult, jong kalkoen(tjie).
Turkish, Turks; – **bath**, Turkse bad, sweetbad; – **delight**, Turkse lekkers; – **towel**, growwe handdoek.
turmalin(e), toermalyn.
turmeric, borrie; kurkuma; – **paper**, kurkumapapier.
turmoil, gewoel, onrus, gejaagdheid, rumoer, verwarring.
turn, v. draai, laat draai; gaan, keer; omkeer, omdraai; omgaan; omblaai, omslaan; verander; (aandag) wy, gee; laat weggaan, laat omdraai; omtrek; word; maak; vertaal, oorsit; suur word, suur maak; – **a key in the lock**, 'n sleutel in die slot (om)draai; **everything –s on his answer**, alles hang van sy antwoord af; **he –s everything upside down, inside out**, hy draai alles om; hy maak alles deurmekaar; **the umbrella –ed inside out**, die sambreel het omgedop; – **the scale**, die deurslag gee; – **the edge of**, stomp maak, laat omlê; – **the flank of an army**, 'n leërmag omtrek; **be –ed 40**, oor die veertig jaar oud wees; **he never –ed a beggar from his door**, hy het nooit 'n bedelaar voor sy deur laat omdraai nie; – **traitor**, verraad pleeg, verraaier word; **the milk will – (sour)**, die melk sal suur word; – **pale**, bleek word; **it –s my stomach**, dit maak my mislik; **success has –ed his head**, voorspoed het sy kop op hol gebring; **he knows how to – a compliment**, hy kan 'n goeie kompliment maak; – **a corner**, 'n hoek omgaan; **we have –ed the corner**, ons is deur die ergste heen, ons het die ergste gehad; – **about**, omdraai; – **ed against him**, teen hom gekant; – **aside**, afwend, wegdraai; – **away**, wegkeer, wegdraai, wegloop; – **back**, terugkeer, terugdraai; – **down**, omdraai, omkeer; afdraai, kleiner draai; omvou; afslaan, van die hand wys; afwys, afstem; – **down a card**, 'n kaart omkeer; – **in**, invou; binnetoe staan; kooi toe gaan, inkruip; – **into French**, in Frans oorsit (vertaal); – **off**, afdraai, afsluit (gas ens.);

klaar maak; in die pad steek, laat loop; uitdraai, wegdraai; ophang; – on, oopdraai, aandraai; he –ed on his heels, hy het op die plek omgedraai; – his back on me, my die rug toekeer; – on the waterworks, begin te huil; – out, wegja; buitekant toe steek (draai); lewer, maak; omkeer, omdraai; 15 men –ed out, 15 man het opgedaag; it –s out that, dit blyk dat; everything –ed out well, alles het goed afgeloop; it –ed out badly, dit het misgeloop; the son dit not – out well, die seun het sleg uitgeval, daar het niks goeds van die seun gekom nie; – out a room, 'n kamer leegmaak; they – out good shoes, hulle maak goeie skoene; you can't – these people out, jy kan nie die mense buitekant die deur sit nie; – over, omgooi, laat omval (omkantel); omblaai; oormaak; I have –ed the matter over and over in my mind. ek het die saak van alle kante beskou; – over a page, omblaai; – round, omdraai; draai om; van opinie verander, 'n ander weg inslaan; – to, (sig) wend tot; begin, aanstalte maak, aanpak; he can – his hand to anything, hy kan enige ding aanvat (aanpak); – to account, voordeel trek uit; – to God, jou tot God wend; – attention to, aandag wy aan (vestig op); he –ed to this sort of work, hy het hierdie soort werk aangepak, hy het hom op hierdie soort werk toegelê; – up, (kaart) omkeer; uitploeë, uitspit, uitgraaf; opdaag; laat opbring; (broekspyp) omslaan; – up the lamp, die lamp opdraai.
turn, n. draai, bog, kromming; wending, omkeer, keerpunt; aard, aanleg, wandelinkie, toertjie; kans, beurt, geleentheid; diens, vriendskap; slag; skok; he took a sudden – to the left, hy het skielik linksweg gedraai; the milk is on the –, die melk is aan suur word; a new – to the conversation, 'n ander wending aan die gesprek; he was of humorous –, hy was humoristies van aard; take a – in the garden, 'n entjie in die tuin gaan loop speak out of your –, 'n entjie jou beurt praat; in –, om die beurt; na mekaar; we must take –s, elkeen van ons moet sy beurt waarneem, elkeen moet sy kans kry; he went hot and cold by –s, hy het beurtelings warm en koud geword; do somebody a good –, iemand 'n diens bewys; be on the –, op die keerpunt staan; the tide is on the –, die gety begin te keer; it gave me quite a –, dit het my erg laat skrik; the meat is done to a –, die vleis is net lekker gaar gemaak; take the second – to the left, links draai op die tweede hoek; one good – deserves another, as die een hand die ander was, word albei skoon; he has a fine – of speed, hy beskik oor 'n goeie vaart; – of a sentence, sinswending.
turn-bench, draaibank.
turn-can, skoorsteenkan.
turn-coat, oorloper, weerhaan.
turn-down, omslaan– . . .
turner, tuimelaar(duif); kunsdraaier.
turnery, draaiwerk.
turning, draai; wending.
turning-point, keerpunt.
turnip, raap.
turnip-tops, raaplowwe.
turnkey, tronkbewaarder, sipier.
turn-out, opkoms; werkstaking; uitrusting; produksie.
turn-over, omkanteling; omset.
turnpike, tolhek, slagboom, draaihek.
turn-screw, skroewedraaier.
turn-side, dronksiekte (by honde).
turn-sole, sonneblom.

turnspit, spit(om)draaier.
turnstile, draaisport, draaihek.
turn-table, draaiskyf.
turn-up, a. omslaan– . . .
turpentine, terpentyn.
turpentine-tree, terpentynboom.
turpitude, laagheid, slegtheid.
turquoise, turkoois.
turret, torinkie; skiettoring.
turreted, met torinkies.
turtle, n. tortelduif.
turtle, n. seeskilpad; turn –, omslaan, omkantel.
turtle-dove, tortelduif.
Tuscan, Toskaans, Toskaner.
Tuscany, Toskane.
tush, interj. ag!, ba!
tush, hoektand.
tusk, slagtand; tand.
tusked, met slagtande.
tussle, n. gestoei, worsteling, bakleiery.
tussle, v. stoei, worstel, baklei.
tussock, graspolletjie; bossie, kuif.
tussore silk, tussor-sy.
tut, interj. ag!, bog!, stil!
tutelage, voogdyskap, voogdy; minderjarigheid, onmondigheid.
tutelar(y), beskerm– . . ., beskermend; – angel, beskermengel.
tutor, n. private onderwyser, tutor; voog; breier, dosent.
tutor, v. onderrig, leer, privaatles gee.
tutorial, a.: – classes, private klasse.
tutorial, n. private klas.
tutorship, voogdyskap; dosentskap.
twaddle, v. klets, sanik, babbel.
twaddle, n. geklets, gesanik, gebabbel.
twaddler, kletsprater, babbelaar.
twaddly, klets– . . .; babbel– . . .
twain, twee; cut in –, aan twee sny.
twang, v. (laat) klink, (laat) tril; tokkel; deur die neus praat.
twang, n. snaarklank; neusklank.
tweak, v. knyp; draai; ruk, pluk.
tweak, n. knyp.
tweed, tweed.
tweedledum: – and tweedledee, peper en koljander (die een is soos die ander).
tweet, tjilp, tjirp.
tweezers, (haar)tangetjie.
twelfth, twaalfde (deel).
twelve, twaalf.
twelvemonth, 'n jaar; this day –, vandag oor 'n jaar; vandag 'n jaar gelede.
twentieth, twintigste (deel).
twenty, twintig.
twentyfold, twintigvoudig.
twerp, skobbejak.
twice, twee maal, twee keer.
twiddle, draai, speel, lol; – one's thumbs, met jou duime speel.
twig, takkie, twyg(ie); waterwysstokkie; hop the –, bokveld toe gaan.
twiggy, vol takkies, takkiesrig.
twilight, skemer(lig), skemerte, skemerig, skemerdonker, skemeraand; vaagheid; – sleep, skemerslaap.
twill, n. gekeperde stof, keper, twill.
twill, v. keper.
twin, a. tweeling– . . .; dubbel; paar-paar; – sisters, tweelingsusters, tweeling; – brother, tweelingbroer; – beds, „tweelingbedde".
twin, n. (een van 'n) tweeling; dubbelganger, ewebeeld; –s, 'n tweeling.
twine, n. tou, seilgare; kronkeling, deureenstrengeling; deurmekaar gevleg.

twine, v. vleg, draai; strengel; inmekaar draai (vleg); – **about, round,** omdraai, omvleg, omstrengel.
twinge, n. steek, pyn; kwelling; **a – of conscience,** gewetenswroeging.
twinge, v. steek; kwel.
twinkle, v. flikker, fonkel; knip(oog).
twinkle, n. oogknip, flikkering, fonkeling.
twinkling, flikkering, fonkeling; **in a –, in the –** **of an eye,** in 'n oogwink.
twirl, v. (in die rondte) draai, swaai; **– one's thumbs,** met jou duime speel.
twirl, n. draai, krul.
twist, n. tou; seilgare; string; twist, katoengaring; roltabak; draai; kronkeling; aard, neiging; **full of turns and –s,** vol draaie en kronkelinge; **he has the – of the wrist,** hy het die slag; **there was a lot of – on the ball,** die bal het baie krul gehad.
twist, v. draai, vleg; kronkel, strengel; krul; verdraai; verwring, vertrek, verrek; **his features –ed with pain,** sy gesig het vertrek van die pyn.
twister, dwarsbalk; vlegter; krulbal.
twit, verwyt, terg, pla.
twitch, v. trek, ruk; vertrek.
twitch, n. trek, ruk; senuweetrekking.
twitter, v. tjilp, tjirp, kwetter; bewe, tril; giggel.
twitter, n. getjilp, getjirp, gekwetter; gegiggel; trilling.
two, twee; **one or –,** een of twee, 'n paar; **cut in –,** middeldeur sny.
two-edged, tweesnydend.
twofold, dubbel, tweevoudig.
two-handed, tweehand- . . .; tweepersoons- . . .
twopence, twee pennies, twee oulap; **I don't care –,** dit kan my niks skeel nie, ek gee g'n flenter om nie.
twopenny, a. twee oulap se . . .; goedkoop, nikswerd.

two-ply, tweedraads-; tweelaag . . .
two-seater, tweepersoonsmotor.
twosome, tweespel, dubbelspel.
two-tongued, vals.
two-seater, tweesitplekrytuig, - motor.
two-stroke, tweeslag-.
tycoon, magnaat.
tympan, timpaan, ysterraam; vlies.
tympanic, trommel- . . .; **– membrane,** trommelvlies.
tympanitis, trommelvliesontsteking.
tympanum, trommelvies.
type, n. tipe, soort, voorbeeld; sinnebeeld; (druk)letter; setsel; **printed in large –,** in groot letter gedruk.
type, v. tik; tipeer.
type-metal, lettermetaal.
type-setter, lettersetter.
typewrite, tik.
typewriter, tikmasjien, skryfmasjien.
typhoid, a. tifeus; **– fever,** ingewandskoors.
typhoon, tifoon.
typhus(-fever), tifus(koors), vlektifus, luiskoors.
typify, tipeer; illustreer, teken.
typist, tikster (tikker), tipis.
typograph, setmasjien.
typographer, tipograaf.
typographic(al), tipografies.
typography, tipografie, drukkuns.
tyrannical, tiranniek (tirannies).
tyrannize, tiranniseer, baasspeel oor.
tyrannous, sien **tyrannical.**
tyranny, tirannie, dwingelandy, baasspelery, wreedheid.
tyrant, tiran, dwingeland.
tyre, sien **tire.**
tyro, sien **tiro.**
Tyrolese, a. Tirolees.
Tyrolese, n. Tiroler.

U

ubiquitous, alomteenwoordig.
ubiquity, alomteenwoordigheid.
u-boat, u-boot, (Duitse) duikboot.
udder, uier.
udometer, reënmeter.
ugh, ga!, ba!, soe!
uglify, lelik maak verlelik.
ugly, a. lelik, wanstaltig, naar; haatlik laag; his conduct has an – look, daar is iets gemeens in sy gedrag; an – customer, 'n gevaarlike klant; – weather, vuil weer, onaangename weer.
uhlan, ulaan.
ukase, oekase, bevelskrif.
ulcer, sweer; verrotte plek, kanker.
ulcerate, sweer, versweer; laat sweer.
ulceration, verswering, sweer.
uliginose, moeras- ...
ulna, ellepyp, ulna.
ulnar, ellepyps- ...
ulster, oorjas, ulster.
ulterior, aan die ander kant; verder, later; geheim, verborge; – motives, bedekte beweegrede, bybedoelinge.
ultimate, uiteindelik, eind- ... , finaal, uiterste, laaste; fundamenteel, primêr; – result, uiteindelike resultaat; – principles, grondbeginsels.
ultimatum, ultimatum; grondbeginsel.
ultimo, van die vorige maand, laaslede.
ultimogeniture, erfopvolgingsreg van die jongste seun.
ultra, n. ekstremis, ultra, heethoof.
ultra, a. ekstremisties, ultra.
ultramarine, a. oorsees.
ultramarine, n. ultramaryn.
ultramontane, ultramontaans.
ultramundane, bo-aards.
ultra-red, ultrarooi.
ultrasonic, ultrasonies.
ultra-violet, ultraviolet.
ululate, skreeu, huil, tjank.
ululation, gehuil, getjank, geskreeu.
umbel, blomskerm.
umbelliferous, skermdraend.
umbellule, skermpie.
umber, n. omber; ombervis.
umber, a. omberkleurig, omberbruin.
umbilical, na(w)el- ... ; – cord, na(w)elstring.
umbilicus, na(w)el; knop(pie).
umbiliform, na(w)elvormig.
umbra, volle skaduwee, slagskaduwee.
umbrage, koelte, skaduwee; aanstoot, beleediging, ergernis; give –, aanstoot gee, vererg; take –, vererg; take –, kwalik neem, beledig voel, kwaad word.
umbrella, sambreel.
umbrella-stand, sambreelstander.
umbrella-tree, kiepersolboom.
umlaut, umlaut.
umpire, n. skeidsregter, arbiter.
umpire, v. as skeidsregter optree.
unabashed, onbeskaam(d); nie uit die veld geslaan nie; verleë nie.
unabated, onverminder(d), onverswak.
unabbreviated, onverkort.
unable, onbekwaam, nie in staat nie.
unabolished, nie afgeskaf nie.
unabridged, onverkort.
unaccented, onbetoon, toonloos.
unacceptable, onaanneemlik; onwelkom.
unaccommodating, onvriendelik, ontoegeeflik; hardkoppig, veeleisend.
unaccompanied, alleen, onvergesel; sonder begeleiding.

unaccomplished, onuitgevoer, onvoltooi(d); sonder talente.
unaccountable, onverklaarbaar; onverantwoordelik.
unaccustomed, ongewoon; – to, ongewend (ongewoond) aan.
unachievable, onbereikbaar, onuitvoerbaar.
unacknowledged, nie erken nie; onbeantwoord.
unacquainted, onbekend.
unadorned, onversier, sonder versiering.
unadulterated, onvervals, eg, suiwer.
unadvisable, ongerade.
unadvisedly, onverstandig, onversigtig.
unaffected, natuurlik, ongedwonge, eg.
unaided, sonder hulp, alleen.
unalarmed, gerus, onbevrees.
unallotted, nie toegeken nie.
unalloyed, onvermeng, suiwer.
unalterable, onveranderlik, vas.
unaltered, onverander(d).
unambiguous, ondubbelsinnig, duidelik.
unambitious, eersugloos; slap, traag.
unamiable, onbeminlik, onvriendelik.
unamusing, onvermaaklik.
unanalysed, onopgelos, onontleed.
unanimated, onbesiel(d), leweloos.
unanimity, eenstemmigheid, eenparigheid, eensgesindheid.
unanimous, eenstemmig, eenparig.
unannounced, onaangekondig, onaangemeld, onverwag.
unanswerable, onbeantwoordbaar; onweerlegbaar.
unanswered, onbeantwoord.
unappeasable, onversoenlik; onbevredigbaar, onversadigbaar.
unappeased, onversoen, onbevredig.
unappreciated, ongewaardeer(d).
unapproachable, ontoeganklik, ongenaakbaar.
unappropriated, nie toegeëien nie, sonder baas; nie geskik nie.
unapproved, nie goedgekeur nie.
unapt, ongeskik, onvanpas; ongeneig.
unarmed, ongewapen(d), ontwapen(d).
unartistic, onartistiek.
unascertained, nie seker nie, onseker.
unashamed, onbeskaam(d), sonder skaamte, onbeskof.
unasked, ongevra(ag), ongenooi; op eie houtjie.
unassailable, onweerlegbaar, onbetwisbaar, onaantasbaar.
unassisted, sonder hulp, alleen.
unassuming, beskeie.
unattached, los, nie verbonde nie.
unattainable, onbereikbaar.
unattempted, onbeproef.
unattended, onvergesel, alleen.
unattractive, onaantreklik.
unauthorized, onwettig, nie gemagtig nie, onbevoeg.
unavailable, nie beskikbaar nie.
unavailing, nutteloos, tevergeefs.
unavenged, ongewreek.
unavoidable, onvermydelik.
unaware, onbewus, onwetend; I was – of it, ek het nie daarvan geweet nie, ek was daar onbewus van.
unawares, onverwags, skielik, onverhoeds; onwetend; take (catch) –, oorval.
unbacked, sonder hulp, nie ondersteun nie; ongeleer, ongedresseer, wys; it is an – horse, daar word nie op die perd gewed nie.
unbalanced, onewewigtig.
unbandaged, onverbind, sonder verband.
unbaptized, ongedoop.

unbearable, ondraaglik, onuitstaanbaar.
unbeaten, onoorwonne; ongebaan.
unbeautiful, onskoon.
unbecoming, onbehoorlik, onbetaamlik, onwelvoeglik; onvanpas.
unbegotten, ongebore.
unbelief, ongeloof.
unbeliever, ongelowige.
unbelieving, ongelowig.
unbeloved, onbemin(d).
unbend, reguit maak; verslap; ontspan; vriendeliker word, ontdooi.
unbending, styf, onbuigsaam; ontoegeeflik, streng, straf.
unbeseeming, ongepas, onbehoorlik.
unbias(s)ed, onbevooroordeeld.
unbiblical, onbybels.
unbidden, ongevra(ag), ongenooi.
unbigoted, gematig, nie dweepsiek nie.
unbind, losmaak, ontbind.
unbleached, ongebleik.
unblemished, onbevlek, vlekloos, onbesmet, skoon, rein.
unblushing, skaamteloos.
unblushingly, op skaamtelose manier.
unbolt, ontgrendel, oopmaak, oopsluit.
unborn, ongebore.
unbosom, ontboesem, die hart uitstort.
unbounded, grensloos, onbegrens.
unbowel, die ingewande uithaal.
unbrace, ontspan; losmaak, losryg.
unbred, ongemanierd, onopgevoed.
unbribable, onomkoopbaar.
unbridle, die toom afhaal; loslaat.
unbridled, onbeteuel(d), toomloos.
unbroken, onafgebroke; ongestoord; heel, nie stukkend nie; ongetem, wys.
unbrotherly, onbroederlik.
unbuckle, losgespe(r), losmaak.
unburden, ontboesem, lug gee aan (die gevoelens); van 'n las bevry; – **oneself**, jou hart uitstort.
unburied, onbegrawe.
unbusinesslike, onprakties, onsaaklik.
unbutton, losknoop.
uncage, uit die hok (kou) laat, loslaat.
uncalled, ongeroep; – **for**, onvanpas, onnodig.
uncanny, geheimsinnig, onheilspellend, spookagtig, angswekkend.
uncared-for, onversorg, verwaarloos.
uncase, uit die sak haal, uithaal.
unceasing, voortdurend, aanhoudend, onophoudelik, onafgebroke.
unceremonious, familiaar; kortaf.
unceremoniously, sonder pligpleginge.
uncertain, onseker, twyfelagtig; veranderlik, ongestadig; onvas.
uncertainty, onsekerheid.
uncertificated, ongesertifiseer(d).
unchain, losmaak, ontketen.
unchallenged, onbestrede, onbetwis; ongehinder; onuitgedaag.
unchangeable, onveranderlik.
uncharitable, onbarmhartig, hard.
unchaste, onkuis.
unchivalrous, onridderlik.
unchristian, onchristelik.
uncircumcized, onbesnede; heidens.
uncivil, onbeleef, onvriendelik, onbeskof.
uncivilised, onbeskaaf, barbaars.
unclad, ongeklee(d).
unclaimed, onopgeëis; nie gelos nie.
unclasp, oopmaak, losmaak, losgespe(r).
uncle, oom; **U. Sam**, Verenigde State (van Amerika).
unclean, vuil; onrein; onkuis.

unclog, oopmaak, skoonmaak.
unclose, oopmaak, ontsluit.
unclothe, uittrek, ontklee.
unclouded, onbewolk.
uncock, in (die) rus sit; die rant (van 'n hoed) afslaan.
uncoil, losdraai, afdraai, afrol, afwen.
uncoined, ongemunt.
uncoloured, ongekleur; onopgesmuk.
uncombed, ongekam, deurmekaar.
uncomely, onbevallig; onbekoorlik.
uncomfortable, ongemaklik, ongerieflik; ontuis, verleë, nie op jou gemak nie.
uncommitted, ongebonde, vry; ongedaan.
uncommon, buitengewoon, ongewoon.
uncommunicative, stil(swyend), terughoudend, teruggetrokke, swygsaam.
uncomplaining, tevrede, gelate.
uncomplicated, eenvoudig.
uncomplimentary, sonder komplimente; onbeleef, onvriendelik.
uncompounded, enkelvoudig, nie samegestel(d) nie.
uncompromising, onbuigsaam, onversetlik, ontoegewend, beginselvas.
unconcern, onverskilligheid, onbekommerdheid, ongevoeligheid.
unconcerned, onverskillig, onbekommerd.
unconditional, onvoorwaardelik.
unconfessed, onbelede; sonder te bieg.
unconfirmed, onbevestig; nie aangeneem nie.
unconformable, ongelykvormig; strydig, uiteenlopend; ongelyklopend, onewewydig.
uncongenial, teenstrydig, ongelyksoortig; onaangenaam, onsimpatiek.
unconnected, onsamehangend, los.
unconquerable, onoorwinlik.
unconquered, onoorwonne.
unconscientious, nie konsensieus nie, gewetenloos, slap, traag.
unconscionable, heeltemal onbillik, geweteloos, onredelik.
unconscious, onbewus; bewusteloos.
unconsidered, ondeurdag; nie in aanmerking geneem.
unconstitutional, ongrondwetlik.
unconstrained, ongedwonge.
uncontaminated, skoon, rein, onbevlek.
uncontemplated, onverwag; onvoorsien.
uncontested, onbetwis; onbestrede.
uncontradicted, onweerlê (onweerlegde); nie teëgespreek nie.
uncontrollable, onbedwingbaar, onbeteuelbaar.
uncontrolled, onbeteuel, bandeloos.
unconventional, vry, natuurlik, sonder pligpleginge (formaliteite).
unconverted, onbekeer(d); onvervyf.
unconvinced, onoortuig.
uncooked, rou, ongekook.
uncork, ontkurk, die prop uittrek.
uncorroborated, nie bevestig nie.
uncorrupted, onbedorwe.
uncoupled, losgekoppel, afgekoppel.
uncourteous, onbeleef, onhoflik.
uncourtly, onhoflik.
uncouth, lomp, baar; ongepoets.
uncover, oopmaak; ontbloot, kaal maak; – **the head**, die hoof ontbloot, die hoed afhaal.
uncoveted, ongevra(ag), nie verlang nie.
uncreated, ongeskape.
uncritical, onkrities, goedgelowig.
uncrossed, ongekruis; vry, onbelemmer.
uncrown, ontkroon.
uncrowned, ongekroon; ontkroon(d).

unction, salwing; salf, oliesel; balsem; genot; vleiery.
unctuous, salwend; vleiend; vetterig.
uncultivated, onbewerk, onbebou; onontwikkel(d).
uncultured, onbeskaaf.
uncurbed, onbeteuel(d), ongebreidel(d).
uncurl, die krulle uithaal; losdraai.
uncurtailed, onverkort; onverminder.
uncut, onoopgesny; ongesny; ongeslyp.
undamaged, onbeskadig.
undated, ongedateer(d), sonder datum.
undaunted, onverskrokke, onversaag; nie ontmoedig nie, nie afgeskrik nie.
undeceive, tot ontnugtering bring.
undecided, onbeslis; besluiteloos.
undecipherable, nie te ontsyfer nie, onleesbaar.
undeclinable, onverbuigbaar.
undefended, onverdedig, onbeskerm.
undefiled, onbesoedel(d) onbevlek.
undefined, ongedefinieer, onbepaal(d).
undelivered, nie afgelewer nie.
undemonstrative, kalm, bedaard, stil.
undeniable, onloënbaar.
undependable, onbetroubaar.
undeplored, onbetreur(d).
under, prep. onder, benede; **speak – one's breath**, fluister, saggies praat; – **sentence of death**, tot die dood veroordeel.
under, adv. onder.
under, a. onder-..., onderste; – **dog**, die ondergeskikte, die man aan die kortste ent.
underbid, laer bieë (bied) as.
underbred, sleg opgevoed, ongemanierd.
undercarriage, onderstel.
undercharge, te min laat betaal; die skoot (lading) te swak maak.
underclothes, **underclothing**, onderklere.
undercurrent, onderstroom.
undercut, v. wegsny; (pryse) afslaan, verminder; 'n opskoot (lugskoot) slaan (in gholf, boks).
undercut, n. op(trek)-skoot.
underdo, halfgaar kook, bak (braai).
underdone, halfgaar, halfrou.
underdrain, sugslote maak, dreineer.
underdress, te dun (te sleg) klee(d).
underestimate, onderskat, te gering ag.
underestimation, onderskatting, geringskatting.
under-expose, te kort belig, onderbelig.
under-exposure, onderbeligting.
underfed, ondervoed.
underfeed, te min kos gee, ondervoed.
underfoot, onder die voete.
undergarment, stuk onderklere, onderkleed.
undergo, ondergaan; deurstaan, uitstaan.
undergradiate, ongegradueerde.
underground, adv. onder die grond.
underground, a. onderaards, ondergronds.
underground, n. ondergrondse spoorweg.
undergrown, onuitgegroei, verpot.
undergrowth, struikgewas, ruigte, boskasie (bosgasie).
underhand, adv. agteraf, stilletjies.
underhand, a. agterbaks, slinks, onderduims; onderlangs.
underlay, v. stut, steun.
underlay, n. onderlêer.
underlet, onder die waarde verhuur; onderverhuur.
underlie, lê onder; ten grondslag lê aan.
underline, onderstreep; beklemtoon.
underlinen, onderklere.
underling, handlanger, ondergeskikte.
underman, te swak beman, onderbeman.
undermentioned, onderstaande.

undermine, uitgrawe, uitkalwe; ondermyn, benadeel.
underneath, onder, benede.
underpay, te min betaal.
underpin, stut.
underplot, by-intrige, byhandeling.
underprivileged, minderbevoorreg.
underproof, benede die vereiste sterkte.
underprop, ondersteun, stut.
underquote, 'n laer prys opgee as.
underrate, onderskat.
under-ripe, halfryp, nie ryp genoeg nie.
under-secretary, ondersekretaris.
undersell, goedkoper verkoop as; onder die waarde verkoop.
undersigned, ondergetekende.
undersized, (te) klein, kleiner as die gewone grootte, onder normaal.
underskirt, onderrok.
understand, begryp, verstaan, vat; hoor; **we – that**, ons verneem dat; **no one could – that from my words**, niemand kon dit uit my woorde aflei nie; **he gave me (I was given) to –**, hy het my laat verstaan (te verstaan gegee).
understanding, a. intelligent.
understanding, n. verstand, intelligensie, begrip; verstandhouding, ooreenkoms; **people without –**, mense sonder verstand; **come to an –**, tot 'n verstandhouding (skikking) kom; **on the –**, op voorwaarde, met dien verstande.
understate, nie alles meedeel nie; te laag opgee, onvoldoende weergee; benede die waarheid bly.
understatement, onderskatting, onvolledige opgawe, onvoldoende beskrywing (uiteensetting).
understock, te min voorraad inslaan; te min vee aanhou.
understood, verstaan; vanselfsprekend
understudy, plaasvervanger.
undertake, onderneem; aanneem; aanpak, aanvat; waarborg.
undertaker, lykbesorger, (begrafnis)ondernemer.
undertaking, onderneming; lykbesorging.
under-timed, te min belig, onderbelig.
undertone, n. fluisterstem, gesmoorde stem, gedempte toon; dowwe tint.
undertone, v. (te) swak fikseer.
undertrump, laer troef, ondertroef.
undervaluation, te lae waardering.
undervalue, onderskat, te laag waardeer.
underwear, onderklere.
underwood, struikgewas, ruigte, bossies.
underworld, die ander wêreld, doderyk, onderwêreld; lae kringe, agterbuurte.
underwrite, onderteken; skeepsassuransies sluit, verseker.
underwriter, versekeraar, assuradeur.
undeserved, onverdien(d).
undeserving, onwaardig.
undesirable, a. ongewens; ongerieflik.
undesirable, n. ongewenste persoon.
undesirous, nie begerig nie.
undetected, onontdek, geheim, verborge.
undetermined, onbeslis, onbepaald.
undeterred, onvervaard, onverskrokke, nie ontmoedig nie, nie afgeskrik nie.
undeveloped, onontwikkel(d).
undeviating, reguit, onwankelbaar.
undigested, onverteer(d).
undignified, onwaardig, sonder waardigheid.
undiluted, onverdun(d).
undiminished, onverminder(d).
undimmed, onverduister(d), nie verdof nie, helder, skerp.

undirected, onbestuur(d); sonder rigting, ongeadresseer(d).
undiscerned, onopgemerk.
undiscerning, sonder deursig, nie skerpsiende nie, kortsigtig.
undischarged, (nog) gelaai, nie afgeskiet nie; onafbetaal; nie ontslaan nie; nie vrygespreek nie.
undisciplined, ongedissiplineer(d), tugloos; ongeoefen.
undiscovered, onontdek.
undisguised, onvermom, sonder vermomming, openhartig, opreg.
undismayed, onverskrokke, onvervaard.
undisputed, onbetwis, onbestrede.
undissolved, onopgelos; nie ontbind nie.
undistinguishable, onherkenbaar, nie te onderskei nie, nie uit mekaar te ken nie, eenders.
undisturbed, ongehinder(d), ongestoor(d); rustig, bedaard, kalm.
undivided, onverdeel(d), geheel.
undivorced, ongeskei, nie geskei nie.
undivulged, geheim, nie openbaar gemaak nie, ongeopenbaar(d).
undo, losmaak, oopmaak; tot niet maak; in die ongeluk stort.
undoing, (die) losmaak (oopmaak); vernietiging; ongeluk, ondergang.
undone, ongedaan; los(gemaak); **what is done, cannot be –**, gedane sake het geen keer nie.
undoubtedly, ongetwyfeld, sonder twyfel.
undraped, nie gedrapeer nie; naak.
undreamt of, ongehoord, ongekend.
undress, v. ontklee, uittrek.
undress, n. gewone drag; huisrok.
undressed, uitgetrek; onaangetrek, ongeklee(d); ontoeberei; ru, skurf.
undrinkable, ondrinkbaar.
undue, oordrewe, buitensporig; onbehoorlik; nog nie verval nie.
undulate, golf, wuif.
undulating, golwend, wuiwend.
undulation, golwing, golwende, beweging.
undulatory, golwend, golwings-. . ., golf-. . .; – theory, golwingsteorie.
unduly, oormatig, bowemate, buiten die maat, te veel.
undutiful, ongehoorsaam.
undying, onsterflik, ewig.
unearned, onverdien(d).
unearth, (wild) opja; op-, uitgrawe, uitspit; aan die lig bring; opspoor.
unearthly, bowenatuurlik, bowenaards; spookagtig, geheimsinnig; onmoontlike (uur).
uneasiness, besorgdheid, ongerustheid.
uneasy, ongemaklik; onrustig; ongerus, besorg, beangs; verontrustend; rusteloos; nie op jou gemak nie.
uneatable, oneetbaar.
unedifying, onstigtelik.
uneducated, onopgevoed, ongeletterd.
unembarrassed, onbelemmer, ongehinder; op jou gemak, nie verleë nie; los, vry.
unemotional, nie emosioneel nie.
unemphatic, sonder nadruk; swak, flou.
unemployed, werkloos; ongebruik.
unemployment, werkloosheid; – **benefit**; werkloosheidsuitkering.
unencumbered, onbelas; vry, los.
unending, eindeloos, oneindig.
unendorsed, nie-geëndosseer.
unenfranchised, nie stemgeregtig nie.
unengaged, vry, nie verloof nie; onbespreek, onbeset.
unenterprising, sonder ondernemingsgees.

unentertaining, vervelend, droog.
unenviable, onbenydenswaardig.
unequal, ongelyk, verskillend; – **to the task**, nie opgewasse vir die taak nie.
unequalled, ongeëwenaard, weergaloos.
unequivocal, duidelik, onomwonde.
unerring, onfeilbaar, raak, sekuur.
unespied, onbespied, ongesien.
unessential, a. onbelangrik, nie essensieel nie.
unessential, n. onbelangrike (onder)deel, bysaak.
unestablished, nie vasgestel nie.
unestimated, onbereken.
unevaporated, onverdamp.
uneven, ongelyk, hobbelagtig, stamperig, skurf, nie glad nie; onewe; ongestadig, onegalig; – **number**, onewe getal.
uneventful, stil; onbelangrik; **it was an – year**, daar het nie veel gedurende die jaar plaasgevind nie.
unexamined, nie ondersoek nie.
unexcelled, onoortroffe.
unexceptionable, onberispelik.
unexecuted, onuitgevoer.
unexhausted, onuitgeput.
unexpected, onverwag.
unexpectedly, onverwags.
unexpensive, nie duur nie, goedkoop.
unexpired, onverstreke, nie om nie.
unexplored, onbekend, nie nagevors nie.
unexposed, beskut, beskerm, nie blootgestel nie; onbelig.
unexpressed, onuitgesproke.
unextinguishable, onuitblusbaar.
unfadable, onverbleikbaar.
unfailing, onfeilbaar; onuitputlik; getrou, (ge-) wis, seker.
unfair, onbillik; oneerlik, partydig.
unfaithful, ontrou, vals.
unfaltering, onwankelbaar, vas, standvastig; sonder om te haper.
unfamiliar, onbekend, vreemd.
unfashionable, nie na die mode nie, ouderwets, ou-modies.
unfasten, losmaak.
unfathomable, onpeilbaar, ondeurgrondelik.
unfavourable, ongunstig.
unfed, ongevoed; ongevoer.
unfeeling, gevoelloos, wreed, ongevoelig.
unfeigned, ongeveins, opreg, eg, waar.
unfeminine, onvroulik.
unfermented, ongegis.
unfetter, van boeie bevry; ontketen.
unfilial, onkinderlik.
unfinished, onvoltooi(d), nie klaar nie.
unfit, onbekwaam, ongeskik; ongepas; **he is – for a doctor**, hy sal nie deug as dokter nie.
unfix, losmaak.
unfixed, los; onbepaald, onseker.
unflagging, onverslap, onvermoeid.
unfledged, sonder vere; onbedrewe, jonk.
unflinching, onverskrokke, onversaag.
unfold, oopmaak, oopvou, uitsprei, ontvou; openbaar maak, aan die lig bring; ontplooi, ontwikkel.
unfolding, ontplooiing, ontwikkeling; openbaarmaking.
unforeseen, onvoorsien.
unforgettable, onvergeetlik.
unforgivable, onvergeeflik.
unforgiving, onversoenlik.
unformed, vormloos; ongevorm.
unfortified, onversterk.
unfortunate, a. ongelukkig, rampspoedig.
unfortunate, n. ongelukkige.
unfounded, ongegrond; vals.

unfrequented, eensaam, stil, verlate.
unfriendly, onvriendelik.
unfruitful, onvrugbaar.
unfulfilled, onvervul(d).
unfurl, ontplooi, ontvou, uitsprei.
unfurnished, ongemeubileer(d).
ungainly, lomp, ongemanierd, onhandig.
ungallant, onhoflik, nie galant nie.
ungarnished, onversier(d), onopgesmuk.
ungenial, onvriendelik, ongesellig; ongunstig, sleg (van weer).
ungentle, onsag, hard, ru; ongemanierd.
ungentlemanly, onhoflik, onfatsoenlik.
ungird, losgord, losmaak.
unglazed, onverglaas; sonder ruite.
unglove, die handskoen uittrek.
ungodly, goddeloos, godvergete.
ungovernable, onregeerbaar, wild, woes.
ungraceful, onbevallig, onaantreklik, lelik, lomp.
ungracious, onvriendelik, onbeleef, koud.
ungrammatical, ongrammatikaal.
ungrateful, ondankbaar, onerkentlik.
ungrounded, ongegrond.
ungrudging, gewillig; gul.
ungual, klou- . . ., klouvormig; nael-.
unguarded, onbedagsaam; onbewaak.
unguent, salf, olie.
unhackneyed, nie-afgesaag.
unhallow, ontheilig.
unhampered, onbelemmer(d), vry.
unhandsome, onknap, lelik; onaardig.
unhandy, lomp, onhandig.
unhappiness, ongeluk; ellende, verdriet.
unhappy, ongelukkig.
unharmed, ongedeerd, onbeskadig.
unharness, uitspan, aftuie.
unhealthy, ongesond.
unheard, ongehoor(d); something – of, iets ongehoords, 'n ongehoorde ding.
unheeded, onopgemerk, veronagsaam.
unhesitating, sonder aarsel, beslis.
unhinge, uithaak, uit die skarniere lig; van stryk bring, deurmekaar maak; his mind became –d, hy het van sy verstand afgeraak.
unhitch, uit-, afhaak, losmaak.
unholy, onheilig, goddeloos; vreeslik.
unhonoured, ongeëer(d).
unhook, uithaak, losmaak.
unhorse, afgooi, uit die saa gooi.
unhurt, ongekwes, onbeseer(d).
unicellular, eensellig.
unicorn, eenhoring; eenhoringkewer.
unification, unifikasie, vereniging.
uniform, a. eenvormig, gelykvormig, dieselfde, uniform; eenparig; gestadig; – motion, eenparige (egalige) beweging.
uniform, n. uniform.
uniform, v. in 'n uniform steek.
uniformity, uniformiteit, eenvormigheid.
unify, verenig, tot een maak.
unilateral, eensydig; – parking, eensyparkering.
unimaginable, ondenkbaar.
unimaginative, sonder verbeeldingskrag
unimpaired, onbeskadig, onverswak.
unimpeachable, onberispelik; onaantasbaar.
unimpeded, onbelemmer(d), onvertraag.
unimportant, onbelangrik.
unimproved, onverbeter; onbewerk.
uninfluenced, nie beïnvloed nie, onpartydig, onbevooroordeeld.
uninformed, nie op hoogte van sake nie.
uninhabitable, onbewoonbaar.
uninhabited, onbewoon.
uninjured, onbeseer, onbeskadig.
uninsured, onverassureer.

unintelligent, dom, bot, onintelligent.
unintelligible, onverstaanbaar, onduidelik, onbegryplik.
unintentional onopsetlik, nie moedswillig nie.
uninteresting, oninteressant, droog.
uninterrupted, ongestoor(d), onafgebroke.
uninvited, ongenooi, ongevra(ag).
uninviting, nie aanloklik nie, afstotend.
union, vereniging, unie; samesmelting; huwelik, verbintenis; eensgesindheid; eenheid; verbond; in perfect –, volkome eensgesind; – is strength, eendrag maak mag.
unionist, unionis.
unique, a. ongeëwenaard, enig, uniek.
unison, harmonie, ooreenstemming; eenstemmigheid, eensgesindheid; in –, eensgesind, eenstemmig; in harmonie.
unit, eenheid.
unitarian, n. unitariër.
unitarian, a. unitaries.
unite, verenig, verbind, saamsmelt; saamspan, saamwerk; saamvoeg; een word.
united, verenig; The U- States, Die Verenigde State; U. Nations (Organisation), Verenigde Volke (-Organisasie).
unity, eenheid; eendrag, eensgesindheid, harmonie, ooreenstemming.
universal, universeel, algemeen; it met with – approval, dit het algemeen byval gevind.
universal joint, kruiskoppelaar.
universalize, algemeen maak.
universality, algemeenheid.
universe, heelal.
university, n. universiteit.
university, a. universitêr, universiteits . . .
unjust, onregverdig, onbillik.
unjustifiable, onverdedigbaar, onverskoonbaar, ongeregverdig.
unkempt, ongekam; slordig, vuil.
unkept, nie bewaar nie, verwaarloos.
unkind, onvriendelik.
unknightly, onridderlik.
unknowable, ondeurgrondelik, onkenbaar.
unknowing, onbewus, onwetend.
unknown, a. onbekend.
unknown, n. onbekende.
unlaboured, natuurlik, spontaan.
unlace, losryg, losmaak.
unladylike, nie soos dit 'n dame betaam nie, onvroulik.
unlamented, onbetreur, onbeween.
unlatch, die knip afhaal, oopmaak.
unlearn, afleer, vergeet, verleer.
unlearned, ongeleerd.
unlearnt, nie geleer nie.
unleavened, ongesuur, ongerys.
unless, tensy, behalwe, as . . . nie.
unlettered, ongeletter(d).
unlicked, ongelek; rou, baar, lomp.
unlike, anders, verskillend; ongelyk; he is – his parents, hy aard nie na sy ouers nie; he plays quite – anyone I have heard before, hy speel heeltemal anders as enigeen wat ek tevore gehoor het.
unlikelihood, onwaarskynlikheid.
unlikely, onwaarskynlik.
unlimited, onbeperk, onbegrens; geweldig baie.
unlink, los-, uitskakel, uithaak.
unload, aflaai, ontlaai, van 'n las bevry; die patroon uithaal, die skoot afhaal; ontslae raak van.
unlock, oop-, ontsluit; onthul.
unlooked-for, onverwag.
unlovely, onbeminlik, onskoon.

unlucky, ongelukkig; vrugteloos; ongelukbringend.
unmade, ongemaak, nog nie klaar nie.
unmake, tot niet maak, vernietig.
unmaimed, onvermink.
unman, ontmoedig; ontman, van bemanning berowe.
unmanageable, onregeerbaar, onhandelbaar, onbeteuelbaar, lastig; **an – child,** 'n ongeseglike (lastige) kind.
unmanlike, onmanlik.
unmanly, lafhartig, onmanlik.
unmannerly, ongemanierd, onbeskof.
unmarked, onopgemerk; ongemerk.
unmarketable, onverkoopbaar.
unmarried, ongetroud.
unmask, ontmasker, die masker afhaal.
unmatched, ongeëwenaard.
unmeaning, betekenisloos.
unmeant, onopsetlik.
unmeasured, ongemeet.
unmelodious, onwelluidend.
unmentionable, onnoembaar.
unmerciful, onbarmhartig, ongenadig, ongevoelig, wreed.
unmerited, onverdien.
unmethodical, onmetodies.
unmindful: – of, sonder om te dink (jou te steur) aan, sonder om rekening te hou met.
unmistakable, onmiskenbaar.
unmitigated, ongestil, onversag, onverminder; deurtrap; **an – blackguard,** 'n deurtrapte skurk.
unmixed, ongemeng, skoon, suiwer.
unmolested, ongemolesteer, ongehinder.
unmoor, die anker lig, losgooi.
unmortgaged, nie onder verband nie, vry, onverbind.
unmotherly, onmoederlik.
unmounted, onberede; ongemonteer.
unmourned, onbetreur onbeween.
unmoved, onbewoë, kalm, koel; onbeweeglik, onwrikbaar, standvastig.
unmurmuring, sonder om te murmureer.
unmusical, onmusikaal; onwelluidend.
unmutilated, onvermink.
unnamed, ongenoem; naamloos.
unnatural, onnatuurlik; gemaak.
unnavigable, onbevaarbaar.
unnecessary, onnodig, oorbodig.
unneighbourly, onbuurskaplik.
unnerve, ontsenu, verswak; uitput.
unnoticed, onopgemerk.
unnumbered, ongenommer; talloos.
unobliging, onvriendelik.
unobservant, onoplettend.
unobserved, onopgemerk.
unobstructed, vry, onbelemmer(d).
unobtainable, onverkrygbaar.
unobtrusive, nie opdringerig nie, beskeie.
onoccupied, vry, nie besig nie; leeg, oop.
unoffending, onskuldig; onskadelik.
unofficial, onoffisieel, nie-amptelik.
unopened, ongeopen, toe.
unopposed, onbestrede; ongehinder.
unorganized, ongeorganiseer(d).
unoriginal, onoorspronklik, ontleen.
unorthodox, onortodoks.
unostentatious, eenvoudig, beskeie, nie opdringerig (opvallend) nie.
unowned, sonder eienaar, baasloos.
unpack, uitpak; afpak, aflaai.
unpaid, onbetaal(d).
unpalatable, onsmaaklik; onaangenaam.
unpardonable, onvergeeflik.

unparliamentary, onparlementêr.
unpatented, ongepatenteer(d).
unpatriotic, onvaderlandsliewend.
unpaved, ongeplavei, ongestraat.
unpeeled, ongeskil.
unpeg, die penne uithaal.
unpensioned, ongepensioeneer(d).
unpeople, ontvolk.
unperceived, ongemerk, onopgemerk.
unperformed, ongedaan, onverrig.
unperturbed, onverstoor(d), (hout)gerus.
unphilosophical, onfilosofies.
unpick, lostrek, lostorring; oopsteek.
unpicked, ongepluk; nog nie gekies nie.
unpin, die spelde uittrek, losspelde.
unpitied, onbeklaag.
unpitying, onbarmhartig, wreed.
unplaced, ongeplaas; nie geplaas nie.
unpleasant, onaangenaam, onplesierig.
unpleasantness, onaangenaamheid.
unploughed, ongeploeg (ongeploeë).
unpointed, sonder punt; sonder leestekens.
unpolished, ongepolys; onbeskaaf, ru.
unpolluted, onbevlek, onbesmet.
unpopular, impopulêr, ongewild.
unpractical, onprakties, onuitvoerbaar.
unpractised, onbedrewe, onervare.
unprecedented, ongehoor(d); ongeëwenaard.
unprejudiced, onbevooroordeeld.
unpremeditated, onopsetlik, onvoorberei; spontaan.
unprepared, onvoorberei, onklaar.
unpresuming, beskeie, nederig.
unpretending, nie aanmatigend nie, beskeie.
unprincipled, beginselloos, geweteloos.
unprinted, ongedruk, onbedruk.
unprivileged, onbevoorreg.
unproductive, onvrugbaar, skraal, nie produktief nie, nie betalend nie.
unprofessional, strydig met die eise van 'n beroep, onprofessioneel.
unprofitable, onvoordelig.
unprogressive, konserwatief, ouderwets.
unprolific, onvrugbaar.
unpromising, weinig belowend.
unpronounceable, onuitspreekbaar.
unpropitious, ongunstig.
unprosperous, onvoorspoedig.
unprotected, onbeskerm, onbeskut.
unproved, onbewese, nie bewys nie.
unprovided, onvoorsien; onversorg.
unprovoked, sonder aanleiding (oorsaak), moedswillig, goedsmoeds.
unpublished, onuitgegee; nog onbekend.
unpunctual, nie op tyd nie, laat.
unpunished, ongestraf.
unqualified, onbevoeg, onbekwaam, ongeskik; ongekwalifiseer(d), ongesertifiseer(d); onbeperk, algeheel, volmondig.
unquelled, nie onderdruk nie, ongedemp.
unquenchable, onversadigbaar, onbevredigbaar, onlesbaar; onblusbaar.
unquestionable, onbetwisbaar, ontwyfelbaar.
unquestioned, onbetwis.
unquestioning, sonder om vrae te stel; onbeperk, onvoorwaardelik, blind.
unquiet, rusteloos, onrustig.
unravel, uitrafel, losmaak, ontwar.
unrazored, ongeskeer.
unread, ongelees; onbelese.
unreadable, onleesbaar.
unready, onbereid; traag; nie klaar nie.
unreal, onwerklik, denkbeeldig, hersenskimmig, onwesenlik.
unreason, dwaasheid, onverstandigheid.

unreasonable, onbillik, onredelik, onverstandig.
unreasoned, onberedeneer(d).
unreclaimed, onontgin; nie opgeëis nie.
unrecognizable, onherkenbaar.
unreconcilable, onversoenlik.
unreconciled, onversoen.
unrecorded, onvermeld.
unredeemed, onvervul (van belofte); nie gelos nie; verlore, nie vrygemaak nie.
unreel, afrol, afdraai, afwen.
unrefined, ongesuiwer(d); onbeskaaf.
unreflecting, gedagteloos, onnadenkend.
unrefuted, onweerlê, onbestrede.
unregarded, veronagsaam.
unregistered, ongeregistreer(d), nie ingeskryf nie (oningeskrewe).
unrelaxed, onverslap, onvermoeid.
unrelenting, onverbiddelik; sonder ophou.
unreliable, onvertroubaar.
unreligious, ongodsdienstig.
unremembered, vergeet.
unremitting, aanhoudend.
unremunerative, onvoordelig, nie lonend nie.
unrepair, bouvalligheid, verwaarlosing.
unrepealed, onherroep.
unrepentant, onboetvaardig
unrepining, sonder klagte, gedwee, geduldig, stil, gelate.
unreplenished, onaangevul.
unrepresented, onverteenwoordig.
unrequited, onbeloon, onbeantwoord.
unreserved, onvoorwaardelik; openhartig, on-gereserveer(d), onbespreek.
unresolved, besluiteloos.
unresponsive, onsimpatiek, stug, terughoudend, nie tegemoetkomend nie.
unrest, onrus; beroering; oproerigheid.
unrestful, onrustig.
unrestrained, onbeteuel(d), onbedwonge; onbeperk.
unrestricted, vry, onbeperk, onbelemmer(d).
unretarded onvertraag.
unrevenged, ongewreek.
unrevised, onhersien.
unrevoked, onherroep.
unrewarded, onbeloon.
unrhythmical, onritmies.
unriddle, ontsyfer, oplos, uitpluis.
unrighteous, onregverdig, goddeloos
unrip, lostrek, losskeur, lostorring.
unripe, onryp, groen.
unrivalled, ongeëwenaard, weergaloos.
unrobe, uittrek, ontklee(d).
unroll, ooprol, afrol.
unromantic, onromanties, prosaïes.
unroofed, dakloos, sonder dak.
unroot, uitruk, ontwortel.
unruffled, kalm, bedaard; glad.
unruly, bandeloos, teuelloos, onregeerbaar; koppig; wild, lastig.
unsaddle, afsaal.
unsafe, onveilig, gevaarlik.
unsaid, ongesê.
unsalable, onverkoopbaar.
unsalaried, onbesoldig.
unsalted, vars, ongesout.
unsanctioned, onbekragtig, nie goedgekeur nie, ongeoorloof.
unsanitary, ongesond.
unsatisfied, ontevrede, onvoldaan.
unsaved, ongered, nie verlos nie, verlore.
unsavoury, onsmaaklik, nie lekker nie; onaangenaam, walglik.
unscalable, onbeklimbaar.
unscared, onverskrokke.

unscarred, sonder littekens.
unscathed, ongedeer, onbeskadig, veilig.
unscientific, onwetenskaplik.
unscrew, losskroewe, losdraai.
unscriptural, onbybels.
unscrupulous, geweteloos, beginselloos.
unseal, die seël verbreek, oopmaak.
unsealed, ongeseël; oopgemaak.
unseasonable, ontydig; ongeleë.
unseasoned, klam, onuitgedroog (van hout); ongekrui, ongepeper.
unseat, ontsetel, uit die saal gooi, afgooi; van 'n sitplek berowe.
unseaworthy, onseewaardig.
unseconded, ongesekondeer(d).
unseeing, onoplettend, blind.
unseemly, onbetaamlik, onwelvoeglik.
unseen, a. onsigbaar, ongesien; – translation, vertaling op sig.
unseen, n. die onbekende, die ongesiene; vertaling op sig, onvoorbereide werk.
unselfish, onselfsugtig, onbaatsugtig.
unsent, ongestuur, nie aangestuur nie.
unseparated, ongeskeie.
unserviceable, ondienlik, onbruikbaar.
unset, nog nie onder nie (son); opgestel (strik, wip); pap, slap, nog nie styf nie; stomp, nie aangesit nie.
unsettle, in die war stuur, deurmekaar maak; van stryk af bring.
unsettled, deurmekaar, in die war; van stryk af; veranderlik, ongestadig; nog nie afgehandel nie; onbetaal, onvereffen; onseker, sonder vaste woonplek; onbewoon; the matter is still –, dis nog 'n onuitgemaakte saak; – weather, ongestadige weer.
unsex, vroulikheid (manlikheid) ontneem.
unshackle, die boeie losmaak, bevry.
unshaken, onwrikbaar, rotsvas.
unshapely, misvorm, vormloos, lelik.
unshaven, ongeskeer.
unsheathe, uit die skede trek.
unsheltered, onbeskut.
unship, aflaai, ontskeep, aan land sit.
unshod, onbeslaan; ongeskoei.
unshoe, die hoefysters aftrek; ontskoei.
unshorn, ongeskeer.
unshrinkable, krimpvry.
unshrinking, onverskrokke, onbevrees.
unsighted, sonder visier; nog nie in sig nie.
unsightly, lelik, mismaak, afsigtelik.
unsigned, ongeteken.
unskilful, onbekwaam, onbedrewe.
unskilled, onervare; ongeskool(d).
unslaked, ongeblus.
unsociable, ongesellig.
unsoiled, ongevlek; onbevlek, skoon.
unsold, onverkoop.
unsolicited, ongevra(ag).
unsolicitous, onbesorg, onbekommerd.
unsolvable, onoplosbaar.
unsolved, onopgelos.
unsophisticated, onskuldig, onbedorwe, eenvoudig; eg, suiwer, onvervals.
unsorted, ongesorteer, deurmekaar.
unsought, ongesoek (ongesog).
unsound, ongesond; onjuis, vals, misleidend; swak; sleg.
unsparing, rojaal, mild, oorvloedig; streng, meedoënloos; he was – in his efforts, hy het geen moeite gespaar nie; – efforts, onvermoeide poginge.
unspeakable, onuitspreeklik; onuitstaanbaar.
unspecified, ongespesifiseer(d).
unspent, onverbruik, nie uitgegee nie.

unspilt, nie gemors nie, ongestort.
unspoilt, onbedorwe.
unsportsmanlike, unsporting, onsportief.
unspotted, ongevlek; skoon, onbeklad.
unsprung, ongeveer.
unstable veranderlik, onvas.
unstained ongeverf; onbesmet.
unstamped, ongefrankeer, sonder seël; ongestempel.
unstarched, ongestyf, sonder stysel.
unstartled, nie verskrik nie, houtgerus.
unstatesmanlike, 'n staatsman onwaardig; ontaktvol.
unsteadfast, onstandvastig.
unsteady, onvas, los; veranderlik, onbestendig, wisselvallig, onseker; **the ladder is –**, die leer staan nie vas nie.
unstinted, ruim, mild, oorvloedig, rojaal.
unstitch, lostrek, die steke uittrek.
unstrained, natuurlik; ongefiltreer; slap.
unstressed, onbeklemtoon, onbetoon.
unstring die snare losmaak (laat skiet); ontspan, verslap.
unstrung, van stryk af, senuweeagtig.
unstudied, natuurlik, ongedwonge.
unstuffed, onopgestop.
unsubdued, onoorwonne; onbeteuel.
unsubmissive, ongehoorsaam, opstandig.
unsubstantial, onstoflik, denkbeeldig, hersenskimmig; onvoedsaam; swak.
unsubstantiated, ongegrond, onbewese.
unsuccessful, ongelukkig; misluk, nie-geslaag, vergeefs; **return –**, onverrigter sake terugkeer.
unsuitable, ongeskik.
unsuited, ongeskik.
unsullied, onbeklad, onbevlek, skoon.
unsupported, nie ondersteun nie, sonder ondersteuning, alleen.
unsurpassed, onoortroffe.
unsurveyed, onopgemeet.
unsusceptible, onvatbaar; onontvanklik.
unsuspected, onverdag; onvermoed.
unsuspecting, argeloos, onskuldig.
unsuspicious, nie agterdogtig nie, argeloos.
unswayed, onbeïnvloed, standvastig
unswept, ongevee (nie uitgevee nie).
unsworn, onbeëdig.
unsymmetrical, onsimmetries, ongelyk.
unsympathetic, onsimpatiek.
unsystematic, onsistematies.
untainted, vlekloos, onbesmet, rein.
untamable, ontembaar.
untamed, ongetem, wild, woes.
untanned, ongelooi.
untarnished, onbevlek, sonder smet.
untasted, ongeproe, onaangeraak.
untaught, ongeleer(d), onkundig.
untaxed, onbelas.
untenable, onhoudbaar.
untenanted, onverhuur, onbewoon.
untended, onversorg; sonder wagter.
unterrified, onverskrokke.
untested, onbeproef.
unthankful, ondankbaar.
unthatched, ongedek.
unthinkable, ondenkbaar.
unthinking, onbedagsaam, onnadenkend.
unthought-of, onverwag, ongedag.
unthread, die draad uit die naald trek.
untidy, slordig; deurmekaar.
untie, losmaak, losknoop.
until, sien **till**, totdat.
untilled, onbewerk, onbebou.
untimely, ontydig; ongeleë; vroegtydig.
untired, onvermoeid.

untiring, onvermoeid.
untitled, sonder titel, ongetitel(d).
unto, aan, tot, vir.
untold, onvertel; talloos, ongetel; ongeken, onberekenbaar.
untorn, ongeskeur, heel.
untouchable, n. paria, onreine.
untouchable, a. on(aan)raakbaar, onrein.
untouched, onaangeroer onaangeraak.
untoward, eiewys, verkeerd; ongelukkig, teenspoedig.
untracked, ongebaan.
untrained, ongeoefen; ongeleer(d), baar.
untrammelled, onbelemmer(d).
untransferable, nie oordraagbaar nie.
untranslatable, onvertaalbaar.
untried, onbeproef; onverhoor(d).
untrimmed, ongeknip; onopgemaak.
untrodden, ongebaan, onbetree.
untroubled, ongestoord; onbewoë.
untrue, onwaar, vals; ontrou.
untruth, onwaarheid, leuen.
untruthful, vals, onopreg, oneerlik.
untune, ontstem, verwar; vals maak.
unturned, nie omgekeer nie.
untutored, ongeleer(d), ongeletter(d).
untwine, losdraai, losmaak.
unused, ongebruik.
unusual, buitengewoon, ongewoon.
unutterable, onuitspreeklik.
unvaccinated, ongeënt.
unvalued, ongewaardeer; ongetakseer.
unvanquished, onoorwonne.
unvaried, onverander(d).
unvarnished, onvernis; suiwer, rein.
unveil, ontsluier, onthul.
unventilated, ongeventileer(d).
unversed, onbedrewe (in).
unviolated, ongeskonde.
unvoiced, onuitgespreek; stemloos.
unwarlike, nie oorlogsugtig nie.
unwarned, ongewaarsku.
unwarped, nie krom (skeef) nie; onbevooroordeeld, onpartydig.
unwarrantable, nie te regverdig nie.
unwarranted, ongewaarborg; ongewettig; verregaand, ongeregverdig.
unwary, onversigtig, onbedag.
unwashed, ongewas.
unwatched, onbespied, onbewaak.
unwatered, onbesproei, nie natgemaak (natgelei) nie; onverdun; dors.
unwavering, onwankelbaar; standvastig.
unweaned, ongespeen.
unwearied, onvermoeid.
unwearying, aanhoudend, volhardend.
unwedded, ongetroud.
unweeded, ongeskoffel, vol onkruid.
unwelcome, onwelkom.
unwell, siek(erig), onwel.
unwept, onbetreur, onbeween.
unwhitewashed, ongewit.
unwholesome, ongesond.
unwieldy, swaar, lastig, lomp.
unwilling, onwillig; ongeneig, ongeneë.
unwind, afdraai, afrol.
unwinking, wakker, waaksaam.
unwisdom, onverstandigheid, dwaasheid.
unwise, onverstandig, onwys, dom.
unwished, ongewens.
unwithered, onverwelk.
unwitting, onbewus, onwetend.
unwomanly, onvroulik.
unwonted, ongewoon, ongewend.
unworkable, onprakties; onbewerkbaar.

unworldly, onwêrelds.
unworn, ongedra, nuut.
unworthy, onwaardig.
unwound, losgedraai, afgerol, afgewen.
unwounded, ongewond, ongedeerd.
unwoven, ongeweef.
unwrap, oopmaak, oopvou.
unwrinkled, sonder rimpels, glad.
unwritten, ongeskryf (ongeskrewe); – **law**, ongeskrewe wet.
unwrought, ru, onbewerk.
unyielding, standvastig; onversetlik.
unyoke, uitspan, die juk afhaal; bevry.
up, adv. op, boontoe, na bo; **high** – **in the air**, hoog in die lug; **four floors** –, vier hoog, vier verdiepings hoër op; **he was had** – **for drunkenness**, hy moes weens dronkenskap voorkom; – **and down**, op en neer; **straight** – **to the door**, reguit na die deur toe; **stand** –, opstaan; – **with you!**, opstaan!; **corn is** –, die prys van koring het gestyg; **I must be** – **and doing**, ek moet aan die werk; **well** – **in mathematics**, goed tuis in matesis; **what is** –?, wat makeer?, wat is aan die gang?; **what tricks have you been** – **to?**, watter streke het jy aangevang?; **is not** – **to much**, beteken nie veel nie; **speak** –, harder praat; **he does not feel** – **to the work**, hy voel hom nie tot die werk in staat nie; **save** –, opspaar; **time is** –, die tyd is om (verstreke); **it is all** – **with him**, dit is klaar met hom; **be** – **against**, te staan kom voor, te doen hê met; **it is** – **to you to go**, dit is jou plig om te gaan; – **to date**, by, op die hoogte van die tyd; modern, nuwerwets.
up, prep. op; – **the hill**, (teen) die heuwel uit; – **hill and down dale**, berg op en berg af.
up, n. –**s and downs**, wisselvallighede, voor- en teenspoed; **on the** – **and** –, aan die opkom.
upbear, oplig, omhoog hou, ondersteun.
upbraid, berisp(e).
upbringing, opvoeding.
upcast, n. (die) opgooi; opwaartse worp.
up-country, na (in) die binneland (onderveld).
upgrowth, groei, ontwikkeling; opslag.
upheaval, opstoting; omwenteling.
uphill, opdraand; moeilik, swaar.
uphold, hooghou; handhaaf; verdedig.
upholster, beklee, oortrek; stoffeer.
upholsterer, bekleër, stoffeerder.
upholstery, bekleding; stoffeerdery; stoffeerkuns.
upkeep, onderhoud, instandhouding.
upland, hoogland.
uplift, v. ophef; oplig.
uplift, n. verheffing.
upon, op, bo-op; by; sien **on**; **we had no evidence to go** –, ons het geen getuienis gehad waarop ons kon gaan nie; **not enough to live** –, nie genoeg om van te lewe nie.
upper, a. bo- . . .; hoër, boonste; – **lip**, bolip; – **storey**, boonste verdieping; **there is something wrong in his** – **storey**, hy het nie al sy varkies in die hok nie; **gain the** – **hand**, die oorhand kry, baasraak; **the** – **ten**, die aristokrate, die élite.
upper, n. bo-leer; **be on one's** –**s**, in die knyp sit; brandarm wees.
uppercut, gesighou.
uppermost, a. hoogste, boonste.
uppermost, adv. bo-op, eerste.
uppish, vrypostig; uit die hoogte.
upraise, ophef, oprig.
upright, a. regop; opreg, eerlik.
upright, n. styl, (stut)paal.
uprising, (die) opstaan; rebellie, oproer.

uproar, lawaai, tumult, geskreeu.
uproarious, luidrugtig, lawaaierig.
uproot, ontwortel, uit die grond ruk.
upset, n. ontsteltenis, verwarring.
upset, v. omgooi; omval, omslaan; ontstel, van die wysie bring; in duie laat val, laat misluk, in die war gooi; **he ate something that** – **him**, hy het iets geëet wat hom laat sleg voel het.
upshot, resultaat, uiteinde, uitslag.
upside-down, onderstebo; deurmekaar.
upstairs, adv. op solder, bo; boontoe.
upstairs, a. boonste, bo- . . .
upstart, parvenu; parmant, snip.
up-stream, stroom op.
upstroke, ophaal.
uptake, (die) optel; begrip; **quick in the** –, vlug van begrip.
upthrow, opstoting; (die) opgooi.
upthrust, (die) oplig, opstoting.
upturn, omkeer; opslaan.
upward, a. opwaarts; **prices show an** – **tendency**, pryse is aan styg.
upward(s), adv. opwaarts, boontoe, na bo; **children of six years old and** –, kinders van ses jaar en ouer (daarbo); – **of 40 motor-cars**, meer as 40 motors.
Ural, Oeral: – **Mountains**, Oeralgebergte.
uranium, uraan.
urban, stedelik, stads- . . .; – **areas**, stedelike wyke.
urbane, hoflik, wellewend, fyn beskaaf.
urbanity, hoflikheid, wellewendheid.
urbanize, verstedelik.
urchin, kleuter; deugniet, rakker, (klein) vabond, kwajong.
ureter, urineleier.
urethra, urinebuis.
urge, aanspoor, aansit, aandring; aanja, aandryf; dwing; nadruk lê op, met nadruk wys op; – **on**, aanspoor, ophits.
urgency, dringendheid, noodsaaklikheid.
urgent, dringend, noodsaaklik, spoedeisend; urgent; **be in** – **need of**, dringend behoefte hê aan; **he was** – **with me for further particulars**, hy het sterk aangedring by my om verdere besonderhede.
uric, urine- . . .; – **acid**, urinesuur.
urinal, urinaal, urineglas; water(aflaat)plek.
urinary, urine- . . .; urinebak, -vat, -kom.
urinate, water, urineer.
urination, (die) water.
urine, water, urine.
urn, vaas, kruik, urn; lykbus; koffiekan, teekan.
urology, urologie, urineleer.
Ursa, die Beer; – **Major**, die Groot Beer; – **Minor**, die Klein Beer.
ursine, beeragtig, beer- . . .
us, ons.
usage, behandeling; gewoonte; gebruik; usansie.
usance, handelsgebruik, uso.
use, n. gebruik; nut; gewoonte; bekendheid, voordeel; **put it to a good** –, goeie gebruik daarvan maak; **be in daily** –, elke dag in gebruik wees; **it is no** – **talking**, dit help (baat) nie om te praat nie; **I have no** – **for it**, ek kan dit nie gebruik nie; **out of** –, in onbruik; **be of** –, nuttig (van nut) wees.
use, v. gebruik, gebruik maak van; behandel; uitoefen, aanwend; verbruik, verteer; – **every means**, elke (moontlike) middel aanwend; **he has** –**d me like a dog**, hy het my soos 'n hond behandel; –**up**, opgebruik, verbruik; uitput.
used, gewoond (gewend); **he** – **to say**, hy het dikwels gesê; **he does not come as often as he** –

(to), hy kom nie so dikwels soos sy gewoonte was nie (soos vroeër nie); **the bell – always to ring at one**, die klok het gewoonlik om eenuur gelui; – **up**, op; uitgeput, klaar, kapot, pootuit.
useful, nuttig; **he is making himself generally –**, hy help oral waar hy kan.
useless, nutteloos; vergeefs; nikswerd.
user, gebruiker; **right of –**, gebruiksreg.
usher, n. seremoniemeester; deurwagter, deurwaarder; plekaanwys(t)er; sien **rod**.
usher, v. binnelei, aankondig, aandien.
usual, gewoon, gebruiklik; **it is – to**, dit is die gewoonte om; **as –**, soos gewoonlik.
usually, gewoonlik, in die reël.
usufruct, vruggebruik.
usufructuary, n. vruggebruiker.
usufructuary, a. vruggebruikers-. . .
usurer, woekeraar.
usurious, woeker-. . ., woekerend.
usurp, wederregtelik (onwettig) in besit neem, (sig) toe-eien, usurpeer.
usurpation, wederregtelike inbesitneming, toe-eiening, usurpasie.
usurper, oorweldiger; indringer.
usuary, woeker, woekerwins.
ut, ut (mus.).
utensil, gereedskap, werktuig; **kitchen –s**, kombuisgereedskap, -goed.
uterine, baarmoeder-. . .
uterus, baarmoeder, uterus.

utilization, gebruikmaking, aanwending.
utilize, gebruik, gebruik maak van, aanwend, bestee.
utilitarian, a. nuttigheids-. . ., utiliteits-. . utilitaristies.
utilitarian, n. utilitaris.
utilitarianism, utilitarisme, nuttigheidsleer.
utility, nut, bruikbaarheid, nuttigheid, utiliteit; nuttige iets; – **man**, – **clothes**, dra(ag)klere. plektoestaner, handlanger, hansie-my-kneg;
utmost, a. uiterste, verste; meeste, grootste.
utmost, n. uiterste (bes).
Utopia, Utopia.
utopian, n. utopis.
utopian, a. utopies.
utricle, sel; holte(tjie), sakkie, blasie.
utter, a. totaal, volkome, algeheel, absoluut; – **misery**, die diepste ellende.
utter, v. uit(er), uitdruk, sê, uitspreek; (vals geld, ens.) in omloop bring; **forging and –ing**, die vervals en uitgee.
utterable, wat uitgedruk kan word.
utterance, uitlating, uitdrukking, uiting; (uit)spraak; voordrag; **give – to**, uiting (uitdrukking) gee aan; **pulpit –s**, kanselredes, kanseluitsprake.
utterly, heeltemal, totaal, volkome.
uttermost, uiterste, verste.
uvula, kleintongetjie, huig.
uvular, van die kleintongetjie, huig-. . .
uxorious, (slaafs) versot op jou vrou, vrousiek.

V

vacancy, vakature, vakante betrekking, oop plek; leë ruimte; ledigheid, lusteloosheid; – for, plek vir.
vacant, vakant, leeg, oop, onbeset; ledig, vry; lusteloos; ydel; dom, leeghoofdig; **the house is still** –, die huis staan nog leeg; **a** – **post**, 'n vakante pos; **his mind seems completely** –, dit lyk of hy totaal niks in sy kop het nie; **a** – **stare**, 'n wesenlose blik.
vacate, uittrek, ontruim; afstand doen van, opgee; nietig verklaar.
vacation, (die) uittrek, ontruiming; afstand; nietigverklaring; vakansie.
vaccinate, (in)ent, vaksineer.
vaccination, (in)enting, vaksinasie.
vaccinator, inenter.
vaccine, vaksien, entstof.
vacillate, slinger, swaai; aarsel, weifel.
vacillation, aarseling, weifeling; swaai.
vacuity, leegheid, leë ruimte; domheid.
vacuous, leeg; dom, onnosel, uitdrukkingloos, wesenloos.
vacuum, vakuum, lugleë ruimte.
vacuum brake, lugrem.
vacuum cleaner, stofsuier.
vacuum gauge, verklikker, drukmeter.
vacuum flask, vakuumglas.
vacuum-tube, lugleë buis.
vade-mecum, vademecum, handleiding.
vagabond, n. rondloper; swerwer.
vagabond, a. (rond)swerwend.
vagabond, v. rondloop, rondtrek.
vagabondage, landlopery.
vagary, gril, gier, luim, nuk, kwint.
vagina, vagina; bladskede.
vagrancy, rondlopery, rondtrekkery.
vagrant, a. rondtrekkend, rondlopend, rondswerwend; los, onsamehangend.
vagrant, n. rondloper, (rond)swerwer.
vague, vaag, onduidelik; onseker, onbepaald; **not the –st notion**, nie die flouste idee nie.
vain, nutteloos, vergeefs; verwaand, ydel; beuselagtig, nietig; **in** –, tevergeefs, vrugteloos; **take a name in** –, 'n naam ydellik gebruik.
vainglorious, verwaand, grootpraterig.
vainglory, verwaandheid, grootpratery.
valance, valence, damas (soort stof); (bed)val(letjie).
vale, vallei, dal; – **of tears**, tranedal.
valediction, vaarwel, afskeidswoorde, afskeid.
valedictory, afskeids- . . ., vaarwel- . . .; n. afskeidstoespraak.
valence, valensie.
valency, sien **valence**.
valerian, balderja(n), (valeriaan).
valet, (lyf)bediende.
valetudinarian, swak, sieklik, sukkelend.
Valhalla, Walhalla, hemel, paradys.
valiant, dapper, moedig, onverskrokke.
valid, gegrond, sterk; geldig, van krag.
validate, geldig verklaar, bekragtig.
validation, bekragtiging.
validity, geldigheid, krag.
valise, handsakkie, valies.
valkyr, **valkyrie**, walkure.
valley, vallei, dal, laagte.
valour, moed, dapperheid, onverskrokkenheid.
valorous, moedig, dapper, heldhaftig.
valuable, kosbaar, waardevol.
valuables, kosbaarhede.
valuation, valuasie; skatting, waardering; **set too high a** – **on**, oorskat.
value, n. waarde, prys; betekenis; **set a high** – **on**, hoog waardeer, veel waarde heg aan; – **in exchange**, koopwaarde, ruilwaarde; – re-

ceived, waarde ontvang; – **for your money**, waarde vir jou geld; **the precise** – **of a word**, die juiste betekenis van 'n woord; **out of** –, te lig (donker).
value, v. waardeer, op prys stel; waarde heg aan; valueer, skat; – **at**, skat (takseer) op.
valueless, waardeloos, nikswerd.
valuer, taksateur, skatter.
valve, klep; skulp, skaal; **sliding** –, skuifklep; –**s of the heart**, hartkleppe; – **adjustment**, klepstelling; – **clearance**, klepspeling; – **cock**, klepkraan; – **stem**, klepsteel; – **tappet**, klepstoter.
valved, met 'n klep (kleppe).
valveless, sonder klep(pe).
valvular, klep- . . .
valvule, kleppie.
vamose, (laat) trap (spat).
vamp, n. oorleer, boleer; lap; geïmproviseerde begeleiding.
vamp, v. nuwe oorleer aansit; lap, heel maak ('n begeleiding) improviseer.
vamp, n. flerrie, koket.
vamp, v. verlok, in haar strik vang.
vamper, lapper, heelmaker, improvisator.
vampire, vampier, bloedsuier; uitsuier.
vampire-bat, vampier.
vampirism, vampirisme; afpersing.
van, n. voorhoede; leiers, voormanne; **in the** – **of civilisation**, op die voorpunt van die beskawing.
van, n. (vervoer)wa; bagasiewa (van 'n trein); goederewa, kondukteurswa.
Vandal, Vandaal.
vandalism, vandalisme, vernielsug.
Vandyke, Van Dyck-skildery; – **beard**, puntbaard.
vane, weerhaan, windwys(t)er; wiek.
vanguard, voorhoede; voorpunt.
vanilla, vanielje.
vanish, verdwyn, wegraak; ophou (om te bestaan), wegsterwe; –**ing point**, verdwynpunt.
vanishing: – **cream**, smeltpommade; – **target**, duikskyf.
vanity, leegheid, holheid, onwerklikheid, nietigheid, verganklikheid; skyn; ydelheid; **all is** –, alles is ydelheid; **Vanity Fair**, Ydelheidskermis.
vanity-bag, poeierkwassakkie, jesebelsakkie.
vanquish, verslaan, oorwen (oorwin).
vantage, voordeel (tennis).
vantage-ground, geskikte (geleë) plek.
vapid, flou, laf, smaakloos.
vapidity, flouheid, lafheid.
vaporific, verdampend.
vaporization, verdamping.
vaporize, (laat) verdamp.
vaporizer, verdamper, verdampingstoestel, vaporisator.
vaporous, dampagtig, damperig.
vapour, n. damp, wasem; stoom.
vapour, v. wasem (ver)damp.
vapour bath, stoombad.
vapourer, windmaker, grootprater.
vapourish, damperig; windmakerig.
vapoury, damperig, dampend, wasemend.
variability, veranderlikheid, wispelturigheid.
variable, a. veranderlik, onbestendig, wispelturig, onvas, ongestadig; wisselbaar, wysigbaar, veranderbaar; – **wind**, veranderlike wind; – **gear**, wisselrat.
variable, n. veranderlike grootheid.
variance, verskil (van mening); stryd, teenstrydigheid; geskil, twis, onenigheid; **beat** –, dit nie eens wees nie; in stryd wees (met).
variant, a. verskillend; veranderlik.

variant, n. wisselvorm, variant.
variation, verandering, afwyking, wysiging, variasie.
varicella, waterpokkies, variselle.
varicoloured, veelkleurig.
varicose, spataar- . . .; – **veins**, knopare, spatare.
varied, verskillend; verander; afwisselend; menigvuldig, veelvuldig.
variegate, bont maak (kleur), afwissel.
variegated, bont(gekleur), gevlek, afgewissel.
variegation, (kleur)afwisseling, bontheid, veelkleurigheid.
variety, verskeidenheid; afwisseling; veelsydigheid; variëteit; soort; – **show**, variété-voorstelling; – **concert**, verskeidenheidskonsert.
variola, kinderpokkies.
various, verskillend; verskeie.
varix, aarswelling, aarspat; spataar.
varlet, page; skelm, vabond.
varmint, duiwelskind, blikskottel.
varnish, n. vernis; glans, blinkheid.
varnish, v. vernis; verbloem.
varsity, universiteit.
vary, verander, wysig, afwissel; afwyk; varieer; verskil; **opinions –**, daar is verskil van mening.
vascular, vaat- . . .; – **tissue**, vaatweefsel.
vase, vaas; blompot.
vassal, leenman, vasal; dienaar, kneg.
vassalage, leenmanskap; onderhorigheid, diensbaarheid, knegskap, slawerny.
vast, ontsaglik, geweldig; reusagtig; eindeloos, wyd uitgestrek.
vat, vat, kuip.
Vatican, Vatikaan.
vaticination, voorspelling.
vaticinator, profeet, voorspeller.
vaudeville, vaudeville.
Vaudois, Waldenser; Waadtlander.
vault, n. gewelf, verwulf; (graf)kelder; **the – of heaven**, die hemelgewelf; **wine –**, wynkelder.
vault, v. oorwelf, verwulf, van 'n gewelf (verwuf) voorsien.
vault, v. spring.
vault, n. spring, sprong.
vaulting-horse, bok.
vaunt, v. spog, grootpraat, roem op.
vaunt, n. grootpraat, gespog, spoggery.
vaunter, grootprater, spogter.
veal, kalfsvleis (-vlees).
Veda, Veda.
Vedic, Vedies.
veer, draai, van koers verander; van opinie verander, omspring; laat skiet; – **round**, draai; van mening (gedrag) verander.
vegetable, a. plante- . . ., plantaardig; groente- . . .; – **kingdom**, planteryk; – **marrow**, murg van groente.
vegetable, plant; groentesoort; –**s**, groente.
vegetal, n. plant, groente.
vegetarian, n. vegetariër, groente-eter.
vegetarian, a. vegetaries; – **food**, vegetariërskos, plantaardige voedsel.
vegetarianism, vegetarisme.
vegetation, plantegroei, planteryk, plantewêreld; gewas, uitwas.
vegetative, groei- . . ., plante- . . .; vegeterend.
vehemence, geweld, krag; drif, onstuimigheid, vuur, hartstog.
vehement, geweldig, kragtig; vurig, onstuimig, driftig.
vehicle, rytuig, vervoermiddel; middel, voertuig.
vehicular, rytuig- . . ., vervoer- . . .; voertuig . . .; – **traffic**, rytuigverkeer.
veil, sluier; gordyn, voorhang(sel); skyn, masker; **raise the –**, die sluier oplig; **draw a – over**,

die sluier laat val oor; **take the –**, die sluier aanneem, non word; **under the – of**, onder die dekmantel van; **the – of the temple**, die voorhangsel van die tempel; **beyond the –**, aan gindse sy van die graf, hiernamaals.
veil, v. met 'n sluier bedek; hul; verberg, verbloem, bedek, bewimpel.
vein, n. aar; stemming, luim; gees; trant; aard, neiging.
vein, v. aar.
veined, geaar, vol are.
veinlet, aartjie.
veiny, vol are.
velar, sagte gehemelte- . . ., velaar.
veld(t), veld.
vellum, kalfsleerperkament; velyn.
velocimeter, snelheidsmeter.
velocipede, velocipede, rywiel.
velocity, snelheid.
velour(s), ferweel, veloer (velours).
velum, sagte verhemelte (gehemelte).
velure, ferweel; ferweelkussinkie.
velvet, n. ferweel (fluweel); **be on –**, dit koninklik hê.
velvet, a. ferweel- . . . (fluweel-), ferweelagtig; – **tread**, sagte tred.
velveteen, katoenferweel.
velveting, ferweelstof; pluis.
velvety, ferweelagtig (fluweelagtig).
venal, omkoopbaar, te koop.
venality, omkoopbaarheid.
venation, aarskikking, aarstelsel.
vend, verkoop, (uit)vent.
vendee, koper.
vender, -or, verkoper; venter.
vendetta, bloedwraak, vendetta.
vendibility, verkoopbaarheid.
vendible, verkoopbaar.
veneer, v. inlê (van hout), fineer; vernis; verbloem, bedek.
veneer, n. fineer(hout); vernis(lagie); **liquid –**, strykvernis.
venerability, eer(bied)waardigheid.
venerable, eer(bied)waardig, agbaar.
venerate, vereer, eerbiedig, eer betoon.
veneration, verering, eerbied, ontsag.
venerator, vereerder.
venereal, geslags- . . .; veneries; – **disease**, veneriese siekte.
venesect, bloedlaat.
Venetian, a. Venesiaans; – **blind**, skuifblinding, skuifhortjies; – **lace**, Venesiaanse kant.
Venetian, n. Venesiaan; skuifblinding.
vengeance, wraak; **with a –**, dat dit gons, dat dit help.
venial, vergeeflik, verskoonbaar.
veniality, vergeeflikheid.
Venice, Venesië.
venison, wild(s)vleis (-vlees).
venom, (ver)gif; venyn.
venomous, giftig; venynig.
venous, -ose, aar- . . ., vol are.
vent, n. gat, luggat, skietgat, opening; anus; uiting; **he gave – to his indignation**, hy het uiting gegee aan sy verontwaardiging.
vent, v. 'n gat (opening) maak; lug, uiting gee aan.
venter, buik, maag; bult.
vent-hole, luggat.
ventiduct, lugpyp.
ventil, (lug)klep, ventiel.
ventilate, ventileer, lug, vars lug inlaat; bespreek, ter sprake bring; – **a grievance**, 'n grief lug.
ventilation, ventilasie, lugtoevoer; bespreking, diskussie; lugting.

**ventilator, **ventilator, luggat, lugrooster.
**ventral, **buik-...., van die buik; – fin, buikvin.
**ventricle, **holte; – of the heart, hartkamer.
**ventricose, -ous, **dikbuikig.
**ventriloquize, **buikspreek.
**ventriloquism, **buiksprekery.
**ventriloquist, **buikspreker.
**venture, **n. waagstuk; risiko; onderneming, spekulasie; **he declined the –, **hy wou dit nie riskeer (waag) nie; **at a –, **op goed geluk af, lukraak.
**venture, **v. wae (waag), riskeer, op die spel sit; durf, die vryheid neem; **I – to differ from you, **ek verstout my (ek wil so vry wees) om van u te verskil; **– an opinion, **waag om jou mening uit te spreek; **he would not – (up)on it, **hy wou dit nie waag nie; hy wou die stoute skoene nie aantrek nie.
**venturesome, **waaghalserig; gewaag.
**venue, **plek (van 'n misdaad); plek waar 'n saak moet voorkom.
**Venus, **Venus.
**veracious, **waarheidliewend; waar.
**veranda(h), **veranda.
**verb, **werkwoord, verbum.
**verbal, **woordelik; mondeling; letterlik; werkwoordelik, verbaal; **– evidence, **mondelinge getuienis; **– noun, **werkwoordelike selfstandige naamwoord.
**verbalize, **verbaliseer.
**verbalism, **woord(e) vittery, verbalisme.
**verbalist, **woord(e)vitter.
**verbatim, **woord vir woord, woordelik.
**verbiage, **omhaal van woorde, woordevloed, woorderykheid.
**verbose, **woorderyk, breedsprakig.
**verbosity, **woorderykheid, omhaal van woorde, breedsprakigheid.
**verdancy, **groenheid, (die) groen.
**verdant, **(gras)groen; grasbedek; baar, groen.
**verdict, **uitspraak; oordeel, beslissing.
**verdigris, **kopergroen.
**verdure, **groenigheid, groenheid, (die) groen, groen gras.
**verdurous, **groen.
**verge, **n. kant, rand; grens; roede, staf; **on the – of seventy, **kort by die sewentig; **he was on the – of betraying his secret, **hy was op die punt om die geheim te verklap; **on the – of death, **op die rand van die dood.
**verge, **v. grens (aan); naby kom; **it –s upon blasphemy, **dit grens aan godslastering.
**verger, **koster; stafdraer.
**verification, **bewys, bevestiging; ondersoek, toets, verifikasie, verifieer, kontroleer, nagaan; vervul, nakom, gestand doen.
**verily, **voorwaar, waarlik.
**verisimilar, **waarskynlik.
**verisimilitude, **waarskynlikheid; skynwaarheid.
**veritable, **waar, eg, werklik.
**verity, **waarheid; werklikheid.
**verjuice, **groenvrugtesap, suurdruiwesap.
**vermeil, **vergulde silwer; goudvernis.
**vermian, **wurm-..., wurmagtig.
**vermicelli, **vermicelli.
**vermicide, **wurmgif.
**vermicular, **wurmagtig, wurmvormig.
**vermiculation, **wurmvormige beweging; beskadiging (vernieling) deur wurms.
**vermiculose, -ous, **vol wurms, wurmstekig; wurmvormig.
**vermiform, **wurmvormig.
**vermifuge, **middel teen wurms.
**vermilion, **vermiljoen.

**vermin, **ongedierte, goggas; gespuis, skorriemorrie.
**verminate, **wemel van ongedierte (goggas); ongedierte laat vermeerder, goggas kweek.
**verminous, **ongedierte-...., van ongedierte, vol goggas.
**verm(o)uth, **vermoet.
**vernacular, **n. landstaal, volkstaal.
**vernacular, **a. van die landstaal, inheems, lands-..., volks-...
**vernacularism, **uitdrukking van die volkstaal.
**vernal, **lente-..., voorjaar-...; **– flowers, **voorjaarsblomme; **– grass, **soetgras; **– equinox, **lente-dag-en-nag-ewening.
**vernier, **vernier, nonius.
**Veronese, **a. van Verona.
**veronica, **veronika, erepprys.
**Veronese, **n. inwoner van Verona.
**verricule, **haarbossie, kuifie.
**verruca, **vrat(jie).
**verruciform, **vratvormig.
**versant, **skuinste, helling, hang.
**versatile, **veelsydig; draaibaar, beweegbaar, beweeglik.
**versatility, **veelsydigheid.
**verse, **versreël; vers, strofe; poësie, gedigte; **blank –, **rymlose verse.
**versed, **bedrewe, ervare; gekonfyt.
**verse-monger, **rymelaar, rymer.
**verset, **voorspel, tussenspel.
**versicle, **versie.
**versicoloured, **bont, veelkleurig.
**versification, **versifikasie, beryming; versbou, verskuns.
**versifier, **versemaker, rymelaar.
**versify, **verse maak, berym, op rym sit.
**version, **vertaling; verklaring, uitleg; voorstelling; lesing.
**verso, **keersy; linkerbladsy.
**verst, **werst (Russiese lengtemaat).
**versus, **teen, versus.
**vertebra, **werwel(been), vertebra.
**vertebral, **werwel-...., vertebraal.
**vertebrate, **a. gewerwel, werwel-...
**vertebrate, **n. gewerwelde dier, werweldier.
**vertebration, **werwelverdeling.
**vertex, **top, toppunt; kruin.
**vertical, **a. vertikaal, haaks, loodreg, van die hoogtepunt; **– angle, **tophoek; **– take-off plane, **vertikaalstyg-vliegtuig; regopstyg-vliegtuig.
**vertical, **n. loodlyn; vertikale vlak; loodregte stand.
**vertically, **vertikaal, loodreg, regaf, regop.
**vertiginous, **duiselig, draaierig.
**vertigo, **duiselig, duiseligheid, vertigo.
**verve, **geesdrif, entoesiasme, vuur, gloed.
**very, **a. eg, waar, opreg; **the veriest simpleton knows it, **selfs die grootste domkop weet dit; **from – shame, **uit pure skaamte; **this is the – spot, **dit is presies die plek, dit is die einste (nimlike) plek; **the – man I am looking for, **net die man wat ek soek; **come here this – minute, **kom hier op die daad (op die plek); **his – servants laugh at him, **selfs sy bediendes lag vir hom.
**very, **adv. baie, erg, uiters, in hoë mate.
**vesica, **blaas; sak.
**vesical, **blaas-...; sak-...
**vesicant, **trekpleister, trekmiddel.
**vesicate, **blare trek.
**vesication, **blaartrekking.
**vesicatory, **a. blaartrekkend.
**vesicatory, **n. trekmiddel, trekpleister.
**vesicle, **blasie, sakkie; selletjie.
**vesicular, vesiculous, **blaasagtig.

vesper, aand; versper; aandster.
vesper-bell, vesperklok.
vespiary, wespenes.
vespine, wesp(e)- ...
vessel, vat; kan, kruik, fles, kom; vaartuig; bloedvat; **a chosen** –, 'n uitverkore vat; **the weaker** –, die swakker(e) vat.
vest, n. onderhemp(ie), frok(kie); onderbaadjie.
vest, v. beklee (met); oordra; oorgaan (op); berus (by); – **a person with powers**, iemand met mag beklee (mag verleen); **–ed rights**, gevestigde regte; **the power is –ed in you**, die mag berus by jou.
vestal, Vestaals; – **virgin**, Vestaalse maagd.
vestibule, (voor)portaal, vestibule.
vestige, spoor, teken, bewys, oorblyfsel; **without a** – **of clothing**, sonder 'n draad klere; **not a** – **of evidence**, geen greintjie bewys nie.
vesting, onderhempgoed; onderbaadjiegoed.
vestiture, hare; skubbe, kors, laag.
vestment, kleed, gewaad; altaardoek.
vest-pocket, – **camera**, miniatuur-kamera.
vestry, konsistorie(kamer); sakristie; kerkraad.
vestry-clerk, kassier (van die kerkraad).
vestryman, kerkraadslid.
vesture, kleding; bedekking.
Vesuvian, Vesuviaans; vulkanies.
vetch, wikke.
veteran, a. oud, ervare, beproef.
veteran, n. veteraan.
veterinary, n. veearts.
veterinary, a. veeartsenykundig; – **college**, veeartsenyskool; – **science**, veeartsenykunde; – **surgeon**, veearts.
veto, n. veto(reg); verbod; **put a – on**, die veto uitspreek oor.
veto, v. die veto uitspreek oor; verbied.
vex, vererg, tretter, pla, kwel, irriteer; **a –ed question**, 'n lastige vraagstuk.
vexation, kwelling, ergernis; plaery.
vexatious, ergerlik, kwellend, lastig.
via, oor, langs, via.
viability, lewensvatbaarheid.
viable, lewensvatbaar.
viaduct, viaduk.
vial, fiool, flessie; **pour out –s of wrath**, fiole van toorn uitgiet, wraak neem.
viameter, mylmeter, afstandmeter.
viand(s), kos, lewensmiddels.
viaticum, reiskoste, reisgeld, reisvoorraad, padkos; viaticum.
vibrant, trillend; vibrerend.
vibrate, tril, vibreer; (heen-en-weer) swaai, slinger; sidder, beef.
vibration, trilling, vibrering (vibrasie); swaai, slingering.
vibrator, triller; vibrator.
vibratory, tril- ..., trillend.
vibrissa, neushaar; bekveer; trilhaar.
vibroscope, trillingmeter.
vicar, vikaris; predikant.
vicarage, vikariaat; vikariswoning.
vicarial, vikaris- ...
vicarious, plaasvervangend.
vice, n. ondeug; gebrek, fout; onsedelikheid.
vice, n. skroef; **bench** –, bankskroef.
vice, v. in 'n skroef vasdraai, vasknel.
vice, prep. in die plek van, vise.
vice-admiral, vise-admiraal.
vice-chairman, vise-voorsitter, ondervoorsitter.
vice-chancellor, vise-kanselier.
vicegerent, a. plaasvervangend.
vicegerent, n. plaasvervanger.
vice-president, vise-voorsitter, ondervoorsitter; vise-president.

vice-principal, vise-prinsipaal, onderhoof.
viceregal, onderkonings- ...
viceroy, onderkoning.
viceroyal, onderkoninklik.
vicinity, nabyheid, buurte, omtrek, omgewing; **in the** – **of R50**, so naasteby R50, naby die R50; **its** – **to town is convenient**, dit is gerieflik dat dit so naby die stad is.
vicious, sleg, bedorwe, boos(aardig); gebrekkig, verkeerd; skerp, venynig; vol streke; befoeterd, kwaai, wys; visieus; – **tendencies**, verkeerde neiginge; – **criticism**, venynige kritiek; – **circle**, noodlottige kringloop.
vicissitude, wisselvalligheid; lotswisseling.
victim, slagoffer, prooi; dupe.
victimization, verongelyking, tekortdoening, (die) slagoffer maak van; opligting, afsettery.
victimize, tot slagoffer maak; verongelyk, onreg aandoen, te kort doen.
victor, oorwinnaar.
victoria, victoria (rytuig); waterlelie.
Victoria, Victoria; – **Falls**, Victoria-waterval.
Victorian, Victoriaan(s).
victorine, pelskraag.
victorious, oorwinnend, seëvierend; oorwinnings- ...; **be** –, die oorwinning behaal, seëvier.
victory, oorwinning, sege (seë), seëpraal; **gain the** – **over**, die oorwinning behaal oor, seëvier oor.
victual, **victuals**, n. kos, voedsel, proviand, lewensmiddele, leeftog.
victual, v. van kos voorsien, proviandeer.
victualler, proviandmeester; proviandskip.
victualling, voedselvoorsiening, proviandering.
vie, wedywer, ding.
Vienna, Wenen.
Viennese, n. Wener, Weense (vrou).
Viennese, a. Weens.
view, n. uitsig; kyk, mening, opinie; plan, oogmerk, doel; oorsig; besigtiging; **he was in full** – **of the people**, die mense kon hom goed sien; **as soon as he came in** –, sodra hy te sien (in sig) was; **pass from** –, uit die gesig verdwyn; **he takes a different** –, hy is 'n ander mening toegedaan; **in** – **of**, met die oog op; **on** –, te sien; **with a** – **to**, met die doel om, met die oog op; **to the** –, voor die oë, in die openbaar, in die publiek; **have in** –, ten doel hê, beoog; **in gedagte hou**.
view, v. bekyk, kyk na, beskou, besien; besigtig.
viewer, kyker, toeskouer; (prente)kyker.
viewless, onsigbaar, sonder uitsig.
viewpoint, oogpunt, standpunt.
vigil, (die) waak, wag; **–s**, nagwaak; **keep** –, waak, wag hou.
vigilance, waaksaamheid; versigtigheid; slaaploosheid; – **committee**, waaksaamheidskomitee.
vigilant, waaksaam.
vigilante, hulpkonstabel; nagwag.
vignette, vinjet; krulversieringe.
vigorous, kragtig, sterk, fors; lewenskragtig; gespierd.
vigour, krag, forsheid, sterkte, energie; vitaliteit, lewenskrag; gespierdheid.
Viking, Wiking.
vile, laag, gemeen, vuil, skandelik; ellendig; waardeloos; sleg, vrot.
vilifier, lasteraar, kwaadprater.
vilify, belaster, beswadder, beskinder, kwaadpraat van, swartsmeer.
villa, villa.
village, dorp.
villager, dorpenaar, dorpsbewoner.

villain, skurk; skobbejak; **play the –**, (die rol van) die skurk speel; **you little –**, jou klein skelm, jou deugniet!
villainous, skurkagtig, gemeen, laag.
villainy, skurkagtigheid, gemeenheid.
villus, haartjie.
vim, pit, fut, krag, energie.
vinaceous, wyn- . . ., wynrooi.
vinaigrette, reukflessie, laventelflessie.
vincible, oorwinlik.
vinculum, verbindingstreep.
vindicate, verdedig, handhaaf; regverdig.
vindication, regverdiging, verdediging.
vindicative, wraakgierig, wraaksugtig.
vindicator, verdediger, handhawer, voorspraak.
vindicatory, verdedigend, handhawend; straffend, straf- . . .
vine, wingerdstok, wynstok; klimop, rankplant; rank, loot.
vinegar, n. asyn.
vinegar, a. asynsuur, asyn- . . .
vinegarish, vinegary, suur, asynagtig.
vine-grower, wynboer, wynbouer.
vinery, broeikas vir wingerdstokke.
vineyard, wingerd.
viniculture, wynbou.
viniculturist, wynbouer.
vinometer, wynmeter.
vinous, wyn- . . ., wynagtig; **– flavour**, wynsmaak.
vintage, druiwe-oes, wynoes; wyn.
vintager, druiwesnyer, druiweplukker.
viol, viola.
viola, altviool, viola.
viola, viooltjie, gesiggie.
violaceous, violetagtig, violetkleurig.
violate, skend, verbreek, oortree; ontheilig; verkrag, onteer; stoor.
violation, skending, verbreking, oortreding; ontheiliging; ontering.
violator, skender, verbreker; verkragter.
violence, geweld, gewelddadigheid; hewigheid; aanranding, verkragting; skending; **do – to**, geweld aandoen; verkrag.
violent, geweldig, onstuimig; driftig, opvlieënd, woes; gewelddadig; **a – death**, 'n gewelddadige dood; **he was in a – temper**, hy was in 'n verskriklike humeur.
violet, n. violetjie (viooltjie); pers.
violet, a. pers, violet.
violin, viool.
violinist, vioolspeler, violis.
violist, altspeler.
violoncellist, tjellospeler.
violoncello, tjello.
viper, adder.
virago, mannetjie(s)vrou, duiwelin, heks, rissiepit, helleveeg.
virescence, groenheid, die groen.
Virgilian, Virgiliaans.
virgin, n. maagd; **the (Blessed) V. (Mary)**, die (Heilige) Maagd Maria.
virgin, s. maagdelik, rein, onbevlek; **– soil**, onbeboude (rou, ongebraakte) grond; **– jungle**, oerwoud; **– honey**, skoon heuning, stroopheuning; **– modesty**, maagdelike beskeidenheid.
virginal, a. maagdelik, rein.
virginal, n.: **pair of –s**, spinet.
Virginia, Virginië (V.S.A.); **– creeper**, wildewingerd.
virginity, maagdelikheid.
Virgo, Maagd (sterrekunde).
viridescence, groenagtigheid.
viridescent, groenagtig, groenwordend.
viridity, groenheid, groen kleur.

virile, manlik; kragtig, fors, gespierd.
virility, manlikheid; krag, gespierdheid.
virose, virous, giftig.
virtu, kunsliefde; **articles of –**, kunsvoorwerpe.
virtual, eintlik, feitlik, virtueel; **he is the – manager**, hy is feitlik die bestuurder.
virtually, feitlik.
virtue, deug, deugsaamheid; kuisheid, reinheid; doeltreffendheid; krag; **patience is a –**, geduld oorwin alles, aanhou wen; **by, in – of**, kragtens.
virtuosity, virtuositeit, meesterlikheid.
virtuoso, virtuoos; kunskenner.
virtuous, deugsaam; kuis, rein.
virulence, venynigheid, kwaadaardigheid.
virulent, giftig; kwaadaardig; venynig.
virus, venyn, (ver)gif, smetstof; venynigheid, kwaadaardigheid, bitsigheid.
visa, sien **visé**, visum.
visage, gelaat.
vis-a-vis, vis-a-vis.
viscera, ingewande, binnegoed.
visceral, ingewands- . . .
viscerate, die ingewande uithaal, ontwei.
viscid, taai, klewerig, dik.
viscidity, taaiheid, klewerigheid.
viscosity, klewerigheid; viskositeit.
viscount, burggraaf.
viscountcy, burggraafskap.
viscountess, burggravin.
viscous, klewerig, taai.
visé, n. visum.
visé, v. viseer.
visibility, sigbaarheid; lig; **– was bad**, dit was moeilik om te sien.
visible, sigbaar; duidelik; te sien.
vision, n. gesig, (die) sien; insig, toekomsblik; gesigsvermoë; uitsig; visioen, visie; droomgesig, droombeeld.
vision, v. in die gees (in die verbeelding) sien, visualiseer, voorstel.
visionary, a. sieners- . . .; denkbeeldig; ingebeeld fantasties.
visionary, n. siener, dromer, dweper.
visit, v. besoek (aflê by), (gaan) kuier (by), visite maak; besoek; inspekteer, visenteer; **– a person with**, iemand besoek met.
visit, n. besoek, kuier, visite; **on a – to friends**, by vriende op besoek; **I paid him a long –**, ek het lank by hom gekuier; **right of –**, visitasiereg.
visitant, trekvoël; besoeker, kuiergas.
visitation, ondersoek, visitasie, inspeksie; besoek; besoeking, beproewing.
visiting, (die) besoek (aflê), kuier; **be on – terms with**, goed genoeg ken om te besoek.
visiting-card, visitekaartjie.
visiting-day, dag vir besoekers, ontvangdag.
visitor, besoeker, kuiergas; **–s**, kuiergaste, (kuier)mense, besoekers; **–s' book**, hotelregister, vreemdelingeboek.
visor, -zor, **visard**, -zard, visier, helmklep, -masker; masker.
vista, gesig, uitsig, vergesig, verskiet.
visual, gesig(s)- . . .; – angle, gesigshoek; **– nerve**, gesigsenuwee.
visualization, voorstelling.
visualize, aanskoulik voorstel, 'n voorstelling maak van, voor die gees roep, veraanskoulik.
vital, a. lewens- . . .; allergrootste; lewensgevaarlik; **– power**, lewenskrag; **– importance**, lewensbelang, die allergrootste belang; **a – question**, 'n lewensvraag; **a – wound**, 'n dodelike wond; **a – error**, 'n fatale fout; **– statistics**,

bevolkingstatistiek; hoofsaaklikste syfers; hoofmate (van 'n vrou).
vital, n. **-s,** lewensdele.
vitalism, vitalisme.
vitality, lewenskrag, vitaliteit.
vitalize, lewe gee; verlewendig, besiel.
vitiate, bederwe, besmet, verpes; vernietig, kragteloos maak; **-d constitution,** ondermynde gestel; **-d air,** verpeste lug; **-d mind,** onrein(e) gemoed; **-d judgment,** onsuiwer oordeel.
vitiation, besmetting; vernietiging.
viticultural, wynbou(ers)- . . .
viticulture, wynbou, wynboerdery.
viticulturist, wynbouer, wynboer.
vitreosity, glasagtigheid.
vitreous, glasagtig, glas- . . .; - **body,** glasliggaam; - **humour,** glasvog.
vitrescence, glaswording, verglasing.
vitric, a. glasagtig, glas- . . .
vitric(s), glas, glasgoed, glaswerk.
vitrifiable, verglaasbaar.
vitrifiction, verglasing.
vitrify, verglaas, tot glas maak.
vitriol, vitrioel; **blue, copper -,** blouvitrioel, kopervitrioel.
vitriolic, vitrioel- . . ., vitrioelagtig; skerp, bitsig, venynig.
vituperate, (uit)skel, slegmaak.
vituperation, (die) uitskel, geskel, slegsêery, slegmakery.
vituperative, (uit)skel: . . ., slegsê- . . .
vivacious, lewendig, lewenslustig, vrolik, opgewek; oorblywend.
vivacity, lewenslustigheid, vrolikheid, opgewektheid, lewendigheid.
vivarium, dieretuin; visdam.
viva voce, mondeling, viva voce.
vivid, helder, duidelik; lewendig; skitterend, glansend, (oog)verblindend; **a - imagination,** 'n lewendige (sterk) verbeeldingskrag.
vivify, verlewendig, lewendig maak, besiel, inspireer, opwek.
viviparous, lewendbarend.
vivisect, lewendig ontleed (oopsny).
vivisection, viviseksie.
vixen, wyfiejakkals; heks, helleveeg.
vixenish, kyfagtig, duiwelagtig.
vizi(e)r, visier.
vocabulary, woordeskat; woordelys.
vocal, stem- . . ., vokaal; mondeling; stemhebbend; **- chords,** stembande; **- music,** vokale musiek (vokaalmusiek); **- performer,** sanger(es).
vocalism, gebruik van die stem; vokalisme, vokaalstelsel.
vocalist, sanger(es).
vocalize, uitspreek, 'n klank vorm; stemhebbend maak; praat, sing.
vocation, roeping; beroep, professie; ambag, werk; **he felt no - (for the ministry),** hy het hom nie geroepe gevoel om predikant te word nie; **he mistook his -,** hy het die verkeerde beroep gekies.
vocational, beroeps- . . ., vak- . . .; - **training,** vakopleiding.
vocative, vokatief.
vociferate, raas, skreeu, tier.
vociferation, geraas, geskreeu.
vociferous, luidrugtig, skreeuend.
vodka, wodka.
vogue, mode; populariteit; **large hats are the -,** groot hoede is in die mode; **it has had a great -,** dit het baie opgang gemaak, dit was danig in die mode; **in -,** in die mode, in swang.

voice, n. stem, spraak; vorm; uitdrukking; **in a loud -,** met luide stem; **he gave - to his indignation,** hy het uitdrukking gegee aan sy verontwaardiging; **I have no - in the matter,** ek het niks te sê in die saak nie; **with one -,** eenstemmig, eenparig; **active, passive -,** bedrywende, lydende vorm.
voice, v. uiting gee aan; stemhebbend maak; (orrel) stem; - **the general sentiment,** die algemene gevoel vertolk (uitdruk).
voiced, stemhebbend.
voiceless, spraakloos, stom; stemloos.
void, a. leeg; vakant; ongeldig, nietig; kragteloos; ontbloot (van); **null and -,** ongeldig, van nul en gener waarde; **a proposal wholly - of sense,** 'n voorstel wat hoegenaamd geen sin het nie.
void, n. (leë) ruimte; leegte, leemte; (die) niet.
void, v. ongeldig verklaar; ontlas; ontruim.
voidance, (die) afsit, ontslag; ontruiming, (die) leegmaak.
voile, voile.
volant, vlieënd; rats, vlug.
volar, (hand)palm- . . .
volatile, vlugtig, vlug- . . .; lewendig, vrolik; onbestendig; ongedurig; **- salts,** vlugsout; **- oil,** vlugtige olie.
volatility, vlugtigheid; onbestendigheid.
volatilization, vlugtigmaking.
volatilize, vlugtig maak, (laat) verdamp.
volcanic, vulkanies.
volcano, vuurspuwende berg, vulkaan.
volition, wil, wilskrag, wilsuiting.
volitional, wils- . . ., van die wil.
volley, n. sarsie, salvo; stroom, (stort)vloed; vlughou, -skoot (tennis); **a - of oaths,** 'n stroom vloeke; **half -,** skephou, -skoot (tennis).
volley, v. in sarsies skiet; losbars, losbreek, lostrek; in die vlug slaan.
volt, n. volt (elektr.).
volt, n. draai, swenking, volte.
voltage, spanning.
voltaic, galvanies, voltaïes; - **battery,** galvaniese battery.
voltaism, galvanisme.
voltameter, voltameter.
voltmeter, voltmeter.
volubility, vlotheid, woorderykheid.
voluble, vlot, glad, woorderyk.
volume, (boek)deel; volume; grootte; omvang; massa; papirusrol; **in three -s,** in drie dele; **the - of his voice,** die omvang van sy stem; **-s of smoke,** rookwolke.
voluminous, uit baie (boek)dele bestaande; lywig, dik, groot, omvangryk; produktief, vrugbaar.
voluntary, a. vrywillig; ongedwonge; opsetlik, moedswillig; **a - school,** 'n vry skool.
voluntary, n. orrelstuk, voor-, tussen-, naspel; vrywilliger.
volunteer, n. vrywilliger.
volunteer, a. vrywilligers- . . .; **- corps,** vrywilligerskorps.
volunteer, v. vrywillig diensneem; vrywillig onderneem; as vrywilliger dien; **- assistance,** hulp aanbied.
voluptuary, n. wellusteling.
voluptuary, a. wellustig.
voluptuous, wellustig, sinlik.
volute, krul; rolslak.
voluted, gekrul, spiraalvormig.
vomit, v. vomeer (vermeer), (uit)braak.
vomit, n. braaksel; braakmiddel.
vomitive, braak- . . .; **- nut,** braakneut.
vomitory, a. braak- . . .
vomitory, n. braakmiddel, vomitief.

voodoo, toordery, toorkuns.
voracious, gulsig, vraatsugtig.
voracity, gulsigheid, vraatsugtigheid.
vortex, maalstroom, draaikolk.
vortical, draai- . . ., draaiend, maal- . . .
vortiginous, warrelend, draaiend.
votaress, vereerster; aanhangster.
votary, aanbidder, geesdriftige aanhanger, bewonderaar, volgeling.
vote, n. stem; stemming; stemreg; stembriefie; mosie; begrotingspos; **without a dissentient –,** sonder 'n teenstem, eenparig; **a – of noconfidence,** 'n mosie van wantroue; **woman must have the –,** vroue moet stemreg kry; **put to the –,** tot stemming bring, laat stem; **take a – on the question,** oor die saak stem.
vote, v. stem, jou stem uitbring; verklaar; voorstel, toestaan; **it was –d a failure,** almal het verklaar dat dit 'n mislukking was; **I – we go home,** ek stel voor dat ons huis toe gaan; **– against,** stem teen; **– down,** afstem; **– for,** stem voor (vir).
voter, kieser, stemgeregtigde; –s' roll, kieserslys.
voting, stemming, (die) stem; **– by ballot,** stemming met geslote briefies.
voting-paper, stembriefie, stembiljet.
votive, votief, gelofte- . . ; **– offering,** dankoffer.
vouch, bevestig, getuig, bewys lewer; waarborg, instaan (vir); **– for the truth of,** instaan vir die waarheid van.
voucher, bewys(stuk), kwitansie, teenblad.
vouchsafe, vergun, toestaan; **he –d me no answer,** hy het hom nie verwaardig om my te antwoord nie.
vow, n. gelofte, eed.
vow, v. 'n gelofte doen; plegtig belowe.
vowel, klinker, vokaal.
vowel gradation, ablaut.
vowel mutation, umlaut.
voyage, n. (see)reis.
voyage, v. 'n seereis maak, reis, vaar.
voyager, seereisiger.
vulcanite, eboniet, vulkaniet.
vulcanization, vulkanisasie.
vulcanize, vulkaniseer.
vulgar, plat, onbeskof, ongepoets, laag, grof; vulgêr; algemeen, alledaags, volks- . . .; **the – era,** die Christelike jaartelling; **– fraction,** gewone breuk.
vulgarism, plat uitdrukking; platheid.
vulgarity, onbeskoftheid, ongepoetstheid, laagheid, platheid, vulgariteit.
vulgarize, gemeengoed maak; verlaag, vulgariseer.
Vulgate, Vulgata.
vulnerability, kwesbaarheid.
vulnerable, kwesbaar, wondbaar.
vulnerary, a. wondhelend, wondheel- . . .
vulnerary, n. wond(heel)middel.
vulpine, jakkalsagtig, jakkals- . . ., skelm, slu, oorlams, slim.
vulture, aasvoël; roofsugtige, skraper.
vulturine, vulturish, vulturous, aasvoëlagtig, aasvoël- . . .; roofsugtig.
vying, sien **vie.**

W

wad, n. prop, stopsel, pluisie; rol.
wad, v. watteer; toestop, opvul.
wadding, watte, kapok, vulsel.
waddle, v. waggel, strompel.
waddle, n. gewaggel, waggelende gang.
wade, v. deurwaad, deurloop; – **into someone**, iemand opdons; – **through**, deurwaad, deursukkel, deurworstel, deurswoeg; – **through a book**, 'n boek deurworstel.
wade, n. (die) deurwaad; geswoeg, gesukkel.
wader, wader; moerasvoël, (poen)snip; –s, kapstewels, waterlaarse.
wading-bird, moerasvoël, (poel)snip.
wafer, wafel(tjie), oblietjie; ouel; hostie.
waffle, wafel.
waffle, v. babbel, klets.
waffle-iron, wafelyster.
waft, v. drywe, waai, swewe, meevoer.
waft, n. swaai, vleuelslag; luggie; vlagie.
wag, v. swaai, waai, kwispel, skud; **the dog –s his tail**, die hond swaai sy stert; **the tail –s the dog**, Klaas is baas, die mindere regeer die meerdere; kinders weet altyd beter; **tongues are –ging**, die tonge is los, pratery is aan die gang; **so the world –s**, dit is die wêreld se beloop.
wag, n. swaai, kwispeling, skud.
wag, n. spotvoël, terggees, grappemaker.
wage, n. loon; gasie, verdienste; besoldiging; **the –s of sin is death**, die besoldiging van die sonde is die dood; **living –**, bestaanbare loon; **a fair day's work for a fair day's –**, loon volgens werk; **flat –**, uniforme loonstandaard.
wage, v. voer, maak; – **war**, oorlog maak (voer).
wager, n. weddenskap.
wager, v. wed.
wage-rate, loonstandaard.
wage(s) fund, loonfonds.
waggery, tergery, korswel, grapmakery.
waggish, ondeund, grapmakerig.
waggle, sien **wag**.
wag(g)on, wa; vragwa, ,,trok".
wag(g)oner, wadrywer, voerman van 'n wa; **the W–**, die Voerman.
wag(g)onette, waentjie.
wagtail, kwikstertjie.
waif, wegloop-dier, goed sonder baas; strandgoed; swerwer; verlatene, daklose kind; **–s and strays**, stukkies en brokkies; hawelose kinders.
wail, v. weeklaag, huil, kerm; **W– Wall**, Klaagmuur.
wail, n. weeklag, jammerklag, gekerm.
wain, wa; **Charlie's W–**, die Groot Beer.
wainscot, n. beskot, lambrisering.
wainscot, v. beklee, lambriseer.
wainscoting, beskot, lambrisering.
waist, middel(lyf); lyfie.
waist-band, broeksband, band van 'n rok.
waist-belt, lyfband, gordband, gordel.
waist-cloth, lendedoek.
waistcoat, onderbaadjie; **sleeved –**, onderbaadjie met moue.
waist-deep, tot aan (by) die middel, pensdiep (van diere).
wait, v. wag; versuim, vertoef; afwag; bedien; **– a minute**, wag 'n bietjie; **keep –ing**, laat wag; **– for**, wag vir (op); **he –ed his opportunity**, hy het sy kans afgewag; **– up**, opbly; **– (up)on**, bedien, oppas; opwagting maak by ('n minister, ens.).
wait, n. (die) wag; loer, hinderlaag; **we had a long –**, ons moes lank wag; **lie in –**, op die loer lê.
waiter, tafelbediende, kelner; skinkbord, presenteertafeltjie; **dumb –**, stomme kneg, dientafel, diener.
waiting, n. (die) wag; (die) bedien, bediening; opwagting; **be in –**, klaar (gereed) staan, byderhand wees; **lady in –**, hofdame; **lord in –**, kamerheer.
waiting, a. wagtend; bedienend.
waiting-room, wagkamer.
waitress, kelnerin, (tafel)bediende, kafeemeisie.
waive, afsien van, laat vaar, afstand doen van.
wake, v. wakker word (maak); ontwaak, opstaan; opwek; wakker skud, aanwakker, aanvuur; **– up there**, word tog wakker, maak jou oë oop, moenie so aan die slaap wees nie; **in his waking hours**, as hy nie slaap nie.
wake, n. (die) waak (by 'n lyk).
wake, kielwater, vaarwater, sog; spoor; **in the – of**, kort agter, op die hakke van; **in die voetspore van**.
wakeful, wakker, slaaploos; waaksaam.
waken, wakker maak (word).
Waldenses, Waldensers.
wale, **weal**, n. dikhou, streep, striem.
wale, **weal**, v. dikhoue slaan, pimpel en pers slaan, striem.
Wales, Wallis.
Walhalla, sien **Valhalla**.
walk, v. loop, stap, wandel; betree; op 'n stappie gaan; voetslaan; **– the boards**, die planke betree; toneelspeler wees; **– the hospitals**, die hospitale besoek, hospitaalwerk doen; **– the streets**, die strate platloop, op straat rondslenter; die baan opgaan; **– a horse**, 'n perd op 'n stappie lei (ry); **– about**, rondloop, rondstap; **– away**, wegloop; **– away from somebody**, van iemand wegloop; iemand ver agterlaat; **– away with something**, maak dat jy met iets wegkom; **– down**, afstap, afloop; **– in**, binnekom; **– into a shop**, 'n winkel binnestap; **– into somebody**, iemand lelik inklim (invlie); **– off**, wegstap, wegloop; **you have –ed me off my legs**, jy het my (skoon) disnis geloop; **the policeman –ed him off**, die konstabel het hom weggebring; **– on**, aanloop, verder loop; **– out**, uitloop; **– over**, oorloop, oorstap; maklik (fluit-fluit) wen; **he –ed over the difficulties**, die moeilikhede was vir hom niks; **– up**, oploop, boontoe loop; **– up to**, na toe loop, op afstap; **– with**, loop by (met); **– with a person**, met iemand saamloop; **– with God**, met God wandel.
walk, n. gang, pas; (die) loop; wandeling; wandelweg, wandelplek, looppad, voetpad, promenade, laan; beroep; stand; **go for, take a –**, 'n entjie gaan loop (stap, wandel); **– of life**, beroep, werk; stand.
walker, wandelaar, loper, stapper, voetganger; loopvoël.
walkie-talkie, loopprater, geselsradio.
walking, n. (die) loop, ens.
walking, a. lopend, loop- . . .; **– dictionary**, wandelende woordeboek.
walking-chair, loopwaentjie, stootstoel(tjie).
walking-dress, looprok, wandelrok.
walking-papers, ontslag, afdanking.
walking-stick, kierie, wandelstok.
walking-tour, looptoer, wandeltoer, staptog.
walk-out, werkstaking.
walk-over, maklike oorwinning; present-wedstryd; **-punte**; **it was a – for him**, hy het fluitfluit gewen, dit was vir hom sommer kinderspeletjies (om te wen); hy het die wedstryd present gekry.
Walkyrie, sien **Valkyrie**.

wall, n. muur; wal; – **of partition**, skeidsmuur, skeidslyn; **run your head against a –**, met jou kop teen die muur loop; **–s have ears**, mure het ore; **with one's back to the –**, in die hoek (nou) gedryf, alleen teen die oornag; **the weakest goes to the –**, die swakste gaan ten onder (moet die onderspit delf).
wall, v. ommuur, 'n muur bou (om); **–ed towns**, ommuurde stede;. – **up**, toebou, toemessel.
wallaby, kangaroetjie, wallaby.
wall-creeper, muurgrawer; klimop.
wall-cress, rotsplant.
wallet, sakkie; sakboekie; portefeulje; kossak, knapsak.
wall-eye, witoog, glasoog.
wall-eyed, witoog- . . ., glasoog- . . .
wall-flower, muurblom (let. en fig.).
Walloon, n. Waals; Waal.
Walloon, a. Waals.
wallop, ransel, uitlooi, 'n loesing gee.
walloping, a. tamaai, yslik, frisgeboud.
walloping, n. afranseling, loesing.
wallow, v. rol, wentel (in die modder, water, ens.); swelg; **he –s in money**, hy kan swem in sy geld.
wallow, n. rolplek.
wall-painting, muurskildering.
wall-paper, plakpapier, behangselpapier.
wall-plate, muurplaat, muurbalk.
walnut, okkerneut; okkerneutboom; okkerneuthout.
walrus, walrus.
waltz, n. v. wals.
wan, bleek, asvaal, flets, vaal.
wand, staf, towerstaf, stok.
wander, swerwe, dwaal, ronddool; verdwaal, verlore raak, wegraak; afdwaal (van die onderwerp); yl, deurmekaar praat; **his mind –s**, hy yl, hy is deurmekaar.
wanderer, (rond)swerwer, swerweling.
wandering, a. swerwend, dwalend, ronddolend; afdwalend; **the W– Jew**, die Wandelende Jood; a – **kidney**, 'n wandelende (los) nier; a – **abscess**, 'n kruipsweer.
wandering(s), n. swerftogte, omswerwing; ylhoofdigheid, afdwaling.
wanderlust, swerflus.
wane, v. taan, verbleek, verminder, verswak, afneem, verflou.
wane, n. verbleking, vermindering, verswakking, afneming; **on the –**, aan die afneem (verminder), aan taan.
want, n. gebrek, skaarste, behoefte, nood, armoede; **be in – of money**, in geldnood verkeer; **for – of**, by gebrek aan; **be in – of a servant**, 'n bediende nodig hê; – **of sense**, gebrek aan verstand; **supply the –s of**, in die behoeftes voorsien van.
want, v. nodig hê, behoefte hê aan, kortkom, kortskiet, makeer, ontbreek; gebrek ly; begeer, verlang, wil hê, wil; **be found –ing**, in gebreke bly; te lig gevind word; **the head is –ing**, die kop ontbreek of makeer; **this –s careful handling**, dit moet sorgvuldig aangepak word; **I don't – to go**, ek wil nie gaan nie; **call me if I am –ed**, roep my as julle my nodig kry; **he is –ed by the police**, die polisie soek (na) hom.
wanting, sonder; – **honesty, nothing can be done**, sonder eerlikheid kan niks uitgevoer word nie.
wanton, a. dartel, uitgelate, vrolik; vol nukke en grille, veranderlik; wild, weelderig, woes; ligsinnig, losbandig, wellustig.
wanton, n. wellusteling, ligtekooi.
wanton, v. baljaar, jakker.
wapiti, wapiti(hert).

war, n. oorlog, stryd, kryg; **civil –**, burgeroorlog; **make, wage –**, oorlog voer; **declare –**, oorlog verklaar; **be at – with**, in oorlog gewikkel wees met, in oorlog verkeer met; **a – to the knife**, 'n stryd op lewe en dood; **art of –**, krygskuns; **carry the – into the enemy's country**, aanvallend optree; **War Office**, Ministerie van Oorlog.
war, v. oorlog (stryd) voer.
war-baby, oorlogskindjie.
warble, v. sing, kweel.
warble, n. gesing, gekweel; lied.
warble, n. rugsweer, skaafplek.
warbler, sangvoël, sanger.
war-cloud, oorlogswolk.
war-cry, oorlogskreet, strydkreet.
ward, n. bewaking; beskerming, bewaring, voogdyskap; pleegkind; (stads)wyk; afdeling, saal, kamer (in 'n hospitaal).
ward, v. bewaar, beskerm; – **off**, afwend, keer, pareer, afweer.
war-dance, oorlogsdans.
warden, voog; bewaarder; opsiener; wykmeester; hoof, direkteur.
warder, bewaarder, wagter, sipier.
wardrobe, klerekas; (voorraad) klere.
wardrobe-mistress, kostumier.
ward-room, offisierskajuit.
wardship, voogdy(skap).
ware, n. goed, ware; **–s**, koopware.
ware, v. oppas vir; vermy.
warehouse, n. loods, pakhuis; winkel.
warehouse, v. bêre, opbêre, wegpak.
warfare, oorlog, kryg, stryd; **after long –**, na lang oorlogvoer.
war-horse, oorlogsperd, strydros.
wariness, versigtigheid.
warlike, oorlogsugtig, krygshaftig, krygs- . . ., oorlogs- . . .
warm, a. warm; heet; verhit; hartstogtelik, emosioneel, vurig; hartlik, innig; vars (van spoor); ryk, welgesteld; – **with wine**, verhit deur wyn; **I'll make it – for him**, ek sal vuurmaak onder hom, ek sal hom opdruk; – **thanks**, innige dank; **a – reception**, 'n hartlike ontvangs; **I was in a – corner**, ek het dit net benoud gekry; **it was – work**, dit het net moeilik gegaan; die werk het met groot gevaar gepaard gegaan.
warm, v. warm maak (word), verwarm; – **yourself at the fire**, vir jou by die vuur verwarm (warm maak); **the room is –ing up**, die kamer word warm; **my heart –s to him**, my hart begin warm klop vir hom.
warm-blooded, warmbloedig.
warm-hearted, hartlik, goedhartig.
warming, afranseling, loesing.
warming-pan, bedwarmer; plektoestaner.
warmonger, oorlogstoker.
warmth, warmte; hartlikheid.
warn, waarsku; in kennis stel, verwittig; vermaan.
warning, waarskuwing, vermaning; inkennisstelling; (die) opsê (opsegging), kennisgewing; **let this be a – to you**, laat dit vir jou as waarskuwing dien; **give –**, waarsku; **take –**, 'n waarskuwing ter harte neem.
warp, n. skering (lengtedrade van 'n weefsel); (die) kromtrek, kromtrekking, skeefheid; ontaarding, verdorwenheid; werptou.
warp, v. krom trek, skeef trek, krom (skeef) word; bederf, (laat) ontaard, versleg; bevooroordeeld maak; verdraai; trek, sleep (van 'n skip); **hardship –ed his disposition**, swaarkry het hom laat ontaard; **his judgment is –ed by self-interest**, eiebelang benewel sy oordeel.

war-paint, oorlogsverf; volle mondering.
war-path, oorlogspad; **be, go on the –,** op die oorlogspad wees, oorlog verklaar; **die stryd aanvaar, strydlustig wees.**
warrant, n. volmag; versekering, waarborg, magbrief, lasbrief, bevelskrif, bevel tot inhegtenisneming; **– of attorney,** prokurasie, volmag.
warrant, v. magtig, volmag gee; waarborg, verseker, garandeer; regverdig; **I'll – you,** dit kan ek jou verseker, dit kan jy my glo.
warrantable, wettig; verdedigbaar.
warrantee, ontvanger van 'n waarborg, gevolmagtigde.
warrantor, warrenter, waarborger; borg; volmaggewer.
warranty, volmag; waarborg, garansie.
warren, boerplek van konyne, konynwerf.
wariror, krygsman, soldaat, kryger.
war-ship, oorlogskip.
war-song, krygslied.
wart, vrat(jie); knoes; **you have painted him with his –s,** jy het nie sy gebreke probeer bedek nie.
warthog, wildevark, vlakvark.
warty, vratterig, vol vratjies.
war-whoop, oorlogskreet.
wary, versigtig, behoedsaam.
was, sien **be.**
wash, v. was, uitwas, afwas, (af)spoel, uitspoel, bespoel; **– one's hands of,** jou hande in onskuld was; **– one's dirty linen in public,** jou huislike moeilikhede (oneningheid) in die openbaar bespreek; **the water had –ed a channel,** die water het 'n sloot gespoel; **this won't –,** dit sal verkleur van die was; dit hou geen steek nie, dit gaan nie op nie; **– away,** uitwas; wegspoel, verspoel; **– down,** afwas; na binne spoel (van kos); **–ed out,** poot-uit, gedaan; **– up,** afwas, was (van skottelgoed, ens.); uitspoel, aan land spoel.
wash, n. (die) was; wasgoed; spoeling; geklots, golfslag; kielwater; spoelgrond, dryfgrond; skottel(goed)water; flou (slegte) tee (drank); waterverf; vernis, vloeistof, water, wasmiddel; **send it to the –,** gooi dit in die was; **come out in the –,** agterna blyk.
washable, wasbaar, wat kan gewas word.
washaway, verpoeling.
wash-basin, waskom.
wash-board, wasplank.
wash-day, wasdag.
washer, wasser; waster.
washerwoman, wasmeid, wasvrou.
wash-hand basin, waskom.
wash-hand-stand, wastafel(tjie).
wash-house, washuis, wasinrigting.
washiness, waterigheid; flouheid.
washing, n. wasgoed.
washing, a. was- . . .
wash-leather, seemsleer.
wash-out, misoes, fiasko; verspoeling; uitspoeling.
wash-stand, wastafel.
wash-tub, wasbalie, wasvat.
washy, waterig, dun, flou; bleek, naar; swak, kragteloos, beroerd.
wasp, perdeby, wesp.
waspish, wespagtig; prikkelbaar, kort van draad, opvlieënd, bitsig.
wast, sien **be.**
wastage, verspilling, (die) vermors, vermorsing; afval; slytasie.
waste, a. woes, woestynagtig; verlate; onbebou, onbewerk; oortollig, ongebruik; **lay –,** verwoes; **lie –,** onbebou (onbewerk) lê; **– land,** onbeboude grond; **– product,** afval(produk); **– paper,** skeurpapier.
waste, v. verspil, verkwis, deurbring, vermors; verwoes; verminder, afneem; wegkwyn; verniel, laat verval; **– time,** tyd verspil; **– money,** geld verkwis; **that water is wasting,** daardie water gaan verlore; **– breath, words,** woorde verspil, tevergeefs praat; **– not, want not,** as jy vandag spaar, sal jy môre hê.
waste, n. woesteny, woestyn, wildernis; verkwisting, verspilling, (die) vermors; afval; vermindering, afneming; verbruik, (die) afslyt, slytasie; verwaarlosing; verval; **it is – of time,** dit is tydverspilling; **run to –,** verlore gaan; **wilful – makes woeful want,** vandag verteer, môre ontbeer; **(cotton) –,** poetskatoen.
waste-basket, snippermandjie.
waste-book, kladboek.
wasteful, verkwistend, spandabel.
wastepaper basket, snippermandjie.
waste-pipe, afvoerpyp, -buis.
waster, deurbringer, verkwister.
wastrel, misbaksel, foutfabrikaat; straatkind; deugniet, niksnuts; deurbringer.
watch, n. wag; waak; waaksaamheid; horlosie; **pass as a – in the night,** gou vergeet wees; **keep –,** (die) wag hou; dophou; **on the –,** op die uitkyk (loer); op wag.
watch, v. waak; wag hou, op wag staan; bewaak, bespied, dophou, in die oog hou; oplet; afwag; **if you don't – it,** as jy nie oppas nie; **– one's time,** jou tyd afwag; **– for,** op die uitkyk (loer) wees na; **– over,** waak oor, wag hou oor.
watch-case, horlosiekas.
watch-chain, horlosieketting.
watch-dog, waghond.
watch-fire, wagvuur, kampvuur.
watchful, waaksaam, op die hoede.
watch-glass, horlosieglas.
watch-guard, horlosieketting.
watch-key, horlosiesleutel.
watchman, nagwag; wagter.
watch-spring, horlosieveer.
watch-tower, wagtoring.
watchword, wagwoord; leuse.
water, n. water; **be in smooth –,** oor alle moeilikhede heen wees; **in deep –s,** swaar beproef, in groot moeilikhede; **still –s run deep,** stille waters diepe grond (onder draai die duiwel rond); **fish in troubled –s,** in troebel water vis; **get into hot –,** in die moeilikheid kom, jou vasloop; **throw cold – on,** kou(e) water gooi op; **cast one's bread upon the –s,** jou brood op die water uitwerp; **it brings the – to one's mouth,** dit laat 'n mens se mond water; **he spends money like –,** hy mors met geld; **make (pass) –,** water, urineer; **tread –,** watertrap; **– on the knee,** water in die knie; **– on the brain,** hoofwatersug, waterhoof; **in low –,** in geldelike nood; **high – mark,** hoogwaterpeil; hoogtepunt; **of the first –,** van die eerste water; **a blunder of the first –,** 'n yslike flater; **– ski,** waterski; **– sprinkler,** sproeier.
water, v. natmaak, nat gooi, nat sprinkel; verdun, water bygooi; ('n perd, ens.) water gee; gaan water suip; water inneem; water (mond, oë) moireer; **–ed silk,** gewaterde sy; **it makes one's mouth –,** dit laat 'n mens watertand; **– down,** verwater.
water-bailiff, waterfiskaal, waterskout.
water-borne, oor die water vervoer, water- . . . , skeeps- . . . ; **– sewerage,** spoelriolering.
water-bottle, kraffie; waterfles.
water-cart, waterkar.

**water-chute, **afglyplank, afglygeut.
**water-closet, **watersekreet, waterkloset.
**water-colour, **waterverf; waterverfskildery; waterverftekening.
**watercourse, **waterloop; watervoor.
**watercress, **bronkors, bronslaai.
**water-cure, **waterkuur, hidropatie.
**water-diviner, **waterwyser.
**waterfall, **waterval.
**water-finder, **waterwyser.
**waterfowl, **waterhoender(s), watervoël(s).
**water-gate, **sluis, vloeddeur.
**water-gauge, **watermeter.
**water-hammer, **waterslag.
**water-hole, **watergat; drinkplek; suipgat.
**water-hose, **waterslang, spuitslang.
**wateriness, **waterigheid, wateragtigheid.
**watering-can, **gieter.
**watering-cart, **waterkar.
**watering-place, **watersuipplek; badplaas, strand.
**water-jacket, **koelmantel.
**water-level, **waterhoogte; waterpas.
**water-line, **waterlyn.
**waterlogged, **vol water geloop (van 'n skip); deurweek (van hout).
**Waterloo: **met his –, sy dreuning teëgekom; sy partuur gekry.
**water-main, **hoofwaterpyp.
**waterman, **veerman.
**watermark, **watermerk.
**watermelon, **waatlemoen.
**water-meter, **watermeter.
**water-mill, **watermeul(e).
**water-plane, **watervliegtuig.
**water-plate, **warmwaterbord.
**water polo, **waterpolo.
**water-power, **waterkrag.
**waterproof, **a. waterdig.
**waterproof, **n. reënjas, -mantel; waterdigte stof; rubberlaken.
**water-rate, **waterbelasting.
**water-resistant, **watervas.
**watershed, **waterskeiding.
**waterside, **waterkant.
**water-skin, **watersak.
**waterspout, **waterhoos; spuier.
**watersprite, **watergees.
**water-supply, **watervoorraad; watervoorsiening.
**watertight, **waterdig.
**water-way, **waterweg; watergang.
**water-wheel, **waterrat.
**waterworks, **waterwerke, waterkering; **turn on the –, **aan die huil gaan.
**watery, **waterig, (pap)nat; te pap gekook; vogtig (oë); dun, flou, verdun; laf, smaakloos; bleek.
**watt, **watt (in elektrisiteit).
**wattle, **latwerk, vlegwerk; lat, spar; lel (bel) (van kalkoen); Autraliese akasia, basboom.
**wattle-work, **latwerk, vlegwerk.
**waul, **miaau, tjank, skreeu.
**wave, **v. golf (golwe); (van hare) onduleer, kartel; wapper; swaai, wuif, waai; wink; – **one's hand, **met die hand wuif.
**wave, **n. golf, brander; golwende lyn (golflyn); golwing; swaai, (die) wuif, waai; haargolf, kartel, ondulering; **permanent –, **blywende (vaste) kartel (ondulering, haargolf).
**waveless, **spieëlglad, stil, kalm.
**wavelet, **golfie, brandertjie.
**waver, **aarsel, weifel, op twee gedagtes hink; begin te wyk, begin moed opgee; flikker; bewe.
**waverer, **weifelaar.
**waveringly, **weifelend, aarselend.
**wavy, **a. golwend, gegolf, krul- . . .

**wax, **n. was; byewas; lak; oorwas, oorsmeer.
**wax, **v. was, groei (van die maan); – **and wane, **groei en afneem; – **fat, merry, indignant, **vet, vrolik, verontwaardig word.
**wax, **v. met was smeer (bestryk).
**wax-candle, **waskers.
**wax-chandler, **waskersmaker, -verkoper.
**wax-cloth, **wasdoek.
**wax-doll, **waspop.
**waxen, **was- . . ., wasagtig.
**wax-light, **waskers, wasliggie.
**wax-palm, **waspalm(boom).
**wax-paper, **waspapier.
**waxwork, **wasbeeld; wasmodellering.
**waxy, **wasagtig; was- . . .
**way, **weg, pad; rigting; wyse, manier, gewoonte, gebruik; toestand; **the – of all flesh, **die weg van alle vlees; **pave the –, **die weg baan, die pad oopmaak; **he asked me that –, **hy het my gevra hoe die pad gaan; **find the –, **die pad kry, regkom; **lose the –, **verdwaal; **the parting of the –s, **die skeiding van die weë; die kruispad; **go one's –, **vertrek, heengaan, weggaan; jou gang gaan; **he came by – of London, **hy het oor Londen gekom; **lead the –, **verloop, die pad wys; die voorbeeld gee, die toon aangee; **it is nothing out of the –, **dit is niks buitengewoons nie; **an out-of-the- – place, **'n afgeleë plek; **he goes out of his – to be rude, **hy lê hom daarop toe om onbeleef te wees; **that is the – to do it, **dit is die manier om dit aan te pak, so moet dit gedoen word; **go one's own –, **jou eie gang gaan, jou nie aan ander steur nie; **have one's own –, **jou sin kry; **it is a long – off, **dit is 'n hele ent daarnatoe; **it went a long – to . . ., **dit het baie daartoe bygedra om . . .; **still a long – off perfection, **op verre na nog nie volmaak nie; **be in the –, **in die pad wees; **get out of the –, **uit die pad staan, padgee; **get something out of the –, **van iets ontslae raak; iets in orde bring; **put a person out of the –, **iemand uit die weg ruim; **clear the –, **opsy staan, padgee; die pad skoonmaak; **on the – home, **op pad huis toe; **by the –, **terloops; tussen hakies; **which – is he going, **waarheen gaan hy?; **look the other –, **'n ander kant opkyk; maak of jy iemand nie sien nie; **the – of the world, **die wêreld se beloop; **make one's –, **jou weg baan; vooruitkom in die wêreld; **under –, **onder weg, in beweging; **not a bad fellow, in some –s, **in sommige opsigte nie 'n slegte kêrel nie; **no – inferior, **hoegenaamd nie slegter nie; **things are in a bad –, **sake staan maar sleg; **in a small –, **op klein skaal; **by – of apology, **by wyse van verontskuldiging; **–s and means, **middele.
**way-bill, **vragbrief, geleibrief.
**wayfarer, **reisiger.
**wayfaring, **a. (rond)reisend, (rond)trekkend.
**waylay, **op die loer lê vir, inwag.
**wayside, **die kant van die pad.
**wayward, **eiewys, eiesinnig, wispelturig.
**way-worn, **vermoeid, moeg van reis.
**we, **ons.
**weak, **swak; tingerig; flou; slap; sieklik; **a – hand, **slegte kaarte; – **tea, **flou tee.
**weaken, **verswak; verslap; flouer maak.
**weak-eyed, **swak (sleg) van oë.
**weak-headed, **swakhoofdig.
**weak-kneed, **swak in die knieë; slap, papbroekig, lamsakkerig.
**weakling, **swakkeling, sukkelaar.
**weakly, **sieklik, swak, tingerig.
**weakness, **swakheid; swak, swakte; **have a – for something, **'n swak hê vir iets.

weak-sighted, swak (sleg) van oë.
weal, welvaart, voorspoed, welsyn, geluk; **the public, general –**, die algemene welsyn; **– or woe**, voor- of teenspoed, wel of wee.
weal, sien **wale**.
wealth, rykdom, vermoë; magdom, oorvloed, weelde; **a – of fruit**, vrugte in oorvloed, 'n magdom van vrugte.
wean, speen; afleer, afwen.
weanling, gespeende kind (dier).
weapon, wapen.
wear, v. dra; (af)slyt, uitslyt, wegslyt; uitput, afmat; (stadig) omgaan (van tyd); **– one's heart on one's sleeve**, die hart op die tong hê; **– a face of joy**, opgeruimd wees; **he –s his years well**, hy dra sy jare goed, hy lyk nog heeltemal jonk vir sy jare; **this –s well**, dit dra goed, dit hou lank; **a worn joke**, 'n afgesaagde grap; **the day –s away**, die dag gaan langsaam om; **– away one's youth in trifles**, jou jeug met nietighede verslyt; **worn away, afgeslyt**; **they succeeded in –ing down the opposition**, hulle het daarin geslaag om die teenstanders uit te put; **– off**, afslyt, wegslyt; verdwyn; **– on**, langsaam verbygaan; **– out**, slyt, afslyt, verslyt; uitput, afmat, gedaan maak; **his patience was worn out at last**, uiteindelik het sy geduld opgeraak; **– out one's welcome**, van iemand se gasvryheid misbruik maak.
wear, n. (die) dra; drag; mode; slytasie; **these clothes are not fit for seaside –**, hierdie klere is nie geskik om aan die strand te dra nie; **fair – and tear**, billike slytasie; **this jacket will stand any amount of –**, hierdie baadjie sal lank dra; **be the worse for –**, verslyt (verslete) wees.
wearable, geskik om te dra, draagbaar.
wearer, draer.
weariness, moegheid, vermoeidheid.
wearing-apparel, klere, aantrekgoed.
wearisome, vermoeiend, afmattend, vervelend (vervelig).
weary, a. vermoeid, moeg; sat; afmattend, vermoeiend, vervelend.
weary, v. vermoei, moeg maak; verveel; moeg word (van).
weasel, wesel.
weasel-faced, met 'n skerp gesig.
weather, n. weer; **under the –**, in die verknorsing; **make bad –**, slegte weer tref; **under stress of –**, as gevolg van stormagtige weer.
weather, v. aan wind en weer blootstel; deurstaan, te bowe kom, veilig deurkom, braveer, trotseer; verweer, verbrokkel, opkrummel (van rotse).
weather-beaten, deur die weer geteister; verweer.
weather-board, skutplank; loefsy.
weather-bound, deur slegte weer opgehou.
weathercock, weerhaan; „verkleurmannetjie".
weather-eye: keep one's – open, goed dophou, 'n oog in die seil hou.
weather forecast, weervoorspelling.
weather-glass, weerglas.
weather prophet, weerprofeet.
weather-vane, weerhaan; „verkleurmannetjie".
weather-worn, verweer.
weave, weef, vleg; dwaal (oor 'n pad); **woven paper**, velynpapier.
weaver, wewer; wewervoël.
web, web; weefsel; spinnerak; swemvlies; groot rol papier; **spider's –**, spinnerak; **a – of lies**, 'n weefsel van leuen en bedrog.
webbed, met swemvliese.
webbing, smal seildoek, seilband.
web-eye, (nael)vlies op die oog.
web-footed, met swempote, swempoot-.

wed, trou; verenig, paar, verbind; **–ded life**, getroude lewe, huwelikslewe; **–ded bliss**, huweliksgeluk; **–ded to**, verknog aan.
wedding, bruilof, trouery, trouplegtigheid; **silver, golden –**, silwer-, goue bruilof.
wedding breakfast, bruilofsmaal.
wedding-cake, bruidskoek.
wedding-card, troukaartjie.
wedding-day, troudag.
wedding-garment, bruilofskleed.
wedding-ring, trouring.
wedge, n. keil, wig; **the thin end of the –**, die eerste stap, die begin.
wedge, v. keil, 'n keil inslaan; oopklowe; vaskeil; **– in**, indruk, inbeur.
wedge-shaped, wigvormig.
wedge-tailed, met 'n spits stert.
wedlock, huwelik, eg; **born in lawful –**, in wetlike eg gebore.
Wednesday, Woensdag.
wee, baie klein; **a – bit**, 'n ou klein bietjie.
weed, n. onkruid, gras, skrale, slappe; gaip, lummel; **ill –s grow apace**, onkruid vergaan nie.
weed, v. onkruid uitroei, skoffel, gras uittrek; **– out**, uitroei; die slegtes uitgooi, uitsoek.
weed-grown, vervuil, vol onkruid.
weeds, onkruid, gras; rougewaad.
weedy, vol onkruid, vervuil; lang, skraal, slap, niksbeduidend.
week, week; **this day –**, vandag oor ag dae.
week-day, week(s)dag, werkdag.
week-end, naweek.
week-ender, naweek-kuiergas.
weekly, a. weekliks, week- . . .
weekly, adv. weekliks, elke week.
weekly, n. weekblad.
weep, huil, ween; beween, betreur; drup; sweet; **– oneself out**, jou uithuil.
weeper, huiler, (be)wener; roukla(g)er, klaagvrou; lanferband, rouband; rousluier; **–s**, roumansjette.
weeping-willow, treurwilg(er).
weevil, kalender.
weevilled, weevily, vol kalander(s).
weft, inslag; weefsel.
weigh, weë (weeg); oorweeg; opweeg (teen); geld; **– the consequences**, die gevolge oorweeg; **– one's words**, jou woorde weë; **– anchor**, die anker lig; **– one argument, against with another**, die een argument teen die ander opweeg; **– down**, neerdruk, afdruk, swaar druk op; **one good argument –s down six bad ones**, een goeie argument weeg op teen ses swakkes; **he is –ed down with cares**, hy gaan gebuk onder sorge; **– out**, afweeg; **– up**, ophys, oplig; **– upon**, neerdruk, swaar druk op.
weighage, weeggeld, -loon.
weigh-bridge, weegbrug, brugbalans.
weighing-machine, groot skaal.
weight, n. gewig; swaarte; las; belang; **this has great – with me**, dit weeg swaar by my; **men of –**, manne van gewig (invloed, gesag).
weight, v. gewig opsit; swaarder maak; beswaar, belas.
weightless, sonder gewig.
weighty, swaar; gewigtig; belangrik; invloedryk, gesaghebbend; weldeurdag.
weir, dam, dwarsmuur (in 'n rivier), wal, weer.
weird, a. bonatuurlik, geheimsinnig, spookagtig, grillerig; eienaardig, raar, vreemd; **the – sisters**, die skikgodinne.
welcome, interj. welkom.

welcome, n. welkom, verwelkoming; **bid one –, iemand welkom heet; give a warm –,** hartlik verwelkom.
welcome, v. welkom heet, verwelkom.
welcome, a. welkom; **make one –,** iemand vriendelik ontvang; **you are –,** tot jou diens, nie te dank nie; **you are – to any service I can do,** ek is heeltemal tot jou (u) diens; **you are – to take steps,** dit staan jou heeltemal vry om stappe te doen.
weld, v. sweis, (aanmekaar) smee; verenig, verbind.
weld, n. las, sweisplek, smeeplek.
weldable, sweisbaar, smeebaar.
welfare, welvaart, welsyn.
well, n. bron, fontein, put; (ink)pot, (ink)koker.
well, v. opwel, ontspruit, ontspring.
well, adv. goed, wel; terdeë; **– done:** knap gedaan!, mooi so!; **you did – to come,** dit was goed van jou om te kom, jy het reg gehandel om te kom; **that is just as –,** dit is ook maar goed; **he gave me clothes as –,** hy het my boonop nog klere gegee; **it may – be that,** dit is heeltemal moontlik dat; **you may – say that,** dit mag jy wel sê; **very –, I shall tell your mamma,** toe maar, ek sal vir jou ma vertel.
well, a. wel, goed; gesond; **– enough,** goed genoeg; taamlik, gangbaar.
well, n: **I wish him –,** ek wens hom die beste toe.
well, interj. wel.
well-balanced, goed gebalanseerd; ewewigtig, besadig.
well-behaved, gehoorsaam, soet, goed opgevoed, met goeie maniere.
well-being, welsyn, welvaart.
well-bred, welopgevoed; volbloed-...
well-chosen, goed gekies (gekose).
well-conducted, van goeie gedrag; goed bestuur, goed gedirigeer.
well-connected, van goeie familie.
well-disposed, vriendelik gesind.
well-doer, weldoener.
well-done, goed gaar; knap gedaan.
well-founded, gegrond.
well-informed, goed ingelig; belese.
well-intentioned, goed bedoel.
well-knit, vasgebou, sterk, gespierd.
well-looking, aanvallig.
well-mannered, welgemanierd, beleef.
well-meaning, welmenend, opreg.
well-meant, goed bedoel, welgemeen.
well-nigh, amper, byna.
well-off, welgesteld.
well-read, belese.
well-set, vas, stewig, gespierd.
well-spent, goed bestee.
well-spoken, welbespraak.
well-timed, tydig, net betyds.
well-to-do, welgesteld.
well-tried, dikwels, beproef.
well-turned, mooi gevorm; mooi uitgedruk, mooi gesê.
well-wisher, (welwillende) vriend.
well-worn, verslyt, afgesaag.
Welsh, a. Wallies, van Wallis; **– rabbit** (rarebit), gebraaide brood met kaas.
Welsh, n. Wallies; inwoner van Wallis.
welsh, **welch**, laat spat.
Welshman, inwoner van Wallis, Walliser.
welt, rand, strokie (leer), kantstrokie; dikhou, striem.
welter, v. rol, wentel.
welter, n. warboel, verwarring, deurmekaarspul; (die) rol.
welterweight, weltergewig.

wen, geswel, keelgeswel.
wench, meisie, nôi, meisiemens; slet; **a buxom –,** 'n frisgeboude nôi.
wend, gaan; **– one's way to,** jou begewe na, op weg gaan na.
werewolf, werw-, weerwolf.
Wesleyan, a. Wesleyaans.
Wesleyan, n. Wesleyaan.
west, n. die weste.
west, a. weste-..., wes-..., westelik.
west, adv. wes, na die weste(kant); **– of,** wes van; **go –, bokveld toe gaan; that's gone –,** dis klaarpraat.
westerly, westelik, weste-...
Western, a. Westelik; Westers; Wes-.
western, a. westelik, wes-, weste-.
Western, n. Westerling; rolprent van die Wilde Weste.
westward, weswaarts.
wet, a. nat, vogtig; reënagtig; **I am – to the skin,** ek het nie 'n droë draad aan my lyf nie, ek is papnat; **a – blanket,** 'n remskoen, jandooi; **he is a real – blanket,** hy kan nie boe of ba sê nie.
wet, v. bevogtig, natmaak; **– one's whistle,** jou keel natmaak, 'n doppie wegslaan, jou keel smeer; **– the bargain,** op die koop drink.
wet, n. (die) nat, nattigheid, vogtigheid; reënagtigheid; sopie.
wether, hamel.
wet-nurse, n. soogvrou.
wet-nurse, v. soog.
wettish, natterig, klam.
whack, v. moker, geweldig slaan.
whack, n. slag, harde hou; deel, porsie.
whacker, knewel, reus, tamaai grote.
whacking, a. tamaai, reusagtig.
whacking, n. loesing, pak.
whale, n. walvis; **a – of a time,** groot pret.
whale, v. op walvisvangs uitgaan.
whalebone, balein.
whaleman, walvisvanger.
whale-oil, walvistraan.
whaler, walvisvaarder, walvisvanger.
whaling, walvisvangs, walvisvaart.
whang, mokerslag, hou.
wharf, n. kaai.
wharf, v. (vas)meer.
wharfage, kaaigeld.
what, a. watter, wat; **– books have you read?** watter boeke het jy gelees?; **– news?** wat is die nuus?; **– matter?** watter verskil maak dit?; wat kom dit daarop aan?; **– good is it?,** wat help dit?; **– manner of man is he?,** hoe 'n kêrel is hy?; **– a fool you are?,** wat 'n gek is jy tog!; **they will give you – help is possible,** hulle sal jou alle moontlike hulp verleen.
what, pron. wat; hoe; hè; –?, hè?; **– ho!,** hallo, hêi; **– though we are poor?,** watter saak maak dit of ons arm is?; **– next?,** wat nou?; nou praat ek geen woord meer nie!; **well, – of it?,** wel, waarom nie?; wat sou dit?; **– is your name?,** hoe is jou naam?; **I know –,** ek het 'n plan; **he knows –s –,** hy weet hoe sake staan; **come – may,** laat kom wat wil, wat ook al mag gebeur; **gone with –,** arrie, maar dis 'n doring van 'n nôi!; **with drink and – with fright,** he did not know much about the facts, deels van die drink en deels van die skrik, het hy nie eintlik geweet wat werklik gebeur het nie; **– if he asks?,** sê nou hy vra?; **– if we were to try?,** hoe sal dit wees as ons probeer?; **and – not,** ensovoorts, en so meer, en wat nie al nie.
what-d'ye-call-him, what's-his-name, dinges, hoesenaam.

whatever, whate'er, wat ook al, al wat; – **I have is yours,** al wat ek het, is joue; **do – you like,** maak net wat jy wil; – **measures,** watter maatreëls ook al; **no doubt –,** hoegenaamd geen twyfel nie.

whatso, whatsoever, whatsoe'er, sien **whatever.**

wheat, koring; **bearded –,** baardkoring.

wheaten, koring-. . .

wheedle, vlei, flikflooi, mooipraat, mooibroodjies bak, lek, pamperlang; – **a person into doing something,** iemand deur mooipraatjies omhaal om iets te doen.

wheedler, vleier, flikflooier.

wheel, n. wiel, rat; swenking; **–s within –s,** magte agter die skerms; ingewikkelde masjinerie; 'n duistere saak, 'n ingewikkelde plan; **Fortune's –,** die rat van die Fortuin; **break on the –,** radbraak; **everything went on –s,** alles het gerol, alles het so glad soos seep gegaan; **the fifth – of a coach,** die vyfde wiel aan die wa; **the man at the –,** die stuurman, die bestuurder.

wheel, v. (laat) swenk; krink, draai; rol, stoot; fiets; draaie maak, in 'n sirkel voortbeweeg.

wheelbarrow, kruiwa.

wheel-base, asafstand.

wheel-chair, rolstoel.

wheel-horse, agterperd.

wheeze, n. gehyg, gefluit (van keel).

wheezy, kortasem, hygerig.

whelp, n. klein hondjie; welp; ongepoetste lummel, stout kind.

whelp, v. kleintjies kry, jong.

when, adv. and conj. wanneer, toe, as; terwyl; – **it rains he stays at home,** as dit reent, bly hy tuis; **he stopped – he saw me,** hy het gaan staan toe hy my sien; **how could you –, you knew that . . .,** hoe kon jy, terwyl jy geweet het dat . . .?

when, pron.: **till – can you stay?,** tot wanneer kan jy bly?; **from –?,** van wanneer af?, sedert wanneer?

when, n.: **he told me the – and the how of it,** hy het my alle besonderhede vertel.

whence, adv. waarvandaan, van waar; **I take it – it comes,** van 'n esel kan jy 'n skop verwag.

whence, pron. waarvandaan; **from – is he,** waarvandaan kom hy?

whene'er, whenever, whensoever, wanneer ook (al); elke keer as.

where, adv. waar; waarheen, waarnatoe; – **are you going?,** waarheen (waarnatoe) gaan jy?; – **shall we be if prices fall now?,** wat word van ons as die pryse nou daal?

where, pron. waarvandaan, waarheen; – **do you come from? – are you going to?** waarvandaan kom jy? waarheen gaan jy?

whereabout(s), adv. waaromtrent, waar.

whereabouts, n. verblyfplek, houplek, loopplek, boerplek.

whereas, aangesien, nademaal, daar, terwyl.

whereat, waarop.

whereby, waardeur, waarby.

where'er, sien **wherever.**

wherefore, waarom, hoekom; daarom.

wherein, waarin.

whereinto, waarin.

whereof, waarvan.

whereon, waarop.

wheresoever, waar ook al.

whereto, waarnatoe, waartoe; waarom.

whereupon, waarop.

wherever, waar ook (al); oral waar.

wherewith, waarmee.

wherewithal: he has not the – to do it, hy beskik nie oor die middele om dit ten uitvoer te bring nie.

whet, slyp, aansit, skerp maak; prikkel, opwek.

whether, a. pron. watter (een).

whether, conj. of; ditsy (hetsy); – **he is here or not,** of hy nou hier is of nie.

whetstone, slypsteen.

whew, maggies!, allawêreld!, soe!

whey, wei, dikmelkwater.

which, a. watter; – **way shall we go?,** watter kant toe sal ons gaan?

which, pron. watter, wie, wat; – **of you?,** wie van julle?; **how am I to know – is –?,** hoe moet ek hulle uit mekaar uit ken?

whichever, whichsoever, wat ook.

whiff, luggie, geurtjie, trekkie; sigaartjie; skif (bootjie); **a – of fresh air,** bietjie vars lug.

Whig, Whig, Liberaal.

while, n. tydjie, rukkie, wyle; **for a –,** 'n rukkie; **in a little –,** gou, binnekort; **once in a –,** af en toe, so nou en dan; **I have not seen him for a long –,** ek het hom lank nie gesien nie; **it is not worth –,** dit is nie die moeite werd nie.

while, v. (die tyd) verdrywe, omkry.

while, conj. terwyl, onderwyl.

whilst, sien **while,** conj.

whim, gril, nuk, gier, streek; windas.

whimper, v. huil, grens; sanik, met 'n huilstem praat; kreun, kla(e); tjank.

whimper, n. gehuil, gegrens, huilstem, gekreun; getjank.

whimsical, vol nukke (grille), wispelturig, kaprisieus; vreemd, raar.

whimsicality, nukke, grille, wispelturigheid.

whimsy, gier, gril, nuk.

whine, v. huil, tjank; met 'n huilstemmetjie praat, kla(e).

whine, n. gehuil, getjank; gekla(e), gekerm.

whinger, dolk, lang mes.

whinny, v. runnik.

whinny, n. gerunnik.

whip, v. (weg)spring, wip; gryp; piets, raps, met die peits gee, wiks, slaan; (eiers) klop, klits, oorhands naai; vasdraai; – **creation,** alles (almal) oortref, almal kafloop (oes); – **in,** regpiets; – **off one's coat,** jou baadjie uitpluk; – **the horses on,** die perde onder die peits kry (aanstoot); – **out one's knife,** jou mes uitpluk; **you must – it out of him,** jy moet dit uit hom uitklop.

whip, n. sweep, peits, karwats; koetsier; hystoestel, katrol; – **of the party,** die „sweep" van die party.

whip-cord, voorslag(riem).

whiphand, die hand wat die sweep vashou; **have the – of,** in jou mag hê, baas wees oor.

whip-lash, voorslag.

whipper, voerman; slaner.

whipper-snapper, kindjie, seuntjie, mannetjie; ja(a)psnoet, snip, parmant.

whippet, (soort) windhond.

whipping, pak (slae).

whipping-boy, „opdokker", sondebok.

whipping-post, geselpaal, slaanpaal.

whipping-top, sweeptol, draaitol.

whip-round, (haastige) kollekte.

whir(r), v. gons, 'n gedruis maak, snor.

whir(r), n. gegons, gedruis, gesnor.

whirl, v. (in die rondte) draai, vinnig draai, (d)warrel, snor.

whirl, n. vinnige draai, draaiing, (d)warreling, gewarrel; **my thoughts are in a –,** alles draai in my kop.

whirligig, draaitol; mallemeule (mallemole),

whirlpool 740 **wild**

draaimeul; draaikewer; sirkelgang; **the – of time,** die lotswisseling.
whirlpool, maalstroom, draaikolk.
whirlwind, (d)warrelwind; **sow wind and reap –,** wie wind saai sal storm maai.
whisk, n. stoffer, besempie; (eier)klopper.
whisk, v. (af)vee, (af)stof, (af)borsel; klop, klits; swaai, draai; wip.
whisker(s), wangbaard, bakbaard; snor.
whiskered, met 'n snor, gesnor(d).
whisky, whisky.
whisper, v. fluister, suutjies praat; influister, toefluister; ruis, ritsel.
whisper, n. (die) fluister, gefluister, fluistering; geruis, geritsel; **talk in a –,** suutjies praat, fluister.
whispering, n. gefluister.
whispering, a. fluisterend; fluister- . . .
whispering-gallery, fluistergewelf, fluistergalery.
whist, whisht, sjt (sjuut)!
whist, whist (kaartspel).
whistle, v. fluit; verklik; – **for the wind,** die wind fluit; **you may – for it,** jy kan maar daarna fluit.
whistle, n. fluit, gefluit; fluitjie.
whistler, fluiter.
whit, iets, 'n ietsie; **no –, not a –, never a –,** nie die minste nie, nie 'n krieseltjie nie.
Whit, Whitsun, Pinkster- . . .; **Whit Monday,** Pinkstermaandag.
white, a. wit; blank; bleek; rein, vlekloos, onskuldig; – **alloy,** witmetaal; – **bear,** ysbeer; – **civilization,** blanke beskawing; – **heat,** gloeihitte; **a – lie,** 'n noodleuentjie; **a – man,** 'n wit man, 'n blanke; 'n witman, 'n man honderd.
white, v. wit, witmaak.
white, n. wit; **dressed in –,** wit aangetrek; **the – of an egg,** die wit van 'n eier; **the – of the eye,** die wit van die oë.
white-collar: – **worker,** kantoorwerker.
white-handed, met onbesoedelde hande.
white-hot, gloeiend-warm.
white-lipped, met bleek lippe.
white-livered, lafhartig, bangbroekig.
whiten, wit word; witmaak.
whitewash, n. witkalk, witklei, witsel.
whitewash, v. wit, afwit; verontskuldig, van skuld vryspreek, van blaam suiwer, goedpraat.
whither, waarheen, waarnatoe.
whiting, witkalk, kryt.
whitleather, aluinleer.
whitlow, fyt.
Whitsun, sien Whit.
Whitsuntide, Pinkster, Pinksterdae.
whittle, v. sny, afsny; – **away, down,** afsnipper, verminder, inkort, besnoei.
Whitworth: – **thread,** Whitworth-draad.
whity, witagtig.
whiz, whizz, v. gons, fluit, sing, sis.
whiz, whizz, n. gegons, gefluit, gesis.
who, wie; wat; **he knows –'s –,** hy ken al die mense; hy is ouer as twaalf.
whoa, sien wo.
whoever, whosoever, wie ook.
whole, a. heel; onbeskadig, ongedeerd, veilig; gesond; **three – days,** drie volle dae; **the – city,** die hele stad.
whole, n. hele, geheel; alles; **on the –,** oor die algemeen; **I cannot tell you the – of it,** ek kan jou nie alles vertel nie; **nature is a –,** die natuur is 'n eenheid, die natuur is een (geheel).
whole-coloured, eenkleurig.
whole-hearted, hartlik; algeheel.
whole-hoofed, eenhoewig.

whole-length, van die kop tot die voete, tot die voete uit, van die volle lengte.
wholesale, n. groothandel.
wholesale, a. groothandel- . . .; op groot skaal; **a – dealer,** 'n groothandelaar; – **prices,** groothandelpryse; **a – slaughter,** 'n slagting (moord) op groot skaal.
wholesale, adv. op groot skaal.
wholesaler, groothandelaar.
wholesome, gesond, heilsaam.
wholly, heeltemal, geheel en al, geheel, volkome; – **yours,** geheel die uwe.
whom, sien who, wat, vir (aan) wie.
whoop, skreeu, roep, hoe; optrek.
whooping-cough, sien **hooping-cough,** kinkhoes.
whop, afransel, klop; oes, kafloop.
whopper, n. yslike kluitjie; 'n groot leuen; kafferpak; 'n yslike.
whopping, n. afranseling, pak.
whopping, a. yslik, tamaai, 'n knewel van 'n . . .; **a - lie,** 'n yslike kluitjie.
whore, hoer.
whorl, draai (van 'n skulp); blaarkrans.
whortleberry, bloubessie.
whose, van wie, wie se, wie s'n.
whoso, whosoever, sien **whoever.**
why, adv. waarom, hoekom.
why, interj. wel, tog, mos; –, **it's Jones,** maar dit is mos Jones!
wick, pit (van 'n lamp).
wicked, goddeloos, boos, sondig, sleg; ondeund, onnutsig.
wickedness, goddeloosheid, sonde.
wicker, n. biesies, matjiesgoed, riet.
wicker, a. gevleg(te), riet- . . .; – **basket,** gevlegte mandjie, rietmandjie; – **chair,** gevlegte stoel, rietstoel; – **work,** vlegwerk.
wicket, hekkie, deurtjie, poortjie; draaisport; orderdeur; baan (krieket); paaltjies (krieket).
wicket-keeper, paaltjie(s)wagter.
wide, wyd, breed, ruim; ver; uitgestrek; **far and –,** wyd en syd, heinde en ver; – **of,** ver van.
wide-awake, wakker, nugter, uitgeslaap, versigtig, geslepe.
widen, wyer maak (word), breër maak.
wide-spread, verbrei, algemeen.
widow, n. weduwee, weduvrou.
widow, v. tot weduwee (wewenaar) maak.
widower, wewenaar.
widowhood, weduweeskap, -staat.
width, wydte, breedte; breedheid, veelomvattendheid, uitgestrektheid.
wield, uitoefen, beheer, bestuur; swaai; hanteer; – **the sceptre,** die septer swaai.
wife, vrou, eggenote.
wifely, vroulik, huisvroulik.
wifie, vroutjie.
wig, n. pruik.
wigged, met 'n pruik, gepruik.
wigging, skrobbering.
wiggle, v. skommel, wikkel, wiebel; kronkel.
wight, skepsel, mens.
wigwam, hut, pondok.
wild, a. wild; woes, dol, rasend; skrikkerig, bang; roekeloos, onverskillig, losbandig; stormagtig, geweldig; verwilderd; onbebou(d); – **beasts,** ongedierte, wilde diere; – **man,** wilde, barbaar; **a – fellow,** 'n onverskillige kêrel; – **locks,** windverwaaide hare; – **run,** wild groei; wild rondloop; **be – about something,** dol wees op iets, dweep met iets; woedend wees oor iets; – **with excitement,** dol (rasend) van opgewondenheid; **I made a – guess,** ek het sommer blindweg geraai; **drive –,** dol (rasend) maak.
wild, adv. blindweg; los en vas (praat).

wild   741   **wing**

wild, n. wildernis, woesteny.
wild boar, wildevark.
wildcat, n. wildekat.
wildcat, a. onbesonne, halsoorkop-.
wild-duck, wilde-eend.
wildebeest, wildebees.
wilderness, wildernis, woesteny.
wildfire, Griekse vuur; like –, soos 'n lopende vuur.
wild goose, wildegans, berggans; a – chase, 'n dwase onderneming, 'n gek spul.
wile, n. (skelm) streek, lis, geslepenheid.
wile, v. verlok, aanlok.
wilful, moedswillig, opsetlik; eiewys.
wiliness, listigheid, sluheid.
will, v. wil, begeer; wens; vermaak; **it shall be as you –,** jy kan jou sin kry; **would it were otherwise,** was dit tog maar anders!; **would God I had died,** was ek tog maar dood!
will, aux. v. sal; **you – hear soon enough,** jy sal gou genoeg hoor; **I – not be caught again,** ek sal my nie weer laat vang nie; **I would not do it for R10,** ek sou dit vir geen R10 doen nie; **children – be children,** kinders is nou eenmaal kinders; **he would get in my light,** hy wou mos aanhou in my lig staan; **he – sit there for hours,** daar sit hy (dan) ure lank; **this – be Waterloo, I suppose,** dit is nou seker Waterloo.
will, n. wil; wilskrag; wens, begeerte; laaste wil, testament; **against my –,** teen my sin; **of my own free –,** uit eie beweging, uit vrye wil; **with a –,** met hart en siel, met lus; **where there's a – there's a way,** wie wil, die kan; waar 'n wil is, is 'n weg; **Thy – be done,** U wil geskied; **what is your –?,** wat verlang u, wat is u begeerte?; **have one's –,** jou sin kry; **at –,** na wens, net wanneer jy wil; **make one's –,** testament maak.
willing, (ge)willig.
will-o'-the-wisp, dwaallig; blinkwater; glipperige kêrel.
willow, n. wilgerboom (wilg).
willow, v. uitpluis, uitkam, uitslaan.
willow, n. wolf, pluismasjien.
willowy, soos 'n wilgerboom; skraal.
will-power, wilskrag.
willynilly, of hy wil of nie.
wilt, v. kwyn, verwelk, verlep word.
wily, listig, slu, geslepe, slim, oulik.
wimple, sluier, kap.
win, v. wen (win); behaal; verdien; bereik; – **a victory,** 'n oorwinning behaal; – **one's spurs,** jou spore verdien; – **one's way,** vooruit beur; – **the field,** die oorwinning behaal, die slag wen; – **the summit,** die top haal (bereik); – **over,** beweeg, oorhaal, ompraat; – **through all difficulties,** alle moeilikhede oorwin (te bowe kom).
win, n. oorwinning; wenslag.
wince, v. (ineen)krimp. terugdeins; (spiere) trek, gril, huiwer, ys; – **under pain,** ineenkrimp van pyn; **without wincing,** sonder om 'n spier te vertrek.
wince, n. krimping, terugdeinsing; gril, huiwering, trekking.
wincey, wol, katoen.
winch, slinger, wen, windas.
wind, n. wind; lug; ruik; asem; blaasinstrumente; **in the teeth of the –,** reg teen die wind (op); **go like the –,** so vinnig soos die wind gaan; **there is something in the –,** daar is iets aan die gang; **find out how the – blows,** lies, kyk van watter kant die wind waai; **take the – out of one's sails,** iemand die loef afsteek; **it's an ill – that blows nobody any good,** geen kwaad sonder baat; **from the four –s,** uit alle rigtinge; **get – of,** 'n snuf in die neus kry, 'n voëltjie hoor fluit; **be troubled with –s,** las van winde hê; **fling, cast to the –s,** oorboord gooi; **get the – up,** in die knyp raak, bang word; **put the – up,** bang maak, die skrik op die lyf ja; **let me recover my –,** laat ek eers weer asem kry; **second –,** tweede asem.
wind, v. blaas (op 'n trompet, ens.); ruik, die ruik (lug) kry van; asem haal, asem skep; uitasem raak; laat asem skep, laat blaas; **a brief rest to – the horses,** 'n klein bietjie rus om die perde te laat blaas; **quite –ed by the climb,** heeltemal uit-asem van die klim.
wind, v. met draaie loop, slinger, kronkel; draai, rol; – **off,** afdraai, afrol, afwen, los draai; – **a person round one's fingers,** iemand na jou pype laat dans; – **a blanket round him,** hom in 'n kombers toedraai; – **up,** oprol, opdraai; ('n horlosie) opwen; **the administration needs –ing up,** die administrasie moet bietjie onder hande geneem word; **expectations were wound up to a high pitch,** die verwagtinge was hoog gespanne; **he wound up by declaring,** hy het geëindig deur te verklaar, ten slotte het hy verklaar; – **up a company,** 'n maatskappy likwideer.
wind, n. draai, bog.
windage, speelruimte.
windbag, grootprater, windsak.
wind-bound, deur teëwinde opgehou.
wind-break, windskut, windskerm.
wind-chest, blaasbalk, lugkas.
wind-colic, windkramp.
wind-egg, windeier.
windfall, afgewaaide vrugte; geluk, meevallertjie.
wind-gall, swelsel, dik plek.
wind-gauge, windmeter.
winding, n. draai, kronkeling, bog.
winding, a. draai- . . ., kronkelend, kronkel- . . .
winding-sheet, doodskleed.
winding staircase, wenteltrap.
wind-instrument, blaasinstrument.
windlass, n. wen, windas.
windlass, v. opwen, ophys, optrek.
windmill, windpomp, windmeul; **fight –s,** teen windmeule veg.
window, venster, raam.
window-dressing, uitstalling, etalering; windmakery, reklame, oëverblindery.
windowed, met vensters.
window-envelope, vensterkoevert.
window-shopping, winkelkykery.
window-sill, vensterbank.
windpipe, lugpyp.
wind-screen, windskerm; – **wiper,** ruitveër; – **washer,** ruitspuit.
wind-tunnel, windtonnel.
windward, n. loefsy, windkant.
windward, a. na die wind gekeer.
windy, winderig; opgeblaas; windmakerig, grootpraterig, opgeblase.
wine, wyn.
winebag, wynsak; wynsuiper, dronkaard.
winebibber, wynsuiper, drinkebroer.
winebottle, wynfles, wynbottel.
wineglass, wynglas, wynkelkie.
winepress, wynpers, persbalie, trapbalie.
wineskin, wynsak.
wine-stone, wynsteen.
wine-vault, wynkelder.
wing, n. vlerk, vleuel; wiek; modderskerm; vlug; **clip one's –s,** iemand bandvat (kortvat); **take under one's –,** onder jou beskerming neem; **on the –s of the wind,** op die vleuels van die wind; **on the –,** in die vlug; aan die gang;

add, lend –s to, verhaas, bespoedig; **take –,** opvlie, die vlerke uitslaan, begin vlie; **the left – of an army,** die linkervleuel van 'n leër.
wing, v. van vlerke (vleuels) voorsien; bevleuel; vlie; in die vlerk skiet, kwes; aanvuur, aanspoor; **–ed words,** gevleuelde woorde; **the bird –s the air,** die voël deurklief die lug.
wing-beat, vleuelslag.
wing-case, vlerkskild.
winged, gevleuel.
wing-nut, vleuelmoer.
wing-spread, vlerkspanning.
wing-footed, gevleuel(d), snel.
wing-stroke, vleuelslag.
wink, v. oë knip, knipoog; wink; flikker; **– at a person,** vir iemand oë knip; **– at,** maak of jy nie sien nie, deur die vingers sien.
wink, n. knipogie; wink; **I could not ge a – of sleep,** ek het nie 'n oog toegemaak nie.
winking, a. knip- . . ., knippend.
winking, n. oogknip.
winkle, alikruikel.
winner, wenner, oorwinnaar.
winning, a. wen- . . .; innemend, bevallig, vriendelik; **the – side,** die wenkant; **the – hit,** die beslissende slag.
winning, n. (die) wen; –s, wins(te).
winning-post, wenpaal.
winnow, (uit)wan, uitwaai, uitkaf, skoongooi; (uit)sif, skei; waai, klap.
winsome, innemend, bevallig, vriendelik.
winter, n. winter; **– quarters,** winterkwartiere.
winter, v. oorwinter.
winter solstice, wintersonnestilstand.
wintry, winter- . . ., winteragtig, koud.
winy, wynagtig, wyn- . . .
wipe, v. (af)vee, afdroë, skoonvee; **– the face,** die gesig afvee; **– one's eyes,** jou oë afvee, jou trane afdroë; **– away,** afvee; **– out,** uitvee; totaal vernietig; **– out a disgrace,** 'n skande uitwis; **– out a deficit,** 'n agterstand inhaal, 'n tekort goedmaak; **– the floor with,** fyngoed maak van, heeltemal kafloop; **– up,** opvee.
wipe, n. veeg; hou, klap; sakdoek.
wiper, (af)veër; doek.
wire, n. draad; telegraafdraad; telegram; **send a –,** 'n telegram stuur, telegrafeer; **by –,** telegrafies; **pull the –s,** in die geheim invloed uitoefen, agter die skerms werk; **– recorder,** draadopnemer.
wire, v. met draad vasmaak; die drade lê (span, bedraad (elek.)); inrye, aan 'n draad rye; (voëls) in 'n strik vang; telegrafeer, sein; **– in,** opdons, alle kragte inspan.
wire-cutter, draadtang, draadskêr.
wire-dancer, koorddanser.
wire-draw, draadtrek; vit, haarklowe.
wire-edge, draad (van mes, ens.).
wire entanglement, draadversperring.
wire-haired, steekhaar- . . .
wireless, n. radio, draadloos, draadlose telegrafie.
wireless, a. draadloos.
wire-netting, netdraad, sifdraad.
wire-puller, 'draadtrekker; konkelaar, knoeier.
wire-rope, staaldraad.
wiring, (die) insit van die drade; (elektriese) geleiding, draad (drade).
wiry, draadagtig, draad- . . .; taai, gespierd, sterk.
wisdom, wysheid; verstand.
wisdom tooth, verstandskies.
wise, a. verstandig, wys; **he came away none the –r,** hy het daar niks te wete gekom nie; **put –,** op die hoogte bring.

wise, n. manier, wyse; **in no –,** hoegenaamd nie.
wiseacre, alweter, slimprater.
wisecrack, kwinkslag; –s, sêgoed.
wish, v. wens, begeer, verlang; **you could not – it better,** beter kon jy dit nie verlang nie; **– one at the devil,** iemand verwens, iemand na die maan wens; **I – to go,** ek wil graag gaan; **– success,** voorspoed toewens.
wish, n. wens, begeerte, verlange; **good –es,** beste wense; **get your –,** jou sin kry; **if –es were horses, beggars might ride,** met wens kom jy nie ver nie; **the – is father to the thought,** die wens is die vader van die gedagte.
wishful, verlangend.
wishing-bone, borsbeentjie, vurkbeentjie, geluksbeentjie.
wish-wash, flou drinkgoed; gesanik.
wisp, bossie, toutjie, hopie (strooi, ens.).
wistaria, wistaria, bloureën.
wistful, hunkerend; peinsend.
wit, v. weet; **God wot,** God weet; **to –,** naamlik, dit wil sê.
wit, n. vernuf, verstand; geestigheid; **past the – of man,** bo die menslike verstand; **out of one's –s,** nie reg by jou verstand nie; buite jouself; **at one's – 's end,** ten einde raad, raad-op; **he has his –s about him,** hy het al sy positiewe bymekaar, hy weet wat hy doen; **he has quick –s,** hy is vlug van begrip (gevat).
wit, n. geestige persoon.
witch, n. (tower)heks, towernares.
witch, v. toor; betower, bekoor.
witchcraft, toordery (towery), toorkuns (towerkuns).
witch-doctor, toordokter.
witchery, toordery (towery); bekoring.
with, met, saam met; by; van; **it rests – you,** dit hang van jou af, dit lê aan jou; **no pen to write –,** geen pen om mee te skrywe nie; **– that,** daarop, hiermee, **tremble – fear,** bewe van vrees; **he is down – fever,** hy lê aan die koors; **– ease,** maklik; **what do you want – me,** wat wil jy van my hê?
withal, boonop, buitendien.
withdraw, wegtrek, opsy trek; terugtrek, herroep; intrek; wegvat, wegneem; verskuiwe; jou verwyder, opsy gaan, eenkant toe gaan, weggaan.
withdrawal, terugtrek(king), intrekking, verskuiwing, verwydering, herroeping.
withe, withy, lat, loot.
wither, (laat) verwelk, verlep word, verdroog, kwyn, agteruitgaan, vergaan; **– one with a look,** iemand middeldeur kyk.
withered, verwelk, verlep, verdor, verdroog; uitgeteer.
withers, skof (van 'n perd).
withhold, weerhou, terughou, weier.
within, adv. binne; van binne; **go –,** binnegaan; **clean – and without,** skoon van binne en (van) buite; **stay –,** in die huis bly, binne bly; **is Mr A. –?,** is mnr. A. tuis?
within, n. binnekant.
within, prep. binne, in; **– doors,** binnenshuis; **safe – the walls,** veilig binnekant die mure; **– bounds,** binne die perke; **a task well – his powers,** 'n taak waartoe hy wel in staat is; **– true – limits,** tot op sekere hoogte waar; **he was – an ace of being drowned,** hy het so bynabyna verdrink; **– a year of his death,** binne 'n jaar na sy dood.
without, adv. buitekant, (van) buite.
without, n. buitekant, buite; **seen from –,** van die buitekant gesien.

without 743 **word**

without, prep, buite, buitekant, sonder; – **a hat**, sonder hoed; **do – something**, sonder iets klaarkom; – **doubt**, ongetwyfeld, sonder enige twyfel; **that goes – saying**, dit spreek vanself.
withstand, weerstaan.
witness, n. getuie, getuienis; **bear – to, of**, getuig van; **call to –**, tot getuie roep.
witness, v. getuig, getuienis aflê; aanskou, sien; as getuie onderteken; – **my poverty**, getuie my armoede.
witness-box, getuiebank.
witticism, geestigheid, kwinkslag.
wittingly, met voorbedagte rade, opsetlik, bewus.
witty, geestig.
wizard, towenaar, waarsêer; a. wonderlik.
wizened, wizen, weazen, verrimpel, uitgedroog, verskrompel.
wo, whoa, hook! hokaai!
wobble, v. slinger, waggel, strompel, aarsel, weifel, onseker wees.
wobble, n. waggelende gang, geslinger; onsekerheid, onvastheid.
woe, wee, nood, ellende, smart; **weal and –**, wel en wee, voor- en teenspoed; – **is me**, wee my; – **be to you**, wee jou (u); –**s**, moeilikhede, ellende(s), rampe, teleurstellinge.
woebegone, treurig, armsalig.
woeful, treurig, droewig.
wold, bosveld, vlakte.
wolf, wolf; vraat, gulsigaard; wanklank, wolf; **cry – too often**, so dikwels vals alarm maak dat niemand jou later glo nie; **keep the – from the door**, sorg dat daar genoeg is om van te lewe, die honger op 'n afstand hou; **a – in sheep's clothing**, 'n wolf in skaapsklere.
wolf-dog, skaaphond, wolfshond.
wolf-hound, wolfshond.
wolfish, wolfagtig, wolf- . . .; gulsig.
wolfram, wolfram.
wolfskin, wolfsvel.
wolf-spider, jagspinnekop.
wolverene, -ine, veelvraat (soort dier).
woman, n. vrou; **there is a – in it**, daar sit 'n vrou agter; **a –'s wit**, vroulike instink; **he is tied to the –'s apron-strings**, hy kan niks doen sonder die vrou nie.
woman, a. vroue- . . .; – **suffrage**, vrouestemreg.
woman-hater, vrouehater.
womanhood, vroulikheid, vroulike staat.
womanish, vrouagtig, verwyf.
womanize, verwyf maak.
womankind, die vroulike geslag, die vrouens, die vroumense.
womanlike, vroulik, soos 'n vrou.
womanly, vroulik.
womb, baarmoeder.
wonder, n. wonder; wonderwerk; verwondering, verbasing; **work –s**, wondere doen; 'n verbasend goeie uitwerking hê; **the child is a –**, dit is 'n wonderkind; **it is no – that**, dit is geen wonder dat; **you are punctual for a –**, jy is waarlik waar op tyd; **we looked at him in silent –**, vol stomme verbasing het ons hom aangestaar.
wonder, v. verwonder, wonder; graag wil weet, nuuskierig wees; verbaas wees; **can you – at it**, kan jy jou daaroor verwonder?, is dit 'n wonder?
wonderful, wonderlik, wonderbaar; merkwaardig, verbasend.
wonderland, wonderland, towerland.
wonderment, verwondering, verbasing.
wonder-struck, wonder-stricken, verbaas, stom van verbasing.
wonder-worker, wonderdoener.

wondrous, wonderlik.
wonky, dronkerig; bewerig.
wont, a. gewoond (gewend); **he was – to stay**, dit was sy gewoonte om te bly.
wont, n. gewoonte, gebruik; **according to his –**, volgens gewoonte.
wonted, gewoon.
woo, die hof maak, vry na; probeer omhaal (ompraat); flikflooi.
wood, bos, woud; hout; **the –s**, die bos(se); **he cannot see the – for the trees**, weens die bome kan hy die bos nie sien nie; **out of the –**, uit die moeilikheid (verleentheid) uit.
woodbine, woodbind, (wilde) kanferfoelie.
woodcock, houtsnip.
woodcut, houtsnee.
woodcutter, houtkapper, houthakker; houtgraveur.
woodcutting, houtsnykuns; houtkappery.
wooded, bosryk, bosagtig.
wooden, (hout) . . ., van hout; dom, bot, suf, wesenloos; styf, lomp, houterig.
wood-engraver, houtgraveur.
wood-engraving, houtgravure; houtgraveerkuns.
wood-fibre, houtvesel(s).
woodland, boswêreld, bosland.
wood-louse, houtluis.
woodman, boswagter.
wood-nymph, bosnimf.
woodpecker, houtkapper, speg.
wood-pigeon, bosduif.
woodsman, bosbewoner.
wood-sorrel, bossuring.
wood-wool, houtwol, skaafsels.
woodwork, houtwerk.
woody, bosagtig, bosryk; houtagtig.
wooer, vryer.
woof, weefsel, inslag.
wool, wol; wolklere; wolhare; **much cry and little –**, veel geskreeu en weinig wol; **go for – and come home shorn**, met die kous op die kop terugkom.
wool-carding, -combing, (die) uitkam van wol, wolkaardery.
wool-dyed, in die wol geverf.
wool-gathering, n. afgetrokkenheid; **go –**, sit en droom, verstrooid wees.
wool-grower, wolboer, skaapboer.
woollen, a. wol- . . ., van wol.
woollen, n. wolstof, wolgoed.
woollen-draper, verkoper van wolgoed.
woolliness, wollerigheid.
woolly, wol) . . ., wolhaar- . . .; vaag; onduidelik (van stem); **the – flock**, die woltrop.
wool-pack, wolbaal.
woolsey, wolkatoen.
word, n. woord; berig, boodskap; wagwoord; bevel; **in a, one –**, kortom, om kort te gaan; **that is hot the – for it**, dit is nie die juiste woord daarvoor nie; dit is nog nie sterk genoeg uitgedruk nie; – **for –**, woord vir woord; **by – of mouth**, mondeling; **take one at his –**, iemand op sy woord glo; iemand aan sy woord hou; **you may take my – for it**, ek gee jou my woord (van eer), daarop kan jy reken; **big –s**, grootpraat, bluf; **fine –s butter no parsnips**, break no bones, are but wind, praat en doen is twee; **have –s with**, woorde hê met, rusie kry met; **may I have a – with you?** mag ek jou bietjie spreek? **suit the action to the –**, die daad by die woord voeg; **you waste –s**, jy praat net verniet; **have the last –**, die laaste woord hê; **say a good – for**, vir iemand 'n goeie woordjie doen; **eat one's –s**, jou woorde terugtrek; – **of command**, bevel; **a – to the wise**, 'n goeie begryper

het 'n halwe woord nodig; **send –**, berig (tyding) stuur, laat weet; **give, pledge one's –**, jou woord gee; **keep one's –**, jou woord hou; **break one's –**, jou woord nie hou nie; **upon my –**, op my woord (van eer); **a man of his –**, 'n man van sy woord; **he is as good as his –**, hy is 'n man van sy woord; **his – is as good as his bond**, jy kan op hom staatmaak; **give the – to**, die bevel gee.
word, v. onder woorde bring; uitdruk, stel, formuleer.
word-building, woordvorming.
wording, bewoording.
word-painter, woordkunstenaar.
word-perfect, rolvas.
word-play, woordspeling.
word-splitting, haarklowery.
wordy, woorde . . .; omslagtig, langdradig, woordryk.
work, n. werk, arbeid; **set to –**, aan die werk gaan (tyg); aan die gang sit; **have one's – cut out for one**, jou hande vol hê; **a – of art**, 'n kunswerk; **make short – of**, gou speel met; **many hands make light –**, vele hande maak ligte werk, vele honde is 'n haas se dood; **out of –**, werkloos, sonder werk; **the –s of a watch**, die (rat)werk van 'n horlosie; **the –s**, die fabriek; verskansing, vesting.
work, v. werk, arbei; (laat) bewerk; uitwerking hê; laat werk; beheer, (be)stuur; hanteer; teweegbring, veroorsaak; gis, rys (suurdeeg, ens.); oplos, uitwerk, bereken, uitreken; deurwerk, knie, brei; **– a typewriter**, met 'n skryfmasjien werk; **–ed by electricity**, deur elektrisiteit gedrywe; **– mischief**, kwaad veroorsaak; **– a change**, 'n verandering teweegbring; **– wonders**, wonder(werk)e verrig; 'n wonderlike uitwerking hê; **the yeast began to –**, die suurdeeg het begin rys (werk); **– a pattern**, 'n patroon uitwerk; **– one's passage**, jou passasie verdien; **– against**, teëwerk, **he is –ing at it**, hy is besig daarmee, hy werk daaraan; **stockings – down**, kouse sak af; **– for a cause**, vir 'n saak werk; **– in**, te pas bring; **he –ed himself into a rage**, hy het hom boos gemaak; **he –ed his audience into enthusiasm**, hy het sy gehoor tot geesdrif opgewek; **– off**, ontslae raak van, kwytraak; van die hand sit; **he –ed off all his old jokes on us**, al sy afgesaagde grappe het hy by ons kom verkoop; **one can't – off a toothache**, tandpyn kan nie oor van werk nie; **– on**, aanhou werk, deurwerk; **– out**, uitwerk; bereken; uitkom; uitput; bewerkstellig, bewerk; **it –s out at 7 rand**, dit kom uit op (te staan op) 7 rand; **the mine is quite –ed out**, die myn is heeltemal uitgeput of uitgewerk; **– together**, meewerk, saamwerk; **– up**, vooruithelp, opwerk; aanhits, aanspoor; opgewonde maak; deurwerk, knie; bywerk; **he –ed up his class**, hy het sy klas opgewerk, onder sy leiding het die klas fluks gevorder; **he –ed up the history of trade unions**, hy het hom in die geskiedenis van vakverenigings ingewerk; **– up a sketch**, 'n skets uitwerk (opwerk); **in a highly wrought-up state**, hoogs gespanne; **– upon**, invloed (uitwerking) hê op.
workability, bewerkbaarheid; uitvoerbaarheid.
workable, bewerkbaar; uitvoerbaar.
workaday, gewoon, alledaags, saai.
work-bag, werksak(kie).
work-box, werkkissie, naaikissie.
workday, werkdag.
worker, werker, arbeider; werkby.
workhouse, armhuis, armegestig.
working, a. werkend, arbeidend, werk- . . .; **a –**

knowledge of the language, 'n gangbare kennis van die taal; **– capital**, bedryfskapitaal; **– expenses**, bedryfskoste; **– man**, werksman, arbeider; **– classes**, arbeiders klasse.
working, n. (die) werk; werking; bedryf; ontginning; myn; steengroef; **the – of his face**, die vertrekking van sy gesig.
working-class, werkende klas, arbeidersklas.
working-day, werkdag.
workless, werkloos, sonder werk.
workman, werksman.
workmanlike, handig, deeglik, knap, saaklik.
workmanship, handigheid, knapheid; afwerking, uitvoering; maaksel; werk.
work-out, oefening; toets.
workshop, werkwinkel, werkplek.
world, wêreld; **the other, next –, the – to come**, die hiernamaals; **bring a child into the –**, 'n kind in die wêreld bring; **she is all the – to me**, sy is vir my alles; **a man of the –**, 'n man van die wêreld; **let the – slide**, sake (maar) hulle gang laat gaan; **all the – and his wife**, almal, iedereen; **what will the – say about it?**, wat sal die mense daarvan sê?; **he lives out of the –**, hy lewe soos 'n kluisenaar; **the – of sport**, die sportwêreld, die gebied van sport; **the – of dreams**, die droomwêreld; **who in the – was it? wie op aarde was dit?**
world language, wêreldtaal.
worldling, wêreldling.
worldly, wêrelds, aards; wêreldsgesind.
worldly-minded, wêreldsgesind.
world-weary, lewensmoeg.
world-wide, alom bekend, wêreld- . . ., **– reputation**, wêreldberoemdheid.
worm, n. wurm; skroefdraad; koeëltrekker; slang (van 'n brandewynketel); **the – of conscience**, gewetensknaging; gewetenswroeging; **I am a – to-day**, ek is vandag nie 'n pyp tabak werd nie; **a – will turn**, selfs 'n lam skop, selfs Job se geduld raak op.
worm, v. kruip; kronkel; van wurms suiwer, wurms uitroei; **– on one's way**, kruip-kruip vooruitkom, inkruip, deurkruip; **he –ed himself into the favour of**, hy het hom ingedring in die guns van; **try to – a secret out**, 'n geheim probeer ontlok.
worm-cast, wurmhopie.
worm-eaten, wurmstekig, deur wurms gevreet; muf, verouderd.
worm-hole, wurmgat.
worm-holed, vol wurmgate, wurmstekig, vermolm, vergaan.
worm-wheel, wurmwiel.
wormwood, (wilde)als; alsem.
wormy, wurmagtig; vol wurms.
worn, moeg, vermoeid; verslete (verslyt), afgeslyt; oud, afgesaag; sien **wear**.
worriment, las; kwelling.
worry, v. lastig val, nie met rus laat nie, peuter, lol, terg, pla(e); knies, kwel; karnuffel, byt, hap; **don't – yourself**, ontstel jou nie; moenie onnodige moeite doen nie; **he is much worried**, hy is baie bekommerd, hy kwel hom baie; hy word baie lastig geval; **he wears a worried look**, dit lyk of iets hom kwel.
worry, n. moeite, las; gelol, plaery; kwelling, besorgdheid, kommer, sorg.
worse, a. erger, slegter; **he is none the – for it**, dit het hom geen kwaad gedoen nie; **he is the – for drink**, hy het te veel gedrink; **be the – for wear**, verslete (verslyt, oud) wees.
worse, n. erger (slegter) dinge, iets ergers; **but – followed**, maar die ergste moes nog kom; **have the –**, die neerlaag ly, die slegste van af-

wor...
worthy, a. waardig, werd; agtenswaardig of such an occasion, woorde wat by s leentheid pas; **a – man**, 'n agtenswaard
worthy, n. waardige persoon, man van a
would, sien **will**, v.
would-be, kastig (kamtig), sogenaam rant- . . ., toekomstig, aanstaande.
wound, n. wond, seerplek.
wound, v. wond, kwes; seermaak, grief, oorsaak.
wounded, a. gewond, gekwes.
wounded, n. (die) gewonde(s).
wound-wort, wondkruid.
wove(n), sien **weave**.
wrack, seegras.
wraith, gees, skim.
wrangle, v. twis, kyf, rusie maak.
wrangle, n. (ge)twis, gekyf, rusie(maker
wrangler, rusiemaker.
wrap, v. toemaak, toedraai; inpak; h **paper**, in papier toedraai; **–ped in mis** die mis; **–ped in darkness**, in duistern **– round**, toemaak, toedraai; **the moth up in her child**, die moeder gaan heel in haar kind, die moeder lewe net kind; **be –ped up in a subject**, heeltema in 'n vak; **mind you – up well**, sorg goed toemaak.
wrap, n. mantel, tjalie, halsdoek, serp; r omhulsel.
wrapper, omslag; buiteblaar, dekblad sigaar); japon; reisdeken.
wrapping, omslag; omhulsel; (die) toed
wrath, toorn, gramskap.
wrathful, toornig.
wreak, wreek, wraak uitoefen op, wra op; **– one's rage upon**, jou woede koel
wreath, krans; kring, ring.
wreathe, omkrans, bekrans; ('n kra draai; kronkel; omstrengel; **his face smiles**, sy gesig was een glimlag.

mag beswyk (wyk); – **to a request,** 'n versoek toestaan.
yield, n. opbrings; oes; produksie.
yielding, toegewend, meegaande; produktief.
yodel, jodel.
yog(h)urt, jogurt.
yoke, n. juk; skouerstuk; (huweliks)band; **submit to the – of,** onder die gesag (juk) buig van.
yoke, v. die juk oplê; (osse) inspan.
yoke-bone, jukbeen.
yoke-fellow, yoke-mate, maat; eggenoot.
yokel, takhaar, plaasjapie, lummel.
yoke-pin, jukskei.
yolk, geel van 'n eier, eiergeel, door (dooier).
yon, daardie.
yonder, a. daardie, ginds, gunters.
yonder, adv. daar(so), (daar)gunter.
yore, die ou-tyd, vanmelewe; **of –,** vanmelewe, vroeër dae.
yorker, duikbal (in krieket).
Yorkshire: – **pudding,** deegtoespys.
you, jy, jou, julle, u; – **fool,** jou gek; **get** – **gone,** maak dat jy wegkom; **what are** – **to do with him?** wat moet ('n) mens met hom aanvang?

young, a. jong; klein; onervare; **her** – **man,** haar kêrel; **the evening is** – **yet,** die aand het nog maar pas begin; **you** – **rascal,** jou klein skelm!
young, n. kleintjie(s); **with –,** dragtig.
youngish, (nog maar) jonk, jongerig.
youngling, jong kind; jong dier.
youngster, kind, seun, snuiter.
your, jou; u.
yours, joue; van u; **you and –,** jy en jou mense (huisgesin), jy en al wat jy het; – **of the 11th,** u brief (skrywe) van die 11de; **no child of –,** nie jou kind nie; – **truly,** hoogagtend, (geheel) die uwe.
yourself, jouself, self; uself; **you said so –,** jy het dit self gesê; **why are you sitting by –?** waarom sit jy so op jou eentjie (alleen)? **do it by –,** dit alleen (sonder hulp) doen; **how's –?** hoe gaan dit nog met jou?; **you are not quite –,** jy is nie op jou stukke nie; **have you hurt –?,** het jy jou seer gemaak?
youth, jeug, jonkheid; jongman; jong mense jong geslag, jongspan.
youthful, jeugdig.
Yule, Kersfees, Kerstyd.

Z

zareba, (om)heining, verskansing.
zeal, ywer, erns, vuur, geesdrif.
zealot, yweraar, dweper; geesdrywer.
zealotry, dweepsug, fanatisme.
zealous, vurig, geesdriftig, ywerig.
zebra, sebra, kwagga, streepesel; – **crossing,** sebra-oorgang.
zenith, senit, toppunt, hoogste punt.
zephyr, sefier, windjie, luggie.
zeppelin, zeppelin, lugskip.
zero, v. op nul bring; op skoot bring, instel (geweer).
zero, nul; nulpunt; vriespunt; zero; – **hour,** aanvalsuur.
zest, graagte, gretigheid, lus; smaak, geur; **do something with –,** iets met lus aanpak; **add a – to,** interessant (boeiend) maak, die genot verhoog van.
zigzag, a. sigsag, sigsagswys, kronkelend.
zigzag, n. sigsagpad, ens., kronkelpad.
zigzag, adv. sigsagsgewys, draai-draai.
zigzag, v. draai-draai loop, kronkel.

zinc, n. sink.
zip, fluit, gons.
zip-fastener, zipper, ritssluiting.
Zion, Sion.
Zionism, Sionisme.
Zionist, Sionis.
zither, (n), siter.
zodiac, diereriem, sodiak.
zodiacal, van die diereriem, sodiakaal.
zone, sone, (aard)gordel, lugstreek; streek.
zoo, dieretuin.
zoological, dierkundig, soologies; – **garden,** dieretuin.
zoologist, dierkundige, sooloog.
zoology, dierkunde, soologie.
zoom, v. zoem.
zoom, n. zoemvlug.
zoophyte, plantdier, soofiet.
Zulu, Zoeloe.
zygoma, jukbeen.
zymosis, gisting; aansteeklike siekte.
zymotic, gistings- . . .; aansteeklik.

Some Common Abbreviations

AA Automobile Association.
a(dj). adjective.
abl. ablative.
a/c account
acc. accusative.
A.D. Anno Domini.
A.D.C. aide-de-camp.
ad. lib. ad libitum (to the extent desired).
adv. adverb.
Adv. Advocate.
Afr. Afrikaans.
alg. algebra.
a.m. ante meridiem (before noon).
Amer. America(n).
anon. anonymous.
appro. approval.
Apr. April.
arr. arrives.
A.S. Anglo-Saxon.
Assoc. Association.
Aug. August.

b. born; bowled.
B.A. Bachelor of Arts.
Bart Baronet.
BBC British Broadcasting Company.
B.C. before Christ.
B.C.L. Bachelor of Civil Law.
B. Comm. Bachelor of Commerce.
B.D. Bachelor of Divinity.
B.E.A. British East Africa.
b.h.p. brake horse-power.
Bros. Brothers.
B.Sc. Bachelor of Science.

C celsius.
°C degree celsius.
c cent.
C.A. Chartered Accountant.
Cantab. Cantabrigian.
cap. capital; caput (chapter).
Capt. Captain.
cf. confer (compare).
cg centigram.
Chron. Chronicles.
C.I.D. Criminal Investigation Department.
c.i.f. cost, insurance and freight.
circ. circa, circiter.
cl centilitre.
cm centimetre.
cm² square centimetre.
cm³ cubic centimetre.
Co. Company.
C.O. Commanding Officer.
c/o care of.
C.O.D. cash on delivery.
Col. Colonel.
col. column.
colloq. colloquial.
comp. comparative.
conj. conjugation.
co-op. co-operative.
Cor. Corinthians.
c.p. candle power.
Cpl Corporal.
Cr. creditor.
cresc. crescendo.
cub. cubic.
cumec cubic metre per second.
c. & b. caught and bowled.

d. died.
Dan. Daniel.
dat. dative.
D.C. da capo (from the beginning).

D.C.L. Doctor of Civil Law.
D.D. Doctor of Divinity.
Dec. December.
deg. degree.
dep. depart; deputy.
Dept Department.
der. derivation.
Deut. Deuteronomy.
dg decigram.
dim. diminuendo; diminutive.
dis. discount.
div. dividend.
dl decilitre.
D.Lit(t). Doctor of Literature.
dm decimetre.
do ditto.
doz. dozen.
D.Phil. Doctor of Philosophy.
Dr debtor; doctor.
dr. drachma.
D.Sc. Doctor of Science.
Du. Dutch.

E East
Ed. Editor(ial).
E. long. East longitude.
E. & O.E. errors and omissions excepted.
Eph. Ephesians.
esp. especially.
Esq. Esquire.
Esth. Esther.
etc. et cetera.
et seq(q). et sequentia (and what follows).
ex. example.
exam. examination.
Exod. Exodus.
Ezek. Ezekiel.

F Fahrenheit.
f. feminine; franc(s); from.
Feb. February.
fig. figure; figurative(ly).
fl. florin(s); Dutch guilder(s).
f.o.b. free on board.
fol. folio.
f.o.r. free on rail.
Fr. French.
fr. franc(s).
F.R.C.S. Fellow of the Royal College of Surgeons.
Frl. Fraulein (Miss).
fut. future.

g. guinea.
g gram(s).
GCM greatest common measure.
G.C.M.G. Grand Cross of St. Michael and St. George.
Gen. General; Genesis.
geog. geography.
geol. geology.
geom. geometry.
G.P. general practitioner.
GPO General Post Office.
gr. grain(s); grammar.
gym. gymnasium; gymnastic costume.

h hour(s).
ha hectare(s).
Hab. Habakuk.
HCF highest common factor.
H.E. His Excellency.

Heb. Hebrew(s).
hg hectogram.
hl hectolitre.
hm hectometre.
H.M. His, Her Majesty.
HMS His, Her Majesty's Ship.
Hon. Sec. Honorary Secretary.
h.p. horse-power.

ib(id). ibidem (in the same place).
I.D.B. Illicit Diamond Buying.
id. idem (the same).
i.e. id est (that is).
incog. incognito.
inf. infra.
inst. instant.
Is. Island (Isle).
Isa. Isaiah.
ital. italics.

Jan. January.
Jer. Jeremiah.
Josh. Joshua.
J.P. Justice of the Peace.
Jr Junior.
Judg. Judges.
jun. junior.

K.C. King's Counsel.
K.C.B. Knight Commander of the Bath.
K.C.M.G. Knight Commander of St. Michael and St. George.
kg kilogram.
kl kilolitre.
km kilometre.
km/h kilometres per hour.
Kt Knight.

l. left; lira (lire).
Lam. Lamentations.
lat. latitude.
l.b.w. leg before wicket.
LCM lowest common multiple.
L.D.S. Licentiate in Dental Surgery.
Lev. Leviticus.
Lieut. Lieutenant.
Litt. D. Litterarum Doctor (Doctor of Letters).
LL.B. Legum Baccalaureus (Bachelor of Laws).
LL.D. Legum Doctor (Doctor of Laws).
loc. cit. loco citato (in the place quoted).
log logarithm; logic(ally).
long. longitude.
Lt Lieutenant.
Ltd Limited.

M. Monsieur.
m. masculine.
m metre(s).
M.A. Master of Arts.
Maj. Major.
Mal. Malachi.
Mar. March.
matric. matriculation.
Matt. Matthew.
M.Com. Master of Commerce.
M.D. Medicinae Doctor (Doctor of Medicine).
MEC Member of Executive Committee.
mem. memento (remember).
memo. memorandum.
Messrs Messieurs.
mg milligram.
Mic. Micah.
min minute(s).
ml millilitre.

Ml megalitre.
M.L.A. Member of Legislative Assembly.
M.L.C. Member of Legislative Council.
Mlle Mademoiselle.
mm millimetre(s).
M.O. Medical Officer of Health.
MP Member of Parliament.
MPC Member of Provincial Council.
Mr Mister.
Mrs Mistress.
m/s metre per second.
MS manuscript.
MSS manuscripts.
Mt Mount.

N North.
n. neuter; nominative; noon; noun.
N.B. nota bene (note well).
n.b. no ball.
N.C.O. non-commissioned officer.
n.d. no date.
(NE) North-East.
Neh. Nehemiah.
nem. con. nemine contradicente (no one objecting).
N. lat. north latitude.
No numero (number).
Nov. November.
N.T. New Testament.
Num. Numbers.
(NW) north-west.

ob. obiit (died).
Obad. Obadiah.
Oct. October.
oct. octavo.
OFS Orange Free State.
OHMS On His, Her Majesty's Service.
O.K. all correct.
op. opus (work).
op. cit. opere citato (cited works).
O.T. Old Testament.

p. page.
par. paragraph.
PAYE pay as you earn.
P.C. Privy Councillor.
p.c. per cent.
pd paid.
per pro. per procurationem (by proxy).
Pet. Peter.
Ph.D. Philosophiae Doctor (Doctor of Philosophy.)
Phil. Philippians.
pl. plate; plural.
p.m. post meridiem (after noon).
PMG Postmaster-General.
P.O. Post Office.
pop. population.
p.p. past (passive) participle; per pro.
Pref. Preface.
pref. preference; prefix.
prep. preparation; preposition.
Pres. President.
Prof. Professor.
pron. pronoun.
pro tem. pro tempore (for the time).
Prov. Proverbs.
prox. proximo (next month).
PS postscript.
Ps. Psalm(s).
pt. part; pint; port.
PTO please turn over.
PWD Public Works Department.

Q.E.D. quod erat demonstrandum (which was to be proved).
Q.E.F. quod erat faciendum (which was to be done).
q.t. quiet.
quot. quotation.
q.v. quod vide (which see).

R. River.
RAC Royal Automobile Club.
RAF Royal Air Force.
R.C. Roman Catholic.
Rd Road.
recd. received.
Ref. Reformed.
regt. regiment.
Rev. Reverend.
R.I.P. requiescat in pace (rest in peace).
R.M. Resident Magistrate.
R.M.S. royal mail steamer.
Rom. Romans.
rom. Roman (type).
R.S.V.P. répondez s'il vous plaît (please reply).
Rt Hon. Right Honourable.
Rt Rev. Right Reverend.

S. Saint; Signor; South.
s. singular; son.
s second(s) (time).
SA South Africa(n).
Sam. Samuel.
SAR South African Railways.
SE south-east.
Sec. Secretary.
sec. second.
sen. senior.
Sept. September.
Sergt (Sgt) Sergeant.
SI Système International de 'Unités.
S. lat. South latitude.
Soc. Society.
sov. sovereign.
sq. square.
Sr Senior.
SSE south-south-east.

SSW south-south-west.
St Saint; Street.
st. stumped.
stg. sterling.
sup. supra; superlative.
suppl. supplement.
supt. superintendent.
s.v. sub voce (under that word).
SW South-West.

TB tuberculosis.
Thess. Thessalonians.
Tim. Timothy.
Tit. Titus.
T.O. Turn Over.
Toc H. Talbot House.
Treas. Treasurer.

UN United Nations.
UNO United Nations Organization.
US(A) United States (of America).
USSR Union of Socialist Soviet Republics.

v. versus; vide (see).
V volt.
Ven. Venerable.
verb. sap. verbum sapienti (a word to the wise).
v.f. very fair.
v.g. very good.
viz videlicet (namely).
vol. volume.
v.v. verses.

W west, watt.
w. wide; with; wicket.
w.c. water closet.
W. long. West longitude.
W/L. wave length.
WSW west-south-west.

Xmas Christmas.

YMCA Young Men's Christian Association.
YWCA Young Women's Christian Association

Zech. Zechariach.
Zeph. Zephaniah.

Geographical Names

Aachen, Aix-la-Chapelle, Aken.
Abyssinia, Abessinië.
Acadia, Akadië.
Adriatic: the –, die Adriatiese See.
Aegean Sea, Egeïese See.
Afghanistan, Afganistan.
Africa, Afrika.
Albania, Albanië.
Alexandria, Alexandrië.
Algeria, Algerië, Algerye.
Algiers, Algiers.
Aliwal North, Aliwal-Noord.
Alps, Alpe.
Alsace, die Elsas.
Alsace-Lorraine, Elsas-Lotharinge.
Amazon, Amasone.
America, Amerika.
Andalusia, Andalusië.
Andes, Andes.
Antarctic Ocean, Suidpoolsee, Suidelike Yssee.
Antilles, Antille; **Lesser** –, Klein Antille.
Antioch, Antiochië.

Antwerp, Antwerpen.
Apennines, Apennyne.
Appalachians, Appalache.
Arabia, Arabië.
Arcadia, Arkadië.
Arctic Ocean, Noordpoolsee, Noordelike Yssee.
Ardennes, Ardenne.
Argentina, the Argentine, Argentinië.
Armenia, Armenië.
Arras, Atrecht.
Asia, Asië.
Asia Minor, Klein-Asië.
Assyria, Assirië.
Athens, Athene.
Atlantic Ocean, Atlantiese Oseaan.
Australia, Australië.
Austria, Oostenryk.
Austria-Hungary, Oostenryk-Hongarye.
Azores, Asore.

Babel, Babylon, Babel, Babilon.
Babylonia, Babilonië.

Baden, Baden.
Bahamas, Bahama-eilande.
Bale, vide **Basel.**
Balearic Islands, Baleare, Baleariese Eilande.
Balkans: the –, die Balkan.
Baltic Sea, Oossee.
Baluchistan, Beloetsjistan.
Basel, Basle, Bâle, Basel.
Basutoland, Basoetoland.
Bavaria, Beiere.
Beaufort West, Beaufort-Wes.
Bechuanaland, Betsjoeanaland.
Belgian Congo: the –, die Belgiese Kongo.
Belgium, België.
Belgrade, Belgrado.
Bengal, Bengale.
Bergen, Bergen (in Holland en in Noorweë).
Berlin, Berlyn.
Bermudas, Bermuda-eilande.
Bethlehem, Bethlehem (in die O V S. en die V S A), Betlehem (in Palestina).
Biscay: Bay of –, Golf van Biskaje.
Black Forest, Swart Woud.
Black Sea, Swart See.
Blue Nile, Blou Nyl.
Boeotia, Beosië.
Bohemia, Boheme.
Bosnia, Bosnië.
Bosp(h)orus: the –, die Bosporus.
Bothnia, Botnië.
Bothnia: Gulf of –, Botniese Golf.
Brazil, Brasilië.
Britain, Brittanje.
Britannia, Britannië.
Brittany, Bretagne.
Bruges, Brugge.
Brunswick, Brunswyk.
Brussels, Brussel.
Bucharest, Boekarest.
Budapest, Boedapest.
Bulgaria, Bulgarye.
Burgundy, Boergondië.
Burma, Birma.
Byzantium, Bisantium.

Cairo, Kaïro.
Calabria, Kalabrië.
California, Kalifornië.
Cambrai, Kameryk.
Cameroons: the –, Kameroen.
Camperdown, Kamperduin.
Canaan, Kanaän.
Canada, Kanada.
Canary Islands, Kanariese Eilande.
Canterbury, Kantelberg.
Cape of Good Hope, Kaap die Goeie Hoop (de Goede Hoop).
Cape Province, Kaapprovinsie, Kaapland.
Cape Town, Kaapstad.
Cape Verde Islands, Kaap-Verdiese Eilande.
Caribbean Sea, Karibiese See.
Caribbees, Karibiese Eilande.
Carinthia, Karintië.
Carpathians, Karpate.
Carrara, Carrara.
Carthage, Carthago.
Caspian Sea, Kaspiese See.
Castile, Kastilië.
Catalonia, Katalonië.
Caucasus, Kaukasus.
Celebes, Celebes.
Ceylon, Ceylon.
Charybdis, Charybdis.
Chile, Chili.
China, China, Sjina.

Cilicia, Cilicië.
Circassia, Cirkassië.
Cleves, Kleef.
Coblenz, Koblentz.
Cochin-China, Cochin-China.
Cologne, Keulen.
Colorado, Colorado.
Congo, Kongo.
Constance, Konstanz.
Constantia, Constantia.
Constantinople, Konstantinopel.
Copenhagen, Kopenhagen.
Cordova, Cordova.
Corinth, Korinthe.
Cornwall, Cornwallis.
Corsica, Korsika, Corsica.
Cracow, Krakau.
Crete, Kreta.
Crimea: the –, die Krim.
Croatia, Kroasië.
Cuba, Kuba.
Curacao, Curacao.
Cyclades, Ciklade.
Cyprus, Ciprus.
Cyrenaica, Cirenaïka.
Cyrene, Cirene.
Czechoslovakia, Tsjeggo-Slowakye.

Dacia, Dacië.
Dalmatia, Dalmasië.
Damascus, Damaskus.
Danube, Donau.
Dardenelles, Dardenelle.
Dead Sea, Dooie See.
Delphi, Delphi.
Dunkirk, Duinkerken.

East Africa, Oos-Afrika.
East Friesland, Oos-Friesland.
East London, Oos-Londen.
Edenburg, Edenburg (in O V S).
Edinburgh, Edinburg (in Skotland).
Edom, Edom.
Egypt, Egipte.
Eire, Eire.
Elysium, Elysium.
England, Engeland.
Ephesus, Efese.
Est(h)onia, Estland.
Ethiopia, Ethiopië.
Etruria, Etrurië.
Euphrates, Eufraat.
Eurasia, Eurasië.
Europe, Europa.

Fiji Islands, Fidji-eilande.
Finland, Finland.
Flanders, Vlaandere.
Florence, Florence.
Flushing, Vlissingen.
France, Frankryk.
Franconia, Franke.
Frankfort, Frankfort.
French Hoek, Franschhoek.
Friesland, Friesland.

Galicia, Galicië.
Galilee, Galilea.
Gambia, Gambia.
Gascony, Gascogne, Gaskonje.
Gaul, Gallië.
G(u)elderland, Guelders, Gelderland.
Geneva, Genève.
Genoa, Genua.

Georgia, Georgië (in Rusland), Georgia (in die V S A.).
Germania, Germanië.
Germany, Duitsland.
Ghana, Ghana.
Ghent, Gent.
Gold Coast, Goudkus.
Granada, Granada.
Great Britain, Groot-Brittanje.
Greece, Griekeland.
Greenland, Groenland.
Griqualand, Griekwaland.
Guinea, Guinee, Guinea.

Hague: The –, Den Haag, 's-Gravenhage.
Hamburg, Hamburg.
Hanover, Hannover (in Duitsland), Hanover (in Suid-Afrika).
Havana, Havana.
Hawaii, Hawaii.
Hebrides, Hebride.
Heligoland, Helgoland.
Helsinki, Helsingfors, Helsingfors.
Helvetia, Helvesië.
Herzegovina, Herzegowina.
Hesperides, Hesperide.
Hesse, Hesse.
Hibernia, Hibernië.
Himilayas, Himalaja.
Hindustan, Hindoestan.
Holland, Holland.
Hungary, Hongarye.

Iberia, Iberië.
Iceland, Ysland.
India, Indië; Further –, Agter-Indië.
Indies: the West –, Wes-Indië; the East –, Oos-Indië; the Dutch East –, Nederlands-Indië.
Ionian Sea, Ioniese See.
Iran, Iran (Persië).
Iraq, Irak.
Ireland, Ierland.
Italy, Italië.
Ivory Coast, Ivoorkus.

Jamaica, Jamaika.
Japan, Japan.
Java, Java.
Jerusalem, Jerusalem.
Jordan, Jordaan.
Judea, Judea.
Jutland, Jutland.

Kalahari, Kalahari.
Kar(r)oo, Karoo; the Great –, die Groot –; the Little –, die Klein –.
Kashmir, Kasjmir.
Kenya, Kenia.
Konigsberg, Koningsbergen.
Korea, Korea.

Laccadives, Lakkadive.
Laced(a)emonia, Lacedemonië.
Ladrones, Diewe-eilande.
Laodic(a)ea, Laodicea.
Lapland, Lapland.
Latvia, Letland.
Lebanon, Libanon.
Leghorn, Livorno.
Levant: the –, die Levant.
Leyden, Leiden.
Libya, Libië.
Liége, Luik.

Lille, Rysel.
Lisbon, Lissabon.
Lithuania, Litaue.
Livonia, Lyfland.
Lombardy, Lombardye.
London, Londen.
Lorraine, Lotharinge.
Lourenco Marques, Lourenco Marques.
Louvain, Leuven.
Lower Egypt, Benede-Egipte.
Lucerne, Luzern.
Luxemburg, Luxemburg.
Lyons, Lyon.

Macedonia, Macedonië.
Madagascar, Madagaskar.
Magdeburg, Maagdenburg.
Mainz, Mayence, Mainz.
Majorca, Majorka.
Malacca, Malakka.
Malawi, Malawi.
Malay Archipelago, Maleise Argipel.
Malaya, die Maleise Skiereiland.
Maldives, Maledive.
Malines, Mechlin, Mechelen.
Manchuria, Mantsjoerye.
Manila, Manila.
Marianas, Mariane.
Marianas, vide Ladrones.
Marseilles, Marseille.
Matabeleland, Matebeleland.
Mecca, Mekka.
Mechlin, vide Malines.
Mediterranean Sea, Middellandse See.
Mesopotamia, Mesopotamië, die Tweestromeland.
Meuse, Maas, Maas.
Mexico, Mexiko.
Milan, Milaan.
Minorca, Minorka.
Moluccas, Molukke.
Mons, Bergen (in België).
Moravia, Morawië.
Morocco, Marokko.
Moscow, Moskou.
Moselle, Moesel.
Mozambique, Mosambiek.
München, München.

Namaqualand, Namakwaland.
Namur, Namen.
Nantes, Nantes.
Naples, Napels.
Nazareth, Nasaret.
Netherlands: the –, Nederland.
Netherlands: the – East Indies, Nederlands-Indië.
Newfoundland, Newfoundland.
New Guinea, Nieu-Guinee (-Guinea).
New Zealand, Nieu-Seeland.
Nice, Nizza.
Nieuport, Nieuwpoort.
Nigeria, Nigerië.
Nile, Nyl.
Nineveh, Ninevé.
Normandy, Normandië.
North America, Noord-Amerika.
North Cape, Noordkaap.
North Carolina, Noord-Carolina.
Northern Rhodesia, Noord-Rhodesië.
North Holland, Noord-Holland.
North Sea, Noordsee.
Norway, Noorweë.
Nova Scotia, Nieu-Skotland.
Nubia, Nubië.
Nuremberg, Neurenberg.

Oceania, Oseanië.
Olives: Mount of –, Olyfberg.
Olympus, Olimpus, Olympus.
Orange River, Oranjerivier, Grootrivier.
Orange Free State, Oranje-Vrystaat.
Orkneys, Orkade, Orkadiese Eilande.
Ostend, Oostende.
Outeniqua Mountains, Outenikwaberge.

Pacific Ocean, Stille Oseaan, Stille Suidsee.
Pakistan, Pakistan.
Palatinate: the –, die Palts.
Palestine, Palestina.
Panama Canal, Panamakanaal.
Paraguay, Paraguay.
Paris, Parys (in Frankryk).
Parnassus, Parnassus, Parnas.
Parys, Parys (in die O V S).
Patagonia, Patagonië.
Peloponnesus, Peloponnesus.
Pennsylvania, Pennsilvanië.
Persia, Persië.
Peru, Peru.
Philippines, Filippyne.
Phoenicia, Fenicië.
Picardy, Pikardië.
Piedmont, Piëmont.
Poland, Pole.
Polar Sea, Poolsee.
Polynesia, Polinesië.
Pomerania, Pommere.
Pompeii, Pompeji.
Portugal, Portugal.
Posen, Posen (provinsie).
Posen, Posen (stad).
Prague, Praag.
Prussia, Pruise.
Punjab, Pandjab.
Pyrenees, Pireneë.

Ratisbon, Regensburg, Regensburg.
Red Sea, Rooi See.
R(h)eims, Reims.
Rhine, Ryn.
Rhodes, Rhodus.
Rhodesia, Rhodesië.
Rhone, Rhone.
Riebeek West, Riebeek-Wes.
Rome, Rome.
Rondebosch, Rondebosch.
Rouen, Rouaan.
R(o)umania, Roemenië.
Rubicon, Rubicon.
Russia, Rusland.

Salonica, Saloniki.
Salt River, Soutrivier.
Sarajevo, Serajevo, Serajevo.
Sarawak, Serawak.
Sardinia, Sardinië.
Savoy, Savoje.
Saxony, Sakse.
Scandinavia, Skandinawië.
Scheldt, Schelde.
Schleswig, Sleswick, Sleeswyk.
Scotland, Skotland.
Scylla, Scylla.
Scythia, Skithië.
Sea Point, Seepunt.
Sekukuniland, Sekoekoensland.
Senegambia, Senegambië.
Serajevo, vide Sarajevo.
Servia, Serwië.
Seville, Sevilla.

Siberia, Siberië.
Sicily, Sicilië.
Silesia, Silesië.
Singapore, Singapoer.
Slavonia, Slawonië.
Slovakia, Slowakye.
Slovenia, Slowenië.
Smyrna, Smirna.
Society Islands, Geselskapseilande.
Solomon Islands, Salomons-eilande.
Somerset East, Somerset-Oos.
Sound: the –, die Sont.
South Africa, Suid-Afrika.
South America, Suid-Amerika.
Southern Rhodesia, Suid-Rhodesië.
South Pacific Ocean, Stille Suidsee.
Soviet Russia, Sowjet-Rusland.
Spain, Spanje.
Spice Islands, Molukke.
Spitzbergen, Spitsberge.
Sporades, Sporade.
Stamboul, Istanbul, Stamboel, Istanboel.
Stellenbosch, Stellenbosch.
St Helena (Bay), St. Helena(-baai).
Stockholm, Stockholm.
Strasbourg, Strassburg, Straatsburg.
Styria, Stiermarke.
Sudan: the –, die Soedan.
Suez, Suez.
Sumatra, Sumatra.
Sunda, Soenda.
Surinam, Suriname.
Swabia (Suabia), Swabe.
Swaziland, Swaziland.
Sweden, Swede.
Switzerland, Switserland.
Syracuse, Sirakuse (op Sicilië), Syracuse (in die V S A)
Syria, Sirië.

Table Bay, Tafelbaai.
Table Mountain, Tafelberg.
Tagus, Taag.
Tanganyika, Tanganjika.
Tangier, Tanger.
Tartary, Tartarye.
Tasmania, Tasmanië.
Texel, Tessel, Texel.
Thames, Teems.
Thebes, Thebe.
Thrace, Thracië.
Thuringia, Turinge.
Tibet, Tibet.
Tierra del Fuego, Vuurland.
Tigris, Tigris, Tiger.
Tongres, Tongeren.
Tournai, Doornik.
Touws River, Touwsrivier.
Transvaal, Transvaal.
Transylvania, Seweburge, Transsilvanië.
Treves, Trier.
Trieste, Triëst.
Troy, Troje.
Turin, Turyn.
Turkey, Turkye.
Tuscany, Toskane.
Tyrol, Tirol.

Uganda, Uganda.
Ukraine: the –, die Oekraïne.
Umbria, Umbrië.
United States (of America), Verenigde State (van Amerika).
Upper Egypt, Bo-Egipte.
Ural Mountains, Oeralgebergte.

Uruguay, Uruguay.
Ushant, Ouessant.

Valais, Wallis (in Switserland).
Van Diemen's Land, Van Diemensland.
Venezuela, Venezuela.
Venice, Venesië.
Vereeniging, Vereeniging.
Vesuvius, Vesuvius.
Victoria, Victoria.
Virginia, Virginië.
Vienna, Wenen.
Vistula, Weichsel.
Vladivostok, Wladiwostok.
Volga, Wolga.
Vosges, Vogese.

Waal, Waal (rivier).
Wales, Wallis (in Brittanje).
Wallachia, Walachye.
Wallonia, Wallonië, die Waleland.

Warsaw, Warschau.
Weenen, Weenen (in Natal).
West Africa, Wes-Afrika.
Western Europe, Wes-Europa.
Westphalia, Wesfale.
White Nile, Wit Nyl.
White Sea, Wit See.
Wurtemburg, Wurtemberg.

Yellow Sea, Geel See.
Ypres, Ieperen.
Yugoslavia, Joego-Slawië.

Zambesi, Zambezi, Zambezi.
Zambia, Zambia.
Zanzibar, Zanzibar.
Zealand, Seeland (in Denemarke).
Zeeland, Seeland (in Nederland).
Zion, Sion.
Zuider (Zuyder) Zee, Suidersee.
Zululand, Zoeloeland.